Standard & Poor's
500 Guide

1996 Edition

Standard & Poor's

McGraw-Hill

New York San Francisco Washington, D.C. Auckland Bogotá
Caracas Lisbon London Madrid Mexico City Milan
Montreal New Delhi San Juan Singapore
Sydney Tokyo Toronto

FOR STANDARD & POOR'S
Vice President, Index Products & Services: Elliott Shurgin
Managing Editor: Shauna Morrison
Business Manager: Richard Albanese

McGraw-Hill
A Division of The McGraw·Hill Companies

2 3 4 5 6 7 8 9 0   AGM/AGM   9 0 0 9 8 7 6

ISBN 0-07-052154-9

*The sponsoring editor for this book was David Conti, and the
production supervisor was Thomas G. Kowalczyk. The front
matter and introduction were set by North Market Street
Graphics.*

Printed and bound by Quebecor Printing.

This book is printed on acid-free paper.

The companies contained in this handbook represented the
components of the S&P 500 Index as of October 20, 1995. Additions to or deletions from the Index will cause its composition
to change over time. Company additions and company deletions from the S&P equity indexes do not in any way reflect an
opinion on the investment merits of the company.

ABOUT THE AUTHOR

Standard & Poor's, a division of The McGraw-Hill Companies, Inc., is the nation's leading securities information company. It provides a broad range of financial services, including the respected debt ratings and stock rankings, advisory services, data guides, and the most closely watched and widely reported gauges of stock market activity—the S&P 500, S&P MidCap 400, S&P SmallCap 600, and the S&P Super Composite 1500 stock price indexes. S&P products are marketed around the world and used extensively by financial professionals and individual investors.

Introduction

by Alan J. Miller, C.F.A.

While he was getting dressed one morning, Art Jones heard a news report on the radio saying that the Dow Jones Industrial Average had risen nine points on the previous day. Later he read in his morning newspaper that more stocks had declined than advanced. "How could that be?" he wondered. "Had the market gone up or down?"

Jenny Martin had been interviewing investment advisors to find someone to manage her stock portfolio and it seemed that everyone she spoke to claimed to have outperformed the market. That struck her as hard to believe and, in fact, all the managers she spoke to did seem to be comparing their results to different benchmarks. How could she tell how well those managers really had done?

"I think the market is really going to take off," Mark Johnson thought, "and I'd like to participate. But I'm afraid that even if I'm right, I could end up buying the wrong stocks and the ones I buy could go down while everything else goes up. I can't afford to diversify by buying 1,000 different companies. I just wish there were some way I could buy the whole market. Is there anything I can do?"

Mary Carter had a question for her accountant. "I'd like to invest in a few high-quality, well-established companies that are selling at reasonable prices," she said. "But with thousands and thousands of different companies around—including many that I just wouldn't be interested in because they're too new or too small—I just wouldn't know where to begin. Is there some way I could cut that number down to manageable size and know that the universe I'm looking at consists only of large capitalization, established companies?"

Andrew Perez is the marketing manager for a nationwide computer company whose products and services are used by many of the largest corporations in the country—and he's always on the lookout for even more customers. What he's really looking for are established companies that are in good financial shape and growing, so that they'll be responsive to his suggestions for upgrading their hardware, purchasing additional software, or engaging in more sophisticated networking—and will have the funds to carry out those plans if he convinces them of their value. But where can he find the names of those companies and the information about them which he requires?

Sally Kennedy is the founder and president of a small company in an industry dominated by a dozen or so major competitors. She'd really like to find out how well those larger companies in her industry are doing. Where can she look?

Six different questions, all leading to the same answer: Turn to the Standard & Poor's 500 Index.

What Is the S&P 500?

For sheer longevity, no other stock market indicators compare with the Dow Jones Industrial Average, which has been around since 1884, and the Standard & Poor's 500 Composite Stock Price Index, which was first introduced in 1923. Over the decades, both indicators have been consistently and widely cited as benchmarks of market performance.

Historically, the two indicators were viewed as complementary measures—but in recent years, the key differences between the DJIA and the S&P 500 Index have come into sharper focus. Today, sophisticated investors realize that the DJIA and the S&P 500 Index cannot be used interchangeably: based on different universes and methodologies, they provide very different pictures of market activity.

The DJIA tracks the stock performance of 30 "blue chip" companies, allowing equal weight to a one point move in each stock, notwithstanding substantial differences in stock prices and company capitalizations. As a result, a 5% move, say, in a $200 stock would have ten times the weight of a 5% move in a $20 stock and companies with larger equity capitalizations would not necessarily be weighted any more heavily than companies with smaller capitalizations. Despite these methodological shortcomings, the DJIA has generally been accepted as a reasonable indicator for the "blue chip" market but, because it contains nothing but "blue chip" stocks, by no stretch of the imagination could it be considered representative of the *overall* market.

The S&P 500, on the other hand, covers a far larger and more varied universe of companies, and hence is a more accurate barometer of the overall stock market.

Standard & Poor's 500 composite stock-price index is widely regarded as the most accurate proxy for the stock market and is used by virtually all professional consultants as the benchmark against which to measure money managers' performance. The index contains a representative sample of common stocks that trade on the New York and American Stock Exchanges as well as on the Nasdaq Stock Market (those issues that are part of the Nasdaq National Market). Moreover, the S&P 500 is part of the U.S. Commerce Department's monthly leading business indicators index and is used as the basis for more than $320 billion in index funds.

As the name indicates, the S&P 500 consists of 500 U.S. stocks, which at the end of the third quarter of 1995 represented about 69% of the total market value of American stocks. Although these are not necessarily the 500 largest companies in the United States, most of the largest companies are included. All of these stocks are widely held and the total market value of the "500" exceeds $4 trillion.

More than 91% (457 issues representing 93% of the market value) of the issues in the index are listed on the New York Stock Exchange. Another 8% (37 issues accounting for 6% of the market value) are traded on the Nasdaq Stock Market and the remaining 1% (6 issues with less than 1% of the market value) are listed on the American Stock Exchange.

But let's take another look at the half-dozen questions raised at the beginning of this introduction.

The Six Questions...Answered

1. Art Jones

If the Dow Jones Industrial Average rose nine points but more stocks declined than advanced, had the market really gone up or down?

In a sense, there really is no one answer to that question because it all depends on how you choose to define "the market." But in another sense, it is probably fair to say that the S&P 500 Index provides as good a picture of what the market "really" does as any index around. It is, after all, an average of 500 companies, not just 30, which makes it a better proxy for the overall market than the Dow Jones Industrial Average. And since, unlike advance-decline indices, the 500 stocks are *capitalization* weighted, it wouldn't be distorted by declines in a large number of small companies which might actually have been more than offset (in terms of total dollars gained or lost by investors) by increases in a smaller number of large companies. So if Art wants to know how the market "really" did, he ought to take a look at the S&P 500.

2. Jenny Martin

If all the investment advisors she talks to claim to have outperformed the market (by comparing their results to different benchmarks), how can she tell how well they've truly done?

Now this question turns out to be somewhat easier than it appeared to be at first blush. For if the S&P 500 really is the best proxy for the overall stock market, then an investment advisor who invests in common stocks can reasonably be measured by comparing his performance to that index. Of course, if the advisor invests only in international stocks, or small capitalization stocks, or long-term bonds, or some other mix of assets, a different benchmark would have to be developed to measure his performance fairly. But for the typical common stock manager, the best benchmark probably is the S&P 500.

3. Mark Johnson

How can he invest in the overall market without taking the risk of investing in the stocks of individual companies?

Consider the alternatives. First, Mark might just invest in an actively managed common stock mutual fund which is broadly diversified among hundreds of companies. If the diversification is broad enough, and if the securities owned are selected at random, the law of averages would suggest that the fund's results would approximate those of the overall market (as measured by the S&P 500).

Unfortunately, however, most funds *aren't* that diversified. They might own a couple of hundred stocks, but probably not 500. And for that reason alone, this approach might not work.

But there is another even more important reason why this approach would not work. It is because the portfolios of *actively managed* funds, by definition, are *not* randomized, but rather are consciously structured by their managers to reflect those managers' best judgments regarding the relative attractiveness of alternative investment vehicles. Thus, those managers *intentionally* overweight some companies (which the fund managers expect to be stellar performers) and underweight others (which they expect to fare relatively poorly).

Now, if the fund managers' judgments turn out to be right, terrific. But suppose they're not? In that case, the fund, despite its being broadly diversified, still may perform substantially worse than the market (as measured by the S&P 500). And remember, that risk—the chance of performing poorly as a result of picking the wrong stocks, even though the market on average did well—is precisely the risk that Mark is seeking to avoid.

No, selecting an *actively* managed fund *wouldn't* solve Mark's problem. But suppose Mark could invest in a *passively* managed fund—one whose managers simply tried to replicate the performance of the market as a whole, without trying to add value (and thereby running the risk of subtracting value instead) through individual stock selection. Would that satisfy Mark's need?

In fact, it would. And, fortunately for Mark, *passively* managed mutual funds which merely seek to replicate the performance of the S&P 500 Index (commonly known as index funds) abound. Indeed, these funds have so grown in popularity (in large part because, strange as it may seem, stock market indices actually have tended to *outperform* a majority of mutual funds and pension plans actively managed by professionals) that, as of 1994 year-end, more than $20 billion was invested in mutual funds indexed to the S&P 500.

But passively managed index funds are not the only option open to Mark. He may make an even more direct bet on the direction of the market by investing in "stock index futures" themselves—or, if he is even more speculatively inclined, in *options* on stock index futures.

Stock index futures are, in effect, futures contracts on the value of the theoretical basket of securities which comprise a stock index. Indices on which futures contracts may be written include the New York Stock Exchange Composite Index (traded on the New York Futures Exchange), the Value Line Composite Index (traded on the Kansas City Board of Trade), and, of course, the Standard & Poor's 500 Index and Standard & Poor's MidCap 400 Index (both traded on the Chicago Mercantile Exchange). Since investors in such indices obviously can't deliver an index of stocks to a futures buyer, settlement of such contracts is in cash.

The Chicago Mercantile Exchange also trades options on Standard & Poor's 500 and MidCap 400 futures contracts. Exercise of one of those options establishes a position in the underlying futures contract. Options on the Standard & Poor's 500 Index are traded on the Chicago Board Options Exchange, and options on the Standard & Poor's Mid-Cap 400 Index are traded on the American Stock Exchange. Unlike options on futures contracts, options on stock indices are settled in cash.

Of course, if Mark thought that the market was likely to decline rather than advance, but didn't want to incur the risk of going short the wrong stocks (those that might turn out to rise even in a falling market), trading in Standard & Poor's 500 Index futures contracts and options on those contracts could serve his purposes too. In that event, he would sell short futures contracts or call options on futures contracts or buy put options on futures contracts, rather than buying futures contracts or call options.

Finally, if Mark discovered a stock which he believed would outperform the market substantially but thought that the overall market itself was just as likely to decline as to rise, the futures contracts and options markets could help him too. In that event, he could buy the stock and short the market (by shorting futures contracts or calls on futures contracts on the S&P 500 Composite Index). If he turned out to be right and the stock did substantially outperform the market, he would do well whether the stock market itself rose or fell: if the stock market rose, the stock would rise even more (on a percentage basis), so he'd make more money on his long position in the stock than he would lose on his short positions in the futures or options markets. On the other hand, if the stock market declined, the stock would decline less (or maybe even rise) and he'd make more money on his short positions in futures contracts or options than he'd lose on the stock itself (or maybe, if he got really lucky, even make money on both).

4. Mary Carter

How can she find individual high-quality, well-established companies from which to select, for investment purposes, those that are selling at reasonable prices?

The components of the S&P 500 Composite Index are just what Mary is looking for. Indeed, as of the end of 1995's third quarter, the "average" S&P 500 company boasted a market value of $8.6 billion.

What Mary should do is to turn to the pages of this book, which include extensive data on all 500 companies in the S&P 500 Composite Index. But before doing so, she should be sure to read the final sections of this introduction—"What You'll Find in This Book" and "How to Use This Book to Select Investments"—in order to learn just how to extract the most value from that data.

5. Andrew Perez

How can Andrew find established companies that are in good financial shape, growing, and have the funds to acquire the hardware or software he'll be recommending to them?

The companies in the S&P 500 Composite Index should be Andrew's starting point, too, and the pages of this book are where he'll find the information on those companies which he requires. But before thumbing through these pages, Andrew, like Mary, would be well advised to refer first to the section titled "What You'll Find in This Book," which appears later in this introduction.

6. Sally Kennedy

How can Sally find out how her major competitors, the larger companies in her industry, are doing?

You guessed it: A good place for Sally to start would be with the companies in this book. If Sally's industry is dominated by a number of large competitors, there is little doubt that most, if not all, will show up here. And here's where she's likely to find a lot of the information on those companies too.

But we're at the point now where we really must try to provide Mary, Andrew, and Sally with more guidance. Art, Jenny, and Mark, you will recall, were primarily concerned with using the Standard & Poor's 500 Composite Index in the aggregate, in order to find out how the market's "really" doing (Art), to measure investment managers' performance (Jenny), or to invest in the market as a whole or hedge individual stock positions (Mark). And we've explained all that.

Mary, Andrew, and Sally, however, are primarily interested in the *components* of the S&P 500, in their quest for companies which might represent good individual investments (Mary), or companies which could turn out to be good potential clients (Andrew), or companies which are important business competitors (Sally). And it is those individual companies which most of this book is about. So it's time to show Mary, Andrew, Sally—and you. . . .

What You'll Find in This Book

In the pages that follow you will find an array of text and statistical data on 500 different companies in 87 industries. This information, dealing with everything from the nature of these companies' basic businesses, recent corporate developments, current outlooks, and select financial information relating to revenues, earnings, dividends, margins, capitalization, and so forth, might initially seem overwhelming. However, it's not that difficult. Just take a few moments to familiarize yourself with what you'll find on these pages.

Please note that during 1995, Standard & Poor's greatly improved the Stock Reports by adding a variety of new features to help you in making investment decisions. At the time this handbook was being prepared, some companies were not yet converted to the enhanced format and are presented in this book in their existing format.

Following is a glossary of terms and definitions used throughout this book. Please refer to this section as you encounter terms which need further clarification.

Enhanced Stock Report Terms

Quantitative Evaluations

S&P Opinion—Buy, hold or sell recommendations are provided using S&P's unique STARS (Stock Appreciation Ranking System), which measures short-term (six- to 12-month) appreciation potential of stocks. STARS performance is measured against the performance of the S&P 500 Index.

STARS Rankings are as follows:

***** Buy—Expected to be among the best performers over the next 12 months.

**** Accumulate—Expected to be an above-average performer.

*** Hold—Expected to be an average performer.

** Avoid—Likely to be a below-average performer.

* Sell—Expected to be a well-below-average performer and fall in price.

Outlook—Using S&P's exclusive proprietary quantitative model, stocks are ranked in one of five Outlook Groups—ranging from Group 5, listing the most undervalued stocks, to Group 1, the most overvalued issues. Group 5 stocks are expected to generally outperform all others. To identify a stock that is in a strengthening or weakening position, a positive (+) or negative (−) Timing Index is placed next to the Outlook ranking. Using these rankings, here's what action should be taken:

5+ = Buy	2+ = Hold if in portfolio
5 = Hold if in portfolio	2− = Sell
4+ = Hold if in portfolio	1+ = Hold if in portfolio
4− = Sell	1− = Sell
3+ = Hold if in portfolio	
3− = Sell	

The Timing Index helps identify the right time to buy stocks, but its most important function is to indicate when it is time to sell. Because Group 5 stocks have historically produced the best results, S&P recommends buying only Group 5 stocks with a positive Timing Index. Then, hold onto each one for as long as it remains in a positive trend (positive Timing Index), even if the ranking falls as the stock appreciates toward overvalued status. This will reduce transaction costs and substantially raise your chances of outperforming the market in the long run. It will also raise the number of transactions which qualify as long-term capital gains for tax purposes.

Fair Value—The price at which a stock should sell today as calculated by S&P's computers using our quantitative model based on the company's earnings, growth potential, return on equity relative to the S&P 500 and its industry group, price to book ratio history, current yield relative to the S&P 500, and other factors. The current fair price is shown given today's S&P 500 level.

Risk—Rates the volatility of the stock's price over the past year.

Technical Evaluation—In researching the past market history of prices and trading volume for each company, S&P's computer models apply special technical methods and formulas to identify and project price trends for the stock. They analyze how the price of the stock is moving and evaluate the interrelationships between the moving averages to ultimately determine buy or sell signals—and to decide whether they're bullish, neutral or bearish for the stock. The date the signals were initiated is also provided so you can take advantage of a recent or ongoing uptrend in price, or see how a stock has performed over time since our last technical signal was generated.

Relative Strength Rank—Shows, on a scale of 1 to 99, how the stock has performed compared with all other companies in S&P's universe of companies on a rolling 13-week basis.

Insider Activity—Gives an insight as to insider sentiment by showing whether directors, officers and key employees—who may have proprietary information not available to the general public—are buying or selling the company's stock during the most recent six months.

Key Stock Statistics

Avg. Daily Vol.—The average daily trading volume of the stock for the past 20 days on a rolling basis, shown in millions.

Market Cap.—The price of the stock multiplied by the number of shares outstanding, shown in billions.

Insider Holdings—The percentage of outstanding shares held by directors, officers and key employees of the company, and others who hold a minimum of 10% of the outstanding shares.

Value of $10,000 Invested 5 years ago—The value today of a $10,000 investment in the stock made five years ago, assuming year-end reinvestment of dividends.

S&P Ranking

The investment process involves assessment of various factors—such as products and industry position, company resources and financial policy—with results that make some common stocks more highly esteemed than others. In this assessment, Standard & Poor's believes that earnings and dividend performance is the end result of the interplay of these factors and that, over the long run, the record of this performance has a considerable bearing on relative quality. The rankings, however, do not reflect all of the factors that may bear on stock quality.

Growth and stability of earnings and dividends are the key elements in Standard & Poor's earnings and dividend rankings for common stocks, which are designed to capsulize the nature of this record in a single symbol. It should be noted, however, that the process also takes into consideration certain adjustments and modifications deemed desirable in establishing such rankings.

These rankings are derived by means of a computerized scoring system based on per share earnings and dividend records of the most recent ten years. Basic scores are computed for earnings and dividends and then adjusted by a set of predetermined modifiers for growth, stability, and cyclicality. Adjusted scores for earnings and dividends are then combined to yield a final score.

The ranking system also makes allowance for the fact that, in general, corporate size imparts certain recognized advantages from an investment standpoint. Minimum size limits (in terms of corporate sales) are set for the various rankings, but exceptions may be made where a score reflects an outstanding earnings-dividend record.

Final scores are then translated into one of the following rankings:

A+   Highest
A   High
A−   Above Average
B+   Average
B   Below Average
B−   Lower

C   Lowest

D   In Reorganization

NR   No Ranking

In some instances, rankings may be modified by special considerations, such as natural disasters, massive strikes, or nonrecurring accounting adjustments.

It is important to note that a ranking is not a forecast of future market price performance, but is basically an appraisal of past performance of earnings and dividends and relative current standing. Consequently, rankings should not be used as market recommendations: a high-score stock may at times be so overpriced as to justify its sale while a low-score stock may be attractively priced for purchase. Rankings based upon earnings and dividend records are no substitute for complete analysis. They cannot take into account the potential effects of management changes, internal company policies not yet fully reflected in the earnings and dividend record, public relations standings, recent competitive shifts, and a host of other factors that may be relevant in investment decision making.

Beta

The beta coefficient is a measure of the volatility of a stock's price relative to the S&P 500 Index (a proxy for the overall market). An issue with a beta of 1.5 for example, tends to move 50% more than the overall market, in the same direction. An issue with a beta of 0.5 tends to move 50% less. If a stock moved exactly as the market moved, it would have a beta of 1.0. A stock with a negative beta tends to move in a direction opposite to that of the overall market.

Per Share Data ($) Tables

Tangible Book Value; Book Value (See also: "Common Equity" under Industrial)—Indicates the theoretical dollar amount per common share one might expect to receive from a company's tangible "book" assets should liquidation take place. Generally, book value is determined by adding the stated value of the common stock, paid-in capital and retained earnings and then subtracting intangible assets (excess cost over equity of acquired companies, goodwill, and patents), preferred stock at liquidating value and unamortized debt discount. Divide that amount by the outstanding shares to get book value per common share.

Cash Flow—Net income plus depreciation, depletion, and amortization, divided by shares used to calculate earnings per common share. (Also see: "Cash Flow" for Industrial Companies.)

Earnings—The amount a company reports as having been earned for the year on its common stock based on generally accepted accounting standards. Earnings may be indicated in terms of *primary* (common stock and common stock equivalents such as stock options and warrants) and *fully diluted* (reflecting dilution in earnings resulting if all contingent issuances of common stock materialized at the outset of the year), and are generally reported from continuing operations, before extraordinary items. INSURANCE companies report *operating earnings* before gains/losses on security transactions and *earnings* after such transactions.

Dividends—Generally total cash payments per share based on the ex-dividend dates over a twelve-month period. May also be reported on a declared basis where this has been established to be a company's payout policy.

Payout Ratio—Indicates the percentage of earnings paid out in dividends. It is calculated by dividing the annual dividend by the earnings. For INSURANCE companies *earnings* after gains/losses on security transactions are used.

Prices High/Low—Shows the calendar year high and low of a stock's market price.

P/E Ratio High/Low—The ratio of market price to earnings—essentially indicates the valuation investors place on a company's earnings. Obtained by dividing the annual earnings into the high and low market price for the year. For INSURANCE companies *operating earnings* before gains/losses on security transactions are used.

Net Asset Value—Appears on investment company reports and reflects the market value of stocks, bonds, and net cash divided by outstanding shares. The % DIFFERENCE indicates the percentage premium or discount of the market price over the net asset value.

Portfolio Turnover—Appears on investment company reports and indicates percentage of total security purchases and sales for the year to overall investment assets. Primarily mirrors trading aggressiveness.

Income/Balance Sheet Data Tables

Banks

Net Interest Income—Interest and dividend income, minus interest expense.

Loan Loss Provision—Amount charged to operating expenses to provide an adequate reserve to cover anticipated losses in the loan portfolio.

Taxable Equivalent Adjustment—Increase to render income from tax-exempt loans and securities comparable to fully taxed income.

Noninterest Income—Service fees, trading and other income, excluding gains/losses on securities transactions.

% Expenses/Op. Revenues—Noninterest expense as a percentage of taxable equivalent net interest income plus noninterest income (before securities gains/losses). A measure of cost control.

Commercial Loans—Commercial, industrial, financial, agricultural loans and leases, gross.

Other Loans—Gross consumer, real estate and foreign loans.

% Loan Loss Reserve—Contra-account to loan assets, built through provisions for loan losses, which serves as a cushion for possible future loan charge-offs.

% Loans/Deposits—Proportion of loans funded by deposits. A measure of liquidity and an indication of bank's ability to write more loans.

Earning Assets—Assets on which interest is earned.

Money Market Assets—Interest-bearing interbank deposits, federal funds sold, trading account securities.

Investment Securities—Federal, state, and local government bonds and other securities.

Gains/Losses on Securities Transactions—Realized losses on sales of securities, usually bonds.

Net Before Taxes—Amount remaining after operating expenses are deducted from income, including gains or losses on security transactions.

Effective Tax Rate—Actual income tax expense divided by net before taxes.

Net Income—The final profit before dividends (common/preferred) from all sources after deduction of expenses, taxes, and fixed charges, but before any discontinued operations or extraordinary items.

Net Interest Margin—A percentage computed by dividing net interest income, on a taxable equivalent basis, by average earning assets. Used as an analytical tool to measure profit margins from providing credit services.

% Return on Revenues—Net income divided by gross revenues.

% Return on Assets—Net income divided by average total assets. An analytical measure of asset-use efficiency and industry comparison.

% Return on Equity—Net income (minus preferred dividend requirements) divided by average common equity. Generally used to measure performance.

Total Assets—Includes interest-earning financial instruments—principally commercial, real estate, consumer loans and leases; investment securities/trading accounts; cash/money market investments; other owned assets.

Cash—Mainly vault cash, interest-bearing deposits placed with banks, reserves required by the Federal Reserve and items in the process of collection—generally referred to as float.

Government Securities—Includes United States Treasury securities and securities of other U.S. government agencies at book or carrying value. A bank's major "liquid asset."

State and Municipal Securities—State and municipal securities owned at book value.

Loans—All domestic and foreign loans (excluding leases), less unearned discount and reserve for possible losses. Generally considered a bank's principal asset.

Deposits—Primarily classified as either *demand* (payable at any time upon demand of depositor) or *time* (not payable within thirty days).

Deposits/Capital Funds—Average deposits divided by average capital funds. Capital funds include capital notes/debentures, other long-term debt, capital stock, surplus, and undivided profits. May be used as a "leverage" measure.

Long-Term Debt—Total borrowings for terms beyond one year including notes payable, mortgages, debentures, term loans, and capitalized lease obligations.

Common Equity—Includes common/capital surplus, undivided profits, reserve for contingencies and other capital reserves.

% Equity to Assets—Average common equity divided by average total assets. Used as a measure of capital adequacy.

% Equity to Loans—Average common equity divided by average loans. Reflects the degree of equity coverage to loans outstanding.

Industrial Companies

Following data is based on Form 10K Annual Report data as filed with SEC.

Revenues—Net sales and other operating revenues. Includes franchise/leased department income for retailers, and royalties for publishers and oil and mining companies. Excludes excise taxes for tobacco, liquor, and oil companies.

Operating Income—Net sales and operating revenues less cost of goods sold and operating expenses (including research and development, profit sharing, exploration and bad debt, but excluding depreciation and amortization).

% Operating Income of Revenues—Net sales and operating revenues divided into operating income. Used as a measure of operating profitability.

Capital Expenditures—The sum of additions at cost to property, plant and equipment and leaseholds, generally excluding amounts arising from acquisitions.

Depreciation—Includes noncash charges for obsolescence, wear on property, current portion of capitalized expenses (intangibles), and depletion charges.

Interest Expense—Includes all interest expense on short/long-term debt, amortization of debt discount/premium and deferred expenses (e.g., financing costs).

Net Before Taxes—Includes operating and nonoperating revenues (including extraordinary items not net of taxes), less all operating and nonoperating expenses, except income taxes and minority interest, but including equity in nonconsolidated subsidiaries.

Effective Tax Rate—Actual income tax charges divided by net before taxes.

Net Income—Profits derived from all sources after deduction of expenses, taxes, and fixed charges, but before any discontinued operations, extraordinary items, and dividends (preferred/common).

% Net Income of Revenues—Net income divided by sales/operating revenues.

Cash Flow—Net income (before extraordinary items and discontinued operations, and after preferred dividends) plus depreciation, depletion, and amortization.

Cash—Includes all cash and government and other marketable securities.

Current Assets—Those assets expected to be realized in cash or used up in the production of revenue within one year.

Current Liabilities—Generally includes all debts/obligations falling due within one year.

Current Ratio—Current assets divided by current liabilities. A measure of liquidity.

Total Assets—Current assets plus net plant and other noncurrent assets (intangibles and deferred items).

% Return on Assets—Net income divided by average total assets on a per common share basis. Used in industry analysis and as a measure of asset-use efficiency.

Long-Term Debt—Debts/obligations due after one year. Includes bonds, notes payable, mortgages, lease obligations, and industrial revenue bonds. Other Long-Term Debt, when reported as a separate account, is excluded. This account generally includes pension and retirement benefits.

Common Equity (See also: "Book Value" under Per Share Data Table)—Common stock plus capital surplus and retained earnings, less any difference between the carrying value and liquidating value of preferred stock.

Total Invested Capital—The sum of stockholders' equity plus long-term debt, capital lease obligations, deferred income taxes, investment credits, and minority interest.

% Long-Term Debt of Invested Capital—Long-term debt divided by total invested capital. Indicates how highly "lever aged" a business might be.

% Return on Equity—Net income less preferred dividend requirements divided by average common shareholders' equity on a per common share basis. Generally used to measure performance and industry comparisons.

Utilities

Operating Revenues—Represents the amount billed to customers by the utility.

Depreciation—Amounts charged to income to compensate for the decline in useful value of plant and equipment.

Maintenance—Amounts spent to keep plants in good operating condition.

Operating Ratio—Ratio of operating costs to operating revenues or the proportion of revenues absorbed by expenses. Obtained by dividing operating expenses including depreciation, maintenance, and taxes by revenues.

Fixed Charges Coverage—The number of times income before interest charges (operating income plus other income) after taxes covers total interest charges and preferred dividend requirements.

Construction Credits—Credits for interest charged to the cost of constructing new plant. A combination of allowance for equity funds used during construction and allowance for borrowed funds used during construction—credit.

Effective Tax Rate—Actual income tax expense divided by the total of net income and actual income tax expense.

Net Income—Amount of earnings for the year which is available for preferred and common dividend payments.

% Return on Revenues—Obtained by dividing net income for the year by revenues.

% Return on Invested Capital—Percentage obtained by dividing income available for fixed charges by average total invested capital.

% Return on Common Equity—Percentage obtained by dividing income available for common stock (net income less preferred dividend requirements) by average common equity.

Gross Property—Includes utility plant at cost, plant work in progress, and nuclear fuel.

Capital Expenditures—Represents the amounts spent on capital improvements to plant and funds for construction programs.

Net Property—Includes items in gross property less provision for depreciation.

% Earned on Net Property—Percentage obtained by dividing operating income by average net property for the year. A measure of plant efficiency.

Total Invested Capital—Sum of total capitalization (common-preferred-debt), accumulated deferred income taxes, accumulated investment tax credits, minority interest, contingency reserves, and contributions in aid of construction.

Total Capitalization—Combined sum of total common equity, preferred stock and long-term debt.

Long-Term Debt—Debt obligations due beyond one year from balance sheet date.

Capitalization Ratios—Reflect the percentage of each type of debt/equity issues outstanding to total capitalization. % DEBT is obtained by dividing total debt by the sum of debt, preferred, common, paid-in capital and retained earnings. % PREFERRED is obtained by dividing the preferred stocks outstanding by total capitalization. % COMMON, divide the sum of common stocks, paid-in capital and retained earnings by total capitalization.

Finally, at the very bottom of the right-hand page, you'll find general information about the company: its address and telephone number, the names of its senior executive officers and directors (usually including the name of the investor contact), the transfer agent and registrar for the stock, and the state in which the company is incorporated.

How to Use This Book to Select Investments

And so, at last, we come to the $64,000 question: Given this vast array of data, how might a businesswoman seeking to find out about her competition, the marketing manager looking for clients, a job seeker, and the investor use it to best serve their respective purposes?

If you are like one of the first three of these individuals—a business-woman, the marketing manager, or the job seeker—your task will be arduous, to be sure, but this book will provide you with an excellent starting point and your payoff can make it all worthwhile. You will have to go through this book page by page, looking for those companies that are in the industries in which you are interested, that are of the size and financial strength that appeal to you, that are located geographically in your territory or where you're willing to relocate, that have been profitable and growing, and so forth. And then you will have to read about just what's going on at those companies by referring to the appropriate "Company Overview," "Business Summary," and "Important Developments" comments in these reports.

Of course, this book won't do it *all* for you. It is, after all, just a start-ing point, not a conclusive summary of everything you might need to know. It is designed to educate, not to render advice or provide recom-mendations. But it will get you pointed in the right direction.

Finally, what about the investor who wants to use this book to find good individual investments from among the 500 stocks in the S&P 500 Index? If you fall into that category, what should you do?

Well, you can approach your quest the same way that the business-woman looking for information about her competitors, the marketing manager, and the job seeker approached theirs—by thumbing through this book page by page, looking for companies with high historic growth rates, generous dividend payout policies, wide profit margins, A+ S&P Rankings, or whatever other characteristics you consider desirable in stocks in which you might invest. In this case, however, we have made your job just a little bit easier.

We have already prescreened the 500 companies in this book for sev-eral of the stock characteristics in which investors generally are most interested, including S&P Earnings and Dividends Rankings, growth records, and dividend payment histories, and we're pleased to present on the next five pages lists of those companies which score highest on the bases of these criteria. So if you, like most investors, find these characteristics important in potential investments, you might want to turn first to the companies on these lists in your search for attractive investments.

Good luck and happy investment returns!

Companies With Five Consecutive Years of Earnings Increases

This table, compiled from a computer screen of the stocks in this handbook, shows companies that have recorded rising per-share earnings for five consecutive years, have a minimum 10% five-year EPS growth rate based on trailing 12-month earnings, have estimated 1995 EPS at least 10% above those reported for 1994, pay dividends and have Standard & Poor's earnings and dividend rankings of A– or better. The list is sorted by the five-year EPS growth rate.

Company	Business	Fiscal Year End	5 Yr. EPS Growth Rate %	EPS $ 1994 Act.	EPS $ 1995 Est.	S&P Stock Rank	Price	P/E on 1995 Est.	% Yield
Home Depot	Bldg mtls,home improv strs	Jan*	26	1.32	1.55	A	38.13	24.6	0.5
Circuit City Stores	Retailer:video eq,appliances	Feb*	25	1.72	1.98	A	35.00	17.7	0.3
Medtronic, Inc	Cardiac pacemakers:med.serv	Apr#	20	1.01	1.27	A+	55.25	43.5	0.4
Great Lakes Chemical	Bromine & brominated chem	Dec	18	4.00	4.50	A+	67.75	15.1	0.6
Coca-Cola Co	Major soft drink/juice co	Dec	17	1.98	2.38	A+	72.38	30.4	1.2
Loral Corp	Military electronic systems	Mar*	17	1.69	1.92	A+	30.75	16.0	1.0
Pep Boys–Man,Mo,Ja	Retail chain: auto parts, etc.	Jan*	17	1.32	1.55	A+	24.00	15.5	0.7
Wal-Mart Stores	Operates discount stores	Jan*	17	1.17	1.30	A+	23.00	17.7	0.8
Albertson's, Inc	Food supermkts: food–drug	Jan*	16	1.65	1.85	A+	34.38	18.6	1.5
UST Inc	Snuff,tobacco,wine,spirits	Dec	16	1.87	2.15	A+	29.88	13.9	4.3
Norwest Corp	Comm'l banking,Minneapolis	Dec	15	2.45	2.80	A–	32.00	11.4	3.0
Johnson & Johnson	Health care products	Dec	14	3.12	3.70	A+	79.75	21.6	1.6
Abbott Laboratories	Diversified health care prod	Dec	13	1.87	2.15	A+	40.38	18.8	2.0
Federal Natl Mtge	Provides residential mtg fds	Dec	13	7.80	8.60	A–	103.00	12.0	2.6
Schering–Plough	Pharmaceut'l/consumer prod	Dec	13	2.41	2.80	A+	54.00	19.3	2.1
Service Corp Intl	Funeral service:cemetery	Dec	13	1.51	1.72	A–	39.63	23.0	1.1
Automatic Data Proc	Computer services	Jun#	12	2.37	2.77	A+	72.88	26.3	0.9
SunTrust Banks	Comm'l bkg,Georgia,FL,Tenn	Dec	12	4.37	4.95	A+	66.88	13.5	2.1
Walgreen Co	Major retail drug chain	Aug#	12	1.14	1.30	A+	28.00	21.5	1.5
McDonald's Corp	Fast food restaurant:franch'g	Dec	11	1.68	1.95	A+	41.50	21.3	0.6
Sysco Corp	Food distr & service systems	Jun#	11	1.18	1.38	A+	30.50	22.1	1.4
Textron, Inc	Aerospace/coml prod/finl svcs	Dec	11	4.80	5.45	A	67.25	12.3	2.3
Amer Greetings Cl'A'	Cards & gift wrappings	Feb*	10	2.00	2.20	A	31.13	14.1	2.0
Amer Intl Group	Major int'l insur hldg co	Dec	10	4.58	5.20	A+	85.25	16.4	0.3
Intl Flavors/Fragr	Dev&mfr flavor&fragr prod	Dec	10	2.03	2.30	A+	48.13	20.9	2.5
SBC Communications	Tel svc:Ark,Kan,Mo,Okl,Tex	Dec	10	2.74	3.05	A	55.25	18.1	2.9
Sigma–Aldrich	Specialty chem prod	Dec	10	2.21	2.65	A+	48.50	18.3	0.7
ConAgra Inc	Prepared foods:agri–products	May#	9	1.81	2.06	A+	39.75	19.3	2.3
Becton, Dickinson	Health care pr:ind'l safety	Sep	8	3.05	3.55	A+	65.63	18.5	1.2
Marsh & McLennan	Insur brokerage & agency serv	Dec	5	5.19	5.75	A+	85.75	14.9	3.7

*Actual 1995 EPS & estimated 1996 EPS; P/E based on estimated 1996 EPS. #Actual 1995 EPS; P/E based on 1995 actual EPS.

Chart based on October 20, 1995 prices and data.

NOTE: All earnings estimates are Standard & Poor's projections.

Rapid Growth Stocks

The stocks listed below have shown strong and consistent earnings growth. Issues of rapidly growing companies tend to carry high price-earnings ratios and offer potential for substantial appreciation. At the same time,though, the stocks are subject to strong selling pressures should growth in earnings slow. Five-year earnings growth rates have been calculated for fiscal years 1990 through 1994 and the most current 12-month earnings.

Company	Business	S&P Stock Rank	Fiscal Year End	— EPS $ — 1994 Act.	1995 Est.	5 Yr. EPS % Growth	Price	P/E on 1995 Est.	% Yield
Abbott Laboratories	Diversified health care prod	A+	Dec	1.87	2.15	13.00	40.38	18.8	2.0
Albertson's, Inc	Food supermkts: food–drug	A+	Jan*	1.65	1.85	16.00	34.38	18.6	1.5
Automatic Data Proc	Computer services	A+	Jun#	2.37	2.77	12.00	72.88	26.3	0.9
Cabletron Systems	Mfr computer interconnectn eq	B	Feb*	2.27	3.00	38.00	76.13	25.4	0.0
Echlin Inc	Auto elec,brake replacem't pts	A–	Aug#	2.06	2.60	29.00	34.38	13.2	2.3
Federal Natl Mtge	Provides residential mtg fds	A–	Dec	7.80	8.60	13.00	103.00	12.0	2.6
First Data	Credit–card processing svcs	NR	Dec	1.87	2.25	16.00	62.75	27.9	0.1
Gillette Co	Shaving, personal care: pens	A+	Dec	1.57	1.80	16.00	48.88	27.2	1.2
Great Lakes Chemical	Bromine & brominated chem	A+	Dec	4.00	4.50	18.00	67.75	15.1	0.6
Home Depot	Bldg mtls,home improv strs	A	Jan*	1.32	1.55	26.00	38.13	24.6	0.5
MBNA Corp	Bank hldg/credit card svc'g	NR	Dec	1.77	2.30	18.00	37.63	16.4	2.2
Medtronic, Inc	Cardiac pacemakers:med.serv	A+	Apr#	1.01	1.27	20.00	55.25	43.5	0.4
Micron Technology	Mfr microcomputer parts	B	Aug#	1.91	3.95	NM	69.38	17.6	0.2
Microsoft Corp	Software for microcomputers	B+	Jun#	1.88	2.32	25.00	95.50	41.2	0.0
Motorola, Inc	Semiconductors:communic eq	A	Dec	2.65	3.14	32.00	64.38	20.5	0.6
Norwest Corp	Comm'l banking,Minneapolis	A–	Dec	2.45	2.80	15.00	32.00	11.4	3.0
Schering–Plough	Pharmaceut'l/consumer prod	A+	Dec	2.41	2.80	13.00	54.00	19.3	2.1
Sysco Corp	Food distr & service systems	A+	Jun#	1.18	1.38	11.00	30.50	22.1	1.4
UST Inc	Snuff,tobacco,wine,spirits	A+	Dec	1.87	2.15	16.00	29.88	13.9	4.3
Wal–Mart Stores	Operates discount stores	A+	Jan*	1.17	1.30	17.00	23.00	17.7	0.8
Walgreen Co	Major retail drug chain	A+	Aug#	1.14	1.30	12.00	28.00	21.5	1.5
Wendy's Intl	Fast food restaurant:franch'g	B+	Dec	0.93	1.10	20.00	20.38	18.5	1.1

*Actual 1995 EPS & estimated 1996 EPS; P/E based on estimated 1996 EPS. #Actual 1995 EPS; P/E based on 1995 actual EPS. NM - Not meaningful, value greater than 100.

Chart based on October 20, 1995 prices and data.

NOTE: All earnings estimates are Standard & Poor's projections.

Stocks With A+ Rankings

Based on the issues in this handbook, this screen shows stocks of all companies with Standard & Poor's earnings and dividend rankings of A+.

Company	Business
Abbott Laboratories	Diversified health care prod
Albertson's, Inc	Food supermkts: food–drug
Amer Home Products	Drugs, food,household/ware
Amer Int'l Group	Major int'l insur hldg co
Anheuser–Busch Cos	Largest U.S. brewer:baking
Archer–Daniels–Midland	Process soybeans:flour mill'r
Automatic Data Proc	Computer services
Banc One Corp	Comml bkg,Ohio,midwest
Becton, Dickinson	Health care pr:ind'l safety
Bristol–Myers Squibb	Pharmaceutical,medical prod
Coca–Cola Co	Major soft drink/juice co
ConAgra Inc	Prepared foods:agri–products
CPC Intl	International food processor
Dillard Dept Str'A'	Dept stores in southwest US
Emerson Electric	Mfr electric/electronic prdts
Genl Electric	Consumer/ind'l prod,broad'cst
Genuine Parts	Distrib auto replacement parts
Gillette Co	Shaving, personal care: pens
Great Lakes Chemical	Bromine & brominated chem
Heinz (H.J.)	Major mfr of processed foods
Illinois Tool Works	Fasteners,tools, plastic items
Intl Flavors/Fragr	Dev&mfr flavor&fragr prod
Interpublic Grp Cos	Worldwide advertis'g agencies
Johnson & Johnson	Health care products
Kellogg Co	Convenience food products
KeyCorp	Commercial bkg,Ohio,Nthn US
Kimberly–Clark	Consumer products:newsprint

Company	Business
Limited Inc	Women's apparel stores
Loral Corp	Military electronic systems
Marsh & McLennan	Insur brokerage & agency serv
May Dept Stores	Large department store chain
McDonald's Corp	Fast food restaurant:franch'g
Medtronic, Inc	Cardiac pacemakers:med.serv
Merck & Co	Ethical drugs/specialty chem
Minnesota Min'g/Mfg	Scotch tapes: coated abrasives
Newell Co	Mfr,mkt consumer products
Nordstrom, Inc	Dept stores:upscale apparel
Pep Boys–Man,Mo,Ja	Retail chain: auto parts, etc.
PepsiCo Inc	Soft drink:snack fd/food svc
Philip Morris Cos	Cigarettes,food prod,brew'g
Pitney Bowes	Postage meters: mailing sys
Raytheon Co	Defense&comm'l electr:constr
Rubbermaid, Inc	Mfr plastic/rubber housewre
Schering–Plough	Pharmaceut'l/consumer prod
Sigma–Aldrich	Specialty chem prod
SunTrust Banks	Comm'l bkg,Georgia,FL,Tenn
Sysco Corp	Food distr & service systems
Torchmark Corp	Insurance:fin'l services
UST Inc	Snuff,tobacco,wine,spirits
Wal–Mart Stores	Operates discount stores
Walgreen Co	Major retail drug chain
Winn–Dixie Stores	Food supermarkets in south
Wrigley, (Wm) Jr	Major chewing gum producer

Chart based on October 20, 1995 prices and data.

Fast-Rising Dividends

Based on the issues in this handbook, the companies below were chosen on the basis of their five-year annual growth rate in dividends from 1990 to the current 12-month indicated rate. All have increased their dividend payments each calendar year from 1990 to their current 12-month indicated rate.

Company	-- $ Divd. -- Paid 1990	Paid 1994	†Ind. Divd. Rate	*Divd. Growth Rate %	Price	% Yield
U.S. HealthCare	0.10	0.72	1.00	59.21	35.75	2.8
Mattel, Inc	0.02	0.18	0.24	59.03	27.12	0.9
Home Depot	0.04	0.15	0.20	40.19	38.12	0.5
Travelers Group	0.18	0.57	0.80	35.27	50.50	1.6
Sysco Corp	0.10	0.36	0.44	34.92	30.50	1.4
Federal Natl Mtge	0.72	2.40	2.72	30.97	103.00	2.6
Hewlett-Packard	0.21	0.55	0.80	30.78	88.75	0.9
Archer-Daniels-Midland	0.05	0.07	0.20	25.04	16.25	1.2
Wal-Mart Stores	0.07	0.16	0.20	24.90	23.00	0.9
UNUM Corp	0.38	0.92	1.06	23.01	54.25	2.0
Cooper Tire & Rubber	0.10	0.23	0.30	22.57	23.62	1.3
Circuit City Stores	0.04	0.09	0.12	22.06	35.00	0.3
Campbell Soup	0.50	1.12	1.24	21.30	52.50	2.4
Medtronic, Inc	0.10	0.19	0.26	21.08	55.25	0.5
Disney (Walt) Co	0.14	0.29	0.36	20.67	57.25	0.6
Philip Morris Cos	1.46	2.85	4.00	20.58	85.62	4.7
Hasbro Inc	0.13	0.27	0.32	20.52	29.50	1.1
Fluor Corp	0.24	0.52	0.60	19.45	56.50	1.1
UST Inc	0.55	1.12	1.30	18.94	29.87	4.4
Pall Corp	0.19	0.37	0.42	18.04	24.12	1.7
Conrail Inc	0.75	1.40	1.70	17.93	70.12	2.4
Norwest Corp	0.42	0.77	0.96	17.80	32.00	3.0
Gillette Co	0.26	0.48	0.60	17.68	48.87	1.2
ConAgra Inc	0.41	0.75	0.95	17.43	39.75	2.4
Coca-Cola Co	0.40	0.78	0.88	17.33	72.37	1.2
Federal Home Loan	0.53	1.04	1.20	17.15	68.62	1.7
Albertson's, Inc	0.23	0.42	0.52	17.10	34.37	1.5
Nucor Corp	0.12	0.17	0.28	16.72	46.12	0.6
Schering-Plough	0.53	0.99	1.16	16.59	54.00	2.1
PepsiCo Inc	0.37	0.68	0.80	16.54	52.62	1.5
Golden West Finl	0.17	0.31	0.34	16.16	52.50	0.6
Automatic Data Proc	0.33	0.56	0.70	15.92	72.87	1.0
Banc One Corp	0.67	1.21	1.36	15.89	36.37	3.7
Abbott Laboratories	0.40	0.74	0.84	15.72	40.37	2.1
Merck & Co	0.64	1.14	1.36	15.64	60.00	2.3
Walgreen Co	0.21	0.35	0.44	15.62	28.00	1.6
Colgate-Palmolive	0.90	1.54	1.88	15.59	70.25	2.7
Great Lakes Che	0.22	0.38	0.46	15.20	67.75	0.7
Pitney Bowes	0.60	1.04	1.20	14.97	42.87	2.8
Amer Stores	0.27	0.46	0.56	14.93	29.50	1.9

Company	-- $ Divd. -- Paid 1990	Paid 1994	†Ind. Divd. Rate	*Divd. Growth Rate %	Price	% Yield
Johnson & Johnson	0.66	1.13	1.32	14.64	79.75	1.7
Jefferson-Pilot	0.99	1.68	1.92	14.62	68.62	2.8
First Union Corp	1.08	1.72	2.08	14.45	52.00	4.0
Illinois Tool Works	0.33	0.54	0.68	14.05	59.00	1.2
Rubbermaid, Inc	0.27	0.46	0.50	13.46	26.12	1.9
Block (H & R)	0.68	1.15	1.28	13.40	41.25	3.1
Mallinckrodt Group	0.33	0.52	0.62	13.30	36.62	1.7
Anheuser-Busch Cos	0.94	1.52	1.76	13.21	65.75	2.7
Amer Greetings Cl'A'	0.34	0.53	0.64	13.05	31.12	2.1
Baxter International	0.62	1.01	1.13	12.74	40.50	2.8
U.S. Bancorp	0.58	0.91	1.12	12.66	31.50	3.6
Amer Intl Group	0.18	0.29	0.34	12.54	85.25	0.4
Heinz (H.J.)	0.87	1.35	1.59	12.26	47.25	3.4
Morgan Stanley Grp	0.75	1.20	1.28	12.21	87.87	1.5
Engelhard Corp	0.20	0.31	0.36	12.17	25.87	1.4
BankAmerica Corp	1.00	1.60	1.84	12.06	62.62	2.9
Pfizer, Inc	0.60	0.94	1.04	11.91	61.00	1.7
Genl Electric	0.94	1.44	1.64	11.90	64.62	2.5
Bankers Trust NY	2.33	3.60	4.00	11.65	64.87	6.2
Wachovia Corp	0.82	1.23	1.44	11.44	47.87	3.0
Warner-Lambert	1.52	2.44	2.60	11.39	87.25	3.0
Winn-Dixie Stores	1.03	1.49	1.80	11.23	63.37	2.8
Bemis Co	0.36	0.54	0.64	11.20	26.00	2.5
Intl Flavors/Fragr	0.72	1.08	1.24	11.20	48.12	2.6
SunTrust Banks	0.86	1.32	1.44	11.20	66.87	2.2
Procter & Gamble	0.93	1.32	1.60	11.02	81.00	2.0
Sherwin-Williams	0.38	0.56	0.64	10.82	36.62	1.7
KeyCorp	0.88	1.28	1.44	10.79	35.75	4.0
Morgan (J.P.)	1.82	2.72	3.00	10.67	79.75	3.8
Interpublic Grp Cos	0.37	0.55	0.62	10.58	40.00	1.6
Providian Corp	0.54	0.80	0.90	10.57	42.12	2.1
Republic New York	0.87	1.26	1.44	10.53	62.12	2.3
Avery Dennison Crp	0.64	0.99	1.08	10.52	44.00	2.5
Allergan, Inc	0.28	0.42	0.48	10.42	31.37	1.5
SAFECO Corp	1.28	1.88	2.12	10.40	67.18	3.2
Pep Boys-Man,Mo,Ja	0.12	0.17	0.19	10.30	24.00	0.8
Luby's Cafeterias	0.43	0.61	0.72	10.24	21.00	3.4
Foster Wheeler	0.48	0.72	0.78	10.18	37.00	2.1
Louisiana Pacific	0.35	0.48	0.56	10.17	24.12	2.3
Bausch & Lomb	0.64	0.93	1.04	10.06	35.87	2.9

†12-month indicated rate. *Five-year annual compounded growth rate.
Chart based on October 20, 1995 prices and data.

Higher Dividends For Ten Years

These companies have all paid higher cash dividends in each of the past ten calendar years and currently yield at least 2%. To be able to increase dividends under the difficult economic conditions that were experienced at times over the past ten years, indicates healthy finances and capable management.

Company	Price	†Ind. Divd. Rate	% Yield
Abbott Laboratories	40.37	0.84	2.1
Air Products & Chem	51.12	1.04	2.0
ALLTEL Corp	30.00	0.96	3.2
Amer Brands	42.25	2.00	4.7
Amer Home Products	88.37	3.00	3.4
Ameritech Corp	53.75	2.00	3.7
AMP Inc	40.37	0.92	2.3
Anheuser-Busch Cos	65.75	1.76	2.7
Avery Dennison Corp	44.00	1.08	2.5
Banc One Corp	36.37	1.36	3.7
Bankers Trust NY	64.87	4.00	6.2
Bard (C.R.)	29.12	0.64	2.2
Baxter International	40.50	1.13	2.8
Bell Atlantic Corp	63.75	2.80	4.4
Bemis Co	26.00	0.64	2.5
Block (H & R)	41.25	1.28	3.1
Boatmen's Bancshares	39.12	1.48	3.8
Bristol-Myers Squibb	76.37	2.96	3.9
Brown-Forman Cl'B'	39.50	0.99	2.5
Campbell Soup	52.50	1.24	2.4
Central & So. West	27.00	1.72	6.4
Chubb Corp	94.50	1.96	2.1
Clorox Co	72.50	2.12	2.9
ConAgra Inc	39.75	0.95	2.4
Consolidated Edison	30.75	2.04	6.6
Dayton Hudson	73.62	1.76	2.4
Deluxe Corp	32.00	1.48	4.6
Dominion Resources	40.50	2.58	6.4
duPont(EI)deNemours	66.75	2.08	3.1
Duke Power	44.75	2.04	4.6

Company	Price	†Ind. Divd. Rate	% Yield
Dun & Bradstreet	59.37	2.64	4.4
Emerson Electric	71.12	1.96	2.8
Exxon Corp	75.75	3.00	4.0
Federal Natl Mtge	103.00	2.72	2.6
First Union Corp	52.00	2.08	4.0
Fleetwood Enterpr	20.50	0.60	2.9
Gannett Co	55.00	1.40	2.5
Genl Electric	64.62	1.64	2.5
Giant Food Cl'A'	31.75	0.74	2.3
Harland (John H.)	22.00	1.02	4.6
Heinz (H.J.)	47.25	1.59	3.4
Honeywell, Inc	43.87	1.04	2.4
Household Intl	62.50	1.36	2.2
Intl Flavors/Fragr	48.12	1.24	2.6
Jefferson–Pilot	68.62	1.92	2.8
Kellogg Co	74.62	1.56	2.1
KeyCorp	35.75	1.44	4.0
Kimberly–Clark	70.62	1.80	2.5
Lilly (Eli)	94.37	2.74	2.9
Lincoln Natl Corp	45.87	1.72	3.7
Louisiana Pacific	24.12	0.56	2.3
Luby's Cafeterias	21.00	0.72	3.4
Marsh & McLennan	85.75	3.20	3.7
Masco Corp	28.12	0.76	2.7
May Dept Stores	40.25	1.14	2.8
McGraw-Hill Cos.	81.25	2.40	3.0
Merck & Co	60.00	1.36	2.3
Minnesota Min'g/Mfg	56.50	1.88	3.3
Monsanto Co	102.62	2.76	2.7
Morgan (J.P.)	79.75	3.00	3.8

Company	Price	†Ind. Divd. Rate	% Yield
NBD Bancorp	39.25	1.32	3.4
Natl Service Indus	30.12	1.12	3.7
NationsBank Corp	70.00	2.00	2.9
Northern States Pwr	47.62	2.70	5.7
PPG Indus	43.50	1.20	2.8
Peoples Energy	28.50	1.80	6.3
Philip Morris Cos	85.62	4.00	4.7
Pitney Bowes	42.87	1.20	2.8
Potlatch Corp	41.87	1.64	3.9
Procter & Gamble	81.00	1.60	2.0
Providian Corp	42.12	0.90	2.1
Quaker Oats	34.75	1.14	3.3
Republic New York	62.12	1.44	2.3
Rockwell Intl	45.87	1.08	2.4
Rohm & Haas	54.87	1.64	3.0
SBC Communications	55.25	1.65	3.0
SAFECO Corp	67.18	2.12	3.2
Schering–Plough	54.00	1.16	2.1
Stanley Works	46.00	1.44	3.1
SunTrust Banks	66.87	1.44	2.2
Supervalu Inc	30.62	0.98	3.2
Temple–Inland	47.87	1.20	2.5
Torchmark Corp	43.62	1.16	2.7
UST Inc	29.87	1.30	4.4
Union Electric	39.50	2.50	6.3
U.S. Bancorp	31.50	1.12	3.6
USLIFE Corp	29.75	0.93	3.1
V.F. Corp	47.87	1.44	3.0
Wachovia Corp	47.87	1.44	3.0
Warner–Lambert	87.25	2.60	3.0

†12-month indicated rate.
Chart based on October 20, 1995 prices and data.

S&P 500 STOCK SCREENS

Stock Reports

In using the Stock Reports in this handbook, please pay particular attention to the dates attached to each evaluation, recommendation, or analysis section. Opinions rendered are as of that date and may change often. It is strongly suggested that before investing in any security you should obtain the current analysis on that issue.

To order the latest Standard & Poor's Stock Report on a company, for as little as $2.00 per report, please call:

S&P Reports On-Demand at 1-800-292-0808.

AMP Inc.

NYSE Symbol **AMP**
In S&P 500

11-OCT-95

Industry:
Electronics/Electric

Summary: The world's largest producer of electronic and electrical connection devices, AMP derives nearly 60% of its revenues from international operations.

S&P Opinion: Hold (★★★)	Recent Price • 37⅞	Yield • 2.5%
	52 Wk Range • 46¼-33¾	12-Mo. P/E • 20.1

Quantitative Evaluations

Outlook
(1 Lowest—5 Highest)
• **4+**

Fair Value
• **40¼**

Risk
• **Low**

Earn./Div. Rank
• **A-**

Technical Eval.
• **Bearish** since 7/95

Rel. Strength Rank
(1 Lowest—99 Highest)
• **21**

Insider Activity
• **Neutral**

Earnings vs. Previous Year
▲=Up ▼=Down ▶=No Change

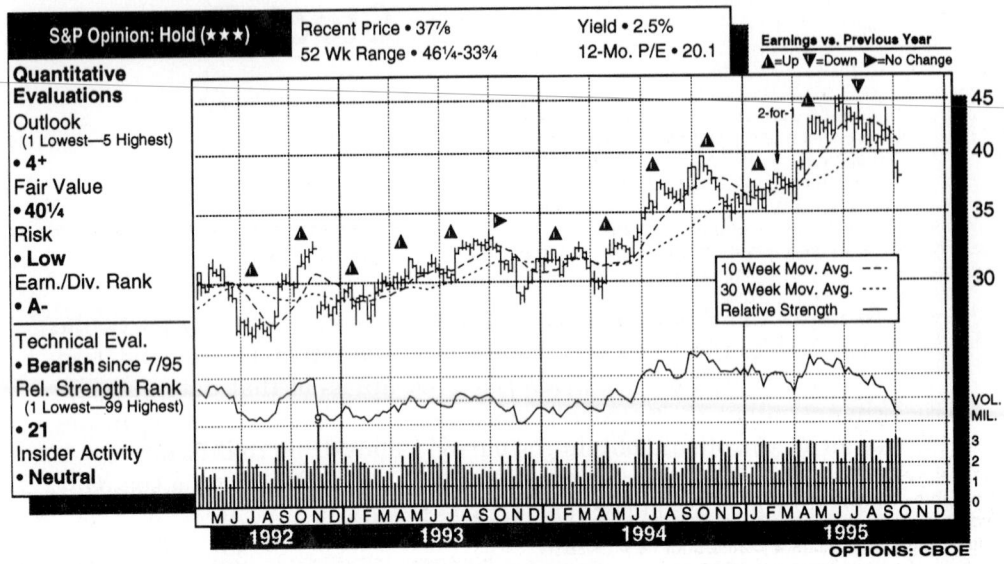

Earnings vs. Previous Year
▲=Up ▼=Down ▶=No Change

10 Week Mov. Avg. - - -
30 Week Mov. Avg. ·····
Relative Strength —

2-for-1

VOL. MIL.

M J J A S O N D J F M A M J J A S O N D J F M A M J J A S O N D J F M A M J J A S O N D
1992 1993 1994 1995

OPTIONS: CBOE

Overview - 11-OCT-95

Sales for 1996 are expected to advance approximately 15%, reflecting the broadly positive effect of stronger economic growth throughout the world, especially in Europe. Sales will also benefit from new product introductions, a further gain in market share, and acquisitions. In addition, the company will expand into value-added assemblies and new geographic markets. Margins should benefit from the higher volume, lessening pressure on prices, and well controlled expenses. Recent efforts to consolidate operations, restrain employment and modernize facilities should assist in expense control.

Valuation - 11-OCT-95

AMP's shares have recently sold off due to a lowering of expectations by analysts and weakness in electronics stocks in general. While the earnings outlook remains favorable and AMP is well positioned in many rapidly growing international markets, its current multiple incorporates this bright outlook. The connector industry remains inherently competitive and vulnerable to economic cycles. In addition, over the long-term the trend towards miniaturization presents a negative. While AMP's targeting of new markets expands the potential markets the company addresses from approximately $25 billion to around $60-80 billion and enhances growth prospects in the years ahead, these efforts are unlikely to have a major impact in the near-term.

Key Stock Statistics

S&P EPS Est. 1995	2.05	Tang. Bk. Value/Share	11.66
P/E on S&P Est. 1995	18.5	Beta	0.72
S&P EPS Est. 1996	2.40	Shareholders	9,200
Dividend Rate/Share	0.92	Market cap. (B)	$ 8.1
Shs. outstg. (M)	217.6	Inst. holdings	76%
Avg. daily vol. (M)	0.946	Insider holdings	NA

Value of $10,000 invested 5 years ago: $ 19,714

Fiscal Year Ending Dec. 31

	1995	% Change	1994	% Change	1993	% Change
Revenues (Million $)						
1Q	1,203	33%	906.1	8%	838.0	2%
2Q	1,336	33%	1,004	14%	882.7	7%
3Q	—	—	1,020	19%	857.4	1%
4Q	—	—	1,097	26%	873.0	3%
Yr.	—	—	4,027	17%	3,451	3%
Income (Million $)						
1Q	104.8	32%	79.55	10%	72.52	3%
2Q	97.52	2%	95.82	27%	75.73	5%
3Q	—	—	93.17	20%	77.40	NM
4Q	—	—	100.9	42%	71.00	NM
Yr.	—	—	369.4	25%	296.7	2%
Earnings Per Share ($)						
1Q	0.50	32%	0.38	10%	0.35	5%
2Q	0.45	-1%	0.46	26%	0.36	6%
3Q	E0.52	17%	0.44	20%	0.37	NM
4Q	E0.58	21%	0.48	41%	0.34	1%
Yr.	E2.05	16%	1.76	25%	1.41	3%

Next earnings report expected: late October

Business Summary - 11-OCT-95

AMP Inc. is the world's leading producer of electrical and electronic connection devices.

More than 100,000 types and sizes of products, including terminals; fiber-optic, printed circuit board and cable connectors ans assemblies; connectorized printed circuit boards; cable and cabling systems; wide and local area network products and systems; and related application tools and machines. The products comprise approximately 235 product families. Nearly 90% of the company's business is in electronic/electrical connection, switching and programming devices and associated application tools and machines.

The company's products have potential uses wherever an electronic, electrical, computer or telecommunications system is involved, and are becoming increasingly critical to the performance of these systems as voice, data and video communications converge. Products are supplied to more than 200,000 original electrical/electronic equipment manufacturers, as well as to customers that install and maintain the equipment.

While the company is seeking to widen its leadership in the terminal and connector product area, it is also steadily diversifying into total interconnection systems and higher value assemblies. This is increasing the potential markets being addressed by the company from approximately $25 billion to around $60-80 billion.

International operations accounted for 58% of sales and 51% of pretax income in 1994.

Research, development and engineering expenditures totaled $456.0 million (11.3% of sales) in 1994, down from $406.0 million (11.8%) in 1993. AMP has been among the top 50 U.S. corporations in patents awarded for many years.

Important Developments

Sep. '95—The company said that its third quarter sales should approach $1.30 billion, up about 15% or more from $1.11 billion in the year earlier period and down slightly from the second quarter. The decrease from the second quarter should reflect seasonal effects, a barely growing Japanese economy, a leveling off in car production in Europe and Japan, and a little higher average value of the dollar against the yen and D-mark from the second quarter. It added that it estimated per share third quarter earnings would be $0.50 to $0.53. Commenting on its full year projections, the company said that sales growth by regions in local currencies for the entire year looked like 12-15% in the Americas and Asia-Pacific and about 20% in Europe.

Capitalization

Long Term Debt: $309,413,000 (6/95).

Per Share Data ($)

(Year Ended Dec. 31)

	1994	1993	1992	1991	1990	1989
Tangible Bk. Val.	11.14	9.80	9.26	9.02	8.46	7.64
Cash Flow	3.19	2.66	2.74	2.34	2.32	2.11
Earnings	1.76	1.42	1.38	1.23	1.35	1.32
Dividends	Nil	0.80	0.76	0.72	0.68	0.60
Payout Ratio	Nil	57%	55%	59%	50%	45%
Prices - High	39¾	33⅝	34⅜	30	27⅝	24¾
- Low	28⅞	27⅜	26⅜	20½	19	20
P/E Ratio - High	23	24	25	24	20	19
- Low	16	19	19	17	14	15

Income Statement Analysis (Million $)

	1994	%Chg	1993	%Chg	1992	%Chg	1991
Revs.	4,027	17%	3,451	3%	3,337	8%	3,095
Oper. Inc.	947	20%	787	-4%	821	16%	706
Depr.	300	15%	262	-9%	288	22%	236
Int. Exp.	20.0	3%	19.5	-34%	29.5	-29%	41.6
Pretax Inc.	594	22%	486	1%	479	13%	424
Eff. Tax Rate	38%	—	39%	—	39%	—	39%
Net Inc.	369	24%	297	2%	290	12%	260

Balance Sheet & Other Fin. Data (Million $)

	1994	1993	1992	1991	1990	1989
Cash	395	407	478	451	460	334
Curr. Assets	2,012	1,644	1,614	1,616	1,618	1,437
Total Assets	3,771	3,118	3,005	3,007	2,929	2,530
Curr. Liab.	1,011	752	845	888	953	725
LT Debt	211	131	42.9	53.0	61.1	69.5
Common Eqty.	2,334	2,056	1,943	1,913	1,793	1,625
Total Cap.	2,595	2,241	2,061	2,043	1,934	1,767
Cap. Exp.	457	330	312	313	338	252
Cash Flow	669	559	578	496	494	451

Ratio Analysis

	1994	1993	1992	1991	1990	1989
Curr. Ratio	2.0	2.2	1.9	1.8	1.7	2.0
% LT Debt of Cap.	8.1	5.8	2.1	2.6	3.2	3.9
% Net Inc.of Revs.	9.2	8.6	8.7	8.4	9.4	10.0
% Ret. on Assets	10.7	9.7	9.7	8.7	10.5	11.5
% Ret. on Equity	16.8	14.8	15.1	14.0	16.8	17.9

Dividend Data

Dividends have been paid since 1951. A dividend reinvestment plan is available.

Amt. of Div. $	Date Decl.	Ex-Div. Date	Stock of Record	Payment Date
0.420	Oct. 26	Nov. 01	Nov. 07	Dec. 01 '94
0.460	Jan. 25	Jan. 31	Feb. 06	Mar. 01 '95
2-for-1	Jan. 25	Mar. 02	Feb. 06	Mar. 01 '95
0.230	Apr. 28	May. 02	May. 08	Jun. 01 '95
0.230	Jul. 26	Aug. 03	Aug. 07	Sep. 01 '95

Data as orig. reptd.; bef. results of disc. opers. and/or spec. items. Per share data adj. for stk. divs. as of ex-div. date.
E-Estimated. NA-Not Available. NM-Not Meaningful. NR-Not Ranked.

Office—Friendship Rd., Harrisburg, PA 17105-3608. **Tel**—(717) 564-0100. **Chrmn**—J. E. Marley. **Pres & CEO**—W. J. Hudson. **Exec VP-CFO**—B. Savidge. **VP-Fin**—R. M. Ripp. **Secy**—D. F. Henschel. **Investor Contact**—William Oakland. **Dirs**—D. F. Baker, R. D. DeNunzio, B. H. Franklin, J. M. Hixon III, W. J. Hudson, J. E. Marley, H. A. McInnes, J. C. Morley, W. F. Raab, P. G. Schloemer, T. Shiina. **Transfer Agents & Registrars**—Chemical Bank, NYC. **Incorporated** in New Jersey in 1941. **Empl**-36,100. **S&P Analyst:** Paul H. Valentine, CFA

STANDARD & POOR'S
STOCK REPORTS

AMR Corp.

NYSE Symbol **AMR**
In S&P 500

25-JUL-95   **Industry:** Air Transport

Summary: This holding company's principal subsidiary is American Airlines. Other activities include a computer reservation system and a general airline services group.

S&P Opinion: Accumulate (★★★★)

Recent Price • 75⅛	Yield • Nil
52 Wk Range • 80¼-48⅛	12-Mo. P/E • 20.1

Quantitative Evaluations

Outlook
(1 Lowest—5 Highest)
• **3+**

Fair Value
• **76⅜**

Risk
• **Low**

Earn./Div. Rank
• **C**

Technical Eval.
• **Bearish** since 3/95

Rel. Strength Rank
(1 Lowest—99 Highest)
• **50**

Insider Activity
• **Neutral**

Earnings vs. Previous Year
▲=Up ▼=Down ▶=No Change

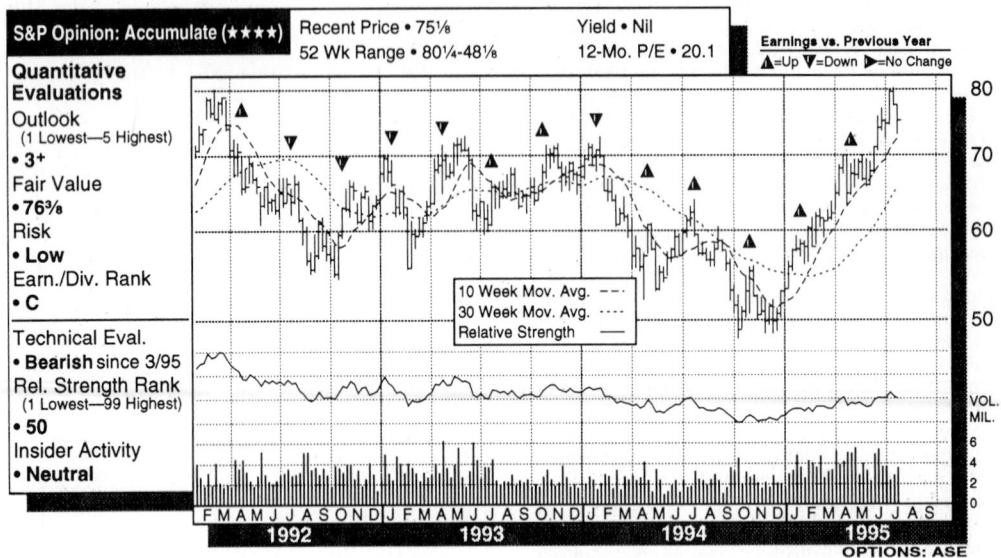

10 Week Mov. Avg. – – –
30 Week Mov. Avg. ·······
Relative Strength ——

OPTIONS: ASE

Overview - 25-JUL-95

Revenues for 1995 are forecast to rise modestly from those of 1994. American Airlines will continue to modify its route system as part of its transitional program. The trend is towards the longer haul and international routes. Capacity is expected to grow slightly, despite a planned reduction in fleet size. Passenger traffic is projected to increase moderately, but lower average fares are anticipated. Unit costs should decline, due to the longer average stage length, lower travel agent commissions and the effects of cost reduction initiatives. Accordingly, margin growth should be fairly healthy. Gains will be limited by greater interest charges, but share earnings will benefit from the reduction of preferred stock.

Valuation - 25-JUL-95

AMR shares have climbed significantly since the beginning of the year, reflecting improved industry traffic and higher average fares. With its size, American should be a major beneficiary of this industry growth. In addition, the carrier is projected to continue its lead in attracting premium (business) traffic. Cost reduction programs should help restrain expenses. To this end, the carrier's ability to secure its planned $750 million in wage concessions is particularly important. Expect the stock to react to news relating to negotiations with its unions. Nevertheless, AMR shares trade at a low cash flow and price multiple.

Key Stock Statistics

S&P EPS Est. 1995	7.50	Tang. Bk. Value/Share	24.87
P/E on S&P Est. 1995	10.0	Beta	1.60
S&P EPS Est. 1996	7.50	Shareholders	17,200
Dividend Rate/Share	Nil	Market cap. (B)	$ 5.6
Shs. outstg. (M)	76.0	Inst. holdings	88%
Avg. daily vol. (M)	0.632	Insider holdings	NA

Value of $10,000 invested 5 years ago: $ 12,952

Fiscal Year Ending Dec. 31

	1995	% Change	1994	% Change	1993	% Change
Revenues (Million $)						
1Q	3,970	4%	3,808	NM	3,814	9%
2Q	4,307	5%	4,101	-3%	4,212	17%
3Q	—	—	4,233	NM	4,199	13%
4Q	—	—	3,995	11%	3,591	NM
Yr.	—	—	16,137	2%	15,816	10%
Income (Million $)						
1Q	38.00	NM	-7.00	NM	-22.00	NM
2Q	192.0	25%	153.0	NM	47.00	NM
3Q	—	—	205.0	64%	125.0	NM
4Q	—	—	-123.0	NM	-246.0	23%
Yr.	—	—	228.0	NM	-96.00	NM
Earnings Per Share ($)						
1Q	0.48	NM	-0.30	NM	-0.43	NM
2Q	2.48	40%	1.77	NM	0.39	NM
3Q	E3.02	—	2.47	73%	1.43	NM
4Q	E1.52	—	-1.70	NM	-3.47	NM
Yr.	E7.50	—	2.26	NM	-2.05	NM

Next earnings report expected: mid October

Business Summary - 25-JUL-95

AMR Corp. is the parent company of American Airlines, the SABRE Group and the AMR Management Services Group.

At the end of 1994, American Airlines provided service to 170 destinations throughout the world. Its domestic hubs are at Dallas/Ft. Worth, Chicago, Nashville, San Juan, and Miami. A substantial reduction in service to the Raleigh/Durham hub was announced in January 1995. American Eagle consists of four regional airlines that provide connecting turboprop service at seven of American's high-traffic cities to smaller markets. The cargo division provides a full range of freight and mail services to shippers throughout the airline's system.

Operating data for American Airlines (passenger- and seat-miles in billions):

	1994	1993	1992
Rev. pass-miles	98.90	97.16	97.43
Avail. seat-miles	152.67	160.89	153.00
Load factor %	64.8	60.4	63.7
Rev. per RPM(cents)	12.97	13.28	12.21
Cost per ASM(cents)	8.34	8.25	---

SABRE Group operates the one of largest computer reservations systems and provides data processing, information management, computer and development services to the travel and other industries.

AMR Management Services provides ground, cargo and cabin services to other airlines, leases aircraft to American Eagle, serves as an investment adviser, and provides training services.

At March 31, 1995, American's fleet totaled 648 jet aircraft, comprising 35 A300-600Rs, 81 B-727-200s, 84 B-757-200s, 30 B-767-200s, 41 B-767-300s, 260 MD-80s, 23 DC-10s, 19 MD-11s and 75 F-100s. American Eagle carriers operated 267 regional aircraft.

Important Developments

Jul. '95—American Airlines' passenger traffic in the first six months of 1994 increased 1.8%, year to year; capacity was down 5.1%, and the load factor rose to 63.7% from 58.8%.

Mar. '95—The company announced plans to reduce annual administrative costs by $93 million in 1996; savings of $38 million were forecast for 1995.

Feb. '95—American Airlines changed its travel agent commission structure by introducing a maximum commission payment of $50 for any round-trip domestic ticket and $25 for any one-way domestic ticket. Total 1994 commissions to agents exceeded $1.3 billion.

Capitalization

Long Term Debt: $7,667,000,000 (3/95), incl. $2.25 billion of capital lease obligations.

Depositary Preferred Stock: 1,592,610 shs. ($50 liquid. pref.); conv. into com. at $79 a sh. Each represents 0.10 sh. of 6% series A conv.

Per Share Data ($) (Year Ended Dec. 31)

	1994	1993	1992	1991	1990	1989
Tangible Bk. Val.	43.50	22.86	22.05	35.28	48.50	55.05
Cash Flow	18.70	13.16	6.74	8.57	10.40	16.33
Earnings	2.26	-2.05	-6.35	-3.54	-0.64	7.16
Dividends	Nil	Nil	Nil	Nil	Nil	Nil
Payout Ratio	Nil	Nil	Nil	Nil	Nil	Nil
Prices - High	72¾	72⅞	80¼	71⅛	70¼	107½
- Low	48⅛	55½	54⅜	44¼	39¾	52⅛
P/E Ratio - High	32	NM	NM	NM	NM	15
- Low	21	NM	NM	NM	NM	7

Income Statement Analysis (Million $)

	1994	%Chg	1993	%Chg	1992	%Chg	1991
Revs.	16,137	3%	15,701	9%	14,396	12%	12,887
Oper. Inc.	2,537	47%	1,731	81%	955	16%	826
Depr.	1,253	8%	1,156	18%	980	19%	821
Int. Exp.	637	-5%	668	3%	651	28%	508
Pretax Inc.	370	NM	-112	NM	-696	NM	-339
Eff. Tax Rate	38%	—	NM	—	NM	—	NM
Net Inc.	228	NM	-96.0	NM	-474	NM	-239

Balance Sheet & Other Fin. Data (Million $)

	1994	1993	1992	1991	1990	1989
Cash	777	586	858	1,249	949	601
Curr. Assets	3,118	2,690	2,868	2,806	2,658	2,091
Total Assets	19,486	19,326	18,706	16,208	13,354	10,877
Curr. Liab.	4,914	4,417	4,720	4,742	4,825	3,479
LT Debt	7,878	7,554	7,838	5,879	3,272	2,306
Common Eqty.	3,302	3,195	3,349	3,794	3,727	3,766
Total Cap.	11,537	12,140	11,383	10,214	7,650	6,874
Cap. Exp.	1,114	2,577	3,881	3,918	2,479	1,897
Cash Flow	1,425	1,000	505	581	648	1,028

Ratio Analysis

	1994	1993	1992	1991	1990	1989
Curr. Ratio	0.6	0.6	0.6	0.6	0.6	0.6
% LT Debt of Cap.	68.3	62.2	68.9	57.6	42.8	33.5
% Net Inc.of Revs.	1.4	NM	NM	NM	NM	4.3
% Ret. on Assets	1.2	NM	NM	NM	NM	4.3
% Ret. on Equity	5.3	NM	NM	NM	NM	12.5

Dividend Data (No dividends have been paid on the common stock since 1980. A "poison pill" stock purchase right was issued in 1986.)

Data as orig. reptd.; bef. results of disc. opers. and/or spec. items. Per share data adj. for stk. divs. as of ex-div. date. E-Estimated. NA-Not Available. NM-Not Meaningful. NR-Not Ranked.

Office—4333 Amon Carter Blvd., Fort Worth, TX 76155. **Tel**—(817) 963-1234. **Chrmn, Pres & CEO**—R. L. Crandall. **EVP-CFO**—D. J. Carty. **Secy**—C. D. MarLett. **Investor Contact**—Linda J. Dill (817-967-2970). **Dirs**—H. P. Allen, D. L. Boren, E. A. Brennan, A. M. Codina, R. L. Crandall, C. F. Edley, C. T. Fisher III, E. G. Graves, D. J. Kelly, A. D. Mc Laughlin, C. H. Pistor Jr., J. M. Rodgers, M. Segall, E. F. Williams Jr. **Transfer Agent & Registrar**—First Chicago Trust Co. of New York, NYC. **Incorporated** in Delaware in 1934; reincorporated in Delaware in 1982. **Empl**-109,208.
S&P Analyst: Joe Victor Shammas

21-OCT-95

Industry:
Telecommunications

Summary: AT&T is the largest U.S. long-distance and cellular telephone company. It also manufactures telecommunications equipment and computers and provides financial services.

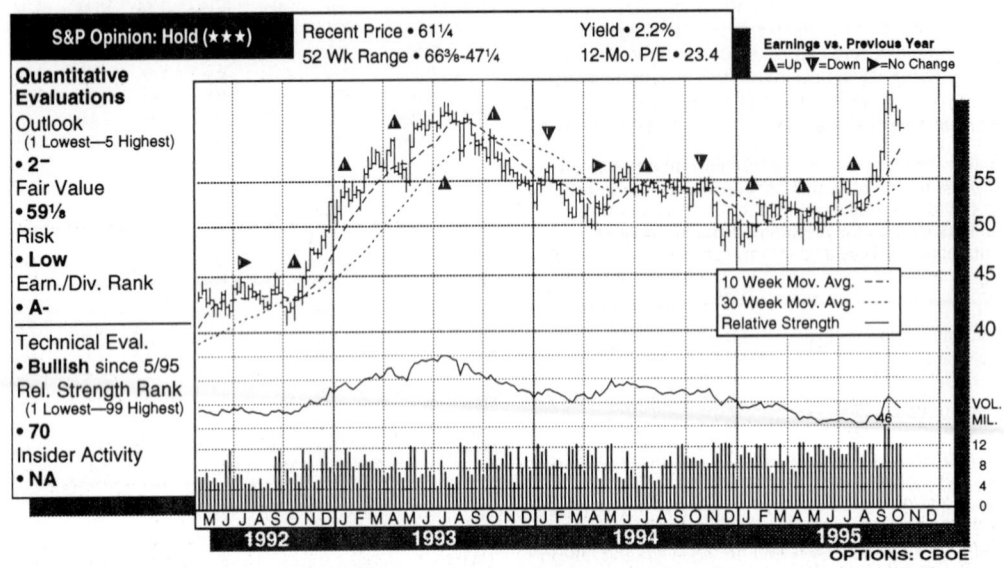

S&P Opinion: Hold (★★★)	Recent Price • 61¼	Yield • 2.2%
	52 Wk Range • 66⅜-47¼	12-Mo. P/E • 23.4

Earnings vs. Previous Year
▲=Up ▼=Down ▶=No Change

Quantitative Evaluations

Outlook
(1 Lowest—5 Highest)
• **2⁻**

Fair Value
• **59⅛**

Risk
• **Low**

Earn./Div. Rank
• **A-**

Technical Eval.
• **Bullish** since 5/95

Rel. Strength Rank
(1 Lowest—99 Highest)
• **70**

Insider Activity
• **NA**

10 Week Mov. Avg. —
30 Week Mov. Avg. ·····
Relative Strength —

1992 1993 1994 1995

VOL. MIL.

OPTIONS: CBOE

Overview - 20-OCT-95

AT&T plans to split into three separate, publicly traded companies. The first will consist of core long-distance operations, wireless services and the credit card business, and will retain the AT&T name. The second company, as yet unnamed, will include equipment manufacturing and Bell Labs. The third will be the troubled Global Information Solutions (GIS) computer unit, formerly known as NCR, which is currently restructuring its operations. The breakup should aid each company by allowing it to focus on its specific business. The equipment unit in particular should benefit from the separation. AT&T's aggressive entry into the toll market and plans to offer local service are penalizing equipment sales, since the regional Bells have become far more reluctant to buy from a competitor.

Valuation - 20-OCT-95

While the shares rose sharply on news of AT&T's breakup plan, they have been relatively flat since then. As part of the plan, AT&T will sell its remaining stake in AT&T Capital Corp., with proceeds to be used to cut debt. An initial public offering of 15% of the equipment unit is expected in 1996's first half, with the full spinoff to be completed by the end of the year. Current shareholders will own shares in each of the three companies. Our 1995 estimate of $2.76 includes a $0.74 charge for the GIS restructuring. While we feel the breakup is an excellent move, it will not be completed until the end of 1996; we expect the shares to be market performers until that time.

Key Stock Statistics

S&P EPS Est. 1995	2.76	Tang. Bk. Value/Share	10.78
P/E on S&P Est. 1995	22.2	Beta	0.63
S&P EPS Est. 1996	3.88	Shareholders	2,302,300
Dividend Rate/Share	1.32	Market cap. (B)	$ 97.2
Shs. outstg. (M)	1586.3	Inst. holdings	36%
Avg. daily vol. (M)	4.098	Insider holdings	NA

Value of $10,000 invested 5 years ago: $ 15,999

Fiscal Year Ending Dec. 31

	1995	% Change	1994	% Change	1993	% Change
Revenues (Million $)						
1Q	18,262	7%	17,097	9%	15,719	2%
2Q	19,512	7%	18,238	12%	16,316	3%
3Q	19,704	6%	18,649	12%	16,662	3%
4Q	—	—	21,110	14%	18,459	5%
Yr.	—	—	75,094	12%	67,156	3%
Income (Million $)						
1Q	1,198	12%	1,074	15%	936.0	6%
2Q	1,355	9%	1,248	24%	1,005	5%
3Q	262.0	-75%	1,050	NM	1,051	9%
4Q	—	—	1,338	36%	982.0	-2%
Yr.	—	—	4,710	19%	3,974	4%
Earnings Per Share ($)						
1Q	0.76	10%	0.69	NM	0.69	3%
2Q	0.85	6%	0.80	8%	0.74	3%
3Q	0.16	-76%	0.67	-14%	0.78	8%
4Q	E0.99	16%	0.85	18%	0.72	-4%
Yr.	E2.76	-8%	3.01	2%	2.94	3%

Next earnings report expected: late January

Business Summary - 03-OCT-95

AT&T Corp. provides domestic and international information movement and management services and products, as well as leasing and financial services. Revenue contributions in recent years were:

	1994	1993
Telecommunication services	58%	60%
Sales of products & systems	28%	26%
Rentals & other services	10%	10%
Financial services & leasing	4%	4%

AT&T's offerings for the information movement and management business combine communications and computing applications and products. The company provides long-distance communication services throughout the U.S. and internationally to virtually all nations and territories. Through the September 1994 acquisition of McCaw Cellular, AT&T is now also the largest U.S. provider of cellular telephone services. In addition, it manufactures a range of customer premises equipment, data communications and computer products, switching and transmission equipment and components for high-technology products and systems.

The company participates in a number of international marketing and manufacturing joint ventures and also holds interests in various international telephone services companies. Bell Laboratories designs and develops new products and carries out basic research.

AT&T Capital Corp. (87% owned) provides direct financing and finance leasing for its own and other companies products. The company also provides consumer credit through the AT&T Universal Card.

Important Developments

Aug. '95—AT&T created three businesses to offer services to facilitate Internet use. They will provide Internet access, help businesses reach customers and complete secure sales transactions on the Internet, and offer content services.
Jun. '95—The McCaw Cellular unit agreed to settle shareholder lawsuits related to its proposed acquisition of the 48% of LIN Broadcasting it does not already own. McCaw would raise the purchase price to $129.50 a share, from its previous offer of the appraised value of $127.50. The transaction was expected to close in late September or early October.
Mar. '95—AT&T placed winning bids totaling $1.7 billion for 21 licenses in the FCC's auction of personal communications services (PCS) licenses.

Capitalization

Long Term Debt: $13,450,000,000 (6/95).
Minority Interests: $1,190,000,000.

Per Share Data ($)

(Year Ended Dec. 31)

	1994	1993	1992	1991	1990	1989
Tangible Bk. Val.	8.07	9.58	13.55	11.90	12.42	11.45
Cash Flow	5.66	5.62	5.57	3.42	5.63	5.62
Earnings	3.01	2.94	2.86	0.40	2.51	2.50
Dividends	1.32	1.32	1.32	1.32	1.32	1.20
Payout Ratio	44%	45%	46%	331%	53%	48%
Prices - High	57⅛	65	53⅛	40⅜	46⅝	47⅜
- Low	47¼	50⅛	36⅝	29	29	28⅛
P/E Ratio - High	19	22	19	NM	19	19
- Low	16	17	13	NM	12	11

Income Statement Analysis (Million $)

	1994	%Chg	1993	%Chg	1992	%Chg	1991
Revs.	75,094	12%	67,156	5%	64,089	2%	63,089
Oper. Inc.	13,137	33%	9,864	NM	9,941	5%	9,451
Depr.	4,136	14%	3,626	NM	3,608	-7%	3,897
Int. Exp.	1,520	169%	566	-22%	725	-10%	805
Pretax Inc.	7,582	22%	6,204	5%	5,902	NM	883
Eff. Tax Rate	37%	—	36%	—	36%	—	41%
Net Inc.	4,710	19%	3,974	4%	3,807	NM	522

Balance Sheet & Other Fin. Data (Million $)

	1994	1993	1992	1991	1990	1989
Cash	1,208	532	1,310	2,148	1,389	1,183
Curr. Assets	37,611	29,738	26,514	24,613	17,776	15,291
Total Assets	79,262	60,766	57,188	53,355	43,775	37,687
Curr. Liab.	30,930	25,334	21,386	20,991	15,089	12,237
LT Debt	11,358	6,812	8,604	8,484	9,118	8,144
Common Eqty.	17,921	13,850	18,921	16,228	14,093	12,738
Total Cap.	34,517	21,789	32,987	29,123	26,935	23,771
Cap. Exp.	5,304	3,701	4,183	4,093	3,667	3,757
Cash Flow	8,846	7,600	7,415	4,419	6,131	6,053

Ratio Analysis

	1994	1993	1992	1991	1990	1989
Curr. Ratio	1.2	1.2	1.2	1.2	1.2	1.2
% LT Debt of Cap.	32.9	31.3	26.1	29.1	33.9	34.3
% Net Inc.of Revs.	6.3	5.9	5.9	0.8	5.3	5.3
% Ret. on Assets	6.3	6.7	6.8	1.0	6.7	7.4
% Ret. on Equity	27.7	24.3	21.4	3.2	20.2	22.3

Dividend Data —Dividends have been paid since 1881. A dividend reinvestment plan is available.

Amt. of Div. $	Date Decl.	Ex-Div. Date	Stock of Record	Payment Date
0.330	Sep. 17	Sep. 26	Sep. 30	Nov. 01 '94
0.330	Dec. 21	Dec. 23	Dec. 30	Feb. 01 '95
0.330	Mar. 15	Mar. 27	Mar. 31	May. 01 '95
0.330	Jun. 21	Jun. 28	Jun. 30	Aug. 01 '95
0.330	Sep. 11	Sep. 27	Sep. 29	Nov. 01 '95

Data as orig. reptd.; bef. results of disc. opers. and/or spec. items. Per share data adj. for stk. divs. as of ex-div. date. E-Estimated. NA-Not Available. NM-Not Meaningful. NR-Not Ranked.

Office—32 Avenue of the Americas, New York, NY 10013-2412. **Tel**—(212) 387-5400. **Chrmn & CEO**—R. E. Allen. **CFO**—R. W. Miller. **Secy**—M. J. Wasser. **Investor Contact**—MaryAnn Nibeojeski. **Dirs**—R. E. Allen, M. K. Eickhoff, W. Y. Elisha, P. M. Hawley, C. A. Hills, B. K. Johnson, D. Lewis, D. F. McHenry, V. A. Pelson, D. S. Perkins, H. B. Schacht, M. I. Sovern, F. A. Thomas, J. D. Williams, T. H. Wyman. **Transfer Offices**—First Chicago Trust Co. of New York, NYC. **Incorporated** in New York in 1885. **Empl**- 304,500. **S&P Analyst:** Kevin J. Gooley

Abbott Laboratories

NYSE Symbol **ABT**
In S&P 500

12-SEP-95

Industry:
Drugs-Generic and OTC

Summary: This company is a leading maker of pharmaceutical, nutritional, and hospital and laboratory products.

S&P Opinion: Accumulate (★★★★)

Recent Price • 39¼	Yield • 2.1%
52 Wk Range • 42⅜-29¾	12-Mo. P/E • 19.5

Quantitative Evaluations

Outlook
(1 Lowest—5 Highest)
• **3+**

Fair Value
• **38¾**

Risk
• **Low**

Earn./Div. Rank
• **A+**

Technical Eval.
• **Bearish** since 7/95

Rel. Strength Rank
(1 Lowest—99 Highest)
• **36**

Insider Activity
• **Neutral**

Earnings vs. Previous Year
▲=Up ▼=Down ▶=No Change

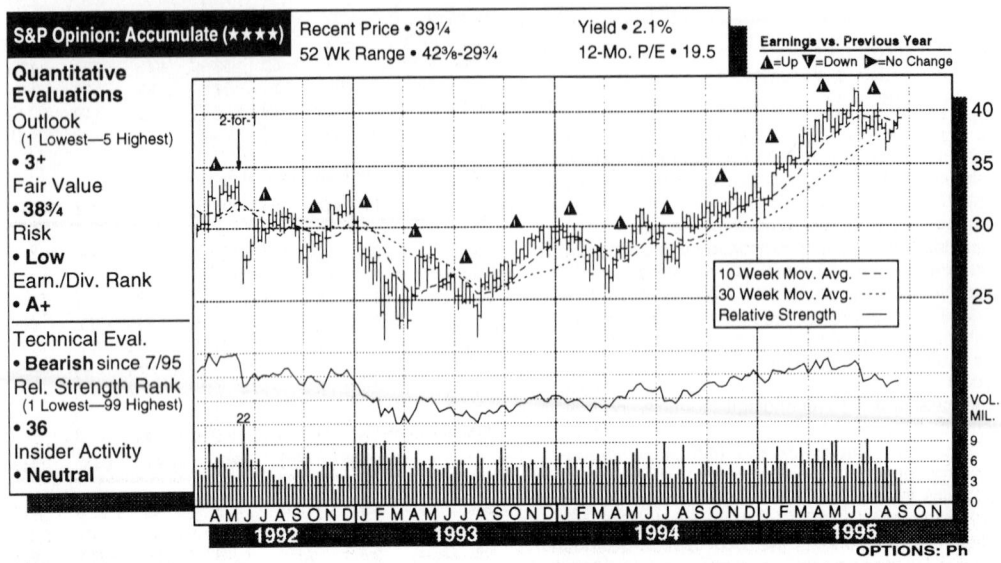

- 10 Week Mov. Avg. – – –
- 30 Week Mov. Avg. ·······
- Relative Strength —

OPTIONS: Ph

Overview - 11-SEP-95

Sales should show further growth in 1996, although at a slower pace than the 11% indicated for 1995 (which was recently boosted by favorable foreign exchange). Pharmaceutical sales are expected to post another respectable gain, bolstered by continued advances in Biaxin antibiotic, Depakote anticonvulsant and Hytrin treatment for enlarged prostates, as well as from new drugs such as Prevacid antiulcer. New products such as the AxSYM immunoassay system and LCX DNA probe tests should also bolster Abbott's diagnostics business. Sales of medical nutritionals should also rise, but sales of infant nutritionals are expected to decline due to the loss of several large WIC contracts.

Valuation - 12-SEP-95

The stock has been an erratic performer in recent months, relecting profit taking after a sustained uptrend and investor concern over expected generic erosion in Hytrin (the drug's patent expires in January 1997) and the loss of several large WIC infant nutritional contracts. However, Abbott should be able to maintain solid double digit profit growth in the years ahead, fortified by its dominant positions in niche pharmaceutical, nutritional and diagnostic products markets; good control over costs; and a proven ability to generate lucrative new cost-saving medical products. Some increase in the $0.21 quarterly dividend is expected in early 1996. The stock is a choice selection for total return in the health care sector.

Key Stock Statistics

S&P EPS Est. 1995	2.15	Tang. Bk. Value/Share	5.34
P/E on S&P Est. 1995	18.3	Beta	0.81
S&P EPS Est. 1996	2.40	Shareholders	86,300
Dividend Rate/Share	0.84	Market cap. (B)	$ 31.0
Shs. outstg. (M)	793.5	Inst. holdings	52%
Avg. daily vol. (M)	1.096	Insider holdings	NA

Value of $10,000 invested 5 years ago: $ 25,916

Fiscal Year Ending Dec. 31

	1995	% Change	1994	% Change	1993	% Change
Revenues (Million $)						
1Q	2,524	14%	2,215	8%	2,046	9%
2Q	2,500	13%	2,204	6%	2,074	9%
3Q	—	—	2,255	9%	2,060	5%
4Q	—	—	2,482	11%	2,228	6%
Yr.	—	—	9,156	9%	8,408	7%
Income (Million $)						
1Q	417.3	14%	366.2	6%	345.5	17%
2Q	424.0	13%	376.6	9%	346.1	9%
3Q	—	—	351.3	11%	316.2	13%
4Q	—	—	422.5	8%	391.3	12%
Yr.	—	—	1,517	8%	1,399	13%
Earnings Per Share ($)						
1Q	0.52	16%	0.45	10%	0.41	17%
2Q	0.53	15%	0.46	10%	0.42	14%
3Q	E0.49	14%	0.43	13%	0.38	15%
4Q	E0.61	15%	0.53	10%	0.48	14%
Yr.	E2.15	15%	1.87	11%	1.69	15%

Next earnings report expected: mid October

Abbott Laboratories

12-SEP-95

Business Summary - 12-SEP-95

Abbott Laboratories is a major diversified health care concern with solid positions in pharmaceuticals; infant and adult nutritionals; and hospital, laboratory and diagnostic products. Contributions by business segment in 1994 were:

	Sales	Profits
Pharmaceutical & nutritional	54%	63%
Hospital & laboratory	46%	37%

Foreign operations accounted for 33% of sales and 30% of profits in 1994. Research and development expenses equaled 10.5% of sales in each of 1994 and 1993.

Pharmaceuticals include the broad-spectrum macrolide antibiotic clarithromycin (sold under Biaxin and other names), erythromycin antibiotic, Depakote anticonvulsant agent, Loftyl vasoactive agent, Hytrin for hypertension and enlarged prostates, Abbokinase anti-thrombolytic drug, Ogen oral estrogen, Survanta lung surfactant and various cough/cold products. Other products include infant formulas (13% of 1994 sales) such as Similac, Isomil and Advance; and adult nutritionals (11%), comprised of Ensure nitrogen formulations, protein formulas, diabetic products and other items. Abbott also sells personal care products such as Selsun Blue dandruff shampoo and Murine eye and ear care items.

Hospital and laboratory products include diagnostic systems for blood banks, hospitals and laboratories; intravenous (I.V.) and irrigation fluids and related administration equipment, including electronic drug delivery systems (9%); drugs and drug delivery systems; anesthetics; critical care products; and other medical specialty items for hospitals and alternate care sites. Diagnostic items include the Spectrum and Quantum clinical chemistry systems; the AxSYM, Commander and IMx lines of diagnostic instruments and chemical reagent used with immunoassay diagnostics; screening tests for hepatitis, AIDS and other infectious diseases; and related items.

Important Developments

Sep. '95—TAP Holdings, the company's joint venture with Takeda Chemical Industries of Japan, signed an agreement with RPMS Technology of London to develop compounds discovered by RPMS to treat H. pylori infection. H. pylori has been linked with duodenal and gastric ulcers. Abbott has also filed for approval to market its popular Biaxin antibiotic to treat H. pylori. Separately, Abbott's directors authorized the repurchase of up to 20 million company common shares.

Capitalization

Long Term Debt: $435,730,000 (6/95).

Per Share Data ($)

(Year Ended Dec. 31)

	1994	1993	1992	1991	1990	1989
Tangible Bk. Val.	5.04	4.48	4.00	3.77	3.30	3.08
Cash Flow	2.50	2.27	1.97	1.72	1.52	1.31
Earnings	1.87	1.69	1.47	1.28	1.11	0.97
Dividends	0.74	0.66	0.58	0.48	0.40	0.34
Payout Ratio	39%	39%	39%	38%	36%	35%
Prices - High	34	30⅞	34¼	34⅞	23¼	17⅝
- Low	25⅜	22⅝	26⅛	19⅝	15⅝	11⅝
P/E Ratio - High	18	18	23	27	21	18
- Low	14	13	18	15	14	12

Income Statement Analysis (Million $)

	1994	%Chg	1993	%Chg	1992	%Chg	1991
Revs.	9,156	9%	8,408	7%	7,852	14%	6,877
Oper. Inc.	2,655	9%	2,442	13%	2,169	12%	1,936
Depr.	511	6%	484	13%	428	13%	379
Int. Exp.	50.0	-7%	54.0	2%	53.0	-17%	64.0
Pretax Inc.	2,167	12%	1,943	12%	1,739	13%	1,544
Eff. Tax Rate	30%	—	28%	—	29%	—	30%
Net Inc.	1,517	8%	1,399	13%	1,239	14%	1,089

Balance Sheet & Other Fin. Data (Million $)

	1994	1993	1992	1991	1990	1989
Cash	315	379	258	146	53.0	49.0
Curr. Assets	3,876	3,586	3,232	2,891	2,461	2,103
Total Assets	8,524	7,689	6,941	6,255	5,563	4,852
Curr. Liab.	3,476	3,095	2,783	2,229	2,001	1,384
LT Debt	287	307	110	125	135	147
Common Eqty.	4,049	3,675	3,348	3,203	2,834	2,726
Total Cap.	4,392	4,033	3,779	3,675	3,378	3,312
Cap. Exp.	929	953	1,007	771	641	573
Cash Flow	2,027	1,883	1,667	1,468	1,322	1,167

Ratio Analysis

	1994	1993	1992	1991	1990	1989
Curr. Ratio	1.1	1.2	1.2	1.3	1.2	1.5
% LT Debt of Cap.	6.5	7.6	2.9	3.4	4.0	4.4
% Net Inc.of Revs.	16.6	16.6	15.8	15.8	15.7	16.0
% Ret. on Assets	18.9	19.3	18.9	18.5	18.8	17.9
% Ret. on Equity	39.7	40.2	38.1	36.2	35.3	33.4

Dividend Data

Dividends have been paid since 1926. A dividend reinvestment plan is available.

Amt. of Div. $	Date Decl.	Ex-Div. Date	Stock of Record	Payment Date
0.190	Sep. 09	Oct. 07	Oct. 14	Nov. 15 '94
0.190	Dec. 09	Jan. 09	Jan. 13	Feb. 15 '95
0.210	Feb. 10	Apr. 07	Apr. 14	May. 15 '95
0.210	May. 19	Jul. 12	Jul. 14	Aug. 15 '95
0.210	Sep. 08	Oct. 11	Oct. 13	Nov. 15 '95

Data as orig. reptd.; bef. results of disc. opers. and/or spec. items. Per share data adj. for stk. divs. as of ex-div. date. E-Estimated. NA-Not Available. NM-Not Meaningful. NR-Not Ranked.

Office—100 Abbott Park Road, Abbott Park, IL 60064. **Tel**—(708) 937-6100. **Chrmn & CEO**—D. L. Burnham. **Pres & COO**—T. R. Hodgson. **SVP & Secy**—J. M. de Lasa. **SVP-Fin & CFO**—G. P. Coughlan. **VP & Treas**—T. C. Freyman. **Investor Contact**—Patricia Bergeron. **Dirs**—F. K. Austen, D. L. Burnham, H. L. Fuller, The Lord Hayhoe PC, T. R. Hodgson, A. F. Jacobson, D. A. Jones, B. Powell, Jr., A. B. Rand, W. A. Reynolds, W. D. Smithburg, J. R. Walter, W. L. Weiss. **Transfer Agent & Registrar**—First National Bank of Boston. **Incorporated** in Illinois in 1900. **Empl**-49,464. **S&P Analyst:** H.B. Saftlas

Advanced Micro Devices

NYSE Symbol **AMD**
In S&P 500

13-OCT-95

Industry: Electronics/Electric

Summary: This company is a leading producer of semiconductors that are used principally by the computer and telecommunications industries.

| S&P Opinion: Accumulate (★★★★) | Recent Price • 27⅜ | Yield • Nil |
| | 52 Wk Range • 39¼-22¼ | 12-Mo. P/E • 10.1 |

Quantitative Evaluations

Outlook
(1 Lowest—5 Highest)
• **5⁻**

Fair Value
• **36¼**

Risk
• **Average**

Earn./Div. Rank
• **B-**

Technical Eval.
• **Bearish** since 4/94

Rel. Strength Rank
(1 Lowest—99 Highest)
• **9**

Insider Activity
• **NA**

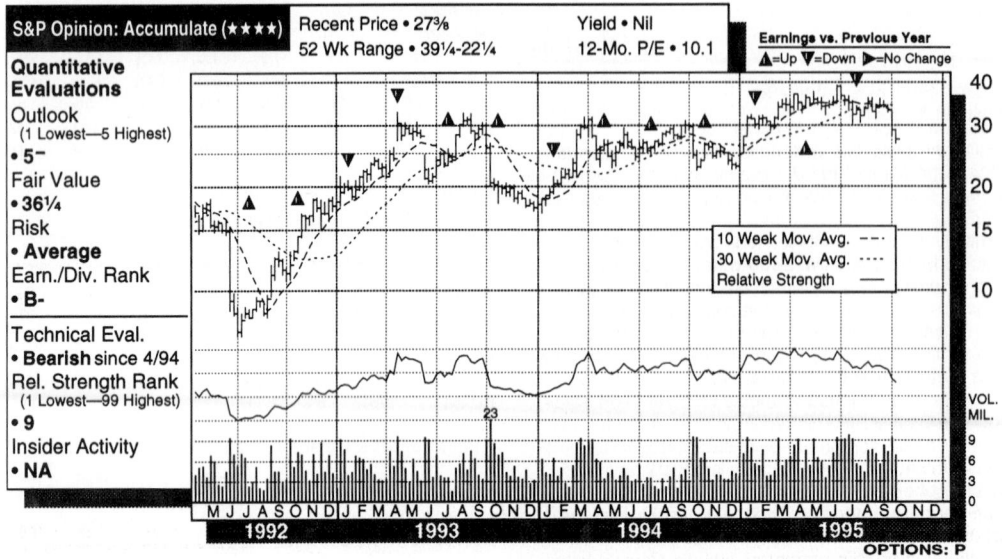

Earnings vs. Previous Year
▲=Up ▼=Down ▶=No Change

10 Week Mov. Avg. - - -
30 Week Mov. Avg. ....
Relative Strength ——

OPTIONS: P

Overview - 13-OCT-95

Sales are expected to increase some 10% in 1996, fueled by strong demand for flash memories, communications and programmable products, offset by lower microprocessor sales. The transition to AMD's new K-5 chip family away from the 486 is expected to slow microprocessor sales. Gross margins should narrow, reflecting price pressures on microprocessors and start-up cost associated with the company's new Fab 25 facility. This will result in higher depreciation expense and research and development costs being allocated to cost of goods sold. Furthermore, the company's purchases of flash memory from its joint venture with Fujitsu carries a higher cost of sales than internally produced products. Operating expenses are expected to be well contained, leading to EPS of $3.65, versus 1995's projection of $2.95.

Valuation - 13-OCT-95

We have upgraded the shares to accumulate from hold, as we believe the shares have become oversold in the mid-$20 range. At these levels, the shares are off more than 30% from the 52-week high and trade at a very low multiple to our 1996 $3.65 estimate. The sell-off is mainly due to delays in introducing AMD's K-5 Pentium compatible chip, now set for 1996's second half, and a steep decline in its 486 business. While we were also disappointed in the delay, AMD's other businesses (75% of sales in 1995's third quarter) are growing sharply and should provide support for the shares. More importantly, we believe investors will revisit the shares as the K-5 introduction approaches.

Key Stock Statistics

S&P EPS Est. 1995	2.95	Tang. Bk. Value/Share	16.38
P/E on S&P Est. 1995	9.3	Beta	1.10
S&P EPS Est. 1996	3.65	Shareholders	9,500
Dividend Rate/Share	Nil	Market cap. (B)	$ 2.9
Shs. outstg. (M)	103.8	Inst. holdings	62%
Avg. daily vol. (M)	1.752	Insider holdings	NA

Value of $10,000 invested 5 years ago: $ 34,774

Fiscal Year Ending Dec. 31

	1995	% Change	1994	% Change	1993	% Change
Revenues (Million $)						
1Q	620.1	21%	513.1	26%	407.4	NM
2Q	626.2	17%	533.3	30%	409.1	17%
3Q	590.4	9%	543.1	30%	418.4	17%
4Q	—	—	545.2	32%	413.4	3%
Yr.	—	—	2,135	30%	1,648	9%
Income (Million $)						
1Q	96.80	14%	84.59	38%	61.45	-28%
2Q	91.99	-1%	93.23	45%	64.35	55%
3Q	56.16	-35%	86.69	41%	61.34	25%
4Q	—	—	40.76	-2%	41.64	-40%
Yr.	—	—	305.3	33%	228.8	-7%
Earnings Per Share ($)						
1Q	0.96	13%	0.85	35%	0.63	-30%
2Q	0.86	-8%	0.93	43%	0.65	51%
3Q	0.52	-40%	0.86	41%	0.61	20%
4Q	E0.62	59%	0.39	-5%	0.41	-44%
Yr.	E2.95	-2%	3.02	31%	2.30	-11%

Next earnings report expected: early January

Advanced Micro Devices

Business Summary - 13-OCT-95

Advanced Micro Devices is the fourth largest U.S. manufacturer of integrated circuits, with a principal focus on microprocessors, applications solutions products and high volume commodity products.

To date, the company has primarily based its microprocessor efforts on the X86 architecture, originally developed by Intel Corp. AMD's strategy has been to serve as an alternative source for X86 microprocessors at comparable prices but with additional customer-driven features. During 1994, 37% of AMD's revenues were derived from the company's AM486DX product family. In mid 1996, the company is expected to offer its next generation of microprocessor products known as the K86. The company's initial K86 product, the K-5, is expected to compete directly against Intel's Pentium family of microprocessors.

Applications solutions products include integrated circuits that work with central processing units to manage selected input/output or other system functions. The company also supplies a range of products designed to add additional functions, improve performance and reduce costs in computer peripheral, interface or mass storage applications. A family of voice/data communications products are also available.

High volume commodity products include programmable logic devices (PLDs) and non-volatile/volatile memory devices. Non-volatile memories retain data when system power is shut off, sheil volatile memories do not. Non-volatile memories include Eraseable programmable read-only memories (EPROMs) and FLASH memory. Volatile memories include Dynamic and Static Random Access Memories (DRAMs and SRAMs). In April 1993, AMD established a joint venture with Fujitsu Ltd. to manufacture flash memories.

Foreign sales accounted for 29% of revenues and 9% of operating income in 1994. R&D spending totaled $280.0 million (13.1% of sales) in 1994.

In January 1995, AMD and Intel reached an agreement to settle all outstanding legal disputes between the two companies, including the granting to AMD of a perpetual license to the microcode in the Intel386 and Intel486 microprocessors. However, AMD does not have the right to copy other Intel microcode. Intel received $58 million as settlement for past damages in the 486 ICE case.

Important Developments

Sep. '95—AMD said that volume production of its new SS/5-75 microprocessor will begin in 1996's second quarter. This chip, an early version of its K-5 architecture, will be marketed as a plug-in replacement for a 75MHz Pentium. The company added that its advanced K-5 products, which offer a 30% performance advantage over Pentium, will be available one quarter after the SS/5-75. A total of three million units of the K-5 architecture are expected to be produced in 1996.

Capitalization

Long Term Debt: $216,378,000 (10/1/95).

Per Share Data ($)

(Year Ended Dec. 31)

	1994	1993	1992	1991	1990	1989
Tangible Bk. Val.	16.38	12.76	9.91	7.27	5.63	6.39
Cash Flow	5.24	4.14	4.23	3.30	0.79	2.10
Earnings	3.02	2.30	2.57	1.53	-0.78	0.44
Dividends	Nil	Nil	Nil	Nil	Nil	Nil
Payout Ratio	Nil	Nil	Nil	Nil	Nil	Nil
Prices - High	31¾	32⅞	21½	17¾	11⅜	10½
- Low	16¾	17	7⅜	4	3½	7⅛
P/E Ratio - High	11	14	8	12	NM	24
- Low	6	7	3	3	NM	16

Income Statement Analysis (Million $)

	1994	%Chg	1993	%Chg	1992	%Chg	1991
Revs.	2,135	30%	1,648	9%	1,514	23%	1,227
Oper. Inc.	729	52%	480	14%	422	59%	265
Depr.	216	23%	175	15%	152	-3%	156
Int. Exp.	10.1	3%	9.8	-58%	23.3	-8%	25.2
Pretax Inc.	470	48%	318	17%	272	88%	145
Eff. Tax Rate	34%	—	28%	—	9.80%	—	NM
Net Inc.	305	33%	229	-7%	245	69%	145

Balance Sheet & Other Fin. Data (Million $)

	1994	1993	1992	1991	1990	1989
Cash	378	488	364	301	115	279
Curr. Assets	987	964	738	626	397	594
Total Assets	2,446	1,929	1,448	1,292	1,112	1,122
Curr. Liab.	592	455	353	455	318	276
LT Debt	76.0	80.0	20.0	42.0	131	126
Common Eqty.	1,563	1,180	874	611	464	518
Total Cap.	1,854	1,475	1,096	836	794	847
Cap. Exp.	549	388	222	111	304	159
Cash Flow	511	393	387	291	64.0	172

Ratio Analysis

	1994	1993	1992	1991	1990	1989
Curr. Ratio	1.7	2.1	2.1	1.4	1.2	2.2
% LT Debt of Cap.	4.1	5.4	1.8	5.0	16.5	14.9
% Net Inc.of Revs.	14.3	13.0	16.2	11.8	NM	4.2
% Ret. on Assets	13.8	13.3	17.5	12.0	NM	4.1
% Ret. on Equity	21.2	20.8	31.0	24.9	NM	7.2

Dividend Data

Prior to the special dividend paid on May 24, 1995, no cash dividends have ever been paid on the common stock. A "poison pill" stock purchase rights plan was adopted in 1990.

Amt. of Div. $	Date Decl.	Ex-Div. Date	Stock of Record	Payment Date
0.010	Apr. 19	Apr. 27	May. 03	May. 24 '95

Data as orig. reptd.; bef. results of disc. opers. and/or spec. items. Per share data adj. for stk. divs. as of ex-div. date. E-Estimated. NA-Not Available. NM-Not Meaningful. NR-Not Ranked. Data for 1994 refl. Intel settlement.

Office—901 Thompson Place (P.O. Box 3453), Sunnyvale, CA 94088-3453. **Tel**—(408) 732-2400. **Chrmn & CEO**—W. J. Sanders III. **Vice Chrmn**—A. Holbrook. **Pres & COO**—R. Previte. **SVP, CFO, Treas & Investor Contact**—Marvin Burkett. **VP & Secy**—T. M. McCoy. **Dirs**—F. Baur, C. M. Blalack, R. G. Brown, A. Holbrook, R. Previte, J. L. Roby, W. J. Sanders III, L. Silverman. **Transfer Agent & Registrar**—First National Bank of Boston. **Incorporated** in Delaware in 1969. **Empl**-11,800. **S&P Analyst:** John D. Coyle, CFA

11

Aetna Life & Casualty

NYSE Symbol **AET**
In S&P 500

16-AUG-95

Industry:
Insurance

Summary: As one of the largest multi-line insurers in the U.S., Aetna has a major presence in the life-health and property-casualty insurance markets; and in the pension and annuity fields.

S&P Opinion: Hold (★★★)	Recent Price • 62⅝	Yield • 4.4%
	52 Wk Range • 64⅞-42¼	12-Mo. P/E • 46.0

Quantitative Evaluations

Outlook
(1 Lowest—5 Highest)
• **3+**

Fair Value
• **61⅝**

Risk
• **Low**

Earn./Div. Rank
• **B-**

Technical Eval.
• **Bearish** since 4/95

Rel. Strength Rank
(1 Lowest—99 Highest)
• **44**

Insider Activity
• **NA**

Earnings vs. Previous Year
▲=Up ▼=Down ▶=No Change

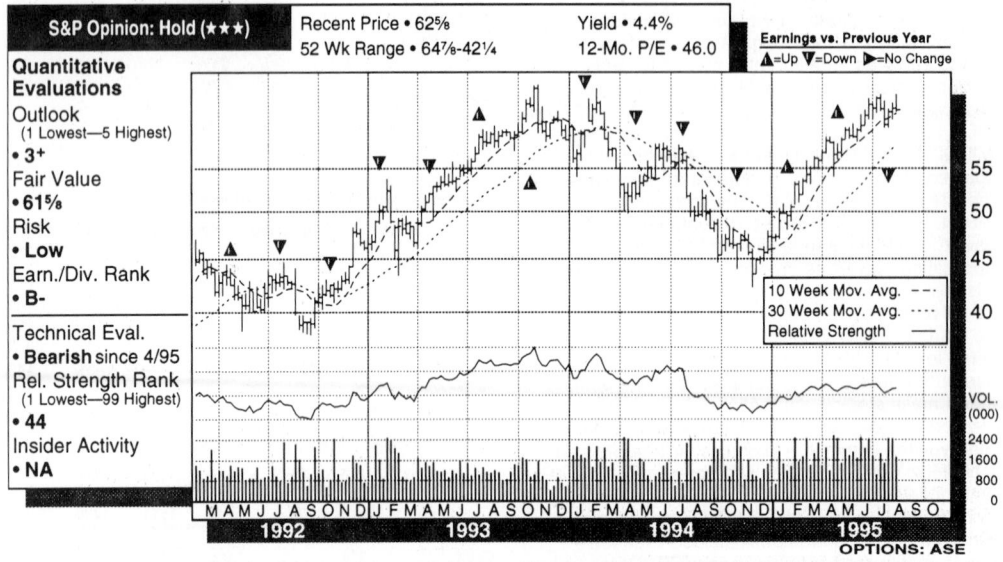

10 Week Mov. Avg. – – –
30 Week Mov. Avg. · · · ·
Relative Strength —

OPTIONS: ASE

Overview - 16-AUG-95

The drop in operating earnings seen during 1995 reflects a second quarter net charge of $4.31 a share made to boost environmental reserves. Despite higher catastrophe losses in 1994, profit comparisons were aided by the absence of net charges of about $1.3 billion taken in 1993. Group health profit growth will be modest, reflecting a shift to lower-margin health plans. P-C premium levels will decline, as AET reduces its exposure to certain lines. This is a plus, long term; however, near-term underwriting results will remain below average. Cost savings of $200 million annually from various cutbacks will help results. Exiting the large-case, fully guaranteed GIC and single-premium annuity lines is a plus, since it frees up capital that can be allocated to higher-return businesses. At year-end 1994, these two lines had $11.9 billion in assets and $997 million in reserves.

Valuation - 16-AUG-95

After a lackluster performance during much of 1994 due to the negative effects of higher interest rates and rising catastrophe losses, AET's shares have rebounded nicely so far in 1995. Much of the recent strength reflects the market's enthusiasm for AET's recent restructuring efforts and heightened speculation that it may even spin off its property-casualty operations. Though these actions leave AET better positioned long term, the shares are fairly valued in the near term, particularly in light of AET's somewhat erratic operating earnings track record.

Key Stock Statistics

S&P EPS Est. 1995	1.35	Tang. Bk. Value/Share	58.76
P/E on S&P Est. 1995	46.4	Beta	1.39
S&P EPS Est. 1996	6.30	Shareholders	29,600
Dividend Rate/Share	2.76	Market cap. (B)	$ 7.0
Shs. outstg. (M)	113.2	Inst. holdings	85%
Avg. daily vol. (M)	0.417	Insider holdings	NA

Value of $10,000 invested 5 years ago: $ 15,279

Fiscal Year Ending Dec. 31

	1995	% Change	1994	% Change	1993	% Change
Revenues (Million $)						
1Q	4,485	4%	4,314	NM	4,294	-5%
2Q	4,447	NM	4,405	2%	4,327	—
3Q	—	—	4,385	2%	4,303	—
4Q	—	—	4,421	5%	4,194	-3%
Yr.	—	—	17,525	2%	17,118	-2%
Income (Million $)						
1Q	160.8	NM	45.70	-67%	139.3	-10%
2Q	-296.9	NM	132.4	-12%	150.8	NM
3Q	—	—	129.4	-43%	225.6	114%
4Q	—	—	160.0	NM	-1,130	NM
Yr.	—	—	467.5	NM	-615.3	NM
Earnings Per Share ($)						
1Q	1.42	NM	0.40	-68%	1.26	-10%
2Q	-2.62	NM	1.17	-14%	1.36	NM
3Q	—	—	1.15	-43%	2.03	114%
4Q	—	—	1.42	NM	-10.09	NM
Yr.	E1.35	-67%	4.14	NM	-5.54	NM

Next earnings report expected: late October

Aetna Life & Casualty

Business Summary - 16-AUG-95

Aetna is the largest investor-owned insurance organization in the U.S. Net profit/losses (in millions; before adjustments) in recent years were:

	1994	1993
Health insurance/managed care	$341.7	$272.2
Life insurance/annuities	159.1	111.4
Property-casualty	58.1	-13.0
Large case pensions	54.4	-822.3
International	71.2	55.0

The health insurance segment (Aetna Health Plans) provides indemnity and managed health care plans (HMOs and PPOs) to employers and employer-sponsored groups. Life insurance, disability, long term care insurance, and certain specialized programs are also offered. At year end 1994, enrollment totaled 15.6 million lives (7 million managed care; 8.6 million indemnity), up from 15 million (5.4; 9.6) at year end 1993. The life insurance segment offers life insurance, annuities and other savings and retirement products to individuals and employer sponsored groups. Assets under management at year end 1994 were $19.4 billion. The p-c sector writes most types of commercial and personal coverage. Earned premiums in 1994 were $4.4 billion, down from $4.7 billion in 1993. The large case pension unit offers retirement and savings products and advisory services. Assets under management at year end 1994 were $46.3 billion, 74% of which were experience rated or non-guaranteed. Fully guaranteed products, which are being discontinued, accounted for the balance.

Important Developments

Jul. '95—AET's sharply lower earnings for the first half of 1995 reflected a second quarter net charge of $488 million ($4.31 a share) taken to boost reserves for environmental losses. This charge offset improved property-casualty operating profits amid lower catastrophe losses. Separately, AET's return to profitability in 1994 was aided by the absence of net charges totaling almost $1.3 billion taken in 1993 to discontinue the sale of certain large-case guaranteed investment contracts (GICs) and single-premium annuities ($825 million); to implement another round of cost cutting that included the elimination of 4,000 jobs ($200 million); and to boost workers' compensation reserves ($259 million).

Capitalization

Long Term Debt: $1,117,900,000 (6/95).
Minority Interest: $275,000,000.

Per Share Data ($)

(Year Ended Dec. 31)

	1994	1993	1992	1991	1990	1989
Tangible Bk. Val.	47.52	62.77	64.07	64.33	61.62	59.33
Oper. Earnings	4.52	-6.07	-0.76	6.28	6.25	4.72
Earnings	4.14	-5.54	-0.05	4.59	5.52	5.69
Dividends	2.76	2.76	2.76	2.76	2.76	2.76
Relative Payout	67%	NM	NM	60%	50%	49%
Prices - High	65¾	66¼	48⅞	49⅛	58⅜	62½
- Low	42¼	43⅜	38	31⅞	29	46⅝
P/E Ratio - High	16	NM	NM	11	11	11
- Low	10	NM	NM	7	5	8

Income Statement Analysis (Million $)

	1994	%Chg	1993	%Chg	1992	%Chg	1991
Life Ins. In Force	288,546	-4%	299,996	-22%	382,542	3%	370,048
Prem.Inc Life A&H	6,863	18%	5,818	3%	5,633	5%	5,370
Prem.Inc Cas/Prop	4,430	-7%	4,757	-8%	5,161	-26%	7,005
Net Invest. Inc.	4,464	-9%	4,919	-3%	5,069	-12%	5,735
Oth. Revs.	1,769	9%	1,624	NM	1,634	50%	1,086
Total Revs.	17,525	2%	17,118	-2%	17,497	-9%	19,196
Pretax Inc.	658	NM	-1,146	NM	-120	NM	417
Net Oper. Inc.	510	NM	-673	NM	-84.0	NM	691
Net Inc.	468	NM	-614	NM	-5.0	NM	505

Balance Sheet & Other Fin. Data (Million $)

	1994	1993	1992	1991	1990	1989
Cash & Equiv.	3,731	2,340	3,182	3,997	2,964	3,515
Premiums Due	1,723	1,665	2,071	2,977	2,772	2,640
Inv Assets Bonds	37,112	41,545	36,347	35,149	34,227	33,252
Inv. Assets Stock	1,656	1,659	1,496	1,122	911	1,348
Inv. Assets Loans	12,377	15,330	18,515	21,229	23,543	23,425
Inv. Assets Total	54,293	61,456	58,797	60,991	63,260	61,191
Deferred Policy Cost	2,015	1,867	1,706	1,663	1,619	1,536
Total Assets	94,173	100,037	89,928	91,988	89,301	87,099
Debt	1,115	1,160	956	1,021	1,012	1,038
Common Eqty.	5,503	7,043	7,238	7,385	7,072	6,937

Ratio Analysis

	1994	1993	1992	1991	1990	1989
Comb. Loss-Exp.Ratio	117.7	117.9	131.0	116.7	114.3	112.3
% Ret. on Revs.	2.7	NM	NM	2.6	3.2	3.3
% Ret. on Equity	7.5	NM	NM	7.0	8.8	9.5
% Invest. Yield	7.7	8.2	8.6	9.2	9.4	9.3

Dividend Data —Dividends have been paid since 1934. A dividend reinvestment plan is available. A "poison pill" stock purchase right was adopted in 1989.

Amt. of Div. $	Date Decl.	Ex-Div. Date	Stock of Record	Payment Date
0.690	Jun. 24	Jul. 25	Jul. 29	Aug. 15 '94
0.690	Sep. 30	Oct. 24	Oct. 28	Nov. 15 '94
0.690	Dec. 09	Jan. 23	Jan. 27	Feb. 15 '95
0.690	Feb. 24	Apr. 24	Apr. 28	May. 15 '95
0.690	Jun. 30	Jul. 26	Jul. 28	Aug. 15 '95

Data as orig. reptd.; bef. results of disc. opers. and/or spec. items. Per share data adj. for stk. divs. as of ex-div. date. E-Estimate. NA-Not Available. NM-Not Meaningful. NR-Not Ranked.

Office—151 Farmington Ave., Hartford, CT 06156. **Tel**—(203) 273-0123. **Chrmn & Pres**—R. E. Compton. **Vice-Chrmn**—R. L. Huber. **Secy**—L. M. Nickerson. **Investor Contact**—Daniel S. Messina. **Dirs**—W. Barnes, R. E. Compton, J. F. Donahue, W. H. Donaldson, B. H. Franklin, E. G. Graves, G. Greenwald, M. H. Jordan, J. D. Kuehler, F. R. O'Keefe Jr., D. M. Roderick. **Transfer Agent & Registrar**—First Chicago Trust Co. of New York, NYC. **Incorporated** in Connecticut in 1853; reincorporated in 1967. **Empl**-40,900. **S&P Analyst:** Catherine A. Seifert

Ahmanson (H.F.) & Co.

NYSE Symbol **AHM**
In S&P 500

16-AUG-95 Industry: Banking

Summary: This company owns Home Savings of America, the largest savings institution in the U.S., with more than 350 branches in five states.

S&P Opinion: Hold (★★★)	Recent Price • 21¼	Yield • 4.0%
	52 Wk Range • 23¾-15¼	12-Mo. P/E • 14.7

Quantitative Evaluations

Outlook
(1 Lowest—5 Highest)
• **3+**

Fair Value
• **21**

Risk
• **Average**

Earn./Div. Rank
• **B**

Technical Eval.
• **Bearish** since 4/95

Rel. Strength Rank
(1 Lowest—99 Highest)
• **34**

Insider Activity
• **Neutral**

Earnings vs. Previous Year
▲=Up ▼=Down ▶=No Change

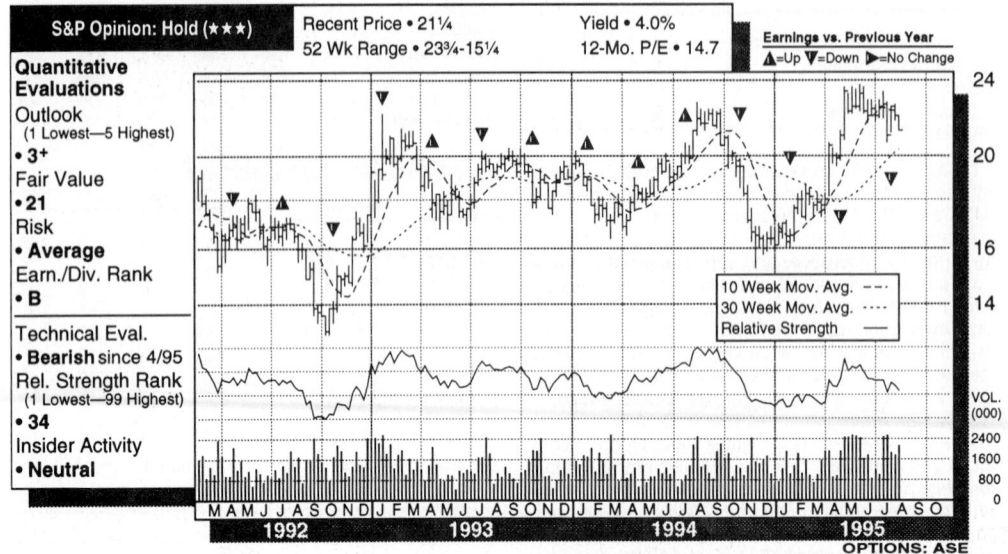

10 Week Mov. Avg. - - - -
30 Week Mov. Avg. · · · ·
Relative Strength ——

OPTIONS: ASE

Overview - 16-AUG-95

AHM is expected to post solid earnings growth in 1996. The main contributor is anticipated expansion of the interest rate spread. As a lender overwhelmingly focused on monthly adjustable-rate mortgages tied to a cost of funds index, the company's spread tends to widen during periods of declining interest rates. Two effects are present. First, deposit costs reprice downwards. And two, because of the lag in reporting the cost of funds index, loan yields remain relatively rich. Mortgage volume could suffer from the shift to a fixed-rate market. Credit quality has been significantly improved through the bulk sale of problem assets, but some deterioration is expected with attempts to diversify lending. Small reductions in overhead cost ratios are likely, partially due to branch consolidations.

Valuation - 16-AUG-95

Ahmanson shares are rated as an average performer. The stock, along with the entire thrift group, has rallied this year with the drop in interest rates, which has positive implications for 1996 profits. The shares trade close to an all-time high and at a slight premium to book value, in line with industry averages. The company is not a takeover play, like a number of other California institutions; new management appears intent on remaining independent and charting its own course. One concern is asset quality. The California economy is still weak, and the company could be hurt by attempts to diversify lending operations. The annual dividend has been flat at $0.88 for more than five years.

Key Stock Statistics

S&P EPS Est. 1995	1.75	Tang. Bk. Value/Share	21.82
P/E on S&P Est. 1995	12.1	Beta	1.95
S&P EPS Est. 1996	2.30	Shareholders	7,400
Dividend Rate/Share	0.88	Market cap. (B)	$ 2.5
Shs. outstg. (M)	117.1	Inst. holdings	94%
Avg. daily vol. (M)	0.412	Insider holdings	NA

Value of $10,000 invested 5 years ago: $ 14,870

Fiscal Year Ending Dec. 31

	1995	% Change	1994	% Change	1993	% Change
Revenues (Million $)						
1Q	930.0	19%	778.7	-6%	827.3	-14%
2Q	1,003	29%	774.8	-7%	833.9	-10%
3Q	—	—	818.9	NM	819.2	-6%
4Q	—	—	1,009	20%	840.8	-3%
Yr.	—	—	3,381	2%	3,321	-9%
Income (Million $)						
1Q	50.70	-8%	55.36	68%	32.86	43%
2Q	62.23	-15%	73.54	NM	-291.0	NM
3Q	—	—	68.53	-2%	69.99	38%
4Q	—	—	39.94	-20%	50.11	NM
Yr.	—	—	237.4	NM	-138.0	NM
Earnings Per Share ($)						
1Q	0.33	-8%	0.36	57%	0.23	44%
2Q	0.42	-19%	0.52	NM	-2.55	NM
3Q	E0.47	NM	0.47	-6%	0.50	25%
4Q	E0.53	130%	0.23	-28%	0.32	NM
Yr.	E1.75	10%	1.59	NM	-1.51	NM

Next earnings report expected: mid October

Ahmanson (H.F.) & Co.

Business Summary - 16-AUG-95

H.F. Ahmanson & Company is the parent of Home Savings of America, the largest U.S. savings institution, based on 1994 year-end assets of $53.7 billion. At December 31, 1994, Home Savings had 357 savings branches located in six states and 82 loan offices located in 12 states. Loans of $36.5 billion at 1994 year-end, down from $38.3 billion a year earlier, were divided:

	1994	1993
One- to four-family units	71%	75%
Apartments	23%	19%
Commercial & industrial real estate	5%	5%
Other	1%	1%

About 95.1% of the company's loan and MBS portfolio at December 31, 1994, consisted of ARMs, the majority of which carry rates that adjust monthly based on changes in the monthly cost of funds index.

Total deposits of $40.7 billion at 1994 year-end were 7% checking, 9% passbook, 15% money-market savings accounts, 68% term accounts under $100,000 and 1% jumbo CDs over $100,000. The average yield on earning assets for 1994 was 6.31% (6.52% for 1993), and the cost of funds was 3.75% (3.64%), for a spread of 2.56% (2.88%).

Nonperforming assets and restructured loans were $843.0 million (1.57% of assets) at year-end 1994, down from $960.3 million (1.89% of assets) a year earlier. Reserves were $400.2 million (0.72% of assets), versus $438.8 million (0.86%) a year earlier. Net chargeoffs in 1994 totaled $215.1 million (0.40% of assets), against $590.7 million (1.16%).

Important Developments

May '95—The company's Home Savings subsidiary agreed to sell its 60 retail branches in New York City, Long Island and Westchester County ($8.3 billion in deposits) and up to $1.5 billion of securities to Green-Point Financial Corp. for $660 million. Closing was expected during the third or fourth quarter of 1995.

Capitalization

FHLB Advances: $2,590,101,000 (6/95).
Other Borrowings: $3,579,604,000.
Preferred Stock: $657,500,000.

Per Share Data ($)

(Year Ended Dec. 31)

	1994	1993	1992	1991	1990	1989
Tangible Bk. Val.	19.70	15.94	17.76	16.63	15.08	14.33
Earnings	1.59	-1.51	1.19	2.06	1.64	1.95
Dividends	0.88	0.88	0.88	0.88	0.88	0.88
Payout Ratio	56%	NM	74%	43%	54%	45%
Prices - High	22¾	22⅛	19½	20⅞	22½	25
- Low	15¼	16¾	13	12	10⅝	15¾
P/E Ratio - High	14	NM	16	10	14	13
- Low	10	NM	11	6	6	8

Income Statement Analysis (Million $)

	1994	%Chg	1993	%Chg	1992	%Chg	1991
Net Int. Inc.	1,297	-3%	1,337	-2%	1,359	5%	1,292
Loan Loss Prov.	177	-69%	575	65%	348	78%	195
Non Int. Inc.	286	195%	97.0	-53%	208	1%	205
Non Int. Exp.	996	-8%	1,079	16%	929	15%	809
Pretax Inc.	411	NM	-219	NM	290	-39%	473
Eff. Tax Rate	42%	—	NM	—	46%	—	48%
Net Inc.	237	NM	-137	NM	156	-37%	246
% Net Int. Marg.	2.64%	—	2.90%	—	3.02%	—	2.71%

Balance Sheet & Other Fin. Data (Million $)

	1994	1993	1992	1991	1990	1989
Total Assets	53,726	50,871	48,141	47,226	51,201	44,652
Loans	48,791	44,624	42,401	42,318	44,839	38,407
Deposits	40,655	38,019	39,273	39,147	38,606	33,086
Capitalization:						
Debt	6,822	3,902	2,662	3,349	7,551	6,186
Equity	2,309	2,292	2,571	2,481	2,342	2,001
Total	9,786	6,851	5,408	6,005	9,893	8,187

Ratio Analysis

	1994	1993	1992	1991	1990	1989
% Ret. on Assets	0.5	NM	0.3	0.5	0.4	0.5
% Ret. on Equity	8.1	NM	5.5	10.0	8.3	10.0
% Loan Loss Resv.	0.8	1.0	1.0	0.7	0.5	0.3
% Risk Based Capital	12.2	12.6	13.0	10.4	9.0	7.1
Price Times Book Value:						
High	1.2	1.4	1.1	1.3	1.5	1.7
Low	0.8	1.1	0.7	0.7	0.7	1.1

Dividend Data

Dividends have been paid since 1968. A stockholder rights plan was adopted in 1988.

Amt. of Div. $	Date Decl.	Ex-Div. Date	Stock of Record	Payment Date
0.220	Jul. 12	Aug. 03	Aug. 09	Sep. 01 '94
0.220	Oct. 04	Nov. 04	Nov. 10	Dec. 01 '94
0.220	Dec. 06	Feb. 03	Feb. 09	Mar. 01 '95
0.220	Mar. 21	May. 04	May. 10	Jun. 01 '95
0.220	Jul. 11	Aug. 10	Aug. 14	Sep. 01 '95

Data as orig. reptd.; bef. results of disc opers. and/or spec. items. Per share data adj. for stk. divs. as of ex-div. date. E-Estimated. NA-Not Available. NM-Not Meaningful. NR-Not Ranked.

Office—4900 Rivergrade Rd., Irwindale, CA 91706. **Tel**—(818) 814-7986. **Chrmn & CEO**—C. R. Rinehart. **Pres & COO**—F. J. Forster. **Exec VP & Secy**—G. G. Gregory. **Exec VP & CFO**—K. M. Twomey. **Sr VP & Investor Contact**—Stephen A. Swartz (818) 814-7986. **Dirs**—W. H. Ahmanson, B. Allumbaugh, H. A. Black, R. M. Bressler, D. R. Carpenter, L. M. Cook, F. J. Forster, P. D. Matthews, D. M. Reyes, C. R. Rinehart, E. A. Sanders, A. W. Schmutz, W. D. Schulte, K. M. Twomey. **Transfer Agent & Registrar**—First Chicago Trust Co. of New York, NYC. **Incorporated** in California in 1928; reincorporated in Delaware in 1985. **Empl**-9,859. **S&P Analyst:** Paul L. Huberman, CFA

Air Products & Chemicals

NYSE Symbol **APD**

In S&P 500

01-SEP-95

Industry:
Chemicals

Summary: This major producer of industrial gases also makes specialty and intermediate chemicals and is developing environmental and energy-related businesses.

S&P Opinion: Accumulate (★★★★)

Recent Price • 54¾	Yield • 1.9%
52 Wk Range • 59%-43⅛	12-Mo. P/E • 17.4

Quantitative Evaluations

Outlook
(1 Lowest—5 Highest)
• **4+**

Fair Value
• **54¾**

Risk
• **Low**

Earn./Div. Rank
• **A**

Technical Eval.
• **Bullish** since 8/95

Rel. Strength Rank
(1 Lowest—99 Highest)
• **27**

Insider Activity
• **Neutral**

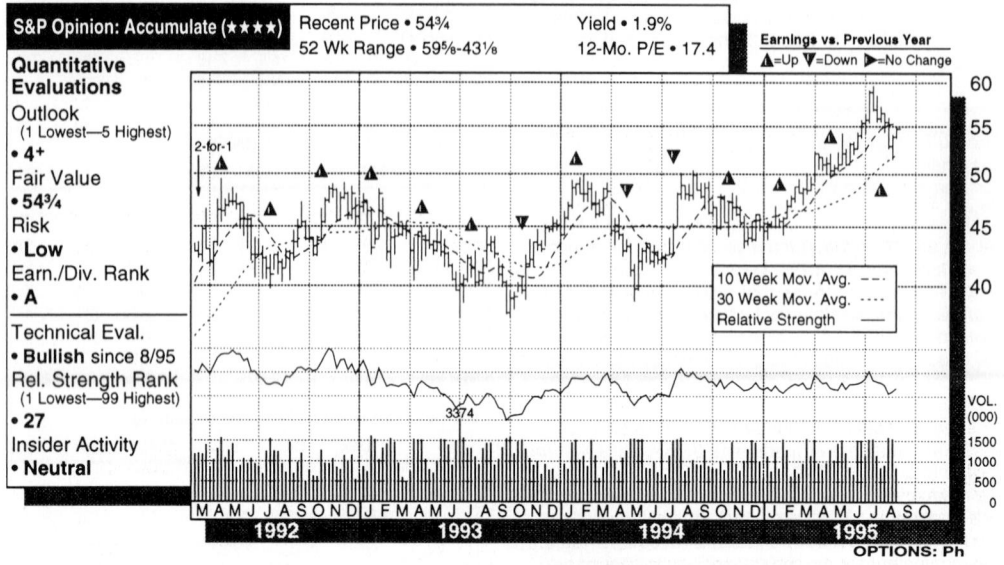

Earnings vs. Previous Year
▲=Up ▼=Down ▶=No Change

10 Week Mov. Avg. — - —
30 Week Mov. Avg. ......
Relative Strength ——

OPTIONS: Ph

Overview - 01-SEP-95

We see earnings in fiscal 1996 benefiting from the projected growing U.S. and European economies, which should result in continued volume gains in the industrial gases and specialty chemicals units. Selling prices for industrial gases in the U.S. should continue to rise modestly, with industrywide price increases and very high operating rates. However, the drop in methanol prices since early 1995 and the absence of merchant sales of ammonia will be limiting factors in 1996. Profits of the environmental business should pick up, assuming the facilities operate well, while a better project mix should help the equipment business return to the black. A cost reduction program will help profitability. A stock repurchase program will boost share earnings comparisons.

Valuation - 01-SEP-95

The shares of this industrial gases producer have been weak in recent weeks, falling from their all time high achieved in early July due to a combination of factors, including the announcement of new industrial gases capacity by a competitor. We feel the concerns of industry oversupply are overblown. Improving fundamentals for the industrial gases industry, including good volume growth and positive pricing momentum due to very high operating rates, make the shares, selling at 17 times our estimated fiscal 1995 earnings per share, attractive for the intermediate term. The dividend has been raised for 13 consecutive years.

Key Stock Statistics

S&P EPS Est. 1995	3.20	Tang. Bk. Value/Share	18.86
P/E on S&P Est. 1995	17.1	Beta	1.34
S&P EPS Est. 1996	3.50	Shareholders	11,100
Dividend Rate/Share	1.04	Market cap. (B)	$ 6.0
Shs. outstg. (M)	111.8	Inst. holdings	82%
Avg. daily vol. (M)	0.309	Insider holdings	NA

Value of $10,000 invested 5 years ago: $ 25,645

Fiscal Year Ending Sep. 30

	1995	% Change	1994	% Change	1993	% Change
Revenues (Million $)						
1Q	920.8	11%	827.3	NM	822.3	8%
2Q	982.9	14%	858.6	3%	833.9	5%
3Q	982.4	13%	868.4	5%	824.8	NM
4Q	—	—	931.0	9%	855.5	2%
Yr.	—	—	3,485	5%	3,328	3%
Income (Million $)						
1Q	86.70	15%	75.10	9%	69.00	7%
2Q	88.60	NM	13.50	-82%	75.30	3%
3Q	100.1	52%	65.80	-7%	70.80	4%
4Q	—	—	79.10	NM	-14.20	NM
Yr.	—	—	233.5	16%	200.9	-27%
Earnings Per Share ($)						
1Q	0.77	17%	0.66	8%	0.61	7%
2Q	0.79	NM	0.12	-82%	0.66	2%
3Q	0.89	53%	0.58	-6%	0.62	3%
4Q	E0.75	7%	0.70	NM	-0.13	NM
Yr.	E3.20	55%	2.06	17%	1.76	-28%

Next earnings report expected: late October

16

Air Products & Chemicals

Business Summary - 29-AUG-95

This major industrial gas producer derived its fiscal 1994 sales and operating profits from the following major business segments:

	Sales	Profits
Industrial gases	56%	70%
Chemicals	34%	27%
Environmental & energy	2%	Nil
Equipment & services	8%	2%

International operations accounted for 24% of sales and 22% of operating income in fiscal 1994.

APD is an international producer of industrial, medical and specialty gases, including nitrogen, oxygen, argon, hydrogen, helium, carbon monoxide, synthesis gas and fluorine compounds for both merchant and tonnage (on-site) customers.

Chemicals include polymers (emulsions, polyvinyl alcohol) for adhesives, coatings, paper and textiles; polyurethane intermediates and additives used in furniture, automotive and construction markets; and amines and specialty and epoxy additives for pesticides, water treatment chemicals, adhesives and coatings. Commodity chemicals (methanol, ammonia and acetic acid) are also produced as raw materials or coproducts.

Environmental and energy activities include landfill gas recovery and ventures in waste-to-energy, cogeneration and flue gas desulfurization.

Equipment and services consist of cryogenic and process equipment for air separation, gas processing, natural gas liquefaction, hydrogen purification and nitrogen rejection; technology licensing; and venture R&D activities.

Important Developments

Jul. '95—APD said that fiscal 1995 third quarter earnings included a nonrecurring gain of $0.06 a share, while the year earlier period included charges totaling $0.14 a share. Excluding nonrecurring items, earnings rose 15%, reflecting continued strong growth in the industrial gases and chemicals businesses. Industrial gases profits rose 7% on worldwide volume growth and improved merchant gas prices of 3% in the U.S. Chemical profits advanced 9% on volume growth of 11% with gains in all major products, and despite lower ammonia profits. Merchant ammonia capacity was shut down in February and is being converted to hydrogen production. Environmental profits declined from those of the 1994 period which included a performance bonus, while the equipment segment reported a breakeven performance, versus a small loss.

Capitalization

Long Term Debt: $1,326,100,000 (6/95).

Per Share Data ($)
(Year Ended Sep. 30)

	1994	1993	1992	1991	1990	1989
Tangible Bk. Val.	18.86	17.85	17.87	15.51	14.53	12.47
Cash Flow	5.22	4.87	5.46	5.12	4.86	4.63
Earnings	2.06	1.76	2.45	2.23	2.08	2.02
Dividends	0.95	0.89	0.82	0.75	0.69	0.63
Payout Ratio	46%	51%	34%	34%	33%	31%
Prices - High	50⅛	48½	49½	37⅛	30½	24⅜
- Low	38¾	37½	36½	25⅝	21½	20
P/E Ratio - High	24	28	20	17	15	12
- Low	19	20	15	12	10	10

Income Statement Analysis (Million $)

	1994	%Chg	1993	%Chg	1992	%Chg	1991
Revs.	3,485	5%	3,328	3%	3,217	10%	2,931
Oper. Inc.	840	-3%	864	6%	812	11%	729
Depr.	360	2%	353	4%	340	5%	325
Int. Exp.	90.0	5%	86.0	-5%	91.0	-15%	107
Pretax Inc.	325	8%	301	-26%	407	12%	363
Eff. Tax Rate	28%	—	33%	—	32%	—	31%
Net Inc.	234	16%	201	-27%	277	11%	249

Balance Sheet & Other Fin. Data (Million $)

	1994	1993	1992	1991	1990	1989
Cash	100	238	117	104	74.0	50.0
Curr. Assets	1,178	1,196	998	901	837	757
Total Assets	5,036	4,762	4,492	4,228	3,900	3,366
Curr. Liab.	1,076	874	719	785	623	494
LT Debt	923	1,016	956	945	954	854
Common Eqty.	2,206	2,102	2,098	1,841	1,688	1,445
Total Cap.	3,552	3,607	3,556	3,263	3,094	2,716
Cap. Exp.	614	495	428	506	468	414
Cash Flow	594	554	617	574	538	508

Ratio Analysis

	1994	1993	1992	1991	1990	1989
Curr. Ratio	1.1	1.4	1.4	1.1	1.3	1.5
% LT Debt of Cap.	26.0	28.2	26.9	29.0	30.8	31.4
% Net Inc.of Revs.	6.7	6.0	8.6	8.5	7.9	8.4
% Ret. on Assets	4.8	4.3	6.4	6.1	6.3	7.0
% Ret. on Equity	10.9	9.5	14.1	14.0	14.6	16.3

Dividend Data

Dividends have been paid since 1954. A dividend reinvestment plan is available. A "poison pill" stock purchase right was adopted in 1988.

Amt. of Div. $	Date Decl.	Ex-Div. Date	Stock of Record	Payment Date
0.245	Sep. 15	Sep. 27	Oct. 03	Nov. 14 '94
0.245	Nov. 18	Dec. 27	Jan. 03	Feb. 13 '95
0.245	Mar. 16	Mar. 28	Apr. 03	May. 12 '95
0.260	May. 17	Jun. 29	Jul. 03	Aug. 14 '95

Data as orig. reptd.; bef. results of disc. opers. and/or spec. items. Per share data adj. for stk. divs. as of ex-div. date. E-Estimated. NA-Not Available. NM-Not Meaningful. NR-Not Ranked.

Office—7201 Hamilton Blvd., Allentown, PA 18195-1501 **Tel**—(610) 481-4911. **Chrmn & Pres**—H. A. Wagner. **Sr VP-Fin**—G. A. White. **VP-Secy**—J. H. Agger. **Investor Contact**—Brennen Arndt. **Dirs**—D. F. Baker, T. H. Barrett, L. P. Bremer III, W. M. Caldwell, R. Cizik, R. M. Davis, T. R. Lautenbach, R. F. M. Lubbers, J. Rodin, T. Shiina, L. D. Thomas, H. A. Wagner. **Transfer Agent & Registrar**—Mellon Securities Trust Co., Pittsburgh. **Incorporated** in Michigan in 1940; reincorporated in Delaware in 1961. **Empl**-13,300. **S&P Analyst:** Richard O'Reilly, CFA

AirTouch Communications

NYSE Symbol **ATI**
In S&P 500

01-NOV-95

Industry:
Telecommunications

Summary: ATI is a leading provider of wireless communications services worldwide. The company was spun off to Pacific Telesis shareholders in April 1994.

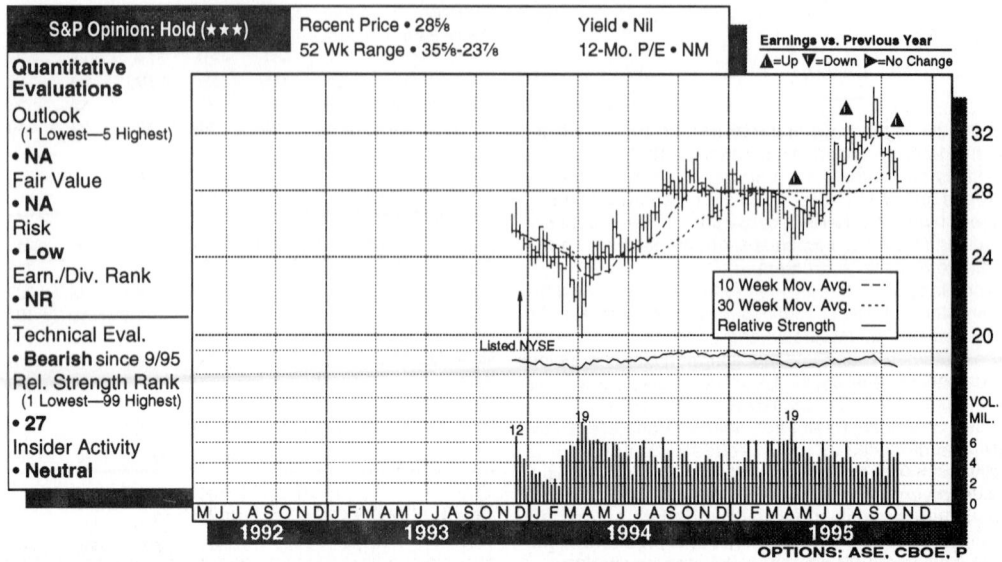

S&P Opinion: Hold (★★★)	Recent Price • 28⅝	Yield • Nil
	52 Wk Range • 35⅝-23⅞	12-Mo. P/E • NM

Earnings vs. Previous Year
▲=Up ▼=Down ▶=No Change

Quantitative Evaluations

Outlook
(1 Lowest—5 Highest)
• **NA**

Fair Value
• **NA**

Risk
• **Low**

Earn./Div. Rank
• **NR**

Technical Eval.
• **Bearish** since 9/95

Rel. Strength Rank
(1 Lowest—99 Highest)
• **27**

Insider Activity
• **Neutral**

10 Week Mov. Avg. ---
30 Week Mov. Avg. ····
Relative Strength —

Listed NYSE

1992 1993 1994 1995

OPTIONS: ASE, CBOE, P

Overview - 01-NOV-95

Expected rapid industrywide growth in demand for mobile telecommunications services should contribute to strong revenue growth through 1996. However, as competition begins to increase with the advent of new services such as enhanced specialized mobile radio (ESMR) and personal communications services (PCS), this growth in demand will be offset by pressures on pricing. The company's efforts to create a national network through an alliance with other cellular operations should help its competitive position, but efforts to be a major player in PCS may prove expensive over the near term. International revenues should continue their strong growth, aided by the company's position as the largest European cellular provider. AirTouch is also a partner in Globalstar, a venture that plans to offer satellite-based wireless services by 1998.

Valuation - 01-NOV-95

The shares have been held back by investor concerns about increasing competition. The company's premier U.S. operations will benefit from its pending alliances, while international operations should make growing contributions in future periods. Despite these strong long-term growth prospects, near-term earnings may be restricted by costs associated with the planned alliance with U S WEST's cellular operations. We recommend holding the shares until the potential impact of these costs becomes clearer.

Key Stock Statistics

S&P EPS Est. 1995	0.30	Tang. Bk. Value/Share	6.05
P/E on S&P Est. 1995	95.4	Beta	NA
S&P EPS Est. 1996	0.45	Shareholders	9,400
Dividend Rate/Share	Nil	Market cap. (B)	$ 14.1
Shs. outstg. (M)	495.0	Inst. holdings	57%
Avg. daily vol. (M)	0.861	Insider holdings	NA

Value of $10,000 invested 5 years ago: NA

Fiscal Year Ending Dec. 31

	1995	% Change	1994	% Change	1993	% Change
Revenues (Million $)						
1Q	367.2	43%	257.3	8%	239.0	—
2Q	395.1	42%	279.2	7%	260.0	—
3Q	407.2	40%	290.4	14%	255.0	—
4Q	—	—	309.3	32%	235.0	—
Yr.	—	—	1,136	15%	988.0	44%
Income (Million $)						
1Q	35.30	28%	27.50	—	—	—
2Q	38.70	17%	33.10	—	—	—
3Q	46.70	36%	34.40	—	—	—
4Q	—	—	3.10	—	—	—
Yr.	—	—	98.10	145%	40.10	NM
Earnings Per Share ($)						
1Q	0.07	17%	0.06	—	--	—
2Q	0.08	14%	0.07	—	--	—
3Q	0.09	29%	0.07	—	--	—
4Q	E0.06	NM	0.01	—	--	—
Yr.	E0.30	50%	0.20	122%	0.09	NM

Next earnings report expected: early February

AirTouch Communications

Business Summary - 31-OCT-95

AirTouch Communications, Inc. (formerly PacTel Corp.) is a leading provider of wireless telecommunications services worldwide. In the U.S., ATI has interests in cellular systems in markets covering approximately 35 million POPs (as adjusted for percentage ownership). Internationally, the company has interests in licenses covering 64.1 million POPs.

At September 30, 1995, the company served 1,915,000 cellular subscribers in the U.S. (based on proportionate interests). The cellular systems serve 10 of the 30 largest U.S. markets. As part of its strategy to build on existing regional networks to increase its geographic footprint, ATI agreed to form a domestic cellular joint venture with U S WEST (USW). The venture will be 70% owned by ATI and will have operations in 21 states. The companies will also form a 50/50 joint venture to pursue personal communications services (PCS) opportunities.

In October 1994, ATI agreed to form a national wireless partnership with U S WEST, Bell Atlantic (BEL) and NYNEX (NYN); the partnership, which will be 50%-owned by the ATI/USW venture, builds on ATI's joint venture with USW. BEL and NYN merged their cellular operations, which cover 55 million potential customers on the East Coast and in the Southwest. Under the agreement, the four companies formed a partnership to bid for PCS licenses that will complement the four companies' existing cellular assets.

ATI has focused its international growth on Europe and Asia, concentrating on countries with favorable demographics such as population growth and per capita income. Major international cellular operations include interests in German, Portuguese and Japanese cellular systems.

The company is the fourth largest provider of paging services in the U.S., providing local, regional and national narrowband data and messaging services in 120 markets in 17 states. At September 30, 1995, domestic paging operations served 1,875,000 customers. International paging interests include holdings in a Portuguese nationwide paging operator and a stake in a Thailand national paging service.

Important Developments

Oct. '95—ATI said it could experience some short-term earnings dilution from the planned merger of its domestic cellular operations with those of U S WEST. Under the first phase of the merger, the companies on November 1 will begin using the same management for various support services for their independently owned cellular operations.

May '95—The FCC denied seven states the authority to continue regulating intrastate cellular rates.

Capitalization

Long Term Debt: $121,900,000 (9/95).
Minority Interests: $145,200,000.

Per Share Data ($)

(Year Ended Dec. 31)

	1994	1993	1992	1991	1990	1989
Tangible Bk. Val.	6.05	5.94	6.76	NA	NA	NA
Cash Flow	0.61	0.50	0.31	NA	NA	NA
Earnings	0.20	0.09	0.01	NA	NA	NA
Dividends	Nil	Nil	NA	NA	NA	NA
Payout Ratio	Nil	Nil	NA	NA	NA	NA
Prices - High	30⅝	27¼	NA	NA	NA	NA
- Low	19⅞	24⅜	NA	NA	NA	NA
P/E Ratio - High	NM	NM	NA	NA	NA	NA
- Low	NM	NM	NA	NA	NA	NA

Income Statement Analysis (Million $)

	1994	%Chg	1993	%Chg	1992	%Chg	1991
Revs.	1,235	17%	1,058	54%	687	—	NA
Oper. Inc.	278	-9%	307	115%	143	—	NA
Depr.	205	18%	174	34%	130	—	NA
Int. Exp.	10.7	-59%	25.8	NM	6.6	—	NA
Pretax Inc.	223	45%	154	NM	42.8	—	NA
Eff. Tax Rate	49%	—	44%	—	94%	—	NA
Net Inc.	98.1	145%	40.1	NM	2.6	—	NA

Balance Sheet & Other Fin. Data (Million $)

	1994	1993	1992	1991	1990	1989
Cash	840	1,461	NA	NA	NA	NA
Curr. Assets	1,266	1,661	NA	NA	NA	NA
Total Assets	4,488	4,077	3,855	NA	NA	NA
Curr. Liab.	530	314	NA	NA	NA	NA
LT Debt	120	69.0	69.7	NA	NA	NA
Common Eqty.	3,460	3,337	3,201	NA	NA	NA
Total Cap.	3,919	3,709	NA	NA	NA	NA
Cap. Exp.	383	397	NA	NA	NA	NA
Cash Flow	303	214	133	NA	NA	NA

Ratio Analysis

	1994	1993	1992	1991	1990	1989
Curr. Ratio	2.4	5.3	NA	NA	NA	NA
% LT Debt of Cap.	3.1	1.8	NA	NA	NA	NA
% Net Inc.of Revs.	7.9	3.8	0.4	NA	NA	NA
% Ret. on Assets	2.3	1.2	NA	NA	NA	NA
% Ret. on Equity	2.9	1.9	NA	NA	NA	NA

Dividend Data —No dividends have been paid. The company does not expect to pay cash dividends for the foreseeable future and intends to retain future earnings for the development of its business.

Data as orig. reptd.; bef. results of disc. opers. and/or spec. items. Per share data adj. for stk. divs. as of ex-div. date. E-Estimated. NA-Not Available. NM-Not Meaningful. NR-Not Ranked.

Office—One California St., San Francisco, CA 94111. **Tel**—(415) 658-2000. **Chrmn & CEO**—S. L. Ginn. **Pres**—C. L. Cox. **Exec VP-CFO**—M. Gyani. **VP-Secy**—M. G. Gill. **Investor Contact**—Barbara Riker. **Dirs**—C. A. Bartz, C. L. Cox, D. G. Fisher, S. L. Ginn, J. R. Harvey, P. Hazen, A. Rock, C. R. Schwab, G. P. Schultz. **Transfer Agent & Registrar**—Bank of New York, NYC. **Incorporated** in California in 1984. **Empl**-4,576. **S&P Analyst:** Kevin J. Gooley

Alberto-Culver

NYSE Symbol **ACV**
In S&P 500

07-AUG-95

Industry:
Cosmetics/Toiletries

Summary: Alberto-Culver produces well known hair care products and other health and beauty aids, and operates Sally Beauty, the world's largest chain of professional beauty supply stores.

S&P Opinion: Accumulate (★★★★)

Recent Price • 30⅛
52 Wk Range • 32½-20¾

Yield • 1.1%
12-Mo. P/E • 16.5

Earnings vs. Previous Year
▲=Up ▼=Down ▶=No Change

Quantitative Evaluations

Outlook
(1 Lowest—5 Highest)
• **4+**

Fair Value
• **31¾**

Risk
• **Low**

Earn./Div. Rank
• **A**

Technical Eval.
• **Bearish** since 9/94

Rel. Strength Rank
(1 Lowest—99 Highest)
• **22**

Insider Activity
• **Neutral**

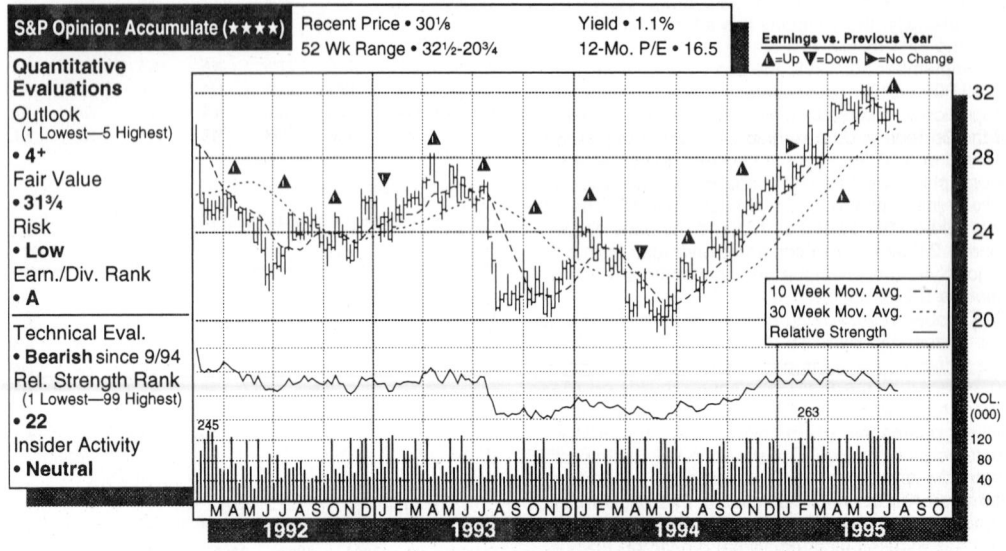

10 Week Mov. Avg. — -
30 Week Mov. Avg. ·····
Relative Strength —

Overview - 07-AUG-95

Sales should advance moderately in fiscal 1996, with increases in each operating division. Sales of personal use and food products should continue to benefit from wider distribution, especially overseas, and new product introductions, including product line extensions. Potential acquisitions of niche products, especially in growing overseas markets, could further aid sales growth. Sales at Sally Beauty should rise on higher same-store sales, new store openings in the U.S., and expansion into Asian markets. Despite high costs for advertising, marketing programs, distribution improvements, and product and package developments, margins should widen on higher volume of personal use and food products and a higher percentage of sales derived from the very profitable Sally Beauty stores.

Valuation - 07-AUG-95

The shares have been trending upward since reaching their most recent low just under 20 in mid-1994. We attribute this rise to an acceleration in the company's earnings, mainly reflecting improved margins due to a higher percentage of sales derived from the very profitable Sally Beauty stores. We expect earnings to increase 12%-15% annually in the near future, as the company pursues overseas growth. Small- to medium-sized acquisitions will boost growth. Based on fiscal 1996's estimated EPS, the shares are trading near the low end of their historical price-earnings range, and should be accumulated for capital appreciation.

Key Stock Statistics

S&P EPS Est. 1995	1.85	Tang. Bk. Value/Share	10.50
P/E on S&P Est. 1995	16.3	Beta	1.12
S&P EPS Est. 1996	2.15	Shareholders	2,900
Dividend Rate/Share	0.32	Market cap. (B)	$0.835
Shs. outstg. (M)	27.7	Inst. holdings	18%
Avg. daily vol. (M)	0.027	Insider holdings	NA

Value of $10,000 invested 5 years ago: $ 14,227

Fiscal Year Ending Sep. 30

	1995	% Change	1994	% Change	1993	% Change
Revenues (Million $)						
1Q	311.5	9%	284.6	6%	269.0	9%
2Q	324.2	7%	302.8	5%	288.5	5%
3Q	357.7	14%	315.0	9%	289.6	4%
4Q	—	—	313.7	4%	300.5	3%
Yr.	—	—	1,216	6%	1,148	5%
Income (Million $)						
1Q	11.20	31%	8.53	NM	8.60	-8%
2Q	12.23	31%	9.31	-17%	11.25	10%
3Q	13.63	11%	12.28	22%	10.06	10%
4Q	—	—	13.95	23%	11.37	15%
Yr.	—	—	44.07	7%	41.27	7%
Earnings Per Share ($)						
1Q	0.40	NM	0.40	33%	0.30	-9%
2Q	0.44	33%	0.33	-15%	0.39	8%
3Q	0.49	11%	0.44	26%	0.35	9%
4Q	E0.52	—	0.50	25%	0.40	14%
Yr.	E1.85	—	1.57	9%	1.44	6%

Next earnings report expected: late October

Alberto-Culver

Business Summary - 07-AUG-95

Business segment contributions in fiscal 1994 were:

	Sales	Profits
Mass marketed products	40%	14%
Institutional	8%	10%
Sally Beauty	52%	76%

International operations accounted for 25% of sales and 13% of profits in fiscal 1994.

Mass marketed products consist of personal use products, food and household aids, and health and hygiene products. Personal use products include hair fixatives, shampoos, hairdressings and conditioners sold under such trademarks as Alberto, Alberto VO5, Bold Hold, Consort, Tresemme, TCB, Alberto One Step and Alberto Balsam; FDS Feminine Deodorant Spray; Alberto VO5 Tropical deodorant; Command after shave lotion; and Beyond Fragrances. Food and household aids include Sugartwin sugar replacement, Mrs. Dash seasonings, Molly McButter butter substitute, Village Saucerie sauce and recipe mixes, Baker's Joy baking spray, Static Guard anti-static spray, and Kleen Guard furniture polish. Health and hygiene products are sold by Swedish-based, wholly owned Cederroth. Major products include Salve adhesive bandages, Seltin salt substitute, Savett wet wipes, Lactacyd liquid soap, and Topz cotton buds.

Institutional products include specialty foods for institutions and restaurants and professional hair care products. Major brands include Milani, Sugartwin, Mrs. Dash, Molly McButter, Diafoods Thick-it, Smithers, Tresemme, TCB and Indola.

Sally Beauty operates the world's largest network of cash-and-carry beauty supply stores carrying a full complement of professional toiletry and salon hair care products. As of December 31, 1994, Sally operated 1,386 outlets in the U.S. and the U.K., up from 1,235 at the end of fiscal 1993.

Important Developments

Jul. '95—ACV attributed its strong third quarter performance to strong sales in Europe, mainly reflecting the acquisition of Swedish-based Molnlycke Toiletries in April. Sales and profits at the company's Alberto-Culver USA unit were relatively unchanged from last year's strong third quarter results, while Sally Beauty Supply recorded good sales and earnings growth.

Capitalization

Long Term Debt: $87,683,000 (6/95).
Class A Common Stock: 10,949,209 shs. ($0.22 par); divd. may exceed Cl. B divd.; 0.10 vote per sh.
Class B Common Stock: 16,766,240 shs. ($0.22 par); conv. sh.-for-sh. into Cl. A.
The Lavin family owns 47% of Cl. B and 12% of Cl. A. Institutions hold 56% of Cl. A and 36% of Cl. B. Shareholders of record: 1,176 Cl. A; 1,344 Cl. B.

Per Share Data ($)

(Year Ended Sep. 30)

	1994	1993	1992	1991	1990	1989
Tangible Bk. Val.	9.85	8.71	7.92	7.23	7.56	5.53
Cash Flow	2.19	2.01	1.91	1.47	1.68	1.42
Earnings	1.57	1.44	1.36	1.06	1.30	1.13
Dividends	0.28	0.28	0.24	0.22	0.19	0.17
Payout Ratio	18%	19%	17%	20%	16%	15%
Prices - High	27⅜	28¼	32	34¼	33¼	26¾
- Low	19⅜	20⅛	21¼	20½	19⅛	16⅜
P/E Ratio - High	17	20	24	32	26	24
- Low	12	14	16	19	15	15

Income Statement Analysis (Million $)

	1994	%Chg	1993	%Chg	1992	%Chg	1991
Revs.	1,216	6%	1,148	5%	1,091	25%	874
Oper. Inc.	94.2	6%	88.7	4%	85.0	39%	61.3
Depr.	17.2	6%	16.2	5%	15.5	36%	11.4
Int. Exp.	8.6	-11%	9.7	-17%	11.7	72%	6.8
Pretax Inc.	71.1	9%	65.1	6%	61.4	28%	48.1
Eff. Tax Rate	38%	—	37%	—	37%	—	37%
Net Inc.	44.1	7%	41.3	7%	38.6	28%	30.1

Balance Sheet & Other Fin. Data (Million $)

	1994	1993	1992	1991	1990	1989
Cash	50.4	73.9	80.2	84.6	75.0	39.3
Curr. Assets	402	401	412	404	329	256
Total Assets	610	593	610	574	437	363
Curr. Liab.	216	196	219	192	137	128
LT Debt	43.0	80.2	84.5	97.8	60.7	68.9
Common Eqty.	327	299	286	249	231	160
Total Cap.	385	388	378	372	296	233
Cap. Exp.	26.2	26.4	21.8	29.7	14.4	17.8
Cash Flow	61.3	57.5	54.1	41.5	45.1	37.1

Ratio Analysis

	1994	1993	1992	1991	1990	1989
Curr. Ratio	1.9	2.0	1.9	2.1	2.4	2.0
% LT Debt of Cap.	11.2	20.7	22.4	26.3	20.5	29.5
% Net Inc.of Revs.	3.6	3.6	3.5	3.4	4.4	4.1
% Ret. on Assets	7.4	6.9	6.5	6.0	8.4	8.8
% Ret. on Equity	14.2	14.2	14.3	12.6	17.3	19.9

Dividend Data (Dividends have been paid since 1967. Payments are identical on Class A and Class B shares.)

Amt. of Div. $	Date Decl.	Ex-Div. Date	Stock of Record	Payment Date
0.070	Jul. 28	Aug. 01	Aug. 05	Aug. 20 '94
0.070	Oct. 27	Oct. 31	Nov. 04	Nov. 20 '94
0.080	Jan. 26	Jan. 30	Feb. 03	Feb. 20 '95
0.080	Apr. 27	May. 01	May. 05	May. 20 '95
0.080	Jul. 27	Aug. 03	Aug. 07	Aug. 20 '95

Data as orig. reptd.; bef. results of disc. opers. and/or spec. items. Per share data adj. for stk. divs. as of ex-div. date. E-Estimated. NA-Not Available. NM-Not Meaningful. NR-Not Ranked.

Office—2525 Armitage Ave., Melrose Park, IL 60160. **Tel**—(708) 450-3000. **Chrmn**—L. H. Lavin. **Pres & CEO**—H. B. Bernick. **VP, Secy & Treas**—B. E. Lavin. **VP-Fin & Investor Contact**—William J. Cernugel. **Dirs**—A. R. Abboud, C. L. Bernick, H. B. Bernick, R. P. Gwinn, L. W. Jennings, B. E. Lavin, L. H. Lavin, H. M. Visotsky, W. W. Wirtz. **Transfer Agent & Registrar**—First National Bank of Boston. **Incorporated** in Delaware in 1961. **Empl**-9,300. **S&P Analyst:** Elizabeth Vandeventer

Albertson's, Inc.

NYSE Symbol **ABS**
In S&P 500

11-AUG-95 Industry:
Retail Stores

Summary: This operator of supermarkets and combination food-drug stores, the fourth largest U.S. food retailer, operates 720 stores in 10 states.

| S&P Opinion: Hold (★★★) | Recent Price • 29¼ | Yield • 1.8% |
| | 52 Wk Range • 32½-26¼ | 12-Mo. P/E • 17.2 |

Quantitative Evaluations

Outlook
(1 Lowest—5 Highest)
• **2⁻**

Fair Value
• **27**

Risk
• **Low**

Earn./Div. Rank
• **A+**

Technical Eval.
• **Bearish** since 5/95

Rel. Strength Rank
(1 Lowest—99 Highest)
• **21**

Insider Activity
• **Favorable**

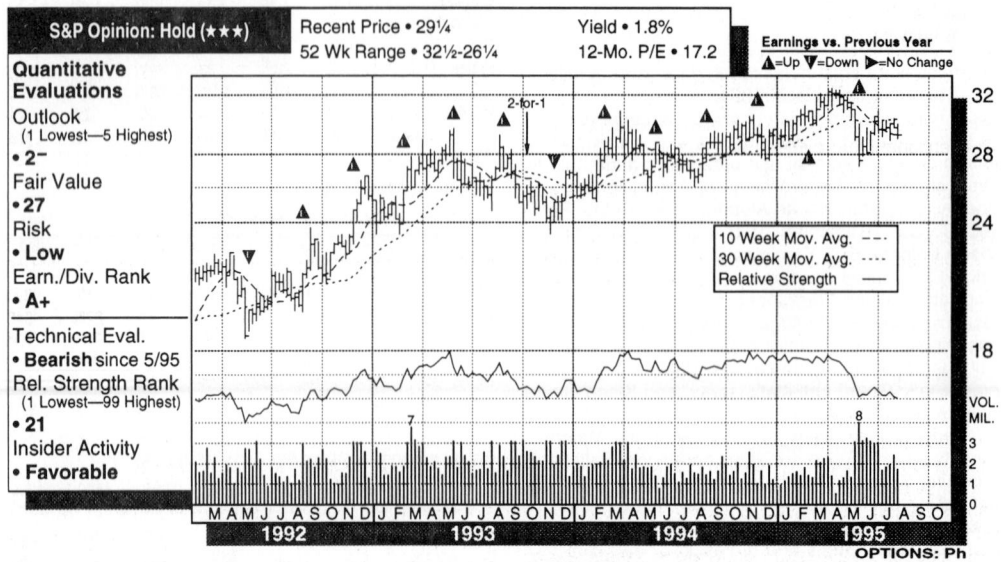

Earnings vs. Previous Year
▲=Up ▼=Down ▶=No Change

10 Week Mov. Avg. - - -
30 Week Mov. Avg. ·····
Relative Strength ——

OPTIONS: Ph

Overview - 11-AUG-95

Revenue gains in 1995-96 should total about 11%, with increases in same-store sales of 1% to 2%. The company plans to add about 43 new stores and re-model 56 units. Gross margins should widen only modestly--most benefits of self-distribution in ware-housing have already been achieved. Operating and administrative expense ratios should improve, on greater efficiencies and higher sales. Operating profit should climb about 11%, as should earnings per share. Strong management and presence in growing geographic areas bode well for future earnings gains. Increased use of technology to lower costs should en-hance ABS's competitive position. Strong cash flow provides ample funds for a $560 million capital spend-ing program and a share buyback of up to five million shares.

Valuation - 11-AUG-95

Earnings gains have slowed from Albertson's enviable record of 18% annual earnings growth over the past decade. Significant financial strength and consistent earnings gains have resulted in a premium P/E multi-ple to that of other supermarket companies. The com-pany's combination store format is best able to gain market share in the highly competitive supermarket in-dustry. But reflecting diminished opportunities for gross margin expansion, earnings gains have slowed some-what and are projected to increase only about 11% this year. We see the shares as fairly valued at this level.

Key Stock Statistics

S&P EPS Est. 1996	1.85	Tang. Bk. Value/Share	6.90
P/E on S&P Est. 1996	15.8	Beta	0.76
S&P EPS Est. 1997	2.05	Shareholders	11,400
Dividend Rate/Share	0.52	Market cap. (B)	$ 7.4
Shs. outstg. (M)	254.0	Inst. holdings	46%
Avg. daily vol. (M)	0.425	Insider holdings	NA

Value of $10,000 invested 5 years ago: $ 22,798

Fiscal Year Ending Jan. 31

	1996	% Change	1995	% Change	1994	% Change
Revenues (Million $)						
1Q	3,083	6%	2,910	7%	2,720	18%
2Q	—	—	2,988	8%	2,768	6%
3Q	—	—	2,928	7%	2,734	6%
4Q	—	—	3,069	NM	3,062	14%
Yr.	—	—	11,895	5%	11,284	11%
Income (Million $)						
1Q	99.3	17%	85.16	15%	74.14	125%
2Q	—	—	93.68	23%	75.87	15%
3Q	—	—	94.33	50%	62.71	-12%
4Q	—	—	144.2	14%	127.0	20%
Yr.	—	—	417.4	23%	339.7	23%
Earnings Per Share ($)						
1Q	0.39	15%	0.34	17%	0.29	132%
2Q	E0.41	—	0.37	23%	0.30	20%
3Q	E0.43	—	0.37	48%	0.25	-7%
4Q	E0.62	—	0.57	14%	0.50	25%
Yr.	E1.85	—	1.65	23%	1.34	29%

Next earnings report expected: late August

Albertson's, Inc.

Business Summary - 11-AUG-95

At February 2, 1995, Albertson's operated 720 stores in 19 western and southern states. The stores consisted of 588 combination food and drug units, 88 conventional units and 44 warehouse stores. About 93% of the square footage was newly built or remodeled during the past 10 years.

Combination food and drug stores range in size from 35,000 to 75,000 sq. ft. Selling space is divided between prescription and proprietary drugs and general merchandise, and regular supermarket products.

Conventional supermarkets range from 15,000 to 35,000 sq. ft. in size and offer a full line of grocery items and, in many locations, feature in-store bakeries and delicatessens.

Warehouse stores vary in size from 17,000 sq. ft. up to 73,000 sq. ft. These no-frills units offer significant savings on meat and produce and from large, bulk packaging.

Retail operations are supported by 11 company-owned distribution centers. About 77% of all products purchased by company stores are supplied from facilities operated by Albertson's.

A $3.4 billion capital spending plan for the five years from 1995 through 1999 includes building 351 new stores and making 242 remodels. Square footage would rise about 8% annually. The balance of the program is earmarked for retail replacement equipment, distribution and new information systems. The company aims for a 12% return on average assets and a 15% annual gain in share earnings.

Important Developments

Jun. '95—Albertson's issued $200 million 6.375% notes due June 1, 2000. Identical store sales increased 0.5% in the first quarter of 1995-96 from a year earlier; total sales rose 6.0%. Gross profit increased as a percentage of sales due to higher utilization of the company's distribution facilities. Operating profit rose 11.3%, year-to-year. Net square footage rose 7.2% in the first quarter from a year earlier. Capital spending in 1995-96 was projected at $590 million, most of which was earmarked for new stores. The company has said that it continues to concentrate on increasing same-store sales, employee training and advancement, controlling expenses, and adding retail store square footage. Directors have authorized the repurchase of up to five million common shares through March 31, 1996.

Capitalization

Long Term Debt: $515,197,000, incl. $130.1 million of capital lease obligs. (4/4/95).

Per Share Data ($) (Year Ended Jan. 31)

	1995	1994	1993	1992	1991	1990
Tangible Bk. Val.	6.65	5.48	5.24	4.54	4.06	3.47
Cash Flow	2.54	2.11	1.70	1.47	1.33	1.14
Earnings	1.65	1.34	1.05	0.97	0.88	0.74
Dividends	0.53	0.35	0.31	0.27	0.23	0.19
Payout Ratio	32%	26%	30%	28%	26%	25%
Cal. Yrs.	1994	1993	1992	1991	1990	1989
Prices - High	$30\frac{7}{8}$	$29\frac{5}{8}$	$26\frac{3}{4}$	$25\frac{3}{4}$	$18\frac{7}{8}$	$15\frac{1}{8}$
- Low	$25\frac{1}{8}$	$23\frac{3}{8}$	$18\frac{3}{8}$	$16\frac{3}{8}$	$12\frac{1}{4}$	$9\frac{1}{8}$
P/E Ratio - High	19	22	26	26	22	21
- Low	15	19	18	17	14	13

Income Statement Analysis (Million $)

	1995	%Chg	1994	%Chg	1993	%Chg	1992
Revs.	11,895	5%	11,284	11%	10,174	17%	8,680
Oper. Inc.	961	16%	826	19%	695	27%	548
Depr.	226	15%	197	15%	172	28%	134
Int. Exp.	66.1	20%	55.2	16%	47.7	70%	28.1
Pretax Inc.	679	23%	552	24%	444	9%	406
Eff. Tax Rate	39%	—	39%	—	38%	—	37%
Net Inc.	417	23%	340	23%	276	7%	258

Balance Sheet & Other Fin. Data (Million $)

	1995	1994	1993	1992	1991	1990
Cash	50.0	62.0	40.0	34.0	23.0	44.0
Curr. Assets	1,190	1,122	1,013	751	677	668
Total Assets	3,622	3,295	2,946	2,216	2,014	1,863
Curr. Liab.	1,095	990	816	652	586	555
LT Debt	512	665	508	152	159	218
Common Eqty.	1,688	1,389	1,388	1,199	1,088	929
Total Cap.	2,202	2,083	1,917	1,360	1,259	1,170
Cap. Exp.	473	456	331	273	255	303
Cash Flow	644	536	448	392	356	305

Ratio Analysis

	1995	1994	1993	1992	1991	1990
Curr. Ratio	1.1	1.1	1.2	1.2	1.2	1.2
% LT Debt of Cap.	23.3	31.9	26.5	11.1	12.6	18.7
% Net Inc.of Revs.	3.5	3.0	2.7	3.0	2.8	2.6
% Ret. on Assets	12.1	11.1	10.7	12.3	12.1	11.4
% Ret. on Equity	27.1	25.0	21.3	22.7	23.2	22.7

Dividend Data (Dividends have been paid since 1960. A poison pill stock purchase rights plan was adopted in 1987.)

Amt. of Div. $	Date Decl.	Ex-Div. Date	Stock of Record	Payment Date
0.110	Sep. 06	Oct. 31	Nov. 04	Nov. 25 '94
0.110	Dec. 05	Jan. 30	Feb. 03	Feb. 25 '95
0.130	Mar. 06	May. 01	May. 05	May. 25 '95
0.130	May. 26	Aug. 02	Aug. 04	Aug. 25 '95

Data as orig. reptd.; bef. results of disc. opers. and/or spec. items. Per share data adj. for stk. divs. as of ex-div. date. E-Estimated. NA-Not Available. NM-Not Meaningful. NR-Not Ranked.

Office—250 Parkcenter Blvd. (P.O. Box 20), Boise, ID 83726. **Tel**—(208) 385-6200. **Chrmn & CEO**—G. G. Michael. **Pres & COO**—J. B. Carley. **SVP-Fin & CFO**—A. C. Olson. **VP, Treas & Investor Contact**—David I. Connolly. **Secy**—Kaye L. O'Riordan. **Dirs**—K. Albertson, A. G. Ames, C. D. Andrus, J. B. Carley, P. I. Corddry, J. B. Fery, C. A. Johnson, C. D. Lein, W. E. McCain, G. G. Michael, B. Rivera, J. B. Scott, W. M. Storey, S. D. Symms. **Transfer Agents & Registrars**—Chemical Trust Co. of California, SF; West One Bank, Idaho, Boise. **Incorporated** in Idaho in 1945; reincorporated in Delaware in 1969. **Empl**-75,000. **S&P Analyst:** Karen J. Sack, CFA

Alcan Aluminium

NYSE Symbol **AL** Options on ASE (Mar-Jun-Sep-Dec) & Toronto (Feb-May-Aug-Nov) In S&P 500

Price	Range	P–E Ratio	Dividend	Yield	S&P Ranking	Beta
Oct. 20'95	1995					
29⅞	36⅝–23⅜	13	¹0.60	2.0%	B–	1.05

Summary

Alcan, one of the world's largest aluminum producers from smelting facilities located mainly in Canada, serves a wide geographic range of markets. Ending an aluminum surplus that existed since 1991, global output cuts and U.S. and European economic growth resulted in demand exceeding supply since mid-1994. Aided by higher fabricated aluminum products prices, profits rose sharply in 1995's first three quarters. Profits should maintain their uptrend in 1996.

Current Outlook

Earnings for 1996 are estimated at $4.00 a share up from 1995's estimated earnings of $2.70.

The quarterly dividend (before 15% Canadian tax) was doubled to $0.15, from $0.07½, in July.

Assuming 2.6% U. S. GDP growth and stable business conditions in the rest of the world, operating revenues should record another solid gain in 1996 on increased volume and shipments for both ingot and fabricated products. The higher volume and price, the likely absence of strike related disruptions and a better spread between ingot and fabricated prices should expand margins and lift operating profits. Aided by lower interest costs and flat tax rate, earnings should increase in 1996.

Oper. Revenues (Million U.S. $)

Quarter:	1995	1994	1993	1992
Mar.	2,399	1,786	1,731	1,836
Jun.	2,449	2,059	1,858	1,957
Sep.	2,288	2,139	1,813	1,958
Dec.	---	2,232	1,830	1,845
	---	8,216	7,232	7,596

Operating revenues for the nine months ended September 30, 1995, rose 19%, year to year, mostly reflecting increases in fabricated aluminum products shipments and prices. Margins widened, and aided by a one-time after tax gain of $24 million, net income advanced to $497 million from $48 million. After preferred dividends, share earnings were $2.13, versus $0.15. Results exclude an extraordinary loss of $1.24 in 1995 for the writedown of the Kemano hydroelectric project.

Common Share Earnings (U.S. $)

Quarter:	1995	1994	1993	1992
Mar.	0.75	d0.13	d0.11	d0.09
Jun.	0.77	0.01	d0.18	d0.15
Sep.	0.61	0.27	d0.08	d0.07
Dec.	E0.57	0.19	d0.17	d0.29
	E2.70	0.34	d0.54	d0.60

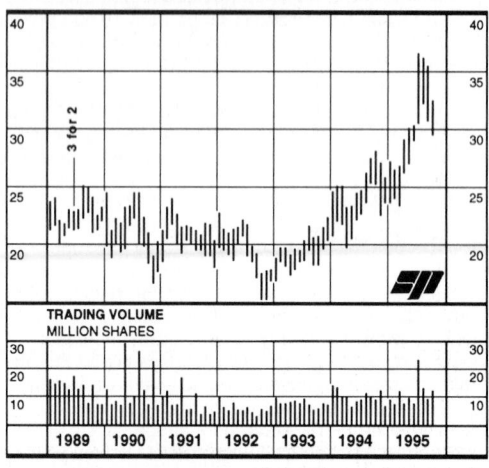

TRADING VOLUME
MILLION SHARES

1989 1990 1991 1992 1993 1994 1995

Important Developments

Oct. '95— AL reported share earnings of $0.61 on a 6.5% gain in sales for 1995's third quarter, versus $0.27 a year earlier. Results exclude an extraordinary loss of $1.24 for the writedown of the Kemano hydroelectric project in 1995. The increase in sales resulted from higher prices for ingot and fabricated products. AL noted that third quarter earnings were not as strong as those recorded earlier in 1995 due to the economic uncertainty in North America and Europe along with inventory destocking by customers. Separately, workers voted to accept the company's contract offer which should enable the AL to restart the three Quebec smelters idled since October 6. The company estimated that it would lose some 40,000 to 50,000 tons of production in the fourth quarter as a result of the strike and incur costs of $40 million to $50 million.

Next earnings report expected in January.

Per Share Data (U.S. $)

Yr. End Dec. 31	1994	1993	1992	1991	³1990	1989	1988	1987	1986	1985
Tangible Bk. Val.	**19.17**	18.28	19.06	21.17	22.19	20.30	18.06	15.05	13.18	12.23
Cash Flow	**2.26**	1.43	1.40	1.67	4.08	5.84	6.20	3.81	3.03	0.26
Earnings²	**0.34**	d0.54	d0.60	d0.25	2.33	3.58	3.85	1.68	0.97	d0.97
Dividends	**0.300**	0.300	0.450	0.860	1.120	1.120	0.586	0.389	0.356	0.489
Payout Ratio	**88%**	NM	NM	NM	48%	31%	15%	23%	39%	NM
Prices—High	**28⅛**	22⅜	22¾	24	24½	25⅛	22¼	25¼	15⅝	13⅞
Low	**19¾**	16⅞	15¼	18	16⅝	20⅛	15⅝	12⅝	12⅜	10⅛
P/E Ratio—	**83–58**	NM	NM	NM	11–7	7–6	6–4	15–7	16–13	NM

Data as orig. reptd. Adj. for stk. divs. of 50% Jun. 1989, 50% Jun. 1987. **1.** In U.S. funds, bef. 15% Can. nonresid. tax. **2.** Bef. spec. item(s) of +0.11 in 1986, +0.16 in 1985. **3.** Reflects merger or acquisition. d-Deficit. E-Estimated. NM-Not Meaningful.

Alcan Aluminium Limited

Income Data (Million U.S. $)

Year Ended Dec. 31	Revs.	Oper. Inc.	% Oper. Inc. of Revs.	Cap. Exp.	Depr.	Int. Exp.	[4]Net Bef. Taxes	Eff. Tax Rate	[2]Net Inc.	% Net Inc. of Revs.	Cash Flow
1994	8,216	876	10.7	264	431	235	211	53.1%	96	1.2	506
1993	7,232	590	8.2	251	443	229	d118	NM	d104	NM	321
1992	7,596	575	7.6	389	449	267	d124	NM	[3]d112	NM	314
1991	7,748	527	6.8	819	429	286	d140	NM	d36	NM	373
[1]1990	8,757	952	10.9	1,255	393	263	670	18.8%	543	6.2	914
1989	8,839	1,421	16.1	1,273	333	180	1,201	29.1%	835	9.4	1,147
1988	8,529	1,800	21.1	660	316	150	1,450	34.3%	931	10.9	1,217
1987	6,797	1,138	16.7	409	296	183	668	34.4%	433	6.4	693
1986	5,956	850	14.3	318	276	217	413	38.7%	[3]218	3.7	494
1985	5,718	581	10.2	569	258	271	d267	NM	d216	NM	42

Balance Sheet Data (Million U.S. $)

Dec. 31	Cash	Assets	Curr. Liab.	Ratio	Total Assets	% Ret. on Assets	Long Term Debt	Common Equity	Total Cap.	% LT Debt of Cap.	% Ret. on Equity
1994	27	2,821	1,384	2.0	9,989	1.0	2,206	4,308	7,809	28.2	1.8
1993	81	2,402	1,335	1.8	9,810	NM	2,322	4,096	7,729	30.0	NM
1992	149	2,655	1,545	1.7	10,146	NM	2,287	4,266	7,909	28.9	NM
1991	205	3,070	1,960	1.6	10,816	NM	2,185	4,730	8,337	26.2	NM
1990	200	3,370	2,148	1.6	10,649	5.4	1,796	4,942	8,109	22.1	11.0
1989	247	3,471	2,095	1.7	9,508	9.2	1,079	4,610	7,020	15.4	18.7
1988	670	3,770	1,655	2.3	8,615	11.7	1,199	4,109	6,598	18.2	23.9
1987	493	3,198	1,159	2.8	7,660	5.9	1,336	3,565	6,135	21.8	11.9
1986	316	2,746	1,086	2.5	7,118	3.0	1,366	3,116	5,557	24.6	7.3
1985	177	2,578	1,126	2.3	6,861	NM	1,600	2,746	5,261	30.4	NM

Data as orig. reptd. **1.** Reflects merger or acquisition. **2.** Bef. spec. items. **3.** Reflects accounting change. **4.** Incl. equity in earns. of nonconsol. subs. d-Deficit. NM-Not Meaningful.

Business Summary

Alcan is one of the world's largest aluminum producers. Shipments in 1994 came to 2,660,000 metric tons, with 66% fabricated products and 34% ingot and ingot products (purchased and resold at little or no profit or loss). Of 1994 total sales, 40% were in the U.S., 34% in Europe, 12% in Canada, and 7% each in the Pacific and South America. Fabricated products and non-aluminum sales by market in 1994 were: containers and packaging (34% of the total), building and construction (22%), electrical (9%), transportation (8%), and other (27%), which includes sales to distributors and sales of chemicals, alumina and bauxite.

Bauxite reserves are estimated to be sufficient to support existing smelter capacity for over 50 years. Mines are located in Brazil, Guinea, Jamaica and Ghana. Alumina plants are located in Canada, Brazil, Guinea, Jamaica, Ireland, the U.K., India and Japan. Alcan also has a 21% interest in an alumina plant in Queensland, Australia.

Consolidated primary capacity at year-end 1994 was 1,561,000 metric tons a year. Smelting capacity in Canada is rated at 1,093,000 tons, with the rest in Brazil, the U.K. and the U.S. In 1994, consolidated primary output was 1,435,000 tons. Alcan has its own hydroelectric facilities in Canada, and electric power outside that country is supplied from a variety of sources.

With full output in 1994 of new can sheet rolling capacity at the Logan plant (Kentucky), expansion of hot and cold rolling capacity at AL's 50%-owned Norf complex (Germany) in the 1994 last half, and mid-1994 acquisition of a cold rolling and finishing plant at Nachterstedt (Germany), AL has become the world's largest producer of rolled products. In December 1994, AL sold most of the assets of its North American building products divisions to Genstar Capital. In August 1994, it sold its 73% stake in Alcan Australia for $245 million.

Dividend Data

Dividends have been paid since 1939. Payments are made in U.S. funds, subject to 15% Canadian tax. A dividend reinvestment plan is available. A "poison pill" stock purchase right was amended in April 1995.

Amt. of Divd. $	Date Decl.	Ex-divd. Date	Stock of Record	Payment Date
0.07½	Oct. 27	Nov. 15	Nov. 21	Dec. 21'94
0.07½	Feb. 9	Feb. 16	Feb. 23	Mar. 23'95
0.07½	Apr. 27	May 15	May 19	Jun. 19'95
0.15	Jul. 27	Aug. 17	Aug. 21	Sep. 21'95

Capitalization

Long Term Debt: $1,865,000,000 (9/95).

Cum. Red. Preference Stock: $353,000,000.

Common Stock: 225,244,908 shs. (no par). Institutions hold 48% (incl. about 10% by Fidelity Management & Research Co. and Fidelity Management Trust Co.).
Shareholders of record: 25,273.

Office—1188 Sherbrooke Street West, Montreal, QC, H3A 3G2. **Tel**—(514) 848-8000. **Pres & CEO**—J. Bougie. **VP & CFO**—S. Thadhani. **VP & Secy**—P. K. Pal. **Investor Contact**—Duncan Curry. **Dirs**—J. R. Evans (Chrmn), S. I. Bata, W. R. C. Blundell, J. Bougie, W. Chippindale, A. E. Gotlieb, J. E. Newall, J. L. Nichol, P. H. Pearse, G. Russell, G. Saint-Pierre. **Transfer Agents**—R-M Trust Co., Montreal, Winnipeg, Regina, Calgary, Vancouver and Toronto, Canada, and London, England; Chemical Bank, NYC. **Incorporated** in Canada in 1928. **Empl**—42,000.

Information has been obtained from sources believed to be reliable, but its accuracy and completeness are not guaranteed. Leo J. Larkin

Alco Standard

NYSE Symbol **ASN**
In S&P 500

09-AUG-95
Industry: Paper/Products

Summary: Alco Standard is the largest U.S. distributor and converter of paper and related products, and is also a major and rapidly growing distributor of office products.

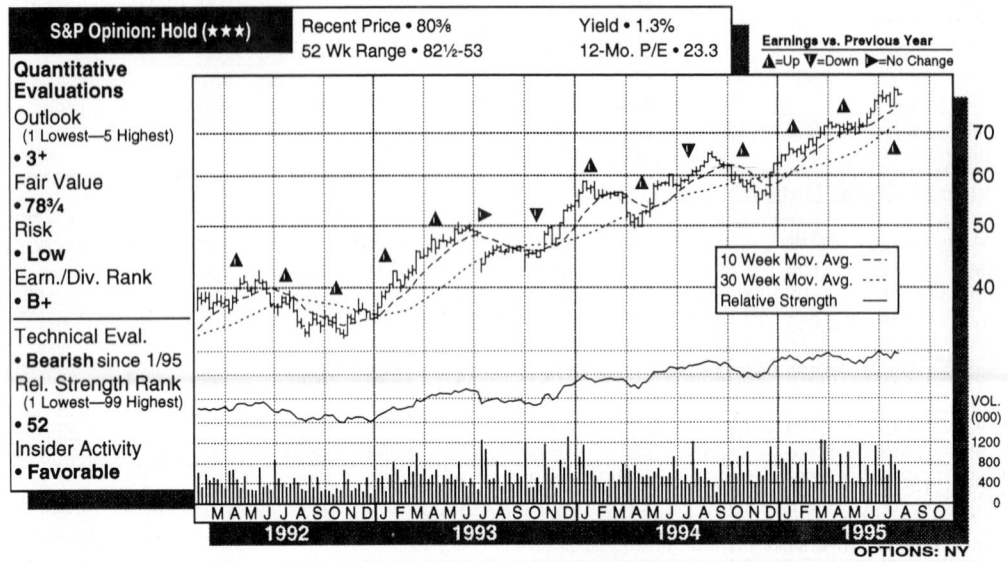

S&P Opinion: Hold (★★★)

| Recent Price • 80⅝ | Yield • 1.3% |
| 52 Wk Range • 82½-53 | 12-Mo. P/E • 23.3 |

Earnings vs. Previous Year
▲=Up ▼=Down ▶=No Change

Quantitative Evaluations

Outlook
(1 Lowest—5 Highest)
• **3+**

Fair Value
• **78¾**

Risk
• **Low**

Earn./Div. Rank
• **B+**

Technical Eval.
• **Bearish** since 1/95

Rel. Strength Rank
(1 Lowest—99 Highest)
• **52**

Insider Activity
• **Favorable**

10 Week Mov. Avg. – – –
30 Week Mov. Avg. ·······
Relative Strength ——

VOL. (000)

OPTIONS: NY

Overview - 09-AUG-95

Fiscal 1995 and 1996 sales should rise strongly, primarily with the continued rapid pace of office products acquisitions and internal growth at Unisource. Benefits from the company's three-year restructuring program should have a positive impact, although the full impact of savings related to the program may not be apparent until fiscal 1997. Savings from the restructuring program should increase as the company completes a new information technology upgrade, which should improve productivity and customer service and create new marketing opportunities with national accounts. Despite continuing competitive pressures and high interest expense, and absent the 1994 restructuring charge, a strong profit advance is expected for fiscal 1995. A further advance is likely in fiscal 1996.

Valuation - 09-AUG-95

ASN's stock is trading near its all-time high, at about 22 times our 1995 earnings estimate and 20 times our fiscal 1996 estimate. This far exceeds the average multiple for S&P 500 stocks and for the S&P Industrials. Although we think an above average multiple is warranted because of the unique nature of ASN's distribution businesses, we think the stock is fully priced at its current valuation. The stock should be an average performer over the next year as ASN continues to pursue its restructuring and growth plans. We would not add to positions at this time.

Key Stock Statistics

S&P EPS Est. 1995	3.55	Tang. Bk. Value/Share	7.42
P/E on S&P Est. 1995	22.6	Beta	1.01
S&P EPS Est. 1996	3.95	Shareholders	NA
Dividend Rate/Share	1.04	Market cap. (B)	$ 4.4
Shs. outstg. (M)	55.0	Inst. holdings	63%
Avg. daily vol. (M)	0.139	Insider holdings	NA

Value of $10,000 invested 5 years ago: $ 26,168

Fiscal Year Ending Sep. 30

	1995	% Change	1994	% Change	1993	% Change
Revenues (Million $)						
1Q	2,182	14%	1,922	33%	1,444	25%
2Q	2,446	24%	1,969	32%	1,491	26%
3Q	2,596	30%	2,001	29%	1,547	25%
4Q	—	—	2,104	7%	1,962	36%
Yr.	—	—	7,996	24%	6,445	31%
Income (Million $)						
1Q	45.47	43%	31.85	29%	24.76	25%
2Q	49.13	29%	38.02	29%	29.54	27%
3Q	58.92	NM	-48.31	NM	30.70	7%
4Q	—	—	49.04	NM	-77.39	NM
Yr.	—	—	17.01	123%	7.62	-93%
Earnings Per Share ($)						
1Q	0.77	28%	0.60	15%	0.52	21%
2Q	0.83	30%	0.64	12%	0.57	10%
3Q	0.99	NM	-0.95	NM	0.58	NM
4Q	E0.96	—	0.83	NM	-1.71	NM
Yr.	E3.55	—	1.10	NM	-0.04	NM

Next earnings report expected: mid October

Alco Standard

Business Summary - 09-AUG-95

Alco Standard is the largest distributor of copiers and the largest marketer and distributor of paper and imaging products and supply systems in North America. Segment contributions in fiscal 1994 were:

	Sales	Profits
Unisource U.S.	64%	41%
Unisource Canada	8%	4%
Alco Office products	28%	55%

Unisource (formerly Paper Corp. of America) was formed to combine the operations of Paper Corp. with the operations of Butler Paper, Crown Paper and Abitibi-Price's paper distribution businesses, all acquired in recent years. Unisource markets and distributes paper and related products, including printing and communications paper for printing, publishing and office use, and paper, plastic and disposable products and supplies for packaging, food service, janitorial and industrial use. It also produces pressure-sensitive and water-activated carton sealing tapes, dispensing equipment, envelopes and food service disposables.

Office products operations include the sale, lease, rental and servicing of photocopiers, facsimile equipment, micrographics equipment and other automated office equipment, office furniture and supplies. In recent years, ASN has acquired numerous U.S. office products dealers and several in Canada. The company also established a base in Europe with sales of about $150 million in fiscal 1994, primarily in the United Kingdom. The company's acquisition plans are primarily focused on expanding in North America and the United Kingdom. Alco Management Services offers facilities management services through office products dealers. The dealers operate customer central reprographic departments, supplying labor, equipment and supplies, for a per-copy fee.

Important Developments

Jul. '95—Through the first three quarters of fiscal 1994-5, Alco Office Products completed 68 acquisitions with annualized revenues of $418 million, while Unisource completed eight acquisitions with revenues of $95 million. Separately, in June ASN agreed to sell Central Products Co., a producer of carton sealing tapes with revenues of $125 million.

Capitalization

Total Debt: $1,368,000,000 (6/95).
Depositary Shares:
Series AA: 4,025,000 shs. ($50 liq. val.); conv. into com. at $44.64 a sh.;
Series BB: 3,400,000 shs. ($77.375 liq. val.); automatic conv. into com. at $94.40 a sh. 10/1/98.

Per Share Data ($)

(Year Ended Sep. 30)

	1994	1993	1992	1991	1990	1989
Tangible Bk. Val.	7.68	2.65	7.69	10.19	10.08	9.39
Cash Flow	2.90	1.63	3.59	3.47	3.50	3.84
Earnings	1.10	-0.04	2.22	1.95	2.19	2.68
Dividends	1.00	0.96	0.92	0.88	0.84	0.76
Payout Ratio	91%	NM	41%	45%	38%	26%
Prices - High	65½	54¾	42⅝	35⅞	37⅞	36⅝
- Low	49½	35¾	33⅛	29	27⅝	25⅜
P/E Ratio - High	60	NM	19	18	17	14
- Low	45	NM	15	15	13	9

Income Statement Analysis (Million $)

	1994	%Chg	1993	%Chg	1992	%Chg	1991
Revs.	7,993	24%	6,438	31%	4,922	4%	4,752
Oper. Inc.	439	29%	339	22%	278	7%	260
Depr.	96.8	22%	79.4	24%	64.1	-6%	68.5
Int. Exp.	71.8	12%	63.9	25%	51.2	6%	48.3
Pretax Inc.	157	NM	25.0	-86%	173	20%	144
Eff. Tax Rate	55%	—	69%	—	40%	—	39%
Net Inc.	71.0	NM	8.0	-92%	104	18%	88.0

Balance Sheet & Other Fin. Data (Million $)

	1994	1993	1992	1991	1990	1989
Cash	53.0	36.0	24.0	120	27.0	38.0
Curr. Assets	NA	NA	NA	NA	NA	NA
Total Assets	3,502	3,349	2,445	2,021	1,738	1,479
Curr. Liab.	1,057	1,020	762	611	576	539
LT Debt	806	1,003	697	464	357	227
Common Eqty.	1,166	819	860	821	686	594
Total Cap.	2,205	2,049	1,587	1,310	1,086	875
Cap. Exp.	108	84.0	58.0	55.0	67.0	75.0
Cash Flow	156	77.0	168	156	145	166

Ratio Analysis

	1994	1993	1992	1991	1990	1989
Curr. Ratio	NA	NA	NA	NA	NA	NA
% LT Debt of Cap.	36.5	49.0	43.9	35.4	32.8	25.9
% Net Inc.of Revs.	0.9	0.1	2.1	1.8	2.1	2.8
% Ret. on Assets	1.9	0.3	4.6	4.5	5.6	8.7
% Ret. on Equity	5.6	NM	12.2	11.2	14.1	20.0

Dividend Data (Dividends have been paid since 1965. A dividend reinvestment plan is available. A "poison pill" stock purchase rights plan was adopted in 1988.)

Amt. of Div. $	Date Decl.	Ex-Div. Date	Stock of Record	Payment Date
0.250	Aug. 09	Aug. 16	Aug. 22	Sep. 10 '94
0.260	Nov. 11	Nov. 15	Nov. 21	Dec. 10 '94
0.260	Jan. 27	Feb. 14	Feb. 21	Mar. 10 '95
0.260	May. 02	May. 16	May. 22	Jun. 10 '95
0.260	Aug. 08	Aug. 17	Aug. 21	Sep. 10 '95

Data as orig. reptd.; bef. results of disc. opers. and/or spec. items. Per share data adj. for stk. divs. as of ex-div. date. E-Estimated. NA-Not Available. NM-Not Meaningful. NR-Not Ranked.

Office—825 Duportail Rd., Wayne, PA 19087-5589 (P.O. Box 834, Valley Forge, PA 19482-0834). **Tel**—(215) 296-8000. **Chrmn**—R. B. Mundt. **Pres & CEO**—J. E. Stuart. **VP & Secy**—J. K. Croney. **Investor Contact**—Suzanne Shenk. **Dirs**—J. M. Buck, Jr., P. J. Darling, W. F. Drake, Jr., J. J. Forese, F. S. Hammer, B. B. Hauptfuhrer, D. G. Mead, R. B. Mundt, P. C. O'Neill, R. G. Sada, J. W. Stratton, J. E. Stuart. **Transfer Agent & Registrar**—National City Bank, Cleveland. **Incorporated** in Ohio in 1952. **Empl**-30,600. **S&P Analyst:** Joshua M. Harari, CFA

Alexander & Alexander

NYSE Symbol **AAL**
In S&P 500

20-SEP-95

Industry:
Insurance

Summary: This insurance broker is being restructured under new management that has cut the common dividend 90%, issued $200 million of preferred stock, and sold non-core assets.

S&P Opinion: Hold (★★★)	Recent Price • 24¾	Yield • 0.4%
	52 Wk Range • 26⅜-18½	12-Mo. P/E • NM

Quantitative Evaluations

Outlook
(1 Lowest—5 Highest)
• **1+**

Fair Value
• **15⅝**

Risk
• **Low**

Earn./Div. Rank
• **B-**

Technical Eval.
• **Bearish** since 8/95

Rel. Strength Rank
(1 Lowest—99 Highest)
• **57**

Insider Activity
• **Neutral**

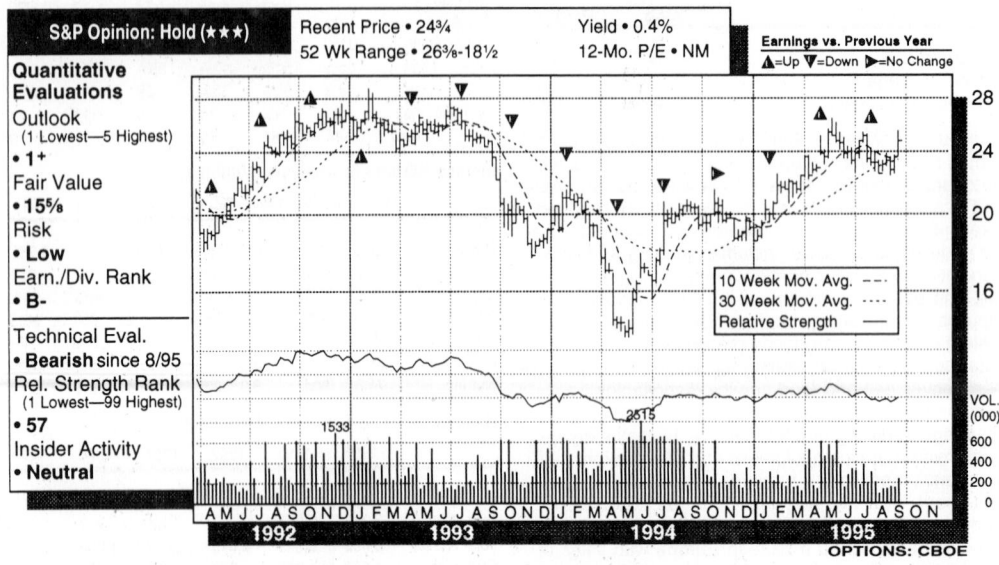

Earnings vs. Previous Year
▲=Up ▼=Down ▶=No Change

10 Week Mov. Avg. - - - -
30 Week Mov. Avg. ....
Relative Strength ———

OPTIONS: CBOE

Overview - 20-SEP-95

A return to profitability is seen for 1995, and sharply higher earnngs are expected for 1996. Results in 1994 were penalized by restructuring charges, weak insurance pricing, and relatively low investment yields. Recent steps, including management changes, a 90% dividend cut, and reinsuring against certain discontinued operations, have started to yield positive results, and will enhance AAL's long-term position. Aggressive cost cutting efforts led to 1994 fourth quarter restructuring and other pretax charges totaling about $164 million. The long-term outlook is aided by an expected firming of U.S. insurance pricing. Prices in certain overseas lines have already firmed, and a record level of catastrophe losses in the U.S. has helped pricing in most property lines. A favorable response by AAL's existing and prospective clients to its restructuring efforts also aids the long term outlook.

Valuation - 20-SEP-95

The shares of this beleagured insurance brokerage and management consulting firm have been fairly strong lately, reflecting hopes that recent restructuring moves, coupled with stronger property casualty insurance pricing, will return the company to solid footing. We share the market's positive view that AAL is on its way to a long-term turnaround. However, the shares, which were recently trading at more than 24X our 1995 EPS estimate of $1.00, are fairly valued for the near-term.

Key Stock Statistics

S&P EPS Est. 1995	1.00	Tang. Bk. Value/Share	NM
P/E on S&P Est. 1995	24.8	Beta	1.02
S&P EPS Est. 1996	1.65	Shareholders	3,200
Dividend Rate/Share	0.10	Market cap. (B)	$ 1.1
Shs. outstg. (M)	44.3	Inst. holdings	73%
Avg. daily vol. (M)	0.037	Insider holdings	NA

Value of $10,000 invested 5 years ago: $ 9,845

Fiscal Year Ending Dec. 31

	1995	% Change	1994	% Change	1993	% Change
Revenues (Million $)						
1Q	324.2	NM	323.0	NM	325.0	1%
2Q	328.1	-2%	335.1	-2%	342.0	-1%
3Q	—	—	332.6	2%	327.0	-4%
4Q	—	—	333.2	-4%	347.8	1%
Yr.	—	—	1,324	-1%	1,342	NM
Income (Million $)						
1Q	41.70	NM	-1.80	NM	10.90	-48%
2Q	22.70	NM	3.80	-68%	11.90	-30%
3Q	—	—	0.10	NM	-4.10	NM
4Q	—	—	-109.3	NM	3.20	-62%
Yr.	—	—	-107.2	NM	23.60	-57%
Earnings Per Share ($)						
1Q	0.80	NM	-0.09	NM	0.22	-57%
2Q	0.37	NM	0.04	-85%	0.26	-37%
3Q	—	—	-0.11	NM	-0.11	NM
4Q	—	—	-2.61	NM	0.03	-85%
Yr.	E1.00	NM	-2.79	NM	0.40	-70%

Next earnings report expected: early November

Business Summary - 19-SEP-95

Alexander & Alexander Services Inc. is a holding company that, through subsidiaries, provides risk management, insurance brokerage, and human resource management consulting serivces on a worldwide basis. Segment contributions (profits in millions) in 1994 were:

	Revs.	Profits
Insurance services	84%	-$12.2
Human resources mgmt. consulting	16%	-19.1
Corporate & other	---	-51.6

About 52% of revenues in 1994 were from the U.S.; the U.K. accounted for 24%, Canada 9%, and other countries 15%.

The insurance services business consists primarily of negotiating and placing property and casualty insurance for clients (mostly corporations) with underwriters worldwide. Compensation is generally by commission, usually as a percentage of the premium paid by the client. Risk surveys and analyses, loss control and cost studies, and claims processing services are also provided.

The Alexander Consulting Group oversees employee benefit and management consulting activities worldwide.

Important Developments

Jul. '95—Results in the first half of 1995 included a net gain of $0.47 a share from the February 1995 sale of Alexsis, Inc., AAL's third party administrator. Year to date results from continuing operations also benefited from a 7.3% rise in revenues and a 3.1% decline in operating expenses. Growth in consulting revenues, contributions from new U.S. retail brokerage business, and higher fiduciary investment income paced the rise in revenues. The decline in operating expenses is the result of a company-wide cost containment effort.

Capitalization

Long Term Debt: $155,400,000 (6/95).
$3.625 Series A Conv. Pfd. Stock: 2,300,000 shs. ($1 stated value).
$4 Series B Conv. Pfd. Stock: 4,300,000 shs. ($50 stated value). Conv. into com. at $17 a sh. All held by American International Group.
Cl. C Common Stock: 366,904 shs. ($1 par); conv. into com. sh.-for-sh.

Per Share Data ($)

(Year Ended Dec. 31)

	1994	1993	1992	1991	1990	1989
Tangible Bk. Val.	-4.02	-0.63	0.13	3.81	4.48	3.18
Cash Flow	-1.62	1.66	2.82	1.51	3.13	3.33
Earnings	-2.79	0.40	1.34	-0.25	1.35	1.45
Dividends	0.32	1.00	1.00	1.00	1.00	1.00
Payout Ratio	NM	250%	75%	NM	74%	68%
Prices - High	22¾	28⅞	27⅝	27⅝	31½	34
- Low	14	17⅝	18	18	16⅛	22⅝
P/E Ratio - High	NM	72	20	NM	23	23
- Low	NM	44	13	NM	12	16

Income Statement Analysis (Million $)

	1994	%Chg	1993	%Chg	1992	%Chg	1991
Revs.	1,324	-1%	1,342	NM	1,350	-1%	1,369
Oper. Inc.	37.0	-65%	107	-27%	147	-1%	149
Depr.	51.2	-6%	54.5	-10%	60.5	-16%	72.2
Int. Exp.	16.0	11%	14.4	-20%	18.0	-19%	22.2
Pretax Inc.	-146	NM	32.0	-69%	104	NM	-3.0
Eff. Tax Rate	NM	—	20%	—	46%	—	NM
Net Inc.	-106	NM	23.6	-57%	54.9	NM	-10.4

Balance Sheet & Other Fin. Data (Million $)

	1994	1993	1992	1991	1990	1989
Cash	989	889	819	835	696	685
Curr. Assets	2,387	2,202	2,061	2,084	2,047	1,893
Total Assets	2,946	2,794	2,643	2,767	2,835	2,605
Curr. Liab.	2,149	2,086	1,937	1,949	1,952	1,744
LT Debt	133	112	125	170	183	216
Common Eqty.	-3.0	161	193	374	431	375
Total Cap.	464	406	389	624	710	694
Cap. Exp.	22.0	26.0	18.0	23.0	42.0	55.0
Cash Flow	-71.0	72.0	115	62.0	127	135

Ratio Analysis

	1994	1993	1992	1991	1990	1989
Curr. Ratio	1.1	1.1	1.1	1.1	1.0	1.1
% LT Debt of Cap.	28.6	27.5	32.1	27.2	25.7	31.1
% Net Inc.of Revs.	NM	1.8	4.1	NM	4.1	4.7
% Ret. on Assets	NM	0.8	2.0	NM	2.0	2.3
% Ret. on Equity	NM	9.8	19.3	NM	13.6	15.8

Dividend Data —Dividends have been paid since 1922. A poison pill stock purchase rights plan was adopted in 1987 and amended in 1994.

Amt. of Div. $	Date Decl.	Ex-Div. Date	Stock of Record	Payment Date
0.025	Jul. 15	Aug. 26	Sep. 01	Sep. 30 '94
0.025	Nov. 17	Nov. 25	Dec. 01	Dec. 30 '94
0.025	Feb. 15	Feb. 23	Mar. 01	Mar. 31 '95
0.025	May. 18	May. 25	Jun. 01	Jun. 30 '95
0.025	Aug. 17	Aug. 30	Sep. 01	Sep. 29 '95

Data as orig. reptd.; bef. results of disc. opers. and/or spec. items. Per share data adj. for stk. divs. as of ex-div. date. E-Estimated. NA-Not Available. NM-Not Meaningful. NR-Not Ranked.

Office—1185 Ave. of the Americas, New York, NY 10036. **Tel**—(212) 840-8500. **Chrmn, Pres & CEO**—F. G. Zarb. **EVP & CFO**—E. F. Kosnik. **VP & Treas**—R. A. Kershaw. **Dirs**—K. Black, Jr., J. A. Bogardus, Jr., R. E. Boni, W. P. Cooke, E. G. Corrigan, J. L. Dionne, G. R. Ford, P. C. Godsoe, A. M. M. Grossart, M. H. Hartigan II, J. B. Hurlock, R. A. Iles, E. F. Kosnick, V. R. McLean, J. D. Robinson, III, W. M. Wilson, F. G. Zarb. **Transfer Agents & Registrars**—First Chicago Trust Co. of New York, NYC; Montreal Trust Co. of Canada, Toronto; R-M Trust Co., Essex, England. **Incorporated** in Maryland in 1922; reincorporated in 1973. **Empl**-12,000. **S&P Analyst:** Catherine A. Seifert

Allergan, Inc.

NYSE Symbol **AGN**
In S&P 500

31-AUG-95

Industry:
Medical equipment/
supply

Summary: This company offers a broad line of contact lens care products, ophthalmic drug and surgical products, and treatments for dermatological and neuromuscular disorders.

S&P Opinion: Hold (★★★)	Recent Price • 30⅜	Yield • 1.6%
	52 Wk Range • 32⅛-24⅞	12-Mo. P/E • 30.7

Earnings vs. Previous Year
▲=Up ▼=Down ▶=No Change

Quantitative Evaluations

Outlook
(1 Lowest—5 Highest)
• **3⁻**

Fair Value
• **30¼**

Risk
• **Average**

Earn./Div. Rank
• **NR**

Technical Eval.
• **Neutral** since 8/95

Rel. Strength Rank
(1 Lowest—99 Highest)
• **51**

Insider Activity
• **Neutral**

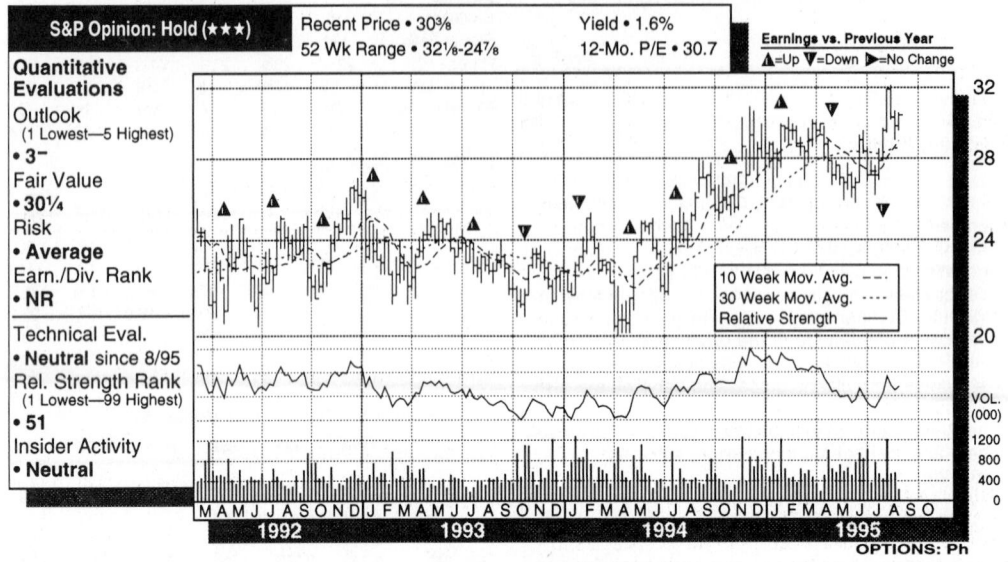

10 Week Mov. Avg. ---
30 Week Mov. Avg. ·····
Relative Strength —

VOL.
(000)

1200
800
400
0

M A M J J A S O N D J F M A M J J A S O N D J F M A M J J A S O N D J F M A M J J A S O
1992 1993 1994 1995

OPTIONS: Ph

Overview - 31-AUG-95

Sales should show further progress in 1996, aided by gains in each core business. Brisk demand should continue for silicone intraocular lenses (AGN has nearly half of this market segment), and for cataract removal products. Aided by new products, ophthalmic pharmaceutical sales should also rise, although gains will probably be restricted by price discounting in the managed care sector. Growth is also seen for contact lens care products, bolstered by anticipated market share gains for the company's new Complete one-bottle disinfection solution. Profitability should benefit from the greater volume, and comparisons will be aided by the absence of a 1995 charge of $0.78 a share related to a retinoid venture.

Valuation - 31-AUG-95

After a somewhat erratic performance in the 1995 first half, the shares have bounced back in the third quarter, buoyed by a respectable gain in second quarter sales and operating earnings. Despite competitive pricing conditions in ophthalmic pharmaceuticals, intraocular lenses and other lines, operating profits should continue to improve in coming quarters, aided by new products and geographic expansion, especially in India and China. Prospects are enhanced by anticipated benefits from promising new retinoid drugs such as tazarotene for psoriasis and acne, and from other products from an aggressive R&D program. The shares are rated a long-term hold.

Key Stock Statistics

S&P EPS Est. 1995	1.10	Tang. Bk. Value/Share	7.42
P/E on S&P Est. 1995	27.6	Beta	1.36
S&P EPS Est. 1996	2.10	Shareholders	17,000
Dividend Rate/Share	0.48	Market cap. (B)	$ 1.9
Shs. outstg. (M)	64.1	Inst. holdings	84%
Avg. daily vol. (M)	0.086	Insider holdings	NA

Value of $10,000 invested 5 years ago: $ 19,080

Fiscal Year Ending Dec. 31

	1995	% Change	1994	% Change	1993	% Change
Revenues (Million $)						
1Q	228.3	9%	210.1	4%	202.8	-3%
2Q	262.2	17%	224.7	8%	207.9	-6%
3Q	—	—	242.2	12%	216.9	-5%
4Q	—	—	270.2	17%	231.3	-3%
Yr.	—	—	947.2	10%	858.9	-4%
Income (Million $)						
1Q	21.70	-2%	22.20	NM	22.30	12%
2Q	-23.00	NM	23.50	NM	23.40	3%
3Q	—	—	30.20	7%	28.30	-6%
4Q	—	—	34.80	14%	30.50	-8%
Yr.	—	—	110.7	6%	104.5	-1%
Earnings Per Share ($)						
1Q	0.34	-3%	0.35	6%	0.33	10%
2Q	-0.36	NM	0.37	6%	0.35	3%
3Q	E0.52	11%	0.47	9%	0.43	-4%
4Q	E0.60	11%	0.54	15%	0.47	-4%
Yr.	E1.10	-36%	1.73	9%	1.58	1%

Next earnings report expected: mid October

Allergan, Inc.

Business Summary - 31-AUG-95

Allergan is a leading producer of ophthalmic drugs, intraocular lenses and other ophthalmic surgical items and contact lens care solutions. Skin care items and other drugs are also offered. Sales by business segment in recent years were:

	1994	1993	1992
Eye care drugs	41%	42%	43%
Optical	36%	38%	40%
Surgical	15%	13%	13%
Allergan Herbert	4%	4%	4%
Botox	4%	3%	---

Foreign operations accounted for 53% of both sales and operating profits in 1994. R&D spending equaled 11.8% of sales in 1994 (11.9% in 1993).

Eye care drugs include prescription and non-prescription products to treat eye diseases and disorders, including glaucoma, inflammation, infection, allergy and dry eye. Important products include Betagan, a beta adrenergic blocking agent used in the initial treatment of glaucoma; and Propine, a drug used when initial drug therapy for glaucoma is inadequate. Other drugs include Acular, a treatment for the relief of seasonal conjunctivitis, and several anti-infective agents.

Optical products consist of OTC contact lens care products, including daily cleaners to remove film and deposits from contact lenses; enzymatic cleaners to remove protein deposits; and disinfecting solutions to destroy harmful microorganisms on contact lens surfaces. Lens care products are sold under the Complete, Lens Plus, Ultrazyme and UltraCare names.

Surgical products include intraocular lenses (IOLs) and surgical adjunct products. IOLs are implanted in the eye after the removal of cataracts. Allergan Herbert offers skin care therapeutic products. Botox is a drug used to treat eye muscle disorders. AGN is studying possible neurological uses for Botox, and is also R&D on receptor-selective retinoids to treat acne, psoriasis and cancer.

Important Developments

Aug. '95—AGN agreed to acquire Herald Pharmacal, a maker of aesthetic skin care products, with annual sales in excess of $15 million. In June, the company filed for FDA approval for tazarotene, a topical retinoid treatment for psoraisis and acne. Also in June, Allergan-Ligand Retinoid Therapeutics (ALRT), a retinoid drug R&D concern, raised $32.5 million by selling units to AGN and Ligand Pharmaceuticals shareholders. AGN also contributed $50 million to ALRT, and Ligand contributed $17.5 million.

Capitalization

Long Term Debt: $240,400,000 (6/95).
Minority Interest: $17,100,000.

Per Share Data ($)

(Year Ended Dec. 31)

	1994	1993	1992	1991	1990	1989
Tangible Bk. Val.	7.50	6.20	5.61	4.69	4.01	2.78
Cash Flow	2.55	2.29	2.20	-0.23	1.87	NA
Earnings	1.73	1.58	1.56	-0.92	1.21	0.86
Dividends	0.42	0.40	0.38	0.33	0.28	0.05
Payout Ratio	24%	25%	24%	NM	23%	6%
Prices - High	30⁷/₈	26³/₈	27¹/₄	25¹/₂	19³/₈	25¹/₂
- Low	20	20³/₄	20³/₈	16³/₄	12¹/₄	15⁵/₈
P/E Ratio - High	18	17	17	NM	16	30
- Low	12	13	13	NM	10	18

Income Statement Analysis (Million $)

	1994	%Chg	1993	%Chg	1992	%Chg	1991
Revs.	947	NM	859	-4%	898	7%	839
Oper. Inc.	209	9%	191	2%	188	2%	184
Depr.	52.3	12%	46.8	9%	42.9	-7%	46.2
Int. Exp.	11.3	20%	9.4	-33%	14.0	-20%	17.4
Pretax Inc.	159	10%	144	NM	144	NM	-48.0
Eff. Tax Rate	29%	—	25%	—	25%	—	NM
Net Inc.	111	6%	105	NM	106	NM	-61.0

Balance Sheet & Other Fin. Data (Million $)

	1994	1993	1992	1991	1990	1989
Cash	131	142	121	127	84.0	84.0
Curr. Assets	486	444	423	422	431	431
Total Assets	1,060	940	886	834	947	936
Curr. Liab.	324	276	268	269	256	367
LT Debt	84.0	105	82.0	97.0	148	96.0
Common Eqty.	603	515	500	445	524	445
Total Cap.	708	642	595	553	672	542
Cap. Exp.	58.3	59.9	65.6	51.0	42.9	63.0
Cash Flow	163	151	149	-15.0	126	99

Ratio Analysis

	1994	1993	1992	1991	1990	1989
Curr. Ratio	1.5	1.6	1.6	1.6	1.7	1.2
% LT Debt of Cap.	11.9	16.3	13.8	17.6	22.0	17.8
% Net Inc.of Revs.	11.7	12.2	11.8	NM	9.2	7.1
% Ret. on Assets	11.1	11.7	12.4	NM	8.7	6.5
% Ret. on Equity	19.9	21.0	22.5	NM	16.8	12.1

Dividend Data —Dividends were initiated in October 1989.

Amt. of Div. $	Date Decl.	Ex-Div. Date	Stock of Record	Payment Date
0.110	Jul. 26	Aug. 22	Aug. 26	Sep. 15 '94
0.110	Oct. 19	Nov. 10	Nov. 17	Dec. 08 '94
0.110	Jan. 24	Feb. 13	Feb. 17	Mar. 10 '95
0.120	Apr. 25	May. 22	May. 26	Jun. 16 '95
0.120	Jul. 25	Aug. 23	Aug. 25	Sep. 15 '95

Data as orig. reptd.; bef. results of disc. opers. and/or spec. items. Per share data adj. for stk. divs. as of ex-div. date.
E-Estimated. NA-Not Available. NM-Not Meaningful. NR-Not Ranked.

Office—2525 Dupont Drive, Irvine, CA 92715-1599. **Tel**—(714) 752-4500. **Chrmn**—G. S. Herbert. **Pres & CEO**—W. C. Shepherd. **EVP & COO**—R. M. Haugen. **VP & Secy**—F. R. Tunney, Jr. **VP & CFO**—A. J. Moyer. **Investor Contact**—Jeff B. D'Eliscu. **Dirs**—H. W. Boyer, T. J. Erickson, H. E. Evans, W. R. Grant, H. E. Greene, Jr., R. M. Haugen, G. S. Herbert, L. J. Kaplan, L. G. McCraw, L. T. Rosso, L. D. Schaeffer, W. C. Shepherd. H. Wendt. **Transfer Agent & Registrar**—First Chicago Trust Co. of New York, NYC. **Incorporated** in California in 1948. **Empl**-4,903. **S&P Analyst:** H. B. Saftlas

AlliedSignal

NYSE Symbol **ALD**
In S&P 500

04-AUG-95

Industry:
Conglomerate/diversified

Summary: AlliedSignal provides a broad range of products and services to the aerospace and automotive industries and makes fibers, chemicals, plastics and other engineered materials.

S&P Opinion: Accumulate (★★★★)

Recent Price • 46	Yield • 1.7%
52 Wk Range • 46⅞-30⅜	12-Mo. P/E • 15.9

Quantitative Evaluations

Outlook
(1 Lowest—5 Highest)
• **3**

Fair Value
• 44¼

Risk
• **Low**

Earn./Div. Rank
• **B+**

Technical Eval.
• **Bearish** since 2/95

Rel. Strength Rank
(1 Lowest—99 Highest)
• **69**

Insider Activity
• **Neutral**

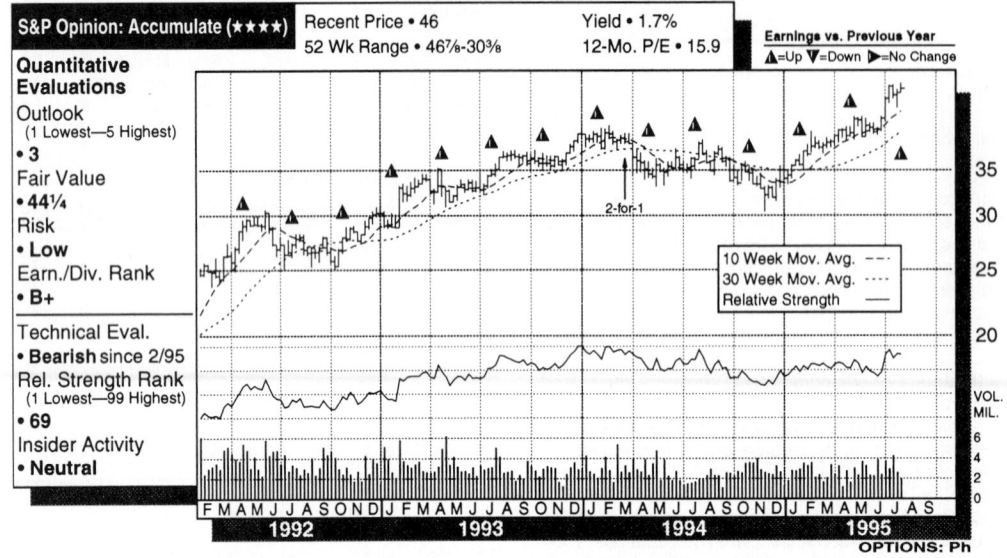

Earnings vs. Previous Year
▲=Up ▼=Down ▶=No Change

2-for-1

10 Week Mov. Avg. ---
30 Week Mov. Avg. ·····
Relative Strength ——

OPTIONS: Ph

Overview - 04-AUG-95

Revenues are expected to rise more than 10% in 1995, as acquisitions aid all segments. Aerospace sales should also benefit from strength in the aftermarket segment. Automotive group revenues are expected to climb, despite declining North American vehicle sales, on higher vehicle content and greater international sales. The engineered materials division is forecast to expand briskly, reflecting improved pricing conditions and volume growth, particularly in fibers (industrial polyesters and nylons), CFC substitutes and engineered plastics. Margin gains will develop as the company extends its highly successful program of productivity improvement.

Valuation - 04-AUG-95

The shares have been in an uptrend since late 1994, as the company achieved stated performance goals. ALD projects annual earnings gains of 13% to 17% for the next two years, driven by new products, international expansion, acquisitions, and further benefits from a productivity program. The ability to slash costs by integrating acquisitions is fundamental to the company's effectiveness. As long as superior earnings growth continues, the shares, which we view as attractive, should outperform the market. We are remain confident that ALD can achieve such growth.

Key Stock Statistics

S&P EPS Est. 1995	3.15	Tang. Bk. Value/Share	6.53
P/E on S&P Est. 1995	14.6	Beta	1.06
S&P EPS Est. 1996	3.55	Shareholders	82,100
Dividend Rate/Share	0.78	Market cap. (B)	$ 13.2
Shs. outstg. (M)	284.3	Inst. holdings	72%
Avg. daily vol. (M)	0.586	Insider holdings	NA

Value of $10,000 invested 5 years ago: $ 31,066

Fiscal Year Ending Dec. 31

	1995	% Change	1994	% Change	1993	% Change
Revenues (Million $)						
1Q	3,419	15%	2,986	3%	2,901	-3%
2Q	3,630	14%	3,187	4%	3,055	NM
3Q	—	—	3,110	11%	2,812	-4%
4Q	—	—	3,534	16%	3,059	NM
Yr.	—	—	12,817	8%	11,827	-2%
Income (Million $)						
1Q	198.0	17%	169.0	16%	146.0	20%
2Q	227.0	16%	196.0	17%	167.0	19%
3Q	—	—	189.0	15%	165.0	22%
4Q	—	—	205.0	15%	178.0	29%
Yr.	—	—	759.0	16%	656.0	23%
Earnings Per Share ($)						
1Q	0.70	17%	0.60	18%	0.51	17%
2Q	0.80	16%	0.69	17%	0.59	19%
3Q	E0.79	—	0.67	16%	0.58	22%
4Q	E0.84	—	0.73	17%	0.63	28%
Yr.	E3.15	—	2.68	16%	2.31	22%

Next earnings report expected: late October

Business Summary - 04-AUG-95

AlliedSignal Inc. is a broadly diversified manufacturer whose operations are conducted under three business segments: aerospace, automotive, and engineered materials. Contributions by segment in 1994 were:

	Sales	Profits
Aerospace	36%	36%
Automotive	38%	32%
Engineered materials	26%	32%

Foreign operations contributed 24% of sales in 1994 (22% in 1993).

Aerospace products include primary propulsion and gas turbine engines, environmental control systems, airborne radar systems, microwave landing systems, avionics, wheels, brakes, controls and other products used in aircraft, spacecraft, missiles, military vehicles and other applications. The division also performs extensive aftermarket activities, providing spare parts, maintenance and repair, and retrofitting services.

The automotive segment's principal business areas are braking systems, engine components, safety restraint systems and the aftermarket. Within each area, the segment offers a wide range of products for passenger cars and light, medium and heavy trucks. Brand names include Bendix, Fram, Autolite and Garrett.

Engineered materials comprise five major divisions: fibers, fluorine products, performance materials, plastics and laminate systems. Other businesses not included in these divisions are the Paxon joint venture (producing high-density polyethylene with Exxon), the Environmental Catalysts joint venture (supplying the catalyst and substrate used in catalytic converters) and Carbon Materials (producing binder pitch).

Important Developments

Jul. '95—ALD agreed to buy Hoechst AG's 96% interest in Riedel-de Haen AG, a European maker of pharmaceutical intermediates, coatings and sealants, and specialty dyes (1994 sales of $250 million).
Jul. '95—The company said it plans to double the capacity of its polyester fibers manufacturing plant in Longlaville, France, by 1997. Earlier, in May, ALD reached an agreement in principle to acquire a 50 million lb. polyester plant from Bridgestone/Firestone. The Hopewell, Va., facility should contribute $100 million to annual sales.
Apr. '95—ALD bought The Budd Co.'s Wheel & Brake division (sales of $250 million) for $160 million.
Oct. '94—The Lycoming Turbine Engine division was purchased from Textron Inc. for $375 million plus the assumption of certain liabilities.

Capitalization

Long Term Debt: $1,317,000,000 (3/95).

Per Share Data ($)

(Year Ended Dec. 31)

	1994	1993	1992	1991	1990	1989
Tangible Bk. Val.	5.77	4.59	4.24	6.82	12.55	11.76
Cash Flow	4.52	4.13	3.66	0.72	3.21	3.07
Earnings	2.68	2.31	1.90	-1.00	1.67	1.77
Dividends	0.67	0.58	0.50	0.80	0.90	0.90
Payout Ratio	25%	25%	27%	NM	52%	49%
Prices - High	40¾	40⅛	31	22½	19	20¼
- Low	30⅜	28¾	20½	13	12½	15⅞
P/E Ratio - High	15	17	16	NM	11	11
- Low	11	12	11	NM	7	9

Income Statement Analysis (Million $)

	1994	%Chg	1993	%Chg	1992	%Chg	1991
Revs.	12,817	8%	11,827	-2%	12,042	2%	11,831
Oper. Inc.	1,675	15%	1,452	14%	1,279	25%	1,026
Depr.	523	2%	514	4%	496	6%	470
Int. Exp.	166	-11%	186	-25%	247	-13%	283
Pretax Inc.	1,141	25%	910	30%	702	NM	-389
Eff. Tax Rate	31%	—	28%	—	24%	—	NM
Net Inc.	759	16%	656	23%	535	NM	-272

Balance Sheet & Other Fin. Data (Million $)

	1994	1993	1992	1991	1990	1989
Cash	508	892	931	238	382	525
Curr. Assets	4,585	4,567	4,919	4,129	4,316	4,141
Total Assets	11,321	10,829	10,756	10,382	10,456	10,132
Curr. Liab.	3,391	3,489	3,505	3,603	3,424	3,227
LT Debt	1,424	1,602	1,777	1,914	2,051	1,903
Common Eqty.	2,982	2,390	2,251	2,983	3,380	3,412
Total Cap.	4,812	4,331	4,440	5,490	6,104	6,037
Cap. Exp.	639	718	691	668	675	541
Cash Flow	1,282	1,170	1,031	197	888	913

Ratio Analysis

	1994	1993	1992	1991	1990	1989
Curr. Ratio	1.4	1.3	1.4	1.1	1.3	1.3
% LT Debt of Cap.	29.6	37.0	40.0	34.9	33.6	31.5
% Net Inc.of Revs.	5.9	5.5	4.4	NM	3.7	4.4
% Ret. on Assets	6.9	6.1	5.0	NM	4.7	5.3
% Ret. on Equity	28.3	28.3	20.1	NM	14.1	16.0

Dividend Data (Dividends have been paid since 1920. A dividend reinvestment plan is available.)

Amt. of Div. $	Date Decl.	Ex-Div. Date	Stock of Record	Payment Date
0.167	Jul. 29	Aug. 15	Aug. 19	Sep. 09 '94
0.167	Oct. 28	Nov. 14	Nov. 18	Dec. 09 '94
0.195	Feb. 07	Feb. 14	Feb. 21	Mar. 10 '95
0.195	Apr. 24	May. 15	May. 19	Jun. 09 '95
0.195	Jul. 21	Aug. 16	Aug. 18	Sep. 08 '95

Data as orig. reptd.; bef. results of disc. opers. and/or spec. items. Per share data adj. for stk. divs. as of ex-div. date. E-Estimated. NA-Not Available. NM-Not Meaningful. NR-Not Ranked.

Office—101 Columbia Rd. (P.O. Box 4000), Morristown, NJ 07962-2497. **Tel**—(201) 455-2000. **Chrmn & CEO**—L. A. Bossidy. **EVPs**—J. W. Barter, D. P. Burnham, F. M. Poses. **SVP & CFO**—R. F. Wallman. **VP & Treas**—N. A. Garvey. **Secy**—P. M. Kreindler. **Investor Contact**—James V. Gelly (201-455-2222). **Dirs**—H. W. Becherer, L. A. Bossidy, E. E. Covert, A. M. Fudge, W. R. Haselton, P. X. Kelley, R. P. Luciano, R. E. Palmer, I. G. Seidenberg, A. C. Sigler, J. R. Stafford, T. P. Stafford, D. C. Staley, R. C. Winters. **Transfer Agent & Registrar**—Bank of New York, NYC. **Incorporated** in Delaware in 1985. **Empl**-87,500. **S&P Analyst:** Joe Victor Shammas

Allstate Corp.

NYSE Symbol **ALL**
In S&P 500

14-AUG-95

Industry:
Insurance

Summary: Allstate is the second largest property-casualty insurer in the U.S. In June 1995 Sears, Roebuck & Co. distributed its remaining 80% interest in ALL to Sears shareholders.

S&P Opinion: Hold (★★★)	Recent Price • 30⅛	Yield • 2.6%
	52 Wk Range • 33⅜-22⅝	12-Mo. P/E • 9.5

Quantitative Evaluations

Outlook
(1 Lowest—5 Highest)
• **NA**

Fair Value
• **NA**

Risk
• **Low**

Earn./Div. Rank
• **NR**

Technical Eval.
• **Bullish** since 6/95

Rel. Strength Rank
(1 Lowest—99 Highest)
• **32**

Insider Activity
• **NA**

Earnings vs. Previous Year
▲=Up ▼=Down ▶=No Change

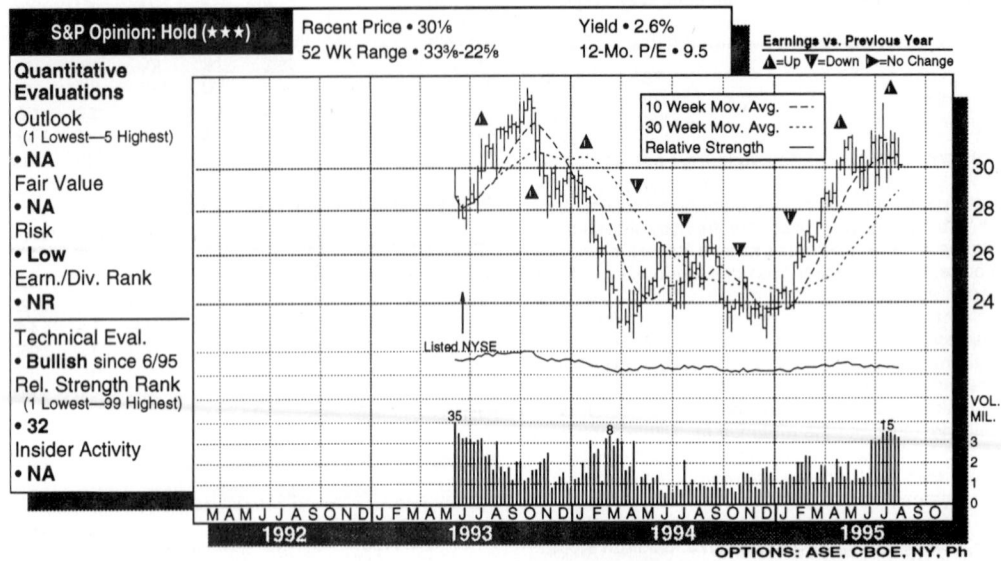

10 Week Mov. Avg. – – –
30 Week Mov. Avg. ·····
Relative Strength ——

Listed NYSE

OPTIONS: ASE, CBOE, NY, Ph

Overview - 14-AUG-95

Written premiums will likely be flat in 1995, due to a planned curtailment of writings in storm-prone areas as ALL seeks to better manage its exposure to catastrophe losses. Underwriting results will benefit from this strategy. The outlook for sharply higher operating earnings in 1995 is skewed by catastrophe losses of $2 billion (including $1.6 billion in pretax losses from the California earthquake) that depressed results in 1994. Though curtailing writings in storm prone areas will aid results, ALL does not utilize catastrophe reinsurance. This puts the company at greater financial risk when catastrophes strike. Partly offsetting this risk is ALL's geographically diverse book of business, strong capital base, and planned expansion into non-standard auto and select commercial lines.

Valuation - 14-AUG-95

After a lackluster performance during 1994 amid concerns over rising interest rates and catastrophe losses, the shares of this leading property-casualty insurer have rebounded nicely so far in 1995. Though the shares trade at about nine times our 1995 operating earnings estimate of $3.40 a share (which excludes realized investment gains or losses and gains from asset sales), they are fairly valued, near term, in light of ALL's above average exposure to catastrophe losses and lack of catastrophe reinsurance. We would look for a pullback of about 10% from current levels as an opportunity to selectively add to positions. A buying opportunity may arise if Sears shareholders opt to sell their recently acquired ALL shares.

Key Stock Statistics

S&P EPS Est. 1995	3.40	Tang. Bk. Value/Share	21.45
P/E on S&P Est. 1995	8.9	Beta	NA
S&P EPS Est. 1996	3.60	Shareholders	5,800
Dividend Rate/Share	0.78	Market cap. (B)	$ 13.5
Shs. outstg. (M)	449.0	Inst. holdings	0%
Avg. daily vol. (M)	2.112	Insider holdings	NA

Value of $10,000 invested 5 years ago: NA

Fiscal Year Ending Dec. 31

	1995	% Change	1994	% Change	1993	% Change
Revenues (Million $)						
1Q	5,573	5%	5,322	—	—	—
2Q	5,671	7%	5,318	—	—	—
3Q	—	—	5,394	1%	5,320	—
4Q	—	—	5,430	3%	5,283	—
Yr.	—	—	21,464	2%	20,946	4%
Income (Million $)						
1Q	541.7	NM	-275.2	—	—	—
2Q	519.1	29%	402.0	—	—	—
3Q	—	—	193.9	NM	0.33	—
4Q	—	—	163.1	-37%	259.0	—
Yr.	—	—	483.8	-63%	1,302	NM
Earnings Per Share ($)						
1Q	1.21	NM	-0.61	NM	0.75	27%
2Q	1.15	29%	0.89	-5%	0.94	77%
3Q	—	—	0.43	-40%	0.72	NM
4Q	—	—	0.37	-35%	0.57	NM
Yr.	E3.40	NM	1.08	-64%	2.99	NM

Next earnings report expected: mid October

Allstate Corp.

Business Summary - 14-AUG-95

Allstate Corp. is a leading U.S. property-liability and life insurer through its Allstate Insurance Co. and Allstate Life Insurance Co. subsidiaries, respectively. Established in 1931 by Sears, Roebuck & Co., Allstate is the second largest property-liability insurer in the U.S. and one of the 20 largest life insurers. It writes business mainly through some 14,500 full-time Allstate agents in the U.S. and Canada.

The company's primary business is the sale of private passenger automobile and homeowners insurance, and it maintains national market shares of about 12% in each of those lines. The personal property and casualty business (PP&C) division, representing 90% of ALL's 1994 property-casualty earned premiums, writes primarily private passenger automobile and homeowners policies. ALL is licensed to write policies in all 50 states and in Canada.

The company's commercial property and casualty business (business insurance), representing 8% of 1993 p-c earned premiums, writes selected commercial lines for small and medium-size businesses, which it markets through its own agents as well as a network of independent agents. Mortgage insurance (which accounted for 2% of 1994 earned premiums) is offered through PMI Mortgage Insurance Co., the third largest mortgage guaranty insurer in the U.S. In April 1995, ALL reduced its stake in PMI to 30% following the initial public offering of 70% of PMI's common stock.

Allstate Life offers life insurance and annuity and pension products countrywide. It reaches a broad market of potential insureds through various distribution channels, including Allstate agents, financial institutions, independent agents and brokers and direct marketing techniques. During 1994, annuities represented 50% of the unit's total premiums and deposits.

Important Developments

Jul. '95—ALL's sharply higher earnings for the first half of 1995 largely reflected 58% lower catastrophe losses of $536 million versus $1.28 billion. The higher 1994 catastrophe losses were largely the result of claims from the Northridge, California earthquake in January 1994. As a result, the combined ratio improved to 100.4% from 114.6% Bottom line results in the 1995 interim were also aided by a $93.4 million net gain on the sale of 70% of The PMI Group, Inc. Results in the 1994 period were restated to reflect the sale of the PMI stake. Earlier, in June, Sears, Roebuck & Co. (NYSE:S) completed the divestiture of its 80.3% interest in ALL effective June 30, 1995. At that date of record, Sears distributed 0.927035 of an ALL common share for every Sears common share held, in a tax free distribution.

Capitalization

Total Debt: $862,000,000 (9/94).

Per Share Data ($)
(Year Ended Dec. 31)

	1994	1993	1992	1991	1990	1989
Tangible Bk. Val.	18.73	22.89	NA	NA	NA	NA
Oper. Earnings	0.78	2.67	-1.40	NA	NA	NA
Earnings	1.08	2.99	-1.15	NA	NA	NA
Dividends	0.72	0.36	NA	NA	NA	NA
Relative Payout	67%	12%	NA	NA	NA	NA
Prices - High	29⅞	34¼	NA	NA	NA	NA
- Low	22⅝	27	NA	NA	NA	NA
P/E Ratio - High	28	11	NA	NA	NA	NA
- Low	21	9	NA	NA	NA	NA

Income Statement Analysis (Million $)

	1994	%Chg	1993	%Chg	1992	%Chg	1991
Life Ins. In Force	NA	—	138,423	12%	124,040	—	NA
Prem.Inc Life A&H	1,053	-2%	1,079	-4%	1,128	-6%	1,197
Prem.Inc Cas/Prop	16,807	3%	16,323	4%	15,738	4%	15,147
Net Invest. Inc.	3,401	2%	3,324	4%	3,201	7%	3,001
Oth. Revs.	202	-8%	220	36%	162	NM	5.0
Total Revs.	21,464	2%	20,946	4%	20,228	5%	19,350
Pretax Inc.	227	-84%	1,376	NM	-1,424	NM	539
Net Oper. Inc.	352	-70%	1,158	NM	-606	NM	719
Net Inc.	484	-63%	1,302	NM	-499	NM	723

Balance Sheet & Other Fin. Data (Million $)

	1994	1993	1992	1991	1990	1989
Cash & Equiv.	778	786	796	NA	NA	NA
Premiums Due	2,316	1,964	1,875	NA	NA	NA
Inv Assets Bonds	38,041	38,888	32,144	NA	NA	NA
Inv. Assets Stock	4,852	4,555	3,837	NA	NA	NA
Inv. Assets Loans	3,234	3,563	3,701	NA	NA	NA
Inv. Assets Total	48,179	48,791	41,731	NA	NA	NA
Deferred Policy Cost	2,074	1,511	1,529	NA	NA	NA
Total Assets	61,369	59,358	52,098	NA	NA	NA
Debt	869	850	1,800	NA	NA	NA
Common Eqty.	8,426	10,300	5,383	NA	NA	NA

Ratio Analysis

	1994	1993	1992	1991	1990	1989
Comb. Loss-Exp.Ratio	111.0	103.0	120.8	107.5	109.9	107.5
% Ret. on Revs.	2.3	6.2	NM	3.7	3.9	4.9
% Ret. on Equity	5.2	16.6	NM	NM	NM	NM
% Invest. Yield	7.0	7.4	NA	NA	NA	NA

Dividend Data
—Dividends were initiated in August 1993.

Amt. of Div. $	Date Decl.	Ex-Div. Date	Stock of Record	Payment Date
0.180	Aug. 10	Sep. 01	Sep. 08	Sep. 29 '94
0.180	Nov. 09	Dec. 02	Dec. 08	Dec. 29 '94
0.195	Feb. 07	Mar. 03	Mar. 09	Mar. 30 '95
0.195	May. 23	Jun. 02	Jun. 08	Jun. 29 '95
0.195	Aug. 09	Aug. 17	Aug. 21	Sep. 28 '95

Data as orig. reptd.; bef. results of disc. opers. and/or spec. items. Per share data adj. for stk. divs. as of ex-div. date. E-Estimate. NA-Not Available. NM-Not Meaningful. NR-Not Ranked.

Office—Allstate Plaza, 2775 Sanders Road, Northbrook, IL 60062. **Tel**—(708) 402-5000. **Chrmn & CEO**—J. D. Choate. **Pres & COO**—E. M. Liddy. **VP-CFO**—N. A. Florek. **VP-Treas**—M. J. Resnick. **VP-Secy**—R. W. Pike. **Dirs**—J. G. Andress, W. L. Batts, E. A. Brennan, J. D. Choate, J. M. Denny, C. F. Edley, W. E. Hedien, W. E. LaMothe, N. C. Reynolds, D. H. Rumsfeld. **Transfer Agent & Registrar**—Harris Trust & Savings Bank, Chicago. **Incorporated** in Delaware in 1992. **Empl-** 49,000. **S&P Analyst:** C. A. Seifert

ALLTEL Corp.

NYSE Symbol **AT**
In S&P 500

26-AUG-95

Industry:
Telecommunications

Summary: ALLTEL Corp. operates one of the largest telephone systems in the U.S., serving some 1.6 million subscriber lines in 22 states.

S&P Opinion: Accumulate (★★★★)	Recent Price • 27¾	Yield • 3.5%
	52 Wk Range • 31⅜-23¼	12-Mo. P/E • 17.6

Quantitative Evaluations

Outlook
(1 Lowest—5 Highest)
• **2⁻**

Fair Value
• **24⅝**

Risk
• **Low**

Earn./Div. Rank
• **A**

Technical Eval.
• **Bullish** since 10/94

Rel. Strength Rank
(1 Lowest—99 Highest)
• **62**

Insider Activity
• **NA**

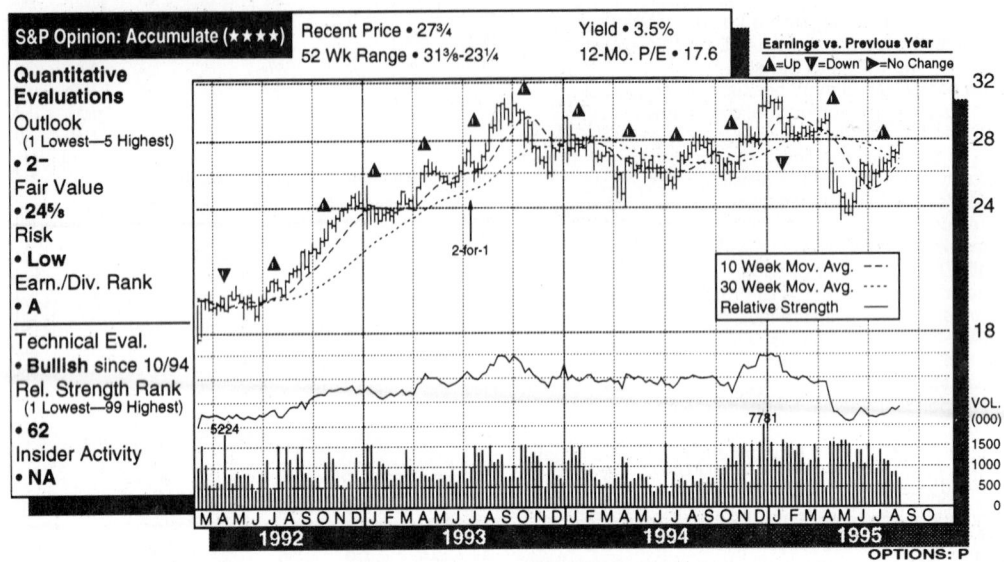

Earnings vs. Previous Year
▲=Up ▼=Down ▶=No Change

2-for-1

10 Week Mov. Avg. - - - -
30 Week Mov. Avg. · · · ·
Relative Strength ——

OPTIONS: P

Overview - 25-AUG-95

ALLTEL should continue to post earnings gains above the industry average, reflecting its successful growth strategy. The company's strategy focuses on diversification while also maximizing the growth prospects for its core telephone businesses. Nontelephone operations are led by the cellular and information services units, which should continue to do well. The cellular unit's customer base is growing rapidly, while a planned staff reduction at its information services unit is expected to reduce operating expenses by about $15 million annually. Meanwhile, telephone operations remain an integral part of AT's strategy. The company is moving to improve its competitive edge through strategic repositioning of operations and cost control.

Valuation - 25-AUG-95

The shares have risen about 16% in the last three months, versus about 7% for the S&P 500, as investors focus on the company's strong growth prospects. Earlier in the year, the shares plunged on slower than anticipated first quarter growth in the information services unit. This was due to a continuing transition to a broader customer base, with less reliance on financial institutions. Following improved second quarter results, investors are now recognizing that this broadening will benefit AT over the long term. With the cellular unit continuing its rapid growth and core telephone operations continuing to post solid results, we recommend the shares for total return.

Key Stock Statistics

S&P EPS Est. 1995	1.85	Tang. Bk. Value/Share	6.34
P/E on S&P Est. 1995	15.0	Beta	0.78
S&P EPS Est. 1996	2.00	Shareholders	93,000
Dividend Rate/Share	0.96	Market cap. (B)	$ 5.2
Shs. outstg. (M)	188.8	Inst. holdings	39%
Avg. daily vol. (M)	0.172	Insider holdings	NA

Value of $10,000 invested 5 years ago: $ 17,303

Fiscal Year Ending Dec. 31

	1995	% Change	1994	% Change	1993	% Change
Revenues (Million $)						
1Q	763.6	8%	709.4	30%	546.7	8%
2Q	786.5	7%	734.6	29%	568.9	9%
3Q	—	—	745.3	30%	571.7	9%
4Q	—	—	772.4	18%	654.8	22%
Yr.	—	—	2,962	26%	2,342	12%
Income (Million $)						
1Q	78.62	9%	71.89	14%	63.16	27%
2Q	98.10	29%	76.19	19%	63.83	11%
3Q	—	—	79.73	21%	65.98	13%
4Q	—	—	43.95	-36%	69.06	9%
Yr.	—	—	271.8	4%	262.0	15%
Earnings Per Share ($)						
1Q	0.41	8%	0.38	13%	0.33	26%
2Q	0.52	30%	0.40	18%	0.34	11%
3Q	E0.45	7%	0.42	20%	0.35	11%
4Q	E0.47	104%	0.23	-36%	0.36	7%
Yr.	E1.85	29%	1.43	3%	1.39	14%

Next earnings report expected: mid October

ALLTEL Corp.

26-AUG-95

Business Summary - 02-MAY-95

ALLTEL Corp. is a diversified telecommunications company. Business segment contributions in 1994:

	Revenue	Profits
Telephone operations	40%	61%
Information services	29%	20%
Product distribution	15%	4%
Cellular	11%	13%
Other	5%	2%

As of December 31, 1994, AT provided local telephone service to over 1,643,000 access lines in 22 states. As part of its strategy to improve the competitive position of its telephone operations through repositioning and cost control, AT may look at exchange or acquisition possibilities in high growth areas.

The information services unit provides outsourcing, software and information processing services to financial, telecommunications and healthcare companies. AT's cellular operations serve some 7.9 million POPs (population adjusted for percent ownership) in 19 states concentrated in the Sun Belt region. Cellular subscribers numbered 469,000 at December 31, 1994. Distribution operations include Alltel Supply, a leading supplier of telecom equipment, and HWC Distribution, which distributes specialty wire and cable products. Other operations include the publication of telephone directories, paging services, and an 8% interest in LDDS Communications Inc., a regional long distance carrier.

Important Developments

Feb. '95—The company reduced its stake in Comdial Corporation, a manufacturer of telecommunications systems, to 6.05%.
Jan. '95—ALLTEL Mobile and BellSouth Mobility signed a definitive agreement involving cellular transactions impacting markets in five states: North and South Carolina, Mississippi, Tennessee and Pennsylvania.
Nov. '94—The company signed a definitive agreement to sell certain telephone and cable television properties to Citizens Utilities. The telephone properties serve approximately 109,000 access lines in Arizona, California, Nevada, New Mexico, Oregon, Tennessee, Utah and West Virgina, and the cable operations serve 7,000 customers. AT will receive approximately $290 million, comprised of cash, assumed debt and 3,600 of Citizens' Pennsylvania telephone access lines. Separately, ALLTEL Mobile signed a definitive agreement to exchange several of its cellular telephone properties in West Virginia and Oklahoma for several cellular properties in Georgia and North Carolina owned by United States Cellular.

Capitalization

Long Term Debt: $1,865,445,000 (3/95).
Red. Cum. Preferred Stock: $7,748,000.
Cum. Preferred Stock: $9,295,000.

Per Share Data ($)

(Year Ended Dec. 31)

	1994	1993	1992	1991	1990	1989
Tangible Bk. Val.	5.96	5.53	4.86	4.58	4.60	4.85
Cash Flow	3.34	2.84	2.54	2.50	2.34	2.40
Earnings	1.43	1.39	1.22	1.17	1.17	1.16
Dividends	0.90	0.82	0.76	0.71	0.65	0.59
Payout Ratio	63%	59%	62%	61%	56%	51%
Prices - High	31⅜	31¼	25	21⅝	19⅝	21
- Low	24	22⅞	17⅞	15⅞	12⅜	11¾
P/E Ratio - High	22	22	20	18	17	18
- Low	17	16	14	14	11	10

Income Statement Analysis (Million $)

	1994	%Chg	1993	%Chg	1992	%Chg	1991
Revs.	2,962	26%	2,342	12%	2,092	20%	1,748
Depr.	362	33%	272	11%	245	13%	217
Maint.	151	15%	131	7%	122	12%	109
Constr. Credits	NA	—	2.0	3%	2.0	4%	1.9
Eff. Tax Rate	38%	—	42%	—	36%	—	33%
Net Inc.	272	4%	262	14%	229	21%	189

Balance Sheet & Other Fin. Data (Million $)

	1994	1993	1992	1991	1990	1989
Gross Prop.	4,697	4,235	3,297	2,913	2,759	2,486
Net Prop.	2,963	2,676	2,062	1,825	1,755	1,615
Cap. Exp.	596	426	367	308	272	231
Total Cap.	3,896	3,575	2,643	2,405	2,265	2,057
Fxd. Chgs. Cov.	4.1	5.4	4.8	4.0	4.5	3.9
Capitalization:						
LT Debt	1,846	1,596	1,018	992	905	799
Pfd.	17.1	18.0	19.1	21.3	23.5	36.1
Common	1,616	1,545	1,295	1,072	1,005	884

Ratio Analysis

	1994	1993	1992	1991	1990	1989
% Ret. on Revs.	9.2	11.2	10.9	10.8	12.3	12.6
% Ret. On Invest.Cap	10.9	11.6	12.7	11.4	12.2	11.5
% Return On Com.Eqty	17.1	18.3	18.8	18.0	19.3	18.2
% Earn. on Net Prop.	16.6	14.0	15.8	14.3	15.2	14.0
% LT Debt of Cap.	53.1	50.5	43.7	47.6	46.8	46.5
Capital. % Pfd.	0.5	0.6	0.8	1.0	1.2	2.1
Capital. % Common	46.4	48.9	55.5	51.4	52.0	51.4

Dividend Data

Dividends have been paid since 1961. A dividend reinvestment plan is available.

Amt. of Div. $	Date Decl.	Ex-Div. Date	Stock of Record	Payment Date
0.220	Jul. 21	Aug. 29	Sep. 02	Oct. 03 '94
0.240	Oct. 24	Nov. 30	Dec. 06	Jan. 03 '95
0.240	Jan. 26	Feb. 17	Feb. 24	Apr. 03 '95
0.240	Apr. 20	Jun. 08	Jun. 12	Jul. 03 '95
0.240	Jul. 20	Sep. 07	Sep. 11	Oct. 03 '95

Data as orig. reptd.; bef. results of disc. opers and/or spec. items. Per share data adj. for stk. divs. as of ex-div. date. E-Estimated. NA-Not Available. NM-Not Meaningful. NR-Not Ranked.

Office—One Allied Drive, Little Rock, AR 72202. Tel—(501) 661-8000. Chrmn, Pres & CEO—J. T. Ford. SVP-Secy—F. X. Frantz. Treas—J. M. Green. VP-Investor Contact—Ron Payne. Dirs—B. W. Agee, M. D. Andreas, J. T. Ford, L. L. Gellerstedt III, W. W. Johnson, E. A. Mahony Jr., J. P. McConnell, G. C. McConnaughey, J. Natori, P. F. Searle, J. E. Steuri, C. H. Tiedemann, R. Townsend, W. H. Zimmer Jr. Transfer Agent & Registrar—KeyCorp Shareholder Services Inc. Incorporated in Delaware. Empl- 16,363. S&P Analyst: Kevin J. Gooley

Aluminum Co. of America

NYSE Symbol AA Options on CBOE (Jan-Apr-Jul-Oct) In S&P 500

Price	Range	P–E Ratio	Dividend	Yield	S&P Ranking	Beta
Nov. 2'95	1995					
51½	60¼–36⅞	9	[1]0.90	[1]1.7%	B–	1.00

Summary

Alcoa, the world's largest aluminum producer, is focusing on boosting returns in aluminum operations. Sustained U.S. and European economic growth, together with a Japanese recovery, should continue to outweigh heavy aluminum exports from Russia and reopening of idled aluminum facilities. Further earnings growth is projected for 1996.

Current Outlook

Earnings for 1996 are projected at $6.00 a share, versus the $4.75 estimated for 1995.

AA makes base dividend payments of $0.22½ quarterly; it also pays 30% of annual earnings above $3.00 a share, spread over the next year's quarters. Extra dividends for 1996 will supplement the base payments, given estimated 1995 income.

Assuming 2.6% GDP growth in the U. S. and stable business conditions in the rest of the world, sales should post another solid increase in 1996 on higher volume and prices. Demand from canned sheet, transportation and building and construction markets should stay firm. Sales will also be boosted by some inventory rebuilding. Aided by continued cost cutting, only moderate increases in raw material costs and flat interest expense, earnings should rise again in 1996.

Sales & Oper. Revenues (Billion $)

Quarter:	1995	1994	1993	1992
Mar.	3.01	2.22	2.11	2.25
Jun.	3.16	2.48	2.41	2.41
Sep.	3.26	2.56	2.23	2.38
Dec.	---	2.64	2.31	2.45
	---	9.90	9.06	9.49

Sales for the nine months ended September 30, 1995, rose 29%, year to year, primarily reflecting higher prices. Margins widened, and aided by the absence of a net plant closing charge of $50 million, net income increased to $639.6 million ($3.58 a share) from $75.1 million ($0.41) in the year-earlier period.

Common Share Earnings ($)

Quarter:	1995	1994	1993	1992
Mar.	1.08	d0.23	0.16	0.32
Jun.	1.23	0.25	0.20	0.01
Sep.	1.27	0.39	0.16	0.26
Dec.	E1.17	2.07	d0.50	d0.47
	E4.75	2.48	0.01	0.12

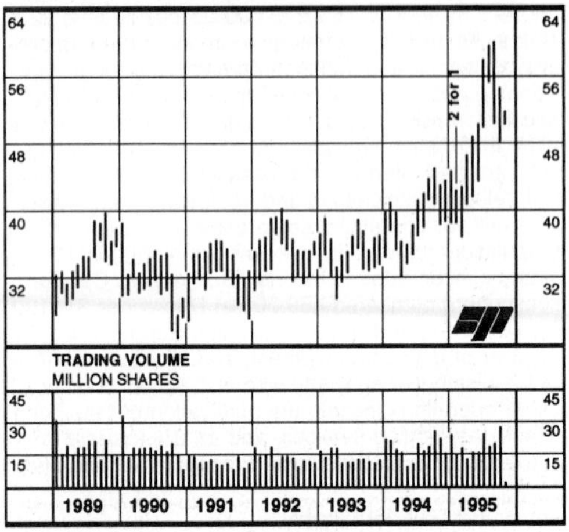

Important Developments

Oct. '95— The company reported share earnings of $1.27 on a 27% increase in sales for 1995's third quarter, versus $0.39 a year earlier. Aluminum product shipments for the quarter totaled 655,000 metric tons, versus 651,000 tons; shipments for the first nine months were 1,936,000 tons, versus 1,912,000 tons. Cash and equivalents totaled $992 million at the end of 1995's third quarter.

Jul. '95— The company announced that it planned to invest $30 million in Europe to manufacture forged aluminum truck wheels and was in the process of selecting a site for the plant. The company noted that demand for its lightweight wheels throughout the world would soon exceed its U.S. production capacity. The new plant will have enough capacity to ensure adequate and timely supplies in Europe.

Next earnings report expected in mid-January.

Per Share Data ($)

Yr. End Dec. 31	1994	1993	1992	1991	1990	1989	1988	[2]1987	1986	1985
Tangible Bk. Val.	**19.85**	18.95	19.63	27.28	28.97	27.97	24.85	20.54	19.72	19.76
Cash Flow	**6.25**	4.04	4.25	4.59	5.70	9.05	8.49	4.69	3.65	2.07
Earnings[3]	**2.48**	0.02	0.12	0.36	1.70	5.34	4.87	1.26	1.54	d0.12
Dividends	**0.80**	0.80	0.80	0.80	[4]0.89	[4]1.50	[4]1.26	0.60	0.60	0.60
Payout Ratio	**32%**	NM	667%	225%	52%	28%	26%	48%	39%	NM
Prices—High	**45⅛**	39 3/16	40 5/16	36 9/16	38⅝	39 13/16	28 11/16	32⅜	23 3/16	20⅜
Low	**32⅛**	29½	30½	26⅞	24 13/16	27⅝	19 5/16	16⅞	16 5/16	14⅞
P/E Ratio—	**18–13**	NM	NM	NM	23–15	7–5	6–4	26–13	15–11	NM

Data as orig. reptd. Adj. for stk. div(s) of 100% Feb. 1995. **1.** See Dividend Data. **2.** Reflects merger or acquisition. **3.** Bef. spec. item(s) of -0.38 in 1994, -6.83 in 1992, -0.14 in 1987, -0.06 in 1986. **4.** Paid from yr.'s earns., incl. yr.-end divd. pd. in next yr. d-Deficit. E-Estimated. NM-Not Meaningful.

Income Data (Million $)

Year Ended Dec. 31	Revs.	Oper. Inc.	% Oper. Inc. of Revs.	Cap. Exp.	Depr.	Int. Exp.	[2]Net Bef. Taxes	Eff. Tax Rate	[3]Net Inc.	% Net Inc. of Revs.	Cash Flow
1994	9,904	1,193	12.0	612	671	108	823	26.7%	443	4.5	1,112
1993	9,056	1,042	11.5	747	705	91	191	NM	5	0.1	708
1992	9,492	1,264	13.3	789	705	117	299	44.3%	[4]22	0.2	726
1991	9,884	1,507	15.2	841	720	166	400	45.4%	63	0.6	781
1990	10,710	2,176	20.3	851	690	205	1,047	37.6%	295	2.8	983
1989	10,910	2,750	25.2	876	655	197	2,166	36.9%	945	8.7	1,598
1988	9,795	2,509	25.6	857	638	230	1,635	36.6%	861	8.8	1,497
[1]1987	7,767	1,601	20.6	856	587	282	522	41.2%	224	2.9	822
1986	4,667	667	14.3	556	357	176	302	12.5%	[4]264	5.7	619
1985	5,163	616	11.9	533	355	187	d112	NM	d17	NM	336

Balance Sheet Data (Million $)

Dec. 31	Cash	Assets	Curr. Liab.	Ratio	Total Assets	% Ret. on Assets	Long Term Debt	Common Equity	Total Cap.	% LT Debt of Cap.	% Ret. on Equity
1994	625	4,153	2,554	1.6	12,353	3.7	1,030	3,943	6,937	14.8	11.7
1993	655	3,703	2,093	1.8	11,597	Nil	1,433	3,528	6,637	21.6	0.1
1992	548	3,248	2,165	1.5	11,023	0.2	855	3,549	6,047	14.1	0.5
1991	626	3,616	2,070	1.7	11,178	0.6	1,131	4,882	8,161	13.9	1.2
1990	636	3,744	2,038	1.8	11,413	2.6	1,295	5,108	8,803	14.7	5.8
1989	805	3,738	2,143	1.7	11,541	8.6	1,316	5,201	8,968	14.7	19.4
1988	507	3,192	1,884	1.7	10,538	8.4	1,525	4,570	8,175	18.7	20.4
1987	264	2,505	1,521	1.6	9,902	2.7	2,458	3,845	7,929	31.0	5.9
1986	204	1,552	944	1.6	6,767	3.9	1,326	3,656	5,475	24.2	7.3
1985	384	1,691	815	2.1	6,354	NM	1,554	3,242	5,276	29.4	NM

Data as orig. reptd. **1.** Reflects merger or acquisition and accounting change. **2.** Incl. equity in earns. of nonconsol. subs. **3.** Bef. spec. items. **4.** Reflects accounting change. d-Deficit. NM-Not Meaningful.

Business Summary

Alcoa is the world's largest producer of aluminum and alumina. It is organized into 22 business units, with 169 operating and sales locations in 26 countries. Segment contributions in 1994 were:

	Revs.	Profits
Alumina & chemicals	15%	64%
Aluminum processing	66%	15%
Non–aluminum products......	19%	21%

The alumina and chemicals segment includes the production and sale of bauxite, alumina and alumina chemicals and transportation services. Aluminum processing comprises the manufacturing and marketing of molten metal, ingot, and aluminum products that are flat-rolled, engineered or finished. Also included are power, transportation and other services. The non-aluminum products segment includes the production and sale of electrical, ceramic, plastic and composite materials products, manufacturing equipment, gold, magnesium products, and steel and titanium forgings.

Most facilities located in the U.S. are owned by the parent company. Alcoa of Australia (60%-owned) and Alcoa Aluminio S.A. (59%-owned) in Brazil are the two largest operating subsidiaries.

Revenues by market in 1994 were derived as follows: packaging, 29%; transportation, 17%; distributors and other, 16%; alumina and chemicals, 15%; building and construction, 14%; and aluminum ingot, 9%.

Dividend Data

Dividends have been paid since 1939. A dividend reinvestment plan is available. In November 1994, the company changed its dividend policy. It boosted the base quarterly dividend to $0.225, from $0.20 (as adjusted). When annual earnings exceed $3 a share, it will pay out 30% of the excess earnings in the next year, in equal quarterly installments together with base dividends, rather than in a single first quarter payment.

Amt. of Divd. $	Date Decl.	Ex–divd. Date	Stock of Record	Payment Date
2–for–1	Nov. 11	Feb. 27	Feb. 3	Feb. 25'95
0.22½	Nov. 11	Jan. 30	Feb. 3	Feb. 25'95
0.22½	Mar. 10	May 1	May 5	May 25'95
0.22½	Jul. 14	Aug. 2	Aug. 4	Aug. 25'95
0.22½	Sep. 14	Nov. 1	Nov. 3	Nov. 25'95

Capitalization

Long Term Debt: $1,432,000,000 (9/95).

Minority Interests: $1,636,900,000.

$3.75 Cum. Pfd. Stock: 557,649 shs. ($100 par).

Common Stock: 178,494,892 shs. ($1 par).
Institutions hold 80%.
Shareholders: 55,200.

Office—425 Sixth Ave., Pittsburgh, PA 15219-1850. **Tel**—(412) 553-4545. **Chrmn & CEO**—P. H. O'Neill. **Secy**—Barbara S. Jeremiah. **EVP & CFO**—J. H. M. Hommen. **Investor Contact**—Edgar M. Cheely, Jr. **Dirs**—K. W. Dam, J. P. Diesel, J. T. Gorman, J. M. Gueron, Sir Ronald Hampel, J. P. Mulroney, P. H. O'Neill, Sir Arvi Parbo, H. B. Schacht, F. N. Shumway, F. A. Thomas, M. v.N. Whitman. **Transfer Agent & Registrar**—First Chicago Trust Co. of New York, Jersey City, NJ. **Incorporated** in Pennsylvania in 1925. **Empl**—61,700.

Information has been obtained from sources believed to be reliable, but its accuracy and completeness are not guaranteed.   Leo Larkin

ALZA Corp.

NYSE Symbol **AZA**
In S&P 500

05-SEP-95

Industry:
Drugs-Generic and OTC

Summary: This company is a leader in the field of controlled release therapeutic drug delivery systems. Earnings are derived from product sales and licensee royalties and fees.

S&P Opinion: Hold (★★★)

Recent Price • 23	Yield • Nil
52 Wk Range • 27-17	12-Mo. P/E • 30.3

Earnings vs. Previous Year
▲=Up ▼=Down ▶=No Change

Quantitative Evaluations

Outlook
(1 Lowest—5 Highest)
• **4⁻**

Fair Value
• **23%**

Risk
• **Average**

Earn./Div. Rank
• **B**

Technical Eval.
• **Bearish** since 7/95

Rel. Strength Rank
(1 Lowest—99 Highest)
• **22**

Insider Activity
• **Neutral**

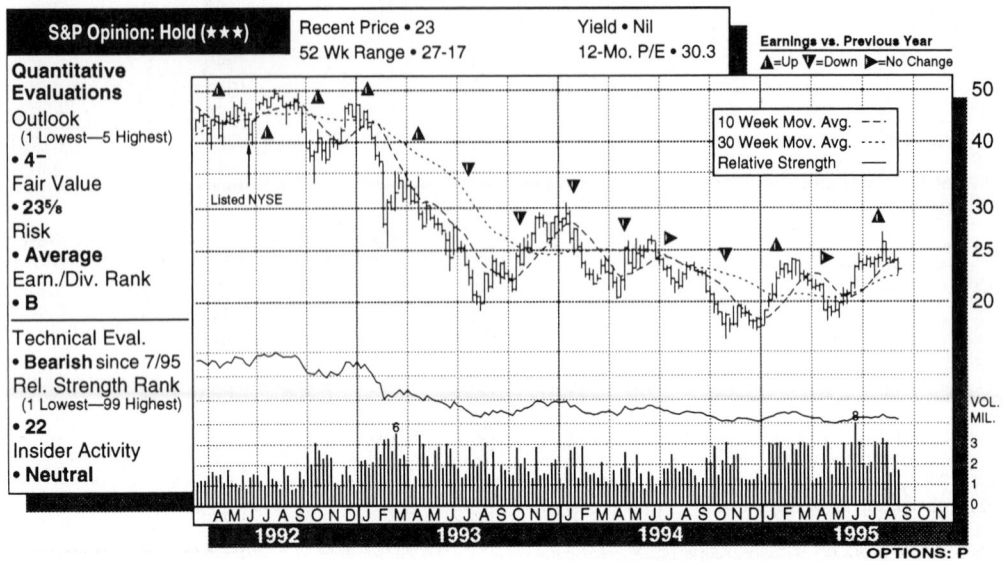

10 Week Mov. Avg. – – –
30 Week Mov. Avg. ·····
Relative Strength ——

Listed NYSE

VOL.
MIL.

OPTIONS: P

Overview - 04-SEP-95

Total revenues are expected to post another respectable advance in 1996. Royalties and fees from licensee sales of drugs produced through ALZA technology should rise, aided by gains for Adalat CR (marketed by Bayer AG), Glucotrol XL (Pfizer), DynaCirc CR (Sandoz), Efidac 24 (Ciba-Geigy) and Actisite periodontal fiber (Procter & Gamble). Royalties from Procardia XL (sold by Pfizer) are being restricted by reserves established for potential retroactive downward revision in royalties (pending resolution of certain patent issues). Sales of ALZA's own proprietary products, most notably Testoderm testosterone patch, are expected to increase, as are R&D revenues. Margins should widen on the greater volume.

Valuation - 04-SEP-95

Although well below past highs, the shares have moved higher in recent months, aided by good second quarter earnings and heightened takeover speculation. Germany's Bayer AG has been rumored to be interested in ALZA. On the other hand, the stock has been adversely affected by negative publicity concerning the older, short-acting form of Procardia and a potential reduction in royalty income from Procardia XL due to a U.S. patent issued to Bayer AG (Procardia XL, the long-acting form of the drug, accounted for 45% of the company's royalty revenues in the first half of 1995). New products in the R&D pipeline offer much long-term promise for ALZA. The shares are rated a long-term hold.

Key Stock Statistics

S&P EPS Est. 1995	0.90	Tang. Bk. Value/Share	4.99
P/E on S&P Est. 1995	25.6	Beta	1.63
S&P EPS Est. 1996	1.05	Shareholders	10,000
Dividend Rate/Share	Nil	Market cap. (B)	$ 1.9
Shs. outstg. (M)	82.3	Inst. holdings	64%
Avg. daily vol. (M)	0.440	Insider holdings	NA

Value of $10,000 invested 5 years ago: $ 10,484

Fiscal Year Ending Dec. 31

	1995	% Change	1994	% Change	1993	% Change
Revenues (Million $)						
1Q	80.24	18%	68.17	-3%	69.94	28%
2Q	83.01	20%	69.15	21%	57.06	-11%
3Q	—	—	66.23	15%	57.80	-10%
4Q	—	—	75.21	52%	49.39	-27%
Yr.	—	—	278.8	19%	234.2	-7%
Income (Million $)						
1Q	17.04	9%	15.62	-25%	20.77	29%
2Q	17.45	18%	14.75	5%	14.09	-16%
3Q	—	—	12.51	-11%	14.13	-27%
4Q	—	—	15.25	NM	-6.12	NM
Yr.	—	—	58.12	36%	42.87	-41%
Earnings Per Share ($)						
1Q	0.21	NM	0.21	-19%	0.26	30%
2Q	0.21	17%	0.18	NM	0.18	-14%
3Q	E0.23	53%	0.15	-17%	0.18	-25%
4Q	E0.25	32%	0.19	NM	-0.08	NM
Yr.	E0.90	27%	0.71	31%	0.54	-40%

Next earnings report expected: late October

Business Summary - 04-SEP-95

ALZA produces, primarily under joint arrangements, a broad range of drug products based on its proprietary therapeutic systems technologies, which are designed to release pre-programmed amounts of medication over extended time periods. In joint efforts, clients pay the company product development costs in return for marketing rights to the product; ALZA receives royalties based on the client's product sales. In some cases, the product is manufactured by the company and in others it is produced by the client. Contributions to revenues in recent years were:

	1994	1993	1992
Royalties & fees	44%	48%	46%
Product sales	25%	23%	30%
Research revenues	25%	20%	16%
Other revenue	6%	9%	8%

R&D outlays equaled 27.3% of total revenues in 1994 and 22.7% in 1993. Export sales accounted for 6.1% of 1994 sales.

Drug delivery systems developed by ALZA include OROS osmotic tablets for precise, controlled drug release; transdermal patches allowing continuous, systemic therapy; fibers for localized treatment of periodontal disease; electrotransport of drugs across intact skin; bioerodible polymers; systems to treat ocular conditions; and other systems.

Commercial products include Procardia XL, a heart drug developed with Pfizer for the treatment of angina and hypertension (royalties from Pfizer accounted for 30% of 1994 revenues); Nicoderm, a transdermal patch used for smoking cessation therapy; Transderm-Scop, which prevents nausea caused by motion sickness; Catapres-TTS, a treatment for high blood pressure; Duragesic, for the management of pain; Volmax, a treatment for asthma; Minipress XT, an anti-hypertensive; and Testoderm testosterone patch. Funded with $250 million from the company, Therapeutic Discovery Corp. (TDC) was formed by ALZA in 1993 to develop drugs based on company technologies. ALZA has the right to license each TDC product, and has an option to purchase all TDC stock.

Important Developments

Jul. '95—ALZA's royalties and fees in the first half of 1995 rose 12%, to $68.2 million, aided by royalties from Bayer AG on sales of Adalat CR (marketed in the U.S. by Pfizer as Procardia XL). Royalties and fees in the first half reflect a reduction of about $5 million to reflect additions to a reserve for a potential reduction in royalty income from Procardia XL due to a U.S. patent issued to Bayer AG.

Capitalization

Long Term Debt: $353,303,000 (6/95) of zero coup. sub. debs. conv. into 12.3 million com. shs.

Per Share Data ($)   (Year Ended Dec. 31)

	1994	1993	1992	1991	1990	1989
Tangible Bk. Val.	4.44	3.76	5.44	4.48	3.39	2.92
Cash Flow	0.87	0.69	1.01	-0.78	0.43	0.34
Earnings	0.71	0.54	0.90	-0.88	0.35	0.27
Dividends	Nil	Nil	Nil	Nil	Nil	Nil
Payout Ratio	Nil	Nil	Nil	Nil	Nil	Nil
Prices - High	30¾	47⅛	55⅛	50⅛	25½	23
- Low	17	19¼	33½	23⅜	16⅝	11¼
P/E Ratio - High	43	87	61	NM	73	83
- Low	24	36	37	NM	48	41

Income Statement Analysis (Million $)

	1994	%Chg	1993	%Chg	1992	%Chg	1991
Revs.	261	19%	220	-4%	229	64%	140
Oper. Inc.	109	4%	105	-5%	111	85%	60.0
Depr.	13.7	11%	12.3	32%	9.3	43%	6.5
Int. Exp.	19.7	-7%	21.1	12%	18.8	4%	18.0
Pretax Inc.	93.0	41%	66.0	-37%	105	NM	-41.4
Eff. Tax Rate	38%	—	35%	—	32%	—	NM
Net Inc.	58.1	35%	42.9	-41%	72.2	NM	-62.1

Balance Sheet & Other Fin. Data (Million $)

	1994	1993	1992	1991	1990	1989
Cash	345	94.0	131	172	302	109
Curr. Assets	492	198	228	249	354	147
Total Assets	806	622	698	580	531	288
Curr. Liab.	56.0	286	39.1	20.8	18.6	16.5
LT Debt	346	2.0	232	218	279	77.0
Common Eqty.	364	307	408	323	220	187
Total Cap.	729	318	646	549	504	266
Cap. Exp.	37.2	23.8	41.4	34.1	24.7	44.2
Cash Flow	71.8	55.1	81.5	-55.6	30.3	22.9

Ratio Analysis

	1994	1993	1992	1991	1990	1989
Curr. Ratio	8.8	0.7	5.8	12.0	19.1	8.9
% LT Debt of Cap.	47.4	0.6	35.9	39.8	55.5	29.0
% Net Inc.of Revs.	22.3	19.5	31.5	NM	24.8	22.9
% Ret. on Assets	8.1	6.2	11.1	NM	6.0	6.8
% Ret. on Equity	17.3	11.4	19.4	NM	12.1	10.8

Dividend Data —No cash dividends have ever been paid. In June 1993, the company distributed to stockholders one Therapeutic Discovery Corp. (TDC) unit for every 10 ALZA shares held of record May 28, 1993. Each unit consisted of one TDC common share and one warrant to buy 0.125 of an ALZA share at $65 a share.

Data as orig. reptd.; bef. results of disc. opers. and/or spec. items. Per share data adj. for stk. divs. as of ex-div. date. E-Estimated. NA-Not Available. NM-Not Meaningful. NR-Not Ranked.

Office—950 Page Mill Rd. (P.O. Box 10950), Palo Alto, CA 94303-0802. **Tel**—(415) 494-5000. **Co-Chrmn**—A. Zaffaroni. **Co-Chrmn & CEO**—E. Mario. **VP & CFO**—B. C. Cozadd. **VP & Treas**—D. R. Hoffmann. **Investor Contact**—M. Boennighausen. **Dirs**—W. G. Davis, M. S. Gerstel, R. J. Glaser, E. Mario, D. O. Morton, R. A. Peterson, J. E. Shaw, I. Stein, J. N. Stern, A. Zaffaroni. **Transfer Agent & Registrar**—First National Bank of Boston. **Incorporated** in California in 1968; reincorporated in Delaware in 1987. **Empl-**1,288. **S&P Analyst:** H. Saftlas

41

Amerada Hess

NYSE Symbol **AHC**
In S&P 500

25-OCT-95

Industry: Oil and Gas

Summary: This integrated oil and natural gas company recently added significant capacity to its major refinery.

S&P Opinion: Buy (★★★★)

Recent Price • 45	Yield • 1.4%
52 Wk Range • 53⅛-43¾	12-Mo. P/E • NM

Quantitative Evaluations

Outlook
(1 Lowest—5 Highest)
• **1⁻**

Fair Value
• **37⅛**

Risk
• **Low**

Earn./Div. Rank
• **B-**

Technical Eval.
• **Bullish** since 8/95

Rel. Strength Rank
(1 Lowest—99 Highest)
• **22**

Insider Activity
• **Neutral**

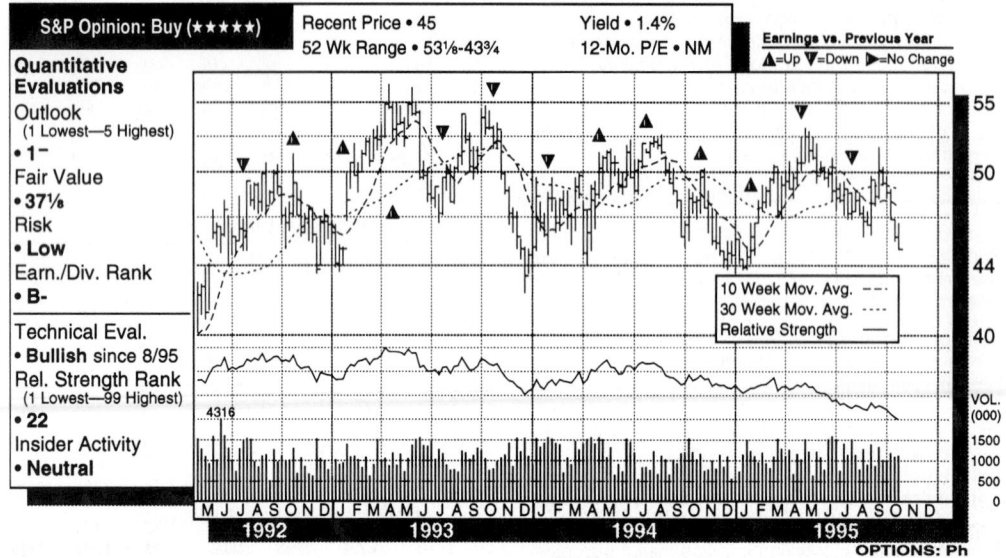

Earnings vs. Previous Year
▲=Up ▼=Down ▶=No Change

10 Week Mov. Avg. — - —
30 Week Mov. Avg. - - - - -
Relative Strength ——

OPTIONS: Ph

Overview - 25-OCT-95

Revenues should rise in the near term, as crude oil, natural gas and refined product volumes increase. Results for 1996 will benefit from a slight upturn in refining margins in the U.S., though we expect to see downstream asset sales and/or rationalizations in the near term. Emphasis on exploration focused on the North Sea, should help reduce AHC's traditional reliance on refining and marketing. The cash position is healthy, following completion of major capital projects in 1993, and continued strong levels of cash flow will help the company reduce long term debt. During 1995, AHC intends to reduce its long term debt to under $3 billion, and seeks a further $350 to $400 million reduction by year-end 1996. Long-term prospects are enhanced by strong North American natural gas business, a recent expansion of refining capacity, and greater overseas oil output.

Valuation - 25-OCT-95

The shares have fluctuated thus far in 1995, reflecting volatility in oil prices and refining margins. Expected profitability for the fourth quarter and lower debt levels are likely to boost the shares in coming months, as promising exploration plays are likely to bring profits to the bottom line. A writedown of inventories in the first quarter clouded a strong fundamental picture. Our projection of 1996 cash flow of $15.50 per share makes us believe that the shares are undervalued at current levels. Increased capacity at the St. Croix refinery contributes to our bullish stance, since we anticipate improved refining margins over the next year.

Key Stock Statistics

S&P EPS Est. 1995	-0.13	Tang. Bk. Value/Share	33.19
P/E on S&P Est. 1995	NM	Beta	0.95
S&P EPS Est. 1996	1.35	Shareholders	13,100
Dividend Rate/Share	0.60	Market cap. (B)	$ 4.1
Shs. outstg. (M)	93.0	Inst. holdings	66%
Avg. daily vol. (M)	0.233	Insider holdings	NA

Value of $10,000 invested 5 years ago: $ 9,978

Fiscal Year Ending Dec. 31

	1995	% Change	1994	% Change	1993	% Change
Revenues (Million $)						
1Q	1,978	6%	1,858	18%	1,578	9%
2Q	1,778	19%	1,488	6%	1,403	-5%
3Q	—	—	1,494	20%	1,246	-12%
4Q	—	—	1,762	7%	1,645	2%
Yr.	—	—	6,602	12%	5,873	-2%
Income (Million $)						
1Q	25.16	-70%	83.66	NM	3.47	NM
2Q	-40.22	NM	-16.70	NM	-145.1	NM
3Q	-104.6	NM	-1.91	NM	-22.41	NM
4Q	—	—	8.70	NM	-133.6	NM
Yr.	—	—	73.70	NM	-297.7	NM
Earnings Per Share ($)						
1Q	0.27	-70%	0.90	NM	0.04	NM
2Q	-0.43	NM	-0.18	NM	-1.57	NM
3Q	-1.13	NM	-0.02	NM	-0.24	NM
4Q	E-0.40	NM	0.09	NM	-1.45	NM
Yr.	E-0.13	NM	0.79	NM	-3.22	NM

Next earnings report expected: late October

Business Summary - 18-OCT-95

Amerada Hess is an integrated oil and gas company. Oil is produced domestically, both onshore and offshore, as well as in Canada, the U.K. and Norwegian sectors of the North Sea, the Middle East, and, most recently, Gabon. Natural gas is produced primarily in the U.S., but also in Canada and the U.K. and Norwegian sectors of the North Sea. Segment profits (in millions) in recent years were:

	1994	1993	1992
Exploration/production	$157	$116	$219
Refining/marketing	95	-293	-129
Corp./other	-178	-91	-82

Net crude and natural gas liquids production in 1994 averaged 250,520 b/d (215,390), of which 27% came from the U.S.. Natural gas production averaged 846.1 MMcf a day (887.3), with 50% in the U.S. Net proved reserves at December 31, 1994, were 644 million bbl. of crude oil and liquids (670 million) and 2,581 Bcf of natural gas (2,653 billion).

Refinery runs averaged 388,000 b/d in 1994 (351,000 b/d in 1993), and refined products sold totaled 386,000 b/d (377,000 b/d). Refineries are located at St. Croix, U.S. Virgin Islands, and Port Reading, N.J. In early 1995, the St. Croix refinery received approval to operate the facility at rates in excess of 100,000 b/d. The fluid catlytic cracking unit has tested successfully at 110,000 b/d.

AMH had several significant exploration successes in 1994, both in the North Sea and in the U.S. Gulf of Mexico. For 1995, the company will expand its exploration budget, focusing on core areas in the North Sea and the U.S. Gulf of Mexico, concentrating on the use of low-cost methods. Deep-water U.S. Gulf exploration, where AMH has under certain circumstance assumed sole ownership of key properties, should remain an important part of the company's strategy.

Important Developments

Sep. '95—Amerada Hess said its subsidiary's refinery in St. Croix was shut down in anticipation of Hurricane Marilyn. Processing units were brought back on line within a three week period.
May '95—J.B. Hess replaced his father, Leon Hess, as the company's chairman and CEO. Leon Hess had run AHC's oil operations for more than 50 years. The company said debt reduction would be one of the new CEO's priorities.

Capitalization

Long Term Debt: $2,873,692,000 (6/95).

Per Share Data ($) (Year Ended Dec. 31)

	1994	1993	1992	1991	1990	1989
Tangible Bk. Val.	33.33	32.71	36.59	38.63	38.34	31.69
Cash Flow	10.77	5.69	9.63	11.26	15.13	12.60
Earnings	0.79	-3.21	0.09	1.04	5.96	5.87
Dividends	0.60	0.60	0.60	0.60	0.60	0.60
Payout Ratio	76%	NM	736%	58%	10%	10%
Prices - High	52⅝	56⅜	51¼	59⅛	56	51⅞
- Low	43¾	42⅜	36⅝	42½	42⅞	31
P/E Ratio - High	67	NM	NM	57	9	9
- Low	55	NM	NM	41	7	5

Income Statement Analysis (Million $)

	1994	%Chg	1993	%Chg	1992	%Chg	1991
Revs.	6,602	13%	5,852	NM	5,875	-6%	6,267
Oper. Inc.	1,312	78%	737	-27%	1,009	4%	973
Depr.	928	12%	825	NM	833	NM	829
Int. Exp.	245	-2%	249	-2%	255	7%	238
Pretax Inc.	236	NM	-222	NM	123	6%	116
Eff. Tax Rate	69%	—	NM	—	94%	—	27%
Net Inc.	74.0	NM	-297	NM	8.0	-90%	84.0

Balance Sheet & Other Fin. Data (Million $)

	1994	1993	1992	1991	1990	1989
Cash	53.0	80.0	141	120	130	120
Curr. Assets	1,722	1,688	2,068	2,476	3,280	1,951
Total Assets	8,338	8,642	8,722	8,841	9,057	6,867
Curr. Liab.	1,201	1,443	1,517	1,851	2,677	1,458
LT Debt	3,235	3,515	3,141	3,023	2,532	2,348
Common Eqty.	3,100	3,029	3,388	3,132	3,106	2,561
Total Cap.	6,882	7,006	7,046	6,790	6,198	5,306
Cap. Exp.	596	1,348	1,558	1,712	1,461	1,561
Cash Flow	1,002	527	841	913	1,226	1,022

Ratio Analysis

	1994	1993	1992	1991	1990	1989
Curr. Ratio	1.4	1.2	1.4	1.3	1.2	1.3
% LT Debt of Cap.	47.0	50.2	44.6	44.5	40.9	44.3
% Net Inc.of Revs.	1.1	NM	0.1	1.3	6.9	8.5
% Ret. on Assets	0.9	NM	0.1	0.9	6.1	7.8
% Ret. on Equity	2.4	NM	0.2	2.7	17.0	20.1

Dividend Data —Common dividends, paid since 1922, were suspended in 1986 and resumed in 1987. A dividend reinvestment plan is available.

Amt. of Div. $	Date Decl.	Ex-Div. Date	Stock of Record	Payment Date
0.150	Dec. 07	Dec. 15	Dec. 21	Jan. 04 '95
0.150	Mar. 01	Mar. 07	Mar. 13	Mar. 31 '95
0.150	Jun. 07	Jun. 15	Jun. 19	Jun. 30 '95
0.150	Sep. 06	Sep. 14	Sep. 18	Sep. 29 '95

Data as orig. reptd.; bef. results of disc. opers. and/or spec. items. Per share data adj. for stk. divs. as of ex-div. date.
E-Estimated. NA-Not Available. NM-Not Meaningful. NR-Not Ranked.

Office—1185 Avenue of the Americas, New York, NY 10036. **Tel**—(212) 997-8500. **Chrmn & CEO**—J. B. Hess. **Pres & COO**—S. Laidlaw. **EVP & CFO**—J. Y. Schreyer. **VP, Secy & Investor Contact**—Carl T. Tursi. **Dirs**—M. B. Bianchi, J. B. Collins II, B. T. Deverin, P. S. Hadley, J. B. Hess, L. Hess, E. E. Holiday, T. H. Kean, C. C. F. Laidlaw, H. W. McCollum, R. B. Oresman, W. A. Pogue, J. Y. Schreyer, R. B. Sellars, W. I. Spencer, R. F. Wright. **Transfer Agents**—Chemical Bank, NYC; First Fidelity Bank, Newark, NJ; R-M Trust Co., Toronto. **Registrar**—Chemical Bank, NYC. **Incorporated** in Delaware in 1920. **Empl**-9,858. **S&P Analyst:** Raymond J. Deacon

Amdahl Corp.

ASE Symbol **AMH**
In S&P 500

02-OCT-95

Industry:
Data Processing

Summary: Amdahl manufactures IBM plug-compatible mainframes and also offers servers, data storage systems, software, and a variety of services. Fujitsu Limited owns 44% of the shares.

S&P Opinion: Hold (★★★)	Recent Price • 9⅞	Yield • Nil
	52 Wk Range • 13⅝-8	12-Mo. P/E • 11.3

Quantitative Evaluations

Outlook
(1 Lowest—5 Highest)
• **4⁻**

Fair Value
• **10½**

Risk
• **High**

Earn./Div. Rank
• **C**

Technical Eval.
• **Neutral** since 8/95

Rel. Strength Rank
(1 Lowest—99 Highest)
• **16**

Insider Activity
• **Neutral**

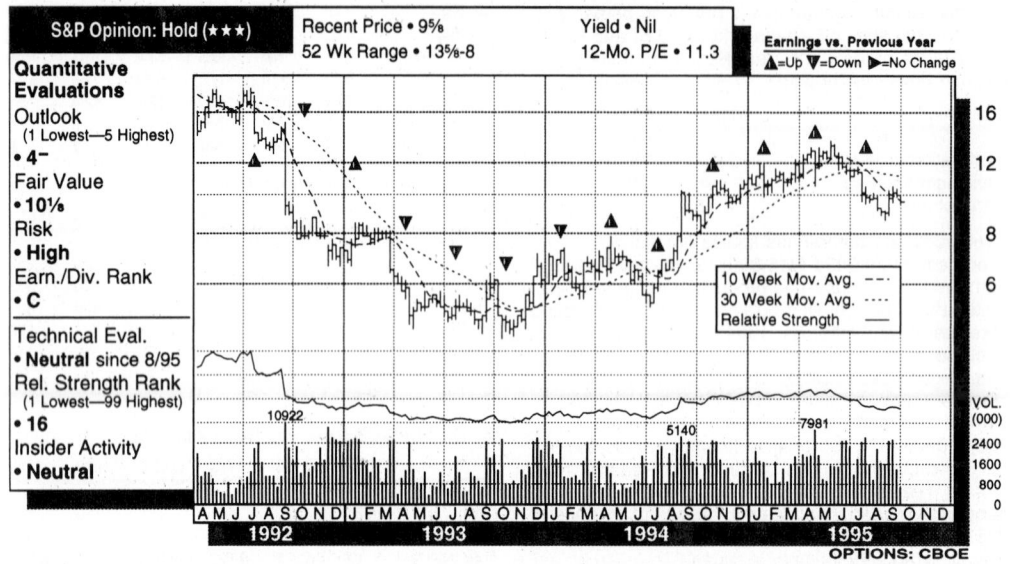

Earnings vs. Previous Year
▲=Up ▼=Down ▶=No Change

10 Week Mov. Avg. ---
30 Week Mov. Avg. ····
Relative Strength —

VOL. (000)

OPTIONS: CBOE

Overview - 02-OCT-95

Mainframe demand was solid in 1995's first half, particularly for upgrades, and the pricing environment was slightly more favorable. These trends are likely to continue through the balance of 1995, as the elimination of excess capacity in the industry has resulted in an improved supply/demand balance. AMH's storage business will continue to underperform until new products are unveiled in early 1995. The rapid growth in software, systems integration and open systems hardware should continue. These emerging businesses accounted for 15% of second quarter revenues. The net result of these factors should be a modest decline in total revenues for the year. Gross margins should widen, reflecting reduced manufacturing overhead and an improved product mix. MG&A expense should rise about 15%, offset by lower R&D spending. EPS are expected to reach $0.95 in 1995 and $1.00 in 1996.

Valuation - 02-OCT-95

The shares continue to languish due to several investor concerns, including the looming 1996 transition to a new family of CMOS mainframes and RAID storage products. We continue to view both factors as potential disruptions to AMH's ongoing turnaround, and represent the basis for our current neutral opinion. Despite more than $5 a share in net cash on the balance sheet and a P/E multiple that is at a significant discount to the S&P 500, we would avoid adding to positions until these transition issues are behind the company.

Key Stock Statistics

S&P EPS Est. 1995	0.95	Tang. Bk. Value/Share	7.96
P/E on S&P Est. 1995	10.1	Beta	1.60
S&P EPS Est. 1996	1.00	Shareholders	26,000
Dividend Rate/Share	Nil	Market cap. (B)	$ 1.1
Shs. outstg. (M)	118.9	Inst. holdings	44%
Avg. daily vol. (M)	0.459	Insider holdings	NA

Value of $10,000 invested 5 years ago: $ 6,936

Fiscal Year Ending Dec. 31

	1995	% Change	1994	% Change	1993	% Change
Revenues (Million $)						
1Q	371.5	-2%	378.8	NM	381.0	-23%
2Q	378.7	-5%	396.9	-14%	463.2	-33%
3Q	—	—	364.2	-7%	393.7	-33%
4Q	—	—	498.7	13%	442.9	-41%
Yr.	—	—	1,639	-2%	1,681	-33%
Income (Million $)						
1Q	20.59	190%	7.11	NM	-248.4	NM
2Q	26.24	110%	12.52	NM	-23.70	NM
3Q	—	—	14.29	NM	-275.7	NM
4Q	—	—	40.89	NM	-40.86	NM
Yr.	—	—	74.80	NM	-588.7	NM
Earnings Per Share ($)						
1Q	0.17	183%	0.06	NM	-2.19	NM
2Q	0.22	100%	0.11	NM	-0.21	NM
3Q	E0.20	67%	0.12	NM	-2.41	NM
4Q	E0.35	3%	0.34	NM	-0.36	NM
Yr.	E0.95	51%	0.63	NM	-5.17	NM

Next earnings report expected: late October

Amdahl Corp.

Business Summary - 02-OCT-95

Amdahl produces large-scale computers that are software and hardware compatible with those of IBM, the dominant factor in the market. It also provides storage and communications products and consulting and educational services. Revenues by product line in recent years were:

	1994	1993
Processor equipment	50%	51%
Maintenance, software, services & leases	34%	31%
Storage products	13%	16%
Servers, communication & other products	3%	2%

Foreign operations contributed 42% of revenues in 1994, up from 38% in each of 1993 and 1992.

The company's 5995 series of mainframes competes with IBM's ES9000 series. Higher performance models began shipping in the 1994 third quarter. AMH also makes high performance direct access storage devices (DASD) and controllers for use with large-scale computers; sells mid-range and larger data servers manufactured by Sun Microsystems and Cray Research; management software for distributed computing networks; Huron software for applications development and business process reengineering; and UTS, a UNIX-based proprietary operating system that runs independently on IBM, Hitachi and AMH mainframes. The company also provides computer maintenance, consulting and educational services.

Fujitsu Ltd. supplies both components and subassemblies for AMH's computer systems. Communication control processors and direct access storage devices are made by Fujitsu to AMH's specifications. AMH and Fujitsu will jointly develop the company's next generation of mainframe computers.

Important Developments

Sep. '95—AMH agreed to acquire Canada-based DMR Group, a leading provider of information technology services, for US$90 million (C$8.25 a share). DMR subsequently received a C$9 a share offer from BDM Int'l Inc. AMH maintains that DMR's principal shareholders have irrevocably agreed to tender their shares to the company.

Sep. '95—AMH announced new RAID (Redundant Arrays of Inexpensive Disks) storage subsystems and CMOS-based System 390 servers. The new RAID series, called Spectris, is compatible with System 390 environments and offers up to 726GB of scaleable disk storage. Spectris is expected to be available in 1996's first quarter. The Server series, called Millennium, can be part of a S/390 Parallel Sysplex environments or function as an independent server. Millennium is expected to ship in mid-1996.

Capitalization

Long Term Debt: $80,000,000 (6/95).

Per Share Data ($)

(Year Ended Dec. 31)

	1994	1993	1992	1991	1990	1989
Tangible Bk. Val.	7.51	6.90	12.12	12.38	12.44	10.80
Cash Flow	1.75	-3.33	1.79	1.38	3.01	2.54
Earnings	0.63	-5.17	-0.06	0.04	1.66	1.39
Dividends	Nil	0.05	0.10	0.10	0.10	0.10
Payout Ratio	Nil	NM	NM	251%	6%	7%
Prices - High	11⅛	8½	20⅝	17⅞	18⅞	23⅜
- Low	5¼	4⅜	6⅝	11⅝	10	10¾
P/E Ratio - High	18	NM	NM	NM	11	17
- Low	8	NM	NM	NM	6	8

Income Statement Analysis (Million $)

	1994	%Chg	1993	%Chg	1992	%Chg	1991
Revs.	1,639	-2%	1,681	-33%	2,525	48%	1,702
Oper. Inc.	197	NM	-32.0	NM	211	79%	118
Depr.	133	-37%	210	NM	208	39%	150
Int. Exp.	9.9	-44%	17.8	-15%	21.0	69%	12.4
Pretax Inc.	80.0	NM	-713	NM	-14.0	NM	7.0
Eff. Tax Rate	6.80%	—	NM	—	NM	—	37%
Net Inc.	75.0	NM	-588	NM	-7.0	NM	4.0

Balance Sheet & Other Fin. Data (Million $)

	1994	1993	1992	1991	1990	1989
Cash	699	253	295	412	593	563
Curr. Assets	1,346	1,125	1,753	1,540	1,595	1,670
Total Assets	1,719	1,672	2,701	2,336	2,327	2,234
Curr. Liab.	661	771	907	631	694	825
LT Debt	99	20.0	222	109	25.0	87.0
Common Eqty.	876	790	1,371	1,378	1,371	1,176
Total Cap.	1,027	870	1,754	1,675	1,598	1,408
Cap. Exp.	68.0	135	403	326	316	306
Cash Flow	208	-378	201	154	341	280

Ratio Analysis

	1994	1993	1992	1991	1990	1989
Curr. Ratio	2.0	1.5	1.9	2.4	2.3	2.0
% LT Debt of Cap.	9.7	2.3	12.6	6.5	1.6	6.2
% Net Inc.of Revs.	4.6	NM	NM	0.3	8.5	7.3
% Ret. on Assets	4.4	NM	NM	0.2	8.0	7.3
% Ret. on Equity	8.9	NM	NM	0.3	14.4	13.8

Dividend Data —Cash dividends, initiated in 1977, were suspended following the August 1993 payment.

Data as orig. reptd.; bef. results of disc. opers. and/or spec. items. Per share data adj. for stk. divs. as of ex-div. date. E-Estimated. NA-Not Available. NM-Not Meaningful. NR-Not Ranked.

Office—1250 E. Arques Ave., Sunnyvale, CA 94088-3470. **Tel**—(408) 746-6000. **Chrmn**—J. C. Lewis. **Pres & CEO**—E. J. Zemke. **SVP, CFO & Secy**—B. J. Ryan. **Investor Contact**—A. William Stewart. **Dirs**—K. Fukagawa, M. R. Hallman, E. F. Heizer, Jr., K. Kojima, J. C. Lewis, B. G. Malkiel, G. R. Packard, W. B. Reinhold, T. Tsuchimoto, J. S. Webb, E. J. Zemke. **Transfer Agent & Registrar**—Bank of New York, NYC. **Incorporated** in Delaware in 1972. **Empl**-5,600. **S&P Analyst:** John D. Coyle, CFA

American Brands

NYSE Symbol **AMB**
In S&P 500

31-JUL-95 **Industry:** Tobacco

Summary: This diversified holding company has interests in a wide variety of consumer businesses, including cigarettes, distilled spirits, office products, hardware, and leisure products.

S&P Opinion: Buy (★★★★★)	Recent Price • 39⅝	Yield • 5.1%
	52 Wk Range • 42⅛-32⅞	12-Mo. P/E • 11.9

Quantitative Evaluations

Outlook
(1 Lowest—5 Highest)
• **4⁻**

Fair Value
• **39⅛**

Risk
• **Low**

Earn./Div. Rank
• **A**

Technical Eval.
• **Bullish** since 12/94

Rel. Strength Rank
(1 Lowest—99 Highest)
• **30**

Insider Activity
• **NA**

Earnings vs. Previous Year
▲=Up ▼=Down ▶=No Change

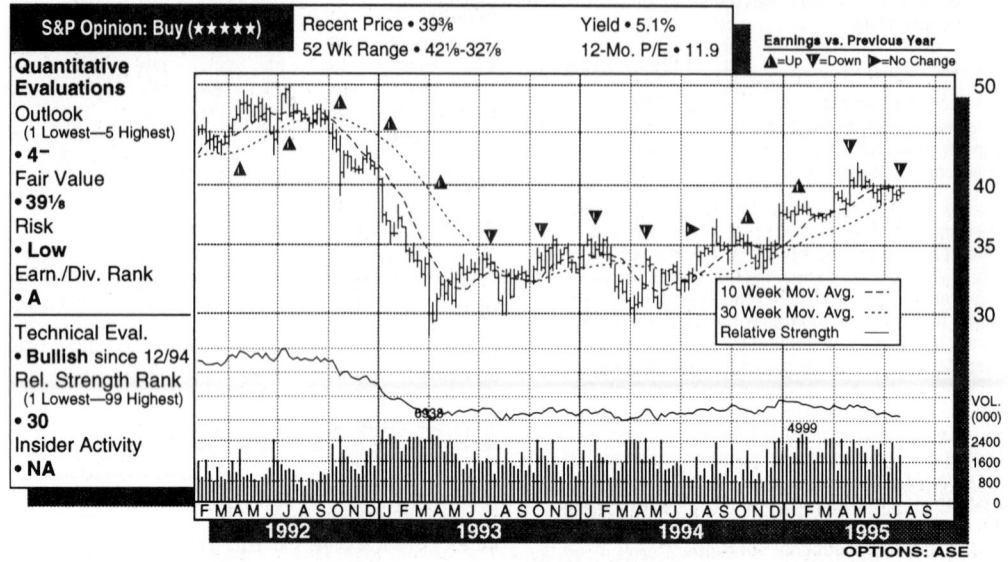

10 Week Mov. Avg. ---
30 Week Mov. Avg. ·····
Relative Strength —

OPTIONS: ASE

Overview - 31-JUL-95

Earnings from ongoing operations through 1996 are expected to advance at a high single-digit pace, with projected gains in all major segments. Although continued competitive industry conditions facing both Gallaher Tobacco and distilled spirits operations will likely restrain gains in these segments, rapid gains from other segments, as well as an improving product mix shift, should more than offset. With interest and related expenses projected to be reduced significantly in 1995 and 1996, combined with fewer shares outstanding, we forecast earnings per share to climb 18% in 1995, and nearly 13% in 1996. While our assumptions exclude major acquisitions, chances are high of such activity near-term.

Valuation - 31-JUL-95

Given our bullish earnings per share forecast through 1996, we view these shares as attractive at current levels. We believe that management's aggressive business restructuring actions over the past year has positioned the company well for sustainable earnings growth in coming years. We expect that a greater focus on core segments, coupled with the elimination of U.S. tobacco uncertainties, should allow for more predictable earnings growth ahead. In addition, funds received from recent divestments gives management substantial flexibility with regard to additive acquisitions and further share buybacks. AMB, at a discount to the S&P 500, and yielding 5%, is a strong total return play for most investors.

Key Stock Statistics

S&P EPS Est. 1995	2.80	Tang. Bk. Value/Share	3.75
P/E on S&P Est. 1995	14.1	Beta	1.00
S&P EPS Est. 1996	3.15	Shareholders	69,400
Dividend Rate/Share	2.00	Market cap. (B)	$ 7.4
Shs. outstg. (M)	188.8	Inst. holdings	60%
Avg. daily vol. (M)	0.357	Insider holdings	NA

Value of $10,000 invested 5 years ago: $ 14,361

Fiscal Year Ending Dec. 31

	1995	% Change	1994	% Change	1993	% Change
Revenues (Million $)						
1Q	1,515	-25%	2,033	-3%	2,090	-2%
2Q	2,595	—	--	—	2,020	-7%
3Q	—	—	--	—	1,980	-12%
4Q	—	—	5,457	148%	2,200	-4%
Yr.	—	—	7,490	-10%	8,290	-6%
Income (Million $)						
1Q	116.6	-10%	129.5	-48%	247.1	NM
2Q	119.1	-22%	151.9	NM	151.3	-25%
3Q	—	—	131.8	55%	85.00	-58%
4Q	—	—	471.9	155%	184.8	-21%
Yr.	—	—	885.1	32%	668.2	-24%
Earnings Per Share ($)						
1Q	0.60	-6%	0.64	-48%	1.22	3%
2Q	0.63	-16%	0.75	NM	0.75	-23%
3Q	E0.67	—	0.65	55%	0.42	-57%
4Q	E0.90	—	2.34	157%	0.91	-21%
Yr.	E2.80	—	4.38	33%	3.30	-23%

Next earnings report expected: late October

American Brands

Business Summary - 31-JUL-95

American Brands derived its 1994 sales and operating profits as follows:

	Sales	Profits
Tobacco products		
Domestic	12%	19%
International	47%	39%
Hardware and home products	10%	13%
Distilled spirits	9%	17%
Office products	8%	6%
Golf & leisure products	4%	6%
Other	10%	1%

Foreign operations accounted for 64% of revenues and 49% of profits in 1994.

The U.S.-based American Tobacco Co. was sold by AMB in December 1994 to B.A.T. Industries p.l.c. AMB retains ownership of U.K.- based Gallaher Ltd., which produces cigarettes, cigars and smoking tobaccos principally in the U.K. under labels including Benson & Hedges, Silk Cut and Berkeley. Gallaher's U.K. market share was about 40% in 1994.

Distilled spirits brands include Jim Beam, Old Grand-Dad, Gilbeys, DeKuyper, and Whyte & Mackay. Hardware and home improvement subsidiaries include Moen, Master Lock, Aristokraft, and Waterloo Industries. Office products include ACCO World supplies and stationary products, and Swingline staplers and fasteners. Specialty products include Titleist, Foot-Joy and Acushnet golf products.

During 1994, AMB sold its American Tobacco, Franklin Life Insurance, and Dollond & Atchinson subsidiaries.

Important Developments

Jul. '95—AMB said income from ongoing operations in 1995's first half rose 7.7%, year to year, to $549 million. Strong growth for international tobacco (+14%), office products (+14%), and golf & leisure products (+11%) helped offset sluggish gains for hardware & home improvement products (+2%) and distilled spirits (+1%). Earnings per share during 1995's first half also benefited from a 24% reduction in interest and related expenses, and 5.2% fewer primary shares, which more than offset a higher effective tax rate (39.3% vs. 36.2%). Management said that it expected a strong 1995 second half, with a particularly strong ongoing earnings per share comparison in the third quarter. AMB anticipated earnings per share in 1995 to exceed 1994's $2.37 ($2.34 fully diluted) from ongoing operations by more than 17%.

Capitalization

Long Term Debt: $1,436,300,000 (6/95).
Conv. Preferred Stock: $15,700,000.

Per Share Data ($)

(Year Ended Dec. 31)

	1994	1993	1992	1991	1990	1989
Tangible Bk. Val.	5.33	2.51	5.33	3.87	2.83	5.29
Cash Flow	5.94	4.83	5.78	5.30	4.28	4.35
Earnings	4.38	3.30	4.29	3.91	2.99	3.26
Dividends	1.99	1.97	1.80	1.59	1.40	1.26
Payout Ratio	45%	60%	42%	41%	48%	39%
Prices - High	38⅜	40⅝	49⅞	47⅝	41⅝	41
- Low	29⅜	28½	39	35⅝	30⅞	30⅝
P/E Ratio - High	9	12	12	12	14	13
- Low	7	9	9	9	10	9

Income Statement Analysis (Million $)

	1994	%Chg	1993	%Chg	1992	%Chg	1991
Revs.	7,490	-10%	8,288	-6%	8,840	6%	8,379
Oper. Inc.	1,557	-7%	1,670	-15%	1,970	11%	1,777
Depr.	314	2%	309	2%	304	8%	281
Int. Exp.	212	-13%	244	-10%	270	2%	264
Pretax Inc.	1,351	26%	1,076	-23%	1,398	13%	1,238
Eff. Tax Rate	35%	—	38%	—	37%	—	35%
Net Inc.	885	32%	668	-24%	884	10%	806

Balance Sheet & Other Fin. Data (Million $)

	1994	1993	1992	1991	1990	1989
Cash	110	142	140	129	154	149
Curr. Assets	4,671	NA	NA	NA	NA	NA
Total Assets	9,794	16,339	14,963	15,116	13,835	11,394
Curr. Liab.	3,116	NA	NA	NA	NA	NA
LT Debt	1,512	2,492	2,407	2,552	2,434	1,717
Common Eqty.	4,622	4,254	4,283	4,163	3,633	2,938
Total Cap.	6,283	6,888	6,947	7,118	6,483	5,042
Cap. Exp.	201	250	289	234	297	257
Cash Flow	1,198	976	1,178	1,073	832	822

Ratio Analysis

	1994	1993	1992	1991	1990	1989
Curr. Ratio	1.5	NA	NA	NA	NA	NA
% LT Debt of Cap.	24.1	36.2	34.6	35.9	37.5	34.1
% Net Inc.of Revs.	11.8	8.1	10.0	9.6	7.2	8.7
% Ret. on Assets	6.8	4.3	5.9	5.5	4.6	5.3
% Ret. on Equity	19.9	15.6	20.8	20.2	17.3	22.4

Dividend Data (Dividends have been paid since 1905. A dividend reinvestment plan is available. A new "poison pill" stock purchase right was adopted in 1987.)

Amt. of Div. $	Date Decl.	Ex-Div. Date	Stock of Record	Payment Date
0.500	Jul. 26	Jul. 29	Aug. 04	Sep. 01 '94
0.500	Oct. 25	Oct. 28	Nov. 03	Dec. 01 '94
0.500	Jan. 31	Feb. 02	Feb. 08	Mar. 01 '95
0.500	Apr. 25	May. 02	May. 08	Jun. 01 '95
0.500	Jul. 25	Aug. 03	Aug. 07	Sep. 01 '95

Data as orig. reptd.; bef. results of disc. opers. and/or spec. items. Per share data adj. for stk. divs. as of ex-div. date. E-Estimated. NA-Not Available. NM-Not Meaningful. NR-Not Ranked.

Office—1700 East Putnam Ave., Old Greenwich, CT 06870-0811. **Tel**—(203) 698-5000. **Chrmn & CEO**—T. C. Hays. **Pres & COO**—J. T. Ludes. **SVP-CFO**—D. L. Bauerlein Jr. **VP-Secy**—L. F. Fernous Jr. **Investor Contact**—Dan Conforti. **Dirs**—W. J. Alley, E. R. Anderson, P. O. Ewers, T. C. Hays, J. W. Johnstone Jr., W. J. Kelley, S. Kirschner, G. R. Lohman, J. T. Ludes, C. H. Pistor Jr., P. M. Wilson. **Transfer Agent**—Co. itself. **Incorporated** in New Jersey in 1904; reincorporated in Delaware in 1985. **Empl**-34,820. **S&P Analyst:** Kenneth A. Shea

American Electric Power

NYSE Symbol **AEP**
In S&P 500

23-AUG-95 | **Industry:** Utilities-Electric | **Summary:** This electric utility holding company operates in Ohio, Indiana, Michigan, Virginia, West Virginia, Kentucky and Tennessee, and is the second largest electric system in the U.S.

S&P Opinion: Hold (★★★)	Recent Price • 34¼	Yield • 7.0%
	52 Wk Range • 35¾-29¼	12-Mo. P/E • 13.0

Quantitative Evaluations

Outlook
(1 Lowest—5 Highest)
• **1+**

Fair Value
• **28⅞**

Risk
• **Low**

Earn./Div. Rank
• **B+**

Technical Eval.
• **Bearish** since 7/95

Rel. Strength Rank
(1 Lowest—99 Highest)
• **34**

Insider Activity
• **Neutral**

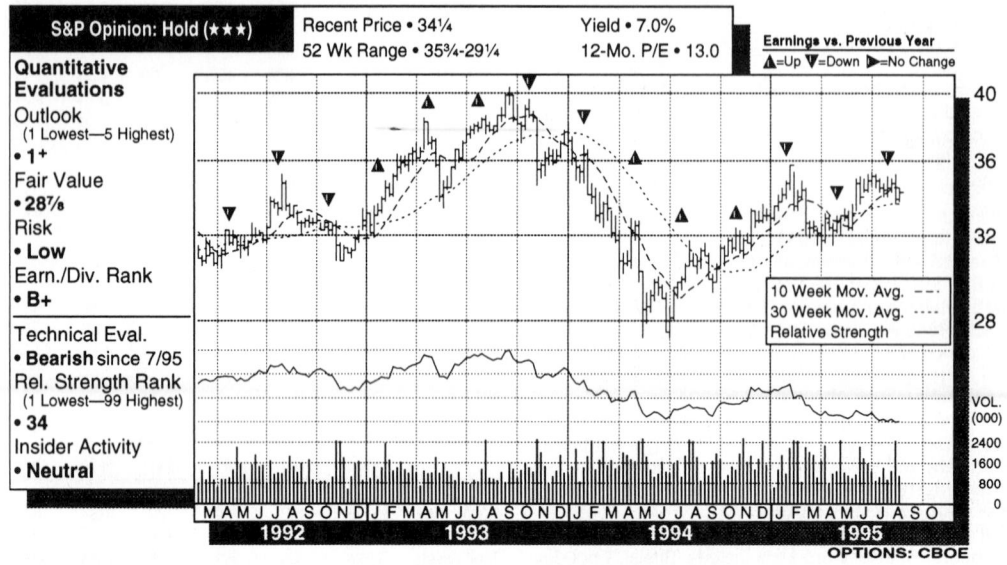

Earnings vs. Previous Year
▲=Up ▼=Down ▶=No Change

10 Week Mov. Avg. ---
30 Week Mov. Avg. ····
Relative Strength —

1992 1993 1994 1995

OPTIONS: CBOE

Overview - 15-AUG-95

Share earnings for 1995 should benefit from somewhat higher electricity sales, assuming continued economic growth in the company's service territories. Ongoing efforts to control operating and maintenance expenses will also contribute to the modest growth we are forecasting. Settlement of the rate case in Ohio is not expected to have a substantial impact on earnings, but does help offset sharply lower sales to other electric utilities. Earnings have also been penalized in the 1995 first half by a return to more normal temperatures compared to unseasonably warm weather a year earlier. Reorganization of the firm by function--separating transmission, distribution and generation organizations--should ease the company's transition to a more competitive environment. However, earnings growth will be modest over the next year and a half.

Valuation - 23-AUG-95

With a only a 3% gain in price since the end of 1994, AEP's shares are greatly underperforming broader market averages, and have not kept pace with electric utility stock prices either. While the shares are currently trading in the mid-range of AEP's historic P/E, prospects for an earnings turnaround are weakend by its large industrial customer base, a segment where rates are most vulnerable to price cutting. Also, AEP's dividend payout ratio is among the highest in the industry, and a dividend increase in the next twelve months does not appear likely.

Key Stock Statistics

S&P EPS Est. 1995	2.80	Tang. Bk. Value/Share	22.67
P/E on S&P Est. 1995	12.2	Beta	0.59
S&P EPS Est. 1996	2.90	Shareholders	194,000
Dividend Rate/Share	2.40	Market cap. (B)	$ 6.4
Shs. outstg. (M)	185.9	Inst. holdings	31%
Avg. daily vol. (M)	0.293	Insider holdings	0%

Value of $10,000 invested 5 years ago: $ 15,549

Fiscal Year Ending Dec. 31

	1995	% Change	1994	% Change	1993	% Change
Revenues (Million $)						
1Q	1.42	NM	1,488	13%	1,321	2%
2Q	1,305	-3%	1,349	11%	1,210	3%
3Q	—	—	1,385	-1%	1,406	10%
4Q	—	—	1,283	-4%	1,331	3%
Yr.	—	—	5,505	4%	5,269	4%
Income (Million $)						
1Q	0.15	NM	152.9	15%	133.1	2%
2Q	96.48	-7%	103.8	20%	86.22	16%
3Q	—	—	139.8	NM	-10.14	NM
4Q	—	—	103.4	-28%	144.6	-7%
Yr.	—	—	500.0	41%	353.8	-24%
Earnings Per Share ($)						
1Q	0.80	-4%	0.83	15%	0.72	1%
2Q	0.52	-7%	0.56	19%	0.47	17%
3Q	E0.76	NM	0.76	NM	-0.06	NM
4Q	E0.72	29%	0.56	-29%	0.79	-7%
Yr.	E2.80	3%	2.71	41%	1.92	-24%

Next earnings report expected: mid October

American Electric Power

Business Summary - 23-AUG-95

American Electric Power is an integrated electric utility holding company serving an area with a population of seven million in portions of Ohio, Indiana, Michigan, Virginia, West Virginia, Kentucky and Tennessee. Based on kilowatt-hours generated, AEP is the second largest utility system in the U.S. Electric revenues by customer class:

	1994	1993	1992	1991
Residential	33%	34%	33%	33%
Commercial	22%	22%	22%	22%
Industrial	30%	29%	30%	29%
Wholesale	13%	13%	13%	15%
Other	2%	2%	3%	1%

Sources of electric generation in 1994 were coal 89%, nuclear 7%, other 1% and purchased power 3%. Peak demand in 1994 was 26,371 mw, and the net internal capability, or capability excluding purchased power arrangements, at peak totaled 23,457 mw.

The 25.4%-owned Zimmer plant began commercial operation in 1991. Zimmer, originally designed as a nuclear station, was abandoned in 1984 and was converted to a 1,300 mw coal-fired plant. In the third quarter of 1993, AEP incurred a $145 million after-tax charge ($0.78 a share) after the Ohio Supreme Court upheld a 1992 order of the Public Utilities Commission of Ohio (PUCO) preventing the recovery of AEP's investment in Zimmer via rates. Under a 1985 settlement, $219 million of Zimmer costs were disallowed.

AEP has made substantial construction commitments although it does not expect to build new generating capacity until the next century. Construction expenditures for 1995 through 1997, primarily for production and distribution facilities, are estimated at $2.1 billion. The capital cost for compliance with the Clean Air Act Amendments of 1990 (CAAA) has been included in this estimate except for the cost of scrubbers for the Gavin plant, which has emitted about 25% of the AEP's systemwide total sulfur dioxide emissions. In 1992, AEP entered into an agreement for construction and lease of the Gavin Plant scrubbers with an unaffiliated firm. AEP believes the cost of compliance with the CAAA should be recoverable from ratepayers.

Important Developments

Jul. '95—AEP announced plans to reduce 1,200 jobs at 16 fossil-fuel plants in five states through the elimination of staffing generating units that shut down for maintenance or scheduled outages.

Jun. '95—AEP's Ohio Power Co. unit, the Ohio PUC staff and other parties jointly reached a settlement agreement that would produce an additional $66 million in annual revenues and fix Ohio Power's Electric Fuel Component rate at 1.456 cents per kwh for a three and one-half year period beginning June 1.

Capitalization

Long Term Debt: $4,579,207,000 (3/95).
Subsid. Preferred Stock: $823,540,000.

Per Share Data ($)

(Year Ended Dec. 31)

	1994	1993	1992	1991	1990	1989
Tangible Bk. Val.	22.67	22.33	22.87	22.79	22.49	22.60
Earnings	2.71	1.92	2.54	2.70	2.65	3.25
Dividends	2.40	2.40	2.40	2.40	2.40	2.36
Payout Ratio	89%	125%	95%	89%	91%	73%
Prices - High	37⅜	40⅜	35¼	34¼	33⅛	33⅜
- Low	27¼	32	30⅜	26⅝	26	25¾
P/E Ratio - High	14	21	14	13	13	10
- Low	10	17	12	10	10	8

Income Statement Analysis (Million $)

	1994	%Chg	1993	%Chg	1992	%Chg	1991
Revs.	5,505	4%	5,269	4%	5,045	NM	5,047
Depr.	572	8%	531	4%	510	NM	508
Maint.	544	4%	523	NM	525	7%	490
Fxd. Chgs. Cov.	2.6	6%	2.5	10%	2.3	-8%	2.4
Constr. Credits	NA	—	NA	—	9.0	-64%	25.0
Eff. Tax Rate	26%	—	32%	—	26%	—	25%
Net Inc.	500	41%	354	-24%	468	-6%	498

Balance Sheet & Other Fin. Data (Million $)

	1994	1993	1992	1991	1990	1989
Gross Prop.	18,175	17,712	17,510	17,148	16,653	16,108
Cap. Exp.	643	592	629	636	671	838
Net Prop.	11,348	11,100	11,228	11,196	11,064	10,843
Capitalization:						
LT Debt	4,687	4,964	5,126	4,793	4,785	4,516
% LT Debt	48	50	51	50	50	47
Pfd.	824	769	765	673	680	701
% Pfd.	8.50	7.80	7.60	6.90	7.00	7.30
Common	4,230	4,152	4,246	4,222	4,167	4,394
% Common	43	42	42	44	43	46
Total Cap.	12,669	12,841	11,754	11,530	11,638	11,619

Ratio Analysis

	1994	1993	1992	1991	1990	1989
Oper. Ratio	83.1	82.4	82.5	81.8	83.3	80.5
% Earn. on Net Prop.	8.3	8.3	7.8	8.2	7.9	8.9
% Ret. on Revs.	9.1	6.7	9.3	9.9	9.6	12.2
% Ret. On Invest.Cap	7.4	6.7	8.5	8.5	8.2	9.4
% Return On Com.Eqty	11.9	8.4	11.1	11.9	11.6	14.6

Dividend Data —Dividends have been paid since 1909. A dividend reinvestment plan is available.

Amt. of Div. $	Date Decl.	Ex-Div. Date	Stock of Record	Payment Date
0.600	Jul. 27	Aug. 04	Aug. 10	Sep. 09 '94
0.600	Oct. 26	Nov. 04	Nov. 10	Dec. 09 '94
0.600	Jan. 25	Feb. 06	Feb. 10	Mar. 10 '95
0.600	Apr. 26	May. 04	May. 10	Jun. 09 '95
0.600	Jul. 26	Aug. 08	Aug. 10	Sep. 08 '95

Data as orig. reptd.; bef. results of disc opers. and/or spec. items. Per share data adj. for stk. divs. as of ex-div. date. E-Estimated. NA-Not Available. NM-Not Meaningful. NR-Not Ranked.

Office—One Riverside Plaza, Columbus, OH 43215. **Tel**—(614) 223-1000. **Chrmn, Pres & CEO**—E. L. Draper Jr. **Secy**—G. P. Maloney. **Treas**—P. J. DeMaria. **Investor Contact**—John Bilacic. **Dirs**—P. J. DeMaria, E. L. Draper Jr., R. M. Duncan, A. G. Hansen, L. A. Hudson Jr., G. P. Maloney, A. E. Peyton, T. F. Reid, D. G. Smith, L. G. Stuntz, M. Tanenbaum, A. H. Zwinger. **Transfer Agent & Registrar**—First Chicago Trust Co. of New York, Jersey City, N.J. **Incorporated** in New York in 1905. **Empl**-19,660. **S&P Analyst:** Jane Collin

American Express

NYSE Symbol **AXP**
In S&P 500

22-SEP-95

Industry:
Finance

Summary: American Express, a leader in travel-related services, is also active in investment services, expense management services and international banking.

S&P Opinion: Buy (★★★★)

Recent Price • 44⅜	Yield • 2.1%	
52 Wk Range • 44⅜-28⅛	12-Mo. P/E • 15.4	

Earnings vs. Previous Year
▲=Up ▼=Down ▶=No Change

Quantitative Evaluations

Outlook
(1 Lowest—5 Highest)
• **3+**

Fair Value
• **43¼**

Risk
• **Low**

Earn./Div. Rank
• **B**

Technical Eval.
• **Bearish** since 3/95

Rel. Strength Rank
(1 Lowest—99 Highest)
• **76**

Insider Activity
• **Neutral**

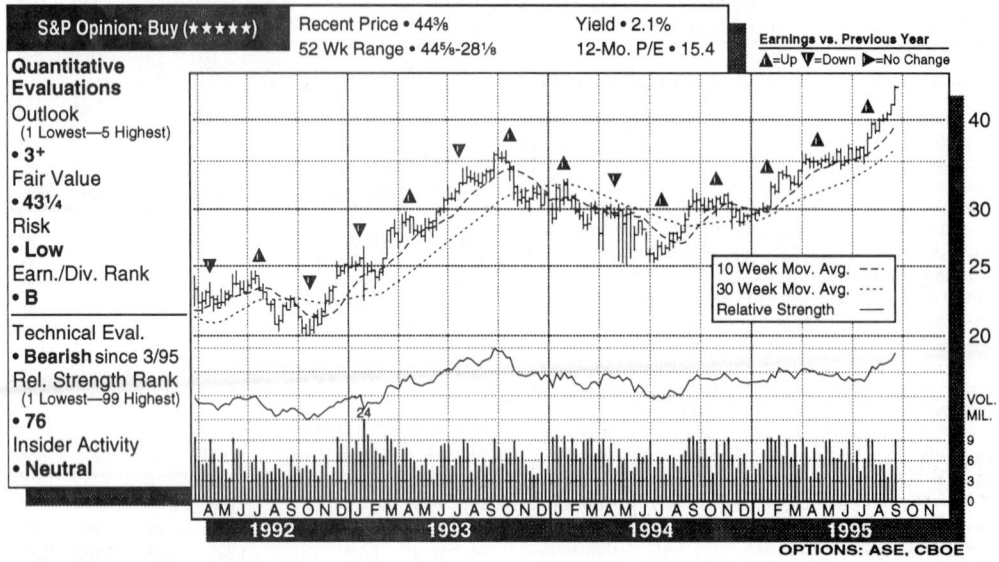

10 Week Mov. Avg. ---
30 Week Mov. Avg. - - -
Relative Strength ——

OPTIONS: ASE, CBOE

Overview - 22-SEP-95

Earnings should continue to benefit from growth in charge card volume, reflecting both higher spending per cardmember and an increase in cards outstanding, as well as improving credit quality. The charge card business is expected to benefit from the introduction of new card products such as co-branded cards and reward innovations targeted to specific market segments. The company's longer range goal is to increase its credit portfolio to $30 billion by the year 2000, from about $9 billion currently. The acquisition of Thomas Cook's travel business will enhance AXP's ability to meet growing global demand for business travel management. Growing sales of annuities, mutual funds and various insurance products should also have a favorable effect. A share buyback program will further aid earnings comparisons.

Valuation - 22-SEP-95

Despite their strong rise thus far in 1995, we still view the shares as undervalued. The company's prospects continue to improve following a corporate restructuring that has fostered the development of new growth opportunities for the charge card business and franchise expansion. In addition, industry trends favor the growing use of credit cards for spending purposes, and AXP has captured nearly 100% of the important travel and entertainment charge spending segments. The shares continue to trade at a discount to both the company's growth rate and the multiple of the broader market.

Key Stock Statistics

S&P EPS Est. 1995	3.25	Tang. Bk. Value/Share	14.27
P/E on S&P Est. 1995	13.7	Beta	1.09
S&P EPS Est. 1996	3.70	Shareholders	60,500
Dividend Rate/Share	0.90	Market cap. (B)	$ 21.0
Shs. outstg. (M)	487.7	Inst. holdings	64%
Avg. daily vol. (M)	1.377	Insider holdings	NA

Value of $10,000 invested 5 years ago: NA

Fiscal Year Ending Dec. 31

	1995	% Change	1994	% Change	1993	% Change
Revenues (Million $)						
1Q	3,771	12%	3,370	NM	3,360	-50%
2Q	3,967	13%	3,506	NM	3,520	-49%
3Q	—	—	3,604	NM	3,580	-47%
4Q	—	—	3,802	2%	3,710	-45%
Yr.	—	—	14,282	NM	14,170	-47%
Income (Million $)						
1Q	353.0	11%	317.0	-55%	701.0	182%
2Q	410.0	14%	359.0	19%	301.0	-3%
3Q	—	—	369.0	18%	312.0	NM
4Q	—	—	335.0	15%	290.7	NM
Yr.	—	—	1,380	-14%	1,605	NM
Earnings Per Share ($)						
1Q	0.70	13%	0.62	-56%	1.41	176%
2Q	0.81	16%	0.70	17%	0.60	-5%
3Q	E0.85	20%	0.71	16%	0.61	NM
4Q	E0.90	38%	0.65	14%	0.57	NM
Yr.	E3.25	21%	2.68	-15%	3.17	NM

Next earnings report expected: late October

American Express

Business Summary - 22-SEP-95

American Express is a major financial services company principally engaged in providing travel-related, financial planning, asset management, expense management and international banking services worldwide. During 1993, it sold 78% of its stake in First Data Corp. Lehman Brothers was spun off to shareholders in May 1994. Segment contributions in 1994 were:

	Revs.	Profits
Travel-related services	72.3%	66.3%
Financial Advisors	23.1%	28.4%
American Express Bank	4.6%	5.3%

Travel Related Services (TRS) markets travelers cheques and the American Express Card, including the Gold Card, the Platinum Card, the Corporate Card, the Purchasing Card and Optima Cards. At year-end 1994, total cards in force worldwide aggregated 36.3 million, up 2.5% from December 31, 1993. Card charge volume in 1994 was about $141 billion, up 13.6% from 1993. TRS also provides vacation and leisure travel services and corporate card and business travel support. Other activities include publishing, direct mail merchandise services, and life insurance.

Financial Advisors (formerly IDS Financial Services) provides financial products including insurance, annuities, limited partnerships and mutual funds, and tax and financial planning services to individuals, businesses and institutions.

American Express Bank Ltd. provides a range of financial services to wealthy entrepreneurs and local financial service institutions through a network of 81 offices in 37 countries.

Important Developments

Sep. '95—The company noted that several major financial institutions had expressed an interest in acquiring its American Express Bank unit. AXP intends to review the inquiries to see what value might be realized from the sale, versus the long term potential of keeping the unit.

Sep. '95—A group including Warren Buffett and Berkshire Hathaway Inc. disclosed that it raised its stake in American Express to 10.1%, from 9.8%.

Mar. '95—Directors authorized the repurchase of up to 40 million common shares (about 8% of the shares outstanding) over the next two to three years. The program is in addition to a September 1994 authorization to buy 20 million shares. Through July 31, 1995, 29.5 million shares were repurchased under the plans at an average price of $32.52.

Capitalization

Long Term Debt: $6,491,000,000 (6/95).

7.75% Conv. Exch. Preferred Stock: $200,000,000.

Per Share Data ($)

(Year Ended Dec. 31)

	1994	1993	1992	1991	1990	1989
Tangible Bk. Val.	12.57	16.81	14.58	14.43	13.21	12.90
Earnings	2.68	3.17	0.83	1.59	0.69	2.70
Dividends	0.93	1.00	1.00	0.96	0.92	0.86
Payout Ratio	35%	32%	120%	60%	133%	32%
Prices - High	33 1/8	36 5/8	25 3/8	30 3/8	35 1/4	39 3/8
- Low	25	22 3/8	20	18	17 1/2	26 3/8
P/E Ratio - High	12	12	31	19	51	15
- Low	9	7	24	11	25	10

Income Statement Analysis (Million $)

	1994	%Chg	1993	%Chg	1992	%Chg	1991
Cards in Force	36.3	3%	35.4	2%	34.7	-5%	36.6
Card Chg Volume	141,000	14%	124,000	5%	118,000	6%	111,000
Premium Income	783	12%	702	-10%	776	9%	711
Commissions	8,591	10%	7,818	-41%	13,188	10%	12,006
Int & Div.	4,120	-16%	4,914	-57%	11,380	NM	11,490
Total Revs.	14,282	NM	14,173	-47%	26,961	5%	25,763
Net Bef. Taxes	1,891	-19%	2,326	NM	775	2%	759
Income Other	1,380	-14%	1,605	NM	436	-45%	789

Balance Sheet & Other Fin. Data (Million $)

	1994	1993	1992	1991	1990	1989
Total Assets	97,006	94,132	175,752	146,441	137,682	130,855
Cash Items	3,433	3,312	5,395	4,876	6,400	7,452
Investment Assets:						
Bonds	23,026	23,026	63,778	49,597	45,670	38,834
Stocks	Nil	Nil	1,693	1,982	1,968	2,136
Loans	29,830	29,904	22,782	24,047	18,213	17,963
Total	54,830	52,930	88,543	76,476	66,100	59,889
Accounts Receiv.	17,147	16,142	32,785	29,882	34,729	34,437
Cust. Deposits	10,013	11,131	21,360	24,778	27,843	31,191
Travel Cheques Outst	5,271	4,800	4,729	4,375	4,225	3,834
Debt	7,162	8,561	15,122	13,292	12,521	14,348
Common Eqty.	6,233	8,234	6,999	6,815	6,135	5,391

Ratio Analysis

	1994	1993	1992	1991	1990	1989
% Ret. on Assets	1.4	1.7	0.3	0.6	0.3	0.8
% Ret. on Equity	18.6	20.5	5.7	11.6	5.3	22.5

Dividend Data —Dividends have been paid since 1870. A dividend reinvestment plan is available.

Amt. of Div. $	Date Decl.	Ex-Div. Date	Stock of Record	Payment Date
0.225	Sep. 26	Oct. 03	Oct. 07	Nov. 10 '94
0.225	Mar. 27	Apr. 03	Apr. 07	May. 10 '95
0.225	May. 22	Jul. 05	Jul. 07	Aug. 10 '95

Data as orig. reptd.; bef. results of disc. opers. and/or spec. items. Per share data adj. for stk. divs. as of ex-div. date. E-Estimated. NA-Not Available. NM-Not Meaningful. NR-Not Ranked.

Office—American Express Tower, World Financial Center, New York, NY 10285. **Tel**—(212) 640-2000. **Chrmn & CEO**—H. Golub. **Vice Chrmn**—K. I. Chenault, J. S. Linen. **Pres**—J. E. Stiefler. **EVP, CFO & Treas**—M. P. Monaco. **Secy**—S. P. Norman. **VP & Investor Contact**—Ronald C. Stovall. **Dirs**—D. F. Akerson, A. L. Armstrong, E. L. Artzt, W. G. Bowen, D. M. Culver, C. W. Duncan, Jr., R. M. Furlaud, H. Golub, B. S. Greenough, F. R. Johnson, V. E. Jordan, Jr., H. A. Kissinger, D. Lewis, A. Papone, R. S. Penske, F. P. Popoff, J. E. Stiefler. **Transfer Agent & Registrar**—Chemical Bank, NYC. **Organized** in Buffalo in 1850; incorporated in 1965. **Empl**-72,412. **S&P Analyst:** Stephen R. Biggar

American General

NYSE Symbol **AGC**
In S&P 500

31-JUL-95

Industry: Insurance

Summary: American General is a diversified financial services concern primarily engaged in the underwriting of life insurance, the sale of annuities, and consumer finance lending.

| S&P Opinion: Buy (★★★★) | Recent Price • 36 | Yield • 3.4% |
| | 52 Wk Range • 36⅞-25% | 12-Mo. P/E • 13.4 |

Quantitative Evaluations

Outlook
(1 Lowest—5 Highest)
• **4**

Fair Value
• **37½**

Risk
• **Low**

Earn./Div. Rank
• **B+**

Technical Eval.
• **Bullish** since 12/94

Rel. Strength Rank
(1 Lowest—99 Highest)
• **57**

Insider Activity
• **Neutral**

Earnings vs. Previous Year
▲=Up ▼=Down ▶=No Change

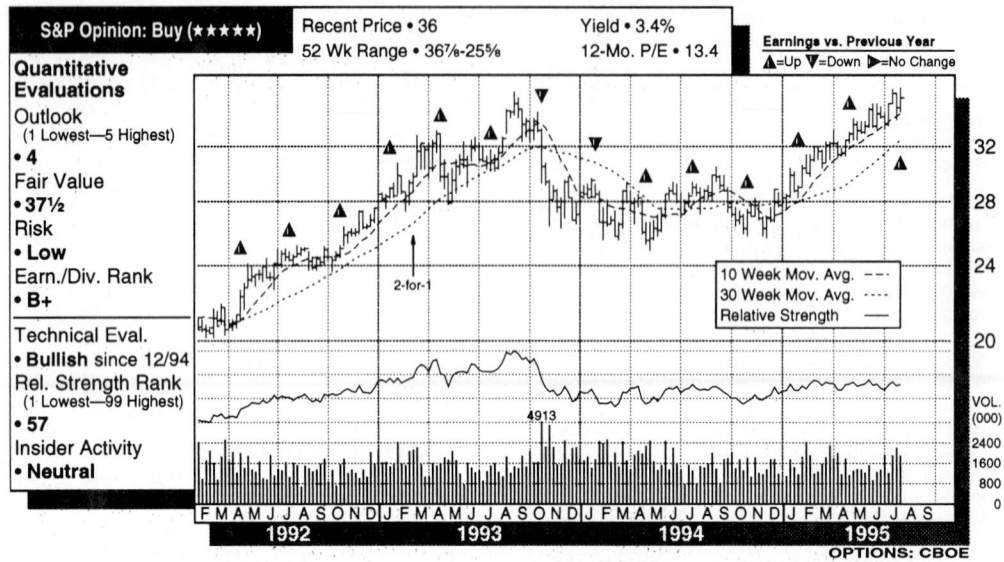

10 Week Mov. Avg. – – –
30 Week Mov. Avg. ······
Relative Strength —

2-for-1

4913

VOL. (000)
2400
1600
800
0

OPTIONS: CBOE

Overview - 31-JUL-95

Operating earnings growth in 1995 will be aided by continued asset increases, greater market penetration, and relatively stable net interest margins in the annuity sector. Growth in receivables amid an economic recovery together with somewhat stable interest rate spreads should aid profit gains in the consumer finance sector. The life insurance outlook is mixed, as expense cutbacks and productivity gains partly offset slowing policy sales. The acquisition of Franklin Life will not likely be dilutive, and will add positively to added growth here. Investment income growth will be modest amid a relatively low interest rate environment. Share earnings will be aided by an aggressive stock buyback plan. From April 1987 through year end 1994, about 50 million shares were repurchased.

Valuation - 31-JUL-95

After a lackluster performance during much of 1994 due the negative effects of higher interest rates and concerns over the disruptive effects of an unsuccessful takeover attempt of rival insurer Unitrin, American General shares have rebounded nicely so far in 1995. Despite their recent appreciation, the shares remain attractive at 10 times our 1995 operating earnings estimate (which excludes realized investment gains or losses) of $3.45 a share, particularly in light of the company's above average growth prospects and sound fundamentals.

Key Stock Statistics

S&P EPS Est. 1995	3.45	Tang. Bk. Value/Share	18.70
P/E on S&P Est. 1995	10.4	Beta	1.27
S&P EPS Est. 1996	3.85	Shareholders	29,600
Dividend Rate/Share	1.24	Market cap. (B)	$ 7.4
Shs. outstg. (M)	204.8	Inst. holdings	74%
Avg. daily vol. (M)	0.374	Insider holdings	NA

Value of $10,000 invested 5 years ago: $ 30,189

Fiscal Year Ending Dec. 31

	1995	% Change	1994	% Change	1993	% Change
Revenues (Million $)						
1Q	1,518	25%	1,214	-38%	1,960	—
2Q	—	—	1,232	2%	1,205	—
3Q	—	—	1,265	4%	1,222	—
4Q	—	—	1,130	-7%	1,215	2%
Yr.	—	—	4,841	NM	4,829	5%
Income (Million $)						
1Q	175.0	9%	160.9	12%	144.1	8%
2Q	180.0	14%	157.7	5%	150.6	18%
3Q	—	—	159.0	34%	118.7	-14%
4Q	—	—	35.00	NM	-163.5	NM
Yr.	—	—	513.0	105%	249.9	-53%
Earnings Per Share ($)						
1Q	0.85	13%	0.75	14%	0.66	8%
2Q	0.88	17%	0.75	7%	0.70	19%
3Q	—	—	0.77	40%	0.55	-13%
4Q	—	—	0.18	NM	-0.76	NM
Yr.	E3.45	—	2.45	113%	1.15	-53%

Next earnings report expected: late October

Business Summary - 31-JUL-95

American General is one of the largest insurance-based financial services holding companies in the U.S. Current operations focus on individual life insurance, annuities and consumer finance. Contributions to 1994 revenue and pretax operating incme (before corporate and other expenses):

	Revs.	Profits
Life insurance	39%	37%
Retirement annuities	31%	26%
Consumer finance	30%	37%

The Life Insurance segment was formed in 1993 through the combination of the home service and special markets life insurance divisions. This unit underwrites and sells permanent and term life insurance to customers, in their homes, through employee agents. Whole, term and interest sensitive life insurance and annuities are also offered to middle and upper middle income customers through agents, brokers and financial institutions. At December 31, 1994, insurance in force exceeded $135 billion.

The Retirement Annuities segment consists of The Variable Annuity Life Insurance Co. (VALIC), one of the largest providers of retirement annuity plans for employees of non-profit organizations. VALIC provides fixed and variable tax-qualified annuity products on a group and individual basis.

The Consumer Finance segment offers various consumer credit related products, including home equity loans, retail financing, credit related insurance and credit cards. At December 31, 1994 receivables outstanding totaled $7.9 billion.

Important Developments

Jul. '95—AGC noted that second quarter 1995 retirement annuity sales at its VALIC subsidiary rose 33%, year to year. But, narrower investment spreads offset the growth in assets, and limited VALIC's operating profit growth to 8.0%. Consumer finance earnings rose 1.6%, as growth in receivables and higher average net portfolio yields were offset by an uptick in the cost of funds and by higher loss provisions. Life insurance operating profits rose 37% (to $86 million from $63 million). The growth primarily reflected contributions from the January 1995 acquisition of The Franklin Life Insurance Co. from American Brands for $1.17 billion in cash. Franklin, primarily an individual life insurer, had about $7.4 billion in assets. In December, AGC acquired 40% of Western National Corp., a life insurer with assets of $8.5 billion, from Conseco, Inc. for $274 million.

Capitalization

Long Term Debt: $5,747,000,000 (3/95).

Per Share Data ($) (Year Ended Dec. 31)

	1994	1993	1992	1991	1990	1989
Tangible Bk. Val.	14.09	21.10	17.01	15.52	14.19	13.97
Oper. Earnings	3.00	1.12	2.41	2.13	1.86	1.55
Earnings	2.45	1.15	2.45	2.13	2.35	1.67
Dividends	1.16	1.10	1.04	1.00	1.40	0.75
Payout Ratio	47%	96%	42%	47%	60%	45%
Prices - High	30½	36½	29⅜	22⅞	25⅜	19¼
- Low	24⅞	26¼	20⅛	14	11¾	14¾
P/E Ratio - High	12	32	12	11	11	12
- Low	10	23	8	7	5	9

Income Statement Analysis (Million $)

	1994	%Chg	1993	%Chg	1992	%Chg	1991
Life Ins. In Force	NA	—	92,634	-8%	101,179	4%	97,534
Premium Income Life	NA	—	668	-5%	703	NM	698
Prem.Inc A & H	NA	—	207	10%	189	4%	182
Premium Income Other	NA	—	58.0	23%	47.0	15%	41.0
Net Invest. Inc.	2,493	2%	2,437	5%	2,327	7%	2,178
Total Revs.	4,841	NM	4,829	5%	4,602	5%	4,395
Pretax Inc.	802	33%	602	-22%	775	14%	678
Net Oper. Inc.	627	157%	244	-53%	524	9%	479
Net Inc.	513	105%	250	-53%	533	11%	480

Balance Sheet & Other Fin. Data (Million $)

	1994	1993	1992	1991	1990	1989
Cash & Equiv.	45.0	6.0	17.0	39.0	91.0	108
Premiums Due	NA	NA	NA	NA	NA	NA
Inv Assets Bonds	25,909	26,546	21,343	17,955	15,954	13,952
Inv. Assets Stock	224	233	390	438	353	1,383
Inv. Assets Loans	3,848	4,188	4,784	5,286	5,508	5,175
Inv. Assets Total	30,697	31,876	27,814	25,025	23,057	21,548
Deferred Policy Cost	2,731	1,637	2,083	1,919	1,823	1,725
Total Assets	46,295	43,982	39,742	36,105	33,808	32,062
Debt	8,926	7,529	7,471	7,224	7,149	6,864
Common Eqty.	3,457	5,137	4,614	4,329	4,138	4,090

Ratio Analysis

	1994	1993	1992	1991	1990	1989
% Ret. on Revs.	10.6	5.2	11.6	10.9	12.5	9.8
% Ret. on Assets	1.1	0.6	1.4	1.4	1.7	1.3
% Ret. on Equity	11.9	5.2	11.9	11.3	13.7	9.8
% Invest. Yield	8.0	8.2	8.8	9.1	9.4	9.4

Dividend Data (Dividends have been paid since 1929. A dividend reinvestment plan is available. A "poison pill" stock purchase right was adopted in 1989.)

Amt. of Div. $	Date Decl.	Ex-Div. Date	Stock of Record	Payment Date
0.290	Jul. 28	Aug. 02	Aug. 08	Sep. 01 '94
0.290	Oct. 27	Nov. 01	Nov. 07	Dec. 01 '94
0.310	Feb. 02	Feb. 08	Feb. 14	Mar. 01 '95
0.310	Apr. 27	May. 03	May. 09	Jun. 01 '95
0.310	Jul. 27	Aug. 03	Aug. 07	Sep. 01 '95

Data as orig. reptd.; bef. results of disc. opers. and/or spec. items. Per share data adj. for stk. divs. as of ex-div. date. E-Estimated. NA-Not Available. NM-Not Meaningful. NR-Not Ranked.

Office—2929 Allen Parkway, Houston, TX 77019. **Tel**—(713) 522-1111. **Chrmn & CEO**—H. S. Hook. **Pres**—J. R. Tuerff. **VP-CFO**—A. P. Young. **VP-Investor Contact**—Robert D. Mrlik. **Dirs**—J. E. Attwell, B. F. Carruth, W. L. Davis Jr., R. M. Devlin, H. S. Hook, L. D. Horner, R. J. V. Johnson, R. E. Smittcamp, A. M. Tatlock, J. R. Tuerff. **Registrar & Transfer Agent**—First Chicago Trust Co. of New York, NYC. **Incorporated** in Texas in 1926. **Empl**-11,500. **S&P Analyst:** Catherine A. Seifert

American Greetings

NASDAQ Symbol **AGREA**
In S&P 500

30-OCT-95

Industry:
Graphic Arts

Summary: American Greetings, founded in 1906, is the world's largest greeting card company. Its products are distributed to 97,000 retail outlets in more than 70 countries.

S&P Opinion: Accumulate (★★★★)

Recent Price • 31⅝	Yield • 2.0%
52 Wk Range • 32⅝-25¾	12-Mo. P/E • 15.3

Quantitative Evaluations

Outlook
(1 Lowest—5 Highest)
• **3+**

Fair Value
• **31**

Risk
• **Low**

Earn./Div. Rank
• **A**

Technical Eval.
• **Bearish** since 8/95

Rel. Strength Rank
(1 Lowest—99 Highest)
• **75**

Insider Activity
• **Neutral**

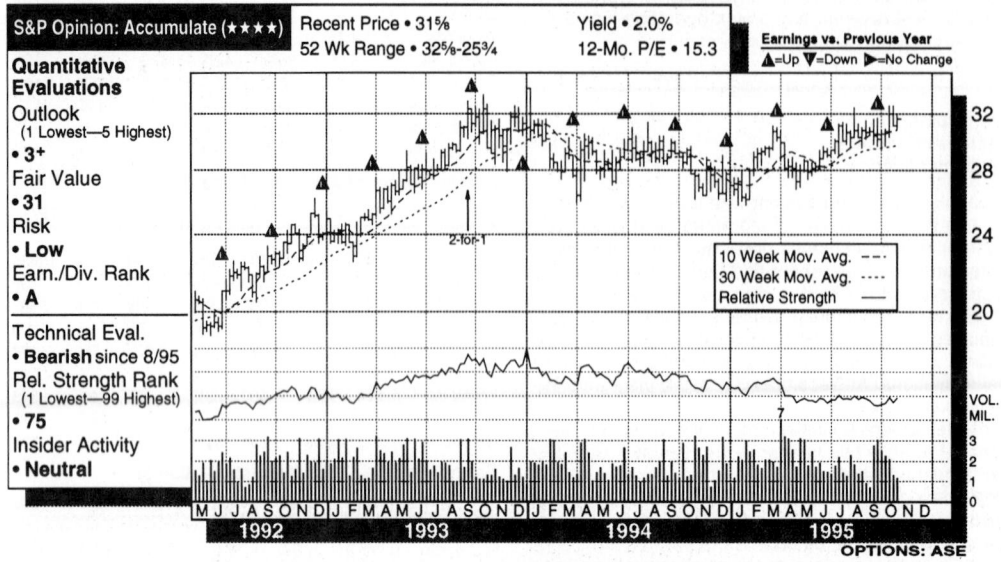

Earnings vs. Previous Year
▲=Up ▼=Down ▶=No Change

10 Week Mov. Avg. ----
30 Week Mov. Avg. ·····
Relative Strength ——

2-for-1

OPTIONS: ASE

Overview - 30-OCT-95

Revenues for the fiscal year to end February 29, 1996, are expected to rise about 6% from those of 1994-95, boosted by firmer pricing and new product introductions. Margins should continue to widen. North American operations are benefiting from broader greeting card lines in the Canadian marketplace and further efficiencies in the U.S. and Canada. The recent turnaround in Europe should continue, aided by a focus on high-margin greeting card product and aggressive management. The outlook for fiscal 1996-97 is also favorable, aided by further widening of product line, growth in CreataCard and online sales, and better European margins. CreataCard sales should continue to grow significantly and after several years of heavy depreciation costs, the product should begin to contribute to profitability in 1996-97.

Valuation - 30-OCT-95

The shares of American Greetings slightly outperformed the general market thus far in 1995 and we expect the widely-held shares to stay in the mainstream in future periods. The company is benefiting from healthy growth in greeting cards, with consumers continuing to choose the most expensive cards which carry higher margins. An improving product mix in the U.S. and Europe, and an expanding presence in drug chains, supermarkets and mass merchandisers also boost prospects. CreataCard should become profitable in late 1996 and strongly profitable beginning in 1997. The annually-raised cash dividends augment total returns on the stock.

Key Stock Statistics

S&P EPS Est. 1996	2.20	Tang. Bk. Value/Share	16.03
P/E on S&P Est. 1996	14.4	Beta	1.01
S&P EPS Est. 1997	2.55	Shareholders	21,000
Dividend Rate/Share	0.64	Market cap. (B)	$ 2.4
Shs. outstg. (M)	74.6	Inst. holdings	84%
Avg. daily vol. (M)	0.337	Insider holdings	NA

Value of $10,000 invested 5 years ago: $ 19,852

Fiscal Year Ending Feb. 28

	1996	% Change	1995	% Change	1994	% Change
Revenues (Million $)						
1Q	438.5	5%	416.0	5%	395.4	5%
2Q	431.2	7%	401.1	3%	388.4	5%
3Q	—	—	551.0	5%	522.5	6%
4Q	—	—	500.4	5%	474.5	6%
Yr.	—	—	1,869	5%	1,781	5%
Income (Million $)						
1Q	37.30	12%	33.16	14%	29.03	14%
2Q	15.03	12%	13.42	23%	10.92	23%
3Q	—	—	58.89	14%	51.47	17%
4Q	—	—	43.32	10%	39.47	16%
Yr.	—	—	148.8	14%	130.9	17%
Earnings Per Share ($)						
1Q	0.50	11%	0.45	14%	0.39	11%
2Q	0.20	11%	0.18	20%	0.15	25%
3Q	E0.84	6%	0.79	13%	0.70	16%
4Q	E0.66	14%	0.58	9%	0.53	13%
Yr.	E2.20	10%	2.00	13%	1.77	14%

Next earnings report expected: mid December

Business Summary - 30-OCT-95

American Greetings Corporation is believed to be the second largest manufacturer of greeting cards and among the four largest producers of gift wrappings in the U.S. and Canada. It also produces a line of giftware items and candles and licenses a family of character properties.

About 5% of total revenues in fiscal 1994-95 were from international sources, primarily Mexico, Canada and Europe. The company does not derive more than 10% of total revenues from any single customer, government agency or export sales.

Greeting cards account for 65% of total sales. Trademarks include CreataCard, Forget Me Not, Carlton Cards, Entre Nous, Kid Zone, Black Impressions, La Flor, Greeting U, Pet Tales, Strawberry Shortcake, Care Bears, Holly Hobbie and Bloomer Bunny.

American Greetings also operates several smaller business units. An independent licensing division licenses characters to more than 200 companies for product marketing. Plus Mark produces Christmas promotional products such as gift wrap, ribbon, bows and boxed Christmas cards. AG Industries produces cabinet fixtures. ACME manufactures picture frames. Carlton Cards produces greeting cards, gift wrap and party goods. Wilhold hair care products are made mainly for women. In June 1993, Magnivision, the leading manufacturer and distributor of nonprescription reading glasses to chain drug stores and other mass retailers in 16 countries, was acquired.

Important Developments

Sep. '95—The company's U.K. subsidiary, Carlton Cards Ltd., sold substantially all of its retail stores to Clinton Cards plc. Clinton is the U.K..'s largest specialty greeting card retailer. The arrangement extends Carlton Cards Ltd.'s long-term supplier relationship with Clinton. AGREA said the transaction will reduce fiscal 1996 earnings by $0.06 a share, but should begin to have a positive contribution in fiscal 1997.
Jul. '95—The company agreed to buy a majority interest in South African greeting card company S.A. Greetings Corporation (PTY) Ltd., a major supplier to chain stores, supermarkets and The Kardies chain of 150 franchised card shops. Terms were not disclosed.

Capitalization

Long Term Debt: $77,175,000 (8/95).
Cl. A Com. Stk.: 70,006,622 shs. ($1 par); one vote per sh.
Institutions hold about 84%.
Shareholders: 21,000.
Cl. B Com. Stk.: 4,585,081 shs. ($1 par); ea. conv. into one Cl. A; 10 votes per sh.
About 59% is closely held.

Per Share Data ($) — (Year Ended Feb. 28)

	1995	1994	1993	1992	1991	1990
Tangible Bk. Val.	15.61	14.21	13.06	12.05	10.39	9.45
Cash Flow	2.92	2.58	2.29	2.13	2.05	2.08
Earnings	2.00	1.77	1.55	1.40	1.30	1.13
Dividends	0.54	0.48	0.42	0.38	0.35	0.33
Payout Ratio	27%	27%	27%	28%	27%	29%
Cal. Yrs.	1994	1993	1992	1991	1990	1989
Prices - High	34	34¼	26¼	20¾	18¾	18⅝
- Low	25⅞	22½	18⅝	15½	13⅜	10¼
P/E Ratio - High	17	19	17	15	14	17
- Low	13	13	12	11	10	9

Income Statement Analysis (Million $)

	1995	%Chg	1994	%Chg	1993	%Chg	1992
Revs.	1,869	6%	1,770	6%	1,672	8%	1,554
Oper. Inc.	303	10%	275	12%	245	17%	210
Depr.	68.4	15%	59.6	11%	53.7	18%	45.5
Int. Exp.	16.9	NM	16.9	-37%	26.9	-12%	30.4
Pretax Inc.	227	9%	209	15%	181	18%	153
Eff. Tax Rate	35%	—	38%	—	38%	—	36%
Net Inc.	149	14%	131	17%	112	15%	97.0

Balance Sheet & Other Fin. Data (Million $)

	1995	1994	1993	1992	1991	1990
Cash	87.0	101	235	194	81.0	123
Curr. Assets	893	850	912	848	738	681
Total Assets	1,762	1,565	1,548	1,438	1,256	1,141
Curr. Liab.	362	376	330	219	254	201
LT Debt	74.0	54.0	169	256	246	235
Common Eqty.	1,160	1,053	953	865	657	605
Total Cap.	1,291	1,170	1,218	1,219	1,001	940
Cap. Exp.	97.0	103	77.1	67.3	45.3	42.9
Cash Flow	217	190	166	143	125	133

Ratio Analysis

	1995	1994	1993	1992	1991	1990
Curr. Ratio	2.5	2.3	2.1	3.9	2.9	3.4
% LT Debt of Cap.	5.8	4.6	13.9	21.0	24.6	25.0
% Net Inc.of Revs.	8.0	7.4	6.7	6.3	5.8	5.6
% Ret. on Assets	8.9	8.3	7.5	6.8	6.9	6.5
% Ret. on Equity	13.4	12.9	12.3	12.1	13.2	12.4

Dividend Data

—Cash has been paid each year since 1950. A dividend reinvestment plan is available.

Amt. of Div. $	Date Decl.	Ex-Div. Date	Stock of Record	Payment Date
0.140	Oct. 31	Nov. 18	Nov. 25	Dec. 09 '94
0.140	Jan. 30	Feb. 17	Feb. 24	Mar. 10 '95
0.140	Apr. 10	May. 22	May. 26	Jun. 09 '95
0.160	Jun. 23	Aug. 23	Aug. 25	Sep. 08 '95

Data as orig. reptd.; bef. results of disc. opers. and/or spec. items. Per share data adj. for stk. divs. as of ex-div. date. E-Estimated. NA-Not Available. NM-Not Meaningful. NR-Not Ranked.

Office—10500 American Rd., Cleveland, OH 44144-2398. **Tel**—(216) 252-7300. **Fax**—(216) 252-6777. **Chrmn & CEO**—M. Weiss. **Pres & COO**—E. Fruchtenbaum. **SVP & CFO**—W. S. Meyer. **Treas**—D. A. Cable. **SVP & Secy**—J. Groetzinger, Jr. **Investor Contact**—John D. Barker (216-252-4864). **Dirs**—S. S. Cowen, E. Fruchtenbaum, H. H. Jacobs, A. B. Ratner, H. H. Stone, I. I. Stone, J. S. Wagner, M. Weiss, M. A. Wolf, A. Zaleznik. **Transfer Agent & Registrar**—Society National Bank, Cleveland. **Incorporated** in Ohio in 1944. **Empl**-21,100. **S&P Analyst:** W. H. Donald

American Home Products

NYSE Symbol **AHP**
In S&P 500

08-SEP-95

Industry:
Drugs-Generic and
OTC

Summary: This leading maker of drugs, hospital supplies and consumer products significantly broadened its sales base with the $9.6 billion acquisition of American Cyanamid in November 1994.

S&P Opinion: Accumulate (★★★★)	Recent Price • 77	Yield • 3.9%
	52 Wk Range • 80¾-57⅛	12-Mo. P/E • 11.1

Quantitative Evaluations

Outlook
(1 Lowest—5 Highest)
• **1+**

Fair Value
• **64**

Risk
• **Low**

Earn./Div. Rank
• **A+**

Technical Eval.
• **Bullish** since 10/94

Rel. Strength Rank
(1 Lowest—99 Highest)
• **24**

Insider Activity
• **Neutral**

Earnings vs. Previous Year
▲=Up ▼=Down ▶=No Change

10 Week Mov. Avg. ---
30 Week Mov. Avg. ......
Relative Strength —

OPTIONS: ASE

Overview - 08-SEP-95

Revenues are expected to show further growth in 1996 from $13.5 billion indicated for 1995. Pharmaceutical sales should benefit from strength overseas and greater contributions from new products such as Effexor antidepressant and Prempro/Premphase hormone replacement therapy. Gains are also seen for agricultural and consumer healthcare lines, aided by new products. However, food sales may remain sluggish. Profitability should benefit from cost streamlining and asset divestiture programs. EPS are estimated at $5.60 for 1996, versus $6.70 indicated for 1995 (including a gain of $2.03 from the sale of a business in the first quarter).

Valuation - 08-SEP-95

The shares have climbed significantly in the past 12 months, reflecting strength in the overall drug group and investor anticipation of benefits from the American Cyanamid acquisition. Cyanamid's pharmaceutical and hospital products lines complement AHP's existing lines, and significant potential exists in terms of cost streamlining, especially in pharmaceutical production, marketing, and R&D. By the end of 1997, the company expects to reduce its debt by about $5 billion, including over $2 billion from asset sales, with the balance from internal funds. The shares, trading at about a market multiple and yielding 3.9%, are recommended for long-term capital gains and rising dividend income.

Key Stock Statistics

S&P EPS Est. 1995	6.70	Tang. Bk. Value/Share	NM
P/E on S&P Est. 1995	11.5	Beta	0.76
S&P EPS Est. 1996	5.60	Shareholders	70,400
Dividend Rate/Share	3.00	Market cap. (B)	$ 23.7
Shs. outstg. (M)	309.9	Inst. holdings	64%
Avg. daily vol. (M)	0.379	Insider holdings	NA

Value of $10,000 invested 5 years ago: $ 17,925

Fiscal Year Ending Dec. 31

	1995	% Change	1994	% Change	1993	% Change
Revenues (Million $)						
1Q	3,491	63%	2,144	2%	2,111	5%
2Q	3,299	67%	1,978	4%	1,909	8%
3Q	—	—	2,259	4%	2,168	3%
4Q	—	—	2,586	22%	2,116	6%
Yr.	—	—	8,966	8%	8,305	5%
Income (Million $)						
1Q	1,023	146%	415.8	4%	401.5	180%
2Q	299.6	NM	300.0	4%	287.5	9%
3Q	—	—	413.0	4%	397.5	4%
4Q	—	—	399.5	4%	382.8	6%
Yr.	—	—	1,528	4%	1,469	28%
Earnings Per Share ($)						
1Q	3.33	149%	1.34	4%	1.29	193%
2Q	0.97	-1%	0.98	5%	0.93	11%
3Q	E1.21	-10%	1.35	5%	1.28	5%
4Q	E1.19	-8%	1.30	6%	1.23	6%
Yr.	E6.70	35%	4.97	5%	4.73	29%

Next earnings report expected: late October

American Home Products

Business Summary - 08-SEP-95

American Home Products is a leading maker of drugs, medical products and food items. Through the November 1994 acquisition of American Cyanamid, it diversified into agricultural products and expanded its drug, vaccine and medical products lines. Pro forma sales (including Cyanamid) in 1994 were derived as follows:

	Sales
Health care products	81%
Agricultural products	12%
Food items	7%

Foreign operations accounted for 38% of pro forma sales in 1994. R&D equaled 9.1% of actual sales, up from 8.0% in 1993.

Prescription drugs (55% of pro forma 1994 sales) include contraceptives such as Triphasal and Norplant, estrogen replacements such as Premarin, Cordorone and other cardiovasculars, Effexor antidepressant and other mental health drugs, analgesics, anti-cancer therapeutics, antibiotics, vaccines, pediatric products, generics and animal health items. Consumer health care items (15%) include Advil and Anacin analgesics, Dimetapp and Robitussin for coughs and colds, Primatene asthma medication, Preparation H and Centrum vitamins. Genetics Institute (65% owned) is a biotechnology concern with interests in orthopedics, hematology, oncology and other areas.

Medical supplies and diagnostic products (11%) include needles and syringes, catheters, enteral pumps and feeding sets, endoscopic instruments, wound closure products and other items. Agricurual chemicals (12%) consist of herbicides such as Pursuit, Scepter and others, as well as other crop protection items. Food products (7%) include Chef Boyardee items, Gulden's mustard, Jiffy-Pop popcorn and other items.

Important Developments

Aug. '95—AHP said it has 35 new drugs and extensions of existing products in its pharmaceutical R&D pipeline, including 20 that are either under regulatory review or in late stages of clinical trials. During 1995, the company expects to receive FDA approval for Prempro/Premphase hormone replacement therapy and Normiflo anticoagulant. New products expected to receive clearance in 1996 include bromfenac analgesic and Lodine ER for the treatment of osteoarthritis. Other promising products in the pipeline are tasosarten, an angiotensin II treatment for hypertension; and zalephon, a sedative/hypnotic agent.

Capitalization

Long Term Debt: $8,726,472,000 (6/95).
$2 Conv. Pfd. Stk.: 35,600 shs. ($2.50 par); ea. conv. into 9 com. shs.

Per Share Data ($)

	(Year Ended Dec. 31)					
	1994	1993	1992	1991	1990	1989
Tangible Bk. Val.	-16.10	10.18	9.11	9.64	7.61	4.48
Cash Flow	5.97	5.51	4.33	4.89	4.49	4.01
Earnings	4.97	4.73	3.66	4.36	3.92	3.54
Dividends	2.92	2.86	2.66	2.38	2.15	1.95
Payout Ratio	58%	60%	72%	55%	55%	55%
Prices - High	67¼	69	84¼	86¼	55⅛	54¾
- Low	55⅜	55½	62¼	46½	43	39⅞
P/E Ratio - High	14	15	23	20	14	15
- Low	11	3	17	11	11	11

Income Statement Analysis (Million $)

	1994	%Chg	1993	%Chg	1992	%Chg	1991
Revs.	8,996	8%	8,305	5%	7,874	11%	7,079
Oper. Inc.	2,484	11%	2,237	6%	2,116	12%	1,884
Depr.	306	27%	241	15%	210	26%	167
Int. Exp.	115	145%	47.0	31%	36.0	16%	31.0
Pretax Inc.	2,030	2%	1,993	16%	1,724	-2%	1,760
Eff. Tax Rate	25%	—	26%	—	33%	—	22%
Net Inc.	1,528	4%	1,469	28%	1,151	-16%	1,375

Balance Sheet & Other Fin. Data (Million $)

	1994	1993	1992	1991	1990	1989
Cash	1,944	2,220	1,982	2,065	1,789	1,208
Curr. Assets	7,821	4,808	4,552	4,119	3,826	3,533
Total Assets	21,675	7,687	7,141	5,939	5,637	5,681
Curr. Liab.	4,618	1,584	1,493	1,270	1,029	1,109
LT Debt	9,973	859	602	105	777	1,896
Common Eqty.	4,254	3,876	3,560	3,298	2,672	1,967
Total Cap.	14,551	5,083	4,534	3,595	3,654	3,883
Cap. Exp.	473	518	428	228	248	251
Cash Flow	1,834	1,710	1,361	1,542	1,410	1,248

Ratio Analysis

	1994	1993	1992	1991	1990	1989
Curr. Ratio	1.7	3.0	3.0	3.2	3.7	3.2
% LT Debt of Cap.	68.5	16.9	13.3	2.9	21.3	48.8
% Net Inc.of Revs.	17.0	17.7	14.6	19.4	18.2	16.3
% Ret. on Assets	10.4	19.9	17.7	23.7	21.7	20.8
% Ret. on Equity	37.8	39.7	33.7	46.0	52.9	42.8

Dividend Data —Dividends have been paid since 1919. A dividend reinvestment plan is available.

Amt. of Div. $	Date Decl.	Ex-Div. Date	Stock of Record	Payment Date
0.750	Oct. 27	Nov. 04	Nov. 11	Dec. 01 '94
0.750	Jan. 26	Feb. 07	Feb. 13	Mar. 01 '95
0.750	Apr. 26	May. 08	May. 12	Jun. 01 '95
0.750	Jul. 27	Aug. 09	Aug. 11	Sep. 01 '95

Data as orig. reptd.; bef. results of disc. opers. and/or spec. items. Per share data adj. for stk. divs. as of ex-div. date.
E-Estimated. NA-Not Available. NM-Not Meaningful. NR-Not Ranked.

Office—Five Giralda Farms, Madison, NJ 07940. **Tel**—(201) 660-5000. **Chrmn & CEO**—J. R. Stafford. **Secy**—C. G. Emerling. **VP-Fin**—J. R. Considine. **Investor Contact**—Claire Ball. **Dirs**—C. Alexander, F. A. Bennack, Jr., R. G. Blount, R. C. Duke, J. D. Feerick, F. Hassan, J. P. Mascotte, M. L. Polan, J. R. Stafford, J. R. Torell III, W. Wrigley. **Transfer Agent & Registrar**—Chemical Bank, NYC. **Incorporated** in Delaware in 1926. **Empl**-74,009. **S&P Analyst:** Herman B. Saftlas

American Int'l Group

NYSE Symbol **AIG**

In S&P 500

13-SEP-95

Industry: Insurance

Summary: AIG is one of the world's leading insurance organizations, providing property, casualty and life insurance and various other financial services in 130 countries and territories.

S&P Opinion: Buy (★★★★★)	Recent Price • 79¾	Yield • 0.4%
	52 Wk Range • 81⅝-58⅝	12-Mo. P/E • 16.3

Quantitative Evaluations

Outlook
(1 Lowest—5 Highest)
• **4+**

Fair Value
• **80¼**

Risk
• **Low**

Earn./Div. Rank
• **A+**

Technical Eval.
• **Bullish** since 8/95

Rel. Strength Rank
(1 Lowest—99 Highest)
• **62**

Insider Activity
• **Favorable**

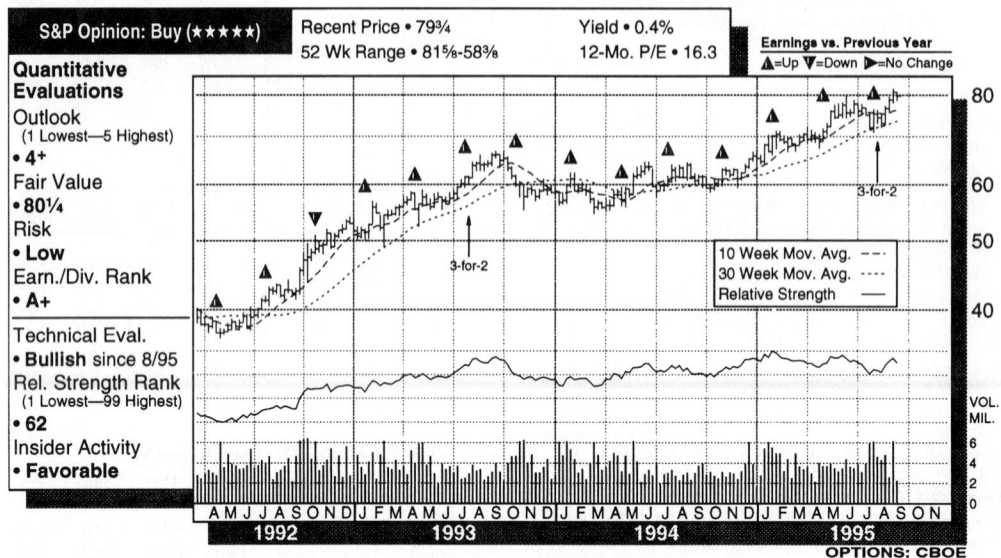

Earnings vs. Previous Year ▲=Up ▼=Down ▶=No Change

10 Week Mov. Avg. – – –
30 Week Mov. Avg. · · · ·
Relative Strength ——

OPTIONS: CBOE

Overview - 13-SEP-95

Solid property-casualty underwriting performance and strong life results should lead to higher earnings in coming periods. Though not immune to the catastrophe losses that have plagued insurers of late, AIG has a substantial capital base and a widely diversified book of business to help mitigate these losses. AIG will also benefit handsomely from an expected upturn in rates in the wake of these losses. Net written premiums will rise 10%-15% in 1995, reflecting both volume and pricing gains, particularly in certain specialty and property lines. This growth will be partly offset by a reduction in certain undesirable lines. Barring a surge in claims, underwriting results should approximate breakeven. Foreign life operations and financial services should continue to perform well.

Valuation - 13-SEP-95

The shares of this bellwether insurer have been very strong lately. After shunning the stock amid concerns over the impact of record catastrophe losses, higher interest rates and environmental related issues, investors have instead begun focusing on AIG's strong market presence, superior underwriting track record and heretofore relatively low valuation. Despite recent appreciation, the shares remain attractive at 14 times our 1996 operating earnings estimate (which excludes realized investment gains) of $5.85 a share, given AIG's superior growth prospects. The shares were split 3-for-2 on July 28, 1995.

Key Stock Statistics

S&P EPS Est. 1995	5.20	Tang. Bk. Value/Share	38.23
P/E on S&P Est. 1995	15.3	Beta	1.15
S&P EPS Est. 1996	5.85	Shareholders	14,700
Dividend Rate/Share	0.34	Market cap. (B)	$ 38.4
Shs. outstg. (M)	474.2	Inst. holdings	54%
Avg. daily vol. (M)	0.832	Insider holdings	NA

Value of $10,000 invested 5 years ago: $ 22,251

Fiscal Year Ending Dec. 31

	1995	% Change	1994	% Change	1993	% Change
Revenues (Million $)						
1Q	5,463	5%	5,226	21%	4,311	-1%
2Q	6,458	15%	5,626	5%	5,339	18%
3Q	—	—	5,675	11%	5,120	10%
4Q	—	—	5,915	10%	5,360	10%
Yr.	—	—	22,442	11%	20,130	9%
Income (Million $)						
1Q	572.2	13%	505.6	6%	475.2	17%
2Q	633.8	15%	549.7	14%	482.0	15%
3Q	—	—	542.5	20%	451.1	33%
4Q	—	—	577.7	13%	510.2	11%
Yr.	—	—	2,176	13%	1,918	18%
Earnings Per Share ($)						
1Q	1.21	14%	1.06	7%	0.99	16%
2Q	1.34	16%	1.16	14%	1.01	15%
3Q	—	—	1.14	20%	0.95	34%
4Q	—	—	1.22	14%	1.07	12%
Yr.	E5.20	14%	4.58	14%	4.03	18%

Next earnings report expected: late October

American Int'l Group

Business Summary - 13-SEP-95

AIG is a holding company whose subsidiaries engage in property, casualty, marine and life insurance underwriting throughout the U.S. and in some 129 other countries. It also offers a variety of financial services, including airline leasing and currency trading. Contributions to revenues in recent years were:

	1994	1993	1992
General insurance	53%	55%	57%
Life insurance	38%	36%	34%
Agency operations	1%	1%	1%
Financial services	8%	8%	8%

International operations accounted for 52% of revenues and 52% of pretax profits in 1994.

General insurance written premiums totaling $10.9 billion in 1994 were derived: commercial casualty 53%, international 33%, pools and associations 5%, personal lines 4%, commercial property 3%, and mortgage guaranty 2%. AIG's general insurance operations are multiline property-casualty companies. The Domestic General-Brokerage division deals principally with insurance brokers representing major industrial and commercial clients. The Agency division provides coverage to small and medium-size businesses and writes selected personal lines. Financial service operations include interest rate and currency swaps, cash management, premium financing, airline leasing and private banking. AIG also owns 46.4% of Transatlantic Holdings, Inc., a reinsurer.

Life insurance subsidiaries offer individual and group life, annuity and accident and health policies. Foreign operations accounted for 96% of the segment's operating income in 1994.

Important Developments

Aug. '95—AIG's higher first half earnings mainly reflected 11% growth in general insurance premiums, and catastrophe losses of $55 million, unchanged from the prior six months. Separately, during 1994, AIG made several strategic investments. In December, it invested $216 million in NYSE-listed 20th Century Industries (TW), buying $200 million of TW convertible preferred stock and warrants to buy 16 million common shares. In July, AIG infused $200 million into Alexander & Alexander Services, Inc., and received 4 million 8% convertible preferred shares.

Capitalization

Total Debt: $18,230,044,000, incl. $4.8 billion of GIC obligations and $10.8 billion of subsid. debt (6/95).
Minority Interest: $300,000,000.

Per Share Data ($)

	1994	1993	1992	1991	1990	1989
Tangible Bk. Val.	34.66	31.95	26.53	23.41	20.15	17.65
Oper. Earnings	4.46	3.88	3.27	3.11	2.95	2.79
Earnings	4.58	4.03	3.40	3.23	3.07	2.95
Dividends	0.29	0.26	0.23	0.21	0.18	0.16
Relative Payout	6%	6%	7%	6%	6%	5%
Prices - High	67⅛	66⅞	54	45⅜	37⅝	39⅞
- Low	54½	49	36½	32	25⅜	23½
P/E Ratio - High	15	17	16	14	12	14
- Low	12	12	11	10	8	8

Income Statement Analysis (Million $)

	1994	%Chg	1993	%Chg	1992	%Chg	1991
Life Ins. In Force	333,379	30%	257,162	22%	210,606	9%	193,226
Prem.Inc Life A&H	6,724	17%	5,746	18%	4,853	20%	4,059
Prem.Inc Cas/Prop	10,287	8%	9,567	4%	9,209	1%	9,104
Net Invest. Inc.	3,184	12%	2,840	11%	2,566	11%	2,303
Oth. Revs.	2,247	13%	1,982	13%	1,761	24%	1,418
Total Revs.	22,442	11%	20,135	9%	18,389	9%	16,884
Pretax Inc.	2,952	13%	2,601	22%	2,137	6%	2,023
Net Oper. Inc.	2,119	15%	1,848	18%	1,561	5%	1,492
Net Inc.	2,176	13%	1,918	18%	1,625	5%	1,553

Balance Sheet & Other Fin. Data (Million $)

	1994	1993	1992	1991	1990	1989
Cash & Equiv.	3,402	6,039	5,568	7,880	7,262	5,008
Premiums Due	8,802	8,364	9,010	9,027	8,793	7,734
Inv Assets Bonds	35,431	30,067	23,613	23,613	20,639	18,049
Inv. Assets Stock	5,099	4,488	2,705	2,291	1,987	2,230
Inv. Assets Loans	5,353	3,577	3,080	2,999	2,629	1,612
Inv. Assets Total	73,388	60,947	56,977	44,404	34,826	26,593
Deferred Policy Cost	5,132	4,249	3,658	3,243	2,777	2,350
Total Assets	114,346	101,015	79,835	69,389	58,143	46,143
Debt	17,519	15,689	13,464	11,922	10,385	5,860
Common Eqty.	16,422	15,224	12,632	11,313	9,754	8,255

Ratio Analysis

	1994	1993	1992	1991	1990	1989
Comb. Loss-Exp.Ratio	98.8	100.1	102.4	100.4	99.6	100.0
% Ret. on Revs.	9.7	9.5	8.8	9.2	9.2	9.7
% Ret. on Equity	13.7	13.8	12.6	14.7	15.9	18.0
% Invest. Yield	4.7	4.8	4.9	5.8	6.6	7.4

Dividend Data

Dividends have been paid each year since 1969.

Amt. of Div. $	Date Decl.	Ex-Div. Date	Stock of Record	Payment Date
0.115	Nov. 14	Feb. 27	Mar. 03	Mar. 17 '95
0.115	Mar. 13	May. 26	Jun. 02	Jun. 16 '95
3-for-2	May. 29	Jul. 31	Jun. 30	Jul. 28 '95
0.085	May. 24	Sep. 06	Sep. 08	Sep. 22 '95
0.085	Sep. 12	Dec. 06	Dec. 08	Dec. 22 '95

Data as orig. reptd.; bef. results of disc. opers. and/or spec. items. Per share data adj. for stk. divs. as of ex-div. date. E-Estimate. NA-Not Available. NM-Not Meaningful. NR-Not Ranked.

Office—70 Pine St., New York, NY 10270. Tel—(212) 770-7000. Chrmn & CEO—M. R. Greenberg. Pres—T. R. Tizzio. Treas—W. N. Dooley. VP & Secy—K. E. Shannon. Investor Contact—Charlene M. Hamrah. Dirs—M. B. Aidinoff, L. M. Bentsen, M. A. Cohen, B. B. Conable, Jr., M. Feldstein, H. Freeman, L. L. Gonda, M. R. Greenberg, C. A. Hills, F. J. Hoenemeyer, J. I. Howell, E. E. Matthews, D. P. Phypers, J. J. Roberts, E. E. Stempel, T. R. Tizzio. Transfer Agent & Registrar—Bank of New York, NYC. Incorporated in Delaware in 1967. Empl-32,000. S&P Analyst: Catherine A. Seifert

American Stores

NYSE Symbol **ASC**
In S&P 500

05-OCT-95 | **Industry:** Retail Stores

Summary: This company, one of the leading U.S. retailers, operates about 1,600 combination food/drug stores, super drug centers, drug stores and food stores in 27 states.

S&P Opinion: Accumulate (★★★★)	Recent Price • 28⅜	Yield • 1.9%
	52 Wk Range • 30¾-23¼	12-Mo. P/E • 11.5

Quantitative Evaluations

Outlook
(1 Lowest—5 Highest)
• **5⁻**

Fair Value
• **32⅛**

Risk
• **Low**

Earn./Div. Rank
• **A**

Technical Eval.
• **Bearish** since 6/95

Rel. Strength Rank
(1 Lowest—99 Highest)
• **55**

Insider Activity
• **Neutral**

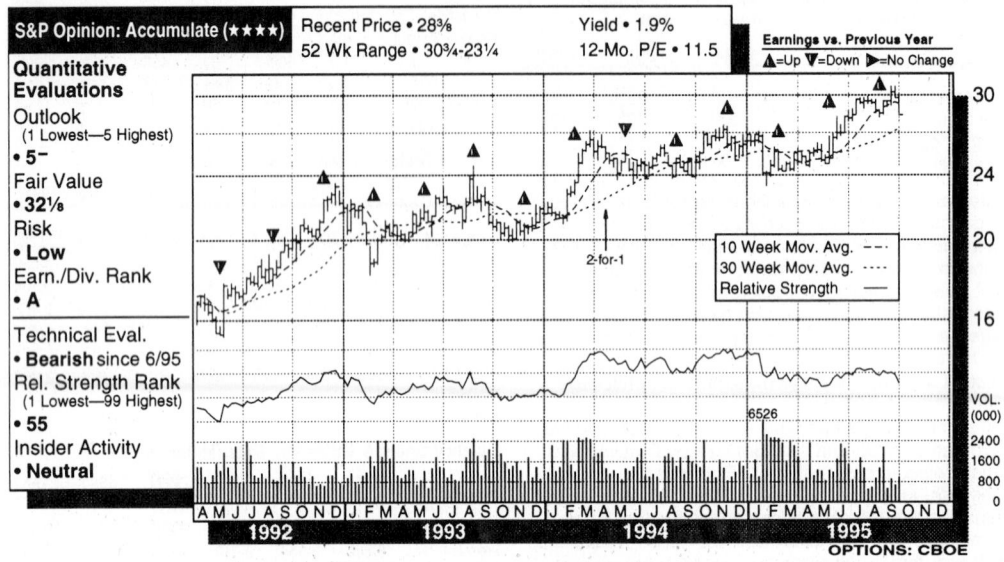

Earnings vs. Previous Year
▲=Up ▼=Down ▶=No Change

10 Week Mov. Avg. – – –
30 Week Mov. Avg. ·······
Relative Strength ——

2-for-1

OPTIONS: CBOE

Overview - 05-OCT-95

Lower revenues in 1995-6 will reflect store closings and the sale of 45 Acme Stores. Operating profit should increase moderately at Lucky Stores, on improved expense ratios, but there is keen pricing competition, particularly in northern California. Same-store sales gains and declining expenses should boost operating income at Eastern food operations (Jewel and Acme). Strong sales gains at Osco Drug and lower expenses should offset downward pressure on gross margins from third-party payment plans. Interest costs will continue to drop, reflecting redemption of subordinated notes and use of strong cash flow to bring debt levels more in line with industry norms. American's transition from a holding to an operating company should aid the bottom line, as expenses are reduced and redundancies eliminated.

Valuation - 05-OCT-95

The shares, which were in a narrow trading range for some time, have inched up in recent months. As economic growth slows, investors seek more defensive issues such as supermarkets. Earnings are projected to increase about 10% this year, excluding special items. Gains should accelerate over the next few years, as the company lowers its cost structure and becomes more efficient. Meanwhile, strong cash flow has enabled American to raise its dividend while maintaining an aggressive capital spending program and repurchasing common shares.

Key Stock Statistics

S&P EPS Est. 1996	2.15	Tang. Bk. Value/Share	3.31
P/E on S&P Est. 1996	13.2	Beta	1.20
S&P EPS Est. 1997	2.45	Shareholders	18,800
Dividend Rate/Share	0.56	Market cap. (B)	$ 4.3
Shs. outstg. (M)	147.5	Inst. holdings	58%
Avg. daily vol. (M)	0.170	Insider holdings	NA

Value of $10,000 invested 5 years ago: $ 22,384

Fiscal Year Ending Jan. 31

	1996	% Change	1995	% Change	1994	% Change
Revenues (Million $)						
1Q	4,362	-5%	4,610	-1%	4,668	-5%
2Q	4,495	-4%	4,669	NM	4,693	NM
3Q	—	—	4,432	-2%	4,532	NM
4Q	—	—	4,647	-5%	4,871	NM
Yr.	—	—	18,355	-2%	18,763	-2%
Income (Million $)						
1Q	53.88	12%	47.96	-15%	56.51	194%
2Q	73.94	7%	69.03	18%	58.50	16%
3Q	—	—	97.93	116%	45.41	6%
4Q	—	—	130.3	28%	101.7	8%
Yr.	—	—	345.2	32%	262.1	27%
Earnings Per Share ($)						
1Q	0.37	9%	0.34	-15%	0.40	186%
2Q	0.50	4%	0.48	17%	0.41	14%
3Q	E0.47	-32%	0.69	116%	0.32	5%
4Q	E0.81	-11%	0.91	27%	0.71	8%
Yr.	E2.15	-11%	2.42	31%	1.85	26%

Next earnings report expected: late November

Business Summary - 05-OCT-95

American Stores Company is one of the largest U.S. retailers. It operates about 1,600 retail units, consisting of combination food/drug stores, super drug centers, drug stores and food stores, in 27 states.

Western food operations consist of Lucky Stores Northern and Southern California divisions and Jewel-Osco - New Mexico. Operations include about 436 stores with 10.9 million sq. ft. of selling space. The stores consist of more than 300 grocery stores, 95 expanded grocery stores, about 21 combination food/drug stores and three drug stores.

Eastern food operations are Jewel Food Stores, headquartered in Illinois, and Acme Markets, headquartered in Pennsylvania. The division currently operates about 380 stores. Star Markets, headquartered in Massachusetts, was sold in September 1994.

Drug store operations accounted for 26% of sales and 31% of operating profit in 1994-5. Drug store operations consist of Osco Drug in Illinois and Sav-on Drugs in California. There are 781 drug stores in operation (including 148 jointly operated Jewel Osco combination stores) with 11.4 million sq. ft. of selling space.

In June 1991, the company sold Alpha Beta Co., which operated 142 stores in southern California, for $241 million. The sale was made to comply with a 1990 consent decree settling antitrust litigation arising from the 1988 acquisition, for $2.4 billion, of Lucky Stores, a California-based supermarket chain with 600 stores. In April 1992, American sold 74 Jewel Osco stores for $325 million.

Important Developments

Aug. '95—Same-store sales rose 1.57%, year to year, in the second quarter of 1995-6. Operating profit at the western food operations rose 6.3%, reflecting both higher margins and lower expenses. Eastern food operations generated a 2.3% increase in operating profit, reflecting strong expense controls. Higher sales, which increased gross margin dollars, and good control of operating expenses as a percentage of sales resulted in a 4.0% increase in operating profit at the drug store operations. Interest expense declined $5.5 million in the second quarter due to lower interest rates and the redemption of convertible subordinated notes. The company repurchased 1.3 million shares in the second quarter under a four million share repurchase program. Capital spending for 1995-6 should approximate $700 million, including 75 new and replacement stores, 80 major remodels and 70 minor remodels.

Capitalization

Long Term Debt: $1,943,666,000 (4/95), incl. $72.1 million of lease obligs.

Per Share Data ($)

	1995	1994	1993	1992	1991	1990
Tangible Bk. Val.	1.96	-0.60	-1.33	-3.03	-4.61	-6.10
Cash Flow	5.27	4.41	3.94	4.23	3.90	3.16
Earnings	2.42	1.85	1.47	1.73	1.32	0.87
Dividends	0.48	0.80	0.36	0.32	0.28	0.25
Payout Ratio	20%	43%	25%	18%	21%	31%
Cal. Yrs.	1994	1993	1992	1991	1990	1989
Prices - High	27¾	24⅝	23½	23⅛	17⅞	18⅛
- Low	20⅞	18⅛	15¼	13	10⅝	13¼
P/E Ratio - High	11	13	16	13	14	21
- Low	9	10	10	7	8	15

(Year Ended Jan. 31)

Income Statement Analysis (Million $)

	1995	%Chg	1994	%Chg	1993	%Chg	1992
Revs.	18,355	-2%	18,763	-2%	19,051	-9%	20,823
Oper. Inc.	1,092	8%	1,014	4%	978	2%	955
Depr.	407	12%	365	5%	346	NM	345
Int. Exp.	175	-9%	193	-10%	215	-20%	268
Pretax Inc.	606	26%	481	24%	389	-14%	451
Eff. Tax Rate	43%	—	46%	—	47%	—	47%
Net Inc.	345	32%	262	27%	206	-14%	240

Balance Sheet & Other Fin. Data (Million $)

	1995	1994	1993	1992	1991	1990
Cash	196	59.6	54.0	71.0	77.0	87.0
Curr. Assets	2,132	1,996	1,999	2,138	2,281	2,261
Total Assets	7,032	6,927	6,545	6,955	7,245	7,398
Curr. Liab.	1,931	2,054	1,895	1,975	2,120	2,240
LT Debt	2,064	2,091	2,176	2,662	3,101	3,399
Common Eqty.	2,051	1,742	1,692	1,516	1,351	1,202
Total Cap.	4,436	4,180	4,012	4,354	4,635	4,707
Cap. Exp.	538	594	386	355	330	552
Cash Flow	752	627	553	585	538	400

Ratio Analysis

	1995	1994	1993	1992	1991	1990
Curr. Ratio	1.1	1.0	1.1	1.1	1.1	1.0
% LT Debt of Cap.	46.5	50.0	54.2	61.1	66.9	72.2
% Net Inc.of Revs.	1.9	1.4	1.1	1.2	0.8	0.5
% Ret. on Assets	4.9	3.9	3.0	3.4	2.5	1.5
% Ret. on Equity	18.2	15.2	12.7	16.7	14.3	9.7

Dividend Data —Dividends have been paid since 1965. A poison pill stock purchase rights plan was adopted in 1988.

Amt. of Div. $	Date Decl.	Ex-Div. Date	Stock of Record	Payment Date
0.120	Sep. 20	Sep. 26	Sep. 30	Oct. 13 '94
0.120	Dec. 05	Dec. 19	Dec. 23	Jan. 06 '95
0.140	Mar. 21	Mar. 27	Mar. 31	Apr. 12 '95
0.140	Jun. 21	Jun. 28	Jul. 01	Jul. 14 '95
0.140	Sep. 20	Sep. 27	Sep. 29	Oct. 12 '95

Data as orig. reptd.; bef. results of disc. opers. and/or spec. items. Per share data adj. for stk. divs. as of ex-div. date. E-Estimated. NA-Not Available. NM-Not Meaningful. NR-Not Ranked.

Office—709 East South Temple, Salt Lake City, UT 84102. **Tel**—(801) 539-0112. **Chrmn & CEO**—V. L. Lund. **Pres & COO**—D. L. Maher. **Exec VP & CFO**—T. Beck. **Secy**—J. Lunt. **Investor Contact**—Meredith Anderson. **Dirs**—H. I. Bryant, L. H. Callister, A. B. Engebretsen, J. B. Fisher, F. R. Gumucio, L. G. Harmon, V. L. Lund, J. E. Masline, M. T. Miller, L. T. Perry, B. S. Preiskel, J. L. Scott, A. W. Skaggs, L. S. Skaggs, A. K. Smith. **Transfer Agent & Registrar**—First Chicago Trust Co. of New York, Jersey City, N.J. **Incorporated** in Utah in 1947; reincorporated in Delaware in 1965. **Empl**-127,000. **S&P Analyst:** Karen J. Sack, CFA

Ameritech

NYSE Symbol **AIT**
In S&P 500

16-SEP-95

Industry:
Telecommunications

Summary: Ameritech is the third largest telephone holding company in the U.S., based on 1994 access lines. AIT provides service in parts of five upper-Midwestern states.

S&P Opinion: Accumulate (★★★★)	Recent Price • 52¼	Yield • 3.8%
	52 Wk Range • 52⅜-38	12-Mo. P/E • 16.3

Quantitative Evaluations

Outlook
(1 Lowest—5 Highest)
• **1+**

Fair Value
• **44¼**

Risk
• **Low**

Earn./Div. Rank
• **A-**

Technical Eval.
• **Bearish** since 4/94

Rel. Strength Rank
(1 Lowest—99 Highest)
• **69**

Insider Activity
• **Neutral**

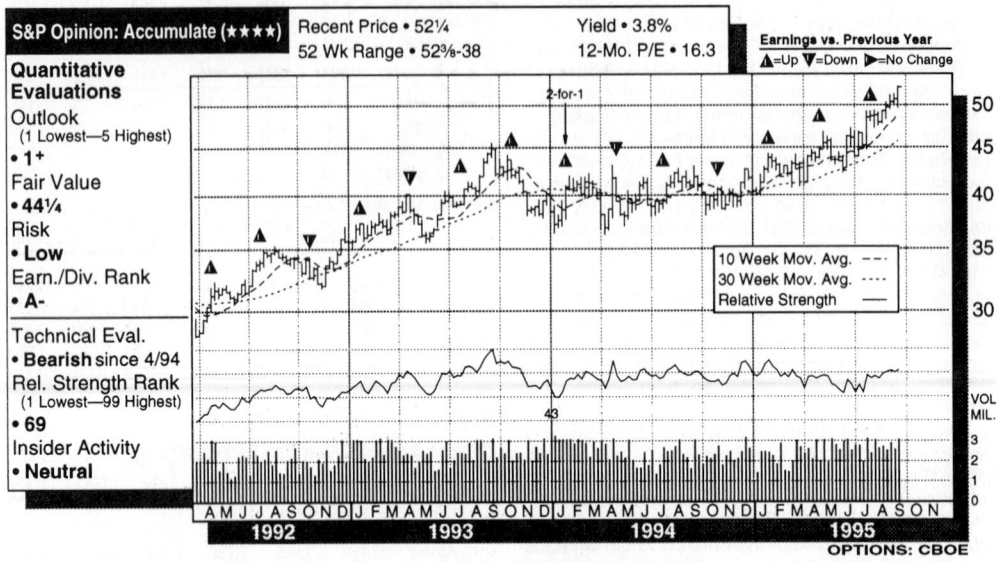

Earnings vs. Previous Year
▲=Up ▼=Down ▶=No Change

10 Week Mov. Avg. – – –
30 Week Mov. Avg. · · · ·
Relative Strength —

OPTIONS: CBOE

Overview - 15-SEP-95

Ameritech is moving to position itself for a competitive telephone market; its strategy focuses on entering complementary lines of business such as cable television and long-distance services while maintaining its focus on its Upper Midwest operating region. AIT's Customers First plan, when fully approved by regulators, will make Ameritech the first Bell company to enter the long-distance market. Meanwhile, the company has been working with state regulators to increase its pricing flexibility while restructuring its operations and upgrading its network to better position telephone operations for competition. These actions should result in continued revenue growth and margin expansion in the core business despite competitive inroads. Cellular operations and investments in international ventures, notably Telecom Corp. of New Zealand, will contribute to long-term earnings gains.

Valuation - 15-SEP-95

The shares have risen sharply in 1995 on continued strong earnings growth and a more favorable outlook for proposed federal telecommunications legislation. The House and Senate have both passed bills allowing the Bell companies earlier entry into the long-distance market; the two versions will now be reconciled in conference committee. The stock's performance should continue to benefit from AIT's successful efforts to position itself for a more competitive market. With a healthy dividend yield, the shares are recommended for both income and growth.

Key Stock Statistics

S&P EPS Est. 1995	3.40	Tang. Bk. Value/Share	12.18
P/E on S&P Est. 1995	15.4	Beta	0.50
S&P EPS Est. 1996	3.60	Shareholders	956,300
Dividend Rate/Share	2.00	Market cap. (B)	$ 29.0
Shs. outstg. (M)	554.2	Inst. holdings	37%
Avg. daily vol. (M)	0.614	Insider holdings	NA

Value of $10,000 invested 5 years ago: $ 20,095

Fiscal Year Ending Dec. 31

	1995	% Change	1994	% Change	1993	% Change
Revenues (Million $)						
1Q	3,146	4%	3,034	8%	2,797	4%
2Q	3,369	6%	3,184	8%	2,951	5%
3Q	—	—	3,170	8%	2,947	5%
4Q	—	—	3,181	5%	3,016	6%
Yr.	—	—	12,570	7%	11,710	5%
Income (Million $)						
1Q	578.9	NM	43.80	-85%	300.0	-11%
2Q	503.5	13%	446.6	15%	389.6	14%
3Q	—	—	250.9	-41%	425.0	29%
4Q	—	—	429.1	8%	398.2	19%
Yr.	—	—	1,170	-23%	1,513	12%
Earnings Per Share ($)						
1Q	1.05	NM	0.08	-86%	0.55	-12%
2Q	0.91	12%	0.81	13%	0.71	12%
3Q	E0.82	78%	0.46	-41%	0.78	27%
4Q	E0.62	-21%	0.78	7%	0.73	17%
Yr.	E3.40	60%	2.13	-23%	2.78	11%

Next earnings report expected: mid October

Ameritech

Business Summary - 15-SEP-95

Ameritech is the third largest U.S. telephone holding company, based on 1994 U.S. access lines. Its telephone subsidiaries provide local exchange service in five Midwestern states to 18.4 million customer access lines.

In October 1994, the Illinois Commerce Commission approved AIT's new regulatory plan. In addition to rate reductions, the plan also caps basic residential service rates at current levels for five years and institutes a price cap formula for non-competitive services. The move to a price cap system instead of traditional rate-of-return regulation will allow AIT to retain more of the profitability improvements from investment in new technology and work force reductions.

Ameritech Mobile provides wireless communications services. At December 31, 1994, 1,299,000 cellular lines and 632,000 pagers were in service.

Other units provide directory advertising and publishing and voice response and voice messaging services; sell, install and maintain business customer premises equipment (CPE) and sell network and central office-based services provided by the Bell Companies; arrange financing and leasing of computer and communications products; develop and invest in new products and technology; and develop international business opportunities.

A consortium led by AIT and Bell Atlantic acquired Telecom Corp. of New Zealand for US$2.45 billion in 1990. The companies sold 31% of Telecom Corp.'s share capital in an international public offering in July 1991. During 1993, AIT reduced its stake to 24.9%.

AIT and the six other Bell companies jointly own Bell Communications Research, which provides technical assistance and consulting to the Bells.

Important Developments

Aug. '95—AIT signed a 25 year contract with China United Telecommunications Corp. to build and help operate a digital cellular network in China. Separately, the company reached tentative three year labor contracts with two of its unions. In another matter, GTE will join the video programming and interactive services venture formed by AIT, SBC Communications, BellSouth and Walt Disney.
May '95—AT&T filed with state regulators to provide local telephone service in Chicago and Grand Rapids as part of AIT's Customers First plan.
Apr. '95—The Justice Department recommended approval of AIT's Customers First plan, which would allow the company to resell long-distance service in Chicago and Grand Rapids in exchange for opening its local markets to competition.

Capitalization

Long Term Debt: $4,571,700,000 (6/95).

Per Share Data ($)

(Year Ended Dec. 31)

	1994	1993	1992	1991	1990	1989
Tangible Bk. Val.	10.98	14.25	12.82	15.06	14.50	14.09
Cash Flow	6.15	6.75	6.30	5.79	5.81	5.70
Earnings	2.13	2.78	2.51	2.20	2.36	2.29
Dividends	1.94	1.86	1.78	1.71	1.61	1.49
Payout Ratio	91%	67%	71%	78%	68%	65%
Prices - High	43⅛	45½	37	34⅞	34⅞	34⅛
- Low	36¼	35	28⅛	27⅞	26¼	23½
P/E Ratio - High	20	16	15	16	15	15
- Low	17	13	11	13	11	10

Income Statement Analysis (Million $)

	1994	%Chg	1993	%Chg	1992	%Chg	1991
Revs.	12,570	7%	11,710	5%	11,153	3%	10,818
Depr.	2,205	2%	2,162	6%	2,031	6%	1,915
Maint.	NA	—	1,729	NM	1,737	5%	1,647
Constr. Credits	13.3	18%	11.3	49%	7.6	-67%	22.9
Eff. Tax Rate	33%	—	32%	—	32%	—	30%
Net Inc.	1,170	-23%	1,513	12%	1,346	15%	1,166

Balance Sheet & Other Fin. Data (Million $)

	1994	1993	1992	1991	1990	1989
Gross Prop.	29,546	29,117	28,370	27,158	26,370	25,092
Net Prop.	13,455	17,366	17,335	16,986	16,652	16,296
Cap. Exp.	2,466	2,564	2,267	2,200	2,154	2,015
Total Cap.	11,370	14,179	14,460	16,187	15,912	16,458
Fxd. Chgs. Cov.	5.0	5.7	4.9	3.9	4.8	5.4
Capitalization:						
LT Debt	4,448	4,090	4,586	4,964	5,074	5,069
Pfd.	Nil	Nil	Nil	Nil	Nil	Nil
Common	6,055	7,845	6,992	8,097	7,732	7,686

Ratio Analysis

	1994	1993	1992	1991	1990	1989
% Ret. on Revs.	9.3	12.9	12.1	10.8	11.8	12.1
% Ret. On Invest.Cap	12.6	14.1	12.1	10.8	10.7	10.1
% Return On Com.Eqty	14.4	20.4	19.8	14.5	16.3	15.8
% Earn. on Net Prop.	9.5	11.0	10.0	8.9	9.9	9.9
% LT Debt of Cap.	42.3	34.3	39.6	38.0	39.6	39.7
Capital. % Pfd.	Nil	Nil	Nil	Nil	Nil	Nil
Capital. % Common	57.7	65.7	60.4	62.0	60.4	60.3

Dividend Data

Dividends were initiated in 1984. A dividend reinvestment plan is available. A "poison pill" stock purchase rights plan was adopted in 1988.

Amt. of Div. $	Date Decl.	Ex-Div. Date	Stock of Record	Payment Date
0.480	Sep. 21	Sep. 26	Sep. 30	Nov. 01 '94
0.500	Dec. 21	Dec. 23	Dec. 30	Feb. 01 '95
0.500	Mar. 15	Mar. 27	Mar. 31	May. 01 '95
0.500	Jun. 21	Jun. 28	Jun. 30	Aug. 01 '95

Office—30 South Wacker Drive, Chicago, IL 60606. **Tel**—(312) 750-5000. **Chrmn, Pres & CEO**—R. C. Notebaert. **EVP & CFO**—Oren G. Shaffer. **Secy**—B. B. Howat. **VP-Investor Contact**—Sari L. Macrie. **Dirs**—R. H. Brown, D. C. Clark, M. R. Goodes, H. H. Gray, J. A. Henderson, S. B. Lubar, L. M. Martin, A. C. Martinez, J. B. McCoy, R. C. Notebaert, J. D. Ong, A. B. Rand, J. A. Unruh. **Transfer Agent & Registrar**—First Chicago Trust Co. of New York, NYC. **Incorporated** in Delaware in 1983. **Empl**- 62,094. **S&P Analyst:** Kevin J. Gooley

Amgen

NASDAQ Symbol **AMGN**
In S&P 500

28-OCT-95

Industry:
Drugs-Generic and
OTC

Summary: This leading biotechnology concern's key products are Epogen and Neupogen, genetically engineered versions of natural hormones that stimulate production of blood components.

S&P Opinion: Accumulate (★★★★)	Recent Price • 47	Yield • Nil
	52 Wk Range • 52⅝-26½	12-Mo. P/E • 33.1

Quantitative Evaluations

Outlook
(1 Lowest—5 Highest)
• **2+**

Fair Value
• **43**

Risk
• **Average**

Earn./Div. Rank
• **B-**

Technical Eval.
• **Bullish** since 5/94

Rel. Strength Rank
(1 Lowest—99 Highest)
• **63**

Insider Activity
• **Unfavorable**

Earnings vs. Previous Year
▲=Up ▼=Down ▶=No Change

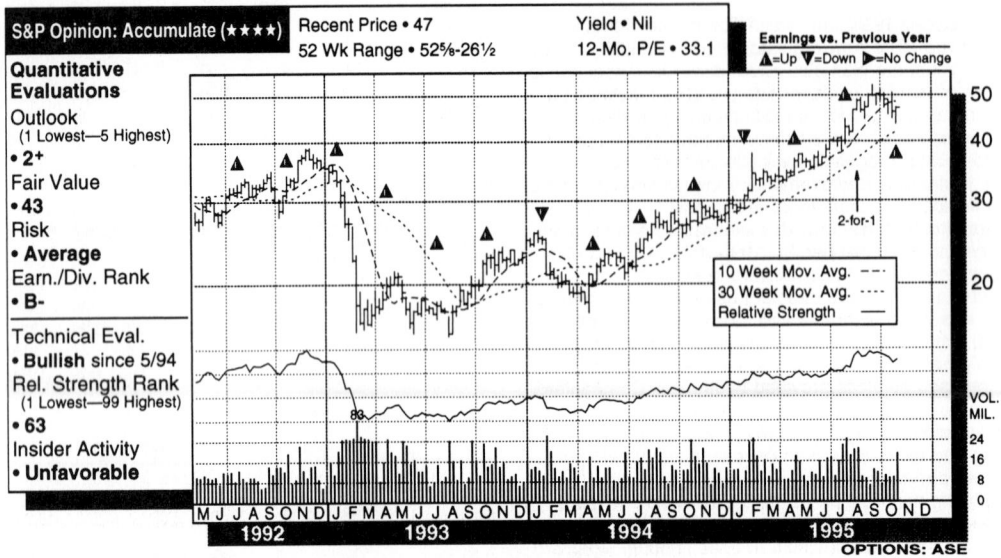

10 Week Mov. Avg. – – –
30 Week Mov. Avg. ·······
Relative Strength ——

2-for-1

OPTIONS: ASE

Overview - 20-OCT-95

Another respectable gain is anticipated for total revenues in 1996. Sales of Epogen red blood cell stimulant (up 23% in the 1995 third quarter) should remain strong, reflecting growth in the U.S. dialysis population and the administration of higher dosing regimens per patient. Despite recent slowing in U.S. volume, worldwide sales of white blood cell stimulant Neupogen (up 7% in the quarter), should improve in coming quarters, aided by further expansion in the chemotherapy market, greater marketing efforts abroad, and new therapeutic indications. Although R&D will remain at relatively high levels, margins should be well maintained, on greater volume and control of operating costs.

Valuation - 20-OCT-95

Shares of this premier biotechnology company are a good selection for investors seeking representation in the volatile biotechnology sector at limited risk. Amgen offers prospects for double-digit sales and earnings growth, an attractive lineup of new products, and takeover appeal (although a successful buyout would probably cost over $14 billion). Although it does not yet have any commercial products, Synergen (acquired in late 1994) enhances the company's R&D base and future financial prospects. Synergen's strength in neurobiology and inflammation fits well with Amgen's core hematology products, and it will provide $200 million of tax loss carryforwards after 1996.

Key Stock Statistics

S&P EPS Est. 1995	1.90	Tang. Bk. Value/Share	5.30
P/E on S&P Est. 1995	24.7	Beta	2.19
S&P EPS Est. 1996	2.20	Shareholders	11,600
Dividend Rate/Share	Nil	Market cap. (B)	$ 12.4
Shs. outstg. (M)	263.5	Inst. holdings	64%
Avg. daily vol. (M)	3.212	Insider holdings	NA

Value of $10,000 invested 5 years ago: $ 115,097

Fiscal Year Ending Dec. 31

	1995	% Change	1994	% Change	1993	% Change
Revenues (Million $)						
1Q	439.4	21%	364.0	17%	310.2	41%
2Q	493.7	19%	414.7	21%	343.1	31%
3Q	493.3	16%	426.4	20%	354.9	17%
4Q	—	—	442.9	21%	365.6	19%
Yr.	—	—	1,648	20%	1,374	26%
Income (Million $)						
1Q	108.6	16%	93.46	16%	80.56	27%
2Q	137.7	28%	107.5	7%	100.2	40%
3Q	145.8	28%	114.0	11%	102.7	15%
4Q	—	—	4.79	-95%	91.10	-32%
Yr.	—	—	319.7	-15%	374.6	5%
Earnings Per Share ($)						
1Q	0.39	18%	0.33	20%	0.28	28%
2Q	0.50	29%	0.39	10%	0.35	43%
3Q	0.52	27%	0.41	14%	0.36	20%
4Q	E0.51	NM	0.02	-95%	0.32	-30%
Yr.	E1.90	66%	1.14	-12%	1.30	7%

Next earnings report expected: early February

Business Summary - 23-OCT-95

Amgen is a leading biotechnology that develops, manufactures and markets products based on advanced cellular and molecular biology. Its two principal products are Neupogen, which had worldwide sales of $829 million in 1994 ($719 million in 1993), and Epogen, which had sales of $721 million in 1994 ($587 million in 1993).

Neupogen is a recombinant version of human granulocyte colony stimulating factor (G-CSF), a protein that stimulates the production of neutrophils (a type of white blood cell that defends the body against bacterial infection). Its principal use is to build neutrophil levels in cancer patients whose natural neutrophils were destroyed by chemotherapy. Neupogen has an estimated 30% of the U.S. myelosuppressive chemotherapy market. Amgen has marketing rights to Neupogen in the U.S., Canada and Australia, and markets the drug jointly with F. Hoffmann-La Roche. The latter has rights to the drug in most other areas (rights in Japan are held by Kirin Brewery).

Epogen is a genetically engineered version of human erythropoietin (EPO), a natural hormone that stimulates the production of red blood cells in bone marrow. The drug's primary market is dialysis patients suffering from severe chronic anemia as a result of their failure to produce adequate amounts of natural EPO. Amgen has EPO rights to the U.S. dialysis market and has licensed Johnson & Johnson U.S. rights to all other indications. Kirin Brewery has EPO rights in Japan, while J&J has EPO rights for most other areas.

Drug products in clinical testing include Infergen (consensus interferon) for hepatitis C; and stem cell factor, an early acting hematopoietic agent that may be useful with high-dose chemotherapy. Amgen and Regeneron Pharmaceuticals are jointly doing R&D on neurotrophic factors that may be used to treat neurodegenerative diseases. Amgen is also studying Neupogen to treat community acquired pneumonia, cancer and various infectious diseases.

Important Developments

Oct. '95—Sales of Epogen rose 23% in the third quarter, while sales of Neupogen were up 7%. U.S. sales of Neupogen increased only 2.2%, reflecting inventory building in the second quarter before the July 4 holiday and ongoing managed care pressures. A Phase III clinical trial of Neupogen for the treatment of moderate pneumonia did not meet its primary endpoint. However, the drug appeared to be efficacious in patients with severe pneumonia. Separately, Amgen plans to file for FDA approval to market Infergen to treat chronic hepatitis C.

Capitalization

Long Term Debt: $177,200,000 (9/95).

Per Share Data ($) (Year Ended Dec. 31)

	1994	1993	1992	1991	1990	1989
Tangible Bk. Val.	4.81	4.36	3.42	2.02	1.57	0.90
Cash Flow	1.41	1.48	1.33	0.42	0.21	0.16
Earnings	1.14	1.30	1.21	0.33	0.13	0.09
Dividends	Nil	Nil	Nil	Nil	Nil	Nil
Payout Ratio	Nil	Nil	Nil	Nil	Nil	Nil
Prices - High	30⅛	35⅞	39⅛	38	10⅝	5
- Low	17⅜	15½	24⅝	9½	3⅝	2⅝
P/E Ratio - High	26	27	32	NM	81	54
- Low	15	12	20	NM	27	28

Income Statement Analysis (Million $)

	1994	%Chg	1993	%Chg	1992	%Chg	1991
Revs.	1,648	20%	1,374	26%	1,093	60%	682
Oper. Inc.	801	29%	619	33%	466	69%	276
Depr.	74.5	52%	48.9	50%	32.5	51%	21.5
Int. Exp.	15.8	56%	10.1	62%	6.2	82%	3.4
Pretax Inc.	588	NM	592	5%	563	NM	158
Eff. Tax Rate	46%	—	37%	—	37%	—	38%
Net Inc.	320	-15%	375	5%	358	NM	97.9

Balance Sheet & Other Fin. Data (Million $)

	1994	1993	1992	1991	1990	1989
Cash	697	723	555	378	157	80.0
Curr. Assets	1,116	1,055	873	590	327	182
Total Assets	1,994	1,766	1,374	866	514	308
Curr. Liab.	536	412	311	295	103	55.0
LT Debt	183	181	130	39.7	12.8	64.7
Common Eqty.	1,274	1,172	934	531	398	188
Total Cap.	1,458	1,353	1,064	571	411	253
Cap. Exp.	131	210	219	117	65.0	44.0
Cash Flow	394	424	390	119	52.0	31.0

Ratio Analysis

	1994	1993	1992	1991	1990	1989
Curr. Ratio	2.1	2.6	2.8	2.0	3.2	3.3
% LT Debt of Cap.	12.6	13.4	12.2	7.0	3.1	25.6
% Net Inc.of Revs.	19.4	27.3	32.7	14.3	9.0	10.0
% Ret. on Assets	17.1	24.0	31.5	14.0	7.7	7.3
% Ret. on Equity	26.3	35.8	48.2	20.7	11.0	10.8

Dividend Data —No cash dividends have been paid. A three-for-one stock split was effected in September 1991, and a two-for-one split was effected in August 1990.

Amt. of Div. $	Date Decl.	Ex-Div. Date	Stock of Record	Payment Date
2-for-1	Jul. 20	Aug. 16	Aug. 01	Aug. 15 '95

Data as orig. reptd.; bef. results of disc. opers. and/or spec. items. Per share data adj. for stk. divs. as of ex-div. date. E-Estimated. NA-Not Available. NM-Not Meaningful. NR-Not Ranked.

Office—1840 Dehavilland Dr., Thousand Oaks, CA 91320-1789. **Tel**—(805) 499-5725. **Chrmn & CEO**—G. M. Binder. **Pres & COO**—K. W. Sharer. **VP & Secy**—G. A. Vandeman. **SVP-Fin & CFO**—R. S. Attiyeh. **Investor Contact**—Sarah H. Crampton. **Dirs**—R. F. Baddour, G. M. Binder, W. K. Bowes, Jr., F. P. Johnson, Jr., S. Lazarus, E. Ledder, G. S. Omenn, J. Pelham, B. H. Semler, K. W. Sharer. **Transfer Agent & Registrar**—American Stock Transfer & Trust Co., NYC. **Incorporated** in California in 1980; reincorporated in Delaware in 1987. **Empl-** 4,012. **S&P Analyst:** H. B. Saftlas

Amoco Corp.

NYSE Symbol **AN**
In S&P 500

30-OCT-95
Industry:
Oil and Gas

Summary: Amoco is a major integrated petroleum and chemicals company.

S&P Opinion: Hold (★★★)	Recent Price • 64	Yield • 3.8%
	52 Wk Range • 69¾-56⅜	12-Mo. P/E • 14.5

Quantitative Evaluations

Outlook
(1 Lowest—5 Highest)
• **2+**

Fair Value
• **62¾**

Risk
• **Low**

Earn./Div. Rank
• **B**

Technical Eval.
• **Bearish** since 11/94

Rel. Strength Rank
(1 Lowest—99 Highest)
• **51**

Insider Activity
• **Neutral**

Earnings vs. Previous Year
▲=Up ▼=Down ▶=No Change

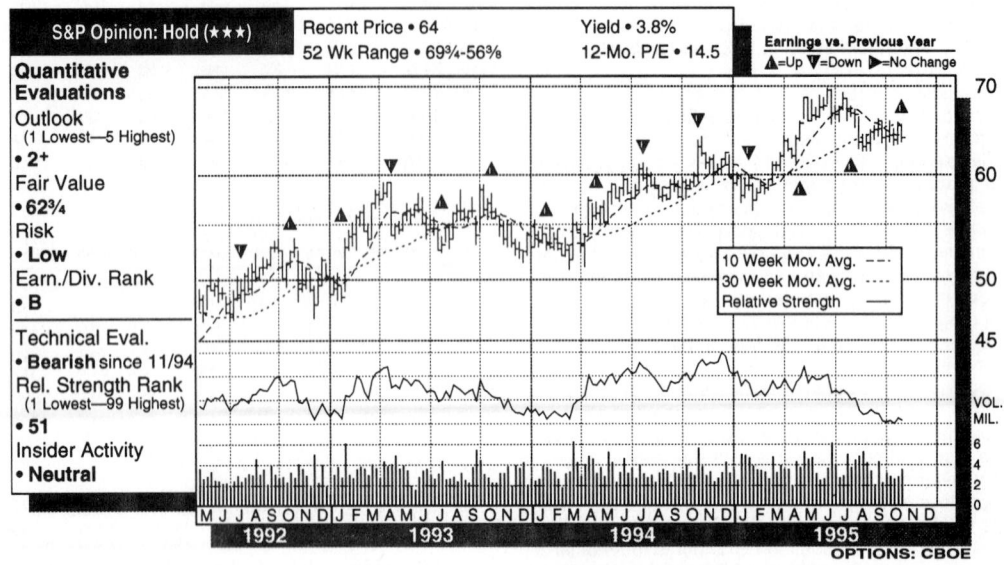

10 Week Mov. Avg. – – –
30 Week Mov. Avg. ‥‥‥
Relative Strength —

OPTIONS: CBOE

Overview - 30-OCT-95

Despite restructuring charges, profits will climb in 1995, paced by chemicals earnings. The company has completed a majority of the work involved in its restructuring, and we believe profitability of its divisions will consequently improve. Expansion in chemicals operations should spur higher earnings in 1995, and stable oil prices should keep margins intact. The outlook is less bright for 1996; chemical earnings will decrease from their peak. Upstream earning should benefit from gradual improvement in natural gas prices forecast through 1997. Downstream, we believe that demand over the next several months will exceed expectations, while industry capacity continues to run at high levels in the U.S. Exploration and development in Alberta should boost earnings in 1995 and 1996.

Valuation - 30-OCT-95

Although the shares are not expected to outperform the market for the remainder of 1995, the dividend should should bolster the stock in the near-term. As long as stable oil and natural gas prices continue to provide robust cash flow to support exploration activities and chemicals segment expansion, the shares should trade within the current range. Amoco's aggressive capital spending jumped to $1.2 billion in the first nine months of 1995, from $739 million in the 1994 perriod. We remain more optimistic about prospects for other companies in this group, which have proven their success at reducing finding and extraction costs on a barrel of oil equivalent basis.

Key Stock Statistics

S&P EPS Est. 1995	4.30	Tang. Bk. Value/Share	29.50
P/E on S&P Est. 1995	14.9	Beta	0.52
S&P EPS Est. 1996	4.65	Shareholders	134,800
Dividend Rate/Share	2.40	Market cap. (B)	$ 31.4
Shs. outstg. (M)	490.9	Inst. holdings	60%
Avg. daily vol. (M)	0.580	Insider holdings	NA

Value of $10,000 invested 5 years ago: $ 14,898

Fiscal Year Ending Dec. 31

	1995	% Change	1994	% Change	1993	% Change
Revenues (Million $)						
1Q	6,756	15%	5,861	-6%	6,233	-1%
2Q	6,814	3%	6,600	2%	6,486	-2%
3Q	7,644	13%	6,760	6%	6,374	-11%
4Q	—	—	5,255	-16%	6,243	-13%
Yr.	—	—	26,048	3%	25,336	-10%
Income (Million $)						
1Q	523.0	31%	398.0	74%	229.0	-25%
2Q	533.0	30%	410.0	-16%	487.0	NM
3Q	599.0	35%	445.0	-14%	520.0	5%
4Q	—	—	536.0	-8%	584.0	7%
Yr.	—	—	1,789	-2%	1,820	114%
Earnings Per Share ($)						
1Q	1.05	31%	0.80	74%	0.46	-25%
2Q	1.08	30%	0.83	-15%	0.98	NM
3Q	1.21	36%	0.89	-15%	1.05	5%
4Q	E0.96	-11%	1.08	-8%	1.17	6%
Yr.	E4.30	19%	3.60	-2%	3.66	114%

Next earnings report expected: late January

Amoco Corp.

Business Summary - 30-OCT-95

Amoco (formerly Standard Oil Co. of Indiana) is a major integrated petroleum and chemical company. A restructuring program was initiated during 1994. Profit contributions by segment in recent years were:

	1994	1993	1992
Exploration & Production	55%	50%	70%
Ref., mkt., & trans.	21%	40%	40%
Chemicals	24%	10%	-10%

Net production of crude oil and natural gas liquids in 1994 averaged 668,000 bbl. a day (678,000 in 1993) and net production of natural gas 4.2 Bcf a day (4.1). Refinery product sales were 1,361,000 b/d (1,312,000 b/d), of which the U.S. represented 86% and Canada 13%. U.S. gasoline sales accounted for 45% of total sales, distillate products for 27%, and other 14%.

Net proved reserves at the end of 1994 were 1,696 million bbl. of crude oil, 509 million bbl. of natural gas liquids, and 18,521 Bcf of natural gas.

The company expects to incur about $200 million in net restructuring costs, in addition to $256 million accrued in the 1994 second quarter. The costs are primarily for system redesign, relocations, work force consolidation, and process redevelopment.

At the end of 1994, Amoco owned or held interests in 59 U.S. natural gas processing plants, of which it operated 33.

The company drilled 41 development and extension wells in the Gulf of Mexico in 1994; 34 were producers. Amoco operated 15 of the wells. The company is committed to several deep water prospects in the Gulf. The Ram/Powell project is expected to begin production in late 1997; the remaining projects are in preliminary stages. Capital and exploration spending for 1995 was projected at $4.2 billion, up from $3.2 billion in 1994.

Important Developments

Oct. '95—The company said it plans to form a limited partnership with Shell Oil Co., combining exploration and production assets in the greater Permian Basin area of West Texas and in southeast New Mexico. Amoco will own 65% of the venture, intended to increase profitability and recoveries from the area.
Aug. '95—Amoco formed a joint venture with FEMSA, the holding company for Oxxo, Mexico's largest convenience store chain (700 sites). In conjunction with Pemex gasoline franchises, the partnership will offer one-stop services of convenience food stores, car washes, quick lubes, and fast-food.

Capitalization

Long Term Debt: $4,223,000,000 (6/95).
Minority Interest: $14,000,000.

Per Share Data ($)

(Year Ended Dec. 31)

	1994	1993	1992	1991	1990	1989
Tangible Bk. Val.	28.97	27.53	26.11	28.52	28.03	26.75
Cash Flow	8.11	8.08	6.63	6.84	8.53	7.97
Earnings	3.60	3.66	1.71	2.36	3.77	3.12
Dividends	2.20	2.20	2.20	2.20	2.04	1.90
Payout Ratio	61%	60%	129%	93%	54%	60%
Prices - High	64⅛	59¼	53¾	55	60⅜	55¾
- Low	50⅞	48⅛	41¾	45⅝	49¼	36¾
P/E Ratio - High	18	16	31	23	16	18
- Low	14	13	24	19	13	12

Income Statement Analysis (Million $)

	1994	%Chg	1993	%Chg	1992	%Chg	1991
Revs.	26,048	3%	25,336	NM	25,280	NM	25,325
Oper. Inc.	4,143	-9%	4,568	31%	3,489	-22%	4,454
Depr.	2,239	2%	2,193	-10%	2,440	9%	2,239
Int. Exp.	318	-6%	338	27%	266	-49%	520
Pretax Inc.	2,491	NM	2,507	150%	1,003	-51%	2,035
Eff. Tax Rate	28%	—	27%	—	15%	—	42%
Net Inc.	1,789	-2%	1,820	114%	850	-28%	1,173

Balance Sheet & Other Fin. Data (Million $)

	1994	1993	1992	1991	1990	1989
Cash	1,789	1,217	1,288	1,583	2,399	1,180
Curr. Assets	6,642	6,094	5,795	6,393	8,216	6,428
Total Assets	29,316	28,486	28,453	30,510	32,209	30,430
Curr. Liab.	5,024	5,343	4,985	6,557	6,799	5,888
LT Debt	4,387	4,037	5,113	4,596	5,249	5,658
Common Eqty.	14,382	13,665	12,960	14,156	14,068	13,684
Total Cap.	21,745	20,718	21,035	22,714	24,047	23,749
Cap. Exp.	2,572	2,817	2,334	3,141	3,021	2,643
Cash Flow	4,028	4,013	3,290	3,412	4,326	4,110

Ratio Analysis

	1994	1993	1992	1991	1990	1989
Curr. Ratio	1.3	1.1	1.2	1.0	1.2	1.1
% LT Debt of Cap.	20.2	19.5	24.3	20.2	21.8	23.8
% Net Inc.of Revs.	6.9	7.2	3.4	4.6	6.8	6.7
% Ret. on Assets	6.2	6.4	2.9	3.8	6.2	5.4
% Ret. on Equity	12.8	13.7	6.3	8.4	13.9	12.0

Dividend Data

—Dividends have been paid since 1894. A dividend reinvestment plan is available.

Amt. of Div. $	Date Decl.	Ex-Div. Date	Stock of Record	Payment Date
0.550	Oct. 25	Nov. 03	Nov. 09	Dec. 10 '94
0.600	Jan. 24	Feb. 02	Feb. 08	Mar. 10 '95
0.600	Apr. 25	May. 04	May. 10	Jun. 10 '95
0.600	Jul. 25	Aug. 07	Aug. 09	Sep. 10 '95
0.600	Oct. 24	Nov. 06	Nov. 08	Dec. 10 '95

Data as orig. reptd.; bef. results of disc. opers. and/or spec. items. Per share data adj. for stk. divs. as of ex-div. date. E-Estimated. NA-Not Available. NM-Not Meaningful. NR-Not Ranked.

Office—200 East Randolph Drive, Chicago, IL 60601. **Tel**—(312) 856-6111. **Chrmn, Pres & CEO**—H. L. Fuller. **EVP & CFO**—J. L. Carl. **Secy**—Patricia A. Brandin. **Investor Contact**—C. K. Koepke. **Dirs**—D. R. Beall, R. S. Block, J. H. Bryan, E. B. Davis, Jr., R. J. Ferris, H. L. Fuller, R. H. Malott, F. A. Maljers, W. E. Massey, M. R. Seger, L. D. Thomas, M. H. Wilson, R. D. Wood. **Transfer Agents & Registrars**—First Chicago Trust Co. of New York, NYC; R-M Trust Co., Toronto. **Incorporated** in Indiana in 1889. **Empl**-43,205. **S&P Analyst:** Raymond J. Deacon

Andrew Corp.

NASDAQ Symbol **ANDW**
In S&P 500

02-OCT-95 **Industry:** Telecommunications

Summary: This company is a global supplier of communications products and systems to commercial, industrial, governmental and military customers.

Quantitative Evaluations		
Outlook (1 Lowest—5 Highest)	Recent Price • 61⅛	Yield • Nil
• **3+**	52 Wk Range • 64½-29⅜	12-Mo. P/E • 39.2

Outlook (1 Lowest—5 Highest)
• **3+**

Fair Value
• **61⅛**

Risk
• **Average**

Earn./Div. Rank
• **B**

Technical Eval.
• **Bullish** since 5/93

Rel. Strength Rank (1 Lowest—99 Highest)
• **57**

Insider Activity
• **Unfavorable**

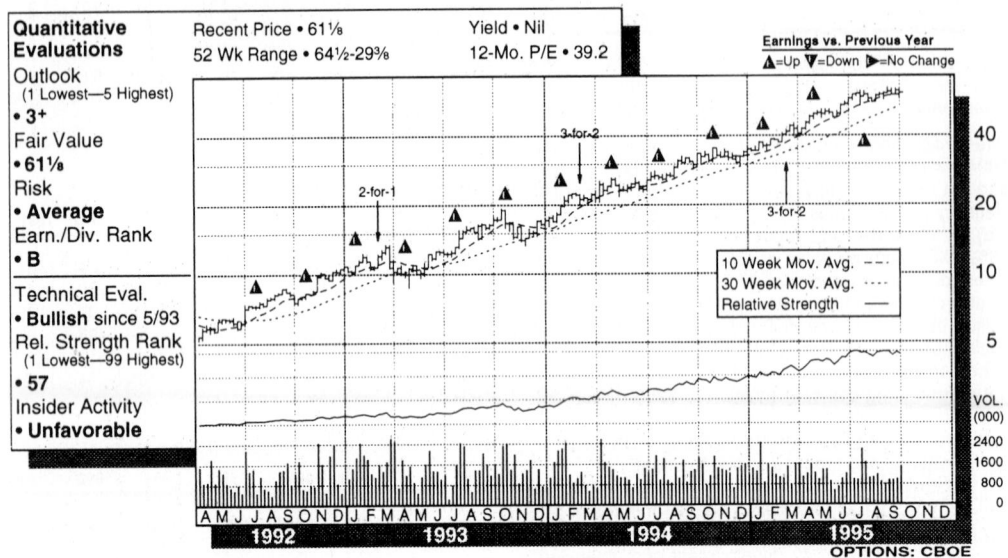

Earnings vs. Previous Year
▲=Up ▼=Down ▶=No Change

10 Week Mov. Avg. -----
30 Week Mov. Avg. ······
Relative Strength —

OPTIONS: CBOE

Business Profile - 02-OCT-95

Andrew continues to be optimistic about the future, especially with products and services for the fast-growth wireless markets, including the emerging personal communications services (PCS). The company expects significant order activity from the PCS market in the second half of calendar 1995. Andrew believes that the wireless communications markets will continue to drive the business in the months and years ahead. The Andrew family controls over 25% of the shares.

Operational Review - 02-OCT-95

Sales for the first nine months of fiscal 1995 increased 15%, year to year, reflecting growth in the international wireless communications market, as well as in the terrestrial microwave and broadcast television markets. Margins widened on a more favorable product mix and more efficient production; pretax income advanced 65%. Including a $1.1 million nonrecurring gain, net income also was up 65%. Total backlog increased 48%, to $151.6 million at June 30, 1995, from $102.4 million a year earlier.

Stock Performance - 29-SEP-95

In the past 30 trading days, ANDW's shares have increased 3%, compared to a 5% rise in the S&P 500. Average trading volume for the past five days was 293,120 shares, compared with the 40-day moving average of 210,290 shares.

Key Stock Statistics

Dividend Rate/Share	Nil	Shareholders	500
Shs. outstg. (M)	38.9	Market cap. (B)	$ 2.4
Avg. daily vol. (M)	0.228	Inst. holdings	58%
Tang. Bk. Value/Share	7.37	Insider holdings	NA
Beta	1.13		

Value of $10,000 invested 5 years ago: $ 112,265

Fiscal Year Ending Sep. 30

	1995	% Change	1994	% Change	1993	% Change
Revenues (Million $)						
1Q	142.6	17%	121.8	21%	101.0	2%
2Q	156.3	10%	142.2	42%	99.9	-8%
3Q	161.3	19%	136.0	23%	110.5	-3%
4Q	—	—	158.6	33%	119.4	NM
Yr.	—	—	558.5	30%	430.8	-3%
Income (Million $)						
1Q	11.23	75%	6.43	35%	4.77	16%
2Q	14.11	55%	9.09	101%	4.53	8%
3Q	18.45	67%	11.07	71%	6.46	10%
4Q	—	—	17.81	47%	12.10	12%
Yr.	—	—	44.40	59%	27.86	11%
Earnings Per Share ($)						
1Q	0.29	70%	0.17	36%	0.12	33%
2Q	0.36	54%	0.23	94%	0.12	23%
3Q	0.47	68%	0.28	66%	0.17	27%
4Q	—	—	0.45	46%	0.31	15%
Yr.	—	—	1.13	56%	0.73	25%

Next earnings report expected: mid November

Business Summary - 02-OCT-95

Andrew Corporation, the successor to a partnership formed in 1937, is a multinational supplier of communications products to commercial, industrial, military and government customers. Its principal products are coaxial cables, special-purpose antennas, microwave antennas, radar and communication reconnaissance systems and connectivity devices.

Contributions to sales in recent fiscal years were:

	1994	1993
Coaxial cable systems & bulk cables	45%	41%
Microwave antenna systems	19%	22%
Special antennas	19%	13%
Earth station antennas	4%	5%
Network products	9%	13%
Defense electronics	3%	5%
Other	1%	1%

International sales accounted for 44% of the total in fiscal 1994.

Coaxial cables are used to carry radio frequency signals, while waveguides (tubular conductors) have their greatest application at higher frequencies, although they are also employed in UHF broadcasting. Semi-flexible cables and waveguides are sold under the trademark HELIAX.

Microwave antenna systems are used in land-based microwave radio networks by the telecommunications industry for telephone, telex, video and data transmission. Other users include pipeline companies, electric utilities and railroads.

Earth station antenna systems are used at land-based terminals to receive signals from, and transmit signals to, communication satellites, for distribution of CATV, UHF and VHF broadcasts. Uses for Andrew's special antennas include cellular systems, FM and TV broadcasting, multipoint distribution services and instructional TV.

Defense electronic products, including electronic scanning and communications receiver systems, are used primarily for intelligence gathering in strategic surveillance operations.

Network products provide connections between different computing systems and are used by businesses, industries and government customers using networked systems.

Important Developments

Jul. '95—Andrew said that orders in the fiscal 1995 third quarter totaled $157.3 million, up 6.4%, year to year. Orders from international markets, including Europe, South America and the Pacific Rim, were particularly strong. Backlog expected to be shipped over the next 12 months was $131.1 million, up 29% from that a year earlier.

Capitalization

Long Term Debt: $49,255,000 (6/95).

Per Share Data ($) (Year Ended Sep. 30)

	1994	1993	1992	1991	1990	1989
Tangible Bk. Val.	6.12	4.73	4.05	3.99	3.52	3.36
Cash Flow	1.70	1.26	1.00	0.90	0.73	0.66
Earnings	1.13	0.72	0.58	0.51	0.40	0.36
Dividends	Nil	Nil	Nil	Nil	Nil	Nil
Payout Ratio	Nil	Nil	Nil	Nil	Nil	Nil
Prices - High	35⅜	19½	10⅞	8⅛	5¾	5⅞
- Low	16	8⅝	5	4½	3½	4
P/E Ratio - High	31	27	19	16	14	16
- Low	14	12	9	9	9	11

Income Statement Analysis (Million $)

	1994	%Chg	1993	%Chg	1992	%Chg	1991
Revs.	558	29%	431	-2%	442	6%	416
Oper. Inc.	98.4	46%	67.3	7%	62.8	9%	57.7
Depr.	21.9	6%	20.7	16%	17.9	3%	17.3
Int. Exp.	5.2	-5%	5.4	-11%	6.1	-6%	6.6
Pretax Inc.	69.4	59%	43.6	9%	40.0	11%	35.9
Eff. Tax Rate	36%	—	36%	—	38%	—	38%
Net Inc.	44.4	59%	27.9	12%	25.0	13%	22.2

Balance Sheet & Other Fin. Data (Million $)

	1994	1993	1992	1991	1990	1989
Cash	40.3	21.7	7.4	17.1	13.8	7.4
Curr. Assets	261	203	190	210	189	166
Total Assets	415	337	314	343	320	266
Curr. Liab.	91.6	63.9	65.4	59.5	53.2	65.9
LT Debt	45.5	50.0	52.6	58.3	63.4	15.6
Common Eqty.	273	220	192	217	199	182
Total Cap.	318	270	245	276	262	198
Cap. Exp.	27.1	17.9	17.8	25.0	25.2	16.3
Cash Flow	66.3	48.5	42.9	39.4	33.3	29.6

Ratio Analysis

	1994	1993	1992	1991	1990	1989
Curr. Ratio	2.8	3.2	2.9	3.5	3.6	2.5
% LT Debt of Cap.	14.3	18.5	21.5	21.1	24.2	7.9
% Net Inc.of Revs.	7.9	6.5	5.7	5.3	5.0	5.4
% Ret. on Assets	11.7	8.4	8.2	6.7	6.3	6.5
% Ret. on Equity	17.9	13.4	13.2	10.7	9.7	9.3

Dividend Data —No cash has been paid. A three-for-two stock split was effected in March 1995.

Amt. of Div. $	Date Decl.	Ex-Div. Date	Stock of Record	Payment Date
3-for-2	Feb. 08	Mar. 09	Feb. 22	Mar. 08 '95

Data as orig. reptd.; bef. results of disc. opers. and/or spec. items. Per share data adj. for stk. divs. as of ex-div. date.
E-Estimated. NA-Not Available. NM-Not Meaningful. NR-Not Ranked.

Office—10500 West 153rd St., Orland Park, IL 60462. **Tel**—(708) 349-3300. **Chrmnm, Pres & CEO**—F. L. English. **VP-Fin, CFO & Investor Contact**—Charles R. Nicholas. **Treas**—M. J. Gittelman. **Secy**—J. F. Petelle. **Dirs**—J. G. Bollinger, J. L. Boyes, G. N. Butzow, K. J. Douglas, F. L. English, D. N. Frey, C. M. Howard, O. J. Wade. **Transfer Agent & Registrar**—Harris Trust & Savings Bank, Chicago. **Incorporated** in Illinois in 1947; reincorporated in Delaware in 1987. **Empl**-3,096. **S&P Analyst:** Alan Aaron

Anheuser-Busch

31-OCT-95 Industry: Beverages

Summary: Anheuser-Busch Cos., Inc. is the parent company of the world's largest brewer, a major bakery goods producer, and an operator of theme parks.

S&P Opinion: Hold (★★★)	Recent Price • 67	Yield • 2.6%
	52 Wk Range • 67⅜-48½	12-Mo. P/E • 16.3

Quantitative Evaluations

Outlook
(1 Lowest—5 Highest)
• **2⁻**

Fair Value
• **63⅞**

Risk
• **Low**

Earn./Div. Rank
• **A+**

Technical Eval.
• **Bullish** since 5/95

Rel. Strength Rank
(1 Lowest—99 Highest)
• **90**

Insider Activity
• **Neutral**

Earnings vs. Previous Year
▲=Up ▼=Down ▶=No Change

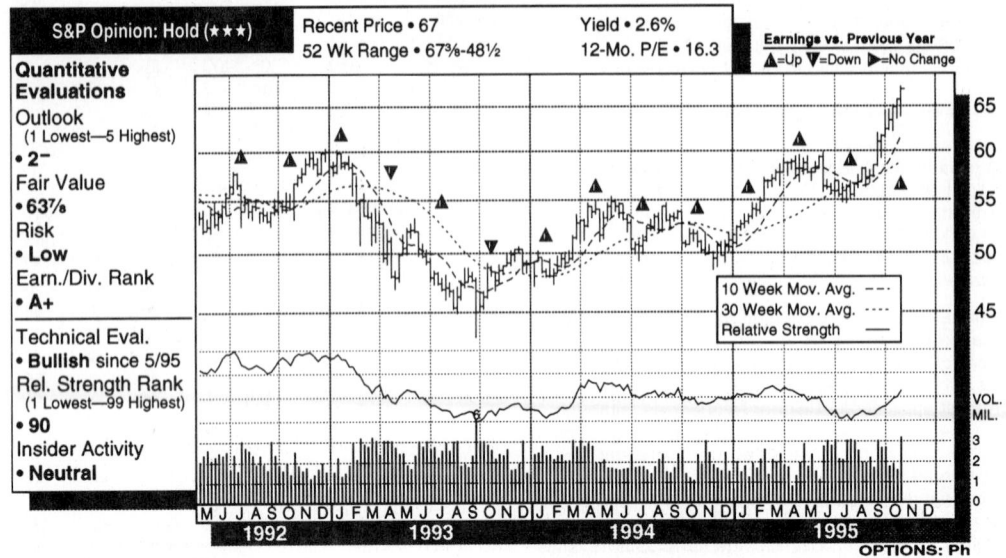

10 Week Mov. Avg. ---
30 Week Mov. Avg. ······
Relative Strength ——

OPTIONS: Ph

Overview - 31-OCT-95

Net sales from ongoing operations should rise at a mid single-digit annual pace through 1996, primarily reflecting modestly greater beer volume. Brewing profit margins are expected to be stable, as benefits from an improved product mix shift (to premium and specialty brews) and cost cutting actions help offset higher brewing and packaging material costs. Also, the planned disposition of various unstrategic company assets (such as the baking, snacks and baseball-related businesses) should allow greater focus and resources behind BUD's core brewing business. Aggressive stock buybacks should continue to boost EPS comparisons.

Valuation - 31-OCT-95

The shares reacted favorably to BUD's late October announcement that it will sell various of its underperforming assets, and further streamline its brewing production system. The moves should allow BUD to become an even more focused and efficient brewer than before. Also, the business disposals should free up a significant amount of funds to be used to better support the company's U.S. brewing business, and to accelerate BUD's push abroad. However, the highly mature U.S. beer market will still pose formidable challenges to BUD's near-term sales growth prospects, and hold earnings per share gains (before special items) to approximately 10% annually over the next few years. The shares are presently adequately valued at about 15 times 1996's $4.50 estimate.

Key Stock Statistics

S&P EPS Est. 1995	4.10	Tang. Bk. Value/Share	15.28
P/E on S&P Est. 1995	16.3	Beta	1.06
S&P EPS Est. 1996	4.50	Shareholders	66,000
Dividend Rate/Share	1.76	Market cap. (B)	$ 17.1
Shs. outstg. (M)	255.5	Inst. holdings	59%
Avg. daily vol. (M)	0.536	Insider holdings	NA

Value of $10,000 invested 5 years ago: $ 20,028

Fiscal Year Ending Dec. 31

	1995	% Change	1994	% Change	1993	% Change
Revenues (Million $)						
1Q	2,757	5%	2,628	5%	2,503	-4%
2Q	3,292	4%	3,169	6%	2,991	1%
3Q	3,436	4%	3,298	4%	3,157	2%
4Q	—	—	2,959	4%	2,854	5%
Yr.	—	—	12,054	5%	11,505	1%
Income (Million $)						
1Q	216.1	6%	204.4	5%	194.1	-10%
2Q	329.1	2%	322.5	5%	308.6	NM
3Q	339.7	3%	329.4	NM	-75.00	NM
4Q	—	—	175.7	5%	166.8	3%
Yr.	—	—	1,032	74%	594.5	-40%
Earnings Per Share ($)						
1Q	0.83	9%	0.76	10%	0.69	-7%
2Q	1.27	5%	1.21	8%	1.12	5%
3Q	1.32	5%	1.26	NM	-0.28	NM
4Q	E0.68	NM	0.68	10%	0.62	7%
Yr.	E4.10	5%	3.91	80%	2.17	-38%

Next earnings report expected: early February

Business Summary - 31-OCT-95

Anheuser-Busch is the largest U.S. brewer. The company is also the parent corporation to a number of subsidiaries that conduct various other businesses. Sales and profit contributions (profits in millions) in 1994 were:

	Sales	Profits
Beer	76%	$1,789
Food products	18%	44
Entertainment	6%	69

Beer brands include Budweiser, Bud Light, Bud Dry Draft, Michelob, Michelob Light, Michelob Dry, Michelob Golden Draft, Busch, Busch Light, Natural Light, Natural Pilsner, King Cobra and O'Doul's (a nonalcoholic malt beverage). The company operates 13 breweries, strategically located across the country, to economically serve its distribution system. Sales in 1994 totaled 88.5 million barrels (up 1.4% from 87.3 million barrels in 1993), or 45.0% of industry sales (44.7% in 1993). Vertically integrated operations include can manufacturing, metalized paper printing and barley malting. Some 96% of barrelage is sold through 900 independent wholesalers.

The food products segment consists mainly of Campbell Taggart Inc., the second largest U.S. producer of bakery goods. Products are marketed mainly under the Colonial, Rainbo or Kilpatricks labels. This segment also includes Eagle Snacks, which produces a line of salted snacks and nut items under the Eagle Snacks and Cape Cod labels.

Entertainment operations include ten theme parks, including Busch Gardens in Florida and Virginia; Sea World parks in Florida, Texas, Ohio and California; and water parks in Florida and Virginia. The segment also includes the St. Louis Cardinals baseball franchise and real estate development interests.

Important Developments

Oct. '95—BUD announced a series of initiatives it would undertake to enhance shareholder value, which, when coupled with its earlier-announced spin-off of Campbell Taggart, would improve its cash position in excess of $200 million. The latest initiatives included: selling BUD's snack food business; consolidating brewing capacity, resulting in the closing of the company's Tampa brewery; selling the St. Louis National baseball club (Cardinals); and lowering beer wholesale inventories in order to achieve greater system-wide efficiencies and reduce costs. Management said that the moves would allow the company to better achieve its three major objectives of increasing its U.S. brewing industry market share, expanding internationally, and supporting the growth of its entertainment and packaging subsidiaries.

Capitalization

Long Term Debt: $3,176,400,000 (6/95).

Per Share Data ($)

(Year Ended Dec. 31)

	1994	1993	1992	1991	1990	1989
Tangible Bk. Val.	15.28	14.08	14.78	13.75	11.14	9.06
Cash Flow	6.28	4.36	5.46	5.12	4.70	4.10
Earnings	3.91	2.17	3.48	3.26	2.96	2.68
Dividends	1.52	1.36	1.20	1.06	0.94	0.80
Payout Ratio	39%	63%	34%	32%	32%	30%
Prices - High	55⅜	60¼	60¾	62	45¼	46
- Low	47⅛	43	51¾	39¼	34	30⅝
P/E Ratio - High	14	28	17	19	15	17
- Low	12	20	15	12	11	11

Income Statement Analysis (Million $)

	1994	%Chg	1993	%Chg	1992	%Chg	1991
Revs.	12,054	5%	11,505	NM	11,394	4%	10,996
Oper. Inc.	2,527	6%	2,385	2%	2,343	4%	2,256
Depr.	628	3%	608	7%	567	6%	534
Int. Exp.	221	6%	208	4%	200	-16%	239
Pretax Inc.	1,707	63%	1,050	-35%	1,615	6%	1,521
Eff. Tax Rate	40%	—	43%	—	38%	—	38%
Net Inc.	1,032	73%	595	-40%	994	6%	940

Balance Sheet & Other Fin. Data (Million $)

	1994	1993	1992	1991	1990	1989
Cash	156	127	215	97.0	95.0	36.0
Curr. Assets	1,862	1,795	1,816	1,628	1,426	1,277
Total Assets	11,045	10,880	10,538	9,987	9,634	9,026
Curr. Liab.	1,669	1,816	1,460	1,403	1,412	1,303
LT Debt	3,078	3,032	2,643	2,645	3,147	3,307
Common Eqty.	4,415	4,255	4,620	4,438	3,679	3,100
Total Cap.	8,752	8,458	8,540	8,584	8,222	7,723
Cap. Exp.	785	777	737	703	899	1,646
Cash Flow	1,660	1,203	1,561	1,474	1,324	1,174

Ratio Analysis

	1994	1993	1992	1991	1990	1989
Curr. Ratio	1.1	1.0	1.2	1.2	1.0	1.0
% LT Debt of Cap.	35.2	35.8	30.9	30.8	38.3	42.8
% Net Inc.of Revs.	8.6	5.2	8.7	8.5	7.8	8.1
% Ret. on Assets	9.6	5.7	9.8	9.5	9.0	9.5
% Ret. on Equity	24.2	13.7	22.2	23.1	24.9	24.8

Dividend Data
Dividends have been paid since 1932. A dividend reinvestment plan is available. A "poison pill" stock purchase right was adopted in 1985.

Amt. of Div. $	Date Decl.	Ex-Div. Date	Stock of Record	Payment Date
0.400	Oct. 26	Nov. 03	Nov. 09	Dec. 09 '94
0.400	Dec. 14	Feb. 03	Feb. 09	Mar. 09 '95
0.400	Apr. 26	May. 03	May. 09	Jun. 09 '95
0.440	Jul. 26	Aug. 07	Sep. 09	Sep. 08 '95
0.440	Oct. 25	Nov. 07	Nov. 09	Dec. 08 '95

Data as orig. reptd.; bef. results of disc. opers. and/or spec. items. Per share data adj. for stk. divs. as of ex-div. date. E-Estimated. NA-Not Available. NM-Not Meaningful. NR-Not Ranked.

Office—1 Busch Place, St. Louis, MO 63118. **Tel**—(314) 577-2000. **Chrmn & Pres**—A. A. Busch III. **EVP & CFO**—J. E. Ritter. **Secy**—JoBeth G. Brown. **Investor Contact**—David Sauerhoff. **Dirs**—P. Aramburuzabala O., R. T. Baker, A. A. Busch III, A. B. Craig III, B. A. Edison, P. M. Flanigan, J. E. Jacob, C. F. Knight, V. R. Loucks, Jr., V. S. Martinez, S. C. Mobley, J. B. Orthwein, D. A. Warner III, W. H. Webster, E. E. Whitacre, Jr. **Transfer Agent & Registrar**—Boatmen's Trust Co., St. Louis. **Incorporated** in Missouri in 1925; reincorporated in Delaware in 1979. **Empl**-42,622. **S&P Analyst:** Kenneth A. Shea

Apple Computer

NASDAQ Symbol **AAPL**

In S&P 500

18-SEP-95

Industry:
Data Processing

Summary: Apple is a leading maker of personal computers and related products. The company has transitioned to a new line of personal computer products powered by the PowerPC microprocessor.

S&P Opinion: Avoid (★★)	Recent Price • 35⅞	Yield • 1.3%
	52 Wk Range • 50⅛-32½	12-Mo. P/E • 9.1

Quantitative Evaluations

Outlook
(1 Lowest—5 Highest)
• **4⁻**

Fair Value
• **47¾**

Risk
• **Average**

Earn./Div. Rank
• **B+**

Technical Eval.
• **Bearish** since 7/95

Rel. Strength Rank
(1 Lowest—99 Highest)
• **2**

Insider Activity
• **Unfavorable**

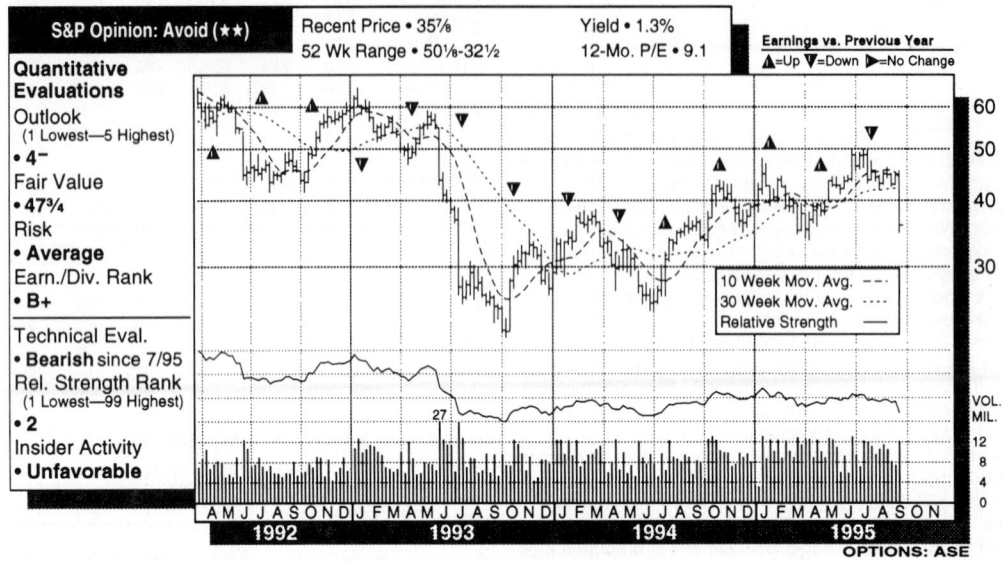

Earnings vs. Previous Year
▲=Up ▼=Down ▶=No Change

10 Week Mov. Avg. — - —
30 Week Mov. Avg. ·········
Relative Strength ———

OPTIONS: ASE

Overview - 18-SEP-95

We have cut our revenue growth expectation for fiscal 1995's fourth quarter to 10% from 20%, due to new product delays and ongoing component shortages. We still believe that revenue growth could approximate 15%-20% in fiscal 1996, as Apple's large installed base upgrades to the new PowerPC systems. However, existing customers could move to Windows 95 depending on its perceived functionality versus Apple's operating system. Gross margins are expected to narrow, reflecting product mix issues near term, and as AAPL seeks to grow its market share. This strategy is entailing a more aggressive pricing stance to compete with Windows/Intel PCs and the licensing of its proprietary OS, which could cannibalize existing products. EPS for fiscal 1996 are expected to be only slightly higher, due to the lower margins.

Valuation - 18-SEP-95

Apple's shares fell sharply on the news that fourth quarter revenues and earnings would fall well below expectations. While the reason for the shortfall appears to be Apple's inability to execute, versus a fundamental slowing in demand, we ultimately believe that it will continue to lose market share in an increasingly Microsoft Windows-dominated world. In addition, we now view the often-rumored takeover possibility of Apple as extremely remote, reflecting the prohibitive price tag ($4.4 billion currently) for what is essentially a niche player in a highly competitive industry. We recommend avoid the shares.

Key Stock Statistics

S&P EPS Est. 1995	3.55	Tang. Bk. Value/Share	23.20
P/E on S&P Est. 1995	10.1	Beta	2.03
S&P EPS Est. 1996	3.60	Shareholders	32,400
Dividend Rate/Share	0.48	Market cap. (B)	$ 4.4
Shs. outstg. (M)	122.7	Inst. holdings	56%
Avg. daily vol. (M)	2.007	Insider holdings	NA

Value of $10,000 invested 5 years ago: $ 10,864

Fiscal Year Ending Sep. 30

	1995	% Change	1994	% Change	1993	% Change
Revenues (Million $)						
1Q	2,832	14%	2,487	24%	2,000	7%
2Q	2,652	28%	2,077	5%	1,974	15%
3Q	2,575	20%	2,150	15%	1,862	7%
4Q	—	—	2,493	16%	2,141	21%
Yr.	—	—	9,189	15%	7,977	13%
Income (Million $)						
1Q	188.0	NM	40.02	-75%	161.3	-3%
2Q	73.00	NM	17.40	-84%	110.9	14%
3Q	103.0	-25%	138.1	NM	-188.0	NM
4Q	—	—	114.7	NM	2.66	-97%
Yr.	—	—	310.2	NM	86.59	-84%
Earnings Per Share ($)						
1Q	1.55	NM	0.34	-74%	1.33	-2%
2Q	0.59	NM	0.15	-84%	0.92	-16%
3Q	0.84	-28%	1.16	NM	-1.63	NM
4Q	E0.60	-37%	0.95	NM	0.02	-98%
Yr.	E3.55	36%	2.61	NM	0.73	-83%

Next earnings report expected: mid October

Business Summary - 18-SEP-95

Apple Computer Inc. makes personal computers and related software and peripherals. Its operating systems are proprietary. In March 1994, Apple launched a new line of computers powered by the PowerPC microprocessor jointly developed by the company, IBM and Motorola. Foreign operations contributed 45% of revenues in each of the past three fiscal years.

The Macintosh product family includes a range of personal computer offerings. The Macintosh LC line is targeted at education and business markets; the Macintosh Performa line is targeted at first-time personal computer users; the Power Macintosh family of computers utilizes the RISC-based PowerPC 601 processor and is generally considered the company's most advanced computer line; and the PowerBook family of notebook-sized personal computers is designed for diverse mobile computing needs. A full line of work group servers and communications products is also available.

During 1994, AAPL introduced eWorld, an on-line service. In January 1995, the company introduced the MessagePad 120, the third generation of its Newton personal digital assistant product. The company also offers a full line of computer peripherals, including printers, disk drives, scanners, modems and color and monochrome monitors.

Operating system software consists of AAPL's proprietary Macintosh system software (System 7.5) and A/UX (the company's implementation of AT&T's UNIX system). Wholly owned Claris Corp. develops and markets applications software.

During 1995, Apple began licensing its proprietary MAC OS to various vendors, including Power Computing Corp. and Radius Inc. In November 1994, Apple, IBM and Motorola reached an agreement on a new common hardware platform for the PowerPC microprocessor allowing users to run a variety of operating systems.

Important Developments

Sep. '95—AAPL said that shipments, revenues and gross margins in fiscal 1995's fourth quarter will be negatively impacted by component shortages, new product delays and pricing pressures on older models. The company also stopped shipments of its newly introduced PowerBook 5300 portable computers due to safety problems with the lithium ion battery. Shipments, when resumed, will include a replacement nickel metal hydride battery.

Aug. '95—The company introduced three new Power Macintosh models, the 7200, 7500 and 8500. These models complement Apple's most powerful model introduced in June, the Power Macintosh 9500. All of the models feature the industry standard Peripheral Component Interconnect (PCI) bus.

Capitalization

Long Term Debt: $303,000,000 (6/30/95).

Per Share Data ($) (Year Ended Sep. 30)

	1994	1993	1992	1991	1990	1989
Tangible Bk. Val.	19.94	17.45	18.46	14.92	12.54	11.77
Cash Flow	4.03	2.12	6.10	4.28	5.39	4.50
Earnings	2.61	0.73	4.33	2.58	3.77	3.53
Dividends	0.48	0.48	0.48	0.48	0.44	0.40
Payout Ratio	18%	64%	11%	19%	12%	11%
Prices - High	43¾	65¼	70	73¼	47¾	50⅜
- Low	24⅝	22	41½	40¼	24¼	32½
P/E Ratio - High	17	89	16	28	13	14
- Low	9	30	10	16	6	9

Income Statement Analysis (Million $)

	1994	%Chg	1993	%Chg	1992	%Chg	1991
Revs.	9,189	15%	7,977	13%	7,087	12%	6,309
Oper. Inc.	563	-6%	597	-42%	1,023	17%	876
Depr.	168	1%	166	-24%	217	6%	204
Int. Exp.	39.7	—	Nil	—	Nil	—	Nil
Pretax Inc.	500	NM	140	-84%	855	71%	500
Eff. Tax Rate	38%	—	38%	—	38%	—	38%
Net Inc.	310	NM	87.0	-84%	530	71%	310

Balance Sheet & Other Fin. Data (Million $)

	1994	1993	1992	1991	1990	1989
Cash	1,258	892	1,436	893	997	809
Curr. Assets	4,476	4,338	3,558	2,864	2,403	2,294
Total Assets	5,303	5,171	4,224	3,494	2,976	2,744
Curr. Liab.	1,944	2,515	1,426	1,217	1,027	895
LT Debt	304	Nil	Nil	Nil	Nil	Nil
Common Eqty.	2,383	2,026	2,187	1,767	1,447	1,486
Total Cap.	3,358	2,656	2,798	2,277	1,949	1,849
Cap. Exp.	160	213	195	218	224	239
Cash Flow	478	253	748	514	678	579

Ratio Analysis

	1994	1993	1992	1991	1990	1989
Curr. Ratio	2.3	1.7	2.5	2.4	2.3	2.6
% LT Debt of Cap.	9.1	Nil	Nil	Nil	Nil	Nil
% Net Inc.of Revs.	3.4	1.1	7.5	4.9	8.5	8.6
% Ret. on Assets	5.8	1.9	13.7	9.5	17.3	18.6
% Ret. on Equity	13.9	4.2	26.8	19.1	33.9	36.1

Dividend Data —Cash payments began in 1987.

Amt. of Div. $	Date Decl.	Ex-Div. Date	Stock of Record	Payment Date
0.120	Nov. 04	Nov. 18	Nov. 25	Dec. 16 '94
0.120	Jan. 26	Feb. 13	Feb. 17	Mar. 10 '95
0.120	Apr. 27	May. 26	Jun. 02	Jun. 23 '95
0.120	Jul. 20	Aug. 16	Aug. 18	Sep. 08 '95

Data as orig. reptd.; bef. results of disc. opers. and/or spec. items. Per share data adj. for stk. divs. as of ex-div. date. E-Estimated. NA-Not Available. NM-Not Meaningful. NR-Not Ranked.

Office—20525 Mariani Ave., Cupertino, CA 95014. **Tel**—(408) 996-1010. **Chrmn—A.** C. Markkula, Jr. **Pres & CEO**—M. H. Spindler. **EVP & CFO**—J. A. Graziano. **Investor Contact**—Bill Slakey (408-974-3488). **Dirs**—G. F. Amelio, P. O. Crisp, B. Goldstein, J. A. Graziano, B. J. Hintz, K. M. Hudson, D. E. Lewis, A. C. Markkula, Jr., M. H. Spindler. **Transfer Agent & Registrar**—First National Bank of Boston. **Incorporated** in California in 1977. **Empl**-11,287. **S&P Analyst:** John D. Coyle, CFA

Applied Materials

NASDAQ Symbol **AMAT**
In S&P 500

18-SEP-95

Industry:
Electronics/Electric

Summary: This company, the world's largest manufacturer of wafer fabrication equipment for the semiconductor industry, produces deposition, etching and ion implantation systems.

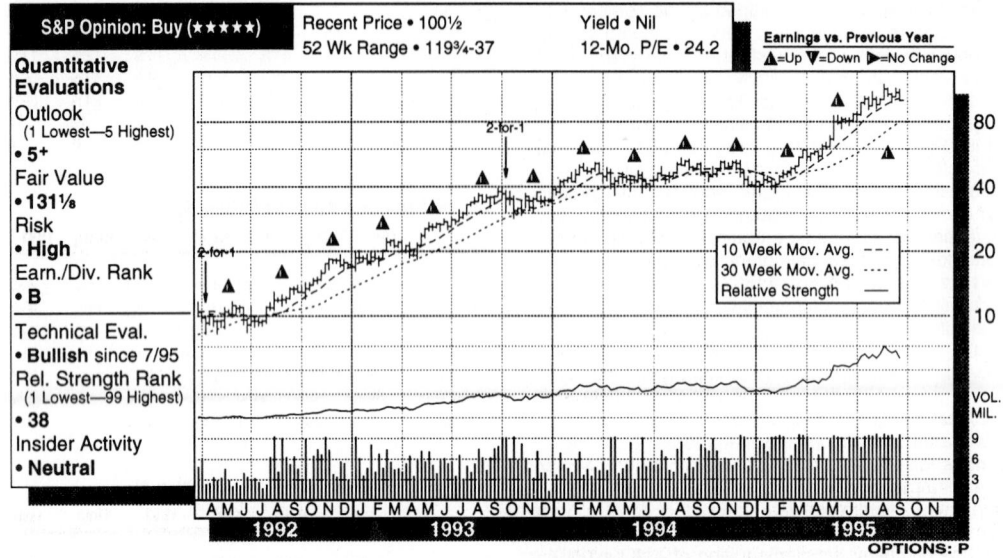

S&P Opinion: Buy (★★★★)	Recent Price • 100½	Yield • Nil
	52 Wk Range • 119¾-37	12-Mo. P/E • 24.2

Quantitative Evaluations

Outlook
(1 Lowest—5 Highest)
• **5+**

Fair Value
• **131⅛**

Risk
• **High**

Earn./Div. Rank
• **B**

Technical Eval.
• **Bullish** since 7/95

Rel. Strength Rank
(1 Lowest—99 Highest)
• **38**

Insider Activity
• **Neutral**

Earnings vs. Previous Year
▲=Up ▼=Down ▶=No Change

10 Week Mov. Avg. – – –
30 Week Mov. Avg. ......
Relative Strength ——

OPTIONS: P

Overview - 18-SEP-95

Fiscal 1996 sales are expected to advance about 50%, as strong demand for semiconductors is elevating worldwide capital spending on new fabs and related semiconductor equipment. Sales in the first half are expected to increase sharply, reflecting a strong backlog position and higher production capacity. We are forecasting more modest growth in the second half, at approximately 30%, which is more in line with projected industry growth rates. Margins are expected to widen, reflecting greater plant efficiencies. Operating expense growth is not expected to keep pace with the sales gains, resulting in additional operating leverage. Long-term prospects should benefit from AMAT's global sales and distribution diversity and new product introductions.

Valuation - 18-SEP-95

We have upgraded the shares to strong buy after AMAT reported third quarter earnings that were much better than expected. Moreover, visibility in the next several quarters is expected to be strong, which should assuage investor concerns about a potential slowdown in the semiconductor business. AMAT is uniquely positioned to benefit from continued capacity expansion that is now occurring in the industry, as it features a broad product line-up and is well diversified in key geographies. With earnings growth of more than 50% expected for fiscal 1996, and some 25%-30% in fiscal 1997, the shares trade at a significant discount to these growth rates. Our six to 12 month target price range is $140-$150.

Key Stock Statistics

S&P EPS Est. 1995	5.10	Tang. Bk. Value/Share	13.58
P/E on S&P Est. 1995	19.7	Beta	2.08
S&P EPS Est. 1996	7.85	Shareholders	1,000
Dividend Rate/Share	Nil	Market cap. (B)	$ 8.9
Shs. outstg. (M)	88.2	Inst. holdings	91%
Avg. daily vol. (M)	2.569	Insider holdings	NA

Value of $10,000 invested 5 years ago: $ 141,052

Fiscal Year Ending Oct. 31

	1995	% Change	1994	% Change	1993	% Change
Revenues (Million $)						
1Q	506.1	49%	340.5	58%	216.0	29%
2Q	675.4	64%	411.3	61%	256.0	42%
3Q	897.7	104%	440.2	56%	281.4	45%
4Q	—	—	467.8	43%	327.4	56%
Yr.	—	—	1,660	54%	1,080	44%
Income (Million $)						
1Q	65.81	76%	37.39	155%	14.69	130%
2Q	93.64	70%	55.07	147%	22.33	138%
3Q	139.2	139%	58.14	106%	28.17	164%
4Q	—	—	63.10	83%	34.51	165%
Yr.	—	—	213.7	114%	99.7	153%
Earnings Per Share ($)						
1Q	0.76	69%	0.45	150%	0.18	100%
2Q	1.08	66%	0.65	141%	0.27	108%
3Q	1.57	131%	0.68	100%	0.34	127%
4Q	E1.65	126%	0.73	74%	0.42	147%
Yr.	E5.10	103%	2.51	107%	1.21	124%

Next earnings report expected: mid November

Business Summary - 18-SEP-95

Applied Materials is the leading producer of wafer fabrication systems for the worldwide semiconductor industry. The company also sells related spare parts and services.

Contributions by geographic area in fiscal 1994 were:

	Sales	Profits
U.S.	37%	36%
Europe	18%	20%
Japan	27%	19%
Asia/Pacific	18%	25%

The company's products are sophisticated systems requiring state-of-the-art technology in wafer processing chemistry and physics, particulate management, automation, process control and software.

A fundamental step in fabricating a semiconductor is deposition, a process of layering either electrically insulating (dielectric) or electrically conductive material on the wafer. The company currently participates in chemical vapor deposition (CVD), physical vapor deposition (PVD) and epitaxial ans polysilicon deposition.

Applied is a leader in etch systems. Before etch processing begins, a wafer is patterned with photoresist during photolithography. Etching then selectively removes material from areas which are not covered by the photoresist.

The company also manufactures ion implantation equipment. During ion implantation, silicon wafers are bombarded by a high-velocity beam of electrically charged ions. These ions penetrate the wafer at selected sites and change the electrical properties of the implanted area.

The company is also a 50% stockholder in Applied Komatsu Technology, Inc., which produces thin film transistor (TFT) manufacturing systems for active-matrix liquid crystal displays.

Important Developments

Sep. '95—AMAT declared a two-for-one stock split on September 14, 1995 for holders of record as of September 26.
Aug. '95—The company announced a shelf registration for up to $266.9 million in medium term notes.
Jul. '95—AMAT was selected by the Malaysian government's ministry of Science and Technology to be a key supplier in the development of that country's semiconductor industry. The company will provide a range of its most advanced Etch, CVD and PVD semiconductor fabrication technologies for a new fab located in Malaysia's capital. Separately, AMAT completed a public offering of 4.025 million common shares at $82.75 a share, including 525,000 shares under an over-allotment option. Proceeds will be used for general corporate purposes.

Capitalization

Long Term Debt: $231,103,000 (7/95).

Per Share Data ($) (Year Ended Oct. 31)

	1994	1993	1992	1991	1990	1989
Tangible Bk. Val.	11.49	7.45	6.06	4.82	4.52	3.92
Cash Flow	3.20	1.67	0.93	0.74	0.74	0.95
Earnings	2.51	1.21	0.54	0.38	0.50	0.77
Dividends	Nil	Nil	Nil	Nil	Nil	Nil
Payout Ratio	Nil	Nil	Nil	Nil	Nil	Nil
Prices - High	54½	40	19⅜	9½	10⅛	8¼
- Low	36¼	16⅛	8⅛	4⅞	4⅛	5⅜
P/E Ratio - High	22	33	36	25	20	11
- Low	14	13	15	13	8	7

Income Statement Analysis (Million $)

	1994	%Chg	1993	%Chg	1992	%Chg	1991
Revs.	1,660	54%	1,080	44%	751	18%	639
Oper. Inc.	396	99%	199	107%	96.1	26%	76.5
Depr.	58.5	55%	37.8	36%	27.7	13%	24.5
Int. Exp.	16.0	13%	14.2	-7%	15.2	9%	14.0
Pretax Inc.	331	121%	150	155%	58.9	46%	40.4
Eff. Tax Rate	35%	—	34%	—	33%	—	35%
Net Inc.	214	115%	100	152%	39.5	51%	26.2

Balance Sheet & Other Fin. Data (Million $)

	1994	1993	1992	1991	1990	1989
Cash	422	266	223	140	72.0	107
Curr. Assets	1,231	776	582	434	367	343
Total Assets	1,703	1,120	854	661	558	434
Curr. Liab.	496	381	248	200	195	143
LT Debt	209	121	118	124	54.0	29.0
Common Eqty.	966	599	474	325	300	254
Total Cap.	1,187	727	599	456	362	290
Cap. Exp.	186	99	67.0	67.0	111	43.0
Cash Flow	272	137	67.2	50.7	50.5	63.6

Ratio Analysis

	1994	1993	1992	1991	1990	1989
Curr. Ratio	2.5	2.0	2.3	2.2	1.9	2.4
% LT Debt of Cap.	17.6	16.7	19.8	27.2	14.8	10.2
% Net Inc.of Revs.	12.9	9.2	5.3	4.1	6.0	10.3
% Ret. on Assets	14.9	10.0	4.9	4.3	6.8	13.2
% Ret. on Equity	26.8	18.4	9.3	8.3	12.1	22.4

Dividend Data

No cash has been paid. A two-for-one stock split was declared on September 14, 1995. Two-for-one stock splits were effected in 1993, 1992 and 1986. A "poison pill" stock purchase rights plan was adopted in 1989.

Amt. of Div. $	Date Decl.	Ex-Div. Date	Stock of Record	Payment Date
2-for-1	Sep. 14	Oct. 13	Sep. 26	Oct. 12 '95

Data as orig. reptd.; bef. results of disc. opers. and/or spec. items. Per share data adj. for stk. divs. as of ex-div. date.
E-Estimated. NA-Not Available. NM-Not Meaningful. NR-Not Ranked.

Office—3050 Bowers Ave., Santa Clara, CA 95054-3299. **Tel**—(408) 727-5555. **Chrmn & CEO**—J. C. Morgan. **Pres**—D. Maydan. **SVP, CFO & Investor Contact**—Gerald F. Taylor. **Secy**—D. A. Slichter. **Treas**—Nancy H. Handel. **Dirs**—M. Armacost, J. W. Bagley, H. M. Dwight Jr., G. B. Farnsworth, P. V. Gerdine, P. R. Low, D. Maydan, J. C. Morgan, A. J. Stein, H. Toyoda. **Transfer Agent**—Harris Trust Co. of California, LA. **Incorporated** in California in 1967; reincorporated in Delaware in 1987. **Empl**-6,497. **S&P Analyst:** John D. Coyle, CFA

STANDARD & POOR'S
STOCK REPORTS

Archer-Daniels-Midland

NYSE Symbol **ADM**
In S&P 500

19-OCT-95

Industry:
Food

Summary: This company is a major processor and merchandiser of agricultural commodities, including oilseeds, corn and wheat.

S&P Opinion: Hold (★★★)	Recent Price • 15¾	Yield • 0.6%
	52 Wk Range • 20⅛-14¼	12-Mo. P/E • 10.4

Quantitative Evaluations

Outlook
(1 Lowest—5 Highest)
• **2+**

Fair Value
• **15⅛**

Risk
• **Low**

Earn./Div. Rank
• **A+**

Technical Eval.
• **Bearish** since 6/95

Rel. Strength Rank
(1 Lowest—99 Highest)
• **47**

Insider Activity
• **Neutral**

Earnings vs. Previous Year
▲=Up ▼=Down ▶=No Change

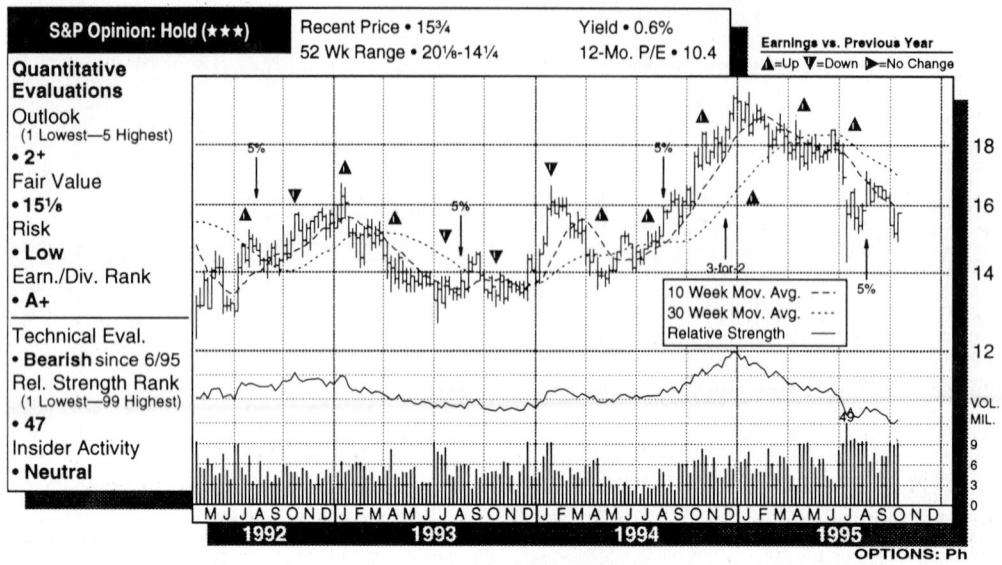

10 Week Mov. Avg. – – –
30 Week Mov. Avg. · · · ·
Relative Strength ——

OPTIONS: Ph

Overview - 19-OCT-95

Sales are expected to rise at a mid single-digit pace in fiscal 1996, driven principally by higher selling prices. With reduced U.S. grain crop sizes and the resultant higher costs of goods sold, pressures on margins are expected to restrain profits during the fiscal year. These pressures should be offset somewhat by increasing export sales and an improving product mix shift that increasingly emphasizes more profitable value-added bioproducts. However, earnings per share in fiscal 1996 are likely to be held in line with record year-earlier results. A more aggressive stance toward share buybacks should be a modest contributing factor to earnings per share.

Valuation - 19-OCT-95

Despite ADM's favorable long-term growth prospects, we believe that the recent government probe into possible company anti-competitive business practices will limit near-term share performance. We expect ADM to achieve steady, albeit unspectacular, earnings growth over the long term, driven principally by growing global demand for the company's grain-based food ingredient products. And, although uncertainties are inherent for constantly changing agricultural market conditions, ADM has shown it is able to grow earnings at a solid pace over the long term. Finances are very sound, which allows the company substantial flexibility with regard to acquisition and/or capital project opportunities. Near-term uncertainties, however, warrant a cautious stance.

Key Stock Statistics

S&P EPS Est. 1996	1.45	Tang. Bk. Value/Share	10.99
P/E on S&P Est. 1996	10.9	Beta	0.96
Dividend Rate/Share	0.09	Shareholders	34,400
Shs. outstg. (M)	532.5	Market cap. (B)	$ 8.6
Avg. daily vol. (M)	2.111	Inst. holdings	52%
		Insider holdings	NA

Value of $10,000 invested 5 years ago: $ 14,012

Fiscal Year Ending Jun. 30

	1996	% Change	1995	% Change	1994	% Change
Revenues (Million $)						
1Q	—	—	3,015	15%	2,614	10%
2Q	—	—	3,222	14%	2,822	11%
3Q	—	—	3,300	10%	3,010	23%
4Q	—	—	3,135	7%	2,929	21%
Yr.	—	—	12,672	11%	11,374	16%
Income (Million $)						
1Q	163.1	6%	154.5	124%	69.06	-45%
2Q	—	—	220.1	51%	146.1	-6%
3Q	—	—	195.7	49%	131.3	1%
4Q	—	—	225.6	64%	137.7	11%
Yr.	—	—	795.9	64%	484.1	-9%
Earnings Per Share ($)						
1Q	0.31	9%	0.29	125%	0.13	-43%
2Q	E0.39	-5%	0.41	54%	0.27	-2%
3Q	E0.35	-3%	0.36	50%	0.24	5%
4Q	E0.39	-7%	0.42	65%	0.25	17%
Yr.	E1.45	-2%	1.48	67%	0.89	-6%

Next earnings report expected: late October

Archer-Daniels-Midland

Business Summary - 18-OCT-95

Archer-Daniels-Midland is primarily engaged in the processing and merchandising of raw agricultural commodities, largely used in the production of consumer foods and beverages. Revenue contributions in recent fiscal years:

	1994-95	1993-94
Oilseed	60%	50%
Corn	20%	26%
Wheat flour	11%	13%
Other	9%	11%

Foreign operations accounted for 28% of net sales and 10% of operating profits in fiscal 1995.

Soybeans, cottonseed, sunflower seeds, canola, peanuts, flaxseed and corn germ are processed to provide vegetable oils and meals principally for the food and feed industries. Crude vegetable oil is sold to others or refined and hydrogenated to produce oils for margarine, shortening, salad oils and other food products.

Corn wet milling products include syrup, starch, glucose, dextrose, crystalline dextrose, high fructose sweeteners, crystalline fructose, corn gluten feed and ethyl alcohol. Dry milled products include ethanol, distilled grains, meal and grits. The most important uses for the company's various corn products are in the food, beverage and pet food industries.

Wheat flour is sold primarily to large bakeries; durum flour is sold primarily to pasta manufacturers; bulgur, a gelatinized wheat food, is sold to both domestic and export food markets.

Other operations include grain merchandising; production of barley malt, cane sugar, animal feeds and various consumer foods; and other products for industrial markets.

Important Developments

Oct. '95—Based on a brief report, net income during fiscal 1996's first quarter rose 5.5%, year to year, to $163.1 million ($0.31 per share), from $154.5 million ($0.28). The results are adjusted for the 5% stock dividend paid in September 1995.

Jul. '95—ADM's gross profits increased by $505 million in fiscal 1995, to $1.6 billion, led by the combined effect of increased sales volumes, higher average selling prices and lower raw material commodity prices. Separately, ADM received a subpoena for documents and testimony concerning certain of its marketing practices, pursuant to a federal grand jury investigation of possible anti-trust law violations.

Capitalization

Long Term Debt: $2,070,095,000 (6/95).

Per Share Data ($)

(Year Ended Jun. 30)

	1995	1994	1993	1992	1991	1990
Tangible Bk. Val.	11.73	9.76	8.63	8.13	7.09	6.27
Cash Flow	2.18	1.54	1.52	1.41	1.28	1.28
Earnings	1.48	0.89	0.94	0.89	0.82	0.85
Dividends	0.10	0.06	0.06	0.54	0.05	0.05
Payout Ratio	7%	7%	6%	6%	6%	5%
Prices - High	20	20⅛	16⅝	18	18¼	13½
- Low	14¼	13½	12⅞	12¼	9⅝	9⅛
P/E Ratio - High	14	23	18	20	22	16
- Low	10	15	13	14	12	11

Income Statement Analysis (Million $)

	1995	%Chg	1994	%Chg	1993	%Chg	1992
Revs.	12,672	11%	11,374	16%	9,811	6%	9,232
Oper. Inc.	1,598	43%	1,121	5%	1,067	2%	1,042
Depr.	385	9%	354	8%	329	12%	294
Int. Exp.	203	2%	199	14%	174	27%	137
Pretax Inc.	1,182	60%	738	-1%	746	-2%	760
Eff. Tax Rate	33%	—	34%	—	28%	—	34%
Net Inc.	796	64%	484	-10%	535	6%	504

Balance Sheet & Other Fin. Data (Million $)

	1995	1994	1993	1992	1991	1990
Cash	1,119	1,335	1,868	1,403	891	829
Curr. Assets	3,713	3,911	3,922	3,213	2,532	2,304
Total Assets	9,757	8,747	8,404	7,525	6,261	5,450
Curr. Liab.	1,172	1,127	960	937	857	676
LT Debt	2,070	2,021	2,039	1,562	980	751
Common Eqty.	5,854	5,045	4,883	4,492	3,922	3,573
Total Cap.	8,463	7,499	7,336	6,540	5,355	4,728
Cap. Exp.	559	514	394	480	468	327
Cash Flow	1,181	839	863	797	728	732

Ratio Analysis

	1995	1994	1993	1992	1991	1990
Curr. Ratio	3.2	3.5	4.1	3.4	3.0	3.4
% LT Debt of Cap.	24.5	27.0	27.8	23.9	18.3	15.9
% Net Inc.of Revs.	6.3	4.3	5.4	5.5	5.5	6.2
% Ret. on Assets	8.7	5.6	6.6	7.3	8.1	9.5
% Ret. on Equity	14.8	9.8	11.3	12.0	12.6	14.6

Dividend Data —Dividends have been paid since 1927.

Amt. of Div. $	Date Decl.	Ex-Div. Date	Stock of Record	Payment Date
0.025	Oct. 20	Oct. 31	Nov. 04	Nov. 28 '94
0.025	Jan. 23	Jan. 30	Feb. 03	Feb. 27 '95
0.025	Apr. 20	May. 01	May. 05	May. 30 '95
0.025	Jul. 19	Aug. 02	Aug. 04	Aug. 28 '95
5%	Jul. 19	Aug. 17	Aug. 21	Sep. 18 '95

Data as orig. reptd.; bef. results of disc. opers. and/or spec. items. Per share data adj. for stk. divs. as of ex-div. date. E-Estimated. NA-Not Available. NM-Not Meaningful. NR-Not Ranked.

Office—4666 Faries Parkway (Box 1470), Decatur, IL 62525. **Tel**—(217) 424-5200. **Chrmn & CEO**—D. O. Andreas. **Pres**—J. R. Randall. **VP & CFO**—D. J. Schmalz. **VP & Secy**—R. P. Reising. **Dirs**—D. O. Andreas, L. W. Andreas, M. D. Andreas, M. L. Andreas, S. M. Archer, Jr., R. Bruce, G. O. Coan, J. H. Daniels, R. A. Goldberg, H. D. Hale, F. R. Johnson, B. Mulrooney, J. R. Randall, Mrs. N. A. Rockefeller, R. S. Strauss, J. K. Vanier, O. G. Webb. **Transfer Agent & Registrar**—Harris Trust and Savings Bank, Chicago. **Incorporated** in Delaware in 1923. **Empl**-14,833. **S&P Analyst:** Kenneth A. Shea

STOCK REPORTS

Armco Inc.

NYSE Symbol **AS**
In S&P 500

19-SEP-95

Industry:
Steel-Iron

Summary: Armco is the second largest U.S. producer of stainless flat-rolled steels and the largest producer of electrical steels. It also makes carbon steels and steel products.

S&P Opinion: Hold (★★★)	Recent Price • 6½ — Yield • Nil
	52 Wk Range • 7¾-5⅞ — 12-Mo. P/E • 12.3

Earnings vs. Previous Year
▲=Up ▼=Down ▶=No Change

Quantitative Evaluations

Outlook
(1 Lowest—5 Highest)
• 1⁻

Fair Value
• 3½

Risk
• Average

Earn./Div. Rank
• C

Technical Eval.
• **Bullish** since 9/95

Rel. Strength Rank
(1 Lowest—99 Highest)
• 39

Insider Activity
• **Neutral**

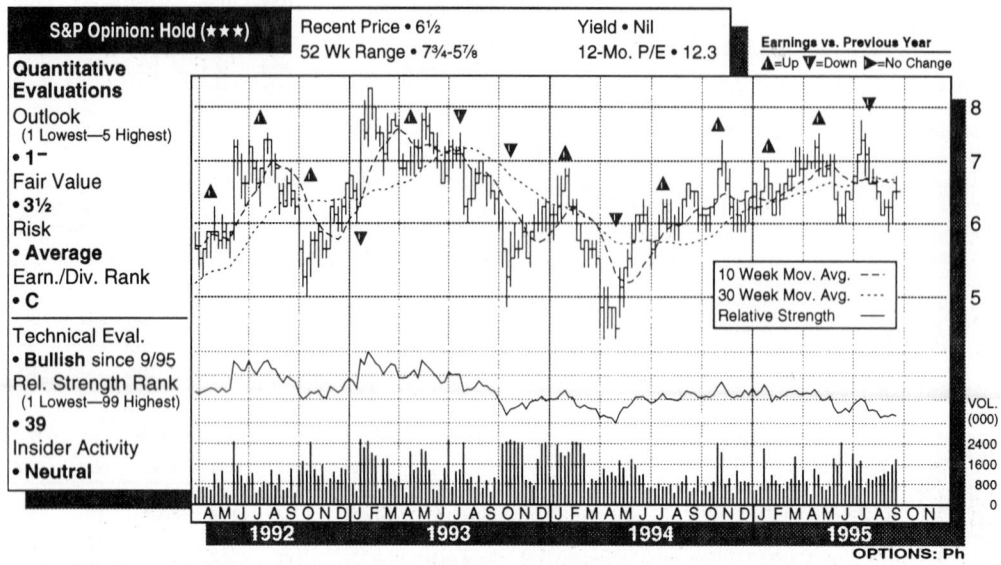

10 Week Mov. Avg. - - -
30 Week Mov. Avg. · · · ·
Relative Strength ——

VOL.
(000)
2400
1600
800
0

OPTIONS: Ph

Overview - 19-SEP-95

We anticipate a 10% rise in sales in 1996, mostly reflecting continued gains in volume and prices in specialty flat rolled and contributions from the refurbished Mansfield plant. To a lesser extent, sales will be lifted by contributions from Douglas Dynamics and a better market for products made by Sawhill Tubular. Aided by an expected increase in prices for both stainless and carbon sheet, greater capacity utilization at all facilities, the likely absence of equipment failures, a return to profitability at Mansfield and only moderate increases in raw material costs, earnings should increase in 1996. The company's long-term sales and earnings growth will benefit from strong secular demand for stainless flat roll, contributions from the reequipped Mansfield plant, possible asset sales and reduction of debt.

Valuation - 19-SEP-95

Despite Armco's appeal as a speculative turnaround play, we continue to rank the shares a hold primarily due to our concern the flat roll stainless market has peaked near term as a result of a slower growing economy and overstocking of inventory by end users. Also, the recent equipment failures at the Mansfield and Butler plants confirm our fears that the company is still capable of negative surprises and diminish near term earnings prospects. We still believe Armco has strong upside potential once everything falls into place, but we prefer to take a wait and see attitude near term.

Key Stock Statistics

S&P EPS Est. 1995	0.15	Tang. Bk. Value/Share	NM
P/E on S&P Est. 1995	43.3	Beta	1.56
S&P EPS Est. 1996	0.80	Shareholders	34,700
Dividend Rate/Share	Nil	Market cap. (B)	$0.703
Shs. outstg. (M)	106.1	Inst. holdings	74%
Avg. daily vol. (M)	0.304	Insider holdings	NA

Value of $10,000 invested 5 years ago: $ 6,519

Fiscal Year Ending Dec. 31

	1995	% Change	1994	% Change	1993	% Change
Revenues (Million $)						
1Q	368.4	-3%	379.6	-11%	427.0	17%
2Q	390.6	10%	354.9	-22%	454.0	-17%
3Q	—	—	368.0	-12%	419.8	-29%
4Q	—	—	335.1	-8%	363.5	-36%
Yr.	—	—	1,438	-14%	1,664	-20%
Income (Million $)						
1Q	2.40	NM	-27.20	NM	-21.10	NM
2Q	35.90	-49%	69.90	NM	-1.40	NM
3Q	—	—	25.40	NM	-188.0	NM
4Q	—	—	9.60	NM	-45.70	NM
Yr.	—	—	77.70	NM	-256.2	NM
Earnings Per Share ($)						
1Q	-0.02	NM	-0.30	NM	-0.25	NM
2Q	0.30	-52%	0.63	NM	-0.06	NM
3Q	E-0.09	NM	0.20	NM	-1.85	NM
4Q	E-0.04	NM	0.05	NM	-0.48	NM
Yr.	E0.15	-74%	0.57	NM	-2.64	NM

Next earnings report expected: mid October

Business Summary - 19-SEP-95

Armco is a diversified maker of carbon and specialty steels and related products. Contributions (profits in million $) by segment in 1994 were as follows:

	Sales	Profits
Specialty flat rolled steel	73%	$126.3
Other steel and fabricated products	27%	-54.9

Specialty flat rolled steel includes businesses that produce stainless and electrical steel sheet and strips and stainless plate through Eastern Stainless Corp. (subsequently divested in late 1994). Raw steelmaking facilities are concentrated in Butler, Pa., with a melt capacity of some 875,000 tons at 1994's year end. Finishing operations are conducted at Butler, Coshocton and Zanesville, Ohio.

Since the acquisition of Cyclops in 1992 some 70% of AS's sales of specialty flat rolled steel have been stainless steel and 30% have been electrical steel. Segment sales by market in 1994 were: automotive, 41%; industrial and electrial equipment, 36%; service centers, 9%; appliance, utensils and cutlery, 3%; other, 11%.

Other steel and fabricated products include steelmaking, fabricating and process plants in Pennsylvania and Ohio; steel tubing companies; a nonresidential construction company and a snowplow manufacturer.

Sales by product line in 1994 were: sheet and strip, 66%; pipe and tubing, 13%; semi-finished steel, 5%; plate, 4%; construction products, 2%; other, 10%.

National Oil-Well, AS's 50% owned joint venture with USX Corp., makes oil field tubular pipe, process pumps and drilling and production equipment used in the oil and gas industry.

Important Developments

Aug. '95—AS announced that unexpected equipment failure at its Mansfield, Ohio, specialty steel plant and hot strip problems at its Butler, Pa. plant will result in lower shipments in both the third and fourth quarters and have an adverse impact on earnings.

May '95— AS and USX Corp. announced that they had signed a letter of intent to sell their jointly owned National-Oilwell partnership. The sale was expected to close during 1995's third quarter. Other terms of the proposed sale were not disclosed.

May '95— AS announced the sale of its stake in AK Steel Holding Corp. AS stated that transaction would yield net proceeds of $27.2 million and also result in a $0.24 gain in 1995's second quarter.

Capitalization

Long Term Debt: $375,400,000 (6/95).

$2.10 Conv.Pfd.Stock: 1,697,231 shs. (no par); red. at $40; conv. into 1.27 com.

$3.625 Conv. Pfd. Stock: 2,700,000 shs. (no par); red at $40; conv. into 6.78 com.

$4.50 Conv. Pfd. Stock: 999,900 shs. ($1 par); conv. into 2.22 com.

Per Share Data ($) (Year Ended Dec. 31)

	1994	1993	1992	1991	1990	1989
Tangible Bk. Val.	-5.57	-6.59	0.94	5.02	9.31	10.76
Cash Flow	1.10	-2.06	-3.79	-3.38	-0.26	2.90
Earnings	0.57	-2.64	-4.37	-3.89	-0.71	2.28
Dividends	Nil	Nil	Nil	Nil	0.40	0.30
Payout Ratio	Nil	Nil	Nil	Nil	NM	13%
Prices - High	7⅜	8⅜	7½	6¼	11¼	13½
- Low	4½	4⅞	4¼	4	3⅞	9½
P/E Ratio - High	13	NM	NM	NM	NM	6
- Low	8	NM	NM	NM	NM	4

Income Statement Analysis (Million $)

	1994	%Chg	1993	%Chg	1992	%Chg	1991
Revs.	1,438	-14%	1,664	-20%	2,074	30%	1,595
Oper. Inc.	130	63%	80.0	-17%	96.0	12%	86.0
Depr.	56.0	-7%	60.0	3%	58.0	29%	45.0
Int. Exp.	38.0	-14%	44.0	-14%	51.0	-39%	84.0
Pretax Inc.	49.0	NM	-263	NM	-453	NM	-335
Eff. Tax Rate	NM	—	NM	—	NM	—	NM
Net Inc.	78.0	NM	-255	NM	-421	NM	-336

Balance Sheet & Other Fin. Data (Million $)

	1994	1993	1992	1991	1990	1989
Cash	229	184	182	333	189	477
Curr. Assets	649	625	784	666	642	884
Total Assets	1,935	1,905	1,960	1,847	2,294	2,489
Curr. Liab.	390	353	472	375	479	427
LT Debt	364	380	403	355	367	423
Common Eqty.	-428	-523	132	484	824	951
Total Cap.	145	76.0	763	927	1,290	1,474
Cap. Exp.	87.0	54.0	68.0	43.0	70.0	170
Cash Flow	116	-213	-373	-298	-23.0	256

Ratio Analysis

	1994	1993	1992	1991	1990	1989
Curr. Ratio	1.7	1.8	1.7	1.8	1.3	2.1
% LT Debt of Cap.	250.4	497.6	52.8	38.3	28.4	28.7
% Net Inc.of Revs.	5.4	NM	NM	NM	NM	8.7
% Ret. on Assets	4.0	NM	NM	NM	NM	7.9
% Ret. on Equity	NM	NM	NM	NM	NM	22.8

Dividend Data —Common dividends were omitted in January 1991, after having been resumed in April 1989. The most recent payment was $0.10 in January 1991. Dividends have been maintained on the preferred stock. A "poison pill" stock purchase rights plan was adopted in 1986.

Data as orig. reptd.; bef. results of disc. opers. and/or spec. items. Per share data adj. for stk. divs. as of ex-div. date.
E-Estimated. NA-Not Available. NM-Not Meaningful. NR-Not Ranked.

Office—1 Oxford Center, 301 Grant St., Pittsburgh, PA 15219-1415. **Tel**—(412) 255-9800. **Chrmn**—J. C. Haley. **Pres & CEO**—J. F. Will. **VP-Treasurer**—J. L. Bertsch. **VP-Secy**—G. R. Hildreth. **Investor Contact**—Frederick P. O'Brien. **Dirs**— J. J. Burns Jr., D. A. Duke, J. C. Haley, P. H. Henson Jr., B. E. Robbins, B. R. Roberts, J. D. Turner, J. F. Will. **Transfer Agent & Registrar**—Fifth Third Bank, Cincinnati, Ohio. **Incorporated** in Ohio in 1917. **Empl**-5,500. **S&P Analyst:** Leo Larkin

Armstrong World Industries

NYSE Symbol **ACK**
In S&P 500

29-SEP-95

Industry:
Home Furnishings

Summary: Armstrong is a leading producer of interior furnishings, including floor coverings, ceiling materials and furniture, for renovation/remodeling and new construction markets.

S&P Opinion: Accumulate (★★★★)	Recent Price • 57	Yield • 2.6%
	52 Wk Range • 60½-36	12-Mo. P/E • 11.7

Quantitative Evaluations

Outlook
(1 Lowest—5 Highest)
• **2⁻**

Fair Value
• **53½**

Risk
• **Average**

Earn./Div. Rank
• **B+**

Technical Eval.
• **Bullish** since 7/95

Rel. Strength Rank
(1 Lowest—99 Highest)
• **36**

Insider Activity
• **Neutral**

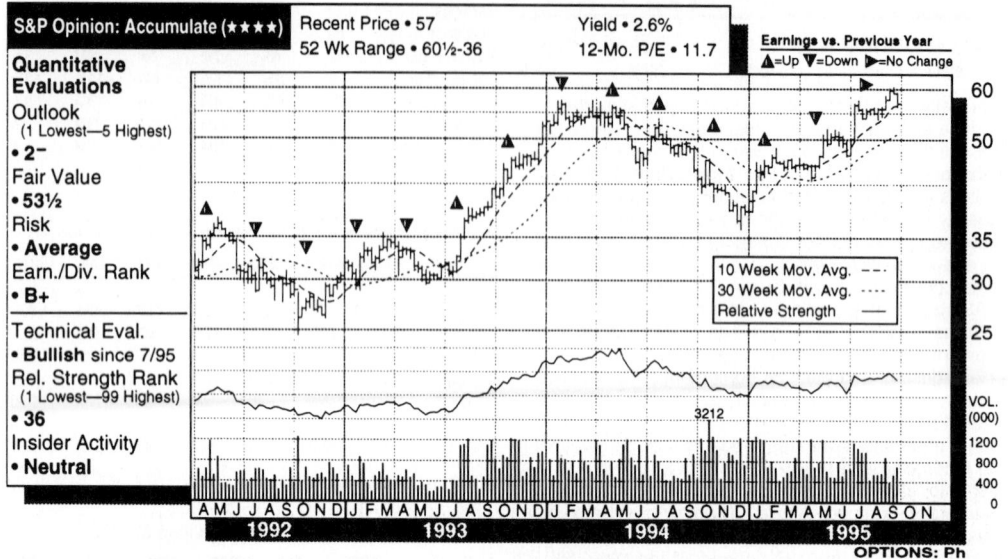

Earnings vs. Previous Year ▲=Up ▼=Down ▶=No Change

10 Week Mov. Avg. - - -
30 Week Mov. Avg. ....
Relative Strength —

3212

VOL. (000)

OPTIONS: Ph

Overview - 28-SEP-95

Sales for 1995 should rise on higher volume at all businesses, reflecting increased share, new products, improved marketing capabilities, and a focus on developing information technologies. A stronger housing market in the U.S., stimulated by lower mortgage rates in mid-1995, should aid demand for residential products. Non-residential products should continue to benefit from stronger European economies. Despite competitive pressures and higher raw material prices, which will be partially offset by higher selling prices, margins should expand on efforts to control expenses including switching suppliers, consolidating operations, reducing scrap, and renegotiating supply contracts. Primary share earnings will be hurt by a one-time restructuring charge of $0.27 and the absence of $0.49 in one-time gains.

Valuation - 28-SEP-95

These shares have maintained their recovery after declining in 1994's second half. We attribute this performance to a strong earnings outlook for 1995 and 1996. ACK's profits (which we estimate on a primary basis) should benefit from stronger domestic nonresidential and European markets, as well as improved demand for residential products in the U.S., thanks to the improved housing market. Results will be enhanced by the company's focus on improving its financial performance. Based on our estimates for 1996, we now consider shares in ACK undervalued, and have raised our opinion on the stock from hold to accumulate.

Key Stock Statistics

S&P EPS Est. 1995	5.15	Tang. Bk. Value/Share	12.70
P/E on S&P Est. 1995	11.1	Beta	1.65
S&P EPS Est. 1996	5.80	Shareholders	8,600
Dividend Rate/Share	1.44	Market cap. (B)	$ 2.1
Shs. outstg. (M)	37.2	Inst. holdings	81%
Avg. daily vol. (M)	0.119	Insider holdings	NA

Value of $10,000 invested 5 years ago: $ 18,574

Fiscal Year Ending Dec. 31

	1995	% Change	1994	% Change	1993	% Change
Revenues (Million $)						
1Q	699.6	9%	642.7	5%	611.9	-4%
2Q	731.4	6%	689.3	10%	629.0	-4%
3Q	—	—	715.3	8%	660.1	NM
4Q	—	—	705.4	13%	624.4	—
Yr.	—	—	2,753	9%	2,525	—
Income (Million $)						
1Q	34.40	-28%	48.00	NM	11.30	-27%
2Q	52.70	-1%	53.30	67%	31.90	63%
3Q	—	—	61.60	46%	42.30	NM
4Q	—	—	47.50	NM	-22.00	NM
Yr.	—	—	210.4	NM	63.50	NM
Earnings Per Share ($)						
1Q	0.82	-30%	1.17	NM	0.21	-34%
2Q	1.31	NM	1.31	72%	0.76	73%
3Q	E1.67	8%	1.54	48%	1.04	NM
4Q	E1.35	15%	1.17	NM	-0.68	NM
Yr.	E5.15	-1%	5.22	NM	1.32	NM

Next earnings report expected: mid October

Armstrong World Industries

Business Summary - 20-SEP-95

Armstrong World Industries is primarily a manufacturer of interior furnishings, including floor coverings, building products and furniture. Contributions by industry segment in 1994 were:

	Sales	Profit
Floor coverings	47%	53%
Building products	23%	24%
Furniture	19%	11%
Industry products & other	11%	12%

The home improvement and refurbishing market accounted for about 43% of sales in 1994, commercial and institutional building for about 42% and new residential building for about 11%; the remainder was to industrial markets. International sales accounted for 24% of total sales and 23% of profits.

A broad range of floor coverings is manufactured. Resilient flooring is made in both sheet and tile form; ceramic tile is produced through American Olean, acquired in 1988.

Building materials consist of ceiling materials for residential, commercial and institutional uses. Most contain features such as noise reduction, fire protection and ease of installation.

Thomasville Furniture makes traditional and contemporary wood and upholstered furniture for residential and commercial use. Industrial products consist of a variety of products (flexible pipe, gasket materials, etc.) for a number of industries.

ACK is involved in asbestos-related litigation, and in various other lawsuits, which are mostly environmentally-related.

Important Developments

Sep. '95—ACK announced that its textile products operation, a part of the industry products market segment, was for sale. The company did not expect the sale to have a significant impact on its corporate results.
Jul. '95—ACK attributed its flat earnings growth in the second quarter to lower North American residential resilient flooring sales, higher flooring raw material costs, and promotional pricing in selected flooring lines.

Capitalization

Long Term Debt: $449,000,000 (6/95), incl. $245.5 million ESOP loan guarantee.
Minority Interest: $8,600,000.
7.25% ESOP Preferred Stock: $261,600,000; conv. into 5,478,416 com. shs.

Per Share Data ($)

(Year Ended Dec. 31)

	1994	1993	1992	1991	1990	1989
Tangible Bk. Val.	17.17	12.88	14.70	16.65	17.01	16.72
Cash Flow	8.66	4.62	1.51	4.77	6.53	6.11
Earnings	5.22	1.32	-2.03	1.11	3.18	3.17
Dividends	1.26	1.20	1.20	1.19	1.14	1.05
Payout Ratio	24%	90%	NM	107%	34%	31%
Prices - High	57½	55¼	37½	34½	38¾	50⅞
- Low	36	28¾	24½	27⅞	18	33⅜
P/E Ratio - High	11	42	NM	31	12	16
- Low	7	22	NM	21	6	11

Income Statement Analysis (Million $)

	1994	%Chg	1993	%Chg	1992	%Chg	1991
Revs.	2,753	9%	2,525	NM	2,550	5%	2,439
Oper. Inc.	467	34%	348	23%	284	-7%	306
Depr.	133	2%	130	-5%	137	NM	136
Int. Exp.	28.3	-26%	38.0	-9%	41.6	-9%	45.8
Pretax Inc.	306	NM	93.0	NM	-61.0	NM	102
Eff. Tax Rate	31%	—	29%	—	NM	—	39%
Net Inc.	210	NM	64.0	NM	-62.5	NM	61.0

Balance Sheet & Other Fin. Data (Million $)

	1994	1993	1992	1991	1990	1989
Cash	12.0	9.0	15.0	8.0	25.0	17.0
Curr. Assets	691	640	713	719	727	724
Total Assets	2,233	1,929	2,010	2,150	2,146	2,033
Curr. Liab.	387	436	546	480	545	401
LT Debt	483	511	527	566	501	450
Common Eqty.	707	547	546	618	631	707
Total Cap.	1,259	1,110	1,122	1,627	1,575	1,603
Cap. Exp.	148	118	116	133	195	231
Cash Flow	325	174	56.0	177	253	277

Ratio Analysis

	1994	1993	1992	1991	1990	1989
Curr. Ratio	1.8	1.5	1.3	1.5	1.3	1.8
% LT Debt of Cap.	38.4	46.0	47.0	34.8	31.8	28.1
% Net Inc.of Revs.	7.6	2.5	NM	2.5	5.7	6.1
% Ret. on Assets	10.1	3.2	NM	2.8	7.3	7.8
% Ret. on Equity	30.5	8.1	NM	6.6	19.8	17.7

Dividend Data

Dividends have been paid since 1934. A dividend reinvestment plan is available. A "poison pill" stock purchase rights plan was adopted in 1986.

Amt. of Div. $	Date Decl.	Ex-Div. Date	Stock of Record	Payment Date
0.320	Oct. 24	Oct. 31	Nov. 04	Dec. 01 '94
0.320	Jan. 23	Jan. 30	Feb. 03	Mar. 01 '95
0.360	Apr. 24	May. 01	May. 05	Jun. 01 '95
0.360	Jul. 31	Aug. 09	Aug. 11	Sep. 01 '95

Data as orig. reptd.; bef. results of disc. opers. and/or spec. items. Per share data adj. for stk. divs. as of ex-div. date.
E-Estimated. NA-Not Available. NM-Not Meaningful. NR-Not Ranked.

Office—313 West Liberty St., P.O. Box 3001, Lancaster, PA 17604. **Tel**—(717) 397-0611. **Chrmn, Pres & CEO**—G. A. Lorch. **SVP-Fin**—W. J. Wimer. **SVP-Secy**—L. A. Pulkrabek. **Investor Contact**—Warren M. Posey. **Dirs**— H. J. Arnelle, V. C. Campbell, E. A. Deaver, U. F. Fairbairn, M. C. Jensen, G. A. Lorch, J. E. Marley, R. F. Patton, J. P. Samper, J. L. Stead. **Transfer Agent & Registrar**—First Chicago Trust Co. of New York, Jersey City, NJ. **Incorporated** in Pennsylvania in 1891. **Empl**-20,600. **S&P Analyst:** Elizabeth Vandeventer

ASARCO Inc.

NYSE Symbol **AR**
In S&P 500

26-SEP-95

Industry:
Mining/Diversified

Summary: ASARCO is one of the world's largest copper producers. It also mines lead, zinc and silver. Other operations include specialty chemicals, crushed stone and environmental services.

S&P Opinion: Hold (★★★)	Recent Price • 31¾	Yield • 2.6%
	52 Wk Range • 36½-23%	12-Mo. P/E • 8.7

Quantitative Evaluations

Outlook
(1 Lowest—5 Highest)
• **5+**

Fair Value
• **38¾**

Risk
• **Average**

Earn./Div. Rank
• **B-**

Technical Eval.
• **Bearish** since 7/95

Rel. Strength Rank
(1 Lowest—99 Highest)
• **19**

Insider Activity
• **Neutral**

Earnings vs. Previous Year
▲=Up ▼=Down ▶=No Change

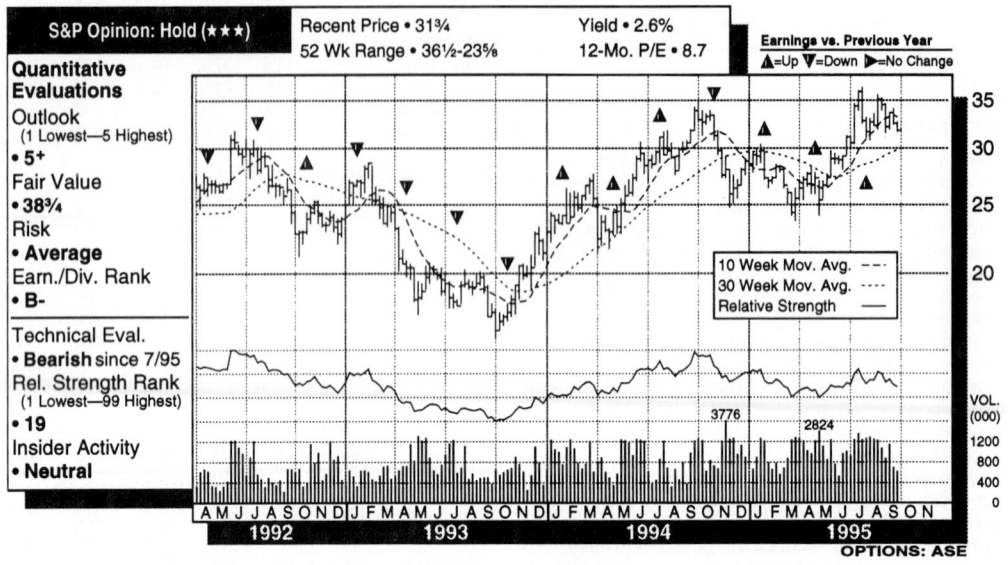

10 Week Mov. Avg. ---
30 Week Mov. Avg. ----
Relative Strength —

OPTIONS: ASE

Overview - 26-SEP-95

Copper volumes are expected to advance about 8% in 1995, reflecting increased equity ownership in Southern Peru Copper Corp. and the return to normal production at the Ray mine in Arizona after flooding conditions required substantial redevelopment work. Copper prices should be higher, year to year, at least through 1995's third quarter. Silver volume will fall, following the sale of its 80% interest in the Quiruvilca mine in Peru. Silver prices will be moderately higher. Volumes and prices for molybdenum will be sharply higher. Good gains are anticipated for specialty chemicals. Interest costs will be higher, reflecting the purchase of a 10.7% stake in Southern Peru Copper.

Valuation - 26-SEP-95

Shares of this important copper and metals producer have climbed sharply since mid-1995, reflecting favorable year-to-year profit comparisons. Additionally, the common dividend was doubled in June. Recently, AR has weakened as investors now anticipate some slippage in copper prices into 1996. AR is attractively priced relative to its book value and recent earnings, but production levels will grow only moderately over the next two years. Consequently, we think the stock will be only an average market performer until a case can be made for higher copper prices.

Key Stock Statistics

S&P EPS Est. 1995	5.60	Tang. Bk. Value/Share	36.19
P/E on S&P Est. 1995	5.7	Beta	0.74
S&P EPS Est. 1996	5.10	Shareholders	12,900
Dividend Rate/Share	0.80	Market cap. (B)	$ 1.3
Shs. outstg. (M)	42.4	Inst. holdings	77%
Avg. daily vol. (M)	0.170	Insider holdings	NA

Value of $10,000 invested 5 years ago: $ 13,139

Fiscal Year Ending Dec. 31

	1995	% Change	1994	% Change	1993	% Change
Revenues (Million $)						
1Q	791.0	79%	443.0	-3%	457.0	NM
2Q	787.5	61%	487.8	17%	418.6	-14%
3Q	—	—	513.0	21%	425.2	-13%
4Q	—	—	588.1	35%	435.5	-8%
Yr.	—	—	2,032	17%	1,736	-9%
Income (Million $)						
1Q	65.11	145%	26.60	NM	-30.90	NM
2Q	56.41	NM	5.36	NM	-24.10	NM
3Q	—	—	-16.15	NM	-3.00	NM
4Q	—	—	48.22	NM	-12.60	NM
Yr.	—	—	64.03	NM	-70.68	NM
Earnings Per Share ($)						
1Q	1.56	144%	0.64	NM	-0.74	NM
2Q	1.34	NM	0.13	NM	-0.58	NM
3Q	E1.40	NM	-0.39	NM	-0.08	NM
4Q	E1.30	13%	1.15	NM	-0.30	NM
Yr.	E5.60	NM	1.53	NM	-1.70	NM

Next earnings report expected: late October

ASARCO Inc.

Business Summary - 26-SEP-95

ASARCO is a major producer of nonferrous metals, has specialty chemicals and crushed stone operations, provides environmental services, and holds interests in foreign mining firms. Business segment contributions in 1994 (profits in million $):

	Sales	Profits
Metals	82%	-$9
Specialty chemicals	14%	13
Aggregates	2%	7
Other	2%	6
Equity in assoc. cos.	---	48

Excluding associated companies, AR's share of mine output in 1994 was 6,143,000 oz. of silver, 286,600 tons of copper, 127,800 tons of lead, and 120,500 tons of zinc. Including purchased materials, refined output was 36,126,000 oz. of silver, 492,600 tons of copper, and 205,800 tons of lead.

Through wholly owned Enthone-OMI, Inc., AR produces specialty chemicals for metal plating and electronics applications. AR's American Limestone unit is a construction aggregates business. Other operations include Encycle and Hydrometrics, which provide environmental services.

Southern Peru Copper Corp. (SPCC), 63% owned (52.3% owned before April 1995), produced 267,800 tons of copper and 2,980,000 ounces of silver in 1994. SPCC is completing a $445 million modernization and expansion, which includes the addition of 40,000 tons of SX-EW copper output a year by late 1995, and the acquisition of the Ilo refinery completed in May 1994. In August 1994, AR exchanged its shares in Mexico Desarrollo Industrial Minero (a privately held company) for 23.6% of the publicly-listed shares of Grupo Mexico (GM), the largest mining firm in Mexico. AR has a 15.4% interest in M.I.M. Holdings Ltd., a major mining company based in Australia.

Important Developments

Aug. '95—AR sold its 80% interest in the Quiruvilca mine in Peru to Pan American Silver Corp. for 500,000 shares of Pan American (worth $3.5 million at recent prices), 500,000 warrants and a life-of-mine royalty of up to 20% of Quiruvilca's profits. In 1994 Quiruvilca accounted for 2,245,600 oz. of AR's silver production or 37%.

Apr. '95—AR sold $150 million of 30-year 8.5% debentures. Proceeds were used to repay, in part, revolving credit borrowings. Those borrowings were used to buy an additional 10.7% interest in Southern Peru Copper Corp. from Newmont Gold for $116.4 million.

Capitalization

Long Term Debt: $1,135,706,000 (6/95).
Minority Interests: $366,145,000.

Per Share Data ($)

(Year Ended Dec. 31)

	1994	1993	1992	1991	1990	1989
Tangible Bk. Val.	36.04	35.27	32.74	36.24	36.78	34.56
Cash Flow	3.51	0.24	1.39	2.94	5.42	7.03
Earnings	1.53	-1.70	-0.70	1.12	3.60	5.50
Dividends	0.40	0.50	0.80	1.60	1.60	1.50
Payout Ratio	26%	NM	NM	143%	44%	27%
Prices - High	34⅞	28⅝	31¾	30½	33	35⅞
- Low	21⅜	16¼	19¾	18¼	22¼	26⅛
P/E Ratio - High	23	NM	NM	27	9	7
- Low	14	NM	NM	16	6	5

Income Statement Analysis (Million $)

	1994	%Chg	1993	%Chg	1992	%Chg	1991
Revs.	2,032	17%	1,736	-9%	1,908	NM	1,910
Oper. Inc.	148	NM	6.0	-96%	149	9%	137
Depr.	83.1	3%	80.6	-7%	86.6	16%	74.9
Int. Exp.	62.5	9%	57.3	12%	51.2	11%	46.2
Pretax Inc.	78.0	NM	-106	NM	-66.0	NM	52.0
Eff. Tax Rate	18%	—	NM	—	NM	—	11%
Net Inc.	64.0	NM	-71.0	NM	-29.0	NM	46.0

Balance Sheet & Other Fin. Data (Million $)

	1994	1993	1992	1991	1990	1989
Cash	18.0	31.0	33.0	35.0	35.0	23.0
Curr. Assets	747	620	687	637	677	579
Total Assets	3,291	3,152	2,946	2,937	2,771	2,441
Curr. Liab.	466	419	421	352	363	338
LT Debt	915	869	784	748	522	334
Common Eqty.	1,517	1,472	1,357	1,495	1,510	1,438
Total Cap.	2,588	2,488	2,246	2,396	2,160	1,907
Cap. Exp.	98.0	112	135	283	241	271
Cash Flow	147	10.0	58.0	121	224	296

Ratio Analysis

	1994	1993	1992	1991	1990	1989
Curr. Ratio	1.6	1.5	1.6	1.8	1.9	1.7
% LT Debt of Cap.	35.3	34.9	34.9	31.2	24.2	17.5
% Net Inc.of Revs.	3.2	NM	NM	2.4	6.8	10.5
% Ret. on Assets	2.0	NM	NM	1.6	5.8	10.0
% Ret. on Equity	4.3	NM	NM	3.1	10.2	16.8

Dividend Data

Dividends were resumed in 1987 after omission since 1984. A "poison pill" stock purchase rights plan was adopted in 1989. A dividend reinvestment plan is available.

Amt. of Div. $	Date Decl.	Ex-Div. Date	Stock of Record	Payment Date
0.100	Oct. 26	Nov. 04	Nov. 11	Dec. 01 '94
0.100	Jan. 25	Jan. 31	Feb. 06	Mar. 01 '95
0.200	Apr. 26	May. 02	May. 08	Jun. 01 '95
0.200	Jul. 26	Aug. 03	Aug. 07	Sep. 01 '95

Data as orig. reptd.; bef. results of disc. opers. and/or spec. items. Per share data adj. for stk. divs. as of ex-div. date.
E-Estimated. NA-Not Available. NM-Not Meaningful. NR-Not Ranked.

Office—180 Maiden Lane, New York, NY 10038-4991. **Tel**—(212) 510-2000. **Chrmn & Pres**—R. de J. Osborne. **VP-Secy**—A. B. Kinsolving. **VP-Fin-CFO**—K. R. Morano. **Treas & Investor Contact**—Thomas J. Findley Jr. **Dirs**—W. C. Butcher, J. C. Cotting, D. C. Garfield, E. G. Gee, H. Holiday Jr., J. W. Kinnear III, F. R. McAllister, M. T. Muse, M. T. Nelligan, J. D. Ong, R. de J. Osborne, J. Wood. **Transfer Agent & Registrar**—Bank of New York, NYC. **Incorporated** in New Jersey in 1899. **Empl**-8,000. **S&P Analyst:** Stephen R. Klein

Ashland Inc.

NYSE Symbol **ASH**
In S&P 500

23-OCT-95
Industry: Oil and Gas

Summary: Ashland Oil is a leading independent petroleum refiner and marketer, and produces a full range of products, including Valvoline motor oil.

| S&P Opinion: Accumulate (★★★★) | Recent Price • 33¼ | Yield • 3.3% |
| | 52 Wk Range • 39⅞-30½ | 12-Mo. P/E • 21.0 |

Quantitative Evaluations

Outlook (1 Lowest—5 Highest)
• **1⁻**

Fair Value
• **29¾**

Risk
• **Low**

Earn./Div. Rank
• **B**

Technical Eval.
• **Bullish** since 9/95

Rel. Strength Rank (1 Lowest—99 Highest)
• **43**

Insider Activity
• **NA**

Earnings vs. Previous Year
▲=Up ▼=Down ▶=No Change

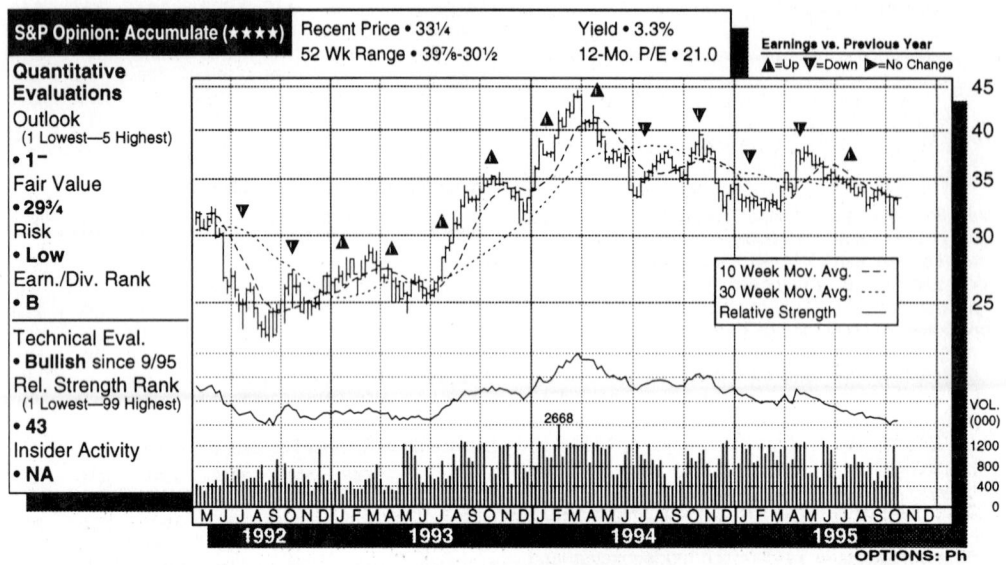

10 Week Mov. Avg. - - -
30 Week Mov. Avg. ·····
Relative Strength ——

2668

VOL. (000)

1992 1993 1994 1995

OPTIONS: Ph

Overview - 23-OCT-95

Revenues in the fiscal 1995 fourth quarter were expected to show an upturn, on improved demand for refined products, greater chemical sales, and improvement at the highway construction group. Stable prices and continued domestic growth were expected to boost gasoline and lubricants demand. Although wholesale gasoline prices were down, retail prices were not expected to drop as precipitously, aiding the SuperAmerica retail division. We are less optimistic about chemical earnings for fiscal 1996 (chemical earnings may peak in the fiscal 1995 fourth quarter), because of further capacity additions in the industry. Although costs to comply with standards imposed by the Clean Air Act will affect earnings, we believe that long-term earnings power will buoy the shares over the next 12 to 15 months.

Valuation - 23-OCT-95

Ashland's shares are highly leveraged to refining margins, although the company has made important efforts to diversify its business in recent years. Although refining margins usually widen with lower feedstock costs, the futures markets have recently eroded industry margins, despite promising fundamentals for gasoline markets. Refinery utilization has been rising, and now exceeds 95%. We believe that, at the margin, rising utilization rates should lead to higher prices for refined products. We view the shares as undervalued at current levels, based on our cash flow and earnings projections.

Key Stock Statistics

S&P EPS Est. 1995	0.19	Tang. Bk. Value/Share	19.98
P/E on S&P Est. 1995	NM	Beta	0.93
S&P EPS Est. 1996	3.15	Shareholders	30,200
Dividend Rate/Share	1.10	Market cap. (B)	$ 2.1
Shs. outstg. (M)	63.6	Inst. holdings	54%
Avg. daily vol. (M)	0.162	Insider holdings	NA

Value of $10,000 invested 5 years ago: $ 10,040

Fiscal Year Ending Sep. 30

	1995	% Change	1994	% Change	1993	% Change
Revenues (Million $)						
1Q	2,498	15%	2,172	-15%	2,555	2%
2Q	3,270	49%	2,200	-8%	2,386	6%
3Q	—	—	2,476	-5%	2,605	NM
4Q	—	—	2,609	5%	2,487	-12%
Yr.	—	—	9,457	-7%	10,199	NM
Income (Million $)						
1Q	35.00	-40%	58.38	136%	24.75	8%
2Q	-29.00	NM	32.92	NM	0.84	NM
3Q	48.00	9%	44.00	-34%	66.54	166%
4Q	—	—	61.00	-9%	67.00	NM
Yr.	—	—	197.0	39%	142.2	NM
Earnings Per Share ($)						
1Q	0.50	-44%	0.90	120%	0.41	5%
2Q	-0.55	NM	0.47	NM	0.01	NM
3Q	0.69	6%	0.65	-20%	0.81	93%
4Q	E-0.45	NM	0.93	-7%	1.00	NM
Yr.	E0.19	-94%	2.94	30%	2.26	NM

Next earnings report expected: late October

Ashland Inc.

23-OCT-95

Business Summary - 23-OCT-95

Ashland is a leading independent petroleum refiner producing a full range of products, including Valvoline brand motor oil. The SuperAmerica Group, the company's marketing subsidiary, offers gasoline and convenience merchandise through 700 stores. The chemical unit manufactures specialty chemicals and plastics. The exploration business participates in energy exploration and production in the U.S. and Nigeria. ASH is also involved in highway construction and coal mining.

Capital spending in fiscal 1994 totaled $376 million, down from fiscal 1993's $432 million. Petroleum expenditures for fiscal 1994 were $155 million, or 41% of the total budget. The company expects capital expenditures to remain in line with depreciation. The decline in capital spending reflects completed environmental requirements at its refineries. Operating profits in recent fiscal years were:

	1994	1993
Petroleum	25%	15%
SuperAmerica	13%	17%
Valvoline	12%	15%
Chemical	28%	29%
Construction	16%	14%
Exploration	6%	10%

In fiscal 1994, ASH processed 338,400 bbl. of oil a day and sold 357,700 b/d of petroleum products. Valvoline product sales came to 17,900 b/d, and SuperAmerica sold some 70,200 b/d of gasoline. Production of oil was 18,700 b/d (in Nigeria) and natural gas 94,300 Mcf a day. Arch Mineral (50% owned) sold 24.3 million tons of coal and Ashland Coal (38%) sold 18.2 million tons.

Important Developments

Sep. '95—Ashland expects to record a $90 million fourth quarter charge to write down oil and gas properties in compliance with FASB 121. It will also take incur a pretax charge of about $40 million in connection with an early retirement program.

Jul. '95—Operating earnings rose in the fiscal 1995 third quarter, as refining margins for gasoline showed improvement. The average refining margin for the quarter was $4.90 per bbl., versus $2.26 per bbl. in the previous quarter. Chemical earnings fell 10%, to $30 million, while Valvoline's operating income declined $10 million. With lower domestic natural gas prices, Ashland Exploration achieved near break-even results.

Capitalization

Long Term Debt: $1,803,000,000 (6/95).
$3.125 Cum. Conv. Pfd. Stock: 6,000,000 shs. ($50 liquid pref.); conv. into 1.546 com.

Per Share Data ($)

(Year Ended Sep. 30)

	1994	1993	1992	1991	1990	1989
Tangible Bk. Val.	19.56	17.90	16.94	23.03	20.94	18.54
Cash Flow	7.75	7.21	3.79	7.32	8.22	6.97
Earnings	2.94	2.26	-1.18	2.56	3.27	1.55
Dividends	1.00	1.00	1.00	1.00	1.00	1.00
Payout Ratio	34%	44%	NM	41%	32%	67%
Prices - High	44½	35⅝	34	35¼	40⅛	43
- Low	33¼	24¼	22½	26⅛	26⅜	33⅛
P/E Ratio - High	15	16	NM	14	12	28
- Low	11	11	NM	10	8	21

Income Statement Analysis (Million $)

	1994	%Chg	1993	%Chg	1992	%Chg	1991
Revs.	9,505	-1%	9,611	NM	9,592	3%	9,303
Oper. Inc.	651	11%	587	159%	227	-60%	561
Depr.	295	2%	290	NM	290	9%	267
Int. Exp.	117	-12%	133	NM	132	6%	125
Pretax Inc.	272	36%	200	NM	-157	NM	193
Eff. Tax Rate	28%	—	29%	—	NM	—	25%
Net Inc.	197	39%	142	NM	-68.0	NM	145

Balance Sheet & Other Fin. Data (Million $)

	1994	1993	1992	1991	1990	1989
Cash	40.0	41.0	53.0	71.0	81.0	70.0
Curr. Assets	2,171	1,973	2,110	2,119	2,143	1,778
Total Assets	5,815	5,552	5,668	5,449	5,118	4,456
Curr. Liab.	1,688	1,619	2,046	1,823	1,806	1,515
LT Debt	1,391	1,399	1,445	1,337	1,235	1,074
Common Eqty.	1,295	1,155	1,086	1,444	1,280	1,141
Total Cap.	3,016	2,898	2,590	3,092	2,839	2,494
Cap. Exp.	376	432	504	445	446	413
Cash Flow	473	426	221	412	457	387

Ratio Analysis

	1994	1993	1992	1991	1990	1989
Curr. Ratio	1.3	1.2	1.0	1.2	1.2	1.2
% LT Debt of Cap.	46.1	48.3	55.8	43.2	43.5	43.1
% Net Inc.of Revs.	2.1	1.5	NM	1.6	2.1	1.1
% Ret. on Assets	3.4	2.5	NM	2.7	3.8	2.0
% Ret. on Equity	14.4	12.2	NM	10.5	15.1	7.7

Dividend Data

—Dividends have been paid since 1936. A dividend reinvestment plan is available. A poison pill stock purchase rights plan was adopted in 1986.

Amt. of Div. $	Date Decl.	Ex-Div. Date	Stock of Record	Payment Date
0.275	Nov. 03	Nov. 21	Nov. 28	Dec. 15 '94
0.275	Jan. 25	Feb. 16	Feb. 23	Mar. 15 '95
0.275	May. 18	May. 25	Jun. 01	Jun. 15 '95
0.275	Jul. 19	Aug. 22	Aug. 24	Sep. 15 '95

Data as orig. reptd.; bef. results of disc. opers. and/or spec. items. Per share data adj. for stk. divs. as of ex-div. date.
E-Estimated. NA-Not Available. NM-Not Meaningful. NR-Not Ranked.

Office—1000 Ashland Drive (P.O. Box 391), Ashland, KY 41114. **Tel**—(606) 329-3333. **Chrmn & CEO**—J. R. Hall. **Pres**—P. W. Chellgren. **SVP & CFO**—J. M. Quin. **SVP & Secy**—T. L. Feazell. **VP & Investor Contact**—William P. Hartl. **Dirs**—J. S. Blanton, T. E. Bolger, S. C. Butler, F. C. Carlucci, P. W. Chellgren, J. B. Farley, E. B. Fitzgerald, R. E. Gomory, J. R. Hall, P. F. Noonan, J. C. Pfeiffer, J. R. Rinehart, M. D. Rose, W. L. Rouse, Jr., R. B. Stobaugh, J. W. Vandeveer. **Transfer Agents**—Mellon Securities Trust Co., NYC; Co.'s office. **Registrars**—Mellon Securities Trust Co., NYC; Bank One, Lexington, KY. **Incorporated** in Kentucky in 1936. **Empl**-31,800. **S&P Analyst:** Raymond J. Deacon

Atlantic Richfield

NYSE Symbol **ARC**
In S&P 500

30-OCT-95

Industry:
Oil and Gas

Summary: ARCO is a major oil producer in Alaska and a leading marketer of gasoline in California and throughout the West. It also has interests in coal and chemicals.

| S&P Opinion: Accumulate (★★★★) | Recent Price • 106⅛ | Yield • 5.2% |
| | 52 Wk Range • 117⅞-100¼ | 12-Mo. P/E • 13.0 |

Quantitative Evaluations

Outlook
(1 Lowest—5 Highest)
• **3+**

Fair Value
• **104**

Risk
• **Low**

Earn./Div. Rank
• **B+**

Technical Eval.
• **Bullish** since 3/94

Rel. Strength Rank
(1 Lowest—99 Highest)
• **43**

Insider Activity
• **NA**

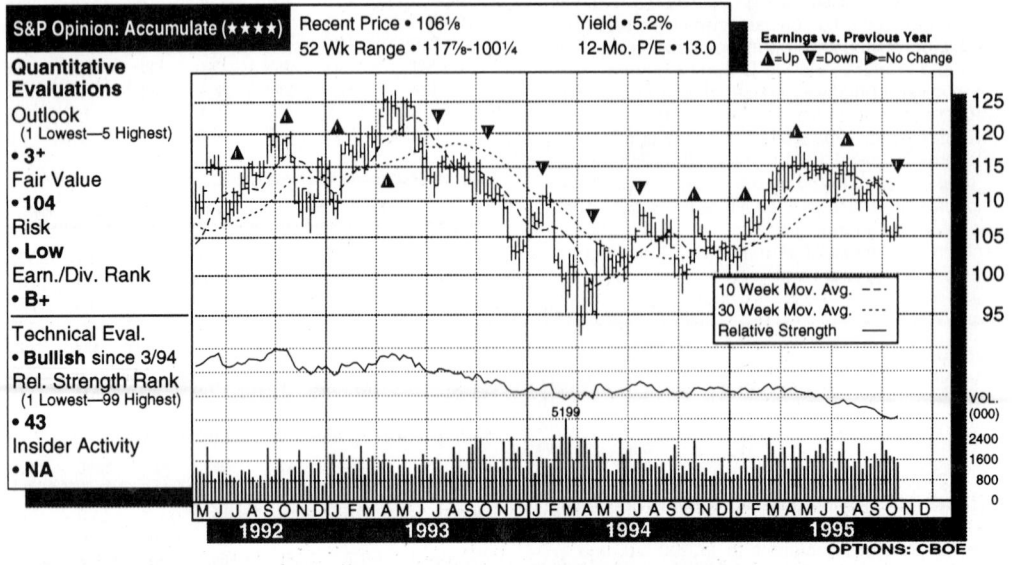

Earnings vs. Previous Year
▲=Up ▼=Down ▶=No Change

10 Week Mov. Avg. - - -
30 Week Mov. Avg. · · · ·
Relative Strength ——

OPTIONS: CBOE

Overview - 30-OCT-95

An earnings uptrend should continue, led by stable oil and natural gas prices and increased volumes. ARCO's strategy has been to integrate Alaskan crude oil production with California refining and marketing. Exploration in Canada continues, and the lifting of the U.S. ban on Alaskan North Slope crude would be a boon. The near-term outlook for refining margins is clouded by environmental issues associated with CARB gasoline requirements in California, where refiners have thus far been unable to recover the additional costs of producing CARB gasoline. Debt levels reflect a plan to cut long-term debt by $1 billion in 1995. We believe ARCO is effectively expanding its exploration and production business overseas.

Valuation - 30-OCT-95

The shares were in a downtrend since mid-1993, reflecting deteriorating earnings power and lower oil prices. ARCO has taken actions, including asset sales, rationalizations and spinoffs, to restore earnings growth, and these efforts led to a rising stock price thus far in 1995. ARC's shares remain cheap, relative to those of the company's peers, based on our 1995 and 1996 EPS and cash flow forecasts. We believe that the high yield from a secure dividend should boost the share price in the near-term. In the long-term, repositioning of the asset base overseas, where there are a number of potentially high reward projects under development, should provide an above-average return.

Key Stock Statistics

S&P EPS Est. 1995	8.25	Tang. Bk. Value/Share	41.10
P/E on S&P Est. 1995	12.9	Beta	0.80
S&P EPS Est. 1996	8.55	Shareholders	100,000
Dividend Rate/Share	5.50	Market cap. (B)	$ 17.1
Shs. outstg. (M)	160.8	Inst. holdings	62%
Avg. daily vol. (M)	0.337	Insider holdings	NA

Value of $10,000 invested 5 years ago: $ 12,756

Fiscal Year Ending Dec. 31

	1995	% Change	1994	% Change	1993	% Change
Revenues (Million $)						
1Q	4,457	17%	3,800	-16%	4,510	4%
2Q	4,046	-3%	4,170	-11%	4,670	3%
3Q	4,514	6%	4,270	-6%	4,550	-6%
4Q	—	—	4,244	-11%	4,760	-4%
Yr.	—	—	16,550	-10%	18,490	NM
Income (Million $)						
1Q	322.0	116%	149.0	-43%	260.0	44%
2Q	391.0	NM	24.00	-91%	271.0	-12%
3Q	315.0	-28%	435.0	NM	68.00	-80%
4Q	—	—	311.0	NM	-330.0	NM
Yr.	—	—	919.0	NM	269.0	-77%
Earnings Per Share ($)						
1Q	1.97	114%	0.92	-43%	1.60	43%
2Q	2.39	NM	0.14	-92%	1.67	-13%
3Q	1.93	-28%	2.67	NM	0.42	-80%
4Q	E1.96	3%	1.90	NM	-2.06	NM
Yr.	E8.25	47%	5.63	NM	1.66	-78%

Next earnings report expected: late January

Atlantic Richfield

Business Summary - 29-OCT-95

Atlantic Richfield (ARCO) is one of the largest U.S.-based integrated oil companies, and has large holdings in petrochemicals and coal. It is uniquely positioned among domestic integrated oil companies, because it supplies all refined product sales with crude oil produced from its North American holdings. Segment profit contributions in recent years were:

	1994	1993
Petro. expl. & production	33%	7%
Petro. refining & marketing	16%	36%
Petro. transportation	13%	21%
Spec. & interm. chemicals	27%	26%
Lyondell Petrochemical	6%	1%
Coal	5%	10%

In 1994, net production of crude oil and natural gas liquids averaged 591,300 bbl. a day in the U.S. (63% from Alaska, primarily the North Slope) and 72,800 b/d foreign; natural gas sales 1.47 Bcf a day; refinery runs 408,300 b/d; domestic petroleum products sales 477,900 b/d (western areas only). ARCO is a leading marketer of gasoline in the five-state region of California, Oregon, Washington, Nevada and Arizona. There were 1,554 retail outlets at December 31, 1994.

Net proved reserves at 1994 year end stood at 2,468 million bbl. of crude and natural gas liquids (91% U.S., 9% foreign) and 8,108 Bcf of natural gas (57%, and 43%, respectively).

The company owns 83% of ARCO Chemical (RCM, NYSE); 82% of Vastar Resources (VRI, NYSE), which owns and operates most of ARCO's domestic natural gas reserves; and 49.9% of Lyondell Petrochemical (LYO, NYSE), which makes and markets basic commodity chemicals, including ethylene and propylene.

Important Developments

Sep. '95—ARCO's chairman said it expects capital spending for the 1995-1999 period to approximate $13 billion. Major portions of the budget will be allocated to developing ARCO's oil discovery in Ecuador, bringing new natural gas onstream in Indonesia, developing the Trent and Tyne gas fields and the Shearwater gas condensate field in the U.K., the addition of a propylene oxide/styrene monomer plant in Rotterdam, and other development projects in Algeria and Qatar. In the U.S., ARCO will make investments in two Alaska projects, including a major enhanced oil recovery project at the Kuparuk River field, will increase funding for Vastar Resources, and continue with exploration and development of natural gas prospects in the Gulf of Mexico, and has plans to expand ARCO's West Coast gasoline marketing.

Capitalization

Long Term Debt: $6,752,000,000 (6/95).
Minority Interest: $453,000,000.
Cum. Conv. Preference Stock: $1,000,000.

Per Share Data ($)

(Year Ended Dec. 31)

	1994	1993	1992	1991	1990	1989
Tangible Bk. Val.	38.28	37.89	41.82	41.76	43.55	38.95
Cash Flow	15.85	11.81	18.12	14.89	20.02	20.76
Earnings	5.63	1.66	7.39	4.39	10.20	11.26
Dividends	5.50	5.50	5.50	5.50	5.00	4.50
Payout Ratio	98%	331%	74%	123%	47%	38%
Prices - High	112 3/8	127 3/4	121 3/4	135 3/4	142 1/4	114 3/8
- Low	92 1/2	100 1/2	98 1/8	99 1/8	105 1/2	80 3/8
P/E Ratio - High	20	77	16	31	14	10
- Low	16	61	13	23	10	7

Income Statement Analysis (Million $)

	1994	%Chg	1993	%Chg	1992	%Chg	1991
Revs.	15,035	-13%	17,189	-2%	17,503	3%	17,037
Oper. Inc.	3,039	3%	2,964	-17%	3,554	2%	3,491
Depr.	1,671	1%	1,652	-5%	1,736	2%	1,701
Int. Exp.	796	3%	771	-12%	877	-10%	971
Pretax Inc.	1,368	116%	634	-67%	1,907	64%	1,160
Eff. Tax Rate	28%	—	52%	—	36%	—	36%
Net Inc.	919	NM	269	-77%	1,193	68%	709

Balance Sheet & Other Fin. Data (Million $)

	1994	1993	1992	1991	1990	1989
Cash	4,385	3,747	2,915	2,549	3,031	3,009
Curr. Assets	6,813	6,231	5,646	5,338	6,048	5,414
Total Assets	24,563	23,894	24,256	24,492	23,864	22,261
Curr. Liab.	4,488	4,335	4,821	5,213	4,260	3,437
LT Debt	7,198	7,089	6,227	5,989	5,997	5,313
Common Eqty.	6,216	6,061	6,650	6,755	7,065	6,469
Total Cap.	16,604	16,382	16,258	16,367	16,895	15,551
Cap. Exp.	1,658	2,070	2,278	3,239	2,718	2,105
Cash Flow	2,587	1,918	2,926	2,407	3,313	3,599

Ratio Analysis

	1994	1993	1992	1991	1990	1989
Curr. Ratio	1.5	1.4	1.2	1.0	1.4	1.6
% LT Debt of Cap.	43.4	43.3	38.3	36.6	35.5	34.2
% Net Inc.of Revs.	6.1	1.6	6.8	4.2	9.4	12.7
% Ret. on Assets	3.8	1.1	4.9	2.9	7.4	9.1
% Ret. on Equity	14.9	4.2	17.7	10.3	25.3	31.6

Dividend Data —Dividends have been paid since 1927. A dividend reinvestment plan is available. A poison pill stock purchase rights plan was adopted in 1986.

Amt. of Div. $	Date Decl.	Ex-Div. Date	Stock of Record	Payment Date
1.375	Jan. 23	Feb. 13	Feb. 17	Mar. 15 '95
1.375	May. 01	May. 15	May. 19	Jun. 15 '95
.10 Spl.	Aug. 01	Aug. 16	Aug. 18	Sep. 15 '95
1.375	Jul. 24	Aug. 16	Aug. 18	Sep. 15 '95
1.375	Oct. 23	Nov. 15	Nov. 17	Dec. 15 '95

Data as orig. reptd.; bef. results of disc. opers. and/or spec. items. Per share data adj. for stk. divs. as of ex-div. date. E-Estimated. NA-Not Available. NM-Not Meaningful. NR-Not Ranked.

Office—515 South Flower St., Los Angeles, CA 90071-2256. **Tel**—(213) 486-3511. **Chrmn**—M. R. Bowlin. **EVP & CFO**—R. J. Arnault. **Secy**—B. G. Whitmore. **Investor Contact**—Chris Noble **Dirs**—R. J. Arnault, F. D. Boren, M. R. Bowlin, L. M. Cook, R. H. Deihl, J. Gavin, H. H. Gray, P. M. Hawley, W. F. Kieschnick, K. Kresa, D. T. McLaughlin, J. B. Slaughter, W. E. Wade, Jr. H. B. Waldron, H. Wendt. **Transfer Agent & Registrar**—First Chicago Trust Co. of New York, Jersey City, NJ. **Incorporated** in Pennsylvania in 1870; reincorporated in Delaware in 1985. **Empl**-23,200. **S&P Analyst:** Raymond J. Deacon

Autodesk, Inc.

NASDAQ Symbol **ACAD**

In S&P 500

17-OCT-95 **Industry:** Data Processing

Summary: Autodesk develops, markets and supports computer-aided design and drafting (CAD) software, including its flagship AutoCAD program, for use on desktop computers and workstations.

S&P Opinion: Accumulate (★★★★)	Recent Price • 37¼	Yield • 0.6%
	52 Wk Range • 53-30¾	12-Mo. P/E • 24.8

Quantitative Evaluations

Outlook
(1 Lowest—5 Highest)
• **4+**

Fair Value
• **40⅛**

Risk
• **Average**

Earn./Div. Rank
• **B+**

Technical Eval.
• **Bearish** since 8/95

Rel. Strength Rank
(1 Lowest—99 Highest)
• **7**

Insider Activity
• **NA**

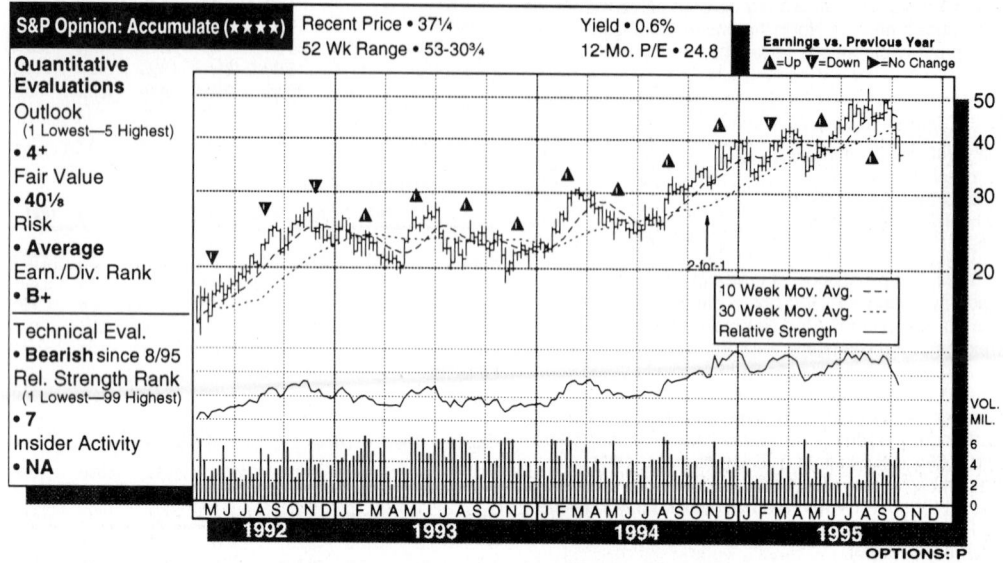

Earnings vs. Previous Year
▲=Up ▼=Down ▶=No Change

2-for-1

10 Week Mov. Avg. ---
30 Week Mov. Avg. ·····
Relative Strength —

VOL. MIL.

1992   1993   1994   1995

OPTIONS: P

Overview - 17-OCT-95

Revenues are expected to rise strongly through fiscal 1996-97, aided by the availability of AutoCAD Release 13, the newest version of the company's flagship software program, and the introduction of other new products, including extension packages for AutoCAD. Strong European and Asia/Pacific markets and firm business in North America and Latin America should boost results. Margins are expected to widen as higher volume and well controlled expenses outweigh expansion costs, particularly in Asia, and an increased proportion of less profitable AutoCAD upgrades and non-AutoCAD products.

Valuation - 17-OCT-95

The shares, which rose sharply in the first half of 1995 on expectations of a strong product cycle associated with AutoCAD Release 13, have slipped of late on concerns this product is selling below expectations. However, the company continues to report impressive financial results, we expect stronger sales of AutoCAD Release 13 in the coming quarters, and sales of other products are robust. Long-term revenue and earnings growth are expected to exceed 20%, driven by demand for more powerful and functional versions of AutoCAD, aided by the introduction of new products. In light of the superior revenue and earnings growth we expect, the stock's premium valuation is deserved. In addition, we believe the multiple attached to earnings could expand as the company continues to diversify its revenue base.

Key Stock Statistics

S&P EPS Est. 1996	2.05	Tang. Bk. Value/Share	7.68
P/E on S&P Est. 1996	18.2	Beta	1.21
S&P EPS Est. 1997	2.40	Shareholders	1,600
Dividend Rate/Share	0.24	Market cap. (B)	$ 1.8
Shs. outstg. (M)	47.0	Inst. holdings	86%
Avg. daily vol. (M)	0.854	Insider holdings	NA

Value of $10,000 invested 5 years ago: $ 20,160

Fiscal Year Ending Jan. 31

	1996	% Change	1995	% Change	1994	% Change
Revenues (Million $)						
1Q	138.7	30%	106.6	1%	105.4	35%
2Q	140.7	28%	110.3	3%	106.9	20%
3Q	—	—	108.2	10%	98.18	NM
4Q	—	—	129.6	27%	102.1	-1%
Yr.	—	—	454.6	12%	405.6	10%
Income (Million $)						
1Q	25.98	58%	16.45	7%	15.44	66%
2Q	26.30	59%	16.59	NM	16.47	56%
3Q	—	—	15.90	6%	14.93	17%
4Q	—	—	7.68	-50%	15.33	37%
Yr.	—	—	56.61	-9%	62.17	42%
Earnings Per Share ($)						
1Q	0.51	55%	0.33	6%	0.31	59%
2Q	0.52	53%	0.34	5%	0.32	51%
3Q	E0.49	53%	0.32	7%	0.30	20%
4Q	E0.53	NM	0.15	-52%	0.32	43%
Yr.	E2.05	80%	1.14	-9%	1.25	42%

Next earnings report expected: mid November

Business Summary - 17-OCT-95

Autodesk, Inc. designs, develops, markets and supports design automation and multimedia software products for use on personal computers and workstations.

The Design Automation Group includes the company's principal product, AutoCAD, a general purpose design and drafting tool. AutoCAD, which accounted for 80% of revenues in fiscal 1994-95, versus 85% in both fiscal 1993-94 and 1992-93, automates the design and drafting process by enabling users to interactively create, store and edit a wide variety of drawings. The drawing data may be exchanged with other applications software, databases and larger computer-based CAD systems. AutoCAD runs in most PC and workstation operating environments, including MS-DOS, Windows, UNIX, and the Apple Macintosh operating system, and supports hundreds of peripheral devices. The software provides users with many of the capabilities of more expensive mainframe or minicomputer-based CAD systems, but at a substantially lower cost. The company also offers add-on and support software packages for AutoCAD.

Other Design Automation products include: AutoCAD LT, a low cost CAD package offering 2-D and basic 3-D drafting capabilities; AutoSketch, a low-cost, entry-level 2D drafting package; AutoCAD Designer, which delivers parametric-feature-based, solid modeling; AutoSurf an easy-to-use surface modeling tool; and AutoCAD Data Extension, an add-on program which incorporates AutoCAD drawings and database records and other documents into one integrated environment.

The company's Multimedia product family focuses on visualization, animation and simulation software. Products include: 3D Studio, 3D modeling software for the PC; Animator Studio, a multimedia animation program; and AutoVision, which helps users create photorealistic still renderings.

Foreign sales accounted for 61% of net revenues in 1994-95 (58% in 1993-94).

Important Developments

Jun. '95—The company's Board of Directors approved a continuation of the company's stock repurchase program and authorized the buy-back of up to 2 million ACAD common shares.

Feb. '95—During the fourth quarter of fiscal 1994-95, the company recorded a charge of approximately $26 million ($0.33 a share) resulting from a judgement in a suit filed by Vermont Microsystems; Autodesk is currently appealing the ruling. In November 1994, Autodesk shipped AutoCAD Release 13, a major upgrade to its flagship design automation software product.

Capitalization

Long Term Debt: None (7/95).

Per Share Data ($)

					(Year Ended Jan. 31)	
	1995	1994	1993	1992	1991	1990
Tangible Bk. Val.	6.85	6.26	5.57	5.44	4.47	3.28
Cash Flow	1.48	1.52	1.11	1.38	1.38	1.07
Earnings	1.14	1.25	0.88	1.15	1.15	0.96
Dividends	0.24	0.48	0.24	0.23	0.20	0.80
Payout Ratio	20%	38%	26%	20%	17%	84%
Cal. Yrs.	1994	1993	1992	1991	1990	1989
Prices - High	41½	28⅜	28¼	31⅛	30⅛	21¾
- Low	21⅛	18½	11⅝	14¾	16	13¼
P/E Ratio - High	36	23	32	27	26	23
- Low	19	15	13	13	14	14

Income Statement Analysis (Million $)

	1995	%Chg	1994	%Chg	1993	%Chg	1992
Revs.	465	11%	419	14%	368	29%	285
Oper. Inc.	130	26%	103	29%	80.0	-12%	91.4
Depr.	17.4	33%	13.1	16%	11.3	NM	11.2
Int. Exp.	NA	—	NA	—	NA	—	NA
Pretax Inc.	89.1	-8%	96.8	39%	69.8	-24%	92.3
Eff. Tax Rate	37%	—	36%	—	37%	—	37%
Net Inc.	56.6	-9%	62.2	42%	43.9	-24%	57.8

Balance Sheet & Other Fin. Data (Million $)

	1995	1994	1993	1992	1991	1990
Cash	240	178	153	171	124	106
Curr. Assets	373	280	249	248	188	145
Total Assets	482	405	358	328	265	194
Curr. Liab.	155	102	84.1	57.0	43.8	31.1
LT Debt	Nil	Nil	Nil	Nil	0.2	0.4
Common Eqty.	323	297	268	267	218	159
Total Cap.	326	302	273	271	221	163
Cap. Exp.	20.0	21.5	11.0	9.9	21.1	13.4
Cash Flow	74.0	75.3	55.2	68.9	67.9	51.8

Ratio Analysis

	1995	1994	1993	1992	1991	1990
Curr. Ratio	2.4	2.7	3.0	4.3	4.3	4.7
% LT Debt of Cap.	Nil	Nil	Nil	Nil	0.1	0.2
% Net Inc.of Revs.	12.2	14.8	11.9	20.3	23.9	26.0
% Ret. on Assets	12.8	16.4	12.9	19.4	24.6	25.3
% Ret. on Equity	18.3	22.1	16.6	23.7	30.0	30.1

Dividend Data —Dividends were initiated in 1989.

Amt. of Div. $	Date Decl.	Ex-Div. Date	Stock of Record	Payment Date
2-for-1	Sep. 08	Oct. 31	Oct. 14	Oct. 28 '94
0.060	Dec. 16	Jan. 09	Jan. 13	Jan. 27 '95
0.060	Mar. 09	Apr. 03	Apr. 07	Apr. 21 '95
0.060	May. 19	Jul. 05	Jul. 07	Jul. 21 '95
0.060	Sep. 15	Oct. 11	Oct. 13	Oct. 27 '95

Data as orig. reptd.; bef. results of disc. opers. and/or spec. items. Per share data adj. for stk. divs. as of ex-div. date. E-Estimated. NA-Not Available. NM-Not Meaningful. NR-Not Ranked.

Office—111 McInnis Parkway, San Rafael, CA 94903. **Tel**—(415) 507-5000. **Chrmn, Pres & CEO**—Carol Bartz. **VP & CFO**—E. B. Herr. **Investor Contact**—Christine Tsingos. **VP & Secy**—Sandra D. Marin. **Dirs**—C. Bartz, M. A. Bertelsen, C. W. Beveridge, J. H. Dawson, G. P. Lutz, M. A. Taylor, M. Topfer. **Transfer Agent**—Harris Trust & Savings Bank, Chicago. **Incorporated** in California in 1982. **Empl**-1,795. **S&P Analyst**: Peter C. Wood, CFA

Automatic Data Processing

NYSE Symbol **AUD**
In S&P 500

16-OCT-95

Industry:
Data Processing

Summary: The largest independent computing service firm in the U.S., AUD has posted 137 consecutive quarters of double-digit share earnings growth; the trend should continue in fiscal 1996.

S&P Opinion: Accumulate (★★★★)

Recent Price • 71½
52 Wk Range • 72⅜-52½

Yield • 1.0%
12-Mo. P/E • 25.1

Quantitative Evaluations

Outlook
(1 Lowest—5 Highest)
• **3+**

Fair Value
• **68⅞**

Risk
• **Low**

Earn./Div. Rank
• **A+**

Technical Eval.
• **Bullish** since 6/94

Rel. Strength Rank
(1 Lowest—99 Highest)
• **80**

Insider Activity
• **Neutral**

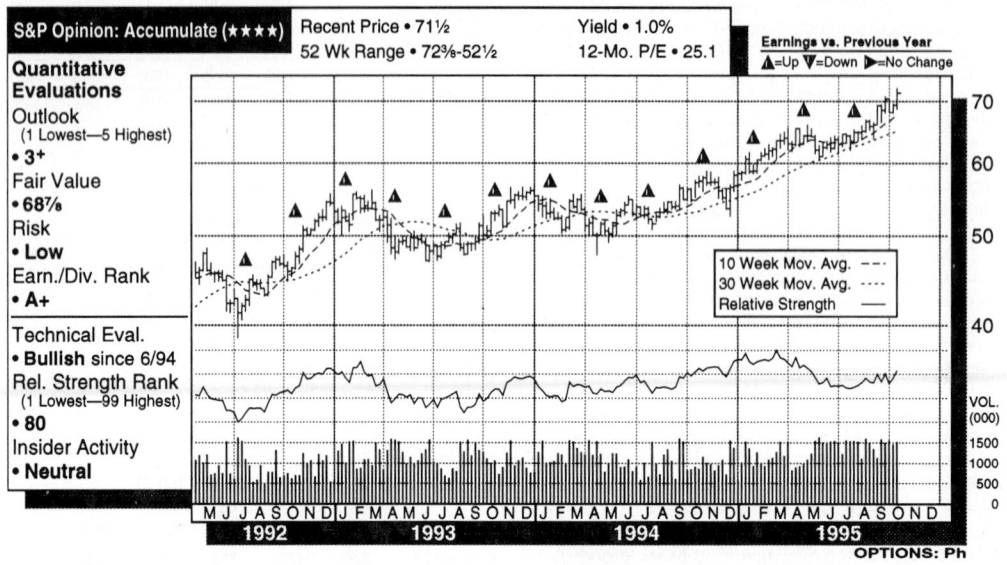

Earnings vs. Previous Year
▲=Up ▼=Down ▶=No Change

10 Week Mov. Avg. - - -
30 Week Mov. Avg. ·····
Relative Strength ——

VOL.
(000)

OPTIONS: Ph

Overview - 16-OCT-95

Revenue growth should accelerate in fiscal 1996, aided by underlying economic strength. The employer services segment should see double digit revenue growth, aided by strong sales activity and increased client retention rates. Brokerage services should continue to grow, aided by a strengthened competitive position and an increased terminal count. Dealer services are expected to continue to benefit from higher auto sales and market share gains. Margins should improve, benefiting from ongoing automation and increased operating efficiencies. A stock repurchase program should help boost share earnings growth. Results should also benefit from a number of recent acquisitions.

Valuation - 16-OCT-95

The shares have been in a long uptrend and now trade near their record highs. AUD should generate annual earnings growth in the mid-teens over the next several years, driven by continued gains in its three major businesses, which account for over 90% of its revenues. Strategic acquisitions should continue to strengthen the company's competitive position. The stock merits a premium valuation in light of the focused business strategy being executed by AUD's strong management team, and the company's record of predictable earnings growth. Although the shares are positioned for further gains, at 22 times our fiscal 1996 estimate we would not aggressively add to positions at this time.

Key Stock Statistics

S&P EPS Est. 1996	3.20	Tang. Bk. Value/Share	9.65
P/E on S&P Est. 1996	22.3	Beta	0.89
S&P EPS Est. 1997	3.70	Shareholders	24,500
Dividend Rate/Share	0.70	Market cap. (B)	$ 10.3
Shs. outstg. (M)	143.9	Inst. holdings	73%
Avg. daily vol. (M)	0.319	Insider holdings	NA

Value of $10,000 invested 5 years ago: $ 30,856

Fiscal Year Ending Jun. 30

	1996	% Change	1995	% Change	1994	% Change
Revenues (Million $)						
1Q	747.1	20%	622.3	13%	552.0	12%
2Q	—	—	672.6	16%	577.7	12%
3Q	—	—	799.0	18%	674.4	10%
4Q	—	—	799.9	20%	664.9	11%
Yr.	—	—	2,894	17%	2,469	11%
Income (Million $)						
1Q	81.90	19%	68.70	17%	58.51	—
2Q	—	—	94.92	18%	80.18	14%
3Q	—	—	125.3	19%	105.0	14%
4Q	—	—	105.9	17%	90.44	14%
Yr.	—	—	394.8	18%	334.1	14%
Earnings Per Share ($)						
1Q	0.57	16%	0.49	17%	0.42	14%
2Q	E0.77	15%	0.67	18%	0.57	14%
3Q	E1.01	16%	0.87	18%	0.74	14%
4Q	E0.85	15%	0.74	16%	0.64	14%
Yr.	E3.20	16%	2.77	17%	2.37	14%

Next earnings report expected: mid January

Automatic Data Processing

Business Summary - 16-OCT-95

AUD provides a broad range of data processing services, including employer services, financial services and specialized services. The company believes it is the largest independent computing services concern in the U.S.

Employer services accounted for 56% of revenues in fiscal 1995. Payroll services, with over 300,000 clients, are the largest contributor, including both payroll processing and a tax filing service.

Brokerage services (23% of revenues) include brokerage processing, order matching, on-line trading, record-keeping, database and stock quotation services and proxy services.

Dealer services (15% of revenues) consist of turnkey systems providing such functions as inventory control, lease management, parts invoicing and repair order billing, to over 13,000 auto and truck dealers in North America and Europe.

Other businesses include claims services, which involves preparing estimates of the cost to repair auto damage and providing related claims management information.

Under an ongoing acquisition program the company acquired: Computer Care, a leading provider of customer service reminder programs to auto dealers, in September 1994; National Bio Systems, a company that helps auto insurers control the costs of accident related medical expenses, and Peachtree Software, a vendor of accounting and payroll software products, both in October 1994; WTR, a benefits consulting and 401-K plan processor, in January 1995; Turbodata, a leading European auto dealer computer service company with 3,000 clients in Belgium, France, Germany and the Netherlands, in March 1995; and Wilco Systems Inc., which specializes in the development of financial and communications systems, in July 1995.

Important Developments

Aug. '95—The company entered into an agreement to acquire GSI, a European computer services company based in Paris, France, for approximately $460 million. The transaction is expected to close in early November and will have a slightly dilutive effect on AUD's earnings per share. Separately, AUD also entered into an agreement to acquire Sandy Corp., a leading performance improvement company that provides consulting, training and communication services to the automotive industry. Each Sandy share will be exchanged for $12 worth of AUD stock and the transaction is valued at approximately $30 million.

Capitalization

Long Term Debt: $390,177,000 (6/95).

Per Share Data ($)

(Year Ended Jun. 30)

	1995	1994	1993	1992	1991	1990
Tangible Bk. Val.	9.65	7.69	6.51	5.29	7.62	7.64
Cash Flow	3.98	3.42	3.07	2.68	2.45	2.21
Earnings	2.77	2.37	2.08	1.84	1.63	1.44
Dividends	0.77	0.54	0.47	0.42	0.36	0.31
Payout Ratio	28%	23%	23%	23%	22%	22%
Prices - High	66	59³/₄	56⁷/₈	55⁵/₈	46³/₈	30¹/₈
- Low	57¹/₂	47⁵/₈	46⁷/₈	38³/₄	25	22⁵/₈
P/E Ratio - High	24	25	27	30	28	21
- Low	21	20	23	21	15	16

Income Statement Analysis (Million $)

	1995	%Chg	1994	%Chg	1993	%Chg	1992
Revs.	2,894	17%	2,469	11%	2,223	15%	1,941
Oper. Inc.	731	19%	615	12%	547	16%	470
Depr.	173	17%	148	6%	140	21%	116
Int. Exp.	24.3	17%	20.8	5%	19.8	61%	12.3
Pretax Inc.	534	20%	446	15%	387	13%	342
Eff. Tax Rate	26%	—	25%	—	24%	—	25%
Net Inc.	395	18%	334	14%	294	15%	256

Balance Sheet & Other Fin. Data (Million $)

	1995	1994	1993	1992	1991	1990
Cash	698	591	368	414	320	396
Curr. Assets	1,211	985	771	734	622	735
Total Assets	3,201	2,706	2,439	2,169	1,565	1,692
Curr. Liab.	543	478	416	367	352	382
LT Debt	390	373	348	333	44.0	53.0
Common Eqty.	2,097	1,691	1,494	1,297	1,053	1,127
Total Cap.	2,506	2,098	1,917	1,693	1,164	1,238
Cap. Exp.	118	111	87.0	56.0	70.0	82.0
Cash Flow	567	482	434	372	342	325

Ratio Analysis

	1995	1994	1993	1992	1991	1990
Curr. Ratio	2.2	2.1	1.9	2.0	1.8	1.9
% LT Debt of Cap.	15.6	17.8	18.1	19.7	3.8	4.3
% Net Inc.of Revs.	13.6	13.5	13.2	13.2	12.9	12.4
% Ret. on Assets	13.4	13.0	12.7	13.6	14.5	12.5
% Ret. on Equity	20.8	21.0	21.0	21.7	21.6	20.3

Dividend Data —Dividends were initiated in 1974.

Amt. of Div. $	Date Decl.	Ex-Div. Date	Stock of Record	Payment Date
0.150	Nov. 15	Dec. 12	Dec. 16	Jan. 01 '95
0.150	Jan. 23	Mar. 13	Mar. 17	Apr. 01 '95
0.175	May. 19	Jun. 14	Jun. 16	Jul. 01 '95
0.175	Aug. 14	Sep. 13	Sep. 15	Oct. 01 '95

Data as orig. reptd.; bef. results of disc. opers. and/or spec. items. Per share data adj. for stk. divs. as of ex-div. date.
E-Estimated. NA-Not Available. NM-Not Meaningful. NR-Not Ranked.

Office—One ADP Blvd., Roseland, NJ 07068. **Tel**—(201) 994-5000. **Chrmn & CEO**—J. S. Weston. **Pres & COO**—A. F. Weinbach. **SVP & Secy**—F. S. Lafer. **VP, CFO & Investor Contact**—F. D. Anderson, Jr. **Dirs**—J. A. Califano, Jr., L. G. Cooperman, G. H. Heilmeier, A. D. Jordan, H. M. Krueger, C. P. Lazarus, F. V. Malek, H. Taub, L. A. Tisch, A. F. Weinbach, J. S. Weston. **Transfer Agent**—Chemical Bank, NYC. **Incorporated** in Delaware in 1961. **Empl**-22,000. **S&P Analyst:** Alan Aaron

Avery Dennison

NYSE Symbol **AVY**
In S&P 500

04-AUG-95

Industry:
Office Equipment

Summary: This company is a leading worldwide manufacturer of pressure sensitive adhesives and materials, office products, labels, retail systems and specialty chemicals.

S&P Opinion: Accumulate (★★★★)	Recent Price • 40 Yield • 2.7%
	52 Wk Range • 43¾-31⅛ 12-Mo. P/E • 17.1

Quantitative Evaluations

Outlook
  (1 Lowest—5 Highest)
• **2**

Fair Value
• **39⅛**

Risk
• **Low**

Earn./Div. Rank
• **B+**

Technical Eval.
• **Bearish** since 9/94

Rel. Strength Rank
  (1 Lowest—99 Highest)
• **20**

Insider Activity
• **Unfavorable**

Earnings vs. Previous Year
▲=Up ▼=Down ▶=No Change

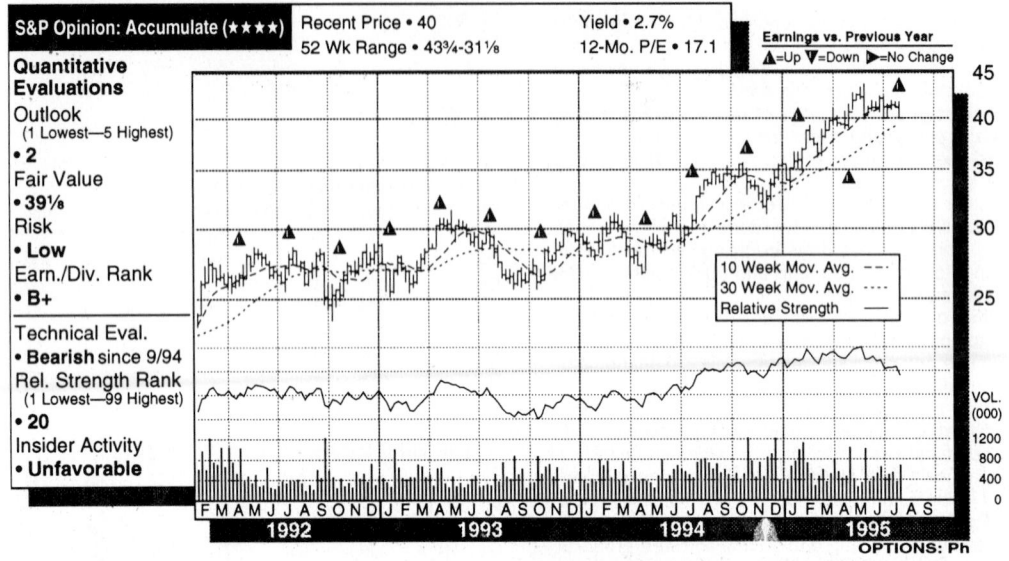

10 Week Mov. Avg. – – –
30 Week Mov. Avg. ·····
Relative Strength ——

OPTIONS: Ph

Overview - 04-AUG-95

S&P projects that sales will advance about 10% for the rest of 1995 and in 1996 as all three segments benefit from the healthy global economy and strong packaging, durable goods, office and retail markets. International sales should also be boosted by favorable currency exchange rates. Market share gains and growth of newer products will also aid sales. Raw material cost increases are expected to slow after the rapid rise since 1994. Profitability should advance on the higher volumes and continuing benefits of cost reduction programs in Europe. Ongoing stock repurchases will aid share earnings comparisons.

Valuation - 03-AUG-95

The shares of this manufacturer of pressure sensitive adhesives and materials have performed well since the beginning of 1995, reflecting continued good gains in sales and earnings. The company intends to focus on its core adhesives and office products businesses and grow through internal as well as geographic expansion. Long-term growth is being driven by the widening use of non-impact printing systems for computers and for product tracking and information needs. The proliferation of high quality graphics on packaging and consumer products is also spurring sales of pressure sensitive labels. The shares are attractive at their current P/E multiple in view of the positive earnings outlook for the company.

Key Stock Statistics

S&P EPS Est. 1995	2.60	Tang. Bk. Value/Share	11.89
P/E on S&P Est. 1995	15.4	Beta	1.34
S&P EPS Est. 1996	2.90	Shareholders	9,600
Dividend Rate/Share	1.08	Market cap. (B)	$ 2.2
Shs. outstg. (M)	53.3	Inst. holdings	66%
Avg. daily vol. (M)	0.101	Insider holdings	NA

Value of $10,000 invested 5 years ago: $ 14,567

Fiscal Year Ending Dec. 31

	1995	% Change	1994	% Change	1993	% Change
Revenues (Million $)						
1Q	773.2	16%	667.7	NM	666.5	NM
2Q	780.5	9%	718.6	9%	662.2	NM
3Q	—	—	733.7	15%	638.1	-3%
4Q	—	—	736.7	15%	641.9	2%
Yr.	—	—	2,857	10%	2,609	NM
Income (Million $)						
1Q	34.50	37%	25.20	14%	22.20	9%
2Q	35.70	28%	27.90	22%	22.80	2%
3Q	—	—	27.80	46%	19.00	2%
4Q	—	—	28.50	48%	19.30	2%
Yr.	—	—	109.4	31%	83.30	4%
Earnings Per Share ($)						
1Q	0.65	44%	0.45	18%	0.38	15%
2Q	0.67	34%	0.50	28%	0.39	5%
3Q	E0.63	—	0.50	52%	0.33	6%
4Q	E0.65	—	0.52	53%	0.34	6%
Yr.	E2.60	—	1.97	37%	1.44	8%

Next earnings report expected: late October

Business Summary - 04-AUG-95

Avery Dennison Corp. is a leading worldwide manufacturer of pressure sensitive adhesives and materials, office products, product identification and control systems, and specialty chemicals. The company was formed through the October 1990 merger of Avery International Corp. and Dennison Manufacturing Corp. Industry segment contributions in 1994:

	Sales	Profits
Adhesives and materials	52%	60%
Office products	27%	26%
Converted products	21%	14%

Foreign operations, primarily in Europe, accounted for 35% of sales and 24% of profits in 1994.

The adhesives and materials group includes pressure sensitive, self-adhesive coated papers, films and foils in roll and sheet form, graphic and decoration films and labels, specialty fastening and bonding tapes, and adhesives, protective coatings and electroconductive resins for industrial, automotive, aerospace, appliance, electronic, medical and consumer markets.

Office products consist of pressure sensitive labels, laser print labels and software, binders, organizing systems, marking devices and numerous other products for office, home and school uses.

Converted products include custom and stock labels and application systems for the industrial, durable goods, cosmetic, consumer packaged goods and electronic data processing markets; self-adhesive postal stamps; and tags, labels, printers, marking and coding systems, application devices, plastic fasteners and cable ties for apparel, retail and industrial markets for use in identification, tracking and control applications.

Important Developments

Jul. '95—AVY reported that sales were up both domestically and internationally in the second quarter, with gains in all three segments. Excluding foreign exchange rate fluctuations, sales were up 6%. Profitability improved on new products and continued cost reduction programs. AVY repurchased 210,000 shares in the second quarter, and had 4.8 million shares remaining for purchase under current authorization. Capital spending for 1995 was budgeted at over $175 million.
Jan. '95—Avery said sales and profits were up significantly in 1994 at both U.S. and international operations, led by the adhesives and materials segment. All three sectors reported increased sales and profits. Separately, AVY said it repurchased 3.2 million common shares in 1994 at a cost of $106 million.

Capitalization

Long Term Debt: $451,200,000 (6/95).

Per Share Data ($) (Year Ended Dec. 31)

	1994	1993	1992	1991	1990	1989
Tangible Bk. Val.	11.07	10.33	11.29	11.07	11.21	9.10
Cash Flow	3.81	3.08	2.88	2.51	1.55	3.10
Earnings	1.97	1.44	1.33	1.02	0.10	1.96
Dividends	0.99	0.90	0.82	0.76	0.64	0.54
Payout Ratio	50%	62%	60%	74%	672%	28%
Prices - High	36	31½	29⅛	25¾	33	33¼
- Low	26⅜	25⅛	23¼	19	15½	21
P/E Ratio - High	18	22	22	25	NM	17
- Low	13	17	17	19	NM	11

Income Statement Analysis (Million $)

	1994	%Chg	1993	%Chg	1992	%Chg	1991
Revs.	2,857	10%	2,609	NM	2,623	3%	2,545
Oper. Inc.	318	17%	271	2%	266	13%	235
Depr.	103	8%	95.4	2%	93.9	2%	92.3
Int. Exp.	45.7	NM	45.5	1%	44.9	5%	42.6
Pretax Inc.	173	31%	132	2%	130	24%	105
Eff. Tax Rate	37%	—	37%	—	39%	—	40%
Net Inc.	109	31%	83.3	4%	80.1	27%	63.0

Balance Sheet & Other Fin. Data (Million $)

	1994	1993	1992	1991	1990	1989
Cash	3.1	5.8	3.9	5.3	6.5	3.1
Curr. Assets	677	615	661	701	847	506
Total Assets	1,763	1,639	1,684	1,740	1,890	1,142
Curr. Liab.	554	473	439	475	548	324
LT Debt	347	311	335	330	376	213
Common Eqty.	729	719	803	825	846	539
Total Cap.	1,116	1,075	1,205	1,235	1,310	818
Cap. Exp.	163	101	88.0	123	149	83.0
Cash Flow	212	179	174	155	96.0	137

Ratio Analysis

	1994	1993	1992	1991	1990	1989
Curr. Ratio	1.2	1.3	1.5	1.5	1.5	1.6
% LT Debt of Cap.	31.1	28.9	27.8	26.7	28.7	26.1
% Net Inc.of Revs.	3.8	3.2	3.1	2.5	0.2	5.0
% Ret. on Assets	6.6	5.1	4.8	3.5	0.3	7.6
% Ret. on Equity	15.5	11.2	10.0	7.6	0.7	16.5

Dividend Data
(Dividends have been paid since 1964. A dividend reinvestment plan is available. A new "poison pill" stock purchase right was issued in 1988.)

Amt. of Div. $	Date Decl.	Ex-Div. Date	Stock of Record	Payment Date
0.240	Jul. 28	Aug. 31	Sep. 07	Sep. 21 '94
0.270	Oct. 27	Dec. 01	Dec. 07	Dec. 14 '94
0.270	Jan. 26	Feb. 23	Mar. 01	Mar. 15 '95
0.270	Apr. 27	Jun. 01	Jun. 07	Jun. 21 '95
0.270	Jul. 27	Sep. 01	Sep. 06	Sep. 20 '95

Data as orig. reptd.; bef. results of disc. opers. and/or spec. items. Per share data adj. for stk. divs. as of ex-div. date. E-Estimated. NA-Not Available. NM-Not Meaningful. NR-Not Ranked.

Office—150 North Orange Grove Blvd., Pasadena, CA 91103. **Tel**—(818) 304-2000. **Chrmn & CEO**—C. D. Miller. **Pres & COO**—P. M. Neal. **SVP-Fin & CFO**—R. G. Jenkins. **VP-Secy**—R. G. van Schoonenberg. **VP-Treas & Investor Contact**—Wayne H. Smith. **Dirs**—D. L. Allison Jr., J. C. Argue, J. T. Bok, F. V. Cahouet, R. M. Ferry, F. D. Frost, C. D. Miller, P. W. Mullin, P. M. Neal, S. R. Petersen, J. B. Slaughter, L. R. Tollenaere. **Transfer Agent & Registrar**—First Interstate Bank, Los Angeles. **Incorporated** in California in 1946; reincorporated in Delaware in 1977. **Empl**-16,250. **S&P Analyst:** Richard O'Reilly, CFA

STOCK REPORTS

Avon Products

NYSE Symbol **AVP**
In S&P 500

27-SEP-95

Industry:
Cosmetics/Toiletries

Summary: This company is the world's leading direct marketer of cosmetics, toiletries, fashion jewelry and fragrances, with over 1.9 million sales representatives worldwide.

S&P Opinion: Accumulate (★★★★)

| Recent Price • 73% | Yield • 2.9% |
| 52 Wk Range • 75%-54 | 12-Mo. P/E • 18.5 |

Quantitative Evaluations

Outlook
(1 Lowest—5 Highest)
• **2+**

Fair Value
• **70½**

Risk
• **Low**

Earn./Div. Rank
• **B+**

Technical Eval.
• **Bullish** since 8/95

Rel. Strength Rank
(1 Lowest—99 Highest)
• **71**

Insider Activity
• **Neutral**

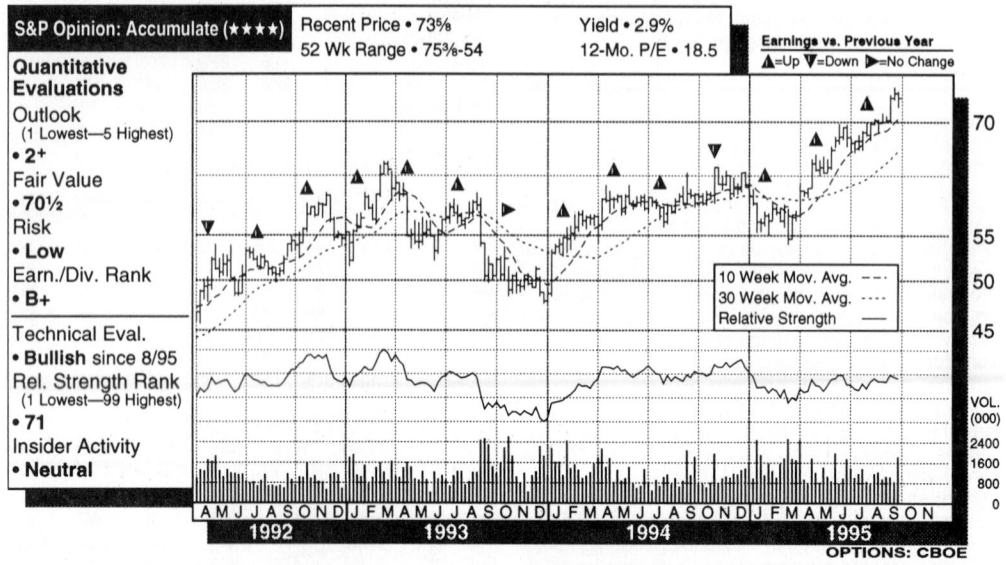

Earnings vs. Previous Year
▲=Up ▼=Down ▶=No Change

10 Week Mov. Avg. - - -
30 Week Mov. Avg. ......
Relative Strength ——

OPTIONS: CBOE

Overview - 27-SEP-95

Sales from ongoing operations for 1995 are expected to show further progress. Domestic sales should increase on demand for existing products, new products, and stepped-up marketing efforts. Sales in the Pacific Rim, Latin America and Europe should continue to improve. Results from Europe will benefit from favorable exchange rates. Margins are expected to expand on the increased volume, a more profitable product mix, cost controls and improved profitability in Japan and Europe. Various one-time charges related to an early retirement program in Japan and severance costs in Europe should be mostly offset by a one-time pretax gain of $25 million. Share earnings will benefit from fewer outstanding shares.

Valuation - 27-SEP-95

AVP's shares are attractively priced, selling at around 14 times estimated 1996 earnings. This multiple is at the low end of its historical range, implying that the shares should outperform the market over the next 12 months. Over the past few years, Avon has reported consistently higher earnings (excluding any one-time charges) on rapid overseas expansion, new products and cost controls. We believe Avon will continue to fulfill investor expectations. The company's recent history of annual dividend increases, along with its current yield (which exceeds 3%), lends additional appeal to this stock.

Key Stock Statistics

S&P EPS Est. 1995	4.30	Tang. Bk. Value/Share	2.83
P/E on S&P Est. 1995	17.1	Beta	1.45
S&P EPS Est. 1996	4.80	Shareholders	26,100
Dividend Rate/Share	2.20	Market cap. (B)	$ 5.1
Shs. outstg. (M)	68.1	Inst. holdings	84%
Avg. daily vol. (M)	0.238	Insider holdings	NA

Value of $10,000 invested 5 years ago: $ 25,332

Fiscal Year Ending Dec. 31

	1995	% Change	1994	% Change	1993	% Change
Revenues (Million $)						
1Q	976.2	10%	886.0	5%	841.9	4%
2Q	1,064	6%	1,007	6%	949.3	7%
3Q	—	—	1,010	6%	957.1	2%
4Q	—	—	1,364	8%	1,259	7%
Yr.	—	—	4,267	6%	4,008	5%
Income (Million $)						
1Q	34.40	17%	29.50	20%	24.60	NM
2Q	80.40	10%	73.20	12%	65.60	10%
3Q	—	—	51.30	-5%	54.00	NM
4Q	—	—	110.1	4%	105.4	2%
Yr.	—	—	264.8	6%	249.6	43%
Earnings Per Share ($)						
1Q	0.50	14%	0.44	29%	0.34	NM
2Q	1.17	15%	1.02	12%	0.91	10%
3Q	E0.89	22%	0.73	-3%	0.75	NM
4Q	E1.74	9%	1.59	9%	1.46	2%
Yr.	E4.30	15%	3.75	8%	3.46	42%

Next earnings report expected: late October

Business Summary - 20-SEP-95

Avon Products is one of the world's leading marketers of beauty care products, fashion jewelry, apparel, and gift and decorative products. The company completed the divestiture of its health care operations in 1990. In the third quarter of 1994, AVP sold its Giorgio prestige fragrance retail business to Procter & Gamble for $150 million in order to focus on growing its direct selling business.

By geographic area, sales and pretax profits from direct selling were derived as follows in 1994:

	Sales	Profits
United States	36%	35%
Americas	33%	47%
Pacific	16%	15%
Europe	15%	3%

Avon products are available in 120 countries around the world, and the company has direct investment operations in 40 countries, on all continents. Together, foreign operations accounted for about 64% of revenues in 1994 and 65% of related pretax profits.

Direct selling operations consist of the sale of cosmetics, toiletries and fragrances (61% of 1994's sales), gift and decorative products (18%), apparel (11%), and fashion jewelry and accessories (10%) direct to the consumer through sales representatives.

At the end of 1994, Avon had some 440,000 active representatives in the U.S. (up from 415,000 in 1993) and 1,460,000 abroad (1,330,000). Almost all representatives are women who sell on a part-time basis. The representatives are independent contractors or independent dealers, and are not agents or employees of Avon. Avon sells products through a combination of direct selling and marketing utilizing its representatives, the mail, or by phone or fax.

Important Developments

Aug. '95—AVP announced that its Chinese subsidiary was planning to build a new $40 million manufacturing plant in China to support the company's aggressive expansion in that country.

Jul. '95—AVP attributed the 11% increase in its second quarter 1995 net income (including a net one-time gain of $3 million) from continuing operations to strong results (excluding any one-time charges) in Brazil, Europe, and the Pacific region. AVP's U.S. operations reported a pretax profit increase of only 2% on a 4% decrease in sales, versus record second quarter results last year.

Capitalization

Long Term Debt: $114,200,000 (6/95).

Per Share Data ($)   (Year Ended Dec. 31)

	1994	1993	1992	1991	1990	1989
Tangible Bk. Val.	2.58	2.34	2.30	1.48	3.97	-1.67
Cash Flow	4.54	4.22	3.18	3.72	3.75	3.20
Earnings	3.75	3.46	2.43	2.92	2.81	2.10
Dividends	1.90	1.70	1.50	4.40	1.00	1.00
Payout Ratio	51%	49%	62%	164%	36%	49%
Prices - High	63⅝	64⅜	60¼	49	38⅛	41¼
- Low	48⅜	47⅝	44	26⅛	22¾	19½
P/E Ratio - High	17	19	25	17	14	20
- Low	13	14	18	9	8	9

Income Statement Analysis (Million $)

	1994	%Chg	1993	%Chg	1992	%Chg	1991
Revs.	4,267	6%	4,008	5%	3,810	6%	3,593
Oper. Inc.	551	8%	511	NM	513	3%	500
Depr.	55.7	2%	54.7	NM	54.2	2%	52.9
Int. Exp.	51.0	13%	45.0	2%	44.0	-55%	97.0
Pretax Inc.	434	4%	418	34%	312	-16%	372
Eff. Tax Rate	38%	—	39%	—	42%	—	42%
Net Inc.	265	6%	250	43%	175	-17%	211

Balance Sheet & Other Fin. Data (Million $)

	1994	1993	1992	1991	1990	1989
Cash	215	232	147	116	380	84.0
Curr. Assets	1,150	1,082	903	896	1,174	1,020
Total Assets	1,978	1,958	1,736	1,729	2,059	2,098
Curr. Liab.	1,141	1,059	1,003	1,031	1,102	963
LT Debt	117	124	178	208	335	674
Common Eqty.	186	314	311	252	375	210
Total Cap.	383	511	548	540	812	989
Cap. Exp.	100	60.0	80.0	65.0	38.0	37.0
Cash Flow	321	304	229	245	213	177

Ratio Analysis

	1994	1993	1992	1991	1990	1989
Curr. Ratio	1.0	1.0	0.9	0.9	1.1	1.1
% LT Debt of Cap.	30.4	24.2	32.4	38.6	41.2	68.1
% Net Inc.of Revs.	6.2	6.2	4.6	5.9	5.7	4.6
% Ret. on Assets	13.7	13.5	10.1	9.7	9.4	6.5
% Ret. on Equity	108.9	79.9	62.2	53.1	54.3	52.6

Dividend Data —Dividends have been paid since 1919. A dividend reinvestment plan is available. A "poison pill" stock purchase right was adopted in 1987.

Amt. of Div. $	Date Decl.	Ex-Div. Date	Stock of Record	Payment Date
0.500	Nov. 03	Nov. 09	Nov. 16	Dec. 01 '94
0.500	Feb. 02	Feb. 08	Feb. 14	Mar. 01 '95
0.500	May. 04	May. 11	May. 17	Jun. 01 '95
0.550	Aug. 02	Aug. 16	Aug. 18	Sep. 01 '95

Data as orig. reptd.; bef. results of disc. opers. and/or spec. items. Per share data adj. for stk. divs. as of ex-div. date.
E-Estimated. NA-Not Available. NM-Not Meaningful. NR-Not Ranked.

Office—9 West 57th St., New York, NY 10019. **Tel**—(212) 546-6015. **Chrmn & CEO**—J. E. Preston. **Pres**—E. J. Robinson. **SVP-CFO**—E. D. Woodbury. **VP-Secy**—W. M. Miller, Jr. **Investor Contact**—Ann Scavullo. **Dirs**—B. Barnes, R. S. Barton, D. B. Burke, E. T. Fogarty, S. C. Gault, G. V. Grune, C. S. Locke, A. S. Moore, R. D. Oliver, J. E. Preston, E. J. Robinson, J. A. Rice, C. C. Selby. **Transfer Agent & Registrar**—First Chicago Trust Co. of New York, NYC. **Incorporated** in New York in 1916. **Empl**-30,400. **S&P Analyst:** E.A. Vandeventer

Baker Hughes

NYSE Symbol **BHI**
In S&P 500

02-AUG-95

Industry:
Oil and Gas

Summary: A leader in the oil well equipment and services industry, this company is the world's largest maker of bits used by the oil and gas industries.

S&P Opinion: Buy (★★★★)

Recent Price • 21⅞	Yield • 2.1%
52 Wk Range • 23¾-16¾	12-Mo. P/E • 27.0

Quantitative Evaluations

Outlook
(1 Lowest—5 Highest)
• 1

Fair Value
• 19⅛

Risk
• **Low**

Earn./Div. Rank
• **B**

Technical Eval.
• **Bearish** since 5/95

Rel. Strength Rank
(1 Lowest—99 Highest)
• 46

Insider Activity
• **NA**

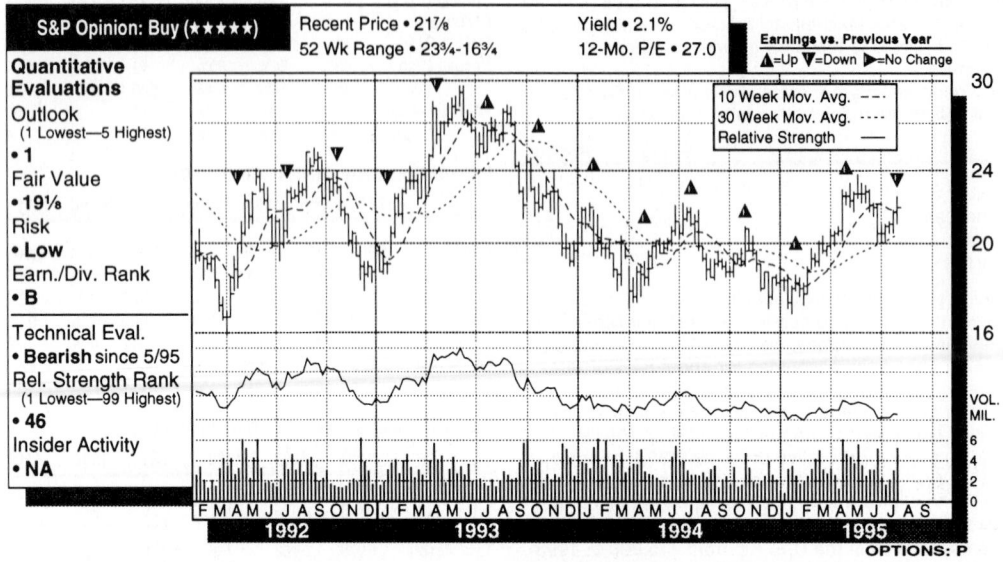

Earnings vs. Previous Year
▲=Up ▼=Down ▶=No Change

10 Week Mov. Avg. – – –
30 Week Mov. Avg. ·····
Relative Strength —

OPTIONS: P

Overview - 02-AUG-95

Revenues should continue to advance near term, reflecting our forecast of a moderate pickup in gas and oil drilling outside the U.S., as well as the company's ability to garner additional market share in its oilfield services segment. However, oil prices have fallen $3/bbl over the past two months. Yet, demand for natural gas is expanding, particularly from the rapidly growing economies such as those of the Pacific Rim. Further restructurings, including asset sales, are anticipated as the company repositions its portfolio of businesses to allow it to focus on its core strengths. Looking beyond 1995, we see average annual earnings growth exceeding 14%.

Valuation - 02-AUG-95

The shares have recently been trading in a narrow range, in spite of the drop in oil prices precipitated by threats of increased production from OPEC. In 1995, the price of natural gas, a primary driver for rig count growth, has seen the impact of mild weather and increased gas production. Average prices are currently forecast to fall from those observed in 1994. However, rig counts should remain stable, due to high levels of gas demand growth. With current low gas price levels, BHI is likely to seek acquisitions that would create further synergies for their business, and lead to further market share gains. The relative age of the oil and gas infrastructure thoughout the world, as well at the increased efficiency attainable with today's equipment bode well for the shares.

Key Stock Statistics

S&P EPS Est. 1995	0.71	Tang. Bk. Value/Share	4.56
P/E on S&P Est. 1995	30.8	Beta	1.14
S&P EPS Est. 1996	1.00	Shareholders	18,200
Dividend Rate/Share	0.46	Market cap. (B)	$ 3.1
Shs. outstg. (M)	141.1	Inst. holdings	72%
Avg. daily vol. (M)	0.609	Insider holdings	NA

Value of $10,000 invested 5 years ago: $ 9,748

Fiscal Year Ending Sep. 30

	1995	% Change	1994	% Change	1993	% Change
Revenues (Million $)						
1Q	606.9	-3%	624.6	-9%	684.0	13%
2Q	652.6	NM	650.0	-6%	692.0	11%
3Q	668.4	13%	590.5	-12%	670.0	4%
4Q	—	—	639.7	-2%	654.8	-2%
Yr.	—	—	2,505	-7%	2,702	6%
Income (Million $)						
1Q	24.23	44%	16.88	NM	4.21	-83%
2Q	28.00	20%	23.29	NM	2.80	-85%
3Q	32.24	-6%	34.44	45%	23.83	NM
4Q	—	—	56.54	102%	28.02	18%
Yr.	—	—	131.1	123%	58.86	NM
Earnings Per Share ($)						
1Q	0.15	50%	0.10	NM	0.01	-94%
2Q	0.18	29%	0.14	—	Nil	—
3Q	0.09	-59%	0.22	47%	0.15	NM
4Q	E0.28	—	0.39	117%	0.18	20%
Yr.	E0.71	—	0.85	150%	0.34	—

Next earnings report expected: mid November

Baker Hughes

Business Summary - 02-AUG-95

Baker Hughes provides a wide range of equipment and services used in the drilling, completion and reworking of oil and gas wells. It also makes process equipment for pumping and treating liquids, and specialty chemicals for water treatment. The company was formed in 1987 through the merger of Baker International Corp. and Hughes Tool Co. Since its inception, BHI has made a series of acquisitions and has disposed of noncore businesses. BHI sold its EnviroTech Measurements & Controls group in March 1994 and its EnviroTech Pumpsystems unit in the fourth quarter of fiscal 1994.

Segment contributions in fiscal 1994 (million $):

	Revs.	Profits
Oilfield products & services	$2,110	$158
Process equipment	297	22

International sales in fiscal 1994 accounted for 48% of revenues. BHI's overseas businesses earned $158 million, while domestic operations earned $60 million loss. The sale of products in fiscal 1994 accounted for $1.8 billion of revenues, and services and rentals totaled $777 million.

Oilfield equipment includes a broad range of rolling cutter and diamond bits and basic drilling rig equipment. The company believes it is the leading maker of rock bits. It also produces drilling fluids for oil and gas wells.

The process equipment segment makes and sells products and provides services used (after oil and gas wells are drilled) to achieve safety and long-term productivity, to provide structural integrity, to protect against pressure and corrosion damage, and to stimulate or rework wells.

Important Developments

Jul. '95—Baker Hughes' third quarter operating earnings (excluding non-recurring items) rose 50% to $32.2 million ($0.21 a share), owing to market share increases and improved margins at Baker Hughes INTEQ (BHI's integrated solutions segment). Net income in the quarter was reduced by $0.12 a share due to the redemption of preferred stock held by Sonat Inc. Oilfield revenues rose 12% on a year to year basis, while worldwide rig counts were down 4%, as drillers were faced with lower natural gas prices. The company noted increased revenues per rig as a driver of earnings growth in the quarter. For the remainder of fiscal 1995, the company expects increased drilling activity in the Western Hemisphere, driven largely by natural gas drilling in Venezuela, Argentina and Columbia, and a modest increase in North Sea activity.

Capitalization

Long Term Debt: $760,167,000 (3/95).

Per Share Data ($) (Year Ended Sep. 30)

	1994	1993	1992	1991	1990	1989
Tangible Bk. Val.	10.21	10.04	10.43	11.17	10.36	6.95
Cash Flow	1.94	1.62	1.12	2.27	1.94	1.46
Earnings	0.85	0.34	Nil	1.26	1.06	0.64
Dividends	0.46	0.46	0.46	0.46	0.46	0.46
Payout Ratio	54%	135%	NM	37%	47%	73%
Prices - High	22⅛	29⅝	25⅜	31	34¾	27⅝
- Low	17	18½	15⅞	17⅞	21¾	13⅝
P/E Ratio - High	26	87	NM	25	33	43
- Low	20	54	NM	14	21	21

Income Statement Analysis (Million $)

	1994	%Chg	1993	%Chg	1992	%Chg	1991
Revs.	2,505	-7%	2,702	6%	2,539	-10%	2,828
Oper. Inc.	361	-5%	380	16%	329	-24%	434
Depr.	154	-14%	179	15%	156	12%	139
Int. Exp.	63.8	-1%	64.7	-5%	68.1	-19%	83.6
Pretax Inc.	226	126%	100	NM	32.0	-85%	212
Eff. Tax Rate	42%	—	41%	—	84%	—	18%
Net Inc.	131	122%	59.0	NM	5.0	-97%	173

Balance Sheet & Other Fin. Data (Million $)

	1994	1993	1992	1991	1990	1989
Cash	69.0	7.0	7.0	52.0	125	116
Curr. Assets	1,400	1,417	1,361	1,358	1,306	1,165
Total Assets	3,000	3,143	3,213	2,906	2,784	2,066
Curr. Liab.	545	496	646	705	630	545
LT Debt	638	936	812	545	612	417
Common Eqty.	1,438	1,411	1,446	1,545	1,424	903
Total Cap.	2,334	2,628	2,523	2,155	2,113	1,502
Cap. Exp.	109	127	138	161	133	145
Cash Flow	273	225	156	312	248	174

Ratio Analysis

	1994	1993	1992	1991	1990	1989
Curr. Ratio	2.6	2.9	2.1	1.9	2.1	2.1
% LT Debt of Cap.	27.3	35.6	32.2	25.3	28.9	27.8
% Net Inc.of Revs.	5.2	2.2	0.2	6.1	5.4	3.6
% Ret. on Assets	4.3	1.8	0.2	6.1	5.5	3.9
% Ret. on Equity	8.4	3.3	NM	11.6	11.1	8.5

Dividend Data (Baker International had paid dividends since 1929 and Hughes Tool since 1973. Payments by the merged company began in 1987. A "poison pill" stock purchase right was adopted in 1988.)

Amt. of Div. $	Date Decl.	Ex-Div. Date	Stock of Record	Payment Date
0.115	Jul. 27	Aug. 02	Aug. 08	Aug. 26 '94
0.115	Oct. 26	Nov. 01	Nov. 07	Nov. 25 '94
0.115	Jan. 25	Jan. 31	Feb. 06	Feb. 24 '95
0.115	Apr. 26	May. 02	May. 08	May. 26 '95
0.115	Jul. 26	Aug. 03	Aug. 07	Aug. 25 '95

Data as orig. reptd.; bef. results of disc. opers. and/or spec. items. Per share data adj. for stk. divs. as of ex-div. date. E-Estimated. NA-Not Available. NM-Not Meaningful. NR-Not Ranked.

Office—3900 Essex Lane, Houston, TX 77027-5177. **Tel**—(713) 439-8600. **Chrmn, Pres & CEO**—J. D. Woods. **VP-CFO & Treas**—E. L. Mattson. **Secy**—L. O'Donnell III. **VP & Investor Contact**—S. B. Gill. **Dirs**—L. M. Alberthal, Jr., G. M. Anderson, V. G. Beghini, J. S. Blanton, H. M. Conger, E. M. Filter, J. B. Foster, R. D. Kinder, J. F. Maher, D. G. Mead, D. C. Trauscht, J. D. Woods. **Transfer Agent & Registrar**—First Chicago Trust Co. of New York, NYC. **Incorporated** in Delaware in 1987. **Empl**-14,700. **S&P Analyst:** Raymond J. Deacon

Ball Corp.

NYSE Symbol **BLL**
In **S&P 500**

08-AUG-95 Industry: Containers

Summary: Ball manufactures metal and glass food and beverage containers and other packaging products, and has interests in aerospace and other technical fields.

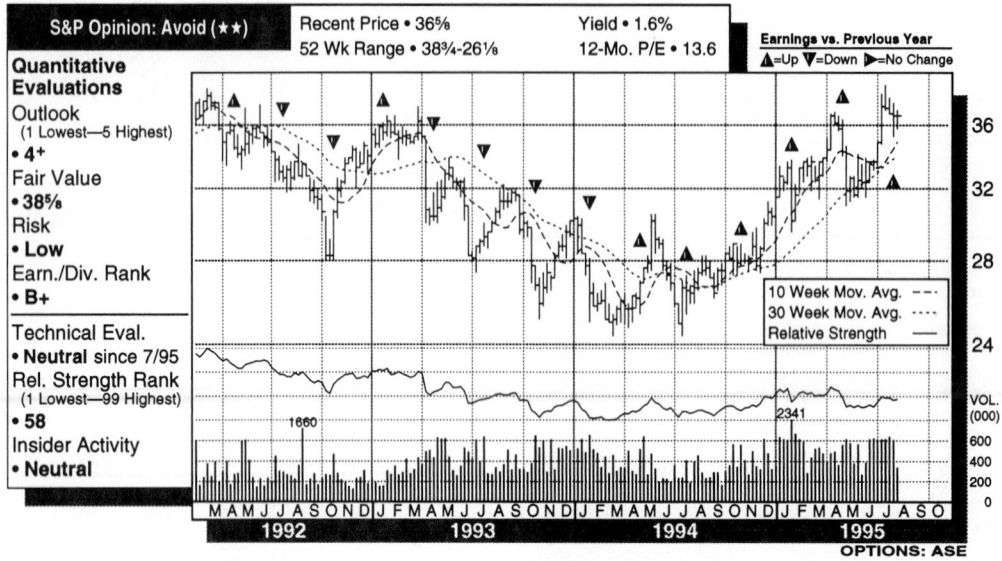

S&P Opinion: Avoid (★★)	Recent Price • 36⅝ — Yield • 1.6%
	52 Wk Range • 38¾-26⅛ — 12-Mo. P/E • 13.6

Earnings vs. Previous Year
▲=Up ▼=Down ▶=No Change

Quantitative Evaluations

Outlook
(1 Lowest—5 Highest)
• **4+**

Fair Value
• **38⅝**

Risk
• **Low**

Earn./Div. Rank
• **B+**

Technical Eval.
• **Neutral** since 7/95

Rel. Strength Rank
(1 Lowest—99 Highest)
• **58**

Insider Activity
• **Neutral**

10 Week Mov. Avg. ---
30 Week Mov. Avg. ·····
Relative Strength —

VOL. (000)

OPTIONS: ASE

Overview - 08-AUG-95

Sales from continuing operations will rise in 1996 due to price increases to offset higher raw materials costs. Only a slight rise in packaging volume is expected. Stable margins are expected as gains in productivity offset materials cost increases not recaptured in price hikes. Aerospace should also advance in 1996 as backlogs have continued to grow. We now expect interest expense to rise due to sharply higher levels of debt and with the impact of LIFO charges, only modestly higher net income is expected. The contribution of BLL's glass container operations to the Saint-Gobain joint venture would remove related sales and expenses from BLL's income statement and replace them with a single line for BLL's share of the income or loss of the joint venture.

Valuation - 08-AUG-95

We continue our avoid recommendation for this stock. Packaging, BLL's largest business, is an industry susceptible to sudden competitive pricing pressures, particularly as declining segments such as glass undergo bouts of erosion. The shift away from glass will continue as newer heat-resistant plastics draw business from hot-fill products. Segregation of glass operations in the Saint-Gobain joint venture may stabilize the results of BLL's 100%-owned operations, but the impact of the joint venture's equity results may add volatility and lessen the predictability of BLL's earnings. We are also concerned that start-up costs for the PET bottle business could stymie earnings growth.

Key Stock Statistics

S&P EPS Est. 1995	2.40	Tang. Bk. Value/Share	17.49
P/E on S&P Est. 1995	15.3	Beta	0.85
S&P EPS Est. 1996	2.55	Shareholders	10,800
Dividend Rate/Share	0.60	Market cap. (B)	$ 1.1
Shs. outstg. (M)	30.2	Inst. holdings	69%
Avg. daily vol. (M)	0.124	Insider holdings	NA

Value of $10,000 invested 5 years ago: $ 13,004

Fiscal Year Ending Dec. 31

	1995	% Change	1994	% Change	1993	% Change
Revenues (Million $)						
1Q	605.6	3%	587.3	10%	534.7	10%
2Q	755.2	12%	676.6	2%	665.5	11%
3Q	—	—	717.5	5%	683.0	20%
4Q	—	—	613.3	10%	557.7	6%
Yr.	—	—	2,595	6%	2,441	12%
Income (Million $)						
1Q	19.60	87%	10.50	15%	9.12	-19%
2Q	21.90	27%	17.20	29%	13.30	-30%
3Q	—	—	23.30	NM	3.80	-82%
4Q	—	—	22.00	NM	-58.70	NM
Yr.	—	—	73.00	NM	-30.40	NM
Earnings Per Share ($)						
1Q	0.63	91%	0.33	6%	0.31	-18%
2Q	0.70	27%	0.55	28%	0.43	-38%
3Q	E0.65	—	0.76	NM	0.10	-87%
4Q	E0.42	—	0.71	NM	-2.02	NM
Yr.	E2.40	—	2.35	NM	-1.24	NM

Next earnings report expected: late October

Ball Corp.

08-AUG-95

Business Summary - 08-AUG-95

Ball manufactures metal and glass containers for the beverage and food industries and provides aerospace and communications systems and services. Contributions in 1994 (profits in million $):

	Sales	Profits
Packaging products	90%	$153.3
Aerospace & Technologies	10%	19.1

Packaging products include aluminum and steel two piece beverage cans and two and three piece steel food cans (61% of 1994 sales); and glass containers for food and beverage packaging (29%). BLL believes it is the third largest producer in each of the three packaging market segments within which it competes. Anheuser-Busch accounted for 11% of 1994 sales. Sales to all Pepsi and Coca-Cola bottlers accounted for 21% of 1994 sales.

In 1995, BLL entered the plastic packaging business by securing its first contract to supply Pepsi with PET bottles in January 1996. A plant will be built in the Los Angeles area. In July 1995, BLL announced plans to build a second PET bottle plant in New York State to supply two customers in New York beginning in early 1996.

Ball Aerospace & Technologies is comprised of five businesses: electro-optics/cryogenics, telecommunications, time/frequency standards, space systems and systems engineering. U.S. government agencies account for about 78% of this segment's sales. Total backlog at June 30, 1995, was $470 million.

Important Developments

Jun. '95—BLL and Group Saint-Gobain agreed to form a glass container manufacturing company in the U.S. with sales of more than $1.5 billion. BLL will transfer the assets of Ball Glass Container Corp. to a new joint venture company to be owned 58% by Saint-Gobain and 42% by BLL. Concurrently, American National Can, a unit of Pechiney S.A., entered into an agreement with the joint venture to sell its Foster-Forbes glass operations to the joint venture. The joint venture will operate 22 plants in 15 states in the U.S., employing 8,500 people and supplying glass containers for food, wine, beer, juice and other beverages.

Capitalization

Long Term Debt: $488,900,000 (6/30/95), incl. ESOP debt.
Series B ESOP Convertible Pfd. Stock: 1,828,000 shs. (stated value $36.75). Conv. into 1.1552 com. shs. Held by ESOP trust.
Minority Interest: $23,200,000.

Per Share Data ($)

(Year Ended Dec. 31)

	1994	1993	1992	1991	1990	1989
Tangible Bk. Val.	15.80	13.75	20.35	17.16	14.81	14.27
Cash Flow	6.46	2.59	6.00	6.82	4.47	3.62
Earnings	2.35	-1.24	2.21	2.42	2.03	1.44
Dividends	0.60	1.24	1.22	1.18	1.14	1.10
Payout Ratio	26%	NM	56%	54%	57%	73%
Prices - High	32⅛	37¼	39½	38¼	34½	34⅜
- Low	24⅜	25⅛	28	25⅝	26	25¼
P/E Ratio - High	14	NM	18	16	17	24
- Low	10	NM	13	11	13	18

Income Statement Analysis (Million $)

	1994	%Chg	1993	%Chg	1992	%Chg	1991
Revs.	2,595	6%	2,441	12%	2,178	-4%	2,267
Oper. Inc.	291	37%	213	-11%	238	-6%	253
Depr.	122	11%	110	11%	99	-3%	102
Int. Exp.	44.5	-7%	47.6	25%	38.2	-10%	42.4
Pretax Inc.	122	NM	-50.0	NM	103	-6%	109
Eff. Tax Rate	37%	—	NM	—	35%	—	37%
Net Inc.	73.0	NM	-32.5	NM	62.9	-5%	66.2

Balance Sheet & Other Fin. Data (Million $)

	1994	1993	1992	1991	1990	1989
Cash	10.4	8.2	14.5	20.8	30.0	10.4
Curr. Assets	698	692	619	634	542	374
Total Assets	1,760	1,796	1,564	1,559	1,308	938
Curr. Liab.	500	451	359	442	323	219
LT Debt	377	513	452	334	405	263
Common Eqty.	605	549	596	487	337	314
Total Cap.	1,066	1,153	1,159	1,074	944	698
Cap. Exp.	95.0	141	110	96.0	34.0	56.0
Cash Flow	192	74.0	156	158	98.0	83.0

Ratio Analysis

	1994	1993	1992	1991	1990	1989
Curr. Ratio	1.4	1.5	1.7	1.4	1.7	1.7
% LT Debt of Cap.	35.4	44.5	39.0	31.1	42.9	37.6
% Net Inc.of Revs.	2.8	NM	2.9	2.9	3.7	2.9
% Ret. on Assets	4.1	NM	4.1	4.3	4.5	4.1
% Ret. on Equity	12.0	NM	9.9	12.7	13.6	9.3

Dividend Data (Dividends have been paid since 1958. A dividend reinvestment plan is available. A "poison pill" stock purchase right was adopted in 1986.)

Amt. of Div. $	Date Decl.	Ex-Div. Date	Stock of Record	Payment Date
0.150	Jul. 27	Aug. 26	Sep. 01	Sep. 15 '94
0.150	Oct. 26	Nov. 25	Dec. 01	Dec. 15 '94
0.150	Jan. 25	Feb. 23	Mar. 01	Mar. 15 '95
0.150	Apr. 27	May. 25	Jun. 01	Jun. 15 '95
0.150	Jul. 26	Aug. 30	Sep. 01	Sep. 15 '95

Data as orig. reptd.; bef. results of disc. opers. and/or spec. items. Per share data adj. for stk. divs. as of ex-div. date. E-Estimated. NA-Not Available. NM-Not Meaningful. NR-Not Ranked.

Office—345 South High St., Muncie, IN 47307-0407. **Tel**—(317) 747-6100. **Chrmn**—A. M. Owsley. **Pres & CEO**—G. A. Sissel. **SVP & CFO**—R. D. Hoover. **Secy**—E. A. Overmyer. **Investor Contact**—Brad Wilkes. **Dirs**—F. A. Bracken, H. M. Dean, J. T. Hackett, J. F. Lehman, J. Nicholson, A. M. Owsley, G. A. Sissel, W. T. Stephens, W. P. Stiritz. **Transfer Agent & Registrar**—First Chicago Trust Co. of New York, Jersey City, NJ. **Incorporated** in Indiana in 1922. **Empl**-12,873. **S&P Analyst:** Joshua M. Harari, CFA

Bally Entertainment

NYSE Symbol **BLY**
In S&P 500

14-AUG-95

Industry: Leisure/Amusement

Summary: This major gaming company operates casino/hotels in Atlantic City and Las Vegas. BLY plans to spin off ownership of its large fitness center business to BLY shareholders.

| S&P Opinion: Hold (★★★) | Recent Price • 12¼ | Yield • Nil |
| | 52 Wk Range • 12⅞-5¼ | 12-Mo. P/E • 49.0 |

Quantitative Evaluations

Outlook
(1 Lowest—5 Highest)
• **1+**

Fair Value
• **10⅜**

Risk
• **Average**

Earn./Div. Rank
• **C**

Technical Eval.
• **Bullish** since 7/95

Rel. Strength Rank
(1 Lowest—99 Highest)
• **71**

Insider Activity
• **NA**

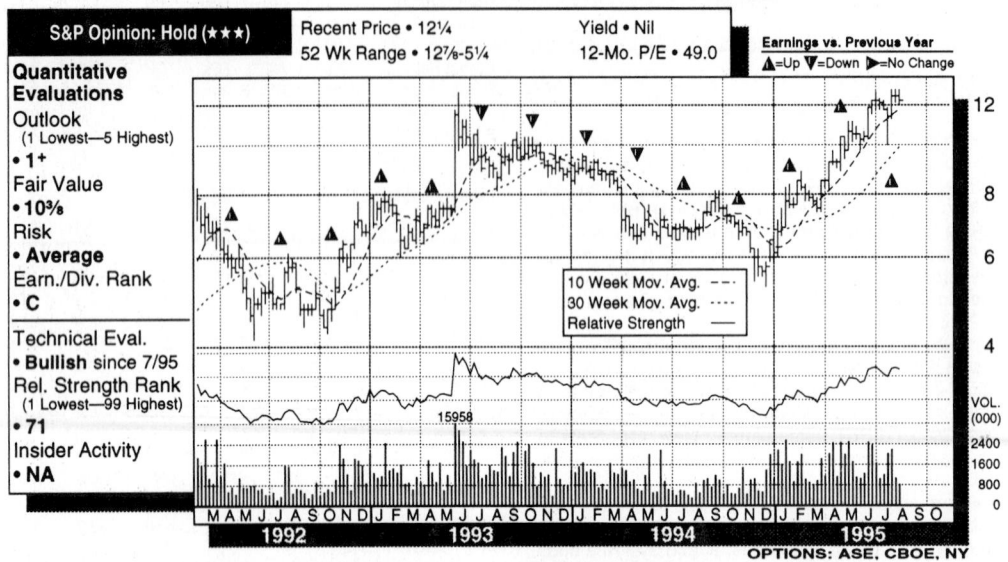

Earnings vs. Previous Year
▲=Up ▼=Down ▶=No Change

10 Week Mov. Avg. ---
30 Week Mov. Avg. ····
Relative Strength —

15958

VOL. (000)
2400
1600
800
0

1992 1993 1994 1995

OPTIONS: ASE, CBOE, NY

Overview - 14-AUG-95

In 1995, we expect BLY's earnings to be helped by further gains from Atlantic City, and the debut of a Louisiana joint venture casino boat. Our $0.55 earnings per share estimate includes likely pre-opening charges related to the Louisiana project and the expected debut of a relocated casino barge in northern Mississippi. In Las Vegas, we look for BLY's customer levels to be boosted by the spring 1995 opening of a nearby monorail system. BLY's longer-term expansion may include a large addition to Bally's Park Place in Atlantic City (possibly opening in early 1997, and a new casino/hotel in Las Vegas. However, BLY's sizable debt level may restrain its ability to successfully pursue some large new gaming projects or acquisitions, particularly without partners.

Valuation - 14-AUG-95

With improving operations in Atlantic City, and growth prospects in newer gaming markets, the stock of this major casino company has gained favor with investors. The company's dependence on the Atlantic City gaming market becomes less worrisome as prospects for approval on casinos in nearby states diminish. Also, we look for the potential spinoff of BLY's large fitness center business to be at least modestly beneficial to BLY shareholders. Overall, we view BLY's stock as having speculative appeal as a holding for capital gains. However, with the stock up sharply from its 1995 low, and the company having a a relatively high cost of capital, we would not be a purchaser of additional shares at this time.

Key Stock Statistics

S&P EPS Est. 1995	0.55	Tang. Bk. Value/Share	2.88
P/E on S&P Est. 1995	22.3	Beta	2.16
S&P EPS Est. 1996	0.80	Shareholders	16,200
Dividend Rate/Share	Nil	Market cap. (B)	$0.576
Shs. outstg. (M)	47.0	Inst. holdings	18%
Avg. daily vol. (M)	0.301	Insider holdings	NA

Value of $10,000 invested 5 years ago: $ 8,956

Fiscal Year Ending Dec. 31

	1995	% Change	1994	% Change	1993	% Change
Revenues (Million $)						
1Q	228.3	8%	212.3	-37%	335.0	NM
2Q	245.0	3%	238.4	-27%	327.9	-1%
3Q	—	—	261.8	-21%	332.5	NM
4Q	—	—	230.3	-29%	324.8	8%
Yr.	—	—	942.3	-29%	1,320	2%
Income (Million $)						
1Q	4.17	NM	-9.70	NM	3.84	-1%
2Q	9.38	52%	6.17	163%	2.35	-44%
3Q	—	—	11.77	NM	-0.32	NM
4Q	—	—	-10.20	NM	-21.90	36%
Yr.	—	—	-1.90	NM	-16.03	NM
Earnings Per Share ($)						
1Q	0.07	NM	-0.22	NM	0.07	40%
2Q	0.17	42%	0.12	NM	0.04	-67%
3Q	E0.28	17%	0.24	NM	-0.02	NM
4Q	E0.04	NM	-0.23	NM	-0.48	NM
Yr.	E0.55	NM	-0.10	NM	-0.40	NM

Next earnings report expected: early November

Business Summary - 14-AUG-95

Bally Entertainment (formerly Bally Manufacturing) is a major leisure-time company whose operations now consist primarily of several casino/hotels, plus a large fitness center business, which BLY is planning to spin off. In July 1995, a BLY joint venture casino boat opened in Lousiana, and BLY is planning to open a relocated Mississippi casino barge in the fall of 1995. During recent years, BLY has been involved in a sizable restructuring, including asset sales and refinancings. BLY no longer has any common stock interest in equipment maker Bally Gaming International.

BLY operates two of the 12 casino/hotels-- Bally's Park Place and The Grand-- in Atlantic City. These facilities have provided most of BLY's operating profit in recent years. Also, BLY (or subsidiaries) own about 80% of the common stock of a reorganized Nevada casino business, whose Las Vegas facility BLY operates.

BLY's relocated Mississippi casino would be in Tunica County (near Memphis, Tenn.), Between late 1993 and early 1995, BLY operated a casino at another Tunica County site.

Also, BLY is the largest health club operator in the U.S., with about 340 fitness centers operating under various names. Ownership of this business, which is now being treated as a discontinued operation, may be spun off to BLY shareholders in 1995.

Important Developments

Jul. '95—A BLY joint venture casino boat opened on Lake Ponchartrain, about eight miles from the French Quarter in New Orleans. Also, in Mississippi, BLY is likely to reopen a casino barge in the fall of 1995, at a new site closer to Memphis, Tenn. In this project, BLY will be a joint venture partner with Lady Luck Gaming Corp. In addition, BLY has announced plans to develop a $420 million casino/hotel project in Las Vegas. The facility, with a Parisian theme, would open in 1997. In Atlantic City, Bally's Park Place may receive a large casino expansion. At BLY's other casino/hotel in Atlantic City--The Grand--casino space was recently expanded by about 30%. Also, BLY's directors have approved a plan to spin off ownership of its fitness center business (now treated as a discontinued operation) to shareholders. This could occur later in 1995.

Capitalization

Long Term Debt: $1,265,790,000 (3/95; excl. $283,234,000 related to fitness center business).
Minority Interest: $25,243,000 (3/95).
8% Conv. Exch. Preferred Stock: About 694,000 shs.; ea. conv. into two com. shs.

Per Share Data ($)

(Year Ended Dec. 31)

	1994	1993	1992	1991	1990	1989
Tangible Bk. Val.	2.88	1.61	2.88	2.12	1.59	8.86
Cash Flow	1.37	1.68	2.17	0.99	-5.96	5.42
Earnings	-0.10	-0.40	-0.05	-1.79	-10.57	0.66
Dividends	Nil	Nil	Nil	Nil	0.22	0.29
Payout Ratio	Nil	Nil	Nil	Nil	NM	45%
Prices - High	9⅝	12¾	8¼	6½	15⅝	29¾
- Low	5¼	6	4⅛	1⅞	2⅛	13½
P/E Ratio - High	NM	NM	NM	NM	NM	45
- Low	NM	NM	NM	NM	NM	20

Income Statement Analysis (Million $)

	1994	%Chg	1993	%Chg	1992	%Chg	1991
Revs.	942	-29%	1,320	7%	1,234	-8%	1,340
Oper. Inc.	207	NM	209	50%	139	49%	93.0
Depr.	69.0	-29%	97.0	5%	92.0	-2%	94.0
Int. Exp.	131	NM	130	3%	126	-20%	158
Pretax Inc.	6.0	NM	-21.0	NM	3.0	NM	-78.0
Eff. Tax Rate	49%	—	NM	—	83%	—	NM
Net Inc.	-2.0	NM	-16.0	NM	1.0	NM	-58.0

Balance Sheet & Other Fin. Data (Million $)

	1994	1993	1992	1991	1990	1989
Cash	184	203	37.0	54.0	72.0	75.0
Curr. Assets	249	438	265	380	519	607
Total Assets	1,936	2,540	1,925	2,120	2,890	3,029
Curr. Liab.	178	390	336	573	1,126	543
LT Debt	1,259	1,484	1,010	978	744	1,701
Common Eqty.	259	329	376	327	331	595
Total Cap.	1,743	2,083	1,503	1,458	1,165	2,404
Cap. Exp.	96.0	97.0	40.0	42.0	204	214
Cash Flow	64.0	78.0	89.0	34.0	-168	146

Ratio Analysis

	1994	1993	1992	1991	1990	1989
Curr. Ratio	1.4	1.1	0.8	0.7	0.5	1.1
% LT Debt of Cap.	72.2	71.3	67.2	67.0	63.9	70.7
% Net Inc.of Revs.	NM	NM	NM	NM	NM	1.3
% Ret. on Assets	NM	NM	NM	NM	NM	0.9
% Ret. on Equity	NM	NM	NM	NM	NM	3.0

Dividend Data —Common dividends were omitted in October 1990. In October 1992, BLY cured an arrearage of Series D preferred stock dividends through the issuance of common stock.

Data as orig. reptd.; bef. results of disc. opers. and/or spec. items. Per share data adj. for stk. divs. as of ex-div. date.
E-Estimated. NA-Not Available. NM-Not Meaningful. NR-Not Ranked.

Office—8700 West Bryn Mawr Ave., Chicago, IL 60631. Tel—(312) 399-1300. Chrmn, CEO & Pres—A. M. Goldberg. EVP, CFO & Treas—L. S. Hillman. Secy—Carol Stone DePaul. Investor Contact—Kent McMillen. Dirs—G. H. Aronoff, B. K. Brunet, A. M. Goldberg, E. M. Halkyard, J. K. Looloian, R. J. Marano, P. L. O'Malley, J. M. Rochford. Transfer Agent & Registrar—Chemical Bank, NYC. Incorporated in Delaware in 1968. Empl- S&P Analyst: Tom Graves, CFA

Baltimore Gas & Electric

NYSE Symbol **BGE**

In S&P 500

23-AUG-95 | **Industry:** Util.-Diversified | **Summary:** This electric and gas utility serves the city of Baltimore and much of central Maryland.

S&P Opinion: Hold (★★★)

| Recent Price • 26⅛ | Yield • 6.0% |
| 52 Wk Range • 26½-20¾ | 12-Mo. P/E • 15.0 |

Quantitative Evaluations

Outlook
(1 Lowest—5 Highest)
• **3+**

Fair Value
• **25¼**

Risk
• **Low**

Earn./Div. Rank
• **A**

Technical Eval.
• **Bearish** since 2/95

Rel. Strength Rank
(1 Lowest—99 Highest)
• **55**

Insider Activity
• **Neutral**

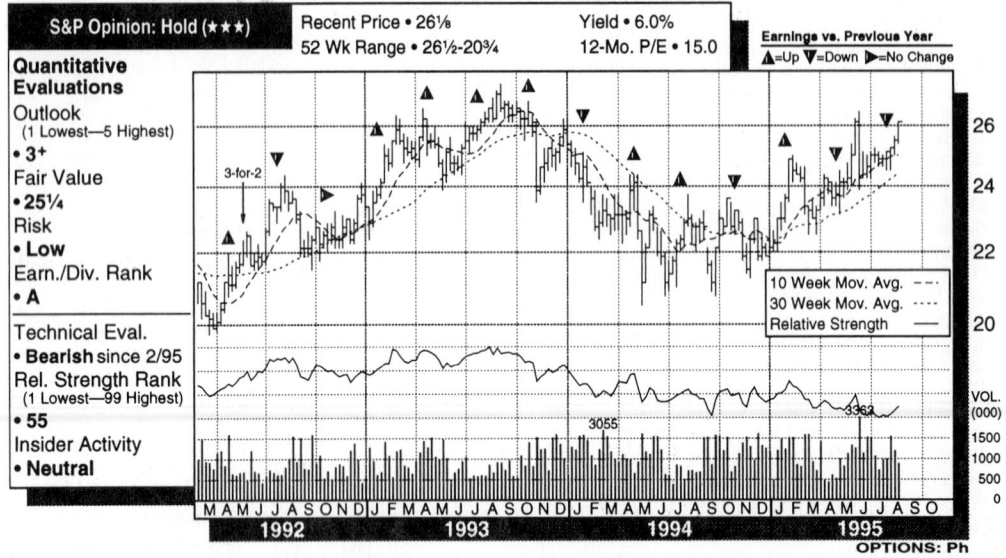

Earnings vs. Previous Year
▲=Up ▼=Down ▶=No Change

10 Week Mov. Avg. - - -
30 Week Mov. Avg. ·····
Relative Strength ——

OPTIONS: Ph

Overview - 23-AUG-95

Share earnings for 1995 should reflect somewhat higher sales of both electricity and gas, owing to a growing residential and commercial customer base. BGE continues to lower operating and maintenance expenses, which, combined with slightly higher profit contributions from diversified businesses, should help widen margins. We also expect earnings comparisons to benefit from the absence of a $0.07 writeoff of a portion of the work in progress at BGE's Perryman site in 1994. The new, cost-effective Perryman and Calvert Cliffs plants coming on stream allow BGE a competitive edge in its service area. The company also benefits from a favorable regulatory environment. The balance sheet is reasonable for a utility, with long-term debt comprising approximately 47% of total capital.

Valuation - 23-AUG-95

The shares have advanced roughly 15% from their 1994 year-end level and are currently near the upper end of their 10-year trading range. The company's stock price improvement primarily reflects the Federal Reserve's easing of interest rates in May, but improvement in the company's fundamentals is also a factor. The service area's low industrial customer base helps insulate BGE from stiff price competition and the company's efforts to lower debt and raise its cash flow should enhance prospects for another above-average dividend increase next Spring. The dividend payout ratio is somewhat below the industry average, so the above-average hikes should continue over the next few years.

Key Stock Statistics

S&P EPS Est. 1995	2.05	Tang. Bk. Value/Share	18.42
P/E on S&P Est. 1995	12.7	Beta	0.61
S&P EPS Est. 1996	2.16	Shareholders	81,100
Dividend Rate/Share	1.56	Market cap. (B)	$ 3.8
Shs. outstg. (M)	147.5	Inst. holdings	39%
Avg. daily vol. (M)	0.262	Insider holdings	0%

Value of $10,000 invested 5 years ago: $ 16,438

Fiscal Year Ending Dec. 31

	1995	% Change	1994	% Change	1993	% Change
Revenues (Million $)						
1Q	715.3	-7%	767.7	12%	683.8	2%
2Q	642.5	-1%	651.2	15%	564.7	4%
3Q	—	—	753.9	-3%	774.1	14%
4Q	—	—	610.3	-6%	646.1	7%
Yr.	—	—	2,783	4%	2,669	7%
Income (Million $)						
1Q	70.85	-14%	82.15	25%	65.80	11%
2Q	50.89	-24%	66.71	19%	55.88	47%
3Q	—	—	126.6	-19%	157.1	26%
4Q	—	—	48.15	55%	31.14	-27%
Yr.	—	—	323.6	4%	309.9	17%
Earnings Per Share ($)						
1Q	0.38	-22%	0.49	29%	0.38	3%
2Q	0.28	-28%	0.39	26%	0.31	55%
3Q	E0.96	22%	0.79	-22%	1.01	20%
4Q	E0.43	65%	0.26	86%	0.14	-36%
Yr.	E2.05	6%	1.93	4%	1.85	13%

Next earnings report expected: late October

Business Summary - 23-AUG-95

Baltimore Gas & Electric provides electric and gas service to a population of some 2.6 million in Maryland. The local economy includes service businesses, heavy industry and the Port of Baltimore. In 1994, electricity accounted for 76% of revenues, gas for 15%, and other activities for 9%. Electric revenues by customer were:

	1994	1993	1992	1991
Residential	44%	44%	43%	44%
Commercial	40%	41%	43%	43%
Industrial	10%	9%	10%	11%
Other	6%	6%	4%	2%

Sources of power in 1994 were coal 56%, nuclear 39%, hydro and gas 3%, oil 3%, and -1% purchased (net). Peak demand in 1994 was 6,038 mw, and capability at time of peak totaled 6,722 mw, for a capacity margin of 10%. Gas sales totaled 108,728,000 DTH in 1994, versus 107,795,000 DTH in 1993.

Construction expenditures for the electric and gas utilities totaled $449 million in 1994. Electric utility outlays include construction of two 5,000 kilowatt diesel generators at Calvert Cliffs Nuclear plant, one of which is to be completed in 1995, and a 140 megawatt (mw) combustion turbine plant the began operating in mid-1995. BGE estimates construction projects for both electric and gas facilities to improve generation, distribution and transmission facilities at $350 million, $340 million and $325 million in 1995, 1996 and 1997, respectively.

Constellation Holdings coordinates BGE's nonutility businesses in energy and environmental projects, real estate, senior living and health care, and investment and financial services. Nonutility operations accounted for earnings of $0.12 a share in 1994, versus $0.08 in 1993.

Important Developments

Aug. '95—The company requested that the Maryland Public Service Commission (PSC) decrease the electric fuel rate by 6.7% ($24 million) as of September 1, 1995. If approved, the new rate would be the 10th consecutive rate decrease and its lowest fuel rate in 12 years. The request is a result of continued strong operating performance at both the company's Calvert Cliffs nuclear plant, and its coal-fired generators, and decreasing fuel costs at the plants. A proposed rate increase in natural gas rates related to BGE's unregulated activities is pending approval in November.

Capitalization

Long Term Debt: $2,579,841,000 (3/95).
Red. Cum. Preference Stock: $279,500,000.
Cum. Pfd. & Pref. Stock: $209,185,000.

Per Share Data ($)

(Year Ended Dec. 31)

	1994	1993	1992	1991	1990	1989
Tangible Bk. Val.	18.42	17.82	17.57	16.94	16.52	16.55
Earnings	1.93	1.85	1.63	1.52	1.09	2.03
Dividends	1.51	1.47	1.43	1.40	1.40	1.38
Payout Ratio	78%	79%	88%	92%	128%	68%
Prices - High	25½	27½	24⅜	22⅞	23⅛	23¼
- Low	20½	22⅜	19¾	17⅛	16¼	19
P/E Ratio - High	13	15	15	15	16	11
- Low	11	12	12	11	12	9

Income Statement Analysis (Million $)

	1994	%Chg	1993	%Chg	1992	%Chg	1991
Revs.	2,783	4%	2,669	7%	2,491	1%	2,459
Depr.	296	25%	237	6%	223	12%	200
Maint.	165	-9%	182	5%	173	NM	174
Fxd. Chgs. Cov.	2.6	-5%	2.8	15%	2.4	14%	2.1
Constr. Credits	33.5	49%	22.5	2%	22.1	-41%	37.5
Eff. Tax Rate	32%	—	31%	—	28%	—	27%
Net Inc.	324	5%	310	17%	264	13%	234

Balance Sheet & Other Fin. Data (Million $)

	1994	1993	1992	1991	1990	1989
Gross Prop.	7,722	7,359	6,947	6,577	6,207	5,706
Cap. Exp.	483	478	389	456	535	447
Net Prop.	5,417	5,197	4,966	4,774	4,513	4,144
Capitalization:						
LT Debt	2,585	2,823	2,377	2,390	2,194	2,077
% LT Debt	45	47	43	47	46	45
Pfd.	489	552	565	568	534	492
% Pfd.	8.40	9.20	10	11	11	11
Common	2,718	2,621	2,535	2,153	2,073	2,001
% Common	47	44	46	42	43	44
Total Cap.	7,097	7,220	6,626	6,165	5,630	5,326

Ratio Analysis

	1994	1993	1992	1991	1990	1989
Oper. Ratio	82.7	81.9	82.7	83.2	85.5	80.3
% Earn. on Net Prop.	9.1	9.5	8.8	8.9	7.2	11.9
% Ret. on Revs.	11.6	11.6	10.6	9.5	8.1	13.8
% Ret. On Invest.Cap	7.2	7.2	7.1	7.5	6.4	8.5
% Return On Com.Eqty	10.6	10.4	9.5	9.0	6.6	12.6

Dividend Data

Cash has been paid each year since 1910. A dividend reinvestment plan is available.

Amt. of Div. $	Date Decl.	Ex-Div. Date	Stock of Record	Payment Date
0.380	Jul. 15	Sep. 06	Sep. 12	Oct. 03 '94
0.380	Oct. 21	Dec. 06	Dec. 12	Jan. 03 '95
0.380	Feb. 17	Mar. 06	Mar. 10	Apr. 03 '95
0.390	May. 19	Jun. 08	Jun. 12	Jul. 03 '95
0.390	Jul. 21	Sep. 07	Sep. 11	Oct. 02 '95

Data as orig. reptd.; bef. results of disc opers. and/or spec. items. Per share data adj. for stk. divs. as of ex-div. date.
E-Estimated. NA-Not Available. NM-Not Meaningful. NR-Not Ranked.

Office—Gas & Electric Building, Charles Center, Baltimore, MD 21201. **Tel**—(410) 783-5920. **Chrmn & CEO**—C. H. Poindexter. **Pres**—E. A. Crooke. **VP-CFO & Secy**—C. W. Shivery. **Investor Contact**—Kevin J. Miller. **Dirs**—H. F. Baldwin, B. B. Byron, J. O. Cole, D. A. Colussy, E. A. Crooke, J. R. Curtiss, J. W. Geckle, M. L. Grass, F. A. Hrabowski III, N. Lampton, G. V. McGowan, C. H. Poindexter, G. L. Russell Jr., M. D. Sullivan. **Transfer Agent & Registrar**—Harris Trust & Savings Bank, Chicago. **Incorporated** in Maryland in 1906. **Empl**-9,648. **S&P Analyst**: Jane Collin

Banc One

NYSE Symbol **ONE**
In S&P 500

23-OCT-95

Industry:
Banking

Summary: This Ohio-based bank holding company, the eighth largest in the U.S., operates more than 1,400 branches in 11 states, mostly in the Central and Southwest regions.

S&P Opinion: Hold (★★★)	Recent Price • 36⅜	Yield • 3.7%
	52 Wk Range • 38½-24⅛	12-Mo. P/E • 14.6

Quantitative Evaluations

Outlook
(1 Lowest—5 Highest)
• **3⁻**

Fair Value
• **37⅞**

Risk
• Average

Earn./Div. Rank
• **A+**

Technical Eval.
• **Bullish** since 4/95

Rel. Strength Rank
(1 Lowest—99 Highest)
• **68**

Insider Activity
• **Neutral**

Earnings vs. Previous Year
▲=Up ▼=Down ▶=No Change

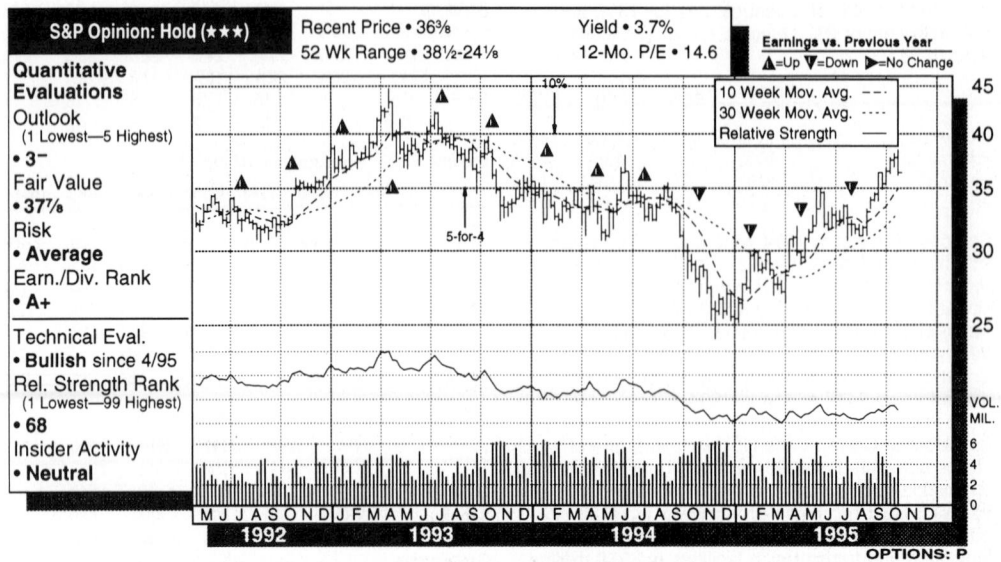

10 Week Mov. Avg. ---
30 Week Mov. Avg. ····
Relative Strength —

OPTIONS: P

Overview - 23-OCT-95

Average earning assets dipped 2.1%, year to year, in the third quarter of 1995, reflecting a run-off in the securities portfolio, but with a 13 basis point increase in the net interest margin due to a more favorable asset mix, net interest income rose 0.6%. The improvement reflects a number of steps ONE has taken to arrest margin pressure, including the purchase of interest rate caps, sale of fixed-rate securities, and issuance of intermediate term CDs. Increased contributions from merchant processing fees and loan servicing income, as well as a continued focus on expense management, should provide much of the expected earnings growth going into 1996. With reserves at 253% of nonperforming loans, the loan loss provision should not be a drag on earnings. Longer-term earnings will benefit from a focus on markets where ONE has a leading presence.

Valuation - 23-OCT-95

After adjusting for nonrecurring charges in 1994, earnings are expected to show only a modest increase in 1995, with more improvement coming in 1996. Efforts to stop margin erosion have largely succeeded, with proceeds from asset sales being reinvested at higher rates. ONE has made good progress in increasing noninterest income and controlling expenses, but pending improved results from core lending operations, the shares, which have rebounded from a late 1994 sell-off, are not expected to outperform the overall market in the near term.

Key Stock Statistics

S&P EPS Est. 1995	3.20	Tang. Bk. Value/Share	18.69
P/E on S&P Est. 1995	11.4	Beta	1.43
S&P EPS Est. 1996	3.60	Shareholders	43,900
Dividend Rate/Share	1.36	Market cap. (B)	$ 14.3
Shs. outstg. (M)	392.4	Inst. holdings	48%
Avg. daily vol. (M)	0.636	Insider holdings	NA

Value of $10,000 invested 5 years ago: $ 22,601

Fiscal Year Ending Dec. 31

	1995	% Change	1994	% Change	1993	% Change
Revenues (Million $)						
1Q	2,179	11%	1,965	13%	1,734	10%
2Q	2,216	10%	2,008	12%	1,789	19%
3Q	2,259	7%	2,113	18%	1,795	20%
4Q	—	—	1,860	2%	1,828	22%
Yr.	—	—	7,857	9%	7,227	20%
Income (Million $)						
1Q	302.5	-7%	327.0	22%	267.5	34%
2Q	307.5	-7%	330.6	17%	281.9	42%
3Q	331.0	17%	283.2	NM	284.9	49%
4Q	—	—	64.38	-78%	286.3	48%
Yr.	—	—	1,005	-10%	1,121	43%
Earnings Per Share ($)						
1Q	0.75	-5%	0.79	13%	0.70	12%
2Q	0.77	-4%	0.80	9%	0.73	16%
3Q	0.83	22%	0.68	-9%	0.75	19%
4Q	E0.85	NM	0.15	-80%	0.75	27%
Yr.	E3.20	32%	2.42	-17%	2.93	23%

Next earnings report expected: mid January

Business Summary - 20-OCT-95

Banc One Corp. is the eighth largest U.S. bank holding company, with assets at September 30, 1995 of $88.4 billion. It is the largest banking organization in Arizona and the second largest in Ohio, Indiana and West Virginia. At September 30, 1995, the company operated 1,408 banking offices through 62 affiliated banks in Ohio, Indiana, Colorado, Wisconsin, Kentucky, Illinois, Texas, Oklahoma, Arizona, Utah and West Virginia. ONE emphasizes retail banking and has extensive credit card processing operations. Lending to middle market corporations is also important. Other affiliates engage in data processing, venture capital, investment and merchant banking, trust, investment management, brokerage, equipment leasing, mortgage banking, credit card, consumer finance, and insurance.

During 1994, average earning assets of $78.3 billion (up 11% from 1993) were divided: net loans and leases 75%, securities 23%, and short-term investments 2%. Average sources of funds were noninterest bearing demand deposits 15%, other demand 11%, time deposits 26%, savings deposits 23%, short-term borrowings 12%, long-term debt 2%, equity 9%, and other 2%.

At year-end 1994, nonperforming assets were $466 million (0.75% of loans and related assets), down from $643 million (1.12%) a year earlier. The reserve for loan losses was 1.45% of total loans and leases, versus 1.68%. Net chargeoffs were 0.53% of average loans in 1994, against 0.73% in 1993.

At September 30, 1995, the company had Tier 1 and total capital ratios of 10.13% and 14.20%, respectively, versus 9.93% and 13.33% at year-end 1994.

Important Developments

Jul. '95—ONE withdrew an offer to acquire Bank of Boston Corp. (NYSE: BKB) for $45 a share following the termination of a proposed merger of equals between BKB and CoreStates Financial Corp. Banc One said it would welcome an opportunity to discuss a possible affiliation with BKB under more normal circumstances.
Jul. '95—The company agreed to acquire Premier Bancorp Inc. (assets of $5.5 billion) for $20.15 a share. Premier Bancorp operates 150 banking offices throughout Louisiana.

Capitalization

Long Term Debt: $2,677,205,000 (9/95).
Conv. Preferred Stock: $249,853,000.

Per Share Data ($) — (Year Ended Dec. 31)

	1994	1993	1992	1991	1990	1989
Tangible Bk. Val.	17.76	17.88	14.80	13.05	11.31	9.65
Earnings	2.42	2.93	2.39	2.12	1.83	1.67
Dividends	1.24	1.07	0.89	0.77	0.69	0.62
Payout Ratio	51%	37%	37%	36%	38%	38%
Prices - High	38	44¾	38⅞	34⅞	21⅞	22¼
- Low	24⅛	32¼	30⅝	16½	12½	13⅜
P/E Ratio - High	16	15	16	16	12	13
- Low	10	11	13	8	7	8

Income Statement Analysis (Million $)

	1994	%Chg	1993	%Chg	1992	%Chg	1991
Net Int. Inc.	4,189	2%	4,090	29%	3,165	79%	1,771
Tax Equiv. Adj.	88.0	11%	79.0	5%	75.0	10%	68.0
Non Int. Inc.	1,681	13%	1,492	29%	1,157	37%	844
Loan Loss Prov.	242	-34%	369	-28%	510	20%	424
% Exp/Op Revs.	65%	—	62%	—	61%	—	55%
Pretax Inc.	64.6	-96%	1,699	46%	1,161	65%	705
Eff. Tax Rate	34%	—	34%	—	33%	—	25%
Net Inc.	1,005	-10%	1,121	44%	781	48%	529
% Net Int. Marg.	5.40%	—	6.29%	—	6.13%	—	6.09%

Balance Sheet & Other Fin. Data (Million $)

	1994	1993	1992	1991	1990	1989
Earning Assets:						
Money Mkt.	NA	NA	NA	NA	NA	NA
Inv. Securities	15,152	17,408	13,884	7,989	5,272	5,133
Com'l Loans	17,958	15,064	13,534	11,055	8,530	7,740
Other Loans	44,035	38,782	25,188	19,142	11,833	10,169
Total Assets	88,923	79,919	61,417	46,293	30,336	26,552
Demand Deposits	14,406	13,675	10,316	6,729	3,729	3,545
Time Deposits	53,684	47,268	38,149	30,328	18,587	17,408
LT Debt	1,694	1,702	1,173	696	525	356
Common Eqty.	7,315	6,784	4,954	3,545	2,876	2,255

Ratio Analysis

	1994	1993	1992	1991	1990	1989
% Ret. on Assets	1.1	1.5	1.3	1.6	1.5	1.4
% Ret. on Equity	13.8	17.8	17.2	17.4	16.4	16.3
% Loan Loss Resv.	1.5	1.7	1.9	1.8	1.6	1.4
% Loans/Deposits	91.1	88.4	79.9	81.5	91.3	85.5
% Equity to Assets	8.2	8.4	7.6	8.7	9.3	8.3

Dividend Data —Dividends have been paid since 1935. A dividend reinvestment plan is available.

Amt. of Div. $	Date Decl.	Ex-Div. Date	Stock of Record	Payment Date
0.310	Oct. 18	Dec. 09	Dec. 15	Jan. 02 '95
0.340	Jan. 24	Mar. 09	Mar. 15	Mar. 31 '95
0.340	Apr. 18	Jun. 13	Jun. 15	Jun. 30 '95
0.340	Jul. 18	Sep. 13	Sep. 15	Sep. 29 '95
0.340	Oct. 17	Dec. 13	Dec. 15	Jan. 02 '96

Data as orig. reptd.; bef. results of disc opers. and/or spec. items. Per share data adj. for stk. divs. as of ex-div. date.
E-Estimated. NA-Not Available. NM-Not Meaningful. NR-Not Ranked.

Office—100 East Broad St., Columbus, OH 43271. **Tel**—(614) 248-5944. **Chrmn & CEO**—J. B. McCoy. **Pres & COO**—R. J. Lehmann. **EVP-Fin**—M. J. McMennamin. **Investor Contact**—Jacqueline R. Spak. **Dirs**—C. E. Exley, Jr., E. G. Gee, J. R. Hall, L. P. Jackson, Jr., J. W. Kessler, R. J. Lehmann, J. B. McCoy, J. G. McCoy, R. L. Scott, T. R. Shackelford, A. Shumate, F. P. Stratton, Jr., R. D. Walter. **Transfer Agent & Registrar**—Bank One, Indianapolis. **Incorporated** in Delaware in 1967; reincorporated in Ohio in 1989. **Empl**-48,800. **S&P Analyst:** Stephen R. Biggar

Bank of Boston

NYSE Symbol **BKB**

In S&P 500

10-AUG-95

Industry:
Banking

Summary: This bank holding company, the 19th largest in the U.S. with assets of $45 billion, owns banks in Massachusetts, Connecticut and Rhode Island.

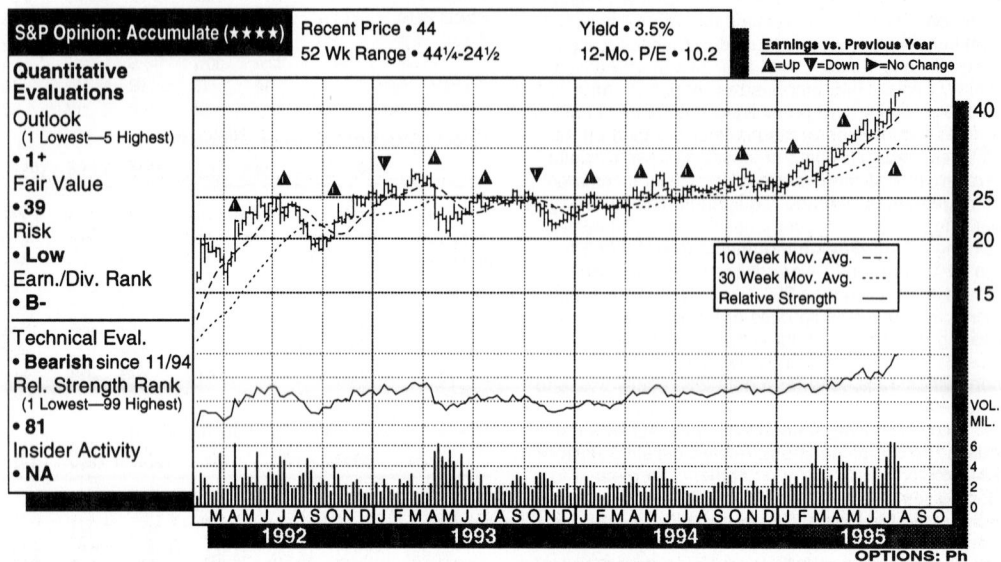

S&P Opinion: Accumulate (★★★★)	Recent Price • 44	Yield • 3.5%
	52 Wk Range • 44¼-24½	12-Mo. P/E • 10.2

Earnings vs. Previous Year
▲=Up ▼=Down ▶=No Change

Quantitative Evaluations

Outlook
(1 Lowest—5 Highest)
• **1+**

Fair Value
• **39**

Risk
• **Low**

Earn./Div. Rank
• **B-**

Technical Eval.
• **Bearish** since 11/94

Rel. Strength Rank
(1 Lowest—99 Highest)
• **81**

Insider Activity
• **NA**

10 Week Mov. Avg. ---
30 Week Mov. Avg. ····
Relative Strength —

VOL.
MIL.

OPTIONS: Ph

Overview - 10-AUG-95

Earnings in 1995 will likely continue to benefit from a focus on global networks and strength in the personal and corporate banking businesses. The net interest margin widened considerably, year to year, in the second quarter of 1995, as loan yields continue to grow at a faster pace than retail deposit rates. Careful attention to expense levels, including staff reductions in existing operations, contributed to an improvement in the operating efficiency ratio (excluding special items) to 57.9% in 1995's second quarter, versus 61.4% a year earlier. A higher revenue base should provide further modest efficiency improvement in 1995. Despite strong credit quality, the provision for loan losses will likely trend upward in 1995 due to management's intent to further strengthen the loan loss reserve.

Valuation - 10-AUG-95

Based on improving fundamentals, the shares are expected to continue to outperform the overall market in the year ahead. BKB's well diversified income stream, widening margins and demonstrated ability to improve efficiency bode well for the future. In addition, the recent sale of its Maine and Vermont banks will allow the company to concentrate on its core three-state market. The subject of several recent, though failed, takeover bids, BKB remains attractive as a potential acquisition target.

Key Stock Statistics

S&P EPS Est. 1995	4.40	Tang. Bk. Value/Share	21.79
P/E on S&P Est. 1995	10.0	Beta	1.56
S&P EPS Est. 1996	4.60	Shareholders	20,700
Dividend Rate/Share	1.48	Market cap. (B)	$ 4.8
Shs. outstg. (M)	111.2	Inst. holdings	70%
Avg. daily vol. (M)	1.359	Insider holdings	NA

Value of $10,000 invested 5 years ago: $ 29,556

Fiscal Year Ending Dec. 31

	1995	% Change	1994	% Change	1993	% Change
Revenues (Million $)						
1Q	1,326	38%	958.8	15%	835.0	—
2Q	1,340	30%	1,032	22%	848.0	—
3Q	—	—	1,285	44%	890.0	—
4Q	—	—	1,270	39%	912.0	—
Yr.	—	—	4,546	30%	3,485	—
Income (Million $)						
1Q	125.3	22%	102.7	105%	50.14	28%
2Q	133.3	41%	94.50	32%	71.40	60%
3Q	—	—	124.0	200%	41.40	-20%
4Q	—	—	120.8	18%	102.5	81%
Yr.	—	—	441.9	61%	274.8	43%
Earnings Per Share ($)						
1Q	1.08	23%	0.88	80%	0.49	2%
2Q	1.11	39%	0.80	33%	0.60	22%
3Q	E1.05	—	1.07	NM	0.30	-44%
4Q	E1.15	—	1.04	18%	0.88	54%
Yr.	E4.40	—	3.79	66%	2.28	9%

Next earnings report expected: mid October

Bank of Boston

Business Summary - 09-AUG-95

Bank of Boston is a New England regional bank holding company with significant international operations. At June 30, 1995, it was the 19th largest bank holding company in the U.S. with $45.3 billion in assets. BKB owns The First National Bank of Boston, as well as other smaller banks in Massachusetts, one in Connecticut and one in Rhode Island. In the first quarter of 1995, the company sold its banks in Vermont and Maine. In addition to traditional strength in corporate banking, BKB focuses on global and personal banking, including investment management and trust operations, commercial real estate lending, and mortgage banking. International operations include financing trade and investment and indigenous banks in Argentina and Brazil.

In 1994, average earning assets of $38.1 billion (up from $34.3 billion in 1993) consisted of loans and lease financing 78%, securities 9%, and other 13%. Average sources of funds were: interest bearing deposits 56%, noninterest bearing deposits 15%, other interest bearing liabilities 17%, notes payable 5%, and stockholders' equity 7%.

At December 31, 1994, nonperforming assets totaled $441 million (1.4% of loans and related assets), down from $659 million (2.3%) a year earlier. The reserve for loan losses was 2.19% of loans and leases (2.68%). Net chargeoffs in 1994 were 0.82% of average loans and leases (0.84% in 1993)

At June 30, 1995, BKB had estimated Tier 1 and total capital ratios of 7.7% and 13.0%, respectively, versus 7.0% and 12.2% at year-end 1994.

Important Developments

Apr. '95—The company noted that during the first quarter of 1995 it recognized a pretax gain of $75 million ($30 million after tax) from the sale of its Maine and Vermont subsidiaries.

Mar. '95—Directors authorized the repurchase of up to $150 million of BKB common stock. The shares would be used for a number of corporate purposes, including employee benefit and director plans, the dividend reinvestment plan, and for the conversion of convertible subordinated debentures. The company noted that it had completed the acquisition of $50 million of common stock under a buyback program announced in November 1994.

Capitalization

Notes Payable: $2,110,000,000 (6/95).
Preferred Stock: $508,000,000.

Per Share Data ($)

(Year Ended Dec. 31)

	1994	1993	1992	1991	1990	1989
Tangible Bk. Val.	17.77	18.93	15.87	13.22	14.32	21.80
Earnings	3.79	2.28	2.10	-0.64	-6.21	0.80
Dividends	0.93	0.40	0.10	0.10	0.82	1.24
Payout Ratio	25%	18%	5%	NM	NM	155%
Prices - High	29¼	29⅛	26⅜	12⅞	20	30⅝
- Low	22⅛	20¼	11¼	3	6	15¾
P/E Ratio - High	8	13	13	NM	NM	38
- Low	6	9	5	NM	NM	20

Income Statement Analysis (Million $)

	1994	%Chg	1993	%Chg	1992	%Chg	1991
Net Int. Inc.	1,585	4%	1,519	38%	1,098	19%	925
Tax Equiv. Adj.	7.0	-13%	8.0	NM	8.0	-53%	17.0
Non Int. Inc.	801	40%	572	-5%	604	-6%	640
Loan Loss Prov.	130	86%	70.0	-30%	100	-70%	328
% Exp/Op Revs.	62%	—	74%	—	76%	—	84%
Pretax Inc.	791	61%	490	46%	336	NM	-80.0
Eff. Tax Rate	44%	—	44%	—	43%	—	NM
Net Inc.	442	61%	275	43%	192	NM	-34.0
% Net Int. Marg.	4.17%	—	4.10%	—	3.90%	—	3.26%

Balance Sheet & Other Fin. Data (Million $)

	1994	1993	1992	1991	1990	1989
Earning Assets:						
Money Mkt.	3,341	2,751	2,539	2,136	2,538	6,389
Inv. Securities	4,700	3,007	2,911	4,754	3,526	2,784
Com'l Loans	13,171	18,169	11,003	11,104	11,996	13,753
Other Loans	18,309	10,613	12,169	11,134	10,601	12,544
Total Assets	44,630	40,588	32,346	32,700	32,529	39,178
Demand Deposits	5,469	5,566	4,482	4,003	4,074	4,048
Time Deposits	25,887	24,049	20,819	20,734	22,435	24,649
LT Debt	2,169	1,973	1,432	1,103	1,182	1,664
Common Eqty.	2,634	2,403	1,792	1,406	1,447	1,888

Ratio Analysis

	1994	1993	1992	1991	1990	1989
% Ret. on Assets	1.0	0.8	0.6	NM	NM	0.2
% Ret. on Equity	16.1	11.8	10.9	NM	NM	2.9
% Loan Loss Resv.	2.2	2.7	3.6	4.2	4.2	3.6
% Loans/Deposits	99.5	97.2	90.4	88.6	83.7	89.6
% Equity to Assets	5.8	5.4	5.0	4.3	4.9	5.3

Dividend Data (Common dividends, paid each year since 1784, were omitted from mid-1991 to late 1992. A dividend reinvestment plan is available. A "poison pill" stock purchase right was issued in 1990.)

Amt. of Div. $	Date Decl.	Ex-Div. Date	Stock of Record	Payment Date
0.220	Jul. 28	Aug. 02	Aug. 08	Aug. 26 '94
0.270	Oct. 21	Nov. 01	Nov. 07	Nov. 25 '94
0.270	Jan. 26	Jan. 31	Feb. 06	Feb. 24 '95
0.270	Apr. 27	May. 02	May. 08	May. 26 '95
0.370	Jul. 27	Aug. 03	Aug. 07	Aug. 25 '95

Data as orig. reptd.; bef. results of disc opers. and/or spec. items. Per share data adj. for stk. divs. as of ex-div. date. E-Estimated. NA-Not Available. NM-Not Meaningful. NR-Not Ranked.

Office—100 Federal St., Boston, MA 02110. **Tel**—(617) 434-2200. **Chrmn, Pres & CEO**—C. K. Gifford. **Vice Chrmn, CFO & Treas**—W. J. Shea. **Vice Chrmn**—E. A. O'Neal. **Investor Contact**—John A. Kahwaty. **Dirs**—W. A. Budd, W. F. Connell, G. L. Countryman, A. F. Emerson, C. K. Gifford, T. J. May, D. F. McHenry, J. D. Monan, P. C. O'Brien, J. W. Rowe, R. A. Smith, W. C. Van Faasen, T. B. Wheeler, A. M. Zeien. **Transfer Agent & Registrar**—The First National Bank of Boston. **Incorporated** in Massachusetts in 1970; Bank chartered under National Bank Act in 1864. **Empl**-18.113. **S&P Analyst:** Stephen R. Biggar

Bank of New York

NYSE Symbol **BK**
In S&P 500

15-AUG-95

Industry:
Banking

Summary: This company, the 15th largest banking organization in the U.S, is a leader in securities processing and also provides a complete range of banking and other financial services.

S&P Opinion: Accumulate (★★★★)

Recent Price • 39	Yield • 3.7%
52 Wk Range • 43⅝-26⅜	12-Mo. P/E • 9.0

Quantitative Evaluations

Outlook
(1 Lowest—5 Highest)
• **3+**

Fair Value
• **38⅞**

Risk
• **Average**

Earn./Div. Rank
• **B**

Technical Eval.
• **Bullish** since 1/95
Rel. Strength Rank
(1 Lowest—99 Highest)
• **39**
Insider Activity
• **Neutral**

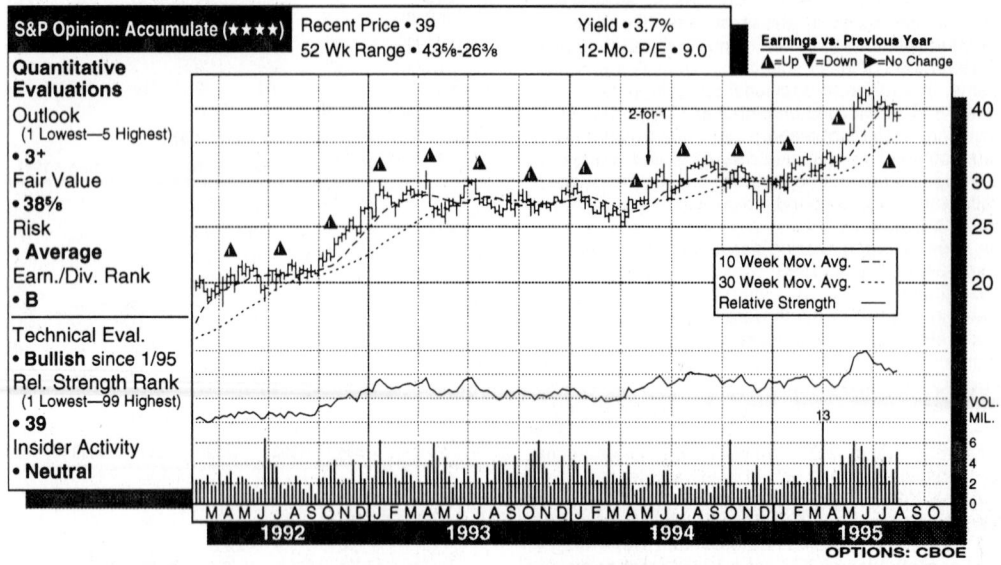

Earnings vs. Previous Year
▲=Up ▼=Down ▶=No Change

10 Week Mov. Avg. ---
30 Week Mov. Avg. ····
Relative Strength —

OPTIONS: CBOE

Overview - 15-AUG-95

Growth in net interest income is expected to continue into 1995, led by strong gains in the credit card portfolio. Managed credit card outstandings at June 30, 1995, increased 15%, year to year, to $7.7 billion, while card accounts rose 9% to 6.0 million. The net interest margin should also widen as a better asset mix results from growth in the higher-yielding credit card portfolio. Asset quality continues to improve and reserves are adequate at 307% of nonperforming loans. However, net charge-offs have exceeded provisions in recent periods, and with the expected growth in the credit card business, there may be pressure to modestly boost the level of provisions. Earnings should also benefit from growth in the securities processing business and well controlled operating expenses.

Valuation - 15-AUG-95

After trading in a relatively tight range for the past two years, the shares have been in a significant uptrend thus far in 1995, as BK's strong growth prospects are becoming more apparent. Favorable trends include a shift in the asset mix to higher-yielding assets, particularly credit cards, and a thriving securities processing business. Given an expected slower growth environment in the quarters ahead, BK's diversity of earnings sources should allow it to achieve a continued strong financial performance. At less than eight times the 1996 per-share earnings estimate of $5.00, the shares appear undervalued.

Key Stock Statistics

S&P EPS Est. 1995	4.55	Tang. Bk. Value/Share	23.20
P/E on S&P Est. 1995	8.6	Beta	1.95
S&P EPS Est. 1996	5.00	Shareholders	26,500
Dividend Rate/Share	1.44	Market cap. (B)	$ 7.5
Shs. outstg. (M)	190.9	Inst. holdings	69%
Avg. daily vol. (M)	0.750	Insider holdings	NA

Value of $10,000 invested 5 years ago: $ 25,752

Fiscal Year Ending Dec. 31

	1995	% Change	1994	% Change	1993	% Change
Revenues ()						
1Q	1,078	10%	976.0	2%	955.0	3%
2Q	1,331	31%	1,019	5%	972.0	10%
3Q	—	—	1,104	15%	963.0	7%
4Q	—	—	1,151	23%	934.0	7%
Yr.	—	—	4,251	11%	3,822	7%
Income ()						
1Q	213.0	20%	178.0	33%	134.0	68%
2Q	226.0	28%	176.0	49%	118.0	36%
3Q	—	—	194.0	28%	151.0	54%
4Q	—	—	201.0	28%	157.0	51%
Yr.	—	—	749.0	34%	559.0	51%
Earnings Per Share ()						
1Q	1.12	21%	0.93	35%	0.68	34%
2Q	1.14	24%	0.92	53%	0.60	8%
3Q	E1.14	—	1.01	29%	0.78	39%
4Q	E1.15	—	1.06	31%	0.81	35%
Yr.	E4.55	—	3.92	37%	2.87	29%

Next earnings report expected: mid October

Bank of New York

Business Summary - 15-AUG-95

The Bank of New York Company, Inc., is the 15th largest bank holding company in the U.S., with assets at June 30, 1995, of approximately $53 billion. Principal operations include securities and other processing services (American Depositary Receipts, corporate trust, stock transfer, master trust, mutual funds custody, securities lending, funds transfer, trade finance, cash management), credit cards (6.0 million card accounts and $7.7 billion of managed outstandings), corporate banking (syndication and loan sales, factoring, commercial finance, leasing), retail banking (379 offices in New York and New Jersey), trust, investment management and private banking (financial planning, trusts and estate settlement, real estate management), and financial market services (foreign exchange trading, risk management products and municipal securities broker/dealer and underwriting activities).

During 1994, average earning assets of $42.9 billion (up 6.2% from 1993) were divided: domestic loans 51%, foreign loans 24%, investment securities 14%, and other 11%. Sources of funds were interest-bearing deposits 50%, interest-free deposits 18%, short-term borrowings 14%, long-term debt 3%, equity 8% and other 7%.

At December 31, 1994, nonperforming assets were $353 million (1.1% of loans and related assets), versus $639 million (2.1%) at year-end 1993. The allowance for loan losses was 2.40% of loans, compared with 3.17%. Net chargeoffs were $354 million (1.11% of average loans in 1994), versus $387 million (1.27%) in 1993.

Important Developments

May '95—BK signed a definitive agreement to acquire the global custody business of J.P. Morgan & Co., including securities lending and the domestic custody business in the U.S. and U.K., for an undisclosed amount. The acquisition will add about $800 billion to the company's $1.65 trillion in custodized assets. Earlier, in April, BK agreed to purchase the securities processing business of BankAmerica Corp. for an undisclosed amount.
May '95—The company sold the mortgage servicing portfolio of its ARCS Mortgage subsidiary, consisting of loans valued at $7.6 billion, to Chase Manhattan Corp.'s mortgage unit for an undisclosed amount. BK will continue to originate loans through its BNY Mortgage Co. unit in New York.
Apr. '95—The company said it completed a 5,000,000 common share buyback program initiated in the first quarter of 1994.

Capitalization

Long Term Debt: $1,710,000,000 (6/95).
Preferred Stock: $111,000,000.
Warrants: To purchase 27,548,872 com. shs. at $31 ea. to 1998.

Per Share Data ()

(Year Ended Dec. 31)

	1994	1993	1992	1991	1990	1989
Tangible Bk. Val.	22.26	20.33	19.85	18.26	18.29	18.33
Earnings	3.92	2.87	2.22	0.64	1.99	0.12
Dividends	1.10	0.85	0.76	0.84	1.06	0.99
Payout Ratio	28%	30%	34%	130%	53%	821%
Prices - High	33¼	31¼	27⅜	18⅛	20⅞	27½
- Low	25	25⅜	15	8¼	6⅝	18⅜
P/E Ratio - High	8	11	12	28	10	NM
- Low	6	9	7	13	3	NM

Income Statement Analysis ()

	1994	%Chg	1993	%Chg	1992	%Chg	1991
Net Int. Inc.	1,717	15%	1,497	22%	1,224	2%	1,198
Tax Equiv. Adj.	46.0	-13%	53.0	-15%	62.0	-17%	75.0
Non Int. Inc.	1,274	-3%	1,319	21%	1,091	14%	956
Loan Loss Prov.	162	-43%	284	-33%	427	-43%	746
% Exp/Op Revs.	54%	—	59%	—	58%	—	59%
Pretax Inc.	1,198	35%	886	58%	559	NM	177
Eff. Tax Rate	37%	—	37%	—	34%	—	31%
Net Inc.	749	34%	559	51%	369	NM	122
% Net Int. Marg.	4.11%	—	3.84%	—	3.55%	—	3.43%

Balance Sheet & Other Fin. Data ()

	1994	1993	1992	1991	1990	1989
Earning Assets:						
Money Mkt.	4,951	1,630	999	2,402	2,661	2,982
Inv. Securities	4,651	5,597	4,648	3,773	3,287	3,829
Com'l Loans	16,085	12,594	12,303	14,484	15,219	16,502
Other Loans	17,868	18,813	15,928	14,336	18,613	20,135
Total Assets	48,879	45,546	40,909	39,426	45,390	48,857
Demand Deposits	8,579	8,690	7,534	6,342	7,355	8,031
Time Deposits	25,512	23,469	21,915	22,632	26,666	26,896
LT Debt	1,774	1,590	1,592	1,200	840	866
Common Eqty.	4,177	3,778	3,210	2,554	2,537	2,489

Ratio Analysis

	1994	1993	1992	1991	1990	1989
% Ret. on Assets	1.5	1.2	0.9	0.3	0.6	0.1
% Ret. on Equity	19.5	15.0	13.5	4.2	13.0	0.7
% Loan Loss Resv.	2.4	3.1	3.7	3.6	3.1	3.1
% Loans/Deposits	97.0	97.6	93.0	96.6	97.0	102.4
% Equity to Assets	7.5	8.3	5.9	5.0	4.3	4.5

Dividend Data (Dividends have been paid since 1785. A dividend reinvestment plan is available.)

Amt. of Div. $	Date Decl.	Ex-Div. Date	Stock of Record	Payment Date
0.320	Oct. 11	Oct. 17	Oct. 21	Nov. 03 '94
0.320	Jan. 10	Jan. 13	Jan. 20	Feb. 02 '95
0.320	Apr. 11	Apr. 17	Apr. 21	May. 04 '95
0.360	Jul. 11	Jul. 19	Jul. 21	Aug. 03 '95

Data as orig. reptd.; bef. results of disc opers. and/or spec. items. Per share data adj. for stk. divs. as of ex-div. date.
E-Estimated. NA-Not Available. NM-Not Meaningful. NR-Not Ranked.

Office—48 Wall St., New York, NY 10286. **Tel**—(212) 495-1784. **Chrmn & CEO**—J. C. Bacot. **Pres**—T. A. Renyi. **Sr EVP-CFO**—D. D. Papageorge. **Secy**—P. C. Miller. **Investor Contacts**—Paul J. Leyden, Andrew M. Merrill. **Dirs**—J. C. Bacot, R. Barth, W. R. Chaney, S. F. Chevalier, A. P. Gammie, R. E. Gomory, A. R. Griffith, E. L. Hennessy Jr., J. C. Malone, D. L. Miller, H. B. Morley, M. T. Muse, C. A. Rein, T. A. Renyi, H. E. Sells, D. C. Staley, W. S. White Jr., S. H. Woolley. **Transfer Agent & Registrar**—The Bank of New York, NYC. **Incorporated** in N.Y. in 1968; The Bank of New York founded in 1784. **Empl**-15,477. **S&P Analyst:** Stephen R. Biggar

BankAmerica Corp.

NYSE Symbol **BAC**
In S&P 500

23-AUG-95

Industry:
Banking

Summary: BankAmerica, the second largest U.S. bank holding company, provides banking and financial services in the U.S. and in selected international markets to consumers and businesses.

S&P Opinion: Accumulate (★★★★)	Recent Price • 54½	Yield • 3.4%
	52 Wk Range • 56⅛-38⅝	12-Mo. P/E • 9.4

Quantitative Evaluations

Outlook
(1 Lowest—5 Highest)
• **3+**

Fair Value
• **54**

Risk
• **Low**

Earn./Div. Rank
• **B**

Technical Eval.
• **Bearish** since 6/95

Rel. Strength Rank
(1 Lowest—99 Highest)
• **44**

Insider Activity
• **NA**

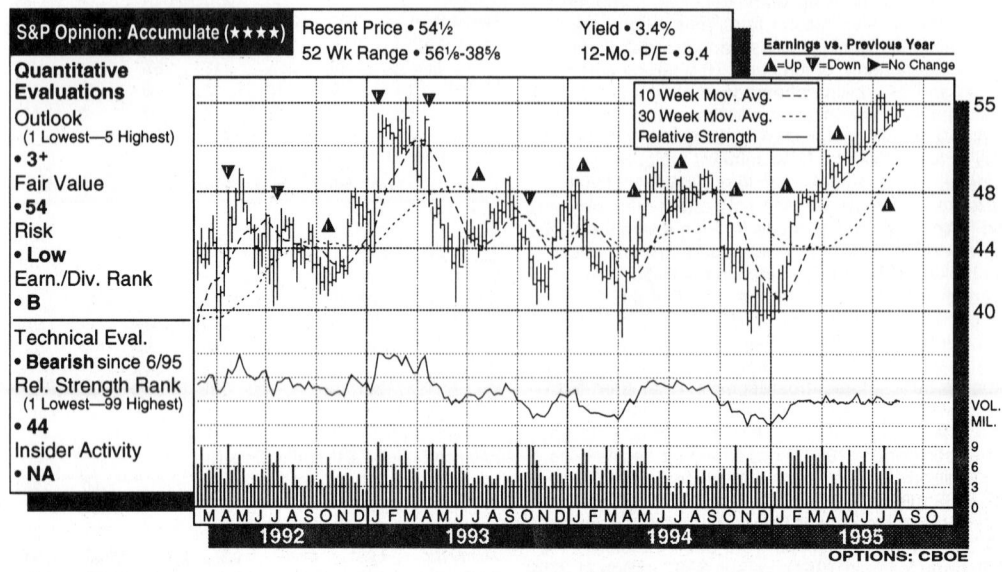

Earnings vs. Previous Year
▲=Up ▼=Down ▶=No Change

10 Week Mov. Avg. – – –
30 Week Mov. Avg. ......
Relative Strength ——

OPTIONS: CBOE

Overview - 23-AUG-95

The outlook for revenue growth in 1995 continues to improve, as recent acquisitions of mortgage servicing and orgination operations, particularly Arbor National, contribute to a nationwide expansion of the mortgage lending business. The August 1994 acquisition of Continental Bank, the consolidation of which was recently completed, will also provide greater access to U.S. wholesale customers, particularly in the Midwest. Increased focus on areas with greater earnings potential, such as the credit card and other consumer lending segments, should also contribute to profit improvement. Credit quality continues to improve, with nonaccrual assets down 12%, year to year, to $2.0 billion at June 30, 1995.

Valuation - 23-AUG-95

Despite a strong rise thus far in 1995, the shares remain attractive on a valuation basis for above-average appreciation in the next six to nine months. Earnings gains have been accented by healthy loan growth particularly in the higher-yielding consumer sector, which has contributed to a wider net interest margin. A continuing favorable banking climate, including flat to declining interest rates, should allow BAC to further improve on its financial performance. Trading at about eight times the 1996 earnings estimate of $6.80 a share, and yielding 3.4%, the shares are poised for additional appreciation.

Key Stock Statistics

S&P EPS Est. 1995	6.10	Tang. Bk. Value/Share	26.14
P/E on S&P Est. 1995	8.9	Beta	1.71
S&P EPS Est. 1996	6.80	Shareholders	162,300
Dividend Rate/Share	1.84	Market cap. (B)	$ 20.3
Shs. outstg. (M)	374.3	Inst. holdings	63%
Avg. daily vol. (M)	0.948	Insider holdings	0%

Value of $10,000 invested 5 years ago: $ 24,685

Fiscal Year Ending Dec. 31

	1995	% Change	1994	% Change	1993	% Change
Revenues (Million $)						
1Q	4,829	27%	3,816	-5%	4,014	39%
2Q	5,127	30%	3,957	NM	3,939	-3%
3Q	—	—	4,228	7%	3,952	-7%
4Q	—	—	4,530	13%	3,995	-2%
Yr.	—	—	16,531	4%	15,900	4%
Income (Million $)						
1Q	611.0	19%	513.0	6%	484.0	60%
2Q	645.0	23%	525.0	8%	488.0	103%
3Q	—	—	547.0	13%	486.0	2%
4Q	—	—	591.0	19%	496.0	5%
Yr.	—	—	2,176	11%	1,954	31%
Earnings Per Share ($)						
1Q	1.46	15%	1.27	7%	1.19	-2%
2Q	1.56	17%	1.33	11%	1.20	90%
3Q	E1.52	12%	1.36	14%	1.19	-2%
4Q	E1.56	11%	1.41	17%	1.21	2%
Yr.	E6.10	14%	5.36	12%	4.79	13%

Next earnings report expected: mid October

BankAmerica Corp.

23-AUG-95

Business Summary - 23-AUG-95

BankAmerica Corp. is the holding company for Bank of America, the second largest U.S. bank and the largest in California, and Seattle-First National Bank, the largest bank in Washington. It also has banking operations in Arizona, Oregon, Nevada, Idaho, Texas, New Mexico, Hawaii and Alaska. In August 1994, the company acquired Illinois-based Continental Bank Corp. (assets of $23 billion). Retail banking services for consumers and small businesses are provided through nearly 2,000 branches and include a full range of deposit and loan products, as well as credit card, home mortgage, manufactured housing financing and consumer finance products. Corporate and international banking includes credit, trade finance, cash management, investment banking and capital-raising services, capital markets products and financial advisory services. Other activities include credit and financial services for the commercial real estate sector, middle-market banking, and personal trust and investment services for private banking clients.

Average earning assets in 1994 of $168.2 billion (up from 1993's $159.0 billion) consisted of residential real estate loans 19%, other consumer loans 19%, commercial and industrial 20%, other domestic loans 7%, foreign loans 11%, investment securities 12%, and temporary investments 12%. Average sources of funds were noninterest-bearing deposits 23%, other domestic deposits 44%, other foreign deposits 11%, short-term borrowings 6%, long-term debt 7%, and stockholders' equity 9%.

At year-end 1994, nonperforming assets were $2.61 billion (1.85% of total loans), down from $3.60 billion (2.84%) a year earlier. The reserve for loan losses was 2.62% of loans, versus 2.77%. Net chargeoffs during 1994 were 0.37% of average loans, versus 0.89% in 1993.

Important Developments

Aug. '95—BankAmerica said it signed a definitive agreement to sell its corporate trust business to First Bank System, Inc. (NYSE; FBS) for an undisclosed amount. Earlier, it reached a definitive agreement to sell its mortgage and asset securities services business to Bankers Trust New York Corp. (NYSE; BT) for an undisclosed amount.

Jul. '95—The company said it repurchased 4.0 million shares of its common stock during the second quarter of 1995 (at an average price of $52.41 a share) under a previously announced stock repurchase program. Year-to-date repurchases under the plan now total 9.6 million shares ($49.45).

Capitalization

Long Term Debt: $16,078,000,000 (6/95).
Preferred Stock: $2,723,000,000.

Per Share Data ($)

(Year Ended Dec. 31)

	1994	1993	1992	1991	1990	1989
Tangible Bk. Val.	25.25	22.35	19.91	30.78	27.21	23.32
Earnings	5.36	4.79	4.24	4.81	3.85	3.79
Dividends	1.60	1.40	1.30	1.20	1.00	0.60
Payout Ratio	30%	29%	31%	25%	26%	16%
Prices - High	50¼	55½	49¾	44¾	33½	36⅜
- Low	38⅜	40⅜	35⅜	23⅛	17½	17
P/E Ratio - High	9	12	12	9	9	10
- Low	7	8	8	5	5	4

Income Statement Analysis (Million $)

	1994	%Chg	1993	%Chg	1992	%Chg	1991
Net Int. Inc.	7,542	1%	7,441	11%	6,718	50%	4,472
Tax Equiv. Adj.	24.0	9%	22.0	NM	22.0	144%	9.0
Non Int. Inc.	4,123	-2%	4,212	16%	3,638	53%	2,375
Loan Loss Prov.	460	-43%	803	-19%	990	23%	805
% Exp/Op Revs.	64%	—	64%	—	65%	—	61%
Pretax Inc.	3,717	8%	3,428	28%	2,682	43%	1,873
Eff. Tax Rate	41%	—	43%	—	44%	—	40%
Net Inc.	2,176	11%	1,954	31%	1,492	33%	1,124
% Net Int. Marg.	4.50%	—	4.71%	—	4.75%	—	4.36%

Balance Sheet & Other Fin. Data (Million $)

	1994	1993	1992	1991	1990	1989
Earning Assets:						
Money Mkt.	19,211	15,500	10,300	7,600	5,700	4,800
Inv. Securities	18,016	19,700	15,300	8,400	6,900	7,100
Com'l Loans	36,869	29,100	28,200	17,600	18,900	18,900
Other Loans	104,043	97,200	96,300	68,800	66,900	57,000
Total Assets	215,475	186,900	180,600	115,500	110,700	98,800
Demand Deposits	36,566	32,900	33,900	18,800	18,700	18,200
Time Deposits	117,828	108,700	104,000	75,300	73,600	63,000
LT Debt	13,558	14,100	16,400	3,820	3,930	4,080
Common Eqty.	15,823	14,200	12,500	6,740	5,810	4,900

Ratio Analysis

	1994	1993	1992	1991	1990	1989
% Ret. on Assets	1.1	1.1	0.9	1.0	0.8	0.8
% Ret. on Equity	13.1	12.9	12.7	17.3	15.5	18.7
% Loan Loss Resv.	2.6	2.8	3.2	2.8	3.4	4.4
% Loans/Deposits	91.3	89.2	90.3	91.8	92.9	93.4
% Equity to Assets	7.3	7.2	6.3	5.4	5.0	4.2

Dividend Data

Common dividends, paid since 1933, were omitted in early 1986 and resumed in 1989.

Amt. of Div. $	Date Decl.	Ex-Div. Date	Stock of Record	Payment Date
0.400	Aug. 01	Aug. 17	Aug. 23	Sep. 15 '94
0.400	Nov. 07	Nov. 16	Nov. 22	Dec. 14 '94
0.460	Feb. 06	Feb. 15	Feb. 22	Mar. 14 '95
0.460	May. 01	May. 18	May. 24	Jun. 14 '95
0.460	Aug. 08	Aug. 22	Aug. 24	Sep. 15 '95

Data as orig. reptd.; bef. results of disc opers. and/or spec. items. Per share data adj. for stk. divs. as of ex-div. date.
E-Estimated. NA-Not Available. NM-Not Meaningful. NR-Not Ranked.

Office—Bank of America Center, San Francisco, CA 94104. **Tel**—(415) 622-3530. **Chrmn, Pres & CEO**—R. M. Rosenberg. **Vice Chrmn & CFO**—L. W. Coleman. **EVP & Secy**—C. A. Sorokin. **Investor Contact**—Eric Durant. **Dirs**—J. F. Alibrandi, J. E. Barad, P. B. Bedford, A. F. Brimmer, R. A. Clarke, L. W. Coleman, T. F. Crull, K. Feldstein, D. E. Guinn, P. M. Hawley, F. L. Hope, Jr., I. E. Lozano, Jr., W. E. Massey, J. M. Richman, R. M. Rosenberg, A. M. Spence. **Transfer Agent & Registrar**—Chemical Trust Co. of California, NYC and SF. **Incorporated** in Delaware in 1968; Bank of America incorporated in California in 1930. **Empl**-95,800. **S&P Analyst:** Stephen R. Biggar

Bankers Trust

NYSE Symbol **BT**
In S&P 500

24-AUG-95 Industry:
Banking

Summary: This bank holding company, the seventh largest in the U.S., focuses on corporate services such as money and securities markets activities, corporate finance and fiduciary services.

S&P Opinion: Avoid (★★)	Recent Price • 66⅛	Yield • 6.1%
	52 Wk Range • 74-49¾	12-Mo. P/E • 31.8

Earnings vs. Previous Year
▲=Up ▼=Down ▶=No Change

Quantitative Evaluations

Outlook
(1 Lowest—5 Highest)
• **3⁻**

Fair Value
• **65¾**

Risk
• **Average**

Earn./Div. Rank
• **A-**

Technical Eval.
• **Bullish** since 12/94

Rel. Strength Rank
(1 Lowest—99 Highest)
• **57**

Insider Activity
• **Neutral**

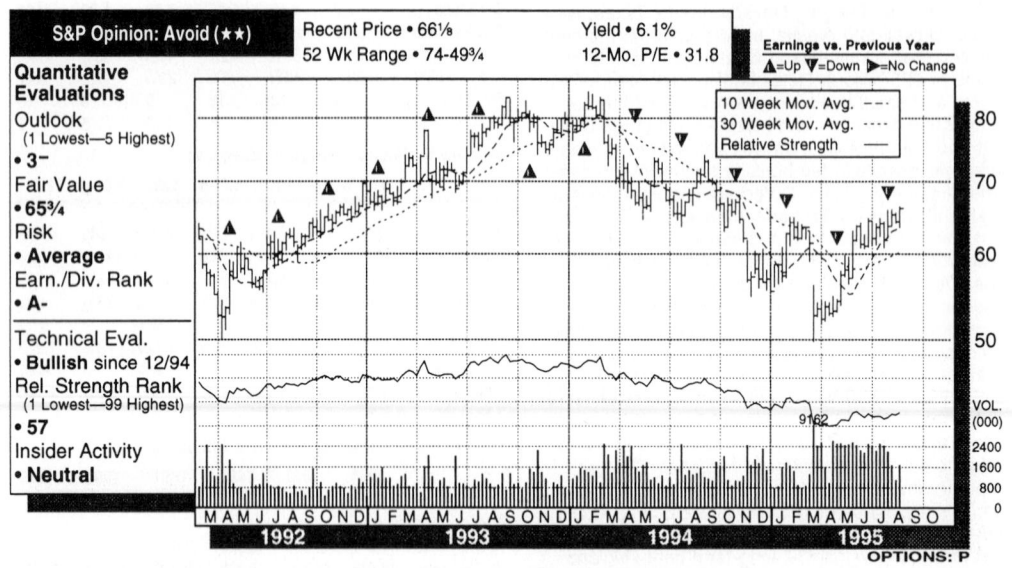

10 Week Mov. Avg.
30 Week Mov. Avg.
Relative Strength

OPTIONS: P

Overview - 24-AUG-95

With a deterioration of market conditions in many Latin American countries, continuing slowness in the market for risk management products, and unsettled global markets, BT is facing a difficult business environment. The company has been investing in businesses with long term profit potential, particularly trust activities, such as securities processing, investment and cash management and employee benefit plan administration, which will provide a more stable source of earnings for the future. In addition, an expense reduction program will help bring costs more in line with the revenue base. Nevertheless, uncertain future conditions for the trading and derivatives business makes it difficult to forecast earnings with any degree of confidence.

Valuation - 24-AUG-95

While a return to profitability was achieved in the second quarter of 1995, BT's earnings remain well below historical levels. An expense reduction program is on track, but the outlook for derivatives and trading revenues, BT's two primary growth drivers in the past, is uncertain. Although speculators banking on the potential break up or sale of the company have propped the shares up in recent periods, we would avoid the shares based on fundamentals and vulnerability to further setbacks.

Key Stock Statistics

S&P EPS Est. 1995	1.70	Tang. Bk. Value/Share	51.38
P/E on S&P Est. 1995	38.9	Beta	1.47
S&P EPS Est. 1996	6.00	Shareholders	23,600
Dividend Rate/Share	4.00	Market cap. (B)	$ 5.1
Shs. outstg. (M)	78.4	Inst. holdings	71%
Avg. daily vol. (M)	0.311	Insider holdings	NA

Value of $10,000 invested 5 years ago: $ 21,092

Fiscal Year Ending Dec. 31

	1995	% Change	1994	% Change	1993	% Change
Revenues (Million $)						
1Q	1,695	-1%	1,716	-2%	1,755	10%
2Q	2,107	11%	1,892	NM	1,899	9%
3Q	—	—	1,914	-9%	2,106	27%
4Q	—	—	1,981	-3%	2,040	31%
Yr.	—	—	7,503	-4%	7,800	19%
Income (Million $)						
1Q	-157.0	NM	164.0	-29%	230.0	31%
2Q	91.00	-50%	181.0	-28%	251.0	22%
3Q	—	—	169.0	-45%	310.0	47%
4Q	—	—	101.0	-64%	279.0	64%
Yr.	—	—	615.0	-43%	1,070	41%
Earnings Per Share ($)						
1Q	-2.11	NM	1.90	-28%	2.64	31%
2Q	0.98	-53%	2.09	-28%	2.90	21%
3Q	E1.35	-32%	1.98	-45%	3.60	47%
4Q	E1.48	24%	1.19	-63%	3.26	65%
Yr.	E1.70	-76%	7.17	-42%	12.40	41%

Next earnings report expected: mid October

Bankers Trust

Business Summary - 24-AUG-95

Bankers Trust New York is the parent of Bankers Trust Co., the seventh largest bank in the U.S. BT concentrates on wholesale banking. The core businesses are client finance, client advisory, client financial risk management, client transaction processing, and trading and positioning. A significant portion of 1994 earnings was derived from client financing and client financial risk management, particularly derivatives contracts related to interest rates, currencies, equities and commodities (or indices thereof), and credit. The BT Securities Corp. subsidiary, which accounts for about 19% of consolidated assets, underwrites and deals in securities and provides financial advisory services. International operations accounted for 60% and 48% of net income and total assets, respectively, in 1994.

During 1994, average earning assets of $76.3 billion (down from $76.8 billion in 1993) were divided: trading account assets 48%, investment securities 9%, commercial and industrial loans 3%, other domestic loans 6%, foreign loans 7%, and other temporary investments 27%. Average sources of funds were noninterest bearing deposits 4%, other domestic deposits 6%, foreign deposits 12%, short-term borrowings 47%, long-term debt 5%, equity 4%, and other 22%.

At year-end 1994, nonperforming assets were $1.43 billion (11.4% of total loans outstanding), up from $1.38 billion (9.10%) a year earlier. The reserve for loan losses was 10.0% of loans, against 8.71%. Net chargeoffs were 0.78% of average loans during 1994, against 2.54% in 1993.

At June 30, 1995, Tier 1 capital was estimated at 8.70% of risk-adjusted assets, versus 8.85% at March 31. Total capital at June 30 was estimated at 14.00% of risk-adjusted assets, down from 14.40%.

Important Developments

Aug. '95—BT reached a definitive agreement to acquire the mortgage and asset securities services business of BankAmerica Corp. for an undisclosed amount.

Jul. '95—The company attributed a return to profitability in the second quarter of 1995 mainly to an improved performance in client-related businesses and a turnaround in trading activities. However, while client derivatives volume remained steady during the quarter, they consisted mainly of low-margin transactions. In response to the lower revenue and reduced market activity in certain businesses, BT has implemented a wide ranging expense reduction program aimed at reducing overall operating expenses by about $200 million in 1995 and $275 million in 1996. The program includes an anticipated staff reduction of 1,400, for which a provision for severance-related costs of $50 million pretax was recorded in the first quarter.

Capitalization

Long Term Debt: $6,621,000,000 (3/95).
Cum. Preferred Stock: $639,000,000.

Per Share Data ($)

(Year Ended Dec. 31)

	1994	1993	1992	1991	1990	1989
Tangible Bk. Val.	55.14	53.10	39.90	35.33	31.19	26.29
Earnings	7.17	12.40	8.82	7.75	7.80	-12.10
Dividends	3.70	3.24	2.88	2.60	2.38	2.14
Payout Ratio	52%	26%	33%	34%	31%	NM
Prices - High	84⅝	83½	70⅛	68	46¾	58¼
- Low	54¾	65¾	50	39½	28½	34½
P/E Ratio - High	12	7	8	9	6	NM
- Low	8	5	6	5	4	NM

Income Statement Analysis (Million $)

	1994	%Chg	1993	%Chg	1992	%Chg	1991
Net Int. Inc.	1,172	-11%	1,314	15%	1,147	56%	737
Tax Equiv. Adj.	83.0	1%	82.0	58%	52.0	63%	32.0
Non Int. Inc.	2,401	-28%	3,351	44%	2,335	-6%	2,476
Loan Loss Prov.	25.0	-73%	93.0	-59%	225	-5%	238
% Exp/Op Revs.	75%	—	64%	—	66%	—	67%
Pretax Inc.	869	-44%	1,550	71%	906	9%	834
Eff. Tax Rate	29%	—	31%	—	16%	—	20%
Net Inc.	615	-43%	1,070	41%	761	14%	667
% Net Int. Marg.	1.64%	—	1.82%	—	1.81%	—	1.46%

Balance Sheet & Other Fin. Data (Million $)

	1994	1993	1992	1991	1990	1989
Earning Assets:						
Money Mkt.	63,391	59,842	40,233	35,768	26,466	22,326
Inv. Securities	7,475	7,073	6,215	6,516	7,030	6,204
Com'l Loans	4,439	6,004	8,271	7,094	8,316	7,219
Other Loans	8,164	9,296	9,144	10,043	13,264	14,040
Total Assets	97,016	92,082	72,448	63,959	63,596	55,658
Demand Deposits	3,826	3,892	4,206	4,042	7,085	6,262
Time Deposits	21,113	18,884	20,865	18,792	21,503	19,958
LT Debt	6,455	5,597	3,992	3,081	2,650	2,435
Common Eqty.	4,309	4,284	3,309	2,912	2,524	2,136

Ratio Analysis

	1994	1993	1992	1991	1990	1989
% Ret. on Assets	0.6	1.3	1.0	1.1	1.0	NM
% Ret. on Equity	14.6	29.7	27.4	28.3	31.8	NM
% Loan Loss Resv.	10.0	8.7	9.4	10.6	10.1	12.9
% Loans/Deposits	50.1	66.7	69.1	74.7	75.1	80.7
% Equity to Assets	3.8	4.1	3.6	3.7	3.1	5.0

Dividend Data —Dividends have been paid since 1904. A dividend reinvestment plan is available. A "poison pill" stock purchase rights plan was adopted in 1988.

Amt. of Div. $	Date Decl.	Ex-Div. Date	Stock of Record	Payment Date
0.900	Sep. 20	Sep. 29	Oct. 05	Oct. 25 '94
1.000	Dec. 20	Dec. 30	Jan. 06	Jan. 25 '95
1.000	Mar. 21	Mar. 30	Apr. 05	Apr. 25 '95
1.000	Jun. 20	Jul. 03	Jul. 06	Jul. 25 '95

Data as orig. reptd.; bef. results of disc opers. and/or spec. items. Per share data adj. for stk. divs. as of ex-div. date. E-Estimated. NA-Not Available. NM-Not Meaningful. NR-Not Ranked.

Office—280 Park Ave., New York, NY 10017. **Tel**—(212) 250-2500. **Chrmn & CEO**—C. S. Sanford, Jr. **Pres**—E. B. Shanks, Jr. **EVP-CFO & Contr**—T. T. Yates. **Secy**—J. T. Byrne, Jr. **VP-Investor Contact**—Mary M. Flournoy (212) 454-3201. **Dirs**—G. B. Beitzel, P. A. Griffiths, W. R. Howell, J. M. Huntsman, V. E. Jordan, Jr., H. Maxwell, D. F. McCullough, N. J. Nicholas, Jr., R. E. Palmer, D. Pineau-Valencienne, C. S. Sanford, Jr., E. B. Shanks, Jr., P. C. Stewart, G. J. Vojta. **Transfer Agent & Registrar**—Harris Trust Co. of New York, Chicago. **Incorporated** in New York in 1966. **Empl**-14,144. **S&P Analyst:** Stephen R. Biggar

Bard (C. R.)

NYSE Symbol **BCR**
In S&P 500

18-SEP-95

Industry:
Medical equipment/
supply

Summary: C. R. Bard produces and markets a wide range of disposable therapeutic and diagnostic medical devices used in cardio-vascular, urological and surgical procedures.

S&P Opinion: Accumulate (★★★★)	Recent Price • 29½ Yield • 2.2%
	52 Wk Range • 31⅞-23 12-Mo. P/E • 19.9

Quantitative Evaluations

Outlook
(1 Lowest—5 Highest)
• **4-**

Fair Value
• **31¼**

Risk
• **Low**

Earn./Div. Rank
• **A-**

Technical Eval.
• **Bullish** since 9/94

Rel. Strength Rank
(1 Lowest—99 Highest)
• **20**

Insider Activity
• **NA**

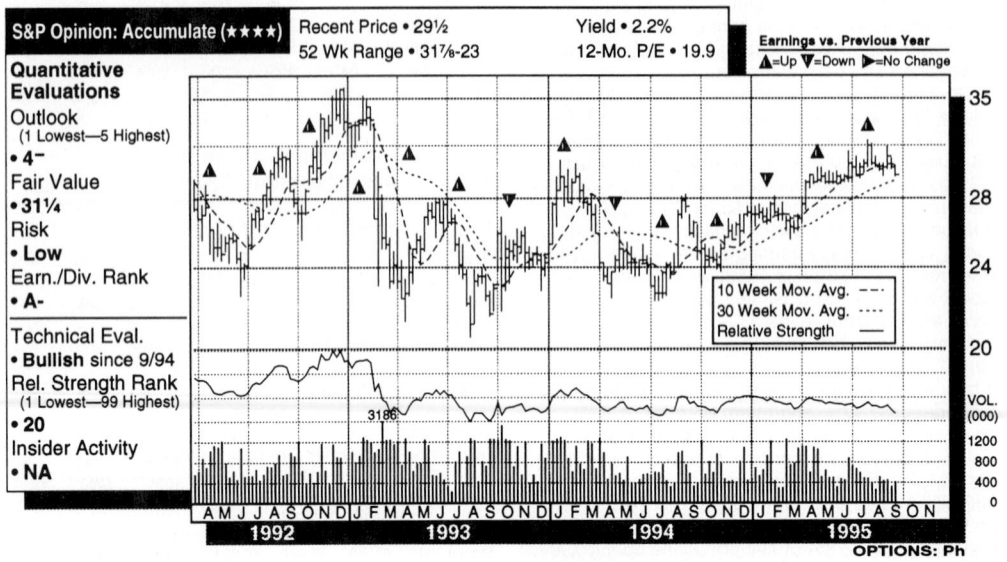

10 Week Mov. Avg. ---
30 Week Mov. Avg. ·····
Relative Strength ——

Earnings vs. Previous Year
▲=Up ▼=Down ▶=No Change

OPTIONS: Ph

Overview - 18-SEP-95

Sales should post further progress in 1996. Despite a more cost-constrained hospital market and rising competitive pressures, domestic cardiovascular sales should benefit from the planned introduction of new state-of-the-art Pronto and ProCross over-the-wire angioplasty catheters now that the FDA's moratorium on new Bard submissions has been lifted. Higher sales are also forecast for urological and surgical products, aided by contributions from acquisitions. Continued forward momentum is also forecast for overseas sales, which climbed 29% in the first half of 1995. Despite a probable rise in interest expense, margins should be well maintained on higher volume and productivity improvements.

Valuation - 18-SEP-95

The shares, which have performed erratically in recent years, have been in an uptrend over the past 12 months, helped by strength in health care issues and the June 1995 lifting of an FDA moratorium on new product submissions from Bard's USCI cardiovascular products unit. The moratorium was imposed in early 1994 following the company's admission of guilt in the past sale of defective catheters. Prospects for the years ahead are bolstered by the planned launch of new angioplasty catheter products, as well as other promising cardiovascular products now under development such as coronary stents and cardiac ablation catheters. We continue to recommend the stock for long-term appreciation.

Key Stock Statistics

S&P EPS Est. 1995	1.95	Tang. Bk. Value/Share	4.07
P/E on S&P Est. 1995	15.1	Beta	1.02
S&P EPS Est. 1996	2.20	Shareholders	8,000
Dividend Rate/Share	0.64	Market cap. (B)	$ 1.5
Shs. outstg. (M)	52.3	Inst. holdings	70%
Avg. daily vol. (M)	0.084	Insider holdings	NA

Value of $10,000 invested 5 years ago: $ 14,916

Fiscal Year Ending Dec. 31

	1995	% Change	1994	% Change	1993	% Change
Revenues (Million $)						
1Q	264.1	7%	247.4	5%	236.0	NM
2Q	277.2	8%	256.3	5%	243.9	NM
3Q	—	—	251.9	3%	243.5	-3%
4Q	—	—	262.6	6%	247.0	-4%
Yr.	—	—	1,018	5%	970.8	-2%
Income (Million $)						
1Q	24.20	6%	22.80	-15%	26.90	60%
2Q	24.10	3%	23.30	15%	20.30	13%
3Q	—	—	22.80	NM	-25.20	NM
4Q	—	—	6.00	-85%	40.10	90%
Yr.	—	—	74.90	21%	62.10	-17%
Earnings Per Share ($)						
1Q	0.47	7%	0.44	-14%	0.51	59%
2Q	0.46	2%	0.45	15%	0.39	15%
3Q	E0.50	14%	0.44	NM	-0.48	NM
4Q	E0.52	NM	0.11	-86%	0.77	93%
Yr.	E1.95	35%	1.44	21%	1.19	-16%

Next earnings report expected: mid October

Bard (C. R.)

Business Summary - 18-SEP-95

C. R. Bard manufactures and distributes medical, surgical, diagnostic and patient care products, most of which are used once and then discarded. Hospitals, physicians and nursing homes account for 90% of sales. Foreign sales (including exports) accounted for 30% of total sales and 36% of operating profits in 1994. R&D spending equaled 6.9% of sales in 1994 (6.8% in 1993).

Cardiovascular products (36% of 1994 sales) include angiographic recanalization devices such as balloon angioplasty catheters, steerable guide wires, guiding catheters, inflation devices and developmental atherectomy and laser devices; electrophysiology products such as temporary pacing catheters, diagnostic and therapeutic electrodes and cardiac mapping systems; a cardiopulmonary support system; and blood oxygenators, cardiotomy reservoirs and other products used in open-heart surgery. After suspension in 1989 and 1990, Bard resumed angioplasty sales in the U.S. during 1991. Catheters include fixed-wire, over-the-wire and rapid exchange models. New cardiovascular products under development include coronary stents and cardiac ablation catheters.

Urological products (29%) include Foley catheters, trays and related urine collection systems used extensively in postoperative bladder drainage; ureteral stents; and specialty devices for prostate cancer detection, ureteroscopy, incontinence and stone removal.

Surgical products (35%) include wound and chest drainage systems; implantable blood vessel replacements; vascular access catheters and ports; irrigation products for endoscopy, laparoscopy and orthopedics; ostomy devices; skin care and wound management products; and percutaneous feeding devices.

Important Developments

Sep. '95—MedChem Products set September 28 as the meeting date for its shareholders to vote on Bard's offer to acquire MedChem for about $102 million in Bard common stock. MedChem, a manufacturer of hemostatic products that arrest bleeding during surgery, vascular access catheters and a wound closure device, has annual sales of about $40 million.
Jun. '95—The FDA lifted the Applications Integrity Policy that had been in effect at Bard's USCI division since early 1994. This action now permits USCI to make new product submissions with the FDA. Also in June, Bard completed the arrangement of a $350 million, five year syndicated credit facility with a group of 15 banks.

Capitalization

Long Term Debt: $199,200,000 (6/95).

Per Share Data ($)

(Year Ended Dec. 31)

	1994	1993	1992	1991	1990	1989
Tangible Bk. Val.	3.35	4.49	6.45	5.81	5.30	5.00
Cash Flow	2.20	1.87	1.82	1.63	1.13	1.51
Earnings	1.44	1.19	1.42	1.08	0.76	1.18
Dividends	0.58	0.54	0.50	0.46	0.42	0.36
Payout Ratio	40%	45%	35%	43%	55%	30%
Prices - High	30½	35¼	35⅞	31¾	22½	26½
- Low	22¼	20½	22½	14⅞	12⅞	8¾
P/E Ratio - High	21	30	25	29	30	22
- Low	15	17	16	14	17	16

Income Statement Analysis (Million $)

	1994	%Chg	1993	%Chg	1992	%Chg	1991
Revs.	1,018	5%	971	-2%	990	13%	876
Oper. Inc.	190	—	167	16%	144	17%	123
Depr.	39.6	12%	35.5	67%	21.2	-28%	29.5
Int. Exp.	15.1	32%	11.4	-10%	12.6	-11%	14.1
Pretax Inc.	103	4%	99	-7%	107	39%	77.0
Eff. Tax Rate	27%	—	37%	—	30%	—	26%
Net Inc.	74.9	21%	62.1	-17%	75.0	31%	57.2

Balance Sheet & Other Fin. Data (Million $)

	1994	1993	1992	1991	1990	1989
Cash	34.2	75.0	49.8	33.8	19.9	11.1
Curr. Assets	428	422	417	374	341	305
Total Assets	958	799	713	658	613	563
Curr. Liab.	365	264	215	190	171	123
LT Debt	78.3	68.5	68.6	68.9	69.8	70.3
Common Eqty.	440	383	392	366	342	334
Total Cap.	518	452	461	435	412	404
Cap. Exp.	34.2	30.7	30.3	31.0	28.2	31.8
Cash Flow	115	97.6	96.2	86.7	60.1	83.5

Ratio Analysis

	1994	1993	1992	1991	1990	1989
Curr. Ratio	1.2	1.6	1.9	2.0	2.0	2.5
% LT Debt of Cap.	15.1	15.2	14.9	15.9	16.9	17.4
% Net Inc.of Revs.	7.4	6.4	7.6	6.5	5.1	8.4
% Ret. on Assets	8.5	8.3	11.0	9.0	6.9	12.2
% Ret. on Equity	18.2	16.1	19.8	16.2	12.1	20.1

Dividend Data —Dividends have been paid since 1960. A dividend reinvestment plan is available. A "poison pill" stock purchase rights plan was adopted in 1985.

Amt. of Div. $	Date Decl.	Ex-Div. Date	Stock of Record	Payment Date
0.150	Oct. 12	Oct. 18	Oct. 24	Nov. 04 '94
0.150	Dec. 14	Jan. 17	Jan. 23	Feb. 03 '95
0.150	Apr. 19	Apr. 25	May. 01	May. 12 '95
0.160	Jul. 12	Jul. 20	Jul. 24	Aug. 04 '95

Data as orig. reptd.; bef. results of disc. opers. and/or spec. items. Per share data adj. for stk. divs. as of ex-div. date. E-Estimated. NA-Not Available. NM-Not Meaningful. NR-Not Ranked.

Office—730 Central Ave., Murray Hill, NJ 07974. **Tel**—(908) 277-8000. **Chrmn, Pres & CEO**—W. H. Longfield. **EVP & COO**—B. F. Smith. **VP & CFO**—W. C. Bopp. **VP & Secy**—R. A. Flink. **VP, Treas & Investor Contact**—Earle L. Parker. **Dirs**—J. F. Abely, Jr., W. T. Butler, R. B. Carey, Jr., D. A. Cronin, Jr., T. K. Dunnigan, R. E. Herzlinger, W. H. Longfield, R. P. Luciano, R. H. McCaffrey, B. F. Smith. **Transfer Agent & Registrar**—First Chicago Trust Co. of New York, NYC. **Incorporated** in New York in 1923; reincorporated in New Jersey in 1972. Empl-8,650. **S&P Analyst:** H. B. Saftlas

Barrick Gold

NYSE Symbol **ABX**
In S&P 500

17-AUG-95

Industry: Mining/Diversified

Summary: With the 1994 acquisition of Lac Minerals, Barrick Gold (formerly American Barrick Resources) is now the largest gold mining company in the world outside South Africa.

S&P Opinion: Hold (★★★)	Recent Price • 25⅛
	52 Wk Range • 27½-19¾

Yield • 0.5%
12-Mo. P/E • 31.4

Quantitative Evaluations

Outlook (1 Lowest—5 Highest)
• **2⁻**

Fair Value
• **22¾**

Risk
• **Average**

Earn./Div. Rank
• **A-**

Technical Eval.
• **Bearish** since 10/94

Rel. Strength Rank (1 Lowest—99 Highest)
• **43**

Insider Activity
• **NA**

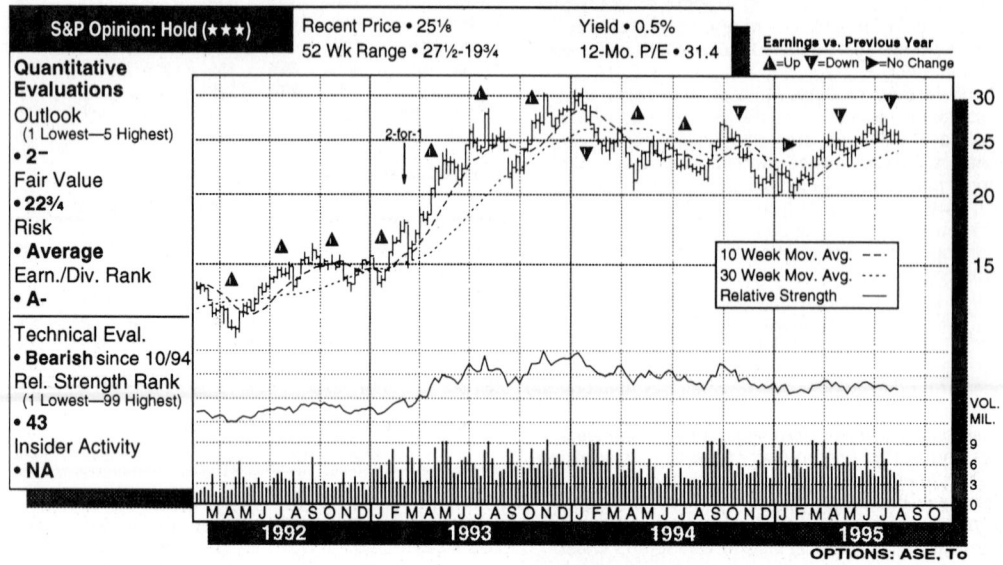

Earnings vs. Previous Year
▲=Up ▼=Down ▶=No Change

10 Week Mov. Avg. ---
30 Week Mov. Avg. ····
Relative Strength ——

OPTIONS: ASE, To

Overview - 17-AUG-95

Gold production is projected to increase nearly 30% in 1995, reflecting the full-year inclusion of the Lac Mineral properties in Chile, Canada and United States. Also boosting volumes will be start up of the new Tambo mine in Chile. Average mining costs could rise moderately, reflecting the acquisition of Lac's higher-cost mines. Additionally, ABX will experience higher costs at the Mercur mine stemming from lower oxide recovery because of hard ore, and higher costs at Bullfrog due to lower quality ore grades. Also restricting margins will be sharply higher exploration outlays. First half price realizations were $405/oz., versus $404/oz. which was higher than spot markets due to hedging. Limiting profit comparisons will be some 16% more shares outstanding, higher interest costs and effective tax rates.

Valuation - 17-AUG-95

Shares of this leading gold producer continue to lag the overall market, reflecting sluggish precious metals' prices. On a relative basis, well-managed ABX continues to outperform other gold stocks. The late 1994 acquisition of Lac Minerals for 66.2 million common shares plus $153 million was a strategic coup, as the deal brings ABX a major property in Chile at a very attractive price. Looking out to 1996, ABX will benefit from the start up of a major new mine in Nevada. While we applaud ABX's extensive use of hedging to reduce price risk, we are neutral on the stock for now until a clear uptrend in gold prices emerges.

Key Stock Statistics

S&P EPS Est. 1995	0.85	Tang. Bk. Value/Share	7.41
P/E on S&P Est. 1995	29.6	Beta	0.07
S&P EPS Est. 1996	0.95	Shareholders	7,300
Dividend Rate/Share	0.12	Market cap. (B)	$ 9.1
Shs. outstg. (M)	353.3	Inst. holdings	34%
Avg. daily vol. (M)	0.936	Insider holdings	NA

Value of $10,000 invested 5 years ago: $ 32,513

Fiscal Year Ending Dec. 31

	1995	% Change	1994	% Change	1993	% Change
Revenues (Million $)						
1Q	300.0	60%	187.3	30%	144.1	77%
2Q	309.8	49%	207.4	18%	175.2	52%
3Q	—	—	216.1	21%	178.1	24%
4Q	—	—	325.2	91%	170.2	-15%
Yr.	—	—	936.1	40%	667.5	24%
Income (Million $)						
1Q	71.00	18%	60.42	31%	46.07	99%
2Q	75.40	21%	62.38	9%	57.16	56%
3Q	—	—	61.26	5%	58.34	18%
4Q	—	—	66.40	28%	51.81	-21%
Yr.	—	—	250.5	17%	213.4	22%
Earnings Per Share ($)						
1Q	0.20	-5%	0.21	31%	0.16	100%
2Q	0.21	-5%	0.22	10%	0.20	54%
3Q	E0.22	10%	0.20	-5%	0.21	17%
4Q	E0.22	22%	0.18	NM	0.18	-22%
Yr.	E0.85	5%	0.81	8%	0.75	21%

Next earnings report expected: mid October

Barrick Gold

Business Summary - 17-AUG-95

Barrick Gold (formerly American Barrick Resources) is the world's third largest gold mining company and largest producer in the Americas. ABX operates mines in the U.S., Canada and Chile. ABX produced 2,326,000 ounces of gold in 1994, versus 1,632,000 oz. in 1993. The average price realized in 1994 was $402/oz., compared with $409/oz. in 1993. The average production cost was $167/oz., versus $170/oz. in 1993. Contributions to gold production (in ounces) by mine in recent years:

	1994	1993
Betze-Post	1,849,500	1,439,900
Mercur	108,100	114,800
Bullfrog	77,100	---
El Indio	70,500	---
Bousquet	68,600	---
Holt-McDermott	59,900	64,200
Doyon	36,100	---
Golden Patricia	28,000	---
Macassa	16,200	---
Pinson	11,600	13,100

Total proven and probable gold reserves at 1994 year-end were 37,600,000 ounces, versus 28,400,000 ounces in 1993. Total reserves were 44,000,000 in 1994 (30,600,000). Included in 1994's total reserves are 12.9 million ounces derived from the September 1994 acquisition of Lac Minerals. ABX paid $152.5 million in cash for Lac and issued 66,200,000 common shares.

In early 1995 ABX commenced production at the new Tambo open pit mine in Chile. Annual production is estimated at 120,000 ounces. Construction is underway at the Meikle underground mine in Nevada. Production, estimated at 400,000 oz./year is expected to commence in 1996's second half. Meikle has total reserves of 6.6 million ounces.

Important Developments

May '95—ABX sold the Macassa mine in Ontario (acquired from Lac Minerals in September 1994) to Kinross Gold Corp. for $42.5 million plus warrants covering 2,500,000 KGC common shares. At 1994 year-end, Macassa had proven and probable gold reserves of 743,000 ounces.
Mar. '95—The Tambo mine (Chile), which provided mill feed to El Indio, became a separate mine with the completion of its own 6,000 metric-ton per day mill. Ore will come from two main pits, Wendy and Kimberly. Tambo is targeted to produce 120,000 ounces of gold in 1995.

Capitalization

Long Term Debt: $232,000,000 (6/95).

Per Share Data ($) (Year Ended Dec. 31)

	1994	1993	1992	1991	1990	1989
Tangible Bk. Val.	7.41	4.16	3.50	2.99	2.41	2.05
Cash Flow	1.15	1.00	0.86	0.52	0.39	0.32
Earnings	0.81	0.75	0.62	0.34	0.23	0.15
Dividends	0.10	0.08	0.07	0.06	0.04	0.03
Payout Ratio	14%	11%	11%	17%	20%	23%
Prices - High	31	30⅜	16⅜	14	12⅜	8⅝
- Low	19⅞	13⅝	11⅛	9¼	7⅝	4⅛
P/E Ratio - High	38	41	26	41	55	57
- Low	25	18	18	27	34	27

Income Statement Analysis (Million $)

	1994	%Chg	1993	%Chg	1992	%Chg	1991
Revs.	936	40%	668	24%	540	57%	345
Oper. Inc.	435	29%	337	17%	288	85%	156
Depr.	106	49%	71.1	3%	69.0	35%	51.3
Int. Exp.	11.4	28%	8.9	-4%	9.3	-1%	9.4
Pretax Inc.	336	24%	270	21%	223	94%	115
Eff. Tax Rate	25%	—	21%	—	22%	—	20%
Net Inc.	251	18%	213	22%	175	89%	92.4

Balance Sheet & Other Fin. Data (Million $)

	1994	1993	1992	1991	1990	1989
Cash	458	348	288	252	312	305
Curr. Assets	656	410	353	328	391	368
Total Assets	3,472	1,634	1,504	1,306	1,147	1,050
Curr. Liab.	289	140	139	112	112	89.0
LT Debt	285	219	317	306	363	419
Common Eqty.	2,617	1,191	993	841	645	526
Total Cap.	3,079	1,489	1,360	1,189	1,035	961
Cap. Exp.	272	165	255	264	170	224
Cash Flow	357	284	244	144	107	76.0

Ratio Analysis

	1994	1993	1992	1991	1990	1989
Curr. Ratio	2.3	2.9	2.5	2.9	3.5	4.1
% LT Debt of Cap.	9.2	14.7	23.3	25.7	35.0	43.6
% Net Inc.of Revs.	26.8	32.0	32.4	26.8	23.1	17.4
% Ret. on Assets	9.1	13.5	12.4	7.4	5.2	3.9
% Ret. on Equity	12.3	19.5	19.0	12.2	9.8	7.5

Dividend Data

—Dividends were initiated in 1987. Semiannual payments in the past 12 months (in U.S. funds) before 15% Canadian nonresident tax:

Amt. of Div. $	Date Decl.	Ex-Div. Date	Stock of Record	Payment Date
0.040	Feb. 08	May. 24	May. 31	Jun. 15 '93
0.040	Sep. 23	Nov. 23	Nov. 30	Dec. 15 '93
0.050	Apr. 22	May. 24	May. 31	Jun. 15 '94
0.050	Sep. 13	Nov. 23	Nov. 30	Dec. 15 '94
0.060	Apr. 18	May. 24	May. 31	Jun. 15 '95

Data as orig. reptd.; bef. results of disc. opers. and/or spec. items. Per share data adj. for stk. divs. as of ex-div. date. E-Estimated. NA-Not Available. NM-Not Meaningful. NR-Not Ranked.

Office—Royal Bank Plaza, South Tower, 200 Bay St., Suite 2700, Toronto, Ontario, Canada M5J 2J3. **Tel**—(416) 861-9911. **Chrmn & CEO**—P. Munk. **Pres & COO**—R. M. Smith. **Secy**—S. E. Veenman. **VP-CFO**—R. Oliphant. **SVP-Investor Contact**—Belle Mulligan. **Dirs**—H. L. Beck, C. W. D. Birchall, M. A. Cohen, P. A. Crossgrove, J. T. Eyton, D. H. Gilmour, A. A. MacNaughton, B. Mulroney, P. Munk, E. N. Ney, J. L. Rotman, R. M. Smith, G. C. Wilkins. **Transfer Agent & Registrar**—R-M Trust Co., Toronto, Mellon Securities Trust Co., Ridgefield Park, NJ. **Incorporated** in Ontario in 1984. **Empl**-5,000. **S&P Analyst:** Stephen R. Klein

Barnett Banks

NYSE Symbol **BBI**
In **S&P 500**

18-OCT-95 | **Industry:** Banking

Summary: Florida's largest bank holding company, and the 22nd largest in the U.S., Barnett operates through more than 600 offices in Florida and Georgia.

S&P Opinion: Hold (★★★)

| Recent Price • 58⅛ | Yield • 3.2% |
| 52 Wk Range • 59½-37¼ | 12-Mo. P/E • 11.3 |

Quantitative Evaluations

Outlook
(1 Lowest—5 Highest)
• **3+**

Fair Value
• **58½**

Risk
• **Low**

Earn./Div. Rank
• **A-**

Technical Eval.
• **Bullish** since 12/94

Rel. Strength Rank
(1 Lowest—99 Highest)
• **74**

Insider Activity
• **NA**

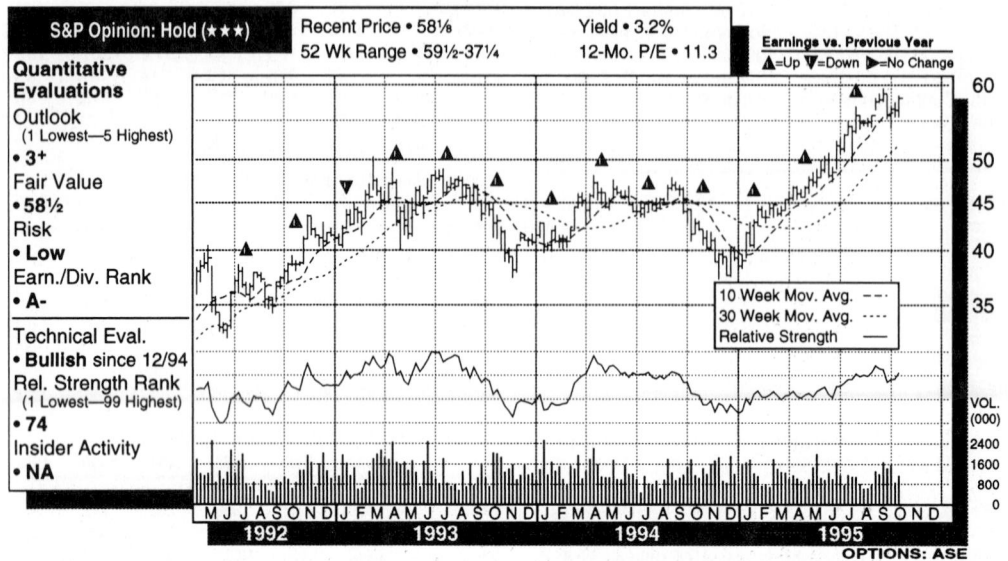

Earnings vs. Previous Year
▲=Up ▼=Down ▶=No Change

10 Week Mov. Avg. — - -
30 Week Mov. Avg. - - - -
Relative Strength —

1992 1993 1994 1995

VOL. (000)
2400
1600
800
0

OPTIONS: ASE

Overview - 18-OCT-95

Loan growth in 1996 is expected in the 8% to 10% range, with the strongest demand in the consumer areas of residential mortgage and installment lending. In addition, the recent acquisition of Glendale Federal Bank's Florida franchise will strengthen BBI's market share and loan gathering efficiency. Further, the inclusion of Glendale's large deposit base has enabled the net interest margin to stabilize. Revenues should receive a boost from the recent acquisitions of EquiCredit Corp. and BancPLUS Financial, although the net effect after expenses is expected to be neutral this year. Credit quality continues to improve, with nonperforming assets down 7%, year to year, to $282.2 million at September 30, 1995, and the allowance for loan losses at 245% of nonperforming loans.

Valuation - 18-OCT-95

The expectation of relatively modest earnings growth in 1995 is the primary factor behind our neutral assessment of the shares. Despite healthy loan growth, the higher level of interest rates in effect for much of this year has reduced the net interest margin, leading to only moderate improvement in net interest income. While the significant buildup of the mortgage banking business through acquisitions makes sense strategically for diversification purposes in the long run, it will have a minimal impact on the bottom line in the intermediate period. Pending earnings surprises on the upside, the shares are expected to track market averages over the near term.

Key Stock Statistics

S&P EPS Est. 1995	5.25	Tang. Bk. Value/Share	24.08
P/E on S&P Est. 1995	11.1	Beta	1.75
S&P EPS Est. 1996	5.50	Shareholders	33,200
Dividend Rate/Share	1.88	Market cap. (B)	$ 5.6
Shs. outstg. (M)	96.5	Inst. holdings	52%
Avg. daily vol. (M)	0.239	Insider holdings	NA

Value of $10,000 invested 5 years ago: $ 20,380

Fiscal Year Ending Dec. 31

	1995	% Change	1994	% Change	1993	% Change
Revenues (Million $)						
1Q	882.2	19%	743.3	-8%	805.5	-12%
2Q	914.1	20%	760.2	-4%	790.6	-10%
3Q	—	—	786.3	NM	788.8	-8%
4Q	—	—	807.7	8%	745.0	-14%
Yr.	—	—	3,097	-1%	3,130	-9%
Income (Million $)						
1Q	128.7	9%	118.0	28%	92.30	35%
2Q	132.2	9%	121.2	16%	104.2	66%
3Q	134.1	9%	123.4	11%	111.1	56%
4Q	—	—	125.4	11%	113.3	NM
Yr.	—	—	488.0	16%	421.0	102%
Earnings Per Share ($)						
1Q	1.27	10%	1.15	28%	0.90	34%
2Q	1.30	9%	1.19	18%	1.01	68%
3Q	1.34	11%	1.21	12%	1.08	57%
4Q	E1.34	8%	1.24	12%	1.11	NM
Yr.	E5.25	10%	4.79	17%	4.10	107%

Next earnings report expected: mid January

Business Summary - 18-OCT-95

Barnett Banks is the largest bank holding company headquartered in Florida and the 22nd largest in the U.S. BBI has a decentralized system of 31 banks with 628 offices in Florida and Georgia. The company ranks first, second or third in share of individual, partnership and corporate bank deposits in all 45 Florida counties in which it operates. In recent years, it has been increasing market share of deposits through both internal growth and acquisitions. BBI held a leading 26.6% deposit market share in Florida at September 30, 1994. In 1993, BBI exchanged its Atlanta banking franchise for Bank South Corp.'s Pensacola, Fla., bank and other considerations. Nonbanking subsidiaries offer trust ($9 billion of assets managed), credit card, mortgage banking ($9.8 billion of residential real estate outstandings) and securities brokerage (40 offices).

In 1994, average earning assets of $34.4 billion ($33.5 billion in 1993) consisted of commercial, financial and agricultural loans 12%, commercial real estate loans 7%, residential mortgages 28%, consumer loans 28%, investment securities 22% and other 3%. Average sources of funds were interest-bearing deposits 69%, demand deposits 14%, short-term borrowings 6%, long-term debt 2%, equity 8% and other 1%.

At December 31, 1994, nonperforming assets were $291 million (1.01% of loans and related assets), down from $458 million (1.74%) a year earlier. The reserve for loan losses was 1.76% of loans, versus 2.01%. Net chargeoffs in 1994 were 0.34% of average loans, against 0.55% in 1993.

Important Developments

Oct. '95—The company acquired Community Bank of the Islands ($85 million in assets), a privately held financial institution in southwestern Florida, for an undisclosed amount.
Sep. '95—BBI reached a definitive agreement to acquire First Financial Bancshares ($132 million in assets), which serves central and eastern Polk County, Fla., through six offices, for $20 million in cash.
Jul. '95—The company noted that it had been authorized to repurchase up to 10 million common shares as part of an ongoing capital management program.
Mar. '95—The company acquired BancPLUS Financial Corp., which originates, acquires, markets and services first mortgage loans secured by residential properties in all 50 states, for $162 million in cash. Based in San Antonio, Tex., BancPLUS originated $1.5 billion in loans in 1994.

Capitalization

Long Term Debt: $1,151,211,000 (9/95).
Cum. Conv. Preferred Stock: $212,999,000.

Per Share Data ($)

	1994	1993	1992	1991	1990	1989
Tangible Bk. Val.	25.02	25.40	21.16	21.03	19.61	22.22
Earnings	4.79	4.10	1.98	1.71	1.61	4.07
Dividends	1.59	1.41	1.32	1.32	1.29	1.16
Payout Ratio	33%	34%	67%	77%	80%	29%
Prices - High	48⅛	50⅜	43⅝	36⅜	37¾	40
- Low	37¼	37⅜	31	15½	14⅛	32¼
P/E Ratio - High	10	12	22	21	23	10
- Low	8	9	16	9	9	8

(Year Ended Dec. 31)

Income Statement Analysis (Million $)

	1994	%Chg	1993	%Chg	1992	%Chg	1991
Net Int. Inc.	1,633	-1%	1,651	-1%	1,676	29%	1,301
Tax Equiv. Adj.	44.0	-11%	49.5	-15%	58.0	-6%	62.0
Non Int. Inc.	556	-7%	599	NM	603	32%	456
Loan Loss Prov.	74.0	-38%	120	-53%	257	-27%	352
% Exp/Op Revs.	61%	—	65%	—	75%	—	69%
Pretax Inc.	738	18%	628	107%	304	87%	163
Eff. Tax Rate	34%	—	33%	—	31%	—	24%
Net Inc.	488	16%	421	102%	208	68%	124
% Net Int. Marg.	4.87%	—	5.07%	—	5.11%	—	4.69%

Balance Sheet & Other Fin. Data (Million $)

	1994	1993	1992	1991	1990	1989
Earning Assets:						
Money Mkt.	35.0	275	NA	NA	NA	156
Inv. Securities	7,683	5,789	6,824	4,944	4,235	3,131
Com'l Loans	4,446	4,087	4,231	4,415	4,530	4,099
Other Loans	24,075	21,843	21,820	19,073	20,609	19,265
Total Assets	41,278	38,331	39,465	32,721	32,214	29,007
Demand Deposits	5,958	6,017	5,955	3,881	3,763	3,407
Time Deposits	29,151	26,617	28,734	24,973	24,963	21,649
LT Debt	777	682	701	710	495	391
Common Eqty.	2,919	2,659	2,341	1,760	1,572	1,691

Ratio Analysis

	1994	1993	1992	1991	1990	1989
% Ret. on Assets	1.3	1.1	0.6	0.4	0.3	0.9
% Ret. on Equity	18.1	16.0	9.1	7.4	6.2	16.0
% Loan Loss Resv.	1.8	2.0	2.1	1.9	1.7	1.1
% Loans/Deposits	81.2	80.1	75.1	81.4	84.4	89.5
% Equity to Assets	6.8	6.4	5.5	4.8	5.3	5.9

Dividend Data —Dividends have been paid since 1945. A dividend reinvestment plan is available. A "poison pill" stock purchase rights plan was adopted in 1990.

Amt. of Div. $	Date Decl.	Ex-Div. Date	Stock of Record	Payment Date
0.410	Nov. 16	Dec. 05	Dec. 09	Jan. 03 '95
0.410	Feb. 15	Mar. 03	Mar. 09	Apr. 03 '95
0.470	May. 17	Jun. 06	Jun. 09	Jul. 03 '95
0.470	Aug. 16	Sep. 06	Sep. 08	Oct. 02 '95

Office—50 North Laura St., Jacksonville, FL 32202-3638; P.O. Box 40789, Jacksonville, FL 32203-0789. **Tel**—(904) 791-7720. **Chrmn & CEO**—C. E. Rice. **Pres & COO**—A. L. Lastinger Jr. **CFO**—C. W. Newman. **Secy**—C. C. Cosby. **Investor Contact**—Gregory M. Delaney. **Dirs**—W. H. Alford, R. Bornstein, J. L. Broadhead, A. R. Carpenter, A. M. Codina, M. M. Criser, J. B. Critchfield, C. H. Golembe, A. L. Lastinger Jr., C. V. McKee, R. Diaz-Oliver, T. L. Rankin, C. E. Rice, F. H. Schultz, S. Turley, J. A. Williams. **Transfer Agent & Registrar**—First Chicago Trust, Jersey City, N.J. **Incorporated** in Florida in 1930; Barnett Bank of Jacksonville chartered in 1877. **Empl**-18,420. **S&P Analyst:** Stephen R. Biggar

Bassett Furniture Industries

NASDAQ Symbol **BSET**

In S&P 500

19-OCT-95

Industry:
Home Furnishings

Summary: Bassett is a leading producer of wood furniture for bedroom, dining room, living room and nursery use, as well as upholstered furniture and other related products.

Quantitative Evaluations	
Outlook (1 Lowest—5 Highest)	• 1⁻
Fair Value	• 21¼
Risk	• **Low**
Earn./Div. Rank	• **B**
Technical Eval.	• **Bullish** since 4/95
Rel. Strength Rank (1 Lowest—99 Highest)	• 35
Insider Activity	• **Neutral**

Recent Price • 25⅜   Yield • 3.2%
52 Wk Range • 30¾-24   12-Mo. P/E • 15.1

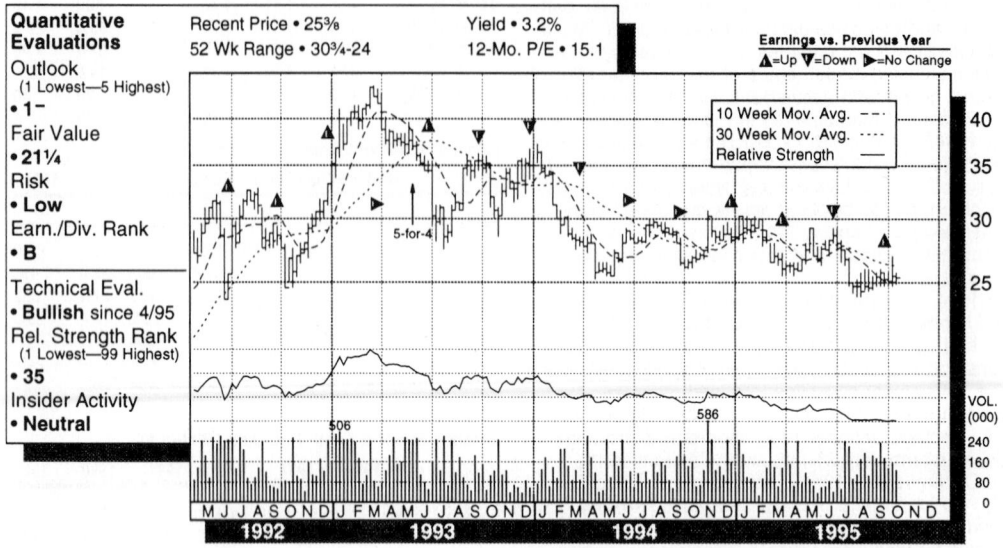

Earnings vs. Previous Year
▲=Up ▼=Down ▶=No Change

10 Week Mov. Avg. ---
30 Week Mov. Avg. ·····
Relative Strength —

Business Profile - 11-OCT-95

This furniture producer's recent results have been impacted by rising interest rates and declining housing starts. While there has been a recent moderation in interest rates and an uptick in housing starts, the company continues to experience raw materials cost pressures but has been unable to pass through such costs to dealers. Earlier in 1995, BSET adjusted production schedules in response to a slowdown in retail sales of household furniture.

Operational Review - 16-OCT-95

Net sales for the nine months ended August 31, 1995, declined 5.2%, year to year, primarily reflecting a slowdown in retail sales of household furniture and incoming orders. Reduced production schedules combined with the inability to pass through any raw material price hikes and market introduction costs also served to depress operating earnings. Higher marketing and merchandising costs incurred in an effort to stimulate sales also negatively impacted results; EPS declined to $1.11, from $1.14.

Stock Performance - 13-OCT-95

In the past 30 trading days, BSET's shares have increased 2%, compared to a 4% rise in the S&P 500. Average trading volume for the past five days was 25,340 shares, compared with the 40-day moving average of 32,785 shares.

Key Stock Statistics

Dividend Rate/Share	0.80	Shareholders	2,200
Shs. outstg. (M)	14.0	Market cap. (B)	$0.351
Avg. daily vol. (M)	0.026	Inst. holdings	45%
Tang. Bk. Value/Share	21.57	Insider holdings	NA
Beta	0.70		

Value of $10,000 invested 5 years ago: $ 15,326

Fiscal Year Ending Nov. 30

	1995	% Change	1994	% Change	1993	% Change
Revenues (Million $)						
1Q	123.6	2%	121.7	1%	120.3	13%
2Q	119.0	-12%	134.6	4%	128.9	13%
3Q	119.2	-5%	125.0	3%	121.2	NM
4Q	—	—	129.3	-3%	133.4	1%
Yr.	—	—	510.6	1%	503.8	6%
Income (Million $)						
1Q	4.90	4%	4.73	-23%	6.18	-1%
2Q	4.98	-35%	7.68	9%	7.06	-99%
3Q	5.78	26%	4.59	-1%	4.65	-20%
4Q	—	—	7.98	NM	7.98	-9%
Yr.	—	—	24.98	-3%	25.87	-6%
Earnings Per Share ($)						
1Q	0.35	6%	0.33	-24%	0.43	NM
2Q	0.35	-34%	0.53	NM	0.53	14%
3Q	0.41	28%	0.32	NM	0.32	-20%
4Q	—	—	0.57	4%	0.55	-10%
Yr.	—	—	1.75	-2%	1.79	-6%

Next earnings report expected: late December

Business Summary - 19-OCT-95

One of the leading wood furniture manufacturers in the U.S., Bassett Furniture Industries produces a full line of furniture for the home, consisting of bedroom and dining suites and accent pieces; occasional tables, wall and entertainment units; upholstered sofas, chairs and love seats (motion and stationary); recliners; and mattresses and box springs.

Bassett's products are distributed through a large number of retailers, including mass merchandisers, independent furniture stores, chain furniture stores, decorator showrooms, warehouse showrooms and specialty stores. In October 1994, Bassett announced the Bassett Direct Plus Dealership Program, under which Bassett retailers open free-standing Bassett stores between 15,000 and 20,000 sq. ft. in size, which would exclusively carry Bassett products. The company believes the cornerstone of the Bassett Direct Dealership Program is the partnership between Bassett and the retailer, designed to create the closest possible working relationship between the two. This is accomplished through a combination of the latest computer technologies such as EDI (Electronic Data Interchange) and BassNET, which are part of a streamlined management system for the retailer.

The company's products are principally sold in the U.S. Sales to J.C. Penney Co. accounted for 13% of revenues in fiscal 1994, versus 12% in fiscal 1993.

The company manufactures its products at more than 40 plants throughout the U.S. In addition, Bassett operates a general office building and two warehouses in Bassett, Va., and a showroom in High Point, N.C.

The company believes that "Solutions by Bassett" is the the answer to the frustrating problems consumers face when trying to decorate a combination living/dining room area. This concept features scaled-down dining suites, along with upholstery, occasional tables, wall units and entertainment pieces. BSET asserts that "Solutions" saves on endless hours spent trying to select the perfect furnishings for this problem area of the home.

Important Developments

Oct. '95—The company said that its order backlog improved in the 1995 third quarter from the depressed levels of the prior quarter. Bassett noted that the increased incoming order rate was recorded throughout all of its divisions.

Capitalization

Long Term Debt: None (8/95).

Per Share Data ($)

(Year Ended Nov. 30)

	1994	1993	1992	1991	1990	1989
Tangible Bk. Val.	20.95	19.99	18.99	17.72	16.89	17.29
Cash Flow	2.36	2.41	2.50	1.92	0.88	1.76
Earnings	1.75	1.79	1.90	1.37	0.34	1.22
Dividends	0.80	0.78	0.64	0.53	0.67	1.07
Payout Ratio	46%	44%	33%	39%	187%	85%
Prices - High	37¼	44	35¼	21¼	20¼	21¼
- Low	25¼	27½	19½	16⅞	15⅛	18½
P/E Ratio - High	21	25	18	15	58	17
- Low	14	15	10	12	43	15

Income Statement Analysis (Million $)

	1994	%Chg	1993	%Chg	1992	%Chg	1991
Revs.	511	1%	504	7%	473	18%	402
Oper. Inc.	33.9	-6%	36.2	-1%	36.7	62%	22.7
Depr.	8.8	-2%	9.0	6%	8.5	8%	7.9
Int. Exp.	Nil	—	Nil	—	Nil	—	Nil
Pretax Inc.	34.8	-5%	36.5	-7%	39.3	46%	26.9
Eff. Tax Rate	28%	—	29%	—	30%	—	26%
Net Inc.	25.0	-3%	25.9	-6%	27.5	39%	19.8

Balance Sheet & Other Fin. Data (Million $)

	1994	1993	1992	1991	1990	1989
Cash	42.3	53.0	50.2	74.0	57.6	76.4
Curr. Assets	199	202	193	202	183	212
Total Assets	340	331	319	291	271	305
Curr. Liab.	35.0	33.2	36.9	29.0	20.1	42.2
LT Debt	Nil	Nil	Nil	Nil	Nil	Nil
Common Eqty.	295	289	274	255	244	263
Total Cap.	296	289	274	255	244	263
Cap. Exp.	10.0	6.2	9.9	7.9	9.1	8.2
Cash Flow	33.8	34.9	36.0	27.7	13.0	27.3

Ratio Analysis

	1994	1993	1992	1991	1990	1989
Curr. Ratio	5.7	6.1	5.2	7.0	9.1	5.0
% LT Debt of Cap.	Nil	Nil	Nil	Nil	Nil	Nil
% Net Inc.of Revs.	4.9	5.1	5.8	4.9	1.2	4.1
% Ret. on Assets	7.5	8.0	9.0	7.1	1.8	6.2
% Ret. on Equity	8.7	9.2	10.4	8.0	2.1	7.2

Dividend Data

—Cash has been paid each year since 1935. A shareholder rights plan was adopted in 1988.

Amt. of Div. $	Date Decl.	Ex-Div. Date	Stock of Record	Payment Date
0.200	Oct. 24	Nov. 10	Nov. 17	Nov. 30 '94
0.200	Feb. 15	Feb. 21	Feb. 27	Mar. 01 '95
0.200	May. 03	May. 11	May. 17	Jun. 01 '95
0.200	Aug. 02	Aug. 16	Aug. 18	Sep. 01 '95

Data as orig. reptd.; bef. results of disc. opers. and/or spec. items. Per share data adj. for stk. divs. as of ex-div. date. E-Estimated. NA-Not Available. NM-Not Meaningful. NR-Not Ranked.

Office—P.O. Box 626, Bassett, VA 24055. **Tel**—(703) 629-6000. **Chrmn & CEO**—R. H. Spilman. **Pres**—G. A. Hunsucker. **EVP-Fin, Treas & Investor Contact**—B. M. Brammer. **Secy**—J. S. Payne. **Dirs**—P. W. Brown, T. E. Capps, A. T. Dickson, P. Fulton, W. H. Goodwin, Jr., G. A. Hunsucker, G. W. Lyles, Jr., J. W. McGlothlin, A. F. Sloan, J. W. Snow, R. H. Spilman. **Transfer Agent & Registrar**—Co.'s office. **Incorporated** in Virginia in 1930. **Empl**-7,800. **S&P Analyst:** Philip D. Wohl

28-AUG-95

Industry:
Medical equipment/
supply

Summary: The world's leading maker of contact lenses and related solutions, Bausch & Lomb also produces ophthalmic drugs, sunglasses and other biomedical and consumer items.

| S&P Opinion: Hold (★★★) | Recent Price • 40¾ | Yield • 2.6% |
| | 52 Wk Range • 42⅞-30⅝ | 12-Mo. P/E • NM |

Quantitative Evaluations

Outlook
(1 Lowest—5 Highest)
• **3+**

Fair Value
• **40**

Risk
• **Low**

Earn./Div. Rank
• **A-**

Technical Eval.
• **Bearish** since 7/95

Rel. Strength Rank
(1 Lowest—99 Highest)
• **32**

Insider Activity
• **Favorable**

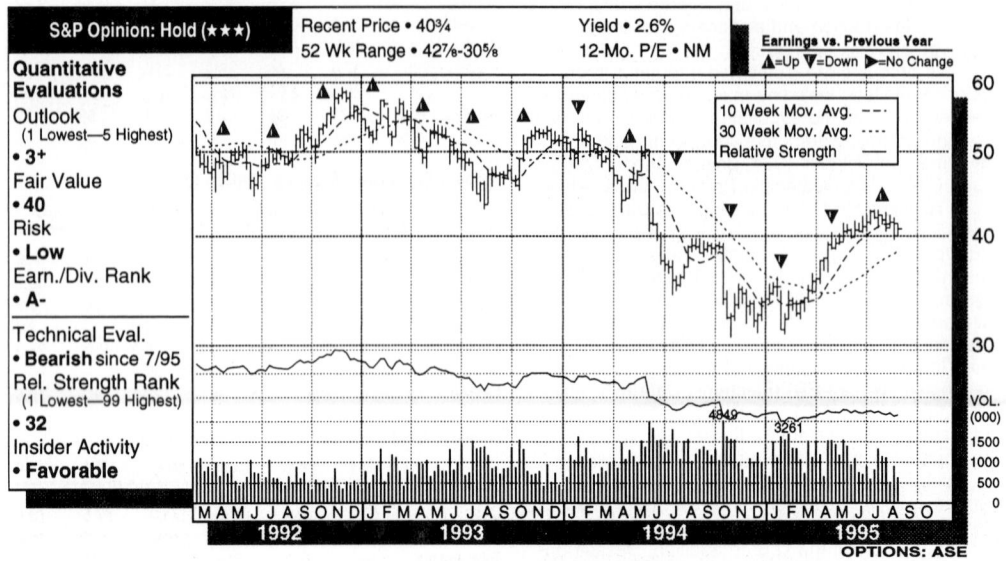

Earnings vs. Previous Year
▲=Up ▼=Down ▶=No Change

10 Week Mov. Avg. – – –
30 Week Mov. Avg. ......
Relative Strength ——

OPTIONS: ASE

Overview - 25-AUG-95

Sales are expected to show further progress in 1996. Despite continuing intense competition in many lines, contact lenses and related products and ophthalmic drugs should show good gains, aided by new products and greater market expansion abroad. Contact lens sales should be bolstered by the launch of Soflens 66, a new high water-contact disposable lens, while brisk demand for Miracle Ear and Mirage should continue to boost sales of hearing aids. Further growth is also seen for the sunglasses and biomedical businesses. Despite ongoing new product and advertising costs, margins should benefit from improving sales, personnel reductions and other cost streamlining moves.

Valuation - 28-AUG-95

The shares have performed well so far in 1995, reflecting recovery from weakness in 1994 triggered by problems related to excess distributor inventories and adverse publicity from an SEC inquiry associated with a past unsuccessful contact lens distributor marketing program. BOL has taken corrective actions to solve these problems and has effected other changes that should enhance future profits, including work force reductions, a $75 million writeoff of goodwill on oral care lines, and the sale of the sports optics business. Earnings should show steady improvement through 1996. Trading at about a market multiple, the shares are rated a long-term hold for total return. Dividends were recently raised about 6%, to $0.26 quarterly.

Key Stock Statistics

S&P EPS Est. 1995	2.70	Tang. Bk. Value/Share	9.40
P/E on S&P Est. 1995	15.1	Beta	1.18
S&P EPS Est. 1996	3.00	Shareholders	9,100
Dividend Rate/Share	1.04	Market cap. (B)	$ 2.3
Shs. outstg. (M)	57.3	Inst. holdings	70%
Avg. daily vol. (M)	0.155	Insider holdings	NA

Value of $10,000 invested 5 years ago: $ 14,024

Fiscal Year Ending Dec. 31

	1995	% Change	1994	% Change	1993	% Change
Revenues (Million $)						
1Q	465.6	6%	438.8	8%	407.6	10%
2Q	535.5	11%	483.3	NM	479.4	7%
3Q	—	—	449.5	-10%	498.8	8%
4Q	—	—	479.0	-1%	486.3	14%
Yr.	—	—	1,851	-1%	1,872	10%
Income (Million $)						
1Q	20.28	-43%	35.66	9%	32.85	15%
2Q	51.59	56%	33.06	-30%	47.03	15%
3Q	—	—	7.69	-86%	55.75	12%
4Q	—	—	-62.93	NM	20.92	-60%
Yr.	—	—	13.48	-91%	156.6	-9%
Earnings Per Share ($)						
1Q	0.34	-43%	0.60	11%	0.54	15%
2Q	0.89	62%	0.55	-29%	0.78	15%
3Q	E0.76	NM	0.13	-86%	0.93	12%
4Q	E0.71	NM	-1.05	NM	0.35	-59%
Yr.	E2.70	NM	0.23	-91%	2.60	-8%

Next earnings report expected: mid October

Bausch & Lomb

Business Summary - 28-AUG-95

Bausch & Lomb, the world's leading maker of contact lenses and related solutions and accessories, also produces ophthalmic drugs, dental plaque removal devices, and optical items. Business segment contributions in 1994 were:

	Sales	Profits
Health care products	66%	53%
Optics	34%	47%

International operations provided 45% of sales and 88% of profits in 1994. R&D spending equaled 3.3% of sales in 1994 and 3.1% in 1993.

Health care products include personal health, medical and biomedical products. Personal health items (36% of 1994 sales) consist of solutions used for the care of contact lenses and relief of eye irritation sold under the Sensitive Eyes, ReNu, Boston and other names; contact lens accessories; over-the-counter drugs; and oral care products, which include the Interplak line of home plaque removal devices and Interjet oral irrigator. Medical products (21%) include contact lenses and lens material, prescription pharmaceuticals, periodontal diagnostic items, and hearing aids. Therapeutic skin care products are also sold. A vision care service plan and other contact lens service programs are also offered.

Biomedical products (9%) include specialized laboratory animals such as rats, mice and guinea pigs from Charles River Laboratories; and biotechnical products and services, primarily for the production of monoclonal antibodies.

The optics segment includes consumer products such as Ray-Ban sunglasses and Bushnell and Bausch & Lomb binoculars, readers, magnifiers, telescopes and riflescopes; and optical thin-film coating services.

Important Developments

Jul. '95—The company said it plans to invest over $30 million to install the next generation of soft contact lens manufacturing technology. The new equipment will significantly reduce unit manufacturing costs of soft contact lens products and substantially increase production capacity. The technology will initially be used to make Soflens 66, a new high-water content disposable lens, which is scheduled to be introduced in the U.S. during 1995. Earnings in the second quarter included a gain of $0.36 a share from the sale of the sports optics division, offset by an $0.18 charge for litigation expenses.

Capitalization

Long Term Debt: $235,323,000 (7/1/95).
Minority Interest: $431,727,000.
Class B Common: 815,231 shs. ($0.08 par).

Per Share Data ($)

(Year Ended Dec. 31)

	1994	1993	1992	1991	1990	1989
Tangible Bk. Val.	8.79	7.95	11.45	10.18	9.35	7.53
Cash Flow	1.89	4.01	4.03	2.56	3.23	2.77
Earnings	0.23	2.60	2.84	1.42	2.19	1.89
Dividends	0.96	0.88	0.80	0.72	0.66	0.58
Payout Ratio	NM	34%	28%	50%	30%	30%
Prices - High	53⅞	57½	60½	60	36½	33
- Low	30⅝	43	44½	31¾	26⅜	20⅜
P/E Ratio - High	NM	22	21	42	17	17
- Low	NM	17	16	22	12	11

Income Statement Analysis (Million $)

	1994	%Chg	1993	%Chg	1992	%Chg	1991
Revs.	1,851	-1%	1,872	10%	1,709	12%	1,520
Oper. Inc.	268	-30%	385	13%	342	8%	316
Depr.	99	17%	84.6	17%	72.0	5%	68.7
Int. Exp.	41.4	21%	34.2	16%	29.5	-24%	38.6
Pretax Inc.	90.0	-63%	242	-8%	263	75%	150
Eff. Tax Rate	59%	—	33%	—	32%	—	40%
Net Inc.	13.0	-92%	157	-8%	171	99%	86.0

Balance Sheet & Other Fin. Data (Million $)

	1994	1993	1992	1991	1990	1989
Cash	233	546	417	412	386	321
Curr. Assets	954	1,402	1,082	965	943	778
Total Assets	2,458	2,512	1,874	1,770	1,677	1,429
Curr. Liab.	677	715	567	609	579	444
LT Debt	290	321	278	196	215	219
Common Eqty.	914	927	898	819	825	713
Total Cap.	1,632	1,669	1,196	1,062	1,090	985
Cap. Exp.	85.0	107	119	89.0	108	100
Cash Flow	113	241	243	155	194	167

Ratio Analysis

	1994	1993	1992	1991	1990	1989
Curr. Ratio	1.4	2.0	1.9	1.6	1.6	1.7
% LT Debt of Cap.	17.7	19.2	23.2	18.4	19.7	22.2
% Net Inc.of Revs.	0.7	8.4	10.0	5.7	9.6	9.4
% Ret. on Assets	0.5	7.2	9.4	5.0	8.5	8.7
% Ret. on Equity	1.5	17.2	20.0	10.4	17.2	17.0

Dividend Data

Dividends have been paid since 1952. A dividend reinvestment plan is available. A "poison pill" stock purchase rights plan was adopted in 1988.

Amt. of Div. $	Date Decl.	Ex-Div. Date	Stock of Record	Payment Date
0.245	Jul. 26	Aug. 26	Sep. 01	Oct. 03 '94
0.245	Oct. 25	Nov. 25	Dec. 01	Jan. 02 '95
0.245	Feb. 28	Mar. 06	Mar. 10	Apr. 03 '95
0.245	Apr. 25	May. 25	Jun. 01	Jul. 03 '95
0.260	Jul. 25	Aug. 30	Sep. 01	Oct. 02 '95

Data as orig. reptd.; bef. results of disc. opers. and/or spec. items. Per share data adj. for stk. divs. as of ex-div. date.
E-Estimated. NA-Not Available. NM-Not Meaningful. NR-Not Ranked.

Office—1 Lincoln First Square, Rochester, NY 14601-0054. **Tel**—(716) 338-6000. **Chrmn & CEO**—D. E. Gill. **SVP-Fin & CFO**—S. C. McCluski. **Secy**—S. A. Hellrung. **Investor Contact**—Franklin T. Jepson. **Dirs**—F. E. Agnew, W. Balderston III, B. R. Boss, D. E. Gill, J. T. Holmes, R. R. McMullin, J. R. Purcell, L. J. Rice, A. W. Trivelpiece, W. H. Waltrip, K. L. Wolfe. **Transfer Agent & Registrar**—First National Bank of Boston. **Incorporated** in New York in 1908. **Empl**-14,000. **S&P Analyst:** H. B. Saftlas

STOCK REPORTS

Baxter International

NYSE Symbol **BAX**
In S&P 500

25-AUG-95

Industry:
Medical equipment/supply

Summary: Baxter is the world's leading maker and distributor of hospital supplies and medical equipment, marketing over 200,000 products to customers in 100 countries worldwide.

S&P Opinion: Accumulate (★★★★)	Recent Price • 37⅛	Yield • 3.0%
	52 Wk Range • 38⅛-23¾	12-Mo. P/E • 16.5

Quantitative Evaluations

Outlook (1 Lowest—5 Highest)
• **2+**

Fair Value
• **35**

Risk
• **Low**

Earn./Div. Rank
• **B+**

Technical Eval.
• **Bullish** since 5/94

Rel. Strength Rank (1 Lowest—99 Highest)
• **60**

Insider Activity
• **Unfavorable**

Earnings vs. Previous Year
▲=Up ▼=Down ▶=No Change

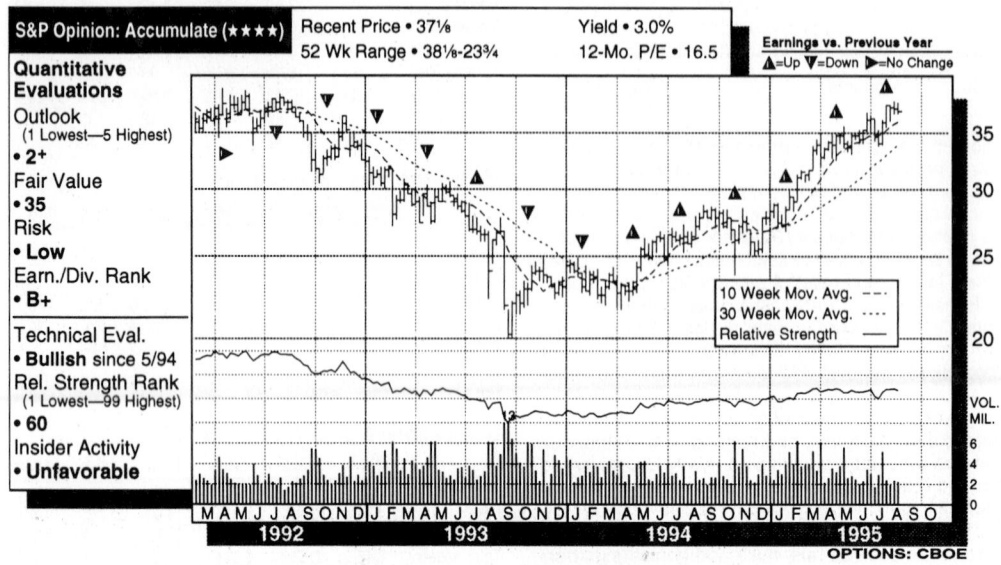

10 Week Mov. Avg. — – –
30 Week Mov. Avg. · · · ·
Relative Strength ——

OPTIONS: CBOE

Overview - 25-AUG-95

Sales are expected to show further growth in 1996. Despite the planned sale of the industrial division (sales of $450 million in 1994), revenues should benefit from expanded penetration in foreign markets, additional contracts, and generally firmer prices. New products, especially in the medical specialties area, should also help. Margins should widen, on the greater volume, an improved product mix, and tight control over marketing and administrative costs. EPS comparisons will be aided by stock repurchase programs. Exciting new high-tech R&D products such as an artificial blood product and a cardiac pump enhance long-term prospects.

Valuation - 25-AUG-95

Like most other health care equities, the shares were strong performers in recent months, reflecting improved prospects for the medical products industry and investor confidence that the company has returned to solid earnings growth, after highly erratic performance in recent years. Baxter aims to achieve sustained annual operational cash flow of $500 million, maintain a net-debt-to-capital ratio of 35% to 40%, repurchase $500 million of common stock in 1995-6, and reduce the marketing and administrative expense-to-sales ratio. Earnings growth over the next few years should be in the high single digits. The shares have appeal for long-term appreciation and rising dividend income.

Key Stock Statistics

S&P EPS Est. 1995	2.35	Tang. Bk. Value/Share	5.14
P/E on S&P Est. 1995	15.8	Beta	1.00
S&P EPS Est. 1996	2.60	Shareholders	77,800
Dividend Rate/Share	1.13	Market cap. (B)	$ 10.4
Shs. outstg. (M)	276.8	Inst. holdings	74%
Avg. daily vol. (M)	0.384	Insider holdings	NA

Value of $10,000 invested 5 years ago: $ 17,436

Fiscal Year Ending Dec. 31

	1995	% Change	1994	% Change	1993	% Change
Revenues (Million $)						
1Q	2,318	6%	2,193	7%	2,041	3%
2Q	2,465	6%	2,316	5%	2,215	6%
3Q	—	—	2,315	4%	2,228	5%
4Q	—	—	2,500	4%	2,395	4%
Yr.	—	—	9,324	5%	8,879	5%
Income (Million $)						
1Q	145.0	11%	131.0	130%	57.00	-48%
2Q	165.0	15%	144.0	9%	132.0	2%
3Q	—	—	149.0	10%	135.0	-9%
4Q	—	—	172.0	NM	-592.0	NM
Yr.	—	—	596.0	NM	-268.0	NM
Earnings Per Share ($)						
1Q	0.52	11%	0.47	135%	0.20	-46%
2Q	0.59	13%	0.52	8%	0.48	4%
3Q	E0.58	9%	0.53	8%	0.49	-6%
4Q	E0.66	8%	0.61	NM	-2.14	NM
Yr.	E2.35	10%	2.13	NM	-0.97	NM

Next earnings report expected: late October

Baxter International

Business Summary - 25-AUG-95

Baxter International is the world's leading manufacturer and marketer of hospital supplies and related medical equipment. The company offers over 200,000 products to health care providers in 100 countries, and also has R&D programs in biotechnology, cardiology, renal therapy and other medical fields. The diagnostics manufacturing business was sold in December 1994. Sales and pretax profits in 1994 were derived as follows:

	Sales	Income
Medical/laboratory products	62%	43%
Medical specialties	38%	57%

Foreign operations accounted for 27% of sales and 59% of pretax income in 1994. R&D spending equaled 3.7% of sales in 1994 and 3.8% in 1993.

Medical/laboratory products include intravenous fluids and pumps, diagnostic testing equipment and reagents, surgical instruments and procedure kits, and a range of disposable and reusable medical products. Self-manufactured products, as well as a significant portion of third party manufactured products, are distributed through Baxter's distribution system to U.S. hospitals, alternate-site facilities, medical laboratories, and industrial and educational facilities.

Medical specialties include specialized items used for treating kidney and heart disease and blood disorders and for collecting and processing blood. Products include dialysis equipment and supplies; prosthetic heart valves and cardiac catheters; blood-clotting therapies; and machines and supplies for collecting, separating and storing blood. This segment also includes the sale of medical products outside the U.S.

Important Developments

Jul. '95—Baxter said it was on track to reach its goal of $500 million in operational cash flow in 1995. The company added that it was ahead of schedule on a two-year, $500 million share repurchase program. It has purchased $255 million of stock since the program was announced in February 1995, while maintaining a ratio of net debt to capital under 40%. Separately, Baxter attributed its second quarter sales gains to a 15% rise in the medical specialties segment. Sales in medical/laboratory products and distribution were flat. Marketing and administrative expenses in the quarter equaled 18.1% of sales, versus 19.8% in the 1994 period. The company plans to sell its Industrial and Life Sciences division to VWR Corp. for about $400 million.

Capitalization

Long Term Debt: $2,508,000,000 (6/95).

Per Share Data ($)

(Year Ended Dec. 31)

	1994	1993	1992	1991	1990	1989
Tangible Bk. Val.	13.18	11.52	13.59	14.45	13.45	13.49
Cash Flow	3.73	0.95	3.39	3.55	1.72	2.51
Earnings	2.13	-0.97	1.99	2.03	-0.05	1.50
Dividends	1.02	1.00	0.86	0.74	0.64	0.56
Payout Ratio	48%	NM	43%	36%	NM	36%
Prices - High	28⅞	32¾	40½	40⅞	29½	25⅞
- Low	21⅝	20	30½	25⅝	20½	17½
P/E Ratio - High	14	NM	20	20	NM	17
- Low	10	NM	15	13	NM	12

Income Statement Analysis (Million $)

	1994	%Chg	1993	%Chg	1992	%Chg	1991
Revs.	9,324	5%	8,879	5%	8,471	-5%	8,921
Oper. Inc.	1,471	-4%	1,525	6%	1,435	-5%	1,515
Depr.	448	-16%	531	36%	390	-9%	427
Int. Exp.	242	4%	232	5%	221	-4%	231
Pretax Inc.	810	NM	-318	NM	766	-8%	830
Eff. Tax Rate	25%	—	NM	—	25%	—	26%
Net Inc.	596	NM	-267	NM	561	-5%	591

Balance Sheet & Other Fin. Data (Million $)

	1994	1993	1992	1991	1990	1989
Cash	471	479	32.0	328	40.0	67.0
Curr. Assets	4,340	4,422	3,589	4,004	3,443	3,424
Total Assets	10,002	10,545	9,155	9,340	8,517	8,503
Curr. Liab.	2,766	2,933	2,368	2,357	2,324	1,859
LT Debt	2,341	2,800	2,433	2,249	1,729	2,052
Common Eqty.	3,720	3,185	3,795	4,034	3,753	3,366
Total Cap.	6,228	6,186	6,402	6,860	6,014	6,563
Cap. Exp.	502	605	640	627	435	385
Cash Flow	1,044	263	946	995	434	709

Ratio Analysis

	1994	1993	1992	1991	1990	1989
Curr. Ratio	1.6	1.5	1.5	1.7	1.5	1.8
% LT Debt of Cap.	37.6	45.3	38.0	32.8	28.7	31.3
% Net Inc.of Revs.	6.4	NM	6.6	6.6	0.5	6.0
% Ret. on Assets	5.7	NM	6.1	6.6	0.4	5.2
% Ret. on Equity	17.1	NM	14.2	14.6	NM	11.8

Dividend Data —Dividends have been paid since 1934. A dividend reinvestment plan is available. A poison pill stock purchase rights plan was adopted in 1989.

Amt. of Div. $	Date Decl.	Ex-Div. Date	Stock of Record	Payment Date
0.262	Aug. 01	Aug. 31	Sep. 07	Oct. 03 '94
0.262	Nov. 14	Dec. 01	Dec. 07	Jan. 02 '95
0.262	Feb. 13	Mar. 09	Mar. 15	Apr. 03 '95
0.283	May. 08	Jun. 12	Jun. 14	Jul. 03 '95
0.283	Jul. 31	Sep. 11	Sep. 13	Oct. 02 '95

Data as orig. reptd.; bef. results of disc. opers. and/or spec. items. Per share data adj. for stk. divs. as of ex-div. date. E-Estimated. NA-Not Available. NM-Not Meaningful. NR-Not Ranked.

Office—One Baxter Parkway, Deerfield, IL 60015. **Tel**—(708) 948-2000. **Chrmn & CEO**—V. R. Loucks, Jr. **SVP & CFO**—H. M. J. Kraemer, Jr. **SVP & Secy**—A. F. Staubitz. **Treas**—A. G. Sieck. **Investor Contact**—N. Jeharajah. **Dirs**—S. S. Cathcart, D. C. K. Chin, J. W. Colloton, S. Crown, J. D. Ebert, M. J. Evans, F. R. Frame, W. B. Graham, D. W. Grainger, M. R. Ingram, A. J. Levine, V. R. Loucks, Jr., G. C. St. Laurent, Jr., M. E. Trout, F. L. Turner. **Transfer Agent & Registrar**—First Chicago Trust Co. of New York, NYC. **Incorporated** in Delaware in 1931. **Empl**-53,500. **S&P Analyst:** H.B. Saftlas

Becton, Dickinson

NYSE Symbol **BDX**
In S&P 500

30-SEP-95

Industry: Medical equipment/ supply

Summary: This company is a major factor in the medical and hospital supply fields, offering a broad range of medical devices and diagnostic products.

S&P Opinion: Accumulate (★★★★)	Recent Price • 62⅞	Yield • 1.3%
	52 Wk Range • 63½-45⅛	12-Mo. P/E • 17.9

Earnings vs. Previous Year
▲=Up ▼=Down ▶=No Change

Quantitative Evaluations

Outlook
(1 Lowest—5 Highest)
• **4+**

Fair Value
• **62¼**

Risk
• **Low**

Earn./Div. Rank
• **A+**

Technical Eval.
• **Bearish** since 3/95

Rel. Strength Rank
(1 Lowest—99 Highest)
• **77**

Insider Activity
• **Neutral**

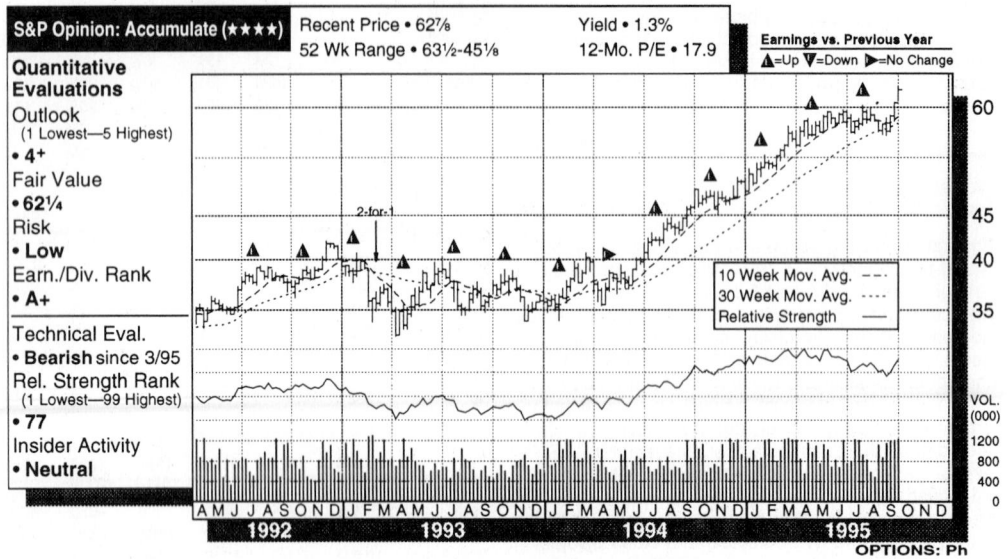

10 Week Mov. Avg. ---
30 Week Mov. Avg. ····
Relative Strength ——

VOL. (000)
1200
800
400
0

1992   1993   1994   1995

OPTIONS: Ph

Overview - 29-SEP-95

Sales from continuing businesses should rise in fiscal 1996. Gains are indicated for both medical supplies and devices and diagnostic systems, bolstered by improved demand for established products and new products. Demand for hypodermic and diabetes care lines should continue to benefit from ongoing conversions to safety products and the trend toward more frequent injections, respectively. With greater market penetration abroad, another healthy gain is indicated for foreign sales. Margins should be well maintained on better volume, an improved product mix and cost streamlining measures. Benefits from increased R&D spending and an expanding presence overseas enhance longer-range prospects.

Valuation - 28-SEP-95

The stock has been a strong performer since mid-1994, buoyed by strength in the health care sector and an improving earnings picture. Despite ongoing managed care pressures, demand for medical products has improved and pricing has firmed with increased hospital spending. The company recently sold its medical gloves business under a program aimed at divesting businesses not achieving acceptable levels of profitability. The corporate policy also includes seeking strategic acquisitions that mesh with existing operations. Cash flow will also be used to buy back shares, which will help Becton achieve its return-on-equity goal (a target of 20% has been set for 1997). The shares are recommended for long-term capital appreciation.

Key Stock Statistics

S&P EPS Est. 1995	3.55	Tang. Bk. Value/Share	17.65
P/E on S&P Est. 1995	17.7	Beta	0.70
S&P EPS Est. 1996	4.05	Shareholders	7,100
Dividend Rate/Share	0.82	Market cap. (B)	$ 4.1
Shs. outstg. (M)	65.9	Inst. holdings	83%
Avg. daily vol. (M)	0.262	Insider holdings	NA

Value of $10,000 invested 5 years ago: $ 22,300

Fiscal Year Ending Sep. 30

	1995	% Change	1994	% Change	1993	% Change
Revenues (Million $)						
1Q	593.5	7%	554.1	-1%	560.0	12%
2Q	692.8	9%	634.8	4%	612.5	3%
3Q	704.1	8%	653.0	4%	625.4	6%
4Q	—	—	717.6	8%	667.0	-2%
Yr.	—	—	2,559	4%	2,465	4%
Income (Million $)						
1Q	33.54	31%	25.70	NM	25.67	18%
2Q	64.93	14%	57.09	-3%	58.97	14%
3Q	66.65	15%	58.07	NM	58.23	5%
4Q	—	—	86.31	13%	76.44	6%
Yr.	—	—	227.2	7%	212.8	6%
Earnings Per Share ($)						
1Q	0.46	39%	0.33	2%	0.32	18%
2Q	0.92	21%	0.76	NM	0.76	15%
3Q	0.95	22%	0.78	4%	0.75	5%
4Q	E1.22	3%	1.18	20%	0.98	6%
Yr.	E3.55	16%	3.05	13%	2.71	5%

Next earnings report expected: early November

Business Summary - 29-SEP-95

Becton, Dickinson manufactures and sells a broad range of medical, diagnostic and other products. Contributions by business segment in fiscal 1994 were:

	Sales	Profits
Medical	56%	71%
Diagnostic	44%	29%

International operations accounted for 44% of sales and 31% of profits in fiscal 1994. R&D expenses equaled 5.6% of sales in both fiscal 1994 and fiscal 1993.

Major products in the medical segment consist of disposable and reusable hypodermic equipment, including disposable hypodermic needles and syringes, diabetes care products and prefillable syringe systems; and intravenous and operating room products, comprised of intravenous and cardiovascular catheters, surgical products and related items. The segment also manufactures specialty needles, suction products, elastic support products, surgical blades and thermometers. BDX is believed to be the world's leading maker of single-use hypodermic needles and syringes. Contract packaging services are also offered. These products are sold through distributors and directly to hospitals, laboratories and other end-users.

Diagnostic products include the Vacutainer line of blood collection equipment, consisting of needles, evacuated tubes and microcollection devices; laboratory ware and supplies; manual and instrumented microbiology products; hematology instruments; and other diagnostic systems, including immunodiagnostic test kits and instrumentation systems.

Important Developments

Sep. '95—The company said it plans to invest up to $12 million (Singapore) over the next five years in R&D activities in Singapore. Becton also plans to invest $25 million with the Suzhou Pharmaceutical Group to form a joint venture that will manufacture and market Becton products in China. In June, BDX sold its medical gloves business (about $100 million in annual sales) to Maxxim Medical. The sale resulted in a pretax loss of $6 million ($0.06 a share) in the third quarter. Favorable foreign exchange boosted earnings in the first nine months of fiscal 1995 by $0.13 a share. In May, BDX purchased the diagnostics unit of MicroProbe Corp. That business makes DNA-based instruments used to test for vaginitis.

Capitalization

Long Term Debt: $565,345,000 (6/95).
ESOP Preferred Stock: $55,122,000.

Per Share Data ($)

(Year Ended Sep. 30)

	1994	1993	1992	1991	1990	1989
Tangible Bk. Val.	17.77	16.43	17.27	15.29	13.52	11.88
Cash Flow	5.16	4.62	4.33	4.38	4.09	3.53
Earnings	3.05	2.71	2.58	2.43	2.34	2.00
Dividends	0.74	0.66	0.60	0.58	0.54	0.50
Payout Ratio	24%	24%	23%	23%	23%	24%
Prices - High	49⅞	40¾	42⅛	40¾	38⅜	31⅛
- Low	34	32⅝	32¼	29	27⅞	24¼
P/E Ratio - High	16	15	16	17	16	16
- Low	11	12	13	12	12	12

Income Statement Analysis (Million $)

	1994	%Chg	1993	%Chg	1992	%Chg	1991
Revs.	2,559	4%	2,465	4%	2,365	9%	2,172
Oper. Inc.	511	15%	444	-4%	464	6%	438
Depr.	155	6%	146	7%	136	10%	124
Int. Exp.	68.4	-9%	74.9	-8%	81.8	-3%	84.4
Pretax Inc.	296	33%	223	-17%	269	NM	267
Eff. Tax Rate	23%	—	4.50%	—	26%	—	29%
Net Inc.	227	7%	213	6%	201	6%	190

Balance Sheet & Other Fin. Data (Million $)

	1994	1993	1992	1991	1990	1989
Cash	179	65.0	100	84.0	73.0	95.0
Curr. Assets	1,327	1,151	1,221	1,032	962	869
Total Assets	3,160	3,088	3,178	2,780	2,594	2,270
Curr. Liab.	678	636	713	531	574	568
LT Debt	669	681	685	739	649	516
Common Eqty.	1,466	1,444	1,536	1,304	1,174	1,071
Total Cap.	2,163	2,140	2,403	2,207	1,969	1,650
Cap. Exp.	123	184	193	215	264	314
Cash Flow	378	355	334	312	292	280

Ratio Analysis

	1994	1993	1992	1991	1990	1989
Curr. Ratio	2.0	1.8	1.7	1.9	1.7	1.5
% LT Debt of Cap.	30.9	31.8	28.5	33.5	33.0	31.3
% Net Inc.of Revs.	8.9	8.6	8.5	8.7	9.1	8.7
% Ret. on Assets	7.5	6.9	6.7	7.1	7.6	7.4
% Ret. on Equity	15.8	13.9	13.9	15.1	16.2	15.8

Dividend Data —Dividends have been paid since 1926. A dividend reinvestment plan is available.

Amt. of Div. $	Date Decl.	Ex-Div. Date	Stock of Record	Payment Date
0.185	Jul. 26	Sep. 02	Sep. 09	Sep. 30 '94
0.205	Nov. 22	Dec. 13	Dec. 19	Jan. 03 '95
0.205	Jan. 24	Mar. 06	Mar. 10	Mar. 31 '95
0.205	May. 23	Jun. 06	Jun. 09	Jun. 30 '95
0.205	Jul. 25	Sep. 06	Sep. 08	Sep. 29 '95

Data as orig. reptd.; bef. results of disc. opers. and/or spec. items. Per share data adj. for stk. divs. as of ex-div. date.
E-Estimated. NA-Not Available. NM-Not Meaningful. NR-Not Ranked.

Office—One Becton Dr., Franklin Lakes, NJ 07417-1880. **Tel**—(201) 847-6800. **Chrmn, Pres & CEO**—C. Castellini. **VP & CFO**—E. J. Ludwig. **Secy**—R. P. Ohlmuller. **VP & Treas**—G. D. Cheatham. **Investor Contact**—Ronald Jasper. **Dirs**—H. N. Beaty, H. P. Becton, C. Castellini, G. M. Edelman, E. B. Fitzgerald, J. W. Galiardo, R. W. Hanselman, T. A. Holmes, F. A. Olson, J. E. Perella, G. M. Shatto, R. S. Troubh. **Transfer Agent & Registrar**—First Chicago Trust Co. of New York, NYC. **Incorporated** in New Jersey in 1906. **Empl**- 18,600. **S&P Analyst:** H. B. Saftlas

Bell Atlantic

NYSE Symbol **BEL**
In S&P 500

28-JUL-95

Industry:
Telecommunications

Summary: In addition to its local telephone operations, this company also provides cellular telephone services and has investments in various international telecommunications ventures.

S&P Opinion: Buy (★★★★)	Recent Price • 58	Yield • 4.8%
	52 Wk Range • 58⅞-48⅜	12-Mo. P/E • 17.5

Quantitative Evaluations

Outlook
(1 Lowest—5 Highest)
• **1**

Fair Value
• **46⅞**

Risk
• **Low**

Earn./Div. Rank
• **A-**

Technical Eval.
• **Bearish** since 2/95

Rel. Strength Rank
(1 Lowest—99 Highest)
• **54**

Insider Activity
• **Unfavorable**

Earnings vs. Previous Year
▲=Up ▼=Down ▶=No Change

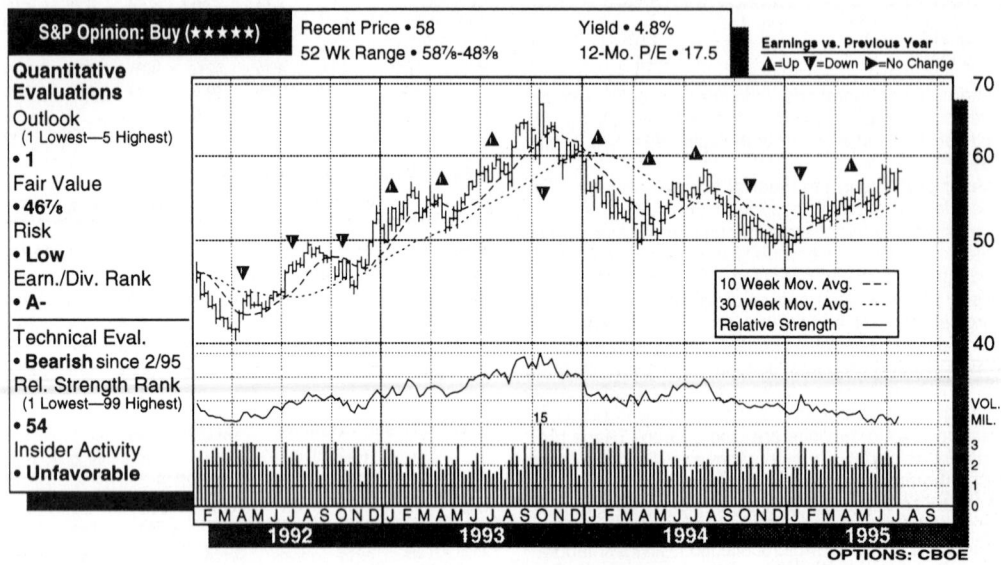

10 Week Mov. Avg. — - —
30 Week Mov. Avg. ·····
Relative Strength ———

VOL. MIL.

OPTIONS: CBOE

Overview - 28-JUL-95

To achieve its goal of being a leading player in a competitive telecommunications market, BEL has sought to leverage its existing investment in its core telephone network while targeting capital expenditures to strategic opportunities such as wireless communications and cable television. These investments will open up faster growth revenue lines and enhance the company's longer-term earnings prospects. On the legislative front, the House version of proposed federal telecommunications legislation would allow the Bell companies into the long-distance market sooner than expected. At the state level, favorable regulatory environments will enable the company to retain operating improvements from investment in new technology and work force reductions. Already among the most efficient of its peers on an operating basis, BEL plans to continue streamlining its operations and reducing costs.

Valuation - 28-JUL-95

The shares have recovered somewhat in 1995, as interest rates have declined and investors have begun focusing more on the company's strong growth prospects. We believe Bell Atlantic is the best positioned of its peers to take advantage of the opening of the cable television market while maximizing the value of its core network. The shares should benefit from the faster growth prospects of cable investments and wireless operations and are an excellent vehicle for capital appreciation.

Key Stock Statistics

S&P EPS Est. 1995	3.85	Tang. Bk. Value/Share	13.93
P/E on S&P Est. 1995	15.1	Beta	0.52
S&P EPS Est. 1996	4.10	Shareholders	990,600
Dividend Rate/Share	2.80	Market cap. (B)	$ 25.5
Shs. outstg. (M)	436.4	Inst. holdings	32%
Avg. daily vol. (M)	0.559	Insider holdings	NA

Value of $10,000 invested 5 years ago: $ 13,720

Fiscal Year Ending Dec. 31

	1995	% Change	1994	% Change	1993	% Change
Revenues (Million $)						
1Q	3,450	NM	3,420	8%	3,163	3%
2Q	3,565	4%	3,430	7%	3,220	2%
3Q	—	—	3,455	5%	3,290	4%
4Q	—	—	3,487	5%	3,317	2%
Yr.	—	—	13,791	6%	12,990	3%
Income (Million $)						
1Q	414.5	5%	395.9	6%	372.2	7%
2Q	447.1	8%	415.4	8%	385.5	22%
3Q	—	—	275.7	-29%	386.7	-2%
4Q	—	—	314.9	-7%	337.2	3%
Yr.	—	—	1,402	-5%	1,482	7%
Earnings Per Share ($)						
1Q	0.95	4%	0.91	7%	0.85	5%
2Q	1.02	7%	0.95	8%	0.88	19%
3Q	E1.01	—	0.63	-29%	0.89	-2%
4Q	E0.87	—	0.72	-6%	0.77	1%
Yr.	E3.85	—	3.21	-5%	3.39	5%

Next earnings report expected: mid October

Bell Atlantic

Business Summary - 28-JUL-95

Bell Atlantic is the second largest U.S. provider of exchange telephone service, based on 1994 U.S. access lines, serving 19 million customer access lines in six East Coast states and Washington, D.C. The telephone units also publish telephone directories and engage in other related activities.

BEL also provides cellular telephone services to 1.7 million subscribers (in controlled markets), primarily in the mid-Atlantic and Northeast regions. In July 1995, BEL and NYNEX completed a merger of their cellular operations. Initially, BEL will own 62.35% of the venture and NYNEX will have 37.65% with the right to purchase an additional 2.35% interest for $500 million; however, the venture will be managed as a 50/50 partnership. BEL and NYN have also formed a national wireless partnership, known as PCS PrimeCo, with AirTouch Communications (ATI) and U S WEST (USW). The partnership, which will be 50%-owned by the BEL/NYN partnership, builds on BEL's merger of its cellular assets with those of NYN. In a previous separate transaction, USW and ATI agreed to form a cellular joint venture that will have operations in 21 states.

Other businesses include paging operations; computer services; CPE equipment sales; computers and communications equipment training services; and financial and real estate services. BEL also owns a minority interest in Bell Communications Research, which provides technical assistance and consulting services to telephone companies.

International operations include a 24.9% interest in Telecom Corp. of New Zealand; a 46% interest in a Mexican cellular company; an interest in a New Zealand pay television company; and an interest in a cellular venture in Czechoslovakia.

Important Developments

Jun. '95—PCS PrimeCo elected to deploy code division multiple access (CDMA) digital technology throughout its planned personal communications services (PCS) network.

May '95—The video company recently formed by BEL, NYNEX and Pacific Telesis will be called Tele-TV. Separately, BEL and NYNEX invested $30 million in wireless cable provider CAI Wireless Systems. The two companies will eventually invest up to $100 million in CAI.

Mar. '95—In FCC auctions for broadband personal communications services licenses, the PCS PrimeCo national wireless partnership placed winning bids totaling $1.1 billion in 11 markets, including Chicago, Dallas and Miami. Separately, BEL won court approval to offer video programming nationwide.

Capitalization

Long Term Debt: $6,700,000,000 (3/95).

Per Share Data ($) (Year Ended Dec. 31)

	1994	1993	1992	1991	1990	1989
Tangible Bk. Val.	13.87	18.60	17.74	19.48	22.40	21.46
Cash Flow	NA	NA	NA	NA	NA	NA
Earnings	3.21	3.39	3.23	3.41	3.38	2.72
Dividends	2.74	2.68	2.58	2.48	2.36	2.20
Payout Ratio	85%	79%	80%	73%	69%	81%
Prices - High	59⅝	69⅛	53⅞	54⅛	57⅛	56⅛
- Low	48⅜	49⅝	40¼	43	39½	34¾
P/E Ratio - High	19	20	17	16	17	21
- Low	15	15	12	13	12	13

Income Statement Analysis (Million $)

	1994	%Chg	1993	%Chg	1992	%Chg	1991
Revs.	13,791	7%	12,900	2%	12,647	3%	12,280
Depr.	2,652	4%	2,545	5%	2,417	5%	2,299
Maint.	NA	—	NA	—	1,875	5%	1,791
Constr. Credits	NA	—	NA	—	NA	—	20.6
Eff. Tax Rate	39%	—	35%	—	32%	—	33%
Net Inc.	1,402	-5%	1,482	7%	1,382	4%	1,332

Balance Sheet & Other Fin. Data (Million $)

	1994	1993	1992	1991	1990	1989
Gross Prop.	33,746	32,330	31,046	31,848	30,784	29,312
Net Prop.	16,938	20,366	20,330	19,962	19,447	18,874
Cap. Exp.	2,699	2,449	2,547	2,545	2,747	3,008
Total Cap.	18,228	22,187	21,830	19,444	21,781	20,905
Fxd. Chgs. Cov.	4.9	4.7	3.9	3.8	4.0	3.8
Capitalization:						
LT Debt	6,806	7,206	7,348	7,960	8,171	7,721
Pfd.	85.0	Nil	Nil	Nil	Nil	Nil
Common	6,081	8,224	7,816	7,831	8,930	8,591

Ratio Analysis

	1994	1993	1992	1991	1990	1989
% Ret. on Revs.	10.2	11.4	10.9	10.8	10.7	9.4
% Ret. On Invest.Cap	9.8	9.5	9.5	9.9	9.2	7.9
% Return On Com.Eqty	19.6	17.3	17.4	15.9	14.8	11.7
% Earn. on Net Prop.	10.2	9.9	9.2	9.4	10.1	8.3
% LT Debt of Cap.	52.5	46.7	48.5	50.4	47.8	47.3
Capital. % Pfd.	0.6	Nil	Nil	Nil	Nil	Nil
Capital. % Common	46.9	53.3	51.5	49.6	52.2	52.7

Dividend Data (Dividends were initiated in 1984. A dividend reinvestment plan is available. A "poison pill" stock purchase rights plan was adopted in 1989.)

Amt. of Div. $	Date Decl.	Ex-Div. Date	Stock of Record	Payment Date
0.690	Aug. 23	Oct. 04	Oct. 11	Nov. 01 '94
0.690	Nov. 22	Jan. 04	Jan. 10	Feb. 01 '95
0.700	Mar. 28	Apr. 04	Apr. 10	May. 01 '95
0.700	Jun. 27	Jul. 06	Jul. 10	Aug. 01 '95

Data as orig. reptd; bef. results of disc. opers. and/or spec. items. Per share data adj. for stk. divs. as of ex-div date. E-Estimated. NA-Not Available. NM-Not Meaningful. NR-Not Ranked.

Office—1717 Arch St., Philadelphia, PA 19103. **Tel**—(215) 963-6000. **Chrmn & CEO**—R. W. Smith. **Vice Chmn**—L. T. Babbio, Jr. and J. G. Cullen. **EVP & CFO**—W. O. Albertini. **VP & Secy**—P. A. Bulliner. **Investor Contact**—Peter D. Crawford. **Dirs**—W. W. Adams, W. O. Albertini, L. T. Babbio, T. E. Bolger, F. C. Carlucci, W. G. Copeland, J. G. Cullen, J. H. Gilliam Jr., T. H. Kean, J. C. Marous Jr., J. F. Maypole, J. Neubauer, T. H. O'Brien, R. L. Ridgway, R. W. Smith, S. Young. **Transfer Agent**—Bank of New York, NYC. **Incorporated** in Delaware in 1983. **Empl**-72,300. **S&P Analyst:** Kevin J. Gooley

BellSouth Corp.

NYSE Symbol **BLS**
In S&P 500

05-SEP-95 | Industry: Telecommunications

Summary: BLS is the largest U.S. telephone holding company, providing local service in nine southeastern states. It has also expanded into wireless and international ventures.

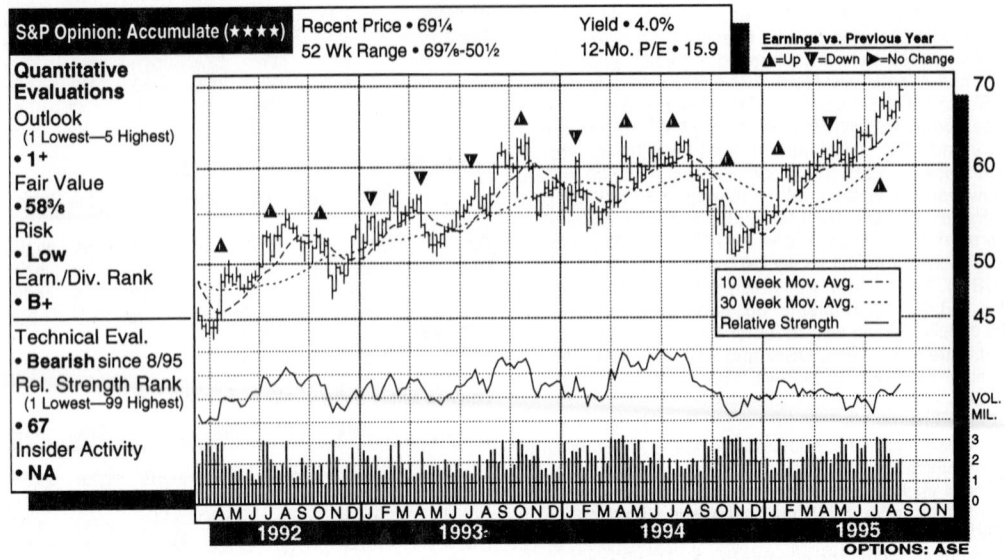

S&P Opinion: Accumulate (★★★★)	Recent Price • 69¼	Yield • 4.0%
	52 Wk Range • 69⅞-50½	12-Mo. P/E • 15.9

Quantitative Evaluations

Outlook
(1 Lowest—5 Highest)
• **1+**

Fair Value
• **58⅜**

Risk
• **Low**

Earn./Div. Rank
• **B+**

Technical Eval.
• **Bearish** since 8/95

Rel. Strength Rank
(1 Lowest—99 Highest)
• **67**

Insider Activity
• **NA**

Earnings vs. Previous Year
▲=Up ▼=Down ▶=No Change

10 Week Mov. Avg. ----
30 Week Mov. Avg. ·····
Relative Strength ——

OPTIONS: ASE

Overview - 05-SEP-95

Continued population inflow to the Sunbelt will help BLS maintain earnings growth, despite increasing competition and a difficult Florida regulatory environment. The company has moved to open its core markets to more competition. It anticipates that this will accelerate development of new services, with increased competition outweighed by greater network usage. Unregulated businesses are growing rapidly; BLS anticipates that such operations will provide about 60% of total revenues by 2000. The majority of growth will come from investments in wireless businesses, including strong domestic cellular operations, a 50% stake in a nationwide wireless data provider, and international cellular investments. The company is also investing in a venture to offer telephone services in the huge German market.

Valuation - 05-SEP-95

We expect the shares to benefit from strong growth in the company's core telephone operations. BLS expects to add 1 million access lines in 1995, up from an impressive 887,000 added in 1994. The 1996 Olympics in Atlanta should further bolster results. In addition, the company's strong position in South America should benefit from U.S. efforts to extend the North American Free Trade Agreement throughout the continent. With a healthy dividend yield, we recommend the shares for long-term total return.

Key Stock Statistics

S&P EPS Est. 1995	4.45	Tang. Bk. Value/Share	21.35
P/E on S&P Est. 1995	15.6	Beta	0.51
S&P EPS Est. 1996	4.80	Shareholders	1,183,600
Dividend Rate/Share	2.76	Market cap. (B)	$ 34.4
Shs. outstg. (M)	496.5	Inst. holdings	30%
Avg. daily vol. (M)	0.386	Insider holdings	NA

Value of $10,000 invested 5 years ago: $ 15,779

Fiscal Year Ending Dec. 31

	1995	% Change	1994	% Change	1993	% Change
Revenues (Million $)						
1Q	4,299	4%	4,124	8%	3,834	3%
2Q	4,390	6%	4,128	6%	3,907	2%
3Q	—	—	4,198	5%	4,015	7%
4Q	—	—	4,395	7%	4,125	5%
Yr.	—	—	16,845	6%	15,880	4%
Income (Million $)						
1Q	547.1	-7%	585.3	42%	411.2	-11%
2Q	556.9	8%	516.5	19%	433.1	-6%
3Q	—	—	499.5	13%	442.4	15%
4Q	—	—	558.5	NM	-252.6	NM
Yr.	—	—	2,160	109%	1,034	-38%
Earnings Per Share ($)						
1Q	1.10	-7%	1.18	42%	0.83	-12%
2Q	1.12	8%	1.04	20%	0.87	-7%
3Q	E1.12	11%	1.01	13%	0.89	14%
4Q	E1.12	NM	1.12	NM	-0.51	NM
Yr.	E4.45	2%	4.35	109%	2.08	-38%

Next earnings report expected: late October

BellSouth Corp.

Business Summary - 05-SEP-95

BellSouth Corporation is the largest U.S. telephone holding company, based on 1994 access lines. The telephone unit provided local exchange telephone service in nine southeastern states to about 20 million customer access lines at March 31, 1995. The telephone operations provided 83% of operating revenues and 90% of net income in 1994.

The company has concentrated on growth of its mobile communications unit both internally and through acquisitions. At March 31, 1995, BLS served 2.3 million cellular subscribers (based on its percentage ownership in each market) and 1.6 million paging customers in the U.S. The company also has interests in international cellular operations (mainly in Latin America) covering about 51.4 million POPs (adjusted); at March 31, 1995, international ventures served some 415,200 subscribers.

In July 1994, BLS won a narrowband PCS (personal communications services) license in the FCC auction for about $47.5 million. With the new license, the MobileComm nationwide paging system, RAM mobile data system and domestic cellular operations, the company believes that it will be able to offer customers the most comprehensive array of wireless services in the U.S. BLS has been exploring applications for the license, with an acknowledgement paging service leading the options; other applications inculde locator services, electronic mail, credit card verification and wireless telemetry.

Operations also include directory advertising and publishing, the sale and service of telecommunications and computer systems and a minority interest in Bell Communications Research.

Important Developments

Aug. '95—GTE will join a venture formed by Disney, BLS, SBC Communications (formerly Southwestern Bell) and Ameritech. Separately, the company and the Communications Workers of America agrred tentatively to a new three-year contract.
May '95—The company's BellSouth Telecommunications unit said it would reduce its work force by 9,000 to 11,000 over the next two years, in addition to previously announced reductions of 10,200, expected to be completed in 1995. Separately, construction began on a PCS network to be operated by BLS and its partners, covering the Carolinas and eastern Tennessee MTAs (major trading areas). The company won licenses for these MTAs in in the FCC's March auction of broadband PCS licenses.

Capitalization

Long Term Debt: $7,456,800,000 (3/95).

Per Share Data ($)

	1994	1993	1992	1991	1990	1989
Tangible Bk. Val.	25.93	24.38	24.19	23.47	24.14	24.97
Cash Flow	10.81	8.34	9.55	9.24	9.53	9.60
Earnings	4.35	2.08	3.38	3.11	3.38	3.55
Dividends	2.76	2.76	2.76	2.74	2.68	2.48
Payout Ratio	63%	133%	82%	88%	79%	70%
Prices - High	63½	63⅞	55½	55	59¼	58⅛
- Low	50½	50⅜	43⅜	45⅜	49	39
P/E Ratio - High	15	31	16	18	18	16
- Low	12	24	13	15	14	11

Income Statement Analysis (Million $)

	1994	%Chg	1993	%Chg	1992	%Chg	1991
Revs.	16,845	6%	15,880	4%	15,202	5%	14,446
Depr.	3,206	3%	3,104	NM	3,100	3%	3,016
Maint.	NA	—	NA	—	4,662	97%	2,366
Constr. Credits	NA	—	NA	—	15.3	-15%	18.1
Eff. Tax Rate	37%	—	36%	—	36%	—	33%
Net Inc.	2,160	109%	1,034	-38%	1,658	10%	1,507

Balance Sheet & Other Fin. Data (Million $)

	1994	1993	1992	1991	1990	1989
Gross Prop.	44,199	41,975	39,801	38,403	36,812	35,982
Net Prop.	25,162	24,856	24,273	24,059	23,907	23,742
Cap. Exp.	3,600	3,486	3,189	3,102	3,191	3,223
Total Cap.	25,893	24,856	25,478	25,340	25,335	25,327
Fxd. Chgs. Cov.	6.1	3.3	4.4	3.8	4.1	4.1
Capitalization:						
LT Debt	7,435	7,381	7,360	7,745	7,781	7,055
Pfd.	Nil	Nil	Nil	Nil	Nil	Nil
Common	14,367	13,494	13,799	13,105	12,666	13,103

Ratio Analysis

	1994	1993	1992	1991	1990	1989
% Ret. on Revs.	12.8	6.5	10.9	10.4	11.4	12.1
% Ret. On Invest.Cap	11.1	6.8	9.5	9.1	9.5	10.0
% Return On Com.Eqty	15.4	6.3	11.9	11.3	12.8	13.7
% Earn. on Net Prop.	11.3	7.0	9.2	8.6	9.5	9.5
% LT Debt of Cap.	34.1	35.4	34.8	37.1	38.1	35.0
Capital. % Pfd.	Nil	Nil	Nil	Nil	Nil	Nil
Capital. % Common	65.9	64.6	65.2	62.9	61.9	65.0

Dividend Data

Dividends were initiated in 1984. A dividend reinvestment plan is available. A poison pill stock purchase rights plan was adopted in 1989.

Amt. of Div. $	Date Decl.	Ex-Div. Date	Stock of Record	Payment Date
0.690	Sep. 26	Oct. 03	Oct. 10	Nov. 01 '94
0.690	Nov. 28	Jan. 05	Jan. 11	Feb. 01 '95
0.690	Feb. 27	Apr. 05	Apr. 11	May. 01 '95
0.690	Jun. 26	Jul. 07	Jul. 11	Aug. 01 '95

Office—1155 Peachtree St., N.E., Atlanta, GA 30309-3610. **Tel**—(404) 249-2000. **Chrmn & CEO**—J. L. Clendenin. **Vice-Chrmn & COO**—F. D. Ackerman. **VP & CFO**—R. M. Dykes. **VP, Secy & Treas**—A. G. Yokley. **Investor Contact**—Nancy Humphries. **Dirs**—F. D. Ackerman, R. V. Anderson, J. H. Blanchard, A. F. Brimmer, J. H. Brown, J. L. Clendenin, A. M. Codina, M. M. Criser, G. B. Davidson, P. B. Davis, J. G. Medlin, Jr., R. B. Smith, C. D. Spangler, Jr., R. A. Terry, T. R. Williams, J. T. Wilson. **Transfer Agent & Registrar**—Chemical Bank, NYC. **Incorporated** in Georgia in 1983. **Empl**-92,100. **S&P Analyst:** Kevin J. Gooley

Bemis Co.

NYSE Symbol **BMS**
In S&P 500

23-OCT-95 | Industry: Containers

Summary: Bemis has become an important producer of a broad range of flexible packaging, packaging equipment and pressure sensitive materials primarily through internal development.

S&P Opinion: Hold (★★★)	Recent Price • 26	Yield • 2.5%	
	52 Wk Range • 30-21%	12-Mo. P/E • 16.8	

Earnings vs. Previous Year
▲=Up ▼=Down ▶=No Change

Quantitative Evaluations

Outlook
(1 Lowest—5 Highest)
• **2⁻**

Fair Value
• **26⅜**

Risk
• **Low**

Earn./Div. Rank
• **A**

Technical Eval.
• **Bearish** since 9/95

Rel. Strength Rank
(1 Lowest—99 Highest)
• **23**

Insider Activity
• **NA**

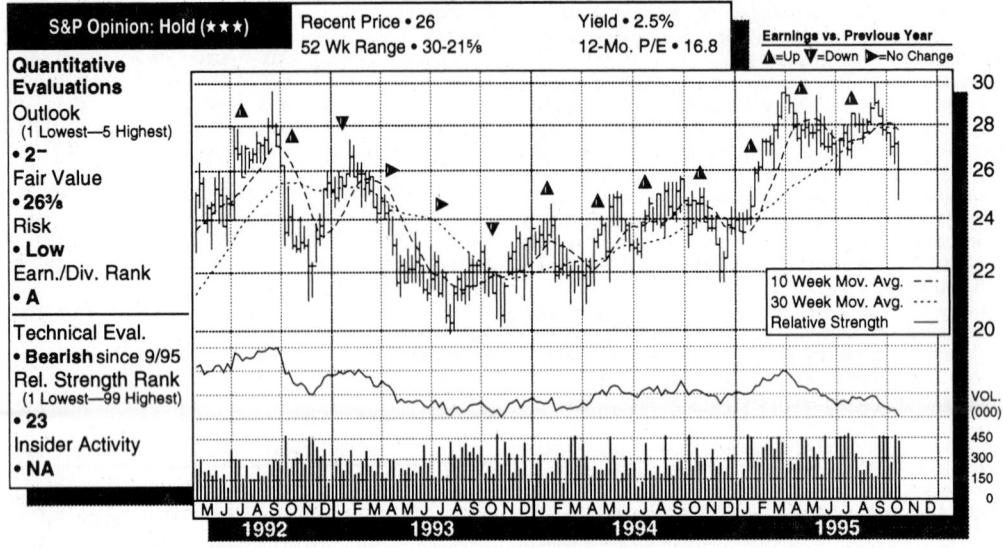

10 Week Mov. Avg. ‑ ‑ ‑
30 Week Mov. Avg. ·····
Relative Strength ——

VOL. (000)
450
300
150
0

Overview - 23-OCT-95

Sales are expected to rise moderately for the remainder of 1995 through 1996 as increased unit volume growth and improving economic conditions are offset by pricing pressures. Efforts to improve manufacturing efficiency and streamline operations, plus increased volume in the pressure sensitive materials and coated and laminated film businesses, should help offset some of the effects of strong price competition and higher raw material costs. The company's strong market position in packaging products should enable it to maintain a steady double-digit growth rate for the next few years. New opportunities with long-term potential exist in snack foods and the medical packaging segment. The company's recent acquisition of Banner Packaging, a flexible packaging manufacturer, should have a minimal impact on near-term results.

Valuation - 23-OCT-95

The shares began to appreciate in early 1995, due in part to improving European results and acquisitions, but have dropped 15% since their mid-year high. Although Bemis has been attempting to keep its prices in line with increased raw materials costs and continues its capital program, sales growth slowed during the third quarter due to a correction in industry inventory levels and price volatility in raw material markets. Although the shares are trading at only 15X our projected 1995 earnings and 13X our estimate for 1996, steep discounts to the rest of the container group, the stock appears to be adequately valued with earnings expected to grow at about 15%.

Key Stock Statistics

S&P EPS Est. 1995	1.65	Tang. Bk. Value/Share	7.84
P/E on S&P Est. 1995	15.8	Beta	1.11
S&P EPS Est. 1996	1.90	Shareholders	5,600
Dividend Rate/Share	0.64	Market cap. (B)	$ 1.3
Shs. outstg. (M)	51.5	Inst. holdings	50%
Avg. daily vol. (M)	0.086	Insider holdings	NA

Value of $10,000 invested 5 years ago: $ 17,122

Fiscal Year Ending Dec. 31

	1995	% Change	1994	% Change	1993	% Change
Revenues (Million $)						
1Q	368.5	14%	323.3	10%	292.6	NM
2Q	383.2	13%	337.7	11%	303.3	2%
3Q	372.5	5%	356.2	19%	299.5	2%
4Q	—	—	373.2	21%	308.1	2%
Yr.	—	—	1,390	16%	1,203	2%
Income (Million $)						
1Q	16.09	18%	13.59	26%	10.75	NM
2Q	21.13	13%	18.68	20%	15.51	NM
3Q	20.83	14%	18.29	NM	0.98	-93%
4Q	—	—	22.23	18%	18.84	14%
Yr.	—	—	72.79	58%	46.08	-20%
Earnings Per Share ($)						
1Q	0.31	19%	0.26	24%	0.21	NM
2Q	0.41	14%	0.36	20%	0.30	NM
3Q	0.40	14%	0.35	NM	0.02	-93%
4Q	E0.53	23%	0.43	19%	0.36	16%
Yr.	E1.65	18%	1.40	57%	0.89	-20%

Next earnings report expected: late January

Business Summary - 20-OCT-95

Bemis manufactures a wide range of consumer and industrial packaging materials, packaging machinery and industrial products. Business segment contributions in 1994:

	Sales	Profits
Flexible packaging	70%	71%
Specialty coated & graphics products	30%	29%

Sales to Europe accounted for 11% of total sales and 8% of profits in 1994, compared with 12% of sales and 5% of profits in 1993.

The company's coated and laminated film products, which include perishable and frozen food packaging, stretch film and carton sealing tape, accounted for 31% of net sales in 1994. BMS also makes multiwall and consumer-size paper bags for products such as seed, feed, flour, cement and chemicals. These packaging products accounted for 15% of 1994 sales. Polyethylene packaging products, including extruded products, printed roll stock and pre-formed bags, represented 16% of sales. BMS also produces packaging systems for a wide range of consumer and industrial products, including toilet tissue, candy, frozen vegetables and pharmaceutical products. Packaging machinery accounted for 8% of 1994 sales.

The specialty coated and graphics products segment manufactures pressure-sensitive materials, which accounted for 29% of 1994 sales. BMS manufactures industrial adhesive products for mounting and bonding, quality roll label and sheet print stock for a variety of applications, including packaging labels, and a line of highly specialized laminates for graphics and photography.

The food industry accounts for approximately 70% of the company's sales.

In the flexible packaging products segment, the company has 30 manufacturing plants, of which six are leased, located in 15 states and one foreign country. In the specialty coated and graphics products area, the company has 10 manufacturing plants, with three leased, located in five states and three foreign countries.

Important Developments

Oct. '95—Bemis acquired Banner Packaging, Inc., a Wisconsin-based flexible packaging manufacturer with annual sales of $60 million. The purchase was made for an undisclosed amount of cash and stock.
Jun. '95—The company offered for public sale $100 million of 6.70% notes, due July 1, 2005, at 99.768. Proceeds will be used to pay off commercial paper.

Capitalization

Long Term Debt: $158,274,000 (9/95).
Minority Interest: $27,461,000.

Per Share Data ($)

(Year Ended Dec. 31)

	1994	1993	1992	1991	1990	1989
Tangible Bk. Val.	7.58	6.75	6.55	6.51	5.26	5.13
Cash Flow	2.38	1.78	2.02	1.95	1.82	1.59
Earnings	1.40	0.89	1.11	1.03	0.99	0.90
Dividends	0.54	0.50	0.46	0.42	0.36	0.30
Payout Ratio	39%	56%	42%	37%	36%	32%
Prices - High	25¾	27⅜	29⅝	20¾	18¾	18¾
- Low	20½	19⅞	19¾	13½	12⅞	11¼
P/E Ratio - High	18	31	27	20	19	21
- Low	15	22	18	13	13	13

Income Statement Analysis (Million $)

	1994	%Chg	1993	%Chg	1992	%Chg	1991
Revs.	1,390	16%	1,203	2%	1,181	3%	1,142
Oper. Inc.	180	22%	148	NM	147	3%	143
Depr.	50.9	10%	46.2	-2%	47.3	NM	47.1
Int. Exp.	8.4	17%	7.2	-4%	7.5	-38%	12.1
Pretax Inc.	121	58%	76.7	-18%	93.7	7%	87.7
Eff. Tax Rate	37%	—	37%	—	35%	—	36%
Net Inc.	72.8	58%	46.1	-20%	57.3	8%	53.0

Balance Sheet & Other Fin. Data (Million $)

	1994	1993	1992	1991	1990	1989
Cash	12.7	8.9	0.1	1.4	9.2	1.4
Curr. Assets	419	337	315	308	344	286
Total Assets	923	790	743	715	756	632
Curr. Liab.	211	184	161	167	194	171
LT Debt	172	123	131	129	171	110
Common Eqty.	418	371	361	329	296	266
Total Cap.	654	551	549	527	533	442
Cap. Exp.	106	91.8	70.7	56.9	73.2	82.6
Cash Flow	124	92.0	105	100	92.0	83.0

Ratio Analysis

	1994	1993	1992	1991	1990	1989
Curr. Ratio	2.0	1.8	2.0	1.8	1.8	1.7
% LT Debt of Cap.	26.3	22.4	23.9	24.5	32.1	24.8
% Net Inc.of Revs.	5.2	3.8	4.8	4.6	4.5	4.4
% Ret. on Assets	8.5	6.0	7.5	7.5	7.3	7.6
% Ret. on Equity	18.5	12.6	15.8	17.1	18.1	18.5

Dividend Data

—Dividends have been paid each year since 1922. A "poison pill" stock purchase rights plan was adopted in 1989.

Amt. of Div. $	Date Decl.	Ex-Div. Date	Stock of Record	Payment Date
0.135	Oct. 20	Nov. 14	Nov. 18	Dec. 01 '94
0.160	Feb. 02	Feb. 08	Feb. 14	Mar. 01 '95
0.160	May. 04	May. 11	May. 17	Jun. 01 '95
0.160	Aug. 03	Aug. 14	Aug. 16	Sep. 01 '95

Data as orig. reptd.; bef. results of disc. opers. and/or spec. items. Per share data adj. for stk. divs. as of ex-div. date. E-Estimated. NA-Not Available. NM-Not Meaningful. NR-Not Ranked.

Office—222 South 9th St., Suite 2300, Minneapolis, MN 55402-4099. **Tel**—(612) 376-3000. **Pres & CEO**—J. H. Roe. **SVP-Secy**—S. W. Johnson. **SVP-CFO, Treas & Investor Contact**—Benjamin R. Field III. **Dirs**—W. H. Buxton, H. J. Curler, J. H. Curler, R. Greenkorn, L. W. Knoblauch, E. S. McBride, N. P. McDonald, R. F. Mlnarik, E. N. Perry, J. H. Roe, W. R. Wallin, R. F. Zicarelli. **Transfer Agent & Registrar**—Norwest Bank Minnesota, South St. Paul. **Incorporated** in Missouri in 1885. **Empl**-8,100. **S&P Analyst:** Stewart Scharf

Beneficial Corp.

NYSE Symbol **BNL**
In S&P 500

26-JUL-95

Industry: Finance

Summary: This financial services holding company specializes in real estate secured, personal unsecured and sales finance loans, and also has interests in related credit insurance.

| S&P Opinion: Hold (★★★) | Recent Price • 45⅞ | Yield • 3.7% |
| | 52 Wk Range • 47-35¼ | 12-Mo. P/E • 17.3 |

Earnings vs. Previous Year
▲=Up ▼=Down ▶=No Change

Quantitative Evaluations

Outlook
(1 Lowest—5 Highest)
• **4⁻**

Fair Value
• **46⅞**

Risk
• **Low**

Earn./Div. Rank
• **B+**

Technical Eval.
• **Bullish** since 7/95

Rel. Strength Rank
(1 Lowest—99 Highest)
• **63**

Insider Activity
• **Neutral**

2-for-1

10 Week Mov. Avg. – – –
30 Week Mov. Avg. · · · ·
Relative Strength ——

VOL.
(000)
1200
800
400
0

F M A M J J A S O N D J F M A M J J A S O N D J F M A M J J A S O N D J F M A M J J A S
1992   1993   1994   1995

OPTIONS: P

Overview - 26-JUL-95

Earnings in 1995 should be driven by growth in finance receivables, cost controls and strong credit quality, although expected losses from the refund anticipation loan (RAL) business will dampen overall profits. Robust demand in the consumer loan segment is expected to lead to gains in finance receivables of about 10%. The RAL business, a particularly profitable venture, will be penalized by collection problems following a recent IRS decision to send tax refund checks directly to taxpayers rather than to BNL to pay off loans. Lending spreads are expected to remain flat, given the rapid turnover of loans and borrowings. With asset quality continuing to improve and conservative reserve levels, the provision for loan losses should rise only modestly with expected loan growth.

Valuation - 26-JUL-95

The shares were downgraded following news that the company's tax refund anticipation loan business, which was particularly profitable, was dealt a second major blow after the IRS decided to issue paper checks to certain consumers filing for the earned income tax credit for which BNL had already funded loans. The IRS had earlier stopped providing information on whether liens against tax refunds existed for customers filing for such loans. To date, at least, collection efforts have been successful in recovering receivables affected by the IRS decision. However, until strong profits resume, the shares are not expected to outperform the broader market.

Key Stock Statistics

S&P EPS Est. 1995	4.00	Tang. Bk. Value/Share	24.61
P/E on S&P Est. 1995	11.3	Beta	1.32
S&P EPS Est. 1996	4.80	Shareholders	15,300
Dividend Rate/Share	1.72	Market cap. (B)	$ 2.4
Shs. outstg. (M)	52.9	Inst. holdings	73%
Avg. daily vol. (M)	0.110	Insider holdings	NA

Value of $10,000 invested 5 years ago: $ 23,251

Fiscal Year Ending Dec. 31

	1995	% Change	1994	% Change	1993	% Change
Revenues (Million $)						
1Q	560.2	4%	537.2	8%	499.6	7%
2Q	594.2	16%	511.1	6%	482.8	7%
3Q	—	—	528.0	11%	477.7	8%
4Q	—	—	561.1	13%	497.4	9%
Yr.	—	—	2,137	9%	1,958	8%
Income (Million $)						
1Q	20.70	-66%	60.90	23%	49.60	14%
2Q	62.80	12%	56.20	16%	48.60	15%
3Q	—	—	51.40	16%	44.50	16%
4Q	—	—	9.20	-79%	43.30	86%
Yr.	—	—	177.7	-4%	186.0	25%
Earnings Per Share ($)						
1Q	0.37	-67%	1.13	23%	0.92	12%
2Q	1.15	10%	1.05	17%	0.90	13%
3Q	E1.20	—	0.95	14%	0.83	15%
4Q	E1.25	—	0.15	-81%	0.80	90%
Yr.	E4.00	—	3.28	-5%	3.45	25%

Next earnings report expected: late October

Beneficial Corp.

Business Summary - 26-JUL-95

Beneficial Corp. is a consumer-oriented financial services company specializing in loans to middle-class Americans for major purchases, education, home improvement, debt consolidation and other uses. It also has interests in related credit insurance, commercial lending, income tax refund anticipation loan and real estate development businesses. Finance receivables of $12.3 billion at year-end 1994, up 12% from $11.0 billion a year earlier, were divided:

	1994	1993
Real estate secured	56%	61%
Personal unsecured	20%	20%
Sales finance	23%	17%
Commercial bank loans	1%	2%

Domestic operations are conducted from 902 offices throughout the U.S.; California accounts for 19% of total worldwide receivables. International operations (15% of receivables) consist of 188 offices: 102 in Canada, 69 in the United Kingdom, and 17 in Germany. Customer accounts increased to 4,400,000 at 1994 year-end, from 3,500,000 at the end of 1993.

Loan and sales finance balances more than two months delinquent were 2.46% of such receivables at 1994 year-end, versus 2.67% a year before. Net chargeoffs in 1994 amounted to $148.7 million (1.28% of average finance receivables), versus $149.1 million (1.42%) in 1993. Credit loss reserves were $331.6 million at the end of 1994 (2.69% of finance receivables), versus $279.0 million (2.53%). The year-end 1994 reserve covered 1994 net chargeoffs 2.2 times, up from 1.9 times for the year-end 1993 reserve.

BNL's Insurance Group, which underwrites life and disability consumer credit insurance, reported net income of $45.1 million in 1994, compared to $44.3 million in 1993.

Important Developments

Feb. '95—BNL announced that a recent decision by the Internal Revenue Service (IRS) to change the manner in which it processes the earned income tax credit portion of certain tax refunds would likely significantly influence earnings of the company's tax refund anticipation loan (RAL) business. Management now believes that the RAL business, which was previously expected to have a pretax profit of about $15 million, will at best break even and at worst generate a pretax loss of up to $80 million. The company recorded a $65 million pretax ($39 million aftertax) loss in the first quarter of 1995 to reflect the best estimate of possible losses for the RAL business.

Capitalization

Long Term Debt: $7,147,000,000 (6/95).
Cum. Preferred Stock: $114,900,000.

Per Share Data ($) (Year Ended Dec. 31)

	1994	1993	1992	1991	1990	1989
Tangible Bk. Val.	24.13	22.55	20.69	21.55	18.90	17.17
Earnings	3.28	3.45	2.75	2.90	2.51	2.51
Dividends	1.62	1.43	1.35	1.27	1.17	1.10
Payout Ratio	49%	41%	49%	44%	47%	44%
Prices - High	44	40½	33⅝	33¼	27½	28⅜
- Low	34½	31¼	28⅛	20¼	17¼	21⅜
P/E Ratio - High	13	12	12	11	11	11
- Low	11	9	10	7	7	9

Income Statement Analysis (Million $)

	1994	%Chg	1993	%Chg	1992	%Chg	1991
Total Revs.	2,137	9%	1,958	8%	1,819	NM	1,810
Int. Exp.	674	6%	633	-2%	643	-6%	684
% Exp/Op Revs.	85%	—	84%	—	86%	—	86%
Pretax Inc.	326	3%	315	25%	252	-2%	258
Eff. Tax Rate	46%	—	41%	—	41%	—	42%
Net Inc.	178	-4%	186	26%	148	NM	149

Balance Sheet & Other Fin. Data (Million $)

	1994	1993	1992	1991	1990	1989
Cash & Secs.	190	182	190	123	248	78.0
Loans	11,991	10,740	9,330	8,330	7,773	6,693
Total Assets	14,378	12,917	11,423	9,972	9,270	7,948
ST Debt	5,974	5,051	3,749	3,354	3,133	2,708
Capitalization:						
Debt	4,825	4,639	4,749	3,902	3,938	3,288
Equity	1,285	1,197	1,093	1,136	870	796
Total	6,225	5,951	5,957	5,153	4,922	4,199
Price Times Book HI	1.8	1.8	1.6	1.5	1.5	1.6
Price Times Book LO	1.4	1.4	1.4	0.9	0.9	1.2

Ratio Analysis

	1994	1993	1992	1991	1990	1989
% Ret. on Revs.	8.3	9.5	8.2	8.2	6.7	7.7
% Ret. on Assets	1.3	1.5	1.4	1.5	1.4	1.6
% Ret. on Equity	13.9	15.8	12.8	14.3	13.4	14.6
Loans/Equity	9.2	8.8	7.9	8.0	8.7	8.5

Dividend Data (Dividends have been paid since 1929. A dividend reinvestment plan is available. An amended "poison pill" stock purchase rights plan was adopted in 1990.)

Amt. of Div. $	Date Decl.	Ex-Div. Date	Stock of Record	Payment Date
0.430	Aug. 18	Aug. 26	Sep. 01	Sep. 30 '94
0.430	Nov. 16	Nov. 25	Dec. 01	Dec. 31 '94
0.430	Feb. 24	Feb. 28	Mar. 06	Mar. 31 '95
0.430	May. 18	May. 25	Jun. 01	Jun. 30 '95

Data as orig. reptd.; bef. results of disc opers. and/or spec. items. Per share data adj. for stk. divs. as of ex-div. date. E-Estimated. NA-Not Available. NM-Not Meaningful. NR-Not Ranked.

Office—301 North Walnut St., Wilmington, DE 19801. **Tel**—(302) 425-2500. **Chrmn & CEO**—F. M. W. Caspersen. **Member, Office of Pres & COO**—D. J. Farris. **Member, Office of Pres & CFO**—A. C. Halvorsen. **VP-Secy**—E. F. Caulfield. **Investor Contact**—Karen Pagonis. **Dirs**—C. W. Bower, R. J. Callander, R. C. Cannada, F. M. W. Caspersen, L. S. Coleman, Jr., D. J. Farris, J. H. Gilliam, Jr., A. C. Halvorsen, R. A. Hernandez, J. R. Hillier, G. L. Holm, T. H. Kean, S. Muller, S. J. Ross, R. A. Tucker, S. M. Wachter, C. H. Watts II, K. M. Worthy. **Transfer Agent and Registrar**—First Chicago Trust Co. of New York, Jersey City, NJ. **Incorporated** in Delaware in 1929. **Empl**-8,500. **S&P Analyst:** Stephen R. Biggar

Bethlehem Steel

NYSE Symbol **BS**
In S&P 500

03-OCT-95

Industry:
Steel-Iron

Summary: Bethlehem is the second largest U.S. steel producer, with products directed largely to the carbon sheet, strip and plate markets.

S&P Opinion: Hold (★★★)

| Recent Price • 14⅛ | Yield • Nil |
| 52 Wk Range • 20⅞-13⅝ | 12-Mo. P/E • 14.0 |

Quantitative Evaluations

Outlook
(1 Lowest—5 Highest)
• **1⁻**

Fair Value
• **12¼**

Risk
• **Average**

Earn./Div. Rank
• **C**

Technical Eval.
• **Bearish** since 7/95

Rel. Strength Rank
(1 Lowest—99 Highest)
• **17**

Insider Activity
• **NA**

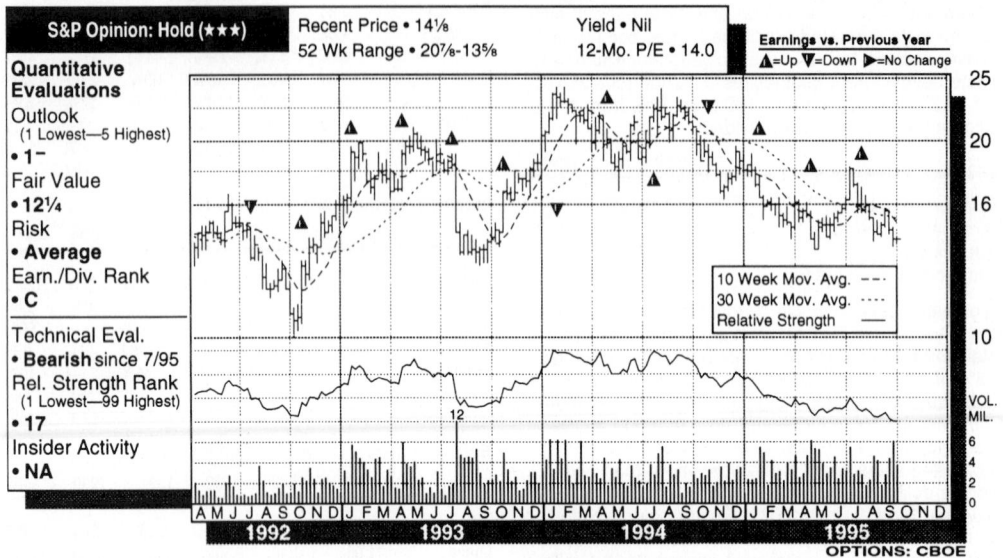

Earnings vs. Previous Year
▲=Up ▼=Down ▶=No Change

10 Week Mov. Avg. ---
30 Week Mov. Avg. ·····
Relative Strength —

1992 1993 1994 1995

VOL. MIL.

OPTIONS: CBOE

Overview - 03-OCT-95

Assuming GDP growth of 2.6% and a rebound in car sales in 1996, we anticipate an 8% increase in sales next year. The projected gain in steel segment sales will reflect a recovery in flat rolled sheet prices, steady demand for plate, rail products and light structurals and a better mix resulting from decreased exports. Improved pricing and mix, higher capacity utilization, much smaller losses in steel-related operations and only moderate increases in raw material costs will lift operating profits. Aided further by lower interest and depreciation charges, earnings should rise again in 1996. The cessation of steelmaking at the structural products plant, greater focus on the medium-size beam market and debt reduction will aid longer-term profitability.

Valuation - 03-OCT-95

BS's shares underperformed the market through late September 1996, falling some 26%, versus a gain of 27% in the S&P 500. BS also underperformed the S&P Steel Index, which was down 11% through August 31, 1995. Despite this poor relative performance and a negative near-term earnings outlook, we are maintaining our hold rating on the shares. We think that the downside risk is limited and that the stock price has likely discounted most of the bad news. Also, with the Steel Index down for two consecutive years, institutional money managers may be examining the group with a view toward a turnaround. However, given its history of disappointing profits vis-a-vis its peers, BS does not warrant an accumulate or buy recommendation yet.

Key Stock Statistics

S&P EPS Est. 1995	1.30	Tang. Bk. Value/Share	1.45
P/E on S&P Est. 1995	10.9	Beta	1.47
S&P EPS Est. 1996	2.20	Shareholders	40,000
Dividend Rate/Share	Nil	Market cap. (B)	$ 1.6
Shs. outstg. (M)	110.4	Inst. holdings	76%
Avg. daily vol. (M)	0.869	Insider holdings	NA

Value of $10,000 invested 5 years ago: $ 8,066

Fiscal Year Ending Dec. 31

	1995	% Change	1994	% Change	1993	% Change
Revenues (Million $)						
1Q	1,241	10%	1,131	11%	1,020	3%
2Q	1,250	2%	1,231	10%	1,117	10%
3Q	—	—	1,233	17%	1,055	5%
4Q	—	—	1,225	8%	1,130	14%
Yr.	—	—	4,819	11%	4,323	8%
Income (Million $)						
1Q	52.50	NM	12.90	NM	-41.30	NM
2Q	60.30	132%	26.00	NM	-5.30	NM
3Q	—	—	10.30	-67%	31.20	NM
4Q	—	—	31.30	NM	-242.6	NM
Yr.	—	—	80.50	NM	-266.3	NM
Earnings Per Share ($)						
1Q	0.38	NM	0.02	NM	-0.53	NM
2Q	0.45	NM	0.14	NM	-0.27	NM
3Q	E0.20	—	Nil	—	0.22	NM
4Q	E0.27	42%	0.19	NM	-2.78	NM
Yr.	E1.30	NM	0.35	NM	-3.37	NM

Next earnings report expected: late October

Business Summary - 03-OCT-95

Bethlehem Steel Corporation is the second largest U.S. steel producer and has fabricating and other operations. Segment contributions (profits in millions) in 1994 were:

	Sales	Profits
Basic steel	98%	$166.0
Steel related	2%	-32.4

Raw steel production totaled 9.8 million tons in 1994, 10.3 million tons in 1993 and 10.5 million in 1992. Shipments were 9.3 million tons in 1994, 9.0 million in 1993 and 8.4 million in 1992. BS used 85% of its production capacity in 1994, versus 90% in 1993 and 66% in 1992.

Steel mill products include sheet, strip and tin mill products (66.1% of total 1994 sales), plates (14.0%), structural shapes and piling (6.7%), rail products (2.8%), bar, rods and semifinished (1.2%) and other steel mill products (1.3%). Other products and services accounted for 5.5%.

Major markets in 1994 included service centers, processors and converters (45.9%), transportation (24.2%), construction (14.7%), containers (5.7%), machinery (4.9%) and other (4.6%).

Steel-related operations include the manufacture and fabrication of a variety of steel products, including forgings and castings. BS's marine construction operations are also part of this segment.

Important Developments

Aug. '95—BS announced that it had signed a two-year agreement with Oil Capital Ltd., a New York-based exploration and production company. Under terms of the agreement, which has automatic one-year renewals subject to termination by either party, BS would provide an initial 300,000 tons of 42-inch-diameter pipe for the proposed construction of a Caspian-to-Mediterranean pipeline. The pact contains an option for BS to provide an additional 300,000 tons as construction progresses. BS said that it could begin making the pipe as early as 1996 if the pipeline gets all the necessary approvals. The company noted that the proposed pipeline has some distance to go before it becomes a reality.

May '95— The U.S. Supreme Court declined to review a decision by the Kentucky Supreme Court that reinstated a 1987 trial verdict against Bethlehem Steel in a dispute over coal rights in Pike County, Ky. The decision could cost Bethlehem $38 million.

Capitalization

Long Term Debt: $615,700,000 (6/95).

Conv. Preferred Stock: $481,200,000 (liquid. pref.); conv. into 20,000,000 com. shs.

ESOP 5% Conv. Preference Stock: $89,000,00 (liquid. pref.); conv. into 2,619,000 com. shs.

Per Share Data ($)   (Year Ended Dec. 31)

	1994	1993	1992	1991	1990	1989
Tangible Bk. Val.	1.45	-5.25	-2.01	2.47	11.96	17.81
Cash Flow	2.81	-0.31	0.46	-7.23	-2.41	7.26
Earnings	0.35	-3.37	-2.73	-10.41	-6.45	2.93
Dividends	Nil	Nil	Nil	0.40	0.40	0.20
Payout Ratio	Nil	Nil	Nil	NM	NM	7%
Prices - High	24¼	21	17¼	18½	21⅛	28½
- Low	16¼	12⅞	10	10¾	10⅝	15¼
P/E Ratio - High	69	NM	NM	NM	NM	10
- Low	46	NM	NM	NM	NM	5

Income Statement Analysis (Million $)

	1994	%Chg	1993	%Chg	1992	%Chg	1991
Revs.	4,819	11%	4,323	8%	4,008	-7%	4,318
Oper. Inc.	395	19%	332	NM	75.0	-13%	86.0
Depr.	261	-6%	278	6%	262	9%	240
Int. Exp.	77.0	7%	72.0	-4%	75.0	4%	72.0
Pretax Inc.	95.0	NM	-350	NM	-238	NM	-764
Eff. Tax Rate	15%	—	NM	—	NM	—	NM
Net Inc.	81.0	NM	-265	NM	-198	NM	-766

Balance Sheet & Other Fin. Data (Million $)

	1994	1993	1992	1991	1990	1989
Cash	160	229	208	84.0	274	531
Curr. Assets	1,569	1,591	961	958	1,203	1,435
Total Assets	5,782	5,877	5,071	4,128	4,382	4,793
Curr. Liab.	1,011	914	893	931	831	838
LT Debt	668	718	727	762	590	656
Common Eqty.	586	120	58.0	361	1,181	1,683
Total Cap.	1,824	1,415	1,106	1,436	2,079	2,658
Cap. Exp.	445	327	329	556	488	421
Cash Flow	299	-29.0	38.0	-549	-182	544

Ratio Analysis

	1994	1993	1992	1991	1990	1989
Curr. Ratio	1.6	1.7	1.1	1.0	1.4	1.7
% LT Debt of Cap.	36.6	50.8	65.7	53.0	28.4	24.7
% Net Inc.of Revs.	1.7	NM	NM	NM	NM	4.7
% Ret. on Assets	1.3	NM	NM	NM	NM	5.3
% Ret. on Equity	10.2	NM	NM	NM	NM	13.9

Dividend Data —Common dividends were omitted in January 1992, after having been resumed in July 1989. Previously, common payments were omitted in October 1985. Dividends have been maintained on the $5 and $2.50 convertible preferred issues. A "poison pill" stock purchase rights plan was adopted in 1988.

Data as orig. reptd.; bef. results of disc. opers. and/or spec. items. Per share data adj. for stk. divs. as of ex-div. date. E-Estimated. NA-Not Available. NM-Not Meaningful. NR-Not Ranked.

Office—1170 Eighth Ave., Bethlehem, PA 18016-7699. **Tel**—(610) 694-2424. **Chrmn & CEO**—C. H. Barnette. **Pres**—R. P. Penny. **Exec VP, CFO & Treas**—G. L. Millenbruch. **Scy**—W. H. Graham **Investor Contact**—Blaise E. Derrico. **Dirs**—C. H. Barnette, B. R. Civiletti, W. H. Clark Jr., J. B. Curcio, T. L. Holton, L. B. Kaden, H. P. Kamen, W. Knowlton, R. McClements Jr., G. L. Millenbruch, R. P. Penny, D. P. Phypers, W. A. Pogue, J. F. Ruffle. **Transfer Agent & Registrar**—First Chicago Trust Co. of New York, NYC. **Incorporated** in Delaware in 1936. **Empl**-19,900. **S&P Analyst:** Leo Larkin

Beverly Enterprises

NYSE Symbol BEV Options on Pacific (Mar-Jun-Sep-Dec) In S&P 500

Price	Range	P–E Ratio	Dividend	Yield	S&P Ranking	Beta
Aug. 3'95	1995					
13⅝	16⅛–10⅞	18	None	None	B–	0.75

Summary

This company is the largest owner/operator of nursing homes in the U.S., operating 712 nursing facilities throughout the country. Beverly plans to spin off about 80% of its institutional pharmacy subsidiary, Pharmacy Corp. of America, to BEV shareholders in a tax-free distribution, while selling the remaining stake in a public offering.

Current Outlook

Profits in 1996 are seen reaching $1.05 a share, up from $0.80 indicated for 1995.

Early resumption of dividends on the common (omitted in 1988) is not expected.

Fundamental trends in the long term care segment are improving, with same-store revenues and operating profits on the rise. As such, BEV should produce good earnings gains in the second half of 1995 and through 1996. The company's strategy of converting leased nursing homes to owned units and expanding ancillary services should aid both the top and bottom lines going forward, as would a successful turnaround at the PCA unit.

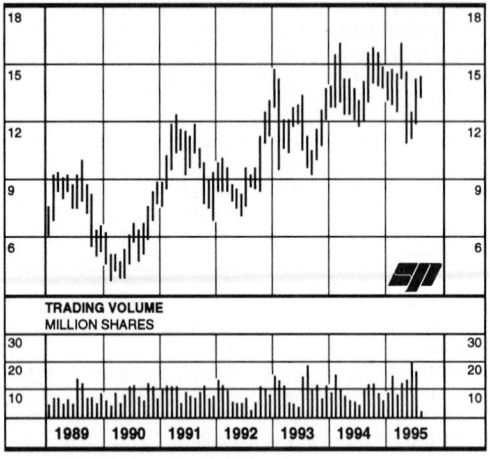

TRADING VOLUME
MILLION SHARES

Revenues (Million $)

Quarter:	1995	1994	1993	1992
Mar.	799	720	694	610
Jun.	794	728	718	624
Sep.		767	732	674
Dec.		769	737	689
		2,984	2,871	2,596

Revenues in the six months ended June 30, 1995, rose 10%, year to year, as growth within the pharmacy and rehabilitation services areas largely reflected acquisitions. Same-facility revenue advanced 8%. Profitability was restricted by a second quarter net operating deficit of $5.0 million ($0.06 a share) at the PCA unit and a net charge of $2.5 million ($0.03) from the sale of four nursing homes. After taxes at 38.0%, versus 33.0%, net income fell 11%, to $26.7 million ($0.31 a share) from $30.0 million ($0.35).

Common Share Earnings ($)

Quarter:	1995	1994	1993	1992
Mar.	0.17	0.15	0.13	0.09
Jun.	0.14	0.19	0.18	0.15
Sep.	E0.23	0.24	d0.04	0.17
Dec.	E0.26	0.20	0.17	d0.38
	E0.80	0.79	0.45	0.04

Important Developments

Jun. '95— BEV acquired Pharmacy Management Services Inc., a leading independent provider of comprehensive medical cost-containment and managed care services to workers' compensation payors and claimants, for a total of about 12,361,184 BEV common shares.

May '95— Beverly postponed the planned IPO and spinoff of its Pharmacy Corp. of America unit due to operational problems, including revenue reductions resulting from lost customers and changes in the pricing structure for its infusion therapy products, as well as higher than expected costs associated with the integration of recent acquisitions. Beverly said it remains intent on spinning off PCA after resolving the operational problems.

Next earnings report expected in mid-October.

Per Share Data ($)

Yr. End Dec. 31	¹1994	1993	1992	¹1991	1990	1989	1988	¹1987	¹1986	¹1985
Tangible Bk. Val.	**4.76**	6.00	5.26	5.28	4.22	4.84	5.05	5.43	6.86	7.10
Cash Flow	**1.68**	1.36	0.95	1.20	1.05	d0.88	0.88	0.73	1.95	2.20
Earnings²	**0.79**	0.45	0.04	0.37	0.19	d1.96	d0.47	d0.58	0.81	1.07
Dividends	**Nil**	Nil	Nil	Nil	Nil	Nil	Nil	0.20	0.20	0.17
Payout Ratio	**Nil**	Nil	Nil	Nil	Nil	Nil	Nil	NM	24%	17%
Prices—High	**16⅛**	14¾	13⅛	12⅜	8⅞	10	7⅞	18⅛	22½	20⅛
Low	**11¾**	9¼	7⅛	6⅞	3¾	5	3¾	6⅝	14⅛	15¼
P/E Ratio—	**20–15**	33–21	NM	33–19	47–20	NM	NM	NM	28–17	19–14

Data as orig. reptd. Adj. for stk. div. of 100% Jun. 1986. **1.** Refl. merger or acq. **2.** Bef. spec. item(s) of -0.03 in 1994, -0.03 in 1993, -0.19 in 1992, +0.04 in 1987, -0.10 in 1986. d-Deficit. E-Estimated. NM-Not Meaningful.

Income Data (Million $)

Year Ended Dec. 31	Revs.	Oper. Inc.	% Oper. Inc. of Revs.	Cap. Exp.	Depr.	Int. Exp.	Net Bef. Taxes	Eff. Tax Rate	[2]Net Inc.	% Net Inc. of Revs.	Cash Flow
[1]1994	2,969	243	8.2	100	77.6	65	115	33.0%	77	2.6	146
1993	2,871	209	7.3	205	71.7	62	90	33.0%	60	2.1	108
1992	2,597	182	7.0	177	68.2	63	8	50.1%	4	0.2	71
[1]1991	2,301	155	6.7	123	65.1	69	42	29.8%	29	1.3	94
1990	2,113	134	6.3	43	54.9	83	20	36.0%	13	0.6	67
1989	2,104	127	6.0	41	58.2	95	d132	NM	d104	NM	d47
1988	2,025	140	6.9	46	72.3	104	d33	NM	d24	NM	47
[1]1987	2,094	97	4.6	101	77.1	103	d60	NM	d33	NM	43
[1]1986	2,019	251	12.4	457	72.1	106	90	43.0%	51	2.5	124
[1]1985	1,691	264	15.6	285	63.2	115	103	42.0%	60	3.5	123

Balance Sheet Data (Million $)

Dec. 31	Cash	Assets	Curr. Liab.	Ratio	Total Assets	% Ret. on Assets	Long Term Debt	Common Equity	Total Cap.	% LT Debt of Cap.	% Ret. on Equity
1994	68	652	410	1.6	2,323	3.5	918	677	1,826	50.3	10.6
1993	74	549	397	1.4	1,994	3.0	707	589	1,518	46.5	6.3
1992	50	519	382	1.4	1,854	0.2	713	494	1,385	51.5	0.6
1991	37	414	328	1.3	1,673	1.7	628	499	1,259	49.9	6.2
1990	18	384	314	1.2	1,623	0.7	695	395	1,238	56.1	3.2
1989	38	589	486	1.2	1,639	NM	599	338	1,086	55.2	NM
1988	63	396	241	1.6	1,844	NM	915	444	1,525	60.0	NM
1987	40	473	907	0.5	2,072	NM	451	489	1,083	41.6	NM
1986	58	425	252	1.7	2,220	2.4	1,111	644	1,913	58.1	8.2
1985	198	507	299	1.7	2,020	3.0	1,036	597	1,697	61.0	10.8

Data as orig. reptd. 1. Refl. merger or acq. 2. Bef. spec. items. d-Deficit. NM-Not Meaningful.

Business Summary

Beverly Enterprises is the largest operator of skilled and intermediate care nursing homes in the U.S. The company also operates retirement living and congregate living projects, home health care units and pharmacies. Revenues in recent years were derived as follows:

	1994	1993	1992
Medicaid room & board	47%	50%	54%
Medicare room & board	11%	11%	11%
Private and Veterans room & board	16%	16%	17%
Ancillary and other	26%	23%	18%

At January 31, 1995, BEV operated 727 skilled and intermediate care nursing facilities, ranging in capacity from 20 to 388 beds, in 33 states and the District of Columbia. Of the total, 409 were owned by the company, 314 were leased and four were managed for others. Patient days totaled 26,766,000 in 1994, down from 29,041,000 in 1993. Average occupancy equaled 88.5% in both 1994 and 1993.

Skilled care facilities provide convalescent, rehabilitative and sustaining care over extended periods of time, while intermediate units offer similar care on a less extensive basis.

American Transitional Hospitals (ATH; acquired in September 1994 for 2,400,000 common shares) operates six acute long term transitional hospitals. ATH also operates eight nursing facilities that provide a more complex level of sub-acute care than BEV's other nursing facilities.

Pharmacy Corp. of America (PCA; formed through the consolidation of several recently-acquired drug distributors), supplies pharmaceuticals and related supplies and services to the company's nursing homes and transitional hospitals, as well as other institutions.

At January 31, 1995, BEV also operated 40 retirement and congregate living projects with about 2,500 apartment units, 65 pharmacies and pharmacy related entities and four home health care agencies.

Dividend Data

Dividends, paid since 1979, were omitted in early 1988. A "poison pill" stock purchase rights plan was adopted in 1994.

Capitalization

Long Term Debt: $901,048,000 (3/95).

$2.75 Cum. Conv. Exch. Pfd. Stk.: 3,000,000 shs. (liq. preference $50 per sh.); conv. into 11.3 million com. shs.

Common Stock: 98,094,942 shs. ($0.10 par). Institutions hold 66%. Shareholders of record: 7,738.

Offices—1200 South Waldron Rd., No. 155, Fort Smith, AR 72903. **Tel**—(501) 452-6712. **Chrmn, Pres & CEO**—D. R. Banks. **EVP-Fin & CFO**—R. D. Woltil. **EVP & Secy**—R. W. Pommerville. **SVP & Treas**—S. Hollingsworth Jr. **Investor Contact**—Bess Bowman. **Dirs**—B.F. Anthony Jr., D.R. Banks, C. Bradbury, J.R. Greene, E.E. Holiday, J.E.M. Jacoby, R.J. Lavizzo-Mourey, L.W. Menk, M.R. Seymann. **Transfer Agent & Registrar**—The Bank of New York, NYC. **Incorporated** in California in 1964; reincorporated in Delaware in 1987. **Empl**—82,000.
Information has been obtained from sources believed to be reliable, but its accuracy and completeness are not guaranteed. Robert M. Gold

Biomet, Inc.

NASDAQ Symbol **BMET**
In S&P 500

24-OCT-95

Industry:
Medical equipment/
supply

Summary: Biomet makes surgical implants for replacement of hip and knee joints, orthopedic support items, fracture fixation devices, and other related medical devices.

S&P Opinion: Accumulate (★★★★)	Recent Price • 17⅝	Yield • Nil
	52 Wk Range • 18½-10¾	12-Mo. P/E • 24.5

Quantitative Evaluations

Outlook
(1 Lowest—5 Highest)
• **2⁻**

Fair Value
• **17**

Risk
• **Average**

Earn./Div. Rank
• **B+**

Technical Eval.
• **Bullish** since 9/94

Rel. Strength Rank
(1 Lowest—99 Highest)
• **86**

Insider Activity
• **Unfavorable**

Earnings vs. Previous Year
▲=Up ▼=Down ▶=No Change

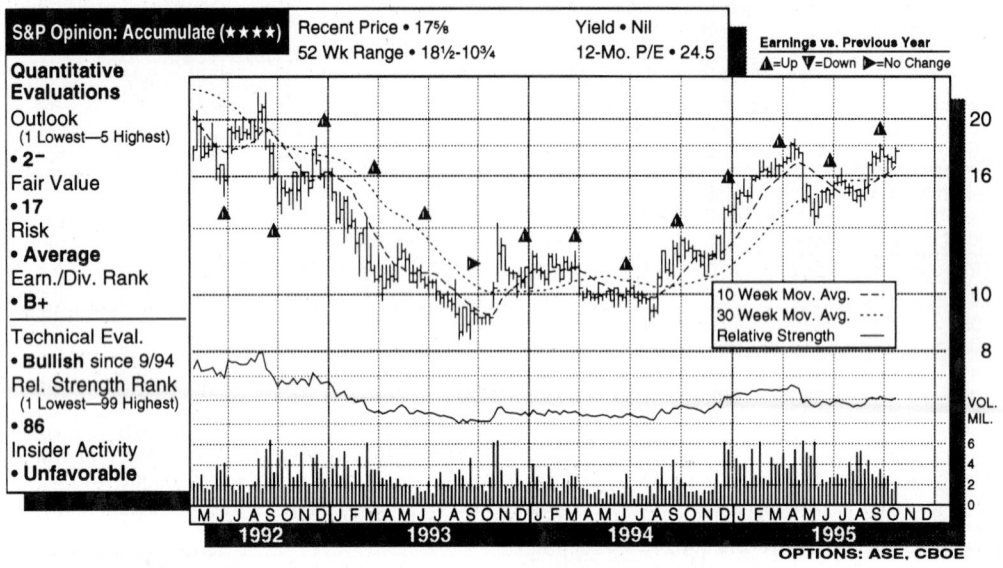

10 Week Mov. Avg. — - -
30 Week Mov. Avg. · · · ·
Relative Strength —

OPTIONS: ASE, CBOE

Overview - 20-OCT-95

Boosted by the full-year inclusion of Kirschner Medical (acquired in November 1994), total sales are expected to climb to $540 million in 1995-6, from 1994-5's $452 million. Results should benefit from gains in established reconstructive and bone growth stimulation products, new hip and knee products and arthroscopic devices, and from an expanded sales force. Biomet expects to launch a new line of external fixation products to replace products that it distributed for Orthofix, an Italian maker of external fixation devices. Despite a projected higher tax rate, margins should widen, on greater volume, and synergies and cost economies related to Kirschner.

Valuation - 20-OCT-95

After a year-long advance through April 1995, the shares have been erratic performers, reflecting profit taking by certain large holders, as well as news of the termination of EBI's distribution agreement with Orthofix. However, Biomet has established itself as a technology leader in the reconstructive implant market, with more than a dozen orthopedic products introduced in the past year. New products, a highly efficient marketing organization, synergies from Kirschner, and increasing penetration of foreign markets should allow sales gains in excess of orthopedic market growth rates in coming years. The shares remain attractive for above-average capital appreciation.

Key Stock Statistics

S&P EPS Est. 1996	0.85	Tang. Bk. Value/Share	3.59
P/E on S&P Est. 1996	20.7	Beta	1.83
Dividend Rate/Share	Nil	Shareholders	13,300
Shs. outstg. (M)	115.3	Market cap. (B)	$ 2.1
Avg. daily vol. (M)	0.440	Inst. holdings	47%
		Insider holdings	NA

Value of $10,000 invested 5 years ago: $ 25,636

Fiscal Year Ending May 31

	1996	% Change	1995	% Change	1994	% Change
Revenues (Million $)						
1Q	127.2	32%	96.23	11%	86.89	11%
2Q	—	—	106.9	18%	90.31	10%
3Q	—	—	120.7	26%	95.66	14%
4Q	—	—	128.5	28%	100.4	11%
Yr.	—	—	452.3	21%	373.3	6%
Income (Million $)						
1Q	20.75	21%	17.11	12%	15.33	—
2Q	—	—	19.41	16%	16.79	6%
3Q	—	—	20.54	14%	18.08	13%
4Q	—	—	22.13	13%	19.61	12%
Yr.	—	—	79.20	13%	69.82	9%
Earnings Per Share ($)						
1Q	0.18	20%	0.15	15%	0.13	NM
2Q	E0.20	18%	0.17	13%	0.15	7%
3Q	E0.22	22%	0.18	13%	0.16	14%
4Q	E0.25	32%	0.19	12%	0.17	13%
Yr.	E0.85	23%	0.69	13%	0.61	9%

Next earnings report expected: mid December

Biomet, Inc.

Business Summary - 24-OCT-95

Biomet designs, makes and markets surgical implants and orthopedic support devices used mostly by orthopedic medical specialists. Its products are used mainly in the surgical replacement of hip and knee joints and in fracture fixation procedures as an aid to healing. Sales in recent years were derived as follows:

	1994-1995	1993-1994	1992-1993
Reconstructive devices	60%	58%	56%
EBI products	22%	24%	25%
Other	18%	18%	19%

Products are distributed in about 100 countries, with foreign operations (including exports) accounting for 24% of 1994-5 sales.

The company's reconstructive devices include implants for partial or total replacement of hips and knees, as well as instruments for use by surgeons in performing such procedures. Hip femoral prostheses consist of a femoral head, neck and stem, cast or machined into a single piece. Most hip systems offered use titanium alloy femoral components and ultrahigh-molecular-weight components. Biomet has an estimated 10% to 11% share of the total U.S. reconstructive device market.

The Electro-Biology, Inc. (EBI) unit produces both invasive and non-invasive electrical stimulation devices used in the treatment of recalcitrant bone fractures, spinal fusion stimulation systems used as an adjunctive treatment in spinal fusion procedures and external fixation products. EBI accounts for half of the domestic electrical stimulation device market.

Other products consist of internal fixation products, arthroscopy products, operating room supplies, orthopedic support products, powered surgical equipment and oral-maxillofacial implants and instruments. Through a venture with U.S. Surgical Corp., the company is also engaged in the development of bioresorbable orthopedic and oral-maxillofacial implants.

Important Developments

Aug. '95—Reconstructive devices sales in the 1995-6 first quarter climbed 33%, year to year, boosted by the inclusion of Kirschner Medical (acquired in November 1994). EBI division sales increased 21%, while sales of other products (including certain Kirschner lines) soared 41%. Kirschner, a maker of joint reconstruction products, surgical instruments and orthopedic support items, was acquired for $38.9 million in cash and stock. Results in the quarter included a charges of $2 million related to patent litigation and $1 million related to the restructuring of Kirschner's implant division, largely offset by a $2.5 million gain on the sale of holdings in American Medical Electronics.

Capitalization

Long Term Debt: None (5/95).

Per Share Data ($)

					(Year Ended May 31)	
	1995	1994	1993	1992	1991	1990
Tangible Bk. Val.	3.59	3.12	2.61	2.05	1.54	1.16
Cash Flow	0.81	0.71	0.66	0.53	0.41	0.32
Earnings	0.69	0.61	0.56	0.46	0.36	0.27
Dividends	Nil	Nil	Nil	Nil	Nil	Nil
Payout Ratio	Nil	Nil	Nil	Nil	Nil	Nil
Cal. Yrs.	1994	1993	1992	1991	1990	1989
Prices - High	14¼	16½	30½	32⅜	9⅝	7
- Low	9	8⅜	13¾	8⅛	4⅞	4
P/E Ratio - High	21	27	54	70	27	26
- Low	13	14	25	18	14	15

Income Statement Analysis (Million $)

	1995	%Chg	1994	%Chg	1993	%Chg	1992
Revs.	452	21%	373	11%	335	22%	275
Oper. Inc.	133	17%	114	12%	102	31%	78.0
Depr.	14.4	20%	12.0	3%	11.7	43%	8.2
Int. Exp.	1.0	75%	0.6	-37%	0.9	12%	0.8
Pretax Inc.	125	17%	107	13%	94.3	23%	76.5
Eff. Tax Rate	37%	—	35%	—	32%	—	32%
Net Inc.	79.2	13%	69.8	9%	64.0	24%	51.8

Balance Sheet & Other Fin. Data (Million $)

	1995	1994	1993	1992	1991	1990
Cash	90.0	141	93.6	74.6	50.7	42.9
Curr. Assets	392	342	271	210	152	115
Total Assets	539	418	354	279	211	155
Curr. Liab.	89.2	53.8	46.7	42.0	33.6	22.6
LT Debt	Nil	Nil	Nil	Nil	Nil	Nil
Common Eqty.	445	357	301	232	173	129
Total Cap.	447	361	304	234	174	130
Cap. Exp.	28.9	6.5	14.9	14.0	11.1	6.5
Cash Flow	93.6	81.9	75.6	60.0	46.0	35.6

Ratio Analysis

	1995	1994	1993	1992	1991	1990
Curr. Ratio	4.4	6.4	5.8	5.0	4.5	5.1
% LT Debt of Cap.	Nil	Nil	Nil	Nil	Nil	Nil
% Net Inc.of Revs.	17.5	18.7	19.1	18.9	18.8	18.4
% Ret. on Assets	16.5	18.1	20.0	21.1	21.5	21.8
% Ret. on Equity	19.8	21.3	23.8	25.5	26.0	26.3

Dividend Data —No cash dividends have been paid. A two-for-one stock split was effected in December 1991.

Data as orig. reptd.; bef. results of disc. opers. and/or spec. items. Per share data adj. for stk. divs. as of ex-div. date. E-Estimated. NA-Not Available. NM-Not Meaningful. NR-Not Ranked.

Office—Airport Industrial Park, P.O. Box 587, Warsaw, IN 46581-0587. **Tel**—(219) 267-6639. **Chrmn**—N. L. Noblitt. **Pres & CEO**—D. A. Miller. **VP-Fin & Treas**—G. D. Hartman. **VP & Secy**—D. P. Hann. **Investor Contact**—J. M. Howie. **Dirs**—J. L. Ferguson, D. P. Hann, M. R. Harroff, T. F. Kearns, Jr., D. A. Miller, J. L. Miller, K. V. Miller, C. E. Niemier, N. L. Noblitt, J. M. Norris, M. T. Quayle, L. G. Tanner. **Transfer Agent**—Lake City Bank, Warsaw. **Incorporated** in Indiana in 1977. **Empl**- 1,855. **S&P Analyst:** H. B. Saftlas

Black & Decker

NYSE Symbol **BDK**
In S&P 500

03-AUG-95 | **Industry:** Building | **Summary:** This company is the world's largest producer of power tools and a leading supplier of household products.

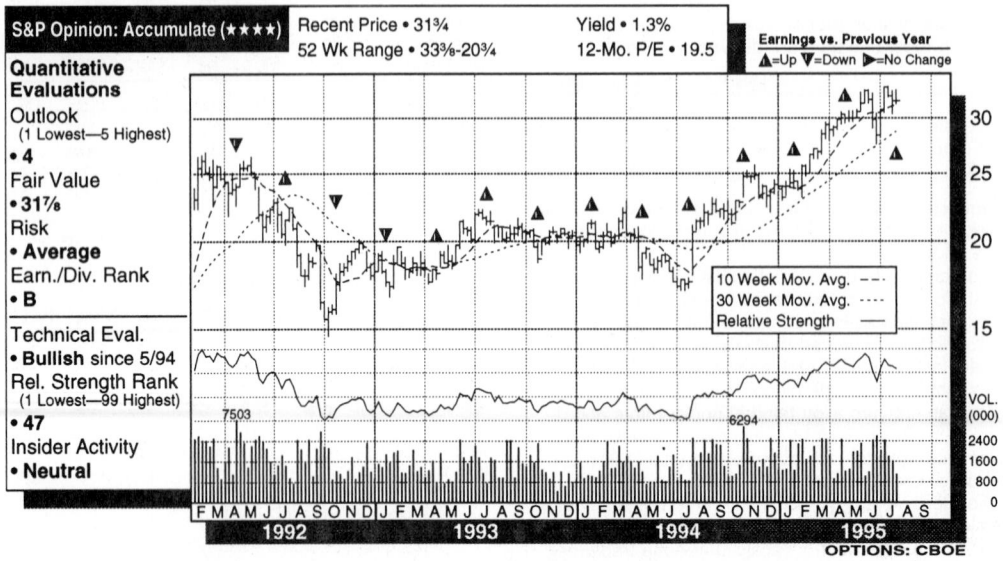

S&P Opinion: Accumulate (★★★★) | Recent Price • 31¾ | Yield • 1.3%
52 Wk Range • 33⅞-20¾ | 12-Mo. P/E • 19.5

Earnings vs. Previous Year
▲=Up ▼=Down ▶=No Change

Quantitative Evaluations

Outlook
(1 Lowest—5 Highest)
• **4**

Fair Value
• **31⅞**

Risk
• **Average**

Earn./Div. Rank
• **B**

Technical Eval.
• **Bullish** since 5/94

Rel. Strength Rank
(1 Lowest—99 Highest)
• **47**

Insider Activity
• **Neutral**

10 Week Mov. Avg. - - -
30 Week Mov. Avg. ·····
Relative Strength —

VOL. (000)
2400
1600
800
0

7503   6294

F M A M J J A S O N D | J F M A M J J A S O N D | J F M A M J J A S O N D | J F M A M J J A S
1992 | 1993 | 1994 | 1995

OPTIONS: CBOE

Overview - 03-AUG-95

Sales should continue to improve in 1995. Volume gains will reflect increased domestic market share and greater domestic demand for nearly all company consumer products. Favorable response to new products, including the DeWalt line of professional power tools, the Quantum line of higher-priced consumer power tools, Titan locksets, and a line of decorative faucets would be positive factors. Products introduced in the past three years now account for as much as 33% of sales in some consumer businesses. Demand in overseas markets should continue to improve. Margins should widen, on productivity gains and cost reduction measures, and interest expense should drop, with lower debt levels. By 1997, the company hopes to have cut operating expenses by $100 million, and to achieve consolidated operating margins of 12%.

Valuation - 28-JUL-95

Since reaching their recent low of 17 in mid-1994, BDK's shares have risen over 85%. We attribute this significant upturn to higher than expected earnings in the second half of 1994 and expectations that earnings will increase 15% to 20% annually in the foreseeable future. This above average growth should result from BDK's successful efforts to boost revenue growth via new products, improve margins, and reduce debt. Based on 1995's earnings estimate, the shares are selling at a premium to the S&P 500; nevertheless, given BDK's growth prospects, we rate the shares "accumulate."

Key Stock Statistics

S&P EPS Est. 1995	1.85	Tang. Bk. Value/Share	NM
P/E on S&P Est. 1995	17.2	Beta	1.78
S&P EPS Est. 1996	2.25	Shareholders	19,700
Dividend Rate/Share	0.40	Market cap. (B)	$ 2.7
Shs. outstg. (M)	85.2	Inst. holdings	80%
Avg. daily vol. (M)	0.329	Insider holdings	NA

Value of $10,000 invested 5 years ago: $ 18,598

Fiscal Year Ending Dec. 31

	1995	% Change	1994	% Change	1993	% Change
Revenues (Million $)						
1Q	1,200	11%	1,085	-1%	1,100	3%
2Q	1,329	9%	1,221	6%	1,156	2%
3Q	—	—	1,323	11%	1,190	NM
4Q	—	—	1,619	13%	1,437	3%
Yr.	—	—	5,248	7%	4,882	2%
Income (Million $)						
1Q	25.70	76%	14.60	5%	13.90	101%
2Q	34.80	51%	23.00	18%	19.50	61%
3Q	—	—	29.30	50%	19.50	97%
4Q	—	—	60.50	43%	42.30	NM
Yr.	—	—	127.4	34%	95.20	NM
Earnings Per Share ($)						
1Q	0.27	93%	0.14	8%	0.13	117%
2Q	0.37	54%	0.24	20%	0.20	67%
3Q	E0.41	—	0.31	55%	0.20	150%
4Q	E0.80	—	0.68	45%	0.47	NM
Yr.	E1.85	—	1.37	37%	1.00	NM

Next earnings report expected: late October

Business Summary - 03-AUG-95

Black & Decker makes a wide range of products sold to residential and commercial markets in over 100 countries. In 1989, it acquired Emhart Corp., a diversified multinational producer of industrial and consumer products and information and electronic systems. Sales by product group in recent years:

	1994	1993
Power tools	31%	30%
Information technology & services	17%	16%
Household products	14%	15%
Security hardware	10%	11%
Commercial/industrial goods	11%	12%
Outdoor products	6%	6%
Accessories	7%	6%
Plumbing products	4%	4%

Domestic sales accounted for 60% of the total in 1994, Europe 24%, and other countries 15%.

Consumer and home improvement products include professional and residential corded and cordless portable electric power tools, such as drills, screwdrivers and saws; bench and stationary tools; small home appliances, such as hand-held vacuums, irons, toasters, coffee makers, food processors and lighting products; corded and cordless lawn and garden products, such as hedge and grass trimmers, mowers, and chain saws; security hardware, such as residential and commercial locksets and deadbolts; various plumbing products, such as faucets, shower valves and bath accessories; and outdoor recreational products, such as steel and composite golf club shafts. Practically all consumer and home improvement products are sold under well-known brand names.

Commercial and industrial products include fastening systems and tools, and high-speed machines for the glass-making industry. Information technology and services are offered by PRC Inc., which provides professional services related to computer systems and software.

Important Developments

Jul. '95—BDK attributed its 8.8% year-to-year sales increase in the 1995 second quarter to strong demand for all products except plumbing products. Operating income expanded 20%, aided by cost reductions and productivity improvement programs. With slightly lower interest expense and a reduced tax rate, net income was up 51%, to $34.8 million, from $23 million.

Capitalization

Long Term Debt: $1,812,100,000 (7/2/95).
7.75% Ser. B Cum. Conv. Pfd. Stk.: 150,000 shs. ($1,000 stated value); ea. conv. into 42.333 com. shs.; Newell Corp. holds 100%.

Per Share Data ($)

(Year Ended Dec. 31)

	1994	1993	1992	1991	1990	1989
Tangible Bk. Val.	12.04	10.72	11.08	14.18	14.94	12.24
Cash Flow	3.91	2.51	1.52	4.03	4.21	2.18
Earnings	1.37	1.00	-1.11	0.81	0.84	0.51
Dividends	0.40	0.40	0.40	0.40	0.40	0.40
Payout Ratio	29%	40%	NM	50%	48%	78%
Prices - High	25¾	22¼	26⅞	19⅝	20⅛	25¼
- Low	17	16⅝	14⅝	8½	8	18⅛
P/E Ratio - High	19	22	NM	24	24	50
- Low	12	17	NM	10	10	36

Income Statement Analysis (Million $)

	1994	%Chg	1993	%Chg	1992	%Chg	1991
Revs.	5,248	7%	4,882	2%	4,780	3%	4,637
Oper. Inc.	607	33%	455	-16%	542	-10%	600
Depr.	214	70%	126	-37%	201	1%	199
Int. Exp.	195	8%	180	-21%	228	-26%	309
Pretax Inc.	190	22%	156	NM	-29.0	NM	108
Eff. Tax Rate	33%	—	39%	—	NM	—	51%
Net Inc.	127	34%	95.0	NM	-73.0	NM	53.0

Balance Sheet & Other Fin. Data (Million $)

	1994	1993	1992	1991	1990	1989
Cash	66.0	82.0	66.0	75.0	84.0	158
Curr. Assets	1,833	1,764	1,783	1,730	1,934	3,105
Total Assets	5,434	5,311	5,392	5,533	5,890	6,258
Curr. Liab.	1,880	1,509	1,490	1,374	1,712	2,426
LT Debt	1,723	2,069	2,109	2,626	2,756	2,630
Common Eqty.	1,019	899	924	877	921	721
Total Cap.	2,938	3,166	3,225	3,693	3,710	3,390
Cap. Exp.	199	210	184	108	113	112
Cash Flow	329	210	116	249	257	129

Ratio Analysis

	1994	1993	1992	1991	1990	1989
Curr. Ratio	1.0	1.2	1.2	1.3	1.1	1.3
% LT Debt of Cap.	58.7	65.4	65.4	71.1	74.3	77.6
% Net Inc.of Revs.	2.4	2.0	NM	1.1	1.1	0.9
% Ret. on Assets	2.4	1.8	NM	0.9	0.8	0.7
% Ret. on Equity	12.0	9.1	NM	5.5	6.1	4.1

Dividend Data

(Dividends have been paid since 1937. A dividend reinvestment plan is available. A poison pill stock purchase rights plan was adopted in 1986.)

Amt. of Div. $	Date Decl.	Ex-Div. Date	Stock of Record	Payment Date
0.100	Jul. 25	Sep. 12	Sep. 16	Sep. 30 '94
0.100	Oct. 24	Dec. 12	Dec. 16	Dec. 30 '94
0.100	Feb. 15	Mar. 13	Mar. 17	Mar. 31 '95
0.100	Apr. 25	Jun. 14	Jun. 16	Jun. 30 '95
0.100	Jul. 24	Sep. 13	Sep. 15	Sep. 29 '95

Data as orig. reptd.; bef. results of disc. opers. and/or spec. items. Per share data adj. for stk. divs. as of ex-div. date. Book val. in Per Share Data table incl. intangibles. E-Estimated. NA-Not Available. NM-Not Meaningful. NR-Not Ranked.

Office—701 East Joppa Rd., Towson, MD 21286. **Tel**—(410) 716-3900. **Chrmn & CEO**—N. D. Archibald. **CFO**—T. M. Schoewe. **VP & Treas**—K. W. Hyle. **VP & Secy**—B. Lucas. **Investor Contact**—Michael J. Allan. **Dirs**—N. D. Archibald, B. L. Bowles, M. Candlish, A. G. Decker, Jr., A. Luiso, J. D. Muncaster, L. R. Pugh, M. H. Willes, M. C. Woodward, Jr. **Transfer Agent & Registrar**—First Chicago Trust Co. of New York, NYC. **Incorporated** in Maryland in 1910. **Empl**-35,800. **S&P Analyst:** Elizabeth Vandeventer

Block (H & R)

NYSE Symbol **HRB**
In S&P 500

17-AUG-95 Industry: Services

Summary: HRB is North America's largest tax service company for individuals, and it also owns CompuServe, a major online computer information service.

S&P Opinion: Accumulate (★★★★)

Recent Price • 37⅛	Yield • 3.4%
52 Wk Range • 47⅝-33	12-Mo. P/E • 36.8

Quantitative Evaluations

Outlook
(1 Lowest—5 Highest)
• **2+**

Fair Value
• **35¾**

Risk
• **Average**

Earn./Div. Rank
• **A+**

Technical Eval.
• **Bullish** since 7/95

Rel. Strength Rank
(1 Lowest—99 Highest)
• **18**

Insider Activity
• **NA**

Earnings vs. Previous Year
▲=Up ▼=Down ▶=No Change

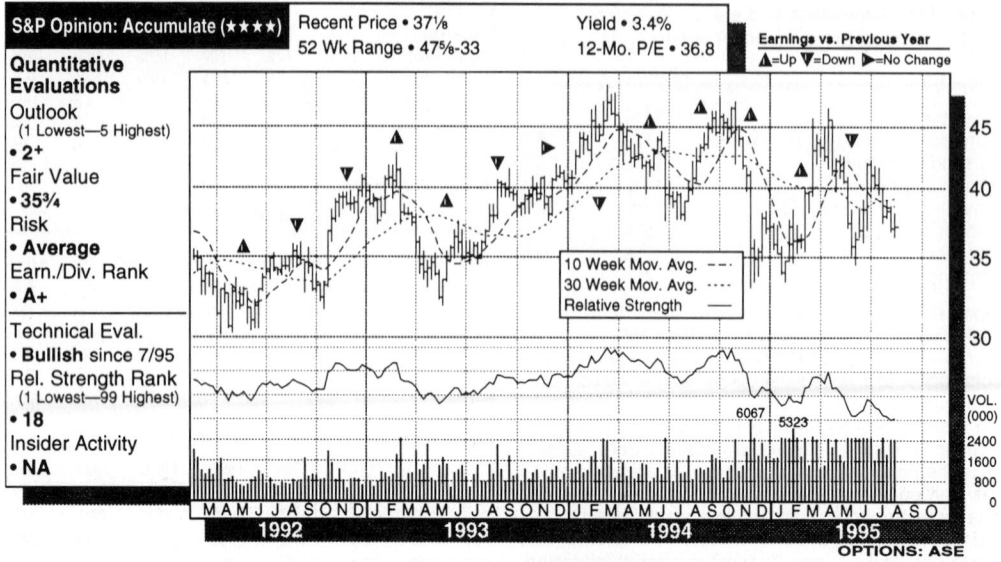

10 Week Mov. Avg. - - -
30 Week Mov. Avg. .....
Relative Strength —

OPTIONS: ASE

Overview - 17-AUG-95

Notwithstanding new pricing initiatives, strong double-digit revenue gains will continue at CompuServe in 1995-6, boosted by new subscribers and customer usage, and from the acquisition of Spry. Significant one-time charges will be partially offset by nonrecurring accounting gains in the tax business. Fewer shares outstanding will also help. Tax services revenues are expected to rebound in 1995-6. Demand for services should be boosted by tax law changes. The stronger revenues will also favorably impact profitability, combined with the absence of problems and charges related to changes in the Refund Anticipation Loan program that heavily penalized fiscal 1995 results. The $0.76 unusual charge related to the purchase of Spry will also be absent. A strong earnings advance is likely in 1996-7, aided by contributions from Spry.

Valuation - 17-AUG-95

We favor HRB for a number of reasons, not least of which is the cushion that the generous cash dividend provides. Cash dividends have been increased in each year since 1962. Notwithstanding ups and downs over the course of any given year, HRB has hit new yearly highs in each of the past six years, and we see no reason for that pattern to change given the outlook for accelerating earnings growth likely in the next several years. The acquisition of Spry Inc., plus pricing, marketing and other initiatives, are major enhancements to CompuServe's competitive lead in the online services business.

Key Stock Statistics

S&P EPS Est. 1996	2.05	Tang. Bk. Value/Share	6.03
P/E on S&P Est. 1996	18.1	Beta	0.78
Dividend Rate/Share	1.28	Shareholders	24,200
Shs. outstg. (M)	104.7	Market cap. (B)	$ 3.9
Avg. daily vol. (M)	0.515	Inst. holdings	78%
		Insider holdings	NA

Value of $10,000 invested 5 years ago: $ 24,287

Fiscal Year Ending Apr. 30

	1995	% Change	1994	% Change	1993	% Change
Revenues (Million $)						
1Q	145.4	41%	103.3	-44%	184.0	3%
2Q	172.9	32%	131.2	-40%	218.0	10%
3Q	268.0	17%	229.4	-26%	309.0	20%
4Q	774.0	NM	774.7	-5%	814.3	10%
Yr.	1,360	10%	1,239	-19%	1,525	11%
Income (Million $)						
1Q	-2.96	NM	-5.44	NM	-7.11	31%
2Q	-1.25	NM	-4.17	NM	-4.01	20%
3Q	8.08	NM	-17.93	NM	8.58	68%
4Q	103.4	-47%	194.4	6%	183.2	10%
Yr.	107.3	-35%	164.0	-9%	180.7	11%
Earnings Per Share ($)						
1Q	-0.03	NM	-0.08	NM	-0.07	NM
2Q	-0.01	NM	-0.04	NM	-0.04	NM
3Q	0.08	NM	-0.17	NM	0.08	60%
4Q	0.98	-46%	1.83	7%	1.71	13%
Yr.	1.01	-34%	1.54	-8%	1.68	13%

Next earnings report expected: late August

Block (H & R)

Business Summary - 10-AUG-95

Segment contributions in 1993-4 were:

	Revs.	Profits
Tax operations	61%	64%
Computer services	35%	33%
Other	4%	3%

HRB operated or franchised more than 9,500 tax preparation offices during the 1994 tax filing season. In addition to the U.S., offices are located in Canada, Europe and Australia. About 18,107,000 taxpayers were served worldwide in 1993-4, down 0.5% from the level of 1992-3; the number of returns prepared was 15,530,000, down 0.3%. HRB maintained its market share in 1993-4, serving 14.7% of U.S. taxpayers either by preparing their tax returns or electronically filing returns prepared by the taxpayer or by another preparer.

CompuServe provides communications and information services to personal computer owners worldwide. At mid June 1995, its roster of active accounts was more than 3.1 million, making it the largest active membership of any online service. Currently, CompuServe is serving up to 60,000 new members each week. Block Financial Corp. is a leading vendor of point-of-sale credit card authorization services, participates in tax refund anticipation loans and sells personal finance software through Block Financial Software (formerly Meca Software, acquired in November 1993).

Through an initial public offering in January 1994, HRB sold wholly owned INTERIM Services, Inc., a major temporary services concern, for a gain of $27.3 million.

Important Developments

Aug. '95—HRB announced a number of investment initiatives for CompuServe that will have a total cost in excess of $70 million in fiscal 1996 and will reduce fiscal year 1996 profitability beginning in the quarter which ended July 31, 1995. The impact will be partially offset by a one-time pretax benefit of about $30 million relating to the accounting treatment of advertising costs. HRB said that the new initiatives should have a significant positive impact on revenues in fiscal 1997 and on earnings beginning in fiscal 1998. The company also resumed a stock buyback program in which seven million shares remain authorized for repurchase.

Jun. '95—HRB said that its fourth quarter earnings included a $0.79 per share ($83.5 million) charge for purchased research and development related to the acquisition of Spry, Inc.

Capitalization

Long Term Debt: None (1/95).

Per Share Data ($)

(Year Ended Apr. 30)

	1995	1994	1993	1992	1991	1990
Tangible Bk. Val.	NA	6.03	4.93	4.61	4.28	3.99
Cash Flow	NA	2.07	2.19	1.89	1.61	1.43
Earnings	1.01	1.54	1.68	1.49	1.31	1.16
Dividends	1.22	1.09	0.97	0.85	0.74	0.61
Payout Ratio	121%	71%	57%	56%	57%	53%
Cal. Yrs.	1994	1993	1992	1991	1990	1989
Prices - High	48¾	42¾	41⅛	38¼	22¾	18¾
- Low	33	31⅞	30⅛	19⅞	15	13⅛
P/E Ratio - High	48	28	24	26	17	16
- Low	33	21	18	13	11	11

Income Statement Analysis (Million $)

	1994	%Chg	1993	%Chg	1992	%Chg	1991
Revs.	1,215	-19%	1,495	12%	1,337	15%	1,163
Oper. Inc.	321	NM	324	15%	282	13%	250
Depr.	57.1	4%	54.7	23%	44.3	34%	33.0
Int. Exp.	3.8	-22%	4.9	-8%	5.3	-50%	10.5
Pretax Inc.	283	-4%	295	12%	264	17%	226
Eff. Tax Rate	42%	—	39%	—	39%	—	38%
Net Inc.	164	-9%	181	12%	162	16%	140

Balance Sheet & Other Fin. Data (Million $)

	1994	1993	1992	1991	1990	1989
Cash	514	335	274	228	240	252
Curr. Assets	700	590	568	648	642	595
Total Assets	1,075	1,006	963	1,036	942	826
Curr. Liab.	336	330	328	437	412	357
LT Debt	Nil	Nil	Nil	Nil	4.9	4.7
Common Eqty.	708	650	614	574	503	446
Total Cap.	708	650	614	582	516	461
Cap. Exp.	83.7	71.9	55.8	38.3	28.4	26.6
Cash Flow	221	235	207	173	153	126

Ratio Analysis

	1994	1993	1992	1991	1990	1989
Curr. Ratio	2.1	1.8	1.7	1.5	1.6	1.7
% LT Debt of Cap.	Nil	Nil	Nil	Nil	1.0	1.0
% Net Inc.of Revs.	13.5	12.1	12.1	12.1	12.0	11.4
% Ret. on Assets	15.8	18.4	16.2	14.1	13.9	13.1
% Ret. on Equity	24.2	28.6	27.3	25.9	26.0	24.1

Dividend Data

Dividends have been raised each year since Block went public in 1962. A shareholder rights plan was adopted in 1988 and amended in 1990.

Amt. of Div. $	Date Decl.	Ex-Div. Date	Stock of Record	Payment Date
0.313	Jun. 22	Sep. 06	Sep. 12	Oct. 03 '94
0.313	Nov. 30	Dec. 07	Dec. 13	Jan. 03 '95
0.313	Feb. 28	Mar. 07	Mar. 13	Apr. 03 '95
0.313	May. 26	Jun. 08	Jun. 12	Jul. 03 '95
0.320	Jun. 21	Sep. 07	Sep. 11	Oct. 02 '95

Data as orig. reptd.; bef. results of disc. opers. and/or spec. items. Per share data adj. for stk. divs. as of ex-div. date. E-Estimated. NA-Not Available. NM-Not Meaningful. NR-Not Ranked.

Office—4410 Main St., Kansas City, MO 64111. **Tel**—(816) 753-6900. **Chrmn**—H. W. Bloch. **Pres & CEO**—R. H. Brown. **VP & CFO**—W. P. Anderson. **Secy**—J. H. Ingraham. **VP Fin, Treas & Investor Contact**—Ozzie Wenich. **Dirs**—G. K. Baum, H. W. Bloch, R. H. Brown, R. E. Davis, H. F. Frigon, R. W. Hale, M. L. Rich, F. L. Salizzoni, A. C. Sorensen, M. I. Sosland. **Transfer Agent & Registrar**—Boatmen's Trust Co., St. Louis. **Incorporated** in Missouri in 1955. **Empl**-3,700. **S&P Analyst:** William H. Donald

Boatmen's Bancshares

NASDAQ Symbol **BOAT**

In S&P 500

31-JUL-95 | **Industry:** Banking

Summary: The largest bank holding company in Missouri, Boatmen's operates more than 500 locations in nine states and is also one of the largest U.S. providers of trust services.

S&P Opinion: Hold (★★★)	Recent Price • 37⅛	Yield • 3.7%
	52 Wk Range • 38-26⅛	12-Mo. P/E • 11.1

Quantitative Evaluations

Outlook
(1 Lowest—5 Highest)
• **3⁻**

Fair Value
• **36½**

Risk
• **Low**

Earn./Div. Rank
• **A**

Technical Eval.
• **Bullish** since 3/95

Rel. Strength Rank
(1 Lowest—99 Highest)
• **64**

Insider Activity
• **Neutral**

Earnings vs. Previous Year
▲=Up ▼=Down ▶=No Change

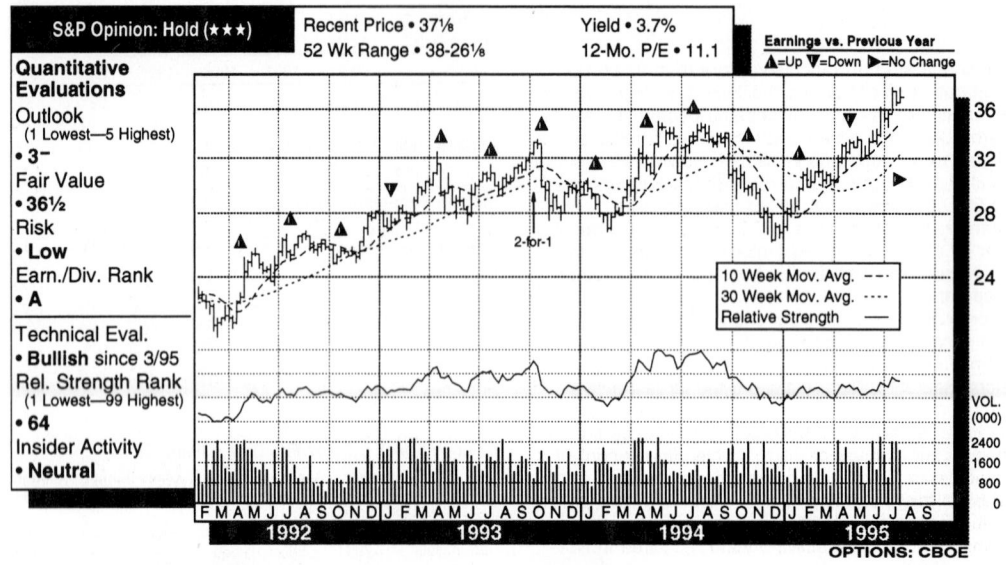

10 Week Mov. Avg. – – –
30 Week Mov. Avg. ·······
Relative Strength ——

2-for-1

VOL. (000)

OPTIONS: CBOE

Overview - 31-JUL-95

BOAT's aggressive growth strategy should continue to add to earnings in 1995, albeit at a slower pace than in recent years. Earnings should also benefit from efficiencies gained through consolidations. The increasing geographic diversification of the company's service territory will also help even out the effects of fluctuations in local economic conditions. The net interest margin narrowed a modest 15 basis points in the first half of 1995, and is expected to remain relatively flat for the next few quarters. Nonperforming assets were down 29%, year to year, to $191 million at June 30, 1995, although loan loss provisions will likely rise with projected loan growth. Expense growth should be moderate as BOAT strives to reduce its efficiency ratio to a target of less than 60% (from 62% in 1994).

Valuation - 31-JUL-95

The shares have risen strongly thus far this year given the higher valuations afforded regional bank stocks, but appear fairly valued at current levels. Earnings growth has tapered off and is only expected at about 3% in 1995 and 7% in 1996. Acquisition activity will likely subside as the company consolidates recent mergers, including $3.5 billion Worthen Banking. With a leading market share in three states of its nine-state territory, and large trust operations, BOAT is well positioned for the longer term, but we would wait to add to holdings until better prospects become more apparent in earnings.

Key Stock Statistics

S&P EPS Est. 1995	3.50	Tang. Bk. Value/Share	18.45
P/E on S&P Est. 1995	10.6	Beta	0.92
S&P EPS Est. 1996	3.75	Shareholders	29,700
Dividend Rate/Share	1.36	Market cap. (B)	$ 4.7
Shs. outstg. (M)	125.9	Inst. holdings	44%
Avg. daily vol. (M)	0.414	Insider holdings	NA

Value of $10,000 invested 5 years ago: $ 30,040

Fiscal Year Ending Dec. 31

	1995	% Change	1994	% Change	1993	% Change
Revenues (Million $)						
1Q	718.4	34%	536.2	7%	500.9	NM
2Q	750.2	33%	563.3	7%	527.2	4%
3Q	—	—	583.2	8%	540.0	6%
4Q	—	—	611.5	14%	538.7	10%
Yr.	—	—	2,294	9%	2,107	5%
Income (Million $)						
1Q	85.37	NM	85.58	8%	79.25	43%
2Q	108.7	23%	88.04	10%	79.72	35%
3Q	—	—	89.70	10%	81.33	12%
4Q	—	—	92.01	19%	77.13	173%
Yr.	—	—	355.3	12%	317.4	47%
Earnings Per Share ($)						
1Q	0.67	-18%	0.82	6%	0.77	33%
2Q	0.84	NM	0.84	9%	0.77	24%
3Q	E0.96	—	0.86	10%	0.78	2%
4Q	E1.02	—	0.88	17%	0.75	159%
Yr.	E3.50	—	3.40	11%	3.07	36%

Next earnings report expected: mid October

Boatmen's Bancshares

Business Summary - 31-JUL-95

Boatmen's Bancshares is the largest bank holding company headquartered in Missouri and is among the 30 largest bank holding companies in the U.S. At June 30, 1995, the company operated more than 500 banking offices locations in Missouri, Kansas, New Mexico, Oklahoma, Iowa, Illinois, Arkansas, Tennessee and Texas. Following the February 1995 acquisition of Worthen Banking Corp., the company has leading market shares in Arkansas, Missouri and New Mexico. Boatmen's trust operations are among the 15 largest in the U.S., with assets under management of approximately $45 billion. Other nonbank subsidiaries include mortgage banking and credit life insurance units, an insurance agency and a credit card bank.

Average earning assets of $24.5 billion in 1994 (up from $22.3 billion in 1993) consisted of: net loans 64%, investment securities 35% and other 1%. Average sources of funds were: demand deposits 16%, savings deposits 8%, interest-bearing deposits 24%, time deposits 27%, short-term borrowings 14%, long-term debt 2%, equity 8% and other 1%.

Nonperforming assets at year-end 1994 were $185.6 million (1.12% of loans and foreclosed property), compared with $285.5 million (1.90%) a year earlier. The reserve for loan losses at 1994 year end was $342.0 million ($341.1 million a year earlier), equal to 2.08% (2.30%) of net loans outstanding. Net chargeoffs were $24.3 million (or 0.15% of average loans) in 1994, compared with $34.0 million (0.24%) in 1993.

Important Developments

Jun. '95—The company reached a definitive agreement to acquire Jonesboro, Ark.-based Citizens Bancshares Corp. (assets of $224 million) for an undisclosed amount.

Apr. '95—Boatmen's acquired West Side Bancshares, Inc. (assets of $145 million) of San Angelo, Texas, for about 600,000 common shares.

Feb. '95—The company acquired Little Rock, Ark.-based Worthen Banking Corp. ($3.5 billion in assets) in a stock transaction valued at about $595 million. Under the agreement, BOAT exchanged one common share for each of Worthen's 17.3 million common shares, including shares issued for stock options. As a result of the acquisition, BOAT now has a dominant market share in Arkansas.

Capitalization

Long Term Debt: $561,738,000 (6/95).
Redeemable Preferred Stock: $1,132,000.

Per Share Data ($) (Year Ended Dec. 31)

	1994	1993	1992	1991	1990	1989
Tangible Bk. Val.	18.69	17.84	16.45	15.59	14.52	15.67
Earnings	3.40	3.07	2.25	2.03	1.95	1.86
Dividends	1.30	1.15	1.10	1.07	1.06	1.03
Payout Ratio	38%	38%	49%	53%	54%	55%
Prices - High	35	33½	28¼	24⅜	17⅞	19¾
- Low	26⅛	26⅞	20¾	14½	12¼	14⅞
P/E Ratio - High	10	11	13	12	9	11
- Low	8	9	9	7	6	8

Income Statement Analysis (Million $)

	1994	%Chg	1993	%Chg	1992	%Chg	1991
Net Int. Inc.	1,024	4%	982	16%	847	51%	562
Tax Equiv. Adj.	34.2	-4%	35.6	NM	35.9	8%	33.2
Non Int. Inc.	520	5%	493	22%	403	50%	268
Loan Loss Prov.	24.3	-60%	60.2	-55%	135	53%	88.5
% Exp/Op Revs.	62%	—	48%	—	65%	—	62%
Pretax Inc.	542	17%	464	51%	307	48%	207
Eff. Tax Rate	34%	—	32%	—	30%	—	28%
Net Inc.	355	12%	317	47%	215	43%	150
% Net Int. Marg.	4.32%	—	4.56%	—	4.40%	—	4.08%

Balance Sheet & Other Fin. Data (Million $)

	1994	1993	1992	1991	1990	1989
Earning Assets:						
Money Mkt.	NA	NA	NA	NA	NA	NA
Inv. Securities	8,091	3,325	6,925	4,333	3,589	2,870
Com'l Loans	7,976	7,491	6,350	5,170	4,744	4,584
Other Loans	8,571	7,335	6,349	4,579	4,512	4,460
Total Assets	28,927	26,654	23,387	17,635	17,469	14,542
Demand Deposits	4,590	4,770	4,032	2,875	2,766	2,411
Time Deposits	17,600	16,134	14,955	10,603	10,900	8,440
LT Debt	553	525	420	279	246	256
Common Eqty.	2,201	2,133	1,793	1,343	1,147	1,086

Ratio Analysis

	1994	1993	1992	1991	1990	1989
% Ret. on Assets	1.3	1.3	1.0	0.9	0.9	0.9
% Ret. on Equity	16.3	16.0	12.5	11.9	12.1	12.0
% Loan Loss Resv.	2.1	2.3	2.3	1.8	1.6	1.5
% Loans/Deposits	74.3	70.9	66.5	71.9	67.2	82.5
% Equity to Assets	7.9	8.0	7.7	7.8	7.6	7.4

Dividend Data (Dividends have been paid each year since 1873. A dividend reinvestment plan is available. A preferred stock purchase rights plan was adopted in 1990.)

Amt. of Div. $	Date Decl.	Ex-Div. Date	Stock of Record	Payment Date
0.340	Aug. 09	Aug. 25	Aug. 31	Oct. 01 '94
0.340	Nov. 08	Nov. 23	Nov. 30	Jan. 01 '95
0.340	Jan. 31	Feb. 23	Mar. 01	Apr. 01 '95
0.340	Apr. 27	May. 25	Jun. 01	Jul. 01 '95

Data as orig. reptd.; bef. results of disc opers. and/or spec. items. Per share data adj. for stk. divs. as of ex-div. date. E-Estimated. NA-Not Available. NM-Not Meaningful. NR-Not Ranked.

Office—One Boatmen's Plaza, 800 Market St., St. Louis, MO 63101. **Tel**—(314) 466-6000. **Chrmn & CEO**—A. B. Craig III. **Pres**—S. B. Hayes III. **EVP & CFO**—J. W. Kienker. **Secy**—D. L. Foulk. **Investor Contact**—Kevin R. Stitt (314-466-7662). **Dirs**—R. L. Battram, B. A. Bridgewater Jr., W. E. Cornelius, A. B. Craig III, I. W. Davis, J. E. Hayes Jr., S. B. Hayes III, L. M. Liberman, J. P. MacCarthy, W. E. Maritz, A. E. Newman, J. E. Ritter, W. P. Stiritz, A. E. Suter, D. D. Sutherland, T. C. Wetterau. **Transfer Agent**—Boatmen's Trust Co., St. Louis. **Incorporated** in Missouri in 1979. **Empl**-14,485. **S&P Analyst:** Stephen R. Biggar

Boeing Co.

NYSE Symbol **BA**
In S&P 500

30-SEP-95 | **Industry:** Aerospace | **Summary:** Boeing is the world's leading manufacturer of commercial jets. It also produces military aircraft and space systems.

S&P Opinion: Hold (★★★)

Recent Price • 68¼	Yield • 1.5%
52 Wk Range • 72⅜-42⅝	12-Mo. P/E • 80.3

Quantitative Evaluations

Outlook
(1 Lowest—5 Highest)
• **1+**

Fair Value
• **47¾**

Risk
• **Low**

Earn./Div. Rank
• **A-**

Technical Eval.
• **Bullish** since 11/93

Rel. Strength Rank
(1 Lowest—99 Highest)
• **58**

Insider Activity
• **Neutral**

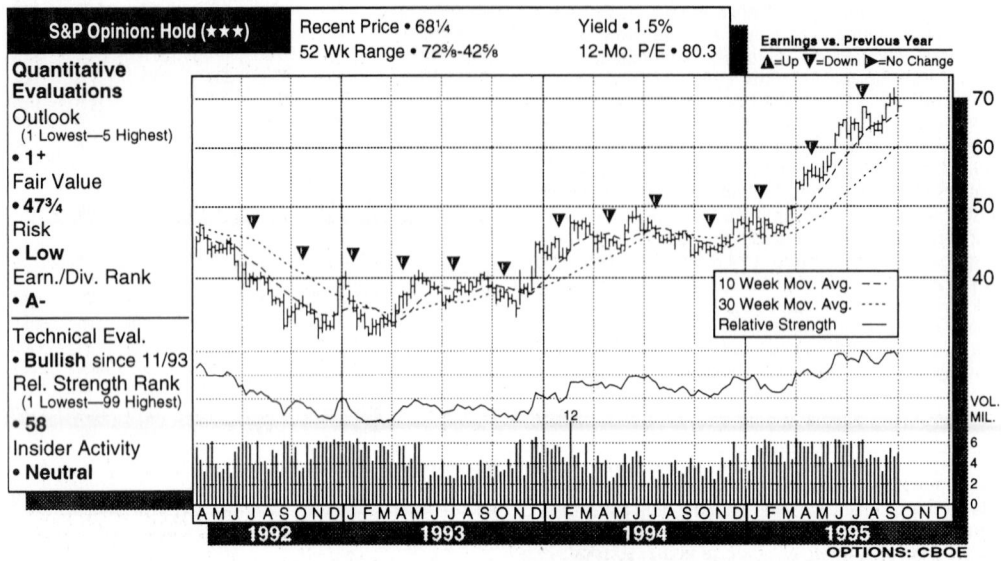

Earnings vs. Previous Year
▲=Up ▼=Down ▶=No Change

10 Week Mov. Avg. ---
30 Week Mov. Avg. ·····
Relative Strength —

VOL. MIL.

OPTIONS: CBOE

Overview - 29-SEP-95

Sales for 1995 are expected to be moderately below those of 1994, reflecting reduced deliveries of commercial aircraft. Second half deliveries should be about the same as the year-earlier period, aided by the new 777. Defense and space revenues are expected to be up modestly, due to Space Station activity. Margins will widen slightly, due to reduced headcount, stringent cost reduction efforts and lower research and development spending. However, initial 777 deliveries will limit margin expansion. Results will be hurt by a $600 million nonrecurring charge to implement a special early retirement program. The tax rate is projected to fall, reflecting the special retirement charge and R&D tax credits.

Valuation - 29-SEP-95

The rally in BA shares since late 1994 coincides with the recovery in the airline industry. International orders have already begun to improve. The company should also benefit from market share gains, spurred by the new 777 and the next-generation 737s. If orders in the first two quarters of 1995 are any judge, Boeing appears to have reversed an unfavorable market share trend. However, margins may thin with recent sale prices estimated to be substantially below list. Plans to reduce costs and increase throughput may offset price concessions. While we view BA shares as long term growth holdings, we feel the run-up in price has reduced their current attractiveness. Accordingly, we rate the shares a hold, and await a weakening of the price to the low 60s.

Key Stock Statistics

S&P EPS Est. 1995	1.25	Tang. Bk. Value/Share	27.86
P/E on S&P Est. 1995	54.6	Beta	0.70
S&P EPS Est. 1996	2.70	Shareholders	101,200
Dividend Rate/Share	1.00	Market cap. (B)	$ 23.4
Shs. outstg. (M)	342.4	Inst. holdings	58%
Avg. daily vol. (M)	1.036	Insider holdings	NA

Value of $10,000 invested 5 years ago: $ 19,458

Fiscal Year Ending Dec. 31

	1995	% Change	1994	% Change	1993	% Change
Revenues (Million $)						
1Q	5,037	-21%	6,345	-5%	6,644	-17%
2Q	5,558	3%	5,396	-32%	7,985	2%
3Q	—	—	5,063	-2%	5,153	-25%
4Q	—	—	5,120	-9%	5,656	-25%
Yr.	—	—	21,924	-14%	25,438	-16%
Income (Million $)						
1Q	181.0	-38%	292.0	-10%	325.0	-23%
2Q	-231.0	NM	222.0	-48%	426.0	-1%
3Q	—	—	185.0	-2%	189.0	-45%
4Q	—	—	157.0	-48%	304.0	-15%
Yr.	—	—	856.0	-31%	1,244	-20%
Earnings Per Share ($)						
1Q	0.53	-38%	0.86	-10%	0.96	-22%
2Q	-0.68	NM	0.65	-48%	1.25	-2%
3Q	E0.60	11%	0.54	-4%	0.56	-45%
4Q	E0.80	74%	0.46	-48%	0.89	-15%
Yr.	E1.25	-50%	2.51	-31%	3.66	-20%

Next earnings report expected: late October

Business Summary - 29-SEP-95

Boeing is the world's leading manufacturer of commercial jets. The commercial transportation division contributed 77% of revenues in 1994 (77% of profits), the defense & space division was 22% (23%), and other industries was 1% (Nil).

International sales made up 54% of revenues in 1994, with 34% going to Asia, 15% to Europe, 4% to Oceania and 1% to the Western Hemisphere and Africa. The U.S. Government accounted for approximately 19% of revenues in 1994.

A total of 270 aircraft were delivered in 1994. As of June 30, 1995, the status (in units) of commercial jet programs was:

	Backlog	1995 Deliveries	Cum. Deliveries
707	0	0	1,010
727	0	0	1,831
737	419	55	2,730
747	105	16	1,062
757	160	27	678
767	127	16	575
777	162	5	5
Total	973	119	7,891

As of June 30, 1995, the total backlog was $62.5 billion (of which $57.6 billion was commercial), versus $66.3 billion ($60.6 billion) at year-end 1994.

Major defense and space programs include the E-3 Airborne Warning and Control System (AWACS) updates, the new 767-based AWACS and B-2 bomber subcontract work. Important development programs include the V-22 Osprey tiltrotor aircraft, the RAH-66 Comanche light helicopter and the F-22 advanced technology fighter. Boeing is manager of NASA's International Space Station program.

Important Developments

Sep. '95—The company said it will postpone delivery of its GE90 powered 777 to allow completion of certification testing. The first 777 (PW4084 powered) was delivered in May 1995.

Jul. '95—International Lease Finance Corp. ordered 54 B-737s, valued at $2.25 billion. Delivery is scheduled to begin in late 1997.

Jul. '95—The company noted that 60 aircraft were delivered to customers in 1995's second quarter, down from 67 in the year-earlier period. However, orders during the period totaled 75 aircraft, versus 43 in 1994. Boeing projects total 1995 deliveries of approximately 235 transports.

Jun. '95—Directors authorized production of a stretched version of the B-777 commercial jetline, designated the 777-300. Earlier, the company had announced customer commitments to order 31 of the long-range twinjets.

Capitalization

Long Term Debt: $2,361,000,000 (6/95).

Per Share Data ($)

(Year Ended Dec. 31)

	1994	1993	1992	1991	1990	1989
Tangible Bk. Val.	28.46	26.41	23.73	23.71	20.30	17.73
Cash Flow	5.87	6.68	7.39	6.97	5.98	3.77
Earnings	2.51	3.66	4.57	4.56	4.01	1.96
Dividends	1.00	1.00	1.00	1.00	0.95	0.78
Payout Ratio	40%	27%	22%	22%	24%	40%
Prices - High	50⅛	44¾	54⅝	53	61⅞	41¼
- Low	42⅛	33⅜	33⅛	41¼	37¾	25¾
P/E Ratio - High	20	12	12	12	15	21
- Low	17	9	7	9	9	13

Income Statement Analysis (Million $)

	1994	%Chg	1993	%Chg	1992	%Chg	1991
Revs.	21,924	-14%	25,438	-16%	30,184	3%	29,314
Oper. Inc.	2,293	-16%	2,716	-9%	3,001	8%	2,780
Depr.	1,142	11%	1,025	7%	961	16%	826
Int. Exp.	217	15%	189	42%	133	133%	57.0
Pretax Inc.	1,143	-37%	1,821	-19%	2,256	2%	2,204
Eff. Tax Rate	25%	—	32%	—	31%	—	29%
Net Inc.	856	-31%	1,244	-20%	1,554	NM	1,567

Balance Sheet & Other Fin. Data (Million $)

	1994	1993	1992	1991	1990	1989
Cash	2,643	3,108	3,614	3,453	3,326	1,863
Curr. Assets	10,414	9,175	8,087	8,829	8,770	8,660
Total Assets	21,463	20,450	18,147	15,784	14,591	13,278
Curr. Liab.	6,827	6,531	6,140	6,276	7,132	6,673
LT Debt	2,603	2,613	1,772	1,313	311	275
Common Eqty.	9,700	8,983	8,056	8,093	6,973	6,131
Total Cap.	12,354	11,771	10,003	9,508	7,459	6,605
Cap. Exp.	795	1,348	2,212	1,878	1,609	1,372
Cash Flow	1,998	2,269	2,515	2,393	2,063	1,302

Ratio Analysis

	1994	1993	1992	1991	1990	1989
Curr. Ratio	1.5	1.4	1.3	1.4	1.2	1.3
% LT Debt of Cap.	21.1	22.2	17.7	13.8	4.2	4.2
% Net Inc.of Revs.	3.9	4.9	5.1	5.3	5.0	3.3
% Ret. on Assets	4.1	6.4	9.2	10.4	10.0	5.2
% Ret. on Equity	9.2	14.6	19.3	20.9	21.2	11.7

Dividend Data

Dividends have been paid since 1942. A "poison pill" stock purchase right was adopted in 1987.

Amt. of Div. $	Date Decl.	Ex-Div. Date	Stock of Record	Payment Date
0.250	Oct. 31	Nov. 04	Nov. 11	Dec. 02 '94
0.250	Dec. 12	Feb. 06	Feb. 10	Mar. 03 '95
0.250	Apr. 24	May. 08	May. 12	Jun. 02 '95
0.250	Jun. 26	Aug. 09	Aug. 11	Sep. 01 '95

Data as orig. reptd.; bef. results of disc. opers. and/or spec. items. Per share data adj. for stk. divs. as of ex-div. date.
E-Estimated. NA-Not Available. NM-Not Meaningful. NR-Not Ranked.

Office—7755 East Marginal Way South, Seattle, WA 98108. **Tel**—(206) 655-2121. **Chrmn & CEO**—F. Shrontz. **Pres**—P. M. Condit. **Sr VP-CFO**—B. E. Givan. **Secy**—H. Howard. **Investor Contact**—Larry Bishop (206-655-2608). **Dirs**—R. A. Beck, J. E. Bryson, P. M. Condit, J. B. Fery, P. E. Gray, H. J. Haynes, S. Hiller Jr., G. M. Keller, D. E. Petersen, C. M. Pigott, F. D. Raines, R. L. Ridgway, F. Shrontz, G. H. Weyerhaeuser. **Transfer Agent & Registrar**—First National Bank of Boston. **Incorporated** in Delaware in 1934. **Empl-** 115,000. **S&P Analyst:** Joe Victor Shammas

Boise Cascade

NYSE Symbol **BCC**
In S&P 500

23-OCT-95

Industry: Paper/Products

Summary: This leading forest products company manufactures paper and paper products, distributes office supplies, and is also a producer of building materials.

S&P Opinion: Accumulate (★★★★)	Recent Price • 36½ Yield • 1.6% 52 Wk Range • 47½-22⅝ 12-Mo. P/E • 7.2

Earnings vs. Previous Year
▲=Up ▼=Down ▶=No Change

Quantitative Evaluations

Outlook
(1 Lowest—5 Highest)
• **2+**

Fair Value
• **36**

Risk
• **Average**

Earn./Div. Rank
• **B-**

Technical Eval.
• **Bearish** since 7/95

Rel. Strength Rank
(1 Lowest—99 Highest)
• **15**

Insider Activity
• **Favorable**

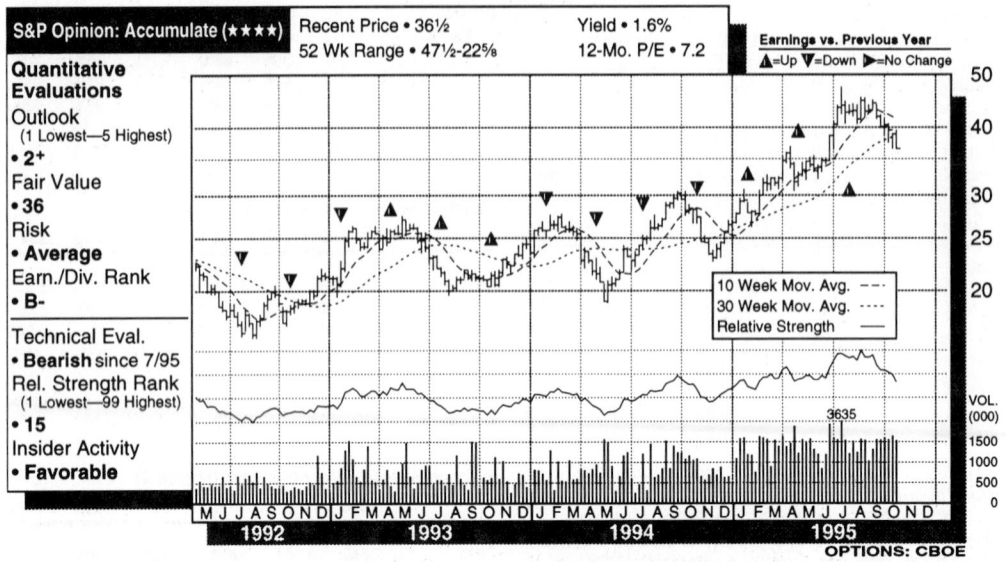

10 Week Mov. Avg. – – –
30 Week Mov. Avg. · · · ·
Relative Strength —

OPTIONS: CBOE

Overview - 19-OCT-95

Sales growth should continue through 1996, but at a moderating pace. Although slower global economies have started to ease demand in several paper grades, an expected economic rebound and the end of inventory adjustments should bring the industry back to life. Sales in BCC's office products division should also be boosted by its ongoing acquisition program. The sluggish building products segment is likely to benefit somewhat from the recent revival of the housing market. Operating margins should improve a bit on solid paper pricing, cost controls and better trends in building products. Although the bottom line will be hurt by the absence of earnings from Rainy River (takeover pending) and the loss of 50% of profits from Boise's Jackson facilities (joint venture pending), much of the EPS dilution will be offset by the use of transaction proceeds to pay down debt and buy back shares.

Valuation - 19-OCT-95

BCC's shares, which have risen strongly since the spring of 1994, have recently been experiencing a correction. The deterioration of investor sentiment has been related to worries about the recent slowdown in paper industry trends, which many feel could be signalling a nearing cyclical peak. We disagree with that sentiment, based on a belief that limited capacity expansion and an anticipated economic rebound will extend the upturn. With lower interest rates also increasing our enthusiasm about prospects in the building materials area, we see Boise's profit growth continuing through 1996 and its shares resuming their uptrend.

Key Stock Statistics

S&P EPS Est. 1995	6.80	Tang. Bk. Value/Share	22.69
P/E on S&P Est. 1995	5.4	Beta	1.14
S&P EPS Est. 1996	7.50	Shareholders	24,800
Dividend Rate/Share	0.60	Market cap. (B)	$ 1.7
Shs. outstg. (M)	47.8	Inst. holdings	76%
Avg. daily vol. (M)	0.458	Insider holdings	NA

Value of $10,000 invested 5 years ago: $ 10,194

Fiscal Year Ending Dec. 31

	1995	% Change	1994	% Change	1993	% Change
Revenues (Million $)						
1Q	1,223	30%	941.0	-4%	984.0	3%
2Q	1,270	27%	1,000	3%	974.0	6%
3Q	1,339	23%	1,090	9%	1,003	7%
4Q	—	—	1,109	11%	996.9	10%
Yr.	—	—	4,140	5%	3,958	7%
Income (Million $)						
1Q	57.04	NM	-37.60	NM	-12.10	NM
2Q	105.9	NM	-19.16	NM	-17.13	NM
3Q	118.5	NM	-31.71	NM	-24.23	NM
4Q	—	—	25.86	NM	-23.68	NM
Yr.	—	—	-62.61	NM	-77.14	NM
Earnings Per Share ($)						
1Q	0.93	NM	-1.35	NM	-0.56	NM
2Q	1.82	NM	-0.86	NM	-0.72	NM
3Q	2.03	NM	-1.19	NM	-0.91	NM
4Q	E2.02	NM	0.32	NM	-0.98	NM
Yr.	E6.80	NM	-3.08	NM	-3.17	NM

Next earnings report expected: mid January

Business Summary - 23-OCT-95

Boise Cascade is an integrated paper and forest products company. Segment contributions (profits in millions) in 1994 were:

	Sales	Profits
Paper & paper products	39%	-$38
Office products	22%	42
Building products	38%	151
Other	1%	5

Paper and paper products manufactured by BCC include uncoated business, printing, forms and converting papers (43% of its pulp and paper capacity); coated papers for magazines, catalogs and direct-mail advertising (14%); newsprint (13%); containerboard, corrugated containers for packaging food and manufactured products, point-of-purchase displays, bulk containers and other specialty corrugated products (19%); and market pulp (11%).

Through its 82%-owned Boise Cascade Office Products unit, BCC distributes over 11,000 products for use in the office, including consumable supplies, furniture and other products. Most of the products offered are purchased from other manufacturers.

Building products include plywood, lumber, particleboard, specialty wood products and engineered wood products, most of which are sold to independent wholesalers and dealers and through BCC's nine wholesale building materials distribution outlets and two satellite locations. Practical capacity at 1994 year-end was 1.9 billion sq. ft. of plywood, 760 million board ft. of lumber, 195 million sq. ft. of particleboard, and four million cubic ft. of engineered wood products.

Important Developments

Oct. '95—BCC reached an agreement to form a joint venture with Brazil-based Companhia Suzano de Papel e Celulose, with the venture to acquire (through cash contribution by Suzano) and operate BCC's pulp and paper mill, timberlands and wastepaper recycling plant in Jackson, Ala. The venture (50%-owned by each) would expand the annual production capacity of the mill to 460,000 tons from 130,000 tons.

Sep. '95—The company's Rainy River Forest Products affiliate (in which it holds a 60% equity stake and 49% voting interest) agreed to merge with the Stone-Consolidated unit of Stone Container Corp. in a transaction where Rainy River shareholders would receive shares and cash valued at about C$750 million (US$549 million). BCC anticipated the receipt of at least US$216 million in cash (80% at closing and the remainder in 1996) from the transaction, and up to 7% of the shares in the combined unit. Rainy River is a Canadian unit that owns two of BCC's former newsprint mills and one uncoated groundwood paper mill.

Capitalization

Long Term Debt: $1,496,600,000 (9/95), incl. $228,212,000 of guaranteed ESOP debt.
Preferred Stock: $337,251,000 (6/95).

Per Share Data ($)   (Year Ended Dec. 31)

	1994	1993	1992	1991	1990	1989
Tangible Bk. Val.	18.76	24.83	29.54	37.21	40.06	40.87
Cash Flow	3.13	3.89	2.22	4.01	7.22	10.99
Earnings	-3.08	-3.17	-4.79	-2.46	1.62	6.19
Dividends	0.60	0.60	0.60	1.29	1.52	1.43
Payout Ratio	NM	NM	NM	NM	94%	21%
Prices - High	30½	27½	25⅜	29¼	46¼	48
- Low	19	19½	16⅜	18⅜	19¾	39¾
P/E Ratio - High	NM	NM	NM	NM	29	8
- Low	NM	NM	NM	NM	12	6

Income Statement Analysis (Million $)

	1994	%Chg	1993	%Chg	1992	%Chg	1991
Revs.	4,140	5%	3,958	7%	3,716	-6%	3,950
Oper. Inc.	350	33%	263	68%	157	-19%	194
Depr.	236	-12%	268	NM	266	9%	245
Int. Exp.	149	NM	149	-12%	170	-7%	182
Pretax Inc.	-65.0	NM	-125	NM	-252	NM	-127
Eff. Tax Rate	NM	—	NM	—	NM	—	NM
Net Inc.	-63.0	NM	-77.0	NM	-153	NM	-79.0

Balance Sheet & Other Fin. Data (Million $)

	1994	1993	1992	1991	1990	1989
Cash	29.5	22.4	20.3	22.0	25.9	25.2
Curr. Assets	918	887	866	933	998	932
Total Assets	4,294	4,513	4,560	4,729	4,785	4,143
Curr. Liab.	658	688	750	652	758	678
LT Debt	1,856	1,840	1,942	2,191	1,935	1,498
Common Eqty.	818	969	1,136	1,422	1,556	1,564
Total Cap.	3,358	3,567	3,578	3,988	3,904	3,380
Cap. Exp.	271	221	283	299	758	699
Cash Flow	119	147	84.0	152	274	463

Ratio Analysis

	1994	1993	1992	1991	1990	1989
Curr. Ratio	1.4	1.3	1.2	1.4	1.3	1.4
% LT Debt of Cap.	55.3	51.6	54.3	54.9	49.5	44.3
% Net Inc.of Revs.	NM	NM	NM	NM	1.8	6.2
% Ret. on Assets	NM	NM	NM	NM	1.7	7.4
% Ret. on Equity	NM	NM	NM	NM	4.8	19.4

Dividend Data —Dividends have been paid since 1935. A new "poison pill" stock purchase right was issued in 1988. A dividend reinvestment plan is available.

Amt. of Div. $	Date Decl.	Ex-Div. Date	Stock of Record	Payment Date
0.150	Dec. 16	Dec. 23	Jan. 01	Jan. 15 '95
0.150	Feb. 02	Mar. 27	Apr. 01	Apr. 15 '95
0.150	Apr. 21	Jun. 28	Jul. 01	Jul. 15 '95
0.150	Jul. 28	Sep. 27	Oct. 01	Oct. 15 '95

Data as orig. reptd.; bef. results of disc. opers. and/or spec. items. Per share data adj. for stk. divs. as of ex-div. date. E-Estimated. NA-Not Available. NM-Not Meaningful. NR-Not Ranked.

Office—1111 W. Jefferson St., P.O. Box 50, Boise, ID 83728-0001. **Tel**—(208) 384-6161. **Chrmn, Pres & CEO**—G. J. Harad. **Sr VP-CFO**—T. Crumley. **VP-Treas**—I. Littman. **Investor Contact**—Vincent Hannity. **Dirs**—A. L. Armstrong, R. E. Coleman, G. J. Harad, R. K. Jaedicke, J. A. McClure, P. J. Phoenix, A. W. Reynolds, J. E. Shaw, F. A. Shrontz, E. W. Spencer, R. H. Waterman Jr., W. W. Woods Jr. **Transfer Agents**—First Chicago Trust Co. of N.Y., NYC; Co.'s office. **Incorporated** in Delaware in 1931. **Empl**-16,618. **S&P Analyst:** Michael W. Jaffe

Boston Scientific

NYSE Symbol **BSX**
In S&P 500

24-OCT-95

Industry:
Medical equipment/
supply

Summary: This maker of medical devices for cardiology, radiology and other fields is rapidly expanding its base in interventional cardiology through acquisitions and new products.

S&P Opinion: Buy (★★★★)	Recent Price • 40	Yield • Nil
	52 Wk Range • 43½-15¼	12-Mo. P/E • NM

Quantitative Evaluations

Outlook
(1 Lowest—5 Highest)
• **2**

Fair Value
• **39**

Risk
• **Average**

Earn./Div. Rank
• **NR**

Technical Eval.
• **Bearish** since 7/95

Rel. Strength Rank
(1 Lowest—99 Highest)
• **86**

Insider Activity
• **NA**

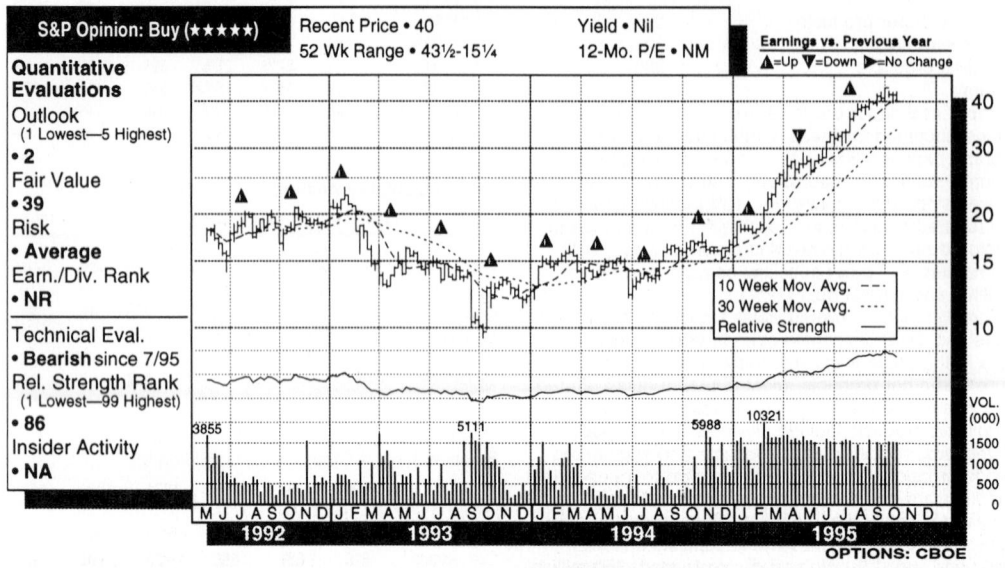

Earnings vs. Previous Year
▲=Up ▼=Down ▶=No Change

10 Week Mov. Avg. ---
30 Week Mov. Avg. ·····
Relative Strength —

OPTIONS: CBOE

Overview - 24-OCT-95

Sales are expected to rise over 35% in 1996, to $1.2 billion, bolstered by gains in established cardiology, radiology and other lines, and by strong growth in recent and pending acquisitions. Acquisitions include cardiac device producers Heart Technology, Meadox Medicals and EP Technologies (now pending), as well as SCIMED Life Systems and two smaller acquisitions in the first quarter. Results in coming quarters should also benefit from an expanded presence in international markets, the launch of a number of new products, productivity enhancements, and synergies from acquisitions. Earnings for 1996 are expected to reach $1.65 a share.

Valuation - 24-OCT-95

The shares have been in a strong uptrend since the start of 1995. In addition to improvement in the overall health care sector, the stock has benefited from investor enthusiasim over the recent acquisition of SCIMED (a leading maker of angioplasty catheters) and Cardiovascular Imaging (ultrasound diagnostics), and the planned purchase of Heart Technology and Meadox Medicals. Heart Technology's unique Rotoblater catheter removes arterial plaque with a spinning diamond coated tip, while Meadox is a leading maker of vascular prostheses used to bypass or replace damaged blood vessels. Benefits from these acquisitions, together with a revitalized R&D program, enhance long-term prospects. We recommend purchase of the stock.

Key Stock Statistics

S&P EPS Est. 1995	0.48	Tang. Bk. Value/Share	3.14
P/E on S&P Est. 1995	83.3	Beta	NA
S&P EPS Est. 1996	1.65	Shareholders	3,000
Dividend Rate/Share	Nil	Market cap. (B)	$ 6.4
Shs. outstg. (M)	151.4	Inst. holdings	47%
Avg. daily vol. (M)	0.336	Insider holdings	NA

Value of $10,000 invested 5 years ago: NA

Fiscal Year Ending Dec. 31

	1995	% Change	1994	% Change	1993	% Change
Revenues (Million $)						
1Q	215.7	105%	105.3	18%	88.94	23%
2Q	227.3	107%	109.9	16%	94.44	24%
3Q	—	—	112.2	17%	95.60	17%
4Q	—	—	121.6	20%	101.1	20%
Yr.	—	—	449.0	18%	380.1	21%
Income (Million $)						
1Q	-68.63	NM	18.03	18%	15.28	24%
2Q	45.92	145%	18.77	12%	16.77	26%
3Q	—	—	19.76	14%	17.33	14%
4Q	—	—	23.18	14%	20.31	30%
Yr.	—	—	79.74	14%	69.69	23%
Earnings Per Share ($)						
1Q	-0.45	NM	0.18	20%	0.15	15%
2Q	0.30	58%	0.19	12%	0.17	21%
3Q	E0.31	55%	0.20	18%	0.17	13%
4Q	E0.32	33%	0.24	14%	0.21	40%
Yr.	E0.48	-41%	0.81	16%	0.70	23%

Next earnings report expected: late October

Boston Scientific

Business Summary - 24-OCT-95

Boston Scientific develops, makes and markets medical devices used in various interventional medical specialties, including cardiology, gastroenterology, pulmonary medicine, radiology, urology and vascular surgery. Its products are used by physicians to perform less invasive procedures, providing effective alternatives to traditional surgery by reducing procedural trauma, complexity, risk to the patient, cost, and recovery time.

Foreign subsidiaries accounted for 15% of sales and 11% of operating profits in 1994. R&D spending was equal to 6.6% of 1994 sales (6.3% in 1993).

BSX sells products designed to treat patients with peripheral vascular disease (disease that appears in blood vessels other than the heart). Products include a broad line of products used in coronary and vascular percutaneous transluminal angioplasty, a procedure to enlarge a blocked artery by means of a balloon-tipped catheter; the Greenfield Vena Cava Filter System, a filter permanently implanted in high risk patients to reduce their incidence of pulmonary embolism; a family of intravascular catheter-directed ultrasound imaging systems for diagnostic use in the blood vessels, heart chambers and coronary arteries; and catheter-based electrophysiology (EP) diagnostic systems.

Non-vascular intervention products consist of catheters and accessories designed to drain fluid collections from the body, various forms of biopsy products and other accessory devices. The line includes products used through a flexible endoscope to treat or diagnose gastrointestinal (GI) disorders; biliary intervention products used used in endoscopic procedures in the gall bladder and bile ducts; devices used to diagnose and treat polyps and other ailments in the lower GI tract; products designed to treat patients with urinary stone disease; and the Dowd Prostate Balloon Dilatation Catheter used to treat a specific patient population suffering from benign propstatic hypertrophy.

Important Developments

Oct. '95—The company said shareholders of Heart Technology (HRTT) would vote in mid-December on its planned acquisition of HRTT for about $500 million in BSX stock. HRTT produces the Rotoblator, a catheter with a spinning diamond-coated tip used to remove arterial plaque. BSX also plans to acquire Meadox Medicals, a producer of vascular replacement devices made of collagen or textiles (for about $425 million in stock), and EP Technologies, a maker of advanced electrophysiology catheters (for $150 million in stock).

Per Share Data ($)

(Year Ended Dec. 31)

	1994	1993	1992	1991	1990	1989
Tangible Bk. Val.	3.14	2.37	2.35	1.48	0.41	NA
Cash Flow	0.91	0.76	0.62	0.48	0.28	0.08
Earnings	0.81	0.70	0.57	0.44	0.25	0.06
Dividends	Nil	Nil	Nil	NA	NA	NA
Payout Ratio	Nil	Nil	Nil	NA	NA	NA
Prices - High	17⅞	23⅝	20⅞	NA	NA	NA
- Low	11⅞	9⅜	14	NA	NA	NA
P/E Ratio - High	22	34	37	NA	NA	NA
- Low	15	13	25	NA	NA	NA

Income Statement Analysis (Million $)

	1994	%Chg	1993	%Chg	1992	%Chg	1991
Revs.	449	18%	380	21%	315	37%	230
Oper. Inc.	139	21%	115	18%	97.2	32%	73.9
Depr.	9.1	43%	6.4	45%	4.4	29%	3.4
Int. Exp.	2.0	-2%	2.1	-27%	2.8	-1%	2.9
Pretax Inc.	129	18%	109	19%	91.6	33%	68.8
Eff. Tax Rate	38%	—	36%	—	38%	—	39%
Net Inc.	79.7	14%	69.7	23%	56.6	36%	41.5

Balance Sheet & Other Fin. Data (Million $)

	1994	1993	1992	1991	1990	1989
Cash	118	103	137	66.1	0.3	NA
Curr. Assets	264	216	236	149	58.0	NA
Total Assets	432	323	299	208	102	86.0
Curr. Liab.	73.7	57.1	42.6	29.2	34.1	NA
LT Debt	8.9	6.0	6.1	23.2	19.1	31.6
Common Eqty.	340	247	249	156	48.0	24.0
Total Cap.	355	266	257	179	67.0	56.0
Cap. Exp.	35.8	35.8	17.6	7.3	3.5	7.3
Cash Flow	88.8	76.1	61.0	44.9	25.9	7.5

Ratio Analysis

	1994	1993	1992	1991	1990	1989
Curr. Ratio	3.6	3.8	5.6	5.1	1.7	NA
% LT Debt of Cap.	2.5	22.0	2.4	13.0	28.3	56.7
% Net Inc.of Revs.	17.8	18.3	18.0	18.0	14.8	4.5
% Ret. on Assets	21.1	22.9	25.3	NA	NA	6.5
% Ret. on Equity	27.2	28.8	32.7	NA	NA	25.1

Capitalization

Long Term Debt: $38,154,000 (9/95).

Dividend Data —Dividends have never been paid.

Data as orig. reptd.; bef. results of disc. opers. and/or spec. items. Per share data adj. for stk. divs. as of ex-div. date. E-Estimated. NA-Not Available. NM-Not Meaningful. NR-Not Ranked.

Office—One Boston Scientific Place, Natick, MA 01760-1537. **Tel**—(508) 650-8000. **Co-Chrmn, Pres & CEO**—P. M. Nicholas. **Co-Chrmn**—J. E. Abele. **EVP** —J. A. Ciffolillo. **SVP-Fin, CFO & Investor Contact**—L. C. Best. **SVP & Secy**—P. W. Sandman. **Dirs**—J. E. Abele, C J. Aschauer, Jr., R. F. Bellows, J. A. Ciffolillo, J. L. Fleishman, L. L. Horsch, N. J. Nicholas, Jr., P. M. Nicholas, D. A. Spencer. **Transfer Agent & Registrar**—First National Bank of Boston. **Incorporated** in Delaware in 1979. **Empl**-2,838. **S&P Analyst:** Herman Saftlas

Briggs & Stratton

NYSE Symbol **BGG**

In S&P 500

14-SEP-95

Industry: Machinery

Summary: This company is the largest producer of small gasoline engines. More than 80% of its engine sales are to manufacturers of lawn and garden equipment.

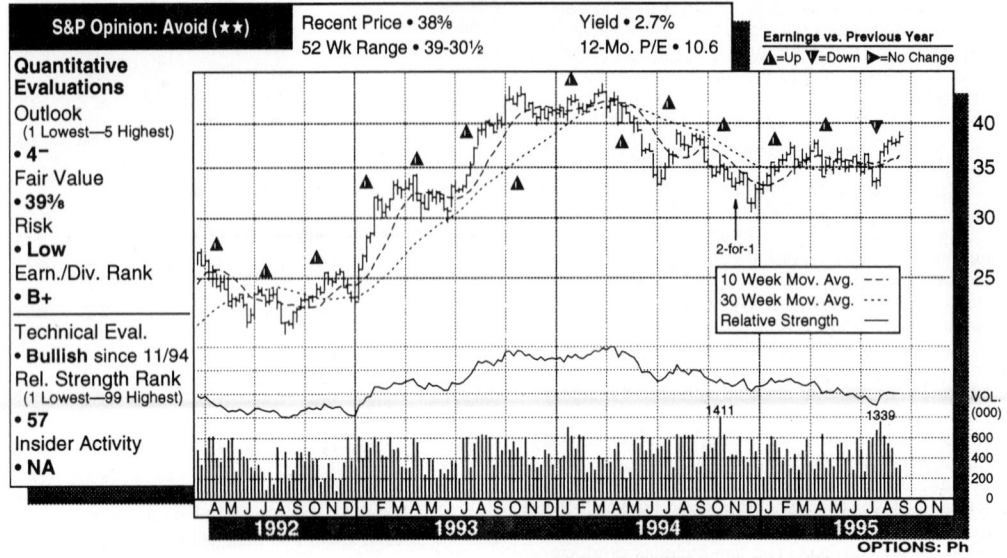

S&P Opinion: Avoid (★★)		
Recent Price • 38⅝		Yield • 2.7%
52 Wk Range • 39-30½		12-Mo. P/E • 10.6

Earnings vs. Previous Year
▲=Up ▼=Down ▶=No Change

Quantitative Evaluations

Outlook
(1 Lowest—5 Highest)
• **4⁻**

Fair Value
• **39⅜**

Risk
• **Low**

Earn./Div. Rank
• **B+**

Technical Eval.
• **Bullish** since 11/94

Rel. Strength Rank
(1 Lowest—99 Highest)
• **57**

Insider Activity
• **NA**

2-for-1

10 Week Mov. Avg. - - -
30 Week Mov. Avg. ·····
Relative Strength ——

1411   1339

VOL. (000)

1992   1993   1994   1995

OPTIONS: Ph

Overview - 14-SEP-95

We anticipate a 5.0% drop in sales for fiscal 1996, as lower volume offsets a small rise in prices. In fiscal 1995 inventory increased 64% while sales rose 4.2% and shipments rose 3.0%. Consequently, a large portion of BGG's sales in fiscal 1996 will come from inventory. With lower production resulting from the inventory drawdown, there will be pressure on gross margins as unabsorbed overhead leads to higher unit costs. Margins will also come under pressure from plant start-up costs. Sales and profit comparisons will be particularly difficult in the fiscal 1996's first two quarters. Longer term, sales and profits will be boosted by a continued shift toward higher margin, greater horsepower engines used for riding units, and a transfer of production to lower cost southern facilities.

Valuation - 14-SEP-95

We upgraded BGG to avoid from sell as fiscal 1995's final quarter (excluding a $0.41 charge) exceeded both our and "Street" estimates. BGG stated that it would be difficult to achieve higher sales and earnings in fiscal 1996 but the market ignored BGG's cautious outlook and the stock rose sharply after earnings were released. Given the very favorable investor psychology toward the shares together with the prospect that BGG will build cash as inventory declines, the company no longer warrants a sell rating. However, we believe earnings estimates for fiscal 1996 are too high and the risk of disappointment remains. Accordingly, we rate the shares avoid.

Key Stock Statistics

S&P EPS Est. 1996	3.00	Tang. Bk. Value/Share	15.00
P/E on S&P Est. 1996	12.8	Beta	0.89
Dividend Rate/Share	1.04	Shareholders	6,200
Shs. outstg. (M)	29.9	Market cap. (B)	$ 1.2
Avg. daily vol. (M)	0.073	Inst. holdings	73%
		Insider holdings	NA

Value of $10,000 invested 5 years ago: NA

Fiscal Year Ending Jun. 30

	1995	% Change	1994	% Change	1993	% Change
Revenues (Million $)						
1Q	227.9	15%	198.6	15%	172.0	9%
2Q	366.7	11%	328.9	8%	305.2	15%
3Q	450.2	17%	386.2	7%	360.9	5%
4Q	295.0	-21%	371.8	23%	301.6	11%
Yr.	1,340	4%	1,286	13%	1,139	9%
Income (Million $)						
1Q	11.42	78%	6.42	—	—	—
2Q	33.71	18%	28.64	22%	23.40	29%
3Q	47.33	33%	35.71	16%	30.82	11%
4Q	12.34	-61%	31.71	75%	18.10	121%
Yr.	104.8	2%	102.5	46%	70.35	37%
Earnings Per Share ($)						
1Q	0.39	80%	0.22	NM	-0.07	NM
2Q	1.17	18%	0.99	22%	0.81	30%
3Q	1.64	33%	1.23	16%	1.07	11%
4Q	0.42	-62%	1.10	76%	0.63	119%
Yr.	3.62	2%	3.54	46%	2.43	37%

Next earnings report expected: mid October

Briggs & Stratton

Business Summary - 13-SEP-95

Briggs & Stratton is the world's largest manufacturer of air-cooled gasoline engines for outdoor power equipment, and of locks for use in automobiles and trucks. Its auto lock business was spun off in February 1995. Contributions by industry segment in fiscal 1994 were:

	Sales	Profits
Engines and parts	93%	93%
Locks	7%	7%

Export sales accounted for 21% of the total in fiscal 1994, up from 22% in fiscal 1993.

Engines are produced in models ranging from 3 to 18 horsepower, with most output concentrated in air cooled aluminum alloy gasoline engines. In fiscal 1994, 85% of OEM engines sales were to makers of lawn and garden equipment; 15% were to manufacturers of other powered equipment, primarily for the construction industry and for agriculture. BGG makes the majority of the components used in its products; raw materials used are aluminum, steel, zinc and brass. Its largest manufacturing plant is located in Wisconsin; engines are also made in Murray, Ky., and Poplar Bluff, Mo.

Engine sales are generally highest in the March quarter and weakest in the September quarter. The June quarter is the least predictable quarter of the fiscal year.

MTD Products Inc., the company's largest customer, accounted for 18% of total sales in fiscal 1994, Tomkins PLC for 12%, and A B Electrolux 12%.

Major engine manufacturing competitors are Tecumseh Products Co., Kohler Co., Onan Corp., Honda Motor Co., Ltd., Kawasaki Heavy Industries, Ltd., Tecnamotor S.p.A. and Toro Co. Inc.

BGG designs, manufactures, sells and services automotive locks and related products for major North American car and truck manufacturers.

Important Developments

Aug. '95—BGG reported share earnings of $0.42 on a 21% decline in sales in fiscal 1995's fourth quarter, versus $1.10 in the 1994 period. Earnings for fiscal 1995's fourth quarter included a $0.41 charge for supplemental retirement benefits. The company stated that it was too early to make a precise forecast for fiscal 1996 but expressed its belief that the outlook for retail sales of outdoor power equipment seemed to be good. It added, however, that it ended the year with unusually high inventory and that engine production would be lower in fiscal 1996. It also noted that it would incur costs for the start-up of four new plants. BGG said that these factors would make it difficult to achieve higher sales and earnings in fiscal 1996.

Capitalization

Long Term Debt: $75,000,000 (6/95).

Per Share Data ($)

(Year Ended Jun. 30)

	1995	1994	1993	1992	1991	1990
Tangible Bk. Val.	NA	13.96	12.45	10.80	9.84	9.38
Cash Flow	NA	5.03	4.09	3.23	2.57	2.60
Earnings	3.62	3.54	2.43	1.78	1.26	1.23
Dividends	1.21	0.90	0.85	0.80	0.80	0.80
Payout Ratio	33%	25%	35%	45%	63%	65%
Prices - High	38	45⅛	44¾	27⅜	22⅜	17
- Low	32¼	33⅛	23⅜	20⅞	12¼	10¼
P/E Ratio - High	10	13	18	15	18	14
- Low	9	9	10	12	10	8

Income Statement Analysis (Million $)

	1994	%Chg	1993	%Chg	1992	%Chg	1991
Revs.	1,286	13%	1,139	9%	1,042	10%	951
Oper. Inc.	215	21%	178	30%	137	36%	101
Depr.	43.0	-11%	48.1	14%	42.1	12%	37.7
Int. Exp.	9.0	-20%	11.3	NM	11.2	NM	11.2
Pretax Inc.	170	49%	114	42%	80.2	51%	53.0
Eff. Tax Rate	40%	—	39%	—	36%	—	31%
Net Inc.	102	45%	70.3	37%	51.5	41%	36.5

Balance Sheet & Other Fin. Data (Million $)

	1994	1993	1992	1991	1990	1989
Cash	221	110	78.9	47.1	9.5	5.7
Curr. Assets	483	353	297	231	202	224
Total Assets	777	656	614	557	535	561
Curr. Liab.	207	158	160	126	118	160
LT Debt	75.0	75.0	75.0	75.0	75.0	75.0
Common Eqty.	404	360	312	285	271	259
Total Cap.	491	485	441	418	405	389
Cap. Exp.	40.8	38.1	40.2	32.0	37.8	79.5
Cash Flow	145	118	93.6	74.2	76.8	20.7

Ratio Analysis

	1994	1993	1992	1991	1990	1989
Curr. Ratio	2.3	2.2	1.9	1.8	1.7	1.4
% LT Debt of Cap.	15.3	15.5	17.0	17.9	18.5	19.3
% Net Inc.of Revs.	8.0	6.2	4.9	3.8	3.5	NM
% Ret. on Assets	14.3	11.1	8.8	6.7	6.5	NM
% Ret. on Equity	26.8	20.9	17.3	13.1	13.3	NM

Dividend Data —Dividends have been paid since 1929. A dividend reinvestment plan is available. A poison pill stock purchase rights plan was adopted in 1989.

Amt. of Div. $	Date Decl.	Ex-Div. Date	Stock of Record	Payment Date
0.250	Nov. 15	Nov. 29	Dec. 05	Jan. 03 '95
0.250	Jan. 18	Feb. 10	Feb. 16	Apr. 03 '95
Stk	Feb. 06	Feb. 28	Feb. 16	Feb. 27 '95
0.250	Apr. 19	May. 22	May. 26	Jun. 28 '95
0.260	Aug. 01	Aug. 29	Aug. 31	Oct. 02 '95

Data as orig. reptd.; bef. results of disc. opers. and/or spec. items. Per share data adj. for stk. divs. as of ex-div. date. E-Estimated. NA-Not Available. NM-Not Meaningful. NR-Not Ranked.

Office—12301 West Wirth St, Wauwatosa, WI 53222. **Tel**—(414) 259-5333. **Chrmn & CEO**—F. P. Stratton, Jr. **Pres & COO**—J. S. Shiely. **EVP, CFO, Secy-Treas & Investor Contact**—Robert H. Eldridge. **Dirs**—M. E. Batten, R. H. Eldridge, P. A. Georgescu, J. L. Murray, C. B. Rogers, Jr., J. S. Shiely, C. I. Story, F. P. Stratton, Jr., E. J. Zarwell. **Transfer Agent & Registrar**—Firstar Trust Co., Milwaukee. **Incorporated** in Delaware in 1924; reincorporated in Wisconsin in 1992. **Empl**-8,628. **S&P Analyst:** Leo Larkin

Bristol-Myers Squibb

STOCK REPORTS

NYSE Symbol **BMY**
In S&P 500

14-SEP-95

Industry:
Drugs-Generic and OTC

Summary: This company is one of the world's largest pharmaceutical concerns. Interests are also held in infant nutritionals, nonprescription medications, medical devices and toiletries.

S&P Opinion: Accumulate (★★★★)		
Recent Price • 67¼	Yield • 4.3%	
52 Wk Range • 69⅞-55¾	12-Mo. P/E • 17.2	

Earnings vs. Previous Year
▲=Up ▼=Down ▶=No Change

Quantitative Evaluations

Outlook
(1 Lowest—5 Highest)
• **3+**

Fair Value
• **65½**

Risk
• **Low**

Earn./Div. Rank
• **A+**

Technical Eval.
• **Bullish** since 9/94

Rel. Strength Rank
(1 Lowest—99 Highest)
• **32**

Insider Activity
• **Neutral**

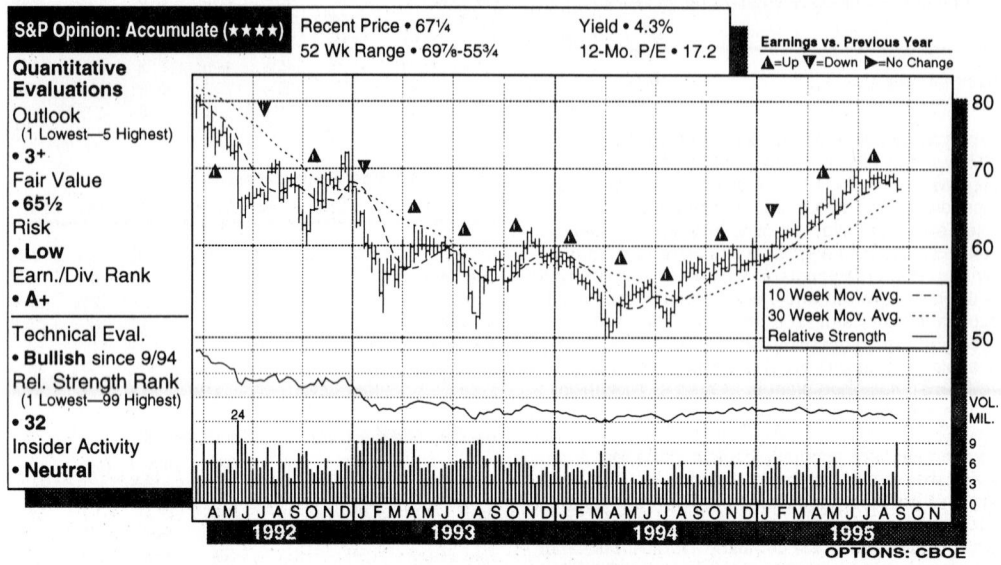

10 Week Mov. Avg. — - —
30 Week Mov. Avg. ·····
Relative Strength ——

OPTIONS: CBOE

Overview - 14-SEP-95

Sales and earnings growth are expected to moderate in 1996. Despite momentum in sales of new drugs such as Taxol anticancer, Serzone antidepressant and Glucophage for non-insulin dependent diabetes, overall pharmaceutical results are expected to be restricted by lower sales of BMY's largest selling drug, Capoten, which loses patent protection in February 1996. Strong gains in recent sales reflected contributions from three major acquisitions in 1994, as well as more favorable foreign exchange. New WIC contracts should boost nutritional product sales in 1996, but most other businesses are likely to show relatively modest growth.

Valuation - 14-SEP-95

Buoyed by strength in pharmaceuticals and an attractive yield, the shares have risen steadily since mid-1994. Renewed investor interest in drug stocks reflects a more favorable regulatory climate in Washington, firmer pricing, and rotation to defensive issues as the outlook becomes more uncertain for cyclicals. In addition to its formidable ethical drug operation, BMY has growing medical devices, OTC medicines and toiletries, and beauty products businesses. Dominant positions in growing markets, global reach, new products, and extensive cost containment programs should allow continued good EPS growth in coming years. We recommend accumulation of the shares for long-term total return.

Key Stock Statistics

S&P EPS Est. 1995	5.05	Tang. Bk. Value/Share	9.88
P/E on S&P Est. 1995	13.3	Beta	1.21
S&P EPS Est. 1996	5.30	Shareholders	163,400
Dividend Rate/Share	2.96	Market cap. (B)	$ 34.6
Shs. outstg. (M)	507.2	Inst. holdings	51%
Avg. daily vol. (M)	1.222	Insider holdings	NA

Value of $10,000 invested 5 years ago: $ 15,084

Fiscal Year Ending Dec. 31

	1995	% Change	1994	% Change	1993	% Change
Revenues (Million $)						
1Q	3,301	16%	2,834	3%	2,755	4%
2Q	3,445	16%	2,970	6%	2,802	2%
3Q	—	—	2,932	2%	2,862	-3%
4Q	—	—	3,247	9%	2,993	6%
Yr.	—	—	11,984	5%	11,413	2%
Income (Million $)						
1Q	657.0	13%	581.0	1%	574.8	8%
2Q	608.0	12%	542.0	4%	520.5	10%
3Q	—	—	620.8	2%	608.0	6%
4Q	—	—	98.64	-61%	255.8	NM
Yr.	—	—	1,842	-6%	1,959	27%
Earnings Per Share ($)						
1Q	1.29	13%	1.14	3%	1.11	8%
2Q	1.20	12%	1.07	6%	1.01	10%
3Q	E1.31	7%	1.22	3%	1.18	7%
4Q	E1.25	NM	0.19	-62%	0.50	NM
Yr.	E5.05	40%	3.62	-5%	3.80	28%

Next earnings report expected: mid October

Bristol-Myers Squibb

Business Summary - 14-SEP-95

Bristol-Myers Squibb ranks among the world's largest pharmaceutical concerns. Sales and profits by product segment in 1994 were as follows:

	Sales	Profits
Pharmaceuticals	58%	86%
Medical devices	14%	-9%
Nonprescription health	17%	17%
Toiletries & beauty aids	11%	6%

Foreign operations provided 41% of sales and 40% of profits in 1994. R&D equaled 9.2% of sales in 1994, versus 9.9% in 1993.

Pharmaceuticals comprise cardiovasculars (23% of total 1994 sales), which include Capoten, Corgard, Pravachol and Monopril; anti-infectives (13%) such as Azactam and Cefzil; anticancer agents such as Taxol (11%); and Videx AIDS therapy, Serzone antidepressant, Buspar anti-anxiety agent and other drug products.

Medical devices consist of orthopedic implants, ostomy care and wound management products, surgical instruments and other items.

Nonprescription health products comprise Enfamil infant formulas and other nutritionals, analgesics such as Bufferin, Excedrin and Nuprin; Comtrex cough/cold remedies; vitamins; and skin care products.

Toiletries and beauty aids encompass the Clairol and Ultress lines of hair care products, Nice 'n Easy and Clairesse hair colorings, Final Net hair spray, Vitalis hair preparation, Ban deodorant, and other products.

Important Developments

Aug. '95—The company said it would invest $20 million in Somatix Therapy Corp., a biotechnology firm that specializes in gene therapy, in return for certain rights in the area of cancer gene therapy.
May '95—The FDA approved BMY's new Glucophage treatment for persons with non-insulin dependent (type II) diabetes for whom diet alone is inadequate to control blood glucose levels. Diabetes affects an estimated 14 million people in the U.S., with 50% undiagnosed. Separately, the company signed a licensing agreement with Taiho Pharmaceuticals of Japan, obtaining exclusive marketing rights to the anticancer drug UFT (tegafur and uracil) in most parts of the world. Under the agreement, BMY will complete U.S. and European Phase III clinical trials for the drug for colorectal cancer and additional indications.

Capitalization

Long Term Debt: $679,000,000 (6/95).
$2 Conv. Pfd. Stock: 20,182 shs. ($1 par); red. at $50; conv. into 4.24 com.

Per Share Data ($)

(Year Ended Dec. 31)

	1994	1993	1992	1991	1990	1989
Tangible Bk. Val.	9.35	10.89	11.32	10.82	9.97	9.24
Cash Flow	4.27	4.40	3.54	4.42	3.79	1.80
Earnings	3.62	3.80	2.97	3.95	3.33	1.43
Dividends	3.66	2.88	2.79	2.49	2.19	2.03
Payout Ratio	101%	76%	94%	63%	66%	143%
Prices - High	61	67¼	90⅛	89⅜	68	58
- Low	50	50⅞	60	61⅛	50½	44
P/E Ratio - High	17	18	30	23	20	41
- Low	14	13	20	15	15	31

Income Statement Analysis (Million $)

	1994	%Chg	1993	%Chg	1992	%Chg	1991
Revs.	11,984	5%	11,413	2%	11,156	NM	11,159
Oper. Inc.	3,549	11%	3,211	NM	3,191	6%	3,012
Depr.	328	6%	308	4%	295	20%	246
Int. Exp.	83.0	17%	71.0	15%	62.0	-9%	68.0
Pretax Inc.	2,555	NM	2,571	29%	1,987	-31%	2,887
Eff. Tax Rate	28%	—	24%	—	23%	—	29%
Net Inc.	1,842	-6%	1,959	27%	1,538	-25%	2,056

Balance Sheet & Other Fin. Data (Million $)

	1994	1993	1992	1991	1990	1989
Cash	2,423	2,729	2,385	1,583	1,958	2,282
Curr. Assets	6,710	6,570	6,621	5,567	5,670	5,552
Total Assets	12,910	12,101	10,804	9,416	9,215	8,497
Curr. Liab.	4,274	3,065	3,300	2,752	2,821	2,659
LT Debt	644	588	176	135	231	237
Common Eqty.	5,703	5,939	6,019	5,793	5,416	5,081
Total Cap.	6,348	6,528	6,196	6,042	5,799	5,381
Cap. Exp.	573	570	647	633	513	555
Cash Flow	2,170	2,267	1,833	2,302	1,992	943

Ratio Analysis

	1994	1993	1992	1991	1990	1989
Curr. Ratio	1.6	2.1	2.0	2.0	2.0	2.1
% LT Debt of Cap.	10.1	9.0	2.8	2.2	4.0	4.4
% Net Inc.of Revs.	15.4	17.2	13.8	18.4	17.0	8.1
% Ret. on Assets	14.8	17.2	15.2	22.2	19.8	8.3
% Ret. on Equity	31.8	33.0	26.1	36.8	33.4	12.9

Dividend Data

—Dividends have been paid since 1933. A dividend reinvestment plan is available.

Amt. of Div. $	Date Decl.	Ex-Div. Date	Stock of Record	Payment Date
0.730	Sep. 12	Oct. 03	Oct. 07	Nov. 01 '94
0.740	Dec. 06	Dec. 30	Jan. 06	Feb. 01 '95
0.740	Mar. 07	Apr. 03	Apr. 07	May. 01 '95
0.740	Jun. 05	Jul. 05	Jul. 07	Aug. 01 '95
0.740	Sep. 12	Oct. 04	Oct. 06	Nov. 01 '95

Data as orig. reptd.; bef. results of disc. opers. and/or spec. items. Per share data adj. for stk. divs. as of ex-div. date.
E-Estimated. NA-Not Available. NM-Not Meaningful. NR-Not Ranked.

Office—345 Park Ave., New York, NY 10022. **Tel**—(212) 546-4000. **Chrmn, Pres & CEO**—C. A. Heimbold, Jr. **EVP**—K. Weg. **Secy**—A. C. Brennan. **VP & Treas**—H. M. Bains, Jr. **Investor Contact**—Jon Morris. **Dirs**—R. E. Allen, M. E. Autera, E. V. Futter, L. V. Gerstner, Jr., C. A. Heimbold, Jr., J. D. Macomber, J. D. Robinson III, A. C. Sigler, L. W. Sullivan, K. E. Weg. **Transfer Agents & Registrars**—Chemical Bank, NYC; Chemical Trust Co., SF. **Incorporated** in Delaware in 1933. **Empl**-49,500. **S&P Analyst:** H.B. Saftlas

Brown-Forman Corp.

NYSE Symbol **BF.B**

In S&P 500

21-SEP-95   **Industry:** Beverages

Summary: This leading distiller and importer of alcoholic beverages markets such brands as Jack Daniel's, Southern Comfort, Korbel and Bolla.

S&P Opinion: Hold (★★★)

Recent Price • 38⅞	Yield • 2.5%
52 Wk Range • 38⅞-26⅛	12-Mo. P/E • 17.7

Earnings vs. Previous Year
▲=Up ▼=Down ▶=No Change

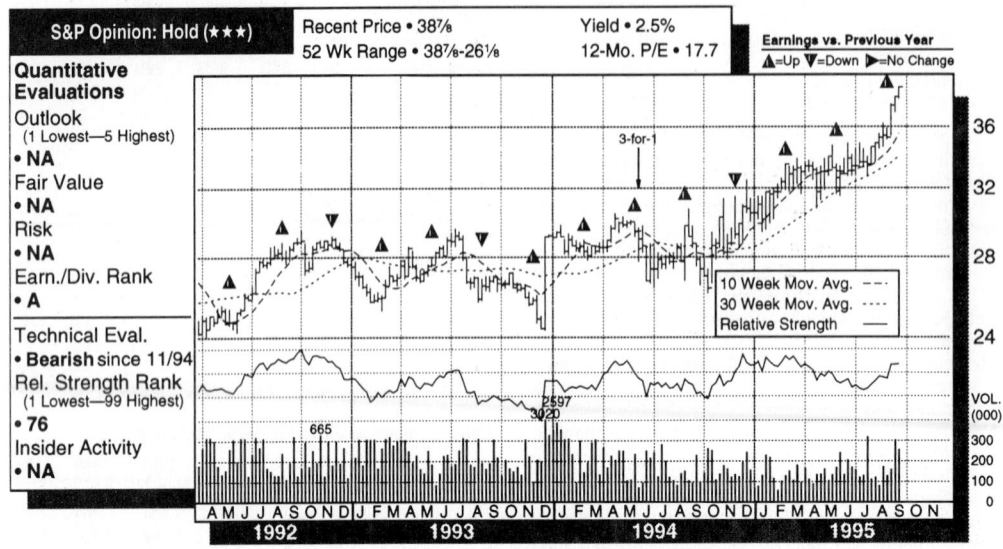

Quantitative Evaluations

Outlook
(1 Lowest—5 Highest)
• **NA**

Fair Value
• **NA**

Risk
• **NA**

Earn./Div. Rank
• **A**

Technical Eval.
• **Bearish** since 11/94

Rel. Strength Rank
(1 Lowest—99 Highest)
• **76**

Insider Activity
• **NA**

Overview - 21-SEP-95

Net sales (excluding excise taxes) in 1995-96 are expected to grow at a high single-digit pace, driven primarily by increased unit volumes for existing alcoholic beverage products, and new product introductions. Operating margins should be sustained, as benefits accruing from the company's improved wines and spirits product mix and from further cost savings arising from recent streamlining initiatives in the consumer durables segment offset increased marketing spending behind international expansion and new products. With interest expense on the modest decline, we expect earnings per share to climb nearly 12% in fiscal 1995-96, to $2.40. In fiscal 1996-97, $2.65 is seen.

Valuation - 21-SEP-95

Given our expectations of approximate 10% annual earnings per share growth through fiscal 1996-97, we view the shares as neutral for near-term performance. In spite of the mature, competitive alcoholic beverage product markets in the U.S., management has done a commendable job in the recent past of growing its sales base, primarily through product line extensions of its well known brands, and from expansion overseas. Assuming management can continue to be successful at both, we believe that further low double-digit EPS can be achieved. The company's consistent high return on shareholder equity, and growing dividend stream makes these relatively low-risk shares an attractive long-term holding.

Key Stock Statistics

S&P EPS Est. 1996	2.40	Tang. Bk. Value/Share	3.94
P/E on S&P Est. 1996	16.2	Beta	0.95
S&P EPS Est. 1997	2.65	Shareholders	4,300
Dividend Rate/Share	0.99	Market cap. (B)	$ 2.7
Shs. outstg. (M)	69.0	Inst. holdings	35%
Avg. daily vol. (M)	0.045	Insider holdings	NA

Value of $10,000 invested 5 years ago: $ 15,693

Fiscal Year Ending Apr. 30

	1996	% Change	1995	% Change	1994	% Change
Revenues (Million $)						
1Q	352.1	—	—	—	322.5	-1%
2Q	—	—	—	—	396.0	NM
3Q	—	—	1,079	NM	348.5	-1%
4Q	—	—	341.8	2%	334.4	-2%
Yr.	—	—	1,420	1%	1,401	NM
Income (Million $)						
1Q	32.15	14%	28.13	-4%	29.45	-16%
2Q	—	—	49.05	-22%	62.52	22%
3Q	—	—	37.69	-3%	38.77	4%
4Q	—	—	33.76	11%	30.33	-7%
Yr.	—	—	148.6	-8%	161.1	3%
Earnings Per Share ($)						
1Q	0.46	12%	0.41	16%	0.35	-17%
2Q	E0.77	8%	0.71	-6%	0.76	22%
3Q	E0.61	13%	0.54	12%	0.48	7%
4Q	E0.56	14%	0.49	11%	0.44	13%
Yr.	E2.40	12%	2.15	5%	2.04	9%

Next earnings report expected: late November

Business Summary - 20-SEP-95

Brown-Forman Corp. (formerly Brown-Forman Distillers) is a leading producer and importer of alcoholic beverages. Operations also include Lenox china, crystal and glassware and Hartmann luggage. Contributions in 1994-95 were:

	Sales	Profits
Wine & spirits	68%	86%
Consumer durables	32%	14%

The major American spirits produced are Jack Daniel's (sales of 4,740,000 nine-liter cases in 1994-95), Southern Comfort (2,175,000) and Early Times (1,440,000). Imported spirits include Canadian Mist (3,055,000). Major wines include Fetzer (1,940,000), Korbel Champagnes (1,060,000) and Bolla (885,000).

Consumer durables consist of Lenox china, crystal and giftware, sold through retail outlets and company-operated stores. This segment also includes Dansk, a producer of tableware and giftware, and Hartmann Luggage.

Sales outside the United States, consisting principally of exports of wines and spirits, amounted to approximately $221.4 million in fiscal 1994-95 (16% of total sales, excluding excise taxes), up from $212.9 million in 1993-94 (16%).

In October 1993, the company sold a credit card transaction processing business.

Important Developments

Aug. '95—During fiscal 1995-96's first quarter, wines and spirits segment sales rose 16%, year to year, led by worldwide sales gains for Jack Daniel's and Southern Comfort, and by strong consumer trial of Tropical Freezes, a new line of semi-frozen cocktails. Consumer durables sales were flat, as gains for Lenox china and crystal products to department and specialty stores were offset by lower revenues from direct marketing and retail divisions. Operating income growth of 10% in the quarter benefited from the increased sales, but was partially offset by higher advertising expenses in international markets, and in the U.S. for the introduction of Tropical Freezes. Net interest expense fell 9.1%, year to year, due to higher investment levels at foreign and offshore subsidiaries, and lower debt levels in the U.S.

Capitalization

Long Term Debt: $243,677,000 (7/95).

$0.40 Cum. Preferred Stock: 11,779,000 shs. ($10 par); red. at $10.25.

Class A Common Stock: 28,988,091 shs. ($0.15 par); voting.

Officers & directors own more than 60%.

Class B Common Stock: 40,008,147 shs. ($0.15 par); nonvoting.

Per Share Data ($) — (Year Ended Apr. 30)

	1995	1994	1993	1992	1991	1990
Tangible Bk. Val.	3.94	2.54	6.37	5.78	5.33	4.42
Cash Flow	2.78	2.63	2.41	2.21	2.13	1.36
Earnings	2.15	2.04	1.88	1.76	1.74	0.96
Dividends	0.97	0.93	0.86	0.78	0.72	0.63
Payout Ratio	45%	45%	46%	44%	41%	65%
Cal. Yrs.	1994	1993	1992	1991	1990	1989
Prices - High	32½	29⅝	30	28⅛	30⅝	29⅜
- Low	26⅛	24⅜	24	21⅝	18⅝	18¾
P/E Ratio - High	15	15	16	16	18	31
- Low	12	12	13	12	11	20

Income Statement Analysis (Million $)

	1995	%Chg	1994	%Chg	1993	%Chg	1992
Revs.	1,420	1%	1,401	NM	1,415	12%	1,260
Oper. Inc.	311	9%	286	-4%	299	10%	271
Depr.	43.5	-5%	46.0	5%	43.8	17%	37.3
Int. Exp.	22.6	31%	17.2	8%	15.9	15%	13.8
Pretax Inc.	247	-4%	257	6%	243	8%	224
Eff. Tax Rate	40%	—	37%	—	36%	—	35%
Net Inc.	149	-7%	161	3%	156	7%	146

Balance Sheet & Other Fin. Data (Million $)

	1995	1994	1993	1992	1991	1990
Cash	62.0	31.0	93.0	67.0	108	106
Curr. Assets	698	650	720	651	622	587
Total Assets	1,286	1,234	1,311	1,194	1,083	1,021
Curr. Liab.	286	281	210	214	190	199
LT Debt	247	299	154	114	112	114
Common Eqty.	534	452	806	723	649	584
Total Cap.	907	865	1,082	956	870	806
Cap. Exp.	51.1	27.4	33.6	52.1	51.5	50.1
Cash Flow	192	207	199	183	177	114

Ratio Analysis

	1995	1994	1993	1992	1991	1990
Curr. Ratio	2.4	2.3	3.4	3.0	3.3	3.0
% LT Debt of Cap.	27.2	34.6	14.3	11.9	12.9	14.2
% Net Inc.of Revs.	10.5	11.5	11.0	11.6	13.0	8.0
% Ret. on Assets	11.8	13.8	12.5	12.9	13.9	8.0
% Ret. on Equity	30.1	28.6	20.4	21.3	23.6	14.3

Dividend Data —Dividends have been paid on Class A shares since 1945 and on Class B since 1960. Dividends are identical on the two classes of stock. A dividend reinvestment plan is available.

Amt. of Div. $	Date Decl.	Ex-Div. Date	Stock of Record	Payment Date
0.237	Jul. 28	Aug. 30	Sep. 06	Oct. 01 '94
0.248	Nov. 17	Nov. 28	Dec. 02	Jan. 01 '95
0.248	Jan. 26	Mar. 03	Mar. 09	Apr. 01 '95
0.248	May. 25	Jun. 06	Jun. 09	Jul. 01 '95
0.248	Jul. 27	Aug. 31	Sep. 05	Oct. 01 '95

Data as orig. reptd.; bef. results of disc. opers. and/or spec. items. Per share data adj. for stk. divs. as of ex-div. date. E-Estimated. NA-Not Available. NM-Not Meaningful. NR-Not Ranked.

Office—850 Dixie Highway, Louisville, KY 40210. **Tel**—(502) 585-1100. **Chrmn**—W. L. L. Brown Jr. **Pres & CEO**—O. Brown II. **SVP & Secy**—M. B. Crutcher. **Treas**—C. A. Sailer. **Investor Contact**—D. Jackson. **Dirs**—G. G. Brown III, O. Brown II, W. L. L. Brown Jr., O. B. Frazier, R. P. Mayer, S. E. O'Neil, J. S. Speed, W. M. Street, J. S. Welch. **Transfer Agent & Registrar**—First Chicago Trust Co. of New York, NYC. **Incorporated** in Delaware in 1933. **Empl**-7,300. **S&P Analyst:** Kenneth A. Shea

Brown Group

NYSE Symbol **BG**
In S&P 500

27-SEP-95

Industry:
Leather/shoes

Summary: Brown Group manufactures, imports, and retails a wide variety of women's, men's and children's shoes.

S&P Opinion: Avoid (★★)	Recent Price • 18⅝ Yield • 5.4%
	52 Wk Range • 35⅜-16 12-Mo. P/E • 29.1

Quantitative Evaluations

Outlook
(1 Lowest—5 Highest)
• **NA**

Fair Value
• **NA**

Risk
• **Low**

Earn./Div. Rank
• **B-**

Technical Eval.
• **Bearish** since 9/95

Rel. Strength Rank
(1 Lowest—99 Highest)
• **4**

Insider Activity
• **Neutral**

Earnings vs. Previous Year
▲=Up ▼=Down ▶=No Change

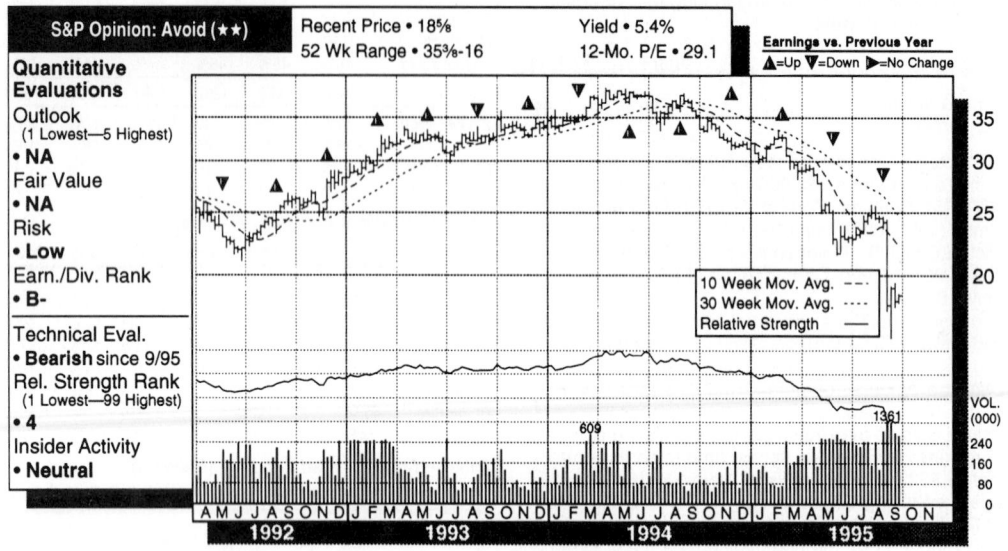

10 Week Mov. Avg. ─ ─ ─
30 Week Mov. Avg. ⋯⋯⋯
Relative Strength ──

Overview - 27-SEP-95

Sales growth from ongoing businesses in fiscal 1995-96 could be under some pressure, mainly in the first half of the year, reflecting soft retail conditions. Sales at Famous Footwear could increase somewhat, however, on store expansion and slightly higher comparable store sales. Despite the benefits from past restructuring efforts, margins are also expected to be under some pressure, particularly in the first half. Earnings will be hurt by a net special charge of $0.41 to close the company's remaining five factories in the U.S. Over the longer term, operations could benefit from the absence of overhead expenses at these factories.

Valuation - 27-SEP-95

These shares have been trending downward since mid-1994, reflecting lower than expected earnings growth beginning in the third quarter of fiscal 1994-95 due to weak retail sales. To make matters worse, BG negatively surprised the investment community by reporting losses in the first and second quarters of fiscal 1995-96, and cutting the dividend to $0.25 from $0.40 with the September 7 dividend announcement. BG's management has done an excellent job restructuring the company, including the recent plans to close the five remaining factories in the U.S., to improve the cost structure and refocus the company for growth. But, until the retail market shows some pick-up, we would avoid this stock.

Key Stock Statistics

S&P EPS Est. 1996	0.60	Tang. Bk. Value/Share	12.51
P/E on S&P Est. 1996	31.0	Beta	0.63
S&P EPS Est. 1997	1.80	Shareholders	6,000
Dividend Rate/Share	1.00	Market cap. (B)	$0.332
Shs. outstg. (M)	17.9	Inst. holdings	56%
Avg. daily vol. (M)	0.200	Insider holdings	NA

Value of $10,000 invested 5 years ago: $ 9,792

Fiscal Year Ending Jan. 31

	1996	% Change	1995	% Change	1994	% Change
Revenues (Million $)						
1Q	357.4	-3%	369.5	-5%	389.1	-11%
2Q	342.9	-3%	353.0	-7%	381.0	-8%
3Q	—	—	406.9	-9%	445.8	-9%
4Q	—	—	322.2	-16%	381.9	-15%
Yr.	—	—	1,462	-9%	1,598	-11%
Income (Million $)						
1Q	-4.41	NM	7.33	64%	4.48	NM
2Q	-8.38	NM	7.53	16%	6.48	19%
3Q	—	—	14.93	16%	12.87	19%
4Q	—	—	3.77	NM	-30.55	NM
Yr.	—	—	33.57	NM	-6.71	NM
Earnings Per Share ($)						
1Q	-0.25	NM	0.42	75%	0.24	NM
2Q	-0.48	NM	0.43	34%	0.32	-16%
3Q	E0.74	-13%	0.85	5%	0.81	9%
4Q	E0.59	181%	0.21	NM	-1.76	NM
Yr.	E0.60	-69%	1.91	NM	-0.39	NM

Next earnings report expected: late November

Business Summary - 27-SEP-95

Brown Group operates in the footwear business. In 1994, it sold its specialty retailing business, comprised of 343 Cloth World stores, to Fabri-Centers of America, Inc., for $62 million. In 1994, BG also closed its Maryland Square catalog business, and completed its withdrawal from the Wohl Leased Shoe Department business. This business involved the management of over 500 shoe departments in department stores.

Footwear operations include manufacturing, importing, foreign sourcing and retailing a wide variety of women's (61% of total footwear sales in 1994-95), men's (23%) and children's (16%) shoes.

Approximately 54% of 1994-95 footwear segment sales were made at footwear retail operations. Through its Pagoda division, BR sources a wide variety of footwear primarily from the Far East and Brazil for other BG divisions and for outside customers, which primarily consist of large discount store operations. During 1994-95, this division was responsible for sourcing 85 million pairs of shoes. BG's Brown Shoe Company division has annual domestic manufacturing capacity of approximately seven million pairs.

Major women's brands include Airstep, Brittania, Connie, DeLiso, Donnay, Dr. Scholl's, Fanfares, Jordache, Life Stride, Maserati, Melange, Naturalizer, NaturalSport, Natural Sold, Penaljo, Revelations and Waikiki; men's brands include Brittania, Britt Gear, Donnay, Dr. Scholl's, Reed St. James, Regal, Remington and UnionBay; and children's brands include Barbie for Girls, Buster Brown, Candie's, Casper, Disney, Disney Babies, Donnay, Fanfares, The Flintstones, G.I. Joe, Jordache, The Lion King, Mickey Unlimited, 101 Dalmatians, Playskool, Remington, Rookie League, UnionBay, Waikiki, Wildcats and YDS.

The company's footwear retail operations include 418 Naturalizer stores, 722 Famous Footwear stores, and 14 F. X. La Salle stores.

Important Developments

Sep. '95—BG reported a $0.07 a share loss, excluding net special charges, in the second quarter of fiscal 1995-96. BG attributed this loss to ongoing soft business at its wholesale units, which was partly offset by higher sales at Famous Footwear. Separately, BG took a special charge of $0.55 a share in order to close its five remaining domestic plants whose products could barely compete with low cost imports. BG could improve its pretax earnings by about $10 million annually due to the overhead reductions made by these plant closings. A part of this charge was offset by a one-time credit of $0.14 associated with inventory liquidation.

Capitalization

Long Term Debt: $57,467,000 (7/29/95), incl. leases.

Per Share Data ($)

(Year Ended Jan. 31)

	1995	1994	1993	1992	1991	1990
Tangible Bk. Val.	13.90	13.27	16.69	18.10	19.47	19.39
Cash Flow	3.17	3.17	1.93	2.68	3.52	3.39
Earnings	1.91	-0.39	0.27	0.92	1.85	1.78
Dividends	1.60	1.60	1.60	1.60	1.60	1.60
Payout Ratio	84%	NM	594%	176%	87%	91%
Cal. Yrs.	1994	1993	1992	1991	1990	1989
Prices - High	38⅞	NA	29	28⅜	30	35½
- Low	30⅝	NA	21	21⅝	19¾	26¾
P/E Ratio - High	20	NA	NM	31	16	20
- Low	16	NA	NM	24	11	15

Income Statement Analysis (Million $)

	1995	%Chg	1994	%Chg	1993	%Chg	1992
Revs.	1,465	-8%	1,598	-11%	1,791	4%	1,728
Oper. Inc.	89.0	20%	74.0	25%	59.0	-9%	65.0
Depr.	22.1	-3%	22.8	-20%	28.4	-6%	30.1
Int. Exp.	15.8	-10%	17.6	5%	16.8	5%	16.0
Pretax Inc.	60.0	NM	-11.8	NM	5.0	-77%	22.0
Eff. Tax Rate	44%	—	NM	—	8.50%	—	30%
Net Inc.	33.6	NM	-6.7	NM	4.7	-70%	15.7

Balance Sheet & Other Fin. Data (Million $)

	1995	1994	1993	1992	1991	1990
Cash	18.9	16.9	21.6	18.7	16.3	22.3
Curr. Assets	479	612	580	514	536	531
Total Assets	637	772	760	705	737	713
Curr. Liab.	220	371	318	217	250	225
LT Debt	133	135	123	145	129	132
Common Eqty.	250	234	289	313	336	339
Total Cap.	396	376	419	468	483	485
Cap. Exp.	32.5	30.2	24.3	24.7	32.6	31.3
Cash Flow	55.7	16.1	33.1	45.8	60.4	58.8

Ratio Analysis

	1995	1994	1993	1992	1991	1990
Curr. Ratio	2.2	1.6	1.8	2.4	2.1	2.4
% LT Debt of Cap.	33.7	36.0	29.4	30.9	26.6	27.3
% Net Inc.of Revs.	2.3	NM	0.3	0.9	1.8	1.7
% Ret. on Assets	4.7	NM	0.6	2.2	4.4	4.3
% Ret. on Equity	13.8	NM	1.5	4.8	9.5	9.2

Dividend Data —Dividends have been paid since 1923. A dividend reinvestment plan is available. A "poison pill" stock purchase rights plan was adopted in 1986.

Amt. of Div. $	Date Decl.	Ex-Div. Date	Stock of Record	Payment Date
0.400	Sep. 08	Sep. 13	Sep. 19	Oct. 01 '94
0.400	Dec. 01	Dec. 06	Dec. 12	Jan. 03 '95
0.400	Mar. 02	Mar. 07	Mar. 13	Apr. 01 '95
0.400	May. 25	May. 30	Jun. 05	Jul. 01 '95
0.250	Sep. 07	Sep. 14	Sep. 18	Oct. 02 '95

Data as orig. reptd.; bef. results of disc. opers. and/or spec. items. Per share data adj. for stk. divs. as of ex-div. date. E-Estimated. NA-Not Available. NM-Not Meaningful. NR-Not Ranked. Fisc. 1995-96 2nd qtr EPS incls. -$0.41 in net spec. charges.

Office—8400 Maryland Ave., St. Louis, MO 63105. **Tel**—(314) 854-4000. **Chrmn, Pres & CEO**—B. A. Bridgewater, Jr. **EVP, CFO & Investor Contact**—H. E. Rich. **VP & Secy**—R. D. Pickle. **Dirs**—J. L. Bower, B. A. Bridgewater, Jr., J. C. Esrey, J. F. Lane, R. A. Liddy, J. D. Macomber, W. E. Maritz, E. C. Meyer, H. E. Rich, M. I. Sosland, D. R. Toll. **Transfer Agent & Registrar**— Boatmen's Trust Co., St. Louis. **Incorporated** in New York in 1913. **Empl**-14,500. **S&P Analyst:** Elizabeth Vandeventer

Browning-Ferris Industries

STOCK REPORTS

NYSE Symbol **BFI**
In S&P 500

09-SEP-95

Industry:
Pollution Control

Summary: BFI is one of the largest providers of solid waste collection, processing, transportation and disposal services for commercial, industrial, governmental and residential customers.

S&P Opinion: Hold (★★★)	Recent Price • 35	Yield • 1.9%
	52 Wk Range • 40%-25%	12-Mo. P/E • 18.7

Earnings vs. Previous Year
▲=Up ▼=Down ▶=No Change

Quantitative Evaluations

Outlook
(1 Lowest—5 Highest)
• **3+**

Fair Value
• **32¾**

Risk
• **Average**

Earn./Div. Rank
• **A-**

Technical Eval.
• **Bearish** since 7/95

Rel. Strength Rank
(1 Lowest—99 Highest)
• **23**

Insider Activity
• **NA**

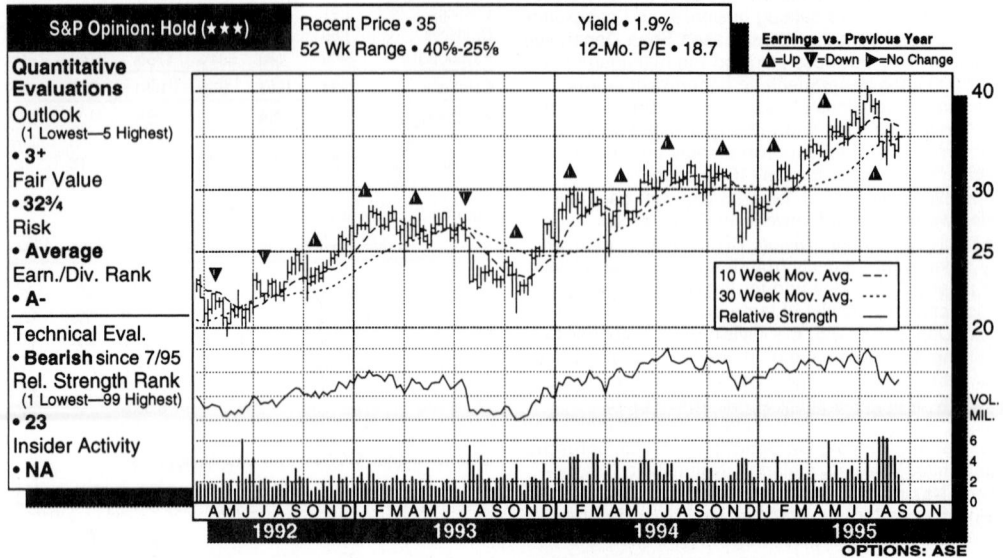

10 Week Mov. Avg. ---
30 Week Mov. Avg. ····
Relative Strength —

OPTIONS: ASE

Overview - 23-AUG-95

BFI should extend its profit growth into fiscal 1996 aided by acquisitions. Collection margins will benefit from higher equipment productivity and contributions from New York City operations. Disposal and transfer volumes from same sites may slow as recent aggressive rate hikes has led to a diversion of business to competing fills and waste-to-energy plants. Margins, however, should improve as legal costs ease. Medical waste volumes should increase moderately though margins should widen as collection costs per unit decline. While recycling growth should remain heady, some softening in prices for corrugated and newspaper is likely after fiscal 1995's sharp increases. International growth may slow, as fiscal 1995 benefited from two major acquisitions. Interest costs will increase.

Valuation - 23-AUG-95

BFI has been a strong performer in 1995 as its profits have been propelled by recent acquisitions. The 1994 acquisitions of Attwoods Plc and Otto Waste Service marked BFI's major thrust into international markets. In fiscal 1995 international revenues will account for more than 25% the firm's total business, up from 11% in fiscal 1993. BFI also is aggressively building a presence in the important New York City collection market where authorities are breaking up the local carting cartels. While long-term prospects are bright, our recent downgrading reflects our discomfort with BFI's premium earnings multiple in view of the cyclical nature of much of its business.

Key Stock Statistics

S&P EPS Est. 1995	1.95	Tang. Bk. Value/Share	4.60
P/E on S&P Est. 1995	17.9	Beta	1.65
S&P EPS Est. 1996	2.20	Shareholders	20,000
Dividend Rate/Share	0.68	Market cap. (B)	$ 7.5
Shs. outstg. (M)	212.9	Inst. holdings	68%
Avg. daily vol. (M)	0.981	Insider holdings	NA

Value of $10,000 invested 5 years ago: $ 10,484

Fiscal Year Ending Sep. 30

	1995	% Change	1994	% Change	1993	% Change
Revenues (Million $)						
1Q	1,293	39%	928.3	9%	848.0	6%
2Q	1,409	43%	984.2	19%	826.0	6%
3Q	1,550	34%	1,161	30%	892.7	7%
4Q	—	—	1,241	34%	928.5	7%
Yr.	—	—	4,315	23%	3,495	6%
Income (Million $)						
1Q	89.57	52%	58.99	13%	52.29	30%
2Q	92.81	50%	61.92	22%	50.84	31%
3Q	106.3	32%	80.81	96%	41.24	-11%
4Q	—	—	82.25	55%	53.08	6%
Yr.	—	—	284.0	44%	197.4	12%
Earnings Per Share ($)						
1Q	0.45	32%	0.34	10%	0.31	19%
2Q	0.47	38%	0.34	13%	0.30	20%
3Q	0.53	29%	0.41	71%	0.24	-20%
4Q	E0.50	19%	0.42	35%	0.31	3%
Yr.	E1.95	28%	1.52	32%	1.15	4%

Next earnings report expected: late October

Business Summary - 29-AUG-95

BFI collects, processes for recycling, transports and disposes of a wide range of commercial, industrial, medical and residential solid wastes. Revenues in recent fiscal years were derived from:

	1994	1993
North American operations:		
Collection	50%	56%
Disposal & transfer	19%	21%
Medical waste	3%	4%
Recycling	8%	6%
Services group	2%	2%
International operations	18%	11%

The company's subsidiaries and affiliates operate in about 400 locations in North America and 250 locations elsewhere. Solid waste collection operations are conducted in approximately 430 locations, primarily in North America, Europe and Australia. As of September 30, 1994, BFI operated 97 active solid waste sanitary landfill sites in North America, with an additional 49 sites overseas. The company also operated 110 transfer stations where solid wastes are compacted for transfer to distant final disposal sites. Medical waste services are provided in approximately 100 of its locations, while recycling services are provided in about 230 locations, serving 5.0 million households. BFI is also involved in resource recovery facilities, and sweeping and portable restroom services. Hazardous waste services were discontinued in fiscal 1990.

From time to time, BFI may be the subject of investigations into alleged antitrust activities in the waste hauling industry and may face fines in connection with hazardous waste sites.

Important Developments

Aug. '95—BFI acquired Metro Health Waste Processing Inc., an operator of a medical waste processing plant in New York City. The transaction reflects BFI's strategy to build a major presence in the New York market.
Jun. '95—BFI sold 11,499,200 units of 7.25% Automatic Common Exchange Securities (ACES) at $35.625 each. Proceeds from the offering will not be received until June 30, 1998 when the ACES are converted into no more than 11.5 million BFI common shares and no less than 9.6 million.

Capitalization

Long Term Debt: $2,278,068,000 (6/95), incl. $345 million of 6.25% debs. conv. into com. at $41 a sh., and $400 million of 6.75% debs. conv. into com. at $52.50 a sh.
7.25% Automatic Common Exchange Securities: 11,499,200 units conv. into common on June 30, 1998 at a rate of 0.833 to 1.0 units per BFI common share.

Per Share Data ($) (Year Ended Sep. 30)

	1994	1993	1992	1991	1990	1989
Tangible Bk. Val.	6.74	6.24	6.52	4.72	4.65	6.26
Cash Flow	3.96	3.37	3.42	2.69	3.67	3.20
Earnings	1.52	1.15	1.11	0.42	1.68	1.74
Dividends	0.68	0.68	0.68	0.68	0.64	0.56
Payout Ratio	45%	59%	65%	159%	38%	32%
Prices - High	32⅞	28⅝	27⅛	30¾	49¼	42¾
- Low	24¼	20⅞	19½	16⅞	20¾	26⅞
P/E Ratio - High	22	25	24	73	29	25
- Low	16	18	18	40	12	15

Income Statement Analysis (Million $)

	1994	%Chg	1993	%Chg	1992	%Chg	1991
Revs.	4,315	23%	3,495	6%	3,287	3%	3,183
Oper. Inc.	1,003	27%	790	10%	717	-8%	782
Depr.	459	21%	380	4%	367	5%	349
Int. Exp.	105	17%	89.6	3%	86.9	5%	83.1
Pretax Inc.	499	53%	327	14%	288	146%	117
Eff. Tax Rate	40%	—	40%	—	39%	—	44%
Net Inc.	284	44%	197	12%	176	171%	65.0

Balance Sheet & Other Fin. Data (Million $)

	1994	1993	1992	1991	1990	1989
Cash	141	232	389	141	139	133
Curr. Assets	1,186	925	1,013	719	772	605
Total Assets	5,797	4,296	4,068	3,656	3,574	3,017
Curr. Liab.	1,179	924	780	715	749	599
LT Debt	1,459	1,079	1,094	1,152	1,193	945
Common Eqty.	2,392	1,533	1,460	1,114	1,162	1,242
Total Cap.	3,951	2,634	2,579	2,292	2,380	2,246
Cap. Exp.	984	665	514	497	481	714
Cash Flow	743	577	543	415	562	484

Ratio Analysis

	1994	1993	1992	1991	1990	1989
Curr. Ratio	1.0	1.0	1.3	1.0	1.0	1.0
% LT Debt of Cap.	36.9	41.0	42.4	50.3	50.1	42.1
% Net Inc.of Revs.	6.6	5.6	5.3	2.0	8.7	10.3
% Ret. on Assets	5.3	4.7	4.3	1.8	7.7	9.9
% Ret. on Equity	13.8	13.0	13.1	5.7	21.1	22.9

Dividend Data —Dividends have been paid since 1950. A dividend reinvestment plan is available. A poison pill stock purchase rights plan was adopted in 1988.

Amt. of Div. $	Date Decl.	Ex-Div. Date	Stock of Record	Payment Date
0.170	Sep. 07	Sep. 13	Sep. 19	Oct. 06 '94
0.170	Dec. 08	Dec. 14	Dec. 20	Jan. 06 '95
0.170	Mar. 02	Mar. 13	Mar. 17	Apr. 07 '95
0.170	Jun. 07	Jun. 14	Jun. 16	Jul. 07 '95

Data as orig. reptd.; bef. results of disc. opers. and/or spec. items. Per share data adj. for stk. divs. as of ex-div. date.
E-Estimated. NA-Not Available. NM-Not Meaningful. NR-Not Ranked.

Office—Browning-Ferris Bldg., 757 N. Eldridge, P.O. Box 3151, Houston, TX 77253. **Tel**—(713) 870-8100. **Chrmn & CEO**—W. D. Ruckelshaus. **Pres & COO**—B. E. Ranck. **SVP & CFO**—J. E. Curtiss. **VP & Secy**—G. K. Burger. **VP & Treas**—H. L. Hirvela. **VP & Investor Contact**—Brett Frazier. **Dirs**—W. T. Butler, C. J. Grayson, Jr., G. Grinstein, N. A. Myers, U. Otto, H. J. Phillips, Sr., B. E. Ranck, J. L. Roberts, Jr., W. D. Ruckelshaus, M. J. Shapiro, R. M. Teeter, L. A. Waters, M. v. N. Whitman, P. S. Willmott. **Transfer Agent & Registrar**—First Chicago Trust Co. of New York, Jersey City, NJ. **Incorporated** in Delaware in 1970. **Empl**- 37,000. **S&P Analyst:** Stephen R. Klein

Brunswick Corp.

NYSE Symbol **BC**
In S&P 500

24-OCT-95

Industry:
Leisure/Amusement

Summary: This company is the world's largest manufacturer of recreational boats and a leading maker of marine engines. Its brands include Bayliner, Sea Ray and Mercury.

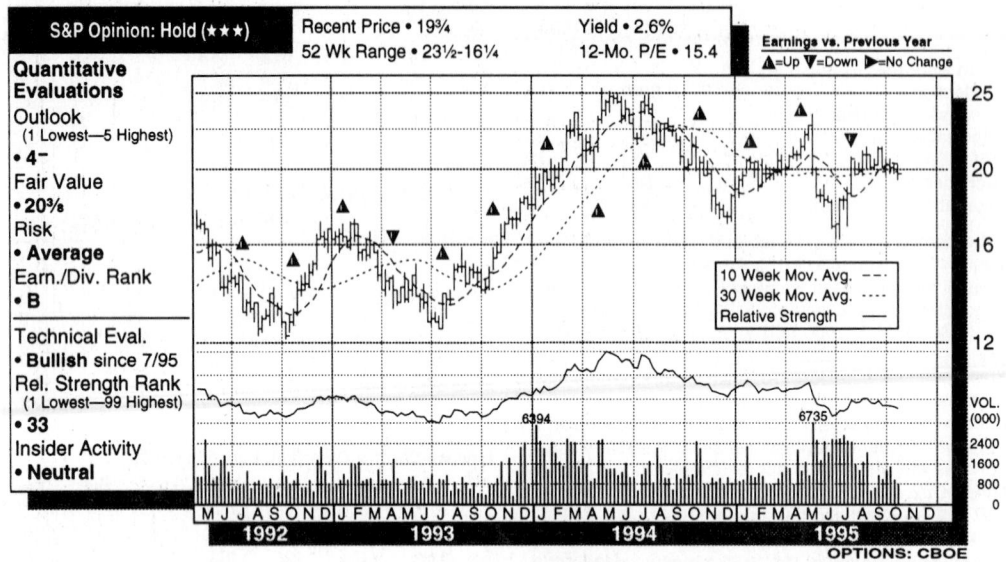

S&P Opinion: Hold (★★★)	Recent Price • 19¾	Yield • 2.6%
	52 Wk Range • 23½-16¼	12-Mo. P/E • 15.4

Quantitative Evaluations

Outlook
(1 Lowest—5 Highest)
• **4⁻**

Fair Value
• **20⅛**

Risk
• **Average**

Earn./Div. Rank
• **B**

Technical Eval.
• **Bullish** since 7/95

Rel. Strength Rank
(1 Lowest—99 Highest)
• **33**

Insider Activity
• **Neutral**

Earnings vs. Previous Year
▲=Up ▼=Down ▶=No Change

10 Week Mov. Avg. - - -
30 Week Mov. Avg. ····
Relative Strength ——

VOL. (000)

OPTIONS: CBOE

Overview - 24-OCT-95

We expect BC to generally maintain its strong market position in the boating and marine engine industry in the remainder of 1995 and in 1996. However, the near-term outlook for consumer spending, particularly on durable goods such as boats, appears less robust than previously expected. In the recreation segment, results in 1995's fourth quarter, as well as in 1996, will get a boost from initial shipments of the new Frameworx bowling scoring system and a recent restructuring. We also expect the company to be looking for acquisitions in the recreation segment. Longer term, a federally mandated transition toward more environmentally friendly products is likely to raise the prices that consumers pay for engine products and could restrain sales in the second half of this decade.

Valuation - 24-OCT-95

The planned divestitures of the unprofitable Circus World Pizza operations and the golf club shaft business should help recreation profits in 1995's fourth quarter and in 1996 as well. We also believe that although consumer spending could slow down, there is enough pent up demand for boats that modest growth in the marine segment is likely in 1996. As a result, we recently raised our 1996 earnings estimate to $1.90 a share from $1.75 and upgraded our opinion on the stock to hold. BC also has a strong balance sheet, which should be helpful if the marine industry faces another cyclical downturn. Our estimate for 1995 includes $0.29 a share in nonrecurring charges.

Key Stock Statistics

S&P EPS Est. 1995	1.37	Tang. Bk. Value/Share	6.09
P/E on S&P Est. 1995	14.4	Beta	1.62
S&P EPS Est. 1996	1.90	Shareholders	25,800
Dividend Rate/Share	0.50	Market cap. (B)	$ 1.9
Shs. outstg. (M)	95.8	Inst. holdings	76%
Avg. daily vol. (M)	0.219	Insider holdings	NA

Value of $10,000 invested 5 years ago: $ 16,601

Fiscal Year Ending Dec. 31

	1995	% Change	1994	% Change	1993	% Change
Revenues (Million $)						
1Q	774.2	22%	634.9	17%	542.8	NM
2Q	839.2	12%	748.2	27%	589.0	8%
3Q	725.7	10%	662.1	23%	539.4	7%
4Q	—	—	654.9	22%	535.6	15%
Yr.	—	—	2,700	22%	2,207	7%
Income (Million $)						
1Q	40.20	52%	26.40	169%	9.80	-13%
2Q	37.10	-33%	55.20	145%	22.50	25%
3Q	34.70	18%	29.40	93%	15.20	32%
4Q	—	—	18.00	157%	7.00	NM
Yr.	—	—	129.0	137%	54.50	37%
Earnings Per Share ($)						
1Q	0.42	50%	0.28	180%	0.10	-23%
2Q	0.38	-34%	0.58	142%	0.24	20%
3Q	0.36	16%	0.31	94%	0.16	33%
4Q	E0.21	11%	0.19	171%	0.07	NM
Yr.	E1.37	1%	1.35	137%	0.57	33%

Next earnings report expected: early February

Brunswick Corp.

Business Summary - 23-OCT-95

Brunswick is the world's largest manufacturer of pleasure boats and is a leading maker of marine engines. It is also engaged in other recreational businesses, including bowling centers, bowling equipment and fishing equipment. In May 1995, BC largely completed the divestiture of other businesses (consisting largely of defense products), which have been treated as discontinued operations. Contributions (profits in millions) from continuing operations in 1994 were:

	Sales	Profits
Marine	74%	$175.6
Recreation	26%	82.8

BC's boat brands include Bayliner, Sea Ray, Maxum, Cobra, Quantum, Robalo, Ciera, Trophy, JAZZ, Laguna, Ski Ray, Sea Rayder, Astro, Fisher, MonArk, ProCraft, Starcraft and Spectrum. The company is also one of the leading makers of marine engines; its brands include Mercury, MerCruiser, Mariner and Force.

The company's recreation segment makes bowling equipment, including lanes, automatic pinsetters, computerized scoring equipment, pins, balls and bags. BC also operates about 126 recreation centers, which largely feature bowling. Other businesses include the manufacture of fishing equipment, golf equipment and electric trolling motors. Fishing equipment brands include Zebco, Quantum, Pro-Staff, Classic and Martin, and trolling motor brands include MotorGuide, Stealth and Thruster. In October 1992, the company acquired the Fishing division of Browning.

In a May 1992 public offering, 6.5 million BC common shares were sold at $16.875 each.

Important Developments

Oct. '95—In 1995's third quarter, BC's sales from its large marine business were up 8.9%, year to year, to $548.7 million, while operating profit totaled $54.2 million, up 12%. In the recreation segment, sales rose 12% to $177.0 million, but profit (before nonrecurring charges) fell 12% to $12.2 million, due to a higher level of research & development spending for new product development and high promotion and start-up costs associated with the company's new Frameworx bowling scoring system. Brunswick noted it had begun shipping Frameworx in July 1995.

Capitalization

Long Term Debt: $315,900,000 (6/95).

Per Share Data ($)

(Year Ended Dec. 31)

	1994	1993	1992	1991	1990	1989
Tangible Bk. Val.	5.41	4.29	4.31	4.03	4.09	2.90
Cash Flow	2.60	1.81	1.68	1.24	2.46	1.00
Earnings	1.35	0.57	0.43	-0.27	0.80	-0.81
Dividends	0.44	0.44	0.44	0.44	0.44	0.44
Payout Ratio	33%	77%	102%	NM	55%	NM
Prices - High	25⅜	18½	17¾	16⅜	16⅛	21½
- Low	17	12½	12⅛	8	6⅜	13
P/E Ratio - High	19	32	41	NM	20	NM
- Low	13	22	28	NM	8	NM

Income Statement Analysis (Million $)

	1994	%Chg	1993	%Chg	1992	%Chg	1991
Revs.	2,700	22%	2,207	7%	2,059	-1%	2,088
Oper. Inc.	330	51%	218	11%	196	47%	133
Depr.	120	2%	118	2%	116	-13%	133
Int. Exp.	28.5	5%	27.2	-9%	29.9	-7%	32.0
Pretax Inc.	198	128%	87.0	40%	62.0	NM	-22.0
Eff. Tax Rate	35%	—	37%	—	36%	—	NM
Net Inc.	129	135%	55.0	38%	40.0	NM	-24.0

Balance Sheet & Other Fin. Data (Million $)

	1994	1993	1992	1991	1990	1989
Cash	203	249	196	102	85.0	22.0
Curr. Assets	1,058	950	865	825	811	779
Total Assets	2,122	1,984	1,908	1,857	1,895	1,985
Curr. Liab.	621	602	503	539	531	563
LT Debt	319	325	305	316	302	462
Common Eqty.	911	804	823	779	824	776
Total Cap.	1,363	1,233	1,302	1,278	1,308	1,384
Cap. Exp.	105	96.0	89.0	82.0	91.0	128
Cash Flow	249	172	156	110	217	89.0

Ratio Analysis

	1994	1993	1992	1991	1990	1989
Curr. Ratio	1.7	1.6	1.7	1.5	1.5	1.4
% LT Debt of Cap.	23.4	26.3	23.4	24.7	23.1	33.4
% Net Inc.of Revs.	4.8	2.5	1.9	NM	2.9	NM
% Ret. on Assets	6.3	2.8	2.0	NM	3.6	NM
% Ret. on Equity	15.0	6.7	4.8	NM	8.8	NM

Dividend Data —Dividends have been paid since 1969. A dividend reinvestment plan is available. A "poison pill" stock purchase rights plan was adopted in 1986 and amended in 1989.

Amt. of Div. $	Date Decl.	Ex-Div. Date	Stock of Record	Payment Date
0.110	Oct. 25	Nov. 16	Nov. 22	Dec. 15 '94
0.125	Feb. 07	Feb. 17	Feb. 24	Mar. 15 '95
0.125	Apr. 26	May. 19	May. 25	Jun. 15 '95
0.125	Jul. 25	Aug. 23	Aug. 25	Sep. 15 '95

Data as orig. reptd.; bef. results of disc. opers. and/or spec. items. Per share data adj. for stk. divs. as of ex-div. date. E-Estimated. NA-Not Available. NM-Not Meaningful. NR-Not Ranked.

Office—1 N. Field Ct., Lake Forest, IL 60045-4811. **Tel**—(708) 735-4700. **Chrmn, Pres & CEO**—P. N. Larson. **Exec VP**—J. M. Charvat. **VP & Secy**—D. M. Yaconetti. **Treas**—R. S. O'Brien. **Investor Contact**—Ross H. Stemer. **Dirs**—M. J. Callahan, J. P. Diesel, D. E. Guinn, G. D. Kennedy, B. K. Koken, P. N. Larson, J. W. Lorsch, B. Martin Musham, R. N. Rasmus, R. W. Schipke. **Transfer Agent & Registrar**—Co.'s office. **Incorporated** in Delaware in 1907. **Empl**-20,800. **S&P Analyst:** Michael V. Pizzi

Burlington Northern Santa Fe

NYSE Symbol **BNI**
In S&P 500

25-SEP-95

Industry:
Railroads

Summary: This company, formed through the September 1995 merger of Burlington Northern and Santa Fe Pacific Corp. operates the nation's largest railroad and has interests in pipelines.

S&P Opinion: Accumulate (★★★★)	Recent Price • 71½ Yield • 1.7%
	52 Wk Range • 76½-45½ 12-Mo. P/E • 13.6

Quantitative Evaluations

Outlook
(1 Lowest—5 Highest)
• **4+**

Fair Value
• **75⅜**

Risk
• **Low**

Earn./Div. Rank
• **NR**

Technical Eval.
• **Bullish** since 2/95

Rel. Strength Rank
(1 Lowest—99 Highest)
• **56**

Insider Activity
• **Neutral**

Earnings vs. Previous Year
▲=Up ▼=Down ▷=No Change

10 Week Mov. Avg. - - - -
30 Week Mov. Avg. · · · · ·
Relative Strength ——

10361

VOL. (000)
2400
1600
800
0

OPTIONS: CBOE

Overview - 25-SEP-95

A solid profit gain is projected for 1995 reflecting improvement at Burlington Northern R.R. and the inclusion of Santa Fe Pacific from late September. Coal traffic will remain strong as utilities switch to low-sulfur Western coal, although competitive pressure on rates will continue. While auto industry sales will be soft, BNI will benefit from a new contract with Toyota. Intermodal should post gains, reflecting the inclusion of Santa Fe and a new contract with Evergreen Lines. Forest products traffic will be hurt by reduced housing construction. Margins should widen, as congestion in western coal fields is alleviated following the completion of double-track projects. Results will also benefit from the installation of more efficient locomotives and lower personal injury claims. Offsetting will be merger-related costs.

Valuation - 25-SEP-95

Despite the significant appreciation in the shares of this western railroad have risen sharply since early 1995, BNI remains conservatively valued based on the near-term profit outlook. Arguably, BNI should command a premium to its group (which it does not) since the merger with Santa Fe Pacific Corp. in September 1995 is expected to yield $560 million in savings after three years. The combined railroad is a powerhouse, holding dominant positions in three of the industry's most attractive markets: western coal, intermodal and grain. Though BNI could take a breather here, we believe it will outperform the market over the next six to 12 months.

Key Stock Statistics

S&P EPS Est. 1995	5.55	Tang. Bk. Value/Share	24.47
P/E on S&P Est. 1995	12.9	Beta	1.49
S&P EPS Est. 1996	6.25	Shareholders	32,000
Dividend Rate/Share	1.20	Market cap. (B)	$ 10.2
Shs. outstg. (M)	142.0	Inst. holdings	53%
Avg. daily vol. (M)	0.586	Insider holdings	NA

Value of $10,000 invested 5 years ago: $ 26,612

Fiscal Year Ending Dec. 31

	1995	% Change	1994	% Change	1993	% Change
Revenues (Million $)						
1Q	1,347	11%	1,210	3%	1,170	-1%
2Q	1,284	8%	1,192	4%	1,142	5%
3Q	—	—	1,249	9%	1,141	-1%
4Q	—	—	1,344	8%	1,246	4%
Yr.	—	—	4,995	6%	4,699	1%
Income (Million $)						
1Q	108.0	24%	87.00	6%	82.00	-10%
2Q	130.0	59%	82.00	14%	72.00	100%
3Q	—	—	115.0	NM	24.00	-61%
4Q	—	—	142.0	20%	118.0	6%
Yr.	—	—	426.0	44%	296.0	-1%
Earnings Per Share ($)						
1Q	1.14	27%	0.90	5%	0.86	-17%
2Q	1.37	61%	0.85	15%	0.74	85%
3Q	E1.40	15%	1.22	NM	0.21	-69%
4Q	E1.64	9%	1.51	21%	1.25	2%
Yr.	E5.55	24%	4.48	46%	3.06	-9%

Next earnings report expected: late October

Burlington Northern Santa Fe

Business Summary - 25-SEP-95

Burlington Northern Santa Fe Corp., created in September 1995 through the merger of Burlington Northern Inc. and Santa Fe Pacific Corp., operates the largest U.S. rail system, consisting more than 31,000 miles of track in 27 western and midwestern states and two Canadian provinces. A 44% interest is held in Santa Fe Pacific Pipeline Partners L.P.

Contributions to rail revenues (Burlington only) by traffic group in recent years were:

	1994	1993	1992
Coal	33%	32%	32%
Agricultural	16%	16%	16%
Intermodal	15%	15%	15%
Forest products	10%	10%	10%
Chemicals	8%	8%	8%
Consumer products	5%	5%	5%
All other	13%	14%	14%

Burlington Northern R.R. is the largest hauler of western low-sulfur coal. More than 90% of its coal shipments originate in the Powder River Basin of Wyoming and Montana. BNI is also the largest rail hauler of grain in North America. Some 50% of grain traffic is moved to export points in the Pacific Northwest, Great Lakes and Texas Gulf.

In 1994, BNI handled 260.6 billion ton-miles of traffic, up from 237.3 billion in 1993, at an average of 1.92 cents per ton-mile (1.98 cents). Productivity in 1994 was 8.49 million ton-miles per worker, up from 7.78 million in 1993. The average haul was 793 miles (778 miles); the operating ratio was 83% (86%). The equipment fleet at 1994 year-end consisted of 2,402 locomotives (1,246 leased), with average age of 14.5 years, and 65,027 freight cars (20,592 leased), averaging 15.0 years.

Important Developments

Sep. '95—On September 22 Burlington Northern Santa Fe Corp. was created reflecting the merger of Burlington Northern, Inc. and Santa Fe Pacific Corp. Some 52.2 million new BNI shares (a 58% increase in total outstanding) were issued to acquire SFX's publicly-held shares. In January BNI paid $500 million for a 16% stake in SFX. The merger creates the nation's largest rail system operating over 31,000 miles in 27 states and two Canadian provinces. The merger, which will provide access to new markets and create new single-line long-haul routes is expected to yield $560 million in savings after three years. SFX, which also has interests in petroleum pipelines, earned $199 million in 1994 on revenues of $2.7 billion.

Capitalization

Long Term Debt: $2,194,000,000 (6/95).

$3.125 Cum. Conv. Pfd Stock: 6,899,657 shs. ($50 liquid. pref.); ea. conv. into 1.0638 com.

Per Share Data ($)

(Year Ended Dec. 31)

	1994	1993	1992	1991	1990	1989
Tangible Bk. Val.	21.21	17.73	15.71	13.76	16.29	14.33
Cash Flow	8.49	6.98	7.15	0.52	7.40	7.28
Earnings	4.48	3.06	3.35	-3.96	2.89	3.19
Dividends	1.20	1.20	1.20	1.20	1.20	1.20
Payout Ratio	27%	39%	36%	NM	41%	37%
Prices - High	66⅝	58⅞	47⅜	41⅞	39¼	32⅜
- Low	46½	42	33¼	26¼	22¼	21⅜
P/E Ratio - High	15	19	14	NM	14	10
- Low	10	14	10	NM	8	7

Income Statement Analysis (Million $)

	1994	%Chg	1993	%Chg	1992	%Chg	1991
Revs.	4,995	6%	4,699	1%	4,630	2%	4,559
Oper. Inc.	1,215	20%	1,013	8%	935	15%	816
Depr.	362	3%	352	4%	338	-3%	347
Int. Exp.	155	7%	145	-22%	186	-18%	226
Pretax Inc.	695	33%	521	15%	452	NM	-489
Eff. Tax Rate	39%	—	43%	—	34%	—	NM
Net Inc.	426	44%	296	-1%	299	NM	-305

Balance Sheet & Other Fin. Data (Million $)

	1994	1993	1992	1991	1990	1989
Cash	27.0	17.0	57.0	16.0	56.0	83.0
Curr. Assets	1,012	891	777	705	625	797
Total Assets	7,592	7,045	6,537	6,324	6,075	6,148
Curr. Liab.	1,447	1,529	1,353	1,422	1,170	1,288
LT Debt	1,697	1,526	1,527	1,834	2,083	2,220
Common Eqty.	1,892	1,574	1,383	1,202	1,241	1,080
Total Cap.	5,390	4,787	4,405	4,123	4,632	4,591
Cap. Exp.	698	676	487	509	401	373
Cash Flow	766	626	634	40.0	567	552

Ratio Analysis

	1994	1993	1992	1991	1990	1989
Curr. Ratio	0.7	0.6	0.6	0.5	0.5	0.6
% LT Debt of Cap.	31.5	31.9	34.7	44.5	45.0	48.3
% Net Inc.of Revs.	8.5	6.3	6.5	NM	4.7	5.3
% Ret. on Assets	5.8	4.3	4.6	NM	3.6	3.9
% Ret. on Equity	23.3	18.5	22.8	NM	19.0	24.1

Dividend Data

Dividends have been paid since 1940. A "poison pill" stock purchase rights plan was adopted in 1986.

Amt. of Div. $	Date Decl.	Ex-Div. Date	Stock of Record	Payment Date
0.300	Jul. 22	Aug. 31	Sep. 07	Oct. 01 '94
0.300	Oct. 20	Nov. 30	Dec. 06	Jan. 01 '95
0.300	Jan. 19	Mar. 02	Mar. 08	Apr. 01 '95
0.300	Apr. 20	Jun. 01	Jun. 07	Jul. 01 '95
0.300	Jul. 20	Sep. 01	Sep. 06	Oct. 01 '95

Data as orig. reptd.; bef. results of disc. opers. and/or spec. items. Per share data adj. for stk. divs. as of ex-div. date. E-Estimated. NA-Not Available. NM-Not Meaningful. NR-Not Ranked.

Office—3800 Continental Plaza, 777 Main St., Fort Worth, TX 76102-5384. **Tel**—(817) 333-2000. **Chrmn**—G. Grinstein. **Pres & CEO**—R. D. Krebs. **SVP & CFO**—D. E. Springer. **Secy**—B. A. Edwards-Adams. **VP & Investor Contact**—Marsha Morgan. **Dirs**—J. F. Alibrandi, J. S. Blanton, J. J. Burns Jr., D. P. Davison, G. Deukmejian, D. J. Evans, G. Grinstein, B. C. Jordan, R. D. Krebs, B. M. Lindig, B. F. Love, R. S. Roberts, M. J. Shapiro, A. R. Weber, R. H. West, J. S. Whisler, E. E. Whitacre Jr., R. B. Woodard, M. B. Yanney. **Transfer Agent & Registrar**—First Chicago Trust Co. of New York. **Incorporated** in Delaware in 1961; reincorporated in Delaware in 1995. **Empl**-45,000. **S&P Analyst**: Stephen R. Klein

18-OCT-95   **Industry:** Oil and Gas

Summary: This holding company is engaged, through its Meridian Oil unit, in exploration, development and production of oil and gas, and in related marketing activities.

S&P Opinion: Avoid (★★)	Recent Price • 36⅝	Yield • 1.5%
	52 Wk Range • 42⅞-33⅛	12-Mo. P/E • NM

Quantitative Evaluations

Outlook (1 Lowest—5 Highest)
• **1−**

Fair Value
• **24¾**

Risk
• **Low**

Earn./Div. Rank
• **NR**

Technical Eval.
• **Bullish** since 12/94

Rel. Strength Rank (1 Lowest—99 Highest)
• **25**

Insider Activity
• **Neutral**

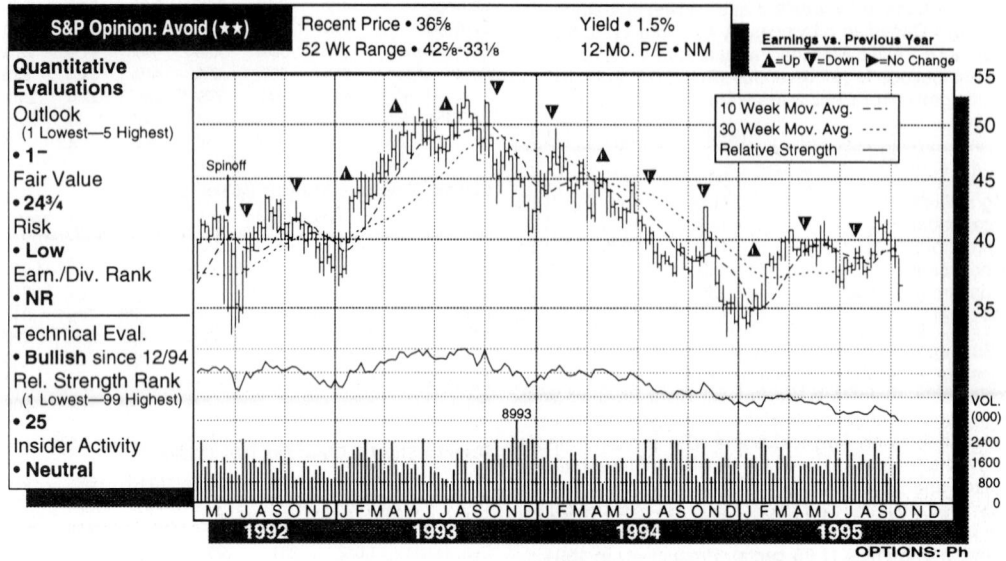

Earnings vs. Previous Year: ▲=Up ▼=Down ▶=No Change

10 Week Mov. Avg. ---
30 Week Mov. Avg. ·····
Relative Strength —

OPTIONS: Ph

Overview - 17-OCT-95

Despite increased production, 1995 revenues will decline, as evidenced by the results of the year's first nine months. A loss will be incurred, though, because of a non-cash charge. Gas prices, although not as depressed as those earlier in 1995 and throughout 1994, remain in a trough, with little likelihood of a breakout. Despite projections by industry publications of demand growth during 1995, supply will be more than adequate, relieving pressure on prices. Even oil prices, which have strengthened from the lows of a year ago and have stabilized recently, are not about to take off. BR, which is essentially a producer, sells its products on the spot and short-term markets, and will be hurt by the effects of a lackluster marketplace that restricts both revenues and income. However, cash flow should continue to be adequate, reflecting a slight shortfall from the previous year.

Valuation - 18-OCT-95

The shares, which have declined after the taking of a non-cash charge related to low gas prices, are unlikely to make any dramatic upward move. With a previously high P/E multiple and low yield, the shares could have been considered overpriced. Performance is unlikely to improve significantly in the next several months, reflecting continued sluggishness in petroleum and natural gas markets. However, BR has significant reserves, and can be regarded as a long-term energy play. The shares could also attract those who believe that natural gas prices will be on the rebound.

Key Stock Statistics

S&P EPS Est. 1995	-2.00	Tang. Bk. Value/Share	20.01
P/E on S&P Est. 1995	NM	Beta	0.33
S&P EPS Est. 1996	0.72	Shareholders	24,700
Dividend Rate/Share	0.55	Market cap. (B)	$ 4.7
Shs. outstg. (M)	126.6	Inst. holdings	68%
Avg. daily vol. (M)	0.295	Insider holdings	NA

Value of $10,000 invested 5 years ago: NA

Fiscal Year Ending Dec. 31

	1995	% Change	1994	% Change	1993	% Change
Revenues (Million $)						
1Q	214.6	-22%	275.0	-13%	316.5	17%
2Q	211.2	-21%	266.0	-15%	312.2	25%
3Q	210.2	-23%	273.0	-12%	309.5	9%
4Q	—	—	241.0	-22%	310.8	-8%
Yr.	—	—	1,055	-16%	1,249	9%
Income (Million $)						
1Q	-4.82	NM	47.72	6%	45.23	51%
2Q	2.18	-93%	33.01	-75%	133.6	NM
3Q	-299.6	NM	20.70	-15%	24.31	-26%
4Q	—	—	52.82	1%	52.05	-46%
Yr.	—	—	154.3	-40%	255.2	35%
Earnings Per Share ($)						
1Q	-0.04	NM	0.37	6%	0.35	52%
2Q	0.02	-92%	0.25	-75%	1.02	NM
3Q	-2.36	NM	0.16	-11%	0.18	-28%
4Q	E0.38	-10%	0.42	5%	0.40	-45%
Yr.	E-2.00	NM	1.20	-38%	1.95	35%

Next earnings report expected: mid January

Burlington Resources

Business Summary - 17-OCT-95

Burlington Resources is a holding company engaged, through its principal subsidiary, Meridian Oil Inc., in exploration, development and production of oil and gas, and in related marketing activities, including aggregation and resale of third party oil and gas. The company was formed by Burlington Northern Inc. (BNI) to consolidate BNI's natural resources operations, and was spun off to BNI shareholders in 1988. In mid-1992, BR spun off its El Paso Natural Gas unit, and also sold nearly all coal operations.

The company undertakes oil and gas operations in the San Juan, Gulf Coast, Permian, Anadarko, Black Warrior and Williston Basins. In 1994, BR established an operating position in the shallow offshore waters of the Gulf of Mexico by acquiring the Diamond Shamrock Offshore Partners Limited Partnership, with an interest in 99 offshore leases. Virtually all company production is from U.S. properties. A number of BR's producing areas have wells that qualify under the Internal Revenue Code for Section 29 tax credits; the company received about $84 million of tax credits in 1994. BR's oil and gas production is sold on the spot market and under short-term contracts at market responsive prices.

Total proved reserves at 1994 year-end were estimated at 184.1 million bbl. of oil (168.2 million in 1993) and 5.5 Tcf of gas (5.2). In 1994 natural gas prices averaged $1.65 per Mcf ($1.87 in 1993) and oil prices averaged $15.66 per barrel ($16.71). Production in 1994 amounted to 1,052 MMcf/d of gas (920 in 1993) and 45.6 Mbbl/d of oil (41.9). In 1994, BR's additions to reserves equaled 212% of its oil and gas production. Capital spending in 1994 climbed to $882 million, from $553 million in 1993, on increased developmental drilling and producing property acquisitions.

In February 1995, BR sold its intrastate natural gas pipeline systems in West Texas and its underground gas storage facility to K N Energy Inc., for about $80 million. In 1992, the company essentially completed a program of selling nonstrategic real estate, minerals and forest products assets and reinvesting net proceeds in oil and gas reserves and in the repurchase of common stock; proceeds from the sales totaled about $1.4 billion.

Important Developments

Oct. '95—Because of an accounting standard adopted during the third quarter, the company generated a non-cash charge, for impairment of properties due to low natural gas prices, of $304 million. After taking the charge, BR reported a loss of $300 million for the quarter. Excluding the charge, third quarter earnings were $4 million, or $0.03 a share, versus $21 million, or $0.16 a share, a year earlier. The decline was attributed to weak natural gas prices, particularly in California.

Capitalization

Long Term Debt: $1,360,403,000 (6/95).

Per Share Data ($) (Year Ended Dec. 31)

	1994	1993	1992	1991	1990	1989
Tangible Bk. Val.	20.30	20.11	18.67	22.11	21.92	22.08
Cash Flow	3.81	4.13	3.38	3.64	3.43	2.74
Earnings	1.20	1.95	1.44	1.48	1.46	0.99
Dividends	0.55	0.55	0.60	0.70	0.70	0.61
Payout Ratio	46%	28%	41%	47%	47%	61%
Prices - High	49⅝	53⅞	43½	43¾	50⅛	53⅝
- Low	33⅛	36½	33	32⅞	36¾	32⅛
P/E Ratio - High	41	28	30	30	34	54
- Low	28	19	23	22	25	32

Income Statement Analysis (Million $)

	1994	%Chg	1993	%Chg	1992	%Chg	1991
Revs.	1,055	-16%	1,249	9%	1,141	-35%	1,754
Oper. Inc.	512	-5%	541	9%	496	-25%	662
Depr. Depl. & Amort.	337	18%	285	11%	256	-11%	289
Int. Exp.	90.0	23%	73.0	-8%	79.0	-35%	122
Pretax Inc.	90.0	-71%	307	41%	218	-15%	256
Eff. Tax Rate	NM	—	17%	—	13%	—	23%
Net Inc.	154	-40%	255	34%	190	-4%	197

Balance Sheet & Other Fin. Data (Million $)

	1994	1993	1992	1991	1990	1989
Cash	20.0	20.0	32.0	17.0	30.0	160
Curr. Assets	266	277	370	760	1,136	893
Total Assets	4,809	4,448	4,470	6,290	6,360	6,098
Curr. Liab.	262	300	346	916	1,070	1,155
LT Debt	1,309	819	1,003	1,548	1,378	718
Common Eqty.	2,568	2,608	2,406	2,907	3,024	3,223
Total Cap.	4,358	3,994	3,977	5,135	5,077	4,694
Cap. Exp.	882	553	315	806	1,083	656
Cash Flow	492	540	446	486	487	408

Ratio Analysis

	1994	1993	1992	1991	1990	1989
Curr. Ratio	1.0	0.9	1.1	0.8	1.1	0.8
% LT Debt of Cap.	30.0	20.5	25.2	30.1	27.1	15.3
% Ret. on Assets	3.4	5.7	3.6	3.2	3.4	2.5
% Ret. on Equity	6.0	10.1	7.2	6.8	6.8	4.8

Dividend Data —BR initiated dividends in 1988. A poison pill stock purchase rights plan was adopted in 1988.

Amt. of Div. $	Date Decl.	Ex-Div. Date	Stock of Record	Payment Date
0.138	Oct. 06	Dec. 05	Dec. 09	Jan. 03 '95
0.138	Jan. 11	Mar. 13	Mar. 17	Apr. 03 '95
0.138	Apr. 06	Jun. 14	Jun. 16	Jul. 03 '95
0.138	Jul. 12	Sep. 13	Sep. 15	Oct. 02 '95
0.138	Oct. 13	Dec. 13	Dec. 15	Jan. 02 '96

Data as orig. reptd.; bef. results of disc opers. and/or spec. items. Per share data adj. for stk. divs. as of ex-div. date. E-Estimated. NA-Not Available. NM-Not Meaningful. NR-Not Ranked.

Office—5051 Westheimer, Suite 1400, Houston, TX 77056. **Tel**—(713) 624-9000. **Chrmn, Pres & CEO**—T. H. O'Leary. **SVP & CFO**—J. E. Hagale. **Secy**—Wendi S. Zerwas. **Investor Contact**—James W. Leahy. **Dirs**—J. V. Byrne, S. P. Gilbert, J. F. McDonald, T. H. O'Leary, D. M. Roberts, W. Scott, Jr., W. E. Wall. **Transfer Agent & Registrar**—First National Bank of Boston. **Incorporated** in Delaware in 1988. **Empl**-1,846. **S&P Analyst:** Michael C. Barr

CBS Inc.

NYSE Symbol **CBS**
In S&P 500

02-AUG-95 **Industry:** Broadcasting

Summary: Operations of this major broadcast company include a TV network, TV stations, and radio interests.

S&P Opinion: Accumulate (★★★★)

Recent Price • 75⅞	Yield • 0.5%
52 Wk Range • 76½-50	12-Mo. P/E • 28.6

Quantitative Evaluations

Outlook
(1 Lowest—5 Highest)
• **1⁻**

Fair Value
• **60%**

Risk
• **Average**

Earn./Div. Rank
• **B**

Technical Eval.
• **Bearish** since 2/95

Rel. Strength Rank
(1 Lowest—99 Highest)
• **78**

Insider Activity
• **NA**

Earnings vs. Previous Year
▲=Up ▼=Down ▶=No Change

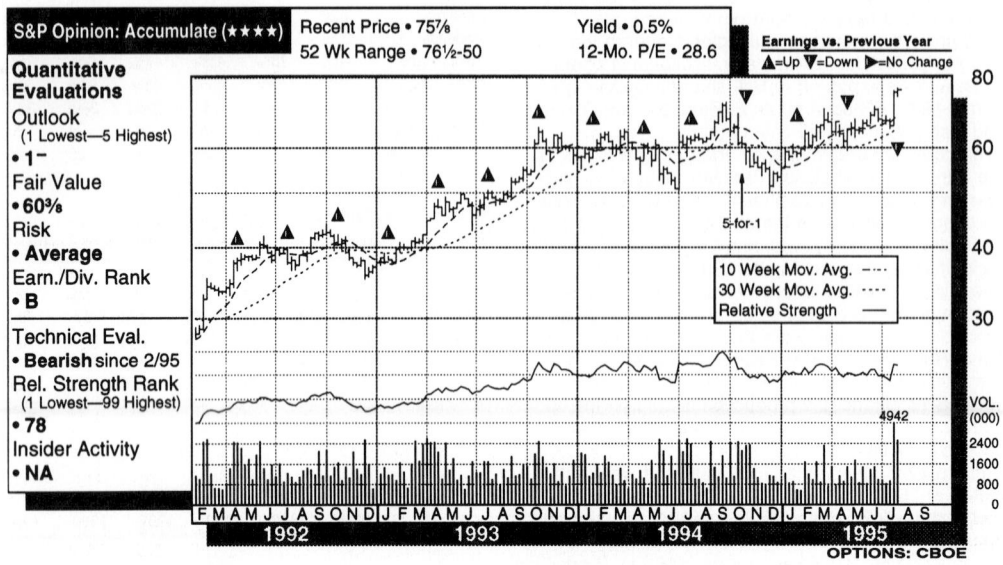

10 Week Mov. Avg. ----
30 Week Mov. Avg. ·····
Relative Strength ——

5-for-1

4942

VOL.
(000)

OPTIONS: CBOE

Overview - 02-AUG-95

As we went to press, Westinghouse Electric Corp. (WX) had agreed to acquire CBS for roughly $81 a share. We expect that other companies such as Seagram and Turner Broadcasting will now be taking a closer look at making an offer for CBS. Meanwhile, we look for CBS's earnings in 1995 to be restrained by lower primetime audiences for the TV network's programming. Also, the TV network is facing higher compensation fees to TV station affiliates, which reflects efforts by CBS to secure national programming distribution through long-term affiliation agreements. However, we expect recent strong demand for advertising time to fuel a resumption of earnings growth in 1995's fourth quarter. Our earnings estimate for 1995 includes a one-time charge of $0.32 a share related to staff reduction costs.

Valuation - 02-AUG-95

Based on takeover prospects, we view this stock as having appeal for aggressive investors. Westinghouse has already agreed to pay roughly $81 a share, and we see a prospect that a higher bid will emerge. CBS's appeal as a takeover candidate should be broadened by the easing of regulatory constraints on the owners of TV broadcast networks, making it more feasible for CBS to be acquired by the parent company of one of the major Hollywood studios. Based solely on earnings prospects (excluding any takeover speculation), we view CBS's stock as amply priced.

Key Stock Statistics

S&P EPS Est. 1995	2.55	Tang. Bk. Value/Share	NM
P/E on S&P Est. 1995	29.8	Beta	0.57
S&P EPS Est. 1996	3.60	Shareholders	10,500
Dividend Rate/Share	0.40	Market cap. (B)	$ 4.8
Shs. outstg. (M)	61.4	Inst. holdings	87%
Avg. daily vol. (M)	0.648	Insider holdings	NA

Value of $10,000 invested 5 years ago: $ 21,276

Fiscal Year Ending Dec. 31

	1995	% Change	1994	% Change	1993	% Change
Revenues (Million $)						
1Q	897.7	-28%	1,247	42%	878.9	-19%
2Q	889.6	NM	882.7	6%	835.8	7%
3Q	—	—	727.1	-3%	752.6	12%
4Q	—	—	855.2	-18%	1,043	8%
Yr.	—	—	3,712	6%	3,510	NM
Income (Million $)						
1Q	21.90	-68%	69.30	28%	54.20	NM
2Q	51.90	-53%	109.3	2%	107.4	56%
3Q	—	—	58.50	-51%	118.3	177%
4Q	—	—	44.50	-4%	46.40	39%
Yr.	—	—	281.6	-14%	326.2	101%
Earnings Per Share ($)						
1Q	0.32	-62%	0.85	21%	0.70	NM
2Q	0.80	-42%	1.37	2%	1.35	51%
3Q	E0.58	—	0.77	-48%	1.48	168%
4Q	E0.85	—	0.69	25%	0.55	29%
Yr.	E2.55	—	3.74	-8%	4.08	94%

Next earnings report expected: mid October

Business Summary - 02-AUG-95

CBS Inc., is a major U.S. broadcaster whose operations include a TV network and ownership of seven TV stations. In 1994, the company repurchased 22% of its common shares, after buying back nearly half of its common stock in early 1991.

Current operations include the CBS Television Network and owned TV stations in New York (WCBS-TV), Chicago (WBBM-TV), Los Angeles (KCBS-TV), Minneapolis (WCCO-TV) and Green Bay, Wis. (WFRV-TV). Also, four other TV stations are expected to be part of a joint venture with Westinghouse Broadcasting Co. The CBS network distributes programming to more than 200 U.S. TV stations, including the owned stations, and to certain foreign affiliated stations. Principal competitors of CBS in the TV network business include ABC (owned by Capital Cities/ABC), NBC (owned by General Electric), and the Fox network (owned by News Corp.).

CBS also owns and operates eight AM and 13 FM radio stations in the following markets: New York (WCBS-AM & FM), Chicago (WBBM-AM & FM), Dallas/Fort Worth (KTXQ-FM, KLRX-FM), Los Angeles (KNX-AM & FM), San Francisco (KCBS-AM & KRQR-FM), Philadelphia (WOGL-AM & FM), Boston (WODS-FM), Houston/Galveston (KLTR-FM), Washington, D.C. (WLTT-FM), St. Louis (KMOX-AM & KLOU-FM), Detroit (WWJ-AM & WJOI-FM), and Minneapolis (WCCO-AM & WLTE-FM). It also operates the CBS Radio Networks, and is a broadcast sales representative for a number of radio stations.

Important Developments

Aug. '95—Westinghouse Electric Corp. (WX) has agreed to acquire CBS for $81 a share in cash, plus a limited amount of additional consideration, depending on when the transaction was completed. Also, completion of the acquisition is likely to require a change in federal regulations, so that a CBS-WX combination could own more TV stations, with wider audience coverage, than is currently allowed. Meanwhile, in 1995's second quarter, CBS's operating profit fell 49%, year to year. This was largely due to lower earnings from the CBS television network, whose results were hurt by weakness in audience levels and increased payments to TV stations affiliated with the network. Also, there was a special charge against operating profit ($0.32 a share after-tax) related to staff reductions.

Capitalization

Total Debt: $507,200,000 (3/95).
$10 Conv. Series B Preference Stock: About 0.9 million shs.

Per Share Data ($)

(Year Ended Dec. 31)

	1994	1993	1992	1991	1990	1989
Tangible Bk. Val.	-0.38	11.06	2.42	3.17	19.48	19.46
Cash Flow	4.69	4.85	2.71	-0.66	1.02	2.65
Earnings	3.74	4.08	2.10	-1.22	0.71	2.31
Dividends	0.40	0.25	0.20	0.20	0.88	0.88
Payout Ratio	11%	6%	10%	NM	132%	37%
Prices - High	72¼	65¼	44⅛	37⅝	41¼	44¼
- Low	50	37¼	27¼	25⅝	30¼	33¼
P/E Ratio - High	19	16	21	NM	58	19
- Low	13	9	13	NM	43	14

Income Statement Analysis (Million $)

	1994	%Chg	1993	%Chg	1992	%Chg	1991
Revs.	3,712	6%	3,510	NM	3,503	15%	3,035
Oper. Inc.	481	14%	423	82%	233	NM	-229
Depr.	68.0	8%	63.0	7%	59.0	2%	58.0
Int. Exp.	61.0	2%	60.0	-28%	83.0	22%	68.0
Pretax Inc.	437	-9%	479	111%	227	NM	-178
Eff. Tax Rate	36%	—	32%	—	28%	—	NM
Net Inc.	282	-13%	326	100%	163	NM	-99.0

Balance Sheet & Other Fin. Data (Million $)

	1994	1993	1992	1991	1990	1989
Cash	102	594	478	486	2,599	1,078
Curr. Assets	948	1,678	1,481	1,520	3,525	1,901
Total Assets	2,160	3,419	3,175	2,799	4,692	4,638
Curr. Liab.	794	1,039	1,117	951	815	821
LT Debt	507	590	870	697	712	796
Common Eqty.	242	1,138	446	354	2,456	2,457
Total Cap.	958	1,974	1,590	1,293	3,474	3,584
Cap. Exp.	73.0	107	72.0	64.0	60.0	99
Cash Flow	339	377	209	-53.0	131	340

Ratio Analysis

	1994	1993	1992	1991	1990	1989
Curr. Ratio	1.2	1.6	1.3	1.6	4.3	2.3
% LT Debt of Cap.	52.9	29.9	54.7	53.9	20.5	22.2
% Net Inc.of Revs.	7.6	9.3	4.6	NM	2.8	10.0
% Ret. on Assets	11.6	9.2	5.4	NM	2.0	6.6
% Ret. on Equity	47.3	38.0	37.1	NM	3.2	12.0

Dividend Data

(Dividends have been paid since 1931. A dividend reinvestment plan is available.)

Amt. of Div. $	Date Decl.	Ex-Div. Date	Stock of Record	Payment Date
5-for-1	—	Oct. 19	Oct. 03	Oct. 18 '94
0.100	Oct. 12	Nov. 17	Nov. 23	Dec. 12 '94
0.100	Feb. 08	Feb. 15	Feb. 22	Mar. 10 '95
0.100	May. 10	May. 18	May. 24	Jun. 09 '95
0.100	Jul. 13	Aug. 21	Aug. 23	Sep. 11 '95

Data as orig. reptd.; bef. results of disc. opers. and/or spec. items. Per share data adj. for stk. divs. as of ex-div. date.
E-Estimated. NA-Not Available. NM-Not Meaningful. NR-Not Ranked.

Office—51 W. 52nd St., New York, NY 10019. **Tel**—(212) 975-4321. **Chrmn, Pres & CEO**—L. A. Tisch. **EVP & CFO**—P. W. Keegan. **EVP & Secy**—E. O. Kaden. **VP & Treas**—L. J. Rauchenberger, Jr. **Investor Contact**—K. Fawcett. **Dirs**—M. C. Bergerac, H. Brown, E. V. Futter, H. A. Kissinger, H. B. Schacht, E. W. Spencer, F. A. Thomas, L. A. Tisch, P. R. Tisch, J. D. Wolfensohn, D. Yankelovich. **Transfer Agent & Registrar**—First Chicago Trust Co. of N.Y., Jersey City, NJ. **Incorporated** in New York in 1927. **Empl**-6,400. **S&P Analyst:** Tom Graves, CFA

24-OCT-95 | Industry: Food

Summary: This international food processor makes a broad line of branded grocery items and is a leading corn refiner.

| S&P Opinion: Accumulate (★★★★) | Recent Price • 67½ | Yield • 2.3% |
| | 52 Wk Range • 69½-50⅞ | 12-Mo. P/E • 19.1 |

Quantitative Evaluations

Outlook
(1 Lowest—5 Highest)
• **2+**

Fair Value
• **65%**

Risk
• **Low**

Earn./Div. Rank
• **A+**

Technical Eval.
• **Bearish** since 6/94

Rel. Strength Rank
(1 Lowest—99 Highest)
• **68**

Insider Activity
• **Unfavorable**

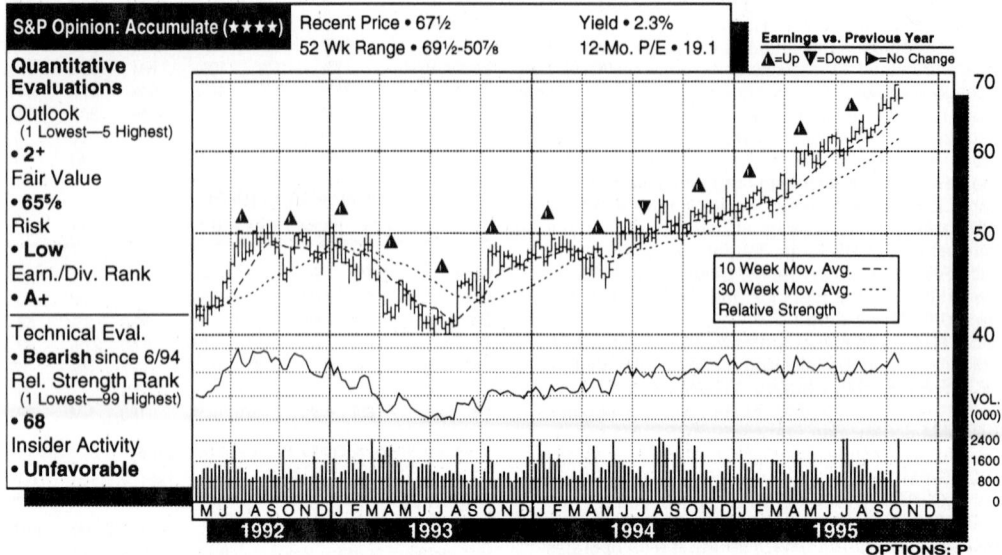

Earnings vs. Previous Year
▲=Up ▼=Down ▶=No Change

10 Week Mov. Avg. - - -
30 Week Mov. Avg. ·······
Relative Strength ———

VOL. (000)
2400
1600
800
0

OPTIONS: P

Overview - 24-OCT-95

Both sales and profits through 1996 are expected to continue their long upward climb, driven mostly by increased global consumer food volumes. North American profits should rise at a mid single-digit annual pace, driven by new product successes and acquisition contributions. European profits should continue to rise at a strong pace, reflecting restructuring benefits and acquisition contributions. Latin American profits, although volatile, should remain in a long-term uptrend, reflecting reduced trade barriers and increased consumption levels. Corn refining profits should increase on favorable market conditions. We expect earnings per share, exclusive of special items, to grow at a 10% to 15% annual pace over the next few years.

Valuation - 24-OCT-95

Given our expectation of 10% to 15% annual earnings per share growth through 1996, we view these high quality, low-risk shares as attractive. Presently trading at only a modest premium to the S&P 500 index, the shares appear to be attractively valued for above average gains ahead. As one of the nation's most international food companies, we expect the stock to continue to command a premium valuation to most other U.S. food companies. The stock has been a strong performer since mid-1993, as strong profit gains from foreign operations have helped offset difficult growth in mature North American markets. Looking ahead, we expect investors to continue to seek out steady earnings growers, like CPC, especially in the midst of a slow U.S. economy.

Key Stock Statistics

S&P EPS Est. 1995	3.65	Tang. Bk. Value/Share	4.42
P/E on S&P Est. 1995	18.5	Beta	0.73
S&P EPS Est. 1996	4.10	Shareholders	32,100
Dividend Rate/Share	1.52	Market cap. (B)	$ 9.8
Shs. outstg. (M)	146.0	Inst. holdings	61%
Avg. daily vol. (M)	0.277	Insider holdings	NA

Value of $10,000 invested 5 years ago: $ 21,096

Fiscal Year Ending Dec. 31

	1995	% Change	1994	% Change	1993	% Change
Revenues (Million $)						
1Q	1,955	12%	1,738	6%	1,636	7%
2Q	2,040	10%	1,856	10%	1,690	1%
3Q	2,046	13%	1,813	9%	1,664	4%
4Q	—	—	2,019	15%	1,748	-2%
Yr.	—	—	7,425	10%	6,738	2%
Income (Million $)						
1Q	111.1	13%	98.09	9%	90.40	2%
2Q	142.0	NM	-14.94	NM	116.9	3%
3Q	142.2	13%	125.4	3%	122.0	4%
4Q	—	—	136.5	9%	125.1	6%
Yr.	—	—	345.1	-24%	454.2	5%
Earnings Per Share ($)						
1Q	0.73	16%	0.63	9%	0.58	5%
2Q	0.96	NM	-0.11	NM	0.76	6%
3Q	0.95	14%	0.83	5%	0.79	7%
4Q	E1.00	11%	0.90	10%	0.82	6%
Yr.	E3.65	62%	2.25	-24%	2.95	6%

Next earnings report expected: early February

CPC International

Business Summary - 24-OCT-95

CPC is a major worldwide producer of branded consumer foods and corn refinery products. The company operates businesses in 59 countries in North America, Europe, Latin America and Asia. Business segment contributions in 1994 were:

	Sales	Profits
Consumer foods	84%	79%
Corn refining	16%	21%

Operations outside North America accounted for 61% of sales (40% Europe; 17% Latin America; 4% Asia) and 57% of profits (31% Europe; 20% Latin America; 6% Asia) in 1994.

Consumer foods include Hellmann's and Best Foods mayonnaise, Mazola corn oil and margarine, Skippy peanut butter, Arnold breads, Thomas' English muffins, Mueller's pasta, Karo and Golden Griddle syrups, Argo and Maizena corn starches and Knorr soups, bouillons and sauces. Products sold in international markets include Knorr soups, sauces, gravies, desserts and prepared meals; seasonings, condiments and spices; corn starch; quick energy products; cheeses and dairy products; mayonnaise, margarine and corn oil. The company also operates a foodservice distribution unit, Caterplan.

Corn wet milling operations produce sweeteners, starches, animal feeds, ethanol and corn oil for industrial uses.

CPC has a total of 143 operating plants, of which 27 are in the U.S., eight in Canada, 42 in Europe, 20 in Africa and the Middle East, 32 in Latin America and 14 in Asia.

Important Developments

Oct. '95—In 1995's first nine months, CPC's worldwide consumer foods profits rose 13%, on 12% greater sales. North American consumer foods profits rose 1.5%, held by heavy marketing spending. European consumer foods profits rose 15%, led by volume growth and favorable currency exchange values. Latin American consumer foods profits rose 60% on the recovery from the year-ago period when results were hurt by difficult operating conditions in Brazil. Asian consumer foods profits were essentially flat, held by continued heavy investment spending. Corn refining profits advanced 5% on increased worldwide volumes. Separately, CPC completed the acquisition of the fresh sweet baked goods and bread business of Kraft Foods, Inc. (1994 sales of $1.2 billion), for $865 million in cash.

Capitalization

Long Term Debt: $915,000,000 (6/95).
Minority Interest: $153,000,000.
Series A ESOP Conv. Pfd. Stock: $192,000,000.

Per Share Data ($)

(Year Ended Dec. 31)

	1994	1993	1992	1991	1990	1989
Tangible Bk. Val.	5.06	6.37	5.40	4.99	3.51	4.04
Cash Flow	4.20	4.56	4.35	4.16	3.87	3.42
Earnings	2.25	2.95	2.78	2.61	2.42	2.11
Dividends	1.38	1.28	1.17	1.10	1.00	0.88
Payout Ratio	61%	43%	42%	42%	41%	40%
Prices - High	55⅝	51⅛	51⅝	46¾	42⅜	36⅞
- Low	44¼	39⅞	39¾	36	31	24¾
P/E Ratio - High	25	17	19	18	18	17
- Low	20	14	14	14	13	12

Income Statement Analysis (Million $)

	1994	%Chg	1993	%Chg	1992	%Chg	1991
Revs.	7,425	10%	6,738	2%	6,599	7%	6,189
Oper. Inc.	1,216	9%	1,111	3%	1,076	5%	1,023
Depr.	288	19%	242	2%	238	2%	234
Int. Exp.	107	-3%	110	-5%	116	-9%	128
Pretax Inc.	615	-22%	790	6%	745	7%	694
Eff. Tax Rate	40%	—	40%	—	40%	—	40%
Net Inc.	345	-24%	455	6%	431	7%	404

Balance Sheet & Other Fin. Data (Million $)

	1994	1993	1992	1991	1990	1989
Cash	125	166	158	216	48.0	107
Curr. Assets	2,215	1,972	2,025	1,792	1,714	1,427
Total Assets	5,668	5,061	5,171	4,510	4,490	3,705
Curr. Liab.	2,088	1,583	1,706	1,360	1,555	1,197
LT Debt	879	898	954	1,016	990	845
Common Eqty.	1,696	1,729	1,633	1,432	1,253	1,018
Total Cap.	2,770	2,804	2,767	2,885	2,706	2,316
Cap. Exp.	401	363	297	282	336	267
Cash Flow	622	685	658	628	584	529

Ratio Analysis

	1994	1993	1992	1991	1990	1989
Curr. Ratio	1.1	1.2	1.2	1.3	1.1	1.2
% LT Debt of Cap.	31.7	32.0	34.5	35.2	36.6	36.5
% Net Inc.of Revs.	4.6	6.7	6.5	6.5	6.5	6.4
% Ret. on Assets	6.5	8.9	8.9	9.0	9.1	9.5
% Ret. on Equity	19.7	26.5	26.0	29.3	32.1	30.2

Dividend Data —Dividends have been paid since 1920. A dividend reinvestment plan is available. A new "poison pill" stock purchase rights plan was adopted in 1991.

Amt. of Div. $	Date Decl.	Ex-Div. Date	Stock of Record	Payment Date
0.340	Sep. 20	Sep. 26	Sep. 30	Oct. 25 '94
0.360	Dec. 20	Dec. 27	Jan. 03	Jan. 25 '95
0.360	Mar. 21	Mar. 27	Mar. 31	Apr. 25 '95
0.360	Jun. 20	Jun. 28	Jun. 30	Jul. 25 '95
0.380	Sep. 18	Sep. 27	Sep. 29	Oct. 25 '95

Data as orig. reptd.; bef. results of disc. opers. and/or spec. items. Per share data adj. for stk. divs. as of ex-div. date.
E-Estimated. NA-Not Available. NM-Not Meaningful. NR-Not Ranked.

Office—International Plaza, Englewood Cliffs, NJ 07632. **Tel**—(201) 894-4000. **Chrmn & Pres**—C. R. Shoemate. **SVP-CFO**—K. Schlatter. **Secy**—J. B. Meagher. **VP & Investor Contact**—John W. Scott. **Dirs**—T. H. Black, A. C. DeCrane, Jr., W. C. Ferguson, R. J. Gillespie, E. R. Gordon, G. V. Grune, L. I. Higdon, Jr., R. G. Holder, E. S. Kraus, A. Labergere, W. S. Norman, C. R. Shoemate. **Transfer Agent & Registrar**—First Chicago Trust Co. of New York, Jersey City, NJ. **Incorporated** in Delaware in 1959. **Empl**-41,900. **S&P Analyst:** Kenneth A. Shea

08-AUG-95 | **Industry:** Railroads

Summary: This company operates a major eastern rail system, a leading containership line and is the largest U.S. barge operator. CSX also provides intermodal services and operates resorts.

S&P Opinion: Accumulate (★★★★)	Recent Price • 83¾	Yield • 2.1%
	52 Wk Range • 87¼-63⅛	12-Mo. P/E • 15.8

Quantitative Evaluations

Outlook
(1 Lowest—5 Highest)
• **2−**

Fair Value
• **76⅜**

Risk
• **Low**

Earn./Div. Rank
• **B**

Technical Eval.
• **Bullish** since 7/95

Rel. Strength Rank
(1 Lowest—99 Highest)
• **52**

Insider Activity
• **NA**

Earnings vs. Previous Year
▲=Up ▼=Down ▶=No Change

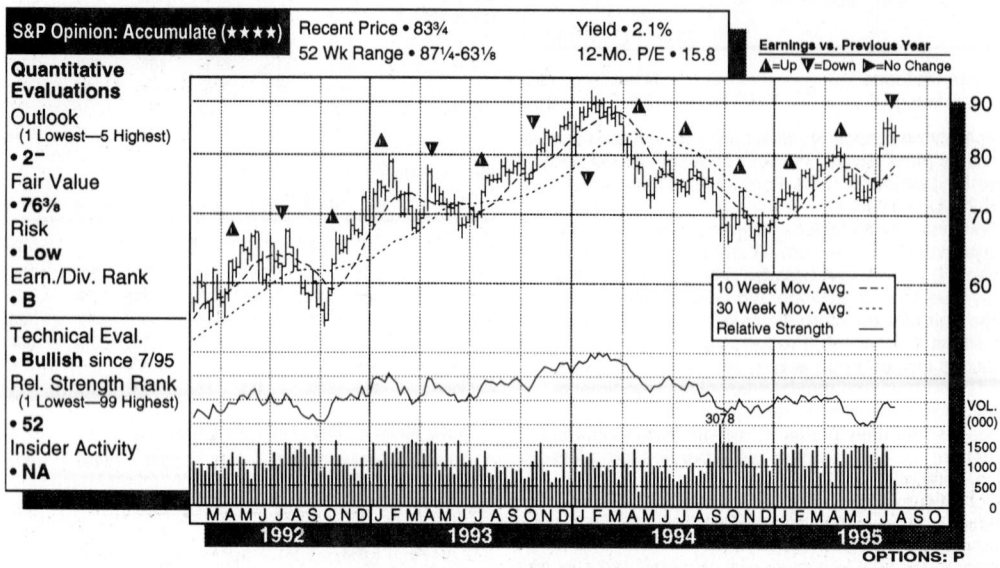

10 Week Mov. Avg. − − −
30 Week Mov. Avg. ·······
Relative Strength —

OPTIONS: P

Overview - 08-AUG-95

Profit comparisons in 1995 will be penalized by the $1.57 a share charge to restructure telecommunication operations and cover relocation and severance costs at Sea-Land. Rail operating profits will benefit from increased grain traffic for export and heavier movements to poultry breeders. Coal volumes may be flat as a soft domestic market is balanced by robust export demand. Margins should benefit from reduced train cycle times and reduced crew sizes. Intermodal profits could fall stemming fierce competition from truckers. Shipping volumes will reflect strong growth in world trade. Operating profits will benefit from the absence of 1994's strike-related costs and savings from the consolidation of administrative offices. Barge profits will benefit from higher rates and increased coal and grain movements and industrial backhaul volumes.

Valuation - 08-AUG-95

Shares of this multimodal transportation firm have rallied sharply in 1995 and are closing in on their early 1994 highs. Renewed interest in railroad issues reflects diminishing concerns about the longevity of the current business cycle (and low valuations). CSX's attraction also lies in the positive turn in the barge industry's fundamentals, savings seen from reflagging part of Sea-Land's fleet and the benefits anticipated from Sea-Land's alliance with Maersk Line. Despite the recent price advance, CSX continues to trade at a large discount to the average stock earnings multiple.

Key Stock Statistics

S&P EPS Est. 1995	5.20	Tang. Bk. Value/Share	36.32
P/E on S&P Est. 1995	16.1	Beta	1.48
S&P EPS Est. 1996	7.70	Shareholders	57,400
Dividend Rate/Share	1.76	Market cap. (B)	$ 8.7
Shs. outstg. (M)	105.2	Inst. holdings	67%
Avg. daily vol. (M)	0.228	Insider holdings	NA

Value of $10,000 invested 5 years ago: $ 27,099

Fiscal Year Ending Dec. 31

	1995	% Change	1994	% Change	1993	% Change
Revenues (Million $)						
1Q	2,468	11%	2,227	5%	2,123	2%
2Q	2,600	10%	2,371	5%	2,264	3%
3Q	—	—	2,470	10%	2,238	1%
4Q	—	—	2,540	10%	2,315	3%
Yr.	—	—	9,608	7%	8,940	2%
Income (Million $)						
1Q	121.0	64%	74.00	NM	-9.00	NM
2Q	19.00	-88%	162.0	5%	154.0	NM
3Q	—	—	177.0	181%	63.00	-51%
4Q	—	—	239.0	58%	151.0	NM
Yr.	—	—	652.0	82%	359.0	NM
Earnings Per Share ($)						
1Q	1.15	62%	0.71	NM	-0.09	NM
2Q	0.18	-88%	1.55	5%	1.48	NM
3Q	E1.90	—	1.68	175%	0.61	-51%
4Q	E1.97	—	2.29	57%	1.46	NM
Yr.	E5.20	—	6.23	80%	3.46	NM

Next earnings report expected: late October

CSX Corp.

Business Summary - 08-AUG-95

Contributions to operating profits (in millions) by business segment were:

	1994	1993	1992
Railroad	$929	$746	$121
Shipping	187	100	134
Intermodal	61	53	-6
Barge	63	45	60
Non-transportation	54	45	41

CSX Transportation operates the nation's third largest rail system, which spans 18,779 miles in 20 states and Ontario. CSX is the nation's largest coal hauler. In 1994 CSX derived 32% of its rail revenues from coal, 15% from chemicals, automobiles (11%) and forest products (10%). CSX handled 4.48 million carloads in 1994 generating an average revenue of $1,032 per load, versus 4.20 million carloads at an average revenue of $1,042 per unit.

Sea-Land Service operates one of the world's largest containership lines. In 1994 it carried 1,288,000 loads (yielding an average $2,302 per load), versus 1,180,305 loads in 1993 ($2,405). Sea-Land calls on 120 ports in 80 countries, employing a fleet of 93 vessels.

CSX Intermodal Inc. provides transcontinental intermodal services, employing most national railroads. It handled 1,283,00 loads in 1994 of which 45% was domestic, versus 1,141,000 loads in 1993 (47%). Logistics and warehousing services are provided by Customized Transportation Inc.

American Commercial Lines is the largest U.S. barge carrier, operating a fleet of 3,295 barges and 117 towboats. Some 22% of barge revenues are derived from transporting coal. The Jeffboat division is engaged in inland marine construction.

Non-transportation business includes the operation of two resorts and real estate activities. CSX also holds an 87% stake in Yukon Pacific Corp. which plans to develop a gas pipeline in Alaska.

Important Developments

Jul. '95—CSX made a $165 million charge against 1995 second quarter net income (1.57 a share). The charge primarily covers costs to write off telecommunication equipment, relocate Sea-Land's headqarters and severance payments associated with the reflagging of five vessels. Sea-Land expects to save $2.5 million annually by operating with lower cost crews under a foreign flag.

May '95—Sea-Land Service and Maersk Line, a major Danish shipping line, agreed to substantially expand their operating alliance. To be phased in gradually, beginning in mid-1996, the alliance covers the sharing of vessels, terminals containers and other assets on all routes served.

Capitalization

Long Term Debt: $2,577,000,000 (6/95).

Per Share Data ($) (Year Ended Dec. 31)

	1994	1993	1992	1991	1990	1989
Tangible Bk. Val.	33.22	27.78	26.54	30.81	35.75	33.05
Cash Flow	11.74	8.96	5.32	4.23	8.44	8.51
Earnings	6.23	3.46	0.19	-0.75	3.63	4.09
Dividends	1.76	1.58	1.52	1.43	1.40	1.28
Payout Ratio	28%	46%	NM	NM	39%	30%
Prices - High	92⅜	88⅛	73⅝	58	38⅛	38⅝
- Low	63⅛	66⅞	54½	29¾	26	29¾
P/E Ratio - High	15	25	NM	NM	11	9
- Low	10	19	NM	NM	7	7

Income Statement Analysis (Million $)

	1994	%Chg	1993	%Chg	1992	%Chg	1991
Revs.	9,608	7%	8,940	2%	8,734	1%	8,636
Oper. Inc.	1,809	15%	1,578	6%	1,492	10%	1,355
Depr.	577	NM	572	9%	527	5%	501
Int. Exp.	310	4%	298	8%	276	-10%	306
Pretax Inc.	1,027	59%	647	NM	8.0	NM	-88.0
Eff. Tax Rate	35%	—	42%	—	NM	—	NM
Net Inc.	652	82%	359	NM	20.0	NM	-76.0

Balance Sheet & Other Fin. Data (Million $)

	1994	1993	1992	1991	1990	1989
Cash	535	499	530	465	609	591
Curr. Assets	1,665	1,571	1,421	1,535	1,725	1,711
Total Assets	13,724	13,420	13,049	12,798	12,804	12,298
Curr. Liab.	2,505	2,275	2,280	2,477	2,303	2,331
LT Debt	2,618	3,133	3,245	2,804	3,025	2,727
Common Eqty.	3,731	3,180	2,975	3,182	3,541	3,247
Total Cap.	8,919	8,654	8,302	8,207	9,100	8,626
Cap. Exp.	875	768	1,041	864	927	815
Cash Flow	1,229	931	547	425	830	862

Ratio Analysis

	1994	1993	1992	1991	1990	1989
Curr. Ratio	0.7	0.7	0.6	0.6	0.7	0.7
% LT Debt of Cap.	29.4	36.7	39.1	34.2	33.2	31.6
% Net Inc.of Revs.	6.8	4.0	0.2	NM	4.4	5.5
% Ret. on Assets	4.8	2.7	0.2	NM	2.9	3.5
% Ret. on Equity	18.8	11.7	0.6	NM	10.5	13.3

Dividend Data (A "poison pill" stock purchase plan was adopted in 1988. A dividend reinvestment plan is available.)

Amt. of Div. $	Date Decl.	Ex-Div. Date	Stock of Record	Payment Date
0.440	Oct. 12	Nov. 18	Nov. 25	Dec. 15 '94
0.440	Feb. 08	Feb. 17	Feb. 24	Mar. 15 '95
0.440	Apr. 25	May. 19	May. 25	Jun. 15 '95
0.440	Jul. 12	Aug. 23	Aug. 25	Sep. 15 '95

Data as orig. reptd.; bef. results of disc. opers. and/or spec. items. Per share data adj. for stk. divs. as of ex-div. date. E-Estimated. NA-Not Available. NM-Not Meaningful. NR-Not Ranked.

Office—One James Center, 901 East Cary St., Richmond, VA 23219-4031. **Tel**—(804) 782-1400. **Chrmn & Pres**—J. W. Snow. **EVP & CFO**—P. R. Goodwin. **VP-Treas**—G. R. Weber. **VP & Secy**—A. A. Rudnick. **Investor Contact**—Kathy Wilson. **Dirs**—E. L. Addison, E. E. Bailey, R. L. Burrus Jr., B. C. Gottwald, J. R. Hall, R. D. Kunisch, H. L. McColl Jr., J. W. McGlothlin, S. J. Morcott, C. E. Rice, W. C. Richardson, F. S. Royal, J. W. Snow. **Transfer Agent & Registrar**—Harris Trust Co., Chicago. **Incorporated** in Virginia in 1978. **Empl-46,747. S&P Analyst:** Stephen R. Klein

CUC International

NYSE Symbol **CU**
In S&P 500

07-OCT-95

Industry:
Services

Summary: CUC International is a membership based consumer company, providing its members a variety of services that offer discounts and convenience.

Quantitative Evaluations

Recent Price • 35
52 Wk Range • 35⅝-18⅞

Yield • Nil
12-Mo. P/E • 46.1

Outlook
(1 Lowest—5 Highest)
• **1+**

Fair Value
• **26⅛**

Risk
• **Low**

Earn./Div. Rank
• **B**

Technical Eval.
• **Bearish** since 9/95

Rel. Strength Rank
(1 Lowest—99 Highest)
• **85**

Insider Activity
• **Neutral**

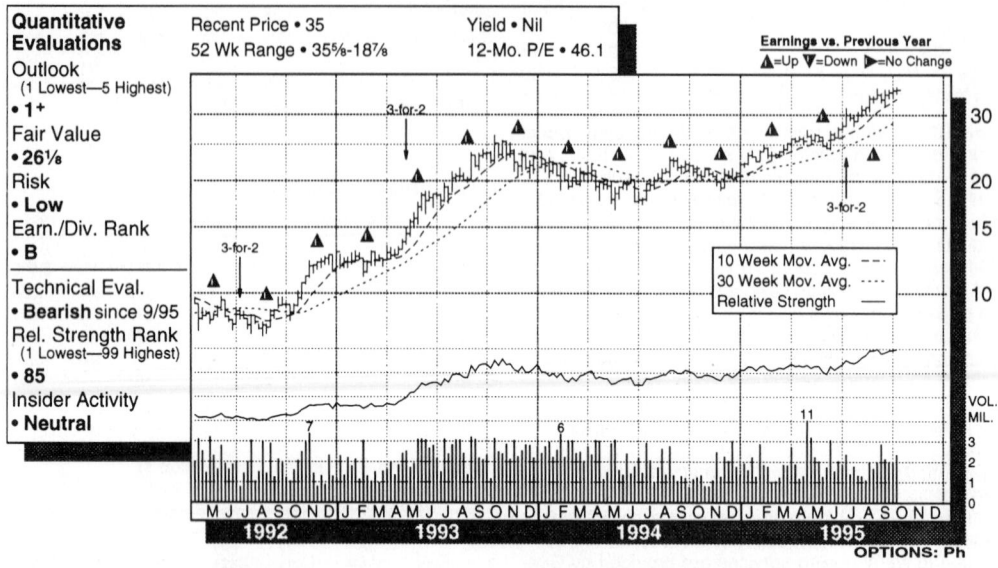

Earnings vs. Previous Year
▲=Up ▼=Down ▶=No Change

10 Week Mov. Avg. — —
30 Week Mov. Avg. · · · ·
Relative Strength —

OPTIONS: Ph

Business Profile - 06-OCT-95

CUC International has expanded its interactive retailing operations this year. The company launched a shopping service on the Internet in September and earlier joined the Microsoft Interactive Television (MITV) Media Partners Program. An agreement with a subsidiary of First Data Corporation will enable CUC to offer its services to small to medium sized credit card issuers, a previously untapped market. The company has made several acquisitions thus far in fiscal 1996.

Operational Review - 06-OCT-95

CUC has been a rapidly growing company, with sales and earnings advancing at annual compound rates of 18% and 40%, respectively, over the past four fiscal years. Continued strong membership trends allowed revenues to increase 23% in the first half of 1995-96. Higher renewal rates widened operating margins, and earnings rose 34%. Long-term debt, comprised of zero coupon convertible securities, is only 2.5% of shareholders' equity.

Stock Performance - 06-OCT-95

In the past 30 trading days, CU's shares have increased 5%, compared to a 4% rise in the S&P 500. Average trading volume for the past five days was 465,080 shares, compared with the 40-day moving average of 431,472 shares.

Key Stock Statistics

Dividend Rate/Share	Nil	Shareholders	2,800
Shs. outstg. (M)	178.6	Market cap. (B)	$ 6.2
Avg. daily vol. (M)	0.420	Inst. holdings	92%
Tang. Bk. Value/Share	1.63	Insider holdings	NA
Beta	1.25		

Value of $10,000 invested 5 years ago: $ 122,206

Fiscal Year Ending Jan. 31

	1996	% Change	1995	% Change	1994	% Change
Revenues (Million $)						
1Q	292.5	19%	245.0	18%	207.0	19%
2Q	316.0	25%	253.0	17%	215.8	19%
3Q	—	—	263.7	19%	222.1	18%
4Q	—	—	281.7	20%	234.4	18%
Yr.	—	—	1,045	19%	879.3	18%
Income (Million $)						
1Q	34.21	29%	26.60	39%	19.07	53%
2Q	38.17	37%	27.96	37%	20.35	51%
3Q	—	—	30.25	33%	22.74	51%
4Q	—	—	32.78	30%	25.22	41%
Yr.	—	—	117.6	35%	87.37	48%
Earnings Per Share ($)						
1Q	0.19	26%	0.15	35%	0.11	42%
2Q	0.21	31%	0.16	33%	0.12	38%
3Q	—	—	0.17	30%	0.13	33%
4Q	—	—	0.19	27%	0.15	29%
Yr.	—	—	0.67	31%	0.51	38%

Next earnings report expected: late November

CUC International

Business Summary - 06-OCT-95

CUC International Inc. is a membership-based consumer services company, providing over 38 million individual customers with access to services such as discount shopping, travel, automobile discounts, dining, home improvement, vacation exchange, credit card and checking account enhancement packages and discount coupon programs. The company also administers insurance package programs that are generally combined with discount shopping and travel memberships for credit union members. Services are provided through individual, wholesale, and discount coupon memberships.

The company's revenues are derived principally from membership fees, which vary depending on the membership program. Fees generally range from $6 to $250 per year. CU arranges with client financial institutions, retailers, oil companies, credit unions, on-line networks, fundraisers and others to market certain membership services directly to the clients' individual account holders. Participating clients receive commissions on initial and renewal memberships, averaging 20% of the net membership fees.

Major membership services offered by the company include Shoppers Advantage, a discount shopping program that provides product price information and home shopping services; Travelers Advantage, a discount travel service program whereby members can obtain information on schedules and rates for major scheduled airlines, hotel chains and car rental agencies and travel packages; and AutoVantage, which offers comprehensive new car summaries and discounts on new domestic and foreign cars purchased through the company's independent dealer network, tire and parts discounts and used car valuations.

Through its Comp-U-Card division, CU offers other membership services, including a dining service, a credit card registration service, Buyers Advantage and a home service. CU also sells enhancement package memberships through client financial institutions, which select a package of CU's products and services to be added to the clients' own services for use by checking account holders.

Important Developments

Sep. '95—The company launched Shopper's Advantage, a shopping service on the Internet featuring more than 250,000 brand name items. Separately, CUC completed the acquisition of North American Outdoor Group, Inc. (NOAG), a one-million-member organization, for about $52 million in stock. In June 1995, CU acquired GETKO Group Inc., which distributes welcome packages to new homeowners, for stock valued at approximately $100 million.

Capitalization

Long Term Debt: $14,031,000 (net of $1,434,000 unamortized original issue discount) of zero coupon notes due 1996, conv. into 10.125 com. shs. per $100 face amount (7/95).

Per Share Data ($)

(Year Ended Jan. 31)

	1995	1994	1993	1992	1991	1990
Tangible Bk. Val.	1.44	0.63	-0.18	-0.47	-0.79	-0.91
Cash Flow	0.80	0.64	0.49	0.27	0.25	0.18
Earnings	0.67	0.51	0.37	0.17	0.16	0.08
Dividends	Nil	Nil	Nil	Nil	Nil	0.99
Payout Ratio	Nil	Nil	Nil	Nil	Nil	NM
Cal. Yrs.	1994	1993	1992	1991	1990	1989
Prices - High	23⁷/₈	26¹/₂	12⁷/₈	9³/₄	4¹/₂	4¹/₈
- Low	16⁵/₈	11¹/₈	7⁵/₈	3⁷/₈	2³/₈	2¹/₁₆
P/E Ratio - High	36	52	34	59	30	56
- Low	25	22	21	24	16	28

Income Statement Analysis (Million $)

	1995	%Chg	1994	%Chg	1993	%Chg	1992
Revs.	1,039	19%	875	18%	739	15%	641
Oper. Inc.	209	26%	166	36%	122	23%	99
Depr.	23.3	4%	22.3	29%	17.3	10%	15.7
Int. Exp.	NA	—	4.8	-45%	8.7	-46%	16.0
Pretax Inc.	191	35%	142	48%	96.1	113%	45.1
Eff. Tax Rate	38%	—	39%	—	39%	—	44%
Net Inc.	118	35%	87.4	49%	58.8	134%	25.1

Balance Sheet & Other Fin. Data (Million $)

	1995	1994	1993	1992	1991	1990
Cash	181	117	28.6	14.4	13.3	12.3
Curr. Assets	504	377	243	205	143	111
Total Assets	768	613	479	322	239	201
Curr. Liab.	109	123	127	133	103	85.0
LT Debt	15.0	22.0	37.0	69.0	101	117
Common Eqty.	443	285	150	-1.0	-22.0	-41.0
Total Cap.	458	307	187	68.0	80.0	78.0
Cap. Exp.	17.6	9.1	4.6	6.7	4.9	4.1
Cash Flow	141	110	76.1	40.8	28.9	19.0

Ratio Analysis

	1995	1994	1993	1992	1991	1990
Curr. Ratio	4.6	3.1	1.9	1.5	1.4	1.3
% LT Debt of Cap.	3.3	7.2	19.9	101.4	126.5	NM
% Net Inc.of Revs.	11.3	10.0	8.0	3.9	3.9	2.2
% Ret. on Assets	16.9	15.8	14.1	7.8	8.0	3.7
% Ret. on Equity	32.0	39.7	NM	NM	NM	20.9

Dividend Data —In June 1989, CU paid special dividends of $1.48 a share in cash and $2.07 face amount ($0.93 discount amount) of zero coupon notes due 1996 as part of a recapitalization plan (data adjusted). A three-for-two stock split was effected in May 1993.

Amt. of Div. $	Date Decl.	Ex-Div. Date	Stock of Record	Payment Date
3-for-2	Jun. 07	Jul. 03	Jun. 19	Jun. 30 '95

Data as orig. reptd.; bef. results of disc. opers. and/or spec. items. Per share data adj. for stk. divs. as of ex-div. date. E-Estimated. NA-Not Available. NM-Not Meaningful. NR-Not Ranked.

Office—707 Summer St., Stamford, CT 06901. **Tel**—(203) 324-9261. **Chrmn & CEO**—W. A. Forbes. **Pres & COO**—E. K. Shelton. **SrVP & CFO**—C. Corigliano. **Secy**—R. T. Tucker. **VP & Investor Contact**—Sandra Morgan (203-965-5114). **Dirs**—B. Burnap, T. B. Donnelley, W. A. Forbes, S. A. Greyser, W. B. King, H. C. McCall, B. C. Perfit, R. P. Rittereiser, S. M. Rumbough Jr., E. K. Shelton. **Transfer Agent & Registrar**—First National Bank of Boston. **Incorporated** in Delaware in 1974. **Empl**- 8,000. **S&P Analyst:** Stephen Madonna, CFA

Cabletron Systems

NYSE Symbol **CS**
In S&P 500

02-OCT-95

Industry:
Data Processing

Summary: CS is a leading provider of intelligent hubs, switching products and management software for Ethernet, Token Ring, FDDI and ATM networking environments.

S&P Opinion: Accumulate (★★★★)

Recent Price • 65⅞	Yield • Nil
52 Wk Range • 69¼-37⅜	12-Mo. P/E • 25.0

Quantitative Evaluations

Outlook
(1 Lowest—5 Highest)
• **5+**

Fair Value
• **92⅜**

Risk
• **Average**

Earn./Div. Rank
• **B**

Technical Eval.
• **Bullish** since 3/95

Rel. Strength Rank
(1 Lowest—99 Highest)
• **90**

Insider Activity
• **Neutral**

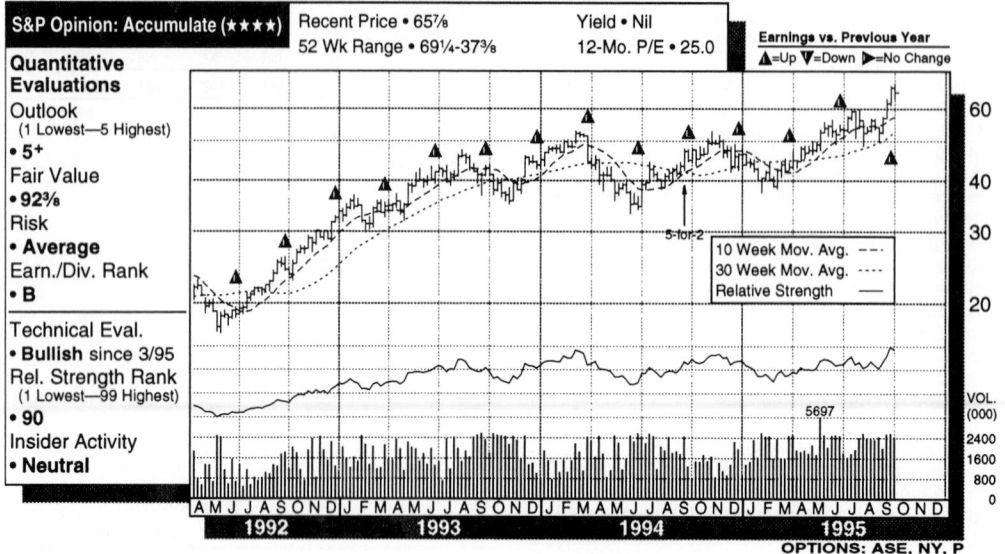

Earnings vs. Previous Year
▲=Up ▼=Down ▶=No Change

5-for-2

10 Week Mov. Avg. – – –
30 Week Mov. Avg. ·······
Relative Strength ——

5697

VOL. (000)
2400
1600
800
0

OPTIONS: ASE, NY, P

Overview - 02-OCT-95

CS's exceptional growth is expected to continue, as demand for networking products remains strong. We are forecasting revenue growth of about 32% in 1995-96, reflecting continued strong demand for intelligent hub products of which CS is the industry leader. In addition, the company's new switching product line-up should find good market acceptance, as end-users are increasingly implementing switches across their networks. Despite ongoing competitive pressures, we believe gross margins will remain stable to slightly higher, aided by the higher-margin switching and software products. Operating costs should remain well controlled, although R&D is expected to rise as a percent of sales. Interest income comparisons are expected to be favorable and earnings for 1995-96 are expected to reach $3.00 a share.

Valuation - 02-OCT-95

We believe recent product announcements adequately address critical new networking technologies and solidify CS's position among the industry's leading players. These announcements, particularly in the fast growing area of switching, should remove investor concerns about CS's technological viability in this fast changing industry. While the pending merger between Chipcom and 3COM could heighten near-term competitive pressures, we believe that CS's leading position will be maintained in the long run. These solid fundamentals along with CS's strong revenue and earnings potential should lead to continued above-average capital gains for shareholders.

Key Stock Statistics

S&P EPS Est. 1996	3.00	Tang. Bk. Value/Share	8.90
P/E on S&P Est. 1996	22.0	Beta	1.23
S&P EPS Est. 1997	3.60	Shareholders	1,800
Dividend Rate/Share	Nil	Market cap. (B)	$ 4.7
Shs. outstg. (M)	71.6	Inst. holdings	59%
Avg. daily vol. (M)	0.648	Insider holdings	NA

Value of $10,000 invested 5 years ago: $ 439,166

Fiscal Year Ending Feb. 28

	1996	% Change	1995	% Change	1994	% Change
Revenues (Million $)						
1Q	240.8	33%	180.7	37%	131.5	49%
2Q	257.3	33%	194.0	37%	141.9	47%
3Q	—	—	210.0	34%	156.5	42%
4Q	—	—	226.0	34%	168.2	37%
Yr.	—	—	810.7	36%	598.1	43%
Income (Million $)						
1Q	48.30	34%	36.16	38%	26.23	49%
2Q	52.77	37%	38.47	36%	28.27	47%
3Q	—	—	41.83	34%	31.17	41%
4Q	—	—	45.52	36%	33.55	37%
Yr.	—	—	162.0	36%	119.2	43%
Earnings Per Share ($)						
1Q	0.68	33%	0.51	37%	0.37	48%
2Q	0.74	37%	0.54	35%	0.40	45%
3Q	E0.77	31%	0.59	34%	0.44	39%
4Q	E0.82	28%	0.64	36%	0.47	36%
Yr.	E3.00	32%	2.27	35%	1.68	42%

Next earnings report expected: mid December

Cabletron Systems

Business Summary - 02-OCT-95

Cabletron Systems, Inc. is a leading vendor of internetworking products, most notably hardware and software connectivity solutions for local area and wide area networks (LANs & WANs). Products are distributed primarily through a direct sales force. Contributions to sales by product line in recent fiscal years:

	1994-95	1993-94	1992-93
Interconnection	91.4%	92.7%	93.9%
Cables	1.2%	1.6%	2.8%
Test equipment & services	7.4%	5.7%	3.3%

Customers outside the U.S. accounted for 28% of sales in 1994-95, up from 27% in 1993-94.

CS's networking approach is based on the strategy called Synthesis, a blueprint for transitioning end users from traditional router-based internetworks to switch-based virtual networks. Synthesis incorporates the company's hub and management technologies with emerging switching technologies. A key component of Synthesis is the company's MMAC-Plus, an intelligent switching hub that, among other things, provides high-speed switching capabilities for shared-access, packet-based LANs. This product is complemented by CS's Multi Media Access Center (MMAC), an intelligent hub that allows the integration of multiple network standards such as Ethernet, Token Ring and FDDI. These products are managed by the company's network management software product called SPECTRUM.

Other interconnection products include multiport repeaters designed to increase the reach of a geographically dispersed LAN; bridges, which perform high-speed filtering and data transmission; stand-alone transceivers, which attach to personal computers in a network enabling the user to communicate with other users in the LAN; and network interface cards (NICs), which provide a high-speed data connection for personal computer platforms.

CS offers cable assemblies and various cables, as well as connectors and accessories for the cable. Test equipment offered is designed to analyze and verify proper installation and operation of the company's products. Services include LAN installation and consulting.

Important Developments

Sep. '95—CS introduced two new modules under its new MMAC SmartSwitch family, including a 24-port Ethernet and a dual port FDDI switch. During the next six months, CS is expected to announce Smart-Switches addressing wiring closet, backbone and enterprise switching applications. The new switches will embrace most key networking technologies, including Token Ring, 100Base-T, VG-ANyLAN and ATM.

Capitalization

Long Term Debt: None (8/95).

Per Share Data ($) (Year Ended Feb. 28)

	1995	1994	1993	1992	1991	1990
Tangible Bk. Val.	8.22	5.94	4.09	2.90	2.01	1.02
Cash Flow	2.63	1.92	1.35	0.93	0.60	0.37
Earnings	2.27	1.68	1.19	0.83	0.54	0.35
Dividends	Nil	Nil	Nil	Nil	Nil	Nil
Payout Ratio	Nil	Nil	Nil	Nil	Nil	Nil
Cal. Yrs.	1994	1993	1992	1991	1990	1989
Prices - High	53	47⅝	34⅛	22⅛	11¾	6¾
- Low	33	29¾	16⅞	10¼	2¾	3¾
P/E Ratio - High	23	28	29	27	22	19
- Low	15	18	14	12	5	11

Income Statement Analysis (Million $)

	1995	%Chg	1994	%Chg	1993	%Chg	1992
Revs.	811	36%	598	43%	418	44%	291
Oper. Inc.	265	37%	194	42%	137	44%	95.0
Depr.	26.4	56%	16.9	44%	11.7	66%	7.1
Int. Exp.	Nil	—	Nil	—	Nil	—	Nil
Pretax Inc.	248	36%	183	41%	130	42%	91.8
Eff. Tax Rate	35%	—	35%	—	36%	—	37%
Net Inc.	162	36%	119	43%	83.5	44%	58.0

Balance Sheet & Other Fin. Data (Million $)

	1995	1994	1993	1992	1991	1990
Cash	245	164	154	90.9	60.5	15.8
Curr. Assets	471	326	285	193	129	73.0
Total Assets	690	499	343	236	154	87.0
Curr. Liab.	96.3	70.7	51.3	30.7	13.5	19.7
LT Debt	Nil	Nil	Nil	Nil	Nil	Nil
Common Eqty.	588	424	289	204	140	67.0
Total Cap.	594	428	292	206	140	68.0
Cap. Exp.	63.1	39.4	28.3	25.5	14.5	10.8
Cash Flow	188	136	95.2	65.1	39.5	24.0

Ratio Analysis

	1995	1994	1993	1992	1991	1990
Curr. Ratio	4.9	4.6	5.5	6.3	9.5	3.7
% LT Debt of Cap.	Nil	Nil	Nil	Nil	Nil	Nil
% Net Inc.of Revs.	20.0	19.9	20.0	20.0	19.9	21.5
% Ret. on Assets	27.2	28.2	28.7	29.7	29.2	34.5
% Ret. on Equity	32.0	33.3	33.8	33.6	34.0	51.8

Dividend Data —The company has never paid a cash dividend. A 2.5-for-1 stock split was effected in September, 1994.

Data as orig. reptd.; bef. results of disc. opers. and/or spec. items. Per share data adj. for stk. divs. as of ex-div. date. E-Estimated. NA-Not Available. NM-Not Meaningful. NR-Not Ranked.

Office—35 Industrial Way, Rochester, NH 03867-0505. **Tel**—(603) 332-9400. **Chrmn, COO & Treas**—C. R. Benson. **Pres & CEO**—S. R. Levine. **CFO**—D. J. Kirkpatrick. **Secy**—M. D. Myerow. **Investor Contact**—Ed Cortes (603-335-6311). **Dirs**—C. R. Benson, P. R. Duncan, S. R. Levine, D. F. McGuinness, M. D. Myerow. **Transfer Agent & Registrar**—State Street Bank & Trust Co., Boston. **Incorporated** in Delaware in 1988. **Empl**-4,870. **S&P Analyst:** John D. Coyle, CFA

Campbell Soup

NYSE Symbol **CPB**
In S&P 500

18-SEP-95

Industry:
Food

Summary: Campbell Soup is a major producer of branded soups and other grocery food products. The Dorrance family controls 58% of the common stock.

S&P Opinion: Accumulate (★★★★)

Recent Price • 48⅜	Yield • 2.6%
52 Wk Range • 51¼-37⅞	12-Mo. P/E • 17.3

Quantitative Evaluations

Outlook
(1 Lowest—5 Highest)
• **4+**

Fair Value
• **47⅛**

Risk
• **Low**

Earn./Div. Rank
• **B**

Technical Eval.
• **Bearish** since 7/95

Rel. Strength Rank
(1 Lowest—99 Highest)
• **49**

Insider Activity
• **NA**

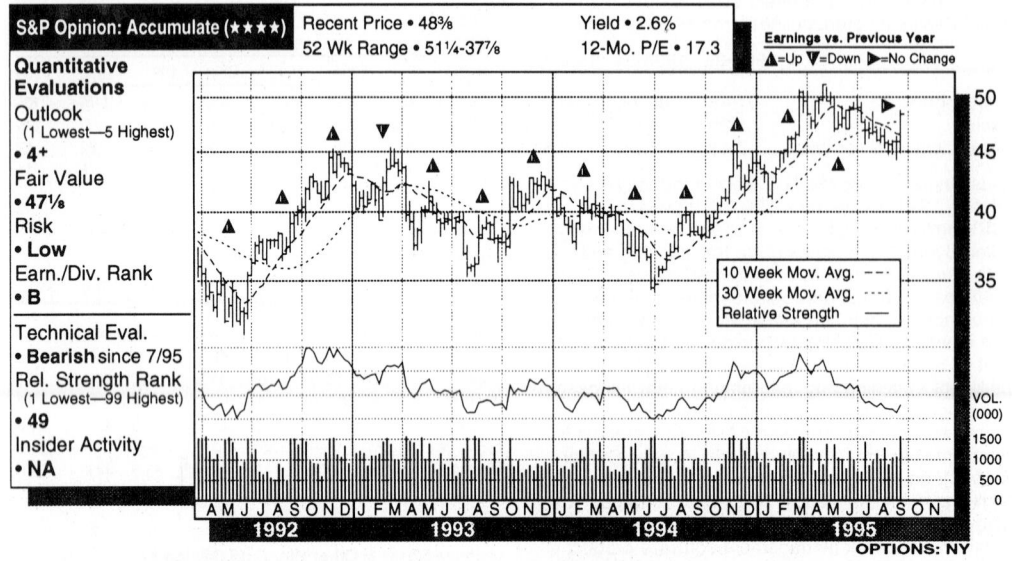

Earnings vs. Previous Year
▲=Up ▼=Down ▶=No Change

10 Week Mov. Avg. - - -
30 Week Mov. Avg. ·····
Relative Strength —

OPTIONS: NY

Overview - 18-SEP-95

Net sales are projected to rise at a high single-digit rate in fiscal 1996, driven by unit volume gains for core soup and grocery products, contributions from recent acquisitions (principally Pace Foods), higher average selling prices, and geographic expansion. Recent divestitures of underperforming businesses and a further improved product mix should help sustain CPB's relatively high operating margins. In spite of modestly dilutive interest and goodwill amortization expenses related to the January 1995 acquisition of Pace, we are confident that earnings will grow at least 10% in fiscal 1996, to $3.10 per share.

Valuation - 18-SEP-95

Recent EPS growth has slowed, reflecting the interest and goodwill dilution related to the January 1995 acquisition of Pace Foods. However, we expect EPS comparisons to return to their more historical, double-digit growth rates by fiscal 1996's second half as the Pace dilution impact wanes. We anticipate that the digestion of Pace and other strategic acquisitions will help support the company's relatively high operating margins for years to come. Rapid debt paydown should continue in fiscal 1996's first half, further bolstering CPB's balance sheet to more normal levels. Future earnings growth should be driven by the further leveraging of Campbell's strong portfolio of brands both in the U.S. and abroad, and additional acquisitions. These low-risk, high quality shares are attractive for purchase for virtually all accounts.

Key Stock Statistics

S&P EPS Est. 1996	3.10	Tang. Bk. Value/Share	2.68
P/E on S&P Est. 1996	15.6	Beta	1.11
Dividend Rate/Share	1.24	Shareholders	43,000
Shs. outstg. (M)	249.6	Market cap. (B)	$ 12.1
Avg. daily vol. (M)	0.274	Inst. holdings	25%
		Insider holdings	NA

Value of $10,000 invested 5 years ago: $ 18,531

Fiscal Year Ending Jul. 31

	1995	% Change	1994	% Change	1993	% Change
Revenues (Million $)						
1Q	1,864	6%	1,763	4%	1,696	10%
2Q	2,040	8%	1,894	6%	1,789	2%
3Q	1,744	11%	1,568	-4%	1,632	6%
4Q	1,630	11%	1,465	NM	1,470	3%
Yr.	7,278	9%	6,690	2%	6,586	5%
Income (Million $)						
1Q	197.4	19%	166.0	6%	156.6	21%
2Q	231.0	14%	203.0	NM	-115.9	NM
3Q	127.0	7%	119.0	10%	108.5	19%
4Q	143.0	NM	142.0	16%	122.0	12%
Yr.	698.0	11%	630.0	145%	257.2	-48%
Earnings Per Share ($)						
1Q	0.79	20%	0.66	6%	0.62	22%
2Q	0.93	15%	0.81	NM	-0.46	NM
3Q	0.51	9%	0.47	9%	0.43	19%
4Q	0.57	NM	0.57	19%	0.48	9%
Yr.	2.80	12%	2.51	146%	1.02	-48%

Next earnings report expected: mid November

Campbell Soup

Business Summary - 15-SEP-95

Campbell Soup Co., through its subsidiaries, manufactures and markets branded convenience food products worldwide. Operations outside the United States accounted for 32% of net sales and 20% of pretax earnings in fiscal 1994 (latest available), consisting of Europe (15% and 6%), Australia (8% and 7%), and Other (9% and 7%). Contributions to sales and operating profits by segment in fiscal 1995 were:

	Sales	Profits
U.S.A.	59%	74%
Bakery & Confectionery	22%	15%
International Grocery	19%	11%

Major U.S. products include both condensed and ready to serve soups (Campbell's, Home Cookin', Chunky, Healthy Request); convenience meals (Swanson, Hungry Man); beans (Homestyle Pork and Beans); juices (Campbell's Tomato, V8); canned spaghetti and gravies (Franco-American); spaghetti sauce (Prego); pickles (Vlasic); refrigerated salad dressings (Marie's); Mexican sauces (Pace); and frozen seafood products (Mrs. Paul's). Foodservice operations serve the away-from-home eating market.

Bakery & Confectionery products include Pepperidge Farm, Inc. in the U.S., a producer of bread, cakes and related products; Belgium-based Biscuits Delacre, a maker of biscuit and chocolate products; and Arnotts Biscuits Ltd. of Australia, a maker of biscuit and bakery products. Godiva Chocolatier (worldwide) and Lamy-Lutti (Europe) serve the candy market.

The International Grocery division consists of soup, grocery and frozen businesses in Canada, Mexico, Argentina, Europe, Australia and Asia. Major brands include Fray Bentos, Betis, Pleybin, Freshbake, and Groko.

Important Developments

Sep. '95—During fiscal 1995, U.S.A. division profits rose 13% (to $885 million), on an 8% sales rise. Acquisitions contributed to half of the sales growth. Bakery & Confectionery profits rose 8% (to $182 million), on 8% higher sales, led by Pepperidge Farm and the confectionery businesses. International Grocery profits rose 12% (to $135 million), on 10% greater sales. Contributions from recently-acquired The Stratford Upon Avon Foods helped offset the negative impact of the devalued Mexican peso. Separately, management said that acquisitions contributed a third of the company's sales growth in fiscal 1995.
Jan. '95—The company acquired Pace Foods Ltd. (estimated 1994 sales and operating earnings of $220 million and $54 million, respectively), a producer of Mexican sauces, for $1.1 billion in cash.

Capitalization

Long Term Debt: $857,000,000 (7/95).

Per Share Data ($)

(Year Ended Jul. 31)

	1995	1994	1993	1992	1991	1990
Tangible Bk. Val.	NA	5.67	4.40	6.31	5.35	5.06
Cash Flow	NA	3.60	1.91	2.74	2.35	0.73
Earnings	2.80	2.51	1.02	1.95	1.58	0.02
Dividends	1.21	1.09	0.91	0.71	0.56	0.49
Payout Ratio	43%	43%	90%	36%	35%	879%
Prices - High	51¼	46	45⅜	45¼	43⅞	31
- Low	41	34¼	35¼	31½	27	21⅞
P/E Ratio - High	18	18	44	23	28	NM
- Low	15	14	35	16	17	NM

Income Statement Analysis (Million $)

	1994	%Chg	1993	%Chg	1992	%Chg	1991
Revs.	6,690	2%	6,586	5%	6,263	NM	6,204
Oper. Inc.	1,323	12%	1,178	8%	1,093	13%	970
Depr.	273	22%	223	12%	200	3%	195
Int. Exp.	85.0	-11%	96.0	-20%	120	-12%	137
Pretax Inc.	963	82%	529	-34%	799	18%	675
Eff. Tax Rate	36%	—	50%	—	39%	—	39%
Net Inc.	630	145%	257	-48%	491	22%	402

Balance Sheet & Other Fin. Data (Million $)

	1994	1993	1992	1991	1990	1989
Cash	96.0	70.0	118	192	103	147
Curr. Assets	1,601	1,686	1,502	1,519	1,666	1,602
Total Assets	4,992	4,898	4,354	4,149	4,116	3,932
Curr. Liab.	1,665	1,851	1,300	1,278	1,298	1,232
LT Debt	560	462	693	773	806	629
Common Eqty.	1,989	1,704	2,028	1,793	1,692	1,778
Total Cap.	2,951	2,435	3,032	2,848	2,789	2,680
Cap. Exp.	421	644	374	361	422	284
Cash Flow	903	480	691	596	189	189

Ratio Analysis

	1994	1993	1992	1991	1990	1989
Curr. Ratio	1.0	0.9	1.2	1.2	1.3	1.3
% LT Debt of Cap.	19.0	19.0	22.9	27.1	28.9	23.5
% Net Inc.of Revs.	9.4	3.9	7.8	6.5	0.1	0.2
% Ret. on Assets	12.7	5.6	11.6	9.8	0.1	0.3
% Ret. on Equity	34.1	13.8	25.8	23.2	0.3	0.7

Dividend Data

—Dividends have been paid since 1902. A dividend reinvestment plan is available.

Amt. of Div. $	Date Decl.	Ex-Div. Date	Stock of Record	Payment Date
0.280	Sep. 22	Sep. 30	Oct. 06	Oct. 31 '94
0.310	Nov. 17	Dec. 30	Jan. 06	Jan. 31 '95
0.310	Mar. 23	Apr. 03	Apr. 07	Apr. 28 '95
0.310	Jun. 22	Jul. 05	Jul. 07	Jul. 31 '95

Data as orig. reptd.; bef. results of disc. opers. and/or spec. items. Per share data adj. for stk. divs. as of ex-div. date. E-Estimated. NA-Not Available. NM-Not Meaningful. NR-Not Ranked.

Office—Campbell Place, Camden, NJ 08103-1799. **Tel**—(609) 342-4800. **Chrmn, Pres & CEO**—D. W. Johnson. **Vice Chrmn**—B. Dorrance. **SVP-Finance**—R. Stubin. **Secy**—J. J. Furey. **Investor Contact**—Leonard F. Griehs. **Dirs**—A. A. App, R. A. Beck, E. M. Carpenter, B. Dorrance, J. T. Dorrance III, T. W. Field Jr., D. W. Johnson, P. E. Lippincott, M. A. Malone, C. H. Mott, R. A. Pfeiffer Jr., G. M. Sherman, D. M. Stewart, G. Strawbridge Jr., R. J. Vlasic, C. C. — Weber. **Transfer Agent & Registrar**—First Chicago Trust Co. of New York, Jersey City, N.J. **Incorporated** in New Jersey in 1922. **Empl**- 44,378. **S&P Analyst:** Kenneth A. Shea

Capital Cities/ABC

NYSE Symbol **CCB**
In S&P 500

01-AUG-95

Industry:
Broadcasting

Summary: This major media company operates the ABC TV network, owns eight TV stations, has equity interests in various cable networks and has a large publishing business.

| S&P Opinion: Hold (★★★) | Recent Price • 96⅛ | Yield • 0.2% |
| | 52 Wk Range • 109½-75⅛ | 12-Mo. P/E • 20.0 |

Earnings vs. Previous Year
▲=Up ▼=Down ▷=No Change

Quantitative Evaluations

Outlook
(1 Lowest—5 Highest)
• **1**

Fair Value
• **88⅜**

Risk
• **Low**

Earn./Div. Rank
• **A**

Technical Eval.
• **Bullish** since 12/92

Rel. Strength Rank
(1 Lowest—99 Highest)
• **89**

Insider Activity
• **Neutral**

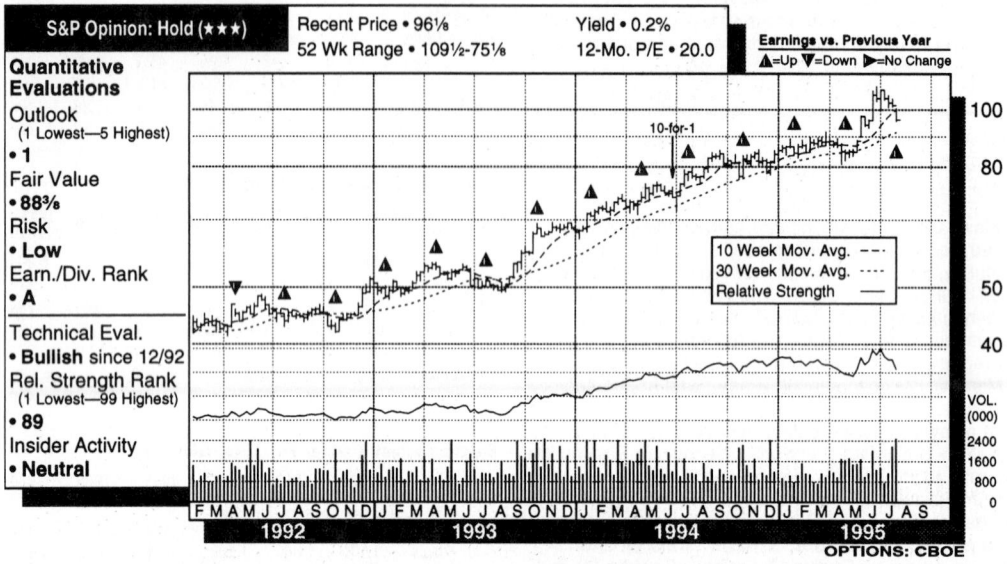

10-for-1

10 Week Mov. Avg. − − −
30 Week Mov. Avg. · · · · ·
Relative Strength ———

VOL.
(000)
2400
1600
800
0

F M A M J J A S O N D J F M A M J J A S O N D J F M A M J J A S O N D J F M A M J J A S O N D J F M A M J J A S
1992   1993   1994   1995

OPTIONS: CBOE

Overview - 01-AUG-95

We expect that this large communications company will be acquired by The Walt Disney Co. (DIS) in 1996. Meanwhile, in 1995, we expect earnings from the ABC television network to benefit from a stronger advertising environment and the favorable audience demographics of various shows broadcast by ABC. However, higher compensation fees to network affiliates will limit the network's overall profit gain. Also, we expect earnings increases in 1995 from CCB's other major U.S. broadcast operations or investments. We look for profit from CCB's publishing operations to be relatively flat, with higher newsprint costs being a restraint. In 1996, we expect CCB's profit gains to be partly fueled by strong demand for advertising time on the ABC television network.

Valuation - 01-AUG-95

With Disney offering to acquire CCB for cash and stock valued at about $125 a share, we do not expect a higher bid from another party to emerge. The stock component of DIS's offer accounts for close to half of the transaction's total value. As a result, we expect fluctuations in DIS's stock price to be a principal factor in CCB's share price during the months ahead. Although we like the combined companies' long-term prospects, we do not advise adding to holdings of either CCB or DIS at this time. We view DIS's current stock price as adequately reflecting the pro forma fiscal 1996 earnings we expect from a DIS-CCB merger.

Key Stock Statistics

S&P EPS Est. 1995	5.20	Tang. Bk. Value/Share	14.60
P/E on S&P Est. 1995	18.5	Beta	0.98
S&P EPS Est. 1996	5.80	Shareholders	9,800
Dividend Rate/Share	0.20	Market cap. (B)	$ 17.9
Shs. outstg. (M)	153.9	Inst. holdings	82%
Avg. daily vol. (M)	0.517	Insider holdings	NA

Value of $10,000 invested 5 years ago: $ 17,115

Fiscal Year Ending Dec. 31

	1995	% Change	1994	% Change	1993	% Change
Revenues (Million $)						
1Q	1,607	14%	1,405	19%	1,178	8%
2Q	1,649	7%	1,538	7%	1,439	3%
3Q	—	—	1,462	12%	1,301	7%
4Q	—	—	1,974	12%	1,755	7%
Yr.	—	—	6,379	12%	5,674	6%
Income (Million $)						
1Q	157.8	36%	116.1	65%	70.49	69%
2Q	208.9	10%	189.5	25%	151.9	3%
3Q	—	—	133.7	71%	78.27	26%
4Q	—	—	240.6	44%	166.7	21%
Yr.	—	—	679.8	45%	467.4	20%
Earnings Per Share ($)						
1Q	1.02	35%	0.76	76%	0.43	71%
2Q	1.36	11%	1.23	34%	0.92	4%
3Q	E0.97	—	0.87	83%	0.47	27%
4Q	E1.85	—	1.56	51%	1.04	24%
Yr.	E5.20	—	4.42	55%	2.85	22%

Next earnings report expected: late October

Business Summary - 31-JUL-95

Capital Cities/ABC, Inc. was formed in 1986 by the merger of American Broadcasting Companies, one of the major television and radio networks, into Capital Cities Communications, a leading independent TV and radio broadcaster.

The broadcast division (83% of revenues and 88% of operating income in 1994) includes the ABC television network, with about 225 primary affiliates; the ABC Radio Networks, with about 3,400 affiliates; eight owned TV stations; and 21 owned radio stations. The TV stations are: WABC-TV, New York; KABC-TV, Los Angeles; WLS-TV, Chicago; WPVI-TV, Philadelphia; KGO-TV, San Francisco; KTRK-TV, Houston; WTVD, Durham-Raleigh; and KFSN-TV, Fresno. CCB's radio holdings include stations in New York (WABC and WPLJ), Los Angeles (KABC and KLOS), Chicago (WLS and WLS-FM) and San Francisco (KGO and KSFO).

CCB also has equity interests in four U.S. cable television channels--ESPN and ESPN-2 (80%), The Arts & Entertainment Network (38%) and Lifetime (50%)--and in a number of overseas filmed entertainment or broadcast companies.

The publishing division (17% of revenues and 12% of income) has seven daily newspapers and a number of weekly papers and shopping guides. CCB's specialized publication segment includes products aimed at various consumer, trade, agricultural and other special-interest markets. Among the publications are W, Los Angeles and Institutional Investor magazines and Women's Wear Daily. In all, CCB's specialized publications include more than 50 products.

Important Developments

Jul. '95—CCB agreed to be acquired The Walt Disney Co. in a cash and stock transaction valued at about $19 billion. CCB shareholders would have the right to receive $65 in cash and one share of DIS common stock in exchange for each CCB share held. Some CCB shareholders may receive a larger proportion of cash, and less DIS stock. The transaction could be completed in early 1996. Meanwhile, in 1995's second quarter, CCB's operating profit from its broadcasting segment was up 5%, helped by stronger advertising demand for the ABC television network. Earnings from CCB's television were down slightly, reflecting the absence of an unusual year-ago credit. From the publishing area, CCB's quarterly earnings declined 2%. CCB's non-operating earnings were helped by a non-recurring gain from the sale of CCB's New England newspapers. Also, as of July 2, 1995, CCB had cash equivalents or short-term investments totaling about $1.45 billion.

Capitalization

Long Term Debt: $610,631,000 (3/95).
Minority Interest: $129,402,000.

Per Share Data ($)

(Year Ended Dec. 31)

	1994	1993	1992	1991	1990	1989
Tangible Bk. Val.	14.86	9.99	10.69	9.28	7.10	6.19
Cash Flow	5.54	3.81	3.29	3.18	3.70	3.61
Earnings	4.42	2.85	2.34	2.23	2.77	2.72
Dividends	0.20	0.02	0.02	0.02	0.02	0.02
Payout Ratio	5%	1%	1%	1%	1%	1%
Prices - High	86½	64⅜	52⅛	50⅜	63¼	56¾
- Low	60¼	47⅝	41	35¾	38	35¼
P/E Ratio - High	20	23	22	23	23	21
- Low	14	17	17	16	14	13

Income Statement Analysis (Million $)

	1994	%Chg	1993	%Chg	1992	%Chg	1991
Revs.	6,379	12%	5,674	6%	5,344	NM	5,382
Oper. Inc.	1,411	38%	1,019	16%	879	-4%	920
Depr.	173	11%	156	-1%	158	NM	158
Int. Exp.	59.0	-16%	70.0	-40%	117	-39%	193
Pretax Inc.	1,205	46%	828	21%	686	4%	662
Eff. Tax Rate	44%	—	44%	—	43%	—	43%
Net Inc.	680	46%	467	20%	389	4%	375

Balance Sheet & Other Fin. Data (Million $)

	1994	1993	1992	1991	1990	1989
Cash	1,019	438	1,198	1,336	1,360	1,141
Curr. Assets	2,716	1,992	2,733	2,824	2,816	2,536
Total Assets	6,768	5,793	6,522	6,696	6,696	6,360
Curr. Liab.	1,044	871	1,095	1,167	896	800
LT Debt	653	662	964	1,372	1,913	1,760
Common Eqty.	4,289	3,572	3,806	3,655	3,368	3,292
Total Cap.	5,305	4,572	5,104	5,291	5,508	5,287
Cap. Exp.	121	105	115	121	141	199
Cash Flow	852	624	547	533	637	643

Ratio Analysis

	1994	1993	1992	1991	1990	1989
Curr. Ratio	2.6	2.3	2.5	2.4	3.1	3.2
% LT Debt of Cap.	12.3	14.5	18.9	25.9	34.7	33.3
% Net Inc.of Revs.	10.7	8.2	7.3	7.0	8.9	9.8
% Ret. on Assets	10.8	7.9	5.9	5.6	7.5	7.9
% Ret. on Equity	17.3	13.1	10.5	10.7	14.7	15.6

Dividend Data

(Dividends were initiated in 1976. A "poison pill" stock purchase right was adopted in 1989.)

Amt. of Div. $	Date Decl.	Ex-Div. Date	Stock of Record	Payment Date
0.050	Sep. 21	Sep. 26	Sep. 30	Nov. 16 '94
0.050	Dec. 21	Dec. 23	Dec. 30	Jan. 31 '95
0.050	Mar. 21	Mar. 27	Mar. 31	May. 17 '95
0.050	Jun. 22	Jun. 28	Jun. 30	Aug. 16 '95

Data as orig. reptd.; bef. results of disc. opers. and/or spec. items. Per share data adj. for stk. divs. as of ex-div. date. E-Estimated. NA-Not Available. NM-Not Meaningful. NR-Not Ranked.

Office—77 West 66th St., New York, NY 10023. **Tel**—(212) 456-7777. **Chrmn & CEO**—T. S. Murphy. **Pres & COO**—R. A. Iger. **Sr VP-CFO**—R. J. Doerfler. **Secy**—P. R. Farnsworth. **VP & Investor Contact**—Joseph M. Fitzgerald. **Dirs**—R. P. Bauman, N. F. Brady, W. E. Buffett, D. B. Burke, F. T. Cary, J. B. Fairchild, L. H. Goldenson, R. A. Iger, F. S. Jones, A. D. Jordan, J. H. Muller Jr., T. S. Murphy, W. Robertson, M. C. Woodward Jr. **Transfer Agent & Registrar**—Harris Trust Co. of New York, NYC. **Incorporated** in New York in 1946. **Empl**-20,200. **S&P Analyst:** Tom Graves, CFA

Carolina Power & Light

NYSE Symbol **CPL**
In S&P 500

24-OCT-95

Industry:
Utilities-Electric

Summary: This Southeastern utility supplies electric power to more than a million customers in a 30,000 square mile area covering east and west North Carolina and central South Carolina.

S&P Opinion: Hold (★★★)	Recent Price • 33	Yield • 5.4%
	52 Wk Range • 34-25	12-Mo. P/E • 14.2

Earnings vs. Previous Year
▲=Up ▼=Down ▶=No Change

Quantitative Evaluations

Outlook
(1 Lowest—5 Highest)
• **2+**

Fair Value
• **31%**

Risk
• **Low**

Earn./Div. Rank
• **A-**

Technical Eval.
• **Bullish** since 12/94

Rel. Strength Rank
(1 Lowest—99 Highest)
• **67**

Insider Activity
• **NA**

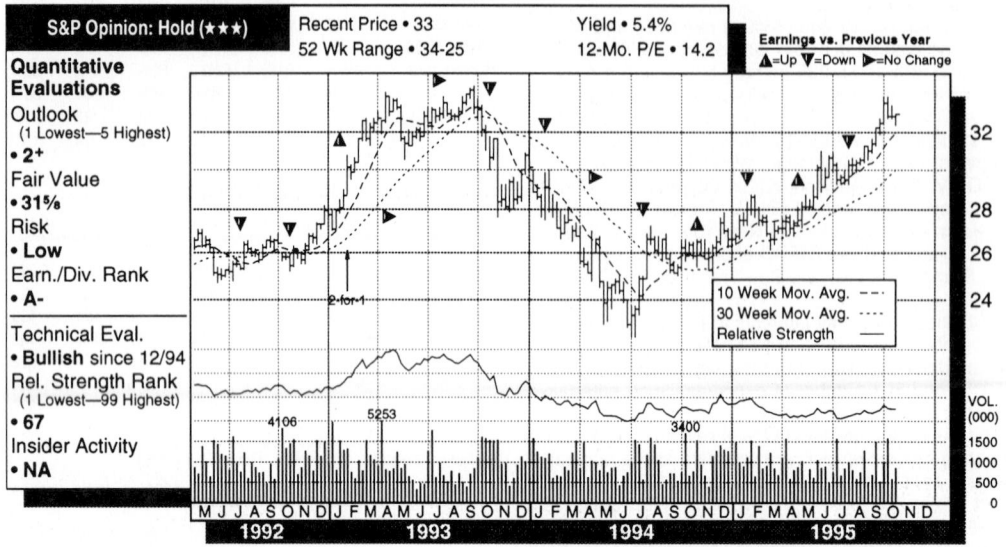

10 Week Mov. Avg. — — —
30 Week Mov. Avg. ....
Relative Strength ———

Overview - 24-OCT-95

Peak demand systemwide rose 5.8% last year, on good growth in the customer count, and we expect the another increase in 1995 due to warmer weather. Assuming continued growth in CPL's economic service area, we expect the company's kilowatt hour sales will advance an average 2.0 at least this year and next. Because CPL's location facilitates the purchase and sale of power with a number of other utilities, it should be able to supply rising demand without adding new generating facilities. CPL's high utilization of low-cost nuclear capacity (nuclear fuel comprised 42% of its total power generation in the first half of this year, versus 30% a year earlier) also gives it a market advantage. The company recently arranged long-term contracts with its wholesale customers and with duPont and Allied, its largest industrial users.

Valuation - 24-OCT-95

CPL's shares have recovered nearly all the ground lost in the steep 1993-94 price decline for electric utilities. We believe the upturn also reflects speculation that the company may be taken over, as were several other small- to mid-size, well managed utilities this summer. The Fed easing of rates last spring also boosted the shares, along with economic growth in CPL's service region. For the future, we expect earnings gains over the next 12 to 15 months and above-average dividend increases to boost CPL's market performance. An ongoing share repurchase program limits downside risk.

Key Stock Statistics

S&P EPS Est. 1995	2.40	Tang. Bk. Value/Share	15.95
P/E on S&P Est. 1995	13.7	Beta	0.65
S&P EPS Est. 1996	2.50	Shareholders	69,700
Dividend Rate/Share	1.76	Market cap. (B)	$ 5.1
Shs. outstg. (M)	155.4	Inst. holdings	31%
Avg. daily vol. (M)	0.242	Insider holdings	NA

Value of $10,000 invested 5 years ago: $ 19,947

Fiscal Year Ending Dec. 31

	1995	% Change	1994	% Change	1993	% Change
Revenues (Million $)						
1Q	728.2	-2%	744.5	5%	707.5	8%
2Q	682.0	NM	687.3	2%	674.6	9%
3Q	875.5	9%	805.5	-6%	854.8	4%
4Q	—	—	639.3	-3%	658.6	NM
Yr.	—	—	2,877	NM	2,895	5%
Income (Million $)						
1Q	98.03	10%	88.82	-6%	94.00	NM
2Q	55.96	-4%	58.22	-17%	69.98	1%
3Q	151.9	26%	120.3	1%	118.6	-18%
4Q	—	—	45.88	-28%	63.87	-10%
Yr.	—	—	313.2	-10%	346.5	-9%
Earnings Per Share ($)						
1Q	0.65	14%	0.57	NM	0.57	NM
2Q	0.36	-3%	0.37	-12%	0.42	NM
3Q	1.02	29%	0.79	10%	0.72	-20%
4Q	E0.37	23%	0.30	-21%	0.38	-17%
Yr.	E2.40	18%	2.03	-3%	2.10	-11%

Next earnings report expected: mid January

Carolina Power & Light

24-OCT-95

Business Summary - 20-OCT-95

Carolina Power & Light provides electric service in eastern and western North Carolina and central South Carolina, areas with a combined population of more than 3.5 million. Electric revenues by customer class in recent years were:

	1994	1993	1992	1991
Residential	32%	33%	32%	32%
Industrial	21%	26%	26%	26%
Commercial	26%	20%	20%	21%
Other	21%	21%	22%	21%

Sources of power generation in 1994 were coal 43%, nuclear 42%, purchased 13%, and other 2%. System peak demand, including purchases, was 10,144 mw in 1994, and system capability totaled 11,209 mw, for a capacity margin of 10.5%.

The company has completed its base load construction program for the foreseeable future. CPL currently projects 2.1% average annual growth in system peak demand over the next 10 years and capacity margins of 13.6% for both 1995 and 1996, assuming normal weather conditions. It plans roughly $287 million in capital outlays from 1995 through 1997 to add new combustion turbine units for use during periods of high demand. The company has long-term purchase contracts with other utilities -- 400 mw of generating capacity from Duke Power through 1996 and 250 mw from Indiana Michigan Power through 2010. It is also obligated to purchase a percentage of North Carolina Eastern Municipal Power Agency's capacity reserve at the Mayo and Harris plants, in which CPL shares an ownership interest, through 1997 and 2007, respectively.

In mid-1994, the Nuclear Regulatory Commission (NRC) named the company's Harris plant one of the seven best-performing nuclear plants in the U.S. In addition, the NRC removed CPL's Brunswick nuclear plant from the list of plants receiving increased regulatory scrutiny.

Important Developments

Oct. '95—CPL reported that it had bought back about 6.8 million of its common shares through September 30, 1995 under a July 1994 authorization to repurchase up to 10 million shares.
Oct. '95—The company noted that increased earnings in the third quarter reflected continued strength in its service area economy, warmer weather than in the year earlier period, and share repurchases.

Capitalization

Long Term Debt: $2,684,408,000 (9/95).
Cum. Preferred Stock: $143,801,000.

Per Share Data ($)

(Year Ended Dec. 31)

	1994	1993	1992	1991	1990	1989
Tangible Bk. Val.	15.95	15.86	15.36	14.53	13.68	13.60
Earnings	2.03	2.10	2.36	2.27	1.58	2.10
Dividends	1.70	1.64	1.58	1.52	1.46	1.42
Payout Ratio	84%	78%	67%	67%	92%	68%
Prices - High	30	34⅝	28¼	27⅛	23⅞	24
- Low	22½	27	24½	21⅝	19	17½
P/E Ratio - High	15	16	12	12	15	11
- Low	11	13	10	10	12	8

Income Statement Analysis (Million $)

	1994	%Chg	1993	%Chg	1992	%Chg	1991
Revs.	2,877	NM	2,895	5%	2,767	3%	2,686
Depr.	398	-4%	414	4%	398	2%	392
Maint.	207	-12%	235	-5%	248	38%	180
Fxd. Chgs. Cov.	3.4	7%	3.2	NM	3.2	9%	3.0
Constr. Credits	9.5	-37%	15.0	36%	11.0	22%	9.0
Eff. Tax Rate	35%	—	35%	—	37%	—	36%
Net Inc.	313	-10%	346	-9%	380	NM	377

Balance Sheet & Other Fin. Data (Million $)

	1994	1993	1992	1991	1990	1989
Gross Prop.	9,546	9,330	9,058	8,798	8,570	8,757
Cap. Exp.	301	389	334	292	316	322
Net Prop.	6,349	6,432	6,426	6,430	6,467	6,676
Capitalization:						
LT Debt	2,531	2,585	2,675	2,734	2,615	2,524
% LT Debt	48	48	50	51	50	48
Pfd.	144	144	144	269	339	350
% Pfd.	2.70	2.70	2.70	5.00	6.50	6.60
Common	2,586	2,632	2,534	2,391	2,254	2,420
% Common	49	49	47	44	43	46
Total Cap.	7,141	7,210	6,673	6,642	6,524	6,658

Ratio Analysis

	1994	1993	1992	1991	1990	1989
Oper. Ratio	84.7	83.8	80.4	78.8	78.7	76.5
% Earn. on Net Prop.	7.0	7.3	8.4	8.8	8.5	8.8
% Ret. on Revs.	10.9	12.0	13.7	14.0	10.7	15.2
% Ret. On Invest.Cap	7.1	8.1	9.2	9.7	9.1	9.3
% Return On Com.Eqty	11.6	13.0	15.4	15.7	15.7	14.6

Dividend Data
—Dividends have been paid since 1937. A dividend reinvestment plan is available.

Amt. of Div. $	Date Decl.	Ex-Div. Date	Stock of Record	Payment Date
0.425	Sep. 22	Oct. 04	Oct. 11	Nov. 01 '94
0.440	Dec. 14	Jan. 04	Jan. 10	Feb. 01 '95
0.440	Mar. 15	Apr. 04	Apr. 10	May. 01 '95
0.440	May. 10	Jul. 06	Jul. 10	Aug. 01 '95
0.440	Sep. 20	Oct. 05	Oct. 10	Nov. 01 '95

Data as orig. reptd.; bef. results of disc opers. and/or spec. items. Per share data adj. for stk. divs. as of ex-div. date.
E-Estimated. NA-Not Available. NM-Not Meaningful. NR-Not Ranked.

Office—411 Fayetteville St., Raleigh, NC 27601. **Tel**—(919) 546-6111. **Chrmn & CEO**—S. H. Smith, Jr. **Pres & COO**—W. Cavanaugh III. **EVP & CFO**—G. E. Harder. **SVP & Secy**—R. E. Jones. **Investor Contact**—Robert F. Drennan, Jr. (919-546-7474). **Dirs**—L. M. Baker, Jr., E. B. Borden, F. J. Capel, W. Cavanaugh III, G. H. V. Cecil, C. W. Coker, R. L. Daugherty, J. R. B. Jackson, R. L. Jones, E. C. Lee, S. H. Smith, Jr., J. T. Wilson. **Transfer Agent & Registrar**—Wachovia Bank of North Carolina, Winston-Salem. **Incorporated** in North Carolina in 1926. **Empl**-7,812. **S&P Analyst:** Jane Collin

STANDARD & POOR'S

STOCK REPORTS

Caterpillar, Inc.

NYSE Symbol **CAT**
In S&P 500

29-SEP-95

Industry:
Machinery

Summary: This company is the world's largest manufacturer of earthmoving machinery and equipment and is a major producer of diesel and natural gas engines and turbines.

S&P Opinion: Hold (★★★)	Recent Price • 58⅞	Yield • 2.4%
	52 Wk Range • 75¼-48¼	12-Mo. P/E • 10.3

Quantitative Evaluations

Outlook
(1 Lowest—5 Highest)
• **2+**

Fair Value
• **56⅝**

Risk
• **Average**

Earn./Div. Rank
• **B**

Technical Eval.
• **Bearish** since 9/95

Rel. Strength Rank
(1 Lowest—99 Highest)
• **7**

Insider Activity
• **Unfavorable**

Earnings vs. Previous Year
▲=Up ▼=Down ▶=No Change

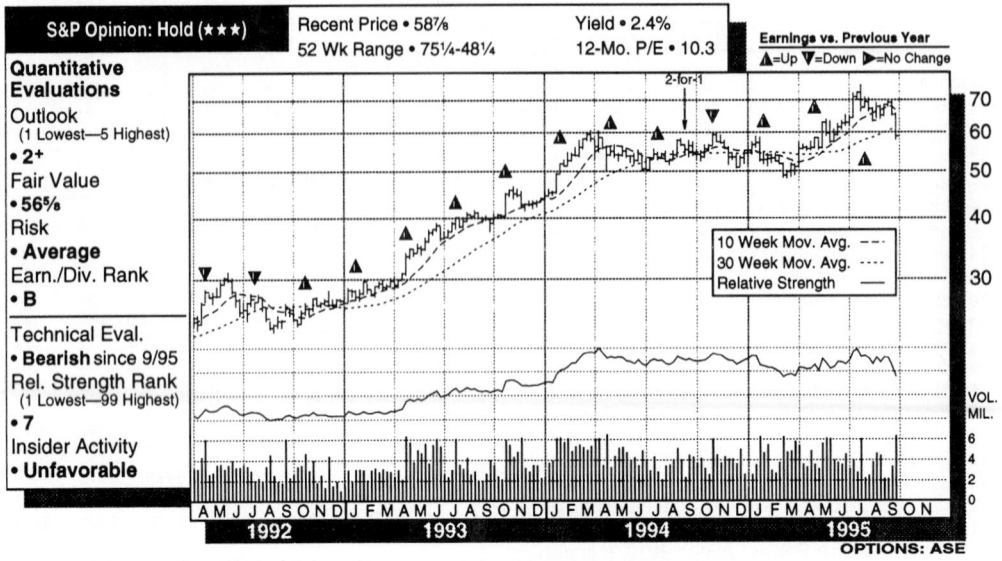

10 Week Mov. Avg. – – –
30 Week Mov. Avg. · · · ·
Relative Strength —

OPTIONS: ASE

Overview - 29-SEP-95

Assuming GDP growth of about 2.6% in 1996 and continued recovery in overseas economies, we anticipate a 10% increase in sales for 1996. Construction equipment sales should rise as dealers rebuild inventories; engine sales will probably decline. Firm prices, an improved product mix, continued high capacity utilization, stable raw material costs, and benefits of a factory modernization program should permit improvement in gross profits and earnings. The benefits of the factory modernization program, debt reduction, new products and aggressive expansion into the market for mining-related equipment in Russia and China will boost long-term sales and profits.

Valuation - 29-SEP-95

Following a sharp decline on news that third quarter earnings would not match 1994's $1.20, CAT's shares through late September were virtually unchanged for the year, versus a 27% gain in the S&P 500. We have lowered our estimates for 1995 and 1996 to reflect the company's announcement. However, we are maintaining our hold rating on the shares. We continue to be very enthusiastic about CAT's long-term prospects and believe the stock is reasonably valued at 9X our revised 1996 estimate. However, we don't think the shares are undervalued; also, they do not warrant an accumulate or strong buy recommendation given the possibility that earnings comparisons may not turn positive until 1996's second quarter.

Key Stock Statistics

S&P EPS Est. 1995	5.40	Tang. Bk. Value/Share	15.79
P/E on S&P Est. 1995	10.9	Beta	1.08
S&P EPS Est. 1996	6.50	Shareholders	33,700
Dividend Rate/Share	1.40	Market cap. (B)	$ 11.4
Shs. outstg. (M)	199.0	Inst. holdings	70%
Avg. daily vol. (M)	0.966	Insider holdings	NA

Value of $10,000 invested 5 years ago: $ 44,859

Fiscal Year Ending Dec. 31

	1995	% Change	1994	% Change	1993	% Change
Revenues (Million $)						
1Q	3,773	15%	3,286	22%	2,697	24%
2Q	4,213	17%	3,605	24%	2,905	12%
3Q	—	—	3,509	23%	2,845	10%
4Q	—	—	3,928	24%	3,168	16%
Yr.	—	—	14,328	23%	11,615	14%
Income (Million $)						
1Q	300.0	56%	192.0	NM	34.00	NM
2Q	323.0	35%	240.0	NM	67.00	NM
3Q	—	—	244.0	-44%	432.0	NM
4Q	—	—	279.0	89%	148.0	NM
Yr.	—	—	955.0	40%	681.0	NM
Earnings Per Share ($)						
1Q	1.50	60%	0.94	NM	0.17	NM
2Q	1.62	37%	1.18	NM	0.33	NM
3Q	E1.05	-13%	1.20	-44%	2.13	NM
4Q	E1.23	-11%	1.38	89%	0.73	NM
Yr.	E5.40	15%	4.70	40%	3.36	NM

Next earnings report expected: late October

Business Summary - 29-SEP-95

The world's largest manufacturer of earthmoving and construction machinery, Caterpillar also makes diesel and natural gas engines and turbines. Segment contributions in 1994:

	Revs.	Profits
Machinery & equipment	68%	73%
Engines	29%	23%
Financial services	3%	4%

Sales outside the U.S. accounted for 49% of consolidated sales in 1994 and 1993, 55% in 1992, 59% in 1991 and 55% in 1990.

Machinery and equipment includes track and wheel tractors, track and wheel loaders, pipelayers, motor graders, wheel tractor scrapers, track and wheel excavators, backhoe loaders, log skidders, log loaders, off-highway trucks, articulated dump trucks, paving products and related parts.

Diesel and natural gas engines range from 54 to 8,000 hp, and are used in earthmoving and construction machines, on-highway trucks and marine, petroleum, agricultural, industrial and other applications. CAT also makes turbines ranging from 1,340 to 15,000 horsepower (1,000 to 11,200 kilowatts).

Worldwide sales by major end use in 1994 were as follows: transportation 28%; energy 22%; housing and forest products 11%; mining 12%; commercial and industrial construction 11%; food and water 4%; and other 12%.

Financial services include providing financing for company and noncompetitive equipment sold through dealers, and extending loans to CAT dealers and customers.

Manufacturing activities are carried on in 26 plants inside the U.S. and 12 locations elsewhere. Products are sold through a worldwide network of 187 independent dealers and one company-owned dealership.

Important Developments

Sep. '95—CAT said it expects 1995's third quarter earnings to trail 1994's third quarter. The company also stated that it plans to reduce production at several of its facilities to maintain dealer and company inventories in line with dealer selling rates. From June through August, dealer machine retail sales exceeded 1994's levels for the same period, and CAT's machine orders from dealers for the same period were down only slightly. CAT noted that in its earlier outlook statements it had predicted reduced business activity in 1995's second half. The company added that its earlier outlook for record sales and profits for 1995 remains unchanged.

Capitalization

Long Term Debt: $5,042,000,000 (6/95).

Per Share Data ($)   (Year Ended Dec. 31)

	1994	1993	1992	1991	1990	1989
Tangible Bk. Val.	13.34	9.06	6.04	19.45	21.63	21.33
Cash Flow	8.05	6.62	2.16	0.94	3.57	4.77
Earnings	4.70	3.36	-1.08	-2.00	1.04	2.45
Dividends	0.45	0.30	0.30	0.60	0.60	0.60
Payout Ratio	10%	9%	NM	NM	58%	24%
Prices - High	60¾	46⅝	31⅛	28⅞	34¼	34½
- Low	50⅝	26⅞	20⅝	18⅞	19⅛	26⅜
P/E Ratio - High	13	14	NM	NM	33	14
- Low	11	8	NM	NM	18	11

Income Statement Analysis (Million $)

	1994	%Chg	1993	%Chg	1992	%Chg	1991
Revs.	14,328	23%	11,615	14%	10,194	NM	10,182
Oper. Inc.	2,321	59%	1,459	113%	685	1%	675
Depr.	680	3%	661	1%	654	10%	593
Int. Exp.	410	-7%	440	-11%	497	6%	469
Pretax Inc.	1,309	81%	723	NM	-331	NM	-555
Eff. Tax Rate	27%	—	5.80%	—	NM	—	NM
Net Inc.	955	40%	681	NM	-217	NM	-403

Balance Sheet & Other Fin. Data (Million $)

	1994	1993	1992	1991	1990	1989
Cash	419	83.0	119	104	110	148
Curr. Assets	7,409	6,071	5,537	5,570	5,901	5,708
Total Assets	16,250	14,807	13,935	12,042	11,951	10,926
Curr. Liab.	5,498	4,671	4,227	3,859	4,259	3,904
LT Debt	4,270	3,895	4,119	3,892	2,890	2,288
Common Eqty.	2,911	2,199	1,575	4,044	4,540	4,474
Total Cap.	7,181	6,118	5,713	8,022	7,430	6,762
Cap. Exp.	694	632	640	774	1,039	1,089
Cash Flow	1,635	1,342	436	189	723	968

Ratio Analysis

	1994	1993	1992	1991	1990	1989
Curr. Ratio	1.3	1.3	1.3	1.4	1.4	1.5
% LT Debt of Cap.	59.5	63.7	72.1	48.5	38.9	33.8
% Net Inc.of Revs.	6.7	5.9	NM	NM	1.8	4.5
% Ret. on Assets	6.2	4.7	NM	NM	1.8	4.8
% Ret. on Equity	37.6	36.0	NM	NM	4.7	11.6

Dividend Data —Dividends have been paid since 1914. A dividend reinvestment plan is available. A "poison pill" stock purchase rights plan was adopted in 1986.

Amt. of Div. $	Date Decl.	Ex-Div. Date	Stock of Record	Payment Date
0.150	Oct. 12	Oct. 18	Oct. 24	Nov. 19 '94
0.250	Dec. 14	Jan. 13	Jan. 20	Feb. 18 '95
0.250	Apr. 12	Apr. 18	Apr. 24	May. 20 '95
0.350	Jun. 07	Jul. 18	Jul. 20	Aug. 19 '95

Data as orig. reptd.; bef. results of disc. opers. and/or spec. items. Per share data adj. for stk. divs. as of ex-div. date. E-Estimated. NA-Not Available. NM-Not Meaningful. NR-Not Ranked.

Office—100 N.E. Adams St., Peoria, IL 61629. **Tel**—(309) 675-1000. **Chrmn & CEO**—D. V. Fites. **Secy**—R. R. Atterbury III. **Treas**—R. W. Wuttke. **Investor Contact**—James F. Masterson. **Dirs**—L. H. Affinito, D. V. Fites, J. W. Fondahl, D. R. Goode, J. P. Gorter, J. R. Junkins, P. A. Magowan, G. R. Parker, G. A. Schaefer, J. I. Smith, J. W. Wogsland, C. K. Yeutter. **Transfer Agent**—First Chicago Trust Co. of New York, NYC. **Incorporated** in California in 1925; reincorporated in Delaware in 1986. **Empl**-54,499. **S&P Analyst:** Leo Larkin

Centex Corp.

NYSE Symbol **CTX**
In S&P 500

04-OCT-95

Industry:
Building

Summary: The leading U.S. homebuilder, Centex sells homes in 20 states across the U.S. It also engages in mortgage banking and general construction contracting.

S&P Opinion: Accumulate (★★★★)	Recent Price • 29	Yield • 0.7%
	52 Wk Range • 31⅜-20⅛	12-Mo. P/E • 17.7

Quantitative Evaluations

Outlook
(1 Lowest—5 Highest)
• **2+**

Fair Value
• **27⅛**

Risk
• **Average**

Earn./Div. Rank
• **B+**

Technical Eval.
• **Bullish** since 5/95

Rel. Strength Rank
(1 Lowest—99 Highest)
• **64**

Insider Activity
• **Neutral**

Earnings vs. Previous Year
▲=Up ▼=Down ▶=No Change

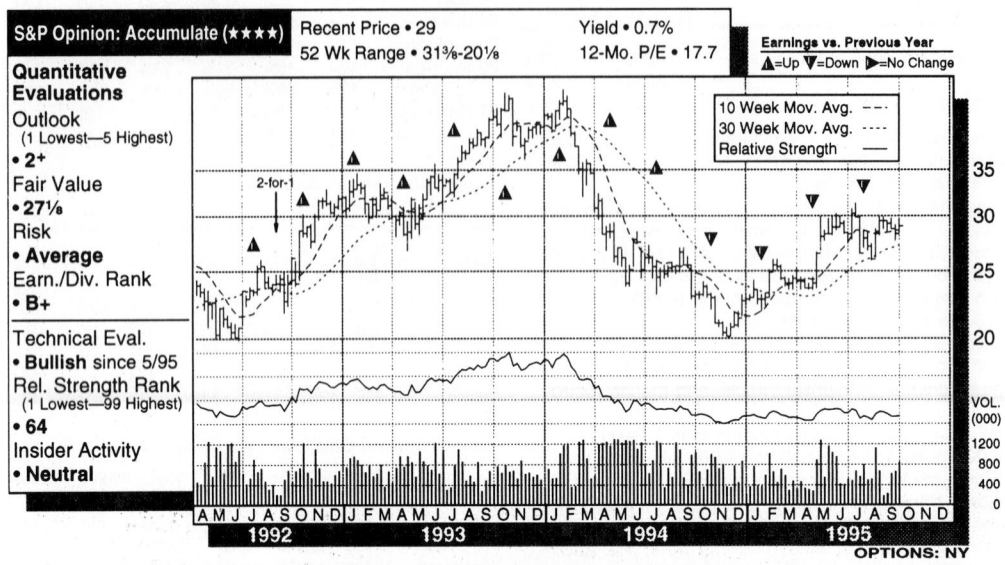

10 Week Mov. Avg. ----
30 Week Mov. Avg. ·····
Relative Strength ——

2-for-1

VOL.
(000)
OPTIONS: NY

Overview - 04-OCT-95

Revenues are likely to be relatively flat in 1995-96. While the order slowdown spurred by a period of tight credit will impact early year home sales, a sharp drop in mortgage rates in recent months has boosted order rates, and should lead to improved sales as the year progresses. Lower interest rates will have a similar effect on revenue trends in the mortgage banking and contracting segments, despite the closing of a large number of mortgage banking offices in the past year and a highly competitive contracting market. Margins are likely to mirror sales trends, but could narrow slightly for the full year, as competitive pressures are likely to continue despite improving industry conditions. The bottom line will be hurt by the absence of a gain on the IPO of Centex Construction Products. EPS computations will be influenced by CTX's repurchase of about 12% of its shares in 1994-95.

Valuation - 04-OCT-95

The shares have enjoyed a nice rebound in 1995 on improving interest rate trends, following a steep drop in 1994 that was stimulated by the Fed's credit tightening program. Industry prospects are likely to improve for a period of time, boosted by the buyer friendly rates, particularly if lower rates are able to spark the moderating economy. With CTX's recent acquisition of an interest in Vista Properties likely to further aid future prospects, Centex's stock should remain in investor favor over the next year.

Key Stock Statistics

S&P EPS Est. 1996	1.75	Tang. Bk. Value/Share	24.02
P/E on S&P Est. 1996	16.6	Beta	1.77
S&P EPS Est. 1997	1.90	Shareholders	2,100
Dividend Rate/Share	0.20	Market cap. (B)	$0.832
Shs. outstg. (M)	28.2	Inst. holdings	75%
Avg. daily vol. (M)	0.127	Insider holdings	NA

Value of $10,000 invested 5 years ago: $ 19,723

Fiscal Year Ending Mar. 31

	1996	% Change	1995	% Change	1994	% Change
Revenues (Million $)						
1Q	701.0	-16%	832.5	19%	698.3	25%
2Q	—	—	855.7	5%	813.5	26%
3Q	—	—	793.2	-5%	833.3	28%
4Q	—	—	796.1	-8%	869.5	34%
Yr.	—	—	3,278	2%	3,214	28%
Income (Million $)						
1Q	7.87	-85%	53.40	NM	17.01	70%
2Q	—	—	16.90	-26%	22.85	26%
3Q	—	—	13.06	-45%	23.59	34%
4Q	—	—	8.89	-59%	21.72	42%
Yr.	—	—	92.25	8%	85.16	40%
Earnings Per Share ($)						
1Q	0.27	-84%	1.67	NM	0.52	63%
2Q	E0.53	-4%	0.55	-21%	0.70	23%
3Q	E0.50	14%	0.44	-39%	0.72	31%
4Q	E0.45	45%	0.31	-53%	0.66	40%
Yr.	E1.75	-42%	3.04	17%	2.60	36%

Next earnings report expected: late October

Centex Corp.

Business Summary - 04-OCT-95

Centex Corp., the largest U.S. homebuilder, also has mortgage banking and construction contracting operations. In April 1994, CTX sold 51% of its construction products subsidiary to the public, while in December 1994, it disposed of its savings and loan operations. Business segment contributions in 1994-95 were:

	Revs.	Profits
Homebuilding	65%	83%
Contracting & construction	32%	-1%
Financial services	3%	7%
Equity int. & other	---	11%

The company builds, sells and finances residential housing and also originates mortgages on homes sold by others. About 95% of the houses sold are single-family detached homes; the remainder are townhomes and low-rise condominiums. Centex markets homes in 20 states across the U.S. Home closings in 1994-95 totaled 12,964, up from 12,563 in 1993-94. The average sales price in 1994-95 was $159,222 ($147,466 in the prior fiscal year).

The company originates mortgage loans, securitizes and sells them in the secondary market and sells mortgage servicing rights. In 1994-95, it provided financing for 66% of CTX home closings, down from 74% in the prior year.

Centex's nationwide construction contracting business provides general contracting services for a diversified range of building types for public and private projects. New contracts in 1994-95 totaled $1.15 billion.

Centex Construction Products (49%-owned) makes and distributes portland cement, aggregates, readymix concrete and gypsum wallboard.

Important Developments

Sep. '95—The company completed the acquisition of equity interests in Vista Properties Inc., ending its bidding war with Lennar Corp. for the Vista stake. The final agreement was part of Vista's prepackaged bankruptcy restructuring, under which Vista's stockholders and noteholders received an aggregate of $115 million, including $85 million provided by Centex and $30 million coming from Vista's cash balance. Vista is a land development concern with a portfolio of more than 35 properties, comprising over 4,000 acres in seven states. The land is zoned, planned or developed for single- and multi-family residential properties (50%), office and industrial (35%) and retail and commercial (15%).

Jul. '95—The company reported that new home orders increased 14% on a year-to-year basis in the second quarter of 1995 (based on unit volume). Order backlog of 4,617 homes at June 30, 1995, was 15% lower than the year-earlier total, but was up 16% from the March 31, 1995, level.

Capitalization

Long Term Debt: $322,054,000 (6/95).

Per Share Data ($)   (Year Ended Mar. 31)

	1995	1994	1993	1992	1991	1990
Tangible Bk. Val.	23.80	21.12	18.57	16.99	16.07	14.86
Cash Flow	3.25	3.20	2.41	1.60	1.92	2.30
Earnings	3.04	2.60	1.91	1.11	1.42	2.01
Dividends	0.20	0.20	0.20	0.20	0.20	0.18
Payout Ratio	7%	8%	10%	18%	14%	10%
Cal. Yrs.	1994	1993	1992	1991	1990	1989
Prices - High	45¾	45¼	32⅞	23⅜	22⅛	21
- Low	20⅛	26¾	19⅞	14	9⅝	13⅝
P/E Ratio - High	15	17	17	21	16	10
- Low	7	10	10	13	7	7

Income Statement Analysis (Million $)

	1995	%Chg	1994	%Chg	1993	%Chg	1992
Revs.	3,278	2%	3,214	28%	2,503	16%	2,166
Oper. Inc.	76.0	-51%	155	44%	108	77%	61.0
Depr.	6.4	-67%	19.6	21%	16.2	5%	15.4
Int. Exp.	NA	—	NA	—	NA	—	NA
Pretax Inc.	146	8%	135	47%	91.8	100%	45.9
Eff. Tax Rate	37%	—	37%	—	34%	—	25%
Net Inc.	92.2	8%	85.2	40%	61.0	76%	34.6

Balance Sheet & Other Fin. Data (Million $)

	1995	1994	1993	1992	1991	1990
Cash	24.0	155	136	272	41.0	26.0
Curr. Assets	NA	NA	NA	NA	NA	NA
Total Assets	2,050	2,580	2,272	2,347	2,032	2,045
Curr. Liab.	1,133	1,613	1,366	1,496	1,289	1,354
LT Debt	221	224	227	230	145	148
Common Eqty.	668	669	578	518	484	448
Total Cap.	916	944	878	819	708	654
Cap. Exp.	10.6	31.9	18.0	18.0	15.0	34.0
Cash Flow	99	105	77.2	50.0	59.0	70.8

Ratio Analysis

	1995	1994	1993	1992	1991	1990
Curr. Ratio	NA	NA	NA	NA	NA	NA
% LT Debt of Cap.	24.2	23.7	25.8	28.1	20.5	22.6
% Net Inc.of Revs.	2.8	2.6	2.4	1.6	1.9	3.0
% Ret. on Assets	4.3	3.5	2.6	1.6	2.1	3.2
% Ret. on Equity	14.6	13.6	11.0	6.8	9.4	14.6

Dividend Data —Dividends were initiated in 1973. A poison pill stock purchase rights plan was adopted in 1986.

Amt. of Div. $	Date Decl.	Ex-Div. Date	Stock of Record	Payment Date
0.050	Aug. 18	Sep. 08	Sep. 14	Oct. 05 '94
0.050	Dec. 01	Dec. 08	Dec. 14	Jan. 06 '95
0.050	Feb. 15	Mar. 09	Mar. 15	Apr. 13 '95
0.050	May. 23	Jun. 13	Jun. 15	Jul. 06 '95
0.050	Aug. 01	Sep. 12	Sep. 14	Oct. 05 '95

Data as orig. reptd.; bef. results of disc. opers. and/or spec. items. Per share data adj. for stk. divs. as of ex-div. date. E-Estimated. NA-Not Available. NM-Not Meaningful. NR-Not Ranked.

Office—3333 Lee Parkway, Dallas, TX 75219. **Tel**—(214) 559-6500. **Chrmn & CEO**—L. E. Hirsch. **Pres**—W. J. Gillilan III. **EVP & CFO**—D. W. Quinn. **VP & Secy**—R. G. Smerge. **VP & Investor Contact**—Sheila E. Gallagher. **Dirs**—A. B. Coleman, D. W. Cook III, J. L. Elek, W. J. Gillian III, L. E. Hirsch, C. W. Murchison III, C. H. Pistor, D. W. Quinn, P. R. Seegers, P. T. Stoffel. **Transfer Agent & Registrar**—Chemical Mellon, Ridgefield Park, NJ. **Incorporated** in Nevada in 1968; predecessor organized in Texas in 1950. **Empl**-6,395. **S&P Analyst:** Michael W. Jaffe

Central & South West

NYSE Symbol **CSR**
In S&P 500

16-AUG-95 | **Industry:** Utilities-Electric | **Summary:** This Dallas-based utility holding company has four utility units serving customers in Texas, Oklahoma, Louisiana and Arkansas.

S&P Opinion: Hold (★★★)	Recent Price • 24½	Yield • 7.0%
	52 Wk Range • 26⅝-20⅛	12-Mo. P/E • 12.0

Earnings vs. Previous Year
▲=Up ▼=Down ▶=No Change

Quantitative Evaluations

Outlook
(1 Lowest—5 Highest)
• **2+**

Fair Value
• **23**

Risk
• **Low**

Earn./Div. Rank
• **A-**

Technical Eval.
• **Bullish** since 1/95

Rel. Strength Rank
(1 Lowest—99 Highest)
• **22**

Insider Activity
• **Neutral**

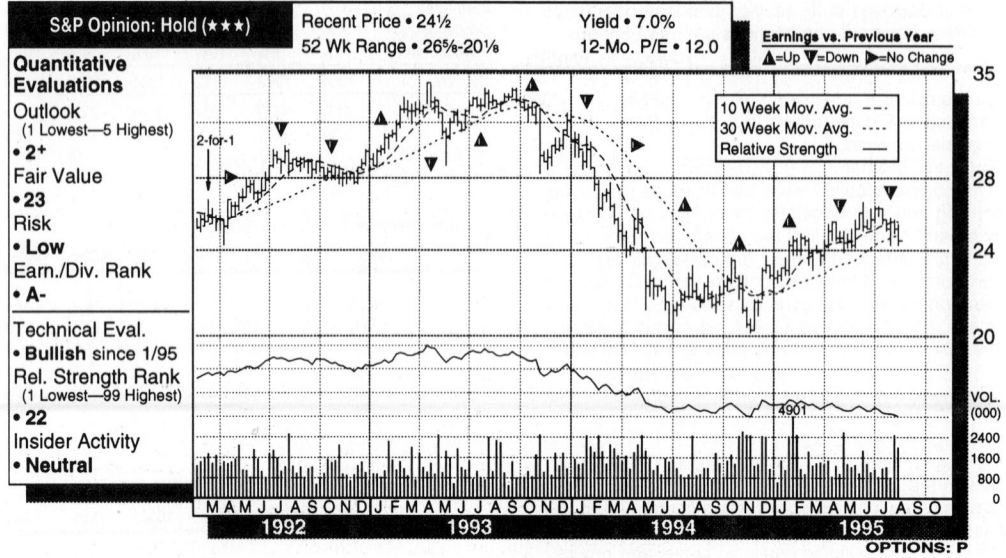

Legend:
10 Week Mov. Avg. ---
30 Week Mov. Avg. .....
Relative Strength —

2-for-1

VOL. (000)
2400
1600
800
0

M A M J J A S O N D | J F M A M J J A S O N D | J F M A M J J A S O N D | J F M A M J J A S O
1992 | 1993 | 1994 | 1995

OPTIONS: P

Overview - 16-AUG-95

Share earnings for 1995 should reflect somewhat higher kilowatt-hour (kwh) sales as a result of continued growth in demand within the company's service territory, a rate increase and well controlled expenses. Sales to commercial and industrial customers are growing rapidly, and fuel and purchased power costs expenses are declining as higher kwh sales allow produciton efficiencies. CSR has reduced maintenance costs as well, and a recent rate increase is also a positive factor. Higher interest costs from new financings and growing depreciation and amortization expenses may be somewhat offsetting, however. Weakening prospects for substantial earnings growth for 1996 are higher taxes and a rate rollback for the Central Power & Light Co. subsidiary expected in late 1995.

Valuation - 16-AUG-95

Appreciation in the shares of this low cost energy producer are likely to be modest in the 1995 second half. Year-to-date gains in the stock have been a modest 7.2% despite the Federal Reserve Board's easing in May. Anticipation of further easing would boost the shares, and the stock has some appeal due to its above average yield. Still, the dividend payout is high relative to the industry average, and we expect only modest growth in the dividend in 1996. However, as greater demand for electricity and better gas prices next year minimize the negative impact of the rate reduction later this year, we expect CSR to be a good total return investment with little downside risk.

Key Stock Statistics

S&P EPS Est. 1995	2.05	Tang. Bk. Value/Share	15.90
P/E on S&P Est. 1995	12.0	Beta	0.46
S&P EPS Est. 1996	2.15	Shareholders	74,000
Dividend Rate/Share	1.72	Market cap. (B)	$ 4.7
Shs. outstg. (M)	191.7	Inst. holdings	44%
Avg. daily vol. (M)	0.357	Insider holdings	NA

Value of $10,000 invested 5 years ago: $ 17,173

Fiscal Year Ending Dec. 31

	1995	% Change	1994	% Change	1993	% Change
Revenues (Million $)						
1Q	658.0	-23%	850.0	5%	810.0	18%
2Q	920.0	1%	908.0	2%	892.0	17%
3Q	—	—	1,070	-6%	1,140	15%
4Q	—	—	795.0	-6%	843.0	-1%
Yr.	—	—	3,623	-2%	3,688	12%
Income (Million $)						
1Q	44.00	-8%	48.00	4%	46.00	-27%
2Q	108.0	NM	107.0	11%	96.00	22%
3Q	—	—	189.0	4%	181.0	3%
4Q	—	—	68.00	NM	-42.00	NM
Yr.	—	—	412.0	47%	281.0	-30%
Earnings Per Share ($)						
1Q	0.20	-13%	0.23	NM	0.23	-23%
2Q	0.54	-2%	0.55	15%	0.48	23%
3Q	E0.96	-1%	0.97	4%	0.93	2%
4Q	E0.35	6%	0.33	NM	-0.25	NM
Yr.	E2.05	-1%	2.08	50%	1.39	-32%

Next earnings report expected: late November

Central & South West

Business Summary - 14-AUG-95

Central & South West Corp. is a public utility holding company. Its subsidiaries, Central Power & Light, Public Service of Oklahoma, Southwestern Electric Power and West Texas Utilities, provide electric (85% of 1994 revenues) and gas (15%) service to more than 1.6 million customers (4.3 million people) in a widely diversified area covering 152,000 square miles in Texas (62% of 1994 electric revenues), Oklahoma (24%), Louisiana (8%) and Arkansas (6%). Electric revenues in recent years were derived as follows:

	1994	1993	1992	1991
Residential	38%	38%	38%	39%
Commercial	27%	27%	28%	28%
Industrial	24%	24%	24%	23%
Other	11%	11%	10%	10%

Sources of electric generation in 1994 were natural gas (44%), coal (36%), lignite (9)%, purchased power (5%) and nuclear (6)%. Peak demand in 1994 was 11,434 mw, and system capability at time of peak totaled 14,177 mw, for a capacity margin of 19%. The company owns 25.2% of the two-unit, 2,500 mw South Texas nuclear project.

Capital outlays for construction in 1994 were $578 million. Based on growth projections, CSR does not plan to add significant generating capaility through the end of the decade and outlays budgeted for construction projects for 1995, 1996 and 1997 range from $385 million to $358 million, mostly to improve and expand distribution facilities.

Non-utility operations include Transok, an Oklahoma natural gas marketing, gathering and transmission company; CSW Energy, a developer of cogeneration projects; CSW Credit, which buys electric utilities' accounts receivable; CSW Leasing, which invests in leveraged leases; and Central and South West Services, which provides professional services for the CSR system.

Important Developments

Jul. '95—CSR reported a 3% year-to-year decline in net income for the six months ended June 30, 1995. It attributed the decrease to a $42 million reserve to cover deferred merger and acquisition costs due to the termination in early June of a plan to merge with El Paso Electric in early June. Also lowering net income were higher interest costs and lower earnings from a non- utility subsidiary that were only partly offset by higher non-fuel revenues. Despite a 2.4% increase in total kilwatt hour sales due to greater demand from the industrial sector, revenues fell 10%, due to a write off of fuel recoveries and reserves for customer refunds.

Capitalization

Long Term Debt: $2,954,000,000 (6/95).
Subsidiary Preferred Stock: $327,000,000.

Per Share Data ($)

(Year Ended Dec. 31)

	1994	1993	1992	1991	1990	1989
Tangible Bk. Val.	15.90	14.45	14.71	14.30	13.80	13.28
Earnings	2.08	1.39	2.03	1.99	1.89	1.63
Dividends	1.70	1.62	1.54	1.46	1.38	1.30
Payout Ratio	82%	117%	76%	73%	73%	80%
Prices - High	30⅞	34¼	30	27⅛	23	20⅛
- Low	20⅛	28¼	24¼	20¾	18⅜	14⅞
P/E Ratio - High	15	25	15	14	12	12
- Low	10	20	12	10	10	9

Income Statement Analysis (Million $)

	1994	%Chg	1993	%Chg	1992	%Chg	1991
Revs.	3,623	-2%	3,687	12%	3,289	8%	3,047
Depr.	356	8%	330	7%	308	6%	291
Maint.	176	-11%	197	16%	170	-6%	181
Fxd. Chgs. Cov.	2.8	14%	2.5	-11%	2.8	NM	2.8
Constr. Credits	NA	—	NA	—	2.0	-60%	5.0
Eff. Tax Rate	28%	—	29%	—	26%	—	28%
Net Inc.	412	47%	281	-30%	404	NM	401

Balance Sheet & Other Fin. Data (Million $)

	1994	1993	1992	1991	1990	1989
Gross Prop.	11,868	11,357	11,190	10,788	10,251	9,634
Cap. Exp.	578	508	425	327	329	331
Net Prop.	7,998	7,807	7,903	7,802	7,550	7,186
Capitalization:						
LT Debt	2,940	2,749	2,647	2,518	2,513	2,537
% LT Debt	47	46	45	44	45	46
Pfd.	327	350	367	389	394	397
% Pfd.	5.20	5.80	6.20	6.80	7.00	7.10
Common	3,052	2,930	2,927	2,834	2,743	2,647
% Common	48	49	49	49	49	47
Total Cap.	8,687	8,299	7,951	7,677	7,528	7,366

Ratio Analysis

	1994	1993	1992	1991	1990	1989
Oper. Ratio	83.6	87.6	82.0	81.4	82.0	80.7
% Earn. on Net Prop.	7.5	5.9	7.5	7.4	6.7	6.9
% Ret. on Revs.	11.4	7.6	12.3	13.2	14.1	13.2
% Ret. On Invest.Cap	8.3	6.8	8.6	8.8	9.5	8.4
% Return On Com.Eqty	13.2	10.6	13.3	13.4	13.2	11.7

Dividend Data —Dividends have been paid since 1947, and increased each year since 1951. A dividend reinvestment plan is available.

Amt. of Div. $	Date Decl.	Ex-Div. Date	Stock of Record	Payment Date
0.425	Jul. 21	Aug. 02	Aug. 08	Aug. 31 '94
0.425	Oct. 20	Nov. 02	Nov. 08	Nov. 30 '94
0.430	Jan. 16	Feb. 02	Feb. 08	Feb. 28 '95
0.430	Apr. 20	May. 02	May. 08	May. 31 '95
0.430	Jul. 20	Aug. 04	Aug. 08	Aug. 31 '95

Data as orig. reptd.; bef. results of disc opers. and/or spec. items. Per share data adj. for stk. divs. as of ex-div. date. E-Estimated. NA-Not Available. NM-Not Meaningful. NR-Not Ranked.

Office—1616 Woodall Rodgers Freeway, Dallas, TX 75202,1234. **Tel**—(214) 777-1000. **Chrmn, Pres & CEO**—E. R. Brooks. **SVP & CFO**—G. D. Rosilier. **Secy**—F. L. Frawley. **Investor Contact**—Sharon R. Peavy. **Dirs**—G. Biggs, M. S. Boren, E. R. Brooks, D. M. Carlton, J. H. Foy, R. W. Lawless, H. D. Mattison, J. L. Powell, T. V. Shockley III, J. C. Templeton, L. D. Ward. **Transfer Agent & Registrar**—Co.'s office. **Incorporated** in Delaware in 1925. **Empl**-8,055. **S&P Analyst:** Jane Collin

Ceridian Corp.

NYSE Symbol **CEN**
In S&P 500

25-SEP-95

Industry:
Data Processing

Summary: Ceridian provides payroll processing and other employer services, media and market research, and systems integration services to commercial and government customers.

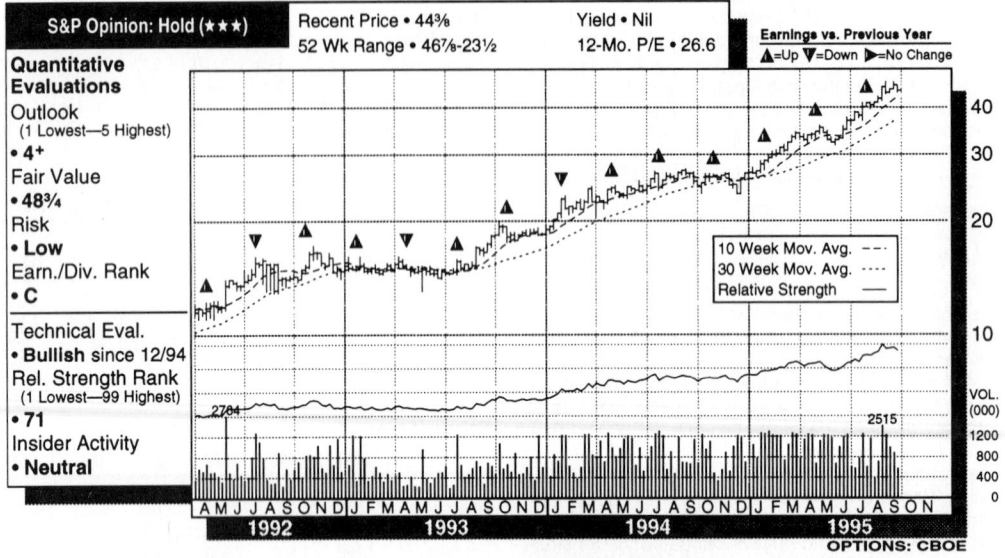

| S&P Opinion: Hold (★★★) | Recent Price • 44⅜ | Yield • Nil | |
| | 52 Wk Range • 46⅞-23½ | 12-Mo. P/E • 26.6 | |

Earnings vs. Previous Year
▲=Up ▼=Down ▶=No Change

Quantitative Evaluations

Outlook
(1 Lowest—5 Highest)
• **4+**

Fair Value
• **48¾**

Risk
• **Low**

Earn./Div. Rank
• **C**

Technical Eval.
• **Bullish** since 12/94

Rel. Strength Rank
(1 Lowest—99 Highest)
• **71**

Insider Activity
• **Neutral**

10 Week Mov. Avg. — – –
30 Week Mov. Avg. ·······
Relative Strength ——

VOL. (000)

OPTIONS: CBOE

Overview - 19-SEP-95

Revenues are expected to continue to grow through 1996. Employer Services should benefit from an expanded product line, continued enhancements to its core payroll product offerings and the recently-announced proposed acquisition of Comdata. Arbitron revenues are expected to be aided by initiatives to expand its services beyond radio ratings. Computing Devices International revenues should benefit from continued growth in its markets. Margins are expected to widen on the higher volume, improved productivity in Employer Services and the maturing of large contracts. Long-term results will be aided by consolidation of the company's data centers.

Valuation - 19-SEP-95

The shares have been in an uptrend for several years, aided by widening margins and ongoing earnings improvement. Ceridian should generate annual earnings growth of at least 20% over the next several years, driven mainly by strength in its Information Services group and gains at Computing Devices International. Strategic acquisitions, including Comdata, should continue to strengthen the company's competitive position. In light of CEN's recent record of earnings growth, and the increased predictability of those earnings in the form of ongoing relationships and longer-term contracts, the shares merit a premium valuation. However, the shares are trading at nearly 20x times our 1996 EPS estimate, and though the potential for further gains still exists, we would not aggressively add to positions at this time.

Key Stock Statistics

S&P EPS Est. 1995	1.85	Tang. Bk. Value/Share	NM
P/E on S&P Est. 1995	24.0	Beta	1.41
S&P EPS Est. 1996	2.30	Shareholders	49,400
Dividend Rate/Share	Nil	Market cap. (B)	$ 2.0
Shs. outstg. (M)	45.7	Inst. holdings	90%
Avg. daily vol. (M)	0.226	Insider holdings	NA

Value of $10,000 invested 5 years ago: NA

Fiscal Year Ending Dec. 31

	1995	% Change	1994	% Change	1993	% Change
Revenues (Million $)						
1Q	257.8	16%	221.3	-1%	224.0	9%
2Q	253.5	16%	218.5	-3%	225.9	15%
3Q	—	—	242.4	16%	208.9	3%
4Q	—	—	234.1	3%	226.9	NM
Yr.	—	—	916.3	3%	886.1	7%
Income (Million $)						
1Q	28.40	28%	22.20	72%	12.90	-38%
2Q	22.00	34%	16.40	95%	8.40	NM
3Q	—	—	19.20	79%	10.70	15%
4Q	—	—	20.80	NM	-54.00	NM
Yr.	—	—	78.60	NM	-22.00	NM
Earnings Per Share ($)						
1Q	0.54	29%	0.42	40%	0.30	-39%
2Q	0.40	38%	0.29	45%	0.20	NM
3Q	E0.41	17%	0.35	40%	0.25	14%
4Q	E0.50	32%	0.38	NM	-1.24	NM
Yr.	E1.85	29%	1.43	NM	-0.52	NM

Next earnings report expected: mid October

Business Summary - 22-SEP-95

In July 1992, Ceridian Corporation (formerly Control Data Corp.) spun off its Computer Products business (named Control Data Systems). Continuing operations consist of two business segments: Information Services and Defense Electronics.

Information Services, which provides technology-based services on a repetitive or subscription basis, consists of two business units: Ceridian Employer Services and The Arbitron Co. Employer Services provides payroll processing, payroll tax filing and training services; payroll, human resources management and benefits administration software; and employee assistance programs. During 1994, payroll processing and payroll tax filing services accounted for 82% of Employer Services total revenue. Arbitron is a leading provider of radio audience measurement information (size and demographics) and also provides electronic media and marketing information to radio and television broadcasters, cable operators, advertising agencies and advertisers.

Through its Computing Devices International unit, CEN develops, manufactures and markets electronic systems, subsystems and components and provides systems integration and other services, primarily to government defense agencies. In addition, Business Information Services runs custom data processing applications for customers (primarily the U.S. Government) and delivers them via a timesharing network.

In January 1995, CEN acquired MediaMAPS, the developer of an integrated database system for radio station marketing and promotion; Paragon Imaging Inc., an imaging software provider for the Department of Defense's intelligence community and service commands; Human Effectiveness Inc., an employee assistance provider; and Payroll Tax Management, a payroll tax filing operation.

Important Developments

Sep. '95—CEN acquired Resumix, Inc., a provider of skills management software and services with projected 1995 revenues of $25 million.
Aug. '95—The company said it reached a definitive agreement to acquire Comdata Holdings Corp. for common and preferred stock of Ceridian; equity consideration will total about $900 million. Comdata, a leading provider of transaction processing and information services to the transportation and gaming industries, has projected 1995 revenues of $300 million. The transaction is expected to be accretive to Ceridian's earnings per share in 1996, and to provide an increasingly positive contribution to earnings thereafter.

Capitalization

Long Term Debt: $12,900,000 (6/95).
5.5% Cum. Exch. Preferred Stock: 47,200 shs. ($5,000 liquid. pref.); conv. into 10,384,000 com. shs.

Per Share Data ($) (Year Ended Dec. 31)

	1994	1993	1992	1991	1990	1989
Tangible Bk. Val.	-3.91	-3.63	-2.36	10.09	10.35	9.31
Cash Flow	2.00	0.07	-0.15	1.66	2.26	-12.53
Earnings	1.43	-0.52	-0.69	-0.21	0.05	-16.11
Dividends	Nil	Nil	Nil	Nil	Nil	Nil
Payout Ratio	Nil	Nil	Nil	Nil	Nil	Nil
Prices - High	27½	19⅞	17¼	13¾	21⅝	24
- Low	18½	13	9⅛	6¾	7⅝	16¼
P/E Ratio - High	19	NM	NM	NM	NM	NM
- Low	13	NM	NM	NM	NM	NM

Income Statement Analysis (Million $)

	1994	%Chg	1993	%Chg	1992	%Chg	1991
Revs.	916	3%	886	7%	830	-46%	1,525
Oper. Inc.	99	25%	79.0	18%	67.0	-28%	93.0
Depr.	26.0	NM	26.0	13%	23.0	-71%	80.0
Int. Exp.	2.0	-88%	16.0	NM	16.0	-36%	25.0
Pretax Inc.	85.0	NM	-18.0	NM	-24.0	NM	2.0
Eff. Tax Rate	7.70%	—	NM	—	NM	—	NM
Net Inc.	79.0	NM	-22.0	NM	-29.0	NM	-9.0

Balance Sheet & Other Fin. Data (Million $)

	1994	1993	1992	1991	1990	1989
Cash	171	216	153	211	351	525
Curr. Assets	346	387	346	792	951	1,274
Total Assets	690	616	530	1,214	1,424	1,861
Curr. Liab.	307	316	298	467	624	843
LT Debt	18.0	16.0	187	183	193	352
Common Eqty.	-50.0	-124	-100	435	446	401
Total Cap.	212	134	92.0	636	655	768
Cap. Exp.	38.0	28.0	19.0	68.0	104	156
Cash Flow	92.0	3.0	-7.0	71.0	96.0	-529

Ratio Analysis

	1994	1993	1992	1991	1990	1989
Curr. Ratio	7.1	1.2	1.2	1.7	1.5	1.5
% LT Debt of Cap.	8.3	12.2	202.9	28.8	29.5	45.9
% Net Inc.of Revs.	8.6	NM	NM	NM	0.2	NM
% Ret. on Assets	11.9	NM	NM	NM	0.2	NM
% Ret. on Equity	NM	NM	NM	NM	0.5	NM

Dividend Data —Common dividends were omitted in 1985, after having been paid since 1977. In July 1992, the company distributed 0.25 of a Control Data Systems common share for each CEN common share held.

Data as orig. reptd.; bef. results of disc. opers. and/or spec. items. Per share data adj. for stk. divs. as of ex-div. date.
E-Estimated. NA-Not Available. NM-Not Meaningful. NR-Not Ranked.

Office—8100 34th Ave. South, Minneapolis, MN 55425. **Tel**—(612) 853-8100. **Chrmn & Pres**—L. Perlman. **VP & Secy**—J. Haveman. **VP & Treas**—R. S. McCambridge. **Investor Contact**—Renee Svendsen (612) 853-2641. **Dirs**—R. M. Davis, A. W. Dawson, R. James, R. G. Lareau, G. R. Lewis, C. Marshall, L. Perlman, C. J. Uhrich, R. W. Vieser, P. S. Walsh. **Transfer Agent & Registrar**—Bank of New York, NYC. **Incorporated** in Delaware in 1912. **Empl**-7,500. **S&P Analyst:** Alan Aaron

16-OCT-95

Industry:
Paper/Products

Summary: Champion is a leading paper manufacturer, with important positions in printing and writing papers, publication papers, pulp and newsprint. CHA also produces lumber and plywood.

S&P Opinion: Buy (★★★★★)

Recent Price • 54⅜	Yield • 0.4%
52 Wk Range • 60¼-32¾	12-Mo. P/E • 8.0

Earnings vs. Previous Year
▲=Up ▼=Down ▶=No Change

Quantitative Evaluations

Outlook
(1 Lowest—5 Highest)
• **2+**

Fair Value
• **48⅜**

Risk
• **Average**

Earn./Div. Rank
• **B-**

Technical Eval.
• **Bearish** since 7/95

Rel. Strength Rank
(1 Lowest—99 Highest)
• **47**

Insider Activity
• **Neutral**

10 Week Mov. Avg. – – –
30 Week Mov. Avg. · · · · ·
Relative Strength —

9052

VOL. (000)

OPTIONS: CBOE

Overview - 16-OCT-95

Sales growth should continue through 1996, although the pace is likely to slow from the torrid rate experienced to date in 1995. While some moderation in global economies and inventory adjustments have slowed certain paper industry segments, CHA's major products are concentrated in some of the industry's strongest sectors. Lack of capacity expansion in those areas should also allow steep price increases to remain in effect. Although wood products sales have been hurt by a sluggish domestic homebuilding market, trends should improve in 1996, as lower long-term interest rates have started to rejuvenate the housing market. Margins should remain firm in 1996, on continued high pulp and paper prices, benefits of a multi-year capital improvement program, cost controls and an easing of difficulties in the wood products area.

Valuation - 16-OCT-95

Champion's shares have appreciated strongly in the past year on very favorable conditions in the paper industry. Although the stock has recently gone through a correction phase, on worries that moderating economic trends will signal the end of the paper industry upturn, we remain enthusiastic about upcoming prospects. Our optimism is based on the belief that little capacity expansion and an anticipated economic rebound will allow the uptrend to continue in paper, and that a rejuvenated housing market will boost the wood products segment. Given our upbeat outlook, we believe the shares are far underpriced in their recent trading range of about five times our 1996 forecast.

Key Stock Statistics

S&P EPS Est. 1995	8.40	Tang. Bk. Value/Share	32.99
P/E on S&P Est. 1995	6.5	Beta	0.56
S&P EPS Est. 1996	10.00	Shareholders	22,200
Dividend Rate/Share	0.20	Market cap. (B)	$ 5.3
Shs. outstg. (M)	96.6	Inst. holdings	79%
Avg. daily vol. (M)	0.830	Insider holdings	NA

Value of $10,000 invested 5 years ago: $ 18,475

Fiscal Year Ending Dec. 31

	1995	% Change	1994	% Change	1993	% Change
Revenues (Million $)						
1Q	1,634	33%	1,226	-3%	1,267	6%
2Q	1,756	41%	1,242	-1%	1,256	2%
3Q	1,841	33%	1,385	11%	1,245	-1%
4Q	—	—	1,465	13%	1,300	5%
Yr.	—	—	5,318	5%	5,069	3%
Income (Million $)						
1Q	131.2	NM	-30.99	NM	-28.06	NM
2Q	187.5	NM	-31.10	NM	-22.34	NM
3Q	235.6	NM	23.12	NM	-53.48	NM
4Q	—	—	102.3	NM	-30.56	NM
Yr.	—	—	63.31	NM	-134.4	NM
Earnings Per Share ($)						
1Q	1.33	NM	-0.41	NM	-0.38	NM
2Q	1.93	NM	-0.41	NM	-0.31	NM
3Q	2.47	NM	0.18	NM	-0.65	NM
4Q	E2.66	161%	1.02	NM	-0.41	NM
Yr.	E8.40	NM	0.38	NM	-1.75	NM

Next earnings report expected: early January

Business Summary - 11-OCT-95

Champion International is one of the leading domestic manufacturers of paper for business communications, commercial printing, publications and newspapers. It also has substantial plywood and lumber manufacturing operations. CHA owns or controls 5.1 million acres of timberlands in the U.S., and has Canadian and Brazilian units with significant timber resources. Segment contributions (profits in millions) in 1994 were:

	Sales	Profits
Paper	79%	$70.9
Wood products	21%	242.3

International operations, principally in Canada and Brazil, accounted for about 18% of sales in 1994.

At December 31, 1994, CHA's printing and writing papers business was operating mills with an annual capacity of 2,058,000 tons of printing and writing papers and bleached paperboard. Its uncoated papers are used for computer forms, copier paper and envelope papers, while coated papers are used in catalogs, magazines and annual reports. Bleached paperboard is converted into milk and juice cartons and ovenable packaging, and is also sold to independent purchasers or exported. At December 31, 1994, CHA's publication papers operations had an annual capacity of about 1,273,000 tons of publication papers, while its newsprint business had an annual capacity of 948,000 tons of newsprint, directory paper and groundwood specialties. CHA also produces unbleached linerboard and kraft paper for multi-wall and grocery bags, and at 1994 year-end had an annual capacity of 403,000 tons of linerboard and 116,000 tons of kraft paper. While certain of the company's mills purchase pulp in the open market, Champion and its 84%-owned Weldwood of Canada unit are net sellers of pulp.

At the end of 1994, CHA had an annual capacity of 843 million sq. ft. of softwood plywood and 416 million board feet of softwood lumber, while Weldwood had a capacity of 425 million sq. ft. of plywood, 762 million board feet of softwood lumber (absent 185 million board feet of annual capacity of two sawmills sold in February 1995) and 160 million sq. ft. of waferboard.

Important Developments

Jun. '95—With Goldman, Sachs & Co. acting as underwriter, the company completed a secondary offering of 5.5 million Champion common shares at $52.45 each. All of the shares were sold for Loews Corp., with Champion repurchasing two million of its shares and the remaining 3.5 milion sold to the public. Earlier in the month, Champion repurchased 7.9 million of its common shares from Berkshire Hathaway Corp. under a right of first refusal, after Berkshire converted its 300,000 CHA preference shares into the common.

Capitalization

Long Term Debt: $2,776,559,000 (9/95).
Minority Interest: $100,774,000.

Per Share Data ($) (Year Ended Dec. 31)

	1994	1993	1992	1991	1990	1989
Tangible Bk. Val.	31.74	31.71	34.01	39.51	39.58	38.60
Cash Flow	5.31	3.03	4.28	3.83	5.60	7.52
Earnings	0.38	-1.75	-0.15	0.14	2.11	4.56
Dividends	0.20	0.20	0.20	0.20	1.10	1.10
Payout Ratio	53%	NM	NM	143%	52%	24%
Prices - High	40	34⅝	30¼	30⅝	33¾	37¾
- Low	28	27⅛	23½	22¼	23⅛	28⅞
P/E Ratio - High	NM	NM	NM	NM	16	8
- Low	NM	NM	NM	NM	11	6

Income Statement Analysis (Million $)

	1994	%Chg	1993	%Chg	1992	%Chg	1991
Revs.	5,318	5%	5,069	3%	4,926	3%	4,786
Oper. Inc.	725	42%	510	5%	484	-7%	521
Depr.	459	4%	443	8%	411	20%	342
Int. Exp.	243	-6%	258	5%	246	-7%	264
Pretax Inc.	106	NM	-157	NM	12.0	-84%	74.0
Eff. Tax Rate	23%	—	NM	—	NM	—	51%
Net Inc.	63.0	NM	-133	NM	14.0	-65%	40.0

Balance Sheet & Other Fin. Data (Million $)

	1994	1993	1992	1991	1990	1989
Cash	91.0	63.0	92.0	172	103	56.0
Curr. Assets	1,179	1,114	1,143	1,162	1,104	1,074
Total Assets	8,964	9,143	9,381	8,656	8,351	7,531
Curr. Liab.	1,034	772	786	794	801	804
LT Debt	2,889	3,316	3,291	2,978	2,689	2,025
Common Eqty.	2,961	2,950	3,159	3,671	3,680	3,589
Total Cap.	7,258	7,698	7,958	7,678	7,375	6,577
Cap. Exp.	329	606	718	661	1,047	994
Cash Flow	494	281	397	354	518	709

Ratio Analysis

	1994	1993	1992	1991	1990	1989
Curr. Ratio	1.1	1.4	1.5	1.5	1.4	1.3
% LT Debt of Cap.	39.8	43.1	41.4	38.8	36.5	30.8
% Net Inc.of Revs.	1.2	NM	0.3	0.8	4.4	8.4
% Ret. on Assets	0.7	NM	0.2	0.5	2.8	6.2
% Ret. on Equity	1.2	NM	NM	0.3	5.4	12.6

Dividend Data —Dividends have been paid since 1940. A dividend reinvestment plan is available.

Amt. of Div. $	Date Decl.	Ex-Div. Date	Stock of Record	Payment Date
0.050	Aug. 18	Sep. 12	Sep. 16	Oct. 12 '94
0.050	Nov. 17	Dec. 12	Dec. 16	Jan. 10 '95
0.050	Feb. 16	Mar. 13	Mar. 17	Apr. 13 '95
0.050	May. 18	Jun. 14	Jun. 16	Jul. 13 '95
0.050	Aug. 17	Sep. 13	Sep. 15	Oct. 12 '95

Data as orig. reptd.; bef. results of disc. opers. and/or spec. items. Per share data adj. for stk. divs. as of ex-div. date. E-Estimated. NA-Not Available. NM-Not Meaningful. NR-Not Ranked.

Office—One Champion Plaza, Stamford, CT 06921. **Tel**—(203) 358-7000. **Chrmn & CEO**—A. C. Sigler. **Pres**—L. C. Heist. **SVP-Finance & Investor Contact**—Frank Kneisel. **VP-Secy**—L. A. Fox. **Dirs**—R. A. Charpie, A. F. Emerson, A. E. Gotlieb, L. C. Heist, S. C. Mobley, H. B. Morley, K. C. Nichols, L. G. Rawl, W. V. Shipley, A. C. Sigler, J. S. Tisch, R. E. Walton, J. L. Weinberg. **Transfer Agent & Registrar**—Chemical Bank, NYC. **Incorporated** in New York in 1937. **Empl**-24,615. **S&P Analyst:** Michael W. Jaffe

Charming Shoppes

NASDAQ Symbol **CHRS**
In S&P 500

22-AUG-95

Industry:
Retail Stores

Summary: This retailer operates over 1,400 specialty stores in 46 states featuring moderately priced apparel in junior, misses and women's sizes.

S&P Opinion: Avoid (★★)	Recent Price • 4⅞	Yield • 1.9%
	52 Wk Range • 9¼-3⅞	12-Mo. P/E • 97.5

Quantitative Evaluations

Outlook
(1 Lowest—5 Highest)
• **2⁻**

Fair Value
• **4⅜**

Risk
• **Average**

Earn./Div. Rank
• **B+**

Technical Eval.
• **Bearish** since 3/94

Rel. Strength Rank
(1 Lowest—99 Highest)
• **11**

Insider Activity
• **Neutral**

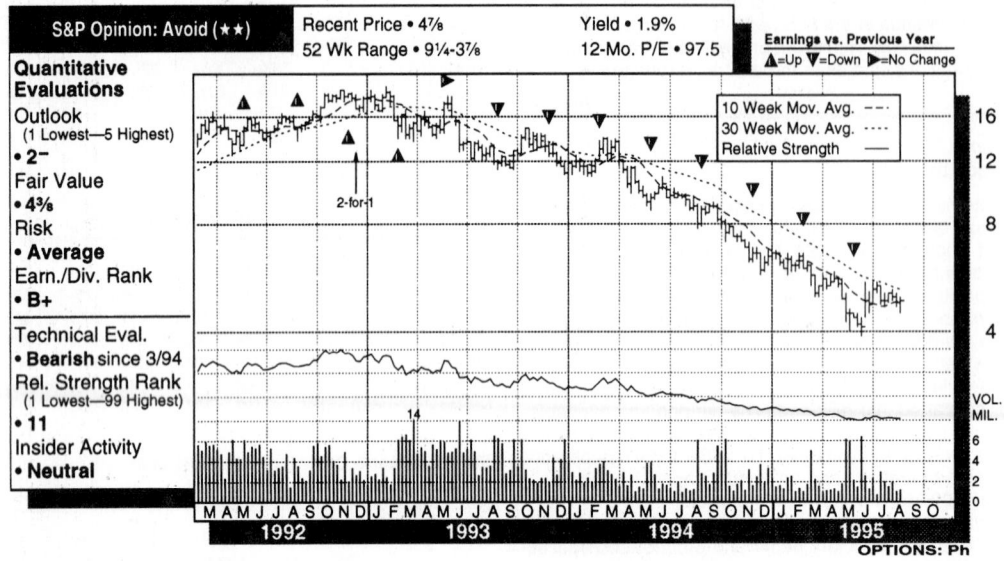

Earnings vs. Previous Year
▲=Up ▼=Down ▶=No Change

- 10 Week Mov. Avg. ---
- 30 Week Mov. Avg. ·····
- Relative Strength —

2-for-1

14

VOL. MIL.

MAMJJASOND JFMAMJJASOND JFMAMJJASOND JFMAMJJASO
1992 · 1993 · 1994 · 1995

OPTIONS: Ph

Overview - 22-AUG-95

The company incurred a loss in the first half of 1995-96 on a drop in sales and higher markdowns to clear out merchandise. Sales should begin to increase in the second half, reflecting the company's new merchandising strategy and refurbished stores. Although a new advertising campaign has now been postponed until the spring of 1996 as the company finetunes its merchandise strategy, gross margins should begin to widen in the second half with fewer markdowns and promotions and also lower occupancy costs reflecting store closings. Expense ratios should be well controlled. The company has cut back its store opening program to about 50 units for 1995-96, with some 45 store closures planned. In light of this cutback and the company's strong balance sheet, the $0.023 quarterly dividend is secure.

Valuation - 22-AUG-95

The shares have fallen dramatically since early 1994. Weak apparel sales, high markdowns and intense competition from other retailers offering low priced merchandise has eroded the company's market share. Steps are being taken to develop a new merchandise strategy. Until sales gains resume, we anticipate that the shares, which are trading slightly below book value, will languish. Given the company's inexpensive strip mall locations and the weak environment for apparel sales, we doubt that the company is a takeover candidate.

Key Stock Statistics

S&P EPS Est. 1996	0.10	Tang. Bk. Value/Share	5.37
P/E on S&P Est. 1996	48.8	Beta	0.83
S&P EPS Est. 1997	0.45	Shareholders	4,200
Dividend Rate/Share	0.09	Market cap. (B)	$0.479
Shs. outstg. (M)	103.0	Inst. holdings	67%
Avg. daily vol. (M)	0.282	Insider holdings	0%

Value of $10,000 invested 5 years ago: $ 9,693

Fiscal Year Ending Jan. 31

	1996	% Change	1995	% Change	1994	% Change
Revenues (Million $)						
1Q	244.3	-18%	298.0	8%	275.3	5%
2Q	270.4	-16%	323.4	5%	308.6	6%
3Q	—	—	306.3	-2%	313.0	8%
4Q	—	—	345.4	-3%	357.2	6%
Yr.	—	—	1,273	1%	1,254	6%
Income (Million $)						
1Q	-4.37	NM	13.96	-14%	16.22	NM
2Q	-3.13	NM	18.06	-12%	20.60	-5%
3Q	—	—	7.51	-50%	15.16	-13%
4Q	—	—	5.16	-78%	23.78	-8%
Yr.	—	—	44.69	-41%	75.76	-7%
Earnings Per Share ($)						
1Q	-0.04	NM	0.13	-13%	0.15	NM
2Q	-0.03	NM	0.17	-11%	0.19	-5%
3Q	E0.10	43%	0.07	-50%	0.14	-13%
4Q	E0.07	40%	0.05	-77%	0.22	-8%
Yr.	E0.10	-76%	0.42	-40%	0.70	-7%

Next earnings report expected: mid November

Charming Shoppes

Business Summary - 22-AUG-95

Charming Shoppes operates a chain of women's specialty stores under the tradenames Fashion Bug and Fashion Bug Plus. At the end of 1994-95, a total of 1,428 stores were in operation in 46 states throughout the East, South and Midwest, with the greatest concentration in Pennsylvania, followed by Ohio, Maryland, New Jersey and Illinois. The stores are located in both enclosed malls and strip shopping centers situated primarily in suburban metropolitan areas and smaller towns. Fashion Bug stores range in size from 6,000 sq. ft. to 16,000 sq. ft.; Fashion Bug Plus stores are generally 3,000 to 5,000 sq. ft.

Fashion Bug stores sell a wide variety of junior, misses, girls' and women's size apparel and accessories at moderate and popular prices. About 75% of the merchandise is private label, primarily under the Stefano and Maggie Lawrence labels. Charming plans to increase the percentage of private label products. The private label program was developed in response to customer demand for better quality merchandise, comparable to certain national brands, but at lower prices. The company also sells men's sportswear, accessories and coats and girls' clothing in many stores. Charming is testing sales of casual footwear in more than 250 stores. Fashion Bug Plus stores, which cater primarily to the large-size woman, often adjoin Fashion Bug stores (double front stores with separate entrances).

Charming's wholly owned contracting and buying subsidiaries, located in Hong Kong, conduct operations throughout the world.

The company encourages sales through its own private label charge card. At 1994-95 year-end, there were 3.5 million active charge accounts, accounting for 39% of sales. Charming's charge card portfolio is administered by Spirit of America National Bank, N.A., wholly owned by CHRS.

Important Developments

Aug. '95—Management attributed the company's second quarter sales decline primarily to a disappointing response to its merchandise assortment and general weakness in women's apparel sales. During the February through July period, the company opened 18 new stores and closed 31, bringing the total number of operating stores to 1,415. During 1995-96, the company plans capital expenditures of $30 million primarily for the construction of some 55 new stores, the remodeling and expansion of existing units, and the completion of the 175,000 sq. ft. expansion of its Greencastle, Ind., distribution center. Upon completion of this expansion, the company will have the capacity to service over 2,000 stores.

Capitalization

Long Term Debt: $17,118,000 (4/29/95).

Per Share Data ($) (Year Ended Jan. 31)

	1995	1994	1993	1992	1991	1990
Tangible Bk. Val.	5.43	5.08	4.35	3.57	2.99	2.63
Cash Flow	0.81	1.03	1.02	0.80	0.63	0.55
Earnings	0.42	0.70	0.75	0.55	0.40	0.36
Dividends	0.09	0.09	0.08	0.06	0.06	0.06
Payout Ratio	21%	13%	11%	11%	15%	17%
Cal. Yrs.	1994	1993	1992	1991	1990	1989
Prices - High	14	19½	19	12⅝	6¼	9½
- Low	5¾	10⅝	10⅝	5⅛	3½	4⅞
P/E Ratio - High	33	28	25	23	16	26
- Low	14	15	14	9	9	13

Income Statement Analysis (Million $)

	1995	%Chg	1994	%Chg	1993	%Chg	1992
Revs.	1,273	2%	1,254	NM	1,254	23%	1,021
Oper. Inc.	98.0	-30%	141	-1%	143	31%	109
Depr.	42.6	17%	36.4	23%	29.6	11%	26.6
Int. Exp.	2.3	-10%	2.6	-14%	3.0	-15%	3.5
Pretax Inc.	63.0	-44%	112	-6%	119	39%	85.5
Eff. Tax Rate	29%	—	32%	—	32%	—	32%
Net Inc.	44.7	-41%	75.8	-7%	81.1	39%	58.3

Balance Sheet & Other Fin. Data (Million $)

	1995	1994	1993	1992	1991	1990
Cash	84.0	98.0	150	107	74.0	74.0
Curr. Assets	432	440	434	396	298	280
Total Assets	841	829	737	637	525	466
Curr. Liab.	240	258	234	214	161	146
LT Debt	17.3	22.3	26.2	31.2	35.9	32.1
Common Eqty.	559	522	445	362	299	262
Total Cap.	601	571	504	423	365	320
Cap. Exp.	75.7	79.0	65.0	46.7	53.7	36.4
Cash Flow	87.0	112	111	84.9	63.8	55.8

Ratio Analysis

	1995	1994	1993	1992	1991	1990
Curr. Ratio	1.8	1.7	1.9	1.9	1.9	1.9
% LT Debt of Cap.	2.9	3.9	5.2	7.4	9.8	10.0
% Net Inc.of Revs.	3.5	6.0	6.9	5.7	4.6	4.5
% Ret. on Assets	5.3	9.7	11.8	10.0	8.1	8.3
% Ret. on Equity	8.3	15.6	20.0	17.5	14.4	14.8

Dividend Data —Cash payments began in 1976. A "poison pill" stock purchase rights plan was adopted in 1989.

Amt. of Div. $	Date Decl.	Ex-Div. Date	Stock of Record	Payment Date
0.023	Sep. 22	Sep. 27	Oct. 03	Oct. 14 '94
0.023	Dec. 08	Dec. 23	Dec. 30	Jan. 16 '95
0.023	Mar. 17	Mar. 27	Mar. 31	Apr. 15 '95
0.023	Jun. 12	Jun. 27	Jun. 29	Jul. 15 '95

Data as orig. reptd.; bef. results of disc. opers. and/or spec. items. Per share data adj. for stk. divs. as of ex-div. date. E-Estimated. NA-Not Available. NM-Not Meaningful. NR-Not Ranked.

Office—450 Winks Lane, Bensalem, PA 19020. **Tel**—(215) 245-9100. **Chrmn & CEO**—D. V. Wachs. **Vice Chrmn, Pres & COO**—P. Wachs. **EVP-Fin & CFO**—I. Szeftel. **VP, Secy, Treas & Investor Contact**—Bernard Brodsky. **Dirs**—J. L. Castle II, M. Kafry, S. Sidewater, D. V. Wachs, P. Wachs. **Transfer Agent & Registrar**—Mellon Bank (East) N.A., Philadelphia. **Incorporated** in Pennsylvania in 1969. **Empl**-16,600. **S&P Analyst:** Karen J. Sack CFA

Chase Manhattan

NYSE Symbol **CMB**
In S&P 500

29-AUG-95 | **Industry:** Banking

Summary: Chase Manhattan has agreed to merge with Chemical Banking in a transaction that will create the largest U.S. bank holding company with nearly $300 billion in assets.

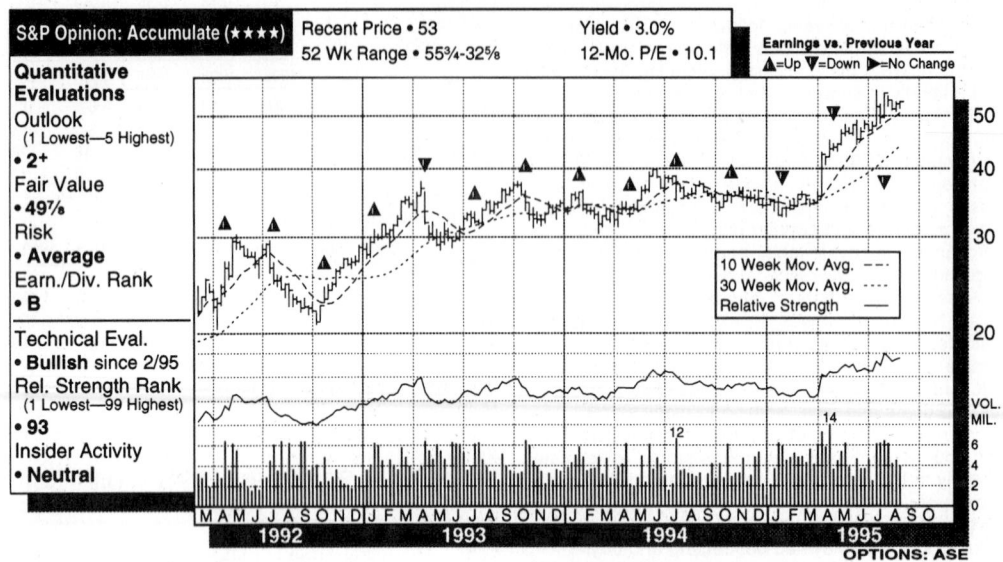

S&P Opinion: Accumulate (★★★★) | Recent Price • 53 | Yield • 3.0%
52 Wk Range • 55¾-32⅝ | 12-Mo. P/E • 10.1

Earnings vs. Previous Year
▲=Up ▼=Down ▶=No Change

Quantitative Evaluations

Outlook
(1 Lowest—5 Highest)
• **2+**

Fair Value
• **49⅞**

Risk
• **Average**

Earn./Div. Rank
• **B**

Technical Eval.
• **Bullish** since 2/95

Rel. Strength Rank
(1 Lowest—99 Highest)
• **93**

Insider Activity
• **Neutral**

10 Week Mov. Avg. — - —
30 Week Mov. Avg. - - - -
Relative Strength ——

VOL.
MIL.

OPTIONS: ASE

Overview - 29-AUG-95

Net interest income will likely trend lower for the balance of 1995, as a modestly higher level of interest-earning assets is offset by continued pressure on the net interest margin given a less favorable mix of funding sources. Noninterest income should improve, following a recent recovery in trading businesses and continued strength in mortgage servicing volumes and consumer banking fees. An aggressive focus on expense control, including a recently announced retirement program and productivity initiatives, is expected to hold expense growth under 2% in 1995. Looking ahead, the proposed combination with Chemical Banking will create a much stronger institution with respect to product offerings, geographic presence, efficiency, capital strength, and capacity for technology investment spending.

Valuation - 29-AUG-95

We share the market's enthusiasm for the proposed merger with Chemical Banking. Apart from substantial expense reductions made possible by the overlap that exists in terms of geographic presence and product offerings between the two companies, the combination will bring much needed economies of scale to succeed in an increasingly competitive banking environment. Performance goals set for the new company of double-digit earnings growth, an efficiency ratio in the low 50s and return on equity of 18% or better, seem reasonable, and selective accumulation of the shares is recommended.

Key Stock Statistics

S&P EPS Est. 1995	5.65	Tang. Bk. Value/Share	32.93
P/E on S&P Est. 1995	9.4	Beta	1.84
S&P EPS Est. 1996	6.50	Shareholders	53,100
Dividend Rate/Share	1.80	Market cap. (B)	$ 10.6
Shs. outstg. (M)	177.6	Inst. holdings	71%
Avg. daily vol. (M)	0.930	Insider holdings	NA

Value of $10,000 invested 5 years ago: $ 22,666

Fiscal Year Ending Dec. 31

	1995	% Change	1994	% Change	1993	% Change
Revenues (Million $)						
1Q	2,714	-8%	2,935	4%	2,819	-2%
2Q	2,858	-8%	3,105	13%	2,751	-1%
3Q	—	—	2,528	-10%	2,814	4%
4Q	—	—	2,619	-14%	3,033	10%
Yr.	—	—	11,187	-2%	11,417	3%
Income (Million $)						
1Q	260.0	-29%	364.0	NM	-347.0	NM
2Q	281.0	-8%	307.0	32%	233.0	53%
3Q	—	—	305.0	14%	267.0	52%
4Q	—	—	229.0	-27%	313.0	85%
Yr.	—	—	1,205	159%	466.0	-27%
Earnings Per Share ($)						
1Q	1.29	-28%	1.80	NM	-2.43	NM
2Q	1.38	-5%	1.46	22%	1.20	45%
3Q	E1.45	-3%	1.49	19%	1.25	33%
4Q	E1.55	41%	1.10	-28%	1.53	76%
Yr.	E5.65	-4%	5.87	NM	1.89	-45%

Next earnings report expected: mid October

Chase Manhattan

Business Summary - 29-AUG-95

This company is the parent of Chase Manhattan Bank, the fifth largest bank in the U.S. Wholesale banking services include global corporate finance, global capital markets, global risk management, and transaction and information processing for multinationals, local corporations, governments and financial institutions. Retail businesses include the second largest commercial bank issuer of credit cards in the U.S., with receivables of about $12 billion, and mortgage origination and servicing. Global private banking services (approximately $67 billion of client assets) are increasingly important. In addition, CMB offers its Vista Family of Mutual Funds to its U.S. clients, and Chase Vista Unit Trust Funds to clients outside the U.S. Regional banking services are provided through 324 branches in New York, Connecticut and New Jersey. International operations in over 50 countries accounted for 32% of average earning assets in 1994.

Average earning assets during 1994 of $94.1 billion (up 7.0% from 1993) were divided: domestic loans 47%, overseas loans 18%, investment securities 8%, trading securities 7%, and other temporary assets 20%. Average sources of funds were: interest-free deposits 25%, other domestic deposits 20%, overseas deposits 27%, short-term borrowings 4%, long-term debt 4%, equity 7% and other 13%.

At year-end 1994, nonperforming assets were $911 million (0.79% of assets), including $251 million of domestic real estate assets (OREO), down from $1.95 billion (1.88%) a year earlier, including $895 million of OREO. The allowance for loan losses was 2.24% of loans in 1994, versus 2.24% in 1993. Net chargeoffs during 1994 were 0.85% of average loans, versus 2.17% in 1993.

Important Developments

Aug. '95—The company and Chemical Banking Corp. (NYSE; CHL) signed a definitive agreement to merge in a transaction whereby 1.04 CHL shares would be exchanged for each share of the new CMB. With $297 billion in assets, the combined entity would be the largest bank holding company in the U.S. Cost savings from the consolidation of certain operations and elimination of redundant expenses, expected to be achieved within three years, are estimated at $1.5 billion, or about 16% of the current expense base of the combined banks. A pretax merger charge of $1.5 billion is expected and includes severance payments of $550 million related to a personnel reduction of about 12,000 and real estate costs of $550 million for the closing of some 100 branches. The transaction is expected to be completed in the first quarter of 1996 and be accretive to earnings in 1997.

Capitalization

Long Term Debt: $5,568,000,000 (6/95).
Preferred Stock: $1,400,000,000.

Per Share Data ($)

(Year Ended Dec. 31)

	1994	1993	1992	1991	1990	1989
Tangible Bk. Val.	32.93	32.23	27.25	24.18	22.45	28.17
Earnings	5.87	1.89	3.46	3.12	-3.31	-7.94
Dividends	1.46	1.20	1.20	1.20	2.16	2.36
Payout Ratio	25%	63%	35%	38%	NM	NM
Prices - High	40	38	30⅜	21⅞	35¾	44⅞
- Low	30⅜	27⅜	17¼	10¼	9¾	28
P/E Ratio - High	7	20	9	7	NM	NM
- Low	5	14	5	3	NM	NM

Income Statement Analysis (Million $)

	1994	%Chg	1993	%Chg	1992	%Chg	1991
Net Int. Inc.	3,689	-5%	3,863	8%	3,564	7%	3,345
Tax Equiv. Adj.	25.0	-14%	29.0	-26%	39.0	-35%	60.0
Non Int. Inc.	2,948	NM	2,949	23%	2,407	9%	2,199
Loan Loss Prov.	500	-68%	1,561	28%	1,220	12%	1,085
% Exp/Op Revs.	67%	—	67%	—	66%	—	68%
Pretax Inc.	1,770	142%	731	-11%	825	28%	644
Eff. Tax Rate	32%	—	36%	—	23%	—	19%
Net Inc.	1,205	159%	466	-27%	639	23%	520
% Net Int. Marg.	3.89%	—	4.33%	—	4.09%	—	3.85%

Balance Sheet & Other Fin. Data (Million $)

	1994	1993	1992	1991	1990	1989
Earning Assets:						
Money Mkt.	29,180	18,828	14,718	11,117	5,537	9,361
Inv. Securities	7,219	9,074	6,180	4,972	6,405	7,506
Com'l Loans	11,287	23,031	13,393	14,428	19,461	19,823
Other Loans	51,980	37,650	49,547	53,941	56,512	58,117
Total Assets	114,038	102,103	95,862	98,197	98,064	107,369
Demand Deposits	14,310	16,690	14,116	15,162	14,481	16,435
Time Deposits	55,646	54,819	53,108	56,355	56,232	52,638
LT Debt	4,839	5,641	5,257	5,732	6,349	6,371
Common Eqty.	6,959	6,723	5,034	4,282	3,890	4,102

Ratio Analysis

	1994	1993	1992	1991	1990	1989
% Ret. on Assets	1.0	0.9	0.6	0.5	NM	NM
% Ret. on Equity	19.9	14.6	15.6	14.0	NM	NM
% Loan Loss Resv.	2.2	2.4	3.1	2.9	3.8	4.3
% Loans/Deposits	90.1	84.9	93.1	94.8	105.7	111.0
% Equity to Assets	4.6	6.6	3.3	3.0	3.1	3.2

Dividend Data —Dividends have been paid since 1848. A dividend reinvestment plan is available.

Amt. of Div. $	Date Decl.	Ex-Div. Date	Stock of Record	Payment Date
0.400	Oct. 18	Oct. 24	Oct. 28	Nov. 15 '94
0.400	Jan. 18	Jan. 25	Jan. 31	Feb. 15 '95
0.450	Apr. 18	Apr. 24	Apr. 28	May. 15 '95
0.450	Jul. 19	Jul. 27	Jul. 31	Aug. 15 '95

Data as orig. reptd.; bef. results of disc opers. and/or spec. items. Per share data adj. for stk. divs. as of ex-div. date. E-Estimated. NA-Not Available. NM-Not Meaningful. NR-Not Ranked.

Office—One Chase Manhattan Plaza, New York, NY 10081. **Tel**—(212) 552-2222. **Chrmn & CEO**—T. G. Labrecque. **Pres & COO**—A. F. Ryan. **Vice Chrmn**—R. J. Boyle. **EVP & CFO**—A. K. Mathrani. **Investor Contact**—William Maletz. **Dirs**—S. V. Berresford, D. Boudreau, R. J. Boyle, M. A. Burns, J. A. Estrada, J. L. Ferguson, H. L. Fuller, W. H. Gray, D. T. Kearns, M. Kruse, T. G. Labrecque, D. E. Lewis, P. W. MacAvoy, J. H. McArthur, D. T. McLaughlin, E. T. Pratt, H. B. Schacht, D. H. Trautlein. **Transfer Agent & Registrar**—Mellon Securities Trust Co., Pittsburgh, Pa. **Incorporated** in Delaware in 1969; bank formed in 1799. **Empl**-35,050. **S&P Analyst:** Stephen R. Biggar

STANDARD & POOR'S
STOCK REPORTS

Chemical Banking

NYSE Symbol **CHL**
In S&P 500

29-AUG-95 Industry:
Banking

Summary: Chemical has agreed to merge with Chase Manhattan Corp. in a transaction that will create the largest U.S. bank holding company with nearly $300 billion in assets.

S&P Opinion: Accumulate (★★★★)	Recent Price • 54⅞	Yield • 3.3%
	52 Wk Range • 54⅞-33⅝	12-Mo. P/E • 10.0

Quantitative Evaluations

Outlook
(1 Lowest—5 Highest)
• **2+**

Fair Value
• **50¼**

Risk
• **Low**

Earn./Div. Rank
• **B-**

Technical Eval.
• **Bullish** since 3/95

Rel. Strength Rank
(1 Lowest—99 Highest)
• **93**

Insider Activity
• **Neutral**

Earnings vs. Previous Year
▲=Up ▼=Down ▶=No Change

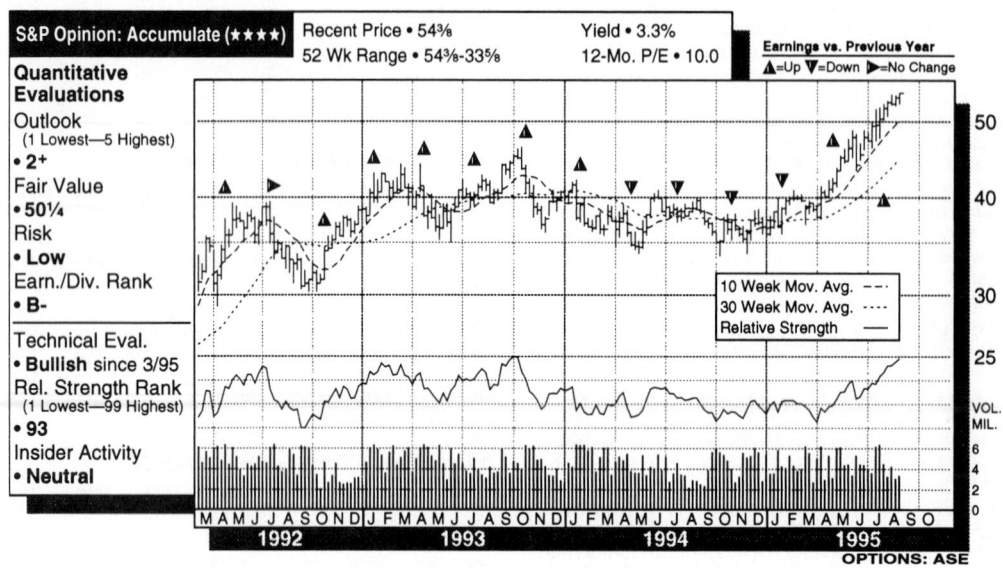

10 Week Mov. Avg. - - -
30 Week Mov. Avg. ·····
Relative Strength —

OPTIONS: ASE

Overview - 29-AUG-95

Net interest income for the balance of 1995 is expected to be flat, as growth in average assets in the 5% - 7% range is offset by narrower spreads in the higher interest rate environment. Competitive loan pricing and greater deposit costs will also restrict margins. A restructuring plan, including a workforce reduction and branch closings, has been cutting costs, although investment spending in higher-growth businesses, particularly credit card and mortgage and consumer finance, is expected to lead to flat expense levels for the year. Looking ahead, the proposed combination with Chase Manhattan will create a much stronger institution with respect to product offerings, geographic presence, efficiency, capital strength, and capacity for technology investment spending.

Valuation - 29-AUG-95

We share the market's enthusiasm for the proposed merger with Chase Manhattan. Apart from substantial expense reductions made possible by the overlap that exists in terms of geographic presence and product offerings between the two companies, the combination will bring much needed economies of scale to succeed in an increasingly competitive banking environment. Performance goals set for the new company of double-digit earnings growth, an efficiency ratio in the low 50s and return on equity of 18% or better, seem reasonable, and selective accumulation of the shares is recommended.

Key Stock Statistics

S&P EPS Est. 1995	6.25	Tang. Bk. Value/Share	38.78
P/E on S&P Est. 1995	8.7	Beta	1.31
S&P EPS Est. 1996	6.90	Shareholders	40,700
Dividend Rate/Share	2.00	Market cap. (B)	$ 14.5
Shs. outstg. (M)	240.9	Inst. holdings	76%
Avg. daily vol. (M)	0.665	Insider holdings	NA

Value of $10,000 invested 5 years ago: $ 27,204

Fiscal Year Ending Dec. 31

	1995	% Change	1994	% Change	1993	% Change
Revenues (Million $)						
1Q	3,536	17%	3,021	NM	3,049	-6%
2Q	3,728	22%	3,068	-3%	3,174	5%
3Q	—	—	3,297	7%	3,077	2%
4Q	—	—	3,299	6%	3,127	9%
Yr.	—	—	12,685	2%	12,427	2%
Income (Million $)						
1Q	396.0	24%	319.0	-15%	374.0	44%
2Q	453.0	27%	357.0	-6%	381.0	59%
3Q	—	—	439.0	-13%	502.0	78%
4Q	—	—	179.0	-48%	347.0	14%
Yr.	—	—	1,294	-18%	1,569	44%
Earnings Per Share ($)						
1Q	1.51	34%	1.13	-7%	1.21	21%
2Q	1.72	34%	1.28	-5%	1.35	63%
3Q	E1.55	-3%	1.60	-13%	1.84	88%
4Q	E1.47	133%	0.63	-49%	1.23	13%
Yr.	E6.25	35%	4.64	-18%	5.63	44%

Next earnings report expected: mid October

Business Summary - 29-AUG-95

Following its December 1991 acquisition of Manufacturers Hanover Corp. (MHC), Chemical Banking is now the fourth largest U.S. bank holding company based on total assets of $178.5 billion at June 30, 1995. Principal bank subsidiaries are Chemical Bank and Texas Commerce Bank N.A.

Global bank operations include worldwide wholesale client management and venture capital activities; acquisition finance, loan syndications, high-yield securities and mergers and acquisitions; securities, foreign exchange and derivatives trading; and cross-border investment banking, local merchant banking and trade finance. Regional bank activities include New York market consumer, commercial and professional banking, retail card services, private banking and Geoserve (cash management, funds transfer, trade, corporate trust and securities services worldwide). Texas Commerce ($20 billion in assets and 115 locations) is a leading provider of financial products and services to businesses and individuals throughout Texas. Real estate activities include the management of the company's commercial real estate portfolio.

Average earning assets in 1994 of $130.0 billion (up from $124.9 billion in 1993) consisted of domestic loans 44%, foreign loans 14%, investment securities 20%, trading account assets 9%, and other temporary assets 13%. Average sources of funds were demand deposits 13%, other domestic deposits 29%, foreign deposits 15%, short-term borrowings 18%, long-term debt 5%, equity 7%, and other 13%.

At year-end 1994, nonperforming assets were $1.14 billion (1.45% of loans), against $3.53 billion (4.68%) a year earlier. The reserve for loan losses was 3.15% of loans, down from 4.01%. Net chargeoffs in 1994 were 1.46% of average loans, versus 1.63% in 1993.

Important Developments

Aug. '95—The company and Chase Manhattan Corp. (NYSE; CMB) signed a definitive agreement to merge in a transaction whereby 1.04 CHL shares would be exchanged for each share of the new CMB. With $297 billion in assets, the combined entity would be the largest bank holding company in the U.S. Cost savings from the consolidation of certain operations and elimination of redundant expenses, expected to be achieved within three years, are estimated at $1.5 billion, or about 16% of the current expense base of the combined banks. A pretax merger charge of $1.5 billion is expected and includes severance payments of $550 million related to a personnel reduction of about 12,000 and real estate costs of $550 million for the closing of some 100 branches. The transaction is expected to be completed in the first quarter of 1996 and be accretive to earnings in 1997.

Capitalization

Long Term Debt: $7,202,000,000 (6/95).
Preferred Stock: $1,250,000,000.

Per Share Data ($) (Year Ended Dec. 31)

	1994	1993	1992	1991	1990	1989
Tangible Bk. Val.	37.88	37.61	32.43	30.98	32.86	34.00
Earnings	4.64	5.63	3.90	0.11	2.38	-8.29
Dividends	1.64	1.37	1.20	1.05	2.29	2.72
Payout Ratio	35%	24%	31%	NM	96%	NM
Prices - High	42⅛	46⅜	39½	30⅛	31⅜	41⅛
- Low	33⅝	35	21⅞	10½	9⅝	28½
P/E Ratio - High	9	8	10	NM	13	NM
- Low	7	6	6	NM	4	NM

Income Statement Analysis (Million $)

	1994	%Chg	1993	%Chg	1992	%Chg	1991
Net Int. Inc.	4,674	NM	4,636	NM	4,598	12%	4,113
Tax Equiv. Adj.	24.0	14%	21.0	-32%	31.0	-34%	47.0
Non Int. Inc.	35.3	-99%	3,882	31%	2,973	9%	2,736
Loan Loss Prov.	550	-56%	1,259	-8%	1,365	1%	1,345
% Exp/Op Revs.	67%	—	62%	—	65%	—	77%
Pretax Inc.	2,212	5%	2,108	59%	1,329	NM	290
Eff. Tax Rate	42%	—	26%	—	18%	—	47%
Net Inc.	1,294	-19%	1,604	48%	1,086	NM	154
% Net Int. Marg.	3.61%	—	3.73%	—	3.82%	—	3.33%

Balance Sheet & Other Fin. Data (Million $)

	1994	1993	1992	1991	1990	1989
Earning Assets:						
Money Mkt.	29,539	28,265	14,009	16,849	6,547	7,821
Inv. Securities	26,997	25,948	23,426	19,763	10,686	9,708
Com'l Loans	24,972	33,620	28,015	31,929	18,927	18,167
Other Loans	54,255	42,238	54,647	52,908	26,682	26,913
Total Assets	171,423	149,888	139,655	138,930	73,019	71,513
Demand Deposits	21,399	23,443	22,813	18,025	13,080	13,397
Time Deposits	75,107	74,834	71,360	74,925	35,871	36,754
LT Debt	6,753	8,192	6,798	5,738	3,233	2,970
Common Eqty.	9,262	9,510	8,003	5,683	3,003	2,801

Ratio Analysis

	1994	1993	1992	1991	1990	1989
% Ret. on Assets	0.8	1.1	0.8	0.1	0.4	NM
% Ret. on Equity	14.8	16.1	16.0	0.4	7.1	NM
% Loan Loss Resv.	3.2	4.0	3.7	3.9	4.6	5.9
% Loans/Deposits	81.6	76.7	87.1	90.6	92.2	88.8
% Equity to Assets	4.7	7.3	4.2	3.4	3.9	3.8

Dividend Data —Dividends have been paid since 1827. A dividend reinvestment plan is available. A "poison pill" stock purchase rights plan was adopted in 1989.

Amt. of Div. $	Date Decl.	Ex-Div. Date	Stock of Record	Payment Date
0.440	Sep. 20	Sep. 30	Oct. 06	Oct. 31 '94
0.440	Dec. 20	Dec. 30	Jan. 06	Jan. 31 '95
0.440	Mar. 21	Mar. 31	Apr. 06	Apr. 30 '95
0.500	Jun. 20	Jul. 03	Jul. 06	Jul. 31 '95

Data as orig. reptd.; bef. results of disc opers. and/or spec. items. Per share data adj. for stk. divs. as of ex-div. date. E-Estimated. NA-Not Available. NM-Not Meaningful. NR-Not Ranked.

Office—270 Park Ave., New York, NY 10017-2036. **Tel**—(212) 270-6000. **Chrmn & CEO**—W. V. Shipley. **Pres**—E. D. Miller. **EVP & CFO**—P. J. Tobin. **Secy**—J. B. Wynne. **Investor Contact**—John Borden. **Dirs**—F. A. Bennack, Jr., M. C. Bergerac, R. W. Bromery, C. W. Duncan, Jr., M. R. Goodes, G. V. Grune, W. B. Harrison, Jr., H. S. Hook, H. L. Kaplan, J. B. Llewellyn, J. P. Mascotte, J. F. McGillicuddy, E. D. Miller, W. V. Shipley, A. C. Sigler, M. I. Sovern, J. R. Stafford, W. B. Thomas, M. v.N. Whitman, R. D. Wood. **Transfer Agent & Registrar**—Chemical Bank, NYC. **Incorporated** in Delaware in 1968; bank started in 1824. **Empl**-42,130. **S&P Analyst:** Stephen R. Biggar

Chevron Corp.

NYSE Symbol **CHV**
In S&P 500

03-AUG-95

Industry:
Oil and Gas

Summary: Chevron is a major integrated oil company, with exploration, production, refining and marketing interests throughout the world.

S&P Opinion: Hold (★★★)	Recent Price • 48¾	Yield • 4.1%
	52 Wk Range • 49¾-37⅞	12-Mo. P/E • 15.0

Earnings vs. Previous Year
▲=Up ▼=Down ▶=No Change

Quantitative Evaluations

Outlook
(1 Lowest—5 Highest)
• **1**

Fair Value
• **40⅞**

Risk
• **Low**

Earn./Div. Rank
• **B**

Technical Eval.
• **Bearish** since 2/95

Rel. Strength Rank
(1 Lowest—99 Highest)
• **43**

Insider Activity
• **Neutral**

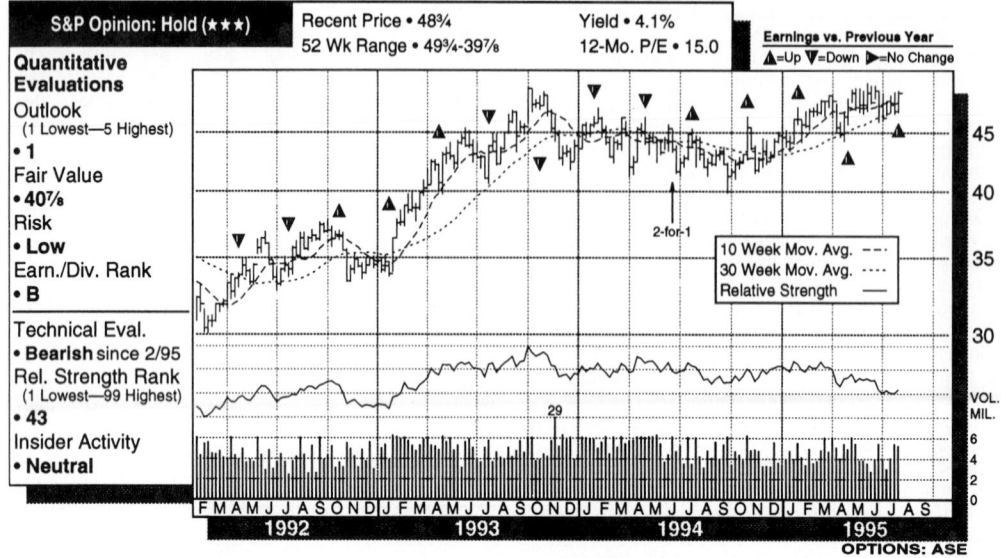

2-for-1

10 Week Mov. Avg. – – –
30 Week Mov. Avg. ·····
Relative Strength —

45
40
35
30

VOL.
MIL.
6
4
2
0

F M A M J J A S O N D | J F M A M J J A S O N D | J F M A M J J A S O N D | J F M A M J J A S
1992 | 1993 | 1994 | 1995

OPTIONS: ASE

Overview - 01-AUG-95

Profits near term are expected to trend higher, benefiting from the company's restructuring program and higher chemical earnings. CHV has been divesting nonstrategic businesses in recent years to streamline its asset base and lower its cost structure. The program has succeeded, and long-term earning power has been enhanced by the more focused business profile. CHV's domestic strategy is to develop natural gas properties, while its refining and marketing operations have been narrowed to western and southern regions of the U.S. Overseas, the company is pioneering exploration and production in the former Soviet Union. Its 50%-owned Caltex subsidiary, a leading refiner and marketer in the Far East, is expanding its manufacturing capacity in robust Pacific Rim markets.

Valuation - 03-AUG-95

Weak domestic natural gas prices and depressed European refined product margins have been overshadowed by the long-awaited turnaround in U.S. refined product margins, which should continue to support the shares at current price levels. The refocused asset base should sustain modest earnings growth longer term. Internal cash generation, now being fueled by strong chemical prices, is impressive and should fund CHV's capital budget without the need for additional borrowings. We believe crude oil prices will remain stable during the remainder of 1995, though gas prices are expected to show modest increases. On this basis, we believe the shares are fairly priced at current levels.

Key Stock Statistics

S&P EPS Est. 1995	3.20	Tang. Bk. Value/Share	22.89
P/E on S&P Est. 1995	15.2	Beta	0.68
S&P EPS Est. 1996	3.60	Shareholders	153,000
Dividend Rate/Share	2.00	Market cap. (B)	$ 32.4
Shs. outstg. (M)	652.0	Inst. holdings	45%
Avg. daily vol. (M)	0.988	Insider holdings	NA

Value of $10,000 invested 5 years ago: $ 18,313

Fiscal Year Ending Dec. 31

	1995	% Change	1994	% Change	1993	% Change
Revenues (Million $)						
1Q	7,859	11%	7,112	-19%	8,736	5%
2Q	9,397	23%	7,620	-9%	8,400	-19%
3Q	—	—	8,176	NM	8,213	-25%
4Q	—	—	7,432	-5%	7,815	-27%
Yr.	—	—	30,340	-8%	33,014	-12%
Income (Million $)						
1Q	459.0	18%	388.0	-23%	501.0	47%
2Q	607.0	136%	257.0	NM	50.00	-84%
3Q	—	—	425.0	1%	420.0	-10%
4Q	—	—	623.0	112%	294.0	-73%
Yr.	—	—	1,693	34%	1,265	-43%
Earnings Per Share ($)						
1Q	0.70	17%	0.60	-22%	0.77	56%
2Q	0.93	138%	0.39	NM	0.08	-84%
3Q	E0.80	—	0.65	NM	0.65	-6%
4Q	E0.90	—	0.96	111%	0.46	-72%
Yr.	E3.20	—	2.60	34%	1.94	-40%

Next earnings report expected: late October

Chevron Corp.

Business Summary - 03-AUG-95

Chevron Corporation (formerly Standard Oil of California) is a major international oil company. Net income (in millions) by business segment in recent years:

	1994	1993
U.S. exploration & production	$518	$566
U.S refining & marketing	40	-170
International expl. & prod.	539	580
International refining & mktg.	239	252
Chemicals	206	143
Coal & other minerals	111	44

In 1994, worldwide production of crude oil and natural gas liquids averaged 992,510 bbl. a day (37% U.S.), production of natural gas 2.6 Bcf a day (79% U.S.), refinery input 1,836,000 b/d and petroleum product sales 2,248,000 b/d. At year-end 1994, CHV had the largest U.S. refining capacity and ranked among the top 10 in worldwide refining capacity, including its share of affiliates' capacity. Principal refined product markets are southeastern, south central and western states. The Caltex Group (equally owned with Texaco Inc.) markets oil in Africa, Asia and Australia and produces oil in Indonesia. Net proved reserves at 1994 year end were 4,167 million bbl. of crude oil and liquids and 9,967 Bcf of natural gas. CHV has boosted 1995 capital and exploratory spending by about 5%. About 70% of the $2.7 billion earmarked for worldwide exploration will be for projects outside the U.S.

Chemical products include benzene, styrene, polystyrene, ethylene, polyethylene, paraxylene and normal alpha olefins, as well as fuel additives. Plants are located in 10 states and in France, Brazil and Japan. An expansion of polystyrene capacity from 530 million to 875 million lbs./yr. at the Cedar Bayou, Texas, facility is scheduled to be completed in 1996.

Important Developments

Jul. '95—Chevron reported seccond quarter net income more than double that of last year. Strong demand for petrochemicals, notably ethylene, styrene and paraxylene, pushed chemical earnings to $175 million, from $49 million. A 14% jump in oil prices boosted international exploration and production earnings 45% to $194 million from $134 million. Refining and marketing earnings benefited from fewer refinery turnarounds and an improvement in U.S. refining margins, which outweighed the impact of the sale of the Port Arthur, Texas, and Philadelphia refineries. The refinery divestitures led to an 18% reduction in refined product sales volumes. During the quarter, Chevron introduced its new gasoline containing Techron, a proprietary fuel additive.

Capitalization

Long Term Debt: $4,451,000,000 (6/95).

Per Share Data ($) (Year Ended Dec. 31)

	1994	1993	1992	1991	1990	1989
Tangible Bk. Val.	22.27	21.40	21.11	21.25	21.15	19.69
Cash Flow	6.33	5.71	7.08	5.58	6.86	4.11
Earnings	2.60	1.95	3.26	1.85	3.05	0.36
Dividends	1.85	1.75	1.65	1.63	1.48	1.40
Payout Ratio	71%	90%	51%	87%	48%	396%
Prices - High	47⅜	49⅜	37¾	40⅛	40⅞	36¾
- Low	39⅞	33¾	30⅛	31¾	31⅝	22¾
P/E Ratio - High	18	25	12	22	13	NM
- Low	15	17	9	17	10	NM

Income Statement Analysis (Million $)

	1994	%Chg	1993	%Chg	1992	%Chg	1991
Revs.	30,340	-6%	32,123	-14%	37,464	3%	36,461
Oper. Inc.	4,925	-4%	5,141	2%	5,028	10%	4,562
Depr.	2,431	NM	2,452	-5%	2,594	NM	2,616
Int. Exp.	419	13%	371	-22%	478	-12%	546
Pretax Inc.	2,803	16%	2,426	-30%	3,463	54%	2,252
Eff. Tax Rate	40%	—	48%	—	36%	—	43%
Net Inc.	1,693	34%	1,265	-43%	2,210	71%	1,293

Balance Sheet & Other Fin. Data (Million $)

	1994	1993	1992	1991	1990	1989
Cash	1,306	2,016	1,695	1,485	1,684	1,628
Curr. Assets	7,591	8,682	8,772	9,031	10,089	8,620
Total Assets	34,407	34,736	33,970	34,636	35,089	33,884
Curr. Liab.	9,392	10,606	9,835	9,480	9,017	7,583
LT Debt	4,128	4,082	4,953	5,991	6,710	7,390
Common Eqty.	14,596	13,997	13,728	14,739	14,836	13,980
Total Cap.	21,398	20,995	21,575	23,707	24,702	24,806
Cap. Exp.	3,112	3,214	3,369	3,665	3,136	3,102
Cash Flow	4,124	3,717	4,804	3,909	4,850	2,813

Ratio Analysis

	1994	1993	1992	1991	1990	1989
Curr. Ratio	0.8	0.8	0.9	1.0	1.1	1.1
% LT Debt of Cap.	19.3	19.4	23.0	25.3	27.2	29.8
% Net Inc.of Revs.	5.6	3.9	5.9	3.5	5.6	0.9
% Ret. on Assets	4.9	3.7	6.7	3.7	6.3	0.7
% Ret. on Equity	11.8	9.1	16.0	8.8	15.1	1.7

Dividend Data (Dividends have been paid since 1912. A dividend reinvestment plan is available. A "poison pill" stock purchase rights plan was adopted in 1988.)

Amt. of Div. $	Date Decl.	Ex-Div. Date	Stock of Record	Payment Date
0.463	Jul. 27	Aug. 04	Aug. 10	Sep. 12 '94
0.463	Oct. 26	Nov. 04	Nov. 10	Dec. 12 '94
0.463	Jan. 25	Feb. 10	Feb. 16	Mar. 10 '95
0.463	Apr. 26	May. 11	May. 17	Jun. 12 '95
0.500	Jul. 26	Aug. 15	Aug. 17	Sep. 11 '95

Data as orig. reptd.; bef. results of disc. opers. and/or spec. items. Per share data adj. for stk. divs. as of ex-div. date. E-Estimated. NA-Not Available. NM-Not Meaningful. NR-Not Ranked.

Office—225 Bush St., San Francisco, CA 94104-4289. **Tel**—(415) 894-7700. **Chrmn & CEO**—K. T. Derr. **Vice Chrmn**—J. N. Sullivan, J. D. Bonney. **Secy**—Lydia I. Beebe. **VP-Fin**—M. R. Klitten. **Investor Contact**—M. J. Foehr. **Dirs**—S. H. Armacost, J. D. Bonney, K. T. Derr, S. Ginn, C. A. Hills, C. M. Pigott, C. Rice, J. N. Sullivan, G. H. Weyerhaeuser, J. A. Young. **Transfer Agent**—Co.'s office. **Registrar**—First Trust California, San Francisco. **Incorporated** in Delaware in 1926. **Empl**-45,758. **S&P Analyst:** Raymond J. Deacon

Chrysler Corp.

NYSE Symbol **C**
In S&P 500

06-NOV-95

Industry:
Auto/Truck mfrs.

Summary: The third largest U.S. automaker, Chrysler is the leader in the minivan and sport utility segments of the motor vehicle markets.

S&P Opinion: Hold (★★★)		
Recent Price • 50¾	Yield • 3.9%	
52 Wk Range • 58⅛-38¼	12-Mo. P/E • 8.4	

Quantitative Evaluations

Outlook
(1 Lowest—5 Highest)
• **2⁻**

Fair Value
• **51**

Risk
• **Average**

Earn./Div. Rank
• **B-**

Technical Eval.
• **Bullish** since 6/95

Rel. Strength Rank
(1 Lowest—99 Highest)
• **35**

Insider Activity
• **Unfavorable**

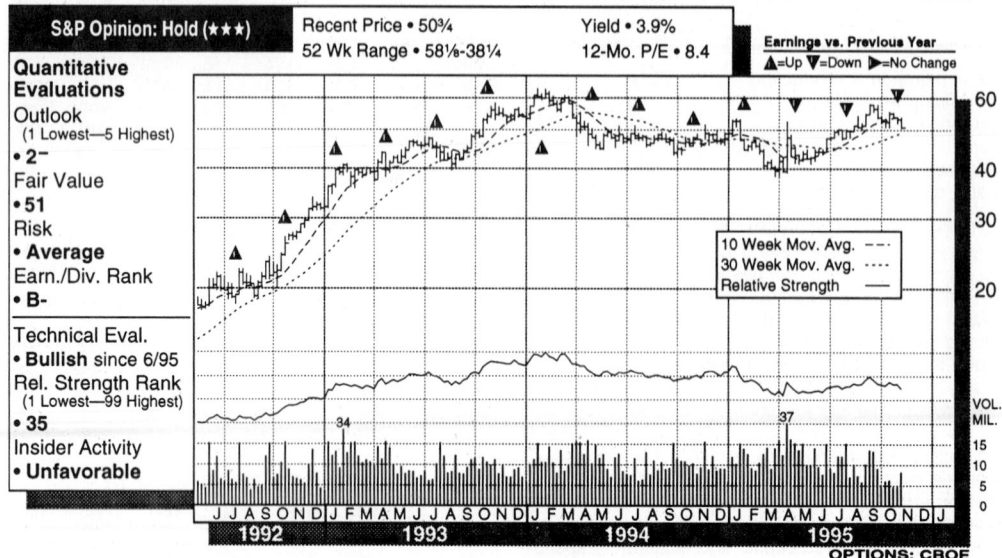

Earnings vs. Previous Year
▲=Up ▼=Down ▶=No Change

10 Week Mov. Avg. ----
30 Week Mov. Avg. .....
Relative Strength —

OPTIONS: CBOE

Overview - 04-NOV-95

Chrysler's vehicle sales should increase in 1996 as minivan production returns to normal levels after 1995's diminished output due to model changeover and production of highly profitable Jeeps and Dodge Ram pickups remains strong. We expect the redesigned minivans to gain market share in 1996. With higher aggregate volume, greater profitability of recently designed models, continued cost controls and low pension expense, we expect earnings to rebound sharply in 1996 due to a decline in new product start-up costs and flat marketing costs. The projected earnings gain should be realized even in a flat to slightly down overall North American market. Further dividend increases are likely and share repurchases are continuing.

Valuation - 02-NOV-95

We maintain our hold recommendation on Chrysler due to mounting evidence that U.S. demand may decline further near term and that the peak of the current business cycle is near. Weak consumer economic indicators including declining consumer confidence, high debt and sluggish income growth do not bode well for early 1996, but we expect improvement by mid-year. Even with the modest downturn, we expect Chrysler's earnings to improve as minivan production returns to normal. Aggressive marketing actions by Chrysler have kept inventories lean. While we think the modest earnings multiple and recent increase in shareholder activism at Chrysler should help support the stock price, we would not add to holdings at this time due to the economic uncertainty.

Key Stock Statistics

S&P EPS Est. 1995	4.30	Tang. Bk. Value/Share	21.80
P/E on S&P Est. 1995	11.8	Beta	0.69
S&P EPS Est. 1996	6.00	Shareholders	143,000
Dividend Rate/Share	2.00	Market cap. (B)	$ 19.4
Shs. outstg. (M)	382.6	Inst. holdings	58%
Avg. daily vol. (M)	1.145	Insider holdings	NA

Value of $10,000 invested 5 years ago: $ 33,803

Fiscal Year Ending Dec. 31

	1995	% Change	1994	% Change	1993	% Change
Revenues (Million $)						
1Q	13,613	3%	13,223	21%	10,904	33%
2Q	12,516	-4%	13,082	19%	11,031	18%
3Q	12,009	3%	11,659	20%	9,713	5%
4Q	—	—	14,260	19%	11,952	17%
Yr.	—	—	52,224	20%	43,600	18%
Income (Million $)						
1Q	592.0	-37%	938.0	77%	530.0	NM
2Q	135.0	-86%	956.0	40%	685.0	NM
3Q	354.0	-46%	651.0	54%	423.0	109%
4Q	—	—	1,168	50%	777.0	118%
Yr.	—	—	3,713	54%	2,415	NM
Earnings Per Share ($)						
1Q	1.59	-38%	2.55	62%	1.57	NM
2Q	0.35	-87%	2.61	40%	1.86	NM
3Q	0.91	-48%	1.76	56%	1.13	82%
4Q	E1.45	-55%	3.20	52%	2.11	88%
Yr.	E4.30	-57%	10.11	49%	6.77	NM

Next earnings report expected: mid January

Chrysler Corp.

Business Summary - 04-NOV-95

Chrysler is the third largest U.S. motor vehicle manufacturer. The company's automotive segment also includes the operations of Electrospace Systems, a worldwide supplier of electronic systems and services, and the car rental operations of Thrifty Rent-A-Car Systems, Snappy Car Rental, Dollar Rent A Car and General Rent-A-Car. The financial segment consists primarily of Chrysler Financial Corp.'s vehicle financing, insurance and other financing services. Segment contributions (profits in millions) in 1994 were:

	Revs.	Profits
Automotive	96%	$5,829
Financial services	4%	315

In 1994, the company had pretax income of $5,239 million in the U.S., $208 million in Canada and $383 million elsewhere.

Chrysler, Plymouth, Dodge and Eagle car models accounted for 9.0% of total U.S. registrations (including foreign-built cars) in 1994, versus 9.8% in 1993, 8.3% in 1992, 8.6% in 1991 and 9.3% in 1990. Comparable figures for trucks (including Jeeps) were 21.7%, 21.4%, 21.1%, 19.5% and 17.3%. Chrysler's combined share of the North American car and truck market was 14.7% in 1994, versus 14.8% in 1993, 13.4% in 1992 and 12.4% in 1991. Vehicles are marketed through some 5,000 dealers.

Of the 2,762,103 Chrysler cars and trucks assembled in 1994, 1,755,903 were built in the U.S., 692,615 in Canada, 34,611 in Japan (by Mitsubishi Motors), 238,888 in Mexico and 40,086 elsewhere.

Important Developments

Nov. '95—Chrysler's board said that it is reviewing its corporate governance policies and the board's composition and is considering approving an anti-greenmail provision in its bylaws. This is in response to a request by the company's largest shareholder, Tracinda Corp., which is controlled by K. Kerkorian. Tracinda is demanding changes in Chrysler's capital structure and dividend policy and has lobbied for the anti-greenmail policy in an effort to prove that it does not want to receive any benefit that would not be given to all shareholders. Tracinda is also demanding the right to appoint three of Chrysler's directors. Earlier in 1995, Tracinda attempted to acquire all of Chrysler's shares but was unable to obtain the necessary financing. Instead, Tracinda increased its holdings to 14.1% of Chrysler's stock.

Capitalization

Long Term Debt: $12,016,000,000 (9/95).
Conv. Preferred Stock: $84,000,000 (liquid. value).

Per Share Data ($)

(Year Ended Dec. 31)

	1994	1993	1992	1991	1990	1989
Tangible Bk. Val.	21.60	4.65	6.95	3.14	6.90	12.63
Cash Flow	15.53	11.52	6.91	3.82	6.55	7.77
Earnings	10.11	6.77	1.47	-2.22	0.30	1.36
Dividends	1.10	0.65	0.60	0.60	1.20	1.20
Payout Ratio	11%	10%	41%	NM	397%	85%
Prices - High	63½	58⅜	33⅞	15⅞	20⅜	29⅝
- Low	43⅛	31¾	11½	9¾	9⅛	18⅛
P/E Ratio - High	6	9	23	NM	68	22
- Low	4	5	8	NM	30	13

Income Statement Analysis (Million $)

	1994	%Chg	1993	%Chg	1992	%Chg	1991
Revs.	50,736	20%	42,260	19%	35,501	26%	28,162
Oper. Inc.	7,223	45%	4,977	90%	2,622	NM	720
Depr.	1,944	19%	1,640	2%	1,610	10%	1,465
Int. Exp.	1,114	-13%	1,280	-19%	1,581	-22%	2,031
Pretax Inc.	5,830	52%	3,838	NM	934	NM	-809
Eff. Tax Rate	36%	—	37%	—	46%	—	NM
Net Inc.	3,713	54%	2,415	NM	505	NM	-537

Balance Sheet & Other Fin. Data (Million $)

	1994	1993	1992	1991	1990	1989
Cash	5,145	4,040	2,357	2,041	1,572	1,269
Total Assets	49,539	43,830	40,653	43,076	46,374	51,038
LT Debt	7,650	6,871	13,434	14,980	12,750	13,966
Total Debt	NA	11,451	15,551	19,438	22,900	27,546
Common Eqty.	9,831	5,974	6,676	6,109	6,849	7,233
Cap. Exp.	3,843	3,028	2,916	2,348	2,045	1,922
Cash Flow	5,577	3,975	2,046	927	1,466	1,806

Ratio Analysis

	1994	1993	1992	1991	1990	1989
% Ret. on Assets	7.9	5.2	1.2	NM	0.1	0.6
% Ret. on Equity	45.9	33.5	6.8	NM	1.0	4.3
% LT Debt of Cap.	41.7	50.1	63.3	68.4	60.4	60.7

Dividend Data —Following a four-year hiatus, dividends were resumed in 1984. A dividend reinvestment plan is available. A "poison pill" stock purchase right was revised in 1994.

Amt. of Div. $	Date Decl.	Ex-Div. Date	Stock of Record	Payment Date
0.400	Dec. 01	Dec. 09	Dec. 15	Jan. 13 '95
0.400	Mar. 02	Mar. 09	Mar. 15	Apr. 14 '95
0.500	May. 17	Jun. 13	Jun. 15	Jul. 14 '95
0.500	Sep. 07	Sep. 13	Sep. 15	Oct. 16 '95

Data as orig. reptd.; bef. results of disc. opers. and/or spec. items. Per share data adj. for stk. divs. as of ex-div. date. E-Estimate. NA-Not Available. NM-Not Meaningful. NR-Not Ranked.

Office—12000 Chrysler Drive, Highland Park, MI 48288. **Tel**—(313) 956-5741. **Chrmn & CEO**—R. J. Eaton. **Vice Chrmn**—T. G. Denomme. **Pres & COO**—R. A. Lutz. **VP & CFO**—G. C. Valade. **VP & Treas**—T. P. Capo. **VP & Secy**—W. J. O'Brien. **Investor Contact**—Sam A. Messina. **Dirs**—L. H. Affinito, R. E. Allen, J. E. Antonini, J. A. Califano Jr., T. G. Denomme, R. J. Eaton, A. J. de Grandpre, E. G. Graves, K. Kresa, R. J. Lanigan, R. A. Lutz, P. A. Magowan, W. G. Milliken, M. T. Stamper, L. R. Wilson. **Transfer Agent & Registrar**—First Chicago Trust Co. of New York, Jersey City, N.J. **Incorporated** in Delaware in 1925. **Empl**-121,000. **S&P Analyst:** Joshua M. Harari, CFA

Chubb Corp.

NYSE Symbol **CB**
In S&P 500

29-JUL-95

Industry:
Insurance

Summary: This large, broadly based property-casualty insurance organization also has interests in life and health insurance and real estate development.

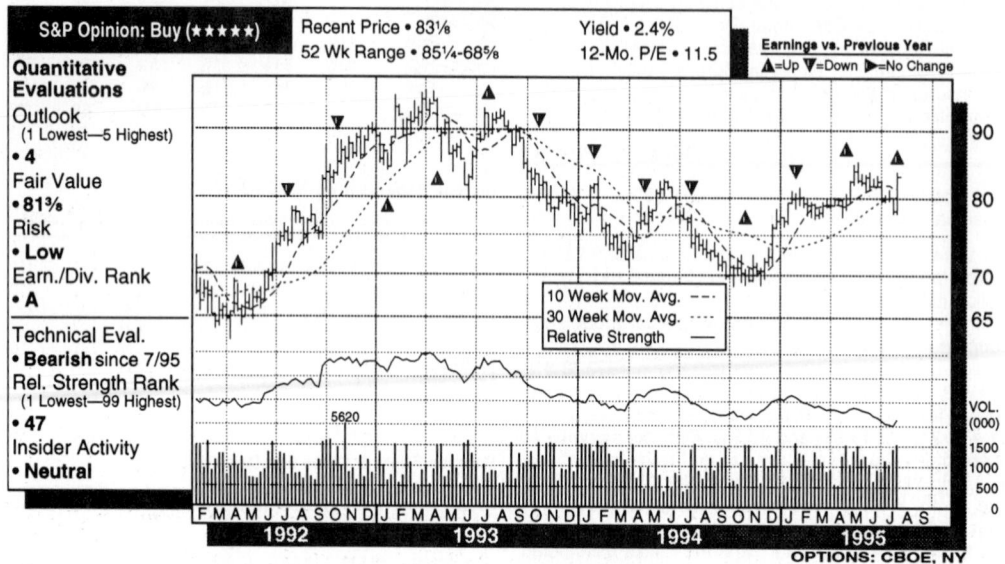

S&P Opinion: Buy (★★★★★)	Recent Price • 83⅛	Yield • 2.4%
	52 Wk Range • 85¼-68⅝	12-Mo. P/E • 11.5

Earnings vs. Previous Year
▲=Up ▼=Down ▶=No Change

Quantitative Evaluations

Outlook
(1 Lowest—5 Highest)
• 4

Fair Value
• 81⅜

Risk
• **Low**

Earn./Div. Rank
• **A**

Technical Eval.
• **Bearish** since 7/95

Rel. Strength Rank
(1 Lowest—99 Highest)
• **47**

Insider Activity
• **Neutral**

10 Week Mov. Avg. ---
30 Week Mov. Avg. ······
Relative Strength —

OPTIONS: CBOE, NY

Overview - 28-JUL-95

Operating earnings growth in 1995 will be aided by an easing of catastrophe losses and by the absence of charges of $358 million taken in late 1993 to cover a $675 million increase in asbestos related reserves. Net written premiums will likely advance 12%-15%, reflecting volume growth and price increases in several lines. Improved underwriting trends emerging in several key lines also bode well for the long-term profit picture. Fundamentally, CB is a solid underwriter poised to benefit from a firming of p-c insurance rates. CB's dominant presence in certain lines of business affords it a greater degree of pricing control. CB's decision to scale back real estate development activities may lead to somewhat erratic real estate profits near term, but long term this is a plus. Investment income growth will be modest amid relatively lower interest rates, but asset writedowns are unlikely.

Valuation - 28-JUL-95

After a lackluster performance during much of 1994 due to the negative effects of higher interst rates, these interest-sensitive shares have rebounded nicely in 1995. Better than expected second quarter operating results fueled much of the recent rise. Despite their appreciation, the shares remain attractive at 12 times our 1995 operating earnings estimate of $7.00 a share (which excludes realized investment gains), given CB's superior growth prospects and solid fundamentals.

Key Stock Statistics

S&P EPS Est. 1995	7.00	Tang. Bk. Value/Share	52.75
P/E on S&P Est. 1995	11.9	Beta	1.14
S&P EPS Est. 1996	7.70	Shareholders	8,800
Dividend Rate/Share	1.96	Market cap. (B)	$ 7.2
Shs. outstg. (M)	87.0	Inst. holdings	70%
Avg. daily vol. (M)	0.280	Insider holdings	NA

Value of $10,000 invested 5 years ago: $ 19,701

Fiscal Year Ending Dec. 31

	1995	% Change	1994	% Change	1993	% Change
Revenues (Million $)						
1Q	1,464	5%	1,396	13%	1,238	5%
2Q	NA	—	1,415	10%	1,284	9%
3Q	—	—	1,429	-9%	1,570	26%
4Q	—	—	1,470	4%	1,408	5%
Yr.	—	—	5,710	4%	5,500	11%
Income (Million $)						
1Q	146.7	100%	73.20	-50%	145.8	2%
2Q	185.0	26%	146.7	-13%	168.5	29%
3Q	—	—	152.7	NM	-130.6	NM
4Q	—	—	155.9	-3%	160.5	-19%
Yr.	—	—	528.5	54%	344.2	-44%
Earnings Per Share ($)						
1Q	1.66	100%	0.83	-49%	1.64	1%
2Q	2.09	27%	1.65	-13%	1.89	28%
3Q	—	—	1.71	NM	-1.42	NM
4Q	—	—	1.76	-2%	1.80	-19%
Yr.	E7.00	—	5.95	52%	3.91	-44%

Next earnings report expected: mid October

McGraw Hill

Business Summary - 28-JUL-95

Chubb Corp. is engaged in property-casualty insurance domestically and abroad and in life and health insurance and real estate development.

In 1994, CB wrote $4.0 billion in property-casualty premiums, of which specialty commercial lines accounted for 37%, standard commercial lines 34%, personal lines 21%, and reinsurance assumed 8%. Written premiums were divided: other specialty commercial 19%, fidelity and surety 18%, commercial multi-peril 15%, commercial casualty 14%, homeowners 11%, reinsurance assumed 8%, workers' compensation 5%, personal auto 5%, and other personal lines 5%. The p-c group operates through more than 3,300 independent agents and some 400 insurance brokers.

The life and health insurance group is composed of Chubb Life Insurance Co. of America and its wholly-owned subsidiaries, Colonial Life Insurance Co. of America, Chubb Sovereign Life Insurance Co., and ChubbHealth, Inc. (a joint venture with Healthsource, Inc. Life insurance in force at year-end 1994 totaled $61.7 billion. The life group offers participating and nonparticipating individual life insurance, as well as group life and health insurance and individual health and annuity contracts on a nonparticipating basis only. Managed care health services are offered in the New York City area through ChubbHealth. Average invested assets of the life and p-c companies totaled $11.3 billion at year-end 1994.

Bellemead Development Corp. (4% of 1994 revenues) develops industrial, commercial and residential real estate, mainly in New Jersey. Bellemead's vacancy rate at year-end 1994 was 9%, versus 10% in 1993 and 14% at year-end 1992.

Important Developments

Jul. '95—The growth in CB's second quarter 1995 operating earnings (to $1.72 a share from $1.54) reflected improved underwriting trends in most lines of business, coupled with higher life/health and real estate profits. These factors offset higher catastrophe losses of $42.7 million, versus $$12.9 million.
Feb. '95—CB's sharply higher net income for 1994 reflected the absence of a $358 million ($3.95 a share) net third quarter 1993 charge to cover a $675 million reserve taken to settle asbestos related claims against Fibreboard Corp. The settlement also called for the establishment of a $1.525 billion trust fund (35% funded by CB, 65% by CNA) to settle claims filed after August 27, 1993.

Capitalization

Long Term Debt: $1,184,600,000 (3/95).

Per Share Data ($) (Year Ended Dec. 31)

	1994	1993	1992	1991	1990	1989
Tangible Bk. Val.	48.09	47.84	44.36	39.88	34.26	29.91
Oper. Earnings	5.50	2.24	5.59	5.83	5.72	4.56
Earnings	5.95	3.91	6.96	6.32	6.07	4.91
Dividends	1.84	1.72	1.60	1.48	1.32	1.16
Relative Payout	31%	44%	23%	23%	22%	24%
Prices - High	83⅛	96⅜	91	78	54¾	49¾
- Low	68⅝	76	62⅜	50	34⅝	28⅞
P/E Ratio - High	14	25	13	12	9	10
- Low	12	19	9	8	6	6

Income Statement Analysis (Million $)

	1994	%Chg	1993	%Chg	1992	%Chg	1991
Life Ins. In Force	61,701	14%	54,283	17%	46,455	12%	41,502
Prem.Inc Life A&H	836	4%	801	16%	689	9%	634
Prem.Inc Cas/Prop	3,776	8%	3,505	11%	3,163	4%	3,037
Net Invest. Inc.	829	4%	800	7%	751	7%	701
Oth. Revs.	268	-32%	393	17%	337	139%	141
Total Revs.	5,710	4%	5,500	11%	4,941	9%	4,513
Pretax Inc.	639	86%	344	-54%	748	9%	684
Net Oper. Inc.	487	152%	193	-61%	493	-3%	509
Net Inc.	528	53%	344	-44%	617	12%	552

Balance Sheet & Other Fin. Data (Million $)

	1994	1993	1992	1991	1990	1989
Cash & Equiv.	221	210	207	199	182	174
Premiums Due	787	720	625	632	633	636
Inv. Assets Bonds	10,722	10,718	10,000	8,660	7,887	7,164
Inv. Assets Stock	642	930	738	1,143	858	869
Inv. Assets Loans	203	194	193	187	170	161
Inv. Assets Total	12,378	11,842	10,932	9,990	8,914	8,194
Deferred Policy Cost	1,136	1,012	929	886	831	779
Total Assets	20,723	19,437	15,019	13,775	12,268	11,179
Debt	1,439	1,369	1,361	1,280	1,076	872
Common Eqty.	4,247	4,196	3,954	3,542	2,883	2,604

Ratio Analysis

	1994	1993	1992	1991	1990	1989
Comb. Loss-Exp.Ratio	99.5	114.8	101.1	99.5	99.7	101.9
% Ret. on Revs.	9.3	5.9	12.5	12.2	12.3	10.5
% Ret. on Equity	12.5	8.4	16.5	17.2	19.0	17.3
% Invest. Yield	6.8	7.0	7.1	7.3	7.8	7.9

Dividend Data (Dividends have been paid since 1902. A "poison pill" stock purchase right was adopted in 1989.)

Amt. of Div. $	Date Decl.	Ex-Div. Date	Stock of Record	Payment Date
0.460	Sep. 09	Sep. 19	Sep. 23	Oct. 11 '94
0.460	Dec. 02	Dec. 12	Dec. 16	Jan. 03 '95
0.490	Mar. 03	Mar. 13	Mar. 17	Apr. 04 '95
0.490	Jun. 12	Jun. 21	Jun. 23	Jul. 11 '95

Data as orig. reptd.; bef. results of disc. opers. and/or spec. items. Per share data adj. for stk. divs. as of ex-div. date.
E-Estimate. NA-Not Available. NM-Not Meaningful. NR-Not Ranked.

Office—15 Mountain View Rd., Warren. NJ 07061-1615. **Tel**—(908) 903-2000. **Chrmn & Pres**—D. R. O'Hare. **VP-Secy**—H. G. Gulick.
VP-Treas—P. J. Sempier. **VP-Investor Contact**—Gail E. Devlin (908) 903-3245. **Dirs**—J. C. Beck, P. Chubb III, J. J. Cohen, H. U. Harder, D. H. Hoag, R. V. Lindsay, T. C. MacAvoy, G. G. Michelson, Jr., D. R. O'Hare, E. G. Procope, W. B. Rudman, Sir David Scholey, R. G. H. Seitz, L. M. Small, R. G. Stone Jr., R. D. Wood. **Transfer Agent & Registrar**—First Chicago Trust Co. of New York, NYC. **Incorporated** in New Jersey in 1967. **Empl**- 11,200. **S&P Analyst:** Catherine A. Seifert

CIGNA Corp.

NYSE Symbol **CI**
In S&P 500

11-OCT-95 | Industry: Insurance

Summary: CIGNA is one of the largest insurance-based financial services concerns, and a major force in the property-casualty, group life/health insurance, and annuity fields.

S&P Opinion: Hold (★★★)	Recent Price • 105⅝	Yield • 3.0%
	52 Wk Range • 108-60¼	12-Mo. P/E • 9.6

Earnings vs. Previous Year
▲=Up ▼=Down ▶=No Change

Quantitative Evaluations

Outlook
(1 Lowest—5 Highest)
• **2+**

Fair Value
• **99½**

Risk
• **Low**

Earn./Div. Rank
• **B+**

Technical Eval.
• **Bearish** since 3/95

Rel. Strength Rank
(1 Lowest—99 Highest)
• **88**

Insider Activity
• **NA**

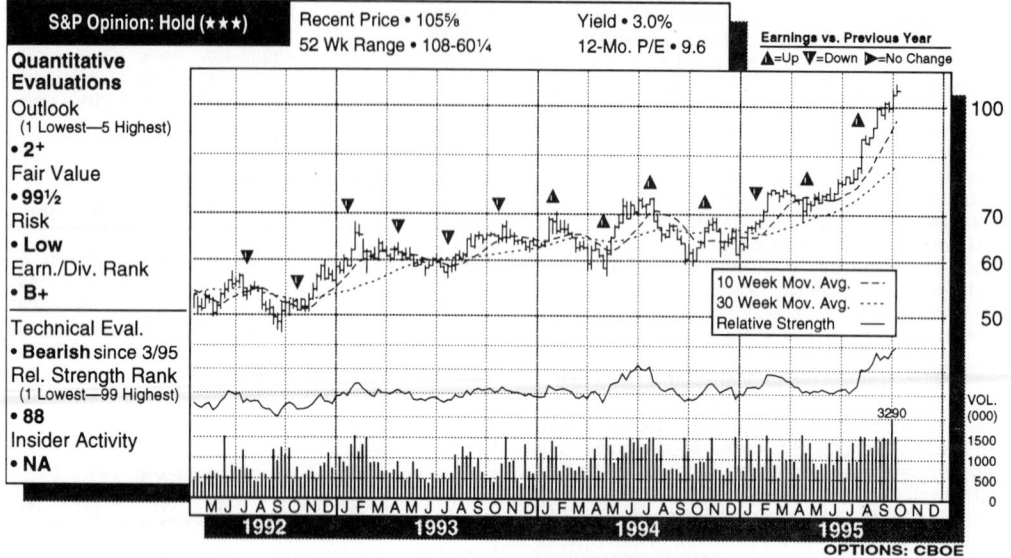

10 Week Mov. Avg. - - -
30 Week Mov. Avg. ·····
Relative Strength —

OPTIONS: CBOE

Overview - 11-OCT-95

The operating loss seen for 1995 reflects a $750 million (about $10.35 a share) net third quarter charge CI is expected to take to cover a $1.2 billion increase to reserves for environmental and asbestos claims. This action, plus the restructuring of the property-casualty division into two units (one focused on ongoing operations and one resposible for "running off" undesirable business), leaves CI better situated long term. However, overall results have been handicapped by the problematic property-casualty unit. The above mentioned actions may set the stage for a sale or spinoff of the property-casualty division. Moreover, further additions to reserves for environmental losses in the "run-off" p-c unit might be necessary in 1996. Employee benefits margins may narrow amid a shift to managed care and higher than expected medical costs, but CI will be a long term player in this arena.

Valuation - 11-OCT-95

After a lackluster preformance during much of 1994 amid the negative effects of higher interest rates and rising catastrophe losses, the shares have rebounded sharply so far in 1995. Increased speculation that CI may restructure some of its operations, particularly its property-casualty division, has fueled some of the stock's recent rise and will likely provide near term support to the share price. However, at almost 11 times our 1996 operating earnings estimate of $10.00 a share (which excludes realized investment gains or losses), the shares are at the upper end of their valuation range and are fairly valued, near term.

Key Stock Statistics

S&P EPS Est. 1995	-2.00	Tang. Bk. Value/Share	78.40
P/E on S&P Est. 1995	NM	Beta	1.36
S&P EPS Est. 1996	10.00	Shareholders	16,400
Dividend Rate/Share	3.04	Market cap. (B)	$ 7.4
Shs. outstg. (M)	72.5	Inst. holdings	86%
Avg. daily vol. (M)	0.479	Insider holdings	NA

Value of $10,000 invested 5 years ago: $ 23,789

Fiscal Year Ending Dec. 31

	1995	% Change	1994	% Change	1993	% Change
Revenues (Million $)						
1Q	4,754	5%	4,531	4%	4,374	-6%
2Q	4,753	5%	4,538	NM	4,563	-2%
3Q	—	—	4,600	2%	4,525	—
4Q	—	—	4,723	-4%	4,940	3%
Yr.	—	—	18,392	NM	18,402	NM
Income (Million $)						
1Q	290.0	154%	114.0	148%	46.00	-57%
2Q	205.0	52%	135.0	53%	88.00	-32%
3Q	—	—	123.0	NM	-94.00	NM
4Q	—	—	182.0	-6%	194.0	NM
Yr.	—	—	554.0	137%	234.0	-31%
Earnings Per Share ($)						
1Q	4.00	153%	1.58	147%	0.64	-57%
2Q	2.82	52%	1.86	52%	1.22	-33%
3Q	—	—	1.70	NM	-1.31	NM
4Q	—	—	2.52	-7%	2.70	NM
Yr.	E-2.00	NM	7.66	136%	3.25	-31%

Next earnings report expected: early November

CIGNA Corp.

11-OCT-95

Business Summary - 06-OCT-95

CIGNA Corp., formed through the 1982 combination of Connecticut General Corp. and INA Corp., is one of the largest investor-owned insurance organizations in the U.S. Contributions (in millions) to operating income in recent years:

	1994	1993
Group life & health	$531	$463
Group retirement & savings	184	182
Indiv. fin'l services	131	123
Property-casualty	-239	-680
Other	-81	-78

The property-casualty group is among the largest in the U.S. Written premiums totaled $4.0 billion in 1994 ($4.2 billion in 1993), of which international lines equaled 38%, workers' compensation 14%, reinsurance (held for sale) 12%, casualty 10%, commercial packages 9%, commercial property 6%, other lines 6%, and personal lines 5%.

The employee life and health benefits segment markets a full line of group life and health insurance products and conducts CI's managed-care operations. Premiums and fees totaled $7.8 billion in 1994 ($7.4 billion in 1993), of which medical indemnity contributed 26%, life indemnity 23%, prepaid medical and dental 36% and other 15%. At year-end 1993 (latest available), CI had 48 HMOs and preferred provider organizations (PPOs) serving 3.6 million members (2.7 million in HMOs and 900,000 in PPOs) in 71 markets. The employee retirement and savings benefits segment provides pension, profit-sharing and retirement savings programs to companies of all sizes. At year end 1994, assets under mamanement here totaled $33.9 billion ($34.5 billion in 1993). Individual financial services businesses market life insurance, disability coverages, investment products and financial planning to small businesses and individuals. CIGNA RE is a life/health reinsurer, part of which was sold in 1994.

Important Developments

Oct. '95—CI announced plans to increase its reserves for environmental and asbestos reserves by $1.2 billion. This action will result in an aftertax third quarter charge of approximately $750 million (or about $10.35 a share). In a related move, CI also plans to restructure its property-casualty insurance unit into two separate operations. One division (which will not have the financial burden associated with environmental or asbestos claims) will manage CI's ongoing p-c operations. The other will be responsible for run-off operations, including those associated with environmental and asbestos claims. The restructuring is set to be completed in the fourth quarter, pending regulatory approval.

Capitalization

Long Term Debt: $1,467,000,000 (6/95).

Per Share Data ($)

(Year Ended Dec. 31)

	1994	1993	1992	1991	1990	1989
Tangible Bk. Val.	64.33	73.78	60.79	61.15	50.43	57.50
Oper. Earnings	7.27	0.14	2.02	5.61	4.40	4.35
Earnings	7.66	3.25	4.70	6.34	4.20	5.68
Dividends	3.04	3.04	3.04	3.04	3.04	2.96
Relative Payout	40%	94%	65%	48%	72%	52%
Prices - High	74	68⅜	60⅞	61¾	60⅝	66¾
- Low	57	56½	47⅛	36	33¼	45⅞
P/E Ratio - High	10	21	13	10	14	12
- Low	7	17	10	6	8	8

Income Statement Analysis (Million $)

	1994	%Chg	1993	%Chg	1992	%Chg	1991
Life Ins. In Force	NA	—	NA	—	574,318	13%	508,756
Prem.Inc Life A&H	8,869	4%	8,516	-7%	9,127	1%	9,019
Prem.Inc Cas/Prop	5,043	-2%	5,136	7%	4,797	-9%	5,276
Net Invest. Inc.	3,946	1%	3,902	NM	3,914	1%	3,860
Oth. Revs.	534	-32%	788	6%	744	25%	595
Total Revs.	18,392	NM	18,402	NM	18,582	NM	18,750
Pretax Inc.	805	NM	165	-8%	179	-69%	584
Net Oper. Inc.	526	NM	NA	—	145	-64%	401
Net Inc.	554	137%	234	-31%	337	-26%	453

Balance Sheet & Other Fin. Data (Million $)

	1994	1993	1992	1991	1990	1989
Cash & Equiv.	2,528	1,975	1,745	2,561	1,877	1,420
Premiums Due	3,986	4,065	3,564	3,931	4,167	3,559
Inv Assets Bonds	31,670	33,112	28,228	26,296	24,918	23,579
Inv. Assets Stock	1,860	1,849	2,321	2,140	1,687	1,316
Inv. Assets Loans	15,325	13,684	12,975	13,024	12,544	11,387
Inv. Assets Total	50,919	50,728	45,082	42,597	40,092	36,967
Deferred Policy Cost	1,128	1,085	1,061	1,056	1,001	961
Total Assets	86,102	84,975	69,827	66,737	63,691	57,779
Debt	1,389	1,235	929	848	832	640
Common Eqty.	5,811	6,575	5,744	5,863	5,242	5,520

Ratio Analysis

	1994	1993	1992	1991	1990	1989
Comb. Loss-Exp.Ratio	123.9	137.4	131.3	117.3	115.9	115.8
% Ret. on Revs.	3.0	1.3	1.8	2.4	1.8	2.9
% Ret. on Equity	8.9	3.8	5.8	8.2	5.9	8.4
% Invest. Yield	7.8	8.1	8.9	9.4	9.7	9.8

Dividend Data

Dividends were paid by Connecticut General since 1867 and by INA since 1874. A dividend reinvestment plan is available.

Amt. of Div. $	Date Decl.	Ex-Div. Date	Stock of Record	Payment Date
0.760	Jul. 27	Sep. 06	Sep. 12	Oct. 10 '94
0.760	Oct. 26	Dec. 07	Dec. 13	Jan. 10 '95
0.760	Feb. 22	Mar. 07	Mar. 13	Apr. 10 '95
0.760	May. 24	Jun. 08	Jun. 12	Jul. 10 '95
0.760	Jul. 26	Sep. 08	Sep. 12	Oct. 10 '95

Data as orig. reptd.; bef. results of disc. opers. and/or spec. items. Per share data adj. for stk. divs. as of ex-div. date. E-Estimate. NA-Not Available. NM-Not Meaningful. NR-Not Ranked.

Office—One Liberty Place, Philadelphia, PA 19192. **Inc.**—in Delaware in 1981. **Tel**—(215) 761-1000. **Chrmn & CEO**—W. H. Taylor. **VP-CFO**—J. G. Stewart. **VP-Treas**—P. H. Rohrkemper. **Secy**—C. J. Ward. **Investor Contact**—R. W. Sullivan. **Dirs**—R. P. Bauman, E. Berezin, R. H. Campbell, A. C. DeCrane Jr., J. F. English Jr., B. M. Fox, F. S. Jones, G. D. Laubach, M. W. Lewis, P. F. Oreffice, C. R. Shoemate, L. W. Sullivan, W. H. Taylor, E. K. Zilkha. **Transfer Agent & Registrar**—First Chicago Trust Co. of New York, NYC. **Empl**-48,341. **S&P Analyst:** Catherine A. Seifert

Cincinnati Milacron

NYSE Symbol **CMZ**

In S&P 500

13-OCT-95

Industry:
Machinery

Summary: This company is a leading manufacturer of machine tools, plastics machinery, computer controls and software for factory automation.

S&P Opinion: Hold (★★★)	Recent Price • 28⅝
	52 Wk Range • 33⅝-19⅞

Yield • 1.3%

12-Mo. P/E • 21.0

Earnings vs. Previous Year
▲=Up ▼=Down ▶=No Change

Quantitative Evaluations

Outlook
(1 Lowest—5 Highest)
• **2+**

Fair Value
• **25¾**

Risk
• **Average**

Earn./Div. Rank
• **B-**

Technical Eval.
• **Bullish** since 7/95

Rel. Strength Rank
(1 Lowest—99 Highest)
• **11**

Insider Activity
• **Neutral**

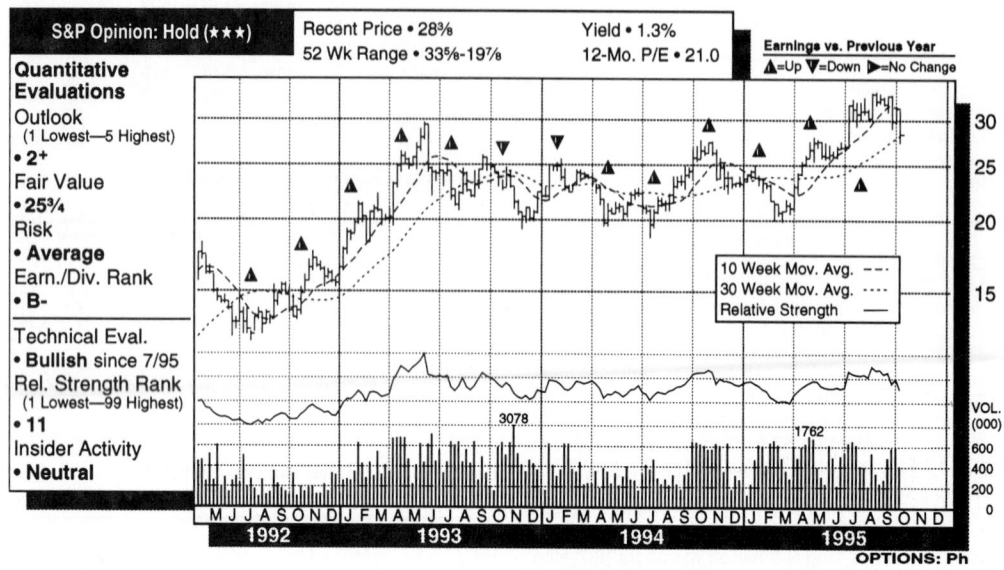

10 Week Mov. Avg. - - -
30 Week Mov. Avg. .....
Relative Strength ——

3078

1762

VOL.
(000)

OPTIONS: Ph

Overview - 13-OCT-95

Based on our forecast of 2.6% GDP growth in 1996 and the impact of acquisitions, we project a 20% sales gain in 1996. The sales increase should occur in plastics machinery and industrial products; the absence of the electronic division may lead to a small decline in machine tools. Gross margins will probably remain unchanged, as the absence of the electronic division offsets improvement in the plastics and industrial products business. Benefiting from well controlled SG&A and lower interest expense, earnings, excluding gains on asset sales, should rise in 1996. Long-term sales and earnings will benefit from a recovery in aerospace, improvement in secular demand for plastics machinery, expansion into the market for metalcutting tools, debt reduction and acquisitions.

Valuation - 13-OCT-95

While we believe CMZ has appeal as an earnings turnaround/restructuring play, we are maintaining our hold rating on the shares near term. The stock price appears to have discounted most of the good news. At current levels, the shares do not warrant an accumulate or buy rating. Through early October, CMZ had risen 24%, versus a 27% increase in the S&P 500. Although CMZ's sales and profits may be more resilent than some other cyclical issues, recent company announcement of disappointing third quarter earnings may put pressure on the stock price. Accordingly, we think there may be a more opportune time to accumulate the shares.

Key Stock Statistics

S&P EPS Est. 1995	3.30	Tang. Bk. Value/Share	5.49
P/E on S&P Est. 1995	8.6	Beta	1.80
S&P EPS Est. 1996	2.15	Shareholders	6,500
Dividend Rate/Share	0.36	Market cap. (B)	$0.916
Shs. outstg. (M)	34.2	Inst. holdings	65%
Avg. daily vol. (M)	0.107	Insider holdings	NA

Value of $10,000 invested 5 years ago: $ 19,373

Fiscal Year Ending Dec. 31

	1995	% Change	1994	% Change	1993	% Change
Revenues (Million $)						
1Q	331.4	35%	245.5	12%	219.0	37%
2Q	413.6	54%	269.3	14%	236.6	27%
3Q	—	—	361.2	20%	300.7	33%
4Q	—	—	321.2	18%	272.7	25%
Yr.	—	—	1,197	16%	1,029	30%
Income (Million $)						
1Q	13.05	162%	4.98	17%	4.27	NM
2Q	8.36	6%	7.88	27%	6.20	124%
3Q	—	—	11.89	NM	-7.81	NM
4Q	—	—	12.96	NM	-47.35	NM
Yr.	—	—	37.71	NM	-45.40	NM
Earnings Per Share ($)						
1Q	0.38	171%	0.14	8%	0.13	NM
2Q	0.24	4%	0.23	21%	0.19	90%
3Q	E0.43	23%	0.35	NM	-0.23	NM
4Q	E2.25	NM	0.38	NM	-1.40	NM
Yr.	E3.30	NM	1.10	NM	-1.41	NM

Next earnings report expected: early November

Cincinnati Milacron

Business Summary - 13-OCT-95

Cincinnati Milacron is a leading producer of machine tools, plastics machinery, computer controls and software for factory automation. Contributions in 1994 were:

	Sales	Profits
Machine tools	28%	1%
Plastics machinery	42%	55%
Industrial products	30%	44%

Sales by industry in 1994 were: automotive/truck (24%), job shops/custom molders (19%), industrial products (16%), construction (10%), electrical (6%), aerospace (5%), packaging (3%) and other (17%).

Foreign operations accounted for 27% of 1994 sales and 35% of operating profit.

The Machine Tools Group includes Advanced Machine Tool Systems, Standard Machine Tool Products and Electronic Systems. Advanced Machine Tool consists of aerospace and special machines, including composites processing equipment; applied production turning centers and centerless grinding machines; and flexible manufacturing cells. Standard machine tools include turning centers, horizontal machining centers and vertical machining centers. The electronic systems division designs and produces computer controls for machine tools and plastics machinery. CMZ intends to sell the electronic systems division by 1995's year end.

Plastics processing machinery includes injection molding machines and extrusion systems. Injection molding includes electric and hydraulic models and reaction injection molding machines. Extrusion systems include twin-screw and single-screw extruders, Sano blown-film and cast-film systems and a variety of blow molding machines.

The Industrial Products Group consists of Cimcool metalworking fluids, precision grinding wheels and Valenite's metalcutting tools.

Important Developments

Sep. '95—CMZ and Trinova Corp. (NYSE, TNV) jointly announced a letter of intent for the sale of CMZ's Electronic Systems Division (ESD) for $105 million in cash subject to post closing adjustments. The unit's sales in 1995 were about $90 million. The transaction was expected to occur before 1995 year-end and include long-term supplier contracts. The company said that the sale would result in a gain of about $1.75 a share.

Jun. '95—The company agreed to acquire Talbot Holdings Ltd., a U.S. supplier of round high-speed metalcutting tools (annual sales of $40 million) for a total of $38 million.

Capitalization

Long Term Debt: $307,800,000.(6/95).
$4 Cum. Pfd. Stk.: 60,000 shs. ($1 par).

Per Share Data ($)

(Year Ended Dec. 31)

	1994	1993	1992	1991	1990	1989
Tangible Bk. Val.	4.04	3.52	4.67	4.49	8.85	9.07
Cash Flow	1.93	-0.60	1.33	-2.17	0.05	1.69
Earnings	1.10	-1.41	0.58	-3.04	-0.87	0.75
Dividends	0.36	0.36	0.36	0.63	0.72	0.72
Payout Ratio	33%	NM	62%	NM	NM	96%
Prices - High	27⅝	29⅝	18¼	15¼	21¼	25⅛
- Low	18⅝	16¼	10⅞	6⅝	8¾	15
P/E Ratio - High	25	NM	31	NM	NM	34
- Low	17	NM	19	NM	NM	20

Income Statement Analysis (Million $)

	1994	%Chg	1993	%Chg	1992	%Chg	1991
Revs.	1,197	16%	1,029	30%	789	5%	754
Oper. Inc.	98.3	35%	72.9	14%	63.9	50%	42.6
Depr.	28.2	8%	26.1	25%	20.9	-13%	24.0
Int. Exp.	17.9	14%	15.7	-18%	19.1	NM	19.1
Pretax Inc.	48.9	NM	-37.2	NM	27.0	NM	-73.4
Eff. Tax Rate	23%	—	NM	—	40%	—	NM
Net Inc.	37.7	NM	-45.4	NM	16.1	NM	-83.1

Balance Sheet & Other Fin. Data (Million $)

	1994	1993	1992	1991	1990	1989
Cash	21.5	18.8	14.9	16.2	45.2	32.9
Curr. Assets	515	484	429	443	490	499
Total Assets	788	730	579	598	693	686
Curr. Liab.	363	369	237	255	236	240
LT Debt	143	108	154	156	157	166
Common Eqty.	152	118	128	123	242	221
Total Cap.	301	232	289	285	414	404
Cap. Exp.	43.0	23.4	17.6	15.5	34.1	33.6
Cash Flow	65.7	-19.5	36.8	-59.3	1.3	41.1

Ratio Analysis

	1994	1993	1992	1991	1990	1989
Curr. Ratio	1.4	1.3	1.8	1.7	2.1	2.1
% LT Debt of Cap.	47.5	46.4	53.5	54.7	38.0	41.1
% Net Inc.of Revs.	3.1	NM	2.0	NM	NM	2.2
% Ret. on Assets	5.0	NM	2.7	NM	NM	2.6
% Ret. on Equity	27.7	NM	12.6	NM	NM	8.2

Dividend Data —Dividends have been paid since 1923. A dividend reinvestment plan is available.

Amt. of Div. $	Date Decl.	Ex-Div. Date	Stock of Record	Payment Date
0.090	Nov. 08	Nov. 18	Nov. 25	Dec. 12 '94
0.090	Feb. 17	Feb. 22	Feb. 28	Mar. 12 '95
0.090	Apr. 25	May. 15	May. 19	Jun. 12 '95
0.090	Jul. 18	Aug. 23	Aug. 25	Sep. 12 '95

Data as orig. reptd.; bef. results of disc. opers. and/or spec. items. Per share data adj. for stk. divs. as of ex-div. date. E-Estimated. NA-Not Available. NM-Not Meaningful. NR-Not Ranked.

Office—4701 Marburg Ave., Cincinnati, OH 45209. **Tel**—(513) 841-8100. **Chrmn & CEO**—D. J. Meyer. **Pres & COO**—R. E. Ross. **VP & CFO**—R. D. Brown. **VP & Secy**—W. F. Taylor. **Investor Contact**—Al Beaupre. **Dirs**—D. F. Allen, N. A. Armstrong, L. J. Everingham, J. A. D. Geier, H. A. Hammerly, D. J. Meyer, J. E. Perrella, R. E. Ross, J. A. Steger, H. C. Stonecipher. **Transfer Agent & Registrar**—Mellon Bank, Pittsburgh. **Incorporated** in Ohio in 1922; reincorporated in Delaware in 1983. **Empl**-8,395. **S&P Analyst:** Leo Larkin

CINergy Corp.

NYSE Symbol **CIN**
In S&P 500

24-AUG-95

Industry:
Utilities-Electric

Summary: This holding company was formed in October 1994 via Cincinnati Gas & Electric Co.'s acquisition of PSI Resources, Inc. (the holding company for Indiana's largest electric utility).

S&P Opinion: Hold (★★★)	Recent Price • 25¾	Yield • 6.7%
	52 Wk Range • 27-20¾	12-Mo. P/E • 19.4

Quantitative Evaluations

Outlook
(1 Lowest—5 Highest)
• **2⁻**

Fair Value
• **23%**

Risk
• **Low**

Earn./Div. Rank
• **B**

Technical Eval.
• **Bearish** since 8/95

Rel. Strength Rank
(1 Lowest—99 Highest)
• **32**

Insider Activity
• **Neutral**

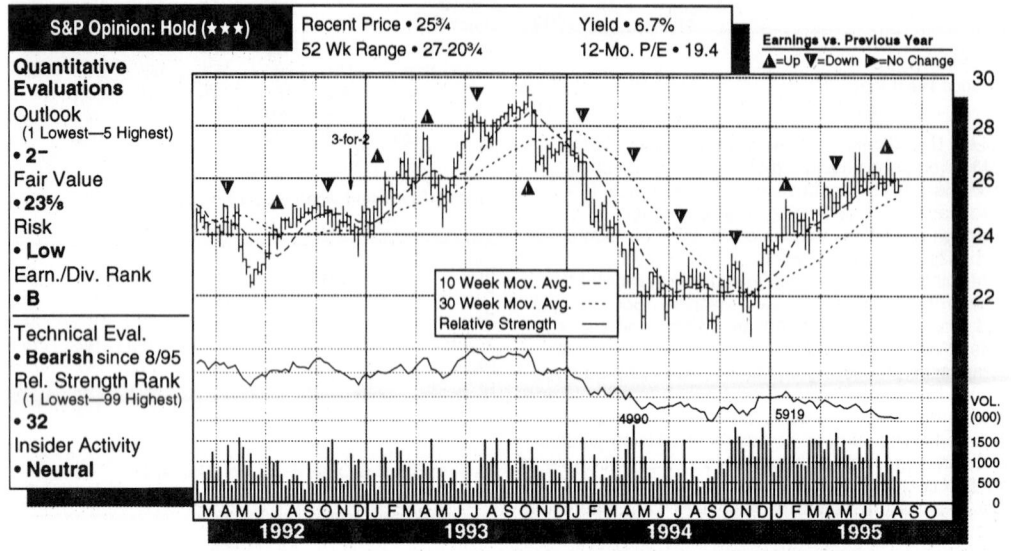

Earnings vs. Previous Year
▲=Up ▼=Down ▶=No Change

10 Week Mov. Avg. — — —
30 Week Mov. Avg. · · · · ·
Relative Strength ——

Overview - 24-AUG-95

Share earnings comparisons for 1995 should reflect higher electricity sales, aided by potentially greater off-system sales, a rate increase at the PSI Resources subsidiary, rate relief for merger costs as well as cost savings from combination of the two utilities. Comparisons will also benefit from the absence of one-time write-offs totaling $0.41, which largely represent merger-related costs. We do not expect that a possible common stock offering will be dilutive, since Indiana regulators have agreed to allow the company to earn a return on a capital structure that included those shares.

Valuation - 24-AUG-95

Shares declined sharply in late 1993 and early 1994 (prior to the acquisition), primarily due to the effect of rising interest rates on dividend yielding issues such as CIN. The stock has rebounded significantly since, largely on investor perceptions that the combination of these two low-cost companies provides a competitive advantage. The merger is expected to result in cost savings for CINergy of $1.5 billion over 10 years, which are to be apportioned via the regulatory process between ratepayers and CIN's shareholders. We believe CIN is well positioned for a period of rising competition within the electric utility industry. While its P/E of 19 is high for the industry, the dividend yield is about average. We do not expect a dividend hike until the company has more fully absorbed the PSI Energy merger.

Key Stock Statistics

S&P EPS Est. 1995	2.10	Tang. Bk. Value/Share	15.40
P/E on S&P Est. 1995	12.3	Beta	0.49
S&P EPS Est. 1996	2.16	Shareholders	85,600
Dividend Rate/Share	1.72	Market cap. (B)	$ 4.0
Shs. outstg. (M)	156.0	Inst. holdings	57%
Avg. daily vol. (M)	0.271	Insider holdings	NA

Value of $10,000 invested 5 years ago: $ 17,934

Fiscal Year Ending Dec. 31

	1995	% Change	1994	% Change	1993	% Change
Revenues (Million $)						
1Q	804.5	-7%	866.0	75%	493.5	10%
2Q	668.4	NM	673.0	83%	367.5	10%
3Q	—	—	692.0	69%	408.6	16%
4Q	—	—	693.4	44%	482.2	15%
Yr.	—	—	2,924	67%	1,752	13%
Income (Million $)						
1Q	101.6	3%	99.0	45%	68.40	2%
2Q	60.03	23%	49.00	23%	39.93	-9%
3Q	—	—	58.00	-3%	59.50	29%
4Q	—	—	-14.66	NM	-176.6	NM
Yr.	—	—	191.1	NM	-8.72	NM
Earnings Per Share ($)						
1Q	0.65	-4%	0.68	-4%	0.71	1%
2Q	0.39	18%	0.33	-13%	0.38	-12%
3Q	E0.60	54%	0.39	-36%	0.61	36%
4Q	E0.46	NM	-0.10	NM	-2.08	NM
Yr.	E2.10	62%	1.30	NM	-0.39	NM

Next earnings report expected: late October

CINergy Corp.

Business Summary - 24-AUG-95

CINergy Corp. is the holding company formed in October 1994 through the merger of Cincinnati Gas & Electric Co. and PSI Resources, Inc. It is the 13th largest investor-owned electric utility in the U.S. in terms of generating capability, serving 1.3 million electric customers and 429,000 gas customers in a 25,000 sq. mile area of Ohio, Indiana and Kentucky. In its order approving the merger, the SEC reserved jurisdiction over the company's ownership of Cincinnati Gas & Electric's gas operations for a period of three years. At the end of the three year period, divestiture of the gas business may be required under the Public Utility Holding Company Act of 1935.

Cincinnati Gas & Electric and its subsidiaries supply electricity and natural gas in the southwestern portion of Ohio and adjacent areas in Kentucky and Indiana. Of 1994 revenues, electricity accounted for some 83% and gas 15%. Cincinnati Gas & Electric's electric revenues by customer in 1994 were: residential 27%, commercial 22%, industrial 31%, and other 20%.

The primary subsidiary of PSI Resources (formerly PSI Holdings) is PSI Energy (formerly Public Service Co. of Indiana), the state's largest electric utility, serving a population of approximately 1.9 million. In February 1995, regulators approved a settlement that permits CIN a 4.3% rate increase for PSI Energy that also apportions savings from the merger between customers and shareholders. Regulators also approved an additional 1.9% rate increase for CIN in March 1995.

Under the Public Utility Holding Company Act, CIN may be required to divest its gas operations, but the company is continuing to pursue SEC approval to retain the business.

Important Developments

Aug. '95—CINergy reported that electric operating revenues in the 1995 first half rose 1.9%, year to year, largely reflecting a May 1994 rate increase and, to a lesser extent, rate increases in the first quarter. The gains were partly offset by lower sales to other utilities and residential customers due to comparatively mild weather this year. Industrial sales grew, however, on firm growth in the primary metals and chemical sectors of its service area. Profitability benefited from sharply lower year-to-year price comparisons for gas and purchased power. Net income advanced 9% but, with 6.9% more shares outstanding, earnings per share were up only 3%, to $1.04 from $1.01.

Capitalization

Long Term Debt: $2,652,382,000 (6/95).
Red. Cum. Preferred Stock: $160,000,000.
Cum. Preferred Stock: $227,915,000.

Per Share Data ($) (Year Ended Dec. 31)

	1994	1993	1992	1991	1990	1989
Tangible Bk. Val.	15.40	17.10	19.01	18.55	17.75	16.59
Earnings	1.30	-0.39	2.04	2.21	2.75	2.89
Dividends	1.39	1.67	1.65	1.65	1.60	1.53
Payout Ratio	107%	NM	81%	75%	58%	53%
Prices - High	27¾	29⅝	26⅝	26¾	21⅛	21⅝
- Low	20¾	23⅞	22¼	18⅝	18⅝	16¼
P/E Ratio - High	21	NM	13	12	8	7
- Low	16	NM	11	8	7	6

Income Statement Analysis (Million $)

	1994	%Chg	1993	%Chg	1992	%Chg	1991
Revs.	2,924	67%	1,752	13%	1,553	2%	1,518
Depr.	294	93%	152	8%	141	8%	131
Maint.	201	84%	109	4%	105	-13%	121
Fxd. Chgs. Cov.	2.3	78%	1.3	-44%	2.3	-21%	2.9
Constr. Credits	18.5	164%	7.0	-61%	18.0	-74%	68.0
Eff. Tax Rate	44%	—	NM	—	25%	—	19%
Net Inc.	191	NM	-8.7	NM	202	-2%	207

Balance Sheet & Other Fin. Data (Million $)

	1994	1993	1992	1991	1990	1989
Gross Prop.	9,363	5,258	5,308	5,110	4,729	4,286
Cap. Exp.	480	199	230	410	467	441
Net Prop.	6,199	3,786	3,945	3,861	3,579	3,203
Capitalization:						
LT Debt	2,715	1,829	1,810	1,734	1,651	1,348
% LT Debt	48	50	48	48	49	47
Pfd.	478	330	330	330	290	241
% Pfd.	8.50	9.00	8.70	9.10	8.70	8.40
Common	2,414	1,519	1,655	1,584	1,399	1,279
% Common	43	41	44	43	42	45
Total Cap.	6,874	4,553	4,250	4,047	3,717	3,236

Ratio Analysis

	1994	1993	1992	1991	1990	1989
Oper. Ratio	84.9	81.8	83.3	86.0	84.2	83.3
% Earn. on Net Prop.	7.2	8.3	6.7	5.7	6.7	7.9
% Ret. on Revs.	6.5	NM	13.0	13.6	16.3	16.7
% Ret. On Invest.Cap	6.7	3.3	8.7	7.8	9.8	10.9
% Return On Com.Eqty	8.2	NM	10.8	12.2	15.9	18.1

Dividend Data —Dividends have been paid since 1853. A dividend reinvestment plan is available.

Amt. of Div. $	Date Decl.	Ex-Div. Date	Stock of Record	Payment Date
0.103	Oct. 25	Oct. 28	Nov. 03	Nov. 15 '94
0.430	Jan. 25	Jan. 31	Feb. 06	Feb. 15 '95
0.430	Apr. 20	Apr. 25	May. 01	May. 15 '95
0.430	Jul. 20	Jul. 27	Jul. 31	Aug. 15 '95

Data as orig. reptd.; bef. results of disc opers. and/or spec. items. Per share data adj. for stk. divs. as of ex-div. date. E-Estimated. NA-Not Available. NM-Not Meaningful. NR-Not Ranked.

Office—139 East Fourth St., Cincinnati, OH 45202. **Tel**—(513) 381-2000. **Chairman & CEO**—J. H. Randolph. **Vice-Chairman, Pres & COO**—J. E. Rogers. **VP-CFO**—J. W. Leonard. **VP-Secy**—C. M. Foley. **Investor Contact**—Julie Janson (513-287-3025). **Dirs**—N. A. Armstrong, J. K. Baker, H. A. Barker, M. G. Browning, C. L. Buenger, P. R. Cox, K. M. Duberstein, J. A. Hillenbrand II, G. C. Juilfs, M. Perelman, T. E. Petry, J. H. Randolph, J. E. Rogers, J. J. Schiff Jr., P. R. Sharp, V. P. Smith, D. S. Taft, O. W. Waddell. **Transfer Agent**—Company's office. **Registrar**—Fifth Third Bank, Cincinnati. **Incorporated** in Ohio in 1837; reincorporated in Delaware in 1994. **Empl**-8,868. **S&P Analyst:** Jane Collin

Circuit City Stores

NYSE Symbol **CC**
In S&P 500

19-OCT-95

Industry:
Retail Stores

Summary: The largest U.S. retailer of brand-name consumer electronics and major appliances, Circuit City has more than 380 stores throughout the U.S.

S&P Opinion: Accumulate (★★★★)		
Recent Price • 36½	Yield • 0.3%	
52 Wk Range • 38-21	12-Mo. P/E • 20.1	

Quantitative Evaluations

Outlook
(1 Lowest—5 Highest)
• **2+**

Fair Value
• **33%**

Risk
• **Average**

Earn./Div. Rank
• **A**

Technical Eval.
• **Bullish** since 7/95

Rel. Strength Rank
(1 Lowest—99 Highest)
• **83**

Insider Activity
• **Neutral**

Earnings vs. Previous Year
▲=Up ▼=Down ▶=No Change

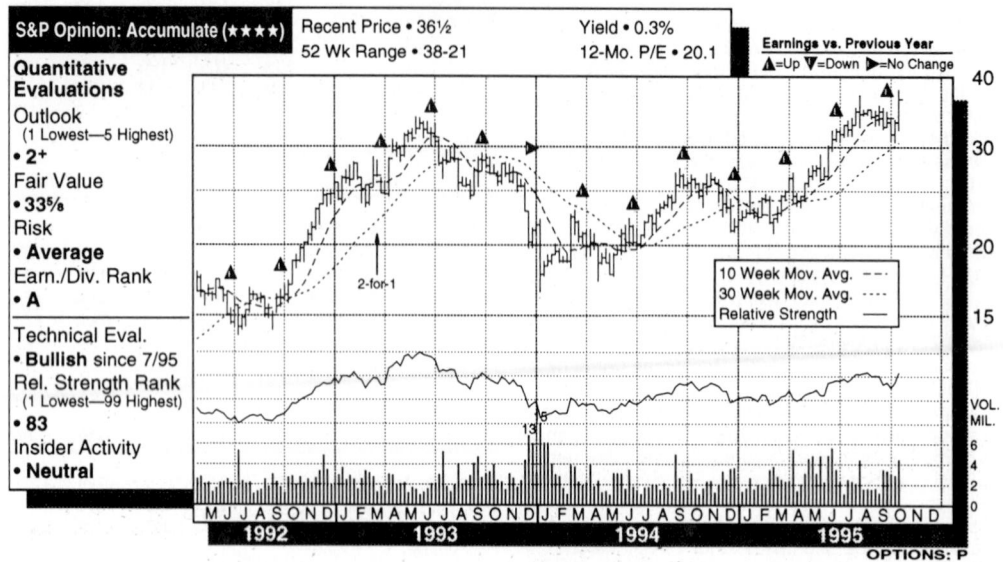

- 10 Week Mov. Avg. ---
- 30 Week Mov. Avg. ····
- Relative Strength —

2-for-1

VOL. MIL.

OPTIONS: P

Overview - 19-OCT-95

We expect revenues of this leading consumer electronics retailer to post healthy double-digit increases for the remainder of 1995-6, fueled by new store openings and growth at existing stores. The pace of same-store sales growth will be somewhat slower than in 1994-5, but should still be in upper-single to low-double digits. Gross margins will continue to narrow, restricted by competitive pricing in key markets and an increased proportion of sales of less profitable computers and music software. Operating expenses should decrease as a percentage of sales, as benefits from economies of scale and cost controls outweigh higher pre-opening and advertising spending.

Valuation - 19-OCT-95

The shares, spurred by positive sales and earnings reports, are up over 75% in 1995, and were recently near their record high. Sales growth should continue to be fueled by the addition of new stores (60 in 1995-6), with an added boost from the August 1995 launch of Windows 95. We remain somewhat cautious about the highly competitive retail environment, which will continue to result in price cutting and narrower margins. Nevertheless, since CC holds the leading position in a potentially explosive consumer electronics market, we advise accumulation for long-term gains on any near-term weakness.

Key Stock Statistics

S&P EPS Est. 1996	1.98	Tang. Bk. Value/Share	9.72
P/E on S&P Est. 1996	18.4	Beta	0.62
S&P EPS Est. 1997	2.40	Shareholders	7,800
Dividend Rate/Share	0.12	Market cap. (B)	$ 3.5
Shs. outstg. (M)	97.2	Inst. holdings	76%
Avg. daily vol. (M)	0.636	Insider holdings	NA

Value of $10,000 invested 5 years ago: $ 34,377

Fiscal Year Ending Feb. 28

	1996	% Change	1995	% Change	1994	% Change
Revenues (Million $)						
1Q	1,392	33%	1,049	31%	799.0	24%
2Q	1,601	31%	1,219	34%	906.7	26%
3Q	—	—	1,405	38%	1,018	26%
4Q	—	—	1,910	36%	1,407	28%
Yr.	—	—	5,583	35%	4,130	26%
Income (Million $)						
1Q	24.62	25%	19.69	14%	17.23	51%
2Q	41.25	14%	36.06	29%	27.97	30%
3Q	—	—	28.44	46%	19.46	17%
4Q	—	—	83.69	24%	67.74	11%
Yr.	—	—	167.9	27%	132.4	20%
Earnings Per Share ($)						
1Q	0.25	25%	0.20	11%	0.18	50%
2Q	0.42	14%	0.37	28%	0.29	26%
3Q	E0.35	21%	0.29	45%	0.20	NM
4Q	E0.98	14%	0.86	23%	0.70	11%
Yr.	E1.98	15%	1.72	26%	1.36	18%

Next earnings report expected: mid December

Circuit City Stores

Business Summary - 19-OCT-95

Circuit City Stores, Inc. is the largest U.S. retailer of brandname consumer electronics and major appliances and a leading retailer of personal computers and music software. At October 5 1995, it operated 381 stores throughout the U.S., with 344 superstores, five consumer electronics stores, and 32 mall units. Revenue sources in recent fiscal years were:

	1994-95	1993-94	1992-93
Television	19%	20%	23%
VCR/Camcorders	14%	17%	19%
Audio	20%	21%	20%
Home office	20%	12%	7%
Other electronics	12%	12%	12%
Appliances	15%	18%	19%

The company operates four superstore formats with square footage and merchandise assortments tailored to population size and volume expectations. The "D" stores, introduced in 1994-5, average 42,000 sq. ft., and offer the largest merchandise assortment serving the most populous trade areas. The "C" format (34,000 sq. ft.) is designed to serve moderately smaller trade areas and provides a highly competitive merchandise assortment. "B" format stores (24,000 sq. ft.) are located in smaller markets that are on the fringes of larger metropolitan markets; and "A" format stores (16,000 sq. ft.) are designed to serve the least populated trade areas.

Five electronics-only stores (4,000 sq. ft.) offer a full line of consumer electronics and a limited selection of major appliances, while 32 Circuit City Express units, which average 3,000 sq. ft., are in shopping malls and carry smaller electronic products.

In late 1993, CC began testing CarMax, a retail superstore format selling late-model used cars. At August 31, 1995, four CarMax stores were in operation.

The company also operates eight mechanized full-line electronics distribution centers designed to serve stores in a 500-mile range.

Important Developments

Oct. '95—Total sales in September climbed 33%, year to year; same-store sales were up 8%. During September, CC opened nine new superstores, including its first in Colorado Springs, Colo., and Salisbury, Md., and one each in Fresno, Santa Barbara and San Diego, Calif., Minneapolis, Minn., Waco, Tex., and Nashville, Tenn.

Sep. '95—In the 1995-6 second quarter, the company opened 15 new superstores, including its first in Denver, Colo., Bloomington and Springfield, Ill.; Midland, College Station and Waco, Tex.;, Winchester, Va.; and Jacksonville, N.C.

Capitalization

Long Term Debt: $299,652,000 (8/95).

Per Share Data ($)

(Year Ended Feb. 28)

	1995	1994	1993	1992	1991	1990
Tangible Bk. Val.	9.10	7.39	6.02	4.78	3.96	3.92
Cash Flow	2.41	1.92	1.58	1.21	0.92	1.09
Earnings	1.72	1.36	1.15	0.82	0.61	0.85
Dividends	0.09	0.08	0.06	0.05	0.05	0.04
Payout Ratio	6%	6%	5%	6%	8%	4%
Cal. Yrs.	1994	1993	1992	1991	1990	1989
Prices - High	27	33⁷/₈	26¹/₈	13	14¹/₂	13¹/₂
- Low	16¹/₂	19³/₄	11¹/₈	5⁵/₈	4¹/₂	8⁷/₈
P/E Ratio - High	16	25	23	16	24	16
- Low	10	15	10	7	7	10

Income Statement Analysis (Million $)

	1995	%Chg	1994	%Chg	1993	%Chg	1992
Revs.	5,583	35%	4,130	26%	3,270	17%	2,790
Oper. Inc.	345	28%	269	22%	221	31%	169
Depr.	66.9	22%	55.0	32%	41.7	17%	35.7
Int. Exp.	13.9	88%	7.4	9%	6.8	-36%	10.7
Pretax Inc.	269	29%	209	19%	175	41%	124
Eff. Tax Rate	38%	—	37%	—	37%	—	37%
Net Inc.	168	27%	132	20%	110	41%	78.2

Balance Sheet & Other Fin. Data (Million $)

	1995	1994	1993	1992	1991	1990
Cash	47.0	75.2	141	71.5	25.2	91.7
Curr. Assets	1,387	997	791	597	450	442
Total Assets	2,004	1,555	1,263	1,000	874	714
Curr. Liab.	706	546	373	279	261	222
LT Debt	179	30.0	82.0	85.0	94.0	94.0
Common Eqty.	877	710	576	448	367	359
Total Cap.	1,056	740	658	533	461	453
Cap. Exp.	375	252	190	110	160	69.0
Cash Flow	235	187	152	114	86.0	100

Ratio Analysis

	1995	1994	1993	1992	1991	1990
Curr. Ratio	2.0	1.8	2.1	2.1	1.7	2.0
% LT Debt of Cap.	16.9	4.0	12.5	16.0	20.5	20.7
% Net Inc.of Revs.	3.0	3.2	3.4	2.8	2.4	3.7
% Ret. on Assets	9.4	9.4	9.7	8.3	7.1	11.9
% Ret. on Equity	21.1	20.6	21.4	19.1	15.5	24.5

Dividend Data —Dividends were initiated in 1979. A poison pill stock purchase rights plan was adopted in 1988.

Amt. of Div. $	Date Decl.	Ex-Div. Date	Stock of Record	Payment Date
0.025	Dec. 15	Dec. 23	Dec. 30	Jan. 16 '95
0.025	Mar. 15	Mar. 24	Mar. 30	Apr. 14 '95
0.030	Jun. 13	Jun. 27	Jun. 29	Jul. 14 '95
0.030	Sep. 15	Sep. 27	Sep. 29	Oct. 16 '95

Data as orig. reptd.; bef. results of disc. opers. and/or spec. items. Per share data adj. for stk. divs. as of ex-div. date. E-Estimated. NA-Not Available. NM-Not Meaningful. NR-Not Ranked.

Office—9950 Mayland Dr., Richmond, VA 23233-1464. **Tel**—(804) 527-4000. **Chrmn, Pres & CEO**—R. L. Sharp. **Vice Chrmn**—A. L. Wurtzel. **SVP, CFO & Secy**—M. T. Chalifoux. **Investor Contact**—Ann M. Collier (804-527-4058). **Dirs**—M. T. Chalifoux, R. N. Cooper, D. D. Drysdale, B. S. Feigin, T. D. Nierenberg, H. G. Robinson, W. J. Salmon, M. Salovaara, R. L. Sharp, E. Villanueva, A. L. Wurtzel. **Transfer Agent & Registrar**—Mellon Securities Trust Co., Pittsburgh. **Incorporated** in Virginia in 1949. **Empl**-30,998. **S&P Analyst:** Maureen C. Carini

Cisco Systems

NASDAQ Symbol **CSCO**
In S&P 500

02-OCT-95 **Industry:** Data Processing

Summary: Cisco offers a complete line of routers and switching products that connect and manage communications among local and wide area computer networks employing a variety of protocols.

S&P Opinion: Accumulate (★★★★)	Recent Price • 69	Yield • Nil
	52 Wk Range • 73⅞-25½	12-Mo. P/E • 45.4

Quantitative Evaluations

Outlook
(1 Lowest—5 Highest)
• **5+**

Fair Value
• **92⅛**

Risk
• **Average**

Earn./Div. Rank
• **B**

Technical Eval.
• **Bullish** since 9/94

Rel. Strength Rank
(1 Lowest—99 Highest)
• **84**

Insider Activity
• **Unfavorable**

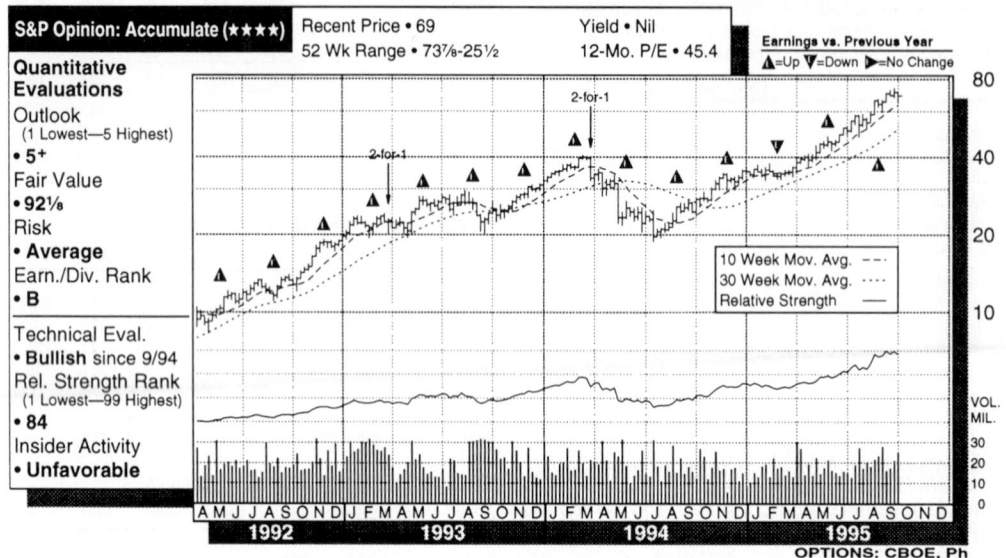

Earnings vs. Previous Year
▲=Up ▼=Down ▶=No Change

10 Week Mov. Avg. – – –
30 Week Mov. Avg. · · · ·
Relative Strength —

OPTIONS: CBOE, Ph

Overview - 02-OCT-95

Sales for fiscal 1996 are expected to grow 50%, which is at the high end of of projected industry growth rates. CSCO continues to be a primary beneficiary of companies' connecting their disparate computer networks through router and switching technology. Recent acquisitions that target emerging markets like ATM and ISDN, are also boosting top line growth. CSCO may experience some gross margin pressures, as its product mix shifts to less profitable low-end routers and switching products. In addition, lower-margin third-party vendor sales are expected to account for a greater portion of the product mix. Operating expenses will continue to increase sharply, as CSCO builds its sales and marketing infrastructure and invests heavily in R&D. Earnings of $2.50 per share are projected for fiscal 1996, versus fiscal 1995's $1.52, which includes a $0.21 second quarter charge.

Valuation - 02-OCT-95

Despite the strong share price performance since mid-1994, we believe CSCO will continue to produce above-average investment returns, as it remains the dominant vendor in the fast growing networking industry. Furthermore, CSCO's strong balance sheet will allow it to make additional acquisitions in emerging technologies and markets and to implement additional share buybacks. Based on these strong fundamentals and a P/E valuation well below its 30% - 50% two-to-three year projected EPS growth rate, the shares are recommended for accumulation.

Key Stock Statistics

S&P EPS Est. 1996	2.50	Tang. Bk. Value/Share	4.37
P/E on S&P Est. 1996	27.6	Beta	1.77
Dividend Rate/Share	Nil	Shareholders	2,400
Shs. outstg. (M)	271.3	Market cap. (B)	$ 18.7
Avg. daily vol. (M)	3.998	Inst. holdings	78%
		Insider holdings	NA

Value of $10,000 invested 5 years ago: NA

Fiscal Year Ending Jul. 31

	1995	% Change	1994	% Change	1993	% Change
Revenues (Million $)						
1Q	392.9	58%	248.5	97%	126.4	99%
2Q	454.9	51%	302.2	108%	145.1	96%
3Q	509.9	54%	331.2	92%	172.4	89%
4Q	621.2	72%	361.2	76%	205.2	86%
Yr.	1,979	59%	1,243	92%	649.0	91%
Income (Million $)						
1Q	98.77	56%	63.49	64%	38.69	150%
2Q	53.49	-31%	77.47	100%	38.69	110%
3Q	125.0	48%	84.34	82%	46.30	99%
4Q	143.7	60%	89.57	67%	53.72	97%
Yr.	421.0	34%	314.9	83%	172.0	104%
Earnings Per Share ($)						
1Q	0.37	54%	0.24	85%	0.13	100%
2Q	0.19	-34%	0.29	93%	0.15	100%
3Q	0.45	41%	0.32	78%	0.18	100%
4Q	0.51	50%	0.34	66%	0.21	86%
Yr.	1.52	28%	1.19	80%	0.66	97%

Next earnings report expected: mid November

Cisco Systems

Business Summary - 29-SEP-95

Cisco Systems develops, manufactures, markets and supports high-performance, multiprotocol internetworking systems that enable customers to build large-scale integrated networks of computer networks. Its products connect and manage communications among local and wide area networks (LANs and WANs) that employ a variety of protocols, media interfaces, network topologies and cabling systems.

International sales accounted for 42% of net sales in fiscal 1994, versus 39% in fiscal 1993.

The company's product family includes backbone and remote access routers, LAN and asynchronous transfer mode (ATM) switches; dial up access servers and network management software. All products support multiprotocol multiple media connectivity in multivendor environments. The company's Internetwork Operating System (IOS) provides a common software platform across all network environments.

High-performance, intelligent routers interconnect networks using different protocols and media. Access routers extend the network to regional sales groups, small satellite offices and individual telecommuters.

The company markets its products in the U.S. mainly through a direct sales force and internationally through distributors in about 74 countries.

In January 1995, CSCO acquired Lightstream Corp., a developer of enterprise-class ATM switching technology, for $120.5 million cash. In December 1994, CSCO acquired Kalpana Inc., a leading worldwide supplier of Ethernet switches, for 6.8 million shares. In October, the company sold a 26.8% interest in its Japanese subsidiary, Nihon Cisco, to 13 leading Japanese companies seeking to develop and expand the internetworking market in Japan. In August 1994, CSCO acquired Newport Systems Solutions, a supplier of software-based routers, in exchange for 4.3 million shares. In September 1993, CSCO acquired Crescendo Communications, a provider of high-performance workgroup solutions, in exchange for 3.4 million (adjusted) shares.

Important Developments

Sep. '95—CSCO agreed to purchase Grand Junction Networks Inc., a leading provider of Fast Ethernet and Ethernet desktop switching products, in exchange for five million shares (indicated value $348 million). Separately, CSCO agreed to issue 81,000 shares (indicated value $5.5 million) to acquire Internet Junction, Inc., a developer of software that connects desktop users to the Internet.

Aug. '95—CSCO agreed to purchase Combinet Inc., a leading maker of ISDN remote-access networking products, in exchange for two million shares.

Capitalization

Long Term Debt: None (7/30/95).

Minority Interest: $40,792,000.

Options: To purchase 19,023,000 shs. at $0.01 to $37 ea. (7/94).

Per Share Data ($)
(Year Ended Jul. 31)

	1995	1994	1993	1992	1991	1990
Tangible Bk. Val.	NA	3.29	1.92	1.02	0.56	0.32
Cash Flow	NA	1.30	0.72	0.36	0.19	0.07
Earnings	1.52	1.19	0.66	0.33	0.17	0.07
Dividends	Nil	Nil	Nil	Nil	Nil	Nil
Payout Ratio	Nil	Nil	Nil	Nil	Nil	Nil
Prices - High	67	40¾	29⅝	20¼	8½	2⅞
- Low	32⅜	18¾	16⅜	8⅛	2⁷⁄₁₆	1⅛
P/E Ratio - High	44	34	45	58	40	45
- Low	21	16	25	24	14	18

Income Statement Analysis (Million $)

	1994	%Chg	1993	%Chg	1992	%Chg	1991
Revs.	1,243	92%	649	91%	340	86%	183
Oper. Inc.	519	87%	277	104%	136	97%	69.0
Depr.	30.8	132%	13.3	106%	6.5	112%	3.0
Int. Exp.	NA	—	NA	—	NA	—	NA
Pretax Inc.	509	85%	275	102%	136	92%	71.0
Eff. Tax Rate	38%	—	38%	—	38%	—	39%
Net Inc.	315	83%	172	104%	84.4	95%	43.2

Balance Sheet & Other Fin. Data (Million $)

	1994	1993	1992	1991	1990	1989
Cash	183	89.0	156	91.0	57.0	4.0
Curr. Assets	508	268	247	141	78.0	16.0
Total Assets	1,054	595	324	154	83.0	17.0
Curr. Liab.	206	120	78.3	26.3	13.2	8.8
LT Debt	Nil	Nil	Nil	Nil	0.1	0.2
Common Eqty.	848	475	246	128	69.0	8.0
Total Cap.	848	475	246	128	69.0	8.0
Cap. Exp.	59.6	33.9	21.6	11.3	4.1	0.3
Cash Flow	346	185	90.8	46.2	14.7	4.3

Ratio Analysis

	1994	1993	1992	1991	1990	1989
Curr. Ratio	2.5	2.2	3.2	5.4	5.9	1.8
% LT Debt of Cap.	Nil	Nil	Nil	Nil	0.2	2.7
% Net Inc.of Revs.	25.3	26.5	24.8	23.6	19.9	15.1
% Ret. on Assets	38.2	37.0	34.7	36.5	23.2	39.2
% Ret. on Equity	47.6	47.2	44.4	43.9	34.8	78.9

Dividend Data —No cash dividends have been paid. Two-for-one stock splits were effected in March of each of the past four years (1991-1994).

Data as orig. reptd.; bef. results of disc. opers. and/or spec. items. Per share data adj. for stk. divs. as of ex-div. date. E-Estimated. NA-Not Available. NM-Not Meaningful. NR-Not Ranked.

Office—170 W. Tasman Drive, San Jose, CA 95134-1706. **Tel**—(408) 526-4000. **Chrmn**—J. P. Morgridge. **Vice Chrmn**—D. T. Valentine. **Pres & CEO**—J. Chambers. **CFO, VP-Fin, Secy & Investor Contact**—L. R. Carter. **Dirs**—C. A. Bartz, J. T. Chambers, M. S. Frankel, J. F. Gibbons, J. P. Morgridge, R. L. Puette, D. H. Ring, M. Son, D. T. Valentine. **Transfer Agent & Registrar**—Bank of Boston. **Incorporated** in California in 1984. **Empl**-2,443. **S&P Analyst:** John D. Coyle, CFA

Citicorp

NYSE Symbol **CCI**
In S&P 500

16-AUG-95 | Industry: Banking

Summary: This company, the parent of Citibank, the largest bank in the U.S., has a substantial worldwide corporate and retail banking presence.

S&P Opinion: Buy (★★★★★)

Recent Price • 64%	Yield • 1.9%
52 Wk Range • 66⅛-38½	12-Mo. P/E • 8.6

Quantitative Evaluations

Outlook
(1 Lowest—5 Highest)
• **2+**

Fair Value
• **59**

Risk
• **Low**

Earn./Div. Rank
• **B-**

Technical Eval.
• **Bullish** since 2/95

Rel. Strength Rank
(1 Lowest—99 Highest)
• **77**

Insider Activity
• **Neutral**

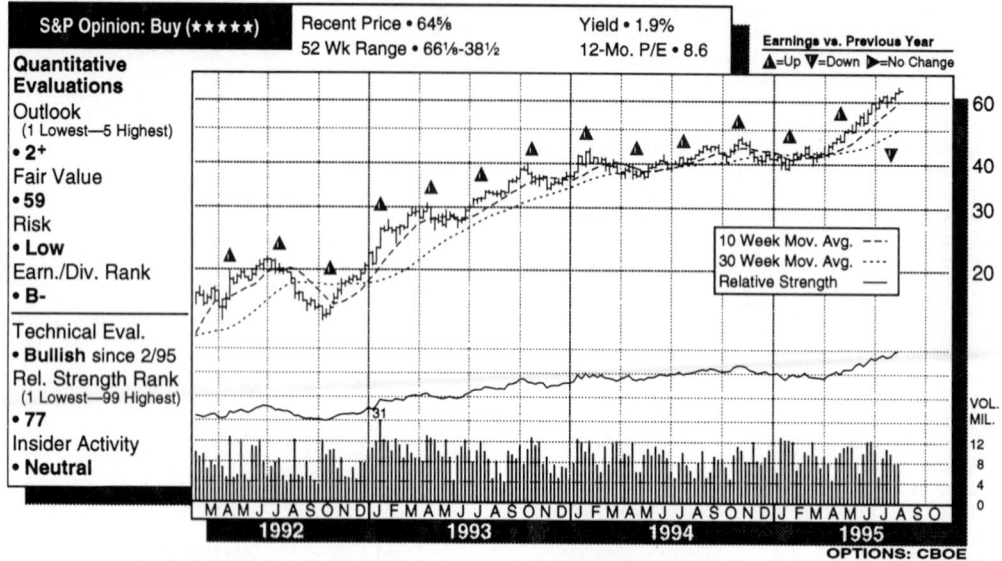

Earnings vs. Previous Year
▲=Up ▼=Down ▶=No Change

10 Week Mov. Avg. ---
30 Week Mov. Avg. ·····
Relative Strength —

OPTIONS: CBOE

Overview - 16-AUG-95

Profits in 1995 should continue to benefit from strength in the global consumer business, reflecting improved credit costs and growth in the domestic credit card operation. Managed U.S. receivables for credit cards rose a strong 20% in the second quarter of 1995, year to year, reflecting CCI's focus on the higher-yielding consumer business. Results from the North American commercial real estate segment have reached near breakeven on improved credit costs and asset sale gains and should continue to improve as total exposure declines further. Global finance profits, lower in 1994 on reduced trading revenues, are also expected to improve as trading revenues strengthen. The absence of deferred tax benefits and a return to normalized venture capital gains will somewhat offset improved core results.

Valuation - 16-AUG-95

After a brief selloff in late 1994 on interest rate worries and news of the Mexican financial crisis, the shares of this major money center bank have risen sharply thus far in 1995. With its far-reaching global presence and focus on high-yielding consumer business, CCI is better positioned than other money center banks to produce continued strong revenue growth in times of relatively weak trading revenues. The early 1995 doubling of the common stock dividend demonstrated management's confidence in future earnings power. Trading at less than nine times expected 1996 earnings, the shares are attractive for further superior capital appreciation.

Key Stock Statistics

S&P EPS Est. 1995	7.30	Tang. Bk. Value/Share	35.28
P/E on S&P Est. 1995	8.9	Beta	1.15
S&P EPS Est. 1996	8.10	Shareholders	60,000
Dividend Rate/Share	1.20	Market cap. (B)	$ 25.3
Shs. outstg. (M)	397.5	Inst. holdings	77%
Avg. daily vol. (M)	1.728	Insider holdings	NA

Value of $10,000 invested 5 years ago: $ 27,987

Fiscal Year Ending Dec. 31

	1995	% Change	1994	% Change	1993	% Change
Revenues (Million $)						
1Q	7,715	-6%	8,234	4%	7,907	-1%
2Q	7,934	-10%	8,788	13%	7,795	NM
3Q	—	—	7,036	-13%	8,095	NM
4Q	—	—	7,592	-10%	8,399	3%
Yr.	—	—	31,650	-2%	32,196	NM
Income (Million $)						
1Q	829.0	36%	609.0	65%	370.0	102%
2Q	853.0	-3%	877.0	97%	446.0	NM
3Q	—	—	894.0	69%	528.0	NM
4Q	—	—	1,042	81%	575.0	105%
Yr.	—	—	3,422	78%	1,919	166%
Earnings Per Share ($)						
1Q	1.71	38%	1.24	75%	0.71	92%
2Q	1.76	-4%	1.83	108%	0.88	NM
3Q	E1.85	-1%	1.87	76%	1.06	NM
4Q	E1.95	-11%	2.20	90%	1.16	119%
Yr.	E7.30	2%	7.15	87%	3.82	183%

Next earnings report expected: mid October

Citicorp

Business Summary - 16-AUG-95

Citicorp, the parent of Citibank, the largest U.S. bank, provides a broad range of financial services to individuals, businesses, governments and financial institutions from over 3,400 locations in 94 countries and territories throughout the world. Its Global Consumer business operates a full-service consumer franchise encompassing branch banking, credit and charge cards, and private banking. The Global Finance business provides a diverse range of wholesale banking services to local and multinational corporate customers, financial institutions and government entities. Contributions by segment in 1994 were:

	Revs. (Mil. $)	Net Inc. (Mil. $)	Return on Assets
Global consumer	$10,386	$1,788	1.67%
Global finance	5,496	1,404	1.01%
North. Amer. comm'l. real estate	81	-298	---
Cross-border Refin. portfolio	205	221	---
Corporate	580	307	---

During 1994, average interest-earning assets of $213 billion (up from $199 billion in 1993) were divided: consumer loans 41%, commercial loans 26%, federal funds sold 8%, investment securities 9%, trading account assets 12% and bank deposits 4%. Average sources of funds were: domestic deposits 14%, foreign deposits 38%, short-term liabilities 14%, long-term debt 7%, noninterest-bearing deposits 21% and shareholders' equity 6%.

At December 31, 1994, cash-basis and renegotiated commercial loans totaled $2.2 billion, down from $4.2 billion a year earlier. Consumer loans delinquent 90 days or more came to $3.3 billion (3.4% of consumer loans), down from $3.6 billion (4.2%). The reserve for loan losses was 3.38% of loans at 1994 year-end, versus 3.15%. Net chargeoffs in 1994 equaled 0.81% of average loans, versus 1.48% in 1993.

At June 30, 1995, Tier 1 capital was estimated at 8.4% (7.1% a year earlier), while total capital was 12.4% (11.6%).

Important Developments

Jul. '95—CCI said it completed the redemption of 39% of its PERCS Conversion Preferred Stock. The company also noted that it initiated a program to buy back up to $3 billion of common or convertible preferred stock over the next 24 months and had repurchased $50 million of its common shares during the second quarter of 1995.

Capitalization

Long Term Debt: $18,712,000,000 (6/95).
Preferred Stock: $4,020,000,000.

Per Share Data ($) (Year Ended Dec. 31)

	1994	1993	1992	1991	1990	1989
Tangible Bk. Val.	33.58	25.09	20.41	19.51	21.63	22.37
Earnings	7.15	3.82	1.35	-3.22	0.57	1.16
Dividends	0.45	Nil	Nil	0.75	1.74	1.58
Payout Ratio	6%	Nil	Nil	NM	305%	137%
Prices - High	47¾	39¾	22½	17½	29⅝	35½
- Low	36⅛	20½	10⅜	8½	10¾	24⅝
P/E Ratio - High	7	10	17	NM	52	31
- Low	5	5	8	NM	19	21

Income Statement Analysis (Million $)

	1994	%Chg	1993	%Chg	1992	%Chg	1991
Net Int. Inc.	8,911	16%	7,690	3%	7,456	3%	7,265
Tax Equiv. Adj.	26.0	73%	15.0	-21%	19.0	-46%	35.0
Non Int. Inc.	7,637	-9%	8,385	3%	8,153	14%	7,155
Loan Loss Prov.	1,881	-28%	2,600	-37%	4,146	7%	3,890
% Exp/Op Revs.	62%	—	66%	—	64%	—	77%
Pretax Inc.	4,611	61%	2,860	102%	1,418	NM	-236
Eff. Tax Rate	26%	—	33%	—	49%	—	-285.70%
Net Inc.	3,422	78%	1,919	166%	722	NM	-913
% Net Int. Marg.	NA	—	3.88%	—	3.76%	—	3.72%

Balance Sheet & Other Fin. Data (Million $)

	1994	1993	1992	1991	1990	1989
Earning Assets:						
Money Mkt.	52,732	29,702	30,020	23,310	19,140	30,490
Inv. Securities	20,703	15,530	15,060	14,710	14,080	14,700
Com'l Loans	13,836	12,931	14,340	16,450	19,650	19,840
Other Loans	139,670	127,139	126,700	136,400	138,900	142,600
Total Assets	250,489	217,000	214,000	217,000	217,000	230,600
Demand Deposits	20,860	20,100	18,800	17,300	16,100	17,700
Time Deposits	134,866	125,000	125,400	129,200	126,300	120,200
LT Debt	17,877	18,100	20,100	23,300	23,200	24,000
Common Eqty.	13,582	10,066	7,970	7,350	8,190	8,240

Ratio Analysis

	1994	1993	1992	1991	1990	1989
% Ret. on Assets	1.5	0.9	0.3	NM	0.1	0.2
% Ret. on Equity	NA	17.8	6.8	NM	2.1	4.3
% Loan Loss Resv.	3.4	3.2	2.8	2.2	2.8	3.0
% Loans/Deposits	97.9	95.8	96.9	103.1	109.7	116.1
% Equity to Assets	NA	4.2	3.3	3.8	3.7	3.9

Dividend Data —Common dividends, paid since 1813, were suspended in late 1991, and reinstated in June 1994.

Amt. of Div. $	Date Decl.	Ex-Div. Date	Stock of Record	Payment Date
0.150	Jul. 19	Jul. 25	Jul. 29	Aug. 17 '94
0.150	Oct. 18	Oct. 25	Oct. 31	Nov. 17 '94
0.300	Jan. 17	Jan. 25	Jan. 31	Feb. 17 '95
0.300	Apr. 18	Apr. 24	Apr. 28	May. 17 '95
0.300	Jul. 18	Jul. 27	Jul. 31	Aug. 17 '95

Data as orig. reptd.; bef. results of disc opers. and/or spec. items. Per share data adj. for stk. divs. as of ex-div. date. E-Estimated. NA-Not Available. NM-Not Meaningful. NR-Not Ranked.

Office—399 Park Ave., New York, NY 10043. **Tel**—(212) 559-1000. **Chrmn & CEO**—J. S. Reed. **EVP**—T. E. Jones. **EVP & Secy**—C. E. Long. **Investor Contact**—Frederick A. Roesch. **Dirs**—D. W. Calloway, C. H. Chandler, P. Chia, P. J. Collins, K. T. Derr, H. J. Haynes, J. S. Reed, W. R. Rhodes, R. L. Ridgway, H. O. Ruding, R. B. Shapiro, F. A. Shrontz, M. H. Simonsen, R. B. Smith, C. J. Steffen, F. A. Thomas, E. S. Woolard, Jr. **Transfer Agents & Registrars**—Citibank, N.A., NYC; First Interstate Bank of California, Calabasas, CA; The First National Bank of Chicago; Montreal Trust Co., Toronto. **Incorporated** in Delaware in 1968; Bank founded in 1812. **Empl**-82,600. **S&P Analyst:** Stephen R. Biggar

Clorox Co.

NYSE Symbol **CLX**
In **S&P 500**

24-AUG-95

Industry:
Household Products

Summary: This company is a diversified producer of household cleaning, grocery and specialty food products.

S&P Opinion: Hold (★★★)	Recent Price • 65½ Yield • 3.2%
	52 Wk Range • 67½-50 12-Mo. P/E • 17.3

Quantitative Evaluations

Outlook
(1 Lowest—5 Highest)
• **3+**

Fair Value
• **63¾**

Risk
• **Low**

Earn./Div. Rank
• **A**

Technical Eval.
• **Bullish** since 8/95

Rel. Strength Rank
(1 Lowest—99 Highest)
• **58**

Insider Activity
• **Neutral**

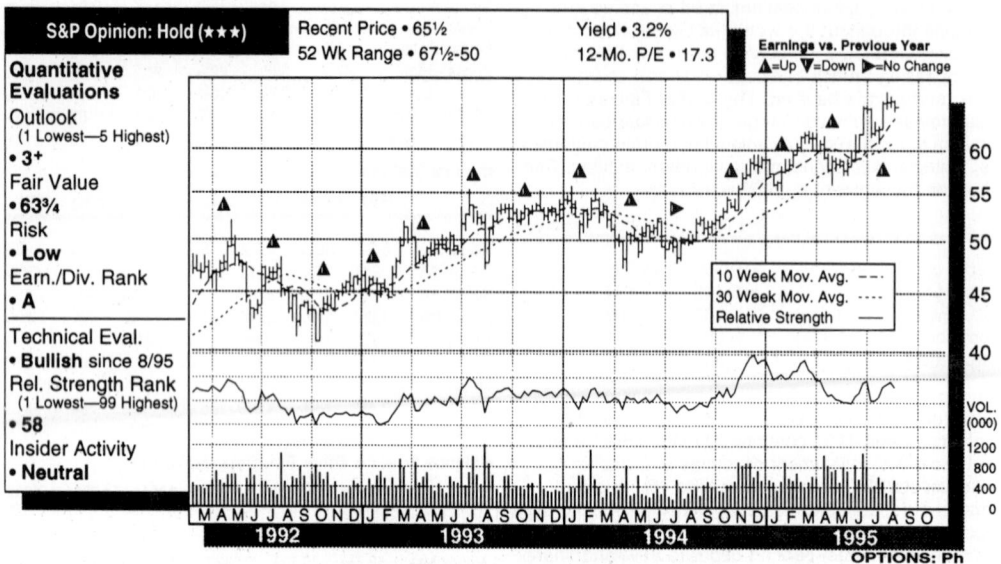

Earnings vs. Previous Year
▲=Up ▼=Down ▶=No Change

- 10 Week Mov. Avg. ---
- 30 Week Mov. Avg. ····
- Relative Strength ——

OPTIONS: Ph

Overview - 24-AUG-95

Sales for fiscal 1996 are expected to continue in a solid uptrend, spurred by higher sales of existing products, contributions from new products (especially in overseas markets) and line extensions of existing products, and potential acquisitions. Sales should be enhanced by ongoing expansion overseas, particularly in Latin America, the Asia/Pacific region, Russia, and Eastern Europe. The company expects 20% of its revenues will be derived from overseas markets by 2000. Margins could widen slightly, aided by efforts to control overhead and operating costs that should offset aggressive new product spending and continued competitive pricing. Share earnings comparisons will benefit from fewer shares outstanding.

Valuation - 24-AUG-95

We feel that these shares are fully-valued, given their current price/earnings ratio, based on fiscal 1996's estimated earnings. As such, we are retaining a neutral opinion on Clorox for now. Like comparable manufacturers of household products, Clorox's stock has underperformed the market this year, most likely as a result of investor preferences to invest in industries offering superior earnings growth. However, over the longer term, we think Clorox's shares could reward investors, reflecting an expected annual earnings growth rate of 12%, the maintenance of a 3% plus dividend yield, and annual increases in the dividend.

Key Stock Statistics

S&P EPS Est. 1996	4.20	Tang. Bk. Value/Share	7.04
P/E on S&P Est. 1996	15.6	Beta	0.95
Dividend Rate/Share	2.12	Shareholders	13,100
Shs. outstg. (M)	53.1	Market cap. (B)	$ 3.5
Avg. daily vol. (M)	0.079	Inst. holdings	53%
		Insider holdings	NA

Value of $10,000 invested 5 years ago: $ 18,900

Fiscal Year Ending Jun. 30

	1995	% Change	1994	% Change	1993	% Change
Revenues (Million $)						
1Q	476.4	6%	449.7	14%	394.7	-6%
2Q	414.5	12%	370.8	13%	327.4	-7%
3Q	499.1	4%	481.9	11%	435.6	-4%
4Q	594.3	11%	534.4	12%	476.6	-3%
Yr.	1,984	8%	1,837	12%	1,634	-5%
Income (Million $)						
1Q	53.18	15%	46.31	—	—	—
2Q	34.10	11%	30.59	12%	27.24	11%
3Q	54.03	9%	49.52	9%	45.42	18%
4Q	59.52	11%	53.58	7%	49.97	NM
Yr.	200.8	12%	180.0	7%	167.9	42%
Earnings Per Share ($)						
1Q	1.00	18%	0.85	4%	0.82	4%
2Q	0.64	12%	0.57	14%	0.50	11%
3Q	1.02	10%	0.93	12%	0.83	17%
4Q	1.13	13%	1.00	NM	1.00	NM
Yr.	3.78	13%	3.35	9%	3.07	41%

Next earnings report expected: mid October

Clorox Co.

Business Summary - 24-AUG-95

Clorox Co. is an international company whose principal products include non-durable household consumer products sold primarily to grocery stores and other retail stores. In fiscal 1993, the company implemented a new strategy for its domestic operations, and as such, sold two non-strategic businesses including the frozen food and bottled water divisions. In its continuing operations, CLX is now focused on developing new products and line extensions of existing products, as well as making strategic acquisitions, such as the early 1994 purchase of S.O.S home cleaning products. Internationally, CLX is expanding its laundry, household cleaning and insecticide business mainly into developing countries, in part through joint ventures and acquisitions.

Clorox's business is divided into three areas, including domestic retail products, international, and institutional. The domestic retail products includes laundry additives, home cleaning products, cat litters, insecticides, charcoal briquets, salad dressings, sauces and water filter systems. Major brand names and products include various laundry and cleaning products using the Clorox name; Liquid-plumr drain unclogger; Formula 409 and Pine Sol cleaning solutions; Soft Scrub abrasive liquid cleanser; Tilex mildew cleaner; Kingsford and Match Light charcoals; Scoop Fresh, Control and Fresh Step cat litters; Combat ant and roach killers; Hidden Valley salad dressings; K. C. Masterpiece barbeque sauce; Kitchen Bouquet browning and seasoning sauce; Salad Crispins mini-croutons; Brita water filter systems; and S.O.S steel wool soap pads and home cleaning products.

The international division includes household products, consisting of laundry additives, home cleaning products and insecticides. Products are sold in more than 90 countries, and are manufactured in over 35 plants in the U.S., Puerto Rico and abroad. The institutional division includes institutional cleaning products and food products.

Important Developments

Aug. '95—CLX attributed the 12% year-to-year gain in its fiscal 1995 net income to a 10% rise in shipments. The strong shipment growth reflected record amounts of established brands shipped, including Clorox liquid bleach, Pine-Sol cleaner, Combat insecticides, Kingsford charcoal briquets, and Brita water filtration products. The strong shipment growth also reflected the introduction of 16 new products and overseas expansion.

Capitalization

Long Term Debt: $253,079,000 (6/95).

Per Share Data ($)

(Year Ended Jun. 30)

	1995	1994	1993	1992	1991	1990
Tangible Bk. Val.	NA	7.30	7.57	6.13	5.36	13.12
Cash Flow	NA	5.69	4.42	3.65	2.48	3.67
Earnings	3.78	3.35	3.07	2.17	0.98	2.80
Dividends	1.92	1.80	1.71	1.59	1.47	1.29
Payout Ratio	51%	54%	56%	74%	151%	45%
Prices - High	67½	59½	55⅜	52	42⅞	45⅜
- Low	55¼	47	44	39½	35	32⅛
P/E Ratio - High	18	18	18	24	43	16
- Low	15	14	14	18	36	11

Income Statement Analysis (Million $)

	1993	%Chg	1992	%Chg	1991	%Chg	1990
Revs.	1,837	12%	1,634	-5%	1,717	4%	1,646
Oper. Inc.	420	21%	348	12%	311	5%	295
Depr.	94.1	28%	73.6	-9%	80.5	-1%	81.4
Int. Exp.	18.4	-3%	18.9	-23%	24.7	-12%	28.2
Pretax Inc.	307	12%	275	30%	211	145%	86.0
Eff. Tax Rate	41%	—	39%	—	44%	—	39%
Net Inc.	180	7%	168	42%	118	123%	53.0

Balance Sheet & Other Fin. Data (Million $)

	1993	1992	1991	1990	1989	1988
Cash	NA	116	69.0	114	125	233
Curr. Assets	504	532	418	467	418	615
Total Assets	1,698	1,649	1,615	1,603	1,138	1,213
Curr. Liab.	376	372	421	348	226	331
LT Debt	216	204	257	400	8.0	7.0
Common Eqty.	909	879	814	784	811	786
Total Cap.	1,258	1,227	1,188	1,247	912	882
Cap. Exp.	36.6	78.0	125	132	157	92.0
Cash Flow	306	242	198	134	201	187

Ratio Analysis

	1993	1992	1991	1990	1989	1988
Curr. Ratio	1.3	1.4	1.0	1.3	1.9	1.9
% LT Debt of Cap.	17.1	16.6	21.6	32.1	0.8	0.8
% Net Inc.of Revs.	9.7	10.3	6.9	3.2	10.4	10.7
% Ret. on Assets	10.7	10.3	7.3	3.8	13.2	12.1
% Ret. on Equity	20.1	19.8	14.7	6.6	19.5	19.2

Dividend Data —Dividends have been paid since 1968. A dividend reinvestment plan is available.

Amt. of Div. $	Date Decl.	Ex-Div. Date	Stock of Record	Payment Date
0.480	Sep. 21	Oct. 24	Oct. 28	Nov. 15 '94
0.480	Jan. 18	Jan. 23	Jan. 27	Feb. 15 '95
0.480	Mar. 15	Apr. 24	Apr. 28	May. 15 '95
0.530	Jul. 18	Jul. 26	Jul. 28	Aug. 15 '95

Data as orig. reptd.; bef. results of disc. opers. and/or spec. items. Per share data adj. for stk. divs. as of ex-div. date. E-Estimated. NA-Not Available. NM-Not Meaningful. NR-Not Ranked.

Office—1221 Broadway, Oakland, CA 94612. **Tel**—(510) 271-7000. **Chrmn & CEO**—G. C. Sullivan. **CFO**—W. F. Ausfahl. **VP-Secy**—E. A. Cutter. **VP-Treas & Investor Contact**—K. M. Rose. **Dirs**—W. F. Ausfahl, D. Boggan Jr., J. W. Collins, U. Fairchild, J. Krautter, J. Manchot, D. O. Morton, E. L. Scarff, L. R. Scott, F. N. Shumway, G. C. Sullivan, J. A. Vohs, C. A. Wolfe. **Transfer Agent & Registrar**—First Chicago Trust Co. of New York, NYC. **Incorporated** in Ohio in 1957; reincorporated in Delaware in 1986. **Empl**-4,850. **S&P Analyst:** Elizabeth Vandeventer

Coastal Corp.

NYSE Symbol **CGP**
In S&P 500

14-AUG-95　**Industry:**
Utilities-Gas

Summary: CGP operates one of the largest U.S. natural gas pipeline systems. Activities also include coal mining, exploration and production, oil refining, and chemicals.

S&P Opinion: Accumulate (★★★★)	Recent Price • 31⅛	Yield • 1.3%
	52 Wk Range • 31¾-24¾	12-Mo. P/E • 15.9

Quantitative Evaluations

Outlook
(1 Lowest—5 Highest)
• **4+**

Fair Value
• **32%**

Risk
• **Low**

Earn./Div. Rank
• **B+**

Technical Eval.
• **Bearish** since 3/95

Rel. Strength Rank
(1 Lowest—99 Highest)
• **45**

Insider Activity
• **Neutral**

Earnings vs. Previous Year
▲=Up ▼=Down ▶=No Change

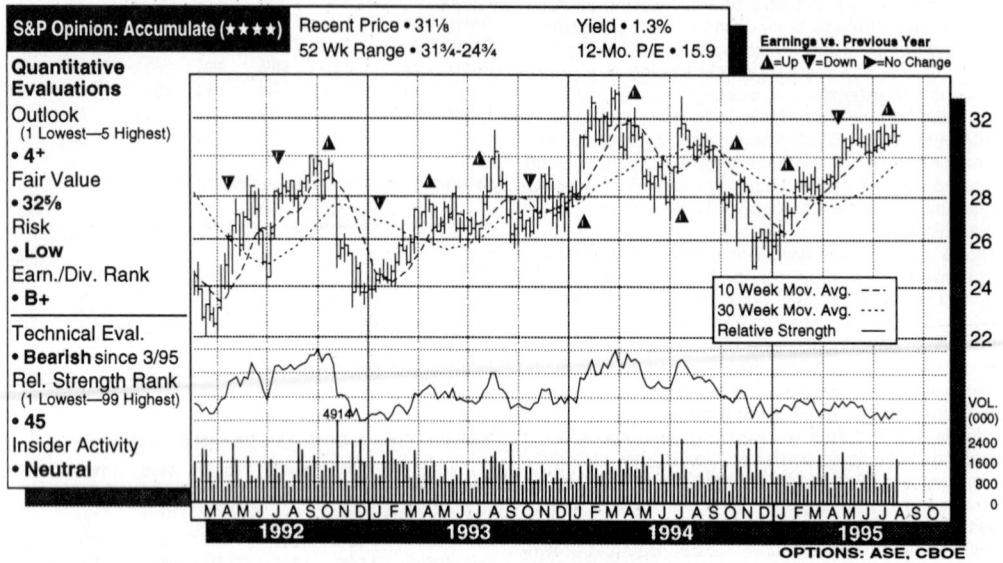

10 Week Mov. Avg. – – –
30 Week Mov. Avg. · · · ·
Relative Strength ——

OPTIONS: ASE, CBOE

Overview - 14-AUG-95

The company is reaping the results of its successful restructuring of two years ago, which enhanced the yield of higher-value petroleum products through low cost modifications in refining and marketing. Earnings in 1995 should benefit from increased natural gas profits, reflecting expansion of the customer base, new services offered to producers and customers, and development of gas marketing operations. Refining and marketing profits should rise, as margins improve from depressed levels and throughput grows on higher demand and expansion of capacity. An expected decline in industry capacity should lead to further refining margin growth over the long-term. Also laying the groundwork for future expansion is the solid nature of Coastal's core segments in natural gas and coal. With this secure base, management can focus on businesses with the most potential for growth.

Valuation - 14-AUG-95

The company's shares have continued their rise from the lows at the end of 1994 and early 1995. At current P/E levels, and with a low yield, there is slight room for further growth, although very limited. Natural gas prices have lost some of the ground that was gained from winter's depressed levels. April and May weather was chilly, fueling demand for gas and resulting in storage levels returning to more normal levels. Summer warm spells have sparked increased air-conditioning usage. Earnings will continue to improve from early 1995's disappointing results.

Key Stock Statistics

S&P EPS Est. 1995	2.20	Tang. Bk. Value/Share	16.71
P/E on S&P Est. 1995	14.1	Beta	0.78
S&P EPS Est. 1996	2.50	Shareholders	37,000
Dividend Rate/Share	0.40	Market cap. (B)	$ 3.3
Shs. outstg. (M)	104.8	Inst. holdings	66%
Avg. daily vol. (M)	0.224	Insider holdings	NA

Value of $10,000 invested 5 years ago: $ 10,266

Fiscal Year Ending Dec. 31

	1995	% Change	1994	% Change	1993	% Change
Revenues ()						
1Q	2,618	-3%	2,701	2%	2,647	4%
2Q	2,614	5%	2,487	-6%	2,632	10%
3Q	—	—	2,676	16%	2,308	-11%
4Q	—	—	2,352	-8%	2,549	NM
Yr.	—	—	10,215	NM	10,136	NM
Income ()						
1Q	57.60	-29%	81.10	NM	25.00	NM
2Q	57.20	33%	43.10	50%	28.80	138%
3Q	—	—	26.60	NM	-11.40	NM
4Q	—	—	81.80	8%	75.90	NM
Yr.	—	—	232.6	97%	118.3	NM
Earnings Per Share ()						
1Q	0.51	-30%	0.73	NM	0.24	NM
2Q	0.50	35%	0.37	48%	0.25	127%
3Q	E0.31	48%	0.21	NM	-0.15	NM
4Q	E0.88	19%	0.74	9%	0.68	NM
Yr.	E2.20	7%	2.05	101%	1.02	NM

Next earnings report expected: late October

Coastal Corp.

Business Summary - 09-AUG-95

Coastal Corp. is a broadly based energy supply company. The company operates principally in the following lines of business: natural gas, refining and marketing, exploration and production, and coal. Its core segments are natural gas and coal. Operating profit contributions (in million $) by segment in recent years were:

	1994	1993	1992	1991
Natural gas systems	431.3	$405.2	$403.1	$402.2
Refining & marketing	153.1	98.0	-192.1	- 99.3
Coal	98.2	95.1	92.8	91.8
Exploration/production	41.8	49.9	45.8	45.2
Other	9.0	-12.8	-19.7	-4.3

CGP owns and operates major natural gas pipeline systems with over 22,000 miles of pipeline--including ANR Pipeline Co., acquired in 1985 for $2.5 billion, Great Lakes Gas Transmission (50%-owned), and Colorado Interstate Gas--that service markets from the Rocky Mountains to the Midwest and Upper Great Lakes areas. Coastal subsidiaries also have interests in 26 underground storage facilities in Colorado, Kansas, Michigan and New York with a working capacity of more than 267 Bcf. Pipeline throughput totaled 1,980 Bcf of gas in 1994, up from 1,908 Bcf in 1993.

The company operates three core refineries that produce a full range of petroleum products. Refinery crude oil throughput averaged 359,000 bbl. per day in 1994, up from 351,000 in 1993. Total capacity at year-end 1994 was 423,000 bbl. per day.

CGP, through ANR Coal Co., also mines and markets coal. At year-end 1994, coal reserves totaled 839 million tons. Gas and oil exploration and production operations are conducted in most of the productive areas of the contiguous U.S. At year-end 1994, proved reserves were estimated at 33.7 million bbl. of oil and 958 Bcf of gas.

Other CGP units are engaged in chemicals, independent power projects, including cogeneration, and trucking operations. In 1994, CGP embarked on an expansion of its power production business, concentrating on leveraging its expertise in emerging international markets.

Important Developments

Aug. '95—A 1979, 20-year purchase contract between Tesoro Petroleum, CGP and KCS Energy, Inc. with Tennessee Gas Pipeline Co. was upheld by the Texas Supreme Court, but with provision for a trial on the issue of what volumes Tennessee Gas must buy under the contract. CGP intends to ask the Court to reconsider its decision on this single issue remanded to the trial court.

Capitalization

Long Term Debt: $3,650,400,000 (3/95).
Common: 104,408,397 shs., also 413,179 shs. of Class A Common, each entitled to 100 votes.

Per Share Data ()

	(Year Ended Dec. 31)					
	1994	1993	1992	1991	1990	1989
Tangible Bk. Val.	16.26	14.40	13.63	19.16	18.58	16.73
Cash Flow	5.50	4.42	2.41	3.79	5.10	4.77
Earnings	2.05	1.02	-1.23	0.92	2.15	1.90
Dividends	0.40	0.40	0.40	0.40	0.40	0.30
Payout Ratio	20%	39%	NM	43%	18%	17%
Prices - High	33¾	31⅜	30	36¾	39⅝	33⅛
- Low	24¾	23½	22	23¾	29¼	22
P/E Ratio - High	16	31	NM	40	18	17
- Low	12	23	NM	26	14	12

Income Statement Analysis ()

	1994	%Chg	1993	%Chg	1992	%Chg	1991
Revs.	10,215	NM	10,136	NM	10,063	5%	9,549
Oper. Inc.	1,034	11%	931	27%	734	-13%	846
Depr.	363	2%	356	-6%	378	26%	301
Int. Exp.	416	-8%	451	-9%	496	8%	460
Pretax Inc.	325	61%	202	NM	-198	NM	158
Eff. Tax Rate	28%	—	41%	—	NM	—	39%
Net Inc.	233	97%	118	NM	-126	NM	96.0

Balance Sheet & Other Fin. Data ()

	1994	1993	1992	1991	1990	1989
Cash	74.0	159	44.0	24.0	71.0	149
Curr. Assets	2,428	2,574	3,028	3,028	3,244	3,194
Total Assets	10,535	10,227	10,580	9,487	9,230	8,773
Curr. Liab.	2,514	2,390	2,612	2,772	2,974	2,879
LT Debt	3,720	3,813	4,306	3,866	3,436	3,248
Common Eqty.	2,248	2,068	1,999	2,030	1,969	1,774
Total Cap.	7,652	7,457	7,692	6,562	6,072	5,727
Cap. Exp.	543	393	574	729	587	428
Cash Flow	578	463	250	397	535	447

Ratio Analysis

	1994	1993	1992	1991	1990	1989
Curr. Ratio	1.0	1.1	1.2	1.1	1.1	1.1
% LT Debt of Cap.	47.0	51.1	56.0	58.9	56.6	56.7
% Net Inc.of Revs.	2.3	1.2	NM	1.0	2.4	2.2
% Ret. on Assets	2.2	1.1	NM	1.0	2.5	2.0
% Ret. on Equity	10.0	5.2	NM	4.8	12.0	11.0

Dividend Data —

Amt. of Div. $	Date Decl.	Ex-Div. Date	Stock of Record	Payment Date
0.100	Feb. 07	Feb. 22	Feb. 28	Apr. 01 '94
0.100	Nov. 03	Nov. 23	Nov. 30	Jan. 01 '95
0.100	Feb. 03	Feb. 22	Feb. 28	Apr. 01 '95
0.100	May. 04	May. 24	May. 31	Jul. 01 '95
0.100	Aug. 03	Aug. 29	Aug. 31	Oct. 01 '95

Data as orig. reptd.; bef. results of disc. opers. and/or spec. items. Per share data adj. for stk. divs. as of ex-div. date. E-Estimated. NA-Not Available. NM-Not Meaningful. NR-Not Ranked.

Office—Nine Greenway Plaza, Houston, TX 77046-0995. **Tel**—(713) 877-1400. **Chrmn & CEO**—O. S. Wyatt, Jr. **Pres & COO**—D. A. Arledge. **Treas**—R. D. Matthews. **SVP & Secy**—A. M. O'Toole. **Investor Contact**—Stirling D. Pack, Jr. **Dirs**—D. A. Arledge, J. M. Bissell, G. L. Brundrett, Jr., H. Burrow, R. D. Chapin, Jr., J. F. Cordes, R. L. Gates, K. O. Johnson, J. S. Katzin, J. H. Marshall II, T. R. McDade, L. D. Wooddy, Jr., O. S. Wyatt, Jr. **Transfer Agents & Registrars**—Bank of New York, NYC; Co's. office, Houston. **Incorporated** in Delaware in 1972. **Empl**-16,300. **S&P Analyst:** Michael C. Barr

Coca-Cola

NYSE Symbol **KO**
In S&P 500

25-OCT-95

Industry:
Beverages

Summary: Coca-Cola is the world's largest soft-drink company and has a sizable fruit juice business. Its bottling interests include a 44% stake in NYSE-listed Coca-Cola Enterprises.

S&P Opinion: Buy (★★★★)

| Recent Price • 72⅝ | Yield • 1.2% |
| 52 Wk Range • 73⅞-48¾ | 12-Mo. P/E • 31.6 |

Quantitative Evaluations

Outlook
(1 Lowest—5 Highest)
• **2+**

Fair Value
• **70⅝**

Risk
• **Low**

Earn./Div. Rank
• **A+**

Technical Eval.
• **Bullish** since 7/94

Rel. Strength Rank
(1 Lowest—99 Highest)
• **83**

Insider Activity
• **Neutral**

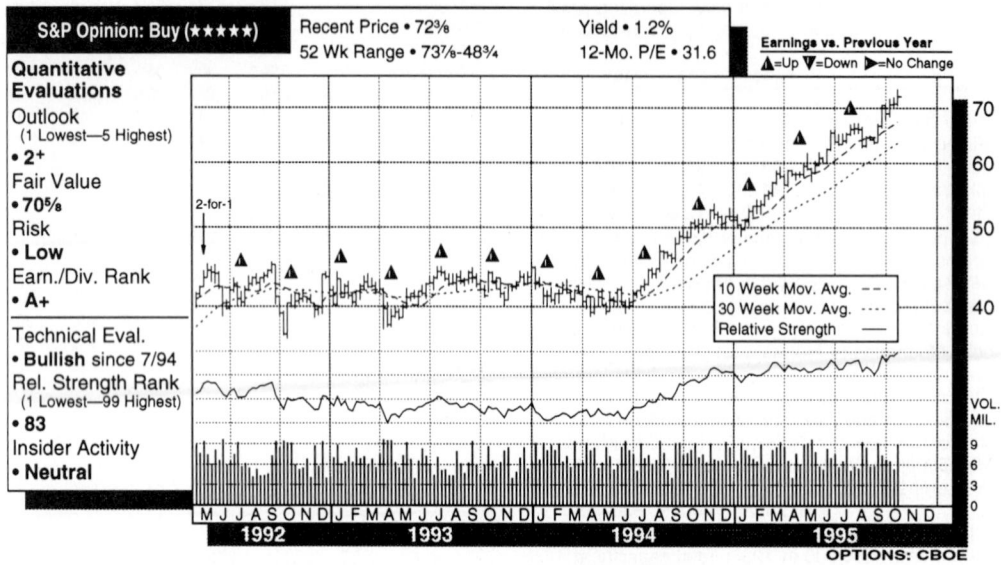

Earnings vs. Previous Year
▲=Up ▼=Down ▶=No Change

2-for-1

10 Week Mov. Avg. ----
30 Week Mov. Avg. ......
Relative Strength ——

VOL.
MIL.

1992 1993 1994 1995

OPTIONS: CBOE

Overview - 20-OCT-95

Revenues are projected to grow at an approximate 15% annual pace through 1996, driven by a projected 8% to 10% annual increase in global soft drink gallon shipments, and higher selling prices. Foreign currency exchange translations may contribute modestly to sales volatility. Operating profit margins should be maintained, as productivity gains and an improving geographic profit mix help offset the possible effect of lower-margin bottler investments. Equity income from bottler interests should trend higher on increased unit case volume growth. Despite reduced tax benefits on income generated in Puerto Rico, active tax management should allow KO's effective tax rate in 1995 and 1996 to remain stable. Ongoing aggressive stock repurchases (about 2% annually) should contribute to an approximate 20% annual earnings per share growth rate through 1996.

Valuation - 20-OCT-95

Despite the stock's rich P/E multiple, which is at or near its historical high, we expect the stock of this premier growth company to advance at an above-average pace over the next 12 months. With expectations of continued slow U.S. economic growth, we expect investors to continue to seek companies with good earnings track records in international markets, like KO. The company's strong balance sheet, high returns on invested capital, and dependable dividend growth will also continue to make this equity attractive over the longer term for virtually all accounts.

Key Stock Statistics

S&P EPS Est. 1995	2.38	Tang. Bk. Value/Share	3.65
P/E on S&P Est. 1995	30.4	Beta	0.83
S&P EPS Est. 1996	2.85	Shareholders	195,000
Dividend Rate/Share	0.88	Market cap. (B)	$ 91.4
Shs. outstg. (M)	1261.2	Inst. holdings	53%
Avg. daily vol. (M)	1.384	Insider holdings	NA

Value of $10,000 invested 5 years ago: $ 40,777

Fiscal Year Ending Dec. 31

	1995	% Change	1994	% Change	1993	% Change
Revenues (Million $)						
1Q	3,854	15%	3,352	10%	3,060	10%
2Q	4,936	14%	4,342	11%	3,899	10%
3Q	4,895	10%	4,461	23%	3,629	3%
4Q	—	—	4,017	19%	3,373	4%
Yr.	—	—	16,172	16%	13,957	7%
Income (Million $)						
1Q	638.0	22%	521.0	15%	454.0	18%
2Q	898.0	18%	758.0	12%	678.0	20%
3Q	802.0	13%	708.0	20%	590.0	9%
4Q	—	—	567.0	22%	466.0	19%
Yr.	—	—	2,554	17%	2,188	16%
Earnings Per Share ($)						
1Q	0.50	25%	0.40	14%	0.35	21%
2Q	0.71	20%	0.59	13%	0.52	21%
3Q	0.64	16%	0.55	22%	0.45	10%
4Q	E0.51	16%	0.44	22%	0.36	20%
Yr.	E2.38	20%	1.98	18%	1.68	17%

Next earnings report expected: late January

Business Summary - 24-OCT-95

Coca-Cola is the world's largest soft-drink company and a major producer of juice and related products. The company holds a 44% interest in Coca-Cola Enterprises, its largest bottler. Segment contributions in 1994 were:

	Revs.	Profits
Soft drinks	89%	97%
Foods	11%	3%

The company manufactures soft drink concentrates and syrups, which are sold to independent (and company-owned) bottlers and fountain wholesalers. Brands include Coca-Cola (best-selling soft drink in the world, including Coca-Cola classic), diet Coke (sold as Coke light in many territories outside the U.S.), Sprite, diet Sprite, Barq's, Mr. PiBB, Mello Yello, Fanta, TAB, Fresca, PowerAde, Minute Maid soft drinks, and other products developed for specific markets, including Georgia brand coffee. KO also has substantial equity positions in bottlers that represent about 43% of the company's U.S. unit case volume.

Coca-Cola Foods is the world's largest marketer and distributor of juice, juice drink, and related products. Brands include Minute Maid, Five Alive, Bright & Early, Hi-C, and Bacardi (under license).

International operations in 1994 accounted for 68% of net operating revenues (26% European Community; 22% Pacific & Canada; 12% Latin America; 5% Northeast Europe/Middle East; 3% Africa) and 79% of operating profits (29% Pacific & Canada; 24% European Community; 17% Latin America; 5% Northeast Europe/Middle East; 4% Africa).

Changes to U.S. tax law enacted in 1993 will limit the future utilization of favorable tax treatment from operations in Puerto Rico, and will exert upward pressure on KO's effective tax rate.

Important Developments

Oct. '95—KO reported that worldwide gallon shipments increased by approximately 10% in 1995's first nine months, with a 5% gain in North America and a 12% rise in international markets. The Latin America group volume gained 11%, Greater Europe group rose 10%, Africa group rose 26%, and Middle and Far East group advanced 12%. Worldwide unit case volume also increased by 9%, reflecting a 6% gain in North America, and a 10% increase in international markets. Management said that KO's first nine month results put the company on track to achieve its long-term goal of average annual international unit volume growth of 8% to 10%. In North America, unit case volume growth continued to reflect gains from core brands (which were helped by packaging innovations), and from contributions from new products, such as Powerade, Minute Maid Juices To Go, Fruitopia and Barq's.

Capitalization

Long Term Debt: $892,000,000 (6/95).

Per Share Data ($) (Year Ended Dec. 31)

	1994	1993	1992	1991	1990	1989
Tangible Bk. Val.	3.59	3.11	2.68	3.10	2.62	2.19
Cash Flow	2.28	1.94	1.67	1.41	1.20	0.98
Earnings	1.98	1.68	1.43	1.21	1.02	0.85
Dividends	0.78	0.68	0.56	0.48	0.40	0.34
Payout Ratio	39%	40%	39%	39%	39%	39%
Prices - High	53½	45⅛	45⅜	40⅞	24½	20¼
- Low	38⅞	37½	35⅝	21⅜	16⅜	10⅞
P/E Ratio - High	27	27	32	34	24	24
- Low	20	22	25	18	16	13

Income Statement Analysis (Million $)

	1994	%Chg	1993	%Chg	1992	%Chg	1991
Revs.	16,172	16%	13,957	7%	13,074	13%	11,572
Oper. Inc.	4,090	17%	3,485	13%	3,080	19%	2,586
Depr.	382	15%	333	7%	310	22%	254
Int. Exp.	199	12%	178	4%	171	-8%	185
Pretax Inc.	3,728	17%	3,185	16%	2,746	15%	2,383
Eff. Tax Rate	32%	—	31%	—	31%	—	32%
Net Inc.	2,554	17%	2,188	16%	1,884	16%	1,618

Balance Sheet & Other Fin. Data (Million $)

	1994	1993	1992	1991	1990	1989
Cash	1,531	1,078	1,063	1,117	1,492	1,182
Curr. Assets	5,205	4,434	4,248	4,144	4,143	3,604
Total Assets	13,873	12,021	11,052	10,222	9,278	8,283
Curr. Liab.	6,177	5,171	5,303	4,118	4,296	3,658
LT Debt	1,426	1,428	1,120	985	536	549
Common Eqty.	5,235	4,584	3,888	4,426	3,774	3,185
Total Cap.	6,841	6,125	5,090	5,611	4,650	4,330
Cap. Exp.	878	808	1,083	792	642	462
Cash Flow	2,936	2,521	2,194	1,872	1,600	1,355

Ratio Analysis

	1994	1993	1992	1991	1990	1989
Curr. Ratio	0.8	0.9	0.8	1.0	1.0	1.0
% LT Debt of Cap.	20.8	23.3	22.0	17.6	11.5	12.7
% Net Inc.of Revs.	15.8	15.7	14.4	14.0	13.5	13.3
% Ret. on Assets	19.9	19.0	17.9	16.6	15.8	15.5
% Ret. on Equity	52.4	51.8	45.7	39.6	39.3	38.5

Dividend Data —Dividends have been paid since 1893. A dividend reinvestment plan is available.

Amt. of Div. $	Date Decl.	Ex-Div. Date	Stock of Record	Payment Date
0.195	Oct. 20	Nov. 25	Dec. 01	Dec. 15 '94
0.220	Feb. 16	Mar. 09	Mar. 15	Apr. 01 '95
0.220	Apr. 20	Jun. 13	Jun. 15	Jul. 01 '95
0.220	Jul. 20	Sep. 13	Sep. 15	Oct. 01 '95
0.220	Oct. 19	Nov. 29	Dec. 01	Dec. 15 '95

Data as orig. reptd.; bef. results of disc. opers. and/or spec. items. Per share data adj. for stk. divs. as of ex-div. date. E-Estimated. NA-Not Available. NM-Not Meaningful. NR-Not Ranked.

Office—1 Coca-Cola Plaza, N.W., Atlanta, GA 30313. **Tel**—(404) 676-2121. **Chrmn & CEO**—R. C. Goizueta. **Pres & COO**—M. D. Ivester. **CFO**—J. E. Chesnut. **Secy**—Susan E. Shaw. **Investor Contact**—Juan D. Johnson. **Dirs**—H. A. Allen, R. W. Allen, C. P. Black, W. E. Buffett, C. W. Duncan, Jr., R. C. Goizueta, M. D. Ivester, S. B. King, D. F. McHenry, P. F. Oreffice, J. D. Robinson III, W. B. Turner, P. V. Ueberroth, J. B. Williams. **Transfer Agent & Registrar**—First Chicago Trust Co. of New York, Jersey City, NJ. **Incorporated** in Delaware in 1919. **Empl**- 33,000. **S&P Analyst:** Kenneth A. Shea

Colgate-Palmolive

NYSE Symbol **CL**
In S&P 500

27-SEP-95 | **Industry:** Household Products | **Summary:** This major consumer products company markets oral care, body care, household surface care, fabric care and animal dietary care products in more than 190 countries and territories.

S&P Opinion: Accumulate (★★★★)	Recent Price • 66½	Yield • 2.9%	Earnings vs. Previous Year
	52 Wk Range • 77⅜-56	12-Mo. P/E • 17.0	▲=Up ▼=Down ▶=No Change

Quantitative Evaluations

Outlook
(1 Lowest—5 Highest)
• **3-**

Fair Value
• **64⅞**

Risk
• **Low**

Earn./Div. Rank
• **B+**

Technical Eval.
• **Bullish** since 10/94

Rel. Strength Rank
(1 Lowest—99 Highest)
• **15**

Insider Activity
• **NA**

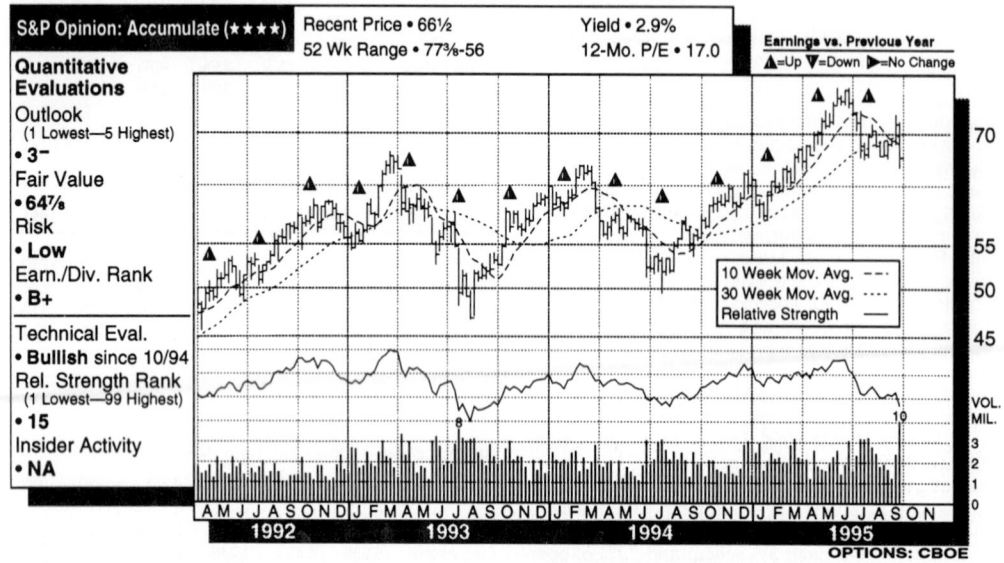

10 Week Mov. Avg. - - -
30 Week Mov. Avg. · · · ·
Relative Strength —

OPTIONS: CBOE

Overview - 27-SEP-95

Despite ongoing pricing pressures in the U.S., sales should continue to advance in 1995, reflecting further overseas expansion, with particular focus on developing countries, and acquisitions. Favorable reactions to new products and existing product relaunches should aid unit growth. Operating margins should expand on a more profitable global product mix and higher sales in more profitable developing countries. Earnings growth, however, will be hurt by reduced profits in Mexico, costs related to changing the distribution at Hill's and various restructuring expenses. Profits will also be hurt by a one-time $369 million ($2.54 a share) aftertax restructuring charge.

Valuation - 27-SEP-95

After reaching an all-time high in mid-1995, the shares of this well-known consumer products company have retreated some 15%. They were hit by the company's announcement in late September that earnings in the second half of 1995 would be lower than street estimates due to various one-time events, even though sales and earnings from most parts of the world were on target. The company also announced restructuring plans that would boost operating efficiencies and improve information technologies. As a result, we lowered our estimates for both 1995 and 1996. Nevertheless, we still like the stock, given the company's well-known global franchise and long-term growth prospects.

Key Stock Statistics

S&P EPS Est. 1995	1.05	Tang. Bk. Value/Share	NM
P/E on S&P Est. 1995	63.3	Beta	0.90
S&P EPS Est. 1996	4.15	Shareholders	44,100
Dividend Rate/Share	1.88	Market cap. (B)	$ 9.6
Shs. outstg. (M)	145.4	Inst. holdings	61%
Avg. daily vol. (M)	0.820	Insider holdings	NA

Value of $10,000 invested 5 years ago: $ 23,844

Fiscal Year Ending Dec. 31

	1995	% Change	1994	% Change	1993	% Change
Revenues (Million $)						
1Q	1,980	12%	1,770	4%	1,703	6%
2Q	2,091	11%	1,891	7%	1,775	-1%
3Q	—	—	1,931	6%	1,823	NM
4Q	—	—	1,996	8%	1,840	4%
Yr.	—	—	7,588	6%	7,141	2%
Income (Million $)						
1Q	156.5	5%	149.6	6%	140.8	24%
2Q	143.2	NM	142.5	NM	142.4	14%
3Q	—	—	151.0	6%	142.8	11%
4Q	—	—	137.1	12%	122.1	11%
Yr.	—	—	580.2	6%	548.1	15%
Earnings Per Share ($)						
1Q	1.05	7%	0.98	15%	0.85	15%
2Q	0.95	2%	0.93	8%	0.86	15%
3Q	E-1.77	NM	1.00	12%	0.89	14%
4Q	E0.82	-10%	0.91	17%	0.78	18%
Yr.	E1.05	-73%	3.82	13%	3.38	16%

Next earnings report expected: early November

Colgate-Palmolive

27-SEP-95

Business Summary - 27-SEP-95

Colgate-Palmolive Company is an international manufacturer and distributor of consumer and industrial products. In 1992, CL acquired for $670 million The Mennen Company, whose brand names include Mennen Speed Stick deodorant, Baby Magic lotion and Mennen Skin Bracer aftershave. In early 1995, the company acquired the Kolynos oral care business from American Home Products for about $1 billion. Kolynos is a multinational business operating in Argentina, Brazil, Colombia, Ecuador, Peru and Uruguay. Contributions to sales and operating profits by region in 1994 were:

	Sales	Profits
North America	31.6%	31.5%
Europe	26.9%	20.8%
Latin America	22.9%	30.7%
Asia & Africa	18.6%	16.9%

Household and personal care products consist of laundry and dishwashing detergents, fabric softeners, cleaners and cleansers, liquid bleach, toothpastes, toothbrushes, bar and liquid soaps, hair care and shave products, oral rinses, deodorants, consumer first-aid products and other items. Oral care products accounted for 26% of sales in 1994 (25% in 1993), followed by personal care 24% (24%), household surface care 17% (17%) and fabric care 18% (19%).

Specialty marketing consists of Hill's pet food and care products, which made up 11% of 1994's sales (11%), and Sterno and other cooking fuel.

Principal global trademarks and trade names include Colgate, Palmolive, Ajax, Fab and Science Diet, in addition to various regional trade names.

Important Developments

Sep. '95—CL announced that results for the second half of 1995 would be lower than analysts' estimates. The company said earnings would be hurt by weakness in Mexico, costs related to changing the distribution at Hill's and expenses associated with restructuring the company. In connection with the restructuring, CL said it would take a one-time $369 million aftertax charge, or $2.54 a share, in the third quarter of 1995. The restructuring, which will occur over a two-year period, will entail closing or reconfiguring 24 of CL's 112 plants and reducing the workforce by 3,000.

Capitalization

Long Term Debt: $2,965,100,000 (6/95).
$4.25 Preferred Stock: $12,500,000.
ESOP Preference Stock: $395,939,375; conv. into 12.2 million com. shs.

Per Share Data ($) — (Year Ended Dec. 31)

	1994	1993	1992	1991	1990	1989
Tangible Bk. Val.	0.88	1.74	7.28	6.92	5.91	8.39
Cash Flow	5.43	4.72	4.14	1.85	3.23	2.70
Earnings	3.82	3.38	2.92	0.77	2.28	1.99
Dividends	1.54	1.34	1.15	1.02	0.90	0.78
Payout Ratio	40%	40%	40%	144%	40%	38%
Prices - High	65⅜	67¼	60⅝	49⅛	37¾	32½
- Low	49½	46¾	45⅛	33⅝	26⅜	22⅛
P/E Ratio - High	17	20	21	64	17	16
- Low	13	14	15	44	12	11

Income Statement Analysis (Million $)

	1994	%Chg	1993	%Chg	1992	%Chg	1991
Revs.	7,588	6%	7,141	2%	7,007	16%	6,060
Oper. Inc.	1,228	10%	1,113	18%	943	27%	744
Depr.	235	12%	210	9%	193	32%	146
Int. Exp.	131	62%	81.0	-7%	87.0	-24%	114
Pretax Inc.	918	6%	864	19%	728	NM	218
Eff. Tax Rate	33%	—	33%	—	35%	—	43%
Net Inc.	580	6%	548	15%	477	NM	125

Balance Sheet & Other Fin. Data (Million $)

	1994	1993	1992	1991	1990	1989
Cash	218	211	221	245	276	524
Curr. Assets	2,178	2,070	1,995	1,858	1,813	1,897
Total Assets	6,142	5,761	5,434	4,511	4,158	3,536
Curr. Liab.	1,529	1,394	1,360	1,262	1,297	989
LT Debt	1,752	1,532	947	851	1,068	1,059
Common Eqty.	1,799	1,851	2,598	1,847	1,348	1,110
Total Cap.	3,870	3,674	3,738	2,928	2,694	2,406
Cap. Exp.	401	364	416	285	385	211
Cash Flow	794	736	649	250	428	367

Ratio Analysis

	1994	1993	1992	1991	1990	1989
Curr. Ratio	1.4	1.5	1.5	1.5	1.4	1.9
% LT Debt of Cap.	45.3	41.7	25.3	29.1	39.7	44.0
% Net Inc.of Revs.	7.6	7.7	6.8	2.1	5.6	5.6
% Ret. on Assets	9.9	10.1	9.2	2.7	8.3	8.5
% Ret. on Equity	31.1	24.7	19.8	6.2	24.4	24.5

Dividend Data —Dividends have been paid since 1895. A dividend reinvestment plan is available. A "poison pill" stock purchase rights plan adopted in 1984 was amended in 1988.

Amt. of Div. $	Date Decl.	Ex-Div. Date	Stock of Record	Payment Date
0.410	Oct. 13	Oct. 19	Oct. 25	Nov. 15 '94
0.410	Jan. 12	Jan. 19	Jan. 25	Feb. 15 '95
0.410	Mar. 09	Apr. 19	Apr. 25	May. 15 '95
0.470	Jul. 13	Jul. 21	Jul. 25	Aug. 15 '95

Data as orig. reptd.; bef. results of disc. opers. and/or spec. items. Per share data adj. for stk. divs. as of ex-div. date. E-Estimated. NA-Not Available. NM-Not Meaningful. NR-Not Ranked.

Office—300 Park Ave., New York, NY 10022. **Tel**—(212) 310-2000. **Chrmn & CEO**—R. Mark. **Pres**—W. S. Shanahan. **CFO**—R. M. Agate. **Sr VP & Secy**—A. D. Hendry. **Investor Contact**—Bina Thompson (212) 310-3072. **Dirs**—V. R. Alden, J. K. Conway, R. E. Ferguson, E. M. Hancock, D. W. Johnson, J. P. Kendall, D. E. Lewis, R. Mark, H. B. Wentz Jr. **Transfer Agent & Registrar**—First Chicago Trust Company of New York, Jersey City, N.J. **Incorporated** in Delaware in 1923. **Empl**-32,800. **S&P Analyst:** Elizabeth Vandeventer

Columbia Gas System

NYSE Symbol **CG**
In S&P 500

15-AUG-95   **Industry:** Utilities-Gas

Summary: CG's subsidiaries are engaged in the production, transmission and distribution of natural gas. In July 1991, the company filed for Chapter 11 bankruptcy protection.

S&P Opinion: Hold (★★★)	Recent Price • 34½	Yield • Nil
	52 Wk Range • 35-22¼	12-Mo. P/E • 8.0

Quantitative Evaluations

Outlook
(1 Lowest—5 Highest)
• **3⁻**

Fair Value
• **34%**

Risk
• **Low**

Earn./Div. Rank
• **D**

Technical Eval.
• **Bullish** since 2/95

Rel. Strength Rank
(1 Lowest—99 Highest)
• **62**

Insider Activity
• **NA**

Earnings vs. Previous Year
▲=Up ▼=Down ▶=No Change

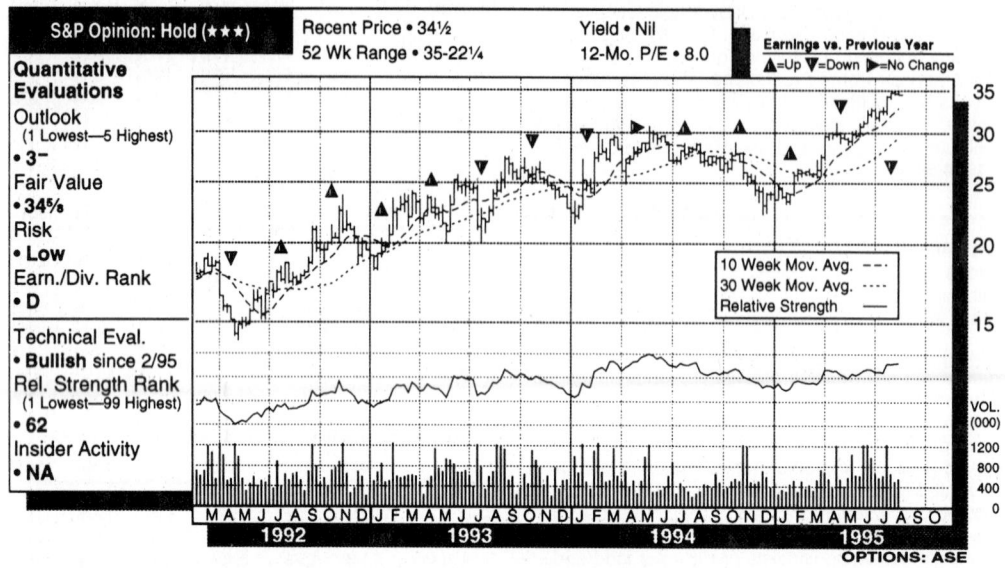

10 Week Mov. Avg. — · —
30 Week Mov. Avg. · · · ·
Relative Strength ——

VOL.
(000)
1200
800
400
0

MAMJJASOND JFMAMJJASOND JFMAMJJASOND JFMAMJJASO
1992   1993   1994   1995

OPTIONS: ASE

Overview - 15-AUG-95

CG anticipates that it could emerge from bankruptcy prior to the end of 1995. Until this occurs, the absence of recorded interest expense on pre-petition debt should boost quarterly results by approximately $0.80 to $0.85 a share. Estimated 1995 earnings of $5.45 a share reflect the impact of this benefit. Bankruptcy-adjusted earnings in 1995 should decrease, reflecting warmer weather in 1995's first half, lower natural gas prices, and reduced oil production. Improved distribution profits will partially offset these negative factors. 1996 share earnings are estimated at $2.60 a share, assuming CG emerges from bankruptcy in 1995. Estimates do not include significant charges ($5 to $10 a share) that CG will incur when it comes out of bankruptcy.

Valuation - 15-AUG-95

CG's shares plummeted and the dividend was omitted after the company filed for bankruptcy protection in 1991. Since 1991, the shares have been steadily rising and have appreciated approximately 47% since the beginning of 1995. The shares are currently trading at about 13 times 1996 estimated earnings of $2.60 a share, assuming that CG emerges from bankruptcy prior to the end of 1995. If the company does come out of bankruptcy in 1995, a dividend could be reinstated in 1996. Based on the recent share price appreciation, the shares are fairly valued and should only be an average market performer over the next 6 to 12 months.

Key Stock Statistics

S&P EPS Est. 1995	5.45	Tang. Bk. Value/Share	31.58
P/E on S&P Est. 1995	6.3	Beta	0.38
S&P EPS Est. 1996	2.60	Shareholders	60,000
Dividend Rate/Share	Nil	Market cap. (B)	$ 1.7
Shs. outstg. (M)	50.6	Inst. holdings	71%
Avg. daily vol. (M)	0.159	Insider holdings	NA

Value of $10,000 invested 5 years ago: $ 7,413

Fiscal Year Ending Dec. 31

	1995	% Change	1994	% Change	1993	% Change
Revenues ()						
1Q	1,052	-9%	1,157	-5%	1,223	18%
2Q	474.7	-9%	520.5	-12%	592.9	14%
3Q	—	—	386.5	-32%	565.5	31%
4Q	—	—	769.0	-24%	1,010	8%
Yr.	—	—	2,833	-16%	3,391	16%
Income ()						
1Q	128.8	-8%	140.2	NM	139.8	NM
2Q	30.90	-35%	47.80	NM	-2.60	NM
3Q	—	—	-15.00	NM	-54.40	42%
4Q	—	—	73.20	5%	69.40	-21%
Yr.	—	—	246.2	62%	152.2	67%
Earnings Per Share ()						
1Q	2.55	-8%	2.77	NM	2.77	NM
2Q	0.61	-36%	0.95	NM	-0.06	NM
3Q	E0.39	NM	-0.30	NM	-1.07	NM
4Q	E1.90	31%	1.45	6%	1.37	-21%
Yr.	E5.45	12%	4.87	62%	3.01	68%

Next earnings report expected: early November

Columbia Gas System

Business Summary - 14-AUG-95

Columbia Gas System is a holding company for sub-sidiaries principally engaged in the production, trans-mission and distribution of natural gas. Other interests include gas marketing, providing supply and fuel man-agement services, the sale of propane, and cogenera-tion projects. On July 31, 1991, CG and its principal pipeline subsidiary, Columbia Gas Transmission Corp., filed for protection under Chapter 11 of the U.S. Bank-ruptcy Code to seek relief from the high-cost gas purchase contracts signed in the early 1980s. Industry segment contributions in 1994 were:

	Revs.	Profits
Gas distribution	56%	34%
Gas transmission	27%	54%
Oil & gas production	6%	8%
Other	11%	4%

CG's five gas distribution units serve more than 1.9 million residential, commercial and industrial custom-ers in Ohio, Pennsylvania, Maryland, Virginia and Ken-tucky. Total gas sales volume in 1994 amounted to 280.5 Bcf, down from 292.3 Bcf in 1993. Gas trans-ported for others totaled 232.5 Bcf, up from 217.5 Bcf.

The company's transmission subsidiaries operate a 23,300 mile pipeline network serving 15 northeastern, mid-Atlantic, midwestern, and southern states and the District of Columbia. CG also operates extensive un-derground storage facilities.

At year-end 1994, proved reserves were estimated at 683.8 Bcf of gas and 12.3 million bbl. of oil and other liquids.

Important Developments

Aug. '95—Columbia Gas Transmission Corp. filed a general rate case that will produce additional annual revenue of about $150 million. The new rates are ex-pected to become effective, subject to refund, Febru-ary 1, 1996. CG's filing proposes a 14.5% return on equity. The increase would be partially offset later in 1996, upon expiration of $90 million in annual surcharges being collected in current rates to reim-burse CG for restructuring and other costs being paid to upstream pipelines under FERC Order 636.

Jul. '95—The Bankruptcy Court for the District of Del-aware scheduled confirmation hearings to begin on November 13, 1995, for the amended Chapter 11 re-organization plans filed by CG and the Columbia Gas Transmission Corp. The company believes that it will emerge from bankruptcy prior to the end of 1995. Sep-arately, Columbia Gas Transmission Corp. said it plans to invest about $350 million, over a three-year period, beginning in 1997, to expand the capacity of its natural gas pipeline system.

Capitalization

Long Term Debt: $4,100,000 (3/95).
Liabilities Subject to Chapter 11 Proceedings: $3,990,700,000.

Per Share Data ()

					(Year Ended Dec. 31)	
	1994	1993	1992	1991	1990	1989
Tangible Bk. Val.	29.03	24.27	21.12	19.77	34.67	35.34
Cash Flow	10.05	7.75	9.08	-10.09	7.47	8.35
Earnings	4.87	3.01	1.79	-15.72	2.21	3.21
Dividends	Nil	Nil	Nil	1.16	2.20	2.00
Payout Ratio	Nil	Nil	Nil	NM	100%	62%
Prices - High	30¾	27½	23⅞	47½	54¾	52¾
- Low	21½	18⅛	14	12⅞	41½	33¾
P/E Ratio - High	6	9	13	NM	25	16
- Low	4	6	8	NM	19	11

Income Statement Analysis ()

	1994	%Chg	1993	%Chg	1992	%Chg	1991
Revs.	2,833	-16%	3,391	16%	2,927	14%	2,577
Oper. Inc.	635	4%	613	15%	531	NM	-800
Depr.	262	9%	240	-35%	368	29%	285
Int. Exp.	15.0	-85%	102	NM	14.0	-90%	140
Pretax Inc.	392	36%	288	79%	161	NM	-1,205
Eff. Tax Rate	37%	—	47%	—	44%	—	NM
Net Inc.	246	62%	152	67%	91.0	NM	-794

Balance Sheet & Other Fin. Data ()

	1994	1993	1992	1991	1990	1989
Cash	1,482	1,340	821	408	8.0	14.0
Curr. Assets	2,485	2,487	2,129	1,825	1,462	1,645
Total Assets	7,165	6,958	6,531	6,332	6,196	5,878
Curr. Liab.	860	1,094	863	829	1,933	1,886
LT Debt	4.3	4.8	5.4	6.1	1,429	1,196
Common Eqty.	1,468	1,227	1,075	1,007	1,758	1,620
Total Cap.	1,855	1,526	1,312	5,176	4,196	3,832
Cap. Exp.	434	355	295	377	628	467
Cash Flow	508	392	459	-509	353	380

Ratio Analysis

	1994	1993	1992	1991	1990	1989
Curr. Ratio	2.9	2.3	2.5	2.2	0.8	0.9
% LT Debt of Cap.	0.2	0.3	0.4	0.5	44.8	42.5
% Net Inc.of Revs.	8.7	4.5	3.1	NM	4.4	4.6
% Ret. on Assets	3.5	2.3	1.4	NM	1.6	2.5
% Ret. on Equity	18.3	13.2	8.7	NM	5.9	9.2

Dividend Data —Dividends, paid since 1943, were omitted in June 1991. The most recent distribution was $0.58 in May 1991.

Data as orig. reptd.; bef. results of disc. opers. and/or spec. items. Per share data adj. for stk. divs. as of ex-div. date. E-Estimated. NA-Not Available. NM-Not Meaningful. NR-Not Ranked.

Office—20 Montchanin Rd., Wilmington, DE 19807. **Tel**—(302) 429-5000. **Chrmn, Pres & CEO**—O. G. Richard III. **SVP & CFO**—M. W. O'Donnell. **SVP & Secy**—D. L. Bell, Jr. **Investor Contact**—Thomas L. Hughes (302-429-5363). **Dirs**—R. F. Albosta, R. H. Beeby, T. S. Blair, W. K. Cadman, J. D. Daly, J. P. Heffernan, R. H. Hillenmeyer, M. T. Hopkins, M. Jozoff, W. E. Lavery, G. P. MacNichol III, G. E. Mayo, D. E. Olesen, E. G. Procope, O. G. Richard III, J. R. Thomas III, W. R. Wilson. **Transfer Agent & Registrar**—Harris Trust Co. of New York, NYC. **Incorporated** in Delaware in 1926. **Empl**-9,935. **S&P Analyst:** Ronald J. Gross

Columbia/HCA Healthcare Corp.

NYSE Symbol **COL**
In S&P 500

23-AUG-95

Industry: Health Care Centers

Summary: Columbia/HCA is the largest domestic provider of health care services, operating about 326 hospitals and 115 outpatient surgery centers in 36 states, England and Switzerland.

S&P Opinion: Accumulate (★★★★)

Recent Price • 49¾	Yield • 0.2%
52 Wk Range • 49⅞-33½	12-Mo. P/E • 24.0

Quantitative Evaluations

Outlook
(1 Lowest—5 Highest)
• **5⁻**

Fair Value
• **65½**

Risk
• **Low**

Earn./Div. Rank
• **NR**

Technical Eval.
• **Bullish** since 12/94

Rel. Strength Rank
(1 Lowest—99 Highest)
• **72**

Insider Activity
• **Neutral**

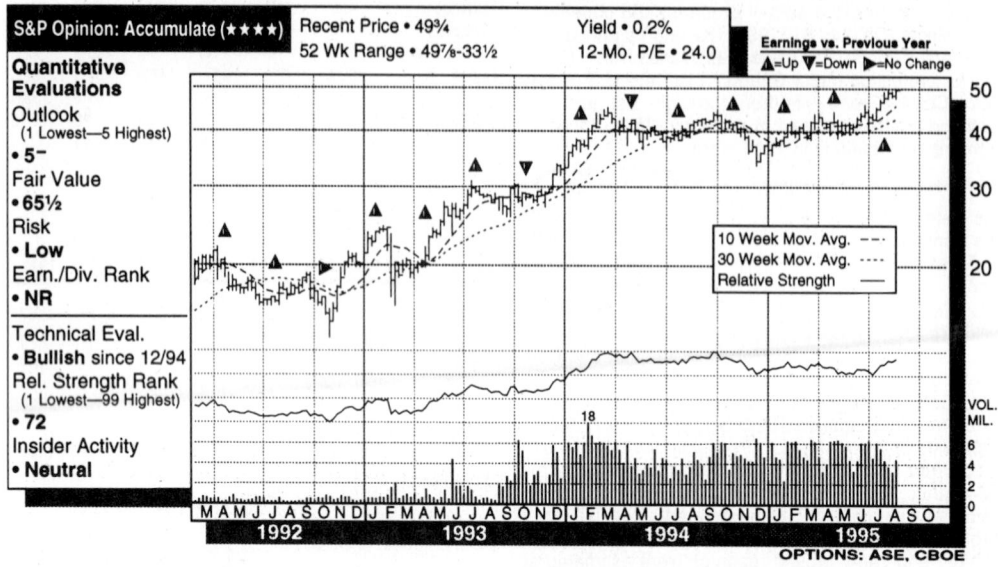

Earnings vs. Previous Year
▲=Up ▼=Down ▶=No Change

10 Week Mov. Avg. ----
30 Week Mov. Avg. ·····
Relative Strength —

VOL. MIL.

OPTIONS: ASE, CBOE

Overview - 22-AUG-95

As the leading provider of health care services in the U.S., Columbia/HCA is well positioned to take advantage of the consolidation of the nation's health care delivery system. The company has aggressively expanded its market presence through acquisitions and joint ventures, and can use its size and operating leverage to negotiate favorable contracts with managed care entities and suppliers. The April 1995 acquisition of HealthTrust Inc. is expected to boost 1995 revenues past $17 billion, and management is seeking to save up to $150 million annually from the elimination of operating redundancies and the refinancing of about $1.7 billion of HealthTrust debt.

Valuation - 22-AUG-95

The release of 1995 second quarter core EPS of $0.70 met our expectations, and provided confidence in our full year estimate of $3.05. In particular, it was encouraging that COL has been able to increase same-facility admissions despite flat admission trends for hospitals nationwide, suggesting that the company's strategies continue to boost market share. Since the beginning of 1995, the company has completed acquisitions and joint ventures of 24 hospitals with 4,700 beds, and has letters of intent for another 22 hospital acquisitions or joint ventures comprising over 5,000 beds. We believe that Columbia/HCA will continue to take market share away from its competitors, and will be the most effective provider in the managed care environment.

Key Stock Statistics

S&P EPS Est. 1995	3.05	Tang. Bk. Value/Share	7.60
P/E on S&P Est. 1995	16.3	Beta	0.97
S&P EPS Est. 1996	3.45	Shareholders	15,600
Dividend Rate/Share	0.12	Market cap. (B)	$ 21.8
Shs. outstg. (M)	442.9	Inst. holdings	57%
Avg. daily vol. (M)	0.755	Insider holdings	1%

Value of $10,000 invested 5 years ago: NA

Fiscal Year Ending Dec. 31

	1995	% Change	1994	% Change	1993	% Change
Revenues (Million $)						
1Q	4,380	58%	2,778	5%	2,654	NM
2Q	4,361	62%	2,689	6%	2,536	NM
3Q	—	—	2,728	10%	2,491	NM
4Q	—	—	2,937	14%	2,571	NM
Yr.	—	—	11,132	9%	10,252	NM
Income (Million $)						
1Q	358.0	161%	137.0	-33%	205.0	NM
2Q	78.00	-62%	205.0	23%	166.0	NM
3Q	—	—	176.0	NM	28.00	NM
4Q	—	—	227.0	29%	176.0	NM
Yr.	—	—	745.0	30%	575.0	NM
Earnings Per Share ($)						
1Q	0.80	100%	0.40	-34%	0.61	126%
2Q	0.70	17%	0.60	22%	0.49	63%
3Q	E0.79	58%	0.50	NM	0.08	-64%
4Q	E0.76	23%	0.62	19%	0.52	37%
Yr.	E3.05	43%	2.13	25%	1.70	44%

Next earnings report expected: early November

Columbia/HCA Healthcare Corp.

Business Summary - 22-AUG-95

Columbia/HCA was formed in February 1994 as a result of a merger between Columbia Healthcare Corporation and HCA-Hospital Corporation of America. In April 1995, the company acquired HealthTrust Inc., an operator of 116 acute care hospitals and other ancillary health care facilities in 22 states. Following the transaction, Columbia/HCA was operating 320 hospitals and over 100 outpatient surgery centers in the U.S., England and Switzerland.

Most of the company's acute care hospitals provide medical and surgical services, including inpatient care, intensive and cardiac care, diagnostic and emergency services, as well as outpatient services such as surgery, laboratory, radiology, respiratory therapy, cardiology and physical therapy. Its psychiatric hospitals provide therapeutic programs tailored to child psychiatric, adolescent psychiatric, alcohol and drug abuse, and adult alcohol or drug abuse patients. Other outpatient or related health care services include ambulatory surgery centers, diagnostic centers, cardiac rehabilitation centers, skilled nursing services and home health/infusion services.

Total hospital admissions in 1994 came to 1,189,400, up from 1,158,400 in 1993. Emergency room visits totaled 3,215,500 (3,139,700). Average daily census in 1994 was 18,524, down from 18,702; the occupancy rate was 44% (45%); and the average length of stay was 5.7 days (5.9). Medicare accounted for 34% of patient revenues in 1994 (34% in 1993), Medicaid for 5% (4%), and other sources for 61% (62%).

Important Developments

Jun. '95—COL refinanced about $1.7 billion of high-cost debt assumed in the acquisition of HealthTrust. Included in the refinancings were $469 million of 10.75% notes, $196 million of 10.25% notes, $291 million of 8.75% debentures and $706 million outstanding on a floating rate credit facility. The company took a charge of $0.21 a share in the second quarter of 1995 related to the transaction, which is expected to lower annual interest charges by $25 million to $30 million.
Apr. '95—Columbia/HCA acquired HealthTrust Inc., an operator of 116 acute care and certain other ancillary health care facilities in 22 states, in return for 82,000,000 COL common shares and the assumption of about $1.7 billion of debt (a total value of about $5 billion).

Capitalization

Long Term Debt: $3,853,000,000 (12/94).
Minority Interest: $258,000,000.
Nonvoting Common Stock: 14,118,999 shs. ($0.01 par).
Shareholders of record: 20,000.

Per Share Data ($)

	1994	1993	1992	1991	1990	1989
Tangible Bk. Val.	7.61	6.65	10.25	6.40	1.30	NA
Cash Flow	3.87	3.33	2.49	2.03	1.65	1.52
Earnings	2.13	1.70	1.18	0.92	0.83	0.48
Dividends	0.09	0.06	Nil	Nil	Nil	NA
Payout Ratio	4%	4%	Nil	Nil	Nil	NA
Prices - High	45¼	33⅞	22	18¾	15½	NA
- Low	33¼	16¼	13¾	9¾	10	NA
P/E Ratio - High	21	20	19	20	19	NA
- Low	16	10	12	11	12	NA

Income Statement Analysis (Million $)

	1994	%Chg	1993	%Chg	1992	%Chg	1991
Revs.	11,132	9%	10,252	NM	807	62%	499
Oper. Inc.	2,214	14%	1,938	NM	115	49%	77.0
Depr.	609	10%	554	NM	28.7	56%	18.4
Int. Exp.	260	-22%	333	NM	49.1	105%	23.9
Pretax Inc.	12.6	-99%	978	NM	52.5	53%	34.3
Eff. Tax Rate	39%	—	40%	—	32%	—	28%
Net Inc.	745	30%	575	NM	25.9	70%	15.2

Balance Sheet & Other Fin. Data (Million $)

	1994	1993	1992	1991	1990	1989
Cash	13.0	224	76.1	29.4	7.9	1.1
Curr. Assets	2,550	2,488	338	166	103	41.0
Total Assets	12,339	10,216	1,072	485	322	138
Curr. Liab.	1,767	1,915	203	98.0	80.0	32.0
LT Debt	3,853	3,335	539	230	172	90.0
Common Eqty.	5,022	3,471	265	118	41.0	5.0
Total Cap.	9,612	7,420	851	380	233	108
Cap. Exp.	975	1,042	344	96.0	108	10.0
Cash Flow	1,354	1,129	54.6	33.6	19.5	10.0

Ratio Analysis

	1994	1993	1992	1991	1990	1989
Curr. Ratio	1.4	1.3	1.7	1.7	1.3	1.3
% LT Debt of Cap.	40.1	44.9	63.3	60.5	74.0	83.3
% Net Inc.of Revs.	6.7	5.6	3.2	3.0	3.4	4.1
% Ret. on Assets	6.4	4.8	3.0	3.4	4.3	NA
% Ret. on Equity	17.0	16.6	12.0	17.6	41.7	NA

Dividend Data —Cash dividends were initiated in November 1993. Recent payments were as follows:

Amt. of Div. $	Date Decl.	Ex-Div. Date	Stock of Record	Payment Date
0.030	Aug. 11	Oct. 26	Nov. 01	Dec. 01 '94
0.030	Dec. 22	Jan. 26	Feb. 01	Mar. 01 '95
0.030	Feb. 13	Apr. 25	May. 01	Jun. 01 '95
0.030	Jun. 13	Jul. 28	Aug. 01	Sep. 01 '95
0.030	Aug. 14	Oct. 30	Nov. 01	Dec. 01 '95

Data as orig. reptd.; bef. results of disc. opers. and/or spec. items. Per share data adj. for stk. divs. as of ex-div. date.
E-Estimated. NA-Not Available. NM-Not Meaningful. NR-Not Ranked.

Office—One Park Plaza, Nashville, Tennessee 37203. **Tel**—(615) 327-9551. **Chrmn**—T. F. Frist, Jr. **Pres & CEO**—R. L. Scott. **COO**—D. T. Vandewater. **SVP-CFO & Treas**—D. C. Colby. **Secy**—Joan O. Kroger. **Investor Contact**—Victor L. Campbell (615-320-2053). **Dirs**—M. Averhoff, T. F. Frist, Jr., J. D. Grissom, C. J. Kane, J. W. Landrum, T. M. Long, D. D. Moore, R. W. Moorhead III, C. F. Pollard, C. E. Reichardt, F. S. Royal, R. L. Scott, R. D. Walter, W. T. Young. **Registrar & Transfer Agent**—National City Bank, Cleveland. **Incorporated** in Nevada in 1990. **Empl**-190,000.
S&P Analyst: Robert M. Gold

Comcast Corp.

NASDAQ Symbol **CMCSK**

In S&P 500

30-OCT-95 | Industry: Broadcasting

Summary: Comcast is the fifth largest cable television system opera-tor in the U.S. Through AMCELL, it is a major provider of cellular telephone services in the Northeast.

S&P Opinion: Accumulate (★★★★)

Recent Price • 18⅞	Yield • 0.5%
52 Wk Range • 22⅝-13¾	12-Mo. P/E • NM

Quantitative Evaluations

Outlook
(1 Lowest—5 Highest)
• **NA**

Fair Value
• **NA**

Risk
• **Average**

Earn./Div. Rank
• **B-**

Technical Eval.
• **Bearish** since 7/95

Rel. Strength Rank
(1 Lowest—99 Highest)
• **30**

Insider Activity
• **NA**

Earnings vs. Previous Year
▲=Up ▼=Down ▶=No Change

10 Week Mov. Avg. – – –
30 Week Mov. Avg. ·····
Relative Strength ——

3-for-2

OPTIONS: Ph

Overview - 30-OCT-95

Revenues and cash flow should advance in 1995, re-flecting acquisitions, strong gains in cellular customers, and the favorable impact on cable revenues of eased FCC rate restrictions. Sharp increases in book charges and interest expense will also reflect acquisi-tions. The outlook for revenues and cash flow in 1996 is even more favorable, reflecting a further easing in regulatory restraints, gains in subscribers (partly re-flecting the Scripps acquisition), and growing demand for a la carte cable services. Ongoing expansion in demand for cellular services will also boost revenues and cash flow. Substantial noncash charges and in-terest costs will lead to further net losses. Ongoing investments in new technologies, programming and overseas expansion have strong promise for future growth and profitability.

Valuation - 30-OCT-95

The stock, having settled back somewhat from a 52-week peak reached in midsummer, has several factors in its favor which should boost performance in the months ahead. The passage of deregulatory leg-islation in Congress in 1995 gives strong promise that some form of cable deregulation will become effective in late 1996. The bills provide for the relaxation of cable rate restrictions, but at the same time, unfetter restraints against telephone competition. Meanwhile, earlier FCC rate relief will serve to boost revenues in 1995, 1996 and 1997. With cash flow growth ex-pected to exceed 15% on average, the shares should provide capital appreciation over the long term.

Key Stock Statistics

S&P EPS Est. 1995	-0.35	Tang. Bk. Value/Share	NM
P/E on S&P Est. 1995	NM	Beta	1.20
Dividend Rate/Share	0.09	Shareholders	4,300
Shs. outstg. (M)	239.8	Market cap. (B)	$ 4.5
Avg. daily vol. (M)	0.870	Inst. holdings	64%
		Insider holdings	NA

Value of $10,000 invested 5 years ago: $ 18,130

Fiscal Year Ending Dec. 31

	1995	% Change	1994	% Change	1993	% Change
Revenues (Million $)						
1Q	663.6	102%	328.7	1%	325.2	65%
2Q	823.6	142%	340.6	NM	340.1	54%
3Q	—	—	345.7	3%	335.4	52%
4Q	—	—	360.2	7%	337.5	29%
Yr.	—	—	1,375	3%	1,338	49%
Income (Million $)						
1Q	-0.63	NM	-15.78	NM	-23.86	NM
2Q	-29.29	NM	-12.76	NM	-17.13	NM
3Q	—	—	-17.25	NM	-35.66	NM
4Q	—	—	-29.55	NM	-22.23	NM
Yr.	—	—	-75.33	NM	-98.87	NM
Earnings Per Share ($)						
1Q	Nil	—	-0.07	NM	-0.11	NM
2Q	-0.12	NM	-0.05	NM	-0.08	NM
3Q	E-0.12	NM	-0.07	NM	-0.17	NM
4Q	E-0.11	NM	-0.13	NM	-0.10	NM
Yr.	E-0.35	NM	-0.32	NM	-0.46	NM

Next earnings report expected: early November

Comcast Corp.

30-OCT-95

Business Summary - 30-OCT-95

Contributions by business segment (profits in millions) in 1994 were:

	Service Income	Oper. Profits
Cable communications	77%	$288.0
Cellular	21%	26.4
Other	2%	-74.6

Based on the 3.0 million subscribers in owned or managed systems as of February 28, 1995, Comcast is the fifth largest U.S. cable system operator. In addition, the company has equity investments in Nextel Communications, Teleport Communications Group, the QVC home shopping network, Turner Broadcasting, Viewer's Choice, E! Entertainment and Music Choice. Comcast is also an equity participant in ventures for cable and telephone systems in Birmingham, London and Cambridge, England. In March 1995, Comcast entered several joint ventures with TCI, Sprint Corp., and Cox Communications to provide wireless and wireline telephony services in the U.S. and elsewhere.

Through American Cellular Network Corp. (AMCELL), cellular telephone services are provided in New Jersey, Delaware, Illinois and Pennsylvania, covering a population of more than 7.5 million.

Important Developments

Oct. '95—Comcast agreed to purchase E. W. Scripps Co.'s cable properties serving nearly 800,000 subscribers in exchange for roughly 78.5 million shares of Comcast's Class A special common stock, valued at about $1.575 billion. The transaction, which is expected to close in the third quarter of 1996, would make Comcast the third largest cable system operator in the U.S.

Dec. '94—The company acquired Maclean Hunter Ltd.'s U.S. cable operations for $1.27 billion in cash. The purchase included 550,000 subscribers, mostly in Fort Lauderdale, Detroit and New Jersey. Comcast also announced that it had formed a joint venture with California Public Employees Retirement Systems (CalPERS) to co-own the purchased systems; the company owns 55% and CalPERS 45%.

Capitalization

Long Term Debt: $6,399,519,000 (6/95), incl. $742,287,000 of notes and debs. conv. into Cl. A spl. com. at $11.02 to $24.50 a sh.

Cl. A Common Stock: 39,074,706 shs. ($1 par). Institutions hold 100%.
Shareholders: 1,854 of record (2/95).

Cl. A Special Common Stock: 191,916,990 shs. ($1 par); nonvoting. Institutions hold 67%.
Shareholders: 2,407 of record (2/95).

Cl. B Common Stock: 8,786,250 shs. ($1 par); 100% owned by R. J. Roberts (controls 78% of the voting stock).

Per Share Data ($)

(Year Ended Dec. 31)

	1994	1993	1992	1991	1990	1989
Tangible Bk. Val.	-3.04	-3.93	-0.89	0.10	-0.13	0.99
Cash Flow	1.11	1.13	0.07	0.05	-0.10	-0.09
Earnings	-0.32	-0.46	-1.08	-0.87	-1.05	-0.93
Dividends	0.09	0.09	0.09	0.09	0.08	0.06
Payout Ratio	NM	NM	NM	NM	NM	NM
Prices - High	24	28⅛	13⅛	12⅛	11¾	13¼
- Low	14	11⅝	9	7¼	5⅛	7¼
P/E Ratio - High	NM	NM	NM	NM	NM	NM
- Low	NM	NM	NM	NM	NM	NM

Income Statement Analysis (Million $)

	1994	%Chg	1993	%Chg	1992	%Chg	1991
Revs.	1,375	3%	1,338	49%	900	25%	721
Oper. Inc.	576	-5%	606	53%	397	28%	309
Depr.	336	-2%	342	47%	232	41%	164
Int. Exp.	313	-10%	347	29%	268	31%	205
Pretax Inc.	-85.0	NM	-84.0	NM	-157	NM	-98.0
Eff. Tax Rate	NM	—	NM	—	NM	—	NM
Net Inc.	-75.0	NM	-99.0	NM	-217	NM	-155

Balance Sheet & Other Fin. Data (Million $)

	1994	1993	1992	1991	1990	1989
Cash	465	680	348	596	206	273
Curr. Assets	609	777	429	645	251	314
Total Assets	6,763	4,948	4,272	2,794	2,457	2,583
Curr. Liab.	661	595	392	264	187	157
LT Debt	4,811	4,163	3,974	2,165	2,002	1,998
Common Eqty.	-726	-869	-181	19.0	-22.0	168
Total Cap.	5,475	3,292	3,792	2,472	2,226	2,376
Cap. Exp.	270	NA	NA	NA	92.0	90.0
Cash Flow	261	243	14.0	9.0	-17.0	-15.0

Ratio Analysis

	1994	1993	1992	1991	1990	1989
Curr. Ratio	0.9	1.3	1.1	2.4	1.3	2.0
% LT Debt of Cap.	87.9	126.4	104.8	87.6	89.9	84.1
% Net Inc.of Revs.	NM	NM	NM	NM	NM	NM
% Ret. on Assets	NM	NM	NM	NM	NM	NM
% Ret. on Equity	NM	NM	NM	NM	NM	NM

Dividend Data —Dividends have been paid since 1977.

Amt. of Div. $	Date Decl.	Ex-Div. Date	Stock of Record	Payment Date
0.023	Sep. 20	Nov. 25	Dec. 01	Dec. 22 '94
0.023	Dec. 15	Feb. 27	Mar. 03	Mar. 24 '95
0.023	Mar. 20	May. 26	Jun. 02	Jun. 23 '95
0.023	Jun. 21	Aug. 30	Sep. 01	Sep. 22 '95
0.023	Sep. 18	Dec. 05	Dec. 07	Dec. 28 '95

Data as orig. reptd.; bef. results of disc. opers. and/or spec. items. Per share data adj. for stk. divs. as of ex-div. date.
E-Estimated. NA-Not Available. NM-Not Meaningful. NR-Not Ranked.

Office—1500 Market St., Philadelphia, PA 19102-2148. **Tel**—(215) 665-1700. **Chrmn**—R. J. Roberts. **Vice Chrmn**—J. A. Brodsky. **Pres**—B. L. Roberts. **SVP, Treas & Investor Contact**—John R. Alchin (215-981-7503). **SVP & Secy**—D. L. Wang. **Dirs**—D. Aaron, G. G. Amsterdam, S. M. Bonovitz, J. A. Brodsky, J. L. Castle, B. L. Roberts, R. J. Roberts, B. C. Watson, I. A. Wechsler, A. Wexler. **Transfer Agent**—Bank of New York, NYC. **Incorporated** in Pennsylvania in 1969. **Empl**-5,391. **S&P Analyst:** William H. Donald

Community Psychiatric Centers

NYSE Symbol **CMY**
In S&P 500

31-JUL-95

Industry: Health Care Centers

Summary: This company delivers a broad range of psychiatric and long-term critical care services through 63 separately licensed facilities in the U.S., Puerto Rico and the U.K.

S&P Opinion: Accumulate (★★★★)	Recent Price • 12¾	Yield • Nil
	52 Wk Range • 15¾-9¼	12-Mo. P/E • 24.5

Quantitative Evaluations

Outlook (1 Lowest—5 Highest)
• **4**

Fair Value
• **14½**

Risk
• **Average**

Earn./Div. Rank
• **B**

Technical Eval.
• **Bearish** since 3/93

Rel. Strength Rank (1 Lowest—99 Highest)
• **59**

Insider Activity
• **Favorable**

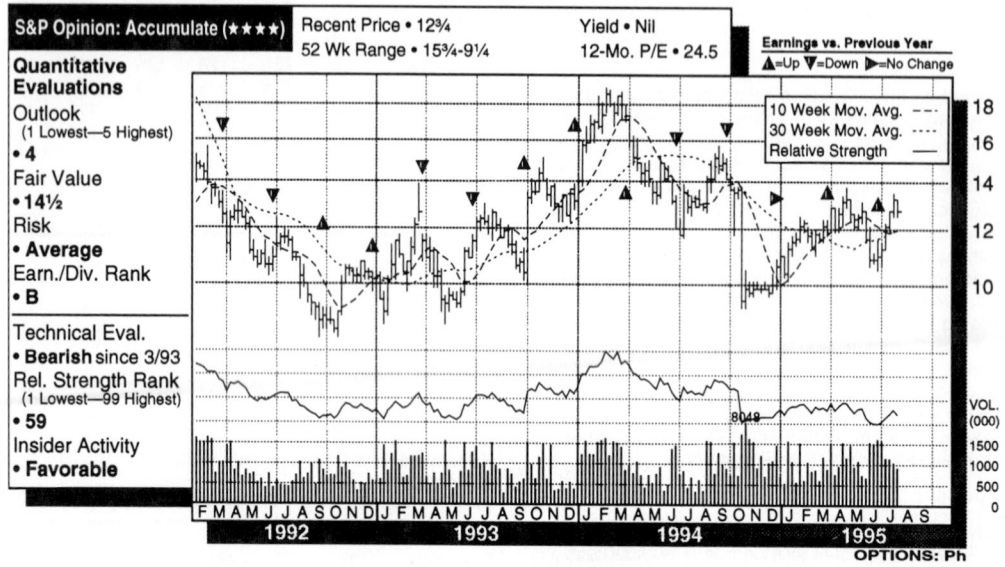

Earnings vs. Previous Year
▲=Up ▼=Down ▶=No Change

10 Week Mov. Avg. – –
30 Week Mov. Avg. - - - -
Relative Strength —

OPTIONS: Ph

Overview - 31-JUL-95

Revenue growth in the second half of fiscal 1995 and into 1996 will come primarily from the Transitional Hospitals Corp. (THC) unit, together with improving business trends in U.K. psychiatric operations. Results from the domestic psychiatric business are likely to remain under pressure on lower lengths of stay. Although costs related to the development of THC continue to be incurred, this business contributed profits of $0.06 a share in the first half of fiscal 1995 on revenues of $90 million (35% of total operating revenues). THC will become increasingly visible as the year progresses.

Valuation - 31-JUL-95

Results substantially exceeded expectations in the second quarter of fiscal 1995, strengthening our view that CMY is one of the more attractive companies in the health care services sector. CMY is changing its focus from psychiatric to long-term hospital care, which offers superior growth and wider operating margins. The U.S. psychiatric business will remain under pressure from managed care entities, restricting overall profit gains. Despite growing pains, THC began to make a positive contribution in the 1995 first half, and we expect momentum to build throughout the year. The shares are currently trading at 18X our revised fiscal 1995 EPS estimate, well below the projected growth rate.

Key Stock Statistics

S&P EPS Est. 1995	0.70	Tang. Bk. Value/Share	10.09
P/E on S&P Est. 1995	18.2	Beta	1.48
S&P EPS Est. 1996	0.85	Shareholders	2,400
Dividend Rate/Share	Nil	Market cap. (B)	$0.557
Shs. outstg. (M)	43.7	Inst. holdings	80%
Avg. daily vol. (M)	0.217	Insider holdings	NA

Value of $10,000 invested 5 years ago: $ 4,672

Fiscal Year Ending Nov. 30

	1995	% Change	1994	% Change	1993	% Change
Revenues (Million $)						
1Q	120.4	30%	92.53	9%	84.69	1%
2Q	136.7	26%	108.8	26%	86.15	-8%
3Q	—	—	105.7	32%	80.01	NM
4Q	—	—	118.4	36%	87.03	NM
Yr.	—	—	424.0	26%	335.6	-3%
Income (Million $)						
1Q	5.93	NM	0.63	NM	-37.94	NM
2Q	9.18	NM	2.39	-32%	3.49	-73%
3Q	—	—	1.67	-59%	4.07	94%
4Q	—	—	5.54	NM	5.49	NM
Yr.	—	—	10.22	NM	-24.89	NM
Earnings Per Share ($)						
1Q	0.14	NM	0.01	NM	-0.88	NM
2Q	0.21	NM	0.06	-25%	0.08	-72%
3Q	E0.15	—	0.04	-56%	0.09	80%
4Q	E0.20	—	0.13	NM	0.13	NM
Yr.	E0.70	—	0.24	NM	-0.58	NM

Next earnings report expected: early October

Community Psychiatric Centers

Business Summary - 31-JUL-95

Community Psychiatric Centers is one of the largest publicly owned operators of acute psychiatric hospitals. It also operates a growing chain of long-term critical care hospitals through its Transitional Hospitals Corp. (THC) division. Psychiatric facilities accounted for 76% of total revenues in fiscal 1994, and THC for 24%.

As of February 1995, CMY operated 48 psychiatric centers with 4,062 licensed beds, located in California (11 centers), 16 other states (24 units), Puerto Rico (one) and the U.K. (13). The units offer drug therapy, alcoholism rehabilitation, and occupational and recreational therapy, generally under the supervision of the patient's doctor.

Total patient days of service in fiscal 1994 totaled 744,657, up from 705,069 in fiscal 1993. Admissions came to 43,919 (39,563). Net revenue per patient day averaged $433.66 ($450.25); average length of stay was 14.2 days (15.6). Patient days in established hospitals (open more than 12 months) totaled 724,078 (656,154).

About 58% of U.S. acute psychiatric revenues in fiscal 1994 were derived from HMOs, PPOs and other managed care providers; 16% from payments from patients and their private insurance plans; 20% from Medicare and Medicaid; and 6% from the CHAMPUS program for military personnel.

Transitional Hospitals Corp. (THC) operates 14 long-term critical care facilities in 11 states throughout the U.S. These units offer care for patients stable enough to leave an acute care hospital, but too ill to return home or move to a nursing facility. Total patient days in THC facilities in fiscal 1994 amounted to 100,485 (23,011 in fiscal 1993). Admissions totaled 2,400 (478), net revenue per patient day amounted to $1,005.43 ($787.49), and average length of stay was 41.0 days (63.7).

Important Developments

Jun. '95—CMY reported net earnings in the second quarter of fiscal 1995 of $7.7 million ($0.18 a share), on revenues of $136.7 million, before a special gain of $1.5 million ($0.03) related to the resolution of certain U.S. psychiatric assets previously restructured in 1993. Highlights of the quarter included strong growth in the U.K. psychiatric division on increased bed capacity, rising patient census levels and increased average revenue per patient day, and contributions from the Transitional Hospitals Corp. division (revenues of $49.1 million and net earnings of $0.03 a share), on higher patient volume and enhanced Medicare reimbursement.

Capitalization

Long Term Debt: $48,419,000 (2/95).

Per Share Data ($)

(Year Ended Nov. 30)

	1994	1993	1992	1991	1990	1989
Tangible Bk. Val.	9.71	9.44	10.16	10.18	9.59	8.07
Cash Flow	0.66	-0.29	0.80	1.23	2.02	1.75
Earnings	0.24	-0.58	0.52	0.98	1.80	1.56
Dividends	0.01	0.18	0.36	0.36	0.36	0.36
Payout Ratio	4%	NM	67%	37%	20%	23%
Prices - High	19	15⅛	15⅝	40	30⅝	35
- Low	9¼	8¾	8⅜	10⅝	19¾	22¼
P/E Ratio - High	79	NM	30	41	17	22
- Low	39	NM	16	11	11	14

Income Statement Analysis (Million $)

	1994	%Chg	1993	%Chg	1992	%Chg	1991
Revs.	424	26%	336	-2%	344	-12%	393
Oper. Inc.	36.0	24%	29.0	-33%	43.0	-64%	119
Depr.	18.6	48%	12.6	NM	12.6	6%	11.9
Int. Exp.	4.8	82%	2.7	9%	2.4	-2%	2.5
Pretax Inc.	17.0	NM	-39.0	NM	37.0	-48%	71.0
Eff. Tax Rate	41%	—	NM	—	37%	—	36%
Net Inc.	10.2	NM	-24.9	NM	23.1	-49%	45.3

Balance Sheet & Other Fin. Data (Million $)

	1994	1993	1992	1991	1990	1989
Cash	51.0	35.6	67.8	79.5	50.4	63.9
Curr. Assets	184	150	167	199	191	161
Total Assets	605	530	541	570	552	475
Curr. Liab.	80.5	55.7	33.1	30.0	37.4	37.7
LT Debt	69.1	40.7	26.3	27.2	28.6	29.7
Common Eqty.	440	422	451	484	461	387
Total Cap.	523	473	502	535	509	433
Cap. Exp.	48.8	59.1	19.4	23.5	46.4	50.4
Cash Flow	28.9	-12.3	35.8	57.2	93.9	81.0

Ratio Analysis

	1994	1993	1992	1991	1990	1989
Curr. Ratio	2.3	2.7	5.0	6.6	5.1	4.3
% LT Debt of Cap.	13.2	8.6	5.2	5.1	5.6	6.9
% Net Inc.of Revs.	2.4	NM	6.7	11.5	22.2	22.5
% Ret. on Assets	1.8	NM	4.3	8.1	16.2	15.0
% Ret. on Equity	2.4	NM	5.1	9.6	19.7	18.6

Dividend Data (Quarterly dividends, paid since 1974, were omitted in April 1993. Special dividends of $0.01 a share were paid in March 1994 and April 1995.)

Amt. of Div. $	Date Decl.	Ex-Div. Date	Stock of Record	Payment Date
0.010	Mar. 07	Mar. 27	Mar. 31	Apr. 14 '95

Data as orig. reptd.; bef. results of disc. opers. and/or spec. items. Per share data adj. for stk. divs. as of ex-div. date. E-Estimated. NA-Not Available. NM-Not Meaningful. NR-Not Ranked.

Office—6600 W. Charleston Blvd., Suite 118, Las Vegas, NV 89102. **Tel**—(702) 259-3600. **Chrmn & CEO**—R. L. Conte. **Secy**—R. Ooley. **EVP & CFO**—Wendy L. Simpson. **Investor Contact**—Suzanne S. Hovdey. **Dirs**—R.L. Conte, D.L. Dennis, H. Fleischmann, J.H. Lindheimer, D.L. Shires, Jr., R.L. Thomas, D.A. Wakefield. **Transfer Agent & Registrar**—Chemical Trust Co. of California, LA. **Incorporated** in California in 1962; reincorporated in Nevada in 1972. **Empl**-9,775. **S&P Analyst:** Robert M. Gold

COMPAQ Computer

NYSE Symbol **CPQ**
In S&P 500

25-OCT-95

Industry:
Data Processing

Summary: Compaq is the leading worldwide manufacturer of desktop and portable computers and PC servers. Products are sold in more than 100 countries through some 38,000 marketing locations.

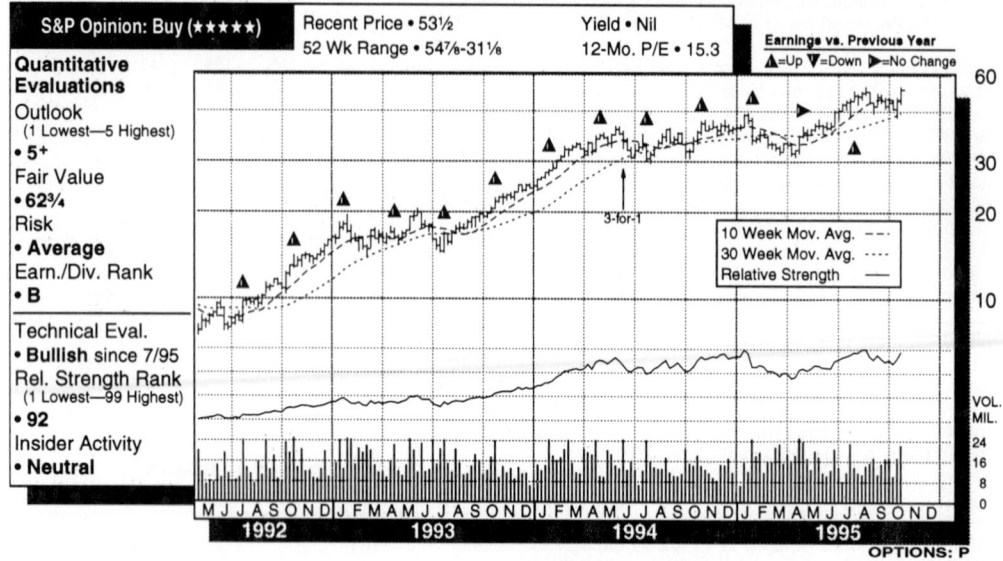

S&P Opinion: Buy (★★★★★)	Recent Price • 53½	Yield • Nil
	52 Wk Range • 54⅞-31⅛	12-Mo. P/E • 15.3

Earnings vs. Previous Year
▲=Up ▼=Down ▶=No Change

Quantitative Evaluations

Outlook
(1 Lowest—5 Highest)
• **5+**

Fair Value
• **62¾**

Risk
• **Average**

Earn./Div. Rank
• **B**

Technical Eval.
• **Bullish** since 7/95

Rel. Strength Rank
(1 Lowest—99 Highest)
• **92**

Insider Activity
• **Neutral**

10 Week Mov. Avg. ---
30 Week Mov. Avg. ....
Relative Strength —

3-for-1

M J J A S O N D J F M A M J J A S O N D J F M A M J J A S O N D J F M A M J J A S O N D
1992   1993   1994   1995

VOL. MIL.

OPTIONS: P

Overview - 25-OCT-95

Revenue growth is projected to remain brisk through 1996, as the outlook for demand in desktops, portables and servers remains strong. Compaq is particularly well positioned in desktops and servers, where it features a completely refreshed product line. The company's portable business should also rebound on the strength of new products. Gross margins are expected to remain under pressure, reflecting continued competitive pricing in desktop and portable markets, offset by CPQ's ongoing dominance in the highly profitable server segment. An upside margin surprise is possible depending on the extent of efficiencies realized from a new build-to-order strategy. Operating costs should remain well controlled.

Valuation - 25-OCT-95

After lowering our opinion to accumulate from buy in early July due to near-term uncertainty, we reinstated our buy recommendation on the shares in mid-July on the strength of second quarter earnings and management's bullish comments about second half prospects. While third quarter results were a little softer than we expected, we believe future prospects remain very bright. CPQ is expected to be a leading beneficiary of the strong acceptance of Windows 95 and strong PC fundamentals in general. As a result, we continue to strongly recommended the shares for their capital appreciation potential.

Key Stock Statistics

S&P EPS Est. 1995	3.90	Tang. Bk. Value/Share	15.81
P/E on S&P Est. 1995	13.7	Beta	1.40
S&P EPS Est. 1996	4.65	Shareholders	7,800
Dividend Rate/Share	Nil	Market cap. (B)	$ 14.4
Shs. outstg. (M)	264.2	Inst. holdings	72%
Avg. daily vol. (M)	3.318	Insider holdings	NA

Value of $10,000 invested 5 years ago: $ 40,377

Fiscal Year Ending Dec. 31

	1995	% Change	1994	% Change	1993	% Change
Revenues (Million $)						
1Q	2,959	30%	2,278	41%	1,611	106%
2Q	3,501	40%	2,499	53%	1,632	97%
3Q	3,594	27%	2,838	63%	1,746	64%
4Q	—	—	3,251	48%	2,202	55%
Yr.	—	—	10,866	51%	7,191	75%
Income (Million $)						
1Q	216.0	1%	213.0	108%	102.4	126%
2Q	246.0	17%	210.0	105%	102.3	NM
3Q	245.0	22%	201.0	88%	106.8	116%
4Q	—	—	243.0	61%	151.0	69%
Yr.	—	—	867.0	88%	462.0	117%
Earnings Per Share ($)						
1Q	0.80	NM	0.80	95%	0.41	132%
2Q	0.90	15%	0.78	93%	0.40	NM
3Q	0.89	19%	0.75	79%	0.42	114%
4Q	E1.25	39%	0.90	55%	0.58	57%
Yr.	E3.90	21%	3.23	77%	1.82	112%

Next earnings report expected: late January

COMPAQ Computer

Business Summary - 25-OCT-95

COMPAQ manufactures personal computers, PC server systems and related products. CPQ products are currently sold in more than 100 countries by over 38,000 organizations, including authorized retailers, value-added resellers (VARs), system integrators, distributors and third party maintainers.

	1994	1993
Desktops	58%	53%
Portables	25%	35%
Servers	17%	12%

Operations outside the U.S. and Canada contributed 50% of revenues in 1994, up from 49% in 1993.

Desktop products include the Deskpro product line, which is designed to deliver high-performance and advanced features to the business user in a networked PC environment; the ProLinea family of products, the leading unit seller in both 1994 and 1993, is a value offering targeted at the business and small office, home office (SOHO) market; and the Presario line of personal computers targeted at the consumer and SOHO markets. In April 1995, CPQ unveiled 12 new Presario models, including the first Pentium-based machines. In March, more than 100 new models of the ProLinea and Deskpro product lines were introduced.

Portable systems include the Compaq Contura family, the company's most popular product line in 1994, which includes the Contura Aero subnotebook computer and the Contura 400 with tilted keyboard and wrist rest. The LTE Elite family is a family of five high-performance notebook computers.

Server offerings include the high-end Rack-Mountable Proliant family and the best-selling ProSignia line for more general-purpose computing needs.

System options include add-on video display monitors, memory upgrades, storage and back-up devices, docking stations, and communication products.

Manufacturing operations are located in Houston, Texas; Erksine, Scotland; Singapore; Jaguariuna, Brazil; and Sheenzhen, China.

Important Developments

Oct. '95—CPQ agreed to acquire Thomas-Conrad Corp., a privately held maker of network interface cards and hubs. Terms were not disclosed. The company also formed an Internetworking Products Group as a result of this planned acquisition. Separately, CPQ selected Digital Equipment as its preferred service and support provider.

Capitalization

Long Term Debt: $300,000,000 (9/95).
Options: To buy 29,388,000 shs. (12/31/94).

Per Share Data ($)

(Year Ended Dec. 31)

	1994	1993	1992	1991	1990	1989
Tangible Bk. Val.	14.07	10.49	8.38	7.64	7.20	4.97
Cash Flow	3.85	2.43	1.50	1.12	2.20	1.58
Earnings	3.23	1.82	0.86	0.50	1.71	1.30
Dividends	Nil	Nil	Nil	Nil	Nil	Nil
Payout Ratio	Nil	Nil	Nil	Nil	Nil	Nil
Prices - High	42⅛	25¼	16⅝	24¾	22⅝	18¾
- Low	24⅛	13⅞	7⅜	7⅜	11⅞	9⅞
P/E Ratio - High	13	14	19	50	13	14
- Low	7	8	9	15	7	8

Income Statement Analysis (Million $)

	1994	%Chg	1993	%Chg	1992	%Chg	1991
Revs.	10,866	51%	7,191	75%	4,100	25%	3,271
Oper. Inc.	1,434	69%	847	76%	482	3%	469
Depr.	168	8%	155	-3%	159	-3%	164
Int. Exp.	74.0	17%	63.0	33%	47.5	8%	43.9
Pretax Inc.	1,172	90%	616	98%	311	79%	174
Eff. Tax Rate	26%	—	25%	—	31%	—	25%
Net Inc.	867	88%	462	117%	213	63%	131

Balance Sheet & Other Fin. Data (Million $)

	1994	1993	1992	1991	1990	1989
Cash	471	627	357	452	435	161
Curr. Assets	5,158	3,291	2,319	1,783	1,688	1,312
Total Assets	6,166	4,084	3,142	2,826	2,718	2,090
Curr. Liab.	2,013	1,244	960	639	644	564
LT Debt	300	Nil	Nil	73.0	73.0	274
Common Eqty.	3,674	2,654	2,007	1,931	1,859	1,172
Total Cap.	4,153	2,840	2,183	2,188	2,074	1,526
Cap. Exp.	357	145	159	160	325	362
Cash Flow	1,035	617	372	295	590	417

Ratio Analysis

	1994	1993	1992	1991	1990	1989
Curr. Ratio	2.6	2.6	2.4	2.8	2.6	2.3
% LT Debt of Cap.	7.2	Nil	Nil	3.3	3.5	17.9
% Net Inc.of Revs.	8.0	6.4	5.2	4.0	12.6	11.6
% Ret. on Assets	16.7	12.5	7.3	4.8	18.2	18.0
% Ret. on Equity	27.0	19.4	11.1	7.0	28.9	33.3

Dividend Data —No cash dividends have been paid on the common stock, and future earnings are expected to be retained for use in operations. A 3-for-1 split was effected on June 7, 1994. A "poison pill" stock purchase right was issued in 1989.

Data as orig. reptd.; bef. results of disc. opers. and/or spec. items. Per share data adj. for stk. divs. as of ex-div. date. E-Estimated. NA-Not Available. NM-Not Meaningful. NR-Not Ranked.

Office—20555 SH 249, Houston, TX 77070. **Tel**—(713) 370-0670. **Pres & CEO**—E. Pfeiffer. **SVP-Fin & CFO**—D. J. White. **SVP & Secy**—W. D. Fargo. **Dirs**— B. M. Rosen (Chrmn), R. T. Enloe III, G. H. Heilmeier, G. E. R. Kinnear II, P. N. Larson, K. L. Lay, E. Pfeiffer, K. Roman. **Co-Transfer Agents & Registrars**—Co. itself; BancBoston Trust Co. of New York. **Incorporated** in Delaware in 1982. **Empl**-14,372. **S&P Analyst:** John D. Coyle, CFA

Computer Associates Int'l

NYSE Symbol **CA**
In S&P 500

17-AUG-95

Industry:
Data Processing

Summary: This company develops, markets and supports standardized software products, including systems software, database management systems and applications software.

S&P Opinion: Buy (★★★★★)

Recent Price • 73⅞	Yield • 0.3%
52 Wk Range • 77½-37½	12-Mo. P/E • 20.4

Quantitative Evaluations

Outlook
(1 Lowest—5 Highest)
• **5+**

Fair Value
• **88¼**

Risk
• **Average**

Earn./Div. Rank
• **B+**

Technical Eval.
• **Bullish** since 8/95

Rel. Strength Rank
(1 Lowest—99 Highest)
• **72**

Insider Activity
• **Neutral**

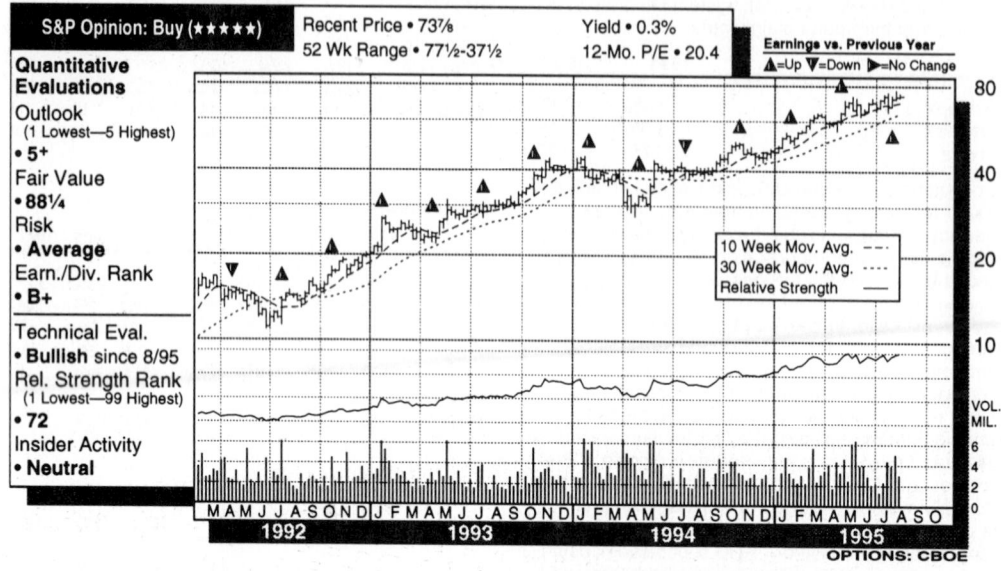

Earnings vs. Previous Year
▲=Up ▼=Down ▶=No Change

10 Week Mov. Avg. — — —
30 Week Mov. Avg. ·······
Relative Strength ———

OPTIONS: CBOE

Overview - 17-AUG-95

Revenues are expected to rise through 1995-96, benefiting from a growing systems software market and aided by new product introductions (particularly of non-mainframe products), acquisitions and increased maintenance contracts. Operating margins are expected to widen, aided by volume efficiencies and stringent cost controls. Operating share earnings should benefit from the higher revenues, wider margins and a stock repurchase program; however, results in the second quarter of 1995-96 are expected to be penalized by a large write-off of R&D costs associated with the acquisition of Legent Corp.

Valuation - 17-AUG-95

The shares have risen sharply over the past three years on rapid revenue and earnings growth stemming from the company's leading position in the growing mainframe systems software market and the introduction of new products serving the enterprise-wide environment of networked computers. Excluding nonrecurring charges, earnings in fiscal 1995-96 are expected to increase over 20% from fiscal 1994-95. However, the multiple attached to earnings is modest. The stock should outperform the market during the upcoming 12 month timeframe, reflecting faster-than-average earnings growth combined with potential expansion of the multiple attached to those earnings.

Key Stock Statistics

S&P EPS Est. 1996	4.25	Tang. Bk. Value/Share	7.98
P/E on S&P Est. 1996	17.4	Beta	1.46
Dividend Rate/Share	0.20	Shareholders	9,000
Shs. outstg. (M)	160.1	Market cap. (B)	$ 12.1
Avg. daily vol. (M)	0.720	Inst. holdings	63%
		Insider holdings	NA

Value of $10,000 invested 5 years ago: $ 60,857

Fiscal Year Ending Mar. 31

	1996	% Change	1995	% Change	1994	% Change
Revenues (Million $)						
1Q	577.5	21%	476.6	13%	423.4	15%
2Q	—	—	623.3	21%	517.0	20%
3Q	—	—	721.0	26%	574.4	15%
4Q	—	—	802.0	27%	633.7	17%
Yr.	—	—	2,623	22%	2,148	17%
Income (Million $)						
1Q	88.55	NM	-85.58	NM	30.75	60%
2Q	—	—	130.4	49%	87.54	86%
3Q	—	—	174.2	40%	124.2	55%
4Q	—	—	212.9	34%	158.8	60%
Yr.	—	—	431.9	8%	401.3	63%
Earnings Per Share ($)						
1Q	0.53	NM	-0.53	NM	0.18	64%
2Q	E0.94	21%	0.78	53%	0.51	82%
3Q	E1.25	20%	1.04	44%	0.72	50%
4Q	E1.53	20%	1.27	37%	0.93	63%
Yr.	E4.25	65%	2.57	10%	2.34	63%

Next earnings report expected: mid October

Business Summary - 17-AUG-95

Computer Associates International designs, develops, markets and supports standardized computer software products for use with a broad range of mainframe, midrange and desktop computers from many different hardware manufacturers.

Until mid-1982, the company was primarily a supplier of systems software for IBM mainframe computers using the VSE operating system. Since then, it has broadened its product line through new software development and a series of acquisitions, and currently offers a portfolio of more than 300 products, including systems management, information management and business management software.

Systems management software enables a customer to more efficiently utilize its data processing hardware, software and personnel resources by providing tools to measure and improve a computer's performance and programmer productivity.

Information management products include database management systems (used to store, retrieve and manipulate data) and applications generators including front-end computer-aided software engineering (CASE) tools.

Business management applications are used in financial, human resource, manufacturing, distribution and banking applications systems.

The company also sells consumer software through its 4Home products division.

CA's products primarily operate on mainframe computers utilizing the VSE, VM and MVS operating system, as well as minicomputers running the VMS operating system. However, the company has enhanced many of its software programs to operate in a networked environment of powerful desktop computers.

Business outside North America accounted for 49% of 1994-5 revenues, versus 46% in 1993-4.

Important Developments

Aug. '95—The company said that it expected to record a $800 million ($5.00 a share) after tax charge in the second quarter of fiscal 1995-6, to reflect expenses, primarily the write-off of purchased R&D, associated with its pending acquisition of Legent Corp. About 91% of Legent's total oustanding shares were validly tendered in CA's $47.95 cash offer which expired July 31, 1995. The acquisition of Legent, primarily a mainframe software vendor, will become effective following the satisfaction of certain conditions, but in no event earlier than November 6, 1995.

Aug. '94—During the first quarter of 1994-5, CA recorded a charge of $249,300,000 ($154,000,000, or $0.94 a share, after taxes) related to the writeoff of purchased R&D associated with the acquisition of The ASK Group, a vendor of database and other software products.

Capitalization

Long Term Debt: $50,489,000 (3/95).

Per Share Data ($)

(Year Ended Mar. 31)

	1995	1994	1993	1992	1991	1990
Tangible Bk. Val.	7.98	6.39	4.83	4.44	5.64	4.99
Cash Flow	3.97	3.46	2.56	1.73	1.45	1.43
Earnings	2.57	2.34	1.44	0.92	0.86	0.85
Dividends	0.20	0.14	0.10	0.10	0.10	Nil
Payout Ratio	8%	6%	7%	11%	12%	Nil
Cal. Yrs.	1994	1993	1992	1991	1990	1989
Prices - High	50⅞	44¼	20¾	11⅞	16⅞	22⅛
- Low	27⅜	20⅛	10⅞	6¼	4⅜	10½
P/E Ratio - High	20	19	14	13	20	26
- Low	11	9	8	7	5	12

Income Statement Analysis (Million $)

	1995	%Chg	1994	%Chg	1993	%Chg	1992
Revs.	2,623	22%	2,148	17%	1,841	22%	1,509
Oper. Inc.	1,190	45%	821	42%	579	43%	405
Depr.	236	23%	192	NM	191	33%	144
Int. Exp.	23.6	80%	13.1	-22%	16.9	72%	9.8
Pretax Inc.	697	11%	627	63%	384	44%	267
Eff. Tax Rate	38%	—	36%	—	36%	—	39%
Net Inc.	432	8%	401	63%	246	51%	163

Balance Sheet & Other Fin. Data (Million $)

	1995	1994	1993	1992	1991	1990
Cash	301	368	229	282	248	110
Curr. Assets	1,148	999	869	904	888	725
Total Assets	3,269	2,492	2,349	2,169	1,599	1,453
Curr. Liab.	848	549	528	593	361	329
LT Debt	50.0	71.0	167	41.0	25.0	26.0
Common Eqty.	1,578	1,243	1,055	988	1,090	990
Total Cap.	2,089	1,613	1,478	1,255	1,238	1,124
Cap. Exp.	35.0	29.0	22.2	15.1	19.2	22.8
Cash Flow	668	593	437	307	268	265

Ratio Analysis

	1995	1994	1993	1992	1991	1990
Curr. Ratio	1.4	1.8	1.6	1.5	2.5	2.2
% LT Debt of Cap.	2.4	4.4	11.3	3.3	2.0	2.3
% Net Inc.of Revs.	16.5	18.7	13.3	10.8	11.8	12.2
% Ret. on Assets	15.1	16.8	11.2	8.7	10.6	11.5
% Ret. on Equity	30.9	35.4	24.7	15.9	15.5	17.3

Dividend Data —Semiannual dividends were initiated in May 1990.

Amt. of Div. $	Date Decl.	Ex-Div. Date	Stock of Record	Payment Date
0.070	Dec. 09	Dec. 14	Dec. 20	Jan. 06 '94
0.100	May. 26	Jun. 14	Jun. 20	Jul. 05 '94
0.100	Dec. 09	Dec. 14	Dec. 20	Jan. 09 '95
0.100	May. 18	Jun. 16	Jun. 20	Jul. 05 '95
3-for-2	Aug. 09	Sep. 06	Aug. 21	Sep. 05 '95

Data as orig. reptd.; bef. results of disc. opers. and/or spec. items. Per share data adj. for stk. divs. as of ex-div. date. E-Estimated. NA-Not Available. NM-Not Meaningful. NR-Not Ranked.

Office—One Computer Associates Plaza, Islandia, NY 11788. **Tel**—(516) 342-5224. **Chrmn & CEO**—C. B. Wang. **Pres**—S. Kumar. **Sr VP & CFO**—P. A. Schwartz. **Sr VP & Secy**—B. A. Frease. **Sr VP & Treas**—I. Zar. **Investor Contact**—Douglas Robinson. **Dirs**—R. M. Artzt, I. Goldstein, R. A. Grasso, S. S. Kenny, S. Kumar, E. C. Lord III, G. E. Martinelli, W. F. P. de Vogel, C. B. Wang. **Transfer Agent**—Mellon Securities Trust Co., Ridgefield Park, N.J. **Incorporated** in Delaware in 1974. **Empl**-7,600. **S&P Analyst:** Peter C. Wood, CFA

STANDARD & POOR'S

STOCK REPORTS

Computer Sciences

NYSE Symbol **CSC**
In S&P 500

26-OCT-95

Industry:
Data Processing

Summary: This leading vendor in the computer services industry provides management consulting, systems development, integration and operations, and other information technology services.

S&P Opinion: Hold (★★★)	Recent Price • 67¾	Yield • Nil
	52 Wk Range • 70¼-41½	12-Mo. P/E • 30.1

Quantitative Evaluations

Outlook
(1 Lowest—5 Highest)
• **3+**

Fair Value
• **68½**

Risk
• **Low**

Earn./Div. Rank
• **B+**

Technical Eval.
• **Bullish** since 10/92

Rel. Strength Rank
(1 Lowest—99 Highest)
• **86**

Insider Activity
• **Neutral**

Earnings vs. Previous Year
▲=Up ▼=Down ▶=No Change

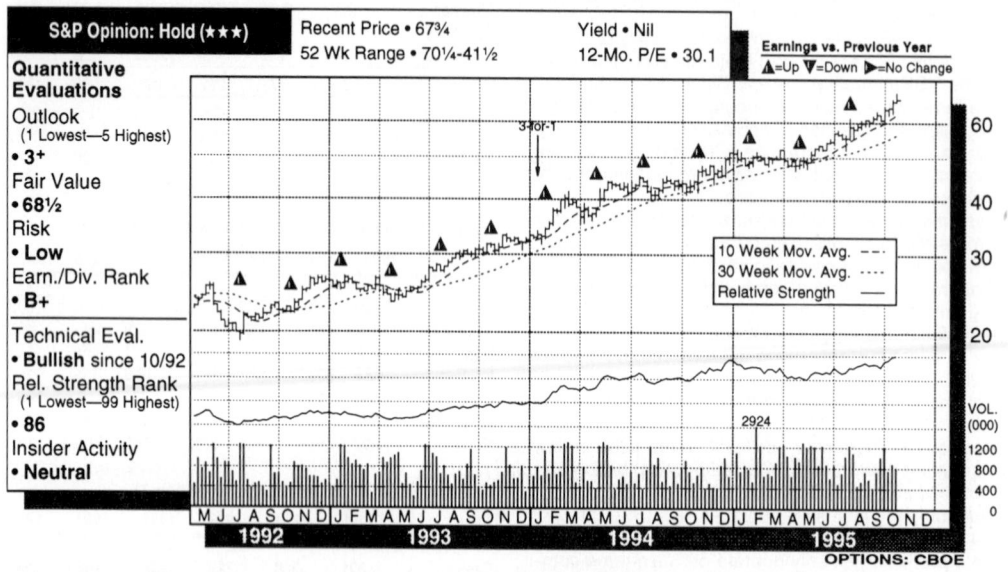

10 Week Mov. Avg. ---
30 Week Mov. Avg. ·····
Relative Strength —

OPTIONS: CBOE

Overview - 26-OCT-95

Revenues are expected to continue to advance in fiscal 1995-96, aided by internal growth and acquisitions. Domestic commercial revenues should be boosted by strong consulting, systems integration and data services outsourcing. International operations should be strong as well, aided by a major outsourcing contract with British Aerospace, together with general economic growth. CSC is also addressing new business opportunities in the federal market. Margins should widen on the higher volume, a better product mix, and well controlled costs. Earnings should benefit from the higher revenues and the expected margin improvement.

Valuation - 26-OCT-95

The shares of this leading computer services company have risen sharply since mid-1993, and are near their record high. CSC's annual earnings growth rate should be in the high-teens over the next several years, aided by a highly predictable revenue stream associated with multi-year contracts. Selective acquisitions should continue to strengthen the company's competitive position. The stock merits a premium valuation, in light of the strong and increasingly predictable sales and earnings growth we project. However, the current P/E multiple is at the top of the historical range, and we believe that the shares are likely only to track the market in coming months.

Key Stock Statistics

S&P EPS Est. 1996	2.50	Tang. Bk. Value/Share	12.52
P/E on S&P Est. 1996	27.1	Beta	1.20
S&P EPS Est. 1997	2.95	Shareholders	7,800
Dividend Rate/Share	Nil	Market cap. (B)	$ 3.7
Shs. outstg. (M)	55.5	Inst. holdings	82%
Avg. daily vol. (M)	0.169	Insider holdings	NA

Value of $10,000 invested 5 years ago: $ 35,194

Fiscal Year Ending Mar. 31

	1996	% Change	1995	% Change	1994	% Change
Revenues (Million $)						
1Q	966.8	31%	738.2	21%	608.1	NM
2Q	1,005	27%	788.5	27%	622.3	1%
3Q	—	—	827.9	33%	621.4	2%
4Q	—	—	1,018	39%	730.9	12%
Yr.	—	—	3,373	31%	2,583	4%
Income (Million $)						
1Q	27.72	27%	21.82	20%	18.16	13%
2Q	30.35	32%	22.92	25%	18.27	7%
3Q	—	—	26.75	23%	21.68	15%
4Q	—	—	39.25	20%	32.83	26%
Yr.	—	—	110.7	22%	90.93	16%
Earnings Per Share ($)						
1Q	0.49	17%	0.42	17%	0.36	13%
2Q	0.53	20%	0.44	22%	0.36	5%
3Q	E0.62	22%	0.51	21%	0.42	13%
4Q	E0.86	19%	0.72	14%	0.63	22%
Yr.	E2.50	20%	2.09	18%	1.77	14%

Next earnings report expected: late October

Computer Sciences

Business Summary - 17-OCT-95

Computer Sciences is one of the largest computer services companies in the U.S., providing a variety of information technology consulting, systems integration and outsourcing to industry and government. Revenues by market in recent fiscal years were derived as follows:

	1994-5	1993-4	1992-3
Federal government	44%	48%	51%
U.S. commercial	35%	39%	38%
State & local government	NM	1%	2%
International	21%	12%	9%

Serving the U.S. federal government market, the company designs, engineers and integrates computer-based systems and communications systems, providing all the hardware, software, training and related elements necessary to develop, operate and maintain a system. It also provides multidisciplinary technical services.

In the U.S. commercial market, CSC provides consulting and technical services in the development and integration of computer and communication systems to nonfederal organizations. The company is also a major provider of outsourcing services, providing clients with comprehensive information technology services, including systems analysis, applications development, network operations and data center management.

The company's international operations, with major offices in the U.K., France, Germany, Belgium, the Netherlands and Australia, provide a wide range of information technology services to commercial and public sector clients. Services span the range of consulting, systems integration and outsourcing.

Important Developments

Jul. '95—CSC announced a contract to provide technical information systems security applications primarily to the Department of Defense. The company is one of three vendors that will compete for a total of $1.095 billion of work, with CSC's portion expected to be in excess of $300 million.

Apr. '95—The company said that revenue increases for the fourth quarter and full fiscal year ended March 31, 1995, reflect the impact of more than $4 billion in new multi-year agreements that CSC began work on during the year. The new business included contracts valued at $1.5 billion with Hughes Aircraft Co.; $1.5 billion with British Aerospace; and $1 billion with NASA.

Apr. '95—In the fourth quarter of fiscal 1994-5, the company acquired a 75% interest in Ploenzke AG, Germany's largest independent computer services firm, for an undisclosed amount.

Capitalization

Long Term Debt: $309,918,000 (6/95).

Per Share Data ($) (Year Ended Mar. 31)

	1995	1994	1993	1992	1991	1990
Tangible Bk. Val.	12.36	8.93	7.66	5.87	6.52	5.98
Cash Flow	5.35	4.31	3.91	3.02	2.17	2.06
Earnings	2.09	1.77	1.55	1.37	1.34	1.36
Dividends	Nil	Nil	Nil	Nil	Nil	Nil
Payout Ratio	Nil	Nil	Nil	Nil	Nil	Nil
Cal. Yrs.	1994	1993	1992	1991	1990	1989
Prices - High	52⅝	33⅜	28	27	19⅜	19½
- Low	31⅝	23⅜	19	15⅞	12¼	15⅜
P/E Ratio - High	25	19	18	20	14	14
- Low	15	13	12	12	9	11

Income Statement Analysis (Million $)

	1995	%Chg	1994	%Chg	1993	%Chg	1992
Revs.	3,373	31%	2,583	4%	2,480	17%	2,113
Oper. Inc.	376	29%	291	11%	263	25%	210
Depr.	173	32%	131	10%	119	46%	81.7
Int. Exp.	28.8	67%	17.2	-16%	20.5	-3%	21.2
Pretax Inc.	174	17%	149	16%	128	17%	109
Eff. Tax Rate	36%	—	39%	—	39%	—	38%
Net Inc.	111	22%	90.9	16%	78.1	15%	68.2

Balance Sheet & Other Fin. Data (Million $)

	1995	1994	1993	1992	1991	1990
Cash	155	127	155	130	137	119
Curr. Assets	1,082	857	748	666	618	557
Total Assets	2,334	1,806	1,454	1,375	1,007	918
Curr. Liab.	778	661	445	401	355	343
LT Debt	310	273	295	349	109	108
Common Eqty.	1,149	806	695	607	526	458
Total Cap.	1,511	1,115	991	956	635	566
Cap. Exp.	193	119	95.4	52.7	27.0	33.8
Cash Flow	283	222	197	150	105	100

Ratio Analysis

	1995	1994	1993	1992	1991	1990
Curr. Ratio	1.4	1.3	1.7	1.7	1.7	1.6
% LT Debt of Cap.	20.5	24.5	29.8	36.5	17.1	19.1
% Net Inc.of Revs.	3.3	3.5	3.2	3.2	3.7	4.4
% Ret. on Assets	5.1	5.5	5.5	5.7	6.7	8.0
% Ret. on Equity	10.9	12.0	11.9	11.9	13.1	15.4

Dividend Data —No cash dividends have been paid since 1969. A "poison pill" stock purchase rights plan was adopted in 1989. A three-for-one stock split was effected in January 1994.

Data as orig. reptd.; bef. results of disc. opers. and/or spec. items. Per share data adj. for stk. divs. as of ex-div. date. E-Estimated. NA-Not Available. NM-Not Meaningful. NR-Not Ranked.

Office—2100 E. Grand Ave., El Segundo, CA 90245. **Tel**—(310) 615-0311. **Chrmn & CEO**—W. R. Hoover. **Pres & COO**—V. B. Honeycutt. **VP & CFO**—L. J. Level. **VP & Secy**—H. D. Fisk. **Investor Contact**—Bruce Plowman. **Dirs**—H. P. Allen, I. W. Bailey II, V. B. Honeycutt, W. R. Hoover, R. C. Lawton, L. J. Level, F. W. McFarlan, J. R. Mellor, A. E. Nashman. **Transfer Agent & Registrar**—Mellon Securities Trust Co., NYC. **Incorporated** in Nevada in 1959. **Empl**-30,000. **S&P Analyst:** Alan Aaron

ConAgra, Inc.

NYSE Symbol **CAG**
In S&P 500

27-SEP-95

Industry:
Food

Summary: ConAgra is the largest independent U.S. food processor, with interests in branded dry grocery and frozen food products, processed meats, flour milling, and grain merchandising.

S&P Opinion: Accumulate (★★★★)

| Recent Price • 39¼ | Yield • 2.1% |
| 52 Wk Range • 39⅜-29¾ | 12-Mo. P/E • 18.6 |

Earnings vs. Previous Year
▲=Up ▼=Down ▶=No Change

Quantitative Evaluations

Outlook
(1 Lowest—5 Highest)
• **4+**

Fair Value
• **40%**

Risk
• **Low**

Earn./Div. Rank
• **A+**

Technical Eval.
• **Bearish** since 9/95

Rel. Strength Rank
(1 Lowest—99 Highest)
• **71**

Insider Activity
• **Neutral**

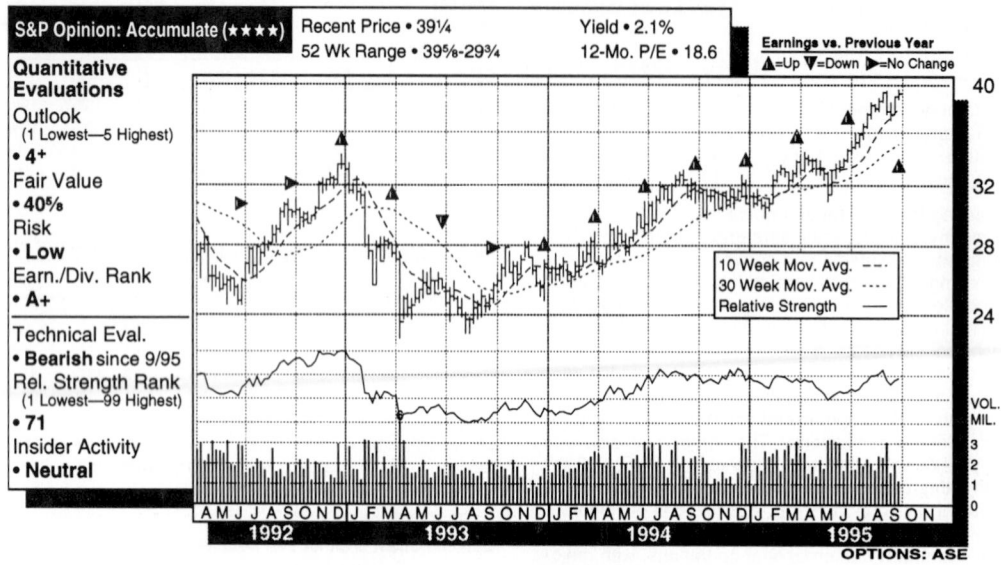

10 Week Mov. Avg. ---
30 Week Mov. Avg. ·····
Relative Strength ——

1992 1993 1994 1995

VOL. MIL.

OPTIONS: ASE

Overview - 26-SEP-95

Sales are expected to continue their long, modest upward climb in fiscal 1996, paced by internal growth and contributions from acquisitions. Solid profit growth for core Grocery/Diversified segment businesses is expected, led by the growing line of Healthy Choice frozen meals and dry grocery items. Refrigerated product segment profits should rise, led by packaged meats, beef, cheese and turkey products businesses. Food Inputs & Ingredients profits should also grow, led by flour milling, grain merchandising and specialty food ingredients businesses. Further shedding of unstrategic assets should contribute to margin enhancement, allowing earnings per share to grow 14% in fiscal 1996, to $2.35.

Valuation - 26-SEP-95

Based on our bullish near-term and longer-term EPS growth outlook, the shares appear attractive at current levels for superior growth ahead. We expect profitability and earnings visibility to be enhanced by a gradual shift toward value-added, branded processed food products, as well as a further pruning of low-margin, unstrategic assets. ConAgra's substantial scale and diversity give it the resources and insulation from changing market conditions not enjoyed by many of its smaller competitors. As a result, its earnings stream tends to be more predictable than that of most of its peers. A modest P/E makes these high quality, low-risk shares attractive for virtually all accounts.

Key Stock Statistics

S&P EPS Est. 1996	2.35	Tang. Bk. Value/Share	0.30
P/E on S&P Est. 1996	16.7	Beta	0.86
Dividend Rate/Share	0.83	Shareholders	31,000
Shs. outstg. (M)	245.6	Market cap. (B)	$ 9.8
Avg. daily vol. (M)	0.368	Inst. holdings	46%
		Insider holdings	NA

Value of $10,000 invested 5 years ago: $ 23,068

Fiscal Year Ending May 31

	1996	% Change	1995	% Change	1994	% Change
Revenues (Million $)						
1Q	6,436	3%	6,246	10%	5,687	3%
2Q	—	—	6,289	-1%	6,355	14%
3Q	—	—	5,758	3%	5,581	10%
4Q	—	—	5,817	-1%	5,888	9%
Yr.	—	—	24,109	3%	23,512	9%
Income (Million $)						
1Q	87.10	13%	76.80	14%	67.60	-3%
2Q	—	—	149.9	12%	134.0	5%
3Q	—	—	118.5	14%	103.7	14%
4Q	—	—	150.4	14%	131.8	28%
Yr.	—	—	495.6	13%	437.1	12%
Earnings Per Share ($)						
1Q	0.36	16%	0.31	15%	0.27	NM
2Q	E0.72	14%	0.63	13%	0.56	8%
3Q	E0.57	16%	0.49	14%	0.43	16%
4Q	E0.70	11%	0.63	15%	0.55	31%
Yr.	E2.35	14%	2.06	14%	1.81	15%

Next earnings report expected: late December

Business Summary - 26-SEP-95

ConAgra is a diversified producer of processed foods, agricultural commodities and other related products. Sales and operating profit contributions by business segment in 1994-5 were:

	Sales	Profits
Grocery/Diversified Products	20%	49%
Refrigerated Foods	56%	32%
Food Inputs & Ingredients	24%	19%

The Grocery/Diversified Products segment consists of those companies that produce branded shelf-stable and frozen food products. Major shelf-stable grocery brands include Hunt's and Healthy Choice tomato products; Wesson oils; Healthy Choice soups; Orville Redenbacher's and Act II popcorn; Peter Pan peanut butter; and Van Camp's canned beans. Major frozen grocery brands include Healthy Choice, Banquet, Marie Callender's, Kid Cuisine, Morton, Chun King and La Choy. Diversified products companies include Lamb-Weston (frozen potatoes); Arrow Industries (maker of private label products); and business interests in seafood, pet products, and frozen microwave products in the U.K.

Refrigerated Foods consists of beef, pork and lamb products (Monfort, Armour); branded processed meats (Armour, Swift Premium, Eckrich, Healthy Choice); poultry (Butterball, Country Pride); cheeses (County Line); and refrigerated dessert toppings (Reddi-Wip).

Food Inputs & Ingredients businesses include crop protection chemicals and fertilizers; grain processing (flour, oat and dry corn milling; barley processing); specialty retailing; and worldwide commodity trading (grains, oilseeds, edible beans and peas, and other commodities).

Important Developments

Sep. '95—During fiscal 1996's first quarter, all three of CAG's major industry segments achieved double-digit operating profit growth. Operating profit for the Grocery/Diversified products segment was led by an acquisition within the Lamb-Weston potato products division, continued growth for Healthy Choice consumer frozen foods, and the acquisition of the Van Camp's bean products business. Refrigerated Foods' operating profits grew, reflecting favorable market conditions for the fresh meat business, and good gains for branded packaged meats; chicken products profits declined, but were expected to improve for the remainder of the year. Food Inputs & Ingredients' profit growth was led by good gains for the grain merchandising and international fertilizers businesses, and the divestment of unhealthy businesses.

Capitalization

Long Term Debt: $2,520,000,000 (5/95).
Red. Preferred Stock: $354,900,000.

Per Share Data ($) (Year Ended May 31)

	1995	1994	1993	1992	1991	1990
Tangible Bk. Val.	0.30	-1.61	-2.45	-2.12	-4.26	4.59
Cash Flow	3.70	3.42	3.07	2.88	2.33	1.90
Earnings	2.06	1.81	1.58	1.50	1.42	1.25
Dividends	0.78	0.70	0.60	0.52	0.44	0.39
Payout Ratio	38%	38%	41%	35%	32%	31%
Cal. Yrs.	1994	1993	1992	1991	1990	1989
Prices - High	33⅛	33⅝	35¾	36½	25½	20⅛
- Low	25½	22¾	24½	22⅜	15⅛	12⅞
P/E Ratio - High	16	19	23	24	18	16
- Low	12	13	16	15	11	10

Income Statement Analysis (Million $)

	1995	%Chg	1994	%Chg	1993	%Chg	1992
Revs.	24,109	3%	23,512	9%	21,519	1%	21,219
Oper. Inc.	1,476	10%	1,337	10%	1,213	NM	1,207
Depr.	376	2%	368	5%	349	9%	319
Int. Exp.	311	8%	289	2%	283	-21%	356
Pretax Inc.	826	15%	720	14%	631	7%	588
Eff. Tax Rate	40%	—	39%	—	38%	—	37%
Net Inc.	496	14%	437	11%	392	5%	372

Balance Sheet & Other Fin. Data (Million $)

	1995	1994	1993	1992	1991	1990
Cash	60.0	452	447	536	967	333
Curr. Assets	5,140	5,143	4,487	4,371	4,343	3,348
Total Assets	10,801	10,722	9,989	9,759	9,420	4,804
Curr. Liab.	3,965	4,753	4,273	4,081	4,087	2,968
LT Debt	2,520	2,207	2,159	2,124	2,093	635
Common Eqty.	2,495	2,227	2,055	2,232	1,817	1,096
Total Cap.	5,895	4,889	4,570	4,713	4,266	1,837
Cap. Exp.	428	395	341	370	332	349
Cash Flow	847	782	716	667	543	350

Ratio Analysis

	1995	1994	1993	1992	1991	1990
Curr. Ratio	1.3	1.1	1.1	1.1	1.1	1.1
% LT Debt of Cap.	42.7	45.1	47.3	45.1	49.1	34.6
% Net Inc.of Revs.	2.1	1.9	1.8	1.8	1.6	1.5
% Ret. on Assets	4.6	4.2	3.8	3.7	4.2	5.1
% Ret. on Equity	20.0	19.4	16.4	16.4	19.0	22.3

Dividend Data —Dividends have been paid since 1976. A dividend reinvestment plan is available. A poison pill stock purchase rights plan was adopted in 1986.

Amt. of Div. $	Date Decl.	Ex-Div. Date	Stock of Record	Payment Date
0.208	Sep. 22	Oct. 31	Nov. 04	Dec. 01 '94
0.208	Dec. 01	Jan. 30	Feb. 03	Mar. 01 '95
0.208	Apr. 10	May. 01	May. 05	Jun. 01 '95
0.208	Jul. 06	Aug. 02	Aug. 04	Sep. 01 '95

Data as orig. reptd.; bef. results of disc. opers. and/or spec. items. Per share data adj. for stk. divs. as of ex-div. date. E-Estimated. NA-Not Available. NM-Not Meaningful. NR-Not Ranked.

Office—One ConAgra Dr., Omaha, NE 68102-5001. **Tel**—(402) 595-4000. **Chrmn & CEO**—P. B. Fletcher. **Treas**—J. P. O'Donnell. **VP & Investor Contact**—Walter H. Casey. **Dirs**—P. B. Fletcher, C. M. Harper, R. A. Krane, G. Rauenhorst, C. E. Reichardt, R. W. Roskens, M. R. Scardino, W. Scott, Jr., W. G. Stocks, J. J. Thompson, F. B. Wells, T. R. Williams, C. K. Yeutter. **Transfer Agent & Registrar**—Chemical Bank, NYC. **Incorporated** in Nebraska in 1919; reincorporated in Delaware in 1975. **Empl**-90,871. **S&P Analyst:** Kenneth A. Shea

Conrail

NYSE Symbol **CRR**

In S&P 500

20-OCT-95   Industry:
Railroads

Summary: This company operates an 11,300-mile railroad in 14 midwestern and northeastern states. Shipments of intermodal, chemicals and autos generate more than half of total revenues.

S&P Opinion: Accumulate (★★★★)	Recent Price • 71½	Yield • 2.4%
	52 Wk Range • 72¼-48¼	12-Mo. P/E • 13.1

Quantitative Evaluations

Outlook
(1 Lowest—5 Highest)
• **1+**

Fair Value
• **64¼**

Risk
• **Low**

Earn./Div. Rank
• **B**

Technical Eval.
• **Bullish** since 7/95

Rel. Strength Rank
(1 Lowest—99 Highest)
• **79**

Insider Activity
• **Neutral**

Earnings vs. Previous Year
▲=Up ▼=Down ▶=No Change

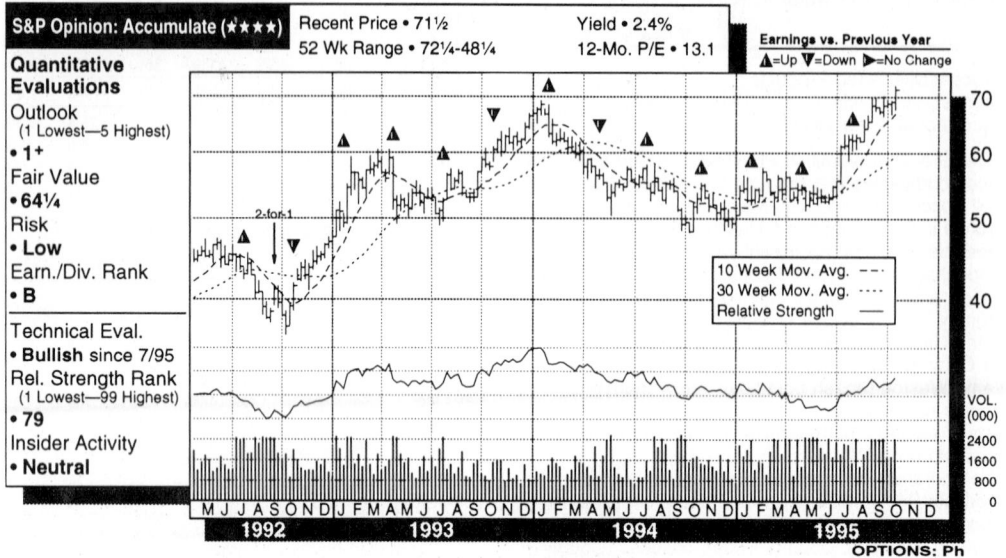

10 Week Mov. Avg. – – –
30 Week Mov. Avg. ·····
Relative Strength —

VOL.
(000)

OPTIONS: Ph

Overview - 20-OCT-95

CRR should extend its profit gain into 1996, reflecting continued moderate growth. Auto shipments are expected to rebound. The reduction of excessive stocks at electric utilities bodes well for coal shipments. Intermodal freight should rebound in 1996 after truckload carriers captured freight through fierce rate discounting. Boosting volumes will be CRR's new double-stack service with Norfolk Southern plus continued growth for their Triple Crown joint venture. Margins should widen as CRR increases locomotive utilization rates, cuts labor costs through its early retirement program and experiences reduced personal injury claims as safety performance improves. Interest expense should decline. Limiting profit comparisons will be the absence of 1995's favorable tax adjustment.

Valuation - 20-OCT-95

The shares of this railroad climbed to record highs in October, propelled by solid profit gains despite sluggish traffic and persistent takeover rumours involving Norfolk Southern. While the economy in 1996 is expected to remain on a slow growth track, CRR has proven adept in managing its costs and should be able to further improve operating margins. CRR continues to send positive signals to investors, such as its 13% dividend hike in July and the repurchase of 1,099,306 of its common shares during 1995's first nine months for $54.58 each. Trading at a discount to the market multiple, we believe CRR offers sound long-term value.

Key Stock Statistics

S&P EPS Est. 1995	5.55	Tang. Bk. Value/Share	36.31
P/E on S&P Est. 1995	12.9	Beta	1.53
S&P EPS Est. 1996	5.95	Shareholders	19,700
Dividend Rate/Share	1.70	Market cap. (B)	$ 5.8
Shs. outstg. (M)	82.8	Inst. holdings	78%
Avg. daily vol. (M)	0.418	Insider holdings	NA

Value of $10,000 invested 5 years ago: $ 34,315

Fiscal Year Ending Dec. 31

	1995	% Change	1994	% Change	1993	% Change
Revenues (Million $)						
1Q	889.0	5%	847.0	4%	816.0	2%
2Q	923.0	-3%	951.0	9%	873.0	4%
3Q	923.0	-3%	949.0	11%	854.0	NM
4Q	—	—	986.0	8%	910.0	6%
Yr.	—	—	3,733	8%	3,453	3%
Income (Million $)						
1Q	55.00	NM	-32.00	NM	46.00	21%
2Q	123.0	22%	101.0	19%	85.00	10%
3Q	116.0	9%	106.0	NM	-3.00	NM
4Q	—	—	149.0	41%	106.0	15%
Yr.	—	—	324.0	38%	234.0	-17%
Earnings Per Share ($)						
1Q	0.66	NM	-0.45	NM	0.52	24%
2Q	1.52	23%	1.24	23%	1.01	12%
3Q	1.44	12%	1.29	NM	-0.07	NM
4Q	E1.94	5%	1.84	45%	1.27	15%
Yr.	E5.55	42%	3.90	42%	2.74	-16%

Next earnings report expected: mid October

Business Summary - 19-OCT-95

Conrail is the parent of Consolidated Rail Corp., which was formed in 1976 through the amalgamation of the Penn Central, Erie Lackawanna, Lehigh and Hudson River, Reading, Central of New Jersey and Lehigh Valley railroads, all of which entered bankruptcy in the late 1960s or early 1970s.

CRR's 11,349-mile rail network (including 1,798 miles of leased lines or trackage rights) spans 14 midwestern and northeastern states, the District of Columbia and the Province of Quebec. Chicago and St. Louis mark the railroad's western gateways, with Boston and Montreal its easternmost points. Operating data for recent years was:

	1994	1993	1992
Carloads (mil.)	4.22	3.90	3.72
Revenue/carload	$885	$887	$900
Operating ratio	83.8%	82.9%	84.0%
Labor ratio	33.7%	35.6%	37.0%

Rail activities consist entirely of freight transportation, having transferred its commuter and intercity passenger service to local authorities at 1982 year-end. Contributions to freight revenues:

	1994	1993	1992
Intermodal	21.2%	19.9%	18.8%
Coal	17.9%	18.0%	21.1%
Chemicals/waste	16.9%	17.4%	17.0%
Automotive	15.9%	15.5%	13.9%
Food & grain	10.2%	10.8%	10.9%
Forest products	9.1%	9.5%	9.9%
Metals	8.9%	8.9%	8.3%

The equipment fleet at the end of 1994 included 2,147 locomotives (having an average age of 16.7 years) and 56,391 freight cars (21.0 years). The percentage of surplus locomotives and freight cars at December 31, 1994, was 1.5%. and 11.7%, respectively.

Important Developments

Sep. '95—Through September 30, 1995 repurchased 1,099,306 of its common shares (1.4% of total outstanding) for $60 million, or $54.58 each. CRR has another $290 million remaining under its multi-year stock repurchase program.
Sep. '95—Conrail launched a joint double-stack container service with Norfolk Southern between New York and Atlanta. CRR said the two railroads had spent $17 million to adjust track heights to facilitate the service.

Capitalization

Long Term Debt: $2,037,000,000 (9/95).
7.51% ESOP Conv. Junior Preferred
Stock: $283,000.000; conv. into 9,821,358 com. shs.

Per Share Data ($) (Year Ended Dec. 31)

	1994	1993	1992	1991	1990	1989
Tangible Bk. Val.	36.70	34.56	34.16	32.23	35.95	30.12
Cash Flow	7.29	6.16	6.80	0.96	5.74	3.15
Earnings	3.90	2.74	3.28	-2.70	2.55	1.09
Dividends	1.40	1.20	1.27	0.85	0.75	0.65
Payout Ratio	36%	44%	30%	NM	26%	59%
Prices - High	69¼	67½	48⅜	42⅜	25¾	24¾
- Low	48⅛	47½	36¼	18⅜	16¼	16
P/E Ratio - High	18	25	15	NM	10	23
- Low	12	17	11	NM	6	15

Income Statement Analysis (Million $)

	1994	%Chg	1993	%Chg	1992	%Chg	1991
Revs.	3,733	8%	3,453	3%	3,345	3%	3,252
Oper. Inc.	968	11%	875	6%	829	8%	765
Depr.	278	-2%	284	-4%	295	-4%	307
Int. Exp.	193	4%	186	8%	173	-5%	182
Pretax Inc.	532	21%	440	-4%	460	NM	-334
Eff. Tax Rate	39%	—	47%	—	39%	—	NM
Net Inc.	324	38%	234	-17%	282	NM	-206

Balance Sheet & Other Fin. Data (Million $)

	1994	1993	1992	1991	1990	1989
Cash	43.0	38.0	40.0	135	153	502
Curr. Assets	1,125	1,062	790	878	838	1,230
Total Assets	8,322	7,948	7,315	7,096	7,245	7,471
Curr. Liab.	1,201	1,075	1,279	1,164	1,054	1,077
LT Debt	1,940	1,959	1,577	1,637	1,680	857
Common Eqty.	2,885	2,750	2,724	2,373	2,641	4,044
Total Cap.	6,068	5,824	4,969	4,727	5,063	5,217
Cap. Exp.	490	650	491	398	381	678
Cash Flow	581	497	556	86.0	538	430

Ratio Analysis

	1994	1993	1992	1991	1990	1989
Curr. Ratio	0.9	1.0	0.6	0.8	0.8	1.1
% LT Debt of Cap.	32.0	33.6	31.7	34.6	33.2	16.4
% Net Inc.of Revs.	8.7	6.8	8.4	NM	7.3	4.3
% Ret. on Assets	4.0	3.1	4.0	NM	4.2	2.0
% Ret. on Equity	10.8	7.8	9.9	NM	9.3	3.7

Dividend Data —Dividend payments began in 1987. A dividend reinvestment plan is available. A "poison pill" stock purchase right was issued in 1989.

Amt. of Div. $	Date Decl.	Ex-Div. Date	Stock of Record	Payment Date
0.375	Nov. 16	Nov. 23	Nov. 30	Dec. 15 '94
0.375	Feb. 15	Feb. 22	Feb. 28	Mar. 15 '95
0.375	May. 17	May. 24	May. 31	Jun. 15 '95
0.425	Aug. 02	Aug. 29	Aug. 31	Sep. 15 '95

Data as orig. reptd.; bef. results of disc. opers. and/or spec. items. Per share data adj. for stk. divs. as of ex-div. date. E-Estimated. NA-Not Available. NM-Not Meaningful. NR-Not Ranked.

Office—2001 Market St., Philadelphia, PA 19101-1417. **Tel**—(215) 209-4000. **Chrmn**—J. A. Hagen. **Pres & CEO**—D. M. LeVan. **SVP Fin**—H. Brown. **VP & Secy**—A. Schimmel. **Investor Contact**—Thomas J. McFadden (215 209-5592). **Dirs**—H. F. Baldwin, C. S. Brinegar, D. B. Burke, K. F. Feldstein, J. A. Hagen, R. S. Hillas, E. B. Jones, D. M. LeVan, D. B. Lewis, J. C. Marous, R. T. Schuler, D. H. Swanson. **Transfer Agent**—First Chicago Trust Co. of New York, Jersey City, NJ. **Incorporated** in Pennsylvania in 1976; reincorporated in Pennsylvania in 1993. **Empl**-24,833. **S&P Analyst:** Stephen R. Klein

Consolidated Edison

NYSE Symbol **ED**
In S&P 500

30-AUG-95

Industry:
Util.-Diversified

Summary: This electric and gas utility serves the commercial and residential economy of New York City. Puchased power is a significant energy source for the company.

S&P Opinion: Hold (★★★)	Recent Price • 28¾	Yield • 7.1%
	52 Wk Range • 30⅞-23	12-Mo. P/E • 9.6

Quantitative Evaluations

Outlook
(1 Lowest—5 Highest)
• **2+**

Fair Value
• **26**

Risk
• **Low**

Earn./Div. Rank
• **A**

Technical Eval.
• **Bullish** since 1/95

Rel. Strength Rank
(1 Lowest—99 Highest)
• **35**

Insider Activity
• **Favorable**

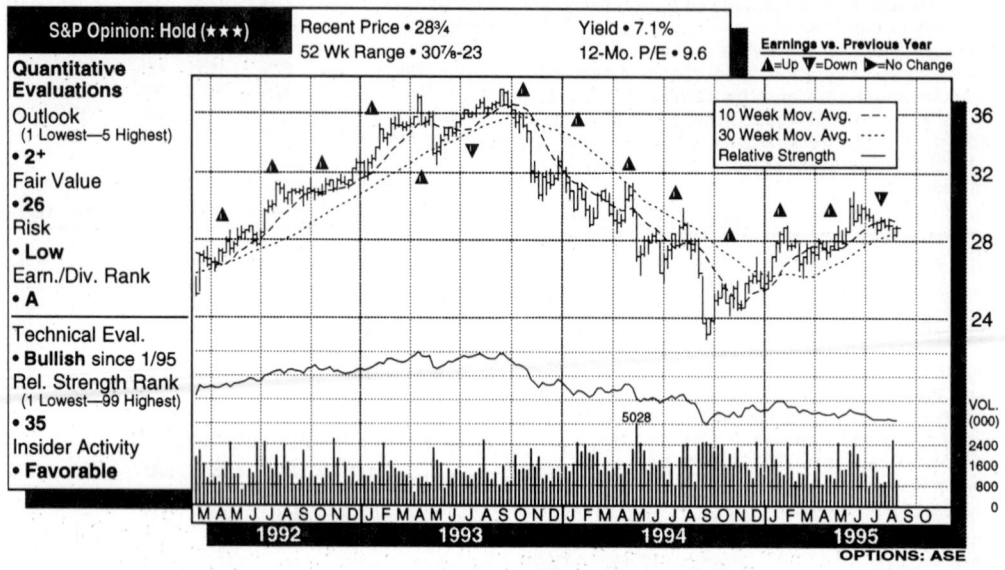

Earnings vs. Previous Year
▲=Up ▼=Down ▶=No Change

10 Week Mov. Avg. — —
30 Week Mov. Avg. ····
Relative Strength —

OPTIONS: ASE

Overview - 28-AUG-95

Share earnings are likely to decline in 1995, due to a freeze on rates and a modest reduction in the allowed return on common equity in the first year of the 3-year adjustable rate agreement effective April 1. Incentive awards under the agreement are less than those earned by the company during 1994. While the company's rates are among the highest in the nation, it appears fairly well insulated from increasing competition within the electric utility industry due to an absence of an industrial customer base. The company's balance sheet is strong; long-term debt comprised a below-industry-average 39.6% of total capital as of June 30, 1995.

Valuation - 28-AUG-95

ED shares fell sharply from late 1993 through most of 1994 due to rising interest rates, a New York state rate cut recommendation and recognition of increasingly competitive markets. The shares have rebounded somewhat this year, aided by investors' anticipation of Fed easing of interest rates. As with most utilities, ED's shares typically do well when interest rates are falling, and decline in periods of rising interest rates. We believe the stock is fairly valued in a range of 10 to 11 times earnings. Its yield is above average for investor-owned utilities, as is its payout ratio based on estimated 1995 earnings; dividend growth over the next few years should modestly exceed that of the group overall.

Key Stock Statistics

S&P EPS Est. 1995	2.75	Tang. Bk. Value/Share	22.34
P/E on S&P Est. 1995	10.5	Beta	0.60
S&P EPS Est. 1996	2.80	Shareholders	159,100
Dividend Rate/Share	2.04	Market cap. (B)	$ 6.8
Shs. outstg. (M)	234.9	Inst. holdings	34%
Avg. daily vol. (M)	0.405	Insider holdings	NA

Value of $10,000 invested 5 years ago: $ 14,421

Fiscal Year Ending Dec. 31

	1995	% Change	1994	% Change	1993	% Change
Revenues (Million $)						
1Q	1,669	-2%	1,698	7%	1,586	9%
2Q	1,460	5%	1,392	NM	1,396	9%
3Q	—	—	1,822	1%	1,800	5%
4Q	—	—	1,461	-2%	1,484	NM
Yr.	—	—	6,373	2%	6,265	6%
Income (Million $)						
1Q	201.0	6%	189.3	23%	153.9	32%
2Q	76.40	-12%	87.21	40%	62.45	-19%
3Q	—	—	339.9	5%	324.8	5%
4Q	—	—	117.9	NM	117.3	17%
Yr.	—	—	734.3	12%	658.5	9%
Earnings Per Share ($)						
1Q	0.82	6%	0.77	24%	0.62	32%
2Q	0.29	-12%	0.33	43%	0.23	-23%
3Q	E1.31	-7%	1.41	4%	1.35	4%
4Q	E0.33	-30%	0.47	2%	0.46	18%
Yr.	E2.75	-8%	2.98	12%	2.66	8%

Next earnings report expected: late October

Consolidated Edison

Business Summary - 30-AUG-95

Consolidated Edison supplies electricity to all of New York City (except part of Queens) and most of Westchester County. Gas and steam services are provided in certain parts of the service area. In 1994, electric sales accounted for 81% of revenues, gas 14%, and steam 4%. Electric revenues in recent years by customer class were:

	1994	1993	1992	1991
Residential	34%	34%	33%	33%
Commercial-industrial	62%	64%	66%	65%
Other	4%	2%	1%	2%

Electric energy sources in 1994, including those for purchased power, were natural gas 35%, nuclear 19%, oil 9%, and hydro and other 5%. Some 32% of 1994's energy requirements were met with purchased power. ED's nuclear capacity is derived from its Indian Point 2 plant in Westchester County. Peak demand in 1994 was 10,384 mw, and capability at peak totaled 13,462 mw, for a capacity margin of 23%. Gas sales in 1994 totaled 108,572,482 dekatherms, up 5.8% from 1993.

The company's near-term generating strategy is to develop conservation programs including demand-side management, implement plant life extension projects, and continue to explore economic power purchases. Based on current demand growth projections, the company does not expect to add any new capacity resources to its system over the next 20 years. ED estimates construction expenditures of $730 million in 1995, down from $758 million in 1994, largely for electric facilities.

Important Developments

Jul. '95—ED reported little year-to-year change in earnings for the 1995 first half. Electric sales volume was off 1.6%, excluding sales to other utilities, firm gas sales fell 9.7%, and steam sales volume dropped 15%, primarily as a result of warmer weather. Revenues stayed even with last year's due to a 1.1% rate increase in April 1994 under a 1992 three-year rate agreement. A new rate agreement effective April 1 this year does not provide for a base load rate increase in the first year, and only limited increases in 1996 and 1997, but does allow recovery of some increases related to employee costs, independent power purchase contracts, demand side management and renewable energy costs and property taxes. Under existing ratemaking procedures, most of the variations in electric sales from the level projected in rate decisions as well as most weather-related variations in gas sales are excluded in determining reported earnings.

Capitalization

Long Term Debt: $3,971,002,000, incl. $46,528,000 of capital lease obligations (6/95).
Red. Cum. Preferred Stock: $100,000,000.
Cum. Preferred Stock: $540,133,000.

Per Share Data ($) (Year Ended Dec. 31)

	1994	1993	1992	1991	1990	1989
Tangible Bk. Val.	21.90	20.89	20.58	20.00	19.56	19.07
Earnings	2.98	2.66	2.46	2.32	2.34	2.49
Dividends	2.00	1.94	1.90	1.86	1.82	1.72
Payout Ratio	67%	73%	77%	80%	78%	69%
Prices - High	32⅜	37¾	32⅞	28¾	29¼	29⅞
- Low	23	30¼	25	22½	19¾	22¼
P/E Ratio - High	11	14	13	12	13	12
- Low	8	11	10	10	8	9

Income Statement Analysis (Million $)

	1994	%Chg	1993	%Chg	1992	%Chg	1991
Revs.	6,373	2%	6,265	6%	5,933	1%	5,873
Depr.	422	4%	404	6%	381	6%	360
Maint.	506	-11%	571	8%	529	2%	521
Fxd. Chgs. Cov.	4.3	9%	3.9	7%	3.6	3%	3.5
Constr. Credits	18.9	78%	10.6	-23%	13.8	-4%	14.4
Eff. Tax Rate	37%	—	36%	—	35%	—	34%
Net Inc.	734	11%	659	9%	604	7%	567

Balance Sheet & Other Fin. Data (Million $)

	1994	1993	1992	1991	1990	1989
Gross Prop.	14,390	13,750	13,191	12,521	11,922	11,366
Cap. Exp.	805	803	830	784	736	630
Net Prop.	10,561	10,156	9,730	9,263	8,815	8,411
Capitalization:						
LT Debt	4,078	3,694	3,494	3,420	3,371	3,150
% LT Debt	41	39	39	40	40	39
Pfd.	640	641	641	633	636	639
% Pfd.	6.40	6.80	7.10	7.30	7.50	7.80
Common	5,313	5,069	4,887	4,608	4,502	4,382
% Common	53	54	54	53	53	54
Total Cap.	12,562	11,965	10,252	9,751	9,517	9,116

Ratio Analysis

	1994	1993	1992	1991	1990	1989
Oper. Ratio	83.7	84.8	85.2	86.2	86.0	85.9
% Earn. on Net Prop.	10.0	9.6	9.3	9.0	9.3	9.5
% Ret. on Revs.	11.5	10.5	10.2	9.7	10.0	10.9
% Ret. On Invest.Cap	8.5	8.5	9.0	8.9	8.9	9.5
% Return On Com.Eqty	13.5	12.5	12.0	11.6	12.0	13.2

Dividend Data —Dividends have been paid since 1885. A dividend reinvestment plan is available.

Amt. of Div. $	Date Decl.	Ex-Div. Date	Stock of Record	Payment Date
0.500	Jul. 26	Aug. 11	Aug. 17	Sep. 15 '94
0.500	Oct. 25	Nov. 09	Nov. 16	Dec. 15 '94
0.510	Jan. 24	Feb. 09	Feb. 15	Mar. 15 '95
0.510	Apr. 25	May. 11	May. 17	Jun. 15 '95
0.510	Jul. 25	Aug. 14	Aug. 16	Sep. 15 '95

Data as orig. reptd.; bef. results of disc opers. and/or spec. items. Per share data adj. for stk. divs. as of ex-div. date. E-Estimated. NA-Not Available. NM-Not Meaningful. NR-Not Ranked.

Office—4 Irving Place, New York, NY 10003. **Tel**—(212) 460-4600. **Chrmn & Pres**—E. R. McGrath. **EVP & CFO**—R. J. McCann. **Secy**—A. M. Bankston. **Investor Contact**—William J. Clifford. **Transfer Agent**—Company's office. **Registrar**—Chemical Bank, NYC. **Incorporated** in New York in 1884. **Empl**-17,097. **S&P Analyst:** Jane Collin

Consolidated Freightways

NYSE Symbol **CNF**
In S&P 500

11-AUG-95 | **Industry:** Trucking | **Summary:** This company operates the third largest U.S. general freight motor carrier, three regional trucking firms, and Emery Worldwide, a leading air freight carrier.

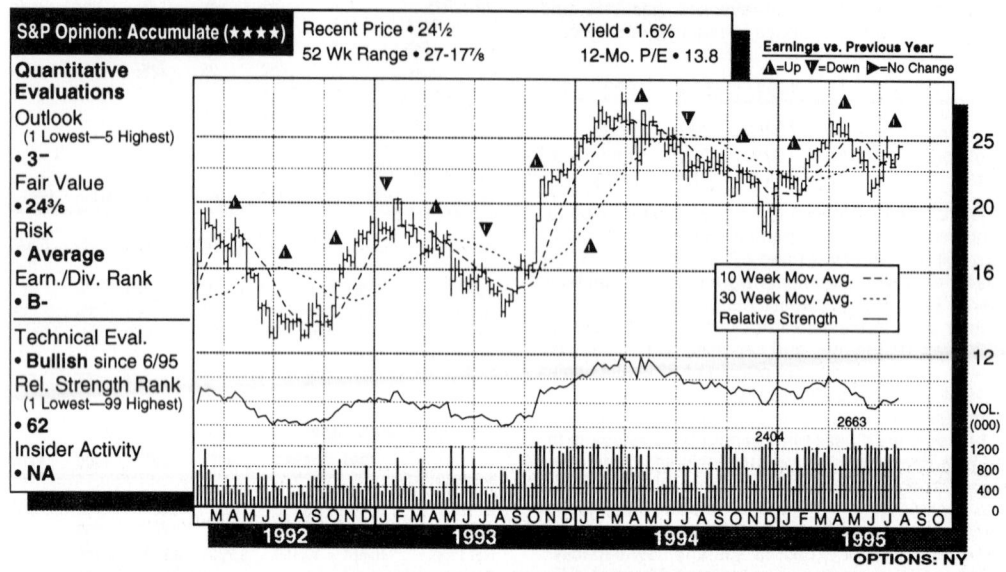

S&P Opinion: Accumulate (★★★★)

Recent Price • 24½	Yield • 1.6%
52 Wk Range • 27-17⅞	12-Mo. P/E • 13.8

Earnings vs. Previous Year
▲=Up ▼=Down ▶=No Change

Quantitative Evaluations

Outlook
(1 Lowest—5 Highest)
• **3**⁻

Fair Value
• **24⅜**

Risk
• **Average**

Earn./Div. Rank
• **B-**

Technical Eval.
• **Bullish** since 6/95

Rel. Strength Rank
(1 Lowest—99 Highest)
• **62**

Insider Activity
• **NA**

10 Week Mov. Avg. – – –
30 Week Mov. Avg. – – –
Relative Strength ——

OPTIONS: NY

Overview - 11-AUG-95

While slower growth is anticipated for Emery's domestic business, international traffic (now Emery's largest market) will continue to expand at a double-digit pace, reflecting an upturn in Europe. Margins will benefit from the operation of more efficient aircraft and savings from the installation of new terminal handling systems. Cargo rates will be flat. Profits at CF Motor-Freight should rebound primarily reflecting the absence of losses stemming from 1994's Teamsters' strike and restructuring/relocation costs incurred during 1994. A weak rate environment will limit CF Motor's recovery. CNF's regional carriers should continue to post double-digit volume gains as a result of territorial expansion. Menlo Logistics will benefit from a major new contract with AT&T. Interest costs and preferred dividend payments will decline.

Valuation - 11-AUG-95

CNF's shares have rebounded in 1995 after a poor performance in 1994. Investors have responded favorably to the resumption of common stock dividends and apparently no longer fear a recession. However, new worries have surfaced: discounting pressure in the long-haul trucking market and sluggish domestic volumes at Emery. These concerns should fade as the economy gets its second wind, providing for sharply higher prices for CNF. The conversion of CNF's $1.54 Depositary Shares in March increased common shares by 19% but is not expected to be dilutive as the issue's dividend payment has been eliminated.

Key Stock Statistics

S&P EPS Est. 1995	2.10	Tang. Bk. Value/Share	5.72
P/E on S&P Est. 1995	11.7	Beta	1.67
S&P EPS Est. 1996	2.65	Shareholders	16,000
Dividend Rate/Share	0.40	Market cap. (B)	$ 1.1
Shs. outstg. (M)	43.3	Inst. holdings	74%
Avg. daily vol. (M)	0.333	Insider holdings	NA

Value of $10,000 invested 5 years ago: $ 9,780

Fiscal Year Ending Dec. 31

	1995	% Change	1994	% Change	1993	% Change
Revenues (Million $)						
1Q	1,296	17%	1,103	11%	993.0	NM
2Q	1,321	25%	1,060	4%	1,020	2%
3Q	—	—	1,236	16%	1,067	3%
4Q	—	—	1,281	15%	1,112	9%
Yr.	—	—	4,680	12%	4,192	3%
Income (Million $)						
1Q	24.17	58%	15.26	85%	8.27	NM
2Q	22.23	NM	5.21	-38%	8.39	-14%
3Q	—	—	20.28	19%	17.08	NM
4Q	—	—	19.55	16%	16.84	NM
Yr.	—	—	60.30	19%	50.57	NM
Earnings Per Share ($)						
1Q	0.50	79%	0.28	180%	0.10	NM
2Q	0.45	NM	0.01	-90%	0.10	-29%
3Q	E0.55	—	0.42	20%	0.35	NM
4Q	E0.60	—	0.40	21%	0.33	NM
Yr.	E2.10	—	1.11	28%	0.87	NM

Next earnings report expected: late October

Consolidated Freightways

Business Summary - 11-AUG-95

Consolidated Freightways provides a broad range of transportation services. Contributions to operating profits (in million $) by business segment:

	1994	1993	1992
CF MotorFreight	-$46.6	$31.7	$27.5
Con-Way Transportation	111.2	71.9	53.7
Emery Worldwide	77.6	16.6	-32.7

CF MotorFreight is one of the largest U.S. general freight carriers, serving the U.S., Puerto Rico and points in Mexico, Canada, Latin America, Europe and Asia through a network of 437 terminals. In 1994, CF handled 11 million shipments weighing an aggregate of 12.7 billion lbs. over an average haul of 1,361 miles. CNF's Menlo Logistics unit provides a variety of logistics services including carrier management, warehousing and order processing.

Con-Way Transportation Services operates three regional motor carriers specializing in overnight and second-day delivery of LTL freight. At 1994 year end, CNF's regional carriers operated 353 terminals. In 1994, CNF's regional carriers handled 8.4 million shipments weighing 9.9 billion lbs. over an average haul of 355 miles. Con-Way Truckload provides door-to-door regional, inter-regional and transcontinental truckload freight services employing company trucks and rail intermodal services. Con-Way also operates as a non-vessel operating common carrier arranging ocean freight transportation for small shipments.

Emery Worldwide provides global air cargo services for parcels and packages of all sizes. In North America Emery operates a fleet of 69 aircraft and 1,300 trucks and vans to provide door-to-door freight service. Service is also provided to 89 nations employing lift capacity on commercial airlines. Emery's freight-sorting hub, in Dayton, has a capacity of 1.2 million pounds of cargo per hour. Emery Worldwide Airlines (7% of air freight revenues), employing a separate fleet of 23 aircraft, provides air cargo service to the U.S. Postal Service under a contract that expires in January 2004.

Important Developments

Aug. '95—CF MotorFreight implemented rate hikes averaging 3.5%. CNF said it needed higher rates to cover higher labor costs, restore margins and provide for capital spending needs. In January CF Motor-Freight lifted its rates some 4.0%.

Apr. '95—CNF's Emery unit was awarded a four-year extension of a contract with General Motors valued at $100 million annually. In January, Emery won a two-year contract from Northern Telecom to handle its North American air freight business.

Capitalization

Long Term Debt: $397,689,000 (3/95).
Series B Pfd. Stk.: 961,032 shs. ($0.01 stated value); ea. conv. into four com. shs. Held by ESOP.

Per Share Data ($) (Year Ended Dec. 31)

	1994	1993	1992	1991	1990	1989
Tangible Bk. Val.	5.72	3.48	2.07	4.00	5.01	6.26
Cash Flow	4.70	4.62	3.36	2.65	3.41	4.10
Earnings	1.11	0.87	-0.58	-1.52	-1.16	0.02
Dividends	0.10	Nil	Nil	Nil	0.53	1.04
Payout Ratio	9%	Nil	Nil	Nil	NM	NM
Prices - High	29¼	24	19⅝	21½	26⅞	37¾
- Low	17⅞	13⅝	12½	9½	10¾	25¼
P/E Ratio - High	26	28	NM	NM	NM	NM
- Low	16	16	NM	NM	NM	NM

Income Statement Analysis (Million $)

	1994	%Chg	1993	%Chg	1992	%Chg	1991
Revs.	4,680	12%	4,192	3%	4,056	NM	4,082
Oper. Inc.	276	8%	256	37%	187	23%	152
Depr.	134	-1%	136	-2%	139	-7%	150
Int. Exp.	29.0	-8%	31.6	-20%	39.4	-19%	48.4
Pretax Inc.	112	23%	91.0	NM	-11.0	NM	-43.0
Eff. Tax Rate	46%	—	45%	—	NM	—	NM
Net Inc.	60.0	18%	51.0	NM	-4.0	NM	-40.0

Balance Sheet & Other Fin. Data (Million $)

	1994	1993	1992	1991	1990	1989
Cash	96.0	139	152	285	218	111
Curr. Assets	1,031	896	863	874	911	861
Total Assets	2,473	2,307	2,293	2,285	2,412	2,392
Curr. Liab.	945	818	710	733	830	756
LT Debt	398	408	505	647	674	652
Common Eqty.	530	487	446	537	577	630
Total Cap.	1,110	1,054	1,132	1,226	1,301	1,363
Cap. Exp.	182	201	149	98.0	142	256
Cash Flow	175	167	118	97.0	119	151

Ratio Analysis

	1994	1993	1992	1991	1990	1989
Curr. Ratio	1.1	1.1	1.2	1.2	1.1	1.1
% LT Debt of Cap.	35.9	38.8	44.7	52.8	51.8	47.8
% Net Inc.of Revs.	1.3	1.2	NM	NM	NM	0.2
% Ret. on Assets	2.5	2.2	NM	NM	NM	0.5
% Ret. on Equity	8.0	6.7	NM	NM	NM	0.1

Dividend Data (A "poison pill" stock purchase rights plan was adopted in 1986. Quarterly dividends on the common were resumed with the February 24, 1995, payment.)

Amt. of Div. $	Date Decl.	Ex-Div. Date	Stock of Record	Payment Date
0.100	Dec. 05	Dec. 23	Dec. 30	Feb. 24 '95
0.100	May. 01	May. 08	May. 12	Jun. 15 '95
0.100	Jul. 25	Aug. 02	Aug. 04	Sep. 15 '95

Data as orig. reptd.; bef. results of disc. opers. and/or spec. items. Per share data adj. for stk. divs. as of ex-div. date.
E-Estimated. NA-Not Available. NM-Not Meaningful. NR-Not Ranked.

Office—3240 Hillview Ave., Palo Alto, CA 94304. **Tel**—(415) 494-2900. **Chrmn & CEO**—D. E. Moffitt. **EVP-CFO**—G. L. Quesnel. **VP-Secy & Investor Contact**—Maryla R. Boonstoppel. **Dirs**—R. Alpert, E. F. Cheit, G. R. Evans, M. G. Gill, R. Jaunich II, G. E. Liener, R. B. Madden, D. E. Moffitt, R. E. Poelman, R. D. Rogers, W. D. Walsh, R. P. Wayman. **Transfer Agent & Registrar**—First Chicago Trust Co. of New York, NYC. **Incorporated** in Delaware in 1958. **Empl**-40,500. **S&P Analyst:** Stephen R. Klein

Consolidated Natural Gas

NYSE Symbol **CNG**
In S&P 500

29-AUG-95

Industry:
Utilities-Gas

Summary: This major integrated natural gas system serves retail customers in Ohio, Pennsylvania and West Virginia, and wholesale customers in New York and the Northeast.

S&P Opinion: Hold (★★★)	Recent Price • 38	Yield • 5.1%
	52 Wk Range • 41⅛-33⅜	12-Mo. P/E • NM

Quantitative Evaluations

Outlook
(1 Lowest—5 Highest)
• **1+**

Fair Value
• **31½**

Risk
• **Low**

Earn./Div. Rank
• **B+**

Technical Eval.
• **Bullish** since 12/94

Rel. Strength Rank
(1 Lowest—99 Highest)
• **44**

Insider Activity
• **Neutral**

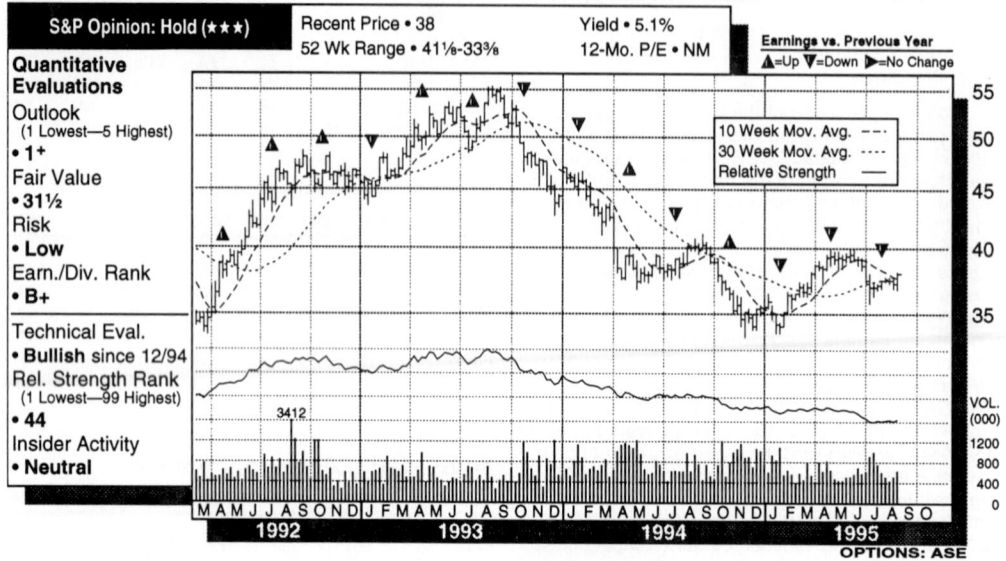

Earnings vs. Previous Year
▲=Up ▼=Down ▶=No Change

10 Week Mov. Avg. ---
30 Week Mov. Avg. ....
Relative Strength —

OPTIONS: ASE

Overview - 29-AUG-95

Gas distribution profits should move up nicely this year, due to rate hikes granted last year, as will transmission results aided by a rate case settlement early this year. The exploration and production area has been weakened severely by wellhead shut-ins, due to weak demand; growth in the company's new electric power marketing activities should be somewhat offsetting. At present, CNG is the fourth largest such marketer in the U.S. Although we expect expansion of gas pipeline facilities to aid future prospects, one-time charges of $2.03 a share to write down uneconomic assets and reduce the headcount in the first half and soft gas prices will severely impair comparisons for 1995. Excluding such charges, earnings through 1995's first half were flat, year to year.

Valuation - 29-AUG-95

CNG's share price appreciation has trailed broader market averages this year, due to slumping natural gas prices. A move up in the third quarter is possible as investors react positively to large writedowns of subpar assets and the focus on cost cutting, which includes a goal of 7% lower operating costs by year end. Despite its decision last year to forego the annual dividend increase after 29 consecutive increases, the dividend appears secure. CNG's aggressive cost reductions and pursuit of more viable markets such as electric power sales should help improve future valuations.

Key Stock Statistics

S&P EPS Est. 1995	2.20	Tang. Bk. Value/Share	23.37
P/E on S&P Est. 1995	17.3	Beta	0.36
S&P EPS Est. 1996	2.30	Shareholders	40,800
Dividend Rate/Share	1.94	Market cap. (B)	$ 3.6
Shs. outstg. (M)	93.3	Inst. holdings	46%
Avg. daily vol. (M)	0.101	Insider holdings	NA

Value of $10,000 invested 5 years ago: $ 9,739

Fiscal Year Ending Dec. 31

	1995	% Change	1994	% Change	1993	% Change
Revenues (Million $)						
1Q	1,192	-2%	1,214	7%	1,132	23%
2Q	665.0	14%	582.0	6%	549.0	23%
3Q	—	—	452.0	-4%	473.0	31%
4Q	—	—	789.0	-23%	1,030	30%
Yr.	—	—	3,036	-5%	3,184	26%
Income (Million $)						
1Q	-21.40	NM	130.9	4%	125.7	13%
2Q	-33.51	NM	3.07	-54%	6.64	NM
3Q	—	—	-24.56	NM	-29.97	NM
4Q	—	—	73.74	-14%	86.11	-11%
Yr.	—	—	183.2	-3%	188.5	-3%
Earnings Per Share ($)						
1Q	-0.23	NM	1.41	4%	1.36	7%
2Q	-0.36	NM	0.03	-57%	0.07	NM
3Q	E-0.21	NM	-0.26	NM	-0.32	NM
4Q	E0.80	1%	0.79	-15%	0.93	-11%
Yr.	E2.20	12%	1.97	-3%	2.03	-7%

Next earnings report expected: early November

Consolidated Natural Gas

Business Summary - 29-AUG-95

Consolidated Natural Gas is engaged in all aspects of the natural gas business, including exploration, production, purchasing, gathering, transmission, storage and distribution. The company also owns substantial coal reserves. Revenue contributions in recent years:

	1994	1993	1992	1991
Regulated gas sales:				
Res./comm.	52%	50%	57%	53%
Commercial	16%	2%	2%	2%
Industrial	2%	13%	7%	16%
Nonregulated gas sales	30%	17%	11%	9%
Other	Nil	18%	23%	20%

The company supplies gas to nearly 1.8 million retail customers in Ohio, Pennsylvania, Virginia and West Virginia through six gas distribution subsidiaries. CNG Transmission operates an interstate pipeline system serving CNG's distribution units, and non-affiliated utilities in the Midwest, the Mid-Atlantic states and the Northeast. Gas volumes sold and transported in 1994 totaled 1,343 Bcf, versus 1,192 Bcf in 1993.

Exploration and production activities are conducted by CNG Producing primarily in the Gulf of Mexico, the Southwest, the Appalachian region, and Canada. Proved reserves at 1994 year-end totaled 972 Bcf of gas, up from 960 Bcf a year earlier, and 46.5 million bbl. of oil and condensate, up from 27.9 million bbl.

Other operations include CNG Gas Services Corp., which arranges gas sales, transportation, storage and other services for large customers; Consolidated Natural Gas Service Co., Inc., which advises, assists and manages activities for other system companies; CNG Coal Co., which holds coal reserves; and CNG Energy Co., which develops opportunities in energy related markets.

Important Developments

Aug. '95—CNG reiterated its goals of attaining 10% annual growth in operating earnings growth starting this year and a return on equity of 12% to 15% for 1995 and 1996. Results for 1995's first half were penalized by milder than usual weather, and by noncash one-time charges in the second quarter of $0.22 a share to write down the value of redundant coal properties, and $0.25 to cover costs of a workforce reduction. In the first quarter, CNG wrote down oil and gas producing properties as a result of low gas wellhead prices, lowering net income $1.56 a share (noncash); in 1995's first half, it sold its gas production at an average price of $1.82 a thousand cubic foot, down from $2.35 a year earlier. Much smaller restructuring costs may also be charged against 1995 third quarter results.

Capitalization

Long Term Debt: $1,297,453,000 (6/95), incl. $250 million of 7.25% debs., conv. into com. at $54 a sh.

Per Share Data ($) (Year Ended Dec. 31)

	1994	1993	1992	1991	1990	1989
Tangible Bk. Val.	23.48	23.30	22.96	21.57	21.28	20.20
Cash Flow	4.97	5.21	5.42	5.22	5.20	5.54
Earnings	1.97	2.03	2.19	1.94	1.91	2.20
Dividends	1.94	1.92	1.90	1.88	1.84	1.76
Payout Ratio	98%	95%	87%	97%	96%	80%
Prices - High	47	55⅜	48⅝	45	52⅞	51½
- Low	33⅞	42⅝	33½	37⅞	41	37⅛
P/E Ratio - High	24	27	22	23	28	23
- Low	17	21	15	20	21	17

Income Statement Analysis (Million $)

	1994	%Chg	1993	%Chg	1992	%Chg	1991
Revs.	3,036	-5%	3,184	26%	2,521	-3%	2,607
Oper. Inc.	623	-4%	652	3%	630	11%	570
Depr.	279	-5%	295	2%	288	1%	285
Int. Exp.	97.0	8%	90.0	-11%	101	-9%	111
Pretax Inc.	266	-8%	288	9%	264	18%	223
Eff. Tax Rate	31%	—	35%	—	26%	—	25%
Net Inc.	183	-3%	188	-4%	195	15%	169

Balance Sheet & Other Fin. Data (Million $)

	1994	1993	1992	1991	1990	1989
Cash	31.9	27.1	43.4	25.0	70.0	27.8
Curr. Assets	1,065	1,043	1,197	1,094	1,235	1,087
Total Assets	5,519	5,410	5,242	5,011	5,006	4,601
Curr. Liab.	1,211	1,113	1,238	1,185	1,239	1,245
LT Debt	1,152	1,159	1,112	1,159	1,129	891
Common Eqty.	2,184	2,176	2,133	1,890	1,845	1,672
Total Cap.	4,128	4,154	3,953	3,789	3,714	3,317
Cap. Exp.	416	341	439	484	402	631
Cash Flow	462	483	483	453	446	457

Ratio Analysis

	1994	1993	1992	1991	1990	1989
Curr. Ratio	0.9	0.9	1.0	0.9	1.0	0.9
% LT Debt of Cap.	27.9	27.9	28.1	30.6	30.4	26.8
% Net Inc.of Revs.	6.0	5.9	7.7	6.5	6.0	6.5
% Ret. on Assets	3.4	3.5	3.7	3.3	3.3	4.2
% Ret. on Equity	8.4	8.7	9.4	9.0	9.1	11.0

Dividend Data —Dividends have been paid since 1944. A dividend reinvestment plan is available.

Amt. of Div. $	Date Decl.	Ex-Div. Date	Stock of Record	Payment Date
0.485	Sep. 13	Oct. 07	Oct. 14	Nov. 15 '94
0.485	Dec. 13	Jan. 09	Jan. 13	Feb. 15 '95
0.485	Mar. 14	Apr. 07	Apr. 14	May. 15 '95
0.485	Jun. 13	Jul. 12	Jul. 14	Aug. 15 '95

Data as orig. reptd.; bef. results of disc. opers. and/or spec. items. Per share data adj. for stk. divs. as of ex-div. date. E-Estimated. NA-Not Available. NM-Not Meaningful. NR-Not Ranked.

Office—CNG Tower, 625 Liberty Ave., Pittsburgh, PA 15222-3199. **Tel**—(412) 227-1000. **Chrmn & CEO**—G. A. Davidson, Jr. **Vice Chrmn & CFO**—L. D. Johnson. **Treas**—R. M. Sable, Jr. **Secy**—L. J. McKeown. **Investor Contact**—James W. Garrett. **Dirs**—W. S. Barrack, J. W. Connolly, G. A. Davidson, Jr., R. J. Groves, L. D. Johnson, P. E. Lego, M. A. McKenna, S. A. Minter, W. R. Peirson, R. P. Simmons, L. Wyse. **Transfer Agent & Registrar**—Society National Bank, Cleveland. **Incorporated** in Delaware in 1942. **Empl**-7,566. **S&P Analyst:** Jane Collin

Cooper Industries

NYSE Symbol **CBE**
In S&P 500

20-SEP-95

Industry:
Manufacturing/Distr

Summary: Cooper Industries is a diversified, worldwide manufacturer of electrical products, tools and hardware, and automotive products.

S&P Opinion: Hold (★★★)		
Recent Price • 36⅛		Yield • 3.6%
52 Wk Range • 42⅛-31⅝		12-Mo. P/E • NM

Quantitative Evaluations

Outlook
(1 Lowest—5 Highest)
• **3⁻**

Fair Value
• **36⅛**

Risk
• **Low**

Earn./Div. Rank
• **A**

Technical Eval.
• **Bullish** since 12/94

Rel. Strength Rank
(1 Lowest—99 Highest)
• **13**

Insider Activity
• **Unfavorable**

Earnings vs. Previous Year
▲=Up ▼=Down ▶=No Change

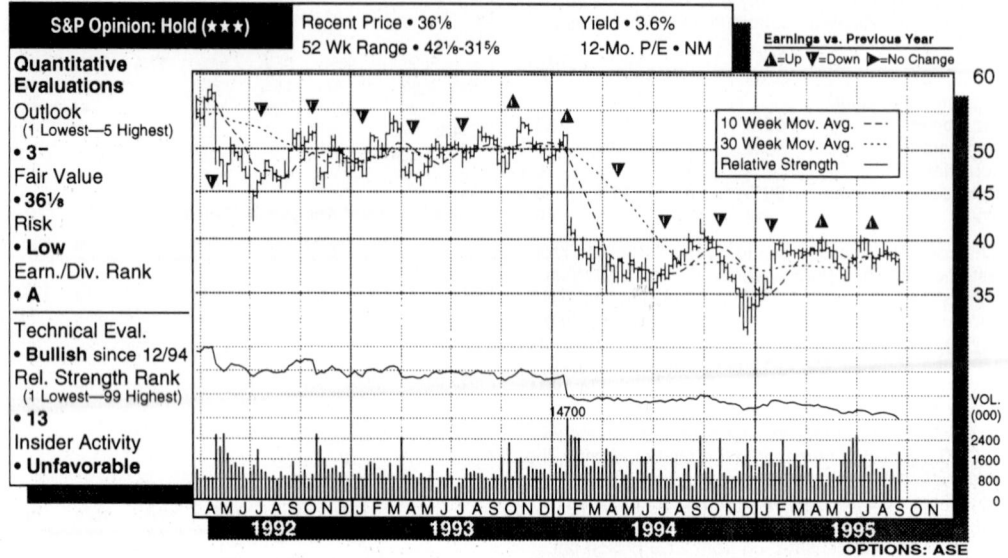

- 10 Week Mov. Avg. – – –
- 30 Week Mov. Avg. · · · ·
- Relative Strength —

OPTIONS: ASE

Overview - 20-SEP-95

Revenues from continuing operations for 1996 are expected to increase from 1995's levels, reflecting continued gains in tools and hardware, and modest growth in electrical and automotive products. Aided by higher capacity utilization, overhead cost reductions, better pricing and a leveling of raw material prices, margins should expand and result in higher earnings in 1996. The divestment of the petroleum and industrial equipment unit in 1995 should reduce the volatility of CBE's earnings over the course of future business cycles. We expect the company to continue to adjust its business mix with selective acquisitions and possibly divestitures. Eventual conversion of CBE's $691 million of convertible debt will reduce interest expense but result in moderate share earnings dilution.

Valuation - 20-SEP-95

Following the spin-off of Cooper-Cameron, the company's former petroleum and industrial equipment segment, CBE is focused on more stable markets for electrical, tool, hardware and automotive products. However, the company is fairly valued at some 15 times projected 1995 earnings and with a large overhang of some $691 million in debt convertible at $41.17 a share, the stock's near term progress could slow. Longer term, conversion of this debt would stabilize CBE's balance sheet and permit pursuit of acquisition opportunities to supplement the moderate growth expected from the current business mix.

Key Stock Statistics

S&P EPS Est. 1995	2.40	Tang. Bk. Value/Share	NM
P/E on S&P Est. 1995	15.1	Beta	1.49
S&P EPS Est. 1996	2.70	Shareholders	35,500
Dividend Rate/Share	1.32	Market cap. (B)	$ 3.9
Shs. outstg. (M)	107.6	Inst. holdings	75%
Avg. daily vol. (M)	0.294	Insider holdings	NA

Value of $10,000 invested 5 years ago: NA

Fiscal Year Ending Dec. 31

	1995	% Change	1994	% Change	1993	% Change
Revenues (Million $)						
1Q	1,123	8%	1,038	-29%	1,471	-2%
2Q	1,268	8%	1,174	-27%	1,612	5%
3Q	—	—	1,136	-29%	1,592	7%
4Q	—	—	1,240	-22%	1,599	-2%
Yr.	—	—	4,588	-27%	6,274	2%
Income (Million $)						
1Q	55.30	6%	52.20	-17%	63.10	-4%
2Q	82.80	4%	79.30	-23%	102.9	-6%
3Q	—	—	75.80	-23%	98.90	10%
4Q	—	—	85.50	-16%	102.2	6%
Yr.	—	—	292.8	-20%	367.1	2%
Earnings Per Share ($)						
1Q	0.48	41%	0.34	-23%	0.44	-4%
2Q	0.71	22%	0.58	-27%	0.79	-6%
3Q	E0.56	2%	0.55	-27%	0.75	12%
4Q	E0.65	3%	0.63	-19%	0.78	7%
Yr.	E2.40	14%	2.10	-24%	2.75	1%

Next earnings report expected: late October

Cooper Industries

Business Summary - 15-SEP-95

Cooper Industries is a diversified, worldwide manufacturer of electrical products, tools and hardware, and automotive products. The company discontinued its electrical power equipment and petroleum and industrial equipment segments in 1994. Industry segment contributions in 1994 were as follows:

	Revs.	Profits
Electrical products	45%	53%
Tools & hardware	20%	16%
Automotive products	35%	31%

Overseas operations accounted for 23% of revenues and 18% of operating earnings in 1994.

The electrical products segment makes electrical and electronic distribution and circuit protection products for use in residential, commercial and industrial construction, and maintenance and repair. It also makes products for use by utilities and industries for primary power distribution and control.

Tools and hardware items are made for use in residential, commercial and industrial construction, maintenance and repair, and for general industrial and consumer use.

The automotive products segment manufactures spark plugs, wiper blades, lamps, brake system components and other products for use by the automotive aftermarket and in automobile assemblies. Additionally, this segment manufactures and distributes suspension, steering, temperature control and driveline components for the automotive aftermarket.

Important Developments

Jul. '95—Second quarter earnings of $0.71 a share were before a charge of $186.6 million ($1.60 a share) related to the spin-off of Cooper Cameron (RON), which was completed on July 17, 1995 with the distribution of 85.5% of RON's common stock. RON is comprised of CBE's discontinued petroleum and industrial equipment business. The spin-off was accomplished through an exchange offer which permitted CBE shareholders to exchange CBE shares for shares in RON on a 1 for 2.25 basis. As a result of the exchange offer, 9.5 million CBE shares were exchanged for 33.7 million RON shares, leaving CBE with approximately 107.5 million common shares outstanding and a 14.5% stake in RON. CBE said the spin-off was implemented to allow financial markets to evaluate its businesses more effectively.

Capitalization

Long Term Debt: $1,886,200,000. (6/95).

Per Share Data ($)
(Year Ended Dec. 31)

	1994	1993	1992	1991	1990	1989
Tangible Bk. Val.	5.02	-3.14	-6.12	0.93	-2.34	-2.23
Cash Flow	4.31	5.40	5.25	5.34	4.96	3.84
Earnings	2.10	2.75	2.71	3.04	2.81	2.51
Dividends	1.32	1.32	1.24	1.16	1.08	1.00
Payout Ratio	63%	48%	46%	38%	38%	41%
Prices - High	52¼	54¾	59⅜	58	46	40
- Low	31⅝	45⅝	41¾	38½	31¼	26⅞
P/E Ratio - High	25	20	22	19	16	16
- Low	15	17	15	13	11	11

Income Statement Analysis (Million $)

	1994	%Chg	1993	%Chg	1992	%Chg	1991
Revs.	4,588	-27%	6,253	2%	6,119	NM	6,155
Oper. Inc.	777	-23%	1,006	6%	945	-13%	1,080
Depr.	199	-34%	303	5%	289	12%	258
Int. Exp.	73.0	-26%	99	-15%	116	-28%	161
Pretax Inc.	505	-19%	625	8%	580	-13%	669
Eff. Tax Rate	42%		41%		38%		41%
Net Inc.	293	-20%	367	2%	361	-8%	393

Balance Sheet & Other Fin. Data (Million $)

	1994	1993	1992	1991	1990	1989
Cash	25.3	13.0	17.8	19.4	13.5	28.5
Curr. Assets	2,100	2,582	2,837	2,909	2,908	2,799
Total Assets	6,401	7,148	7,576	7,149	7,168	6,745
Curr. Liab.	1,333	1,703	1,650	1,711	1,866	1,782
LT Debt	1,362	1,254	1,816	1,479	1,684	1,829
Common Eqty.	2,741	2,351	2,117	2,648	2,353	1,979
Total Cap.	4,103	4,239	4,683	5,167	5,020	4,743
Cap. Exp.	209	275	274	266	240	191
Cash Flow	492	617	598	600	550	404

Ratio Analysis

	1994	1993	1992	1991	1990	1989
Curr. Ratio	1.6	1.5	1.7	1.7	1.6	1.6
% LT Debt of Cap.	33.2	29.6	38.8	28.6	33.6	38.6
% Net Inc.of Revs.	6.4	5.9	5.9	6.4	5.8	5.2
% Ret. on Assets	4.6	5.0	4.9	5.4	5.2	4.7
% Ret. on Equity	10.2	14.4	12.9	13.5	14.3	13.6

Dividend Data

Dividends have been paid since 1947. A dividend reinvestment plan is available. A "poison pill" stock purchase rights plan was adopted in 1987.

Amt. of Div. $	Date Decl.	Ex-Div. Date	Stock of Record	Payment Date
0.330	Aug. 02	Sep. 07	Sep. 13	Oct. 03 '94
0.330	Nov. 01	Dec. 01	Dec. 07	Jan. 02 '95
0.330	Feb. 14	Feb. 23	Mar. 01	Apr. 03 '95
0.330	Apr. 25	Jun. 09	Jun. 13	Jul. 03 '95
0.330	Aug. 01	Sep. 12	Sep. 14	Oct. 02 '95

Data as orig. reptd.; bef. results of disc. opers. and/or spec. items. Per share data adj. for stk. divs. as of ex-div. date.
E-Estimated. NA-Not Available. NM-Not Meaningful. NR-Not Ranked.

Office—1001 Fannin, Suite 4000, Houston, TX 77002. **Tel**—(713) 739-5400. **Chrmn**—R. Cizik. **Pres & CEO**—H. J. Riley, Jr. **SVP-Fin & CFO**—D. B. McWilliams. **SVP & Secy**—D. K. Schumacher. **Investor Contact**—Richard J. Bajenski. **Dirs**—W. L. Batts, R. Cizik, C. J. Grum, L. A. Hill, H. S. Hook, C. S. Nicandros, F. A. Olson, J. D. Ong, H. J. Riley, Jr., Sir Ralph H. Robins, A. T. Young. **Transfer Agent & Registrar**—First Chicago Trust Co. of New York, NYC. **Incorporated** in Ohio in 1929. **Empl**-40,800. **S&P Analyst:** Joshua M. Harari, CFA

Cooper Tire & Rubber

NYSE Symbol **CTB**
In S&P 500

09-AUG-95 **Industry:** Rubber

Summary: The fourth largest U.S. tire maker, Cooper supplies tires exclusively for the replacement market. It also manufactures original equipment automotive components.

S&P Opinion: Accumulate (★★★★)	Recent Price • 25¼	Yield • 1.2%
	52 Wk Range • 29⅝-21⅝	12-Mo. P/E • 16.7

Quantitative Evaluations

Outlook
(1 Lowest—5 Highest)
• **1⁻**

Fair Value
• **22**

Risk
• **Low**

Earn./Div. Rank
• **A**

Technical Eval.
• **Bearish** since 1/95

Rel. Strength Rank
(1 Lowest—99 Highest)
• **42**

Insider Activity
• **NA**

Earnings vs. Previous Year
▲=Up ▼=Down ▶=No Change

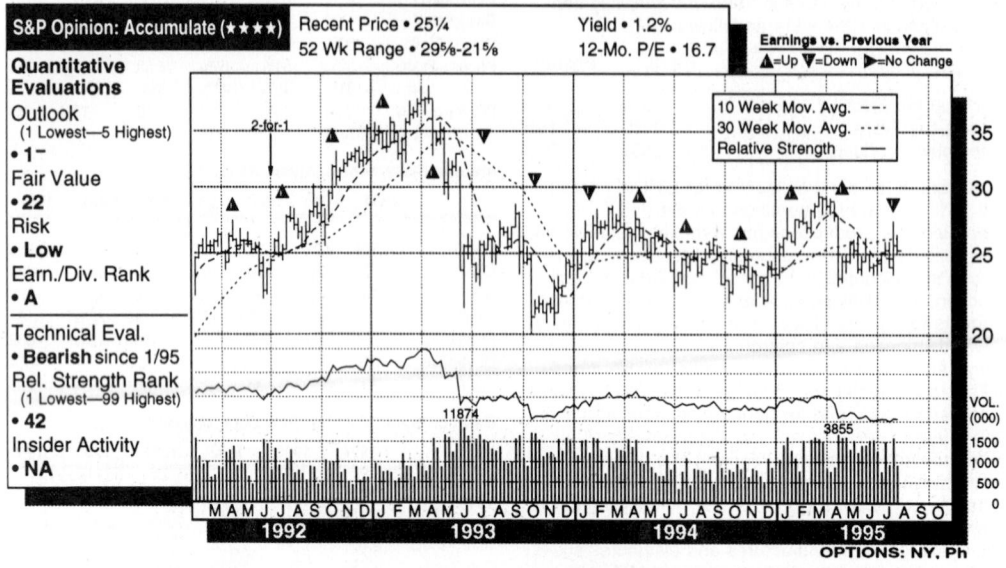

- 10 Week Mov. Avg. ---
- 30 Week Mov. Avg. ·····
- Relative Strength —

OPTIONS: NY, Ph

Overview - 09-AUG-95

Sales should advance in 1996, reflecting the additional replacement tire business from Sears, Pep Boys and other customers, greater demand for engineered products due to new contracts. More price increases are likely to pass through higher materials costs and restore margins. Results should be aided by greater operating efficiencies due to high capacity utilization. Favorable long-term trends include a growing car and truck population and a continued rise in miles driven per vehicle. Efforts to expand export sales from a relatively small base are developing nicely, aided by weakness in the U.S. dollar versus certain foreign currencies. Local production of engineered rubber products in Europe is possible if original equipment customers are interested.

Valuation - 09-AUG-95

Despite lower first half earnings, due largely to a lag in the pass-through of higher raw materials costs, we believe that CTB remains on a strong long term growth trend. Aided by recent customer additions, expanded tire output at the Albany, Ga., plant, and strong OEM demand for non-tire parts, CTB should report a stronger second half and enjoy a strong earnings rise in 1996. With international opportunities under evaluation, we expect the company to maintain its outstanding long-term earnings growth record. We believe the stock is an attractive portfolio addition for steady, above average growth at its present trading level of around 14 times estimated 1996 earnings.

Key Stock Statistics

S&P EPS Est. 1995	1.50	Tang. Bk. Value/Share	8.18
P/E on S&P Est. 1995	16.8	Beta	1.74
S&P EPS Est. 1996	1.75	Shareholders	7,600
Dividend Rate/Share	0.30	Market cap. (B)	$ 2.1
Shs. outstg. (M)	83.6	Inst. holdings	64%
Avg. daily vol. (M)	0.280	Insider holdings	NA

Value of $10,000 invested 5 years ago: $ 32,717

Fiscal Year Ending Dec. 31

	1995	% Change	1994	% Change	1993	% Change
Revenues (Million $)						
1Q	365.4	11%	329.1	18%	280.1	4%
2Q	371.4	13%	329.3	13%	292.6	-4%
3Q	—	—	383.5	18%	326.1	7%
4Q	—	—	361.3	23%	294.9	NM
Yr.	—	—	1,403	18%	1,194	2%
Income (Million $)						
1Q	27.22	3%	26.51	5%	25.20	34%
2Q	24.66	-10%	27.46	14%	24.02	-4%
3Q	—	—	35.45	41%	25.16	-17%
4Q	—	—	39.10	40%	27.84	-18%
Yr.	—	—	128.5	26%	102.2	-6%
Earnings Per Share ($)						
1Q	0.33	3%	0.32	7%	0.30	30%
2Q	0.29	-12%	0.33	14%	0.29	-3%
3Q	E0.40	—	0.42	40%	0.30	-17%
4Q	E0.48	—	0.47	42%	0.33	-20%
Yr.	E1.50	—	1.54	26%	1.22	-6%

Next earnings report expected: early September

Cooper Tire & Rubber

09-AUG-95

Business Summary - 08-AUG-95

Cooper Tire & Rubber is the fourth largest tire manufacturer in the U.S., and the ninth largest worldwide. Its tires are sold exclusively to the replacement tire market. Other rubber products include inner tubes, vibration control products, hose and hose assemblies, automotive body and window sealing systems, and specialty seating components. The 10 largest customers accounted for 53% of sales in 1994, versus 55% in 1993 and 1992. A single customer provided 13%, 14% and 15% of sales in 1994, 1993 and 1992, respectively. Exports account for 6% of the 1994 total, versus 5% in 1993. CTB believes that its shipments of automobile and truck tires amounted to approximately 10%, 10%, 11%, 10%, 8.3% and 7.7% of all those made in the U.S. in 1994, 1993, 1992, 1991, 1990 and 1989, respectively.

A complete line of replacement automobile and truck tires and heavy-duty inner tubes is manufactured in a wide range of sizes and types. A variety of engineered rubber products are manufactured. These can be broadly categorized as torsional springs, body-frame/cradle isolators, body sealing, chassis-suspension components, suspension strut/spring isolators, power-train isolators, and hoses. Lines under development include color-matched body seals, which will be supplied for several General Motors 1996 models, and high pressure air conditioning and power steering hoses, which require a different manufacturing process than current low pressure hose products.

Tires are made at four plants and sold nationally in the replacement tire market, primarily through more than 2,000 independent dealers and distributors under the Cooper, Falls Mastercraft and Starfire house brandnames and under private label brands. The independent marketing channel accounted for about two-thirds of all replacement passenger tires sold in the U.S. in recent years. Two plants are dedicated to production of tubes, and three plants produce engineered rubber products, which are sold to GM, Ford and Chrysler and eight foreign-owned or joint-venture vehicle manufacturing operations in North America.

Important Developments

May '95—CTB announced plans to invest $112 million to expand warehousing and tire production capability. About half of the expenditure will be devoted to boosting radial passenger tire production and customer service capability at the Albany, Ga., plant. The balance will add warehouse space and increase passenger tire production at the Findlay, Ohio, and Tupelo, Miss., plants.

Capitalization

Long Term Debt: $33,370,000 (6/30/95).

Per Share Data ($)

(Year Ended Dec. 31)

	1994	1993	1992	1991	1990	1989
Tangible Bk. Val.	7.65	6.30	5.52	5.14	4.47	3.77
Cash Flow	2.20	1.78	1.75	1.35	1.14	1.00
Earnings	1.54	1.22	1.30	0.96	0.81	0.71
Dividends	0.23	0.20	0.17	0.13	0.10	0.09
Payout Ratio	15%	16%	13%	14%	13%	12%
Prices - High	29½	39⅝	35⅝	26⅜	10½	9¾
- Low	21⅝	20	22⅛	7⅛	6¼	5⅝
P/E Ratio - High	19	32	27	27	13	14
- Low	14	16	17	8	8	8

Income Statement Analysis (Million $)

	1994	%Chg	1993	%Chg	1992	%Chg	1991
Revs.	1,403	18%	1,194	2%	1,175	17%	1,001
Oper. Inc.	264	25%	212	1%	209	31%	160
Depr.	55.6	20%	46.4	22%	38.1	19%	32.0
Int. Exp.	3.8	-17%	4.7	-7%	5.0	-40%	8.3
Pretax Inc.	208	27%	164	-4%	170	37%	124
Eff. Tax Rate	38%	—	38%	—	36%	—	36%
Net Inc.	129	26%	102	-6%	108	36%	79.4

Balance Sheet & Other Fin. Data (Million $)

	1994	1993	1992	1991	1990	1989
Cash	103	25.8	55.1	24.4	10.1	49.6
Curr. Assets	455	332	315	262	268	249
Total Assets	1,040	890	797	671	616	520
Curr. Liab.	152	127	140	117	101	99
LT Debt	33.6	38.7	48.1	53.5	91.0	65.7
Common Eqty.	662	550	471	440	369	310
Total Cap.	725	608	526	532	494	405
Cap. Exp.	78.0	117	110	86.0	100	73.0
Cash Flow	184	149	146	111	94.0	82.0

Ratio Analysis

	1994	1993	1992	1991	1990	1989
Curr. Ratio	3.0	2.6	2.3	2.2	2.7	2.5
% LT Debt of Cap.	4.6	6.4	9.1	10.1	18.4	16.2
% Net Inc.of Revs.	9.2	8.6	9.2	7.9	7.4	6.7
% Ret. on Assets	13.3	12.1	14.7	12.3	11.7	12.1
% Ret. on Equity	21.2	20.0	23.7	19.6	19.5	20.5

Dividend Data

(Dividends have been paid since 1950. A "poison pill" stock purchase rights plan was adopted in 1988.)

Amt. of Div. $	Date Decl.	Ex-Div. Date	Stock of Record	Payment Date
0.060	Nov. 10	Nov. 18	Nov. 25	Dec. 19 '94
0.060	Feb. 14	Feb. 28	Mar. 06	Mar. 31 '95
0.060	May. 02	May. 26	Jun. 02	Jun. 30 '95
0.075	Jul. 24	Aug. 30	Sep. 01	Sep. 30 '95

Data as orig. reptd.; bef. results of disc. opers. and/or spec. items. Per share data adj. for stk. divs. as of ex-div. date. E-Estimated. NA-Not Available. NM-Not Meaningful. NR-Not Ranked.

Office—Lima & Western Aves., Findlay, OH 45840. **Tel**—(419) 423-1321. **Chrmn & Pres**—P. Rooney. **EVP-CFO & Investor Contact**—J. Alec Reinhardt. **Secy**—S. C. Kaiman. **Dirs**—D. A. Davis, E. D. Dunford, J. Fahl, D. J. Gormley, I. W. Gorr, J. M. Magliochetti, A. H. Meltzer, J. A. Reinhardt, P. W. Rooney, L. F. Winbigler. **Transfer Agent & Registrar**—KeyCorp Shareholder Services, Cleveland. **Incorporated** in Delaware in 1930. **Empl**-7,815. **S&P Analyst:** Joshua M. Harari, CFA

Coors (Adolph) Co.

NASDAQ Symbol **ACCOB**
In S&P 500

09-SEP-95

Industry:
Beverages

Summary: Adolph Coors Co. is the parent company of the third larg-est U.S. brewer, with an approximate 10% market share.

S&P Opinion: Avoid (★★)		
Recent Price • 17½	Yield • 2.9%	
52 Wk Range • 20½-14¾	12-Mo. P/E • 15.8	

Quantitative Evaluations

Outlook
(1 Lowest—5 Highest)
• **3⁻**

Fair Value
• **17⅛**

Risk
• **Low**

Earn./Div. Rank
• **B-**

Technical Eval.
• **Bearish** since 6/95

Rel. Strength Rank
(1 Lowest—99 Highest)
• **44**

Insider Activity
• **NA**

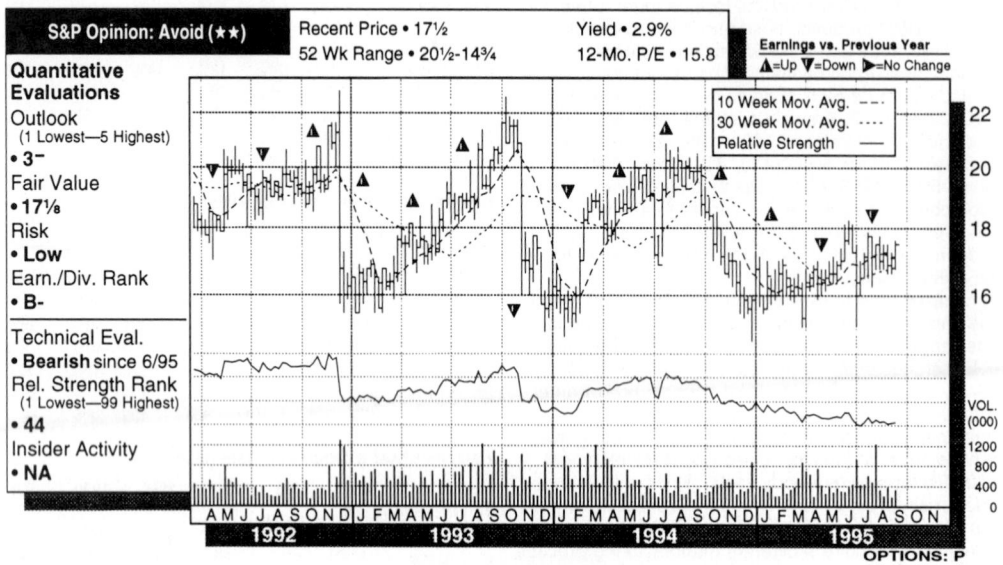

Earnings vs. Previous Year
▲=Up ▼=Down ▶=No Change

10 Week Mov. Avg. ‐ ‐ ‐
30 Week Mov. Avg. ‐‐‐‐
Relative Strength ─

VOL. (000)

1200
800
400
0

1992   1993   1994   1995

OPTIONS: P

Overview - 07-SEP-95

Net sales are expected to grow at a low single-digit annual rate through 1996, led principally by modestly higher volumes and an improving product mix toward premium brands. Near-term margins may continue to be under pressure from higher packaging costs, particularly for aluminum and corrugated box board. The company will try to offset these pressures through the continued emphasis of high-margin new products, such as Zima Gold, Coors Special Lager and Coors Red Light, and through further cost cutting actions. Earnings per share for 1995 are likely to fall signifi-cantly short of 1994's $1.27 (before nonrecurring items). A modest earnings recovery is possible in 1996.

Valuation - 07-SEP-95

Given our expectations of uninspiring earnings trends for the foreseeable future, we would avoid the shares until there is evidence of a material recovery in operat-ing profitability. With only a modest 10% share of the highly competitive, mature U.S. brewing industry, Coors faces material competitive disadvantages re-lated primarily to economies of scale. This disadvan-tage is particularly acute in times of sharply higher raw materials costs, as has been the case recently. Thus, the company's future success hinges largely on new product success, product mix improvement, and pro-ductivity gains. Despite the stock's low valuation to cash flow and tangible book value, we advise avoiding the stock for now.

Key Stock Statistics

S&P EPS Est. 1995	0.90	Tang. Bk. Value/Share	17.06
P/E on S&P Est. 1995	19.4	Beta	0.32
S&P EPS Est. 1996	1.10	Shareholders	5,500
Dividend Rate/Share	0.50	Market cap. (B)	$0.672
Shs. outstg. (M)	38.4	Inst. holdings	36%
Avg. daily vol. (M)	0.054	Insider holdings	NA

Value of $10,000 invested 5 years ago: $ 10,381

Fiscal Year Ending Dec. 31

	1995	% Change	1994	% Change	1993	% Change
Revenues (Million $)						
1Q	326.6	3%	318.5	8%	296.0	4%
2Q	399.5	-8%	432.2	5%	412.9	1%
3Q	—	—	555.6	4%	535.6	4%
4Q	—	—	356.4	6%	337.3	NM
Yr.	—	—	1,663	5%	1,582	2%
Income (Million $)						
1Q	0.09	-99%	6.93	49%	4.66	NM
2Q	15.18	-37%	23.91	27%	18.89	26%
3Q	—	—	17.34	81%	9.59	-61%
4Q	—	—	9.94	NM	-75.06	NM
Yr.	—	—	58.12	NM	-41.93	NM
Earnings Per Share ($)						
1Q	Nil	—	0.18	50%	0.12	NM
2Q	0.40	-37%	0.63	26%	0.50	25%
3Q	E0.45	NM	0.45	80%	0.25	-62%
4Q	E0.05	-81%	0.26	NM	-1.97	NM
Yr.	E0.90	-41%	1.52	NM	-1.10	NM

Next earnings report expected: late October

Coors (Adolph) Co.

Business Summary - 07-SEP-95

Adolph Coors Co., through its subsidiary, Coors Brewing Co., produces and markets beer and other malt-based beverages.

Major products include the following beer brands: Original Coors, Coors Light, Coors Extra Gold, Coors Artic Ice, Coors Artic Ice Light, Coors Dry, non-alcoholic Coors Cutter, Keystone, Keystone Light, Keystone Dry, Keystone Ice and Keystone Amber Light in all 50 states and the District of Columbia. Other malt beverage products, which are sold in most states, include George Killian's Irish Red, Winterfest, Zima Clearmalt, and Zima Gold. In 1994, the company sold 20.4 million barrels of malt beverage products, up 2.7% from the level of 1993.

Coors has three domestic production facilities: the first, the world's largest single-site brewery, is in Golden, Colo.; the second, a packaging and brewing facility, is in Memphis, Tenn.; the third facility, which currently operates as a packaging plant and distribution facility, is near Elkton, Va. Significant portions of the company's aluminum can, glass bottle and malt requirements are produced in its own facilities.

Coors has a licensing agreement with Molson Breweries of Canada Ltd. for that company to brew and distribute Original Coors and Coors Light in Canada. A similar agreement allows Asahi Breweries Ltd. to brew and distribute Original Coors in Japan.

Important Developments

Jul. '95—ACCOB placed privately $100 million of debt carrying maturities of 7 and 10 years, with a weighted average interest rate of 6.8%. Net company proceeds were earmarked for debt paydown and for seasonal working capital needs.

Jun. '95—Total company sales volume of malt beverages for the 24 weeks ended June 11, 1995, amounted to 8,826,000, down 2.7% from the year-earlier level. Management attributed the lower net income reported for 1995's first half primarily to higher aluminum and other packaging material costs, and a less profitable sales mix (significantly lower Zima Clearmalt volumes). ACCOB said that its core beer volume was up about 1% in 1995's first half, year to year.

Capitalization

Long Term Debt: $131,000,000 (6/11/95).
Cl. A Common Stock: 1,260,000 shs. ($1 par).
Cl. B Common Stock: 37,160,679 shs. (no par); nonvoting.
The Coors family controls 33% of Cl. B & all of Cl. A.
Institutions hold about 37% of Cl. B.
Shareholders: 5,541 of record (3/95).

Per Share Data ($) (Year Ended Dec. 31)

	1994	1993	1992	1991	1990	1989
Tangible Bk. Val.	17.06	16.21	17.81	28.64	28.59	28.12
Cash Flow	4.67	2.02	4.00	4.45	4.56	3.66
Earnings	1.52	-1.10	0.95	0.64	1.05	0.36
Dividends	0.50	0.50	0.50	0.50	0.50	0.50
Payout Ratio	33%	NM	53%	78%	48%	140%
Prices - High	20⅞	22½	22⅞	24¼	27⅜	24⅜
- Low	14¾	15	15½	17⅜	17⅛	17⅜
P/E Ratio - High	14	NM	24	38	26	68
- Low	10	NM	16	27	16	48

Income Statement Analysis (Million $)

	1994	%Chg	1993	%Chg	1992	%Chg	1991
Revs.	1,663	5%	1,582	2%	1,551	-19%	1,917
Oper. Inc.	215	10%	196	4%	188	-3%	194
Depr.	121	2%	119	4%	114	-20%	142
Int. Exp.	17.8	-14%	20.6	-5%	21.6	23%	17.6
Pretax Inc.	104	82%	57.0	-3%	59.0	157%	23.0
Eff. Tax Rate	44%	—	NM	—	39%	—	NM
Net Inc.	58.1	NM	-41.9	NM	35.7	49%	23.9

Balance Sheet & Other Fin. Data (Million $)

	1994	1993	1992	1991	1990	1989
Cash	27.0	82.0	40.0	15.0	64.0	44.0
Curr. Assets	355	384	382	543	522	456
Total Assets	1,372	1,351	1,373	1,986	1,762	1,531
Curr. Liab.	380	377	269	432	321	262
LT Debt	131	175	220	220	110	Nil
Common Eqty.	674	632	685	1,099	1,092	1,061
Total Cap.	872	860	985	1,479	1,383	1,252
Cap. Exp.	160	122	115	355	302	150
Cash Flow	179	77.0	150	166	169	135

Ratio Analysis

	1994	1993	1992	1991	1990	1989
Curr. Ratio	0.9	1.0	1.4	1.3	1.6	1.7
% LT Debt of Cap.	14.9	20.3	22.3	14.9	8.0	Nil
% Net Inc.of Revs.	3.5	NM	2.3	1.2	2.1	0.7
% Ret. on Assets	4.3	NM	2.1	1.3	2.3	0.8
% Ret. on Equity	8.9	NM	4.0	2.2	3.6	1.2

Dividend Data —Dividends are paid on the Class B common stock.

Amt. of Div. $	Date Decl.	Ex-Div. Date	Stock of Record	Payment Date
0.125	Aug. 11	Aug. 25	Aug. 31	Sep. 15 '94
0.125	Nov. 18	Nov. 23	Nov. 30	Dec. 15 '94
0.125	Feb. 17	Feb. 22	Feb. 28	Mar. 15 '95
0.125	May. 12	May. 24	May. 31	Jun. 15 '95
0.125	Aug. 25	Aug. 29	Aug. 31	Sep. 15 '95

Data as orig. reptd.; bef. results of disc. opers. and/or spec. items. Per share data adj. for stk. divs. as of ex-div. date. E-Estimated. NA-Not Available. NM-Not Meaningful. NR-Not Ranked.

Office—Golden, CO 80401. **Tel**—(303) 279-6565. **Chrmn**—W. K. Coors. **V-Chrmn & CEO**—P. H. Coors. **Pres & COO**—W. L. Kielly III. **Secy**—P. J. Smith. **Investor Contact**—Becky Winning (303-277-7152). **Dirs**—J. Coors, P. H. Coors, W. K. Coors, J. B. Llewellyn, L. G. Nogales, W. R. Sanders. **Transfer Agent**—First National Bank of Boston. **Incorporated** in Colorado in 1913. **Empl-** 6,300. **S&P Analyst:** Kenneth A. Shea

CoreStates Financial

NYSE Symbol **CFL**
In S&P 500

05-SEP-95 Industry:
Banking

Summary: This multi-bank holding company delivers financial services primarily in Pennsylvania, Delaware and New Jersey, as well as selected services worldwide.

S&P Opinion: Hold (★★★)	Recent Price • 37¼ Yield • 3.7%
	52 Wk Range • 37⅞-22⅞ 12-Mo. P/E • 13.4

Quantitative Evaluations

Outlook
(1 Lowest—5 Highest)
• **4+**

Fair Value
• **38¾**

Risk
• **Low**

Earn./Div. Rank
• **B+**

Technical Eval.
• **Bullish** since 12/94

Rel. Strength Rank
(1 Lowest—99 Highest)
• **60**

Insider Activity
• **Neutral**

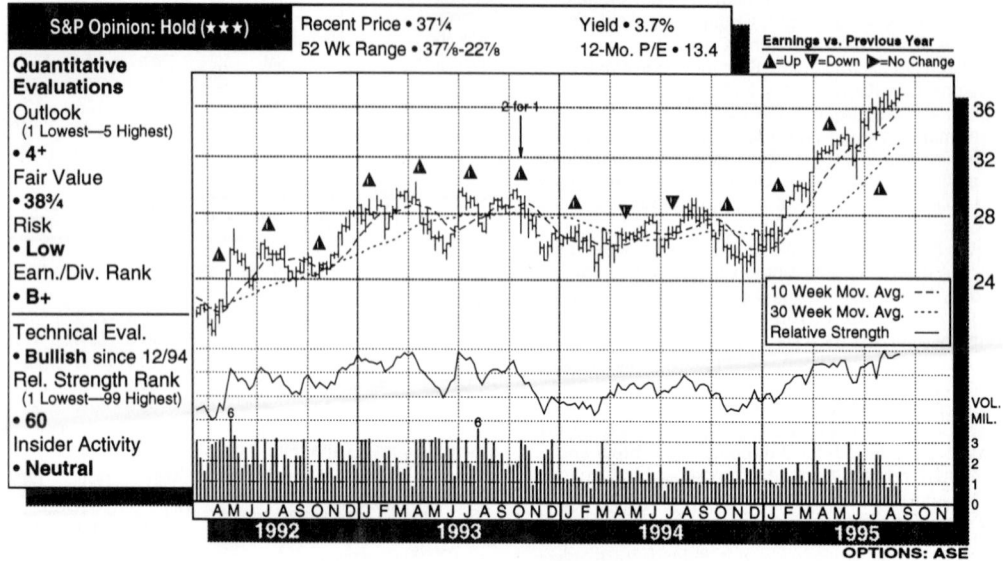

Earnings vs. Previous Year
▲=Up ▼=Down ▶=No Change

10 Week Mov. Avg. ---
30 Week Mov. Avg. ····
Relative Strength —

VOL.
MIL.

OPTIONS: ASE

Overview - 05-SEP-95

Net interest income is expected to increase 6% to 8% in 1995 on modest loan growth and a wider net interest margin. CFL has consistently maintained better margins than its peer group, reflecting wide spreads in credit card and middle market lending and a large base of low-cost deposit funds. The loan loss provision should stabilize, following an early 1994 jump resulting from the acquisition of Constellation Bancorp. Revenues from the Electronic Payment Services joint venture, which provides ATM and point-of-sale processing, are growing rapidly, and should offset flat fee-based revenues. Acquisition activity will likely subside, as the company focuses on integrating recent purchases. Earnings comparisons will benefit from the absence of merger-related charges, which came to about $1.17 a share in 1994.

Valuation - 05-SEP-95

The shares received a boost earlier this year on investor enthusiasm for a process redesign program aimed at enhancing customer focus and improving productivity. While the process redesign will allow the company to become more competitive in the long run, the near-term outlook for relatively modest loan growth and a slowdown in acquisition activity while recent purchases are digested remain a concern. At just over nine times the 1996 earnings estimate, the shares are trading in line with those of other regional banks. However, at nearly 2.3 times June 30 book value, the shares are at a considerable premium to regional bank peers.

Key Stock Statistics

S&P EPS Est. 1995	3.15	Tang. Bk. Value/Share	16.15
P/E on S&P Est. 1995	11.8	Beta	1.46
S&P EPS Est. 1996	4.00	Shareholders	43,300
Dividend Rate/Share	1.36	Market cap. (B)	$ 5.2
Shs. outstg. (M)	139.5	Inst. holdings	58%
Avg. daily vol. (M)	0.233	Insider holdings	NA

Value of $10,000 invested 5 years ago: $ 22,405

Fiscal Year Ending Dec. 31

	1995	% Change	1994	% Change	1993	% Change
Revenues (Million $)						
1Q	713.3	19%	600.8	23%	487.8	-7%
2Q	721.8	16%	621.5	24%	500.0	-2%
3Q	—	—	621.7	20%	516.3	NM
4Q	—	—	712.8	40%	509.5	-13%
Yr.	—	—	2,497	24%	2,014	-6%
Income (Million $)						
1Q	55.37	NM	-30.00	NM	73.32	24%
2Q	126.0	100%	63.09	-24%	83.29	25%
3Q	—	—	104.2	21%	86.01	27%
4Q	—	—	111.5	31%	85.31	23%
Yr.	—	—	248.8	-24%	327.9	25%
Earnings Per Share ($)						
1Q	0.38	NM	-0.21	NM	0.63	22%
2Q	0.89	102%	0.44	-38%	0.71	23%
3Q	E0.92	24%	0.74	1%	0.73	25%
4Q	E0.96	23%	0.78	7%	0.73	23%
Yr.	E3.15	80%	1.75	-38%	2.80	23%

Next earnings report expected: mid October

CoreStates Financial

Business Summary - 05-SEP-95

Philadelphia-based CoreStates Financial Corp is a multibank holding company. Its primary banking subsidiaries are CoreStates Bank, N.A. (which operates under names including Philadelphia National Bank, First Pennsylvania Bank and Hamilton Bank), CoreStates Bank of Delaware and CoreStates New Jersey National Bank. The units provide wholesale banking services, including international products, and consumer financial services which include retail banking, credit cards, trust and investment management services and electronic payment services. Nonbank affiliates include Congress Financial Corp., a majority-owned commercial financing and factoring business, and Electronic Payment Services, a consumer electronic transaction processing joint venture. A growing portion of earnings comes from electronic and paper transactions, including cash management and high-volume consumer financial transactions, which include checks, credit cards and the rapidly growing debit card transactions, such as those generated by the company's MAC automated teller machine network and point-of-sale processing. CFL also engages in discount brokerage, investment advisory and lease financing.

Average earning assets in 1994 of $24.3 billion (up from $24.2 billion in 1993) were divided: commercial loans 34%, real estate loans 26%, consumer loans 11%, other loans 10%, investment securities 12% and temporary investments 7%. Average sources of funds were: noninterest-bearing demand deposits 22%, consumer deposits 27%, other deposits 25%, short-term borrowings 7%, long-term debt 6%, equity 8% and other 5%.

At the end of 1994, nonperforming assets totaled $310.9 million (1.51% of loans and related assets), down from $438.7 million (2.20%) a year earlier. The reserve for loan losses was 2.44% of loans, versus 2.28%. Net chargeoffs were 1.13% of average loans in 1994 and 0.60% in 1993.

Important Developments

Mar. '95—CFL announced a corporate-wide process redesign plan to restructure its banking services around customers and give employees more authority to make decisions to benefit customers. The project includes a workforce reduction of 2,800 and is expected to contribute about $0.16 a share to earnings in 1995 and reach an annualized benefit of $0.90 a share by the fourth quarter of 1996. A related pretax restructuring charge of $110 million was recorded in the first quarter of 1995. Directors also authorized an expansion of the company's stock repurchase program from a maximum of 2% of shares outstanding to 5% per year. During the first half of 1995, the company repurchased 8,100,000 common shares.

Capitalization

Long Term Debt: $1,822,045,000 (6/95).

Per Share Data ($)

(Year Ended Dec. 31)

	1994	1993	1992	1991	1990	1989
Tangible Bk. Val.	16.22	16.68	14.58	14.03	12.71	15.79
Earnings	1.75	2.80	2.27	2.09	1.03	2.52
Dividends	1.24	1.14	1.02	0.97	0.96	0.87
Payout Ratio	71%	41%	45%	46%	93%	35%
Prices - High	29⅛	30¼	29	24⅜	22⅝	25¼
- Low	22⅞	25⅛	21	12	11⅜	19⅛
P/E Ratio - High	17	11	13	12	22	10
- Low	13	9	9	6	11	8

Income Statement Analysis (Million $)

	1994	%Chg	1993	%Chg	1992	%Chg	1991
Net Int. Inc.	1,389	24%	1,118	6%	1,057	NM	1,048
Tax Equiv. Adj.	21.3	-11%	24.0	-14%	28.0	-18%	34.0
Non Int. Inc.	549	9%	503	-6%	533	-4%	554
Loan Loss Prov.	247	147%	100	-16%	119	-37%	188
% Exp/Op Revs.	67%	—	63%	—	68%	—	65%
Pretax Inc.	392	-20%	488	25%	390	18%	331
Eff. Tax Rate	37%	—	33%	—	33%	—	31%
Net Inc.	249	-24%	328	25%	262	15%	228
% Net Int. Marg.	5.80%	—	5.82%	—	5.61%	—	5.58%

Balance Sheet & Other Fin. Data (Million $)

	1994	1993	1992	1991	1990	1989
Earning Assets:						
Money Mkt.	2,483	1,282	1,875	1,718	1,261	493
Inv. Securities	2,881	2,732	2,610	2,091	1,914	1,580
Com'l Loans	10,690	10,252	8,412	8,044	8,685	6,062
Other Loans	9,837	5,420	7,057	6,984	8,181	6,030
Total Assets	29,325	23,666	23,699	21,624	23,520	16,849
Demand Deposits	6,362	6,008	5,820	5,077	4,937	3,594
Time Deposits	15,678	10,945	11,442	10,964	11,645	7,847
LT Debt	1,791	1,455	1,243	1,143	787	602
Common Eqty.	2,350	1,959	1,704	1,539	1,380	1,246

Ratio Analysis

	1994	1993	1992	1991	1990	1989
% Ret. on Assets	0.9	1.4	1.2	1.0	0.5	1.2
% Ret. on Equity	11.0	18.3	16.3	15.6	7.6	16.8
% Loan Loss Resv.	2.4	2.1	2.1	2.3	2.4	1.5
% Loans/Deposits	93.1	96.5	89.6	93.7	101.7	105.7
% Equity to Assets	8.2	7.9	7.2	6.6	6.5	7.2

Dividend Data

Cash was paid in each year since 1884 by Philadelphia National. Dividend reinvestment and share purchase plans are available.

Amt. of Div. $	Date Decl.	Ex-Div. Date	Stock of Record	Payment Date
0.300	Jul. 19	Aug. 30	Sep. 06	Oct. 01 '94
0.340	Nov. 15	Nov. 30	Dec. 06	Jan. 01 '95
0.340	Feb. 21	Mar. 01	Mar. 07	Apr. 01 '95
0.340	May. 16	May. 31	Jun. 06	Jul. 01 '95
0.340	Jul. 18	Aug. 31	Sep. 05	Oct. 01 '95

Data as orig. reptd.; bef. results of disc opers. and/or spec. items. Per share data adj. for stk. divs. as of ex-div. date. E-Estimated. NA-Not Available. NM-Not Meaningful. NR-Not Ranked.

Main Office—Broad and Chestnut Sts., P.O. Box 7618, Philadelphia, PA 19101-7618. **Tel**—(215) 973-3827. **Chrmn & CEO**—T. A. Larsen. **Pres & COO**—C. L. Coltman III. **CFO**—D. C. Carney. **SVP & Secy**—M. R. O'Leary. **Investor Contact**—William R. Wolf (215-786-7640). **Dirs**—G. A. Butler, R. H. Campbell, N. G. Harris, C. E. Hughes, S. A. Jackson, E. E. Jones, T. A. Larsen, H. Lotman, G. Lynett, P. A. McFate, J. A. Miller, M. Miller, Jr., S. W. Naidoff, S. S. Preston III, J. M. Seabrook, J. L. Shane, R. W. Smith, H. A. Sorgenti, P. S. Strawbridge. **Transfer Agent & Registrar**—First Chicago Trust Co. of New York, Jersey City, NJ. **Empl**—15,745. **Empl- S&P Analyst:** Stephen R. Biggar

Corning Inc.

NYSE Symbol **GLW**
In S&P 500

13-OCT-95

Industry: Glass/products

Summary: Corning's businesses are concentrated in laboratory services, fiber optics, specialty materials and consumer products.

S&P Opinion: Hold (★★★)

| Recent Price • 26⅞ | Yield • 2.7% |
| 52 Wk Range • 37⅜-24⅛ | 12-Mo. P/E • NM |

Quantitative Evaluations

Outlook
(1 Lowest—5 Highest)
• **4‾**

Fair Value
• **27¼**

Risk
• **Low**

Earn./Div. Rank
• **A-**

Technical Eval.
• **Bearish** since 4/95

Rel. Strength Rank
(1 Lowest—99 Highest)
• **9**

Insider Activity
• **Unfavorable**

Earnings vs. Previous Year
▲=Up ▼=Down ►=No Change

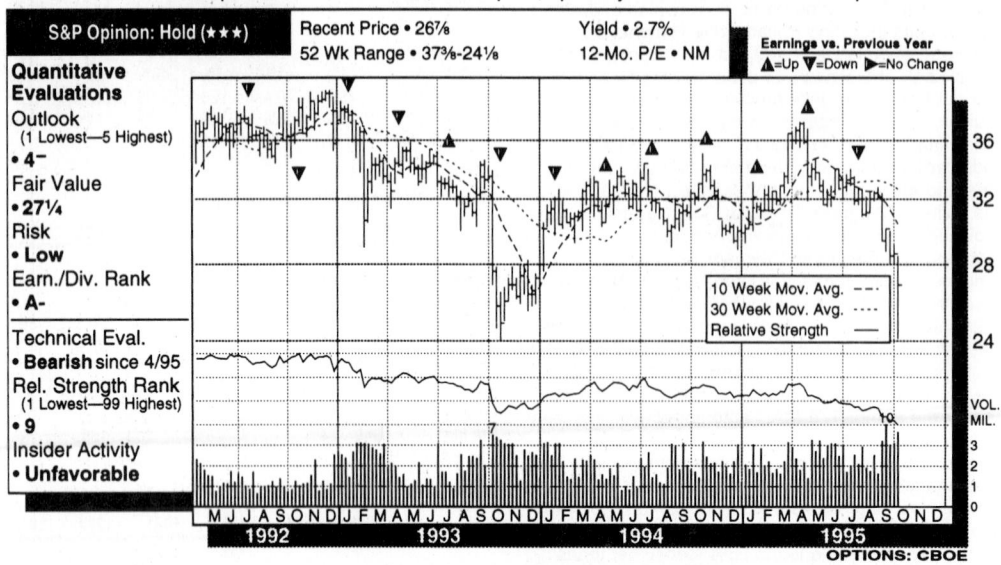

10 Week Mov. Avg. ---
30 Week Mov. Avg. ·····
Relative Strength —

OPTIONS: CBOE

Overview - 13-OCT-95

Revenues should rise about 8% in 1996, led by communications, which is benefiting from strong demand for fiber optics. Specialty materials should grow substantially, led by brisk demand for automobile pollution-control devices. However, laboratory services sales will rise only modestly due to a highly competitive market. Consumer products should rebound somewhat from depressed levels, spurred by a more focused product line. Equity earnings should benefit from stronger worldwide economies. Profitability should be restored despite continued pricing pressures at laboratory services due to the higher volume and the favorable impact of a restructuring, as well as from the absence of a $1.62 charge for writing off 50%-owned Dow Corning and $0.35 in other charges.

Valuation - 05-OCT-95

We recently downgraded Corning to "hold" from "accumulate" following management's announcement that it expected extended weakness in its Clinical Labs unit and that the turnaround in its consumer business would be further delayed. These negatives are likely to largely offset positive trends in its other businesses and sharply reduces the company's earnings visibility over the intermediate term. On a longer-term basis the shares of this well managed company are likely to recover as the company exploits the strong positions it holds in its businesses. In addition, the writing off of its investment in Dow Corning, which filed for bankruptcy in May 1995 due to litigation related to its discontinued breast implant business, removed a cloud from the shares.

Key Stock Statistics

S&P EPS Est. 1995	-0.29	Tang. Bk. Value/Share	2.59
P/E on S&P Est. 1995	NM	Beta	0.48
S&P EPS Est. 1996	1.60	Shareholders	15,000
Dividend Rate/Share	0.72	Market cap. (B)	$ 6.0
Shs. outstg. (M)	229.8	Inst. holdings	58%
Avg. daily vol. (M)	0.961	Insider holdings	NA

Value of $10,000 invested 5 years ago: $ 14,161

Fiscal Year Ending Dec. 31

	1995	% Change	1994	% Change	1993	% Change
Revenues (Million $)						
1Q	1,123	17%	956.6	16%	827.6	9%
2Q	1,307	18%	1,109	22%	912.8	4%
3Q	—	—	1,453	20%	1,207	9%
4Q	—	—	1,281	17%	1,091	9%
Yr.	—	—	4,799	19%	4,039	8%
Income (Million $)						
1Q	79.40	37%	58.00	16%	49.80	-23%
2Q	-297.2	NM	111.4	24%	89.80	34%
3Q	—	—	76.90	NM	-33.90	NM
4Q	—	—	35.00	NM	-120.9	NM
Yr.	—	—	281.3	NM	-15.20	NM
Earnings Per Share ($)						
1Q	0.35	25%	0.28	8%	0.26	-24%
2Q	-1.32	NM	0.54	15%	0.47	34%
3Q	E0.36	NM	0.36	NM	-0.18	NM
4Q	E0.32	129%	0.14	NM	-0.64	NM
Yr.	E-0.29	NM	1.32	NM	-0.09	NM

Next earnings report expected: mid October

Corning Inc.

13-OCT-95

Business Summary - 10-AUG-95

Corning Inc. is a diversified worldwide manufacturing and service company. Contributions in 1994 were:

	Sales	Profits
Specialty materials	18%	22%
Communications	31%	48%
Laboratory services	35%	22%
Consumer products	16%	8%

International business in 1994 accounted for 7% of sales and 13% of pretax income.

Specialty materials include Celcor ceramic substrates for auto pollution-control devices, headlamp glass and technical ceramics.

Communications products consist primarily of the manufacture of optical fibers and cable and glass for televisions and computer terminals.

Laboratory services include clinical testing, industrial laboratory services and environmental testing.

Consumer products include housewares.

Companies in which GLW holds equity interests had revenues of $3.5 billion and net income of $102.7 million in 1994. The company's share of the net income was $48.7 million. However, the largest company in which GLW has an interest, 50%-owned Dow Corning Corp., a producer of silicones, had sales of $2.2 billion and a loss of $6.8 million. Dow Corning filed for bankruptcy in May 1995, due to litigation concerning its discontinued breast implant business. GLW subsequently fully reserved against its investment in Dow Corning and no longer recognizes earnings from the company.

Important Developments

Jun. '95—The company said that its second quarter charge for Dow Corning reflected it fully reserving against its investment in Dow Corning, from which it will no longer recognize earnings. Adjusting for the elimination of Dow Corning's earnings and before special charges, the company said that its second quarter earnings per share increased 12% from an adjusted $0.43 per share in 1994. The company said that it continued to see solid growth and strong profit improvement in most of its core businesses, including opto-electronics, pharmaceutical testing services, environmental products and video displays. On the other hand, results in clinical testing services and consumer products were disappointing.

Capitalization

Long Term Debt: $1,520,300,000 (6/95).
Minority Interest: $275,100,000.
6% Monthly Income Preferred Securities: 7,475,000 shs. Ea. conv. into 1.2821 com.
8% Series B Conv. Pfd. Stock: 256,717 shs.; held by or on behalf of employees.

Per Share Data ($)

(Year Ended Dec. 31)

	1994	1993	1992	1991	1990	1989
Tangible Bk. Val.	3.75	3.37	8.16	9.40	9.01	9.08
Cash Flow	2.92	1.37	2.72	2.90	2.93	2.31
Earnings	1.32	-0.09	1.40	1.66	1.54	1.40
Dividends	0.69	0.68	0.62	0.68	0.46	0.52
Payout Ratio	52%	NM	44%	42%	30%	38%
Prices - High	35	39	40⅜	43⅛	25⅞	21¾
- Low	27⅝	24	28¾	21	17⅜	16
P/E Ratio - High	27	NM	29	26	17	16
- Low	21	NM	21	13	11	11

Income Statement Analysis (Million $)

	1994	%Chg	1993	%Chg	1992	%Chg	1991
Revs.	4,799	19%	4,035	8%	3,744	14%	3,287
Oper. Inc.	1,028	35%	763	5%	730	12%	654
Depr.	338	21%	280	13%	248	NM	248
Int. Exp.	122	30%	94.0	36%	68.9	14%	60.4
Pretax Inc.	508	NM	37.0	-90%	380	-13%	439
Eff. Tax Rate	34%	—	96%	—	24%	—	25%
Net Inc.	281	NM	-15.0	NM	266	-14%	311

Balance Sheet & Other Fin. Data (Million $)

	1994	1993	1992	1991	1990	1989
Cash	161	161	133	208	133	353
Curr. Assets	1,726	1,472	1,289	1,229	1,098	1,169
Total Assets	6,023	5,232	4,286	3,853	3,512	3,361
Curr. Liab.	1,074	1,020	824	708	640	682
LT Debt	1,406	1,586	816	700	611	625
Common Eqty.	2,263	1,686	1,804	2,019	1,850	1,711
Total Cap.	4,305	3,543	2,888	2,935	2,667	2,466
Cap. Exp.	387	443	377	345	417	377
Cash Flow	618	263	512	557	547	430

Ratio Analysis

	1994	1993	1992	1991	1990	1989
Curr. Ratio	1.6	1.4	1.6	1.7	1.7	1.7
% LT Debt of Cap.	32.7	44.8	28.2	23.9	22.9	25.3
% Net Inc.of Revs.	5.9	NM	7.1	9.5	9.7	10.5
% Ret. on Assets	4.7	NM	6.5	8.2	8.5	8.1
% Ret. on Equity	13.4	NM	13.8	15.6	16.3	15.4

Dividend Data —Dividends have been paid since 1881. A dividend reinvestment plan is available. A "poison pill" stock purchase rights plan was adopted in 1986.

Amt. of Div. $	Date Decl.	Ex-Div. Date	Stock of Record	Payment Date
0.180	Dec. 07	Dec. 13	Dec. 19	Dec. 30 '94
0.180	Feb. 01	Feb. 28	Mar. 06	Mar. 31 '95
0.180	Apr. 27	May. 30	Jun. 05	Jun. 30 '95
0.180	Jul. 19	Aug. 31	Sep. 05	Sep. 29 '95

Office—Houghton Park, Corning, NY 14831. **Tel**—(607) 974-9000. **Fax**—(607) 974-8551. **Chrmn & CEO**—J. R. Houghton. **Pres**—R. G. Ackerman. **Vice Chrmn-CFO**—V. C. Campbell. **Secy**—A. J. Peck Jr. **Investor Contact**—Richard B. Klein (607-974-8313). **Dirs**—R. G. Ackerman, R. Barker, M. L. Bundy, V. C. Campbell, B. B. Conable Jr., D. A. Duke, J. H. Foster, G. Gund, J. M. Hennessy, J. R. Houghton, V. E. Jordan Jr., J. W. Kinnear, J. J. O'Connor, C. A. Rein, H. Rosovsky, H. O. Ruding, W. O. — Smithburg, R. G. Stone Jr. **Transfer Agent & Registrar**—Harris Trust & Savings Bank, Chicago. **Incorporated** in New York in 1936. **Empl**- 43,000. **S&P Analyst:** Paul Valentine, CFA

Crane Co.

NYSE Symbol **CR**
In S&P 500

29-JUL-95 **Industry:** Conglomerate/diversified

Summary: Crane is a diversified manufacturer of engineered products for the aerospace, fluid handling, automatic merchandising and construction industries.

S&P Opinion: Hold (★★★)

Recent Price • 37	Yield • 2.0%
52 Wk Range • 39½-24¾	12-Mo. P/E • 16.9

Quantitative Evaluations

Outlook
(1 Lowest—5 Highest)
• **3**

Fair Value
• **36⅜**

Risk
• **Low**

Earn./Div. Rank
• **B+**

Technical Eval.
• **Bearish** since 6/95

Rel. Strength Rank
(1 Lowest—99 Highest)
• **50**

Insider Activity
• **Neutral**

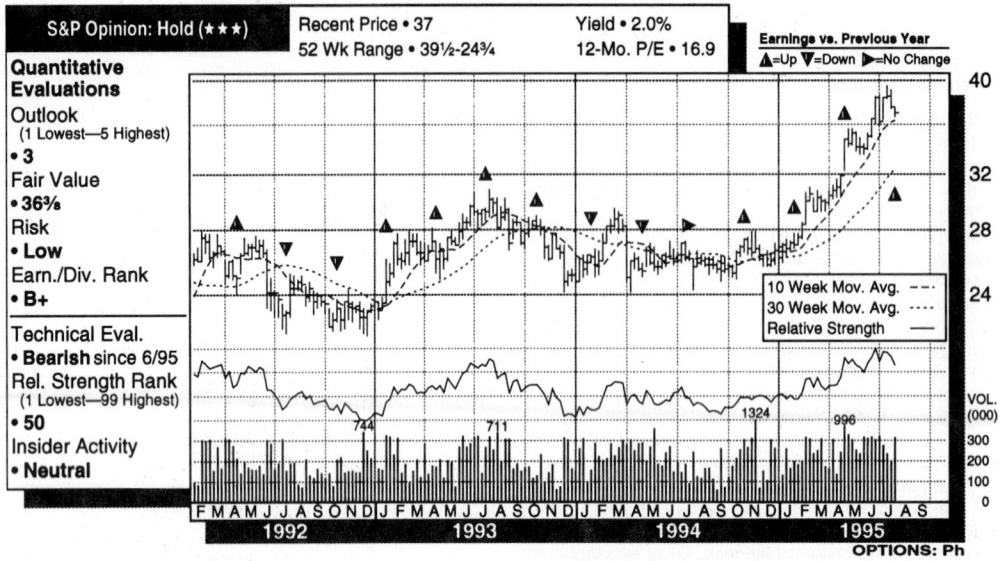

Earnings vs. Previous Year
▲=Up ▼=Down ▶=No Change

10 Week Mov. Avg. – – –
30 Week Mov. Avg. ......
Relative Strength ——

VOL. (000)

OPTIONS: Ph

Overview - 28-JUL-95

We expect a 12% gain in sales for 1995, reflecting the inclusion of Mark Controls and ELDEC for a full year, a stronger market for valves, a cyclical recovery in markets served by National Rejectors, market share gains at National Vendors and higher aerospace sales. Aided by lower costs of integrating acquisitions, the divestiture of an unprofitable unit in wholesale distribution and lower costs at National Rejectors, margins should widen and operating income should increase. Aided further by lower interest expense, earnings should rise in 1995. Assuming 2.6% GDP growth in the U.S. in 1996, sales and earnings should rise again. Acquisitions, market share gains and an eventual cyclical upturn in the aerospace industry should boost long-term sales and profits.

Valuation - 28-JUL-95

While we are optimistic about the long-term prospects for Crane's stock, we are maintaining our hold rating near term. We believe Crane is fairly valued on our 1995 estimate and that the potential for significant price gains from current levels is limited. Accordingly, we cannot justify either an accumulate or strong buy recommendation given the poor risk/reward ratio. Through the end of July, CR rose 38%, versus a 21% gain in the S&P 500. While the shares may continue to rise, we remain neutral for now. Based on projected earnings gains and prospects for growth via acquisitions, current owners should continue to hold for intermediate-term gains.

Key Stock Statistics

S&P EPS Est. 1995	2.40	Tang. Bk. Value/Share	3.49
P/E on S&P Est. 1995	15.4	Beta	1.00
S&P EPS Est. 1996	2.70	Shareholders	6,500
Dividend Rate/Share	0.75	Market cap. (B)	$ 1.1
Shs. outstg. (M)	30.2	Inst. holdings	50%
Avg. daily vol. (M)	0.064	Insider holdings	NA

Value of $10,000 invested 5 years ago: $ 18,802

Fiscal Year Ending Dec. 31

	1995	% Change	1994	% Change	1993	% Change
Revenues (Million $)						
1Q	432.6	30%	331.7	6%	312.3	NM
2Q	451.5	5%	428.7	27%	337.7	NM
3Q	—	—	451.1	33%	337.9	NM
4Q	—	—	441.9	37%	322.3	2%
Yr.	—	—	1,653	26%	1,310	NM
Income (Million $)						
1Q	13.28	79%	7.41	-31%	10.77	20%
2Q	20.12	28%	15.67	NM	15.73	NM
3Q	—	—	16.00	25%	12.76	21%
4Q	—	—	16.86	75%	9.64	-32%
Yr.	—	—	55.93	14%	48.89	101%
Earnings Per Share ($)						
1Q	0.44	76%	0.25	-31%	0.36	24%
2Q	0.66	27%	0.52	NM	0.52	NM
3Q	E0.65	—	0.53	26%	0.42	24%
4Q	E0.65	—	0.56	75%	0.32	-32%
Yr.	E2.40	—	1.86	15%	1.62	105%

Next earnings report expected: late October

Business Summary - 25-APR-95

Crane Co. is a diversified maker of engineered products and the nation's largest distributor of doors, windows and millwork. Industry segment contributions in 1994 (profits in $ million):

	Sales	Profits
Fluid Handling	18%	$19.1
Aerospace	10%	31.3
Engineered Materials	12%	23.0
Crane Controls	5%	4.4
Merchandising Systems	10%	23.2
Wholesale Distribution	44%	20.0
Other	1%	-0.7

Operations outside the U.S. accounted for 20% of sales and 5% of operating profits in 1994.

The fluid handling unit consists of a valve business that serves the global market and pumps used in the chemical, general industrial and commercial industries.

Aerospace makes electronically controlled anti-skid braking systems for aircraft; the unit also makes position indication and control systems and power systems.

Engineered materials manufactures fiberglass reinforced plastic panels, corrosion resistant, plastic lined pipes, fittings and valves used in process industries, high pressure fittings and hoses, high voltage, high frequency capacitors and plumbing products.

Crane contols produces pressure and temperature switches, directional valve controls, balancing and shower valves, electronic and rotational speed sensors.

Merchandising systems makes vending machines for the automated merchandising industry in the U. S. and manufactures coin validation systems for the automatic vending market in Europe.

Wholesale distribution consists mostly of Huttig Sash & Door, which is the nation's largest distributor of doors, windows, molding and trim and related building products.

Important Developments

Mar. '95—Crane said it intended to file a petition of certiorari to the U.S. Supreme Court. This followed an earlier decision by an appeals court which denied CR's petition for a rehearing of a decision reinstating a complaint alleging that the company and its former CF&I Steel Corp. unit had violated the False Claims Act. The complaint alleges failure to disclose CF&I's unfunded pension liabilities in connection with the 1985 spinoff of CF&I to CR's shareholders. A district court had dismissed the complaint because of lack of subject matter jurisdiction. CR said it believes that the complaint will ultimately be dismissed.

Capitalization

Long Term Debt: $331,289,000 (12/94).

Per Share Data ($)
(Year Ended Dec. 31)

	1994	1993	1992	1991	1990	1989
Tangible Bk. Val.	3.11	9.74	9.06	9.77	10.14	7.47
Cash Flow	3.03	2.42	1.56	2.17	2.68	2.37
Earnings	1.86	1.62	0.79	1.42	1.96	1.72
Dividends	0.75	0.75	0.75	0.75	0.75	0.71
Payout Ratio	40%	46%	95%	53%	38%	40%
Prices - High	29½	30⅞	27⅞	30	27¾	25
- Low	24⅛	22⅝	21¾	18¾	17¾	15
P/E Ratio - High	16	19	35	21	14	15
- Low	13	14	28	13	9	9

Income Statement Analysis (Million $)

	1994	%Chg	1993	%Chg	1992	%Chg	1991
Revs.	1,653	26%	1,310	NM	1,307	NM	1,303
Oper. Inc.	145	32%	110	2%	108	5%	103
Depr.	35.5	46%	24.3	3%	23.7	NM	23.7
Int. Exp.	24.2	112%	11.4	-21%	14.5	26%	11.5
Pretax Inc.	91.0	14%	80.0	—	NA	—	72.0
Eff. Tax Rate	39%	—	39%	—	37%	—	38%
Net Inc.	55.9	14%	48.9	101%	24.3	-46%	45.0

Balance Sheet & Other Fin. Data (Million $)

	1994	1993	1992	1991	1990	1989
Cash	2.1	12.6	49.0	23.0	8.0	6.0
Curr. Assets	480	394	379	377	392	398
Total Assets	1,008	744	630	630	665	655
Curr. Liab.	244	272	174	170	174	184
LT Debt	331	106	111	84.0	104	119
Common Eqty.	328	291	271	300	317	284
Total Cap.	692	403	386	404	470	450
Cap. Exp.	28.0	64.0	23.0	21.0	33.0	33.0
Cash Flow	91.4	73.2	48.0	68.7	86.0	77.2

Ratio Analysis

	1994	1993	1992	1991	1990	1989
Curr. Ratio	2.0	1.4	2.2	2.2	2.2	2.2
% LT Debt of Cap.	47.9	26.2	28.8	20.8	22.1	26.5
% Net Inc.of Revs.	3.4	3.7	1.9	3.5	4.4	3.8
% Ret. on Assets	6.4	7.1	3.9	7.0	9.6	8.5
% Ret. on Equity	18.0	17.4	8.6	14.7	21.1	20.3

Dividend Data
(Dividends have been paid since 1939. A dividend reinvestment plan is available. A new "poison pill" stock purchase right was adopted in 1988.)

Amt. of Div. $	Date Decl.	Ex-Div. Date	Stock of Record	Payment Date
0.188	Aug. 22	Aug. 30	Sep. 06	Sep. 14 '94
0.188	Oct. 24	Nov. 29	Dec. 05	Dec. 14 '94
0.188	Feb. 27	Mar. 03	Mar. 09	Mar. 14 '95
0.188	May. 08	May. 31	Jun. 06	Jun. 14 '95

Data as orig. reptd.; bef. results of disc. opers. and/or spec. items. Per share data adj. for stk. divs. as of ex-div. date. E-Estimated. NA-Not Available. NM-Not Meaningful. NR-Not Ranked.

Office—100 First Stamford Place, Stamford, CT 06902. **Tel**—(203) 363-7300. **Chrmn & Pres**—R. S. Evans. **VP-Fin, CFO & Investor Contact**—David S. Smith. **VP & Secy**—P. R. Hundt. **Dirs**—M. Anathan III, E. T. Bigelow, Jr., R. S. Evans, D. R. Gardner, J. Gaulin, R. S. Forte, D. C. Minton, C. J. Queenan, Jr., B. Yavitz. **Transfer Agent & Registrar**—First Chicago Trust Co. of New York, NYC. **Incorporated** in Illinois in 1865; reincorporated in Delaware in 1985. **Empl**- 10,700. **S&P Analyst:** Leo Larkin

Cray Research

NYSE Symbol **CYR**
In S&P 500

07-NOV-95

Industry:
Data Processing

Summary: This company is the leading manufacturer of supercomputers -- large-scale, high-speed computer systems for scientific and engineering applications.

S&P Opinion: Hold (★★★)	Recent Price • 22⅝	Yield • Nil
	52 Wk Range • 29¼-14⅝	12-Mo. P/E • NM

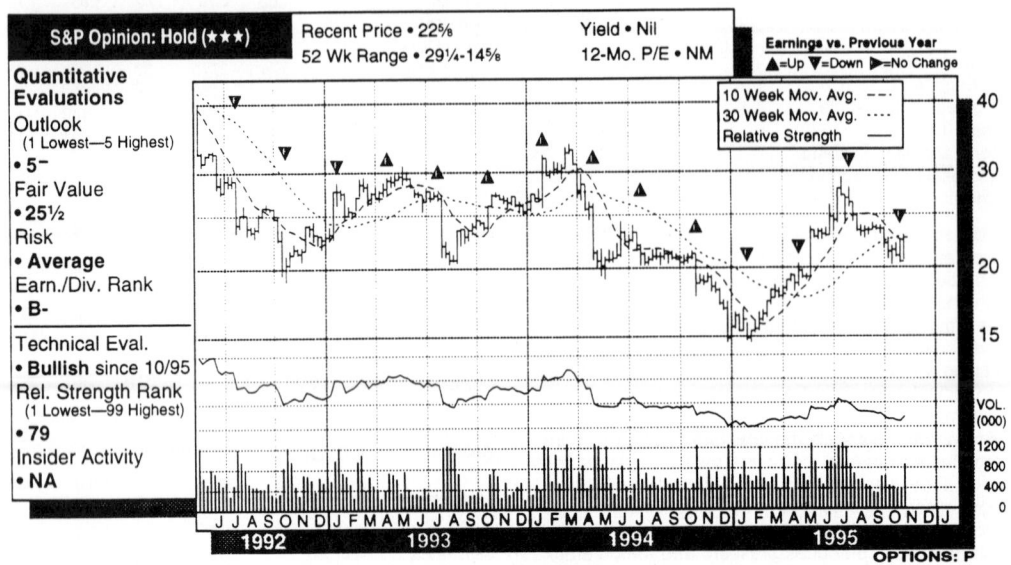

Earnings vs. Previous Year
▲=Up ▼=Down ▶=No Change

10 Week Mov. Avg. ---
30 Week Mov. Avg. ....
Relative Strength ——

OPTIONS: P

Quantitative Evaluations

Outlook
(1 Lowest—5 Highest)
• **5**-

Fair Value
• **25½**

Risk
• **Average**

Earn./Div. Rank
• **B**-

Technical Eval.
• **Bullish** since 10/95

Rel. Strength Rank
(1 Lowest—99 Highest)
• **79**

Insider Activity
• **NA**

Overview - 07-NOV-95

Revenues are likely to advance approximately 25% in 1996, reflecting a continuation of current order rates. The gain should be led by the ramping up of the new Triton family (T90), which replaces the older C90 series and begins shipping in the fourth quarter of 1995. A continued strong reception for the low-end J90 series should also boost revenues. More generally, the company's efforts to expand the markets it serves should also assist growth. Service revenues are expected to grow approximately 15%. Profitability should be restored due to the higher revenues and cost savings from restructuring actions taken in 1995, as well the absence of the restructuring charges themselves.

Valuation - 07-NOV-95

The shares have gradually weakened since the company reported a greater than expected second quarter loss and indicated that second half results would fall below Wall Street's expectations. While the company is attempting to engineer a turnaround through the addition of a new CEO, new product introductions and cost reductions, the shares are likely to languish until concrete evidence of additional progress becomes evident. Pending greater visibility of a turnaround, the shares are only ranked as a "hold."

Key Stock Statistics

S&P EPS Est. 1995	NA	Tang. Bk. Value/Share	25.26
P/E on S&P Est. 1995	NM	Beta	0.95
S&P EPS Est. 1996	NA	Shareholders	5,800
Dividend Rate/Share	Nil	Market cap. (B)	$0.598
Shs. outstg. (M)	25.4	Inst. holdings	76%
Avg. daily vol. (M)	0.105	Insider holdings	NA

Value of $10,000 invested 5 years ago: $ 5,801

Fiscal Year Ending Dec. 31

	1995	% Change	1994	% Change	1993	% Change
Revenues (Million $)						
1Q	131.1	-47%	248.9	23%	202.6	23%
2Q	139.7	-35%	215.8	15%	187.7	1%
3Q	169.2	-23%	219.9	9%	202.0	-8%
4Q	—	—	237.1	-22%	302.6	33%
Yr.	—	—	921.6	3%	894.9	12%
Income (Million $)						
1Q	-48.29	NM	21.95	46%	15.02	NM
2Q	-138.9	NM	8.20	31%	6.24	NM
3Q	-13.54	NM	16.04	5%	15.26	134%
4Q	—	—	9.50	-61%	24.33	NM
Yr.	—	—	55.70	-8%	60.86	NM
Earnings Per Share ($)						
1Q	-1.90	NM	0.84	45%	0.58	NM
2Q	-5.51	NM	0.32	33%	0.24	NM
3Q	-0.54	NM	0.62	7%	0.58	132%
4Q		NM	0.38	-59%	0.93	NM
Yr.		NM	2.16	-7%	2.33	NM

Next earnings report expected: late January

Cray Research

Business Summary - 07-NOV-95

Cray Research is the largest manufacturer of large-scale, high-speed computers, known as supercomputers, used primarily by scientists and engineers for physical simulation in applications such as weather forecasting, aircraft and automotive design and seismic analysis. During 1993, the company entered the commercial market with a line of high-end business servers.

The installed systems base at recent year-ends was as follows:

	1994	1993	1992	1991
Installed base	638	505	446	309

International operations contributed 47% of revenues in both 1994 and 1993. U.S. government agencies provided 36% of 1994 revenues.

The CRAY J90 series, introduced in September 1994 as a follow-on to the Cray EL series, is the company's entry level super-computer system with configurations of from four to 32 CPUs and with a price range of $220,000 to $2.7 million.

The CRAY C90 series and its follow-on, the Cray T90 series, are high-end lines of parallel vector processor (PVP) supercomputer systems. The T90 was launched in February 1995 with general availability expected in the second half of 1995. Configurations on the T90 range from 1 to 32 CPUs with a price range of $2.5 million to $35 million.

In September 1993, CYR unveiled the CRAY T3D, its first massively parallel processing system, which can use up to 2,048 DEC Alpha RISC microprocessors.

In October 1993, CYR announced the CS6400 line of superservers, which run on up to 64 Sun Microsystems superSPARC RISC microprocessors. This line is aimed at commercial data processing markets.

The company offers a complete line of services including product maintenance, consulting and technical support.

Software products include operating systems, compilers and aplications software. Storage products are also available.

Important Developments

Oct. '95—CYR noted that backlog at September 30, 1995, amounted to $355 million, double the year-earlier period, and that it expected earnings for the fourth quarter of 1995 to improve on an operating basis, although it intends to report an operating loss for the full year before restructuring charges. The company said actions taken during 1995 are setting the stage for profitability in 1996, particularly in the second half of the year. CYR also intends to take an additional restructuring charge in the fourth quarter of 1995.

Capitalization

Long Term Debt: $92,703,000 (6/95).

Per Share Data ($)

(Year Ended Dec. 31)

	1994	1993	1992	1991	1990	1989
Tangible Bk. Val.	32.54	30.00	27.76	28.53	24.05	21.11
Cash Flow	7.04	6.80	4.04	8.02	7.70	6.23
Earnings	2.16	2.33	-0.56	4.15	4.02	3.02
Dividends	Nil	Nil	Nil	Nil	Nil	Nil
Payout Ratio	Nil	Nil	Nil	Nil	Nil	Nil
Prices - High	33¾	30⅞	49½	52¼	51¼	65⅞
- Low	14⅝	20⅜	19	29	20	29⅜
P/E Ratio - High	16	13	NM	13	13	22
- Low	7	9	NM	7	5	10

Income Statement Analysis (Million $)

	1994	%Chg	1993	%Chg	1992	%Chg	1991
Revs.	922	3%	895	12%	798	-7%	862
Oper. Inc.	209	2%	205	38%	149	-46%	276
Depr.	126	8%	117	-4%	122	8%	113
Int. Exp.	9.0	5%	8.5	-9%	9.3	19%	7.8
Pretax Inc.	78.0	-7%	84.0	NM	-16.0	NM	167
Eff. Tax Rate	28%	—	28%	—	NM	—	32%
Net Inc.	56.0	-8%	61.0	NM	-15.0	NM	113

Balance Sheet & Other Fin. Data (Million $)

	1994	1993	1992	1991	1990	1989
Cash	56.0	78.0	55.0	37.0	67.0	68.0
Curr. Assets	534	627	505	558	387	457
Total Assets	1,182	1,170	1,021	1,079	944	956
Curr. Liab.	238	272	184	207	204	217
LT Debt	106	105	106	107	105	144
Common Eqty.	829	779	723	759	629	594
Total Cap.	935	885	829	866	735	739
Cap. Exp.	142	124	171	157	172	197
Cash Flow	182	178	107	226	223	191

Ratio Analysis

	1994	1993	1992	1991	1990	1989
Curr. Ratio	2.2	2.3	2.7	2.7	1.9	2.1
% LT Debt of Cap.	11.3	11.9	12.8	12.4	14.4	19.5
% Net Inc.of Revs.	6.0	6.8	NM	13.1	14.0	11.3
% Ret. on Assets	4.8	5.6	NM	11.1	12.3	9.3
% Ret. on Equity	7.0	8.1	NM	16.2	19.1	14.3

Dividend Data —No cash dividends have been paid.

Office—655A Lone Oak Drive, Eagan, MN 55121. Tel—(612) 683-7100. Chrmn & CEO—J. P. Samper. Pres. & COO—R. H. Ewald. EVP-Sales—M. J. Lindseth. CFO—L. L. Betterley. Secy—D. E. Frasch. Investor Relations—Brad Allen. Dirs—L. E. Eaton, R. H. Ewald, C. M. Hapka, P. G. Heasley, R. G. Potter, J. P. Samper, J. H. Suwinski. Transfer Agents & Registrars—Norwest Bank Minnesota, South St. Paul; Chemical Bank, NYC. Incorporated in Delaware in 1972. Empl-4,960. S&P Analyst: Paul H. Valentine, CFA

Crown Cork & Seal

NYSE Symbol **CCK**
In S&P 500

04-AUG-95 Industry:
Containers

Summary: One of the largest producers of metal and plastic containers, crowns and closures, Crown Cork & Seal also produces packaging machinery.

S&P Opinion: Sell (★)	
Recent Price • 45¼	Yield • Nil
52 Wk Range • 50⅝-33½	12-Mo. P/E • 33.5

Quantitative Evaluations

Outlook
(1 Lowest—5 Highest)
• **3⁻**

Fair Value
• **44**

Risk
• **Low**

Earn./Div. Rank
• **B+**

Technical Eval.
• **Bullish** since 9/94

Rel. Strength Rank
(1 Lowest—99 Highest)
• **17**

Insider Activity
• **NA**

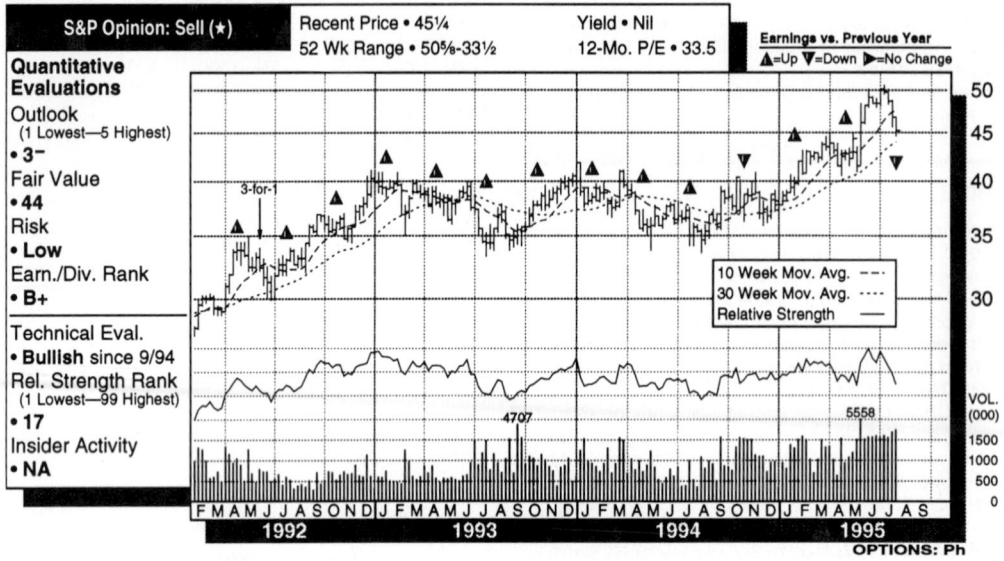

Earnings vs. Previous Year
▲=Up ▼=Down ►=No Change

10 Week Mov. Avg. ---
30 Week Mov. Avg. ·····
Relative Strength —

OPTIONS: Ph

Overview - 03-AUG-95

Although sales should rise in 1995 due to stiff price increases. Volumes have been below projections and raw materials costs have been increasing faster than CCK is able to pass through price increases to customers. Margins have deteriorated and will remain under pressure for the remainder of 1995 and should result in lower earnings. Looking to the longer term, the merger with Carnaud Metalbox will present substantial opportunities for the merged entity to reduce combined overhead costs and develop significant competitive advantage versus its smaller competitors worldwide. Growth opportunities will be presented by the ability to serve global customers as they expand in developing parts of the world and leverage can be gained in areas such as materials purchasing, engineering, research and development, and SG&A.

Valuation - 03-AUG-95

We recently downgraded the stock to sell because we expect a near term decline in the stock price. The company is experiencing deterioration in its margins as a result of the sharp rise in raw materials costs and particularly aluminum. Compounding the cost pressures for the second half of 1995 are tempered volume projections, the possibility of restructuring charges related to the consolidation of CCK with CarnaudMetalbox, and the uncertain outcome of the annual bidding for contracts for the following year which occurs in autumn.

Key Stock Statistics

S&P EPS Est. 1995	2.25	Tang. Bk. Value/Share	3.18
P/E on S&P Est. 1995	20.1	Beta	0.55
Dividend Rate/Share	Nil	Shareholders	6,000
Shs. outstg. (M)	90.2	Market cap. (B)	$ 4.1
Avg. daily vol. (M)	0.531	Inst. holdings	63%
		Insider holdings	NA

Value of $10,000 invested 5 years ago: $ 25,553

Fiscal Year Ending Dec. 31

	1995	% Change	1994	% Change	1993	% Change
Revenues (Million $)						
1Q	1,127	19%	943.0	3%	913.1	9%
2Q	1,386	22%	1,135	-3%	1,169	15%
3Q	—	—	1,283	12%	1,146	12%
4Q	—	—	1,091	17%	935.2	4%
Yr.	—	—	4,452	7%	4,163	10%
Income (Million $)						
1Q	36.50	9%	33.60	14%	29.40	11%
2Q	52.20	-19%	64.80	14%	56.60	16%
3Q	—	—	-7.50	NM	59.70	18%
4Q	—	—	40.10	14%	35.20	18%
Yr.	—	—	131.0	-28%	180.9	16%
Earnings Per Share ($)						
1Q	0.41	8%	0.38	9%	0.35	17%
2Q	0.58	-21%	0.73	12%	0.65	16%
3Q	E0.77	—	-0.08	NM	0.68	17%
4Q	E0.49	—	0.45	13%	0.40	14%
Yr.	E2.25	—	1.47	-29%	2.08	16%

Next earnings report expected: late October

Business Summary - 02-AUG-95

Crown Cork & Seal manufactures aluminum, steel and plastic containers, crowns, aluminum and plastic closures, and filling, packaging and handling machinery. In 1994, about 78% of sales and operating profits were derived from metal packaging and other operations, while 22% was derived from plastic packaging. As of December 1994, CCK had 82 plants in the U.S. and 70 elsewhere.

Contributions by geographic region in 1994 were:

	Sales	Profits
United States	66.7%	62.1%
Europe	14.4%	16.6%
North and Central America	10.5%	6.1%
All other	8.4%	15.2%

CCK makes a wide variety of aerosol, filling and packing cans for the food, citrus, brewing, soft drink, oil, paint, toiletries, drug, chemical, anti-freeze and pet food industries. Cans are made from tinplate and aluminum, and range in size from less than five ounces to five gallons. A wide variety of caps and closures are made for food and nonfood items.

Plastic products include a wide variety of polyethylene terephthalate (PET), polyvinyl chloride (PVC) and polyethylene (HDPE) containers and closures for an assortment of applications, including the packaging of beverages, liquor, water, food, personal care items, dish detergent, automotive, household and industrial chemicals, toiletries and cosmetics. CCK also manufactures polypropylene medical disposal devices and closures and PET preforms.

Machinery lines include bottle washers and rinsers, bottle and can warmers, bottle fillers-crowners for carbonated beverages, can fillers for carbonated beverages, and process equipment.

Important Developments

May '95—CCK agreed to acquire CarnaudMetalbox (CMB), a major European packaging manufacturer, to form a concern with sales of $10 billion. CCK signed an exchange offer with CMB's largest shareholder who controls 32% of CMB's stock. An offer will commence in Europe in which each share of CMB can be exchanged for FF225 cash or securities comprised of CCK common stock (75% of equity election) and mandatorily convertible preferred stock (25%). The total offer is valued at $5.2 billion. After the merger, CCK will initiate a quarterly cash dividend of $0.20 and will raise it to $0.25 per share in the first quarter of 1996. The convertible preferred stock will pay a 4.5% dividend and have a 9.75% conversion premium. The preferred stock can be converted at any time into 0.91 shares of CCK common and is mandatorily convertible in four years.

Capitalization

Long Term Debt: $1,163,700,000 (3/95).
Minority Interest: $79,800,000.

Per Share Data ($)

(Year Ended Dec. 31)

	1994	1993	1992	1991	1990	1989
Tangible Bk. Val.	2.60	1.48	1.59	6.69	10.99	7.24
Cash Flow	3.92	4.28	3.43	2.83	2.42	1.98
Earnings	1.47	2.08	1.79	1.48	1.24	1.19
Dividends	Nil	Nil	Nil	Nil	Nil	Nil
Payout Ratio	Nil	Nil	Nil	Nil	Nil	Nil
Prices - High	41⅞	41⅞	41⅛	31	22⅜	19
- Low	33½	33¼	27⅜	18¼	16½	14⅝
P/E Ratio - High	28	20	23	21	18	16
- Low	23	16	15	12	13	12

Income Statement Analysis (Million $)

	1994	%Chg	1993	%Chg	1992	%Chg	1991
Revs.	4,452	7%	4,163	10%	3,781	NM	3,807
Oper. Inc.	617	10%	562	19%	471	17%	401
Depr.	218	14%	192	35%	142	20%	118
Int. Exp.	99	10%	89.8	16%	77.4	1%	76.6
Pretax Inc.	199	-30%	285	9%	261	21%	215
Eff. Tax Rate	28%	—	34%	—	39%	—	39%
Net Inc.	131	-28%	181	17%	155	21%	128

Balance Sheet & Other Fin. Data (Million $)

	1994	1993	1992	1991	1990	1989
Cash	43.5	54.2	26.9	20.2	21.8	14.4
Curr. Assets	1,606	1,325	1,302	1,149	983	656
Total Assets	4,781	4,217	3,825	2,983	2,596	1,655
Curr. Liab.	1,483	1,281	1,135	761	736	594
LT Debt	1,090	892	940	585	484	94.0
Common Eqty.	1,365	1,252	1,144	1,084	951	811
Total Cap.	2,566	2,217	2,326	1,863	1,562	1,037
Cap. Exp.	440	271	151	185	506	342
Cash Flow	349	373	298	246	209	156

Ratio Analysis

	1994	1993	1992	1991	1990	1989
Curr. Ratio	1.1	1.0	1.1	1.5	1.3	1.1
% LT Debt of Cap.	42.5	40.2	404.0	31.4	31.0	9.1
% Net Inc.of Revs.	2.9	4.3	4.1	3.4	3.5	4.9
% Ret. on Assets	2.9	4.4	4.6	4.6	5.0	6.7
% Ret. on Equity	10.0	14.9	14.0	12.6	12.1	12.6

Dividend Data (After not paying cash dividends since 1956, the company now intends to initiate payments following the merger with CarnaudMetalbox. A "poison pill" stock purchase right was adopted in 1995.)

Data as orig. reptd.; bef. results of disc. opers. and/or spec. items. Per share data adj. for stk. divs. as of ex-div. date. E-Estimated. NA-Not Available. NM-Not Meaningful. NR-Not Ranked.

Office—9300 Ashton Rd., Philadelphia, PA 19136. **Tel**—(215) 698-5100. **Chrmn & Pres**—W. J. Avery. **EVP-Secy**—R. L. Krzyzanowski. **EVP-CFO**—A. W. Rutherford. **SVP-Treas & Investor Contact**—Craig R. L. Calle. **Dirs**— W. J. Avery, H. E. Butwel, C. F. Casey, F. X. Dalton, F. J. Dunleavy, C. C. Hilinski, R. L. Krzyzanowski, J. C. Mandeville, M. J. McKenna, A. W. Rutherford, J. D. Scott, R. J. Siebert, H. A. Sorgenti, E. P. Stuart. **Transfer Agent & Registrar**—First Chicago Trust Co. of New York, NYC. **Incorporated** in New York in 1927; reincorporated in Pennsylvania in 1989. **Empl**-22,373. **S&P Analyst:** Joshua M. Harari, CFA

Cummins Engine

NYSE Symbol **CUM**
In S&P 500

04-AUG-95

Industry:
Auto parts/equipment

Summary: Cummins is the leading manufacturer of diesel engines for heavy-duty trucks and has a growing midrange engine business.

S&P Opinion: Avoid (★★)	Recent Price • 42½	Yield • 2.4%
	52 Wk Range • 48⅝-35⅞	12-Mo. P/E • 6.5

Quantitative Evaluations

Outlook
(1 Lowest—5 Highest)
• **5**

Fair Value
• **53⅞**

Risk
• **Low**

Earn./Div. Rank
• **B-**

Technical Eval.
• **Bearish** since 11/94

Rel. Strength Rank
(1 Lowest—99 Highest)
• **13**

Insider Activity
• **Neutral**

Earnings vs. Previous Year
▲=Up ▼=Down ▶=No Change

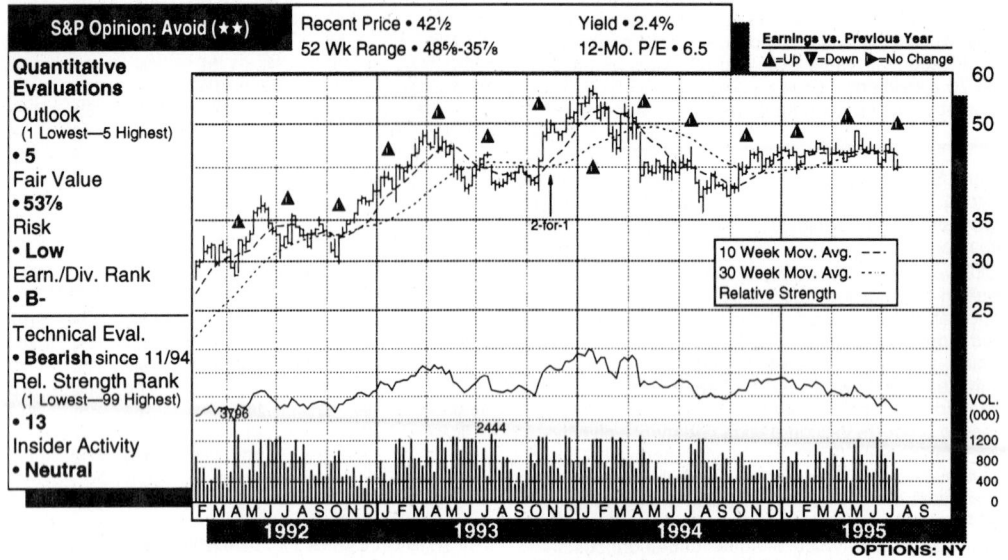

10 Week Mov. Avg. ‑ ‑ ‑
30 Week Mov. Avg. · · · ·
Relative Strength ——

2-for-1

VOL. (000)

OPTIONS: NY

Overview - 04-AUG-95

Although the overall heavy-duty truck order backlog in North America remains strong, heavy-duty engine shipments could decline in 1996 as orders have turned down modestly in recent months. Midrange engine sales continue to grow, but the pace may moderate as shipments to Ford and Chrysler flatten due to lower North American vehicle demand. CUM should continue to benefit from expanded use of B and C series engines in foreign truck models. Component, power generation, marine, government and industrial markets are also strong. Productivity gains and lower interest costs will not outweigh the effect of a full tax rate, and we expect earnings to decline in 1996 after peaking in 1995.

Valuation - 04-AUG-95

Although earnings should rise in 1995 to about $6.60 a share, the stock market has traditionally been reluctant to reward cyclical companies with anything more than a modest earnings multiple of peak year earnings. We believe that 1995 will be the peak earnings year for this cyclical diesel engine manufacturer and think that a multiple expansion is unlikely this year. Trading at about 5.9 times expected 1995 earnings, the shares are likely to mark time before declining in 1996 when earnings are expected to drop.

Key Stock Statistics

S&P EPS Est. 1995	6.60	Tang. Bk. Value/Share	28.20
P/E on S&P Est. 1995	6.4	Beta	1.03
S&P EPS Est. 1996	6.00	Shareholders	4,800
Dividend Rate/Share	1.00	Market cap. (B)	$ 1.6
Shs. outstg. (M)	40.5	Inst. holdings	82%
Avg. daily vol. (M)	0.177	Insider holdings	NA

Value of $10,000 invested 5 years ago: $ 18,653

Fiscal Year Ending Dec. 31

	1995	% Change	1994	% Change	1993	% Change
Revenues (Million $)						
1Q	1,334	21%	1,099	5%	1,048	19%
2Q	1,361	13%	1,205	10%	1,093	15%
3Q	—	—	1,156	17%	988.3	9%
4Q	—	—	1,278	14%	1,118	10%
Yr.	—	—	4,737	12%	4,248	13%
Income (Million $)						
1Q	67.00	23%	54.60	33%	41.10	NM
2Q	69.00	4%	66.20	37%	48.20	156%
3Q	—	—	61.90	52%	40.70	195%
4Q	—	—	70.20	33%	52.60	78%
Yr.	—	—	252.9	38%	182.6	172%
Earnings Per Share ($)						
1Q	1.63	21%	1.35	21%	1.12	NM
2Q	1.69	7%	1.58	19%	1.33	165%
3Q	E1.50	—	1.48	33%	1.11	NM
4Q	E1.78	—	1.68	18%	1.42	80%
Yr.	E6.60	—	6.11	23%	4.95	180%

Next earnings report expected: mid October

Cummins Engine

Business Summary - 03-AUG-95

Cummins is the leading maker of heavy-duty and midrange diesel engines, engine components and power systems for use in truck, bus, marine, power generation, military vehicle, construction, mining, logging, agriculture and rail applications. Sales contributions by market in recent years:

	1994	1993
Heavy-duty truck	30%	29%
Midrange truck	11%	11%
Power generation	22%	23%
Bus & light commercial	12%	12%
Industrial products	11%	10%
Components, marine & gov't.	14%	15%

Every major U.S. truck manufacturer offers Cummins engines as standard or optional equipment. Sales of heavy-duty, midrange and high-horsepower engines were 304,300 in 1994, 263,000 in 1993, 222,000 in 1992 and 200,600 in 1991. CUM's share of the North American heavy-duty diesel truck engine market was about 34% in 1994, 35% in 1993, 37% in 1992 and 38% in 1991, down from 46% in 1990 and over 50% in the prior nine years.

Components include Fleetguard filtration products; Holset turbochargers, air compressors and vibration products; and Cummins Electronics engine controls and on-board business information systems.

Power generation includes alternators, small gasoline engines, Onan generator sets, heat exchangers and electronic and drivetrain components.

In 1994, the U.S. accounted for 58% of sales, Europe/U.K. 14%, Asia/Far East 13%, Latin America 7%, Canada 7%, and Africa/Middle East 2%.

Important Developments

Jul. '95—CUM continued to benefit from solid demand in the second quarter of 1995 with positive year-to-year comparisons in every market segment in unit shipments and dollar revenues. CUM's share of the North American heavy duty diesel engine market increased to 35% in the first half of 1995. CUM continued to benefit from growth in international markets for diesel engines and power generation products. Midrange truck market sales increased 20% on increased sales to Ford for medium duty trucks. Power generation sales were up about 4%, bus and light commercial vehicle sales rose 23%, industrial market sales advanced 20%, and core technology companies (Fleetguard, Holset and Cummins Electronics) sales were up 13%.

Capitalization

Long Term Debt: $154,000,000 (6/95), incl. $51.0 million guarantee of ESOP debt.

Per Share Data ($)

(Year Ended Dec. 31)

	1994	1993	1992	1991	1990	1989
Tangible Bk. Val.	25.78	18.41	11.22	17.15	18.69	19.89
Cash Flow	9.19	8.40	5.54	1.81	-1.43	5.54
Earnings	6.11	4.95	1.77	-2.48	-7.23	-0.76
Dividends	0.63	0.28	0.10	0.35	1.10	1.10
Payout Ratio	10%	6%	6%	NM	NM	NM
Prices - High	57⅝	54⅜	40½	27¼	27¾	36⅛
- Low	35⅞	37⅜	26⅝	16¼	15⅝	24
P/E Ratio - High	9	11	23	NM	NM	NM
- Low	6	8	15	NM	NM	NM

Income Statement Analysis (Million $)

	1994	%Chg	1993	%Chg	1992	%Chg	1991
Revs.	4,737	12%	4,248	13%	3,749	10%	3,406
Oper. Inc.	435	18%	370	46%	253	85%	137
Depr.	128	5%	122	NM	123	-3%	127
Int. Exp.	17.5	-52%	36.3	-11%	41.0	-4%	42.5
Pretax Inc.	294	43%	205	170%	76.0	NM	-46.0
Eff. Tax Rate	14%	—	11%	—	12%	—	NM
Net Inc.	253	38%	183	173%	67.0	NM	-66.0

Balance Sheet & Other Fin. Data (Million $)

	1994	1993	1992	1991	1990	1989
Cash	147	77.0	54.0	52.0	80.0	73.0
Curr. Assets	1,298	1,072	996	908	991	975
Total Assets	2,706	2,391	2,231	2,041	2,086	2,031
Curr. Liab.	840	700	724	689	728	750
LT Debt	155	190	412	443	411	406
Common Eqty.	1,073	709	386	509	554	407
Total Cap.	1,248	1,028	929	1,137	1,145	1,095
Cap. Exp.	238	184	139	124	147	138
Cash Flow	381	297	182	54.0	-35.0	116

Ratio Analysis

	1994	1993	1992	1991	1990	1989
Curr. Ratio	1.5	1.5	1.4	1.3	1.4	1.3
% LT Debt of Cap.	12.4	18.4	44.4	39.0	35.9	37.1
% Net Inc.of Revs.	5.3	4.3	1.8	NM	NM	NM
% Ret. on Assets	9.6	7.5	2.9	NM	NM	NM
% Ret. on Equity	27.5	30.6	12.1	NM	NM	NM

Dividend Data
(Dividends have been paid since 1948. A dividend reinvestment plan is available. A "poison pill" stock purchase rights plan was adopted in 1986.)

Amt. of Div. $	Date Decl.	Ex-Div. Date	Stock of Record	Payment Date
0.250	Oct. 11	Nov. 25	Dec. 01	Dec. 15 '94
0.250	Feb. 14	Feb. 23	Mar. 01	Mar. 15 '95
0.250	Apr. 04	May. 25	Jun. 01	Jun. 15 '95
0.250	Jul. 03	Aug. 30	Sep. 01	Sep. 15 '95

Data as orig. reptd.; bef. results of disc. opers. and/or spec. items. Per share data adj. for stk. divs. as of ex-div. date. E-Estimated. NA-Not Available. NM-Not Meaningful. NR-Not Ranked.

Office—500 Jackson St, Columbus, IN 47202. Tel—(812) 377-5000. Chrmn & CEO—J. A. Henderson. Pres & COO—T. Solso. VP & CFO—P.B. Hamilton. Secy—M. R. Gerstle. Investor Contact—Michele C. Heid. Dirs—H. Brown, K. R. Dabrowski, R. J. Darnall, W. Y. Elisha, H. H. Gray, J. A. Henderson, D. G. Mead, J. I. Miller, W. I. Miller, D. S. Perkins, W. D. Ruckelshaus, H. B. Schacht, T. M. Solso, F. A. Thomas, J. L. Wilson. Transfer Agent & Registrar—First Chicago Trust Co. of New York, Jersey City, NJ. Incorporated in Indiana in 1919. Empl-25,600. S&P Analyst: Joshua M. Harari, CFA

Cyprus Amax Minerals

NYSE Symbol **CYM**
In S&P 500

31-JUL-95

Industry:
Mining/Diversified

Summary: This firm is a leading U.S. copper and coal producer, the world's largest producer of molybdenum and lithium, holds significant interests in gold, and explores for gold and copper.

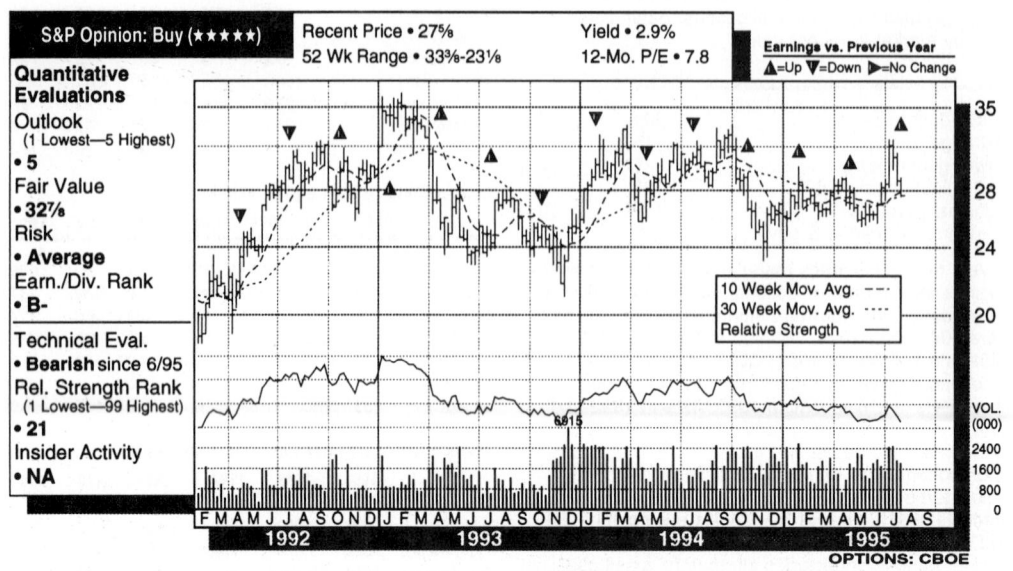

| S&P Opinion: Buy (★★★★★) | Recent Price • 27⅜ | Yield • 2.9% |
| | 52 Wk Range • 33⅞-23⅛ | 12-Mo. P/E • 7.8 |

Quantitative Evaluations

Outlook
(1 Lowest—5 Highest)
• **5**

Fair Value
• **32⅞**

Risk
• **Average**

Earn./Div. Rank
• **B-**

Technical Eval.
• **Bearish** since 6/95

Rel. Strength Rank
(1 Lowest—99 Highest)
• **21**

Insider Activity
• **NA**

Earnings vs. Previous Year
▲=Up ▼=Down ▶=No Change

10 Week Mov. Avg. -- --
30 Week Mov. Avg. .....
Relative Strength —

OPTIONS: CBOE

Overview - 31-JUL-95

Mainly as a result of increases in average annual copper and molybdenum prices, net income is likely to climb in 1995 (before a $400 million pretax writedown of coal assets). Copper profits should advance substantially in the absence of residual negative effects of heavy rain, and on greater copper output, lower unit production costs (primarily reflecting larger molybdenum byproduct credits) and higher realized prices. Earnings from primary molybdenum mines are likely to rise dramatically on higher prices. Coal income will probably improve moderately, reflecting heavier output. Lithium profits are likely to slightly exceed 1994's record as aluminum smelters are restarted. With ongoing cost cuts, earnings should rise sharply. Going forward, exploration emphasis will be on gold and copper.

Valuation - 31-JUL-95

CYM's shares should benefit from increases during the next few years in output of copper (to one billion lbs. from estimated 1995's 675 million), coal (to 100 million tons from 1995's 86 million) and gold including Amax Gold (to one million oz. from 1995's 245,000). We see copper demand continuing to exceed supply and, thus, copper prices staying in an uptrend through mid-1996. Molybdenum prices in 1995 and 1996 may average around levels at which molybdenum is a major earnings contributor to CYM. The bringing onstream of El Abra in 1997 will help to soften any cyclical downturn.

Key Stock Statistics

S&P EPS Est. 1995	4.50	Tang. Bk. Value/Share	25.85
P/E on S&P Est. 1995	6.1	Beta	1.03
S&P EPS Est. 1996	4.75	Shareholders	48,000
Dividend Rate/Share	0.80	Market cap. (B)	$ 2.6
Shs. outstg. (M)	92.7	Inst. holdings	68%
Avg. daily vol. (M)	0.489	Insider holdings	NA

Value of $10,000 invested 5 years ago: $ 12,550

Fiscal Year Ending Dec. 31

	1995	% Change	1994	% Change	1993	% Change
Revenues (Million $)						
1Q	807.0	37%	588.4	57%	374.7	-6%
2Q	875.0	26%	697.0	54%	453.6	12%
3Q	—	—	771.0	96%	393.6	-9%
4Q	—	—	732.0	35%	541.7	33%
Yr.	—	—	2,788	58%	1,764	7%
Income (Million $)						
1Q	97.00	NM	18.70	62%	11.56	NM
2Q	134.0	NM	32.00	-61%	82.03	NM
3Q	—	—	48.00	NM	14.30	-64%
4Q	—	—	67.00	NM	-7.70	NM
Yr.	—	—	166.0	66%	100.2	NM
Earnings Per Share ($)						
1Q	1.00	NM	0.15	-38%	0.24	NM
2Q	1.39	NM	0.30	-83%	1.73	NM
3Q	E1.00	—	0.47	57%	0.30	-67%
4Q	E1.11	—	0.68	NM	-0.14	NM
Yr.	E4.50	—	1.59	-14%	1.85	NM

Next earnings report expected: late October

Cyprus Amax Minerals

31-JUL-95

Business Summary - 31-JUL-95

CYM is a leading copper, molybdenum, coal and lithium producer with interests in gold. Segments in 1994:

	Revs.	Op. Inc.
Copper/molybdenum	47%	59%
Coal	45%	30%
Other	8%	11%

Cyprus Climax Metals, the second largest U.S. copper company, produced 648 million pounds in 1994 from mines mainly in Arizona. With the Henderson molybdenum mine (Colo.) and by-product molybdenum from copper, it is the world's largest molybdenum producer; 1994's output was 57 million lbs. In March 1994, 91.5% of the Cerro Verde mine (Peru) was bought for $31 million. Cathode output by late 1995 will be expanded to an annual rate of 100 million lbs. of copper, from 32 million lbs. produced in 1994 after acquisition. In June 1995, CYM and Codelco (Chile's state-owned copper company) finalized $750 million in financing for the El Abra (Chile) copper deposit. CYM is funding a further $300 million in debt. Construction began in January 1995 on the oxide project which is expected to reach an annual rate of 500 million lbs. of cathodes by mid-1997. CYM owns 51% of El Abra. CYM's year-end 1994 copper and molybdenum reserves were 23.8 and 2.1 billion lbs., respectively.

Cyprus Amax Coal is the second largest U.S. coal producer, with 1994 output of 75 million tons from Colorado, Illinois, Indiana, Kentucky, Pennsylvania, Tennessee, Utah, West Virginia and Wyoming, holding 1994 year-end reserves of 2.5 billion tons. CYM's 40% share of Oakbridge Limited represented 4 million tons of 1994 production. Oakbridge (43% owned since 1995) is an Australian coal mining firm with six mines and reserves of 171 million tons (as CYM's share). About 77% of U.S. output was sold under contract.

Cyprus Foote Mineral is the world's largest and lowest-cost producer of lithium carbonate used in aluminum smelting, greases, plastics, synthetic rubber and drugs. In 1994, output totaled 32 million lbs. from facilities in Nevada and Chile. Amax Gold (47% owned since July 1995) operates mines in California, Nevada and Chile, which produced 241,000 oz. in 1994. It is expected to produce over 625,000 oz. in 1997.

Important Developments

Jun. '95—CYM said that partners in the Kubaka gold project (50% owned by a CYM unit) in eastern Russia signed loan agreements totaling $100 million for development. Construction has begun at the site of the mine, which should produce 310,000 oz./year when operational in 1997.

Capitalization

Long Term Debt: $1,506,000,000 (6/95).

$4 Series A Cum. Preferred Stock: 4,666,635 shs. ($50 liquid. pref.); conv. into 2.057 com.

Per Share Data ($)

(Year Ended Dec. 31)

	1994	1993	1992	1991	1990	1989
Tangible Bk. Val.	22.64	24.16	19.52	28.02	27.94	30.92
Cash Flow	4.31	4.58	-3.17	3.60	5.03	8.46
Earnings	1.59	1.85	-6.31	0.72	2.38	6.06
Dividends	0.90	0.80	0.85	0.80	0.80	0.60
Payout Ratio	57%	43%	NM	112%	32%	10%
Prices - High	33⅜	36⅜	32	25⅜	28½	33
- Low	23⅛	21	18½	17½	13⅞	21⅜
P/E Ratio - High	21	20	NM	35	12	5
- Low	15	11	NM	24	6	4

Income Statement Analysis (Million $)

	1994	%Chg	1993	%Chg	1992	%Chg	1991
Revs.	2,788	58%	1,764	7%	1,641	NM	1,657
Oper. Inc.	583	74%	336	NM	-65.0	NM	174
Depr.	253	74%	145	13%	128	14%	112
Int. Exp.	107	157%	41.6	110%	19.8	-12%	22.4
Pretax Inc.	221	69%	131	NM	-328	NM	54.0
Eff. Tax Rate	25%	—	24%	—	NM	—	20%
Net Inc.	166	66%	100	NM	-245	NM	43.0

Balance Sheet & Other Fin. Data (Million $)

	1994	1993	1992	1991	1990	1989
Cash	139	96.0	90.0	79.0	39.0	44.0
Curr. Assets	1,041	1,008	584	578	565	503
Total Assets	5,407	5,625	1,683	1,966	1,919	1,841
Curr. Liab.	618	967	258	279	229	252
LT Debt	1,391	1,347	232	239	246	108
Common Eqty.	2,096	2,212	923	1,094	1,088	1,183
Total Cap.	3,845	3,735	1,175	1,595	1,614	1,528
Cap. Exp.	359	266	156	190	208	349
Cash Flow	401	243	-128	140	203	329

Ratio Analysis

	1994	1993	1992	1991	1990	1989
Curr. Ratio	1.7	1.0	2.3	2.1	2.5	2.0
% LT Debt of Cap.	36.2	36.1	19.8	15.0	15.2	7.1
% Net Inc.of Revs.	6.0	5.7	NM	2.6	5.9	14.0
% Ret. on Assets	3.0	2.3	NM	2.2	5.9	14.5
% Ret. on Equity	7.2	4.9	NM	2.6	8.4	21.8

Dividend Data

(Quarterly dividends were initiated in 1988. A dividend reinvestment plan is available. A "poison pill" stock purchase right was amended in 1993.)

Amt. of Div. $	Date Decl.	Ex-Div. Date	Stock of Record	Payment Date
0.200	Aug. 25	Oct. 03	Oct. 10	Nov. 01 '94
0.100	Dec. 01	Dec. 06	Dec. 12	Dec. 23 '94
0.200	Dec. 01	Jan. 04	Jan. 10	Feb. 01 '95
0.200	Feb. 16	Apr. 04	Apr. 10	May. 01 '95
0.200	Jun. 22	Jul. 06	Jul. 10	Aug. 01 '95

Data as orig. reptd.; bef. results of disc. opers. and/or spec. items. Per share data adj. for stk. divs. as of ex-div. date. E-Estimated. NA-Not Available. NM-Not Meaningful. NR-Not Ranked.

Office—9100 East Mineral Circle, Englewood, CO 80112. **Tel**—(303) 643-5000. **Co-Chrmn, Pres & CEO**—M. H. Ward. **SVP-Secy & GC**—P. C. Wolf. **SVP-CFO**—G. J. Malys. **VP-Treas & Investor Contact**—Frank J. Kane. **Dirs**—A. Born (Co-Chrmn), L. G. Alvarado, G. S. Ansell, W. C. Bousquette, T. V. Falkie, A. M. Gray, J. C. Huntington Jr., M. A. Morphy, R. A. Schnabel, T. M. Solso, J. H. Stookey, J. A. Todd Jr., B. B. Turner, M. H. Ward. **Transfer Agent & Registrar**—Society National Bank, Denver, Colo. **Incorporated** in Delaware in 1969. **Empl**-9,500. **S&P Analyst:** A.M. Sorrentino, CFA

DSC Communications

NASDAQ Symbol **DIGI**
In S&P 500

16-SEP-95 **Industry:** Telecommunications

Summary: This company manufactures digital switching, transmission, access and private network system products for the telecommunications industry.

S&P Opinion: Accumulate (★★★★)	Recent Price • 56⅝	Yield • Nil
	52 Wk Range • 62½-26⅞	12-Mo. P/E • 35.0

Earnings vs. Previous Year
▲=Up ▼=Down ▶=No Change

Quantitative Evaluations

Outlook (1 Lowest—5 Highest)
• **1+**

Fair Value
• **53**

Risk
• **High**

Earn./Div. Rank
• **B**

Technical Eval.
• **Bullish** since 8/94

Rel. Strength Rank (1 Lowest—99 Highest)
• **79**

Insider Activity
• **Unfavorable**

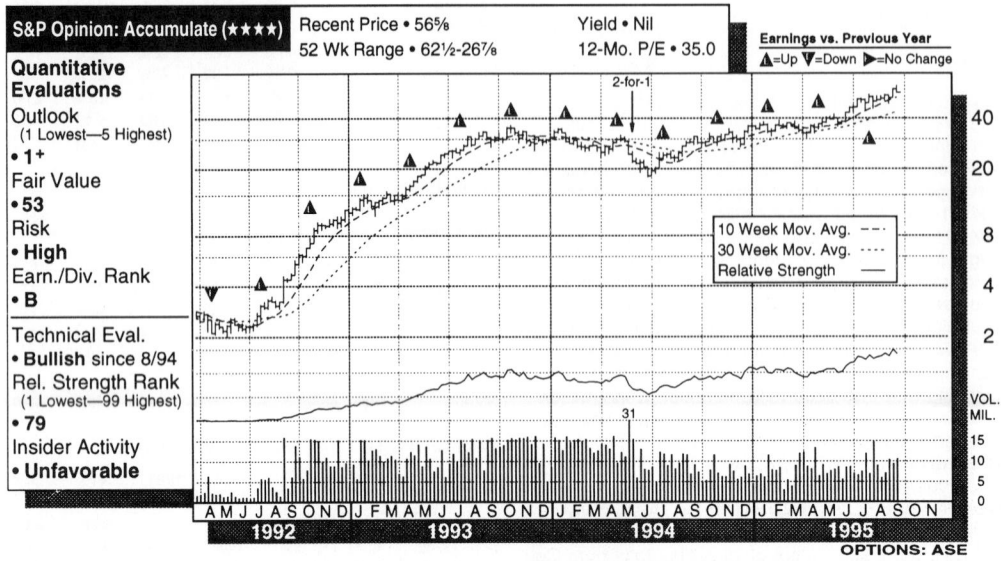

10 Week Mov. Avg. ---
30 Week Mov. Avg. ·····
Relative Strength —

2-for-1

VOL. MIL.

OPTIONS: ASE

Overview - 15-SEP-95

Revenues are expected to grow at a double-digit rate in the next few years, reflecting higher volume shipments of access products, as well as growth in switching and transmission products as telephone companies accelerate capital expenditures. The increase will be aided by the introduction of the Airspan-2000 wireless access product, which should do especially well in developing countries. Revenues should also benefit from efforts to target nontraditional markets, such as cable television operators, and an increased international presence. Profitability should benefit as the higher sales base, operating efficiencies and a more favorable revenue mix offset a high level of research and development expenditures.

Valuation - 15-SEP-95

DSC's shares have had a tremendous runup recently, soaring more than 80% from their low in mid-April. However, despite this move, the shares are still trading on a P/E basis at a discount to the industry's projected annual growth rate of approximately 30%. DSC's better-than-expected results have been driven by sharply higher sales of switching products, especially in the analog cellular market. Future prospects will continue to benefit as carriers upgrade their networks in order to offer more advanced services. The recent acquisition of NKT Elektronik A/S not only broadens the company's product line, but gives DSC an expanded presence in the rapidly growing international market.

Key Stock Statistics

S&P EPS Est. 1995	1.85	Tang. Bk. Value/Share	7.11
P/E on S&P Est. 1995	30.6	Beta	0.62
S&P EPS Est. 1996	2.35	Shareholders	3,600
Dividend Rate/Share	Nil	Market cap. (B)	$ 6.5
Shs. outstg. (M)	114.7	Inst. holdings	89%
Avg. daily vol. (M)	1.894	Insider holdings	NA

Value of $10,000 invested 5 years ago: $ 78,103

Fiscal Year Ending Dec. 31

	1995	% Change	1994	% Change	1993	% Change
Revenues (Million $)						
1Q	318.0	58%	200.9	29%	156.0	51%
2Q	360.0	57%	229.6	36%	168.7	31%
3Q	—	—	260.6	39%	188.0	32%
4Q	—	—	312.1	43%	217.9	35%
Yr.	—	—	1,003	37%	730.8	36%
Income (Million $)						
1Q	41.92	42%	29.60	160%	11.37	NM
2Q	51.96	43%	36.28	99%	18.24	NM
3Q	—	—	43.20	85%	23.29	NM
4Q	—	—	53.55	86%	28.76	119%
Yr.	—	—	162.6	99%	81.66	NM
Earnings Per Share ($)						
1Q	0.36	44%	0.25	108%	0.12	NM
2Q	0.44	42%	0.31	82%	0.17	NM
3Q	E0.48	30%	0.37	72%	0.22	169%
4Q	E0.57	24%	0.46	80%	0.25	82%
Yr.	E1.85	33%	1.39	83%	0.76	NM

Next earnings report expected: mid October

DSC Communications

Business Summary - 15-SEP-95

DSC Communications Corporation designs, manufactures and markets digital switching, transmission and private network system products. Revenues in recent years were derived as follows:

	1994	1993	1992
Switching products	52%	45%	54%
Access products	27%	28%	8%
Transmission products	NA	19%	24%
Other	NA	8%	14%

In recent periods, the switching division has focused on market opportunities such as the burgeoning demand for high-speed switch-based and video-on-demand services and increased utilization of network-based intelligence, service programmability and interconnectivity. Switching and intelligent network products include tandem switches that are generally used to interconnect bundles of local or long-distance telephone lines; the DEX MegaHub product line; switching products based on Signaling System No.7 (SS7), an international standard for interswitching system communications; BASIS and iBSS products, which allow higher bandwidth transmission; and cellular telephone switches.

The access products division develops and markets equipment for use in the local loop--the connection of the customer to the telephone network. Offerings include next-generation digital loop carrier and fiber in the loop products.

Transmission products consist of digital cross-connect systems for switching, multiplexing and termination of digital transmission services; broadband platforms; echo and compression products; and network management systems.

Other products include customer premise products that allow corporate customers with high-capacity networks to integrate multiple media and directly access public networks and various transmission products for wide area networks.

In 1994, three customers accounted for 46% of sales.

Important Developments

Sep. '95—DSC said it is supplying switches to Motorola for deployment in PCS PrimeCo's new personal communications services (PCS) networks.
Jun. '95—The company signed a multimillion-dollar agreement to immediately provide Telefonos de Mexico with MegaHub Signal Transfer Point equipment.
Jan. '95—DSC acquired NKT Elektronik A/S for about $145 million. Denmark-based NKT is one of western Europe's leading suppliers of Synchronous Digital Hierarchy (SDH) optical transmission equipment, with an estimated 17% of that market.

Capitalization

Long Term Debt: $206,483,000 (6/95).

Per Share Data ($)

(Year Ended Dec. 31)

	1994	1993	1992	1991	1990	1989
Tangible Bk. Val.	6.15	5.16	1.59	1.30	2.58	3.16
Cash Flow	1.85	1.18	0.57	-0.83	0.68	0.70
Earnings	1.39	0.76	0.13	-1.31	0.24	0.40
Dividends	Nil	Nil	Nil	Nil	Nil	Nil
Payout Ratio	Nil	Nil	Nil	Nil	Nil	Nil
Prices - High	37⁷/₈	36¹/₂	11¹/₂	4⁷/₈	8³/₈	8⁵/₈
- Low	17⁷/₈	10³/₈	1¹³/₁₆	1¹³/₁₆	2³/₁₆	3³/₈
P/E Ratio - High	27	48	88	NM	36	21
- Low	13	14	14	NM	9	8

Income Statement Analysis (Million $)

	1994	%Chg	1993	%Chg	1992	%Chg	1991
Revs.	1,003	37%	731	36%	536	16%	461
Oper. Inc.	268	73%	155	89%	82.0	NM	6.0
Depr.	53.7	21%	44.3	13%	39.2	-2%	39.8
Int. Exp.	3.7	-49%	7.2	-68%	22.5	-14%	26.2
Pretax Inc.	223	105%	109	NM	17.0	NM	-106
Eff. Tax Rate	27%	—	25%	—	31%	—	NM
Net Inc.	163	99%	82.0	NM	12.0	NM	-107

Balance Sheet & Other Fin. Data (Million $)

	1994	1993	1992	1991	1990	1989
Cash	271	314	70.0	26.0	35.0	68.0
Curr. Assets	738	602	275	307	405	364
Total Assets	1,269	900	548	600	759	570
Curr. Liab.	345	195	196	302	252	130
LT Debt	25.0	57.0	129	109	209	179
Common Eqty.	851	618	203	175	279	254
Total Cap.	876	675	349	297	499	433
Cap. Exp.	141	71.0	21.8	22.3	68.1	50.5
Cash Flow	216	126	50.8	-68.5	58.2	58.9

Ratio Analysis

	1994	1993	1992	1991	1990	1989
Curr. Ratio	2.1	3.1	1.4	1.0	1.6	2.8
% LT Debt of Cap.	2.9	8.4	36.8	36.7	41.9	41.3
% Net Inc.of Revs.	16.2	11.2	2.2	NM	3.9	8.0
% Ret. on Assets	14.8	10.3	2.0	NM	3.0	6.8
% Ret. on Equity	21.9	18.8	6.0	NM	7.6	14.4

Dividend Data —No cash has been paid. A two-for-one stock split was effected in May 1994.

Data as orig. reptd.; bef. results of disc. opers. and/or spec. items. Per share data adj. for stk. divs. as of ex-div. date.
E-Estimated. NA-Not Available. NM-Not Meaningful. NR-Not Ranked.

Office—1000 Coit Rd., Plano, TX 75075-5813. **Tel**—(214) 519-3000. **Chrmn, Pres & CEO**—J. L. Donald. **VP & Secy**—G. B. Brunt. **Sr VP & CFO**—G. F. Montry. **VP & Treas**—C. J. Ornes. **Dirs**—C. M. Brown Jr., F. J. Cummiskey, R. J. Dempsey, J. L. Donald, Sir John Fairclough, J. L. Fischer, R. S. Folsom, G. F. Montry, J. M. Nolan. **Transfer Agent & Registrar**—Society National Bank, Dallas. **Incorporated** in Delaware in 1976. **Empl**- 5,414. **S&P Analyst:** Alan Aaron

Dana Corp.

NYSE Symbol **DCN**
In S&P 500

31-JUL-95

Industry:
Auto parts/equipment

Summary: Dana manufactures truck and car components and parts for both original equipment manufacturers and distribution in the automotive aftermarket.

S&P Opinion: Avoid (★★)

Recent Price • 29%	Yield • 3.1%
52 Wk Range • 32⅛-19⅝	12-Mo. P/E • 11.4

Quantitative Evaluations

Outlook
(1 Lowest—5 Highest)
• **3**

Fair Value
• **28¼**

Risk
• **Average**

Earn./Div. Rank
• **B**

Technical Eval.
• **Bearish** since 7/95

Rel. Strength Rank
(1 Lowest—99 Highest)
• **58**

Insider Activity
• **Unfavorable**

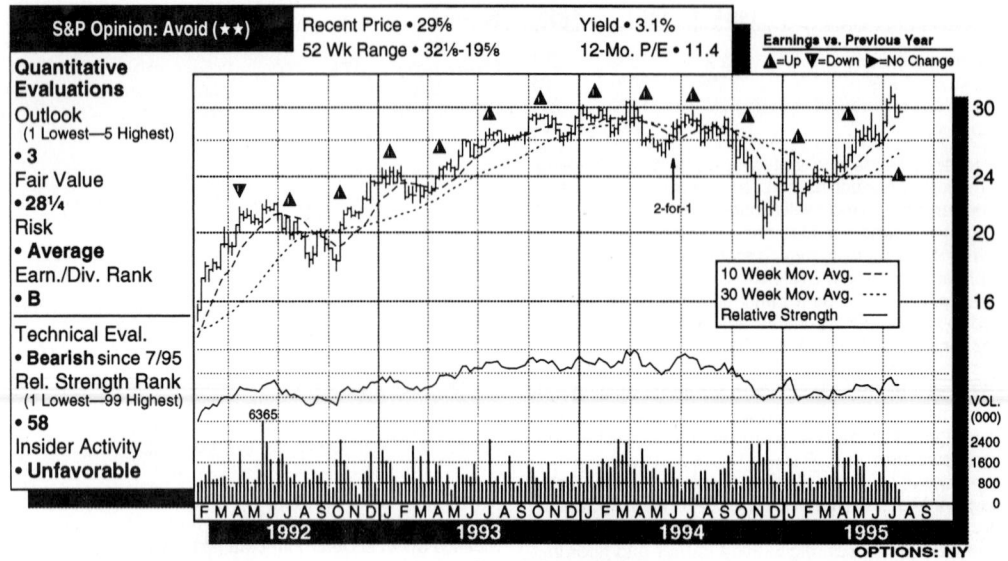

Earnings vs. Previous Year
▲=Up ▼=Down ▶=No Change

10 Week Mov. Avg. - - -
30 Week Mov. Avg. ····
Relative Strength —

2-for-1

OPTIONS: NY

Overview - 31-JUL-95

Improvement in foreign vehicular markets is expected in 1996, and should offset a flattening or even mild downturn in the North American original equipment vehicle markets. Vehicle component shipments should benefit from an overall increase in global vehicle assemblies. Demand for replacement parts, which has been sluggish thus far in 1995, should rebound with the continued use of aging vehicles and a return to more normal weather patterns in North America. Over the long term, international operations should continue to grow, fueled by acquisitions and continuation of a trend to outsourcing by global car and truck producers. The company's long-term goal remains to derive 50% of sales from foreign markets and 50% from domestic sales, and a similar split between original equipment sales and distribution.

Valuation - 31-JUL-95

Although earnings should continue to rise modestly in 1996, the U.S. economy is approaching a cyclical peak. With heavy duty truck orders already declining, related parts sales should turn down in 1996. Furthermore, light vehicle sales are not likely to rise substantially from the levels of 1994 and 1995, making it unlikely that DCN's earnings multiple will expand from the 10 to 11 range of recent months. The stock has underperformed the broader S&P 500 Index since early 1994 and we think it may continue to do so until the next recession. We recommend investors avoid the stock.

Key Stock Statistics

S&P EPS Est. 1995	2.75	Tang. Bk. Value/Share	9.67
P/E on S&P Est. 1995	10.8	Beta	1.13
S&P EPS Est. 1996	3.00	Shareholders	28,300
Dividend Rate/Share	0.92	Market cap. (B)	$ 3.0
Shs. outstg. (M)	101.2	Inst. holdings	76%
Avg. daily vol. (M)	0.159	Insider holdings	NA

Value of $10,000 invested 5 years ago: $ 21,432

Fiscal Year Ending Dec. 31

	1995	% Change	1994	% Change	1993	% Change
Revenues (Million $)						
1Q	1,924	21%	1,597	21%	1,324	12%
2Q	1,969	15%	1,712	21%	1,418	14%
3Q	—	—	1,610	25%	1,291	9%
4Q	—	—	1,695	19%	1,428	13%
Yr.	—	—	6,614	21%	5,460	12%
Income (Million $)						
1Q	59.20	24%	47.70	103%	23.50	NM
2Q	89.10	31%	68.00	86%	36.60	167%
3Q	—	—	52.90	59%	33.30	169%
4Q	—	—	59.60	70%	35.10	63%
Yr.	—	—	228.2	78%	128.5	198%
Earnings Per Share ($)						
1Q	0.59	22%	0.49	90%	0.25	NM
2Q	0.88	28%	0.69	73%	0.40	150%
3Q	E0.63	—	0.54	50%	0.36	167%
4Q	E0.65	—	0.60	60%	0.38	60%
Yr.	E2.75	—	2.31	66%	1.39	184%

Next earnings report expected: early September

Business Summary - 31-JUL-95

Dana manufactures automotive components and industrial products for original equipment (OE) and aftermarket distribution. Segment contributions (profits in millions) in 1994 were:

	Revenues	Profits
Vehicular products	79%	$520.1
Industrial lines	19%	56.9
Financial services	2%	11.6

Dana's international operations contributed 25% of revenues and 21.5% of operating income in 1994. Ford contributed 16% of consolidated sales in 1994, 18% in 1993 and 17% in 1992. Chrysler accounted for 12% of sales in 1994, 11% in 1993 and 9% in 1992.

Consolidated sales by market in 1994 were: 35% light trucks and cars OE, 21% heavy trucks OE, 16% automotive distribution, 10% mobile off-highway/industrial distribution, 8% truck parts distribution, 7% mobile off-highway OE and 3% industrial equipment OE.

Vehicular products consist primarily of the manufacture and marketing of drivetrain components, such as axles, driveshafts, clutches and transmissions; engine parts, such as pistons, piston rings, seals, filters and gaskets; chassis products, such as vehicular frames and cradles and heavy-duty side rails; fluid power components, such as pumps motors and control valves; and industrial products, such as electrical and mechanical brakes and clutches, drives and motion control devices.

Diamond Financial Holdings provides leasing and finance and property development financial services through subsidiaries.

Important Developments

Jul. '95—Sales gains for the first half of 1995 by market area were: highway vehicle original equipment component sales up 23.0%, mobile off-highway original equipment components up 28.7%, industrial original equipment components up 13.6%, automotive aftermarket distribution up 5.7%, truck parts aftermarket distribution up 6.9%, and mobile off-highway/industrial distribution up 9.0%. In the second quarter of 1995, DCN completed the acquisition of the 43% of Hayes-Dana it did not already own at C$18.50 per share or about C$125 million. Previously 57%-owned, Hayes-Dana is a Canadian manufacturer and distributor of vehicular and industrial components.

Capitalization

Long Term Debt: $1,186,500,000 (6/95).
Minority Interest: $152,200,000.

Per Share Data ($)   (Year Ended Dec. 31)

	1994	1993	1992	1991	1990	1989
Tangible Bk. Val.	6.77	5.63	5.09	9.45	12.78	12.47
Cash Flow	4.45	3.51	2.67	2.51	2.66	3.21
Earnings	2.31	1.39	0.49	0.17	0.93	1.62
Dividends	0.83	0.80	0.80	0.80	0.80	0.80
Payout Ratio	36%	58%	163%	487%	86%	50%
Prices - High	30¾	30⅛	24⅛	18¼	19⅛	21½
- Low	19⅝	22	13⅜	12⅛	10	16½
P/E Ratio - High	13	22	49	NM	21	13
- Low	8	16	27	NM	11	10

Income Statement Analysis (Million $)

	1994	%Chg	1993	%Chg	1992	%Chg	1991
Revs.	6,763	21%	5,588	11%	5,036	10%	4,591
Oper. Inc.	738	26%	585	42%	411	10%	372
Depr.	211	8%	196	2%	192	NM	193
Int. Exp.	113	-18%	137	-18%	168	-16%	200
Pretax Inc.	416	70%	244	NM	58.0	—	NM
Eff. Tax Rate	38%	—	37%	—	NM	—	NM
Net Inc.	228	77%	129	NM	43.0	NM	13.0

Balance Sheet & Other Fin. Data (Million $)

	1994	1993	1992	1991	1990	1989
Cash	48.2	50.0	42.0	50.0	42.0	71.0
Curr. Assets	NA	NA	NA	NA	NA	NA
Total Assets	5,111	4,632	4,343	4,179	4,513	5,225
Curr. Liab.	NA	NA	NA	NA	NA	NA
LT Debt	870	846	1,043	1,207	1,152	1,165
Common Eqty.	940	801	707	989	1,049	1,020
Total Cap.	1,962	1,789	1,878	2,512	2,572	2,560
Cap. Exp.	337	178	114	150	228	235
Cash Flow	439	324	235	206	219	262

Ratio Analysis

	1994	1993	1992	1991	1990	1989
Curr. Ratio	NA	NA	NA	NA	NA	NA
% LT Debt of Cap.	44.3	47.3	55.5	48.1	44.8	45.5
% Net Inc.of Revs.	3.4	2.3	0.9	0.3	1.4	2.6
% Ret. on Assets	4.7	2.8	1.0	0.3	1.6	2.6
% Ret. on Equity	26.2	16.5	4.8	1.3	7.3	13.3

Dividend Data (Dividends have been paid since 1936. A dividend reinvestment plan is available. A "poison pill" stock purchase right was adopted in 1986.)

Amt. of Div. $	Date Decl.	Ex-Div. Date	Stock of Record	Payment Date
0.210	Jul. 22	Aug. 26	Sep. 01	Sep. 15 '94
0.210	Oct. 17	Nov. 25	Dec. 01	Dec. 15 '94
0.210	Feb. 13	Feb. 23	Mar. 01	Mar. 15 '95
0.230	Apr. 18	May. 25	Jun. 01	Jun. 15 '95
0.230	Jul. 17	Aug. 30	Sep. 01	Sep. 15 '95

Data as orig. reptd.; bef. results of disc. opers. and/or spec. items. Per share data adj. for stk. divs. as of ex-div. date.
E-Estimated. NA-Not Available. NM-Not Meaningful. NR-Not Ranked.

Office—4500 Dorr St., Toledo, OH 43697. **Tel**—(419) 535-4500. **Chrmn & Pres**—S. J. Morcott. **CFO & Treas**—J. E. Ayers. **Secy**—M. J. Strobel. **Investor Contact**—Steve Superits (800) 537-8823 or (419) 535-4636. **Dirs**—B. F. Bailar, E. M. Carpenter, E. Clark, R. Fridholm, G. H. Hiner, M. R. Marks, S. J. Morcott, J. D. Stevenson, T. B. Sumner Jr. **Transfer Agent & Registrar**—Chemical Bank, NYC. **Incorporated** in Virginia in 1916. **Empl**-40,000. **S&P Analyst:** Joshua M. Harari, CFA

Darden Restaurants

NYSE Symbol DRI   In S&P 500

Price	Range	P–E Ratio	Dividend	Yield	S&P Ranking	Beta
Nov. 6'95	1995					
11½	12–9⅛	NM	¹0.08	¹0.7%	NR	NA

Summary

The largest full-service restaurant company, Darden operates the Red Lobster and Olive Garden chains. DRI closed its China Coast restaurants in August 1995. Formerly part of General Mills, Inc. (GIS), Darden was spun off to GIS shareholders in May 1995 on a share-for-share basis. Darden's common shares were listed on the NYSE.

Business Summary

Darden Restaurants, Inc. operates more than 1,150 restaurants in the Red Lobster and Olive Garden chains. In August 1995, DRI closed its restaurants in the China Coast chain.

DRI became a separate publicly-owned company in May 1995 when ownership of the business was spun off by former parent company General Mills, Inc. (GIS). DRI is named after William B. Darden, who founded the Red Lobster chain in 1968.

Red Lobster is the largest U.S. chain of full-service, seafood-specialty restaurants. As of August 27, 1995, DRI was operating 713 units. The menu features fresh fish, shrimp, crab, lobster, scallops, and other seafood, served in a casual atmosphere. Also, there are several non-seafood entrees available. Dinner entree prices at Red Lobster restaurants range from about $6.69 to $18.99, with the availability or price of certain fresh fish and lobster items dependent upon market conditions. Lunch entree prices range from about $4.29 to $6.99. Also, Red Lobster offers a lower-priced children's menu.

Olive Garden is the largest U.S. chain of casual, full-service Italian restaurants. As of August 27, 1995, DRI was operating about 475 Olive Garden restaurants. The menu offers recipes from northern and southern Italy, including specialties such as veal piccata, fettuccine alfredo, baked lasagna, manicotti and chicken marsala. Other entrees include marinated chicken breasts grilled Venetian-style, and other veal, beef, and seafood dishes. Dinner entre prices at Olive Garden restaurants range about $6.95 to $14.25, and lunch entree prices range from about $4.25 to $8.75. Also, DRI is testing The Olive Garden Cafe concept, which is a limited menu cafe in food court settings at re-

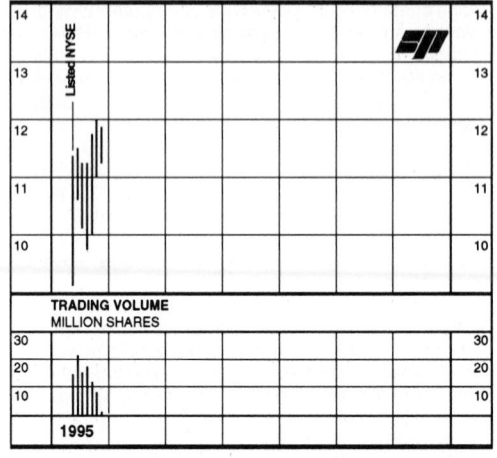

gional shopping malls. Such units are serviced by nearby full-service Olive Garden restaurants.

Important Developments

Sep. '95— DRI said that in fiscal 1996's first quarter, earnings before unusual items increased 5%, to $0.21 a share. This excludes a $0.28 a share charge ($44.8 million after-tax) related to the closing of DRI's China Coast restaurants, of which 51 were open in May 1995. More than half of the China Coast units are to be converted to restaurants in other DRI chains. Also, DRI's first quarter same-store sales in the Red Lobster chain declined 1.0%, but were up 3.8% in the Olive Garden business.

Next earnings report expected in mid-December.

Per Share Data ($)

Yr. End May 31	³1995	³1994
Tangible Bk. Val.	7.37	6.61
Cash Flow	1.17	1.54
Earnings²	0.31	0.75
Dividends	Nil	NA
Payout Ratio	Nil	NA
Calendar Years	1994	1993
Prices—High	NA	NA
Low	NA	NA
P/E Ratio—	NA	NA

Data as orig. reptd. Prior to 1995 data as reptd. in Information Statement dated May 5, 1995. **1.** See Dividend Data. **2.** Bef. spec. item(s) of +0.03 in 1994. **3.** Pro forma. NA-Not Available. NM-Not Meaningful.

Darden Restaurants, Inc.

Income Data (Million $)

Year Ended May 31	Revs.	Oper. Inc.	% Oper. Inc. of Revs.	Cap. Exp.	Depr.	Int. Exp.	Net Bef. Taxes	Eff. Tax Rate	Net Inc.	% Net Inc. of Revs.	Cash Flow
[2]1995	3,163	316	10.0	358	135	26.1	59.8	17.7%	49.2	1.6	185
[2]1994	2,963	331	11.2	335	125	22.6	188.0	36.3%	[1]120.0	4.0	245

Balance Sheet Data (Million $)

May 31	Cash	Assets	Curr. Liab.	Ratio	Total Assets	% Ret. on Assets	Long Term Debt	Common Equity	Total Cap.	% LT Debt of Cap.	% Ret. on Equity
1995	20.1	308	517	0.6	2,113	NA	304	1,174	1,580	19.2	NA
[2]1994	17.7	250	403	0.6	1,859	NA	304	1,052	1,447	21.0	NA

Data as reptd. in Information Statement dated May 5, 1995. **1.** Bef. spec. items. **2.** Pro forma. NA-Not Available.

Net Sales (Million $)

13 Weeks:	1995–96	[1]1994–95	[1]1993–94	[1]1992–93
Aug.	836	788	742	677
Nov.		733	674	623
Feb.		803	755	711
May		838	791	727
		3,162	2,963	2,737

Sales in the three months ended August 27, 1995, increased 6.1%, year to year, including a 10% rise from the Olive Garden chain and a 4% increase from the Red Lobster business. Including a $75 million pretax charge related to the closing of DRI's China Coast restaurant chain, a pretax loss of $23.0 million contrasted with income of $50.8 million. After a tax credit of $10.9 million, against taxes at 38.1%, there was a net loss of $12.1 million ($0.08 a share), versus income of $31.4 million ($0.20). The year-ago results are considered pro forma, since DRI's businesses were part of General Mills until May 28, 1995.

In the fiscal year ended May 28, 1995, DRI's pro forma sales were up 6.7% from those of the prior year. Sales from the Red Lobster buisness (about 60% of the total) were up 4%, while Olive Garden sales (about 38% of the total) increased 8%. Excluding $99.3 million in restructuring charges, operating profit (including depreciation, amortization, and SG&A expense) was down 13%, to $181 million. This partly reflected lower earnings frpom Olive Garden and a larger loss from the China Coast business. Including the restructuring charges ($0.37 a share after-tax), net income was down 59%, to $49.2 million $0.31 a share), from $119.9 million ($0.75). Results for fiscal 1993-94 exclude a special credit of $0.03 a share from accounting changes.

Common Share Earnings ($)

13 Weeks:	1995–96	[1]1994–95	[1]1993–94	[1]1992–93
Aug.	d0.08	---	---	---
Nov.		---	---	---
Feb.		[2]0.21	---	---
May		0.11	---	---
	0.31	0.75	0.56	

Dividend Data

A cash dividend was initiated with the September 1995 declaration of an $0.08 a share annual dividend, which is to be paid in two installments. Also, a "poison pill" stock purchase right was adopted in 1995.

Amt. of Divd. $	Date Decl.	Ex–divd. Date	Stock of Record	Payment Date
0.04	Sep. 18	Oct. 5	Oct. 10	Nov. 1'95
0.04	Sep. 18	Apr. 8	Apr. 10	May 1'96

Finances

At the end of August 1995, DRI closed its China Coast restaurants, which resulted in an after-tax charge of $45 million charge ($0.28 a share) in fiscal 1995-96's first quarter. In addition, the China Coast chain had a first quarter operating loss of more than $7 million, or more than twice the year-ago level. The closing of the China Coast chain and the conversion of some units to restaurants in other DRI chains is expected to help DRI's cash flow and to reduce capital spending related to new units during the next several years.

In June 1995, DRI filed a shelf registration with the SEC for $500 million of long-term debt. The company expected this shelf registration to meet its debt requirements for several years.

On May 28, 1995, General Mills, Inc. (GIS) spun off its restaurant business, Darden Restaurants Inc., to its shareholders. GIS shareholders received one Darden common share for each GIS common share held as of the May 15, 1995, record date.

Capitalization

Long Term Debt: $303,748,000 (8/27/95).

Common Stock: 158,540,000 shs. (no par).

---

1. Pro forma. **2.** 39 wks. d-Deficit.

Office—5900 Lake Ellenor Drive, Orlando, FL 32809. **Tel**—(407) 245-4000. **Chrmn & CEO**—J. R. Lee. **Pres & COO**—J. J. O'Hara. **SVP-Fin**—J. D. Smith. **SVP & Investor Contact**—E. L. Blood. **Dirs**—H. B. Atwater, J. P. Birkelund, D. B. Burke, J. R. Lee, B. S. Murphy, J. J. O'Hara, M. D. Rose, J. A. Smith, B. Sweatt. **Transfer Agent & Registrar**—Norwest Bank, St. Paul, Minn. **Incorporated** in Florida in 1995. **Empl**—118,000.

Information has been obtained from sources believed to be reliable, but its accuracy and completeness are not guaranteed. Tom Graves, CFA

Data General

NYSE Symbol **DGN**
In S&P 500

22-AUG-95 Industry: Data Processing

Summary: Data General provides enterprise servers, storage systems and services primarily based on industry standard technology.

S&P Opinion: Hold (★★★)	Recent Price • 10%
	52 Wk Range • 12-6¾

Yield • Nil
12-Mo. P/E • NM

Quantitative Evaluations

Outlook
(1 Lowest—5 Highest)
• **1**⁻

Fair Value
• **8⅞**

Risk
• **High**

Earn./Div. Rank
• **C**

Technical Eval.
• **Bearish** since 7/95

Rel. Strength Rank
(1 Lowest—99 Highest)
• **72**

Insider Activity
• **NA**

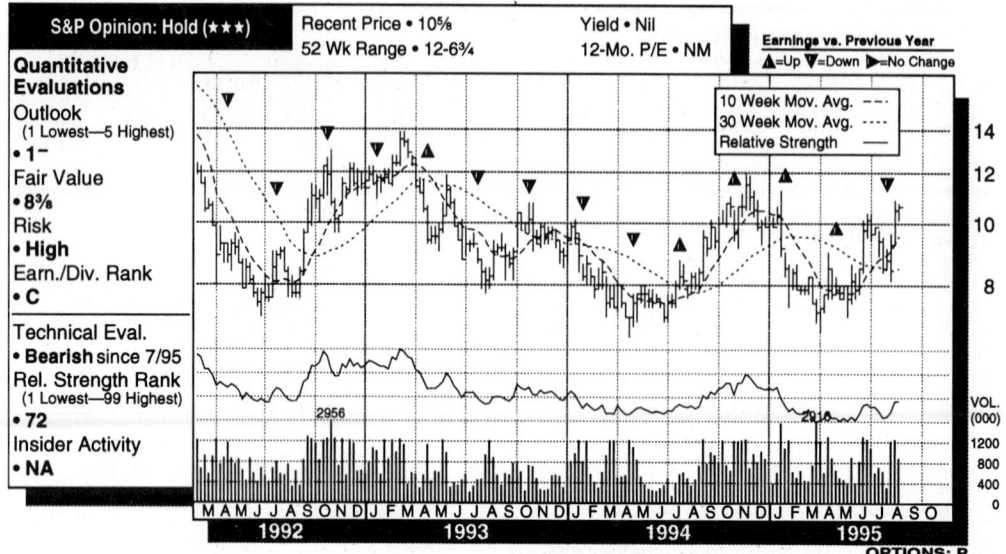

Earnings vs. Previous Year
▲=Up ▼=Down ▶=No Change

10 Week Mov. Avg. – – –
30 Week Mov. Avg. ·······
Relative Strength ——

VOL. (000)

OPTIONS: P

Overview - 22-AUG-95

Revenues should increase 15% in fiscal 1996, reflecting a 22% gain in product sales and a 3% increase in service revenues. Product sales growth should be led by a estimated 50% increase in sales of the CLARiiON storage line to $225 million. The sales increase of the AViiON server line is expected to approximate the mid-teens growth projected for the industry. Sales will be somewhat restrained by the transition to the new Intel-based line of AViiON servers. While growth in the installed base will aid service revenues, a continued decline in revenues from servicing minicomputers, which accounts for 45% of service revenues, will be somewhat offsetting. Profitability is anticipated to be restored due to the higher volume, improved margins on product sales and cost reductions associated with the recent restructuring, as well as the absence of the $43.0 million restructuring charge itself.

Valuation - 22-AUG-95

The shares have recently turned in a strong performance due to better than expected sales of the CLARiiON storage line in the third quarter and excitement over the October introduction of the Intel-based AViiON line. The shares should be able to maintain their recent gains as sales of the CLARiiON storage line accelerate further and the introduction of the Intel-based AViiOn system approaches. However, the company's erratic earnings record over the past decade and relatively modest earnings projections for 1996 are likely to exert a restraining influence.

Key Stock Statistics

S&P EPS Est. 1995	-1.50	Tang. Bk. Value/Share	8.92
P/E on S&P Est. 1995	NM	Beta	2.05
S&P EPS Est. 1996	0.35	Shareholders	12,500
Dividend Rate/Share	Nil	Market cap. (B)	$0.372
Shs. outstg. (M)	37.2	Inst. holdings	80%
Avg. daily vol. (M)	0.204	Insider holdings	0%

Value of $10,000 invested 5 years ago: $ 8,500

Fiscal Year Ending Sep. 30

	1995	% Change	1994	% Change	1993	% Change
Revenues (Million $)						
1Q	282.2	8%	261.2	-7%	280.0	-5%
2Q	283.8	NM	282.9	6%	267.5	-2%
3Q	280.5	-1%	283.8	12%	252.4	-3%
4Q	—	—	292.6	5%	278.4	-3%
Yr.	—	—	1,121	4%	1,078	-3%
Income (Million $)						
1Q	24.20	NM	-21.09	NM	0.80	-80%
2Q	-11.10	NM	-48.00	NM	-7.60	NM
3Q	-61.40	NM	-12.36	NM	-16.40	NM
4Q	—	—	-6.20	NM	-37.20	NM
Yr.	—	—	-87.69	NM	-60.48	NM
Earnings Per Share ($)						
1Q	0.63	NM	-0.60	NM	0.02	-83%
2Q	-0.30	NM	-1.35	NM	-0.22	NM
3Q	-1.65	NM	-0.34	NM	-0.47	NM
4Q	E-0.18	NM	-0.17	NM	-1.06	NM
Yr.	E-1.50	NM	-2.45	NM	-1.73	NM

Next earnings report expected: late October

Business Summary - 22-AUG-95

Data General designs, manufactures, sells and supports multi-user computer systems, servers and mass storage devices. Products and services include database servers, communications and networking servers, workstations, desktop and portable systems, mass storage devices, software and a service/support network. Product sales accounted for 65% of revenues in fiscal 1994 and service for 35%. International business contributed 45% of revenues in fiscal 1994 (46% in fiscal 1993).

DGN's computer systems are grouped into the following product families: 32-bit AViiON systems and workstations; 32-bit ECLIPSE MV systems; CLARiiON mass storage subsystems based on RAID technology; DASHER personal computers; and WALKABOUT laptop and notebook computer systems. AViiON, CLARiiON and to a lesser extent ECLIPSE MV, are the core of the company's current computer business.

Introduced in 1989, AViiON systems are based on the open systems platform of the Motorola 88000 RISC microprocessor and the VME I/O bus. AViiON offerings range from entry-level workstations to high-performance, general-purpose systems and servers. ECLIPSE MV computers use medium, large, and very large scale integration and run DGN's proprietary AOS/VS operating system. CLARiiON mass storage subsystems are based on Redundant Array of Inexpensive Disk (RAID) technology, providing an architecture that speeds access to data while safeguarding it. The DASHER II family consists of personal computers compatible with AViiON, ECLIPSE MV and industry standard architectures.

At July 1, 1995, the company had $182.3 million in cash, temporary investments and marketable securities.

Restructuring charges of $35 million, $25 million, $48 million and $71 million were recognized in fiscal 1994, 1993, 1992 and 1990, respectively.

A pre-tax net gain of $44.5 million was realized in fiscal 1995's first quarter for a software infringement and trade secret suit.

Important Developments

Aug. '95—DGN said that it incurred a $43.0 million restructuring charge in the third quarter for a workforce reduction and other cost reduction activities primarily related to real estate. It added that during the third quarter its revenues for its AViiON server line declined due to a combination of sales force and product transition issues. However, it added that it experienced significant growth in its Open CLARiiON storage line, which posted a revenue increase of more than 70% over the second quarter. DGN also noted that it remained on target for an October introduction of its Intel-based AViiON systems.

Capitalization

Long Term Debt: $154,900,000 (7/1/95).

Per Share Data ($)

(Year Ended Sep. 30)

	1994	1993	1992	1991	1990	1989
Tangible Bk. Val.	8.47	10.51	13.27	15.50	13.21	17.68
Cash Flow	-0.30	0.52	0.66	5.40	-1.45	-0.62
Earnings	-2.45	-1.73	-1.91	2.62	-4.65	-4.10
Dividends	Nil	Nil	Nil	Nil	Nil	Nil
Payout Ratio	Nil	Nil	Nil	Nil	Nil	Nil
Prices - High	11	13⅞	18⅛	22½	13¼	19½
- Low	6⅝	7¾	7⅛	3¾	3½	11¾
P/E Ratio - High	NM	NM	NM	9	NM	NM
- Low	NM	NM	NM	1	NM	NM

Income Statement Analysis (Million $)

	1994	%Chg	1993	%Chg	1992	%Chg	1991
Revs.	1,121	4%	1,078	-3%	1,116	-9%	1,229
Oper. Inc.	32.0	-42%	55.0	-28%	76.0	-56%	174
Depr.	77.0	-3%	79.0	-6%	84.0	-8%	91.0
Int. Exp.	14.0	-5%	14.8	2%	14.5	15%	12.6
Pretax Inc.	-86.0	NM	-55.0	NM	-59.0	NM	92.0
Eff. Tax Rate	NM	—	NM	—	NM	—	6.40%
Net Inc.	-88.0	NM	-60.0	NM	-63.0	NM	86.0

Balance Sheet & Other Fin. Data (Million $)

	1994	1993	1992	1991	1990	1989
Cash	190	192	216	241	75.0	129
Curr. Assets	598	612	684	691	596	710
Total Assets	822	866	940	944	909	1,040
Curr. Liab.	327	303	328	285	444	442
LT Debt	157	158	162	165	57.0	71.0
Common Eqty.	309	377	450	494	405	522
Total Cap.	466	535	612	659	462	593
Cap. Exp.	93.0	95.0	94.0	83.0	85.0	91.0
Cash Flow	-11.0	18.0	22.0	176	-43.0	-18.0

Ratio Analysis

	1994	1993	1992	1991	1990	1989
Curr. Ratio	1.8	2.0	2.1	2.4	1.3	1.6
% LT Debt of Cap.	33.7	29.6	26.5	25.0	12.3	11.9
% Net Inc.of Revs.	NM	NM	NM	7.0	NM	NM
% Ret. on Assets	NM	NM	NM	9.1	NM	NM
% Ret. on Equity	NM	NM	NM	18.7	NM	NM

Dividend Data —No dividends have been paid. A "poison pill" stock purchase right was adopted in 1986.

Data as orig. reptd.; bef. results of disc. opers. and/or spec. items. Per share data adj. for stk. divs. as of ex-div. date. E-Estimated. NA-Not Available. NM-Not Meaningful. NR-Not Ranked.

Office—4400 Computer Drive, Westboro, MA 01580. **Tel**—(508) 898-5000. **Pres & CEO**—R. L. Skates. **VP-CFO**—A. W. DeMelle. **Secy**—C. E. Kaplan. **Investor Contact**—David P. Roy. **Dirs**—F. R. Adler, F. Colloredo-Mansfeld, J. G. McElwee, R. L. Skates, W. N. Thorndike, D. H. Trautlein, R. L. Tucker. **Transfer Agent & Registrar**—First Chicago Trust Co. of New York, NYC. **Incorporated** in Delaware in 1968. **Empl**-5,800. **S&P Analyst:** Paul H. Valentine, CFA

Dayton Hudson

NYSE Symbol **DH**
In S&P 500

26-OCT-95 **Industry:** Retail Stores

Summary: This diversified retailer derives more than 75% of its operating income from its 645 Target and 293 Mervyn's discount chains. It also operates 64 department stores.

S&P Opinion: Hold (★★★)		
Recent Price • 73⅝	Yield • 2.5%	
52 Wk Range • 85¼-63¼	12-Mo. P/E • 14.5	

Earnings vs. Previous Year
▲=Up ▼=Down ▶=No Change

Quantitative Evaluations

Outlook
(1 Lowest—5 Highest)
• **4⁻**

Fair Value
• **75¼**

Risk
• **Low**

Earn./Div. Rank
• **A**

Technical Eval.
• **Bullish** since 7/95

Rel. Strength Rank
(1 Lowest—99 Highest)
• **26**

Insider Activity
• **Neutral**

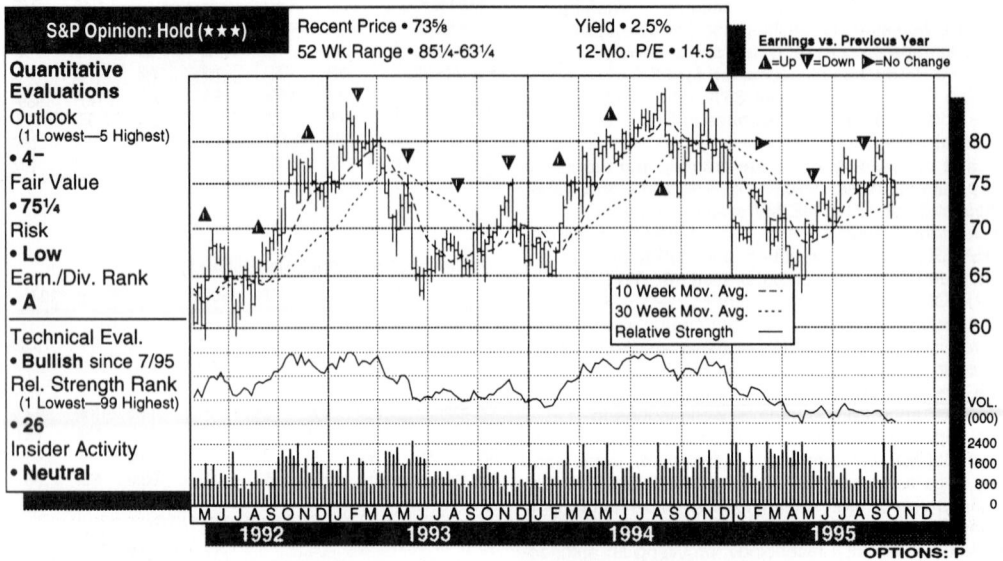

10 Week Mov. Avg. – – –
30 Week Mov. Avg. ····
Relative Strength —

VOL. (000)

OPTIONS: P

Overview - 26-OCT-95

Revenues for FY 96 (Jan.), should increase 8%-10%, mostly reflecting 60 to 70 new Target stores and also 11 new Mervyn's and one new department store; same-store sales should increase about 10% at Target with declines at Mervyn's and a slight increase at the department stores. Operating profits at Target should show strong gains, but a sharp drop is possible at Mervyn's and a modest decline at the department stores. Gross margins will narrow, reflecting competitive pricing, and expense ratios widen on the weak sales volume. Interest expense should increase as a higher debt level is used to fund the company's $1.3 billion capital expenditure program. The company's financial objective is a 15% annual gain in earnings per share.

Valuation - 26-OCT-95

The shares should remain in a narrow trading range as the important holiday selling season approaches, reflecting concerns surrounding consumer spending and competitive pricing. The company expects a turnaround in its ailing Mervyn's division, following a more aggressive price strategy and increased fashion and selling space. We believe that in spite of these initiatives, Mervyn's operating profit will lag expectations. The closure or selling of this division would be a plus for the share price. Also, from time to time, the shares get a boost from speculation that the company plans to sell its department store division, although management has denied this. We remain neutral on the shares for the near-term.

Key Stock Statistics

S&P EPS Est. 1996	5.15	Tang. Bk. Value/Share	41.98
P/E on S&P Est. 1996	14.3	Beta	0.79
S&P EPS Est. 1997	6.20	Shareholders	12,200
Dividend Rate/Share	1.76	Market cap. (B)	$ 5.0
Shs. outstg. (M)	71.8	Inst. holdings	80%
Avg. daily vol. (M)	0.338	Insider holdings	NA

Value of $10,000 invested 5 years ago: $ 13,260

Fiscal Year Ending Jan. 31

	1996	% Change	1995	% Change	1994	% Change
Revenues (Million $)						
1Q	4,757	6%	4,470	11%	4,040	9%
2Q	5,236	9%	4,802	12%	4,287	8%
3Q	—	—	5,046	9%	4,625	7%
4Q	—	—	6,998	11%	6,281	6%
Yr.	—	—	21,311	11%	19,233	7%
Income (Million $)						
1Q	11.00	-72%	39.00	30%	30.00	-14%
2Q	28.00	-43%	49.00	104%	24.00	-43%
3Q	—	—	67.00	56%	43.00	-25%
4Q	—	—	279.0	NM	278.0	12%
Yr.	—	—	434.0	16%	375.0	-2%
Earnings Per Share ($)						
1Q	0.10	-79%	0.48	37%	0.35	-13%
2Q	0.32	-48%	0.62	121%	0.28	-45%
3Q	E0.70	-19%	0.86	59%	0.54	-23%
4Q	E4.05	6%	3.81	NM	3.81	18%
Yr.	E5.15	-11%	5.77	16%	4.99	NM

Next earnings report expected: mid November

Dayton Hudson

Business Summary - 21-OCT-95

This diversified retailer operated 960 stores in 33 states at January 28, 1995. Segment contributions in fiscal 1994-95 were:

	Revs.	Profits
Target	64%	61%
Mervyn's	21%	17%
Department stores	15%	22%

Target is an upscale discount store offering low prices on a broad assortment of mid-range fashion and basic hardlines. At 1994-95 year end, it operated 611 stores; total retail square footage totaled 64 million square feet.

Mervyn's is a moderately priced department store chain specializing in apparel and soft goods. At the end of 1994-95, it operated 286 stores in 15 states; total retail square footage amounted to 23 million.

Dayton Hudson Department Store Co. operates 21 Hudson's, 19 Dayton's and 23 Marshall Field's stores in nine states. Retail area totaled 14 million sq. ft. at the end of 1994-95. The company is emphasizing tailoring merchandise assortments to each trade area.

Capital expenditures in 1994 totaled $1.1 billion, of which 77% were made by Target, 13% Mervyn's, 9% by department stores. During 1994-95, Target added 60 new stores and Mervyn's opened 12. Over the past five years, Target's square footage has grown at a compound annual rate of 10%.

Important Developments

Oct. '95—Management said same store sales for the five weeks ended September 30, 1995 rose 5.3%, reflecting strong performance at Target, while sales at Mervyn's and the department stores were below plan. Operating profit in the second quarter of 1995-96 fell 15% from a year earlier. Target's operating profit increased moderately in the second quarter, while Mervyn's was nil. Operating profit at the department stores declined. Management said that the increased emphasis on national brands, more merchandise on sale each week, increased advertising, a broader assortment of merchandise and the introduction of a California theme into merchandise and advertising would result in steadily improved operating performance at Mervyn's beginning in the third quarter.

Capitalization

Long Term Debt: $4,969,000,000 (7/29/95).
6.5% ESOP Conv. Preferred Stock: $355,000,000. Conv. into 4,166,750 com. shs.

Per Share Data ($)

(Year Ended Jan. 31)

	1995	1994	1993	1992	1991	1990
Tangible Bk. Val.	42.45	38.27	34.83	31.32	28.82	24.73
Cash Flow	13.14	11.92	11.42	9.59	10.58	9.48
Earnings	5.77	4.99	5.02	3.86	5.41	5.37
Dividends	1.68	1.60	1.52	1.44	1.32	1.12
Payout Ratio	29%	32%	30%	37%	24%	19%
Cal. Yrs.	1994	1993	1992	1991	1990	1989
Prices - High	86 7/8	85	79 1/4	80 1/4	79 1/2	67
- Low	64 7/8	62 5/8	58	53 3/4	46 1/4	38 3/4
P/E Ratio - High	15	17	16	21	15	12
- Low	11	13	12	14	9	7

Income Statement Analysis (Million $)

	1995	%Chg	1994	%Chg	1993	%Chg	1992
Revs.	21,311	11%	19,233	7%	17,927	11%	16,115
Oper. Inc.	1,671	6%	1,573	4%	1,507	18%	1,276
Depr.	531	7%	498	8%	459	12%	410
Int. Exp.	439	-3%	453	2%	446	10%	407
Pretax Inc.	714	18%	607	NM	611	29%	472
Eff. Tax Rate	39%	—	38%	—	37%	—	36%
Net Inc.	434	16%	375	-2%	383	27%	301

Balance Sheet & Other Fin. Data (Million $)

	1995	1994	1993	1992	1991	1990
Cash	147	321	117	96.0	92.0	103
Curr. Assets	4,959	4,511	4,414	4,032	3,658	3,107
Total Assets	11,697	10,778	10,337	9,485	8,524	6,684
Curr. Liab.	3,390	3,075	2,964	2,580	2,422	2,195
LT Debt	4,488	4,279	4,330	4,227	3,682	2,510
Common Eqty.	3,043	2,737	2,486	2,231	2,048	1,753
Total Cap.	7,725	7,167	6,923	6,524	5,755	4,264
Cap. Exp.	1,095	978	938	1,009	678	603
Cash Flow	946	856	818	686	754	723

Ratio Analysis

	1995	1994	1993	1992	1991	1990
Curr. Ratio	1.5	1.5	1.5	1.6	1.5	1.4
% LT Debt of Cap.	58.1	59.7	62.5	64.8	64.0	58.9
% Net Inc.of Revs.	2.0	1.9	2.1	1.9	2.8	3.0
% Ret. on Assets	3.9	3.5	3.9	3.3	5.4	6.5
% Ret. on Equity	14.3	13.7	15.2	12.9	20.2	23.7

Dividend Data —Dividends have been paid since 1965. A dividend reinvestment plan is available. A "poison pill" stock purchase right was adopted in 1986.

Amt. of Div. $	Date Decl.	Ex-Div. Date	Stock of Record	Payment Date
0.420	Oct. 12	Nov. 14	Nov. 20	Dec. 10 '94
0.420	Jan. 11	Feb. 13	Feb. 20	Mar. 10 '95
0.440	Apr. 12	May. 15	May. 20	Jun. 10 '95
0.440	Jun. 14	Aug. 16	Aug. 20	Sep. 10 '95
0.440	Oct. 11	Nov. 16	Nov. 20	Dec. 10 '95

Data as orig. reptd.; bef. results of disc. opers. and/or spec. items. Per share data adj. for stk. divs. as of ex-div. date. E-Estimated. NA-Not Available. NM-Not Meaningful. NR-Not Ranked.

Office—777 Nicollet Mall, Minneapolis, MN 55402. **Tel**—(612) 370-6948. **Chrmn & CEO**—R. J. Ulrich. **Pres**—S. E. Watson. **VP & Secy**—J. T. Hale. **SVP & Treas**—D. A. Scovanner. **Investor Contact**—Susan Kahn (612-370-6735). **Dirs**—R. V. Araskog, R. A. Burnett, L. D. DeSimone, R. A. Enrico, W. W. George, R. L. Hale, B. R. Hollander, M. J. Hooper, M. P. McPherson, S. D. Trujillo, R. J. Ulrich, J. R. Walter, S. E. Watson. **Transfer Agent & Registrar**—First Chicago Trust Co. of New York, NYC. **Incorporated** in Minnesota in 1902. **Empl**-194,000. **S&P Analyst:** Karen J. Sack, CFA

Dean Witter, Discover

NYSE Symbol DWD Options on ASE & CBOE & Pacific & Phila (Jan-Apr-Jul-Oct) In S&P 500

Price	Range	P–E Ratio	Dividend	Yield	S&P Ranking	Beta
Aug. 2'95	1995					
49⅞	50⅞–33½	11	0.64	1.3%	NR	NA

Summary

Formerly a unit of Sears, Roebuck, this company has two principal lines of business: credit services and securities. Credit services consist primarily of the issuance and marketing of the Discover credit card; the securities business is conducted through Dean Witter Reynolds, a full service securities firm. Share earnings for 1995 and 1996 are expected to benefit from continued growth in credit card loans outstanding and higher asset management and administration fees.

Current Outlook

Earnings for 1996 are projected at $5.55 a share, up from the $5.00 estimated for 1995.

The minimum expectation is for the quarterly dividend to continue at $0.16 a share.

Profits are expected to post a healthy increase in 1996. Credit services income should benefit from growth in the credit card loan portfolio, reflecting new customer accounts and merchant locations, as well as increased usage. Spreads are expected to widen slightly, based on lower funding costs associated with a drop in market interest rates. Spreads will remain extremely wide despite intensified competition from other issuers. Credit losses are quite low, but may increase with rapid expansion of the customer base. The securities segment, which is more cyclical, is also expected to post higher profits. Commission income should benefit from expansion in the number of account executives. Also, Dean Witter in comparison to many other brokers obtains a high percentage of its income from relatively stable asset management operations.

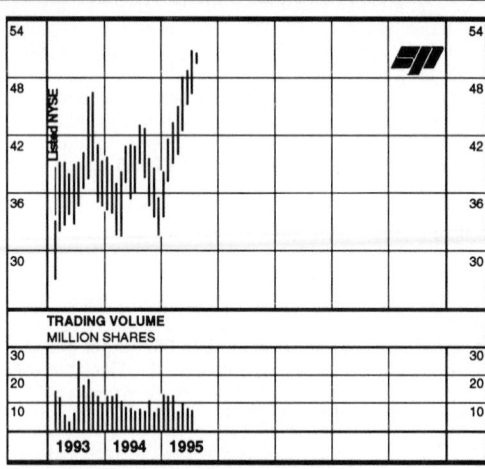

TRADING VOLUME
MILLION SHARES

Total Revenues (Million $)

Quarter:	1995	1994	1993	1992
Mar.	1,841	1,592	1,383	---
Jun.	1,947	1,581	1,424	---
Sep.	---	1,641	1,496	---
Dec.	---	1,788	1,519	---
	---	6,603	5,822	5,184

Revenues in the six months ended June 30, 1995, advanced 19%, year to year, reflecting growth in credit card loan balances outstanding and higher merchant and cardmember fees, partially offset by a sharp drop in underwriting revenue from closed-end mutual funds. Margins narrowed, and the gain in pretax income was held to 9.6%. After taxes at 38.5%, against 38.9%, net income was up 10%. Share earnings were $2.71, against $2.44.

Common Share Earnings ($)

Quarter:	1995	1994	1993	1992
Mar.	1.31	1.23	0.92	---
Jun.	1.39	1.21	0.92	---
Sep.	E1.05	1.08	1.01	---
Dec.	E1.25	0.82	0.81	---
	E5.00	4.35	3.66	¹2.65

Important Developments

Jul. '95— DWD said that managed loans increased by $5.7 billion or 26% over last year to a record $27.1 billion at June 30, 1995. Assets under management or administration at the end of the second quarter of 1995 were $73.3 billion, up $6.4 billion for the year to date, primarily due to higher net asset values for equity and fixed income funds.

Next earnings report expected in mid-October.

Per Share Data ($)

Yr. End Dec. 31	1994	1993	1992
Tangible Bk. Val.	23.35	19.36	15.06
Earnings²	4.35	3.66	2.65
Dividends	0.50	0.30	NA
Payout Ratio	11%	8%	NA
Prices—High	43⅛	46½	NA
Low	31½	27	NA
P/E Ratio—	10–7	13–7	NA

Data as orig. reptd. **1.** Pro forma. **2.** Bef. spec. items of -0.12 in 1993, -0.17 in 1992. NA-Not Available. E-Estimated.

Income Data (Million $)

Year Ended Dec. 31	Commis- sions	Int. Inc.	Total Revs.	Int. Exp.	% Exp./ Revs.	Net Bef. Taxes	Eff. Tax Rate	[1]Net Inc.	Revs.	% Return On [2]Assets	[2]Equity
1994	874	2,507	6,603	1,049	81.6	1,215	39.0%	741	11.2	2.5	19.5
1993	904	1,909	5,822	815	82.9	996	39.4%	604	10.4	2.3	19.6
1992	722	1,975	5,184	966	87.1	703	37.5%	439	8.5	1.8	17.6
1991	697	2,047	4,882	1,082	88.6	556	38.0%	345	7.1	1.6	17.5
1990	667	2,095	4,506	1,178	91.0	404	42.3%	233	5.2	1.2	13.2
1989	NA	NA	3,942	1,112	92.5	297	44.1%	166	4.2	0.9	10.1
1988	NA	NA	3,733	1,190	96.0	150	42.9%	86	2.3	0.5	5.7

Balance Sheet Data (Million $)

Dec. 31	Total Assets	Cash Items	Rec.	Secs. Owned	Sec. Borrowed	Due Brokers & Cust.	Other Liabs.	Debt	Capitalization Equity	Total
1994	31,859	2,829	21,597	1,739	7,448	6,018	8,993	5,293	4,108	9,401
1993	27,662	2,553	17,403	2,429	7,047	5,907	8,090	3,140	3,477	6,617
1992	23,822	2,448	16,964	1,876	8,728	5,000	7,421	Nil	2,673	2,673
1991	22,751	1,800	16,292	2,378	8,375	4,168	7,073	1,039	2,096	3,135
1990	20,839	NA	16,219	1,181	NA	NA	NA	NA	1,841	NA
1989	18,945	NA	15,626	1,066	NA	NA	NA	NA	1,688	NA
1988	17,598	NA	14,475	811	NA	NA	NA	NA	1,588	NA

Data as orig. reptd. **1.** Bef. spec. items. **2.** As reptd. by co. prior to 1994. NA-Not Available.

Business Summary

Dean Witter, Discover & Co. is a balanced financial services organization that provides a broad range of nationally marketed credit and investment products, with a primary focus on the individual. Earnings contributions in recent years:

	1994	1993	1992
Credit services	56%	53%	55%
Securities	44%	47%	45%

Credit services consist primarily of the issuance, marketing and servicing of the Discover Card, a proprietary general purpose credit card. Since nationwide introduction of the Discover Card in 1986, the company has become the largest single issuer of general purpose domestic credit or charge cards as measured by cardholders, with about 32.1 million Discover accounts representing 42.7 million cardholders and about $23 billion of managed loans as of December 31, 1994. Discover has the largest domestic merchant base of any single credit card. Total transactions using the Discover Card have grown rapidly. In 1994, total transactions using Discover were about $39.4 billion, compared with $32.8 billion in 1993. SPS Transaction Services, Inc. (74%-owned) is involved in the electronic processing of point-of-sale transactions for retailers and the development of private label credit card programs.

DWD's securities business is conducted through Dean Witter Reynolds Inc. (acquired by Sears in 1981), a full service securities firm. Dean Witter has a particular focus on serving the investment needs of individual clients. It has the third largest account executive sales organization in the domestic securities industry, with 8,044 account executives located in 353 branch offices servicing the investment needs of over 3 million individual and institutional clients. Total client assets as of December 31, 1994, were about $180.4 billion. Dean Witter Intercapital Inc., a wholly owned subsidiary, is one of the largest asset management operations in the U. S., with total assets of $66.9 billion under management or administration at year end 1994, versus $71.2 billion a year earlier.

Dividend Data

Dividends were initiated in May 1993.

Amt of Divd. $	Date Decl.	Ex-divd. Date	Stock of Record	Payment Date
0.12½	Oct. 25	Nov. 25	Dec. 1	Jan. 3'95
0.16	Jan. 20	Feb. 23	Mar. 1	Apr. 3'95
0.16	Apr. 21	May 25	Jun. 1	Jul. 3'95
0.16	Jul. 21	Aug. 30	Sep. 1	Oct. 2'95

Finances

At March 31, 1995, Dean Witter's net capital of $614.2 million was 24.19% of aggregate debit balances and $503.9 million in excess of the required minimum.

Capitalization

Long Term Borrowings: $5,667,900,000 (3/95).

Common Stock: 170,354,089 shs. ($0.01 par). Institutions hold about 72%.

Office—Two World Trade Center, New York, NY 10048. **Tel**—(212) 392-2222. **Chrmn & CEO**—P. J. Purcell. **EVP-CFO**—T. C. Schneider. **EVP-Secy**—C. A. Edwards. **Investor Contact**—Amy Pappas (212-392-6170). **Dirs**—E. A. Brennan, A. C. DeCrane, Jr., R. M. Gardiner, C. R. Kidder, M. A. Miles, S. C. Mobley, P. J. Purcell, C. B. Rogers, Jr. **Transfer Agent & Registrar**—Dean Witter Trust Co., Jersey City. **Incorporated** in Delaware in 1981. **Empl**—28,475.

Deere & Co.

NYSE Symbol **DE**
In S&P 500

12-SEP-95   **Industry:** Machinery

Summary: This company, the world's largest producer of farm equipment, is also an important maker of construction machinery and lawn and garden equipment.

S&P Opinion: Hold (★★★)	Recent Price • 87⅞	Yield • 2.8%
	52 Wk Range • 95¼-61¼	12-Mo. P/E • 10.5

Quantitative Evaluations

Outlook
(1 Lowest—5 Highest)
• **2+**

Fair Value
• **83**

Risk
• **Low**

Earn./Div. Rank
• **B**

Technical Eval.
• **Bearish** since 8/95

Rel. Strength Rank
(1 Lowest—99 Highest)
• **34**

Insider Activity
• **NA**

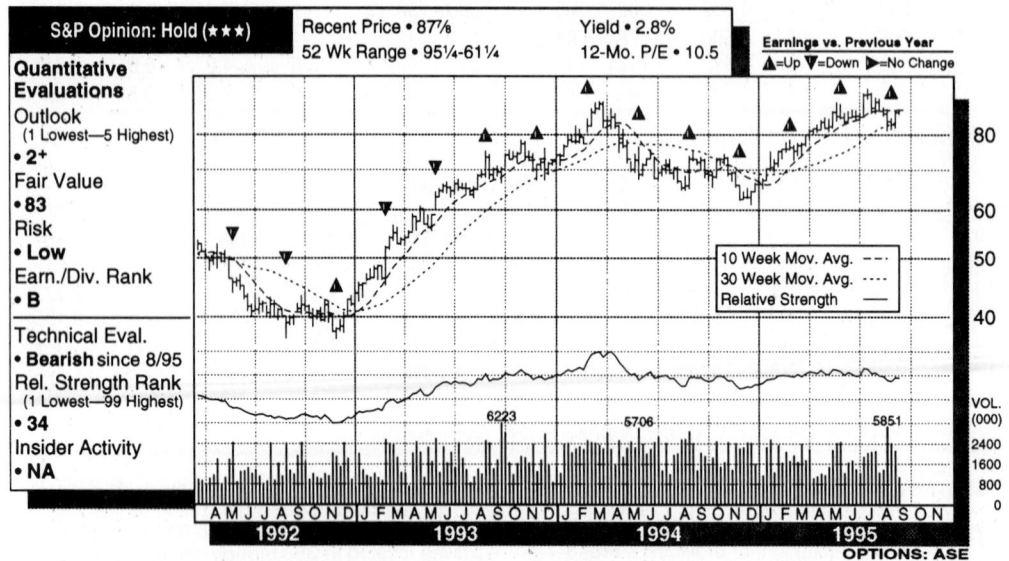

Earnings vs. Previous Year
▲=Up ▼=Down ▶=No Change

10 Week Mov. Avg. — — —
30 Week Mov. Avg. ·······
Relative Strength ——

VOL. (000)

OPTIONS: ASE

Overview - 12-SEP-95

We anticipate a 10% revenue increase in fiscal 1996, reflecting higher volume and prices. Our forecast depends on continued high levels of farm income and 2.6% GDP growth in 1996. However, sales gains will trail the fiscal 1995 rate of increase, reflecting slower economic growth and some slippage in farm income from the 1995 level. With continued high utilization of production facilities, only modest increases in raw material costs, and a favorable product mix, operating profit from equipment segments should advance. Aided by lower interest expense, earnings should rise again in fiscal 1996. Greater overseas demand for U.S. wheat and corn crops, together with the continued introduction of new products, will enhance long-term sales and profit growth.

Valuation - 12-SEP-95

While DE's shares are not overvalued, based on our fiscal 1996 EPS estimate, we rate them only a near-term hold. Through mid-September 1995, the stock had risen 32% from the level at 1994 year-end, more than the S&P 500 and far above the gain for its peer group. With slower economic growth, an unfavorable fiscal 1995 fourth quarter comparison and the possibility that fiscal 1996 could represent peak earnings, we believe that the shares have little upside potential from current levels. Also, DE shares have a tendency to weaken in the second half of the calendar year. The stock will probably be available at lower levels later in the year.

Key Stock Statistics

S&P EPS Est. 1995	8.30	Tang. Bk. Value/Share	29.73
P/E on S&P Est. 1995	10.6	Beta	1.08
S&P EPS Est. 1996	9.60	Shareholders	23,400
Dividend Rate/Share	2.40	Market cap. (B)	$ 7.6
Shs. outstg. (M)	86.7	Inst. holdings	87%
Avg. daily vol. (M)	0.584	Insider holdings	NA

Value of $10,000 invested 5 years ago: $ 17,622

Fiscal Year Ending Oct. 31

	1995	% Change	1994	% Change	1993	% Change
Revenues (Million $)						
1Q	2,106	22%	1,727	21%	1,424	-2%
2Q	2,840	15%	2,460	17%	2,105	13%
3Q	2,700	16%	2,327	14%	2,049	17%
4Q	—	—	2,516	16%	2,176	15%
Yr.	—	—	9,030	16%	7,754	11%
Income (Million $)						
1Q	138.4	59%	87.00	NM	-37.00	NM
2Q	237.0	25%	189.3	NM	21.00	-52%
3Q	180.1	14%	157.7	73%	91.00	NM
4Q	—	—	169.6	55%	109.5	NM
Yr.	—	—	603.6	NM	184.4	NM
Earnings Per Share ($)						
1Q	1.60	57%	1.02	NM	-0.48	NM
2Q	2.74	25%	2.20	NM	0.27	-53%
3Q	2.07	14%	1.82	53%	1.19	NM
4Q	E1.89	-4%	1.97	40%	1.41	NM
Yr.	E8.30	18%	7.01	193%	2.39	NM

Next earnings report expected: early December

Business Summary - 12-SEP-95

Deere & Co. is a leading manufacturer of farm equipment and a broad range of earthmoving and forestry machinery. Through subsidiaries (unconsolidated prior to fiscal 1989), the company finances the sale and leasing of equipment and provides credit, insurance and health care products. Revenues and operating income by industry segment in fiscal 1994 were:

	Revenues	Profits
Farm equipment	52%	51%
Industrial equipment	18%	12%
Lawn and grounds care	14%	15%
Finance and interest income	6%	16%
Ins., health care and other	10%	6%

Operations outside the U.S. and Canada accounted for 20% of revenues and $83 million in operating income, versus 20% of revenues and a $130 million operating loss in fiscal 1993.

Farm equipment includes a full range of agricultural equipment for the farming industry, including tractors; tillage, soil preparation, planting and harvesting machinery; and crop handling equipment.

Industrial equipment includes a broad range of machines used in earthmoving and forestry, including wheel and crawler tractors and attachments; crawler dozers and loaders; four-wheel-drive loaders; elevating scrapers; motor graders; excavators; log skidders; and tree harvesting equipment.

Lawn and grounds care equipment (formerly part of farm equipment) includes smaller tractors for lawn, garden and utility purposes; riding and walk-behind mowers; and other outdoor power products.

Through John Deere Credit Co., John Deere Finance Co. Ltd., John Deere Insurance Group, John Deere Insurance Co. of Canada and Heritage National Healthplan the company finances the sale and lease of equipment and provides credit, insurance and health care products.

Important Developments

Aug. '95—DE reported share earnings of $2.07 on a 16% gain in revenues for fiscal 1995's third quarter, versus $1.82 a year earlier. Earnings for fiscal 1995's first three quarters totaled $6.41 on a 17% gain in revenues, versus $5.04 for the first three quarters of fiscal 1994. Worldwide production tonnage was up 6.0% in the quarter and 8.0% for the first nine months of fiscal 1995. DE stated that due to a planned reduction in parts inventories and interest waiver programs aimed at cutting dealer used goods inventories, fiscal 1995's fourth quarter production and earnings would trail fiscal 1994's fourth quarter. The company noted that despite the unfavorable fourth quarter comparison, earnings for fiscal 1995 would reach record levels.

Capitalization

Long Term Debt: $2,377,100,000 (7/95).

Per Share Data ($)

(Year Ended Oct. 31)

	1994	1993	1992	1991	1990	1989
Tangible Bk. Val.	26.32	20.92	30.30	32.33	36.37	35.81
Cash Flow	10.05	5.69	3.72	2.68	8.17	7.69
Earnings	7.01	2.39	0.49	-0.27	5.42	5.06
Dividends	2.05	2.00	2.00	2.00	2.00	1.30
Payout Ratio	29%	84%	408%	NM	37%	26%
Prices - High	90⅞	78⅜	54	57⅜	78⅜	64¼
- Low	61¼	42⅜	36¾	39⅞	37½	44
P/E Ratio - High	13	33	NM	NM	14	13
- Low	9	18	NM	NM	7	9

Income Statement Analysis (Million $)

	1994	%Chg	1993	%Chg	1992	%Chg	1991
Revs.	8,934	17%	7,654	12%	6,847	-1%	6,926
Oper. Inc.	1,390	54%	904	53%	589	-16%	701
Depr.	262	3%	255	4%	246	10%	224
Int. Exp.	303	-18%	369	-11%	415	-8%	452
Pretax Inc.	936	NM	282	NM	52.0	NM	-25.0
Eff. Tax Rate	36%	—	35%	—	28%	—	NM
Net Inc.	604	NM	184	NM	37.0	NM	-20.0

Balance Sheet & Other Fin. Data (Million $)

	1994	1993	1992	1991	1990	1989
Cash	245	338	217	279	185	204
Curr. Assets	NA	NA	NA	NA	NA	NA
Total Assets	12,781	11,352	11,446	11,649	10,664	9,145
Curr. Liab.	NA	NA	NA	NA	NA	NA
LT Debt	2,054	2,549	2,477	2,217	1,799	1,696
Common Eqty.	2,558	2,085	2,650	2,836	3,008	2,780
Total Cap.	4,625	4,642	5,152	5,128	4,978	4,622
Cap. Exp.	331	313	349	352	376	272
Cash Flow	866	439	283	204	620	578

Ratio Analysis

	1994	1993	1992	1991	1990	1989
Curr. Ratio	NA	NA	NA	NA	NA	NA
% LT Debt of Cap.	44.4	54.9	48.1	43.2	36.1	36.6
% Net Inc.of Revs.	6.8	2.4	0.5	NM	5.3	5.3
% Ret. on Assets	5.0	1.5	0.3	NM	4.1	5.3
% Ret. on Equity	25.9	7.3	1.4	NM	14.2	14.4

Dividend Data

Dividends have been paid since 1937. A dividend reinvestment plan is available. Shareholders vote November 15, on a proposed 3-for-1 stock split.

Amt. of Div. $	Date Decl.	Ex-Div. Date	Stock of Record	Payment Date
0.550	Aug. 31	Sep. 26	Sep. 30	Nov. 01 '94
0.550	Dec. 07	Dec. 23	Dec. 31	Feb. 01 '95
0.550	Feb. 22	Mar. 27	Mar. 31	May. 01 '95
0.550	May. 31	Jun. 28	Jun. 30	Aug. 01 '95
0.600	Aug. 31	Sep. 27	Sep. 30	Nov. 01 '95

Data as orig. reptd.; bef. results of disc. opers. and/or spec. items. Per share data adj. for stk. divs. as of ex-div. date. E-Estimated. NA-Not Available. NM-Not Meaningful. NR-Not Ranked.

Office—John Deere Rd, Moline, IL 61265. **Tel**—(309) 765-8000. **Chrmn & CEO**—H. W. Becherer. **Pres**—D. H. Stowe, Jr. **EVP & CFO**—E. L. Schotanus. **Secy**—F. S. Cottrell. **Investor Contact**—Marie Z. Ziegler. **Dirs**—H. W. Becherer, J. R. Block, L. A. Hadley, R. E. Herzlinger, S. C. Johnson, A. L. Kelly, A. Santamarina, W. A. Schreyer, D. H. Stowe, Jr., J. R. Walter, A. R. Weber. **Transfer Agent & Registrar**—Chemical Bank, NYC. **Incorporated** in Delaware in 1958; business est. in 1837. **Empl**-34,252. **S&P Analyst:** Leo Larkin

STOCK REPORTS

Delta Air Lines

NYSE Symbol DAL
In S&P 500

09-AUG-95 **Industry:** Air Transport

Summary: DAL, the third largest U.S. airline, operates a route system serving 153 cities in 43 states and 57 cities in 32 foreign countries.

S&P Opinion: Hold (★★★)

Recent Price • 76
52 Wk Range • 81¼-42¾

Yield • 0.3%
12-Mo. P/E • 18.7

Earnings vs. Previous Year
▲=Up ▼=Down ▶=No Change

Quantitative Evaluations

Outlook
(1 Lowest—5 Highest)
• **1+**

Fair Value
• **59¼**

Risk
• **Average**

Earn./Div. Rank
• **B-**

Technical Eval.
• **Bearish** since 1/95

Rel. Strength Rank
(1 Lowest—99 Highest)
• **51**

Insider Activity
• **NA**

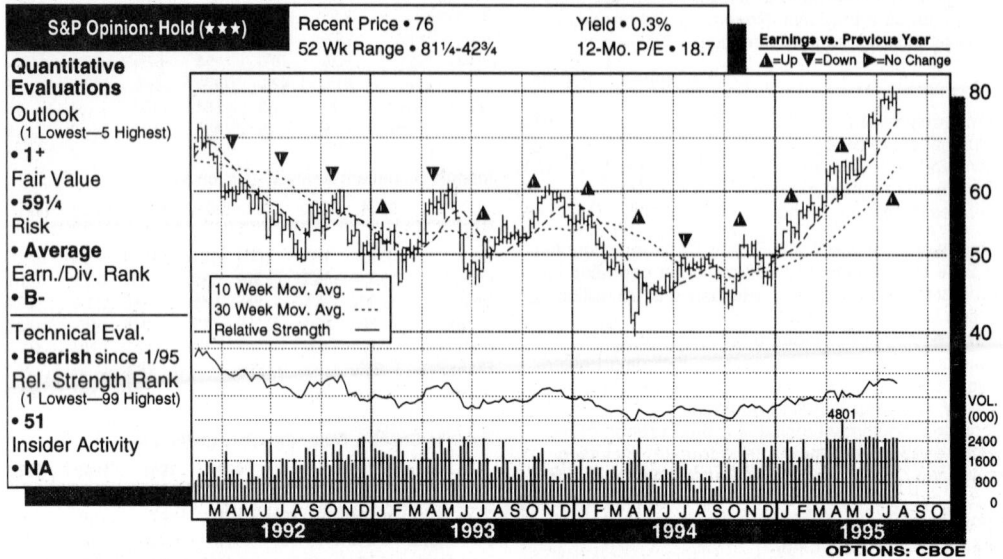

10 Week Mov. Avg. ---
30 Week Mov. Avg. ····
Relative Strength —

VOL. (000)

OPTIONS: CBOE

Overview - 09-AUG-95

Profitability is expected to continue in fiscal 1996. Revenues are forecast to remain at about $12.2 billion, as slightly lower average fares offset robust traffic growth. Earnings improvement will reflect reduced operating costs. Savings will come from decreased salary costs, commission expenses, aircraft leasing fees and maintenance charges. An expected increase in the average stage length (flight distance) will also result in lower unit costs. Although cash levels are high, interest charges are not expected to decline much, because of a shift of certain operating to capital leases.

Valuation - 09-AUG-95

Since late 1994, the shares are up even more than the strong S&P airline index. Although improved pricing helped restore profitability, substantial benefits also came from cost reductions. DAL aims to cut operating costs by $2 billion by mid-1997 (targeting a unit operating cost of 7.5 cents per ASM). Although some gains may be manipulative, real progress has been made. Negotiation of a new pilots union contract may present an obstacle. Results may benefit from the 1996 Olympics, which will be held in Atlanta (a company hub). However, significant dilution will likely occur if the share price consistently exceeds $82, because DAL will then be able to call its Series C preferred stock for redemption.

Key Stock Statistics

S&P EPS Est. 1996	6.00	Tang. Bk. Value/Share	NM
P/E on S&P Est. 1996	12.7	Beta	1.36
S&P EPS Est. 1997	7.50	Shareholders	26,300
Dividend Rate/Share	0.20	Market cap. (B)	$ 3.8
Shs. outstg. (M)	50.8	Inst. holdings	77%
Avg. daily vol. (M)	0.660	Insider holdings	NA

Value of $10,000 invested 5 years ago: $ 11,968

Fiscal Year Ending Jun. 30

	1995	% Change	1994	% Change	1993	% Change
Revenues (Million $)						
1Q	3,157	-2%	3,220	5%	3,064	19%
2Q	2,919	-3%	3,017	5%	2,875	10%
3Q	2,902	-1%	2,943	NM	2,927	4%
4Q	3,216	1%	3,179	2%	3,132	11%
Yr.	12,194	-1%	12,359	3%	11,997	11%
Income (Million $)						
1Q	72.00	19%	60.34	NM	-125.0	NM
2Q	-18.00	NM	-141.0	NM	-144.0	-23%
3Q	-11.00	NM	-77.88	NM	-152.0	NM
4Q	251.0	NM	-249.8	NM	6.00	NM
Yr.	294.0	NM	-408.4	NM	-414.7	NM
Earnings Per Share ($)						
1Q	1.00	54%	0.65	NM	-3.07	NM
2Q	-0.79	NM	-3.36	NM	-3.46	NM
3Q	-0.66	NM	-2.10	NM	-3.61	NM
4Q	4.49	NM	-5.50	NM	-0.41	NM
Yr.	4.07	NM	-10.32	NM	-10.54	NM

Next earnings report expected: late October

Business Summary - 09-AUG-95

Delta Air Lines, Inc. operates a route system that covers most of the U.S. and extends to 32 other countries. At September 12, 1994, it served 153 domestic cities in 43 states, the District of Columbia, Puerto Rico and the U.S. Virgin Islands and 57 international cities. International operations accounted for 23% of revenues in fiscal 1994, up from 21% in fiscal 1993 and 18 in fiscal 1992. The November 1991 acquisition of the trans-Atlantic routes of Pan Am added 21 international destinations in 18 countries.

The airline's major domestic hubs are in Atlanta, Dallas/Ft. Worth, Salt Lake City and Cincinnati. Smaller hubs are in Los Angeles and Orlando. About 85% of flights are involved in hub-and-spoke operations.

Operating data for recent fiscal years (passenger- and seat-miles in billions) was:

	1995	1994	1993
Rev. pass. miles	86.36	85.21	82.41
Avail. seat miles	130.53	131.78	132.28
Load factor (%)	66.2	64.7	62.3
Rev. per RPM (cents)	13.09	13.28	13.44
Cost per ASM (cents)	8.84	9.72	9.50

At March 31, 1995, Delta had 544 aircraft: 11 A310s, 134 B-727s, 69 B-737s, 85 B-757s, 55 B-767s, 56 L-1011s, 11 MD-11s, 120 MD-88s and 3 MD-90s. A total of 115 planes were on order, with 212 on option. Delta also holds a 38% interest in the WORLDSPAN computer reservations system.

Important Developments

Aug. '95—DAL said passenger traffic in July 1995 slid 5.1%, year to year. Capacity was down only 0.4%; the load factor fell to 69.0%, from 72.4%. The company noted that the negative comparison reflected 1994's record traffic, when most markets experienced lower fares. DAL is seeing a corresponding improvement in passenger mile yield.
Jul. '95—The company said it reached its unit operating costs goal in the fiscal 1995 fourth quarter, and reiterated its commitment to reaching 8.0 cents per ASM by the June 1996 quarter.
Feb. '95—DAL changed its travel agency commission program, introducing a maximum commission payment of $50 for any round-trip and $25 for any one-way domestic ticket. It estimated that the cap would affect about 20% of tickets issued by travel agents.

Capitalization

Long Term Debt: $2,827,000,000 (3/95).
ESOP $4.32 Preferred Stock: $125,000,000; excl. $368,000,000 of unearned compensation; ful. conv. into approx. 5.9 million com. shs.
$3.50 Depositary Preferred Stock: 23,000,000 shs. ($1 par); ea. sh. represents 0.001 sh. of Ser. C pfd. stk; ea. Ser. C sh. conv. into 0.7605 com.

Per Share Data ($)

(Year Ended Jun. 30)

	1995	1994	1993	1992	1991	1990
Tangible Bk. Val.	NA	NM	25.28	16.01	33.49	39.25
Cash Flow	NA	5.38	4.55	2.22	4.02	15.18
Earnings	4.07	-10.32	-10.54	-10.60	-7.73	5.79
Dividends	0.20	0.20	0.70	1.20	1.20	1.70
Payout Ratio	5%	NM	NM	NM	NM	28%
Prices - High	79⅞	57⅞	61⅜	75¼	78¾	80⅞
- Low	50¼	39½	45¾	47¾	55½	52½
P/E Ratio - High	20	NM	NM	NM	NM	NM
- Low	12	NM	NM	NM	NM	NM

Income Statement Analysis (Million $)

	1994	%Chg	1993	%Chg	1992	%Chg	1991
Revs.	12,359	3%	11,997	11%	10,837	18%	9,171
Oper. Inc.	757	192%	259	NM	-33.0	NM	71.0
Depr.	678	-10%	752	18%	635	22%	521
Int. Exp.	304	27%	239	8%	221	36%	163
Pretax Inc.	-659	NM	-650	NM	-785	NM	-499
Eff. Tax Rate	NM	—	NM	—	NM	—	NM
Net Inc.	-408	NM	-414	NM	-505	NM	-323

Balance Sheet & Other Fin. Data (Million $)

	1994	1993	1992	1991	1990	1989
Cash	1,302	1,180	50.0	764	68.0	530
Curr. Assets	3,223	2,822	1,698	1,892	1,018	1,475
Total Assets	11,896	11,871	10,162	8,411	7,227	6,484
Curr. Liab.	3,536	2,973	3,543	2,155	1,833	1,763
LT Debt	3,228	3,717	2,833	2,059	1,315	703
Common Eqty.	1,467	1,863	1,466	2,006	2,118	2,620
Total Cap.	4,797	5,714	5,047	4,956	4,466	3,890
Cap. Exp.	1,032	1,714	2,481	2,059	1,538	1,244
Cash Flow	269	227	110	178	747	848

Ratio Analysis

	1994	1993	1992	1991	1990	1989
Curr. Ratio	0.9	0.9	0.5	0.9	0.6	0.8
% LT Debt of Cap.	67.3	65.1	56.1	41.5	29.4	18.1
% Net Inc.of Revs.	NM	NM	NM	NM	3.5	5.7
% Ret. on Assets	NM	NM	NM	NM	4.6	7.5
% Ret. on Equity	NM	NM	NM	NM	12.5	19.1

Dividend Data (Dividends have been paid since 1949. A dividend reinvestment plan is available. A poison pill stock purchase rights plan was adopted in 1986.)

Amt. of Div. $	Date Decl.	Ex-Div. Date	Stock of Record	Payment Date
0.050	Jul. 28	Aug. 04	Aug. 10	Sep. 01 '94
0.050	Oct. 27	Nov. 03	Nov. 09	Dec. 01 '94
0.050	Jan. 26	Feb. 02	Feb. 08	Mar. 01 '95
0.050	Apr. 27	May. 04	May. 10	Jun. 01 '95
0.050	Jul. 28	Aug. 08	Aug. 10	Sep. 01 '95

Data as orig. reptd.; bef. results of disc. opers. and/or spec. items. Per share data adj. for stk. divs. as of ex-div. date.
E-Estimated. NA-Not Available. NM-Not Meaningful. NR-Not Ranked.

Office—Hartsfield Atlanta International Airport, Atlanta, GA 30320. **Tel**—(404) 715-2600. **Chrm, Pres & CEO**—R. W. Allen. **Secy**—M. E. Raines. **SVP & CFO**—T. J. Roeck, Jr. **Dirs**—R. W. Allen, E. L. Artzt, H. A. Biedenharn III, J. L. Broadhead, E. H. Budd, G. D. Busbee, R. E. Cartledge, M. J. Evans, G. Grinstein, J. Hill, Jr., A. Young. **Transfer Agent & Registrar**—First Chicago Trust Co. of New York, Jersey City, NJ. **Incorporated** in Louisiana in 1930; reincorporated in Delaware in 1967. **Empl**-71,412. **S&P Analyst:** Joe Victor Shammas

Deluxe Corp.

NYSE Symbol **DLX**
In S&P 500

20-SEP-95

Industry:
Graphic Arts

Summary: This major printer of bank checks also produces computer forms, provides software and services to financial institutions, and is a direct marketer of consumer products.

S&P Opinion: Accumulate (★★★★)

Recent Price • 33½	Yield • 4.4%
52 Wk Range • 34-25¾	12-Mo. P/E • 20.2

Earnings vs. Previous Year
▲=Up ▼=Down ▶=No Change

Quantitative Evaluations

Outlook
(1 Lowest—5 Highest)
• **1**⁻

Fair Value
• **23%**

Risk
• **Low**

Earn./Div. Rank
• **A**

Technical Eval.
• **Bearish** since 12/92

Rel. Strength Rank
(1 Lowest—99 Highest)
• **61**

Insider Activity
• **Neutral**

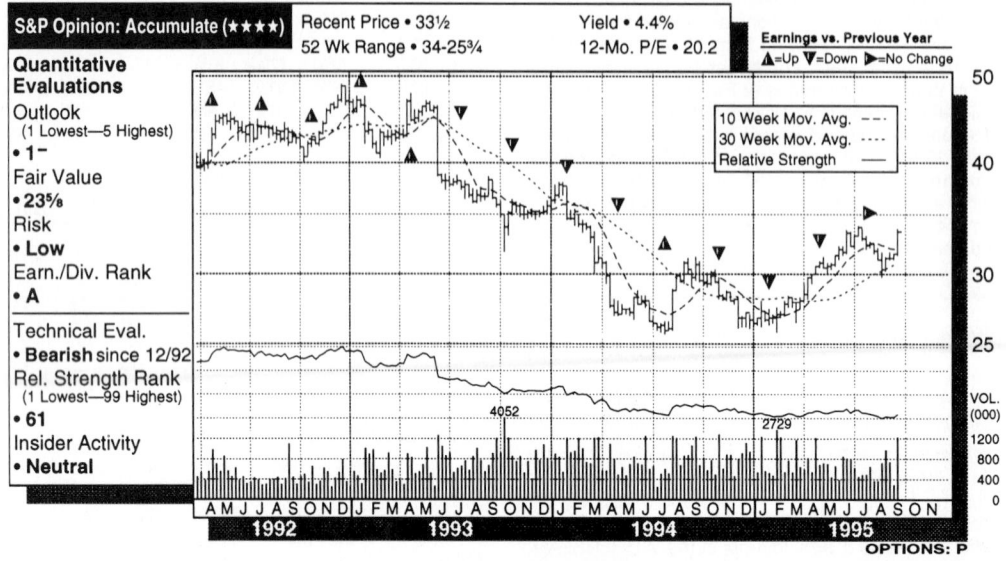

10 Week Mov. Avg. — – –
30 Week Mov. Avg. ·······
Relative Strength ——

OPTIONS: P

Overview - 20-SEP-95

Strong double-digit gains for business systems, electronic payment systems and consumer specialty products sales should continue through 1996. At the end of 1994, revenues from newer businesses exceeded financial institution check sales for the first time. Thus, softness in check printing revenues will have less impact on revenues and profitability. Although operating margins remain under pressure from increased international selling expenses, acquisition costs and startup spending, a resumption of earnings growth is tentatively projected for 1996, aided by improved business conditions. In the long-term, check sales will continue to reflect the impact of consolidations by banks and financial institutions, as well as strong competition.

Valuation - 20-SEP-95

Near-term earnings may be restricted by cost of recent acquisitions and a secular softening in the traditional check and financial forms businesses. A decision by directors in August 1995 not to increase the quarterly dividend interrupted a 34-year tradition of raising the payout. Although the decision may have been good business practice, it served as a dampening factor on the stock. Nevertheless, the yield of about 4.5% provided by the current dividend makes DLX an attractive holding for the short-term.

Key Stock Statistics

S&P EPS Est. 1995	1.70	Tang. Bk. Value/Share	5.48
P/E on S&P Est. 1995	19.7	Beta	0.81
S&P EPS Est. 1996	2.00	Shareholders	23,900
Dividend Rate/Share	1.48	Market cap. (B)	$ 2.8
Shs. outstg. (M)	82.6	Inst. holdings	65%
Avg. daily vol. (M)	0.160	Insider holdings	NA

Value of $10,000 invested 5 years ago: $ 12,076

Fiscal Year Ending Dec. 31

	1995	% Change	1994	% Change	1993	% Change
Revenues (Million $)						
1Q	465.6	8%	430.0	6%	406.0	5%
2Q	442.5	7%	412.3	14%	362.9	NM
3Q	—	—	478.9	29%	372.0	NM
4Q	—	—	478.9	9%	441.2	7%
Yr.	—	—	1,748	11%	1,582	3%
Income (Million $)						
1Q	33.84	-11%	38.04	-27%	51.79	6%
2Q	29.73	NM	29.60	NM	2.25	-95%
3Q	—	—	33.30	-10%	37.00	-27%
4Q	—	—	40.00	-21%	50.83	-9%
Yr.	—	—	140.9	NM	141.9	-30%
Earnings Per Share ($)						
1Q	0.41	-11%	0.46	-26%	0.62	7%
2Q	0.36	NM	0.36	NM	0.03	-95%
3Q	E0.41	3%	0.40	-11%	0.45	-25%
4Q	E0.52	6%	0.49	-20%	0.61	-9%
Yr.	E1.70	NM	1.71	NM	1.71	-29%

Next earnings report expected: late October

Business Summary - 20-SEP-95

Deluxe Corp. (formerly Deluxe Check Printers) prints and sells checks and related forms for financial institutions and their customers. Operations have been expanded in recent years to include electronic funds transfer (EFT) processing, new account verification services, computer and business forms, office products, and direct marketing of selected consumer products.

The payment systems division (62% of sales and 90% of operating income in 1994) prints checks, deposit tickets and related transaction forms. DLX accounts for 53% of the U.S. check printing market. Data Systems is the largest U.S. third-party processor of automated teller machine (ATM) transactions and is the leading processor of interchange transactions for shared ATM networks. Chex Systems, Inc. provides new account verification services to financial institutions. Sales Development Systems provides training and marketing services to the financial industry.

The business systems division (19% of sales and no contribution to profits) is a major supplier of short-run computer and business forms (including checks and related supplies) and record-keeping systems to small businesses and professional practices.

The consumer specialty products division (19% of sales and 10% of income) was formed with the 1987 acquisition of Looart Press, Inc. and its operating unit, Current, Inc. Current is the largest U.S. direct-mail marketer of greeting cards, stationery and related consumer specialty products. Some 40% of the division's sales occur in the fourth quarter.

Important Developments

Aug. '95—Directors maintained the quarterly dividend at $0.37 a share. The dividend, which had increased for 34 consecutive years, was traditionally raised at the August meeting of the directors, but management recommended that it be held at the current level, in view of the company's current earnings and continuing investments needed for long-term business development. DLX noted that its repositioning has taken longer than expected, and that lower earnings during the transition moved the dividend payout beyond an appropriate level. It added that the current dividend will be maintained until earnings growth resumes.
Apr. '95—DLX launched a new line of tamper-resistant checks.

Capitalization

Long Term Debt: $113,897,000 (6/95).

Per Share Data ($)

(Year Ended Dec. 31)

	1994	1993	1992	1991	1990	1989
Tangible Bk. Val.	5.90	6.15	7.77	6.93	5.88	5.47
Cash Flow	2.76	2.58	3.21	3.08	2.64	2.31
Earnings	1.71	1.71	2.42	2.18	2.03	1.79
Dividends	1.46	1.42	1.34	1.22	1.10	0.98
Payout Ratio	85%	83%	55%	56%	54%	55%
Prices - High	38	47⅞	49	48½	35⅞	35¾
- Low	25⅝	31¾	38⅛	32⅝	26⅝	24
P/E Ratio - High	22	28	20	22	18	20
- Low	15	19	16	15	13	13

Income Statement Analysis (Million $)

	1994	%Chg	1993	%Chg	1992	%Chg	1991
Revs.	1,748	10%	1,582	3%	1,534	4%	1,474
Oper. Inc.	320	-9%	353	-9%	389	7%	364
Depr.	86.4	20%	72.3	9%	66.6	-12%	76.0
Int. Exp.	11.3	10%	10.3	-33%	15.4	87%	8.2
Pretax Inc.	241	2%	236	-27%	325	10%	295
Eff. Tax Rate	42%	—	40%	—	38%	—	38%
Net Inc.	141	NM	142	-30%	203	11%	183

Balance Sheet & Other Fin. Data (Million $)

	1994	1993	1992	1991	1990	1989
Cash	78.0	222	381	317	114	45.0
Curr. Assets	421	522	611	539	344	263
Total Assets	1,256	1,252	1,200	1,099	924	847
Curr. Liab.	290	298	224	208	199	168
LT Debt	111	111	116	111	12.0	10.0
Common Eqty.	814	801	830	748	676	631
Total Cap.	966	954	975	891	725	679
Cap. Exp.	126	62.1	71.6	76.0	64.0	88.4
Cash Flow	227	214	269	259	223	198

Ratio Analysis

	1994	1993	1992	1991	1990	1989
Curr. Ratio	1.4	1.8	2.7	2.6	1.7	1.6
% LT Debt of Cap.	11.5	11.6	11.8	12.4	1.6	1.5
% Net Inc.of Revs.	8.1	9.0	13.2	12.4	12.2	11.6
% Ret. on Assets	11.2	11.7	17.7	18.1	19.6	18.7
% Ret. on Equity	17.5	17.5	25.7	25.7	26.5	25.5

Dividend Data —Dividends have been paid since 1921. A poison pill stock purchase rights plan was adopted in 1988.

Amt. of Div. $	Date Decl.	Ex-Div. Date	Stock of Record	Payment Date
0.370	Nov. 11	Nov. 15	Nov. 21	Dec. 05 '94
0.370	Feb. 06	Feb. 14	Feb. 21	Mar. 06 '95
0.370	May. 08	May. 16	May. 22	Jun. 05 '95
0.370	Aug. 14	Aug. 17	Aug. 21	Sep. 05 '95

Data as orig. reptd.; bef. results of disc. opers. and/or spec. items. Per share data adj. for stk. divs. as of ex-div. date.
E-Estimated. NA-Not Available. NM-Not Meaningful. NR-Not Ranked.

Office—1080 West County Rd. F (P.O. Box 64399), Shoreview, MN 55126-8201 (55164-0399). **Tel**—(612) 483-7111. **Chrmn**—H. V. Haverty. **Pres & CEO**—J. A. Blanchard III. **EVP & COO**—J. K. Twogood. **SVP & Secy**—J. H. LeFevre. **SVP, CFO & Investor Contact**—Charles M. Osborne (612-483-7355). **Dirs**—E. W. Asplin, J. A. Blanchard III, B. B. Grogan, H. V. Haverty, A. F. Jacobson, H. W. Lurton, W. MacMillan, E. R. Olson, J. J. Renier, J. Schreiner, J. K. Twogood. **Transfer Agent & Registrar**—Norwest Bank Minnesota, South St. Paul. **Incorporated** in Minnesota in 1920. **Empl**-18,000. **S&P Analyst:** William H. Donald

Detroit Edison

NYSE Symbol **DTE**
In S&P 500

14-AUG-95

Industry:
Utilities-Electric

Summary: This electric utility serves southeastern Michigan, an area that contains 20% of U.S. automakers and many other heavy industrial producers.

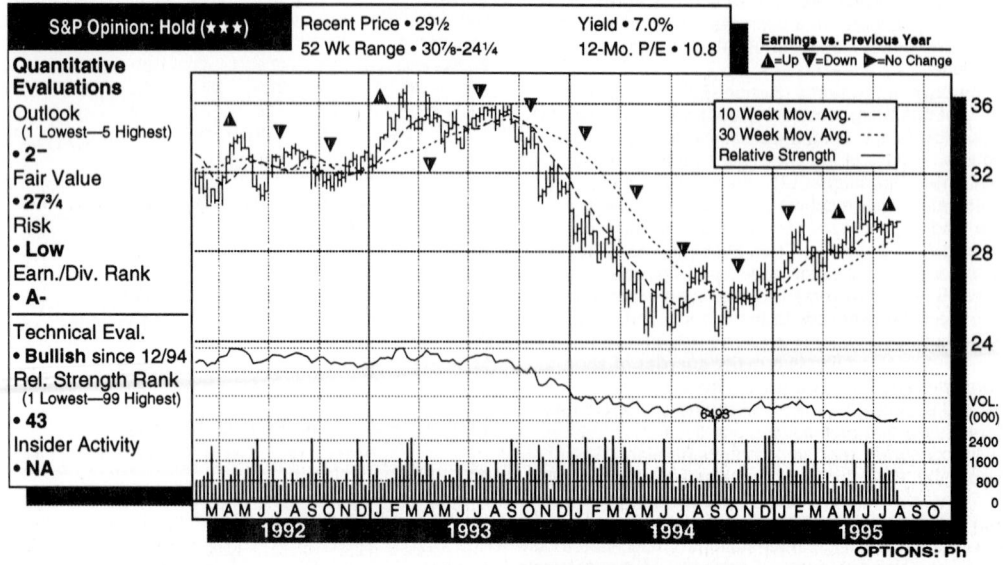

S&P Opinion: Hold (★★★)	Recent Price • 29½	Yield • 7.0%
	52 Wk Range • 30⅞-24¼	12-Mo. P/E • 10.8

Quantitative Evaluations

Outlook
(1 Lowest—5 Highest)
• **2⁻**

Fair Value
• **27¾**

Risk
• **Low**

Earn./Div. Rank
• **A-**

Technical Eval.
• **Bullish** since 12/94

Rel. Strength Rank
(1 Lowest—99 Highest)
• **43**

Insider Activity
• **NA**

Earnings vs. Previous Year
▲=Up ▼=Down ▶=No Change

10 Week Mov. Avg. ---
30 Week Mov. Avg. ·····
Relative Strength —

OPTIONS: Ph

Overview - 11-AUG-95

Earnings are likely to rise only very modestly in 1995, restricted by a slightly lower revenue stream. Increasing electric intensity in DTE's service area is raising kwh sales and providing greater production efficiencies, and we expect a recent substantial reduction in rates to price-sensitive automakers, securing power supply contracts for 20% of kwh sales through 2004, to raise DTE's competitive profile. The return to service of Fermi 2 should reduce costly power purchases, but somewhat higher capital spending, combined with lower auto production rates and sizeable regulatory rate cuts in 1993 and 1994, are negative factors. Overall, cost reduction and control will be the primary drivers of earnings growth in 1995 and 1996.

Valuation - 11-AUG-95

Recent stock price gains compare poorly to those of the broader market averages. As a comparatively high-cost generator of electricity, the company's ability to produce healthy cash flows is important to its ability to maintain its above-average payout. DTE recently exchanged $4.2 million of depository shares for $105 million of low-cost quarterly income debt securities to improve its after-tax cash flow. Although it is commited to reducing long term debt, planned retirements and projected internally funded capital spending reduce the likelihood of a near-term dividend increase. However, the current dividend should be secure. With above-average yield and below-average P/E, the shares offer good total return.

Key Stock Statistics

S&P EPS Est. 1995	2.72	Tang. Bk. Value/Share	22.88
P/E on S&P Est. 1995	10.8	Beta	0.52
S&P EPS Est. 1996	2.80	Shareholders	151,100
Dividend Rate/Share	2.06	Market cap. (B)	$ 4.3
Shs. outstg. (M)	144.9	Inst. holdings	38%
Avg. daily vol. (M)	0.203	Insider holdings	NA

Value of $10,000 invested 5 years ago: $ 16,990

Fiscal Year Ending Dec. 31

	1995	% Change	1994	% Change	1993	% Change
Revenues (Million $)						
1Q	880.3	-2%	899.6	3%	874.8	-2%
2Q	856.0	-2%	872.7	4%	835.2	-3%
3Q	—	—	944.4	-3%	976.3	7%
4Q	—	—	802.7	-8%	869.0	-2%
Yr.	—	—	3,519	-1%	3,555	NM
Income (Million $)						
1Q	113.5	NM	112.9	-17%	135.2	-13%
2Q	91.56	5%	87.28	-15%	102.7	-18%
3Q	—	—	124.4	-19%	153.4	-1%
4Q	—	—	95.38	-27%	130.7	-13%
Yr.	—	—	419.9	-20%	521.9	-11%
Earnings Per Share ($)						
1Q	0.73	1%	0.72	-16%	0.86	-15%
2Q	0.58	7%	0.54	-16%	0.64	-20%
3Q	E0.81	—	0.80	-19%	0.99	-2%
4Q	E0.60	—	0.61	-27%	0.84	-14%
Yr.	E2.72	—	2.67	-20%	3.34	-12%

Next earnings report expected: late October

Detroit Edison

Business Summary - 14-AUG-95

Detroit Edison supplies electricity to more than 1.9 million customers in southeastern Michigan. Electric revenues by customer class in recent years were:

	1994	1993	1992	1991
Residential	32%	32%	31%	32%
Commercial	42%	40%	40%	40%
Industrial	21%	20%	21%	20%
Other	5%	8%	8%	8%

Power sources in 1994 were coal and other fossil fuel, 86%, and purchased power, 14%. Peak demand in 1994 was 9,684 mw, and system capability at time of peak totaled 10,212 mw, for a capacity margin of 6.2%. In 1994, sales to autmotive and auto-related customers comprised 11% of total operating revenues; the 30 largest industrial customers accounted for 18%. Capital outlays in 1994 were $363 million, and are estimated at $394 million for 1995, to improve production, transmission and distribution facilities, general projects and capitalized overhead.

DTE's Fermi 2 nuclear plant began operating commercially in January 1988. In early 1988, the company wrote off disallowed Fermi 2 costs of $2.35 a share; removal of its Greenwood oil plant from the rate base resulted in a charge of $0.49 a share. After a December 1988 rate settlement, DTE recorded an additional charge of $3.81 a share, mostly for disallowed Fermi 2 costs. In February 1990, the company bought the 11% stake in Fermi 2 that it did not already own, for $539.6 million. Net plant investment at the end of 1994 totaled $3.1 billion.

Important Developments

Jun. '95—DTE said its Fermi 2 nuclear plant was operating at 80% of capacity, following a three-week refueling outage. The plant was restarted in December 1994, after an extended shutdown due to a turbine failure in late 1993, and is expected to run at reduced capacity until the next refueling in September 1996, when new low pressure turbines will be installed, raising capacity about 20 mw. In May, the company formed an alliance to share resources, materials and services with eight other nuclear utilities and an engineering and construction firm to cut plant operating costs. In April, DTE announced plans to form a holding company to provide greater financial flexibility through better definition and separation of its regulated and unregulated businesses. Separately, in March 1995, DTE received approvals for special contracts signed in late 1994 that will secure automaker business within its service area by providing annual rate reductions of $30 to $50 million through 2004.

Capitalization

Long Term Debt: $3,926,950,000 (6/95), incl. cap. lease obligs.
Cum. Pfd. Stk.: $379,946,000

Per Share Data ($) (Year Ended Dec. 31)

	1994	1993	1992	1991	1990	1989
Tangible Bk. Val.	22.66	21.24	20.78	18.96	17.19	15.79
Earnings	2.67	3.34	3.79	3.64	3.26	2.65
Dividends	2.06	2.06	1.98	1.88	1.78	1.68
Payout Ratio	77%	62%	52%	52%	55%	63%
Prices - High	30¼	37⅛	35¼	35⅜	30¼	25⅞
- Low	24¼	29⅞	30¼	27¾	23½	17⅛
P/E Ratio - High	11	11	9	10	9	10
- Low	9	9	8	8	7	6

Income Statement Analysis (Million $)

	1994	%Chg	1993	%Chg	1992	%Chg	1991
Revs.	3,519	-1%	3,555	NM	3,558	NM	3,592
Depr.	476	10%	433	2%	423	3%	412
Maint.	262	4%	251	-5%	263	-9%	290
Fxd. Chgs. Cov.	3.0	-3%	3.2	4%	3.0	13%	2.7
Constr. Credits	3.7	23%	3.0	NM	3.0	-25%	4.0
Eff. Tax Rate	39%	—	37%	—	35%	—	32%
Net Inc.	420	-20%	522	-11%	588	4%	568

Balance Sheet & Other Fin. Data (Million $)

	1994	1993	1992	1991	1990	1989
Gross Prop.	13,046	12,717	13,223	12,791	12,487	11,700
Cap. Exp.	378	399	416	272	230	243
Net Prop.	8,586	8,651	9,014	8,992	9,053	8,678
Capitalization:						
LT Debt	3,951	3,972	4,129	4,388	5,050	4,692
% LT Debt	53	52	55	58	63	63
Pfd.	380	381	334	353	376	399
% Pfd.	5.00	5.00	4.40	4.70	4.70	5.30
Common	3,326	3,296	3,114	2,848	2,588	2,370
% Common	44	43	41	38	32	32
Total Cap.	10,019	9,994	9,265	9,202	9,525	8,860

Ratio Analysis

	1994	1993	1992	1991	1990	1989
Oper. Ratio	79.6	76.3	73.2	74.0	73.4	76.6
% Earn. on Net Prop.	8.3	9.8	10.6	10.3	9.9	8.6
% Ret. on Revs.	11.9	14.7	16.5	15.8	15.6	13.3
% Ret. On Invest.Cap	7.1	9.0	10.7	10.8	10.8	10.4
% Return On Com.Eqty	11.8	15.2	18.6	19.5	19.1	16.8

Dividend Data (Dividends have been paid since 1909. A dividend reinvestment plan is available.)

Amt. of Div. $	Date Decl.	Ex-Div. Date	Stock of Record	Payment Date
0.515	Jul. 25	Sep. 15	Sep. 21	Oct. 15 '94
0.515	Dec. 05	Dec. 13	Dec. 19	Jan. 15 '95
0.515	Feb. 28	Mar. 16	Mar. 22	Apr. 15 '95
0.515	May. 22	Jun. 19	Jun. 21	Jul. 15 '95
0.515	Jul. 25	Sep. 19	Sep. 21	Oct. 15 '95

Data as orig. reptd.; bef. results of disc opers. and/or spec. items. Per share data adj. for stk. divs. as of ex-div. date. E-Estimated. NA-Not Available. NM-Not Meaningful. NR-Not Ranked.

Office—2000 Second Ave., Detroit, MI 48226. **Tel**—(313) 237-8000. **Chrmn & CEO**—J. E. Lobbia. **Pres & COO**—A. F. Earley, Jr. **EVP & CFO**—L. G. Garberding. **Secy**—Susan M. Beale. **Investor Contact**—Ron Giaier (313-237-7880). **Dirs**—T. E. Adderley, L. Bauder, D. Bing, A. F. Earley, Jr., L. G. Garberding, A. D. Gilmour, T. S. Leipprandt, J. E. Lobbia, P. S. Longe, E. A. Miller, D. E. Richardson, A. E. Schwartz, W. Wegner. **Transfer Agent & Registrar**—Co.'s office. **Incorporated** in New York in 1903; reincorporated in Michigan in 1967. **Empl**-8,400. **S&P Analyst:** Jane Collin

Dial Corp

NYSE Symbol **DL**
In S&P 500

10-OCT-95 **Industry:**
Conglomerate/diversified

Summary: This company makes branded consumer household and food products, operates commercial and institutional foodservice outlets and provides varied consumer and commercial services.

S&P Opinion: Accumulate (★★★★)	Recent Price • 25	Yield • 2.6%
	52 Wk Range • 26⅜-19¼	12-Mo. P/E • 14.8

Quantitative Evaluations

Outlook
(1 Lowest—5 Highest)
• **2⁻**

Fair Value
• **22⅞**

Risk
• **Low**

Earn./Div. Rank
• **B+**

Technical Eval.
• **Bullish** since 8/95

Rel. Strength Rank
(1 Lowest—99 Highest)
• **53**

Insider Activity
• **NA**

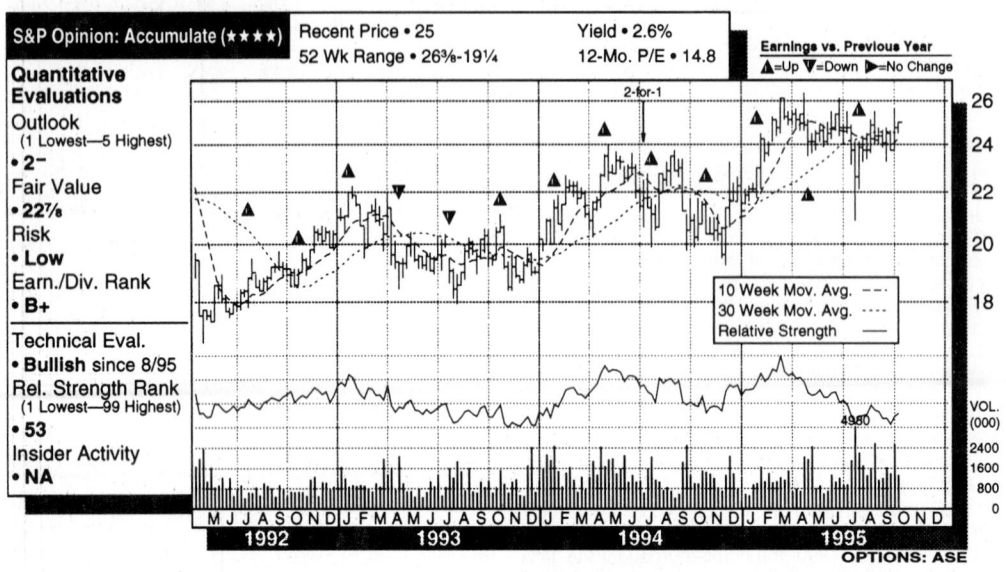

Earnings vs. Previous Year
▲=Up ▼=Down ▶=No Change

2-for-1

10 Week Mov. Avg. ---
30 Week Mov. Avg. ....
Relative Strength —

1992 1993 1994 1995

VOL. (000)

OPTIONS: ASE

Overview - 10-OCT-95

Revenues from ongoing operations should continue to trend higher in 1995. Growth will be driven by new consumer household cleaning and food product introductions and higher sales of existing products, particularly moderately priced laundry products. Revenues should increase in all of the service businesses. Earnings growth should continue to outpace sales growth in 1995, on continued cost-cutting efforts and higher volume. Further operating efficiencies are expected from the consolidation of existing operations and past acquisitions. Margins should also benefit from actions to improve operating results at Premier Cruise Lines. Earnings will be hurt by a one-time $130 million ($1.47 a share) aftertax restructuring charge.

Valuation - 10-OCT-95

Dial should generate strong earnings growth in the years ahead, driven by improvement in all of its business segments. The consumer products division should benefit from improved relationships with its customers and increased focus on expanding its rapidly growing value-priced product lines. The company's active acquisition program should boost results at this division. The service businesses--aircraft catering and convention and travel services--are benefiting from leading market positions and a turnaround in the travel and leisure spending cycle. The shares, which are off slightly from their all-time high, are recommended for accumulation.

Key Stock Statistics

S&P EPS Est. 1995	0.34	Tang. Bk. Value/Share	NM
P/E on S&P Est. 1995	73.5	Beta	1.21
S&P EPS Est. 1996	2.10	Shareholders	54,900
Dividend Rate/Share	0.64	Market cap. (B)	$ 2.3
Shs. outstg. (M)	93.2	Inst. holdings	54%
Avg. daily vol. (M)	0.394	Insider holdings	NA

Value of $10,000 invested 5 years ago: NA

Fiscal Year Ending Dec. 31

	1995	% Change	1994	% Change	1993	% Change
Revenues (Million $)						
1Q	858.2	9%	784.9	23%	638.0	-19%
2Q	901.9	-3%	932.0	20%	774.0	-15%
3Q	—	—	912.5	18%	770.4	-10%
4Q	—	—	917.5	12%	817.9	-3%
Yr.	—	—	3,547	18%	3,000	-11%
Income (Million $)						
1Q	21.51	25%	17.21	54%	11.16	-2%
2Q	47.47	8%	43.93	32%	33.38	NM
3Q	—	—	45.43	22%	37.18	15%
4Q	—	—	34.28	20%	28.55	NM
Yr.	—	—	140.3	27%	110.3	NM
Earnings Per Share ($)						
1Q	0.24	20%	0.20	54%	0.13	-4%
2Q	0.54	8%	0.50	32%	0.38	-4%
3Q	E-0.88	NM	0.52	18%	0.44	16%
4Q	E0.44	13%	0.39	15%	0.34	NM
Yr.	E0.34	-79%	1.61	26%	1.28	NM

Next earnings report expected: late October

Dial Corp

Business Summary - 10-OCT-95

The Dial Corp (formerly Greyhound Dial) is a diversified holding company providing varied products and services for consumers and businesses. The Greyhound Lines U.S. bus operation was divested in 1987. In 1993, Dial acquired Renuzit air fresheners, United Exposition Services Co., Andrews Bartlett & Associates, Inc. exposition services, Gelco Convention Services, Inc. and United Airlines Catering Kitchens. Segment contributions from continuing operations in 1994 were:

	Revs.	Profits
Consumer products	43%	48%
Services	57%	52%

Consumer products include Dial, Tone and other soaps, Dial antiperspirants and deodorants and Breck hair care products; Purex, Trend and Dutch laundry detergents and Brillo soap pads; and food products such as Armour Star and Treet canned meats and Lunch Bucket shelf-stable microwaveable meals. Services provided to consumer markets include Dobbs International Services Inc. in-flight catering, a money order business, travel and tour operations, gift shops, drug stores, cruise ships and duty-free shops. Business market services include contract food services, convention exhibit services and aircraft ground handling services.

In March 1992, Dial spun off its financial services group as a new entity called GFC Financial Corp., and in August 1993, Dial sold publicly its transportation segment, Motor Coach Industries International, through a public offering.

Important Developments

Sep. '95—Dial announced that it would take a $130 million ($1.47 a share) aftertax restructuring charge in the third quarter. About $94 million of the charge would be used to close six plants and reduce the workforce by 15%, or 700 people, in the consumer products group. The remaining $36 million would be used to write down the assets of Premier Cruise Lines. Dial stated that savings from these actions should make positive contributions to the company over the coming years.

Jul. '95—Dial attributed the 9.4% increase in its second-quarter net income mainly to higher operating income at the airline catering and services division and at the travel, leisure and payment services division and to a one-time gain of $3.5 million (pretax) at the convention services division. Operating income was up only 2.3% at the consumer products division due to a previously reported program to effect reductions of trade customers' inventories.

Capitalization

Long Term Debt: $752,768,000 (6/95).
Minority Interest: $23,634,000.
$4.75 Red. Preferred Stock: 382,352 shs. (no par).

Per Share Data ($)

(Year Ended Dec. 31)

	1994	1993	1992	1991	1990	1989
Tangible Bk. Val.	-3.20	-3.17	3.81	11.30	12.65	5.53
Cash Flow	2.87	2.45	1.43	1.24	2.55	2.47
Earnings	1.61	1.28	0.32	0.12	1.45	1.38
Dividends	0.59	0.56	0.60	0.70	0.68	0.66
Payout Ratio	37%	44%	208%	NM	46%	49%
Prices - High	24	22¼	25⅜	23⅛	16⅛	18⅞
- Low	19¼	18	16¾	12⅜	9½	14⅜
P/E Ratio - High	15	17	79	NM	11	14
- Low	12	14	52	NM	7	10

Income Statement Analysis (Million $)

	1994	%Chg	1993	%Chg	1992	%Chg	1991
Revs.	3,547	18%	3,000	-11%	3,389	2%	3,310
Oper. Inc.	396	22%	325	-2%	333	5%	318
Depr.	110	10%	100	7%	93.3	4%	89.3
Int. Exp.	61.0	22%	50.0	-17%	60.0	-10%	67.0
Pretax Inc.	225	29%	175	197%	59.0	2%	58.0
Eff. Tax Rate	36%	—	35%	—	44%	—	72%
Net Inc.	140	27%	110	NM	28.0	155%	11.0

Balance Sheet & Other Fin. Data (Million $)

	1994	1993	1992	1991	1990	1989
Cash	694	546	685	707	824	859
Curr. Assets	1,244	1,053	1,294	1,336	NA	NA
Total Assets	3,781	3,281	3,281	3,592	5,431	5,205
Curr. Liab.	2,057	1,749	1,694	1,755	1,958	1,832
LT Debt	722	625	705	504	1,939	1,797
Common Eqty.	523	437	358	907	993	1,040
Total Cap.	1,308	1,137	1,153	1,505	3,123	3,041
Cap. Exp.	109	115	118	135	108	107
Cash Flow	249	209	120	99	202	193

Ratio Analysis

	1994	1993	1992	1991	1990	1989
Curr. Ratio	0.6	0.6	0.8	0.8	NA	NA
% LT Debt of Cap.	55.2	54.9	61.1	33.5	62.1	59.1
% Net Inc.of Revs.	4.0	3.7	0.8	0.3	3.3	3.1
% Ret. on Assets	4.0	3.4	0.7	0.2	2.2	2.1
% Ret. on Equity	28.9	27.7	3.8	1.0	11.4	10.5

Dividend Data

Dividends have been paid since 1936. A dividend reinvestment plan is available. A "poison pill" stock purchase rights plan was adopted in 1986.

Amt. of Div. $	Date Decl.	Ex-Div. Date	Stock of Record	Payment Date
0.150	Nov. 17	Nov. 25	Dec. 01	Jan. 03 '95
0.150	Feb. 16	Mar. 06	Mar. 10	Apr. 03 '95
0.150	May. 09	May. 25	Jun. 01	Jul. 03 '95
0.160	Aug. 17	Aug. 30	Sep. 01	Oct. 02 '95

Data as orig. reptd.; bef. results of disc. opers. and/or spec. items. Per share data adj. for stk. divs. as of ex-div. date.
E-Estimated. NA-Not Available. NM-Not Meaningful. NR-Not Ranked.

Office—Dial Tower, Phoenix, AZ 85077. **Tel**—(602) 207-5600. **Fax**—(602) 207-5900. **Chrmn & CEO**—J. W. Teets. **Pres & COO**—A. S. Patti. **VP-Fin & Treas**—R. G. Nelson. **VP-Secy**—F. G. Emerson. **Investor Contact**—Roger Bedier. **Dirs**—J. T. Ford, T. L. Gossage, D. E. Guinn, J. Hay, J. K. Hofer, A. S. Patti, J. F. Reichert, L. J. Rice, D. C. Stanfill, J. W. Teets, A. T. Young. **Transfer Agent**—First National Bank of Boston. **Incorporated** in Delaware in 1926; reincorporated in Delaware in 1992. **Empl**-32,519. **S&P Analyst:** E. A. Vandeventer

Digital Equipment

NYSE Symbol **DEC**
In S&P 500

26-OCT-95

Industry:
Data Processing

Summary: Digital Equipment is a leading worldwide provider of computers and related equipment and software.

S&P Opinion: Hold (★★★)

Recent Price • 51¾
52 Wk Range • 55¼-29

Yield • Nil
12-Mo. P/E • 28.0

Earnings vs. Previous Year
▲=Up ▼=Down ▶=No Change

Quantitative Evaluations

Outlook
(1 Lowest—5 Highest)
• **2+**

Fair Value
• **48⅜**

Risk
• **Average**

Earn./Div. Rank
• **C**

Technical Eval.
• **Neutral** since 9/95

Rel. Strength Rank
(1 Lowest—99 Highest)
• **97**

Insider Activity
• **Neutral**

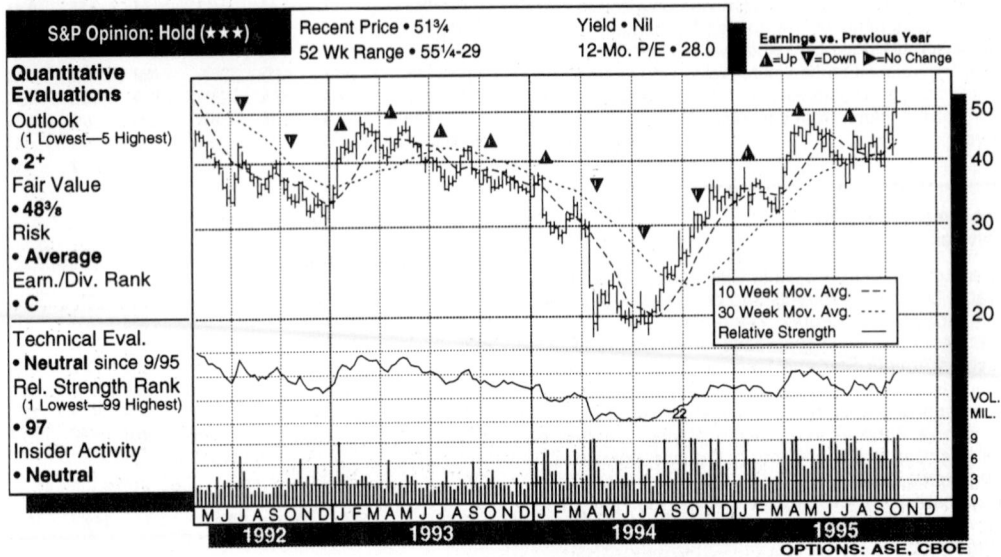

10 Week Mov. Avg. - - -
30 Week Mov. Avg. ····
Relative Strength —

VOL.
MIL.

1992　1993　1994　1995

OPTIONS: ASE, CBOE

Overview - 26-OCT-95

A strong product line-up coupled with a more stream-lined cost structure should allow for sustained profitability through fiscal 1996. Sales growth is expected to accelerate for the balance of the year, reflecting strong demand for Alpha-powered workstations and servers and Intel PCs. Alpha systems rose 40%, year to year; PCs advanced 32%. Because of this strong demand, we are raising our revenue growth forecast for the year to 11% (14% excluding divestitures), up from mid-single digits. Gross margins are expected to stabilize in the 32%-33% range, as a stronger product mix offsets a lower margin mix of service revenues. Operating expenses should grow, reflecting efforts to spur demand creation, but at a rate much lower than revenue growth.

Valuation - 26-OCT-95

The shares, which bottomed in mid-1994, have risen sharply as DEC now seems positioned for sustained profitability. Although aggressive cost cutting has been the primary catalyst behind the improved earnings, DEC is now consistently seeing strong sales growth for 64-bit Alpha products, which account for about 25% of product revenues. New product offerings in this area have extended DEC's price/performance advantage over competitive offerings while an August agreement with Microsoft should solidify the platform. Nevertheless, the shares have moved sharply higher since July and we believe they adequately reflect DEC's improved financial outlook. As a result, we recommend deferring additional purchases at this time.

Key Stock Statistics

S&P EPS Est. 1996	3.90	Tang. Bk. Value/Share	23.51
P/E on S&P Est. 1996	13.3	Beta	1.02
S&P EPS Est. 1997	4.50	Shareholders	68,600
Dividend Rate/Share	Nil	Market cap. (B)	$ 8.1
Shs. outstg. (M)	150.4	Inst. holdings	65%
Avg. daily vol. (M)	2.125	Insider holdings	NA

Value of $10,000 invested 5 years ago: $ 6,310

Fiscal Year Ending Jun. 30

	1996	% Change	1995	% Change	1994	% Change
Revenues (Million $)						
1Q	3,271	5%	3,122	4%	3,015	-9%
2Q	—	—	3,473	7%	3,254	-12%
3Q	—	—	3,467	6%	3,259	-6%
4Q	—	—	3,750	-4%	3,923	NM
Yr.	—	—	13,813	3%	13,451	-6%
Income (Million $)						
1Q	48.17	NM	-195.1	NM	-103.2	—
2Q	—	—	18.88	NM	-72.14	NM
3Q	—	—	73.74	NM	-183.3	NM
4Q	—	—	159.8	NM	-1,745	NM
Yr.	—	—	57.31	NM	-2,104	NM
Earnings Per Share ($)						
1Q	0.26	NM	-1.44	NM	-0.76	NM
2Q	E1.00	NM	0.07	NM	-0.53	NM
3Q	E1.20	173%	0.44	NM	-1.34	NM
4Q	E1.40	39%	1.01	NM	-12.64	NM
Yr.	E3.90	NM	0.15	NM	-15.43	NM

Next earnings report expected: mid January

Digital Equipment

Business Summary - 26-OCT-95

Digital Equipment is a leading maker of computers and associated peripheral equipment, related software and supplies. Revenues in recent fiscal years were derived as follows:

	1995	1994	1993	1992
Product sales	55%	53%	53%	55%
Service & other	45%	47%	47%	45%

Countries outside of the U.S. accounted for 60% of revenues in fiscal 1995.

DEC's 64-bit, open computing architecture, Alpha AXP, supports multiple operating systems (OpenVMS, Digital Unix and Windows NT) and is the foundation for its high performance computer system family. The company offers a complete line of Alpha-based products, ranging from chips and boards to high performance workstations and servers to larger general purpose computer systems.

DEC also offers a full range of Intel-based and industry compatible personal computers, servers and network hardware and desktop integration products. These products support Microsoft Windows, Windows NT and Windows 95 operating systems.

The company's VAX offerings include a line of VAX-station workstations, and high performance servers. All VAX systems use the same 32-bit architecture and VMS operating system, making all computers fully compatible.

Other products include a family of peripheral and data storage products, video terminals, printers and network components, such as hubs, routers and switches.

DEC designs, or acquires from third parties and distributes under license, software products for its computer systems and for systems of other vendors. It also provides a comprehensive portfolio of consulting, systems integration and support services.

In July 1994, a $1.2 billion charge was incurred, for elimination of 20,000 jobs and paring of utilized space by 10 million sq. ft.

Important Developments

Oct. '95—DEC was selected by Compaq Computer to provide worldwide service and support for Compaq's enterprise computing efforts.

Aug. '95—Microsoft announced that it will invest $50 million to $100 million in Digital's service and support organization to help support Windows NT-based computers. Microsoft also said that NT would be available on DEC's Alpha chip at the same time it is available on Intel semiconductors.

Capitalization

Long Term Debt: $1,012,742,000 (9/95).
Preferred Stock: 4,000,000 shs. ($1 par).

Per Share Data ($)

					(Year Ended Jun. 30)	
	1995	1994	1993	1992	1991	1990
Tangible Bk. Val.	NA	22.96	36.19	38.58	61.82	66.76
Cash Flow	NA	-10.47	3.43	-12.63	1.37	6.65
Earnings	0.15	-15.43	-1.93	-18.50	-5.08	0.59
Dividends	Nil	Nil	Nil	Nil	Nil	Nil
Payout Ratio	Nil	Nil	Nil	Nil	Nil	Nil
Prices - High	49½	38⅛	49¼	65½	83	95⅛
- Low	31⅛	18¼	32¾	30⅜	48½	45½
P/E Ratio - High	NM	NM	NM	NM	NM	NM
- Low	NM	NM	NM	NM	NM	NM

Income Statement Analysis (Million $)

	1994	%Chg	1993	%Chg	1992	%Chg	1991
Revs.	13,451	-6%	14,371	3%	13,931	NM	13,911
Oper. Inc.	-1.1	NM	461	NM	97.0	-93%	1,296
Depr.	681	-3%	699	-5%	733	-7%	784
Int. Exp.	73.4	44%	50.8	32%	38.5	-14%	44.6
Pretax Inc.	-2,019	NM	-223	NM	-2,077	NM	-519
Eff. Tax Rate	NM	—	NM	—	NM	—	NM
Net Inc.	-2,104	NM	-250	NM	-2,309	NM	-616

Balance Sheet & Other Fin. Data (Million $)

	1994	1993	1992	1991	1990	1989
Cash	1,181	1,643	1,337	1,924	2,009	1,655
Curr. Assets	6,888	6,883	7,121	7,654	7,622	6,895
Total Assets	10,580	10,950	11,284	11,875	11,655	10,668
Curr. Liab.	5,056	3,919	5,106	4,091	3,290	2,394
LT Debt	1,011	1,018	42.0	150	150	136
Common Eqty.	3,276	4,885	4,931	7,624	8,182	8,036
Total Cap.	4,295	5,903	4,996	7,784	8,365	8,274
Cap. Exp.	682	529	710	738	1,028	1,223
Cash Flow	-1,434	447	-1,576	167	833	1,732

Ratio Analysis

	1994	1993	1992	1991	1990	1989
Curr. Ratio	1.4	1.8	1.4	1.9	2.3	2.9
% LT Debt of Cap.	23.5	17.2	0.8	1.9	1.8	1.6
% Net Inc.of Revs.	NM	NM	NM	NM	0.6	8.4
% Ret. on Assets	NM	NM	NM	NM	0.7	10.5
% Ret. on Equity	NM	NM	NM	NM	0.9	14.1

Dividend Data —No cash dividends have ever been paid. A "poison pill" stock purchase rights plan was adopted in 1989.

Data as orig. reptd.; bef. results of disc. opers. and/or spec. items. Per share data adj. for stk. divs. as of ex-div. date. E-Estimated. NA-Not Available. NM-Not Meaningful. NR-Not Ranked.

Office—111 Powdermill Rd., Maynard, MA 01754-1499. **Tel**—(508) 493-5111. **Chrmn, Pres & CEO**—R. B. Palmer. **VP-Fin & CFO**—W. M. Steul. **VP & Treas**—I. B. Jacobs. **Investor Contact**—Bob Hult (508-493-7182). **Dirs**—V. R. Alden, P. Caldwell, C. H. Chandler, F. P. Doyle, A. de Vitry, R. R. Everett, K. F. Feldstein, T. P. Gerrity, R. B. Palmer, T. L. Phillips, D. C. Staley. **Transfer Agent & Registrar**—First Chicago Trust Co., NYC. **Incorporated** in Massachusetts in 1957. **Empl**-61,700. **S&P Analyst:** John D. Coyle, CFA

Dillard Department Stores

NYSE Symbol **DDS**
In S&P 500

11-SEP-95 | Industry: Retail Stores

Summary: This company operates over 230 department stores located primarily in the Southwest and Midwest. Members of the Dillard family control the supervoting Class B common stock.

S&P Opinion: Hold (★★★)	Recent Price • 32¾	Yield • 0.4%
	52 Wk Range • 32¾-24	12-Mo. P/E • 14.4

Quantitative Evaluations

Outlook
(1 Lowest—5 Highest)
• **2⁻**

Fair Value
• **29⅜**

Risk
• **Average**

Earn./Div. Rank
• **A+**

Technical Eval.
• **Bullish** since 5/95

Rel. Strength Rank
(1 Lowest—99 Highest)
• **70**

Insider Activity
• **Neutral**

Earnings vs. Previous Year
▲=Up ▼=Down ▶=No Change

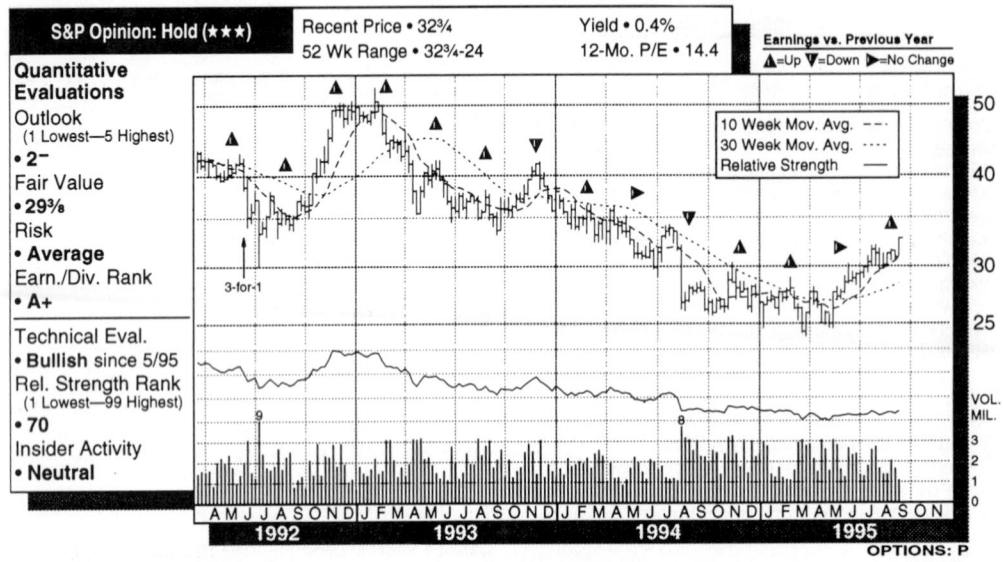

10 Week Mov. Avg. – – –
30 Week Mov. Avg. ·······
Relative Strength ——

3-for-1

VOL. MIL.

AMJJASOND JFMAMJJASOND JFMAMJJASOND JFMAMJJASON
1992   1993   1994   1995

OPTIONS: P

Overview - 08-SEP-95

Sales increases in 1995-6 should come from new and acquired stores, with a moderate 2% to 3% gain in same-store sales. Gross margins should remain about level as an increase in sales of higher-margin private label items is offset by competitive pricing. Improved inventory management should result in fewer markdowns. Expense ratios should benefit from stringent cost controls. The company has historically grown through acquisitions, and with a few regional department store chains struggling, another acquisition could be on the horizon. The company's strong balance sheet leaves ample room for further borrowing to finance the purchase of a department store chain.

Valuation - 11-SEP-95

The share price perked up in recent months from its downtrend that began in 1993. Weak earnings gains have reflected stronger competition from other chains and slower square footage increases. Certain companies, such as Sears and JCPenney, have expanded their offerings of value-priced merchandise. The absence of acquisitions in the past two and a half years has slowed square footage growth. The company, with its strong MIS capabilities, squeezes excess costs from an acquired department store chain immediately. Acquisitions become additive to earnings in the first year they are acquired. Although sales gains should be only moderate in 1995, earnings should increase, and the possibility of an acquisition suggests that the shares be held.

Key Stock Statistics

S&P EPS Est. 1996	2.45	Tang. Bk. Value/Share	20.95
P/E on S&P Est. 1996	13.4	Beta	0.71
S&P EPS Est. 1997	2.70	Shareholders	6,900
Dividend Rate/Share	0.12	Market cap. (B)	$ 3.7
Shs. outstg. (M)	113.0	Inst. holdings	80%
Avg. daily vol. (M)	0.310	Insider holdings	NA

Value of $10,000 invested 5 years ago: $ 14,042

Fiscal Year Ending Jan. 31

	1996	% Change	1995	% Change	1994	% Change
Revenues (Million $)						
1Q	1,327	3%	1,284	10%	1,163	12%
2Q	1,310	11%	1,184	7%	1,105	13%
3Q	—	—	1,334	9%	1,228	5%
4Q	—	—	1,744	7%	1,635	6%
Yr.	—	—	5,546	8%	5,131	9%
Income (Million $)						
1Q	48.38	NM	48.30	NM	48.17	7%
2Q	38.60	14%	33.76	-14%	39.24	8%
3Q	—	—	50.80	20%	42.38	-5%
4Q	—	—	118.9	7%	111.3	NM
Yr.	—	—	251.8	4%	241.1	2%
Earnings Per Share ($)						
1Q	0.43	NM	0.43	NM	0.43	7%
2Q	0.34	13%	0.30	-14%	0.35	6%
3Q	E0.48	7%	0.45	18%	0.38	-5%
4Q	E1.20	14%	1.05	6%	0.99	1%
Yr.	E2.45	10%	2.23	4%	2.14	1%

Next earnings report expected: early November

Dillard Department Stores

Business Summary - 11-SEP-95

At the end of 1994-5, Dillard was operating 229 conventional department stores, ranging in size from 30,000 to 370,000 sq. ft. Most were located in suburban shopping centers in 21 states in the Southwest, Midwest and West. The heaviest concentrations of stores were in Texas, Florida, Louisiana, Missouri, Oklahoma, Ohio, North Carolina and Arizona.

Much of Dillard's growth has been through acquisitions. Its strategy is to enter or further penetrate markets where it can become the dominant conventional department store operator. Over the past 10 years, the company has more than tripled its store base, with much of the growth coming from acquisitions. Stores with low occupancy costs, where there is an opportunity to generate higher profits on lower volumes, have been emphasized. The company also acquires stores that are successful, but not dominant in their markets, and expands their operations to establish a dominant position. In 1994-5, the company's efforts were concentrated on updating and expanding existing businesses. Square footage totaled 35.3 million feet at the end of 1994-5, up 6.5% from a year earlier. Some 65% of the stores are owned rather than leased.

The stores feature brand name goods, in the middle to upper-middle price range. Prices are based on an everyday low price strategy that replaces storewide sales events. Sales per square foot in 1994-5 amounted to $157, up from $147 in 1993-4.

Important Developments

Aug. '95—Same-store sales for the month ended August 26, 1995, rose 2%; overall sales increased 5%. Same-store sales rose 4% in the second quarter of 1995-6. Gross margins narrowed but expenses remained constant at 26.16% of net sales. Merchandise inventories were 7% higher than a year ago, reflecting seven new stores in 1994 and four in the first half of 1995-6; on a comparable-store basis, inventories were up 2%. On June 1, 1995, the company issued $100 million of 6.875% notes due 2005; proceeds were used to reduce short-term debt. In 1995, the company plans to build 11 stores, of which two will be replacement stores, and to remodel and expand eight additional stores.

Capitalization

Long Term Debt: $1,174,966,000 (7/95), incl. some $21 million of capital lease obligs.

$5 Cum. Preferred Stock: 4,400 shs. ($100 par).

Class A Common Stock: 109,028,595 shs. (no par). Institutions own 82%

Class B Common Stock: 4,017,061 shs. (no par). W.D. Co. (controlled by Dillard family) owns 99%. Elects two-thirds of directors.

Per Share Data ($)

(Year Ended Jan. 31)

	1995	1994	1993	1992	1991	1990
Tangible Bk. Val.	20.55	18.42	16.28	14.19	12.31	10.23
Cash Flow	3.91	3.65	3.31	2.85	2.57	2.29
Earnings	2.23	2.14	2.11	1.84	1.67	1.45
Dividends	0.12	0.08	0.08	0.07	0.07	0.06
Payout Ratio	5%	4%	4%	4%	4%	4%
Cal. Yrs.	1994	1993	1992	1991	1990	1989
Prices - High	37⅝	52⅞	51½	45⅝	32	24¾
- Low	25½	33⅛	30	27½	20⅝	13¾
P/E Ratio - High	17	25	24	25	19	17
- Low	11	15	14	15	12	9

Income Statement Analysis (Million $)

	1995	%Chg	1994	%Chg	1993	%Chg	1992
Revs.	5,729	8%	5,312	9%	4,883	17%	4,184
Oper. Inc.	721	3%	702	11%	633	16%	544
Depr.	190	11%	171	26%	136	20%	113
Int. Exp.	124	-5%	131	7%	122	8%	113
Pretax Inc.	406	2%	400	7%	375	16%	322
Eff. Tax Rate	38%	—	40%	—	37%	—	36%
Net Inc.	252	5%	241	2%	236	15%	206

Balance Sheet & Other Fin. Data (Million $)

	1995	1994	1993	1992	1991	1990
Cash	51.1	51.2	92.6	41.6	38.2	54.1
Curr. Assets	2,525	2,457	2,367	2,089	1,855	1,526
Total Assets	4,578	4,430	4,107	3,499	3,008	2,496
Curr. Liab.	759	796	690	737	663	533
LT Debt	1,201	1,270	1,414	1,038	871	772
Common Eqty.	2,323	2,081	1,832	1,583	1,364	1,094
Total Cap.	3,819	3,634	3,418	2,761	2,345	1,963
Cap. Exp.	253	317	344	288	292	207
Cash Flow	442	412	372	319	281	234

Ratio Analysis

	1995	1994	1993	1992	1991	1990
Curr. Ratio	3.3	3.1	3.4	2.8	2.8	2.9
% LT Debt of Cap.	31.4	34.9	41.4	37.6	37.1	39.4
% Net Inc.of Revs.	4.4	4.5	4.8	4.9	4.9	4.7
% Ret. on Assets	5.6	5.6	6.2	6.3	6.5	6.2
% Ret. on Equity	11.4	12.3	13.8	13.9	14.6	15.4

Dividend Data —Dividends have been paid since 1969.

Amt. of Div. $	Date Decl.	Ex-Div. Date	Stock of Record	Payment Date
0.030	Sep. 12	Sep. 26	Sep. 30	Oct. 31 '94
0.030	Nov. 30	Dec. 23	Dec. 31	Feb. 01 '95
0.030	Mar. 21	Mar. 27	Mar. 31	May. 01 '95
0.030	Jun. 19	Jun. 28	Jun. 30	Aug. 01 '95
0.030	Aug. 16	Sep. 27	Sep. 30	Nov. 01 '95

Data as orig. reptd.; bef. results of disc. opers. and/or spec. items. Per share data adj. for stk. divs. as of ex-div. date. E-Estimated. NA-Not Available. NM-Not Meaningful. NR-Not Ranked.

Office—1600 Cantrell Rd. (P.O. Box 486), Little Rock, AR 72203. **Tel**—(501) 376-5200. **Chrmn & CEO**—W. Dillard. **Vice Chrmn**—E. R. Kemp. **Pres & COO**—W. Dillard II. **VP, CFO & Investor Contact**—James I. Freeman. **Dirs**—C. N. Clyde, Jr., R. C. Connor, D. Corbusier, W. D. Davis, A. Dillard, M. Dillard, W. Dillard, W. Dillard II, J. I. Freeman, J. P. Hammerschmidt, W. B. Harrison, Jr., J. M. Hessels, J. H. Johnson, E. R. Kemp, W. Sutton. **Transfer Agent & Registrar**—Boatmen's Trust Co., St. Louis. **Incorporated** in Delaware in 1964. **Empl**-37,832. **S&P Analyst:** Karen J. Sack, CFA

Disney (Walt)

NYSE Symbol **DIS**
In S&P 500

02-AUG-95

Industry:
Leisure/Amusement

Summary: The businesses of this diverse company include filmed entertainment, theme parks, and consumer products.

S&P Opinion: Hold (★★★)

| Recent Price • 57⅜ | Yield • 0.6% |
| 52 Wk Range • 60-37¾ | 12-Mo. P/E • 22.7 |

Quantitative Evaluations

Outlook
(1 Lowest—5 Highest)
• **2**

Fair Value
• **51⅝**

Risk
• **Low**

Earn./Div. Rank
• **A**

Technical Eval.
• **Bearish** since 6/95

Rel. Strength Rank
(1 Lowest—99 Highest)
• **51**

Insider Activity
• **Neutral**

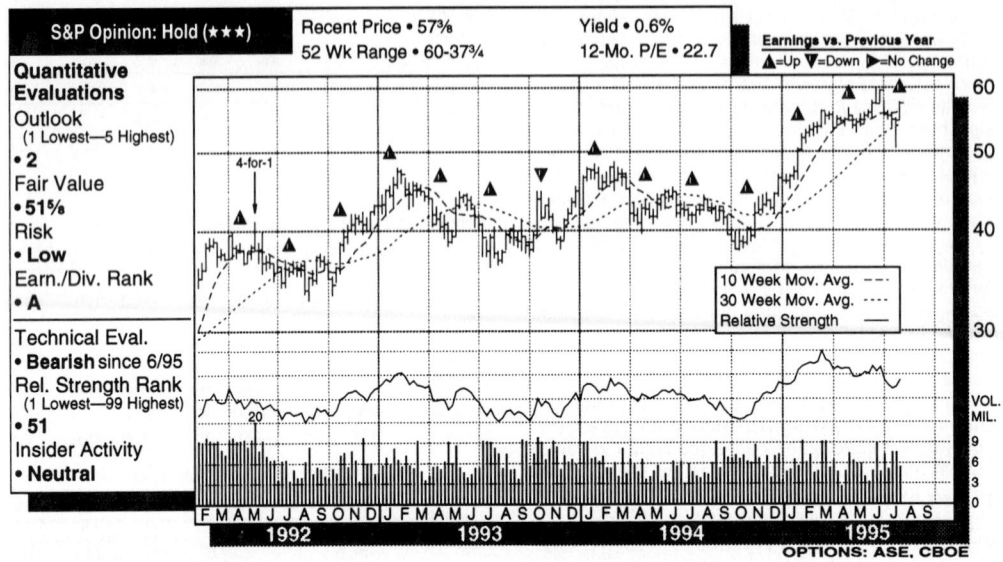

Earnings vs. Previous Year
▲=Up ▼=Down ▶=No Change

10 Week Mov. Avg. ― ― ―
30 Week Mov. Avg. ･ ･ ･ ･ ･
Relative Strength ―――

OPTIONS: ASE, CBOE

Overview - 02-AUG-95

We expect DIS to acquire broadcast company Capital Cities/ABC in the first half of 1996. On a pro forma basis, we look for the acquisition to dilute DIS's reported earnings per share in fiscal 1996 by about $0.40, principally due to non-cash goodwill expense. If this goodwill cost is excluded, we expect the acquisition will add to profits, leading to adjusted per share earnings of about $3.25. In fiscal 1996, we expect profits to be helped by the video releases of "Cinderella," and "The Santa Clause," Disney's current theatrical hit "Pocahontas," plus relatively strong advertising demand for the ABC television network.

Valuation - 02-AUG-95

We expect the stock price of this premier entertainment company to receive further support from the pending acquisition of Capital Cities/ABC (CCB). However, we view the shares as adequately valued at 19x our adjusted per share earnings estimate for fiscal 1996. Disney's stock has already risen sharply in 1995, helped by improved earnings and the strong response to the release of the "The Lion King" video. With its strong franchise in family entertainment, Disney is well situated for the multi-media age ahead. However, after recent problems related to theme park development, we remain somewhat concerned about Disney's long-term ability to meet investors' expectations of earnings growth.

Key Stock Statistics

S&P EPS Est. 1995	2.65	Tang. Bk. Value/Share	11.62
P/E on S&P Est. 1995	21.7	Beta	1.23
S&P EPS Est. 1996	2.65	Shareholders	3,100
Dividend Rate/Share	0.36	Market cap. (B)	$ 32.0
Shs. outstg. (M)	520.8	Inst. holdings	51%
Avg. daily vol. (M)	1.240	Insider holdings	NA

Value of $10,000 invested 5 years ago: $ 21,162

Fiscal Year Ending Sep. 30

	1995	% Change	1994	% Change	1993	% Change
Revenues (Million $)						
1Q	3,302	21%	2,727	14%	2,391	25%
2Q	2,923	28%	2,276	12%	2,026	24%
3Q	2,764	17%	2,354	22%	1,937	3%
4Q	—	—	2,698	24%	2,175	5%
Yr.	—	—	10,055	18%	8,529	14%
Income (Million $)						
1Q	482.4	31%	368.6	42%	260.3	25%
2Q	315.5	27%	248.4	21%	204.9	25%
3Q	318.2	19%	267.5	3%	259.1	17%
4Q	—	—	225.9	NM	-77.78	NM
Yr.	—	—	1,110	65%	671.3	-18%
Earnings Per Share ($)						
1Q	0.91	34%	0.68	36%	0.50	28%
2Q	0.60	33%	0.45	15%	0.39	26%
3Q	0.60	22%	0.49	2%	0.48	17%
4Q	E0.54	—	0.42	NM	-0.15	NM
Yr.	E2.65	—	2.04	66%	1.23	-19%

Next earnings report expected: late October

Business Summary - 02-AUG-95

Walt Disney Co. (formerly Walt Disney Productions) is engaged in the ownership and operation of theme parks and related businesses, and is a major supplier of filmed entertainment. Business segment contributions in fiscal 1994 (excluding an adverse impact from the Euro Disney project, of which DIS now owns approximately 39%) were:

	Revs.	Profits
Theme parks/resorts	34%	35%
Filmed entertainment	48%	44%
Consumer products	18%	22%

Theme parks/resorts include Disneyland in Anaheim, Calif., and the Orlando, Fla.-based Walt Disney World Complex, which contains the Magic Kingdom and resort hotels, Walt Disney Village, Epcot (Environmental Prototype Community of Tomorrow) Center and the Disney-MGM Studio Theme Park (opened to the public in May 1989). In April 1992, the Euro Disney theme park complex (originally 49% owned) opened near Paris, France. Euro Disney has been losing money, and a financial restructuring plan was implemented in 1994. Tokyo Disneyland, which has been open since April 1983, is owned and operated by Oriental Land Co., Ltd., pursuant to a licensing agreement with the company. DIS also earns royalties on certain revenues generated by the Tokyo park.

Filmed entertainment consists of the production and distribution of motion pictures for the theatrical, television, cable and home video markets. Movie financing has come, in part, from limited partnerships. The company also creates TV programming, owns a pay cable TV service called The Disney Channel, and owns a Los Angeles television station. Consumer products include licensing of products, a growing chain of retail stores, and publishing activity.

Important Developments

Jul. '95—DIS agreed to acquire Capital Cities/ABC (CCB) in a cash-and-stock transaction valued at about $19 billion. Shareholders of CCB, which has various broadcasting and publishing interests, will have the right to receive $65 in cash and one common share of Disney for each CCB share held. The transaction may be completed in the first half of 1996. Meanwhile in fiscal 1995's third quarter, profit from DIS's theme park segment was up, 27%, year to year. This excludes the direct impact of DIS's Euro Disney investment, from which there was a loss of $14.4 million (down from a year-ago $52.8 million). Also, consumer product earnings rose 23%, while filmed entertainment was down 8%. Earlier, in June, DIS announced plans to open a new theme park, called Disney's Wild Animal Kingdom, in the spring of 1998 at Walt Disney World Resort in Florida.

Capitalization

Total Debt: $3,665,400,000 (12/94).

Per Share Data ($)

(Year Ended Sep. 30)

	1994	1993	1992	1991	1990	1989
Tangible Bk. Val.	9.92	8.68	8.24	6.80	5.96	4.95
Cash Flow	4.99	3.12	2.94	2.69	2.48	2.12
Earnings	2.04	1.23	1.52	1.20	1.50	1.28
Dividends	0.28	0.23	0.19	0.16	0.13	0.11
Payout Ratio	13%	19%	13%	13%	8%	8%
Prices - High	48⅝	48¾	45¼	32½	34⅛	34⅛
- Low	37¾	36	28½	23⅜	21½	16¼
P/E Ratio - High	24	40	39	27	23	27
- Low	19	29	19	20	14	13

Income Statement Analysis (Million $)

	1994	%Chg	1993	%Chg	1992	%Chg	1991
Revs.	10,055	18%	8,529	14%	7,504	21%	6,182
Oper. Inc.	3,412	32%	2,589	26%	2,047	14%	1,799
Depr.	1,608	56%	1,028	35%	760	-4%	795
Int. Exp.	172	-7%	184	21%	152	7%	142
Pretax Inc.	1,703	59%	1,074	-18%	1,302	28%	1,019
Eff. Tax Rate	35%	—	38%	—	37%	—	38%
Net Inc.	1,110	65%	671	-18%	817	28%	637

Balance Sheet & Other Fin. Data (Million $)

	1994	1993	1992	1991	1990	1989
Cash	187	363	765	886	820	381
Curr. Assets	NA	NA	NA	NA	NA	NA
Total Assets	12,826	11,751	10,862	9,429	8,022	6,657
Curr. Liab.	NA	NA	NA	NA	NA	NA
LT Debt	2,107	1,131	1,608	1,818	1,330	375
Common Eqty.	5,508	5,030	4,705	3,871	3,489	3,044
Total Cap.	8,554	6,834	7,201	6,443	5,822	4,482
Cap. Exp.	1,026	814	599	954	727	785
Cash Flow	2,719	1,700	1,576	1,431	1,362	1,167

Ratio Analysis

	1994	1993	1992	1991	1990	1989
Curr. Ratio	NA	NA	NA	NA	NA	NA
% LT Debt of Cap.	24.6	16.5	22.3	28.2	27.2	19.2
% Net Inc.of Revs.	11.0	7.9	10.9	10.3	14.1	15.3
% Ret. on Assets	9.1	5.9	8.0	7.3	11.4	11.9
% Ret. on Equity	21.3	13.7	19.0	17.4	25.5	25.9

Dividend Data (Dividends have been paid since 1957.)

Amt. of Div. $	Date Decl.	Ex-Div. Date	Stock of Record	Payment Date
0.075	Sep. 26	Oct. 07	Oct. 14	Nov. 18 '94
0.075	Nov. 21	Jan. 03	Jan. 09	Feb. 17 '95
0.090	Jan. 23	Apr. 07	Apr. 14	May. 19 '95
0.090	Jun. 26	Jul. 06	Jul. 10	Aug. 18 '95

Data as orig. reptd.; bef. results of disc. opers. and/or spec. items. Per share data adj. for stk. divs. as of ex-div. date. FY 1993 results incl. large non-recurring charge related to Euro Disney investment. E-Estimated. NA-Not Available. NM-Not Meaningful. NR-Not Ranked.

Office—500 South Buena Vista St., Burbank, CA 91521. Tel—(818) 560-1000. Chrmn, Pres & CEO—M. D. Eisner. EVP & CFO—S. F. Bollenbach. Investor Contact—W. M. Webb. Dirs—S. F. Bollenbach, R. F. Bowers, R. E. Disney, M. D. Eisner, S. P. Gold, S. M. Litvack, I. E. Lozano, Jr., G. J. Mitchell, R. A. Nunis, I. E. Russell, R. A. M. Stern, E. C. Walker, R. L. Watson, G. L. Wilson. Transfer Agent & Registrar—Co.'s office, North Hollywood, Cal. Incorporated in California in 1938; reincorporated in Delaware in 1987. Empl-65,000. S&P Analyst: Tom Graves, CFA

Dominion Resources

STOCK REPORTS

NYSE Symbol **D**
In S&P 500

31-AUG-95

Industry:
Utilities-Electric

Summary: Dominion Resources is a utility holding company whose main unit, Virginia Electric & Power Co., provides electric service in Virginia and, to a lesser extent, in North Carolina.

S&P Opinion: Hold (★★★)	Recent Price • 37	Yield • 7.1%
	52 Wk Range • 39¼-34⅞	12-Mo. P/E • 16.4

Quantitative Evaluations

Outlook
(1 Lowest—5 Highest)
• **1**⁻

Fair Value
• **32¾**

Risk
• **Low**

Earn./Div. Rank
• **A-**

Technical Eval.
• **Bearish** since 6/95

Rel. Strength Rank
(1 Lowest—99 Highest)
• **34**

Insider Activity
• **Neutral**

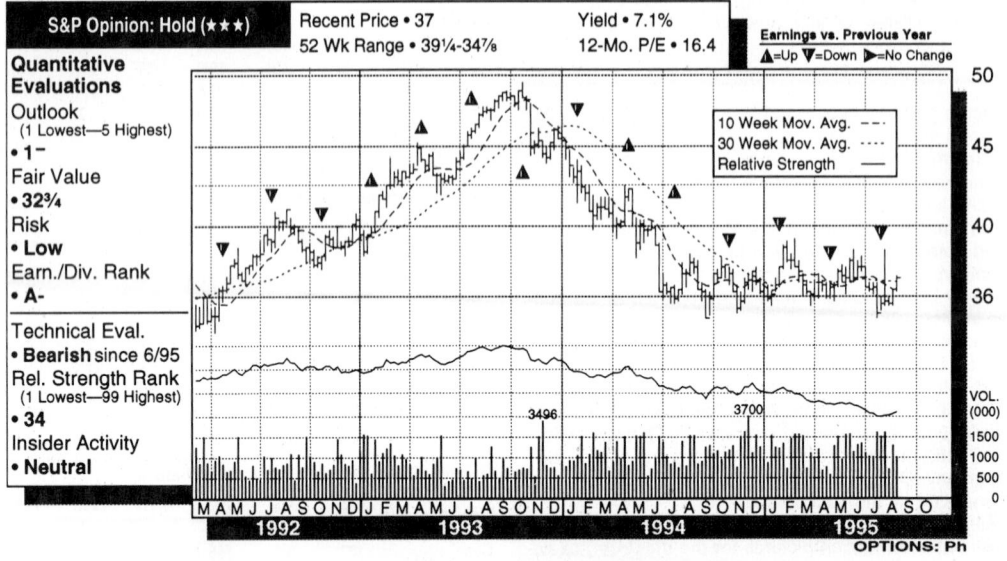

Earnings vs. Previous Year
▲=Up ▼=Down ▶=No Change

10 Week Mov. Avg. ‑ ‑ ‑
30 Week Mov. Avg. ....
Relative Strength ——

3496   3700

VOL. (000)

OPTIONS: Ph

Overview - 28-AUG-95

Efforts to control both operating costs and capital outlays have helped Virginia Power reduce generation costs. D expects its voluntary separation and early retirement programs in 1994 to yield savings of nearly $190 million through the end of the century. To increase competitiveness, it has proposed lower pricing for its large industrial customers, which will likely be supported by slightly higher electricity sales, and a full year of cost savings from workforce reductions. Lower gas sales and prices could impede progress from non-utility operations. While we expect only modest earnings comparisons this year in the absence of one-time gains from the sale of Black Warrior Trust units, longer-term, the outlook is favorable due to economic strength in the company's service territory, Dominion's strong cash flow, and projected profit contributions from new non-regulated businesses.

Valuation - 28-AUG-95

D's share price fell more steeply than most of its peers in 1993 and 1994, as falling gas prices exacerbated fears over growing industry competition. Weak earnings growth has limited D's rebound this year, but, longer term, we believe its relatively small industrial customer base should help shield it from a severe competitive threat. The dividend payout is above the industry average and we see only a modest increase this year. However, ongoing cost cutting should help raise earnings and market performance in coming periods.

Key Stock Statistics

S&P EPS Est. 1995	2.92	Tang. Bk. Value/Share	26.51
P/E on S&P Est. 1995	12.7	Beta	0.22
S&P EPS Est. 1996	3.00	Shareholders	235,000
Dividend Rate/Share	2.58	Market cap. (B)	$ 6.3
Shs. outstg. (M)	173.5	Inst. holdings	39%
Avg. daily vol. (M)	0.355	Insider holdings	NA

Value of $10,000 invested 5 years ago: $ 16,742

Fiscal Year Ending Dec. 31

	1995	% Change	1994	% Change	1993	% Change
Revenues (Million $)						
1Q	1,129	-3%	1,167	6%	1,106	17%
2Q	1,043	-6%	1,110	10%	1,005	15%
3Q	—	—	1,210	-6%	1,287	19%
4Q	—	—	1,005	-3%	1,036	16%
Yr.	—	—	4,491	1%	4,434	17%
Income (Million $)						
1Q	108.5	-23%	141.4	15%	122.5	30%
2Q	78.10	-43%	136.2	32%	103.1	68%
3Q	—	—	161.3	-19%	199.0	33%
4Q	—	—	39.30	-57%	92.00	-26%
Yr.	—	—	478.2	-7%	516.6	20%
Earnings Per Share ($)						
1Q	0.63	-25%	0.84	14%	0.74	25%
2Q	0.45	-44%	0.80	27%	0.63	66%
3Q	E1.09	16%	0.94	-22%	1.20	30%
4Q	E0.75	NM	0.23	-58%	0.55	-29%
Yr.	E2.92	4%	2.81	-10%	3.12	17%

Next earnings report expected: late October

Business Summary - 31-AUG-95

Dominion Resources is a utility holding company whose main subsidiary, Virginia Electric & Power Co., provides electric service in Virginia and to a lesser extent in North Carolina. The company's Virginia and North Carolina service territory, characterized by government installations, high-technology centers and financial services businesses, has one of the strongest economies in the nation. Electric revenues by customer class in recent years were:

	1994	1993	1992	1991
Residential	44%	43%	42%	43%
Commercial	27%	28%	29%	29%
Industrial	11%	11%	11%	11%
Other	18%	18%	18%	17%

Sources of electric generation in 1994 were 36% coal, 34% nuclear, 26% purchased and interchanged, and 4% oil, gas and other. Peak demand in 1994 was 14,877 mw and capability at peak totaled 16,659 mw for a capacity margin of 20%. Dominion purchases power from cogenerators and independent power producers. It plans to meet future load through the construction of generating units and additional purchases from nonutility generators. The company may need new peaking power generation by 2000, but it does not expect to require new base load generation until the middle of the next decade.

Through three non-utility subsidiaries, the company is also involved in the development of non-utility power projects, the acquisition and development of natural gas reserves, residential real estate development, and investment management. In 1994, non-utility operations accounted for 7.1% of revenues and 6.5% of net income.

Important Developments

Aug. '95—D attributed the decline in earnings in the 1995 first half to $1.08 a share from $1.64 a year earlier to lower retail sales. Some $0.29 a share of the reduction was from abnormally mild weather, particularly in the first quarter; the remainder was due to lower income from Dominion Capital's hydroeletric facility, and lower gas prices. Contributing factors also included the loss of income from oil and gas properties in the Black Warrier Trust, which was sold in 1994. Separately, D announced a reorganization of its units and employee cutbacks to reduce costs. In May, the Virginia State Corporation Commission ordered Virginia Power to refund a disputed $8.3 million in excess fuel costs costs borne by ratepayers as a result of a coal hauling contract with CSX Corp., and to renegotiate its contract with CSX and pursue other alternatives to reduce coal transportation charges.

Capitalization

Long Term Debt: $4,780,100,000 (6/95).
Subsid. Red. Preferred Stock: $221,100,000.
Subsid. Preferred Stock: $594,000,000.

Per Share Data ($)

(Year Ended Dec. 31)

	1994	1993	1992	1991	1990	1989
Tangible Bk. Val.	26.51	26.38	25.21	24.41	23.41	22.67
Earnings	2.81	3.12	2.66	2.94	2.92	2.76
Dividends	2.55	2.48	2.40	2.31	2.23	2.15
Payout Ratio	91%	79%	92%	79%	78%	79%
Prices - High	45⅜	49½	41	38⅛	32⅝	32
- Low	34⅞	38¼	34⅛	29⅞	27⅝	27
P/E Ratio - High	16	16	15	13	11	12
- Low	12	12	13	10	9	10

Income Statement Analysis (Million $)

	1994	%Chg	1993	%Chg	1992	%Chg	1991
Revs.	4,491	1%	4,434	17%	3,791	NM	3,786
Depr.	533	5%	510	13%	450	NM	450
Maint.	263	-6%	279	NM	281	-8%	305
Fxd. Chgs. Cov.	2.6	-5%	2.8	8%	2.5	4%	2.4
Constr. Credits	6.4	25%	5.1	-46%	9.5	-19%	11.8
Eff. Tax Rate	26%	—	29%	—	32%	—	31%
Net Inc.	478	-14%	559	18%	475	-7%	511

Balance Sheet & Other Fin. Data (Million $)

	1994	1993	1992	1991	1990	1989
Gross Prop.	15,415	15,009	14,147	13,388	12,684	12,148
Cap. Exp.	721	1,127	941	815	827	938
Net Prop.	10,245	10,207	9,687	9,278	8,959	8,733
Capitalization:						
LT Debt	4,711	4,751	4,404	4,393	4,396	4,547
% LT Debt	47	48	47	49	50	52
Pfd.	816	829	829	735	758	782
% Pfd.	8.10	8.20	8.90	8.20	8.60	9.00
Common	4,586	4,436	4,131	3,878	3,624	3,421
% Common	45	44	44	43	41	39
Total Cap.	12,016	11,897	11,173	10,237	10,013	10,023

Ratio Analysis

	1994	1993	1992	1991	1990	1989
Oper. Ratio	76.9	79.3	78.2	76.6	75.8	77.1
% Earn. on Net Prop.	10.2	9.2	8.8	9.7	9.7	9.9
% Ret. on Revs.	10.6	12.6	12.5	13.5	14.3	12.7
% Ret. On Invest.Cap	8.8	9.9	9.8	11.2	11.3	10.8
% Return On Com.Eqty	10.6	11.9	10.5	12.1	12.5	12.2

Dividend Data

Dividends have been paid since 1925. A dividend reinvestment plan is available.

Amt. of Div. $	Date Decl.	Ex-Div. Date	Stock of Record	Payment Date
0.635	Jul. 15	Aug. 24	Aug. 30	Sep. 20 '94
0.645	Oct. 24	Nov. 23	Dec. 01	Dec. 20 '94
0.645	Feb. 17	Feb. 24	Mar. 02	Mar. 20 '95
0.645	Apr. 21	May. 25	Jun. 01	Jun. 20 '95
0.645	Jul. 21	Aug. 29	Aug. 31	Sep. 20 '95

Data as orig. reptd.; bef. results of disc opers. and/or spec. items. Per share data adj. for stk. divs. as of ex-div. date. E-Estimated. NA-Not Available. NM-Not Meaningful. NR-Not Ranked.

Office—901 East Byrd St. (P.O. Box 26532), Richmond, VA 23261-6532. **Tel**—(804) 775-5700. **Chrmn & CEO**—T. E. Capps. **Pres & COO**—T. L. Baucom. **VP & Treas**—L. R. Robertson. **VP & Secy**—J. K. Davis, Jr. **Investor Contact**—William C. Hall, Jr. (804-775-5813). **Dirs**—J. B. Adams, Jr., T. L. Baucom, J. B. Bernhardt, W. W. Berry, T. E. Capps, B. C. Gottwald, J. W. Harris, B. J. Lambert III, R. L. Leatherwood, H. L. Lindsay, Jr., K. A. Randall, W. T. Roos, F. S. Royal, J. B. Sack, R. L. Sharp, S. D. Simmons, J. W. Snow, R. H. Spilman, W. G. Thomas, D. A. Wollard **Transfer Agent & Registrar**—Mellon Security Transfer Services, Ridgefield, NJ. **Incorporated** in Virginia in 1909. **Empl**-10,789. **S&P Analyst:** Jane Collin

Donnelley (R.R.)

NYSE Symbol **DNY**
In S&P 500

01-AUG-95

Industry:
Graphic Arts

Summary: The largest commercial printer in the U.S., this company specializes in the production of catalogs, inserts, magazines, books, directories, financial and computer documentation.

S&P Opinion: Accumulate (★★★★)

Recent Price • 37⅝	Yield • 1.9%
52 Wk Range • 38¾-27⅞	12-Mo. P/E • 20.7

Quantitative Evaluations

Outlook
(1 Lowest—5 Highest)
• **2**

Fair Value
• **35⅛**

Risk
• **Low**

Earn./Div. Rank
• **A-**

Technical Eval.
• **Bullish** since 7/95

Rel. Strength Rank
(1 Lowest—99 Highest)
• **51**

Insider Activity
• **Neutral**

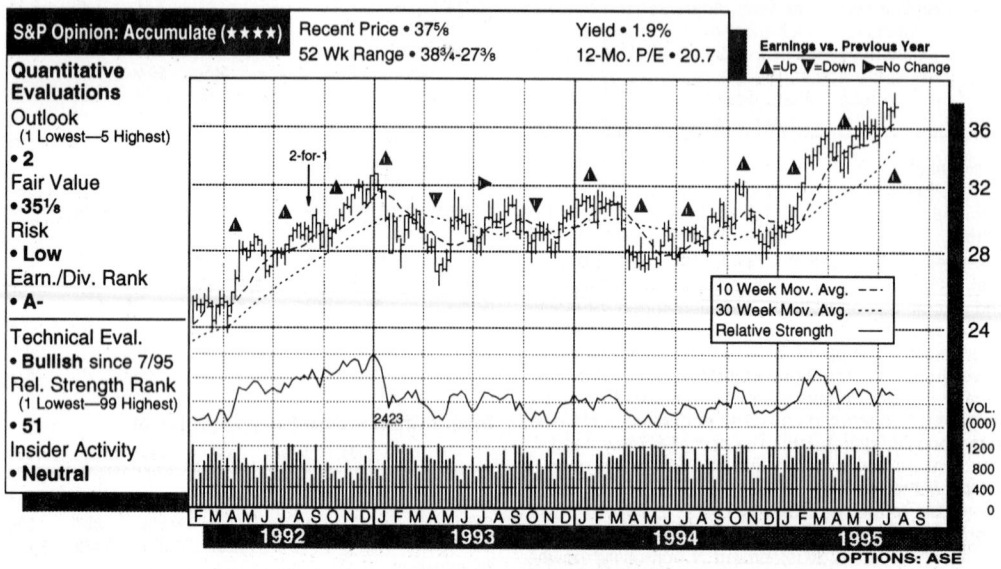

Earnings vs. Previous Year
▲=Up ▼=Down ▶=No Change

10 Week Mov. Avg. - - -
30 Week Mov. Avg. ·····
Relative Strength ——

OPTIONS: ASE

Overview - 01-AUG-95

Double-digit sales growth in 1995 and 1996 will reflect acquisitions, new business opportunities (such as formation of the new Digital division), and stronger demand from current customers. Market share will also increase, aided by business gains such as the Southwestern Bell Yellow Pages. Geographical expansion is continuing, particularly in South America, Central Europe and Asia. A strategic alliance was recently formed in India, where a fragmented $4.4 billion printing market is growing 15% annually. Comparisons will benefit from moderating LIFO charges, but startup expenses and sharply higher interest charges will limit gains in net income in 1995. A stronger EPS advance is likely in 1996, aided by a slower rise in startup and expansion costs.

Valuation - 01-AUG-95

Despite possible short-lived market setbacks over the next several years, the general outlook for the stock is good. Revenue and cash flow are in strong uptrends, although gains in net income are being restricted by heavy investment spending. DNY's business mix is growing more diversified, with heavy emphasis on new digital technologies, which provide a degree of underlying stability to operations, as well as faster growth. Aggressive expansion into fast-growing markets around the world, as well as the company's demonstrated dedication to anticipating customer needs for state-of-the-art services, also serve to bolster a favorable long-term outlook.

Key Stock Statistics

S&P EPS Est. 1995	2.00	Tang. Bk. Value/Share	7.28
P/E on S&P Est. 1995	18.8	Beta	1.15
S&P EPS Est. 1996	2.35	Shareholders	10,400
Dividend Rate/Share	0.72	Market cap. (B)	$ 5.7
Shs. outstg. (M)	153.5	Inst. holdings	73%
Avg. daily vol. (M)	0.216	Insider holdings	NA

Value of $10,000 invested 5 years ago: $ 16,384

Fiscal Year Ending Dec. 31

	1995	% Change	1994	% Change	1993	% Change
Revenues (Million $)						
1Q	1,318	23%	1,071	12%	960.0	2%
2Q	1,491	33%	1,117	12%	994.0	-1%
3Q	—	—	1,243	11%	1,124	8%
4Q	—	—	1,458	11%	1,310	8%
Yr.	—	—	4,889	11%	4,388	5%
Income (Million $)						
1Q	46.84	9%	42.80	NM	-22.11	NM
2Q	64.46	10%	58.34	11%	52.77	-2%
3Q	—	—	80.07	15%	69.45	-4%
4Q	—	—	87.40	11%	78.81	8%
Yr.	—	—	268.6	50%	178.9	-24%
Earnings Per Share ($)						
1Q	0.31	11%	0.28	NM	-0.14	NM
2Q	0.42	11%	0.38	12%	0.34	NM
3Q	E0.60	—	0.52	16%	0.45	-4%
4Q	E0.67	—	0.57	12%	0.51	9%
Yr.	E2.00	—	1.75	51%	1.16	-23%

Next earnings report expected: late October

Business Summary - 01-AUG-95

R. R. Donnelley & Sons, also known as The Lakeside Press, provides a wide range of services in print and digital media. It is the largest U.S. commercial printer, with 20% of the market. Sales by product segment in recent years were:

	1994	1993	1992	1991
Catalogs	31%	32%	35%	39%
Magazines	18%	18%	17%	17%
Directories	14%	14%	16%	16%
Books	13%	13%	11%	11%
Documentation	12%	12%	10%	8%
Financial	5%	6%	5%	4%
Other	7%	5%	65%	5%

DNY is a major supplier of print and digital media services in the U.K. and also provides services in Latin America, other locations in Europe and in Asia. International operations provided over 11% of 1994 revenues, but less than 1% of operating earnings.

The company prints catalogs, preprinted inserts, magazines, telephone directories, financial references, transportation guides and directory needs of schools and industry. DNY is a leading book printer in virtually every category. Other services include printing of financial documents and corporate literature, computer and communications services related to graphic arts and design, and cartographic services. The company has an international satellite system that lets customers transmit data electronically between New York and London and between Singapore and London.

DNY provides services to more than 5,000 customers. No single customer accounted for for than 3% of sales in 1994. The 10 largest customers accounted for 21% of sales in 1994, down from 30% in 1984.

Important Developments

Jun. '95—Tata Press Ltd., one of India's leading commercial printers, approved the company's acquisition of a 25% equity position in Tata. The strategic alliance is part of DNY's plan to raise international sales to 20% of the total by 2000, from 1994's 11%.

Apr. '95—DNY merged Global Software Services, a $650 million software manufacturing, distribution and fulfillment business, with Corporate Software's $650 million distribution and support network. Terms were not disclosed, but the company retained an 80% interest in the new entity, Stream International. Earlier, DNY acquired the manufacturing assets of Novell Inc.'s Lindon, Utah, diskette replication and assembly facility. It also agreed to print the directories of Southwestern Bell Yellow Pages, Inc. beginning in 1995. Total revenues will be about $2.5 billion over 10 years.

Capitalization

Long Term Debt: $1,327,510 (3/95).

Per Share Data ($)   (Year Ended Dec. 31)

	1994	1993	1992	1991	1990	1989
Tangible Bk. Val.	7.13	8.76	9.03	8.25	7.32	7.73
Cash Flow	3.78	2.94	3.17	2.88	2.71	2.42
Earnings	1.75	1.16	1.51	1.32	1.46	1.43
Dividends	0.60	0.54	0.51	0.50	0.48	0.44
Payout Ratio	34%	47%	34%	38%	33%	31%
Prices - High	32½	32¾	33¾	25⅝	26⅜	25⅝
- Low	26⅞	26⅛	23¾	19½	17⅛	17⅛
P/E Ratio - High	19	28	22	19	18	18
- Low	15	23	16	15	12	12

Income Statement Analysis (Million $)

	1994	%Chg	1993	%Chg	1992	%Chg	1991
Revs.	4,889	11%	4,388	5%	4,193	7%	3,915
Oper. Inc.	773	12%	690	4%	664	10%	605
Depr.	313	14%	275	7%	258	23%	210
Int. Exp.	63.7	23%	51.9	18%	43.9	-21%	55.9
Pretax Inc.	39.5	-86%	277	-23%	361	13%	320
Eff. Tax Rate	32%	—	35%	—	35%	—	36%
Net Inc.	269	50%	179	-24%	235	15%	205

Balance Sheet & Other Fin. Data (Million $)

	1994	1993	1992	1991	1990	1989
Cash	21.0	11.0	12.0	99	123	110
Curr. Assets	1,353	1,110	1,022	NA	NA	726
Total Assets	4,452	3,654	3,410	3,404	3,343	2,507
Curr. Liab.	802	685	612	727	677	412
LT Debt	1,212	673	523	528	647	63.0
Common Eqty.	1,978	1,844	1,849	1,730	1,596	1,446
Total Cap.	3,478	2,790	2,772	2,640	2,624	1,874
Cap. Exp.	425	307	228	288	425	237
Cash Flow	582	454	493	415	406	376

Ratio Analysis

	1994	1993	1992	1991	1990	1989
Curr. Ratio	1.7	1.6	1.7	NA	NA	1.8
% LT Debt of Cap.	34.9	24.1	18.8	20.0	24.7	3.3
% Net Inc.of Revs.	5.5	4.1	5.6	5.2	6.5	7.1
% Ret. on Assets	6.6	5.1	6.9	6.1	7.7	9.1
% Ret. on Equity	14.1	9.7	13.1	12.3	14.9	16.2

Dividend Data (Dividends have been paid since 1911 and increased each year since 1971. A dividend reinvestment plan is available. A poison pill stock purchase rights plan was adopted in 1986.)

Amt. of Div. $	Date Decl.	Ex-Div. Date	Stock of Record	Payment Date
0.160	Jul. 29	Aug. 08	Aug. 12	Sep. 01 '94
0.160	Oct. 27	Nov. 04	Nov. 11	Dec. 01 '94
0.160	Jan. 26	Jan. 31	Feb. 06	Mar. 01 '95
0.160	Apr. 27	May. 08	May. 12	Jun. 01 '95
0.180	Jul. 27	Aug. 09	Aug. 11	Sep. 01 '95

Data as orig. reptd.; bef. results of disc. opers. and/or spec. items. Per share data adj. for stk. divs. as of ex-div. date.
E-Estimated. NA-Not Available. NM-Not Meaningful. NR-Not Ranked.

Office—77 West Wacker Drive, Chicago, IL 60601-1696. **Tel**—(312) 326-8000. **Chrmn & CEO**—J. R. Walter. **Vice Chrmn**—J. R. Donnelley. **Secy**—Deborah M. Regan. **EVP & CFO**—F. R. Jarc (until 8/31/95). **SVP, Treas & Investor Contact**—Ronald G. Eidell (312-326-8375). **Dirs**—M. L. Collins, J. R. Donnelley, C. C. Haffner III, T. S. Johnson, R. M. Morrow, M. B. Puckett, J. M. Richman, W. D. Sanders, J. L. Stead, B. L. Thomas, J. R. Walter, H. B. White, S. M. Wolf. **Transfer Agent & Registrar**—First Chicago Trust Co. of New York, NYC. **Incorporated** in Delaware in 1956. **Empl**-41,000. **S&P Analyst:** William H. Donald

27-JUL-95 | Industry: Manufacturing/Distr

Summary: Dover makes a broad range of products, ranging from elevators to electronic circuitry assembly equipment, for the electronic, building, petroleum, aerospace and other industries.

S&P Opinion: Hold (★★★)

Recent Price • 77	Yield • 1.3%
52 Wk Range • 77⅛-49¾	12-Mo. P/E • 17.8

Earnings vs. Previous Year
▲=Up ▼=Down ▶=No Change

Quantitative Evaluations

Outlook
(1 Lowest—5 Highest)
• **3+**

Fair Value
• **76¾**

Risk
• **Low**

Earn./Div. Rank
• **A-**

Technical Eval.
• **Bullish** since 7/95

Rel. Strength Rank
(1 Lowest—99 Highest)
• **77**

Insider Activity
• **Neutral**

10 Week Mov. Avg. — - -
30 Week Mov. Avg. - - - -
Relative Strength —

VOL. (000)
600
400
200
0

F M A M J J A S O N D J F M A M J J A S O N D J F M A M J J A S O N D J F M A M J J A S
1992 1993 1994 1995

OPTIONS: ASE

Overview - 27-JUL-95

We anticipate a 25% gain in sales for 1995, reflecting a continuation of the economic recovery, the favorable impact of acquisitions and a 35% increase in incoming orders. We project gains in all segments. Increased volume, only moderate increases in raw material costs, reorganization of Dover Elevator's North American operations and the absence of writeoffs and unusual expenses in the elevator segment should boost margins and operating income. Assuming an unchanged tax rate, earnings should increase again in 1995. Continued acquisitions, market share improvement of existing businesses, new products and greater emphasis on overseas sales in the elevator segment will boost long term sales and earnings growth.

Valuation - 27-JUL-95

Although we are very positive on Dover long term we are maintaining our hold recommendation on shares near term because we don't believe the upside potential from current levels justifies an accumulate or buy recommendation. Through late July the stock has risen a breathtaking 51% since 1994's year end, more than double the gain in the S&P 500. While the shares are not excessively valued on 1995's earnings, we prefer to stay on the sidelines for now. Based on the company's strong management and excellent financial results over the years, current owners should continue to hold for long-term gains.

Key Stock Statistics

S&P EPS Est. 1995	4.95	Tang. Bk. Value/Share	7.42
P/E on S&P Est. 1995	15.6	Beta	1.14
S&P EPS Est. 1996	5.30	Shareholders	10,000
Dividend Rate/Share	1.04	Market cap. (B)	$ 4.4
Shs. outstg. (M)	56.7	Inst. holdings	65%
Avg. daily vol. (M)	0.089	Insider holdings	NA

Value of $10,000 invested 5 years ago: $ 23,572

Fiscal Year Ending Dec. 31

	1995	% Change	1994	% Change	1993	% Change
Revenues (Million $)						
1Q	854.1	25%	680.7	20%	567.0	4%
2Q	948.2	25%	761.2	28%	594.5	4%
3Q	—	—	804.5	25%	642.2	13%
4Q	—	—	838.9	23%	680.5	17%
Yr.	—	—	3,085	24%	2,484	9%
Income (Million $)						
1Q	59.80	40%	42.57	26%	33.76	12%
2Q	78.89	50%	52.44	32%	39.76	27%
3Q	—	—	51.87	22%	42.36	26%
4Q	—	—	55.49	31%	42.37	25%
Yr.	—	—	202.4	28%	158.3	23%
Earnings Per Share ($)						
1Q	1.06	43%	0.74	25%	0.59	16%
2Q	1.39	51%	0.92	31%	0.70	30%
3Q	E1.20	—	0.91	23%	0.74	28%
4Q	E1.30	—	0.97	31%	0.74	23%
Yr.	E4.95	—	3.54	28%	2.77	24%

Next earnings report expected: mid October

Business Summary - 24-JUL-95

Dover manufactures a variety of specialized industrial products that are marketed to the building, petroleum, electronics, aerospace and other industries. Segment contributions in 1994:

	Sales	Profits
Dover Elevator Int'l	26%	13%
Dover Technologies	20%	21%
Dover Resources	17%	24%
Dover Industries	22%	23%
Dover Diversified	15%	19%

Foreign business accounted for 17% of sales and 13% of operating profit in 1994.

Dover Elevator International makes geared and gearless traction elevators, hydraulic elevators and replacement parts, and provides installation and repair services.

Dover Technologies makes electronic circuitry assembly equipment, automated soldering and board handling equipment, and microwave and R.F. filters.

Dover Resources makes pumps for the delivery of fuel oil, equipment for natural gas compressors, sucker rods, pumps, valves and fittings, gasoline nozzles and fittings, and liquid filtration systems.

Dover Industries makes automotive lifts, food preparation equipment, solid waste compaction equipment, and auto collision measuring and repair systems.

Dover Diversified makes plate/frame heat exchangers, industrial/marine fluid film bearings, and electromechanical actuators.

Important Developments

Jul. '95— DOV reported share earnings of $1.39 for 1995's second quarter on a 25% year-to-year increase in sales versus earnings of $0.92 a year earlier. All five segments recorded sales and earnings gains for the quarter; all but the elevator unit recorded higher earnings for 1995's first half. Dover stated that it expected 1995's second quarter to be the highest quarterly earnings for 1995. The company added that earnings for 1995's second half would exceed 1994's second half but would decline from 1995's second quarter rate due to the current economic slowdown in the U. S., the $20 million reduction in the backlog at Universal Instruments and dilution from acquisitions completed in the second quarter and possible acquisitions in the second half. Dover completed acquisitions totaling $99 million in 1995's first half, with $83 million occurring in the second quarter. Dover said that it would achieve continued earnings growth in 1996 assuming forecasts for a soft landing for the U. S. economy proved to be accurate.

Capitalization

Long Term Debt: $253,345,000 (3/95).

Per Share Data ($) (Year Ended Dec. 31)

	1994	1993	1992	1991	1990	1989
Tangible Bk. Val.	7.42	5.68	7.81	8.96	7.37	7.51
Cash Flow	5.21	4.12	3.56	3.57	3.81	3.52
Earnings	3.54	2.77	2.23	2.15	2.55	2.28
Dividends	0.98	0.90	0.86	0.82	0.76	0.70
Payout Ratio	28%	32%	38%	38%	29%	30%
Prices - High	66⅞	61⅞	47⅝	43¾	41¼	39½
- Low	49¾	45	38¼	34½	27½	27¼
P/E Ratio - High	19	22	21	20	16	17
- Low	14	16	17	16	11	12

Income Statement Analysis (Million $)

	1994	%Chg	1993	%Chg	1992	%Chg	1991
Revs.	3,085	24%	2,484	9%	2,272	3%	2,196
Oper. Inc.	421	27%	331	18%	281	13%	249
Depr.	95.8	24%	77.0	NM	77.5	-9%	85.4
Int. Exp.	36.5	64%	22.3	11%	20.1	-13%	23.2
Pretax Inc.	307	25%	246	23%	200	-2%	204
Eff. Tax Rate	34%	—	36%	—	36%	—	37%
Net Inc.	202	28%	158	22%	129	NM	128

Balance Sheet & Other Fin. Data (Million $)

	1994	1993	1992	1991	1990	1989
Cash	145	96.0	101	127	152	176
Curr. Assets	1,133	904	774	756	815	823
Total Assets	2,071	1,774	1,426	1,357	1,468	1,406
Curr. Liab.	772	596	572	475	608	577
LT Debt	254	252	1.2	6.3	21.0	26.7
Common Eqty.	996	870	805	828	788	747
Total Cap.	1,252	1,142	828	870	846	810
Cap. Exp.	84.9	48.7	47.8	50.4	52.7	70.4
Cash Flow	298	235	207	214	233	223

Ratio Analysis

	1994	1993	1992	1991	1990	1989
Curr. Ratio	1.5	1.5	1.4	1.6	1.3	1.4
% LT Debt of Cap.	20.3	22.1	0.1	0.7	2.5	3.3
% Net Inc.of Revs.	6.6	6.4	5.7	5.8	7.0	6.8
% Ret. on Assets	10.6	9.9	9.4	9.2	11.0	10.6
% Ret. on Equity	21.8	18.9	16.1	16.0	20.7	19.8

Dividend Data (Dividends have been paid since 1955. A "poison pill" stock purchase rights plan was adopted in 1987.)

Amt. of Div. $	Date Decl.	Ex-Div. Date	Stock of Record	Payment Date
0.260	Aug. 05	Aug. 24	Aug. 30	Sep. 15 '94
0.260	Nov. 04	Nov. 21	Nov. 28	Dec. 15 '94
0.260	Feb. 03	Feb. 22	Feb. 28	Mar. 15 '95
0.260	May. 02	May. 22	May. 27	Jun. 15 '95

Data as orig. reptd.; bef. results of disc. opers. and/or spec. items. Per share data adj. for stk. divs. as of ex-div. date. E-Estimated. NA-Not Available. NM-Not Meaningful. NR-Not Ranked.

Office—280 Park Ave., New York, NY 10017. **Tel**—(212) 922-1640. **Chrmn**—G. L. Roubos. **Pres & CEO**—T. L. Reece. **Secy**—R. G. Kuhbach. **VP-Fin & Investor Contact**—John F. McNiff. **Dirs**—D. H. Benson, M. O. Bryant, J. M. Ergas, R. Fleming, J. F. Fort, J. L. Koley, A. J. Ormsby, T. L. Reece, G. L. Roubos, D. G. Thomas, J. W. Yochum. **Transfer Agent & Registrar**—Harris Trust Co. of New York, NYC. **Incorporated** in Delaware in 1947. **Empl**-22,992. **S&P Analyst:** Leo Larkin

Dow Chemical

NYSE Symbol **DOW**
In S&P 500

31-OCT-95 **Industry:** Chemicals

Summary: The second largest chemical company in the U.S., DOW produces basic chemicals and plastics, industrial specialties, and agricultural and household products.

S&P Opinion: Buy (★★★★)	Recent Price • 70¾ 52 Wk Range • 78-60¾

Yield • 4.3%
12-Mo. P/E • 10.3

Quantitative Evaluations

Outlook
(1 Lowest—5 Highest)
• **3+**

Fair Value
• **71¾**

Risk
• **Low**

Earn./Div. Rank
• **B**

Technical Eval.
• **Bullish** since 7/95

Rel. Strength Rank
(1 Lowest—99 Highest)
• **33**

Insider Activity
• **Neutral**

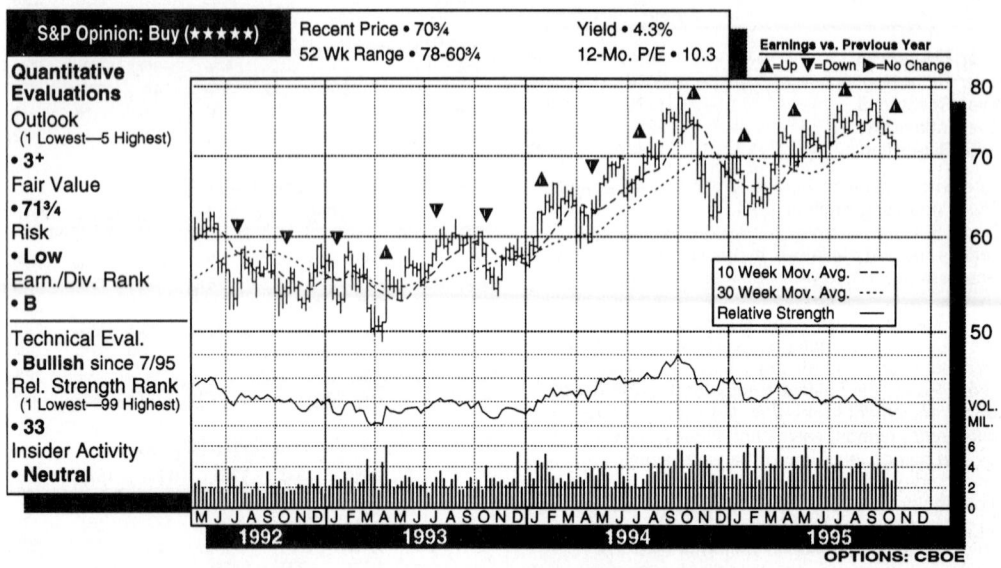

Earnings vs. Previous Year
▲=Up ▼=Down ▶=No Change

10 Week Mov. Avg. – – –
30 Week Mov. Avg. · · · ·
Relative Strength —

OPTIONS: CBOE

Overview - 31-OCT-95

We expect sales and profits of the chemicals and plastics businesses to climb further in 1996, boosted by a projected resurgence of the U.S. economy and continued gains in European and Asian markets. Following softness in the 1995 second half, caused by customer inventory reductions, selling prices should firm during 1996, as chemical industry supply/demand fundamentals strengthen. Prospects for further gains in the consumer segment reflect introduction of a new insecticide, and the absence of plant startup costs for household cleaners. Lower interest expense and the repurchase of 15% of the shares outstanding by early 1996 will aid EPS comparisons. The absence of equity in income of 50%-owned Dow Corning will be a modest negative factor.

Valuation - 31-OCT-95

The shares have declined about 10% from their mid-September high, reflecting increased investor concerns regarding the chemicals industry and soft selling prices. The stock is up only modestly in 1995, underperforming the overall stock market. At a current P/E of about 8X our projected 1996 EPS, the shares are attractive, in view of our positive outlook for DOW and the chemical industry as a whole. Although we see no long-term material impact, the company continues to be affected by the breast implant issue involving 50%-owned Dow Corning Co., and by possible direct liability by DOW.

Key Stock Statistics

S&P EPS Est. 1995	7.30	Tang. Bk. Value/Share	13.58
P/E on S&P Est. 1995	9.7	Beta	0.83
S&P EPS Est. 1996	8.50	Shareholders	96,700
Dividend Rate/Share	3.00	Market cap. (B)	$ 18.8
Shs. outstg. (M)	269.0	Inst. holdings	56%
Avg. daily vol. (M)	0.789	Insider holdings	NA

Value of $10,000 invested 5 years ago: $ 12,939

Fiscal Year Ending Dec. 31

	1995	% Change	1994	% Change	1993	% Change
Revenues (Million $)						
1Q	5,962	31%	4,541	4%	4,363	-6%
2Q	5,517	12%	4,934	2%	4,822	NM
3Q	4,884	-3%	5,046	15%	4,370	-8%
4Q	—	—	5,494	22%	4,505	-5%
Yr.	—	—	20,015	11%	18,060	-5%
Income (Million $)						
1Q	584.0	NM	173.0	-57%	402.0	126%
2Q	334.0	33%	251.0	68%	149.0	-23%
3Q	571.0	97%	290.0	109%	139.0	-9%
4Q	—	—	224.0	NM	-46.00	NM
Yr.	—	—	938.0	46%	644.0	133%
Earnings Per Share ($)						
1Q	2.04	NM	0.62	-58%	1.47	126%
2Q	1.22	34%	0.91	69%	0.54	-24%
3Q	2.15	107%	1.04	108%	0.50	-9%
4Q	E1.89	136%	0.80	NM	-0.18	NM
Yr.	E7.30	117%	3.37	45%	2.33	135%

Next earnings report expected: late January

Dow Chemical

Business Summary - 31-OCT-95

Dow Chemical is a major diversified chemical company. Segment contributions in 1994 were:

	Sales	Profits
Chemicals & performance products	23%	23%
Plastic products	38%	44%
Hydrocarbons	10%	3%
Consumer specialties	29%	30%

Foreign operations accounted for 50% of sales and 45% of operating income in 1994.

Chemicals include inorganics (chlorine, caustic soda, chlorinated solvents, ethylene dichloride, vinyl chloride, magnesium metals) and organics (phenols, acetone, ethylene oxide/glycol, propylene oxide/glycol, and glycerine). Performance products consist of latexes, surfactants, antimicrobials, superabsorbents, cellulose ethers, chelating agents, ion exchange resins, separation membrane systems, heat transfer fluids, lubricants, solvents, and plastic lined pipes.

Plastics include high-, low- and linear low-density polyethylenes, polystyrene resins, polycarbonates, ABS, adhesives, elastomers, polyurethanes, polyols, isocyanates, epoxy resins, and fabricated products (polystyrene and polyethylene foams and films).

Hydrocarbons and energy includes olefins, aromatics, styrene, and power and steam.

Consumer specialties include agricultural products (herbicides and insecticides) and consumer products (Handi-Wrap and Saran Wrap plastic films, Ziploc bags, Spray'n Wash, Dow Bathroom and Fantastik cleaners, and personal and hair care products). In July 1995, Dow sold its pharmaceuticals businesses, including a 71% interest in Marion Merrell Dow.

Important Developments

Oct. '95—The company plans to appeal a Nevada jury verdict against it totaling $14.1 million. The lawsuit was the first involving silicon gel breast implants made by Dow Corning in which DOW was the sole defendant. In May, 1995 Dow Corning Corp. filed for Chapter 11 bankruptcy protection. In the 1995 second quarter, DOW recorded a charge of $338 million ($1.24 a share) to write off its entire investment in 50%-owned Dow Corning.

Oct. '95—DOW said it had one of its best third quarters, on the strength of margin restoration and cost reductions. The company noted that although prices for certain products had softened since mid-year, it expects overall prices to be higher in the fourth quarter than in the 1994 period. Separately, DOW had repurchased 17.7 million common shares to date in 1995.

Capitalization

Long Term Debt: $5,026,000,000 (9/95).

Minority Interest: $1,852,000,000.

7.75% ESOP Preferred Stock: $131,000,000 (red. value). Conv. into 1.5 million com. shs.

Per Share Data ($)

(Year Ended Dec. 31)

	1994	1993	1992	1991	1990	1989
Tangible Bk. Val.	13.71	13.09	13.46	18.95	16.81	14.70
Cash Flow	8.77	7.89	6.47	8.76	9.91	13.03
Earnings	3.37	2.33	0.99	3.46	5.10	9.20
Dividends	2.60	2.60	2.60	2.60	2.60	2.37
Payout Ratio	77%	112%	263%	75%	51%	26%
Prices - High	79¼	62	62⅞	58	75¾	72¼
- Low	56½	49	51	44⅛	37	55½
P/E Ratio - High	24	27	64	17	15	8
- Low	17	21	52	13	7	6

Income Statement Analysis (Million $)

	1994	%Chg	1993	%Chg	1992	%Chg	1991
Revs.	20,015	11%	18,060	-5%	18,971	NM	18,807
Oper. Inc.	3,795	25%	3,044	-5%	3,197	-6%	3,391
Depr.	1,490	-2%	1,522	2%	1,489	4%	1,435
Int. Exp.	603	-9%	666	-14%	773	10%	704
Pretax Inc.	2,052	35%	1,525	75%	872	-48%	1,688
Eff. Tax Rate	38%	—	40%	—	31%	—	30%
Net Inc.	938	46%	644	133%	276	-71%	942

Balance Sheet & Other Fin. Data (Million $)

	1994	1993	1992	1991	1990	1989
Cash	1,134	837	606	536	299	289
Curr. Assets	8,693	7,652	7,443	7,719	8,019	7,340
Total Assets	26,545	25,505	25,360	24,727	23,953	22,166
Curr. Liab.	6,618	5,651	5,641	6,135	5,754	6,484
LT Debt	5,303	5,902	6,191	6,079	5,209	3,855
Common Eqty.	8,212	8,034	8,064	9,441	8,728	7,957
Total Cap.	16,687	16,763	16,515	17,053	15,499	13,187
Cap. Exp.	1,183	1,414	1,608	1,931	2,228	2,066
Cash Flow	2,421	2,159	1,758	2,370	2,674	3,522

Ratio Analysis

	1994	1993	1992	1991	1990	1989
Curr. Ratio	1.3	1.4	1.3	1.3	1.4	1.1
% LT Debt of Cap.	31.8	35.2	37.5	35.6	33.6	29.2
% Net Inc.of Revs.	4.7	3.6	1.5	5.0	7.0	14.1
% Ret. on Assets	5.6	2.5	1.1	3.9	6.0	13.1
% Ret. on Equity	11.4	7.9	3.1	10.3	16.5	33.0

Dividend Data —Dividends have been paid since 1911. A dividend reinvestment plan is available.

Amt. of Div. $	Date Decl.	Ex-Div. Date	Stock of Record	Payment Date
0.650	Sep. 08	Sep. 26	Sep. 30	Oct. 28 '94
0.650	Nov. 10	Dec. 23	Dec. 30	Jan. 30 '95
0.650	Feb. 09	Mar. 27	Mar. 31	Apr. 28 '95
0.750	May. 11	Jun. 28	Jun. 30	Jul. 28 '95
0.750	Sep. 14	Sep. 27	Sep. 29	Oct. 30 '95

Data as orig. reptd.; bef. results of disc. opers. and/or spec. items. Per share data adj. for stk. divs. as of ex-div. date. E-Estimated. NA-Not Available. NM-Not Meaningful. NR-Not Ranked.

Office—2030 Dow Center, Midland, MI 48674. **Tel**—(517) 636-1000. **Chrmn**—F. P. Popoff. **Pres & CEO**—W. S. Stavropoulos. **VP & CFO**—J. P. Reinhard. **Secy**—D. J. Roberts. **Investor Contact**—Teri S. LeBeau. **Dirs**—J. K. Barton, A. J. Butler, D. T. Buzzelli, A. J. Carbone, F. P. Corson, W. D. Davis, M. L. Dow, J. L. Downey, E. C. Falla, B. H. Franklin, A. D. Gilmour, F. W. Lyons, Jr., W.J. Neely, M. D. Parker, F. P. Popoff, J. P. Reinhard, H. T. Shapiro, E. J. Sosa, W. S. Stavropoulos, P. G. Stern. **Transfer Agent & Registrar**—KeyCorp, Cleveland. **Incorporated** in Delaware in 1947. **Empl**-53,700. **S&P Analyst**: Richard O'Reilly, CFA

Dow Jones & Co.

NYSE Symbol **DJ**
In S&P 500

25-OCT-95 Industry:
Publishing

Summary: Dow Jones publishes The Wall Street Journal, Barron's, provides newswire, news retrieval, and financial information services, and publishes general circulation newspapers.

S&P Opinion: Hold (★★★)	Recent Price • 35½	Yield • 2.6%
	52 Wk Range • 38½-28⅛	12-Mo. P/E • 18.3

Quantitative Evaluations

Outlook
(1 Lowest—5 Highest)
• **2−**

Fair Value
• **32½**

Risk
• **Low**

Earn./Div. Rank
• **A**

Technical Eval.
• **Bearish** since 3/95

Rel. Strength Rank
(1 Lowest—99 Highest)
• **36**

Insider Activity
• **Unfavorable**

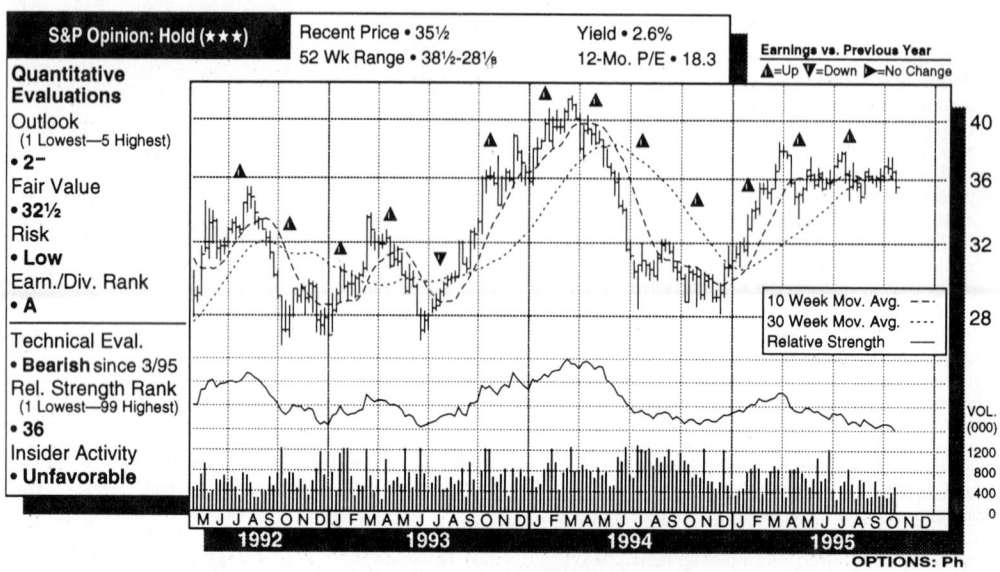

Earnings vs. Previous Year
▲=Up ▼=Down ▶=No Change

10 Week Mov. Avg. ---
30 Week Mov. Avg. ....
Relative Strength —

VOL. (000)

OPTIONS: Ph

Overview - 20-OCT-95

Revenue growth in 1995 and 1996 will reflect higher advertising rates and some improvement in linage anticipated at The Wall Street Journal, international publications, Barron's and community newspapers, as well as modest gains in circulation revenue. Double-digit increases for electronic information services should continue, paced by Telerate's exceptional growth. Despite operating efficiencies, margins will be impacted by sharply higher newsprint and television-related costs. Interest expense will advance, but significantly improved equity and other income (plus lower taxes in 1995) will boost the bottom line. Easing newsprint price pressures should contribute to wider operating margins in 1996.

Valuation - 21-OCT-95

We believe that DJ shares are reasonably valued and form a conservative holding for long-term capital gains and rising dividend income. Although the shares are selling at a higher P/E than appears warranted based on 9% and 13% EPS growth projected for 1995 and 1996, the stock is an attractive long-term holding. Earnings gains should accelerate in the next upturn of the cyclical financial markets, as well as during the next newsprint down cycle. The company has strong franchises in its well-known business publications, and the long-term outlook for information services is excellent, driven by aggressive expansion in new products and services.

Key Stock Statistics

S&P EPS Est. 1995	2.00	Tang. Bk. Value/Share	1.98
P/E on S&P Est. 1995	17.8	Beta	0.87
S&P EPS Est. 1996	2.25	Shareholders	10,700
Dividend Rate/Share	0.92	Market cap. (B)	$ 3.4
Shs. outstg. (M)	96.9	Inst. holdings	38%
Avg. daily vol. (M)	0.077	Insider holdings	NA

Value of $10,000 invested 5 years ago: $ 12,558

Fiscal Year Ending Dec. 31

	1995	% Change	1994	% Change	1993	% Change
Revenues (Million $)						
1Q	545.4	9%	499.2	8%	463.0	6%
2Q	577.0	10%	524.2	8%	487.0	4%
3Q	549.3	10%	501.0	7%	468.7	7%
4Q	—	—	566.6	11%	512.7	8%
Yr.	—	—	2,091	8%	1,932	6%
Income (Million $)						
1Q	46.43	8%	43.18	40%	30.95	15%
2Q	49.32	7%	46.02	16%	39.81	-5%
3Q	33.84	NM	33.75	14%	29.65	51%
4Q	—	—	58.23	24%	47.14	58%
Yr.	—	—	181.2	23%	147.6	25%
Earnings Per Share ($)						
1Q	0.48	12%	0.43	39%	0.31	15%
2Q	0.51	11%	0.46	15%	0.40	-2%
3Q	0.35	3%	0.34	13%	0.30	58%
4Q	E0.66	10%	0.60	28%	0.47	57%
Yr.	E2.00	9%	1.83	24%	1.48	26%

Next earnings report expected: late January

Dow Jones & Co.

Business Summary - 23-OCT-95

Dow Jones & Co. publishes The Wall Street Journal and Barron's National Business and Financial Weekly, provides information services and publishes general circulation newspapers. International operations accounted for 29% of consolidated revenues and 38% of operating profit in 1994. Segment contributions in 1994 were:

	Revs.	Profits
Information services	47%	53%
Business publications	41%	37%
Community newspapers	12%	10%

The Wall Street Journal, a financial and business daily (average 1994 worldwide circulation of 1,914,387) is published in 16 U.S. editions and separate editions of The Asian Wall Street Journal and The Wall Street Journal/Europe. Barron's (circulation 278,333) is a weekly magazine covering business and finance.

Information services include newswires, radio and TV programming, a news retrieval service offering 60 separate databases and database software. Telerate is a major supplier of computerized financial information and transaction services.

Ottaway Newspapers publishes 21 community newspapers, with combined average circulation of 551,454. DJ also holds equity or other interests in international business and financial wire services, newspapers, publications and newsprint mills.

Important Developments

Aug. '95—A 50/50 partnership of DJ and ITT Corp. agreed to purchase WNYC-TV Channel 31 from the City of New York for $207 million cash ($103.5 million each). Upon closing, expected in early 1996, the station will be relaunched as WBIS+, programming local business and sports.

Feb. '95—DJ acquired a majority stake in IDD Enterprises L.P. Terms were not disclosed. New York-based IDD publishes Investment Dealers' Digest and 16 other magazines, newsletters and directories targeted toward the financial industry niche markets. Its software and information products are available to investment banks and other institutions. It also serves the personal investor market through the Internet and other on-line distribution points.

Capitalization

Long Term Debt: $303,278,000 (6/95).

Class B Common Stock: 22,019,244 shs. ($1 par); limited transferability; conv. sh.-for-sh. into com.; 10 votes per sh.

Shareholders of record: 4,500.

Bancroft family members control 42% of com. and 75% of Cl. B com., representing 67% voting control.

Per Share Data ($)

(Year Ended Dec. 31)

	1994	1993	1992	1991	1990	1989
Tangible Bk. Val.	1.83	1.45	0.58	0.14	-0.37	-1.04
Cash Flow	3.90	3.37	2.94	2.53	2.91	4.72
Earnings	1.83	1.48	1.17	0.71	1.06	3.15
Dividends	0.84	0.80	0.76	0.76	0.76	0.72
Payout Ratio	46%	54%	65%	106%	72%	23%
Prices - High	41⅞	39	35⅜	30⅝	33¾	42½
- Low	28⅛	26¾	24½	21⅝	18⅛	29¼
P/E Ratio - High	23	26	30	43	32	13
- Low	15	18	21	30	17	9

Income Statement Analysis (Million $)

	1994	%Chg	1993	%Chg	1992	%Chg	1991
Revs.	2,091	8%	1,932	6%	1,818	5%	1,725
Oper. Inc.	564	12%	505	10%	460	8%	424
Depr.	205	8%	189	6%	179	-2%	183
Int. Exp.	16.9	-25%	22.6	-26%	30.4	-26%	41.2
Pretax Inc.	339	19%	286	22%	234	47%	159
Eff. Tax Rate	47%	—	49%	—	50%	—	55%
Net Inc.	181	22%	148	25%	118	64%	72.0

Balance Sheet & Other Fin. Data (Million $)

	1994	1993	1992	1991	1990	1989
Cash	11.0	6.0	16.0	36.0	18.0	46.0
Curr. Assets	310	268	249	272	248	269
Total Assets	2,446	2,350	2,372	2,471	2,591	2,688
Curr. Liab.	531	471	462	457	404	411
LT Debt	296	261	335	448	608	719
Common Eqty.	1,482	1,493	1,449	1,436	1,435	1,405
Total Cap.	1,777	1,759	1,798	1,963	2,143	2,238
Cap. Exp.	222	161	126	106	123	175
Cash Flow	386	336	298	255	293	475

Ratio Analysis

	1994	1993	1992	1991	1990	1989
Curr. Ratio	0.6	0.6	0.5	0.6	0.6	0.7
% LT Debt of Cap.	16.6	14.8	18.6	22.8	28.4	32.1
% Net Inc.of Revs.	8.7	7.6	6.5	4.2	6.2	18.8
% Ret. on Assets	7.7	6.3	4.9	2.8	4.0	13.2
% Ret. on Equity	12.4	10.1	8.2	5.0	7.5	24.7

Dividend Data —Dividends have been paid since 1906. A dividend reinvestment plan is available. Payments on the common and Class B shares in the past 12 months were:

Amt. of Div. $	Date Decl.	Ex-Div. Date	Stock of Record	Payment Date
0.210	Oct. 19	Oct. 26	Nov. 01	Dec. 01 '94
0.230	Jan. 18	Jan. 26	Feb. 01	Mar. 01 '95
0.230	Apr. 19	Apr. 25	May. 01	Jun. 01 '95
0.230	Jun. 21	Jul. 28	Aug. 01	Sep. 01 '95
0.230	Oct. 18	Oct. 30	Nov. 01	Dec. 01 '95

Data as orig. reptd.; bef. results of disc. opers. and/or spec. items. Per share data adj. for stk. divs. as of ex-div. date. E-Estimated. NA-Not Available. NM-Not Meaningful. NR-Not Ranked.

Office—200 Liberty St., New York, NY 10281. **Tel**—(212) 416-2000. **Chrmn & CEO**—P. R. Kann. **Pres & COO**—K. L. Burenga. **Sr VP & Secy**—P. G. Skinner. **VP-Fin & CFO**—K. J. Roche. **Treas**—L. E. Doherty. **Investor Contact**—Roger May. **Dirs**—R. V. Araskog, B. Bancroft, K. L. Burenga, W. C. Cox, Jr., I. O. Hockaday, Jr., V. E. Jordan, Jr., P. R. Kann, D. K. P. Li, R. C. McPherson, J. A. Ottaway, Jr., D. E. Petersen, W. H. Phillips, J. Q. Riordan, M. S. Robes, C. Salinas de — Gortari, C. M. Valenti, R. D. Wood. **Transfer Agent & Registrar**—Chemical Bank, NYC. **Incorporated** in Delaware in 1949. **Empl-** 10,006. **S&P Analyst:** William H. Donald

Dresser Industries

NYSE Symbol **DI**
In S&P 500

15-AUG-95 | **Industry:** Oil and Gas | **Summary:** Dresser supplies products and services primarily to the oil and natural gas exploration and refined product manufacturing industries.

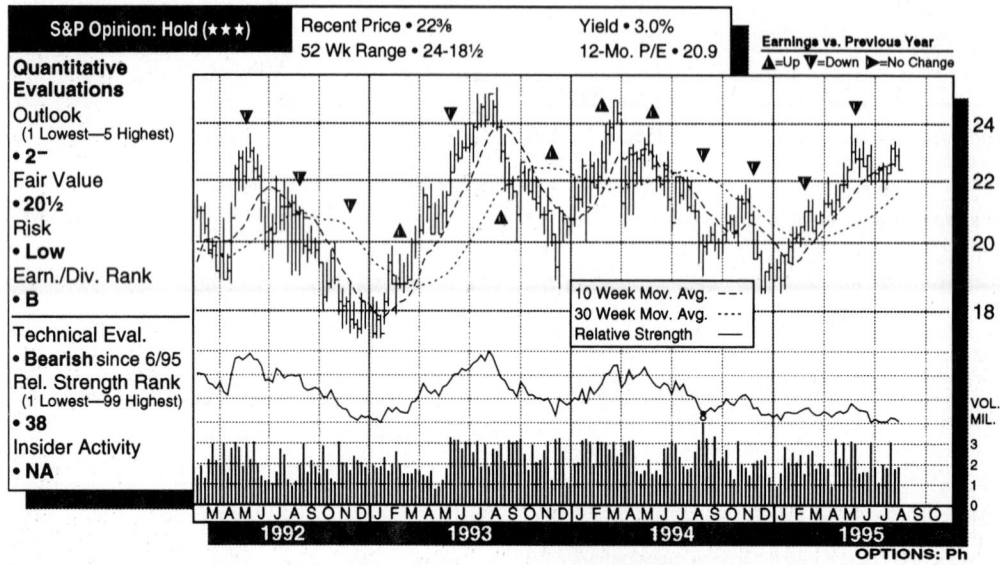

S&P Opinion: Hold (★★★)	Recent Price • 22⅝		Yield • 3.0%	
	52 Wk Range • 24-18½		12-Mo. P/E • 20.9	

Earnings vs. Previous Year
▲=Up ▼=Down ▶=No Change

Quantitative Evaluations

Outlook (1 Lowest—5 Highest)
• **2⁻**

Fair Value
• **20½**

Risk
• **Low**

Earn./Div. Rank
• **B**

Technical Eval.
• **Bearish** since 6/95

Rel. Strength Rank (1 Lowest—99 Highest)
• **38**

Insider Activity
• **NA**

10 Week Mov. Avg. ---
30 Week Mov. Avg. ····
Relative Strength —

OPTIONS: Ph

Overview - 15-AUG-95

Earnings will fall in 1995, following the sale of Dresser's stake in Western Atlas. Longer-term, proceeds from the sale may be used to finance further acquisitions, which will benefit future period earnings. Planned increases in capital expenditure budgets by most oil and gas exploration companies, as well as favorable economic conditions in developing countries, will fuel growth in the Drilling & Production Services segment in 1995. A pick-up in North Sea exploration activities should be a major contributor to this growth. High backlogs in the oilfield services segment will hit the bottom line in 1996, though we expect only modest backlog growth on weak U.S. natural gas prices.

Valuation - 15-AUG-95

The shares have recently consolidated following a run-up that began in December 1994. With oil prices falling nearly $3 a barrel over the past three months and gas prices suffering from excess supply, the shares are not expected to outperform the market in the near term. The current valuation, based on expected 1995 and 1996 EPS and book value, appears reasonable, though we believe a fallback in the share price to the high teens by year end 1995 is possible. However, an upturn in refining margins that should occur in 1995 may lift the shares, as higher margins are likely to translate into increased demand for oil pumps and valves. The opening up of Latin American and Far East markets to oil and natural gas exploration will have positive long-term benefits for the company.

Key Stock Statistics

S&P EPS Est. 1995	1.15	Tang. Bk. Value/Share	5.23
P/E on S&P Est. 1995	19.5	Beta	1.53
S&P EPS Est. 1996	1.35	Shareholders	16,400
Dividend Rate/Share	0.68	Market cap. (B)	$ 4.1
Shs. outstg. (M)	182.4	Inst. holdings	73%
Avg. daily vol. (M)	0.429	Insider holdings	NA

Value of $10,000 invested 5 years ago: $ 11,888

Fiscal Year Ending Oct. 31

	1995	% Change	1994	% Change	1993	% Change
Revenues ()						
1Q	1,300	—	--	—	924.0	4%
2Q	1,261	—	--	—	1,067	14%
3Q	—	—	3,891	NM	1,065	11%
4Q	—	—	1,416	22%	1,160	15%
Yr.	—	—	5,307	26%	4,216	11%
Income ()						
1Q	38.60	-80%	195.3	NM	24.90	144%
2Q	45.10	-17%	54.50	NM	9.50	-31%
3Q	—	—	30.20	-33%	45.30	55%
4Q	—	—	81.80	52%	53.90	NM
Yr.	—	—	361.8	171%	133.6	91%
Earnings Per Share ()						
1Q	0.21	-81%	1.08	NM	0.14	75%
2Q	0.25	-14%	0.29	NM	0.02	-80%
3Q	E0.31	94%	0.16	-38%	0.26	24%
4Q	E0.38	-16%	0.45	-10%	0.50	NM
Yr.	E1.15	-42%	1.98	115%	0.92	77%

Next earnings report expected: mid August

Dresser Industries

15-AUG-95

Business Summary - 15-AUG-95

Dresser makes highly engineered products for the energy and natural resource industries, and engages in project management for hydrocarbon energy-related activities utilized in oil and gas drilling, refining and marketing, production and transmission, and power generation. The company is repositioning its mix of business with divestitures, joint ventures and acquisitions. Foreign sales comprised 43% of fiscal 1994 revenues. Revenues and profits in fiscal 1994 were:

	Revs.	Profits
Oilfield services	31%	34%
Energy processing	45%	47%
Engineering services	24%	19%

The oilfield segment provides a broad range of products and technical services for oil and gas well exploration, development, production and drilling. Major operating units include: Security, which makes drill bits; Baroid, a supplier of drilling equipment, which was acquired in January 1994; Wheatley TXT Corp., a maker of pumps, valves and metering equipment, which was acquired in August 1994; and Bradero Price, an international pipecoating operation.

The energy processing segment makes products for hydrocarbon processors, transporters and refiners, including electrical generator systems, turbines, compressors, valves and controls, pumps, power systems, and measure and control devices. The Dresser-Rand unit, 51% owned, makes compressors and turbines and 49% owned Ingersol-Dresser manufactures pumps. The engineering segment participates in projects involving liquefied natural gas plants and receiving terminals, refining and petrochemical activities, and ammonia/fertilizer facilities.

Important Developments

Aug. '95—Dresser's $1.6 billion Malaysian liquefied natural gas (LNG) expansion project at Bintulu, Sarawak, to result in the world's largest LNG complex, is said to be ahead of schedule for construction of a third gas processing train to liquefy natural gas for storage and loading into LNG supertankers. The third train is now planned for start-up by the end of 1995. The additional three trains will bring capacity at the complex to a record 15.8 million metric tons a year. A fifth 65,000-cubic-meter storage tank also was added to store the increased LNG production from natural gas reserves 70 miles offshore Sarawak. The project is a joint venture with JGC Corporation together with Sime Engineering Sdn. Bhd. of Malaysia.

Capitalization

Long Term Debt: $464,100,000 (4/95).
Minority Interest: $58,300,000 (4/95).

Per Share Data ()

(Year Ended Oct. 31)

	1994	1993	1992	1991	1990	1989
Tangible Bk. Val.	5.30	2.77	4.17	10.45	10.43	10.03
Cash Flow	3.16	2.08	1.24	1.80	1.96	1.89
Earnings	1.98	0.92	0.52	1.04	1.29	1.21
Dividends	0.68	0.60	0.60	0.60	0.55	0.45
Payout Ratio	34%	65%	115%	58%	43%	37%
Prices - High	24⅞	25⅜	23⅝	28½	28⅛	24
- Low	18½	17¼	17¼	16¼	16½	14½
P/E Ratio - High	13	28	45	27	22	20
- Low	9	19	33	16	13	12

Income Statement Analysis ()

	1994	%Chg	1993	%Chg	1992	%Chg	1991
Revs.	5,307	26%	4,216	11%	3,797	-19%	4,670
Oper. Inc.	555	42%	391	83%	214	-28%	298
Depr.	216	36%	159	61%	99	-2%	101
Int. Exp.	49.3	80%	27.4	-8%	29.7	-25%	39.4
Pretax Inc.	619	147%	251	74%	144	-40%	239
Eff. Tax Rate	36%	—	33%	—	45%	—	36%
Net Inc.	362	185%	127	81%	70.0	-50%	140

Balance Sheet & Other Fin. Data ()

	1994	1993	1992	1991	1990	1989
Cash	515	239	155	285	361	455
Curr. Assets	2,197	1,615	1,407	1,608	1,757	1,766
Total Assets	4,324	3,642	3,188	3,251	3,309	3,056
Curr. Liab.	1,367	1,433	1,318	1,063	1,099	972
LT Debt	461	308	25.0	222	232	238
Common Eqty.	1,632	944	949	1,761	1,764	1,608
Total Cap.	2,177	1,403	1,125	2,087	2,094	1,927
Cap. Exp.	187	140	89.0	147	124	80.0
Cash Flow	578	285	169	241	266	255

Ratio Analysis

	1994	1993	1992	1991	1990	1989
Curr. Ratio	1.6	1.1	1.1	1.5	1.6	1.8
% LT Debt of Cap.	21.2	22.0	2.2	10.7	11.1	12.4
% Net Inc.of Revs.	6.8	3.0	1.8	3.0	3.9	4.1
% Ret. on Assets	7.9	3.7	2.2	4.3	5.5	5.5
% Ret. on Equity	25.0	13.4	5.1	8.0	10.3	10.5

Dividend Data —Dividends have been paid since 1948. A dividend reinvestment plan is available. A new "poison pill" stock purchase rights plan was adopted in 1989.

Amt. of Div. $	Date Decl.	Ex-Div. Date	Stock of Record	Payment Date
0.170	Jul. 22	Aug. 26	Sep. 01	Sep. 20 '94
0.170	Nov. 17	Nov. 25	Dec. 01	Dec. 20 '94
0.170	Jan. 20	Feb. 23	Mar. 01	Mar. 20 '95
0.170	May. 16	May. 25	Jun. 01	Jun. 20 '95
0.170	Jul. 20	Aug. 30	Sep. 01	Sep. 20 '95

Data as orig. reptd.; bef. results of disc. opers. and/or spec. items. Per share data adj. for stk. divs. as of ex-div. date. Quarterly Revs. for third qtr. of 1994 are for nine mos. E-Estimated. NA-Not Available. NM-Not Meaningful. NR-Not Ranked.

Office—2001 Ross Ave., Dallas, TX 75201. **Tel**—(214) 740-6000. **Chrmn & CEO**—J. J. Murphy. **Vice Chrmn & CFO**—B. S. St. John. **Pres & COO**—W. E. Bradford. **VP-Secy**—R. Morris. **Investor Contact**—D. Galletly. **Dirs**—W. E. Bradford, S. B. Casey, Jr., S. A. Earle, L. S. Eagleburger, R. Fulgham, J. Gavin, R. L. Hunt, J. L. Martin, J. J. Murphy, L. H. Olmer, J. A. Precourt, B. D. St. John, R. W. Vieser. **Transfer Agents**—Co.'s office; Harris Trust Co., NYC. **Registrars**—Chemical Shareholder Services Group, Dallas; Harris Trust Co., NYC. **Incorporated** in Delaware in 1956. **Empl**-25,926. **S&P Analyst:** Raymond J. Deacon

Duke Power

NYSE Symbol **DUK**
In S&P 500

12-OCT-95 **Industry:** Utilities-Electric

Summary: One of the nation's largest investor-owned electric utilities, DUK serves the Piedmont region of North and South Carolina. It also conducts a variety of diversified operations.

S&P Opinion: Hold (★★★)	Recent Price • 43¾	Yield • 4.6%
	52 Wk Range • 44¼-37⅜	12-Mo. P/E • 14.3

Quantitative Evaluations

Outlook
(1 Lowest—5 Highest)
• **1+**

Fair Value
• **35%**

Risk
• **Low**

Earn./Div. Rank
• **A-**

Technical Eval.
• **Bullish** since 4/95

Rel. Strength Rank
(1 Lowest—99 Highest)
• **83**

Insider Activity
• **Neutral**

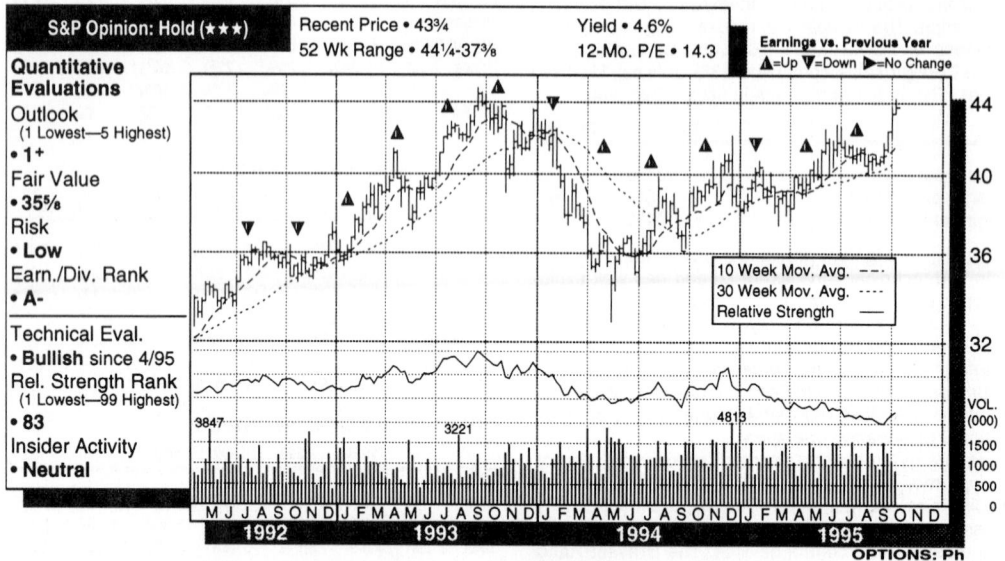

Earnings vs. Previous Year
▲=Up ▼=Down ▶=No Change

10 Week Mov. Avg. ---
30 Week Mov. Avg. ----
Relative Strength ——

OPTIONS: Ph

Overview - 12-OCT-95

Share earnings for 1995 should reflect only modestly higher revenues as the positive effect of regional economic growth on electricity sales is largely offset by an expected decrease in wholesale sales. Results should benefit from the absence of a one-time net charge of $0.26 a share (consisting of a $0.15 workforce reduction charge, a $0.14 charge for certain contingencies and a $0.03 investment gain) and from cost savings from last year's workforce reduction. However, these positive factors will be partly offset by higher depreciation and amortization expenses and an expected resumption of contributions to the Duke Charitable Foundation.

Valuation - 12-OCT-95

Although this well-managed utility benefits from a strong position in one of the more vibrant utility markets in the U.S., growing rate competition is likely to suppress earnings growth over the next several years. Solid financial underpinnings are allowing DUK to invest in plant upgrading and expansion, and to resolve environmental issues, but we expect resulting growth in depreciation and amortization will stifle earnings progress through 1996. Moreover, with the dividend payout limited to 65% of earnings, increases in future dividends are not likely to be as great as in the past. As a result we expect the shares will generally perform in line with the overall market.

Key Stock Statistics

S&P EPS Est. 1995	3.10	Tang. Bk. Value/Share	20.91
P/E on S&P Est. 1995	14.1	Beta	0.43
S&P EPS Est. 1996	3.15	Shareholders	129,600
Dividend Rate/Share	2.04	Market cap. (B)	$ 9.1
Shs. outstg. (M)	204.9	Inst. holdings	40%
Avg. daily vol. (M)	0.257	Insider holdings	NA

Value of $10,000 invested 5 years ago: $ 20,432

Fiscal Year Ending Dec. 31

	1995	% Change	1994	% Change	1993	% Change
Revenues (Million $)						
1Q	1,111	1%	1,099	9%	1,008	3%
2Q	1,052	-3%	1,083	10%	987.0	10%
3Q	—	—	1,273	-1%	1,290	13%
4Q	—	—	1,034	4%	996.9	6%
Yr.	—	—	4,489	5%	4,282	8%
Income (Million $)						
1Q	201.3	16%	173.6	23%	141.7	33%
2Q	137.5	7%	128.0	5%	122.5	41%
3Q	—	—	243.7	NM	241.4	27%
4Q	—	—	93.52	-23%	120.8	-3%
Yr.	—	—	638.9	2%	626.4	23%
Earnings Per Share ($)						
1Q	0.92	16%	0.79	25%	0.63	40%
2Q	0.61	9%	0.56	6%	0.53	47%
3Q	E1.06	-6%	1.13	NM	1.12	32%
4Q	E0.51	28%	0.40	-23%	0.52	-5%
Yr.	E3.10	8%	2.88	3%	2.80	27%

Next earnings report expected: late October

Duke Power

Business Summary - 03-OCT-95

Duke Power supplies electricity to more than 1.7 million customers in the Piedmont region of North Carolina and South Carolina. The company's largest customer is the textile industry, which accounted for 12% of electric revenues in 1994; electricity sold at wholesale to municipalities and other utilities comprised 8% of total sales. Electric revenues by customer class in recent years were:

	1994	1993	1992	1991
Residential	32%	33%	33%	33%
Commercial	24%	24%	24%	24%
Industrial	29%	28%	30%	30%
Other	15%	15%	13%	13%

Power sources in 1994 were nuclear 60%, coal 38%, and hydro and other 2%. Peak demand was 16,070 mw in 1994; capability totaled 17,945 mw, for a capacity margin of 12%. DUK projects demand growth of 2.1% a year through 2009.

Plant construction cost $309 million in 1994 and is estimated at $3 billion for 1995 through 1999 to replace generators and complete the Lincoln Turbine Station, which will add 1,184 mw of generating capacity. Two of its 16 facilities began operating in May 1995, 10 will be in service late in 1995, and four in mid-1996. Funding is to come largely from internally generated cash and debt issues.

Diversified operations, reorganized as Associated Enterprises Group (AEG), comprised 8% of net income in 1994 and consist of Church Street Capital Corp., internal investment managers; Duke Fluor Daniel and Duke Engineering, which design and build coal-fired and other generating plants in the U.S. and abroad; Crescent Resources, a real estate developer; Nantahala Power and Light Co., a small, franchised utility; and Duke Energy, which develops, owns and operates advanced fossil-fuel generating plants in the U.S. and abroad. DUK also markets power with Louis Dreyfus Electric Power, the largest power marketer in the U.S.

Important Developments

Jul. '95—DUK reported a decrease in 1995 first half revenues of 1% from the year earlier level, to $2.16 billion from $2.18 billion, due largely to lower demand from wholesale customers. Earnings available for common shares rose 13%, however, primarily reflecting lower fuel costs due to higher levels of nuclear generation as a percentage of total generation. Retail kilowatt-hour sales in the second quarter were up 3.3%, with gains for general service sales of 4.7% and overall industrial sales up 3%.

Capitalization

Long Term Debt: $3,587,859,000 (6/95).
Red. Cum. Pfd. Stock: $278,029,000.

Per Share Data ($)

(Year Ended Dec. 31)

	1994	1993	1992	1991	1990	1989
Tangible Bk. Val.	20.91	19.91	19.52	19.30	18.35	17.60
Earnings	2.88	2.80	2.21	2.60	2.40	2.56
Dividends	1.92	1.84	1.76	1.68	1.60	1.52
Payout Ratio	67%	66%	80%	65%	67%	59%
Prices - High	43	44⅞	37½	35	32⅜	28¼
- Low	32⅞	35⅜	31⅜	26¾	25½	21⅜
P/E Ratio - High	15	16	17	13	13	11
- Low	11	12	14	10	11	8

Income Statement Analysis (Million $)

	1994	%Chg	1993	%Chg	1992	%Chg	1991
Revs.	4,489	5%	4,282	8%	3,961	4%	3,817
Depr.	460	-6%	488	NM	491	14%	432
Maint.	NA	—	375	-7%	403	14%	355
Fxd. Chgs. Cov.	4.1	-2%	4.2	34%	3.1	-11%	3.5
Constr. Credits	27.4	1%	27.1	28%	21.2	-70%	70.0
Eff. Tax Rate	38%	—	40%	—	37%	—	34%
Net Inc.	639	2%	626	23%	508	-13%	584

Balance Sheet & Other Fin. Data (Million $)

	1994	1993	1992	1991	1990	1989
Gross Prop.	14,489	13,760	14,953	14,337	13,617	12,689
Cap. Exp.	772	655	588	807	1,052	1,060
Net Prop.	9,264	8,924	8,882	8,699	8,450	7,917
Capitalization:						
LT Debt	3,567	3,285	3,202	3,160	3,103	2,822
% LT Debt	40	39	39	40	41	40
Pfd.	780	781	780	731	742	675
% Pfd.	8.80	9.30	9.60	9.20	9.70	9.40
Common	4,533	4,338	4,151	4,066	3,817	3,657
% Common	51	52	51	51	50	51
Total Cap.	11,501	10,895	9,798	9,558	9,241	8,685

Ratio Analysis

	1994	1993	1992	1991	1990	1989
Oper. Ratio	82.6	81.0	81.7	81.5	82.5	80.6
% Earn. on Net Prop.	8.6	9.2	8.2	8.2	7.9	9.2
% Ret. on Revs.	14.2	14.6	12.8	15.3	14.6	15.7
% Ret. On Invest.Cap	7.9	8.5	8.4	9.1	8.8	9.5
% Return On Com.Eqty	13.3	12.5	11.1	13.5	13.1	14.7

Dividend Data

—Dividends have been paid since 1926. A dividend reinvestment plan is available.

Amt. of Div. $	Date Decl.	Ex-Div. Date	Stock of Record	Payment Date
0.490	Oct. 25	Nov. 14	Nov. 18	Dec. 16 '94
0.490	Jan. 31	Feb. 13	Feb. 17	Mar. 16 '95
0.490	Apr. 27	May. 08	May. 12	Jun. 16 '95
0.510	Jul. 24	Aug. 16	Aug. 18	Sep. 18 '95

Data as orig. reptd.; bef. results of disc opers. and/or spec. items. Per share data adj. for stk. divs. as of ex-div. date.
E-Estimated. NA-Not Available. NM-Not Meaningful. NR-Not Ranked.

Office—422 South Church St., Charlotte, NC 28242. **Tel**—(704) 594-0887. **Chrmn & CEO**—W. H. Grigg. **Pres & COO**—R. B. Priory. **VP & CFO**—R. J. Osborne. **Secy**—E. T. Ruff. **Treas & Investor Contact**—Sue A. Becht. **Dirs**—G. A. Bernhardt, C. C. Bowles, R. J. Brown, W. A. Coley, S. C. Griffith Jr., W. H. Grigg, P. H. Henson, G. D. Johnson Jr., J. V. Johnson, W. W. Johnson, M. Lennon, J. G. Martin, B. Mickel, R. B. Priory, R. M. Robinson, II. **Transfer Agent**—Co.'s office. **Registrar**—First Union National Bank of North Carolina, Charlotte. **Incorporated** in New Jersey in 1917; reincorporated in North Carolina in 1964. **Empl**-17,025. **S&P Analyst:** Jane Collin

Dun & Bradstreet

NYSE Symbol **DNB**
In S&P 500

23-OCT-95

Industry:
Publishing

Summary: This company is the world's largest marketer of information, software and services for business decision making. Its businesses include Moody's, Nielsen and IMS International.

|---|---|
| **S&P Opinion: Accumulate (★★★★)** | Recent Price • 59⅝ 52 Wk Range • 59⅝-48½ |
| | Yield • 4.4% 12-Mo. P/E • 15.9 |

Quantitative Evaluations

Outlook
(1 Lowest—5 Highest)
• **3⁻**

Fair Value
• **58¾**

Risk
• **Low**

Earn./Div. Rank
• **A**

Technical Eval.
• **Bullish** since 7/95

Rel. Strength Rank
(1 Lowest—99 Highest)
• **65**

Insider Activity
• **Neutral**

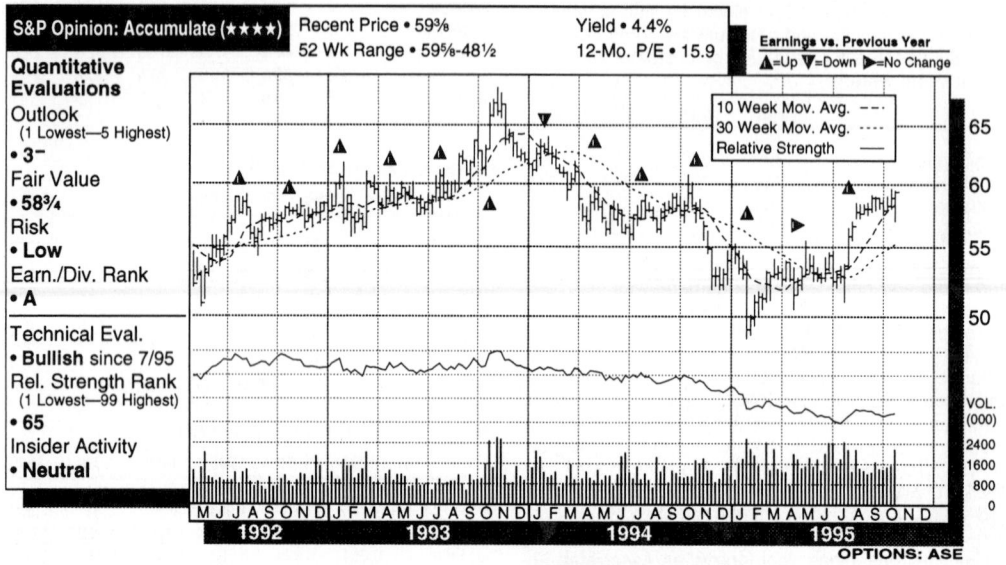

Earnings vs. Previous Year
▲=Up ▼=Down ▶=No Change

10 Week Mov. Avg. ---
30 Week Mov. Avg. ····
Relative Strength —

VOL.
(000)
2400
1600
800
0

1992 1993 1994 1995

OPTIONS: ASE

Overview - 23-OCT-95

Revenue growth was much stronger than originally expected through the first nine months of 1995, rising roughly 11%. That pace should continue through 1996 as DNB continues to focus on growing its revenues. Revenues are benefiting from improvements at Moody's, A. C. Nielsen, IMS, Gartner Group, Nielsen Media Research, Dataquest, DBIS and D&B Software. Profitability, while benefiting from aggressive cost-cutting measures, will be squeezed by accelerated investment spending. Profitability will also be limited by the revenue shift toward newer products and services, which typically have lower margins. Interest costs will also be sharply higher. Restructuring and ongoing productivity measures will continue to benefit earnings through 1997.

Valuation - 23-OCT-95

DNB moved up surprisingly fast over the summer and is likely to move ahead of its previous high (60) in the months ahead, reflecting the market's pleasure with DNB's obvious success in its commitment to accelerate revenue growth. Gains in net income are likely to be modest, however, in the mid single digits through 1996, due to expansion costs and other factors. Although the company has reiterated its intention to gradually reduce the dividend payout ratio, apparently by reducing annual increases, the generous cash dividend remains DNB's strong draw. Combined with modest capital gains, the dividend provides an attractive total return.

Key Stock Statistics

S&P EPS Est. 1995	3.80	Tang. Bk. Value/Share	NM
P/E on S&P Est. 1995	15.6	Beta	0.88
S&P EPS Est. 1996	4.05	Shareholders	15,500
Dividend Rate/Share	2.64	Market cap. (B)	$ 10.1
Shs. outstg. (M)	169.5	Inst. holdings	75%
Avg. daily vol. (M)	0.325	Insider holdings	NA

Value of $10,000 invested 5 years ago: $ 16,580

Fiscal Year Ending Dec. 31

	1995	% Change	1994	% Change	1993	% Change
Revenues (Million $)						
1Q	1,220	11%	1,099	3%	1,071	-3%
2Q	1,307	10%	1,185	2%	1,162	NM
3Q	1,333	11%	1,203	4%	1,158	-3%
4Q	—	—	1,408	7%	1,319	2%
Yr.	—	—	4,896	4%	4,710	NM
Income (Million $)						
1Q	108.9	NM	108.7	3%	105.2	7%
2Q	146.2	1%	144.6	4%	138.8	8%
3Q	171.5	3%	166.7	5%	158.6	6%
4Q	—	—	209.5	NM	26.20	-85%
Yr.	—	—	629.5	47%	428.7	-23%
Earnings Per Share ($)						
1Q	0.64	NM	0.64	8%	0.59	7%
2Q	0.86	1%	0.85	9%	0.78	8%
3Q	1.01	3%	0.98	10%	0.89	6%
4Q	E1.29	5%	1.23	NM	0.15	-85%
Yr.	E3.80	3%	3.70	53%	2.42	-22%

Next earnings report expected: late January

Business Summary - 23-OCT-95

Dun & Bradstreet is the world's largest marketer of business information and related services. Its operations include:

Marketing Information Services (42% of revenues and 27% of operating profits in 1994). This division, which includes Nielsen North America, Nielsen Media and IMS International, provides market-planning, media and retail goods measurements, market research, information, sales promotion evaluations and other services.

Risk Management and Business Marketing Information Services (33% and 43%). D&B Information Services provides information on U.S. businesses and provides marketing information on businesses and furnishes risk-assessment and receivables-management services in 34 countries. D&B Receivable Recovery Systems provides debt-management and collection services. American Credit Indemnity insures against excessive bad-debt losses. Moody's Investors Service publishes financial manuals and issues debt ratings. Interactive Data provides equity and bond market information.

Software Services (8% and a nominal operating profit). This business segment consists of Dun & Bradstreet Software, Sales Technologies and Erisco.

Directory Information Services (9% and 21%). Donnelley Directory publishes yellow pages directories of 36 telephone companies in the U.S. Donnelley Information Publishing publishes and manages proprietary telephone directories.

Other Business Services (8% and 9%). Various units provide marketing, information, administrative, management and numerous other services to businesses and industries worldwide.

International operations accounted for 41% of revenues in 1994.

Important Developments

Aug. '95—DNB sold Interactive Data Corp., a leading provider of securities information and related analytical services, to the Financial Times Group of Pearson PLC for $201 million.

Jun. '95—DNB reported that its D-U-N-S Number, a unique identifier for the 38 million businesses in its worldwide data base, was selected by the European Commission as a standard for electronic commerce involving European businesses. Separately, DNB said it will begin to offer franchise opportunities for businesses wishing to sell DNB's commercial accounts receivable services.

Jan. '95—DNB said that during 1994 it committed to spend over $300 million on 30 strategic acquisitions and equity investments as part of an aggressive program to fuel revenue growth. The company plans to accelerate investments by 25% in 1995.

Capitalization

Long Term Debt: None (6/95).

Per Share Data ($)

(Year Ended Dec. 31)

	1994	1993	1992	1991	1990	1989
Tangible Bk. Val.	-0.28	-0.27	6.14	5.79	5.24	5.62
Cash Flow	5.61	4.01	4.72	4.35	4.34	4.44
Earnings	3.70	2.42	3.10	2.85	2.80	3.14
Dividends	2.56	2.40	2.25	2.15	2.09	1.93
Payout Ratio	69%	99%	73%	75%	73%	61%
Prices - High	64	68½	59⅛	58	48⅝	60¼
- Low	51⅞	55¾	50⅝	39⅛	36⅛	41¼
P/E Ratio - High	17	28	19	20	17	19
- Low	14	23	16	14	13	13

Income Statement Analysis (Million $)

	1994	%Chg	1993	%Chg	1992	%Chg	1991
Revs.	4,896	4%	4,710	NM	4,751	2%	4,643
Oper. Inc.	1,249	12%	1,111	3%	1,075	5%	1,020
Depr.	324	15%	282	-2%	289	8%	268
Int. Exp.	39.0	58%	24.7	-25%	32.8	-38%	52.7
Pretax Inc.	879	49%	588	-26%	795	9%	731
Eff. Tax Rate	28%	—	27%	—	30%	—	30%
Net Inc.	630	47%	429	-23%	554	9%	509

Balance Sheet & Other Fin. Data (Million $)

	1994	1993	1992	1991	1990	1989
Cash	362	669	540	311	338	760
Curr. Assets	1,981	2,122	1,930	1,767	1,786	2,013
Total Assets	5,464	5,170	4,915	4,777	4,754	5,184
Curr. Liab.	2,187	2,044	1,645	1,527	1,676	1,721
LT Debt	Nil	Nil	Nil	Nil	Nil	Nil
Common Eqty.	1,319	1,111	2,156	2,161	2,080	2,185
Total Cap.	1,528	1,197	2,156	2,161	2,090	2,580
Cap. Exp.	273	236	197	226	300	311
Cash Flow	953	710	842	776	789	830

Ratio Analysis

	1994	1993	1992	1991	1990	1989
Curr. Ratio	0.9	1.0	1.2	1.2	1.1	1.2
% LT Debt of Cap.	Nil	Nil	Nil	Nil	Nil	Nil
% Net Inc.of Revs.	12.9	9.1	11.7	11.0	10.5	13.6
% Ret. on Assets	11.9	8.7	11.4	10.7	10.4	11.6
% Ret. on Equity	51.9	27.0	25.7	24.0	24.3	27.6

Dividend Data

Dividends have been paid since 1934. A "poison pill" stock purchase rights plan was adopted in 1988.

Amt. of Div. $	Date Decl.	Ex-Div. Date	Stock of Record	Payment Date
0.650	Oct. 19	Nov. 14	Nov. 18	Dec. 09 '94
0.650	Jan. 18	Feb. 13	Feb. 17	Mar. 10 '95
0.660	Apr. 19	May. 15	May. 19	Jun. 09 '95
0.660	Jul. 19	Aug. 16	Aug. 18	Sep. 08 '95
0.660	Oct. 18	Nov. 16	Nov. 20	Dec. 08 '95

Data as orig. reptd.; bef. results of disc. opers. and/or spec. items. Per share data adj. for stk. divs. as of ex-div. date. E-Estimated. NA-Not Available. NM-Not Meaningful. NR-Not Ranked.

Office—200 Nyala Farms, Westport, Conn. 06880. **Tel**—(203) 834-4200. **Chrmn**—C. W. Moritz. **Pres & CEO**—R. E. Weissman. **EVP & CFO**—N. L. Trivisonno. **VP & Secy**—S. A. Forsberg. **VP & Investor Contact**—Frank L. Alexander. **Dirs**—H. Adams Jr., C. L. Alexander Jr., M. J. Evans, R. J. Lanigan, V. R. Loucks Jr., J. R. Meyer, J. R. Peterson, M. B. Puckett, M. R. Quinlan, V. Taylor, R. E. Weissman. **Transfer Agent & Registrar**—First Chicago Trust Co. of New York, NYC. **Incorporated** in Delaware in 1930. **Empl**-47,100. **S&P Analyst:** William H. Donald

du Pont (E.I.) de Nemours

NYSE Symbol **DD**
In **S&P 500**

22-AUG-95 **Industry:** Chemicals

Summary: This broadly diversified company is the largest U.S. chemicals manufacturer; it also owns Conoco, a large international integrated petroleum company.

S&P Opinion: Accumulate (★★★★)

| Recent Price • 64⅞ | Yield • 3.2% |
| 52 Wk Range • 72⅝-50¾ | 12-Mo. P/E • 13.1 |

Earnings vs. Previous Year
▲=Up ▼=Down ▶=No Change

Quantitative Evaluations

Outlook (1 Lowest—5 Highest)
• 2+

Fair Value
• 62¼

Risk
• Low

Earn./Div. Rank
• B+

Technical Eval.
• Neutral since 4/95

Rel. Strength Rank (1 Lowest—99 Highest)
• 21

Insider Activity
• Neutral

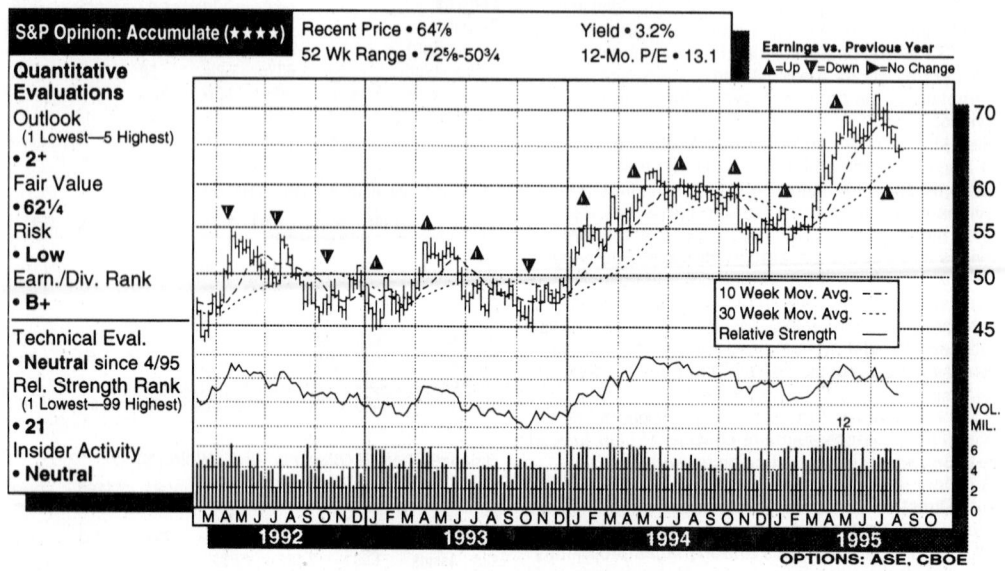

10 Week Mov. Avg. ---
30 Week Mov. Avg. ....
Relative Strength —

OPTIONS: ASE, CBOE

Overview - 16-AUG-95

S&P projects that the modestly expanding U.S. economy and healthier automobile and construction markets will boost domestic volumes in DD's chemicals, fibers and polymers units in the second half of 1995 and into 1996. European and Asian markets are also expected to be much stronger. Price increases for pigments, polymers and fibers will be positive factors, offsetting higher raw material costs. Earnings will be further boosted by ongoing productivity programs. Conoco should report higher earnings in the second half of 1995 versus 1994, reflecting better refining margins and operating rates. The buyback in early April of most of Seagram's interest in DD will positively affect share earnings comparisons, despite increased interest expense.

Valuation - 22-AUG-95

We continue to recommend the purchase of DD's stock, largely on the positive EPS impact we anticipate from the repurchase in early April of almost all of the 24% interest held by Seagram Co. Expected asset sales may include poorly performing businesses. DD should continue to report favorable profit comparisons in the second half, reflecting price increases for key products, strong gains in Europe and Asia, and a stronger performance by Conoco on better refining results. The quarterly dividend was recently boosted a healthy 11%. The shares remain attractive at their current earnings multiple and dividend yield.

Key Stock Statistics

S&P EPS Est. 1995	5.70	Tang. Bk. Value/Share	19.46
P/E on S&P Est. 1995	11.4	Beta	1.10
S&P EPS Est. 1996	6.00	Shareholders	172,000
Dividend Rate/Share	2.08	Market cap. (B)	$ 36.3
Shs. outstg. (M)	555.0	Inst. holdings	58%
Avg. daily vol. (M)	1.174	Insider holdings	18%

Value of $10,000 invested 5 years ago: $ 19,433

Fiscal Year Ending Dec. 31

	1995	% Change	1994	% Change	1993	% Change
Revenues (Million $)						
1Q	10,502	14%	9,190	1%	9,070	NM
2Q	11,329	11%	10,161	6%	9,550	-2%
3Q	—	—	9,845	7%	9,231	-5%
4Q	—	—	10,137	10%	9,251	NM
Yr.	—	—	39,333	6%	37,098	-2%
Income (Million $)						
1Q	959.0	49%	642.0	30%	493.0	12%
2Q	938.0	18%	792.0	53%	516.0	86%
3Q	—	—	647.0	NM	-680.0	NM
4Q	—	—	646.0	173%	237.0	NM
Yr.	—	—	2,727	NM	566.0	-42%
Earnings Per Share ($)						
1Q	1.40	49%	0.94	29%	0.73	14%
2Q	1.70	47%	1.16	53%	0.76	85%
3Q	E1.30	37%	0.95	NM	-1.01	NM
4Q	E1.30	37%	0.95	171%	0.35	NM
Yr.	E5.70	43%	4.00	NM	0.83	-42%

Next earnings report expected: late October

du Pont (E.I.) de Nemours

Business Summary - 22-AUG-95

Contributions by industry segment in 1994:

	Sales	Profits
Petroleum expl. & production	8%	16%
Petroleum ref., mkt. & trans.	35%	6%
Chemicals	10%	12%
Fibers	17%	23%
Polymers	16%	23%
Diversified businesses	14%	20%

Foreign operations accounted for 47% of sales and 36% of net income in 1994.

Conoco is a major international integrated petroleum company with proved developed reserves at 1994 year end of 706 million bbl. of oil and 2,496 bcf of natural gas. Refinery capacity is 595,000 bbl. per day.

Commodity and specialty chemicals include pigments, fluoroproducts, acids, peroxygens and polymer intermediates. DD is a leading producer of man-made fibers (polyester, nylon, Lycra spandex, Kevlar aramid) for textiles, carpets and industrial uses; and polymers, elastomers, films, and fabricated and automotive products. Diversified businesses include agricultural pesticides, electronic materials (photoresists and semiconductor materials), imaging systems (films and printing systems), medical products (X-ray, imaging, biological and diagnostics products, and pharmaceuticals), and 50% owned Consol Energy (coal operations).

Important Developments

Jul. '95—Second quarter earnings benefited by $0.23 a share from the repurchase in April 1995 of 156 million common shares (23% of those then outstanding) at $56.25 each from The Seagram Co. for a total of $8.8 billion (consisting of $1 billion in cash, $7.3 billion in notes, and warrants valued at $440 million). To help fund the repurchase, DD in May sold, through public and private offerings, 27.34 million shares for net proceeds of $1.75 billion. DD also sold 24 million shares to a Flexitrust program. These shares will be used over the next several years to satisfy employee benefit program requirements. DD plans to use cash flow as well as asset sales of up to $2 billion to reduce debt. DD intends to sell its medical products business (with annual sales of $1 billion) and to sell publicly its electronic photomask business. DD expects its debt-to-capital ratio to return to its target range of 35% to 40% by year-end 1996.

Capitalization

Long Term Debt: $6,277,000,000 (3/95).
Minority Interest: $209,000,000.
$3.50-$4.50 Cum. Preferred Stock: 2,372,594 shs. (no par) in 2 series.

Per Share Data ($) (Year Ended Dec. 31)

	1994	1993	1992	1991	1990	1989
Tangible Bk. Val.	18.15	15.81	16.40	23.81	22.97	21.41
Cash Flow	8.37	5.86	5.62	6.40	7.57	7.39
Earnings	4.00	0.83	1.43	2.08	3.40	3.53
Dividends	1.82	1.76	1.74	1.68	1.62	1.45
Payout Ratio	45%	212%	122%	81%	47%	41%
Prices - High	$62\frac{3}{8}$	$53\frac{7}{8}$	$54\frac{7}{8}$	50	$42\frac{3}{8}$	$42\frac{1}{8}$
- Low	$48\frac{1}{4}$	$44\frac{1}{2}$	$43\frac{1}{2}$	$32\frac{3}{4}$	$31\frac{3}{8}$	$28\frac{3}{4}$
P/E Ratio - High	16	65	38	24	12	12
- Low	12	54	30	16	9	8

Income Statement Analysis (Million $)

	1994	%Chg	1993	%Chg	1992	%Chg	1991
Revs.	34,137	4%	32,732	-12%	37,208	-2%	38,151
Oper. Inc.	6,944	13%	6,166	27%	4,837	-22%	6,200
Depr.	2,976	-13%	3,411	21%	2,818	-3%	2,901
Int. Exp.	702	-11%	788	-6%	837	-12%	949
Pretax Inc.	4,382	NM	958	-47%	1,811	-36%	2,818
Eff. Tax Rate	38%	—	41%	—	46%	—	50%
Net Inc.	2,727	NM	566	-42%	975	-31%	1,403

Balance Sheet & Other Fin. Data (Million $)

	1994	1993	1992	1991	1990	1989
Cash	1,109	1,240	1,674	468	611	692
Curr. Assets	11,108	10,899	12,228	10,874	12,233	11,344
Total Assets	36,892	37,053	38,870	36,117	38,128	34,715
Curr. Liab.	7,565	9,439	10,226	7,493	10,023	9,348
LT Debt	6,376	6,531	7,193	6,456	5,663	4,149
Common Eqty.	12,585	10,993	11,528	16,502	16,181	15,561
Total Cap.	20,889	19,414	20,937	26,363	25,523	23,107
Cap. Exp.	3,050	3,655	4,397	5,026	5,383	4,285
Cash Flow	5,693	3,967	3,783	4,294	5,120	5,178

Ratio Analysis

	1994	1993	1992	1991	1990	1989
Curr. Ratio	1.5	1.2	1.2	1.5	1.2	1.2
% LT Debt of Cap.	30.5	33.6	34.4	24.5	22.2	18.0
% Net Inc.of Revs.	8.0	1.7	2.6	3.7	5.8	7.1
% Ret. on Assets	7.4	1.5	2.6	3.8	6.4	7.7
% Ret. on Equity	23.0	4.9	6.9	8.5	14.7	16.4

Dividend Data —Dividends have been paid since 1904. A dividend reinvestment plan is available.

Amt. of Div. $	Date Decl.	Ex-Div. Date	Stock of Record	Payment Date
0.470	Jul. 27	Aug. 09	Aug. 15	Sep. 12 '94
0.470	Oct. 26	Nov. 08	Nov. 15	Dec. 14 '94
0.470	Jan. 25	Feb. 09	Feb. 15	Mar. 14 '95
0.520	Apr. 26	May. 09	May. 15	Jun. 12 '95
0.520	Jul. 26	Aug. 11	Aug. 15	Sep. 12 '95

Data as orig. reptd.; bef. results of disc. opers. and/or spec. items. Per share data adj. for stk. divs. as of ex-div. date. E-Estimated. NA-Not Available. NM-Not Meaningful. NR-Not Ranked.

Office—1007 Market St., Wilmington, DE 19898. **Tel**—(302) 774-1000. **Chrmn & CEO**—E. S. Woolard Jr. **Secy**—L. B. Lancaster. **SVP-CFO**—C. H. Henry. **Investor Contact**—John W. Himes. **Dirs**— P. N. Barnevik, A. F. Brimmer, E. B. du Pont, L. C. Duemling, C. M. Harper, J. A. Krol, C. S. Nicandros, W. K. Reilly, H. R. Sharp III, C. M. Vest, E. S. Woolard Jr. **Transfer Agent**—Co's. office. **Registrar**—Wilmington Trust Co. **Incorporated** in Delaware in 1915. **Empl**-107,000. **S&P Analyst:** Richard O'Reilly, CFA

EG&G Inc.

NYSE Symbol **EGG**
In S&P 500

17-AUG-95 Industry:
Specialty instruments

Summary: This technologically diversified company provides advanced scientific and technical products and services worldwide.

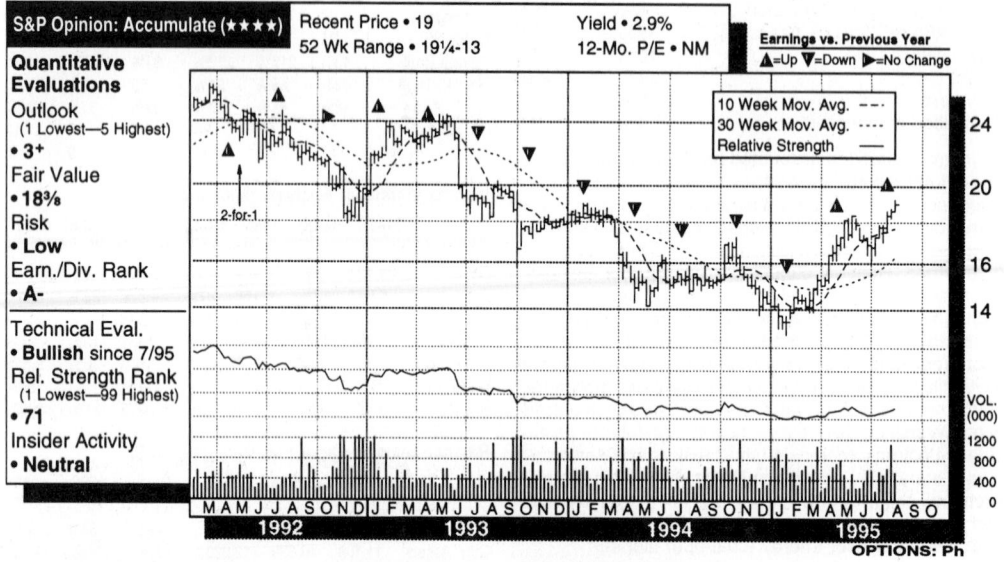

S&P Opinion: Accumulate (★★★★)

Recent Price • 19	Yield • 2.9%
52 Wk Range • 19¼-13	12-Mo. P/E • NM

Earnings vs. Previous Year
▲=Up ▼=Down ▶=No Change

Quantitative Evaluations

Outlook
(1 Lowest—5 Highest)
• **3+**

Fair Value
• **18%**

Risk
• **Low**

Earn./Div. Rank
• **A-**

Technical Eval.
• **Bullish** since 7/95

Rel. Strength Rank
(1 Lowest—99 Highest)
• **71**

Insider Activity
• **Neutral**

10 Week Mov. Avg. ---
30 Week Mov. Avg. ····
Relative Strength —

2-for-1

VOL.
(000)

OPTIONS: Ph

Overview - 17-AUG-95

Revenues for 1996 should increase approximately 10%. The increase should be led by optoelectronics, which should continue to benefit from strong demand from the photography industry and greater sales of sensors used in air bags and in medical products. Instruments should achieve significant growth due to greater market penetration and increased sales of reagents sold with instruments. Technical services growth is likely to be modest due to a flattening of automobile industry sales and essentially unchanged revenues from managing the Kennedy Space Center. The mechanical components segment is likely to grow in line with the economy. Margins should benefit from an improved product mix and $17 million in additional savings from the restructuring begun in 1994. Share earnings should benefit from fewer shares outstanding due to the share repurchase program.

Valuation - 17-AUG-95

The shares have recently been reaching new 52-week highs as the company's operating performance has matched the company's earlier projections and its restructuring program has been smoothly implemented. We believe these trends should continue to exert a positive influence. In addition, the shares will also benefit from EG&G's favorable position in many technologically exciting markets. Lastly, the continuing stock repurchase program should provide support for the shares.

Key Stock Statistics

S&P EPS Est. 1995	1.00	Tang. Bk. Value/Share	5.72
P/E on S&P Est. 1995	19.0	Beta	0.98
S&P EPS Est. 1996	1.30	Shareholders	14,100
Dividend Rate/Share	0.56	Market cap. (B)	$ 1.0
Shs. outstg. (M)	53.1	Inst. holdings	75%
Avg. daily vol. (M)	0.138	Insider holdings	NA

Value of $10,000 invested 5 years ago: $ 13,141

Fiscal Year Ending Dec. 31

	1995	% Change	1994	% Change	1993	% Change
Revenues (Million $)						
1Q	338.2	4%	325.7	-50%	648.9	NM
2Q	342.3	4%	329.9	-50%	662.0	-5%
3Q	—	—	336.9	-55%	746.3	NM
4Q	—	—	340.1	-47%	640.7	-7%
Yr.	—	—	1,333	-51%	2,698	-3%
Income (Million $)						
1Q	9.35	20%	7.81	-59%	19.11	6%
2Q	12.34	37%	8.98	-57%	21.07	-3%
3Q	—	—	-56.94	NM	15.21	-31%
4Q	—	—	8.04	-67%	24.18	-6%
Yr.	—	—	-32.11	NM	79.57	-9%
Earnings Per Share ($)						
1Q	0.17	21%	0.14	-59%	0.34	6%
2Q	0.23	44%	0.16	-57%	0.37	-5%
3Q	E0.25	NM	-1.03	NM	0.27	-31%
4Q	E0.35	133%	0.15	-65%	0.43	-7%
Yr.	E1.00	NM	-0.58	NM	1.41	-10%

Next earnings report expected: mid October

Business Summary - 17-AUG-95

EG&G is a technologically diversified company. Industry segment contributions (profits in million $) in 1994 were:

	Sales	Profits
Technical services	46%	$46.1
Instruments	21%	-49.6
Mechanical components	17%	18.8
Optoelectronics	16%	8.7

About 42% of 1994 sales were to U.S. government agencies. Foreign operations accounted for 23% of revenues and a $33.7 million operating profit.

The company's technical services segment supplies engineering, scientific, management, and technical support services to a broad range of government and industry customers. The largest contributors in this segment are automotive testing and the operation of the Kennedy Space Center.

The company develops and manufactures hardware and associated software for applications in medical diagnostics, biochemical and medical research, materials analyses, environmental monitoring, industrial process management, and airport and industrial security.

Mechanical components include high reliability advanced seals and bellows products, fans, blowers, precision components for aerospace applications, and heat management devices.

The optoelectronics segment designs and manufactures optical sensors ranging from simple photo cells to sophisticated imaging systems, light sources that include flashlamps and laser diodes, and complex devices for weapons' trigger systems.

During the third quarter of 1994, the company announced a plan to exit the Department of Energy (DOE) business that related to managing government facilities engaged in nuclear energy research, weapons production and testing. Three of the four remaining DOE contracts expire at the end of 1995, while the fourth expires at the end of the 1996 third quarter. The company also initiated a repositioning plan intended to result in pretax savings of approximately $30 million in 1996. The plan resulted in pretax charges of $30.4 million in 1994.

Important Developments

Jul. '95—The company said that its increase in earnings in the second quarter primarily reflected a 66% gain in operating income at mechanical components in the absence of a year-earlier charge, and a 61% increase at optoelectronics, which reflected strong demand for flashlamps for single use cameras. EGG added that through July 2, 1995, it had repurchased 2.4 million shares in 1995 as part of an outstanding authorization to purchase 13.3 million shares.

Capitalization

Long Term Liabilities: $71,100,000 (7/95).

Per Share Data ($) (Year Ended Dec. 31)

	1994	1993	1992	1991	1990	1989
Tangible Bk. Val.	5.77	6.03	6.11	5.34	4.28	3.96
Cash Flow	0.08	2.08	2.20	2.06	1.83	1.64
Earnings	-0.58	1.41	1.56	1.46	1.30	1.20
Dividends	0.56	0.52	0.50	0.42	0.38	0.34
Payout Ratio	NM	37%	32%	29%	29%	28%
Prices - High	19	24½	26¾	25	20½	18¼
- Low	13¾	15¾	17⅞	15½	14	14¼
P/E Ratio - High	NM	17	17	17	16	15
- Low	NM	11	11	11	11	12

Income Statement Analysis (Million $)

	1994	%Chg	1993	%Chg	1992	%Chg	1991
Revs.	1,333	-51%	2,698	-3%	2,789	4%	2,689
Oper. Inc.	97.0	-39%	159	-4%	166	4%	159
Depr.	36.8	-3%	37.8	4%	36.3	8%	33.7
Int. Exp.	5.4	-14%	6.3	-12%	7.2	-18%	8.8
Pretax Inc.	-17.0	NM	122	NM	121	NM	120
Eff. Tax Rate	NM	—	35%	—	28%	—	33%
Net Inc.	-32.1	NM	79.6	-9%	87.8	8%	81.2

Balance Sheet & Other Fin. Data (Million $)

	1994	1993	1992	1991	1990	1989
Cash	75.7	72.2	69.8	63.0	34.2	28.6
Curr. Assets	481	465	483	456	408	407
Total Assets	793	769	750	698	675	643
Curr. Liab.	282	237	235	241	258	256
LT Debt	0.8	1.5	2.0	2.3	7.0	8.9
Common Eqty.	445	478	474	421	370	349
Total Cap.	446	479	476	423	381	361
Cap. Exp.	37.3	27.9	22.4	26.6	19.8	23.3
Cash Flow	5.0	117	124	115	104	95.0

Ratio Analysis

	1994	1993	1992	1991	1990	1989
Curr. Ratio	1.7	2.0	2.1	1.9	1.6	1.6
% LT Debt of Cap.	0.2	0.3	0.4	0.5	1.8	2.5
% Net Inc.of Revs.	NM	2.9	3.1	3.0	3.0	4.2
% Ret. on Assets	NM	10.5	12.1	11.8	11.4	12.0
% Ret. on Equity	NM	16.8	19.6	20.5	20.9	20.8

Dividend Data—Dividends have been paid since 1965. A dividend reinvestment plan is available. A "poison pill" stock purchase rights plan was adopted in 1987.

Amt. of Div. $	Date Decl.	Ex-Div. Date	Stock of Record	Payment Date
0.140	Jul. 27	Oct. 17	Oct. 21	Nov. 10 '94
0.140	Oct. 26	Jan. 13	Jan. 20	Feb. 10 '95
0.140	Jan. 25	Apr. 17	Apr. 21	May. 10 '95
0.140	May. 24	Jul. 19	Jul. 21	Aug. 10 '95
0.140	Jul. 26	Oct. 18	Oct. 20	Nov. 10 '95

Data as orig. reptd.; bef. results of disc. opers. and/or spec. items. Per share data adj. for stk. divs. as of ex-div. date. E-Estimated. NA-Not Available. NM-Not Meaningful. NR-Not Ranked.

Office—45 William St., Wellesley, MA 02181. **Tel**—(617) 237-5100. **Fax**—(617) 431-4255. **Chrmn, Pres & CEO**—J. M. Kucharski. **SVP & CFO**—T. J. Sauser. **VP & Clerk**—M. Gross. **Investor Contact**—Deborah S. Lorenz. **Dirs**—D. W. Freed, R. F. Goldhammer, J. B. Gray, K. F. Hansen, J. M. Kucharski, G. E. Marshall, W. F. Pounds, S. Rubinovitz, J. L. Thompson, G. R. Tod, J. F. Turley. **Transfer Agent**—Bank of Boston. **Incorporated** in Massachusetts in 1947. **Empl**-32,000. **S&P Analyst:** Paul H. Valentine, CFA

Eastern Enterprises

NYSE Symbol EFU Options on Phila (Jan-Apr-Jul-Oct)   In S&P 500

Price	Range	P–E Ratio	Dividend	Yield	S&P Ranking	Beta
Oct. 12'95	1995					
31½	32⅝–25¼	15	1.40	4.4%	B+	0.65

Summary

Eastern Enterprises operates a gas utility in Boston, provides barge service, and has a 13% equity interest in U.S. Filter Corp. In July 1994 directors authorized the repurchase, from time to time, of 2,000,000 EFU common shares. In August 1995, EFU said it would invest in two new natural gas projects expected to provide additional supply to meet anticipated growing seasonal and year-round needs in northeast markets. Following a return to profitability in 1994, profits advanced in the first half of 1995 due primarily to higher profits at Midland Enterprises.

Business Summary

Eastern Enterprises' operating income (in million $) in recent years was derived as follows:

	1994	1993	1992
Gas	$65.8	$49.1	$63.1
Barge	35.8	33.0	38.3
Water products	---	–0.4	–0.2

The Boston Gas (BG) subsidiary distributes natural gas to 511,500 residential, industrial and commercial customers in Boston and 73 communities in eastern and central Massachusetts. Total throughput in 1994 was 144.4 billion cubic feet (BCF), versus 144.8 BCF in 1993. Non-interruptible (firm) gas sales in 1994 were 95.5 BCF, versus 95.3 BCF in 1993. In 1994, sales to residential customers accounted for 44% of non-interruptible volumes, commercial 26%, industrial 5%, and transportation 25%. Some 70% of BG supplies are purchased under long-term contracts.

The Midland Enterprises subsidiary is a leading barge operator, providing service on the Ohio and Mississippi Rivers, the Gulf Intracoastal Waterway and the Gulf of Mexico. Midland, operating with a fleet of 2,378 dry barges and 90 towboats, transported 69.6 million tons in 1994. Coal accounts for about 60% of total tonnage. Midland also performs repair work on marine equipment, operates two coal terminals and one phosphate terminal and a marine supply facility. EFU's barge construction operation was sold in June 1994.

EFU exited the water products industry in April 1995 when it sold its WaterPro Supplies Corp. unit for about $52 million. EFU continued to own about 13% of U.S. Filter, a leading manufacturer of water and wastewater treatement equipment and systems.

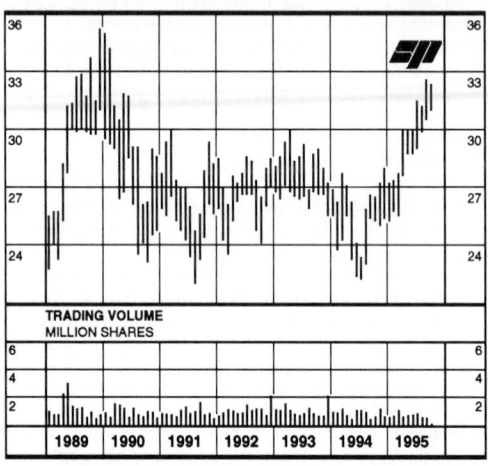

TRADING VOLUME
MILLION SHARES

Important Developments

Aug. '95— EFU said it would invest in two new natural gas projects expected to provide additional supply to meet anticipated growing seasonal and year-round needs in northeast markets. EFU agreed in principle to become a substantial equity partner in the EnergyPlus natural gas service project, with Panhandle Eastern Corp., that is to include a new centralized LNG liquefaction facility with storage capacity of up to 4 billion cu. ft. and up to 400 million cu. ft. per day of vaporization capacity. In addition, EFU agreed in principle to be a 10% equity participant in the $670 million Maritimes and Northeast Pipeline Project, a 650 mile high pressure gas delivery system to transport natural gas from Nova Scotia to the Boston area.

Next earnings report expected in late October.

Per Share Data ($)

Yr. End Dec. 31	1994	1993	1992	1991	1990	1989	1988	[1]1987	1986	1985
Tangible Bk. Val.	**18.33**	16.75	18.88	18.19	19.79	18.81	20.41	19.52	18.74	19.26
Cash Flow	**4.70**	1.19	4.04	3.36	4.51	4.00	3.61	3.37	3.13	1.95
Earnings[2]	**1.87**	d1.43	1.67	1.30	2.77	2.43	2.18	2.05	0.82	d0.55
Dividends	**1.40**	1.40	1.40	1.40	1.40	1.40	1.30	1.30	1.30	1.30
Payout Ratio	75%	NM	84%	107%	49%	57%	59%	63%	157%	NM
Prices—High	**28**	30	28⅝	30	35	35¼	26¾	33¼	30⅞	28⅝
Low	**22¼**	25½	23½	22	23⅛	22¾	21¾	19	22¼	21½
P/E Ratio—	**15–12**	NM	17–14	23–17	13–8	15–9	12–10	16–9	38–27	NM

Data as orig. reptd. **1.** Reflects accounting change. **2.** Bef. spec. item(s) of -2.02 in 1993, +0.37 in 1992, -0.38 in 1991 & bef. results of disc. opers. of +0.59 in 1994, -1.06 in 1985. E-Estimated. d-Deficit. NM-Not Meaningful.

Income Data (Million $)

Year Ended Dec. 31	Revs.	Oper. Inc.	% Oper. Inc. of Revs.	Cap. Exp.	Depr.	Int. Exp.	Net Bef. Taxes	Eff. Tax Rate	[4]Net Inc.	% Net Inc. of Revs.	Cash Flow
[1]1994	925	156	16.9	58	58.9	37.5	[3]65.3	37.5%	38.9	4.2	98
1993	1,100	136	12.4	64	59.0	35.1	[3]d15.2	NM	d32.2	NM	27
1992	1,091	150	13.7	83	53.6	35.2	63.4	39.6%	37.9	3.5	91
1991	993	121	12.2	112	46.5	34.9	47.1	37.6%	[2]29.4	3.0	76
1990	950	129	13.6	97	40.3	32.2	[3]88.6	27.8%	64.0	6.7	104
1989	840	113	13.5	90	36.4	30.6	[3]74.2	23.8%	56.6	6.7	93
1988	672	98	14.6	63	33.1	26.4	[3]63.1	19.7%	50.7	7.5	84
[2]1987	677	97	14.3	41	30.5	23.6	[3]61.2	22.3%	47.6	7.0	78
1986	1,156	143	12.4	71	53.3	40.5	[3]41.6	54.1%	[2]19.1	1.7	72
[1]1985	1,325	127	9.6	78	57.5	42.4	[3]d40.6	NM	d12.7	NM	45

Balance Sheet Data (Million $)

Dec. 31	Cash	Assets	Curr. Liab.	Ratio	Total Assets	% Ret. on Assets	Long Term Debt	Common Equity	Total Cap.	% LT Debt of Cap.	% Ret. on Equity
1994	61	343	212	1.6	1,339	2.9	419	374	914	45.9	10.7
1993	52	363	285	1.3	1,380	NM	388	364	872	44.5	NM
1992	105	387	206	1.9	1,425	2.7	406	518	1,075	37.8	7.4
1991	107	340	208	1.6	1,333	2.3	359	503	993	36.1	5.8
1990	158	386	178	2.2	1,199	5.5	332	513	976	34.0	12.8
1989	38	256	177	1.4	1,149	5.1	309	498	933	33.1	11.6
1988	112	317	146	2.2	1,087	4.8	308	473	903	34.1	11.0
1987	70	229	134	1.7	1,005	4.4	253	452	846	29.9	10.7
1986	138	322	196	1.6	1,135	1.6	348	432	880	39.6	4.4
1985	38	281	214	1.3	1,210	NM	406	443	942	43.1	NM

Data as orig. reptd. 1. Excludes disc. opers. 2. Reflects accounting change. 3. Incl. equity in earns. of nonconsol. subs. 4. Bef. results of disc. opers. and spec. item(s). d-Deficit. NM-Not Meaningful.

Revenues (Million $)

Quarter:	1995	1994	1993	1992
Mar.	367	372	368	357
Jun.	199	192	260	250
Sep.		139	196	203
Dec.		221	276	281
		925	1,100	1,091

Revenues for the first half of 1995 rose only 0.3%, year to year, reflecting a 12% sales gain for Midland Enterprises and a 3.0% decline for Boston Gas. Profits were up 87% for Midland which more than offset a 9.7% decrease for Boston Gas. Overall operating profit rose 9.3%. After other expenses (net), pretax income was up 9.2%. With taxes at 38.1%, versus 39.3%, net income increased 11%, to $1.86 a share on 3.4% fewer average shares outstanding, from $1.62 (before $0.04 gain from discontinued operations).

Common Share Earnings ($)

Quarter:	1995	1994	1993	1992
Mar.	1.51	1.38	1.02	1.32
Jun.	0.35	0.24	0.14	0.32
Sep.		d0.27	d0.93	d0.15
Dec.		0.52	d1.66	0.18
		1.87	d1.43	1.67

Dividend Data

Dividends have been paid since 1974. A dividend reinvestment plan is available. A "poison pill" stock purchase rights plan was adopted in 1990.

Amt of Divd. $	Date Decl.	Ex-divd. Date	Stock of Record	Payment Date
0.35	Oct. 27	Nov. 25	Dec. 1	Jan. 2'95
0.35	Feb. 23	Feb. 28	Mar. 6	Apr. 3'95
0.35	May 25	May 30	Jun. 5	Jul. 5'95
0.35	Jul. 28	Aug. 30	Sep. 1	Oct. 3'95

Capitalization

Long Term Debt: $362,935,000 (6/95).

Subsid. Preferred Stock: $29,245,000.

Common Stock: 20,151,668 shs. ($1 par). Institutions hold some 75%. Shareholders of record: 6,600.

Eastman Chemical

NYSE Symbol **EMN**
In S&P 500

12-SEP-95

Industry:
Chemicals

Summary: This major international chemical concern, spun off by Eastman Kodak at 1993 year end, should continue to benefit from tight industry supply conditions.

S&P Opinion: Accumulate (★★★★)

Recent Price • 66⅞	Yield • 2.6%
52 Wk Range • 67⅛-45¼	12-Mo. P/E • 11.4

Quantitative Evaluations

Outlook
(1 Lowest—5 Highest)
• **NA**

Fair Value
• **NA**

Risk
• **Low**

Earn./Div. Rank
• **NR**

Technical Eval.
• **Bullish** since 12/94

Rel. Strength Rank
(1 Lowest—99 Highest)
• **45**

Insider Activity
• **Neutral**

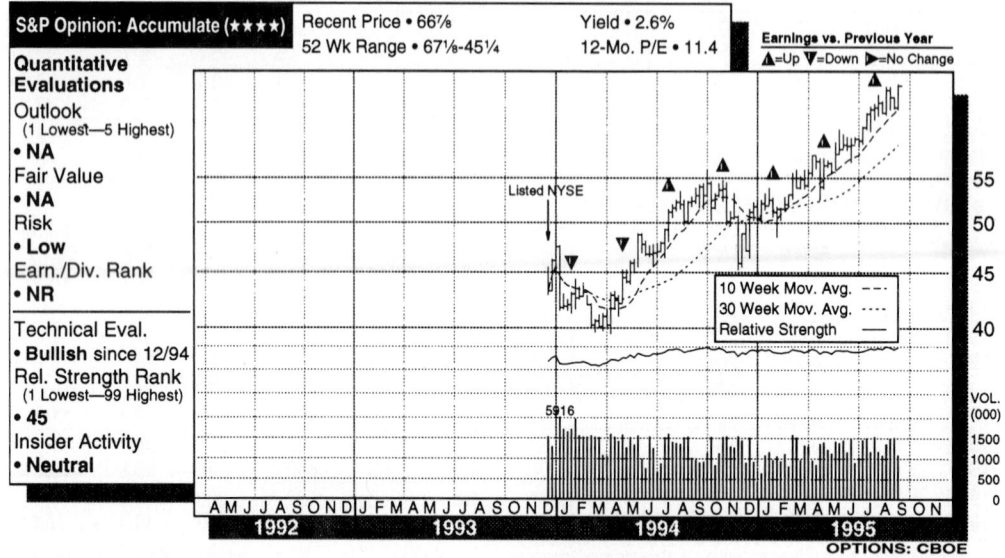

Earnings vs. Previous Year
▲=Up ▼=Down ▶=No Change

Listed NYSE

10 Week Mov. Avg. - - -
30 Week Mov. Avg. · · · ·
Relative Strength ——

5916

VOL. (000)
1500
1000
500
0

55
50
45
40

AMJJASOND 1992 | JFMAMJJASOND 1993 | JFMAMJJASOND 1994 | JFMAMJJASON 1995

OPTIONS: CBOE

Overview - 11-SEP-95

Sales and profits should continue to advance going into 1996, in large part reflecting higher selling prices for PET polyester, filter tow, and various intermediate chemicals and solvents as a result of tight industry supply conditions. While prices for polyethylene have declined since early summer, they remain at very healthy levels. Volume growth should remain strong, aided by the expected start-up of new PET capacity in January 1996. We project that domestic markets will begin to pick up by late 1995, and Europe and Asia should also continue to advance. An aggressive stock repurchase program will also boost EPS comparisons. Capital spending in 1996 may exceed $600 million, including for several PET facilities.

Valuation - 11-SEP-95

Despite a good performance so far in 1995, up 30% to date, the stock is still attractive at a multiple of 11 times our 1995 EPS estimate. The company should see continued strong earnings going into 1996, with rising prices and wider margins for major product lines such as PET polyester and filter tow, through polyethylene prices have soften in recent months. Long-term prospects are enhanced by EMN's leading share of the PET market, which is seeing double-digit volume growth, and by possible acquisitions. The annual dividend, recently raised by 5%, provides a reasonable yield.

Key Stock Statistics

S&P EPS Est. 1995	6.15	Tang. Bk. Value/Share	17.50
P/E on S&P Est. 1995	10.9	Beta	NA
S&P EPS Est. 1996	7.00	Shareholders	107,700
Dividend Rate/Share	1.68	Market cap. (B)	$ 5.3
Shs. outstg. (M)	81.3	Inst. holdings	67%
Avg. daily vol. (M)	0.310	Insider holdings	NA

Value of $10,000 invested 5 years ago: NA

Fiscal Year Ending Dec. 31

	1995	% Change	1994	% Change	1993	% Change
Revenues (Million $)						
1Q	1,232	25%	983.0	4%	941.0	1%
2Q	1,321	26%	1,047	3%	1,012	7%
3Q	—	—	1,130	16%	970.0	NM
4Q	—	—	1,169	19%	980.0	2%
Yr.	—	—	4,329	11%	3,903	2%
Income (Million $)						
1Q	132.0	136%	56.00	-26%	76.00	—
2Q	158.0	90%	83.00	-10%	92.00	—
3Q	—	—	93.00	52%	61.00	—
4Q	—	—	104.0	174%	38.00	—
Yr.	—	—	336.0	26%	267.0	21%
Earnings Per Share ($)						
1Q	1.58	132%	0.68	-4%	0.71	—
2Q	1.90	90%	1.00	11%	0.90	-43%
3Q	E1.40	25%	1.12	96%	0.57	-12%
4Q	E1.27	2%	1.25	NM	0.28	-43%
Yr.	E6.15	52%	4.05	65%	2.46	-10%

Next earnings report expected: late October

Eastman Chemical

Business Summary - 12-SEP-95

Eastman Chemical Co. is a leading international chemical company with a broad portfolio of plastics, chemical and fiber products. The company, formerly the Eastman Chemical division of Eastman Kodak Co., was spun off to Kodak shareholders on December 31, 1993. Business segment contributions in 1994 were:

	Sales	Profits
Performance segment	60%	60%
Industrial segment	40%	40%

Foreign operations accounted for 21% of sales and 2% of profits in 1994.

The performance segment consists of polyester plastics (41% of 1994 segment sales) used for packaging applications, including polyethylene terephthalate (PET) for containers such as soft drink bottles; coatings and paint raw materials (21%), including solvents, alcohols, glycols and resins; and fine chemicals (13%) used in photographic products, home care products and custom chemicals. The segment also includes performance plastics (polyolefins, modified polyesters, cellulosics and alloys) for value added end uses; polymer modifiers and additives; and nutritional supplements and food emulsifiers.

The industrial segment consists of acetate filter tow (31% of 1994 segment sales) used for filtered cigarettes; intermediate chemicals (33%), including acetyl and oxo chemicals and plasticizers used for polymers, agricultural chemicals, industrial intermediates and additives, and pharmaceuticals; and polyethylene and polypropylene (sold November 1994) resins (29%) used in films, extrusion coatings, fibers and injection molding applications. Acetate yarn (7%) is produced for the textile industry.

EMN's largest customer is Eastman Kodak Co., which acccounted for 7% of sales in 1994.

Important Developments

Jul. '95—EMN announced plans to build a PET plant with annual capacity of 130,000 tons in the Netherlands by early 1998. By the end of 1998, EMN plans to double annual PET capacity to 3.4 billion lbs. A Mexican plant with annual capacity of 120,000 tons will begin production in early 1996, while a plant of similar size will go into production in Spain in 1997. EMN also plans to construct two other PET plants with capacity of 130,000 tons, one in North America and the other in Latin America. EMN also plans to build its first wholly owned Asian facility, a polyester co-polymer plant in Malaysia, with startup planned for late 1997. Separately, EMN repurchased $106 million of common stock in the second quarter as part of a $200 million stock repurchase program.

Capitalization

Long Term Debt: $1,289,000,000 (6/95).

Per Share Data ($)

(Year Ended Dec. 31)

	1994	1993	1992	1991	1990	1989
Tangible Bk. Val.	15.59	NA	NA	NA	NA	NA
Cash Flow	8.04	NA	6.86	NA	NA	NA
Earnings	4.05	2.46	2.72	3.69	3.91	NA
Dividends	1.60	Nil	NA	NA	NA	NA
Payout Ratio	40%	Nil	NA	NA	NA	NA
Prices - High	56	48⅛	NA	NA	NA	NA
- Low	39½	42⅞	NA	NA	NA	NA
P/E Ratio - High	14	20	NA	NA	NA	NA
- Low	10	17	NA	NA	NA	NA

Income Statement Analysis (Million $)

	1994	%Chg	1993	%Chg	1992	%Chg	1991
Revs.	4,329	11%	3,903	2%	3,811	5%	3,614
Oper. Inc.	965	—	NA	—	814	—	NA
Depr.	329	—	NA	—	337	—	NA
Int. Exp.	98.0	17%	84.0	-16%	100	—	NA
Pretax Inc.	550	64%	336	-5%	355	—	NA
Eff. Tax Rate	39%	—	39%	—	38%	—	NA
Net Inc.	336	65%	204	-8%	221	-26%	300

Balance Sheet & Other Fin. Data (Million $)

	1994	1993	1992	1991	1990	1989
Cash	90.0	141	16.0	NA	NA	NA
Curr. Assets	1,273	1,103	1,089	NA	NA	NA
Total Assets	4,375	4,341	4,319	4,010	3,760	NA
Curr. Liab.	800	469	2,212	NA	NA	NA
LT Debt	1,195	1,801	Nil	NA	NA	NA
Common Eqty.	1,295	1,061	1,101	1,165	948	NA
Total Cap.	2,815	2,862	1,395	NA	NA	NA
Cap. Exp.	281	NA	NA	NA	NA	NA
Cash Flow	665	NA	558	NA	NA	NA

Ratio Analysis

	1994	1993	1992	1991	1990	1989
Curr. Ratio	1.6	2.4	0.5	NA	NA	NA
% LT Debt of Cap.	42.5	62.9	Nil	NA	NA	NA
% Net Inc.of Revs.	7.8	5.2	5.8	8.3	9.2	NA
% Ret. on Assets	7.7	NA	NA	7.7	NA	NA
% Ret. on Equity	28.5	NA	NA	28.4	NA	NA

Dividend Data

Dividends were initiated in March 1994. A dividend reinvestment plan is available. A poison pill stock purchase rights plan is in effect.

Amt. of Div. $	Date Decl.	Ex-Div. Date	Stock of Record	Payment Date
0.400	Sep. 01	Sep. 12	Sep. 16	Oct. 03 '94
0.400	Dec. 01	Dec. 12	Dec. 16	Jan. 02 '95
0.400	Mar. 02	Mar. 10	Mar. 16	Apr. 03 '95
0.400	Jun. 01	Jun. 14	Jun. 16	Jul. 03 '95
0.420	Sep. 07	Sep. 14	Sep. 18	Oct. 02 '95

Data as orig. reptd.; bef. results of disc. opers. and/or spec. items. Per share data adj. for stk. divs. as of ex-div. date. Statistical data pro forma prior to 1994. E-Estimated. NA-Not Available. NM-Not Meaningful. NR-Not Ra

Office—100 North Eastman Rd., Kingsport, TN 37660-5075. **Tel**—(423) 229-2000. **Chrmn & CEO**—E. W. Deavenport, Jr. **VP & CFO**—H. V. Stephens. **VP & Secy**—J. C. Bracy. **Investor Contact**—John R. Porter III. **Dirs**—H. J. Arnelle, D. F. Baker, R. W. Bourne, Jr., C. A. Campbell, Jr., M. von Clemm, E. W. Deavenport, Jr., L. Liu, M. R. Marks, G. B. Mitchell, J. A. White. **Transfer Agent & Registrar**—First Chicago Trust Co. of New York, Jersey City, NJ. **Incorporated** in Delaware in 1993. **Empl**-17,495. **S&P Analyst:** Richard O'Reilly, CFA

Eastman Kodak

NYSE Symbol **EK**

In S&P 500

18-OCT-95

Industry: Leisure/Amusement

Summary: This major photography company, which is under the leadership of a new chairman and CEO, divested its non-imaging businesses in 1994. Proceeds were largely used to reduce debt.

S&P Opinion: Accumulate (★★★★)	Recent Price • 57¼	Yield • 2.7%
	52 Wk Range • 64½-44¼	12-Mo. P/E • 16.7

Quantitative Evaluations

Outlook
(1 Lowest—5 Highest)
• **2+**

Fair Value
• **55¾**

Risk
• **Low**

Earn./Div. Rank
• **B**

Technical Eval.
• **Bearish** since 4/95

Rel. Strength Rank
(1 Lowest—99 Highest)
• **54**

Insider Activity
• **NA**

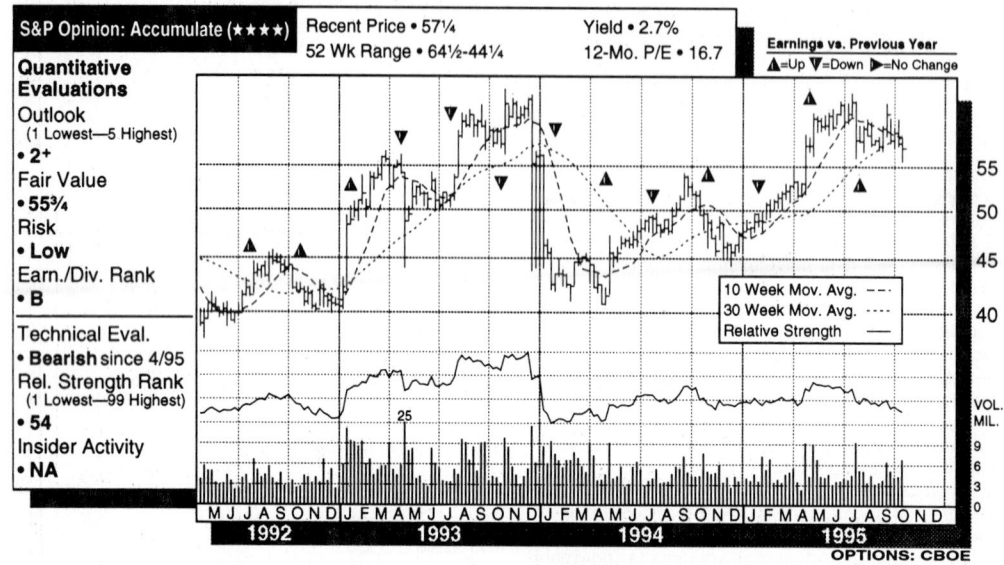

Earnings vs. Previous Year
▲=Up ▼=Down ▶=No Change

10 Week Mov. Avg. — – –
30 Week Mov. Avg. – – – –
Relative Strength ———

VOL. MIL.

OPTIONS: CBOE

Overview - 17-OCT-95

In 1995, we expect EK sales growth to come largely from volume gains, favorable translation of foreign currency, and the fuller inclusion of the Qualex photo finishing business. We look for 1995 profits to be helped by the absence of year-ago unusual charges, benefits from currency fluctuation and productivity gains, and a smaller loss related to the newer digital electronics area. Longer-term, we expect EK's results to benefit from development of overseas markets; the debut of a new consumer film system; and greater effectiveness in translating research efforts into new products.

Valuation - 17-OCT-95

We view this stock as having appeal for capital gains. Near-term, we expect the shares to get support from a recent authorization by EK to repurchase up to $1 billion of its common stock. Also, we are generally impressed by the early efforts of new Chairman/CEO George Fisher. Following his experience at Motorola, Mr. Fisher seems well-suited to provide leadership for EK's new product efforts. Following the divestiture of various health care and household product businesses, EK's focus is increasingly on various imaging businesses. Over the long-term, we look for electronic imaging products to be of growing significance and value to EK. However, during at least the next few years, we expect products based on silver halide film to remain of great importance.

Key Stock Statistics

S&P EPS Est. 1995	3.85	Tang. Bk. Value/Share	11.51
P/E on S&P Est. 1995	14.9	Beta	0.51
S&P EPS Est. 1996	4.20	Shareholders	151,300
Dividend Rate/Share	1.60	Market cap. (B)	$ 20.4
Shs. outstg. (M)	341.8	Inst. holdings	60%
Avg. daily vol. (M)	1.094	Insider holdings	NA

Value of $10,000 invested 5 years ago: $ 17,577

Fiscal Year Ending Dec. 31

	1995	% Change	1994	% Change	1993	% Change
Revenues (Million $)						
1Q	3,137	14%	2,755	-22%	3,540	-20%
2Q	3,992	17%	3,425	-20%	4,265	-18%
3Q	3,877	10%	3,529	-15%	4,133	-20%
4Q	—	—	3,848	-14%	4,480	-17%
Yr.	—	—	13,557	-17%	16,364	-19%
Income (Million $)						
1Q	262.0	81%	145.0	54%	94.00	-35%
2Q	377.0	28%	295.0	-3%	304.0	-16%
3Q	338.0	75%	193.0	NM	-127.0	NM
4Q	—	—	-79.00	NM	204.0	-32%
Yr.	—	—	554.0	17%	475.0	-52%
Earnings Per Share ($)						
1Q	0.77	75%	0.44	52%	0.29	-36%
2Q	1.11	26%	0.88	-5%	0.93	-16%
3Q	0.99	74%	0.57	NM	-0.39	NM
4Q	E0.99	NM	-0.23	NM	0.62	-33%
Yr.	E3.85	133%	1.65	15%	1.44	-53%

Next earnings report expected: mid January

Business Summary - 18-OCT-95

Eastman Kodak is the largest producer of photographic products in the world. In 1994, EK divested various businesses that are not related to imaging. Segment contributions from continuing operations (profits before restructuring charges) in 1994 were:

	Sales	Profits
Consumer	44%	65%
Commercial	56%	35%

Sales to customers outside the U.S. accounted for about 53% of sales in both 1994 and 1993.

EK's consumer imaging segment includes products that are used to capture, record, or display a consumer-oriented image. This includes films, photographic papers, processing services, photographic chemicals, cameras, and projectors. In 1994, EK acquired the portion of the Qualex film processing business that it did not already own.

EK also has businesses that serve the imaging and information needs of commercial customers. This includes films, photographic papers and plates, chemicals, processing equipment, audiovisual equipment, copiers, microfilm products, applications software, printers, other business equipment, and service agreements to support certain products.

Proceeds from asset sales have helped EK to sharply reduce its debt level. Much of the non-imaging health care businesses divested by EK in 1994 were originally acquired through the $5.1 billion acquisition of Sterling Drug Inc. in 1988. Also, ownership of a large chemicals (Eastman Chemical) business was spun off to EK shareholders in about January 1994.

Separately, in 1994, 1993 and 1992, EK had restructuring charges of $0.75, $1.16 and $0.43 a share, respectively (excluding Eastman Chemical Co.).

Important Developments

Oct. '95—EK's directors authorized the repurchase of up to $1 billion of common stock, and a contribution of $500 million of common stock to EK's U.S. pension plan. As of September 30, 1995, EK had cash and marketable securities totaling $1.33 billion. Also, EK's earnings comparison in 1995's third quarter was helped by volume and productivity gains; the absence of about $0.18 a share of unusual charges in the year-ago period; and a benefit of about $0.04 a share from a downward revision of EK's 1995 estimated full-year tax rate. Excluding the impact of an acquisition and a favorable benefit from foreign currency translation, EK's sales in the quarter were up about 4%.

Capitalization

Long-term Debt: $653,000,000 (9/95).

Per Share Data ($) (Year Ended Dec. 31)

	1994	1993	1992	1991	1990	1989
Tangible Bk. Val.	10.01	-2.89	6.60	5.40	7.05	6.36
Cash Flow	4.28	4.83	7.79	4.60	6.20	5.72
Earnings	1.65	1.44	3.06	0.05	2.17	1.63
Dividends	1.60	2.00	2.00	2.00	2.00	2.00
Payout Ratio	97%	139%	65%	823%	92%	123%
Prices - High	56⅜	65	50¾	49¾	43⅞	52⅜
- Low	40⅝	40¼	37¾	37⅝	33¾	40
P/E Ratio - High	34	45	17	NM	20	32
- Low	25	28	12	NM	16	25

Income Statement Analysis (Million $)

	1994	%Chg	1993	%Chg	1992	%Chg	1991
Revs.	13,557	-17%	16,364	-19%	20,183	4%	19,419
Oper. Inc.	2,545	-18%	3,122	-19%	3,874	NM	3,852
Depr.	883	-21%	1,111	-28%	1,539	4%	1,477
Int. Exp.	177	-72%	635	-30%	907	-3%	931
Pretax Inc.	1,002	17%	856	-47%	1,601	NM	11.0
Eff. Tax Rate	45%	—	45%	—	38%	—	NM
Net Inc.	554	17%	475	-52%	994	NM	17.0

Balance Sheet & Other Fin. Data (Million $)

	1994	1993	1992	1991	1990	1989
Cash	2,068	1,966	560	924	916	1,279
Curr. Assets	7,683	8,021	7,405	8,258	8,608	8,591
Total Assets	14,968	20,325	23,138	24,170	24,125	23,652
Curr. Liab.	5,735	4,910	5,998	6,899	7,163	6,573
LT Debt	660	6,853	7,202	7,597	6,989	7,376
Common Eqty.	4,017	3,356	6,557	6,104	6,737	6,642
Total Cap.	4,772	10,288	14,828	15,191	15,556	15,708
Cap. Exp.	1,153	1,082	2,092	2,135	2,037	2,118
Cash Flow	1,437	1,586	2,533	1,494	2,012	1,855

Ratio Analysis

	1994	1993	1992	1991	1990	1989
Curr. Ratio	1.3	1.6	1.2	1.2	1.2	1.3
% LT Debt of Cap.	13.8	66.6	48.6	50.0	44.9	47.0
% Net Inc.of Revs.	4.1	2.9	4.9	0.1	3.7	2.9
% Ret. on Assets	3.1	2.2	4.2	0.1	2.9	2.3
% Ret. on Equity	14.8	9.5	15.7	0.3	10.5	7.9

Dividend Data

Dividends have been paid since 1902. A dividend reinvestment plan is available.

Amt. of Div. $	Date Decl.	Ex-Div. Date	Stock of Record	Payment Date
0.400	Nov. 11	Nov. 25	Dec. 01	Jan. 03 '95
0.400	Feb. 10	Feb. 23	Mar. 01	Apr. 03 '95
0.400	Apr. 21	May. 25	Jun. 01	Jul. 03 '95
0.400	Jul. 14	Aug. 30	Sep. 01	Oct. 02 '95

Data as orig. reptd.; bef. results of disc. opers. and/or spec. items. Per share data adj. for stk. divs. as of ex-div. date. E-Estimated. NA-Not Available. NM-Not Meaningful. NR-Not Ranked.

Office—343 State St., Rochester, NY 14650. **Tel**—(716) 724-4000. **Chrmn, Pres, & CEO**—G. M. C. Fisher. **EVP-CFO**—H. L. Kavetas. **Treas**—J. J. Greene, Jr. **Secy**—J. P. Haag. **Investor Contact**—David L. Fiedler. **Dirs**—R. S. Braddock, M. L. Collins, A. F. Emerson, G. M. C. Fisher, R. C. Goizueta, P. E. Gray, K. Kaske, J. J. Phelan Jr., W. J. Prezzano, L. J. Thomas, R. A. Zimmerman. **Transfer Agent & Registrar**—First Chicago Trust Co., NYC. **Incorporated** in New Jersey in 1901. **Empl**-96,300. **S&P Analyst:** Tom Graves, CFA

Eaton Corp.

NYSE Symbol **ETN**
In S&P 500

29-AUG-95

Industry:
Auto parts/equipment

Summary: ETN produces a wide range of automotive, industrial, commercial and defense products, including truck transmissions and axles, engine components, electrical equipment and controls.

S&P Opinion: Hold (★★★)	Recent Price • 54	Yield • 3.0%
	52 Wk Range • 62½-43⅞	12-Mo. P/E • 10.7

Earnings vs. Previous Year
▲=Up ▼=Down ▶=No Change

Quantitative Evaluations

Outlook
(1 Lowest—5 Highest)
• **4+**

Fair Value
• **55**

Risk
• **Average**

Earn./Div. Rank
• **B+**

Technical Eval.
• **Bearish** since 10/93

Rel. Strength Rank
(1 Lowest—99 Highest)
• **12**

Insider Activity
• **Neutral**

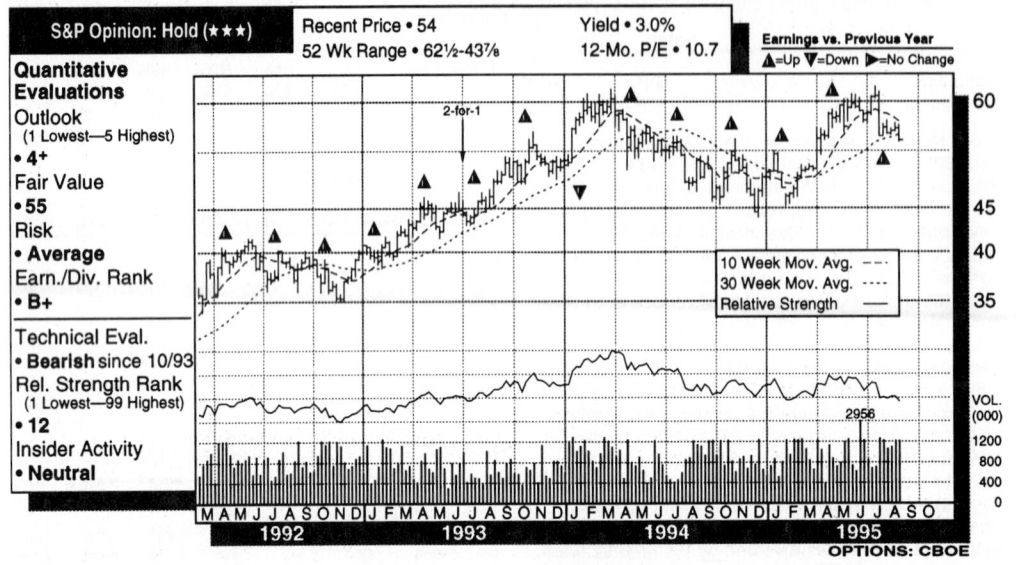

- 10 Week Mov. Avg. - - -
- 30 Week Mov. Avg. ----
- Relative Strength —

2-for-1

2956

VOL.
(000)
1200
800
400
0

60
45
40
35

MAMJJASOND|JFMAMJJASOND|JFMAMJJASOND|JFMAMJJASO
1992 | 1993 | 1994 | 1995

OPTIONS: CBOE

Overview - 29-AUG-95

Sales should continue to rise in 1996, despite the apparent peaking of the North American vehicle markets. Growth will be driven by increased dollar content per vehicle assembled and international market expansion in automotive, increased demand for distribution and controls products, and continued robust growth in semiconductor equipment. With the consolidation of the Westinghouse distribution and controls business complete, earnings growth in the controls segment should accelerate. Productivity gains in most business lines, along with lower interest expense as long term debt is reduced, should lead to higher earnings. Longer term, the company is focusing its expansion plans on the Far East and Latin America, which are expected to be the leading growth areas of the world over the next decade.

Valuation - 29-AUG-95

Although ETN's acquisition of the distribution and controls business from Westinghouse in 1994 is proving to be a coup, ETN remains heavily exposed to the cyclical vehicular, consumer durables and capital goods markets. This exposure has traditionally led to an earnings multiple below that of the S&P 500. With the North American heavy duty truck market peaking and perhaps headed for a downturn next year, and light duty vehicle markets already weakening, we do not think the stock's discount to the S&P 500 will be closed this year. We expect that the stock will be an average performer during the next 12 months.

Key Stock Statistics

S&P EPS Est. 1995	5.40	Tang. Bk. Value/Share	12.00
P/E on S&P Est. 1995	10.0	Beta	1.20
S&P EPS Est. 1996	5.75	Shareholders	14,800
Dividend Rate/Share	1.60	Market cap. (B)	$ 4.2
Shs. outstg. (M)	77.9	Inst. holdings	74%
Avg. daily vol. (M)	0.244	Insider holdings	NA

Value of $10,000 invested 5 years ago: $ 22,448

Fiscal Year Ending Dec. 31

	1995	% Change	1994	% Change	1993	% Change
Revenues (Million $)						
1Q	1,731	26%	1,371	26%	1,086	14%
2Q	1,758	14%	1,545	35%	1,147	13%
3Q	—	—	1,531	45%	1,053	11%
4Q	—	—	1,605	44%	1,115	16%
Yr.	—	—	6,052	38%	4,401	14%
Income (Million $)						
1Q	108.0	46%	74.00	48%	50.00	56%
2Q	110.0	28%	86.00	62%	53.00	29%
3Q	—	—	84.00	91%	44.00	57%
4Q	—	—	89.00	197%	30.00	-19%
Yr.	—	—	333.0	85%	180.0	31%
Earnings Per Share ($)						
1Q	1.39	38%	1.01	33%	0.76	65%
2Q	1.41	25%	1.13	47%	0.77	29%
3Q	E1.20	9%	1.10	75%	0.63	58%
4Q	E1.40	22%	1.15	180%	0.41	-23%
Yr.	E5.40	23%	4.40	71%	2.57	29%

Next earnings report expected: early September

Eaton Corp.

Business Summary - 29-AUG-95

Eaton Corp. is a major industrial company primarily operating in the vehicular components and electrical and electronic controls markets. Segment contributions in 1994:

	Sales	Profits
Vehicle components	47%	60%
Electrical/electronic controls	51%	40%
Defense	2%	---

In 1994, sales were derived 75% from the U.S. and 25% from overseas, while 83% of profits were from the U.S. and 17% from outside the U.S.

Truck components accounted for 30% of total sales in 1994, automobile components for 10%, and off-highway vehicle components for 7%. Truck transmissions and axles are the principal product lines; other products include retarders, power take-offs, antilock brakes, locking differentials, engine valves, valve lifters, tire pressure control systems, tire valves, leaf springs, viscous fan drives, fans, fan shrouds, power steering pumps, emission control valves, superchargers, thermostats, hose tubing, motors, and couplings.

Electrical and electronic control products are divided into three groups: industrial and commercial controls (30% of total sales), automotive and appliance controls (14%), and specialty controls (7%). Controls include electromechanical and electronic control components and systems; sensors and human interface devices; programmable controllers; switches; relays; counters; electrical adjustable speed drives; low-voltage distribution equipment; aerospace power controls; fasteners and thermostats; semiconductor wafer fabrication equipment; automated materials handling systems; and golf grips.

In 1993, ETN decided to retain its previously discontinued defense electronics unit. Products include strategic countermeasures, tactical jamming systems, electronic intelligence, electronic support measures, and radar surveillance.

Important Developments

May '95—In separate transactions, ETN acquired IKU Group of The Netherlands, which is a supplier of electric mirror actuators for automotive manfacturers, and the Emwest electrical switchgear and controls unit of Email Ltd. of Australia. IKU's customers include every major mirror manufacturer in the U.S., Europe and Korea. Emwest expands the company's presence in the emerging Pacific Region markets. The acquisitions had combined sales of about $110 million in 1994. The purchase price for these two acquisitions and other small transactions made in 1995 was $112 million.

Capitalization

Long Term Debt: $1,181,000,000 (6/95).

Per Share Data ($) (Year Ended Dec. 31)

	1994	1993	1992	1991	1990	1989
Tangible Bk. Val.	10.49	11.61	9.71	12.56	12.36	10.65
Cash Flow	7.26	5.19	4.45	3.19	4.45	4.54
Earnings	4.40	2.57	1.99	0.92	2.39	2.79
Dividends	1.20	1.15	1.10	1.10	1.05	1.00
Payout Ratio	27%	45%	55%	121%	42%	35%
Prices - High	62⅛	55⅜	41⅝	33⅛	32¼	33¾
- Low	43⅞	38¼	30⅞	23⅜	20⅜	26½
P/E Ratio - High	14	22	21	36	13	12
- Low	10	15	16	25	9	9

Income Statement Analysis (Million $)

	1994	%Chg	1993	%Chg	1992	%Chg	1991
Revs.	6,052	38%	4,401	14%	3,869	14%	3,381
Oper. Inc.	776	38%	563	41%	399	21%	329
Depr.	216	19%	182	7%	170	10%	155
Int. Exp.	101	16%	87.0	-3%	90.0	5%	86.0
Pretax Inc.	488	86%	262	47%	178	117%	82.0
Eff. Tax Rate	32%	—	31%	—	23%	—	24%
Net Inc.	333	85%	180	31%	137	121%	62.0

Balance Sheet & Other Fin. Data (Million $)

	1994	1993	1992	1991	1990	1989
Cash	41.0	300	216	122	217	193
Curr. Assets	1,846	1,466	1,318	1,186	1,296	1,291
Total Assets	4,682	3,268	3,096	3,087	3,013	3,052
Curr. Liab.	1,102	787	655	699	633	616
LT Debt	1,053	649	833	795	755	836
Common Eqty.	1,680	1,105	948	1,153	1,140	1,145
Total Cap.	2,733	1,754	1,795	2,084	2,060	2,148
Cap. Exp.	267	227	172	170	202	212
Cash Flow	549	362	307	217	315	341

Ratio Analysis

	1994	1993	1992	1991	1990	1989
Curr. Ratio	1.7	1.9	2.0	1.7	2.0	2.1
% LT Debt of Cap.	38.5	37.0	46.4	38.1	36.7	38.9
% Net Inc.of Revs.	5.5	4.1	3.5	1.8	4.6	5.7
% Ret. on Assets	8.1	5.6	4.4	2.0	5.8	6.9
% Ret. on Equity	23.1	17.3	12.9	5.4	15.4	18.3

Dividend Data —Dividends have been paid since 1923. A dividend reinvestment plan is available. A "poison pill" stock purchase rights plan was adopted in 1995.

Amt. of Div. $	Date Decl.	Ex-Div. Date	Stock of Record	Payment Date
0.300	Jul. 27	Aug. 02	Aug. 08	Aug. 25 '94
0.300	Oct. 26	Nov. 01	Nov. 07	Nov. 25 '94
0.300	Jan. 25	Jan. 31	Feb. 06	Feb. 24 '95
0.400	Apr. 26	May. 02	May. 08	May. 25 '95
0.400	Jul. 26	Aug. 03	Aug. 07	Aug. 25 '95

Data as orig. reptd.; bef. results of disc. opers. and/or spec. items. Per share data adj. for stk. divs. as of ex-div. date. E-Estimated. NA-Not Available. NM-Not Meaningful. NR-Not Ranked.

Office—Eaton Center, Cleveland, OH 44114-2584. **Tel**—(216) 523-5000. **Chrmn**—W. E. Butler. **Vice Chrmn & CEO**—S. R. Hardis. **Pres & COO**—A. M. Cutler. **VP-CFO**—A. T. Dillon. **VP-Treas**—J. M. Carmont. **Secy**—E. R. Franklin. **Investor Contact**—William C. Hartman. **Dirs**—N. A. Armstrong, W. E. Butler, A. M. Cutler, P. B. Davis, E. Green, S. R. Hardis, C. E. Hugel, J. R. Miller, F. C. Moseley, V. A. Pelson, A. W. Reynolds, J. S. Rodewig, G. L. Tooker. **Transfer Agent & Registrar**—KeyCorp Shareholder Services, Cleveland. **Incorporated** in Ohio in 1916. **Empl**-51,000. **S&P Analyst:** Joshua M. Harari, CFA

Echlin Inc.

NYSE Symbol **ECH**
In S&P 500

16-OCT-95

Industry:
Auto parts/equipment

Summary: This company produces and distributes automotive aftermarket electrical, brake, fuel and emission systems.

| S&P Opinion: Buy (★★★★★) | Recent Price • 34¾ | Yield • 2.4% |
| | 52 Wk Range • 39⅜-26¾ | 12-Mo. P/E • 13.4 |

Quantitative Evaluations

Outlook
(1 Lowest—5 Highest)
• **5+**

Fair Value
• **46⅜**

Risk
• **Low**

Earn./Div. Rank
• **A-**

Technical Eval.
• **Bearish** since 7/93

Rel. Strength Rank
(1 Lowest—99 Highest)
• **33**

Insider Activity
• **Neutral**

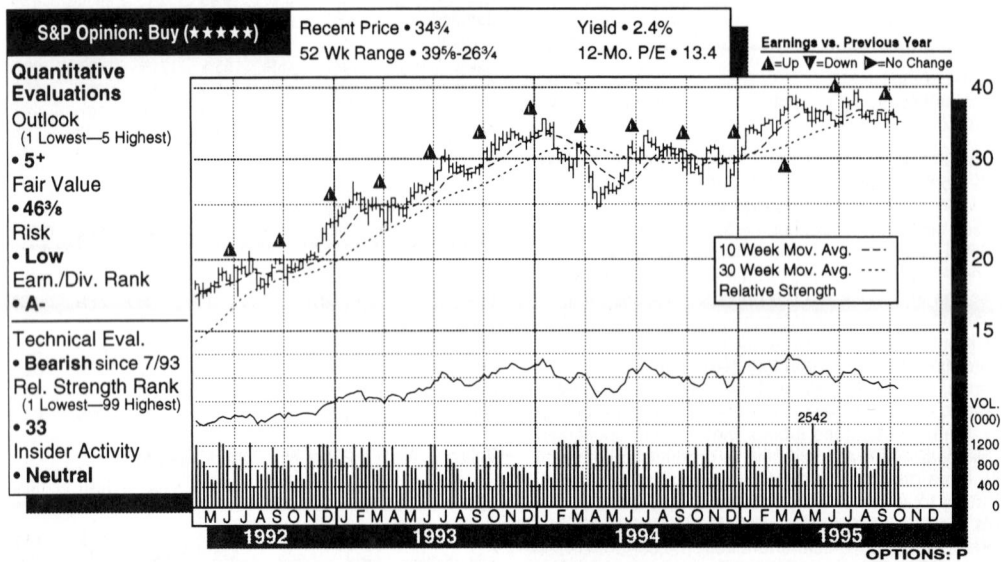

Earnings vs. Previous Year
▲=Up ▼=Down ▶=No Change

10 Week Mov. Avg. ---
30 Week Mov. Avg. ·····
Relative Strength —

2542

VOL. (000)
1200
800
400
0

MJJASOND J FMAM JJASOND J FMAM JJASOND J FMAM JJASOND
1992   1993   1994   1995

OPTIONS: P

Overview - 16-OCT-95

Fiscal 1996 sales should benefit from contributions by acquisitions and price increases, as well as from greater penetration of more rapidly expanding overseas markets. ECH's goal is to boost sales 15% annually by focusing on faster-wearing parts such as brakes, and on costlier items such as electronic components and emissions control parts, supplemented by acquisitions. Over the next few years, growth in emissions-related parts will be sparked by new and more stringent emissions testing regulations, which will tend to increase the frequency and extent of repairs required to keep vehicles in compliance. Aided by continuing cost-cutting efforts and strength in important foreign markets, fiscal 1996 earnings should rise.

Valuation - 16-OCT-95

Despite the likelihood of further significant earnings improvement, the shares continue to trade at a modest multiple of 12X fiscal 1996 estimated earnings, a significant discount to the S&P 500 Index and to that of ECH's peers. We rate the company a strong buy, particularly in view of the relative stability of its largely aftermarket base of business. We believe that the company's expanding foreign operations put it in a good position to participate in the faster growing regions of the world, and eventually to become a dominant international player in aftermarket parts distribution. The cash dividend is secure, and should rise steadily over the long term, supported by strong cash flow and a solid balance sheet.

Key Stock Statistics

S&P EPS Est. 1996	3.00	Tang. Bk. Value/Share	13.52
P/E on S&P Est. 1996	11.6	Beta	1.45
Dividend Rate/Share	0.82	Shareholders	5,200
Shs. outstg. (M)	59.6	Market cap. (B)	$ 2.1
Avg. daily vol. (M)	0.223	Inst. holdings	78%
		Insider holdings	NA

Value of $10,000 invested 5 years ago: $ 27,318

Fiscal Year Ending Aug. 31

	1996	% Change	1995	% Change	1994	% Change
Revenues (Million $)						
1Q	—	—	600.6	20%	499.3	8%
2Q	—	—	648.1	30%	497.1	13%
3Q	—	—	745.1	22%	610.0	17%
4Q	—	—	724.0	16%	623.0	20%
Yr.	—	—	2,718	22%	2,229	15%
Income (Million $)						
1Q	—	—	31.80	32%	24.09	26%
2Q	—	—	28.99	33%	21.76	33%
3Q	—	—	47.77	22%	39.01	31%
4Q	—	—	45.87	27%	36.22	28%
Yr.	—	—	154.4	28%	121.1	29%
Earnings Per Share ($)						
1Q	E0.65	20%	0.54	32%	0.41	24%
2Q	E0.60	25%	0.48	30%	0.37	32%
3Q	E0.90	11%	0.81	23%	0.66	29%
4Q	E0.85	10%	0.77	24%	0.62	29%
Yr.	E3.00	15%	2.60	26%	2.06	29%

Next earnings report expected: mid December

Business Summary - 16-OCT-95

Echlin Inc. is a worldwide manufacturer of automotive products primarily for the aftermarket. Sales by product class in recent fiscal years were:

	1994	1993
Brake system parts	47%	45%
Engine system parts	28%	30%
Other vehicle parts	23%	22%
Nonautomotive products	2%	3%

Brake parts include master cylinders; master cylinder push rods; brake shoes, drums, wheel cylinders and hardware for drum brakes; disc pads, rotors and calipers for disc brakes; hydraulic brake repair kits; and hoses and controllers for electrical brakes. Wheel oil seals, compressors, valves, power boosters, pressure converters, antilock brake systems, air brake actuating products, spring brakes, connectors and slack adjusters are produced for the heavy-duty brake market. Engine system parts include complete distributors and caps, ignition coils, control modules, sensors, actuators, voltage regulators, wires, cables, carburetor and emission control parts, starter drives, fuel pumps and injection systems, starter drives, solenoids, and EGR and PCV valves.

Other vehicle parts include new and remanufactured clutches, engine mounts, power steering, oil and water pumps, timing gears and chains, steering and suspension components, windshield wiper systems, shifters, gaskets, traction bars and high-performance accessories. Nonautomotive items include small engine parts, fork lift truck replacement parts, security access control products and industrial wires and cables.

Fiscal 1994 sales were derived 76% from North America, 19% from Europe and 5% from other countries; operating income was derived 83% from North America, 16% from Europe and 1% from elsewhere. Members of the National Automotive Parts Association (NAPA), including Genuine Parts Co., accounted for 10.3% of fiscal 1994 sales, versus 10.8% in fiscal 1993.

Important Developments

Oct. '95—ECH agreed to acquire American Electronic Components, Inc. (AEC) for 1.5 million common shares. With sales of $40 million, AEC manufactures motor vehicle electronic components, including Hall Effect, variable reluctance and inertia sensors used in braking, drive train and on-board diagnostic systems, and automotive switches, relays and other electromechanical products.

Capitalization

Long Term Debt: $482,169,000 (8/95).

Per Share Data ($)

(Year Ended Aug. 31)

	1995	1994	1993	1992	1991	1990
Tangible Bk. Val.	NA	13.52	12.13	12.34	11.63	11.87
Cash Flow	NA	3.14	2.56	2.15	1.76	1.62
Earnings	2.60	2.06	1.60	1.15	0.75	0.85
Dividends	0.79	0.73	0.70	0.70	0.70	0.70
Payout Ratio	30%	35%	44%	61%	94%	83%
Prices - High	39⅝	35¼	34⅝	23⅝	14⅞	16⅜
- Low	29⅞	24½	22½	13½	9⅞	9⅜
P/E Ratio - High	15	17	22	21	20	19
- Low	11	12	14	12	13	11

Income Statement Analysis (Million $)

	1994	%Chg	1993	%Chg	1992	%Chg	1991
Revs.	2,229	15%	1,944	9%	1,783	6%	1,686
Oper. Inc.	254	26%	202	26%	160	23%	130
Depr.	64.2	14%	56.4	6%	53.0	-2%	54.0
Int. Exp.	23.5	21%	19.4	-12%	22.1	-24%	29.0
Pretax Inc.	178	29%	138	47%	94.0	54%	61.2
Eff. Tax Rate	32%	—	32%	—	32%	—	32%
Net Inc.	121	29%	93.6	46%	64.3	54%	41.7

Balance Sheet & Other Fin. Data (Million $)

	1994	1993	1992	1991	1990	1989
Cash	53.8	28.6	29.8	33.0	19.6	17.7
Curr. Assets	913	739	730	728	762	682
Total Assets	1,577	1,263	1,241	1,192	1,192	1,034
Curr. Liab.	425	357	313	249	252	245
LT Debt	297	158	201	253	236	108
Common Eqty.	799	714	694	649	662	641
Total Cap.	1,152	906	928	943	940	789
Cap. Exp.	75.6	47.7	51.7	59.6	66.0	70.0
Cash Flow	185	150	118	96.0	93.0	82.0

Ratio Analysis

	1994	1993	1992	1991	1990	1989
Curr. Ratio	2.1	2.1	2.3	2.9	3.0	2.8
% LT Debt of Cap.	25.8	17.4	21.6	26.8	25.0	13.6
% Net Inc.of Revs.	5.4	4.8	3.6	2.5	2.9	3.1
% Ret. on Assets	8.5	7.3	5.3	3.5	4.2	4.2
% Ret. on Equity	16.0	13.0	9.5	6.3	7.2	7.0

Dividend Data —Dividends have been paid since 1950.

Amt. of Div. $	Date Decl.	Ex-Div. Date	Stock of Record	Payment Date
0.190	Sep. 13	Oct. 03	Oct. 07	Oct. 18 '94
0.190	Dec. 15	Dec. 29	Jan. 05	Jan. 18 '95
0.205	Apr. 03	Apr. 05	Apr. 11	Apr. 18 '95
0.205	Jun. 28	Jul. 05	Jul. 07	Jul. 18 '95
0.205	Sep. 27	Oct. 05	Oct. 10	Oct. 18 '95

Data as orig. reptd.; bef. results of disc. opers. and/or spec. items. Incl. merger or acq. in 1994, 1991 and 1990. Per share data adj. for stk. divs. as of ex-div. date. E-Estimated. NA-Not Available. NM-Not Meaningful. NR-Not Ranked.

Office—100 Double Beach Rd., Branford, CT 06405. **Tel**—(203) 481-5751. **Chrmn & CEO**—F. J. Mancheski. **Pres & COO**—C. S. Greer. **VP & Secy**—J. P. Leckerling. **VP & Treas**—J. A. Onorato. **Investor Contact**—Paul R. Ryder. **Dirs**—D. A. Bromley, J. F. Creamer, Jr., M. P. DeVane, J. E. Echlin, Jr., C. S. Greer, J. F. Gustafson, D. C. Jensen, T. O. Jones, F. J. Mancheski, P. S. Myers, F. R. O'Keefe, Jr., J. G. Rivard. **Transfer Agent & Registrar**—Bank of Boston. **Incorporated** in Connecticut in 1959. **Empl**-20,600. **S&P Analyst:** Joshua M. Harari, CFA

Echo Bay Mines

ASE Symbol ECO Options on Pacific & Vancouver (Jan-Apr-Jul-Oct) In S&P 500

Price	Range	P-E Ratio	Dividend	Yield	S&P Ranking	Beta
Aug. 21'95	1995					
11	11⅜–8⅝	NM	[1]0.08	0.7%	B–	–0.29

Summary

Echo Bay is a large North American gold mining company. In recent years ECO has substantially increased its exploration outlays. In June 1995 ECO agreed to purchase a 75% stake in the promising Kingking gold project in the Phillipines. Lower gold output combined with flat prices and higher costs should yield a small net loss in 1995.

Current Outlook

A $0.30 a share loss is projected for 1995, versus a $0.07 a share profit in 1994.

Dividends should continue at $0.03¾ semiannually.

Gold production is expected to fall in 1995 as ECO encounters lower-grade ores at the McCoy/Cove mine and 50%-owned Round Mountain property. Partly offsetting will be increased output at Kettle River reflecting the switch over to the higher-grade Lamefoot deposit. Unit costs will rise significantly reflecting increased exploration and development expenditures and accruals for mine reclamation. Additionally, the mining of lower grade ore and the move deeper into the Lupin mine will boost costs. Gold prices are expected to be flat. Increased interest income will be offset by increased preferred dividend payments.

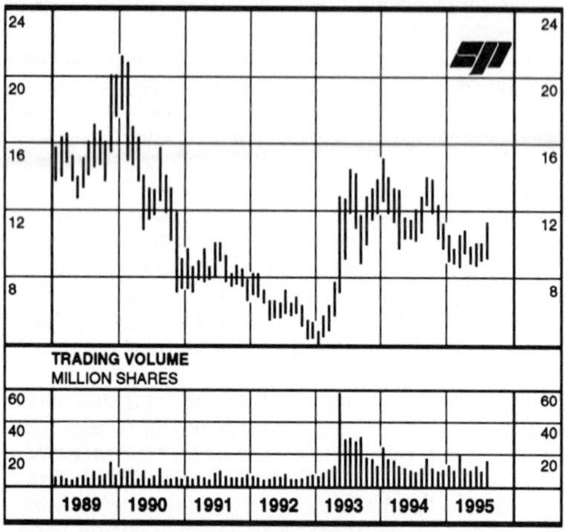

Total Revenues (Million $)

Quarter:	1995	1994	1993	1992
Mar.	84.2	103.1	83.8	71.0
Jun.	90.6	95.8	94.0	86.3
Sep.		89.1	92.0	75.3
Dec.		89.6	96.7	79.8
		377.6	366.5	312.4

Revenues for 1995's first half fell 12%, year to year on a 21% decline in gold production. After preferred dividends a $24.6 million loss ($0.22 a share), contrasted with a $13.2 million profit ($0.12).

Common Share Earnings ($)

Quarter:	1995	1994	1993	1992
Mar.	d0.10	0.10	d0.02	d0.02
Jun.	d0.12	0.02	0.03	Nil
Sep.	Ed0.05	Nil	Nil	d0.04
Dec.	Ed0.03	d0.05	0.02	d0.24
	Ed0.30	0.07	0.03	d0.30

Important Developments

Aug. '95— Pretax income for 1995's second quarter included a $3.2 million gain on the sale of ECO's 50% stake in the Kensington project in Alaska and a $2.1 million gain on the sale of its 24.8% stake in Muscocho Exploration Ltd.

Jul. '95— ECO lifted its holdings in TVI Pacific Inc. to 18.4% with the purchase of an additional 6.7 million TVI common shares for $5.0 million. In June ECO and TVI agreed to purchase the Kingking copper-gold project from Benguet Corp. The partners will pay Benguet $20 million in 1995, $10 million in 1996 and $67 million in 1997 when a feasibility study is completed. The Kingking property contains an estimated 3.8 million ounces of gold and 2.2 billion lbs. of copper.

Next earnings report expected in early November.

Per Share Data ($)

Yr. End Dec. 31	1994	1993	1992	1991	1990	1989	1988	1987	1986	1985
Tangible Bk. Val.	**4.52**	4.58	4.19	4.67	4.47	5.14	5.02	3.81	2.67	1.77
Cash Flow	**0.83**	0.87	0.48	0.81	d0.12	0.83	1.16	0.99	0.70	0.43
Earnings	**0.07**	0.03	d0.30	0.07	d0.60	0.16	0.56	0.52	0.31	0.17
Dividends	**0.075**	0.075	0.075	0.075	0.075	0.073	0.070	0.061	0.047	0.043
Payout Ratio	**107%**	250%	NM	107%	NM	45%	13%	12%	16%	26%
Prices—High	**15⅛**	14½	8¼	10⅛	21¼	20⅛	24	30⅛	12	7⅝
Low	**9¾**	4⅛	4⅜	6⅝	7⅛	12¾	13	11½	6⅜	3⅞
P/E Ratio—	**NM**	NM	NM	NM	NM	NM	43–23	58–22	39–21	46–23

Data as orig. reptd. Adj. for stk. divs. of 100% Jul. 1987. **1.** In U.S. $, subj. to 15% non-resident tax. d-Deficit. E-Estimated. NM-Not Meaningful.

Echo Bay Mines Ltd.

Income Data (Million $)

Year Ended Dec. 31	Revs.	Oper. Inc.	% Oper. Inc. of Revs.	Cap. Exp.	Depr.	Int. Exp.	Net Bef. Taxes	Eff. Tax Rate	Net Inc.	% Net Inc. of Revs.	Cash Flow
1994	378	105	27.8	36	85.5	6.1	19.5	11.3%	8.0	2.1	93.6
1993	367	107	29.3	32	90.4	3.4	18.1	24.8%	3.6	1.0	94.0
1992	312	78	25.0	88	82.1	7.2	d27.2	NM	d31.7	NM	50.3
1991	316	93	29.4	62	75.2	8.0	11.2	39.2%	6.8	2.2	82.0
1990	339	77	22.6	89	47.8	10.4	[2]d65.0	NM	d59.7	NM	d11.8
1989	297	103	34.8	210	55.3	16.3	[2]21.8	26.4%	16.0	5.4	71.3
1988	268	99	37.2	296	40.0	14.1	[2]70.4	22.7%	54.4	20.3	94.4
1987	212	86	40.7	55	22.9	5.2	[2]62.4	22.3%	48.5	22.9	71.4
1986	124	50	40.2	41	17.7	1.7	[2]32.4	20.0%	25.9	20.8	43.6
[1]1985	79	28	34.8	23	11.4	0.7	16.2	20.4%	12.9	16.3	24.3

Balance Sheet Data (Million $)

Dec. 31	Cash	Assets	Curr. Liab.	Ratio	Total Assets	% Ret. on Assets	Long Term Debt	Common Equity	Total Cap.	% LT Debt of Cap.	% Ret. on Equity
1994	202.0	244.0	58	4.2	882	0.9	148	510	803	18.5	1.6
1993	252.0	296.0	148	2.0	990	0.4	157	514	821	19.1	0.7
1992	60.3	105.0	74	1.4	937	NM	246	440	843	29.2	NM
1991	Nil	56.2	70	0.8	875	0.7	268	492	786	34.1	1.4
1990	11.1	68.4	104	0.7	909	NM	328	443	796	41.1	NM
1989	2.7	57.0	102	0.6	992	1.7	338	510	887	38.1	3.2
1988	11.0	72.1	71	1.0	864	7.4	250	497	780	32.0	12.5
1987	27.8	73.1	53	1.4	579	9.6	111	362	506	22.0	15.8
1986	5.6	41.4	48	0.9	414	7.6	78	243	338	23.1	12.8
1985	16.2	35.6	25	1.4	242	6.4	36	148	196	18.6	10.5

Data as orig. reptd. **1.** Refl. merger or acq. **2.** Incl. equity in earns. of nonconsol. subs. d-Deficit. NM-Not Meaningful.

Business Summary

Echo Bay (ECO) is a major North American gold mining company with interests in four operating mines and exploration and development properties in the Americas and Africa. Its share of 1994 gold output was 817,946 ounces, versus 873,900 ounces in 1993. Silver production in 1994 was 10,443,200 oz., compared with 12,454,200 oz. in 1993.

ECO's McCoy/Cove property (Nevada) produced 359,360 oz. of gold and 10,443,151 oz. of silver in 1994, at cash production costs of $199/gold equivalent oz. A decrease of 9.2% and 16% in gold and silver output, respectively, from 1994's record levels reflected lower mill recoveries and throughputs.

The company has a 50% interest in the Round Mountain mine (Nevada), one of the world's largest heap leach gold mines. In 1994, ECO's share of gold production was 211,752 oz. at cash production costs of $180 an oz. ECO and its partners are investing $60 million for an on-site mill, which would increase gold recoveries from the highest-grade nonoxidized ore.

The Lupin mine is located at Contwoyto Lake, Northwest Territories, 56 miles from the Arctic Circle. In 1994, output totaled 180,052 oz. at cash production costs of $280/oz. Prospects for adding significantly to reserves in the future are less rosy each year at this mature mine as the ore grade declines with depth and also becomes more erratic.

ECO's Kettle River property (Wash.) produced 66,782 oz. in 1994, at cash production costs of $259/oz. Mining began at the higher-grade Lamefoot, deposit in late 1994.

Cash production costs in 1994 averaged $214 an oz., the same as in 1993. At year-end 1994, reserves of producing mines totaled 6.9 million oz. of gold and 82.7 million oz. of silver, against year-end 1993's reserves of 7.3 million and 105.1 million oz. of gold and silver, respectively.

Dividend Data

Payments are in U.S. funds, subject to a 15% non-resident tax to U.S. shareholders. A "poison pill" stock purchase rights plan was adopted in 1994.

Amt. of Divd. $	Date Decl.	Ex–divd. Date	Stock of Record	Payment Date
0.03¾	Nov. 10	Dec. 7	Dec. 13	Dec. 31'94
0.03¾	May 10	Jun. 13	Jun. 15	Jun. 30'95

Capitalization

Long Term Debt: $119,121,000 (6/95).

$1.75 Echo Bay Finance Cum. Pfd.: 5,750,000 shs., ea. conv. into 2.985 com. shs.

Common Stock: 112,826,000 shs. (no par).
Institutions own some 26%.
Shareholders: About 67,700.

Office—370-17th St., Suite 4050, Denver, CO 80202. **Tel**—(303) 592-8000. **Chrmn**—R. F. Calman. **Pres & CEO**—R. C. Kraus. **EVP & COO**—R. C. Armstrong. **SVP-Fin & CFO**—P. H. Cheesbrough. **VP & Treas**—R. W. Jenner. **Secy**—R. L. Leclerc. **Investor Contact**—Ted Sheldon. **Dirs**—J. N. Abell, L. C. Burns, R. F. Calman, P. Clarke, L. A. Ferrer, J. G. Christy, R. C. Kraus, R. L. Leclerc, J. F. McOuat, M. E. Sloan, D. W. Strangway, R. G. P. Styles, R. W. Wolcott, Jr., J. Zigarlick, Jr. **Transfer Agents & Registrars**—Montreal Trust Co. of Canada, Toronto et al; Mellon Securities Transfer Services, Ridgefield Park, NJ; Royal Bank of Canada Europe Ltd., London, England. **Reincorporated** in Canada in 1980. **Empl**—1,771.

Stephen R. Klein

Ecolab Inc.

NYSE Symbol **ECL**
In S&P 500

16-OCT-95

Industry:
Chemicals

Summary: Ecolab is the leading worldwide marketer of cleaning, sanitizing and maintenance products and services for the hospitality, institutional and industrial markets.

S&P Opinion: Accumulate (★★★★)

Recent Price • 28
52 Wk Range • 28⅝-19¼

Yield • 1.8%
12-Mo. P/E • 21.5

Earnings vs. Previous Year
▲=Up ▼=Down ▶=No Change

Quantitative Evaluations

Outlook
 (1 Lowest—5 Highest)
• **2⁻**

Fair Value
• **25⅝**

Risk
• **Low**

Earn./Div. Rank
• **B**

Technical Eval.
• **Bearish** since 3/95

Rel. Strength Rank
 (1 Lowest—99 Highest)
• **72**

Insider Activity
• **Neutral**

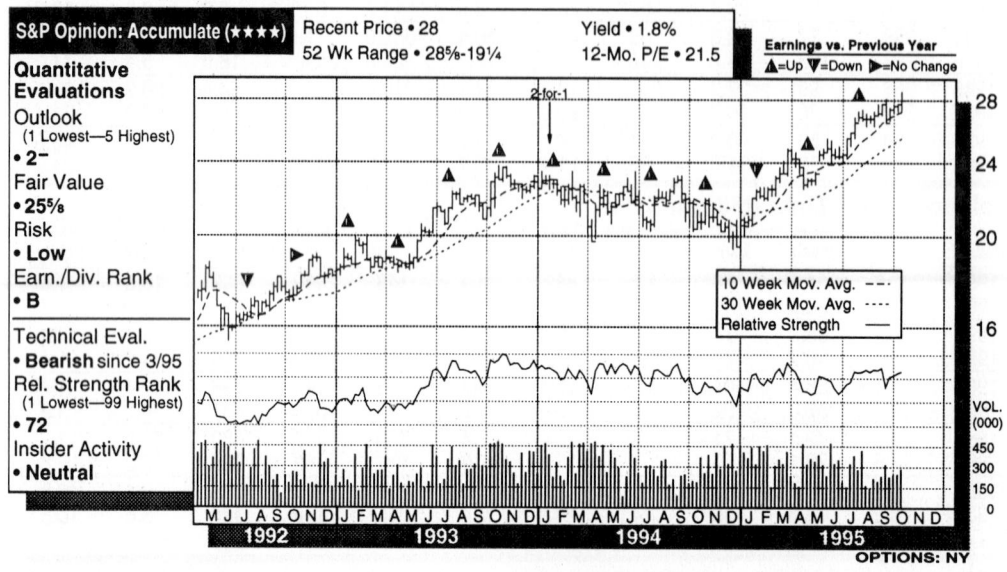

10 Week Mov. Avg. – – –
30 Week Mov. Avg. · · · · ·
Relative Strength ——

28
24
20
16

VOL.
(000)
450
300
150
0

1992 1993 1994 1995

OPTIONS: NY

Overview - 16-OCT-95

S&P projects that sales and earnings will advance further in 1995 on continued worldwide gains in the core businesses, aided by good economic growth and by sales force, product line and market share expansions. International sales growth will be boosted by ongoing growth in Asia and a better comparison is likely in Brazil. Acquisitions should contribute to the gains. Profitability will likely be limited by higher raw material costs. Interest expense will rise in the second half of the year due to the use of cash for a stock buyback, and the tax rate should be about 40%. Earnings of the European joint venture will likely decline due to soft market conditions. The recent stock buyback of 5.2% of the outstanding common shares through a self tender offer will modestly boost share earnings.

Valuation - 16-OCT-95

ECL's shares have risen 33% year to date, boosted by the announcement of the stock buyback program in May 1995. S&P's "accumulate" ranking on the shares reflects the company's attractive long term growth prospects in international markets and strong positive cash flow. The recently completed stock buyback of 5% of the outstanding shares will modestly add to EPS growth. The shares are attractive despite a premium P/E multiple compared to the overall market.

Key Stock Statistics

S&P EPS Est. 1995	1.50	Tang. Bk. Value/Share	6.27
P/E on S&P Est. 1995	18.7	Beta	0.35
S&P EPS Est. 1996	1.75	Shareholders	4,900
Dividend Rate/Share	0.50	Market cap. (B)	$ 1.8
Shs. outstg. (M)	64.4	Inst. holdings	47%
Avg. daily vol. (M)	0.049	Insider holdings	NA

Value of $10,000 invested 5 years ago: $ 22,332

Fiscal Year Ending Dec. 31

	1995	% Change	1994	% Change	1993	% Change
Revenues (Million $)						
1Q	309.6	13%	274.9	14%	240.8	3%
2Q	333.4	11%	299.2	16%	257.8	4%
3Q	—	—	320.4	16%	275.5	6%
4Q	—	—	313.1	17%	267.4	2%
Yr.	—	—	1,208	16%	1,042	4%
Income (Million $)						
1Q	18.39	11%	16.62	32%	12.63	12%
2Q	25.84	9%	23.76	24%	19.16	34%
3Q	—	—	28.49	22%	23.35	16%
4Q	—	—	15.69	-25%	20.79	12%
Yr.	—	—	84.56	11%	75.92	18%
Earnings Per Share ($)						
1Q	0.27	8%	0.25	25%	0.20	11%
2Q	0.38	9%	0.35	17%	0.30	30%
3Q	E0.45	7%	0.42	14%	0.37	16%
4Q	E0.40	74%	0.23	-30%	0.33	12%
Yr.	E1.50	20%	1.25	4%	1.20	18%

Next earnings report expected: late October

Ecolab Inc.

Business Summary - 16-OCT-95

Ecolab (formerly Economics Laboratory) provides cleaning, sanitizing and maintenance products and services for the hospitality, institutional and industrial markets. Geographic contributions in 1994 were:

	Sales	Profits
U.S.	78%	90%
International	22%	10%

In the U.S., Ecolab is the leading supplier of institutional cleaners and sanitizers for warewashing, laundry, kitchen cleaning and general housekeeping, product dispensing equipment and dishwashing racks and related kitchen sundries to the foodservice, lodging and healthcare industries. It also provides institutional and commercial pest elimination and prevention services, janitorial products (floor care, disinfectants, odor control and hand care products) and textile care products for large institutional and commercial laundries. Kay Chemical (acquired December 1994) supplies cleaning and sanitizing products for the fast-food restaurant industry. The Klenzade division provides cleaning and sanitizing products and services to dairy, poultry and swine farms, dairy plants, and food and beverage processors.

Ecolab also provides institutional cleaning, textile, janitorial and Klenzade products and services in Canada, Latin America and the Asia/Pacific region. The 50%-owned Henkel-Ecolab joint venture (formed in 1991) provides cleaning and sanitizing services for European institutional and industrial markets. Sales were $777 million in 1994. Equity income in the venture was $11.0 million in 1994.

Important Developments

Oct. '95—ECL acquired Western Water Management, Inc., a manufacturer of water treatment products, with sales of $12 million in 1994. ECL said that this represented its third, and largest, water care acquisition.
Jun. '95—ECL repurchased 3.55 million common shares (about 5.3% of shares then outstanding) at $25.00 per share through a self-tender offer. ECL had offered to repurchase 3 million shares at a price ranging from $21.75 to $25.00 per share. The company said that it may buyback up to 2.45 million additional shares, to complete the remaining portion of the 6 million share repurchase program announced in May, 1995.
Feb. '95—Earnings in 1994 included an after tax charge of $8 million ($0.12 a share) for costs related to the December 1994 merger with Kay Chemical Co. for 4.46 million common shares.

Capitalization

Long Term Debt: $130,150,000 (6/95).

Per Share Data ($)

(Year Ended Dec. 31)

	1994	1993	1992	1991	1990	1989
Tangible Bk. Val.	6.27	5.34	5.02	4.24	0.60	1.28
Cash Flow	2.24	2.00	1.78	1.76	2.73	1.38
Earnings	1.25	1.20	1.03	0.96	0.98	0.05
Dividends	0.46	0.79	0.36	0.35	0.33	0.33
Payout Ratio	36%	66%	35%	42%	34%	NM
Prices - High	23½	23⅞	19⅛	16¾	15⅝	17⅞
- Low	19¼	18⅛	13⅜	9¾	8⅜	12½
P/E Ratio - High	19	20	19	18	16	NM
- Low	15	15	13	10	9	NM

Income Statement Analysis (Million $)

	1994	%Chg	1993	%Chg	1992	%Chg	1991
Revs.	1,208	16%	1,042	4%	1,005	9%	918
Oper. Inc.	212	23%	172	4%	165	7%	154
Depr.	66.9	33%	50.2	5%	47.7	9%	43.6
Int. Exp.	16.2	-36%	25.2	-37%	39.7	10%	36.2
Pretax Inc.	135	24%	109	19%	91.6	8%	84.7
Eff. Tax Rate	37%	—	31%	—	30%	—	34%
Net Inc.	84.6	11%	75.9	18%	64.3	15%	55.7

Balance Sheet & Other Fin. Data (Million $)

	1994	1993	1992	1991	1990	1989
Cash	98.0	48.0	36.0	78.0	28.0	122
Curr. Assets	401	298	254	284	249	400
Total Assets	1,020	863	832	922	926	1,043
Curr. Liab.	254	196	188	238	234	257
LT Debt	105	126	208	319	205	225
Common Eqty.	462	374	344	298	343	406
Total Cap.	567	500	552	617	657	741
Cap. Exp.	88.0	68.0	57.0	53.0	64.0	63.0
Cash Flow	151	126	112	95.0	129	76.0

Ratio Analysis

	1994	1993	1992	1991	1990	1989
Curr. Ratio	1.6	1.5	1.4	1.2	1.1	1.6
% LT Debt of Cap.	18.6	25.1	37.8	51.7	31.1	30.4
% Net Inc.of Revs.	7.0	7.3	6.4	6.1	3.9	0.2
% Ret. on Assets	8.7	9.0	7.3	5.2	5.9	0.3
% Ret. on Equity	19.6	21.1	19.9	13.7	13.2	0.7

Dividend Data—Dividends have been paid since 1936. A dividend reinvestment plan is available.

Amt. of Div. $	Date Decl.	Ex-Div. Date	Stock of Record	Payment Date
0.110	Aug. 17	Sep. 14	Sep. 20	Oct. 17 '94
0.125	Dec. 19	Dec. 23	Dec. 30	Jan. 17 '95
0.125	Feb. 27	Mar. 08	Mar. 14	Apr. 17 '95
0.125	May. 12	Jun. 23	Jun. 27	Jul. 17 '95
0.125	Aug. 18	Sep. 15	Sep. 19	Oct. 16 '95

Data as orig. reptd.; bef. results of disc. opers. and/or spec. items. Per share data adj. for stk. divs. as of ex-div. date.
E-Estimated. NA-Not Available. NM-Not Meaningful. NR-Not Ranked.

Office—Ecolab Center, St. Paul, MN 55102. **Tel**—(612) 293-2233. **Chrmn**—P. M. Grieve. **Pres & CEO**—A. L. Schuman. **Vice Chrmn & CFO**—M. E. Shannon. **VP & Secy**—K. A. Iverson. **VP & Treas**—S. L. Fritze. **Investor Contact**—Michael J. Monahan. **Dirs**—R. S. Block, R. G. Cleary, P. M. Grieve, J. J. Howard, J. W. Levin, R. F. Richards, R. L. Schall, R. Schulz, A. L. Schuman, M. E. Shannon, P. L. Smith, H. Uytherhoeven, A. Woeste. **Transfer Agent & Registrar**—First Chicago Trust Co. of New York, Jersey City, N.J. **Incorporated** in Delaware in 1924. **Empl**-8,206. **S&P Analyst:** Richard O'Reilly, CFA

Emerson Electric

NYSE Symbol **EMR**
In S&P 500

11-OCT-95

Industry:
Electronics/Electric

Summary: Emerson Electric is a long-established manufacturer of electrical and electronic products.

S&P Opinion: Accumulate (★★★★)	Recent Price • 69⅝	Yield • 2.8%
	52 Wk Range • 75⅜-58⅛	12-Mo. P/E • 17.3

Quantitative Evaluations

Outlook
(1 Lowest—5 Highest)
• **1+**

Fair Value
• **61⅜**

Risk
• **Low**

Earn./Div. Rank
• **A+**

Technical Eval.
• **Bearish** since 1/95

Rel. Strength Rank
(1 Lowest—99 Highest)
• **45**

Insider Activity
• **NA**

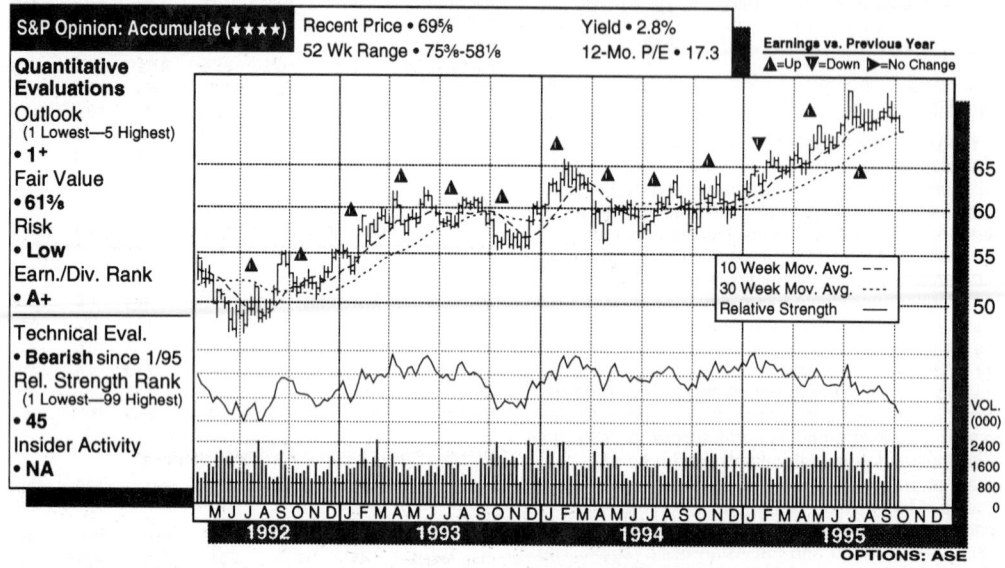

Earnings vs. Previous Year
▲=Up ▼=Down ▶=No Change

10 Week Mov. Avg. – – –
30 Week Mov. Avg. · · · ·
Relative Strength ——

OPTIONS: ASE

Overview - 11-OCT-95

Sales for fiscal 1996 are expected to advance about 15%, reflecting broadbased demand for the company's products throughout the world. Faster growth in the U.S. economy following the current slowdown should be especially positive. International sales and exports are also likely to remain especially strong, due to the company's marketing initiatives and brisk underlying demand. Sales should also benefit from the company's focus on more rapid sales growth through new product development and global expansion. Further acquisitions are also likely to extend the gain. Margins should widen somewhat, with well controlled expenses reflecting the company's Best Cost Producer strategy.

Valuation - 11-OCT-95

Emerson Electric is likely to remain a high quality investment in the electrical equipment industry, as its talented management team extends its long string of earnings and dividend increases. A shift by management over the past 18 months to faster sales growth is especially favorable with a maturing U.S. economy and excellent opportunities for growth in international markets. The long-term outlook is enhanced by our expectation that capital spending will experience good secular growth in the years ahead. All of these factors point to continued appreciation in Emerson Electric's shares. However, any signs that the U.S. economy is weakening could cause the shares to be volatile over the short term.

Key Stock Statistics

S&P EPS Est. 1995	4.08	Tang. Bk. Value/Share	10.60
P/E on S&P Est. 1995	17.1	Beta	1.17
S&P EPS Est. 1996	4.50	Shareholders	31,800
Dividend Rate/Share	1.96	Market cap. (B)	$ 15.7
Shs. outstg. (M)	224.5	Inst. holdings	64%
Avg. daily vol. (M)	0.468	Insider holdings	NA

Value of $10,000 invested 5 years ago: $ 20,760

Fiscal Year Ending Sep. 30

	1995	% Change	1994	% Change	1993	% Change
Revenues (Million $)						
1Q	2,285	14%	2,010	1%	1,984	9%
2Q	2,514	19%	2,117	3%	2,057	7%
3Q	2,630	17%	2,244	7%	2,092	6%
4Q	—	—	2,238	10%	2,041	2%
Yr.	—	—	8,607	5%	8,174	6%
Income (Million $)						
1Q	224.7	-24%	294.0	80%	163.2	7%
2Q	227.1	17%	194.3	9%	177.7	6%
3Q	239.5	15%	208.0	11%	187.2	7%
4Q	—	—	208.2	16%	180.0	7%
Yr.	—	—	904.5	28%	708.1	7%
Earnings Per Share ($)						
1Q	0.91	-31%	1.31	79%	0.73	7%
2Q	1.02	17%	0.87	10%	0.79	5%
3Q	1.07	15%	0.93	12%	0.83	6%
4Q	E1.08	16%	0.93	16%	0.80	7%
Yr.	E4.08	NM	4.04	28%	3.15	6%

Next earnings report expected: early November

Emerson Electric

Business Summary - 11-OCT-95

Emerson Electric is a diversified manufacturer of a broad range of electrical and electronic products. Industry segment contributions in fiscal 1994 were:

	Sales	Profits
Commercial & industrial	57%	53%
Appliance & construction-related	43%	47%

International operations accounted for 31% of sales and 20% of operating income in fiscal 1994.

The commercial and industrial segment includes process control instrumentation, valves and systems, industrial motors and drives, industrial machinery, equipment and components, and electronic products. These products are sold to commercial and industrial distributors and end-users for manufacturing and heavy commercial applications.

Products used in process industries include various types of instrumentation, valves and control systems for measurement and control of fluid flow. The company also manufacturers electronic measurement and data acquisition equipment for use in industrial processing. Beginning with a line of electric motors for industrial and heavy commercial applications, Emerson's products for industrial automation include certain kinds of integral horsepower motors, gear drives, pump motors, alternators and electronic variable speed drives.

Many other commercial and industrial products are also manufactured.

The appliance and construction-related components segment consists of fractional-horsepower motors, appliance components, heating, ventilating and air-conditioning components, and tools. These products are sold to distributors and original equipment manufacturers for inclusion in end-products and systems that are ultimately sold through commercial and residential building construction channels.

Important Developments

Aug. '95—The company said that during its third quarter, it experienced strong sales growth led by capital goods businesses, including industrial motors and drives, process, industrial components and equipment. Tools, heating, ventilating and air conditioning and electronics also reported strong sales. Sales of the appliance components business rose slightly, while sales of the fractional motor business were unchanged as international gains were offset by a slowing domestic market. During the quarter, the company completed the acquisition of Intellution Inc., a leading developer and worldwide supplier of PC-based packaged software for industrial and process applications.

Capitalization

Long Term Debt: $275,800,000 (6/95).

Per Share Data ($)

(Year Ended Sep. 30)

	1994	1993	1992	1991	1990	1989
Tangible Bk. Val.	11.09	9.26	11.68	9.83	8.74	10.24
Cash Flow	5.66	4.66	4.08	3.96	3.78	3.52
Earnings	4.04	3.15	2.96	2.83	2.75	2.63
Dividends	1.56	1.44	1.38	1.32	1.26	1.12
Payout Ratio	39%	46%	47%	47%	46%	42%
Prices - High	$65\frac{7}{8}$	$62\frac{3}{8}$	58	55	$44\frac{3}{8}$	$39\frac{7}{8}$
- Low	$56\frac{1}{8}$	$52\frac{3}{4}$	$46\frac{3}{4}$	$36\frac{7}{8}$	$30\frac{3}{4}$	$29\frac{1}{2}$
P/E Ratio - High	16	20	20	19	16	15
- Low	14	17	16	13	11	11

Income Statement Analysis (Million $)

	1994	%Chg	1993	%Chg	1992	%Chg	1991
Revs.	8,607	5%	8,174	6%	7,706	4%	7,427
Oper. Inc.	1,739	7%	1,618	12%	1,444	3%	1,405
Depr.	365	7%	341	35%	253	NM	254
Int. Exp.	89.0	-25%	119	31%	91.0	-19%	113
Pretax Inc.	1,428	28%	1,112	7%	1,044	4%	1,003
Eff. Tax Rate	37%	—	36%	—	37%	—	37%
Net Inc.	904	28%	708	7%	663	5%	632

Balance Sheet & Other Fin. Data (Million $)

	1994	1993	1992	1991	1990	1989
Cash	113	102	80.0	102	98.0	113
Curr. Assets	3,338	3,074	2,977	2,989	3,139	2,851
Total Assets	8,215	7,815	6,627	6,364	6,376	5,408
Curr. Liab.	2,617	2,693	1,812	2,094	2,336	1,533
LT Debt	280	438	448	450	496	419
Common Eqty.	4,342	3,915	3,730	3,257	2,990	3,073
Total Cap.	4,622	4,536	4,178	3,707	3,486	3,492
Cap. Exp.	332	306	346	311	310	286
Cash Flow	1,269	1,049	916	886	845	788

Ratio Analysis

	1994	1993	1992	1991	1990	1989
Curr. Ratio	1.3	1.1	1.6	1.4	1.3	1.9
% LT Debt of Cap.	6.1	9.7	10.7	12.1	14.2	12.0
% Net Inc.of Revs.	10.5	8.7	8.6	8.5	8.1	8.3
% Ret. on Assets	11.3	9.8	10.2	9.9	10.4	11.3
% Ret. on Equity	22.0	18.5	19.0	20.2	20.2	20.1

Dividend Data —Dividends have been paid since 1947. A dividend reinvestment plan is available. A "poison pill" stock purchase rights plan was adopted in 1988.

Amt. of Div. $	Date Decl.	Ex-Div. Date	Stock of Record	Payment Date
0.430	Nov. 01	Nov. 17	Nov. 23	Dec. 09 '94
0.430	Feb. 07	Feb. 13	Feb. 20	Mar. 10 '95
0.430	May. 02	May. 15	May. 19	Jun. 09 '95
0.490	Aug. 01	Aug. 16	Aug. 18	Sep. 11 '95

Data as orig. reptd.; bef. results of disc. opers. and/or spec. items. Per share data adj. for stk. divs. as of ex-div. date. E-Estimated. NA-Not Available. NM-Not Meaningful. NR-Not Ranked.

Office—8000 W. Florissant Ave., St. Louis, MO 63136. **Tel**—(314) 553-2000. **Chrmn & CEO**—C. F. Knight. **COO**—A. E. Suter. **Pres**—J. J. Adorjan. **Sr VP & CFO**—W. J. Galvin. **Sr VP & Secy**—W. W. Withers. **Investor Contact**—Craig Ashmore. **Dirs**—J. J. Adorjan, L. L. Browning Jr., A. A. Busch III, D. C. Farrell, J. A. Frates, R. B. Horton, C. F. Knight, G. A. Lodge, V. R. Loucks Jr., R. B. Loynd, B. A. Schriever, R. W. Staley, A. E. Suter, W. M. Van Cleave, E. E. Whitacre Jr., E. F. Williams Jr. **Transfer Agent & Registrar**—Boatmen's Trust Co., St. Louis. **Incorporated** in Missouri in 1890. **Empl**-73,900. **S&P Analyst:** Paul H. Valentine, CFA

Engelhard Corp.

NYSE Symbol **EC**
In S&P 500

25-AUG-95 Industry: Chemicals

Summary: Engelhard is a leading producer of catalysts, pigments and additives, and engineered materials. It also provides precious metals management services.

S&P Opinion: Sell (★)	Recent Price • 30	Yield • 1.2%
	52 Wk Range • 32½-13⅞	12-Mo. P/E • 33.7

Earnings vs. Previous Year
▲=Up ▼=Down ▶=No Change

Quantitative Evaluations

Outlook (1 Lowest—5 Highest)
• **5+**

Fair Value
• **35%**

Risk
• **Average**

Earn./Div. Rank
• **B**

Technical Eval.
• **Bullish** since 6/95

Rel. Strength Rank (1 Lowest—99 Highest)
• **40**

Insider Activity
• **Neutral**

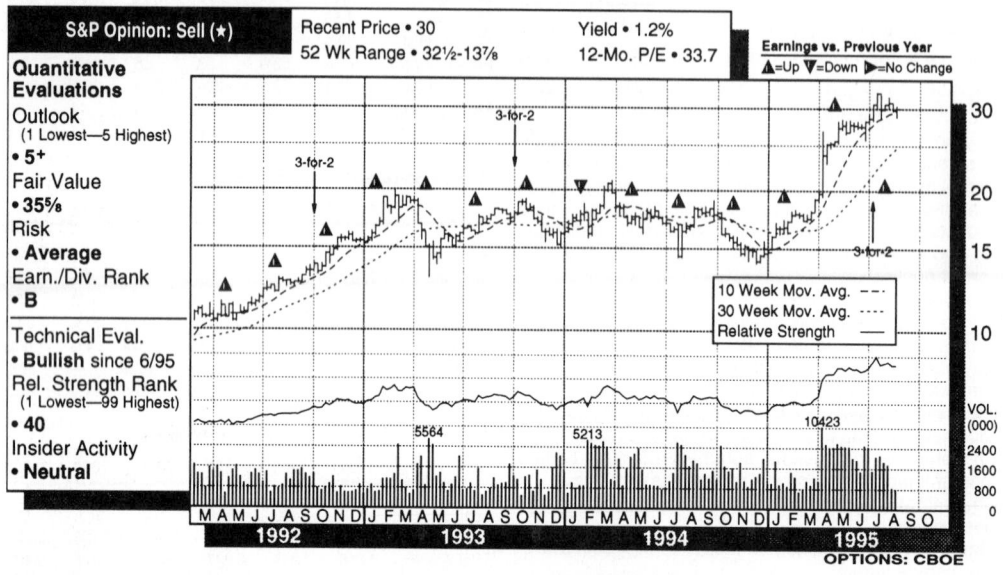

10 Week Mov. Avg. – – –
30 Week Mov. Avg. ·······
Relative Strength ——

OPTIONS: CBOE

Overview - 25-AUG-95

Profits in 1995 are expected to benefit from additional manufacturing cost savings in all three business segments and a reduction in the heavy investment spending in new catalyst and desiccant air-conditioning technology. Catalysts will also advance on higher volumes and prices for petroleum and automotive catalysts. A new petroleum catalyst manufacturing plant should be a positive contributor in 1995. Pigments are expected to be aided by stronger demand from the key paper, plastics and paint markets and the startup of new capacity in mid-1995. Fabricated products should remain healthy on strong demand. Equity income will likely rise sharply as two major ventures turn into the black.

Valuation - 25-AUG-95

This company's stock jumped in 1995's second quarter following its announcement of the PremAir catalyst system in April, as well as in response to favorable analyst recommendations. However, we feel the market has greatly overreacted to the potential of the PremAir system, which will not be commercially available until 1997 at the earliest for use in model year 1998 cars. We feel the shares are overvalued at about 31 times estimated 1995 earnings, a high premium to the overall stock market. Dividends have been raised for 13 consecutive years, and a three-for-two stock split was effected in mid-1995.

Key Stock Statistics

S&P EPS Est. 1995	0.96	Tang. Bk. Value/Share	4.63
P/E on S&P Est. 1995	31.3	Beta	1.14
S&P EPS Est. 1996	1.17	Shareholders	8,700
Dividend Rate/Share	0.36	Market cap. (B)	$ 4.2
Shs. outstg. (M)	143.2	Inst. holdings	52%
Avg. daily vol. (M)	0.253	Insider holdings	NA

Value of $10,000 invested 5 years ago: $ 59,154

Fiscal Year Ending Dec. 31

	1995	% Change	1994	% Change	1993	% Change
Revenues (Million $)						
1Q	694.5	25%	557.7	14%	490.2	-22%
2Q	721.1	14%	633.4	12%	563.2	-12%
3Q	—	—	578.6	4%	558.1	-5%
4Q	—	—	616.1	14%	539.3	-1%
Yr.	—	—	2,386	11%	2,151	-10%
Income (Million $)						
1Q	27.61	21%	22.75	3%	22.18	-1%
2Q	36.72	15%	31.87	12%	28.47	11%
3Q	—	—	29.72	8%	27.58	15%
4Q	—	—	33.64	NM	-61.56	NM
Yr.	—	—	118.0	NM	16.67	-83%
Earnings Per Share ($)						
1Q	0.19	21%	0.16	6%	0.15	3%
2Q	0.26	18%	0.22	13%	0.20	17%
3Q	E0.24	16%	0.21	7%	0.19	21%
4Q	E0.27	17%	0.23	NM	-0.43	NM
Yr.	E0.96	17%	0.82	NM	0.11	-83%

Next earnings report expected: late October

Business Summary - 25-AUG-95

Engelhard Corporation primarily produces specialty chemicals and engineered materials and provides precious metals management services. Contributions by segment in 1994 were:

	Sales	Profits
Catalysts & chemicals	25%	47%
Pigments & additives	16%	35%
Engineered materials & precious metals management	59%	18%

International operations accounted for 34% of sales and 20% of operating profits in 1994.

The catalysts and chemicals segment includes catalysts, chemicals and process technologies for the petroleum refining, chemical, petrochemical, pharmaceutical, food processing, automobile, aircraft, power generation, process and environmental protection industries.

Pigments and additives consist of kaolin-based coatings and extender pigments for a wide variety of papers, including printing, writing, newsprint and paperbroad; and pigments and additives, thickeners and absorbents used in plastics, paints, inks and rubber.

Engineered materials consist of fabricated precious metal (platinum, gold and silver) products and coatings for industrial, instrument, electronic, medical, jewelry, coinage and investment markets. EC is also engaged in secondary refining to recover precious metals and in precious metals dealing and management.

Important Developments

Jul. '95—EC said that all three of its business segments posted significantly higher profits in the 1995 second quarter, with strong gains in auto emission systems, chemical catalysts and pigments. EC said it was continuing to invest heavily in its growth projects.
Jun. '94—EC formed with CLAL (Groupe FIMALAC), France, an equally owned joint venture for refining and manufacturing precious-metal-containing products. The venture combines most of the assets of CLAL and most of EC's engineered materials group in Europe and Asia Pacific and the engineered materials businesses conducted at two plants in the U.S. The venture has annual revenues of more than $1 billion. Most of the precious metals purchased by the joint venture will be supplied by EC's metals management group. Separately, EC and Ford Motor Co. began testing EC's PremAir air catalyst system in a fleet of Ford cars. PremAir reduces ground-level ozone and carbon monoxide.

Capitalization

Long Term Debt: $111,831,000 (3/95).

Per Share Data ($)   (Year Ended Dec. 31)

	1994	1993	1992	1991	1990	1989
Tangible Bk. Val.	4.31	3.69	4.38	5.00	4.72	4.24
Cash Flow	1.30	0.57	1.15	1.09	0.96	-0.06
Earnings	0.82	0.11	0.67	0.58	0.47	-0.51
Dividends	0.31	0.35	0.25	0.22	0.20	0.17
Payout Ratio	37%	NM	37%	38%	43%	NM
Prices - High	21	20	16¼	10⅛	7	7⅝
- Low	13⅞	12⅞	9¼	5	5	5⅛
P/E Ratio - High	26	NM	24	17	15	NM
- Low	17	NM	14	9	11	NM

Income Statement Analysis (Million $)

	1994	%Chg	1993	%Chg	1992	%Chg	1991
Revs.	2,385	11%	2,149	-10%	2,397	-1%	2,430
Oper. Inc.	247	19%	207	-3%	214	4%	206
Depr.	69.1	5%	65.9	-11%	73.8	-5%	77.8
Int. Exp.	22.0	61%	13.7	-17%	16.6	-25%	22.2
Pretax Inc.	157	NM	-5.0	NM	134	14%	118
Eff. Tax Rate	25%	—	NM	—	25%	—	25%
Net Inc.	118	NM	17.0	-83%	100	14%	87.9

Balance Sheet & Other Fin. Data (Million $)

	1994	1993	1992	1991	1990	1989
Cash	26.0	26.0	31.0	36.0	47.0	41.0
Curr. Assets	574	517	569	576	618	653
Total Assets	1,441	1,279	1,279	1,256	1,320	1,340
Curr. Liab.	549	463	366	378	482	475
LT Debt	112	112	114	115	119	220
Common Eqty.	615	531	647	757	710	637
Total Cap.	726	646	773	878	838	865
Cap. Exp.	98.0	NA	54.0	46.0	80.0	87.0
Cash Flow	187	83.0	174	166	145	-9.0

Ratio Analysis

	1994	1993	1992	1991	1990	1989
Curr. Ratio	1.0	1.1	1.6	1.5	1.3	1.4
% LT Debt of Cap.	15.4	17.4	14.7	13.0	14.3	25.5
% Net Inc.of Revs.	4.9	0.8	42.0	3.6	2.4	NM
% Ret. on Assets	8.7	1.3	8.0	6.8	5.3	NM
% Ret. on Equity	20.7	2.9	14.4	12.0	10.4	NM

Dividend Data —Dividends have been paid since 1981. A dividend reinvestment plan is available.

Amt. of Div. $	Date Decl.	Ex-Div. Date	Stock of Record	Payment Date
0.120	Sep. 01	Sep. 07	Sep. 13	Sep. 30 '94
0.120	Nov. 03	Dec. 07	Dec. 13	Dec. 30 '94
0.120	Mar. 02	Mar. 08	Mar. 14	Mar. 31 '95
0.090	May. 04	Jun. 12	Jun. 14	Jun. 30 '95
3-for-2	May. 04	Jul. 03	Jun. 14	Jun. 30 '95

Data as orig. reptd.; bef. results of disc. opers. and/or spec. items. Per share data adj. for stk. divs. as of ex-div. date. E-Estimated. NA-Not Available. NM-Not Meaningful. NR-Not Ranked.

Office—101 Wood Ave. South, Iselin, NJ 08830-0770. **Tel—**(908) 205-6000. **Chrmn & CEO—**O. R. Smith. **Pres—**L. D. LaTorre. **Sr VP-CFO—**R. L. Guyett. **VP-Secy—**A. A. Dornbusch II. **Treas—**M. A. Sperduto. **Investor Contact—**Francis X. Vitale Jr. **Dirs—**L. Alvarado, M. H. Antonini, R. L. Guyett, L. D. LaTorre, A. W. Lea, J. V. Napier, N. T. Pace, R. F. Richards, H. R. Slack, O. R. Smith, D. G. Watson. **Transfer Agent & Registrar—**Mellon Securities Trust Co., Ridgefield Park, N.J. **Incorporated** in Delaware in 1938. **Empl-**5,830. **S&P Analyst:** Richard O'Reilly, CFA

Enron Corp.

NYSE Symbol **ENE**
In S&P 500

03-OCT-95 | **Industry:** Utilities-Gas

Summary: ENE operates the largest U.S. natural gas pipeline system, and engages in oil and gas exploration and production, and in liquid products extraction, marketing and transportation.

S&P Opinion: Hold (★★★)	Recent Price • 33½	Yield • 2.3%
	52 Wk Range • 36⅞-26¾	12-Mo. P/E • 17.0

Quantitative Evaluations

Outlook
(1 Lowest—5 Highest)
• **3+**

Fair Value
• **32⅞**

Risk
• **Low**

Earn./Div. Rank
• **B+**

Technical Eval.
• **Bullish** since 8/95

Rel. Strength Rank
(1 Lowest—99 Highest)
• **46**

Insider Activity
• **Neutral**

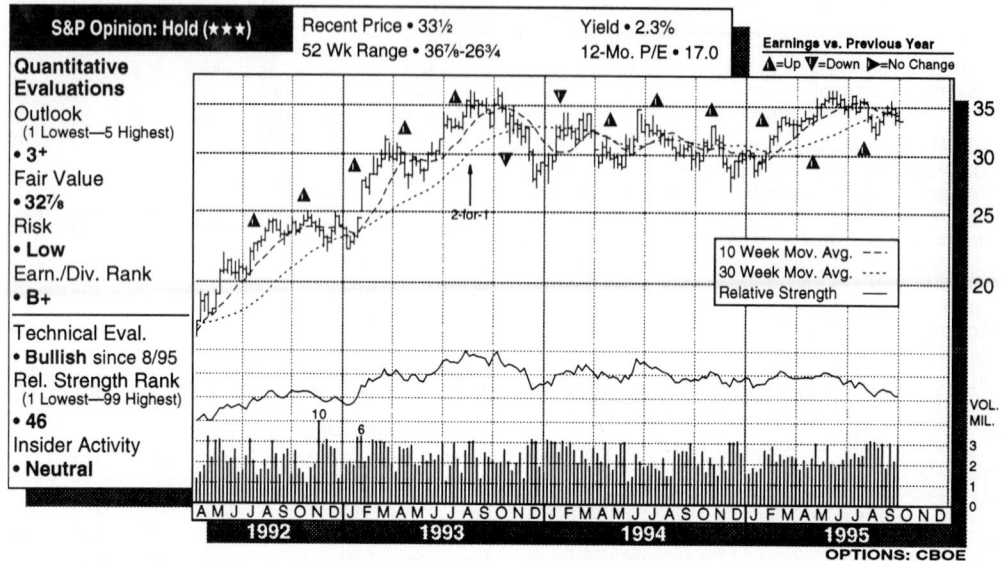

Earnings vs. Previous Year
▲=Up ▼=Down ▶=No Change

10 Week Mov. Avg. — – –
30 Week Mov. Avg. ·····
Relative Strength —

2-for-1

OPTIONS: CBOE

Overview - 03-OCT-95

Share earnings for 1995 should benefit from the company's largest backlog ever at Enron Development Corp., and a significant profit contribution from Enron Capital & Trade Resources (formerly Enron Gas Services Group) as a result of an ongoing restructuring in the electric utility industry and power marketing activities. Enron Oil & Gas (80%-owned) should post higher earnings, aided primarily by higher production in both Trinidad and India, while significant cost reductions at Enron Operations Corp. are expected to continue. In addition, Enron Global Power & Pipelines should also report a higher earnings contribution. The company has hedged a significant level of anticipated 1995 natural gas production, reducing the downside from falling gas prices this year.

Valuation - 03-OCT-95

Over the past year and a half or so, the shares have remained in a relatively narrow trading range that is down only moderately from the highs that were reached in the second half of 1993. While the stock is trading at a premium to the average for its peer group of natural gas pipeline companies (based on 1995 earnings estimates), it appears warranted given the company's chances of attaining its stated goal of at least 15% growth in earnings per share in both 1995 and 1996. The dividend was raised 6.7% in December 1994. This represented the fourth consecutive year that the dividend was raised. Further hikes are expected both this year and next.

Key Stock Statistics

S&P EPS Est. 1995	2.10	Tang. Bk. Value/Share	10.89
P/E on S&P Est. 1995	16.0	Beta	0.32
S&P EPS Est. 1996	2.25	Shareholders	27,000
Dividend Rate/Share	0.80	Market cap. (B)	$ 8.7
Shs. outstg. (M)	252.0	Inst. holdings	55%
Avg. daily vol. (M)	0.556	Insider holdings	NA

Value of $10,000 invested 5 years ago: $ 27,685

Fiscal Year Ending Dec. 31

	1995	% Change	1994	% Change	1993	% Change
Revenues (Million $)						
1Q	2,304	-6%	2,450	32%	1,857	24%
2Q	2,149	13%	1,898	NM	1,907	46%
3Q	—	—	1,997	3%	1,934	29%
4Q	—	—	2,560	13%	2,274	13%
Yr.	—	—	8,905	12%	7,972	26%
Income (Million $)						
1Q	195.0	13%	173.1	18%	146.2	26%
2Q	94.05	24%	75.60	23%	61.25	22%
3Q	—	—	96.00	NM	21.00	-68%
4Q	—	—	108.8	5%	104.1	-1%
Yr.	—	—	453.4	36%	332.5	-1%
Earnings Per Share ($)						
1Q	0.79	13%	0.70	17%	0.60	11%
2Q	0.37	23%	0.30	25%	0.24	14%
3Q	E0.44	16%	0.38	NM	0.07	-73%
4Q	E0.50	16%	0.43	2%	0.42	-2%
Yr.	E2.10	17%	1.80	36%	1.32	-8%

Next earnings report expected: mid October

Enron Corp.

Business Summary - 20-SEP-95

Enron is involved in gathering, transportation and wholesale marketing of natural gas; exploration for and production of oil and gas; production and marketing of natural gas liquids and refined petroleum products; the development, construction and operation of natural gas fired power plants internationally; and the non-price regulated purchasing and marketing of long-term energy related commitments. Segment contributions in 1994 were:

	Revs.	Profits
Transportation & Operation	10.4%	43.1%
Domestic gas & power svcs.	79.8%	21.6%
International gas & power	4.4%	9.5%
Exploration & production	5.4%	25.7%

Enron operates interstate pipelines from Texas to the Canadian border and across the southern U.S. from Florida to California. ENE also holds a 13% interest in Northern Border Partners, L.P., which owns a 70% interest in the Northern Border Pipeline system, and has an interest in an Argentine pipeline company. Natural gas facilities include about 44,000 miles of transmission and gathering lines, 111 mainline compressor stations, four underground gas storage fields and two liquefied natural gas storage facilities. System net throughput in 1994 totaled 8,250 BBtu/d, up from 8,000 BBtu/d in 1993. Enron Gas Services is involved in natural gas and liquids marketing, domestic power development and marketing, and producer finance activities in North America.

Exploration and production activities are conducted through 80%-owned Enron Oil & Gas Co. (EOG). At year-end 1994, EOG estimated net proved natural gas reserves were 1,910 Bcf; net proved crude oil, condensate and natural gas liquids reserves totaled 37 million bbl. EOG's main producing areas are the Big Piney area in Wyoming, South Texas, the Matagorda Trend located offshore Texas, the Canyon Trend in West Texas, southwest New Mexico and offshore Trinidad.

Important Developments

Sep. '95—The company expects no material impact on earnings as a result of its decision to delay its purchase of gas from the J-Block field in the North Sea. The company said it is ready to perform all legal obligations under its agreement with J-Block owners, including future potential prepayments for gas to be taken in later years.

Aug. '95—Enron said it had very strong legal defenses available under its project contracts, in reponse to comments by the Chief Minister in the Maharashtra State Assembly regarding the scrapping of Phase II of the Dabhol Power Project.

Capitalization

Long Term Debt: $3,417,664,000 (6/95).

Per Share Data ($)

(Year Ended Dec. 31)

	1994	1993	1992	1991	1990	1989
Tangible Bk. Val.	10.89	9.93	9.97	8.43	8.02	7.69
Cash Flow	3.61	3.24	3.07	2.89	2.65	2.77
Earnings	1.80	1.32	1.43	1.08	0.88	1.01
Dividends	0.76	0.71	0.66	0.63	0.62	0.62
Payout Ratio	42%	54%	50%	59%	71%	62%
Prices - High	34⅝	37	25⅛	19¼	15¾	15¼
- Low	26¾	22¼	15⅝	12⅜	12⅝	8⅞
P/E Ratio - High	19	28	18	18	18	15
- Low	15	17	11	12	14	9

Income Statement Analysis (Million $)

	1994	%Chg	1993	%Chg	1992	%Chg	1991
Revs.	8,984	13%	7,972	26%	6,325	-53%	13,520
Oper. Inc.	1,157	8%	1,076	10%	981	14%	864
Depr.	441	-4%	458	27%	361	-1%	366
Int. Exp.	273	-9%	300	-8%	327	-16%	391
Pretax Inc.	671	35%	498	12%	446	30%	344
Eff. Tax Rate	25%	—	27%	—	21%	—	27%
Net Inc.	453	36%	333	NM	336	39%	242

Balance Sheet & Other Fin. Data (Million $)

	1994	1993	1992	1991	1990	1989
Cash	132	140	142	217	214	109
Curr. Assets	1,909	2,019	2,126	1,805	2,137	1,632
Total Assets	11,966	11,504	10,664	10,072	9,849	9,105
Curr. Liab.	2,297	2,676	2,642	2,280	2,421	1,606
LT Debt	2,805	2,661	2,459	3,109	2,983	3,184
Common Eqty.	2,740	2,474	2,364	1,706	1,619	1,548
Total Cap.	8,746	7,555	6,966	6,939	6,789	6,924
Cap. Exp.	661	688	589	707	629	480
Cash Flow	880	774	675	583	533	551

Ratio Analysis

	1994	1993	1992	1991	1990	1989
Curr. Ratio	0.8	0.8	0.8	0.8	0.9	1.0
% LT Debt of Cap.	34.0	35.2	35.3	44.7	43.9	46.0
% Net Inc.of Revs.	5.0	4.2	5.3	1.8	1.5	2.3
% Ret. on Assets	3.8	2.9	2.9	2.4	2.1	2.5
% Ret. on Equity	16.7	12.7	14.4	13.0	11.2	13.2

Dividend Data —Dividends have been paid since 1935. A dividend reinvestment plan is available.

Amt. of Div. $	Date Decl.	Ex-Div. Date	Stock of Record	Payment Date
0.200	Oct. 11	Nov. 25	Dec. 01	Dec. 20 '94
0.200	Feb. 14	Feb. 28	Mar. 06	Mar. 20 '95
0.200	May. 02	May. 25	Jun. 01	Jun. 20 '95
0.200	Aug. 08	Aug. 30	Sep. 01	Sep. 20 '95

Data as orig. reptd.; bef. results of disc. opers. and/or spec. items. Per share data adj. for stk. divs. as of ex-div. date. E-Estimated. NA-Not Available. NM-Not Meaningful. NR-Not Ranked.

Office—1400 Smith St., Houston, TX 77002-7369. **Tel**—(713) 853-6161. **Chrmn & CEO**—K. L. Lay. **Pres**—R. D. Kinder. **Secy**—Peggy B. Menchaca. **VP & Treas**—K. S. Huneke. **Investor Contacts**—Mark E. Koenig, Edmund P. Segner III. **Dirs**—R. A. Belfer, N. P. Blake, Jr., J. H. Duncan, J. H. Foy, W. L. Gramm, R. K. Jaedicke, R. D. Kinder, K. L. Lay, C. A. LeMaistre, J. A. Urquhart, Lord J. Wakeham, C. E. Walker, H. S. Winokur Jr. . **Transfer Agent & Registrar**—First Chicago Trust Co. of New York, NYC. **Incorporated** in Delaware in 1930. **Empl**-6,955. **S&P Analyst:** Raymond J. Deacon

ENSERCH Corp.

NYSE Symbol **ENS**
In **S&P 500**

10-SEP-95

Industry:
Utilities-Gas

Summary: This diversified Dallas-based concern operates a large, primarily intrastate, natural gas utility, and is also engaged in oil and gas exploration and production.

S&P Opinion: Hold (★★★)	Recent Price • 16½	Yield • 1.2%
	52 Wk Range • 18⅝-12⅛	12-Mo. P/E • 13.4

Quantitative Evaluations

Outlook
(1 Lowest—5 Highest)
• **2+**

Fair Value
• **15⅞**

Risk
• **Average**

Earn./Div. Rank
• **B**

Technical Eval.
• **Bearish** since 3/95

Rel. Strength Rank
(1 Lowest—99 Highest)
• **18**

Insider Activity
• **NA**

Earnings vs. Previous Year
▲=Up ▼=Down ▶=No Change

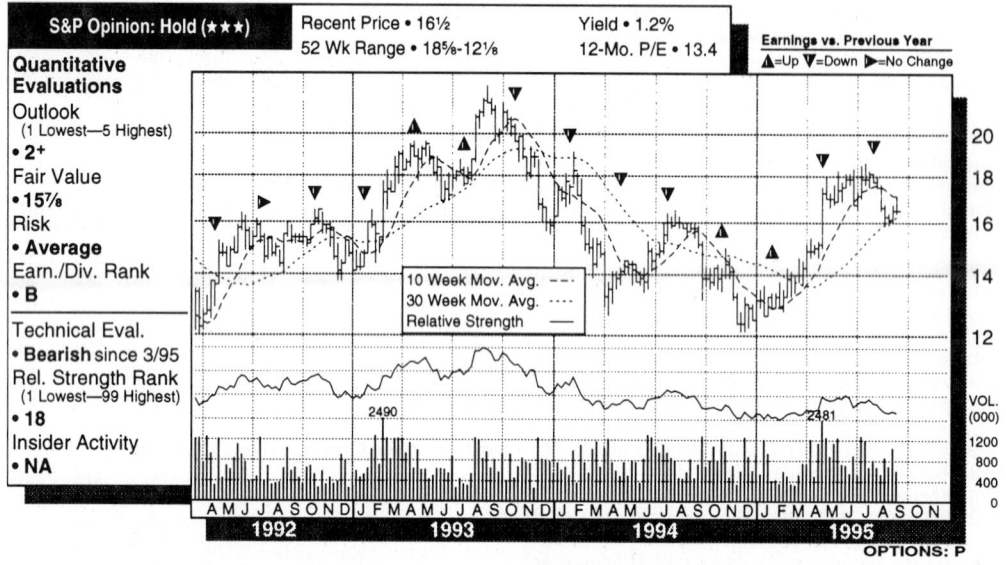

10 Week Mov. Avg. --·
30 Week Mov. Avg. ····
Relative Strength —

VOL. (000)

OPTIONS: P

Overview - 10-SEP-95

Earnings per share of $1.05 in 1994 included a $1.05 income tax credit. After removing the effect of the tax credit, earnings from continuing operations should improve in 1995 to $0.45 a share. Results should benefit from improved contributions from the gas processing operations and slightly higher pipeline profits. Natural gas distribution profits should continue to benefit from an increase in gas sales to higher-margin residential and commercial customers and future growth in deliveries to industrial and electric generation customers. However, exploration and production profits are expected to be penalized by the continuation of depressed natural gas prices.

Valuation - 08-SEP-95

Along with the rest of the industry, ENS's shares fell substantially in 1994, reflecting increased interest rates and depressed natural gas prices. Although the main source of profits remains the utility segment, with ENS's increased emphasis on exploration and production, the shares are expected to be very sensitive to movements in the price of gas. Although the earnings outlook is improving and long-term prospects appear bright, with only a modest increase in natural gas prices expected in 1995 and the shares trading at a hefty 20-times our 1996 EPS estimate of $0.85, the stock is likely to be only an average performer over the next 6-12 months.

Key Stock Statistics

S&P EPS Est. 1995	0.45	Tang. Bk. Value/Share	10.71
P/E on S&P Est. 1995	36.7	Beta	0.91
S&P EPS Est. 1996	0.85	Shareholders	19,600
Dividend Rate/Share	0.20	Market cap. (B)	$ 1.1
Shs. outstg. (M)	68.4	Inst. holdings	71%
Avg. daily vol. (M)	0.166	Insider holdings	NA

Value of $10,000 invested 5 years ago: $ 7,473

Fiscal Year Ending Dec. 31

	1995	% Change	1994	% Change	1993	% Change
Revenues (Million $)						
1Q	547.9	-3%	565.7	-41%	958.0	23%
2Q	396.2	13%	350.1	-48%	672.0	15%
3Q	—	—	439.7	-35%	677.0	15%
4Q	—	—	501.9	-7%	542.0	-38%
Yr.	—	—	1,857	-2%	1,902	-33%
Income (Million $)						
1Q	30.39	-14%	35.36	-8%	38.28	11%
2Q	-14.51	NM	-11.97	NM	5.35	NM
3Q	—	—	-14.97	NM	-27.36	NM
4Q	—	—	73.25	NM	-30.98	NM
Yr.	—	—	81.68	NM	-14.71	NM
Earnings Per Share ($)						
1Q	0.41	-15%	0.48	-9%	0.53	10%
2Q	-0.26	NM	-0.22	NM	0.03	NM
3Q	E-0.30	NM	-0.27	NM	-0.39	NM
4Q	E0.60	-43%	1.05	NM	-0.51	NM
Yr.	E0.45	-57%	1.05	NM	-0.41	NM

Next earnings report expected: late October

ENSERCH Corp.

Business Summary - 10-SEP-95

ENSERCH is a diversified energy company. Segment contributions in 1994 (profits in million $) were:

	Revs.	Profits
Transmission & distribution	90%	$63.2
Exploration & production	4%	25.6
Natural gas liquids	4%	1.0
Power & other	2%	- 2.4

Lone Star Gas, ENS's regulated gas utility segment, transmits and distributes natural gas to 1.28 million customers in 550 cities and towns in Texas, including the 11-county Dallas/Fort Worth area. Enserch Gas Co. purchases and sells natural gas to gas marketing companies, industrial and electric-generation customers and to unaffiliated pipeline and local distribution companies. Total gas sales volume in 1994 came to 545.5 Bcf, versus 413.5 Bcf in 1993. Gas transported was 389.4 Bcf in 1994 (371.1).

Enserch Exploration Inc. is engaged in the exploration for and the development, production and marketing of natural gas and crude oil throughout Texas, offshore the Gulf of Mexico, onshore in the Gulf Coast and Rocky Mountain areas and in various other areas in the U.S. At 1994 year end, proved reserves were 1,042 Bcf of gas and 50.6 million bbl. of oil and natural gas liquids. ENS estimated the present value of future cash flows of its reserves at $827 million at December 31, 1994.

Enserch Processing Co. processes natural gas for the recovery of natural gas liquids. Enserch Development Corp. develops business opportunities in the area of independent power, including cogeneration. In October 1994, ENS sold Enserch Environmental Corp., thereby completing the divestiture of its engineering and construction segment.

Important Developments

Jun. '95—ENS and Grupo Tribasa, S.A. de C.V., an infrastructure development company, agreed to form a joint venture company to develop electric power generation facilities and natural gas pipeline systems in Mexico. Separately, Enserch Gas Marketing acquired the assets of Sunrise Energy Services, Inc., a non-regulated merchant of natural gas and natural gas services, for $8.0 million. In addition, Enserch Exploration acquired the capital stock of DALEN Corp., a company whose assets include gas and oil properties, for $340 million in cash. Also, ENSERCH exchanged 1,204,098 shares of ENS common stock for 100% of the outstanding shares of DGS Holdings Corp., a major marketer of natural gas and natural gas services.

Capitalization

Long Term Debt: $848,718,000 (6/95), incl. $90.75 million of 6.375% debs. conv. into com. at $26.88 a sh.

Adj. Rate Preferred Stock: $175,000,000.

Per Share Data ($)

(Year Ended Dec. 31)

	1994	1993	1992	1991	1990	1989
Tangible Bk. Val.	10.84	9.70	8.72	9.67	10.28	10.02
Cash Flow	2.94	1.76	1.90	2.14	3.02	2.86
Earnings	1.05	-0.41	-0.39	0.07	1.03	0.93
Dividends	0.20	0.20	0.80	0.80	0.80	0.80
Payout Ratio	19%	NM	NM	NM	77%	92%
Prices - High	19⅛	22⅝	16½	20½	28⅛	27½
- Low	12⅛	14⅛	10⅜	12¾	18½	18⅝
P/E Ratio - High	18	NM	NM	NM	27	30
- Low	12	NM	NM	NM	18	20

Income Statement Analysis (Million $)

	1994	%Chg	1993	%Chg	1992	%Chg	1991
Revs.	1,857	-2%	1,902	-33%	2,825	NM	2,835
Oper. Inc.	214	-2%	218	-22%	280	4%	268
Depr.	127	-12%	145	-3%	150	11%	135
Int. Exp.	73.0	-14%	85.0	-26%	115	-3%	119
Pretax Inc.	13.0	NM	-7.0	NM	-15.0	NM	30.0
Eff. Tax Rate	NM	—	NM	—	NM	—	37%
Net Inc.	81.7	NM	-15.0	NM	-13.0	NM	19.0

Balance Sheet & Other Fin. Data (Million $)

	1994	1993	1992	1991	1990	1989
Cash	2.9	19.2	48.6	19.0	17.2	15.5
Curr. Assets	491	508	847	770	913	868
Total Assets	2,846	2,760	3,146	3,163	3,264	3,254
Curr. Liab.	652	703	845	812	849	891
LT Debt	805	719	949	930	967	898
Common Eqty.	725	647	605	686	724	701
Total Cap.	1,986	1,862	2,062	2,123	2,191	2,065
Cap. Exp.	260	236	150	229	205	187
Cash Flow	197	117	125	139	196	171

Ratio Analysis

	1994	1993	1992	1991	1990	1989
Curr. Ratio	0.8	0.7	1.0	0.9	1.1	1.0
% LT Debt of Cap.	40.5	38.6	46.1	43.8	44.1	43.5
% Net Inc.of Revs.	4.4	NM	NM	0.7	2.9	2.6
% Ret. on Assets	2.9	NM	NM	0.6	2.5	2.1
% Ret. on Equity	10.2	NM	NM	0.7	9.4	8.4

Dividend Data —A dividend reinvestment plan is available. A "poison pill" stock purchase rights plan was adopted in 1986.

Amt. of Div. $	Date Decl.	Ex-Div. Date	Stock of Record	Payment Date
0.050	Aug. 02	Aug. 15	Aug. 19	Sep. 06 '94
0.050	Oct. 24	Nov. 14	Nov. 18	Dec. 05 '94
0.050	Feb. 14	Feb. 17	Feb. 24	Mar. 06 '95
0.050	May. 09	May. 15	May. 19	Jun. 05 '95
0.050	Aug. 01	Aug. 16	Aug. 18	Sep. 05 '95

Data as orig. reptd.; bef. results of disc. opers. and/or spec. items. Per share data adj. for stk. divs. as of ex-div. date. E-Estimated. NA-Not Available. NM-Not Meaningful. NR-Not Ranked.

Office—ENSERCH Center, 300 South St. Paul St., Dallas, TX 75201-5598. **Tel**—(214) 651-8700. **Chrmn, Pres & CEO**—D. W. Biegler. **CFO**—M. E. Rescoe. **Secy**—M. G. Fortado. **Treas**—A. E. Gallatin. **VP & Investor Contact**—Benjamin A. Brown. **Dirs**—F. S. Addy, D. W. Biegler, W. B. Boyd, B. A. Bridgewater, Jr., O. C. Donald, L. E. Fouraker, P. M. Geren, Jr., M. J. Girouard, J. M. Haggar, T. W. Luce III, W. C. McCord, D. S. Natalicio, W. R. Wallace. **Transfer Agent & Registrar**—Harris Trust Co. of New York. **Incorporated** in Texas in 1942. **Empl**-4,200. **S&P Analyst:** Ronald J. Gross

Entergy Corp.

NYSE Symbol **ETR**
In S&P 500

28-AUG-95

Industry:
Utilities-Electric

Summary: In December 1993, Entergy, which serves parts of Arkansas, Louisiana, Mississippi and Missouri, merged with Gulf States Utilities, which serves parts of Louisiana and Texas.

S&P Opinion: Hold (★★★)	Recent Price • 24	Yield • 7.5%
	52 Wk Range • 25½-20	12-Mo. P/E • 15.9

Quantitative Evaluations

Outlook
(1 Lowest—5 Highest)
• **4⁻**

Fair Value
• **24**

Risk
• **Low**

Earn./Div. Rank
• **B**

Technical Eval.
• **Bullish** since 3/95

Rel. Strength Rank
(1 Lowest—99 Highest)
• **34**

Insider Activity
• **Neutral**

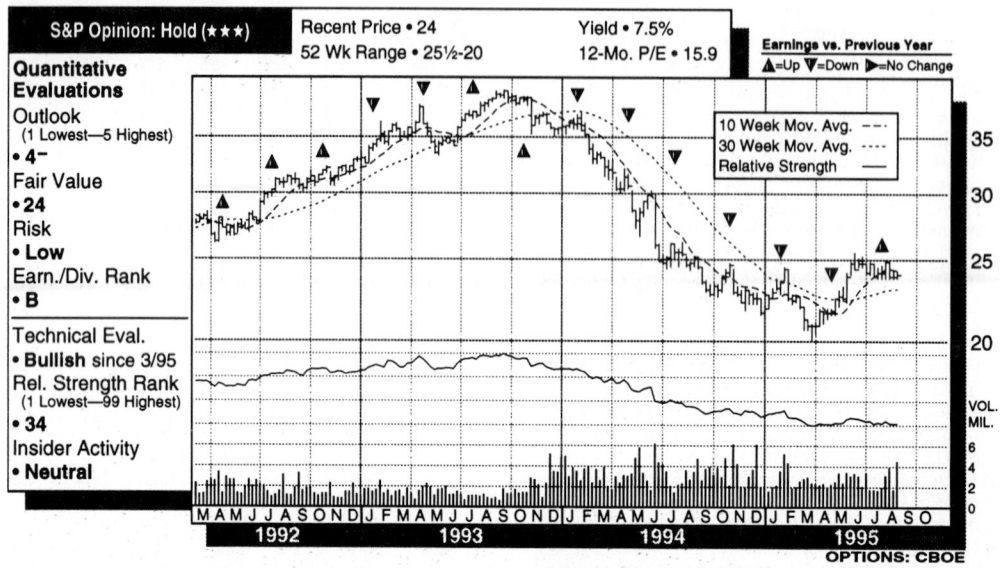

Earnings vs. Previous Year
▲=Up ▼=Down ▶=No Change

10 Week Mov. Avg. ----
30 Week Mov. Avg. ····
Relative Strength ——

VOL. MIL.

OPTIONS: CBOE

Overview - 28-AUG-95

Share earnings for 1995 should reflect good growth in kwh sales, aided by unusually hot weather and good growth in its service area. Operating and maintenance costs should be at least flat, due to greater production efficiencies and planned reductions in overhead and operating costs estimated at 2%. Earnings comparisons will benefit from the absence of $0.67 of charges, but rate case decisions will have a negative impact on revenues and earnings progress; several in 1995 have mandated reductions. An emerging framework for rate decisions in Texas that would allow ETR to allocate profits (and losses) more equitably between consumers and shareholders would be beneficial in the longer term.

Valuation - 22-AUG-95

The shares have fallen sharply from their highs in late 1993, due to the effect of higher interest rates on dividend yielding issues such as ETR, and also on rising competition within the electric utility industry. The stock has recovered in a better interest rate environment in 1995, but progress has not kept pace with that of the utility segment or the S&P 500. With only modest earnings growth projected for the next several years, and the company's commitment to retain cash to repay debt rather than raise its dividend, we expect little price appreciation in the shares. Still, downside risk is minimal, and the dividend, currently yielding well above the industry average, appears secure.

Key Stock Statistics

S&P EPS Est. 1995	2.20	Tang. Bk. Value/Share	27.74
P/E on S&P Est. 1995	10.9	Beta	0.62
S&P EPS Est. 1996	2.25	Shareholders	103,100
Dividend Rate/Share	1.80	Market cap. (B)	$ 5.5
Shs. outstg. (M)	227.7	Inst. holdings	68%
Avg. daily vol. (M)	0.651	Insider holdings	NA

Value of $10,000 invested 5 years ago: $ 14,057

Fiscal Year Ending Dec. 31

	1995	% Change	1994	% Change	1993	% Change
Revenues (Million $)						
1Q	1,346	-4%	1,406	52%	926.4	1%
2Q	1,572	NM	1,586	48%	1,070	12%
3Q	—	—	1,806	28%	1,411	14%
4Q	—	—	1,165	8%	1,078	7%
Yr.	—	—	5,963	33%	4,485	9%
Income (Million $)						
1Q	56.33	-20%	70.74	23%	57.31	-40%
2Q	162.7	13%	144.3	10%	130.9	59%
3Q	—	—	143.2	-39%	233.4	14%
4Q	—	—	-16.43	NM	36.49	-34%
Yr.	—	—	341.8	-25%	458.1	5%
Earnings Per Share ($)						
1Q	0.25	-19%	0.31	-6%	0.33	-39%
2Q	0.71	13%	0.63	-16%	0.75	63%
3Q	E1.09	73%	0.63	-53%	1.34	16%
4Q	E0.15	NM	-0.07	NM	0.21	-34%
Yr.	E2.20	48%	1.49	-43%	2.62	6%

Next earnings report expected: late October

Entergy Corp.

Business Summary - 28-AUG-95

Entergy Corp. (formerly Middle South Utilities) is the holding company for Arkansas Power & Light, Louisiana Power & Light, Mississippi Power & Light and New Orleans Public Service, which provide electricity to more than 2.4 million retail customers. On December 31, 1993, ETR acquired Gulf States Utilities (GSU), which serves parts of Louisiana and Texas and owns 70% of the River Bend nuclear plant, for $2.3 billion. The company also owns System Energy Resources, which has a 90% interest in the Grand Gulf 1 nuclear plant. Excluding GSU, revenues in 1994 were 97% electric and 3% gas. Electric revenue sources in recent years were:

	1994	1993	1992	1991
Residential	37%	36%	36%	37%
Commercial	26%	24%	25%	25%
Industrial	32%	27%	27%	27%
Other	5%	13%	12%	11%

Power sources in 1994 were nuclear 30%, gas 34%, coal 13%, oil 1%, and purchased power 22%. Peak demand in 1994 was 18,029 mw and system capability at time of peak was 20,884 mw, for a capacity margin of 14%.

In 1994, ETR's total outlays to expand its business were $472 million, largely for investments in power generation abroad and to expand its energy services unit, and it plans to invest up to $150 million a year through 1997 to expand nonregulated businesses. ETR has no plans to construct new generating capacity, but estimates yearly outlays to upgrade existing facilities in the mid-$500 million range for the next three years.

Important Developments

Aug. '95—Revenues in the 1995 first half fell modestly, largely due to regulatory rate reductions. The reductions were offset by good growth in total electricity sales as warmer weather and a more active service area economy allowed greater operating efficiencies. Lower costs for debt service, preferred dividends and fewer shares outstanding also aided results. In a May rate case, the PUC of Texas (PUCT) ordered the company to lower GSU's Texas retail revenues by $37 million, a decrease from an earlier recommendation of a $53 million base rate cut.

Capitalization

Long Term Debt: $7,035,128,000 (3/95).
Subsidiary Preference Stock: $150,000,000.
Subsidiary Preferred Stock: $826,653,000.

Per Share Data ($)

(Year Ended Dec. 31)

	1994	1993	1992	1991	1990	1989
Tangible Bk. Val.	27.74	27.16	24.23	23.31	22.01	20.50
Earnings	1.49	2.62	2.48	2.64	2.44	-2.31
Dividends	1.80	1.65	1.45	1.25	1.05	0.90
Payout Ratio	121%	63%	58%	47%	43%	NM
Prices - High	37⅜	39⅞	33⅝	29⅞	23⅝	23¼
- Low	21¼	32½	26⅛	21⅞	18	15½
P/E Ratio - High	25	15	14	11	10	NM
- Low	14	12	11	8	7	NM

Income Statement Analysis (Million $)

	1994	%Chg	1993	%Chg	1992	%Chg	1991
Revs.	5,963	33%	4,485	9%	4,116	2%	4,051
Depr.	657	48%	444	4%	425	7%	399
Maint.	NA	—	307	2%	302	7%	283
Fxd. Chgs. Cov.	1.6	-33%	2.4	13%	2.1	NM	2.1
Constr. Credits	21.8	56%	14.0	17%	12.0	-20%	15.0
Eff. Tax Rate	24%	—	36%	—	34%	—	34%
Net Inc.	342	-25%	458	5%	438	-9%	482

Balance Sheet & Other Fin. Data (Million $)

	1994	1993	1992	1991	1990	1989
Gross Prop.	23,557	23,180	15,051	14,813	14,591	14,297
Cap. Exp.	676	512	427	397	400	370
Net Prop.	15,917	16,022	10,736	10,812	10,928	10,998
Capitalization:						
LT Debt	7,367	7,679	5,326	5,493	6,072	6,347
% LT Debt	49	50	52	53	56	56
Pfd.	1,001	900	705	690	642	681
% Pfd.	6.90	5.90	6.80	6.60	5.90	6.10
Common	6,351	6,536	4,279	4,208	4,121	4,220
% Common	44	43	42	41	38	38
Total Cap.	19,959	19,917	12,088	12,348	12,677	12,893

Ratio Analysis

	1994	1993	1992	1991	1990	1989
Oper. Ratio	82.1	77.9	76.7	73.7	73.7	73.1
% Earn. on Net Prop.	6.7	7.4	8.9	9.8	9.6	9.0
% Ret. on Revs.	5.7	10.2	10.6	11.9	12.0	NM
% Ret. On Invest.Cap	5.5	6.3	8.7	9.3	9.2	1.9
% Return On Com.Eqty	5.3	12.6	10.3	11.6	11.5	NM

Dividend Data —Common dividends were omitted from August 1985 to September 1988. A dividend reinvestment plan is available.

Amt. of Div. $	Date Decl.	Ex-Div. Date	Stock of Record	Payment Date
0.450	Jul. 29	Aug. 08	Aug. 12	Sep. 01 '94
0.450	Oct. 28	Nov. 04	Nov. 10	Dec. 01 '94
0.450	Jan. 27	Feb. 06	Feb. 10	Mar. 01 '95
0.450	Mar. 25	May. 08	May. 12	Jun. 01 '95
0.450	Jul. 28	Aug. 09	Aug. 11	Sep. 01 '95

Data as orig. reptd.; bef. results of disc opers. and/or spec. items. Per share data adj. for stk. divs. as of ex-div. date. E-Estimated. NA-Not Available. NM-Not Meaningful. NR-Not Ranked.

Office—1039 Loyola Ave., New Orleans, LA 70113. **Tel**—(504) 529-5262. **Chrmn & CEO**—E. Lupberger. **Pres**—J. L. Maulden. **SVP & CFO**—G. D. McInvale. **Investor Contact**—M. Stuart Ball. **VP & Secy**—W. J. Regan, Jr., **VP & Secy**—M. G. Thompson. **Dirs**—W. F. Blount, J. A. Cooper, Jr., L. J. Fjeldstad, N. C. Francis, K. Hodges, Jr., R. v.d. Luft, E. Lupberger, K. R. McKee, P. W. Murrill, J. R. Nichols, E. H. Owen, J. N. Palmer, R. D. Pugh, W. J. Regan, Jr., H. D. Shackelford, W. C. Smith, B. A. Steinhagen. **Transfer Agent & Registrar**—Mellon Securities Trust Co., Ridgefield Park, N.J. **Incorporated** in Delaware in 1994; in Florida in 1949. **Empl**-16,037. **S&P Analyst:** Jane Collin

Exxon Corp.

NYSE Symbol **XON**
In S&P 500

30-OCT-95 | **Industry:** Oil and Gas | **Summary:** Exxon is a major factor in the world crude oil, natural gas and chemical industries.

S&P Opinion: Accumulate (★★★★)

Recent Price • 74⅝	Yield • 4.0%
52 Wk Range • 76¾-59⅛	12-Mo. P/E • 13.9

Quantitative Evaluations

Outlook
(1 Lowest—5 Highest)
• **1+**

Fair Value
• **67¾**

Risk
• **Low**

Earn./Div. Rank
• **B+**

Technical Eval.
• **Bearish** since 4/95

Rel. Strength Rank
(1 Lowest—99 Highest)
• **74**

Insider Activity
• **Neutral**

Earnings vs. Previous Year
▲=Up ▼=Down ▶=No Change

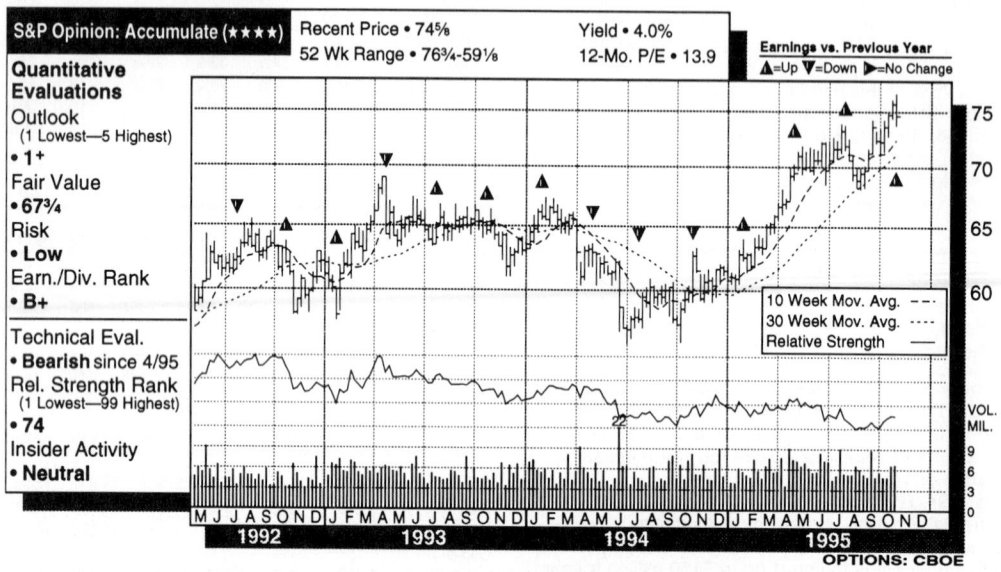

- 10 Week Mov. Avg. – – –
- 30 Week Mov. Avg. ·····
- Relative Strength ——

VOL. MIL.

M J J A S O N D J F M A M J J A S O N D J F M A M J J A S O N D J F M A M J J A S O N D
1992 / 1993 / 1994 / 1995

OPTIONS: CBOE

Overview - 30-OCT-95

Exxon is positioned to exploit growth opportunities worldwide. Debt service is modest while internal cash generation will exceed the capital expenditure program, an internationally focused program consisting mainly of a well-diversified portfolio of exploration and development projects. The chemical segment will likely continue to post strong results through 1995's fourth quarter. However, earnings will falter in the following two quarters, as demand and prices are likely to taper off, though additional ethylene capacity is scheduled to come onstream in 1997. Our forecast for natural gas demand growth worldwide for the next several years bodes well. Share repurchases and increased production volumes should boost earnings into 1996.

Valuation - 30-OCT-95

Investors are focusing on the company's excellent long-term earnings power. While natural gas fundamentals in Europe do not make us optimistic about prices, we are forecasting growth in international volumes in other parts of the world. Barring a surprise at the November OPEC meeting, oil prices are expected to remain stable at $18 through 1995, rising to $18.50 in 1996. Meanwhile, recently announced projects for gas storage in Europe and exploration in Kazakhstan should offer superior returns. We also believe downstream margins in the U.S. will firm in the final quarter of 1995. The shares appear undervalued on a cash-flow basis, and are recommended for above average capital appreciation and income.

Key Stock Statistics

S&P EPS Est. 1995	5.08	Tang. Bk. Value/Share	28.76
P/E on S&P Est. 1995	14.7	Beta	0.66
S&P EPS Est. 1996	5.30	Shareholders	606,600
Dividend Rate/Share	3.00	Market cap. (B)	$ 92.7
Shs. outstg. (M)	1241.8	Inst. holdings	41%
Avg. daily vol. (M)	1.135	Insider holdings	NA

Value of $10,000 invested 5 years ago: $ 19,468

Fiscal Year Ending Dec. 31

	1995	% Change	1994	% Change	1993	% Change
Revenues (Million $)						
1Q	29,779	16%	25,624	-5%	26,900	-2%
2Q	31,667	17%	27,102	-2%	27,600	NM
3Q	30,969	6%	29,237	7%	27,400	-10%
4Q	—	—	30,165	9%	27,700	-9%
Yr.	—	—	112,128	2%	109,500	-5%
Income (Million $)						
1Q	1,660	43%	1,160	-2%	1,185	-11%
2Q	1,630	84%	885.0	-28%	1,235	33%
3Q	1,500	30%	1,155	-15%	1,360	21%
4Q	—	—	1,900	27%	1,500	7%
Yr.	—	—	5,100	-3%	5,280	10%
Earnings Per Share ($)						
1Q	1.33	45%	0.92	-2%	0.94	-11%
2Q	1.30	86%	0.70	-29%	0.98	34%
3Q	1.20	30%	0.92	-16%	1.09	20%
4Q	E1.25	-18%	1.53	28%	1.20	7%
Yr.	E5.08	25%	4.07	-3%	4.21	10%

Next earnings report expected: late January

McGraw Hill

Business Summary - 27-OCT-95

Exxon and the Royal Dutch/Shell Group are generally regarded as the two leading factors in the world petroleum industry. XON also has a major presence in chemicals, coal and minerals.

Profits	1994	1993
U.S. exploration/production	15%	16%
U.S. refining & marketing	5%	8%
Foreign expl. & prod.	35%	40%
Foreign refin. & mktg.	21%	26%
U.S. chemical	8%	5%
Foreign chemical	9%	3%
Coal & other	7%	2%

Net crude oil and natural gas liquids production in 1994 averaged 1,709,000 bbl. a day, of which 33% was from the U.S. Record output from the North Sea boosted 1994 production by 2.5%. Natural gas available for sale was 5,978 million cubic feet a day (34% U.S.). Refinery runs were 3,412,000 b/d in 1994 (27% U.S.), and petroleum product sales amounted to 5,028,000 b/d (24% U.S.).

Net proved reserves at the end of 1994 stood at 6,148 million bbl. of crude oil (6,250 million bbl. at 1993 year end) and 42,228 Bcf of natural gas (42,251 Bcf). Capital and exploration expenditures for 1994 were $7.8 billion, of which $4.0 billion was used for exploration and production, down 12% from the 1993 level. In 1995, Exxon's capital budget will exceed the 1994 level.

Exxon seeks to capitalize on fast-growing demand in the Asia-Pacific region, where the market for liquid natural gas (LNG) is projected to double by 2010. The multi-billion dollar Natuna LNG project typifies this strategy. Downstream efforts in the Asia-Pacific market will focus on refinery expansions and upgrades, which are planned for Thailand's Sriracha refinery, as well as a refinery in Singapore. The company is also aggressively pursuing exploration opportunities in China and Russia.

Important Developments

Sep. '95—Exxon announced it will invest about $600 million in the development of three large underground natural gas storage facilities in Germany and the Netherlands. The new facilities will provide nearly 120 billion cubic feet of gas storage volume and more than 6 billion cubic feet per day of withdrawal capacity to help meet seasonal gas demand swings. Also in September, XON agreed to acquire a 50% interest in Oryx's Mertvyi Kultuk exploration block (12,200 sq. mi.) in Kazakhstan and the associated production sharing contract.

Capitalization

Long Term Debt: $8,550,000,000 (6/95).

ESOP Conv. Preferred Stock: $613,000,000.

Per Share Data ($) — (Year Ended Dec. 31)

	1994	1993	1992	1991	1990	1989
Tangible Bk. Val.	29.68	28.05	27.23	28.16	26.52	24.18
Cash Flow	8.11	8.04	7.89	8.42	8.36	6.26
Earnings	4.07	4.21	3.82	4.45	3.96	2.32
Dividends	2.91	2.88	2.83	2.68	2.47	2.30
Payout Ratio	71%	68%	74%	60%	62%	99%
Prices - High	67⅜	69	65½	61⅞	55⅛	51⅝
- Low	56⅛	57¾	53¾	49⅝	44⅞	40½
P/E Ratio - High	17	16	17	14	14	22
- Low	14	14	14	11	11	17

Income Statement Analysis (Million $)

	1994	%Chg	1993	%Chg	1992	%Chg	1991
Revs.	99,683	2%	97,825	-5%	103,160	NM	102,847
Oper. Inc.	11,942	-1%	12,063	1%	11,928	-8%	13,006
Depr.	5,015	5%	4,759	-6%	5,044	2%	4,935
Int. Exp.	1,178	12%	1,055	-8%	1,148	NM	1,141
Pretax Inc.	8,037	-3%	8,302	10%	7,534	-13%	8,685
Eff. Tax Rate	34%	—	33%	—	33%	—	34%
Net Inc.	5,100	-3%	5,280	10%	4,810	-14%	5,600

Balance Sheet & Other Fin. Data (Million $)

	1994	1993	1992	1991	1990	1989
Cash	1,775	1,652	1,515	1,587	1,379	2,016
Curr. Assets	16,460	14,859	16,424	17,012	18,336	16,576
Total Assets	87,862	84,145	85,030	87,560	87,707	83,219
Curr. Liab.	19,493	18,590	19,663	20,854	24,025	21,984
LT Debt	8,831	8,506	8,637	8,582	7,687	9,275
Common Eqty.	36,861	34,840	33,824	34,974	33,025	30,238
Total Cap.	59,849	56,632	56,523	58,925	56,260	54,735
Cap. Exp.	6,643	6,919	7,225	7,262	6,474	12,002
Cash Flow	10,069	9,985	9,793	10,466	10,428	7,909

Ratio Analysis

	1994	1993	1992	1991	1990	1989
Curr. Ratio	0.8	0.8	0.8	0.8	0.8	0.8
% LT Debt of Cap.	14.8	15.0	15.3	14.6	13.7	16.9
% Net Inc.of Revs.	5.1	5.4	4.7	5.4	4.7	3.4
% Ret. on Assets	5.9	6.2	5.6	6.4	5.9	3.8
% Ret. on Equity	14.1	15.2	13.8	16.3	15.6	9.6

Dividend Data —Dividends have been paid since 1882. A dividend reinvestment plan is available.

Amt. of Div. $	Date Decl.	Ex-Div. Date	Stock of Record	Payment Date
0.750	Oct. 26	Nov. 07	Nov. 14	Dec. 10 '94
0.750	Jan. 25	Feb. 06	Feb. 10	Mar. 10 '95
0.750	Apr. 26	May. 09	May. 15	Jun. 10 '95
0.750	Jul. 26	Aug. 10	Aug. 14	Sep. 11 '95
0.750	Oct. 25	Nov. 09	Nov. 13	Dec. 11 '95

Data as orig. reptd.; bef. results of disc. opers. and/or spec. items. Per share data adj. for stk. divs. as of ex-div. date. Revs. in Income Statement Analysis tbl. excl. excise taxes. E-Estimated. NA-Not Available. NM-Not Meaningful. NR-Not Ranked.

Office—225 East John W. Carpenter Freeway, Irving, TX 75062-2298. **Tel**—(214) 444-1000. **Chrmn & CEO**—L. R. Raymond. **Secy & VP-Investor Relations**—T. P. Townsend. **VP & Treas**—E. A. Robinson. **Dirs**—R. W. Bromery, D. W. Calloway, J. Hay, J. R. Houghton, W. R. Howell, P. E. Lippincott, H. J. Longwell, M. C. Nelson, L. R. Raymond, C. R. Sitter, J. H. Steele, R. E. Wilhelm, J. D. Williams. **Transfer Agent**—Bank of Boston. **Incorporated** in New Jersey in 1882. **Empl**-91,000. **S&P Analyst:** Raymond J. Deacon

FMC Corp.

NYSE Symbol **FMC**
In S&P 500

07-AUG-95

Industry: Chemicals

Summary: FMC is a major producer of industrial, specialty and agricultural chemicals, defense-related systems, petroleum and industrial machinery, and gold and silver.

S&P Opinion: Hold (★★★)	Recent Price • 73¼	Yield • Nil
	52 Wk Range • 75⅜-56	12-Mo. P/E • 14.5

Quantitative Evaluations

Outlook
(1 Lowest—5 Highest)
• **1+**

Fair Value
• **51⅛**

Risk
• **Low**

Earn./Div. Rank
• **B-**

Technical Eval.
• **Bearish** since 3/95

Rel. Strength Rank
(1 Lowest—99 Highest)
• **77**

Insider Activity
• **NA**

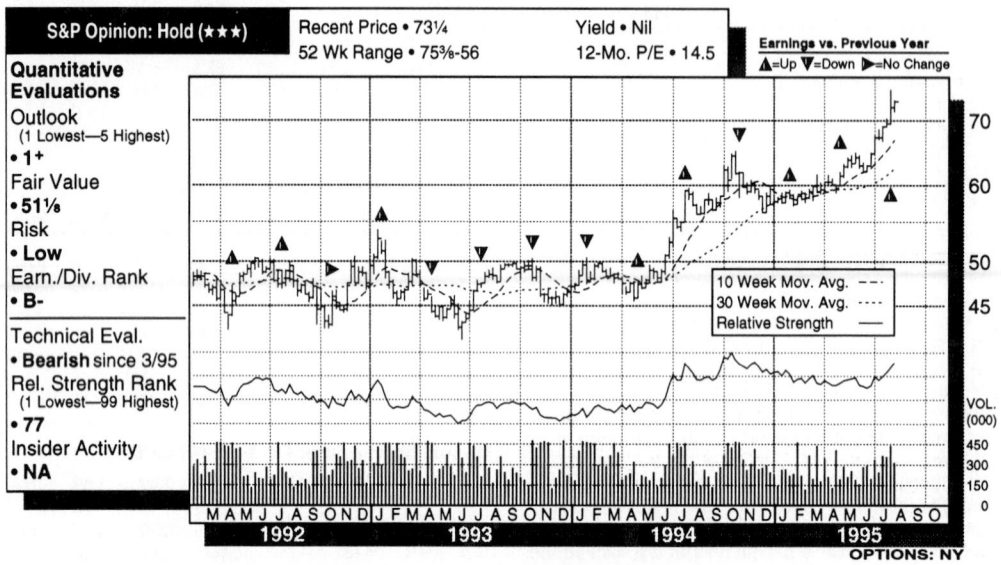

Earnings vs. Previous Year
▲=Up ▼=Down ▶=No Change

10 Week Mov. Avg. - - - -
30 Week Mov. Avg. ········
Relative Strength ──

VOL. (000)

OPTIONS: NY

Overview - 07-AUG-95

We see earnings for 1995 rising on gains in most businesses. Industrial chemicals profits will rise further on increasing prices for soda ash and peroxides, while performance chemicals should also advance, with better showings by pesticides, food and pharmaceutical ingredients and lithium. Machinery is expected to be boosted by the 1994 acquisitions of several petroleum and aircraft equipment companies, a solid backlog of orders, and cost reductions in the food machinery unit. Defense profits may be unchanged on higher foreign sales and favorable one-time contract settlements. Gold should turn profitable in the second half, following the start-up of the Beartrack mine. Restructuring actions implemented since 1994 are expected to reduce annual costs by about $70 million. The recent acquisition of Moorco will result in modest dilution in the second half.

Valuation - 07-AUG-95

After lagging the overall market during the first half of 1995, FMC's stock has been strong in recent weeks, largely in response to better than expected earnings, At its current P/E multiple, we recommend holding the stock. Earnings will continue to advance on the projected strength in many of FMC's late cycle product lines and healthy economic activity outside the U.S. FMC intends to remain a highly diversified company, though the gold unit may be a candidate for divestiture.

Key Stock Statistics

S&P EPS Est. 1995	5.70	Tang. Bk. Value/Share	11.36
P/E on S&P Est. 1995	12.9	Beta	0.75
S&P EPS Est. 1996	6.00	Shareholders	12,400
Dividend Rate/Share	Nil	Market cap. (B)	$ 2.7
Shs. outstg. (M)	36.5	Inst. holdings	67%
Avg. daily vol. (M)	0.073	Insider holdings	NA

Value of $10,000 invested 5 years ago: $ 20,780

Fiscal Year Ending Dec. 31

	1995	% Change	1994	% Change	1993	% Change
Revenues (Million $)						
1Q	1,032	14%	908.0	NM	901.7	-3%
2Q	1,128	6%	1,063	9%	979.0	-8%
3Q	—	—	1,015	10%	926.5	-5%
4Q	—	—	1,039	10%	946.5	-6%
Yr.	—	—	4,011	7%	3,754	-6%
Income (Million $)						
1Q	52.44	14%	46.09	2%	45.40	-17%
2Q	77.70	15%	67.32	8%	62.55	-3%
3Q	—	—	34.70	-2%	35.30	-16%
4Q	—	—	25.30	NM	-102.3	NM
Yr.	—	—	173.4	NM	41.00	-79%
Earnings Per Share ($)						
1Q	1.40	13%	1.24	NM	1.23	-17%
2Q	2.06	13%	1.82	8%	1.69	-3%
3Q	E1.20	—	0.93	-2%	0.95	-17%
4Q	E1.04	—	0.68	NM	-2.77	NM
Yr.	E5.70	—	4.66	NM	1.11	-79%

Next earnings report expected: mid October

Business Summary - 07-AUG-95

FMC, an industrial conglomerate, derived its 1994 sales and operating profits as follows:

	Sales	Profits
Performance chemicals	26%	34%
Industrial chemicals	21%	26%
Precious metals	2%	-2%
Defense systems	27%	35%
Machinery & equipment	24%	7%

International operations accounted for 23% of sales and 25% of pretax income in 1994.

Performance chemicals include insecticides and herbicides; lithium compounds; pharmaceutical ingredients; food additives, stabilizers and thickeners; and flame retardants and water additives.

Industrial chemicals includes natural soda ash and derivatives, peroxides, phosphorus, zeolites, silicates and sulfur derivatives. FMC Gold (80% owned) produces gold and silver.

United Defense (60% owned, formed January, 1994) includes tracked military and combat ground vehicles, naval gun and missile launching systems and steel components for the U.S. and foreign governments.

Machinery and equipment include food machinery (harvesting, preparation, processing, packaging and handling equipment and systems); energy equipment (wellhead and completion equipment, subsea equipment, valves, pumps and loading arms, and marine terminals), and transportation machinery (airline loading and de-icing equipment, conveyor equipment, bulk and unit material-handling equipment and systems and automotive service equipment).

Important Developments

Jul. '95—FMC said that second quarter results continued to show the positive earnings momentum in its commercial markets. Profits for performance chemicals declined, reflecting the loss of agricultural chemicals sales due to an unusually wet spring, higher prices of raw materials for food ingredients, and problems with a plant start-up.

Jun. '95—FMC acquired Moorco International Inc. (MRC) for $312 million. MRC, a maker of fluid measurement and pressure control equipment for the petroleum and process industries, has annual sales of $200 million. Separately, FMC sold a 20% interest in its soda ash business for $150 million to Nippon Sheet Glass Co. and Sumitomo Corp. FMC expects a $100 million gain on the transaction in the third quarter. The two companies will also invest in FMC's two-phased solution mining project.

Capitalization

Long Term Debt: $998,313,000 (3/95).
Minority Interest: $112,674,000.

Per Share Data ($)

(Year Ended Dec. 31)

	1994	1993	1992	1991	1990	1989
Tangible Bk. Val.	11.41	5.99	6.10	8.79	4.30	-2.05
Cash Flow	10.59	7.13	11.62	10.97	10.16	9.85
Earnings	4.66	1.11	5.23	4.77	4.30	4.35
Dividends	Nil	Nil	Nil	Nil	Nil	Nil
Payout Ratio	Nil	Nil	Nil	Nil	Nil	Nil
Prices - High	65⅛	54	53¼	51⅝	38¾	49
- Low	45½	41½	42½	29½	25⅜	31⅝
P/E Ratio - High	14	49	10	11	9	11
- Low	10	37	8	6	6	7

Income Statement Analysis (Million $)

	1994	%Chg	1993	%Chg	1992	%Chg	1991
Revs.	4,011	7%	3,754	-6%	3,974	2%	3,899
Oper. Inc.	535	18%	452	-17%	542	-1%	550
Depr.	221	NM	222	-6%	235	4%	225
Int. Exp.	73.0	-1%	74.0	-24%	97.0	-24%	128
Pretax Inc.	314	NM	40.0	-86%	283	9%	259
Eff. Tax Rate	25%	—	NM	—	31%	—	32%
Net Inc.	173	NM	41.0	-79%	193	12%	173

Balance Sheet & Other Fin. Data (Million $)

	1994	1993	1992	1991	1990	1989
Cash	98.0	78.0	24.0	44.0	93.0	95.0
Curr. Assets	1,376	1,160	1,123	1,180	1,295	1,312
Total Assets	3,352	2,813	2,827	2,816	2,959	2,819
Curr. Liab.	1,269	1,156	1,124	1,193	1,255	1,194
LT Debt	901	750	844	929	1,159	1,326
Common Eqty.	417	217	219	310	150	-71.0
Total Cap.	1,417	1,010	1,118	1,424	1,475	1,369
Cap. Exp.	356	215	314	217	380	281
Cash Flow	394	263	428	398	366	355

Ratio Analysis

	1994	1993	1992	1991	1990	1989
Curr. Ratio	1.1	1.0	1.0	1.0	1.0	1.1
% LT Debt of Cap.	63.6	74.2	75.4	65.3	78.5	96.8
% Net Inc.of Revs.	4.3	1.1	4.8	4.4	4.2	4.6
% Ret. on Assets	5.6	1.4	6.8	6.0	5.4	5.6
% Ret. on Equity	54.6	18.7	72.1	75.0	NM	NM

Dividend Data (Dividends, paid since 1935, were eliminated as part of the 1986 recapitalization in which each public stockholder received $80 cash and one share of the recapitalized company for each FMC share held. For accounting purposes, the recapitalization was treated as a 5.667-for-1 stock split and repurchase of 4.667 of the new shares issued to each public shareholder. FMC financed the plan with $2 billion of debt. A "poison pill" stock purchase right was adopted in 1988.)

Data as orig. reptd.; bef. results of disc. opers. and/or spec. items. Per share data adj. for stk. divs. as of ex-div. date.
E-Estimated. NA-Not Available. NM-Not Meaningful. NR-Not Ranked.

Office—200 East Randolph Drive, Chicago, IL 60601. **Tel**—(312) 861-6000. **Chrmn & CEO**—R. N. Burt. **Pres**—L. D. Brady. **EVP & CFO**—M. J. Callahan. **Secy**—R. L. Day. **Treas**—C. A. Francis. **Investor Contact**—Lisa Azzarello (312) 861-6921. **Dirs**—W. W. Boeschenstein, L. D. Brady, B. A. Bridgewater Jr., P. A. Buffler, R. N. Burt, A. J. Costello, P. L. Davies Jr., J. A. Francois-Poncet, R. H. Malott, E. C. Meyer, W. F. Reilly, J. R. Thompson, C. Yeutter. **Transfer Agent & Registrar**—Harris Trust & Savings Bank, Chicago. **Incorporated** in Delaware in 1928. **Empl**-21,344. **S&P Analyst:** Richard O'Reilly, CFA

FPL Group

NYSE Symbol **FPL**
In S&P 500

15-AUG-95

Industry:
Utilities-Electric

Summary: This electric utility holding company's primary unit is Florida Power & Light Co., which provides electricity to most of the territory along Florida's east and lower west coasts.

S&P Opinion: Accumulate (★★★★)	Recent Price • 38⅝	Yield • 4.5%
	52 Wk Range • 39¼-29⅞	12-Mo. P/E • 12.7

Quantitative Evaluations

Outlook
(1 Lowest—5 Highest)
• **2+**

Fair Value
• **34⅞**

Risk
• **Low**

Earn./Div. Rank
• **B**

Technical Eval.
• **Bullish** since 9/94

Rel. Strength Rank
(1 Lowest—99 Highest)
• **51**

Insider Activity
• **Neutral**

Earnings vs. Previous Year
▲=Up ▼=Down ▶=No Change

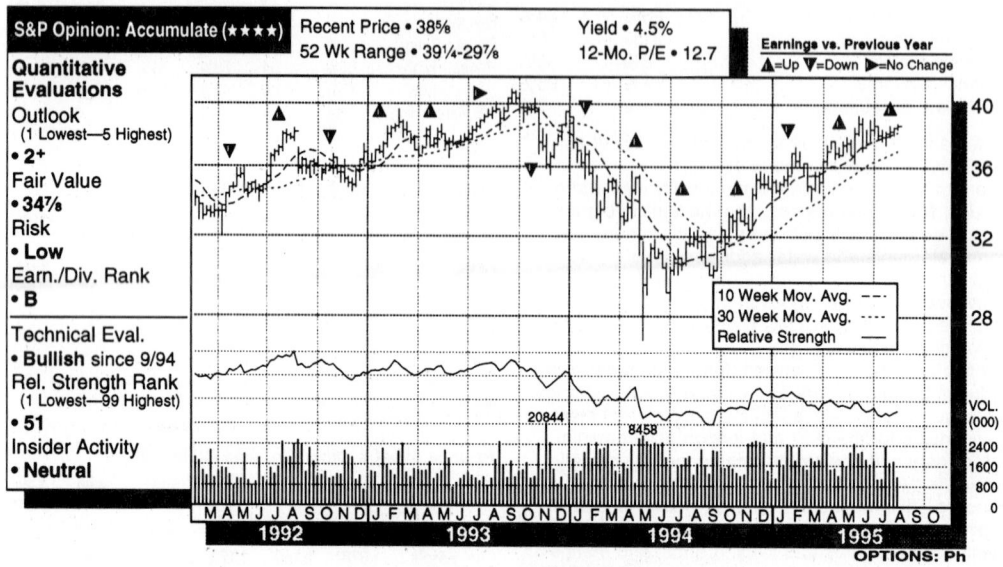

```
10 Week Mov. Avg.  ---
30 Week Mov. Avg.  ····
Relative Strength  —
```

VOL. (000)

OPTIONS: Ph

Overview - 15-AUG-95

Share earnings in 1995 should continue to benefit from rising electricity sales due to customer demand growth that substantially exceeds the national average. Also, results should continue to benefit from well-controlled expenses, due partly to the absence of planned nuclear plant outages. FPL is about half way through a 10-million, three-year share repurchase program initiated in May 1994 which will also boost per-share comparisons this year and in 1996. Modestly offsetting these positive factors is higher depreciation expense resulting from FPL's increased asset base. Longer-term, prospects should be enhanced by activities to reduce fuel costs. The balance sheet is sound, with long-term debt below the nation's average for electric utilities at 44% of total capital.

Valuation - 15-AUG-95

The shares have rebounded well from their bottom in May 1994 after the unexpected 32% dividend cut. The cut is part of FPL's strategy to strengthen share values as well as position itself competitively in a fast changing environment. The payout ratio, which is below average compared to its peers despite a recent 4.8% rate hike, now affords the company greater flexibility to discount prices as competition arises. FPL's competitive position is also enhanced by reasonable rates and a very low industrial customer base. We expect the dividend to continue to grow at a rate well above average for the next several years.

Key Stock Statistics

S&P EPS Est. 1995	3.05	Tang. Bk. Value/Share	22.50
P/E on S&P Est. 1995	12.7	Beta	0.50
S&P EPS Est. 1996	3.15	Shareholders	80,600
Dividend Rate/Share	1.76	Market cap. (B)	$ 7.2
Shs. outstg. (M)	185.1	Inst. holdings	43%
Avg. daily vol. (M)	0.345	Insider holdings	NA

Value of $10,000 invested 5 years ago: $ 14,932

Fiscal Year Ending Dec. 31

	1995	% Change	1994	% Change	1993	% Change
Revenues ()						
1Q	1,177	NM	1,178	4%	1,132	4%
2Q	1,467	2%	1,442	7%	1,350	7%
3Q	—	—	1,512	-6%	1,603	2%
4Q	—	—	1,290	5%	1,231	-3%
Yr.	—	—	5,423	2%	5,316	2%
Income ()						
1Q	99.8	6%	94.44	3%	91.95	24%
2Q	138.3	10%	125.8	14%	110.6	7%
3Q	—	—	222.2	58%	140.5	-25%
4Q	—	—	76.19	-11%	85.73	-15%
Yr.	—	—	518.7	21%	428.8	-8%
Earnings Per Share ()						
1Q	0.57	8%	0.53	6%	0.50	16%
2Q	0.79	13%	0.70	17%	0.60	NM
3Q	E1.27	2%	1.25	67%	0.75	-29%
4Q	E0.42	-2%	0.43	-4%	0.45	-20%
Yr.	E3.05	5%	2.91	27%	2.30	-13%

Next earnings report expected: late October

FPL Group

Business Summary - 15-AUG-95

FPL Group is the holding company for Florida Power & Light Co., which provides electricity to some 6.5 million people in 35 counties, including most of the territory along Florida's east and lower west coasts. Electric revenues by class of customer in recent years were:

	1994	1993	1992	1991
Residential	56%	56%	55%	55%
Commercial	36%	37%	36%	37%
Industrial	4%	4%	4%	5%
Other	4%	3%	5%	3%

Sources of power in 1994 were oil 31%, nuclear 26%, gas 20%, coal 6%, and purchased power 17%. Summer peak load in 1994 was 15,179 mw, and capability at time of peak was 18,146 mw, for a capacity margin of 26%. Energy sales are projected to increase about 2.6% annually for the next five years.

Capital requirements, consisting primarily of expenditures to meet increased electricity usage and growth in the customer base, for 1995 have been forecast at $712 for 1995, down from $759 million in 1994. For the period from 1995 through 1999, FPL expects capital outlays to total $3 billion. The company does not anticipate construction of new generating plants before the year 2004.

FPL owns ESI Energy Inc., which currently participates in 27 independent, largely alternative energy, power production projects; Turner Foods, a leading citrus grove operator, and several smaller operations. In 1990, FPL exited most of its non-energy related businesses. Write offs for the divestitures were $5.54 in 1990 and $0.83 in 1991.

In May 1994, as part of a change in fiscal strategy to strengthen FPL's share value and be more competitive in a rapidly changing business environment, directors authorized repurchase of 10 million shares over the next three years, and set the dividend payout ratio at 60% to 65% of prior year's earnings. As a result, the quarterly dividend was reduced to $0.42 a share from $0.62.

Important Developments

Jul. '95—FPL attributed the 11% growth in earnings per share for the 1995 first half to much warmer than average weather, customer growth and ongoing cost reductions. Results also benefited from a roughly 2% decrease in average shares outstanding.

Capitalization

Long Term Debt: $3,579,446,000 (3/95).
Subsid. Red. Preferred Stock: $54,000,000.
Subsid. Preferred Stock: $451,250,000.

Per Share Data () (Year Ended Dec. 31)

	1994	1993	1992	1991	1990	1989
Tangible Bk. Val.	22.50	21.58	19.84	18.60	19.48	24.47
Earnings	2.91	2.30	2.65	2.31	-2.86	3.12
Dividends	1.88	2.47	2.43	2.39	2.34	2.26
Payout Ratio	65%	107%	92%	103%	NM	72%
Prices - High	39⅛	41	38⅜	37¼	36½	36¾
- Low	26⅞	35½	32	28⅛	26⅛	29
P/E Ratio - High	13	18	14	16	NM	12
- Low	9	15	12	12	NM	9

Income Statement Analysis ()

	1994	%Chg	1993	%Chg	1992	%Chg	1991
Revs.	5,423	2%	5,316	2%	5,193	-1%	5,249
Depr.	724	21%	598	8%	554	7%	518
Maint.	NA	—	NA	—	358	-12%	405
Fxd. Chgs. Cov.	3.2	7%	3.0	-3%	3.1	25%	2.5
Constr. Credits	24.0	-64%	66.2	15%	57.8	70%	34.0
Eff. Tax Rate	37%	—	37%	—	36%	—	29%
Net Inc.	519	21%	429	-8%	467	69%	276

Balance Sheet & Other Fin. Data ()

	1994	1993	1992	1991	1990	1989
Gross Prop.	16,390	15,881	14,972	13,771	12,962	12,167
Cap. Exp.	906	1,248	1,270	1,197	1,038	783
Net Prop.	10,203	10,289	9,866	9,081	8,456	8,079
Capitalization:						
LT Debt	4,050	4,020	4,280	3,948	3,863	3,465
% LT Debt	47	46	49	51	51	47
Pfd.	545	548	551	496	521	519
% Pfd.	6.30	6.30	6.40	6.40	6.90	7.00
Common	4,197	4,101	3,836	3,354	3,161	3,452
% Common	49	47	44	43	42	46
Total Cap.	10,917	10,722	10,732	9,674	9,516	9,384

Ratio Analysis

	1994	1993	1992	1991	1990	1989
Oper. Ratio	84.5	86.4	85.1	86.6	100.8	88.0
% Earn. on Net Prop.	8.2	7.2	8.2	8.1	NM	9.3
% Ret. on Revs.	9.6	8.1	9.0	7.2	NM	6.6
% Ret. On Invest.Cap	7.8	7.0	8.0	7.8	NM	10.2
% Return On Com.Eqty	12.5	10.8	13.0	11.5	NM	12.2

Dividend Data —Dividends have been paid since 1944. A dividend reinvestment plan is available. A "poison pill" stock purchase rights plan was adopted in 1986.

Amt. of Div. $	Date Decl.	Ex-Div. Date	Stock of Record	Payment Date
0.420	Aug. 15	Aug. 22	Aug. 26	Sep. 15 '94
0.420	Nov. 15	Nov. 18	Nov. 25	Dec. 15 '94
0.440	Feb. 13	Feb. 17	Feb. 24	Mar. 15 '95
0.440	May. 15	May. 22	May. 26	Jun. 15 '95
0.440	Aug. 14	Aug. 23	Aug. 25	Sep. 15 '95

Data as orig. reptd.; bef. results of disc opers. and/or spec. items. Per share data adj. for stk. divs. as of ex-div. date. E-Estimated. NA-Not Available. NM-Not Meaningful. NR-Not Ranked.

Office—700 Universe Blvd., Juno Beach, FL 33408. **Tel**—(407) 694-4647. **Chrmn & CEO**—J. L. Broadhead. **EVP & CFO**—M. W. Yackira. **Secy**—D. P. Coyle. **Investor Contact**—Scott Dudley. **Dirs**—H. J. Arnelle, R. M. Beall II, D. Blumberg, J. L. Broadhead, J. H. Brown, M. M. Criser, B. F. Dolan, W. D. Dover, P. J. Evanson, A. Fanjul, D. Lewis, F. V. Malek, P. R. Tregurtha. **Transfer Agent & Registrar**—Bank of Boston. **Incorporated** in Florida in 1925; reincorporated in Florida in 1984. **Empl**-12,100. **S&P Analyst:** Jane Collin

Federal Express

NYSE Symbol **FDX**
In S&P 500

07-OCT-95 | **Industry:** Transportation | **Summary:** This company offers a wide range of express delivery services for the transportation of documents, packages and freight, using an integrated air-ground transportation system.

| S&P Opinion: Buy (★★★★) | Recent Price • 81½ | Yield • Nil | Earnings vs. Previous Year |
| | 52 Wk Range • 84-53½ | 12-Mo. P/E • 14.8 | ▲=Up ▼=Down ▶=No Change |

Quantitative Evaluations

Outlook
(1 Lowest—5 Highest)
• **5+**

Fair Value
• **103⅞**

Risk
• **Low**

Earn./Div. Rank
• **B-**

Technical Eval.
• **Bearish** since 8/95

Rel. Strength Rank
(1 Lowest—99 Highest)
• **89**

Insider Activity
• **Neutral**

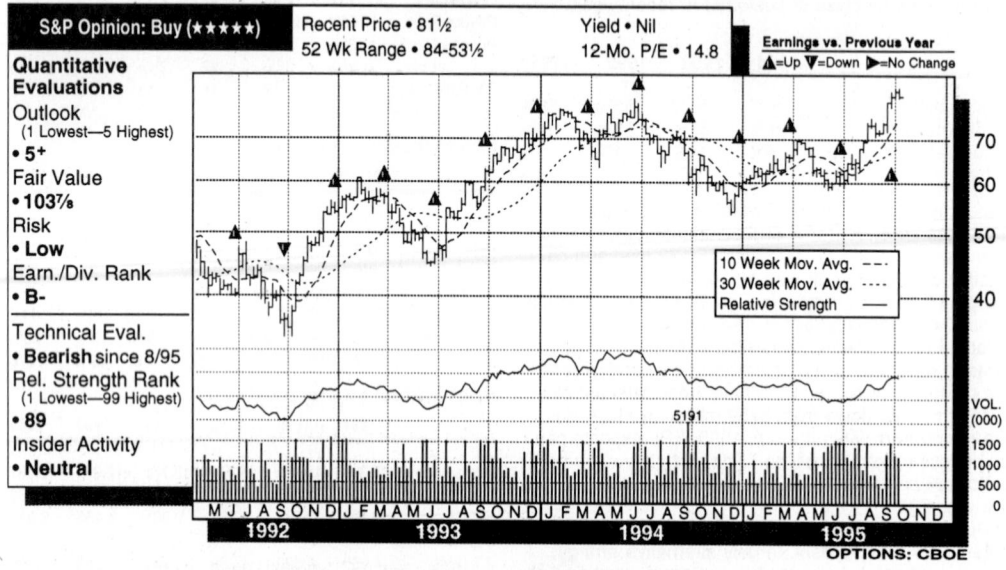

10 Week Mov. Avg. ----
30 Week Mov. Avg. ····
Relative Strength ——

5191

OPTIONS: CBOE

Overview - 06-OCT-95

Revenues in 1995-6 are expected to rise more than 10% from those of 1994-5. Domestic express volume should continue to expand, although faster growth is forecast for less costly standard overnight and second-day delivery services. International volume growth is also projected to be robust, particularly in the international priority category. Price increases, announced in early 1995, should alleviate domestic yield pressure and offset the effect of the less favorable product mix. Profits from international operations should increase with the new Subic Bay facility and the introduction of intra-Asia overnight service. Results will benefit from a continuing strong focus on automation and cost control.

Valuation - 06-OCT-95

The shares have rebounded in recent months on signs that pricing in the very competitive domestic market has improved and on a slowdown in the shift toward less profitable products. In addition, with the new Subic Bay facility, FedEx can develop its intra-Asia overnight delivery operations. The long-term trend of the international air delivery industry is positive as trade barriers come down and international trade increases. While a sustained halt to economic growth may depress the shares, we estimate the chance of such an event as unlikely. Accordingly, given our forecast for long-term earnings growth, we view the shares as very attractive at around 14 times our estimate of 1995-6 earnings.

Key Stock Statistics

S&P EPS Est. 1996	5.75	Tang. Bk. Value/Share	33.02
P/E on S&P Est. 1996	14.2	Beta	1.09
Dividend Rate/Share	Nil	Shareholders	7,900
Shs. outstg. (M)	56.2	Market cap. (B)	$ 4.6
Avg. daily vol. (M)	0.256	Inst. holdings	75%
		Insider holdings	NA

Value of $10,000 invested 5 years ago: $ 17,814

Fiscal Year Ending May 31

	1996	% Change	1995	% Change	1994	% Change
Revenues (Million $)						
1Q	2,453	10%	2,231	11%	2,016	8%
2Q	—	—	2,359	11%	2,122	8%
3Q	—	—	2,333	12%	2,077	7%
4Q	—	—	2,470	9%	2,265	11%
Yr.	—	—	9,392	11%	8,479	9%
Income (Million $)						
1Q	75.30	23%	61.14	86%	32.85	NM
2Q	—	—	86.14	44%	59.69	69%
3Q	—	—	63.11	102%	31.17	NM
4Q	—	—	87.20	8%	80.66	45%
Yr.	—	—	297.6	46%	204.4	86%
Earnings Per Share ($)						
1Q	1.33	23%	1.08	80%	0.60	NM
2Q	E1.60	5%	1.53	43%	1.07	65%
3Q	E1.20	7%	1.12	104%	0.55	NM
4Q	E1.62	5%	1.54	8%	1.43	42%
Yr.	E5.75	9%	5.27	44%	3.65	82%

Next earnings report expected: mid December

Business Summary - 06-OCT-95

Federal Express Corporation is the world's largest all-cargo airline. Contributions by geographical area in 1994-5 were:

	Revs.	Profits
Domestic	73%	79%
International	27%	21%

The company offers four domestic overnight delivery services: FedEx First Overnight, FedEx Priority Overnight, FedEx Standard Overnight and FedEx Overnight Freight. Two U.S. domestic second-day services are also available for less-urgent shipments: FedEx 2Day and FedEx 2Day Freight. In 1995, the company introduced FedEx SameDay for packages that cannot wait until the next day to be delivered.

The company also offers various international document and package delivery services and international freight services.

National sorting facilities are located in Memphis, Tenn., and Indianapolis, Ind. Regional hubs are at Newark, N.J. and Oakland, Calif., and major metropolitan sorting facilities are in Los Angeles, Calif., Chicago, Ill., and Anchorage, Alaska. International sorting facilities are at Subic Bay (Philippines), Tokyo, Paris and London. The company is also developing a regional hub in Fort Worth, expected to become operational in 1997.

As of June 30, 1995, the operating fleet consisted of 501 aircraft divided:nine A300s, 17 A310s, 158 B-727s, five B-747s, 35 DC-10s, 13 MD-11s, 32 F-27s and232 Cessna 208s. There were commitments to purchase 16 A300s, two A310s, 12 MD-11s and 32 208s and options to purchase up to 44 additional A300s.

The company also operated approximately 35,900 ground transport vehicles, including pickup and delivery vans and trucks and over-the-road tractors and trailers. A portion of volume is handled entirely by ground transport.

Important Developments

Sep. '95—The company started its intra-Asia overnight delivery service using its new Subic Bay hub.
Sep. '95—Federal Express introduced FedEx First Overnight for next day delivery by 8:00 a.m. In July 1995, the company began offering FedEx Sameday, a same-day delivery service.
Aug. '95—FDX said it had received government approval of its request to purchase all-cargo route authority to serve China from Evergreen International Airlines. Under this authority, Federal Express said it will become the sole U.S.-based express carrier with aviation rights to China. The transfer is subject to approval from the Chinese government.

Capitalization

Long Term Debt: $1,324,711,000 (5/95).

Per Share Data ($) — (Year Ended May 31)

	1995	1994	1993	1992	1991	1990
Tangible Bk. Val.	33.02	27.02	22.64	20.18	21.40	19.95
Cash Flow	16.81	14.05	12.27	8.59	10.13	11.19
Earnings	5.27	3.65	2.01	-2.11	0.11	2.18
Dividends	Nil	Nil	Nil	Nil	Nil	Nil
Payout Ratio	Nil	Nil	Nil	Nil	Nil	Nil
Cal. Yrs.	1994	1993	1992	1991	1990	1989
Prices - High	80¾	72½	56⅛	44½	58	57⅞
- Low	53½	44⅜	34⅜	31⅜	29½	42⅛
P/E Ratio - High	15	20	28	NM	NM	27
- Low	10	12	17	NM	NM	19

Income Statement Analysis (Million $)

	1995	%Chg	1994	%Chg	1993	%Chg	1992
Revs.	9,392	11%	8,479	9%	7,808	3%	7,550
Oper. Inc.	1,244	12%	1,113	20%	926	11%	834
Depr.	652	12%	583	4%	562	-3%	577
Int. Exp.	142	-22%	182	-9%	200	-1%	203
Pretax Inc.	522	38%	378	85%	204	NM	-146
Eff. Tax Rate	43%	—	46%	—	46%	—	NM
Net Inc.	298	46%	204	85%	110	NM	-113

Balance Sheet & Other Fin. Data (Million $)

	1995	1994	1993	1992	1991	1990
Cash	358	393	155	78.0	118	98.0
Curr. Assets	1,869	1,762	1,440	1,206	1,283	1,315
Total Assets	6,433	5,992	5,793	5,463	5,672	5,675
Curr. Liab.	1,779	1,536	1,449	1,385	1,494	1,240
LT Debt	1,325	1,632	1,882	1,798	1,827	2,148
Common Eqty.	2,246	1,925	1,671	1,580	1,669	1,649
Total Cap.	3,627	3,560	3,626	3,501	3,713	4,096
Cap. Exp.	1,061	1,089	867	771	986	1,145
Cash Flow	950	787	672	443	540	595

Ratio Analysis

	1995	1994	1993	1992	1991	1990
Curr. Ratio	1.1	1.1	1.0	0.9	0.9	1.1
% LT Debt of Cap.	36.5	45.8	51.9	51.3	49.2	56.6
% Net Inc.of Revs.	3.2	2.4	1.4	NM	0.1	1.7
% Ret. on Assets	4.8	3.4	1.9	NM	0.1	2.1
% Ret. on Equity	14.3	11.3	6.7	NM	0.4	7.3

Dividend Data —No dividends have ever been paid on the common stock.

Data as orig. reptd.; bef. results of disc. opers. and/or spec. items. Per share data adj. for stk. divs. as of ex-div. date. E-Estimated. NA-Not Available. NM-Not Meaningful. NR-Not Ranked.

Office—2005 Corporate Ave., Memphis, TN 38132. **Tel**—(901) 369-3600. **Chrmn, Pres & CEO**—F. W. Smith. **Sr VP & CFO**—A. B. Graf. **Secy**—K. R. Masterson. **Investor Contact**—Tom L. Holland (901) 395-3468. **Dirs**—R. H. Allen, H. H. Baker Jr., A. J. A. Bryan, R. L. Cox, R. D. DeNunzio, J. L. Estrin, P. Greer, J. R. Hyde III, C. T. Manatt, G. J. Mitchell, J. W. Smart Jr., F. W. Smith, J. I. Smith, P. S. Willmott. **Transfer Agent & Registrar**—First Chicago Trust Co. of New York, Jersey City, N.J. **Incorporated** in Delaware in 1971. **Empl**- 108,000. **S&P Analyst:** Joe Victor Shammas

Federal Home Loan Mortgage

STOCK REPORTS

NYSE Symbol **FRE**
In S&P 500

07-AUG-95 Industry:
Finance

Summary: Federal Home Loan Mortgage ("Freddie Mac"), a corporate instrumentality of the U.S. government, buys mortgages from lenders and pools and packages the mortgages into securities.

S&P Opinion: Accumulate (★★★★)	Recent Price • 63½	Yield • 1.9%
	52 Wk Range • 73⅛-47	12-Mo. P/E • 11.5

Quantitative Evaluations

Outlook
 (1 Lowest—5 Highest)
• **5⁻**

Fair Value
• **78¾**

Risk
• **Low**

Earn./Div. Rank
• **NR**

Technical Eval.
• **Bullish** since 1/95

Rel. Strength Rank
 (1 Lowest—99 Highest)
• **13**

Insider Activity
• **NA**

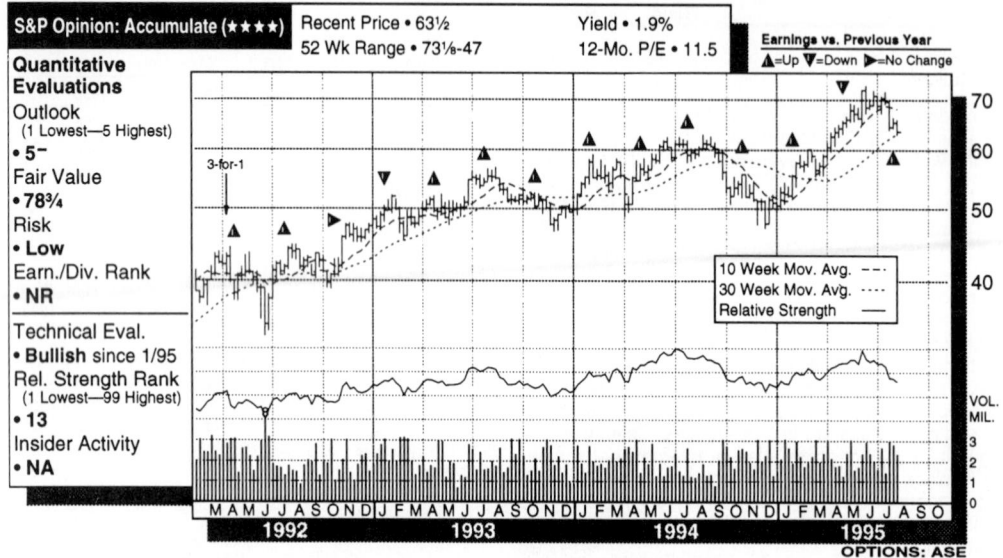

Earnings vs. Previous Year
▲=Up ▼=Down ▶=No Change

10 Week Mov. Avg. ---
30 Week Mov. Avg. ·····
Relative Strength ——

OPTIONS: ASE

Overview - 07-AUG-95

Share earnings are projected to increase steadily over the next three to five years, reflecting anticipated growth in the two business segments: securities and retained mortgages. The securities business should continue to benefit from an increased volume of mortgages securitized as well as increases in the overall level of mortgage debt. FRE earns an average fee of about 0.24% for securitizing a mortgage. At the end of June 1995, it earned this fee on a mortgage principal balance of $459 billion. The company's retained portfolio business, represented by $85 billion of mortgages held for its own account, earns attractive profits because the portfolio can be financed at low rates, given FRE's quasi-agency status. About 60% of new mortgage originations are sold into the secondary market.

Valuation - 07-AUG-95

Freddie Mac shares are a solid, long-term core holding with attributes that would interest a value investor. Trading at a P/E of 10 on 1996 earnings, the company could be reasonably expected to grow earnings in low double digit rates on average for the foreseeable future, aided by expansion of the retained mortgage portfolio it holds for its own account. Freddie's advantage is that it can finance purchases of mortgages at quasi-agency rates. The company also generates impressive returns: return on equity was 22% in 1995's second quarter. The excellent ROE can be partially explained by FRE's highly efficient operations and that fact that it competes in essentially a two-company market.

Key Stock Statistics

S&P EPS Est. 1995	5.80	Tang. Bk. Value/Share	25.80
P/E on S&P Est. 1995	10.9	Beta	2.50
S&P EPS Est. 1996	6.60	Shareholders	NA
Dividend Rate/Share	1.20	Market cap. (B)	$ 11.5
Shs. outstg. (M)	180.8	Inst. holdings	85%
Avg. daily vol. (M)	0.473	Insider holdings	NA

Value of $10,000 invested 5 years ago: $ 31,666

Fiscal Year Ending Dec. 31

	1995	% Change	1994	% Change	1993	% Change
Revenues (Million $)						
1Q	2,130	35%	1,574	35%	1,165	9%
2Q	2,033	25%	1,626	23%	1,318	20%
3Q	—	—	1,779	29%	1,382	25%
4Q	—	—	1,944	22%	1,591	34%
Yr.	—	—	6,923	27%	5,456	22%
Income (Million $)						
1Q	258.0	-7%	277.0	37%	202.0	43%
2Q	264.0	6%	249.0	38%	180.0	9%
3Q	—	—	249.0	25%	200.0	24%
4Q	—	—	252.0	24%	204.0	32%
Yr.	—	—	1,027	31%	786.0	26%
Earnings Per Share ($)						
1Q	1.34	-7%	1.44	36%	1.06	36%
2Q	1.37	6%	1.29	37%	0.94	7%
3Q	E1.51	—	1.29	25%	1.03	24%
4Q	E1.58	—	1.30	25%	1.04	30%
Yr.	E5.80	—	5.32	31%	4.07	24%

Next earnings report expected: mid October

Business Summary - 03-AUG-95

Federal Home Loan Mortgage Corp. ("Freddie Mac") is a corporate instrumentality of the U.S. government, established in 1970 primarily for the purpose of increasing mortgage credit for housing. Its principal activity is the purchase of conventional mortgage loans and the resale of those mortgages in the form of guaranteed mortgage securities. FRE obtains its income from fees received for guaranteeing principal and interest payments on mortgage-backed securities, float income resulting from the lag between when payment is received from mortgagors and subsequently passed on to investors, and interest income on its own mortgage portfolio.

In 1994, FRE purchased $124.2 billion of mortgages, down from $229.7 billion in 1993 and $191.1 billion in 1992. The company issued $117.1 billion in mortgage-backed securities in 1994, $208.7 billion in 1993 and $179.2 billion in 1992. At the end of 1994, mortgage participation and guaranteed mortgage certificates outstanding totaled $461 billion, up from $439 billion a year earlier. Net mortgages retained at December 31, 1994, totaled $72.3 billion, up 30% from $55.7 billion a year earlier.

Freddie Mac has financed the majority of its conventional and FHA/VA mortgage purchases through the sale of Participation Certificates (PCs). PCs represent undivided interests in first lien, fixed-rate or adjustable-rate, conventional or FHA/VA, residential mortgages and provide for monthly payment of interest and pass-through of principal. In addition, the company includes under its Guarantor Program purchases of mortgages (on an individually negotiated basis) in exchange for PCs.

Freddie Mac has issued securities which divide the cash flows of the underlying mortgages or PCs into classes having various features relating to stated maturities or weighted average lives; whether all principal or all interest is to be received; and whether the coupon (if any) on the security is fixed or variable rate.

Important Developments

Jul. '95—Freddie Mac said that in the second quarter of 1995 it increased the pace of profitable retained portfolio purchases, reduced real estate owned balances through aggressive loss mitigation activities and provided lenders with tools to improve the quality of new originations.

Capitalization

Short Term Debt: $55,040,000,000 (6/95).
Long Term Debt: $53,444,000,000 (6/95).
Noncum. Preferred Stock: $837,300,000.

Per Share Data ($)

(Year Ended Dec. 31)

	1994	1993	1992	1991	1990	1989
Tangible Bk. Val.	25.80	19.80	16.68	14.25	11.86	10.63
Earnings	5.32	4.07	3.29	3.08	2.30	2.19
Dividends	1.04	0.88	0.76	0.67	0.53	0.53
Payout Ratio	20%	22%	23%	22%	23%	24%
Prices - High	62⅞	56¾	49¼	46⅜	27⅜	35
- Low	47	45¼	33¾	14¾	10⅛	16¼
P/E Ratio - High	12	14	15	15	12	16
- Low	9	11	10	5	4	7

Income Statement Analysis (Million $)

	1994	%Chg	1993	%Chg	1992	%Chg	1991
Int. Mtgs.	4,528	37%	3,296	26%	2,608	12%	2,332
Int. Invest.	1,287	14%	1,127	23%	917	-16%	1,095
Int. Exp.	4,703	32%	3,571	26%	2,830	3%	2,744
Guaranty Fees	1,108	7%	1,033	10%	936	18%	792
Loan Loss Prov.	200	-33%	300	-37%	473	10%	431
Admin. Exp.	379	5%	361	10%	329	15%	287
Pretax Inc.	1,482	31%	1,128	25%	901	13%	800
Eff. Tax Rate	31%	—	30%	—	31%	—	31%
Net Inc.	1,027	31%	786	26%	622	12%	555

Balance Sheet & Other Fin. Data (Million $)

	1994	1993	1992	1991	1990	1989
Mtges.	72,295	55,732	33,523	26,537	21,395	21,329
Inv.	17,808	18,223	12,542	9,956	11,012	5,765
Cash & Equiv.	11,442	3,216	6,453	7,987	4,859	5,397
Total Assets	106,199	83,880	59,502	46,860	40,579	35,462
ST Debt	47,303	17,999	12,854	17,239	19,959	16,673
LT Debt	48,984	31,994	16,777	13,023	10,982	9,474
Equity	4,300	3,574	3,008	2,566	2,136	1,916

Ratio Analysis

	1994	1993	1992	1991	1990	1989
% Ret. on Assets	1.1	1.1	1.2	1.3	1.1	1.3
% Ret. on Equity	24.4	21.4	21.2	23.6	20.4	25.0
Equity/Assets Ratio	4.2	4.6	5.2	5.4	5.3	5.0
Price Times Book Value:						
High	2.4	2.9	2.5	3.3	2.3	3.3
Low	1.8	2.3	1.7	1.0	0.9	1.5

Dividend Data (Dividends on the common stock began in 1989.)

Amt. of Div. $	Date Decl.	Ex-Div. Date	Stock of Record	Payment Date
0.260	Sep. 09	Sep. 13	Sep. 19	Sep. 30 '94
0.260	Dec. 02	Dec. 06	Dec. 12	Dec. 30 '94
0.300	Mar. 03	Mar. 07	Mar. 13	Mar. 31 '95
0.300	Jun. 02	Jun. 08	Jun. 12	Jun. 30 '95

Data as orig. reptd.; bef. results of disc opers. and/or spec. items. Per share data adj. for stk. divs. as of ex-div. date.
E-Estimated. NA-Not Available. NM-Not Meaningful. NR-Not Ranked.

Office—8200 Jones Branch Drive, McLean, VA 22102. **Tel**—(703) 903-2000. **Chrmn & CEO**—L. C. Brendsel. **Pres**—D. W. Glenn. **VP & Secy**—M. E. Mater. **Investor Contact**—Paul Scarpetta (703-903-2798). **Dirs**—L. C. Brendsel, J. DeConcini, J. C. Etling, D. W. Glenn, G. D Gould, J. M. Hultin, B. C. Jordan, H. Kaufman, J. B. McCoy, J. F. Montgomery, J. B. Nutter, R. E. Palmer, R. F. Poe, D. J. Schuenke, C. Seix, W. J. Turner, H. F. Woods. **Transfer Agent & Registrar**—Chemical Mellon, NYC. **Incorporated** under the laws of the United States in 1970. **Empl**-3,000. **S&P Analyst:** Paul L. Huberman, CFA

Federal Nat'l Mtge. Ass'n

NYSE Symbol **FNM**
In S&P 500

08-SEP-95 | **Industry:** Finance | **Summary:** "Fannie Mae," a U.S. government-sponsored company, uses mostly borrowed funds to buy a variety of mortgages, thereby creating a secondary market for mortgage lenders.

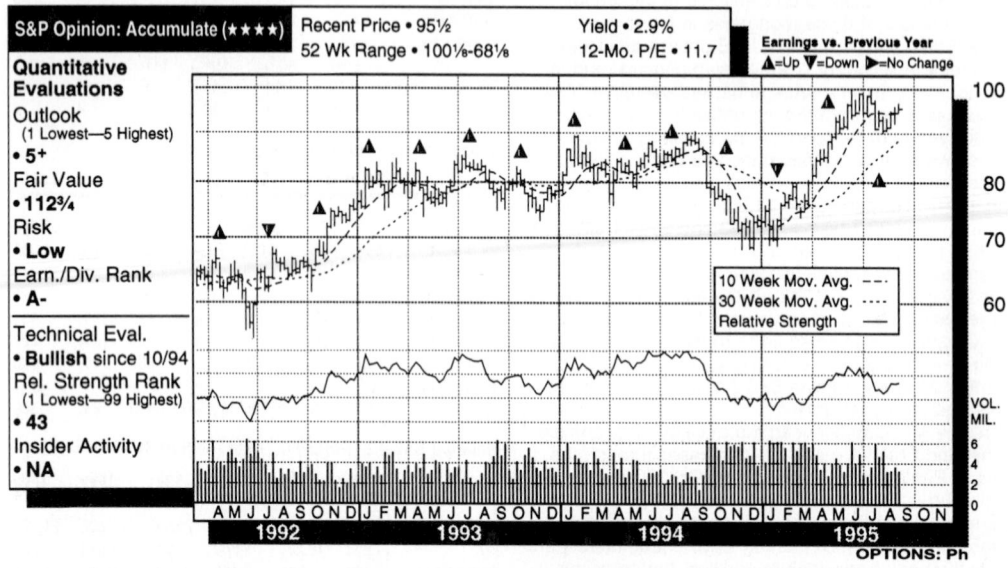

S&P Opinion: Accumulate (★★★★)	Recent Price • 95½	Yield • 2.9%
	52 Wk Range • 100⅛-68⅛	12-Mo. P/E • 11.7

Quantitative Evaluations

Outlook
(1 Lowest—5 Highest)
• **5+**

Fair Value
• **112¾**

Risk
• **Low**

Earn./Div. Rank
• **A-**

Technical Eval.
• **Bullish** since 10/94

Rel. Strength Rank
(1 Lowest—99 Highest)
• **43**

Insider Activity
• **NA**

Earnings vs. Previous Year
▲=Up ▼=Down ▶=No Change

10 Week Mov. Avg. ---
30 Week Mov. Avg. ·····
Relative Strength —

OPTIONS: Ph

Overview - 07-SEP-95

Fannie Mae should increase its earnings per share 8%-12% a year for the foreseeable future. This outlook reflects projected growth in the mortgage portfolio Fannie Mae holds for its own account (about two-thirds of profits). FNM should expand this portfolio about 15% in 1996, based on projected growth on the order of 7% to 9% in mortgage debt outstanding and FNM's plans to increase its purchases of mortgage-backed securities. The mortgage-backed securities segment (about one-third of net income) has shown steady growth, reflecting the fact that about 60% of newly originated mortgages are sold into the secondary market. Stronger housing markets are expected to result in lower aggregate credit loss provisioning. Fannie Mae's steadily increasing capital base bolsters its profit outlook.

Valuation - 31-AUG-95

Fannie Mae, one of the largest companies in the U. S., is a solid core holding. The company faces only one major competitor, and its stock is selling at a P/E ratio of about 10 on projected 1996 earnings per share of $9.50, well below the market's P/E. It enjoys a favorable long-term growth outlook, aided by projected increases in mortgage debt, the company's access to low-cost debt, and an improving capital position. In 1995's second quarter, the company generated a robust ROE of about 23%. Future dividend hikes are likely.

Key Stock Statistics

S&P EPS Est. 1995	8.60	Tang. Bk. Value/Share	34.97
P/E on S&P Est. 1995	11.1	Beta	1.71
S&P EPS Est. 1996	9.50	Shareholders	11,000
Dividend Rate/Share	2.72	Market cap. (B)	$ 26.0
Shs. outstg. (M)	272.8	Inst. holdings	86%
Avg. daily vol. (M)	0.641	Insider holdings	NA

Value of $10,000 invested 5 years ago: $ 32,092

Fiscal Year Ending Dec. 31

	1995	% Change	1994	% Change	1993	% Change
Revenues (Million $)						
1Q	5,290	23%	4,304	50%	2,863	-17%
2Q	5,452	21%	4,496	15%	3,897	7%
3Q	—	—	4,735	16%	4,071	11%
4Q	—	—	5,038	19%	4,222	12%
Yr.	—	—	18,573	16%	16,053	10%
Income (Million $)						
1Q	564.0	3%	545.0	23%	443.6	14%
2Q	577.8	6%	543.0	9%	498.6	21%
3Q	—	—	535.0	1%	527.8	25%
4Q	—	—	518.0	-3%	532.4	24%
Yr.	—	—	2,132	4%	2,042	24%
Earnings Per Share ($)						
1Q	2.06	4%	1.99	13%	1.76	25%
2Q	2.10	6%	1.98	9%	1.81	21%
3Q	E2.17	11%	1.95	1%	1.93	25%
4Q	E2.27	20%	1.89	-3%	1.94	24%
Yr.	E8.60	10%	7.80	5%	7.44	24%

Next earnings report expected: mid October

Business Summary - 08-SEP-95

Federal National Mortgage Association is a stock-holder-owned corporation chartered by the U.S. Congress for the purpose of providing a secondary market for mortgage loans. Although converted to private status in 1970, it remains subject to certain federal regulation: five of its 18 directors are appointed by the president of the U.S.; its debt securities have the status of federal agency securities. Revenues from the company's retained mortgage portfolio account for close to two-thirds of net income.

The company buys and holds mortgages in its portfolio, financing these investments with equity and borrowed funds. FNM also earns guaranty fees from the purchase of mortgages which are then issued as Guaranteed Mortgage-Backed Securities (MBS) and sold to investors. In 1994, FNM issued $130.6 billion of these securities, versus $221.4 billion in 1993, and at year-end 1994, $530.3 billion ($495.5 billion) was outstanding. The effective guaranty fee rate on the issuance of MBS was 0.225% in 1994, up from 0.213% in 1993.

FNM purchased $62.4 billion of mortgages in 1994 ($92.0 billion in 1993) at an average yield of 7.75% (6.89%), and issued $603.3 billion of debt at an average cost of 4.76%, versus $336.3 billion at an average cost of 3.39%. Gross mortgages of $222.1 billion at year-end 1994 (up 16% from $190.9 billion a year ago) were 49% long-term fixed rate, 31% intermediate fixed-rate, 8% adjustable rate, 5% conventional apartment, 5% government-insured single family, and 2% other.

Fannie Mae's approach to managing interest rate risk is to acquire and maintain a portfolio of assets and liabilities that have similar expected durations. Duration measures the weighted-average life of a financial instrument's discounted future cash flows, as well as the sensitivity of the market price of the instrument to changes in interest rates. Credit risk results from the possibility FNM will not recover amounts due from borrowers, lenders or mortgage insurers on loans in its mortgage portfolio or on loans backing MBS it guarantees.

Important Developments

Jul. '95—Fannie Mae said its net mortgage portfolio was $231 billion at the end of the second quarter of 1995, compared with $222 billion at the end of the first quarter.

Capitalization

Short Term Debt: $126,429,000,000 (6/95).
Long Term Debt: $144,507,600,000 (6/95).

Per Share Data ($)

	1994	1993	1992	1991	1990	1989
Tangible Bk. Val.	34.97	29.55	24.79	20.32	16.54	12.52
Earnings	7.80	7.44	6.01	5.33	4.50	3.14
Dividends	2.40	1.84	1.38	1.04	0.72	0.43
Payout Ratio	31%	25%	23%	20%	16%	14%
Prices - High	90⅜	86⅛	77¼	69⅝	44⅝	46⅜
- Low	68⅛	72⅞	55⅛	32⅜	24⅞	16¾
P/E Ratio - High	12	12	13	13	10	15
- Low	9	10	9	6	6	5

Income Statement Analysis (Million $)

	1994	%Chg	1993	%Chg	1992	%Chg	1991
Int. Mtgs.	15,851	14%	13,957	10%	12,651	9%	11,603
Int. Invest.	1,496	71%	876	NM	884	-11%	990
Int. Exp.	14,524	18%	12,300	7%	11,476	6%	10,815
Guaranty Fees	1,083	13%	961	15%	834	24%	675
Loan Loss Prov.	155	-11%	175	-45%	320	-14%	370
Admin. Exp.	525	19%	443	16%	381	19%	319
Pretax Inc.	3,146	5%	3,005	26%	2,382	14%	2,081
Eff. Tax Rate	32%	—	32%	—	31%	—	30%
Net Inc.	2,141	5%	2,042	24%	1,649	13%	1,455

Balance Sheet & Other Fin. Data (Million $)

	1994	1993	1992	1991	1990	1989
Mtges.	220,525	189,892	156,021	126,486	113,875	107,756
Inv.	46,335	21,396	14,786	10,999	9,868	6,656
Cash & Equiv.	231	977	5,193	3,194	4,178	5,214
Total Assets	272,508	216,979	180,978	147,072	133,113	124,315
ST Debt	112,602	71,950	56,404	34,608	38,453	36,346
LT Debt	144,628	129,162	109,896	99,329	84,950	79,718
Equity	9,541	8,052	6,774	5,547	3,941	2,991

Ratio Analysis

	1994	1993	1992	1991	1990	1989
% Ret. on Assets	0.9	1.0	1.0	1.0	0.9	0.7
% Ret. on Equity	24.3	27.5	26.8	30.7	33.8	30.7
Equity/Assets Ratio	3.6	3.7	3.8	3.4	2.7	2.2
Price Times Book Value:						
High	2.6	2.9	3.1	3.4	2.7	3.7
Low	1.9	2.5	2.2	1.6	1.5	1.3

Dividend Data

—Dividends have been paid since 1956. A dividend reinvestment plan is available.

Amt. of Div. $	Date Decl.	Ex-Div. Date	Stock of Record	Payment Date
0.600	Oct. 18	Oct. 25	Oct. 31	Nov. 25 '94
0.680	Jan. 17	Jan. 25	Jan. 31	Feb. 25 '95
0.680	Apr. 18	Apr. 24	Apr. 28	May. 25 '95
0.680	Jul. 18	Jul. 27	Jul. 31	Aug. 25 '95

Data as orig. reptd.; bef. results of disc opers. and/or spec. items. Per share data adj. for stk. divs. as of ex-div. date.
E-Estimated. NA-Not Available. NM-Not Meaningful. NR-Not Ranked.

Office—3900 Wisconsin Ave. N.W., Washington, DC 20016. **Tel**—(202) 752-7000. **Chrmn & CEO**—J. A. Johnson. **Pres**—L. M. Small. **EVP-CFO**—J. T. Howard. **EVP-Secy**—C. S. Bernstein. **Investor Contact**—Elizabeth Snyder (202-752-7115). **Dirs**—F. M. Beck, R. E. Birk, E. Broad, W. M. Daley, T. P. Gerrity, J. A. Johnson, T. A. Leonard, V. A. Mai, A. McLaughlin, R. D. Parsons, F. D. Raines, J. R. Sasso, A. Shusta, L. M. Small, C. J. Sumner, J. H. Villarreal, K. H. Williams. **Transfer Agent & Registrar**—Chemical Bank, NYC. **Incorporated** under the laws of the United States in 1938. **Empl**-3,400. **S&P Analyst:** Paul L. Huberman, CFA

Federal Paper Board

NYSE Symbol **FBO**
In S&P 500

08-SEP-95

Industry: Containers

Summary: This company manufactures bleached and recycled paperboard, market pulp, uncoated free-sheet paper, wood products, foodservice disposables and folding cartons.

S&P Opinion: Hold (★★★)

Recent Price • 40¼	Yield • 3.8%
52 Wk Range • 41½-25⅝	12-Mo. P/E • 10.6

Quantitative Evaluations

Outlook (1 Lowest—5 Highest)
• **5⁺**

Fair Value
• **46⅞**

Risk
• **Low**

Earn./Div. Rank
• **B**

Technical Eval.
• **Bearish** since 7/95

Rel. Strength Rank (1 Lowest—99 Highest)
• **80**

Insider Activity
• **Unfavorable**

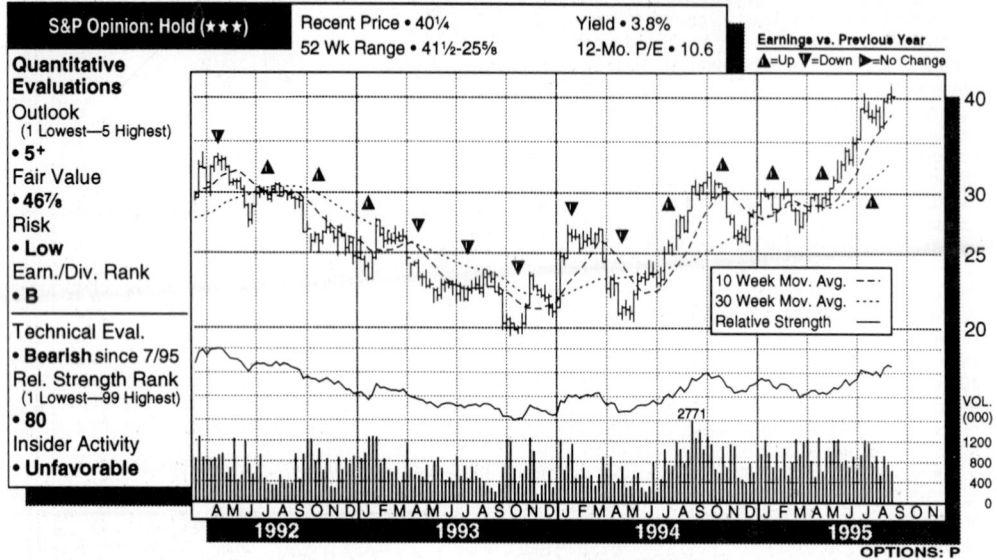

Earnings vs. Previous Year
▲=Up ▼=Down ▶=No Change

10 Week Mov. Avg. ---
30 Week Mov. Avg. ·····
Relative Strength —

2771

VOL. (000)

OPTIONS: P

Overview - 08-SEP-95

Sales should rise strongly in 1995, with relatively healthy global economies continuing to generate favorable demand for pulp, paper and paperboard, and the tight supply situation allowing steep prices to remain in effect. A slight sales gain is also likely in the wood products area, as the recent drop in long-term interest rates should improve building materials markets as the year progresses. Margins should widen significantly on the favorable paper industry conditions, along with cost savings and efficiencies from capital investments and company-wide cost reduction programs. Those factors should outweigh the impact of lower sales prices for lumber and higher log costs in the wood products segment, along with steep raw materials costs encountered in the converting and recycled paperboard businesses in early 1995 (wastepaper costs have trended downward since spring).

Valuation - 08-SEP-95

The company's shares have appreciated substantially since the early part of 1994, as the long-awaited paper industry upturn finally materialized in the latter part of the year. Although moderating U.S. economic conditions cause worries about an approaching industry peak, limited capacity expansion in recent years should allow industry strength to extend into 1996. However, we would not add to our positions until the upturn gives the appearance of continuing through 1997, as the shares' recent trading range of about six to seven times our 1996 EPS forecast is equivalent to their peak in the last paper industry upcycle.

Key Stock Statistics

S&P EPS Est. 1995	5.50	Tang. Bk. Value/Share	16.31
P/E on S&P Est. 1995	7.3	Beta	1.44
S&P EPS Est. 1996	6.25	Shareholders	5,700
Dividend Rate/Share	1.60	Market cap. (B)	$ 1.9
Shs. outstg. (M)	45.8	Inst. holdings	85%
Avg. daily vol. (M)	0.152	Insider holdings	NA

Value of $10,000 invested 5 years ago: $ 19,706

Fiscal Year Ending Dec. 31

	1995	% Change	1994	% Change	1993	% Change
Revenues (Million $)						
1Q	435.8	36%	319.5	NM	319.8	NM
2Q	463.4	33%	348.0	6%	329.6	-4%
3Q	—	—	373.9	15%	324.0	-4%
4Q	—	—	528.3	28%	412.9	-9%
Yr.	—	—	1,570	13%	1,386	-5%
Income (Million $)						
1Q	46.90	NM	-3.30	NM	9.10	-44%
2Q	58.00	NM	12.00	22%	9.80	-61%
3Q	—	—	15.20	NM	-5.97	NM
4Q	—	—	48.10	NM	7.87	-47%
Yr.	—	—	72.00	NM	20.80	-75%
Earnings Per Share ($)						
1Q	1.07	NM	-0.11	NM	0.18	-50%
2Q	1.32	NM	0.25	25%	0.20	-65%
3Q	E1.40	NM	0.32	NM	-0.18	NM
4Q	E1.71	57%	1.09	NM	0.14	-55%
Yr.	E5.50	NM	1.55	NM	0.34	-81%

Next earnings report expected: late September

Federal Paper Board

Business Summary - 08-SEP-95

FBO produces paperboard, pulp, uncoated free-sheet paper, lumber and other wood products, and disposable foodservice and specialty packaging products. Segment contributions in 1994 were:

	Sales	Profits
Paper, paperboard & pulp	62%	67%
Wood products	16%	30%
Converting operations	22%	3%

Exports accounted for 13% of 1994 sales.

The majority of the paperboard produced at the company's mills is converted into packaging for consumer goods or used in printing applications such as menus, greeting cards and brochure covers. FBO's bleached paperboard is also used by the company's converting operations to produce folding cartons, paper cups and other disposable foodservice products, while its recycled paperboard is converted into packaging products by outside customers and its own carton plants. FBO's mills produced about 1,133,000 tons of paperboard in 1994. Paperboard accounted for 41% of total company sales in 1994.

During 1994, FBO produced 1,421,000 tons of pulp, with 864,000 tons used to produce paperboard at the company's mills, and the remainder marketed to others. About 67% of market pulp shipped was sold in export markets, with the product accounting for 12% of FBO's sales in 1994. Uncoated free-sheet paper (9% of sales) made at a mill in Scotland is marketed throughout Europe.

Wood products include dimensional lumber and wood chips. Federal's five lumber plants produced 618.2 million board ft. of lumber in 1994. FBO owns and leases 692,000 acres of timberlands in the Southeast.

Converting operations produce paper and plastic cups, plastic lids, containers and packaging. FBO also makes folding cartons used in the packaging of food, laundry soap, tobacco, medical products, hardware and other items.

Important Developments

Aug. '95—FBO's redemption call for its $2.875 cumulative preferred stock (announced on July 10) expired on August 9. As of mid-July, about 1.5 million of Federal's 2.2 million preferred shares had been converted into FBO common stock, at the conversion ratio of 1.8182 common shares for each preferred share held.
Jul. '95—In reporting very favorable earnings comparisons in the second quarter of 1995, which was related almost entirely to strength in the bleached paperboard, pulp and uncoated free sheet businesses, FBO said it remained optimistic that profits would continue strong in the second half.

Capitalization

Long Term Debt: $857,154,000 (6/17/95).
$1.20 Conv. Preferred Stock: 52,000 shs. ($1 par); ea. conv. into 5.02 com. shs.

Per Share Data ($)

(Year Ended Dec. 31)

	1994	1993	1992	1991	1990	1989
Tangible Bk. Val.	16.31	15.98	16.74	16.09	15.46	16.69
Cash Flow	5.01	3.77	5.36	4.86	4.97	6.76
Earnings	1.55	0.34	1.82	1.83	2.74	5.00
Dividends	1.05	1.00	1.00	1.00	1.00	0.95
Payout Ratio	68%	294%	55%	55%	36%	19%
Prices - High	32	27¾	33⅞	32⅞	27⅜	29⅞
- Low	20⅜	19½	24⅛	17⅜	13⅛	19⅝
P/E Ratio - High	21	82	19	18	10	6
- Low	13	57	13	9	5	4

Income Statement Analysis (Million $)

	1994	%Chg	1993	%Chg	1992	%Chg	1991
Revs.	1,570	13%	1,386	-5%	1,461	2%	1,435
Oper. Inc.	352	23%	287	-20%	361	NM	362
Depr.	146	1%	144	-2%	147	20%	123
Int. Exp.	95.0	3%	92.0	-4%	96.0	-12%	109
Pretax Inc.	101	102%	50.0	-63%	136	-6%	144
Eff. Tax Rate	29%	—	59%	—	39%	—	43%
Net Inc.	72.0	NM	21.0	-75%	83.0	1%	82.0

Balance Sheet & Other Fin. Data (Million $)

	1994	1993	1992	1991	1990	1989
Cash	0.3	0.3	0.3	0.5	1.0	3.1
Curr. Assets	357	310	316	291	354	321
Total Assets	2,610	2,570	2,573	2,493	2,448	1,882
Curr. Liab.	338	278	227	211	234	194
LT Debt	921	974	1,030	1,077	1,092	686
Common Eqty.	809	792	825	780	742	670
Total Cap.	2,193	2,230	2,293	2,236	2,183	1,669
Cap. Exp.	139	161	149	227	509	400
Cash Flow	212	158	222	197	199	267

Ratio Analysis

	1994	1993	1992	1991	1990	1989
Curr. Ratio	1.1	1.1	1.4	1.4	1.5	1.7
% LT Debt of Cap.	42.0	43.7	44.9	48.2	50.0	41.1
% Net Inc.of Revs.	4.6	1.5	5.7	5.7	8.7	15.7
% Ret. on Assets	2.8	0.8	3.2	3.3	5.5	12.6
% Ret. on Equity	8.2	1.8	9.3	9.7	15.6	33.4

Dividend Data

—Dividends have been paid since 1948. A dividend reinvestment plan is available.

Amt. of Div. $	Date Decl.	Ex-Div. Date	Stock of Record	Payment Date
0.250	Sep. 19	Sep. 26	Sep. 30	Oct. 15 '94
0.300	Dec. 20	Dec. 23	Dec. 31	Jan. 15 '95
0.300	Mar. 21	Mar. 27	Mar. 31	Apr. 15 '95
0.400	Jun. 20	Jun. 28	Jun. 30	Jul. 15 '95

Data as orig. reptd.; bef. results of disc. opers. and/or spec. items. Per share data adj. for stk. divs. as of ex-div. date.
E-Estimated. NA-Not Available. NM-Not Meaningful. NR-Not Ranked.

Office—75 Chestnut Ridge Rd., Montvale, NJ 07645. **Tel**—(201) 391-1776. **Pres & CEO**—J. R. Kennedy. **EVP, Treas & Secy**—Q. J. Kennedy. **Dirs**—R. D. Baldwin, T. L. Cassidy, W. R. Clerihue, J. T. Flynn, E. J. Kelly, J. L. Kelsey, J. R. Kennedy, Q. J. Kennedy, W. M. Massey, Jr. **Transfer Agent & Registrar**—American Stock Transfer & Trust Co., NYC. **Incorporated** in New York in 1916; reincorporated in North Carolina in 1994. **Empl**-6,900. **S&P Analyst:** Michael W. Jaffe

First Chicago

NYSE Symbol **FNB**
In S&P 500

17-AUG-95 | Industry: Banking

Summary: This bank holding company, the 10th largest in the U.S., recently agreed to combine its operations with those of Detroit-based NBD Bancorp in a merger of equals.

S&P Opinion: Hold (★★★)	Recent Price • 61¾	Yield • 3.9%
	52 Wk Range • 64⅛-42⅝	12-Mo. P/E • 8.5

Earnings vs. Previous Year
▲=Up ▼=Down ▶=No Change

Quantitative Evaluations

Outlook
(1 Lowest—5 Highest)
• **4+**

Fair Value
• **66½**

Risk
• **Low**

Earn./Div. Rank
• **B-**

Technical Eval.
• **Bearish** since 6/95

Rel. Strength Rank
(1 Lowest—99 Highest)
• **59**

Insider Activity
• **NA**

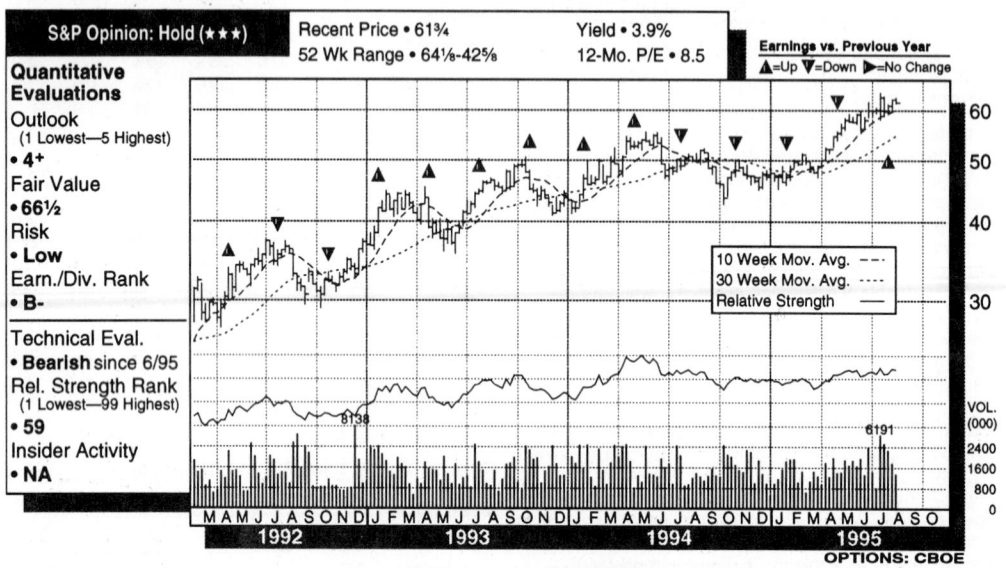

10 Week Mov. Avg. ---
30 Week Mov. Avg. ·····
Relative Strength —

VOL.
(000)
2400
1600
800
0

M A M J J A S O N D J F M A M J J A S O N D J F M A M J J A S O N D J F M A M J J A S O
1992   1993   1994   1995

OPTIONS: CBOE

Overview - 17-AUG-95

Earnings are expected to rise modestly in 1995, as growth in the credit card segment and an increase in middle market lending help boost the level of interest earning assets. The net interest margin, down 22 basis points in the first half of 1995, is expected to remain relatively stable going forward, as FNB maintains a neutral interest rate risk position. Growth in market driven revenues, mostly from equity securities gains, and higher credit card fee revenues should boost noninterest income. Credit quality has improved, and reserves now stand at a hefty 538% of nonperforming loans. Venture capital operations are an important, but volatile, contributor to earnings. Through the sale of investments and hedging using equity derivatives, the company seeks to reduce volatility related to its venture capital portfolio.

Valuation - 17-AUG-95

With its pending merger with NBD Bancorp, FNB is striving to become the leading provider of banking services to a broad array of customers in the Midwest. The opportunity for cost savings of the combined company, due to their geographic overlap, could be significant, but uncertainty exists over whether such savings can be achieved and in what time frame. In any case, we would hold the shares at current levels until evidence is clear that the merged entity is able to generate superior shareholder value.

Key Stock Statistics

S&P EPS Est. 1995	7.20	Tang. Bk. Value/Share	45.16
P/E on S&P Est. 1995	8.6	Beta	1.99
S&P EPS Est. 1996	7.60	Shareholders	14,800
Dividend Rate/Share	2.40	Market cap. (B)	$ 5.6
Shs. outstg. (M)	90.0	Inst. holdings	81%
Avg. daily vol. (M)	0.351	Insider holdings	NA

Value of $10,000 invested 5 years ago: $ 23,074

Fiscal Year Ending Dec. 31

	1995	% Change	1994	% Change	1993	% Change
Revenues (Million $)						
1Q	1,557	32%	1,181	3%	1,150	1%
2Q	1,595	34%	1,187	3%	1,152	12%
3Q	—	—	1,299	-4%	1,354	26%
4Q	—	—	1,428	22%	1,171	4%
Yr.	—	—	5,095	6%	4,827	11%
Income (Million $)						
1Q	195.1	NM	193.8	8%	179.1	195%
2Q	187.4	11%	168.7	NM	168.5	147%
3Q	—	—	153.8	-46%	284.1	NM
4Q	—	—	173.4	NM	172.8	27%
Yr.	—	—	689.7	-14%	804.5	NM
Earnings Per Share ($)						
1Q	2.03	NM	2.05	4%	1.97	82%
2Q	1.95	14%	1.71	-6%	1.81	NM
3Q	E1.60	4%	1.54	-51%	3.14	NM
4Q	E1.62	-8%	1.76	-3%	1.81	18%
Yr.	E7.20	2%	7.04	-20%	8.78	NM

Next earnings report expected: mid October

Business Summary - 17-AUG-95

First Chicago Corp., the 10th largest U.S. bank holding company, provides a broad range of banking, fiduciary, financial and other services domestically and overseas. Consumer banking operations serve local consumers and small businesses through more than 80 retail banking branches. It serves consumers nationwide through First Card, one of the largest U.S. issuers of bank credit cards. The company is also a leading provider of banking services to large corporations, governments, institutions and investors in Chicago and the Midwest, and is among the top U.S. banking companies serving national and international customers. Activities also include venture capital. In July 1994, Lake Shore Bancorp, a Chicago-based bank holding company with assets of about $1.2 billion, was acquired in exchange for about 6.2 million common shares. Contributions to net income (in million $) in 1994 were:

	1994
Credit card	$309
Corporate & institutional	134
Middle market	74
Venture capital	95
Community banking	22
Other	56

Average earning assets in 1994 of $52.6 billion (up 8.5% from 1993) were divided: domestic loans 41%, foreign loans 3%, investment securities 5%, trading account assets 9% and other temporary investments 42%. Average sources of funds were demand deposits 11%, savings and time deposits 20%, foreign deposits 15%, short-term borrowings 32%, long-term debt 4%, equity 7%, and other 11%.

At year-end 1994, nonperforming assets declined to $158 million (0.6% of loans and related assets) from $277 million (1.2%) a year earlier. The reserve for loan losses was 2.8% of loans, versus 3.0%. Net chargeoffs were $151 million (0.6% of average loans) in 1994, versus $182 million (0.8%) in 1993.

Important Developments

Jul. '95—First Chicago and NBD Corp. (NYSE; NBD) signed a definitive agreement providing for a merger of equals. Following the proposed stock transaction, it is expected that FNB and NBD shareholders will hold 50.1% and 49.9%, respectively, of the common equity of the combined company, which will be named First Chicago NBD Corp. With $120 billion in assets, the combined entity will have dominant market share position in Illinois, Michigan and Indiana. The transaction is expected to be completed in the first quarter of 1996, subject to regulatory and shareholder approvals.

Capitalization

Long Term Debt: $2,271,000,000 (6/95).
Preferred Stock: $611,000,000.

Per Share Data ($) (Year Ended Dec. 31)

	1994	1993	1992	1991	1990	1989
Tangible Bk. Val.	NA	40.54	33.18	34.90	36.25	34.82
Earnings	7.04	8.78	-2.08	1.15	3.35	5.10
Dividends	1.95	1.30	1.20	2.00	2.00	1.80
Payout Ratio	28%	15%	NM	174%	60%	35%
Prices - High	55½	50⅝	37¾	28¾	38¼	49⅝
- Low	41⅛	35½	22⅞	15⅝	13⅛	29¼
P/E Ratio - High	8	6	NM	25	11	10
- Low	6	4	NM	14	4	6

Income Statement Analysis (Million $)

	1994	%Chg	1993	%Chg	1992	%Chg	1991
Net Int. Inc.	1,331	9%	1,225	4%	1,183	10%	1,080
Tax Equiv. Adj.	24.2	-37%	38.2	12%	34.0	-11%	38.0
Non Int. Inc.	1,645	37%	1,202	-6%	1,275	9%	1,166
Loan Loss Prov.	224	-17%	270	-71%	916	108%	440
% Exp/Op Revs.	64%	—	54%	—	79%	—	75%
Pretax Inc.	1,063	-18%	1,300	NM	-199	NM	164
Eff. Tax Rate	35%	—	38%	—	NM	—	29%
Net Inc.	690	-14%	805	NM	-114	NM	116
% Net Int. Marg.	2.58%	—	2.61%	—	2.61%	—	2.51%

Balance Sheet & Other Fin. Data (Million $)

	1994	1993	1992	1991	1990	1989
Earning Assets:						
Money Mkt.	26,335	19,356	16,320	13,337	12,604	9,296
Inv. Securities	2,592	2,256	2,400	1,853	1,810	2,253
Com'l Loans	8,833	7,299	8,327	10,331	11,023	10,221
Other Loans	17,114	17,096	14,365	15,330	16,683	19,504
Total Assets	65,900	52,560	49,281	48,963	50,779	47,907
Demand Deposits	7,647	8,184	7,575	6,200	7,065	5,614
Time Deposits	24,019	20,002	22,165	25,891	25,478	27,321
LT Debt	2,271	2,065	1,705	1,725	1,428	1,351
Common Eqty.	NA	3,503	2,732	2,401	2,393	2,273

Ratio Analysis

	1994	1993	1992	1991	1990	1989
% Ret. on Assets	1.1	1.6	NM	0.2	0.5	0.7
% Ret. on Equity	20.8	23.6	NM	4.0	11.4	19.3
% Loan Loss Resv.	2.8	3.0	3.5	3.5	3.6	4.3
% Loans/Deposits	81.9	82.0	76.3	80.0	85.1	90.3
% Equity to Assets	4.8	6.1	3.9	3.7	3.6	3.5

Dividend Data

Dividends have been paid since 1936. A dividend reinvestment plan is available. A poison pill stock purchase rights plan was adopted in 1988.

Amt. of Div. $	Date Decl.	Ex-Div. Date	Stock of Record	Payment Date
0.500	Jul. 08	Aug. 29	Sep. 02	Oct. 01 '94
0.550	Nov. 11	Nov. 28	Dec. 02	Jan. 01 '95
0.550	Feb. 10	Feb. 27	Mar. 03	Apr. 01 '95
0.550	May. 12	Jun. 06	Jun. 09	Jul. 01 '95
0.600	Jul. 14	Sep. 06	Sep. 08	Oct. 01 '95

Data as orig. reptd.; bef. results of disc opers. and/or spec. items. Per share data adj. for stk. divs. as of ex-div. date.
E-Estimated. NA-Not Available. NM-Not Meaningful. NR-Not Ranked.

Office—One First National Plaza, Chicago, IL 60670. **Tel**—(312) 732-4000. **Chrmn & CEO**—R. L. Thomas. **Vice Chrmn**—D. J. Vitale. **Pres & COO**—L. F. Mullin. **EVP & CFO**—R. A. Rosholt. **EVP & Secy**—S. I. Goldberg. **Investor Contact**—Susan L. Temple. **Dirs**—J. H. Bryan, D. L. Buntrock, J. S. Crown, D. V. Fites, D. P. Jacobs, A. J. McKenna, R. M. Morrow, L. F. Mullin, E. L. Neal, J. J. O'Connor, J. K. Pearlman, J. F. Reichert, P. G. Ryan, A. Simmons, R. W. Stone, R. L. Thomas, D. J. Vitale. **Transfer Agent & Registrar**—First Chicago Trust Co. of New York, Jersey City, NJ. **Incorporated** in Delaware in 1969; Bank chartered in 1863. **Empl**-17,630. **S&P Analyst:** Stephen R. Biggar

First Data

STOCK REPORTS

NYSE Symbol **FDC**
In S&P 500

21-SEP-95 **Industry:** Data Processing

Summary: FDC provides information processing and related services to the transaction card, mutual fund, teleservices, receivables and information management industries.

Quantitative Evaluations

Recent Price • 61⅜
52 Wk Range • 61¾-44¾

Yield • 0.2%
12-Mo. P/E • 30.7

Outlook
(1 Lowest—5 Highest)
• **3**

Fair Value
• **59⅝**

Risk
• **Low**

Earn./Div. Rank
• **NR**

Technical Eval.
• **Bullish** since 7/94

Rel. Strength Rank
(1 Lowest—99 Highest)
• **65**

Insider Activity
• **Neutral**

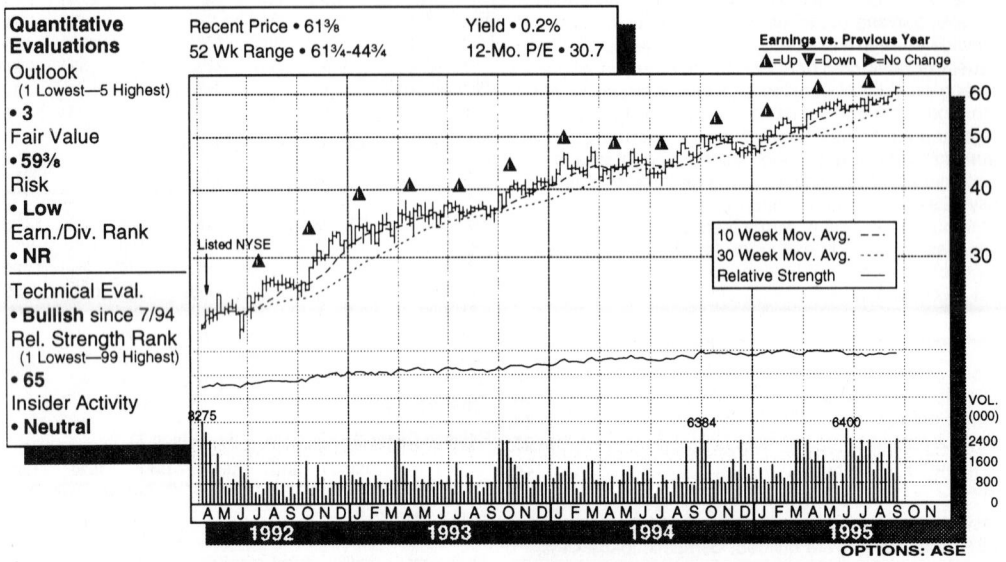

Earnings vs. Previous Year
▲=Up ▼=Down ▶=No Change

10 Week Mov. Avg. — - —
30 Week Mov. Avg. ·······
Relative Strength ———

OPTIONS: ASE

Business Profile - 21-SEP-95

FDC continues to benefit from two trends. The first is an accelerating shift toward the use of credit cards and other card products to replace cash and checks. The second, the outsourcing business, reflects the fact that banks and oil companies, among others, are increasingly outsourcing non-core services. A planned merger with NYSE-listed First Financial Management should produce synergies and cost cutting opportunities.

Operational Review - 21-SEP-95

Revenues in the first half of 1995 rose 20%, year to year, paced by strong growth in the transaction card processing and payment instruments businesses. Despite interest expense and depreciation and amortization charges, net income was also up 20%, to $0.94 a share, from $0.81. FDC maintains its goal of increasing EPS at least 20% annually.

Stock Performance - 15-SEP-95

In the past 30 trading days, FDC's shares have increased 7%, compared to a 4% rise in the S&P 500. Average trading volume for the past five days was 662,100 shares, compared with the 40-day moving average of 403,541 shares.

Key Stock Statistics

Dividend Rate/Share	0.12	Shareholders	800
Shs. outstg. (M)	118.8	Market cap. (B)	$ 7.4
Avg. daily vol. (M)	0.441	Inst. holdings	101%
Tang. Bk. Value/Share	NM	Insider holdings	NA
Beta	NA		

Value of $10,000 invested 5 years ago: NA

Fiscal Year Ending Dec. 31

	1995	% Change	1994	% Change	1993	% Change
Revenues (Million $)						
1Q	437.5	16%	376.0	8%	347.0	23%
2Q	502.6	23%	410.0	8%	379.0	29%
3Q	—	—	432.0	13%	381.0	25%
4Q	—	—	434.4	13%	383.0	19%
Yr.	—	—	1,652	11%	1,490	24%
Income (Million $)						
1Q	50.21	15%	43.70	20%	36.30	21%
2Q	57.95	24%	46.55	19%	39.05	25%
3Q	—	—	53.93	20%	44.76	22%
4Q	—	—	63.97	21%	52.92	22%
Yr.	—	—	208.1	20%	173.1	22%
Earnings Per Share ($)						
1Q	0.45	15%	0.39	18%	0.33	14%
2Q	0.49	17%	0.42	20%	0.35	21%
3Q	—	—	0.48	20%	0.40	21%
4Q	—	—	0.58	21%	0.48	23%
Yr.	—	—	1.87	20%	1.56	20%

Next earnings report expected: late October

Business Summary - 21-SEP-95

First Data Corp. provides high-quality, high-volume information processing and related services. Prior to the April 1992 initial public offering, the company was wholly owned by American Express Co.

The company's oldest and largest unit, First Data Resources (FDR), is a third-party processor of Master-Card and VISA card transactions in the U.S., Mexico and the U.K. It also provides processing and other services to several oil and retail card clients. As a cardholder processor, FDR performs credit card-related transactions, including embossing, transaction reporting, settlement and billing services, as well as certain security and related services, for card-issuing financial institutions. FDR accounted for 45% of FDC's 1994 revenues.

The Integrated Payment Systems unit provides payment instrument transaction processing services to financial institutions and retail consumers. Integrated Marketing Services provides clients with recurring, value-added computer-based information processing services. The Shareholder Services Group provides mutual funds with shareholder servicing and record-keeping services. The Health Systems Group provides management information systems and services to about 600 acute care hospitals. ACB Business Services, Inc. operates a receivables management service nationwide, serving clients engaged in health care, travel and entertainment card, retail, banking and oil and gas activities.

FDR competes with other third-party cardholder and merchant processors, such as Total System Services, Inc., Maryland Bank, N.A., EDS Corp., and Financial Card Services. Its major non-bank competitors for merchant processing are National BankCard Corp. (a unit of First Financial Management Corp.), Card Establishment Services Inc., National Data Corp. and National Processing Co.

In January 1995, FDC agreed to merge with NYSE-listed First Financial Management Corp. (FFM) by issuing about 117 million common shares to FFM shareholders. FFM had 1994 income of $160 million, on revenues of $2.2 billion. Ownership of the combined company would be split almost evenly between FDC and FFM shareholders. The transaction is expected to be completed in late 1995 or early 1996.

Important Developments

Sep. '95—FDC said it would exercise the prepayment option on its 8.39% Series A senior notes due 1996 and 9.27% Series B senior notes due 2001. The prepayment date will be October 12, 1995.

Capitalization

Long Term Debt: $611,489,000 (3/95).

Per Share Data ($)

	1994	1993	1992	1991	1990	1989
Tangible Bk. Val.	9.43	8.66	7.22	NA	NA	NA
Cash Flow	3.16	2.62	2.19	1.93	1.63	1.46
Earnings	1.87	1.56	1.30	1.13	0.99	0.94
Dividends	0.12	0.12	0.06	NA	NA	NA
Payout Ratio	6%	8%	5%	NA	NA	NA
Prices - High	50⅝	42¼	34⅜	NA	NA	NA
- Low	40½	31¼	21¼	NA	NA	NA
P/E Ratio - High	27	27	26	NA	NA	NA
- Low	22	20	16	NA	NA	NA

(Year Ended Dec. 31)

Income Statement Analysis (Million $)

	1994	%Chg	1993	%Chg	1992	%Chg	1991
Revs.	1,652	11%	1,490	24%	1,205	17%	1,026
Oper. Inc.	526	17%	450	37%	329	20%	274
Depr.	144	22%	118	21%	97.5	18%	82.7
Int. Exp.	41.3	NM	41.4	22%	34.0	11%	30.6
Pretax Inc.	356	22%	291	25%	232	21%	191
Eff. Tax Rate	42%	—	41%	—	39%	—	38%
Net Inc.	208	20%	173	23%	141	19%	118

Balance Sheet & Other Fin. Data (Million $)

	1994	1993	1992	1991	1990	1989
Cash	1,188	698	329	335	154	NA
Curr. Assets	NA	NA	NA	NA	NA	NA
Total Assets	5,419	4,148	3,916	3,172	2,376	2,035
Curr. Liab.	NA	NA	NA	NA	NA	NA
LT Debt	429	521	351	444	165	200
Common Eqty.	1,015	954	794	567	499	476
Total Cap.	1,444	1,476	1,145	1,010	664	676
Cap. Exp.	155	84.9	62.2	59.1	58.2	49.9
Cash Flow	352	291	239	201	170	152

Ratio Analysis

	1994	1993	1992	1991	1990	1989
Curr. Ratio	NA	NA	NA	NA	NA	NA
% LT Debt of Cap.	29.7	35.3	30.7	43.9	24.8	29.5
% Net Inc.of Revs.	12.6	11.6	11.7	11.5	12.1	14.6
% Ret. on Assets	4.4	4.3	3.9	4.3	4.7	5.4
% Ret. on Equity	21.4	19.8	20.3	22.1	21.1	23.0

Dividend Data —Dividends were initiated in July 1992.

Amt. of Div. $	Date Decl.	Ex-Div. Date	Stock of Record	Payment Date
0.030	Sep. 28	Oct. 05	Oct. 12	Oct. 26 '94
0.030	Dec. 07	Dec. 14	Dec. 20	Jan. 13 '95
0.030	Mar. 15	Mar. 28	Apr. 03	Apr. 17 '95
0.030	May. 18	Jun. 29	Jul. 03	Jul. 17 '95
0.030	Jul. 26	Sep. 28	Oct. 02	Oct. 16 '95

Data as orig. reptd.; bef. results of disc. opers. and/or spec. items. Per share data adj. for stk. divs. as of ex-div. date.
E-Estimated. NA-Not Available. NM-Not Meaningful. NR-Not Ranked.

Office—11718 Nicholas St., Omaha, NE 68154. **Tel**—(402) 222-8545. **Chrmn & CEO**—H. C. Duques. **EVP, CFO & Investor Contact**—Walter M. Hoff. **Dirs**—B. Burdetsky, H. C. Duques, C. F. Jones, R. J. Levenson, J. D. Robinson III, C. T. Russell, B. L. Schwartz, G. K. Staglin. **Transfer Agent & Registrar**—Norwest Bank Minnesota, South St. Paul. **Incorporated** in Delaware in 1992. **Empl**-22,000. **S&P Analyst:** Mike Cavanaugh

First Fidelity Bancorp.

NYSE Symbol **FFB**

In S&P 500

07-AUG-95 Industry:
Banking

Summary: This bank holding company, the 27th largest in the U.S. with assets of $35 billion, recently agreed to be acquired by First Union Corp. in a stock transaction.

S&P Opinion: Hold (★★★)	Recent Price • 64⅝	Yield • 3.1%
	52 Wk Range • 64½-40½	12-Mo. P/E • 12.0

Quantitative Evaluations

Outlook
(1 Lowest—5 Highest)
• **2⁻**

Fair Value
• **60⅝**

Risk
• **Low**

Earn./Div. Rank
• **B**

Technical Eval.
• **Bullish** since 6/95

Rel. Strength Rank
(1 Lowest—99 Highest)
• **82**

Insider Activity
• **Neutral**

Earnings vs. Previous Year
▲=Up ▼=Down ▶=No Change

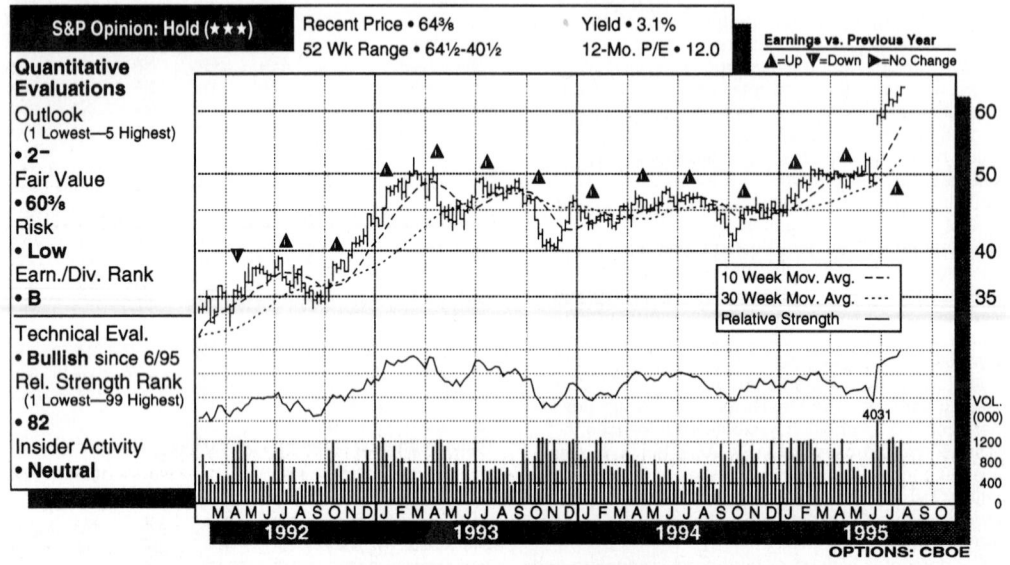

10 Week Mov. Avg. ---
30 Week Mov. Avg. ····
Relative Strength —

OPTIONS: CBOE

Overview - 07-AUG-95

Net interest income may trend down slightly in 1995, as modest growth in average earning assets is offset by narrower margins in the higher interest rate environment. Much of the projected earnings gain should come from noninterest income sources, reflecting a focus on enhancing trust income and investment product offerings, and a continued emphasis on controlling noninterest expenses, which are expected to be held flat, excluding acquisitions. Credit quality has steadily improved over the past year, with nonperforming assets down 35%, year to year, to $276.1 million at June 30, 1995. With reserves built to 295% of nonperforming loans and a favorable loss experience in recent periods, the loan loss provision should trend down in 1995.

Valuation - 07-AUG-95

Given that FFB shares are now linked to the prospects of First Union, the stock is likely to continue to trade at a modest discount to the targeted acquisition price until completion of the merger sometime in the fourth quarter of 1995. We view the acquisition as beneficial to both parties, with the surviving First Union receiving a healthy amount of low-cost deposits as well as a chance to enter the Northeast market and cross-sell many of its banking products to FFB customers. The shares are a worthwhile hold for a tax-free exchange into First Union shares, which are rated accumulate.

Key Stock Statistics

S&P EPS Est. 1995	5.55	Tang. Bk. Value/Share	27.38
P/E on S&P Est. 1995	11.6	Beta	1.35
S&P EPS Est. 1996	5.90	Shareholders	29,900
Dividend Rate/Share	2.00	Market cap. (B)	$ 5.2
Shs. outstg. (M)	80.8	Inst. holdings	33%
Avg. daily vol. (M)	0.305	Insider holdings	NA

Value of $10,000 invested 5 years ago: $ 35,317

Fiscal Year Ending Dec. 31

	1995	% Change	1994	% Change	1993	% Change
Revenues (Million $)						
1Q	684.5	11%	617.8	3%	599.5	-5%
2Q	691.9	11%	623.0	2%	608.2	NM
3Q	—	—	639.3	4%	612.7	3%
4Q	—	—	673.0	11%	608.3	-2%
Yr.	—	—	2,553	5%	2,429	-1%
Income (Million $)						
1Q	112.9	4%	108.9	18%	92.61	41%
2Q	115.3	3%	111.6	14%	97.93	28%
3Q	—	—	115.0	13%	101.5	23%
4Q	—	—	115.6	11%	104.4	16%
Yr.	—	—	451.1	14%	396.5	26%
Earnings Per Share ($)						
1Q	1.32	5%	1.26	14%	1.11	35%
2Q	1.37	6%	1.29	12%	1.15	21%
3Q	E1.40	—	1.33	14%	1.17	14%
4Q	E1.45	—	1.34	10%	1.22	12%
Yr.	E5.55	—	5.21	13%	4.63	19%

Next earnings report expected: mid October

First Fidelity Bancorp.

Business Summary - 03-AUG-95

First Fidelity Bancorporation, the 27th largest bank holding company in the U.S., was formed in 1988 through the merger of First Fidelity, headquartered in New Jersey, and Fidelcor, based in Pennsylvania. At 1994 year end, FFB operated about 700 branch offices in Connecticut, Maryland, New Jersey, New York and Pennsylvania. FFB's principal lines of business are wholesale banking (middle market), community business banking (small businesses), trust and private banking, and consumer banking. Nonbank subsidiaries provide securities brokerage services, mortgage banking, insurance brokerage services, consumer leasing, and community development assistance. The company also provides investment management and advisory services to individuals and corporations.

During 1994, average earning assets of $30.3 billion (up 6.8% from 1993) were divided: commercial loans 22%, consumer loans 20%, mortgage loans 30%, investment securities 26% and other 2%. Average sources of funds were: demand deposits 16%, consumer deposits 64%, other deposits 2%, short-term borrowings 6%, long-term debt 2%, equity 8% and other 2%.

At December 31, 1994, nonperforming assets were 1.38% of loans and related assets, down from 2.30% a year earlier. The reserve for loan losses was 2.52% of total loans, versus 2.82%. Net chargeoffs during 1994 were 0.55% of average loans, against 1.23% in 1993.

Banco Santander, S.A. owns 28.1% of the company's voting stock and has regulatory approval to increase its ownership to 30%.

Important Developments

Jun. '95—First Fidelity agreed to be acquired by First Union Corp. (NYSE; FTU) in a stock transaction valued at about $5.4 billion. Under the agreement, each FFB share would be exchanged for 1.35 shares of FTU. The acquisition would create the sixth largest bank holding company in the U.S. with $124 billion in assets and more than 2,000 offices along the East Coast from Connecticut to Florida. The transaction, expected to close by 1995 year-end, is subject to shareholder and regulatory approvals.

Jun. '95—The company acquired 24 branches and $1.1 billion in deposits in Maryland of Household Bank, FSB, a subsidiary of Household International, Inc., for an approximate $76 million premium.

Capitalization

Long Term Debt: $676,750,000 (6/95).
Preferred Stock: $219,219,000, incl. about 4.8 million shs. of $2.15 Series B Preferred Stock, each conv. into 0.7801 com.

Per Share Data ($)

	1994	1993	1992	1991	1990	1989
Tangible Bk. Val.	22.97	25.65	22.94	20.66	18.05	19.58
Earnings	5.21	4.63	3.89	3.37	-0.33	2.51
Dividends	1.76	1.44	1.23	1.20	1.40	2.00
Payout Ratio	34%	31%	32%	36%	NM	80%
Prices - High	48¼	52⅜	46	34½	24¼	34
- Low	40½	40⅛	30½	14	11⅝	21⅜
P/E Ratio - High	9	11	12	10	NM	14
- Low	8	9	8	4	NM	9

Income Statement Analysis (Million $)

	1994	%Chg	1993	%Chg	1992	%Chg	1991
Net Int. Inc.	1,404	4%	1,354	12%	1,209	14%	1,056
Tax Equiv. Adj.	28.0	-18%	34.0	-13%	39.0	-19%	48.0
Non Int. Inc.	399	6%	376	15%	328	-4%	340
Loan Loss Prov.	79.0	-47%	148	-35%	228	-23%	298
% Exp/Op Revs.	58%	—	58%	—	58%	—	60%
Pretax Inc.	672	17%	574	45%	396	41%	280
Eff. Tax Rate	33%	—	31%	—	21%	—	21%
Net Inc.	451	14%	396	26%	314	42%	221
% Net Int. Marg.	4.72%	—	4.88%	—	4.63%	—	4.20%

Balance Sheet & Other Fin. Data (Million $)

	1994	1993	1992	1991	1990	1989
Earning Assets:						
Money Mkt.	197	1,145	3,602	3,576	779	268
Inv. Securities	7,968	7,899	6,333	6,280	6,684	7,937
Com'l Loans	8,196	7,877	6,686	7,479	8,730	10,028
Other Loans	15,915	13,747	11,945	10,163	10,199	10,058
Total Assets	36,216	33,763	31,480	30,215	29,110	30,728
Demand Deposits	5,394	5,347	5,370	4,628	4,438	4,705
Time Deposits	23,513	22,796	21,635	20,591	18,643	18,168
LT Debt	814	613	529	638	928	780
Common Eqty.	2,647	2,508	2,025	1,713	1,325	1,408

Ratio Analysis

	1994	1993	1992	1991	1990	1989
% Ret. on Assets	1.3	1.3	1.1	0.8	NM	0.6
% Ret. on Equity	18.4	18.8	18.2	16.6	NM	11.6
% Loan Loss Resv.	2.5	2.8	3.3	3.5	3.0	2.0
% Loans/Deposits	82.3	76.0	68.1	68.8	80.3	85.8
% Equity to Assets	6.9	6.3	5.4	4.3	4.1	4.4

Dividend Data (Dividends have been paid since 1812. A dividend reinvestment plan is available. A "poison pill" stock purchase right was adopted in 1989.)

Amt. of Div. $	Date Decl.	Ex-Div. Date	Stock of Record	Payment Date
0.420	Jul. 21	Jul. 26	Aug. 01	Aug. 05 '94
0.500	Oct. 17	Oct. 25	Oct. 31	Nov. 08 '94
0.500	Jan. 19	Jan. 24	Jan. 30	Feb. 07 '95
0.500	Apr. 18	Apr. 24	Apr. 28	May. 05 '95
0.500	Jul. 20	Jul. 27	Jul. 31	Aug. 07 '95

Data as orig. reptd.; bef. results of disc opers. and/or spec. items. Per share data adj. for stk. divs. as of ex-div. date. E-Estimated. NA-Not Available. NM-Not Meaningful. NR-Not Ranked.

Offices—2673 Main St., P.O. Box 6980, Lawrenceville, NJ 08648. **Tel**—(201) 565-3200. **Chrmn, Pres & CEO**—A. P. Terracciano. **Vice Chrmn & CFO**—W. Schoellkopf. **EVP-Secy**—J. L. Mitchell. **Investor Contact**—Laura A. Schaible. **Dirs**—L. E. Azzato, E. E. Barr, R. K. Bullard II, L. A. Butz, L. R. Campbell Jr., J. G. Christy, J. G. Cullen, G. de Las Heras, E. J. Ferland, A. M. Goldberg, L. E. Goodman, F. M. Henry, J. R. Inciarte, J. R. Kennedy, R. J. Marano, J. D. Morrisey Jr., J. Neubauer, P. C. Palmieri, D. C. Parcells, W. Schoellkopf, R. M. Scott, R. Stafford, S. Stallard, A. P. Terracciano, B. C. Watson. **Transfer Agent & Registrar**—First Fidelity Bancorporation, NYC. **Incorporated** in New Jersey in 1987; First National State Bank founded in 1812. **Empl**-12,533. **S&P Analyst:** Stephen R. Biggar

First Interstate Bancorp

NYSE Symbol I
In S&P 500

23-OCT-95

Industry:
Banking

Summary: First Interstate, the 14th largest bank holding company in the U.S., recently received a proposal to be acquired by Wells Fargo & Co. in a stock transaction.

S&P Opinion: Hold (★★★)		
Recent Price • 137¾	Yield • 2.3%	
52 Wk Range • 141⅜-66⅞	12-Mo. P/E • 12.5	

Quantitative Evaluations

Outlook
(1 Lowest—5 Highest)
• **2⁻**

Fair Value
• **97⅞**

Risk
• **Low**

Earn./Div. Rank
• **B**

Technical Eval.
• **Bearish** since 3/95

Rel. Strength Rank
(1 Lowest—99 Highest)
• **99**

Insider Activity
• **Neutral**

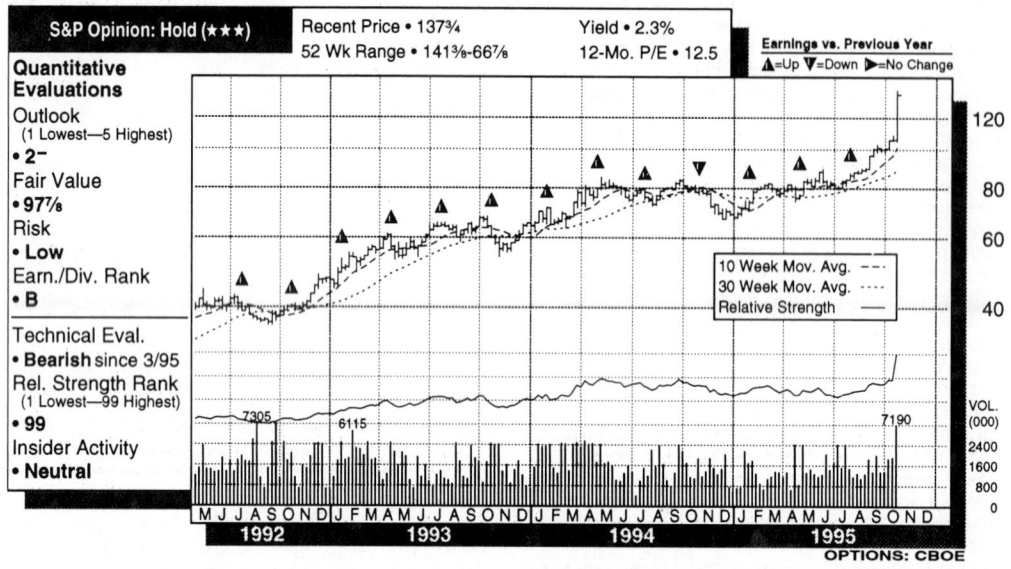

Earnings vs. Previous Year
▲=Up ▼=Down ▶=No Change

10 Week Mov. Avg. ---
30 Week Mov. Avg. ····
Relative Strength —

OPTIONS: CBOE

Overview - 23-OCT-95

Earnings growth into 1996 is expected to be driven by continued strong gains in earning assets, aided by acquisitions and a healthy service territory, and excellent credit quality. The net interest margin is expected to be relatively stable in the near term given the likelihood of flat to slightly lower interest rates. A $141 million restructuring charge taken in 1994 to better position the company for interstate banking is expected to result in annual expense savings of $167 million by mid-1996, primarily from a permanent work force reduction of about 3,000. Asset quality remains strong, and with the allowance for loan losses at 605% of nonperforming loans, additional loan loss provisions are not expected for the next several quarters.

Valuation - 23-OCT-95

Following a sharp run-up on news of a merger proposal from Wells Fargo, the shares were downgraded to hold, reflecting our belief that the acquisition price of 2.8 times I's book value more than adequately captures the inherent value in the shares. Judging from I's initial negative response to the proposal, completion of the merger will likely face a protracted uphill battle. Nevertheless, the combination could create a formidable and very efficient competitor, but with uncertainty particularly with regard to revenue growth prospects, we would not add to positions at this time. Conservative investors may wish to take profits at current levels.

Key Stock Statistics

S&P EPS Est. 1995	11.25	Tang. Bk. Value/Share	46.13
P/E on S&P Est. 1995	12.2	Beta	1.48
S&P EPS Est. 1996	12.25	Shareholders	25,000
Dividend Rate/Share	3.20	Market cap. (B)	$ 10.5
Shs. outstg. (M)	76.0	Inst. holdings	68%
Avg. daily vol. (M)	0.614	Insider holdings	NA

Value of $10,000 invested 5 years ago: $ 43,985

Fiscal Year Ending Dec. 31

	1995	% Change	1994	% Change	1993	% Change
Revenues (Million $)						
1Q	1,190	21%	985.7	NM	985.6	-10%
2Q	1,219	17%	1,043	7%	970.6	-7%
3Q	1,203	10%	1,093	12%	972.9	-2%
4Q	—	—	1,125	16%	969.3	NM
Yr.	—	—	4,246	9%	3,898	-5%
Income (Million $)						
1Q	212.0	15%	184.1	54%	119.5	97%
2Q	219.9	6%	208.2	53%	136.0	111%
3Q	237.8	83%	130.0	-14%	150.4	100%
4Q	—	—	211.3	36%	155.4	89%
Yr.	—	—	733.5	31%	561.4	99%
Earnings Per Share ($)						
1Q	2.66	20%	2.21	60%	1.38	89%
2Q	2.73	15%	2.38	49%	1.60	113%
3Q	2.96	99%	1.49	-17%	1.80	120%
4Q	E2.90	9%	2.65	39%	1.90	109%
Yr.	E11.25	29%	8.71	30%	6.68	107%

Next earnings report expected: mid January

First Interstate Bancorp

Business Summary - 23-OCT-95

First Interstate Bancorp is the 14th largest banking organization in the U.S., with 16 banks in 13 Western states, including First Interstate Bank of California, the third largest bank in that state. Activities are primarily concentrated in California, Texas and Washington. Combined retail banking operations are conducted through approximately 1,100 branches. Lending to small, middle-market and selected large corporations and trust operations are also important. Nonbank subsidiaries include asset-based commercial financing, asset management and investment counseling, bank card operations, mortgage banking and venture capital. First Interstate also has a business development agreement with Standard Chartered PLC, a multinational banking company.

During 1994, average earning assets of $45.6 billion (up from $42.5 billion in 1993) were divided: commercial loans 18%, real estate loans 18%, consumer loans 26%, investment securities 35%, and other 3%. Average sources of funds were: non-interest bearing deposits 29%, other consumer deposits 56%, other time deposits 2%, short-term borrowings 1%, long-term debt 3%, equity 7%, and other 2%.

At December 31, 1994, the reserve for loan losses was 2.81% of loans, against 3.85% a year earlier. Nonperforming assets were $258 million (0.78% of net loans), down from $309 million (1.19%). Net charge-offs during 1994 were 0.46% of average loans, against 0.90% in 1993.

At September 30, 1995, Tier 1 and total capital ratios were estimated at 7.3% and 10.3%, respectively, versus 7.2% and 10.2% at 1994 year end.

Important Developments

Oct. '95—First Interstate received an unsolicited merger proposal from Wells Fargo & Co. (NYSE; WFC), which contemplates merging the two companies in a transaction whereby each I share would be exchanged for 0.625 shares of WFC. The company said it has been exploring a wide range of strategic alternatives and would respond to the merger proposal when appropriate.

Jul. '95—The company acquired Tomball National Bancshares (assets of $98 million) and its Texas National Bank subsidiary for $7.7 million in cash.

Apr. '95—Directors authorized the repurchase of up to 7.6 million company common shares, representing about 10% of those outstanding. Through September 30, 1995, the company had repurchased 781,300 of its common shares.

Capitalization

Long Term Debt: $1,368,000,000 (9/95).

Preferred Stock: $350,000,000.

Per Share Data ($)

(Year Ended Dec. 31)

	1994	1993	1992	1991	1990	1989
Tangible Bk. Val.	34.03	41.36	30.82	26.44	32.84	27.45
Earnings	8.71	6.68	3.23	-5.24	6.79	-3.89
Dividends	2.75	1.60	1.20	1.80	3.00	2.98
Payout Ratio	32%	24%	37%	NM	44%	NM
Prices - High	85	68	48¼	42½	45⅞	70⅜
- Low	62⅜	44½	29¼	20	15⅝	40¾
P/E Ratio - High	10	10	15	NM	7	NM
- Low	7	7	9	NM	2	NM

Income Statement Analysis (Million $)

	1994	%Chg	1993	%Chg	1992	%Chg	1991
Net Int. Inc.	2,327	12%	2,072	3%	2,015	-4%	2,092
Tax Equiv. Adj.	21.4	43%	15.0	-17%	18.0	-31%	26.0
Non Int. Inc.	1,033	8%	954	4%	914	-20%	1,142
Loan Loss Prov.	Nil	—	113	-64%	314	-61%	810
% Exp/Op Revs.	65%	—	67%	—	75%	—	84%
Pretax Inc.	1,183	34%	881	119%	403	NM	-265
Eff. Tax Rate	38%	—	36%	—	30%	—	NM
Net Inc.	734	31%	561	99%	282	NM	-287
% Net Int. Marg.	5.14%	—	4.91%	—	4.89%	—	5.04%

Balance Sheet & Other Fin. Data (Million $)

	1994	1993	1992	1991	1990	1989
Earning Assets:						
Money Mkt.	269	1,943	4,441	4,721	1,851	4,464
Inv. Securities	13,851	16,542	13,913	8,496	6,667	7,696
Com'l Loans	9,294	8,124	7,890	9,422	12,943	16,221
Other Loans	24,089	17,909	17,013	18,998	21,567	22,481
Total Assets	55,813	51,461	50,863	48,922	51,357	59,051
Demand Deposits	16,599	15,425	14,615	12,526	13,131	13,046
Time Deposits	31,828	29,276	29,060	28,908	30,009	33,421
LT Debt	1,388	1,533	2,702	3,108	3,178	3,719
Common Eqty.	3,086	3,198	2,569	1,980	2,408	1,729

Ratio Analysis

	1994	1993	1992	1991	1990	1989
% Ret. on Assets	1.4	1.1	0.6	NM	0.8	NM
% Ret. on Equity	24.1	17.3	13.6	NM	19.3	NM
% Loan Loss Resv.	2.8	3.8	4.3	4.5	3.0	3.8
% Loans/Deposits	68.7	58.1	56.9	68.0	79.2	82.2
% Equity to Assets	5.5	6.0	4.7	3.6	3.8	3.6

Dividend Data —Dividends have been paid since 1958. A dividend reinvestment plan is available. A "poison pill" stock purchase rights plan was adopted in 1988.

Amt. of Div. $	Date Decl.	Ex-Div. Date	Stock of Record	Payment Date
0.750	Oct. 17	Nov. 01	Nov. 07	Nov. 30 '94
0.750	Jan. 17	Jan. 31	Feb. 06	Feb. 24 '95
0.750	Apr. 18	May. 02	May. 08	May. 31 '95
0.800	Jul. 18	Aug. 03	Aug. 07	Aug. 31 '95
0.800	Oct. 17	Nov. 02	Nov. 06	Nov. 30 '95

Data as orig. reptd.; bef. results of disc opers. and/or spec. items. Per share data adj. for stk. divs. as of ex-div. date. E-Estimated. NA-Not Available. NM-Not Meaningful. NR-Not Ranked.

Office—633 West Fifth St., Los Angeles, CA 90071; P.O. Box 54068, Los Angeles, CA 90054. **Tel**—(213) 614-3001. **Chrmn & CEO**—W. E. B. Siart. **Pres & COO**—W. S. Randall. **EVP-Fin**—T. P. Marrie. **SVP-Secy**—E. S. Garlock. **EVP-Investor Contact**—Christine M. McCarthy. **Dirs**—J. E. Bryson, E. M. Carson, J. P. Cobb, R. P. Davidson, M. Du Bain, D. C. Frisbee, G. M. Keller, T. L. Lee, H. M. Messmer, Jr., W. F. Miller, W. S. Randall, S. B. Sample, F. N. Shumway, W. E. B. Siart, R. J. Stegemeier, D. M. Tellep. **Transfer Agent & Registrar**—First Interstate Bank of California, LA. **Incorporated** in Delaware in 1957. **Empl**-27,394. **S&P Analyst:** Stephen R. Biggar

First Mississippi

NYSE Symbol **FRM**
In S&P 500

07-OCT-95 Industry:
Chemicals

Summary: This company has interests in industrial and specialty chemicals, nitrogen fertilizer, and technology-based ventures. FRM plans to spin off 81%-owned FirstMiss Gold.

S&P Opinion: Accumulate (★★★★)	Recent Price • 37½	Yield • 1.1%
	52 Wk Range • 40⅛-19½	12-Mo. P/E • 13.4

Quantitative Evaluations

Outlook
(1 Lowest—5 Highest)
• **2+**

Fair Value
• **38¼**

Risk
• **Average**

Earn./Div. Rank
• **B**

Technical Eval.
• **Bullish** since 8/94

Rel. Strength Rank
(1 Lowest—99 Highest)
• **83**

Insider Activity
• **Unfavorable**

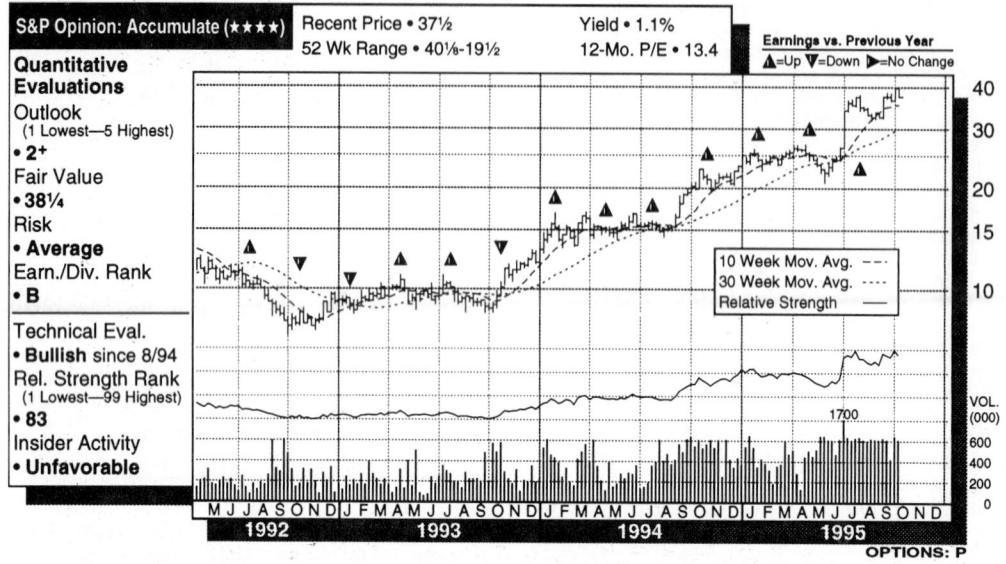

Earnings vs. Previous Year
▲=Up ▼=Down ▶=No Change

10 Week Mov. Avg. – – –
30 Week Mov. Avg. · · · ·
Relative Strength ———

OPTIONS: P

Overview - 06-OCT-95

We see chemical profits in fiscal 1996 continuing to advance on growing contributions from specialties and custom manufacturing, while aniline will be helped by a recent capacity expansion and expected pickups in the housing and durable goods markets. Fertilizer profits should remain very strong with prices remaining at current high levels and favorable feedstock costs. The combustion and plasma segment may turn profitable, reflecting a high order backlog and lower development costs. Results at 81%-owned FirstMiss Gold should improve as output from the new high-grade underground mine reaches 1,200 tons per day by January 1996. The spin-off of the gold unit to shareholders will occur in late October 1995.

Valuation - 27-SEP-95

The stock has been a strong performer since mid-1994, due to increased results of the fertilizer and chemicals segments and improved prospects for FirstMiss Gold (currently valued at about $16 per FRM share). We recommend purchase of the stock, in view of the potentially higher value of the gold unit resulting from the development of the high grade Turquoise Ridge deposit. The rest of FRM is selling at only about 7 times estimated EPS for fiscal 1996. We expect that the specialty chemicals business will continue to grow in fiscal 1996, while the combustion and plasma segment may finally turn profitable. The fertilizer cycle could continue to be strong in 1996 on higher crop acreage and application rates.

Key Stock Statistics

S&P EPS Est. 1996	3.25	Tang. Bk. Value/Share	11.37
P/E on S&P Est. 1996	11.5	Beta	0.24
Dividend Rate/Share	0.40	Shareholders	6,100
Shs. outstg. (M)	20.6	Market cap. (B)	$0.772
Avg. daily vol. (M)	0.139	Inst. holdings	64%
		Insider holdings	NA

Value of $10,000 invested 5 years ago: NA

Fiscal Year Ending Jun. 30

	1995	% Change	1994	% Change	1993	% Change
Revenues (Million $)						
1Q	156.9	38%	113.3	10%	102.7	-27%
2Q	144.0	24%	115.9	11%	104.6	-21%
3Q	176.3	36%	129.6	25%	103.6	-16%
4Q	165.6	11%	149.4	25%	119.1	-8%
Yr.	642.8	26%	508.2	18%	429.9	-18%
Income (Million $)						
1Q	15.02	NM	0.80	-54%	1.74	-67%
2Q	12.94	NM	3.07	NM	-0.65	NM
3Q	19.65	NM	4.85	NM	-0.07	NM
4Q	10.17	14%	8.94	NM	1.65	45%
Yr.	57.79	NM	17.66	NM	2.68	-37%
Earnings Per Share ($)						
1Q	0.74	NM	0.04	-56%	0.09	-67%
2Q	0.63	NM	0.15	NM	0.04	-60%
3Q	0.95	NM	0.24	—	Nil	—
4Q	0.49	11%	0.44	NM	0.08	33%
Yr.	2.80	NM	0.88	NM	0.13	-38%

Next earnings report expected: late October

First Mississippi

Business Summary - 06-OCT-95

This diversified company has interests in chemicals, fertilizer, and technology-based ventures, and plans to spin-off its gold unit. Segment contributions in fiscal 1995 (profits in million $) were:

	Sales	Profits
Chemicals	33%	$40.0
Fertilizer	37%	86.3
Gold	11%	-16.3
Other	19%	-6.2

About 7% of fiscal 1995 sales were exports.

First Chemical produces aniline, nitrated aromatics, aromatic amines, and specialty intermediate and electronic chemicals. A 23% interest is held in Melamine Chemicals, Inc.

Triad Chemical (50% owned) operates at Donaldsonville, La., an ammonia plant (annual capacity of 420,000 tons) and a urea plant (520,000). Wholly owned AMPRO operates an ammonia plant (446,000 tons) at Donaldsonville.

FirstMiss Gold Inc. (81% owned) has a gold mine and mill and heap-leach operations at Getchell, Nev. Underground ore production began in mid-fiscal 1995. Proved reserves were 1,434,900 oz. at June 30, 1995.

Other operations include thermal plasma energy systems and equipment for aluminum recovery, waste treatment and steel production; industrial burners, flares and incinerators; and steel melting and casting operations. In fiscal 1993, FRM discontinued operations in oil and gas, coal and several technology businesses.

Important Developments

Sep. '95—Directors approved the spin-off of 81%-owned FirstMiss Gold Inc. (FRMG). Each FRM shareholder of record October 10, 1995 will receive 0.7 of a share of FRMG for each FRM share held. The action followed the pre-feasibility study of FRMG's Turquoise Ridge gold deposit, which brings FRMG's reserves to 2.7 million ounces. FRMG estimated that the capital required to bring the initial phase of the Turquoise Ridge underground mine into commercial production of 2,000 tons per day would be about $85 million. Initial production would commence in mid-1998.

Jul. '95—FRM achieved record earnings in fiscal 1995 on record fertilizer and chemical profits, despite write-downs and operating losses in the gold business. Combustion and thermal plasma losses were less than half those of fiscal 1994.

Capitalization

Long Term Debt: $84,406,000 (6/95).
Minority Interests: $6,001,000.

Per Share Data ($)

(Year Ended Jun. 30)

	1995	1994	1993	1992	1991	1990
Tangible Bk. Val.	11.40	8.85	8.05	9.50	9.56	9.65
Cash Flow	4.48	2.28	1.53	2.88	2.20	2.00
Earnings	2.80	0.88	0.13	0.21	0.27	0.22
Dividends	0.43	0.30	0.30	0.30	0.30	0.30
Payout Ratio	15%	34%	223%	141%	111%	135%
Prices - High	38	25	13¼	14⅞	12⅜	17⅜
- Low	20¾	12¾	8⅜	7¼	7¾	7⅞
P/E Ratio - High	14	28	NM	71	46	79
- Low	7	14	NM	35	29	36

Income Statement Analysis (Million $)

	1995	%Chg	1994	%Chg	1993	%Chg	1992
Revs.	643	27%	508	18%	430	-18%	525
Oper. Inc.	127	87%	67.8	56%	43.4	-35%	66.5
Depr.	34.6	22%	28.3	1%	27.9	-47%	53.0
Int. Exp.	9.7	-4%	10.1	-22%	13.0	31%	9.9
Pretax Inc.	87.2	182%	30.9	NM	3.9	-51%	7.9
Eff. Tax Rate	38%	—	39%	—	44%	—	37%
Net Inc.	57.8	NM	17.7	NM	2.7	-36%	4.2

Balance Sheet & Other Fin. Data (Million $)

	1995	1994	1993	1992	1991	1990
Cash	41.1	5.0	15.9	19.1	8.2	9.1
Curr. Assets	200	139	131	136	125	150
Total Assets	452	378	384	468	476	512
Curr. Liab.	90.3	60.0	80.7	76.0	93.0	96.0
LT Debt	84.4	104	114	154	143	166
Common Eqty.	233	178	161	188	188	190
Total Cap.	347	296	289	382	374	410
Cap. Exp.	54.9	20.0	41.0	36.0	47.0	65.0
Cash Flow	92.4	45.9	30.5	57.2	43.4	39.8

Ratio Analysis

	1995	1994	1993	1992	1991	1990
Curr. Ratio	2.2	2.3	1.6	1.8	1.3	1.6
% LT Debt of Cap.	24.3	35.1	39.3	40.4	38.1	40.5
% Net Inc.of Revs.	9.0	3.5	0.6	0.8	1.0	0.9
% Ret. on Assets	13.9	4.6	0.6	0.9	1.1	0.9
% Ret. on Equity	28.1	10.4	1.5	2.2	2.8	2.3

Dividend Data —Dividends have been paid since 1973. A dividend reinvestment plan is available. A "poison pill" stock purchase rights plan was adopted in 1989.

Amt. of Div. $	Date Decl.	Ex-Div. Date	Stock of Record	Payment Date
0.087	Nov. 11	Nov. 23	Nov. 30	Dec. 15 '94
0.087	Feb. 28	Mar. 09	Mar. 15	Mar. 30 '95
0.100	May. 23	Jun. 02	Jun. 08	Jun. 23 '95
0.100	Aug. 23	Aug. 31	Sep. 05	Sep. 20 '95
Stk.	Sep. 28	Oct. 23	Oct. 10	Oct. 20 '95

Data as orig. reptd.; bef. results of disc. opers. and/or spec. items. Per share data adj. for stk. divs. as of ex-div. date. E-Estimated. NA-Not Available. NM-Not Meaningful. NR-Not Ranked.

Office—700 North St., P.O. Box 1249, Jackson, MS 39215-1249. **Tel**—(601) 948-7550. **Chrmn & CEO**—J. K. Williams. **Pres**—T. G. Tepas. **VP & CFO**—R. M. Summerford. **Secy & Investor Contact**—James L. McArthur. **Dirs**—R. P. Anderson, P. A. Becker, J. W. Crook, J. E. Fligg, R. P. Guyton, C. P. Moreton, P. W. Murrill, W. A. Percy II, M. T. Reed, Jr., L. R. Speed, R. G. Turner, J. K. Williams. **Transfer Agents**—KeyCorp Shareholder Srvices, Cleveland, Ohio; Co. offices. **Registrars**—KeyCorp Shareholder Services, Cleveland; Deposit Guaranty National Bank, Jackson, Miss. **Incorporated** in Mississippi in 1957. **Empl-** 1,215. **S&P Analyst:** Richard O'Reilly, CFA

First Union Corp.

NYSE Symbol **FTU**
In S&P 500

12-AUG-95

Industry:
Banking

Summary: This North Carolina-based bank holding company, the ninth largest in the U.S., recently agreed to acquire New Jersey-based First Fidelity Bancorp. in a stock transaction.

S&P Opinion: Accumulate (★★★★)	Recent Price • 49⅞	Yield • 4.2%
	52 Wk Range • 51½-39	12-Mo. P/E • 9.7

Quantitative Evaluations

Outlook
(1 Lowest—5 Highest)
• **1** ⁻

Fair Value
• **40⅝**

Risk
• **Low**

Earn./Div. Rank
• **A**

Technical Eval.
• **Bearish** since 5/95

Rel. Strength Rank
(1 Lowest—99 Highest)
• **62**

Insider Activity
• **Neutral**

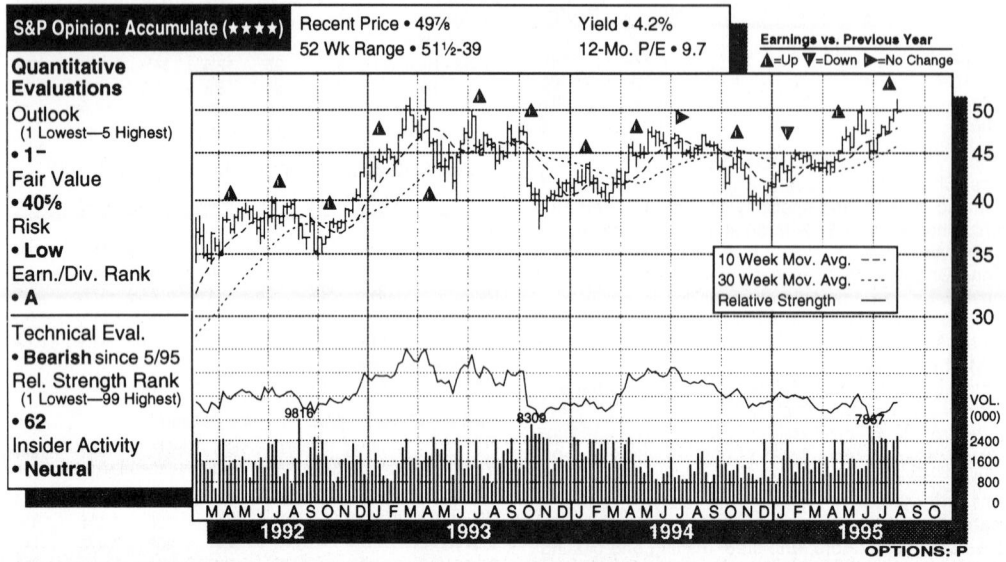

Earnings vs. Previous Year
▲=Up ▼=Down ▶=No Change

10 Week Mov. Avg. – – –
30 Week Mov. Avg. · · · ·
Relative Strength —

OPTIONS: P

Overview - 11-AUG-95

Net interest income should trend higher in 1995 as a rise in earning assets due to acquisitions and strong loan growth offsets pressure on the net interest margin in the higher interest rate environment. Increased contributions from noninterest income sources, particularly the capital management businesses, are also expected, aided by the mid-1994 acquisition of Lieber & Co., which substantially boosted the level of mutual fund assets under management. FTU also intends to expand the range of financial products offered and become more active in the private placement, foreign exchange, and debt and underwriting markets. Credit quality continues to improve, with nonperforming assets down 14%, year to year, to $569 million at June 30, 1995.

Valuation - 11-AUG-95

Acquisitions and a still robust Southeast regional service territory should provide above-average earnings growth in the year ahead. We view the acquisition of First Fidelity as beneficial, with FTU receiving a healthy amount of low-cost deposits, the ability to cross-sell many of its banking products to a new set of customers, as well as a chance to become the dominant and preferred East Coast regional bank. Trading at a modest valuation of around eight times the 1996 earnings estimate of $6.25 a share, and yielding 4.1%, the shares are attractive for both capital appreciation and rising dividend income.

Key Stock Statistics

S&P EPS Est. 1995	5.70	Tang. Bk. Value/Share	23.86
P/E on S&P Est. 1995	8.8	Beta	1.27
S&P EPS Est. 1996	6.25	Shareholders	54,200
Dividend Rate/Share	2.08	Market cap. (B)	$ 8.6
Shs. outstg. (M)	172.0	Inst. holdings	57%
Avg. daily vol. (M)	0.584	Insider holdings	NA

Value of $10,000 invested 5 years ago: $ 30,691

Fiscal Year Ending Dec. 31

	1995	% Change	1994	% Change	1993	% Change
Revenues (Million $)						
1Q	1,753	21%	1,443	5%	1,371	-2%
2Q	1,882	25%	1,509	6%	1,424	1%
3Q	—	—	1,610	10%	1,465	6%
4Q	—	—	1,691	13%	1,495	10%
Yr.	—	—	6,254	9%	5,755	4%
Income (Million $)						
1Q	236.9	6%	222.5	11%	200.0	85%
2Q	249.1	9%	229.6	1%	226.8	81%
3Q	—	—	241.8	24%	195.4	33%
4Q	—	—	231.6	19%	195.3	45%
Yr.	—	—	925.4	13%	817.5	110%
Earnings Per Share ($)						
1Q	1.32	4%	1.27	9%	1.17	44%
2Q	1.45	10%	1.32	NM	1.32	47%
3Q	E1.45	—	1.35	21%	1.12	6%
4Q	E1.48	—	1.04	-7%	1.12	18%
Yr.	E5.70	—	4.98	5%	4.73	27%

Next earnings report expected: mid October

First Union Corp.

Business Summary - 11-AUG-95

First Union is an interstate bank holding company headquartered in North Carolina, where it conducts banking operations through 276 offices. At June 30, 1995, FTU had assets of $83.1 billion, and was the ninth largest bank holding company in the U.S. Since 1985, FTU has expanded into Florida (552 offices), Georgia (154), Tennessee (54), South Carolina (66), Virginia (177), Maryland (26) and the District of Columbia (33). Based on share of deposits, FTU is the largest banking organization in North Carolina and the second largest in Florida. Mortgage banking operations ($34 billion of mortgages serviced) are conducted through 18 offices in 9 states. In addition, First Union operates 184 home equity lending offices, trust operations ($23 billion under management) and other consumer financial services.

Average earning assets of $65.5 billion in 1994 (up from $59.9 billion in 1993) were divided: commercial loans 34%, residential real estate loans 21%, consumer loans 20%, investment securities 16%, securities available for sale 4%, and other assets 5%. Average sources of funds were: interest-free deposits 14%, savings and money-market accounts 31%, time deposits 28% (average total interest-bearing deposits of $43.2 billion were up 6.2% from 1993), short-term borrowings 13%, long-term debt 4%, equity 8%, and other 2%.

At year-end 1994, the reserve for loan losses was 1.81% of loans, against 2.18% a year earlier. Nonperforming assets were $558 million (1.03% of loans and related assets; excludes Southeast Banks segregated assets), versus $916 million (1.95%). Net chargeoffs during 1994 of $163 million represented 0.33% of average loans, versus $252 million (0.58%) in 1993.

Important Developments

Jun. '95—The company signed a definitive agreement to acquire New Jersey-based First Fidelity Bancorporation (NYSE; FFB) in a stock transaction valued at about $5.4 billion. Under the agreement, each FFB common share would be exchanged for 1.35 common shares of FTU. The acquisition would create the eighth largest bank holding company in the U.S., with $124 million in assets and more than 2,000 offices along the East Coast from Connecticut to Florida. The transaction, expected to close by 1995 year-end, is subject to shareholder and regulatory approvals.

Important Developments

Apr. '95—Directors authorized the repurchase of up to 15 million FTU common shares.

Capitalization

Long Term Debt: $5,376,283,000 (6/95).

Per Share Data ($)

(Year Ended Dec. 31)

	1994	1993	1992	1991	1990	1989
Tangible Bk. Val.	23.04	23.69	20.62	16.08	14.54	15.51
Earnings	4.98	4.73	3.72	2.55	2.52	2.40
Dividends	1.72	1.50	1.28	1.12	1.08	1.00
Payout Ratio	35%	32%	34%	44%	43%	42%
Prices - High	48	53⅛	44⅞	31	22	27
- Low	39	37¼	29⅛	13½	13¾	19⅝
P/E Ratio - High	10	11	12	12	9	11
- Low	8	8	8	5	5	8

Income Statement Analysis (Million $)

	1994	%Chg	1993	%Chg	1992	%Chg	1991
Net Int. Inc.	3,034	10%	2,766	38%	2,008	36%	1,476
Tax Equiv. Adj.	92.7	-8%	101	11%	91.0	-15%	107
Non Int. Inc.	1,166	NM	1,165	38%	843	13%	746
Loan Loss Prov.	100	-55%	222	-11%	250	-48%	482
% Exp/Op Revs.	62%	—	63%	—	64%	—	63%
Pretax Inc.	1,415	16%	1,221	69%	722	82%	396
Eff. Tax Rate	35%	—	33%	—	29%	—	20%
Net Inc.	925	13%	818	59%	515	61%	319
% Net Int. Marg.	4.78%	—	4.78%	—	4.98%	—	4.27%

Balance Sheet & Other Fin. Data (Million $)

	1994	1993	1992	1991	1990	1989
Earning Assets:						
Money Mkt.	3,523	1,716	1,945	1,357	1,683	452
Inv. Securities	11,482	14,437	9,934	6,595	8,055	6,120
Com'l Loans	17,521	14,196	10,120	10,260	9,220	7,347
Other Loans	37,181	33,014	23,529	22,160	17,316	14,668
Total Assets	77,314	70,787	51,327	46,085	40,781	32,131
Demand Deposits	10,524	10,861	8,053	6,662	5,140	3,964
Time Deposits	48,435	42,881	31,337	29,936	22,540	17,535
LT Debt	3,429	3,062	2,522	2,039	1,191	872
Common Eqty.	5,398	5,176	3,800	2,981	2,532	2,076

Ratio Analysis

	1994	1993	1992	1991	1990	1989
% Ret. on Assets	1.3	1.2	1.1	0.8	0.8	0.8
% Ret. on Equity	16.5	16.5	14.2	10.8	11.1	12.8
% Loan Loss Resv.	1.8	2.2	2.1	2.0	1.7	1.2
% Loans/Deposits	91.6	87.2	84.7	87.7	94.8	101.6
% Equity to Assets	7.5	7.1	7.1	6.4	6.3	6.6

Dividend Data

(Dividends have been paid since 1914. A dividend reinvestment plan is available. A "poison pill" stock purchase right was adopted in 1990.)

Amt. of Div. $	Date Decl.	Ex-Div. Date	Stock of Record	Payment Date
0.460	Jun. 21	Aug. 25	Aug. 31	Sep. 15 '94
0.460	Oct. 18	Nov. 23	Nov. 30	Dec. 15 '94
0.460	Feb. 21	Feb. 23	Mar. 01	Mar. 15 '95
0.460	Apr. 18	May. 24	May. 31	Jun. 15 '95
0.520	Jun. 19	Aug. 29	Aug. 31	Sep. 15 '95

Data as orig. reptd.; bef. results of disc opers. and/or spec. items. Per share data adj. for stk. divs. as of ex-div. date. E-Estimated. NA-Not Available. NM-Not Meaningful. NR-Not Ranked.

Office—Two First Union Center, Charlotte, NC 28288-0570. **Tel**—(704) 374-6565. **Chrmn & CEO**—E. E. Crutchfield Jr. **Pres**—J. R. Georgius. **EVP-CFO**—R. T. Atwood. **EVP-Secy**—M. A. Cowell Jr. **SVP-Investor Contact**—Barbara K. Massa. **Dirs**—G. A. Bernhardt, W. W. Bradley, R. J. Brown, E. E. Crutchfield Jr., R. D. Davis, R. S. Dickson, B. F. Dolan, R. Dowd Sr., J. R. Georgius, W. H. Goodwin Jr., B. S. Halsey, H. H. Haworth, T. E. Hemby Jr., L. G. Herring, J. A. Laughery, M. — Lennon, R. D. Lovett, H. D. Perry Jr., R. N. Reynolds, R. G. Shaw, L. L. Smith, D. L. Trogdon, J. D. Uible, B. J. Walker, K. G. Younger. **Transfer Agent & Registrar**—First Union National Bank of North Carolina, Charlotte. **Incorporated** in North Carolina in 1967; bank chartered in 1908. **Empl**- 31,858. **S&P Analyst:** Stephen R. Biggar

Fleet Financial

NYSE Symbol **FLT**

In S&P 500

25-JUL-95

Industry:
Banking

Summary: This company has reached a definitive agreement to merge with Shawmut National Corp. in a transaction that would create the ninth largest U.S. bank holding company.

S&P Opinion: Hold (★★★)	Recent Price • 35⅝	Yield • 4.5%
	52 Wk Range • 40½–29⅞	12-Mo. P/E • 8.6

Quantitative Evaluations

Outlook
(1 Lowest—5 Highest)
• **4⁻**

Fair Value
• **36½**

Risk
• **Low**

Earn./Div. Rank
• **B+**

Technical Eval.
• **Bearish** since 6/95

Rel. Strength Rank
(1 Lowest—99 Highest)
• **32**

Insider Activity
• **NA**

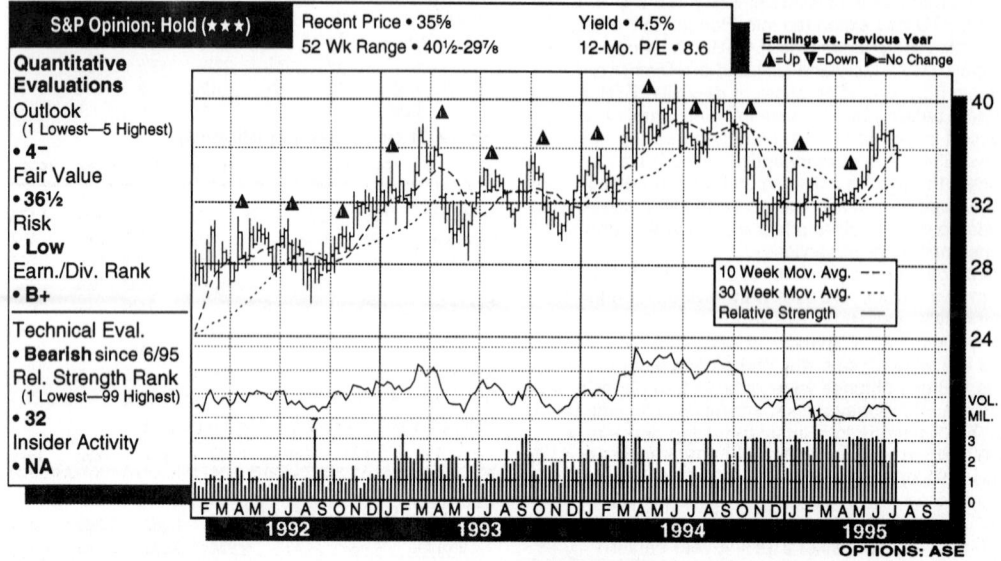

Earnings vs. Previous Year
▲=Up ▼=Down ▶=No Change

10 Week Mov. Avg. ‒ ‒ ‒
30 Week Mov. Avg. ‒‒‒‒
Relative Strength ——

40
32
28
24
VOL. MIL.
3
2
1
0

F M A M J J A S O N D J F M A M J J A S O N D J F M A M J J A S O N D J F M A M J J A S
1992   1993   1994   1995

OPTIONS: ASE

Overview - 25-JUL-95

Factoring in the acquisition of Shawmut National and its related expenses, earnings should continue to rise in 1995. Efficiencies gained from the acquisition will not appear until late 1996, although a $400 million charge for consolidation and staff reductions needed to position the combined company will be taken up front. There will also be offsetting revenue reductions from expected divestitures. While there are benefits to the position of having leading deposit share in several New England states, loan growth in the area is not expected to keep pace with other stronger regions. The acquisition also adds substantial uncertainty to our earnings forecast, since the ultimate amount of branches and operations to be sold in order to satisfy anti-trust regulators is an unknown.

Valuation - 25-JUL-95

We share the market's skepticism about the proposed deal to merge with Shawmut National and downgraded the issue to a hold on the news. While there can be substantial synergies realized given the two companies' overlapping territories, and the expected $400 million savings from consolidations and workforce cutbacks seems reasonable, the lack of diversification given a heavy concentration in the relatively weak New England economy remains a concern. In addition, anti-trust regulators will likely force the shedding of a fair amount of operations, to the benefit of competitors, in areas where markets would be overly dominated.

Key Stock Statistics

S&P EPS Est. 1995	4.30	Tang. Bk. Value/Share	25.05
P/E on S&P Est. 1995	8.3	Beta	1.58
S&P EPS Est. 1996	4.60	Shareholders	38,200
Dividend Rate/Share	1.60	Market cap. (B)	$ 5.0
Shs. outstg. (M)	141.4	Inst. holdings	65%
Avg. daily vol. (M)	0.571	Insider holdings	NA

Value of $10,000 invested 5 years ago: $ 17,973

Fiscal Year Ending Dec. 31

	1995	% Change	1994	% Change	1993	% Change
Revenues (Million $)						
1Q	1,174	10%	1,067	-5%	1,124	-2%
2Q	1,289	18%	1,090	-9%	1,193	NM
3Q	—	—	1,137	-9%	1,246	-1%
4Q	—	—	1,134	2%	1,114	-11%
Yr.	—	—	4,445	-5%	4,677	-4%
Income (Million $)						
1Q	164.1	21%	136.0	28%	106.3	111%
2Q	172.2	16%	148.0	25%	118.7	68%
3Q	—	—	164.0	29%	127.1	66%
4Q	—	—	165.0	21%	136.0	65%
Yr.	—	—	613.0	26%	488.0	74%
Earnings Per Share ($)						
1Q	1.02	29%	0.79	18%	0.67	116%
2Q	1.05	17%	0.90	25%	0.72	60%
3Q	E1.10	—	1.01	29%	0.78	59%
4Q	E1.12	—	1.05	24%	0.85	60%
Yr.	E4.30	—	3.75	25%	3.01	69%

Next earnings report expected: mid October

Fleet Financial

Business Summary - 25-JUL-95

Fleet Financial Group (formerly Fleet/Norstar Financial Group) is the 17th largest U.S. bank holding company. The company's operations are organized into four functional lines of business, the revenues and net income from which were derived as follows in 1994:

	Revs.	Net Inc.
Commercial banking	27%	28%
Consumer banking	42%	35%
Investment services/asset collection	8%	12%
Financial	23%	25%

Commercial banking includes a broad range of commercial and corporate lending, as well as government banking, commercial real estate, asset-based lending, and leasing. Consumer banking (1,100 offices in 38 states) includes retail and community banking, consumer finance, and processing businesses such as mortgage banking and student loan processing. Investment services and asset collection consists of investment management, private banking, discount brokerage, equity capital and asset collection. The financial segment includes the results of the treasury group and the securities portfolio and trading group. Principal subsidiary banks are located in New York, Massachusetts, Rhode Island, Connecticut, Maine and New Hampshire.

At December 31, 1994, nonperforming assets totaled $518 million (1.88% of loans and related assets), down from $601 million (2.27%) a year earlier. The reserve for loan losses was 3.46% of loans and related assets, down from 3.80%. Net charge-offs during 1994 were $104 million, or 0.39% of average loans, versus $290 million (1.11%) in 1993.

Important Developments

Jun. '95—Shareholders approved a proposed merger with Shawmut National Corp. (NYSE; SNC) in a transaction whereby each SNC common share would be exchanged for 0.8922 FLT common shares. The merger would create the ninth largest U.S. bank holding company with assets of $81 billion and leading deposit share in Connecticut, Maine, Massachusetts, New Hampshire and Rhode Island. A related restructuring charge of $400 million for consolidation and workforce reductions will be taken in 1995, although the company expects to trim $400 million of annual expenses within 15 months of the acquisition. The transaction is expected to be completed in the fourth quarter of 1995.

Capitalization

Long Term Debt: $3,804,913,000 (6/95).
Preferred Stock: $378,815,000.

Per Share Data ($) (Year Ended Dec. 31)

	1994	1993	1992	1991	1990	1989
Tangible Bk. Val.	13.55	20.27	12.06	13.33	10.85	13.64
Earnings	3.75	3.01	1.78	0.67	-0.75	3.34
Dividends	1.40	1.02	0.82	0.80	1.25	1.31
Payout Ratio	37%	34%	46%	119%	NM	39%
Prices - High	41 3/8	37 7/8	33 7/8	26 3/8	27 5/8	30 7/8
- Low	29 7/8	28 1/4	24 1/4	9 5/8	8 7/8	23 3/4
P/E Ratio - High	11	13	19	39	NM	9
- Low	8	9	14	14	NM	7

Income Statement Analysis (Million $)

	1994	%Chg	1993	%Chg	1992	%Chg	1991
Net Int. Inc.	1,982	-3%	2,051	5%	1,954	39%	1,404
Tax Equiv. Adj.	40.0	21%	33.0	11%	29.8	-35%	46.0
Non Int. Inc.	1,174	-20%	1,465	19%	1,229	32%	933
Loan Loss Prov.	62.0	-77%	271	-44%	486	-5%	509
% Exp/Op Revs.	65%	—	68%	—	74%	—	78%
Pretax Inc.	1,023	25%	821	58%	518	NM	153
Eff. Tax Rate	39%	—	40%	—	44%	—	36%
Net Inc.	613	26%	488	74%	280	186%	98.0
% Net Int. Marg.	4.65%	—	5.02%	—	4.81%	—	4.05%

Balance Sheet & Other Fin. Data (Million $)

	1994	1993	1992	1991	1990	1989
Earning Assets:						
Money Mkt.	NA	Nil	NM	463	2,264	1,081
Inv. Securities	11,244	14,123	12,660	10,624	5,270	5,524
Com'l Loans	12,675	12,333	12,517	12,199	12,117	12,765
Other Loans	15,355	13,977	16,217	16,751	10,121	11,535
Total Assets	48,757	47,923	46,939	45,445	32,507	33,441
Demand Deposits	6,890	6,473	6,483	6,517	3,433	3,613
Time Deposits	27,916	24,612	26,252	28,729	19,758	18,063
LT Debt	3,457	3,444	3,812	2,511	2,314	1,649
Common Eqty.	3,001	3,138	2,397	2,460	1,941	2,160

Ratio Analysis

	1994	1993	1992	1991	1990	1989
% Ret. on Assets	1.3	1.1	0.6	0.3	NM	1.3
% Ret. on Equity	19.0	16.1	10.4	3.9	NM	17.7
% Loan Loss Resv.	3.4	3.8	3.6	3.6	3.3	1.5
% Loans/Deposits	80.5	84.6	87.8	80.2	92.5	107.8
% Equity to Assets	6.5	7.5	5.8	5.6	6.0	6.9

Dividend Data (Dividends have been paid since 1791. A dividend reinvestment plan is available. A "poison pill" stock purchase right was adopted in 1990.)

Amt. of Div. $	Date Decl.	Ex-Div. Date	Stock of Record	Payment Date
0.350	Jul. 20	Aug. 29	Sep. 03	Oct. 01 '94
0.400	Oct. 19	Nov. 28	Dec. 03	Jan. 01 '95
0.400	Feb. 15	Feb. 27	Mar. 03	Apr. 01 '95
0.400	Apr. 19	May. 26	Jun. 03	Jul. 01 '95

Data as orig. reptd.; bef. results of disc opers. and/or spec. items. Per share data adj. for stk. divs. as of ex-div. date. E-Estimated. NA-Not Available. NM-Not Meaningful. NR-Not Ranked.

Office—50 Kennedy Plaza, Providence, RI 02903. **Tel**—(401) 278-5800. **Chrmn, Pres & CEO**—T. Murray. **EVP & CFO**—E. M. McQuade. **SVP & Secy**—W. C. Mutterperl. **Investor Contact**—Robert W. Lougee, Jr. **Dirs**—W. Barnet III, B. R. Boss, P. J. Choquette, Jr., J. F. Hardymon, R. M. Kavner, L. Keeney, R. C. Kennedy, R. R. McMullin, A. C. Milot, T. Murray, T. D. O'Connor, M. B. Picotte, J. A. Reeves, J. R. Riedman, J. S. Scott. **Transfer Agent & Registrar**—Fleet National Bank, Rhode Island. **Incorporated** in Delaware in 1968. **Empl**-21,500. **S&P Analyst:** Stephen R. Biggar

Fleetwood Enterprises

NYSE Symbol **FLE**
In S&P 500

11-OCT-95

Industry: Auto/Truck mfrs.

Summary: Fleetwood is the largest U.S. manufacturer of recreational vehicles and manufactured housing.

S&P Opinion: Hold (★★★)	Recent Price • 20	Yield • 3.1%
	52 Wk Range • 24⅛-17¾	12-Mo. P/E • 11.9

Quantitative Evaluations

Outlook
(1 Lowest—5 Highest)
• **4⁻**

Fair Value
• **21¼**

Risk
• **Average**

Earn./Div. Rank
• **B+**

Technical Eval.
• **Bearish** since 7/95

Rel. Strength Rank
(1 Lowest—99 Highest)
• **37**

Insider Activity
• **NA**

Earnings vs. Previous Year
▲=Up ▼=Down ▶=No Change

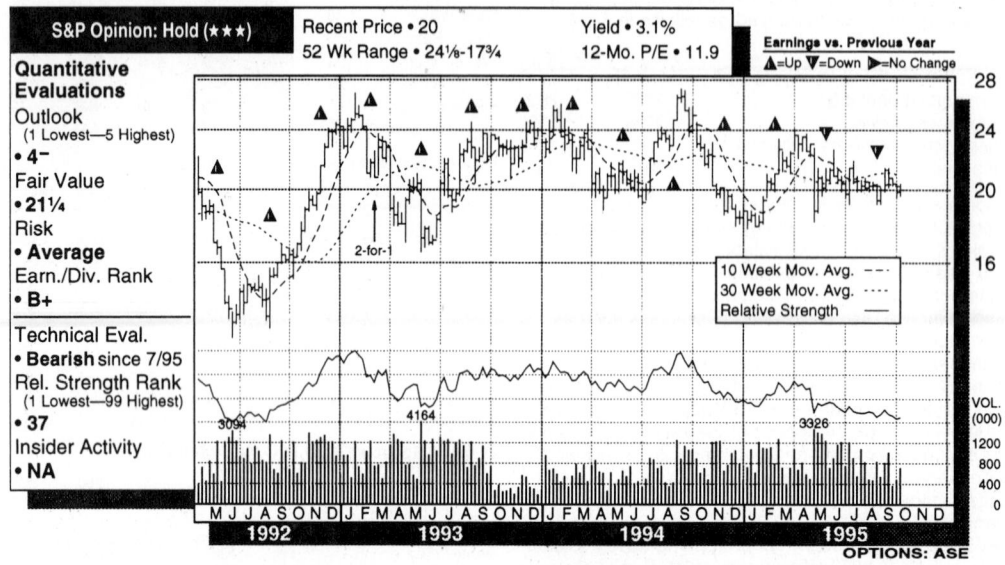

10 Week Mov. Avg. – – –
30 Week Mov. Avg. ·······
Relative Strength ——

2-for-1

OPTIONS: ASE

Overview - 11-OCT-95

Sales growth should continue in 1995-96, but at a slower pace, with most of the gain likely to be sustained in manufactured housing. The division should be aided by growing acceptance of factory-built homes as a lower cost housing alternative, combined with Fleetwood's strong marketing effort, which has enabled it to gain market share in 14 consecutive years. However, the moderating economy is likely to reduce FLE's growth pace in the sector. The RV segment's outlook appears less favorable, as consumers tend to reduce discretionary spending in periods of less robust economic growth. Operating margins are likely to narrow somewhat, as cost controls are outweighed by troubles related to a tougher economic environment, including competitive pricing pressures and the need for greater sales efforts.

Valuation - 11-OCT-95

The shares of Fleetwood have weakened since the spring of 1995, driven by the company's announcements about deteriorating conditions in its RV segment. Although lower interest rates should eventually boost Fleetwood's businesses, current indications lead us to believe that trends will be slowing in both of its operating segments in upcoming periods. While the company's lackluster near-term prospects would currently discourage us from purchasing FLE shares, we believe that most of the troubles are already reflected in its stock price, and we would continue to hold shares of this industry leader for better days ahead.

Key Stock Statistics

S&P EPS Est. 1996	1.75	Tang. Bk. Value/Share	13.55
P/E on S&P Est. 1996	11.4	Beta	1.40
Dividend Rate/Share	0.60	Shareholders	2,000
Shs. outstg. (M)	46.1	Market cap. (B)	$0.904
Avg. daily vol. (M)	0.102	Inst. holdings	66%
		Insider holdings	NA

Value of $10,000 invested 5 years ago: $ 19,473

Fiscal Year Ending Apr. 30

	1996	% Change	1995	% Change	1994	% Change
Revenues (Million $)						
1Q	718.6	-6%	764.3	42%	537.4	14%
2Q	—	—	710.4	25%	567.5	20%
3Q	—	—	661.4	21%	548.6	23%
4Q	—	—	719.5	NM	715.9	29%
Yr.	—	—	2,856	21%	2,369	22%
Income (Million $)						
1Q	22.80	-22%	29.25	93%	15.13	5%
2Q	—	—	21.21	24%	17.08	9%
3Q	—	—	18.28	51%	12.11	12%
4Q	—	—	15.89	-31%	23.12	47%
Yr.	—	—	84.63	26%	67.43	19%
Earnings Per Share ($)						
1Q	0.49	-22%	0.63	91%	0.33	3%
2Q	E0.40	-11%	0.45	22%	0.37	9%
3Q	E0.38	-3%	0.39	50%	0.26	13%
4Q	E0.48	41%	0.34	-32%	0.50	47%
Yr.	E1.75	-4%	1.82	25%	1.46	19%

Next earnings report expected: late November

Fleetwood Enterprises

Business Summary - 06-OCT-95

Fleetwood Enterprises is the largest U.S. producer of recreational vehicles and manufactured housing. Manufacturing operations are conducted principally in 19 states, and to a much lesser extent, in Canada and Europe. Segment contributions in 1994-95 were:

	Sales	Profits
Recreational vehicles	48%	33%
Manufactured housing	48%	59%
Finance/supply/other	4%	8%

Fleetwood's motor homes, which are self-propelled vehicles used primarily for vacations, camping and other leisure activities, are sold under the American Eagle, Bounder, Coronado, Flair, Jamboree, Pace Arrow, Southwind, Tioga and American Dream names. Conventional motor homes made by FLE are fully self-contained, sleep four to eight people and range in length from 22 ft. to 39 ft. The company also sells compact motor homes ranging from 21 ft. to 31 ft.

Travel trailers produced by FLE are designed to be towed by pickup trucks, vans or other vehicles and are similar in use and features to motor homes. The company also makes slide-in truck campers, which fit in the bed of pickup trucks, and additionally manufactures folding trailers.

Manufactured housing products are factory-built homes that are transported to homesites in one or more sections and are installed utilizing their own chassis on either temporary or permanent foundations. About 60% of such homes produced in the U.S. are placed on individually owned lots, with the remainder located on leased sites in manufactured housing communities. Homes built by FLE range in size from 480 to 2,450 sq. ft. and are priced from $10,000 to $110,000, with most selling for under $25,000.

Important Developments

Aug. '95—The company experienced a 22% year over year earnings decline in the first quarter of 1995-96, on a 6.0% drop in revenues. The sales and earnings weakness was related to shrinking demand for motor homes and travel trailers in the recreational vehicles segment, which Fleetwood attributed to dealer and retail customer concerns about the U.S. economy; the 1995-96 quarter was also one week shorter. In addition to the sluggish RV sales, FLE's bottom line was hurt by narrower RV margins resulting from competitive pricing pressures, higher marketing and sales promotion costs and production inefficiencies at several plant locations. The company also noted that sales in the manufactured housing segment were up 2.7% in the quarter, although shipment volume fell 4% to 17,634 homes.

Capitalization

Commercial Paper & Long Term Debt: $289,093,000 (7/95).

Per Share Data ($) (Year Ended Apr. 30)

	1995	1994	1993	1992	1991	1990
Tangible Bk. Val.	13.20	11.88	11.01	10.26	9.78	9.51
Cash Flow	2.34	1.90	1.61	1.26	1.08	1.54
Earnings	1.82	1.46	1.23	0.88	0.69	1.21
Dividends	0.56	0.50	0.47	0.44	0.42	0.38
Payout Ratio	31%	34%	38%	49%	60%	31%
Cal. Yrs.	1994	1993	1992	1991	1990	1989
Prices - High	27¼	26⅞	24⅝	18⅜	14⅝	15⅜
- Low	17⅞	16½	12¾	10¼	7⅞	11
P/E Ratio - High	15	18	20	21	21	13
- Low	10	11	10	12	11	9

Income Statement Analysis (Million $)

	1995	%Chg	1994	%Chg	1993	%Chg	1992
Revs.	2,856	21%	2,369	22%	1,942	22%	1,589
Oper. Inc.	183	31%	140	21%	116	NM	116
Depr.	24.1	18%	20.4	18%	17.3	1%	17.1
Int. Exp.	25.6	41%	18.2	7%	17.0	1%	16.8
Pretax Inc.	142	27%	112	23%	91.3	42%	64.1
Eff. Tax Rate	41%	—	41%	—	38%	—	37%
Net Inc.	84.6	26%	67.4	19%	56.6	41%	40.2

Balance Sheet & Other Fin. Data (Million $)

	1995	1994	1993	1992	1991	1990
Cash	40.6	37.3	34.8	28.0	15.0	19.0
Curr. Assets	NA	NA	NA	NA	NA	NA
Total Assets	1,345	1,224	1,062	915	765	817
Curr. Liab.	NA	NA	NA	409	302	364
LT Debt	145	180	150	Nil	Nil	Nil
Common Eqty.	608	546	503	468	428	424
Total Cap.	752	726	653	468	428	424
Cap. Exp.	68.0	72.9	42.2	25.7	19.2	33.1
Cash Flow	109	87.8	73.9	57.4	47.9	69.9

Ratio Analysis

	1995	1994	1993	1992	1991	1990
Curr. Ratio	NA	NA	NA	NA	NA	NA
% LT Debt of Cap.	19.3	24.8	23.0	Nil	Nil	Nil
% Net Inc.of Revs.	3.0	2.8	2.9	2.5	2.2	3.6
% Ret. on Assets	6.6	5.9	5.7	4.7	3.9	7.3
% Ret. on Equity	14.7	12.8	11.6	8.8	7.2	13.5

Dividend Data —Dividends have been paid since 1965. A "poison pill" stock purchase rights plan was adopted in 1988.

Amt. of Div. $	Date Decl.	Ex-Div. Date	Stock of Record	Payment Date
0.140	Sep. 13	Oct. 03	Oct. 07	Nov. 09 '94
0.140	Dec. 13	Dec. 30	Jan. 06	Feb. 08 '95
0.140	Mar. 14	Apr. 03	Apr. 07	May. 10 '95
0.150	Jun. 13	Jul. 05	Jul. 07	Aug. 09 '95
0.150	Sep. 12	Oct. 04	Oct. 06	Nov. 08 '95

Data as orig. reptd.; bef. results of disc. opers. and/or spec. items. Per share data adj. for stk. divs. as of ex-div. date. E-Estimated. NA-Not Available. NM-Not Meaningful. NR-Not Ranked.

Office—3125 Myers St., Riverside, CA 92503-5527. **Tel**—(909) 351-3500. **Chrmn & CEO**—J. C. Crean. **Pres**—G. F. Kummer. **VP & Secy**—W. H. Lear. **VP, CFO & Investor Contact**—Paul M. Bingham. **Dirs**—W. F. Beran, A. Crean, J. C. Crean, J. L. Doti, T. A. Fuentes, G. F. Kummer, D. M. Lawson, W. W. Weide. **Transfer Agent & Registrar**—First National Bank of Boston. **Incorporated** in California in 1950; reincorporated in Delaware in 1977. **Empl**-18,000. **S&P Analyst:** Michael W. Jaffe

Fleming Cos.

NYSE Symbol **FLM**
In S&P 500

27-OCT-95 **Industry:** Food

Summary: Fleming, one of the largest food wholesalers in the U.S., is in the process of consolidating facilities and re-engineering operating processes to increase efficiency.

| S&P Opinion: Avoid (★★) | Recent Price • 23¾ | Yield • 5.2% |
| | 52 Wk Range • 29⅞-19⅛ | 12-Mo. P/E • 18.4 |

Quantitative Evaluations

Outlook (1 Lowest—5 Highest)
• **3−**

Fair Value
• **23½**

Risk
• **Low**

Earn./Div. Rank
• **B+**

Technical Eval.
• **Bearish** since 7/95

Rel. Strength Rank (1 Lowest—99 Highest)
• **18**

Insider Activity
• **NA**

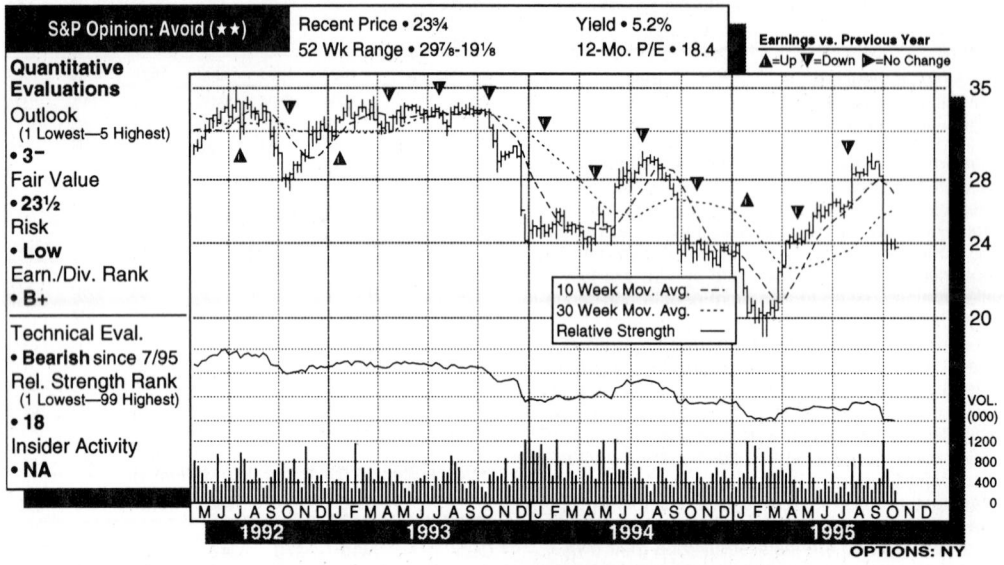

Earnings vs. Previous Year
▲=Up ▼=Down ▶=No Change

10 Week Mov. Avg. - - -
30 Week Mov. Avg. ·······
Relative Strength ——

VOL. (000)

1992 1993 1994 1995

OPTIONS: NY

Overview - 27-OCT-95

Sales should increase only modestly in 1996 as the company rolls out its new marketing system to customers. The company's objective is to lower product costs to retail customers while providing the company with a fair and adequate return for the products and its services. To achieve this objective the company is making major organizational changes and investing in new technology. But the costs of re-engineering the company will continue to keep operating expenses and interest costs high. The re-engineering is expected to result in $65 million of pretax savings annually. The new organizational structure will not be substantially completed until late 1996. Earnings should begin to benefit from these dramatic changes in the company's operations in 1997.

Valuation - 27-OCT-95

The shares of this food distribution company fell following the announcement of lower than expected third quarter and full year 1995 earnings. Earnings gains are a ways off as significant costs are being incurred in connection with Fleming's transformation into a more efficient low-cost food marketing and distribution company. We would avoid the shares until management has its new operating systems on a solid footing. The lofty 5.0% dividend yield, however, should limit the downside.

Key Stock Statistics

S&P EPS Est. 1995	1.30	Tang. Bk. Value/Share	2.92
P/E on S&P Est. 1995	18.3	Beta	0.30
S&P EPS Est. 1996	1.60	Shareholders	11,500
Dividend Rate/Share	1.20	Market cap. (B)	$0.869
Shs. outstg. (M)	37.6	Inst. holdings	76%
Avg. daily vol. (M)	0.090	Insider holdings	NA

Value of $10,000 invested 5 years ago: $ 9,959

Fiscal Year Ending Dec. 31

	1995	% Change	1994	% Change	1993	% Change
Revenues (Million $)						
1Q	5,485	36%	4,032	NM	4,045	3%
2Q	4,020	39%	2,884	-3%	2,965	NM
3Q	3,896	-6%	4,142	41%	2,936	NM
4Q	—	—	4,696	49%	3,147	1%
Yr.	—	—	15,753	20%	13,092	1%
Income (Million $)						
1Q	19.55	-20%	24.40	-35%	37.38	-3%
2Q	14.74	-21%	18.60	-31%	26.84	1%
3Q	3.67	35%	2.72	-87%	20.31	-11%
4Q	—	—	10.46	NM	-47.04	NM
Yr.	—	—	56.17	50%	37.48	-68%
Earnings Per Share ($)						
1Q	0.52	-21%	0.66	-35%	1.02	-6%
2Q	0.39	-22%	0.50	-32%	0.73	-3%
3Q	0.10	43%	0.07	-87%	0.55	-14%
4Q	E0.29	4%	0.28	NM	-1.28	NM
Yr.	E1.30	-14%	1.51	48%	1.02	-69%

Next earnings report expected: late February

Business Summary - 27-OCT-95

Fleming Companies is one of the largest food whole-salers in the U.S., having grown over the past decade mainly through acquisitions. At year-end 1994, the company served 3,700 retail food stores in 43 states, the Caribbean, Mexico, and Central and South American countries with a wide variety of inventory, including groceries, meats, produce, frozen foods, dairy products and general merchandise.

The company is going through an extensive re-engineering process for which it took a $101.3 million charge in the fourth quarter of 1993. The primary objectives are: to lower the cost of goods to its retail customers; to align the retailers, manufacturers and Fleming's business systems through technology; to maximize marketing capabilities by using its size and purchasing power; and to lower system costs through shared efficiencies. The company consists of four core business units: customer management; retail services; category marketing; and product supply. These replace the geographic division structure of the past.

Retail stores served by the company range in size from small convenience outlets to conventional supermarkets to large superstores, combination units and price-impact stores. These units aggregated 100.6 million sq. ft. at year-end 1994.

The stores served can be divided into four classes: independent supermarkets (52%); corporate-owned chains (30%); company-owned chains (13%); and voluntary chains, licensed to do business under a common name (5%).

FLM offers a wide variety of support services to its retail customers designed to provide modern systems and programs to support the operation of their business.

Important Developments

Oct. '95—Sales in the third quarter of 1995, in the food distribution segment fell 7.4% to $3.2 billion year to year; operating earnings rose 10% to $58.9 million. Retail food sales were $0.7 billion, up 4.9%, year-to-year; operating earnings decreased 11.8% to $9.1 million. While the company said it made more progress in achieving its reengineering objectives than originally planned, expenses incurred in the third quarter were higher than anticipated. Other factors which hurt third quarter earnings included soft sales, costs associated with financing certain customers and higher equity investment losses. Management said that more than 40% of its sales base has the new flexible marketing plan installed.

Capitalization

Long Term Debt: $1,705,853,000 (7/15/95), incl. $364,328,000 of capital lease obligations.

Per Share Data ($) (Year Ended Dec. 31)

	1994	1993	1992	1991	1990	1989
Tangible Bk. Val.	2.42	15.93	16.19	14.44	9.98	7.18
Cash Flow	5.42	3.77	5.33	4.22	5.78	4.78
Earnings	1.51	1.02	3.33	2.06	3.06	2.54
Dividends	1.20	1.20	1.20	1.14	1.03	1.00
Payout Ratio	79%	118%	37%	58%	34%	40%
Prices - High	30	34⅜	35⅛	40⅝	37⅝	40
- Low	22⅝	23¾	27¼	29⅞	28	27½
P/E Ratio - High	20	34	11	20	12	16
- Low	15	23	8	15	9	11

Income Statement Analysis (Million $)

	1994	%Chg	1993	%Chg	1992	%Chg	1991
Revs.	15,753	20%	13,092	1%	12,938	NM	12,902
Oper. Inc.	329	12%	293	-16%	348	NM	350
Depr.	146	45%	101	41%	71.8	-1%	72.7
Int. Exp.	121	55%	78.0	-4%	81.1	-13%	93.5
Pretax Inc.	112	56%	72.0	-63%	195	67%	117
Eff. Tax Rate	50%	—	48%	—	39%	—	38%
Net Inc.	56.0	51%	37.0	-69%	119	65%	72.3

Balance Sheet & Other Fin. Data (Million $)

	1994	1993	1992	1991	1990	1989
Cash	28.4	1.6	4.7	21.1	21.3	37.2
Curr. Assets	1,820	1,361	1,403	1,343	1,208	1,141
Total Assets	4,608	3,103	3,118	2,956	2,768	2,689
Curr. Liab.	1,324	919	875	915	830	778
LT Debt	1,995	1,004	1,038	952	981	692
Common Eqty.	1,079	1,060	1,060	957	764	692
Total Cap.	3,125	2,092	2,138	1,935	1,839	1,774
Cap. Exp.	150	56.0	114	82.0	69.0	137
Cash Flow	202	139	191	142	160	140

Ratio Analysis

	1994	1993	1992	1991	1990	1989
Curr. Ratio	1.4	1.5	1.6	1.5	1.5	1.5
% LT Debt of Cap.	63.8	48.0	48.6	49.2	53.4	55.8
% Net Inc.of Revs.	0.4	0.3	0.9	0.6	0.8	0.7
% Ret. on Assets	1.4	1.2	3.8	2.3	3.5	3.0
% Ret. on Equity	5.2	3.5	11.6	7.5	12.7	11.1

Dividend Data —Dividends have been paid since 1927. A dividend reinvestment plan is available. A "poison pill" stock purchase rights plan was adopted in 1986.

Amt. of Div. $	Date Decl.	Ex-Div. Date	Stock of Record	Payment Date
0.300	Oct. 18	Nov. 14	Nov. 18	Dec. 09 '94
0.300	Jan. 24	Feb. 13	Feb. 20	Mar. 10 '95
0.300	May. 04	May. 15	May. 19	Jun. 09 '95
0.300	Jun. 21	Aug. 16	Aug. 18	Sep. 08 '95
0.300	Oct. 25	Nov. 16	Nov. 20	Dec. 08 '95

Data as orig. reptd.; bef. results of disc. opers. and/or spec. items. Per share data adj. for stk. divs. as of ex-div. date. E-Estimated. NA-Not Available. NM-Not Meaningful. NR-Not Ranked.

Office—6301 Waterford Blvd., P.O. Box 26647, Oklahoma City, OK 73118. **Tel**—(405) 840-7200. **Chrmn & CEO**—R. E. Stauth. **Pres & COO**—W. Dowd. **VP Treas & Investor Contact**—J. M. Thompson (405-841-8170). **Dirs**—A. R. Dykes, C. B. Hallett, J. G. Harlow, Jr., L. M. Jones, E. C. Joullian, III, H. L. Leach, J. A. McMillan, G. A. Osborn, R. E. Stauth, E. D. Werries. **Transfer Agent & Registrar**—Liberty National Bank & Trust Co., Oklahoma City. **Incorporated** in Kansas in 1915; reincorporated in Oklahoma in 1981. **Empl**-42,400. **S&P Analyst:** Karen J. Sack, CFA

Fluor Corp.

NYSE Symbol **FLR**
In S&P 500

24-OCT-95

Industry:
Building

Summary: Fluor is one of the world's largest international engineering, construction and related services companies, and has investments in coal.

S&P Opinion: Accumulate (★★★★)	Recent Price • 56½	Yield • 1.1%
	52 Wk Range • 59½-41¼	12-Mo. P/E • 21.6

Quantitative Evaluations

Outlook
(1 Lowest—5 Highest)
• **4+**

Fair Value
• **60%**

Risk
• **Low**

Earn./Div. Rank
• **B**

Technical Eval.
• **Bearish** since 7/95

Rel. Strength Rank
(1 Lowest—99 Highest)
• **49**

Insider Activity
• **NA**

Earnings vs. Previous Year
▲=Up ▼=Down ▶=No Change

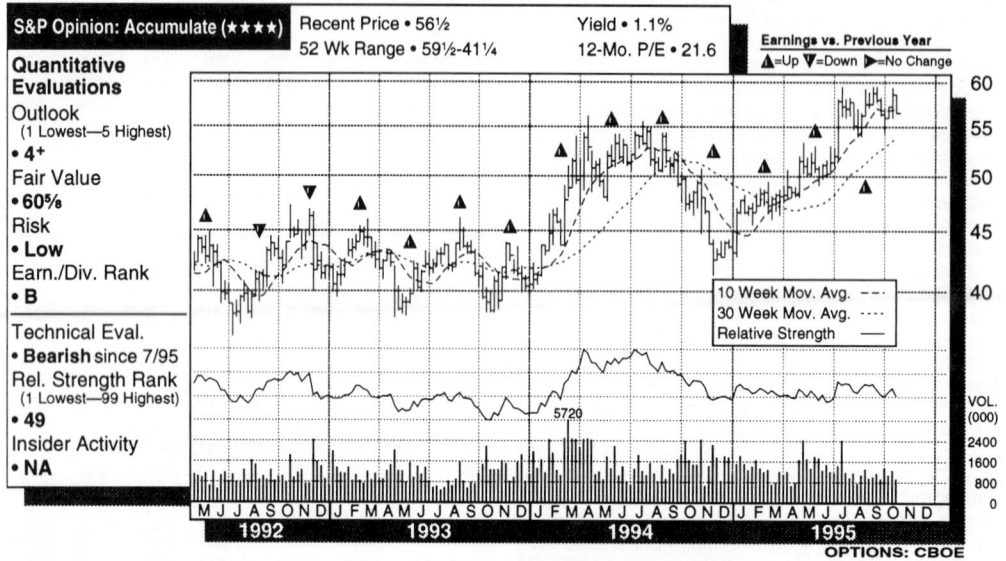

10 Week Mov. Avg. – – –
30 Week Mov. Avg. ·······
Relative Strength —

5720

VOL. (000)

OPTIONS: CBOE

Overview - 24-OCT-95

Assuming 2.6% GDP growth in the U. S. and stable business conditions worldwide, we expect a 10% rise in fiscal 1996's revenues on continued gains in engineering and construction and another increase in coal. Margins in E&C will expand as a result of a more favorable mix of business and a higher volume of work performed. Coal margins will benefit from higher volume as a result of a recovery in steam coal and continued strength in metallurgical coal. Aided by better margins, operating income should exceed the gain in sales. With only a slight decline in interest income and an unchanged tax rate, earnings should rise again fiscal 1996. Longer term sales and earnings growth in E&C will benefit from stronger overseas economies; the coal unit will grow as a result of increased secular demand for cleaner burning coal. Fluor has ample ability to grow via acquisitions and joint ventures.

Valuation - 24-OCT-95

Following a strong gain through June, FLR's shares have been locked in a narrow trading range through late October. Through October the shares are up 32% versus a 27% gain in the S&P 500 and a 23% gain in the S&P E&C index. We remain enthusiastic over FLR's long term prospects based on its very strong position in the E&C industry and in coal together with its rock solid finances. However, we continue to believe that the shares only warrant an accumulate recommendation. FLR is not undervalued at 17X our fiscal 1996 estimate and the upside from current levels is limited.

Key Stock Statistics

S&P EPS Est. 1995	2.80	Tang. Bk. Value/Share	14.79
P/E on S&P Est. 1995	20.2	Beta	1.57
S&P EPS Est. 1996	3.30	Shareholders	15,600
Dividend Rate/Share	0.60	Market cap. (B)	$ 4.7
Shs. outstg. (M)	83.0	Inst. holdings	65%
Avg. daily vol. (M)	0.224	Insider holdings	NA

Value of $10,000 invested 5 years ago: $ 16,286

Fiscal Year Ending Oct. 31

	1995	% Change	1994	% Change	1993	% Change
Revenues (Million $)						
1Q	2,060	NM	2,058	14%	1,807	16%
2Q	2,229	7%	2,080	4%	2,006	30%
3Q	2,437	24%	1,963	6%	1,844	11%
4Q	—	—	2,385	9%	2,193	20%
Yr.	—	—	8,485	8%	7,850	19%
Income (Million $)						
1Q	50.30	14%	44.00	23%	35.68	11%
2Q	55.32	16%	47.74	14%	42.00	18%
3Q	60.20	25%	48.31	18%	40.84	4%
4Q	—	—	52.40	8%	48.30	71%
Yr.	—	—	192.4	15%	166.8	23%
Earnings Per Share ($)						
1Q	0.61	15%	0.53	23%	0.43	10%
2Q	0.66	14%	0.58	14%	0.51	16%
3Q	0.72	24%	0.58	16%	0.50	4%
4Q	E0.81	29%	0.63	7%	0.59	69%
Yr.	E2.80	21%	2.32	14%	2.03	23%

Next earnings report expected: late November

Fluor Corp.

Business Summary - 23-OCT-95

Fluor provides engineering, construction and other services to a wide range of clients worldwide. It also mines coal. Contributions in fiscal 1994 were:

	Revs.	Profits
Engineering & construction	91%	73%
Coal	9%	27%

In fiscal 1994, non-U.S. operations accounted for 28% of revenues and 20% of operating profits.

The Fluor Daniel group provides engineering, construction and related services on a worldwide basis to clients in four business groups: process, industrial, power and government, and diversified services. Services provided include feasibility studies, conceptual design, engineering and procurement, project and construction management, construction, operation, maintenance and plant operations, technical services, quality control, site evaluation, environmental, and project financing services.

Backlog in engineering and construction at October 31, 1994 stood at $14.0 billion, versus $14.8 billion a year earlier. Some 51% of fiscal 1994's year end backlog consisted of projects outside the U. S. versus 39% in fiscal 1993. New awards totaled $8.1 billion, versus $8.0 billion a fiscal 1993's year end.

Coal operations are conducted through A.T. Massey Coal Co., which produces, processes and sells bituminous coal of steam and metallurgical grades from 16 mining complexes. In fiscal 1994, production of steam and metallurgical coal was 17,120 tons and 7,333 tons, respectively, versus 16,048 and 5,163 tons, in fiscal 1993. As of fiscal 1994 year end, total recoverable reserves were estimated at 1,411,265 short tons, of which 1,053,154 were proven recoverable reserves and 358,111 tons were probable recoverable reserves.

Important Developments

Aug. '95— FLR reported share earnings of $0.72 on a 24% increase in revenues for fiscal 1995's third quarter, versus $0.58 in the fiscal 1994 period. E&C revenues rose 25% while coal revenues increased 22%. Operating profits for E&C rose 10% on better margins. The company noted that the gain in E&C profit was mostly the result of an increase in the volume of work performed. Operating profits in coal advanced 28% as increased volume and pricing for metallurgical coal offset softer market conditions for steam coal resulting from unusually mild weather. New awards for the quarter totaled $2.61 billion, versus $2.29 billion in last year's third quarter; backlog at the end of the quarter totaled $14.6 billion, versus $14.9 billion a year earlier.

Capitalization

Long Term Debt: $26,516,000 (7/95).

Per Share Data ($)

(Year Ended Oct. 31)

	1994	1993	1992	1991	1990	1989
Tangible Bk. Val.	14.79	12.72	10.81	12.58	10.75	9.03
Cash Flow	3.70	3.28	3.22	3.21	2.93	2.38
Earnings	2.32	2.03	1.65	1.83	1.71	1.35
Dividends	0.52	0.48	0.40	0.32	0.24	0.14
Payout Ratio	22%	24%	24%	17%	14%	10%
Prices - High	56¼	46⅛	48⅛	54¾	49¼	37¾
- Low	40⅛	38	36⅝	32⅛	29	21⅝
P/E Ratio - High	24	23	29	30	29	28
- Low	17	19	22	18	17	16

Income Statement Analysis (Million $)

	1994	%Chg	1993	%Chg	1992	%Chg	1991
Revs.	8,485	8%	7,850	19%	6,601	-2%	6,742
Oper. Inc.	413	19%	346	NM	343	27%	271
Depr.	114	11%	103	-19%	127	11%	114
Int. Exp.	17.0	-15%	20.0	-17%	24.0	85%	13.0
Pretax Inc.	303	25%	242	13%	215	-6%	228
Eff. Tax Rate	37%	—	31%	—	37%	—	35%
Net Inc.	192	15%	167	24%	135	-9%	149

Balance Sheet & Other Fin. Data (Million $)

	1994	1993	1992	1991	1990	1989
Cash	492	312	343	370	271	235
Curr. Assets	1,258	1,309	1,139	1,160	1,223	1,036
Total Assets	2,825	2,589	2,365	2,421	2,476	2,154
Curr. Liab.	1,021	931	845	848	984	798
LT Debt	30.0	67.0	72.0	88.0	72.0	76.0
Common Eqty.	1,220	1,044	881	1,020	864	720
Total Cap.	1,296	1,162	1,016	1,218	1,040	885
Cap. Exp.	237	172	287	160	156	139
Cash Flow	307	270	262	263	238	192

Ratio Analysis

	1994	1993	1992	1991	1990	1989
Curr. Ratio	1.2	1.4	1.3	1.4	1.2	1.3
% LT Debt of Cap.	2.3	5.7	7.1	7.2	6.9	8.6
% Net Inc.of Revs.	2.3	2.1	2.0	2.2	1.9	1.7
% Ret. on Assets	7.1	6.7	5.6	6.1	6.0	5.1
% Ret. on Equity	17.0	17.3	14.2	15.8	17.5	16.3

Dividend Data —Common dividends were resumed in September 1988, after omission since early 1987. A "poison pill" stock purchase rights plan was adopted in 1987. A dividend reinvestment plan is available.

Amt. of Div. $	Date Decl.	Ex-Div. Date	Stock of Record	Payment Date
0.150	Dec. 07	Dec. 14	Dec. 20	Jan. 10 '95
0.150	Mar. 15	Mar. 22	Mar. 28	Apr. 18 '95
0.150	Jun. 13	Jun. 23	Jun. 27	Jul. 18 '95
0.150	Sep. 11	Sep. 22	Sep. 26	Oct. 17 '95

Data as orig. reptd.; bef. results of disc. opers. and/or spec. items. Per share data adj. for stk. divs. as of ex-div. date. E-Estimated. NA-Not Available. NM-Not Meaningful. NR-Not Ranked.

Office—3333 Michelson Drive, Irvine, CA 92730. **Tel**—(714) 975-2000. **Chrmn & CEO**—L. G. McCraw. **SVP-Secy**—P. J. Trimble. **VP & CFO**—J. M. Conaway. **Investor Contact**—Lila J. Churney (714-975-3909). **Dirs**—C. A. Campbell, Jr., H. K. Coble, P. J. Fluor, D. P. Gardner, W. R. Grant, B. R. Inman, R. V. Lindsay, V. S. Martinez, L. G. McCraw, B. Mickel, M. A. Seger. **Transfer Agent & Registrar**—Chemical Trust Co. of California, Los Angeles; Chemical Bank, NYC. **Incorporated** in California in 1924; reincorporated in Delaware in 1978. **Empl**-39,807. **S&P Analyst:** Leo Larkin

Ford Motor

NYSE Symbol **F**
In S&P 500

02-AUG-95 | **Industry:** Auto/Truck mfrs. | **Summary:** Ford is the world's second largest producer of cars and trucks and has a rapidly growing financial services operation.

S&P Opinion: Hold (★★★) | Recent Price • 29¼ | Yield • 4.2%
| 52 Wk Range • 32⅞-24⅝ | 12-Mo. P/E • 5.4

Quantitative Evaluations

Outlook
(1 Lowest—5 Highest)
• **4⁻**

Fair Value
• **29⅞**

Risk
• **Low**

Earn./Div. Rank
• **B-**

Technical Eval.
• **Bullish** since 4/95

Rel. Strength Rank
(1 Lowest—99 Highest)
• **25**

Insider Activity
• **Neutral**

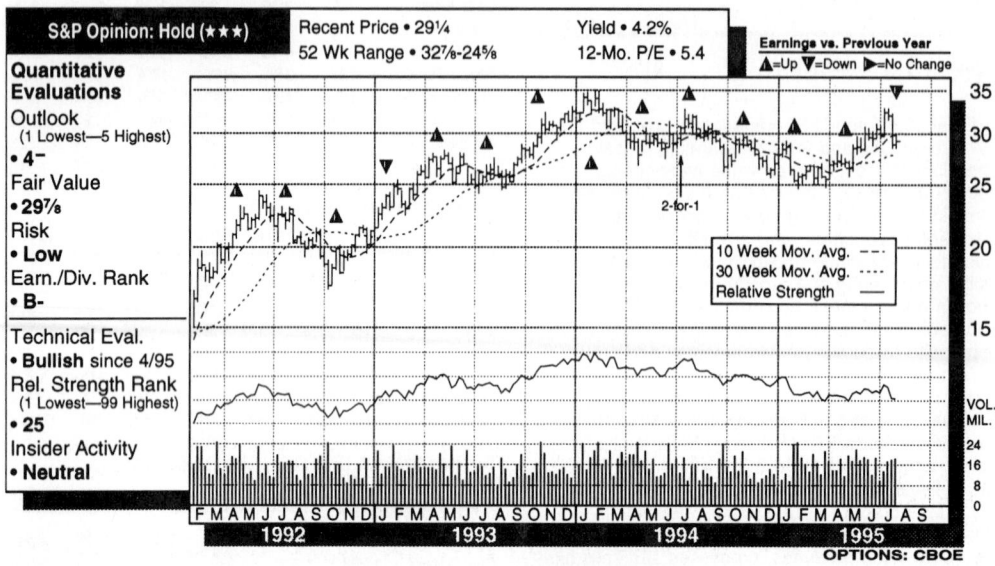

Earnings vs. Previous Year
▲=Up ▼=Down ▶=No Change

10 Week Mov. Avg. - - -
30 Week Mov. Avg. ·····
Relative Strength ——

OPTIONS: CBOE

Overview - 31-JUL-95

Although auto industry sales in North America are declining, and volume is up only modestly in Europe, Ford is benefiting from increased truck production capacity. Despite significant downtime for changeover of the Taurus and Sable production lines, Ford's market share increased in the first half of 1995. With the prospective return to full production of Ford's perennial best selling mid-sized cars, further market share improvement is expected. Aided by cost-cutting efforts related to implementation of the Ford 2000 project to reorganize Ford's approach to product development and a profit at Jaguar, worldwide automotive profits should stabilize in a sluggish economic environment. Financial services should continue to grow steadily, led by rising volume at Ford Motor Credit's vehicle financing operation and the Associates' consumer credit subsidiary.

Valuation - 31-JUL-95

We continue a hold opinion on Ford due to mounting evidence that North American industry volume will peak at a lower level than previously envisioned. First half 1995 North American vehicle sales weakened and production plans continue to be pared. Although earnings should rebound in 1996 due to return of full production of the Taurus and Sable mid-size cars, the North American vehicle market is flattening and we do not think an expansion of the earnings multiple is in store. We expect the stock to be an average performer during the next 12 months and we would not add to positions at this time.

Key Stock Statistics

S&P EPS Est. 1995	5.65	Tang. Bk. Value/Share	15.50
P/E on S&P Est. 1995	5.2	Beta	1.26
S&P EPS Est. 1996	6.00	Shareholders	260,400
Dividend Rate/Share	1.24	Market cap. (B)	$ 29.4
Shs. outstg. (M)	1026.9	Inst. holdings	48%
Avg. daily vol. (M)	4.031	Insider holdings	NA

Value of $10,000 invested 5 years ago: $ 18,041

Fiscal Year Ending Dec. 31

	1995	% Change	1994	% Change	1993	% Change
Revenues (Million $)						
1Q	34,783	14%	30,400	14%	26,760	9%
2Q	36,389	8%	33,770	15%	29,420	10%
3Q	—	—	30,660	25%	24,500	5%
4Q	—	—	33,643	21%	27,840	10%
Yr.	—	—	128,439	18%	108,520	8%
Income (Million $)						
1Q	1,550	71%	904.0	58%	572.0	NM
2Q	1,572	-8%	1,711	121%	775.0	100%
3Q	—	—	1,124	143%	463.0	NM
4Q	—	—	1,569	118%	719.0	NM
Yr.	—	—	5,308	110%	2,529	NM
Earnings Per Share ($)						
1Q	1.44	73%	0.83	63%	0.51	183%
2Q	1.45	-11%	1.63	126%	0.72	106%
3Q	E1.01	—	1.04	160%	0.40	NM
4Q	E1.75	—	1.47	126%	0.65	NM
Yr.	E5.65	—	4.97	119%	2.27	NM

Next earnings report expected: late October

Ford Motor

Business Summary - 01-AUG-95

Ford is the world's second largest motor vehicle manufacturer. It produces cars and trucks, many of the vehicles' plastic, glass and electronic components, and replacement parts. Financial services include Ford Motor Credit (financing and insurance), and ICA Mortgage Corp. (mortgage banking). Ford Holdings (75% owned) owns The Associates Corp., USL Capital (formerly U.S. Leasing), Ford Leasing Development, American Road Insurance and Ford Motor Land Development. Ford also owns 100% of Hertz Corp. (car rental). On September 30, 1994, Ford sold First Nationwide Financial, its savings and loan subsidiary.

In 1994, automotive net income was $3.82 billion. U.S. income was $3.04 billion, versus a $1.48 billion loss in 1993. Outside the U.S., there was income of $784 million, versus a $542 million loss. Foreign income included $388 million in Europe excluding Jaguar, and $395 million elsewhere. Financial services net income was $1.48 billion in 1994 after a $440 million charge for First Nationwide, down from $1.59 billion.

Various Ford, Mercury, Lincoln and Jaguar models accounted for a 21.8% share of cars sold in U.S. markets (including foreign-built) in 1994, compared with 22.3% in 1993, 21.8% in 1992, 20.1% in 1991, 21.1% in 1990, 22.3% in 1989, 21.7% in 1988 and 20.2% in 1987. Comparable figures for trucks were 30.1%, 30.5%, 29.7%, 28.9%, 29.3%,, 28.8% and 29.0%. Vehicle factory sales totaled 6,639,000 cars and trucks in 1994, of which 4,276,000 were in the U.S., versus 5,965,000 and 3,824,000, respectively, in 1993.

Important Developments

Jul. '95—In the 1995 second quarter, F's worldwide automotive operations earned $1.1 billion, versus $1.2 billion in the 1994 period. In the U.S., automotive operations earned $663 million, down from $888 million, and foreign automotive operations earned $437 million, versus $314 million. Financial services operations earned $472 million, compared with $509 million. F's combined U.S. car and truck market share in the second quarter of 1995 was 26.2%, compared with 25.0% in the second quarter of 1994, 26.6% in the first quarter of 1995, and 25.2% for all of 1994. U.S. retail incentives averaged $760 per vehicle, compared with $705 per unit in the first quarter of 1995, $550 in the second quarter of 1994, and $710 for all of 1994.

Capitalization

Total Debt: $143,362,000,000 (6/30/95).
Minority Interest in Ford Hldgs: $1,976,000,000.
Conv. Pfd. Stock: Liquidation pref. of $2.8 billion.
Class B Stock: 71,000,000 shs. ($1 par). All held by the Ford family and their interests. Cl. B has 40% of voting power but is otherwise equal to the common stock.

Per Share Data ($) (Year Ended Dec. 31)

	1994	1993	1992	1991	1990	1989
Tangible Bk. Val.	17.85	12.20	4.68	14.21	16.59	17.55
Cash Flow	14.21	9.85	6.21	3.68	6.20	8.64
Earnings	4.97	2.28	-0.73	-2.40	0.93	4.11
Dividends	0.91	0.80	0.80	0.98	1.50	1.50
Payout Ratio	18%	35%	NM	NM	165%	37%
Prices - High	35⅛	33⅛	24½	18⅞	24⅝	28⅜
- Low	25⅝	21½	13⅞	11¾	12½	20¾
P/E Ratio - High	7	15	NM	NM	26	7
- Low	5	9	NM	NM	13	5

Income Statement Analysis (Million $)

	1994	%Chg	1993	%Chg	1992	%Chg	1991
Revs.	128,439	18%	108,448	8%	100,132	13%	88,286
Oper. Inc.	25,408	39%	18,228	31%	13,877	18%	11,762
Depr.	9,336	25%	7,468	11%	6,756	17%	5,778
Int. Exp.	7,744	6%	7,289	-8%	7,917	-14%	9,219
Pretax Inc.	8,789	120%	4,003	NM	-126	NM	-2,586
Eff. Tax Rate	38%	—	34%	—	NM	—	NM
Net Inc.	5,308	110%	2,529	NM	-501	NM	-2,257

Balance Sheet & Other Fin. Data (Million $)

	1994	1993	1992	1991	1990	1989
Cash	13,822	12,307	12,217	12,928	8,247	11,932
Total Assets	219,354	198,938	180,545	174,429	173,662	160,893
LT Debt	65,207	54,984	49,436	50,218	45,332	38,921
Total Debt	123,868	111,976	98,504	97,413	95,519	82,871
Common Eqty.	18,259	12,174	11,353	20,390	23,238	22,728
Cap. Exp.	9,470	6,814	5,790	5,847	7,163	6,767
Cash Flow	14,357	9,709	6,044	3,498	5,740	8,064

Ratio Analysis

	1994	1993	1992	1991	1990	1989
% Ret. on Assets	2.5	1.3	NM	NM	0.5	2.6
% Ret. on Equity	32.7	18.9	NM	NM	3.7	17.6
% LT Debt of Cap.	70.3	72.8	72.3	65.5	62.4	59.0

Dividend Data (Dividends have been paid since 1947 except for six quarterly omissions in 1982-3. A dividend reinvestment plan is available.)

Amt. of Div. $	Date Decl.	Ex-Div. Date	Stock of Record	Payment Date
0.225	Jul. 14	Jul. 27	Aug. 02	Sep. 01 '94
0.260	Oct. 13	Oct. 26	Nov. 01	Dec. 01 '94
0.260	Jan. 12	Jan. 24	Jan. 30	Mar. 01 '95
0.310	Apr. 13	Apr. 26	May. 02	Jun. 01 '95
0.310	Jul. 13	Jul. 31	Aug. 02	Sep. 01 '95

Data as orig. reptd.; bef. results of disc. opers. and/or spec. items. Per share data adj. for stk. divs. as of ex-div. date. E-Estimate. NA-Not Available. NM-Not Meaningful. NR-Not Ranked.

Office—The American Rd., Dearborn, MI 48121. **Tel**—(313) 322-3000. **Chrmn & CEO**—A. Trotman. **Vice Chrmn**—L. R. Ross. **VP-CFO**—J. M. Devine. **Secy**—J. M. Rintamaki. **Investor Contact**—Mel Stephens. **Dirs**—C. H. Chandler, M. D. Dingman, E. B. Ford II, W. C. Ford, W. C. Ford, Jr., R. C. Goizueta, I. O. Hockaday, Jr., M. J. Kravis, D. Lewis, E. R. Marram, K. H. Olsen, C. E. Reichardt, L. R. Ross, A. J. Trotman, C. R. Wharton, Jr. **Transfer Agent & Registrar**—Chemical Bank, NYC. **Incorporated** in Delaware in 1919. **Empl**-337,778. **S&P Analyst:** Joshua M. Harari, CFA

Foster Wheeler

NYSE Symbol **FWC**
In S&P 500

25-OCT-95

Industry: Building

Summary: This international company offers a broad range of design, engineering, construction, manufacturing, management, real estate development and environmental services.

S&P Opinion: Accumulate (★★★★)

Recent Price • 37	Yield • 2.1%
52 Wk Range • 39½-26⅝	12-Mo. P/E • 18.9

Earnings vs. Previous Year
▲=Up ▼=Down ▶=No Change

Quantitative Evaluations

Outlook
(1 Lowest—5 Highest)
• **3⁻**

Fair Value
• 37⅛

Risk
• **Average**

Earn./Div. Rank
• A

Technical Eval.
• **Bearish** since 9/95

Rel. Strength Rank
(1 Lowest—99 Highest)
• 57

Insider Activity
• **Neutral**

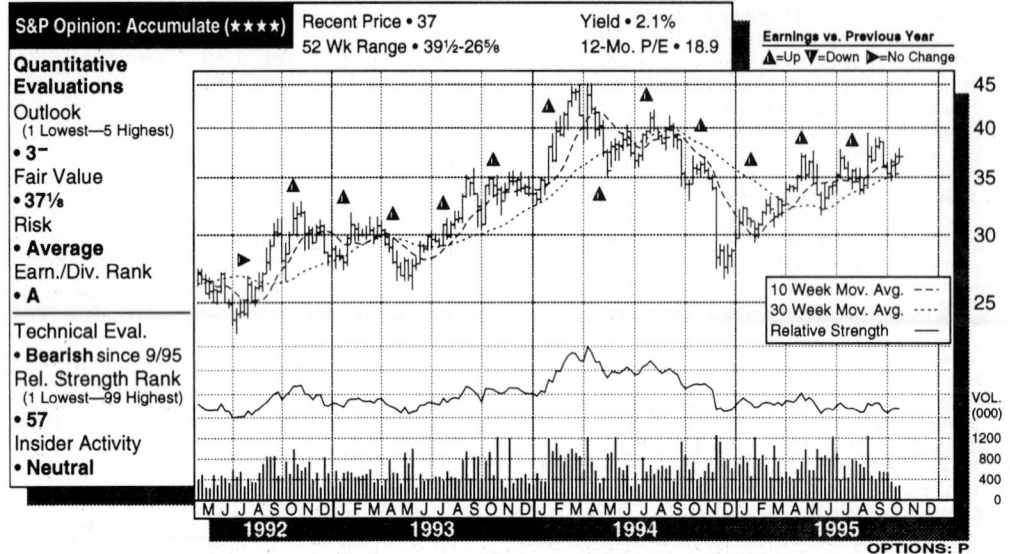

10 Week Mov. Avg. - - -
30 Week Mov. Avg. - - -
Relative Strength ——

VOL. (000)
1200 800 400 0

1992   1993   1994   1995

OPTIONS: P

Overview - 25-OCT-95

Assuming 2.6% U.S. GDP growth and stable business conditions in the rest of the world, we anticipate a 20% increase in operating revenues in 1996. Part of the increase will reflect existing backlog and the balance will come from the inclusion of Enserch Environmental and Ahlstrom Pyropower for the entire year. Margins in engineering and construction and energy equipment will probably be unchanged from 1995 while power systems should improve. With overall margins just about flat, the rise in operating income and earnings excluding charges will lag the gain in sales. Comparisions in 1996's second half will be more favorable as costs for integrating acquisitions lessen. Acquisitions, increased environmental work and a secular increase in the global demand for power will boost long-term sales and profits.

Valuation - 25-OCT-95

We continue to rate shares of FWC "accumulate" based on our expectation of an acceleration in revenue and earnings growth in 1996 and beyond. On a P/E basis FWC is selling at a small discount to the P/E's of other E&C companies we follow. Through mid-October FWC was up 27% versus a 23% gain in the S&P E&C index and a 27% rise the S&P 500 following an increase in the stock price in mid August. Prior to that time, FWC had lagged both the market and E&C index. We believe the share price should begin to outperform the market as it becomes apparent that investors have underestimated the company's long-term growth potential.

Key Stock Statistics

S&P EPS Est. 1995	1.25	Tang. Bk. Value/Share	11.74
P/E on S&P Est. 1995	29.6	Beta	1.90
S&P EPS Est. 1996	2.35	Shareholders	7,700
Dividend Rate/Share	0.78	Market cap. (B)	$ 1.3
Shs. outstg. (M)	35.9	Inst. holdings	65%
Avg. daily vol. (M)	0.061	Insider holdings	NA

Value of $10,000 invested 5 years ago: $ 20,098

Fiscal Year Ending Dec. 31

	1995	% Change	1994	% Change	1993	% Change
Revenues (Million $)						
1Q	643.7	35%	478.0	-19%	587.0	21%
2Q	686.2	18%	579.6	-10%	647.0	11%
3Q	—	—	542.6	-12%	616.4	-6%
4Q	—	—	670.9	-9%	733.5	-4%
Yr.	—	—	2,271	-12%	2,583	4%
Income (Million $)						
1Q	17.88	16%	15.40	21%	12.73	24%
2Q	18.89	13%	16.66	14%	14.56	19%
3Q	—	—	14.68	21%	12.15	27%
4Q	—	—	18.66	2%	18.26	36%
Yr.	—	—	65.41	13%	57.70	27%
Earnings Per Share ($)						
1Q	0.50	16%	0.43	19%	0.36	24%
2Q	0.53	13%	0.47	15%	0.41	21%
3Q	E0.45	10%	0.41	21%	0.34	26%
4Q	E-0.23	NM	0.52	2%	0.51	34%
Yr.	E1.25	-32%	1.83	13%	1.62	27%

Next earnings report expected: late October

Foster Wheeler

Business Summary - 25-OCT-95

Foster Wheeler offers design, engineering and construction services through its worldwide subsidiaries to the chemical, petroleum refining and power generating industries. It also provides hazardous waste management. Revenues and pretax income in 1994 were derived as follows:

	Revs.	Profits
Engineering & construction	69%	50%
Energy equipment	24%	38%
Power systems	7%	12%

Operations outside of North America accounted for 46% of 1994's revenues and 56% of pretax profit.

The engineering and construction group designs, engineers and constructs process plants and fired heaters for oil refineries, synthetic fuels, chemical producers. E&C also provides environmental services for hazardous and mixed waste investigation and remediation, pollution control systems, wastewater treatment and other environmental services.

The energy equipment group designs and fabricates steam generators and condensers, mass transfer equipment, tower packings, industrial wire mesh for the power generation and chemical separations industries worldwide. It also provides natural gas processing and engineering and construction.

Power systems is engaged in the owning/leasing for third parties of solid waste-to-energy and cogeneration plants. Waste-to-energy projects take approximately two to three years from award of a contract and the signing of a service agreement with a commnuity to the beginning of construction.

Corporate and financial services consist of the company's insurance, trading and real estate operations and miscellaneous manufacturing.

Important Developments

Oct. '95—FWC announced that it had completed the acquisition of Ahlstrom Pyropower Sector for some $200 million. The final price is contingent upon Ahlstrom Pyropower's performance for the balance of 1995. Ahlstrom Pyropower's sales are expected to reach $350 million in 1995; it has a current backlog of $550 million and 1,500 employees. Ahlstrom Pyropower is based in San Diego and manufactures fluidized bed combustion systems and provides boiler and plant operations and maintainence systems. FWC plans to incur a fourth quarter reorganization charge of about $46 million pretax to reduce capacity and employment levels. FWC expects the acquisition to make a positive contribution to earnings in 1996.

Capitalization

Long Term Debt: $515,618,000 (6/95).

Per Share Data ($)

(Year Ended Dec. 31)

	1994	1993	1992	1991	1990	1989
Tangible Bk. Val.	10.83	11.10	10.52	14.72	14.11	12.86
Cash Flow	3.05	2.84	2.49	2.20	1.76	1.44
Earnings	1.83	1.62	1.28	1.22	1.08	0.95
Dividends	0.72	0.65	0.59	0.53	0.49	0.44
Payout Ratio	39%	40%	46%	44%	45%	46%
Prices - High	45⅛	35⅞	32⅞	34	28¾	22
- Low	26⅝	25⅞	23	20¼	17¾	14¼
P/E Ratio - High	25	22	26	28	27	23
- Low	15	16	18	17	16	15

Income Statement Analysis (Million $)

	1994	%Chg	1993	%Chg	1992	%Chg	1991
Revs.	2,234	-14%	2,583	4%	2,495	25%	1,992
Oper. Inc.	165	25%	132	-1%	134	46%	92.0
Depr.	43.7	NM	43.7	NM	43.3	25%	34.7
Int. Exp.	35.4	5%	33.8	-6%	35.9	11%	32.4
Pretax Inc.	112	13%	99	41%	70.3	10%	63.8
Eff. Tax Rate	37%	—	39%	—	32%	—	28%
Net Inc.	65.4	13%	57.7	27%	45.5	5%	43.3

Balance Sheet & Other Fin. Data (Million $)

	1994	1993	1992	1991	1990	1989
Cash	354	377	271	233	191	221
Curr. Assets	1,113	983	925	838	750	671
Total Assets	2,063	1,806	1,763	1,635	1,441	1,181
Curr. Liab.	891	779	721	572	565	404
LT Debt	467	397	427	441	282	241
Common Eqty.	456	400	387	538	514	467
Total Cap.	953	824	841	1,006	823	727
Cap. Exp.	39.0	28.0	56.0	119	154	170
Cash Flow	109	101	88.8	78.0	62.4	50.9

Ratio Analysis

	1994	1993	1992	1991	1990	1989
Curr. Ratio	1.2	1.3	1.3	1.5	1.3	1.7
% LT Debt of Cap.	49.0	48.2	50.8	43.9	34.2	33.2
% Net Inc.of Revs.	2.9	2.2	1.8	2.2	2.3	2.7
% Ret. on Assets	3.4	3.2	2.7	2.8	2.9	2.9
% Ret. on Equity	15.2	14.6	9.8	8.2	7.8	7.3

Dividend Data —Dividends have been paid since 1960. A dividend reinvestment plan is available. A "poison pill" stock purchase rights plan was adopted in 1987.

Amt. of Div. $	Date Decl.	Ex-Div. Date	Stock of Record	Payment Date
0.185	Oct. 24	Nov. 08	Nov. 15	Dec. 15 '94
0.185	Jan. 31	Feb. 09	Feb. 15	Mar. 15 '95
0.195	Apr. 25	May. 09	May. 15	Jun. 15 '95
0.195	Jul. 25	Aug. 11	Aug. 15	Sep. 15 '95

Data as orig. reptd.; bef. results of disc. opers. and/or spec. items. Per share data adj. for stk. divs. as of ex-div. date. E-Estimated. NA-Not Available. NM-Not Meaningful. NR-Not Ranked.

Office—Perryville Corporate Park, Clinton, NJ 08809-4000. **Tel**—(908) 730-4000. **Chrmn, Pres & CEO**—R. J. Swift. **EVP & CFO**—D. J. Roberts. **VP & Secy**—J. E. Deones. **Dirs**—E. D. Atkinson, L. E. Azzato, L. E. Boren, M. C. Goss, K. A. DeGhetto, J. A. Hinds, E. J. Ferland, H. E. Kennedy, J. J. Melone, F. E. Perkins, D. J. Roberts, R. J. Swift, J. Timko, Jr., C. Y. C. Tse, R. Van Buren. **Transfer Agent & Registrar**—Mellon Securities Trust Co., Pittsburgh. **Incorporated** in New York in 1927. **Empl**-11,685. **S&P Analyst:** Leo Larkin

Freeport-McM. Copper & Gold

NYSE Symbol FCX.B Options on Phila (Mar-Jun-Sep-Dec) In S&P 500

Price	Range	P–E Ratio	Dividend	Yield	S&P Ranking	Beta
Aug. 21'95	1995					
24¼	27⅜–23⅜	36	0.60	2.5%	NR	0.18

Summary

This company owns 81.3% of P.T. Freeport Indonesia (PT-FI), which explores for, mines and mills copper, gold and silver in Indonesia. In July 1995 Freeport-McMoran Inc. (FTX) distributed its 84.2% stake in FCXB to FTX shareholders. In mid-1995 FTX also sold 23.9 million of the Class A shares to RTZ Corp., a major international mining concern and formed a venture with that firm to develop Freeport-McMoran Copper & Gold's Indonesian concession.

Current Outlook

Earnings for 1995 are estimated at $0.90 a share, up sharply from 1994's $0.38 (after an $0.08 gain). Dividends, at $0.15 quarterly, are not expected to be increased before late 1996.

Gold volumes are expected to increase significantly in 1995 reflecting the completion of a mill expansion and better grade ores. Gold prices are likely to be flat. Copper volumes also will benefit from the mill expansion. Copper margins will widen reflecting higher prices, lower production and delivery costs and the assumption of exploration costs by RTZ Corp. Silver production and prices are expected to be higher. Rio Tinto Minera will operate at a loss, as its smelter was shut down for half of 1995's second quarter as part of its expansion program. Limiting comparisons will be higher interest expense as FCX no longer capitalizes costs related to its mill expansion.

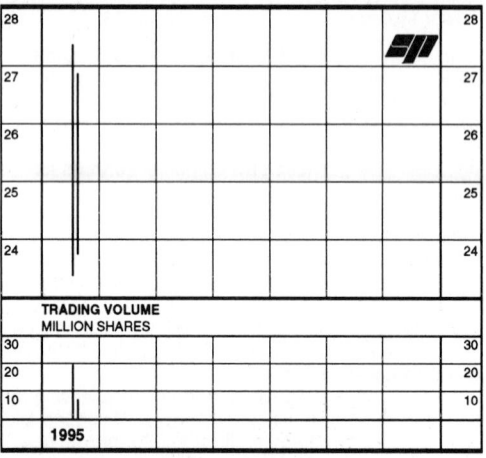

Revenues (Million $)

Quarter:	1995	1994	1993	1992
Mar.	409	266	134	107
Jun.	421	281	215	242
Sep.		313	262	157
Dec.		351	316	209
	1,212	926	714	

Revenues for 1995's first half climbed 51%, year to year. Net income was up 132%. After higher preferred dividends, per share earnings were $0.41, versus $0.11.

[1]Common Share Earnings ($)

Quarter:	1995	1994	1993	1992
Mar.	0.21	0.07	0.02	0.10
Jun.	0.20	0.05	d0.11	0.27
Sep.	E0.25	0.07	0.10	0.12
Dec.	E0.24	0.20	0.15	0.17
	E0.90	0.38	0.16	0.66

Important Developments

Jul. '95— Freeport-McMoran Inc. (FTZ) distributed to its shareholders all 117,909,323 FCXB shares (84.2%) it held. In July FTZ sold 2,400,000 FCXA shares to RTZ Corporation PLC, a major international mining firm for $20.90 each; FTZ sold 21,500,000 FCXA shares to RTZ in May also at $20.90 each. The transactions reflect a far reaching partnership formed between RTZ and FCX in May. Under the terms of that agreement, RTZ will invest $100 million towards exploration in FCX's Indonesian concessions and obtain a 40% share of the cash flow derived from any new projects or expansions emerging from that investment. Later, RTZ will invest another $750 million for exploration and development but will receive 100% of the cash flow until its $750 million is repaid and receive a 40% share thereafter.

Next earnings report expected in late October.

Per Share Data ($)

Yr. End Dec. 31	1994	[2]1993	1992	1991	1990	1989	1988	1987
Tangible Bk. Val.	**1.68**	1.86	2.16	0.95	1.15	0.84	0.82	NA
Cash Flow	**0.75**	0.50	0.91	0.77	0.74	0.72	0.68	NA
Earnings[3]	**0.38**	0.16	0.66	0.56	0.54	0.58	0.55	0.26
Dividends	**0.600**	0.600	0.600	0.550	0.690	0.557	0.159	NA
Payout Ratio	**158%**	379%	91%	98%	128%	96%	29%	NA
Prices—High	**NA**	NA	NA	NA	NA	NA	NA	NA
Low	**NA**	NA	NA	NA	NA	NA	NA	NA
P/E Ratio—	**NA**	NA	NA	NA	NA	NA	NA	NA

Data as orig. reptd. Adj. for stk. div(s) of 100% Jun. 1992, 100% Apr. 1990, 100% May 1989. **1.** Based on comb. Cl. A & Cl. B com shs. **2.** Refl. merger or acquis. **3.** Based on comb. Cl.A & Cl.B com shs. bef. spec. item(s) of -0.05 in 1993, -0.03 in 1991. d-Deficit. E-Estimated. NA-Not Available.

Income Data (Million $)

Year Ended Dec. 31	Revs.	Oper. Inc.	% Oper. Inc. of Revs.	Cap. Exp.	Depr.	Int. Exp.	Net Bef. Taxes	Eff. Tax Rate	[1]Net Inc.	% Net Inc. of Revs.	Cash Flow
1994	1,212	323	26.6	743	75.1	35.1	[2]279	44.2%	130	10.7	154
[3]1993	926	244	26.3	760	67.9	39.8	[2]137	49.2%	61	6.6	100
1992	714	325	45.5	437	48.3	42.9	[2]265	39.2%	130	18.2	171
1991	468	216	46.2	246	38.4	39.8	160	28.5%	102	21.8	140
1990	434	240	55.3	188	35.5	21.7	192	44.5%	93	21.3	128
1989	368	228	62.0	138	24.6	7.3	206	43.6%	99	26.8	123
1988	335	221	66.0	66	20.9	5.4	200	44.5%	94	28.1	115
1987	190	100	52.9	29	23.3	3.6	75	32.5%	43	22.8	NA

Balance Sheet Data (Million $)

Dec. 31	Cash	Assets	Curr. Liab.	Ratio	Total Assets	% Ret. on Assets	Long Term Debt	Common Equity	Total Cap.	% LT Debt of Cap.	% Ret. on Equity
1994	44.0	603	432.0	1.4	3,040	5.0	526	346	2,396	21.9	21.5
1993	14.0	428	288.0	1.5	2,117	3.1	212	373	1,641	12.9	7.9
1992	372.0	661	169.0	3.9	1,694	8.9	645	422	1,510	42.7	40.5
1991	80.8	510	41.7	12.2	1,158	11.1	632	173	964	65.6	53.5
1990	44.4	156	67.5	2.3	675	16.6	294	209	605	48.6	51.1
1989	60.3	136	62.5	2.2	415	28.0	130	144	351	37.0	69.6
1988	64.2	135	61.4	2.2	291	NA	40	140	229	17.5	NA
1987	37.4	89	34.6	2.6	198	23.4	40	97	162	24.7	43.7

Data as orig. reptd. **1.** Bef. spec. item(s). **2.** Incl. equity in earns. of nonconsol. subs. **3.** Refl. merger or acquis. NA-Not Available.

Business Summary

Freeport-McMoRan Copper & Gold owns 81.3% of P.T. Freeport Indonesia, Inc. (PT-FI), which explores for, mines and mills copper, gold and silver on Irian Jaya, the western Indonesian half of the island of New Guinea. PT-FI's original 24,700 acre mining area and a nearby 4.8 million acre exploration area are covered by a 30-year contract of work (with two 10-year extensions permitted), signed with the Indonesian government in 1991. In 1994, 80%-owned P.T. IRJA Eastern Minerals and the Government signed a 30-year contract of work, with two 10-year extensions allowed, covering an adjacent 2.5 million-acre area.

Mill throughput in 1994 averaged 72,500 metric tons a day, versus 1993's 62,300. PT-FI achieved record 1994 sales of 701 million lbs. of copper (average realization $1.02/lb.) and 794,700 oz. of gold ($381/oz.). At year-end 1994, proved and probable copper and gold reserves were 28.0 billion lbs. and 39.6 million oz., respectively.

In mid-1995 mining and milling capacity was expanded to 118,000 tons/day to an annual output rate of about 1.1 billion lbs. of copper and 1.5 million oz. of gold.

In early 1995 FCX reached an agreement with Mitsubishi Materials Corp. and Fluor Daniel Inc. to build a 200,000 metric ton copper smelter/refinery in Gresik, East Java, Indonesia. FCX would have a 10% interest in the $550 million facility which is expected to commence production in late 1998.

Wholly owned Rio Tinto Minera, S.A. (RTM) operates a Spanish copper smelter with annual production capacity of 150,000 metric tons of metal. In July 1994, RTM accepted a $270 million project financing, primarily to raise capacity to 270,000 tons by early 1996.

Dividend Data

Dividends have been paid since 1988.

Capitalization

Long Term Debt: $831,139,000 (6/95).

$1.25 Cum. Preferred Stock: 14,000,000 shs., ea. conv. into 0.835 of a Cl. A com. sh.

Gold Depositary Preferred Stock: 6,000,000 shs., ea. redeemable 8/1/03 in cash for the value of 0.1 oz. of gold; 4,305,580 Series II shs., ea. redeemable 2/1/06 in cash for the value of 0.1 oz. of gold.

Silver Depositary Pfd. Stk.: 4,760,000 shs., ea. redeemable in eight annual installments for the value of 0.5 oz. of silver from 8/1/99 through 8/1/06.

$1.75 Depositary Preference Stock: 8,976,000 shs., ea. conv. into 1.021 of a Cl. A com. sh.

Class A Com. Stock: 84,680,708 shs. ($0.10 par). RTZ Corporation hold 28%. Shareholders of record: 19,873.

Class B Common Stock: 139,980,763 shs. ($0.10 par).

Office—First Interstate Bank Building, One East First St., Suite 1600, Reno, NV 89501. **Tel**—(504) 582-4000. **Chrmn**—J. R. Moffett. **Vice Chrmn**—R. L. Latiolais. **Pres & CEO**—G. A. Mealey. **SVP & CFO**—R. C. Adkerson. **Secy**—M. C. Kilanowski, Jr. **Investor Contact**—Craig E. Saporito. **Dirs**—R. W. Bruce III, T. B. Coleman, W. H. Cunningham, R. A. Day, L. O. Erdahl, R. Grossman, W. B. Harrison,Jr., H. A. Kissinger, B. L. Lackey, R. L. Latiolais, G. K. McDonald, G. A. Mealey, J. R. Moffett, G. Putnam, B. M. Ranklin, Jr., B. C. Schmidt, W. F. Siegel, E. E. Smith, E. Umene, J. T. Wharton, W. W. Woods, Jr. **Transfer Agent & Registrar**—Mellon Securities Trust Co., Ridgefield Park, NJ. **Incorporated** in Delaware in 1987. **Empl**—7,324.

Fruit of the Loom

NYSE Symbol **FTL**
In S&P 500

24-AUG-95 Industry:
Textiles

Summary: This leading international basic apparel maker emphasizes value-priced branded products for consumers of all ages.

| S&P Opinion: Avoid (★★) | Recent Price • 24⅝ | Yield • Nil |
| | 52 Wk Range • 29⅞-19⅞ | 12-Mo. P/E • 35.7 |

Quantitative Evaluations

Outlook
(1 Lowest—5 Highest)
• **2⁻**

Fair Value
• **23¾**

Risk
• **Average**

Earn./Div. Rank
• **NR**

Technical Eval.
• **Bearish** since 12/93

Rel. Strength Rank
(1 Lowest—99 Highest)
• **52**

Insider Activity
• **Neutral**

Earnings vs. Previous Year
▲=Up ▼=Down ▶=No Change

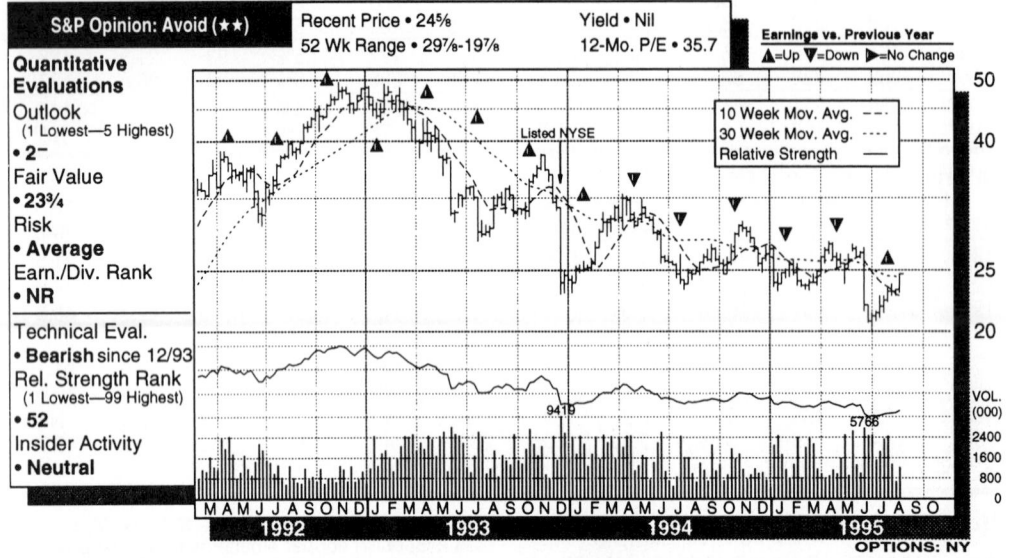

- 10 Week Mov. Avg. — —
- 30 Week Mov. Avg. ......
- Relative Strength ——

Listed NYSE

VOL. (000)

OPTIONS: NY

Overview - 24-AUG-95

Sales are expected to maintain their upward momentum in 1995. Increased market share in North
America, wider distribution in Europe, expansion of activewear and casualwear product lines, new product
introductions, and expanded offerings of existing product line should all contribute to sales growth. Margins
should remain under pressure, reflecting problems in
the screen print business and the inability to fully pass
on higher raw material prices. Comparisons will benefit
from the absence of $68 million of pretax charges re-
lated to inventory and goodwill writeoffs.

Valuation - 24-AUG-95

Shares of this maker of basic apparel have traded in a
narrow range since early 1994, reflecting earnings
pressure resulting from higher raw material prices,
manufacturing inefficiencies, uneven demand, and
special charges. Results at the screen print business,
once believed to be a high growth area, have been
particularly disappointing. As a result, 1995 first half
earnings were lower than expected, and we expect
second half earnings to continue under pressure.
Athough we currently fell that 1996 earnings could recover somewhat, they are not expected to reach
1994's record level. We therefore recommend that investors avoid the shares.

Key Stock Statistics

S&P EPS Est. 1995	2.05	Tang. Bk. Value/Share	3.19
P/E on S&P Est. 1995	12.0	Beta	1.45
S&P EPS Est. 1996	2.45	Shareholders	43,200
Dividend Rate/Share	Nil	Market cap. (B)	$ 1.8
Shs. outstg. (M)	75.9	Inst. holdings	76%
Avg. daily vol. (M)	0.213	Insider holdings	NA

Value of $10,000 invested 5 years ago: $ 16,554

Fiscal Year Ending Dec. 31

	1995	% Change	1994	% Change	1993	% Change
Revenues (Million $)						
1Q	528.2	21%	438.2	2%	429.0	1%
2Q	724.8	14%	635.2	21%	523.0	-2%
3Q	—	—	640.4	32%	484.2	7%
4Q	—	—	584.0	30%	448.3	NM
Yr.	—	—	2,298	22%	1,884	2%
Income (Million $)						
1Q	16.50	-34%	25.10	-43%	44.10	22%
2Q	39.70	3%	38.70	-34%	58.40	2%
3Q	—	—	40.20	-17%	48.60	5%
4Q	—	—	-43.70	NM	61.70	26%
Yr.	—	—	60.30	-72%	212.8	13%
Earnings Per Share ($)						
1Q	0.22	-33%	0.33	-43%	0.58	21%
2Q	0.52	2%	0.51	-34%	0.77	3%
3Q	E0.55	4%	0.53	-17%	0.64	5%
4Q	E0.76	NM	-0.58	NM	0.81	27%
Yr.	E2.05	159%	0.79	-72%	2.80	13%

Next earnings report expected: mid October

Business Summary - 24-AUG-95

Fruit of the Loom (FTL) is a vertically integrated, leading international producer of basic, value-priced apparel, emphasizing branded products for consumers ranging from infants to senior citizens. It is the successor to Northwest Industries, which was acquired by William Farley in 1985. In late 1993, the company acquired Salem Sportswear, a maker of licensed sportswear, for $157.6 million. During 1994, it purchased the sportswear unit of Jostens, Inc., Artex, for $45 million; the assets of The Gitano Group, Inc., a jeans and sportswear manufacturer, for $91.4 million; and Daniel Young International, which does business under the Pro Player brand, for $55.7 million.

FTL offers a broad array of men's and boys' basic and fashion underwear; women's and girls' underwear; infants' and toddlers' apparel; family socks; activewear for the imprint market; casualwear; licensed sports apparel; and jeanswear.The company owns the Fruit of the Loom, BVD, Gitano, Best, Screen Stars and Lofteez trademarks which are used on underwear, activewear and sportswear. FTL also owns the Salem, Salem Sportswear, Office Fan and Pro Player trademarks for its licensed sportswear business. Licensed brands include Munsingwear, Wilson, Kangaroo, Botany 500 and John Henry trademarks used on underwear and certain activewear. The company also licenses cartoon character logos (i.e. Little Mermaid). In addition, it has a licensing agreement with Warnaco and other companies, which produce apparel with the Fruit of the Loom logo.

In 1994, foreign sales accounted for 14.2% of total sales and 8.5% of operating profits.

FTL sells its products to more than 22,000 customers, including all major discount and mass merchandisers, wholesale clubs and screen printers. Products are sold by a nationally organized direct sales force of full-time employees. In 1994, the largest two customers accounted for 15.6% and 11.8% of total sales, respectively.

Capital spending, primarily on acquisitions, totaled $246.4 million in 1994. The company anticipates capital spending of $125 to $140 million in 1995, largely to enhance distribution and yarn capabilities and to establish offshore assembly operations.

Important Developments

Jul. '95—FTL attributed a small earnings increase in the 1995 second quarter to a 14% increase in sales, led by strong volume of men's and boys' underwear, childrenswear, ladies and girls' underwear and family socks. Strength in these areas offset disappointing results in the screenprint T-shirt business.

Capitalization

Long Term Debt: $1,640,600 (6/95).

Per Share Data ($)

(Year Ended Dec. 31)

	1994	1993	1992	1991	1990	1989
Tangible Bk. Val.	2.11	2.00	0.59	-1.97	-7.18	-9.04
Cash Flow	2.67	4.25	3.71	2.81	2.47	2.27
Earnings	0.79	2.80	2.48	1.60	1.25	1.17
Dividends	Nil	Nil	Nil	Nil	Nil	Nil
Payout Ratio	Nil	Nil	Nil	Nil	Nil	Nil
Prices - High	33	49¼	49⅝	28	15⅜	16
- Low	23	22⅞	26½	7⅝	6⅛	6⅛
P/E Ratio - High	42	18	20	18	12	14
- Low	29	8	11	5	5	5

Income Statement Analysis (Million $)

	1994	%Chg	1993	%Chg	1992	%Chg	1991
Revs.	2,298	22%	1,884	2%	1,855	14%	1,628
Oper. Inc.	436	-11%	492	-2%	503	25%	403
Depr.	143	30%	110	18%	93.2	11%	83.8
Int. Exp.	104	42%	73.0	-11%	82.0	-29%	115
Pretax Inc.	134	-63%	367	15%	320	59%	201
Eff. Tax Rate	548%	—	42%	—	41%	—	45%
Net Inc.	60.0	-72%	213	13%	189	70%	111

Balance Sheet & Other Fin. Data (Million $)

	1994	1993	1992	1991	1990	1989
Cash	49.4	74.2	57.4	31.4	59.6	16.7
Curr. Assets	1,077	943	744	656	629	453
Total Assets	3,164	2,734	2,282	2,115	2,151	1,878
Curr. Liab.	332	251	434	370	495	350
LT Debt	1,440	1,194	756	811	1,014	988
Common Eqty.	1,126	1,047	855	689	418	327
Total Cap.	2,609	2,292	1,611	1,500	1,432	1,445
Cap. Exp.	246	263	189	74.0	158	85.0
Cash Flow	203	323	282	195	153	140

Ratio Analysis

	1994	1993	1992	1991	1990	1989
Curr. Ratio	3.2	3.8	1.7	1.8	1.3	1.3
% LT Debt of Cap.	55.2	52.1	46.9	54.1	70.8	68.4
% Net Inc.of Revs.	2.6	11.3	10.2	6.8	5.4	5.5
% Ret. on Assets	2.0	8.5	8.5	4.7	3.8	3.9
% Ret. on Equity	5.5	22.4	24.3	18.6	20.7	24.6

Dividend Data —The company does not anticipate paying dividends in the next several years.

Data as orig. reptd.; bef. results of disc. opers. and/or spec. items. Per share data adj. for stk. divs. as of ex-div. date. E-Estimated. NA-Not Available. NM-Not Meaningful. NR-Not Ranked.

Office—233 South Wacker Dr., 5000 Sears Tower, Chicago, IL 60606. **Tel**—(312) 876-1724. **Chrmn & CEO**—W. Farley. **Pres & COO**—J. B. Holland. **EVP & CFO**—L. K. Switzer. **VP & Treas**—E. C. Shanks. **Investor Contact**—Mark Steinkrauss. **Dirs**—O. A. Al Askari, D. S. Bookshester, W. Farley, J. B. Holland, L. W. Jennings, H. A. Johnson, R. C. Lappin, A. L. Weil, B. Wolfson. **Transfer Agent & Registrar**—Chemical Bank, NYC. **Incorporated** in Delaware in 1985. **Empl**-37,500. **S&P Analyst:** Elizabeth Vandeventer

GTE Corp.

NYSE Symbol **GTE**
In S&P 500

31-JUL-95

Industry:
Telecommunications

Summary: GTE is the largest U.S.-based local telephone holding company and the second largest cellular carrier.

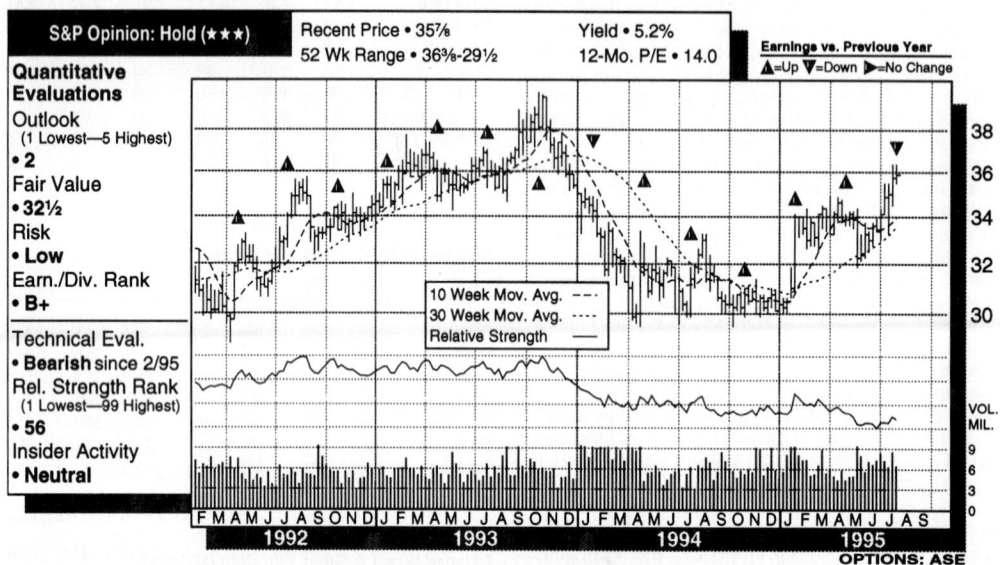

S&P Opinion: Hold (★★★)	Recent Price • 35⅞	Yield • 5.2%
	52 Wk Range • 36⅜-29½	12-Mo. P/E • 14.0

Earnings vs. Previous Year
▲=Up ▼=Down ▶=No Change

Quantitative Evaluations

Outlook
(1 Lowest—5 Highest)
• 2

Fair Value
• 32½

Risk
• Low

Earn./Div. Rank
• B+

Technical Eval.
• **Bearish** since 2/95

Rel. Strength Rank
(1 Lowest—99 Highest)
• 56

Insider Activity
• **Neutral**

10 Week Mov. Avg. - - -
30 Week Mov. Avg. ·····
Relative Strength ——

OPTIONS: ASE

Overview - 28-JUL-95

As traditional telephone services face increasing competition, GTE is seeking faster growth opporunties by upgrading its core network to provide data transport and video services. The company is also aggressively moving to rationalize costs for a more competitive environment. Growth prospects in the near-term will be led by strong wireless operations. Through alliances with other wireless carriers and PCS investments, GTE hopes to increase wireless coverage across its telephone operating markets, leveraging its investment in its core network and its brand awareness. The company continues to invest overseas, with the goal of doubling international revenues, to $5 billion, in five years. International ventures should make growing contributions to profits.

Valuation - 28-JUL-95

The shares have lagged the S&P 500 in 1995, reflecting concerns about increasing competition in California, the company's largest market. The opening of that market to toll competition will limit earnings growth in 1995. In addition, state regulators have proposed opening the entire local market to competition. However, long-term results will benefit from completion of an aggressive restructuring program, cutting annual costs by $1 billion, and from rapid cellular subscriber growth. With a healthy dividend yield, the shares are an attractive holding for total return.

Key Stock Statistics

S&P EPS Est. 1995	2.55	Tang. Bk. Value/Share	8.72
P/E on S&P Est. 1995	14.1	Beta	0.69
S&P EPS Est. 1996	2.78	Shareholders	562,000
Dividend Rate/Share	1.88	Market cap. (B)	$ 34.8
Shs. outstg. (M)	970.0	Inst. holdings	42%
Avg. daily vol. (M)	1.537	Insider holdings	NA

Value of $10,000 invested 5 years ago: $ 13,747

Fiscal Year Ending Dec. 31

	1995	% Change	1994	% Change	1993	% Change
Revenues (Million $)						
1Q	4,762	NM	4,750	-2%	4,830	NM
2Q	5,045	2%	4,960	NM	4,920	-3%
3Q	--	—	5,000	1%	4,940	NM
4Q	--	—	5,250	4%	5,060	-1%
Yr.	--	—	19,940	NM	19,750	-1%
Income (Million $)						
1Q	545.0	8%	504.0	10%	460.0	19%
2Q	582.0	-2%	595.0	36%	438.0	8%
3Q	—	—	659.0	18%	558.0	22%
4Q	—	—	693.0	NM	-466.0	NM
Yr.	—	—	2,451	148%	990.0	-45%
Earnings Per Share ($)						
1Q	0.56	8%	0.52	8%	0.48	12%
2Q	0.60	-3%	0.62	35%	0.46	2%
3Q	E0.67	—	0.69	17%	0.59	13%
4Q	E0.72	—	0.72	NM	-0.50	NM
Yr.	E2.55	—	2.55	148%	1.03	-47%

Next earnings report expected: mid October

Business Summary - 31-JUL-95

GTE is the largest U.S.-based telephone holding company. Other units are in unregulated telecom and other businesses. Segment contributions to 1994 sales and operating income were:

	Sales	Income
Telephone operations	80%	92%
Telecommunications products and services	20%	8%

In the U.S., GTE provides local exchange telephone service through over 17 million access lines in portions of 29 states. The company is moving to improve the competitive position of its telephone operations by selling or trading non-strategic operations. Through a 20.4% interest in the Venezuelan national telephone company, GTE provides local, national and international long-distance services in that country. Other subsidiaries provide telephone service through about 3 million access lines in Canada and the Dominican Republic.

GTE has formed a marketing alliance with Southwestern Bell (SBC) for wireless and associated wired telecommunications services in Texas. The agreement essentially allows each company to compete as an additional cellular brand on the other's cellular network. The alliance will increase the value of GTE's cellular assets in Texas by extending its wireless reach to more of its wireline operating territory and through increased traffic generated on its network by SBC.

The telecommunications products and services segment provides directory advertising; intelligence and electronic defense systems; specialized telecommunications services and systems; aircraft-passenger telecommunications; and cellular telephone service in the U.S., Canada, Venezuela, Argentina and the Dominican Republic. At December 31, 1994, GTE provided cellular service to about 2,339,000 subscribers in the U.S.

In December 1994, GTE agreed to buy the approximately 10 million publicly held shares of Contel Cellular for $25.50 each. GTE acquired 90% of Contel Cellular in its 1991 merger with Contel Corp.

Important Developments

Jul. '95—California state regulators voted to allow full competition in the state's local telephone market, beginning January 1, 1996.

Mar. '95—Bidding was completed in the first phase of FCC auctions for broadband personal communications services (PCS) licenses. GTE won licenses in Atlanta, Seattle, Cincinnati and Denver. Separately, the company chose AT&T and General Instrument to equip a $200 million project to bring cable television services to 900,000 telephone customers in three markets.

Capitalization

Long Term Debt: $12,072,000,000 (3/95).
Minority Interest: $2,132,000,000.
Red. Cum. Preferred Stock: $107,000,000.
Cum. Preferred Stock: $10,000,000.

Per Share Data ($)

(Year Ended Dec. 31)

	1994	1993	1992	1991	1990	1989
Tangible Bk. Val.	8.63	7.75	8.30	9.75	11.52	12.01
Cash Flow	6.13	4.65	5.58	5.38	6.40	6.04
Earnings	2.55	1.03	1.95	1.69	2.26	2.08
Dividends	1.88	1.83	1.76	1.64	1.52	1.40
Payout Ratio	74%	178%	94%	98%	68%	68%
Prices - High	35¼	39⅞	35¾	35	36	35⅝
- Low	29½	34⅛	28⅞	27½	23½	21½
P/E Ratio - High	14	39	18	21	16	17
- Low	12	33	15	16	10	10

Income Statement Analysis (Million $)

	1994	%Chg	1993	%Chg	1992	%Chg	1991
Revs.	19,944	NM	19,748	-1%	19,984	2%	19,621
Depr.	3,432	NM	3,419	4%	3,289	1%	3,254
Maint.	NA	—	2,136	2%	2,097	-5%	2,206
Constr. Credits	28.0	-30%	40.0	-7%	43.0	-23%	56.0
Eff. Tax Rate	37%	—	34%	—	34%	—	29%
Net Inc.	2,451	148%	990	-45%	1,787	17%	1,529

Balance Sheet & Other Fin. Data (Million $)

	1994	1993	1992	1991	1990	1989
Gross Prop.	44,287	43,099	43,354	41,846	34,890	NA
Net Prop.	26,631	26,362	27,300	26,969	22,327	NA
Cap. Exp.	4,192	3,893	3,909	3,965	3,453	NA
Total Cap.	27,899	27,002	28,994	33,807	26,787	24,986
Fxd. Chgs. Cov.	4.4	3.4	2.8	2.5	2.7	NA
Capitalization:						
LT Debt	12,163	13,019	14,182	16,049	NA	NA
Pfd.	1,741	1,373	1,363	1,785	1,818	NA
Common	10,473	9,482	9,964	10,854	8,647	NA

Ratio Analysis

	1994	1993	1992	1991	1990	1989
% Ret. on Revs.	12.3	5.0	8.9	7.8	8.4	8.1
% Ret. On Invest.Cap	13.9	8.2	10.4	9.6	10.5	NA
% Return On Com.Eqty	23.3	10.0	16.9	14.5	18.1	NA
% Earn. on Net Prop.	12.5	7.4	12.0	11.5	12.5	NA
% LT Debt of Cap.	37.4	54.5	55.6	56.0	53.4	NA
Capital. % Pfd.	5.3	5.8	5.3	6.2	8.1	NA
Capital. % Common	32.1	39.7	39.1	37.8	38.5	NA

Dividend Data

(Dividends have been paid since 1936. A dividend reinvestment plan is available. A poison pill stock purchase rights plan was adopted in 1986.)

Amt. of Div. $	Date Decl.	Ex-Div. Date	Stock of Record	Payment Date
0.470	Aug. 04	Aug. 16	Aug. 22	Oct. 01 '94
0.470	Nov. 10	Nov. 16	Nov. 22	Jan. 01 '95
0.470	Jan. 13	Feb. 14	Feb. 21	Apr. 01 '95
0.470	Apr. 19	May. 16	May. 22	Jul. 01 '95

Office—One Stamford Forum, Stamford, CT 06904. **Tel**—(203) 965-2000. **Chrmn & CEO**—C. R. Lee. **Pres**—K. B. Foster. **SVP-Fin & CFO**—J. M. Kelly. **Secy**—M. Drost. **VP & Treas**—J. Murphy. **Dirs**—E. L. Artzt, J. R. Barker, E. H. Budd, K. B. Foster, J. L. Johnson, R. W. Jones, J. L. Ketelson, C. R. Lee, M. T. Masin, S. O. Moose, R. E. Palmer, H. Sloan, R. D. Storey. **Transfer Agents & Registrars**—First National Bank of Boston. **Incorporated** in New York in 1935. **Empl**- 111,000. **S&P Analyst:** Kevin J. Gooley

Gannett Co.

NYSE Symbol **GCI**
In S&P 500

26-JUL-95 Industry:
Publishing

Summary: This leading newspaper publisher also has interests in broadcasting (10 television stations and 11 radio stations) and is the largest outdoor advertising company in North America.

S&P Opinion: Hold (★★★)

Recent Price • 53¾
52 Wk Range • 56⅜-46⅛

Yield • 2.5%
12-Mo. P/E • 15.8

Earnings vs. Previous Year
▲=Up ▼=Down ▶=No Change

Quantitative Evaluations

Outlook
(1 Lowest—5 Highest)
• **4⁻**

Fair Value
• **58⅝**

Risk
• **Low**

Earn./Div. Rank
• **A**

Technical Eval.
• **Bearish** since 6/95

Rel. Strength Rank
(1 Lowest—99 Highest)
• **45**

Insider Activity
• **Neutral**

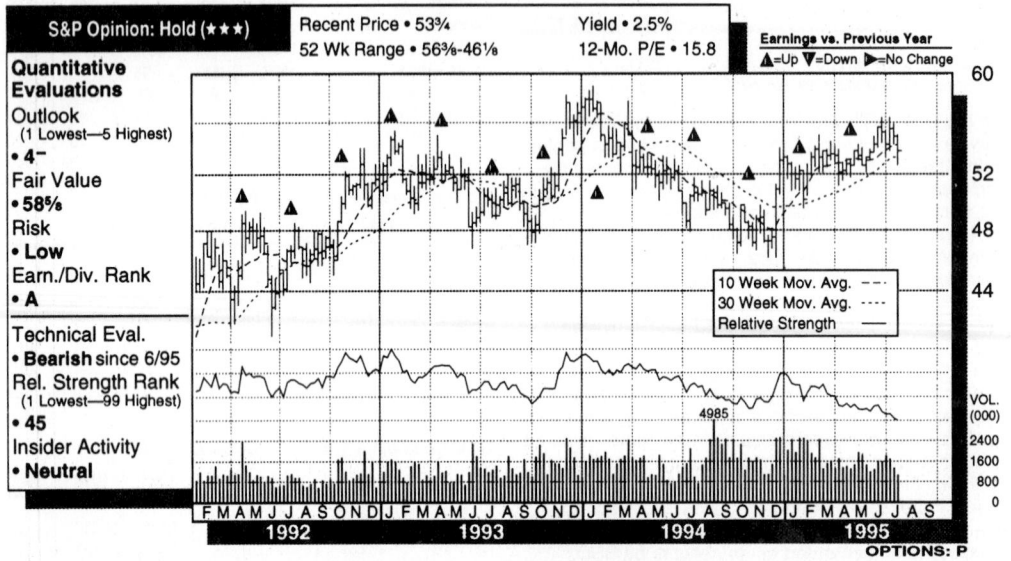

10 Week Mov. Avg. ---
30 Week Mov. Avg. ····
Relative Strength ——

4985

VOL.
(000)
2400
1600
800
0

60
52
48
44

F M A M J J A S O N D J F M A M J J A S O N D J F M A M J J A S O N D J F M A M J J A S
1992   1993   1994   1995

OPTIONS: P

Overview - 26-JUL-95

We expect revenues to rise roughly 5% in 1995, largely on broadcasting and newspaper gains. Ongoing operating efficiencies will boost profitability, but significant increases in newsprint prices over the course of the year will have a major effect on newspaper operations. Interest costs are expected to be higher. Fewer average shares outstanding will benefit share profits, which we project will gain 11%, to $3.60. The pace of newspaper advertising appears to have peaked, but newsprint pricing may have reached a cyclical peak as well. TV, radio and outdoor advertising remain strong, however, and healthy demand should continue through 1996. The purchase of Multimedia Inc., at over 12 times cash flow, could dilute 1996 earnings by roughly $0.30 a share.

Valuation - 26-JUL-95

We view GCI, which is selling a little below its 52-week high, as fairly valued in the short run, even though the stock is selling near a five-year low price-earnings ratio. The planned purchase of Multimedia Inc. at a reasonable multiple of 12 times 1994's cash flow will stall near-term earnings momentum, but is viewed as a smart long-term move. The purchase will boost GCI's broadcast media properties, and give it entree into cable operations, television programming and syndication. Multimedia's assets provide GCI with needed diversity and a more profitable and faster growing business mix. The generous dividend provides a nice cushion under the stock's price.

Key Stock Statistics

S&P EPS Est. 1995	3.60	Tang. Bk. Value/Share	2.94
P/E on S&P Est. 1995	14.9	Beta	1.24
Dividend Rate/Share	1.36	Shareholders	15,000
Shs. outstg. (M)	140.1	Market cap. (B)	$ 7.7
Avg. daily vol. (M)	0.309	Inst. holdings	69%
		Insider holdings	NA

Value of $10,000 invested 5 years ago: $ 14,350

Fiscal Year Ending Dec. 31

	1995	% Change	1994	% Change	1993	% Change
Revenues (Million $)						
1Q	913.8	4%	876.6	4%	844.7	7%
2Q	1,014	5%	966.9	3%	937.8	5%
3Q	—	—	932.4	6%	876.5	3%
4Q	—	—	1,049	7%	982.6	5%
Yr.	—	—	3,825	5%	3,642	5%
Income (Million $)						
1Q	86.21	10%	78.71	19%	66.34	22%
2Q	139.4	6%	131.8	16%	113.7	16%
3Q	—	—	105.5	19%	88.78	12%
4Q	—	—	149.4	16%	129.0	13%
Yr.	—	—	465.4	17%	397.8	15%
Earnings Per Share ($)						
1Q	0.62	15%	0.54	17%	0.46	21%
2Q	1.00	11%	0.90	15%	0.78	15%
3Q	E0.81	—	0.74	21%	0.61	11%
4Q	E1.17	—	1.07	22%	0.88	11%
Yr.	E3.60	—	3.23	19%	2.72	13%

Next earnings report expected: mid October

Business Summary - 26-JUL-95

Contributions to operating revenues and operating income by business segment in 1994 were:

	Revs.	Income
Newspaper publishing	83%	83%
Broadcasting	11%	15%
Outdoor advertising	6%	2%

Newspaper operations consist of 82 dailies in 35 states, Guam and the Virgin Islands, and over 50 nondailies in nine states and Washington, D.C. Total average daily circulation in 1994 exceeded 6.3 million, including USA TODAY, the second largest U.S. newspaper. The company also publishes USA WEEKEND, a newspaper magazine. Other operations include solicitation of national and major local advertisers principally for GCI's newspapers, and provision of news services.

Ten network-affiliated TV stations and 11 radio stations are owned in 20 major U.S. markets. The TV stations are: WXIA, Atlanta; KVUE, Austin; KUSA, Denver; KARE, Minneapolis/St. Paul; KOCO, Oklahoma City; KPNX, Phoenix; WUSA, Washington, D.C.; WFMY, Greensboro/Winston-Salem/High Point; WTLV, Jacksonville; and KTHV, Little Rock.

The outdoor advertising group is the largest in North America, with operations in 11 states and Canada. Other operations include research, marketing, printing, news and broadcast program production.

Important Developments

Jul. '95—GCI agreed to acquire Multimedia Inc. MMEDC) for over $1.71 billion in cash, plus the assumption of $530 million in debt. MMEDC, with 1994 operating income of $189.4 million and operating revenues of $630.5 million, owns 11 daily and 49 non-daily newspapers; owns five network-affiliated TV stations in Cincinnati, St. Louis, Knoxville, Cleveland and Macon, plus two radio stations; operates cable TV systems in Kansas, Oklahoma, Illinois, Indiana and North Carolina, with roughly 450,000 subscribers; provides security monitoring services to over 67,000 security alarm customers; and produces and syndicates TV programming including Donahue, Sally Jessy Raphael, Jerry Springer, Rush Limbaugh, Susan Powter, Dennis Prager, and NewsTalk Television, a cable television network. Consummation of the transaction is subject to approval by MMEDC's shareholders and obtaining regulatory approvals.

Capitalization

Long Term Debt: $624,842,000 (3/95).

Per Share Data ($)

(Year Ended Dec. 31)

	1994	1993	1992	1991	1990	1989
Tangible Bk. Val.	2.51	2.77	1.49	0.91	3.80	3.23
Cash Flow	4.67	4.15	3.77	3.33	3.57	3.64
Earnings	3.23	2.72	2.40	2.00	2.36	2.47
Dividends	1.34	1.30	1.26	1.24	1.21	1.11
Payout Ratio	41%	48%	53%	59%	51%	45%
Prices - High	59	58¼	54	47	44½	49⅞
- Low	46⅛	46¾	41¼	35⅛	29½	34½
P/E Ratio - High	18	21	23	24	19	20
- Low	14	17	17	18	13	14

Income Statement Analysis (Million $)

	1994	%Chg	1993	%Chg	1992	%Chg	1991
Revs.	3,825	5%	3,642	5%	3,469	3%	3,382
Oper. Inc.	1,022	11%	924	13%	815	7%	759
Depr.	209	NM	210	6%	198	-1%	200
Int. Exp.	46.2	-10%	51.5	-3%	53.3	-30%	76.0
Pretax Inc.	782	17%	668	16%	574	14%	503
Eff. Tax Rate	47%	—	41%	—	40%	—	40%
Net Inc.	465	17%	398	15%	346	15%	302

Balance Sheet & Other Fin. Data (Million $)

	1994	1993	1992	1991	1990	1989
Cash	44.3	75.5	73.3	70.7	56.2	55.6
Curr. Assets	651	758	631	636	669	671
Total Assets	3,707	3,824	3,609	3,684	3,826	3,783
Curr. Liab.	527	455	432	444	500	478
LT Debt	767	851	1,081	1,335	849	922
Common Eqty.	1,822	1,908	1,580	1,539	2,063	1,996
Total Cap.	2,754	2,964	2,754	3,129	3,177	3,167
Cap. Exp.	151	182	173	213	205	210
Cash Flow	674	607	544	501	571	588

Ratio Analysis

	1994	1993	1992	1991	1990	1989
Curr. Ratio	1.2	1.7	1.5	1.4	1.3	1.4
% LT Debt of Cap.	27.9	28.7	39.2	42.7	26.7	29.1
% Net Inc.of Revs.	12.2	10.9	10.0	8.9	11.0	11.3
% Ret. on Assets	12.7	10.6	9.5	8.4	10.0	10.5
% Ret. on Equity	25.6	22.6	22.1	17.7	18.7	21.0

Dividend Data

(Dividends have been paid since 1929. A dividend reinvestment plan is available. A "poison pill" stock purchase rights plan was adopted in 1990.)

Amt. of Div. $	Date Decl.	Ex-Div. Date	Stock of Record	Payment Date
0.340	Aug. 23	Sep. 12	Sep. 16	Oct. 01 '94
0.340	Oct. 25	Dec. 12	Dec. 16	Jan. 03 '95
0.340	Feb. 21	Mar. 06	Mar. 10	Apr. 01 '95
0.340	May. 02	Jun. 06	Jun. 09	Jul. 01 '95

Data as orig. reptd.; bef. results of disc. opers. and/or spec. items. Per share data adj. for stk. divs. as of ex-div. date.
E-Estimated. NA-Not Available. NM-Not Meaningful. NR-Not Ranked.

Office—1100 Wilson Blvd., Arlington, VA 22234. **Tel**—(703) 284-6000. **Chrmn, Pres & CEO**—J. J. Curley. **Vice Chrmn & CFO**—D. H. McCorkindale. **Secy**—T. L. Chapple. **SVP & Treas**—J. L. Thomas. **Investor Contact**—Susan Watson (703-284-6914). **Dirs**—A. F. Brimmer, M. A. Brockaw, R. Carter, P. B. Clark, J. J. Curley, S. T. K. Ho, D. Lewis, J. P. Louis, D. H. McCorkindale, R. D. Melton, T. A. Reynolds Jr., C. T. Rowan, D. D. Wharton. **Transfer Agent & Registrar**—Norwest Bank Minnesota. **Incorporated** in New York in 1923; reincorporated in Delaware in 1972. **Empl**-36,000. **S&P Analyst:** William H. Donald

Gap (The)

NYSE Symbol **GPS**
In S&P 500

16-AUG-95

Industry: Retail Stores

Summary: This specialty apparel retailer operates The Gap Stores, Banana Republic, and Old Navy Clothing Co., offering casual clothing to upper, moderate and value-oriented market segments.

S&P Opinion: Accumulate (★★★★)

Recent Price • 32¾	Yield • 1.4%
52 Wk Range • 44¾-28⅞	12-Mo. P/E • 16.1

Earnings vs. Previous Year
▲=Up ▼=Down ▶=No Change

Quantitative Evaluations

Outlook
(1 Lowest—5 Highest)
• **5⁻**

Fair Value
• **44½**

Risk
• Average

Earn./Div. Rank
• A

Technical Eval.
• **Bearish** since 7/95

Rel. Strength Rank
(1 Lowest—99 Highest)
• **19**

Insider Activity
• **Unfavorable**

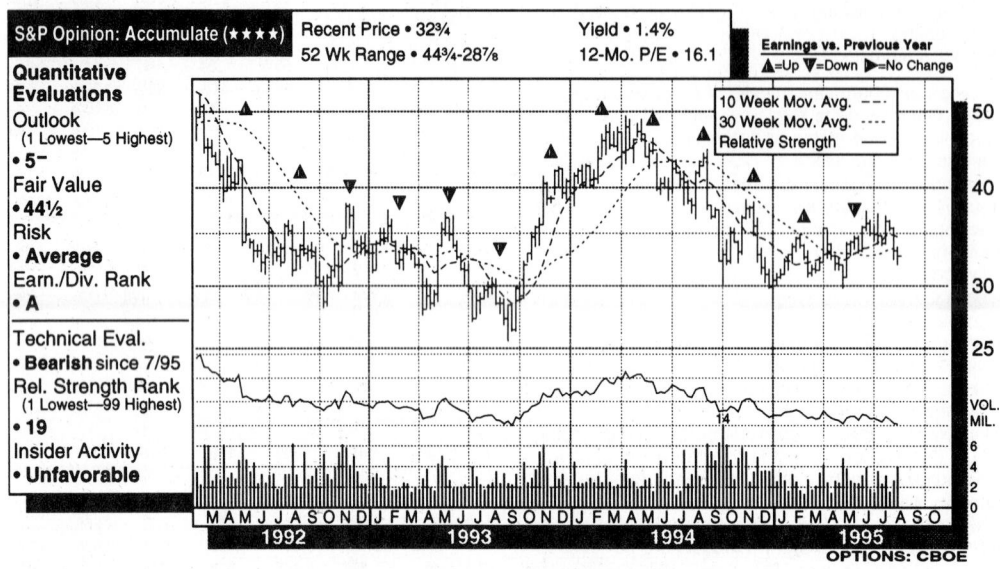

10 Week Mov. Avg. — — ·
30 Week Mov. Avg. ·······
Relative Strength ———

M A M J J A S O N D J F M A M J J A S O N D J F M A M J J A S O N D J F M A M J J A S O
1992 1993 1994 1995

OPTIONS: CBOE

Overview - 16-AUG-95

Same-store sales should advance only modestly in 1995-96, but with a 25% increase in square footage and strong sales gains at Old Navy stores, company sales could increase 16%. Gross margins should narrow with continued competitive pricing. Margin comparisons are difficult since the company had strong increases in gross profit margin over the past two years from improved inventory management, which resulted in more merchandise sold at full price than at markdowns. Expense ratios should benefit from larger, more productive stores. The rollout of Old Navy Clothing Co., value priced stores, product extensions, such as shoes and personal care items, and international expansion should aid long-term growth. The company has no long-term debt and its strong cash flow will be used to fund its capital expenditure program and to repurchase shares.

Valuation - 16-AUG-95

The shares have been in a trading range so far in 1995. But with the weak first half behind, we anticipate renewed interest in this company as the market begins to focus on the second half of 1995, where earnings comparisons are easy, and on 1996. In addition, as the earnings potential of the company's Old Navy concept unfolds, we anticipate an acceleration in the company's earnings P/E. We believe that the company's core growth rate is about 18%.

Key Stock Statistics

S&P EPS Est. 1996	2.30	Tang. Bk. Value/Share	9.61
P/E on S&P Est. 1996	14.2	Beta	1.30
S&P EPS Est. 1997	2.75	Shareholders	6,600
Dividend Rate/Share	0.48	Market cap. (B)	$ 4.8
Shs. outstg. (M)	144.1	Inst. holdings	43%
Avg. daily vol. (M)	0.547	Insider holdings	NA

Value of $10,000 invested 5 years ago: $ 27,116

Fiscal Year Ending Jan. 31

	1996	% Change	1995	% Change	1994	% Change
Revenues (Million $)						
1Q	848.7	13%	752.0	17%	643.6	9%
2Q	868.5	12%	773.1	12%	693.2	13%
3Q	—	—	988.3	10%	898.7	9%
4Q	—	—	1,210	14%	1,060	14%
Yr.	—	—	3,723	13%	3,296	11%
Income (Million $)						
1Q	50.11	-21%	63.48	53%	41.51	-8%
2Q	32.41	-27%	44.35	55%	28.66	-24%
3Q	—	—	93.65	19%	78.92	27%
4Q	—	—	118.8	9%	109.3	66%
Yr.	—	—	320.2	24%	258.4	23%
Earnings Per Share ($)						
1Q	0.35	-20%	0.44	52%	0.29	-9%
2Q	0.22	-27%	0.30	50%	0.20	-23%
3Q	E0.72	13%	0.64	19%	0.54	26%
4Q	E1.01	23%	0.82	9%	0.75	63%
Yr.	E2.30	5%	2.20	24%	1.78	21%

Next earnings report expected: mid November

Business Summary - 11-AUG-95

The Gap, Inc. is a specialty retailer whose major division is The Gap Stores. As of January 28, 1995, the company operated a total of 1,508 stores: 892 Gap, 369 GapKids, 188 Banana Republic and 59 Old Navy Clothing Co.

Gap Stores feature fashion tops, shorts, sweaters, jackets and accessories with a more updated look, and basic jeans and sweaters geared to 20- to 45-year-olds. Stores continue to refine and to expand the merchandise mix. The company purchases merchandise from over 1,000 suppliers located domestically and overseas; 30% of unit purchases were domestic and the remaining 70% were foreign. In 1994-95, about 18% of total merchandise came from Hong Kong. All suppliers manufacture Gap's private-label merchandise to company specifications.

GapKids was introduced in 1986 to provide well-designed, comfortable clothing for boys and girls aged two through 12. The concept was expanded, opening both freestanding stores and departments within existing Gap locations. In 1990, a line of natural-fiber clothing for infants and toddlers, named baby-Gap, was introduced.

Banana Republic (acquired 1983) is a specialty retailer of classic, casual men's and women's fashions, designed for ages 20 to 50. Historically, Banana Republic has offered an imaginative, theatrical backdrop appropriate to travel theme clothing.

The company changed the name of its Gap Warehouse units, introduced in 1993, to Old Navy Clothing Co. This division offers basic and fashion casual clothing at lower price points than Gap and Banana Republic stores.

In recent years, the company has increased the average size of new units and expanded existing stores to include new product lines, such as babyGap, shoes and personal care products.

Important Developments

Aug. '95—Gap said that lower initial merchandise margins and comparable store sales, combined with a continued challenging retail environment, contributed to the drop in second quarter 1995-96 earnings. Same store sales decreased 4% in the second quarter. The company planned to open 175 - 200 stores in 1995-96 for an increase in square footage of about 25%. Capital expenditures are projected at $275 to $300 million in 1995-96. The company operated about 10 million square feet at July 29, 1995, an increase of 23% over a year ago. In October 1994, directors authorized a repurchase program of up to nine million common shares over a two year period. Under this program, a total 2.7 million shares were repurchased by April 29, 1995.

Capitalization

Long Term Debt: None (8/95).

Per Share Data ($) (Year Ended Jan. 31)

	1995	1994	1993	1992	1991	1990
Tangible Bk. Val.	9.50	7.76	6.16	4.76	3.14	2.28
Cash Flow	3.36	2.62	2.12	2.11	1.38	0.96
Earnings	2.20	1.78	1.47	1.62	1.02	0.69
Dividends	0.46	0.38	0.32	0.30	0.22	0.17
Payout Ratio	21%	21%	22%	19%	22%	24%
Cal. Yrs.	1994	1993	1992	1991	1990	1989
Prices - High	49⅜	59¼	59⅜	56¼	18⅛	15⅜
- Low	28⅞	28⅛	28⅛	16⅜	9¾	8⅞
P/E Ratio - High	22	40	40	35	18	22
- Low	13	19	19	10	10	13

Income Statement Analysis (Million $)

	1995	%Chg	1994	%Chg	1993	%Chg	1992
Revs.	3,723	13%	3,296	11%	2,960	18%	2,519
Oper. Inc.	687	26%	547	25%	438	-1%	444
Depr.	168	38%	122	30%	94.2	34%	70.1
Int. Exp.	NA	—	0.8	-78%	3.8	7%	3.5
Pretax Inc.	529	24%	425	25%	340	-8%	371
Eff. Tax Rate	40%	—	39%	—	38%	—	38%
Net Inc.	320	24%	258	22%	211	-8%	230

Balance Sheet & Other Fin. Data (Million $)

	1995	1994	1993	1992	1991	1990
Cash	588	544	243	193	67.0	39.0
Curr. Assets	1,056	956	691	566	365	317
Total Assets	2,004	1,763	1,379	1,147	777	579
Curr. Liab.	500	462	335	330	264	187
LT Debt	Nil	75.0	75.0	77.5	5.0	17.5
Common Eqty.	1,375	1,126	888	678	466	338
Total Cap.	1,375	1,201	963	755	471	355
Cap. Exp.	233	223	211	245	208	93.0
Cash Flow	488	380	305	300	196	136

Ratio Analysis

	1995	1994	1993	1992	1991	1990
Curr. Ratio	2.1	2.1	2.1	1.7	1.4	1.7
% LT Debt of Cap.	Nil	6.2	7.8	10.3	1.1	4.9
% Net Inc.of Revs.	8.6	7.8	7.1	9.1	7.5	6.2
% Ret. on Assets	17.0	16.4	16.6	23.8	21.3	18.4
% Ret. on Equity	25.6	25.6	26.8	40.1	35.9	31.8

Dividend Data —Cash has been paid each year since 1976.

Amt. of Div. $	Date Decl.	Ex-Div. Date	Stock of Record	Payment Date
0.120	May. 24	May. 27	Jun. 03	Jun. 13 '94
0.120	Aug. 24	Aug. 29	Sep. 02	Sep. 12 '94
0.120	Nov. 21	Nov. 28	Dec. 02	Dec. 27 '94
0.120	Feb. 28	Mar. 02	Mar. 08	Mar. 17 '95
0.120	May. 23	May. 26	Jun. 02	Jun. 12 '95

Data as orig. reptd.; bef. results of disc. opers. and/or spec. items. Per share data adj. for stk. divs. as of ex-div. date. E-Estimated. NA-Not Available. NM-Not Meaningful. NR-Not Ranked.

Office—One Harrison, San Francisco, CA 94105. Tel—(415) 952-4400. Chrmn & CEO—D. G. Fisher. Pres & COO—M. S. Drexler. EVP & CFO—R. J. Fisher. SVP-Fin & Investor Contact—Warren R. Hashagen. Secy—Anne B. Gust. Dirs—A. D. P. Bellamy, J. G. Bowes, M. S. Drexler, D. F. Fisher, D. G. Fisher, R. J. Fisher, L. J. Fjeldstad, W. A. Hasler, J. M. Lillie, C. R. Schwab, B. Walker Jr. Transfer Agent & Registrar—Harris Trust Co. of California, Chicago. Incorporated in California in 1969. Empl-44,000. S&P Analyst: Karen J. Sack CFA

General Dynamics

NYSE Symbol **GD**
In S&P 500

24-AUG-95 Industry: Aerospace

Summary: This defense contractor is the sole domestic military tank manufacturer and one of two U.S. nuclear submarine manufacturers.

S&P Opinion: Accumulate (★★★★)	Recent Price • 51⅝ 52 Wk Range • 52½-38¼

Yield • 2.9%
12-Mo. P/E • 12.8

Quantitative Evaluations

Outlook
(1 Lowest—5 Highest)
• **1+**

Fair Value
• **44¾**

Risk
• **Low**

Earn./Div. Rank
• **B**

Technical Eval.
• **Bearish** since 7/95

Rel. Strength Rank
(1 Lowest—99 Highest)
• **77**

Insider Activity
• **NA**

Earnings vs. Previous Year
▲=Up ▼=Down ▶=No Change

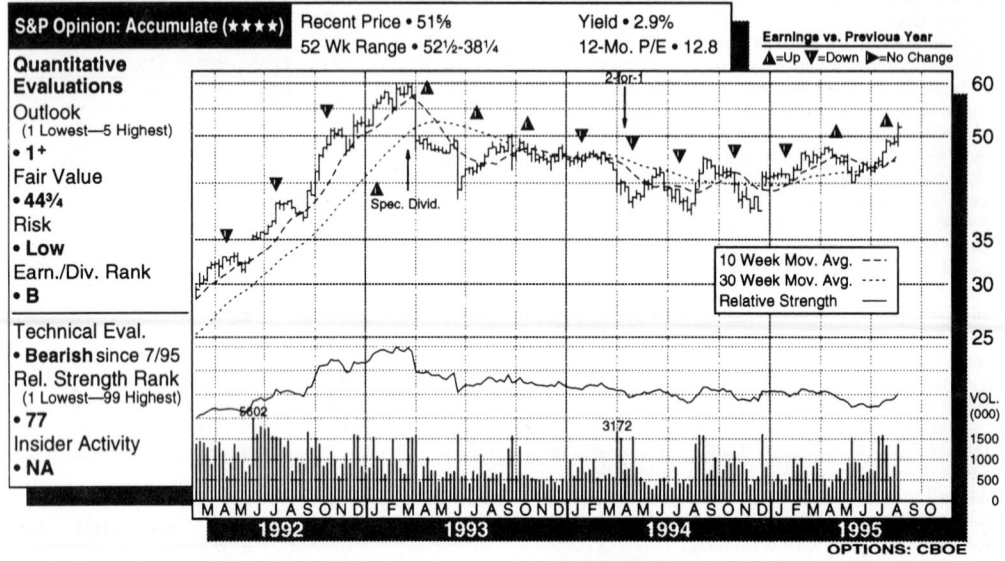

10 Week Mov. Avg. – – –
30 Week Mov. Avg. ⋯⋯
Relative Strength ——

OPTIONS: CBOE

Overview - 24-AUG-95

Revenues in 1995 are likely to decrease moderately from those of 1994. Submarine revenues should be off, as the final SSN 688 boat will be delivered during the year. Operating profit could rise on higher earnings rates. Armored vehicle revenues should also reflect a decline in total deliveries, offset in part by revenues from the Army upgrade program. Margins will reflect higher earnings rates and profits from the SINCGARS radio program. Other operations could be about unchanged. Interest income should increase from a higher average cash balance.

Valuation - 24-AUG-95

In recent years, GD's balance sheet has strengthened, and excess cash has been returned to shareholders through share repurchase and special dividends. However, divested operations and reduced government expenditures have eroded sales during this period, and share price increases suffered. Optimism that the decline is over has lifted GD of late. While there is uncertainty whether Congress will approve funding for the third Seawolf, navy submarine needs could support revenues for many years. Also, as the sole U.S. supplier of tanks, GD will likely provide the next upgrade. In addition, results should be lifted by expansion into foreign markets and other military programs (e.g. SINCGARS and AAAV).

Key Stock Statistics

S&P EPS Est. 1995	3.80	Tang. Bk. Value/Share	22.41
P/E on S&P Est. 1995	13.6	Beta	0.52
S&P EPS Est. 1996	4.00	Shareholders	24,500
Dividend Rate/Share	1.50	Market cap. (B)	$ 3.3
Shs. outstg. (M)	63.0	Inst. holdings	59%
Avg. daily vol. (M)	0.187	Insider holdings	NA

Value of $10,000 invested 5 years ago: $ 40,913

Fiscal Year Ending Dec. 31

	1995	% Change	1994	% Change	1993	% Change
Revenues (Million $)						
1Q	753.0	-6%	800.0	-7%	858.0	1%
2Q	703.0	-14%	820.0	6%	774.0	-9%
3Q	—	—	714.0	-8%	776.0	-9%
4Q	—	—	724.0	-7%	779.0	-14%
Yr.	—	—	3,058	-4%	3,187	-8%
Income (Million $)						
1Q	60.00	9%	55.00	34%	41.00	37%
2Q	61.00	9%	56.00	-2%	57.00	58%
3Q	—	—	54.00	-25%	72.00	148%
4Q	—	—	58.00	-9%	64.00	-58%
Yr.	—	—	223.0	-17%	270.0	9%
Earnings Per Share ($)						
1Q	0.95	10%	0.86	-19%	1.06	NM
2Q	0.97	10%	0.88	-12%	1.00	144%
3Q	E0.94	11%	0.85	-29%	1.20	164%
4Q	E0.94	2%	0.92	-9%	1.01	-59%
Yr.	E3.80	8%	3.51	-18%	4.27	30%

Next earnings report expected: mid October

Business Summary - 22-AUG-95

General Dynamics is a leading defense contractor specializing in the production of nuclear submarines and armored vehicles. Business units relating to missiles, aviation and space products have been divested in recent years. Contributions by segment in 1994 were:

	Sales	Profits
Nuclear submarines	55%	54%
Armored vehicles	39%	44%
Other	6%	2%

The U.S. government contributed 94% of total sales in 1994, including the 22% sold to the government for resale to foreign governments.

Nuclear submarines include the SSN 688 attack submarine, the Trident ballistic missile submarine and the Seawolf attack submarine. The division also performs overhaul and repair work on submarines as well as a broad range engineering work, including the design of the New Attack Submarine (NSSN). At the end of 1994, the backlog was comprised of one SSN 688, three Trident, and three Seawolf submarines.

Land Systems produces the M-1 series of main battle tanks for the U.S. and foreign governments. It also provides engineering and upgrade work as well as support for existing armored vehicles. In addition, the division is the second source producer of the Single Channel Ground and Airborne Radio System (SINC-GARS) for the U.S. Army.

Other activities are the AMSEA ship positioning operation, the Freeman Energy coal mining company and Patriots LNG tanker leasing subsidiaries.

Discontinued operations include the building materials group, Marblehead Lime Co. and commercial aircraft subcontracting. The tactical aircraft business, producer of the F-16 fighter, was sold in early 1993. Cessna Aircraft, the missile division, and the electronics group were sold in 1992.

Important Developments

Aug. '95—GD agreed to buy Bath Iron Works, a privately-owned shipyard, for $300 million in cash. The builder of surface combatant ships, with a backlog of approximately $2 billion, is estimated to reach $830 million of revenues, and $48 million of operating income in 1995.
Mar. '95—Land systems delivered to the Marine Corps the on-shore test rig for the Advanced Amphibious Assault Vehicle (AAAV). This follows the successful demonstration last year of the off-shore capability of the company's AAAV design. GD said the marines are expected to select a sole-source contractor early next year.

Capitalization

Long Term Debt: $188,000,000 (7/2/95).

Per Share Data ($)

(Year Ended Dec. 31)

	1994	1993	1992	1991	1990	1989
Tangible Bk. Val.	20.89	18.81	30.31	23.62	18.12	25.15
Cash Flow	4.13	5.16	4.02	8.08	-3.53	7.82
Earnings	3.51	4.27	3.28	4.46	-7.67	3.51
Dividends	1.35	0.90	0.73	0.50	0.50	0.50
Payout Ratio	38%	21%	22%	11%	NM	14%
Prices - High	47⅝	60	54	27¼	23⅛	30¼
- Low	38	40¼	26¾	10⅛	9½	21¼
P/E Ratio - High	14	14	16	6	NM	9
- Low	11	9	8	2	NM	6

Income Statement Analysis (Million $)

	1994	%Chg	1993	%Chg	1992	%Chg	1991
Revs.	3,058	-4%	3,187	-8%	3,472	-60%	8,751
Oper. Inc.	360	-1%	365	58%	231	-67%	692
Depr.	39.0	-30%	56.0	NM	56.0	-82%	303
Int. Exp.	5.0	25%	4.0	-60%	10.0	-83%	58.0
Pretax Inc.	343	-17%	413	82%	227	-31%	331
Eff. Tax Rate	35%	—	35%	—	NM	—	NM
Net Inc.	223	-17%	270	9%	248	-34%	374

Balance Sheet & Other Fin. Data (Million $)

	1994	1993	1992	1991	1990	1989
Cash	1,059	585	945	820	115	14.0
Curr. Assets	1,797	1,654	3,655	4,319	3,927	3,990
Total Assets	2,673	2,635	4,222	6,207	6,537	6,549
Curr. Liab.	626	775	1,948	3,109	2,918	2,078
LT Debt	196	201	38.0	365	900	906
Common Eqty.	1,316	1,177	1,874	1,980	1,510	2,126
Total Cap.	1,512	1,378	1,912	2,345	2,414	3,671
Cap. Exp.	23.0	14.0	18.0	82.0	321	419
Cash Flow	262	326	304	674	-294	653

Ratio Analysis

	1994	1993	1992	1991	1990	1989
Curr. Ratio	2.9	2.1	1.9	1.4	1.3	1.9
% LT Debt of Cap.	13.0	14.6	2.0	15.6	37.3	24.7
% Net Inc.of Revs.	7.3	8.5	7.1	4.3	NM	2.9
% Ret. on Assets	8.4	7.8	5.6	5.8	NM	4.6
% Ret. on Equity	17.8	17.6	14.9	21.4	NM	14.5

Dividend Data —Dividends were resumed in 1979.

Amt. of Div. $	Date Decl.	Ex-Div. Date	Stock of Record	Payment Date
0.350	Aug. 03	Oct. 07	Oct. 14	Nov. 10 '94
0.350	Nov. 02	Jan. 09	Jan. 13	Feb. 10 '95
0.375	Mar. 08	Apr. 10	Apr. 17	May. 12 '95
0.375	May. 03	Jul. 12	Jul. 14	Aug. 11 '95
0.375	Aug. 02	Oct. 11	Oct. 13	Nov. 10 '95

Data as orig. reptd.; bef. results of disc. opers. and/or spec. items. Per share data adj. for stk. divs. as of ex-div. date.
E-Estimated. NA-Not Available. NM-Not Meaningful. NR-Not Ranked.

Office—3190 Fairview Park Drive, Falls Church, VA 22042. **Tel**—(703) 876-3000. **Chrmn & CEO**—J. R. Mellor. **EVP**—N. D. Chabraja. **VP & CFO**—M. J. Mancuso. **Secy**—E. A. Klobasa. **VP-Treas**—D. H. Fogg. **Investor Contact**—W. Raymond A. Lewis (703-876-3190). **Dirs**—F. C. Carlucci, N. D. Chabraja, J. S. Crown, L. Crown, C. H. Goodman, J. R. Mellor, G. R. Sullivan, C. A. H. Trost. **Transfer Agent & Registrar**—First Chicago Trust Co. of New York. **Incorporated** in Delaware in 1952. **Empl**-20,400. **S&P Analyst:** Joe Victor Shammas

General Electric

NYSE Symbol **GE**
In S&P 500

25-OCT-95

Industry: Electronics/Electric

Summary: General Electric's major businesses include aircraft engines, medical systems, power systems, broadcasting, appliances, lighting and financial services.

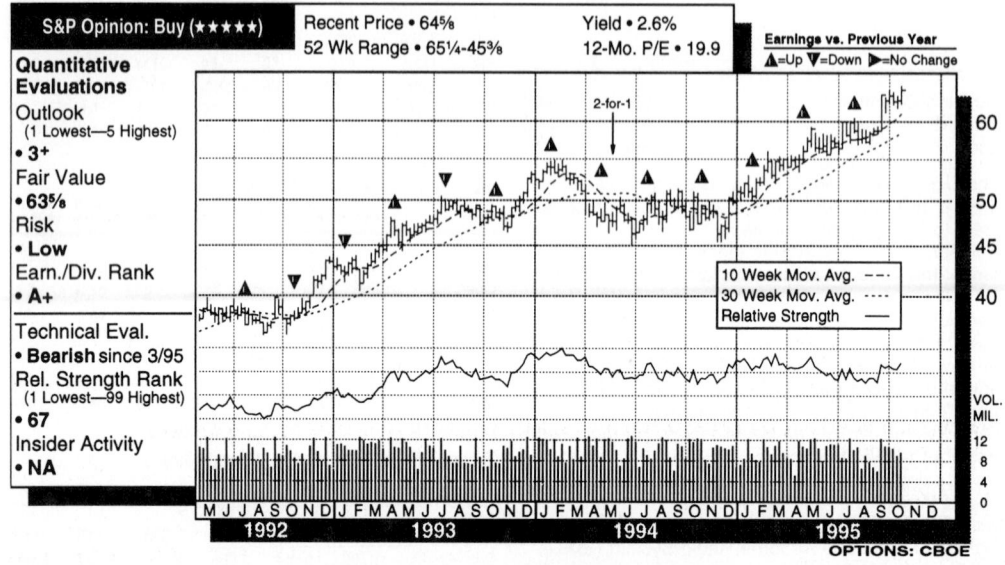

S&P Opinion: Buy (★★★★)	Recent Price • 64⅝		Yield • 2.6%
	52 Wk Range • 65¼-45⅝		12-Mo. P/E • 19.9

Quantitative Evaluations

Outlook
(1 Lowest—5 Highest)
• **3+**

Fair Value
• **63⅝**

Risk
• **Low**

Earn./Div. Rank
• **A+**

Technical Eval.
• **Bearish** since 3/95

Rel. Strength Rank
(1 Lowest—99 Highest)
• **67**

Insider Activity
• **NA**

Earnings vs. Previous Year
▲=Up ▼=Down ▶=No Change

10 Week Mov. Avg. — —
30 Week Mov. Avg. - - - -
Relative Strength ——

OPTIONS: CBOE

Overview - 18-OCT-95

Revenues are expected to increase approximately 12% in 1996, reflecting the positive impact of a stronger economy and favorable cyclical trends in key businesses. Broadcasting and aircraft engines should benefit from favorable cyclical trends in their businesses. Financial services should continue to expand, aided by aggressive marketing and acquisitions. Materials and industrial products and systems should further benefit from additional economic growth. An expanding economy is also expected to lead to a rebound for appliances. Somewhat offsetting is likely to be continued weakness in medical and power generation. Margins should widen on the higher volume, improved manufacturing efficiencies and well controlled costs. A share repurchase program should extend the gain in share earnings.

Valuation - 18-OCT-95

General Electric's shares have recovered to record levels in recent months on strong earnings and a bright outlook. The company is entering favorable cycles in several of its key businesses, including aircraft engines and broadcasting. Financial services should also continue to provide consistent growth. A growing economy should support improved results in other operations. A $5 billion, two year share buyback also enhances the outlook for the shares. A rising dividend further adds to the appeal of the shares. The shares are ranked a "buy."

Key Stock Statistics

S&P EPS Est. 1995	3.90	Tang. Bk. Value/Share	9.48
P/E on S&P Est. 1995	16.6	Beta	1.20
S&P EPS Est. 1996	4.30	Shareholders	460,000
Dividend Rate/Share	1.64	Market cap. (B)	$106.0
Shs. outstg. (M)	1682.4	Inst. holdings	52%
Avg. daily vol. (M)	1.913	Insider holdings	NA

Value of $10,000 invested 5 years ago: $ 23,540

Fiscal Year Ending Dec. 31

	1995	% Change	1994	% Change	1993	% Change
Revenues (Million $)						
1Q	15,126	20%	12,657	-2%	12,900	4%
2Q	17,809	21%	14,768	NM	14,761	4%
3Q	17,341	20%	14,481	-3%	14,858	5%
4Q	—	—	17,791	-2%	18,087	11%
Yr.	—	—	60,108	NM	60,562	6%
Income (Million $)						
1Q	1,372	13%	1,219	12%	1,085	13%
2Q	1,726	11%	1,554	137%	656.0	-42%
3Q	1,610	11%	1,457	21%	1,206	21%
4Q	—	—	1,685	14%	1,477	22%
Yr.	—	—	5,915	34%	4,424	3%
Earnings Per Share ($)						
1Q	0.81	14%	0.71	12%	0.63	13%
2Q	1.02	12%	0.91	136%	0.39	-42%
3Q	0.96	13%	0.85	21%	0.71	21%
4Q	E1.11	12%	0.99	14%	0.87	22%
Yr.	E3.90	13%	3.46	34%	2.59	3%

Next earnings report expected: mid January

General Electric

Business Summary - 25-OCT-95

General Electric is a diversified company with interests in services, technology and manufacturing. Industry segment contributions in 1994:

	Revs.	Profits
Aircraft engines	9%	10%
Appliances	10%	8%
Broadcasting	6%	6%
Industrial products and systems	15%	15%
Materials	9%	11%
Power generation	10%	14%
Technical products/services	7%	9%
Financial services	33%	24%
Other	1%	4%

Foreign operations, including exports, accounted for 21% of sales and 13% of operating income in 1993.

Aircraft engines and related replacement parts are produced for military and commercial aircraft, for naval ships for propulsion, and as industrial power sources.

Appliances include refrigerators, ranges, microwave ovens, freezers, dishwashers, clothes washers and dryers, and room air conditioners.

Broadcasting consists primarily of the National Broadcasting Company (NBC).

Industrial products and systems encompasses lighting products, electrical distribution and control equipment for industrial and commercial construction, transportation systems, motors, industrial automation products and GE Supply.

Materials include high-performance engineered plastics, silicones, superabrasives and laminates.

Power generation and related services are provided for the generation, transmission and distribution of electricity.

Technical products and services consist of technology operations providing products, systems and services to a variety of customers.

Financial services primarily consist of GE Capital Services (including General Electric Credit Corp. and Employers Reinsurance Corp.).

Important Developments

Oct. '95—The company said that eleven of its twelve businesses had increased revenues in the third quarter with six achieving double-digit increases. It added that its operating margin rose to 13.4%, up from last year's 12.8%. Led by NBC, plastics and aircraft engines, five businesses achieved double digit increases in operating profit. Earnings from continuing operations at GE Capital Services rose 16%. However, operating profits declined at power systems. In addition, GE said that it had purchased $2.6 billion of shares under a two-year, $5 billion share repurchase program.

Capitalization

Long Term Debt: $49,800,000,000 (9/95).
Minority Interest: $2,600,000,000.

Per Share Data ($)

(Year Ended Dec. 31)

	1994	1993	1992	1991	1990	1989
Tangible Bk. Val.	8.80	9.05	8.16	6.87	7.07	6.67
Cash Flow	5.34	4.50	4.16	4.18	3.84	3.42
Earnings	3.46	2.59	2.51	2.55	2.42	2.18
Dividends	1.85	1.26	1.16	1.04	0.96	0.85
Payout Ratio	53%	38%	46%	41%	39%	39%
Prices - High	54⅞	53½	43¾	39⅛	37¾	32⅜
- Low	45	40½	36⅜	26½	25	21¾
P/E Ratio - High	16	21	17	15	16	15
- Low	13	16	14	10	10	10

Income Statement Analysis (Million $)

	1994	%Chg	1993	%Chg	1992	%Chg	1991
Revs.	59,316	NM	59,827	6%	56,274	-5%	59,379
Oper. Inc.	16,194	NM	16,241	7%	15,205	-4%	15,887
Depr.	3,207	-2%	3,261	16%	2,818	NM	2,832
Int. Exp.	5,024	-29%	7,057	2%	6,943	-7%	7,504
Pretax Inc.	8,831	31%	6,726	6%	6,326	-3%	6,508
Eff. Tax Rate	31%	—	32%	—	31%	—	31%
Net Inc.	5,915	34%	4,424	3%	4,305	-3%	4,435

Balance Sheet & Other Fin. Data (Million $)

	1994	1993	1992	1991	1990	1989
Cash	2,591	3,218	3,129	1,971	1,975	2,258
Curr. Assets	NA	NA	NA	NA	NA	NA
Total Assets	194,484	251,506	192,876	168,259	153,884	128,344
Curr. Liab.	72,854	155,729	120,475	102,611	93,022	73,902
LT Debt	36,979	28,270	25,376	22,682	21,043	16,110
Common Eqty.	26,387	25,824	23,459	21,683	21,680	20,890
Total Cap.	70,418	60,859	54,719	49,392	47,746	41,544
Cap. Exp.	7,492	4,739	4,824	5,000	4,523	5,474
Cash Flow	9,122	7,685	7,123	7,267	6,811	6,195

Ratio Analysis

	1994	1993	1992	1991	1990	1989
Curr. Ratio	NA	NA	NA	NA	NA	NA
% LT Debt of Cap.	52.5	46.5	46.4	45.9	44.1	38.8
% Net Inc.of Revs.	10.0	7.4	7.7	7.5	7.5	7.3
% Ret. on Assets	2.7	2.0	2.4	2.8	3.1	3.3
% Ret. on Equity	22.7	18.0	19.2	20.6	20.6	20.0

Dividend Data —Dividends have been paid since 1899 and boosted each year since 1975. A dividend reinvestment plan is available.

Amt. of Div. $	Date Decl.	Ex-Div. Date	Stock of Record	Payment Date
0.360	Sep. 16	Sep. 26	Sep. 30	Oct. 25 '94
0.410	Dec. 16	Dec. 23	Dec. 30	Jan. 25 '95
0.410	Feb. 10	Mar. 01	Mar. 07	Apr. 25 '95
0.410	Jun. 23	Jun. 30	Jul. 05	Jul. 25 '95
0.410	Sep. 15	Sep. 27	Sep. 29	Oct. 25 '95

Data as orig. reptd.; bef. results of disc. opers. and/or spec. items. Per share data adj. for stk. divs. as of ex-div. date.
E-Estimated. NA-Not Available. NM-Not Meaningful. NR-Not Ranked.

Office—3135 Easton Turnpike, Fairfield, CT 06431. **Tel**—(203) 373-2459. **Chrmn & CEO**—J. F. Welch Jr. **VP-Secy**—B. W. Heineman Jr. **VP-Fin**—D. D. Dammerman. **Investor Contact**—Jay Ireland (203-373-2816). **Dirs**—H. B. Atwater Jr., D. W. Calloway, S. S. Cathcart, D. D. Dammerman, L. E. Fouraker, P. Fresco, C. X. Gonzalez, H. H. Henley Jr., D. C. Jones, R. E. Mercer, G. G. Michelson, R. S. Penske, B. S. Preiskel, F. H. T. Rhodes, A. C. Sigler, D. A. Warner III, J. F. Welch Jr. **Transfer Agent & Registrar**—Bank of New York, NYC. **Incorporated** in New York in 1892. **Empl**-221,000. **S&P Analyst:** Paul Valentine, CFA

General Mills

NYSE Symbol **GIS**
In S&P 500

21-SEP-95 Industry:
Food

Summary: This company is a major producer of packaged consumer food products, including Big G cereals and Betty Crocker desserts/baking mixes.

| S&P Opinion: Hold (★★★) | Recent Price • 51⅞ | Yield • 3.5% |
| | 52 Wk Range • 64⅝-47¼ | 12-Mo. P/E • 23.2 |

Earnings vs. Previous Year
▲=Up ▼=Down ►=No Change

Quantitative Evaluations

Outlook
(1 Lowest—5 Highest)
• **1⁻**

Fair Value
• **41⅞**

Risk
• **Low**

Earn./Div. Rank
• **A**

Technical Eval.
• **Bearish** since 6/95

Rel. Strength Rank
(1 Lowest—99 Highest)
• **44**

Insider Activity
• **Unfavorable**

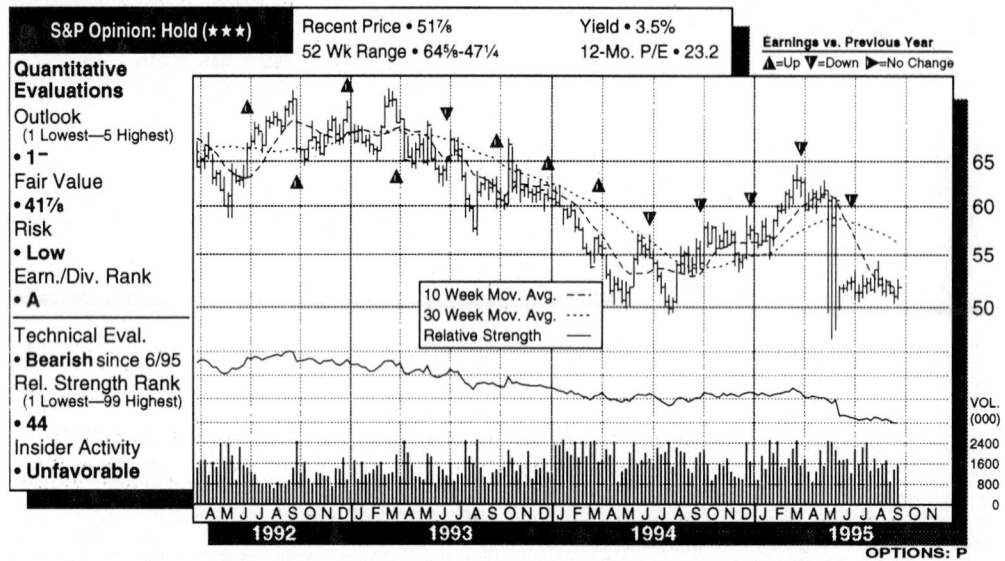

10 Week Mov. Avg. ---
30 Week Mov. Avg. ····
Relative Strength —

VOL. (000)
2400
1600
800
0

A M J J A S O N D J F M A M J J A S O N D J F M A M J J A S O N D J F M A M J J A S O N
1992 · 1993 · 1994 · 1995

OPTIONS: P

Overview - 21-SEP-95

Sales from continuing operations are expected to rise at an approximate 10% annual pace through the fiscal year ending May 1997, driven primarily by increased volumes of new and existing products, and growing international sales contributions. Margins should benefit from recent restructuring actions aimed at boosting manufacturing efficiencies, and from an improving product mix shift, but heavy marketing support behind new and existing products may be somewhat offsetting. Assuming a steady reduction in interest expense, and an effective tax rate of approximately 37%-38%, earnings per share could reach $3.00 in fiscal 1995-96. In fiscal 1996-97, $3.25 is seen.

Valuation - 21-SEP-95

Based on our projection of modest earnings growth for the foreseeable future, we view the shares as fully valued at present levels. Although management took aggressive steps during fiscal 1994-95 to "rightsize" the company for sustainable growth (through the divestment of its restaurant operations, reduction of cereal production capacity, and reduced trade promotion spending), we believe that the increasingly competitive U.S. ready-to-eat cereal market will limit the company's pricing flexibility in this important market for the foreseeable future. The shares, trading at an approximate 15% premium to the S&P 500, appear poised for market performance ahead.

Key Stock Statistics

S&P EPS Est. 1996	3.00	Tang. Bk. Value/Share	0.13
P/E on S&P Est. 1996	17.3	Beta	0.92
S&P EPS Est. 1997	3.25	Shareholders	25,000
Dividend Rate/Share	1.88	Market cap. (B)	$ 8.6
Shs. outstg. (M)	158.5	Inst. holdings	64%
Avg. daily vol. (M)	0.333	Insider holdings	NA

Value of $10,000 invested 5 years ago: NA

Fiscal Year Ending May 31

	1996	% Change	1995	% Change	1994	% Change
Revenues (Million $)						
1Q	1,276	10%	1,157	-45%	2,090	3%
2Q	—	—	1,417	-35%	2,182	4%
3Q	—	—	1,224	-42%	2,101	4%
4Q	—	—	1,229	-43%	2,144	7%
Yr.	—	—	5,027	-41%	8,517	5%
Income (Million $)						
1Q	136.9	16%	118.0	-29%	165.8	4%
2Q	—	—	134.8	-4%	140.7	2%
3Q	—	—	20.20	-86%	145.0	3%
4Q	—	—	-13.30	NM	18.40	-73%
Yr.	—	—	259.7	-45%	469.9	-7%
Earnings Per Share ($)						
1Q	0.86	15%	0.75	-28%	1.04	7%
2Q	E0.90	6%	0.85	-3%	0.88	4%
3Q	E0.75	NM	0.13	-86%	0.91	6%
4Q	E0.49	NM	-0.09	NM	0.12	-71%
Yr.	E3.00	83%	1.64	-44%	2.95	-5%

Next earnings report expected: mid December

General Mills

Business Summary - 21-SEP-95

General Mills is a leading producer of consumer packaged food products. In May 1995, GIS sold its Gorton's seafood products division. In June 1995, GIS spun off to shareholders its restaurant operations.

Major food products include Big G ready-to-eat breakfast cereals (Cheerios, Wheaties, Lucky Charms, Total); baking mixes (Betty Crocker, Bisquick); convenience foods (Betty Crocker dry packaged dinner mixes, Potato Buds instant mashed potatoes); snack products and beverages (Pop Secret microwave popcorn, Bugles snacks, grain and fruit snack products, Squeezit single-serving fruit juice drinks); and other products, including Yoplait and Colombo yogurt. The company also engages in grain merchandising, produces its own ingredient flour requirements and sells flour to bakeries. Products are also made and sold in Canada and Europe, Japan, Korea and Latin America. Products are distributed to retail food chains, co-ops and wholesalers.

Cereal Partners Worldwide, a joint venture with Nestle, S.A., markets breakfast cereals in more than 40 countries and republics around the world, including France, Spain, Portugal, Italy, Ireland, Germany, the U.K., Mexico and the Philippines. GIS has a 50% equity interest in CPW.

Snack Ventures Europe, a joint venture with PepsiCo, Inc., manufactures and sells snack foods in Holland, France, Belgium, Spain, Portugal, Greece, and Italy, and late in fiscal 1995 began expansion into Estonia, Hungary, Russia and Slovakia. GIS has a 40.5% equity interest in SVE.

Important Developments

Sep. '95—Management said that fiscal 1995-96's first quarter results benefited from strong unit volume growth across the company, continuing benefits from productivity efforts, and improving profitability from international activities. Total domestic retail packaged foods unit volume grew more than 12%, led by an 18% unit volume increase for Big G cereals (In the previous year's period, volume fell 21% due to disruptions resulting from improper fumigation of oats by a contractor). Volume trends for GIS' other dry grocery businesses benefited from the company's January 1995 shift to new promotional practices. Internationally, Cereal Partners Worldwide unit volumes rose 25%, leading to market share gains in most markets. Snack Ventures Europe unit volumes rose 15%, reflecting product line additions in established markets, and SVE's expansion into new markets in Eastern Europe.

Capitalization

Long Term Debt: $1,334,900,000 (8/95).

Per Share Data ($)

(Year Ended May 31)

	1995	1994	1993	1992	1991	1990
Tangible Bk. Val.	0.13	6.27	7.15	7.79	6.26	4.57
Cash Flow	2.86	4.86	4.76	4.51	4.15	3.37
Earnings	1.64	2.95	3.10	3.05	2.82	2.28
Dividends	1.88	1.88	1.68	1.48	1.28	1.10
Payout Ratio	115%	63%	43%	49%	46%	48%
Cal. Yrs.	1994	1993	1992	1991	1990	1989
Prices - High	62¼	74⅛	75⅞	73⅝	52	38⅜
- Low	49⅜	56⅞	58¾	43½	31⅜	25⅛
P/E Ratio - High	38	25	24	24	18	17
- Low	30	19	19	14	11	11

Income Statement Analysis (Million $)

	1995	%Chg	1994	%Chg	1993	%Chg	1992
Revs.	5,027	-41%	8,517	5%	8,135	5%	7,778
Oper. Inc.	881	-32%	1,303	10%	1,188	4%	1,145
Depr.	191	-37%	304	12%	271	12%	242
Int. Exp.	126	3%	122	22%	100	12%	89.5
Pretax Inc.	405	-46%	753	-11%	844	NM	845
Eff. Tax Rate	36%	—	38%	—	40%	—	40%
Net Inc.	260	-45%	470	-7%	506	NM	506

Balance Sheet & Other Fin. Data (Million $)

	1995	1994	1993	1992	1991	1990
Cash	13.0	Nil	100	1.0	40.0	71.0
Curr. Assets	897	1,129	1,077	1,035	1,082	910
Total Assets	3,358	5,198	4,651	4,305	3,902	3,290
Curr. Liab.	1,221	1,832	1,559	1,372	1,272	1,173
LT Debt	1,401	1,417	1,268	921	879	689
Common Eqty.	141	1,151	1,219	1,371	1,114	810
Total Cap.	1,960	3,178	2,944	2,726	2,448	1,926
Cap. Exp.	157	560	624	695	555	540
Cash Flow	451	774	777	748	678	550

Ratio Analysis

	1995	1994	1993	1992	1991	1990
Curr. Ratio	0.7	0.6	0.7	0.8	0.9	0.8
% LT Debt of Cap.	71.5	44.6	43.1	33.8	35.9	35.8
% Net Inc.of Revs.	5.2	5.5	6.2	6.5	6.5	5.8
% Ret. on Assets	6.4	9.6	11.5	12.3	12.8	12.0
% Ret. on Equity	40.2	39.9	39.7	40.7	48.0	48.2

Dividend Data—Dividends have been paid since 1898. A dividend reinvestment plan is available. A "poison pill" stock purchase rights plan was adopted in 1986.

Amt. of Div. $	Date Decl.	Ex-Div. Date	Stock of Record	Payment Date
0.470	Dec. 12	Jan. 04	Jan. 10	Feb. 01 '95
0.470	Feb. 27	Apr. 04	Apr. 10	May. 01 '95
Stk	—	May. 30	May. 15	May. 27 '95
0.470	Jun. 26	Jul. 06	Jul. 10	Aug. 01 '95
0.470	Sep. 18	Oct. 05	Oct. 10	Nov. 01 '95

Data as orig. reptd.; bef. results of disc. opers. and/or spec. items. Per share data adj. for stk. divs. as of ex-div. date. E-Estimated. NA-Not Available. NM-Not Meaningful. NR-Not Ranked.

Office—Number One General Mills Blvd., Minneapolis, MN 55426. **Tel**—(612) 540-2311. **Chrmn & CEO**—S. W. Sanger. **Pres**—C. W. Gaillard. **SVP & Secy**—S. S. Marshall. **SVP & Investor Contact**—Dean Belbas. **Dirs**—R. M. Bressler, L. D. DeSimone, W. T. Esrey, C. W. Gaillard, J. R. Hope, K. A. Macke, G. Putnam, M. D. Rose, S. W. Sanger, A. M. Spence, D. A. Terrell, C. A. Wurtele. **Transfer Agent & Registrar**—Norwest Stock Transfer, South St. Paul, Minn. **Incorporated** in Delaware in 1928. **Empl**-9,882. **S&P Analyst:** Kenneth A. Shea

General Motors

NYSE Symbol **GM**
In S&P 500

03-NOV-95

Industry:
Auto/Truck mfrs.

Summary: GM is the world's largest producer of cars and trucks, and has significant finance, aerospace, defense and computer services operations.

S&P Opinion: Hold (★★★)	

Quantitative Evaluations

Outlook
(1 Lowest—5 Highest)
• **1⁻**

Fair Value
• **38⅞**

Risk
• **Average**

Earn./Div. Rank
• **B-**

Technical Eval.
• **Bearish** since 8/95

Rel. Strength Rank
(1 Lowest—99 Highest)
• **33**

Insider Activity
• **Neutral**

Recent Price • 44
52 Wk Range • 51⅞-36⅛

Yield • 2.7%
12-Mo. P/E • 5.4

Earnings vs. Previous Year
▲=Up ▼=Down ▶=No Change

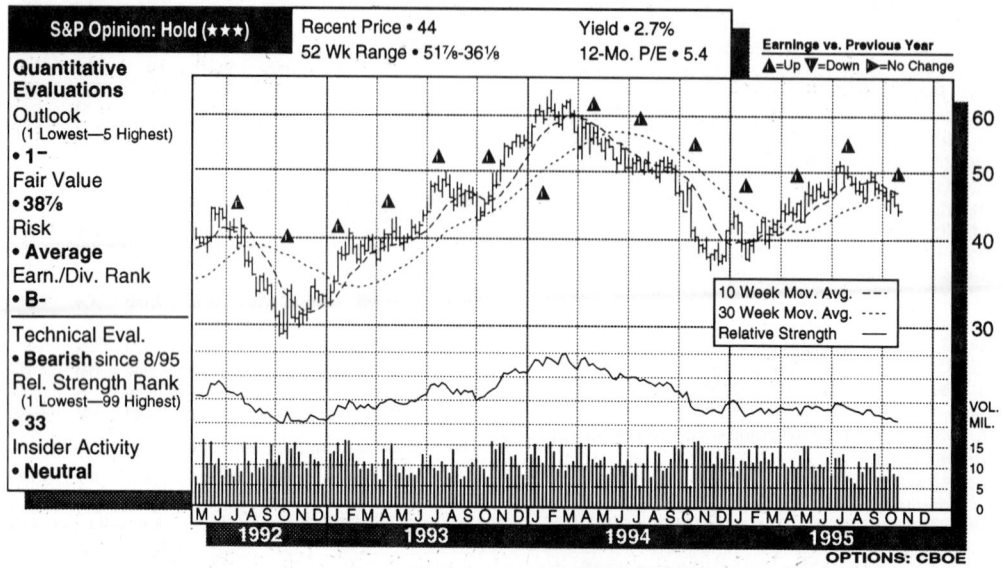

10 Week Mov. Avg. - - - -
30 Week Mov. Avg. · · · · ·
Relative Strength ——

OPTIONS: CBOE

Overview - 03-NOV-95

GM's vehicle sales in 1996 could fall slightly as flat overseas shipments and a continued decline in North America overshadow increases in emerging markets. Retail sales should continue to account for a larger share of North American vehicle deliveries as fleet sales have stabilized after a planned reduction over several years. North American operations should remain profitable as streamlining efforts continue and a more profitable product mix of newly designed and more competitive vehicles enter production. Foreign profits should also rise, despite continued uncertainty caused by currency swings in Europe and parts of Latin America. Overall, with the continued gradual increase in operating efficiency, modest earnings growth appears likely.

Valuation - 03-NOV-95

We are maintaining a neutral opinion on GM due to mounting evidence that U.S. demand may decline further near term and that the peak of the current business cycle is near. U.S. sales have been weak in 1995 and automakers are cutting production. Weak consumer economic indicators including declining confidence, high debt and sluggish income growth do not bode well for early 1996, but we expect improvement by mid-year. With the unsettled outlook, the stock is trading at a modest multiple of our 1996 earnings estimate which should limit the downside. However, we would not add to positions until it becomes more certain that a recession will not occur.

Key Stock Statistics

S&P EPS Est. 1995	7.00	Tang. Bk. Value/Share	NM
P/E on S&P Est. 1995	6.3	Beta	0.56
S&P EPS Est. 1996	8.00	Shareholders	782,000
Dividend Rate/Share	1.20	Market cap. (B)	$ 33.1
Shs. outstg. (M)	747.4	Inst. holdings	58%
Avg. daily vol. (M)	1.773	Insider holdings	NA

Value of $10,000 invested 5 years ago: $ 13,125

Fiscal Year Ending Dec. 31

	1995	% Change	1994	% Change	1993	% Change
Revenues (Million $)						
1Q	43,285	15%	37,495	7%	35,000	9%
2Q	44,146	9%	40,392	10%	36,658	4%
3Q	37,463	9%	34,510	15%	30,138	3%
4Q	—	—	42,553	14%	37,268	4%
Yr.	—	—	154,951	12%	138,220	4%
Income (Million $)						
1Q	2,154	34%	1,612	NM	513.2	NM
2Q	2,270	18%	1,923	116%	889.1	NM
3Q	642.4	16%	552.0	NM	-112.9	NM
4Q	—	—	1,572	34%	1,176	NM
Yr.	—	—	5,659	129%	2,466	NM
Earnings Per Share ($)						
1Q	2.51	35%	1.86	NM	0.42	NM
2Q	2.39	7%	2.23	142%	0.92	NM
3Q	0.42	5%	0.40	NM	-0.49	NM
4Q	E1.68	-3%	1.74	36%	1.28	NM
Yr.	E7.00	13%	6.20	191%	2.13	NM

Next earnings report expected: late January

General Motors

Business Summary - 03-NOV-95

General Motors is the world's largest manufacturer of cars and trucks. Net income by segment in 1994 and 1993 was divided as follows ($ in millions):

	1994	1993
North American Automotive	$690	-$982
International Automotive	1,582	1,225
GM Acceptance Corp.	920	981
Electronic Data Systems	822	724
GM Hughes Electronics	1,049	922
Other	-162	-404

Chevrolet, Buick, Cadillac, Oldsmobile, Pontiac, Saturn and GEO models accounted for 34.3% of total new U.S. car registrations (including imports) in 1994, versus 34.4% in 1993, 34.6% in 1992 and 35.6% in 1991 and 1990. Comparable figures for Chevrolet, GMC, Pontiac and Oldsmobile trucks were 30.9%, 31.4%, 33.3%, 34.0% and 35.7%, respectively. Worldwide wholesale sales were 8,328,000 vehicles in 1994 and 7,785,000 in 1993. GM's car and truck market share in Europe was 12.4% in 1994 versus 12.3% in 1993.

General Motors Acceptance Corp. provides vehicle financing, insurance and other financial services. Electronic Data Systems provides computer services. GM Hughes Electronics manufactures defense electronic, weapons system and automotive electronics, and operates a direct broadcast satellite television system. Other products includes locomotives; drilling, marine and stationary engines; and automated production and test equipment.

Important Developments

Oct. '95—GM's 1995 third quarter consolidated net income totaled $642 million, up from the $552 million reported for the comparable 1994 quarter. The 1995 total included a loss of $93 million (versus a year-earlier loss of $363 million) from North American Automotive Operations (NAO), and income of $111 million ($232 million) from International Automotive Operations (IO), $254 million ($245 million) from GM Acceptance Corp., $246 million ($216 million) from EDS, $256 million ($244 million) from GM Hughes Electronics and a $132 million loss ($22 million loss) from other operations. Worldwide vehicle sales during the third quarter totaled 1,848,000 compared with 1,790,000 in the 1994 quarter.

Capitalization

Total Debt: $77,885,100,000 (9/30/95).
Class E Com. Stk: 442,811,864 shs. ($0.10 par).
Class H Com. Stock: 96,308,464 shs. ($0.10 par).

Per Share Data ($)

(Year Ended Dec. 31)

	1994	1993	1992	1991	1990	1989
Tangible Bk. Val.	12.14	-16.55	-11.48	25.86	29.52	43.48
Cash Flow	20.72	16.26	9.00	4.64	8.87	18.80
Earnings	6.20	2.13	-4.85	-8.85	-4.09	6.33
Dividends	0.80	0.80	1.40	1.60	3.00	3.00
Payout Ratio	13%	38%	NM	NM	NM	47%
Prices - High	65⅜	57⅛	44⅜	44⅜	50½	50½
- Low	36⅛	32	28⅝	26¾	33⅛	39⅛
P/E Ratio - High	11	27	NM	NM	NM	8
- Low	6	15	NM	NM	NM	6

Income Statement Analysis (Million $)

	1994	%Chg	1993	%Chg	1992	%Chg	1991
Revs.	152,172	12%	135,696	3%	131,590	8%	122,081
Oper. Inc.	21,565	26%	17,059	30%	13,143	7%	12,257
Depr.	10,025	6%	9,442	5%	8,959	13%	7,916
Int. Exp.	5,466	-4%	5,718	-22%	7,349	-12%	8,346
Pretax Inc.	8,353	NM	2,575	NM	-3,332	NM	5,892
Eff. Tax Rate	32%	—	4.30%	—	NM	—	NM
Net Inc.	5,659	129%	2,466	NM	-2,620	NM	-4,991

Balance Sheet & Other Fin. Data (Million $)

	1994	1993	1992	1991	1990	1989
Cash	10,939	13,791	7,790	4,282	3,689	5,170
Total Assets	198,598	188,200	191,012	184,325	180,236	173,297
LT Debt	38,123	33,846	39,956	40,683	38,510	36,969
Total Debt	73,730	70,441	82,592	94,022	95,634	93,425
Common Eqty.	9,155	1,191	1,399	26,238	28,736	33,464
Cap. Exp.	17,465	15,175	12,874	12,897	10,932	10,647
Cash Flow	15,363	11,551	6,032	2,853	5,338	11,358

Ratio Analysis

	1994	1993	1992	1991	1990	1989
% Ret. on Assets	2.9	1.3	NM	NM	NM	2.5
% Ret. on Equity	102.6	161.3	NM	NM	NM	12.5
% LT Debt of Cap.	74.2	84.8	84.2	58.2	53.9	49.6

Dividend Data —Dividends have been paid since 1915. A dividend reinvestment plan is available.

Amt. of Div. $	Date Decl.	Ex-Div. Date	Stock of Record	Payment Date
0.200	Nov. 07	Nov. 10	Nov. 17	Dec. 10 '94
0.200	Feb. 06	Feb. 10	Feb. 16	Mar. 10 '95
0.300	May. 01	May. 05	May. 11	Jun. 10 '95
0.300	Aug. 07	Aug. 15	Aug. 17	Sep. 09 '95

Data as orig. reptd.; bef. results of disc. opers. and/or spec. items. Per share data adj. for stk. divs. as of ex-div. date. Quarterly tables reflect total revenues. E-Estimate. NA-Not Available. NM-Not Meaningful. NR-Not Ranked

Office—3044 West Grand Blvd., Detroit, MI 48202-3091. **Tel**—(313) 556-5000. **Chrmn**—J. G. Smale. **Pres & CEO**—J. F. Smith, Jr. **Secy**—S. A. Vickery. **VP & CFO**—J. M. Losh. **Institutional Contact**—Stephane Bello (212-418-6270). **Stockholder Contact**—(313-556-2044). **Dirs**—A. L. Armstrong, J. H. Bryan, T. E. Everhart, C. T. Fisher III, J. W. Marriott, Jr., A. D. McLaughlin, P. H. O'Neill, E. T. Pratt, Jr., J. G. Smale, J. F. Smith, Jr., L. W. Sullivan, D. Weatherstone, T. H. Wyman. **Transfer Agent & Registrar**—First Chicago Trust Co. of New York, Jersey City, NJ. **Incorporated** in Delaware in 1916. **Empl**-700,000. **S&P Analyst:** Joshua M. Harari, CFA

General Public Utilities

NYSE Symbol **GPU**
In S&P 500

12-OCT-95

Industry: Utilities-Electric

Summary: This holding company, one of the 20 largest electric utilities in the U.S., serves 1.9 million customers in New Jersey and Pennsylvania.

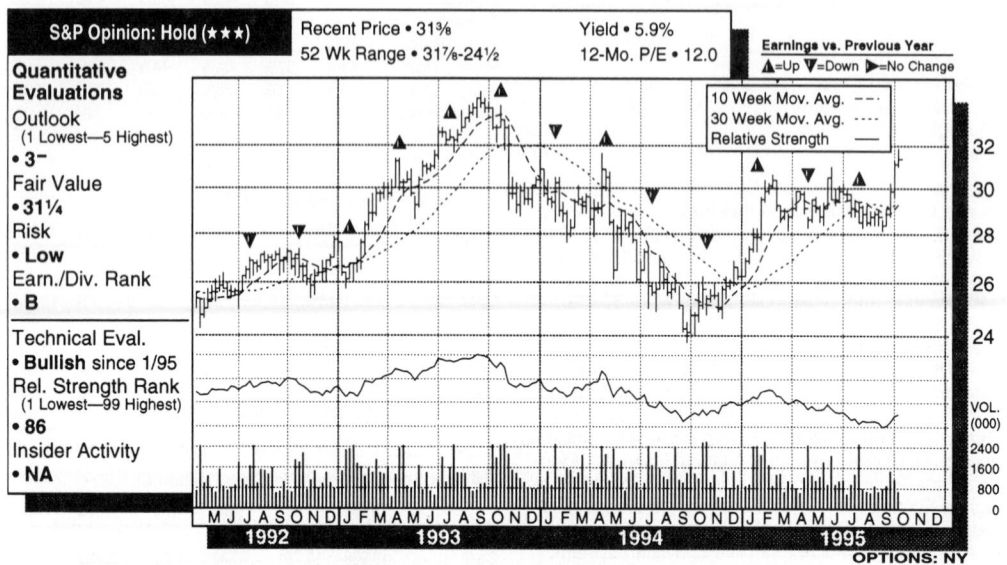

S&P Opinion: Hold (★★★)

Recent Price • 31⅜
52 Wk Range • 31⅞-24½

Yield • 5.9%
12-Mo. P/E • 12.0

Earnings vs. Previous Year
▲=Up ▼=Down ▶=No Change

Quantitative Evaluations

Outlook
(1 Lowest—5 Highest)
• 3-

Fair Value
• 31¼

Risk
• **Low**

Earn./Div. Rank
• **B**

Technical Eval.
• **Bullish** since 1/95

Rel. Strength Rank
(1 Lowest—99 Highest)
• 86

Insider Activity
• **NA**

10 Week Mov. Avg. — – –
30 Week Mov. Avg. ·······
Relative Strength ——

Overview - 12-OCT-95

EPS growth in 1995 from the level of 1994 (before one-time charges) is likely to be modest, in the absence of a $0.23 tax refund. Negative factors include flat to lower revenues, reflecting 1995's mild winter, and more shares outstanding. However, an ongoing program to control costs (in 1994, GPU reduced its work force 11% and consolidated management staff at two Pennsylvania operating subsidiaries) and the amendment or buy out of non-utility generators' long-term supply contracts should add to near-term results. In the long-term, earnings prospects will be challenged by relatively high rates at the Jersey Central Power & Light subsidiary.

Valuation - 12-OCT-95

GPU's shares have moved up 18.6% in the year to date, reflecting investors' anticipation of lower interest rates earlier in the year. Earnings per share comparisons will be hurt in 1995 by additional preferred dividend obligations from a May 1995 issue, and by a $30 million common share offering in June. However, efforts to buy out high cost purchased power contracts and to lower other fuel expense are helping to lower its overall cost structure. In addition, sound finances and a dividend payout below the industry average allowed a 4.4% dividend boost this year, well above the electric utility industry average of 1.5%. We expect above-average dividend increases to continue in the future, helping the shares keep pace with their peers.

Key Stock Statistics

S&P EPS Est. 1995	2.80	Tang. Bk. Value/Share	23.08
P/E on S&P Est. 1995	11.2	Beta	0.63
S&P EPS Est. 1996	2.90	Shareholders	48,000
Dividend Rate/Share	1.88	Market cap. (B)	$ 3.7
Shs. outstg. (M)	116.3	Inst. holdings	63%
Avg. daily vol. (M)	0.237	Insider holdings	NA

Value of $10,000 invested 5 years ago: $ 18,581

Fiscal Year Ending Dec. 31

	1995	% Change	1994	% Change	1993	% Change
Revenues (Million $)						
1Q	914.0	-2%	937.2	6%	881.2	-1%
2Q	864.7	-1%	873.5	1%	863.2	6%
3Q	—	—	994.7	NM	990.2	11%
4Q	—	—	844.1	-2%	861.5	3%
Yr.	—	—	3,650	1%	3,596	5%
Income (Million $)						
1Q	75.50	-39%	122.9	55%	79.32	8%
2Q	60.98	NM	-125.3	NM	58.57	38%
3Q	—	—	111.3	-12%	126.5	52%
4Q	—	—	54.83	75%	31.29	-41%
Yr.	—	—	163.7	-45%	295.7	17%
Earnings Per Share ($)						
1Q	0.65	-39%	1.07	49%	0.72	9%
2Q	0.53	NM	-1.09	NM	0.52	37%
3Q	E1.05	8%	0.97	-15%	1.14	50%
4Q	E0.57	21%	0.47	74%	0.27	-43%
Yr.	E2.80	97%	1.42	-46%	2.65	17%

Next earnings report expected: mid October

General Public Utilities

Business Summary - 12-OCT-95

General Public Utilities is an electric utility holding company whose subsidiaries (Jersey Central Power & Light, Metropolitan Edison, and Pennsylvania Electric) serve 1.9 million customers. Electric revenues in recent periods by customer class were:

	1994	1993	1992	1991
Residential	42%	42%	41%	41%
Commercial	34%	34%	33%	33%
Industrial	22%	22%	23%	23%
Other	2%	2%	3%	3%

Power requirements in 1994 were derived 35% from coal and 22% from nuclear, with 41% purchased and 2% other. Purchased power will represent a substantial share of capacity well into the future. System capability at time of peak in 1994 was 10,071 mw, and peak demand was 8,521 mw, for a reserve at peak demand of 18%.

An accident that shut down the 880 mw Three Mile Island Unit 2 (TMI-2) nuclear unit in 1979 caused significant financial difficulties. Regulators removed both TMI-1 and TMI-2 from the rate base. In 1985, TMI-1 resumed operation was returned to the rate base. GPU's recoverable investment in TMI-2 was $275 million. GPU completed the clean-up of TMI-2 in 1990 at a cost of $973 million. Auditors noted uncertainties associated with the TMI-2 accident in the company's 1994 financial statements.

Capital spending in 1994 totaled $586 million, primarily for construction to maintain and improve existing generation facilities and for the transmission and distribution system. For 1995, it budgeted expenditures of $482 million to continue system development. GPU expects to generate two-thirds of its capital needs through internally generated funds.

Important Developments

Sep. '95—The Federal Energy Regulatory Commission accepted GPU's proposal to charge rates for transmission service based on factors it believes will more fairly distribute costs among all users, including competitors who access the system. The factors include distance, quantity, voltage level and points of origination and destination of the power transported. Separately, The Pennsylvania Supreme Court restored a March 1993 Pennsylvia Public Utility Commission decision that allows it to recover Three Mile Island Unit 2 decommission costs from subsidiaries. As a result, GPU will take a $0.07 a share charge in the third quarter to cover costs not included in its $0.91 writeoff in 1994 for costs it had then deemed unrecoverable.

Capitalization

Long Term Debt: $2,525,840,000 (6/95).
Preferred Stock: 98,116.
Red. Preferred Stock: $134,000,000.
Subsid. Red. Preferred Stock: $330,000,000.

Per Share Data ($) (Year Ended Dec. 31)

	1994	1993	1992	1991	1990	1989
Tangible Bk. Val.	22.33	22.65	21.44	20.77	19.79	18.58
Earnings	1.42	2.65	2.27	1.96	2.51	2.51
Dividends	1.77	1.65	1.58	1.45	1.25	1.00
Payout Ratio	125%	62%	69%	74%	50%	40%
Prices - High	31⅝	34¾	27⅞	27¼	23⅝	23⅝
- Low	23¾	25¾	24¼	21¾	19¼	18⅛
P/E Ratio - High	22	13	12	14	9	9
- Low	17	10	11	11	8	7

Income Statement Analysis (Million $)

	1994	%Chg	1993	%Chg	1992	%Chg	1991
Revs.	3,650	2%	3,596	5%	3,434	2%	3,372
Depr.	354	-2%	360	6%	340	-13%	389
Maint.	NA	—	NA	—	NA	—	239
Fxd. Chgs. Cov.	2.6	-13%	3.0	4%	2.9	15%	2.5
Constr. Credits	11.8	19%	9.9	-21%	12.6	-12%	14.4
Eff. Tax Rate	32%	—	38%	—	38%	—	35%
Net Inc.	164	-45%	296	17%	252	16%	218

Balance Sheet & Other Fin. Data (Million $)

	1994	1993	1992	1991	1990	1989
Gross Prop.	9,415	8,923	8,546	8,094	7,909	7,968
Cap. Exp.	586	496	460	467	491	487
Net Prop.	6,267	5,994	5,829	5,572	5,512	5,307
Capitalization:						
LT Debt	2,345	2,320	2,222	1,992	1,936	1,889
% LT Debt	44	44	44	42	42	43
Pfd.	453	308	465	465	500	400
% Pfd.	8.40	5.90	9.20	9.80	11	9.20
Common	2,573	2,610	2,379	2,306	2,197	2,063
% Common	48	50	47	48	47	47
Total Cap.	6,966	6,798	6,037	5,734	5,578	5,393

Ratio Analysis

	1994	1993	1992	1991	1990	1989
Oper. Ratio	86.6	85.3	86.9	87.6	84.6	84.5
% Earn. on Net Prop.	8.0	9.0	7.9	7.6	8.5	8.7
% Ret. on Revs.	4.5	8.2	7.3	6.5	9.3	9.7
% Ret. On Invest.Cap	5.9	8.2	8.1	7.9	9.0	9.3
% Return On Com.Eqty	6.3	11.9	10.7	9.7	12.3	13.8

Dividend Data —Common dividends, omitted since 1980, were resumed in 1987. Dividends were maintained on subsidiary preferred stock. A dividend reinvestment plan is available.

Amt. of Div. $	Date Decl.	Ex-Div. Date	Stock of Record	Payment Date
0.450	Oct. 06	Oct. 24	Oct. 28	Nov. 30 '94
0.450	Dec. 01	Jan. 23	Jan. 27	Feb. 22 '95
0.470	Apr. 06	Apr. 24	Apr. 28	May. 31 '95
0.470	Jun. 01	Jul. 26	Jul. 28	Aug. 30 '95
0.470	Oct. 05	Oct. 25	Oct. 27	Nov. 29 '95

Data as orig. reptd.; bef. results of disc opers. and/or spec. items. Per share data adj. for stk. divs. as of ex-div. date. E-Estimated. NA-Not Available. NM-Not Meaningful. NR-Not Ranked.

Office—100 Interpace Parkway, Parsippany, NJ 07054-1149. **Tel**—(201) 263-6500. **Chrmn, Pres & CEO**—J. R. Leva. **SVP & CFO**—J. G. Graham. **VP & Treas**—T. G. Howson, **Secy**—Mary A. Nalewako. **Investor Contact**—Joanne M. Barbieri. **Dirs**—L. J. Appell, Jr., D. J. Bainton, T. H. Black, H. F. Henderson, Jr., J. R. Leva, J. M. Pietruski, C. A. Rein, P. R. Roedel, C. A. H. Trost, P. K. Woolf. **Transfer Agent**—Chemical Bank, NYC. **Incorporated** in New York; reincorporated in Pennsylvania in 1969. **Empl**-10,555. **S&P Analyst:** Jane Collin

General Re

NYSE Symbol **GRN**
In S&P 500

18-OCT-95

Industry: Insurance

Summary: General Re is the largest property-casualty reinsurer in the U.S. Other subsidiaries are engaged in property-casualty reinsurance overseas and in other financial services.

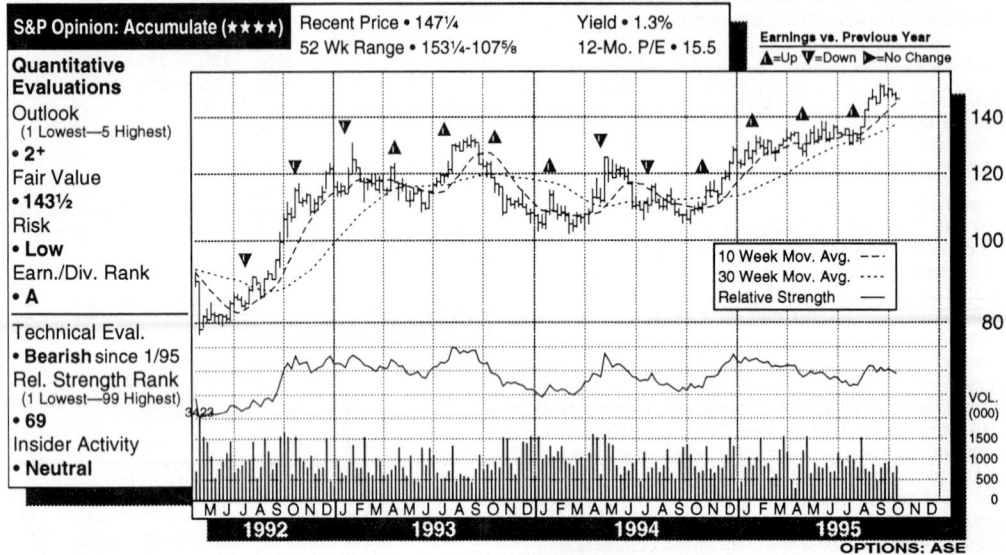

S&P Opinion: Accumulate (★★★★)	Recent Price • 147¼	Yield • 1.3%
	52 Wk Range • 153¼-107⅝	12-Mo. P/E • 15.5

Quantitative Evaluations

Outlook
(1 Lowest—5 Highest)
• **2+**

Fair Value
• **143½**

Risk
• **Low**

Earn./Div. Rank
• **A**

Technical Eval.
• **Bearish** since 1/95

Rel. Strength Rank
(1 Lowest—99 Highest)
• **69**

Insider Activity
• **Neutral**

Earnings vs. Previous Year
▲=Up ▼=Down ▶=No Change

10 Week Mov. Avg. – – –
30 Week Mov. Avg. · · · ·
Relative Strength —

OPTIONS: ASE

Overview - 18-OCT-95

Written premium growth in 1995 will easily top 25%, reflecting growth internationally and a continuation of the improved market conditions that emerged in 1994. Though GRN's primary market is the U.S., a recently announced joint venture with a European insurer will give GRN increased access to the faster growing overseas market. Primarily a casualty reinsurer, GRN has not received the strong price increases that property lines reinsurers (especially those that write catastrophe reinsurance) have garnered in the wake of recent record catastrophe losses. However, these losses have forced primary insurers to rethink their risk retention strategies, and have increased the demand for reinsurance. Assuming "normal" catastrophe loss experience, underwriting results should approach breakeven. Share buybacks (over 21.9 million from mid-1987 to year-end 1994) will aid share earnings.

Valuation - 18-OCT-95

Despite trading close to their 52-week high, the shares of this top notch reinsurer have some additional upside potential, given the company's above-average premium and earnings growth prospects. Thanks to a conservative strategy, General Re's underwriting record is superior to that of the industry overall. Reinsurance stocks tend to trade at higher P/E multiples than those of primary insurers. Although the shares are trading at approximately 14 times our conservative 1996 operating earnings estimate, they remain attractively valued. We would look for any near-term pullback to add to positions.

Key Stock Statistics

S&P EPS Est. 1995	9.10	Tang. Bk. Value/Share	69.59
P/E on S&P Est. 1995	16.2	Beta	0.81
S&P EPS Est. 1996	10.25	Shareholders	4,200
Dividend Rate/Share	1.96	Market cap. (B)	$ 12.3
Shs. outstg. (M)	82.0	Inst. holdings	84%
Avg. daily vol. (M)	0.167	Insider holdings	NA

Value of $10,000 invested 5 years ago: $ 18,507

Fiscal Year Ending Dec. 31

	1995	% Change	1994	% Change	1993	% Change
Revenues (Million $)						
1Q	1,207	18%	1,024	11%	925.4	9%
2Q	1,943	117%	896.0	6%	843.4	2%
3Q	—	—	935.0	3%	904.2	8%
4Q	—	—	982.6	11%	887.0	2%
Yr.	—	—	3,837	8%	3,560	5%
Income (Million $)						
1Q	183.1	87%	97.90	-40%	163.0	11%
2Q	214.2	21%	177.0	-6%	189.0	19%
3Q	—	—	191.0	10%	174.1	25%
4Q	—	—	199.9	17%	171.1	13%
Yr.	—	—	665.3	-5%	696.8	17%
Earnings Per Share ($)						
1Q	2.20	91%	1.15	-39%	1.89	13%
2Q	2.58	22%	2.12	-4%	2.20	22%
3Q	—	—	2.29	13%	2.03	25%
4Q	—	—	2.41	20%	2.00	14%
Yr.	E9.10	14%	7.97	-2%	8.11	19%

Next earnings report expected: early November

Business Summary - 18-OCT-95

General Re Corp. (formerly General Reinsurance) is the parent of General Reinsurance Group, the largest reinsurance organization in the U.S. Operations are conducted in the U.S., Canada and more than 30 foreign countries. Segment contributions to pretax income, before equity earnings:

	1994	1993	1992
Domestic	93%	98%	97%
Overseas	7%	2%	3%

Consolidated net premiums written in 1994 totaled $3.0 billion ($2.52 billion in 1993), of which domestic operations accounted for about 86%. Of domestic premiums written, direct reinsurance accounted for 87%, excess and surplus lines 7%, and direct excess and alternative markets 4%.

Through the use of reinsurance, primary insurers can limit their exposure to risk, and usually write more business than their surplus levels would normally permit. Most of GRN's business is written on an excess of loss basis, which means that its liability arises only after the loss incurred by the primary insurer exceeds a specified amount.

Domestic p-c operations are conducted through General Reinsurance Corp., General Star Companies, and Genesis Companies. General Re Financial Products (established in 1990) offers interest rate and cross currency swaps and fixed income option products. In December 1994, in a move that will further increase its access to the overseas reinsurance markets, GRN invested DM 902 million and formed an alliance with Cologne Re via a joint venture with its parent, Colonia Konzern AG.

Important Developments

Aug. '95—GRN's worldwide net premium volume in the first half of 1995 advanced 73%, year to year, to $2.6 billion from $1.5 billion. The 17% rise in domestic written premiums likely reflected increased demand and better pricing for most types of reinsurance. International written premiums surged to $1.2 billion from $298 million. The growth primarily reflected contributions (recorded on a one-quarter lag) from the December 1994 joint venture with European reinsurer Cologne Re. Domestic underwriting results were aided by lower catastrophe losses, and the combined (loss and expense) ratio improved to 99.3%, from 106.2%. The combined ratio for international operations rose to 101.6% in the first half of 1995 from 100.0% in the 1994 period.

Capitalization

Total Debt: $156,000,000 (6/95).
Minority Interest: $1,194,000,000.
ESOP 7.25% Conv. Preferred Stock: $148,000,000.

Per Share Data ($) (Year Ended Dec. 31)

	1994	1993	1992	1991	1990	1989
Tangible Bk. Val.	59.35	56.68	49.90	45.16	37.50	34.31
Oper. Earnings	7.43	7.01	5.30	6.37	6.35	6.08
Earnings	7.97	8.11	6.84	7.46	6.89	6.52
Dividends	1.92	1.88	1.80	1.68	1.52	1.36
Payout Ratio	24%	23%	26%	23%	22%	21%
Prices - High	129⅛	133⅜	123½	102¾	93¼	96¼
- Low	101¾	104¾	77½	83¾	69	54⅜
P/E Ratio - High	16	16	18	14	14	15
- Low	13	13	11	11	10	8

Income Statement Analysis (Million $)

	1994	%Chg	1993	%Chg	1992	%Chg	1991
Premium Income	2,788	14%	2,446	5%	2,319	3%	2,241
Net Invest. Inc.	749	NM	755	NM	755	NM	752
Oth. Revs.	300	-16%	359	15%	313	46%	214
Total Revs.	3,837	8%	3,560	5%	3,387	6%	3,207
Pretax Inc.	794	-10%	885	23%	721	-9%	793
Net Oper. Inc.	621	3%	604	30%	465	-17%	562
Net Inc.	665	-5%	697	17%	596	-9%	657

Balance Sheet & Other Fin. Data (Million $)

	1994	1993	1992	1991	1990	1989
Cash & Equiv.	514	300	245	244	228	219
Premiums Due	1,421	798	670	588	551	577
Inv. Assets Bonds	14,174	11,441	9,376	9,015	8,224	7,458
Inv. Assets Stock	2,977	2,726	2,157	1,827	1,286	1,342
Inv. Assets Loans	Nil	Nil	Nil	Nil	Nil	Nil
Inv. Assets Total	18,898	14,167	11,532	10,842	9,510	8,799
Deferred Policy Cost	324	153	155	157	149	139
Total Assets	29,597	18,469	13,280	12,416	11,033	10,390
Debt	188	453	209	316	277	278
Common Eqty.	4,859	4,761	4,227	3,911	3,270	3,084

Ratio Analysis

	1994	1993	1992	1991	1990	1989
Prop&Cas Loss	70.7	70.6	78.8	72.5	68.2	70.6
Prop&Cas Expense	30.6	30.9	29.6	29.7	30.8	29.0
Prop&Cas Comb.	101.3	101.5	108.4	102.2	99.0	99.6
% Ret. on Revs.	17.3	19.6	17.6	20.5	20.5	21.6
% Return on Equity	13.6	15.5	14.7	18.1	19.0	20.7

Dividend Data —Except for 1933, dividends have been paid each year since 1926. A dividend reinvestment plan is available. A "poison pill" stock purchase rights plan was adopted in 1991.

Amt. of Div. $	Date Decl.	Ex-Div. Date	Stock of Record	Payment Date
0.480	Dec. 14	Dec. 16	Dec. 22	Dec. 30 '94
0.490	Feb. 08	Mar. 17	Mar. 23	Mar. 31 '95
0.490	Jun. 13	Jun. 20	Jun. 22	Jun. 30 '95
0.490	Sep. 14	Sep. 21	Sep. 25	Sep. 29 '95

Data as orig. reptd.; bef. results of disc. opers. and/or spec. items. Per share data adj. for stk. divs. as of ex-div. date. E-Estimated. NA-Not Available. NM-Not Meaningful. NR-Not Ranked.

Office—Financial Centre, 695 East Main St., P.O. Box 10351, Stamford, CT 06904. **Tel**—(203) 328-5000. **Chrmn & Pres**—R. E. Ferguson. **VP-Secy**—C. F. Barr. **VP-CFO**—J. P. Brandon. **Investor Contact**—Deborah Nelson. **Dirs**—L. W. Benson, W. M. Cabot, J. C. Etling, R. E. Ferguson, W. C. Ferguson, D. J. Kirk, K. Koplovitz, E. H. Malone, A. W. Mathieson, D. E. McKinney, S. A. Ross, W. F. Williams. **Transfer Agent & Registrar**—American Stock Transfer & Trust Co., NYC. **Incorporated** in New York in 1921; reincorporated in Delaware in 1972. **Empl**-2,379. **S&P Analyst:** Catherine A. Seifert

General Signal

NYSE Symbol **GSX**
In S&P 500

23-AUG-95

Industry:
Electronics/Electric

Summary: General Signal is a leading producer of capital goods for the process control, electrical and telecommunications industries.

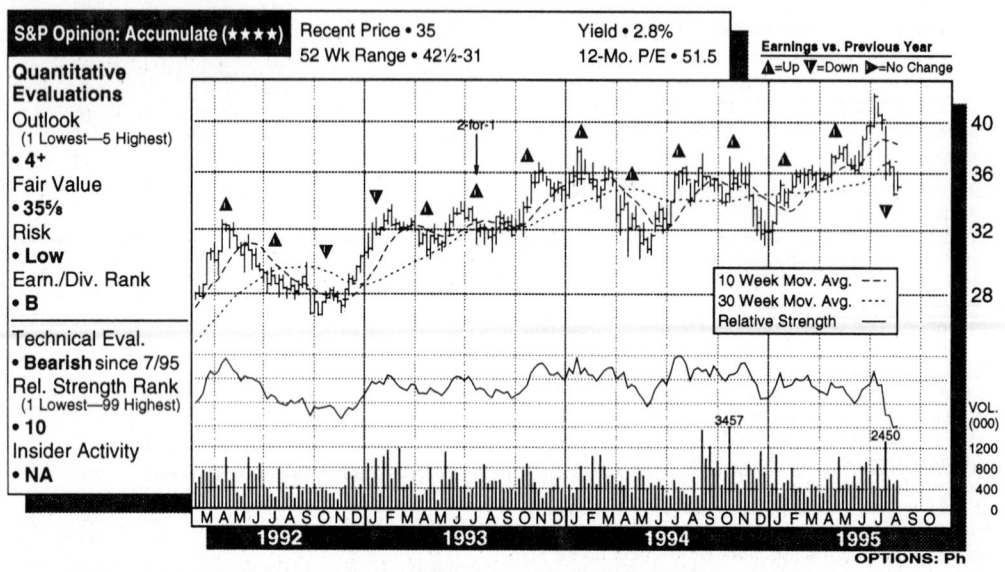

S&P Opinion: Accumulate (★★★★)	Recent Price • 35	Yield • 2.8%
	52 Wk Range • 42½-31	12-Mo. P/E • 51.5

Quantitative Evaluations

Outlook
(1 Lowest—5 Highest)
• **4+**

Fair Value
• **35%**

Risk
• **Low**

Earn./Div. Rank
• **B**

Technical Eval.
• **Bearish** since 7/95

Rel. Strength Rank
(1 Lowest—99 Highest)
• **10**

Insider Activity
• **NA**

Earnings vs. Previous Year
▲=Up ▼=Down ▶=No Change

10 Week Mov. Avg. - - -
30 Week Mov. Avg. ·····
Relative Strength ——

OPTIONS: Ph

Overview - 23-AUG-95

Sales for 1996 are projected to increase about 16% from those of 1995, giving effect to the pending pooling of interest acquisition of Data Switch. In addition, the purchase acquisitions of MagnaTek Electric and Best Power will add approximately $115 million to revenues. Growth should be led by process controls and electrical controls, which should benefit from further economic growth and rising capital spending. Sales of industrial technology, which are highly dependent on automotive sales and the awarding of a major contract from the Post Office, are expected to rise only modestly. The company's continuing focus on improving margins should allow for a higher level of profitability. Somewhat offsetting is likely to be a two percentage point increase in the tax rate.

Valuation - 23-AUG-95

General Signal's shares recently sold off on weaker than expected second quarter earnings even before giving effect to the one-time acquisition-related charge. However, we continue to believe these shares are an excellent vehicle to participate in increasing capital spending. Over the past half dozen years, the company has become a much more efficient business by focusing on productivity improvements and reducing its operating units from 24 to 11. It is also seeking to increase shareholder value through a "bolt-on" acquisition strategy. These factors should produce steadily rising earnings that should result in a higher valuation in the years ahead.

Key Stock Statistics

S&P EPS Est. 1995	2.50	Tang. Bk. Value/Share	8.00
P/E on S&P Est. 1995	14.0	Beta	1.06
S&P EPS Est. 1996	3.00	Shareholders	16,100
Dividend Rate/Share	0.96	Market cap. (B)	$ 1.6
Shs. outstg. (M)	47.3	Inst. holdings	85%
Avg. daily vol. (M)	0.137	Insider holdings	0%

Value of $10,000 invested 5 years ago: $ 17,420

Fiscal Year Ending Dec. 31

	1995	% Change	1994	% Change	1993	% Change
Revenues (Million $)						
1Q	411.0	20%	342.4	-9%	377.0	-8%
2Q	421.4	11%	378.6	-2%	387.0	-8%
3Q	—	—	390.0	5%	373.0	-9%
4Q	—	—	416.7	6%	393.8	4%
Yr.	—	—	1,528	NM	1,530	-5%
Income (Million $)						
1Q	27.30	23%	22.20	27%	17.48	17%
2Q	23.40	-8%	25.30	31%	19.27	21%
3Q	—	—	27.50	22%	22.55	41%
4Q	—	—	29.10	NM	4.86	NM
Yr.	—	—	104.1	56%	66.60	NM
Earnings Per Share ($)						
1Q	0.58	23%	0.47	12%	0.42	8%
2Q	0.50	-6%	0.53	20%	0.44	10%
3Q	E0.69	19%	0.58	12%	0.52	27%
4Q	E0.73	18%	0.62	NM	0.10	NM
Yr.	E2.50	14%	2.20	50%	1.47	NM

Next earnings report expected: mid October

Business Summary - 23-AUG-95

General Signal is a broadly diversified manufacturer. Business segment contributions (profits in millions $) in 1994:

	Sales	Profits
Process controls	40%	$66.8
Electrical controls	40%	30.7
Industrial technology	20%	47.4
Special items	Nil	46.2

Foreign operations accounted for 12% of sales and 6.3% of operating income in 1994 before dispositions and special items.

Process controls products include pumps, industrial fluid mixers, agitators, coal feeder equipment, industrial valves, consistency transmitters, ultra-low temperature laboratory freezers, special refrigerators, and CO_2 incubators, industrial and laboratory ovens and furnaces.

Electrical control products include power systems, power supplies, power conditioners/regulators, transformers, electrical conduit and cable fittings, enclosures and controls, industrial lighting, heat-trace systems, and firestop products, fire detection systems, low voltage systems service, emergency lighting, exit signs, signaling devices, flexible wiring systems, electric motors, radio frequency transmission and pressurization equipment and systems.

The industrial technology segment includes metal components and assemblies for automobiles and bicycles, electronic fareboxes, turnstiles, vending equipment, performance monitoring and test equipment for telecommunications and other industries.

Important Developments

Jul. '95—GSX said that excluding one-time acquisition-related charges for Best Power Technology, Inc., per share earnings for the second quarter increased to $0.60 from $0.53. It added that orders rose 5% in the second quarter, led by a 16.2% gain at process controls. Electrical controls orders rose 3.3%, while industrial technology orders declined 15.9%.

Jul. '95—GSX completed the acquisition of MagneTek Electric, Inc., the medium-power transformer business of MagneTek, Inc. Earlier in the month, the company said that it expected to complete the acquisition of Data Switch Corp., a leading supplier of telecommunications switch equipment, during the third quarter. In June GSX completed the acquisition of Best Power Technology, Inc., a leading supplier of uninterruptible power supply products. These companies had combined sales of about $135 million.

Capitalization

Long Term Debt: $487,200,000 (6/95), incl. $100,000,000 of 5.75% sub. notes due 2002, conv. into com. at $39.50 a sh.

Per Share Data ($)

(Year Ended Dec. 31)

	1994	1993	1992	1991	1990	1989
Tangible Bk. Val.	7.51	7.20	4.79	6.70	5.90	8.89
Cash Flow	3.08	2.35	1.36	2.88	0.97	3.72
Earnings	2.20	1.47	0.24	1.66	-0.35	2.06
Dividends	0.91	0.90	0.90	0.90	0.90	0.90
Payout Ratio	42%	61%	387%	54%	NM	44%
Prices - High	38	36¾	32⅝	27	29¾	29
- Low	30⅛	30⅛	25⅞	17⅝	15¾	22⅞
P/E Ratio - High	17	25	NM	16	NM	14
- Low	14	20	NM	11	NM	11

Income Statement Analysis (Million $)

	1994	%Chg	1993	%Chg	1992	%Chg	1991
Revs.	1,528	NM	1,530	-5%	1,618	NM	1,611
Oper. Inc.	168	5%	160	-2%	164	4%	158
Depr.	41.7	5%	39.6	-10%	44.0	-7%	47.2
Int. Exp.	11.8	-28%	16.5	-39%	27.1	-16%	32.2
Pretax Inc.	160	70%	94.0	NM	14.0	-84%	89.0
Eff. Tax Rate	35%	—	30%	—	32%	—	29%
Net Inc.	104	55%	67.0	NM	9.0	-86%	64.0

Balance Sheet & Other Fin. Data (Million $)

	1994	1993	1992	1991	1990	1989
Cash	Nil	1.0	16.0	18.0	8.0	24.0
Curr. Assets	717	595	678	602	714	774
Total Assets	1,343	1,225	1,226	1,180	1,295	1,324
Curr. Liab.	357	326	336	358	403	445
LT Debt	269	191	358	290	398	331
Common Eqty.	548	525	365	476	450	506
Total Cap.	817	717	723	809	879	870
Cap. Exp.	74.8	55.1	49.3	48.1	68.8	62.0
Cash Flow	146	106	53.0	111	37.0	142

Ratio Analysis

	1994	1993	1992	1991	1990	1989
Curr. Ratio	2.0	1.8	2.0	1.7	1.8	1.7
% LT Debt of Cap.	32.9	26.7	49.5	35.8	45.2	38.1
% Net Inc.of Revs.	6.8	4.4	0.6	4.0	NM	4.1
% Ret. on Assets	8.1	4.9	0.8	5.2	5.8	5.8
% Ret. on Equity	19.5	13.8	2.2	13.8	NM	16.2

Dividend Data

—Dividends have been paid since 1940. A dividend reinvestment plan is available. A "poison pill" stock purchase right was adopted in 1986.

Amt. of Div. $	Date Decl.	Ex-Div. Date	Stock of Record	Payment Date
0.225	Sep. 22	Oct. 03	Oct. 07	Oct. 18 '94
0.240	Dec. 08	Dec. 30	Jan. 06	Jan. 17 '95
0.240	Mar. 16	Apr. 05	Apr. 11	Apr. 20 '95
0.240	Jun. 15	Jul. 10	Jul. 12	Jul. 20 '95

Data as orig. reptd.; bef. results of disc. opers. and/or spec. items. Per share data adj. for stk. divs. as of ex-div. date. E-Estimated. NA-Not Available. NM-Not Meaningful. NR-Not Ranked.

Offices—High Ridge Park, Stamford, CT 06904. **Tel**—(203) 329-4100. **Chrmn & CEO**—E. M. Carpenter. **Pres & COO**—M. D. Lockhart. **VP-Fin & CFO**—T. D. Martin. **VP-Secy**—E. J. Smith Jr. **VP-Investor Contact**—Nino J. Fernandez. **Dirs**—R. E. Bailey, V. C. Campbell, E. M. Carpenter, U. F. Fairbairn, R. E. Ferguson, J. P. Horgan, C. R. Kidder, R. J. Kogan, M. D. Lockhart, N. R. Owen, R. W. Schmitt, J. R. Selby. **Transfer Agent**—The Bank of New York, NYC. **Incorporated** in New York in 1904. **Empl**-12,200. **S&P Analyst:** Paul H. Valentine, CFA

STOCK REPORTS

Genuine Parts

NYSE Symbol **GPC**
In S&P 500

28-AUG-95 | **Industry:** Auto parts/equipment | **Summary:** This company is a leading wholesale distributor of automotive replacement parts, industrial parts and supplies, and office products.

S&P Opinion: Hold (★★★)	Recent Price • 39⅝	Yield • 3.2%
	52 Wk Range • 40⅜-33⅞	12-Mo. P/E • 16.4

Quantitative Evaluations

Outlook (1 Lowest—5 Highest)
• **2⁻**

Fair Value
• **35⅞**

Risk
• **Low**

Earn./Div. Rank
• **A+**

Technical Eval.
• **Bullish** since 7/95

Rel. Strength Rank (1 Lowest—99 Highest)
• **57**

Insider Activity
• **NA**

Earnings vs. Previous Year
▲=Up ▼=Down ▶=No Change

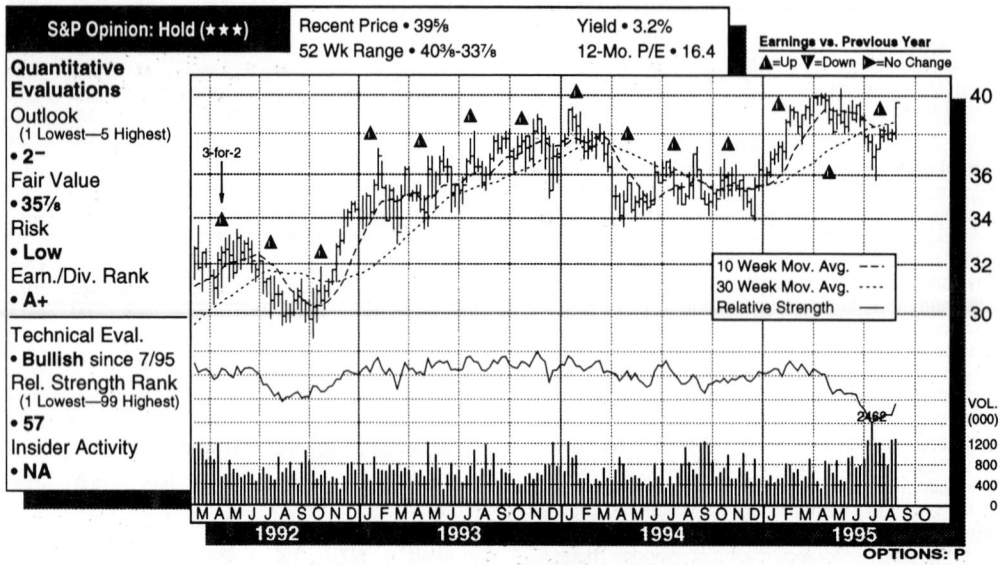

3-for-2

10 Week Mov. Avg. ---
30 Week Mov. Avg. ·····
Relative Strength —

VOL. (000)

OPTIONS: P

Overview - 28-AUG-95

Near-term prospects have moderated somewhat, due to weak economic growth and delays in start-up of new emissions testing programs in the U.S. Longer-term prospects for GPC's automotive replacement parts segment are enhanced by the rising number and increasing complexity of vehicles. Today, the average car in the U.S. is eight years old and the average truck is older. Despite the improved quality of new vehicles, the growing number of older vehicles together with an increase in the percentage of those vehicles that will be subject to emissions inspection will fuel a rise in demand for parts needed to return them to original specifications. GPC also benefits from expansion of its market share, as long-term consolidation in the industry drives out smaller participants.

Valuation - 28-AUG-95

We have downgraded the stock to hold, due to delayed implementation of new emissions testing programs which shaved off some of the anticipated growth in demand for auto parts for 1995. Although GPC still trades at the low end of its average P/E range, and is still attractive for value investors, we expect only average performance near term. Among the catalysts that we think are needed for the stock to outperform is increased demand for replacement parts which may not occur until the new emissions tests are in place in late 1996 or early 1997. However, with a solid balance sheet, little debt and strong cash flow, this A+ ranked stock remains a sound holding.

Key Stock Statistics

S&P EPS Est. 1995	2.55	Tang. Bk. Value/Share	13.01
P/E on S&P Est. 1995	15.5	Beta	0.64
S&P EPS Est. 1996	2.85	Shareholders	7,900
Dividend Rate/Share	1.26	Market cap. (B)	$ 4.9
Shs. outstg. (M)	122.8	Inst. holdings	66%
Avg. daily vol. (M)	0.298	Insider holdings	NA

Value of $10,000 invested 5 years ago: $ 16,960

Fiscal Year Ending Dec. 31

	1995	% Change	1994	% Change	1993	% Change
Revenues (Million $)						
1Q	1,281	10%	1,162	12%	1,038	19%
2Q	1,309	7%	1,220	10%	1,106	19%
3Q	—	—	1,268	11%	1,145	19%
4Q	—	—	1,208	10%	1,095	21%
Yr.	—	—	4,858	11%	4,384	20%
Income (Million $)						
1Q	69.04	10%	62.89	12%	56.39	20%
2Q	74.93	6%	71.01	8%	65.91	20%
3Q	—	—	72.92	16%	63.02	13%
4Q	—	—	81.72	11%	73.55	18%
Yr.	—	—	288.5	11%	258.9	18%
Earnings Per Share ($)						
1Q	0.56	10%	0.51	13%	0.45	10%
2Q	0.61	7%	0.57	8%	0.53	10%
3Q	E0.63	7%	0.59	16%	0.51	4%
4Q	E0.75	14%	0.66	12%	0.59	7%
Yr.	E2.55	9%	2.33	12%	2.08	8%

Next earnings report expected: mid October

Genuine Parts

Business Summary - 28-AUG-95

Genuine Parts Company is the leading independent distributor of automotive replacement parts, operating (as of January 1, 1995) 64 NAPA ware-house-distribution centers in the U.S., about 700 owned jobbing stores, six Rayloc automotive parts rebuilding plants and three Balkamp distribution centers. It also owns 20% of UAP Inc. GPC and UAP contributed their Canadian automotive operations to a partnership formed in 1990.

Contributions by industry segment in 1994 were:

	Sales	Profits
Automotive parts & supplies	55.5%	61.6%
Industrial parts & supplies	27.2%	22.6%
Office products	17.4%	15.8%

The automotive parts group serves 5,800 NAPA Auto Parts jobbing stores, including about 722 company-owned stores, which sell to garages, service stations, car and truck dealers, fleet operators, leasing companies, bus and truck lines, etc. Approximately 125,000 different replacement items are stocked. Rebuilt parts are distributed under the Rayloc brand name. Balkamp is a majority-owned subsidiary which purchases, packages and distributes service and supply items under the Balkamp name to NAPA distribution centers.

Motion Industries, the industrial parts and supplies segment, distributes over 200,000 items, including industrial bearings, mechanical, electrical and fluid power transmission equipment, hydraulic and pneumatic products, material handling components, agricultural and irrigation equipment, and related parts and supplies from some 330 locations in 36 states, including 315 branches, 11 service centers and five distribution centers.

The office products group (S.P. Richards Co.) distributes over 18,000 items, including information processing supplies and office furniture, machines and supplies to office supply dealers, from 37 full line distribution centers and four furniture distribution centers in 27 states.

Important Developments

Jul. '95—All of GPC's segments contributed to improved earnings in 1995's second quarter. Automotive sales rose 5%, while office products advanced 8% and industrial climbed 13%. For the first half, automotive sales rose 5%, office products 10% and industrial 16%. GPC opened its 38th office products distribution center in Pittsburgh, Pa. in June. In May, Horizon Data Supplies, a computer supplies distributor in Reno, Nev. with sales of $27 million, was acquired.

Capitalization

Long Term Debt: $11,184,000 (6/30/95).
Minority Interests: $26,512,000.

Per Share Data ($)

(Year Ended Dec. 31)

	1994	1993	1992	1991	1990	1989
Tangible Bk. Val.	12.45	11.63	10.78	9.85	9.02	8.36
Cash Flow	2.63	2.36	2.19	2.08	2.03	1.93
Earnings	2.33	2.08	1.92	1.81	1.79	1.72
Dividends	1.15	1.06	0.99	0.97	0.92	0.80
Payout Ratio	49%	51%	52%	53%	51%	47%
Prices - High	39⅜	39	34¾	32⅞	28½	29
- Low	33⅝	32⅞	29	23¼	22⅛	23¼
P/E Ratio - High	17	19	18	18	16	17
- Low	14	16	15	13	12	14

Income Statement Analysis (Million $)

	1994	%Chg	1993	%Chg	1992	%Chg	1991
Revs.	4,858	11%	4,384	19%	3,669	7%	3,435
Oper. Inc.	502	11%	453	20%	379	6%	359
Depr.	37.4	9%	34.4	11%	31.1	4%	29.8
Int. Exp.	1.3	-16%	1.6	-14%	1.8	-66%	5.4
Pretax Inc.	477	11%	428	20%	356	6%	337
Eff. Tax Rate	39%	—	39%	—	38%	—	38%
Net Inc.	289	12%	259	18%	220	6%	208

Balance Sheet & Other Fin. Data (Million $)

	1994	1993	1992	1991	1990	1989
Cash	82.0	188	173	186	145	170
Curr. Assets	1,596	1,506	1,277	1,179	1,099	1,056
Total Assets	2,029	1,871	1,597	1,467	1,352	1,292
Curr. Liab.	422	353	309	291	269	245
LT Debt	11.4	12.3	13.0	12.7	16.4	43.1
Common Eqty.	1,526	1,445	1,235	1,127	1,033	972
Total Cap.	1,607	1,517	1,288	1,176	1,083	1,047
Cap. Exp.	66.0	57.5	31.2	27.9	44.5	53.2
Cash Flow	326	293	251	238	235	224

Ratio Analysis

	1994	1993	1992	1991	1990	1989
Curr. Ratio	3.8	4.3	4.1	4.1	4.1	4.3
% LT Debt of Cap.	0.7	0.8	1.0	1.1	1.5	4.1
% Net Inc.of Revs.	5.9	5.9	6.0	6.0	6.2	6.3
% Ret. on Assets	14.9	14.4	14.3	14.7	15.7	16.4
% Ret. on Equity	19.5	18.6	18.6	19.2	20.8	21.7

Dividend Data —Dividends have been paid since 1948. A dividend reinvestment plan is available. A "poison pill" stock purchase rights plan was adopted in 1989.

Amt. of Div. $	Date Decl.	Ex-Div. Date	Stock of Record	Payment Date
0.287	Aug. 15	Sep. 02	Sep. 09	Oct. 01 '94
0.287	Nov. 30	Dec. 05	Dec. 09	Jan. 02 '95
0.315	Feb. 21	Mar. 06	Mar. 10	Apr. 01 '95
0.315	Apr. 18	Jun. 06	Jun. 09	Jul. 01 '95
0.315	Aug. 22	Sep. 06	Sep. 08	Oct. 01 '95

Data as orig. reptd.; bef. results of disc. opers. and/or spec. items. Per share data adj. for stk. divs. as of ex-div. date. E-Estimated. NA-Not Available. NM-Not Meaningful. NR-Not Ranked.

Office—2999 Circle 75 Pkwy, Atlanta, GA 30339. **Tel**—(404) 953-1700. **Chrmn & CEO**—L. L. Prince. **Pres**—T. C. Gallagher. **Secy**—C. Yancey. **SVP-Fin & Investor Contact**—Jerry W. Nix. **Dirs**—J. R. Courim, B. Currey, Jr., J. Douville, T. C. Gallagher, J. H. Lanier, G. E. Larned, W. A. Parker, Jr., L. L. Prince, J. J. Scalley, A. S. Shepherd, L. G. Steiner, J. B. Williams. **Transfer Agent & Registrar**—Trust Co. Bank, Atlanta. **Incorporated** in Georgia in 1928. **Empl**-21,300. **S&P Analyst:** Joshua M. Harari, CFA

Georgia-Pacific

NYSE Symbol **GP**
In S&P 500

01-SEP-95   **Industry:** Building

Summary: One of the world's largest forest products companies, GP produces wood panels, lumber, uncoated paper, pulp and containerboard, and owns over six million acres of timberland.

S&P Opinion: Accumulate (★★★★)	Recent Price • 90⅝	Yield • 2.2%
	52 Wk Range • 95¾-66⅛	12-Mo. P/E • 10.8

Quantitative Evaluations

Outlook
(1 Lowest—5 Highest)
• **2+**

Fair Value
• **81⅝**

Risk
• **Low**

Earn./Div. Rank
• **B-**

Technical Eval.
• **Bearish** since 9/94

Rel. Strength Rank
(1 Lowest—99 Highest)
• **56**

Insider Activity
• **NA**

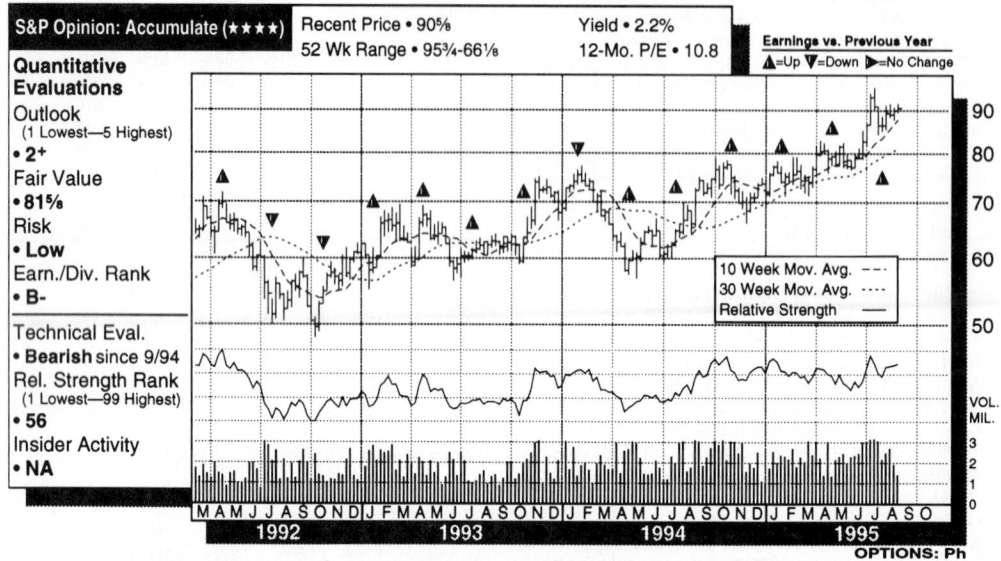

Earnings vs. Previous Year
▲=Up ▼=Down ▶=No Change

10 Week Mov. Avg. ---
30 Week Mov. Avg. - - -
Relative Strength —

VOL.
MIL.

OPTIONS: Ph

Overview - 01-SEP-95

Sales growth should be solid in 1995, as relatively healthy global economies should continue to generate favorable demand for pulp and paper products, with tight supply conditions allowing steep prices to remain in effect. Although the domestic economy has been moderating, limited capacity expansion in recent years should enable the industry upturn to extend into 1996. The building products segment should begin to benefit from the recent plunge in long-term interest rates, but first half weakness is likely to result in lower full year sales in the segment. Margins should widen significantly on favorable pricing trends and cost reduction programs in the pulp and paper segment. While margins of the building products segment are likely to narrow on modestly lower sales and higher log prices, its performance should be aided by the completion of certain cost saving capital projects.

Valuation - 01-SEP-95

After declining in early 1994 on worries about the effect of the Fed's credit tightening program on building markets, GP's shares have climbed since mid-1994 on strengthening conditions in paper markets. With limited capacity expansion likely to extend the paper industry's upturn into 1996, and with the recent drop in long-term interest rates expected to improve conditions in the construction industry, GP's profit gains should continue into 1996. Although a good amount of GP's earnings prospects have been factored into its stock price, the shares still appear undervalued, trading at about 7X our 1996 EPS forecast.

Key Stock Statistics

S&P EPS Est. 1995	11.90	Tang. Bk. Value/Share	14.80
P/E on S&P Est. 1995	7.6	Beta	1.21
S&P EPS Est. 1996	13.25	Shareholders	44,000
Dividend Rate/Share	2.00	Market cap. (B)	$ 8.2
Shs. outstg. (M)	91.0	Inst. holdings	70%
Avg. daily vol. (M)	0.368	Insider holdings	NA

Value of $10,000 invested 5 years ago: $ 21,867

Fiscal Year Ending Dec. 31

	1995	% Change	1994	% Change	1993	% Change
Revenues (Million $)						
1Q	3,477	18%	2,942	NM	2,944	4%
2Q	3,700	16%	3,187	NM	3,205	5%
3Q	—	—	3,267	10%	2,982	-3%
4Q	—	—	3,342	4%	3,199	10%
Yr.	—	—	12,738	3%	12,330	4%
Income (Million $)						
1Q	232.0	NM	56.00	37%	41.00	NM
2Q	265.0	NM	14.00	180%	5.00	25%
3Q	—	—	87.00	NM	-28.00	NM
4Q	—	—	169.00	NM	-36.00	NM
Yr.	—	—	326.00	NM	-18.00	NM
Earnings Per Share ($)						
1Q	2.59	NM	0.63	34%	0.47	NM
2Q	2.95	NM	0.16	167%	0.06	50%
3Q	E3.11	NM	0.98	NM	-0.33	NM
4Q	E3.25	72%	1.89	NM	-0.41	NM
Yr.	E11.90	NM	3.66	NM	-0.21	NM

Next earnings report expected: mid October

Business Summary - 01-SEP-95

Georgia-Pacific is one of the world's leading manufacturers and distributors of building products, pulp and paper. Industry segment contributions in 1994 were:

	Sales	Profits
Building products	60%	81%
Pulp & paper	40%	14%
Other	---	5%

Sales outside the U.S. represented less than 10% of total sales in each of the past three years. No single customer accounted for more than 10% of GP's sales in any year during that period.

GP is the leading manufacturer and distributor of building products in the U.S. Building products include wood panels (25% of total company sales in 1994), lumber (21%) and chemicals, gypsum products and other (14%). These products are sold through a large network of distribution centers throughout the U.S.

Products manufactured by Georgia-Pacific in its pulp and paper division include containerboard and packaging (17% of total company sales in 1994), communication papers (also called uncoated free sheet, 10%), tissue (6%), market pulp (6%) and other (1%). Envelope manufacturing operations were sold in February 1994. The company's pulp, paper and paperboard capacity of 8.7 million tons represents approximately 8% of the total annual capacity in the U.S.

As of December 31, 1994, GP owned more than six million acres of timberland in North America. Approximately 70% of its timber is located in the South, 20% in the East and 10% in the West. Fee-owned timberlands and other timber (controlled through long-term contracts) supply a substantial portion of the company's wood fiber requirements.

Important Developments

Aug. '95—Directors authorized a common share repurchase program, utilizing excess cash flow during periods when GP's total debt is below $5.5 billion.
Jul. '95—The company reported record earnings in the second quarter of 1995, as exceptional results continued in its pulp and paper business. GP noted that although domestic demand was slowed late in the quarter by seasonal factors, the downturn was offset by greater reliance on exports. Georgia added that although price increases in the segment were not likely to continue at the pace experienced since last fall, the business was still performing extremely well. The strength of the pulp and paper segment easily outweighed difficulties in the building products division, which was hurt by the general slowdown in the overall economy and in new home construction. However, GP said it had grown much more optimistic about the segment's prospects, given the recent uptrend in demand and prices that lower interest rates had generated.

Capitalization

Long Term Debt: $4,224,000,000 (6/95).

Per Share Data ($) (Year Ended Dec. 31)

	1994	1993	1992	1991	1990	1989
Tangible Bk. Val.	9.03	5.98	7.00	9.00	10.76	30.30
Cash Flow	12.70	9.18	9.12	8.74	13.06	13.30
Earnings	3.66	-0.21	-0.69	-0.40	4.28	7.42
Dividends	1.60	1.60	1.60	1.60	1.60	1.45
Payout Ratio	44%	NM	NM	NM	38%	19%
Prices - High	79	75	72	60¼	52⅛	62
- Low	56¾	55	48¼	36¼	25⅜	36⅝
P/E Ratio - High	22	NM	NM	NM	12	8
- Low	16	NM	NM	NM	6	5

Income Statement Analysis (Million $)

	1994	%Chg	1993	%Chg	1992	%Chg	1991
Revs.	12,738	3%	12,330	4%	11,847	3%	11,524
Oper. Inc.	1,773	28%	1,385	3%	1,339	4%	1,283
Depr.	805	-2%	823	-3%	848	8%	784
Int. Exp.	460	-11%	516	-9%	567	-5%	598
Pretax Inc.	572	NM	23.0	NM	-74.0	NM	259
Eff. Tax Rate	43%	—	178%	—	NM	—	113%
Net Inc.	326	NM	-18.0	NM	-60.0	NM	-34.0

Balance Sheet & Other Fin. Data (Million $)

	1994	1993	1992	1991	1990	1989
Cash	53.0	41.0	55.0	48.0	58.0	23.0
Curr. Assets	1,862	1,646	1,607	1,562	1,766	1,829
Total Assets	10,728	10,545	10,890	10,622	12,060	7,056
Curr. Liab.	2,325	2,064	2,452	2,722	2,535	924
LT Debt	3,904	4,157	4,019	3,743	5,218	2,336
Common Eqty.	2,620	2,402	2,508	2,736	2,975	2,717
Total Cap.	7,578	7,654	7,729	7,274	9,121	5,894
Cap. Exp.	894	467	384	528	3,789	499
Cash Flow	1,131	805	788	750	1,114	1,185

Ratio Analysis

	1994	1993	1992	1991	1990	1989
Curr. Ratio	0.8	0.8	0.7	0.6	0.7	2.0
% LT Debt of Cap.	51.5	54.3	52.0	51.5	57.2	39.6
% Net Inc.of Revs.	2.6	NM	NM	NM	2.9	6.5
% Ret. on Assets	3.1	NM	NM	NM	3.8	9.8
% Ret. on Equity	13.0	NM	NM	NM	12.8	25.8

Dividend Data

Cash has been paid each year since 1927. A dividend reinvestment plan is available. A "poison pill" stock purchase rights plan was adopted in 1989.

Amt. of Div. $	Date Decl.	Ex-Div. Date	Stock of Record	Payment Date
0.400	Jul. 29	Aug. 15	Aug. 19	Sep. 06 '94
0.400	Oct. 30	Nov. 08	Nov. 15	Dec. 05 '94
0.400	Feb. 01	Feb. 13	Feb. 17	Mar. 13 '95
0.500	May. 02	May. 15	May. 19	Jun. 12 '95
0.500	Aug. 01	Aug. 16	Aug. 18	Sep. 11 '95

Data as orig. reptd.; bef. results of disc. opers. and/or spec. items. Per share data adj. for stk. divs. as of ex-div. date. E-Estimated. NA-Not Available. NM-Not Meaningful. NR-Not Ranked.

Office—133 Peachtree St., N.E., Atlanta, GA 30303. **Tel**—(404) 652-4000. **Chrmn & CEO**—A. D. Correll. **SVP & CFO**—J. F. McGovern. **Secy**—K. F. Khoury. **Investor Contact**—Richard A. Good (404-652-4720). **Dirs**—R. Carswell, J. P. Cobb, A. D. Correll, J. Evans, D. V. Fites, H. C. Fruehauf Jr., R. V. Giordano, D. R. Goode, T. M. Hahn Jr., M. D. Ivester, F. Jungers, R. E. McNair, L. W. Sullivan, J. B. Williams. **Transfer Agent & Registrar**—First Chicago Trust Co. of New York, NYC. **Incorporated** in Georgia. in 1927. **Empl**-47,000. **S&P Analyst:** Michael W. Jaffe

STANDARD & POOR'S

STOCK REPORTS

Giant Food

ASE Symbol **GFS.A**
In S&P 500

07-SEP-95

Industry:
Retail Stores

Summary: This regional supermarket operator is the leading chain in the competitive metropolitan Washington, D.C., market. J. Sainsbury PLC, a U.K. food retailer, has a 50% voting interest.

S&P Opinion: Hold (★★★)	Recent Price • 31⅝	Yield • 2.3%
	52 Wk Range • 32⅝-20¾	12-Mo. P/E • 18.9

Quantitative Evaluations

Outlook
(1 Lowest—5 Highest)
• **NA**

Fair Value
• **NA**

Risk
• **NA**

Earn./Div. Rank
• **A-**

Technical Eval.
• **Bullish** since 7/95

Rel. Strength Rank
(1 Lowest—99 Highest)
• **70**

Insider Activity
• **NA**

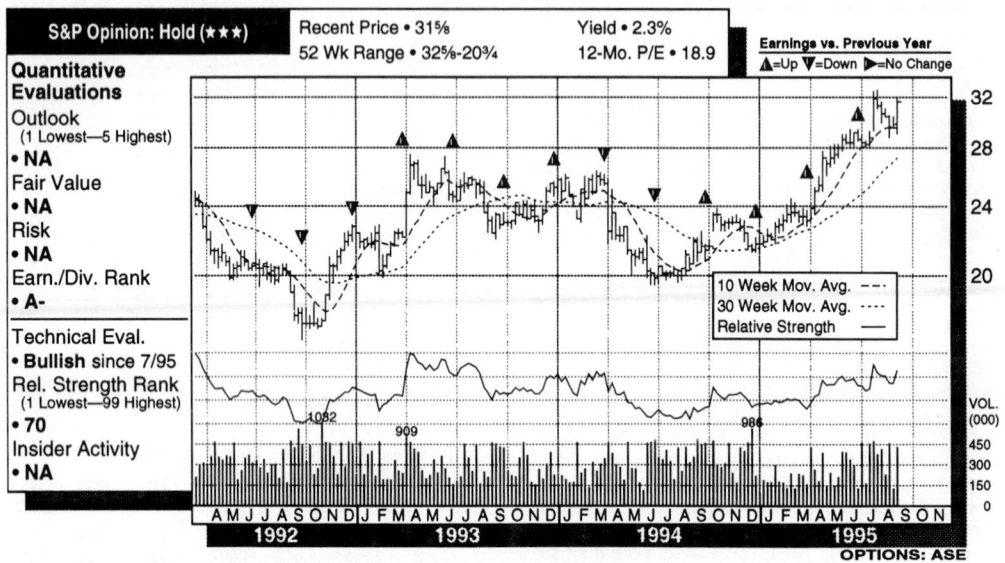

Earnings vs. Previous Year
▲=Up ▼=Down ▶=No Change

10 Week Mov. Avg. ---
30 Week Mov. Avg. ⋯⋯
Relative Strength —

VOL. (000)

OPTIONS: ASE

Overview - 07-SEP-95

Sales for 1995-96 should benefit mostly from new store openings and continued emphasis on promotional pricing; same-store sales gains should be in the 1.5% to 2.0% range. Gross margins should widen slightly, but will continue to be restricted by competitive pricing to retain market share and the lack of food price inflation. Expense ratios will reflect higher labor costs and expenses related to new store openings. Over the longer term, the company's entry into new markets -- Delaware, New Jersey and Pennsylvania -- should result in sales gains and improved expense ratios as costs are spread over a wider store base. Giant is conservatively financed and its dividend has been raised annually over the past decade.

Valuation - 07-SEP-95

The share price began to rise in late 1994 from depressed levels when the company's founding family sold its stake to Sainsbury, a U.K. supermarket chain. There was some speculation that Sainsbury might take the company private. The shares appear to be fully valued at current levels with a 10% gain in earnings projected for 1995-96 and about that percentage the following year. Over the longer term, Giant's aggressive expansion plans in new trade areas, emphasis on promotional programs and new product offerings should continue to provide solid earnings gains.

Key Stock Statistics

S&P EPS Est. 1996	1.75	Tang. Bk. Value/Share	13.16
P/E on S&P Est. 1996	18.1	Beta	0.83
S&P EPS Est. 1997	1.90	Shareholders	40,000
Dividend Rate/Share	0.74	Market cap. (B)	$ 1.9
Shs. outstg. (M)	59.3	Inst. holdings	42%
Avg. daily vol. (M)	0.073	Insider holdings	NA

Value of $10,000 invested 5 years ago: $ 12,921

Fiscal Year Ending Feb. 28

	1996	% Change	1995	% Change	1994	% Change
Revenues (Million $)						
1Q	869.2	5%	830.0	2%	813.5	1%
2Q	856.5	4%	826.4	4%	795.8	2%
3Q	—	—	834.8	4%	799.1	3%
4Q	—	—	1,205	4%	1,159	4%
Yr.	—	—	3,696	4%	3,567	3%
Income (Million $)						
1Q	22.11	8%	20.41	-10%	22.67	19%
2Q	17.77	21%	14.67	NM	14.60	22%
3Q	—	—	18.56	5%	17.72	29%
4Q	—	—	40.52	12%	36.30	-1%
Yr.	—	—	94.16	3%	91.30	12%
Earnings Per Share ($)						
1Q	0.37	9%	0.34	-11%	0.38	19%
2Q	0.30	20%	0.25	4%	0.24	20%
3Q	E0.34	10%	0.31	3%	0.30	30%
4Q	E0.74	7%	0.69	13%	0.61	-2%
Yr.	E1.75	10%	1.59	4%	1.53	12%

Next earnings report expected: late November

Business Summary - 07-SEP-95

At February 27, 1995, Giant Food operated a chain of 161 supermarkets, mostly in the Washington, D.C., metropolitan area and in or near Baltimore. It also operated three freestanding drug stores.

The majority of the company's stores are located in shopping centers. Food/pharmacy combination units totaled 116 at 1994-95 year end. At the end of 1994-95, Giant operated 6.8 million sq. ft. of food and food/drug retail space, up 4.0% from a year earlier.

Giant owns and operates three distribution facilities, with about 1,200,000 sq. ft., in Landover, Md., and also operates a dry grocery warehouse, a frozen food distribution center and an ice cream manufacturing facility. The company produces for sale in its stores bakery products and dairy products, ice cream, soft drinks and ice cubes. Giant also operates vending machines. Transfer sales from these and other activities totaled $429 million in 1994-95, with pretax profits of $51 million.

The company plans to spend $209 million for property, plant and equipment in 1995-96.

Through its GFS Realty Inc. subsidiary, Giant owns 16 shopping centers and three freestanding stores.

Important Developments

Aug. '95—Earnings rose 21%, year to year, in the 12 weeks ended August 12; net income was 2.07% of sales. Total sales rose 3.6% in the second quarter, while same-store sales increased 1.7%. The company credited the increase in sales to effective promotional programs as well as efforts to emphasize perishables, including a locally grown presentation of produce. Sales rose 4.2% in the first half of 1995-96 (24 weeks); net income was 2.31% of sales. The company opened two new stores in the second quarter and has plans for four more by fiscal year end. New stores and expansions will increase square footage by 7% in 1995-96. Another 11 stores are slated to be built in 1997-98, of which five will be in New Jersey and four in Pennsylvania.

Capitalization

Long Term Debt: $198,000,000 (5/95), incl. $140,946,000 of capital lease obligs.
Options: To buy 3,124,035 shs. at an avg. price of $23.56 a sh. (2/95).

Per Share Data ($) (Year Ended Feb. 28)

	1995	1994	1993	1992	1991	1990
Tangible Bk. Val.	12.75	11.97	11.11	10.42	9.42	8.25
Cash Flow	3.25	3.20	2.96	3.01	3.40	2.99
Earnings	1.59	1.53	1.37	1.47	2.01	1.80
Dividends	0.72	0.70	0.68	0.66	0.60	0.50
Payout Ratio	45%	46%	50%	45%	30%	26%
Cal. Yrs.	1994	1993	1992	1991	1990	1989
Prices - High	26⅜	27½	26¼	31¼	29⅞	36¼
- Low	19½	19⅞	16⅞	19¾	21⅛	22⅛
P/E Ratio - High	17	18	19	21	15	20
- Low	12	13	12	14	11	12

Income Statement Analysis (Million $)

	1995	%Chg	1994	%Chg	1993	%Chg	1992
Revs.	3,696	4%	3,567	3%	3,473	NM	3,490
Oper. Inc.	266	-2%	271	9%	248	-1%	251
Depr.	99	-1%	100	5%	94.9	3%	91.9
Int. Exp.	25.6	-6%	27.2	-2%	27.7	2%	27.1
Pretax Inc.	155	2%	152	15%	132	-7%	142
Eff. Tax Rate	39%	—	40%	—	38%	—	39%
Net Inc.	94.0	3%	91.0	11%	82.0	-6%	87.0

Balance Sheet & Other Fin. Data (Million $)

	1995	1994	1993	1992	1991	1990
Cash	250	228	185	151	168	182
Curr. Assets	556	506	462	405	422	422
Total Assets	1,417	1,358	1,297	1,251	1,175	1,081
Curr. Liab.	367	341	307	296	296	275
LT Debt	199	227	248	256	245	242
Common Eqty.	755	713	663	621	556	493
Total Cap.	976	982	958	929	856	787
Cap. Exp.	102	139	75.0	181	168	153
Cash Flow	193	191	176	179	201	179

Ratio Analysis

	1995	1994	1993	1992	1991	1990
Curr. Ratio	1.5	1.5	1.5	1.4	1.4	1.5
% LT Debt of Cap.	20.4	23.1	25.9	27.6	28.7	30.7
% Net Inc.of Revs.	2.5	2.6	2.3	2.5	3.5	3.3
% Ret. on Assets	6.8	6.9	6.4	7.1	10.6	10.5
% Ret. on Equity	12.9	13.3	12.7	14.7	22.8	23.6

Dividend Data —Cash has been paid each year since 1960. A dividend reinvestment plan is available. Recent Class A payments were:

Amt. of Div. $	Date Decl.	Ex-Div. Date	Stock of Record	Payment Date
0.180	Oct. 13	Oct. 31	Nov. 04	Dec. 02 '94
0.180	Jan. 12	Jan. 30	Feb. 03	Mar. 03 '95
0.185	Apr. 27	May. 08	May. 12	Jun. 02 '95
0.185	Jul. 13	Aug. 02	Aug. 04	Sep. 01 '95

Data as orig. reptd.; bef. results of disc. opers. and/or spec. items. Per share data adj. for stk. divs. as of ex-div. date.
E-Estimated. NA-Not Available. NM-Not Meaningful. NR-Not Ranked.

Office—6300 Sheriff Rd., Landover, MD 20785; P.O. Box 1804, Washington, D.C. 20013. Tel—(301) 341-4100. Chrmn & CEO—I. Cohen. Pres—P. L. Manos. SVP-Fin, Secy, Treas, CFO & Investor Contact—David B. Sykes. Dirs—D. Adriano, H. Beckner, I. Cohen, P. F. O'Malley, D. Sainsbury, D. B. Sykes, C. M. Unseld. Transfer Agent & Registrar—American Stock Transfer & Trust Co., NYC. Incorporated in Delaware in 1935. Empl-25,000. S&P Analyst: Karen Sack, CFA

Giddings & Lewis

NASDAQ Symbol **GIDL**
In S&P 500

STANDARD & POOR'S
STOCK REPORTS

17-OCT-95 | Industry: Machinery

Summary: Giddings & Lewis is one of the world's largest suppliers and integrators of industrial automation and machine tools.

S&P Opinion: Hold (★★★)

| Recent Price • 16¾ | Yield • 0.7% |
| 52 Wk Range • 18⅞-13¾ | 12-Mo. P/E • 11.4 |

Earnings vs. Previous Year
▲=Up ▼=Down ▶=No Change

Quantitative Evaluations

Outlook
(1 Lowest—5 Highest)
• **4⁻**

Fair Value
• **18⅝**

Risk
• **Average**

Earn./Div. Rank
• **NR**

Technical Eval.
• **Bearish** since 8/95

Rel. Strength Rank
(1 Lowest—99 Highest)
• **40**

Insider Activity
• **Neutral**

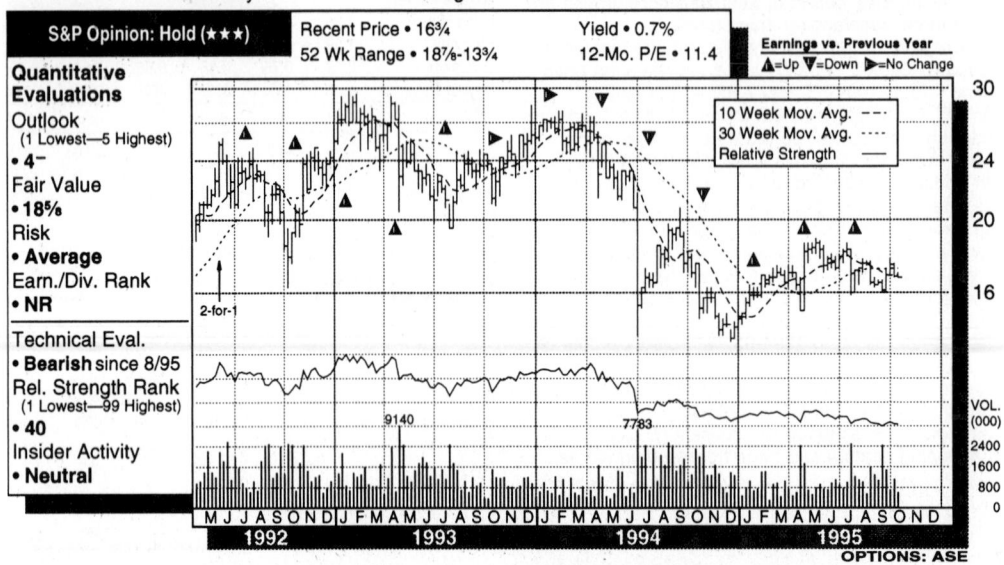

10 Week Mov. Avg. – – –
30 Week Mov. Avg. · · · ·
Relative Strength ——

2-for-1

9140   7783

VOL. (000)
2400
1600
800
0

M J J A S O N D J F M A M J J A S O N D J F M A M J J A S O N D J F M A M J J A S O N D
1992   1993   1994   1995

OPTIONS: ASE

Overview - 17-OCT-95

Based on our forecast for 2.6% GDP growth in the U.S. and stable business conditions in Europe, we project a 10% gain in sales for 1996. Increased shipments of the new RAM machines, inclusion of the Fadal acquisition for the entire year and greater demand in Europe will help boost volume. Assuming much less lower margin project work, stable raw material costs and firm pricing, gross margins should expand. Aided further by a probable decline in SG&A as a percent of sales, only a small rise in interest costs and an unchanged tax rate, earnings should advance in 1996. Acquisitions, new products and the eventual adoption of GIDL's revolutionary new machine, the VARIAX, will boost long-term sales and profit potential. Also, long term demand for GIDL's machines will be lifted by a trend toward increased outsourcing in European manufacturing.

Valuation - 17-OCT-95

While the downside for the shares seems limited, we are maintaining our hold recommendation on the stock. Through early October the shares are up 14% versus a 26% gain the the S&P 500. A series of earnings disappointments has hurt the stock price since June 1994. With the Fadal acquisition and the prospect for less pressure on project work, earnings may be turning the corner. However, given the string of negative surprises, we are reluctant to rate the shares buy or accumulate until we see evidence that the worst is over with respect to gross margins. For now, we prefer to take a wait and see attitude toward the shares.

Key Stock Statistics

S&P EPS Est. 1995	0.95	Tang. Bk. Value/Share	8.69
P/E on S&P Est. 1995	17.6	Beta	1.67
S&P EPS Est. 1996	1.30	Shareholders	2,500
Dividend Rate/Share	0.12	Market cap. (B)	$0.576
Shs. outstg. (M)	34.4	Inst. holdings	76%
Avg. daily vol. (M)	0.183	Insider holdings	NA

Value of $10,000 invested 5 years ago: $ 20,907

Fiscal Year Ending Dec. 31

	1995	% Change	1994	% Change	1993	% Change
Revenues (Million $)						
1Q	154.6	26%	123.0	-12%	140.3	NM
2Q	171.1	18%	144.8	7%	135.8	-9%
3Q	—	—	166.1	36%	122.0	-22%
4Q	—	—	185.5	55%	119.4	-32%
Yr.	—	—	619.5	20%	517.5	-17%
Income (Million $)						
1Q	7.10	3%	6.87	-33%	10.23	39%
2Q	9.32	29%	7.23	-37%	11.48	37%
3Q	—	—	9.81	-12%	11.09	13%
4Q	—	—	23.97	120%	10.90	9%
Yr.	—	—	47.88	10%	43.71	23%
Earnings Per Share ($)						
1Q	0.21	5%	0.20	-39%	0.33	43%
2Q	0.27	29%	0.21	-38%	0.34	26%
3Q	E0.23	-21%	0.29	-12%	0.33	NM
4Q	E0.24	-66%	0.70	119%	0.32	NM
Yr.	E0.95	-32%	1.40	7%	1.31	13%

Next earnings report expected: late October

Giddings & Lewis

Business Summary - 11-OCT-95

Giddings & Lewis is the leading domestic designer and manufacturer of large, high-precision automated machine tools and automated assembly systems. Revenues in recent years were derived as follows:

	1994	1993
Automation technology	26.3%	32.6%
Integrated automation	43.2%	37.7%
Automation measurement/control	10.0%	10.9%
European operations	20.5%	18.8%

Automation technology consists primarily of large, high-precision, computer numerically controlled machine tools and associated products and services. Products include horizontal and vertical machining centers, horizontal and vertical lathes, horizontal boring, drilling and milling machines, cellular and flexible manufacturing systems, fixtures, and cutting tools and drill point grinders. Standalone machines accounted for 37% this unit's revenues in 1994. Cellular and flexible manufacturing systems accounted for 21% of revenues, while parts and related services accounted for 33%.

The integrated automation group includes flexible transfer lines, flexible machining systems, automotive framing and welding systems. It also supplies automated assembly systems, including dials, synchronous and nonsynchronous transport systems and special handling, testing and measurement systems and complete multi-unit production systems. Flexible transfer lines were 65.9% of this unit's revenues in 1994. Automated assembly systems accounted for 27.2% of revenues in 1994.

The automation measurement and control group makes coordinate measurement devices, gaging products, meteorological instruments, programmable industrial controls, and multilayered, high density printed circuit boards.

The European operations group makes and sells products from all three product lines.

Important Developments

Apr. '95—GIDL announced the acquisition of Fadal Engineering Co., Inc. for some $180 million in cash. Fadal, a private Chatsworth, Calif.-based company, manufactures small numerically controlled vertical machining centers (VMCs) for a broad base of customers. Fadal's sales in 1994 totaled $138 million, of which some 10.6% were international. Fadal has an installed base of 9,500 machines and has been consistently profitable.

Capitalization

Long Term Debt: None (7/95).
Options: To buy 697,676 shs. at $7.00 to $28.00 a sh.

Per Share Data ($)

(Year Ended Dec. 31)

	1994	1993	1992	1991	1990	1989
Tangible Bk. Val.	11.67	10.06	7.08	4.44	6.31	5.39
Cash Flow	1.85	1.75	1.66	1.24	1.17	NA
Earnings	1.40	1.31	1.16	0.92	0.87	0.83
Dividends	0.12	0.09	0.11	0.08	0.08	0.02
Payout Ratio	9%	7%	9%	10%	9%	2%
Prices - High	28	29¾	26¾	15⅛	10⅝	9
- Low	13¾	19½	14¾	7⅝	6⅛	7
P/E Ratio - High	20	23	23	17	12	11
- Low	10	15	13	8	7	8

Income Statement Analysis (Million $)

	1994	%Chg	1993	%Chg	1992	%Chg	1991
Revs.	619	20%	517	-17%	623	91%	327
Oper. Inc.	69.1	-8%	74.8	13%	66.1	74%	37.9
Depr.	15.4	4%	14.8	4%	14.2	99%	7.1
Int. Exp.	2.0	-53%	4.2	-55%	9.2	NM	1.5
Pretax Inc.	77.6	11%	70.0	52%	46.0	53%	30.1
Eff. Tax Rate	38%	—	38%	—	23%	—	29%
Net Inc.	47.9	10%	43.7	24%	35.2	65%	21.3

Balance Sheet & Other Fin. Data (Million $)

	1994	1993	1992	1991	1990	1989
Cash	24.1	53.9	8.5	12.1	23.8	10.8
Curr. Assets	463	387	407	338	132	121
Total Assets	687	614	627	560	182	163
Curr. Liab.	155	129	197	179	45.0	49.0
LT Debt	Nil	Nil	68.2	50.6	Nil	Nil
Common Eqty.	485	436	326	215	135	115
Total Cap.	485	436	398	326	136	115
Cap. Exp.	16.7	18.8	13.6	10.6	10.1	6.3
Cash Flow	63.3	58.5	47.1	27.5	24.8	27.1

Ratio Analysis

	1994	1993	1992	1991	1990	1989
Curr. Ratio	3.0	3.0	2.1	1.9	2.9	2.5
% LT Debt of Cap.	Nil	Nil	17.1	15.5	Nil	Nil
% Net Inc.of Revs.	7.7	8.4	5.7	6.5	7.6	9.1
% Ret. on Assets	7.4	6.6	5.6	5.4	10.7	NA
% Ret. on Equity	10.4	10.9	11.5	10.7	14.8	NA

Dividend Data

—Dividends were initiated in November 1989.

Amt. of Div. $	Date Decl.	Ex-Div. Date	Stock of Record	Payment Date
0.030	Oct. 26	Nov. 17	Nov. 23	Dec. 16 '94
0.030	Feb. 15	Mar. 06	Mar. 10	Mar. 31 '95
0.030	Apr. 26	Jun. 06	Jun. 09	Jun. 30 '95
0.01 Spl.	Aug. 23	Sep. 05	Sep. 08	Sep. 29 '95
0.030	Aug. 23	Sep. 06	Sep. 08	Sep. 29 '95

Data as orig. reptd.; bef. results of disc. opers. and/or spec. items. Per share data adj. for stk. divs. as of ex-div. date.
E-Estimated. NA-Not Available. NM-Not Meaningful. NR-Not Ranked.

Office—142 Doty St., Fond du Lac, WI 54935. Tel—(414) 921-9400. Fax—(414) 929-4522. Chrmn & CEO—J. R. Coppola. VP, CFO & Secy—R. C. Kleinfeldt. Treas—D. E. Barnett. Dirs—A. J. Baciocco, Jr., J. A. Becker, J. R. Coppola, R.M. Davis, C. H. Folley, B. F. Garmer III, J. W. Guffey, Jr., R. C. Kleinfeldt, B. R. Stuart. Transfer Agent & Registrar—Firstar Trust Co., Milwaukee. Incorporated in Wisconsin in 1989. Empl-3,788. S&P Analyst: Leo Larkin

Gillette Co.

NYSE Symbol **G**
In S&P 500

30-OCT-95

Industry:
Cosmetics/Toiletries

Summary: Gillette is a well-known global manufacturer of razors and blades, hair care products, toiletries, writing instruments and small appliances.

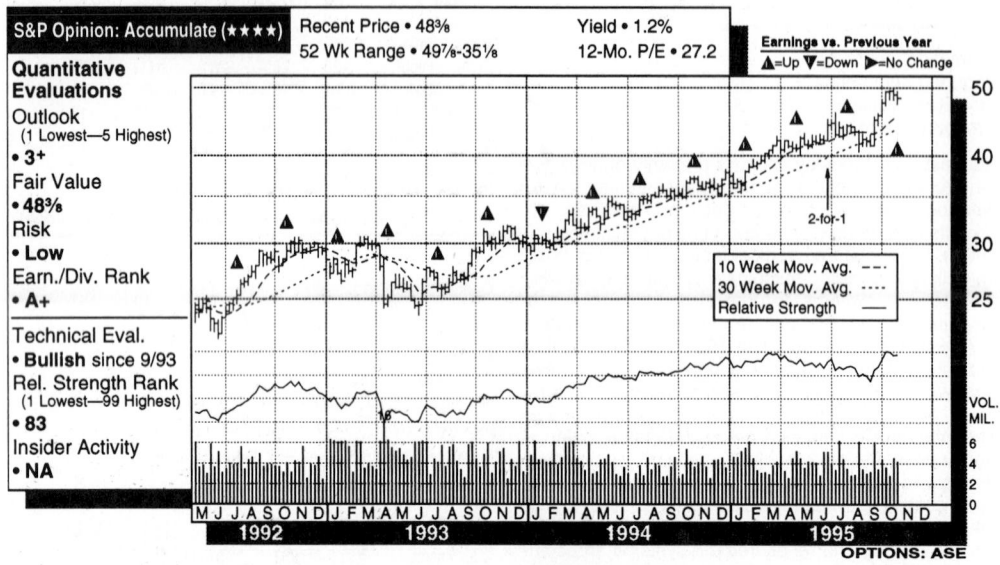

S&P Opinion: Accumulate (★★★★)	Recent Price • 48⅜	Yield • 1.2%
	52 Wk Range • 49⅞-35⅛	12-Mo. P/E • 27.2

Quantitative Evaluations

Outlook
(1 Lowest—5 Highest)
• **3+**

Fair Value
• **48⅜**

Risk
• **Low**

Earn./Div. Rank
• **A+**

Technical Eval.
• **Bullish** since 9/93

Rel. Strength Rank
(1 Lowest—99 Highest)
• **83**

Insider Activity
• **NA**

Earnings vs. Previous Year
▲=Up ▼=Down ▶=No Change

2-for-1

10 Week Mov. Avg. – – –
30 Week Mov. Avg. ·······
Relative Strength ——

OPTIONS: ASE

Overview - 30-OCT-95

Sales should continue to rise in 1996, reflecting higher volume in all divisions. Results will benefit from greater market share for most existing products, reflecting strong product support, and from 25-35 new product introductions. The greatest volume growth will occur in international markets, as the company penetrates untapped markets and continues to expand in Asia and Latin America. Potential acquisitions could boost revenue growth. Margins could expand somewhat, on a more profitable product mix, higher volume, manufacturing efficiencies, and improved results from Mexico.

Valuation - 30-OCT-95

The shares of this leading consumer products company have trended upward since mid-1993, reflecting strong earnings growth. Although the P/E multiple on estimated 1996 EPS is substantially higher than that of the S&P 500, we believe that it is warranted, given Gillette's well-known franchise, leading positions in nearly all of its markets, high overseas exposure, and stable earnings growth. In addition, the company's most profitable and largest business, blades and razors, continues to widen its margins, on higher volume and a more profitable product mix. We advise accumulation of the shares for long-term gains.

Key Stock Statistics

S&P EPS Est. 1995	1.85	Tang. Bk. Value/Share		2.93
P/E on S&P Est. 1995	26.1	Beta		1.34
S&P EPS Est. 1996	2.15	Shareholders		28,900
Dividend Rate/Share	0.60	Market cap. (B)		$ 21.5
Shs. outstg. (M)	443.4	Inst. holdings		68%
Avg. daily vol. (M)	0.746	Insider holdings		NA

Value of $10,000 invested 5 years ago: $ 42,559

Fiscal Year Ending Dec. 31

	1995	% Change	1994	% Change	1993	% Change
Revenues (Million $)						
1Q	1,536	13%	1,361	12%	1,217	NM
2Q	1,601	14%	1,407	14%	1,237	3%
3Q	1,670	11%	1,503	12%	1,340	7%
4Q	—	—	1,799	11%	1,617	7%
Yr.	—	—	6,070	12%	5,411	5%
Income (Million $)						
1Q	196.1	20%	164.0	15%	142.3	10%
2Q	193.1	19%	162.2	20%	134.7	12%
3Q	202.2	17%	172.2	19%	145.0	13%
4Q	—	—	199.9	NM	4.90	-96%
Yr.	—	—	698.3	64%	426.9	-17%
Earnings Per Share ($)						
1Q	0.44	19%	0.37	16%	0.32	10%
2Q	0.43	18%	0.36	20%	0.31	11%
3Q	0.46	19%	0.39	18%	0.32	12%
4Q	E0.52	16%	0.45	NM	0.01	-97%
Yr.	E1.85	18%	1.57	64%	0.96	-17%

Next earnings report expected: late January

Gillette Co.

Business Summary - 30-OCT-95

Gillette is a global maker of razors and blades, hair care products, toiletries, writing instruments and small appliances. Segment contributions in 1994 were:

	Sales	Profits
Blades & razors	39%	69%
Braun products	19%	16%
Toiletries & cosmetics	13%	6%
Stationery products	22%	7%
Oral-B dental items	7%	2%

International operations (including Canada) provided 68% of 1994 sales, and 70% of profits.

Blade and razor products include the Trac II, Atra and Sensor twin-bladed razor and cartridge systems; the Super Stainless Steel and Platinum Plus double-edged blades; and the Daisy, Good News and Micro Trac disposable razors.

Braun AG, the leading producer of electric shavers in Germany, also makes household and personal care appliances. Toiletries and cosmetics include deodorants such as Right Guard, Dry Idea and Soft & Dri; shampoos, sprays and other hair care products sold under the White Rain, Silkience and other names; skin care and shaving cream products; and Jafra skin care and cosmetics.

Stationery products include Parker Pen, Paper Mate, Flair, Eraser Mate and Waterman writing instruments and Liquid Paper and other correction fluids. Oral-B dental products include toothbrushes, toothpastes, rinses and related items.

Important Developments

Oct. '95—Gillette attributed the 18% increase in 1995 third quarter net income to favorable responses to new products, geographic expansion, and solid volume of existing products. The company said that sales and profits improved at all divisions, except for toiletries and cosmetics. While sales at this division were up, profits were hurt by the devaluation of the Mexican peso which negatively affected Jafra sales and profits. Sep. '95—Gillette bought Warner-Lambert Co.'s PRO toothbrush business for an undisclosed price. In 1994, this business had sales of about $40 million.

Capitalization

Long Term Debt: $554,500,000 (6/95).
Minority Interest: $19,200,000.
ESOP 8% Cum. Conv. Pfd. Stk.: $97,800,000.

Per Share Data ($)

(Year Ended Dec. 31)

	1994	1993	1992	1991	1990	1989
Tangible Bk. Val.	2.43	1.17	2.34	1.50	-0.19	-0.49
Cash Flow	2.05	1.39	1.64	1.42	1.22	1.02
Earnings	1.57	0.96	1.16	0.97	0.80	0.68
Dividends	0.48	0.40	0.35	0.30	0.26	0.23
Payout Ratio	31%	42%	30%	32%	33%	35%
Prices - High	38¼	31⅞	30⅝	28⅛	16⅜	12½
- Low	28⅞	23¾	22	14⅛	10⅞	8¼
P/E Ratio - High	24	33	26	29	20	18
- Low	18	25	19	15	14	12

Income Statement Analysis (Million $)

	1994	%Chg	1993	%Chg	1992	%Chg	1991
Revs.	6,070	12%	5,411	5%	5,163	10%	4,684
Oper. Inc.	1,442	13%	1,276	8%	1,178	12%	1,054
Depr.	215	14%	189	-10%	211	9%	193
Int. Exp.	61.0	2%	60.0	-28%	83.0	-28%	115
Pretax Inc.	1,104	62%	683	-18%	830	20%	694
Eff. Tax Rate	37%	—	38%	—	38%	—	38%
Net Inc.	698	63%	427	-17%	513	20%	427

Balance Sheet & Other Fin. Data (Million $)

	1994	1993	1992	1991	1990	1989
Cash	46.0	39.0	40.0	57.0	81.0	137
Curr. Assets	2,747	2,528	2,336	2,178	2,094	1,855
Total Assets	5,494	5,102	4,190	3,887	3,671	3,114
Curr. Liab.	1,783	1,760	1,561	1,485	1,308	1,061
LT Debt	715	840	554	742	1,046	1,041
Common Eqty.	1,963	1,434	1,462	1,057	165	70.0
Total Cap.	2,937	2,507	2,169	2,020	2,037	1,807
Cap. Exp.	400	352	321	286	255	223
Cash Flow	909	611	720	602	488	396

Ratio Analysis

	1994	1993	1992	1991	1990	1989
Curr. Ratio	1.5	1.4	1.5	1.5	1.6	1.7
% LT Debt of Cap.	24.4	33.5	25.5	36.7	51.3	57.6
% Net Inc.of Revs.	11.5	7.9	9.9	9.1	8.5	7.5
% Ret. on Assets	13.2	9.2	12.7	10.7	10.8	9.5
% Ret. on Equity	40.8	29.1	39.1	65.8	263.6	NM

Dividend Data

Dividends have been paid since 1906. A dividend reinvestment plan is available. A poison pill stock purchase rights plan was adopted in 1986.

Amt. of Div. $	Date Decl.	Ex-Div. Date	Stock of Record	Payment Date
0.250	Dec. 16	Jan. 26	Feb. 01	Mar. 03 '95
0.300	Apr. 20	Apr. 25	May. 01	Jun. 05 '95
2-for-1	Apr. 20	Jun. 23	Jun. 01	Jun. 22 '95
0.150	Jul. 20	Jul. 28	Aug. 01	Sep. 05 '95
0.150	Oct. 19	Oct. 30	Nov. 01	Dec. 05 '95

Data as orig. reptd.; bef. results of disc. opers. and/or spec. items. Per share data adj. for stk. divs. as of ex-div. date. E-Estimated. NA-Not Available. NM-Not Meaningful. NR-Not Ranked.

Office—Prudential Tower Bldg., Boston, MA 02199. **Tel**—(617) 421-7000. **Chrmn & CEO**—A. M. Zeien. **Vice Chrmn**—J. E. Mullaney. **SVP-Fin & CFO**—T. F. Skelly. **Secy**—Jill C. Richardson. **VP-Investor Relations**—Robert DiCenso. **Dirs**—W. E. Buffett, W. H. Gantz, M. B. Gifford, C. R. Goldberg, M. C. Hawley, H. H. Jacobi, J. E. Mullaney, R. R. Pivirotto, J. M. Steta, A. B. Trowbridge, J. F. Turley, A. M. Zeien. **Transfer Agent & Registrar**—First National Bank of Boston. **Incorporated** in Delaware in 1917. **Empl**-32,800. **S&P Analyst:** E. A. Vandeventer

Golden West Financial

NYSE Symbol **GDW**
In S&P 500

23-OCT-95 | Industry: Banking

Summary: Golden West Financial is the holding company for World Savings & Loan, the nation's third largest savings and loan with assets of $34.6 billion at September 30, 1995.

S&P Opinion: Accumulate (★★★★)	Recent Price • 52½ Yield • 0.6% 52 Wk Range • 57½-34¼ 12-Mo. P/E • 14.3

Earnings vs. Previous Year
▲=Up ▼=Down ▶=No Change

Quantitative Evaluations

Outlook
(1 Lowest—5 Highest)
• **2+**

Fair Value
• **54¼**

Risk
• **Low**

Earn./Div. Rank
• **B+**

Technical Eval.
• **Bearish** since 7/95

Rel. Strength Rank
(1 Lowest—99 Highest)
• **79**

Insider Activity
• **Neutral**

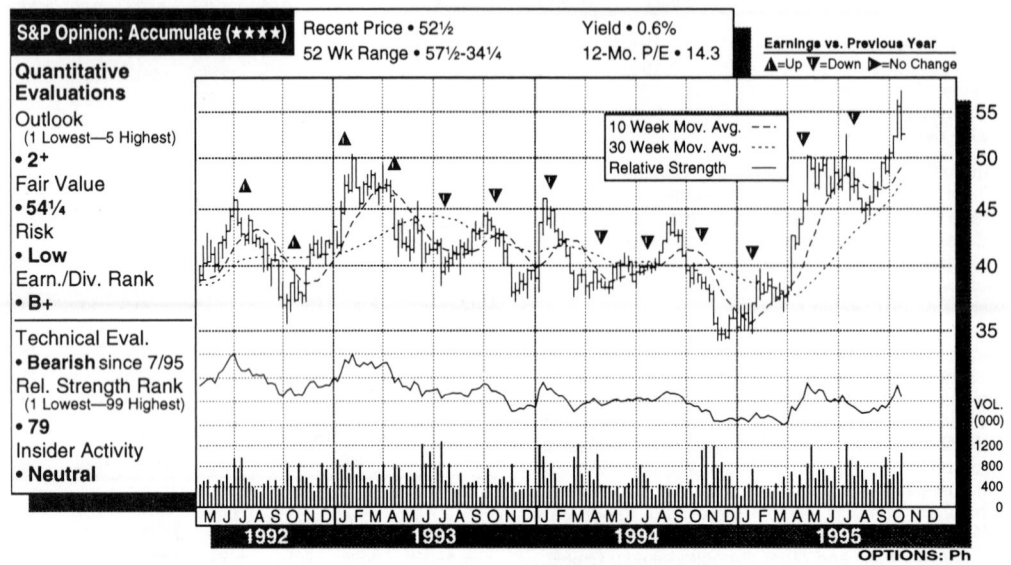

10 Week Mov. Avg. — - -
30 Week Mov. Avg. ......
Relative Strength ——

VOL.
(000)
1200
800
400
0

M J J A S O N D J F M A M J J A S O N D J F M A M J J A S O N D J F M A M J J A S O N D
1992 1993 1994 1995

OPTIONS: Ph

Overview - 23-OCT-95

Profits are expected to improve into 1996, based on expansion of the company's interest rate spread, the difference between the rate earned on loans and investments and the rate paid on deposits and other borrowings. Loan yields are expected to benefit from the repricing of the company's ARM loans to market rates. On the funding side, the recent drop in interest rates means GDW can afford to offer savers lower rates. With a modest recovery in the California economy, the provision or set-aside for loan losses should drop. Loan volume is down, but the company is still growing its balance sheet slowly. Cost ratios are expected to remain extremely low. Share buybacks will bolster per-share earnings comparisons.

Valuation - 23-OCT-95

The stock is rated as accumulate. Under S&P's forecast for declining interest rates, S & L shares, particularly those of standout performers and institutional favorites such as Golden West, should do well. Also, the company has regained the growth momentum it lost in 1993 and 1994, reporting three consecutive quarters of higher earnings through September 30, 1995. Profits in 1996 should improve further, aided by expansion of the interest rate spread and an extremely low cost structure. Lastly, although the Street generally does not regard GDW as a takeover play, the high level of inside ownership suggests management would consider a bid.

Key Stock Statistics

S&P EPS Est. 1995	3.95	Tang. Bk. Value/Share	34.02
P/E on S&P Est. 1995	13.3	Beta	2.27
S&P EPS Est. 1996	4.75	Shareholders	1,900
Dividend Rate/Share	0.34	Market cap. (B)	$ 3.1
Shs. outstg. (M)	58.7	Inst. holdings	66%
Avg. daily vol. (M)	0.143	Insider holdings	NA

Value of $10,000 invested 5 years ago: $ 20,267

Fiscal Year Ending Dec. 31

	1995	% Change	1994	% Change	1993	% Change
Revenues (Million $)						
1Q	562.9	22%	463.1	-2%	474.9	-10%
2Q	613.4	31%	468.9	-3%	485.5	-6%
3Q	631.8	32%	478.0	-2%	488.3	-2%
4Q	—	—	504.0	4%	483.5	NM
Yr.	—	—	1,914	NM	1,932	-5%
Income (Million $)						
1Q	50.93	-22%	65.30	-9%	71.58	2%
2Q	53.56	-14%	61.94	-12%	70.58	-5%
3Q	63.38	13%	56.13	-12%	63.77	-9%
4Q	—	—	47.09	-31%	67.92	-3%
Yr.	—	—	230.4	-16%	273.9	-3%
Earnings Per Share ($)						
1Q	0.87	-15%	1.02	-9%	1.12	2%
2Q	0.91	-7%	0.98	-11%	1.10	-5%
3Q	1.08	19%	0.91	-9%	1.00	-9%
4Q	E1.09	38%	0.79	-25%	1.06	-4%
Yr.	E3.95	6%	3.71	-13%	4.28	-4%

Next earnings report expected: late January

Golden West Financial

Business Summary - 17-OCT-95

Golden West Financial is the holding company for World Savings & Loan, the third largest savings and loan in the U.S., based on assets of $31.7 billion at December 31, 1994. At year-end 1994 the company's savings network included 117 branches in California, 59 in Colorado (seven of which were subsequently sold in January 1995 with $153 million in deposits), 20 in Florida, 14 in Texas, 10 in Kansas, nine in Arizona, and eight in New Jersey. GDW also has 198 mortgage origination offices in 22 states. Loans receivable of $27.3 billion at December 31, 1994, up 13% from $24.2 billion a year earlier, were divided:

	1994	1993
One-to-four family	85%	84%
Apartments	14%	16%
Commercial & sav. accts	1%	Nil
Other	Nil	Nil

New real estate loans originated in 1994 and 1993 amounted to $6.64 billion and $6.41 billion, respectively. The portion of the mortgage portfolio (excluding MBS) composed of rate sensitive loans was 89% at year-end 1994. The one year gap (difference between assets and liabilities maturing/repricing within one year as a percentage of assets) at December 31, 1994 was 9.6%.

Of the $19.2 billion of total deposits at December 31, 1994, checking, passbook and money market accounts represented 17%, time deposits maturing within one year 27%, time deposits maturing in one to two years 29%, time deposits maturing in two to three years 10%, and other 20%. The yield on earning assets for 1994 was 6.57% (6.92% in 1993), the cost of funds was 4.33% (4.45%) , and the spread was 2.24% (2.47%).

Nonperforming assets and troubled loans restructured amounted to $428 million (1.35% of total assets at year-end 1994), down from $431 million (1.50%) a year earlier. The allowance for loan losses was $124 million (0.39% of assets) at December 31, 1994, versus $107 million (0.37%).

Important Developments

Oct. '95—Management said that during the third quarter GDW focused on obtaining financial market borrowings as some customers began seeking higher returns elsewhere in unisured investments.

Capitalization

FHLB Borrowings: $5,976,515,000 (9/95).
Other Borrowings: $3,186,218,000.

Per Share Data ($)

(Year Ended Dec. 31)

	1994	1993	1992	1991	1990	1989
Tangible Bk. Val.	31.81	30.17	24.45	19.88	14.41	11.50
Earnings	3.71	4.28	4.46	3.76	2.87	2.51
Dividends	0.31	0.27	0.23	0.19	0.17	0.15
Payout Ratio	8%	6%	5%	5%	6%	6%
Prices - High	46	50⅜	46¼	44¼	35¼	33¾
- Low	34¼	37⅛	35½	22¼	17⅝	15⅜
P/E Ratio - High	12	12	10	12	12	13
- Low	9	9	8	6	6	6

Income Statement Analysis (Million $)

	1994	%Chg	1993	%Chg	1992	%Chg	1991
Net Int. Inc.	721	-2%	733	2%	717	13%	632
Loan Loss Prov.	63.0	-4%	65.8	52%	43.2	43%	30.2
Non Int. Inc.	37.5	-40%	62.0	51%	41.1	53%	26.9
Non Int. Exp.	303	11%	273	8%	252	4%	242
Pretax Inc.	390	-15%	457	-2%	464	20%	387
Eff. Tax Rate	41%	—	40%	—	39%	—	38%
Net Inc.	230	-16%	274	-4%	284	19%	239
% Net Int. Marg.	2.43%	—	2.61%	—	2.83%	—	2.66%

Balance Sheet & Other Fin. Data (Million $)

	1994	1993	1992	1991	1990	1989
Total Assets	31,684	28,829	25,890	24,298	22,562	19,521
Loans	28,265	25,435	23,760	22,088	20,216	16,990
Deposits	19,219	17,422	16,486	16,819	14,372	11,787
Capitalization:						
Debt	8,874	8,178	6,515	4,973	5,234	5,889
Equity	2,000	2,066	1,727	1,449	1,220	1,046
Total	10,874	10,244	8,242	6,422	6,455	6,935

Ratio Analysis

	1994	1993	1992	1991	1990	1989
% Ret. on Assets	0.8	1.0	1.1	1.0	0.9	0.9
% Ret. on Equity	11.1	14.4	17.9	17.9	16.0	16.3
% Loan Loss Resv.	0.4	0.4	0.3	0.2	0.1	0.1
% Risk Based Capital	13.5	17.4	16.3	15.0	11.6	11.6
Price Times Book Value:						
High	1.4	1.7	1.9	2.2	2.4	2.9
Low	1.1	1.2	1.5	1.1	1.2	1.3

Dividend Data

—Dividends, which had been paid since 1977 prior to omission in 1982, were resumed in 1983.

Amt. of Div. $	Date Decl.	Ex-Div. Date	Stock of Record	Payment Date
0.085	Nov. 02	Nov. 08	Nov. 15	Dec. 12 '94
0.085	Feb. 01	Feb. 09	Feb. 15	Mar. 10 '95
0.085	May. 03	May. 09	May. 15	Jun. 12 '95
0.085	Aug. 02	Aug. 10	Aug. 14	Sep. 11 '95

Data as orig. reptd.; bef. results of disc opers. and/or spec. items. Per share data adj. for stk. divs. as of ex-div. date.
E-Estimated. NA-Not Available. NM-Not Meaningful. NR-Not Ranked.

Office—1901 Harrison St., Oakland, CA 94612. **Tel**—(510) 446-3420. **Co-Chrmn & Co-CEO**—H. M. Sandler. **Co-Chrmn & Co-CEO**—M. O. Sandler. **Pres**—R. W. Kettell. **VP-CFO & Investor Contact**—J. L. Helvey (510) 446-3405. **VP-Secy**—R. C. Rowe. **Dirs**—L. J. Galen, P. A. King, W. P. Kruer, W. D. McKee, B. A. Osher, K. T. Rosen, P. Sack, H. M. Sandler, M. O. Sandler. **Transfer Agent & Registrar**—First Interstate Bank, SF. **Reincorporated** in Delaware in 1975. **Empl- S&P Analyst:** Paul L. Huberman, CFA

Goodrich (B.F.)

NYSE Symbol **GR**
In S&P 500

10-AUG-95

Industry:
Aircraft manufacturing/
components

Summary: This company provides aircraft systems, components and services and manufactures a wide range of specialty chemicals.

S&P Opinion: Accumulate (★★★★)	Recent Price • 56	Yield • 4.0%
	52 Wk Range • 56½-40¾	12-Mo. P/E • 13.6

Earnings vs. Previous Year
▲=Up ▼=Down ▶=No Change

Quantitative Evaluations

Outlook
(1 Lowest—5 Highest)
• **1+**

Fair Value
• **42¾**

Risk
• **Low**

Earn./Div. Rank
• **B-**

Technical Eval.
• **Bearish** since 4/95

Rel. Strength Rank
(1 Lowest—99 Highest)
• **61**

Insider Activity
• **Neutral**

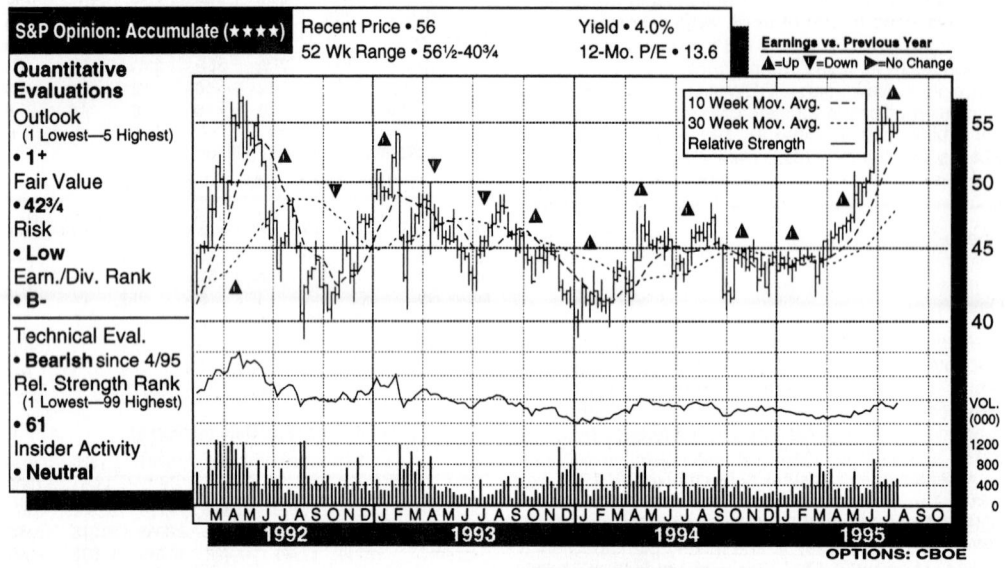

10 Week Mov. Avg. ----
30 Week Mov. Avg. ····
Relative Strength ——

OPTIONS: CBOE

Overview - 10-AUG-95

Sales for 1995 are expected to rise about 10% from those of 1994, despite the sale of Arrowhead. Chemical operations should achieve double-digit growth, primarily on volume and price gains in the plastics and additives segments. Aerospace revenues are forecast to increase more modestly, reflecting a recovery in demand for replacement parts and MRO (maintenance, repair and overhaul) services. Margins are expected to widen on the higher volume, a more favorable product mix and improved prices in the chemicals division. Nonrecurring gains, including a litigation settlement, will outweigh slightly higher interest expense.

Valuation - 10-AUG-95

Goodrich's stock price is influenced by factors affecting both the specialty chemicals and aerospace industries. In recent months, GR shares have surged, reflecting the recovery in the airline industry and optimism that margin pressures in the chemical sector may abate. Adding to the stock's performance has been a generous $2.20-a-share annual dividend. Although operating cash flow has not funded capital expenditures for several years (nor is it expected to do so this year), payments are relatively safe given GR's debt level. The sale of Arrowhead is also a plus. We anticipate further stock gains to result from improved margins in the chemical sector and increased demand from OEMs.

Key Stock Statistics

S&P EPS Est. 1995	4.10	Tang. Bk. Value/Share	8.27
P/E on S&P Est. 1995	13.7	Beta	1.35
S&P EPS Est. 1996	3.90	Shareholders	12,800
Dividend Rate/Share	2.20	Market cap. (B)	$ 1.4
Shs. outstg. (M)	25.9	Inst. holdings	85%
Avg. daily vol. (M)	0.084	Insider holdings	NA

Value of $10,000 invested 5 years ago: $ 17,833

Fiscal Year Ending Dec. 31

	1995	% Change	1994	% Change	1993	% Change
Revenues (Million $)						
1Q	594.0	18%	502.4	33%	376.5	-38%
2Q	600.6	11%	540.5	19%	452.7	-31%
3Q	—	—	561.5	12%	500.8	-23%
4Q	—	—	594.8	22%	488.3	-20%
Yr.	—	—	2,199	21%	1,818	-28%
Income (Million $)						
1Q	17.60	NM	4.90	NM	-6.90	NM
2Q	44.30	139%	18.50	NM	6.00	-48%
3Q	—	—	23.30	50%	15.50	NM
4Q	—	—	19.00	NM	0.70	NM
Yr.	—	—	65.70	NM	15.30	NM
Earnings Per Share ($)						
1Q	0.61	NM	0.11	NM	-0.35	NM
2Q	1.63	155%	0.64	NM	0.15	-59%
3Q	E0.91	—	0.82	55%	0.53	NM
4Q	E0.95	—	0.66	NM	-0.05	NM
Yr.	E4.10	—	2.24	NM	0.28	NM

Next earnings report expected: mid October

Goodrich (B.F.)

Business Summary - 10-AUG-95

The B.F.Goodrich Company provides aircraft systems, components and services and manufactures a wide range of specialty chemicals. The Geon PVC business was sold in 1993. Contributions by segment in 1994:

	Sales	Profits
Aerospace products	47%	65%
Specialty chemicals	46%	32%
Other	7%	3%

Operations outside North America accounted for 11% of sales and 5% of profits in 1994.

The aerospace segment provides aircraft landing systems (landing gear, wheels and brakes), sensors and integrated systems (fuel sensors, ignition systems, electromechanical actuators and windshield wiper systems), safety systems (evacuation slides and rafts, de-icing systems, navigation, collision avoidance systems, weather detection systems and lighting components) and maintenance repair and overhaul services. About 76% of aerospace sales are to the commercial market and about 62% are derived from replacement parts and services.

Specialty chemicals include: the specialty plastics group, which manufactures thermoplastic polyurethanes, low-combustibility plastics and thermoset resins; the specialty additives group, which manufactures synthetic thickeners and emulsifiers, controlled-release and suspension agents, polymer emulsions, dissolvable films, rubber and lubricant additives and plastic and adhesive modifiers; and the sealants, coatings and adhesives group. The water systems and services group was sold in May 1995.

Other operations include the production of chlor-alkali and olefin products. These products include chlorine, caustic soda, hydrogen, ethylene, propylene and other olefins.

Important Developments

Jul. '95—GR said aerospace operating income was up 21%, year to year, on an 8.1% gain in sales in the second quarter. Specialty chemicals income fell 9.6%, despite a 10% increase in sales. Income from other operations rose sharply as revenues jumped 44%.
Jun. '95—Goodrich called for redemption its $3.50 preferred stock for $50.70 per share, plus accrued dividends. Financing was provided by proceeds from a new preferred issuance.
May '95—The Arrowhead Industrial Water division, which had 1994 sales of $44 million, was sold for $80 million cash. Goodrich recorded a pretax gain of $5.0 million on the sale.

Capitalization

Long Term Debt: $419,700,000 (3/95), incl. lease obligs.
$3.50 Conv. Preferred Stock: 2,200,000 shs. ($1 par); ea. conv. into 0.909 com. (3/95).

Per Share Data ($)

(Year Ended Dec. 31)

	1994	1993	1992	1991	1990	1989
Tangible Bk. Val.	8.28	8.00	18.44	34.31	42.68	39.91
Cash Flow	6.59	4.15	4.32	1.43	8.33	10.33
Earnings	2.24	0.28	-0.69	-3.50	4.23	6.43
Dividends	2.20	2.20	2.20	2.20	2.12	2.00
Payout Ratio	98%	NM	NM	NM	50%	31%
Prices - High	48⅜	54¼	58⅛	47⅝	47⅜	69
- Low	39	39½	38⅞	36	29½	38½
P/E Ratio - High	22	NM	NM	NM	11	11
- Low	17	NM	NM	NM	7	6

Income Statement Analysis (Million $)

	1994	%Chg	1993	%Chg	1992	%Chg	1991
Revs.	2,199	21%	1,818	-28%	2,526	2%	2,472
Oper. Inc.	292	49%	196	-2%	201	7%	188
Depr.	112	12%	100	-22%	128	2%	125
Int. Exp.	48.0	12%	43.0	-12%	49.0	7%	46.0
Pretax Inc.	109	NM	15.0	NM	-16.0	NM	-109
Eff. Tax Rate	40%	—	Nil	—	NM	—	NM
Net Inc.	66.0	NM	15.0	NM	-9.0	NM	-81.0

Balance Sheet & Other Fin. Data (Million $)

	1994	1993	1992	1991	1990	1989
Cash	36.0	33.0	97.0	61.0	154	276
Curr. Assets	879	794	797	776	857	1,040
Total Assets	2,469	2,360	2,452	2,271	2,366	2,274
Curr. Liab.	638	469	566	530	610	486
LT Debt	427	487	403	344	207	289
Common Eqty.	813	784	718	1,104	1,249	1,167
Total Cap.	1,350	1,386	1,252	1,566	1,635	1,638
Cap. Exp.	129	232	204	211	244	266
Cash Flow	170	107	111	36.0	211	261

Ratio Analysis

	1994	1993	1992	1991	1990	1989
Curr. Ratio	1.4	1.7	1.4	1.5	1.4	2.1
% LT Debt of Cap.	31.6	35.1	32.2	22.0	12.7	17.6
% Net Inc.of Revs.	3.0	0.8	NM	NM	4.8	7.1
% Ret. on Assets	2.7	0.6	NM	NM	5.0	7.9
% Ret. on Equity	7.2	0.9	NM	NM	8.9	14.7

Dividend Data (Dividends have been paid since 1939. A dividend reinvestment plan is available. A "poison pill" stock purchase rights plan was adopted in 1987.)

Amt. of Div. $	Date Decl.	Ex-Div. Date	Stock of Record	Payment Date
0.550	Oct. 17	Dec. 05	Dec. 09	Jan. 03 '95
0.550	Feb. 21	Mar. 06	Mar. 10	Apr. 03 '95
0.550	Apr. 17	Jun. 06	Jun. 09	Jul. 03 '95
0.550	Jul. 17	Sep. 06	Sep. 08	Oct. 02 '95

Data as orig. reptd.; bef. results of disc. opers. and/or spec. items. Per share data adj. for stk. divs. as of ex-div. date.
E-Estimated. NA-Not Available. NM-Not Meaningful. NR-Not Ranked.

Office—3925 Embassy Parkway, Akron, OH 44333. **Tel**—(216) 374-3985. **Chrmn, Pres & CEO**—J. D. Ong. **Exec VP & CFO**—D. L. Tobler. **VP & Secy**—N. J. Calise. **Investor Contact**—John Atkinson (216) 374-2556. **Dirs**—J. G. Brown, G. A. Davidson Jr., J. J. Glasser, T. H. O'Leary, J. D. Ong, J. A. Pichler, A. M. Rankin Jr., I. M. Ross, D. L. Tobler, W. L. Wallace, J. L. Weinberg, A. T. Young. **Transfer Agent & Registrar**—Bank of New York, NYC. **Incorporated** in New York in 1912. **Empl**-12,456. **S&P Analyst:** Joe Victor Shammas

Goodyear Tire & Rubber

NYSE Symbol **GT**

In S&P 500

28-AUG-95	Industry: Rubber	**Summary:** Goodyear is the largest manufacturer of tires in the U.S., and one of the largest worldwide. Other operations include rubber and plastic products, chemicals and an oil pipeline.

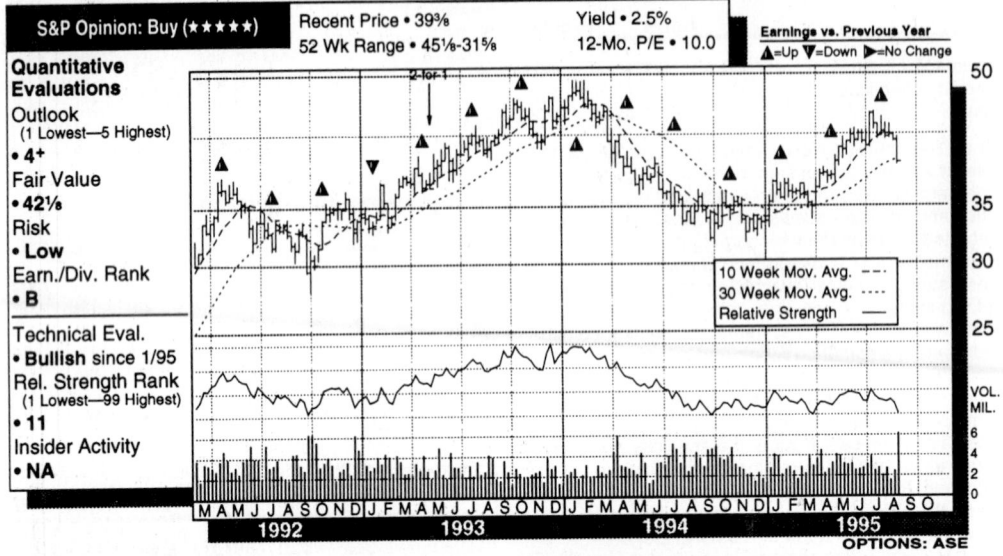

S&P Opinion: Buy (★★★★)	Recent Price • 39⅝ 52 Wk Range • 45⅛-31⅝	Yield • 2.5% 12-Mo. P/E • 10.0

Quantitative Evaluations

Outlook
(1 Lowest—5 Highest)
• **4+**

Fair Value
• **42⅛**

Risk
• **Low**

Earn./Div. Rank
• **B**

Technical Eval.
• **Bullish** since 1/95

Rel. Strength Rank
(1 Lowest—99 Highest)
• **11**

Insider Activity
• **NA**

Earnings vs. Previous Year
▲=Up ▼=Down ▶=No Change

10 Week Mov. Avg. ‒ ‒ ‒
30 Week Mov. Avg. ······
Relative Strength —

OPTIONS: ASE

Overview - 28-AUG-95

Sales for 1996 should rise modestly on a 2% to 3% increase in worldwide original equipment tire demand, and a strong rise in sales of replacement tires. Price increases impemented in 1995 should relieve pressures on margins and any decline in raw materials prices could have a substantial positive impact on margins and earnings. Profits should be boosted by aggressive efforts to contain selling, general and administrative expenses, and to generate further productivity gains as in recent years. The turnaround at All-American Pipeline that began in 1994 is continuing as operating levels have climbed to about 66% of capacity. Longer term, initiatives to boost sales in emerging and more rapidly growing Southeast Asian markets should pay off and recovery of the depressed Mexican economy could also help.

Valuation - 28-AUG-95

GT's shares have weakened on fears that a strong U.S. dollar could weaken foreign profits. We think the concerns are overblown. We expect GT to continue to exploit its large foreign market position and leading share of the U.S. replacement tire market, as well as the relative financial weakness of some of its competitors. Trading at less than 10 times expected 1995 earnings and a little more than two times book value, the stock is a tremendous value. With a steadily strengthening balance sheet and a commitment to a healthy dividend payout, the stock is highly attractive and among the most undervalued automotive suppliers.

Key Stock Statistics

S&P EPS Est. 1995	4.15	Tang. Bk. Value/Share	20.19
P/E on S&P Est. 1995	9.5	Beta	1.18
S&P EPS Est. 1996	4.75	Shareholders	36,300
Dividend Rate/Share	1.00	Market cap. (B)	$ 6.0
Shs. outstg. (M)	152.3	Inst. holdings	70%
Avg. daily vol. (M)	0.697	Insider holdings	NA

Value of $10,000 invested 5 years ago: $ 21,217

Fiscal Year Ending Dec. 31

	1995	% Change	1994	% Change	1993	% Change
Revenues (Million $)						
1Q	3,243	11%	2,910	3%	2,814	1%
2Q	3,351	10%	3,052	2%	3,000	-2%
3Q	—	—	3,116	7%	2,913	-3%
4Q	—	—	3,211	10%	2,916	NM
Yr.	—	—	12,288	6%	11,643	-1%
Income (Million $)						
1Q	133.3	15%	116.0	33%	87.10	32%
2Q	173.8	6%	163.2	7%	152.2	42%
3Q	—	—	151.3	11%	136.2	49%
4Q	—	—	136.5	21%	113.2	10%
Yr.	—	—	567.0	16%	488.7	33%
Earnings Per Share ($)						
1Q	0.88	14%	0.77	28%	0.60	29%
2Q	1.15	6%	1.08	3%	1.05	40%
3Q	E1.12	12%	1.00	9%	0.92	44%
4Q	E1.00	11%	0.90	18%	0.76	6%
Yr.	E4.15	11%	3.75	13%	3.33	30%

Next earnings report expected: late October

Goodyear Tire & Rubber

Business Summary - 28-AUG-95

Goodyear is the world's largest rubber fabricator. Segment contributions in 1994:

	Sales	Profits
Tires & related products	85.6%	84.7%
General rubber/chemical/ plastic products	13.8%	14.3%
Oil transportation	0.6%	1.0%

In 1994, the U.S. accounted for 58% of sales and $591.5 million of operating income, while foreign operations contributed 42% of sales and $601.8 million of earnings. Foreign earnings were from Europe ($212.0 million), Latin America ($278.2 million), Asia ($81.3 million) and Canada ($30.3 million).

Transportation-related products include new tires and inner tubes, retreads, repair materials, automotive belts and hose, molded parts and foam cushioning, auto repairs and services, and other accessories. Sales of new tires alone contributed 77% of total sales in 1994. Replacement volume is significantly higher than sales to the original equipment market.

The 1,750-mile All-American Pipeline carries oil from offshore California wells to Texas refineries; it operated at a loss from its completion in 1989 until 1994 when it generated an $11.8 million profit resulting from an increase in throughput. The pipeline is expected to operate at about 66% of capacity in 1995 and be profitable.

General product lines include various kinds of automotive and industrial belts and hose, molded products, foam cushioning accessories, tank tracks, organic chemicals used in rubber and plastic processing, synthetic rubber and rubber latices, and other products.

Important Developments

Aug. '95—GT said that it was cooperating in a U.S. Justice Department investigation into the domestic tire industry for possible anti-competitive practices. This follows several rounds of tire price hikes instituted in the first half of 1995 by most tire manufacturers which were attributed to higher raw materials prices, including particularly sharp advances in the cost of natural and synthetic rubber and carbon black. Raw materials account for about half the cost of tires, and tire prices traditionally have been volatile when raw materials costs were fluctuating.

Feb. '95—GT said that it expected capital expenditures of approximately $650 million and research and development expenditures of some $340 million in 1995.

Capitalization

Long Term Debt: $1,278,900,000 (6/95).
Minority Interest: $149,700,000.

Per Share Data ($)

	1994	1993	1992	1991	1990	1989
Tangible Bk. Val.	16.44	13.90	11.21	17.87	17.94	18.54
Cash Flow	6.46	5.99	5.69	4.31	3.23	4.96
Earnings	3.75	3.33	2.57	0.62	-0.33	1.64
Dividends	0.75	0.57	0.28	0.20	0.90	0.90
Payout Ratio	20%	18%	11%	38%	NM	55%
Prices - High	49¼	47¼	38⅛	27⅛	23¼	29⅞
- Low	31⅝	32⅝	26	8⅜	6½	21⅛
P/E Ratio - High	13	14	15	44	NM	18
- Low	8	10	10	14	NM	13

(Year Ended Dec. 31)

Income Statement Analysis (Million $)

	1994	%Chg	1993	%Chg	1992	%Chg	1991
Revs.	12,288	6%	11,643	-1%	11,785	8%	10,907
Oper. Inc.	1,492	4%	1,431	9%	1,312	23%	1,063
Depr.	410	4%	393	-12%	446	NM	442
Int. Exp.	135	-19%	167	-30%	237	-27%	326
Pretax Inc.	890	10%	812	24%	653	125%	290
Eff. Tax Rate	34%	—	37%	—	40%	—	68%
Net Inc.	567	16%	489	33%	367	NM	75.0

Balance Sheet & Other Fin. Data (Million $)

	1994	1993	1992	1991	1990	1989
Cash	266	228	304	235	277	215
Curr. Assets	3,623	3,263	3,310	3,119	3,324	3,272
Total Assets	9,123	8,436	8,564	8,511	8,964	8,460
Curr. Liab.	2,572	2,524	2,646	2,393	2,294	2,200
LT Debt	1,109	1,066	1,471	2,038	3,286	2,963
Common Eqty.	2,803	2,301	1,930	2,731	2,098	2,144
Total Cap.	4,056	3,489	3,530	5,488	6,120	5,895
Cap. Exp.	523	432	367	346	575	783
Cash Flow	977	882	813	516	377	573

Ratio Analysis

	1994	1993	1992	1991	1990	1989
Curr. Ratio	1.4	1.3	1.3	1.3	1.4	1.5
% LT Debt of Cap.	27.3	30.5	41.7	37.1	53.7	50.3
% Net Inc.of Revs.	4.6	4.2	3.1	0.7	NM	1.7
% Ret. on Assets	6.4	5.6	4.3	0.8	NM	2.2
% Ret. on Equity	22.2	22.7	15.6	2.8	NM	9.1

Dividend Data —Dividends have been paid since 1937. A dividend reinvestment plan is available.

Amt. of Div. $	Date Decl.	Ex-Div. Date	Stock of Record	Payment Date
0.200	Aug. 02	Aug. 10	Aug. 16	Sep. 15 '94
0.200	Nov. 01	Nov. 09	Nov. 16	Dec. 15 '94
0.200	Jan. 04	Feb. 10	Feb. 16	Mar. 15 '95
0.250	Apr. 10	May. 10	May. 16	Jun. 15 '95
0.250	Aug. 01	Aug. 14	Aug. 16	Sep. 15 '95

Office—1144 East Market St., Akron, OH 44316-0001. **Tel**—(216) 796-2121. **Chrmn & CEO**—S. C. Gault. **Pres & COO**—S. F. Gibara. **VP-CFO**—R. W. Tieken. **VP-Secy**—J. Boyazis. **VP-Treas**—R. W. Hauman. **Investor Contact**—Dianne C. Davis. **Dirs**—J. G. Breen, W. E. Butler, T. H. Cruikshank, S. C. Gault, S. F. Gibara, G. G. Michelson, S. A. Minter, C. W. Parry, A. Pytte, G. H. Schofield, W. C. Turner, H. M. Wells. **Transfer Agent & Registrar**—First Chicago Trust Co. of New York, Jersey City, N.J. **Incorporated** in Ohio in 1898. **Empl**-89,000. **S&P Analyst:** Joshua M. Harari, CFA

Grace (W.R.)

NYSE Symbol **GRA**
In S&P 500

10-OCT-95

Industry:
Chemicals

Summary: Grace, the world's largest producer of specialty chemicals (including plastics packaging, catalysts and container sealants), plans to spin off its health care business.

S&P Opinion: Buy (★★★★★)	Recent Price • 65⅞ Yield • 0.8%
	52 Wk Range • 71⅝-35¼ 12-Mo. P/E • 20.3

Quantitative Evaluations

Outlook
(1 Lowest—5 Highest)
• **1+**

Fair Value
• **59⅛**

Risk
• **Average**

Earn./Div. Rank
• **B-**

Technical Eval.
• **Bullish** since 4/94

Rel. Strength Rank
(1 Lowest—99 Highest)
• **40**

Insider Activity
• **Favorable**

Earnings vs. Previous Year
▲=Up ▼=Down ▶=No Change

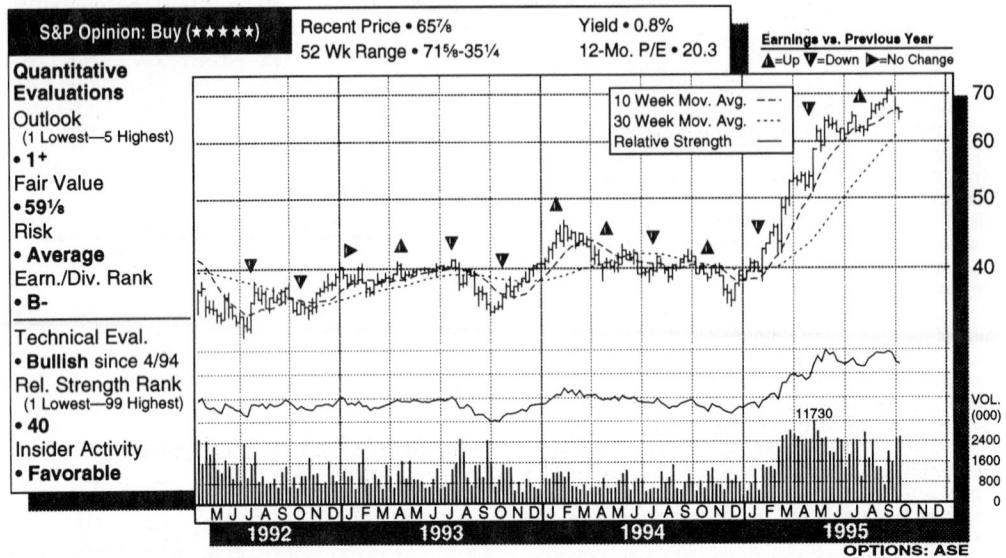

10 Week Mov. Avg. – – –
30 Week Mov. Avg. · · · ·
Relative Strength —

11730

VOL. (000)

OPTIONS: ASE

Overview - 06-OCT-95

We expect that operating earnings of the specialty chemicals business (as currently constituted) will continue to advance at a good pace, led by the packaging and catalysts units. Earnings in 1996 will also benefit from overhead cost reductions projected at over $100 million a year, while interest expense should decline as a result of lower debt. Possible special charges and further restructuring actions could have a meaningful impact on reported results. The health care business (now reported as a discontinued operation in anticipation of its spin-off in the fourth quarter of 1995) will also continue to advance, aided by acquisitions and foreign expansion.

Valuation - 06-OCT-95

S&P strongly recommends the purchase of this stock as a restructuring play. GRA's moves to improve shareholder value include the planned tax-free spin-off of the health care unit in November, and the possible sale of the smaller chemical businesses. Major cost reductions are also being implemented. We see the combined value of the two new companies at over $80 a share. After the spin-off, GRA will be a financially stronger company, allowing for acquisitions and stock repurchases. The dividend was just cut to make the post spin-off payout rate consistent with GRA's peer companies. The stock has surged since early 1995 on investors' expectations of such moves in the wake of the turmoil ensuing from the resignation in March of the highly regarded CEO J.P. Bolduc, and the bid to buy National Medical Care by that unit's management.

Key Stock Statistics

S&P EPS Est. 1995	2.00	Tang. Bk. Value/Share	10.96
P/E on S&P Est. 1995	32.9	Beta	1.12
S&P EPS Est. 1996	3.00	Shareholders	18,500
Dividend Rate/Share	0.50	Market cap. (B)	$ 6.2
Shs. outstg. (M)	96.5	Inst. holdings	79%
Avg. daily vol. (M)	0.546	Insider holdings	NA

Value of $10,000 invested 5 years ago: $ 24,847

Fiscal Year Ending Dec. 31

	1995	% Change	1994	% Change	1993	% Change
Revenues (Million $)						
1Q	853.4	-21%	1,077	9%	986.2	-19%
2Q	936.8	-24%	1,237	13%	1,094	-18%
3Q	—	—	1,307	15%	1,136	-19%
4Q	—	—	1,473	24%	1,192	-24%
Yr.	—	—	5,093	16%	4,408	-20%
Income (Million $)						
1Q	26.20	-31%	38.20	35%	28.30	27%
2Q	48.10	NM	-134.3	NM	53.90	-10%
3Q	—	—	76.00	NM	-236.4	NM
4Q	—	—	103.4	-64%	285.2	NM
Yr.	—	—	83.30	-38%	134.0	69%
Earnings Per Share ($)						
1Q	0.27	-34%	0.41	17%	0.35	40%
2Q	0.51	NM	-1.43	NM	0.60	-10%
3Q	E0.52	-36%	0.81	NM	-2.56	NM
4Q	E0.70	-36%	1.10	-64%	3.05	NM
Yr.	E2.00	127%	0.88	-40%	1.46	66%

Next earnings report expected: late October

Grace (W.R.)

Business Summary - 06-OCT-95

W. R. Grace & Co. is the world's largest specialty chemicals company, with interests in health care. Contributions by segment in 1994 were:

	Sales	Profits
Specialty chemicals	63%	58%
Health care	37%	42%

Foreign operations accounted for 33% of sales and 26% of profits in 1994.

The specialty chemicals business consists of plastic packaging products (28% of total 1994 sales), catalysts (petroleum refining and petrochemical) and silica-based products (12%), construction materials (8%), water treatment and process chemicals (6%), and container sealing compounds (7%). Other products (2%) include drying equipment for graphic arts, and specialty polymers.

National Medical Care, Inc. (NMC) provides kidney dialysis services (26%), home infusion and respiratory therapy services (5%), and medical products (6%). GRA classified NMC as a discontinued operation in the 1995 second quarter, and announced plans to spin off NMC to shareholders in November 1995.

The cocoa and chocolate products, cattle breeding, battery separators, printing products, engineered materials, and electromagnetic radiation control businesses were classified as discontinued operations in 1993. Most of these units were sold in 1994.

In 1993, Grace sold the oil and gas operations of Grace Energy Corp. (classified as discontinued in 1992). The sale of Colowyo Coal Co. was completed in 1994.

Important Developments

Oct. '95—Directors approved the repurchase of up to 10 million common shares. GRA was also pursuing options for its Dearborn water treatment chemicals unit, including the outright sale of the unit or strategic alliances. GRA also said that its cost management study should be completed in October. In June, GRA announced plans to spin off its National Medical Care (NMC) unit to shareholders. GRA expected that the spin-off, subject to various conditions, would be tax-free and take place in the fourth quarter. NMC had sales of $1.9 billion in 1994. NMC was expected to pay GRA a special cash dividend of about $1.2 billion, which GRA expects to apply substantially to reduce debt. Following the spin-off, NMC does not expect to pay a dividend. GRA reduced its post spin-off dividend to be consistent with the payout of peer companies. Constantine Hampers, CEO of NMC, will continue in that position after the spin-off. In May, GRA received a proposal from Hampers to purchase NMC for $3.5 billion.

Capitalization

Long Term Debt: $1,280,900,000 (6/95).
Preferred Stock: $7,400,000.

Per Share Data ($)

(Year Ended Dec. 31)

	1994	1993	1992	1991	1990	1989
Tangible Bk. Val.	6.06	8.54	11.73	17.10	15.68	14.12
Cash Flow	3.66	3.53	3.58	5.95	5.75	5.97
Earnings	0.88	1.46	0.88	2.51	2.36	3.01
Dividends	1.40	1.40	1.40	1.40	1.40	1.40
Payout Ratio	159%	96%	159%	57%	60%	47%
Prices - High	46¾	41¼	45	40¾	33⅝	39⅛
- Low	35¼	34⅜	32	23⅜	17	25⅛
P/E Ratio - High	53	16	51	16	14	13
- Low	40	13	36	9	7	8

Income Statement Analysis (Million $)

	1994	%Chg	1993	%Chg	1992	%Chg	1991
Revs.	5,093	16%	4,408	-20%	5,518	-9%	6,049
Oper. Inc.	775	27%	608	-4%	632	-15%	742
Depr.	261	38%	189	-22%	241	-20%	300
Int. Exp.	119	34%	89.0	-34%	134	-34%	202
Pretax Inc.	139	-37%	221	-1%	224	-38%	359
Eff. Tax Rate	40%	—	39%	—	65%	—	39%
Net Inc.	83.0	-38%	134	70%	79.0	-64%	219

Balance Sheet & Other Fin. Data (Million $)

	1994	1993	1992	1991	1990	1989
Cash	78.0	48.0	63.0	207	116	109
Curr. Assets	2,229	1,975	2,091	1,990	2,380	2,166
Total Assets	6,231	6,109	5,599	6,007	6,227	5,619
Curr. Liab.	2,232	1,993	1,640	1,622	1,680	1,589
LT Debt	1,099	1,174	1,355	1,793	1,964	1,638
Common Eqty.	1,492	1,510	1,538	2,018	1,905	1,723
Total Cap.	2,696	2,789	3,293	4,068	4,144	3,611
Cap. Exp.	445	310	398	489	554	515
Cash Flow	344	323	320	519	494	509

Ratio Analysis

	1994	1993	1992	1991	1990	1989
Curr. Ratio	1.0	1.0	1.3	1.2	1.4	1.4
% LT Debt of Cap.	40.8	42.1	41.1	44.1	47.4	45.4
% Net Inc.of Revs.	1.6	3.0	1.4	3.6	3.0	4.2
% Ret. on Assets	1.3	2.3	1.4	3.5	3.4	4.7
% Ret. on Equity	5.5	8.6	4.4	11.0	11.1	15.6

Dividend Data

—Dividends have been paid since 1934. A dividend reinvestment plan is available. A "poison pill" stock purchase rights plan was adopted in 1987.

Amt. of Div. $	Date Decl.	Ex-Div. Date	Stock of Record	Payment Date
0.350	Oct. 06	Oct. 28	Nov. 03	Dec. 10 '94
0.350	Jan. 05	Jan. 27	Feb. 02	Mar. 10 '95
0.350	Apr. 06	Apr. 28	May. 04	Jun. 12 '95
0.350	Jul. 06	Aug. 01	Aug. 03	Sep. 11 '95
0.125	Oct. 05	Oct. 31	Nov. 02	Dec. 11 '95

Data as orig. reptd.; bef. results of disc. opers. and/or spec. items. Per share data adj. for stk. divs. as of ex-div. date. E-Estimated. NA-Not Available. NM-Not Meaningful. NR-Not Ranked.

Office—One Town Center Rd., Boca Raton, FL 33486-1010. **Tel**—(407) 362-2000. **Chrmn, Pres & CEO**—A. L. Costello. **SVP & CFO**—P. D. Houchin. **Secy**—R. B. Lamm. **VP & Investor Contact**—Peter B. Martin. **Dirs**—A. L. Costello, G. C. Dacey, E. W. Duffy, H. A. Eckmann, J. W. Frick, T. L. Gossage, C. L. Hampers, T. A. Holmes, G. J. Humphrey, V. A. Kamsky, P. S. Lynch, R. C. Macauley, J. E. Phipps, E. J. Sullivan. **Transfer Agent**—Chemical Bank, NYC. **Incorporated** in Connecticut in 1899; reincorporated in New York in 1988. **Empl**-37,900. **S&P Analyst:** Richard O'Reilly, CFA

Grainger (W.W.)

NYSE Symbol **GWW**
In S&P 500

18-OCT-95

Industry:
Electronics/Electric

Summary: Grainger is a leading distributor of equipment, components and supplies to commercial, industrial, contractor and institutional markets.

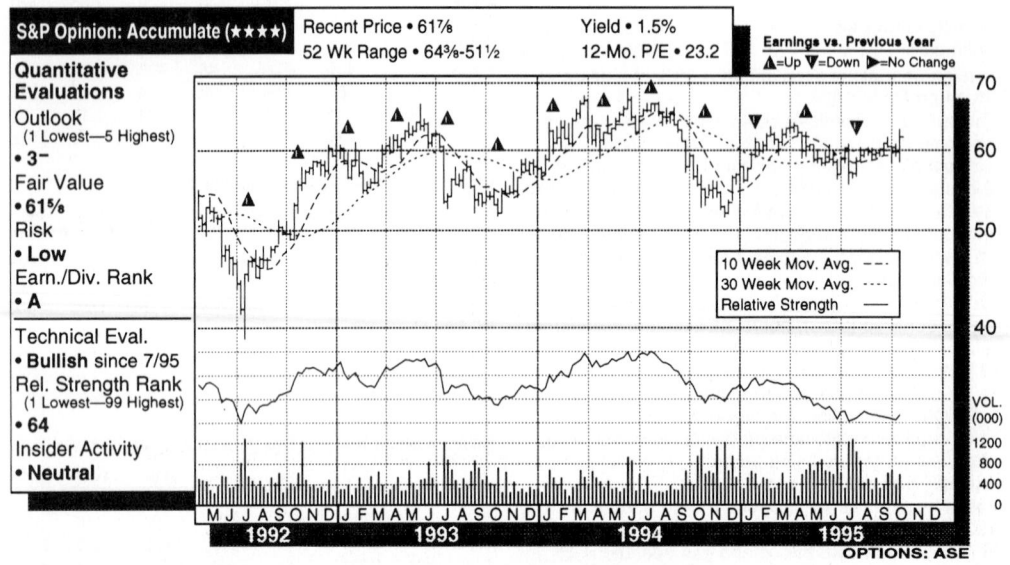

S&P Opinion: Accumulate (★★★★)	Recent Price • 61⅞ Yield • 1.5%
	52 Wk Range • 64⅜-51½ 12-Mo. P/E • 23.2

Earnings vs. Previous Year
▲=Up ▼=Down ►=No Change

Quantitative Evaluations

Outlook
(1 Lowest—5 Highest)
• **3⁻**

Fair Value
• **61⅝**

Risk
• **Low**

Earn./Div. Rank
• **A**

Technical Eval.
• **Bullish** since 7/95

Rel. Strength Rank
(1 Lowest—99 Highest)
• **64**

Insider Activity
• **Neutral**

10 Week Mov. Avg. – – –
30 Week Mov. Avg. ·······
Relative Strength ——

OPTIONS: ASE

Overview - 18-OCT-95

Sales in 1996 should advance 10%, aided by the stronger economy, expansion of the distribution network, and the introduction of new products. In addition, the company's National Accounts program that targets large original equipment manufacturers should aid sales growth. The integration of three units into the company's core business is also likely to stimulate sales growth, as is the acquisition of several smaller distribution companies that will add to volume. Margins should widen on the higher volume, aggressive management of costs and lower infrastructure investment spending, as well as lower amortization of goodwill and other acquisition related expenses.

Valuation - 18-OCT-95

Fueled by a better than expected third quarter, these shares have rebounded sharply following a selloff on disappointing second quarter earnings. While softness in the economy means that another earnings disappointment can't be totally precluded, the fundamentals appear more likely to continue to improve and allow the shares to reach new highs. We are particularly encouraged by the substantial sales gains the company is making in its National Accounts program, which targets large original equipment manufacturers. The sales growth and the widening of margins we project should allow the multiple on these shares to widen.

Key Stock Statistics

S&P EPS Est. 1995	3.65	Tang. Bk. Value/Share	21.07
P/E on S&P Est. 1995	17.0	Beta	1.01
S&P EPS Est. 1996	4.15	Shareholders	2,200
Dividend Rate/Share	0.92	Market cap. (B)	$ 3.1
Shs. outstg. (M)	50.8	Inst. holdings	60%
Avg. daily vol. (M)	0.109	Insider holdings	NA

Value of $10,000 invested 5 years ago: $ 20,681

Fiscal Year Ending Dec. 31

	1995	% Change	1994	% Change	1993	% Change
Revenues (Million $)						
1Q	806.8	14%	706.4	17%	606.2	14%
2Q	813.5	6%	768.5	16%	660.4	9%
3Q	850.0	9%	779.3	12%	698.8	11%
4Q	—	—	768.8	16%	663.0	11%
Yr.	—	—	3,023	15%	2,628	11%
Income (Million $)						
1Q	46.87	13%	41.54	21%	34.19	21%
2Q	39.48	-7%	42.32	19%	35.45	-2%
3Q	49.13	14%	43.05	11%	38.71	4%
4Q	—	—	0.97	-98%	40.92	14%
Yr.	—	—	127.9	-14%	149.3	9%
Earnings Per Share ($)						
1Q	0.92	14%	0.81	25%	0.65	23%
2Q	0.77	-7%	0.83	22%	0.68	1%
3Q	0.96	14%	0.84	12%	0.75	7%
4Q	E1.00	NM	0.02	-98%	0.80	18%
Yr.	E3.65	46%	2.50	-13%	2.88	12%

Next earnings report expected: early February

Business Summary - 18-OCT-95

W.W. Grainger is a nationwide distributor of equipment, components, and supplies to the commercial, industrial, contractor, and institutional markets.

The company's core branch-based business, Grainger, is a nationwide distributor of air compressors, air conditioning and refrigeration equipment and components, air tools and paint spraying equipment, blowers, computer supplies, electric motors, fans, gas engine driven power plants, gearmotors, heating equipment and controls, hydraulic equipment, janitorial supplies, lighting fixtures and components, liquid pumps, material handling and storage equipment, motor controls, office equipment, outdoor equipment, plant and office maintenance equipment, power and hand tools, power generating plants, power transmission components, safety products, and shop tools, as well as other items.

Grainger is also an important resource for both product and procurement process information.

An important selling tool is the company's general catalog, which lists approximately 61,800 items. The Grainger division also operates 342 branch locations in 50 states and Puerto Rico. Approximately 29% of the Grainger division's 1994 sales consisted of items bearing the company's registered trademarks.

During 1994, Grainger completed the integration of its sanitary supply business into its core branch-based business, while it began the integration of of its safety products and production consumable products businesses into its core business. These efforts are to be completed in 1995.

Grainger sells principally to contractors, service shops, industrial and commercial maintenance departments, manufacturers, hotels, and health care and educational facilities.

Important Developments

Jul. '95—GWW said that the increase in its third quarter sales primarily reflected the continuing effects of its market initiatives and an increase in sales of seasonal products. The market initiatives included new product additions, the expansion of branch facilities, adding Zone Distribution centers, and the National Accounts program. The company added that sales to its National Accounts customers, which represent large original equipment manufacturers within its core branch-based business, increased about 23% in the third quarter over the year earlier level. The company added that its margins widened primarily due to a favorable product mix in non-seasonal product categories, well controlled expenses and lower amortization of goodwill and other acquisition related expenses.

Capitalization

Long Term Debt: $4,405,000 (9/95).

Per Share Data ($) (Year Ended Dec. 31)

	1994	1993	1992	1991	1990	1989
Tangible Bk. Val.	18.65	16.11	15.10	16.26	15.07	13.43
Cash Flow	3.80	4.02	3.50	3.07	2.91	2.81
Earnings	2.50	2.88	2.58	2.37	2.31	2.20
Dividends	0.78	0.71	0.65	0.61	0.57	0.50
Payout Ratio	31%	24%	25%	25%	24%	23%
Prices - High	69⅛	66¾	61	55½	39¼	33⅛
- Low	51½	51⅝	39	30¼	27¼	26¼
P/E Ratio - High	28	23	24	23	17	15
- Low	21	18	15	13	12	12

Income Statement Analysis (Million $)

	1994	%Chg	1993	%Chg	1992	%Chg	1991
Revs.	3,023	15%	2,628	11%	2,364	14%	2,077
Oper. Inc.	368	18%	311	12%	278	15%	242
Depr.	66.7	13%	59.2	21%	49.1	30%	37.8
Int. Exp.	3.8	27%	3.0	-12%	3.4	6%	3.2
Pretax Inc.	229	-8%	250	10%	227	9%	209
Eff. Tax Rate	44%	—	40%	—	40%	—	39%
Net Inc.	128	-14%	149	9%	137	7%	128

Balance Sheet & Other Fin. Data (Million $)

	1994	1993	1992	1991	1990	1989
Cash	15.0	3.0	45.0	141	147	81.0
Curr. Assets	964	824	794	854	829	755
Total Assets	1,535	1,377	1,311	1,217	1,162	1,065
Curr. Liab.	459	381	315	280	269	262
LT Debt	1.0	6.2	6.9	11.3	14.5	2.8
Common Eqty.	1,033	942	931	860	815	732
Total Cap.	1,049	971	979	921	881	793
Cap. Exp.	120	99	77.4	32.8	35.0	35.2
Cash Flow	195	208	186	166	160	153

Ratio Analysis

	1994	1993	1992	1991	1990	1989
Curr. Ratio	2.1	2.2	2.5	3.0	3.1	2.9
% LT Debt of Cap.	0.1	0.6	0.7	1.2	1.6	0.4
% Net Inc.of Revs.	4.2	5.7	5.8	6.1	6.6	6.9
% Ret. on Assets	8.8	11.3	10.9	10.9	11.4	11.9
% Ret. on Equity	12.9	16.2	15.4	15.4	16.4	17.5

Dividend Data

Dividends have been paid since 1965. A "poison pill" stock purchase rights plan was adopted in 1989.

Amt. of Div. $	Date Decl.	Ex-Div. Date	Stock of Record	Payment Date
0.200	Oct. 26	Nov. 01	Nov. 07	Dec. 01 '94
0.200	Jan. 25	Jan. 31	Feb. 06	Mar. 01 '95
0.230	Apr. 26	May. 02	May. 08	Jun. 01 '95
0.230	Aug. 02	Aug. 10	Aug. 14	Sep. 01 '95

Data as orig. reptd.; bef. results of disc. opers. and/or spec. items. Per share data adj. for stk. divs. as of ex-div. date.
E-Estimated. NA-Not Available. NM-Not Meaningful. NR-Not Ranked.

Office—5500 West Howard St., Skokie, IL 60077. **Tel**—(708) 982-9000. **Chrmn**—D. W. Grainger. **Pres & CEO**—R. L. Keyser. **VP Fin**—P. O. Loux. **VP-Investor Contact**—Robert D. Pappano. **VP-Secy**—J. M. Baisley. **Dirs**—G. R. Baker, R. E. Elberson, J. D. Fluno, W. H. Gantz, D. W. Grainger, R. L. Keyser, J. W. McCarter Jr., J. D. Slavik, H. B. Smith Jr., F. L. Turner. **Transfer Agent & Registrar**—The First National Bank of Boston. **Incorporated** in Illinois in 1928. **Empl**-11,343. **S&P Analyst:** Paul H. Valentine, CFA

Great Atlantic & Pacific

NYSE Symbol **GAP**

In S&P 500

17-OCT-95

Industry:
Retail Stores

Summary: This company operates more than 1,050 conventional supermarkets and larger superstores throughout the U.S. and in Ontario Canada.

| S&P Opinion: Hold (★★★) | Recent Price • 21⅞ | Yield • 0.9% | **Earnings vs. Previous Year** |
| | 52 Wk Range • 29-17⅜ | 12-Mo. P/E • NM | ▲=Up ▼=Down ▶=No Change |

Quantitative Evaluations

Outlook
(1 Lowest—5 Highest)
• **3+**

Fair Value
• **21⅞**

Risk
• **Average**

Earn./Div. Rank
• **B-**

Technical Eval.
• **Bearish** since 5/95

Rel. Strength Rank
(1 Lowest—99 Highest)
• **4**

Insider Activity
• **Favorable**

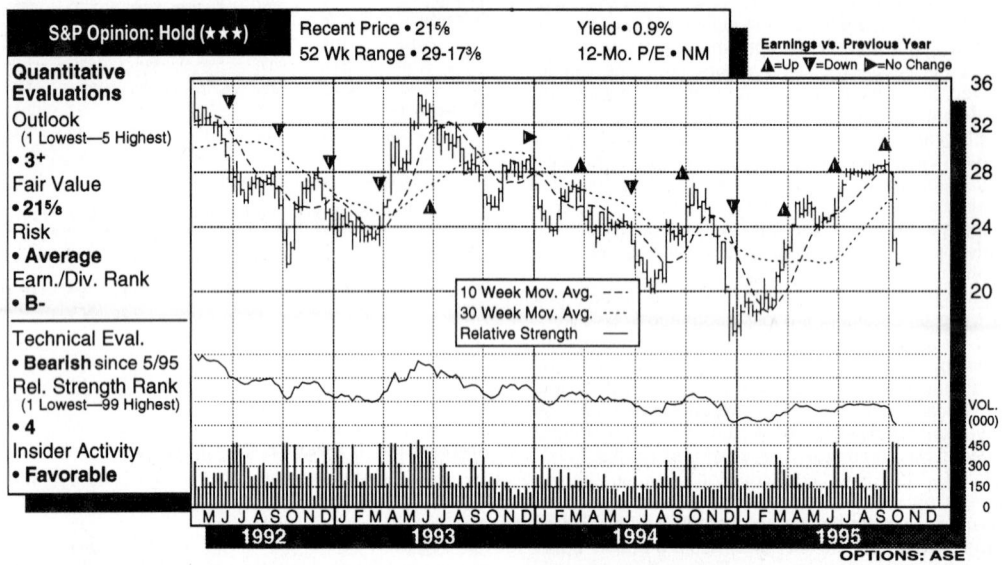

10 Week Mov. Avg. — — —
30 Week Mov. Avg. ········
Relative Strength ——

1992 1993 1994 1995

OPTIONS: ASE

Overview - 16-OCT-95

Same-store sales might be headed for a slight decline in 1995-96, as the company faces increased competition in its markets, and as conversion of its units to the superstore format continues at a slow pace. Sluggish consumer spending will also impact sales. Consumers, who appear to value price and selection over convenience, have sought out the lower-priced, better-stocked superstores of GAP's competitors. Over time, however, the closing of smaller, less-productive units and store remodeling should boost profits. The lone bright spot for the company has been the improved results at its Canadian operations, which have rebounded from depressed levels brought about by various labor disputes.

Valuation - 16-OCT-95

The company's shares have increased nearly 25% in calendar 1995, and now seem fairly valued following the recent decline in comparable-store sales and increased competiton in many of its markets. The combination of better pricing and a conversion of stores to a superstore format should eventually restore profitability in markets where GAP is struggling. The popularity of private brands such as America's and Master Choice should continue to aid margins. GAP trades at around 19x our 1995-96 earnings estimate of $1.15 a share, which has been scaled down over the past few months due to a slowdown in the company's markets.

Key Stock Statistics

S&P EPS Est. 1996	1.15	Tang. Bk. Value/Share	20.59
P/E on S&P Est. 1996	18.8	Beta	1.02
S&P EPS Est. 1997	1.30	Shareholders	11,800
Dividend Rate/Share	0.20	Market cap. (B)	$0.822
Shs. outstg. (M)	38.2	Inst. holdings	37%
Avg. daily vol. (M)	0.098	Insider holdings	NA

Value of $10,000 invested 5 years ago: $ 4,306

Fiscal Year Ending Feb. 28

	1996	% Change	1995	% Change	1994	% Change
Revenues (Million $)						
1Q	3,136	-3%	3,225	-2%	3,279	-1%
2Q	2,341	-2%	2,391	NM	2,399	-1%
3Q	—	—	2,346	NM	2,343	-2%
4Q	—	—	2,370	NM	2,363	NM
Yr.	—	—	10,332	NM	10,384	-1%
Income (Million $)						
1Q	14.55	101%	7.25	-57%	17.05	NM
2Q	9.38	55%	6.06	2%	5.96	-22%
3Q	—	—	-185.7	NM	0.38	-10%
4Q	—	—	5.78	NM	-19.43	NM
Yr.	—	—	-166.6	NM	3.96	NM
Earnings Per Share ($)						
1Q	0.38	100%	0.19	-58%	0.45	NM
2Q	0.25	56%	0.16	7%	0.15	-25%
3Q	E0.27	NM	-4.86	NM	0.01	NM
4Q	E0.25	67%	0.15	NM	-0.51	NM
Yr.	E1.15	NM	-4.36	NM	0.10	NM

Next earnings report expected: mid December

Great Atlantic & Pacific

Business Summary - 17-OCT-95

Great Atlantic & Pacific operates conventional supermarkets and larger superstores selling food and general merchandise in 22 states, the District of Columbia and Ontario, Canada. At September 26, 1995, there were 1,063 stores in operation. The stores carry the trade names A&P, Super Fresh, Family Mart, Kohl's, Waldbaum's, Food Emporium, Food Mart, Sav-A-Center, Futurestore, Farmer Jack, Dominion, Compass Foods and Miracle Food Mart. The company operates its stores with merchandise, pricing and identities tailored to appeal to different market segments.

GAP has expanded and diversified geographically mainly through the acquisition of other supermarket chains. The company has closed over 600 outmoded stores in the past 10 years (it closed 63 in fiscal 1995-96's first 28 weeks). Its five-year development program includes 175 new stores. Retail square footage will be increased by about 3% in each of the next five years. In 1995-96 GAP plans to open 30 new supermarkets (18 opened in the first half) and expand or remodel 51 (9); 35 new supermarkets are projected for fiscal 1996-97, with 30 opening each year thereafter for several years. The company's concentration will be on larger stores in the 50,000 to 65,000 sq. ft. range.

The company intends to improve the use of technology over the several years through scanning and other technological advances to improve customer service, store operations and merchandising.

In support of its retail operations, the company operates two coffee roasting plants, two bakeries, one delicatessen food kitchen and an ice cream plant. It also sells coffee and ice cream products to other retailers.

GAP's U.S. stores offer America's Choice and Master Choice, private premium label merchandise, which are strong contributors to operating margins and the company believes they are an important part of future growth. Private label sales accounted for 23% of total grocery sales in the fiscal year ended February 25, 1995, up from 2.0% in the prior year.

Important Developments

Sep. '95—The company said that 1995-96 second quarter sales declined because of sluggish consumer spending and low levels of retail food inflation. Comparable-store sales fell 0.5% in the period. During the first 28 weeks of fiscal 1996, GAP opened 18 new stores, remodeled or expanded 9 existing stores, and closed 63 stores. GAP noted that it continued to implement its store format restructuring program in Canada, and sales and profitability had improved appreciably there during the repositioning period.

Capitalization

Long Term Debt: $737,506,000 (6/17/95), incl. $142.1 million of lease obligs.

Per Share Data ($)

(Year Ended Feb. 28)

	1995	1994	1993	1992	1991	1990
Tangible Bk. Val.	20.28	26.02	27.06	32.79	31.96	27.49
Cash Flow	NA	6.11	3.27	7.65	9.15	8.54
Earnings	-4.36	0.10	-2.58	1.85	3.95	3.84
Dividends	0.65	0.80	0.80	0.80	0.77	0.68
Payout Ratio	NM	NM	NM	43%	20%	18%
Cal. Yrs.	1994	1993	1992	1991	1990	1989
Prices - High	27⅜	35	35¼	57¾	61¾	65⅜
- Low	17⅞	22½	21⅜	25½	37¾	44¼
P/E Ratio - High	NM	NM	NM	31	16	17
- Low	NM	NM	NM	14	10	12

Income Statement Analysis (Million $)

	1995	%Chg	1994	%Chg	1993	%Chg	1992
Revs.	10,332	NM	10,384	-1%	10,499	-9%	11,591
Oper. Inc.	349	17%	298	-13%	341	-20%	426
Depr.	235	2%	230	3%	224	NM	222
Int. Exp.	73.0	15%	63.3	-5%	66.4	-18%	81.4
Pretax Inc.	-128	NM	7.0	NM	-171	NM	124
Eff. Tax Rate	NM	—	40%	—	NM	—	43%
Net Inc.	-166	NM	4.0	NM	-99.0	NM	71.0

Balance Sheet & Other Fin. Data (Million $)

	1995	1994	1993	1992	1991	1990
Cash	129	124	110	55.7	28.5	35.1
Curr. Assets	1,194	1,230	1,221	1,175	1,212	1,076
Total Assets	2,895	3,099	3,091	3,213	3,307	2,832
Curr. Liab.	1,096	1,151	1,165	1,002	1,096	996
LT Debt	759	707	596	692	753	563
Common Eqty.	775	994	1,034	1,253	1,221	1,092
Total Cap.	1,652	1,802	1,772	2,114	2,127	1,744
Cap. Exp.	215	261	252	168	467	221
Cash Flow	69.0	234	125	292	350	326

Ratio Analysis

	1995	1994	1993	1992	1991	1990
Curr. Ratio	1.1	1.1	1.0	1.2	1.1	1.1
% LT Debt of Cap.	45.9	39.2	33.7	32.7	35.4	32.3
% Net Inc.of Revs.	NM	Nil	NM	0.6	1.3	1.3
% Ret. on Assets	NM	0.1	NM	2.2	4.9	5.4
% Ret. on Equity	NM	0.4	NM	5.7	13.0	14.2

Dividend Data —Quarterly dividends, omitted since 1978, were resumed in 1986.

Amt. of Div. $	Date Decl.	Ex-Div. Date	Stock of Record	Payment Date
0.200	Oct. 04	Oct. 07	Oct. 14	Nov. 01 '94
0.050	Dec. 06	Jan. 05	Jan. 11	Feb. 01 '95
0.050	Mar. 14	Apr. 06	Apr. 12	May. 01 '95
0.050	Jul. 11	Jul. 19	Jul. 21	Aug. 07 '95
0.050	Oct. 03	Oct. 12	Oct. 16	Nov. 01 '95

Data as orig. reptd.; bef. results of disc. opers. and/or spec. items. Per share data adj. for stk. divs. as of ex-div. date. E-Estimated. NA-Not Available. NM-Not Meaningful. NR-Not Ranked.

Office—2 Paragon Drive, Montvale, NJ 07645. **Tel**—(201) 573-9700. **Chrmn & CEO**—J. Wood. **Pres & COO**—C. W. E. Haub. **Vice Chrmn, CFO, Treas & Investor Contact**—Fred Corrado (201) 930-4100. **VP & Secy**—P. R. Brooker. **Dirs**—R. Baumeister, F. Corrado, C. F. Edley, C. W. E. Haub, H. Haub, B. B. Hauptfuhrer, P. C. Nagel Jr., E. C. Siess, F. Teelen, H. W. Van Baalen, R. L. Wetzel, J. Wood. **Transfer Agent & Registrar**—American Stock Transfer & Trust Co., NYC. **Incorporated** in Maryland in 1925. **Empl**-92,000. **S&P Analyst:** Philip D. Wohl

Great Lakes Chemical

NYSE Symbol **GLK**
In S&P 500

04-OCT-95

Industry:
Chemicals

Summary: This company is the world's leading producer of specialty chemicals for use as flame retardants, polymer stabilizers, water treatment chemicals and petroleum additives.

S&P Opinion: Accumulate (★★★★)	Recent Price • 67⅝	Yield • 0.7%
	52 Wk Range • 69⅞-51¾	12-Mo. P/E • 15.7

Quantitative Evaluations

Outlook
(1 Lowest—5 Highest)
• **5⁻**

Fair Value
• **79**

Risk
• **Low**

Earn./Div. Rank
• **A+**

Technical Eval.
• **Bullish** since 7/95

Rel. Strength Rank
(1 Lowest—99 Highest)
• **58**

Insider Activity
• **Neutral**

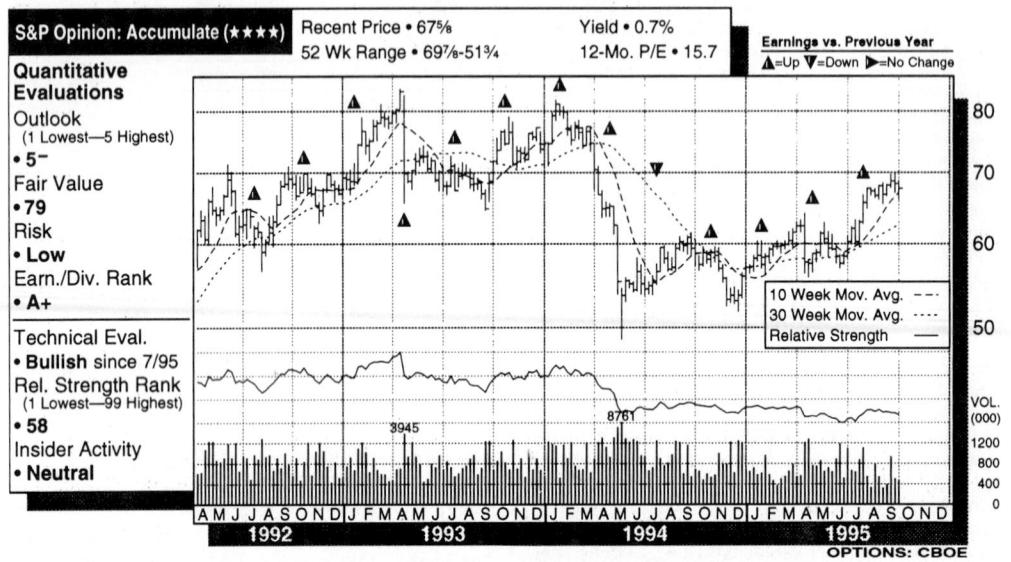

Earnings vs. Previous Year
▲=Up ▼=Down ▶=No Change

10 Week Mov. Avg. - - -
30 Week Mov. Avg. ·····
Relative Strength —

3945

8761

VOL. (000)

1992   1993   1994   1995

OPTIONS: CBOE

Overview - 04-OCT-95

Sales and earnings for 1996 are expected to benefit from continuing growth in the flame retardant, polymer additives and water treatment chemicals businesses, aided by new applications and manufacturing capacity expansions. The furfural business should continue to rebound, aided by a better pricing environment. Octel's profits should advance modestly, reflecting growth in fuel additives and as higher worldwide prices for lead antiknocks offset modestly declining volumes. Possible acquisitions would also boost growth. Earnings comparisons will benefit from ongoing stock repurchases, in addition to the 7.4 million shares acquired since 1993.

Valuation - 04-OCT-95

Largely in response to strong second quarter EPS, GLK's shares rose about 12% in the third quarter, a far better performance than the modest rise seen in the first half of 1995. The shares remain well below the all time high set in 1993. We recently downgraded our opinion of the stock to accumulate from buy due to the strong performance. We expect earnings growth of about 10% for the rest of 1995 and for 1996 as recent acquisitions make a greater profit contribution and the bromine, polymer additives and water treatment chemicals businesses continue to grow. The shares are attractive at the current multiple to the EPS estimate for 1996 and in view of the company's good long-term prospects.

Key Stock Statistics

S&P EPS Est. 1995	4.50	Tang. Bk. Value/Share	13.50
P/E on S&P Est. 1995	15.0	Beta	1.24
S&P EPS Est. 1996	5.00	Shareholders	4,900
Dividend Rate/Share	0.46	Market cap. (B)	$ 4.4
Shs. outstg. (M)	64.7	Inst. holdings	77%
Avg. daily vol. (M)	0.116	Insider holdings	NA

Value of $10,000 invested 5 years ago: $ 29,590

Fiscal Year Ending Dec. 31

	1995	% Change	1994	% Change	1993	% Change
Revenues (Million $)						
1Q	569.0	27%	449.0	4%	430.0	25%
2Q	640.8	22%	526.0	14%	462.0	21%
3Q	—	—	525.0	12%	470.0	28%
4Q	—	—	565.0	31%	430.0	6%
Yr.	—	—	2,065	15%	1,792	20%
Income (Million $)						
1Q	68.33	2%	66.88	4%	64.24	21%
2Q	78.47	16%	67.75	-3%	70.11	19%
3Q	—	—	72.34	6%	68.50	14%
4Q	—	—	71.71	3%	69.94	15%
Yr.	—	—	278.7	2%	272.8	17%
Earnings Per Share ($)						
1Q	1.02	9%	0.94	4%	0.90	20%
2Q	1.20	25%	0.96	-2%	0.98	18%
3Q	E1.15	10%	1.05	9%	0.96	14%
4Q	E1.13	8%	1.05	7%	0.98	15%
Yr.	E4.50	13%	4.00	5%	3.82	17%

Next earnings report expected: late October

Great Lakes Chemical

04-OCT-95

Business Summary - 04-OCT-95

Great Lakes Chemical is the world's leading producer of certain specialty chemicals for such applications as flame retardants, water treatment chemicals and petroleum additives. Contributions to sales:

	1994	1993
Petroleum additives	30%	32%
Water treatment chemicals	18%	21%
Intermediates/fine chemicals	13%	13%
Flame retardants	13%	13%
Polymer stabilizers	8%	5%
Specialized services/mfg.	18%	16%

Foreign operations accounted for 55% of sales and 68% of pretax income in 1994.

U.K.-based Octel Associates (88% owned) is the world's leading producer of a wide range of transportation fuel additives, including lead antiknock octane boosters, cetane improvers, detergents, anti-oxidants, stabilizers and corrosion inhibitors.

Water treatment chemicals include bromine and chlorine-based specialty biocides for recreational and industrial water treatment.

Specialty chemicals include bromine and furfural and derivative products, fine chemicals, and various agricultural products.

Bromine-based flame retardants and polymer stabilizers (antioxidants, UV absorbers) are used to enhance the performance of a wide variety of polymer systems.

The specialized services and manufacturing segment includes fluorine chemicals and fire extinguishants; custom chemical manufacturing; petroleum and environmental services; toxicological services; engineered surface treatments; and international trading.

Important Developments

Jul. '95—GLK said that all of its business units in the second quarter posted doubled digit growth from the 1994 period. GLK also noted that since 1993 it had repurchased about 7.4 million common shares, including 2.8 million in 1995.

Mar. '95—GLK exchanged its 2.2 million common shares (17% interest) in Huntsman Chemical Corp. (HCC) for $58.7 million of 14% preferred stock. In December 1994, Great Lakes received a $130 million dividend from HCC. HCC's other shareholder elected to receive HCC stock, reducing GLK's interest in HCC from 40%. GLK used the proceeds to repurchase common stock. Separately, GLK announced plans for a major expansion of its bromine production capacity in 1995. In late 1994, GLK acquired Olin Corp.'s trichlor dry sanitizer plant in Lake Charles, La., and the petroleum additives business (sales about $60 million) of DuPont for $50 million.

Capitalization

Long Term Debt: $305,929,000 (6/95).
Minority Interest: $29,806,000.

Per Share Data ($) (Year Ended Dec. 31)

	1994	1993	1992	1991	1990	1989
Tangible Bk. Val.	13.37	12.84	10.55	9.47	7.65	6.11
Cash Flow	5.47	5.09	4.32	3.13	2.73	2.36
Earnings	4.00	3.82	3.27	2.23	2.00	1.76
Dividends	0.39	0.35	0.31	0.27	0.23	0.19
Payout Ratio	10%	9%	10%	12%	12%	11%
Prices - High	82	84	71⅜	58	34	24
- Low	48¾	64½	50¼	30⅜	20⅜	14⅛
P/E Ratio - High	20	22	22	26	17	14
- Low	12	17	15	14	10	8

Income Statement Analysis (Million $)

	1994	%Chg	1993	%Chg	1992	%Chg	1991
Revs.	2,065	15%	1,792	20%	1,496	14%	1,308
Oper. Inc.	541	5%	515	18%	438	22%	360
Depr.	102	13%	90.0	20%	74.9	17%	63.8
Int. Exp.	11.9	45%	8.2	-34%	12.4	NM	12.3
Pretax Inc.	436	5%	415	15%	361	13%	320
Eff. Tax Rate	28%	—	27%	—	28%	—	21%
Net Inc.	279	2%	273	17%	233	48%	157

Balance Sheet & Other Fin. Data (Million $)

	1994	1993	1992	1991	1990	1989
Cash	145	180	141	81.0	60.6	30.4
Curr. Assets	980	857	773	641	608	447
Total Assets	2,111	1,901	1,732	1,649	1,406	1,097
Curr. Liab.	428	368	431	303	307	210
LT Debt	144	61.0	46.0	140	76.0	114
Common Eqty.	1,311	1,257	1,053	900	744	591
Total Cap.	1,557	1,410	1,182	1,230	1,001	841
Cap. Exp.	123	79.3	69.4	90.7	73.6	80.1
Cash Flow	381	363	308	221	191	165

Ratio Analysis

	1994	1993	1992	1991	1990	1989
Curr. Ratio	2.3	2.3	1.8	2.1	2.0	2.1
% LT Debt of Cap.	9.2	4.3	3.9	11.4	7.6	13.5
% Net Inc.of Revs.	13.5	15.2	15.6	12.0	13.2	15.5
% Ret. on Assets	14.3	15.0	13.7	10.3	11.2	13.9
% Ret. on Equity	22.3	23.6	23.8	19.1	21.1	22.8

Dividend Data —Dividends have been paid since 1973. A "poison pill" stock purchase rights plan was adopted in 1989.

Amt. of Div. $	Date Decl.	Ex-Div. Date	Stock of Record	Payment Date
0.100	Sep. 26	Sep. 29	Oct. 05	Nov. 01 '94
0.100	Dec. 07	Dec. 23	Jan. 01	Jan. 31 '95
0.105	Mar. 06	Mar. 27	Apr. 01	May. 02 '95
0.105	Jun. 13	Jun. 28	Jul. 01	Aug. 01 '95
0.115	Sep. 05	Sep. 28	Oct. 02	Oct. 31 '95

Data as orig. reptd.; bef. results of disc. opers. and/or spec. items. Per share data adj. for stk. divs. as of ex-div. date.
E-Estimated. NA-Not Available. NM-Not Meaningful. NR-Not Ranked.

Office—One Great Lakes Blvd., West Lafayette, IN 47906-0200. **Tel**—(317) 497-6100. **Chrmn**—M. M. Hale. **Pres & CEO**—R. B. McDonald. **EVP-Fin & CFO**—R. T. Jeffares. **Treas & Secy**—R. R. Ferguson. **Investor Contact**—William P. Blake. **Dirs**—W. H. Congleton, J. S. Day, T. M. Fulton, M. M. Hale, L. H. Johnstone, L. E. Lataif, R. H. Leet, R. B. McDonald. **Transfer Agent & Registrar**—Harris Trust & Savings Bank, Chicago. **Incorporated** in Michigan in 1933; reincorporated in Delaware in 1970. **Empl**-8,500. **S&P Analyst**: Richard O'Reilly, CFA

STANDARD & POOR'S

STOCK REPORTS

Great Western Financial

NYSE Symbol **GWF**
In S&P 500

20-OCT-95

Industry:
Banking

Summary: This diversified financial services company operates more than 1,200 mortgage lending, retail banking and consumer finance offices throughout the U.S.

S&P Opinion: Hold (★★★)	Recent Price • 25⅛	Yield • 3.7%
	52 Wk Range • 25⅝-15½	12-Mo. P/E • 15.1

Quantitative Evaluations

Outlook
(1 Lowest—5 Highest)
• **2+**

Fair Value
• **23⅜**

Risk
• **Average**

Earn./Div. Rank
• **B-**

Technical Eval.
• **Bearish** since 5/95

Rel. Strength Rank
(1 Lowest—99 Highest)
• **88**

Insider Activity
• **Neutral**

Earnings vs. Previous Year
▲=Up ▼=Down ▶=No Change

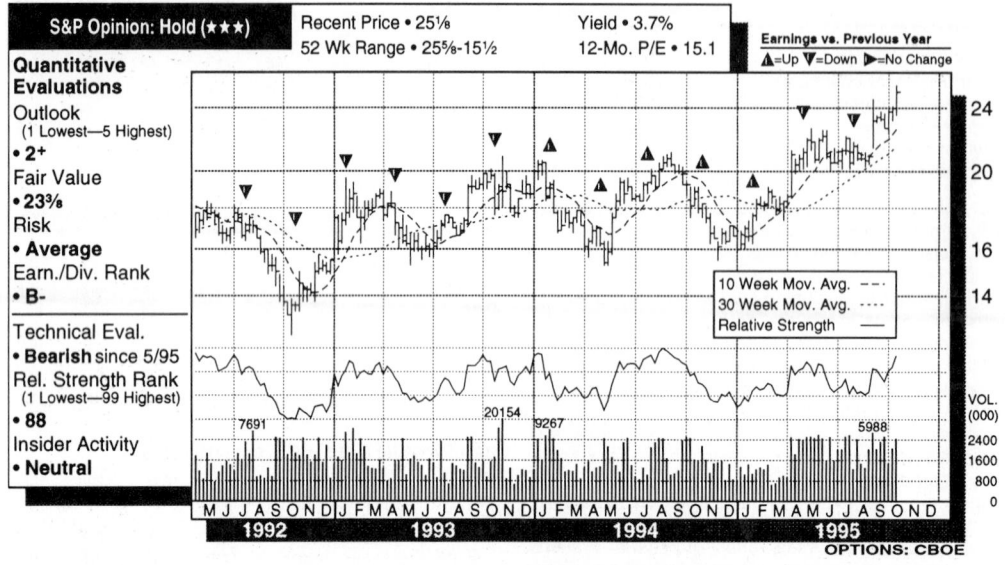

10 Week Mov. Avg. – – –
30 Week Mov. Avg. ·····
Relative Strength ——

OPTIONS: CBOE

Overview - 10-AUG-95

Profits are expected to rise sharply in 1996. A large part of the advance can be attributed to anticipated expansion of the interest rate spread, the difference between the rate GWF earns on its loans and other assets less the rate it pays out on deposits and other borrowings. Based on projected lower interest through mid-1996, deposit costs should (1) reprice downwards and (2) reprice downwards faster than the yields on GWF's loans. The latter effect derives from the fact that the index on which a majority of GWF's ARM loans are based lags changes in market interest rates. Slower loan growth is anticipated with the increased popularity of fixed rate mortgages. A modest recovery in the California economy could help asset quality. GWF's cost structure is higher than its peers.

Valuation - 18-OCT-95

Although we view Great Western as a consolidation candidate, the shares have rallied to a 77% premium over book value, higher than the 50% premium the typical thrift receives in a takeover. The rally was sparked by a surprise bid for a Southern California bank by Wells Fargo. Some takeover premium in terms of the P/E ratio could still be justified, but with a number of thrift institutions open to bids, its doubtful the company will receive its price. The shares could be supported by earnings momentum we see carrying into 1996, primarily due to expansion of the interest rate spread.

Key Stock Statistics

S&P EPS Est. 1995	1.55	Tang. Bk. Value/Share	14.11
P/E on S&P Est. 1995	16.2	Beta	2.25
S&P EPS Est. 1996	2.40	Shareholders	13,500
Dividend Rate/Share	0.92	Market cap. (B)	$ 3.4
Shs. outstg. (M)	135.9	Inst. holdings	86%
Avg. daily vol. (M)	0.517	Insider holdings	NA

Value of $10,000 invested 5 years ago: $ 19,214

Fiscal Year Ending Dec. 31

	1995	% Change	1994	% Change	1993	% Change
Revenues (Million $)						
1Q	827.2	17%	707.5	-2%	721.8	-33%
2Q	882.5	23%	715.2	-3%	741.0	-13%
3Q	915.3	24%	736.0	NM	736.4	-7%
4Q	—	—	838.9	23%	683.6	8%
Yr.	—	—	2,998	4%	2,883	-9%
Income (Million $)						
1Q	43.48	-12%	49.48	9%	45.21	-10%
2Q	50.44	-10%	55.86	6%	52.59	-24%
3Q	68.54	20%	57.23	NM	-17.53	NM
4Q	—	—	88.67	NM	-18.22	NM
Yr.	—	—	251.2	NM	62.05	15%
Earnings Per Share ($)						
1Q	0.28	-13%	0.32	7%	0.30	-19%
2Q	0.32	-16%	0.38	9%	0.35	-31%
3Q	0.45	18%	0.38	NM	-0.18	NM
4Q	E0.50	-18%	0.61	NM	-0.19	NM
Yr.	E1.55	-8%	1.69	NM	0.28	-7%

Next earnings report expected: mid January

Business Summary - 20-OCT-95

Great Western Financial Corp. is a diversified financial services company operating more than 1,200 mortgage lending, retail banking and consumer finance offices throughout the U.S.. It owns Great Western Bank, one of largest thrifts in the U.S., with some 419 branches in California and Florida. Consumer finance operations are conducted through over 500 offices in 24 states. Banking operations accounted for 75% of profits in 1994 (1% in 1993), and consumer finance 25% (99%).

Loans receivable were divided as follows at the end of 1994 and 1993:

	1994	1993
Single-family	59%	72%
Apartments	4%	5%
Commercial	4%	4%
Consumer	6%	6%
Mortgage-backed securities	24%	9%
Other	3%	4%

At 1994 year end, ARMs were 96% of the real estate loan portfolio. The one-year gap (difference between asset and liabilities repricing/maturing within one year as a percentage of assets) was 9.5%. Nonperforming assets and restructured loans at 1994 year end equaled $846 million (1.98% of assets), down from $1.13 billion (2.90%) a year earlier. The reserve for losses at December 31, 1994, totaled $438 million (1.04% of assets), down from $502 million (1.31%) a year earlier. Net chargeoffs in 1994 amounted to $271 million (0.64% of assets), compared with $454 million in 1993 (1.18%).

Of deposits of $28.7 billion at 1994 year end, 42% were transaction accounts, 5% accounts up to six months, 18% accounts of six months, 33% accounts over six months and deferred compensation, and 2% were wholesale. The average yield on earning assets in 1994 was 7.17% (7.54% in 1993), and the average cost of funds was 3.67% (3.75%), for a spread of 3.50% (3.79%).

Important Developments

Oct. '95—Management said that the company's interest rate spread, the difference between its yield on interest-earning assets and its cost of interest-bearing liabilities, rose to 3.01% during the third quarter from 2.83% in the second quarter of 1995. At September 30, 1995, nonperforming assets were $762 million, compared with $759 million at June 30, 1995.

Capitalization

FHLB Advances: $115,000,000 (6/95).
Other Borrowings: $4,120,000,000.
Preferred Stock: 1,177,500 shs., incl. 517,500 shs. conv. into com. at $20.40 a sh.

Per Share Data ($)

(Year Ended Dec. 31)

	1994	1993	1992	1991	1990	1989
Tangible Bk. Val.	13.59	12.80	14.01	14.37	13.64	13.69
Earnings	1.69	0.28	0.30	2.25	1.50	0.78
Dividends	0.92	0.92	0.91	0.87	0.83	0.79
Payout Ratio	54%	329%	303%	39%	55%	101%
Prices - High	21⅛	20⅞	20	21¼	21⅛	25⅛
- Low	15¼	15¼	12½	11	8½	14⅝
P/E Ratio - High	12	75	67	9	14	32
- Low	9	54	42	5	6	19

Income Statement Analysis (Million $)

	1994	%Chg	1993	%Chg	1992	%Chg	1991
Net Int. Inc.	1,322	-4%	1,383	-3%	1,422	12%	1,265
Loan Loss Prov.	207	-55%	463	10%	420	180%	150
Non Int. Inc.	368	82%	202	NM	62.9	-73%	234
Non Int. Exp.	1,076	4%	1,030	6%	970	15%	844
Pretax Inc.	407	NM	92.0	-4%	96.0	-81%	505
Eff. Tax Rate	38%	—	33%	—	44%	—	41%
Net Inc.	251	NM	62.0	15%	54.0	-82%	298
% Net Int. Marg.	3.50%	—	3.79%	—	3.89%	—	3.92%

Balance Sheet & Other Fin. Data (Million $)

	1994	1993	1992	1991	1990	1989
Total Assets	42,218	38,348	38,439	39,600	39,406	37,176
Loans	37,648	33,851	33,753	35,116	34,767	33,187
Deposits	34,999	31,532	30,909	30,570	29,649	23,784
Capitalization:						
Debt	3,822	3,479	4,151	5,592	6,539	10,275
Equity	2,190	2,129	2,155	2,192	2,076	1,988
Total	6,306	5,903	6,601	7,914	8,615	12,263

Ratio Analysis

	1994	1993	1992	1991	1990	1989
% Ret. on Assets	0.7	0.2	0.1	0.8	0.5	0.3
% Ret. on Equity	10.4	1.7	1.8	13.9	9.5	5.0
% Loan Loss Resv.	1.2	1.5	1.3	0.7	0.8	0.7
% Risk Based Capital	11.7	11.7	10.7	9.3	8.9	NA
Price Times Book Value:						
High	1.6	1.6	1.4	1.5	1.5	1.8
Low	1.1	1.2	0.9	0.8	0.6	1.1

Dividend Data

—Dividends have been paid since 1972. A dividend reinvestment plan is available.

Amt. of Div. $	Date Decl.	Ex-Div. Date	Stock of Record	Payment Date
0.230*	Oct. 25	Oct. 31	Nov. 04	Nov. 30 '94
0.230	Jan. 24	Jan. 30	Feb. 03	Feb. 28 '95
0.230	Apr. 25	May. 01	May. 05	May. 31 '95
0.230	Jul. 25	Aug. 02	Aug. 04	Aug. 31 '95

Data as orig. reptd.; bef. results of disc opers. and/or spec. items. Per share data adj. for stk. divs. as of ex-div. date. E-Estimated. NA-Not Available. NM-Not Meaningful. NR-Not Ranked.

Office—9200 Oakdale Ave., Chatsworth, CA 91311. **Tel**—(818) 775-3411. **Chrmn**—J. F. Montgomery. **Pres & CEO**—J. F. Maher. **Exec VP & Secy**—J. L. Erikson. **Exec VP, CFO & Investor Contact**—Carl F. Geuther (818) 852-3436. **Dirs**—D. Alexander, H. F. Christie, S. E. Frank, J. V. Giovenco, F. A. Gryp, E. Hernandez Jr., J. F. Maher, C. D. Miller, J. F. Montgomery, A. E. Siegel, W. B. Wood Jr. **Transfer Agent & Registrar**—First Interstate Bank, Ltd., Los Angeles. **Incorporated** in Delaware in 1955. **Empl**-15,644. **S&P Analyst:** Paul L. Huberman, CFA

Halliburton Co.

NYSE Symbol **HAL**
In S&P 500

30-OCT-95

Industry:
Oil and Gas

Summary: Halliburton provides products used in oil and natural gas development and production; through its Brown & Root subsidiary, HAL offers engineering and construction services.

S&P Opinion: Buy (★★★★)	Recent Price • 40¾	Yield • 2.5%
	52 Wk Range • 45¼-32⅝	12-Mo. P/E • 20.8

Quantitative Evaluations

Outlook
(1 Lowest—5 Highest)
• **1+**

Fair Value
• **37½**

Risk
• **Average**

Earn./Div. Rank
• **B-**

Technical Eval.
• **Bearish** since 8/95

Rel. Strength Rank
(1 Lowest—99 Highest)
• **45**

Insider Activity
• **NA**

Earnings vs. Previous Year
▲=Up ▼=Down ▶=No Change

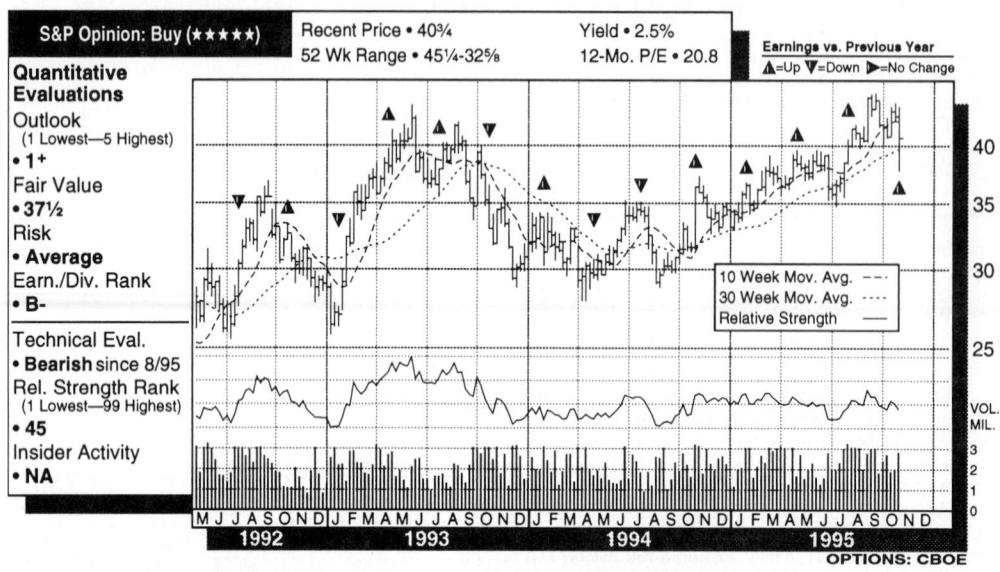

10 Week Mov. Avg. – – –
30 Week Mov. Avg. · · · ·
Relative Strength —

OPTIONS: CBOE

Overview - 30-OCT-95

Shareholders should benefit from the upcoming 1995 spin-off of the insurance segment, which will allow Halliburton to focus on core businesses. Halliburton has succeeded in cutting costs, resulting in higher after-tax margins and increased profitability. HAL returned to profitability in 1994 and will have further operating gains in 1995 and 1996, reflecting operating efficiencies and a focus on core competencies. With nearly half its revenues tied to the oil and gas industry, we believe the company will see benefits from growth in worldwide energy demand. A joint venture in China to produce flow measurement equipment, and a further pickup in industry spending for energy related construction and chemical plant capacity additions should benefit results.

Valuation - 30-OCT-95

Improving fundamentals for the oil services industry helped the shares rise through much of 1995, though a retreat in oil prices from the $20 a barrel high reached in the second quarter, has caused HAL's shares to pull back. Fears that OPEC may raise their production quota at the November meeting have taken their toll on the oil service sector, in our view unnecessarily. With recent forecasts showing world energy demand growing faster than anticipated, fueled mainly by increased consumption in Asia and South America, we believe the outlook for HAL is positive, with the shares undervalued on a cash flow and earnings basis.

Key Stock Statistics

S&P EPS Est. 1995	2.00	Tang. Bk. Value/Share	15.69
P/E on S&P Est. 1995	20.4	Beta	0.99
S&P EPS Est. 1996	2.50	Shareholders	17,400
Dividend Rate/Share	1.00	Market cap. (B)	$ 4.7
Shs. outstg. (M)	114.2	Inst. holdings	76%
Avg. daily vol. (M)	0.465	Insider holdings	NA

Value of $10,000 invested 5 years ago: $ 11,289

Fiscal Year Ending Dec. 31

	1995	% Change	1994	% Change	1993	% Change
Revenues (Million $)						
1Q	1,322	-4%	1,376	-12%	1,559	-7%
2Q	1,445	1%	1,425	-11%	1,597	-2%
3Q	1,490	6%	1,405	-9%	1,541	-2%
4Q	—	—	1,533	-7%	1,653	-2%
Yr.	—	—	5,741	-10%	6,351	-3%
Income (Million $)						
1Q	39.10	120%	17.80	-5%	18.80	94%
2Q	56.20	NM	-19.20	NM	22.90	64%
3Q	68.80	33%	51.70	NM	-160.7	NM
4Q	—	—	127.5	NM	-42.00	NM
Yr.	—	—	177.8	NM	-161.0	NM
Earnings Per Share ($)						
1Q	0.34	113%	0.16	-11%	0.18	100%
2Q	0.49	NM	-0.17	NM	0.20	54%
3Q	0.60	33%	0.45	NM	-1.41	NM
4Q	E0.57	-49%	1.12	NM	-0.37	NM
Yr.	E2.00	28%	1.56	NM	-1.43	NM

Next earnings report expected: early February

Halliburton Co.

Business Summary - 27-OCT-95

Halliburton is the largest factor in oilfield well cementing, completion and stimulation and, through its Brown & Root unit, is a major participant in industrial and marine engineering/construction. It also has a small insurance unit. The company sold a number of non-core businesees during 1994. Profits and losses in recent years, including restructuring charges (in million $):

	1994	1993
Energy services	$191.1	-$147.7
Engineering & construction	67.2	79.3
Insurance services	-0.4	-42.2

Some 41% of 1994 revenues came from operations outside the U.S., down from 44% in 1993. HAL is expanding its overseas exposure in China and the former Soviet Union.

The company provides an extensive array of oilfield equipment and services, including well cementing, completion and stimulation services, drilling muds, pressure control, production testing services, wireline services and measurement while drilling services. Halliburton Drilling Systems was formed in early 1993 by combining the drilling systems businesses acquired from Smith International, Inc. with HAL's existing services such as measurement while drilling and surface data logging.

Brown & Root engages in an extensive range of design, engineering and construction activities, including power plants, refineries and petrochemical facilities. B&R's marine construction activities include the laying and burying of marine pipelines and the fabrication and erection of offshore production platforms for the petroleum industry. The company also engages in environmental consulting and waste management services. Year end backlog rose 14% during 1994.

Important Developments

Oct. '95—Halliburton reported income from operations of $0.60 a share, up from $0.43 the prior year. The company's insurance operations were considered discontinued for financial statement purposes, due to the previously announced agreement to spin off the segment to shareholders by year-end 1995. Engineering and construction services business segment earnings rose 55%, while energy services earnings were up 8%. Charges for provisions related to HAL's exit from the insurance business led to a $0.59 a share charge to earnings.

Aug. '95—Halliburton named Dick Cheney as president and chief executive officer effective October 1, 1995.

Capitalization

Long Term Debt: $644,100,000 (6/95), incl. $354.1 million (net of $374.1 million unamortized debt discount) of zero coupon sub. debs. due 2006, conv. into 6.824 com. shs. per $1,000 principal amt.

Minority Interest: $700,000.

Per Share Data ($)

(Year Ended Dec. 31)

	1994	1993	1992	1991	1990	1989
Tangible Bk. Val.	15.15	14.58	16.60	18.99	19.88	18.72
Cash Flow	3.85	1.13	1.55	2.53	3.75	3.22
Earnings	1.56	-1.43	-1.15	0.25	1.85	1.26
Dividends	1.00	1.00	1.00	1.00	1.00	1.00
Payout Ratio	64%	NM	NM	402%	54%	80%
Prices - High	37¼	44	36⅞	55¼	58¾	44½
- Low	27⅞	25¾	21¾	25½	38¾	27½
P/E Ratio - High	24	NM	NM	NM	32	35
- Low	18	NM	NM	NM	21	22

Income Statement Analysis (Million $)

	1994	%Chg	1993	%Chg	1992	%Chg	1991
Revs.	5,648	-10%	6,275	-4%	6,525	-6%	6,976
Oper. Inc.	446	NM	448	9%	412	39%	296
Depr.	262	-9%	288	NM	289	18%	244
Int. Exp.	47.0	-6%	50.0	-7%	54.0	2%	53.0
Pretax Inc.	291	NM	-188	NM	-130	NM	93.0
Eff. Tax Rate	39%	—	NM	—	NM	—	69%
Net Inc.	178	NM	-160	NM	-123	NM	27.0

Balance Sheet & Other Fin. Data (Million $)

	1994	1993	1992	1991	1990	1989
Cash	507	133	256	331	168	402
Curr. Assets	NA	NA	NA	NA	NA	NA
Total Assets	5,268	5,403	4,736	5,017	4,544	4,263
Curr. Liab.	950	1,067	1,017	999	897	715
LT Debt	623	598	603	651	190	198
Common Eqty.	1,942	1,888	1,907	2,165	2,247	2,119
Total Cap.	2,570	2,489	2,522	2,875	2,544	2,421
Cap. Exp.	235	247	316	426	332	202
Cash Flow	439	127	166	270	400	342

Ratio Analysis

	1994	1993	1992	1991	1990	1989
Curr. Ratio	NA	NA	NA	NA	NA	NA
% LT Debt of Cap.	24.2	24.0	23.9	22.6	7.4	8.2
% Net Inc.of Revs.	3.1	NM	NM	0.4	2.9	2.4
% Ret. on Assets	3.3	NM	NM	0.6	4.5	3.0
% Ret. on Equity	9.3	NM	NM	1.2	9.0	6.3

Dividend Data

Dividends have been paid since 1947. A "poison pill" stock purchase rights plan was adopted in 1986.

Amt. of Div. $	Date Decl.	Ex-Div. Date	Stock of Record	Payment Date
0.250	Nov. 08	Nov. 25	Dec. 01	Dec. 22 '94
0.250	Feb. 16	Feb. 24	Mar. 02	Mar. 23 '95
0.250	May. 16	May. 25	Jun. 01	Jun. 22 '95
0.250	Jul. 20	Aug. 29	Aug. 31	Sep. 21 '95

Data as orig. reptd.; bef. results of disc. opers. and/or spec. items. Per share data adj. for stk. divs. as of ex-div. date.
E-Estimated. NA-Not Available. NM-Not Meaningful. NR-Not Ranked.

Office—3600 Lincoln Plaza, 500 North Akard St., Dallas, TX 75201-3391. **Tel**—(214) 978-2600. **Chrmn, CEO & Pres**—D. Cheney. **VP-Fin**—J. H. Blurton. **VP-Secy**—S. S. Keith. **VP-Investor Contact**—Guy T. Marcus. **Dirs**—A. L. Armstrong, R. W. Campbell, D. Cheney, Lord Clitheroe, R. L. Crandall, W. R. Howell, D. P. Jones, C. J. Silas, R. T. Staubach, R. J. Stegemeir, E. L. Williamson. **Transfer Agent & Registrar**—Chemical Bank, NYC. **Incorporated** in Delaware in 1924. **Empl**-57,200. **S&P Analyst:** Raymond J.Deacon

Handleman Co.

NYSE Symbol **HDL**
In S&P 500

14-AUG-95

Industry:
Leisure/Amusement

Summary: This company is a leading distributor (rack jobber) of home entertainment products.

S&P Opinion: Sell (★)	Recent Price • 9¾ Yield • 4.5% 52 Wk Range • 12-9½ 12-Mo. P/E • 11.6

Quantitative Evaluations

Outlook
(1 Lowest—5 Highest)
• **2⁻**

Fair Value
• **9¼**

Risk
• **Low**

Earn./Div. Rank
• **A-**

Technical Eval.
• **Bullish** since 7/95

Rel. Strength Rank
(1 Lowest—99 Highest)
• **12**

Insider Activity
• **NA**

Earnings vs. Previous Year
▲=Up ▼=Down ▶=No Change

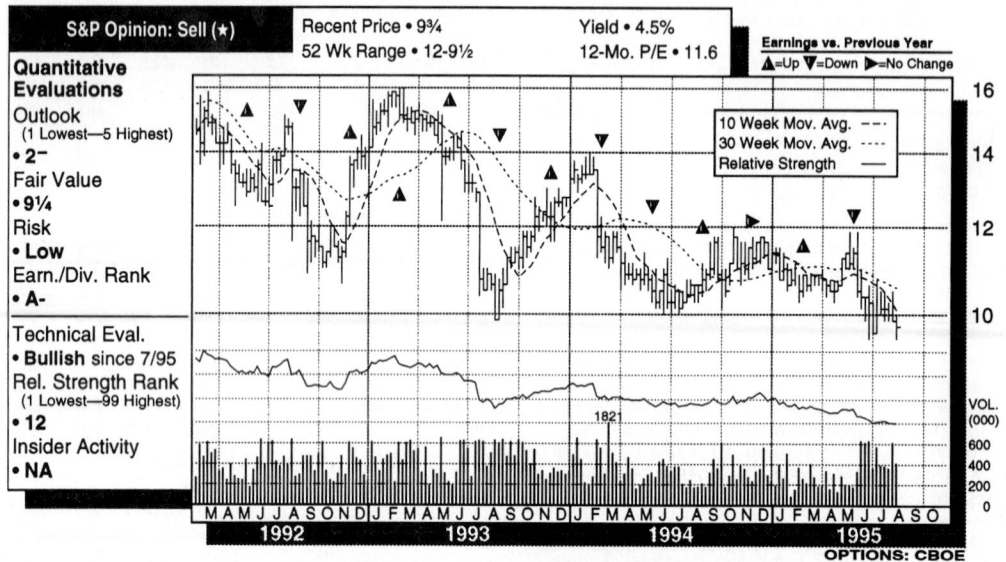

10 Week Mov. Avg. ----
30 Week Mov. Avg. -----
Relative Strength ——

OPTIONS: CBOE

Overview - 14-AUG-95

We expect HDL's music sales in the year ahead to be helped by continued growth of audio compact discs (CDs) as a mass-merchant product. Also, the trend toward consumers purchasing, rather than renting, videos, should benefit HDL. We look for software sales to get a boost from strong sales of home computers. However, over the long term, for the types of products supplied by HDL, there is some threat that consumers will increasingly buy them at home entertainment "superstores," or through delivery to homes through cable or telephone wires, rather than at mass merchants. Also, there is a risk that suppliers of home entertainment products will increasingly sell videos and music directly to mass merchandisers, bypassing HDL. We expect HDL's business strategy to include further efforts to own or license exclusive rights to various products.

Valuation - 14-AUG-95

Following a recent indication that earnings in the first quarter of fiscal 1995-96 would be surprisingly weak, we continue to advise steering clear of this stock. In part, this reflects concern about HDL's sales reliance on two large customers, and the long-term prospect of consumers receiving the types of products furnished by HDL through alternative means of distribution. Also, we are skeptical about HDL's ability to carve out a sizable presence as an owner (or exclusive licensee) of entertainment software.

Key Stock Statistics

S&P EPS Est. 1996	0.75	Tang. Bk. Value/Share	9.29
P/E on S&P Est. 1996	13.0	Beta	1.10
Dividend Rate/Share	0.44	Shareholders	3,600
Shs. outstg. (M)	33.6	Market cap. (B)	$0.328
Avg. daily vol. (M)	0.091	Inst. holdings	75%
		Insider holdings	NA

Value of $10,000 invested 5 years ago: $ 5,597

Fiscal Year Ending Apr. 30

	1995	% Change	1994	% Change	1993	% Change
Revenues (Million $)						
1Q	212.5	10%	194.0	-8%	212.0	27%
2Q	347.2	8%	322.5	NM	321.9	15%
3Q	362.9	21%	300.0	-11%	335.7	10%
4Q	303.5	21%	250.1	NM	251.9	-6%
Yr.	1,226	15%	1,067	-5%	1,122	10%
Income (Million $)						
1Q	0.90	NM	-2.77	NM	4.53	-18%
2Q	15.48	NM	15.45	8%	14.36	14%
3Q	11.10	10%	10.08	-30%	14.32	19%
4Q	0.55	-89%	4.89	-54%	10.53	7%
Yr.	28.02	1%	27.66	-37%	43.74	9%
Earnings Per Share ($)						
1Q	0.03	NM	-0.08	NM	0.14	-18%
2Q	0.46	NM	0.46	7%	0.43	13%
3Q	0.33	10%	0.30	-30%	0.43	19%
4Q	0.02	-87%	0.15	-53%	0.32	7%
Yr.	0.84	1%	0.83	-37%	1.32	9%

Next earnings report expected: late August

Handleman Co.

14-AUG-95

Business Summary - 08-AUG-95

Handleman Co. is one of North America's largest independent distributors of prerecorded music, prerecorded videocassettes, books and home computer software to retail chains throughout the U.S. and Canada.

Contributions to sales in recent fiscal years were:

	1994-95	1993-94
Prerecorded music	53%	54%
Prerecorded video	38%	36%
Books	5%	6%
Software	4%	4%

The company's two largest customers-- Kmart Corp. and Wal-Mart-- account for about 67% of HDL's sales.

Services provided by HDL to retailers include product selection, marketing assistance and product exchanges. Lieberman Enterprises, formerly the company's largest competitor, was acquired in 1991-92.HDL also owns master recordings of a number of public domain movies, and has distribution rights to various video and music titles. HDL's North Coast Entertainment unit, which includes HDL's proprietary products and sales at licensed retail departments, had fiscal 1994-95 sales of $106 million, up 53% from the year before. The growth came largely from acquisitions made in 1994-95.

HDL's competition includes some manufacturers that distribute products directly to retailers, and independent distributors. Also, competition facing HDL's customers includes record and book clubs and specialty retailers.

Important Developments

Aug. '95—HDL expects a loss in fiscal 1995-96's seasonally slow first quarter of $0.18 to $0.21 a share. Profits will be hurt by an unexpected rise in customer returns, partly due to key customers reducing overall store inventories. HDL said that it was taking steps to reduce SG&A expenses. Earlier, in fiscal 1994-95's fourth quarter, HDL had a $5.5 million pretax charge ($0.10 a share, after-tax), related to costs associated with a transition to a new automated distribution facility in the Midwest. The charge largely relates to estimated losses on the sale of buildings currently being used for distribution. There is likely to be some temporary duplication of facilities later in fiscal 1995-96, but the new automated center is expected to improve future efficiency and quality of service. HDL may have another facility realignment charge-- related to establishment of a third new automated distribution-- in 1995-96's fourth quarter.

Capitalization

Long Term Debt: $146,200,000 (4/95).

Per Share Data ($)

(Year Ended Apr. 30)

	1995	1994	1993	1992	1991	1990
Tangible Bk. Val.	NA	8.96	8.69	7.84	7.08	6.73
Cash Flow	NA	1.70	1.97	2.04	1.20	NA
Earnings	0.84	0.83	1.32	1.21	0.72	1.13
Dividends	0.44	0.44	0.41	0.40	0.40	0.39
Payout Ratio	52%	53%	31%	33%	56%	35%
Cal. Yrs.	1994	1993	1992	1991	1990	1989
Prices - High	14	16	15⅞	18¾	22¾	24
- Low	10	9⅞	10⅝	10¼	8⅛	13¾
P/E Ratio - High	17	19	12	15	32	21
- Low	12	12	8	8	11	12

Income Statement Analysis (Million $)

	1994	%Chg	1993	%Chg	1992	%Chg	1991
Revs.	1,067	-5%	1,122	10%	1,020	45%	703
Oper. Inc.	83.0	-17%	100	-2%	102	50%	68.0
Depr.	29.1	34%	21.7	-22%	27.8	75%	15.9
Int. Exp.	7.0	-12%	8.0	-10%	8.9	NM	2.7
Pretax Inc.	46.1	-36%	71.7	9%	65.6	70%	38.5
Eff. Tax Rate	40%	—	39%	—	39%	—	39%
Net Inc.	27.7	-37%	43.7	9%	40.0	70%	23.5

Balance Sheet & Other Fin. Data (Million $)

	1994	1993	1992	1991	1990	1989
Cash	10.6	57.3	57.3	7.9	17.5	24.8
Curr. Assets	477	490	485	294	296	258
Total Assets	641	656	655	424	414	330
Curr. Liab.	261	257	255	170	176	120
LT Debt	76.0	106	136	16.0	16.0	11.0
Common Eqty.	299	289	261	234	220	196
Total Cap.	380	399	400	254	239	210
Cap. Exp.	28.7	32.5	20.0	16.1	37.5	24.5
Cash Flow	56.8	65.5	67.8	39.4	50.8	53.6

Ratio Analysis

	1994	1993	1992	1991	1990	1989
Curr. Ratio	1.8	1.9	1.9	1.7	1.7	2.1
% LT Debt of Cap.	20.1	26.5	33.9	6.3	6.6	5.2
% Net Inc.of Revs.	2.6	3.9	3.9	3.3	5.1	6.4
% Ret. on Assets	4.3	6.7	7.4	5.6	9.9	13.3
% Ret. on Equity	9.4	15.9	16.1	10.3	17.6	22.9

Dividend Data

Dividends have been paid since 1963. A dividend reinvestment plan is available.

Amt. of Div. $	Date Decl.	Ex-Div. Date	Stock of Record	Payment Date
0.110	Jun. 15	Jun. 22	Jun. 28	Jul. 11 '94
0.110	Sep. 08	Sep. 20	Sep. 26	Oct. 11 '94
0.110	Dec. 08	Dec. 20	Dec. 27	Jan. 10 '95
0.110	Mar. 08	Mar. 20	Mar. 24	Apr. 10 '95
0.110	Jun. 14	Jun. 26	Jun. 28	Jul. 10 '95

Data as orig. reptd.; bef. results of disc. opers. and/or spec. items. Per share data adj. for stk. divs. as of ex-div. date. E-Estimated. NA-Not Available. NM-Not Meaningful. NR-Not Ranked.

Office—500 Kirts Blvd., Troy, MI 48084-5299. **Tel**—(810) 362-4400. **Chrmn**—D. Handleman. **Pres & CEO**—S. Strome. **SVP-Fin, CFO & Secy**—R. J. Morris. **VP-Treas & Investor Contact**—Larry A. Edwards. **Dirs**—R. H. Cummings, J. F. Daly, D. Handleman, V. G. Istock, J. B. Nicholson, L. E. Reuss, A. E. Schwartz, S. Strome, G. R. Whitaker, Jr. **Transfer Agent & Registrar**—Continental Stock Transfer & Trust Co., NYC. **Incorporated** in Michigan in 1946; reincorporated in Michigan in 1979. **Empl**-4,100. **S&P Analyst:** Tom Graves, CFA

Harcourt General

STOCK REPORTS

NYSE Symbol **H**
In S&P 500

21-SEP-95

Industry:
Conglomerate/diversified

Summary: This diversified company is a major publisher, owns about 65% of retailer The Neiman Marcus Group, and operates a professional services business.

| S&P Opinion: Accumulate (★★★★) | Recent Price • 40% | Yield • 1.7% |
| | 52 Wk Range • 45¾-32⅛ | 12-Mo. P/E • 19.0 |

Earnings vs. Previous Year
▲=Up ▼=Down ▶=No Change

Quantitative Evaluations

Outlook
(1 Lowest—5 Highest)
• **5+**

Fair Value
• **48⅛**

Risk
• **Low**

Earn./Div. Rank
• **B+**

Technical Eval.
• **Bearish** since 8/95

Rel. Strength Rank
(1 Lowest—99 Highest)
• **19**

Insider Activity
• **Unfavorable**

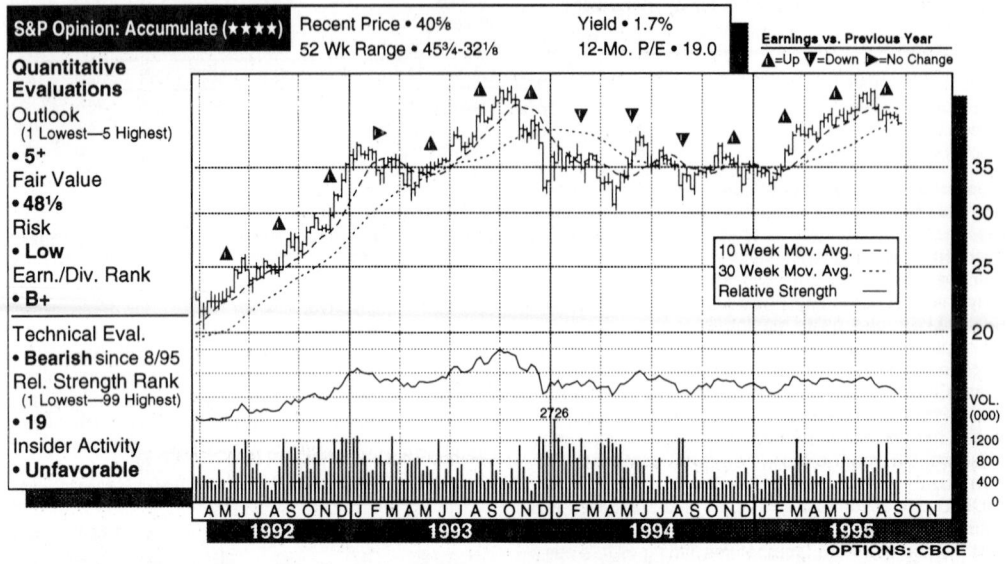

10 Week Mov. Avg. — — —
30 Week Mov. Avg. - - - -
Relative Strength ——

VOL. (000)
1200
800
400
0

1992 1993 1994 1995

OPTIONS: CBOE

Overview - 21-SEP-95

In fiscal 1996, we expect Harcourt's profit from its retailing segment (65%-owned Neiman Marcus Group) to rise about 10%, including increases from both the Neiman Marcus and Bergdorf Goodman store operations. This would follow a smaller overall rise in fiscal 1995, when a sizable profit decline from NMG's mail order business largely offset improvement elsewhere. In Harcourt's publishing business, we expect profit growth of about 5%, helped by gains from secondary school textbooks, and professional publishing. Also, Harcourt's per share earnings could get a modest boost from repurchases of common stock. During the past decade, Harcourt General-- formerly known as General Cinema Corp.-- has gone through various changes in its asset mix; past operations included a large presence in soft drink bottling, a sizable movie theater chain, and insurance businesses.

Valuation - 21-SEP-95

Based on the company's favorable long-term record of building asset value, this stock is attractive for capital appreciation. Even after a large stock buyback in 1995, Harcourt has a sizable cash position, and we expect the company to be looking for further potential acquisitions, particularly in the publishing area. Longer term, we expect Harcourt to have various growth opportunities for its publishing assets in the evolving multi-media world. Also, we look for the 65%-owned Neiman Marcus Group to continue building on its franchise in the high-end retailing business.

Key Stock Statistics

S&P EPS Est. 1995	2.29	Tang. Bk. Value/Share	5.71
P/E on S&P Est. 1995	17.7	Beta	0.74
S&P EPS Est. 1996	2.45	Shareholders	1,500
Dividend Rate/Share	0.68	Market cap. (B)	$ 3.0
Shs. outstg. (M)	72.7	Inst. holdings	52%
Avg. daily vol. (M)	0.175	Insider holdings	NA

Value of $10,000 invested 5 years ago: NA

Fiscal Year Ending Oct. 31

	1995	% Change	1994	% Change	1993	% Change
Revenues (Million $)						
1Q	663.3	-6%	703.8	-13%	810.0	-8%
2Q	774.5	-7%	832.7	-10%	930.0	NM
3Q	813.3	NM	815.1	-19%	1,010	2%
4Q	—	—	802.7	-12%	907.2	NM
Yr.	—	—	3,154	-14%	3,656	-2%
Income (Million $)						
1Q	13.60	130%	5.92	-81%	31.81	18%
2Q	12.74	NM	2.92	-50%	5.81	NM
3Q	95.95	111%	45.52	-57%	106.8	51%
4Q	—	—	43.16	40%	30.87	55%
Yr.	—	—	97.52	-41%	165.5	45%
Earnings Per Share ($)						
1Q	0.17	143%	0.07	-79%	0.34	NM
2Q	0.16	NM	0.04	-43%	0.07	NM
3Q	1.29	126%	0.57	-55%	1.28	44%
4Q	E0.72	33%	0.54	38%	0.39	56%
Yr.	E2.29	88%	1.22	-41%	2.08	44%

Next earnings report expected: early December

Business Summary - 21-SEP-95

This diversified company (formerly General Cinema Corp.) includes publishing, retailing and professional services. H sold its insurance businesses for $400 million in October 1994. Segment contributions (excluding the insurance business, but including the discontinued Contempo Casuals business) in fiscal 1994 were:

	Revs.	Profits
Publishing	29%	64%
Retailing	66%	28%
Professional services	4%	8%

H's publishing business largely comes from the 1991 acquisition of Harcourt Brace & Company. This pooling-of-interests acquisition generated special charges, plus interest expense stemming from debt that has since been retired.

Also, H has about a 65% equity interest (about 51% voting power) in The Neiman-Marcus Group (NMG), which includes the Neiman-Marcus retail chains and two Bergdorf Goodman stores in New York City. NMG is planning to sell its Contempo Casual retail business. Operating results of NMG are consolidated with those of Harcourt with a three-month lag.

H's professional services segment (formerly part of publishing) includes Drake Beam Morin, which provides career transition, employee outplacement and human resource consulting services. H's theater business was spun off in December 1993.

Important Developments

Aug. '95—In fiscal 1995's third quarter, higher profit from H's publishing segment more than offset declines elsewhere. Retail earnings, which exclude results from the divested Contempo Casuals business, were hurt by weak results from the NM Direct mail order business. Meanwhile, Harcourt's directors have authorized the repurchase of an additional 2.5 million common shares. This followed completion of a self-tender offer in April 1995, through which H repurchased about 5.4 million shares for about $219 million ($40.50 per share). The self-tender reduced the number of H shares outstanding by about 7%. As of July 31, 1995, Harcourt had cash equivalents and short-term securities totaling about $493 million, a portion of which came from the sale of H's insurance business for $400 million in October 1994.

Capitalization

Notes & Debentures: $823,956,000 (7/95).
Series A Cum. Conv. Pfd. Stock: About 1,406,000 shs. ($1 par); ea. conv. into 1 com.; pays com. div. plus $0.0075 quarterly.
Class B Stock: 20,803,041 shs. ($1 par) (3/95); ea. conv. into 1 com. on one-time basis; pays div. 10% less than com. div.; 10 votes per sh. in certain cases. Largely owned by Smith family.

Per Share Data ($) (Year Ended Oct. 31)

	1994	1993	1992	1991	1990	1989
Tangible Bk. Val.	7.93	8.30	6.49	0.34	20.36	19.52
Cash Flow	3.27	4.20	3.64	0.12	2.33	2.20
Earnings	1.22	2.08	1.44	-3.88	1.51	1.43
Dividends	0.61	0.57	0.53	0.49	0.45	0.41
Payout Ratio	50%	27%	37%	NM	29%	27%
Prices - High	39½	46⅛	36⅝	24¾	27	28½
- Low	30¼	31¼	18	16½	16½	23⅛
P/E Ratio - High	32	22	25	NM	18	20
- Low	25	15	13	NM	11	16

Income Statement Analysis (Million $)

	1994	%Chg	1993	%Chg	1992	%Chg	1991
Revs.	3,209	-13%	3,692	NM	3,715	3%	3,616
Oper. Inc.	436	-10%	484	17%	415	67%	248
Depr.	163	-4%	169	-3%	174	-45%	315
Int. Exp.	86.0	1%	85.0	-1%	86.0	-75%	349
Pretax Inc.	152	-42%	262	40%	187	NM	-359
Eff. Tax Rate	36%	—	37%	—	39%	—	NM
Net Inc.	98.0	-41%	165	45%	114	NM	-292

Balance Sheet & Other Fin. Data (Million $)

	1994	1993	1992	1991	1990	1989
Cash	820	619	566	1,859	1,634	1,688
Curr. Assets	2,021	NA	NA	NA	2,197	2,208
Total Assets	3,242	5,977	5,287	6,208	3,068	3,404
Curr. Liab.	875	NA	NA	NA	581	1,082
LT Debt	1,123	924	902	870	747	680
Common Eqty.	1,040	1,042	910	453	1,609	1,528
Total Cap.	2,367	2,175	2,032	1,481	2,431	2,264
Cap. Exp.	196	179	202	172	106	138
Cash Flow	261	335	288	9.0	172	163

Ratio Analysis

	1994	1993	1992	1991	1990	1989
Curr. Ratio	2.3	NA	NA	NA	3.8	2.0
% LT Debt of Cap.	47.5	42.5	44.4	58.7	30.7	30.0
% Net Inc.of Revs.	3.0	4.5	3.0	NM	5.1	5.5
% Ret. on Assets	2.1	2.9	2.0	NM	3.4	4.0
% Ret. on Equity	9.3	16.9	16.7	NM	7.0	9.8

Dividend Data —Dividends have been paid since 1953. A dividend reinvestment plan is available.

Amt. of Div. $	Date Decl.	Ex-Div. Date	Stock of Record	Payment Date
0.160	Sep. 16	Oct. 11	Oct. 17	Oct. 31 '94
0.160	Dec. 15	Jan. 06	Jan. 12	Jan. 31 '95
0.160	Mar. 10	Apr. 17	Apr. 22	Apr. 28 '95
0.160	Jun. 16	Jul. 12	Jul. 14	Jul. 31 '95
0.170	Sep. 20	Oct. 11	Oct. 13	Oct. 31 '95

Data as orig. reptd.; bef. results of disc. opers. and/or spec. items. Per share data adj. for stk. divs. as of ex-div. date.
E-Estimated. NA-Not Available. NM-Not Meaningful. NR-Not Ranked.

Office—27 Boylston St., Chestnut Hill, MA 02167. **Tel**—(617) 232-8200. **Chrmn**—Richard A. Smith. **Pres & CEO**—R. J. Tarr Jr. **SVP-CFO**—J. R. Cook. **Sr VP-Secy**—E. P. Geller. **VP & Investor Contact**—Peter Farwell. **Dirs**—W. F. Connell, J. M. Greenberg, H. W. Jarvis, L. M. Martin, M. Segall, Richard A. Smith, Robert A. Smith, P. Stern, S. Stoneman, R. J. Tarr Jr., H. Uyterhoeven, C. R. Wharton. **Transfer Agent & Registrar**—First National Bank of Boston. **Incorporated** in Delaware in 1950. **Empl**-20,972. **S&P Analyst:** Tom Graves, CFA

Harland (John H.)

NYSE Symbol **JH**
In S&P 500

19-SEP-95 **Industry:** Graphic Arts

Summary: This leading supplier of bank checks, business documents and forms also produces optical mark reading and optical character recognition forms and equipment.

S&P Opinion: Hold (★★★)	Recent Price • 22⅛	Yield • 4.6%
	52 Wk Range • 23⅝-19⅛	12-Mo. P/E • 13.3

Quantitative Evaluations

Outlook
(1 Lowest—5 Highest)
• **5⁻**

Fair Value
• **26¾**

Risk
• **Low**

Earn./Div. Rank
• **A**

Technical Eval.
• **Bearish** since 3/95

Rel. Strength Rank
(1 Lowest—99 Highest)
• **24**

Insider Activity
• **NA**

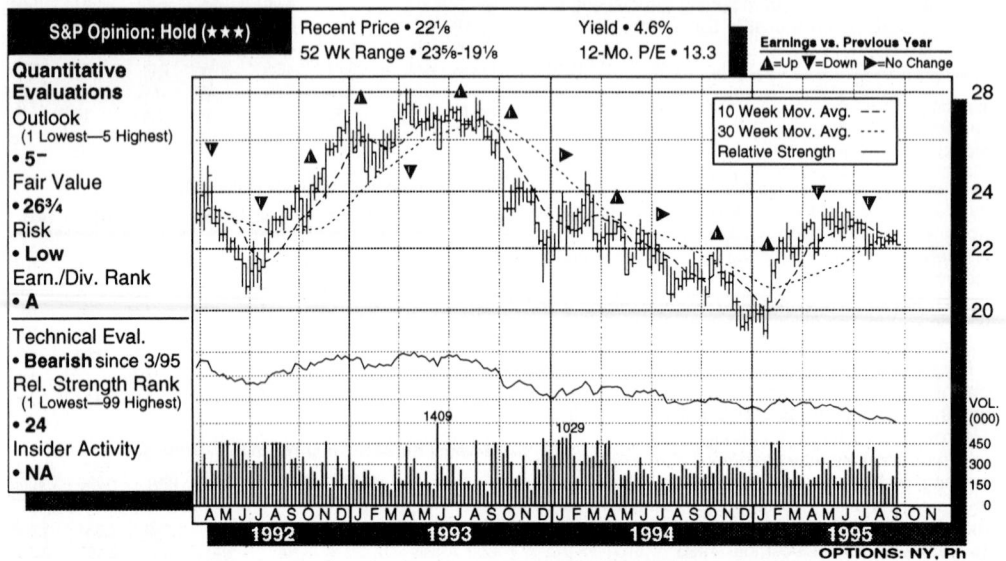

Earnings vs. Previous Year
▲=Up ▼=Down ▶=No Change

10 Week Mov. Avg. ----
30 Week Mov. Avg. ·····
Relative Strength ——

1409   1029

VOL. (000)
450
300
150
0

A M J J A S O N D J F M A M J J A S O N D J F M A M J J A S O N D J F M A M J J A S O N
1992   1993   1994   1995

OPTIONS: NY, Ph

Overview - 19-SEP-95

We expect a small rise in net sales in 1995, as acquisitions and stronger sales of optical mark reading equipment and scannable forms outweigh lower check revenues. Healthy direct marketing group sales, represented by The Check Store, which started up in 1994, will also help. Profitability will benefit from cost-cutting and efficiency measures, wider margins on direct marketing business, and less dilution from earlier acquisitions. Interest expense should be little changed. Stock repurchases will provide a modest boost to EPS. In 1996 and beyond, check sales and profitability will continue to be affected by consolidations among banks and financial institutions. Competition from other printers, particularly discounters, will also remain fierce.

Valuation - 19-SEP-95

The shares, which have been in a narrow trading range for the past six months, are likely to remain only average performers in coming months. Relatively low market valuations of check printers reflect the negative impact on revenues and profits of a shrinking customer base and intense competition. Nevertheless, JH's revenues are growing, and its operating margins should continue to improve, aided by diversification, acquisitions, new products and markets, efficiencies and stock buybacks. These factors provide a cushion for the stock. The dividend, which currently provides a yield of about 4.5%, and has been raised each year since 1953, adds to the stock's long-term appeal.

Key Stock Statistics

S&P EPS Est. 1995	1.77	Tang. Bk. Value/Share	3.84
P/E on S&P Est. 1995	12.5	Beta	0.71
S&P EPS Est. 1996	1.90	Shareholders	7,800
Dividend Rate/Share	1.02	Market cap. (B)	$0.676
Shs. outstg. (M)	30.5	Inst. holdings	59%
Avg. daily vol. (M)	0.044	Insider holdings	NA

Value of $10,000 invested 5 years ago: $ 12,633

Fiscal Year Ending Dec. 31

	1995	% Change	1994	% Change	1993	% Change
Revenues (Million $)						
1Q	138.3	6%	131.0	-2%	133.5	29%
2Q	136.1	4%	130.8	NM	130.0	14%
3Q	—	—	129.1	NM	129.9	14%
4Q	—	—	130.3	3%	126.1	11%
Yr.	—	—	521.3	NM	519.5	17%
Income (Million $)						
1Q	12.76	-2%	12.99	NM	13.12	-12%
2Q	12.47	-3%	12.84	-9%	14.13	-3%
3Q	—	—	13.13	-1%	13.32	-3%
4Q	—	—	12.28	3%	11.96	-12%
Yr.	—	—	51.24	-2%	52.52	-7%
Earnings Per Share ($)						
1Q	0.42	-2%	0.43	10%	0.39	-5%
2Q	0.41	-2%	0.42	NM	0.42	5%
3Q	E0.47	9%	0.43	2%	0.42	8%
4Q	E0.47	17%	0.40	3%	0.39	NM
Yr.	E1.77	5%	1.68	4%	1.62	2%

Next earnings report expected: late October

438

Harland (John H.)

Business Summary - 19-SEP-95

John H. Harland is mainly a financial stationer, engaged primarily in printing checks and related items. With about 30% of the market, it is among the three largest U.S. printers of magnetic ink character recognition (MICR) encoded personalized checks. The company's size was expanded significantly with the January 1993 purchase of Rocky Mountain Bank Note and the February 1992 acquisition of Interchecks, Inc.

The company's principal products are MICR encoded checks designed to be processed on automatic sorting and posting equipment, deposit tickets and related forms for financial institutions and their customers. JH also produces customer-designed printed, lithographed and engraved business forms and other stationery items for banks and other accounts. In early 1994, it began to market checks directly to consumers through a new subsidiary as a means of augmenting financial institution sales. The direct check market is growing 10% to 12% annually.

Scantron Corp. (acquired in 1988) designs, develops and produces optical mark reading (OMR) equipment and scannable forms used to score tests and tabulate data. Datascan, headquartered in Switzerland, is a leading producer of OMR equipment and optical character recognition (OCR) check reader equipment.

JH entered a third line of business with the January 1994 purchase of Marketing Profiles, Inc., a database marketing and consulting firm that provides software products and related marketing services to the financial industry.

Important Developments

Sep. '95—The company received an exclusive five-year contract from Intuit, Inc. to produce computer checks and forms for Quicken software. JH said that Quicken accounts for about 70% of the personal finance software market. As a result of this contract, Intuit will be JH's second largest customer. In order to meet production demands of its growing computer checks and forms business and enhance customer support on the West Coast, the company's Financial Services group acquired the dataPRINT division of Data Print, Inc. Terms were not disclosed.
Jul. '95—Scantron purchased Quality Computers & Applications Inc., a mail-order retailer of software and hardware to the educational technology market, which had 1994 revenues in excess of $10 million.

Capitalization

Long Term Debt: $114,773,000 (6/95).

Per Share Data ($) (Year Ended Dec. 31)

	1994	1993	1992	1991	1990	1989
Tangible Bk. Val.	3.34	4.25	6.42	7.99	7.92	7.26
Cash Flow	3.04	2.70	2.42	1.94	2.08	2.01
Earnings	1.68	1.62	1.59	1.33	1.52	1.54
Dividends	0.98	0.94	0.90	0.86	0.78	0.68
Payout Ratio	58%	58%	57%	65%	51%	44%
Prices - High	$24\frac{3}{4}$	$28\frac{1}{8}$	$27\frac{1}{4}$	$24\frac{3}{8}$	$26\frac{1}{8}$	25
- Low	$19\frac{3}{8}$	$20\frac{7}{8}$	$20\frac{1}{2}$	$17\frac{7}{8}$	$17\frac{7}{8}$	$19\frac{1}{2}$
P/E Ratio - High	15	17	17	18	17	16
- Low	12	13	13	13	12	13

Income Statement Analysis (Million $)

	1994	%Chg	1993	%Chg	1992	%Chg	1991
Revs.	521	NM	519	17%	445	17%	379
Oper. Inc.	134	10%	122	8%	113	4%	109
Depr.	41.5	18%	35.1	18%	29.7	31%	22.6
Int. Exp.	7.8	—	NA	—	NA	—	NA
Pretax Inc.	85.1	NM	85.7	-3%	88.3	11%	79.7
Eff. Tax Rate	40%	—	39%	—	36%	—	38%
Net Inc.	51.2	-2%	52.5	-7%	56.6	14%	49.8

Balance Sheet & Other Fin. Data (Million $)

	1994	1993	1992	1991	1990	1989
Cash	15.3	28.1	19.3	71.4	44.6	78.9
Curr. Assets	117	135	111	150	138	163
Total Assets	414	356	340	352	357	321
Curr. Liab.	79.3	44.0	59.5	35.1	28.4	24.0
LT Debt	115	112	12.6	11.7	12.6	11.3
Common Eqty.	203	184	256	292	296	273
Total Cap.	323	302	271	308	323	294
Cap. Exp.	37.5	27.1	18.7	17.5	29.0	28.7
Cash Flow	92.8	87.6	86.3	72.4	78.0	76.0

Ratio Analysis

	1994	1993	1992	1991	1990	1989
Curr. Ratio	1.5	3.1	1.9	4.3	4.9	6.8
% LT Debt of Cap.	35.6	37.0	4.7	3.8	3.9	3.8
% Net Inc.of Revs.	9.8	10.1	12.7	13.2	15.4	16.8
% Ret. on Assets	13.3	15.9	17.0	14.2	16.9	18.9
% Ret. on Equity	26.5	25.4	21.4	17.1	20.2	22.5

Dividend Data —Dividends, paid since 1932, have been increased each year since 1953. A poison pill stock purchase rights plan was adopted in 1989.

Amt. of Div. $	Date Decl.	Ex-Div. Date	Stock of Record	Payment Date
0.245	Oct. 28	Nov. 10	Nov. 17	Dec. 01 '94
0.255	Jan. 27	Feb. 10	Feb. 16	Mar. 02 '95
0.255	Apr. 28	May. 12	May. 18	Jun. 01 '95
0.255	Jul. 28	Aug. 15	Aug. 17	Aug. 31 '95

Data as orig. reptd.; bef. results of disc. opers. and/or spec. items. Per share data adj. for stk. divs. as of ex-div. date. E-Estimated. NA-Not Available. NM-Not Meaningful. NR-Not Ranked.

Office—2939 Miller Rd. (P.O. Box 105250), Decatur, GA 30035 (30348). **Tel**—(404) 981-9460. **Chrmn, Pres & CEO**—R. R. Woodson. **VP, Treas & CFO**—W. M. Dollar. **VP, Secy & Investor Contact**—Victoria P. Weyand (404-593-5127). **Dirs**—J. P. Baranco, L. L. Gellerstedt, Jr., E. J. Hawie, J. J. McMahon, G. H. Northrop, H. G. Pattillo, L. L. Prince, J. H. Weitnauer Jr., R. R. Woodson, R. A. Yellowlees. **Transfer Agent & Registrar**—Trust Co. Bank, Atlanta. **Incorporated** in Georgia in 1923. **Empl**-7,000. **S&P Analyst:** William H. Donald

Harnischfeger Industries

NYSE Symbol **HPH**
In S&P 500

10-OCT-95 | Industry: Machinery

Summary: This company produces heavy capital goods equipment, including power cranes, electric shovels, material-handling equipment and papermaking machinery.

S&P Opinion: Accumulate (★★★★)	Recent Price • 32¼	Yield • 1.3%
	52 Wk Range • 39⅜-24½	12-Mo. P/E • 28.8

Quantitative Evaluations

Outlook
(1 Lowest—5 Highest)
• **1⁺**

Fair Value
• **28⅝**

Risk
• **Low**

Earn./Div. Rank
• **B**

Technical Eval.
• **Bearish** since 9/95

Rel. Strength Rank
(1 Lowest—99 Highest)
• **13**

Insider Activity
• **Neutral**

Earnings vs. Previous Year
▲=Up ▼=Down ▶=No Change

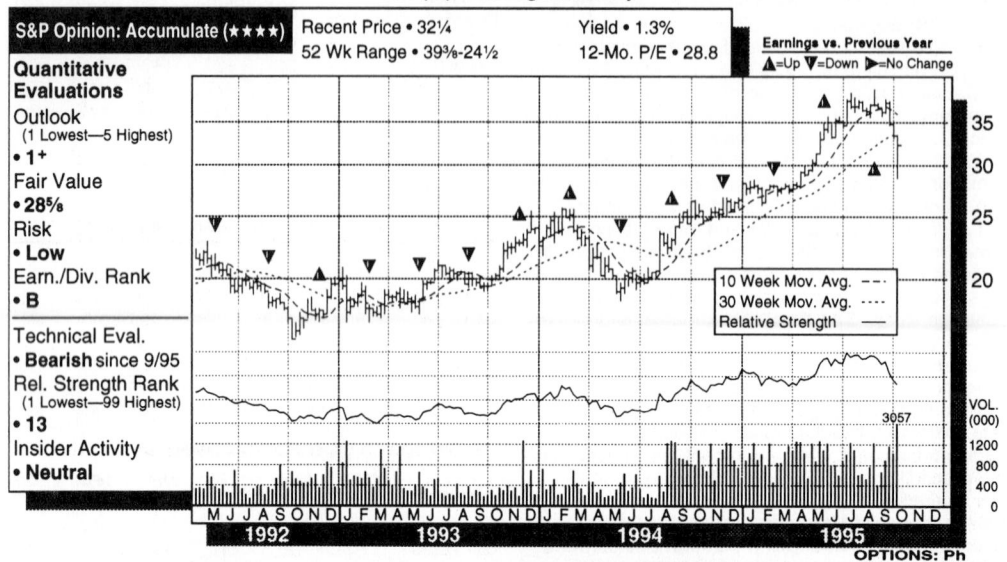

10 Week Mov. Avg. – – –
30 Week Mov. Avg. · · · · ·
Relative Strength ———

OPTIONS: Ph

Overview - 10-OCT-95

Based on our projection of 2.6% GDP growth in 1996, we anticipate a 20% rise in sales for fiscal 1996, reflecting volume and price gains in all three segments. The rate of sales increase in fiscal 1996 will trail 1995's rate due to absence of large acquisitions. Gross margins will expand as a result of high capacity utilization, more parts sales, higher prices and only a small increase in raw material costs. Aided by well-controlled SG&A and an unchanged tax rate, earnings should rise again in fiscal 1996. New products, additional acquisitions, expected gains in market share in existing businesses will boost long-term sales and profit growth. Sales of spare parts and machine rebuilds stemming from HPH's large installed base will also lift long-term earnings.

Valuation - 10-OCT-95

After having risen 40% through late August, HPH's shares were up just 18% through early October. The stock has been under pressure since Caterpillar Inc. disclosed that its third-quarter earnings would not meet analysts' estimates. We surmise that HPH is being viewed more cautiously in light of CAT's announcement. Another factor that may be hurting the stock is HPH's hostile offer for Dobson Park. Nevertheless, we are maintaining our accumulate rating on the shares. HPH is more of a late-cycle play than CAT or Deere & Co.; we think HPH's earnings will not peak until 1997 at the earliest. Revenues and earnings should continue to provide upside surprises and push the shares higher.

Key Stock Statistics

S&P EPS Est. 1995	1.80	Tang. Bk. Value/Share	6.61
P/E on S&P Est. 1995	17.9	Beta	1.23
S&P EPS Est. 1996	2.30	Shareholders	3,500
Dividend Rate/Share	0.40	Market cap. (B)	$ 1.5
Shs. outstg. (M)	48.6	Inst. holdings	68%
Avg. daily vol. (M)	0.309	Insider holdings	NA

Value of $10,000 invested 5 years ago: $ 17,080

Fiscal Year Ending Oct. 31

	1995	% Change	1994	% Change	1993	% Change
Revenues (Million $)						
1Q	477.0	92%	248.0	-12%	282.0	-14%
2Q	541.0	108%	260.5	-19%	321.1	-13%
3Q	580.4	103%	285.3	-8%	310.1	-5%
4Q	—	—	345.8	8%	321.5	-9%
Yr.	—	—	1,140	-8%	1,235	-10%
Income (Million $)						
1Q	2.51	29%	1.95	NM	0.56	-95%
2Q	21.05	NM	2.81	-24%	3.68	-73%
3Q	37.61	NM	4.42	NM	-45.10	NM
4Q	—	—	9.94	-57%	23.16	12%
Yr.	—	—	19.12	NM	-17.70	NM
Earnings Per Share ($)						
1Q	0.06	-25%	0.08	NM	0.02	-94%
2Q	0.46	NM	0.11	-15%	0.13	-72%
3Q	0.81	NM	0.17	NM	-1.78	NM
4Q	E0.47	27%	0.37	-59%	0.91	25%
Yr.	E1.80	143%	0.74	NM	-0.67	NM

Next earnings report expected: late November

Harnischfeger Industries

Business Summary - 10-OCT-95

Harnischfeger Industries makes papermaking machinery, mining equipment and material handling equipment. HPH discontinued its systems business in fiscal 1994. Contributions in fiscal 1994:

	Sales	Profits
Papermaking machinery	64%	50%
Mining equipment	26%	31%
Material handling equip.	10%	19%

Foreign operations accounted for 23% of sales and 36% of operating profits in fiscal 1994.

Through Beloit Corp. (80% owned) and Measurex Corp. (10% owned), HPH manufactures papermaking machinery systems and related products for the pulp and paper industries. Beloit operates on a global basis, with manufacturing facilities in the U. S. and five other countries. Activities are divided into three categories: design, manufacture and installation of equipment, rebuilds and servicing and sale of ancillary equipment and replacement parts. Beloit has the industry's largest installed equipment base, consisting of approximately 1,200 machines.

In December 1994, HPH reduced its stake in Measurex Corp. from 20% to 10%.

HPH's Mining Equipment is the world's largest producer of electric mining shovels and also makes electric and diesel-electric crawler and walker draglines, buckets, hydraulic mining excavators and blasthole drills. The products are used in mines, quarries, and earthmoving operations in the the digging and loading of materials such as coal, copper, iron ore and other materials.

Material Handling Equipment segment makes overhead cranes, electric wire rope and chain hoists and for a variety of users as well as container handling cranes for use in ports.

Important Developments

Sep. '95—HPH commenced an $265 million takeover offer for Britain's Dobson Park Industries PLC. Dobson rejected the offer, stating that it was unwelcome and materially understated Dobson's current worth and potential. The offer came a week after HPH held unsuccessful talks with Dobson Park in an effort to acquire the U.K.-based maker of mining equipment, industrial electronic control systems, toys and plastics. HPH stated that while it believed the offer was fair, it would not rule out a higher bid. HPH added that it would not get carried away with the fever of the deal and would acquire other suppliers to the mining industry if the offer for Dobson Park fails.

Capitalization

Long Term Debt: $467,296,000 (7/95).
Minority Interest: $90,012,000 (7/95).

Per Share Data ($)

(Year Ended Oct. 31)

	1994	1993	1992	1991	1990	1989
Tangible Bk. Val.	12.03	12.69	16.55	16.21	14.99	12.51
Cash Flow	2.41	0.89	3.20	3.16	3.12	2.37
Earnings	0.74	-0.67	1.95	2.08	2.18	1.66
Dividends	0.40	0.40	0.40	0.40	0.20	0.20
Payout Ratio	54%	NM	21%	19%	9%	12%
Prices - High	28⅜	25½	22⅞	22	25	22⅜
- Low	18½	17⅛	16⅛	16	12⅜	15
P/E Ratio - High	38	NM	12	11	11	13
- Low	25	NM	8	8	6	9

Income Statement Analysis (Million $)

	1994	%Chg	1993	%Chg	1992	%Chg	1991
Revs.	1,139	-8%	1,243	-11%	1,391	-13%	1,601
Oper. Inc.	89.0	3%	86.0	-42%	148	-3%	152
Depr.	43.6	6%	41.3	13%	36.6	9%	33.6
Int. Exp.	26.4	-5%	27.7	42%	19.5	23%	15.9
Pretax Inc.	27.0	NM	-27.0	NM	102	-18%	125
Eff. Tax Rate	20%	—	NM	—	35%	—	36%
Net Inc.	19.1	NM	-17.7	NM	56.7	-12%	64.6

Balance Sheet & Other Fin. Data (Million $)

	1994	1993	1992	1991	1990	1989
Cash	153	126	171	220	240	216
Curr. Assets	719	656	880	943	1,010	895
Total Assets	1,439	1,334	1,508	1,507	1,576	1,370
Curr. Liab.	468	424	463	567	644	534
LT Debt	243	243	245	112	115	121
Common Eqty.	486	503	591	594	583	514
Total Cap.	827	866	979	847	827	747
Cap. Exp.	35.1	63.0	53.1	46.7	60.7	51.6
Cash Flow	63.0	24.0	93.0	98.0	100	77.0

Ratio Analysis

	1994	1993	1992	1991	1990	1989
Curr. Ratio	1.5	1.5	1.9	1.7	1.6	1.7
% LT Debt of Cap.	29.4	28.1	25.0	13.2	13.9	16.2
% Net Inc.of Revs.	1.7	NM	4.1	4.0	3.9	3.6
% Ret. on Assets	1.3	NM	3.9	4.3	4.8	4.2
% Ret. on Equity	3.7	NM	9.9	11.3	12.9	11.1

Dividend Data

Common dividends were resumed in 1988 since omission in mid-1982. A "poision pill" stock purchase right was adopted in 1989.

Amt. of Div. $	Date Decl.	Ex-Div. Date	Stock of Record	Payment Date
0.100	Aug. 01	Sep. 20	Sep. 26	Oct. 07 '94
0.100	Dec. 08	Dec. 19	Dec. 23	Jan. 06 '95
0.100	Mar. 14	Mar. 21	Mar. 27	Apr. 07 '95
0.100	Jun. 12	Jun. 22	Jun. 26	Jul. 07 '95
0.100	Aug. 15	Sep. 21	Sep. 25	Oct. 06 '95

Data as orig. reptd.; bef. results of disc. opers. and/or spec. items. Per share data adj. for stk. divs. as of ex-div. date. E-Estimated. NA-Not Available. NM-Not Meaningful. NR-Not Ranked.

Office—13400 Bishops Lane, Brookfield, WI 53005. **Tel**—(414) 671-4400. **Chrmn. & CEO**—J. T. Grade. **EVP & COO**—J. N. Hanson. **EVP-Fin & CFO**—F. M. Corby Jr. **EVP-Secy**—K. T. Lundgren. **Dirs**—D. M. Alvarado, J. D. Correnti, D. H. Davis Jr., H. L. Davis, R. M. Gerrity, J. T. Grade, R. B. Hoffman, C. Inoue, R. C. Joynes, H. V. Kohler Jr., J. Labruyere, R. F. Schnoes, D. Taylor. **Transfer Agent & Registrar**—First National Bank of Boston. **Incorporated** in Wisconsin in 1910; reincorporated in Delaware in 1971. **Empl**-11,200. **S&P Analyst:** Leo Larkin

Harrah's Entertainment

NYSE Symbol HET Options on CBOE (Feb-May-Aug-Nov) In S&P 500

Price	Range	P–E Ratio	Dividend	Yield	S&P Ranking	Beta
Oct. 20'95	1995					
26⅞	45⅞–24¾	33	None	None	NR	1.41

Summary

This company (formerly known as Promus Cos.) is one of the largest casinos companies in the U.S., with gaming operations in at least eight states. Ownership of HET's non-casino hotel business was spun off to shareholders in mid-1995. The spunoff business— called Promus Hotel Corp.— now trades as a separate publicly owned company on the NYSE.

Current Outlook

Earnings for 1996 are estimated at $1.60 a share, up from the $1.38 expected for 1995.

Initiation of cash dividends is not expected.

Earnings for 1996 are expected to be helped by the debut of several new managed casinos, plus expansions of current gaming projects. Our earnings estimate excludes any preopening charges related to new facilities. Also, we look for HET's profits to be hurt by its involvement in a land-based New Orleans casino project, but we are projecting that the negative impact will decline from 1995's expected level. HET is a joint venture partner and manager of the New Orleans facility.

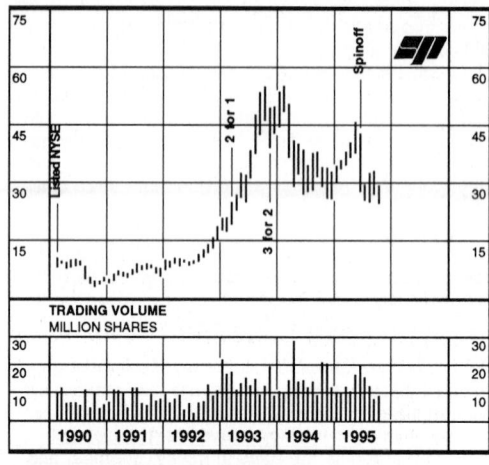

Revenues (Million $)

Quarter:	1995	1994	1993	1992
Mar.	356	290	269	258
Jun.	389	339	316	281
Sep.	426	367	347	316
Dec.		344	320	258
		1,339	1,252	1,113

Revenues from continuing operations for the nine months ended September 30, 1995, increased 18%, year to year. Operating profit was up 21% (13% if preopening charges in the 1994 period are excluded). Helped by a gain on the sale of an equity interest, income from continuing operations rose 40%, to $1.12 a share from $0.80, excluding income from discontinued operations of $0.21 and $0.29 in the respective periods, and special charges of $0.21 and $0.08, respectively.

Common Share Earnings ($)

Quarter:	1995	1994	1993	1992
Mar.	0.28	0.22	0.12	0.05
Jun.	0.35	0.30	0.22	0.14
Sep.	0.50	[1]0.29	0.39	0.27
Dec.	E0.26	d0.31	0.19	0.03
	E1.38	0.49	0.89	0.51

Important Developments

Oct. '95— If unusual items are excluded, HET's earnings per share in 1995 third quarter would have been up close to 20% (about $0.43 vs. $0.36). Much of this growth was generated by a 77% profit increase from HET's riverboat casino division. This more than offset an adverse impact from HET's involvement in a land-based New Orleans casino. Also, HET new facilities planned by HET include expansions in Atlantic City, North Kansas City, and Las Vegas. A pair of new casinos to be managed by HET— in the state of Washington and in New Zealand— are expected between late 1995 and early 1996. Another could open in North Carolina in late 1996. Meanwhile, in June 1995, HET completed a spinoff of its non-casino hotel business, with HET stockholders receiving one share of Promus Hotel Corp. (PRH)) for each two HET shares owned.

Next earnings report expected in late January.

Per Share Data ($)

Yr. End Dec. 31	1994	1993	1992	1991	1990	1989	1988
Tangible Bk. Val.	[3]6.09	[3]4.75	[3]3.68	[3]3.16	[3]1.96	NA	NM
Cash Flow	1.17	1.68	1.22	1.05	1.03	NA	NA
Earnings[5]	0.49	0.89	0.51	0.33	0.30	[2]0.33	[2]0.24
Dividends	Nil	Nil	Nil	Nil	[4]10.00	NM	NM
Payout Ratio	Nil	Nil	Nil	Nil	NM	NM	NM
Prices—High	55¼	55	18¾	9⅛	10²¹⁄₃₂	NM	NM
Low	25⅞	17¹⁵⁄₃₂	7⅜	3⅞	2³¹⁄₃₂	NM	NM
P/E Ratio—	NM	62–20	37–15	27–12	36–10	NM	NM

Data as orig. reptd., data for 1988 as reptd. in proxy statement/prospectus dated 12-13-89. Adjtd. for stk. div(s). of 50% Nov. 1993, 100% Mar. 1993. **1.** Nine mos. **2.** After pro forma interest expenses related to $15/share special div. in Feb. 1990 **3.** Incl. intangibles. **4.** Special. **5.** Bef. spec. item(s) of -0.08 in 1994, -0.05 in 1993, +0.01 in 1992. d-Deficit. E-Estimated. NM-Not Meaningful. NA-Not Available.

Income Data (Million $)

Year Ended Dec. 31	Revs.	Oper. Inc.	% Oper. Inc. of Revs.	Cap. Exp.	Depr.	Int. Exp.	Net Bef. Taxes	Eff. Tax Rate	[3]Net Inc.	% Net Inc. of Revs.	Cash Flow
1994	1,339	340	25.4	219	70.6	82	[2]139.0	54.1%	50.0	3.7	121
1993	1,252	356	28.5	239	80.7	110	[2]170.0	43.1%	92.0	7.3	173
1992	1,113	281	25.2	118	71.7	121	[2]88.0	41.8%	51.0	4.6	123
1991	1,031	246	23.9	174	65.3	137	[2]52.0	42.5%	30.0	2.9	95
1990	1,004	210	20.9	173	57.0	129	[2]44.1	47.0%	23.4	2.3	80
[1]1989	945	NA	NA	NA	NA	132	45.0	43.7%	25.6	2.7	NA
[1]1988	871	182	20.8	NA	44.8	122	26.1	33.0%	17.5	2.0	NA

Balance Sheet Data (Million $)

Dec. 31	Cash	Assets	Curr. Liab.	Ratio	Total Assets	% Ret. on Assets	Long Term Debt	Common Equity	Total Cap.	% LT Debt of Cap.	% Ret. on Equity
1994	85.0	172	295	0.6	1,738	2.8	727	623	1,376	52.9	8.6
1993	62.0	164	252	0.6	1,793	5.4	840	536	1,454	57.7	19.0
1992	43.8	137	157	0.9	1,597	3.3	877	428	1,352	64.9	12.8
1991	34.6	103	223	0.5	1,523	1.8	835	375	1,244	67.1	9.3
1990	40.3	110	204	0.5	1,433	NA	904	213	1,174	76.9	NA
[1]1989	NA	109	173	0.6	1,342	NA	914	176	1,123	81.4	NA
[4]1988	33.9	128	135	0.9	1,334	NA	895	222	1,153	77.6	NA

Data as orig. reptd.; data for 1988 as reptd. in proxy statement/prospectus dated 12-13-89. 1. Pro forma to reflect 1990 spinoff of Promus Companies common shares to Holiday Corp. shareholders and related transactions. 2. Incl. equity in earns. of nonconsol. subs. 3. Bef. spec. item(s). 4. As of 9-29-89, pro forma. NA-Not Available.

Business Summary

Harrah's Entertainment, Inc. (formerly Promus Companies) is a major gaming company which was created in connection with a 1989 restructuring of Holiday Corp. On June 30, 1995, ownership of Promus Cos.' non-casino hotel business—largely consisting of the Embassy Suite, Hampton and Homewood Suites lodging chains— was spun off to shareholders.

Contributions to operating profit (in millions of dollars, before preopening costs and corporate expense) from various HET divisions or areas in recent years were:

Division	1994	1993
Riverboats	$127	$28
Northern Nevada	76	77
Southern Nevada	75	79
Atlantic City	74	68
New Orleans	−9	—
Development costs	−22	−10
Other	−8	−5
Total	313	237

HET's Riverboat Division includes the operation of six casino boats, located in Joliet, Ill. (two); Vicksburg and Tunica, Miss.; Shreveport, La.; and North Kansas City, Mo. Future development is expected to include a casino boat project in Maryland Heights, Mo., and a second gaming riverboat in North Kansas City.

In Northern Nevada, HET operates Harrah's Reno, a casino/hotel with about 565 lodging rooms (including suites) and 58,300 sq. ft. of casino space; Harrah's Lake Tahoe (534 rooms, 63,200 sq. ft.);

and Bill's Lake Tahoe Casino (18,000 sq. ft.) In Southern Nevada, HET operates Harrah's Las Vegas, a casino/hotel with 1,713 guest rooms and about 80,000 sq. ft. of casino space; and Harrah's Laughlin, which has 1,658 rooms and about 47,000 sq. ft. of casino space. Also, Harrah's Atlantic City has about 780 hotel rooms and 65,700 sq. ft. of casino space. Other operations include a temporary land-based casino in New Orleans which opened in May 1995. HET manages the facility and currently has a 53% equity interest in the project. A larger, permanent casino is expected to open there in mid-1996. Also, HET manages an Ak-Chin Indian casino in Arizona, and two partly owned casinos in Colorado.

Gaming projects under development include a riverboat casino project in Maryland Heights, Md.; a partly-owned casino/hotel in Auckland, New Zealand; and an Indian casino in Washington state. Also, HET owns about 14% of Sodak Gaming, Inc.

Dividend Data

In mid-1995, shareholders of Promus Cos. received one share of Promus Hotel Corp. for each two shares of Promus Cos. held. The distribution was to holders of record as of June 21, 1995; the ex-dividend date was July 3, 1995.

Capitalization

Long Term Debt: $730,068,000 (6/30/95).

Minority Interest: $19,682,000 (6/30/95).

Common Stock: 102,531,830 shs. ($0.10 par). Institutions hold about 63%.
Shareholders of record: About 16,993 (1/95).

Office—1023 Cherry Rd., Memphis, TN 38117. **Tel**—(901) 762-8600. **Chrmn**—M. D. Rose. **Pres & CEO**—P. G. Satre. **SVP**—C. V. Reed **SVP & CFO**—C. A. Ledsinger, Jr **Investor Contact**—Charles Atwood (901-762-8852). **Dirs**—J. L. Barksdale, S. Clark-Jackson, J. B. Farley, J. M. Henson, M. D. Rose, W. J. Salmon, P. G. Satre, B. A. Sells, E. N. Williams, S. Young. **Transfer Agent & Registrar**—Bank of New York, NYC. **Incorporated** in Delaware in 1989.

Harris Corp.

NYSE Symbol **HRS**
In S&P 500

28-AUG-95

Industry: Electronics/Electric

Summary: Harris makes advanced electronic systems, semiconductors, communications equipment and systems, and office equipment.

S&P Opinion: Accumulate (★★★★)	Recent Price • 58⅝	Yield • 2.3%
	52 Wk Range • 59-37¾	12-Mo. P/E • 14.8

Quantitative Evaluations

Outlook (1 Lowest—5 Highest)
• **5+**

Fair Value
• **68¾**

Risk
• **Low**

Earn./Div. Rank
• **B+**

Technical Eval.
• **Bearish** since 7/95

Rel. Strength Rank (1 Lowest—99 Highest)
• **73**

Insider Activity
• **Unfavorable**

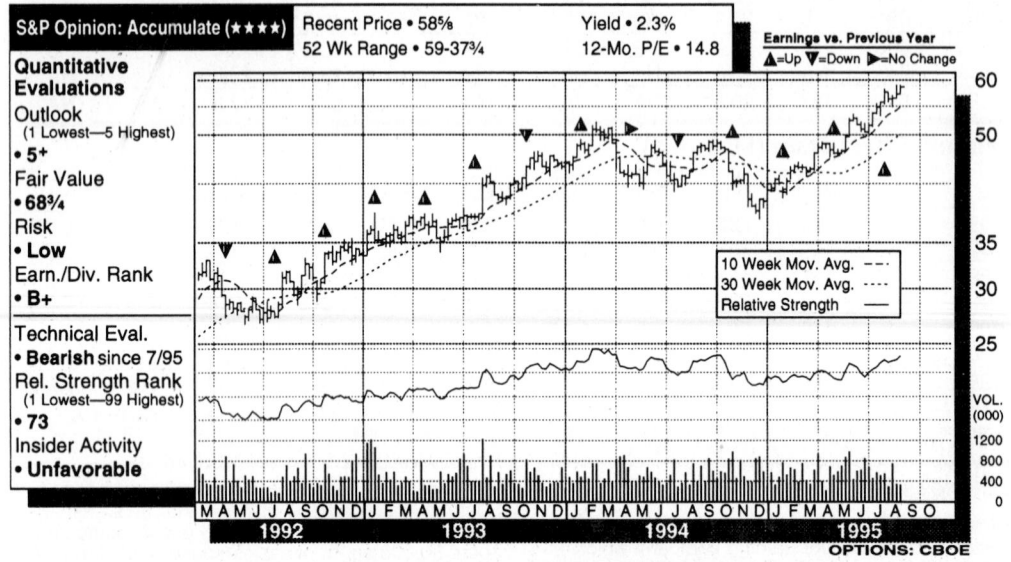

Earnings vs. Previous Year
▲=Up ▼=Down ▶=No Change

10 Week Mov. Avg. - - -
30 Week Mov. Avg. ·····
Relative Strength ——

OPTIONS: CBOE

Overview - 28-AUG-95

Earnings through fiscal 1996 should benefit from favorable operating trends in the company's four core business segments and improving worldwide economies. The semiconductor segment has been consistently profitable over the last several years, and should continue to benefit from the introduction of newer and higher margin products and ongoing industry strength. The electronic systems segment is expected to benefit from the resolution of delays in the development of a new energy-management system. Continued strong gains are also expected in the communications segment, fueled by international expansion. Lanier Worldwide's profits should benefit from continued market expansion and restructured European operations. The company's long-term goal is to realize a 12% return on investment in each of its four segments.

Valuation - 28-AUG-95

Shares of Harris Corp. have performed strongly this year as operating trends have been generally favorable with strength in all segments except for electronic systems. With these favorable trends expected to continue throughout 1996 and a turnaround anticipated at electronic systems as shipment delays are resolved, the favorable earnings momentum should continue. In addition, the price/earnings multiple remains modest in light of the bright prospects. The shares are ranked an "accumulate."

Key Stock Statistics

S&P EPS Est. 1996	4.20	Tang. Bk. Value/Share	26.53
P/E on S&P Est. 1996	14.0	Beta	1.64
Dividend Rate/Share	1.36	Shareholders	10,600
Shs. outstg. (M)	38.9	Market cap. (B)	$ 2.3
Avg. daily vol. (M)	0.083	Inst. holdings	82%
		Insider holdings	NA

Value of $10,000 invested 5 years ago: $ 21,288

Fiscal Year Ending Jun. 30

	1995	% Change	1994	% Change	1993	% Change
Revenues (Million $)						
1Q	816.1	6%	769.1	6%	728.0	6%
2Q	872.3	8%	807.5	5%	767.0	1%
3Q	859.9	3%	838.3	13%	744.0	1%
4Q	932.6	1%	921.2	7%	859.0	4%
Yr.	3,481	4%	3,336	8%	3,099	3%
Income (Million $)						
1Q	28.80	17%	24.70	—	—	—
2Q	34.80	16%	30.00	18%	25.39	32%
3Q	38.00	15%	33.00	20%	27.47	28%
4Q	52.90	55%	34.20	-9%	37.50	52%
Yr.	154.5	27%	121.9	10%	111.1	28%
Earnings Per Share ($)						
1Q	0.73	18%	0.62	-44%	1.10	NM
2Q	0.88	17%	0.75	17%	0.64	31%
3Q	0.98	18%	0.83	NM	0.83	51%
4Q	1.36	56%	0.87	-8%	0.95	9%
Yr.	3.95	29%	3.07	9%	2.82	26%

Next earnings report expected: mid October

Harris Corp.

Business Summary - 28-AUG-95

Harris focuses on four major core businesses: advanced electronic systems, semiconductors, communications, and office equipment distribution. Sales to the U.S. government accounted for 35% of total sales in fiscal 1994 (latest available). Segment contributions in fiscal 1995:

	Sales	Profits
Electronic systems	30%	27%
Semiconductors	19%	24%
Communications	21%	19%
Lanier Worldwide	30%	30%

The electronic systems segment is engaged in research, development, design and production of a broad range of high-technology systems for government and commercial organizations in the U.S. and overseas. Applications include defense, air traffic control, avionics, satellite communications, space exploration, mobile radio networks, simulation, energy management, law enforcement, electronic systems testing and newspaper composition.

The semiconductor segment produces digital and analog integrated circuits and discrete semiconductors for power, signal processing, data acquisition and logic applications.

The communications segment makes products characterized by three principal communication technologies: broadcast, including radio and television products and transmission systems; two-way radio and complete turnkey communication systems; and telecommunications.

Lanier Worldwide, Inc. sells and services office equipment and business communication products.

In October 1994, HRS spun off its Computer Systems division, a maker of security systems and software with revenues of $60 million. One share of Harris Computer Systems (Nasdaq: NHWK) was distributed for every 20 HRS shares held.

Important Developments

Aug. '95—HRS acquired Micro Computer Systems Inc., a maker of telecommunciations test equipment.
Jul. '95—The company said that its sales for fiscal 1994-95 were restrained by the absence of sales of Harris Computer Systems Division, which has been spun-off to shareholders. It added that its earnings growth was led by a 37% increase in earnings at the semiconductor sector despite lower military shipments. Communications earnings rose 19%, while Lanier Worldwide achieved a 27% increase in earnings. These gains more than offset a 12% dip in earnings at electronic systems due to delays in the development and shipment of a new energy-management system.

Capitalization

Long Term Debt: $475,900,000 (6/95).

Per Share Data ($)

(Year Ended Jun. 30)

	1995	1994	1993	1992	1991	1990
Tangible Bk. Val.	NA	26.01	24.71	23.51	22.58	23.55
Cash Flow	NA	6.74	6.62	6.46	5.20	7.95
Earnings	3.95	3.07	2.82	2.24	0.50	3.30
Dividends	1.24	1.12	1.04	1.04	1.04	0.96
Payout Ratio	31%	36%	37%	46%	208%	29%
Prices - High	58¼	52¼	47⅜	35½	28⅞	36⅛
- Low	40½	41⅜	33⅝	26⅝	18¼	13¾
P/E Ratio - High	15	17	17	16	58	11
- Low	10	13	12	12	37	4

Income Statement Analysis (Million $)

	1994	%Chg	1993	%Chg	1992	%Chg	1991
Revs.	3,336	8%	3,099	3%	3,004	-1%	3,040
Oper. Inc.	376	13%	333	6%	314	-5%	331
Depr.	146	-3%	150	-9%	165	-10%	184
Int. Exp.	58.6	-3%	60.2	-9%	66.1	-15%	77.5
Pretax Inc.	194	14%	170	36%	125	NM	10.0
Eff. Tax Rate	37%	—	35%	—	30%	—	NM
Net Inc.	122	10%	111	28%	87.0	NM	19.0

Balance Sheet & Other Fin. Data (Million $)

	1994	1993	1992	1991	1990	1989
Cash	139	132	124	59.0	138	189
Curr. Assets	1,698	1,571	1,533	1,496	1,585	1,534
Total Assets	2,677	2,542	2,484	2,486	2,625	2,558
Curr. Liab.	805	778	764	853	1,194	1,238
LT Debt	662	612	613	563	301	315
Common Eqty.	1,188	1,141	1,068	1,028	1,083	947
Total Cap.	1,872	1,764	1,719	1,633	1,431	1,320
Cap. Exp.	135	149	122	133	193	110
Cash Flow	268	261	252	204	314	232

Ratio Analysis

	1994	1993	1992	1991	1990	1989
Curr. Ratio	2.1	2.0	2.0	1.8	1.3	1.2
% LT Debt of Cap.	35.3	34.7	35.6	34.5	21.0	23.8
% Net Inc.of Revs.	3.7	3.6	2.9	0.6	4.3	5.2
% Ret. on Assets	4.7	4.4	3.5	0.8	5.0	5.5
% Ret. on Equity	10.5	10.0	8.3	1.9	12.7	12.1

Dividend Data —Dividends have been paid since 1941. A dividend reinvestment plan is available. A "poison pill" stock purchase right was adopted in 1986.

Amt. of Div. $	Date Decl.	Ex-Div. Date	Stock of Record	Payment Date
Stk	—	Oct. 11	Oct. 07	Oct. 07 '94
0.310	Oct. 28	Nov. 14	Nov. 18	Dec. 02 '94
0.310	Feb. 24	Mar. 01	Mar. 07	Mar. 17 '95
0.310	Apr. 28	May. 23	May. 30	Jun. 09 '95
0.340	Aug. 25	Sep. 01	Sep. 06	Sep. 15 '95

Data as orig. reptd.; bef. results of disc. opers. and/or spec. items. Per share data adj. for stk. divs. as of ex-div. date.
E-Estimated. NA-Not Available. NM-Not Meaningful. NR-Not Ranked.

Office—1025 West NASA Blvd., Melbourne, FL 32919. **Tel**—(407) 727-9100. **Chrmn & CEO**—J. T. Hartley. **Pres & COO**—P. W. Farmer. **SVP-CFO**—B. R. Roub. **VP-Secy**—R. L. Ballantyne. **Investor Contact**—Jim Burke. **Dirs**—R. Cizik, L. E. Coleman, R. D. DeNunzio, J. L. Dionne, P. W. Farmer, C. J. Grayson, Jr., J. T. Hartley, K. Katen, W. F. Raab, A. Trowbridge. **Transfer Agent & Registrar**—Society National Bank, Cleveland. **Incorporated** in Delaware in 1926. **Empl**-28,200. **S&P Analyst:** Paul H. Valentine, CFA

Hasbro Inc.

ASE Symbol **HAS**
In S&P 500

20-OCT-95

Industry:
Leisure/Amusement

Summary: Hasbro, one of the world's largest toy companies, has a broadly diversified line sold under the Kenner, Milton Bradley, Parker Brothers and Playskool brand names.

S&P Opinion: Accumulate (★★★★)

Recent Price • 30¾
52 Wk Range • 35¼-27⅞

Yield • 1.1%
12-Mo. P/E • 17.4

Earnings vs. Previous Year
▲=Up ▼=Down ▶=No Change

Quantitative Evaluations

Outlook
(1 Lowest—5 Highest)
• **3⁻**

Fair Value
• **30**

Risk
• **Low**

Earn./Div. Rank
• **B+**

Technical Eval.
• **Bullish** since 7/95

Rel. Strength Rank
(1 Lowest—99 Highest)
• **24**

Insider Activity
• **NA**

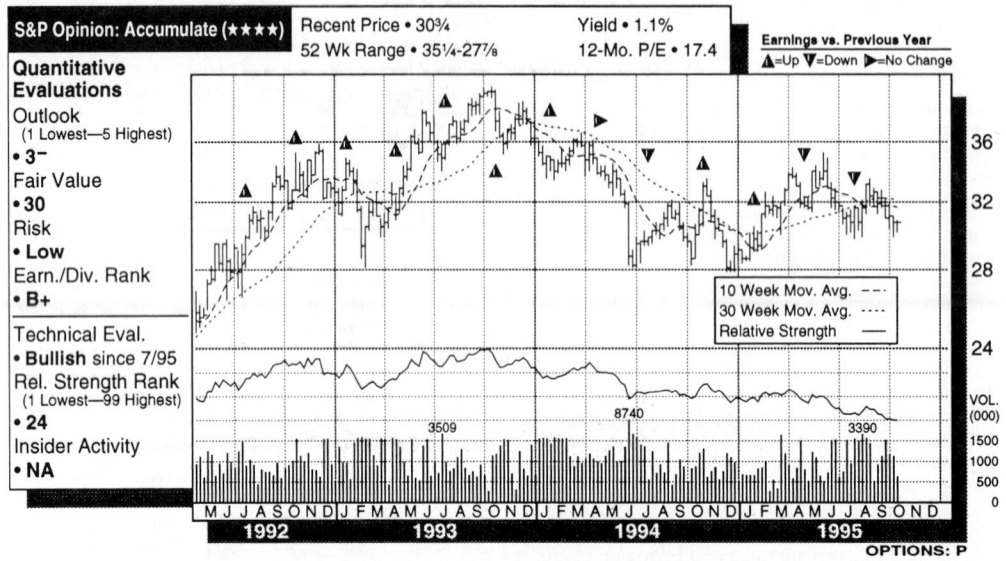

10 Week Mov. Avg. ---
30 Week Mov. Avg. ·····
Relative Strength —

VOL. (000)

3509   8740   3390

1500
1000
500
0

M J J A S O N D J F M A M J J A S O N D J F M A M J J A S O N D J F M A M J J A S O N D
1992   1993   1994   1995

OPTIONS: P

Overview - 20-OCT-95

Sales are projected to advance 12% in 1996, as they benefit from a rejuvenated product line that is the first product line created since the restructuring of the domestic toy group. The company will continue to implement its intensive brand management strategies not only on its classic product lines, but also on new properties based on licenses. Sales are also likely to be augmented by acquisitions. International revenues should grow as the company further penetrates those markets. Margins should expand as the full benefits of a consolidation of manufacturing facilities is realized and in the absence of a $31.0 million ($0.22 a share) charge for the abandonment of efforts to develop a virtual reality game system.

Valuation - 19-OCT-95

Shares of this leading toy and game maker have languished recently following several disappointing quarters and caution about the third quarter earnings outlook. While they are likely to trade in a narrow range in the last two months during the seasonally weak period for toy stocks, they represent excellent longer-term value. Hasbro has leading positions in board games, pre-school toys and other market segments that should allow it to achieve substantial earnings progress in the years ahead. A more responsive management structure and an active acquisition program also bodes well. The multiple of these shares on 1996's estimated earnings is modest for a leading consumer products company.

Key Stock Statistics

S&P EPS Est. 1995	1.93	Tang. Bk. Value/Share	6.44
P/E on S&P Est. 1995	15.9	Beta	1.32
S&P EPS Est. 1996	2.55	Shareholders	5,000
Dividend Rate/Share	0.32	Market cap. (B)	$ 2.6
Shs. outstg. (M)	87.8	Inst. holdings	68%
Avg. daily vol. (M)	0.257	Insider holdings	NA

Value of $10,000 invested 5 years ago: $ 25,838

Fiscal Year Ending Dec. 31

	1995	% Change	1994	% Change	1993	% Change
Revenues (Million $)						
1Q	526.5	8%	489.1	NM	487.0	8%
2Q	481.9	8%	444.3	-14%	515.5	6%
3Q	—	—	796.2	-2%	812.4	5%
4Q	—	—	940.6	NM	932.2	12%
Yr.	—	—	2,670	-3%	2,747	8%
Income (Million $)						
1Q	21.68	-19%	26.72	NM	26.58	14%
2Q	-14.89	NM	1.63	-94%	27.15	20%
3Q	—	—	75.15	NM	75.55	12%
4Q	—	—	75.81	7%	70.73	8%
Yr.	—	—	179.3	-10%	200.0	12%
Earnings Per Share ($)						
1Q	0.25	-17%	0.30	NM	0.30	15%
2Q	-0.17	NM	0.02	-93%	0.30	15%
3Q	E0.75	-12%	0.85	1%	0.84	12%
4Q	E1.10	28%	0.86	10%	0.78	7%
Yr.	E1.93	-4%	2.01	-9%	2.22	10%

Next earnings report expected: early February

Hasbro Inc.

Business Summary - 20-OCT-95

Hasbro Inc. is one of the world's largest manufacturers and marketers of traditional toys.

The Hasbro Toy Group markets all of the company's domestic infant, preschool, activity, boys and girls products. The infant and preschool items are principally marketed under the Playskool brand and are specifically designed for preschool children, toddlers and infants. The preschool line includes such well known products as Lincoln Logs, Tinkertoy, Mr. Potato Head, In-Line Skates, 1-2-3 Bike and the "Busy" line of toys. Playskool's line of infant and juvenile items consists of products for very young children, including the 1-2-3 High Chair, Musical Dream Screen and the Steady Steps line of walkers.

Activity items for both girls and boys include the Fantasic Sticker Maker, Play-Doh and the Easy Bake Oven.

Girls' items include Raggedy Ann and Raggedy Andy, the Littlest Pet Shop and the Baby Check-Up and Baby All Gone dolls.

In boys' toys, the company offers a wide range of products, many of which are tied to entertainment properties, including Batman. Other boys' toys include G.I. Joe, the Tonka line of trucks and vehicles, and the Super Soaker line of water products, which was acquired in 1995.

The Hasbro Game Group is the world's dominant game company and markets its products under the Milton Bradley and Parker Brothers brand names. Its games include Monopoly, Boggle, The Game of Life, Stratego and Candy Land, as well as jigsaw puzzles.

The company conducts its international operations through subsidiaries in more than 25 countries that sell a representative range of the products marketed in the United States together with some items that are sold only internationally. International operations accounted for 43% of sales and 43% of operating income in 1994.

Important Developments

Aug. '95—The company formed a joint venture with DreamWorks SKG, a recently formed motion pciture studio, to produce toys and games emanating from their creative efforts.
Jul. '95—Hasbro said that its second quarter results included a $31.1 million ($0.22 a share) pre-tax charge related to the discontinuance of efforts to develop a virtual reality game system. However, the company noted that revenues of its European units grew 14% in constant currency and 26% after adjusting for the impact of the stronger dollar. Sales of the games group grew more than 21%. Acquisitions also aided comparisons.

Capitalization

Long Term Debt: $149,993,000 (7/95).

Per Share Data ($)

	1994	1993	1992	1991	1990	1989
Tangible Bk. Val.	7.08	7.01	4.76	3.52	7.46	6.21
Cash Flow	2.96	2.95	2.71	1.54	1.48	1.69
Earnings	2.01	2.22	2.01	0.94	1.03	1.04
Dividends	0.27	0.23	0.19	0.15	0.13	0.10
Payout Ratio	13%	10%	9%	16%	12%	10%
Prices - High	36⅝	40⅛	35⅞	27¼	14⅜	16¼
- Low	27⅞	28⅛	23⅛	10⅛	7½	10⅛
P/E Ratio - High	18	18	18	29	14	16
- Low	14	13	12	11	7	10

(Year Ended Dec. 31)

Income Statement Analysis (Million $)

	1994	%Chg	1993	%Chg	1992	%Chg	1991
Revs.	2,670	-3%	2,747	8%	2,541	19%	2,141
Oper. Inc.	394	-9%	432	12%	387	33%	290
Depr.	85.4	31%	65.3	5%	62.1	18%	52.5
Int. Exp.	30.8	3%	29.8	-17%	35.9	-16%	42.6
Pretax Inc.	292	-10%	325	11%	292	100%	146
Eff. Tax Rate	39%	—	39%	—	39%	—	44%
Net Inc.	179	-11%	200	12%	179	119%	81.7

Balance Sheet & Other Fin. Data (Million $)

	1994	1993	1992	1991	1990	1989
Cash	137	186	126	121	289	278
Curr. Assets	1,252	1,301	1,117	1,025	862	807
Total Assets	2,378	2,293	2,083	1,950	1,285	1,246
Curr. Liab.	764	748	701	594	358	384
LT Debt	150	201	206	380	57.0	58.0
Common Eqty.	1,395	1,277	1,106	955	868	802
Total Cap.	1,545	1,477	1,312	1,336	925	860
Cap. Exp.	111	100	90.4	56.0	36.2	50.3
Cash Flow	265	265	241	134	129	150

Ratio Analysis

	1994	1993	1992	1991	1990	1989
Curr. Ratio	1.6	1.7	1.6	1.7	2.4	2.1
% LT Debt of Cap.	9.7	13.6	15.7	28.5	6.2	6.7
% Net Inc.of Revs.	6.7	7.3	7.0	3.8	5.9	6.5
% Ret. on Assets	7.7	9.1	8.8	5.0	7.2	7.4
% Ret. on Equity	13.4	16.7	17.3	8.9	10.9	11.4

Dividend Data —Cash has been paid each year since 1981.

Amt. of Div. $	Date Decl.	Ex-Div. Date	Stock of Record	Payment Date
0.070	Aug. 05	Oct. 31	Nov. 04	Nov. 18 '94
0.070	Dec. 06	Jan. 30	Feb. 03	Feb. 17 '95
0.080	Feb. 21	May. 01	May. 05	May. 19 '95
0.080	May. 11	Aug. 02	Aug. 04	Aug. 18 '95
0.080	Aug. 23	Nov. 01	Nov. 03	Nov. 17 '95

Data as orig. reptd.; bef. results of disc. opers. and/or spec. items. Per share data adj. for stk. divs. as of ex-div. date.
E-Estimated. NA-Not Available. NM-Not Meaningful. NR-Not Ranked.

Office—1027 Newport Ave., P.O. Box 1059, Pawtucket, RI 02862-1059. **Tel**—(401) 431-8697. **Chrmn & CEO**—A. G. Hassenfeld. **Vice Chrmn**—B. J. Alperin. **EVP, CFO & Investor Contact**—John T. O'Neill. **SVP & Secy**—D. M. Robbins. **Dirs**—B. J. Alperin, A. R. Batkin, G. R. Ditomassi, Jr., H. P. Gordon, A. Grass, A. G. Hassenfeld, S. Hassenfeld, M. J. Kravis, M. W. Offit, N. T. Pace, E. J. Rosenwald, Jr., C. Spielvogel, H. Taub, P. R. Tisch, A. J. Vrrecchia, P. Wolfowitz. **Transfer Agent & Registrar**—First National Bank of Boston. **Incorporated** in Rhode Island in 1926. **Empl**-12,500.
S&P Analyst: Paul H. Valentine, CFA

Heinz (H.J.)

NYSE Symbol **HNZ**
In S&P 500

11-SEP-95

Industry:
Food

Summary: H.J. Heinz Co. produces a wide variety of food products worldwide, with major presence in the U.S. in condiments, canned tuna, pet food and frozen potatoes and meals.

S&P Opinion: Accumulate (★★★★)	Recent Price • 43¾	Yield • 3.3%
	52 Wk Range • 47-35½	12-Mo. P/E • 17.8

Quantitative Evaluations

Outlook
(1 Lowest—5 Highest)
• **1+**

Fair Value
• **37⅛**

Risk
• **Low**

Earn./Div. Rank
• **A+**

Technical Eval.
• **Bearish** since 8/94

Rel. Strength Rank
(1 Lowest—99 Highest)
• **39**

Insider Activity
• **Unfavorable**

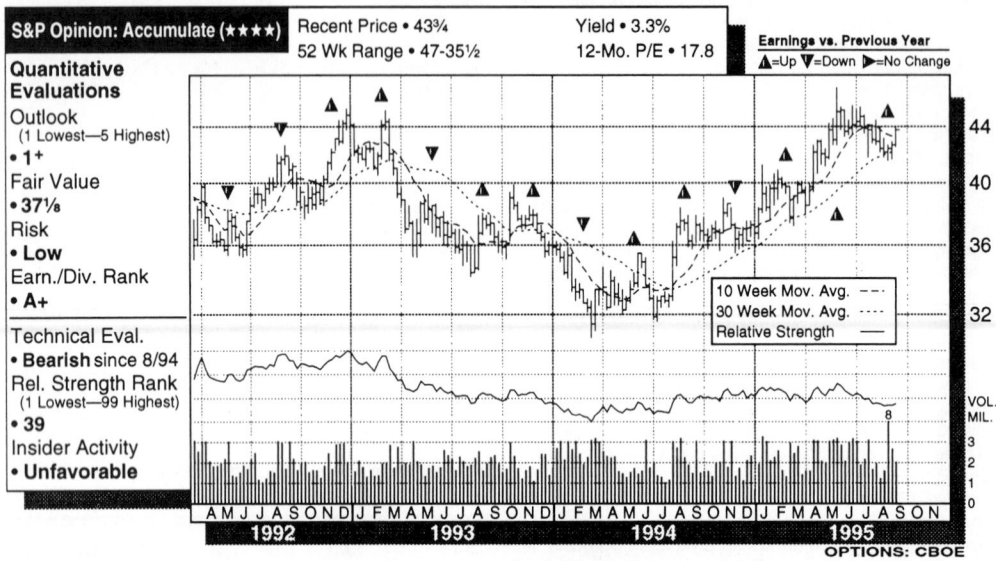

Earnings vs. Previous Year
▲=Up ▼=Down ▶=No Change

10 Week Mov. Avg. ----
30 Week Mov. Avg. ·····
Relative Strength ——

OPTIONS: CBOE

Overview - 11-SEP-95

Sales are expected to advance by about 15% in fiscal 1995-96, driven primarily by contributions from recent acquisitions, and by unit volume growth for core products. Gross margins should benefit in the near-term from growing synergies realized from the recent acquisitions, as well as from other cost saving initiatives. Operating profitability, however, may be pressured by the greater acquisition-related goodwill charges, and by heavier marketing spending behind new and existing products. Current unfavorable net interest expense comparisons will likely ease as acquisition-related debt is repaid. Assuming only modest share repurchases, earnings per share (from continuing operations) are expected to grow by about 11% to 14% annually through fiscal 1996-97.

Valuation - 11-SEP-95

Given our outlook of fairly predictable 11% to 14% annual earnings per share growth through fiscal 1996-97, we view these low-risk shares as attractive for accumulation at current levels. We expect that recent management actions (such as restructuring, acquisitions and divestments) taken to build on core businesses position the company well for both sustainable top-line and bottom-line growth ahead. Also, weakened competition facing HNZ's Star-Kist and Weight Watchers International businesses should also bolster near-term gains. Although the shares have recovered sharply from early-1994 levels, we anticipate that the company's projected earnings momentum will push the shares even higher in coming months.

Key Stock Statistics

S&P EPS Est. 1996	2.70	Tang. Bk. Value/Share	0.52
P/E on S&P Est. 1996	16.2	Beta	0.78
S&P EPS Est. 1997	3.00	Shareholders	59,400
Dividend Rate/Share	1.44	Market cap. (B)	$ 10.7
Shs. outstg. (M)	243.5	Inst. holdings	63%
Avg. daily vol. (M)	0.729	Insider holdings	NA

Value of $10,000 invested 5 years ago: $ 14,798

Fiscal Year Ending Apr. 30

	1996	% Change	1995	% Change	1994	% Change
Revenues (Million $)						
1Q	2,094	21%	1,736	10%	1,583	1%
2Q	—	—	1,975	9%	1,808	4%
3Q	—	—	1,954	14%	1,710	-3%
4Q	—	—	2,421	24%	1,945	-4%
Yr.	—	—	8,087	15%	7,047	NM
Income (Million $)						
1Q	174.5	13%	154.7	2%	152.2	6%
2Q	—	—	139.6	-28%	193.1	25%
3Q	—	—	138.3	8%	128.6	-21%
4Q	—	—	158.4	23%	129.1	85%
Yr.	—	—	591.0	-2%	602.9	14%
Earnings Per Share ($)						
1Q	0.70	13%	0.62	5%	0.59	7%
2Q	E0.64	14%	0.56	-25%	0.75	25%
3Q	E0.64	14%	0.56	12%	0.50	-19%
4Q	E0.72	13%	0.64	25%	0.51	89%
Yr.	E2.70	13%	2.38	1%	2.35	15%

Next earnings report expected: early December

Business Summary - 11-SEP-95

H.J. Heinz manufactures an extensive line of processed food products throughout the world. Sales and profit contributions by geographic region in fiscal 1994-95:

	Sales	Profits
North America	62%	62%
Europe	23%	24%
Asia/Pacific	12%	11%
Other	3%	3%

Food products include Heinz-brand ketchup, sauces and other condiments (21% of 1994-95 sales); tuna (Star-Kist) and other seafood products (9%); baby food (9%); frozen potato products (Ore-Ida); pet food (9-Lives, Amore, Kozy Kitten cat food, Kibbles N' Bits, Ken-L-Ration, Cycle dog food, Jerky Treats, Meaty Bones dog snacks); lower-calorie products (Weight Watchers frozen entrees and desserts); soup (Chef Francisco); sauces/pastes, condiments and pickles, beans, coated products, pasta, bakery products, chicken, frozen pizza and pizza components, full calorie frozen dinners and entrees (The Budget Gourmet), vegetables, ice cream and ice cream novelties; edible oils, vinegar, margarine/shortening, and juices.

HNZ also operates and franchises weight control classes and operates other related programs and activities through its Weight Watchers International subsidiary.

Important Developments

Sep. '95—HNZ attributed its 21% year to year sales gain in fiscal 1995-96's first quarter to acquisitions (12%), volume gains (5%), favorable foreign currency exchange translations (3%), and price increases (1%). HNZ added that significant volume increases during the quarter occurred in Star-Kist tuna, Ore-Ida frozen potatoes, Heinz baby food, Heinz pasta, Ore-Ida Bagel Bites, and bakery products. Sharply greater net interest expense during the quarter (+80%) was due mainly to higher borrowings resulting from acquisitions and higher short-term interest rates. Separately, management said that the recently-acquired brands, combined with organic growth of HNZ's brands, "will provide the opportunity for double-digit earnings growth in fiscal 1996 and beyond."

Capitalization

Long Term Debt: $2,326,785,000 (5/3/95).
$1.70 Third Cum. Conv. Preferred Stk.: 35,800 shs. ($10 par); ea. conv. into nine com. shs.

Per Share Data ($) (Year Ended Apr. 30)

	1995	1994	1993	1992	1991	1990
Tangible Bk. Val.	0.51	4.00	3.73	4.67	5.88	4.89
Cash Flow	3.64	3.31	2.93	3.19	2.87	2.53
Earnings	2.38	2.35	2.04	2.35	2.13	1.90
Dividends	1.41	1.29	1.17	1.05	0.93	0.81
Payout Ratio	59%	55%	56%	42%	42%	41%
Cal. Yrs.	1994	1993	1992	1991	1990	1989
Prices - High	39	45¼	45½	48⅝	37	35⅞
- Low	30¾	34⅛	35⅛	31½	27½	22½
P/E Ratio - High	16	19	22	20	17	19
- Low	13	15	17	13	13	12

Income Statement Analysis (Million $)

	1995	%Chg	1994	%Chg	1993	%Chg	1992
Revs.	8,087	15%	7,047	NM	7,103	8%	6,582
Oper. Inc.	1,471	24%	1,189	-7%	1,285	17%	1,097
Depr.	315	27%	248	7%	232	9%	212
Int. Exp.	211	42%	149	2%	146	1%	144
Pretax Inc.	938	2%	922	29%	716	-27%	984
Eff. Tax Rate	37%	—	35%	—	26%	—	35%
Net Inc.	591	-2%	603	14%	530	-17%	638

Balance Sheet & Other Fin. Data (Million $)

	1995	1994	1993	1992	1991	1990
Cash	207	142	224	273	314	241
Curr. Assets	2,823	2,292	2,623	2,280	2,120	2,014
Total Assets	8,247	6,381	6,821	5,932	4,935	4,487
Curr. Liab.	2,564	1,692	2,866	2,844	1,430	1,280
LT Debt	2,327	1,727	1,009	178	717	875
Common Eqty.	2,472	2,338	2,321	2,367	2,274	1,886
Total Cap.	5,148	4,314	3,526	2,881	3,337	3,072
Cap. Exp.	342	275	431	331	345	355
Cash Flow	906	850	762	850	761	669

Ratio Analysis

	1995	1994	1993	1992	1991	1990
Curr. Ratio	1.1	1.4	0.9	0.8	1.5	1.6
% LT Debt of Cap.	45.2	40.0	28.6	6.2	21.5	28.5
% Net Inc.of Revs.	7.3	8.6	7.5	9.7	8.5	8.3
% Ret. on Assets	8.1	9.2	8.3	11.9	11.9	12.0
% Ret. on Equity	24.6	26.2	22.6	27.8	27.0	27.7

Dividend Data —Dividends have been paid since 1911. A dividend reinvestment plan is available.

Amt. of Div. $	Date Decl.	Ex-Div. Date	Stock of Record	Payment Date
0.360	Sep. 13	Sep. 19	Sep. 23	Oct. 10 '94
0.360	Dec. 07	Dec. 15	Dec. 21	Jan. 10 '95
0.360	Mar. 08	Mar. 15	Mar. 21	Apr. 10 '95
0.360	Jun. 14	Jun. 22	Jun. 26	Jul. 10 '95

Data as orig. reptd.; bef. results of disc. opers. and/or spec. items. Per share data adj. for stk. divs. as of ex-div. date. E-Estimated. NA-Not Available. NM-Not Meaningful. NR-Not Ranked.

Office—600 Grant St., Pittsburgh, PA 15219. **Tel**—(412) 456-5700. **Chrmn, Pres & CEO**—A. J. F. O'Reilly. **V-Chrmn**—J. J. Bogdanovich. **Treas**—P. F. Renne. **Secy**—B. E. Thomas Jr. **Investor Contact**—John Mazur (412-456-6014). **Dirs**—J. J. Bogdanovich, N. F. Brady, R. M. Cyert, T. S. Foley, E. E. Holiday, S. C. Johnson, W. R. Johnson, D. R. Keough, A. Lippert, L. J. McCabe, A. J. F. O'Reilly, L. Ribolla, H. J. Schmidt, D. W. Sculley, E. B. Sheldon, W. P. Snyder III, W. C. Springer, S. D. Wiley, D. R. Williams. **Transfer Agent & Registrar**—Mellon Bank, Pittsburgh. **Incorporated** in Pennsylvania in 1900. **Empl**-42,200. **S&P Analyst:** Kenneth A. Shea

Helmerich & Payne

NYSE Symbol **HP**
In S&P 500

15-AUG-95 Industry:
Oil and Gas

Summary: Helmerich & Payne is a leading contract driller in the U.S. and in Latin America. HP is also engaged in the production of oil and natural gas.

S&P Opinion: Hold (★★★)	Recent Price • 28%	Yield • 1.8%
	52 Wk Range • 31⅜-24½	12-Mo. P/E • 39.8

Earnings vs. Previous Year
▲=Up ▼=Down ▶=No Change

Quantitative Evaluations

Outlook
(1 Lowest—5 Highest)
• **1+**

Fair Value
• **24⅛**

Risk
• **Low**

Earn./Div. Rank
• **B**

Technical Eval.
• **Bearish** since 5/95

Rel. Strength Rank
(1 Lowest—99 Highest)
• **24**

Insider Activity
• **Neutral**

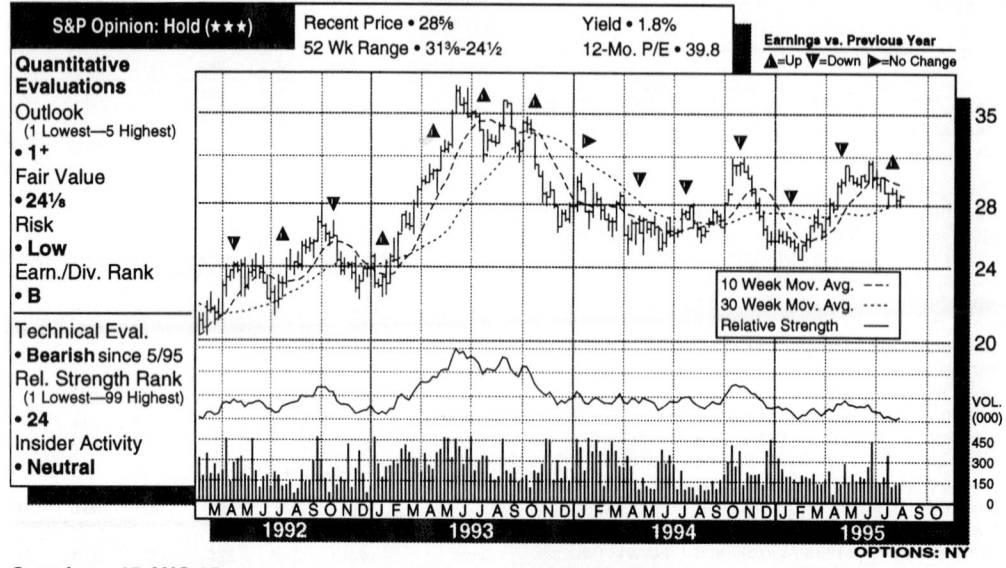

10 Week Mov. Avg. — - —
30 Week Mov. Avg. - - - -
Relative Strength ——

OPTIONS: NY

Overview - 15-AUG-95

Revenues should fall moderately, as a decline in domestic oilfield activity offsets international expansion in rig count. The company is highly leveraged to crude oil markets, and with prices expected remain in their current narrow trading range, earnings comparisons for the year will also be unfavorable. Simultaneously, near-term natural gas price fundamentals look negative, though we believe an upturn in prices by late 1995 is possible, as producers increase storage levels. Growth in chemical segment earnings will continue through 1995, though at a slower pace than in 1994. The decision to retire all remaining long-term debt in fiscal 1995's first quarter will translate into marginal earnings growth, though the company may have to sell a portion of its investment securities portfolio to fund its fiscal 1995 capital expenditures.

Valuation - 15-AUG-95

The shares have been rising on the expectation of a turnaround in natural gas prices, and in view of strong contributions from HP's chemical business. The P/E ratio is well above those of its peers, as investors have focused on expanded drilling activity in Venezuela and Colombia. With dayrates rising, drilling industry fundamentals have now turned the corner after ten years of marginal profitability. Falling natural gas prices had led to a sharp drop in the share price during the final months of 1994. We believe the stock is fairly valued on an earnings and cash flow basis, and expect excess supplies of natural gas to impede the stock's performance through 1995.

Key Stock Statistics

S&P EPS Est. 1995	0.75	Tang. Bk. Value/Share	22.87
P/E on S&P Est. 1995	38.2	Beta	0.57
S&P EPS Est. 1996	1.05	Shareholders	2,100
Dividend Rate/Share	0.50	Market cap. (B)	$0.704
Shs. outstg. (M)	24.7	Inst. holdings	69%
Avg. daily vol. (M)	0.035	Insider holdings	NA

Value of $10,000 invested 5 years ago: $ 9,278

Fiscal Year Ending Sep. 30

	1995	% Change	1994	% Change	1993	% Change
Revenues ()						
1Q	79.94	-3%	82.19	NM	83.00	27%
2Q	79.30	-10%	87.88	5%	83.35	46%
3Q	78.76	NM	78.70	7%	73.61	31%
4Q	—	—	80.23	7%	75.14	23%
Yr.	—	—	329.0	4%	315.1	31%
Income ()						
1Q	4.42	-39%	7.25	NM	7.21	42%
2Q	5.82	-6%	6.16	-15%	7.27	NM
3Q	4.58	-2%	4.66	-5%	4.93	65%
4Q	—	—	2.90	-43%	5.13	NM
Yr.	—	—	20.97	-15%	24.55	126%
Earnings Per Share ()						
1Q	0.18	-40%	0.30	NM	0.30	43%
2Q	0.24	-4%	0.25	-17%	0.30	NM
3Q	0.18	50%	0.12	-40%	0.20	67%
4Q	E0.15	—	0.18	-14%	0.21	NM
Yr.	E0.75	—	0.86	-15%	1.01	124%

Next earnings report expected: NA

Helmerich & Payne

Business Summary - 15-AUG-95

Helmerich & Payne is a diversified energy company involved in contract drilling and oil and gas exploration and production. It also participates in chemicals manufacturing and real estate development, and has equity investments in other publicly held firms. Segment contributions in fiscal 1994 (profits in million $):

	Revs.	Profits
Contract drilling	56%	$20.5
Oil/gas expl. & production	18%	3.2
Energy services	16%	1.5
Real estate	2%	4.5
Chemical	6%	6.0
Other	2%	-5.4

HP's drilling segment has a U.S. fleet of 47 rigs composed of 36 land rigs and 11 offshore rigs. The average U.S. rig utilization rate in fiscal 1994 was 69%, up from 53% in fiscal 1993. International rig utilization averaged 88% in fiscal 1994, versus 68%. Foreign rigs of 29 land units were located primarily in Venezuela, and also in Colombia and Ecuador.

Oil and gas properties are located mostly in Louisiana, Kansas, Texas, Wyoming and Oklahoma. Crude oil output in fiscal 1994 averaged 2,431 barrels per day, up from 2,399 b/d in fiscal 1993. Natural gas produced was 72,953 Mcf per day, versus 78,023 Mcf/d. Oil reserves at September 30, 1994, were 6.7 million barrels, down from 6.9 million bbl. a year earlier. Natural gas reserves were 290.7 Bcf, down from 289.4 Bcf.

The chemical division, Natural Gas Odorizing, Inc. makes warning odorants used in natural and liquefied gas. HP also produces a number of related products used as feedstocks and sulfiding agents.

Helmerich & Payne Properties is one of the largest owners and managers of industrial and commercial real estate in Tulsa, Okla.

Important Developments

Jul. '95—Commenting on its fiscal 1995 third quarter profits, the company said results suffered from significantly lower gas prices. Average prices for natural gas fell 25% versus the prior year. Production volumes of natural gas fell 10%, causing exploration and production segment profits to slide to $19.8 million, from $25.1 million. Earlier in the year, the company ceased operations in both Yemen and Trinidad, a move which offset a slight improvement in Venezuelan and Colombian operations. Contract drilling results suffered from lower gas prices as well, though profits rose to $6.2 million, from $5.9 million. Chemical profits reached $629,000, up from $583,000.

Capitalization

Long Term Debt: None (3/95).

Per Share Data () (Year Ended Sep. 30)

	1994	1993	1992	1991	1990	1989
Tangible Bk. Val.	21.22	20.66	20.07	20.06	19.58	18.34
Cash Flow	3.33	3.17	2.50	2.66	3.84	2.73
Earnings	0.86	1.01	0.45	0.88	1.97	0.94
Dividends	0.49	0.48	0.46	0.46	0.44	0.42
Payout Ratio	56%	48%	103%	53%	23%	45%
Prices - High	31⅜	37½	27⅞	29¼	37¾	34½
- Low	24¾	22¼	19⅛	18	24	20⅜
P/E Ratio - High	36	37	62	33	19	37
- Low	29	22	43	20	12	22

Income Statement Analysis ()

	1994	%Chg	1993	%Chg	1992	%Chg	1991
Revs.	323	6%	306	33%	230	21%	190
Oper. Inc.	84.8	-2%	86.8	34%	65.0	18%	55.0
Depr.	60.4	15%	52.6	6%	49.6	15%	43.1
Int. Exp.	0.4	-58%	0.9	55%	0.6	50%	0.4
Pretax Inc.	31.2	-26%	41.9	110%	20.0	-41%	34.0
Eff. Tax Rate	33%	—	41%	—	44%	—	37%
Net Inc.	21.0	-15%	24.6	128%	10.8	-49%	21.2

Balance Sheet & Other Fin. Data ()

	1994	1993	1992	1991	1990	1989
Cash	38.0	71.0	51.0	70.0	134	121
Curr. Assets	123	150	133	142	201	168
Total Assets	625	611	586	575	583	591
Curr. Liab.	46.7	46.4	35.9	34.0	53.9	53.9
LT Debt	Nil	3.6	8.0	6.0	6.0	49.0
Common Eqty.	524	509	493	491	479	443
Total Cap.	569	557	541	539	526	535
Cap. Exp.	103	50.6	81.0	99	41.0	56.0
Cash Flow	81.4	77.1	60.5	64.0	93.0	66.0

Ratio Analysis

	1994	1993	1992	1991	1990	1989
Curr. Ratio	2.6	3.2	3.7	4.2	3.7	3.1
% LT Debt of Cap.	Nil	0.6	1.5	1.1	1.1	9.2
% Net Inc.of Revs.	6.5	8.0	4.7	11.2	23.9	15.1
% Ret. on Assets	3.4	4.1	1.9	3.7	8.0	3.9
% Ret. on Equity	4.1	4.9	2.2	4.4	10.2	5.2

Dividend Data (Dividends have been paid since 1959. A "poison pill" stock purchase right was adopted in 1986.)

Amt. of Div. $	Date Decl.	Ex-Div. Date	Stock of Record	Payment Date
0.125	Sep. 07	Nov. 08	Nov. 15	Dec. 01 '94
0.125	Dec. 07	Feb. 09	Feb. 15	Mar. 01 '95
0.125	Mar. 01	May. 09	May. 15	Jun. 01 '95
0.125	Jun. 07	Aug. 11	Aug. 15	Sep. 01 '95

Data as orig. reptd.; bef. results of disc. opers. and/or spec. items. Per share data adj. for stk. divs. as of ex-div. date. E-Estimated. NA-Not Available. NM-Not Meaningful. NR-Not Ranked.

Office—Utica at 21st St., Tulsa, OK 74114. **Tel**—(918) 742-5531. **Chrmn**—W. H. Helmerich III. **Pres & CEO**—H. Helmerich. **VP-Secy**—S. R. Mackey. **VP-Fin & Investor Contact**—D. E. Fears. **Dirs**—W. L. Armstrong, G. A. Cox, G. S. Dotson, C. W. Flint Jr., H. Helmerich, W. H. Helmerich III, G. A. Schaefer, H. W. Todd, J. D. Zeglis. **Transfer Agent & Registrar**—Liberty National Bank and Trust Co. of Oklahoma City. **Incorporated** in Delaware in 1940. **Empl**-2,787. **S&P Analyst:** Raymond J. Deacon

Hercules Inc.

NYSE Symbol **HPC**
In S&P 500

20-SEP-95

Industry: Chemicals

Summary: Following the March 1995 sale of its aerospace business to Alliant Techsystems, Hercules is now primarily a producer of specialty chemicals.

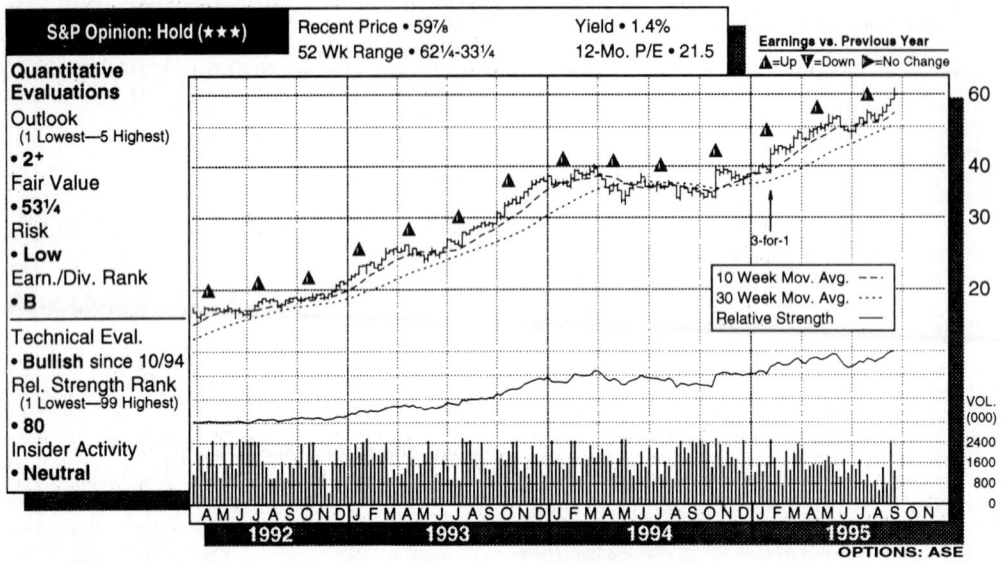

| S&P Opinion: Hold (★★★) | Recent Price • 59⅞ | Yield • 1.4% |
| | 52 Wk Range • 62¼-33¼ | 12-Mo. P/E • 21.5 |

Quantitative Evaluations

Outlook
(1 Lowest—5 Highest)
• **2+**

Fair Value
• **53¼**

Risk
• **Low**

Earn./Div. Rank
• **B**

Technical Eval.
• **Bullish** since 10/94

Rel. Strength Rank
(1 Lowest—99 Highest)
• **80**

Insider Activity
• **Neutral**

Earnings vs. Previous Year
▲=Up ▼=Down ▶=No Change

3-for-1

10 Week Mov. Avg. — — —
30 Week Mov. Avg. - - - -
Relative Strength —

VOL. (000)

OPTIONS: ASE

Overview - 18-SEP-95

Following the March 1995 sale of the company's aerospace business to Alliant Techsystems, annual sales should be about $2.3 billion. We project a continuing advance for chemicals earnings for the rest of 1995 and 1996, as a result of strength in core water-soluble polymers, food gums, resins, paper chemicals and fibers units. Overhead costs have been sharply reduced since early 1995. EPS will benefit from ongoing common stock buybacks (since initiating repurchases in 1991, HPC had acquired 42.4 million shares (as adjusted) through the 1995 second quarter). We believe that the transaction with Alliant Techsystems will be additive to earnings in 1996. Further sales of assets may have meaningful impact on reported earnings.

Valuation - 18-SEP-95

The stock has more than quadrupled since 1991, spurred by cost reductions and divestitures initiated by new management. The sale of the aerospace business in early 1995 nearly completes the company's portfolio changes, and it will now focus on building its core specialty chemical businesses through internal growth and acquisitions. Excess cash flow from operations and possible divestitures will be used to continue a stock repurchase program. Although HPC's outlook is promising, we are neutral on the shares, because of their premium multiple to those of other specialty chemical companies, and would not recommend adding to current holdings.

Key Stock Statistics

S&P EPS Est. 1995	2.80	Tang. Bk. Value/Share	10.26
P/E on S&P Est. 1995	21.4	Beta	1.13
S&P EPS Est. 1996	3.15	Shareholders	19,200
Dividend Rate/Share	0.84	Market cap. (B)	$ 6.7
Shs. outstg. (M)	111.5	Inst. holdings	78%
Avg. daily vol. (M)	0.334	Insider holdings	NA

Value of $10,000 invested 5 years ago: $ 55,807

Fiscal Year Ending Dec. 31

	1995	% Change	1994	% Change	1993	% Change
Revenues (Million $)						
1Q	693.0	2%	680.0	1%	672.0	-10%
2Q	614.3	-13%	706.0	NM	710.7	NM
3Q	—	—	681.0	NM	676.0	-5%
4Q	—	—	754.1	6%	714.7	3%
Yr.	—	—	2,821	2%	2,773	-3%
Income (Million $)						
1Q	89.39	71%	52.34	19%	43.88	19%
2Q	79.10	22%	64.65	18%	54.74	27%
3Q	—	—	66.03	28%	51.50	12%
4Q	—	—	91.14	56%	58.28	39%
Yr.	—	—	274.2	32%	208.4	24%
Earnings Per Share ($)						
1Q	0.76	78%	0.43	27%	0.34	28%
2Q	0.70	30%	0.54	29%	0.42	35%
3Q	E0.69	25%	0.55	36%	0.40	19%
4Q	E0.65	-16%	0.77	67%	0.46	45%
Yr.	E2.80	22%	2.29	41%	1.62	32%

Next earnings report expected: late October

Hercules Inc.

Business Summary - 19-SEP-95

Following the sale of its aerospace business, Hercules is primarily a producer of specialty chemicals. Industry segment contributions in 1994 (profits in millions) were:

	Sales	Profits
Chemical specialties	38%	$197
Food & functional products	34%	148
Aerospace	26%	98
Other	2%	-24

International operations contributed 32% of sales and 40% of profits in 1994.

Specialty chemicals consist of paper chemicals (sizing agents, emulsions, defoamers), resins (rosin and hydrocarbon resins, fatty acids, peroxides and cross-linkers used in adhesives, inks and toners, rubbers, and household products), and polypropylene fibers and yarns for personal care and home furnishings.

Food ingredients include food gums and aroma chemicals used in foods and beverages, and the 50% owned Tastemaker flavors venture. Aqualon water-soluble polymers and coatings are used in paints, adhesives, paper, cosmetics, personal care products, drugs, foods and beverages, inks and oil well drilling. Electronics and printing products includes photoresists and printing plate systems.

In March 1995, HPC sold its aerospace business (solid-propellant rocket motors and components, electronic equipment, ordnance, smokeless powders, and composite structures for the defense, aerospace and sport shooting markets) to Alliant Techsystems, Inc. (ATK), for $252 million and a 27% interest in ATK.

Other operations consisted of Metton liquid molding resins (sold in October 1994) and polypropylene packaging films (sold in April 1994).

Important Developments

Jul. '95—Share earnings in the 1995 first half included a gain of $0.16 from the March 1995 sale of HPC's aerospace businesses (excluding composite materials) to Alliant Techsystems (ATK) for $252 million and 3.86 million ATK common shares (a 27% interest). The businesses sold had profits of $110 million in 1994, on revenues of $657 million. Proceeds were to be used for a stock buyback program. The company has repurchased 42.4 million common shares (as adjusted) since 1991. During 1994, HPC sold its packaging films and liquid molding resins business units for a total of $173 million in cash, and also sold a 22% interest in an Indian investment.

Capitalization

Long Term Debt: $208,188,000 (6/95), incl. $47.1 million conv. into about 3.5 million com. shs.

Per Share Data ($) (Year Ended Dec. 31)

	1994	1993	1992	1991	1990	1989
Tangible Bk. Val.	11.10	11.17	13.38	13.70	13.78	13.59
Cash Flow	3.52	2.94	2.48	1.91	2.00	2.17
Earnings	2.29	1.62	1.23	0.67	0.68	-0.70
Dividends	0.75	0.75	0.75	0.75	0.75	0.75
Payout Ratio	32%	46%	61%	110%	110%	NM
Prices - High	40½	38¼	21¼	16¾	13⅞	17⅜
- Low	32⅛	21⅛	14⅞	10⅝	8½	12¾
P/E Ratio - High	18	24	17	25	20	NM
- Low	14	13	12	16	13	NM

Income Statement Analysis (Million $)

	1994	%Chg	1993	%Chg	1992	%Chg	1991
Revs.	2,813	1%	2,773	-3%	2,865	-2%	2,929
Oper. Inc.	578	2%	564	12%	503	11%	455
Depr.	148	-12%	169	-2%	172	-4%	180
Int. Exp.	36.0	-14%	41.9	-14%	49.0	-29%	69.3
Pretax Inc.	408	34%	305	19%	256	54%	166
Eff. Tax Rate	33%	—	32%	—	35%	—	43%
Net Inc.	274	32%	208	24%	168	77%	95.0

Balance Sheet & Other Fin. Data (Million $)

	1994	1993	1992	1991	1990	1989
Cash	112	155	54.0	179	225	70.0
Curr. Assets	1,152	1,227	1,232	1,411	1,600	1,534
Total Assets	2,941	3,162	3,228	3,467	3,700	3,653
Curr. Liab.	767	884	757	764	908	918
LT Debt	307	317	431	483	601	576
Common Eqty.	1,295	1,368	1,746	1,918	1,942	1,897
Total Cap.	1,731	1,811	2,302	2,555	2,660	2,615
Cap. Exp.	164	149	150	214	272	293
Cash Flow	422	378	340	275	287	300

Ratio Analysis

	1994	1993	1992	1991	1990	1989
Curr. Ratio	1.5	1.4	1.6	1.8	1.8	1.7
% LT Debt of Cap.	17.7	17.5	18.7	18.9	22.6	22.0
% Net Inc.of Revs.	9.7	7.5	5.9	3.2	3.0	NM
% Ret. on Assets	9.2	6.7	5.2	2.7	2.6	NM
% Ret. on Equity	21.1	13.9	9.5	4.9	5.0	NM

Dividend Data —Dividends have been paid since 1913. A dividend reinvestment plan is available. A poison pill stock purchase rights plan was adopted in 1987.

Amt. of Div. $	Date Decl.	Ex-Div. Date	Stock of Record	Payment Date
0.560	Nov. 04	Nov. 28	Dec. 02	Dec. 21 '94
3-for-1	Dec. 08	Jan. 31	Jan. 09	Jan. 30 '95
0.210	Dec. 08	Feb. 27	Mar. 03	Mar. 24 '95
0.210	Apr. 27	May. 26	Jun. 02	Jun. 23 '95
0.210	Jul. 28	Sep. 06	Sep. 08	Sep. 22 '95

Data as orig. reptd.; bef. results of disc. opers. and/or spec. items. Per share data adj. for stk. divs. as of ex-div. date. E-Estimated. NA-Not Available. NM-Not Meaningful. NR-Not Ranked.

Office—Hercules Plaza, Wilmington, DE 19894-0001. **Tel**—(302) 594-5000. **Chrmn, Pres & CEO**—T. L. Gossage. **Secy**—I. J. Floyd. **EVP & CFO**—R. K. Elliott. **Treas**—J. M. King. **VP-Investor Contact**—James R. Rapp. **Dirs**—M. Caspari, R. K. Elliott, R. M. Fairbanks III, T. L. Gossage, E. E. Holiday, R. G. Jahn, G. N. Kelley, R. L. MacDonald, Jr., H. E. McBrayer, P. A. Sneed, L. M. Thomas. **Transfer Agents & Registrars**—Chemical Bank, NYC; Wilmington Trust Co., Wilmington. **Incorporated** in Delaware in 1912. **Empl**-8,500. **S&P Analyst:** Richard O'Reilly, CFA

Hershey Foods

NYSE Symbol **HSY**
In S&P 500

27-SEP-95

Industry: Food

Summary: Hershey is the leading U.S. producer of chocolate and confectionery products. Through its Hershey Pasta Group, it is also the second largest U.S. pasta maker.

S&P Opinion: Accumulate (★★★★)	Recent Price • 63½	Yield • 2.3%
	52 Wk Range • 64¾-44⅛	12-Mo. P/E • 27.6

Quantitative Evaluations

Outlook
(1 Lowest—5 Highest)
• **2+**

Fair Value
• **59**

Risk
• **Low**

Earn./Div. Rank
• **A**

Technical Eval.
• **Neutral** since 9/95

Rel. Strength Rank
(1 Lowest—99 Highest)
• **74**

Insider Activity
• **Neutral**

Earnings vs. Previous Year
▲=Up ▼=Down ▶=No Change

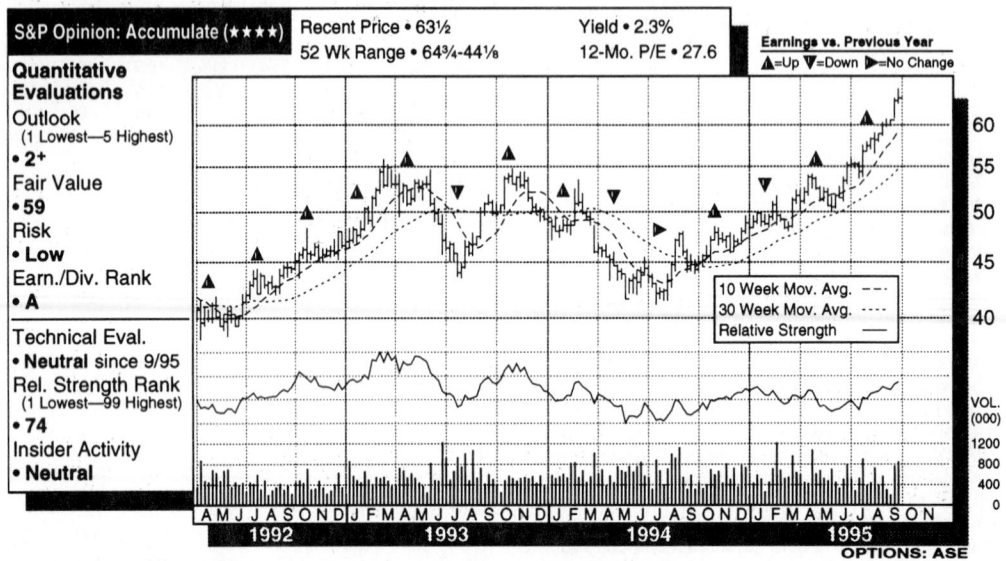

10 Week Mov. Avg. – – –
30 Week Mov. Avg. - - - -
Relative Strength ———

VOL. (000)

OPTIONS: ASE

Overview - 27-SEP-95

Net sales are projected to rise at an approximate 5% to 10% annual pace through 1996, driven primarily by core product volume gains and, to a lesser extent, selected price increases. Near-term cost levels should benefit from 1994's restructuring actions and increased throughput from highly efficient new manufacturing capacity. These benefits, in addition to controlled levels of promotions and advertising for core confectionery brands, should contribute to operating margin expansion. Decreased emphasis on dilutive international expansion and an increasingly aggressive share buyback policy will also contribute to our earnings-per-share growth (before unusual items) forecast of 10% to 14% annually over the next few years.

Valuation - 27-SEP-95

Given our projection of steady, 10% to 14% annual earnings-per-share growth over the next few years, we believe that the shares are attractively valued at current levels. The shares have over the years commanded a premium to the S&P 500's P/E multiple (and HSY's EPS growth rate) because of the company's long record of earnings growth, and relatively conservative level of indebtedness. With expectations of a somewhat soft U.S. economy through 1996, these defensive shares should continue to trade at a premium to the market for the foreseeable future. These high-quality, low-risk shares are principally suited for conservative, long-term growth accounts.

Key Stock Statistics

S&P EPS Est. 1995	3.40	Tang. Bk. Value/Share	11.73
P/E on S&P Est. 1995	18.7	Beta	1.15
S&P EPS Est. 1996	3.85	Shareholders	34,300
Dividend Rate/Share	1.44	Market cap. (B)	$ 4.9
Shs. outstg. (M)	77.7	Inst. holdings	33%
Avg. daily vol. (M)	0.111	Insider holdings	NA

Value of $10,000 invested 5 years ago: $ 20,217

Fiscal Year Ending Dec. 31

	1995	% Change	1994	% Change	1993	% Change
Revenues (Million $)						
1Q	867.5	-2%	883.9	-2%	897.8	12%
2Q	722.3	7%	676.0	9%	618.4	NM
3Q	—	—	966.5	3%	935.7	13%
4Q	—	—	1,080	4%	1,036	7%
Yr.	—	—	3,606	3%	3,488	8%
Income (Million $)						
1Q	60.63	14%	53.02	-50%	105.1	78%
2Q	33.32	32%	25.33	-3%	26.03	-25%
3Q	—	—	81.06	10%	73.97	11%
4Q	—	—	24.82	-73%	92.18	12%
Yr.	—	—	184.2	-38%	297.2	23%
Earnings Per Share ($)						
1Q	0.70	15%	0.61	-47%	1.16	78%
2Q	0.38	31%	0.29	NM	0.29	-26%
3Q	E1.05	13%	0.93	13%	0.82	11%
4Q	E1.27	NM	0.29	-72%	1.04	14%
Yr.	E3.40	60%	2.12	-36%	3.31	23%

Next earnings report expected: late October

Hershey Foods

Business Summary - 26-SEP-95

Hershey Foods Corporation, primarily through its Hershey Chocolate U.S.A., Hershey International and Hershey Pasta Group divisions and its Hershey Canada Inc. subsidiary, produces and distributes a broad line of chocolate, confectionery and pasta products.

The company makes chocolate and confectionery products in various packaged forms and markets them under more than 50 brands. Principal chocolate and confectionery products in the U.S. are: Hershey's, Hershey's with almonds and Cookies 'N' Mint bars; Hugs and Kisses (both also with almonds) chocolates; Kit Kat wafer bars; Mr. Goodbar chocolate bars; Reese's Pieces candies; Rolo caramels in milk chocolate; Skor toffee bars; Y&S Twizzlers licorice; and Amazin' Fruit gummy bears fruit candy. Grocery products include Hershey's chocolate chips, cocoa and syrup; and Reese's peanut butter and peanut butter chips. Hershey's chocolate milk is produced and sold under license by about 20 independent dairies throughout the U.S., using a chocolate milk mix manufactured by HSY. The most significant raw material used in the production of the company's chocolate and confectionery products is cocoa beans.

HSY also makes pasta products throughout most of the U.S. and markets its products on a regional basis under several brand names, including San Giorgio, Ronzoni, Skinner, P&R, Light 'n Fluffy and American Beauty.

The company has various international arrangements, the investment in which changes from time to time, but which in the aggregate are not material to HSY.

Important Developments

Aug. '95—HSY purchased 9,049,773 shares (about 10%) of its common stock outstanding from Hershey Trust Co., for approximately $500 million. The Hershey Trust retained 99.4% of all Class B common shares (which carry 10 votes per share), giving the trust 76.1% voting power of both classes of common stock (from 77.1%).

Jul. '95—Sales and operating income in 1995's first half rose 2% and 19%, respectively, against the same period a year earlier. HSY attributed most of the profit gain to manufacturing efficiencies associated with higher sales at Hershey Chocolate North America and Hershey Pasta Group, and continued productivity improvements.

Jan. '95—HSY said new confectionery products, international acquisitions and pasta price increases were primary sources of sales growth for the company in 1994.

Capitalization

Long Term Debt: $154,089,000 (7/2/95).

Class B Stock: 15,242,979 shs. ($1 par); 10 votes each; div. about 10% lower than com.

Milton Hershey School owns 99%.

Per Share Data ($)

(Year Ended Dec. 31)

	1994	1993	1992	1991	1990	1989
Tangible Bk. Val.	11.39	10.72	11.81	10.13	9.16	8.25
Cash Flow	3.60	4.43	3.63	3.24	3.08	2.50
Earnings	2.12	3.31	2.69	2.43	2.39	1.90
Dividends	1.25	1.14	1.03	0.94	0.99	0.74
Payout Ratio	59%	34%	38%	39%	41%	39%
Prices - High	53½	55⅞	48⅜	44½	39⅝	36⅞
- Low	41⅛	43½	38¼	35⅛	28¼	24¾
P/E Ratio - High	25	17	18	18	17	19
- Low	19	13	14	14	12	13

Income Statement Analysis (Million $)

	1994	%Chg	1993	%Chg	1992	%Chg	1991
Revs.	3,606	3%	3,488	8%	3,220	11%	2,899
Oper. Inc.	604	8%	557	9%	513	11%	463
Depr.	129	29%	100	18%	84.4	16%	72.7
Int. Exp.	40.3	15%	34.9	-17%	41.8	5%	39.7
Pretax Inc.	333	-35%	511	27%	401	10%	363
Eff. Tax Rate	45%	—	42%	—	40%	—	40%
Net Inc.	184	-38%	297	22%	243	10%	220

Balance Sheet & Other Fin. Data (Million $)

	1994	1993	1992	1991	1990	1989
Cash	27.0	16.0	203	71.0	27.0	52.0
Curr. Assets	949	889	940	744	662	568
Total Assets	2,891	2,855	2,673	2,342	2,079	1,814
Curr. Liab.	796	814	737	471	341	286
LT Debt	157	166	174	283	273	216
Common Eqty.	1,441	1,412	1,465	1,335	1,244	1,117
Total Cap.	1,792	1,751	1,843	1,790	1,671	1,475
Cap. Exp.	139	212	250	226	179	162
Cash Flow	313	397	327	292	278	226

Ratio Analysis

	1994	1993	1992	1991	1990	1989
Curr. Ratio	1.2	1.1	1.3	1.6	1.9	2.0
% LT Debt of Cap.	8.8	9.5	9.5	15.8	16.4	14.7
% Net Inc.of Revs.	5.1	8.5	7.5	7.6	7.9	7.1
% Ret. on Assets	6.4	10.9	9.7	9.9	11.1	9.6
% Ret. on Equity	13.0	21.0	17.3	17.0	18.3	16.1

Dividend Data

—Dividends have been paid since 1930. A dividend reinvestment plan is available.

Amt. of Div. $	Date Decl.	Ex-Div. Date	Stock of Record	Payment Date
0.325	Nov. 01	Nov. 15	Nov. 21	Dec. 15 '94
0.325	Feb. 07	Feb. 17	Feb. 24	Mar. 15 '95
0.325	Apr. 24	May. 17	May. 23	Jun. 15 '95
0.360	Aug. 01	Aug. 23	Aug. 25	Sep. 15 '95

Data as orig. reptd.; bef. results of disc. opers. and/or spec. items. Per share data adj. for stk. divs. as of ex-div. date. E-Estimated. NA-Not Available. NM-Not Meaningful. NR-Not Ranked.

Office—100 Crystal A Drive, Hershey, PA 17033. **Tel**—(717) 534-6799. **Chrmn & CEO**—K. L. Wolfe. **Pres**—J. P. Viviano. **Sr VP-Fin**—W. F. Christ. **Investor Contact**—James A. Edris. **Dirs**—H. O. Beaver Jr., T. C. Graham, B. Guiton Hill, J. C. Jamison, S. C. Mobley, F. I. Neff, R. J. Pera, J. M. Pietruski, V. A. Sarni, J. P. Viviano, K. L. Wolfe. **Transfer Agent & Registrar**—Chemical Bank, NYC. **Incorporated** in Delaware in 1927. **Empl**-15,600. **S&P Analyst:** Kenneth A. Shea

Hewlett-Packard

STOCK REPORTS

NYSE Symbol **HWP**
In S&P 500

22-AUG-95 **Industry:**
Specialty instruments

Summary: Hewlett-Packard is a leading manufacturer of computer products, including printers, servers, workstations and PCs. The company also features a vast service and support network.

| S&P Opinion: Accumulate (★★★★) | Recent Price • 83½ | Yield • 1.0% |
| | 52 Wk Range • 85⅜-41¾ | 12-Mo. P/E • 19.6 |

Quantitative Evaluations

Outlook
(1 Lowest—5 Highest)
• **4+**

Fair Value
• **83½**

Risk
• **Low**

Earn./Div. Rank
• **A**

Technical Eval.
• **Bearish** since 8/95

Rel. Strength Rank
(1 Lowest—99 Highest)
• **68**

Insider Activity
• **Unfavorable**

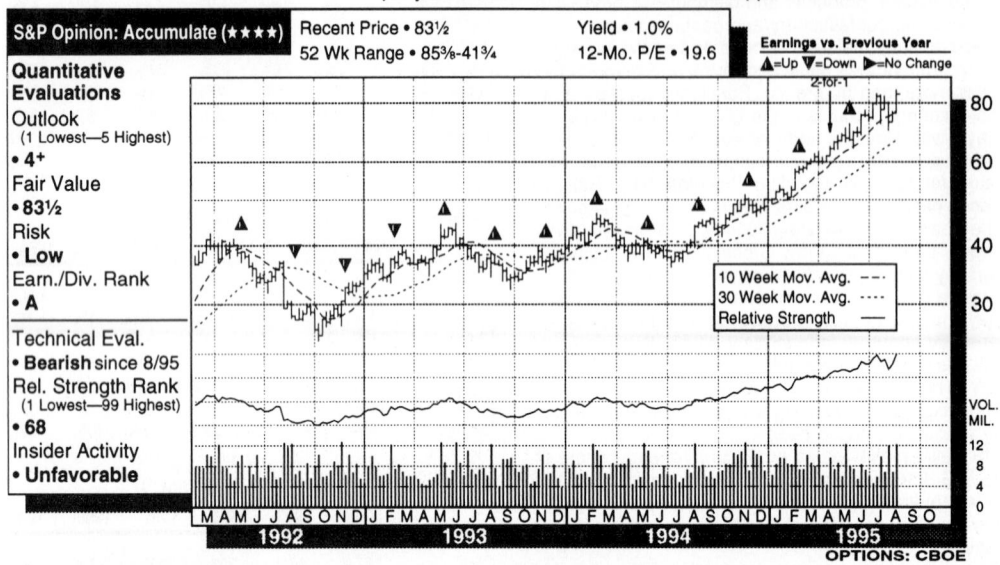

Earnings vs. Previous Year
▲=Up ▼=Down ▶=No Change

10 Week Mov. Avg. – – –
30 Week Mov. Avg. ....
Relative Strength ——

OPTIONS: CBOE

Overview - 22-AUG-95

HWP is coming off is fourth consecutive quarter of explosive EPS growth, fueled by strong demand in all product lines and geographies areas and cost control efforts. We expect a continued strong performance through fiscal 1996, led by demand for HWP's multi-user servers, ink-jet and laser and printers and personal computers. Server sales are benefiting from the ongoing transition to open client-server technology from proprietary systems, while strong consumer and international demand and new product cycles are fueling PC and printer sales. Gross margins are likely to remain under pressure, due to ongoing competition and product mix shifts to more consumer-oriented channels. However, expense control efforts are expected to offset the margin erosion and lead to favorable earnings comparisons.

Valuation - 22-AUG-95

HWP is emerging as the dominant computer vendor in the world, a fact underscored by record results in recent periods. Investors have taken notice of this performance, boosting the stock price from the mid 30's in mid-1994 to near record levels today. We believe HWP will remain a significant force in the computer industry's most visible segments, reflecting its strategy of targeting existing and emerging product categories with powerful offerings at aggressive price points. This competitive positioning and a below market valuation based on our fiscal 1996 estimate, should allow for above average capital appreciation potential for shareholders.

Key Stock Statistics

S&P EPS Est. 1995	4.60	Tang. Bk. Value/Share	21.42
P/E on S&P Est. 1995	18.2	Beta	1.96
S&P EPS Est. 1996	6.05	Shareholders	72,800
Dividend Rate/Share	0.80	Market cap. (B)	$ 40.9
Shs. outstg. (M)	511.5	Inst. holdings	62%
Avg. daily vol. (M)	1.867	Insider holdings	0%

Value of $10,000 invested 5 years ago: $ 37,620

Fiscal Year Ending Oct. 31

	1995	% Change	1994	% Change	1993	% Change
Revenues (Million $)						
1Q	7,304	29%	5,682	24%	4,573	18%
2Q	7,428	19%	6,254	23%	5,096	22%
3Q	7,739	28%	6,053	22%	4,961	23%
4Q	—	—	7,002	23%	5,687	32%
Yr.	—	—	24,991	23%	20,317	24%
Income (Million $)						
1Q	602.0	64%	368.0	41%	261.0	-14%
2Q	577.0	41%	408.0	18%	347.0	7%
3Q	576.0	66%	347.0	28%	271.0	44%
4Q	—	—	476.0	60%	298.0	NM
Yr.	—	—	1,599	36%	1,177	34%
Earnings Per Share ($)						
1Q	1.15	62%	0.71	38%	0.51	-13%
2Q	1.10	41%	0.78	13%	0.69	9%
3Q	1.09	64%	0.66	25%	0.53	41%
4Q	E1.25	37%	0.91	55%	0.59	NM
Yr.	E4.60	50%	3.07	32%	2.33	33%

Next earnings report expected: mid November

STANDARD & POOR'S

STOCK REPORTS

Hewlett-Packard

22-AUG-95

Business Summary - 22-AUG-95

Hewlett-Packard Company produces a broad range of electronic instruments and systems for measurement, analysis and computation. The company derived 23% of its fiscal 1994 revenues from providing service for its equipment, systems and peripherals. Orders originating outside of the U.S. accounted for 54% of total orders in both fiscal 1994 and fiscal 1993.

Key computer products, services and support (79% of fiscal 1994 revenues) include the HP 3000 series, which runs the proprietary MPE operating systems and is sold for business applications; the 9000 line of UNIX-based technical computers, including workstations; and the HP Vectra series of IBM-compatible personal computers. Both the 3000 and 9000 families are based on the company's Precision Architecture reduced instruction set computing (PA-RISC) microprocessor design. The company offers software programming services, network services, distributed systems services and data management services. Peripheral products include printers, such as the HP LaserJet and DeskJet families; plotters and page scanners; video display terminals; and disk and tape drives.

Electronic test and measurement instrumentation, systems and services (11%) include voltmeters and multimeters, counters, oscilloscopes and logic analyzers, signal generators and specialized communications test equipment.

Medical electronic equipment and services (4%) include continuous monitoring systems for critical care patients, medical data management systems and fetal monitors.

Analytical instrumentation and services (3%) include gas and liquid chromatographs, mass spectrometers and spectrophotometers.

Electronic components (3%) include microwave semiconductor and optoelectronic devices sold primarily to original equipment manufacturers.

Important Developments

Jul. '95—HWP unveiled a new line of home-printers that retail for as little as $279. The new models, the DeskJet 600 and 600C printers for PCs and the Desk-Writer 600 for Macintosh computers, can also be upgraded to color at any time with the purchase of a kit.
Jun. '95—The company introduced several new products, including the NetServer LS line of single and multi-processor servers that are powered by the Pentium microprocessor and which feature the industry standard PCI bus; the Vectra XM Series 3 PCs, which feature remote management capabilities along with networking and security features; and the new J-Class of workstations powered by the company's PA-7200 microprocessor.

Capitalization

Long Term Debt: $665,000,000 (7/95).

Per Share Data ($)   (Year Ended Oct. 31)

	1994	1993	1992	1991	1990	1989
Tangible Bk. Val.	18.44	15.60	13.72	14.45	13.03	10.61
Cash Flow	5.00	3.79	3.08	2.62	2.54	2.68
Earnings	3.07	2.33	1.74	1.51	1.53	1.76
Dividends	0.55	0.45	0.36	0.24	0.21	0.18
Payout Ratio	18%	19%	21%	16%	14%	10%
Prices - High	51¼	44⅝	42½	28¾	25¼	30¾
- Low	36	32¼	25⅛	15	12½	20⅛
P/E Ratio - High	17	19	24	19	16	17
- Low	12	14	14	10	8	11

Income Statement Analysis (Million $)

	1994	%Chg	1993	%Chg	1992	%Chg	1991
Revs.	24,991	23%	20,317	24%	16,410	13%	14,494
Oper. Inc.	3,555	36%	2,622	20%	2,183	16%	1,890
Depr.	1,006	35%	743	10%	673	21%	555
Int. Exp.	155	28%	121	26%	96.0	-26%	130
Pretax Inc.	2,423	36%	1,783	35%	1,325	18%	1,127
Eff. Tax Rate	34%	—	34%	—	34%	—	33%
Net Inc.	1,599	36%	1,177	34%	881	17%	755

Balance Sheet & Other Fin. Data (Million $)

	1994	1993	1992	1991	1990	1989
Cash	2,478	1,644	1,035	1,120	1,106	926
Curr. Assets	12,509	10,236	7,679	6,716	6,510	5,731
Total Assets	19,567	16,736	13,700	11,973	11,395	10,075
Curr. Liab.	8,230	6,868	5,094	4,063	4,443	3,743
LT Debt	547	667	425	188	139	474
Common Eqty.	9,926	8,511	7,499	7,269	6,363	5,446
Total Cap.	10,473	9,209	7,973	7,700	6,763	6,168
Cap. Exp.	1,257	1,489	1,032	862	955	915
Cash Flow	2,605	1,920	1,554	1,310	1,305	1,264

Ratio Analysis

	1994	1993	1992	1991	1990	1989
Curr. Ratio	1.5	1.5	1.5	1.7	1.5	1.5
% LT Debt of Cap.	5.2	7.2	5.3	2.4	2.1	7.7
% Net Inc.of Revs.	6.4	5.8	5.4	5.2	5.6	7.0
% Ret. on Assets	8.8	7.7	6.9	6.4	6.8	9.4
% Ret. on Equity	17.3	14.7	11.9	10.9	12.4	16.5

Dividend Data —Dividends have been paid since 1965.

Amt. of Div. $	Date Decl.	Ex-Div. Date	Stock of Record	Payment Date
0.300	Nov. 18	Dec. 15	Dec. 21	Jan. 11 '95
0.300	Jan. 20	Mar. 16	Mar. 22	Apr. 12 '95
2-for-1	Feb. 16	Apr. 17	Mar. 24	Apr. 13 '95
0.200	Feb. 16	Jun. 19	Jun. 21	Jul. 12 '95
0.200	Jul. 21	Sep. 18	Sep. 20	Oct. 11 '95

Data as orig. reptd.; bef. results of disc. opers. and/or spec. items. Per share data adj. for stk. divs. as of ex-div. date. E-Estimated. NA-Not Available. NM-Not Meaningful. NR-Not Ranked.

Office—3000 Hanover St., Palo Alto, CA 94304. **Tel**—(415) 857-1501. **Chrmn, Pres & CEO**—L. E. Platt. **Exec VP-Fin & CFO**—R. P. Wayman. **Secy**—D. C. Nordlund. **Investor Contact**—Steve Beitler. **Dirs**—T. E. Everhart, J. B. Fery, J.-P. G. Gimon, R. A. Hackborn, H. J. Haynes, W. B. Hewlett, S. M. Hufstedler, G. A. Keyworth II, D. M. Lawrence, P. F. Miller Jr., S. P. Orr, D. W. Packard, D. E. Petersen, L. E. Platt, R. P. Wayman. **Transfer Agent & Registrar**—Harris Trust & Savings Bank, Chicago. **Incorporated** in California in 1947. **Empl**-98,600. **S&P Analyst:** John D. Coyle, CFA

457

Hilton Hotels

NYSE Symbol **HLT**
In S&P 500

23-OCT-95

Industry:
Hotels/Motels/Inns

Summary: Hilton owns, manages or franchises about 240 hotels, including five wholly owned casino/hotels in Nevada.

S&P Opinion: Hold (★★★)	Recent Price • 68	Yield • 1.8%
	52 Wk Range • 79¾-57	12-Mo. P/E • 22.3

Earnings vs. Previous Year
▲=Up ▼=Down ▶=No Change

Quantitative Evaluations

Outlook
 (1 Lowest—5 Highest)
 • **3⁻**

Fair Value
 • **66⅞**

Risk
 • **Average**

Earn./Div. Rank
 • **B+**

Technical Eval.
 • **Bullish** since 10/95

Rel. Strength Rank
 (1 Lowest—99 Highest)
 • **63**

Insider Activity
 • **NA**

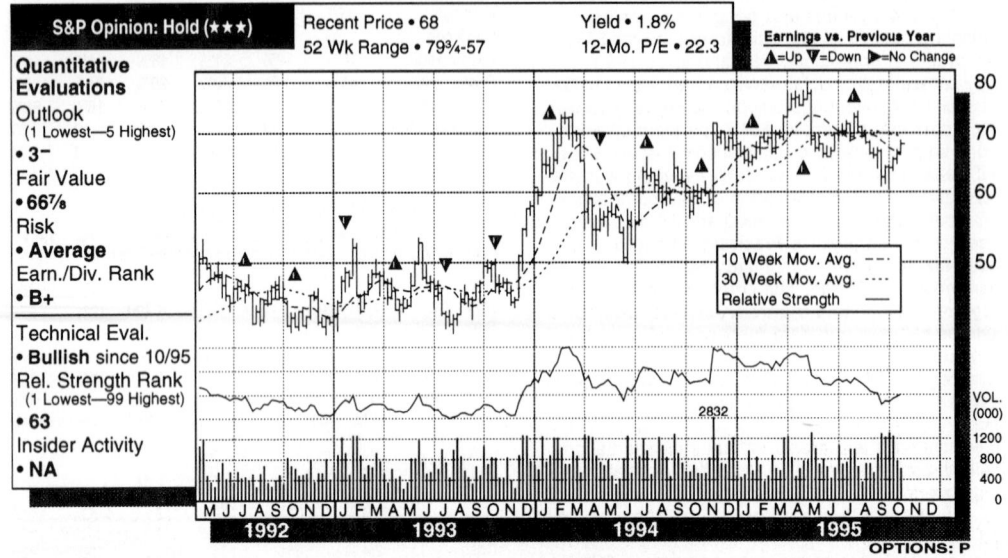

10 Week Mov. Avg. ‒ ‒ ‒
30 Week Mov. Avg. ......
Relative Strength ‒‒‒

VOL. (000)

OPTIONS: P

Overview - 23-OCT-95

In the first half of 1996, we expect HLT to complete a restructuring, whereby ownership of the gaming business is spun off to shareholders. Meanwhile, in 1995, we look for earnings from HLT's non-casino hotel business to rise about 40%, including a modest benefit from a recent accounting adjustment. We expect both occupancy and room rates to be higher at hotels owned or managed by HLT, In the gaming segment, we look for 1995 earnings to be no better than flat, even with a favorable accounting adjustment. Restraining factors include construction projects at the Flamingo Hilton-Las Vegas during the first eight months of the year, and recent profit weakness at HLT's New Orleans casino riverboat, which may be sold. Also, fluctuation in HLT's winning percentage at high-stakes baccarat play (largely at the Las Vegas Hilton) can add to the volatility of quarterly results.

Valuation - 23-OCT-95

Investors were disappointed that HLT did not make more progress in selling part or all of the company. If such a transaction is to occur, we view British company Ladbroke plc (holder of international rights to the Hilton name) as the most logical acquirer of HLT's non-casino hotel business. However, we are not counting on a major portion of HLT being acquired, near term. Based on our 1996 earnings estimate for the company as currently constituted, we consider the stock to be adequately valued, and we do not advise adding to holdings.

Key Stock Statistics

S&P EPS Est. 1995	3.20	Tang. Bk. Value/Share	24.70
P/E on S&P Est. 1995	21.3	Beta	1.04
S&P EPS Est. 1996	3.70	Shareholders	5,600
Dividend Rate/Share	1.20	Market cap. (B)	$ 3.3
Shs. outstg. (M)	48.3	Inst. holdings	44%
Avg. daily vol. (M)	0.261	Insider holdings	NA

Value of $10,000 invested 5 years ago: $ 9,515

Fiscal Year Ending Dec. 31

	1995	% Change	1994	% Change	1993	% Change
Revenues (Million $)						
1Q	381.9	13%	338.8	2%	331.6	20%
2Q	424.2	11%	381.2	10%	345.2	17%
3Q	385.7	1%	380.9	10%	346.7	7%
4Q	—	—	405.3	10%	370.0	10%
Yr.	—	—	1,506	8%	1,394	13%
Income (Million $)						
1Q	32.00	41%	22.70	-2%	23.11	4%
2Q	52.90	56%	33.90	26%	26.80	-17%
3Q	24.80	-8%	27.00	32%	20.50	-10%
4Q	—	—	38.10	18%	32.30	22%
Yr.	—	—	121.7	19%	102.7	-1%
Earnings Per Share ($)						
1Q	0.66	40%	0.47	-2%	0.48	4%
2Q	1.09	56%	0.70	25%	0.56	-18%
3Q	0.51	-9%	0.56	30%	0.43	-10%
4Q	E0.94	19%	0.79	18%	0.67	22%
Yr.	E3.20	27%	2.52	18%	2.14	-1%

Next earnings report expected: mid January

Business Summary - 23-OCT-95

Hilton Hotels Corporation owns and manages hotels throughout the U.S. and franchises the Hilton name to other hotel operators. HLT also has a sizable gaming segment, primarily in Nevada, which accounted for 52% ($159 million) of operating profit in 1994. HLT is planning to spin off the gaming business as a separate publicly owned company.

At year-end 1994, HLT's non-casino hotel business included 18 hotels that it fully owned or leased, about 40 additional hotels that it managed and 162 hotels operated by franchisees. Of the managed properties, HLT had equity interests in about 15. HLT's 219 non-casino properties, which are largely in the U.S., had a total of about 80,372 rooms. Fully owned hotels include the Waldorf-Astoria in New York City, and properties in which HLT has equity interests include the Hilton Hawaiian Village (50%). HLT's international hotel business is operated under the Conrad Hotels name. Hotels bearing the Hilton name outside the U.S. are connected to British company Ladbroke, plc. HLT's hotel segment operating profit totaled $146.2 million in 1994.

HLT gaming properties included five wholly owned casino/hotels in Nevada--two in Las Vegas, two in Reno and one in Laughlin--and two managed facilities in Queensland, Australia, and another in Istanbul, Turkey. HLT owns a minority interest in these three international properties. The five Nevada casino/hotels have about 11,000 rooms and more than 350,000 sq. ft. of gaming space. Also, HLT has a 50% equity interest in a New Orleans riverboat casino project, a one-third interest in a consortium that opened a Windsor, Ontario, casino in May 1994, and a HLT gaming project in Kansas City is expected to open in mid-1996.

Important Developments

Oct. '95—In 1995's third quarter, HLT's profit from its gaming segment declined 55%, year to year, including an adverse impact from a much lower win percentage in baccarat at the Las Vegas Hilton, and profit weakness at HLT's casino riverboat in New Orleans. However, earnings from HLT's non-casino hotel business were up 43%, including strong results from owned properties in New York and Chicago. Meanwhile, HLT is looking to spin off ownership of its gaming business in a tax-free transaction. Subject to various approvals, HLT is seeking to complete the spinoff in early 1996. In 1995's third quarter, unusual charges connected to HLT's proposed restructuring (or related items) were more than offset by a low tax rate. Also, a new HLT gaming project in Kansas City, Mo., estimated to cost $86 million, is expected to open around mid-1996.

Capitalization

Long Term Debt: $1,035,200,000 (6/95).

Per Share Data ($)

(Year Ended Dec. 31)

	1994	1993	1992	1991	1990	1989
Tangible Bk. Val.	23.45	22.11	21.02	20.06	19.44	18.40
Cash Flow	5.14	4.47	4.26	3.96	4.12	3.79
Earnings	2.52	2.14	2.17	1.76	2.34	2.27
Dividends	1.20	1.20	1.20	1.20	1.15	1.00
Payout Ratio	48%	56%	55%	68%	49%	44%
Prices - High	74	61	53¼	49⅞	84⅜	115½
- Low	49¾	41½	39¾	34¼	26⅜	48⅜
P/E Ratio - High	29	29	25	28	36	51
- Low	20	19	18	19	11	21

Income Statement Analysis (Million $)

	1994	%Chg	1993	%Chg	1992	%Chg	1991
Revs.	1,456	7%	1,358	13%	1,203	11%	1,082
Oper. Inc.	354	12%	316	7%	294	18%	249
Depr.	127	13%	112	12%	100	6%	94.0
Int. Exp.	92.7	13%	82.4	15%	71.8	13%	63.3
Pretax Inc.	201	25%	161	1%	159	29%	123
Eff. Tax Rate	39%	—	36%	—	35%	—	31%
Net Inc.	122	18%	103	NM	104	24%	84.0

Balance Sheet & Other Fin. Data (Million $)

	1994	1993	1992	1991	1990	1989
Cash	393	479	511	350	100	445
Curr. Assets	674	727	676	502	285	610
Total Assets	2,926	2,675	2,659	2,187	1,927	2,216
Curr. Liab.	328	278	365	195	241	587
LT Debt	1,252	1,113	1,087	789	527	487
Common Eqty.	1,128	1,057	1,003	953	923	883
Total Cap.	2,504	2,310	2,237	1,912	1,624	1,555
Cap. Exp.	254	157	221	78.0	202	332
Cash Flow	249	215	204	178	198	184

Ratio Analysis

	1994	1993	1992	1991	1990	1989
Curr. Ratio	2.1	2.6	1.9	2.6	1.2	1.0
% LT Debt of Cap.	50.0	48.2	48.6	41.3	32.4	31.3
% Net Inc.of Revs.	8.4	7.6	8.6	7.8	10.3	11.5
% Ret. on Assets	4.3	3.8	4.3	4.1	5.5	5.3
% Ret. on Equity	11.1	10.0	10.6	9.0	12.5	12.9

Dividend Data —Dividends have been paid since 1946.

Amt. of Div. $	Date Decl.	Ex-Div. Date	Stock of Record	Payment Date
0.300	Nov. 17	Dec. 05	Dec. 09	Dec. 23 '94
0.300	Jan. 19	Feb. 27	Mar. 03	Mar. 17 '95
0.300	May. 11	May. 26	Jun. 02	Jun. 16 '95
0.300	Jul. 21	Aug. 30	Sep. 01	Sep. 15 '95

Data as orig. reptd.; bef. results of disc. opers. and/or spec. items. Per share data adj. for stk. divs. as of ex-div. date. E-Estimated. NA-Not Available. NM-Not Meaningful. NR-Not Ranked.

Office—9336 Civic Center Dr., Beverly Hills, CA 90210. Tel—(310) 278-4321. Chrmn & CEO—B. Hilton. Pres & COO—R. C. Avansino Jr. Sr VP-Fin—M. J. Scanlon. Investor Contact—Marc A. Grossman. Dirs—R. C. Avansino Jr., A. S. Crown, G. R. Dillon, B. Hilton, E. M. Hilton, D. H. Huckestein, R. L. Johnson, D. R. Knab, B. V. Lambert, D. F. Tuttle, S. D. Young Jr. Transfer Agent & Registrar—Chemical Bank, NYC. Incorporated in Delaware in 1946. Empl-43,000. S&P Analyst: Tom Graves, CFA

Home Depot

NYSE Symbol **HD**
In S&P 500

10-OCT-95

Industry:
Retail Stores

Summary: This company operates a chain of more than 380 retail warehouse-type stores, selling a wide variety of home improvement products for the do-it-yourself and home remodeling markets.

| S&P Opinion: Accumulate (★★★★) | Recent Price • 38⅞ | Yield • 0.5% |
| | 52 Wk Range • 50-38 | 12-Mo. P/E • 27.2 |

Quantitative Evaluations

Outlook
(1 Lowest—5 Highest)
• **5⁻**

Fair Value
• **48**

Risk
• **Low**

Earn./Div. Rank
• **A**

Technical Eval.
• **Bearish** since 4/95

Rel. Strength Rank
(1 Lowest—99 Highest)
• **25**

Insider Activity
• **Neutral**

Earnings vs. Previous Year
▲=Up ▼=Down ▶=No Change

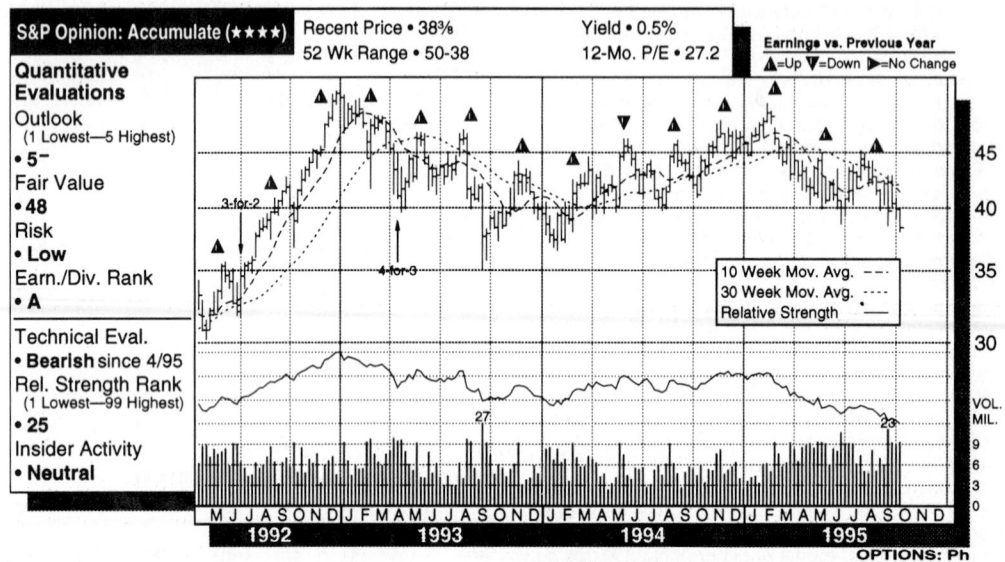

- 10 Week Mov. Avg. – – –
- 30 Week Mov. Avg. - - - -
- Relative Strength —

OPTIONS: Ph

Overview - 10-OCT-95

Although revenue growth has slowed from the robust 30%-plus gains of 1994, we continue to expect increases in the 20-25% range for the remainder of 1995-96. Revenues will continue to be aided by the company's ongoing aggressive expansion program, which is expected to add 84 new stores during the year, including seven in Canada. Same-store sales are expected to be positive, although somewhat restricted by a slowing economy and the cannibalization of existing stores. Margins are likely to trend lower for the rest of 1995-96, due to a shift in sales mix toward less profitable commodity building materials, and higher pre-opening costs. HD's superior fundamentals and well controlled merchandising and operating focus should continue to spur steady revenue and earnings growth.

Valuation - 10-OCT-95

The shares of this leading do-it-yourself home improvement retailer have fallen nearly 25% from their high reached earlier in the year, and were recently languishing near a 52-week low. A slowing economy has curtailed home construction and consequently has resulted in lower industry-wide demand for building materials. Unfavorable weather conditions in certain of the company's key markets also hurt same-store sales comparisons during the first half. With the company's outstanding earnings record and superior fundamentals, we believe HD shares remain attractive as a long-term investment.

Key Stock Statistics

S&P EPS Est. 1996	1.55	Tang. Bk. Value/Share	9.10
P/E on S&P Est. 1996	24.8	Beta	1.04
S&P EPS Est. 1997	1.95	Shareholders	63,100
Dividend Rate/Share	0.20	Market cap. (B)	$ 18.5
Shs. outstg. (M)	476.3	Inst. holdings	55%
Avg. daily vol. (M)	2.759	Insider holdings	NA

Value of $10,000 invested 5 years ago: $ 47,901

Fiscal Year Ending Jan. 31

	1996	% Change	1995	% Change	1994	% Change
Revenues (Million $)						
1Q	3,569	24%	2,872	32%	2,180	33%
2Q	4,152	26%	3,287	34%	2,454	32%
3Q	—	—	3,240	40%	2,317	26%
4Q	—	—	3,077	35%	2,287	26%
Yr.	—	—	12,477	35%	9,239	29%
Income (Million $)						
1Q	157.8	13%	139.7	31%	106.8	34%
2Q	212.9	20%	178.0	32%	134.5	32%
3Q	—	—	140.8	36%	103.4	23%
4Q	—	—	146.0	30%	112.7	16%
Yr.	—	—	604.5	32%	457.4	26%
Earnings Per Share ($)						
1Q	0.34	10%	0.31	-9%	0.34	89%
2Q	0.45	15%	0.39	30%	0.30	30%
3Q	E0.39	26%	0.31	35%	0.23	21%
4Q	E0.37	16%	0.32	28%	0.25	19%
Yr.	E1.55	17%	1.32	31%	1.01	25%

Next earnings report expected: mid November

Business Summary - 10-OCT-95

Home Depot operates retail warehouse-type stores selling a wide assortment of building materials and home improvement products primarily to the do-it-yourself and home remodeling markets. At the end of July 1995, it was operating 362 stores in 28 states, mostly in California, Florida and Texas, and 17 stores in Canada.

Sales by product group in 1994-95 were as follows: plumbing, heating, lighting and electrical supplies (28%); building materials, lumber, and floor and wall coverings (34%); hardware and tools (13%); seasonal and specialty items (15%); and paint and other (11%).

The average store is 103,000 sq. ft. in size, with an additional 20,000 to 28,000 sq. ft. of garden center and storage space. New stores average 102,000 sq. ft. in size. The stores stock about 40,000 to 50,000 product items.

The operating strategy is to provide a broad range of merchandise at competitive prices, utilizing knowledge-able service-oriented personnel and aggressive advertising.

In 1994-95, the company opened 70 new stores, closed one store, and relocated seven existing stores.

In March 1994, HD acquired a 75% interest in Canada's Aikenhead's Home Improvement Warehouse chain from Molson Cos. Ltd., for $160 million. It also has the right to acquire the remaining 25% in six years through a put-call option. Known as Home Depot Canada, the chain operated seven warehouse-style stores in Ontario and opened two new stores in Alberta and one in British Columbia in April 1994. Home Depot Canada opened an additional five stores during 1994-95.

EXPO Design Centers, targeted to the upscale homeowner, offer approximately 125,000-150,000 square feet of selling space, with a focus on upscale interior design products. The company currently operates three EXPO stores, and expects to open its fourth location in the second half of 1995-96.

In October 1994, HD began to test a new prototype store called Home Depot Crossroads, which will carry traditional merchandise, as well as items for farmers and ranchers. The first Crossroads store opened in the second quarter of 1995-96.

Important Developments

Aug. '95—In the second quarter of 1995-96, HD opened 20 new stores, including one in Canada. In addition, the company opened its first CrossRoads store in Quincy, Il. During the remainder of the year, the company expects to open 44 additional stores and relocate one more.

Capitalization

Long Term Debt: $86,564,000 (7/95).

Per Share Data ($)

	1995	1994	1993	1992	1991	1990
Tangible Bk. Val.	7.40	6.22	5.15	3.95	1.87	1.42
Cash Flow	1.54	1.20	0.96	0.73	0.54	0.38
Earnings	1.32	1.01	0.82	0.60	0.45	0.32
Dividends	0.15	0.12	0.08	0.05	0.04	0.02
Payout Ratio	11%	12%	10%	9%	8%	8%
Cal. Yrs.	1994	1993	1992	1991	1990	1989
Prices - High	48¼	50⅞	51½	35⅛	14½	8½
- Low	36½	35	29¾	11⅝	7⅝	4¼
P/E Ratio - High	48	50	63	58	32	27
- Low	36	35	36	19	17	13

Income Statement Analysis (Million $)

	1995	%Chg	1994	%Chg	1993	%Chg	1992
Revs.	12,477	35%	9,239	29%	7,148	39%	5,137
Oper. Inc.	1,117	41%	793	29%	615	42%	434
Depr.	130	51%	85.9	31%	65.6	25%	52.3
Int. Exp.	53.5	20%	44.6	-8%	48.6	102%	24.0
Pretax Inc.	980	33%	737	28%	576	45%	396
Eff. Tax Rate	38%	—	38%	—	37%	—	37%
Net Inc.	605	32%	457	26%	363	46%	249

Balance Sheet & Other Fin. Data (Million $)

	1995	1994	1993	1992	1991	1990
Cash	58.0	431	414	395	137	135
Curr. Assets	2,133	1,967	1,562	1,158	714	566
Total Assets	5,778	4,701	3,932	2,510	1,640	1,118
Curr. Liab.	1,214	973	755	534	413	292
LT Debt	983	882	844	271	531	303
Common Eqty.	3,442	2,814	2,304	1,691	683	512
Total Cap.	4,496	3,724	3,164	1,969	1,222	825
Cap. Exp.	1,101	900	437	432	398	205
Cash Flow	734	543	428	301	196	132

Ratio Analysis

	1995	1994	1993	1992	1991	1990
Curr. Ratio	1.8	2.0	2.1	2.2	1.7	1.9
% LT Debt of Cap.	21.9	23.7	26.7	13.7	43.4	36.7
% Net Inc.of Revs.	4.8	5.0	5.1	4.9	4.3	4.1
% Ret. on Assets	11.5	10.5	11.0	11.0	11.7	12.2
% Ret. on Equity	19.2	17.8	17.8	19.9	27.0	24.8

Dividend Data —Dividends were initiated in 1987. A dividend reinvestment plan is available.

Amt. of Div. $	Date Decl.	Ex-Div. Date	Stock of Record	Payment Date
0.040	Nov. 16	Dec. 01	Dec. 07	Dec. 21 '94
0.040	Feb. 17	Feb. 22	Feb. 28	Mar. 24 '95
0.050	May. 31	Jun. 08	Jun. 12	Jun. 26 '95
0.050	Aug. 18	Sep. 07	Sep. 11	Sep. 25 '95

Data as orig. reptd.; bef. results of disc. opers. and/or spec. items. Per share data adj. for stk. divs. as of ex-div. date. E-Estimated. NA-Not Available. NM-Not Meaningful. NR-Not Ranked.

Office—2727 Paces Ferry Rd., Atlanta, GA 30339. **Tel**—(404) 433-8211. **Chrmn, CEO & Secy**—B. Marcus. **Pres**—A. M. Blank. **EVP & CAO**—R. M. Brill. **CFO**—M. L. Day. **Investor Contact**—L. Fogel. **Dirs**—A. M. Blank, F. Borman, R. M. Brill, B. R. Cox, M. A. Hart III, J. W. Inglis, D. R. Keough, K. G. Langone, B. Marcus, M. F. Wilson. **Transfer Agent & Registrar**—First National Bank of Boston. **Incorporated** in Delaware in 1978. **Empl**-67,000. **S&P Analyst:** Maureen C. Carini

Homestake Mining

NYSE Symbol HM Options on CBOE (Jan-Apr-Jul-Oct) In S&P 500

Price	Range	P–E Ratio	Dividend	Yield	S&P Ranking	Beta
Aug. 16'95	1995					
16⅝	19⅛–14¾	59	0.20	1.2%	B–	–0.19

Summary

This company is one of the world's largest gold producers, with operations in the U.S., Canada and Australia. In August 1995, HM revealed plans to buy the 18.5% publicly-held minority interests of its Australian affiliate for 9,775,000 common shares. Gold output should rise moderately in 1995, reflecting the start up of the Eskay Creek mine in British Columbia.

Current Outlook

Profits for 1995 are estimated at $0.35 a share, versus 1994's $0.57 (including $0.23 of unusual gains).

Dividends are expected to continue at $0.05 quarterly.

Gold volumes should rise moderately as the startup of Eskay Creek in January outweighs lower production at most of HM's other mines. Higher output is seen at the Homestake mine as the installation of a new ventilation shaft permits access to higher grade ores found at deeper levels. Operating costs will rise, reflecting increased accurals for reclamation work and higher costs at Round Mountain due to lower grade ore. Exploration costs will be sharply higher, reflecting increased activity at Ruby Hill in Nevada and near El Hueso in Chile. Prices are expected to be flat. Penalizing comparisons will be a sharply higher tax rate and the absence of 1994's nonrecurring gains.

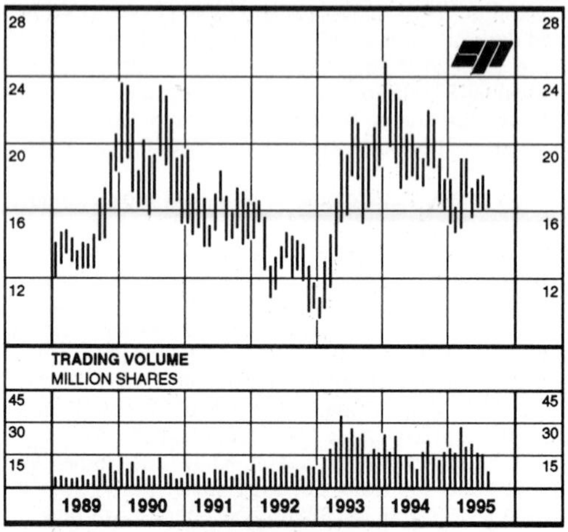

Revenues (Million $)

Quarter:	1995	1994	1993	1992
Mar.	180	172	170	180
Jun.	196	202	187	168
Sep.		167	180	180
Dec.		164	185	156
		705	722	684

Revenues for 1995's first half rose 0.3%, year to year. Net income fell 69% Share earnings were $0.13, versus $0.42.

Common Share Earnings ($)

Quarter:	1995	1994	1993	1992
Mar.	0.05	0.18	0.04	d0.01
Jun.	0.08	0.24	0.08	d0.20
Sep.	E0.10	0.08	0.16	d0.89
Dec.	E0.12	0.07	0.09	d0.20
	E0.35	0.57	0.38	d1.31

Important Developments

Aug. '95— HM revealed plans to swap 9,755,000 HM common shares (or 7%) for the 18.5% publicly held shares in Homestake Gold of Australia (HGAL). HGAL owns the Kalgoorlie mine which contain reserves of 4.7 million ounces of gold.

Jul. '95— HM acquired a 10% stake in Navan Resources plc, an Irish mining firm for $24 million. HM also acquired an option from Navan to buy that firm's 50% stake in the Chelopech gold-copper mine in Bulgaria. The purchase price would be $48 million. Chelopech is estimated to contain 4.5 million ounces of gold and 1.1 billion lbs. of copper. In a separate development, in June HM acquired 5% of Zoloto Mining Ltd. for $1.0 million and took an option for another 62% of that firm for an additional $15 million.

Next earnings report expected in late October.

Per Share Data ($)

Yr. End Dec. 31	1994	1993	[3]1992	1991	1990	1989	[1]1988	1987	1986	1985
Tangible Bk. Val.	**4.27**	3.74	3.40	6.72	8.14	8.15	7.76	7.22	5.73	5.74
Cash Flow	**1.12**	1.14	d0.43	d0.29	0.56	0.88	1.26	2.09	0.84	0.86
Earnings[2]	**0.57**	0.38	d1.31	d1.01	d0.19	0.18	0.65	1.51	0.23	0.24
Dividends	**0.175**	0.100	0.200	0.200	0.200	0.200	0.200	0.125	0.100	0.100
Payout Ratio	**31%**	26%	NM	NM	NM	112%	31%	8%	43%	42%
Prices—High	**24⅞**	22⅞	16⅝	19⅝	23⅝	20⅝	19	24⅛	14⅞	14¼
Low	**16⅛**	9⅝	10	13⅞	15¼	12	12⅛	12⅜	10⅛	10⅛
P/E Ratio—	**44–28**	60–25	NM	NM	NM	NM	29–19	16–8	64–44	60–43

Data as orig. reptd. Adj. for stk. divs. of 100% Nov. 1987. **1.** Refl. merger or acq. **2.** Bef. spec. items of -0.29 in 1991, +0.03 in 1988 & results of disc. ops. of +0.40 in 1990, +0.37 in 1989. **3.** Reflects merger or acqu. and acctg. change. d-Deficit. E-Estimated. NM-Not Meaningful.

Homestake Mining Company

Income Data (Million $)

Year Ended Dec. 31	Revs.	Oper. Inc.	% Oper. Inc. of Revs.	Cap. Exp.	Depr.	Int. Exp.	[4]Net Bef. Taxes	Eff. Tax Rate	[5]Net Inc.	% Net Inc. of Revs.	Cash Flow
1994	659	141	21.4	89	76	10.8	95	8.1%	78	11.8	154
1993	704	168.0	23.9	58	103.0	9.1	61	9.4%	52	7.5	156
[2,3]1992	660	d27.8	NM	63	117.0	16.9	d189	NM	d176	NM	d58
1991	387	d61.7	NM	138	71.3	5.6	d131	NM	[3]d100	NM	d29
[1]1990	482	74.0	15.3	112	74.5	11.8	d14	NM	[3]d19	NM	56
[1]1989	398	54.9	13.8	86	68.4	14.2	26	33.6%	18	4.4	86
[2]1988	346	57.0	16.5	112	59.1	4.1	81	20.6%	63	18.3	122
1987	306	63.1	20.7	39	56.7	1.9	213	31.1%	146	47.9	203
1986	312	50.9	16.3	44	59.4	1.8	26	11.6%	23	7.2	82
1985	298	30.2	10.1	82	61.9	2.0	13	NM	[3]23	7.8	85

Balance Sheet Data (Million $)

Dec. 31	Cash	Assets	Curr. Liab.	Ratio	Total Assets	% Ret. on Assets	Long Term Debt	Common Equity	Total Cap.	% LT Debt of Cap.	% Ret. on Equity
1994	205	343	97	3.5	1,202	6.7	185	589	994	18.6	14.1
1993	135	238	104.0	2.3	1,121	4.6	189.0	515	923	20.5	10.7
1992	71	179	156.0	1.2	1,145	NM	205.0	465	901	22.8	NM
1991	158	265	83.2	3.2	927	NM	48.2	669	770	6.3	NM
1990	312	412	95.8	4.3	1,081	NM	72.4	807	940	7.7	NM
1989	262	388	89.4	4.3	1,094	1.7	93.1	800	972	9.6	2.2
1988	222	307	64.4	4.8	984	6.7	60.3	757	887	6.8	8.7
1987	339	409	73.7	5.5	915	18.2	35.0	703	810	4.3	23.2
1986	104	174	39.4	4.4	693	3.3	35.0	554	627	5.6	4.1
1985	90	209	45.9	4.5	712	3.3	35.0	567	636	5.5	4.1

Data as orig. reptd. 1. Excl. disc. ops. 2. Refl. merger or acq. 3. Refl. acctg. change. 4. Incl. equity in earns. of nonconsol. subs. 5. Bef. spec. items and results of disc. opers. d-Deficit. NM-Not Meaningful. NA-Not Available.

Business Summary

Homestake Mining is one of the world's largest gold producers, with expected 1995 consolidated output of 1.9 million oz. (versus 1994's 1.7 million). Year-end 1994 reserves were 17.9 million oz. (against 18.4 million a year earlier), including 8.0 million in the U.S., 5.3 million in Canada and 4.7 million in Australia. HM also has 51.5 million ounces of silver reserves. The bulk of its production is derived from three gold districts—the Black Hills of South Dakota, the Hemlo camp in Ontario and the Kalgoorlie operations of Western Australia.

The Homestake mine (S.D.) produced 393,900 oz. in 1994. Other U.S. operations include the Mc-Laughlin mine (Calif.), which produced 250,500 oz. in 1994, and 25% of the Round Mountain mine (Nev.), which contributed 105,900 oz. HM's share of 1994 output of the Sante Fe, Marigold and Pinson mines equaled 62,500 oz.

Combined output from HM's 50% of the Williams and David Bell mines and a 25% net profits royalty interest in the Quarter Claim mine, all of the Hemlo district, was 326,500 oz. in 1994. Boundaries of adjacent mines now restrict David Bell from fully replacing reserves. The company has other Canadian operations, including the Nickel Plate mine and an interest in the Snip mine, which produced a total of 133,700 oz. in 1994. HM holds 50.6% of the very-high-grade Eskay Creek, B.C., deposit, which contains reserves of 2.3 million oz. of gold and 102 million oz. of silver. Mine construction was completed in December 1994. HM is forecasting 1995 output of about 170,000 oz. of gold and 7.3 million oz. of silver. Cash costs, including smelters' costs, will be some $185/oz. of gold equivalent.

HM's 82%-owned Homestake Gold of Australia (HGA) owns 50% of the Kalgoorlie operations, which comprise Australia's largest gold mining complex. The Super Pit is the major source of HGA's gold output (352,100 oz. in 1994). HM's El Hueso mine (Chile) contributed 56,400 oz. in 1994; mining ceased in February 1995, but leaching will continue through 1995.

Dividend Data

Dividends have been paid since 1946. A dividend reinvestment plan is available. A "poison pill" stock purchase right was adopted in 1987.

Amt. of Divd. $	Date Decl.	Ex-divd. Date	Stock of Record	Payment Date
0.05	Sep. 22	Oct. 26	Nov. 1	Nov. 15'94
0.05	Jan. 27	Feb. 1	Feb. 7	Feb. 21'95
0.05	Mar. 24	Apr. 19	Apr. 25	May 9'95
0.05	Jul. 28	Aug. 8	Aug. 10	Aug. 24'95

Capitalization

Long Term Debt: $185,000,000 (6/95).

Minority Interest: $90,690,000.

Common Stock: 137,953,936 shs. ($1 par).
Institutions hold about 43%.

Office—650 California St., San Francisco, CA 94108-2788. Tel—(415) 981-8150. Chrmn & CEO—H. M. Conger. Pres & COO—J. E. Thompson. VP-Fin & CFO—G. G. Elam. VP & Secy—W. Kirk. Dirs—M. N. Anderson, R. H. Clark Jr., H. M. Conger, G. R. Durham, D. W. Fuerstenau, H. G. Grundstedt, W. A. Humphrey, R. K. Jaedicke, J. Neerhout Jr., S. T. Peeler, C. A. Rae, B. A. Schepman, J. E. Thompson. Transfer Agent & Registrar—First National Bank of Boston. Incorporated in California in 1877; reincorporated in Delaware in 1984. Empl—1,956.

Honeywell Inc.

NYSE Symbol HON Options on CBOE (Feb-May-Aug-Nov) In S&P 500

Price	Range	P-E Ratio	Dividend	Yield	S&P Ranking	Beta
Aug. 24'95	1995					
42¾	46–30¾	18	1.00	2.3%	B	1.03

Summary

Honeywell is a major manufacturer of automation and control systems for homes, buildings, industry and aerospace. Distribution and/or marketing capabilities extend to 95 countries worldwide. Weakness in the aerospace industry restrained earnings in 1994. However, a recovery in the sector, together with strengthening demand for homes, buildings, and industrial products, should boost 1995 results.

Current Outlook

Earnings for 1995 are estimated at $2.50 a share, up from the $2.15 of 1994.

The dividend is expected to be increased from the current $0.25 quarterly rate.

Sales in 1995 are forecast to rise more than 10% from those of 1994. The largest gains will come in the home and building operation, which is benefiting from the worldwide economic recovery, as well as from acquisitions and a number of new products. Industrial sales should also improve, reflecting strong international demand for automation services and sensor equipment. The aviation segment is expected to achieve robust growth, due to military retrofit programs and the strong business/commuter aircraft market. Margins are projected to widen on higher volumes as well as from cost reduction efforts.

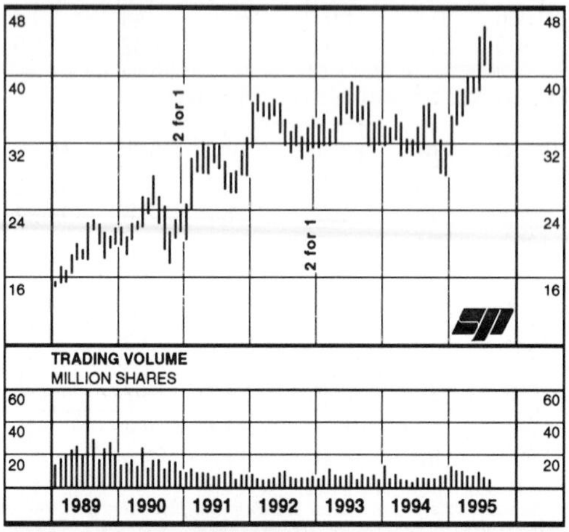

Sales (Million $)

Quarter:	1995	1994	1993	1992
Mar.	1,479	1,348	1,440	1,482
Jun.	1,656	1,464	1,452	1,486
Sep.	---	1,508	1,452	1,550
Dec.	---	1,738	1,620	1,705
	---	6,057	5,963	6,223

Sales in the 26 weeks ended July 2, 1995, rose 11%, year to year. Margins widened and pretax income climbed 15%. After taxes at 34.0%, versus 35.5%, net income advanced 18%, to $0.97 a share, from $0.80.

Common Share Earnings ($)

Quarter:	1995	1994	1993	[1]1992
Mar.	0.43	0.36	0.42	0.82
Jun.	0.54	0.44	0.53	0.58
Sep.	E0.63	0.54	0.60	1.25
Dec.	E0.90	0.81	0.85	0.23
	E2.50	2.15	2.40	2.88

Important Developments

Jul. '95— HON reported that sales were up across all businesses and order momentum was strong in the second quarter of 1995. By segment, revenues from home and building products advanced 18%; sales of industrial products rose 6.7%; and space and aviation sales increased 11%. Profits for the three divisions were up 24%, 9% and 38%, respectively.

Mar. '95— The company acquired a Spain-based company specializing in the installation and maintenance of building management systems. Earlier in the year, Honeywell had announced the completion of several acquisitions across Europe. The combined companies, with annual revenues of over $50 million, will enhance the service offerings of Honeywell Europe's home and building control division.

Next earnings report expected in mid-October.

Per Share Data ($)

Yr. End Dec. 31	1994	1993	1992	1991	1990	1989	[1]1988	1987	[2]1986	1985
Tangible Bk. Val.[3]	**14.57**	13.48	13.10	13.26	11.99	11.99	10.04	13.20	12.17	13.19
Cash Flow	**3.97**	4.15	4.64	4.05	4.01	4.69	d0.89	2.93	1.32	3.39
Earnings[4]	**2.15**	2.40	2.88	2.35	2.45	3.23	d2.56	1.44	0.07	1.51
Dividends	**0.970**	0.908	0.841	0.769	0.703	0.566	0.525	0.507	0.500	0.488
Payout Ratio	**45%**	38%	29%	32%	27%	16%	NM	34%	708%	32%
Prices—High	**36⅞**	39⅜	37 15/16	32¾	28⅛	22⅞	19	22⅝	21	21⅝
Low	**28¼**	31	30 9/16	20½	17¾	14⅞	13⅝	12¼	14⅝	13⅝
P/E Ratio—	**17–13**	16–13	13–10	14–9	11–7	7–5	NM	16–9	NM	14–9

Data as orig. reptd. Adj. for stk. divs. of 100% Dec. 1992, 100% Dec. 1990. **1.** Refl. acctg. change. **2.** Refl. merger or acq. **3.** Incl. intangibles. **4.** Bef. results of disc. opers. of +0.07 in 1990, +0.32 in 1989, -2.28 in 1986, 0.04 in 1985, & spec. item(s) of -1.10 in 1992. E-Estimated. d-Deficit. NM-Not Meaningful.

Income Data (Million $)

Year Ended Dec. 31	Revs.	Oper. Inc.	% Oper. Inc. of Revs.	Cap. Exp.	Depr.	Int. Exp.	[4]Net Bef. Taxes	Eff. Tax Rate	[5]Net Inc.	% Net Inc. of Revs.	Cash Flow
1994	6,057	717	11.8	262	235	76	370	24.6%	279	4.6	514
1993	5,963	766	12.8	232	235	68	479	32.7%	322	5.4	558
1992	6,223	761	12.2	244	243	90	635	37.0%	[2]400	6.4	643
1991	6,193	795	12.8	240	239	89	509	35.0%	331	5.3	570
1990	6,309	787	12.5	252	236	106	516	28.0%	372	5.9	608
[1]1989	6,059	722	11.9	268	248	135	676	18.6%	[2]550	9.1	798
[2]1988	7,148	406	5.7	328	283	254	d201	NM	d435	NM	d152
1987	6,679	766	11.5	312	262	125	412	38.4%	254	3.8	516
[1,3]1986	5,378	511	9.5	548	225	80	40	67.6%	13	0.2	238
1985	6,625	772	11.6	535	344	104	394	30.1%	275	4.2	619

Balance Sheet Data (Million $)

Dec. 31	Cash	Assets	Curr. Liab.	Ratio	Total Assets	% Ret. on Assets	Long Term Debt	Common Equity	Total Cap.	% LT Debt of Cap.	% Ret. on Equity
1994	275	2,649	2,072	1.3	4,886	6.0	502	1,855	2,396	20.9	15.6
1993	256	2,550	1,856	1.4	4,598	6.9	504	1,773	2,305	21.9	18.4
1992	346	2,708	1,969	1.4	4,870	8.4	512	1,790	2,450	20.9	22.2
1991	508	2,699	2,095	1.3	4,807	7.0	640	1,851	2,543	25.2	18.8
1990	368	2,582	2,175	1.2	4,746	7.9	616	1,697	2,349	26.2	21.9
1989	254	2,801	2,416	1.2	5,258	11.0	693	1,918	2,638	26.3	31.2
1988	180	2,764	2,394	1.2	5,089	NM	801	1,731	2,569	31.2	NM
1987	405	2,607	2,096	1.2	5,285	5.0	678	2,245	3,004	22.6	11.8
1986	120	1,987	2,221	0.9	5,139	0.3	585	2,221	2,873	20.4	0.5
1985	497	2,671	1,549	1.2	5,034	5.7	653	2,567	3,417	19.1	11.2

Data as orig. reptd. 1. Excl. disc. op. 2. Refl. acctg. change. 3. Refl. merger or acquis. 4. Incl. equity in earns. of nonconsol. subs. 5. Bef. results of disc. ops. and spec. items. d-Deficit. NM-Not Meaningful.

Business Summary

Honeywell is a major manufacturer of automation and control systems, components, software, products and services for the home, commercial building, industrial and aerospace markets. Contributions by segment in 1994:

	Revs.	Profits
Homes & buildings	44%	45%
Industrial	30%	39%
Space & aviation	24%	16%
Other	2%	Nil

In 1994, international operations contributed 37% of revenues (34% in 1993) and 34% of operating profits (32%).

The homes and buildings segment makes and installs energy management systems, thermostats, fire and security controls and other automatic environmental controls.

The industrial unit provides computer-based systems, sensors and various automation and control products for industrial automation. The division also furnishes services, including product and component testing and instrument maintenance, repair and calibration.

The space and aviation systems group provides control and guidance systems for commercial and military aircraft and space satellite applications.

Other activities include system analysis and design of integrated circuits.

Defense and marine systems operations were spun off to HON shareholders in 1990 as a new company called Alliant Techsystems.

Dividend Data

Dividends have been paid since 1928. A dividend reinvestment plan is available. A "poison pill" stock purchase rights plan was adopted in 1986.

Amt. of Divd. $	Date Decl.	Ex-divd. Date	Stock of Record	Payment Date
0.25	Nov. 14	Nov. 18	Nov. 25	Dec. 12'94
0.25	Feb. 21	Feb. 27	Mar. 3	Mar. 20'95
0.25	Apr. 18	May 22	May 26	Jun. 12'95
0.25	Jul. 18	Aug. 23	Aug. 25	Sep. 11'95

Capitalization

Long Term Debt: $543,900,000 (7/2/94).

Common Stock: 127,059,761 shs. ($1.50 par).
Institutions hold 71%.
Shareholders of record: 31,829 (3/95)

Office—Honeywell Plaza, Minneapolis, MN 55408. **Tel**—(612) 951-1000. **Chrmn & CEO**—M. R. Bonsignore. **Pres & COO**—D. L. Moore. **VP & CFO**—W. M. Hjerpe. **VP & Secy**—S. Ueland, Jr. **Investor Contact**—Mike Robinson (612-951-2122). **Dirs**—A. J. Baciocco, Jr., E. E. Bailey, M. R. Bonsignore, E. H. Clark, Jr., W. H. Donaldson, R. D. Fullerton, J. J. Howard, III, B. Karatz, D. L. Moore, A. B. Rand, S. G. Rothmeier, M. W. Wright. **Transfer Agent & Registrar**—Chemical Bank, NYC. **Incorporated** in Delaware in 1927. **Empl**—50,800.

Information has been obtained from sources believed to be reliable, but its accuracy and completeness are not guaranteed. Joe Victor Shammas

Household International

NYSE Symbol HI Options on ASE (Jan-Apr-Jul-Oct) In S&P 500

Price	Range	P–E Ratio	Dividend	Yield	S&P Ranking	Beta
Oct. 26'95 55	1995 61⅜–35⅞	13	1.36	2.5%	B+	2.17

Summary

Household International is a major provider of consumer finance and banking services and consumer insurance and investment products. Its core business is Household Finance Corp., which is the oldest and largest independent consumer finance company in the U.S. After being constrained for two years by high chargeoffs, earnings were up substantially in 1993 and 1994 on improved results in the bankcard and consumer finance businesses. Further earnings gains are anticipated throughout 1996.

Current Outlook

Earnings for 1995 are estimated at $4.15 a share, up from the $3.52 reported for 1994. An increase to $4.90 is expected for 1996.

In July 1995, the dividend was raised 7.9%, to $0.34 quarterly from $0.31½.

Earnings growth into 1996 should be driven by further gains in managed receivables, a focus on more profitable businesses and expense reduction efforts. Receivables growth is expected to continue in the 8% to 10% range, aided by gains at HFC and in bankcard outstandings. The sale of certain businesses and a restructuring of consumer banking operations should allow the company to concentrate on its most profitable ventures. HI has also taken steps to improve its efficiency ratio, from 60% at the end of 1994 to its target of 55% as of the third quarter of 1995. Credit quality remains strong, with both delinquencies and charge-offs at manageable levels. Overall, earnings are expected to advanced about 18% in 1996.

Review of Operations

Net interest margin in the three months ended September 30, 1995, declined 3.3%, year to year, as strong growth in finance receivables was outweighed by greater funding costs. The provision for credit losses on owned receivables was 8.6% higher, at $188.2 million. Other revenues advanced 24%, led by substantially higher securitization and investment income. Costs and expenses rose 6.6%, and pretax income expanded 33%. After taxes at 35.0%, versus 31.4%, net income climbed 26%. Following preferred dividends, share earnings were $1.11 ($1.10 fully diluted), against $0.90.

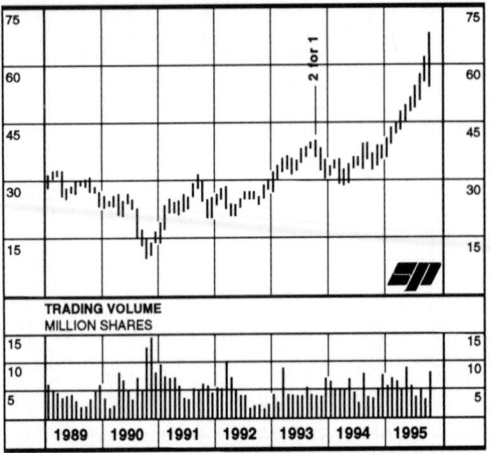

Important Developments

Oct. '95— The company noted that during the third quarter of 1995 it sold consumer banking operations in Ohio and Indiana, resulting in an after-tax gain of about $29 million. Early in the fourth quarter, HI sold its Alexander Life Insurance subsidiary and the bulk of its individual and annuity product lines. The company noted that the businesses sold earned lower returns than available in its consumer lending operations and that the sales would positively impact operating earnings going forward.

Jan. '95— HI sold its Household Financial Services Ltd. (Australia) unit, which offered revolving open-end loans, to the Avco Financial Services subsidiary of Textron Inc. for an undisclosed amount.

Next earnings report expected in late January.

Common Share Earnings ($)

Quarter:	1995	1994	1993	1992
Mar.	0.91	0.74	0.62	0.34
Jun.	1.00	0.81	0.67	0.45
Sep.	1.11	0.90	0.72	0.55
Dec.	E1.15	1.07	0.90	0.63
	E4.15	3.52	2.91	1.97

Per Share Data ($)

Yr. End Dec. 31	1994	1993	1992	1991	1990	1989	1988	1987	1986	1985
Tangible Bk. Val.	15.35	16.78	13.52	12.72	12.55	16.91	16.80	13.71	13.70	13.43
Earnings[1]	3.52	2.91	1.97	1.58	3.03	2.94	2.49	2.79	1.43	1.41
Dividends	1.230	1.170	1.145	1.115	1.085	1.070	1.035	0.965	0.918	0.890
Payout Ratio	35%	40%	58%	71%	36%	36%	42%	35%	64%	63%
Prices—High	39¾	40½	30¼	31½	26⅝	32¾	30½	31¼	26¼	21¹¹⁄₁₆
Low	28½	27	20¾	13¾	9¹¹⁄₁₆	23³⁄₁₆	19¾	16¼	19⁹⁄₁₆	16⅛
P/E Ratio—	11–8	14–9	15–11	20–9	9–3	11–8	12–8	11–6	18–14	15–11

Data as orig. reptd. Adj. for stk. div. of 100% Oct. 1993. 1. Bef. results of disc. opers. of +0.30 in 1989, +0.91 in 1988, +1.27 in 1986, +0.42 in 1985, bef. spec. item(s) of -0.45 in 1986. E-Estimated.

Income Data (Million $)

Year Ended Dec. 31	Total Revs.	Int. Exp.	% Exp./ Op. Revs.	Net Bef. Taxes	Eff. Tax Rate	[1]Net Inc.	% Return On— Revs.	Assets	Equity
1994	4,603	1,243	88.5	528	30.4%	368	8.0	1.1	16.0
1993	4,455	1,150	89.9	451	33.7%	299	6.7	0.9	14.2
1992	4,181	1,420	93.4	278	31.3%	191	4.6	0.6	10.6
1991	4,594	1,887	95.6	200	25.0%	150	3.3	0.5	9.0
1990	4,320	2,026	91.9	349	32.5%	235	5.4	0.8	17.7
1989	3,490	1,708	90.5	333	34.4%	218	6.3	0.9	18.4
1988	2,637	1,219	88.9	292	37.2%	184	7.0	1.0	15.9
1987	3,441	893	NA	341	35.1%	222	6.4	1.5	19.4
1986	2,741	681	NA	162	14.8%	138	5.0	1.2	8.9
1985	3,383	643	NA	232	27.5%	168	5.0	1.6	9.2

Balance Sheet Data (Million $)

Dec. 31	Total Assets	Cash & Secs.	[2]Loans	[2]Loans/ Equity	ST Debt	Capitalization— [4]Debt	[3]Equity	Total	Price Times Book Value HI	LO
1994	34,338	9,546	20,556	9.4–1	4,372	10,274	2,200	13,117	2.6–1.9	
1993	32,961	9,113	19,563	10.5–1	5,642	9,114	2,078	11,531	2.4–1.6	
1992	31,128	7,646	18,961	11.8–1	5,253	9,015	1,608	10,959	2.2–1.5	
1991	29,982	6,710	18,987	[3]14.2–1	4,142	9,595	1,525	11,624	2.5–1.1	
1990	29,455	5,332	22,194	[3]16.6–1	5,681	9,561	1,344	11,374	2.1–0.8	
1989	26,163	4,367	20,017	[3]15.3–1	6,865	7,916	1,194	9,490	1.9–1.4	
1988	21,032	3,359	16,123	[3]13.5–1	5,702	6,560	1,174	7,734	1.8–1.2	
1987	16,986	2,243	13,096	[3]10.4–1	NA	6,265	1,008	7,356	2.3–1.4	
1986	13,207	2,542	9,400	[3]5.8–1	NA	4,872	1,159	6,115	1.9–1.4	
1985	11,929	1,662	7,115	[3]4.0–1	NA	4,176	1,627	5,979	1.6–1.2	

Data as orig. reptd. **1.** Bef. spec. items. **2.** Finance receivables. **3.** Common. **4.** Incl. current portion. NA-Not Available.

Business Summary

Household International Inc. is a major provider of consumer finance and banking services. It also offers consumer insurance and investment products. Total receivables owned of $20.6 billion at 1994 year end, up from $20.5 billion a year earlier, were divided:

	1994	1993
First mortgage	17%	17%
Home equity	13%	14%
Other secured	3%	4%
Bankcard	23%	21%
Merchant participation	13%	13%
Consumer unsecured	25%	21%
Other	6%	10%

Household Finance Corp., the oldest and largest independent consumer finance company in the U.S., had $11.0 billion in receivables owned or serviced at year-end 1994. It provides consumers with a broad range of secured and unsecured lending products for home improvement, education, debt consolidation, travel and leisure. Home equity loans and unsecured lines of credit are areas of significant focus. It services 1.3 million customer accounts through 460 branch offices and two regional processing centers in the U.S.

Household Credit Services is the sixth largest issuer of VISA/Mastercard in the U. S., with 1994 year-end receivables owned or serviced of $10.9 billion and 11.4 million customer accounts.

Household Retail Services ($2.7 billion in receivables), a provider of private label credit cards, is HI's merchant-based retail finance business. Household Bank, f.s.b. ($6.6 billion in deposits at year-end 1994) is a full service consumer bank. During the fourth quarter of 1994, the company discontinued its domestic traditional first mortgage origination business to focus on more profitable ventures.

Dividend Data

Dividends have been paid since 1929. A dividend reinvestment plan is available.

Amt. of Divd. $	Date Decl.	Ex–divd. Date	Stock of Record	Payment Date
0.31½	Dec. 20	Dec. 23	Dec. 30	Jan. 15'95
0.31½	Mar. 14	Mar. 27	Mar. 31	Apr. 15'95
0.31½	May 10	Jun. 28	Jun. 30	Jul. 15'95
0.34	Jul. 11	Sep. 27	Sep. 29	Oct. 15'95

Capitalization

Long Term Debt: $10,803,100,000 (6/95).

Preferred Stock: $320,000,000.

Common Stock: 99,500,000 shs. ($1 par).
Institutions hold approximately 69%.
Shareholders of record: 14,379.

Office—2700 Sanders Rd., Prospect Heights, IL 60070-2799. **Tel**—(708) 564-5000. **Chrmn**—D. C. Clark. **Pres & CEO**—W. F. Aldinger. **SVP-CFO**—D. A. Schoenholz. **Investor Contact**—Michael H. Morgan (708-564-6053). **Dirs**—W. F. Aldinger, D. C. Clark, R. J. Darnall, G. G. Dillon, J. A. Anderson, M. J. Evans, C. F. Freidheim Jr., L. E. Levy, G. A. Lorch, J. D. Nichols, G. P. Osler, J. B. Pitblado, A. E. Rasmussen, S. J. Stewart, L. W. Sullivan, R. C. Tower. **Transfer Agent & Registrar**—Harris Trust and Savings Bank, Chicago. **Incorporated** in Delaware in 1925. **Empl**—15,500.

Stephen R. Biggar

Houston Industries

NYSE Symbol **HOU**

In S&P 500

29-AUG-95

Industry: Utilities-Electric

Summary: This utility holding company owns Houston Lighting & Power Co., the ninth largest utility in the U.S. and invests in nonregulated foreign utilities and power generation projects.

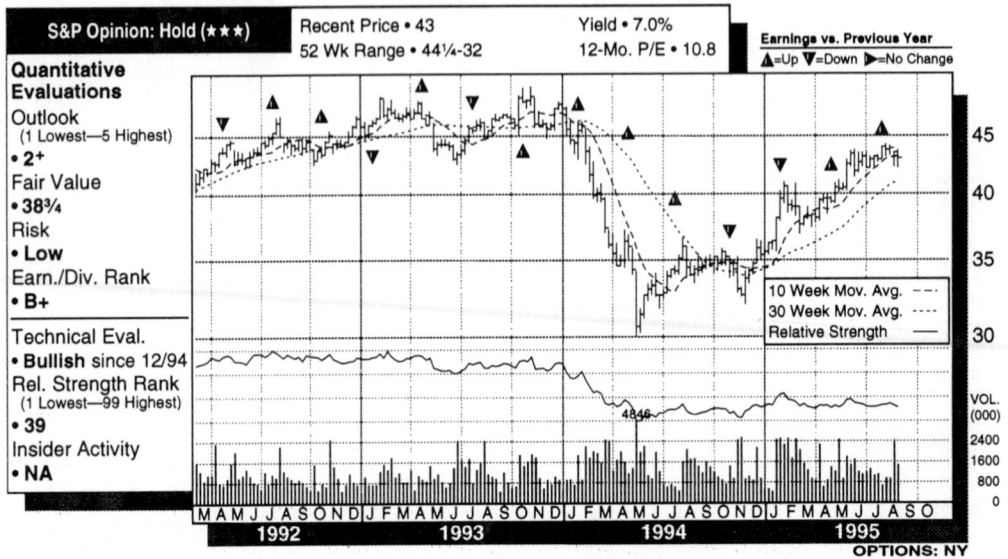

S&P Opinion: Hold (★★★)	Recent Price • 43	Yield • 7.0%	
	52 Wk Range • 44¼-32	12-Mo. P/E • 10.8	

Quantitative Evaluations

Outlook
(1 Lowest—5 Highest)
• **2+**

Fair Value
• **38¾**

Risk
• **Low**

Earn./Div. Rank
• **B+**

Technical Eval.
• **Bullish** since 12/94

Rel. Strength Rank
(1 Lowest—99 Highest)
• **39**

Insider Activity
• **NA**

Earnings vs. Previous Year
▲=Up ▼=Down ▶=No Change

10 Week Mov. Avg. — — —
30 Week Mov. Avg. ········
Relative Strength ———

Overview - 22-AUG-95

Share earnings may rise modestly in 1995, as good growth in residential and industrial kwh sales is weakened by an expected reduction in rate and price discounting to a few large customers. Results should also reflect higher franchise taxes, additional O&M costs related to planned outages at both STP units, and higher amortization and de-commissioning costs under the recent rate agreement. Partially offsetting these negative factors are substantial dividend income and lower interest expense from the sale of KBLCOM Inc. in July, as well as a tax benefit, and the absence of a year earlier $0.38 one-time charge related to the rate proceeding. The estimate for 1995 excludes an expected gain of about $5.30 a share from the sale of KBLCOM.

Valuation - 29-AUG-95

The stock has risen 35% since the beginning of the year as investors viewed positively the sale of KBLCOM. The deal gives HOU a substantial equity position in media giant Time Warner (over 6% if HOU's entire preferred holding is converted), $37 million a year in after-tax dividend income and considerable flexibility in its ability to deal with increasing competition in electric power markets. It also provides it an opportunity to expand utility operations--HOU is rumored to be looking to purchase an electric utility in the UK. We would not expect the market to reward an acquisition near term, but longer term, prospects would be enhanced by such a move.

Key Stock Statistics

S&P EPS Est. 1995	3.40	Tang. Bk. Value/Share	17.81
P/E on S&P Est. 1995	12.6	Beta	0.52
S&P EPS Est. 1996	3.70	Shareholders	66,700
Dividend Rate/Share	3.00	Market cap. (B)	$ 5.6
Shs. outstg. (M)	131.3	Inst. holdings	44%
Avg. daily vol. (M)	0.282	Insider holdings	NA

Value of $10,000 invested 5 years ago: $ 18,293

Fiscal Year Ending Dec. 31

	1995	% Change	1994	% Change	1993	% Change
Revenues (Million $)						
1Q	746.2	-15%	882.0	2%	866.0	-10%
2Q	978.2	-8%	1,067	NM	1,068	-9%
3Q	—	—	1,216	-14%	1,417	NM
4Q	—	—	837.1	-14%	974.0	-9%
Yr.	—	—	4,002	-7%	4,324	-6%
Income (Million $)						
1Q	114.5	198%	38.38	42%	27.06	NM
2Q	133.3	NM	133.8	34%	100.2	-17%
3Q	—	—	236.0	-9%	260.4	9%
4Q	—	—	10.67	-62%	28.36	23%
Yr.	—	—	407.5	-2%	416.0	22%
Earnings Per Share ($)						
1Q	0.93	NM	0.29	38%	0.21	NM
2Q	1.08	6%	1.02	32%	0.77	-17%
3Q	E1.23	-36%	1.92	-4%	2.00	8%
4Q	E0.16	78%	0.09	-59%	0.22	22%
Yr.	E3.40	2%	3.32	4%	3.20	22%

Next earnings report expected: late October

Business Summary - 29-AUG-95

Houston Industries is a holding company whose primary subsidiary, Houston Lighting & Power Co., supplies electricity along the Texas Gulf Coast. Electric operations accounted for 94% of revenues in 1994 and cable television 6%. HOU sold its cable television subsidiary, KBLCOM, in July 1995 to Time Warner, Inc. Electric revenues by customer class in recent years were:

	1994	1993	1992	1991
Residential	40%	39%	38%	40%
Commercial	26%	24%	24%	24%
Industrial	30%	29%	30%	31%
Other	4%	8%	8%	5%

Power requirements in 1994 were derived from gas 34%, coal and lignite 43%, nuclear 7%, and purchased and interchanged 16%. Peak load in 1994 was 11,245 mw and capability totaled 14,386 mw, for a capacity margin of 22%.

HOU and other major parties to a rate case pending before the PUC of Texas reached a settlement agreement in principle in December 1994 that called for HOU to cut utility base rates by $62 million, cut its fuel rate factor by $132 million, refund $145 million of fuel revenues to customers, and also cut base rates by $173 million to reflect the expiration of cogneration firm capacity contracts.

Important Developments

Jul. '95—HOU closed the sale of its cable television subsidiary, KBLCOM Inc. to Time Warner (NYSE: TWX), in a deal valued at roughly $2.4 billion. The sale gives HOU one million shares of TWX common and 11 million shares of TWX convertible preferred (convertible into 22.9 million TWX common shares) that pay a $3.75 a share annual dividend. HOU also received $620 million in cash and will report a $740 million gain on the sale. The gain is about $90 million higher than previously announced due to appreciation in the value of Time Warner common stock since the announcement of the deal.

Jul. '95—The company attributed the 60% increase in share earnings for the 1995 first half to $2.00 from $1.22 a year earlier primarily to the recognition of a tax benefit from its sale of KBLCOM, which added $0.73 a share to 1995 results. The credit was partly offset by a $36.8 million charge for the estimated effects of its pending rate case setlement. Kilowatt hour sales increased 4% in the residential sector and 5% in commercial business.

Capitalization

Long Term Debt: $3,074,653,000 (3/95).
Subsidiary Preferred Stock: $473,255,000.

Per Share Data ($)

(Year Ended Dec. 31)

	1994	1993	1992	1991	1990	1989
Tangible Bk. Val.	17.81	16.23	16.30	17.63	19.06	19.18
Earnings	3.32	3.20	2.63	3.28	2.67	3.32
Dividends	3.00	3.00	2.98	2.96	2.96	2.96
Payout Ratio	90%	94%	113%	90%	111%	89%
Prices - High	47¾	49¾	46⅞	44⅜	37⅛	35⅞
- Low	30	42½	40⅛	34⅝	30⅝	26¾
P/E Ratio - High	14	16	14	14	14	11
- Low	9	13	12	11	11	8

Income Statement Analysis (Million $)

	1994	%Chg	1993	%Chg	1992	%Chg	1991
Revs.	4,002	-7%	4,324	-6%	4,596	3%	4,444
Depr.	484	4%	465	NM	465	7%	435
Maint.	248	-14%	290	13%	257	11%	231
Fxd. Chgs. Cov.	2.5	3%	2.4	14%	2.1	-8%	2.3
Constr. Credits	10.0	43%	7.0	-42%	12.0	-25%	16.0
Eff. Tax Rate	33%	—	34%	—	30%	—	31%
Net Inc.	407	-2%	416	22%	340	-18%	417

Balance Sheet & Other Fin. Data (Million $)

	1994	1993	1992	1991	1990	1989
Gross Prop.	13,018	12,554	12,282	12,018	11,682	11,537
Cap. Exp.	418	333	336	376	358	389
Net Prop.	9,329	9,198	9,190	9,279	9,254	9,433
Capitalization:						
LT Debt	4,223	4,243	4,441	4,869	4,612	4,758
% LT Debt	52	53	54	56	52	53
Pfd.	473	519	558	460	568	568
% Pfd.	5.90	6.50	6.70	5.20	6.40	6.30
Common	3,369	3,274	3,285	3,449	3,647	3,676
% Common	42	41	40	39	41	41
Total Cap.	10,560	10,458	10,529	10,602	10,531	10,659

Ratio Analysis

	1994	1993	1992	1991	1990	1989
Oper. Ratio	80.2	81.7	83.1	81.6	81.4	85.3
% Earn. on Net Prop.	8.6	8.6	8.4	8.8	8.3	5.9
% Ret. on Revs.	10.2	9.6	7.4	9.4	8.1	10.9
% Ret. On Invest.Cap	7.3	8.0	7.4	8.5	7.3	7.5
% Return On Com.Eqty	12.3	12.8	12.8	12.0	9.4	11.7

Dividend Data

—Dividends have been paid since 1922. A dividend reinvestment plan is available.

Amt. of Div. $	Date Decl.	Ex-Div. Date	Stock of Record	Payment Date
0.750	Jun. 01	Aug. 10	Aug. 16	Sep. 10 '94
0.750	Sep. 07	Nov. 09	Nov. 16	Dec. 10 '94
0.750	Dec. 07	Feb. 10	Feb. 16	Mar. 10 '95
0.750	Mar. 01	May. 10	May. 16	Jun. 10 '95
0.750	Jun. 07	Aug. 14	Aug. 16	Sep. 09 '95

Data as orig. reptd.; bef. results of disc opers. and/or spec. items. Per share data adj. for stk. divs. as of ex-div. date. E-Estimated. NA-Not Available. NM-Not Meaningful. NR-Not Ranked.

Office—5 Post Oak Park, 4400 Post Oak Parkway, Houston, TX 77027. **Tel**—(713) 629-3000. **Chrmn & CEO**—D. D. Jordan. **Pres & COO**—R. S. Letbetter. **VP-Treas**—W. A. Cropper. **VP-Secy**—H. R. Kelly. **Investor Contact**—Dan N. Bulla. **Dirs**—M. Carroll, J. T. Cater, R. J. Cruikshank, L. F. Deily, J. M. Hendrie, L. W. Hogan, H. W. Horne, D. D. Jordan, R. S. Letbetter, A. F. Schilt, K. L. Schnitzer Sr., J. T. Trotter, B. Wolfe. **Transfer Agent & Registrar**—Co.'s office. **Incorporated** in Texas in 1906; reincorporated in Texas in 1976. **Empl**-11,498. **S&P Analyst:** Jane Collin

ITT Corp.

NYSE Symbol ITT Options on CBOE (Mar-Jun-Sep-Dec) In S&P 500

	Price	Range	P–E Ratio	Dividend	Yield	S&P Ranking	Beta
	Aug. 9'95	1995					
	118½	121⅞–86⅝	11	1.98	1.7%	B+	1.34

Summary

This conglomerate produces automotive products and electronic components, and engages in hotel and insurance activities. Earnings gains in 1995 will be aided by internal growth, the effects of a 12 million share repurchase, and contributions from an aggressive acquisition plan. In June 1995 ITT announced plans to split into three separate entities (insurance, manufacturing, and hotels/entertainment).

Current Outlook

Excluding realized investment gains or losses and asset sale gains, operating earnings could rise to $9.00 a share in 1995, up from the $6.65 reported for 1994. Earnings could rise to $10.25 in 1996.
A modest increase in the $0.49½ quarterly dividend is likely.

A firming of some rates and the positive effects of a restructuring aid the outlook for insurance in 1995 and beyond. An economic upturn and contributions from acquisitions will aid the hospitality sector's profit outlook. Profit growth in the automotive sector will be aided by increased volume and contributions from an acquisition. Cost cuts and higher sales volume should benefit most other manufacturing operations.

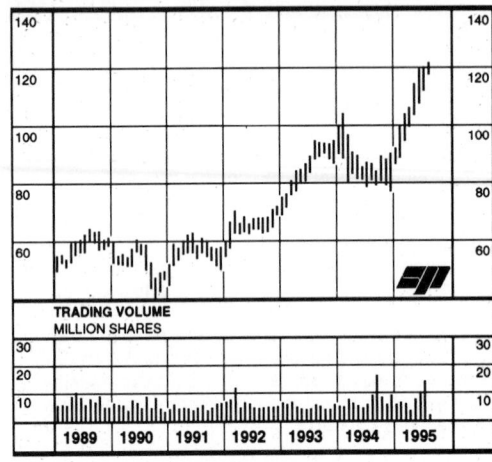

TRADING VOLUME
MILLION SHARES

Sales & Revenues (Billion $)

Quarter:	1995	1994	1993	1992
Mar.	6.54	5.21	5.39	5.09
Jun.	6.95	6.00	5.84	5.36
Sep.		5.67	5.55	5.50
Dec.		6.70	5.98	5.71
		23.62	22.76	21.65

Revenues from continuing operations for the six months ended June 30, 1995 rose 20%, year to year (1994 restated). Aided by a $403 million ($3.76 a share) gain on the sale of assets, net income from continuing operations surged to $791 million from $388 million. Primary share earnings were $7.20 on 10% fewer shares ($6.91 of operating income), versus $3.13 ($2.85); before income from discontinued operations of $0.46, versus $0.61.

Common Share Earnings ($)

Quarter:	1995	1994	1993	1992
Mar.	---	1.39	1.37	1.08
Jun.	¹7.20	1.84	2.15	0.84
Sep.		1.75	2.03	0.94
Dec.		2.12	1.74	d5.33
		7.10	7.29	d2.47

Important Developments

Jun. '95— ITT announced plans to split up into three separate, publicly owned entities by year-end 1995. The three units planned are: ITT Hartford (insurance), ITT Industries, Inc. (automotove, defense, electronics and fluid technology), and new ITT Corp. (ITT Sheraton, Caesars World, Madison Square Garden, ITT World Directories, and ITT Educational Serivvces). ITT shareholders will likely receive one share in each of the three newly created companies for every ITT common share held.

Mar. '95— ITT acquired Caesars World, Inc. (CAW) for $67.50 a share, or about $1.7 billion. Later in March, ITT, in partnership with Cablevision Systems Corp., purchased Madison Square Garden Properties, Inc. from Viacom Inc. for $1.075 billion. Contributions from these acquisitions, plus the repurchase of over 12 million shares in 1994, will aid earnings in 1995.

Next earnings report expected in late October.

Per Share Data ($)

Yr. End Dec. 31	1994	1993	1992	1991	1990	1989	²1988	1987	1986	³1985
Tangible Bk. Val.	50.41	64.08	59.93	69.47	64.01	55.42	56.33	53.83	45.92	40.91
Cash Flow	12.30	12.08	2.38	10.65	11.97	9.88	9.34	9.50	5.51	5.06
Earnings⁴	7.10	7.29	d2.47	6.42	8.06	6.52	5.99	7.20	3.45	1.84
Dividends	1.980	1.980	1.840	1.720	1.630	1.510	1.308	1.063	1.000	1.000
Payout Ratio	28%	27%	NM	26%	19%	21%	21%	14%	28%	54%
Prices—High	104¼	94⅞	72⅛	63	60⅞	64½	54⅞	66⅜	59½	38⅞
Low	77	69	54¾	44⅞	40¼	49¾	43¼	41¾	35⅜	28⅜
P/E Ratio—	15–11	13–9	NM	10–7	8–5	10–8	9–7	9–6	17–10	21–15

Data as orig. reptd. **1.** Six mos. **2.** Reflects merger or acquisition and acctg. change. **3.** Reflects merger or acquisition. **4.** Bef. results of disc. oper. of +1.57 in 1994, +0.44 in 1993, -0.78 in 1990, -0.29 in 1988, +0.08 in 1986, +0.05 in 1985 & spec. item(s) of -0.10 in 1994, -0.41 in 1993, -5.46 in 1992, -0.44 in 1987, -0.30 in 1986. d-Deficit. NM-Not Meaningful.

Income Data (Million $)

Year Ended Dec. 31	Revs.	Oper. Inc.	% Oper. Inc. of Revs.	Cap. Exp.	Depr.	Int. Exp.	Net Bef. Taxes	Eff. Tax Rate	[6]Net Inc.	% Net Inc. of Revs.	Cash Flow
[1]1994	23,620	2,678	9.2	727	[4]592	413	1,259	30.9%	852	3.6	1,414
[1]1993	22,762	2,502	11.0	505	576	[4]920	1,282	26.9%	910	4.0	1,450
1992	21,651	1,374	6.3	646	553	[4]1,050	[5]d498	NM	d270	NM	279
[1]1991	20,421	2,288	11.2	791	535	[4]1,073	[5]990	12.3%	817	4.0	1,299
[1]1990	20,604	2,274	11.0	742	506	[4]1,079	[5]1,385	19.4%	1,056	5.1	1,508
1989	20,054	2,560	12.8	604	485	[4]1,105	[5]1,237	20.4%	922	4.6	1,364
[2]1988	19,355	2,369	12.2	524	500	[4]949	[5]1,117	19.2%	858	4.4	1,336
1987	8,551	936	10.9	461	364	[4]343	[5]1,371	18.2%	1,085	12.7	1,425
[1]1986	7,596	617	8.1	389	335	379	[5]1,145	49.7%	[7]528	7.0	836
[3]1985	11,871	1,023	8.6	643	460	541	[5]468	33.7%	286	2.4	719

Balance Sheet Data (Million $)

Dec. 31	Cash	Assets	Curr. Liab.	Ratio	Total Assets	% Ret. on Assets	Long Term Debt	Common Equity	Total Cap.	% LT Debt of Cap.	% Ret. on Equity
1994	4,816	NA	NA	NA	100,854	1.0	3,340	5,326	8,979	37.2	13.5
1993	4,321	NA	NA	NA	70,560	1.4	9,561	7,534	17,407	54.9	12.0
1992	5,659	NA	NA	NA	58,764	NM	9,517	7,136	17,013	55.9	NM
1991	2,853	NA	NA	NA	53,867	1.6	[8]9,539	7,949	18,712	51.0	10.0
1990	3,017	NA	NA	NA	49,043	2.3	[8]7,245	7,308	15,791	45.9	14.7
1989	2,927	NA	NA	NA	45,503	2.2	[8]6,875	6,803	14,932	46.0	12.8
1988	3,443	NA	NA	NA	41,941	3.1	4,638	7,527	12,673	36.6	11.4
1987	802	3,644	2,259	1.6	13,354	8.4	2,478	7,312	10,403	23.8	15.6
1986	759	3,629	2,450	1.5	12,920	3.9	2,527	6,526	9,762	25.9	8.1
1985	200	5,010	3,847	1.3	14,272	2.1	2,577	5,849	9,226	27.9	4.6

Data as orig. reptd.; Finance subs. consol. aft. 1987. **1.** Excl. disc. opers. **2.** Reflects merger or acquisition and acctg. change. **3.** Excl. disc. opers. and reflects merger or acquisition. **4.** Net of int. income. **5.** Incl. equity in earns. of nonconsol. subs. **6.** Bef. results of disc. opers. and spec. item(s). **7.** Reflects acctg. change. **8.** Incl. curr. portion. d-Deficit. NM-Not Meaningful. NA-Not Available.

Business Summary

ITT is a widely diversified conglomerate. Segment contributions to revenues and profits (in million $, excluding equity income and certain nonrecurring items) from continuing operations in 1994:

	Revs.	Profits
Products:		
Automotive	20%	20%
Defense & Electronics.....	7%	5%
Fluid technology	5%	6%
Services:		
Insurance	47%	50%
Communications	4%	9%
Hotels/Entertainment	17%	10%

The U.S. accounted for 67% of revenues in 1994 (65% in 1993), Western Europe for 25% (26% in 1993), and Canada and other for 8% (9%).

ITT supplies components to automotive manufacturers; makes electronic products; produces fluid control systems; and builds defense technology products. Pulp and timber operations conducted by Rayonier Inc. were spun off to ITT shareholders in early 1994.

The Hartford Group offers property-casualty and life insurance. Other units compile telephone directories and operate Sheraton hotels and casinos. The sale of ITT Financial, a consumer and commercial lender, was completed in June 1995. ITT sold its 30% stake in Alcatel N.V. in 1992.

Dividend Data

Dividends have been paid since 1951. A dividend reinvestment plan is available.

Amt. of Divd. $	Date Decl.	Ex-divd. Date	Stock of Record	Payment Date
0.49½	Jul. 26	Aug. 2	Aug. 8	Oct. 1'94
0.49½	Oct. 11	Nov. 4	Nov. 10	Jan. 1'95
0.49½	Feb. 7	Feb. 13	Feb. 17	Apr. 1'95
0.49½	May 9	May 15	May 19	Jul. 1'95

Capitalization

Total Debt: $9,270,000,000 (3/95).

Cum. Preferred Stock: $652,000,000.

Common Stock: 105,706,553 shs. ($1 par). Institutions hold approximately 72%. Shareholders of record: 56,000 (2/95).

Office—1330 Ave. of the Americas, New York, NY 10019. **Tel**—(212) 258-1000. **Chrmn & Pres**—R. V. Araskog. **EVP-CFO**—R. A. Bowman. **SVP-Treas**—A. N. Reese. **VP-Secy**—G. L. Carr. **VP-Investor Contact**—Ralph D. Allen. **Dirs**—B. B. Anderson, R. V. Araskog, N. D. Archibald, R. A. Burnett, M. David-Weill, S. P. Gilbert, H. Gluck, P. G. Kirk, Jr., E. C. Meyer, B. F. Payton, M. E. White. **Transfer Agent**—Company's office, Secaucus, N. J. **Registrar**—Chemical Bank, NYC. **Incorporated** in Maryland in 1920; reincorporated in Delaware in 1968. **Empl**—110,000.

Information has been obtained from sources believed to be reliable, but its accuracy and completeness are not guaranteed. Catherine A. Seifert

Illinois Tool Works

NYSE Symbol **ITW**
In S&P 500

23-SEP-95

Industry:
Conglomerate/diversified

Summary: Illinois Tool Works makes industrial components and other specialty products for high-volume manufacturing. Primary markets include the auto, food and construction industries.

S&P Opinion: Hold (★★★)

Recent Price • 59¼
52 Wk Range • 65½-39⅝

Yield • 1.1%
12-Mo. P/E • 20.2

Quantitative Evaluations

Outlook
(1 Lowest—5 Highest)
• **4+**

Fair Value
• **63⅝**

Risk
• **Low**

Earn./Div. Rank
• **A+**

Technical Eval.
• **Bearish** since 8/95

Rel. Strength Rank
(1 Lowest—99 Highest)
• **43**

Insider Activity
• **Unfavorable**

Earnings vs. Previous Year
▲=Up ▼=Down ▶=No Change

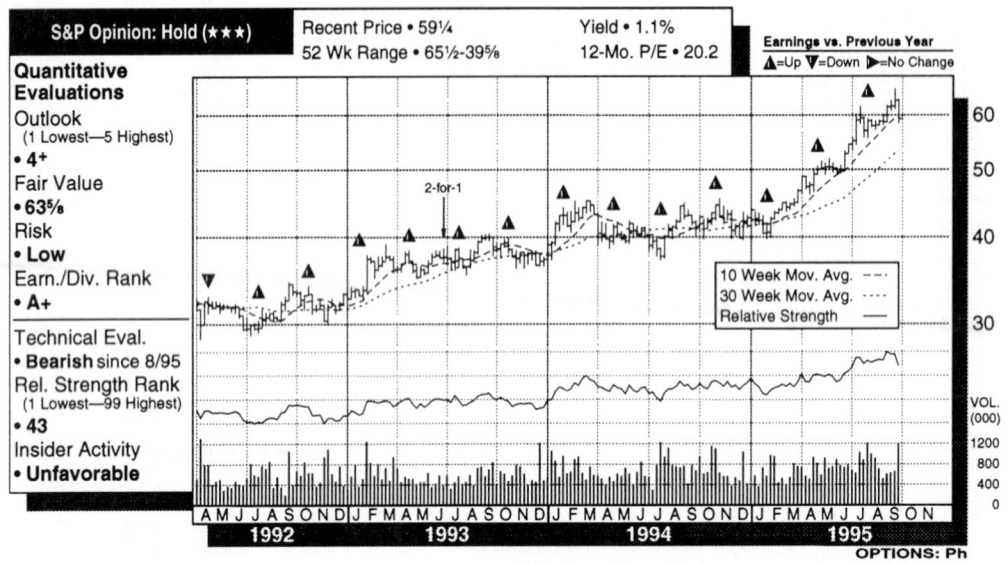

10 Week Mov. Avg. —
30 Week Mov. Avg. ⋯
Relative Strength —

VOL.
(000)

OPTIONS: Ph

Overview - 22-SEP-95

Assumimg GDP growth of 2.6% and a continuation of the recovery in Europe, we anticipate 15% to 20% revenue growth in 1996. Our economic forecast assumes an increase in both car sales and housing starts from 1995's levels. Growth will also reflect contributions from acquisitions and probable gains in market share. Continued high capacity utilization, firm pricing and stability in raw material costs should aid margins and lift gross profits. Assuming level interest expense, well controlled SG&A, lower costs for integrating acquisitions and a flat tax rate, earnings should continue to advance in 1996. Acquisitions, constant improvement in core businesses, market share gains and introduction of new products should boost long-term sales and earnings.

Valuation - 22-SEP-95

Although shares of this well-managed diversified manufacturer may continue to rise, we are maintaining our hold rating on ITW because we believe the potential upside from current levels is not sufficient to add to holdings. Through late September, ITW shares have risen 38%, versus a 24% increase in the S&P 500. The stock has also performed respectably vis a vis other diversified manufacturers. Through August 31, the diversified industrials group was up 33%. Nevertheless, we feel the easy money has been made in this stock and the risk/reward ratio at current levels does not warrant an accumulate or buy recommendation.

Key Stock Statistics

S&P EPS Est. 1995	3.20	Tang. Bk. Value/Share	10.92
P/E on S&P Est. 1995	18.5	Beta	0.86
S&P EPS Est. 1996	3.80	Shareholders	3,600
Dividend Rate/Share	0.68	Market cap. (B)	$ 7.0
Shs. outstg. (M)	117.3	Inst. holdings	70%
Avg. daily vol. (M)	0.156	Insider holdings	NA

Value of $10,000 invested 5 years ago: $ 28,460

Fiscal Year Ending Dec. 31

	1995	% Change	1994	% Change	1993	% Change
Revenues (Million $)						
1Q	929.1	20%	771.4	3%	750.0	12%
2Q	1,091	24%	881.0	6%	829.3	16%
3Q	—	—	870.9	12%	779.5	10%
4Q	—	—	937.9	17%	800.3	12%
Yr.	—	—	3,461	10%	3,159	12%
Income (Million $)						
1Q	75.03	47%	50.92	21%	42.03	4%
2Q	106.3	50%	70.73	29%	54.78	7%
3Q	—	—	71.40	40%	50.95	4%
4Q	—	—	84.74	44%	58.80	14%
Yr.	—	—	277.8	34%	206.6	8%
Earnings Per Share ($)						
1Q	0.66	47%	0.45	20%	0.38	4%
2Q	0.91	47%	0.62	27%	0.49	7%
3Q	E0.74	17%	0.63	40%	0.45	2%
4Q	E0.89	19%	0.75	44%	0.52	13%
Yr.	E3.20	31%	2.45	34%	1.83	6%

Next earnings report expected: mid October

Business Summary - 22-SEP-95

Illinois Tool Works is a leading producer of highly engineered fasteners, components, assemblies and systems. Segment contributions in 1994 were:

	Sales	Profits
Engineered components	53%	55%
Industrial systems & consumables	47%	45%

Foreign operations accounted for 36% of total revenues and 28% of operating profits in 1994.

The engineered components segment consists of the following: automotive and specialty components (metal and plastic fasteners, components and assemblies used in auto and industrial applications); construction products and engineered polymers (fasteners and fastening systems used in wood, metal and concrete/masonry construction applications, and advanced-technology adhesives and polymers used in construction, industrial and consumer markets); and Miller (arc welding equipment and related accessories for metalworking, construction, maintenance and other applications).

The industrial systems and consumables segment includes: consumer packaging products and systems (plastic multipacking and application systems, resealable packaging products, and marking, labeling and identification systems); industrial packaging systems (packaging application equipment and systems, including steel and plastic strapping, wire-tieing equipment, and hot melt adhesive application equipment); specialty packaging (stretch film and carton sealing tape, paper packaging systems and hot melt adhesive application equipment); and finishing systems (electrostatic and conventional, liquid and powder finishing spray guns equipment and systems).

Backlog at December 31, 1994 totaled $355 million, versus $301 million a year earlier.

Important Developments

Sep. '95— ITW announced that it would end its efforts to acquire Elco Industries Inc. Earlier, the company submitted a proposal to acquire Elco.
Jul. '95—ITW reported share earnings of $0.91 on a 24% increase in revenues for 1995's second quarter, versus $0.62 a year earlier. In the engineered components segment, revenues rose 19% and operating income advanced 29%. The company attributed the gain to Miller's domestic business, domestic construction business and European automotive. Revenues in industrial systems and components increased 29% and operating income was up 50%. The improvement in this segment was due mostly to gains in the consumer and industrial packaging businesses.

Capitalization

Long Term Debt: $282,775,000 (6/95).

Per Share Data ($)
(Year Ended Dec. 31)

	1994	1993	1992	1991	1990	1989
Tangible Bk. Val.	9.46	7.35	8.26	7.18	6.80	5.11
Cash Flow	3.62	2.99	2.81	2.62	2.59	2.30
Earnings	2.45	1.83	1.72	1.63	1.67	1.53
Dividends	0.69	0.49	0.45	0.40	0.33	0.27
Payout Ratio	28%	27%	26%	25%	20%	18%
Prices - High	45½	40½	35⅜	34¾	28¾	23¾
- Low	37	32½	28½	22⅞	19⅝	16½
P/E Ratio - High	19	22	21	21	17	16
- Low	15	18	17	14	12	11

Income Statement Analysis (Million $)

	1994	%Chg	1993	%Chg	1992	%Chg	1991
Revs.	3,461	10%	3,159	12%	2,812	7%	2,640
Oper. Inc.	624	22%	510	10%	463	12%	414
Depr.	132	NM	132	8%	122	10%	111
Int. Exp.	26.9	-23%	35.0	-18%	42.9	-3%	44.3
Pretax Inc.	450	34%	336	8%	310	8%	288
Eff. Tax Rate	38%	—	39%	—	38%	—	37%
Net Inc.	278	34%	207	8%	192	6%	181

Balance Sheet & Other Fin. Data (Million $)

	1994	1993	1992	1991	1990	1989
Cash	76.9	35.4	31.2	93.1	46.8	30.9
Curr. Assets	1,263	1,094	1,005	1,088	1,143	824
Total Assets	2,580	2,337	2,204	2,257	2,150	1,688
Curr. Liab.	628	546	513	646	528	384
LT Debt	273	376	252	307	431	334
Common Eqty.	1,542	1,259	1,340	1,212	1,092	871
Total Cap.	1,884	1,727	1,646	1,578	1,585	1,278
Cap. Exp.	131	120	115	170	192	162
Cash Flow	410	338	314	291	282	247

Ratio Analysis

	1994	1993	1992	1991	1990	1989
Curr. Ratio	2.0	2.0	2.0	1.7	2.2	2.1
% LT Debt of Cap.	14.5	21.8	15.3	19.5	27.2	26.2
% Net Inc.of Revs.	8.0	6.5	6.8	6.8	7.2	7.5
% Ret. on Assets	11.3	9.1	8.6	8.1	9.4	10.6
% Ret. on Equity	19.8	15.8	15.0	15.6	18.4	20.1

Dividend Data
—Dividends have been paid since 1933. A dividend reinvestment plan is available.

Amt. of Div. $	Date Decl.	Ex-Div. Date	Stock of Record	Payment Date
0.150	Aug. 05	Sep. 26	Sep. 30	Oct. 25 '94
0.150	Oct. 21	Dec. 23	Dec. 30	Jan. 25 '95
0.150	Feb. 17	Mar. 27	Mar. 31	Apr. 25 '95
0.150	May. 08	Jun. 28	Jun. 30	Jul. 25 '95
0.170	Aug. 04	Sep. 27	Sep. 29	Oct. 25 '95

Data as orig. reptd.; bef. results of disc. opers. and/or spec. items. Per share data adj. for stk. divs. as of ex-div. date. E-Estimated. NA-Not Available. NM-Not Meaningful. NR-Not Ranked.

Office—3600 West Lake Avenue, Glenview, IL 60025-5811. Tel—(708) 724-7500. Chrmn & CEO—J. D. Nichols. Pres—W. J. Farrell. SVP & Secy—S. S. Hudnut. Investor Contact—Linda Williams. Dirs—J. W. Becton, Jr., S. S. Cathcart, S. Crown, H. R. Crowther, W. J. Farrell, R. M. Jones, G. D. Kennedy, R. H. Leet, R. C. McCormack, J. D. Nichols, P. B. Rooney, H. B. Smith, Jr., O. J. Wade, C. A. H. Waller. Transfer Agent & Registrar—Harris Trust and Savings Bank, Chicago. Incorporated in Delaware in 1961. Empl- 19,500. S&P Analyst: Leo Larkin

Inco Ltd.

NYSE Symbol **N** Options on Toronto (Feb-May-Aug-Nov) & ASE (Jan-Apr-Jul-Oct) In S&P 500

Price	Range	P–E Ratio	Dividend	Yield	S&P Ranking	Beta
Oct. 24'95 29⅞	1995 37¾–23½	14	[1]0.40	1.4%	B–	0.84

Summary

This leading nickel producer, which supplies 32% of world market-economy demand, is also a major producer of high-nickel and other alloys, makes high-performance alloy components, and is an important copper producer. Assuming stable business conditions throughout the world in 1996 and higher stainless steel production, earnings should rise again in 1996, following the substantial gain expected for 1995.

Current Outlook

Earnings for 1996 are projected at $3.25 a share, versus the $2.05 estimated for 1995.

Dividends at $0.10 quarterly (before 15% Canadian tax) are the minimum expected.

Assuming 2.6% U. S. GDP growth and stable business conditions in the rest of the world, sales should post another strong gain in 1996. Continued high levels of stainless steel production and firm demand for copper should lift prices and volumes. Aided by lower unit costs, the likely absence of equipment problems and better pricing, earnings should rise again in 1996 despite some dilution from Voisey Bay. Strong secular demand for stainless steel will boost the company's long-term sales and earnings prospects.

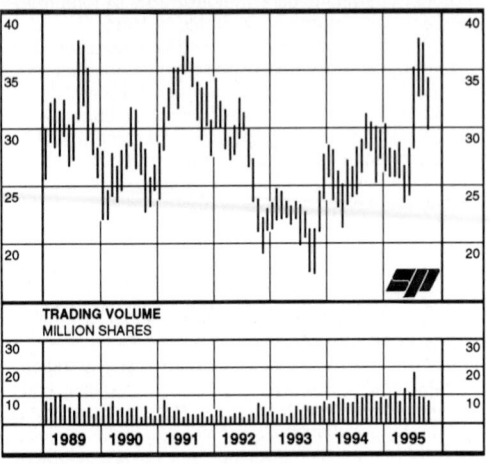

TRADING VOLUME
MILLION SHARES

Net Sales (Million $)

Quarter:	1995	1994	1993	1992
Mar.	881	524	543	680
Jun.	856	590	604	666
Sep.	830	603	468	601
Dec.		767	516	612
		2,484	2,130	2,559

Sales for the nine months ended September 30, 1995, rose 50%, year to year (1994 restated), on higher metals prices and increased volume of shipments of nickel, copper, precious metals and nickel alloys. Although third quarter production was adversely affected by start-up problems and other factors, margins widened significantly, and with interest expense down 2.9%, net income of $166.2 million ($1.37 a share after preferred dividends) contrasted with a net loss of $75.8 million ($0.68) in the year-earlier period.

Common Share Earnings ($)

Quarter:	1995	1994	1993	1992
Mar.	0.60	d0.53	d0.22	0.01
Jun.	0.47	d0.07	d0.03	d0.03
Sep.	0.33	0.02	0.83	0.09
Dec.	E0.65	0.73	d0.36	d0.28
	E2.05	0.15	0.22	d0.21

Important Developments

Oct. '95— The company announced that third quarter production was hurt by start-up and equipment problems which resulted in a 12 million ton production shortfall. It said that the problems had been corrected and production of 111 million tons was planned for the fourth quarter. However, the lower production adversely affected nickel unit production costs in the third quarter.

Jun. '95— The company bought a 25% interest in the Voisey Bay nickel, copper and cobalt discovery and related claim areas in Labrador from Diamond Fields Resources, for $387 million of 6.5% preferred stock, plus C$25 million to fund a feasibility study and further exploration. It also purchased 2,000,000 Diamond Fields common shares (7%) from three holders, for $68 million in cash and 1.4 million common shares.

Next earnings report expected in late January.

Per Share Data ($)

Yr. End Dec. 31	[4]1994	1993	1992	1991	1990	1989	1988	1987	1986	1985
Tangible Bk. Val.	15.08	14.57	14.71	15.70	15.78	12.33	6.51	10.33	9.56	9.68
Cash Flow	2.32	2.46	2.13	2.96	6.19	8.95	8.18	2.55	1.24	1.72
Earnings[2]	0.15	0.22	d0.21	0.74	4.18	7.11	6.50	1.09	d0.16	0.28
Dividends	0.40	0.40	0.85	1.00	1.00	0.85	[3]10.70	0.20	0.20	0.20
Payout Ratio	NM	182%	NM	137%	24%	12%	165%	18%	NM	73%
Prices—High	31¼	27¾	34⅜	38	31⅞	37⅝	35⅛	24	16⅞	15⅜
Low	21⅜	17⅜	19⅛	23⅞	22⅛	25⅝	17⅞	11¾	10½	10⅜
P/E Ratio—	NM	NM	NM	51–32	8–5	5–4	5–3	22–11	NM	55–37

Data as orig. reptd. **1.** In U.S. funds, bef. 15% nonresident Canadian tax. **2.** Bef. spec. item(s) of +0.42 in 1988. **3.** Incl. 10.00 spec. divd. **4.** Refl. acctg. change. d-Deficit. E-Estimated. NM-Not Meaningful.

Income Data (Million $)

Year Ended Dec. 31	Revs.	Oper. Inc.	% Oper. Inc. of Revs.	Cap. Exp.	Depr.	Int. Exp.	[1]Net Bef. Taxes	Eff. Tax Rate	[2]Net Inc.	% Net Inc. of Revs.	Cash Flow
[3]1994	2,484	310	12.5	139	252	89	d13	NM	22	0.9	270
1993	2,130	164	7.7	186	246	99	25	NM	28	1.3	270
1992	2,559	366	14.3	234	253	113	22	93.7%	d18	NM	230
1991	2,999	478	16.0	440	235	120	122	11.9%	83	2.8	312
1990	3,108	798	25.7	573	209	112	693	32.6%	441	14.2	645
1989	3,948	1,546	39.2	389	194	138	1,314	39.2%	753	19.1	942
1988	3,263	1,473	45.1	229	177	92	1,268	45.5%	691	21.2	862
1987	1,789	426	23.8	138	153	101	199	37.0%	125	7.0	266
1986	1,452	228	15.7	139	144	94	27	99.3%	[3]Nil	Nil	127
1985	1,491	299	20.1	93	143	102	27	48.6%	52	3.5	171

Balance Sheet Data (Million $)

Dec. 31	Cash	Assets	Curr. Liab.	Ratio	Total Assets	% Ret. on Assets	Long Term Debt	Common Equity	Total Cap.	% LT Debt of Cap.	% Ret. on Equity
1994	164	1,418	498	2.8	4,016	0.5	922	1,767	2,977	31.0	1.0
1993	47	1,184	492	2.4	3,890	0.7	946	1,607	2,814	33.6	1.5
1992	35	1,140	542	2.1	4,161	NM	1,081	1,608	3,026	35.7	NM
1991	31	1,432	924	1.5	4,478	1.9	991	1,668	3,006	33.0	4.6
1990	70	1,354	720	1.9	4,058	11.4	893	1,648	2,828	31.6	29.7
1989	115	1,350	759	1.8	3,666	19.6	925	1,289	2,398	38.6	75.9
1988	657	1,921	2,052	0.9	4,079	19.5	674	689	1,507	44.7	76.8
1987	34	996	524	1.9	2,994	4.2	811	1,084	2,204	36.8	10.9
1986	25	905	470	1.9	2,976	Nil	941	996	2,257	41.7	NM
1985	21	1,001	496	2.0	3,083	1.7	859	987	2,330	36.9	2.9

Data as orig. reptd. 1. Incl. equity in earns. of nonconsol. subs. 2. Bef. spec. items. 3. Reflects accounting change. d-Deficit. NM-Not Meaningful.

Business Summary

Inco produces 32% of the nickel for the world's market-economy nations, as well as copper and other metals and metals products. Contributions in 1994 were:

	Sales	Profits
Primary metals	75%	81%
Alloys & engineered prdts....	22%	21%
Other business	3%	-2%

Inco mined 14 million short tons of ore in 1994. Nickel and copper production at facilities worldwide was 345 million and 192 million lbs., respectively. Primary nickel accounted for 77% of 1994 group sales, refined copper 13%, precious metals 5%, and other metals 5%. At year-end 1994, the company had proven and probable reserves in Canada of 379 million short tons containing 5.37 million tons of nickel and 3.78 million tons of copper. Inco owns 58% of P.T. International Nickel Indonesia, which produces nickel in matte, an intermediate product, to Japan for further refining. At the end of 1994, reserves of P.T. Inco were 120 million short tons containing 2.2 million tons of nickel.

Products businesses, serving aerospace, energy and other markets, include Inco Alloys International, one of the world's largest suppliers of high-nickel alloys; and Inco Engineered Products, which makes precision-machined components from nickel-based and titanium-based alloys.

Other business includes reclamation facilities, corrosion testing and consulting, construction materials and a venture capital portfolio.

Dividend Data

Dividends have been paid since 1934. Payments are in U.S. funds, subject to 15% Canadian tax. A dividend reinvestment plan is available. A poison pill stock purchase rights plan was adopted in 1988.

Amt. of Divd. $	Date Decl.	Ex-divd. Date	Stock of Record	Payment Date
0.10	Feb. 15	Feb. 21	Feb. 27	Mar. 17'95
0.10	Apr. 18	Apr. 25	May 1	Jun. 1'95
0.10	Jul. 24	Aug. 1	Aug. 3	Sep. 1'95
0.10	Oct. 23	Oct. 31	Nov. 2	Dec. 1'95

Capitalization

Long Term Debt: $807,100,000 (9/95), incl. $172.5 million debs. conv. into com. at $38.25 a sh., and $172.5 million debs. conv. into com. at $30 a sh.

Minority Interest: $257,200,000.

6.5% Pfd. Stock: $386,700,000 (face value), conv. from June 29, 2000, in 13.3 million com. shs.; 100% owned by Diamond Field Resources.

Common Stock: 118,635,000 shs. (no par). Institutions hold 54%. Shareholders of record: 28,691.

Offices—Royal Trust Tower, Toronto-Dominion Centre, Toronto, ON Canada M5K 1N4; One New York Plaza, New York, NY 10004. **Tel**—(416) 361-7511; NYC-(212) 612-5500. **Chrmn & CEO**—M. D. Sopko. **Pres**—S. M. Hand. **Vice Chrmn & CFO**—I. McDougall. **EVP & Secy**—S. F. Feiner. **VP & Treas**—A. J. Sabatino. **Investor Contact**—N. Kurt Barnes. **Dirs**—G. A. Barton, M. Bélanger, P. Crawford, J. A. Erola, W. F. Glavin, S. M. Hand, C. H. Hantho, I. McDougall, G. T. Richardson, R. J. Richardson, M. D. Sopko, F. H. Telmer, R. M. Thomson. **U.S. Transfer Agent & Registrar**—Mellon Securities Trust Co., NYC. **Incorporated** in Canada in 1916. **Empl**—15,709.

Information has been obtained from sources believed to be reliable, but its accuracy and completeness are not guaranteed.   Leo Larkin

Ingersoll-Rand

NYSE Symbol **IR**
In S&P 500

27-OCT-95

Industry:
Machinery

Summary: This major producer of air compressors also has an important stake in other nonelectrical machinery, including equipment for the construction and auto industries.

S&P Opinion: Hold (★★★)	Recent Price • 35¾	Yield • 2.1%
	52 Wk Range • 42⅜-28⅜	12-Mo. P/E • 15.0

Quantitative Evaluations

Outlook
  (1 Lowest—5 Highest)
• **4+**

Fair Value
• **37½**

Risk
• **Low**

Earn./Div. Rank
• **B+**

Technical Eval.
• **Bearish** since 7/95

Rel. Strength Rank
  (1 Lowest—99 Highest)
• **27**

Insider Activity
• **Neutral**

Earnings vs. Previous Year
▲=Up ▼=Down ▶=No Change

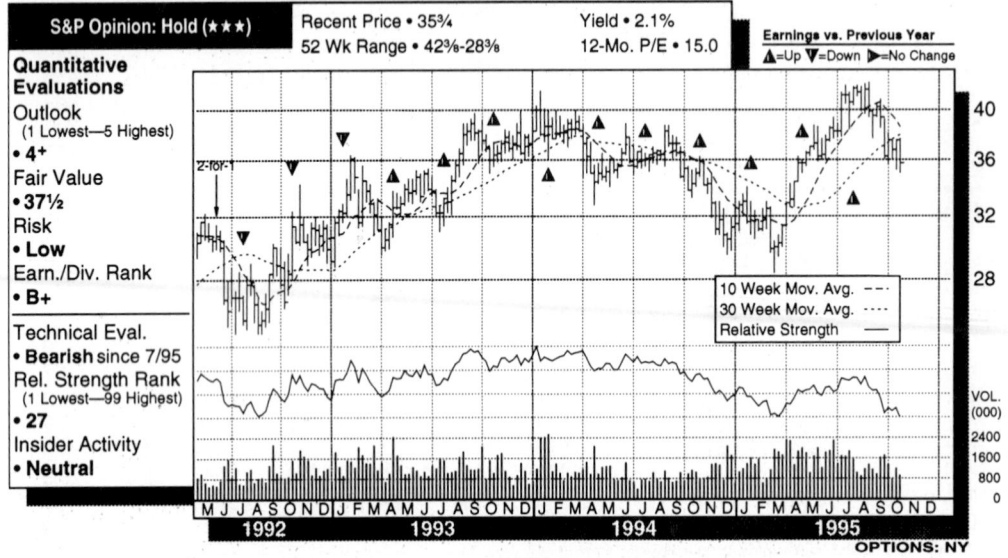

10 Week Mov. Avg. -- -
30 Week Mov. Avg. ....
Relative Strength —

VOL.
(000)

OPTIONS: NY

Overview - 26-OCT-95

Based upon the S&P forecast for 2.5% GDP growth in the U.S., stable conditions in Europe and the inclusion of Clark Equipment for the entire year, we anticipate a 25% sales gain in 1996. Assuming a rise in U.S. car output, sales in the bearings, locks and tools unit will increase from 1995's levels. Steady construction activity along with the addition of Clark will boost standard machinery. The engineered equipment unit will improve, on greater pump industry demand and continued strength in pulp and paper. Aided by firm prices and stable raw material costs, gross margins should widen. Benefiting further from an increase in profits from Dresser-Rand, only a small increase in interest expense and lower costs for integrating acquisitions, earnings should rise again in 1996. Acquisitions and expanded product offerings for construction machinery should boost long-term sales and earnings.

Valuation - 26-OCT-95

IR's shares have been volatile through most of 1995. After dropping to a low of $28 3/8 in February, the shares rebounded to the $42 level by late August. Through late October, the stock is virtually unchanged for 1995 at the $35 level. Although the stock is not overvalued on based upon a multiple of 1996's estimate and our long-term view of the shares remains favorable, we continue to rate the stock a hold. Based on both near and intermediate-term prospects, we believe there is little upside potential at present. Accordingly, we don't believe the shares warrant an accumulate or buy rating.

Key Stock Statistics

S&P EPS Est. 1995	2.45	Tang. Bk. Value/Share	3.48
P/E on S&P Est. 1995	14.6	Beta	1.59
S&P EPS Est. 1996	2.90	Shareholders	15,600
Dividend Rate/Share	0.74	Market cap. (B)	$ 3.7
Shs. outstg. (M)	105.9	Inst. holdings	66%
Avg. daily vol. (M)	0.211	Insider holdings	NA

Value of $10,000 invested 5 years ago: $ 16,310

Fiscal Year Ending Dec. 31

	1995	% Change	1994	% Change	1993	% Change
Revenues (Million $)						
1Q	1,186	17%	1,010	6%	952.1	11%
2Q	1,392	22%	1,144	14%	1,007	11%
3Q	1,521	37%	1,114	14%	973.5	8%
4Q	—	—	1,240	14%	1,089	NM
Yr.	—	—	4,507	12%	4,021	6%
Income (Million $)						
1Q	46.27	40%	33.00	34%	24.60	19%
2Q	66.65	29%	51.57	43%	35.94	10%
3Q	61.80	28%	48.38	37%	35.20	17%
4Q	—	—	78.18	15%	67.80	109%
Yr.	—	—	211.1	29%	163.5	41%
Earnings Per Share ($)						
1Q	0.44	42%	0.31	29%	0.24	20%
2Q	0.63	29%	0.49	44%	0.34	10%
3Q	0.58	26%	0.46	39%	0.33	14%
4Q	E0.80	8%	0.74	14%	0.65	110%
Yr.	E2.45	23%	2.00	28%	1.56	41%

Next earnings report expected: late January

Ingersoll-Rand

Business Summary - 26-OCT-95

Ingersoll-Rand is a diversified producer of capital goods. Its primary business involves the design and manufacture of compressed air systems. Sales and operating profits in 1994 were derived as follows:

	Sales	Profits
Standard machinery	32%	30%
Engineered equipment	21%	8%
Bearings, locks & tools	47%	62%

International operations accounted for 38% of sales and 19% of operating profits in 1994.

Standard machinery includes air compressors, vacuum pumps, air drying and filtering systems, portable and packaged air compressors, pavement millers, rock drills, blasthole drills and water-well drills.

Engineered equipment consists of centrifugal and reciprocating pumps, pulp and paper processing equipment, pelletizing equipment, filters, aerators and dewatering systems.

Bearings, locks and tools include needle bearings, tapered roller bearings, precision components, air-powered tools, hoists and winches, air motors and air starters, automated assembly and test systems, door locks, electronic access systems, door closers and exit devices.

Dresser-Rand, an equally owned joint venture with Dresser Industries, makes gas turbines, gas compressors, power recovery systems, reciprocating gas engines and steam turbines. Dresser-Rand contributed income of $24.6 million in 1994, versus $33.1 million in 1993.

Ingersoll-Dresser Pump Co. (IDP), formed in 1992, is owned 51% by the company and 49% by Dresser.

Important Developments

Oct. '95—IR reported share earnings of $0.58 on a 37% increase in sales for 1995's third quarter, versus $0.46 a year earlier. Excluding the Clark acquisition, sales rose 8.0%. Earnings for 1995's third quarter were hurt by problems at the Door Hardware unit and lower than expected earnings from Dresser Pump Company. Incoming orders for the quarter totaled about $1.55 billion, up 37% from a year earlier. Excluding $325 million from Clark, orders were up 8.0% over 1994.

May '95—IR acquired Clark Equipment Co. in a transaction valued at $1.5 billion. Following the expiration of a cash tender, Clark will be merged into a company unit. Clark, a South Bend, Ind.-based maker of components and construction equipment, had net income of $62.8 million in 1994, on $947 million in sales.

Capitalization

Long Term Debt: $1,287,826,000 (6/95).
Minority Interest: $158,244,000.

Per Share Data ($)

(Year Ended Dec. 31)

	1994	1993	1992	1991	1990	1989
Tangible Bk. Val.	13.34	11.82	11.28	14.74	15.05	13.37
Cash Flow	3.26	2.73	2.23	2.68	2.81	2.83
Earnings	2.00	1.56	1.11	1.46	1.78	1.89
Dividends	0.72	0.70	0.69	0.66	0.63	0.58
Payout Ratio	36%	45%	62%	45%	36%	31%
Prices - High	41⅝	39⅞	34¼	27½	30¼	25⅛
- Low	29½	28¾	25	17½	14¼	16⅞
P/E Ratio - High	21	26	31	19	17	13
- Low	15	18	23	12	8	9

Income Statement Analysis (Million $)

	1994	%Chg	1993	%Chg	1992	%Chg	1991
Revs.	4,507	12%	4,021	6%	3,784	6%	3,586
Oper. Inc.	510	21%	420	13%	372	-5%	393
Depr.	133	7%	124	6%	117	-8%	127
Int. Exp.	47.0	-14%	54.8	-5%	57.6	-9%	63.5
Pretax Inc.	343	29%	265	79%	148	-37%	235
Eff. Tax Rate	35%	—	34%	—	46%	—	36%
Net Inc.	211	29%	164	41%	116	-23%	151

Balance Sheet & Other Fin. Data (Million $)

	1994	1993	1992	1991	1990	1989
Cash	211	234	230	138	52.0	139
Curr. Assets	2,003	1,902	1,968	1,682	1,697	1,599
Total Assets	3,597	3,375	3,388	2,980	2,983	2,595
Curr. Liab.	1,040	1,024	1,080	778	964	676
LT Debt	316	314	356	376	265	280
Common Eqty.	1,531	1,350	1,293	1,633	1,556	1,377
Total Cap.	2,001	1,810	1,795	2,146	1,952	1,886
Cap. Exp.	159	132	132	185	195	155
Cash Flow	344	287	232	277	290	291

Ratio Analysis

	1994	1993	1992	1991	1990	1989
Curr. Ratio	1.9	1.9	1.8	2.2	1.8	2.4
% LT Debt of Cap.	15.8	17.4	19.8	17.5	13.6	14.8
% Net Inc.of Revs.	4.7	4.1	3.1	4.2	5.0	5.9
% Ret. on Assets	6.1	4.8	3.6	5.0	6.6	8.0
% Ret. on Equity	14.6	12.3	7.9	9.4	12.5	14.8

Dividend Data —Dividends have been paid since 1910. A dividend reinvestment plan is available. A poison pill stock purchase rights plan was adopted in 1988.

Amt. of Div. $	Date Decl.	Ex-Div. Date	Stock of Record	Payment Date
0.185	Nov. 02	Nov. 09	Nov. 16	Dec. 01 '94
0.185	Feb. 01	Feb. 09	Feb. 15	Mar. 01 '95
0.185	May. 03	May. 11	May. 17	Jun. 01 '95
0.185	Aug. 02	Aug. 14	Aug. 16	Sep. 01 '95

Data as orig. reptd.; bef. results of disc. opers. and/or spec. items. Per share data adj. for stk. divs. as of ex-div. date. E-Estimated. NA-Not Available. NM-Not Meaningful. NR-Not Ranked.

Office—200 Chestnut Ridge Rd., Woodcliff Lake, NJ 07675. **Tel**—(201) 573-0123. **Chrmn, CEO & Pres**—J. E. Perrella. **Secy**—R. G. Heller. **SVP, CFO & Investor Contact**—Thomas F. McBride (201-573-3486). **Dirs**—D. J. Bainton, T. H. Black, B. T. Byrne, J. P. Flannery, C. J. Horner, H. W. Lictenberger, A. H. Massad, J. E. Perrella, J. E. Phipps, D. E. Procknow, C. E. Ritchie, O. R. Smith, R. J. Swift. **Transfer Agent & Registrar**—Bank of New York, NYC. **Incorporated** in New Jersey in 1905. **Empl**-35,932. **S&P Analyst:** Leo Larkin

Inland Steel Industries

NYSE Symbol **IAD**
In S&P 500

07-OCT-95   **Industry:** Steel-Iron

Summary: The fifth largest integrated steelmaker in the U.S., Inland also operates steel service centers.

| **S&P Opinion: Hold (★★★)** | Recent Price • 21⅞ | Yield • 0.9% |
| | 52 Wk Range • 39½-21¼ | 12-Mo. P/E • 7.0 |

Quantitative Evaluations

Outlook
(1 Lowest—5 Highest)
• **2⁻**

Fair Value
• **20½**

Risk
• **Average**

Earn./Div. Rank
• **C**

Technical Eval.
• **Bearish** since 11/94

Rel. Strength Rank
(1 Lowest—99 Highest)
• **4**

Insider Activity
• **Neutral**

Earnings vs. Previous Year
▲=Up ▼=Down ▶=No Change

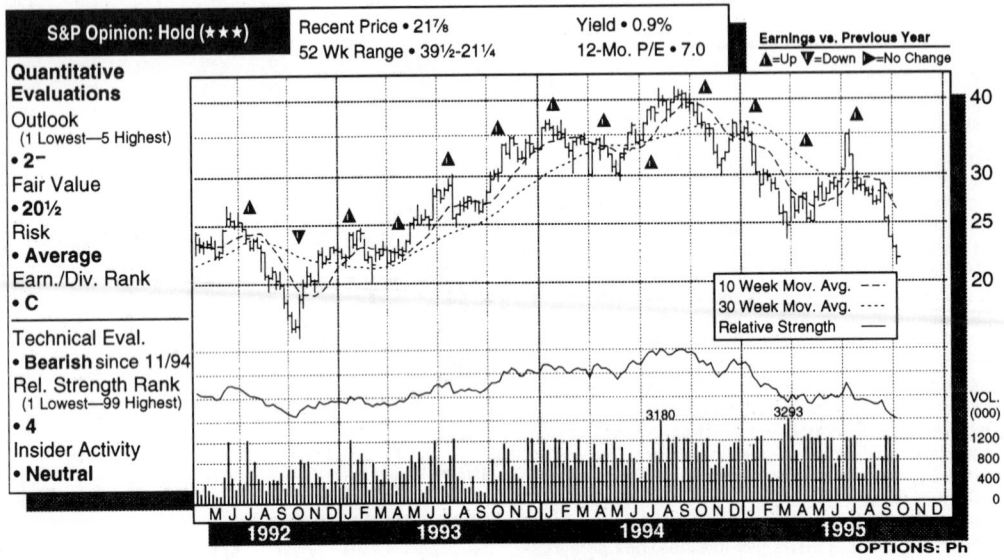

10 Week Mov. Avg. — — —
30 Week Mov. Avg. - - - -
Relative Strength ——

VOL. (000)

OPTIONS: Ph

Overview - 06-OCT-95

Based on a forecast of 2.6% GDP growth, higher car sales and lower imports of flat roll products, we anticipate sales gains of about 2.7% in 1996, reflecting higher prices and volume in both units. We expect a 2.0% increase in shipments in the integrated steel unit and an 2.6% rise in prices. We look for a 5.0% increase in shipments in the distribution unit and a 1.1% rise in prices. Higher capacity utilization rates, an improved mix, increased prices and stable raw material costs will boost operating profit per ton. Benefiting further from an unchanged tax rate and lower preferred dividend expense, IAD should report higher earnings in 1996. Longer term, profits will benefit from aggressive debt reduction, an improved product mix and development of an export business.

Valuation - 06-OCT-95

Inland's shares have severely underperformed the market through late September, falling 33%, versus a 27% increase in the S&P 500 and an 11% decline in the S&P Steel Index through August 31. Announcement of a negative earnings outlook for the third quarter accounts for most of the recent selling pressure in the shares. Given the extent of the slide and the likelihood that the stock price now reflects most of the bad news, we are maintaining our hold recommendation on the shares. While we expect higher earnings in 1996, we would resist the urge to bottom fish at current levels, given the company's history of negative surprises.

Key Stock Statistics

S&P EPS Est. 1995	2.50	Tang. Bk. Value/Share	7.39
P/E on S&P Est. 1995	8.8	Beta	0.85
S&P EPS Est. 1996	3.80	Shareholders	16,000
Dividend Rate/Share	0.20	Market cap. (B)	$ 1.1
Shs. outstg. (M)	48.7	Inst. holdings	71%
Avg. daily vol. (M)	0.244	Insider holdings	NA

Value of $10,000 invested 5 years ago: $ 6,942

Fiscal Year Ending Dec. 31

	1995	% Change	1994	% Change	1993	% Change
Revenues (Million $)						
1Q	1,258	17%	1,076	14%	941.5	5%
2Q	1,274	12%	1,136	14%	996.4	10%
3Q	—	—	1,130	16%	972.0	13%
4Q	—	—	1,156	18%	978.3	18%
Yr.	—	—	4,497	16%	3,888	11%
Income (Million $)						
1Q	44.02	NM	9.19	NM	-31.38	NM
2Q	57.88	81%	32.00	NM	-2.49	NM
3Q	—	—	30.66	81%	16.96	NM
4Q	—	—	35.94	NM	-20.70	NM
Yr.	—	—	107.4	NM	-37.59	NM
Earnings Per Share ($)						
1Q	0.84	NM	0.03	NM	-1.12	NM
2Q	1.08	89%	0.57	NM	-0.30	NM
3Q	E0.18	-67%	0.54	116%	0.25	NM
4Q	E0.40	-39%	0.66	NM	-0.79	NM
Yr.	E2.50	38%	1.81	NM	-1.96	NM

Next earnings report expected: mid October

Inland Steel Industries

07-OCT-95

Business Summary - 06-OCT-95

Inland Steel Industries, Inc. is the fifth largest integrated steel producer in the U.S. and the owner of two major steel service centers. Contributions by segment in 1994 were:

	Sales	Profits
Integrated steel	51%	60%
Steel service center	49%	40%

Raw steel production in 1994 was 5,310,000 net tons (5,003,000 in 1993); shipments totaled 5,170,000 tons (4,835,000). Steel shipments by market were: steel service centers 29%, automotive 32%, steel converters 12%, appliances 9%, machinery 8%, construction 2% and other 8%.

Steel shipments by product class were: sheet, strip, plate and semifinished 88% and bars and related 12%.

Service center operations consist of Joseph T. Ryerson & Son, Inc. and J. M. Tull Metals Company, Inc., with 54 locations nationwide. Ryerson and Tull provide all types, shapes and sizes of carbon, alloy and stainless steel, aluminum, nickel, brass, copper and industrial plastics to manufacturers. They also provide processing services such as sawing, cutting to length, slitting, shearing, flame cutting, laser cutting, drilling, grinding, roll forming, perforating, punching and welding. Shipments were 2,330,000 tons in 1994, versus 2,080,000 tons in 1993.

IAD and Nippon Steel are partners in two joint ventures. IAD owns 60% of the I/N Tek continuous cold rolling facility located in New Carlisle, Ind., and 50% of the I/N Kote facility. I/N Tek reached its design capacity of 1,000,000 tons in 1992; I/N Kote reached its design capacity of 900,000 tons in 1993.

Important Developments

Sep. '95—Inland announced that it would discontinue its plate operations by the end of 1995. The said that costs for the closure had already been provided for and that there would be no charge to earnings.
Sep. '95—IAD said it expects 1995's third-quarter earnings will decline from those of 1994's third quarter. The company attributed the shortfall to a decrease in contract business, which it said would have a negative effect on volume, mix and operating profit per ton. Earlier, in July, IAD stated that weak backlogs and a decision to advance maintenance work on facitities would hurt third-quarter earnings.

Capitalization

Long Term Debt: $696,900,000 (6/95).
9.48% Red. Preferred Stock: $185,000,000; held by Nippon Steel (represents 11% voting power).

Per Share Data ($)

(Year Ended Dec. 31)

	1994	1993	1992	1991	1990	1989
Tangible Bk. Val.	7.39	0.45	1.76	25.88	35.76	39.52
Cash Flow	5.00	1.75	-1.89	-6.06	2.30	6.85
Earnings	1.81	-1.96	-5.83	-9.88	-1.41	3.15
Dividends	Nil	Nil	Nil	0.15	1.40	1.40
Payout Ratio	Nil	Nil	Nil	NM	NM	43%
Prices - High	42	35	27	26⅛	36⅜	48½
- Low	29⅜	20	16¼	17⅜	20½	31⅜
P/E Ratio - High	23	NM	NM	NM	NM	15
- Low	16	NM	NM	NM	NM	10

Income Statement Analysis (Million $)

	1994	%Chg	1993	%Chg	1992	%Chg	1991
Revs.	4,497	16%	3,888	11%	3,494	3%	3,405
Oper. Inc.	380	139%	159	NM	-97.0	NM	-1.0
Depr.	139	5%	132	2%	130	10%	118
Int. Exp.	72.5	-10%	80.9	24%	65.1	8%	60.3
Pretax Inc.	170	NM	-74.0	NM	-258	NM	-380
Eff. Tax Rate	37%	—	NM	—	NM	—	NM
Net Inc.	107	NM	-38.0	NM	-158	NM	-274

Balance Sheet & Other Fin. Data (Million $)

	1994	1993	1992	1991	1990	1989
Cash	107	251	138	47.0	58.0	237
Curr. Assets	1,082	1,099	927	779	916	1,185
Total Assets	3,353	3,436	3,147	2,698	2,935	3,009
Curr. Liab.	565	603	486	456	520	482
LT Debt	706	777	874	765	692	578
Common Eqty.	678	505	397	1,015	1,320	1,526
Total Cap.	1,438	1,401	1,380	2,039	2,290	2,403
Cap. Exp.	182	106	64.0	140	268	197
Cash Flow	218	62.0	-62.0	-186	74.0	244

Ratio Analysis

	1994	1993	1992	1991	1990	1989
Curr. Ratio	1.9	1.8	1.9	1.7	1.8	2.5
% LT Debt of Cap.	49.1	55.5	63.3	37.5	30.2	24.0
% Net Inc.of Revs.	2.4	NM	NM	NM	NM	2.9
% Ret. on Assets	3.0	NM	NM	NM	NM	4.0
% Ret. on Equity	12.9	NM	NM	NM	NM	7.5

Dividend Data —Dividends on the common stock, omitted in 1985 and resumed in 1988, were omitted again in 1991; payments resumed in early 1995. A new "poison pill" stock purchase rights plan was adopted in 1989.

Amt. of Div. $	Date Decl.	Ex-Div. Date	Stock of Record	Payment Date
0.050	Mar. 22	Apr. 04	Apr. 10	May. 01 '95
0.050	May. 24	Jul. 06	Jul. 10	Aug. 01 '95
0.050	Sep. 28	Oct. 04	Oct. 06	Nov. 01 '95

Data as orig. reptd.; bef. results of disc. opers. and/or spec. items. Per share data adj. for stk. divs. as of ex-div. date. E-Estimated. NA-Not Available. NM-Not Meaningful. NR-Not Ranked.

Office—30 W. Monroe St., Chicago, IL 60603. **Tel**—(312) 346-0300. **Chrmn, Pres & CEO**—R. J. Darnall. **Sr VP-Fin**—E. L. Mason. **Secy**—G. A. Ranney Jr. **Investor Contact**—M. Robert Weidner III. **Dirs**—A. R. Abboud, J. W. Cozad, R. J. Darnall, J. A. Henderson, R. B. McKersie, M. S. Nelson Jr., D. S. Perkins, J. I. Smith, N. H. Teeters, A. R. Weber. **Transfer Agent & Registrar**—Harris Trust & Savings Bank, Chicago. **Incorporated** in Delaware in 1917. **Empl-** 15,479. **S&P Analyst:** Leo Larkin

Intel Corp.

NASDAQ Symbol **INTC**
In S&P 500

19-OCT-95 Industry:
Electronics/Electric

Summary: Intel is the world's largest manufacturer of microprocessors, the central processing unit of a PC. Various other products that enhance a PCs capabilities are also produced.

S&P Opinion: Buy (★★★★)		
Recent Price • 62¾	Yield • 0.2%	
52 Wk Range • 78⅜-28¾	12-Mo. P/E • 18.0	

Quantitative Evaluations

Outlook
(1 Lowest—5 Highest)
• **2+**

Fair Value
• **60⅞**

Risk
• **Average**

Earn./Div. Rank
• **B**

Technical Eval.
• **Bearish** since 8/95

Rel. Strength Rank
(1 Lowest—99 Highest)
• **87**

Insider Activity
• **NA**

Earnings vs. Previous Year
▲=Up ▼=Down ▶=No Change

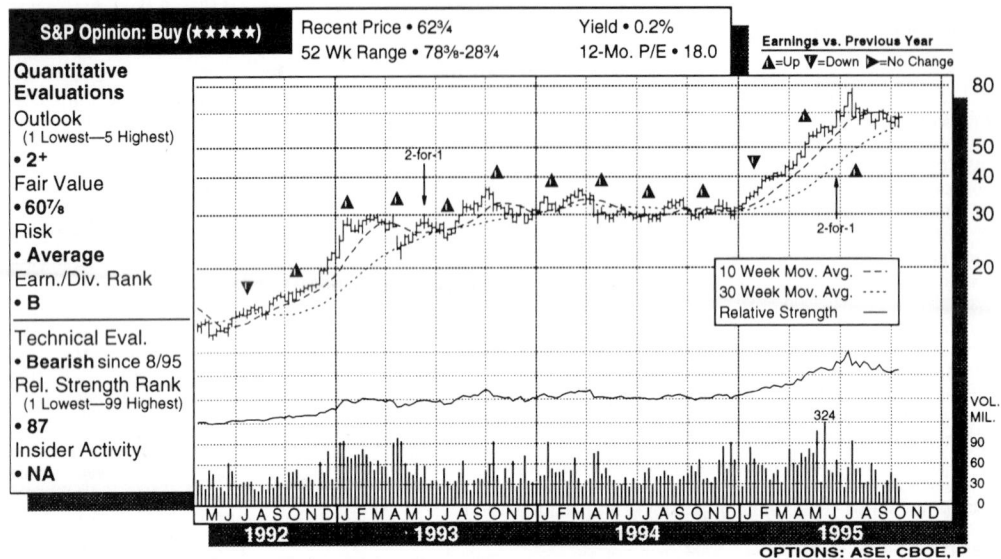

10 Week Mov. Avg. – – –
30 Week Mov. Avg. ····
Relative Strength ——

OPTIONS: ASE, CBOE, P

Overview - 19-OCT-95

Revenues are expected to increase more than 45% in 1995's fourth quarter and some 25% to 30% in 1996, driven by continued strong demand for personal computers (PCs). Growth is being fueled by the rapid market transition to PCs that feature the Pentium microprocessor away from the company's earlier generation 486 family. The recent release of Windows 95 and the introduction of INTC's next generation microprocessor, Pentium Pro, should also sustain strong growth through 1996. Margins are expected to narrow, reflecting increased sales of less profitable board level products, but should remain in the high 40% to low 50% range through 1996. Research and development and marketing costs will grow sharply, as INTC seeks to strengthen its franchise. Nevertheless, strong EPS gains are expected in 1996.

Valuation - 18-OCT-95

We are maintaining our strong buy opinion on the shares following impressive third quarter results and continued favorable prospects for the fourth quarter and into 1996. Intel is increasing its dominance as the world's leading chip maker through aggressive pricing, new product introductions and powerful manufacturing capabilities. Because of this dominant stance, INTC will be a major beneficiary of the strong PC demand that is expected to occur over the next several years. This powerful positioning should lead to strong sales and earnings gains, renewed investor confidence and expansion of the company's below market P/E.

Key Stock Statistics

S&P EPS Est. 1995	4.18	Tang. Bk. Value/Share	11.22
P/E on S&P Est. 1995	15.0	Beta	1.53
S&P EPS Est. 1996	5.10	Shareholders	39,900
Dividend Rate/Share	0.16	Market cap. (B)	$ 55.8
Shs. outstg. (M)	823.5	Inst. holdings	69%
Avg. daily vol. (M)	8.957	Insider holdings	NA

Value of $10,000 invested 5 years ago: $ 73,493

Fiscal Year Ending Dec. 31

	1995	% Change	1994	% Change	1993	% Change
Revenues (Million $)						
1Q	3,577	34%	2,660	31%	2,024	63%
2Q	3,894	41%	2,770	30%	2,130	61%
3Q	4,171	46%	2,863	28%	2,240	57%
4Q	—	—	3,228	35%	2,389	29%
Yr.	—	—	11,521	31%	8,782	50%
Income (Million $)						
1Q	889.0	44%	617.0	13%	548.0	198%
2Q	879.0	37%	640.0	13%	568.5	167%
3Q	931.0	41%	659.0	13%	584.4	143%
4Q	—	—	372.0	-37%	594.0	38%
Yr.	—	—	2,288	NM	2,295	115%
Earnings Per Share ($)						
1Q	1.02	46%	0.70	13%	0.62	188%
2Q	0.99	36%	0.73	12%	0.65	160%
3Q	1.05	38%	0.76	14%	0.66	138%
4Q	E1.12	160%	0.43	-36%	0.68	36%
Yr.	E4.18	60%	2.62	NM	2.60	110%

Next earnings report expected: mid January

Business Summary - 19-OCT-95

Intel designs, develops, manufacturers and markets advanced microcomputer components and related products at various levels of integration. Foreign business accounted for 49% of sales and 19% of operating income in 1994.

Intel's products strategy is twofold: the company offers to OEMs (original equipment manufacturers) a wide range of PC (personal computer) building-block products to meet their needs, and offers to PC users products that expand the capability of their systems and networks.

The company introduced the first microprocessor in 1971, and remains the world's largest maker of such devices. A microprocessor is the central processing unit of a PC that processes system data and controls other devices in the system. Intel's 32-bit processors include the flagship Pentium family and the 486 family. Intel's sixth generation processor, Pentium Pro, is expected to offer substantial performance benefits over Pentium models upon its release in 1995's fourth quarter.

Other products manufactured include chipsets, which support and extend the graphic and other capabilities of microprocessors; embedded chips which provide the computing power in devices other than PC's and workstations, including wireless communications devices, printers, copiers, fax machines etc; flash memory chips used to store computer programs and data entered by users; computer modules and boards, which serve as the basic building block for personal computers for various OEM manufacturers.

Intel also offers a number of networking products including its EtherExpress family of adapters and network managment products sold under the LANDesk product line. The company's ProShare personal conferencing products allow two users to view and manipulate the same documents simultaneously and, in some cases, see the other user. The company's scalable parallel processing systems (SPP) utilize multiple microprocessors working together to solve the most computationally intensive problems.

Important Developments

Sep. '95—Intel named its next generation microprocessor, previously codenamed P6, the Pentium Pro. The microprocessor, to be introduced in 1995's fourth quarter, will be targeted for use in workstations, high-end desktop systems and servers. Separately, Intel was selected by the Department of Energy to build a supercomputer powered by Pentum Pro chips to solve complex problems for scientists. More than 9,000 Pentium Pros will power the new system.

Capitalization

Long Term Debt: $401,000,000 (9/95).
Warrants: To buy 12,500,000 shs. at prices ranging from $55 a sh. to $63 a sh. through 12/95, as adjusted.

Per Share Data ($)

(Year Ended Dec. 31)

	1994	1993	1992	1991	1990	1989
Tangible Bk. Val.	11.22	8.97	6.51	5.42	4.50	3.46
Cash Flow	3.79	3.41	1.85	1.48	1.17	0.84
Earnings	2.62	2.60	1.24	0.98	0.80	0.52
Dividends	0.11	0.17	0.03	Nil	Nil	Nil
Payout Ratio	4%	7%	2%	Nil	Nil	Nil
Prices - High	36¾	37⅛	22⅞	14⅞	13	9
- Low	28	21⅜	11⅝	9½	7	5¾
P/E Ratio - High	14	14	18	15	16	17
- Low	11	8	9	10	9	11

Income Statement Analysis (Million $)

	1994	%Chg	1993	%Chg	1992	%Chg	1991
Revs.	11,521	31%	8,782	50%	5,844	22%	4,779
Oper. Inc.	4,863	18%	4,109	101%	2,043	36%	1,498
Depr.	1,028	43%	717	38%	518	24%	418
Int. Exp.	84.0	45%	58.0	-12%	66.0	-25%	88.0
Pretax Inc.	3,603	2%	3,530	125%	1,569	31%	1,195
Eff. Tax Rate	37%	—	35%	—	32%	—	32%
Net Inc.	2,288	NM	2,295	115%	1,067	30%	819

Balance Sheet & Other Fin. Data (Million $)

	1994	1993	1992	1991	1990	1989
Cash	2,410	3,136	2,835	2,277	1,785	1,090
Curr. Assets	6,167	5,802	4,691	3,604	3,119	2,163
Total Assets	13,816	11,344	8,089	6,292	5,376	3,994
Curr. Liab.	3,024	2,433	1,842	1,228	1,314	921
LT Debt	392	426	2.5	363	345	412
Common Eqty.	9,267	7,500	5,445	4,418	3,592	2,549
Total Cap.	10,048	8,223	5,874	4,924	4,063	3,073
Cap. Exp.	2,441	1,933	1,228	948	680	422
Cash Flow	3,316	3,012	1,584	1,237	943	628

Ratio Analysis

	1994	1993	1992	1991	1990	1989
Curr. Ratio	2.0	2.4	2.5	2.9	2.4	2.3
% LT Debt of Cap.	3.9	5.2	4.2	7.4	8.5	13.4
% Net Inc.of Revs.	19.9	26.1	18.3	17.1	16.6	12.5
% Ret. on Assets	18.3	23.6	14.7	13.9	13.4	10.3
% Ret. on Equity	27.4	35.5	35.5	20.2	20.5	16.7

Dividend Data

Cash dividends were initiated in September 1992. A "poison pill" stock purchase rights plan was adopted in 1989.

Amt. of Div. $	Date Decl.	Ex-Div. Date	Stock of Record	Payment Date
0.060	Nov. 08	Jan. 26	Feb. 01	Mar. 01 '95
0.060	Mar. 23	Apr. 25	May. 01	Jun. 01 '95
2-for-1	Apr. 28	Jun. 19	May. 19	Jun. 16 '95
0.040	Apr. 28	Jul. 28	Aug. 01	Sep. 01 '95
0.040	Sep. 20	Oct. 30	Nov. 01	Dec. 01 '95

Data as orig. reptd.; bef. results of disc. opers. and/or spec. items. Per share data adj. for stk. divs. as of ex-div. date.
E-Estimated. NA-Not Available. NM-Not Meaningful. NR-Not Ranked.

Office—2200 Mission College Blvd., Santa Clara, CA 95052-8119. **Tel**—(408) 765-8080. **Chrmn**—G. E. Moore. **Pres & CEO**—A. S. Grove. **EVP & COO**—C. R. Barrett. **Investor Contact**—Gordon Casey. **VP & CFO**—A. D. Bryant, **VP & Secy**—F. T. Dunlap, Jr. **Dirs**—C. R. Barrett, W. H. Chen, A. S. Grove, D. J. Guzy, R. Hodgson, S. Kaplan, G. E. Moore, M. Palevsky, A. Rock, J. E. Shaw, L. L. Vadasz, D. B. Yoffie, C. E. Young. **Transfer Agent & Registrar**—Harris Trust and Savings Bank. **Incorporated** in California in 1968. **Empl**- 36,000. **S&P Analyst:** John D. Coyle, CFA

STOCK REPORTS

Intergraph Corp.

NASDAQ Symbol **INGR**
In S&P 500

29-AUG-95

Industry: Data Processing

Summary: This company develops and sells software, hardware, and services for technical professionals, particularly those in CAD/CAM/CAE and GIS disciplines.

S&P Opinion: Hold (★★★)

Recent Price • 12¼	Yield • Nil	
52 Wk Range • 14⅜-7⅜	12-Mo. P/E • NM	

Earnings vs. Previous Year
▲=Up ▼=Down ▶=No Change

Quantitative Evaluations

Outlook
(1 Lowest—5 Highest)
• **3**

Fair Value
• **11¼**

Risk
• **High**

Earn./Div. Rank
• **C**

Technical Eval.
• **Bearish** since 7/95

Rel. Strength Rank
(1 Lowest—99 Highest)
• **64**

Insider Activity
• **Neutral**

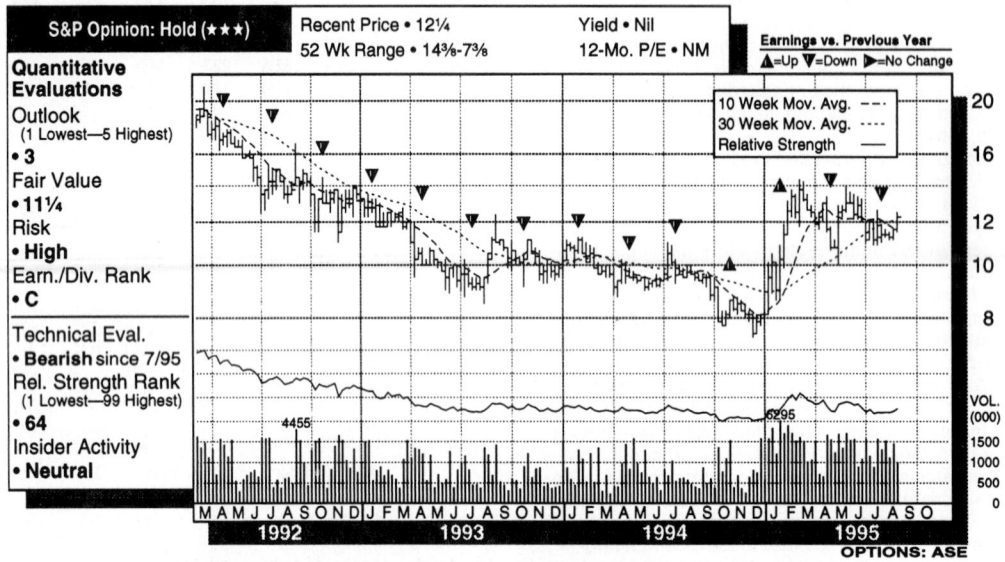

10 Week Mov. Avg. – –
30 Week Mov. Avg. – – –
Relative Strength —

OPTIONS: ASE

Overview - 29-AUG-95

Intergraph sales are expected to rise significantly in 1996 as its gains wider acceptance for its Intel-based workstations that run Microsoft's Windows NT operating system. While the company's product transition has been prolonged, these new systems appear to significantly expand its opportunities in the market. In addition, it is anticipated that industry sales will also remain strong. A 17% increase in orders for new systems during the second quarter reinforces our belief that sales will rise significantly in 1996. However, margin pressure will continue due to aggressive pricing in the market. Nevertheless, profitability should be restored due to the higher volume and a projected $100 million cost savings from the recent restructuring, as well as the absence of the $7.5 million restructuring charge itself.

Valuation - 29-AUG-95

Following a sharp advance in the shares early in 1995 due to indications that the product transition to Intel-based workstations running software on Microsoft's Windows NT had been completed, the shares have more recently languished as poor operating results have dulled the earlier optimism. We remain skeptical towards the shares given the prolonged product transition and continuing losses. Furthermore, sustained profitability at a high level is not assured given the intense industry competition. Therefore, the shares are ranked a "hold."

Key Stock Statistics

S&P EPS Est. 1995	-0.60	Tang. Bk. Value/Share	10.81
P/E on S&P Est. 1995	NM	Beta	1.67
S&P EPS Est. 1996	0.75	Shareholders	6,400
Dividend Rate/Share	Nil	Market cap. (B)	$0.570
Shs. outstg. (M)	46.1	Inst. holdings	41%
Avg. daily vol. (M)	0.239	Insider holdings	NA

Value of $10,000 invested 5 years ago: $ 7,101

Fiscal Year Ending Dec. 31

	1995	% Change	1994	% Change	1993	% Change
Revenues (Million $)						
1Q	257.3	7%	240.1	-15%	282.1	2%
2Q	260.2	7%	242.4	-3%	249.1	-14%
3Q	—	—	262.2	5%	250.6	-17%
4Q	—	—	296.7	10%	268.5	-13%
Yr.	—	—	1,041	NM	1,050	-11%
Income (Million $)						
1Q	-22.47	NM	-14.05	NM	-10.17	NM
2Q	-21.96	NM	-20.16	NM	-18.61	NM
3Q	—	—	-17.50	NM	-19.84	NM
4Q	—	—	-18.51	NM	-69.92	NM
Yr.	—	—	-70.22	NM	-118.5	NM
Earnings Per Share ($)						
1Q	-0.49	NM	-0.31	NM	-0.21	NM
2Q	-0.48	NM	-0.45	NM	-0.40	NM
3Q	E0.10	NM	-0.39	NM	-0.43	NM
4Q	E0.27	NM	-0.41	NM	-1.54	NM
Yr.	E-0.60	NM	-1.56	NM	-2.56	NM

Next earnings report expected: late October

Intergraph Corp.

29-AUG-95

Business Summary - 29-AUG-95

Intergraph Corp. manufactures and markets interactive computer graphics systems. Contributions to revenues in recent years follow:

	1994	1993
Systems	64%	64%
Maintenance and services	36%	36%

INGR's systems combine graphics workstations, servers, and peripheral hardware with operating system and application-specific software programs authored by it and others that perform such functions as design, drafting, mapping, modeling, analysis and documentation. Major markets for its products are architecture, engineering, and construction (AEC), mapping/geographic information systems (GIS), and mechanical design, engineering, and manufacturing (MDEM). The relative contributions of these product families to total system revenue for 1994 and 1993 were AEC 34%, GIS 42%, MDEM 16%, and all other applications (8%).

System hardware consists of workstations and servers based largely on Intel-based systems (74% of sales in 1994). It also produces systems based on the company's microprocessor with a UNIX operating system. In addition, the company has developed interoperability products that allow Windows NT and UNIX applications to work together in a mixed environment.

Software is developed to provide graphics and database management capabilities on INGR systems, advanced compilers for INGR systems, and utilities to enable interoperability with systems from other vendors. Sales of Windows based software represented 48% of software revenues in 1994.

Maintenance and services revenue consists of revenues from maintenance of company's systems and from company training, consulting and other servies.

International revenues provided 39% of the total in 1994, and accounted for a $50.6 million operating loss. The U.S. Government accounted for about 16% of revenues.

Important Developments

Jul. '95—The company said that having completed major transitions in both handware and software products, it found itself with a cost structure that is out of line with current revenue and margin assumptions. In view of that and in an effort to restore profitability and adapt to changing markets, it had undertaken a program to be completed over the next 12 months to reduce expenses by an estimated $100 million per year that resulted in a second quarter restructuring charge of $7.5 million. The restructuring will involve the elimination of approximately 600 positions and the divestiture of non-strategic operations. In addition, the company said that it had sold one of its unprofitable business units during the quarter.

Capitalization

Long Term Debt: $27,008,000 (6/95).

Per Share Data ($)

(Year Ended Dec. 31)

	1994	1993	1992	1991	1990	1989
Tangible Bk. Val.	11.66	12.98	15.49	15.80	14.35	12.58
Cash Flow	0.08	-1.15	1.54	2.87	2.40	2.37
Earnings	-1.56	-2.56	0.18	1.47	1.28	1.48
Dividends	Nil	Nil	Nil	Nil	Nil	Nil
Payout Ratio	Nil	Nil	Nil	Nil	Nil	Nil
Prices - High	11¼	13½	22⅜	31½	23½	22¾
- Low	7⅞	8½	11	13	10½	13¾
P/E Ratio - High	NM	NM	NM	21	18	15
- Low	NM	NM	NM	9	8	9

Income Statement Analysis (Million $)

	1994	%Chg	1993	%Chg	1992	%Chg	1991
Revs.	1,041	NM	1,050	-11%	1,177	-2%	1,195
Oper. Inc.	2.0	NM	-9.0	NM	95.0	-42%	165
Depr.	73.6	13%	65.4	NM	65.7	-4%	68.1
Int. Exp.	2.4	12%	2.1	-31%	3.0	44%	2.1
Pretax Inc.	-74.0	NM	-172	NM	12.0	-89%	112
Eff. Tax Rate	NM	—	NM	—	32%	—	37%
Net Inc.	-70.0	NM	-118	NM	8.4	-88%	71.1

Balance Sheet & Other Fin. Data (Million $)

	1994	1993	1992	1991	1990	1989
Cash	62.0	76.0	93.0	116	90.0	91.0
Curr. Assets	575	585	648	710	640	574
Total Assets	840	855	987	997	907	808
Curr. Liab.	292	236	217	208	197	160
LT Debt	23.4	17.5	19.8	23.4	16.9	7.1
Common Eqty.	522	589	737	755	682	630
Total Cap.	548	619	769	789	710	648
Cap. Exp.	68.0	66.2	83.4	91.6	79.6	74.1
Cash Flow	3.0	-53.0	74.0	139	118	128

Ratio Analysis

	1994	1993	1992	1991	1990	1989
Curr. Ratio	2.0	2.5	3.0	3.4	3.2	3.6
% LT Debt of Cap.	4.3	2.8	2.6	3.0	2.4	1.1
% Net Inc.of Revs.	NM	NM	0.7	5.9	6.0	9.2
% Ret. on Assets	NM	NM	0.9	7.4	7.5	10.3
% Ret. on Equity	NM	NM	1.1	9.9	9.8	13.1

Dividend Data —No cash has been paid. A "poison pill" stock purchase rights plan was adopted in 1993.

Data as orig. reptd.; bef. results of disc. opers. and/or spec. items. Per share data adj. for stk. divs. as of ex-div. date. E-Estimated. NA-Not Available. NM-Not Meaningful. NR-Not Ranked.

Office—Huntsville, AL 35894-0001. **Tel**—(205) 730-2000. **Chrmn & CEO**—J. W. Meadlock. **EVP & CFO**—L. J. Laster. **Secy**—J. R. Wynn. **Treas & Investor Contact**—James Dorton. **Dirs**—R. E. Brown, L. J. Laster, J. W. Meadlock, N. B. Meadlock, K. H. Schonrock, Jr., J. F. Taylor, Jr., R. E. Thurber. **Transfer Agent & Registrar**—Harris Trust and Savings Bank, Chicago. **Incorporated** in Alabama in 1969; reincorporated in Delaware in 1984. **Empl**-9,200. **S&P Analyst:** Paul H. Valentine, CFA

Int'l Business Machines

STOCK REPORTS

NYSE Symbol **IBM**
In S&P 500

19-OCT-95

Industry:
Data Processing

Summary: IBM, the world's largest technology company, offers a diversified line of computer hardware equipment, application and system software and related services.

S&P Opinion: Buy (★★★★)

| Recent Price • 92½ | Yield • 1.0% |
| 52 Wk Range • 114⅝-68 | 12-Mo. P/E • 9.7 |

Quantitative Evaluations

Outlook
(1 Lowest—5 Highest)
• **4+**

Fair Value
• **105¾**

Risk
• **Low**

Earn./Div. Rank
• **B-**

Technical Eval.
• **Bullish** since 11/93

Rel. Strength Rank
(1 Lowest—99 Highest)
• **39**

Insider Activity
• **Neutral**

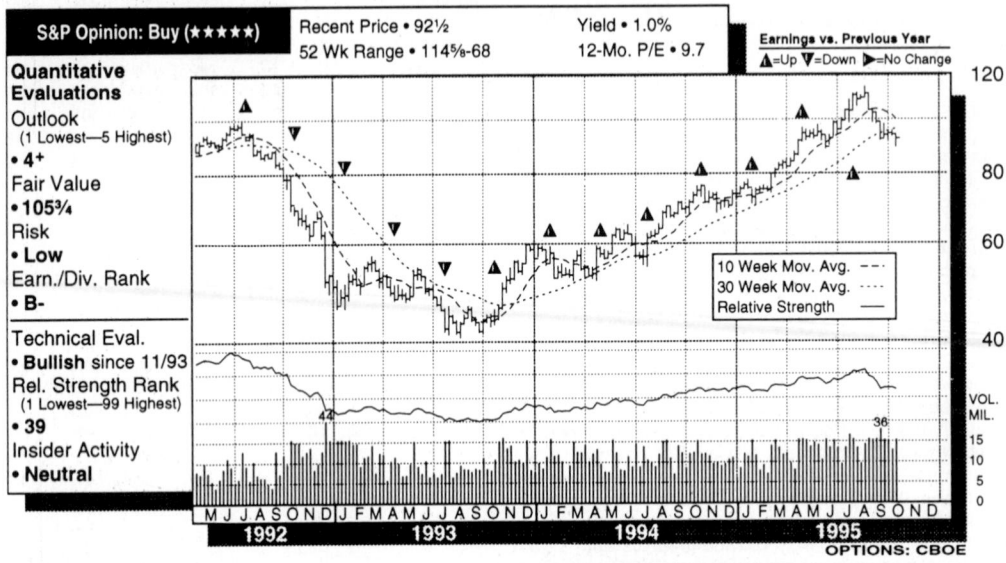

Earnings vs. Previous Year
▲=Up ▼=Down ▶=No Change

10 Week Mov. Avg. ---
30 Week Mov. Avg. ·····
Relative Strength —

OPTIONS: CBOE

Overview - 19-OCT-95

We are forecasting high-single digit revenue growth for the balance of 1995 and into 1996. Growth in 1996 will be fueled by double-digit gains for services, OEM business, RS/6000 workstations, AS/400 minicomputers and PCs. Offsetting will be flat-to-down mainframe revenue and low single-digit gains in maintenance, software and rentals and financing. Margins are expected to narrow, reflecting continued price pressures. Operating expenses will grow at a slower rate than revenues, helped by a recently announced restructuring charge that could eliminate 5,000 to 10,000 additional personnnel. Earnings are expected to reach $12.65 in 1996, although additional buybacks could boost this estimate.

Valuation - 19-OCT-95

We remain bullish on IBM despite concerns about longer term revenue growth prospects. While its third quarter performance did little to assuage these concerns, IBM is committed to revenue growth and, more importantly, to boosting shareholder value. Despite the inconsistent revenue performance, IBM has done a credible job stabilizing key business units and has taken the necessary steps to transition away from mainframes. Profitability has also improved greatly, which is fueling substantial cash flow generation. When coupled with a strong balance sheet, it is clear IBM has the opportunity to grow revenues in several ways. As a result, we strongly recommend the shares for purchase as they remain significantly undervalued in relation to IBM's earnings potential.

Key Stock Statistics

S&P EPS Est. 1995	10.90	Tang. Bk. Value/Share	37.18
P/E on S&P Est. 1995	8.5	Beta	0.69
S&P EPS Est. 1996	12.65	Shareholders	705,300
Dividend Rate/Share	1.00	Market cap. (B)	$ 54.8
Shs. outstg. (M)	568.7	Inst. holdings	51%
Avg. daily vol. (M)	2.702	Insider holdings	NA

Value of $10,000 invested 5 years ago: $ 12,440

Fiscal Year Ending Dec. 31

	1995	% Change	1994	% Change	1993	% Change
Revenues (Million $)						
1Q	15,735	18%	13,373	2%	13,058	-7%
2Q	17,531	14%	15,351	-1%	15,519	-4%
3Q	16,754	9%	15,431	5%	14,743	NM
4Q	—	—	19,897	3%	19,396	NM
Yr.	—	—	64,052	2%	62,716	-3%
Income (Million $)						
1Q	1,289	NM	392.0	NM	-285.0	NM
2Q	1,716	149%	689.0	NM	-8,035	NM
3Q	1,302	83%	710.0	NM	-48.00	NM
4Q	—	—	1,230	NM	382.0	NM
Yr.	—	—	3,021	NM	-7,986	NM
Earnings Per Share ($)						
1Q	2.12	NM	0.64	NM	-0.50	NM
2Q	2.97	161%	1.14	NM	-14.10	NM
3Q	2.30	95%	1.18	NM	-0.12	NM
4Q	E3.50	70%	2.06	NM	0.62	NM
Yr.	E10.90	117%	5.02	NM	-14.02	NM

Next earnings report expected: mid October

Int'l Business Machines

Business Summary - 19-OCT-95

IBM is the largest manufacturer of data processing equipment and systems. Industry segment contributions to revenues in recent years:

	1994	1993
Hardware	51%	50%
Software	18%	18%
Services	15%	13%
Maintenance	11%	12%
Rentals & financing	5%	7%

Foreign operations contributed 59% of revenues in 1994.

Hardware products include high-end and mid-range processors (15% of 1994 revenues); personal computers and RISC System/6000 workstation products (18%); display-based terminals, consumer and financial systems (2%); storage (6%); printers and telecommunication devices (3%); and OEM hardware (5%). Software (18%) includes applications and systems software. Services (15%) include consulting, education, systems development, managed operations and availability services. Maintenance (11%) represents separately billed maintenance services. Rentals and financing (7%) is comprised of financing revenue associated with purchasing and leasing products.

In November, IBM, Apple Computer and Motorola reached an agreement on a new common hardware platform for the PowerPC microprocessor that will allow users to run a variety of operating systems, including IBM's OS/2 for the PowerPC and its version of Unix, AIX, Apple's MAC OS, Microsoft's Windows NT, and Sun Microsystems' Solaris. Prototypes of the systems will be available in 1995, and shipments are expected to begin in 1996.

In February, directors authorized the repurchase of up to $2.5 billion in IBM common shares over an unspecified time frame.

During 1994's first quarter, IBM sold its Federal Systems Co. (FSC) division to Loral Corp. for a net gain of $248 million ($0.43 a share).

Net restructuring charges totaled $8.9 billion in 1993 ($14.02 a share), $8.3 billion in 1992 ($14.51) and $2.9 billion in 1991 ($5.03), reflecting actions taken to cut costs and capacity.

Important Developments

Oct. '95—IBM will take an $800 million charge in 1995's fourth quarter to cover additional work force reductions and the consolidation of leased space and related actions.

Jul. '95—IBM completed the acquisition of Lotus Development Corp for $64 a share cash ($3.5 billion).

Capitalization

Long Term Debt: $10,436,000,000 (9/95).

Preferred Stock: $231,000,000.

Per Share Data ($)

(Year Ended Dec. 31)

	1994	1993	1992	1991	1990	1989
Tangible Bk. Val.	37.20	30.90	47.86	64.39	74.29	66.33
Cash Flow	12.20	-5.80	-3.63	8.02	17.88	13.76
Earnings	5.02	-14.02	-12.03	-0.99	10.51	6.47
Dividends	1.00	1.58	4.84	4.84	4.84	4.73
Payout Ratio	20%	NM	NM	NM	46%	72%
Prices - High	76⅜	59⅞	100⅜	139¾	123⅛	130⅞
- Low	51⅜	40⅝	48¾	83½	94½	93⅜
P/E Ratio - High	15	NM	NM	NM	12	20
- Low	10	NM	NM	NM	9	14

Income Statement Analysis (Million $)

	1994	%Chg	1993	%Chg	1992	%Chg	1991
Revs.	64,052	2%	62,716	-3%	64,523	NM	64,792
Oper. Inc.	9,202	83%	5,018	-39%	8,199	-14%	9,489
Depr.	4,197	-11%	4,710	-2%	4,793	-7%	5,149
Int. Exp.	1,247	-5%	1,319	-10%	1,461	-7%	1,566
Pretax Inc.	5,155	NM	-8,796	NM	-9,025	NM	121
Eff. Tax Rate	41%	—	NM	—	NM	—	566%
Net Inc.	3,021	NM	-7,986	NM	-6,864	NM	-563

Balance Sheet & Other Fin. Data (Million $)

	1994	1993	1992	1991	1990	1989
Cash	10,554	7,133	5,649	5,151	4,551	4,961
Curr. Assets	41,338	39,202	39,692	40,969	38,920	35,875
Total Assets	81,091	81,113	86,705	92,473	87,568	77,734
Curr. Liab.	29,226	33,150	36,737	33,624	25,276	21,700
LT Debt	12,548	15,245	12,853	13,231	11,943	10,825
Common Eqty.	22,288	18,613	27,624	37,006	42,832	38,509
Total Cap.	37,842	36,786	42,507	52,164	58,636	52,614
Cap. Exp.	3,078	3,154	4,751	6,502	6,548	6,410
Cash Flow	7,134	-3,323	-2,071	4,385	10,237	7,998

Ratio Analysis

	1994	1993	1992	1991	1990	1989
Curr. Ratio	1.4	1.2	1.1	1.2	1.5	1.7
% LT Debt of Cap.	53.2	41.4	30.2	25.4	20.4	20.6
% Net Inc.of Revs.	4.7	NM	NM	NM	8.7	6.0
% Ret. on Assets	3.7	NM	NM	NM	7.3	5.0
% Ret. on Equity	14.3	NM	NM	NM	14.8	9.8

Dividend Data

—Dividends have been paid since 1916. A dividend reinvestment plan is available.

Amt. of Div. $	Date Decl.	Ex-Div. Date	Stock of Record	Payment Date
0.250	Oct. 24	Nov. 04	Nov. 10	Dec. 10 '94
0.250	Jan. 31	Feb. 06	Feb. 10	Mar. 10 '95
0.250	Apr. 25	May. 04	May. 10	Jun. 10 '95
0.250	Jul. 25	Aug. 08	Aug. 10	Sep. 09 '95

Data as orig. reptd.; bef. results of disc. opers. and/or spec. items. Per share data adj. for stk. divs. as of ex-div. date. E-Estimated. NA-Not Available. NM-Not Meaningful. NR-Not Ranked.

Office—Old Orchard Rd., Armonk, NY 10504. **Tel**—(914) 765-1900. **Chrmn & CEO**—L. V. Gerstner, Jr. **SVP & CFO**—G. R. Thoman. **Treas**—J. Serkes **Secy**—J. E. Hickey. **Investor Contact**—H. Parke, III (914-765-5008). **Stockholder Relations Dept**—Tel: (914-765-5019). **Dirs**—H. Brown, J. E. Burke, F. Gerber, L. V. Gerstner, Jr., N. O. Keohane, C. F. Knight, T. S. Murphy, L. A. Noto, J. B. Slaughter, G. R. Thoman, A. Trotman, L. C. van Wachem, C. M. Vest, E. S. Woolard, Jr., **Transfer Agent & Registrar**— First Chicago Trust Co. of New York, NYC. **Incorporated** in New York in 1911. **Empl-219,839. S&P Analyst:** John D. Coyle, CFA

Int'l Flavors & Fragrances

NYSE Symbol **IFF**
In S&P 500

15-SEP-95

Industry:
Cosmetics/Toiletries

Summary: IFF, which derives more than two-thirds of sales and earnings from foreign operations, is a leading producer of flavors and fragrances used in a wide variety of consumer goods.

S&P Opinion: Accumulate (★★★★)

Recent Price • 47⅞	Yield • 2.5%
52 Wk Range • 53⅜-40⅜	12-Mo. P/E • 21.5

Quantitative Evaluations

Outlook
(1 Lowest—5 Highest)
• **1+**

Fair Value
• **35⅛**

Risk
• **Low**

Earn./Div. Rank
• **A+**

Technical Eval.
• **Bullish** since 6/94

Rel. Strength Rank
(1 Lowest—99 Highest)
• **28**

Insider Activity
• **Neutral**

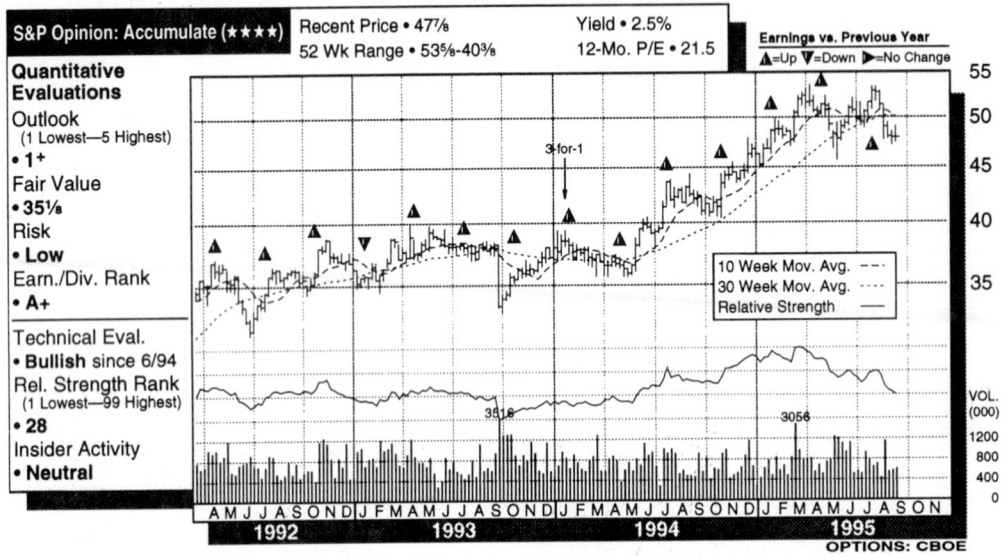

Earnings vs. Previous Year
▲=Up ▼=Down ▶=No Change

10 Week Mov. Avg. — — —
30 Week Mov. Avg. ‥‥‥‥
Relative Strength ———

VOL. (000)

OPTIONS: CBOE

Overview - 15-SEP-95

We expect sales to advance about 11% in each of 1995 and 1996, reflecting continued rising sales volumes of flavors, fragrances and aromas in most parts of the world, especially in less developed countries, stemming from growing consumer demand for personal care, detergent, household, food and beverage products. A continuing high level of new product introductions by customers will be beneficial, but growth in the North American fine fragrance market may remain sluggish, because of a slow retail environment. The stronger U.S. dollar over the past few months should also modestly restrict sales growth in the latter half of 1995. Share earnings comparisons will be helped by an ongoing stock repurchase program.

Valuation - 15-SEP-95

The shares have been excellent performers over the past several years, reflecting steady growth in sales and net income over the past decade. In addition, dividends have been raised annually for the past 34 years, a record that should continue in 1995. The stock has been declining since mid-summer, reflecting investor concerns regarding the possible adverse impact of a stronger U.S. dollar. We recommend accumulation of the stock for long-term appreciation and rising dividend income. IFF's premium P/E is justified, in view of the company's strong growth prospects.

Key Stock Statistics

S&P EPS Est. 1995	2.30	Tang. Bk. Value/Share	10.06
P/E on S&P Est. 1995	20.8	Beta	0.96
S&P EPS Est. 1996	2.60	Shareholders	5,300
Dividend Rate/Share	1.24	Market cap. (B)	$ 5.5
Shs. outstg. (M)	111.3	Inst. holdings	55%
Avg. daily vol. (M)	0.175	Insider holdings	NA

Value of $10,000 invested 5 years ago: $ 24,501

Fiscal Year Ending Dec. 31

	1995	% Change	1994	% Change	1993	% Change
Revenues (Million $)						
1Q	373.6	15%	323.5	5%	309.0	9%
2Q	394.3	14%	345.2	7%	321.3	9%
3Q	—	—	341.7	14%	298.6	2%
4Q	—	—	304.8	17%	259.6	2%
Yr.	—	—	1,315	11%	1,189	6%
Income (Million $)						
1Q	69.96	19%	58.94	5%	56.23	12%
2Q	75.70	17%	64.92	7%	60.93	11%
3Q	—	—	58.91	19%	49.64	NM
4Q	—	—	43.26	21%	35.67	62%
Yr.	—	—	226.0	12%	202.5	15%
Earnings Per Share ($)						
1Q	0.63	19%	0.53	8%	0.49	12%
2Q	0.68	17%	0.58	9%	0.53	12%
3Q	E0.57	8%	0.53	20%	0.44	3%
4Q	E0.42	8%	0.39	22%	0.32	68%
Yr.	E2.30	13%	2.03	14%	1.78	16%

Next earnings report expected: late October

Int'l Flavors & Fragrances

Business Summary - 15-SEP-95

International Flavors & Fragrances is a leading maker of products used by other manufacturers to impart or improve flavor or fragrance in a wide variety of consumer goods. Contributions in 1994 by geographic area were:

	Sales	Profits
U.S.	32%	30%
Western Europe	41%	47%
Other	27%	23%

Fragrance products (59% of 1994 sales) are used in the manufacture of soaps, detergents, cosmetic creams, lotions and powders, lipsticks, aftershave lotions, deodorants, hair preparations, air fresheners, perfumes and colognes and other consumer products. Cosmetics (including perfumes and toiletries) and household products (soaps and detergents) are the company's two largest customer groups.

Flavor products (41% of 1994 sales) are sold principally to the food, beverage and other industries for use in such consumer products as soft drinks, candies, cake mixes, desserts, prepared foods, dietary foods, dairy products, drink powders, pharmaceuticals, oral care products, alcoholic beverages and tobacco.

The company uses both synthetic and natural ingredients in its compounds. A substantial portion of the company's synthetic production is sold to others, including such chemicals as phenyl ethyl alcohol, ionones, alpha amyl cinnamic aldehyde and various synthetic musks.

Important Developments

Jul. '95—Sales in the 1995 second quarter rose 14%, year to year; excluding foreign exchange rates, sales were up 8%. Fragrance sales rose 10%, while flavor sales advanced 19%. North American sales increased 9%, while European sales climbed 19%. Sales in the rest of the world grew 14%.

Feb. '95—IFF reported strong growth in 1994, including an excellent fourth quarter. It met its goals for the year, with good sales increases in both flavors and fragrances in all geographic areas, and said it expected continued strength in 1995. Both fragrance and flavor sales rose 11%. North American sales rose 11%, while European sales were up 9%. Sales in the rest of the world grew 13%. Capital spending for 1995 was budgeted at $105 million, versus $103 million spent in 1994. The company also said it had completed about two-thirds of the repurchase of 7.5 million common shares, authorized in 1992.

Capitalization

Long Term Debt: $15,603,000 (6/95).

Per Share Data ($)

(Year Ended Dec. 31)

	1994	1993	1992	1991	1990	1989
Tangible Bk. Val.	9.04	7.96	8.48	8.39	7.84	6.70
Cash Flow	2.35	2.09	1.83	1.73	1.62	1.43
Earnings	2.03	1.78	1.53	1.47	1.37	1.22
Dividends	1.12	1.02	0.93	0.83	0.73	0.66
Payout Ratio	55%	57%	61%	56%	54%	54%
Prices - High	47⅞	39⅞	38¾	35	25	25⅞
- Low	35⅝	33	31½	22⅞	18¼	16⅛
P/E Ratio - High	24	22	25	24	18	21
- Low	18	19	20	16	13	13

Income Statement Analysis (Million $)

	1994	%Chg	1993	%Chg	1992	%Chg	1991
Revs.	1,315	11%	1,189	6%	1,126	11%	1,017
Oper. Inc.	385	13%	341	7%	318	12%	284
Depr.	36.4	4%	35.1	3%	34.0	16%	29.4
Int. Exp.	13.5	-22%	17.4	40%	12.4	31%	9.5
Pretax Inc.	360	11%	324	15%	282	5%	269
Eff. Tax Rate	37%	—	38%	—	37%	—	37%
Net Inc.	226	12%	202	14%	177	5%	169

Balance Sheet & Other Fin. Data (Million $)

	1994	1993	1992	1991	1990	1989
Cash	302	311	430	410	376	289
Curr. Assets	964	879	965	918	853	724
Total Assets	1,400	1,225	1,268	1,217	1,129	970
Curr. Liab.	260	227	195	181	158	140
LT Debt	14.3	Nil	Nil	Nil	Nil	Nil
Common Eqty.	1,008	892	977	960	898	765
Total Cap.	1,037	903	984	982	919	782
Cap. Exp.	101	82.3	51.1	53.3	41.2	33.4
Cash Flow	262	238	211	198	185	163

Ratio Analysis

	1994	1993	1992	1991	1990	1989
Curr. Ratio	3.7	3.9	5.0	5.1	5.4	5.2
% LT Debt of Cap.	1.4	Nil	Nil	Nil	Nil	Nil
% Net Inc.of Revs.	17.2	17.0	15.7	16.6	16.3	15.9
% Ret. on Assets	17.3	16.5	14.2	14.4	14.9	14.9
% Ret. on Equity	23.9	22.0	18.2	18.2	18.8	18.9

Dividend Data —Dividends have been paid since 1956. A poison pill stock purchase rights plan was adopted in 1990.

Amt. of Div. $	Date Decl.	Ex-Div. Date	Stock of Record	Payment Date
0.270	Sep. 13	Sep. 21	Sep. 27	Oct. 10 '94
0.310	Dec. 13	Dec. 21	Dec. 28	Jan. 10 '95
0.310	Feb. 14	Mar. 21	Mar. 27	Apr. 11 '95
0.310	May. 11	Jun. 23	Jun. 27	Jul. 11 '95
0.310	Sep. 12	Sep. 25	Sep. 27	Oct. 11 '95

Data as orig. reptd.; bef. results of disc. opers. and/or spec. items. Per share data adj. for stk. divs. as of ex-div. date. E-Estimated. NA-Not Available. NM-Not Meaningful. NR-Not Ranked.

Office—521 W. 57th St., New York, NY 10019. **Tel**—(212) 765-5500. **Chrmn & Pres**—E. P. Grisanti. **VP & Secy**—S. A. Block. **VP-Fin, Treas & Investor Contact**—Thomas H. Hoppel. **Dirs**—M. Hayes Adame, R. Chandler Duke, R. M. Furlaud, E. P. Grisanti, T. H. Hoppel, H. R. Kirkpatrick, H. G. Reid, G. Rowe Jr., S. M. Rumbough, Jr., H. P. van Ameringen, H. C. van Baaren, W. D. Van Dyke III. **Transfer Agent & Registrar**—Bank of New York, NYC. **Incorporated** in New York in 1909. **Empl**-4,573. **S&P Analyst:** Richard O'Reilly, CFA

International Paper

NYSE Symbol **IP**
In S&P 500

17-OCT-95

Industry:
Paper/Products

Summary: This worldwide producer of printing papers, packaging and forest products also operates specialty businesses and a broadly based paper distribution network.

S&P Opinion: Accumulate (★★★★)	Recent Price • 38	Yield • 2.6%
	52 Wk Range • 45¾-34	12-Mo. P/E • 9.3

Quantitative Evaluations

Outlook
(1 Lowest—5 Highest)
• **5+**

Fair Value
• **46⅛**

Risk
• **Low**

Earn./Div. Rank
• **B+**

Technical Eval.
• **Bearish** since 7/95

Rel. Strength Rank
(1 Lowest—99 Highest)
• **21**

Insider Activity
• **Neutral**

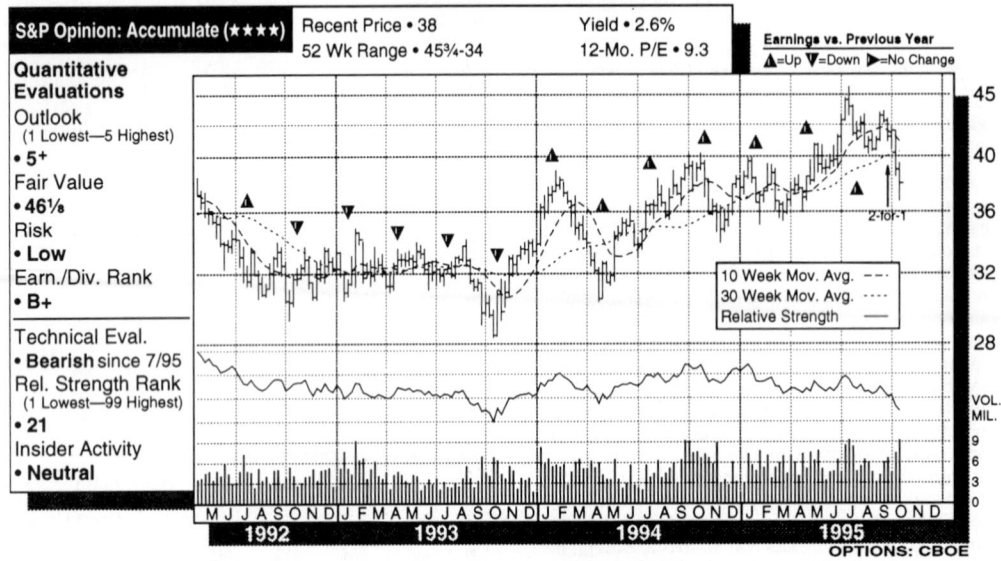

Earnings vs. Previous Year
▲=Up ▼=Down ▶=No Change

10 Week Mov. Avg. —·—
30 Week Mov. Avg. ·····
Relative Strength ——

OPTIONS: CBOE

Overview - 16-OCT-95

Sales growth should continue through 1996, although at a slower pace than generated to date in 1995. Relatively healthy global economies and little industry capacity expansion in recent years (in all areas except containerboard) should keep demand firm and prices high in most paper grades. Although moderating economic trends and inventory adjustments have eased demand for containerboard and uncoated printing paper in recent months, an expected economic pick-up should improve conditions in those areas. Sales will also be boosted by the full-year consolidation of Carter Holt Harvey and the start-up of several new facilities. Forest products sales, which have been sluggish, should be boosted by the recent interest rate stimulated revival of the housing market. Margins should be favorable, on steep paper and packaging prices, better wood products trends and cost control measures.

Valuation - 16-OCT-95

With investors worried that moderating economic trends will bring an end to IP's recent strong earnings growth, the company's volatile shares have experienced a downturn since mid-1995, and have had an overall flat performance in the past year. Although slowdowns in certain of IP's paper markets have tempered our enthusiasm a bit, we continue to anticipate solid earnings growth through 1996. We also believe that an anticipated economic rebound will perk up IP's troubled paper grades, but would be a less aggressive purchaser of IP stock until those events appear more certain.

Key Stock Statistics

S&P EPS Est. 1995	4.85	Tang. Bk. Value/Share	23.17
P/E on S&P Est. 1995	7.8	Beta	0.79
S&P EPS Est. 1996	6.00	Shareholders	29,800
Dividend Rate/Share	1.00	Market cap. (B)	$ 9.7
Shs. outstg. (M)	254.6	Inst. holdings	74%
Avg. daily vol. (M)	1.449	Insider holdings	NA

Value of $10,000 invested 5 years ago: $ 15,523

Fiscal Year Ending Dec. 31

	1995	% Change	1994	% Change	1993	% Change
Revenues (Million $)						
1Q	4,492	32%	3,414	2%	3,362	NM
2Q	5,084	40%	3,633	4%	3,506	3%
3Q	5,100	34%	3,792	11%	3,405	-2%
4Q	—	—	4,127	21%	3,412	NM
Yr.	—	—	14,966	9%	13,685	NM
Income (Million $)						
1Q	246.0	NM	76.00	19%	64.00	-38%
2Q	316.0	NM	91.00	18%	77.00	-32%
3Q	328.0	195%	111.0	131%	48.00	-52%
4Q	—	—	154.0	54%	100.0	NM
Yr.	—	—	432.0	49%	289.0	104%
Earnings Per Share ($)						
1Q	0.98	NM	0.31	17%	0.26	-40%
2Q	1.24	NM	0.36	18%	0.31	-34%
3Q	1.27	185%	0.44	128%	0.19	-52%
4Q	E1.36	121%	0.62	52%	0.40	NM
Yr.	E4.85	180%	1.73	48%	1.17	100%

Next earnings report expected: early January

Business Summary - 16-OCT-95

IP is one of the world's largest producers of paper, paperboard and packaging products. It also distributes paper and office supply products, and produces pulp, lumber, panels and specialty products. Segment contributions in 1994 (profits in millions) were:

	Sales	Profits
Printing papers	28%	$20
Packaging	22%	293
Distribution	22%	74
Specialty products	17%	268
Forest products	11%	378

Sales outside the U.S., including exports, accounted for 30% of the total in 1994.

Uncoated papers produced include reprographic and printing papers, grades sold for conversion into envelopes and forms, and premium writing papers. IP's coated papers are used in magazines and other publications, and its bristols products are used to produce folders, tags, posters and tickets. It also produces pulp, fluff and dissolving pulp.

The packaging segment produces containerboard, corrugated boxes, and agricultural packaging. Its premium bleached board is used for folding cartons, liquid packaging and food service products, and its aseptic packaging systems help keep perishable liquids fresh without refrigeration. It also offers kraft papers.

IP distributes fine paper, printing and industrial products and building materials, primarily made by others, through some 280 centers (mostly in the U.S.).

Specialty products include photosensitive films; nonwoven fabrics; panel products; pressure-sensitive base papers; and adhesives, inks and chemical products. IP also engages in oil and gas exploration.

The company controls 6.1 million acres of timberland through a majority interest in IP Timberlands, Ltd., and sells lumber, panels and oriented strand board. IP also holds a majority stake in New Zealand-based Carter Holt Harvey, a forest products concern with substantial assets in Chile; IP had boosted its stake in Carter to 50% from 24% in April 1995, through the acquisition of shares from Brierly Investments and open market purchases (totaling NZ $1.708 billion).

Important Developments

Sep. '95—The company announced that it was initiating a paper machine modernization and rebuild project at a mill in Jay, Maine, which was slated to increase annual production capacity of coated freesheet paper by 200,000 tons (IP currently has nominal production capacity for coated freesheet). The project was scheduled for completion and start-up in the fourth quarter of 1996.

Capitalization

Long Term Debt: $5,641,000,000 (6/95).

Per Share Data ($)

(Year Ended Dec. 31)

	1994	1993	1992	1991	1990	1989
Tangible Bk. Val.	22.84	22.08	22.08	21.84	22.54	21.52
Cash Flow	5.27	4.81	4.08	4.97	5.66	6.37
Earnings	1.73	1.17	0.59	1.80	2.60	3.86
Dividends	0.84	0.84	0.84	0.84	0.84	0.76
Payout Ratio	49%	72%	145%	47%	32%	20%
Prices - High	40¼	35	39¼	39⅛	29⅞	29⅜
- Low	30⅜	28⅜	29¼	25¼	21⅜	22⅝
P/E Ratio - High	23	30	67	22	11	8
- Low	18	24	50	14	8	6

Income Statement Analysis (Million $)

	1994	%Chg	1993	%Chg	1992	%Chg	1991
Revs.	14,966	9%	13,685	NM	13,598	7%	12,703
Oper. Inc.	1,898	11%	1,708	NM	1,701	NM	1,713
Depr.	885	-1%	898	6%	850	21%	700
Int. Exp.	367	14%	322	11%	289	-18%	351
Pretax Inc.	664	33%	500	143%	206	-68%	638
Eff. Tax Rate	35%	—	42%	—	31%	—	38%
Net Inc.	432	49%	289	104%	142	-64%	399

Balance Sheet & Other Fin. Data (Million $)

	1994	1993	1992	1991	1990	1989
Cash	270	242	225	238	256	102
Curr. Assets	4,830	4,401	4,366	4,131	3,939	3,096
Total Assets	17,836	16,631	16,459	14,941	13,669	11,582
Curr. Liab.	4,034	4,009	4,531	3,727	3,155	2,730
LT Debt	4,464	3,601	3,096	3,351	3,096	2,324
Common Eqty.	6,514	6,225	6,189	5,739	5,632	5,147
Total Cap.	12,590	11,440	10,702	10,134	9,863	8,493
Cap. Exp.	1,114	954	1,368	1,197	1,409	1,345
Cash Flow	1,317	1,187	992	1,099	1,222	1,394

Ratio Analysis

	1994	1993	1992	1991	1990	1989
Curr. Ratio	1.2	1.1	1.0	1.1	1.2	1.1
% LT Debt of Cap.	35.5	31.5	28.9	33.1	31.4	27.4
% Net Inc.of Revs.	2.9	2.1	1.0	3.1	4.4	7.6
% Ret. on Assets	2.5	1.7	0.9	2.8	4.5	8.3
% Ret. on Equity	6.7	4.6	2.3	6.9	10.5	17.6

Dividend Data

—Dividends have been paid since 1946. A dividend reinvestment plan is available.

Amt. of Div. $	Date Decl.	Ex-Div. Date	Stock of Record	Payment Date
0.420	Nov. 08	Nov. 14	Nov. 18	Dec. 15 '94
0.420	Feb. 14	Feb. 17	Feb. 24	Mar. 15 '95
0.420	May. 09	May. 15	May. 19	Jun. 15 '95
0.500	Jul. 11	Aug. 16	Aug. 18	Sep. 15 '95
2-for-1	Jul. 11	Sep. 18	Aug. 18	Sep. 15 '95

Data as orig. reptd.; bef. results of disc. opers. and/or spec. items. Per share data adj. for stk. divs. as of ex-div. date. E-Estimated. NA-Not Available. NM-Not Meaningful. NR-Not Ranked.

Office—Two Manhattanville Rd., Purchase, NY 10577. **Tel**—(914) 397-1500. **Chrmn & CEO**—J. A. Georges. **Pres & COO**—J. T. Dillon. **SVP & CFO**—M. M. Parrs. **VP & Secy**—J. W. Guedry. **Investor Contact**—Carol Tutundgy. **Dirs**—W. C. Butcher, J. T. Dillon, R. J. Eaton, S. C. Gault, J. A. Georges, T. C. Graham, A. G. Hansen, D. F. McHenry, P. F. Noonan, J. C. Pfeiffer, E. T. Pratt, Jr., C. R. Shoemate, R. B. Smith. **Transfer Agent & Registrar**—Chemical Bank, NYC. **Incorporated** in New York in 1941. **Empl**-70,000. **S&P Analyst:** Michael W. Jaffe

Interpublic Group

STOCK REPORTS

NYSE Symbol **IPG**
In S&P 500

24-AUG-95

Industry:
Advertising/Communi-
cations

Summary: Interpublic is one of the world's largest advertising agency systems. It is also involved in the production, distribution, and
syndication of TV shows for the international market.

S&P Opinion: Accumulate (★★★★)

| Recent Price • 38⅞ | Yield • 1.6% |
| 52 Wk Range • 40-29½ | 12-Mo. P/E • 23.4 |

**Quantitative
Evaluations**

Outlook
(1 Lowest—5 Highest)
• **3+**

Fair Value
• **38¼**

Risk
• **Low**

Earn./Div. Rank
• **A+**

Technical Eval.
• **Bullish** since 8/95

Rel. Strength Rank
(1 Lowest—99 Highest)
• **54**

Insider Activity
• **Neutral**

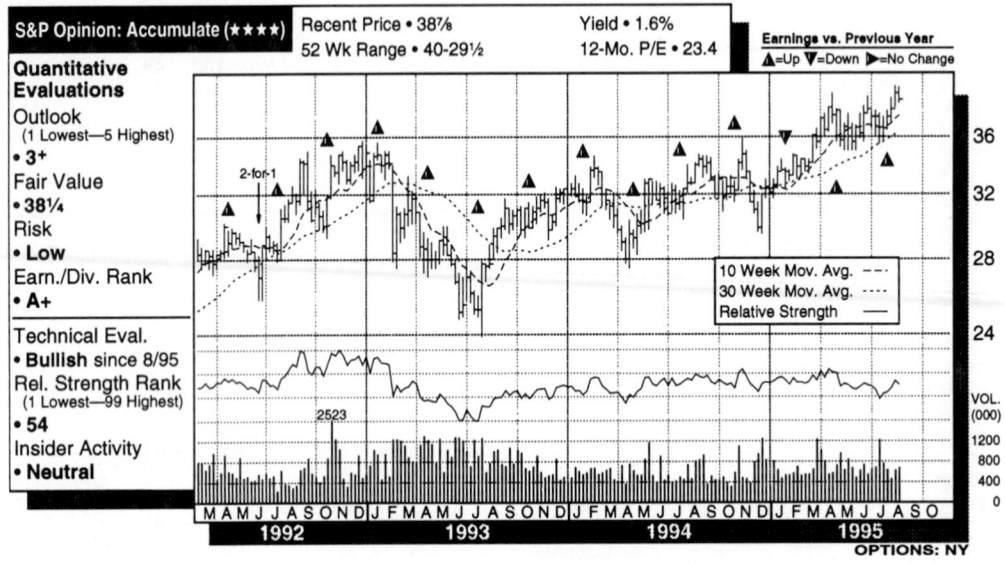

Earnings vs. Previous Year
▲=Up ▼=Down ▶=No Change

10 Week Mov. Avg. ---
30 Week Mov. Avg. ·····
Relative Strength —

2-for-1

2523

VOL.
(000)
1200
800
400
0

OPTIONS: NY

Overview - 24-AUG-95

Gross income should continue to improve through
1995, rising more than 10% for the year (before currency translations), aided by gains in net new business and acquisitions. In addition to a robust U.S.
market, strong growth will come from Latin America
and Pacific Rim markets, as well as from recovering
European markets. Margins will benefit from ongoing
cost-control measures. Profit comparisons will also
benefit from the absence of nonrecurring restructuring
charges. Stabilization of the inflation rate in Brazil
could add up to $0.10 a share to the bottom line.
Aided by continuing advertising health in most geographical markets, and acquisitions, gross income
should again advance more than 10% in 1996. Net
income will benefit from operating efficiencies, as well
as the healthy revenue gains.

Valuation - 24-AUG-95

IPG, the largest of the publicly-held ad agency systems, outperformed the general market in the first half
of 1995 and also did slightly better than its peers.
Strong earnings gains are likely to continue at least
through 1996, aided by a robust advertising climate,
acquisitions and operating efficiencies. The stock,
which is currently undervalued based on the earnings
outlook for 1996, should continue to do well in the
periods ahead. Longer term, IPG is favored for dependable earnings and dividend growth prospects, and
thus, total return.

Key Stock Statistics

S&P EPS Est. 1995	2.25	Tang. Bk. Value/Share	0.80
P/E on S&P Est. 1995	17.3	Beta	1.34
S&P EPS Est. 1996	2.65	Shareholders	5,800
Dividend Rate/Share	0.62	Market cap. (B)	$ 3.0
Shs. outstg. (M)	78.1	Inst. holdings	82%
Avg. daily vol. (M)	0.130	Insider holdings	NA

Value of $10,000 invested 5 years ago: $ 26,113

Fiscal Year Ending Dec. 31

	1995	% Change	1994	% Change	1993	% Change
Revenues (Million $)						
1Q	460.4	9%	421.0	8%	389.8	-3%
2Q	557.2	12%	497.5	3%	483.8	NM
3Q	—	—	440.5	7%	411.0	-6%
4Q	—	—	625.3	23%	509.3	-5%
Yr.	—	—	1,984	11%	1,794	-3%
Income (Million $)						
1Q	15.18	17%	12.99	18%	11.03	14%
2Q	63.77	18%	54.10	10%	48.99	13%
3Q	—	—	17.40	18%	14.69	18%
4Q	—	—	30.75	-39%	50.58	9%
Yr.	—	—	115.3	-8%	125.3	12%
Earnings Per Share ($)						
1Q	0.20	18%	0.17	13%	0.15	15%
2Q	0.82	14%	0.72	11%	0.65	12%
3Q	E0.29	26%	0.23	15%	0.20	18%
4Q	E0.95	138%	0.40	-40%	0.67	8%
Yr.	E2.25	47%	1.53	-8%	1.67	11%

Next earnings report expected: late October

Interpublic Group

Business Summary - 24-AUG-95

The Interpublic Group of Companies is one of the world's largest advertising agency systems. The advertising agency functions of the company are conducted in more than 100 countries through McCann-Erickson Worldwide, Lintas Worldwide, The Lowe Group, Campbell Mithun Esty (50%-owned), Western International Media and other affiliated companies.

The principal functions of the company's advertising agencies are to plan and create advertising programs for clients and to place the advertising in various media, such as radio, television, magazines and newspapers. The usual advertising agency commission is 15% of the gross charge (billings) for advertising space or time, but discounting is common. During 1994, the two largest clients together accounted for about 18% of income from commissions and fees.

Operations outside the U.S. accounted for 63% of income from commissions and fees and 62% of income before taxes and unallocated expenses in 1994.

In addition to advertising agency activities, IPG is involved in publishing, market research, sales promotion, public relations, product development and other related services. IPG owns a significant minority interest in All American Communications, a diversified international producer and distributor of TV programming and recorded music, a worldwide provider of syndication, and is by far the largest international game show syndicator. In January 1995, IPG purchased a minority interest in CKS Group, a leading marketing communications and new media firm.

Important Developments

Jul. '95—IPG said that its agency systems gained $452 million in net new business in the first six months of 1995, versus $341 million in the corresponding year earlier period. In all of 1994, net new business was $693 million, down from $772 million in 1993.

Apr. '95—IPG acquired a 50% equity interest in Campbell Mithun Esty (CME) for $20 million. CME is the nation's 23rd largest agency, with 1994 billings of $500 million. Separately, IPG acquired Newspaper Services of America, the leading provider of print media market analysis and placement services. Terms were not disclosed.

Oct. '94—IPG acquired Western International Media, the leading media buying service, purchasing more than $1.6 billion in advertising.

Capitalization

Long Term Debt: $248,462,000 (3/95), incl. $111,170,000 of sub. debs. conv. into com. at $44.90 a sh.

Minority Interests: $13,120,000.

Per Share Data ($) (Year Ended Dec. 31)

	1994	1993	1992	1991	1990	1989
Tangible Bk. Val.	0.62	0.97	1.50	1.80	1.77	3.55
Cash Flow	2.37	2.48	2.28	2.04	1.75	1.50
Earnings	1.53	1.67	1.50	1.30	1.19	1.05
Dividends	0.54	0.49	0.45	0.41	0.37	0.32
Payout Ratio	36%	29%	30%	33%	34%	31%
Prices - High	35⅞	35⅝	35¾	28⅝	19	19
- Low	27½	23⅞	25¾	16⅞	14⅝	12¼
P/E Ratio - High	23	21	24	22	16	18
- Low	18	14	17	13	12	12

Income Statement Analysis (Million $)

	1994	%Chg	1993	%Chg	1992	%Chg	1991
Revs.	1,916	10%	1,740	-4%	1,804	10%	1,635
Oper. Inc.	278	5%	265	7%	248	8%	230
Depr.	63.9	4%	61.3	4%	59.2	10%	53.9
Int. Exp.	32.9	25%	26.4	-20%	33.2	NM	33.5
Pretax Inc.	205	-12%	233	11%	210	12%	187
Eff. Tax Rate	42%	—	43%	—	44%	—	47%
Net Inc.	115	-8%	125	12%	112	18%	94.6

Balance Sheet & Other Fin. Data (Million $)

	1994	1993	1992	1991	1990	1989
Cash	442	322	291	276	216	123
Curr. Assets	2,675	2,003	1,915	2,032	1,915	1,373
Total Assets	3,793	2,870	2,623	2,784	2,584	1,741
Curr. Liab.	2,595	1,836	1,690	1,854	1,769	1,210
LT Debt	242	226	200	170	144	37.0
Common Eqty.	649	564	511	587	510	368
Total Cap.	904	803	728	774	668	417
Cap. Exp.	55.9	78.8	36.9	46.6	37.2	45.6
Cash Flow	179	187	171	148	118	101

Ratio Analysis

	1994	1993	1992	1991	1990	1989
Curr. Ratio	1.0	1.1	1.1	1.1	1.1	1.1
% LT Debt of Cap.	26.8	28.1	27.5	22.0	21.6	8.8
% Net Inc.of Revs.	6.0	7.2	6.2	5.8	6.0	5.8
% Ret. on Assets	3.4	4.6	4.1	3.5	3.6	4.2
% Ret. on Equity	18.7	23.3	20.4	17.0	17.8	20.3

Dividend Data —Dividends have been paid since 1971. A "poison pill" stock purchase rights plan was adopted in 1989. A dividend reinvestment plan is available.

Amt. of Div. $	Date Decl.	Ex-Div. Date	Stock of Record	Payment Date
0.140	Jul. 19	Aug. 24	Aug. 30	Sep. 15 '94
0.140	Oct. 20	Nov. 22	Nov. 29	Dec. 15 '94
0.140	Feb. 16	Feb. 21	Feb. 27	Mar. 15 '95
0.155	May. 16	May. 23	May. 30	Jun. 15 '95
0.155	Jul. 13	Aug. 28	Aug. 30	Sep. 15 '95

Data as orig. reptd.; bef. results of disc. opers. and/or spec. items. Per share data adj. for stk. divs. as of ex-div. date. E-Estimated. NA-Not Available. NM-Not Meaningful. NR-Not Ranked.

Office—1271 Avenue of the Americas, New York, NY 10020. **Tel**—(212) 399-8000. **Chrmn & Pres**—P. H. Geier Jr. **VP-Secy**—C. Rudge. **Exec VP-Fin & Investor Contact**—Eugene P. Beard. **Dirs**—E. P. Beard, L. V. Cheney, P. H. Geier Jr., F. B. Lowe, L. H. Olsen, K. L. Robbins, J. P. Samper, J. J. Sisco. **Transfer Agent & Registrar**—First Chicago Trust Co. of New York, NYC. **Incorporated** in Delaware in 1930. **Empl**-18,100. **S&P Analyst:** William H. Donald

James River

NYSE Symbol **JR**
In S&P 500

03-OCT-95

Industry:
Paper/Products

Summary: James River is a leading producer of consumer and commercial tissue products, and also makes food and consumer packaging. Communications paper operations were recently spun off.

S&P Opinion: Hold (★★★)	Recent Price • 32	Yield • 1.9%
	52 Wk Range • 37⅜-19⅞	12-Mo. P/E • NM

Quantitative Evaluations

Outlook
  (1 Lowest—5 Highest)
• **1⁺**

Fair Value
• **27**

Risk
• **Average**

Earn./Div. Rank
• **B-**

Technical Eval.
• **Bearish** since 8/95

Rel. Strength Rank
  (1 Lowest—99 Highest)
• **33**

Insider Activity
• **Unfavorable**

Earnings vs. Previous Year
▲=Up ▼=Down ▶=No Change

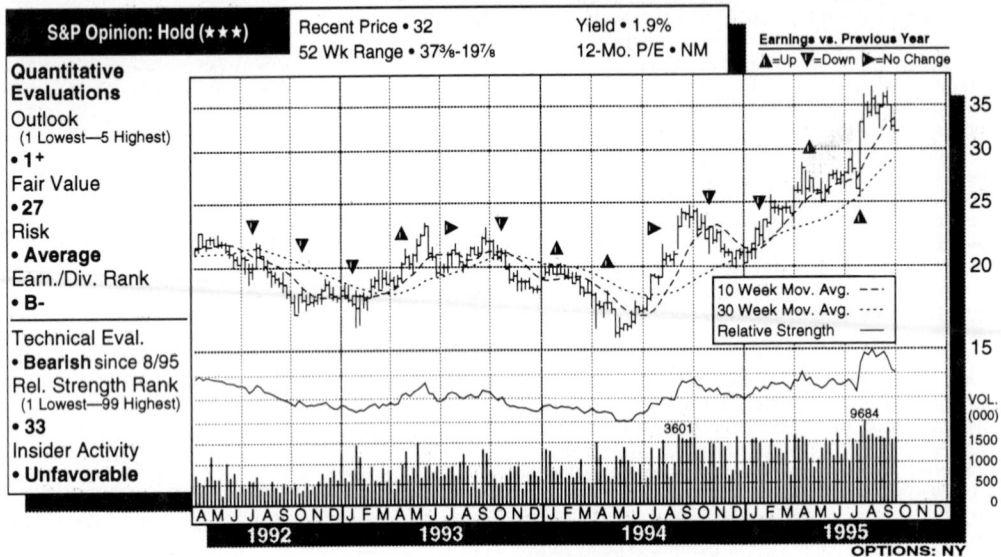

10 Week Mov. Avg. ---
30 Week Mov. Avg. ·····
Relative Strength —

OPTIONS: NY

Overview - 03-OCT-95

Sales from continuing operations should be sharply higher in 1995 on the full-year consolidation of European consumer operations and an improvement in comparable operations. Comparative sales should be boosted by stronger demand in the consumer products area, across-the-board price hikes, including the first in the domestic consumer tissue industry in several years, and new product introductions. Operating margins should widen considerably on the more favorable pricing trends, along with benefits of the early stages of JR's aggressive restructuring program. Those factors should outweigh the impact of continued high raw materials costs. Interest charges are likely to be higher on additional borrowings from the purchase of the European business stake, but debt will be paid down with cash received in the spinoff. Higher preferred dividends will trim share earnings.

Valuation - 03-OCT-95

James River's shares have risen sharply since mid-1994, as worries about economic moderation improved investor sentiment toward consumer products companies. Its stock price also benefited from investor excitement over a program to focus on core operations and reduce debt, and the shares received a very strong bounce after JR outlined details of its ongoing restructuring initiatives at an analysts meeting in late July 1995. Although JR's business outlook should continue to improve through 1996, we believe that prospect is already in its share price, and the stock is fairly priced in its recent trading range.

Key Stock Statistics

S&P EPS Est. 1995	1.35	Tang. Bk. Value/Share	8.05
P/E on S&P Est. 1995	23.7	Beta	1.29
S&P EPS Est. 1996	2.50	Shareholders	19,300
Dividend Rate/Share	0.60	Market cap. (B)	$ 2.6
Shs. outstg. (M)	82.4	Inst. holdings	72%
Avg. daily vol. (M)	0.624	Insider holdings	NA

Value of $10,000 invested 5 years ago: NA

Fiscal Year Ending Dec. 31

	1995	% Change	1994	% Change	1993	% Change
Revenues (Million $)						
1Q	1,637	48%	1,106	NM	1,114	-2%
2Q	1,812	51%	1,198	NM	1,198	-3%
3Q	—	—	1,445	22%	1,184	-3%
4Q	—	—	1,669	44%	1,155	1%
Yr.	—	—	5,417	16%	4,650	-2%
Income (Million $)						
1Q	22.14	NM	-7.09	NM	-10.13	NM
2Q	41.76	NM	12.90	-6%	13.74	33%
3Q	—	—	-0.10	NM	1.19	-61%
4Q	—	—	-18.67	NM	-5.14	NM
Yr.	—	—	-12.96	NM	-0.35	NM
Earnings Per Share ($)						
1Q	0.09	NM	-0.19	NM	-0.22	NM
2Q	0.33	NM	0.06	NM	0.06	NM
3Q	E0.43	NM	-0.18	NM	-0.08	NM
4Q	E0.50	NM	-0.41	NM	-0.16	NM
Yr.	E1.35	NM	-0.72	NM	-0.40	NM

Next earnings report expected: late October

Business Summary - 02-OCT-95

James River is a leading manufacturer of consumer products, including towel and tissue and disposable food and beverage service products. It also makes food and consumer packaging products. In August 1995, JR spun off its communications paper business. Segment contributions (operating profits in millions) in 1994 were:

	Sales	Profits
Consumer products		
North America	43%	$143
Europe	11%	7
Food & consumer packaging	29%	97
Communications papers	17%	-36

Consumer products include bathroom tissue, household roll towels, wipes, paper and plastic cups, paper plates, napkins and plastic cutlery. JR markets its products in both retail and commercial markets. Retail brands include Quilted Northern, Marina and Nice 'n Soft bathroom tissue; Brawny paper towels; Vanity Fair premium food service products; and Dixie plates, cups and cutlery. Commercial towel, tissue and food service products, sold to fast-food chains and distributors, are used in restaurants, hotels, offices, factories and schools. The company began to consolidate its European consumer products business, Jamon N.V., after boosting its stake in the unit to 86% from 43% in July 1994; on an annualized basis, Jamon would have contributed 23% of sales in 1994.

The company provides retail packaging for food and other consumer products that have high-volume distribution. Packaging products include folding cartons, such as ice cream cartons, cereal boxes and microwave packages; flexible packaging, such as snack food packaging, bread bags, and frozen vegetable and cheese packages; and barrier papers, including food wrap and cereal box liners.

Important Developments

Aug. '95—The company completed the spinoff of most of its communications paper business and the specialty paper-based portion of its food and consumer packaging division. Under terms of the spinoff, James River stockholders received one share of the new company, named Crown Vantage Inc., for each 10 JR shares held. James River was to receive $500 million in cash plus $100 million in notes as a return of its capital investment in the businesses.
Jul. '95—The company outlined details of its ongoing restructuring initiatives and cost reduction programs. When fully implemented, the programs are expected to generate up to $640 million in cost savings by 1998, and result in the elimination of about 4,400 jobs in North America and Europe.

Capitalization

Long Term Debt: $2,857,331,000 (6/95).
Minority Interest: $167,812,000.
Preferred Stock: $740,269,000.

Per Share Data ($)

(Year Ended Dec. 31)

	1994	1993	1992	1991	1990	1989
Tangible Bk. Val.	7.48	16.30	18.00	24.76	24.99	24.65
Cash Flow	4.16	3.97	2.54	4.22	2.34	6.13
Earnings	-0.72	-0.40	-1.82	0.66	-0.08	2.45
Dividends	0.60	0.60	0.60	0.70	0.30	0.60
Payout Ratio	NM	NM	NM	106%	NM	24%
Prices - High	24¾	23⅜	23⅜	29¼	29¼	34⅜
- Low	15⅝	16¼	17	17	18½	25¾
P/E Ratio - High	NM	NM	NM	44	NM	14
- Low	NM	NM	NM	26	NM	11

Income Statement Analysis (Million $)

	1994	%Chg	1993	%Chg	1992	%Chg	1991
Revs.	5,417	16%	4,650	-2%	4,728	4%	4,562
Oper. Inc.	566	20%	472	16%	406	-24%	536
Depr.	398	11%	358	NM	356	22%	292
Int. Exp.	189	32%	143	-11%	161	-5%	170
Pretax Inc.	-10.0	NM	17.0	NM	-187	NM	133
Eff. Tax Rate	NM	—	114%	—	NM	—	41%
Net Inc.	-13.0	—	Nil	—	-121	NM	78.0

Balance Sheet & Other Fin. Data (Million $)

	1994	1993	1992	1991	1990	1989
Cash	59.0	24.0	375	85.0	32.0	76.0
Curr. Assets	1,976	1,282	1,697	1,533	1,911	1,454
Total Assets	7,924	5,851	6,336	5,627	5,741	5,818
Curr. Liab.	1,569	781	928	705	789	812
LT Debt	2,668	1,943	2,154	1,758	1,802	1,771
Common Eqty.	1,421	1,514	1,659	2,221	2,212	2,203
Total Cap.	5,579	4,341	4,713	4,808	4,813	4,886
Cap. Exp.	352	331	470	467	NA	575
Cash Flow	340	325	208	345	NA	501

Ratio Analysis

	1994	1993	1992	1991	1990	1989
Curr. Ratio	1.3	1.6	1.8	2.2	2.4	1.8
% LT Debt of Cap.	47.8	44.8	45.7	36.6	37.4	36.3
% Net Inc.of Revs.	NM	NM	NM	1.7	1.4	3.7
% Ret. on Assets	NM	NM	NM	1.4	1.4	3.9
% Ret. on Equity	NM	NM	NM	2.4	2.4	9.4

Dividend Data

Dividends have been paid since 1973. A dividend reinvestment plan is available. A "poison pill" stock purchase rights plan was adopted in 1989. In August 1995, shares of Crown Vantage were distributed to JR stockholders.

Amt. of Div. $	Date Decl.	Ex-Div. Date	Stock of Record	Payment Date
0.150	Jan. 19	Mar. 13	Mar. 17	Mar. 31 '95
0.150	Apr. 20	Jun. 14	Jun. 16	Jun. 30 '95
Stk.	Aug. 16	Aug. 29	Aug. 25	Aug. 28 '95
0.150	Jul. 20	Sep. 13	Sep. 15	Sep. 29 '95
0.150	Sep. 21	Dec. 13	Dec. 15	Dec. 29 '95

Data as orig. reptd.; bef. results of disc. opers. and/or spec. items. Per share data adj. for stk. divs. as of ex-div. date.
E-Estimated. NA-Not Available. NM-Not Meaningful. NR-Not Ranked.

Office—120 Tredegar St., Richmond, VA 23219. **Tel**—(804) 644-5411. **Chrmn**—R. C. Williams. **Pres & CEO**—M. L. Marsh. **SVP & Secy**—C. A. Cutchins IV. **SVP-Fin & CFO**—S. E. Hare. **Investor Contact**—Celeste C. Gunter. **Dirs**—W. T. Burgin, W. H. Clark Jr., W. T. Comfort Jr., W. V. Daniel, B. C. Gottwald, R. M. O'Neil, J. T. Piemont, A. M. Whittemore, R. C. Williams. **Transfer Agent & Registrar**—Wachovia Bank of North Carolina, Winston-Salem. **Incorporated** in Virginia in 1969. **Empl**-33,800. **S&P Analyst:** Michael W. Jaffe

Jefferson-Pilot

NYSE Symbol **JP**
In S&P 500

01-NOV-95

Industry:
Insurance

Summary: Jefferson-Pilot provides an array of insurance and communications products and services. The bulk of revenues and income is derived from life and health insurance operations.

S&P Opinion: Hold (★★★)	Recent Price • 66	Yield • 2.9%
	52 Wk Range • 69½-50⅝	12-Mo. P/E • 12.5

Earnings vs. Previous Year
▲=Up ▼=Down ▶=No Change

Quantitative Evaluations

Outlook
(1 Lowest—5 Highest)
• **1+**

Fair Value
• **51⅞**

Risk
• **Low**

Earn./Div. Rank
• **A**

Technical Eval.
• **Bullish** since 5/94

Rel. Strength Rank
(1 Lowest—99 Highest)
• **77**

Insider Activity
• **Neutral**

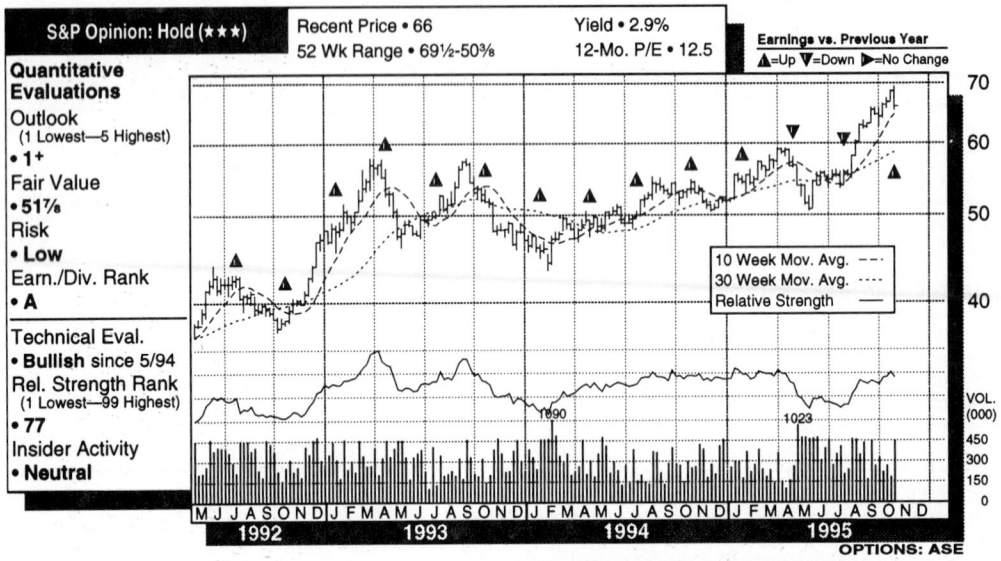

10 Week Mov. Avg. ---
30 Week Mov. Avg. ....
Relative Strength —

VOL.
(000)
450
300
150
0

M J J A S O N D J F M A M J J A S O N D J F M A M J J A S O N D J F M A M J J A S O N D
1992   1993   1994   1995

OPTIONS: ASE

Overview - 01-NOV-95

The forecast for higher operating earnings (from continuing businesses) in coming periods is predicated on continued strong individual life insurance premium growth. JP's recent growth here has been the result of robust sales of individual annuities and interest-sensitive life insurance products. Although many of these products increase JP's risk to interest rate changes, this risk is manageable. Steps taken to increase agent productivity and reduce expenses will also aid profit margins here. Margins in the group insurance area may come under pressure from adverse disability claim trends and increased price competition in traditional medical coverages. An improved advertising market augurs well for the communications group. Investment income growth will be modest amid a relatively lower interest rate environment, but asset writedowns are unlikely.

Valuation - 01-NOV-95

The shares of this life and health insurer have trended upward almost steadily since early 1994, bucking the trend of share price erosion amid rising interest rates that plagued many other life insurers during most of 1994. Though JP's earnings growth prospects are enhanced by a focus on its core insurance and communications businesses following the sale of several nonstrategic assets in early 1995, the shares are fairly valued near term at almost 15 times our 1995 operating earnings estimate of $4.50 a share.

Key Stock Statistics

S&P EPS Est. 1995	4.50	Tang. Bk. Value/Share	40.73
P/E on S&P Est. 1995	14.7	Beta	0.58
S&P EPS Est. 1996	5.00	Shareholders	10,700
Dividend Rate/Share	1.92	Market cap. (B)	$ 3.1
Shs. outstg. (M)	47.5	Inst. holdings	39%
Avg. daily vol. (M)	0.056	Insider holdings	NA

Value of $10,000 invested 5 years ago: $ 28,054

Fiscal Year Ending Dec. 31

	1995	% Change	1994	% Change	1993	% Change
Revenues (Million $)						
1Q	315.2	3%	307.3	NM	306.7	2%
2Q	328.9	5%	314.5	2%	308.1	4%
3Q	—	—	312.5	3%	302.7	1%
4Q	—	—	334.6	2%	329.2	7%
Yr.	—	—	1,269	2%	1,247	4%
Income (Million $)						
1Q	51.87	-1%	52.40	5%	49.94	1%
2Q	51.12	-9%	56.28	8%	52.24	8%
3Q	65.43	15%	56.90	8%	52.47	7%
4Q	—	—	64.31	NM	64.63	14%
Yr.	—	—	229.9	5%	219.3	8%
Earnings Per Share ($)						
1Q	1.07	NM	1.08	9%	0.99	3%
2Q	1.07	-8%	1.16	12%	1.04	11%
3Q	1.38	18%	1.17	13%	1.04	8%
4Q	—	—	1.33	2%	1.30	16%
Yr.	E4.50	-5%	4.73	8%	4.36	9%

Next earnings report expected: early February

Business Summary - 01-NOV-95

Jefferson-Pilot Corp. is a holding company whose principal insurance subsidiary is Jefferson-Pilot Life Insurance Co.. As of early 1995, the company sold Jefferson-Pilot Title Insurance Co. and Jefferson-Pilot Fire & Casualty Co. JP also owns and operates radio and television stations, and produces televised sports programs. Jefferson-Pilot Communications Co., a provider of electronic data services, was also sold in early 1995. Segment contributions from continuing operations in 1994:

	Revs.	Profits
Life/health Insurance	81%	73%
Communications	14%	10%
Investment gains & other	5%	17%

Jefferson Pilot Life Insurance Co. underwrites an array of life insurance products, including whole life, term life, annuity and endowment policies, on an individual and group basis. Products are marketed through a general agency system that utilizes the services of career agents, home service agents, and independent marketing organizations. Accident and health insurance is also offered, mostly on a group basis.

Jefferson-Pilot Communication Co. owns and operates three television and 14 radio stations (as of 9/30/95) in North Carolina, South Carolina, Virginia, Georgia, Florida, Colorado and California. Other operations include a sports production and syndication business and a co-op advertising business.

Important Developments

Oct. '95—JP acquired Alexander Hamilton Life Insurance Company of America from Household International, Inc. (NYSE: HI) for $575 million. Later in the month JP filed a registration statement with the SEC covering the issuance of up to $300 million of debt securities. Proceeds were earmarked for, among other things, the repayment of bank debt incurred in the acquisition of Alexander Hamilton Life.

May '95—JP acquired the life insurance and annuity business of Kentucky Central Life and Health Insurance Co. (KC). JP assumed assets of $869 million and recorded a liability of $1.1 billion in connection with the acquisiiton of KC, which was seized by state regulators in 1993.

Capitalization

Short Term Notes Payable: $76,500,000 (9/95).

Per Share Data ($)

(Year Ended Dec. 31)

	1994	1993	1992	1991	1990	1989
Tangible Bk. Val.	NA	34.25	32.88	29.84	25.47	25.67
Oper. Earnings	3.93	3.62	3.36	2.99	2.59	2.23
Earnings	4.73	4.36	3.99	3.43	2.94	2.43
Dividends	1.68	1.51	1.30	1.09	0.99	0.89
Relative Payout	36%	35%	33%	32%	34%	37%
Prices - High	55⅛	57⅞	49½	39⅛	29⅞	30⅜
- Low	43⅜	45½	33⅜	22⅞	21⅝	19⅞
P/E Ratio - High	12	13	12	11	10	12
- Low	9	10	8	7	7	8

Income Statement Analysis (Million $)

	1993	%Chg	1992	%Chg	1991	%Chg	1990
Life Ins. In Force	41,591	2%	40,843	6%	38,460	NM	38,465
Prem.Inc Life A&H	NA	—	NA	—	NA	—	NA
Prem.Inc Cas/Prop	NA	—	NA	—	NA	—	NA
Net Invest. Inc.	370	2%	361	2%	353	3%	342
Oth. Revs.	NA	—	NA	—	NA	—	NA
Total Revs.	1,247	4%	1,202	2%	1,173	NM	1,163
Pretax Inc.	322	13%	286	17%	245	10%	222
Net Oper. Inc.	158	-8%	171	12%	153	10%	139
Net Inc.	219	6%	206	17%	176	11%	158

Balance Sheet & Other Fin. Data (Million $)

	1993	1992	1991	1990	1989	1988
Cash & Equiv.	101	223	226	185	232	211
Premiums Due	60.5	42.6	40.1	39.3	44.4	38.5
Inv Assets Bonds	3,222	2,816	2,580	2,341	2,243	2,101
Inv. Assets Stock	833	838	784	610	780	618
Inv. Assets Loans	798	782	769	767	743	747
Inv. Assets Total	4,917	4,493	4,189	3,774	3,818	3,518
Deferred Policy Cost	278	260	249	236	221	215
Total Assets	5,641	5,236	4,925	4,455	4,530	4,174
Debt	Nil	Nil	Nil	Nil	Nil	Nil
Common Eqty.	1,733	1,687	1,563	1,353	1,475	1,336

Ratio Analysis

	1993	1992	1991	1990	1989	1988
Comb. Loss-Exp.Ratio	NA	NA	NA	NA	NA	NA
% Ret. on Revs.	17.6	16.9	15.0	13.6	12.1	8.0
% Ret. on Equity	12.9	12.5	12.1	11.1	9.9	7.6
% Invest. Yield	NA	NA	NA	NA	NA	NA

Dividend Data —Dividends have been paid since 1913. A dividend reinvestment plan is available. A "poison pill" stock purchase rights plan was adopted in 1988.

Amt. of Div. $	Date Decl.	Ex-Div. Date	Stock of Record	Payment Date
0.430	Nov. 07	Nov. 14	Nov. 18	Dec. 02 '94
0.430	Nov. 07	Feb. 06	Feb. 10	Mar. 03 '95
0.480	Feb. 13	May. 08	May. 12	Jun. 02 '95
0.480	May. 08	Aug. 16	Aug. 18	Sep. 01 '95
0.480	Aug. 08	Nov. 08	Nov. 10	Dec. 01 '95

Data as orig. reptd.; bef. results of disc. opers. and/or spec. items. Per share data adj. for stk. divs. as of ex-div. date. E-Estimate. NA-Not Available. NM-Not Meaningful. NR-Not Ranked.

Office—100 North Greene St., Greensboro, NC 27401. **Tel**—(910) 691-3000. **Pres & CEO**—D. A. Stonecipher. **VP-CFO & Treas**—D. R. Glass. **VP-Secy**—J. D. Hopkins. **Dirs**— T. M. Belk, W. E. Blackwell, E. B. Borden, W. H. Cunningham, C. R. Ferguson, R. G. Greer, G. W. Henderson, III, A. L. Holton Jr., H. L. McColl Jr., C. W. McCoy, E. S. Melvin, W. P. Payne, D. S. Russell Jr., R. H. Spilman, D. A. Stonecipher, M. A. Walls. **Transfer Agent & Registrar**—First Union National Bank, Charlotte. **Incorporated** in North Carolina in 1968. **Empl**-4,265. **S&P Analyst:** Catherine A. Seifert

Johnson & Johnson

NYSE Symbol **JNJ**
In S&P 500

24-OCT-95

Industry:
Medical equipment/
supply

Summary: The world's largest and most comprehensive health care company, J&J offers a broad line of drugs, consumer products and other medical and dental items.

S&P Opinion: Buy (★★★★)	Recent Price • 79¾	Yield • 1.6%
	52 Wk Range • 79¾-51¼	12-Mo. P/E • 22.2

Quantitative Evaluations

Outlook
(1 Lowest—5 Highest)
• **3+**

Fair Value
• **80%**

Risk
• **Low**

Earn./Div. Rank
• **A+**

Technical Eval.
• **Bullish** since 5/94

Rel. Strength Rank
(1 Lowest—99 Highest)
• **91**

Insider Activity
• **Neutral**

Earnings vs. Previous Year
▲=Up ▼=Down ▶=No Change

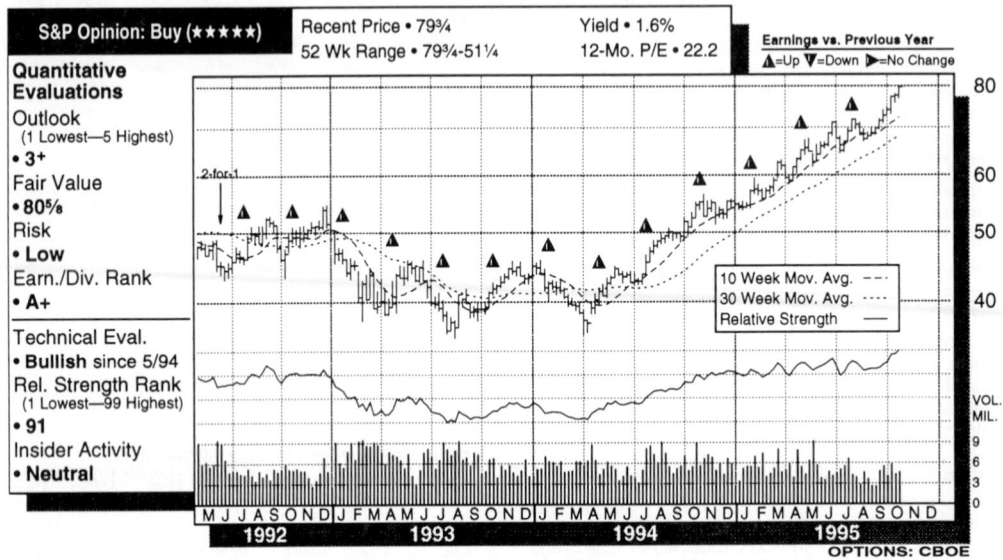

10 Week Mov. Avg. – – –
30 Week Mov. Avg. ‥‥‥
Relative Strength ———

2-for-1

VOL. MIL.

1992 1993 1994 1995

OPTIONS: CBOE

Overview - 24-OCT-95

Sales should post another creditable advance in 1996. Volume should be augmented by sales of new drugs such as Risperdal anti-psychotic, Propulsid gastrointestinal, Sporanox antifungal and Ultram pain reliever, and new medical devices such as the Palmaz-Schatz coronary stent. The stent, used to prevent reocclusion of arteries after angioplasty, has experienced robust growth, with 1996 sales expected to exceed $500 million. The planned acquisition of Cordis Corp. would add nearly $550 million in annual volume. Consumer sales should also rise, on growth in Neutrogena and Pepcid AC for heartburn. Despite a projected higher tax rate, margins should widen, on greater volume and productivity gains.

Valuation - 24-OCT-95

The shares have risen strongly in 1995, on better than expected earnings and renewed investor confidence in medical stocks. Health care issues have benefited from an improved regulatory climate and by their defensive characteristics. Despite competitive conditions in global health care markets, J&J should continue to achieve good earnings growth in coming years, aided by preeminent positions in key markets, geographic expansion, and new product development. Despite their premium multiple, we recommend purchase of the shares for total long-term return. Some increase in the $0.33 quarterly dividend is expected in the spring of 1996.

Key Stock Statistics

S&P EPS Est. 1995	3.70	Tang. Bk. Value/Share	8.92
P/E on S&P Est. 1995	21.6	Beta	1.33
S&P EPS Est. 1996	4.15	Shareholders	104,700
Dividend Rate/Share	1.32	Market cap. (B)	$ 52.3
Shs. outstg. (M)	647.7	Inst. holdings	60%
Avg. daily vol. (M)	0.942	Insider holdings	NA

Value of $10,000 invested 5 years ago: $ 29,912

Fiscal Year Ending Dec. 31

	1995	% Change	1994	% Change	1993	% Change
Revenues (Million $)						
1Q	4,496	22%	3,690	4%	3,560	6%
2Q	4,762	22%	3,916	11%	3,541	4%
3Q	4,738	17%	4,038	15%	3,506	NM
4Q.	—	—	4,090	16%	3,531	NM
Yr.	—	—	15,734	11%	14,138	3%
Income (Million $)						
1Q	654.0	20%	544.0	8%	503.0	11%
2Q	661.0	18%	559.0	13%	495.0	10%
3Q	623.0	19%	525.0	16%	454.0	10%
4Q	—	—	378.0	13%	335.0	9%
Yr.	—	—	2,006	12%	1,787	10%
Earnings Per Share ($)						
1Q	1.02	20%	0.85	10%	0.77	13%
2Q	1.02	19%	0.86	15%	0.75	10%
3Q	0.96	17%	0.82	17%	0.70	11%
4Q	E0.70	19%	0.59	13%	0.52	11%
Yr.	E3.70	19%	3.12	14%	2.74	11%

Next earnings report expected: late January

Johnson & Johnson

Business Summary - 24-OCT-95

Johnson & Johnson is one of the world's leading manufacturers of health care products. Sales and operating profits in 1994 were derived as follows:

	Sales	Profits
Pharmaceuticals	33%	56%
Professional	34%	29%
Consumer	33%	15%

Foreign operations accounted for 50% of sales and 48% of profits in 1994. R&D spending equaled 8.1% of sales in 1994, versus 8.4% in 1993.

Pharmaceuticals consist of more than 80 prescription drugs, contraceptives, therapeutics and veterinary products, including Ortho-Novum oral contraceptives; Propulsid gastrointestinal; Duragesic transdermal patch for pain; Hismanal antihistamine; Nizoral, Terazol and Sporanox antifungals; EPO anti-anemia agent (sold under the Eprex and Procrit names); Imodium antidiarrheal; Retin-A for acne; and Risperdal for the treatment of schizophrenia.

Professional items include ligatures and sutures, mechanical wound closure products, diagnostic products, dental items, coronary stents, surgical dressings, surgical apparel and accessories, endoscopic surgical instruments, intraocular lenses, hyaluronic acid and other medical products.

Consumer products encompass baby toiletries, first-aid products and nonprescription drugs. Among the company's better known products are Johnson's baby powder, shampoo, oil and lotion; Tylenol analgesic; Stayfree, Carefree and Sure & Natural feminine hygiene products; Band-Aid adhesive bandages; Reach toothbrushes; and Neutrogena skin care and beauty products.

Important Developments

Oct. '95—The company began a cash tender offer of $100 a share for all Cordis Corp. common shares. J&J said it would prefer to effect a tax-free exchange of $105 in stock for each Cordis share. The aggregate cost (net of cash) would be about $1.6 billion for the cash tender and $1.7 billion for a negotiated stock swap. Cordis,a leader in the fields of balloon angioplasty catheters and coronary angiographic equipment, earned $50 million on revenues of $443 million in the 12 months through June 1995. Its products are considered a good strategic fit with J&J's Palmaz-Schatz coronary stent, used to reduce arterial reocclusion after angioplasty.

Capitalization

Long Term Debt: $2,138,000,000 (6/30/95).

Per Share Data ($)

(Year Ended Dec. 31)

	1994	1993	1992	1991	1990	1989
Tangible Bk. Val.	7.34	7.22	6.80	7.34	6.30	5.17
Cash Flow	4.25	3.69	3.31	2.94	2.43	2.16
Earnings	3.12	2.74	2.46	2.20	1.72	1.63
Dividends	1.13	1.01	0.89	0.77	0.65	0.56
Payout Ratio	36%	37%	36%	35%	38%	34%
Prices - High	56½	50⅜	58¾	58¾	37⅛	29¾
- Low	36	35⅝	43	32¾	25⅝	20¾
P/E Ratio - High	18	18	24	26	22	18
- Low	12	13	17	15	15	13

Income Statement Analysis (Million $)

	1994	%Chg	1993	%Chg	1992	%Chg	1991
Revs.	15,734	11%	14,138	3%	13,753	10%	12,447
Oper. Inc.	3,531	17%	3,011	6%	2,837	7%	2,657
Depr.	724	17%	617	10%	560	14%	493
Int. Exp.	186	7%	174	-2%	177	1%	175
Pretax Inc.	2,681	15%	2,332	6%	2,207	8%	2,038
Eff. Tax Rate	25%	—	23%	—	26%	—	28%
Net Inc.	2,006	12%	1,787	10%	1,625	11%	1,461

Balance Sheet & Other Fin. Data (Million $)

	1994	1993	1992	1991	1990	1989
Cash	704	476	878	792	931	583
Curr. Assets	6,680	5,217	5,423	4,933	4,664	3,776
Total Assets	15,668	12,242	11,884	10,513	9,506	7,919
Curr. Liab.	4,266	3,212	3,427	2,689	2,623	1,927
LT Debt	2,199	1,493	1,365	1,301	1,316	1,170
Common Eqty.	7,122	5,568	5,171	5,626	4,900	4,148
Total Cap.	9,451	7,183	6,627	6,927	6,216	5,318
Cap. Exp.	937	975	1,103	987	830	750
Cash Flow	2,730	2,404	2,185	1,954	1,617	1,440

Ratio Analysis

	1994	1993	1992	1991	1990	1989
Curr. Ratio	1.6	1.6	1.6	1.8	1.8	2.0
% LT Debt of Cap.	23.3	20.8	20.6	18.8	21.2	22.0
% Net Inc.of Revs.	12.7	12.6	11.8	11.7	10.2	11.1
% Ret. on Assets	14.4	15.0	14.6	14.6	13.1	14.4
% Ret. on Equity	31.6	33.6	30.4	27.8	25.3	28.3

Dividend Data —Dividends have been paid since 1905. A dividend reinvestment plan is available.

Amt. of Div. $	Date Decl.	Ex-Div. Date	Stock of Record	Payment Date
0.290	Oct. 17	Nov. 08	Nov. 15	Dec. 06 '94
0.290	Jan. 03	Feb. 08	Feb. 14	Mar. 07 '95
0.330	Apr. 27	May. 10	May. 16	Jun. 06 '95
0.330	Jul. 17	Aug. 11	Aug. 15	Sep. 05 '95
0.330	Oct. 16	Nov. 10	Nov. 14	Dec. 05 '95

Data as orig. reptd.; bef. results of disc. opers. and/or spec. items. Per share data adj. for stk. divs. as of ex-div. date. E-Estimated. NA-Not Available. NM-Not Meaningful. NR-Not Ranked.

Office—One Johnson & Johnson Plaza, New Brunswick, NJ 08933. **Tel**—(908) 524-0400. **Chrmn & CEO**—R. E. Larsen. **Vice Chrmn**—R. N. Wilson. **VP-Fin & CFO**—C. H. Johnson. **Secy**—P. S. Galloway. **Treas**—Joann H. Heisen. **Investor Contact**—Annie H. Lo (908-524-6491). **Dirs**—Sir James W. Black, G. N. Burrow, J. G. Cooney, P.M. Hawley, C. H. Johnson, A. D. Jordan, A. G. Langbo, R. S. Larsen, P. N. Larson, J. S. Mayo, T. S. Murphy, P. J. Rizzo, M. F. Singer, R. B. Smith, R. N. Wilson. **Transfer Agent & Registrar**—First Chicago Trust Co. of New York, Jersey City, NJ. **Incorporated** in New Jersey in 1887. **Empl**-81,500. **S&P Analyst:** H.B. Saftlas

Johnson Controls

NYSE Symbol **JCI**
In S&P 500

08-AUG-95 Industry: Building

Summary: This company supplies building controls and energy management systems, automotive seating and batteries, and plastic soft-drink bottles and containers.

S&P Opinion: Hold (★★★)

Recent Price • 60
52 Wk Range • 61½-45¾

Yield • 2.6%
12-Mo. P/E • 14.1

Earnings vs. Previous Year
▲=Up ▼=Down ▶=No Change

Quantitative Evaluations

Outlook
(1 Lowest—5 Highest)
• 4+

Fair Value
• 60⅝

Risk
• **Low**

Earn./Div. Rank
• **B+**

Technical Eval.
• **Bullish** since 4/95

Rel. Strength Rank
(1 Lowest—99 Highest)
• 60

Insider Activity
• **NA**

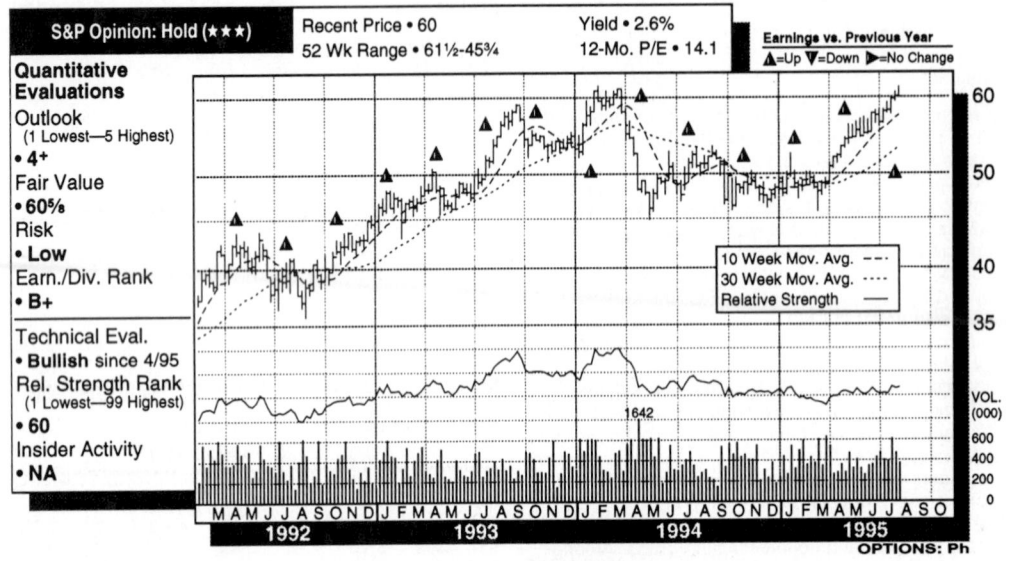

10 Week Mov. Avg. — · —
30 Week Mov. Avg. · · · · ·
Relative Strength ——

1642

VOL. (000)
600
400
200
0

M A M J J A S O N D J F M A M J J A S O N D J F M A M J J A S O N D J F M A M J J A S O
1992   1993   1994   1995

OPTIONS: Ph

Overview - 08-AUG-95

Sales should advance in fiscal 1996, reflecting continued growth in automotive seating, plastics products, retrofit controls and facility management business. Battery sales comparisons should improve with addition of new accounts and with weather conditions more favorable to battery replacement. With ongoing cost reductions in the battery unit, and despite flattening margins in seating and controls, earnings should rise. Longer term, JCI expects to expand its share of the automotive seating business in Europe and North America. The facilities management unit's importance to results should grow over time as new customers are added. This business offers lower building operating costs to its customers through its building management services.

Valuation - 08-AUG-95

Although JCI's earnings should rise in 1996, the stock is trading at about 12X estimated 1996 earnings, which is a fair multiple considering the valuations of comparable diversified, cyclical and capital goods companies. Earnings should continue to grow modestly even in a cyclical downturn in North America, as JCI benefits from secular growth in the automotive seating business. We expect the stock to be an average performer in the near term, but it is a worthwhile total return holding for stable dividend growth and long term capital appreciation.

Key Stock Statistics

S&P EPS Est. 1995	4.50	Tang. Bk. Value/Share	17.94
P/E on S&P Est. 1995	13.3	Beta	1.59
S&P EPS Est. 1996	5.00	Shareholders	33,200
Dividend Rate/Share	1.56	Market cap. (B)	$ 2.5
Shs. outstg. (M)	40.8	Inst. holdings	64%
Avg. daily vol. (M)	0.092	Insider holdings	NA

Value of $10,000 invested 5 years ago: $ 22,330

Fiscal Year Ending Sep. 30

	1995	% Change	1994	% Change	1993	% Change
Revenues (Million $)						
1Q	1,858	17%	1,585	5%	1,511	24%
2Q	2,051	22%	1,682	16%	1,445	22%
3Q	2,181	24%	1,758	10%	1,594	22%
4Q	—	—	1,846	13%	1,632	12%
Yr.	—	—	6,871	11%	6,182	20%
Income (Million $)						
1Q	41.20	8%	38.10	10%	34.60	22%
2Q	32.30	27%	25.50	20%	21.30	29%
3Q	55.30	21%	45.60	8%	42.20	16%
4Q	—	—	56.00	23%	45.60	9%
Yr.	—	—	165.2	20%	137.9	12%
Earnings Per Share ($)						
1Q	0.95	9%	0.87	18%	0.74	12%
2Q	0.73	30%	0.56	33%	0.42	17%
3Q	1.28	21%	1.06	13%	0.94	11%
4Q	E1.54	—	1.31	24%	1.06	8%
Yr.	E4.50	—	3.80	20%	3.16	10%

Next earnings report expected: late October

Johnson Controls

Business Summary - 07-AUG-95

Johnson Controls is a leading manufacturer of automated building controls, batteries, automotive seating and plastics. Contributions by segment in fiscal 1994 were:

	Sales	Income
Automotive	41.8%	39.4%
Controls	32.9%	25.9%
Plastics	14.5%	19.8%
Batteries	10.7%	15.0%

The automotive segment manufactures complete seats and seating components for North American and European car and light-truck manufacturers. The company offers customers complete design, manufacturing and just-in-time delivery capabilities.

The controls segment manufactures, installs and services controls and control systems, principally for non-residential buildings, that are used for temperature and energy management, fire safety and security maintenance. The segment also includes custom engineering, installation and servicing of process control systems and a growing facilities management business that provides operations and maintenance services for more than 9,000 buildings.

The plastics segment is a leading U.S. producer of polyethylene terephthalate (PET) plastic soft-drink bottles. It also makes hot-fill plastic food and drink containers and plastic blowmolding machinery for packaging production.

The battery segment makes lead-acid batteries primarily for the automotive replacement market and for original equipment manufacturers.

The U.S. government accounted for 9% of sales in fiscal 1994, versus 10% in fiscal 1993. The three major U.S. auto companies account for between 4% and 12% of total sales each.

Important Developments

Jun. '95—JCI said that it was in advanced negotiations for the acquisition of Roth Freres Companies, a major supplier of seating and interior components to the European automotive industry with sales of some US$600 million. Roth Freres has plants in Strasbourg-Meinau and Schweighouse, France which produce foam cushions, headrests, headliners, interior door trim and shelves, and joint ventures that supply complete seats in France, Belgium and the Netherlands. Primary customers include Renault, Peugeot, Mitsubishi and Volvo. JCI has operated joint ventures with Roth Freres which have sales of US$375 million annually that are accounted on an equity basis.

Capitalization

Long Term Debt: $639,500,000 (6/95).

Per Share Data ($)

(Year Ended Sep. 30)

	1994	1993	1992	1991	1990	1989
Tangible Bk. Val.	25.52	22.49	25.51	22.51	21.86	20.38
Cash Flow	10.10	9.00	8.18	7.17	6.74	6.42
Earnings	3.80	3.16	2.86	2.19	2.13	2.55
Dividends	1.44	1.36	1.28	1.24	1.20	1.16
Payout Ratio	38%	43%	45%	57%	56%	48%
Prices - High	61¾	59⅛	46⅛	36⅝	32¼	46¾
- Low	44⅞	43	34⅝	21⅞	17⅛	27⅞
P/E Ratio - High	16	19	16	17	15	18
- Low	12	14	12	10	8	11

Income Statement Analysis (Million $)

	1994	%Chg	1993	%Chg	1992	%Chg	1991
Revs.	6,871	11%	6,182	20%	5,157	13%	4,559
Oper. Inc.	624	16%	537	12%	479	12%	426
Depr.	258	8%	238	12%	213	8%	197
Int. Exp.	46.6	-8%	50.7	-4%	52.6	-13%	60.4
Pretax Inc.	326	30%	251	10%	228	30%	176
Eff. Tax Rate	43%	—	45%	—	46%	—	46%
Net Inc.	165	20%	138	12%	123	29%	95.0

Balance Sheet & Other Fin. Data (Million $)

	1994	1993	1992	1991	1990	1989
Cash	133	87.7	96.0	92.0	54.0	27.0
Curr. Assets	1,779	1,532	1,524	1,376	1,291	1,101
Total Assets	3,807	3,231	3,180	2,841	2,799	2,415
Curr. Liab.	1,516	1,285	1,245	1,105	1,099	838
LT Debt	670	500	503	491	483	445
Common Eqty.	1,039	911	1,023	891	861	803
Total Cap.	1,873	1,591	1,761	1,636	1,609	1,502
Cap. Exp.	348	298	237	156	298	224
Cash Flow	414	367	328	284	266	238

Ratio Analysis

	1994	1993	1992	1991	1990	1989
Curr. Ratio	1.2	1.2	1.2	1.2	1.2	1.3
% LT Debt of Cap.	35.8	31.5	28.6	30.0	30.0	29.6
% Net Inc. of Revs.	2.4	2.2	2.4	2.1	2.1	2.6
% Ret. on Assets	4.7	4.3	4.1	3.4	3.5	4.2
% Ret. on Equity	16.0	13.2	11.9	9.9	10.1	11.0

Dividend Data

(Dividends have been paid since 1901. A dividend reinvestment plan is available. A "poison pill" stock purchase rights plan was adopted in 1984.)

Amt. of Div. $	Date Decl.	Ex-Div. Date	Stock of Record	Payment Date
0.360	Jul. 27	Sep. 02	Sep. 09	Sep. 30 '94
0.390	Nov. 16	Dec. 05	Dec. 09	Jan. 03 '95
0.390	Jan. 25	Feb. 27	Mar. 03	Mar. 31 '95
0.390	May. 25	Jun. 06	Jun. 09	Jun. 30 '95
0.390	Jul. 26	Sep. 06	Sep. 08	Sep. 29 '95

Data as orig. reptd.; bef. results of disc. opers. and/or spec. items. Per share data adj. for stk. divs. as of ex-div. date. E-Estimated. NA-Not Available. NM-Not Meaningful. NR-Not Ranked.

Office—5757 North Green Bay Ave., P.O. Box 591, Milwaukee, WI 53201-0591. **Tel**—(414) 228-1200. **Chrmn, Pres & CEO**—J. H. Keyes. **Secy**—J. P. Kennedy. **VP & CFO**—S. A. Roell. **Investor Contact**—Denise M. Zutz. **Dirs**—W. F. Andrews, R. L. Barnett, F. L. Brengel, P. A. Brunner, R. A. Cornog, W. D. Davis, J. H. Keyes, S. J. Morcott, M. R. Seger, D. Taylor, R. F. Teerlink, G. R. Whitaker Jr., R. D. Ziegler. **Transfer Agent & Registrar**—Firstar Trust Co., Milwaukee. **Incorporated** in Wisconsin in 1900. **Empl**-54,800. **S&P Analyst**: Joshua M. Harari, CFA.

Jostens, Inc.

NYSE Symbol **JOS**
In S&P 500

30-AUG-95

Industry:
Jewelry, silverware, time pieces, china

Summary: Jostens produces class rings, yearbooks and recognition products for schools and businesses. It also offers school photography.

S&P Opinion: Buy (★★★★★)	Recent Price • 22⅞	Yield • 3.7%
	52 Wk Range • 23¾-16⅞	12-Mo. P/E • 20.4

Quantitative Evaluations

Outlook
(1 Lowest—5 Highest)
• **3+**

Fair Value
• **22½**

Risk
• **Low**

Earn./Div. Rank
• **B+**

Technical Eval.
• **Bearish** since 9/94

Rel. Strength Rank
(1 Lowest—99 Highest)
• **75**

Insider Activity
• **NA**

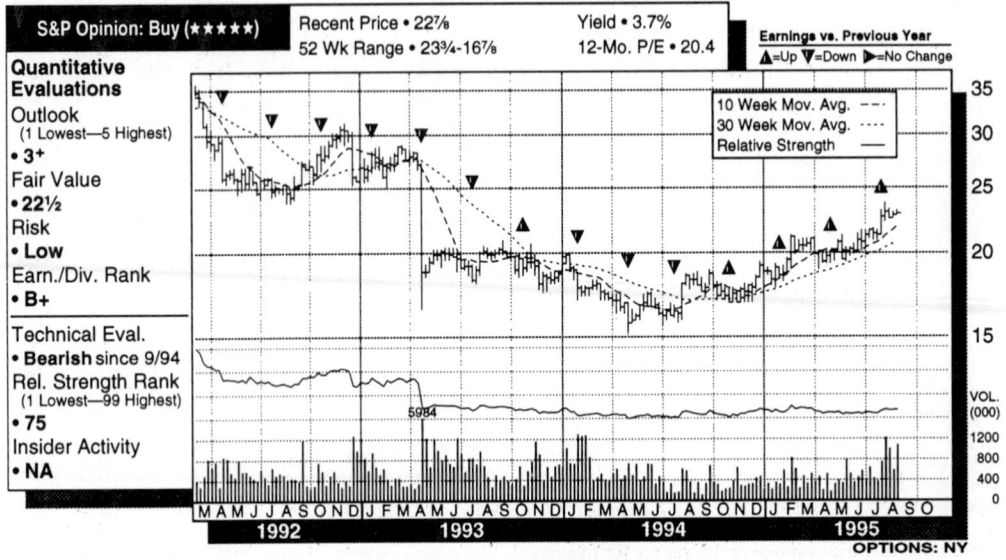

Earnings vs. Previous Year
▲=Up ▼=Down ▶=No Change

10 Week Mov. Avg.
30 Week Mov. Avg.
Relative Strength

5984

VOL. (000)

OPTIONS: NY

Overview - 30-AUG-95

Revenues from school and recognition products should grow in fiscal 1996, aided by favorable demographics for school products and contributions from a multiyear contract with AT&T, together with several other large corporate accounts in the recognition business. The sale of the Jostens Learning Corp. curriculum software unit will allow management to focus on expanding core operations. Proceeds from the sale will be used to buy back about 13% of JOS stock outstanding, contributing significantly to fiscal 1996 earnings per share. Management's objectives for fiscal 1996 include revenue growth, "decent" EPS growth and improving operations at the recognition division.

Valuation - 30-AUG-95

The share price has rebounded sharply from the low of 1994, reflecting the return to profitability in fiscal 1995. The company recently sold the unprofitable curriculum software unit, thereby eliminating its drag on earnings. The core business should benefit from favorable demographics and the absence of distractions from the software unit. Proceeds from the sale will be used to purchase about 13% of the common shares outstanding. Cash flow is strong, the dividend is secure and the price-to-earnings ratio, based on a conservative projection of $1.40 per share for fiscal 1996, is in the lower half of its historical range. In light of favorable long-term prospects, we recommend purchase of this above-average yielding stock for total return.

Key Stock Statistics

S&P EPS Est. 1996	1.40	Tang. Bk. Value/Share	4.67
P/E on S&P Est. 1996	16.3	Beta	1.45
Dividend Rate/Share	0.88	Shareholders	9,700
Shs. outstg. (M)	45.5	Market cap. (B)	$ 1.1
Avg. daily vol. (M)	0.218	Inst. holdings	74%
		Insider holdings	NA

Value of $10,000 invested 5 years ago: $ 9,969

Fiscal Year Ending Jun. 30

	1995	% Change	1994	% Change	1993	% Change
Revenues (Million $)						
1Q	131.6	-12%	149.0	-3%	154.0	8%
2Q	189.9	-4%	198.0	-11%	222.0	-5%
3Q	163.1	3%	158.7	-14%	185.0	11%
4Q	270.4	-16%	321.9	-9%	353.8	5%
Yr.	665.1	-20%	827.3	-10%	914.8	4%
Income (Million $)						
1Q	1.95	34%	1.45	71%	0.85	-70%
2Q	11.71	105%	5.71	-42%	9.88	-36%
3Q	8.51	NM	-9.25	NM	5.46	-47%
4Q	30.47	NM	-24.26	NM	-24.14	NM
Yr.	55.87	NM	-26.35	NM	-7.95	NM
Earnings Per Share ($)						
1Q	0.04	33%	0.03	50%	0.02	-71%
2Q	0.26	100%	0.13	-41%	0.22	-42%
3Q	0.18	NM	-0.20	NM	0.12	-52%
4Q	0.67	NM	-0.54	NM	-0.53	NM
Yr.	1.23	NM	-0.58	NM	-0.18	NM

Next earnings report expected: mid October

Jostens, Inc.

Business Summary - 30-AUG-95

Jostens, Inc. provides products and services that help people recognize achievements and affiliations throughout their lives. Products and services include class rings, yearbooks, graduation products, student photography packages, customized business performance and service awards, sports awards and customized affinity products.

Sales in recent fiscal years were derived as follows:

	1994	1993	1992
School products	66%	59%	59%
Jostens Learning	21%	22%	24%
Recognition	13%	10%	10%
Sportswear	---	9%	7%

School products include class rings (representing about 27% of the segment's fiscal 1994 sales); graduation products such as announcements, diplomas, caps and gowns (23%); student yearbooks (35%); school photography (5%); and other businesses, including commercial printing and the direct marketing of customized products to university alumni and members of sororities, fraternities and other affinity groups (10%).

The recognition segment makes motivation and recognition products, including specialized jewelry, rings, watches, plaques and engraved certificates.

The company recently sold Jostens Learning Corp. (JLC) to an investment partnership led by Bain Capital and Dun & Bradstreet. JLC develops, markets and services computer learning systems for use in elementary and secondary schools. Jostens plans to sell Wicat Systems, a provider of computer-based training systems and coursework for commercial and industrial markets, primarily in the aviation and military industries.

Important Developments

Aug. '95—Jostens announced that will repurchase up to 6.1 million of its common shares through a modified "Dutch auction" tender offer. Under the offer, shareholders will have until September 1, 1995, to tender shares in a price range of $21.50 to $24.50 per share.
Jun. '95—The company sold Jostens Learning Corp. to an investment group led by Bain Capital and Dun & Bradstreet for $50 million cash, a $36 million note maturing in eight years and a separate $4 million note convertible into 19% of the equity of JLC. Jostens intends to sell the Wicat Systems division.

Capitalization

Long Term Debt: $53,899,000 (6/95).

Per Share Data ($) (Year Ended Jun. 30)

	1995	1994	1993	1992	1991	1990
Tangible Bk. Val.	NA	4.59	5.97	6.60	5.85	4.94
Cash Flow	NA	0.28	0.59	2.02	2.14	1.98
Earnings	1.23	-0.58	-0.18	1.50	1.58	1.51
Dividends	0.88	0.88	0.87	0.83	0.78	0.70
Payout Ratio	72%	NM	NM	56%	50%	47%
Prices - High	23¾	20	29	37⅜	38⅝	33
- Low	17¾	15⅛	16½	23¾	28½	22½
P/E Ratio - High	19	NM	NM	25	24	22
- Low	14	NM	NM	16	18	15

Income Statement Analysis (Million $)

	1994	%Chg	1993	%Chg	1992	%Chg	1991
Revs.	827	-10%	915	4%	876	2%	860
Oper. Inc.	61.0	-42%	106	-17%	128	-5%	135
Depr.	38.9	11%	34.9	64%	21.3	-7%	23.0
Int. Exp.	6.8	19%	5.7	-34%	8.7	-15%	10.2
Pretax Inc.	-34.0	NM	-5.0	NM	98.0	-4%	102
Eff. Tax Rate	NM	—	NM	—	37%	—	37%
Net Inc.	-26.3	NM	-7.9	NM	61.4	-4%	64.2

Balance Sheet & Other Fin. Data (Million $)

	1994	1993	1992	1991	1990	1989
Cash	108	14.0	45.0	16.0	27.0	68.0
Curr. Assets	396	379	370	336	296	290
Total Assets	570	583	565	530	473	453
Curr. Liab.	223	199	164	191	158	154
LT Debt	54.0	55.0	55.0	32.0	53.0	75.0
Common Eqty.	257	313	327	296	257	222
Total Cap.	317	385	401	340	316	299
Cap. Exp.	15.2	20.9	19.6	23.4	18.7	17.8
Cash Flow	12.6	26.9	82.7	87.1	79.1	74.0

Ratio Analysis

	1994	1993	1992	1991	1990	1989
Curr. Ratio	1.8	1.9	2.3	1.8	1.9	1.9
% LT Debt of Cap.	17.1	14.3	13.8	9.3	16.9	25.1
% Net Inc.of Revs.	NM	NM	7.0	7.5	7.6	7.8
% Ret. on Assets	NM	NM	11.2	12.7	12.9	12.0
% Ret. on Equity	NM	NM	19.6	23.0	24.9	26.1

Dividend Data
—Cash has been paid each year since 1960. A dividend reinvestment plan is available. A shareholder rights plan was adopted in 1988.

Amt. of Div. $	Date Decl.	Ex-Div. Date	Stock of Record	Payment Date
0.220	Jun. 29	Aug. 09	Aug. 15	Sep. 01 '94
0.220	Oct. 28	Nov. 08	Nov. 15	Dec. 01 '94
0.220	Jan. 26	Feb. 09	Feb. 15	Mar. 01 '95
0.220	Apr. 20	May. 09	May. 15	Jun. 01 '95
0.220	Aug. 04	Aug. 11	Aug. 15	Sep. 01 '95

Data as orig. reptd.; bef. results of disc. opers. and/or spec. items. Per share data adj. for stk. divs. as of ex-div. date.
E-Estimated. NA-Not Available. NM-Not Meaningful. NR-Not Ranked.

Office—5501 Norman Center Dr., Minneapolis, MN 55437. **Tel**—(612) 830-3300. **Chrmn**—R. P. Jensen. **Pres & CEO**—R. C. Buhrmaster. **Sr VP-Secy**—O. E. Fisher Jr. **VP-Treas & Investor Contact**—Robb L. Prince. **Dirs**—L. H. Affinito, W. A. Andres, F. D. Bjork, R. C. Buhrmaster, M. L. Jackson, R. P. Jensen, J. W. Stodder. **Transfer Agent & Registrar**—Norwest Bank Minnesota, South St. Paul. **Incorporated** in Minnesota in 1906. **Empl**-8,000. **S&P Analyst:** Efraim Levy

Kmart Corp.

NYSE Symbol **KM**
In S&P 500

26-OCT-95 Industry: Retail Stores

Summary: Kmart operates some 2,163 discount stores in the U.S. and Puerto Rico. The company also operates stores in Canada, the Czech Republic, Slovakia, Mexico, and Singapore.

S&P Opinion: Avoid (★★)	Recent Price • 9⅞	Yield • 4.8%
	52 Wk Range • 16¾-9⅞	12-Mo. P/E • 49.4

Quantitative Evaluations

Outlook
(1 Lowest—5 Highest)
• 3⁻

Fair Value
• 9⅞

Risk
• Average

Earn./Div. Rank
• A⁻

Technical Eval.
• **Bearish** since 8/95

Rel. Strength Rank
(1 Lowest—99 Highest)
• 3

Insider Activity
• **NA**

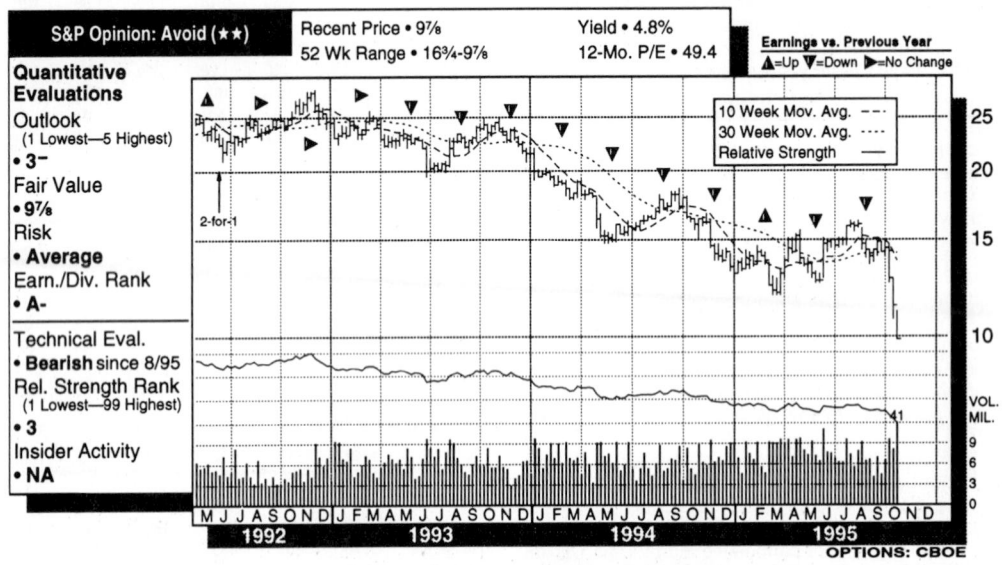

Earnings vs. Previous Year
▲=Up ▼=Down ▶=No Change

10 Week Mov. Avg. – –
30 Week Mov. Avg. ⋯⋯
Relative Strength —

2-for-1

OPTIONS: CBOE

Overview - 26-OCT-95

Kmart is taking many steps to try to stem the erosion in its marketshare caused by other discounters, such as Wal-Mart, Target and Caldor. Underperforming stores are being closed, corporate overhead cut, and nonstrategic assets reduced; the dividend and capital expenditures have also been reduced. The company has implemented new inventory systems and is upgrading its distribution system. In order to improve its balance sheet and cash position, the company has sold off nonstrategic assets and majority stakes in three of its specialty units. Recent sales trends have improved but sales gains have been generated by promotions and as a result the company has posted a net loss in the first half of 1995-96.

Valuation - 26-OCT-95

The share price has fallen precipitously due to continued promotional pricing, which has eroded margins, and speculation about the company's financial position. The company has bolstered its balance sheet by the sale of $3.5 billion in assets in the past year and a half. Kmart has also made progress in lowering its cost structure and has closed some 200 unproductive stores. But with cut-throat pricing in retailing and too many stores competing for the same consumer dollar, we anticipate further store closings. A turnaround for this company appears to be a ways off.

Key Stock Statistics

S&P EPS Est. 1996	0.40	Tang. Bk. Value/Share	12.23
P/E on S&P Est. 1996	24.7	Beta	1.61
S&P EPS Est. 1997	1.00	Shareholders	94,100
Dividend Rate/Share	0.48	Market cap. (B)	$ 4.6
Shs. outstg. (M)	459.4	Inst. holdings	62%
Avg. daily vol. (M)	4.442	Insider holdings	NA

Value of $10,000 invested 5 years ago: $ 7,648

Fiscal Year Ending Jan. 31

	1996	% Change	1995	% Change	1994	% Change
Revenues (Million $)						
1Q	7,797	7%	7,276	-19%	9,027	9%
2Q	8,503	2%	8,340	-18%	10,198	12%
3Q	—	—	8,170	-16%	9,768	10%
4Q	—	—	10,527	3%	10,267	-10%
Yr.	—	—	34,313	NM	34,557	-8%
Income (Million $)						
1Q	-28.00	NM	16.00	-68%	50.00	-57%
2Q	23.00	-73%	86.00	-16%	102.0	-39%
3Q	—	—	29.00	-69%	94.00	-23%
4Q	—	—	129.0	NM	-615.0	NM
Yr.	—	—	260.0	NM	-328.0	NM
Earnings Per Share ($)						
1Q	-0.06	NM	0.03	-73%	0.11	-91%
2Q	0.05	-72%	0.18	-18%	0.22	-41%
3Q	E-0.02	NM	0.06	-70%	0.20	-26%
4Q	E0.43	59%	0.27	NM	-1.35	NM
Yr.	E0.40	-27%	0.55	NM	-0.73	NM

Next earnings report expected: mid November

Kmart Corp.

Business Summary - 26-OCT-95

Kmart operated 2,316 Kmart discount stores in 50 states and Puerto Rico at January 25, 1995. Internationally, the company has stores in Canada, the Czech Republic and Slovakia and has formed joint ventures in Singapore and Mexico. The specialty retail group consisted of 166 Builders Square do-it-yourself improvement centers and a 13% stake in Borders Group, Inc., the balance of which was spun off to shareholders in April 1995. In addition, the company retained 25% and 30% stakes in OfficeMax, Inc. and The Sports Authority, Inc. respectively.

In January 1994, directors approved a restructuring plan to complete a program to modernize its Kmart stores, and recorded a pretax charge of $865 million in the fourth quarter of 1993-94. In November 1994, the company sold its 21.5% interest in Coles Meyer Ltd., an Australian retailer, for $928 million. Kmart sold a 75% interest in OfficeMax Inc. and a 70% interest in Sports Authority, Inc. in initial public offerings; net proceeds totaling $642 million. The company sold its PACE Membership Warehouse unit and PayLess Drug stores in early 1994.

Kmart has targeted a number of areas for improvement in 1995, including improving its merchandise flow and decreasing out-of-stock inventory. Capital expenditures have been reduced and some $475 million in cost reductions will be reflected in 1995. The company plans to close 72 stores in 1995, on top of 110 store closing in recent months. All U.S. Kmart footwear departments are operated under license agreements with the Meldisco subsidiary of Melville Corp. Equity income from 49%-owned Meldisco footwear departments, OfficeMax and Sports Authority was $80 million in 1994-95.

Important Developments

Oct. '95—In response to heavy trading volume in KM's common shares and speculation about the company's financial position, KM said that current liabilities and long-term debt have been reduced by over $2 billion at mid-year 1995 from a year earlier. Merchandise shipments are being received on a normal basis and payments to vendors are being made on schedule. Same store sales in U.S. Kmart stores increased 5.5% in the five weeks ended September 28, 1995. Even though both hardlines and softlines posted sales gains over the prior year, margins were hurt by increased pricing pressures, continuing efforts to clear older merchandise and poor performance at Builders Square. As a result, KM anticipates that third quarter 1995-96 earnings will be well below the year earlier level.

Capitalization

Long Term Debt: $3,681,000,000 (7/95), incl. $1,725,000,000 of lease obligs.

Series C Preferred Stock: 654,815 shs. Ea. sh. conv. into 6.49 common shs.

Per Share Data ($)

(Year Ended Jan. 31)

	1995	1994	1993	1992	1991	1990
Tangible Bk. Val.	12.25	10.40	13.16	12.65	11.74	11.35
Cash Flow	2.05	0.59	3.37	3.21	3.13	1.96
Earnings	0.55	-0.73	2.06	2.02	1.89	0.81
Dividends	0.96	0.95	0.91	0.88	0.85	0.78
Payout Ratio	175%	NM	43%	43%	45%	96%
Cal. Yrs.	1994	1993	1992	1991	1990	1989
Prices - High	22	25¾	28⅛	24¾	18⅝	22½
- Low	12½	19½	20⅞	12⅞	11¾	16¼
P/E Ratio - High	40	NM	14	12	10	28
- Low	23	NM	10	6	6	20

Income Statement Analysis (Million $)

	1995	%Chg	1994	%Chg	1993	%Chg	1992
Revs.	34,025	NM	34,353	-9%	37,942	9%	34,792
Oper. Inc.	1,344	-23%	1,755	-26%	2,361	14%	2,077
Depr.	724	6%	684	NM	685	24%	552
Int. Exp.	511	2%	501	9%	460	15%	401
Pretax Inc.	294	NM	-549	NM	1,426	10%	1,301
Eff. Tax Rate	39%	—	NM	—	34%	—	34%
Net Inc.	260	NM	-327	NM	941	10%	859

Balance Sheet & Other Fin. Data (Million $)

	1995	1994	1993	1992	1991	1990
Cash	480	449	611	565	278	353
Curr. Assets	9,187	9,847	10,509	8,990	7,896	7,984
Total Assets	17,029	17,504	18,931	15,999	13,899	13,145
Curr. Liab.	5,626	5,724	5,495	4,308	4,377	4,299
LT Debt	3,778	3,947	4,935	3,925	3,299	3,029
Common Eqty.	5,900	4,950	6,393	5,905	5,384	4,972
Total Cap.	9,810	10,040	12,739	11,050	8,840	8,101
Cap. Exp.	1,259	1,208	1,435	1,329	974	689
Cash Flow	936	269	1,545	1,367	1,253	784

Ratio Analysis

	1995	1994	1993	1992	1991	1990
Curr. Ratio	1.6	1.7	1.9	2.1	1.8	1.9
% LT Debt of Cap.	38.5	39.3	38.7	35.5	37.3	37.4
% Net Inc.of Revs.	0.8	NM	2.5	2.5	2.3	1.1
% Ret. on Assets	1.5	NM	5.4	5.7	5.6	2.6
% Ret. on Equity	3.9	NM	13.9	14.4	14.6	6.5

Dividend Data —Dividends have been paid since 1913. A "poison pill" stock purchase rights plan was adopted in 1988. A dividend reinvestment plan is available.

Amt. of Div. $	Date Decl.	Ex-Div. Date	Stock of Record	Payment Date
0.240	Oct. 18	Nov. 04	Nov. 10	Dec. 12 '94
0.240	Jan. 17	Feb. 03	Feb. 09	Mar. 13 '95
0.120	Apr. 25	May. 05	May. 11	Jun. 12 '95
0.120	Jul. 18	Aug. 08	Aug. 10	Sep. 11 '95
0.120	Oct. 17	Nov. 07	Nov. 09	Dec. 11 '95

Data as orig. reptd.; bef. results of disc. opers. and/or spec. items. Per share data adj. for stk. divs. as of ex-div. date. E-Estimated. NA-Not Available. NM-Not Meaningful. NR-Not Ranked.

Office—3100 West Big Beaver Rd., Troy, MI 48084-3163. **Tel**—(810) 643-1000. **Chrmn, Pres & CEO**—F. Hall. **EVP & CFO**—T. F. Murasky. **VP & Secy**—Nancy W. LaDuke. **Investor Contact**—Robert M. Burton. **Dirs**—L. H. Affinito, J. A. Califano, W. D. Davis, E. C. Falla, J. P. Flannery, F. Hall, D. B. Harper, F. J. McDonald, J. R. Munro, D. S. Perkins, G. M. Shatto. **Transfer Agent & Registrar**—First National Bank of Boston. **Incorporated** in Michigan in 1916. **Empl**-358,000. **S&P Analyst:** Karen J. Sack, CFA

Kaufman & Broad Home

NYSE Symbol **KBH**
In S&P 500

16-SEP-95 | **Industry:** Building | **Summary:** This regional homebuilder has concentrated on medium-sized developments near major metropolitan areas in California and France. KBH recently expanded into other areas of the U.S.

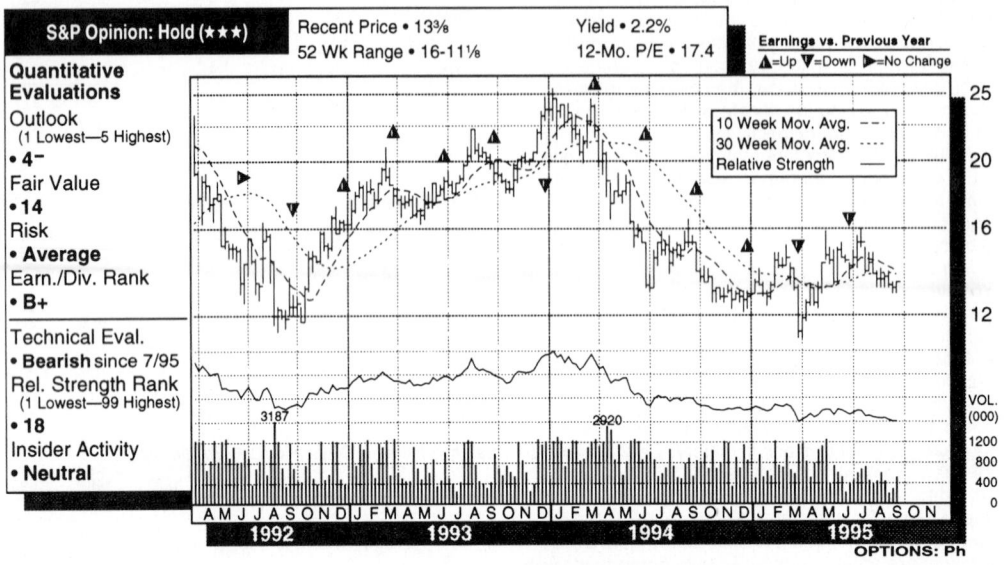

S&P Opinion: Hold (★★★)	Recent Price • 13⅜	Yield • 2.2%
	52 Wk Range • 16-11⅛	12-Mo. P/E • 17.4

Earnings vs. Previous Year
▲=Up ▼=Down ▶=No Change

Quantitative Evaluations

Outlook (1 Lowest—5 Highest)
• **4⁻**

Fair Value
• **14**

Risk
• **Average**

Earn./Div. Rank
• **B+**

Technical Eval.
• **Bearish** since 7/95

Rel. Strength Rank (1 Lowest—99 Highest)
• **18**

Insider Activity
• **Neutral**

Chart legend:
10 Week Mov. Avg. — —
30 Week Mov. Avg. ·······
Relative Strength ——

3187   2920

VOL. (000)

OPTIONS: Ph

Overview - 15-SEP-95

Revenues should be slightly lower in fiscal 1995, hurt largely by a sluggish California market and very poor weather in that area in the first half. However, the sales decline should be limited by KBH's expansion into new domestic areas, along with the improvement in real estate markets being generated by the "buyer-friendly" mortgage rates that have predominated since the spring of 1995. Operating margins should be narrower, with challenging industry conditions likely to continue to necessitate greater efforts to stimulate home sales. Offsetting those factors to an extent will be aggressive cost cutting measures initiated by KBH, including staff cutbacks expected to reduce annual operating expenses by $10 million. Earnings will continue to be restricted by substantial balance sheet leverage.

Valuation - 15-SEP-95

The company's shares enjoyed a bounce after long-term interest rates plunged in May 1995, but much of that appreciation was subsequently erased, as KBH's predominant California housing market has remained rather sluggish. Despite that problem, a better interest rate picture and KBH's successful expansion into Southwestern markets make us more optimistic about the company's upcoming earnings prospects. Given those factors, Kaufman & Broad's stock appears fairly priced in its recent trading range of about 13 times our fiscal 1996 EPS forecast.

Key Stock Statistics

S&P EPS Est. 1995	0.75	Tang. Bk. Value/Share	12.37
P/E on S&P Est. 1995	17.8	Beta	2.04
S&P EPS Est. 1996	1.00	Shareholders	2,300
Dividend Rate/Share	0.30	Market cap. (B)	$0.433
Shs. outstg. (M)	32.4	Inst. holdings	59%
Avg. daily vol. (M)	0.076	Insider holdings	NA

Value of $10,000 invested 5 years ago: $ 11,057

Fiscal Year Ending Nov. 30

	1995	% Change	1994	% Change	1993	% Change
Revenues (Million $)						
1Q	229.8	-11%	256.9	14%	224.9	22%
2Q	315.5	-3%	326.0	2%	320.0	36%
3Q	—	—	348.9	9%	319.9	10%
4Q	—	—	404.5	8%	373.0	-3%
Yr.	—	—	1,336	8%	1,238	13%
Income (Million $)						
1Q	0.44	-95%	8.85	103%	4.37	28%
2Q	3.84	-66%	11.25	24%	9.10	129%
3Q	—	—	10.78	-6%	11.46	95%
4Q	—	—	15.67	5%	14.99	NM
Yr.	—	—	46.55	17%	39.92	42%
Earnings Per Share ($)						
1Q	0.01	-95%	0.22	83%	0.12	20%
2Q	0.10	-64%	0.28	27%	0.22	100%
3Q	E0.25	-7%	0.27	4%	0.26	63%
4Q	E0.39	NM	0.39	15%	0.34	-17%
Yr.	E0.75	-35%	1.16	21%	0.96	23%

Next earnings report expected: late September

Kaufman & Broad Home

Business Summary - 15-SEP-95

Kaufman and Broad Home is the largest single family homebuilder in California and one of the largest builders in France. It recently expanded into Nevada, Arizona, Colorado, Utah, New Mexico and Mexico, and builds on a limited basis in Toronto. KBH generally constructs homes in medium-sized developments close to major metropolitan areas, catering mainly to first-time home buyers. KBH also provides mortgage banking services to its domestic home buyers. Contributions by geographic location (operating profits in millions) in fiscal 1994:

	Sales	Profits
United States	88%	$91.3
France	11%	5.0
Other	1%	-2.0

Unit deliveries in fiscal 1994 were 7,824, versus 6,764 in fiscal 1993 and 4,953 in fiscal 1992.

Homebuilding activity in southern California is concentrated in the Los Angeles, San Diego, Kern, San Bernardino, Riverside and Orange County markets. In northern California, KBH focuses on the San Francisco Bay-San Jose, Monterey Bay, Sacramento, Central Valley and Fresno regions. Most of KBH's communities consist of detached homes, which in fiscal 1994 sold at an average price of $165,900.

French operations concentrate on the metropolitan Paris market. In early 1994, KBH's two French homebuilding divisions, one focusing on entry-level buyers and one on the upwardly mobile executive market, were consolidated into one division. The single-family detached and attached homes sold by the division had an average selling price of $182,300 in fiscal 1994. While still serving both markets, the consolidated division would place greater focus on the entry-level market. The company also develops commercial office buildings and high-density residential projects in Paris.

Important Developments

Jun. '95—The company experienced a 10% year over year gain in net orders in the second quarter of 1995, boosted by a near quadrupling of orders in U.S. states other than California, as KBH benefited from its expansion into the Southwest. Those gains outweighed a 15% decline in the sluggish California market and a much lower total in France, which was affected by anticipation of a May 1995 presidential election. Order backlog at May 31, 1995, amounted to 1,651 units (valued at $275.6 million), up considerably from 1,285 units ($198.5 million) a year earlier.

Capitalization

Total Debt: $886,660,000 (5/95).
$1.52 Depositary Stock: 6,500,000 shs.; rep. one-fifth of Series B mandatory conv. prem. pfd. sh.

Per Share Data ($)

(Year Ended Nov. 30)

	1994	1993	1992	1991	1990	1989
Tangible Bk. Val.	12.46	12.76	9.20	8.97	8.45	6.76
Cash Flow	1.00	0.90	0.87	0.89	1.37	2.57
Earnings	1.16	0.96	0.78	0.80	1.25	2.44
Dividends	0.30	0.30	0.30	0.30	0.30	4.80
Payout Ratio	26%	31%	37%	33%	21%	166%
Prices - High	25½	24¾	25	18¼	15¼	21¾
- Low	12⅛	16	11⅜	8¾	5⅜	9⅞
P/E Ratio - High	22	26	32	23	12	9
- Low	10	17	15	11	4	4

Income Statement Analysis (Million $)

	1994	%Chg	1993	%Chg	1992	%Chg	1991
Revs.	1,336	8%	1,238	13%	1,094	-10%	1,221
Oper. Inc.	115	-6%	122	22%	100	-17%	120
Depr.	3.4	30%	2.6	-24%	3.5	5%	3.3
Int. Exp.	62.6	-6%	66.4	-10%	73.8	-10%	82.2
Pretax Inc.	75.0	1%	74.0	30%	57.0	-12%	65.0
Eff. Tax Rate	37%	—	33%	—	30%	—	26%
Net Inc.	46.6	17%	39.9	41%	28.2	6%	26.5

Balance Sheet & Other Fin. Data (Million $)

	1994	1993	1992	1991	1990	1989
Cash	55.0	75.0	66.0	51.0	28.0	117
Curr. Assets	NA	NA	NA	NA	NA	NA
Total Assets	1,454	1,339	1,432	1,373	1,544	1,487
Curr. Liab.	NA	NA	NA	NA	NA	NA
LT Debt	677	476	727	582	600	726
Common Eqty.	403	443	318	258	234	187
Total Cap.	1,115	964	1,132	949	937	968
Cap. Exp.	Nil	Nil	Nil	Nil	Nil	Nil
Cash Flow	40.1	37.6	31.6	29.8	43.8	84.2

Ratio Analysis

	1994	1993	1992	1991	1990	1989
Curr. Ratio	NA	NA	NA	NA	NA	NA
% LT Debt of Cap.	60.7	49.4	64.2	61.3	64.0	74.9
% Net Inc.of Revs.	3.5	3.2	2.6	2.2	2.9	6.4
% Ret. on Assets	3.4	2.9	1.8	1.8	2.6	7.8
% Ret. on Equity	9.0	9.2	9.0	10.6	18.9	37.9

Dividend Data —Dividends were initiated in 1985.

Amt. of Div. $	Date Decl.	Ex-Div. Date	Stock of Record	Payment Date
0.075	Nov. 04	Nov. 08	Nov. 15	Nov. 25 '94
0.075	Jan. 27	Feb. 08	Feb. 14	Feb. 24 '95
0.075	Mar. 24	May. 08	May. 12	May. 23 '95
0.075	Jun. 30	Aug. 10	Aug. 14	Aug. 29 '95

Data as orig. reptd.; bef. results of disc. opers. and/or spec. items. Per share data adj. for stk. divs. as of ex-div. date. E-Estimated. NA-Not Available. NM-Not Meaningful. NR-Not Ranked.

Office—10990 Wilshire Blvd., Los Angeles, CA 90024. **Tel**—(310) 231-4000. **Chrmn & CEO**—B. Karatz. **SVP & CFO**—M. F. Henn. **Investor Contact**—Bill Hollinger (310) 443-8023. **Dirs**—R. W. Burkle, J. Evans, R. R. Irani, A. Jeancourt-Galignani, J. A. Johnson, B. Karatz, G. Nafilyan, L. G. Nogales, L. Pollack, S. C. Sigoloff. **Transfer Agent & Registrar**—Chemical Trust Company of California, Los Angeles. **Incorporated** in Delaware in 1981. **Empl**- 1,330. **S&P Analyst:** Michael W. Jaffe

Kellogg Co.

NYSE Symbol **K**
In S&P 500

01-AUG-95

Industry:
Food

Summary: Kellogg is the world's leading producer of ready-to-eat cereal products, with a dominant 42% global market share. The W.K. Kellogg Foundation Trust holds 34% of the stock.

S&P Opinion: Avoid (★★)	Recent Price • 73	Yield • 2.1%
	52 Wk Range • 73⅞-51⅛	12-Mo. P/E • 23.0

Quantitative Evaluations

Outlook
(1 Lowest—5 Highest)
• **3**

Fair Value
• **70%**

Risk
• **Low**

Earn./Div. Rank
• **A+**

Technical Eval.
• **Bullish** since 3/95

Rel. Strength Rank
(1 Lowest—99 Highest)
• **66**

Insider Activity
• **Favorable**

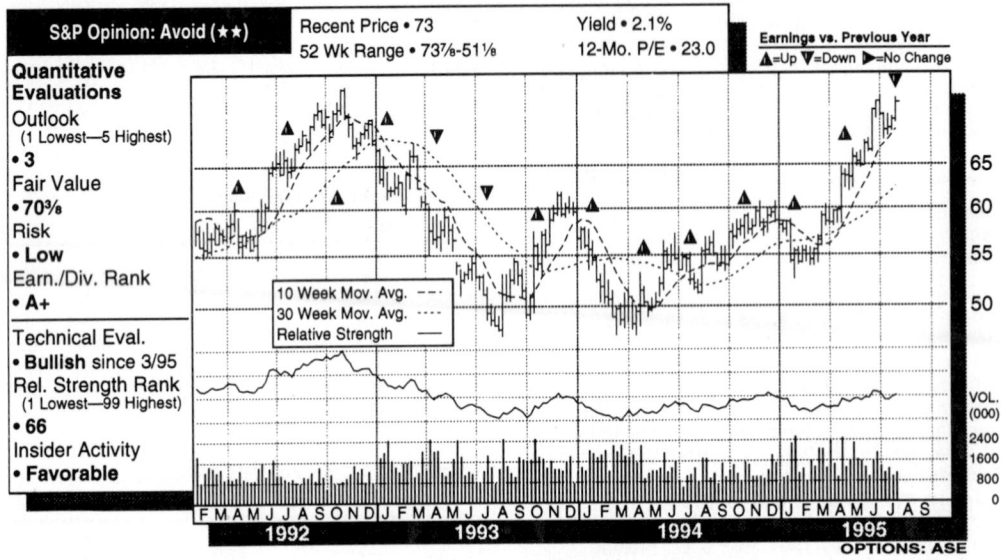

Earnings vs. Previous Year
▲=Up ▼=Down ▶=No Change

10 Week Mov. Avg. - - -
30 Week Mov. Avg. ······
Relative Strength —

OPTIONS: ASE

Overview - 01-AUG-95

Net sales are projected to grow at an annual rate of 7% to 10% through 1996, driven principally by global cereal volume growth and modest price increases. Rising material costs (such as packaging) should be largely offset by cost containment programs, allowing stable gross margins. However, operating margins may be restricted by higher expenses incurred in support of new products and international market expansion, and in response to possible competitive promotional activity. Currency exchange translations will add modestly to quarterly earnings volatility. Aggressive share repurchases will contribute to our projection of steady annual EPS growth (before special items) of 8% to 12% over the next few years.

Valuation - 01-AUG-95

Based on projected annual EPS growth of 8% to 12% over the next few years, the shares appears amply valued. As a result of the company's dominant global share of the growing, relatively high margin (for food) ready-to-eat cereal industry, over the past few years the shares have commanded a substantial premium to the P/E multiple of the S&P 500. However, we believe that this premium may narrow in coming months, reflecting investor concerns about an increasingly price competitive U.S. cereal market, as well as growing international competition. Nevertheless, with K's low debt levels and low business risk profile, the shares remain a good choice for low-risk accounts.

Key Stock Statistics

S&P EPS Est. 1995	3.35	Tang. Bk. Value/Share	8.41
P/E on S&P Est. 1995	21.8	Beta	0.76
S&P EPS Est. 1996	3.80	Shareholders	29,700
Dividend Rate/Share	1.56	Market cap. (B)	$ 15.8
Shs. outstg. (M)	219.8	Inst. holdings	75%
Avg. daily vol. (M)	0.229	Insider holdings	NA

Value of $10,000 invested 5 years ago: $ 24,364

Fiscal Year Ending Dec. 31

	1995	% Change	1994	% Change	1993	% Change
Revenues (Million $)						
1Q	1,716	7%	1,611	6%	1,518	NM
2Q	1,780	10%	1,617	5%	1,542	-3%
3Q	—	—	1,742	4%	1,669	NM
4Q	—	—	1,592	2%	1,566	10%
Yr.	—	—	6,562	4%	6,295	2%
Income (Million $)						
1Q	196.0	7%	183.9	3%	179.2	-6%
2Q	135.9	-10%	151.5	6%	142.7	-13%
3Q	—	—	216.7	59%	135.9	-32%
4Q	—	—	153.3	3%	149.5	17%
Yr.	—	—	705.4	4%	680.7	NM
Earnings Per Share ($)						
1Q	0.89	10%	0.81	7%	0.76	-5%
2Q	0.62	-9%	0.68	10%	0.62	-9%
3Q	E1.05	—	0.96	7%	0.90	7%
4Q	E0.79	—	0.70	6%	0.66	22%
Yr.	E3.35	—	3.15	7%	2.94	3%

Next earnings report expected: late October

Kellogg Co.

Business Summary - 01-AUG-95

Kellogg is the world's leading producer of ready-to-eat cereal products, with an approximate 36% market share in North America and 42% globally (both measured by volume). Sales and profit contributions by geographic region in 1994 were:

	Sales	Profits
U.S.	59%	61%
Europe	25%	24%
Other	16%	15%

Products are manufactured in 19 countries and distributed in nearly 160. Ready-to-eat cereals include Corn Flakes, Rice Krispies, Special K, Frosted Flakes, All-Bran, Corn Pops, Raisin Bran, Bran Flakes, Honey Smacks, Froot Loops, Cocoa Krispies, Apple Jacks, Frosted Mini-Wheats, Nutri-Grain cereals, Bran Buds, Product 19, Cracklin Oat Bran, Cinnamon Mini-Buns, Crispix, Double Dip Crunch, Froot Loops, Fruitful Bran, Apple Raisin Crisp, Just Right, Common Sense, Nut & Honey Crunch, Low Fat Granola, and Mueslix. Cereals are generally marketed under the Kellogg's name and sold principally to the grocery trade through direct sales forces for resale to consumers. K's primary noncereal products are Eggo frozen waffles, Pop-Tarts toaster pastries, and Nutri-Grain Bars.

The company's U.S. manufacturing facilities include five cereal plants and warehouses, in Battle Creek, Mich.; Lancaster, Pa.; Memphis, Tenn.; Omaha, Neb.; and San Leandro, Calif. Other non-cereal foods are also manufactured in the U.S. at various plant locations. Manufacturing facilities outside the U.S. are in Argentina, Australia, Brazil, Canada, Columbia, Denmark, Germany, Great Britain, Guatemala, India, Italy, Japan, Latvia, Mexico, South Africa, South Korea, Spain and Venezuela. A new plant in China is expected to begin operation in mid-1995.

Important Developments

Aug. '95—K said that it was considering the closure of its San Leandro, California, cereal manufacturing plant. If closed, K estimated resultant annual savings at $20 million to $30 million.

Jul. '95—K reported increases in net sales and operating profit (before nonrecurring charges) in 1995's first half of 8.3% and 8.4%, respectively, driven primarily by increased global cereal volumes and cost reduction actions. During the second quarter, the company incurred a pretax charge amounting to $52.8 million ($33.0 million after tax, or $0.15 per share) related to productivity and operational streamlining initiatives in the U.S. and international locations. K believed that such actions would generate annual pretax savings of approximately $20 million beginning in 1996.

Capitalization

Long Term Debt: $718,900,000 (3/95).

Per Share Data ($) (Year Ended Dec. 31)

	1994	1993	1992	1991	1990	1989
Tangible Bk. Val.	8.13	7.26	7.97	8.77	7.62	6.56
Cash Flow	4.29	4.09	3.83	3.44	2.91	2.42
Earnings	3.15	2.94	2.86	2.51	2.08	1.73
Dividends	1.40	1.32	1.20	1.08	0.96	0.86
Payout Ratio	44%	45%	42%	43%	46%	50%
Prices - High	60¾	67⅞	75⅜	67	38¾	40⅞
- Low	47⅜	47¼	54⅜	35	29⅜	28⅞
P/E Ratio - High	19	23	26	27	19	24
- Low	15	16	19	14	14	17

Income Statement Analysis (Million $)

	1994	%Chg	1993	%Chg	1992	%Chg	1991
Revs.	6,562	4%	6,295	2%	6,191	7%	5,787
Oper. Inc.	1,419	6%	1,334	3%	1,294	3%	1,251
Depr.	256	-3%	265	14%	232	4%	223
Int. Exp.	52.3	29%	40.4	20%	33.6	-45%	60.7
Pretax Inc.	1,130	9%	1,034	-3%	1,070	9%	984
Eff. Tax Rate	38%	—	34%	—	36%	—	38%
Net Inc.	705	4%	681	NM	683	13%	606

Balance Sheet & Other Fin. Data (Million $)

	1994	1993	1992	1991	1990	1989
Cash	266	98.0	126	178	101	80.0
Curr. Assets	1,434	1,245	1,237	1,173	1,041	906
Total Assets	4,467	4,237	4,015	3,926	3,749	3,390
Curr. Liab.	1,185	1,215	1,071	1,324	1,110	1,037
LT Debt	719	522	315	15.0	296	371
Common Eqty.	1,808	1,713	1,945	2,160	1,902	1,634
Total Cap.	2,725	2,424	2,445	2,514	2,544	2,295
Cap. Exp.	354	450	474	334	321	509
Cash Flow	962	946	914	829	703	590

Ratio Analysis

	1994	1993	1992	1991	1990	1989
Curr. Ratio	1.2	1.0	1.2	0.9	0.9	0.9
% LT Debt of Cap.	26.4	21.5	12.9	0.6	11.6	16.2
% Net Inc.of Revs.	10.7	10.8	11.0	10.5	9.7	9.1
% Ret. on Assets	16.4	16.8	17.3	15.8	14.2	12.7
% Ret. on Equity	40.6	38.0	33.5	29.9	28.6	27.2

Dividend Data (Dividends have been paid since 1923. A dividend reinvestment plan is available.)

Amt. of Div. $	Date Decl.	Ex-Div. Date	Stock of Record	Payment Date
0.360	Jul. 22	Aug. 26	Sep. 01	Sep. 15 '94
0.360	Nov. 09	Nov. 25	Dec. 01	Dec. 15 '94
0.360	Feb. 08	Feb. 23	Mar. 01	Mar. 15 '95
0.360	Apr. 21	May. 25	Jun. 01	Jun. 15 '95
0.390	Jul. 28	Aug. 30	Sep. 01	Sep. 15 '95

Data as orig. reptd.; bef. results of disc. opers. and/or spec. items. Per share data adj. for stk. divs. as of ex-div. date. E-Estimated. NA-Not Available. NM-Not Meaningful. NR-Not Ranked.

Office—One Kellogg Square, P.O. Box 3599, Battle Creek, MI 49016-3599. **Tel**—(616) 961-2000. **Chrmn & CEO**—A. G. Langbo. **SVP & Secy**—R. M. Clark. **Treas & Investor Contact**—John Bolt. **Dirs**—N. A. Brown, C. X. Gonzalez, G. Gund, W. E. LaMothe, A. G. Langbo, R. G. Mawby, A. McLaughlin, J. R. Munro, H. A. Poling, D. Rumsfeld, T. P. Smucker, D. D. Wharton, J. L. Zabriskie. **Transfer Agent & Registrar**—Harris Trust & Savings Bank, Chicago. **Incorporated** in Delaware in 1922. **Empl**-15,657. **S&P Analyst:** Kenneth A. Shea

Kerr-McGee

NYSE Symbol **KMG**
In S&P 500

14-SEP-95 **Industry:** Oil and Gas

Summary: This integrated oil and natural gas company also engages in chemical production and coal mining. Remaining refining and marketing assets will be sold in 1995.

S&P Opinion: Hold (★★★)	Recent Price • 56	Yield • 2.8%	Earnings vs. Previous Year
	52 Wk Range • 58¼-43¾	12-Mo. P/E • 24.0	▲=Up ▼=Down ▷=No Change

Quantitative Evaluations

Outlook
(1 Lowest—5 Highest)
• **1+**

Fair Value
• **46¾**

Risk
• **Low**

Earn./Div. Rank
• **B**

Technical Eval.
• **Bearish** since 5/95

Rel. Strength Rank
(1 Lowest—99 Highest)
• **58**

Insider Activity
• **Neutral**

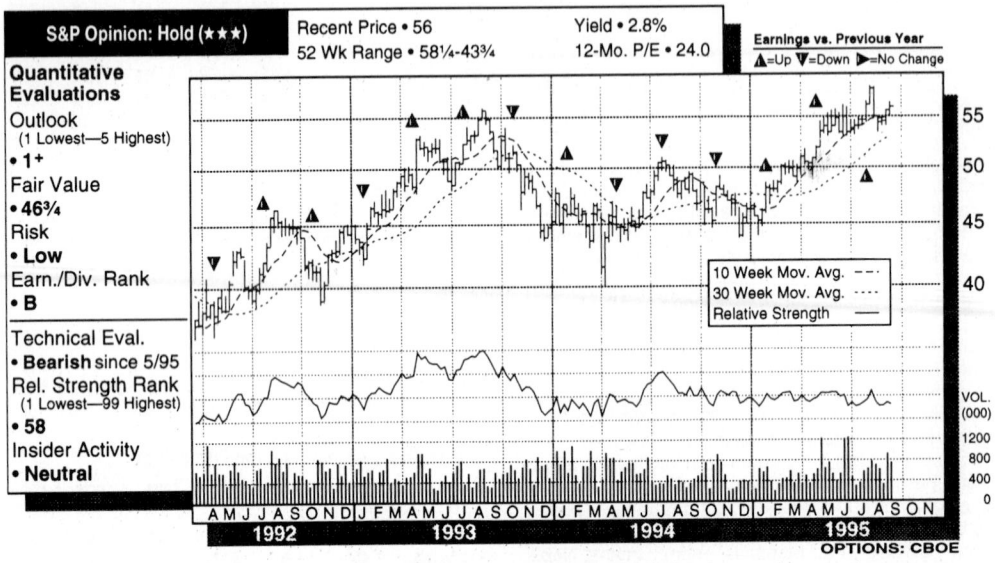

10 Week Mov. Avg. – – –
30 Week Mov. Avg. ·······
Relative Strength ——

VOL. (000)

OPTIONS: CBOE

Overview - 14-SEP-95

Revenues from continuing operations should consolidate in the near-term, reflecting higher crude oil volumes and gains in chemical volumes and prices. The company will use $300 million from the sale of its refining assets to repurchase about 10% of its common shares, with the remaining $100 million to be used for debt reduction. KMG has been shifting its asset base overseas, where economic growth and exploration prospects are more favorable. A concentration on reducing finding and extraction costs should benefit results over the next two years, though the recent drop in natural prices will lead to the sale of non-strategic assets.

Valuation - 14-SEP-95

The shares have trended higher following the announcement that Kerr-McGee made aggreements on the sale of its refining assets. The recent pickup in oil prices may offset the drop in cash flow caused by lower natural gas prices, however, we do not expect the shares to outperform the market over the coming months. The shares appear fairly valued on both an earnings and a cash flow basis at current prices. Improvement in oil and gas volumes, gradually higher gas prices, and improved chemical segment results should buoy the shares over the next twelve months. Plans for exploration in the North Sea and coal acquisitions overseas over the next several years offer considerable upside potential for the shares.

Key Stock Statistics

S&P EPS Est. 1995	2.70	Tang. Bk. Value/Share	27.64
P/E on S&P Est. 1995	20.7	Beta	0.66
S&P EPS Est. 1996	3.00	Shareholders	11,000
Dividend Rate/Share	1.64	Market cap. (B)	$ 3.0
Shs. outstg. (M)	51.8	Inst. holdings	76%
Avg. daily vol. (M)	0.157	Insider holdings	NA

Value of $10,000 invested 5 years ago: $ 13,387

Fiscal Year Ending Dec. 31

	1995	% Change	1994	% Change	1993	% Change
Revenues (Million $)						
1Q	463.9	-42%	800.9	2%	783.5	NM
2Q	456.7	-47%	864.8	2%	845.8	-3%
3Q	—	—	858.2	5%	819.2	-5%
4Q	—	—	829.5	NM	832.6	-4%
Yr.	—	—	3,353	2%	3,281	-3%
Income (Million $)						
1Q	36.80	70%	21.60	-11%	24.40	88%
2Q	44.70	47%	30.40	-10%	33.70	5%
3Q	—	—	17.70	-6%	18.80	-35%
4Q	—	—	20.40	NM	0.20	NM
Yr.	—	—	90.00	17%	77.10	NM
Earnings Per Share ($)						
1Q	0.71	69%	0.42	-16%	0.50	92%
2Q	0.86	48%	0.58	-17%	0.70	3%
3Q	E0.57	63%	0.35	-10%	0.39	-35%
4Q	E0.56	44%	0.39	—	Nil	—
Yr.	E2.70	55%	1.74	11%	1.57	NM

Next earnings report expected: late October

Kerr-McGee

Business Summary - 13-SEP-95

Kerr-McGee is engaged in crude oil and natural gas production and marketing, and has large holdings in chemicals and coal mining. In April 1995, the company adopted a plan to dispose of its refining and marketing business, and listed these operations as discontinued as of that date. Net operating profits (in million $) in recent years were derived as follows:

	1994	1993
Exploration/production	$49	$52
Refining & marketing	22	-19
Chemicals	59	44
Coal	34	58
Other	-1	-3

In 1994, crude oil and condensate production averaged 67,300 bbl. daily (53,200 b/d in 1993), natural gas sales were 271 Mmcf/d (286), crude refinery runs were 146,000 b/d (140,000), and petroleum product sales 233,400 b/d (238,600). Net proved reserves at the end of 1994 were 191 million bbl. of crude oil and condensate (199 million) and 849.2 Bcf of natural gas (708.3). KMG added proved oil and gas reserves equal to 136% of its worldwide production for the year. KMG also produced 25,607,000 tons of coal (23,325,000 in 1993).

Kerr-McGee's 1995 oil and gas exploration budget calls for 50% to be allocated to the Gulf of Mexico, 20% for onshore North America, 15% for the North Sea, and 20% for other international. Major initiatives in the chemicals segment include leveraging upon growth in pigment demand. The segment's largest and most profitable product is titanium dioxide pigment, a white opacifier used primarily in the paint, paper and cosmetics industries. By year end 1996, titanium dioxide capacity is expected to reach 220,000 tons, up from 1995 capacity of 185,000 tons.

Important Developments

Aug. '95—Simultaneous with its announcement of a $300 million common share repurchase, and a $100 million reduction of long term debt, the company hiked its dividend 8%. In response to falling natural gas prices, the company also said that in the third quarter it will take a $100-$125 million charge to write down oil and gas properties, and expects to be selling certain non-strategic properties by the end of 1996. Also in August, KMG was awarded all 17 blocks offshore Louisiana on which the company was the bidder. KMG will be the operator on all of the blocks.
Jul. '95—KMG and its partners were awarded three offshore production licenses covering four blocks in the U.K. sector of the North Sea.

Capitalization

Long Term Debt: $661,000,000 (6/95).

Per Share Data ($)

(Year Ended Dec. 31)

	1994	1993	1992	1991	1990	1989
Tangible Bk. Val.	29.73	29.27	27.96	31.43	30.77	29.44
Cash Flow	8.41	8.08	5.92	8.40	8.83	9.00
Earnings	1.74	1.57	-0.53	2.10	2.26	2.58
Dividends	1.52	1.52	1.52	1.50	1.41	1.27
Payout Ratio	87%	97%	NM	71%	60%	50%
Prices - High	51	56	46⅜	46⅞	53⅝	52
- Low	40	41¾	35⅝	35⅛	42⅜	37⅞
P/E Ratio - High	29	36	NM	22	24	20
- Low	23	27	NM	17	19	14

Income Statement Analysis (Million $)

	1994	%Chg	1993	%Chg	1992	%Chg	1991
Revs.	3,353	2%	3,281	-3%	3,382	3%	3,274
Oper. Inc.	513	10%	467	72%	272	-44%	488
Depr.	345	7%	321	3%	312	3%	304
Int. Exp.	69.0	3%	67.0	-17%	81.0	-14%	94.0
Pretax Inc.	132	12%	118	NM	-64.0	NM	166
Eff. Tax Rate	38%	—	35%	—	NM	—	39%
Net Inc.	90.0	17%	77.0	NM	-26.0	NM	102

Balance Sheet & Other Fin. Data (Million $)

	1994	1993	1992	1991	1990	1989
Cash	82.0	94.0	57.0	192	453	86.0
Curr. Assets	963	866	917	951	1,192	878
Total Assets	3,698	3,547	3,521	3,421	3,473	3,332
Curr. Liab.	890	787	707	608	720	550
LT Debt	673	590	792	926	805	858
Common Eqty.	1,543	1,512	1,350	1,516	1,491	1,476
Total Cap.	2,395	2,274	2,308	2,609	2,541	2,596
Cap. Exp.	1.0	451	373	514	506	506
Cash Flow	435	398	286	406	440	439

Ratio Analysis

	1994	1993	1992	1991	1990	1989
Curr. Ratio	1.1	1.1	1.3	1.6	1.7	1.6
% LT Debt of Cap.	28.1	25.9	34.3	35.5	31.7	33.1
% Net Inc.of Revs.	2.7	2.3	NM	3.1	3.1	4.1
% Ret. on Assets	2.5	2.1	NM	3.0	3.4	3.8
% Ret. on Equity	5.9	5.2	NM	6.8	7.7	8.5

Dividend Data —Dividends have been paid since 1941. A dividend direct purchase and reinvestment plan is available.

Amt. of Div. $	Date Decl.	Ex-Div. Date	Stock of Record	Payment Date
0.380	Nov. 08	Nov. 28	Dec. 02	Jan. 03 '95
0.380	Jan. 10	Feb. 27	Mar. 03	Apr. 03 '95
0.380	May. 09	May. 26	Jun. 02	Jul. 03 '95
0.380	Jul. 11	Aug. 30	Sep. 01	Oct. 02 '95
0.410	Sep. 12	Dec. 04	Dec. 06	Jan. 02 '96

Data as orig. reptd.; bef. results of disc. opers. and/or spec. items. Per share data adj. for stk. divs. as of ex-div. date. E-Estimated. NA-Not Available. NM-Not Meaningful. NR-Not Ranked.

Office—Kerr-McGee Center (P.O. Box 25861), Oklahoma City, OK 73125. **Tel**—(405) 270-1313. **Chrmn & CEO**—F. A. McPherson. **Pres & COO**—L. R. Corbett. **SVP & CFO**—J. C. Linehan. **SVP & Secy**—T. J. McDaniel. **VP & Investor Contact**—A. Barry Brandt (405-270-3125). **Dirs**—B. E. Bidwell, E. H. Clark, Jr., L. R. Corbett, M. C. Jischke, R. S. Kerr, Jr., F. A. McPherson, W. C. Morris, J. J. Murphy, J. J. Nevin, F. M. Walters. **Transfer Agent & Registrar**—Liberty Bank & Trust Co., Oklahoma City. **Incorporated** in Delaware in 1932. **Empl**-5,524. **S&P Analyst:** Raymond J. Deacon

KeyCorp

NYSE Symbol **KEY**
In S&P 500

06-SEP-95 | **Industry:** Banking

Summary: This multiregional bank holding company, headquartered in Cleveland, was formed in March 1994 through the merger of Albany, N.Y.-based KeyCorp into Ohio-based Society Corp.

| S&P Opinion: Hold (★★★) | Recent Price • 31 | Yield • 4.6% |
| | 52 Wk Range • 32¾-23⅝ | 12-Mo. P/E • 9.5 |

Earnings vs. Previous Year
▲=Up ▼=Down ▶=No Change

Quantitative Evaluations

Outlook
(1 Lowest—5 Highest)
• 3⁻

Fair Value
• 30⅞

Risk
• **Low**

Earn./Div. Rank
• **A+**

Technical Eval.
• **Bearish** since 6/95

Rel. Strength Rank
(1 Lowest—99 Highest)
• 44

Insider Activity
• **Neutral**

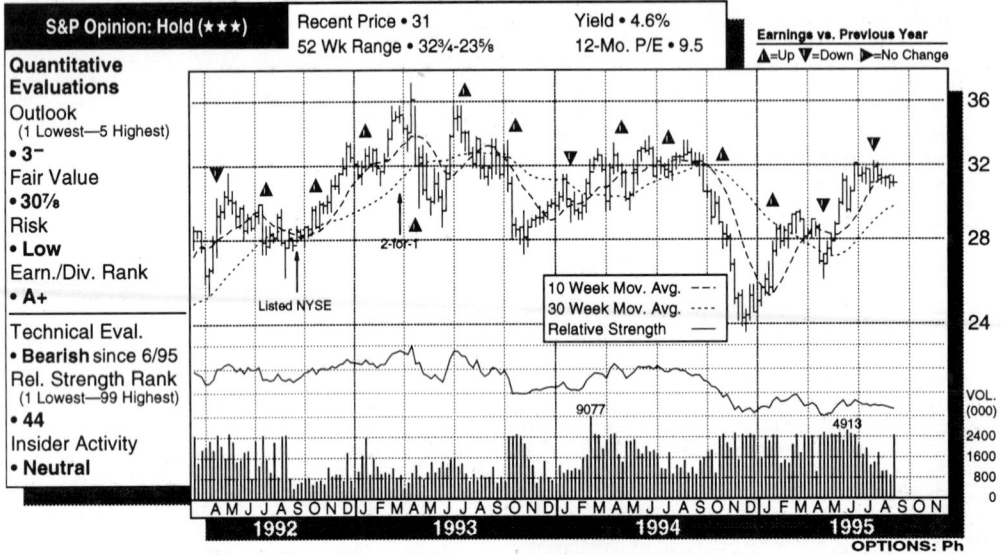

10 Week Mov. Avg. ---
30 Week Mov. Avg. ----
Relative Strength —

OPTIONS: Ph

Overview - 06-SEP-95

Net interest income is expected to be flat to slightly lower in 1995, as strong loan growth in the Rocky Mountain area is offset by a narrower net interest margin due to higher interest rates and competitive pricing. KEY has been taking aggressive steps to reduce its interest rate sensitivity, including securitizing and selling fixed-rate loans and realigning its available-for-sale investment portfolio. Fees from noninterest income sources have been hurt by higher interest rates, but proceeds from the recent sale of the mortgage banking unit will be reinvested in areas with more stable and greater growth potential. Good control of operating expenses and improved asset quality, which will cut credit costs, should mostly offset otherwise weak comparisons.

Valuation - 06-SEP-95

Despite the expectation of relatively healthy loan growth, KEY's modest liability-sensitive position will penalize the net interest margin and lead to flat to lower net interest income in 1995. A restructuring of the balance sheet to minimize sensitivity to interest rates was essentially completed early in 1995, although the company expects to continue to allow certain fixed-rate securities to mature without reinvestment. The recent launch of a new strategic program to both enhance revenue from faster growing areas and improve overhead ratios better positions KEY for the long term, but with only modest earnings improvement expected in the near term, the shares appear adequately valued.

Key Stock Statistics

S&P EPS Est. 1995	3.35	Tang. Bk. Value/Share	16.73
P/E on S&P Est. 1995	9.3	Beta	1.20
S&P EPS Est. 1996	3.75	Shareholders	35,900
Dividend Rate/Share	1.44	Market cap. (B)	$ 7.2
Shs. outstg. (M)	227.5	Inst. holdings	45%
Avg. daily vol. (M)	0.297	Insider holdings	NA

Value of $10,000 invested 5 years ago: $ 23,115

Fiscal Year Ending Dec. 31

	1995	% Change	1994	% Change	1993	% Change
Revenues (Million $)						
1Q	1,416	11%	1,272	NM	1,270	101%
2Q	1,522	14%	1,330	NM	1,318	113%
3Q	—	—	1,374	3%	1,340	130%
4Q	—	—	1,397	9%	1,288	123%
Yr.	—	—	5,373	3%	5,216	119%
Income (Million $)						
1Q	173.9	-17%	208.6	10%	189.9	NM
2Q	199.0	-10%	221.8	13%	196.9	125%
3Q	—	—	229.3	14%	200.8	142%
4Q	—	—	193.8	58%	122.3	41%
Yr.	—	—	853.5	20%	709.9	136%
Earnings Per Share ($)						
1Q	0.71	-16%	0.85	10%	0.77	114%
2Q	0.83	-7%	0.89	10%	0.81	9%
3Q	E0.85	-8%	0.92	12%	0.82	19%
4Q	E0.96	22%	0.79	61%	0.49	-32%
Yr.	E3.35	-3%	3.45	19%	2.89	15%

Next earnings report expected: mid October

Business Summary - 06-SEP-95

KeyCorp, the 11th largest bank holding company in the U.S. with $67.5 billion of assets at June 30, 1995, was formed through the March 1994 merger of KeyCorp, an Albany, N.Y.-based bank holding company, into Society Corp., an Ohio-based bank holding company, which then changed its name to KeyCorp. Through its bank and trust company subsidiaries, the company provides a wide range of banking, fiduciary and other financial services to corporate, individual and institutional customers through more than 1,400 branch and affiliate offices in 25 states.

Services include consumer banking, investment management and trust, corporate banking, securities brokerage and private banking, and customized financial services.

During 1994, average earning assets of $56.9 billion (up from $51.6 billion a year earlier) were divided: loans 75%, investment securities 16%, securities available for sale 7% and other 2%. Average sources of funds were noninterest-bearing deposits 13%, savings and other demand deposits 33%, time deposits 24%, foreign deposits 5%, short-term borrowings 12%, long-term debt 4%, equity 7%, and other 2%.

Total nonperforming assets were $339.8 million (0.73% of loans and related assets) at 1994 year end, down from $500.1 million (1.24%) a year earlier. The allowance for loan losses was $830.3 million (1.80% of loans), versus $802.7 million (2.00%) at the end of 1993. Net charge-offs were 0.26% of average loans in 1994, compared to 0.56% in 1993.

Important Developments

Jul. '95—KEY said that during the second quarter of 1995, it made progress on several strategic initiatives, including the creation of a new operating platform for its national consumer finance business and the implementation of the initial phase of reconfiguring the branch delivery system in two of its markets. It also repurchased 11.7 million common shares during the quarter to be used for various purposes, including the financing of the AutoFinance Group purchase.

Apr. '95—The company acquired Spears, Benzak, Salomon & Farrell, Inc., a New York-based investment management concern with $3.2 billion of assets under management, for 1,910,000 common shares.

Mar. '95—KeyCorp sold its residential mortgage loan servicing operations, which serviced about $28 billion of residential mortgage loans, and recorded a $72.3 million gain on the transaction in the first quarter of 1995. Separately, the company signed a definitive agreement to acquire AutoFinance Group, Inc., a Chicago-based consumer finance concern, for about $325 million in common stock.

Capitalization

Long Term Debt: $4,019,600,000 (6/95).
Preferred Stock: $160,000,000.

Per Share Data ($) (Year Ended Dec. 31)

	1994	1993	1992	1991	1990	1989
Tangible Bk. Val.	15.23	14.47	15.75	16.91	15.34	16.58
Earnings	3.45	2.89	2.51	2.45	2.32	2.32
Dividends	1.28	1.12	0.98	0.92	0.88	0.80
Payout Ratio	37%	39%	39%	38%	38%	35%
Prices - High	33¾	37¼	33½	26¼	17⅝	20¼
- Low	23⅝	27¼	24¼	15¼	12	16½
P/E Ratio - High	10	13	13	11	8	9
- Low	7	9	10	6	5	7

Income Statement Analysis (Million $)

	1994	%Chg	1993	%Chg	1992	%Chg	1991
Net Int. Inc.	2,695	NM	2,679	137%	1,130	64%	687
Tax Equiv. Adj.	58.8	-7%	63.1	129%	27.6	29%	21.4
Non Int. Inc.	895	-8%	973	98%	492	126%	218
Loan Loss Prov.	125	-41%	212	44%	147	84%	79.9
% Exp/Op Revs.	59%	—	64%	—	63%	—	65%
Pretax Inc.	1,283	18%	1,084	147%	439	88%	234
Eff. Tax Rate	34%	—	35%	—	31%	—	30%
Net Inc.	853	20%	710	136%	301	85%	163
% Net Int. Marg.	4.84%	—	5.31%	—	5.33%	—	5.19%

Balance Sheet & Other Fin. Data (Million $)

	1994	1993	1992	1991	1990	1989
Earning Assets:						
Money Mkt.	NA	NA	779	761	347	846
Inv. Securities	12,797	12,849	5,607	3,563	3,165	1,868
Com'l Loans	12,498	10,668	5,354	3,382	3,487	2,634
Other Loans	34,082	30,729	10,848	6,275	6,587	4,175
Total Assets	66,798	59,631	24,978	15,445	15,110	10,903
Demand Deposits	9,136	8,826	3,659	1,967	2,023	1,583
Time Deposits	39,428	37,673	14,999	9,568	10,095	6,841
LT Debt	3,570	1,764	886	177	183	122
Common Eqty.	4,538	4,234	1,808	1,117	1,005	721

Ratio Analysis

	1994	1993	1992	1991	1990	1989
% Ret. on Assets	1.4	1.2	1.3	1.1	1.0	1.1
% Ret. on Equity	19.6	17.8	18.2	15.4	16.1	16.1
% Loan Loss Resv.	1.8	1.9	3.1	1.7	1.8	1.3
% Loans/Deposits	95.9	89.0	86.8	83.7	83.1	80.8
% Equity to Assets	6.8	6.8	6.8	7.1	6.3	6.8

Dividend Data —Dividends have been paid since 1963; the old KeyCorp paid dividends since 1841. A dividend reinvestment plan is available. A shareholder rights plan is in place.

Amt. of Div. $	Date Decl.	Ex-Div. Date	Stock of Record	Payment Date
0.320	Jul. 21	Aug. 25	Aug. 31	Sep. 15 '94
0.320	Nov. 17	Nov. 25	Dec. 01	Dec. 15 '94
0.360	Jan. 19	Feb. 22	Feb. 28	Mar. 15 '95
0.360	May. 18	May. 23	May. 30	Jun. 15 '95
0.360	Aug. 11	Aug. 25	Aug. 29	Sep. 15 '95

Office—127 Public Square, Cleveland, OH 44114-1306. **Tel**—(216) 689-6300. **Chrmn**—V. J. Riley Jr. **Pres & CEO**—R. W. Gillespie. **SVP-CFO**—J. W. Wert. **SVP-Investor Contact**—Jay S. Gould. **Dirs**—H. D. Barclay, W. G. Bares, A. C. Bersticker, T. A. Commes, K. M. Curtis, J. C. Dimmer, L. J. Fjeldstad, R. W. Gillespie, S. R. Hardis, H. S. Hemingway, C. R. Hogan, L. A. Leser, S. A. Minter, M. T. Moore, J. C. Morley, R. W. Pogue, V. J. Riley Jr., R. A. Schumacher, R. B. Stafford, D. W. Sullivan, P. G. Ten Eyck II, N. B. Veeder. **Transfer Agent & Registrar**—KeyCorp Shareholder Services, Cleveland. **Incorporated** in Ohio in 1958. **Empl**-30,370. **S&P Analyst:** Stephen R. Biggar

Kimberly-Clark

NYSE Symbol **KMB**

In S&P 500

15-SEP-95

Industry:
Household Products

Summary: KMB makes consumer and personal care products, including Huggies diapers and Kleenex tissues, with operations to be substantially expanded by the pending purchase of Scott Paper.

S&P Opinion: Accumulate (★★★★)

Recent Price • 64⅞	Yield • 2.7%
52 Wk Range • 68¼-47	12-Mo. P/E • 20.0

Quantitative Evaluations

Outlook
(1 Lowest—5 Highest)
• **3+**

Fair Value
• **64⅝**

Risk
• **Low**

Earn./Div. Rank
• **A+**

Technical Eval.
• **Bullish** since 4/95

Rel. Strength Rank
(1 Lowest—99 Highest)
• **64**

Insider Activity
• **NA**

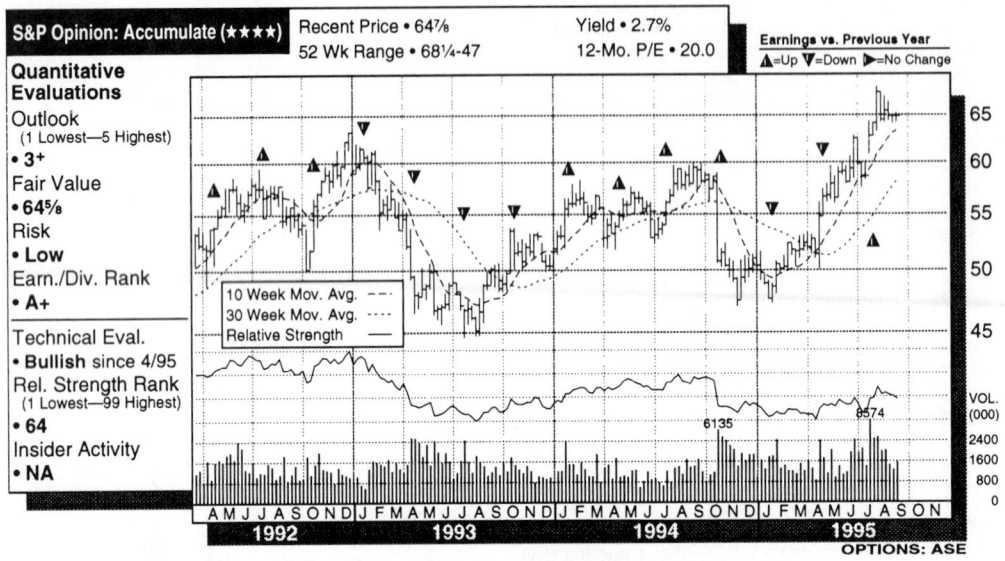

Earnings vs. Previous Year
▲=Up ▼=Down ▶=No Change

OPTIONS: ASE

Overview - 15-SEP-95

Assuming that the planned acquisition of Scott Paper is completed as expected in the final quarter of 1995, the combined firm is likely to have solidly higher sales in 1996. The sales growth should be driven largely by Scott's strong European marketing organization, along with the benefits of the broader product mixture of the merged company, with the firm garnering much shelf space through the combination of KMB's premium products and SPP's value-priced lines. The recent uptrend in consumer tissue pricing should also boost top line growth. Margins should widen substantially, as KMB will quickly take actions to eliminate redundant overhead costs, consolidate workforces and streamline manufacturing facilities. The above factors will easily outweigh any earnings dilution from the planned spin-off of tobacco-related businesses and the reduction of airline operations to a minority interest.

Valuation - 15-SEP-95

Kimberly-Clark's shares have performed favorably in 1995, on improving conditions in consumer tissue markets and investor excitement over the pending takeover of Scott Paper. The complementary nature of the companies' product lines and marketing organizations, along with considerable cost savings to be generated through the integration of operations, leads us to forecast strong earnings growth in 1996. With the shares recently trading at about 13 times our 1996 EPS estimate, further stock appreciation is likely.

Key Stock Statistics

S&P EPS Est. 1995	3.80	Tang. Bk. Value/Share	17.07
P/E on S&P Est. 1995	17.1	Beta	0.92
S&P EPS Est. 1996	5.00	Shareholders	25,600
Dividend Rate/Share	1.80	Market cap. (B)	$ 10.9
Shs. outstg. (M)	160.4	Inst. holdings	62%
Avg. daily vol. (M)	0.389	Insider holdings	NA

Value of $10,000 invested 5 years ago: $ 21,150

Fiscal Year Ending Dec. 31

	1995	% Change	1994	% Change	1993	% Change
Revenues (Million $)						
1Q	2,015	13%	1,777	4%	1,702	-2%
2Q	2,152	18%	1,830	6%	1,726	-1%
3Q	—	—	1,837	3%	1,781	NM
4Q	—	—	1,921	9%	1,764	-3%
Yr.	—	—	7,364	6%	6,973	-2%
Income (Million $)						
1Q	108.7	-20%	136.2	9%	124.8	-6%
2Q	163.3	8%	151.5	14%	133.3	NM
3Q	—	—	141.8	28%	111.2	-18%
4Q	—	—	105.6	-25%	141.6	NM
Yr.	—	—	535.1	5%	510.9	48%
Earnings Per Share ($)						
1Q	0.68	-20%	0.85	9%	0.78	-5%
2Q	1.02	9%	0.94	13%	0.83	-1%
3Q	E1.00	14%	0.88	28%	0.69	-18%
4Q	E1.10	67%	0.66	-25%	0.88	NM
Yr.	E3.80	14%	3.33	5%	3.18	49%

Next earnings report expected: mid October

Business Summary - 14-SEP-95

Kimberly-Clark produces a wide variety of household and personal care products, and additionally manufactures newsprint and premium business, correspondence and specialty papers. KMB also provides air transportation services. Operations would be substantially expanded by the pending acquisition of Scott Paper Co. Product line contributions in 1994:

	Sales	Profits
Class I products	80%	76%
Class II products	15%	22%
Class III products	5%	2%

Operations outside of North America accounted for about 22% of sales and 2.4% of operating profits in 1994. The company has extensive operations in Europe, the Far East and Latin America.

Class I products include tissue products for household, commercial, institutional and industrial uses; infant, child, feminine and incontinence care products; industrial and commercial wipers; health care products; and related items. Familiar brand names include Kleenex, Kotex, New Freedom, Huggies, Pull-Ups and Hi-Dri. KMB had a 31% share of the $3.9 billion U.S. diaper market in 1994, a 45% share of the $1.3 billion facial tissue market, a 28% share of the $2.1 billion feminine pad/tampon market, a 77% share of the $485 million training pants market, and a 52% share of the $455 million incontinence care market.

Class II contains newsprint, printing papers, premium business and correspondence papers, and technical papers. In May 1995, KMB announced that it would spin-off the segment's tobacco papers business.

Class III comprises aircraft services through Midwest Express Airlines (the public stock offering of 70%-80% of Midwest Express is pending), commercial air transportation, and other products and services.

Important Developments

Jul. '95—Kimberly reached a definitive agreement to acquire Scott Paper Co. (SPP), with Scott shareholders to receive .765 KMB shares for each SPP share held (.780 if the pending spin-off of Kimberly's tobacco papers business precedes the merger). The combination would create the second largest household and personal care products company in the U.S. and the world's leading tissue manufacturer. The merger was expected to be completed in the fourth quarter of 1995, subject to regulatory approval, and would be accounted for on a pooling-of-interests basis. Wayne R. Sanders would retain his positions as chairman and CEO of KMB, while Albert J. Dunlap, who holds those titles at Scott, would resign from the firm and serve as a board advisor. Scott is best known for its ScotTissue and Cottonelle bathroom tissue, Viva paper towels and Scotties facial tissue.

Capitalization

Long Term Debt: $965,900,000 (6/95).

Per Share Data ($) (Year Ended Dec. 31)

	1994	1993	1992	1991	1990	1989
Tangible Bk. Val.	16.20	15.27	13.63	15.74	14.14	12.93
Cash Flow	5.37	5.01	3.95	4.84	4.21	3.94
Earnings	3.33	3.18	2.15	3.18	2.70	2.63
Dividends	1.76	1.72	1.64	1.52	1.36	1.30
Payout Ratio	53%	54%	76%	48%	50%	49%
Prices - High	60	62	63¼	52¼	42⅞	37¾
- Low	47	44⅝	46¼	38	30¾	28¾
P/E Ratio - High	18	19	29	16	16	14
- Low	14	14	22	12	11	11

Income Statement Analysis (Million $)

	1994	%Chg	1993	%Chg	1992	%Chg	1991
Revs.	7,364	6%	6,973	-2%	7,091	5%	6,777
Oper. Inc.	1,149	5%	1,096	1%	1,082	7%	1,007
Depr.	330	11%	296	2%	289	9%	266
Int. Exp.	139	5%	132	12%	118	NM	117
Pretax Inc.	828	2%	811	49%	545	-28%	757
Eff. Tax Rate	33%	—	35%	—	34%	—	31%
Net Inc.	535	5%	511	48%	345	-32%	508

Balance Sheet & Other Fin. Data (Million $)

	1994	1993	1992	1991	1990	1989
Cash	24.0	35.0	41.0	43.0	60.0	164
Curr. Assets	1,810	1,675	1,683	1,475	1,397	1,443
Total Assets	6,716	6,381	6,029	5,650	5,284	4,923
Curr. Liab.	2,059	1,909	1,823	1,433	1,466	1,293
LT Debt	930	933	995	875	729	745
Common Eqty.	2,596	2,457	2,191	2,520	2,260	2,086
Total Cap.	4,218	4,042	3,797	4,128	3,711	3,580
Cap. Exp.	485	655	691	537	659	696
Cash Flow	865	807	634	774	672	635

Ratio Analysis

	1994	1993	1992	1991	1990	1989
Curr. Ratio	0.9	0.9	0.9	1.0	1.0	1.1
% LT Debt of Cap.	22.0	23.1	26.2	21.2	19.6	20.8
% Net Inc.of Revs.	7.3	7.3	4.9	7.5	6.7	7.4
% Ret. on Assets	8.2	8.2	5.9	9.3	8.5	9.2
% Ret. on Equity	21.2	22.0	14.6	21.3	20.0	21.4

Dividend Data —Dividends have been paid since 1935. A dividend reinvestment plan is available. A "poison pill" stock purchase rights plan was adopted in 1988.

Amt. of Div. $	Date Decl.	Ex-Div. Date	Stock of Record	Payment Date
0.440	Jul. 27	Sep. 02	Sep. 09	Oct. 04 '94
0.440	Nov. 18	Dec. 05	Dec. 09	Jan. 03 '95
0.450	Feb. 17	Mar. 06	Mar. 10	Apr. 04 '95
0.450	Apr. 20	Jun. 06	Jun. 09	Jul. 05 '95
0.450	Aug. 01	Sep. 06	Sep. 08	Oct. 03 '95

Data as orig. reptd.; bef. results of disc. opers. and/or spec. items. Per share data adj. for stk. divs. as of ex-div. date.
E-Estimated. NA-Not Available. NM-Not Meaningful. NR-Not Ranked.

Office—P.O. Box 619100, D/FW Airport Station, Dallas, TX 75261-9100. **Tel**—(214) 830-1200. **Chrmn & CEO**—W. R. Sanders. **SVP & CFO**—J. W. Donehower. **VP & Secy**—D. M. Crook. **Investor Contact**—Tina S. Barry. **VP & Treas**—W. A. Gamron. **Dirs**—J. F. Bergstrom, P. S. J. Cafferty, P. J. Collins, W. O. Fifield, C. X. Gonzalez, J. G. Grosklaus, L. E. Levy, F. A. McPherson, L. Johnson Rice, W. R. Sanders, W. R. Schmitt, R. L. Tobias. **Transfer Agent & Registrar**—First National Bank of Boston. **Incorporated** in Delaware in 1928. **Empl**-42,707. **S&P Analyst:** Michael W. Jaffe

King World Productions

NYSE Symbol **KWP**
In S&P 500

23-OCT-95

Industry:
Filmed Entertainment

Summary: This company is a leading distributor of first-run syndicated television programs, including "Wheel of Fortune," "Jeopardy!" and "The Oprah Winfrey Show."

S&P Opinion: Hold (★★★)	Recent Price • 35⅞	Yield • Nil	Earnings vs. Previous Year
	52 Wk Range • 44½-32½	12-Mo. P/E • 14.4	▲=Up ▼=Down ▶=No Change

Quantitative Evaluations

Outlook
(1 Lowest—5 Highest)
• **4+**

Fair Value
• **37⅜**

Risk
• **Low**

Earn./Div. Rank
• **B+**

Technical Eval.
• **Bullish** since 9/95

Rel. Strength Rank
(1 Lowest—99 Highest)
• **23**

Insider Activity
• **NA**

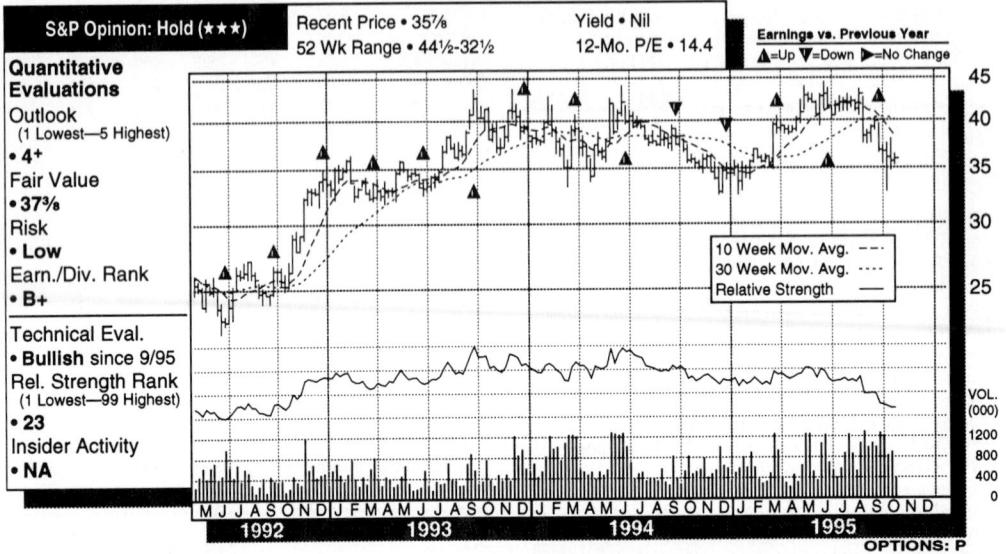

10 Week Mov. Avg. ---
30 Week Mov. Avg. ····
Relative Strength —

VOL. (000)
1200
800
400
0

1992 1993 1994 1995

OPTIONS: P

Overview - 20-OCT-95

In fiscal 1996, we expect revenues and earnings to be helped by KWP having more advertising time to sell and modest growth in license fees. KWP has an additional minute of advertising time to sell for each episode of "Oprah," and another 30 seconds per episode on its two magazine shows, "Inside Edition" and "American Journal." During at least the next several years, we expect distribution of "Wheel of Fortune," "Jeopardy!" and "Oprah" to again generate most of KWP's revenues and earnings. Also, we look for KWP to have a pretax gain of about $9 million in fiscal 1996's first quarter related to the sale of a Buffalo TV station. This is not included in our earnings estimate.

Valuation - 20-OCT-95

We view these shares as having modest appeal, largely based on the sizable amount of free cash flow that the company genetrates and the stock's relatively low P/E. However, we are concerned about KWP's profit dependence on its three primary shows, and we see a difficult environment for launching successful new syndicated programming in the future. For the 1996-97 broadcast season, KWP may seek to introduce one or two new programs, including a high-profile version of the game show "Hollywood Squares" with several partners. However, we don't currently see this prospect as sufficient basis to be enthused about the stock. Also, in the future, KWP and other independent distributors may be facing additional competition from shows produced or distributed by network broadcast companies.

Key Stock Statistics

S&P EPS Est. 1995	3.00	Tang. Bk. Value/Share	14.82
P/E on S&P Est. 1995	12.0	Beta	0.65
S&P EPS Est. 1996	3.35	Shareholders	800
Dividend Rate/Share	Nil	Market cap. (B)	$ 1.3
Shs. outstg. (M)	36.7	Inst. holdings	63%
Avg. daily vol. (M)	0.164	Insider holdings	NA

Value of $10,000 invested 5 years ago: $ 14,114

Fiscal Year Ending Aug. 31

	1995	% Change	1994	% Change	1993	% Change
Revenues (Million $)						
1Q	147.1	-24%	193.1	14%	169.7	-15%
2Q	143.7	5%	137.1	21%	113.1	-6%
3Q	142.6	28%	111.9	27%	87.94	3%
4Q	—	—	38.62	-63%	103.6	6%
Yr.	—	—	480.7	1%	474.3	-6%
Income (Million $)						
1Q	27.87	-28%	38.77	NM	38.50	5%
2Q	29.89	23%	24.29	NM	24.05	13%
3Q	29.22	50%	19.51	5%	18.65	13%
4Q	—	—	5.78	-72%	20.73	NM
Yr.	—	—	88.30	-13%	101.9	7%
Earnings Per Share ($)						
1Q	0.75	-26%	1.02	4%	0.98	4%
2Q	0.80	25%	0.64	3%	0.62	13%
3Q	0.78	50%	0.52	6%	0.49	17%
4Q	E0.67	NM	0.15	-73%	0.55	4%
Yr.	E3.00	29%	2.33	-12%	2.65	9%

Next earnings report expected: mid November

King World Productions

23-OCT-95

Business Summary - 19-OCT-95

KWP distributes and produces television programming. The majority of KWP's revenues comes from the distribution of three programs--"Wheel of Fortune," "Jeopardy!" and "The Oprah Winfrey Show." Each of these shows is among the top-rated (in terms of viewership) syndicated TV shows in the U.S. Also, KWP produces and distributes "Inside Edition." Two newer KWP programs, "American Journal" and a talk show starring Rolonda Watts began airing in September 1993 and January 1994, respectively. In addition, KWP has acquired rights to the "Hollywood Squares" game show and has a 10% equity interest in Crystal Dynamics, a videogame software company.

Merv Griffin Enterprises is producer of "Wheel of Fortune" and "Jeopardy!" KWP has exclusive distribution rights for these shows so long as KWP has sufficient broadcast commitments to cover their production and distribution costs. The agreements prohibit KWP from distributing, on a similar basis, game shows of other producers while it is distributing "Wheel of Fortune" and "Jeopardy!" "The Oprah Winfrey Show" is produced by a business controlled by Ms. Winfrey.

KWP's revenues from distribution of first-run syndicated programs come from two sources. KWP typically receives license fees from individual TV stations and receives an amount of commercial time that KWP sells to advertisers. KWP also distributes a library of movies and other TV programs to domestic TV stations. These include various Sherlock Holmes and Charlie Chan films and "The Little Rascals."

Also, as of July 6, 1995, KWP had authorization to repurchase up to 301,200 additional common shares. Thus far in fiscal 1995, KWP has bought back 180,500 shares, for an aggregate cost of approximately $6.14 million (on average, about $34.02 per share).

Important Developments

Oct. '95—Oprah Winfrey has agreed to continue hosting and producing her popular KWP-distributed talk show through at least the 1997-98 broadcast season. Also, for the 1996-97 broadcast season, KWP may seek to supply a new version of the Hollywood Squares game and/or a new lifestyle show directed at young audiences. Meanwhile, at the end of fiscal 1995's third quarter, KWP had cash or equivalents totaling about $509 million, an increase of $79 million from nine months earlier. The company has authorization to repurchase up to 301,200 KWP common shares. Also, KWP's results for the past three quarters reflect an accounting change related to when revenue from various KWP TV shows is recognized. This change does not affect KWP's cash flow, but causes some incompatibility in year-to-year comparisons of financial results.

Capitalization

Long Term Debt: None (5/95).

Per Share Data ($)
(Year Ended Aug. 31)

	1994	1993	1992	1991	1990	1989
Tangible Bk. Val.	12.49	10.57	8.98	6.35	3.87	1.65
Cash Flow	2.35	2.69	2.46	2.50	2.29	2.04
Earnings	2.33	2.65	2.43	2.38	2.15	1.94
Dividends	Nil	Nil	Nil	Nil	Nil	Nil
Payout Ratio	Nil	Nil	Nil	Nil	Nil	Nil
Prices - High	44⅛	43¾	35¼	34½	30	27⅛
- Low	33¼	31¾	22⅛	21½	18⅛	15¼
P/E Ratio - High	19	17	15	14	14	14
- Low	14	12	9	9	8	8

Income Statement Analysis (Million $)

	1994	%Chg	1993	%Chg	1992	%Chg	1991
Revs.	481	1%	474	-6%	503	6%	476
Oper. Inc.	128	-16%	152	-1%	154	-3%	159
Depr.	0.5	-63%	1.4	27%	1.1	-78%	5.1
Int. Exp.	Nil	—	Nil	—	Nil	—	11.7
Pretax Inc.	141	-13%	163	4%	157	2%	154
Eff. Tax Rate	37%	—	37%	—	40%	—	40%
Net Inc.	88.0	-14%	102	7%	94.9	2%	93.2

Balance Sheet & Other Fin. Data (Million $)

	1994	1993	1992	1991	1990	1989
Cash	342	300	311	242	153	47.0
Curr. Assets	405	428	428	364	269	156
Total Assets	570	536	498	501	407	302
Curr. Liab.	110	141	155	238	144	123
LT Debt	Nil	Nil	Nil	Nil	90.7	89.5
Common Eqty.	459	394	343	242	146	62.0
Total Cap.	459	394	343	263	261	177
Cap. Exp.	0.6	1.7	0.3	4.3	4.2	2.9
Cash Flow	89.0	103	96.0	98.3	89.6	77.1

Ratio Analysis

	1994	1993	1992	1991	1990	1989
Curr. Ratio	3.7	3.0	2.8	1.5	1.9	1.3
% LT Debt of Cap.	Nil	Nil	Nil	Nil	34.7	50.6
% Net Inc.of Revs.	18.4	21.5	18.9	19.6	18.5	18.5
% Ret. on Assets	16.1	19.9	19.0	20.5	23.7	35.0
% Ret. on Equity	20.8	28.0	32.4	47.9	80.6	265.6

Dividend Data —No cash dividends have been paid.

Data as orig. reptd.; bef. results of disc. opers. and/or spec. items. Per share data adj. for stk. divs. as of ex-div. date. E-Estimated. NA-Not Available. NM-Not Meaningful. NR-Not Ranked.

Office—1700 Broadway, New York, NY 10019. **Tel**—(212) 315-4000. **Chrmn**—Roger King. **Pres & CEO**—M. King. **VP-Secy**—D. King. **CFO & Investor Contact**—S. A. LoCascio. **Dirs**—J. Chaseman, D. King, M. King, Richard King, Roger King, R. S. Konecky, S. W. Palley, J. M. Rupp. **Transfer Agent**—First Chicago Trust Co. of New York, NYC. **Incorporated** in Delaware in 1984. **Empl**-430. **S&P Analyst:** Tom Graves, CFA

Knight-Ridder

NYSE Symbol **KRI**
In S&P 500

05-AUG-95 | Industry: Publishing

Summary: Knight-Ridder is one of the largest newspaper publishers in the U.S., and also provides business news and information and electronic retrieval services in over 135 countries.

S&P Opinion: Hold (★★★)	Recent Price • 56	Yield • 2.6%
	52 Wk Range • 59⅛-46½	12-Mo. P/E • 13.3

Quantitative Evaluations

Outlook
(1 Lowest—5 Highest)
• **4+**

Fair Value
• **57**

Risk
• **Low**

Earn./Div. Rank
• **A-**

Technical Eval.
• **Bearish** since 3/95

Rel. Strength Rank
(1 Lowest—99 Highest)
• **33**

Insider Activity
• **NA**

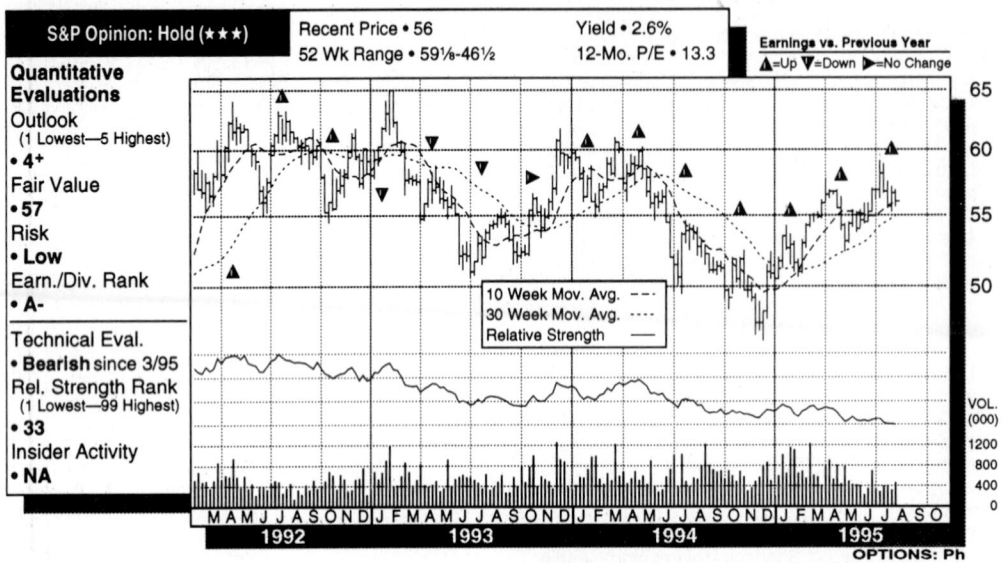

Earnings vs. Previous Year
▲=Up ▼=Down ▶=No Change

10 Week Mov. Avg. – – –
30 Week Mov. Avg. ·····
Relative Strength ——

VOL. (000)

M A M J J A S O N D J F M A M J J A S O N D J F M A M J J A S O N D J F M A M J J A S O
1992 • 1993 • 1994 • 1995

OPTIONS: Ph

Overview - 01-AUG-95

The rise in revenues in 1995 will probably be less than 5%, partly due to the sale of the Journal of Commerce (JOC), which contributed about $60 million to revenues in 1994. In addition, retooling and repricing measures at Dialog will slow revenue growth through much of the year. Slowing advertising momentum has forced us to reduce our expected rise in newspaper revenues to 5%-6%, from 7%. Newspaper operating margins will be pressured by sharply higher newsprint costs, in spite of operating efficiencies in other areas. BIS' margins will be restrained by the pricing and retooling measures. Equity earnings from newsprint and cable operations should advance sharply. Other income includes a $1.07 per share capital gain from the sale of JOC.

Valuation - 01-AUG-95

The stock has pretty much been trading in place in recent months, and not much headway is expected from KRI in the near term, which is understandable given that earnings growth is moderating, and much of the gain in per-share earnings is stemming from stock buybacks. In addition, the market has apparently taken a "wait and see" attitude with regard to the next several quarters which will be affected by retooling and restructuring actions at Dialog. We view KRI's attempts to reposition and restructure BIS' operations as positives that will provide stronger returns longer term. The generous dividend provides a nice cushion under the stock.

Key Stock Statistics

S&P EPS Est. 1995	4.40	Tang. Bk. Value/Share	7.71
P/E on S&P Est. 1995	12.7	Beta	1.13
S&P EPS Est. 1996	3.80	Shareholders	10,700
Dividend Rate/Share	1.48	Market cap. (B)	$ 2.8
Shs. outstg. (M)	49.9	Inst. holdings	68%
Avg. daily vol. (M)	0.076	Insider holdings	NA

Value of $10,000 invested 5 years ago: $ 11,138

Fiscal Year Ending Dec. 31

	1995	% Change	1994	% Change	1993	% Change
Revenues (Million $)						
1Q	674.6	7%	630.9	8%	583.9	5%
2Q	687.5	4%	661.5	6%	621.7	5%
3Q	—	—	642.6	8%	593.1	5%
4Q	—	—	713.9	9%	652.7	5%
Yr.	—	—	2,649	8%	2,451	5%
Income (Million $)						
1Q	35.67	17%	30.37	31%	23.14	-7%
2Q	94.12	88%	50.12	18%	42.50	-8%
3Q	—	—	37.24	19%	31.25	NM
4Q	—	—	53.16	4%	51.21	17%
Yr.	—	—	170.9	15%	148.1	1%
Earnings Per Share ($)						
1Q	0.69	25%	0.55	31%	0.42	-9%
2Q	1.88	104%	0.92	19%	0.77	-8%
3Q	E0.73	—	0.69	21%	0.57	NM
4Q	E1.10	—	0.99	6%	0.93	18%
Yr.	E4.40	—	3.15	18%	2.68	1%

Next earnings report expected: late October

Knight-Ridder

Business Summary - 01-AUG-95

Knight-Ridder (formerly Knight-Ridder Newspapers) derived 81% of revenues and 94% of operating profits from newspaper publishing in 1994. It is also engaged in electronic distribution of commodity and financial news and market quotes and selected computerized information retrieval services.

KRI owns 28 daily newspapers in 15 states, with average daily and Sunday circulations of 3.47 million and 4.59 million, respectively. The larger papers include the Miami Herald, Philadelphia Inquirer, Philadelphia Daily News, Detroit Free Press, San Jose Mercury and San Jose News. KRI also publishes six nondaily suburban newspapers and partially owns three other dailies.

The Business Information Services (BIS) division accounted for 19% of revenues and 6% of operating profits in 1994. Operations include the Dialog and Data-Star information retrieval services; real-time financial news and pricing information through such products as FuturesCenter, MoneyCenter and TradeCenter; daily coverage of transportation and trade issues; and real-time steamship tariff and cargo information through the Journal of Commerce, other publications and electronic services. BIS serves subscribers in over 100 countries. Its major competitors worldwide are Bloomberg, Dow Jones-Telerate and Reuters.

KRI also owns 49.5% of the voting and 65% of the nonvoting common stock of Seattle Times Co.; has interests in two newsprint mills; has interests in TKR Cable Co.; and is part owner of a newspaper advertising sales company.

Important Developments

Jun. '95—Directors authorized a three-million share repurchase program. About 1.9 million shares remain to be purchased under two previous authorizations in 1994 for three million shares each.
Apr. '95—KRI completed the sale of The Journal of Commerce for $115 million. After-tax proceeds from the sale were earmarked for debt reduction and share repurchases.
Mar. '95—TKR Cable, a joint venture with Tele-Communications Inc., agreed to purchase systems serving about 147,000 subscribers in central and northern New Jersey from Sammons Communications for about $268 million.

Capitalization

Long Term Debt: $566,000,000 (3/95).

Per Share Data ($)

	1994	1993	1992	1991	1990	1989
Tangible Bk. Val.	9.57	9.62	8.77	8.16	3.32	3.33
Cash Flow	5.50	4.92	4.69	4.67	5.10	5.49
Earnings	3.15	2.68	2.65	2.55	2.94	3.43
Dividends	1.46	1.40	1.40	1.40	1.34	1.24
Payout Ratio	46%	52%	53%	57%	44%	36%
Prices - High	61	65	64⅛	57½	58	58⅜
- Low	46½	50⅝	51½	43¾	37	42⅞
P/E Ratio - High	19	24	24	23	20	17
- Low	15	19	19	17	13	13

(Year Ended Dec. 31)

Income Statement Analysis (Million $)

	1994	%Chg	1993	%Chg	1992	%Chg	1991
Revs.	2,649	8%	2,451	5%	2,330	4%	2,237
Oper. Inc.	459	12%	409	2%	402	14%	353
Depr.	128	3%	124	10%	113	3%	110
Int. Exp.	44.6	-1%	45.1	-14%	52.4	-24%	68.8
Pretax Inc.	300	20%	249	2%	245	17%	210
Eff. Tax Rate	40%	—	38%	—	38%	—	37%
Net Inc.	171	16%	148	1%	146	11%	132

Balance Sheet & Other Fin. Data (Million $)

	1994	1993	1992	1991	1990	1989
Cash	9.3	23.0	97.1	26.2	26.2	60.6
Curr. Assets	423	401	461	370	389	416
Total Assets	2,447	2,431	2,458	2,333	2,270	2,135
Curr. Liab.	421	406	405	336	314	346
LT Debt	412	410	496	557	804	661
Common Eqty.	1,225	1,243	1,182	1,149	895	917
Total Cap.	1,776	1,793	1,795	1,908	1,886	1,737
Cap. Exp.	67.0	71.0	101	167	246	125
Cash Flow	299	272	259	242	259	288

Ratio Analysis

	1994	1993	1992	1991	1990	1989
Curr. Ratio	1.0	1.0	1.1	1.1	1.2	1.2
% LT Debt of Cap.	23.2	22.9	27.6	29.2	42.6	38.0
% Net Inc.of Revs.	6.5	6.0	6.3	5.9	6.5	7.9
% Ret. on Assets	7.1	6.1	6.0	5.5	6.9	8.1
% Ret. on Equity	14.1	12.2	12.4	12.5	16.8	21.0

Dividend Data
(Dividends have been paid since 1941. A dividend reinvestment plan is available. A "poison pill" stock purchase right was adopted in 1986.)

Amt. of Div. $	Date Decl.	Ex-Div. Date	Stock of Record	Payment Date
0.370	Sep. 22	Sep. 30	Oct. 06	Oct. 14 '94
0.370	Dec. 15	Dec. 22	Dec. 29	Jan. 06 '95
0.370	Mar. 24	Apr. 03	Apr. 07	Apr. 14 '95
0.370	Jun. 22	Jul. 03	Jul. 06	Jul. 14 '95

Data as orig. reptd.; bef. results of disc. opers. and/or spec. items. Per share data adj. for stk. divs. as of ex-div. date. E-Estimated. NA-Not Available. NM-Not Meaningful. NR-Not Ranked.

Office—One Herald Plaza, Miami, FL 33132. **Tel**—(305) 376-3800. **Chrmn & CEO**—P. A. Ridder. **Pres**—J. C. Fontaine. **VP & Secy**—D. C. Harris. **Sr VP & CFO**—R. Jones. **VP & Investor Contact**—Polk Laffoon IV (305) 376-3838. **Dirs**—J. R. Challinor, A. H. Chapman Jr., J. C. Fontaine, P. C. Goldmark Jr., B. B. Hauptfuhrer, J. Hill Jr., W. S. Lee, C. P. McColough, B. R. Morris, T. L. Phillips, E. Ridder, P. A. Ridder, R. F. Singleton, R. L. Tobias, B. K. Toomey, G. F. — Valdes-Fauli, J. L. Weinberg. **Transfer Agent & Registrar**—Chemical Bank, NYC. **Incorporated** in Ohio in 1974. **Empl-** 21,000. **S&P Analyst:** William H. Donald

Kroger Co.

NYSE Symbol **KR**
In S&P 500

11-SEP-95

Industry:
Retail Stores

Summary: This operator of supermarkets and convenience stores is one of the largest chains in the U.S., with over 1,300 supermarkets and more than 900 convenience stores.

S&P Opinion: Buy (★★★★★)

| Recent Price • 32⅞ | Yield • Nil |
| 52 Wk Range • 33¼-21¾ | 12-Mo. P/E • 13.0 |

Earnings vs. Previous Year
▲=Up ▼=Down ▶=No Change

Quantitative Evaluations

Outlook
(1 Lowest—5 Highest)
• **3⁻**

Fair Value
• **32⅝**

Risk
• **Low**

Earn./Div. Rank
• **B**

Technical Eval.
• **Bullish** since 6/95

Rel. Strength Rank
(1 Lowest—99 Highest)
• **68**

Insider Activity
• **Neutral**

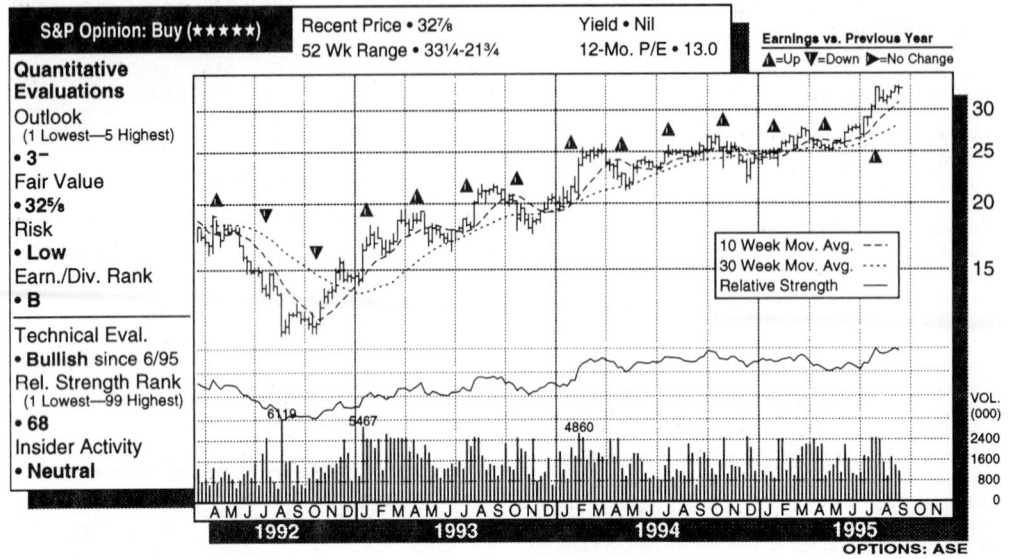

10 Week Mov. Avg. — · —
30 Week Mov. Avg. - - - -
Relative Strength ——

OPTIONS: ASE

Overview - 06-SEP-95

Sales should advance over 5% in 1995, benefiting from new and remodeled stores, as retail square footage increases about 5.4%. Same-store sales should edge up about 2%. Gross margins should widen, reflecting increased sales of higher-margin private label products, improved buying, and lower transportation costs. Expenses should rise as a percentage of sales, due to greater employee benefit costs and new store expenses. Operating cash flow should climb about 8%. Interest expense should decline as the company pays down high interest debt. Share earnings gains will be restricted by more shares outstanding due to increasing employee ownership and the conversion of debentures. Share earnings are projected at $2.70 (primary; $2.50 fully diluted).

Valuation - 11-SEP-95

The share price has risen steadily since late 1992, as the company established a stronger financial footing. Kroger continues to post solid same-store sales gains and healthy increases in operating income. The company, which is still highly leveraged, has proved its ability to generate strong cash flow to pay down debt in a timely fashion. Kroger is now in a position to generate consistent increases in cash flow. As a result, Kroger has boosted its capital spending program, adding new square footage and remodeling stores. As the supermarket industry comes back into favor, reflecting its defensive quality, we anticipate a P/E multiple expansion, based on a 14% jump in 1995 EPS.

Key Stock Statistics

S&P EPS Est. 1995	2.70	Tang. Bk. Value/Share	NM
P/E on S&P Est. 1995	12.2	Beta	1.47
S&P EPS Est. 1996	3.15	Shareholders	59,400
Dividend Rate/Share	Nil	Market cap. (B)	$ 4.0
Shs. outstg. (M)	122.5	Inst. holdings	59%
Avg. daily vol. (M)	0.270	Insider holdings	NA

Value of $10,000 invested 5 years ago: $ 22,288

Fiscal Year Ending Dec. 31

	1995	% Change	1994	% Change	1993	% Change
Revenues (Million $)						
1Q	5,465	3%	5,329	3%	5,174	3%
2Q	5,653	5%	5,394	1%	5,329	5%
3Q	—	—	6,650	3%	6,479	2%
4Q	—	—	5,586	3%	5,402	-19%
Yr.	—	—	22,959	3%	22,384	1%
Income (Million $)						
1Q	64.48	16%	55.69	89%	29.46	40%
2Q	82.46	18%	69.98	136%	29.62	NM
3Q	—	—	51.20	103%	25.21	NM
4Q	—	—	92.04	6%	86.51	26%
Yr.	—	—	268.9	57%	170.8	69%
Earnings Per Share ($)						
1Q	0.56	12%	0.50	67%	0.30	30%
2Q	0.71	15%	0.62	130%	0.27	NM
3Q	E0.51	13%	0.45	96%	0.23	188%
4Q	E0.92	15%	0.80	1%	0.79	7%
Yr.	E2.70	14%	2.37	48%	1.60	44%

Next earnings report expected: mid October

Kroger Co.

Business Summary - 11-SEP-95

The Kroger Co. operates supermarkets and convenience stores, as well as manufacturing facilities. As part of a late 1988 recapitalization, shareholders received a special dividend of $40 a share in cash, plus $17 principal amount of debentures (valued at about $8). The company is focusing on its core business of combination (food/drug) and convenience stores, and has sold or closed certain businesses and underperforming assets.

As of December 31, 1994, the company operated 1,301 supermarkets in 25 states and 932 convenience stores in 16 states. Combination stores range from 40,000 to 80,328 sq. ft. At year-end 1994, combination stores accounted for 58% of the store base and 71% of the supermarket square footage. Kroger's 458 superstores have limited specialty departments, no pharmacy, and are smaller than combo units.

As of December 31, 1994, Dillon Cos. operated 240 supermarkets, principally in Colorado, Kansas, Missouri and Arizona, under names including Dillon Food Stores, King Soopers, Gerbes Supermarkets, Fry's Food Stores and City Market. Dillon convenience stores operate under the trade names Kwik Shop, Quik Stop Markets, Time Saver Stores, Tom Thumb Food Stores, Turkey Hill Minit Markets, Loaf N'Jug and Mini Mart.

The company also operates 37 food processing facilities that supply more than 4,000 private label products to the supermarkets.

Capital expenditures totaled $534 million in 1994, up 42% from 1993. Retail square footage increased by 4.7% in 1994.

Important Developments

Sep. '95—The company said that all of its 6.38% convertible junior subordinated notes were converted into about 10.7 million common shares. This will reduce interest expense and improve leverage ratios. Food sales in the second quarter of 1995 increased 4.8%, year to year; identical-store food sales rose 1.5%. Operating cash flow increased 11.8%. Net operating working capital declined by $199.6 million to $53.7 million. Management attributed the strong second quarter performance to the implementation of new technology, which controlled distribution and logistics costs, and to better than expected sales in new stores. The company plans to increase square footage by 5.4% in 1995, including some 90 new store projects and expansions and 65 remodels. Capital expenditures should approximate $625 million in 1995 and net interest expense $320 million to $325 million.

Capitalization

Long Term Debt: $3,702,956,000 (6/17/95), incl. lease obligs.

Per Share Data ($)

(Year Ended Dec. 31)

	1994	1993	1992	1991	1990	1989
Tangible Bk. Val.	-19.90	-23.32	-30.13	-32.04	-34.18	-36.06
Cash Flow	4.81	3.97	3.74	3.71	3.72	2.66
Earnings	2.37	1.60	1.11	1.12	0.96	-0.23
Dividends	Nil	Nil	Nil	Nil	Nil	Nil
Payout Ratio	Nil	Nil	Nil	Nil	Nil	Nil
Prices - High	26⅞	21¾	21⅛	24½	17	19¾
- Low	19⅜	14	11¼	12⅝	10⅝	8⅜
P/E Ratio - High	11	14	19	22	18	NM
- Low	8	9	10	11	11	NM

Income Statement Analysis (Million $)

	1994	%Chg	1993	%Chg	1992	%Chg	1991
Revs.	22,959	3%	22,384	1%	22,145	4%	21,351
Oper. Inc.	1,027	8%	954	7%	889	-5%	934
Depr.	278	10%	253	5%	241	3%	234
Int. Exp.	331	-16%	392	-17%	475	-11%	535
Pretax Inc.	421	48%	284	64%	173	2%	169
Eff. Tax Rate	36%	—	40%	—	42%	—	40%
Net Inc.	269	57%	171	69%	101	NM	101

Balance Sheet & Other Fin. Data (Million $)

	1994	1993	1992	1991	1990	1989
Cash	27.0	121	104	4.0	55.0	115
Curr. Assets	2,152	2,226	2,168	1,992	1,950	2,048
Total Assets	4,708	4,480	4,303	4,114	4,119	4,242
Curr. Liab.	2,395	2,251	2,174	2,087	2,062	2,069
LT Debt	3,889	4,135	4,473	4,408	4,558	4,724
Common Eqty.	-2,153	-2,459	-2,699	-2,748	-2,859	-2,964
Total Cap.	1,908	1,858	2,051	1,928	1,970	2,053
Cap. Exp.	534	395	245	226	229	131
Cash Flow	547	424	342	335	322	217

Ratio Analysis

	1994	1993	1992	1991	1990	1989
Curr. Ratio	0.9	1.0	1.0	1.0	0.9	1.0
% LT Debt of Cap.	203.8	222.5	218.1	228.6	231.4	NM
% Net Inc.of Revs.	1.2	0.8	0.5	0.5	0.4	NM
% Ret. on Assets	5.8	3.6	2.4	2.4	2.0	NM
% Ret. on Equity	NM	NM	NM	NM	NM	NM

Dividend Data —Following special distributions of $40 a share in October 1988 and $17 a share principal amount of 15.5% debentures in December 1988, Kroger has no plans to resume quarterly dividends, which had been paid since 1902. A "poison pill" stock purchase rights plan was adopted in 1986.

Data as orig. reptd.; bef. results of disc. opers. and/or spec. items. Per share data adj. for stk. divs. as of ex-div. date.
E-Estimated. NA-Not Available. NM-Not Meaningful. NR-Not Ranked.

Office—1014 Vine St., Cincinnati, OH 45202. **Tel**—(513) 762-4000. **Chrmn & CEO**—J. A. Pichler. **Pres & COO**—D. B. Dillon. **VP & Secy**—P. W. Heldman. **VP, Treas & Investor Contact**—L. Turner. **Dirs**—R. V. Anderson, R. L. Bere, R. B. Carey, Jr., J. L. Clendenin, D. B. Dillon, Jr., R. W. Dillon, L. Everingham, J. T. LaMacchia, P. Shontz Longe, T. B. Morton, Jr., T. H. O'Leary, J. D. Ong, K. D. Ortega, J. A. Pichler, M. R. Seger, J. D. Woods. **Transfer Agent & Registrar**—First Chicago Trust Co. of New York, NYC. **Incorporated** in Ohio in 1902. **Empl**-200,000. **S&P Analyst:** Karen J. Sack, CFA

Laidlaw Inc.

NYSE Symbol **LDW.B**
In S&P 500

29-AUG-95

Industry:
Pollution Control

Summary: This Canadian-based company is North America's third largest solid waste management firm, the largest hazardous waste management company and the largest school bus operator.

S&P Opinion: Hold (★★★)	Recent Price • 9¼	Yield • 1.3%
	52 Wk Range • 10⅛-7	12-Mo. P/E • 22.6

Earnings vs. Previous Year
▲=Up ▼=Down ▶=No Change

Quantitative Evaluations

Outlook
(1 Lowest—5 Highest)
• **NA**

Fair Value
• **NA**

Risk
• **NA**

Earn./Div. Rank
• **B+**

Technical Eval.
• **Bullish** since 7/94

Rel. Strength Rank
(1 Lowest—99 Highest)
• **32**

Insider Activity
• **NA**

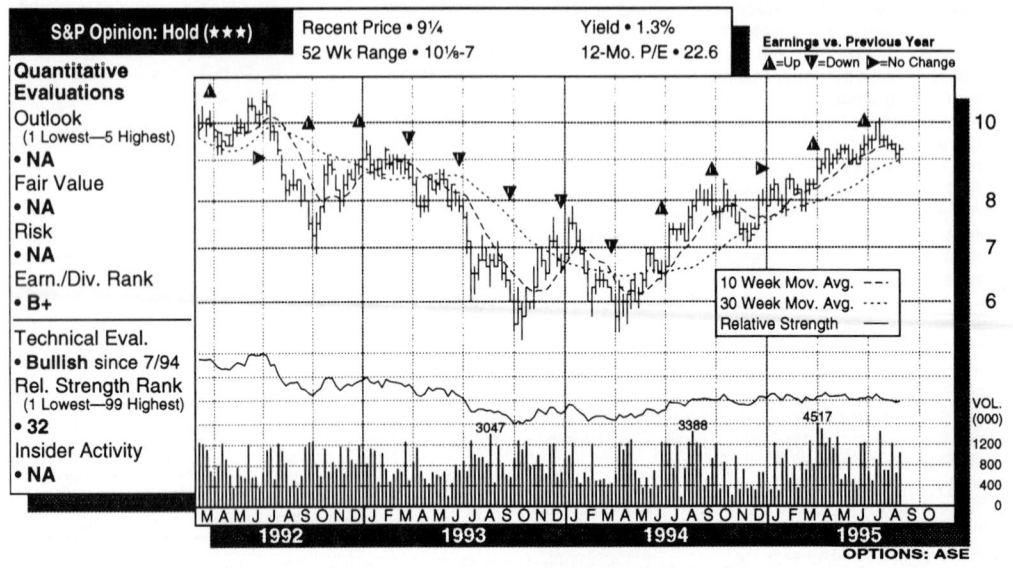

10 Week Mov. Avg. – – –
30 Week Mov. Avg. ·······
Relative Strength ——

VOL.
(000)
1200
800
400
0

M A M J J A S O N D J F M A M J J A S O N D J F M A M J J A S O N D J F M A M J J A S O
1992 1993 1994 1995

OPTIONS: ASE

Overview - 29-AUG-95

Profits from solid waste operations in fiscal 1996 should grow moderately, reflecting increased volumes and low single-digit price increases. Growth could be higher should LDW expand its portfolio of landfills through acquisitions. The growth rate for recycling is expected to slow as prices for newspaper and corrugated board slip from recent highs. LDW's hazardous waste business will benefit from the full-year inclusion of USPCI (acquired December 1994). Offsetting will be pricing pressure in its government services operations. Strong gains are anticipated from passenger services, reflecting the pending acquisition of CareLine and full-year inclusion of Mayflower (acquired in March 1995). Limiting EPS comparisons will be the additional 18,000,000 B shares to be issued for CareLine, increased interest expense and absence of equity income from Attwoods.

Valuation - 29-AUG-95

This Canadian-based company has grown rapidly in recent years through acquisitions. The pending acquisition of CareLine should yield material synergies with LDW's MedTrans unit. Positive contributions also are anticipated from the March 1995 acquisition of Mayflower. With revenues from the U.S. and European operations now 84% of LDW's total, changes in the value of the Canadian dollar no longer significantly influence profits. Though LDW's fundamental picture is favorable, the shares carry greater risk as they trade at a premium to the market multiple.

Key Stock Statistics

S&P EPS Est. 1995	0.50	Tang. Bk. Value/Share	3.43
P/E on S&P Est. 1995	18.5	Beta	0.93
S&P EPS Est. 1996	0.60	Shareholders	8,100
Dividend Rate/Share	0.16	Market cap. (B)	$ 2.6
Shs. outstg. (M)	277.2	Inst. holdings	29%
Avg. daily vol. (M)	0.218	Insider holdings	NA

Value of $10,000 invested 5 years ago: $ 4,559

Fiscal Year Ending Aug. 31

	1995	% Change	1994	% Change	1993	% Change
Revenues (Million $)						
1Q	569.7	4%	546.2	6%	513.0	-2%
2Q	597.0	15%	520.4	11%	469.0	2%
3Q	733.4	27%	579.1	7%	543.8	5%
4Q	—	—	482.6	3%	467.5	10%
Yr.	—	—	2,128	7%	1,993	3%
Income (Million $)						
1Q	38.20	NM	38.05	-22%	48.89	20%
2Q	27.20	60%	16.97	-40%	28.08	NM
3Q	50.30	29%	38.94	NM	-33.60	NM
4Q	—	—	-3.12	NM	-335.0	NM
Yr.	—	—	90.83	NM	-291.6	NM
Earnings Per Share ($)						
1Q	0.14	NM	0.14	-22%	0.18	13%
2Q	0.10	67%	0.06	-40%	0.10	-9%
3Q	0.18	29%	0.14	NM	-0.12	NM
4Q	E0.08	NM	-0.01	NM	-1.21	NM
Yr.	E0.50	52%	0.33	NM	-1.05	NM

Next earnings report expected: early November

Laidlaw Inc.

29-AUG-95

Business Summary - 29-AUG-95

Canada-based Laidlaw Inc. provides solid and hazardous waste services, as well as passenger services. Contributions in fiscal 1994 were:

	Revs.	Profits
Solid waste services	35%	38%
Hazardous waste services	24%	20%
Passenger services	41%	42%

Operations in the U.S. and Europe accounted for 78% of revenues in fiscal 1994.

LDW is the third largest solid waste services company in North America, conducting waste collection, compaction, disposal, recycling, resource recovery, transportation and transfer services for commercial, industrial and residential customers in 18 states and seven Canadian provinces. It operates 32 landfills with unused permitted capacity of about 152 million cubic yards. LDW provides collection services for about 228,000 commercial and industrial customers and some 2.4 million residences and operates 12 transfer stations and 26 materials recovery facilities.

As a result of the December 1994 acquisition of United States Pollution Control Industries (USPCI), Laidlaw is North America's largest hazardous waste management company. Services are provided from 100 locations in 26 states and seven Canadian provinces and in Mexico. There are 11 secure hazardous waste landfills, a land treatment facility for nonhazardous industrial wastes and three incinerators for liquid wastes.

The largest school bus operator in North America, LDW provides transportation for about 1.6 million students per day. It is also the second largest provider of healthcare transportation services. The company also owns 24% of ADT Ltd., a security and vehicle auction firm.

Important Developments

Jul. '95—LDW agreed to acquire CareLine Inc., the third largest provider of ambulance services in the U.S. for some 18,000,000 Class B shares. CRLN has annual revenues of about $225 million.
Mar. '95—Laidlaw completed the acquisition of Mayflower Group Inc., the second largest school bus service company in the U.S., for $157 million. Mayflower has annual revenues of about $250 million and operates approximately 7,200 school buses.

Capitalization

Long Term Debt: $1,703,500,000 (5/95).
5% Cum. Conv. First Pref. Stock: 633,070 shs. (no par); ea. conv. into 1.5 Cl. B shs. at C$8 a sh.
Class A Stock: 47,632,092 shs. (no par). Canadian Pacific Ltd. owns 47%.
Class B Nonvoting Stock: 229,609,268 shs. (no par); has priorities over Cl. A in payment of divs.

Per Share Data ($)

(Year Ended Aug. 31)

	1994	1993	1992	1991	1990	1989
Tangible Bk. Val.	3.90	3.86	5.40	4.82	6.23	4.82
Cash Flow	1.17	-0.22	1.38	-0.48	1.92	1.70
Earnings	0.33	-1.05	0.52	-1.35	1.10	1.00
Dividends	0.12	0.12	0.14	0.27	0.23	0.19
Payout Ratio	36%	NM	28%	NM	21%	21%
Prices - High	8½	9½	11¼	20¼	24⅝	23¾
- Low	5½	5⅜	6⅞	7¼	15½	12⅝
P/E Ratio - High	26	NM	22	NM	22	24
- Low	17	NM	13	NM	14	13

Income Statement Analysis (Million $)

	1994	%Chg	1993	%Chg	1992	%Chg	1991
Revs.	2,128	7%	1,993	3%	1,926	2%	1,882
Oper. Inc.	459	6%	435	-7%	467	NM	463
Depr.	235	1%	232	NM	230	6%	216
Int. Exp.	117	10%	106	-13%	122	-8%	133
Pretax Inc.	121	NM	-317	NM	169	NM	-303
Eff. Tax Rate	25%	—	NM	—	18%	—	NM
Net Inc.	91.0	NM	-291	NM	138	NM	-328

Balance Sheet & Other Fin. Data (Million $)

	1994	1993	1992	1991	1990	1989
Cash	200	212	132	125	208	70.0
Curr. Assets	614	654	524	520	540	305
Total Assets	3,633	3,575	3,659	3,595	3,895	2,651
Curr. Liab.	392	407	349	316	318	211
LT Debt	1,403	1,377	1,261	1,508	1,435	899
Common Eqty.	1,576	1,544	1,950	1,672	1,907	1,330
Total Cap.	3,037	2,974	3,310	3,279	3,577	2,440
Cap. Exp.	329	319	229	248	597	442
Cash Flow	326	-61.0	368	-117	447	346

Ratio Analysis

	1994	1993	1992	1991	1990	1989
Curr. Ratio	1.6	1.6	1.5	1.6	1.7	1.4
% LT Debt of Cap.	46.2	46.3	38.1	46.0	40.1	36.8
% Net Inc.of Revs.	4.3	NM	7.2	NM	15.3	14.9
% Ret. on Assets	2.5	NM	3.6	NM	7.8	9.3
% Ret. on Equity	5.8	NM	7.3	NM	15.3	18.4

Dividend Data —Dividends on the Class A and Class B shares have been paid since 1975 and 1969, respectively. Declarations on the Class A and Class B shares in the past 12 months, in Canadian funds and before 15% nonresident tax, were:

Amt. of Div. $	Date Decl.	Ex-Div. Date	Stock of Record	Payment Date
0.040	Oct. 13	Oct. 26	Nov. 01	Nov. 15 '94
0.040	Jan. 10	Jan. 26	Feb. 01	Feb. 15 '95
0.040	Apr. 13	Apr. 24	Apr. 28	May. 15 '95
0.040	Jul. 13	Jul. 28	Aug. 01	Aug. 15 '95

Data as orig. reptd.; in U.S. funds; based on Canadian GAAP; bef. results of disc. opers. and/or spec. items. Per share data adj. for stk. divs. as of ex-div. date. E-Estimated. NA-Not Available. NM-Not Meaningful. NR-Not Ranked.

Office—3221 North Service Rd., Burlington, ON L7R 3Y8, Canada. **Tel**—(905) 336-1800. **Chrmn**—P. N. T. Widdrington. **Pres & CEO**—J. R. Bullock. **Sr VP & CFO**—L. W. Haworth. **VP & Investor Contact**—Tag Watson. **Secy**—W. R. Cottick. **Dirs**—J. R. Bullock, W. P. Cooper, W. A. Farlinger, R. K. Gamey, D. M. Green, A. S. Kingsmill, D. P. O'Brien, G. Ritchie, W. W. Stinson, S. M. Thompson, P. N. T. Widdrington. **Transfer Agents & Registrars**—R-M Trust Co., Toronto; Mellon Securities Trust Co., NYC. **Incorporated** in Ontario in 1966. **Empl**-54,000. **S&P Analyst:** Stephen R. Klein

Lilly (Eli)

NYSE Symbol **LLY**
In S&P 500

20-SEP-95

Industry:
Drugs-Generic and
OTC

Summary: This major worldwide prescription drugmaker produces Prozac antidepressant, Ceclor and other antibiotics, diabetic care items, and animal health and agricultural products.

S&P Opinion: Accumulate (★★★★)	Recent Price • 85⅜	Yield • 2.9%
	52 Wk Range • 86½-56⅛	12-Mo. P/E • 18.6

Quantitative Evaluations

Outlook
(1 Lowest—5 Highest)
• **2+**

Fair Value
• **80⅛**

Risk
• **Low**

Earn./Div. Rank
• **A**

Technical Eval.
• **Bullish** since 7/95

Rel. Strength Rank
(1 Lowest—99 Highest)
• **81**

Insider Activity
• **Neutral**

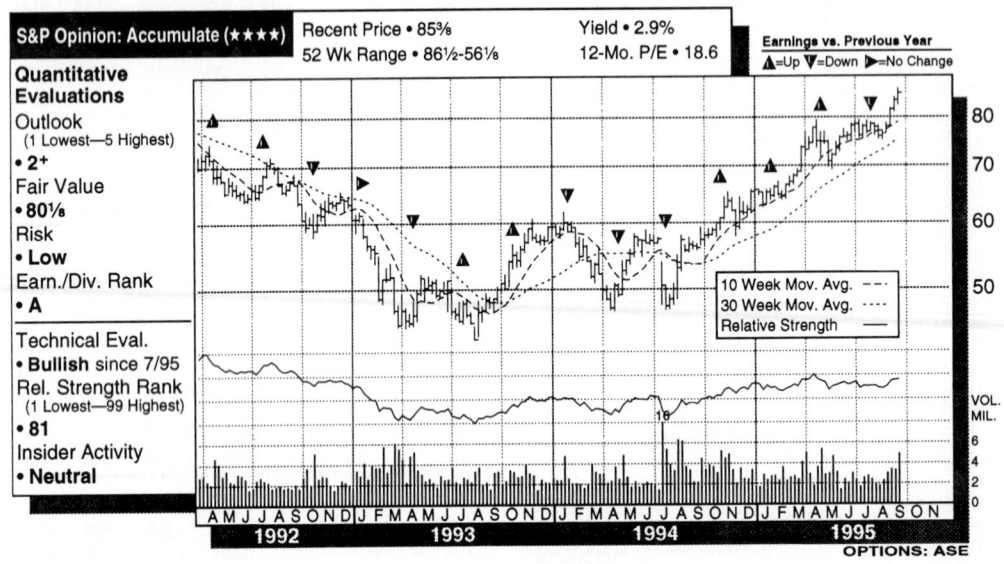

Earnings vs. Previous Year
▲=Up ▼=Down ▶=No Change

10 Week Mov. Avg. – – –
30 Week Mov. Avg. ·······
Relative Strength —

VOL.
MIL.

OPTIONS: ASE

Overview - 20-SEP-95

Sales should post further progress in 1996. Although generic erosion is expected to cause another decline in sales of Ceclor antibiotic, volume should benefit from forward momentum in sales of Prozac antidepressant (which rose 30% in the first half of 1995), Humatrope diabetes treatment, Lorabid antibiotic and other lines. Volume should also be augmented by increased revenues from PCS Health Systems, a large pharmaceutical benefits management company acquired in November 1994. Margins in 1996 should widen on the better volume, much less dilution from PCS and benefits from cost streamlining and productivity improvement programs. Per share profits should also be boosted by reduced average shares outstanding.

Valuation - 20-SEP-95

Together with those of other drug companies, the shares have been in a sustained uptrend over the past 12 months. Strength in the stock also reflects investor appreciation of restructuring moves that included the purchase of PCS Health Systems and the divestiture of the medical devices business (completed with the recent divestiture of Guidant Corp). Long-term prospects are enhanced by significant benefits from integration with PCS's growing managed care network, and contributions from an impressive new drug pipeline that includes treatments for cancer, diabetes, schizophrenia and osteoporosis. The shares are recommended for above-average total return.

Key Stock Statistics

S&P EPS Est. 1995	4.55	Tang. Bk. Value/Share	5.55
P/E on S&P Est. 1995	18.8	Beta	1.12
S&P EPS Est. 1996	5.15	Shareholders	5,900
Dividend Rate/Share	2.58	Market cap. (B)	$ 25.7
Shs. outstg. (M)	272.8	Inst. holdings	69%
Avg. daily vol. (M)	0.973	Insider holdings	NA

Value of $10,000 invested 5 years ago: $ 14,938

Fiscal Year Ending Dec. 31

	1995	% Change	1994	% Change	1993	% Change
Revenues (Million $)						
1Q	1,717	31%	1,309	-16%	1,560	NM
2Q	1,615	20%	1,347	-14%	1,561	6%
3Q	—	—	1,507	-2%	1,531	4%
4Q	—	—	1,548	-14%	1,801	9%
Yr.	—	—	5,712	-11%	6,452	5%
Income (Million $)						
1Q	374.8	25%	300.7	-19%	373.5	-16%
2Q	310.0	-3%	319.2	-8%	346.8	2%
3Q	—	—	295.6	NM	294.4	NM
4Q	—	—	269.6	NM	-523.6	NM
Yr.	—	—	1,185	141%	491.0	-41%
Earnings Per Share ($)						
1Q	1.30	25%	1.04	-18%	1.27	-16%
2Q	1.07	-3%	1.10	-7%	1.18	2%
3Q	E1.06	4%	1.02	2%	1.00	NM
4Q	E1.12	20%	0.93	NM	-1.77	NM
Yr.	E4.55	11%	4.10	146%	1.67	-41%

Next earnings report expected: mid October

Lilly (Eli)

Business Summary - 20-SEP-95

Eli Lilly is a leading producer of prescription pharmaceuticals. In September 1995, the company completed a two-year program of divesting its medical instruments businesses with the divestiture of an 80% interest in Guidant Corp. via an exchange offer. Shareholders exchanged 16.5 million Lilly shares for 57.6 million Guidant shares. Foreign operations contributed 43% of sales and 38% of pretax profits in 1994. R&D outlays equaled 14.7% of sales in 1994 (14.5% in 1993).

The most important drugs are central nervous system agents (32% of 1994 sales) such as Prozac antidepressant, Darvon analgesic and Nalfon nonsteroidal antiarthritic; anti-infectives (29%), which include Ceclor, Keflex, Kefzol and Lorabid orals, and injectables such as Mandol, Nebcin, Vancocin HCl, Tazidime and Kefzol; diabetic care items (13%), of which Humulin insulin and Iletin are the largest; and gastrointestinals (9%) such as Axid antiulcer. Animal health products (8%) include cattle feed additives, antibiotics and related products. Other products (9%) consist of Dobutrex for congestive heart failure, Humatrope hormone and other drugs. PCS Health Systems, a pharmacy benefits management concern, was purchased in November 1994.

Dow Elanco, owned 40% by the company and 60% by Dow Chemical, produces herbicides and other plant science products. Lilly's equity in the earnings of this joint venture is included in other income.

Important Developments

Sep. '95—Lilly completed the disposal of its medical device businesses with the divestiture of its remaining 80% interest in Guidant Corp. Through an exchange offer that expired September 18, shareholders exchanged 16,504,298 Lilly common shares for 57,600,000 Guidant common shares. The transaction reduced the number of Lilly shares about 5.7%. A 20% interest in Guidant had been sold publicly in December 1994. Guidant had 1994 sales of $862 million, and profits of $92 million. Guidant's results were classified by Lilly as discontinued operations since 1994.
Jul. '95—The FDA approved Gemzar, a drug for the treatment of pancreatic cancer. Important new drugs in the R&D pipeline also include olanzapine, a first-line therapy for schizophrenia; raloxifine, a treatment for osteoporosis; and Humulog, a rapid-acting human insulin.

Capitalization

Long Term Debt: $2,102,100,000 (6/95).

Per Share Data ($)

(Year Ended Dec. 31)

	1994	1993	1992	1991	1990	1989
Tangible Bk. Val.	3.23	14.22	15.14	15.52	11.22	11.85
Cash Flow	5.59	3.02	4.06	5.53	4.67	3.93
Earnings	4.10	1.67	2.81	4.50	3.90	3.20
Dividends	2.50	2.42	2.20	2.00	1.64	1.35
Payout Ratio	61%	145%	78%	44%	42%	42%
Prices - High	66¼	62	87¾	85⅛	90⅜	68½
- Low	47⅛	43⅝	57¾	67½	58¾	42⅜
P/E Ratio - High	16	37	31	19	23	21
- Low	11	26	21	15	15	13

Income Statement Analysis (Million $)

	1994	%Chg	1993	%Chg	1992	%Chg	1991
Revs.	5,712	-11%	6,452	5%	6,167	8%	5,726
Oper. Inc.	2,227	NM	2,224	6%	2,089	NM	2,079
Depr.	432	9%	398	8%	368	18%	311
Int. Exp.	129	33%	97.0	-11%	109	23%	88.9
Pretax Inc.	1,699	142%	702	-41%	1,182	-37%	1,879
Eff. Tax Rate	30%	—	30%	—	30%	—	30%
Net Inc.	1,185	141%	491	-41%	828	-37%	1,315

Balance Sheet & Other Fin. Data (Million $)

	1994	1993	1992	1991	1990	1989
Cash	747	987	728	782	751	652
Curr. Assets	3,962	3,697	3,006	2,939	2,501	2,274
Total Assets	14,507	9,624	8,673	8,299	7,143	5,848
Curr. Liab.	5,670	2,928	2,399	2,272	2,818	1,329
LT Debt	2,126	835	582	396	277	270
Common Eqty.	5,356	4,569	4,892	4,966	3,467	3,757
Total Cap.	7,670	5,531	5,644	5,777	4,096	4,327
Cap. Exp.	577	634	913	1,142	1,007	555
Cash Flow	1,617	889	1,106	1,625	1,352	1,135

Ratio Analysis

	1994	1993	1992	1991	1990	1989
Curr. Ratio	0.7	1.3	1.3	1.3	0.9	1.7
% LT Debt of Cap.	27.7	15.1	10.3	6.8	6.8	6.2
% Net Inc.of Revs.	20.7	7.6	13.4	23.0	21.7	22.5
% Ret. on Assets	9.8	5.4	9.8	16.3	17.7	16.8
% Ret. on Equity	23.9	10.4	16.8	30.0	31.9	26.7

Dividend Data —Dividends have been paid since 1885. A dividend reinvestment plan is available. A poison pill stock purchase rights plan was adopted in 1988.

Amt. of Div. $	Date Decl.	Ex-Div. Date	Stock of Record	Payment Date
0.625	Oct. 17	Nov. 08	Nov. 15	Dec. 12 '94
0.645	Dec. 19	Feb. 09	Feb. 15	Mar. 10 '95
0.645	Apr. 17	May. 09	May. 15	Jun. 12 '95
0.645	Jul. 17	Aug. 11	Aug. 15	Sep. 11 '95

Data as orig. reptd.; bef. results of disc. opers. and/or spec. items. Per share data adj. for stk. divs. as of ex-div. date. E-Estimated. NA-Not Available. NM-Not Meaningful. NR-Not Ranked.

Office—Lilly Corporate Center, Indianapolis, IN 46285. **Tel**—(317) 276-2000. **Chrmn & CEO**—R. L. Tobias. **VP-Fin, CFO**—J. M. Cornelius. **VP & Treas**—E. A. Miller. **Secy**—D. P. Carmichael. **Investor Contact**—T. W. Grein (317-276-2506). **Dirs**—S. C. Beering, J. M. Cornelius, J. W. Cozad, A. G. Gilman, C. La Force, Jr., K. L. Lay, B. F. Love, F. G. Prendergast, K. P. Siefert, R. L. Tobias, A. M. Watanabe, A. O. Way, R. D. Wood. **Transfer Agent & Registrar**—Co's office. **Incorporated** in Indiana in 1901. **Empl**-24,900. **S&P Analyst:** H. B. Saftlas

Limited (The)

NYSE Symbol **LTD**
In S&P 500

20-OCT-95 Industry:
Retail Stores

Summary: The Limited is one of the largest specialty and mail order retailers of women's apparel in the U.S. with over 5,048 stores.

S&P Opinion: Buy (★★★★)	Recent Price • 21⅛ Yield • 1.9%
	52 Wk Range • 23¼-16⅝ 12-Mo. P/E • 17.3

Quantitative Evaluations

Outlook
(1 Lowest—5 Highest)
• **3⁻**

Fair Value
• **21¼**

Risk
• **Average**

Earn./Div. Rank
• **A+**

Technical Eval.
• **Bullish** since 8/95

Rel. Strength Rank
(1 Lowest—99 Highest)
• **79**

Insider Activity
• **Favorable**

Earnings vs. Previous Year
▲=Up ▼=Down ▶=No Change

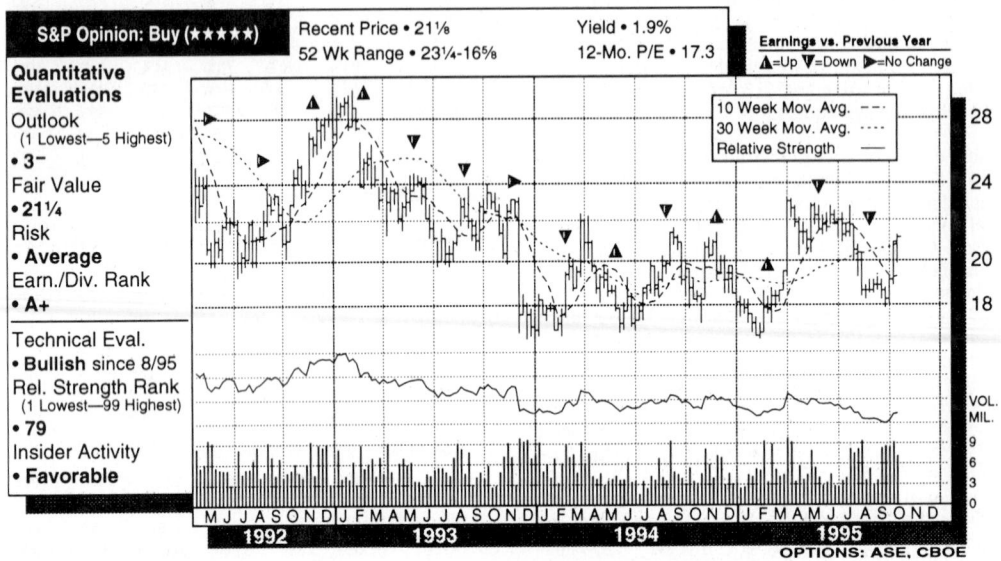

10 Week Mov. Avg. – – –
30 Week Mov. Avg. ·····
Relative Strength —

OPTIONS: ASE, CBOE

Overview - 20-OCT-95

In 1995-96, sales gains should remain strong in the lingerie and personal care products businesses which, with their high operating margins, will show a growing profitability. The company has been aggressively expanding these stores, while pruning the number of women's apparel units. Sales gains in the women's apparel businesses should improve moderately in the second half, reflecting increased spending on apparel, greater advertising and better merchandising; operating income should advance on the higher sales volume and better inventory management, resulting in fewer markdowns. The company has been buying back common shares under a share repurchase program of up to $500 million.

Valuation - 20-OCT-95

The share price has been moving up, reflecting a higher valuation for the company as its businesses are appraised individually and modest sales improvement in the women's apparel businesses. The strong profitability of the non-apparel businesses has been masked by the weak women's apparel units and the spinoff of these units will allow each business to reflect its appropriate growth multiple. Our estimates suggest the lingerie and personal care products businesses is worth $14 per LTD share, $7 for the women's apparel businesses and $3 for the other businesses, including Structure, Abercrombie & Fitch, and Mast Industries, the company's overseas sourcing operation. In sum, we value the company at $24.

Key Stock Statistics

S&P EPS Est. 1996	1.30	Tang. Bk. Value/Share	7.80
P/E on S&P Est. 1996	16.3	Beta	0.87
S&P EPS Est. 1997	1.50	Shareholders	74,300
Dividend Rate/Share	0.40	Market cap. (B)	$ 7.5
Shs. outstg. (M)	358.1	Inst. holdings	55%
Avg. daily vol. (M)	1.607	Insider holdings	NA

Value of $10,000 invested 5 years ago: $ 13,228

Fiscal Year Ending Jan. 31

	1996	% Change	1995	% Change	1994	% Change
Revenues (Million $)						
1Q	1,588	7%	1,482	-2%	1,519	7%
2Q	1,719	8%	1,585	-6%	1,689	13%
3Q	—	—	1,715	6%	1,617	NM
4Q	—	—	2,539	5%	2,421	NM
Yr.	—	—	7,321	1%	7,245	4%
Income (Million $)						
1Q	39.21	-17%	47.28	7%	44.23	-14%
2Q	48.76	-9%	53.83	-21%	68.23	-15%
3Q	—	—	90.49	10%	82.22	3%
4Q	—	—	256.8	31%	196.3	-20%
Yr.	—	—	448.3	15%	391.0	-14%
Earnings Per Share ($)						
1Q	0.11	-15%	0.13	8%	0.12	-14%
2Q	0.14	-7%	0.15	-21%	0.19	-14%
3Q	E0.18	-28%	0.25	9%	0.23	NM
4Q	E0.87	21%	0.72	33%	0.54	-33%
Yr.	E1.30	4%	1.25	16%	1.08	-14%

Next earnings report expected: early November

Business Summary - 20-OCT-95

The Limited, Inc., is a leading specialty retailer. As of January 28, 1995, it was operating 4,867 women's apparel shops across the U.S. The company operates 12 retail divisions. The largest businesses are Lerner New York (846), Lane Bryant (812), Express (716), Limited Stores (709), and Victoria's Secret (601); newer businesses include Structure (466), Bath & Body Works (318), Limited Too (210), Cacique (114), Abercrombie & Fitch (67), Penhaligon's (4), and Henri Bendel (4). Apparel is also distributed through four catalog divisions.

In March 1995, management announced a plan to reconfigure the company, including splitting existing operations into two new public companies, each of which would be about 85% owned by The Limited Inc. Shareholders would receive a cash distribution as a result of the initial public offerings. In May, the company filed with the SEC for an initial public offering of Intibrands Inc., consisting of Victoria Secret's Stores and Catalogue, Bath & Body Works, Cacique, Penhaligon's and Gryphon divisions.. The other new company would be comprised of the women's fashion businesses: Express; Limited; Lerner New York; and Lane Bryant. New ventures and the other businesses, including Structure: Abercrombie & Fitch Co.; The Limited Too; Henri Bendel; and Mast Industries, would continue to be wholly owned by LTD.

Mast Industries is a contract manufacturer and importer of women's apparel, supplying company stores. During 1994-5, the company purchased merchandise from about 4,000 suppliers and factories throughout the world. About 55% of the company's merchandise is purchased in foreign markets.

Important Developments

Oct. '95—Same store sales for the five weeks ended September 30, 1995, rose 1%. Management said in its second quarter earnings release that based on current trends, third quarter earnings could be down 25% to 30% from 1994-95. The company sees profit opportunities in the fourth quarter, even at current sales levels, however; significant operating leverage is inherent in the women's apparel businesses in the final quarter of the fiscal year. The company plans to sell a 16% stake in Intimate Brands Inc., a newly formed company composed of LTD's intimate apparel and personal care products businesses; the initial public offering price per share is estimated at $14 to $17. At a later date, the company planned to spin off its women's fashion apparel businesses and sell a majority interest in its credit card bank.

Capitalization

Long Term Debt: $650,000,000 (7/95).

Per Share Data ($)   (Year Ended Jan. 31)

	1995	1994	1993	1992	1991	1990
Tangible Bk. Val.	7.72	6.82	6.25	5.19	4.33	3.45
Cash Flow	2.00	1.79	1.93	1.72	1.61	1.40
Earnings	1.25	1.08	1.25	1.11	1.10	0.96
Dividends	0.36	0.36	0.28	0.28	0.24	0.16
Payout Ratio	29%	33%	22%	25%	22%	17%
Cal. Yrs.	1994	1993	1992	1991	1990	1989
Prices - High	22⅜	30	32⅞	31⅝	25⅝	20
- Low	16¾	16⅝	19¼	17⅝	11¾	12⅝
P/E Ratio - High	18	28	26	28	23	21
- Low	13	15	15	16	11	13

Income Statement Analysis (Million $)

	1995	%Chg	1994	%Chg	1993	%Chg	1992
Revs.	7,545	2%	7,420	5%	7,086	13%	6,281
Oper. Inc.	1,067	11%	957	-8%	1,036	11%	935
Depr.	268	4%	258	4%	247	11%	223
Int. Exp.	65.4	2%	63.9	2%	62.4	-2%	63.9
Pretax Inc.	744	15%	645	-13%	745	13%	660
Eff. Tax Rate	40%	—	39%	—	39%	—	39%
Net Inc.	448	15%	391	-14%	455	13%	403

Balance Sheet & Other Fin. Data (Million $)

	1995	1994	1993	1992	1991	1990
Cash	243	321	41.2	33.7	13.2	21.7
Curr. Assets	2,548	2,221	1,784	1,604	1,365	1,164
Total Assets	4,570	4,135	3,846	3,419	2,872	2,418
Curr. Liab.	798	707	721	520	481	478
LT Debt	650	650	542	714	540	446
Common Eqty.	2,761	2,441	2,268	1,877	1,560	1,240
Total Cap.	3,717	3,366	3,084	2,858	2,355	1,901
Cap. Exp.	320	296	430	523	429	320
Cash Flow	716	649	702	626	581	507

Ratio Analysis

	1995	1994	1993	1992	1991	1990
Curr. Ratio	3.2	3.1	2.5	3.1	2.8	2.4
% LT Debt of Cap.	17.5	19.3	17.6	25.0	23.0	23.4
% Net Inc.of Revs.	5.9	5.3	6.4	6.4	7.4	7.3
% Ret. on Assets	10.3	9.9	12.5	12.8	15.0	15.2
% Ret. on Equity	17.2	16.7	22.0	23.4	28.4	31.7

Dividend Data —Dividends have been paid since 1970.

Amt. of Div. $	Date Decl.	Ex-Div. Date	Stock of Record	Payment Date
0.090	Nov. 21	Nov. 28	Dec. 02	Dec. 13 '94
0.100	Jan. 30	Feb. 27	Mar. 03	Mar. 14 '95
0.100	May. 15	May. 26	Jun. 02	Jun. 13 '95
0.100	Aug. 18	Sep. 06	Sep. 08	Sep. 19 '95

Office—Two Limited Parkway, Columbus, OH 43216; P.O. Box 16000, Columbus 43230. **Tel**—(614) 479-7000. **Chrmn & Pres**—L. H. Wexner. **Secy**—Bella Wexner. **VP & CFO**—K. B. Gilman. **VP & Investor Contact**—Alfred S. Dietzel. **Dirs**—E. M. Freedman, E. G. Gee, K. B. Gilman, T. G. Hopkins, D. T. Kolat, C. Malone, D. B. Shackelford, A. R. Tessler, M. Trust, M. A. Weiss, B. Wexner, L. H. Wexner, R. Z. Zimmerman. **Transfer Agent & Registrar**—First Chicago Trust Co. of New York, NYC. **Incorporated** in Ohio in 1967; reincorporated in Delaware in 1982. **Empl**-105,600. **S&P Analyst:** Karen J. Sack, CFA

Lincoln National Corp.

NYSE Symbol **LNC**
In S&P 500

29-JUL-95

Industry: Insurance

Summary: LNC is one of the 10 largest multi-line insurance holding companies in the U.S., offering property-casualty, individual life, life-health reinsurance, and annuity products.

S&P Opinion: Hold (★★★)		
Recent Price • 41⅛	Yield • 4.2%	
52 Wk Range • 46¼-34⅝	12-Mo. P/E • 10.6	

Quantitative Evaluations

Outlook
(1 Lowest—5 Highest)
• **3**

Fair Value
• **39⅛**

Risk
• **Low**

Earn./Div. Rank
• **B+**

Technical Eval.
• **Bearish** since 3/95

Rel. Strength Rank
(1 Lowest—99 Highest)
• **17**

Insider Activity
• **Neutral**

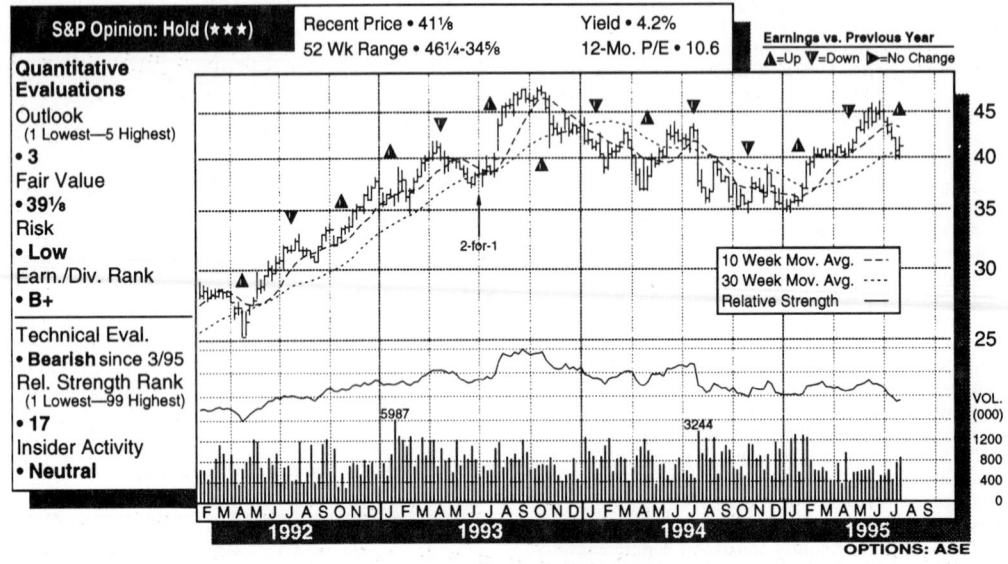

Earnings vs. Previous Year
▲=Up ▼=Down ▶=No Change

10 Week Mov. Avg. ─·─
30 Week Mov. Avg. ·····
Relative Strength ──

2-for-1

VOL. (000)

OPTIONS: ASE

Overview - 28-JUL-95

Operating earnings growth in coming periods is predicated on continued favorable deposit growth and interest rate spreads in the individual life and annuity area. Though property-casualty (p-c) premiums may decline, long-term profitability here is aided by tighter underwriting standards. Pricing in some p-c lines is firming, which also bodes well for the long-term profit picture. Higher catastrophe losses may plague near-term profitability, though. Moreover, LNC's high-cost agency distribution system makes competing in the price competitive standard commercial and personal lines markets difficult. A continuation of the improved underwriting trends that aided life/health reinsurance profit growth in 1994 bodes well for the longer-term outlook here. Further profit gains were masked by continued (albeit stabilizing) losses in the individual disability reinsurance line.

Valuation - 28-JUL-95

After a lackluster performance during most of 1994 due to the negative effects of higher interest rates, these interest-sensitive shares began to recover in early 1995, then dipped in late June amid reports that higher storm losses would negatively impact second quarter operating profits. Despite trading at about 10 times our 1995 operating earnings estimate of $4.15 a share, we believe that, given the lackluster outlook for LNC's property-casualty and individual disability units, the shares are fairly valued, near term.

Key Stock Statistics

S&P EPS Est. 1995	4.15	Tang. Bk. Value/Share	33.78
P/E on S&P Est. 1995	9.9	Beta	1.00
S&P EPS Est. 1996	4.65	Shareholders	13,700
Dividend Rate/Share	1.72	Market cap. (B)	$ 3.9
Shs. outstg. (M)	94.6	Inst. holdings	75%
Avg. daily vol. (M)	0.137	Insider holdings	NA

Value of $10,000 invested 5 years ago: $ 17,469

Fiscal Year Ending Dec. 31

	1995	% Change	1994	% Change	1993	% Change
Revenues (Million $)						
1Q	1,484	-26%	2,007	NM	2,003	—
2Q	1,646	7%	1,544	-19%	1,902	—
3Q	—	—	1,562	-33%	2,327	—
4Q	—	—	1,871	-12%	2,121	5%
Yr.	—	—	6,984	-16%	8,297	3%
Income (Million $)						
1Q	134.8	-11%	151.0	119%	69.00	-32%
2Q	117.9	152%	46.80	-63%	127.2	82%
3Q	—	—	58.38	-69%	187.5	64%
4Q	—	—	93.73	197%	31.55	-59%
Yr.	—	—	349.9	-16%	415.3	14%
Earnings Per Share ($)						
1Q	1.30	-11%	1.46	112%	0.69	-37%
2Q	1.13	151%	0.45	-63%	1.23	64%
3Q	—	—	0.56	-69%	1.82	48%
4Q	—	—	0.90	190%	0.31	-62%
Yr.	—	—	3.37	-17%	4.06	4%

Next earnings report expected: late October

Business Summary - 28-JUL-95

Lincoln National Corp. is a holding company which, through its subsidiaries, provides life-health insurance, annuities, and property-casualty insurance in the U.S. and abroad. Based on assets, it is among the 10 largest publicly held insurance organizations in the U.S. Operating income (in millions) by segment:

	1994	1993
Individual life/Annuities	$185.8	$175.3
Employee benefits	14.1	54.3
Property-casualty	158.8	133.9
Life-health reinsur.	66.6	18.9
Corporate & other	-35.5	-38.9

Lincoln National Life Insurance Co. (the fourth largest stockholder-owned life insurer in the U.S.) sells fixed and variable annuities, plus an array of traditional and interest-sensitive life insurance products. Other subsidiaries include First Penn and American States Life. Security-Connecticut was sold in early 1994. Lincoln National Life Reinsurance Co. and its affiliates are a leading life/health reinsurance organization.

The employee benefits division offers group life and health insurance to small businesses. LNC sold 71% of this unit in a March 1994 IPO of EMPHESYS Financial Group.

Property-casualty operations are conducted through American States Insurance Co. and its subsidiaries. Personal lines (automobile and homeowners coverage) accounted for 40% of the $1.7 billion of premiums written in 1993. Of that amount, over 82% consisted of preferred risk policies. A full spectrum of commercial lines coverage, marketed to small and mid-size businesses, made up the remaining 60% of 1994 premiums written.

Important Developments

Jul. '95—LNC's lower second quarter 1995 operating income of $0.75 a share versus $0.84 a share in the year-earlier interim primarily reflected an 85% plunge in property-casualty operating profits (to $5.4 million from $36.4 million). The sharp decline was largely due to higher aftertax catastrophe losses of $29.5 million, versus $11.2 million. Net income was boosted by investment gains of $39.4 million, versus year-ago losses of $40.7 million.

Apr. '95—LNC acquired the investment management firm Delaware Management Holdings, Inc. for about $305 million, plus contingent payments of up to $22.5 million. Later in the month, LNC increased its presence in the U.K. by acquiring Laurentian Financial Group plc for $237 million. Laurentian is the holding company for a U.K.-based life insurer.

Capitalization

Long Term Debt: $419,152,000 (3/95).

Preferred Stock: $311,295,000.

Per Share Data ($) (Year Ended Dec. 31)

	1994	1993	1992	1991	1990	1989
Tangible Bk. Val.	27.34	37.48	28.22	25.31	22.58	21.51
Oper. Earnings	3.75	3.36	2.63	1.89	2.56	2.30
Earnings	3.37	4.06	3.91	2.30	2.15	3.03
Dividends	1.64	1.52	1.46	1.36	1.30	1.24
Relative Payout	49%	37%	37%	59%	61%	41%
Prices - High	44⅜	48¼	38⅛	27⅝	30⅝	31½
- Low	34⅝	34¾	25¼	19	15⅜	21⅜
P/E Ratio - High	13	12	10	12	14	10
- Low	10	9	6	8	7	7

Income Statement Analysis (Million $)

	1994	%Chg	1993	%Chg	1992	%Chg	1991
Life Ins. In Force	NA	—	233,766	7%	217,985	-15%	255,557
Prem.Inc Life A&H	NA	—	3,515	9%	3,216	-28%	4,488
Prem.Inc Cas/Prop	NA	—	1,841	-12%	2,083	-7%	2,242
Net Invest. Inc.	2,011	-6%	2,147	8%	1,987	10%	1,799
Oth. Revs.	514	-35%	786	5%	748	17%	640
Total Revs.	6,984	-16%	8,289	3%	8,034	-12%	9,169
Pretax Inc.	376	-36%	588	38%	425	114%	199
Net Oper. Inc.	390	13%	344	43%	241	—	NA
Net Inc.	350	-16%	415	14%	363	75%	208

Balance Sheet & Other Fin. Data (Million $)

	1994	1993	1992	1991	1990	1989
Cash & Equiv.	1,471	1,123	1,452	972	1,142	1,014
Premiums Due	565	602	792	926	1,008	828
Inv Assets Bonds	21,644	23,964	20,331	17,849	14,211	13,077
Inv. Assets Stock	1,039	1,080	923	1,025	834	868
Inv. Assets Loans	3,406	3,896	3,699	3,675	3,715	3,511
Inv. Assets Total	26,971	29,732	25,525	22,987	19,112	17,782
Deferred Policy Cost	2,444	2,011	2,118	1,972	1,594	1,402
Total Assets	49,330	48,380	39,672	34,095	27,597	25,070
Debt	420	335	423	253	379	379
Common Eqty.	2,730	3,761	2,636	2,461	2,236	2,185

Ratio Analysis

	1994	1993	1992	1991	1990	1989
Comb. Loss-Exp.Ratio	105.7	107.5	112.7	111.9	109.2	106.7
% Ret. on Revs.	5.0	5.0	4.5	2.3	2.3	3.3
% Ret. on Equity	10.3	13.0	13.6	8.3	8.2	12.2
% Invest. Yield	7.1	7.8	8.2	8.5	9.0	9.7

Dividend Data (Dividends have been paid since 1920. A dividend reinvestment plan is available.)

Amt. of Div. $	Date Decl.	Ex-Div. Date	Stock of Record	Payment Date
0.410	Aug. 11	Oct. 03	Oct. 10	Nov. 01 '94
0.430	Nov. 10	Jan. 04	Jan. 10	Feb. 01 '95
0.430	Mar. 09	Apr. 04	Apr. 10	May. 01 '95
0.430	May. 11	Jul. 06	Jul. 10	Aug. 01 '95

Data as orig. reptd.; bef. results of disc. opers. and/or spec. items. Per share data adj. for stk. divs. as of ex-div. date.
E-Estimate. NA-Not Available. NM-Not Meaningful. NR-Not Ranked.

Office—200 East Berry St., Fort Wayne, IN 46802. **Tel**—(219) 455-2000. **Chrmn & CEO**—I. M. Rolland. **Pres**—R. A. Anker. **Secy**—C. S. Womack. **Treas**—M. A. Roesler. **VP-Investor Contact**—Daniel W. Weber. **Dirs**—R. A. Anker, J. P. Barrett, T. D. Bell, Jr., D. R. Efroymson, H. L. Kavetas, M. L. Lachman, L. J. McKernan, E. L. Neal, J. M. Pietruski, I. M. Rolland, J. S. Ruckelshaus, G. A. Walker, G. R. Whitaker, Jr. **Transfer Agent & Registrar**—First National Bank of Boston. **Incorporated** in Indiana in 1905; reincorporated in 1968. **Empl**- 8,995. **S&P Analyst:** Catherine A. Seifert

STANDARD & POOR'S
STOCK REPORTS

Liz Claiborne

NYSE Symbol **LIZ**
In S&P 500

06-OCT-95

Industry: Textiles

Summary: Liz Claiborne designs and markets men's and women's apparel that is made by independent suppliers and sold through department and specialty stores throughout the world.

S&P Opinion: Hold (★★★)	Recent Price • 25¼	Yield • 1.7%
	52 Wk Range • 26-14⅜	12-Mo. P/E • 22.7

Quantitative Evaluations

Outlook
(1 Lowest—5 Highest)
• **1+**

Fair Value
• **22**

Risk
• **Average**

Earn./Div. Rank
• **A-**

Technical Eval.
• **Bullish** since 3/95

Rel. Strength Rank
(1 Lowest—99 Highest)
• **92**

Insider Activity
• **Neutral**

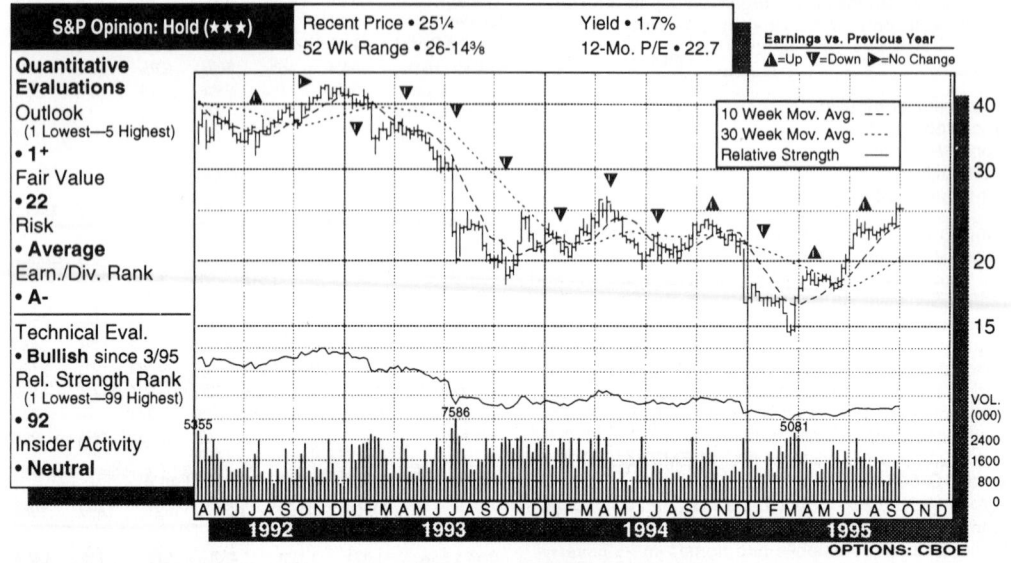

Earnings vs. Previous Year
▲=Up ▼=Down ▶=No Change

10 Week Mov. Avg. – – –
30 Week Mov. Avg. ·······
Relative Strength —

OPTIONS: CBOE

Overview - 05-OCT-95

Sales for 1995 could be flat or decline slightly, reflecting ongoing weak demand for the company's core sportswear line. On a more positive note, sales of many products, including bridgewear, dresses, larger size clothing, home furnishings, accessories and menswear, should improve on good demand. International growth and deeper market penetration of moderately-priced apparel could also make greater contributions to sales. Full-year margins are expected to widen from 1994's depressed level, on fewer markdown prices, restructuring efforts, focus on reducing expenses, and the absence of 1994's one-time $0.24-a-share restructuring charge. Share earnings comparisons will benefit from fewer outstanding shares, reflecting an ongoing stock buyback program.

Valuation - 05-OCT-95

Since reaching a recent low of 14 3/8 in early 1995, these shares have rebounded on expectations that earnings growth is resuming, after several years of flat to declining growth. Like many other apparel companies over the past few years, LIZ has been hurt by sluggish demand for apparel in general, a highly promotional retail environment, and a change in consumer tastes for more moderately-priced casual apparel. LIZ announced several programs in 1995 which could return it to positive earnings growth. Until there is a clear sign that these programs are working, however, we are retaining a neutral opinion on these shares.

Key Stock Statistics

S&P EPS Est. 1995	1.45	Tang. Bk. Value/Share	12.67
P/E on S&P Est. 1995	17.4	Beta	1.18
S&P EPS Est. 1996	1.65	Shareholders	14,100
Dividend Rate/Share	0.45	Market cap. (B)	$ 2.0
Shs. outstg. (M)	75.0	Inst. holdings	86%
Avg. daily vol. (M)	0.285	Insider holdings	NA

Value of $10,000 invested 5 years ago: $ 11,436

Fiscal Year Ending Dec. 31

	1995	% Change	1994	% Change	1993	% Change
Revenues (Million $)						
1Q	527.1	-3%	541.4	2%	531.0	-5%
2Q	474.9	-3%	490.0	-3%	506.9	7%
3Q	—	—	616.8	NM	621.9	NM
4Q	—	—	514.7	-5%	544.1	NM
Yr.	—	—	2,163	-2%	2,204	NM
Income (Million $)						
1Q	28.09	2%	27.44	-33%	41.04	-35%
2Q	17.02	7%	15.90	-49%	31.09	-21%
3Q	—	—	42.89	12%	38.26	-41%
4Q	—	—	-3.37	NM	14.89	-71%
Yr.	—	—	82.85	-34%	125.3	-43%
Earnings Per Share ($)						
1Q	0.37	6%	0.35	-30%	0.50	-32%
2Q	0.23	15%	0.20	-47%	0.38	-19%
3Q	E0.51	-7%	0.55	17%	0.47	-39%
4Q	E0.34	NM	-0.04	NM	0.19	-70%
Yr.	E1.45	37%	1.06	-31%	1.54	-41%

Next earnings report expected: late October

Liz Claiborne

Business Summary - 05-OCT-95

Liz Claiborne designs and markets a wide range of women's apparel and related items, designed for the work and leisure-time needs of the career woman. LIZ also designs men's apparel. Products are manufactured to the company's specifications in the U.S. and abroad and are sold through leading department and specialty stores. Contributions to sales in recent years:

	1994	1993	1992
Women's sportswear	43.1%	48.6%	52.3%
Accessories	8.1%	7.4%	6.2%
Elisabeth	5.9%	6.2%	6.9%
Women's dresses & suits	5.3%	5.6%	7.4%
Outlet stores	6.0%	5.3%	4.9%
Retail stores	6.5%	4.9%	4.0%
Liz & Co.	3.3%	3.9%	4.1%
Dana Buchman	4.9%	3.9%	3.2%
Cosmetics	3.6%	3.8%	3.1%
Men's sportswear	4.4%	3.5%	4.0%
Russ Group	4.8%	3.4%	0.9%
Shoes	2.7%	2.4%	2.0%
Jewelry	1.3%	1.0%	0.8%
Licensing	0.1%	0.1%	0.1%

LIZ's better sportswear products are conceived of and marketed as "designer" items and are offered under the company's various trademarks, including Liz Claiborne, Collection, Lizsport, Lizwear, Elisabeth and Liz & Co. Products are less expensive than designer lines. LIZ also produces a higher-priced "bridge" line of clothing under the Dana Buchman label and clothing in larger sizes under the Elisabeth label. Moderately priced apparel is produced by the Russ division.

At the end of 1994, LIZ operated 29 Liz Claiborne stores, 21 Elisabeth stores, one Dana Buchman store, and 70 outlet stores. The company began expanding operations overseas in 1991 and, as of 1994 year-end, was selling products in more than 50 markets outside the U.S., making up 5.7% of total sales.

Important Developments

Sep. '95—LIZ announced that its board approved the repurchase of up to an added $50 million in common shares, bringing total authorizations under the company's stock purchase program up to $500 million. As of mid-September, LIZ had purchased about 17.3 million commmon shares under the program at an aggregate price of about $450 million.

Aug. '95—LIZ announced that it would lower its trade discount to retailers for women's apparel to 8%, the industry standard, from 10%, as of January 1, 1996. The company said it expected to garner more than $20 million in revenue annually from this move, which it would use toward a national advertising campaign.

Capitalization

Long Term Debt: $1,175,000 (7/1/95).

Per Share Data ($)

(Year Ended Dec. 31)

	1994	1993	1992	1991	1990	1989
Tangible Bk. Val.	12.77	12.41	12.05	10.67	8.39	6.94
Cash Flow	1.50	1.93	2.95	2.92	2.62	2.05
Earnings	1.06	1.54	2.61	2.61	2.37	1.87
Dividends	0.45	0.44	0.39	0.32	0.24	0.19
Payout Ratio	42%	28%	15%	12%	10%	10%
Prices - High	$26\frac{5}{8}$	$42\frac{7}{8}$	$47\frac{7}{8}$	$50\frac{3}{4}$	35	$27\frac{3}{4}$
- Low	$15\frac{3}{8}$	18	$31\frac{7}{8}$	$28\frac{1}{4}$	$20\frac{1}{4}$	$16\frac{1}{2}$
P/E Ratio - High	25	28	18	19	15	15
- Low	15	12	12	11	9	9

Income Statement Analysis (Million $)

	1994	%Chg	1993	%Chg	1992	%Chg	1991
Revs.	2,163	-2%	2,204	NM	2,194	9%	2,007
Oper. Inc.	186	-13%	215	-39%	351	-3%	361
Depr.	35.0	8%	32.3	13%	28.5	6%	27.0
Int. Exp.	NA	—	NA	—	NA	—	NA
Pretax Inc.	131	-34%	199	-42%	342	-3%	351
Eff. Tax Rate	37%	—	37%	—	36%	—	37%
Net Inc.	83.0	-34%	125	-43%	219	-2%	223

Balance Sheet & Other Fin. Data (Million $)

	1994	1993	1992	1991	1990	1989
Cash	330	309	426	472	432	373
Curr. Assets	1,023	1,004	1,110	1,014	853	746
Total Assets	1,290	1,236	1,285	1,175	985	849
Curr. Liab.	303	254	270	250	244	209
LT Debt	1.2	1.3	1.4	1.6	15.1	15.6
Common Eqty.	983	978	998	910	713	612
Total Cap.	986	982	1,015	925	740	639
Cap. Exp.	70.6	91.4	34.7	56.0	38.1	38.2
Cash Flow	118	158	247	250	227	180

Ratio Analysis

	1994	1993	1992	1991	1990	1989
Curr. Ratio	3.4	3.9	4.1	4.1	3.5	3.6
% LT Debt of Cap.	0.1	0.1	0.1	0.2	2.0	2.4
% Net Inc.of Revs.	3.8	5.7	10.0	11.1	11.9	11.7
% Ret. on Assets	6.6	10.2	18.0	20.6	22.8	22.2
% Ret. on Equity	8.5	13.0	23.3	27.4	31.6	30.7

Dividend Data —Dividends have been paid since 1984.

Amt. of Div. $	Date Decl.	Ex-Div. Date	Stock of Record	Payment Date
0.112	Oct. 13	Nov. 04	Nov. 11	Dec. 05 '94
0.112	Jan. 11	Feb. 08	Feb. 14	Mar. 06 '95
0.112	Mar. 23	May. 02	May. 08	Jun. 02 '95
0.112	Jun. 22	Aug. 09	Aug. 11	Sep. 05 '95

Data as orig. reptd.; bef. results of disc. opers. and/or spec. items. Per share data adj. for stk. divs. as of ex-div. date. E-Estimated. NA-Not Available. NM-Not Meaningful. NR-Not Ranked.

Office—1441 Broadway, New York, NY 10018. **Tel**—(212) 354-4900. **Chrmn**—J. A. Chazen. **Pres & CEO**—P. Charron. **Sr VP-Fin & CFO**—S. M. Miller. **Secy**—K. P. Kopelman. **Investor Contact**—Walter Krieger. **Dirs**—L. Abraham, L. Boxer, P. R. Charron, J. A. Chazen, A. M. Fudge, J. J. Gordon, S. Kamin, K. Koplovitz, L. Lowenstein. **Registrar & Transfer Agent**—First Chicago Trust Co. of New York, NYC. **Incorporated** in Delaware in 1981; predecessor incorporated in New York in 1976. **Empl**-8,000. **S&P Analyst:** Elizabeth Vandeventer

Lockheed Martin

NYSE Symbol **LMT** Options on Pacific & Phila (Mar-Jun-Sep-Dec) In S&P 500

Price	Range	P–E Ratio	Dividend	Yield	S&P Ranking	Beta
Oct. 31'95	1995					
68	70–50	23	¹1.40	¹2.1%	NR	0.91

Summary

Formed through the merger of Lockheed Corp. and Martin Marietta Corp. on March 15, 1995, this company is one of the world's leading diversified technology companies, with operations in space and missile systems, electronics, aircraft, information systems, and a broad range of services. The Department of Defense and NASA account for a substantial portion of revenues. Despite declining defense budgets, Lockheed Martin should achieve increased earnings (excluding merger expenses) from cost reduction efforts and an improved competitive position. LMT's shares began trading on the NYSE on March 16.

Current Outlook

Earnings for 1996 are estimated at $6.00 a share, compared with the $3.30 projected for 1995 (after about $2.30 in merger related expenses).

Dividends should continue at $0.35 quarterly.

Revenues for 1996 are expected to rise moderately from those forecast for 1995. The space segment is projected to benefit from increased commercial launches. Aeronautics and information and technology segments should continue their steady growth, but electronics systems will remain weak. Margins are expected to widen from cost reduction measures. Aiding comparative results will be the absence of approximately $690 million in merger-related charges, and the addition of one-time gains from the sale of assets.

Revenues (Million $)

Quarter:	1995	1994	1993	1992
Mar.	5,644	5,036	3,649	---
Jun.	5,606	5,562	5,935	---
Sep.	5,551	5,704	5,913	---
Dec.	---	6,604	6,900	---
	---	22,906	22,397	16,030

Revenues for the nine months ended September 30, 1995, rose 3.1% from the pro forma year-earlier level. Margins widened, but comparative results were hurt by $690 million in merger related expenses and the absence of $168 million in one-time gains. Net income declined 53%, to $1.72 a share ($1.67 fully diluted) from $3.97 ($3.60), excluding a special charge of $0.20 a share in 1994.

Common Share Earnings ($)

Quarter:	1995	1994	1993	1992
Mar.	0.65	1.25	---	---
Jun.	d0.36	1.19	---	---
Sep.	1.43	1.16	---	---
Dec.	E1.58	1.23	---	---
	E3.30	5.32	3.99	3.31

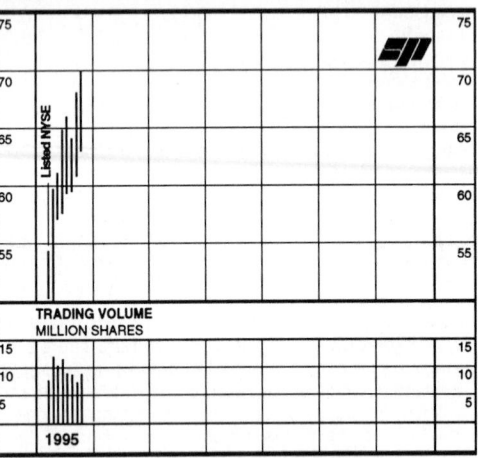

TRADING VOLUME MILLION SHARES

1995

Important Developments

Jun. '95— Lockheed Martin unveiled a consolidation plan designed to yield annual savings of $1.8 billion by 1999. Total cost to implement the consolidation plan, which will be largely completed over the next two years, is approximately $1.7 billion, including a $690 million charge taken in 1995.

Aug. '95— LMT announced segment results for the nine months of 1995. Revenues from the space and strategic missiles segment increased 15%, year to year, and earnings rose 37%. Revenues from information and technology services advanced 10%, and earnings were up 42%. Sales of aeronautics were unchanged, yet earnings rose 16%. Electronics revenues were down 19%, and earnings fell 22%. In other operations, revenues were up 17%, and earnings advanced 25%.

Next earnings report expected in February.

Per Share Data ($)

Yr. End Dec. 31	⁴1994	⁴1993	⁴1992	⁴1991
Tangible Bk. Val.	1.43	d3.15	NA	NA
Cash Flow	10.33	8.75	6.34	NA
Earnings³	²5.32	²3.99	3.31	3.05
Dividends	NA	NA	NA	NA
Payout Ratio	NA	NA	NA	NA
Prices—High	NA	NA	NA	NA
Low	NA	NA	NA	NA
P/E Ratio—	NA	NA	NA	NA

Data as orig. reptd. **1.** See Dividend Data. **2.** Ful. dil.: 4.83 in 1994, 3.75 in 1993. **3.** Bef. spec. item(s) of -0.20 in 1994, -5.15 in 1992. **4.** Major merger resulted in formation of a new co. d-Deficit. E-Estimated. NA-Not Available.

Lockheed Martin Corporation

Income Data (Million $)

Year Ended Dec. 31	Revs.	Oper. Inc.	% Oper. Inc. of Revs.	Cap. Exp.	Depr.	Int. Exp.	Net Bef. Taxes	Eff. Tax Rate	[1]Net Inc.	% Net Inc. of Revs.	Cash Flow
[2]1994	22,906	2,716	11.9	509	937	304	1,675	37.0%	1,055	4.6	1,932
[2]1993	22,397	2,476	11.1	536	936	278	1,306	36.5%	829	3.7	1,720
[2]1992	16,030	1,733	10.8	498	594	177	1,004	35.4%	649	4.0	1,243

Balance Sheet Data (Million $)

Dec. 31	Cash	Assets	Curr. Liab.	Ratio	Total Assets	% Ret. on Assets	Long Term Debt	Common Equity	Total Cap.	% LT Debt of Cap.	% Ret. on Equity
[2]1994	639	8,143	5,635	1.4	18,049	6.0	3,594	5,086	9,680	37.1	21.8

Data as orig. reptd. **1.** Bef. spec. items. **2.** Pro forma.

Business Summary

Lockheed Martin Corp. is a leading international diversified technology company created by the merger of Lockheed Corp. and Martin Marietta Corp. on March 15, 1995. Operations include aeronautics, space and missile systems, electronics, information systems, and a broad range of services. Pro forma contributions by business segment in 1994 were:

	Sales	Profit
Aeronautics	31%	26%
Space and strategic missiles	29%	24%
Electronics	18%	23%
Information and technology services	19%	11%
Energy, materials and other .	3%	16%

The Department of Defense accounted for 63% of pro forma 1994 sales, while NASA and other governmental agencies comprised another 9%. International sales contributed 17%.

Major programs of the aeronautics segment include the F-16 multirole fighter, the C-130 military transport aircraft, the F-22 air superiority fighter, and the P-3 maritime patrol aircraft.

Major programs of the space and strategic missiles segment include the Titan and Atlas expendable launch vehicles and the Trident submarine-launched fleet ballistic missile. Also produced are defense space systems and commercial/civil space systems.

The electronics segment provides complete air defense capabilities for the Aegis cruisers and destroyers; the LANTIRN aircraft targeting system; the Hellfire missile; the warfare and mission planning system for the F-22; as well as various radio frequency, infrared, and electro-optic countermeasures systems.

Information and technology services segment includes activities for NASA (comprised of the manufacture of the orbiter's external tank and space shuttle processing), information processing systems, simulation/automation systems, and various commercial electronic applications (including computer plotters, printers and digitizers).

Other operations are comprised of energy and environment activities, which performs extensive project management and systems integration for the Department of Energy, and publicly-traded Martin Marietta Materials (81%-owned), which produces aggregates and magnesia specialties.

Dividend Data

Lockheed Martin initiated cash dividends on the common shares at a $0.35 quarterly rate, with the first payment on June 30, 1995.

Amt. of Divd. $	Date Decl.	Ex-divd. Date	Stock of Record	Payment Date
0.35	Apr. 28	May 25	Jun. 1	Jun. 30'95
0.35	Jul. 27	Aug. 30	Sep. 1	Sep. 29'95
0.35	Oct. 26	Nov. 29	Dec. 1	Dec. 29'95

Finances

On March 15, 1995, Lockheed Corp., engaged primarily in the research, design and production of military aircraft, space systems, missiles and electronic systems, merged with Martin Marietta Corp., a leader in defense electronics, missiles and space systems, to form Lockheed Martin Corp. Former Lockheed Corp. (LK) shareholders received 1.63 common shares of Lockheed Martin for each LK share owned. Former Martin Marietta (MM) shareholders exchanged their MM shares for LMT common stock on a share-for-share basis.

Capitalization

Long Term Debt: $3,243,000,000; excluding ESOP guarantee of $364,000,000 (9/95).

$3 Conv. Preferred Stock: 20,000,000 shs. ($50 liq. pref.); conv. into com. at $34.5525 a sh.; owned by General Electric Co.

Common Stock: 200,289,477 shs. ($1 par).
Institutions hold about 60%.
Shareholders of record: 45,000 (6/95).

Office—6801 Rockledge Dr., Bethesda, MD 20817. **Tel**—(301) 897-6000. **Chrmn & CEO**—D. M. Tellep. **Pres**—N. R. Augustine. **SVP & CFO**—M. C. Bennett. **Secy**—Lillian M. Trippett. **VP & Investor Contact**—James R. Ryan (301-897-6584). **Dirs**—N. R. Augustine, M. C. Bennett, L. V. Cheney, A. J. Clark, E. I. Colodny, L. M. Cook, J. L. Everett III, H. I. Flournoy, J. F. Gibbons, E. L. Hennessy Jr., E. E. Hood Jr., C. B. Hurtt, G. S. King, L. O. Kitchen, G. S. Macklin, V. N. Marafino, E. F. Murphy, A. E. Murray, D. S. Potter, F. Savage, D. M. Tellep, C. A. H. Trost, J. R. Ukropina, D. C. Yearley. **Transfer Agent & Registrar**—First Chicago Trust Co. of New York. **Incorporated** in Delaware in 1995. **Empl**—173,000.

Joe Victor Shammas

Loews Corp.

NYSE Symbol LTR Options on CBOE (Mar-Jun-Sep-Dec) In S&P 500

Price	Range	P–E Ratio	Dividend	Yield	S&P Ranking	Beta
Oct. 25'95	1995					
146	155⅜–86⅝	10	2.00	1.3%	A–	0.95

Summary

This conglomerate derives most of its revenues from life and property-casualty insurance (through 84%-owned CNA Financial Corp.) and the sale of cigarettes (through Lorillard). Loews also owns about 18% of CBS Inc. In May 1995, CNA acquired Continental Corp. (NYSE:CIC) for some $1.1 billion, creating the sixth largest insurance organization in the U.S. A 2-for-1 stock split is pending.

Current Outlook

Operating earnings (before realized capital gains and losses and before giving effect to the pending 2-for-1 split) are estimated at $12.00 a share for 1995, up from the $8.70 reported for 1994. Operating earnings could rise to $14.00 a share in 1996. The quarterly dividend should continue at $0.25 after the pending 2-for-1 stock split.

Operating earnings growth in 1995 will be aided by lower catastrophe losses and improved workers' compensation underwriting trends at CNA. The growth will be modest compared with 1994's results, which reflected the absence of $4.21 a share in special reserve charges that depressed 1993 results. Insurance premium growth will be modest, as improvements in some sectors of the workers' compensation market are offset by competitive standard commercial lines pricing. The acquisition of Continental Corp. (NYSE:CIC) by CNA offers some synergies, but may necessitate additional reserve bolstering. Cigarette margins will come under pressure from escalating price competition, partially offset by higher unit sales. Share repurchases will aid per-share earnings comparisons.

Total Revenues (Billion $)

Quarter:	1995	1994	1993	1992
Mar.	3.70	3.21	3.54	3.40
Jun.	4.52	3.39	3.38	3.44
Sep.		3.55	3.42	3.42
Dec.		3.37	3.35	3.43
		13.52	13.69	13.69

Revenues for the six months ended June 30, 1995, rose 25%, year to year. Margins widened, largely due to improved underwriting trends at 84% owned CNA Financial, and net income advanced to $634 million from $54 million. Share earnings were $10.76 on 3.3% fewer shares ($6.69 of operating income; $4.07 of investment gains), compared with $0.89 ($3.83 of operating income; $2.94 of investment losses).

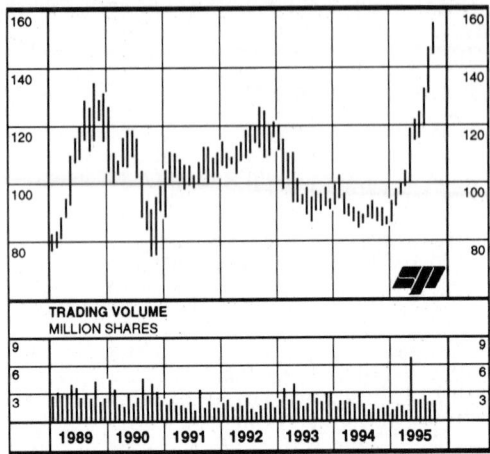

TRADING VOLUME
MILLION SHARES

Common Share Earnings ($)

Quarter:	1995	1994	1993	1992
Mar.	3.64	d0.10	5.25	3.24
Jun.	7.12	1.00	3.16	4.16
Sep.		2.24	d1.40	1.98
Dec.		1.34	2.20	d9.53
		4.45	9.27	d0.33

Important Developments

Aug. '95— LTR's first half 1995 results included contributions from the May acquisition of Continental Corp. (NYSE: CIC) by 84% owned CNA Financial Corp. (NYSE: CNA). CNA acquired CIC for $20 a share in cash, or about $1.1 billion. Separately, LTR expects to reap a $575 million pretax gain on the sale of its CBS Inc. (NYSE: CBS) holdings. Westinghouse Electric (NYSE: WX) has offered to acquire CBS for $81 a share.

Next earnings report expected in early November.

Per Share Data ($)

Yr. End Dec. 31	1994	1993	1992	1991	1990	1989	1988	1987	1986	1985
Tangible Bk. Val.	91.24	99.08	81.68	81.56	69.77	61.45	51.59	40.72	34.58	28.39
Oper. Earnings	8.70	2.06	[1]d3.72	[1]10.19	[1]10.77	[1]10.79	[1]9.81	[1]7.54	[1]NA	[1]NA
Earnings[1,2]	4.45	9.27	d0.33	13.14	11.01	12.07	11.70	8.41	6.69	6.17
Dividends	1.00	1.00	1.00	1.00	1.00	1.00	1.00	1.00	1.00	3.00
Relative Payout	22%	11%	NM	8%	9%	8%	9%	12%	15%	49%
Prices—High	102¾	120¼	126½	112⅞	126⅞	135	83⅛	96¼	72⅜	56¼
Low	84½	86¾	103½	88½	75	77	62	58	53¾	33
P/E Ratio—	23–19	13–9	NM	9–7	12–7	11–6	7–5	11–7	11–8	9–5

Data as orig. reptd. Adj. for stk. divs. of 200% Mar. 1985. 1. Bef. results of disc. opers. of +0.24 in 1988, +0.51 in 1987, +1.06 in 1985 & spec. item(s) of +2.20 in 1992. 2. Aft. gains/losses on sec. trans. d-Deficit. E-Estimated. NM-Not Meaningful. NA-Not Available.

Income Data (Million $)

Year Ended Dec. 31	Life Ins. In Force	Premium Income Life A & H	Cas./ Prop.	Net Invest. Inc.	Oth. Revs.	Total Revs.	Comb. Loss–Exp. Ratio	Net Bef. Taxes	Net Oper. Inc.	[1]Net Inc.	[2]Revs.	[2]Equity
1993	112,248	2,392	6,274	1,378	3,643	13,687	123.5	689	132	594	4.3	10.2
1992	105,212	2,393	6,352	1,992	2,955	13,691	141.9	d518	d244	d22	NM	NM
1991	98,678	2,269	6,654	2,149	2,548	13,620	113.8	1,231	701	904	6.6	16.9
1990	89,262	2,082	6,295	1,666	2,594	12,637	112.9	932	788	805	6.4	16.3
1989	85,919	2,037	5,394	1,625	2,381	11,437	113.6	952	811	907	7.9	20.5
1988	NA	NA	NA	1,549	NA	10,865	NA	1,322	NA	890	8.2	24.5
1987	NA	NA	NA	1,168	NA	9,324	NA	704	NA	656	7.0	21.3
1986	NA	NA	NA	1,205	NA	8,626	NA	685	NA	546	6.3	20.4
1985	NA	NA	NA	1,060	NA	6,700	NA	606	NA	503	7.5	22.6
1984	NA	NA	NA	735	NA	5,603	NA	321	NA	329	5.4	16.5

Balance Sheet Data (Million $)

Dec. 31	Cash & Equiv.	Premiums Due	[3]Bonds	Stocks	Loans	Total	% Invest. Yield	Deferred Policy Costs	Total Assets	Debt	Common Equity
1993	156	4,077	17,658	1,240	295	27,290	5.3	979	45,850	2,196	6,127
1992	105	4,223	23,127	860	330	24,376	8.2	887	40,492	1,760	5,527
1991	102	4,318	22,740	653	373	23,919	9.8	853	39,195	1,945	5,667
1990	83	4,579	18,615	880	403	19,931	8.7	826	34,736	1,826	5,041
1989	63	3,885	18,918	609	431	19,282	9.4	762	32,451	1,866	4,810
1988	40	2,598	14,362	466	473	15,335	10.9	663	25,830	1,393	4,028
1987	72	2,130	12,063	564	523	13,200	9.5	611	22,209	1,453	3,252
1986	101	1,872	10,374	341	628	11,388	11.2	559	19,024	1,265	2,917
1985	58	1,474	8,905	585	833	10,360	11.9	509	16,120	771	2,442
1984	59	1,203	6,011	598	771	7,420	10.1	374	12,557	395	2,007

Data as orig. reptd. 1. Bef. results of disc. opers. 2. Based on oper. earns. prior to 1985. 3. Incl. short-term invest. d-Deficit. NM-Not Meaningful. NA-Not Available.

Business Summary

Loews Corporation is a highly diversified concern, with the bulk of revenues in 1994 from insurance and tobacco operations. Segment contributions (in million $) in 1994 were:

	Revs.	Profits
Property–casualty ins.	$8,089	–$108
Life insurance	2,904	93
Cigarettes	1,916	584
Hotels	217	49
Watches/timing devices	151	4
Drilling	304	–14
Equity in CBS Inc.	46	46
Investment income & other	–111	–109

CNA Financial Corp. (84% owned as of 1994 year-end) is engaged in property and casualty insurance, as well as life, accident and health insurance. (For coverage of CNA, please see Standard NYSE Stock Report No. 413.)

Lorillard, Inc. is the fourth largest producer of tobacco products in the U.S., with a market share of 7.5%. Lorillard's flagship brands, Newport and Kent, accounted for 82% of this unit's sales in 1994.

The hotel division operates 14 hotels (nine owned or leased) in the U.S., Canada and Monaco. Bul-

ova Corp. (97% owned) distributes and sells watches, clocks, and components to the consumer market. Bulova's industrial and defense segment was sold for $20.8 million in January 1995.

Loews owns about 18% of CBS Inc. Wholly owned Diamond M-Odeco Drilling Inc. owns 38 offshore drilling rigs and 10 land rigs and equipment.

Dividend Data

Dividends have been paid since 1967.

Amt. of Divd. $	Date Decl.	Ex-divd. Date	Stock of Record	Payment Date	
0.25	Jan. 17	Jan. 30	Feb. 3	Mar. 1	'95
0.25	Apr. 18	May 1	May 5	Jun. 1	'95
0.25	Jul. 18	Aug. 2	Aug. 4	Sep. 1	'95
2-for-1	Oct. 17	Dec. 4	Nov. 3	Dec. 1	'95
0.25	Oct. 17	Nov. 1	Nov. 3	Dec. 1	'95

Capitalization

Long Term Debt: $4,225,267,000 (6/95).

Minority Interest: $1,077,330,000.

Common Stock: 58,916,400 shs. ($1 par).
The Tisch family controls some 26%; institutions hold about 52% (incl. some Tisch family shares). Shareholders of record: 4,100 (2/95).

Office—667 Madison Ave., New York, NY 10021-8087. **Tel**—(212) 545-2000. **Co-Chrmn & Co-CEO**—L. A. Tisch, P. R. Tisch. **Pres**—J. S. Tisch. **VP-CFO**—R. E. Posner. **VP-Secy**—B. Hirsh. **Treas**—J. J. Kenny. **Dirs**—C. B. Benenson, J. Brademas, B. Myerson, E. J. Noha, G. R. Scott, A. H. Tisch, J. M. Tisch, J. S. Tisch, L. A. Tisch, P. R. Tisch. **Transfer Agent & Registrar**—Chemical Banking Corp., NYC. **Incorporated** in New York in 1954; reincorporated in Delaware in 1970. **Empl**—25,400.

Information has been obtained from sources believed to be reliable, but its accuracy and completeness are not guaranteed. Catherine A. Seifert

Longs Drug Stores

NYSE Symbol **LDG**
In S&P 500

02-OCT-95

Industry:
Retail Stores

Summary: This company operates one of the largest drug store chains in North America, with over 320 stores in the western United States and Hawaii.

S&P Opinion: Hold (★★★)			
Recent Price • 41½		Yield • 2.7%	
52 Wk Range • 42¼-30¼		12-Mo. P/E • 17.3	

Earnings vs. Previous Year
▲=Up ▼=Down ▶=No Change

Quantitative Evaluations

Outlook
(1 Lowest—5 Highest)
• **2+**

Fair Value
• **35⅞**

Risk
• **Low**

Earn./Div. Rank
• **A-**

Technical Eval.
• **Bearish** since 8/95

Rel. Strength Rank
(1 Lowest—99 Highest)
• **84**

Insider Activity
• **NA**

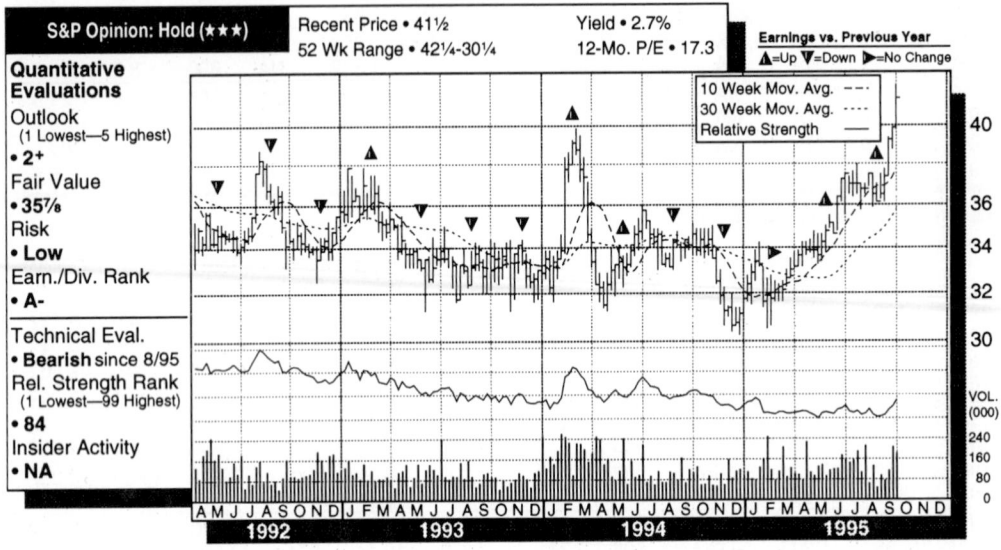

10 Week Mov. Avg. – – –
30 Week Mov. Avg. · · · ·
Relative Strength —

Overview - 02-OCT-95

We project sales to advance in the mid-to-upper-single digits for the second half of 1995-96, primarily reflecting new store openings. Gross margins are expected to trend lower, reflecting an industry-wide move toward lower prescription prices negotiated with third party plans. However, careful attention to costs and the completion of new information systems should reduce expense ratios. Share earnings should benefit from a repurchase program for up to two million common shares.

Valuation - 02-OCT-95

Following modest revenue and earnings growth in the first half of 1995-96, the shares of this leading drug store chain continued to rebound from their lowest level since 1992, and surged to a 52-week high. Comparisons with 1994-95 are being aided by the weak results last year, when earnings were hurt by higher costs due to the rollout of new systems for ordering and handling merchandise. Although we expect earnings to continue to post positive gains for the remainder of the year, any sales or earnings disappointment could cause a pullback in the stock price. Trading in line with the price earnings ratio of the retail drug store index, we see LDG shares as fully valued.

Key Stock Statistics

S&P EPS Est. 1996	2.52	Tang. Bk. Value/Share	25.69
P/E on S&P Est. 1996	16.5	Beta	0.63
S&P EPS Est. 1997	2.70	Shareholders	15,400
Dividend Rate/Share	1.12	Market cap. (B)	$0.831
Shs. outstg. (M)	20.0	Inst. holdings	45%
Avg. daily vol. (M)	0.030	Insider holdings	NA

Value of $10,000 invested 5 years ago: $ 11,114

Fiscal Year Ending Jan. 31

	1996	% Change	1995	% Change	1994	% Change
Revenues (Million $)						
1Q	639.8	3%	622.3	2%	608.0	NM
2Q	646.4	3%	626.3	3%	609.3	NM
3Q	—	—	614.5	3%	597.2	NM
4Q	—	—	695.2	2%	684.7	3%
Yr.	—	—	2,558	2%	2,499	NM
Income (Million $)						
1Q	13.30	2%	13.02	19%	10.92	-20%
2Q	12.49	4%	12.03	-7%	12.96	-4%
3Q	—	—	6.42	-28%	8.94	-4%
4Q	—	—	17.25	2%	16.93	3%
Yr.	—	—	48.73	-2%	49.75	-6%
Earnings Per Share ($)						
1Q	0.65	3%	0.63	19%	0.53	-21%
2Q	0.62	7%	0.58	-8%	0.63	-5%
3Q	E0.35	13%	0.31	-28%	0.43	-4%
4Q	E0.90	8%	0.83	NM	0.83	4%
Yr.	E2.52	7%	2.35	-2%	2.41	-7%

Next earnings report expected: mid November

Longs Drug Stores

Business Summary - 02-OCT-95

As of March 31, 1995, Longs Drug Stores was operating 324 super drug stores in five western states. Most of the stores were in California (278), with the balance in Hawaii (32), Nevada (six), Colorado (six) and Alaska (two).

Each store is centered around three service departments--pharmacy, cosmetics and photo. The majority of the merchandise consists of nationally advertised brands, but many items are sold under the company's private label. Most stores range in size from 15,000 to 25,000 sq. ft. In the past five years, store size was about 19,000 sq. ft., with 67% devoted to selling space. Sales per store averaged $8.2 million in 1994-95.

Operations are decentralized, with each store manager responsible for purchasing and pricing. Autonomy permits the matching of the merchandise with the special requirements of each store's market.

In 1989-90, Longs embarked on a 10-year, $100 million program to develop a retail information system. The system would enable each store to purchase merchandise at a lower cost, establish electronic data links with suppliers, and improve inventory control. Greater productivity, lower merchandise costs and improved merchandising information should result from this program.

At the end of 1994-95, 118 stores were in company-owned buildings on company-owned land. An additional 42 stores were in company-owned buildings on leased land. Land and buildings for the remaining 164 units were leased.

Important Developments

Aug. '95—To enhance its position in the growing managed health care area, the company formed a wholly-owned subsidiary, Integrated Health Concepts (IHC), a pharmacy benefit management company. IHC will offer a broad range of pharmacy benefit management services, including plan design development, pharmacy provider network management, on-line claims adjudication, and prospective and retrospective drug utilization review services. In addition, the subsidiary will provide access to a fully integrated mail service pharmacy and home health care services.
Aug. '95—LDG opened nine stores during the first half of 1995-96, including the six Hawaii stores acquired from PayLess Drug Stores in April. Two underperforming locations were closed.

Capitalization

Long Term Debt: $9,775,000 of guaranteed profit sharing plan debt (7/95).

Per Share Data ($) (Year Ended Jan. 31)

	1995	1994	1993	1992	1991	1990
Tangible Bk. Val.	25.49	24.19	22.45	20.70	18.80	16.68
Cash Flow	4.18	4.02	3.96	3.85	3.99	3.90
Earnings	2.35	2.41	2.58	2.71	2.94	3.01
Dividends	1.12	1.12	1.11	1.07	1.02	0.94
Payout Ratio	48%	46%	43%	39%	35%	31%
Cal. Yrs.	1994	1993	1992	1991	1990	1989
Prices - High	39⅞	37⅞	40	44⅜	44⅞	48½
- Low	30¼	31¼	32½	30⅞	33¼	34½
P/E Ratio - High	17	16	16	16	15	16
- Low	13	13	13	11	11	11

Income Statement Analysis (Million $)

	1995	%Chg	1994	%Chg	1993	%Chg	1992
Revs.	2,558	2%	2,499	NM	2,475	5%	2,366
Oper. Inc.	119	3%	115	NM	116	NM	115
Depr.	37.8	15%	33.0	16%	28.4	22%	23.3
Int. Exp.	NA	—	NA	—	NA	—	NA
Pretax Inc.	81.0	-1%	82.0	-6%	87.0	-4%	91.0
Eff. Tax Rate	40%	—	40%	—	39%	—	39%
Net Inc.	48.7	-2%	49.8	-6%	53.0	-4%	55.4

Balance Sheet & Other Fin. Data (Million $)

	1995	1994	1993	1992	1991	1990
Cash	57.5	42.5	16.1	12.0	9.7	24.6
Curr. Assets	427	390	343	326	313	286
Total Assets	828	795	709	673	623	567
Curr. Liab.	258	247	206	205	198	185
LT Debt	11.2	13.8	16.3	18.5	20.5	22.4
Common Eqty.	524	500	458	423	379	336
Total Cap.	570	548	503	468	426	381
Cap. Exp.	39.2	61.7	55.4	59.7	52.0	43.4
Cash Flow	86.5	82.7	81.4	78.7	81.0	79.5

Ratio Analysis

	1995	1994	1993	1992	1991	1990
Curr. Ratio	1.7	1.6	1.7	1.6	1.6	1.5
% LT Debt of Cap.	2.0	2.5	3.2	4.0	4.8	5.9
% Net Inc.of Revs.	1.9	2.0	2.1	2.3	2.6	2.9
% Ret. on Assets	6.0	6.6	7.7	8.5	10.0	11.4
% Ret. on Equity	9.5	10.3	12.0	13.7	16.7	18.9

Dividend Data —Dividends have been paid since 1961. A "poison pill" stock purchase rights plan was adopted in 1986.

Amt. of Div. $	Date Decl.	Ex-Div. Date	Stock of Record	Payment Date
0.280	Aug. 17	Aug. 24	Aug. 30	Oct. 07 '94
0.280	Nov. 16	Nov. 22	Nov. 29	Jan. 10 '95
0.280	Feb. 23	Mar. 01	Mar. 07	Apr. 10 '95
0.280	May. 17	May. 23	May. 30	Jul. 10 '95
0.280	Aug. 15	Aug. 25	Aug. 29	Oct. 10 '95

Data as orig. reptd.; bef. results of disc. opers. and/or spec. items. Per share data adj. for stk. divs. as of ex-div. date. E-Estimated. NA-Not Available. NM-Not Meaningful. NR-Not Ranked.

Office—141 North Civic Drive, Walnut Creek, CA 94596. **Tel**—(510) 937-1170. **Chrmn & CEO**—R. M. Long. **Pres**—S. D. Roath. **VP & Secy**—O. D. Jones. **VP, Treas & Investor Contact**—Clay E. Selland. **Dirs**—R. M. Brooks, W. G. Combs, D. G. DeSchane, E. E. Johnston, R. M. Long, M. S. Metz, R. A. Plomgren, S. D. Roath, G. H. Saito, H. R. Somerset, D. L. Sorby, T. R. Sweeney, F. E. Trotter. **Transfer Agent & Registrar**—Chemical Trust Co. of California, SF. **Incorporated** in California in 1946; reincorporated in Maryland in 1985. **Empl**-15,500. **S&P Analyst:** Maureen C. Carini

Loral Corp.

NYSE Symbol LOR Options on CBOE (Jan-Apr-Jul-Oct) In S&P 500

Price	Range	P-E Ratio	Dividend	Yield	S&P Ranking	Beta
Aug. 22'95	1995					
55⅜	57¼–36⅜	16	0.64	1.2%	A+	0.63

Summary

Loral is a major manufacturer of electronic warfare, communications and training systems, space systems and tactical weapons. To offset the impact of shrinking defense budgets, significant acquisitions have been made in recent years, strengthening core operations and broadening the types of defense and commercial systems produced. The recent purchase of the Unisys Defense Systems operation will significantly boost sales and earnings growth. In July 1995, LOR announced plans to pay a 2-for-1 stock split in September 1995.

Current Outlook

Earnings for the fiscal year ending March 31, 1996, are projected at $3.85 a share, up from 1994-5's $3.38.

Quarterly dividends was raised to $0.16, from $0.15, with the July announcement.

Sales for 1995-6 are projected to gain about 20%, primarily reflecting the inclusion of Unisys Defense Systems. With total bookings strong in the current fiscal year, a high level of deliveries in electronic combat, training and command, control and communications programs should continue. Effective control of operating costs should aid margins, but interest expense will be substantially higher. Defense Systems will contribute to earnings growth in 1995-6.

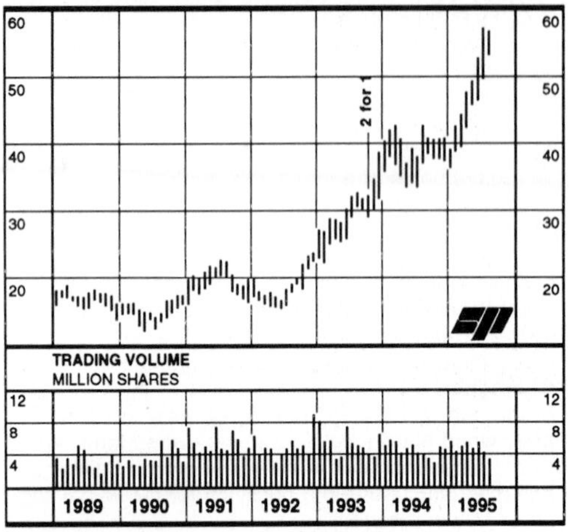

Net Sales (Million $)

Quarter:	1995–96	1994–95	1993–94	1992–93
Jun.	1,504	1,345	849	681
Sep.	---	1,345	837	739
Dec.	---	1,335	902	941
Mar.	---	1,459	1,421	974
	---	5,484	4,009	3,335

Sales in the three months ended June 30, 1995, rose 12%, year to year, reflecting the inclusion of Unisys Defense Systems. Margins widened, and operating income increased 29%. After higher interest charges, taxes at 38.0%, versus 37.9%, and greater equity interests, net income advanced 26%, to $0.80 a share, from $0.65.

Common Share Earnings ($)

Quarter:	1995–96	1994–95	1993–94	1992–93
Jun.	0.80	0.65	0.49	0.36
Sep.	E0.96	0.78	0.56	0.47
Dec.	E1.02	0.83	0.68	0.53
Mar.	E1.07	1.12	1.00	0.69
	E3.85	3.38	2.72	2.07

Important Developments

Jul. '95— Loral said it was awarded a contract to install an electronic mail and messaging system for the Department of Defense, in an opportunity worth in excess of $1 billion. Separately, the backlog at June 30, 1995, totaled $7.22 billion, versus $6.41 billion a year earlier.

May '95— Loral acquired Unisys Corp.'s Defense Systems, a leading systems integrator, for about $798 million in cash.

Apr. '95— The company received an FAA contract, valued at $955 million, to upgrade the U.S. air traffic control system.

Feb. '95— Globalstar Telecommunications Ltd. (GSTRF), purchased a 21.3% interest in Globalstar L.P. with the $200 million proceeds of a public stock offering.

Next earnings report expected in late October.

Per Share Data ($)

Yr. End Mar. 31	1995	[1]1994	[1]1993	1992	[1]1991	[1]1990	1989	1988	1987	[1]1986
Tangible Bk. Val.	**4.64**	Nil	7.77	10.97	7.26	6.10	6.09	2.26	0.24	4.75
Cash Flow	**5.63**	4.41	3.71	4.11	3.51	2.73	2.31	2.82	1.76	1.64
Earnings[2]	**3.38**	2.72	2.07	2.00	1.78	1.54	1.21	1.51	1.18	1.11
Dividends	**0.590**	0.545	0.495	0.470	0.430	0.390	0.350	0.315	0.290	0.255
Payout Ratio	**17%**	20%	26%	25%	25%	26%	30%	21%	25%	23%
Calendar Years	**1994**	1993	1992	1991	1990	1989	1988	1987	1986	1985
Prices—High	**42¾**	38¾	23 21/32	22¾	17 7/16	18 15/16	20¼	24⅝	24⅜	19½
Low	**33½**	22¼	15 5/16	16 1/16	12 1/16	13¾	15¼	12½	16 15/16	12⅛
P/E Ratio—	**13–10**	14–8	11–7	11–8	10–7	12–9	17–13	16–8	21–14	18–11

Data as orig. reptd. Adj. for stk div(s). of 100% Oct. 1993. **1.** Refl. merger or acq. **2.** Bef. results of disc. opers. of +0.02 in 1990, +0.55 in 1989 & spec. item(s) of -3.26 in 1994. E-Estimated.

Loral Corporation

Income Data (Million $)

Year Ended Mar. 31	Revs.	Oper. Inc.	% Oper. Inc. of Revs.	Cap. Exp.	Depr.	Int. Exp.	[3]Net Bef. Taxes	Eff. Tax Rate	[4]Net Inc.	% Net Inc. of Revs.	Cash Flow
1995	5,484	757	13.8	123	192	[6]106.0	471	38.7%	288	5.3	481
[1]1994	4,009	543	13.6	673	142	47.5	364	37.2%	228	5.7	370
[1]1993	3,335	423	12.7	214	126	53.4	256	36.9%	[5]159	4.8	285
1992	2,882	421	14.6	82	129	61.8	240	37.2%	122	4.2	250
[1]1991	2,127	304	14.3	288	88	58.9	163	37.6%	90	4.2	179
[1]1990	1,274	214	16.8	194	65	40.4	123	37.0%	78	6.1	143
[2]1989	1,187	188	15.8	41	55	39.5	95	36.4%	60	5.1	116
1988	1,441	246	17.0	51	65	61.7	122	39.0%	74	5.2	139
1987	690	134	19.4	321	29	12.5	99	41.8%	[5]57	8.3	86
[1]1986	664	119	18.0	71	26	9.0	91	41.9%	53	8.0	79

Balance Sheet Data (Million $)

Mar. 31	Cash	Assets	Curr. Liab.	Ratio	Total Assets	% Ret. on Assets	Long Term Debt	Common Equity	Total Cap.	% LT Debt of Cap.	% Ret. on Equity
1995	126	1,553	1,017	1.5	4,810	5.7	1,316	1,688	3,003	43.8	18.6
1994	238	1,845	1,290	1.4	5,176	5.4	1,624	1,381	3,005	54.0	17.7
1993	117	1,365	755	1.8	3,228	4.8	491	1,188	1,679	29.2	12.8
1992	191	1,204	608	2.0	2,659	4.2	562	997	1,880	29.9	13.4
1991	75	1,177	720	1.6	2,532	4.4	784	672	1,677	46.7	14.3
1990	105	749	436	1.7	1,535	5.2	419	585	1,039	40.3	14.0
1989	87	898	435	2.1	1,461	4.2	423	518	979	43.2	12.6
1988	27	631	326	1.9	1,415	5.0	584	438	1,055	55.3	18.1
1987	43	606	360	1.7	1,467	5.3	667	363	1,052	63.4	17.0
1986	55	378	229	1.7	696	8.9	132	309	467	28.3	18.5

Data as orig. reptd. 1. Refl. merger or acq. 2. Excl. disc. ops. 3. Incl. equity in earns. of nonconsol. subs. 4. Bef. results of disc. ops. & spec. items. 5. Refl. acctg. change. 6. Net.

Business Summary

Loral primarily designs, develops and manufactures defense electronic systems. Principal product areas include command, control, communications and intelligence (C3I)/reconnaissance; electronic combat; tactical weapons; systems integration; training and simulation; and telecommunications and space.

C3I/reconnaissance systems provide systems integration, operations management, information processing and display hardware and software, secure communications and telemetry. Electronic combat products include airborne radar and missile warning systems, electronic and infrared countermeasures and integrated systems. Tactical weapons include complete missiles and guidance and fire control systems for missiles.

Systems integration activities involve the integration of complex computer hardware and software systems principally for federal and foreign government organizations. Training systems include battlefield environment simulators, aircraft simulators, weapons systems trainers, laser-based combat training (MILES) and electronic warfare systems.

Space Systems/Loral (51%-owned) produces satellites and instruments for space communications and earth sensing and provides services for space missions. Globalstar, L.P. (32.3%-owned) is constructing, and will operate, a satellite-based digital telephone system.

U.S. and foreign governments are the principal users of the company's products. Foreign sales accounted for 19% of 1994-5 revenues. Defense contracts comprised 79%.

In 1993-4, LOR acquired IBM's Federal Systems Co. In 1992-3, LOR purchased the missile business of LTV Aerospace and Defense (renamed Loral Vought). In 1990-1, Ford Aerospace (renamed Loral Aerospace Holdings and Space Systems/Loral) was acquired.

Dividend Data

Dividends were initiated in 1976. In July 1995, LOR announced plans to pay a 2-for-1 stock split in September 1995.

Amt. of Divd. $	Date Decl.	Ex-divd. Date	Stock of Record	Payment Date
0.15	Sep. 23	Nov. 23	Nov. 30	Dec. 15'94
0.15	Dec. 13	Feb. 22	Feb. 28	Mar. 15'95
0.15	Mar. 13	May 22	May 26	Jun. 15'95
0.16	Jul. 25	Aug. 28	Aug. 30	Sep. 15'95

Capitalization

Total Debt: $2,123,750,000 (6/95).

Common Stock: 85,667,936 shs. ($0.25 par).
Institutions hold 76%.
Shareholders of record: 4,600 (6/95).

Office—600 Third Ave., New York, NY 10016. Tel—(212) 697-1105. Chrmn & CEO—Bernard L. Schwartz. Pres & COO—F. C. Lanza. SVP & Secy—M. B. Targoff. SVP-Fin—M. P. DeBlasio. VP & Investor Contact—Joanne Hvala (212-697-1105). Dirs—H. Gittis, R. B. Hodes, G. Kekst, F. C. Lanza, C. Lazarus, M. Ruderman, B. L. Schwartz, E. D. Shapiro, A. M. Shinn, A. L. Simon, T. J. Stanton, Jr., D. Yankelovich. Transfer Agent & Registrar—The Bank of New York, NYC. Incorporated in New York in 1948. Empl—28,900.

Information has been obtained from sources believed to be reliable, but its accuracy and completeness are not guaranteed. Joe Victor Shammas

537

Louisiana Land

NYSE Symbol **LLX**

In S&P 500

31-OCT-95 | **Industry:** Oil and Gas

Summary: Louisiana Land is an independent crude oil and gas producer. U.S. holdings are offshore along the Gulf Coast and onshore primarily in Louisiana and Wyoming.

S&P Opinion: Sell (★)	Recent Price • 35⅝	Yield • 0.7%
	52 Wk Range • 46¼-31¼	12-Mo. P/E • NM

Quantitative Evaluations

Outlook
(1 Lowest—5 Highest)
• **1⁻**

Fair Value
• **27⅛**

Risk
• **Low**

Earn./Div. Rank
• **B-**

Technical Eval.
• **Bearish** since 6/95

Rel. Strength Rank
(1 Lowest—99 Highest)
• **30**

Insider Activity
• **NA**

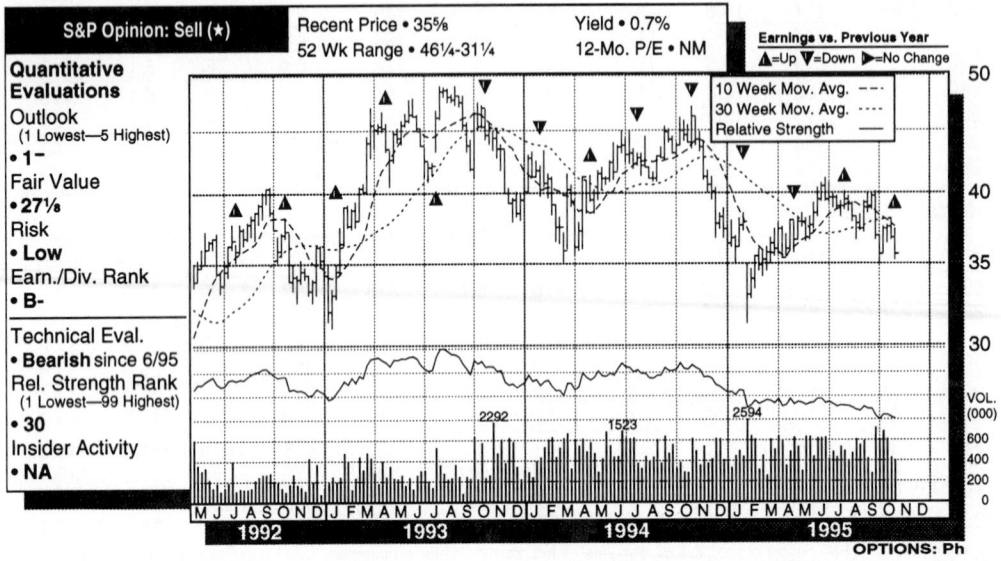

Earnings vs. Previous Year ▲=Up ▼=Down ▶=No Change

10 Week Mov. Avg. — —
30 Week Mov. Avg. ......
Relative Strength —

OPTIONS: Ph

Overview - 31-OCT-95

Louisiana Land is seeking a coherent strategy to allow the company to reach sustained profitability within a low commodity price framework. Debt reduction will be a priority over the next twelve months. Improved site evaluation techniques being used in Louisiana have shown little bottom-line impact, though longer-term production prospects may improve as a result of international volume improvement. Should excess North Sea natural gas production continue, we are likely to lower our 1996 estimates during the fourth quarter. Recent earnings reports have benefited from hedging strategies implemented during 1994. However, cash flow growth over the next 18 months will be restricted by marginally improved commodity prices.

Valuation - 31-OCT-95

The shares have recovered to some degree, following the announcement in early 1995 that LLX would seek to dispose of all of its Canadian oil and gas assets, and close its Calgary office. The company also cut its annual dividend from $1.00 to $0.25, primarily in response to plummeting natural gas prices. We are forecasting gas prices will average $1.60 Mcf in 1995, up from a weak second quarter level. In addition, near-term fundamentals for oil remain weak, due to recent comments from OPEC regarding the possibility of production increases. The November OPEC meeting may have a substantial impact on exploration and production equities, particularly if OPEC does not roll over the current quota.

Key Stock Statistics

S&P EPS Est. 1995	0.49	Tang. Bk. Value/Share	10.84
P/E on S&P Est. 1995	72.7	Beta	0.61
S&P EPS Est. 1996	1.15	Shareholders	13,000
Dividend Rate/Share	0.24	Market cap. (B)	$ 1.2
Shs. outstg. (M)	33.5	Inst. holdings	87%
Avg. daily vol. (M)	0.132	Insider holdings	NA

Value of $10,000 invested 5 years ago: $ 9,262

Fiscal Year Ending Dec. 31

	1995	% Change	1994	% Change	1993	% Change
Revenues (Million $)						
1Q	193.1	-7%	206.7	11%	186.9	2%
2Q	213.1	12%	190.7	-2%	194.7	1%
3Q	212.0	7%	197.9	2%	193.5	-7%
4Q	—	—	206.2	-14%	240.3	18%
Yr.	—	—	801.5	-2%	815.4	4%
Income (Million $)						
1Q	3.50	-44%	6.20	130%	2.70	NM
2Q	6.40	NM	0.60	-89%	5.60	17%
3Q	1.80	NM	-11.30	NM	-1.80	NM
4Q	—	—	-222.4	NM	6.20	-47%
Yr.	—	—	-226.9	NM	12.70	NM
Earnings Per Share ($)						
1Q	0.11	-42%	0.19	111%	0.09	NM
2Q	0.19	NM	0.02	-90%	0.20	18%
3Q	0.05	NM	-0.34	NM	-0.06	NM
4Q	E0.14	NM	-6.64	NM	0.19	-54%
Yr.	E0.49	NM	-6.80	NM	0.43	NM

Next earnings report expected: late January

Business Summary - 31-OCT-95

LLX is an independent crude oil and natural gas producer. The company also owns a refinery in Mobile, Ala., and processes natural gas. It operates onshore in the continental U.S. and offshore in the Gulf of Mexico. The company has working interests in oil and gas properties in Canada, the North Sea, the Middle East, Africa, Indonesia and Colombia. In early 1995, the company announced plans to sell nonstrategic assets, including remaining Canadian oil and gas assets. Contributions to profits in recent years (in million $):

	1994	1993
Domestic petroleum	.-$265.7	$79.2
North Sea petroleum	5.5	-7.7
Other foreign petroleum	-30.7	16.5

In 1994, production of crude and condensate averaged 40,776 b/d (34,785 in 1993), plant products 3,033 b/d (2,758 b/d), and natural gas 277.0 Mmcf/d (219.9 Mmcf/d). Refined product sales were 52,904 b/d in 1994 (54,530 b/d). Worldwide proved reserves at 1994 year-end stood at 97.1 MMBbls of oil and 983.7 Bcf of natural gas. In 1994, additions to proved reserves exceeded production by 115%.

Exploration and capital spending in 1994 totaled $235 million, of which $90 million was related to exploration. In 1994, the company completed three exploratory wells in the Fresh Water Bayou Field (33% net interest) in Vermilion Parish, La. Pipeline constraints limited production to 55 Mmcf/d of gas and 320 b/d of condensate from two of the wells.

Important Developments

Oct. '95—LL&E attributed higher third quarter earnings to increased international volumes and lower unit costs, which offset lower domestic natural gas prices. The company said that substantially all of the third quarter gain in volumes was due to a short-term increase in T-Block production, to entitlement adjustments from concessions offshore Indonesia, and to rising production at the Brae field in the North Sea.
Sep. '95—Louisiana Land & Exploration announced the succesful completion of two development wells in the Fresh Water Bayou Field in Vermilion Parish, La. Both of the wells were completed ahead of schedule and under budget. LL&E owns a 35% working interest in the Fresh Water Bayou field. Also in September, LL&E announced a non-commercial find on the one-million acre Ramla block, offshore Tunisia. The company will plug the well, and commence with additional exploration drilling on the block in 1996.

Capitalization

Long Term Debt: $736,000,000 (6/95).

Per Share Data ($)

(Year Ended Dec. 31)

	1994	1993	1992	1991	1990	1989
Tangible Bk. Val.	10.56	18.00	14.70	15.78	15.91	14.83
Cash Flow	-0.74	4.83	3.72	4.85	5.89	5.55
Earnings	-6.80	0.43	-0.04	0.74	1.94	1.60
Dividends	1.00	1.00	1.00	1.00	1.00	1.00
Payout Ratio	NM	NM	NM	135%	51%	60%
Prices - High	47⅛	49	40½	43½	53⅝	45½
- Low	35⅛	31	25	29⅝	39½	31⅛
P/E Ratio - High	NM	NM	NM	59	28	28
- Low	NM	NM	NM	40	20	19

Income Statement Analysis (Million $)

	1994	%Chg	1993	%Chg	1992	%Chg	1991
Revs.	783	2%	770	NM	766	-4%	797
Oper. Inc.	172	25%	138	2%	135	-2%	138
Depr. Depl. & Amort.	202	55%	130	21%	107	-8%	116
Int. Exp.	47.9	2%	47.0	25%	37.5	-5%	39.5
Pretax Inc.	-345	NM	25.0	NM	-2.0	NM	33.0
Eff. Tax Rate	NM	—	48%	—	NM	—	37%
Net Inc.	-226	NM	13.0	NM	-1.0	NM	21.0

Balance Sheet & Other Fin. Data (Million $)

	1994	1993	1992	1991	1990	1989
Cash	12.5	33.3	40.5	26.7	29.9	5.5
Curr. Assets	184	190	153	187	187	185
Total Assets	1,478	1,839	1,209	1,253	1,226	1,199
Curr. Liab.	191	175	173	162	160	197
LT Debt	740	735	343	347	346	367
Common Eqty.	352	600	417	447	449	416
Total Cap.	1,132	1,486	908	927	927	896
Cap. Exp.	237	182	190	189	183	151
Cash Flow	-25.0	143	105	137	167	163

Ratio Analysis

	1994	1993	1992	1991	1990	1989
Curr. Ratio	1.0	1.1	0.9	1.1	1.2	0.9
% LT Debt of Cap.	65.3	49.4	37.8	37.5	37.3	40.9
% Ret. on Assets	NM	0.8	NM	1.7	4.5	3.7
% Ret. on Equity	NM	2.3	NM	4.7	12.7	10.8

Dividend Data —Dividends have been paid since 1935. A "poison pill" stock purchase rights plan was adopted in 1986. A dividend reinvestment plan is available.

Amt. of Div. $	Date Decl.	Ex-Div. Date	Stock of Record	Payment Date
0.250	Nov. 10	Nov. 25	Dec. 01	Dec. 15 '94
0.060	Jan. 30	Feb. 23	Mar. 01	Mar. 15 '95
0.060	May. 11	May. 25	Jun. 01	Jun. 15 '95
0.060	Jul. 13	Aug. 30	Sep. 01	Sep. 15 '95

Data as orig. reptd.; bef. results of disc opers. and/or spec. items. Per share data adj. for stk. divs. as of ex-div. date. Revs. in Income Statement Analysis tbl. excl. other income. Results in 1994 reflect large 4Q asset write-down. E-Estimated. NA-Not Available. NM-Not Meaningful. NR-Not Ranked.

Office—909 Poydras St., New Orleans, LA 70112. **Tel**—(504) 566-6500. **Chrmn, Pres & CEO**—H. L. Steward. **EVP & COO**—R. A. Bachmann. **SVP-CFO**—L. A. Raspino. **VP & Secy**—F. J. Plaeger II. **Investor Contact**—Randy Pick. **Dirs**—L. C. Adams, R. A. Bachmann, R. E. Howson, E. M. Kelly, K. W. Orce, V. A. Rice, O. R. Smith, H. L. Steward, A. R. Taylor, W. R. Timken, Jr., C. A. H. Trost, E. L. Williamson. **Transfer Agent & Registrar**—First Chicago Trust Co. of New York, Jersey City, NJ. **Incorporated** in Maryland in 1926. Empl-825. **S&P Analyst:** Raymond J. Deacon

Louisiana-Pacific

NYSE Symbol **LPX**
In S&P 500

19-SEP-95 **Industry:** Building

Summary: This major forest products company produces lumber, plywood, oriented strand board, other building products and pulp.

S&P Opinion: Hold (★★★)		
Recent Price • 24½	Yield • 2.3%	
52 Wk Range • 34⅞-20⅞	12-Mo. P/E • 10.3	

Earnings vs. Previous Year
▲=Up ▼=Down ▶=No Change

Quantitative Evaluations

Outlook
(1 Lowest—5 Highest)
• **3⁻**

Fair Value
• **25⅜**

Risk
• **Average**

Earn./Div. Rank
• **B+**

Technical Eval.
• **Bullish** since 6/95

Rel. Strength Rank
(1 Lowest—99 Highest)
• **23**

Insider Activity
• **NA**

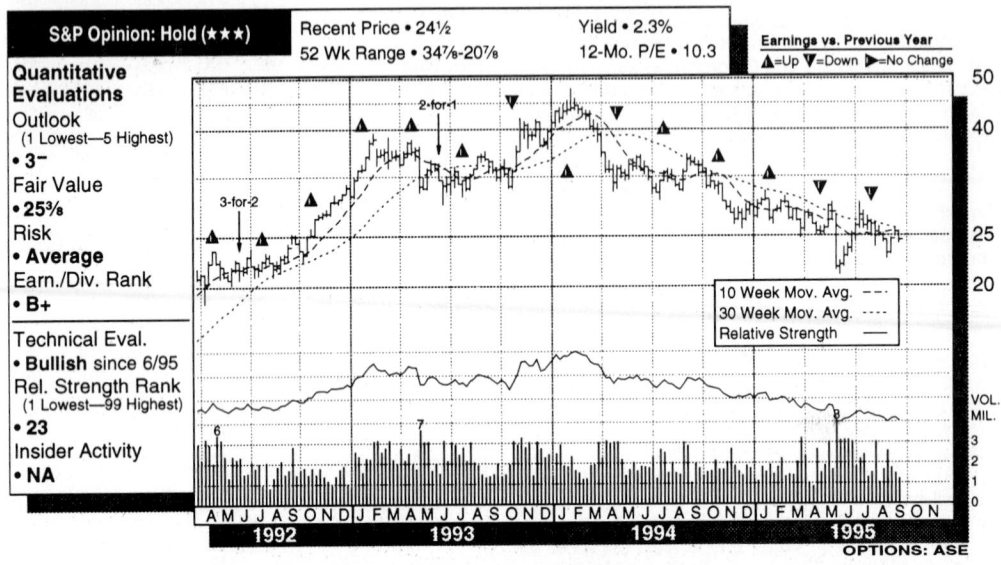

10 Week Mov. Avg. — — —
30 Week Mov. Avg. ……
Relative Strength ——

VOL. MIL.

OPTIONS: ASE

Overview - 19-SEP-95

Modestly lower sales are likely in 1995, as relatively high interest rates led to weak wood products sales in the first half, with the greatest demand and price weakness experienced in lumber. With the fall in long-term interest rates in the spring of 1995 stimulating an improvement in building markets, wood products sales should pick up in the second half, largely on more favorable pricing in certain categories; the greatest gains have been in OSB, although new industry capacity could pressure OSB prices over the next year. LPX's top line should also benefit from strong demand and prices in the much smaller pulp division. Margins are likely to narrow, but improved housing trends should allow wood products margins to bounce back from first half difficulties, and strong gains should be recorded in pulp. The bottom line might also be hurt by legal matters.

Valuation - 19-SEP-95

LPX's shares have fallen about 50% since early 1994, as the Fed's credit tightening program (which ended in early 1995) brought about a slowdown in construction activity and weaker demand for building materials. In addition, news about LPX's expected indictment for alleged violations of environmental laws and fraud (the indictment occurred in June 1995), caused a steep plunge in its stock price in May 1995. Although the recent drop in interest rates could lead to an improvement in industry conditions, we would wait until LPX's legal prospects are clearer before purchasing shares.

Key Stock Statistics

S&P EPS Est. 1995	2.10	Tang. Bk. Value/Share	16.54
P/E on S&P Est. 1995	11.7	Beta	1.41
S&P EPS Est. 1996	2.40	Shareholders	25,600
Dividend Rate/Share	0.56	Market cap. (B)	$ 2.7
Shs. outstg. (M)	107.8	Inst. holdings	50%
Avg. daily vol. (M)	0.356	Insider holdings	NA

Value of $10,000 invested 5 years ago: $ 19,135

Fiscal Year Ending Dec. 31

	1995	% Change	1994	% Change	1993	% Change
Revenues (Million $)						
1Q	686.8	-2%	698.0	8%	649.0	36%
2Q	709.3	-8%	774.7	30%	596.6	11%
3Q	—	—	818.4	30%	629.4	-2%
4Q	—	—	748.4	18%	636.1	20%
Yr.	—	—	3,040	21%	2,511	15%
Income (Million $)						
1Q	54.30	-36%	85.20	-3%	87.70	144%
2Q	26.30	-68%	81.90	25%	65.70	49%
3Q	—	—	95.10	129%	41.50	-25%
4Q	—	—	84.70	42%	59.50	45%
Yr.	—	—	346.9	36%	254.4	44%
Earnings Per Share ($)						
1Q	0.50	-35%	0.77	-4%	0.80	139%
2Q	0.25	-67%	0.75	25%	0.60	48%
3Q	E0.65	-24%	0.86	126%	0.38	-26%
4Q	E0.70	-9%	0.77	43%	0.54	44%
Yr.	E2.10	-33%	3.15	36%	2.32	42%

Next earnings report expected: mid October

Business Summary - 19-SEP-95

Louisiana-Pacific is a major forest products firm, producing lumber, panel and other building products and pulp. Industry segment contributions (operating profits in millions) in 1994 were:

	Sales	Profits
Building products	93%	$636
Pulp	7%	-5

Export sales accounted for 12% of the total in 1994, up from 10% in 1993.

LPX operates 131 plants and mills throughout the U.S., and in Canada, Mexico and Ireland. Products are distributed mainly through distributors and home centers, and through company-owned distribution centers. The company is one of the three largest lumber producers in the U.S., with 19 western sawmills (with annual production capacity of 1.2BBF) and 27 southern sawmills (annual capacity 1.1 BBF). Lumber accounted for 28% of the company's sales in 1994.

Panel products include plywood and a variety of reconstituted panel products such as Inner-Seal oriented strand board, industrial particleboard, medium-density fiberboard and hardboard. LPX is the largest U.S. producer of oriented strand board. The company's reconstituted panel product lines accounted for 34% of its sales in 1994, while plywood sales represented 14%. Other building products (17% of sales) include fiber gypsum wallboard, windows, doors, hardwood veneers, engineered I-joists and cellulose insulation.

LPX has three pulp mills in Alaska, California and British Columbia, with a combined annual capacity of about 600 million short tons.

At December 31, 1994, the company owned about 1,607,700 acres of timberland in the U.S.

Important Developments

Jul. '95—Citing a lack of confidence in its executive team, LPX requested and accepted the resignations of three officers and directors, including Harry A. Merlo, who had been chairman and president. Donald L. Kayser, a board member and former executive of the company, accepted an interim appointment as chairman and CEO; Lee Simpson, a former board member and officer, accepted an interim assignment as president and was reappointed to the board. The changes were primarily stimulated by a variety of lawsuits instituted against LPX over the past year, which center around its oriented strand board (OSB) products. The most recent proceeding involved a federal grand jury indictment in June 1995, for alleged violations of environmental laws and fraud at an OSB mill in Colorado. Other major litigation against LPX includes class action lawsuits in Florida and Washington, which both allege that the company's OSB products are defective and its warranties are inadequate.

Capitalization

Long Term Debt: $184,500,000 (6/95).

Per Share Data ($)

(Year Ended Dec. 31)

	1994	1993	1992	1991	1990	1989
Tangible Bk. Val.	16.33	14.26	12.46	11.15	10.84	10.31
Cash Flow	4.94	3.99	3.14	1.90	2.19	2.91
Earnings	3.15	2.32	1.63	0.51	0.82	1.68
Dividends	0.49	0.43	0.39	0.36	0.35	0.33
Payout Ratio	15%	19%	24%	70%	41%	19%
Prices - High	48	42⅛	31½	15½	15⅛	14½
- Low	25¾	28¾	14⅝	8⅞	6¾	9⅜
P/E Ratio - High	15	18	19	30	18	9
- Low	8	12	9	17	8	6

Income Statement Analysis (Million $)

	1994	%Chg	1993	%Chg	1992	%Chg	1991
Revs.	3,040	21%	2,511	15%	2,185	28%	1,702
Oper. Inc.	756	23%	616	34%	461	80%	256
Depr.	197	8%	183	12%	163	9%	150
Int. Exp.	14.5	-11%	16.3	-39%	26.6	-39%	43.8
Pretax Inc.	560	31%	428	51%	283	NM	87.0
Eff. Tax Rate	38%	—	41%	—	38%	—	36%
Net Inc.	347	37%	254	44%	177	NM	56.0

Balance Sheet & Other Fin. Data (Million $)

	1994	1993	1992	1991	1990	1989
Cash	316	262	228	191	209	353
Curr. Assets	694	614	539	461	509	654
Total Assets	2,716	2,466	2,206	2,107	2,104	2,032
Curr. Liab.	345	317	296	260	196	180
LT Debt	210	289	386	493	589	530
Common Eqty.	1,849	1,571	1,361	1,204	1,167	1,177
Total Cap.	2,329	2,125	1,902	1,837	1,897	1,842
Cap. Exp.	352	290	202	202	375	260
Cash Flow	544	438	340	206	225	313

Ratio Analysis

	1994	1993	1992	1991	1990	1989
Curr. Ratio	2.0	1.9	1.8	1.8	2.6	3.6
% LT Debt of Cap.	9.0	13.6	20.3	26.8	31.0	28.7
% Net Inc.of Revs.	11.4	10.1	8.1	3.3	5.1	9.6
% Ret. on Assets	13.3	10.8	8.2	2.7	4.5	10.0
% Ret. on Equity	20.1	17.3	13.7	4.7	8.0	16.5

Dividend Data

Dividends have been paid since 1973. A dividend reinvestment plan is available. A poison pill stock purchase rights plan was adopted in 1988.

Amt. of Div. $	Date Decl.	Ex-Div. Date	Stock of Record	Payment Date
0.125	Oct. 31	Nov. 10	Nov. 17	Dec. 01 '94
0.125	Jan. 30	Feb. 08	Feb. 14	Mar. 01 '95
0.140	May. 01	May. 12	May. 18	Jun. 01 '95
0.140	Jul. 24	Aug. 11	Aug. 15	Sep. 01 '95

Data as orig. reptd.; bef. results of disc. opers. and/or spec. items. Per share data adj. for stk. divs. as of ex-div. date. E-Estimated. NA-Not Available. NM-Not Meaningful. NR-Not Ranked.

Incorporated—in Delaware in 1972. **Office**—111 S.W. Fifth Ave., Portland, OR 97204-3699. **Tel**—(503) 221-0800. **Chrmn & CEO**—D. R. Kayser. **Pres & COO**—L. Simpson. **VP-Fin, CFO, Treas & Investor Contact**—William L. Hebert. **Dirs**—P. S. du Pont IV, B. G. Hill, D. R. Kayser, F. I. Neff, L. Simpson, C. E. Yeager. **Transfer Agent & Registrar**—First Chicago Trust Co. of New York, Jersey City, NJ. **Empl**-13,000. **S&P Analyst:** Michael W. Jaffe

Lowe's Companies

NYSE Symbol **LOW**
In S&P 500

07-SEP-95 **Industry:** Retail Stores

Summary: This company retails building materials and supplies, lumber, hardware and appliances through more than 350 stores, mainly in the South Atlantic and South Central U.S. regions.

S&P Opinion: Accumulate (★★★★)	Recent Price • 33½	Yield • 0.5%
	52 Wk Range • 41⅜-26	12-Mo. P/E • 22.0

Earnings vs. Previous Year
▲=Up ▼=Down ▶=No Change

Quantitative Evaluations

Outlook
  (1 Lowest—5 Highest)
• **5⁻**

Fair Value
• **37⅞**

Risk
• **Average**

Earn./Div. Rank
• **A-**

Technical Eval.
• **Bullish** since 5/95

Rel. Strength Rank
  (1 Lowest—99 Highest)
• **26**

Insider Activity
• **Neutral**

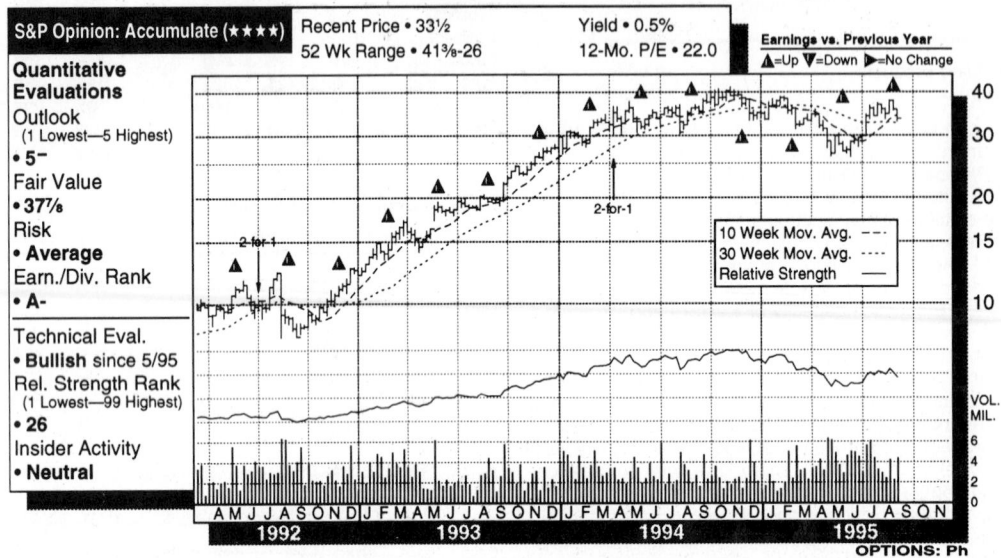

10 Week Mov. Avg. — - —
30 Week Mov. Avg. ....
Relative Strength ———

OPTIONS: Ph

Overview - 07-SEP-95

Sales and earnings growth slowed in the first half of 1995-96, as cooler than expected spring weather restricted demand for home construction materials. Lower lumber prices, a slowing economy and higher interest rates also impacted results. With interest rates moderating, and improved weather, we expect sales to rebound during the second half of the year. Same-store sales growth should return to the mid-single digit levels. Margins will continue to trend higher, owing to the success of newer and larger stores that offer a broader selection of merchandise. Larger volumes generated at these stores and subsequent operating efficiencies, combined with a continuing shift in the product mix away from building commodities to the higher-margin retail customer, should benefit earnings comparisons.

Valuation - 07-SEP-95

LOW's shares were beaten down nearly 30% earlier in the year, following weaker than expected results in the first quarter, which fueled fears that higher interest rates were slowing the economy and would curtail home construction and sales, and consequently demand for building materials. With interest rates stabilizing, pent-up consumer demand should aid comparisons for the rest of 1995-96. The company's penetration of new markets, its favorable merchandise mix, and well controlled costs should also allow an expansion of the price earnings multiple. At a P/E below our projected growth rate, the shares remain attractive for long-term appreciation.

Key Stock Statistics

S&P EPS Est. 1996	1.65	Tang. Bk. Value/Share	9.31
P/E on S&P Est. 1996	20.3	Beta	1.47
S&P EPS Est. 1997	2.05	Shareholders	7,400
Dividend Rate/Share	0.18	Market cap. (B)	$ 5.4
Shs. outstg. (M)	160.1	Inst. holdings	62%
Avg. daily vol. (M)	0.699	Insider holdings	NA

Value of $10,000 invested 5 years ago: $ 48,353

Fiscal Year Ending Jan. 31

	1996	% Change	1995	% Change	1994	% Change
Revenues (Million $)						
1Q	1,635	17%	1,397	41%	992.1	12%
2Q	1,978	20%	1,647	33%	1,242	17%
3Q	—	—	1,579	36%	1,158	17%
4Q	—	—	1,487	30%	1,146	26%
Yr.	—	—	6,111	35%	4,538	18%
Income (Million $)						
1Q	58.93	14%	51.75	76%	29.45	24%
2Q	85.01	19%	71.35	59%	44.96	51%
3Q	—	—	54.19	71%	31.65	67%
4Q	—	—	46.27	80%	25.73	109%
Yr.	—	—	223.6	70%	131.8	56%
Earnings Per Share ($)						
1Q	0.37	6%	0.35	75%	0.20	25%
2Q	0.53	13%	0.47	54%	0.31	53%
3Q	E0.42	24%	0.34	58%	0.22	65%
4Q	E0.33	14%	0.29	66%	0.17	119%
Yr.	E1.65	15%	1.44	62%	0.89	53%

Next earnings report expected: mid November

Lowe's Companies

Business Summary - 06-SEP-95

Lowe's Companies is a retail distributor, at discount prices, of building materials, consumer durables and home center products for the do-it-yourself and home construction markets. As of August 31, 1995, it was operating 352 retail stores in 22 states, principally in the South Atlantic and South Central regions of the U.S.

Contributions to sales by product line in recent fiscal years:

	1994-95	1993-94
Structural lumber	15%	17%
Building materials	20%	21%
Home decoration & lights	20%	18%
Kitchen, bath & laundry	11%	11%
Heating, cooling & water systems	6%	6%
Home entertainment	4%	5%
Yard, patio & garden	12%	11%
Tools	6%	6%
Special orders	6%	6%

At January 31, 1995, Lowe's had total sales floor space of 18,604,368 sq. ft., a 25% increase over fiscal 1993. The average sales floor size was 55,370 sq. ft., versus 45,578 sq. ft. a year earlier, with the company planning to continue expanding the size of its stores.

In an effort to reduce the effect of construction cycles, Lowe's has worked on increasing its focus on its retail business in recent years. Building materials sales are seasonal, with the largest portion occurring in the spring and summer months.

In February 1994, in order to focus its marketing effort on homebuilding contractors, LOW established its 18 contractor yards as a separate, wholly-owned subsidiary, operating as "The Contractor Yard." At April 30, 1995, the company was operating 25 contractor yards.

Expansion plans for 1995-96 envision about 50 to 55 new stores, with 60% in new markets and the balance in relocations, for approximately 5.3 million square feet of additional retail space.

Important Developments

Aug. '95—Sales for the four weeks ended August 25, 1995, increased 11%, year-to-year, fueled by contributions from new stores; same-store sales slid 4%.
Aug. '95—Lowe's said that it expects to open 19 new stores in new markets and relocate 10 additional stores during the balance of 1995-96.

Capitalization

Long Term Debt: $690,273,000 (4/95).

Per Share Data ($)

(Year Ended Jan. 31)

	1995	1994	1993	1992	1991	1990
Tangible Bk. Val.	8.90	5.91	5.02	4.59	4.68	4.33
Cash Flow	2.15	1.44	1.05	0.44	0.82	0.82
Earnings	1.44	0.89	0.58	0.05	0.48	0.51
Dividends	0.17	0.32	0.15	0.14	0.13	0.12
Payout Ratio	12%	36%	25%	305%	27%	24%
Cal. Yrs.	1994	1993	1992	1991	1990	1989
Prices - High	41⅜	29⅞	12¾	9¼	12⅜	8
- Low	26⅝	12	8	5¾	4⅝	5¼
P/E Ratio - High	29	34	22	NM	26	16
- Low	18	13	14	NM	10	10

Income Statement Analysis (Million $)

	1995	%Chg	1994	%Chg	1993	%Chg	1992
Revs.	6,111	35%	4,538	18%	3,846	26%	3,056
Oper. Inc.	481	62%	297	41%	211	40%	151
Depr.	110	37%	80.5	15%	69.8	20%	58.3
Int. Exp.	44.8	68%	26.6	37%	19.4	-3%	19.9
Pretax Inc.	344	74%	198	57%	126	NM	5.0
Eff. Tax Rate	35%	—	34%	—	33%	—	NM
Net Inc.	224	70%	132	56%	84.7	NM	6.5

Balance Sheet & Other Fin. Data (Million $)

	1995	1994	1993	1992	1991	1990
Cash	268	108	54.8	30.8	50.1	55.6
Curr. Assets	1,557	1,084	746	770	616	596
Total Assets	3,106	2,202	1,609	1,441	1,203	1,147
Curr. Liab.	946	681	500	589	338	308
LT Debt	681	592	314	114	159	168
Common Eqty.	1,420	874	733	669	683	646
Total Cap.	2,150	1,492	1,063	788	865	840
Cap. Exp.	414	337	243	140	91.0	92.0
Cash Flow	333	212	155	65.0	123	121

Ratio Analysis

	1995	1994	1993	1992	1991	1990
Curr. Ratio	1.6	1.6	1.5	1.3	1.8	1.9
% LT Debt of Cap.	31.7	39.7	29.5	14.4	18.4	20.0
% Net Inc.of Revs.	3.7	2.9	2.2	0.2	2.5	2.8
% Ret. on Assets	8.2	6.9	5.6	0.5	6.1	6.7
% Ret. on Equity	18.9	16.3	12.1	1.0	10.8	12.1

Dividend Data —Dividends were initiated in 1961. A dividend reinvestment plan is available. A "poison pill" stock purchase right was adopted in 1988. A 2-for-1 stock split was effected in March 1994.

Amt. of Div. $	Date Decl.	Ex-Div. Date	Stock of Record	Payment Date
0.045	Sep. 26	Oct. 11	Oct. 17	Oct. 31 '94
0.045	Dec. 12	Jan. 10	Jan. 17	Jan. 31 '95
0.045	Mar. 20	Apr. 07	Apr. 15	Apr. 29 '95
0.045	Jun. 01	Jul. 13	Jul. 17	Jul. 31 '95

Data as orig. reptd.; bef. results of disc. opers. and/or spec. items. Per share data adj. for stk. divs. as of ex-div. date. E-Estimated. NA-Not Available. NM-Not Meaningful. NR-Not Ranked.

Office—State Highway 268 East (P.O. Box 1111), North Wilkesboro, NC 28659 (28656). **Tel**—(910) 651-4000. **Chrmn**—R. L. Strickland. **Pres & CEO**—L. G. Herring. **COO**—R. L. Tillman. **SVP-Secy**—W. C. Warden Jr. **SVP-CFO & Treas**—H. B. Underwood II. **Investor Contacts**—W. Cliff Oxford, Clarrissa S. Felts. **Dirs**—W. A. Andres, J. M. Belk, G. E. Cadwgan, C. A. Farmer, L. G. Herring, P. Kulynych, R. B. Long, C. B. Malone, R. G. Schwartz, R. L. Strickland, R. L. Tillman. **Transfer Agent & Registrar**—Wachovia Bank of North Carolina, Winston-Salem. **Incorporated** in North Carolina in 1952. **Empl**-37,555. **S&P Analyst:** Maureen C. Carini

Luby's Cafeterias

NYSE Symbol **LUB**
In S&P 500

22-SEP-95 | Industry: Food serving | **Summary:** This company owns and operates more than 180 cafeterias, primarily in Texas.

S&P Opinion: Hold (★★★)

Recent Price • 20⅞
52 Wk Range • 24⅝-18½

Yield • 3.4%
12-Mo. P/E • 13.6

Quantitative Evaluations

Outlook
(1 Lowest—5 Highest)
• **1⁻**

Fair Value
• **18⅜**

Risk
• **Low**

Earn./Div. Rank
• **A**

Technical Eval.
• **Bullish** since 5/95

Rel. Strength Rank
(1 Lowest—99 Highest)
• **63**

Insider Activity
• **NA**

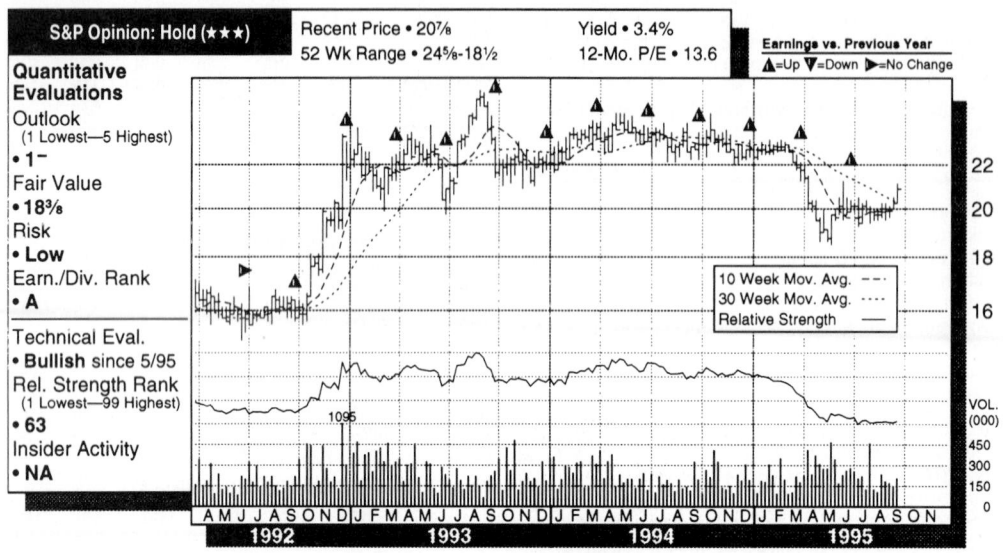

Earnings vs. Previous Year
▲=Up ▼=Down ▶=No Change

10 Week Mov. Avg. — ‑ ‑
30 Week Mov. Avg. · · · ·
Relative Strength —

Overview - 22-SEP-95

Sales growth for LUB in the year ahead is expected to come principally from more cafeterias being open. In fiscal 1996, we look for the opening of 16 to 18 units, and for one cafeteria to close. This would follow the debut of 12 units (including two conversions at former Wyatt's Cafeteria locations) in fiscal 1995. We look for overall sales to be bolstered by menu price increases, which should offset potential weakness at LUB units located near the Mexican border. Also, tighter labor markets are likely to put near-term pressure on LUB's hourly wage costs. However, we estimate that overall fiscal 1996 earnings will be up about 10%. In fiscal 1995, we expect LUB's earnings improvement to be limited by a much larger contribution to a company profit-sharing plan.

Valuation - 22-SEP-95

We view the stock of this cafeteria company as adequately valued, based on the moderate earnings growth we estimate for the year ahead. Also, with LUB having a sizable presence in the Southwest, investors' enthusiasm could be restrained by concerns about economic problems in nearby Mexico. Roughly 20 of LUB's cafeterias are located relatively close to the Mexican border, and weakness in the purchasing power of the Mexican peso could continue to hurt sales at these units. On a more positive note, there have been encouraging results from LUB's limited presence in the competitive Florida market. In general, cafeterias appear relatively well suited to areas where there is a sizable population of older or retired people.

Key Stock Statistics

S&P EPS Est. 1995	1.55	Tang. Bk. Value/Share	8.02
P/E on S&P Est. 1995	13.5	Beta	0.19
S&P EPS Est. 1996	1.70	Shareholders	4,200
Dividend Rate/Share	0.72	Market cap. (B)	$0.495
Shs. outstg. (M)	23.3	Inst. holdings	44%
Avg. daily vol. (M)	0.037	Insider holdings	NA

Value of $10,000 invested 5 years ago: $ 13,700

Fiscal Year Ending Aug. 31

	1995	% Change	1994	% Change	1993	% Change
Revenues (Million $)						
1Q	101.4	8%	94.17	6%	88.60	9%
2Q	100.6	7%	93.72	6%	88.30	7%
3Q	106.9	6%	101.1	7%	94.79	3%
4Q	—	—	101.8	6%	96.07	6%
Yr.	—	—	390.7	6%	367.8	6%
Income (Million $)						
1Q	8.68	NM	8.61	10%	7.85	19%
2Q	8.58	NM	8.58	7%	8.01	11%
3Q	9.91	-5%	10.39	7%	9.71	7%
4Q	—	—	10.20	2%	9.96	2%
Yr.	—	—	37.77	6%	35.53	9%
Earnings Per Share ($)						
1Q	0.35	9%	0.32	10%	0.29	21%
2Q	0.36	9%	0.33	14%	0.29	12%
3Q	0.42	5%	0.40	11%	0.36	9%
4Q	E0.42	5%	0.40	8%	0.37	3%
Yr.	E1.55	7%	1.45	11%	1.31	10%

Next earnings report expected: early October

Luby's Cafeterias

Business Summary - 22-SEP-95

Luby's is one of the largest cafeteria chain companies in the U.S. As of May 1995, LUB was operating 184 cafeterias, including 135 in Texas, 11 in Arizona, nine in Oklahoma, eight in Tennessee, five in Florida, four each in New Mexico and Arkansas, three in Kansas, two each in Missouri and Louisiana, and one Mississippi. In fiscal 1996, LUB is expected to open 14 or 15 cafeterias, following the debut of about 12 in fiscal 1995.

A typical Luby's cafeteria seats 250 to 300 persons and contains 9,000 to 10,500 sq. ft. of floor space. The cafeterias cater primarily to shoppers and office or store personnel for lunch and to families for dinner. In recent years, the estimated cost of constructing, equipping and furnishing a new Luby's cafeteria in a freestanding building under normal conditions (including land acquisition costs) was $2.3 million to $2.6 million. With a new prototype being utilized, the initial investment for a typical new location is about $2.35 million.

Luby's cafeterias are typically open for lunch and dinner, seven days a week. Although there is broad use of certain recipes, menus are not uniform in all outlets on any particular day. They are prepared to reflect local and seasonal food preferences and to take advantage of special food purchasing opportunities. About 30% of LUB's units are in Houston, San Antonio, Dallas or Austin, Tex.

As of May 31, 1995, LUB had cash and equivalents totaling $11.3 million, and $61 million of short-term borrowings. Also, as of late 1994, LUB owned the underlying land and buildings in which 99 of its cafeterias were located; 78 were at leased locations.

Important Developments

Sep. '95—Based on interpretation of monthly data, LUB's comparable unit sales for fiscal 1995's fourth quarter were up about 3%, year to year. Higher tray averages should have more than offset a modest decline in customer counts. We expect that LUB's overall menu prices are up roughly 3.5% from those of the year-ago period. This should help to offset some likely labor cost pressure, and currency-related sales weakness at cafeterias located near the border with Mexico. The value of the peso had declined sharply relative to the U.S. dollar, which hurts the purchasing power of Mexicans visiting the U.S. In fiscal 1995's second quarter, LUB's comparable-unit sales were up 0.5%. This was prior to a June 1995 increase in some menu prices. Also, during fiscal 1995, LUB was a sizable repurchaser of its common stock.

Capitalization

Long Term Debt: None (5/95).

Per Share Data ($)

(Year Ended Aug. 31)

	1994	1993	1992	1991	1990	1989
Tangible Bk. Val.	8.50	8.78	8.01	7.40	6.68	5.95
Cash Flow	2.06	1.87	1.72	1.66	1.59	1.44
Earnings	1.45	1.31	1.19	1.18	1.17	1.08
Dividends	0.60	0.54	0.50	0.46	0.43	0.37
Payout Ratio	41%	41%	42%	39%	36%	35%
Prices - High	24⅝	25⅞	23½	20¾	21¼	18⅞
- Low	21⅝	19¾	14	12	15⅝	15⅜
P/E Ratio - High	17	20	20	18	18	18
- Low	15	15	12	10	13	14

Income Statement Analysis (Million $)

	1994	%Chg	1993	%Chg	1992	%Chg	1991
Revs.	391	6%	368	6%	346	5%	328
Oper. Inc.	74.8	7%	70.1	10%	63.7	6%	60.3
Depr.	15.7	2%	15.4	6%	14.5	12%	13.0
Int. Exp.	0.3	-12%	0.3	NM	0.3	18%	0.3
Pretax Inc.	60.4	7%	56.2	11%	50.5	3%	48.8
Eff. Tax Rate	38%	—	37%	—	36%	—	34%
Net Inc.	37.8	6%	35.5	9%	32.6	NM	32.3

Balance Sheet & Other Fin. Data (Million $)

	1994	1993	1992	1991	1990	1989
Cash	10.9	34.3	12.3	14.2	12.3	15.3
Curr. Assets	18.1	43.8	18.4	21.2	18.4	21.9
Total Assets	290	302	274	261	235	210
Curr. Liab.	56.4	43.3	38.9	40.4	32.5	28.6
LT Debt	Nil	Nil	1.4	1.9	2.3	2.8
Common Eqty.	214	239	217	203	183	163
Total Cap.	230	254	233	218	201	180
Cap. Exp.	26.3	17.8	27.1	28.8	33.7	30.0
Cash Flow	53.5	50.9	47.0	45.3	43.5	39.3

Ratio Analysis

	1994	1993	1992	1991	1990	1989
Curr. Ratio	0.3	1.0	0.5	0.5	0.6	0.8
% LT Debt of Cap.	Nil	Nil	0.6	0.8	1.2	1.6
% Net Inc.of Revs.	9.7	9.7	9.4	9.9	10.3	10.4
% Ret. on Assets	13.3	12.3	12.3	13.0	14.4	14.9
% Ret. on Equity	17.4	15.6	15.6	16.8	18.6	19.2

Dividend Data

—Quarterly dividends have been paid since fiscal 1965 (since March 1973 on the publicly held shares).

Amt. of Div. $	Date Decl.	Ex-Div. Date	Stock of Record	Payment Date
0.165	Jul. 20	Sep. 02	Sep. 09	Sep. 26 '94
0.165	Oct. 10	Dec. 12	Dec. 16	Jan. 03 '95
0.165	Jan. 13	Mar. 06	Mar. 10	Mar. 27 '95
0.165	Mar. 27	Jun. 06	Jun. 09	Jun. 26 '95
0.180	Jul. 26	Sep. 06	Sep. 08	Sep. 25 '95

Data as orig. reptd.; bef. results of disc. opers. and/or spec. items. Per share data adj. for stk. divs. as of ex-div. date.
E-Estimated. NA-Not Available. NM-Not Meaningful. NR-Not Ranked.

Office—2211 Northeast Loop 410, P.O. Box 33069, San Antonio, TX 78265-3069. Tel—(210) 654-9000. Chrmn—J. B. Lahourcade. Pres & CEO—R. Erben. Secy—J. R. Hale. Exec VP & CFO—J. E. Curtis, Jr. Investor Contact—Laura M. Bishop. Dirs—L. F. Cavazos, J. E. Curtis, Jr., D. B. Daviss, R. Erben, R. R. Hemminghaus, J. B. Lahourcade, W. E. Robson, W. J. Salmon, G. H. Wenglein, J. Winik. Transfer Agent & Registrar—American Stock Transfer & Trust Co. Incorporated in Texas in 1959; reincorporated in Delaware in 1991. Empl-10,100. S&P Analyst: Tom Graves, CFA

MBNA Corp.

NYSE Symbol **KRB**
In S&P 500

08-SEP-95

Industry:
Banking

Summary: The nation's second largest lender through bank credit cards and leading issuer of affinity cards, MBNA also provides retail deposit and financial transaction processing services.

| S&P Opinion: Buy (★★★★★) | Recent Price • 35¾ | Yield • 2.4% |
| | 52 Wk Range • 37-21⅛ | 12-Mo. P/E • 17.9 |

Quantitative Evaluations

Outlook
(1 Lowest—5 Highest)
• **5+**

Fair Value
• **47⅝**

Risk
• **Average**

Earn./Div. Rank
• **NR**

Technical Eval.
• **Bullish** since 1/95

Rel. Strength Rank
(1 Lowest—99 Highest)
• **46**

Insider Activity
• **Neutral**

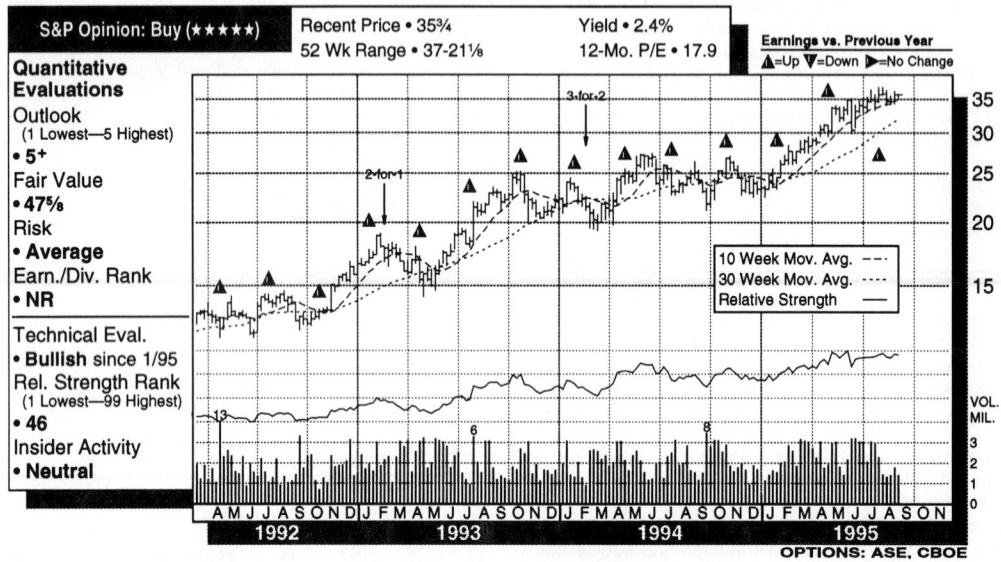

Earnings vs. Previous Year
▲=Up ▼=Down ▶=No Change

10 Week Mov. Avg. ---
30 Week Mov. Avg. ·····
Relative Strength ——

OPTIONS: ASE, CBOE

Overview - 08-SEP-95

Industry trends favoring the growing use of credit cards and a rapidly expanding cardholder base should translate into solid earnings gains into 1996. MBNA's unique marketing strategy includes the targeting of individual membership organizations and developing co-branding relationships with commercial firms. Cardholders are thus encouraged to use the company's credit card over competing cards by showing support for endorsing firms or to receive various economic incentives for using the card. Highlights for 1995's second quarter included a 60% year-to-year jump in managed loans and only a modest rise in the delinquency rate, which nonetheless remains below peer levels. Despite an anticipated slowdown in overall consumer spending, MBNA's superior receivables growth prospects and ability to control credit costs should allow it to generate further strong earnings growth.

Valuation - 08-SEP-95

Despite their substantial rise thus far in 1995, the shares remain attractive, given the company's strong earnings growth potential and expanding market share position. Earnings should continue to be driven by a combination of exceptional credit card receivables growth, aided by successful marketing strategies, good control of credit costs and greater operating efficiency. Trading at only 12 times estimated 1996 earnings, and with earnings gains in excess of 25% expected in each of the next two years, the shares are recommended for purchase.

Key Stock Statistics

S&P EPS Est. 1995	2.30	Tang. Bk. Value/Share	6.42
P/E on S&P Est. 1995	15.5	Beta	NA
S&P EPS Est. 1996	2.90	Shareholders	1,400
Dividend Rate/Share	0.84	Market cap. (B)	$ 5.3
Shs. outstg. (M)	148.5	Inst. holdings	80%
Avg. daily vol. (M)	0.296	Insider holdings	NA

Value of $10,000 invested 5 years ago: NA

Fiscal Year Ending Dec. 31

	1995	% Change	1994	% Change	1993	% Change
Revenues (Million $)						
1Q	536.4	38%	389.7	27%	307.4	5%
2Q	—	—	423.8	24%	340.4	19%
3Q	—	—	492.8	37%	359.3	24%
4Q	—	—	547.5	42%	385.7	27%
Yr.	—	—	1,853	33%	1,393	19%
Income (Million $)						
1Q	68.73	31%	52.34	25%	41.82	17%
2Q	76.83	32%	58.24	26%	46.06	20%
3Q	—	—	73.76	30%	56.64	21%
4Q	—	—	82.26	30%	63.28	22%
Yr.	—	—	266.6	28%	207.8	20%
Earnings Per Share ($)						
1Q	0.46	31%	0.35	25%	0.28	17%
2Q	0.51	31%	0.39	26%	0.31	22%
3Q	E0.64	31%	0.49	29%	0.38	21%
4Q	E0.70	27%	0.55	31%	0.42	21%
Yr.	E2.30	30%	1.77	28%	1.38	20%

Next earnings report expected: mid October

MBNA Corp.

Business Summary - 08-SEP-95

MBNA Corp. is a bank holding company that was formed in December 1990 to conduct the credit card business formerly conducted by a subsidiary of MNC Financial, Inc. KRB conducts the credit card business through its MBNA America Bank N.A. subsidiary.

The company is one of the world's largest lenders through bank credit cards, and is the leading issuer of affinity credit cards, marketed primarily through endorsements of membership associations and financial institutions. At December 31, 1994, the company's credit cards were endorsed by 3,700 organizations. Credit cards issued to affinity group members often carry custom graphics and the name and logo of the endorsing group.

MBNA offers two general types of credit cards--premium (gold) and standard--issued under either the MasterCard or Visa name. The premium card is marketed to members of endorsing organizations, customers of endorsing financial institutions, and to MBNA's qualifying standard card customers. Premium card usage and average account balances are usually higher than those of standard card customers. The company uses the standard card for new customer acquisition and future premium account development.

In addition to its credit card products, the company accepts deposits, primarily money market deposits and certificates of deposit, and offers individual loans, principally unsecured lines of credit that can be accessed by check, and home equity loans. It also provides card processing and financial transaction processing services. In 1993, MBNA chartered a bank in the United Kingdom to enter new European markets. As of December 31, 1994, the company had $6.6 billion in deposits, compared with $5.2 billion a year earlier.

Total managed loans at December 31, 1994, amounted to $18.74 billion, a 52% increase over year-end 1993. During 1994, the company added 4.5 million new accounts (5.6 million new customers). Delinquency on total managed loans was 3.03%, and net credit losses on average managed loans outstanding for the year ended December 31, 1994, were 2.59%.

Important Developments

Jul. '95—At June 30, 1995, total managed loans were $22.7 billion (including $15.5 billion in securitized loans), up from $14.2 billion ($8.8 billion) a year earlier. A record 4.1 million new cardholders (3.3 million new accounts) were added in the first half of 1995. Delinquency on total managed loans rose to 3.23% at June 30, 1995, from 3.15% a year earlier, while net chargeoffs for the first half were 1.78%, versus 2.15% in the year-earlier period.

Capitalization

Long Term Debt: $1,787,000,000 (3/95).

Per Share Data ($)

(Year Ended Dec. 31)

	1994	1993	1992	1991	1990	1989
Tangible Bk. Val.	5.85	4.79	4.09	3.71	NA	NA
Earnings	1.77	1.38	1.15	1.00	0.87	0.70
Dividends	0.72	0.64	0.59	0.53	NA	NA
Payout Ratio	41%	46%	51%	53%	NA	NA
Prices - High	27⅜	25¼	16¾	13½	NA	NA
- Low	19¼	14¼	11⅞	7⅝	NA	NA
P/E Ratio - High	15	18	14	14	NA	NA
- Low	11	10	10	8	NA	NA

Income Statement Analysis (Million $)

	1994	%Chg	1993	%Chg	1992	%Chg	1991
Net Int. Inc.	532	12%	474	32%	358	49%	240
Tax Equiv. Adj.	1.6	NM	1.6	11%	1.5	17%	1.3
Non Int. Inc.	1,014	37%	740	28%	577	7%	540
Loan Loss Prov.	108	10%	99	1%	97.5	12%	86.7
% Exp/Op Revs.	64%	—	64%	—	60%	—	59%
Pretax Inc.	441	132%	190	-30%	272	16%	235
Eff. Tax Rate	40%	—	NM	—	37%	—	36%
Net Inc.	267	28%	208	20%	173	16%	149
% Net Int. Marg.	7.61%	—	8.76%	—	7.20%	—	5.20%

Balance Sheet & Other Fin. Data (Million $)

	1994	1993	1992	1991	1990	1989
Earning Assets:						
Money Mkt.	268	31.0	81.0	475	439	50.0
Inv. Securities	2,002	1,409	1,265	1,293	102	102
Com'l Loans	Nil	Nil	Nil	Nil	Nil	Nil
Other Loans	5,707	3,726	3,979	3,486	3,240	2,261
Total Assets	9,672	7,320	6,455	6,009	4,580	2,859
Demand Deposits	101	71.0	70.0	65.0	87.0	126
Time Deposits	6,531	5,171	4,498	5,029	4,115	1,617
LT Debt	1,564	780	471	Nil	0.6	27.4
Common Eqty.	920	769	661	592	219	262

Ratio Analysis

	1994	1993	1992	1991	1990	1989
% Ret. on Assets	3.2	3.2	3.0	2.8	3.9	4.1
% Ret. on Equity	32.7	30.0	28.6	37.0	49.0	37.2
% Loan Loss Resv.	1.8	2.6	2.5	2.8	3.0	3.6
% Loans/Deposits	86.1	71.1	87.1	68.4	77.1	129.7
% Equity to Assets	9.7	10.5	10.4	7.6	7.9	11.1

Dividend Data —Dividends were initiated in 1991.

Amt. of Div. $	Date Decl.	Ex-Div. Date	Stock of Record	Payment Date
0.180	Jul. 13	Sep. 12	Sep. 16	Oct. 01 '94
0.180	Oct. 11	Dec. 12	Dec. 16	Jan. 01 '95
0.210	Jan. 17	Mar. 13	Mar. 18	Apr. 01 '95
0.210	Apr. 13	Jun. 14	Jun. 16	Jul. 01 '95
0.210	Jul. 13	Sep. 13	Sep. 15	Oct. 01 '95

Data as orig. reptd.; bef. results of disc opers. and/or spec. items. Per share data adj. for stk. divs. as of ex-div. date. E-Estimated. NA-Not Available. NM-Not Meaningful. NR-Not Ranked.

Office—400 Christiana Rd., Newark, DE 19713. **Tel**—(800) 441-7048; (302) 453-9930. **Chrmn & CEO**—A. Lerner. **Pres**—C. M. Cawley. **EVP-CFO & Treas**—M. S. Kaufman. **EVP-Secy**—J. W. Scheflen. **Sr EVP-Investor Contact**—David W. Spartin (800-362-6255; 302-456-8588). **Dirs**—J. H. Berick, C. M. Cawley, B. R. Civiletti, A. Lerner, R. D. Lerner, S. L. Markowitz, M. Rosenthal. **Transfer Agent & Registrar**—National City Bank, Cleveland. **Incorporated** in Maryland in 1990. **Empl**-9,000. **S&P Analyst:** Stephen R. Biggar

MCI Communications

NASDAQ Symbol **MCIC**

In S&P 500

11-SEP-95

Industry:
Telecommunications

Summary: The second largest U.S. long-distance telephone carrier, MCI has a strategic plan that includes profitably growing its core business, expanding globally and entering new markets.

S&P Opinion: Accumulate (★★★★)

Recent Price • 23⅞	Yield • 0.2%
52 Wk Range • 28⅜-17¼	12-Mo. P/E • 18.0

Quantitative Evaluations

Outlook
(1 Lowest—5 Highest)
• **5⁻**

Fair Value
• **32½**

Risk
• **Average**

Earn./Div. Rank
• **B**

Technical Eval.
• **Bearish** since 7/95

Rel. Strength Rank
(1 Lowest—99 Highest)
• **57**

Insider Activity
• **Neutral**

Earnings vs. Previous Year
▲=Up ▼=Down ▶=No Change

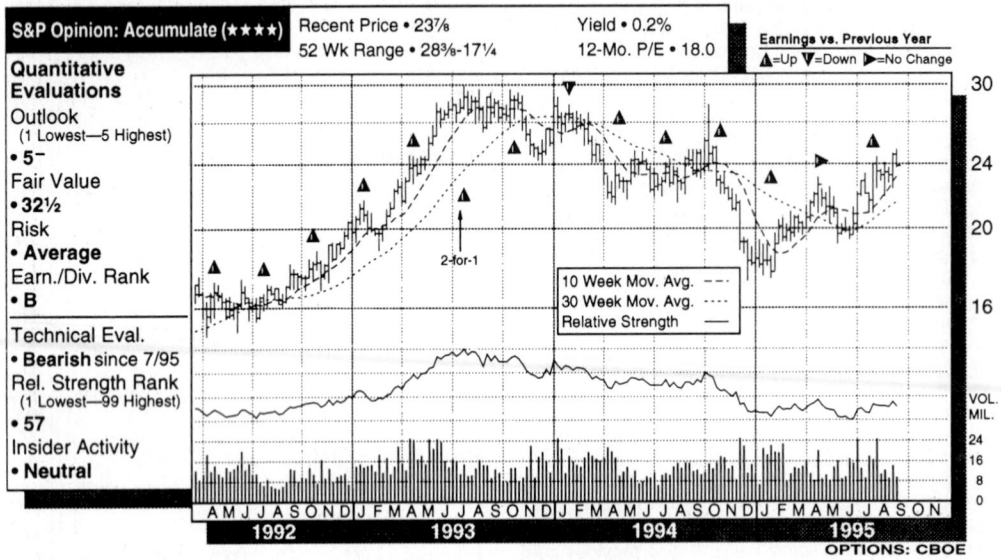

10 Week Mov. Avg. ---
30 Week Mov. Avg. ·····
Relative Strength —

2-for-1

VOL. MIL.

OPTIONS: CBOE

Overview - 08-SEP-95

With long-distance marketshare at nearly 20% and competition fierce, calling volume growth rates will slow. However, aided by more stable average prices and better control of access charges, margins should continue to expand. The alliance with British Telecom (BT) gives MCI a leading edge in the growing market serving multinational corporations while BT's cash infusion will fund expansion into new markets. Entry into local markets and plans to resell wireless services will expand the range of MCI's services while also giving it better control of its cost base. The investment in News Corp. will further broaden the company's product offerings. We believe MCI's strategy will yield continued earnings growth despite the prospect of increased competition within its core market; however, 1995 EPS growth will be limited by the additional shares issued in the BT transaction.

Valuation - 08-SEP-95

The shares have climbed 30% in 1995, compared to 25% for the S&P 500. A planned restructuring will make this efficient company even stronger. MCI will cut 3,000 employees, resulting in a pretax charge of between $600 million and $800 million in the third quarter. Our 1995 estimate of $1.55 excludes the charge. The company will also consolidate its core communications business into one unit, while its ventures and alliances will be placed in a separate unit. The leaner cost base and entry into new markets make the shares attractive for capital appreciation.

Key Stock Statistics

S&P EPS Est. 1995	1.55	Tang. Bk. Value/Share	12.30
P/E on S&P Est. 1995	15.4	Beta	0.89
S&P EPS Est. 1996	1.73	Shareholders	52,300
Dividend Rate/Share	0.05	Market cap. (B)	$ 16.2
Shs. outstg. (M)	677.8	Inst. holdings	56%
Avg. daily vol. (M)	2.270	Insider holdings	NA

Value of $10,000 invested 5 years ago: $ 11,031

Fiscal Year Ending Dec. 31

	1995	% Change	1994	% Change	1993	% Change
Revenues (Million $)						
1Q	3,561	11%	3,221	15%	2,810	12%
2Q	3,706	12%	3,309	13%	2,929	12%
3Q	—	—	3,407	12%	3,054	14%
4Q	—	—	3,400	9%	3,128	13%
Yr.	—	—	13,338	12%	11,921	13%
Income (Million $)						
1Q	244.0	17%	209.0	24%	168.0	19%
2Q	260.0	21%	215.0	21%	178.0	19%
3Q	—	—	220.0	26%	174.0	9%
4Q	—	—	151.0	41%	107.0	-33%
Yr.	—	—	795.0	27%	627.0	3%
Earnings Per Share ($)						
1Q	0.36	NM	0.36	16%	0.31	22%
2Q	0.38	3%	0.37	16%	0.32	21%
3Q	E0.40	5%	0.38	27%	0.30	3%
4Q	E0.41	86%	0.22	22%	0.18	-40%
Yr.	E1.55	17%	1.32	18%	1.12	1%

Next earnings report expected: mid October

Business Summary - 29-AUG-95

MCI Communications is the second largest carrier (after AT&T) of long-distance voice and data communication services in the U.S. The company also provides international telephone service to virtually all countries and territories worldwide.

MCI has laid out a series of initiatives under which it intends to leverage its existing strengths to profitably grow its core business, expand internationally and explore new market opportunities. The initial step of the plan is accelerated deployment of advanced technologies to upgrade MCI's network. MCI also plans to spend $2 billion over the next five years to enter the local telephone market.

The company is expanding globally through a series of strategic alliances led by its alliance with British Telecom. During 1992, MCI formed an alliance with Stentor, a group of major Canadian telephone companies, to build the first fully integrated international network to link the U.S. and Canada. In early 1994, MCI announced a joint venture with 45%-owned Grupo Financiero Banamex-Accival (Banacci), to provide long-distance services when the Mexican long-distance market is opened to competition in 1996.

In September 1994, British Telecommunications (BT) purchased 108.5 million Class A common shares for $3.5B and converted its preferred stake (purchased for $830 million in June 1993) into 27.5 million Class A shares. Following the purchase and conversion, BT holds a 20% voting stake in the company. Under its purchase agreement, BT may name three directors, is prohibited from raising its stake for 10 years, and must hold its common shares for at least four years. MCI will remain operationally independent. The companies plan to invest over $1 billion in a new joint venture, Concert, to provide advanced communications services to multinational corporations worldwide. Concert is 75%-owned by BT but the venture will be operated as an equal partnership.

Important Developments

Aug. '95—The company will resell cellular service from AT&T's McCaw unit, GTE, BellSouth, Frontier Corp. and NewPar, a joint venture of AirTouch Communications and Cellular Communications Inc.
May '95—MCI agreed to invest up to $2 billion in News Corp. over the next four years. The companies plan a global joint venture to create and distribute electronic information, education and entertainment to businesses and consumers. Separately, MCI agreed to acquire cellular reseller Nationwide Cellular Service for about $190 million.

Capitalization

Long Term Debt: $2,936,000,000 (3/95).
Class A Common Stock: 135,998,930 shs. ($0.10 par).
All held by British Telecom, constituting 20% of voting rights.
Com. Stock: 543,724,065 shs. ($0.10 par).

Per Share Data ($) (Year Ended Dec. 31)

	1994	1993	1992	1991	1990	1989
Tangible Bk. Val.	13.24	8.71	5.99	4.94	3.82	3.19
Cash Flow	3.26	2.81	2.69	2.44	1.98	2.43
Earnings	1.32	1.12	1.11	1.01	0.53	1.13
Dividends	0.05	0.05	0.05	0.05	0.05	Nil
Payout Ratio	4%	4%	4%	5%	9%	Nil
Prices - High	29	29⅞	20½	16	22½	24¼
- Low	17¼	18¾	14¾	9	9¼	10⅞
P/E Ratio - High	22	27	18	16	42	21
- Low	13	17	13	9	17	10

Income Statement Analysis (Million $)

	1994	%Chg	1993	%Chg	1992	%Chg	1991
Revs.	13,338	12%	11,921	13%	10,562	25%	8,433
Oper. Inc.	2,780	17%	2,370	13%	2,101	14%	1,837
Depr.	1,176	24%	952	13%	843	13%	746
Int. Exp.	231	-3%	239	-11%	270	NM	270
Pretax Inc.	1,280	22%	1,045	9%	963	14%	848
Eff. Tax Rate	38%	—	40%	—	37%	—	35%
Net Inc.	795	27%	627	3%	609	11%	551

Balance Sheet & Other Fin. Data (Million $)

	1994	1993	1992	1991	1990	1989
Cash	2,268	165	232	51.0	231	197
Curr. Assets	4,888	2,601	2,181	1,758	1,811	1,421
Total Assets	16,366	11,276	9,678	8,834	8,249	6,338
Curr. Liab.	3,137	3,201	2,464	2,300	2,422	1,717
LT Debt	2,997	2,366	3,432	3,104	3,147	2,241
Common Eqty.	9,004	4,712	3,150	2,559	1,940	1,595
Total Cap.	13,193	8,006	7,140	6,408	5,647	4,476
Cap. Exp.	2,897	2,190	1,371	1,381	1,274	1,052
Cash Flow	1,970	1,578	1,432	1,268	1,013	1,229

Ratio Analysis

	1994	1993	1992	1991	1990	1989
Curr. Ratio	1.6	0.8	0.9	0.8	0.7	0.8
% LT Debt of Cap.	22.7	29.6	48.1	48.4	55.7	50.1
% Net Inc.of Revs.	6.0	5.3	5.8	6.5	3.9	9.3
% Ret. on Assets	5.2	5.9	6.5	6.4	4.1	9.8
% Ret. on Equity	10.6	15.7	20.5	23.0	15.2	44.5

Dividend Data

—Cash dividends are paid semi-annually. A "poison pill" stock purchase rights plan was adopted in September 1994.

Amt. of Div. $	Date Decl.	Ex-Div. Date	Stock of Record	Payment Date
0.025	Nov. 03	Nov. 14	Nov. 18	Dec. 09 '94
0.025	May. 10	May. 26	Jun. 02	Jun. 23 '95

Data as orig. reptd.; bef. results of disc. opers. and/or spec. items. Per share data adj. for stk. divs. as of ex-div. date.
E-Estimated. NA-Not Available. NM-Not Meaningful. NR-Not Ranked.

Offices—1801 Pennsylvania Ave. NW, Washington, DC 20006. **Tel**—(202) 872-1600. **Chrmn & CEO**—B. C. Roberts, Jr. **Pres & COO**—G. H. Taylor. **CFO**—D. L. Maine. **Secy**—C. Bolton-Smith, Jr. **Investor Contact**—Mike Kraft. **Dirs**—C. L. Alexander, Jr., J. Areen, M. H. Bader, M. L. Hepher, R. M. Jones, G. S. Macklin, A. T. Mockett, B. C. Roberts, Jr., R. B. Sayford, G. H. Taylor, J. Whittaker, J. R. Worthington. **Transfer Agent & Registrar**—Mellon Securities Trust Co., NYC. **Incorporated** in Del. in 1968. **Empl**-40,667. **S&P Analyst:** Kevin J. Gooley

Mallinckrodt Group

NYSE Symbol **MKG**
In S&P 500

17-OCT-95

Industry:
Medical equipment/
supply

Summary: This company (formerly IMCERA Group, Inc.) is a major producer of medical products, specialty chemicals, and animal health and nutrition products.

| S&P Opinion: Hold (★★★) | Recent Price • 38⅞ | Yield • 1.4% | Earnings vs. Previous Year |
| | 52 Wk Range • 41⅞-29 | 12-Mo. P/E • 16.8 | ▲=Up ▼=Down ▶=No Change |

Quantitative Evaluations

Outlook
 (1 Lowest—5 Highest)
• **4+**

Fair Value
• **40%**

Risk
• **Low**

Earn./Div. Rank
• **B**

Technical Eval.
• **Bearish** since 9/95

Rel. Strength Rank
 (1 Lowest—99 Highest)
• **54**

Insider Activity
• **Neutral**

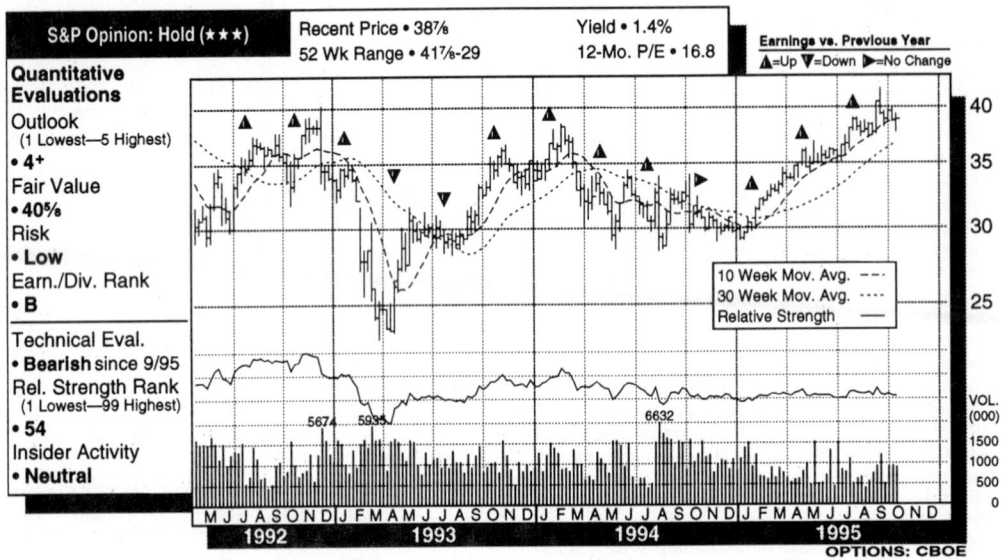

10 Week Mov. Avg. — ‑ ‑
30 Week Mov. Avg. ‑ ‑ ‑ ‑
Relative Strength ——

5674   5935   6632

VOL.
(000)
1500
1000
500

1992   1993   1994   1995

OPTIONS: CBOE

Overview - 13-OCT-95

We are projecting that operating earnings will rise strongly in all three segments in fiscal 1996. Chemicals profits will climb on the expected positive contribution by J.T. Baker (acquired in February 1995), and on further strong gains for the flavors venture. The medical business should also advance on continued growth of newer products and the full year benefits of a restructuring and cost reduction program implemented in mid-1994, offsetting increased price competition for imaging products. The veterinary unit will benefit from modest sales growth resulting from new product introductions; the animal feed ingredients business will be helped by two price increases announced since early 1995. A stock repurchase program will also boost EPS comparisons.

Valuation - 13-OCT-95

MKG's stock has been an average market performer this year, rising about 28% year to date. The shares have been boosted by a more favorable environment for the health care industry, as well as the company's earnings growth prospects of about 15% per year. However, the shares remain well below their all-time high reached in early 1992. We recommend holding the shares, currently selling at about 14 times estimated fiscal 1996 EPS, in view of the company's promising longer term prospects.

Key Stock Statistics

S&P EPS Est. 1996	2.70	Tang. Bk. Value/Share	8.23
P/E on S&P Est. 1996	14.4	Beta	1.70
Dividend Rate/Share	0.56	Shareholders	10,100
Shs. outstg. (M)	76.8	Market cap. (B)	$ 3.0
Avg. daily vol. (M)	0.154	Inst. holdings	76%
		Insider holdings	NA

Value of $10,000 invested 5 years ago: $ 24,108

Fiscal Year Ending Jun. 30

	1995	% Change	1994	% Change	1993	% Change
Revenues (Million $)						
1Q	487.7	10%	444.9	7%	417.0	9%
2Q	516.3	11%	466.3	6%	441.0	5%
3Q	569.1	17%	486.7	11%	439.9	1%
4Q	639.0	18%	542.2	9%	498.4	6%
Yr.	2,212	14%	1,940	8%	1,796	5%
Income (Million $)						
1Q	34.70	-2%	35.30	28%	27.60	NM
2Q	40.60	11%	36.70	31%	28.00	8%
3Q	48.10	12%	42.90	40%	30.60	-6%
4Q	60.70	NM	-7.50	NM	-199.9	NM
Yr.	184.1	71%	107.4	NM	-113.8	NM
Earnings Per Share ($)						
1Q	0.45	NM	0.45	25%	0.36	3%
2Q	0.52	11%	0.47	31%	0.36	9%
3Q	0.62	13%	0.55	41%	0.39	-7%
4Q	0.78	NM	-0.10	NM	-2.59	NM
Yr.	2.37	72%	1.38	NM	-1.48	NM

Next earnings report expected: mid October

Mallinckrodt Group

Business Summary - 13-OCT-95

Mallinckrodt Group (formerly IMCERA Group, following a name change from International Minerals & Chemical) has interests in medical products, specialty chemicals, and animal health and nutrition products. Contributions by product segment in fiscal 1995 were:

	Sales	Profits
Mallinckrodt Medical	46%	64%
Mallinckrodt Chemicals	26%	19%
Mallinckrodt Veterinary	28%	17%

Foreign operations accounted for 37% of sales and 43% of profits in fiscal 1995.

Medical products include X-ray contrast and ultrasound media (Optiray, Hexabrix, Ultraject, Albunex), catheters and interventional products, radiopharmaceuticals (Technescan, OctreoScan), and temperature, blood gas and vital sign monitoring systems and products (Mon-A-Therm, GEM-STAT, HemoCue, tracheal tubes).

Specialty chemicals include analgesics (APAP) and medicinal narcotics, peptides, catalysts, specialty inorganics, stearates (processing aids), and laboratory chemicals; and the 50%-owned Tastemaker flavors venture (equity income was $25.3 million in fiscal 1995).

Veterinary products include mineral feed ingredients, growth promotants (Ralgro, Clinacox), biologicals, antimicrobials, parasiticides, anesthetics, prostaglandins, and surgical products for livestock, poultry and companion animals.

In July 1991, MKG completed the sale of its 38% interest in IMC Fertilizer Group Inc.

Important Developments

Sep. '95—MKG said that it planned to repurchase up to $250 million of its common stock over the next five years. Separately, the company agreed to acquire Syntro Corp., a biotechnology company focused on the development of innovative vaccines for the animal health market, for about $40.4 million.

Aug. '95—MKG said that the February, 1995 acquisition of J.T. Baker for $100 million resulted in modest earnings dilution in fiscal 1995. J.T. Baker, a manufacturer of laboratory, process and microelectronic chemicals with annual sales of $140 million, nearly doubled the size of the company's process and laboratory chemicals business. MKG said that the restructuring of the medical business was on track, including a workforce reduction of 600 positions. Annual cost savings of $40 million are anticipated in the medical unit, with most savings to be achieved in fiscal 1996.

Capitalization

Long Term Debt: $501,500,000 (6/95).

4% Cum. Preferred Stock: 98,330 shs. ($100 par).

Per Share Data ($)

(Year Ended Jun. 30)

	1995	1994	1993	1992	1991	1990
Tangible Bk. Val.	15.12	6.93	5.84	16.02	14.28	11.97
Cash Flow	3.99	2.73	-0.23	2.80	2.32	1.79
Earnings	2.37	1.38	-1.48	1.65	1.37	0.84
Dividends	0.67	0.49	0.43	0.38	0.33	0.33
Payout Ratio	28%	35%	NM	23%	26%	41%
Prices - High	39	38½	36⅝	46⅝	43⅜	25
- Low	29⅛	28⅜	23	28⅞	22⅜	16
P/E Ratio - High	16	28	NM	28	32	30
- Low	12	21	NM	18	16	19

Income Statement Analysis (Million $)

	1995	%Chg	1994	%Chg	1993	%Chg	1992
Revs.	2,212	14%	1,940	8%	1,796	5%	1,703
Oper. Inc.	447	15%	390	24%	315	3%	306
Depr.	125	19%	105	9%	96.0	8%	89.0
Int. Exp.	57.0	43%	39.8	-9%	43.6	10%	39.6
Pretax Inc.	295	73%	171	NM	-132	NM	203
Eff. Tax Rate	38%	—	37%	—	NM	—	37%
Net Inc.	184	72%	107	NM	-113	NM	129

Balance Sheet & Other Fin. Data (Million $)

	1995	1994	1993	1992	1991	1990
Cash	62.0	88.0	51.0	68.0	362	132
Curr. Assets	1,020	932	837	804	1,132	725
Total Assets	2,721	2,434	2,178	2,051	2,250	2,131
Curr. Liab.	748	671	633	452	723	414
LT Debt	502	522	428	264	328	754
Common Eqty.	1,161	1,005	900	1,213	1,074	815
Total Cap.	1,750	1,575	1,364	1,530	1,460	1,632
Cap. Exp.	161	172	188	150	123	173
Cash Flow	309	212	-18.0	218	164	117

Ratio Analysis

	1995	1994	1993	1992	1991	1990
Curr. Ratio	1.4	1.4	1.3	1.8	1.6	1.8
% LT Debt of Cap.	28.7	33.1	31.4	17.3	22.4	46.2
% Net Inc.of Revs.	8.3	5.5	NM	7.6	5.9	4.1
% Ret. on Assets	7.2	4.5	NM	6.0	4.2	2.7
% Ret. on Equity	17.0	11.2	NM	11.2	9.8	6.9

Dividend Data—Dividends were resumed in 1971. A dividend reinvestment plan is available. A "poison pill" stock purchase rights plan was adopted in 1986.

Amt. of Div. $	Date Decl.	Ex-Div. Date	Stock of Record	Payment Date
0.140	Oct. 21	Dec. 12	Dec. 16	Dec. 31 '94
0.140	Feb. 16	Mar. 13	Mar. 17	Mar. 31 '95
0.140	Apr. 24	Jun. 14	Jun. 16	Jun. 30 '95
0.140	Aug. 18	Sep. 13	Sep. 15	Sep. 29 '95

Data as orig. reptd.; bef. results of disc. opers. and/or spec. items. Per share data adj. for stk. divs. as of ex-div. date. Bk. val. figs. in Per Share Data tbl. incl. intangibles in 1992, 1991, 1990, 1989. E-Estimated. NA-Not Available. NM-Not Meaningful. NR-Not Ranked.

Office—7733 Forsyth Blvd., St. Louis, MO 63105-1820. **Tel**—(314) 854-5200. **Chrmn, Pres & CEO**—C. R. Holman. **VP & Secy**—R. A. Keller. **SVP & CFO**—M. A. Rocca. **Investor Contact**—Coleman N. Lannum. **Dirs**—R. F. Bentele, W. L. Davis, R. G. Evens, A. Flamm, C. R. Holman, R. S. Karmel, C. B. Malone, M. Moskin, H. M. Pinet, B. M. Rushton, D. R. Toll, A. Viscusi. **Transfer Agent & Registrar**—First Chicago Trust Co. of New York, Jersey City, NJ. **Incorporated** in New York in 1909. **Empl**-10,300. **S&P Analyst:** Philip J. Birbara

Manor Care

NYSE Symbol **MNR**
In S&P 500

18-SEP-95

Industry:
Health Care Centers

Summary: Manor Care primarily operates nursing home facilities in 28 states. It also owns, operates and franchises hotels and has an 82% stake in an operator of institutional pharmacies.

S&P Opinion: Accumulate (★★★★)	Recent Price • 34⅞	Yield • 0.3%
	52 Wk Range • 35⅝-25¼	12-Mo. P/E • 23.1

Quantitative Evaluations

Outlook
(1 Lowest—5 Highest)
• **3+**

Fair Value
• **33¼**

Risk
• **Low**

Earn./Div. Rank
• **A-**

Technical Eval.
• **Bullish** since 10/93

Rel. Strength Rank
(1 Lowest—99 Highest)
• **73**

Insider Activity
• **NA**

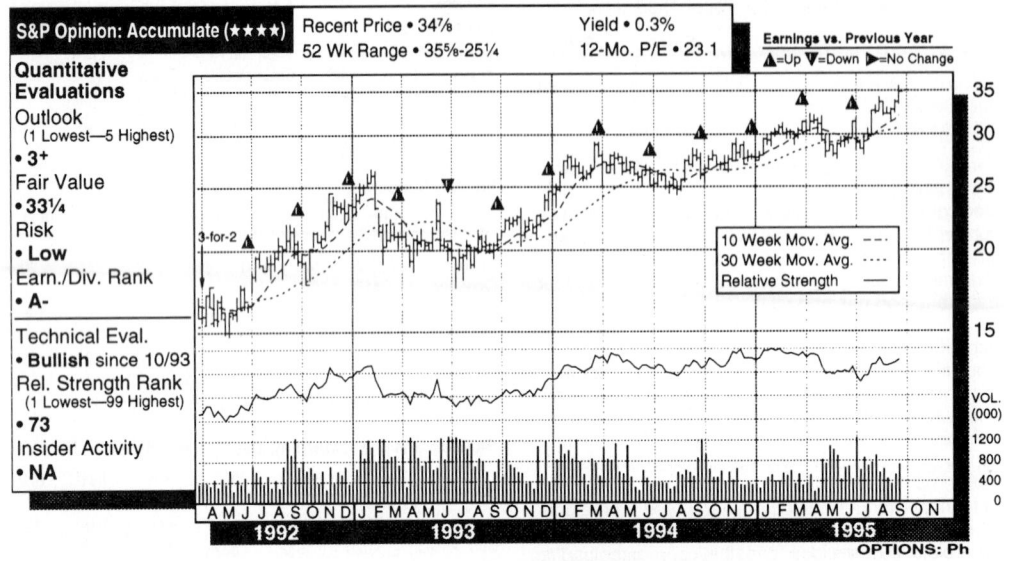

Earnings vs. Previous Year
▲=Up ▼=Down ▶=No Change

10 Week Mov. Avg. — - —
30 Week Mov. Avg. ·····
Relative Strength ——

OPTIONS: Ph

Overview - 15-SEP-95

Revenues in fiscal 1995 rose strongly, reflecting continued gains in both the healthcare and lodging operations. The revenue advance, coupled with well-contained operating costs and a lower tax rate, generated a 21% net earnings increase (per-share profits rose 17%). Aided by a restructuring implemented during fiscal 1995, Manor can now focus its efforts on emerging, higher-margined areas in the health care marketplace such as subacute care, assisted living, home care, institutional pharmacy and rehabilitation therapy. When combined with strong fundamentals in the nursing home business, we anticipate another year of strong earnings gains in fiscal 1996, with share profits expected to rise 16%-20%.

Valuation - 13-SEP-95

Based on our $1.75 EPS estimate for fiscal 1996 (May), MNR should outperform its health care peers over the next six to twelve months. The stock has typically traded at a premium to the market multiple, due to its long track record of above-average profit gains. As such, we believe the shares continue to represent a good investment for those seeking to participate in the long term healthcare segment. In addition, the alliance with In Home Health confirms our belief that the company will pursue a strategy of expanding its presence in fast-growing, higher-margined businesses such as home health care, where it can leverage its medical resources to provide services such as skilled nursing, hospice, infusion therapy and rehabilitation.

Key Stock Statistics

S&P EPS Est. 1996	1.75	Tang. Bk. Value/Share	9.01
P/E on S&P Est. 1996	19.9	Beta	0.90
Dividend Rate/Share	0.09	Shareholders	3,100
Shs. outstg. (M)	62.4	Market cap. (B)	$ 2.2
Avg. daily vol. (M)	0.113	Inst. holdings	54%
		Insider holdings	NA

Value of $10,000 invested 5 years ago: $ 32,026

Fiscal Year Ending May 31

	1995	% Change	1994	% Change	1993	% Change
Revenues (Million $)						
1Q	321.4	13%	284.6	16%	245.0	9%
2Q	324.3	14%	284.6	12%	254.0	12%
3Q	322.1	13%	284.1	16%	244.9	10%
4Q	354.3	14%	309.8	17%	265.6	10%
Yr.	1,322	14%	1,163	15%	1,010	10%
Income (Million $)						
1Q	24.36	23%	19.76	—	—	—
2Q	25.01	24%	20.24	17%	17.28	41%
3Q	18.74	20%	15.65	32%	11.85	29%
4Q	26.38	16%	22.71	31%	17.30	-50%
Yr.	94.49	21%	78.36	26%	62.38	-6%
Earnings Per Share ($)						
1Q	0.39	15%	0.34	21%	0.28	56%
2Q	0.40	18%	0.34	13%	0.30	43%
3Q	0.30	20%	0.25	19%	0.21	31%
4Q	0.42	17%	0.36	20%	0.30	-50%
Yr.	1.51	17%	1.29	18%	1.09	-6%

Next earnings report expected: late September

Business Summary - 15-SEP-95

Manor Care is a holding company whose subsidiaries include Manor Healthcare Corp., one of the largest U.S. nursing home operators, Choice Hotels International, the world's largest franchise motel chain and majority-owned Vitalink Pharmacy Services Inc., an operator of institutional pharmacies. Contributions by business segment in 1994-5 were:

	Revs.	Profits
Health care	77%	74%
Lodging	23%	26%

Manor Care owns, operates or manages 179 nursing centers (including 18 medical and physical rehabilitation centers) which provide high acuity services, skilled nursing care, intermediate nursing care, custodial care and assisted living, primarily for residents over the age of 65. Manor Care and its subsidiaries also own and operate a 172-bed acute care hospital in Mesquite, Texas. In addition, MNR has an 82.3% stake in Vitalink Pharmacy Services Inc., a publicly-traded company that owns and operates 18 institutional pharmacies in 13 states.

Manor's nursing centers range in bed capacity from 52 to 240 beds, have an aggregate bed capacity of 23,830 beds, and achieved an average occupancy rate of 90% in 1994-5. Private pay patients accounted for 53% of nursing home occupancy and 61% of nursing home revenues in 1994-5; Medicaid patients for 36% and 23%, respectively; and Medicare patients for 11% and 16%.

Through the lodging division, Manor franchises approximately 3,400 hotels (open or under development) containing more than 287,000 guest rooms. Facilities, operating under the Quality, Comfort, Clarion, Sleep, Rodeway, Econo Lodge and Friendship Inns names, are primarily in the U.S. but also in more than 30 other countries worldwide.

Important Developments

Sep. '95—MNR agreed to buy six retirement projects located in Florida, Ohio, Illinois, Indiana and California, from Beverly Enterprises. Terms were not disclosed. **May '95**—Manor agreed to form an alliance with In Home Health Inc., a leading provider of home health care services (skilled nursing, infusion therapy, hospice, rehabilitation and personal care). Under the agreement, In Home will conduct a self-tender offer for 6.4 milion of its common shares (about 40% of those outstanding) and Manor will buy voting convertible stock for $20 million. Manor will also receive three-year warrants to buy another 6.0 million In Home common shares.

Capitalization

Long Term Debt: $367,300,000 (5/95).

Per Share Data ($)

(Year Ended May 31)

	1995	1994	1993	1992	1991	1990
Tangible Bk. Val.	9.01	7.52	5.13	4.09	3.03	3.83
Cash Flow	2.73	2.39	2.15	2.16	1.45	1.22
Earnings	1.51	1.29	1.09	1.16	0.56	0.46
Dividends	0.11	0.09	0.09	0.09	0.09	0.09
Payout Ratio	7%	7%	8%	8%	16%	19%
Cal. Yrs.	1994	1993	1992	1991	1990	1989
Prices - High	29⅝	26⅝	24½	19	11⅞	11⅜
- Low	23¼	17½	14½	10⅜	6⅞	8¼
P/E Ratio - High	20	21	22	16	21	25
- Low	15	14	13	9	12	18

Income Statement Analysis (Million $)

	1995	%Chg	1994	%Chg	1993	%Chg	1992
Revs.	1,322	14%	1,163	15%	1,010	10%	916
Oper. Inc.	260	16%	224	15%	195	11%	175
Depr.	76.2	15%	66.5	9%	61.0	7%	57.0
Int. Exp.	29.0	-9%	32.0	-19%	39.7	-12%	44.9
Pretax Inc.	164	20%	137	36%	101	-6%	107
Eff. Tax Rate	40%	—	43%	—	38%	—	38%
Net Inc.	94.5	21%	78.4	26%	62.4	-6%	66.6

Balance Sheet & Other Fin. Data (Million $)

	1995	1994	1993	1992	1991	1990
Cash	75.1	60.5	80.8	83.1	30.3	46.7
Curr. Assets	230	183	194	182	131	148
Total Assets	1,416	1,187	1,107	1,015	944	868
Curr. Liab.	201	166	180	172	119	122
LT Debt	367	277	380	374	456	419
Common Eqty.	625	534	362	305	245	222
Total Cap.	1,215	949	868	792	795	718
Cap. Exp.	119	91.0	90.0	63.0	64.0	81.0
Cash Flow	171	145	123	124	83.0	70.0

Ratio Analysis

	1995	1994	1993	1992	1991	1990
Curr. Ratio	1.1	1.1	1.1	1.1	1.1	1.2
% LT Debt of Cap.	30.3	29.2	43.8	47.2	57.4	58.3
% Net Inc.of Revs.	7.2	6.7	6.2	7.3	3.9	3.8
% Ret. on Assets	7.3	6.6	5.9	6.8	3.6	3.1
% Ret. on Equity	16.3	16.9	18.7	24.2	13.8	12.6

Dividend Data —Dividends have been paid since 1975.

Amt. of Div. $	Date Decl.	Ex-Div. Date	Stock of Record	Payment Date
0.022	Nov. 04	Nov. 08	Nov. 15	Nov. 25 '94
0.022	Jan. 17	Feb. 09	Feb. 15	Feb. 27 '95
0.022	Apr. 27	May. 09	May. 15	May. 26 '95
0.022	Jun. 26	Aug. 11	Aug. 15	Aug. 25 '95

Data as orig. reptd.; bef. results of disc. opers. and/or spec. items. Per share data adj. for stk. divs. as of ex-div. date. E-Estimated. NA-Not Available. NM-Not Meaningful. NR-Not Ranked.

Office—10750 Columbia Pike, Silver Spring, MD 20901. **Tel**—(301) 681-9400. **Chrmn, Pres & CEO**—S. Bainum Jr. **Vice Chrmn**—S. Bainum. **SVP & Secy**—J. H. Rempe. **SVP, CFO & Treas**—J. A. MacCutcheon. **Investor Contact**—Leigh Comas. **Dirs**—J. R. Anderson, S. Bainum, S. Bainum Jr., R. E. Herzlinger, W. H. Longfield, F. V. Malek, J. E. Robertson. **Transfer Agent & Registrar**—Chemical Bank, NYC. **Incorporated** in Delaware in 1968; reincorporated in Delaware in 1981. **Empl**-27,812. **S&P Analyst:** Robert M. Gold

Marsh & McLennan

NYSE Symbol **MMC**
In S&P 500

19-OCT-95 | **Industry:** Insurance

Summary: This holding company owns Marsh & McLennan, the world's largest insurance brokerage concern. Employee benefit consulting and investment management services are also provided.

S&P Opinion: Accumulate (★★★★)	Recent Price • 86⅞ Yield • 3.8%
	52 Wk Range • 89⅜-71¼ 12-Mo. P/E • 16.6

Earnings vs. Previous Year
▲=Up ▼=Down ▶=No Change

Quantitative Evaluations

Outlook
(1 Lowest—5 Highest)
• **2+**

Fair Value
• **84¼**

Risk
• **Low**

Earn./Div. Rank
• **A+**

Technical Eval.
• **Bearish** since 3/95

Rel. Strength Rank
(1 Lowest—99 Highest)
• **47**

Insider Activity
• **Neutral**

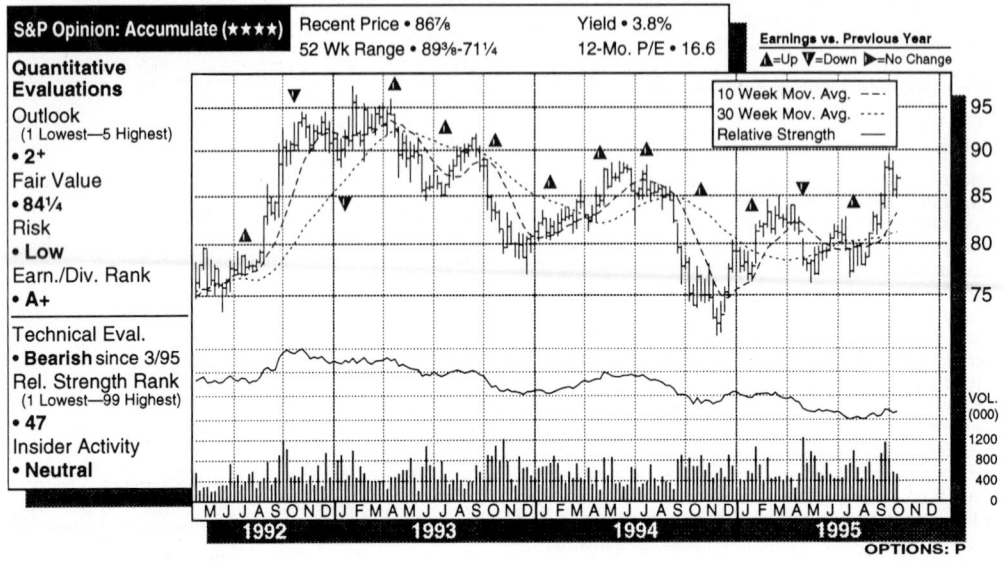

10 Week Mov. Avg. – – –
30 Week Mov. Avg. ⋯⋯
Relative Strength —

OPTIONS: P

Overview - 19-OCT-95

Earnings growth in coming periods is predicated on an upturn in U.S. insurance pricing. Prices in certain lines overseas have firmed, and the record level of catastrophe losses incurred in the U.S. during the past several years augurs well for a pricing turn (albeit a modest one). An economic recovery will likely spur demand for consulting services. Interest income growth will remain under pressure in a relatively low interest rate environment, but the attendant upturn in the securities markets will aid results at Putnam. While growth in assets under management may slow, Putnam will continue to be an important profit contributor. Stock buybacks, including a 3 million authorization made in September, will aid per share results.

Valuation - 19-OCT-95

After dipping in early 1995 amid somewhat disappointing first quarter earnings (which included several unusual items that skewed year-to-year comparisons), the shares of this leading insurance broker have recently trended upward. Despite their recent rally, though, the shares remain attractive at approximately 14 times our 1996 earnings estimate. Insurance brokerage stocks tend to trade at higher multiples than insurance underwriters. Moreover, MMC's dominant market position, strong global franchise and increasingly diversified earnings base merit a higher multiple. We would look for any near-term pullback of 5%-10% to add to positions.

Key Stock Statistics

S&P EPS Est. 1995	5.75	Tang. Bk. Value/Share	11.95
P/E on S&P Est. 1995	15.1	Beta	0.67
S&P EPS Est. 1996	6.00	Shareholders	10,900
Dividend Rate/Share	3.20	Market cap. (B)	$ 6.1
Shs. outstg. (M)	72.6	Inst. holdings	67%
Avg. daily vol. (M)	0.141	Insider holdings	NA

Value of $10,000 invested 5 years ago: $ 13,512

Fiscal Year Ending Dec. 31

	1995	% Change	1994	% Change	1993	% Change
Revenues (Million $)						
1Q	955.2	5%	910.2	9%	833.9	8%
2Q	935.2	11%	840.5	7%	783.3	7%
3Q	—	—	826.9	8%	766.4	5%
4Q	—	—	857.4	10%	779.8	11%
Yr.	—	—	3,435	9%	3,163	8%
Income (Million $)						
1Q	124.8	-5%	130.7	22%	107.4	6%
2Q	101.8	6%	95.70	11%	86.30	9%
3Q	—	—	83.40	10%	76.10	10%
4Q	—	—	72.20	15%	62.60	15%
Yr.	—	—	382.0	15%	332.4	9%
Earnings Per Share ($)						
1Q	1.71	-3%	1.77	21%	1.46	4%
2Q	1.40	8%	1.30	10%	1.18	5%
3Q	—	—	1.14	10%	1.04	7%
4Q	—	—	0.98	17%	0.84	14%
Yr.	E5.75	11%	5.19	15%	4.52	7%

Next earnings report expected: late October

Business Summary - 19-OCT-95

Through subsidiaries, Marsh & McLennan Companies provides professional advice and related services in the areas of insurance and reinsurance, consulting and investment management to clients worldwide. Revenue contributions in recent years:

	1994	1993
Insurance services	55%	57%
Consulting	27%	27%
Investment management	18%	16%

In 1994, 35% of revenues and 29% of operating profits were derived from international operations.

Marsh & McLennan, Inc. advises clients in risk assessment and represents them in the design and implementation of arrangements that transfer risk to insurance underwriters or through alternative funding methods. Services include risk management counseling and administrative services for captive insurance companies. Reinsurance services are provided worldwide through Guy Carpenter & Co., Inc. Seabury & Smith, Inc. designs, distributes and administers a wide range of insurance and financial services. The Frizzell Group designs and administers insurance programs in the United Kingdom. Marsh & McLennan Risk Capital Corp. develops and invests in startup insurance and reinsurance ventures.

William M. Mercer is the world's leading employee benefit consulting firm. Mercer Management Consulting provides management consulting services. National Economic Research Associates provides consulting services on a broad range of microeconomic issues, including antitrust and trade regulation.

The Boston-based Putnam organization conducts investment management activities, with over $95 billion of assets under management at December 31, 1994.

Important Developments

Aug. '95—First half 1995 revenue growth of 8.0% reflected 14% higher consulting revenues, 13% growth in asset management fees, and a 3.7% rise in insurance services revenues. Margins narrowed on 11% higher expenses, paced by costs associated with systems automation initiatives and staff additions. Separately, in September, MMC authorized the repurchase of up to 3 million common shares.

Feb. '95—MMC's revenue growth in 1994 reflected 5.4% higher revenues in its largest segment, insurance services. Growth was mostly the result of contributions from new business and firmer property rates in certain storm-prone areas. However, competitive market conditions kept casualty insurance rates under pressure.

Capitalization

Long Term Debt: $411,100,000 (6/95).

Per Share Data ($)

(Year Ended Dec. 31)

	1994	1993	1992	1991	1990	1989
Tangible Bk. Val.	10.38	9.54	5.66	8.67	8.97	8.03
Cash Flow	6.83	6.15	5.76	5.73	5.58	5.34
Earnings	5.19	4.52	4.21	4.18	4.15	4.10
Dividends	2.80	2.70	2.65	2.60	2.55	2.55
Payout Ratio	54%	60%	63%	61%	61%	61%
Prices - High	88¾	97⅝	94½	87¼	81	89¾
- Low	71¼	77	71¼	69⅛	59¾	55⅛
P/E Ratio - High	17	22	22	21	20	22
- Low	14	17	17	17	14	13

Income Statement Analysis (Million $)

	1994	%Chg	1993	%Chg	1992	%Chg	1991
Revs.	3,435	9%	3,163	8%	2,937	6%	2,779
Oper. Inc.	791	11%	713	9%	653	7%	611
Depr.	121	NM	120	7%	112	NM	113
Int. Exp.	50.6	10%	46.1	20%	38.3	-2%	39.1
Pretax Inc.	632	13%	559	8%	519	-2%	527
Eff. Tax Rate	40%	—	41%	—	42%	—	42%
Net Inc.	382	15%	332	9%	304	NM	306

Balance Sheet & Other Fin. Data (Million $)

	1994	1993	1992	1991	1990	1989
Cash	295	332	371	349	305	293
Curr. Assets	1,446	1,312	1,260	1,039	1,053	911
Total Assets	3,831	3,547	3,088	2,382	2,411	2,035
Curr. Liab.	1,392	1,110	1,017	736	733	625
LT Debt	409	410	411	318	320	319
Common Eqty.	1,461	1,365	1,103	1,035	1,085	873
Total Cap.	1,870	1,775	1,525	1,358	1,417	1,206
Cap. Exp.	149	99	83.0	81.0	155	161
Cash Flow	503	452	416	419	409	384

Ratio Analysis

	1994	1993	1992	1991	1990	1989
Curr. Ratio	1.0	1.2	1.2	1.4	1.4	1.5
% LT Debt of Cap.	21.9	23.1	27.0	23.4	22.6	26.5
% Net Inc.of Revs.	11.1	10.5	10.3	11.0	11.2	12.1
% Ret. on Assets	10.4	10.0	11.0	12.9	13.6	15.2
% Ret. on Equity	27.0	26.9	28.1	29.2	30.8	36.0

Dividend Data

—Dividends have been paid since 1923. A "poison pill" stock purchase rights plan was adopted in 1987.

Amt. of Div. $	Date Decl.	Ex-Div. Date	Stock of Record	Payment Date
0.725	Sep. 20	Oct. 04	Oct. 11	Nov. 15 '94
0.725	Nov. 15	Jan. 05	Jan. 11	Feb. 15 '95
0.725	Mar. 16	Apr. 05	Apr. 11	May. 15 '95
0.725	May. 16	Jul. 07	Jul. 11	Aug. 14 '95
0.800	Sep. 21	Oct. 06	Oct. 11	Nov. 14 '95

Data as orig. reptd.; bef. results of disc. opers. and/or spec. items. Per share data adj. for stk. divs. as of ex-div. date. E-Estimated. NA-Not Available. NM-Not Meaningful. NR-Not Ranked.

Office—1166 Avenue of the Americas, NYC 10036. **Tel**—(212) 345-5000. **Chrmn**—A. J. C. Smith. **Vice Chrmn**—P. L. Wroughton. **VP-Secy**—G. F. Van Gundy. **SVP-CFO**—F. J. Borelli. **Investor Contact**—J. M. Bischoff. **Dirs**—L. W. Bernard, R. H. Blum, F. J. Borelli, R. Clements, P. Coster, R. J. Groves, R. E. Heckert, R. S. Hickok, D. D. Holbrook, R. M. G. Husson, L. J. Lasser, R. M. Morrow Jr., G. Putnam, A. S. Simmons, J. T. Sinnott, A. J. C. Smith, F. J. Tasco, R. J. Ventres, P. L. Wroughton. **Transfer Agent & Registrar**—Harris Trust Co. of New York. **Incorporated** in Delaware in 1923; reincorporated in Delaware in 1969. **Empl**-26,100. **S&P Analyst:** Catherine A. Seifert

23-OCT-95

Industry:
Hotels/Motels/Inns

Summary: This major lodging and food service company, spun off by Marriott Corp. in October 1993, should continue to benefit from cyclical upturns in the U.S. economy and hotel industry.

| S&P Opinion: Hold (★★★) | Recent Price • 37⅝ | Yield • 0.7% |
| | 52 Wk Range • 39¾-25⅞ | 12-Mo. P/E • 21.6 |

Quantitative Evaluations

Outlook
(1 Lowest—5 Highest)
• **2+**

Fair Value
• **36½**

Risk
• **Low**

Earn./Div. Rank
• **NR**

Technical Eval.
• **Bearish** since 7/95

Rel. Strength Rank
(1 Lowest—99 Highest)
• **56**

Insider Activity
• **Neutral**

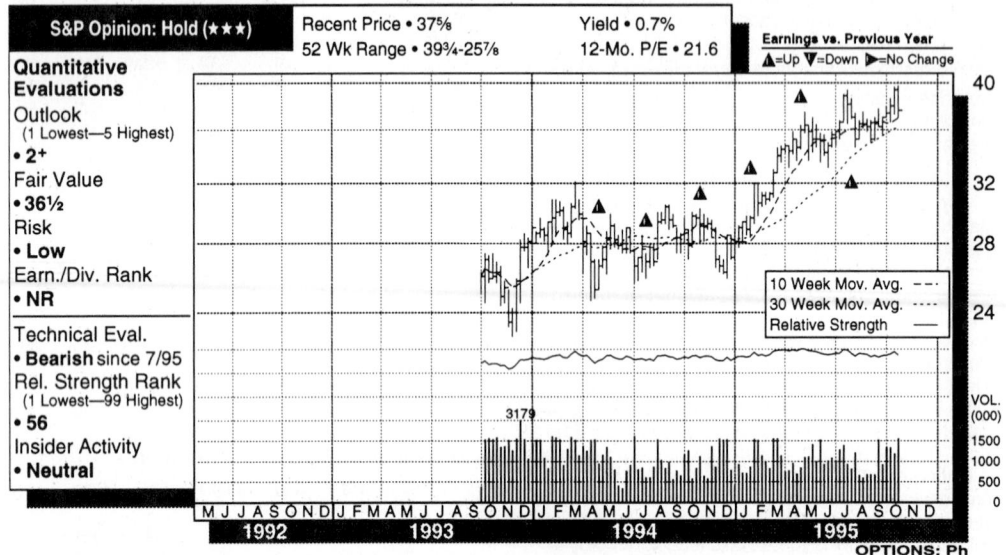

Earnings vs. Previous Year
▲=Up ▼=Down ►=No Change

10 Week Mov. Avg. ---
30 Week Mov. Avg. ·····
Relative Strength —

OPTIONS: Ph

Overview - 20-OCT-95

The lodging business of this major management company is well situated to benefit from a cyclical upturn in the U.S. hotel industry. With its four chains, MAR is able to offer accommodations to travelers who are looking for various levels of service and price considerations. We expect MAR's hotels to continue producing occupancy levels that exceed the industry average. Also, over at least the near-term, we look for revenues to be boosted by impressive gains in average room rates. We expect that improved operating results at managed hotels will generate higher incentives fees for MAR. Overall, in 1996, we project double-digit profit growth from both MAR's lodging and contract service segments. MAR became a publicly owned company in October 1993, when it was spun off to shareholders of Marriott Corp. (now Host Marriott Corp.).

Valuation - 20-OCT-95

We view the stock price of this company as adequately reflecting the double-digit profit improvement projected for 1995 and 1996. Longer-term, we expect the above-average occupancy levels of MAR's various lodging chains should be helpful to the company to add new management agreements and franchises, including conversions from other lodging chains. Also, MAR's growing involvement in the operation of retirement communities and time-sharing resorts fits well with U.S. demographic patterns. The shares have appeal as a long-term holding, but we do not advise buying additional shares at this time.

Key Stock Statistics

S&P EPS Est. 1995	1.85	Tang. Bk. Value/Share	4.21
P/E on S&P Est. 1995	20.3	Beta	NA
S&P EPS Est. 1996	2.10	Shareholders	61,200
Dividend Rate/Share	0.28	Market cap. (B)	$ 4.7
Shs. outstg. (M)	125.3	Inst. holdings	49%
Avg. daily vol. (M)	0.293	Insider holdings	NA

Value of $10,000 invested 5 years ago: NA

Fiscal Year Ending Dec. 31

	1995	% Change	1994	% Change	1993	% Change
Revenues (Million $)						
1Q	2,013	5%	1,916	3%	1,865	5%
2Q	2,112	7%	1,982	5%	1,892	3%
3Q	1,926	6%	1,813	5%	1,728	3%
4Q	—	—	2,704	5%	2,577	3%
Yr.	—	—	8,415	4%	8,062	3%
Income (Million $)						
1Q	52.00	21%	43.00	23%	35.00	17%
2Q	59.00	23%	48.00	17%	41.00	24%
3Q	46.00	24%	37.00	28%	29.00	38%
4Q	—	—	72.00	29%	56.00	19%
Yr.	—	—	200.0	24%	161.0	23%
Earnings Per Share ($)						
1Q	0.40	25%	0.32	10%	0.29	—
2Q	0.45	25%	0.36	13%	0.32	—
3Q	0.35	25%	0.28	17%	0.24	—
4Q	E0.66	20%	0.55	28%	0.43	—
Yr.	E1.85	23%	1.51	19%	1.27	13%

Next earnings report expected: early February

Marriott International

Business Summary - 20-OCT-95

This lodging and food service management company was spun off to shareholders of the former Marriott Corp. (now called Host Marriott Corp.) in October 1993.

The company's lodging business includes the operation or franchising of more than 800 properties in the Marriott, Courtyard, Residence Inn and Fairfield Inn hotel chains. Lodging contributed 72% of MAR's segment operating profit in 1994. Many of the hotels operated by MAR are owned by Host Marriott Corp. or by related partnerships.

At year-end 1994, MAR operated 165 full-service hotels with 76,745 rooms, and was the franchisor of 94 such properties with 29,509 rooms. In the more moderately priced Courtyard chain, it operated 195 hotels (28,551 rooms), and was the franchisor of 36 properties (5,042 rooms). In the Residence Inn chain, which focuses on extended-stay customers, there were 107 hotels (13,547 rooms). In addition, there were 82 Residence Inn franchise properties, with 9,517 rooms. The lower-priced Fairfield Inn chain included 57 properties (7,121 rooms) managed by MAR, and 118 franchises (10,354 rooms). MAR also has a sizable vacation time-share business.

In April 1995, MAR acquired, a 49% interest in The Ritz-Carlton Hotel Company LLC, which owns the management agreements on various Ritz-Carlton properties. The Ritz-Carlton system currently has about 31 hotels and resorts, with more than 10,000 rooms. MAR expected to acquire the remaining 51% equity interest during the next several years, for a price based on cash flow of the Ritz-Carlton business.

MAR's contract services business includes food service and facilities management for accounts at locations such as offices, industrial sites, health care facilities, and schools in the U.S. and Canada. MAR also distributes food and supplies both to its own operations and to unaffiliated customers, and operates 19 retirement communities, which are largely owned by others.

Important Developments

Sep. '95—In 1995's third quarter, operating profit from the lodging segment increased 21%, year to year, and contract service earnings rose 27%. In each of MAR's four lodging businesses, revenue per available room rose at least 6% for comparable units. In the quarter, MAR had higher incentive management fees and franchise fees, increased earnings from its vacation ownership business, and income from MAR's recent investment in the Ritz-Carlton Hotel Company LLC. In MAR contract services segment, profit was up 27% in the seasonally slow third quarter.

Capitalization

Long Term Debt: $799,000,000 (6/16/95).

Per Share Data ($)

(Year Ended Dec. 31)

	1994	1993	1992	1991	1990	1989
Tangible Bk. Val.	3.17	2.31	NA	NA	NA	NA
Cash Flow	2.40	2.05	NA	NA	NA	NA
Earnings	1.51	1.26	1.12	NA	NA	NA
Dividends	0.28	0.14	NM	NA	NA	NA
Payout Ratio	19%	11%	NM	NA	NA	NA
Prices - High	32⅛	29	NM	NA	NA	NA
- Low	24⅝	22¾	NM	NA	NA	NA
P/E Ratio - High	21	23	NM	NA	NA	NA
- Low	16	18	NM	NA	NA	NA

Income Statement Analysis (Million $)

	1994	%Chg	1993	%Chg	1992	%Chg	1991
Revs.	8,415	13%	7,430	-5%	7,787	—	NA
Oper. Inc.	462	19%	389	—	NA	—	NA
Depr.	117	22%	96.0	—	NA	—	NA
Int. Exp.	36.0	20%	30.0	-49%	59.0	—	NA
Pretax Inc.	342	24%	275	18%	233	—	NA
Eff. Tax Rate	42%	—	42%	—	42%	—	NA
Net Inc.	200	26%	159	17%	136	—	NA

Balance Sheet & Other Fin. Data (Million $)

	1994	1993	1992	1991	1990	1989
Cash	204	238	181	NA	NA	NA
Curr. Assets	1,232	1,295	1,284	NA	NA	NA
Total Assets	3,207	3,092	3,048	NA	NA	NA
Curr. Liab.	1,398	1,402	1,365	NA	NA	NA
LT Debt	506	564	902	NA	NA	NA
Common Eqty.	767	696	375	NA	NA	NA
Total Cap.	1,273	1,260	1,277	NA	NA	NA
Cap. Exp.	115	63.0	NA	NA	NA	NA
Cash Flow	317	255	NA	NA	NA	NA

Ratio Analysis

	1994	1993	1992	1991	1990	1989
Curr. Ratio	0.9	0.9	0.9	NA	NA	NA
% LT Debt of Cap.	39.7	44.8	70.6	NA	NA	NA
% Net Inc.of Revs.	2.4	2.1	1.7	NA	NA	NA
% Ret. on Assets	6.4	NA	NA	NA	NA	NA
% Ret. on Equity	27.7	NA	NA	NA	NA	NA

Dividend Data —Dividends were initiated in 1993.

Amt. of Div. $	Date Decl.	Ex-Div. Date	Stock of Record	Payment Date
0.070	Nov. 03	Dec. 22	Dec. 29	Jan. 13 '95
0.070	Feb. 02	Mar. 24	Mar. 30	Apr. 24 '95
0.070	May. 12	Jun. 28	Jun. 30	Jul. 17 '95
0.070	Aug. 03	Sep. 21	Sep. 25	Oct. 16 '95

Data as orig. reptd.; bef. results of disc. opers. and/or spec. items. Per share data adj. for stk. divs. as of ex-div. date. E-Estimated. NA-Not Available. NM-Not Meaningful. NR-Not Ranked. Data pro forma prior to 1994. Quarters

Office—Marriott Drive, Washington, D.C., 20058. **Tel**—(301) 380-3000. **Chrmn & Pres**—J. W. Marriott, Jr. **EVP & CFO**—M. A. Stein. **Investor Contact**—Laura Paugh (301-380-7418). **Dirs**—G. M. Grosvenor, J. W. Marriott, Jr., R. E. Marriott, F. D. McKenzie, H. J. Pearce, W. M. Romney, R. W. Sant, L. M. Small. **Transfer Agent & Registrar**—First Chicago Trust Co. of New York, Jersey City, NJ. **Incorporated** in 1993. **Empl**-163,000. **S&P Analyst:** Tom Graves, CFA

Masco Corp.

NYSE Symbol **MAS**
In S&P 500

11-OCT-95   Industry:
Building

Summary: Masco Corp. produces brand name building and home improvement products, and furniture and home furnishings products. It also owns various equity investments in other companies.

S&P Opinion: Hold (★★★)	Recent Price • 27¾	Yield • 2.8%
	52 Wk Range • 29½-21¼	12-Mo. P/E • 22.6

Earnings vs. Previous Year
▲=Up ▼=Down ▶=No Change

Quantitative Evaluations

Outlook
(1 Lowest—5 Highest)
• **3⁻**

Fair Value
• **27½**

Risk
• **Average**

Earn./Div. Rank
• **B**

Technical Eval.
• **Bearish** since 3/95

Rel. Strength Rank
(1 Lowest—99 Highest)
• **48**

Insider Activity
• **NA**

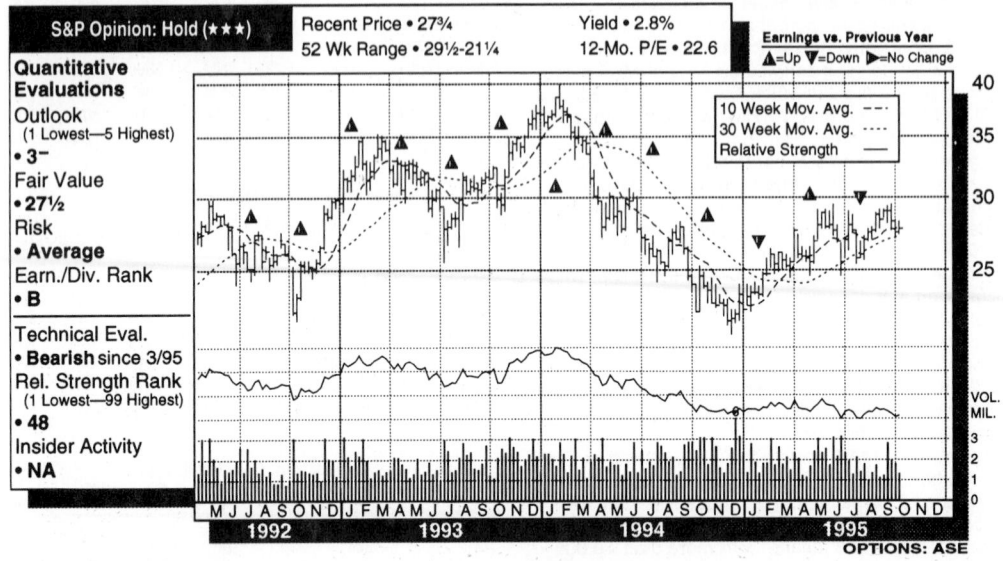

- 10 Week Mov. Avg. – – –
- 30 Week Mov. Avg. ·······
- Relative Strength —

OPTIONS: ASE

Overview - 05-OCT-95

Sales from continuing operations are expected to continue rising in 1995, reflecting ongoing share increases with major retailers such as Home Depot and acquisitions. Despite continuing pricing pressures, margins are expected to widen on higher volume, greater productivity, and expansion and cost reduction programs. If the home furnishings division is divested in 1995, earnings could be hurt by a substantial one-time non-cash charge related to the divestiture. Over the long term, however, the divestiture should boost earnings growth, as the company focuses on its more profitable home improvement and building products business.

Valuation - 11-OCT-95

Although MAS stock has picked up since 1994 year end, the shares remain significantly depressed after reaching a high of almost 40 in early 1994. We believe investors are concerned that demand for the company's products remains relatively weak, and that margins are under pressure. In addition, MAS stock has been hurt by the company's early June announcement that 1995 earnings were likely to fall below most consensus estimates. As a result, we are neutral on the stock over the near term. Longer term, however, we remain optimistic that MAS's earnings will increase at a minimum of 12%-15% annually, as the company increases its market share, adds new product lines, and focuses on its profitable home improvement and building products business.

Key Stock Statistics

S&P EPS Est. 1995	1.75	Tang. Bk. Value/Share	9.52
P/E on S&P Est. 1995	15.9	Beta	1.67
S&P EPS Est. 1996	2.15	Shareholders	6,500
Dividend Rate/Share	0.76	Market cap. (B)	$ 4.4
Shs. outstg. (M)	160.3	Inst. holdings	61%
Avg. daily vol. (M)	0.358	Insider holdings	NA

Value of $10,000 invested 5 years ago: $ 13,211

Fiscal Year Ending Dec. 31

	1995	% Change	1994	% Change	1993	% Change
Revenues (Million $)						
1Q	1,226	17%	1,050	11%	946.0	11%
2Q	1,208	8%	1,120	18%	948.0	9%
3Q	—	—	1,150	17%	982.0	9%
4Q	—	—	1,148	14%	1,010	11%
Yr.	—	—	4,468	15%	3,886	10%
Income (Million $)						
1Q	74.40	14%	65.30	20%	54.50	34%
2Q	63.40	-10%	70.10	32%	53.30	10%
3Q	—	—	72.10	29%	55.70	10%
4Q	—	—	-13.80	NM	57.60	34%
Yr.	—	—	193.7	-12%	221.1	21%
Earnings Per Share ($)						
1Q	0.47	12%	0.42	17%	0.36	33%
2Q	0.40	-9%	0.44	26%	0.35	9%
3Q	E0.46	2%	0.45	25%	0.36	9%
4Q	E0.42	NM	-0.09	NM	0.38	31%
Yr.	E1.75	43%	1.22	-16%	1.45	20%

Next earnings report expected: early November

Masco Corp.

Business Summary - 11-OCT-95

Masco Corp. manufactures building, home improvement, home furnishings and consumer products. Segment contributions in 1994 were:

	Sales	Profits
Building & home improvement products	56%	85%
Home furnishings & consumer specialty products	44%	15%

The company is one of the largest U.S. manufacturers of brand name consumer products for home building and improvement. Products include faucets (Delta, Peerless, Artistic Brass and Sherle Wagner); plumbing supplies (Brass-Craft, Home Plumber and Plumb Shop); and kitchen and bathroom cabinets (Merillat, Kraftmaid, Starmark and Fieldstone). Masco also manufactures kitchen appliances (Thermador); bathroom and spa items (Aqua Glass, Huppe and Hot Spring Spa); and locks and builder's hardware (Baldwin, Weiser, Saflok and Winfield). The Zenith Products Corporation, American Shower & Bath Corporation, NewTeam Group and Melard Manufacturing Corporation, all acquired in 1994, produce plumbing products and bath accessories. MAS also expanded its kitchen cabinet business in 1994 by the acquisition in Germany of Alma Kuchen Aloys Meyer GmbH and Co.

Through a series of acquisitions, MAS has become a leading home furnishings supplier. Products include high-end furniture sold under the Henredon trademark; medium high-end furniture sold under the Drexel and Heritage names; furniture sold under the Universal, Benchcraft and Lineage names; and furniture made through the Lexington Furniture Industries Group. MAS also makes upholstery and other fabrics, mirrors, lamps, and other decorative accessories. The Berkline Corporation, acquired in mid-1994, produces motion furniture. In addition, MAS owns equity investments in other companies, including MascoTech (formerly Masco Industries; 44%). In late 1991, Masco Capital Corp. become a wholly owned subsidiary when MAS paid Masco Industries $50 million for the latter's 50% interest.

Important Developments

Aug. '95—MAS reported that second quarter operating margins of home improvement and building products fell to 17.5% from 20.5%, year to year, while operating margins of home furnishings fell to 4.7% from 5.3%. Both divisions were hurt by a less profitable product mix and plant start-up costs.
Jun. '95—MAS began exploring alternatives with respect to a possible divestiture, initial public offering or spin-off of the home furnishings division.

Capitalization

Long Term Debt: $1,684,290 (6/95), incl. $178 million of debs. conv. into com. at $42.28 a sh.

Per Share Data ($)

(Year Ended Dec. 31)

	1994	1993	1992	1991	1990	1989
Tangible Bk. Val.	8.87	9.12	8.26	11.91	12.01	11.94
Cash Flow	1.98	2.21	1.96	0.98	1.52	1.99
Earnings	1.22	1.45	1.21	0.30	0.91	1.42
Dividends	0.71	0.65	0.61	0.57	0.54	0.50
Payout Ratio	71%	45%	51%	192%	57%	35%
Prices - High	39⅞	38⅞	30	26½	26¾	31⅛
- Low	21¼	25½	22	17	14¼	23¾
P/E Ratio - High	33	27	25	88	29	22
- Low	17	18	18	57	16	17

Income Statement Analysis (Million $)

	1994	%Chg	1993	%Chg	1992	%Chg	1991
Revs.	4,468	15%	3,886	10%	3,525	12%	3,141
Oper. Inc.	630	21%	520	10%	473	35%	351
Depr.	121	4%	116	2%	114	11%	103
Int. Exp.	105	NM	106	5%	101	-20%	127
Pretax Inc.	323	-11%	363	19%	305	NM	98.0
Eff. Tax Rate	40%	—	39%	—	40%	—	54%
Net Inc.	194	-12%	221	21%	183	NM	45.0

Balance Sheet & Other Fin. Data (Million $)

	1994	1993	1992	1991	1990	1989
Cash	71.0	125	54.0	70.0	69.0	113
Curr. Assets	1,891	1,644	1,466	1,376	1,365	1,393
Total Assets	4,390	4,021	3,987	3,786	3,761	3,641
Curr. Liab.	601	490	492	514	552	540
LT Debt	1,593	1,418	1,487	1,369	1,334	1,153
Common Eqty.	2,113	1,998	1,887	1,799	1,774	1,858
Total Cap.	3,705	3,417	3,374	3,168	3,108	3,012
Cap. Exp.	191	167	123	119	193	193
Cash Flow	314	337	298	148	232	310

Ratio Analysis

	1994	1993	1992	1991	1990	1989
Curr. Ratio	3.1	3.4	3.0	2.7	2.5	2.6
% LT Debt of Cap.	43.0	41.5	44.1	43.2	42.9	38.3
% Net Inc.of Revs.	4.3	5.7	5.2	1.4	4.3	7.0
% Ret. on Assets	4.5	5.5	4.7	1.2	3.8	6.3
% Ret. on Equity	9.3	11.4	9.9	2.5	7.8	12.2

Dividend Data —Dividends have been paid since 1944.

Amt. of Div. $	Date Decl.	Ex-Div. Date	Stock of Record	Payment Date
0.180	Sep. 08	Oct. 07	Oct. 14	Nov. 14 '94
0.180	Dec. 09	Dec. 30	Jan. 06	Feb. 06 '95
0.180	Mar. 15	Apr. 03	Apr. 07	May. 08 '95
0.180	Jun. 30	Jul. 12	Jul. 14	Aug. 07 '95
0.190	Sep. 28	Oct. 11	Oct. 13	Nov. 13 '95

Data as orig. reptd.; bef. results of disc. opers. and/or spec. items. Per share data adj. for stk. divs. as of ex-div. date.
E-Estimated. NA-Not Available. NM-Not Meaningful. NR-Not Ranked.

Office—21001 Van Born Rd., Taylor, MI 48180. **Tel**—(313) 274-7400. **Chrmn & CEO**—R. A. Manoogian. **Pres**—W. B. Lyon. **VP & Secy**—E. A. Gargaro, Jr. **SVP-Fin**—R. G. Mosteller. **Treas & Investor Contact**—John C. Nicholls, Jr. **Dirs**—L. Bauder, E. L. Koning, W. B. Lyon, A. Manoogian (Chrmn Emeritus), R. A. Manoogian, J. A. Morgan, A. Simone, P. W. Stroh. **Transfer Agents & Registrars**—NDB Bank, Detroit; Mellon Securities Trust Co., Ridgefield Park, N.J. **Incorporated** in Delaware in 1962. **Empl**-51,300. **S&P Analyst:** Elizabeth Vandeventer

Mattel, Inc.

NYSE Symbol **MAT**
In S&P 500

20-OCT-95

Industry: Leisure/Amusement

Summary: Recent acquisitions have made this company, best known for its Barbie dolls, the world's largest toy maker.

S&P Opinion: Accumulate (★★★★)

Recent Price • 28½	Yield • 0.9%	
52 Wk Range • 30⅝-19⅝	12-Mo. P/E • 22.6	

Quantitative Evaluations

Outlook
(1 Lowest—5 Highest)
• **4+**

Fair Value
• **29½**

Risk
• **Low**

Earn./Div. Rank
• **B**

Technical Eval.
• **Bullish** since 2/95

Rel. Strength Rank
(1 Lowest—99 Highest)
• **32**

Insider Activity
• **Neutral**

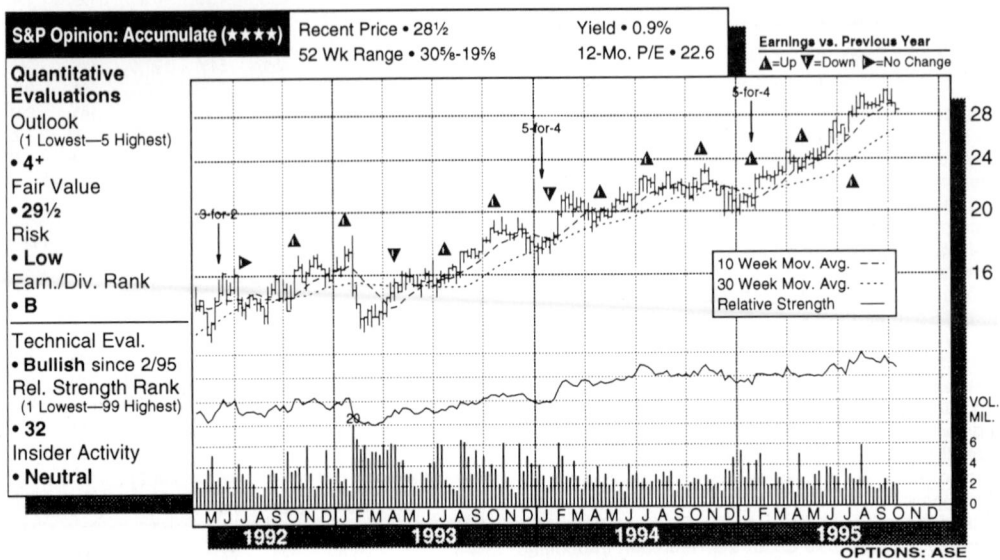

Earnings vs. Previous Year
▲=Up ▼=Down ▶=No Change

10 Week Mov. Avg. – – –
30 Week Mov. Avg. · · · ·
Relative Strength ——

OPTIONS: ASE

Overview - 20-OCT-95

Sales should advance 15% in 1996. The company's aggressive brand management techniques should allow it to continue to increase its market share in foreign countries. In addition, MAT is introducing a line of entertainment and educational software that will considerably expand its market. Fisher-Price will also be introducing a line of computers, developed in conjunction with Compaq Computer. In addition, growth should continue in core brands in the U.S. Margins should widen, aided by price hikes moderating cost increases. EPS should benefit from fewer shares outstanding.

Valuation - 20-OCT-95

The shares are likely to rise in the long-term, as MAT grows through intensive brand management, international expansion, and new product introductions. In addition, the company is likely to continue an active acquisition strategy. An expansion of the stock's multiple to a level more in line with that of leading consumer products companies is anticipated, as investors focus on MAT's consistent sales and earnings growth over the past several years. However, for the near-term, the shares may remain in a narrow range, reflecting seasonal weakness of toy stocks in the last two months of the year. In addition, company forecasts of a strong fourth quarter are viewed skeptically by some investors, because of sluggish retail sales.

Key Stock Statistics

S&P EPS Est. 1995	1.60	Tang. Bk. Value/Share	3.29
P/E on S&P Est. 1995	17.8	Beta	0.70
S&P EPS Est. 1996	1.90	Shareholders	37,000
Dividend Rate/Share	0.24	Market cap. (B)	$ 6.1
Shs. outstg. (M)	221.6	Inst. holdings	79%
Avg. daily vol. (M)	0.627	Insider holdings	NA

Value of $10,000 invested 5 years ago: $ 43,924

Fiscal Year Ending Dec. 31

	1995	% Change	1994	% Change	1993	% Change
Revenues (Million $)						
1Q	543.6	12%	487.3	2%	477.2	46%
2Q	763.5	17%	650.3	13%	576.6	43%
3Q	1,176	13%	1,037	16%	896.7	48%
4Q	—	—	1,030	37%	753.9	48%
Yr.	—	—	3,205	19%	2,704	46%
Income (Million $)						
1Q	26.96	12%	24.07	30%	18.48	25%
2Q	67.50	18%	57.08	40%	40.77	74%
3Q	151.3	15%	131.8	26%	104.7	49%
4Q	—	—	42.86	NM	-28.00	NM
Yr.	—	—	255.8	88%	135.9	-6%
Earnings Per Share ($)						
1Q	0.12	15%	0.10	30%	0.08	-11%
2Q	0.30	21%	0.25	35%	0.18	25%
3Q	0.67	16%	0.58	18%	0.49	7%
4Q	E0.51	168%	0.19	NM	-0.14	NM
Yr.	E1.60	43%	1.12	81%	0.62	-32%

Next earnings report expected: early February

Mattel, Inc.

Business Summary - 20-OCT-95

Mattel is the world's largest manufacturer and marketer of toys.

In recent years, the company has focused on its core product lines, which accounted for 80% of sales in 1994. The largest product line is the long-lived Barbie line of fashion dolls and accessories, which accounted for 34% of total pro forma sales in 1994. Fisher-Price preschool and juvenile products accounted for 28%, while Disney toys represented 13% and Hot Wheels 5%.

Other toys include See 'n Say toys, large dolls, including the Li'l Miss line, the Uno and Ship-Bo games, the rights to Scrabble in certain markets outside of the U.S., activity toys marketed under the Nickelodeon brand name, sports toys sold under the Avia brand name, Power Wheels battery-operated ride-on vehicles, and Hula Hoops and Frisbees marketed under the Wham-O trademark. In addition, toys based on the movie Lion King were introduced in 1994.

An aggressive new product introduction program, including new items in existing lines and new product lines, is being implemented in 1995.

Foreign operations accounted for 50% of sales and 47% of operating income in 1994.

The company has pursued an aggressive acquisition policy in recent years. In July 1994, it bought a majority of shares of J. W. Spear & Sons PLC, which holds the rights to Scrabble and other games outside of the U.S. In May 1994, it acquired Kransco, a toymaker with $175 million in sales, whose leading product line is Power Wheels battery-operated ride-on vehicles. In November 1993, MAT purchased Fisher-Price, a leading maker of preschool and infant toys and juvenile products, for about 48.8 million common shares (as adjusted through 1994).

Important Developments

Jul. '95—MAT said that despite increased material costs and a sluggish retail environment in certain markets, it achieved strong earnings in the third quarter, paced by excellent consumer and retail trade reception for its core product line. It added that growth was broadbased, with a 15% increase in the U.S. and a 10% gain in international markets. Excluding a 75% drop in Mexican sales, international sales rose 20%. The company also announced plans to repurchase all of its 12.5%, Series F convertible preference stock, for about $75 million. The stock would have been convertible into 2.6 million common shares.

Capitalization

Long Term Debt: $263,262,000 (9/95).

Per Share Data ($)

(Year Ended Dec. 31)

	1994	1993	1992	1991	1990	1989
Tangible Bk. Val.	2.81	3.07	2.68	2.21	1.81	1.25
Cash Flow	1.68	1.04	1.33	1.17	0.95	0.82
Earnings	1.12	0.62	0.92	0.79	0.61	0.54
Dividends	0.24	0.15	0.12	0.07	0.03	Nil
Payout Ratio	21%	24%	13%	8%	5%	Nil
Prices - High	23⅝	19⅝	17¼	14¼	9	7⅛
- Low	16½	13⅛	12¾	6¼	5¼	3¼
P/E Ratio - High	21	32	19	18	15	13
- Low	15	21	14	8	9	6

Income Statement Analysis (Million $)

	1994	%Chg	1993	%Chg	1992	%Chg	1991
Revs.	3,205	19%	2,704	46%	1,848	14%	1,622
Oper. Inc.	673	30%	518	59%	325	10%	295
Depr.	124	35%	92.0	45%	63.6	10%	57.7
Int. Exp.	55.4	-12%	62.6	14%	55.0	3%	53.6
Pretax Inc.	394	66%	237	10%	216	14%	189
Eff. Tax Rate	35%	—	43%	—	33%	—	38%
Net Inc.	256	88%	136	-6%	144	22%	118

Balance Sheet & Other Fin. Data (Million $)

	1994	1993	1992	1991	1990	1989
Cash	260	524	295	197	198	220
Curr. Assets	1,544	1,471	872	709	627	603
Total Assets	2,459	2,000	1,260	1,061	930	830
Curr. Liab.	916	783	413	400	331	336
LT Debt	360	328	287	185	168	178
Common Eqty.	1,052	791	534	438	328	214
Total Cap.	1,446	1,146	823	629	566	463
Cap. Exp.	163	101	75.3	49.3	84.4	85.0
Cash Flow	375	223	203	176	141	120

Ratio Analysis

	1994	1993	1992	1991	1990	1989
Curr. Ratio	1.7	1.9	2.1	1.8	1.9	1.8
% LT Debt of Cap.	24.9	28.6	34.9	29.4	29.7	38.3
% Net Inc.of Revs.	8.0	5.0	7.8	7.3	6.2	6.4
% Ret. on Assets	11.3	7.2	12.3	11.7	10.3	10.4
% Ret. on Equity	26.8	16.9	28.4	30.4	33.5	46.0

Dividend Data —Dividends on the common stock were resumed in May 1990. A new poison pill stock purchase rights plan was adopted in 1992.

Amt. of Div. $	Date Decl.	Ex-Div. Date	Stock of Record	Payment Date
0.060	Nov. 11	Dec. 15	Dec. 21	Jan. 04 '95
5-for-4	Dec. 23	Jan. 23	Jan. 06	Jan. 20 '95
0.060	Feb. 10	Mar. 17	Mar. 23	Apr. 05 '95
0.060	May. 10	Jun. 20	Jun. 22	Jul. 06 '95
0.060	Aug. 25	Sep. 19	Sep. 21	Oct. 03 '95

Data as orig. reptd.; bef. results of disc. opers. and/or spec. items. Per share data adj. for stk. divs. as of ex-div. date. E-Estimated. NA-Not Available. NM-Not Meaningful. NR-Not Ranked.

Office—333 Continental Blvd., El Segundo, CA 90245-5012. **Tel**—(310) 252-2000. **Chrmn & CEO**—J. W. Amerman. **Pres**—J. E. Barad. **EVP-Fin**—F. Luzuriaga. **VP & Secy**—N. Mansour. **Investor Contact**—Michael Salop. **Dirs**—J. W. Amerman, J. E. Barad, H. Brown, J. A. Eskridge, T. M. Friedman, R. M. Loeb, E. H. Malone, E. N. Ney, W. D. Rollnick, J. L. Vogelstein, L. F. Williams. **Transfer Agent & Registrar**—First National Bank of Boston. **Incorporated** in California in 1948; reincorporated in Delaware in 1968. **Empl**-22,000. **S&P Analyst:** Paul H. Valentine, CFA

May Department Stores

NYSE Symbol **MA**
In S&P 500

19-OCT-95

Industry:
Retail Stores

Summary: May Department Stores is one of the largest retailing companies in the U.S., operating 315 department stores and a nationwide chain of more than 4,580 shoe stores.

S&P Opinion: Hold (★★★)

Recent Price • 43½	Yield • 2.8%
52 Wk Range • 45⅝-32¼	12-Mo. P/E • 14.0

Quantitative Evaluations

Outlook
(1 Lowest—5 Highest)
• **5⁻**

Fair Value
• **52⅝**

Risk
• **Low**

Earn./Div. Rank
• **A+**

Technical Eval.
• **Bullish** since 7/95

Rel. Strength Rank
(1 Lowest—99 Highest)
• **21**

Insider Activity
• **Neutral**

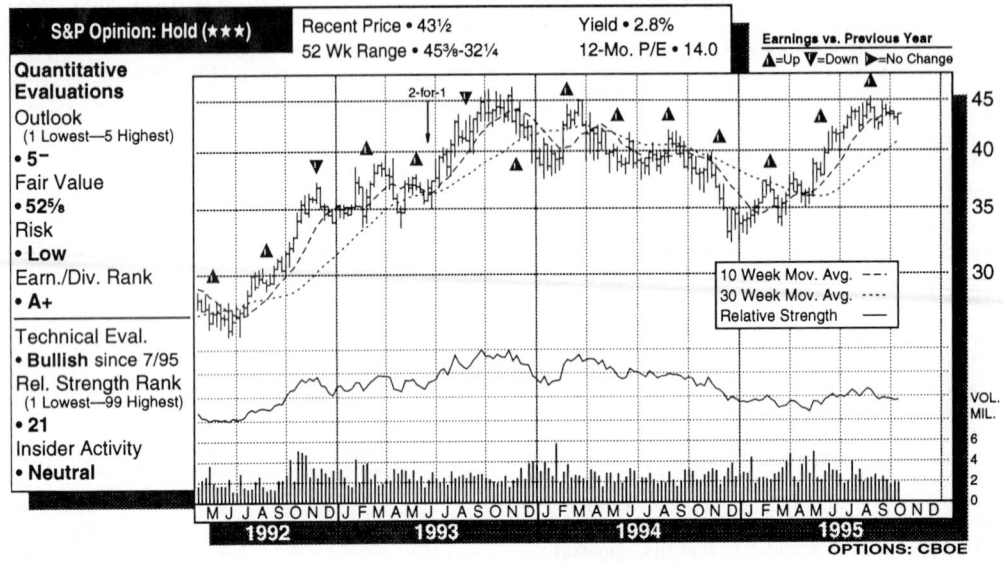

Earnings vs. Previous Year
▲=Up ▼=Down ▶=No Change

10 Week Mov. Avg. — — —
30 Week Mov. Avg. ·······
Relative Strength ———

OPTIONS: CBOE

Overview - 18-OCT-95

Sales for 1995-96 should reflect 4% growth in comparable-store sales and the opening of 23 new department stores and some 365 Payless Shoe stores. Gross margins should remain about level as the consumer continues to be highly price sensitive. SG&A expenses should decline as a percentage of sales, reflecting the consolidation of some backoffice functions, which should result in lower payroll costs. May has one of the lowest expense structures in the department store industry. This and moderate sales gains should continue to boost earnings. Sales and earnings gains should be stronger in the second half with easier comparisons. The company has grown over the years through acquisitions and more are a possibility, either through small groups of stores or even a large regional chain.

Valuation - 18-OCT-95

The shares of May, one of the stronger players in the rapidly consolidating department store industry, have rebounded from their lows of earlier in 1995. Continued promotional pricing should put pressure on earnings in the holiday season and as a result, the shares may languish in the near term. Recent acquisitions will improve May's competitive position in the mid-Atlantic region. We expect the company to continue to make acquisitions of smaller, weaker players and benefit from the economies of scale. The company's balance sheet is strong and the dividend, which has been raised frequently, yields 2.6%.

Key Stock Statistics

S&P EPS Est. 1996	3.35	Tang. Bk. Value/Share	14.74
P/E on S&P Est. 1996	13.0	Beta	0.83
S&P EPS Est. 1997	3.75	Shareholders	46,000
Dividend Rate/Share	1.14	Market cap. (B)	$ 10.0
Shs. outstg. (M)	249.4	Inst. holdings	72%
Avg. daily vol. (M)	0.418	Insider holdings	NA

Value of $10,000 invested 5 years ago: $ 21,316

Fiscal Year Ending Jan. 31

	1996	% Change	1995	% Change	1994	% Change
Revenues (Million $)						
1Q	2,787	6%	2,620	8%	2,422	1%
2Q	2,948	9%	2,706	5%	2,586	4%
3Q	—	—	2,945	5%	2,814	5%
4Q	—	—	3,950	7%	3,707	3%
Yr.	—	—	12,223	6%	11,529	3%
Income (Million $)						
1Q	114.0	2%	112.0	17%	96.00	19%
2Q	141.0	8%	130.0	11%	117.0	-70%
3Q	—	—	139.0	5%	133.0	NM
4Q	—	—	401.0	10%	365.0	14%
Yr.	—	—	782.0	10%	711.0	18%
Earnings Per Share ($)						
1Q	0.44	2%	0.43	23%	0.35	17%
2Q	0.55	10%	0.50	11%	0.45	-70%
3Q	E0.59	9%	0.54	6%	0.51	NM
4Q	E1.77	11%	1.59	10%	1.44	20%
Yr.	E3.35	9%	3.06	10%	2.77	23%

Next earnings report expected: early November

May Department Stores

Business Summary - 19-OCT-95

May Department Stores became one of the largest U.S. retailing companies through its 1986 acquisition of Associated Dry Goods. At the end of fiscal 1994-95, the company operated 314 department stores in 29 states and the District of Columbia. In addition, May operates Volume Shoe Corp., the largest U. S. chain of self-service family shoe stores; at 1994-95 year-end, the company operated 4,435 stores in 49 states and the District of Columbia. Segment contributions in 1994-95 were:

	Sales	Profits
Department stores	82%	86%
Specialty	18%	14%

The company operates department stores in most of the major markets of the U.S. and some smaller ones. Stores include Lord & Taylor, Foley's, Robinsons-May, Hecht's, Famous-Barr, Filene's, Kaufmann's and Meier & Frank. The company's specialty business consisted of Payless ShoeSource outlets.

May's capital budget for 1995-1999 totaled $5 billion, of which $3.2 billion was earmarked to open 125 new department stores, adding 20.3 million square feet to the existing 52 million square feet. An additional 1,200 Payless ShoeSource and 900 Payless Kids stores are planned, adding 4.8 million sq. ft. to the existing 14.9 sq. ft. The plan includes $480 million to expand and remodel 100 department stores and $100 million to improve its distribution centers.

In 1989, MA sold its Caldor discount chain and its Loehmann's division. Venture, a Midwest discount chain, was spun off to shareholders in 1990-91.

Important Developments

Oct. '95—Same-store sales in MA's department stores rose 3.6% in the five weeks ended September 30, while declining 0.2% at its Payless ShoeSource division. In the first half of 1995-96, same-store sales at department stores rose 3.7% but declined 3.0% at Payless. Gross margins narrowed in the second quarter of 1995-96, while expense ratios improved; operating income rose 6.9%. Effective August 28, 1995, the company purchased 14 John Wanamaker stores in the Philadelphia area and three Woodward & Lothrop stores in the Washington D.C. area for about $415 million, including $175 million for inventory and receivables. The Philadelphia stores will be converted into Hecht's and the Washington D.C. area stores into Lord & Taylor's.

Capitalization

Long Term Debt: $3,057,000,000 (7/29/95).
ESOP Preference Shares: $370,000,000.

Per Share Data ($) (Year Ended Jan. 31)

	1995	1994	1993	1992	1991	1990
Tangible Bk. Val.	14.22	12.16	10.26	7.08	7.44	8.64
Cash Flow	4.56	4.16	3.64	3.29	3.11	2.85
Earnings	3.06	2.77	2.35	2.01	1.94	1.88
Dividends	1.01	0.92	0.82	0.80	0.77	0.69
Payout Ratio	33%	33%	35%	40%	39%	34%
Cal. Yrs.	1994	1993	1992	1991	1990	1989
Prices - High	45⅛	46½	37¼	30¼	29⅝	26⅜
- Low	32¼	33⅜	25⅞	18¾	18⅞	17⅜
P/E Ratio - High	15	17	16	15	15	14
- Low	11	12	11	9	10	9

Income Statement Analysis (Million $)

	1995	%Chg	1994	%Chg	1993	%Chg	1992
Revs.	12,223	6%	11,529	3%	11,150	5%	10,615
Oper. Inc.	1,914	8%	1,770	13%	1,571	12%	1,400
Depr.	374	8%	347	8%	321	NM	319
Int. Exp.	257	-2%	263	-14%	306	-14%	354
Pretax Inc.	1,296	10%	1,178	49%	791	NM	796
Eff. Tax Rate	40%	—	40%	—	24%	—	35%
Net Inc.	782	10%	711	18%	603	17%	515

Balance Sheet & Other Fin. Data (Million $)

	1995	1994	1993	1992	1991	1990
Cash	55.0	46.0	172	207	80.0	92.0
Curr. Assets	4,910	4,679	4,654	4,574	4,377	4,053
Total Assets	9,472	8,800	8,545	8,728	8,295	7,802
Curr. Liab.	1,895	1,771	1,975	1,522	1,742	1,994
LT Debt	2,815	2,822	2,879	3,918	3,565	3,003
Common Eqty.	4,135	3,639	3,181	2,400	2,467	2,319
Total Cap.	7,388	6,847	6,394	7,043	6,781	6,051
Cap. Exp.	937	700	404	512	548	522
Cash Flow	1,137	1,039	906	816	776	763

Ratio Analysis

	1995	1994	1993	1992	1991	1990
Curr. Ratio	2.6	2.6	2.4	3.0	2.5	2.0
% LT Debt of Cap.	38.9	41.2	45.0	55.6	52.6	49.6
% Net Inc.of Revs.	6.4	6.2	5.4	4.9	5.0	5.4
% Ret. on Assets	8.6	8.2	7.0	6.0	6.2	7.1
% Ret. on Equity	19.6	20.3	19.6	22.1	24.3	20.6

Dividend Data —Dividends have been paid since 1911. A "poison pill" stock purchase right was adopted in 1986. A dividend reinvestment plan is available.

Amt. of Div. $	Date Decl.	Ex-Div. Date	Stock of Record	Payment Date
0.260	Nov. 01	Nov. 25	Dec. 01	Dec. 15 '94
0.260	Feb. 01	Feb. 23	Mar. 01	Mar. 15 '95
0.285	Feb. 21	May. 25	Jun. 01	Jun. 15 '95
0.285	May. 19	Aug. 30	Sep. 01	Sep. 15 '95

Data as orig. reptd.; bef. results of disc. opers. and/or spec. items. Per share data adj. for stk. divs. as of ex-div. date. E-Estimated. NA-Not Available. NM-Not Meaningful. NR-Not Ranked.

Office—611 Olive St., St. Louis, MO 63101-1799. **Tel**—(314) 342-6300. **Chrmn & CEO**—D. C. Farrell. **Pres & CFO**—J. T. Loeb. **Secy**—R. A. Brickson. **Sr VP-Treas & Investor Contact**—J. R. Kniffen. **Dirs**—R. L. Battram, D. C. Farrell, T. A. Hays, H. L. Kaplan, J. T. Loeb, E. H. Meyer, R. E. Palmer, A. E. Pearson, M. R. Quinlan, W. P. Stiritz, R. D. Storey, M. L. Weidenbaum, E. E. Whitacre Jr. **Transfer Agent & Registrar**—Bank of New York, NYC. **Incorporated** in New York in 1910. **Empl**-119,000. **S&P Analyst:** Karen J. Sack, CFA

Maytag Corp.

NYSE Symbol **MYG**
In S&P 500

24-AUG-95 **Industry:**
Electronics/Electric

Summary: MYG produces appliances under the Maytag, Magic Chef, Admiral and Jenn-Air names, and floor care products under the Hoover name. The Dixie-Narco division makes vending equipment.

S&P Opinion: Hold (★★★)		
Recent Price • 15⅞	Yield • 3.2%	
52 Wk Range • 18¾-14	12-Mo. P/E • 96.1	

Earnings vs. Previous Year
▲=Up ▼=Down ▶=No Change

Quantitative Evaluations

Outlook
(1 Lowest—5 Highest)
• **3⁻**

Fair Value
• **15**

Risk
• **Low**

Earn./Div. Rank
• **B-**

Technical Eval.
• **Bullish** since 9/92

Rel. Strength Rank
(1 Lowest—99 Highest)
• **22**

Insider Activity
• **Neutral**

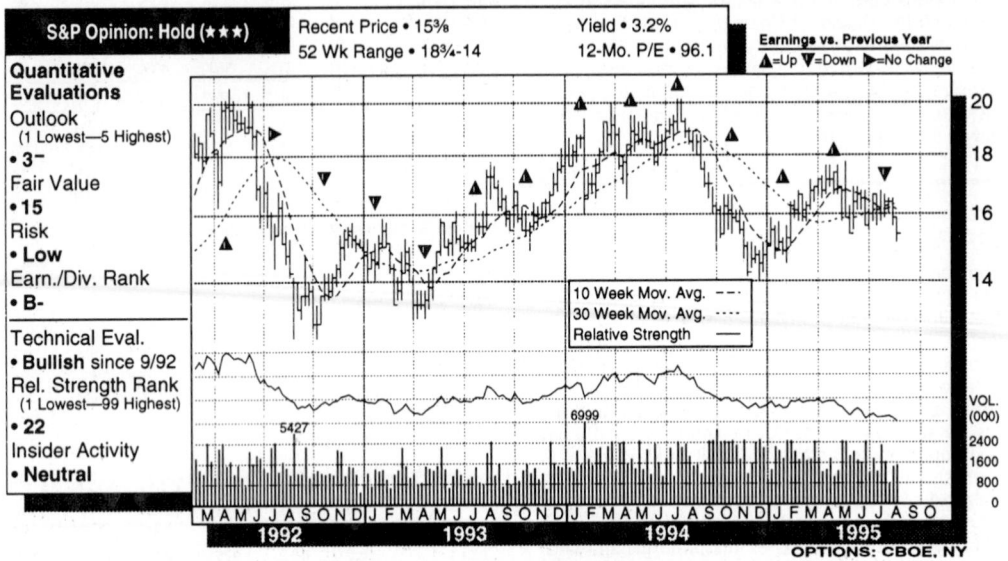

10 Week Mov. Avg. – – –
30 Week Mov. Avg. ⋯⋯⋯
Relative Strength —

5427   6999

VOL. (000)
2400
1600
800
0

1992 1993 1994 1995

OPTIONS: CBOE, NY

Overview - 24-AUG-95

Sales from continuing operations could be under some pressure in 1995 on soft demand for appliances in North America. However, sales of the premium Jenn-Air and Maytag brands should increase on strong marketing efforts, favorable reactions to new products including an "intelligent dishwasher" and faster-cooking ranges, and increased market share within the medium-to-upper priced appliance category. Sales of floor care products vending machines should also increase on new product introductions. Despite a more profitable product mix, margins are likely to narrow on the inability to pass on higher raw material prices and an extremely competitive market in the low-to-medium priced market. Interest charges should be lower. Earnings comparisons will be hurt by various one-time charges.

Valuation - 24-AUG-95

The overall appliance industry has increasingly weakened this year, which we attribute to the disappointing results reported by Maytag for the second quarter. As a result, we lowered our 1995 earnings estimate for Maytag, as well as downgraded our recommendation to a hold. Both sales and margins at the company are under pressure, and it is likely that results in the second half of 1995 will also be under pressure, barring any major boom in the economy. Earnings growth should resume in 1996. However, we feel the stock is adequately priced, given our 1996 earnings estimate and uncertainty regarding the state of the appliance industry next year.

Key Stock Statistics

S&P EPS Est. 1995	0.14	Tang. Bk. Value/Share	3.51
P/E on S&P Est. 1995	NM	Beta	1.13
S&P EPS Est. 1996	1.55	Shareholders	32,500
Dividend Rate/Share	0.50	Market cap. (B)	$ 1.7
Shs. outstg. (M)	107.6	Inst. holdings	66%
Avg. daily vol. (M)	0.235	Insider holdings	NA

Value of $10,000 invested 5 years ago: $ 9,973

Fiscal Year Ending Dec. 31

	1995	% Change	1994	% Change	1993	% Change
Revenues (Million $)						
1Q	820.1	4%	790.6	10%	717.0	-5%
2Q	803.5	-8%	870.4	16%	753.3	-2%
3Q	—	—	848.9	10%	770.2	5%
4Q	—	—	862.6	16%	746.7	-5%
Yr.	—	—	3,373	13%	2,987	-2%
Income (Million $)						
1Q	39.53	28%	31.00	NM	-10.55	NM
2Q	-101.2	NM	41.14	93%	21.31	13%
3Q	—	—	61.03	165%	23.04	NM
4Q	—	—	17.97	3%	17.47	55%
Yr.	—	—	151.1	195%	51.27	NM
Earnings Per Share ($)						
1Q	0.37	28%	0.29	NM	-0.10	NM
2Q	-0.95	NM	0.39	95%	0.20	11%
3Q	E0.37	-35%	0.57	159%	0.22	NM
4Q	E0.35	106%	0.17	6%	0.16	45%
Yr.	E0.14	-90%	1.42	196%	0.48	NM

Next earnings report expected: late October

Maytag Corp.

Business Summary - 24-AUG-95

Maytag is engaged in two industry segments: appliances (94% of sales and 94% of operating profits in 1994) and vending equipment (6% and 6%, respectively). Approximately 16% of 1994's sales were made outside of North America. In mid-1995, Maytag sold its Hoover Europe division to Candy S.p.A., a European producer of household appliances.

Home appliances include laundry equipment, gas and electric ranges, refrigerators, freezers, dishwashers, food waste disposals and floor care products. Important trademarks include Maytag, Magic Chef (acquired in 1986), Admiral, Jenn-Air, Hardwick, Norge and Hoover (acquired in 1989). The company sold its Toastmaster subsidiary in 1987, its Magic Chef air conditioning unit in 1988, and its microwave and dehumidifier businesses in 1992.

Maytag's products are sold to all major market segments, including the replacement market, the commercial laundry market, the new home and apartment building market, the manufactured housing (mobile home) market, the recreational vehicle market, the private-label market, and the household/commercial floor care market. Most products are sold directly to dealers and through independent distributors, mass merchandisers and large national department stores.

Dixie-Narco produces soft-drink vending equipment and money changers. Its products are sold to all major bottlers.

Maycor Appliance Parts and Service Co. provides consolidated service and parts distribution for most of Maytag's appliance brands. Maytag International Inc. handles the sales of appliances and licensing of certain home appliance brands in markets outside of North America. Maytag Financial Services provides financing programs to certain customers in North America.

Important Developments

Jul. '95—Maytag attributed the decline in net income (excluding nonrecurring items) for the second quarter of 1995 to lower unit volumes of major appliances, the inability to pass on raw material price increases, and competitive pressures. Sales at the North American appliance group declined 3.6%, while operating income was down 8.3%. Sales at Dixie Narco declined 1.7%, but operating income increased 3.7%. Following a one-time after tax charge of $135 million in connection with the sale of the Hoover Europe division and excluding a special charge of $3.4 million, Maytag reported a loss of $101.1 million ($0.95 a share), versus net income of $41.1 million ($0.39 a share). Excluding the nonrecurring items, 1995's second quarter share earnings would have been $0.32.

Capitalization

Long Term Debt: $568,864,000 (6/95).

Per Share Data ($)

(Year Ended Dec. 31)

	1994	1993	1992	1991	1990	1989
Tangible Bk. Val.	3.14	2.50	2.54	6.32	6.31	5.51
Cash Flow	2.53	1.53	0.90	1.62	1.75	2.01
Earnings	1.42	0.48	-0.08	0.75	0.94	1.27
Dividends	0.50	0.50	0.50	0.50	0.95	0.95
Payout Ratio	35%	104%	NM	67%	102%	76%
Prices - High	20⅛	18⅝	20⅝	16½	20⅝	26¾
- Low	14	13	12½	10⅜	9⅞	18⅞
P/E Ratio - High	14	39	NM	22	22	21
- Low	10	27	NM	14	11	15

Income Statement Analysis (Million $)

	1994	%Chg	1993	%Chg	1992	%Chg	1991
Revs.	3,373	13%	2,987	-2%	3,041	2%	2,971
Oper. Inc.	442	34%	331	19%	277	-9%	304
Depr.	119	6%	112	9%	103	11%	93.0
Int. Exp.	74.6	-1%	75.4	NM	75.0	NM	75.2
Pretax Inc.	241	168%	90.0	NM	8.0	-93%	123
Eff. Tax Rate	37%	—	43%	—	NM	—	36%
Net Inc.	151	196%	51.0	NM	-8.0	NM	79.0

Balance Sheet & Other Fin. Data (Million $)

	1994	1993	1992	1991	1990	1989
Cash	110	31.7	57.0	48.8	69.6	39.3
Curr. Assets	1,130	1,057	1,016	1,077	1,169	1,140
Total Assets	2,504	2,469	2,501	2,535	2,587	2,436
Curr. Liab.	534	651	563	568	556	489
LT Debt	663	725	789	809	858	877
Common Eqty.	732	587	599	1,011	1,015	938
Total Cap.	1,433	1,356	1,477	1,895	1,944	1,875
Cap. Exp.	79.0	96.0	120	143	141	128
Cash Flow	270	163	95.0	172	185	208

Ratio Analysis

	1994	1993	1992	1991	1990	1989
Curr. Ratio	2.1	1.6	1.8	1.9	2.1	2.3
% LT Debt of Cap.	46.3	53.4	53.4	42.7	44.1	46.8
% Net Inc.of Revs.	4.5	1.7	NM	2.7	3.2	4.3
% Ret. on Assets	6.1	2.1	NM	3.1	3.9	6.2
% Ret. on Equity	22.9	8.6	NM	7.8	10.1	16.1

Dividend Data

Dividends have been paid since 1946. A dividend reinvestment plan is available. A "poison pill" stock purchase rights plan was adopted in 1988.

Amt. of Div. $	Date Decl.	Ex-Div. Date	Stock of Record	Payment Date
0.125	Aug. 11	Aug. 26	Sep. 01	Sep. 15 '94
0.125	Nov. 10	Nov. 25	Dec. 01	Dec. 15 '94
0.125	Feb. 09	Feb. 23	Mar. 01	Mar. 15 '95
0.125	May. 11	May. 25	Jun. 01	Jun. 15 '95
0.125	Aug. 10	Aug. 30	Sep. 01	Sep. 15 '95

Data as orig. reptd.; bef. results of disc. opers. and/or spec. items. Per share data adj. for stk. divs. as of ex-div. date. E-Estimated. NA-Not Available. NM-Not Meaningful. NR-Not Ranked.

Office—403 West 4th St. North, Newton, IA 50208. Tel—(515) 792-8000. Fax—(515) 791-8395. Chrmn & CEO—L. A. Hadley. Secy—J. E. Bennett. EVP-CFO—J. P. Cunningham, Jr. Treas—D. D. Urbani. Investor Contact—James G. Powell. Dirs—B. R. Allen, E. C. Cazier Jr., H. L. Clark Jr., L. Crown, L. A. Hadley, W. R. Hicks, R. D. Ray, B. G. Rethore, W. A. Reynolds, J. A. Sivright, N.E. Stearns Jr., F. G. Steingraber, C. J. Uhrich, P. S. Willmott. Transfer Agent & Registrar—First National Bank of Boston. Incorporated in Delaware in 1925. Empl-19,772. S&P Analyst: Elizabeth Vandeventer

McDermott International

NYSE Symbol **MDR**
In S&P 500

06-NOV-95 **Industry:** Oil and Gas

Summary: McDermott is engaged in the power generation systems market. It also constructs marine production and transportation structures for the oil and natural gas industry.

S&P Opinion: Sell (★)	Recent Price • 16	Yield • 6.3%
	52 Wk Range • 29⅛-15⅝	12-Mo. P/E • 42.1

Earnings vs. Previous Year
▲=Up ▼=Down ▶=No Change

Quantitative Evaluations

Outlook
(1 Lowest—5 Highest)
• **3⁻**

Fair Value
• **15¾**

Risk
• **Low**

Earn./Div. Rank
• **B-**

Technical Eval.
• **Bullish** since 10/95

Rel. Strength Rank
(1 Lowest—99 Highest)
• **4**

Insider Activity
• **NA**

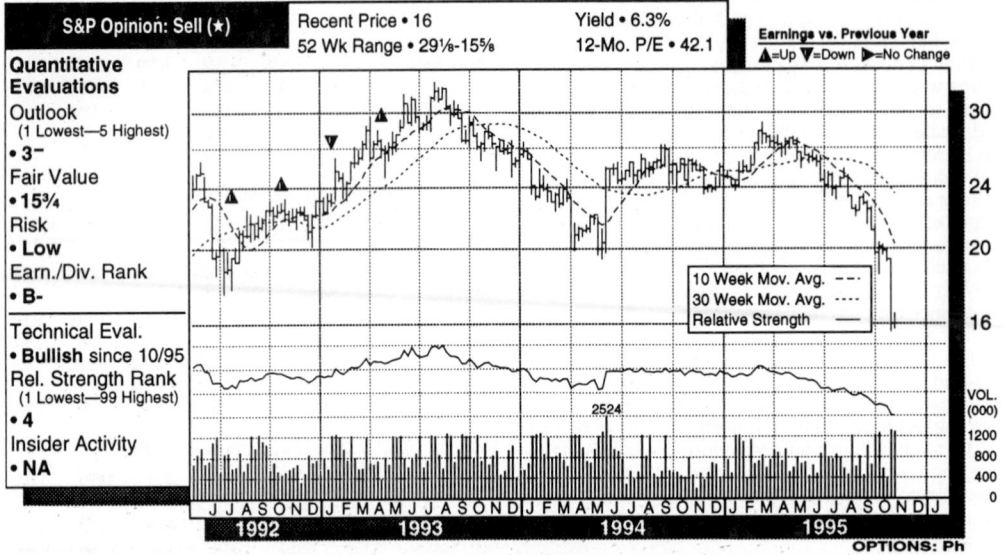

10 Week Mov. Avg. — —
30 Week Mov. Avg. - - - -
Relative Strength ——

2524

VOL. (000)

OPTIONS: Ph

Overview - 06-NOV-95

Operating revenues, before restructuring moves, are expected to fall through year-end 1996, following the January 1994 acquisition of Offshore Pipelines and the divestiture of a minority interest in J. Ray McDermott. Marine construction segment earnings, which have suffered from weaker demand in Southeast Asia, the Middle East and the Gulf of Mexico, will remain flat, as competitive conditions in this market are expected to continue. Power generation earnings should fall during the remainder of 1995 and into 1996, although demand from abroad and growth in the domestic cogeneration market augur well for growth in coming years. Given recent price cuts by McDermott and its competitors in the marine construction segment, we believe further downward earnings revisions are possible.

Valuation - 06-NOV-95

The shares have fallen sharply on negative earnings trends in the marine construction business. The company has been reducing prices in an attempt to win market share, causing margins to deteriorate, and earnings have suffered. With oil prices expected to be volatile in the near term in anticipation of the November 21 OPEC meeting and with gas prices depressed due to an oversupply in the U.S., near-term fundamentals are not promising. The shares will also continue to suffer because of lower income from the power generation systems business, where margins have been under pressure from weak domestic power generation construction.

Key Stock Statistics

S&P EPS Est. 1996	0.70	Tang. Bk. Value/Share	3.43
P/E on S&P Est. 1996	22.9	Beta	0.66
S&P EPS Est. 1997	1.40	Shareholders	6,700
Dividend Rate/Share	1.00	Market cap. (B)	$0.868
Shs. outstg. (M)	54.3	Inst. holdings	78%
Avg. daily vol. (M)	0.276	Insider holdings	NA

Value of $10,000 invested 5 years ago: $ 9,119

Fiscal Year Ending Mar. 31

	1996	% Change	1995	% Change	1994	% Change
Revenues (Million $)						
1Q	816.5	-75%	3,235	—	--	—
2Q	806.8	-75%	3,256	—	--	—
3Q	—	—	3,350	—	--	—
4Q	—	—	844.3	—	--	—
Yr.	—	—	3,044	-75%	12,251	—
Income (Million $)						
1Q	8.83	183%	3.12	-54%	6.81	108%
2Q	9.05	NM	-3.26	NM	29.61	52%
3Q	—	—	29.81	94%	15.38	-26%
4Q	—	—	-18.79	NM	11.78	-56%
Yr.	—	—	10.88	-88%	89.96	34%
Earnings Per Share ($)						
1Q	0.12	NM	0.02	—	--	—
2Q	0.13	NM	-0.10	—	--	—
3Q	E0.20	-61%	0.51	—	--	—
4Q	E0.25	NM	-0.39	—	--	—
Yr.	E0.70	NM	0.05	-98%	2.87	122%

Next earnings report expected: late January

Business Summary - 06-NOV-95

McDermott International, Inc. supplies fossil-fuel and nuclear steam generating systems and equipment to the electric power generation industry and nuclear reactor components to the U.S. Navy. Through its marine construction services segment, MDR designs, engineers, builds and installs marine pipelines, offshore structures and subsea production systems for development drilling and production, and onshore construction and maintenance services. In January 1995, MDR contributed a majority of its marine construction services business to J. Ray McDermott, S.A. (NYSE: JRM), a Panamanian corporation, and acquired Offshore Pipelines. MDR retained a 64% interest in JRM following the $370 million transaction. Fiscal 1994-5 contributions:

	Revs.	Profits
Power generation	54%	32%
Marine construction	46%	68%

MDR is involved in the market for providing power through cogeneration and refuse-fueled power plants. The company is an equipment supplier, an operations and maintenance contractor, and has ownership interests in this field. The company also is a major supplier of nuclear steam generating equipment, including critical heat exchangers and replacement recirculating steam generators, in the Canadian, U.S. and international markets.

MDR builds fixed platforms, which are fastened to the seafloor by pilings driven through their structural legs, installed in water depths of more than 1,000 feet. The segment is also capable of building and installing tension-leg platforms, floating production systems and subsea templates. JRM owns 50% of the HeereMac joint-venture, which provides heavy-lift marine installation services worldwide.

Important Developments

Oct. '95—Second-quarter results improved despite competitive North Sea and Southeast Asian markets, which affected marine construction profits. Increased North Sea revenues reflected significant amounts of revenue associated with purchased equipment and subcontract activities. Equity income from marine construction joint ventures also declined, although the company believes growing backlogs of these ventures will result in increased profits in coming periods. Stagnant domestic utility markets restrained growth in the B&W Power Generation Group's results, while Engineering & Construction results were hurt by cost overruns for a U.S. customer.

Capitalization

Long Term Debt: $567,717,000 (6/95).
Minority Interest: $345,568,000.
Ser. C $2.875 Cum. Conv. Pfd. Stk: 2,875,000 shs. (liquid pref. $50); ea. conv. into 1.4184 com.
Subsid. $2.60 Cum. Pfd. Stk: 2,932,160 shs.

Per Share Data ($)

(Year Ended Mar. 31)

	1995	1994	1993	1992	1991	1990
Tangible Bk. Val.	3.24	20.20	6.07	11.00	9.50	11.72
Cash Flow	2.20	NA	3.63	4.48	0.39	0.33
Earnings	0.05	2.87	1.29	1.75	-1.97	-2.68
Dividends	1.00	1.57	1.00	1.00	1.00	1.00
Payout Ratio	NM	55%	78%	57%	NM	NM
Cal. Yrs.	1994	1993	1992	1991	1990	1989
Prices - High	27½	NA	26	28½	34½	26¼
- Low	19⅜	NA	16	15¼	21⅝	14⅝
P/E Ratio - High	NM	NA	20	16	NM	NM
- Low	NM	NA	12	9	NM	NM

Income Statement Analysis (Million $)

	1995	%Chg	1994	%Chg	1993	%Chg	1992
Revs.	3,044	-75%	12,251	NM	3,173	-10%	3,524
Oper. Inc.	122	-59%	296	53%	193	-20%	240
Depr.	116	73%	67.2	-45%	122	-3%	126
Int. Exp.	60.0	81%	33.2	-64%	92.0	-12%	105
Pretax Inc.	3.0	-99%	233	85%	126	-12%	143
Eff. Tax Rate	NM	—	40%	—	32%	—	30%
Net Inc.	11.0	-92%	131	96%	67.0	-17%	81.0

Balance Sheet & Other Fin. Data (Million $)

	1995	1994	1993	1992	1991	1990
Cash	219	624	319	72.0	204	135
Curr. Assets	1,451	2,551	1,356	1,175	1,217	1,180
Total Assets	4,752	3,447	3,093	3,126	3,314	3,336
Curr. Liab.	1,491	1,557	1,240	1,136	1,503	1,193
LT Debt	579	459	583	765	640	873
Common Eqty.	567	1,161	460	704	567	643
Total Cap.	1,642	1,674	1,272	1,796	1,574	1,891
Cap. Exp.	98.0	NA	82.0	76.0	139	127
Cash Flow	118	198	189	206	17.0	12.0

Ratio Analysis

	1995	1994	1993	1992	1991	1990
Curr. Ratio	1.0	1.6	1.1	1.0	0.8	1.0
% LT Debt of Cap.	35.3	27.4	45.8	42.6	40.6	46.2
% Net Inc.of Revs.	0.4	1.1	2.1	2.3	NM	NM
% Ret. on Assets	0.3	NA	2.1	2.3	NM	NM
% Ret. on Equity	0.5	NA	11.4	11.8	NM	NM

Dividend Data —Dividends have been paid since 1955. A "poison pill" stock purchase right was adopted in 1986.

Amt. of Div. $	Date Decl.	Ex-Div. Date	Stock of Record	Payment Date
0.250	Nov. 08	Dec. 09	Dec. 15	Jan. 01 '95
0.250	Feb. 07	Mar. 09	Mar. 15	Apr. 01 '95
0.250	Jun. 12	Jun. 13	Jun. 15	Jul. 01 '95
0.250	Aug. 08	Sep. 13	Sep. 15	Oct. 01 '95

Data as orig. reptd.; bef. results of disc. opers. and/or spec. items. Per share data adj. for stk. divs. as of ex-div. date. E-Estimated. NA-Not Available. NM-Not Meaningful. NR-Not Ranked.

Office—1450 Poydras St., New Orleans, LA 70112-6050. **Tel**—(504) 587-5400. **Chrmn & CEO**—R. E. Howson. **Sr VP & CFO**—B. A. Hattox. **Sr VP & Secy**—L. R. Purtel. **VP & Investor Contact**—George A. Stoddart (504) 587-5682. **Dirs**—T. D. Barrow, T. H. Black, J. F. Bookout, P. J. Burguieres, J. L. Dutt, B. A. Hattox, R. E. Howson, J. A. Hunt, J. W. Johnstone, J. H. Macdonald, W. McCollam Jr., J. A. Morgan, J. N. Turner. **Transfer Agent & Registrar**—First Chicago Trust Co. of New York, NYC. **Incorporated** in Panama in 1959. **Empl**-25,200. **S&P Analyst:** Raymond J. Deacon

McDonald's Corp.

NYSE Symbol **MCD**
In S&P 500

30-OCT-95

Industry:
Food serving

Summary: MCD is the largest fast-food restaurant company in the U.S. and the world. Some 37% of its more than 15,000 restaurants are outside the U.S.

| S&P Opinion: Hold (★★★) | Recent Price • 41¾ | Yield • 0.6% |
| | 52 Wk Range • 42-27¾ | 12-Mo. P/E • 22.1 |

Quantitative Evaluations

Outlook
(1 Lowest—5 Highest)
• **4+**

Fair Value
• **42¾**

Risk
• **Low**

Earn./Div. Rank
• **A+**

Technical Eval.
• **Bearish** since 7/95

Rel. Strength Rank
(1 Lowest—99 Highest)
• **88**

Insider Activity
• **Neutral**

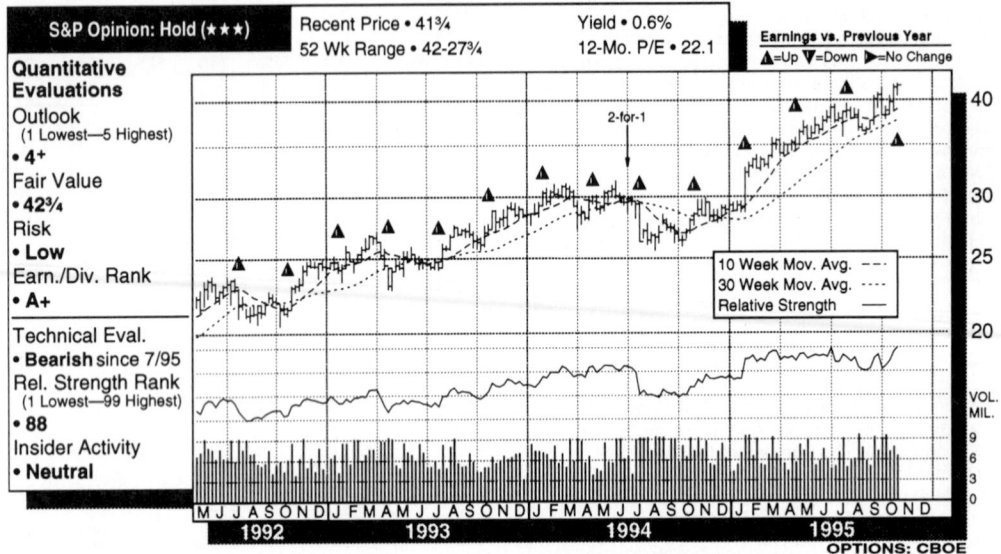

Earnings vs. Previous Year
▲=Up ▼=Down ▶=No Change

2-for-1

10 Week Mov. Avg. - - -
30 Week Mov. Avg. ....
Relative Strength —

VOL. MIL.

1992 1993 1994 1995

OPTIONS: CBOE

Overview - 30-OCT-95

In 1996 and beyond, we expect further double-digit annual earnings growth from the international operations of this well-managed company. In various foreign markets, additional benefits from economies of scale are likely as MCD's presence continues to grow. Earnings from outside the U.S. have recently been accounting for more than half of the company's operating profit. In the U.S., MCD has successfully implemented a value-oriented strategy, and we expect at least a modest profit increase in the year ahead. MCD's access to consumers is being extended by development of smaller satellite locations at numerous sites.
Long-term, we see MCD facing the challenge of an aging U.S. population increasingly shifting to casual dining restaurants that offer more amenities and a fuller menu.

Valuation - 30-OCT-95

The stock of this highly successful restaurant company is increasingly a proxy for investors' expectations for worldwide economic growth. MCD has proven its ability to introduce and expand its food-service concept in foreign markets; currently, about 37% of MCD's more than 15,000 restaurants are located outside the U.S. We expect MCD's overall earnings to grow 12% to 14% annually during the next few years. Also, we look for the the stock to get some near-term support from continuation of a large share repurchase program by the company. We view the stock as an attractive long-term holding, with the shares offering both growth and defensive characteristics.

Key Stock Statistics

S&P EPS Est. 1995	1.95	Tang. Bk. Value/Share	9.01
P/E on S&P Est. 1995	21.4	Beta	1.05
S&P EPS Est. 1996	2.20	Shareholders	529,300
Dividend Rate/Share	0.27	Market cap. (B)	$ 29.0
Shs. outstg. (M)	694.0	Inst. holdings	58%
Avg. daily vol. (M)	1.768	Insider holdings	NA

Value of $10,000 invested 5 years ago: $ 25,415

Fiscal Year Ending Dec. 31

	1995	% Change	1994	% Change	1993	% Change
Revenues (Million $)						
1Q	2,161	20%	1,796	9%	1,654	2%
2Q	2,468	22%	2,029	8%	1,878	6%
3Q	2,580	16%	2,225	14%	1,944	2%
4Q	—	—	2,270	18%	1,932	6%
Yr.	—	—	8,321	12%	7,408	4%
Income (Million $)						
1Q	280.7	15%	243.4	11%	218.3	16%
2Q	379.7	18%	322.3	12%	288.8	14%
3Q	400.1	14%	349.8	13%	310.9	8%
4Q	—	—	308.9	17%	264.5	16%
Yr.	—	—	1,224	13%	1,083	13%
Earnings Per Share ($)						
1Q	0.39	20%	0.32	14%	0.29	12%
2Q	0.52	18%	0.44	13%	0.39	13%
3Q	0.56	17%	0.48	13%	0.43	8%
4Q	E0.48	12%	0.43	19%	0.36	18%
Yr.	E1.95	16%	1.68	16%	1.45	12%

Next earnings report expected: late January

McDonald's Corp.

30-OCT-95

Business Summary - 23-OCT-95

McDonald's operates, licenses and services the world's largest chain of fast-food restaurants. At December 31, 1994, there were 9,744 units in the U.S. and 5,461 in more than 60 other countries or overseas territories. Of the international units, 69% were in Japan, Canada, Germany, England, Australia and France.

Contributions by geographic area in 1994 were United States 50% of revenues, 50% of profits, Europe/Africa/Middle East 31% revenues, 30% of profits, Canada 7% of revenues, 5% of profits, Asia/Pacific 9% of revenues, 11% of profits, and Latin America 3% of revenues, 4% of profits.

Units in operation at year end were:

	1994	1993	1992	1991
Company	3,083	2,699	2,551	2,547
Franchisees	10,458	9,832	9,237	8,735
Affiliates	1,664	1,462	1,305	1,136
Total	15,205	13,993	13,093	12,418

MCD restaurants offer a substantially uniform menu, including hamburgers, french fries, chicken, fish, specialty sandwiches, beverages and desserts. Most units also serve breakfast.

MCD owns or leases a substantial amount of the real estate used by franchisees in their operations. Fees from franchisees to MCD typically include rents and service fees, often totaling at least 11.5% of sales. Licensees make sizable investments in startup costs.

Important Developments

Oct. '95—In 1995's third quarter, U.S. systemwide sales (including franchises) rose 4.7%, year to year, while sales in international markets were up 24% (19% if currency fluctuation is excluded). International operating profit increased 25% (19% if adjusted for currency), while U.S. profit was up 2%. Overall, foreign currency fluctuation contributed about $0.01 a share to MCD's third quarter earnings, and about $0.05 to earnings in 1995's first nine months. As of September 30, 1995, there were 16,099 MCD restaurants open worldwide, up 10% from a year earlier. Of these, about 37% were outside the U.S. In addition, MCD had 1,304 satellite units open worldwide. Also, as of September 30, 1995, MCD had repurchased about $800 million of common stock under a three-year $1 billion authorization announced in January 1994.

Capitalization

Long Term Debt: $3,976,700,000 (6/95).
Preferred Stock: $542,900,000 (6/95).

Per Share Data ($)

(Year Ended Dec. 31)

	1994	1993	1992	1991	1990	1989
Tangible Bk. Val.	8.60	7.32	6.63	6.22	5.29	4.17
Cash Flow	2.57	2.15	1.98	1.81	1.71	1.50
Earnings	1.68	1.45	1.30	1.17	1.10	0.98
Dividends	0.23	0.21	0.20	0.18	0.17	0.15
Payout Ratio	14%	15%	15%	15%	15%	15%
Prices - High	31½	29⅝	25¼	20	19¼	17½
- Low	25½	22¾	19⅛	13⅛	12½	11½
P/E Ratio - High	19	20	19	17	18	18
- Low	15	16	15	11	11	12

Income Statement Analysis (Million $)

	1994	%Chg	1993	%Chg	1992	%Chg	1991
Revs.	8,321	12%	7,408	4%	7,133	7%	6,695
Oper. Inc.	2,801	16%	2,415	5%	2,290	13%	2,022
Depr.	629	28%	493	NM	493	8%	457
Int. Exp.	326	-3%	336	-15%	393	-6%	418
Pretax Inc.	1,887	13%	1,676	16%	1,448	11%	1,299
Eff. Tax Rate	35%	—	35%	—	34%	—	34%
Net Inc.	1,224	13%	1,083	13%	959	12%	860

Balance Sheet & Other Fin. Data (Million $)

	1994	1993	1992	1991	1990	1989
Cash	180	186	437	220	143	137
Curr. Assets	741	663	865	646	549	495
Total Assets	13,592	12,035	11,681	11,349	10,668	9,175
Curr. Liab.	2,451	1,102	1,545	1,288	1,199	1,017
LT Debt	2,935	3,489	3,176	4,267	4,429	3,901
Common Eqty.	6,446	6,350	5,984	4,537	3,984	3,349
Total Cap.	10,930	10,744	9,911	9,837	9,306	8,064
Cap. Exp.	1,539	1,354	1,171	1,129	1,613	1,556
Cash Flow	1,806	1,528	1,437	1,297	1,232	1,113

Ratio Analysis

	1994	1993	1992	1991	1990	1989
Curr. Ratio	0.3	0.6	0.6	0.5	0.5	0.5
% LT Debt of Cap.	26.9	32.5	32.0	43.4	47.6	48.4
% Net Inc.of Revs.	14.7	14.6	13.4	12.8	12.1	12.0
% Ret. on Assets	9.6	9.3	8.3	7.8	8.1	8.5
% Ret. on Equity	19.3	17.0	17.4	19.7	21.6	21.8

Dividend Data —Dividends were initiated in 1976. A dividend reinvestment plan is available. A new "poison pill" stock purchase rights plan was adopted in 1988.

Amt. of Div. $	Date Decl.	Ex-Div. Date	Stock of Record	Payment Date
0.060	Nov. 15	Nov. 23	Nov. 30	Dec. 16 '94
0.060	Jan. 19	Feb. 22	Feb. 28	Mar. 17 '95
0.067	May. 26	May. 30	Jun. 05	Jun. 16 '95
0.067	Jul. 11	Aug. 29	Aug. 31	Sep. 15 '95

Data as orig. reptd.; bef. results of disc. opers. and/or spec. items. Per share data adj. for stk. divs. as of ex-div. date. E-Estimated. NA-Not Available. NM-Not Meaningful. NR-Not Ranked.

Office—McDonald's Plaza, Oak Brook, IL 60521. **Tel**—(708) 575-3000. **Chrmn & CEO**—M. R. Quinlan. **Vice Chrmn & CFO**—J. M. Greenberg. **Broker Inquiries**—Tel. 708-575-5137. **Shareholder Services**—Tel. 708-575-6413. **Dirs**—H. Adams Jr., R. M. Beavers Jr., J. R. Cantalupo, G. C. Gray, J. M. Greenberg, D. R. Keough, D. G. Lubin, A. J. McKenna, M. R. Quinlan, E. H. Rensi, T. Savage, P. D. Schrage, B. F. Smith, R. W. Stone, R. N. Thurston, F. L. Turner, B. B. Vedder Jr. **Transfer Agent & Registrar**—First Chicago Trust Company, Jersey City, N.J. **Incorporated** in Delaware in 1965. **Empl**-167,000. **S&P Analyst:** Tom Graves, CFA

McDonnell Douglas

NYSE Symbol **MD**
In S&P 500

02-OCT-95

Industry:
Aerospace

Summary: This leading manufacturer of fighter aircraft for the U.S. military is also a producer of missiles, space systems and commercial jetliners.

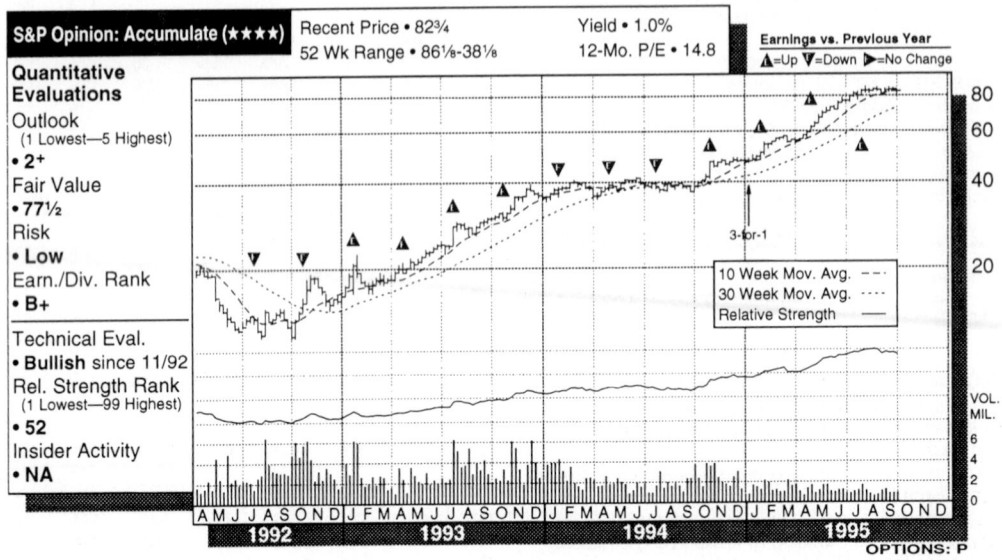

S&P Opinion: Accumulate (★★★★)

Recent Price • 82¾	Yield • 1.0%
52 Wk Range • 86⅛-38⅛	12-Mo. P/E • 14.8

Earnings vs. Previous Year
▲=Up ▼=Down ▶=No Change

Quantitative Evaluations

Outlook
(1 Lowest—5 Highest)
• **2+**

Fair Value
• **77½**

Risk
• **Low**

Earn./Div. Rank
• **B+**

Technical Eval.
• **Bullish** since 11/92

Rel. Strength Rank
(1 Lowest—99 Highest)
• **52**

Insider Activity
• **NA**

3-for-1

10 Week Mov. Avg. — -
30 Week Mov. Avg. — —
Relative Strength — —

VOL. MIL.

1992 1993 1994 1995

OPTIONS: P

Overview - 29-SEP-95

Sales for 1995 should increase in the high single digits from those of 1994, primarily reflecting commercial sales. The group will benefit from a pickup in deliveries of MD-80s and MD-90s; deliveries of MD-11s will be about unchanged. Military aircraft sales should show a modest rise as increases in some models offset declining rates for others. Missiles and space revenues will be off slightly, reflecting winding-down of certain programs. Margins should continue to widen. Interest expense is anticipated to fall, and share earnings are expected to benefit from fewer shares outstanding.

Valuation - 29-SEP-95

MD has demonstrated that it can earn a profit with low-volume commercial jet production, but it has not be able to secure enough orders to launch the MD-95. Major airlines must still be convinced that MD will be a long-term participant in the commercial jet market. Military aircraft might get a boost if the DOD announces a need for 80-120 C-17s or if Congress buys more fighters. Although the strategic direction of the missiles and helicopter businesses might need to be reassessed, due to reduced defense spending and/or increased competition, we believe the planned Delta III satellite launcher could become a major product in the large-payload rocket market. Accordingly, we view the shares, trading at 14 times our estimate of 1995 earnings, as attractive.

Key Stock Statistics

S&P EPS Est. 1995	6.00	Tang. Bk. Value/Share	34.75
P/E on S&P Est. 1995	13.8	Beta	0.10
S&P EPS Est. 1996	6.75	Shareholders	24,700
Dividend Rate/Share	0.80	Market cap. (B)	$ 9.3
Shs. outstg. (M)	113.0	Inst. holdings	54%
Avg. daily vol. (M)	0.194	Insider holdings	NA

Value of $10,000 invested 5 years ago: $ 47,313

Fiscal Year Ending Dec. 31

	1995	% Change	1994	% Change	1993	% Change
Revenues (Million $)						
1Q	3,333	13%	2,953	-18%	3,617	-11%
2Q	3,922	21%	3,250	-15%	3,810	-21%
3Q	—	—	3,461	NM	3,428	-12%
4Q	—	—	3,512	-3%	3,632	-22%
Yr.	—	—	13,176	-9%	14,487	-17%
Income (Million $)						
1Q	159.0	19%	134.0	-25%	179.0	NM
2Q	169.0	22%	138.0	-19%	170.0	NM
3Q	—	—	161.0	13%	142.0	NM
4Q	—	—	165.0	NM	-132.0	NM
Yr.	—	—	598.0	67%	359.0	-49%
Earnings Per Share ($)						
1Q	1.38	21%	1.14	-26%	1.53	NM
2Q	1.48	27%	1.17	-19%	1.44	NM
3Q	E1.52	12%	1.36	12%	1.21	NM
4Q	E1.62	17%	1.39	NM	-1.12	NM
Yr.	E6.00	19%	5.05	65%	3.06	-49%

Next earnings report expected: mid October

McDonnell Douglas

02-OCT-95

Business Summary - 29-SEP-95

McDonnell Douglas Corporation is a leading producer of military and commercial aircraft. Sales and operating earnings by segment in 1994 were:

	Sales	Profits
Military aircraft	59%	66%
Commercial aircraft	24%	4%
Missiles/space/electronics	14%	25%
Financial services & other	3%	5%

Sales to the U.S. Government, including foreign military sales, accounted for 70% of 1994 sales, versus 63% in 1993.

Military aircraft include the F/A-18 multi-role aircraft for the U.S. Navy and Marines and for Canada, Australia, Spain, Switzerland and Finland; the F-15 fighter for the USAF and several foreign nations; the AV-8B Harrier II VSTOL plane for the U.S. Marine Corps and foreign nations; the C-17 military transport; and the T-45 trainer for the Navy. MD also makes the AH-64 helicopter for the U.S. Army and several foreign nations.

Commercial aircraft include several models of the MD-80, the MD-90 derivative of the MD-80 and the three-engined MD-11 widebody.

Missiles, space and electronics programs include the U.S. Navy's Harpoon antiship missile, the Tomahawk cruise missile, the Standoff Land Attack Missile (SLAM), the Delta launch vehicle and a variety of defense electronic products and systems.

Financial services include commercial aircraft financing and commercial equipment leasing.

Important Developments

Aug. '95—Twelve C-17 transports completed a 30-day Reliability, Maintainability and Availability Evaluation. During the intensive evaluation, launch reliability and utilization rates easily exceeded required target rates. A decision by the Department of Defense on whether to purchase additional C-17s is expected in late 1995.
Jul. '95—Britain awarded a $4 billion contract for 67 Apache army attack helicopters to McDonnell Douglass and U.K.-based Westland Group.
May '95—Hughes Electronics agreed to buy at least 10 launches, beginning 1998, as the first customer of MD's Delta III. If all options are exercised, the deal could be worth $1.5 billion.
Mar. '95—The company delivered its first two MD-90 commercial jetliners.

Capitalization

Long Term Debt: $2,649,000,000 (6/95), incl. current maturities.
Minority Interest: $69,000,000.

Per Share Data ($)

(Year Ended Dec. 31)

	1994	1993	1992	1991	1990	1989
Tangible Bk. Val.	33.17	28.93	25.70	33.65	30.58	28.17
Cash Flow	7.28	5.66	9.52	7.28	7.03	3.92
Earnings	5.05	3.06	5.99	3.08	2.39	-0.32
Dividends	0.55	0.47	0.47	0.47	0.94	0.94
Payout Ratio	11%	15%	8%	15%	39%	NM
Prices - High	48⅝	39½	26	26⅞	21¼	31½
- Low	34⅛	16⅛	11⅜	8⅞	11⅜	19⅞
P/E Ratio - High	10	13	4	9	9	NM
- Low	7	5	2	3	5	NM

Income Statement Analysis (Million $)

	1994	%Chg	1993	%Chg	1992	%Chg	1991
Revs.	13,162	-9%	14,474	-17%	17,373	-6%	18,432
Oper. Inc.	1,419	5%	1,349	52%	889	-44%	1,576
Depr.	264	-14%	308	-25%	411	-15%	483
Int. Exp.	270	24%	217	-56%	493	2%	485
Pretax Inc.	920	100%	459	-58%	1,086	74%	624
Eff. Tax Rate	35%	—	22%	—	36%	—	43%
Net Inc.	598	67%	359	-49%	698	97%	355

Balance Sheet & Other Fin. Data (Million $)

	1994	1993	1992	1991	1990	1989
Cash	421	86.0	82.0	229	226	119
Curr. Assets	NA	NA	NA	NA	NA	NA
Total Assets	12,216	12,026	13,781	14,841	14,965	13,397
Curr. Liab.	NA	NA	NA	NA	NA	NA
LT Debt	2,143	2,465	2,391	3,009	3,466	2,654
Common Eqty.	3,872	3,413	3,022	3,877	3,514	3,287
Total Cap.	6,084	5,950	5,413	6,886	6,980	5,941
Cap. Exp.	NA	NA	NA	NA	NA	864
Cash Flow	862	667	1,109	838	808	450

Ratio Analysis

	1994	1993	1992	1991	1990	1989
Curr. Ratio	NA	NA	NA	NA	NA	NA
% LT Debt of Cap.	35.2	41.4	44.2	43.7	49.7	44.7
% Net Inc.of Revs.	4.5	2.5	4.0	1.9	1.7	NM
% Ret. on Assets	5.0	2.8	4.8	2.4	1.9	NM
% Ret. on Equity	16.5	11.1	20.0	9.6	8.1	NM

Dividend Data —Dividends have been paid since 1950.

Amt. of Div. $	Date Decl.	Ex-Div. Date	Stock of Record	Payment Date
0.200	Oct. 28	Nov. 28	Dec. 02	Jan. 03 '95
3-for-1	Oct. 28	Jan. 04	Dec. 02	Jan. 03 '95
0.200	Jan. 27	Feb. 27	Mar. 03	Apr. 03 '95
0.200	Apr. 28	Jun. 06	Jun. 09	Jul. 03 '95
0.200	Jul. 21	Aug. 30	Sep. 01	Oct. 02 '95

Data as orig. reptd.; bef. results of disc. opers. and/or spec. items. Per share data adj. for stk. divs. as of ex-div. date. E-Estimated. NA-Not Available. NM-Not Meaningful. NR-Not Ranked.

Office—P.O. Box 516, St. Louis, MO 63166-0516. **Tel**—(314) 232-0232. **Chrmn**— J. F. McDonnell. **Pres & CEO**—H. C. Stonecipher. **VP & Secy**—S. N. Frank. **Sr VP & CFO**—J. F. Palmer. **Investor Contact**—Robert M. Bokern (314) 232-6358. **Dirs**—J. H. Biggs, B. A. Bridgewater Jr., B. B. Byron, W. E. Cornelius, W. H. Danforth, K. M. Duberstein, W. S. Kanaga, J. F. McDonnell, J. S. McDonnell III, G. A. Schaefer, R. L. Thompson, H. S. Stonecipher, P. R. Vagelos. **Transfer Agent & Registrar**—First Chicago Trust Co., NYC. **Incorporated** in Maryland in 1939. **Empl**-64,092. **S&P Analyst:** Joe Victor Shammas

McGraw-Hill Companies

NYSE Symbol **MHP**

In S&P 500

01-NOV-95 Industry: Publishing

Summary: The McGraw-Hill Companies is a leading information services organization serving worldwide markets in education, business, industry, the professions and government.

S&P Opinion: No Opinion	Recent Price • 82⅜	Yield • 2.9%
	52 Wk Range • 84¾-63⅝	12-Mo. P/E • 18.4

Quantitative Evaluations

Outlook
(1 Lowest—5 Highest)
• **2+**

Fair Value
• **79¾**

Risk
• **Low**

Earn./Div. Rank
• **NR**

Technical Eval.
• **Bearish** since 9/95

Rel. Strength Rank
(1 Lowest—99 Highest)
• **70**

Insider Activity
• **NA**

Earnings vs. Previous Year
▲=Up ▼=Down ▶=No Change

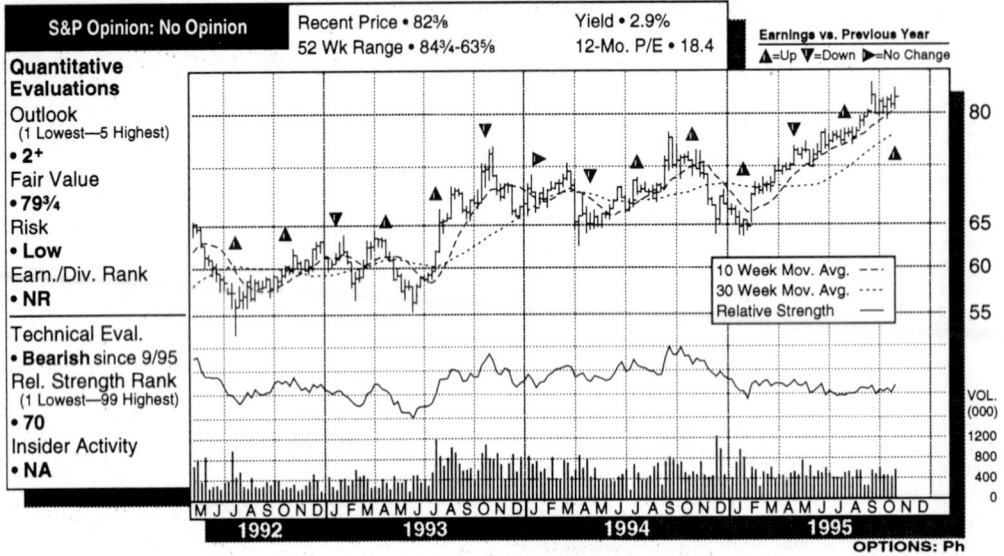

10 Week Mov. Avg. - - -
30 Week Mov. Avg. ·····
Relative Strength ——

VOL. (000)

OPTIONS: Ph

Overview - 01-NOV-95

Revenue gains anticipated for 1996 will largely reflect contributions from financial services, and information and media services. Although the school-age population will continue to grow, a slowdown in state adoptions will negatively impact el-hi publishing. Profitability will benefit from ongoing efficiency measures, but improvement will be limited by the cost of investments in new products and services. The company affirmed that it is on target to achieve its growth objectives for the full year 1995. Operating income in the nine months through September 30, 1995, advanced nearly 14% on a 5.9% rise in revenues. Educational and professional publishing profits climbed 21%; financial services profits rose 6.9%; and information and media services profits advanced 15%.

Valuation - 31-OCT-95

The consensus opinion among analysts who follow MHP calls for earnings gains of roughly 11% in both 1995 and 1996. At nearly 19 times trailing 12-month earnings, the stock currently trades at a multiple much higher than projected growth rates, and at a premium to the overall market. MHP's valuation stems from a number of positive factors, including the perception that the company's strong franchises have significant underlying value. Costs of expanding international markets, acquisitions and ongoing investments in new products and services, have combined with cyclical factors to moderate MHP's earnings gains. Consistent annual increases in the cash dividend, which has been raised in each year since 1974, also buoy the stock.

Key Stock Statistics

S&P EPS Est.	NA	Tang. Bk. Value/Share	NM
P/E on S&P Est.	NA	Beta	0.70
Dividend Rate/Share	2.40	Shareholders	6,500
Shs. outstg. (M)	49.9	Market cap. (B)	$ 4.1
Avg. daily vol. (M)	0.089	Inst. holdings	64%
		Insider holdings	NA

Value of $10,000 invested 5 years ago: $ 17,901

Fiscal Year Ending Dec. 31

	1995	% Change	1994	% Change	1993	% Change
Revenues (Million $)						
1Q	568.5	2%	559.8	20%	467.0	3%
2Q	712.8	10%	648.3	32%	490.9	1%
3Q	904.3	6%	855.5	54%	555.0	4%
4Q	—	—	697.3	2%	682.6	18%
Yr.	—	—	2,761	26%	2,195	7%
Income (Million $)						
1Q	13.95	-7%	14.97	-2%	15.25	23%
2Q	52.84	10%	48.04	11%	43.18	17%
3Q	105.8	17%	90.16	NM	-91.87	NM
4Q	—	—	49.95	11%	44.88	NM
Yr.	—	—	203.1	NM	11.44	-93%
Earnings Per Share ($)						
1Q	0.28	-7%	0.30	-3%	0.31	24%
2Q	1.06	9%	0.97	10%	0.88	17%
3Q	2.12	16%	1.82	NM	-1.87	NM
4Q	—	—	1.01	11%	0.91	NM
Yr.	—	—	4.10	NM	0.23	-93%

Next earnings report expected: early February

Business Summary - 31-OCT-95

The McGraw-Hill Companies, Inc., is a leading provider of information products and services to business, professional and educational markets worldwide through books, magazines, newsletters, software, on-line data services, CD-ROMs, facsimile and television broadcasting. Segment contributions in 1994 were:

	Revs.	Profits
Information & media services	31%	24%
Educational and professional publishing	42%	28%
Financial services	27%	48%

International operations accounted for 13% of revenues and 9% of operating profits in 1994.

Information and media services include Business Week magazine, as well as other magazines, newsletters, directories, and video and online products serving the construction, computer and communications, aerospace and defense, energy, health care and process industries. Also included are four network-affiliated TV stations in Denver, Indianapolis, San Diego and Bakersfield.

Educational and professional publishing includes college publishing, medical, international, legal, and professional book operations. The group also includes the Macmillan/McGraw-Hill School Publishing Co., which operated as a 50%-owned joint venture from its formation in 1989 until October 1993, when MHP acquired the remaining 50%.

Financial services include Standard & Poor's, DRI/McGraw-Hill, commodity services, J. J. Kenny Co., and international trade and logistics management services.

Important Developments

Jun. '95—Corel Corporation, a major developer and marketer of PC graphics and SCSI software, signed a book publishing agreement with Osborne/McGraw-Hill, a unit of MHP's Professional Publishing Group, to develop a new line of books that focus on Corel's family of software products. Between five and eight books are scheduled to be published by Osborne over the next year and a half under the new CorelPRESS imprint.

Jun. '95—Standard & Poor's introduced its new Bank Loan Ratings (BLRs), the first rating scale designed specifically to serve the $665 billion syndicated bank loan market. The BLRs are designed to measure both whether an issuer will pay on time and how well protected from loss the lender is in the event the issuer defaults.

Capitalization

Long Term Debt: $657,705,000 (6/95).

$1.20 Conv. Preference Stock: 1,514 shs. ($10 par); red. at $40; ea. conv. into 3.3 com. shs.

Per Share Data ($)

(Year Ended Dec. 31)

	1994	1993	1992	1991	1990	1989
Tangible Bk. Val.	-1.21	-4.01	7.23	8.60	7.48	9.60
Cash Flow	6.16	1.92	4.65	4.51	4.90	2.23
Earnings	4.10	0.23	3.13	3.03	3.53	0.82
Dividends	2.32	2.28	2.24	2.20	2.16	2.05
Payout Ratio	57%	NM	72%	73%	61%	251%
Prices - High	77¼	75¼	66½	64¾	61⅛	86⅛
- Low	62½	55¼	53	49¾	39⅞	53½
P/E Ratio - High	19	NM	21	21	17	NM
- Low	15	NM	17	16	11	NM

Income Statement Analysis (Million $)

	1994	%Chg	1993	%Chg	1992	%Chg	1991
Revs.	2,761	26%	2,195	7%	2,050	6%	1,943
Oper. Inc.	477	27%	376	5%	358	5%	342
Depr.	102	23%	82.9	12%	74.3	3%	72.1
Int. Exp.	51.7	42%	36.3	-3%	37.6	-20%	47.0
Pretax Inc.	345	NM	66.0	-75%	267	3%	258
Eff. Tax Rate	41%	—	83%	—	43%	—	43%
Net Inc.	203	NM	11.0	-93%	153	3%	148

Balance Sheet & Other Fin. Data (Million $)

	1994	1993	1992	1991	1990	1989
Cash	8.0	48.0	13.0	17.0	21.0	35.0
Curr. Assets	1,124	1,132	911	942	961	840
Total Assets	3,009	3,084	2,508	2,525	2,534	2,208
Curr. Liab.	1,008	1,069	841	819	845	793
LT Debt	658	758	359	437	508	378
Common Eqty.	913	823	909	999	954	880
Total Cap.	1,700	1,700	1,377	1,619	1,579	1,298
Cap. Exp.	77.1	49.8	55.9	51.2	95.8	58.0
Cash Flow	305	94.0	227	220	239	109

Ratio Analysis

	1994	1993	1992	1991	1990	1989
Curr. Ratio	1.1	1.1	1.1	1.2	1.1	1.1
% LT Debt of Cap.	38.7	44.6	26.0	27.0	32.1	29.1
% Net Inc.of Revs.	7.4	0.5	7.5	7.6	8.9	2.2
% Ret. on Assets	6.7	0.4	6.1	5.8	7.3	2.0
% Ret. on Equity	23.3	1.3	16.1	15.1	18.8	4.4

Dividend Data —Dividends have been paid since 1937, and raised each year since 1974. A dividend reinvestment plan is available. A new "poison pill" stock purchase right was issued in 1989.

Amt. of Div. $	Date Decl.	Ex-Div. Date	Stock of Record	Payment Date
0.580	Oct. 19	Nov. 21	Nov. 28	Dec. 12 '94
0.600	Jan. 25	Feb. 17	Feb. 24	Mar. 10 '95
0.600	Apr. 26	May. 22	May. 26	Jun. 12 '95
0.600	Jul. 26	Aug. 24	Aug. 28	Sep. 12 '95
0.600	Oct. 25	Nov. 24	Nov. 28	Dec. 12 '95

Data as orig. reptd.; bef. results of disc. opers. and/or spec. items. Per share data adj. for stk. divs. as of ex-div. date.
E-Estimated. NA-Not Available. NM-Not Meaningful. NR-Not Ranked.

Office—1221 Avenue of the Americas, New York, NY 10020. **Tel**—(212) 512-2000. **Chrmn & CEO**—J. L. Dionne. **Pres & COO**—H. W. McGraw, III. **Senior EVP & Secy**—R. N. Landes. **Senior EVP & Gen Counsel**—K. M. Vittor. **EVP & CFO**—R. J. Bahash. **SVP & Investor Contact**—Donald S. Rubin (212-512-4321). **Dirs**—J. L. Dionne, V. Gregorian, J. T. Hartley, G. B. Harvey, R. H. Jenrette, D. Johnston, P. O. Lawson-Johnston, L. K. Lorimer, H. W. McGraw III, R. P. McGraw, L. D. Rice, P. J. Rizzo, J. H. Ross, A. O. Way. **Transfer Agents**—Chemical Bank, NYC; Chemical Trust Co. of California. **Incorporated** in New York in 1925. **Empl**-15,339. **S&P Analyst:** William H. Donald

Mead Corp.

NYSE Symbol **MEA**
In S&P 500

09-AUG-95

Industry:
Paper/Products

Summary: This major integrated producer of white papers, paper-board and converted products also makes construction materials and operates a large paper distribution business.

| S&P Opinion: Hold (★★★) | Recent Price • 62¼ | Yield • 1.8% |
| | 52 Wk Range • 64⅛-43⅜ | 12-Mo. P/E • 4.8 |

Earnings vs. Previous Year
▲=Up ▼=Down ▶=No Change

Quantitative Evaluations

Outlook
(1 Lowest—5 Highest)
• **5+**

Fair Value
• **73¾**

Risk
• **Low**

Earn./Div. Rank
• **B-**

Technical Eval.
• **Bearish** since 9/94

Rel. Strength Rank
(1 Lowest—99 Highest)
• **73**

Insider Activity
• **Neutral**

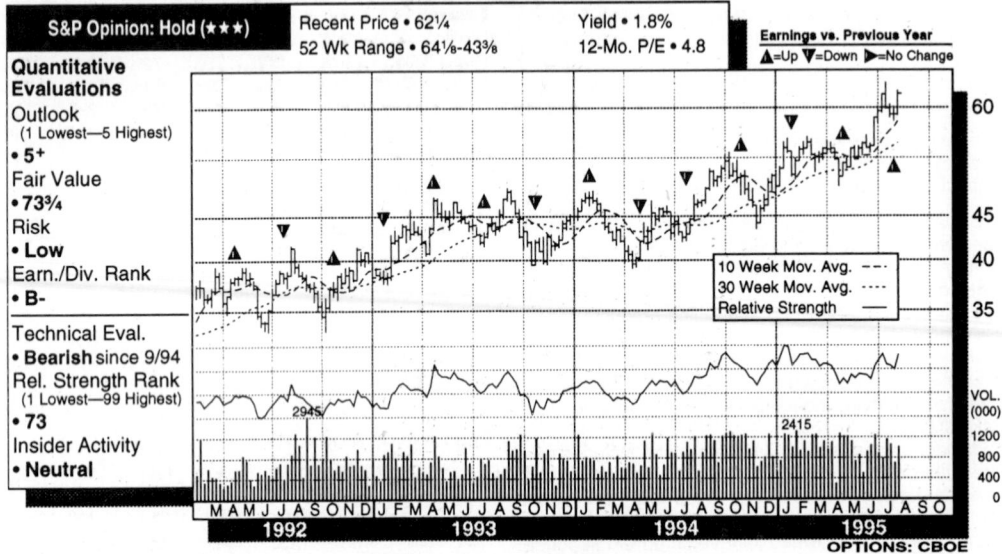

10 Week Mov. Avg. ----
30 Week Mov. Avg. ----
Relative Strength —

OPTIONS: CBOE

Overview - 09-AUG-95

Sales from continuing operations should be solidly higher in 1995, as growth in global economies continues to stimulate strong pulp and paper demand, and tight supply conditions lead to ongoing steep product prices. Sales should rise in both the manufacturing and distribution segments. Operating margins should widen, on the favorable pricing trends and improved production efficiencies. Joint venture profits are expected to fall, with weak lumber prices and higher wood costs likely to outweigh strength in the pulp area. Interest charges should be much lower, as MEA vastly improved its balance sheet with proceeds from the late 1994 sale of Mead Data Central. Mead's bottom line will also benefit from the absence of various one-time items, which reduced earnings from continuing operations by $0.77 a share in 1994. Mead's share repurchase program will aid EPS comparisons.

Valuation - 09-AUG-95

Mead's shares have been in an uptrend since late 1990. The early gains were stimulated by an improving economy and investor enthusiasm for Mead's operating strategy, while appreciation in the past year reflected a long-awaited upturn in industry conditions. Although the recent slowing of U.S. economic growth causes worries about an industry cycle peak, we expect tight supply conditions and strong export markets to allow industry strength to continue through 1996. However, the shares seem fairly priced in their recent trading range of about 9X our 1996 EPS estimate, given the growing level of economic uncertainty.

Key Stock Statistics

S&P EPS Est. 1995	6.30	Tang. Bk. Value/Share	35.92
P/E on S&P Est. 1995	9.9	Beta	1.43
S&P EPS Est. 1996	7.25	Shareholders	17,900
Dividend Rate/Share	1.12	Market cap. (B)	$ 3.5
Shs. outstg. (M)	56.3	Inst. holdings	70%
Avg. daily vol. (M)	0.177	Insider holdings	NA

Value of $10,000 invested 5 years ago: $ 19,613

Fiscal Year Ending Dec. 31

	1995	% Change	1994	% Change	1993	% Change
Revenues (Million $)						
1Q	1,241	23%	1,008	-11%	1,136	4%
2Q	1,442	24%	1,166	-8%	1,263	3%
3Q	—	—	1,208	-4%	1,262	NM
4Q	—	—	1,176	4%	1,130	NM
Yr.	—	—	4,558	-5%	4,790	2%
Income (Million $)						
1Q	61.70	NM	15.90	-38%	25.60	45%
2Q	102.2	129%	44.70	-5%	47.20	NM
3Q	—	—	41.60	39%	30.00	-20%
4Q	—	—	-12.60	NM	21.30	25%
Yr.	—	—	89.60	-28%	124.1	NM
Earnings Per Share ($)						
1Q	1.07	NM	0.27	-37%	0.43	39%
2Q	1.87	153%	0.74	-5%	0.78	NM
3Q	E1.71	—	0.68	36%	0.50	-21%
4Q	E1.65	—	-0.18	NM	0.36	24%
Yr.	E6.30	—	1.52	-27%	2.08	NM

Next earnings report expected: mid October

Business Summary - 08-AUG-95

Mead Corp. is a major producer of paper, paperboard and wood products. It also distributes school, office and industrial supplies. In December 1994, Mead sold its electronic publishing business. Segment contributions from continuing operations in 1994 (profits before significant non-recurring items):

	Sales	Profits
Paper	25%	45%
Packaging & paperboard	28%	43%
Distribution & school/office products	47%	12%

The company makes copier paper, uncoated and coated paper for commercial printing, form bond, carbonless paper and papers for conversion by customers into business forms, greeting cards, bank checks and other products. It makes web coated offset paper used in books, magazines, catalogs and advertising, and produces cotton content and premium sulfite paper, premium recycled papers, technical and specialty papers, and decorative laminating papers. It also sells market pulp.

Mead produces packaging and packaging systems primarily for the beverage market. It manufactures coated natural kraft products used by the beverage packaging industry and by makers of folding cartons for soap, food, hardware and apparel. The company also sells corrugated shipping containers and corrugating medium.

The Zellerbach unit distributes printing papers, industrial supplies and packaging materials and equipment. These products are sold nationally through a network of wholesale locations and printer-supply retail outlets. Mead also makes and distributes school and office supplies.

Northwood Forest Industries (50% owned) manufactures bleached softwood kraft pulp, lumber and plywood products. Northwood Panelboard (50%) produces oriented structural board. Sales to the North American market represent 80% of wood product sales.

Important Developments

Jul. '95—Mead reported that it completed its $350 million stock repurchase program (authorized in October 1994) in the second quarter of 1995, with a total of 6.7 million shares acquired in the plan; in April 1995, directors authorized the buyback of an additional five million shares. During the prior quarter, Mead essentially completed its debt reduction program, with a total of $610 million of short- and long-term debt retired in the first quarter of 1995 and the final quarter of 1994. All of the programs were funded with proceeds from the $1.5 billion sale of the Mead Data Central Electronic Publishing division to Reed Elselvier plc in December 1994.

Capitalization

Long Term Debt: $710,700,000 (7/2/95).

Per Share Data ($)

(Year Ended Dec. 31)

	1994	1993	1992	1991	1990	1989
Tangible Bk. Val.	35.85	20.79	19.78	21.17	21.77	20.98
Cash Flow	4.44	6.84	5.20	5.32	4.82	6.18
Earnings	1.52	2.08	0.63	1.29	1.71	3.33
Dividends	1.00	1.00	1.00	1.00	0.97	0.85
Payout Ratio	66%	48%	159%	77%	53%	25%
Prices - High	53¼	48½	41⅝	37¼	39½	46⅝
- Low	39⅛	37½	33⅛	24½	19½	34¼
P/E Ratio - High	35	23	66	29	23	14
- Low	26	18	53	19	11	10

Income Statement Analysis (Million $)

	1994	%Chg	1993	%Chg	1992	%Chg	1991
Revs.	4,558	-5%	4,790	2%	4,703	3%	4,579
Oper. Inc.	370	-33%	554	6%	521	11%	469
Depr.	188	-34%	283	5%	269	14%	236
Int. Exp.	107	8%	99	-2%	101	-15%	119
Pretax Inc.	112	-45%	202	NM	62.0	-52%	130
Eff. Tax Rate	20%	—	39%	—	39%	—	42%
Net Inc.	89.6	-28%	124	NM	38.0	-50%	76.0

Balance Sheet & Other Fin. Data (Million $)

	1994	1993	1992	1991	1990	1989
Cash	484	9.0	18.0	25.0	21.0	21.0
Curr. Assets	1,894	1,131	1,129	1,093	982	985
Total Assets	4,863	4,165	4,031	3,986	3,889	3,750
Curr. Liab.	1,088	712	730	746	693	700
LT Debt	958	1,369	1,332	1,316	1,257	950
Common Eqty.	2,183	1,578	1,495	1,478	1,531	1,681
Total Cap.	3,534	3,258	3,103	3,043	3,082	2,961
Cap. Exp.	365	347	271	266	455	616
Cash Flow	278	408	307	312	300	416

Ratio Analysis

	1994	1993	1992	1991	1990	1989
Curr. Ratio	1.7	1.6	1.5	1.5	1.4	1.4
% LT Debt of Cap.	27.1	42.0	42.9	43.2	40.8	32.1
% Net Inc.of Revs.	2.0	2.6	0.8	1.7	2.2	4.7
% Ret. on Assets	2.0	3.0	0.9	1.9	2.9	5.9
% Ret. on Equity	4.8	8.0	2.5	5.0	6.9	13.5

Dividend Data (Dividends have been paid since 1940. A dividend reinvestment plan is available. A poison pill stock purchase rights plan was adopted in 1986.)

Amt. of Div. $	Date Decl.	Ex-Div. Date	Stock of Record	Payment Date
0.250	Aug. 04	Aug. 09	Aug. 15	Sep. 01 '94
0.250	Oct. 31	Nov. 04	Nov. 10	Dec. 01 '94
0.250	Jan. 26	Jan. 31	Feb. 06	Mar. 01 '95
0.280	Apr. 27	May. 02	May. 08	Jun. 01 '95
0.280	Aug. 03	Aug. 10	Aug. 14	Sep. 01 '95

Data as orig. reptd.; bef. results of disc. opers. and/or spec. items. Per share data adj. for stk. divs. as of ex-div. date.
E-Estimated. NA-Not Available. NM-Not Meaningful. NR-Not Ranked.

Office—Courthouse Plaza N.E., Dayton, OH 45463. Tel—(513) 495-6323. Chrmn, Pres & CEO—S. C. Mason. Secy—G. J. Maly, Jr. VP & CFO—W. R. Graber. Treas—J. T. Matthews. Investor Contact—Mark Pomerleau. Dirs—J. C. Bogle, J. G. Breen, W. E. Hoglund, B. C. Jordan, J. A. Krol, S. C. Mason, C. S. Mechem Jr., P. F. Miller, Jr., W. S. Shanahan, T. B. Stanley, Jr., L. J. Styslinger, Jr. Transfer Agent & Registrar—First National Bank of Boston. Incorporated in Ohio in 1930. Empl-16,100. S&P Analyst: Michael W. Jaffe

Medtronic, Inc.

NYSE Symbol **MDT**
In S&P 500

26-AUG-95

Industry:
Medical equipment/
supply

Summary: The world's leading producer of implantable cardiac pace-makers, this company also makes implantable defibrillators, heart valves, and other cardiac and neurological products.

S&P Opinion: Buy (★★★★)	Recent Price • 92⅝	Yield • 0.6%
	52 Wk Range • 94¾-47½	12-Mo. P/E • 32.5

Quantitative Evaluations

Outlook
(1 Lowest—5 Highest)
• **2+**

Fair Value
• **88⅜**

Risk
• **Low**

Earn./Div. Rank
• **A+**

Technical Eval.
• **Bullish** since 4/92

Rel. Strength Rank
(1 Lowest—99 Highest)
• **86**

Insider Activity
• **Neutral**

Earnings vs. Previous Year
▲=Up ▼=Down ▶=No Change

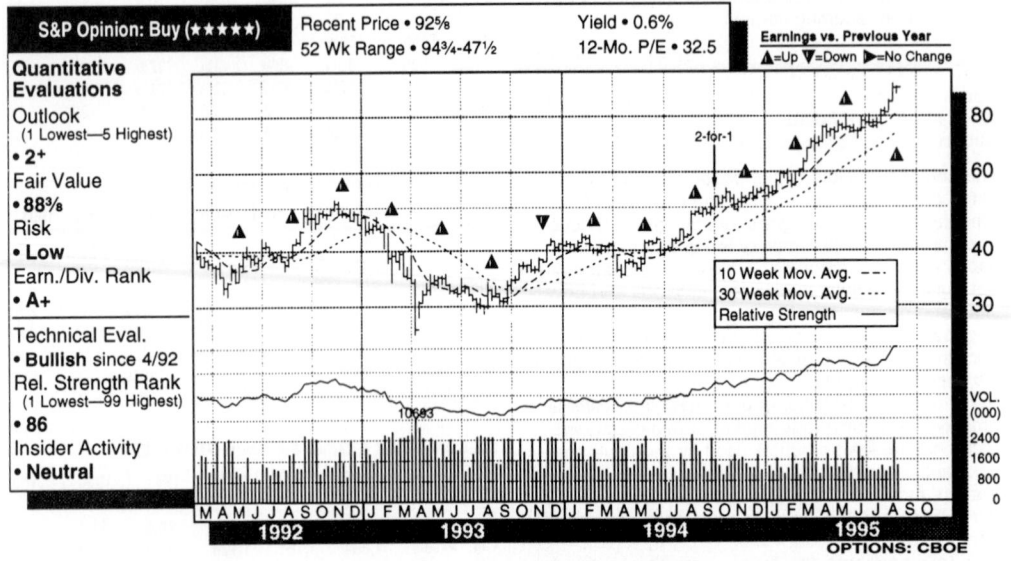

10 Week Mov. Avg. — - —
30 Week Mov. Avg. - - - -
Relative Strength —

OPTIONS: CBOE

Overview - 24-AUG-95

Sales should produce another healthy advance in 1995-6. Despite heightened cost consciousness in major medical markets, volume should benefit from continued strong demand for MDT's state-of-the-art pacemakers and other cardiac and neurological products. Respectable sales gains are indicated for both domestic and international segments of the business. Approved by the FDA in March, the company's new implantable Jewel defibrillator should significantly bolster its tachyarrhythmia (rapid heart beat) management business, and new products will also boost sales of pacemakers and neurological and interventional vascular product lines. Margins should widen, on greater volume and improved productivity.

Valuation - 25-AUG-95

The shares have been in a steady uptrend over the past 12 months, on strength in the medical sector and acceleration of sales and earning growth. MDT holds nearly 50% of the world bradycardia pacing market, which is growing at 4% to 5% a year. The company's new Jewel defibrillator, approved by the FDA in March 1995, is expected to significantly bolster MDT's position in the tachyarrhythmia treatment segment, which is growing about 30% annually. With Jewel well established in Europe, the company holds over 50% of that market. Projected rapid earnings growth appears to justify the rich multiple enjoyed by the shares, which remain attractive for long-term appreciation.

Key Stock Statistics

S&P EPS Est. 1996	3.80	Tang. Bk. Value/Share	8.41
P/E on S&P Est. 1996	24.4	Beta	1.15
Dividend Rate/Share	0.52	Shareholders	21,900
Shs. outstg. (M)	115.5	Market cap. (B)	$ 10.7
Avg. daily vol. (M)	0.315	Inst. holdings	70%
		Insider holdings	NA

Value of $10,000 invested 5 years ago: $ 58,579

Fiscal Year Ending Apr. 30

	1996	% Change	1995	% Change	1994	% Change
Revenues (Million $)						
1Q	523.8	30%	403.8	22%	331.3	NM
2Q	—	—	408.1	23%	332.1	NM
3Q	—	—	413.7	20%	344.6	12%
4Q	—	—	516.7	31%	393.0	10%
Yr.	—	—	1,742	25%	1,391	5%
Income (Million $)						
1Q	99.8	53%	65.08	24%	52.50	—
2Q	—	—	69.72	24%	56.20	—
3Q	—	—	71.38	25%	56.91	19%
4Q	—	—	87.82	32%	66.74	15%
Yr.	—	—	294.0	27%	232.4	10%
Earnings Per Share ($)						
1Q	0.86	54%	0.56	23%	0.46	18%
2Q	E0.93	52%	0.61	24%	0.49	-3%
3Q	E0.95	53%	0.62	25%	0.50	24%
4Q	E1.06	39%	0.76	31%	0.58	18%
Yr.	E3.80	49%	2.55	26%	2.02	13%

Next earnings report expected: mid November

Medtronic, Inc.

Business Summary - 04-MAY-95

Medtronic is the world's leading producer of implantable cardiac pacemakers, with about half of the $1.6 billion worldwide bradycardia pacing market. Other cardiovascular and neurological products are also sold. Sales by business segment in 1993-4 were:

	Sales
Pacemakers and related products and services	67%
Nonpacing cardiovascular items	24%
Other products	9%

Foreign operations provided 42% of sales and 37% of profits in 1993-4. R&D equaled 11.2% of sales in 1993-4, up from 10.0% in 1992-3.

Cardiac pacemakers consist of implantable pulse generators (IPGs) that generate electrical impulses and leads that conduct these impulses to the heart. The pulse generator is implanted under the skin and is connected to the heart by a lead. MDT's product line includes pacemakers that can be noninvasively programmed by a physician to adjust sensing, electrical pulse intensity, duration, rate and other factors, as well as pacers that can sense in both the upper and lower chambers of the heart and produce impulses appropriate to heart activity. Pacemakers are sold under the Thera, Elite, Activitrax, Minix, Minuet, Legend and other names.

Nonpacing cardiovascular products include the Jewel line of implantable cardioverter-defibrillator (ICD) devices to treat rapid heart beating, prosthetic heart valves, membrane oxygenators, therapeutic catheters such as angioplasty catheters, vascular grafts and related items. Other products include implantable neurostimulation systems, external neurostimulation devices, a drug administration system, electrodes and cables and various related items.

Important Developments

Mar. '95—The FDA approved the company's Jewel line of five implantable cardioverter-defibrillators for treatment of tachyarrhythmia or dangerously fast cardiac rhythms. The Jewel devices are smaller than competing defibrillators, allowing them to be implanted in the upper chest area with a single incision, instead of in the abdomen, simplifying implant surgery and reducing hospital stays.

Feb. '95—The FDA approved MDT's new Falcon single-operator exchange balloon catheter for coronary angioplasty. In January, the FDA cleared the company's new Thera line of cardiac pacemakers. Thera pacemakers are microprocessor-based with common programming commands, featuring ease of use and better diagnostic feedback than older pacers.

Capitalization

Long Term Liabilities: $109,558,000 (1/95).

Per Share Data ($) (Year Ended Apr. 30)

	1995	1994	1993	1992	1991	1990
Tangible Bk. Val.	11.56	9.06	7.28	6.70	5.74	4.99
Cash Flow	3.48	2.57	2.24	1.86	1.52	1.29
Earnings	2.55	2.03	1.78	1.36	1.13	1.01
Dividends	0.68	0.34	0.28	0.25	0.21	0.17
Payout Ratio	27%	17%	15%	18%	18%	17%
Cal. Yrs.	1994	1993	1992	1991	1990	1989
Prices - High	55⅞	47¾	52¼	47⅛	23	17¾
- Low	34⅝	25⅞	31⅝	19¼	14¾	9⅝
P/E Ratio - High	22	24	29	35	20	18
- Low	14	13	18	14	13	10

Income Statement Analysis (Million $)

	1995	%Chg	1994	%Chg	1993	%Chg	1992
Revs.	1,742	25%	1,391	5%	1,328	13%	1,177
Oper. Inc.	543	37%	396	19%	332	9%	305
Depr.	107	70%	63.0	15%	54.7	-8%	59.4
Int. Exp.	9.0	10%	8.2	-21%	10.4	-22%	13.4
Pretax Inc.	442	27%	347	11%	313	29%	243
Eff. Tax Rate	34%	—	33%	—	33%	—	34%
Net Inc.	294	27%	232	9%	212	31%	162

Balance Sheet & Other Fin. Data (Million $)

	1995	1994	1993	1992	1991	1990
Cash	324	181	156	110	113	52.0
Curr. Assets	1,104	846	775	696	612	479
Total Assets	1,947	1,623	1,286	1,163	1,024	856
Curr. Liab.	456	439	348	309	292	260
LT Debt	14.2	20.2	10.9	8.6	7.9	8.0
Common Eqty.	1,335	1,053	841	796	683	541
Total Cap.	1,385	1,090	857	823	706	566
Cap. Exp.	96.9	86.0	87.4	77.2	73.7	58.5
Cash Flow	401	295	266	221	170	139

Ratio Analysis

	1995	1994	1993	1992	1991	1990
Curr. Ratio	2.4	1.9	2.2	2.3	2.1	1.8
% LT Debt of Cap.	1.0	1.9	1.3	1.0	1.1	1.4
% Net Inc.of Revs.	16.9	16.7	15.9	13.7	13.1	13.0
% Ret. on Assets	16.5	15.9	17.5	14.8	13.6	13.4
% Ret. on Equity	24.7	24.5	26.2	21.9	20.9	21.3

Dividend Data —Dividends were initiated in 1977.

Amt. of Div. $	Date Decl.	Ex-Div. Date	Stock of Record	Payment Date
2-for-1	Aug. 31	Sep. 30	Sep. 15	Sep. 29 '94
0.103	Sep. 22	Oct. 07	Oct. 14	Oct. 28 '94
0.103	Dec. 01	Dec. 30	Jan. 06	Jan. 27 '95
0.103	Mar. 08	Apr. 03	Apr. 07	Apr. 30 '95
0.130	Jun. 29	Jul. 05	Jul. 07	Jul. 28 '95

Data as orig. reptd.; bef. results of disc. opers. and/or spec. items. Per share data adj. for stk. divs. as of ex-div. date. E-Estimated. NA-Not Available. NM-Not Meaningful. NR-Not Ranked.

Office—7000 Central Ave. N.E., Minneapolis, MN 55432. **Tel**—(612) 574-4000; 1-800-328-2518. **Chrmn**—W. R. Wallin. **Vice Chrmn**—G. D. Nelson. **Pres & CEO**—W. W. George. **SVP & Secy**—R. E. Lund. **SVP & CFO**—R. L. Ryan. **VP & Treas**—M. J. Boris. **Investor Contact**—Dale Beumer (612-574-3038). **Dirs**—F. C. Blodgett, A. D. Collins, Jr., W. W. George, A. M. Gotto, Jr., B. P. Healy, V. H. Heath, T. E. Holloran, E. W. Martin, G. D. Nelson, R. L. Schall, J. W. Schuler, G. W. Simonson, G. M. Sprenger, R. A. Swalin, W. R. Wallin. **Transfer Agent & Registrar**—Norwest Bank Minnesota, South St. Paul. **Incorporated** in Minnesota in 1957. **Empl-** 8,709. **S&P Analyst:** H.B. Saftlas

Mellon Bank

NYSE Symbol **MEL**
In S&P 500

06-SEP-95 Industry:
Banking

Summary: Following the August 1994 acquisition of The Dreyfus Corp., this Pittsburgh-based bank holding company is the second largest investment management company in the U.S.

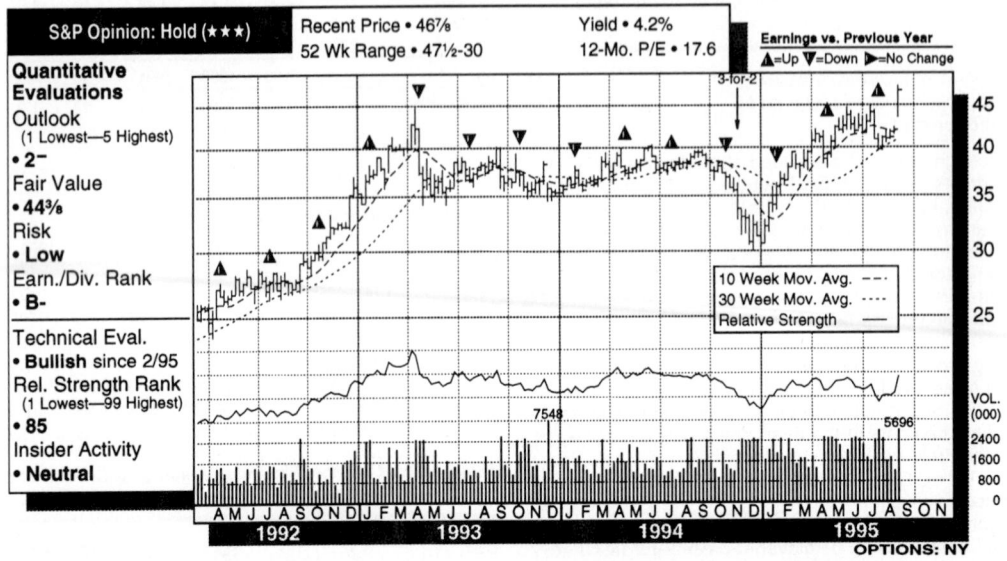

S&P Opinion: Hold (★★★)

Recent Price • 46⅞
52 Wk Range • 47½–30

Yield • 4.2%
12-Mo. P/E • 17.6

Earnings vs. Previous Year
▲=Up ▼=Down ▶=No Change

Quantitative Evaluations

Outlook
(1 Lowest—5 Highest)
• **2−**

Fair Value
• **44⅜**

Risk
• **Low**

Earn./Div. Rank
• **B−**

Technical Eval.
• **Bullish** since 2/95

Rel. Strength Rank
(1 Lowest—99 Highest)
• **85**

Insider Activity
• **Neutral**

3-for-2

10 Week Mov. Avg. – – –
30 Week Mov. Avg. · · · ·
Relative Strength —

VOL.
(000)

7548

5696

OPTIONS: NY

Overview - 06-SEP-95

Earnings gains in 1995 should reflect modest loan growth, a better asset mix and well controlled operating costs, aided by the absence of Dreyfus merger-related expenses. Loan growth should be driven by advances in the higher-yielding credit card segment, led by contributions from the Cornerstone product (introduced in early 1994), while margins will likely expand as low-yielding money market assets are replaced with loans. A lower level of mutual fund assets managed (caused by a reduction in institutional money market assets and bond funds) led to a drop in noninterest income in the first half of 1995, but with the mutual fund business regaining momentum, this trend should reverse. The efficiency ratio could also improve, given a focus on more profitable businesses and well controlled operating expenses.

Valuation - 06-SEP-95

The shares have rallied strongly thus far in 1995, in part reflecting speculation of a possible takeover or merger. Fundamentally, our principal cause for concern with the shares remains continued pressure on trust and investment management fees, by far MEL's lead source of noninterest income, following a decline in assets under management. The mutual fund business, however, is showing a resurgence, encouraged by a stable interest rate environment and renewed growth in money market funds. With an above-average yield and MEL's strong capital position, the shares are a worthwhile long-term holding.

Key Stock Statistics

S&P EPS Est. 1995	4.45	Tang. Bk. Value/Share	16.15
P/E on S&P Est. 1995	10.5	Beta	1.25
S&P EPS Est. 1996	5.00	Shareholders	23,100
Dividend Rate/Share	2.00	Market cap. (B)	$ 7.0
Shs. outstg. (M)	146.5	Inst. holdings	64%
Avg. daily vol. (M)	0.519	Insider holdings	NA

Value of $10,000 invested 5 years ago: $ 30,959

Fiscal Year Ending Dec. 31

	1995	% Change	1994	% Change	1993	% Change
Revenues (Million $)						
1Q	1,083	13%	960.0	20%	799.0	2%
2Q	1,112	16%	959.0	27%	758.0	6%
3Q	—	—	977.0	16%	843.0	9%
4Q	—	—	1,061	27%	837.0	19%
Yr.	—	—	3,957	22%	3,237	9%
Income (Million $)						
1Q	170.0	9%	156.0	NM	34.00	-60%
2Q	172.0	9%	158.0	60%	99.0	10%
3Q	—	—	78.00	-32%	114.0	-27%
4Q	—	—	41.00	-64%	114.0	9%
Yr.	—	—	433.0	20%	361.0	-17%
Earnings Per Share ($)						
1Q	1.08	12%	0.96	NM	0.21	-77%
2Q	1.09	12%	0.97	10%	0.88	-6%
3Q	E1.12	167%	0.42	-58%	1.00	-42%
4Q	E1.16	NM	0.07	-93%	1.00	-7%
Yr.	E4.45	84%	2.42	-22%	3.09	-33%

Next earnings report expected: mid October

Mellon Bank

Business Summary - 06-SEP-95

Mellon Bank Corp., the 24th largest U.S. bank holding company, provides a wide range of financial products and services in domestic and selected international markets through banking subsidiaries in Pennsylvania, Massachusetts, Delaware, Maryland and New Jersey. Services include retail banking (1,060 domestic locations), commercial banking, trust and investment management, residential real estate loan financing, mortgage servicing, mutual fund and various securities-related activities. In August 1994, The Dreyfus Corp. was acquired in exchange for 32.3 million common shares. MEL became the largest U.S. bank manager of mutual funds and the second largest investment management concern, with $200 billion of managed assets. The New Jersey market was entered through the September 1994 purchase of Glendale Bancorporation (assets of $245 million).

At year-end 1994, earning assets of $32.3 billion (up from $30.7 billion a year earlier) were divided: loans 78%, investment securities 16%, money market and other short term investments 6%. Average sources of funds were noninterest-bearing deposits 18%, domestic interest-bearing deposits 48%, foreign deposits 6%, short-term borrowings 8%, long-term debt 5%, equity 11%, and other 4%.

At year-end 1994, nonperforming assets were $239 million (0.89% of loans and related assets), down from $341 million (1.39%) a year earlier. The reserve for loan losses was 2.27% of loans, down from 2.45%. Net chargeoffs in 1994 were 0.27% of average loans, versus 0.64% in 1993.

Important Developments

Aug. '95—The company reached an agreement to purchase the Pennsylvania corporate trust portfolio of CoreStates Financial Corp. for an undisclosed amount.
Jul. '95—Directors authorized the buyback of up to 2.5 million common shares. In the first half of 1995, the company repurchased 2.7 million shares under an earlier 3 million share buyback program.
Jun. '95—MEL purchased 3,750,000 of its common shares and warrants for an additional 4.5 million shares from a unit of American Express Co. for $213 million. The shares and warrants had been issued in a May 1993 transaction involving the acquisition of Boston Co.

Capitalization

Long Term Debt: $1,868,000,000 (6/95).
Preferred Stock: $435,000,000.

Per Share Data ($)

(Year Ended Dec. 31)

	1994	1993	1992	1991	1990	1989
Tangible Bk. Val.	15.48	14.85	15.21	14.17	11.46	22.35
Earnings	2.42	3.09	4.64	3.11	1.89	2.22
Dividends	1.57	1.01	0.93	0.93	0.93	0.93
Payout Ratio	65%	33%	20%	30%	49%	42%
Prices - High	40⅜	44⅞	37	25⅜	20	25⅜
- Low	30	34⅛	22½	14⅜	11¾	16⅝
P/E Ratio - High	17	15	8	8	11	11
- Low	12	11	5	5	6	8

Income Statement Analysis (Million $)

	1994	%Chg	1993	%Chg	1992	%Chg	1991
Net Int. Inc.	1,508	15%	1,307	13%	1,154	18%	974
Tax Equiv. Adj.	13.0	30%	10.0	-17%	12.0	-56%	27.0
Non Int. Inc.	1,652	29%	1,276	50%	851	11%	770
Loan Loss Prov.	70.0	-44%	125	-32%	185	-26%	250
% Exp/Op Revs.	75%	—	74%	—	72%	—	71%
Pretax Inc.	711	19%	600	22%	492	60%	308
Eff. Tax Rate	39%	—	40%	—	11%	—	9.10%
Net Inc.	433	20%	361	-17%	437	56%	280
% Net Int. Marg.	4.71%	—	4.39%	—	4.44%	—	3.93%

Balance Sheet & Other Fin. Data (Million $)

	1994	1993	1992	1991	1990	1989
Earning Assets:						
Money Mkt.	883	1,583	1,376	1,240	947	4,924
Inv. Securities	5,125	5,012	5,738	5,744	4,614	3,453
Com'l Loans	10,830	9,809	8,765	8,928	8,784	9,956
Other Loans	15,903	14,664	11,191	10,175	9,954	9,442
Total Assets	38,644	36,139	31,574	29,355	28,762	31,467
Demand Deposits	5,979	6,914	5,640	4,597	5,133	4,351
Time Deposits	21,591	22,526	19,490	17,857	17,582	16,993
LT Debt	1,568	1,990	1,587	1,501	1,420	1,799
Common Eqty.	3,672	2,721	2,077	1,638	1,292	1,223

Ratio Analysis

	1994	1993	1992	1991	1990	1989
% Ret. on Assets	1.1	1.0	1.5	1.0	0.6	0.6
% Ret. on Equity	9.5	11.9	20.4	15.4	9.0	11.5
% Loan Loss Resv.	2.3	2.5	2.5	3.1	2.8	3.1
% Loans/Deposits	97.0	88.9	79.4	85.1	82.5	90.9
% Equity to Assets	9.9	7.5	6.3	5.2	4.6	3.7

Dividend Data —Dividends have been paid since 1895. A dividend reinvestment plan is available. A "poison pill" stock purchase rights plan was adopted in 1989.

Amt. of Div. $	Date Decl.	Ex-Div. Date	Stock of Record	Payment Date
0.675	Sep. 20	Oct. 25	Oct. 31	Nov. 15 '94
3-for-2	Sep. 20	Nov. 16	Nov. 01	Nov. 15 '94
0.450	Jan. 13	Jan. 25	Jan. 31	Feb. 15 '95
0.500	Apr. 18	Apr. 24	Apr. 28	May. 15 '95
0.500	Jul. 18	Jul. 27	Jul. 31	Aug. 15 '95

Data as orig. reptd.; bef. results of disc opers. and/or spec. items. Per share data adj. for stk. divs. as of ex-div. date. E-Estimated. NA-Not Available. NM-Not Meaningful. NR-Not Ranked.

Office—One Mellon Bank Center, Pittsburgh, PA 15258-0001. **Tel**—(412) 234-5000. **Chrmn, Pres & CEO**—F. V. Cahouet. **Vice Chrmn, CFO & Treas**—S. G. Elliott. **Secy**—J. M. Gockley. **Investor Contact**—Donald MacLeod. **Dirs**—B. C. Borgelt, C. R. Brown, F. V. Cahouet, J. W. Connolly, C. A. Corry, C. F. Fetterolf, I. J. Gumberg, P. Hutchinson, R. E. Lee, A. W. Mathieson, E. J. McAniff, R. Mehrabian, S. P. Mellon, D. S. Shapira, W. K. Smith, H. Stein, J. L. Thomas, W. W. von Schack, W. J. Young. **Transfer Agent & Registrar**—Mellon Bank, Pittsburgh. **Incorporated** in 1971; bank originally chartered in 1902. **Empl**-25,000. **S&P Analyst:** Stephen R. Biggar

Melville Corp.

NYSE Symbol **MES**
In S&P 500

27-OCT-95

Industry:
Retail Stores

Summary: Melville is one of the largest diversified specialty retailers in the U.S., selling footwear, apparel, health and beauty aids, toys and household items.

S&P Opinion: Hold (★★★)	Recent Price • 34⅜	Yield • 4.8%	
	52 Wk Range • 39⅞-29½	12-Mo. P/E • 18.4	

Earnings vs. Previous Year
▲=Up ▼=Down ▶=No Change

Quantitative Evaluations

Outlook
(1 Lowest—5 Highest)
• **2⁻**

Fair Value
• **32⅛**

Risk
• **Low**

Earn./Div. Rank
• **A-**

Technical Eval.
• **Bearish** since 3/95

Rel. Strength Rank
(1 Lowest—99 Highest)
• **24**

Insider Activity
• **NA**

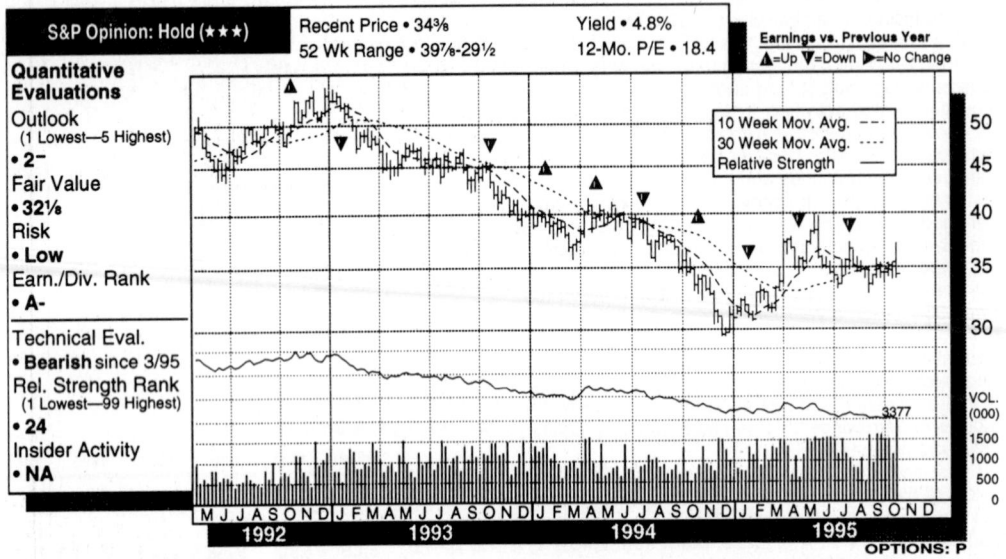

10 Week Mov. Avg. ---
30 Week Mov. Avg. ····
Relative Strength —

VOL.
(000)
3377

1992 1993 1994 1995

OPTIONS: P

Overview - 26-OCT-95

In the light of disappointing financial results and pressure from institutional investors, management has announced a restructuring of the company's portfolio of retail operations into three publicly traded companies. Management believes that the benefits of this plan are that: the company, focused on specific industry segment of retailing, will be able to respond faster to industry conditions; each company will be valued as an individual entity; and the significant cost savings from the reduction of corporate overhead, consolidation of operations and the closing of unprofitable stores will increase profitability. Any reduction in the dividend will be used to strengthen the balance sheets of the new companies, permitting acceleration of investments in the businesses without the need for significant outside financing.

Valuation - 25-OCT-95

The share price declined slightly following the company's announcement of a restructuring. Given the weak retail sales environment and heavy promotional pricing, retail stocks are out of favor. We believe that the current market price of the shares reflects the breakup value of the company. CVS is the crown jewel of MES' portfolio of retail companies, alone worth some $20 a share. We see little downside risk at this price level and would retain our shares in anticipation of an improved retail environment in 1996.

Key Stock Statistics

S&P EPS Est. 1995	-5.60	Tang. Bk. Value/Share	17.45
P/E on S&P Est. 1995	NM	Beta	1.10
Dividend Rate/Share	1.52	Shareholders	7,200
Shs. outstg. (M)	105.1	Market cap. (B)	$ 3.3
Avg. daily vol. (M)	0.445	Inst. holdings	87%
		Insider holdings	NA

Value of $10,000 invested 5 years ago: $ 9,604

Fiscal Year Ending Dec. 31

	1995	% Change	1994	% Change	1993	% Change
Revenues (Million $)						
1Q	2,492	5%	2,380	17%	2,033	-1%
2Q	2,770	10%	2,507	-1%	2,537	2%
3Q	2,814	3%	2,737	16%	2,355	-1%
4Q	—	—	3,661	4%	3,510	NM
Yr.	—	—	11,286	8%	10,435	NM
Income (Million $)						
1Q	-26.45	NM	-2.51	NM	-21.69	NM
2Q	31.08	-32%	45.60	-39%	74.53	-3%
3Q	-2.48	NM	51.72	25%	41.50	-25%
4Q	—	—	212.7	-10%	237.4	NM
Yr.	—	—	307.5	-7%	331.8	113%
Earnings Per Share ($)						
1Q	-0.29	NM	-0.06	NM	-0.24	—
2Q	0.25	-36%	0.39	-42%	0.67	—
3Q	-0.06	NM	0.45	29%	0.35	-66%
4Q	E-5.50	NM	1.97	-11%	2.22	NM
Yr.	E-5.60	NM	2.75	-8%	3.00	124%

Next earnings report expected: late February

Melville Corp.

Business Summary - 26-OCT-95

Melville is one of the largest diversified specialty retailers in the U.S. The company ended 1994 with a total of 7,378 stores, up from 7,282 a year earlier. Contributions by product line in 1994 were:

	Sales	Profits
Apparel	33%	25%
Drug, health & beauty aids	38%	35%
Footwear	16%	25%
Toys & household items	13%	15%

Apparel is sold through the Marshalls, Wilsons Suede and Leather and Bob's divisions. At 1994 year end, the company operated 484 Marshalls stores, 628 Wilsons and 20 Bob's units.

Footwear is sold through stores under the Thom McAn and Footaction trade names. As part of the 1992 strategic realignment program, Melville closed more than half of the Thom McAn chain. At year-end 1994, Thom McAn operated 323 units, Footaction operated 439 stores and 2,778 Meldisco leased shoe departments, mainly in Kmart stores.

As of December 31, 1994, the company operated 1,328 prescription drug and health and beauty aids stores in 15 states and the District of Columbia, under the CVS name. Melville also operated 996 toy and hobby stores in 50 states and Puerto Rico, under the name Kay-Bee Toys. The household furnishings division includes 145 Linens 'n Things stores and 237 This End Up stores that sell casual crate-designed furniture in 32 states.

Important Developments

Oct. '95—MES plans to break up the company into three publicly traded businesses: chain drug holding, which will include CVS, as well as Linens 'n Things and Bob's; footwear, including Meldisco, Footaction and Thom McAn; and Kay-Bee toy stores. The footwear businesses and Kay-Bee will be spun off to shareholders by the end of 1996. While the chain drug holding company will initially include Linens 'n Things and Bob's, Melville believes that these businesses have the potential to become stand-alone companies in the long term. The company agreed to sell its Marshalls division to TJX Companies, Inc. for about $550 million and plans to sell Wilsons and This End Up. The company will record after-tax fourth quarter charges of $585 million related to writeoffs and severance costs and $195 million for the divestiture of Marshalls.

Capitalization

Long Term Debt: $332,056,000 (9/95).
Minority Interest: $73,887,000 (7/95).
$4 Cum. Preferred Stock: 13,298 shs. ($100 par).
$3.90 ESOP Conv. Preference Stock: $339,942,000; conv. into about 6.5 million com. shs.

Per Share Data ($)

(Year Ended Dec. 31)

	1994	1993	1992	1991	1990	1989
Tangible Bk. Val.	18.18	16.94	15.56	12.22	9.83	9.36
Cash Flow	4.71	4.82	3.27	4.67	4.80	4.55
Earnings	2.75	3.00	1.34	3.20	3.59	3.56
Dividends	1.52	1.52	1.48	1.44	1.42	1.30
Payout Ratio	55%	51%	111%	45%	40%	35%
Prices - High	41⅝	54¾	55	55¼	57⅝	53⅝
- Low	29½	38⅞	42½	38½	32⅝	36⅞
P/E Ratio - High	15	18	41	17	16	15
- Low	11	13	32	12	9	10

Income Statement Analysis (Million $)

	1994	%Chg	1993	%Chg	1992	%Chg	1991
Revs.	11,286	8%	10,435	NM	10,433	6%	9,886
Oper. Inc.	817	NM	809	-11%	909	11%	822
Depr.	206	7%	192	-4%	201	32%	152
Int. Exp.	34.1	32%	25.8	-3%	26.7	-14%	31.2
Pretax Inc.	578	-4%	600	79%	335	-48%	640
Eff. Tax Rate	38%	—	37%	—	38%	—	38%
Net Inc.	307	-8%	332	113%	156	-55%	347

Balance Sheet & Other Fin. Data (Million $)

	1994	1993	1992	1991	1990	1989
Cash	117	81.0	145	79.0	111	369
Curr. Assets	2,650	2,398	2,442	2,370	2,113	1,875
Total Assets	4,735	4,272	4,214	4,085	3,662	3,032
Curr. Liab.	1,643	1,328	1,381	1,330	1,202	855
LT Debt	350	365	375	384	395	390
Common Eqty.	2,369	2,228	2,060	1,735	1,495	1,261
Total Cap.	2,924	2,790	2,575	2,662	2,427	2,176
Cap. Exp.	421	387	304	253	231	203
Cash Flow	497	507	341	483	493	490

Ratio Analysis

	1994	1993	1992	1991	1990	1989
Curr. Ratio	1.6	1.8	1.8	1.8	1.8	2.2
% LT Debt of Cap.	12.0	13.1	14.6	14.4	16.3	17.9
% Net Inc.of Revs.	2.7	3.2	1.5	3.5	4.4	5.3
% Ret. on Assets	6.8	7.8	3.7	8.9	11.5	14.2
% Ret. on Equity	12.6	14.7	6.8	20.4	26.8	26.7

Dividend Data —Dividends have been paid since 1916.

Amt. of Div. $	Date Decl.	Ex-Div. Date	Stock of Record	Payment Date
0.380	Oct. 12	Oct. 18	Oct. 24	Nov. 01 '94
0.380	Jan. 11	Jan. 18	Jan. 24	Feb. 01 '95
0.380	Apr. 11	Apr. 18	Apr. 24	May. 01 '95
0.380	Jul. 13	Jul. 20	Jul. 24	Aug. 01 '95
0.380	Oct. 11	Oct. 20	Oct. 24	Nov. 01 '95

Data as orig. reptd.; bef. results of disc. opers. and/or spec. items. Per share data adj. for stk. divs. as of ex-div. date. E-Estimated. NA-Not Available. NM-Not Meaningful. NR-Not Ranked.

Office—1 Theall Rd., Rye, NY 10580. Tel—(914) 925-4000. Chrmn & CEO—S. P. Goldstein. Pres & COO—H. Rosenthal. VP-Fin—C. E. Alberini. Secy—A. V. Richards. Dirs—H. L. Battle, Jr., A. J. Bloostein, W. D. Cornwell, J. J. Creedon, S. P. Goldstein, M. H. Jordan, W. H. Joyce, T. R. Lautenbach, T. Levitt, D. F. McCullough, H. Rosenthal, I. G. Seidenberg, P. C. Stewart, M. C. Woodward, Jr. Transfer Agent & Registrar—Chemical Bank, NYC. Incorporated in New York in 1914. Empl-105,000. S&P Analyst: Karen J. Sack, CFA

Mercantile Stores

NYSE Symbol **MST**
In S&P 500

26-OCT-95

Industry:
Retail Stores

Summary: This company operates 103 department stores in 42 predominantly southern and midwestern markets under locally prominent names. Over 40% of the shares are closely held.

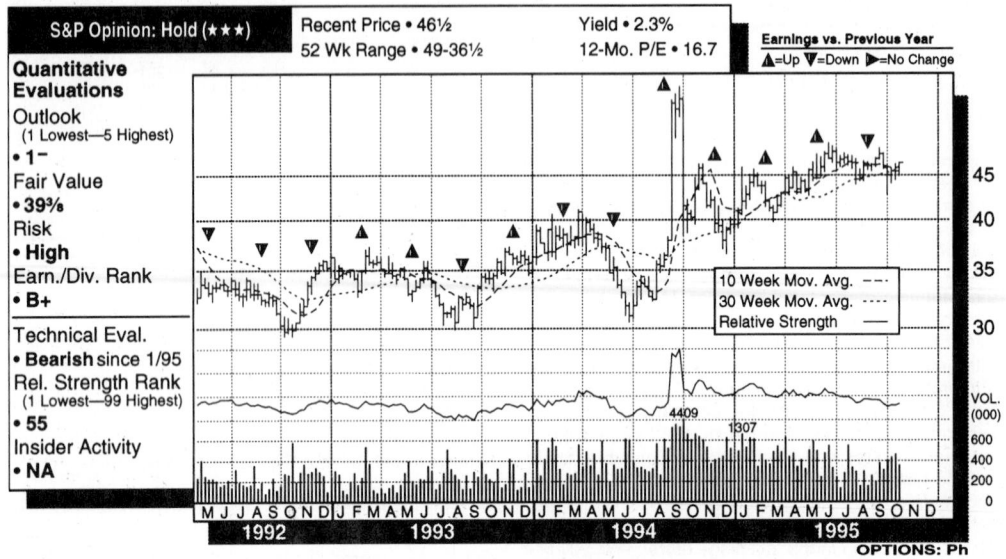

S&P Opinion: Hold (★★★)	
Recent Price • 46½	Yield • 2.3%
52 Wk Range • 49-36½	12-Mo. P/E • 16.7

Earnings vs. Previous Year
▲=Up ▼=Down ▶=No Change

Quantitative Evaluations

Outlook
(1 Lowest—5 Highest)
• **1⁻**

Fair Value
• **39⅜**

Risk
• **High**

Earn./Div. Rank
• **B+**

Technical Eval.
• **Bearish** since 1/95

Rel. Strength Rank
(1 Lowest—99 Highest)
• **55**

Insider Activity
• **NA**

10 Week Mov. Avg. - - -
30 Week Mov. Avg. ·····
Relative Strength ——

OPTIONS: Ph

Overview - 26-OCT-95

Sales should increase moderately in 1995-96, on modest gains in same-store sales, the addition of new units, and remodels. Gross margins should remain about level, restricted by continued competitive pricing. SG&A expenses should decrease as a percentage of sales, reflecting cost controls and the consolidation of divisions, which cut payroll costs. Interest expense will be little changed. Results will reflect the absence of a charge of $0.08 a share, related to the consolidation of two divisions. However, the lack of apparel inflation in 1994-95 led to a LIFO inventory credit of $0.22 a share in the fourth quarter. This will make fourth quarter comparisons more difficult this year.

Valuation - 26-OCT-95

Reflecting weak apparel sales, the shares have been in a narrow trading range in recent months. A plethora of retail outlets and competitive pricing will continue to create a difficult sales environment. Better inventory management, cost controls and a store remodeling program should continue to boost earnings. The shares, however, appear fairly valued based on the company's operations. In November 1994, the company terminated merger talks. In the rapidly consolidating department store industry, cost savings can be generated by economies of scale, and a merger of this closely held company is still a possibility.

Key Stock Statistics

S&P EPS Est. 1996	2.90	Tang. Bk. Value/Share	37.94
P/E on S&P Est. 1996	16.0	Beta	0.91
S&P EPS Est. 1997	3.40	Shareholders	9,900
Dividend Rate/Share	1.06	Market cap. (B)	$ 1.7
Shs. outstg. (M)	36.8	Inst. holdings	46%
Avg. daily vol. (M)	0.081	Insider holdings	NA

Value of $10,000 invested 5 years ago: $ 13,956

Fiscal Year Ending Jan. 31

	1996	% Change	1995	% Change	1994	% Change
Revenues (Million $)						
1Q	602.9	2%	593.0	4%	572.3	-3%
2Q	642.5	4%	619.3	NM	615.4	2%
3Q	—	—	679.5	4%	654.1	NM
4Q	—	—	928.6	5%	888.1	NM
Yr.	—	—	2,820	3%	2,730	NM
Income (Million $)						
1Q	9.95	11%	9.00	-22%	11.48	40%
2Q	6.50	-34%	9.80	NM	-1.33	NM
3Q	—	—	26.21	28%	20.54	11%
4Q	—	—	59.51	6%	55.96	2%
Yr.	—	—	104.5	21%	86.64	NM
Earnings Per Share ($)						
1Q	0.27	12%	0.24	-23%	0.31	41%
2Q	0.18	-33%	0.27	NM	-0.04	NM
3Q	E0.75	6%	0.71	27%	0.56	12%
4Q	E1.70	5%	1.62	7%	1.52	-6%
Yr.	E2.90	2%	2.84	21%	2.35	NM

Next earnings report expected: early November

Business Summary - 20-OCT-95

As of January 28, 1995, Mercantile Stores operated 103 department stores in 17 states under 13 locally prominent trade names and two specialty stores. The company maintains a partnership position in five operating shopping centers ventures.

All stores carry a wide assortment of goods. The company has developed and marketed private-label goods and offers well-known national brands, recently augmented by the addition of higher-quality designer apparel. Capital spending in 1994-95 totaled $93.6 million, with about 75% allocated for store remodeling and upgrading of merchandise presentation.

The chain store divisions are: Bacons/ McAlpin's/ Lion/ Root's in Tennessee and Alabama; Castner Knott Co. in Tennessee, Alabama and Kentucky; Gayfers/ J. B. White in Alabama, Georgia, Mississippi and South Carolina; Gayfers/Maison Blanche in Alabama, Mississippi, Louisiana, and Florida; Jones/ Joslins/ Hennssy's / de Lendrecie's / Glass Block in Missouri, Kansas, Colorado, Wyoming, Montana, North Dakota and Minnesota.

Store space at January 28, 1995, totaled 16,484,000 sq. ft. Average sales per sq. ft. came to $173 in 1994-95, up from $169 in 1993-94. A typical store is 170,000 square feet.

Over the past three years the company has increased the efficiency of its operations by reducing the number of store groups from eleven to five. Merchandise planning and accounting have been centralized in the company's Cincinnati headquarters.

Important Developments

Oct. '95—Sales for the five weeks ended September 30, 1995, rose 5.2%; same store sales for the same period fell 0.1%. Excluding the impact of the credit operations, net income for the second quarter of 1995-96 rose 21.5%. During the second quarter, MST continued to underwrite the startup costs associated with the assumption of full responsibility for its private label credit card, including the full establishment of a bad debt reserve. Capital expenditures for 1995 are estimated at $110 million; about 60% are earmarked for remodeling and upgrading stores, 25% for new stores and the balance for support functions for the new credit card center. In November 1994, the company said talks regarding a possible merger or business combination with an unnamed party had been terminated.

Capitalization

Long Term Debt: $257,616,000 (7/95).

Per Share Data ($) (Year Ended Jan. 31)

	1995	1994	1993	1992	1991	1990
Tangible Bk. Val.	38.01	36.18	34.81	33.97	31.87	29.24
Cash Flow	5.37	4.89	4.91	5.01	5.07	5.02
Earnings	2.84	2.35	2.36	3.10	3.36	3.54
Dividends	1.02	1.02	1.02	1.01	0.96	0.89
Payout Ratio	36%	43%	43%	33%	29%	25%
Cal. Yrs.	1994	1993	1992	1991	1990	1989
Prices - High	57	37¼	42⅛	42½	45⅜	50½
- Low	30½	29⅞	29⅜	26¾	24¼	37½
P/E Ratio - High	24	16	18	14	14	14
- Low	13	13	12	9	7	11

Income Statement Analysis (Million $)

	1995	%Chg	1994	%Chg	1993	%Chg	1992
Revs.	2,835	3%	2,749	NM	2,751	11%	2,470
Oper. Inc.	283	11%	254	-8%	276	—	273
Depr.	93.5	NM	93.5	NM	94.0	33%	70.6
Int. Exp.	28.1	-22%	36.2	2%	35.5	52%	23.4
Pretax Inc.	173	20%	144	NM	143	-23%	186
Eff. Tax Rate	40%	—	40%	—	39%	—	39%
Net Inc.	105	21%	87.0	NM	87.0	-24%	114

Balance Sheet & Other Fin. Data (Million $)

	1995	1994	1993	1992	1991	1990
Cash	114	195	217	122	45.0	71.0
Curr. Assets	1,219	1,269	1,265	1,171	1,117	1,113
Total Assets	1,982	2,032	2,008	1,673	1,597	1,548
Curr. Liab.	262	367	273	182	182	240
LT Debt	261	272	390	207	208	199
Common Eqty.	1,401	1,335	1,283	1,251	1,174	1,077
Total Cap.	1,662	1,607	1,673	1,465	1,389	1,279
Cap. Exp.	94.0	106	111	80.0	83.0	107
Cash Flow	198	108	181	185	187	185

Ratio Analysis

	1995	1994	1993	1992	1991	1990
Curr. Ratio	4.7	3.5	4.6	6.4	6.1	4.6
% LT Debt of Cap.	15.7	16.9	23.3	14.1	15.0	15.6
% Net Inc.of Revs.	3.7	3.2	3.2	4.6	5.2	5.6
% Ret. on Assets	5.2	4.3	4.7	7.0	7.9	8.7
% Ret. on Equity	7.6	6.6	6.9	9.4	11.0	12.7

Dividend Data —Dividends have been paid since 1940.

Amt. of Div. $	Date Decl.	Ex-Div. Date	Stock of Record	Payment Date
0.255	Oct. 05	Nov. 23	Nov. 30	Dec. 15 '94
0.255	Feb. 01	Feb. 22	Feb. 28	Mar. 15 '95
0.265	Apr. 06	May. 24	May. 31	Jun. 15 '95
0.265	Aug. 02	Aug. 29	Aug. 31	Sep. 15 '95
0.265	Oct. 05	Nov. 28	Nov. 30	Dec. 15 '95

Data as orig. reptd.; bef. results of disc. opers. and/or spec. items. Per share data adj. for stk. divs. as of ex-div. date. E-Estimated. NA-Not Available. NM-Not Meaningful. NR-Not Ranked.

Office—9450 Seward Rd., Fairfield, OH 45014. **Tel**—(513) 881-8000. **Chrmn & CEO**—D. L. Nichols. **SVP & CFO**—J. M. McVicker. **Secy**—D. F. Murphy. **Treas & Investor Contact**—William A. Carr. **Dirs**—H. K. H. Brodie, J. A. Herdeg, T. J. Malone, R. C. McPherson, G. H. Milliken, M. K. Milliken, R. Milliken, G. S. Moore, D. L. Nichols, F. G. Rodgers, R. K. Smith. **Transfer Agent & Registrar**—Harris Trust Co. of New York, NYC. **Incorporated** in Delaware in 1919. **Empl**-30,500. **S&P Analyst**: Karen J. Sack, CFA

Merck & Co.

NYSE Symbol **MRK**
In S&P 500

14-SEP-95

Industry:
Drugs-Generic and OTC

Summary: Merck is one of the world's largest producers of prescription pharmaceuticals. Its Medco Containment subsidiary is the leading pharmacy benefits management firm.

S&P Opinion: Buy (★★★★)

Recent Price • 51¾	Yield • 2.6%	
52 Wk Range • 52⅜-33¼	12-Mo. P/E • 20.5	

Earnings vs. Previous Year
▲=Up ▼=Down ▶=No Change

Quantitative Evaluations

Outlook
(1 Lowest—5 Highest)
• **3+**

Fair Value
• **51¼**

Risk
• **Low**

Earn./Div. Rank
• **A+**

Technical Eval.
• **Bullish** since 8/94

Rel. Strength Rank
(1 Lowest—99 Highest)
• **55**

Insider Activity
• **NA**

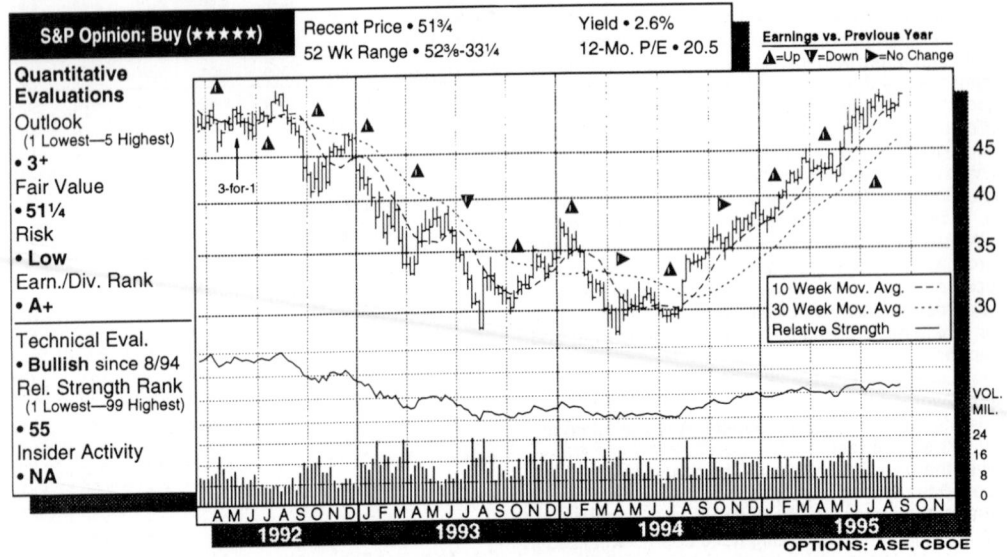

10 Week Mov. Avg. — —
30 Week Mov. Avg. ·····
Relative Strength —

VOL. MIL.

OPTIONS: ASE, CBOE

Overview - 14-SEP-95

Further sales progress is seen for 1996. Although the divestiture of Medco's behavioral care unit (1994 sales of $300 million) is planned, volume should be augmented by growth in key drug lines such as Vasotec cardiovascular, Zocor cholesterol-lowering agent and Proscar for enlarged prostates. New products such as Cozaar antihypertensive, Varivax chicken pox vaccine, Fosomax for osteoporosis, and Trusopt glaucoma treatment should also boost sales. Gains are also forecast for Medco's continuing businesses, aided by new accounts. Although likely to remain dilutive near-term, Medco has enhanced Merck's position in the fast-growing managed care market, and should provide important synergies in coming years.

Valuation - 14-SEP-95

Merck, the premier U.S. drugmaker, has continued to lead an uptrend in drug stocks in recent periods, with the the shares up over 70% from their mid-1994 low. Renewed interest in the pharmaceutical sector reflects a more friendly political climate in Washington, drug patent extensions under GATT legislation, and investor rotation to defensive issues. Although not likely to regain its former high double-digit pace, the company should continue to post creditable EPS growth in coming years, aided by global marketing strengths, an impressive new drug pipeline, and benefits from the Medco acquisition. The stock is recommended for superior long-term capital appreciation.

Key Stock Statistics

S&P EPS Est. 1995	2.70	Tang. Bk. Value/Share	3.21
P/E on S&P Est. 1995	19.2	Beta	1.19
S&P EPS Est. 1996	3.05	Shareholders	82,300
Dividend Rate/Share	1.36	Market cap. (B)	$ 64.3
Shs. outstg. (M)	1236.7	Inst. holdings	50%
Avg. daily vol. (M)	1.965	Insider holdings	NA

Value of $10,000 invested 5 years ago: $ 23,007

Fiscal Year Ending Dec. 31

	1995	% Change	1994	% Change	1993	% Change
Revenues (Million $)						
1Q	3,817	9%	3,514	48%	2,380	7%
2Q	4,136	9%	3,792	47%	2,574	8%
3Q	—	—	3,792	49%	2,544	3%
4Q	—	—	3,872	29%	3,001	15%
Yr.	—	—	14,970	43%	10,498	9%
Income (Million $)						
1Q	757.4	12%	675.2	10%	613.8	14%
2Q	858.1	12%	764.1	NM	172.6	-74%
3Q	—	—	784.8	11%	705.7	9%
4Q	—	—	773.0	15%	674.2	11%
Yr.	—	—	2,997	38%	2,166	-11%
Earnings Per Share ($)						
1Q	0.61	13%	0.54	NM	0.54	12%
2Q	0.69	13%	0.61	NM	0.15	-73%
3Q	E0.69	11%	0.62	NM	0.62	13%
4Q	E0.71	16%	0.61	9%	0.56	6%
Yr.	E2.70	13%	2.38	27%	1.87	-12%

Next earnings report expected: mid October

Business Summary - 14-SEP-95

Merck is a leading maker of prescription drugs. An important part of its business is conducted through the Merck-Medco managed care division (acquired in November 1993), which manages pharmacy benefits for more than 40 million Americans. A specialty chemicals business was sold in February 1995.

Operations outside of North America accounted for 29% of sales and pretax income in 1994. R&D spending equaled 8.2% of sales in 1994 and 11.2% in 1993.

Important drug categories include cardiovasculars (36% of total 1994 sales), including Vasotec ACE inhibitor, Mevacor and Zocor cholesterol-lowering agents (Merck has about 40% of the worldwide cholesterol-lowering market), Vaseretic and Prinivil; anti-ulcerants (10%) such as Prilosec and Pepcid; antibiotics (6%), of which Primaxin, Mefoxin and Noroxin are the largest; vaccines/biologicals (3%), which include M-M-R II (measles, mumps and rubella vaccine live), Recombivax HB recombinant hepatitis B vaccine, and Varivax vaccine against chicken pox; and ophthalmologicals (3%) such as Timoptic; anti-inflammatories/analgesics (2%).

Other drugs (3%) consist of Proscar for the treatment of enlarged prostates and treatments for Parkinson's disease and other ailments. Animal health and agricultural products (7%) include Ivomec, an antiparasitic agent; Heartgard-30 to prevent canine heartworm disease; and coccidiostats to treat poultry disease.

Other human health care sales (27%) consist of Medco's sales of non-Merck products and Medco human health services. The company also has several joint ventures. These include prescription drug ventures with Astra AB of Sweden and duPont, and an over-the-counter drug alliance with Johnson & Johnson.

Important Developments

Aug. '95—Merck filed a New Drug Application with the FDA for Quadramet, a treatment for severe and chronic pain that it plans to market through a joint venture with DuPont. Earlier, in July, an FDA panel recommended approval for the company's new Fosomax drug to treat osteoporosis. New products launched in 1995 include Cozaar, an antihypertensive; Varivax, a vaccine against chicken pox; and Trusopt, a treatment for glaucoma. Products in the R&D pipeline include treatments for asthma, unstable angina, migraine and AIDS. In July, Merck signed a definitive agreement to sell Medco's behavorial care business for $340 million. The Kelco specialty chemicals business was sold in February for $1.1 billion.

Capitalization

Long Term Debt: $916,100,000 (6/95).
Minority Interest: $1,357,700,000 (6/95).

Per Share Data ($)

	1994	1993	1992	1991	1990	1989
Tangible Bk. Val.	3.15	2.69	4.24	4.06	3.12	2.78
Cash Flow	2.92	2.20	2.37	2.04	1.72	1.43
Earnings	2.38	1.87	2.12	1.83	1.52	1.26
Dividends	1.16	1.06	0.96	0.79	0.67	0.57
Payout Ratio	49%	57%	45%	43%	44%	45%
Prices - High	39½	44⅛	56⅝	55¾	30⅜	27
- Low	28⅛	28⅝	40½	27⅞	22⅜	18¾
P/E Ratio - High	17	24	27	30	20	21
- Low	12	15	19	15	15	15

Income Statement Analysis (Million $)

	1994	%Chg	1993	%Chg	1992	%Chg	1991
Revs.	14,970	43%	10,498	9%	9,663	12%	8,603
Oper. Inc.	5,075	19%	4,262	13%	3,782	13%	3,352
Depr.	670	78%	377	30%	290	19%	243
Int. Exp.	124	46%	84.7	17%	72.7	6%	68.7
Pretax Inc.	4,509	43%	3,153	-12%	3,596	13%	3,192
Eff. Tax Rate	32%	—	30%	—	31%	—	33%
Net Inc.	2,997	38%	2,166	-11%	2,447	15%	2,122

Balance Sheet & Other Fin. Data (Million $)

	1994	1993	1992	1991	1990	1989
Cash	2,270	1,542	1,094	1,412	1,197	1,144
Curr. Assets	6,922	5,735	4,400	4,311	3,766	3,410
Total Assets	21,857	19,928	11,086	9,499	8,030	6,757
Curr. Liab.	5,449	5,896	3,617	2,814	2,827	1,907
LT Debt	1,146	1,121	496	494	124	118
Common Eqty.	11,139	10,022	5,003	4,916	3,834	3,521
Total Cap.	14,735	12,650	6,215	6,296	4,764	4,459
Cap. Exp.	1,009	1,013	1,067	1,042	671	433
Cash Flow	3,667	2,543	2,737	2,364	2,013	1,702

Ratio Analysis

	1994	1993	1992	1991	1990	1989
Curr. Ratio	1.3	1.0	1.2	1.5	1.3	1.8
% LT Debt of Cap.	7.8	8.9	8.0	7.8	2.6	2.6
% Net Inc.of Revs.	20.0	20.6	25.3	24.7	23.2	22.8
% Ret. on Assets	14.4	13.5	23.9	24.2	24.3	23.3
% Ret. on Equity	28.4	27.9	49.6	48.5	48.9	47.0

Dividend Data
—Dividends have been paid since 1935. A dividend reinvestment plan is available.

Amt. of Div. $	Date Decl.	Ex-Div. Date	Stock of Record	Payment Date
0.300	Jul. 26	Sep. 02	Sep. 09	Oct. 01 '94
0.300	Nov. 23	Dec. 02	Dec. 08	Jan. 02 '95
0.300	Feb. 28	Mar. 03	Mar. 09	Apr. 03 '95
0.300	May. 23	Jun. 02	Jun. 08	Jul. 03 '95
0.340	Jul. 25	Sep. 05	Sep. 07	Oct. 02 '95

Data as orig. reptd.; bef. results of disc. opers. and/or spec. items. Per share data adj. for stk. divs. as of ex-div. date. E-Estimated. NA-Not Available. NM-Not Meaningful. NR-Not Ranked.

Office—One Merck Drive, P.O. Box 100, Whitehouse Station, NJ 08889. **Tel**—(908) 423-1000. **Chrmn, Pres & CEO**—R. V. Gilmartin. **Secy**—C. A. Colbert. **VP & CFO**—J. C. Lewent. **Treas**—C. Dorsa. **Investor Contact**—James Hinrichs (908-423-6883). **Dirs**—H. B. Atwater, Jr., Sir Derek Birkin, L. A. Bossidy, W. G. Bowen, J. B. Cole, C. K. Davis, L. C. Elam, C. E. Exley, Jr., R. V. Gilmartin, W. N. Kelley, S. O. Thier, D. Weatherstone. **Transfer Agent & Registrar**—Norwest Bank Minnesota. **Incorporated** in New Jersey in 1934. **Empl**-47,500. **S&P Analyst:** H. B. Saftlas

Meredith Corp.

NYSE Symbol **MDP**
In S&P 500

30-OCT-95 Industry:
Publishing

Summary: Meredith derives the bulk of its earnings from publishing magazines (primarily Better Homes and Gardens and Ladies' Home Journal) and ownership of six TV stations.

| S&P Opinion: Hold (★★★) | Recent Price • 34⅞ | Yield • 1.1% |
| | 52 Wk Range • 42½-22¼ | 12-Mo. P/E • 25.6 |

Earnings vs. Previous Year
▲=Up ▼=Down ▶=No Change

Quantitative Evaluations

Outlook
(1 Lowest—5 Highest)
• **2+**

Fair Value
• **36**

Risk
• **Average**

Earn./Div. Rank
• **B**

Technical Eval.
• **Bullish** since 12/92

Rel. Strength Rank
(1 Lowest—99 Highest)
• **34**

Insider Activity
• **Neutral**

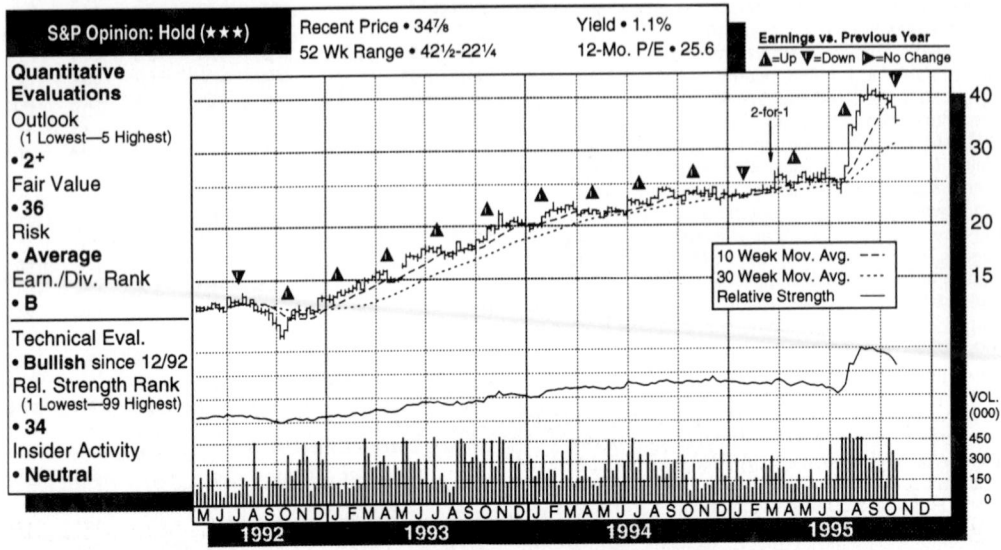

10 Week Mov. Avg. ----
30 Week Mov. Avg. ·····
Relative Strength ——

1992   1993   1994   1995

Overview - 30-OCT-95

Revenues from continuing operations are expected to advance in fiscal 1996, boosted by stronger contributions from broadcasting and magazines. Advertising will benefit from rate increases, a healthy advertising climate generally, and by Olympics and national election advertising. Comparisons will also benefit from several TV station acquisitions. Circulation revenues should also rise, reflecting the increasing popularity of home/gardening/lifestyle publications. Aggressive expansion in licensing will continue. Margins will remain under pressure from higher paper costs, sluggish book sales, and one-time restructuring charges in the book and magazine operations. Interest costs should also trend downward.

Valuation - 30-OCT-95

Meredith's earnings from continuing operations are projected to advance roughly 25% in the fiscal year ending June 1996. In addition, the company plans to sell the remainder of its recently discontinued, 70%-owned cable operation. The absence of cable strengthens MDP's balance sheet and frees up funds for other uses, including acquisitions and debt reduction. With demographic trends in its favor, and stronger contributions from broadcasting and licensing, the longer-term outlook for revenues and profits is quite positive. Nevertheless, the stock, which has been in a healthy uptrend for over two years, appears to be near saturation level. We recommend refraining from additional purchases for the time being.

Key Stock Statistics

S&P EPS Est. 1996	1.60	Tang. Bk. Value/Share	NM
P/E on S&P Est. 1996	21.8	Beta	0.99
Dividend Rate/Share	0.40	Shareholders	3,500
Shs. outstg. (M)	27.5	Market cap. (B)	$0.958
Avg. daily vol. (M)	0.061	Inst. holdings	53%
		Insider holdings	NA

Value of $10,000 invested 5 years ago: $ 22,398

Fiscal Year Ending Jun. 30

	1996	% Change	1995	% Change	1994	% Change
Revenues (Million $)						
1Q	207.7	4%	200.1	10%	182.3	3%
2Q	—	—	214.9	5%	204.6	8%
3Q	—	—	230.4	12%	205.8	3%
4Q	—	—	239.1	16%	206.8	2%
Yr.	—	—	884.5	11%	799.5	4%
Income (Million $)						
1Q	9.51	-11%	10.67	NM	3.44	—
2Q	—	—	8.92	-22%	11.50	144%
3Q	—	—	10.18	41%	7.22	35%
4Q	—	—	10.08	102%	4.99	-3%
Yr.	—	—	39.85	47%	27.15	46%
Earnings Per Share ($)						
1Q	0.34	-13%	0.39	NM	0.12	9%
2Q	E0.37	16%	0.32	-20%	0.40	158%
3Q	E0.45	22%	0.37	45%	0.25	46%
4Q	E0.44	22%	0.36	100%	0.18	6%
Yr.	E1.60	11%	1.44	52%	0.95	56%

Next earnings report expected: late January

Meredith Corp.

30-OCT-95

Business Summary - 30-OCT-95

Contributions by business segment in fiscal 1995:

	Revs.	Profits
Publishing	77%	51%
Broadcasting	14%	44%
Real estate	3%	2%
Cable	6%	3%

Meredith publishes 18 subscription-based magazines, including Better Homes and Gardens, Successful Farming, WOOD, Ladies' Home Journal, Country Home, Traditional Home and Midwest Living. Special-interest publications include 40 home/gardening/lifestyle products. MDP has licensed Wal-Mart Stores to operate Better Homes and Gardens Garden Centers in over 2,100 stores. Multicom Publishing is licensed to develop and publish CD-ROM titles based on MDP's editorial products. Reader's Digest Association received a license in July 1995 to market MDP-trademarked products.

The company owns six TV stations: KVVU (a FOX affiliate), Henderson, Nev.; KCTV (CBS), Kansas City, Mo.; KPHO (CBS), Phoenix, Ariz.; WNEM (CBS), Bay City-Saginaw-Flint, Mich.; WSMV (NBC), Nashville; and WOFL (FOX), Orlando-Daytona Beach, Fla. The purchase of a seventh station, WOGX (FOX), in Ocala, Fla., is pending.

MDP publishes some 250 home and family service books. The books are marketed through retail centers, direct mail and book clubs. MDP also operates a national real estate marketing service that licenses selected real estate firms to exclusive territories.

Important Developments

Oct. '95—MDP announced plans to sell its cable segment within the next year and classified it as a discontinued operation. Negotiations are in progress for the sale of its 70%-owned Minneapolis system, which serves 120,000 subscribers. A small North Dakota system was sold in March.

Jul. '95—Reader's Digest Association (RDA) acquired rights from the company to develop and directly market MDP books and other merchandise. The 16 1/2 year agreement also gives RDA access to MDP's 60 million-name mailing list. As part of the arrangement, MDP will combine its book and magazine publishing units and will eliminate 50 book-related positions. MDP's magazine and retail book operations will continue to operate independently of RDA. Terms were not disclosed.

Capitalization

Long Term Debt: $166,079,000 (6/95).

Class B Common Stock: 6,729,025 shs. ($1 par); 10 votes per sh.; transfer restricted; conv. sh.-for-sh. into com.

Meredith interests hold over 50% voting control.
Institutions hold about 56% of com. and Cl. B.
Shareholders of record: 2,000.

Per Share Data ($)

(Year Ended Jun. 30)

	1995	1994	1993	1992	1991	1990
Tangible Bk. Val.	-6.81	-3.10	-2.89	2.92	4.89	3.57
Cash Flow	2.75	2.17	1.67	0.57	1.22	0.45
Earnings	1.44	0.96	0.61	0.03	0.68	-0.04
Dividends	0.36	0.34	0.32	0.32	0.32	0.32
Payout Ratio	25%	36%	51%	NM	47%	NM
Prices - High	29⅛	23⅜	21¾	14⅛	15⅛	18⅛
- Low	22⅝	19⅜	13⅛	11	10⅝	10⅜
P/E Ratio - High	20	24	36	NM	22	NM
- Low	16	20	22	NM	16	NM

Income Statement Analysis (Million $)

	1995	%Chg	1994	%Chg	1993	%Chg	1992
Revs.	885	11%	800	4%	769	7%	718
Oper. Inc.	112	23%	91.3	25%	73.3	83%	40.1
Depr.	36.4	6%	34.3	6%	32.4	85%	17.5
Int. Exp.	15.1	30%	11.6	17%	9.9	NM	0.7
Pretax Inc.	77.1	42%	54.2	64%	33.1	NM	1.8
Eff. Tax Rate	48%	—	50%	—	48%	—	47%
Net Inc.	39.8	46%	27.2	46%	18.6	NM	1.0

Balance Sheet & Other Fin. Data (Million $)

	1995	1994	1993	1992	1991	1990
Cash	17.0	50.0	40.0	84.0	128	5.0
Curr. Assets	262	298	287	223	309	201
Total Assets	882	864	901	593	594	617
Curr. Liab.	288	280	282	124	148	186
LT Debt	166	127	132	38.0	Nil	0.3
Common Eqty.	241	258	284	301	343	310
Total Cap.	462	460	487	360	363	328
Cap. Exp.	24.7	20.8	16.1	6.7	9.1	12.3
Cash Flow	76.3	61.5	51.0	18.5	41.0	16.7

Ratio Analysis

	1995	1994	1993	1992	1991	1990
Curr. Ratio	0.9	1.1	1.0	1.8	2.1	1.1
% LT Debt of Cap.	36.0	27.6	27.1	10.6	Nil	0.1
% Net Inc.of Revs.	4.5	3.4	2.4	0.1	3.1	NM
% Ret. on Assets	4.6	3.0	2.6	0.2	3.9	NM
% Ret. on Equity	16.0	10.0	6.6	0.3	7.3	NM

Dividend Data —Dividends have been paid since 1947.

Amt. of Div. $	Date Decl.	Ex-Div. Date	Stock of Record	Payment Date
0.180	Nov. 15	Nov. 23	Nov. 30	Dec. 15 '94
0.200	Jan. 30	Feb. 22	Feb. 28	Mar. 15 '95
2-for-1	Jan. 30	Mar. 17	Mar. 01	Mar. 16 '95
0.100	May. 10	May. 24	May. 31	Jun. 15 '95
0.100	Aug. 09	Aug. 29	Aug. 31	Sep. 15 '95

Data as orig. reptd.; bef. results of disc. opers. and/or spec. items. Per share data adj. for stk. divs. as of ex-div. date.
E-Estimated. NA-Not Available. NM-Not Meaningful. NR-Not Ranked.

Office—1716 Locust St., Des Moines, IA 50309-3023. **Tel**—(515) 284-3000. **Chrmn & CEO**—J. D. Rehm. **Pres**—W. T. Kerr. **VP-Secy**—T. L. Slaughter. **VP-Fin & Investor Contact**—Larry D. Hartsook. **Dirs**—H. M. Baum, R. A. Burnett, P. M. Grieve, F. B. Henry, J. W. Johnson, W. T. Kerr, R. E. Lee, R. S. Levitt, E. T. Meredith III, N. L. Reding, J. D. Rehm, S. Uehling. **Transfer Agent & Registrar**—Registrar & Transfer Co., Cranford, N.J. **Incorporated** in Iowa in 1905. **Empl**-2,400. **S&P Analyst:** William H. Donald

Merrill Lynch

NYSE Symbol **MER**
In S&P 500

20-OCT-95 Industry: Securities

Summary: Merrill Lynch is one of the largest and most diversified securities firms in the world.

S&P Opinion: No Opinion	Recent Price • 64⅛	Yield • 1.7%	Earnings vs. Previous Year
	52 Wk Range • 64¾-32¼	12-Mo. P/E • 13.6	▲=Up ▼=Down ▶=No Change

Quantitative Evaluations

Outlook
(1 Lowest—5 Highest)
• **2+**

Fair Value
• **61⅛**

Risk
• **Average**

Earn./Div. Rank
• **B+**

Technical Eval.
• **Bullish** since 2/95

Rel. Strength Rank
(1 Lowest—99 Highest)
• **51**

Insider Activity
• **NA**

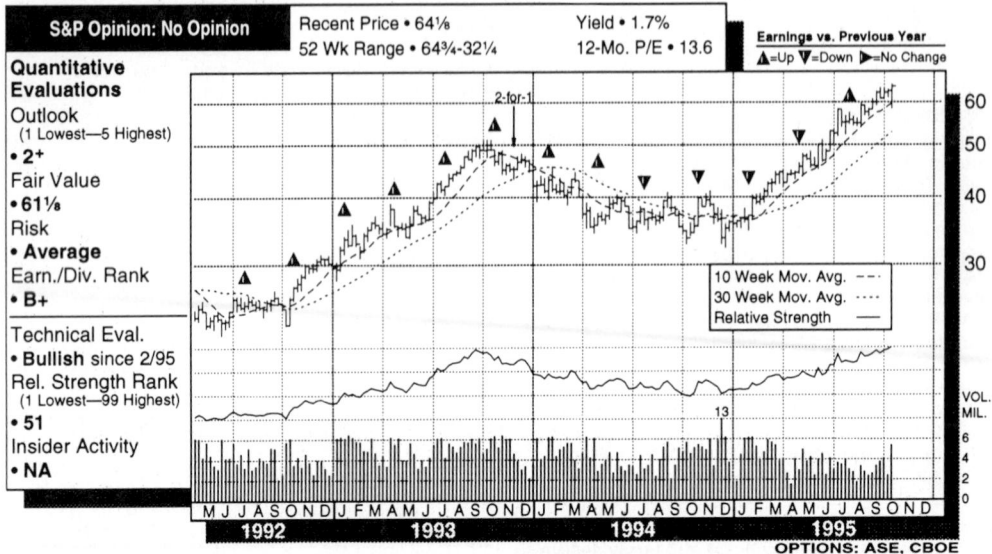

10 Week Mov. Avg. ---
30 Week Mov. Avg. ····
Relative Strength —

VOL.
MIL.

OPTIONS: ASE, CBOE

Overview - 27-JUL-95

Profits for 1996 are expected to advance. Commissions are anticipated to improve on higher retail investor trading. Interest and dividends (net) should also climb, mainly due to the effect of projected lower interest rates on MER's cost of financing its securities inventory. Principal transactions income should improve, reflecting an anticipated stronger bond market. Merrill does not use its capital to profit from short-term price changes to the extent certain of its competitors do. Investment banking revenues are expected to recover, based on increased issuer activity. Asset management operations, a source of stable fees, should make a stronger contribution. MER has made considerable progress in reducing its earnings sensitivity to market conditions.

Valuation - 17-OCT-95

Price to tangible book value is the preferred measure to use to value brokerage stocks because their highly liquid balance sheets are readily marked to market. Also, the traditional price earnings ratio tends to make the stocks appear underpriced at market tops and overpriced at market lows. As of late October 1995, the shares were trading at about twice tangible book value, well above its average price to book of some 50% over the past four years. As the bellwether stock in the brokerage group, the shares deserve a premium to the group.

Key Stock Statistics

S&P EPS Est. 1995	5.50	Tang. Bk. Value/Share	29.24
P/E on S&P Est. 1995	11.7	Beta	1.88
S&P EPS Est. 1996	6.65	Shareholders	12,200
Dividend Rate/Share	1.04	Market cap. (B)	$ 10.5
Shs. outstg. (M)	176.0	Inst. holdings	56%
Avg. daily vol. (M)	0.807	Insider holdings	NA

Value of $10,000 invested 5 years ago: $ 55,959

Fiscal Year Ending Dec. 31

	1996	% Change	1995	% Change	1994	% Change
Revenues (Million $)						
1Q	—	—	5,204	10%	4,739	20%
2Q	—	—	5,585	25%	4,480	13%
3Q	—	—	5,431	20%	4,530	9%
4Q	—	—	—	—	4,484	NM
Yr.	—	—	—	—	18,233	10%
Income (Million $)						
1Q	—	—	227.3	-39%	371.8	9%
2Q	—	—	282.8	12%	251.8	-27%
3Q	—	—	300.4	30%	231.6	-36%
4Q	—	—	—	—	161.6	-53%
Yr.	—	—	—	—	1,017	-27%
Earnings Per Share ($)						
1Q	E1.60	48%	1.08	-36%	1.68	11%
2Q	E1.70	21%	1.40	19%	1.18	-23%
3Q	E1.75	19%	1.47	34%	1.10	-30%
4Q	E1.60	3%	1.55	104%	0.76	-50%
Yr.	E6.65	21%	E5.50	16%	4.75	-23%

Next earnings report expected: late January

Merrill Lynch

Business Summary - 20-OCT-95

Merrill Lynch & Co. is a diversified financial services company which, through subsidiaries, provides investment, financing, insurance and related services. Its chief subsidiary, Merrill Lynch, Pierce, Fenner & Smith (MLPF&S), is one of the largest in the securities industry. Revenues in recent years were derived:

	1994	1993
Commissions	30%	27%
Int. & divs. (net)	10%	10%
Principal trans.	24%	28%
Invest. banking	13%	17%
Asset mgmt.	18%	15%
Other	5%	3%

MLPF&S, directly and through subsidiaries, is a broker in securities, option contracts, commodity and financial futures contracts, and selected insurance products; a dealer in corporate and municipal securities; and an investment banker. MER manages mutual funds, provides investment advisory services, and engages in international banking outside the U.S.

At 1994 year-end, the MLPF&S unit had about 7.1 million customer accounts (6.9 million a year earlier). In the U. S. and Canada, these accounts were served by about 12,300 retail financial consultants and institutional account executives in more than 500 offices worldwide. In the rest of the world these accounts were served by about 1,125 retail financial consultants and institutional account executives. Assets in private clients accounts totaled $568 billion at year-end 1994, versus $557 billion.

At June 30, 1995, MLPF&S's regulatory net capital of $1,615 million was 12% of aggregate debit balances and was $1,347 million in excess of the minimum required.

Important Developments

Oct. '95—The company said that assets in Private Client accounts worldwide grew to $675 billion at the end of the 1995 third quarter, up 5% and 18%, respectively, from the end of the preceding quarter and the year-earlier quarter. Third quarter 1995 results included about $7 million of integration costs associated with the Smith New Court acquisition. MER acquired Smith New Court, a U.K. securities firm, during the quarter for about $842 million.

Capitalization

Long Term Debt: $15,703,594,000 (6/95).
Preferred Stock: $618,800,000 (liquid. pref.).

Per Share Data ($) (Year Ended Dec. 31)

	1994	1993	1992	1991	1990	1989
Tangible Bk. Val.	27.67	23.27	19.54	16.06	13.47	13.78
Cash Flow	NA	NA	NA	NA	NA	NA
Earnings	4.75	6.14	4.18	3.01	0.79	-1.17
Dividends	0.89	0.70	0.57	0.50	0.50	0.50
Payout Ratio	19%	11%	14%	17%	63%	NM
Prices - High	45 5/8	51 1/8	33 3/8	30 1/2	13 5/8	18 3/8
- Low	32 1/4	28	22 1/4	9 5/8	8 1/8	11 3/4
P/E Ratio - High	10	8	8	10	17	NM
- Low	7	5	5	3	10	NM

Income Statement Analysis (Million $)

	1994	%Chg	1993	%Chg	1992	%Chg	1991
Commissions	2,871	NM	2,894	21%	2,400	12%	2,138
Int. Inc.	9,578	35%	7,099	22%	5,807	NM	5,761
Total Revs.	18,233	10%	16,588	24%	13,428	9%	12,363
Int. Exp.	8,609	43%	6,030	25%	4,835	-5%	5,106
Pretax Inc.	1,730	-29%	2,425	50%	1,621	59%	1,017
Eff. Tax Rate	41%	—	43%	—	41%	—	32%
Net Inc.	1,017	-27%	1,394	46%	952	37%	696

Balance Sheet & Other Fin. Data (Million $)

	1994	1993	1992	1991	1990	1989
Total Assets	163,749	152,910	107,024	86,259	68,130	63,942
Cash Items	7,265	5,853	4,676	4,429	5,829	4,360
Receivables	91,917	82,516	57,084	43,075	32,260	31,645
Secs. Owned	52,739	51,549	31,669	24,908	17,284	15,721
Sec. Borrowed	78,304	79,632	51,180	38,698	27,341	28,558
Due Brokers & Cust.	16,247	18,434	12,290	13,184	13,219	10,064
Other Liabs.	48,517	35,899	28,114	22,595	18,002	15,272
Capitalization:						
Debt	14,863	13,469	10,871	7,964	6,342	6,897
Equity	5,199	5,292	4,269	3,518	2,925	2,851
Total	20,681	18,955	15,140	11,483	9,267	10,048

Ratio Analysis

	1994	1993	1992	1991	1990	1989
% Ret. on Revs.	5.6	8.4	7.1	5.6	1.7	NM
% Ret. on Assets	0.6	1.0	0.8	0.8	0.3	NM
% Ret. on Equity	18.6	27.3	22.0	20.8	5.8	NM

Dividend Data —Dividends have been paid since 1971. A dividend reinvestment plan is available. A "poison pill" stock purchase right was adopted in 1987.

Amt. of Div. $	Date Decl.	Ex-Div. Date	Stock of Record	Payment Date
0.230	Oct. 24	Oct. 31	Nov. 04	Nov. 23 '94
0.230	Jan. 26	Jan. 30	Feb. 03	Feb. 22 '95
0.260	Apr. 25	May. 02	May. 08	May. 24 '95
0.260	Jul. 21	Aug. 02	Aug. 04	Aug. 23 '95

Data as orig. reptd.; bef. results of disc opers. and/or spec. items. Per share data adj. for stk. divs. as of ex-div. date. E-Estimated. NA-Not Available. NM-Not Meaningful. NR-Not Ranked.

Office—World Financial Center, North Tower, New York, NY 10281-1123. **Tel**—(212) 449-1000. **Chrmn & CEO**—D. P. Tully. **Pres & COO**—D. H. Komansky. **SVP-CFO**—J. M. Willett, Jr. **Secy**—G. T. Russo. **Investor Contact**—William Hartman. **Dirs**—W. O. Bourke, W. H. Clark, J. K. Conway, S. L. Hammerman, R. A. Hanson, E. H. Harbison, Jr., G. B. Harvey, W. R. Hoover, D. H. Komansky, R. P. Luciano, A. L. Peters, J. J. Phelan, Jr., D. P. Tully, W. L. Weiss. **Transfer Agents & Registrars**—Co.'s office; Chemical Bank, NYC. **Incorporated** in Delaware in 1973. **Empl**-45,400. **S&P Analyst:** Paul L. Huberman, CFA

Microsoft Corp.

NASDAQ Symbol **MSFT**

In S&P 500

25-JUL-95

Industry: Data Processing

Summary: Microsoft develops and markets a diverse line of systems and applications microcomputer software, including the MS-DOS and Windows operating environment for IBM and compatible PCs.

S&P Opinion: Hold (★★★)	Recent Price • 92	Yield • Nil
	52 Wk Range • 109¼-49¼	12-Mo. P/E • 39.7

Earnings vs. Previous Year
▲=Up ▼=Down ▶=No Change

Quantitative Evaluations

Outlook
(1 Lowest—5 Highest)
• **1+**

Fair Value
• **89%**

Risk
• **Low**

Earn./Div. Rank
• **B+**

Technical Eval.
• **Bullish** since 3/94

Rel. Strength Rank
(1 Lowest—99 Highest)
• **69**

Insider Activity
• **Unfavorable**

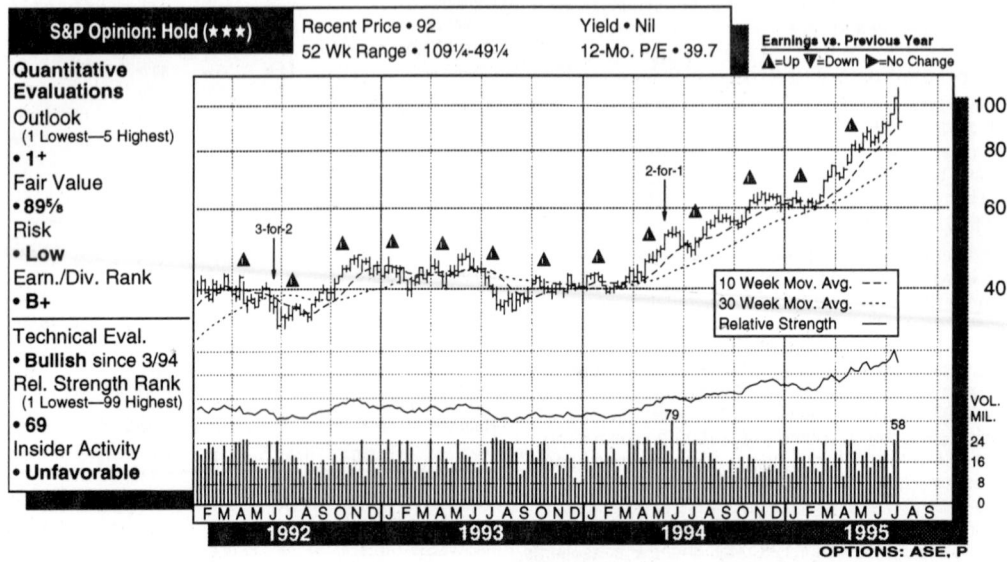

10 Week Mov. Avg. - - -
30 Week Mov. Avg. ......
Relative Strength ——

OPTIONS: ASE, P

Overview - 25-JUL-95

Revenues should continue to advance strongly through fiscal 1996, reflecting the continued popularity of Windows, Microsoft's graphical operating environment that runs with the MS-DOS operating system, and associated applications, aided by higher PC shipments. Strong acceptance of the Microsoft Office suite of applications, including Word and Excel, should continue to aid results. New products, including Windows 95, the successor to the Windows operating environment, which is expected to ship in August 1995, as well as new consumer offerings and contributions from acquisitions, should also boost revenue growth. Margins should narrow somewhat, reflecting continued high R&D and marketing costs.

Valuation - 25-JUL-95

The stock has risen sharply since mid-1993, reflecting strong earnings gains, powered by the company's dominant position in PC operating systems and leading position in PC business applications. The shares have been particularly strong this year on anticipation of Windows 95. The strong product cycle associated with this major upgrade, combined with new consumer software and on-line services products, are expected to aid earnings growth. However, the shares trade above our estimate of the company's long term growth rate. Although Microsoft's earnings prospects are bright, we believe the stock is fairly valued and should perform in line with the market in coming months.

Key Stock Statistics

S&P EPS Est. 1996	2.95	Tang. Bk. Value/Share	8.42
P/E on S&P Est. 1996	31.2	Beta	1.24
Dividend Rate/Share	Nil	Shareholders	27,800
Shs. outstg. (M)	585.6	Market cap. (B)	$ 54.8
Avg. daily vol. (M)	6.739	Inst. holdings	40%
		Insider holdings	NA

Value of $10,000 invested 5 years ago: $ 95,169

Fiscal Year Ending Jun. 30

	1995	% Change	1994	% Change	1993	% Change
Revenues (Million $)						
1Q	1,247	27%	983.0	20%	818.0	41%
2Q	1,482	31%	1,129	20%	938.0	38%
3Q	1,587	28%	1,244	30%	958.0	41%
4Q	1,621	25%	1,293	24%	1,039	27%
Yr.	5,937	28%	4,649	24%	3,753	36%
Income (Million $)						
1Q	316.0	32%	239.0	—	—	—
2Q	373.0	29%	289.0	22%	236.0	35%
3Q	396.0	55%	256.0	5%	243.0	36%
4Q	368.0	2%	362.0	37%	265.0	26%
Yr.	1,453	27%	1,146	20%	953.0	35%
Earnings Per Share ($)						
1Q	0.51	29%	0.39	13%	0.35	40%
2Q	0.60	28%	0.47	21%	0.39	30%
3Q	0.63	50%	0.42	5%	0.40	33%
4Q	0.58	-2%	0.59	36%	0.43	23%
Yr.	2.32	23%	1.88	20%	1.57	31%

Next earnings report expected: late October

Business Summary - 25-JUL-95

Microsoft develops, markets and supports microcomputer software, including operating systems, languages and application programs, as well as books, hardware and multimedia products. Revenues by product group in recent fiscal years were:

	1995	1994	1993
Systems software	35%	33%	34%
Applications software	61%	63%	60%
Hardware & other	4%	4%	6%

Products are distributed through four primary channels: OEM (28% of fiscal 1995 revenues); U.S. and Canadian resellers (32%); European resellers (25%); and other international resellers (15%).

Microsoft markets proprietary microcomputer operating systems, including MS-DOS, Windows, Windows for Workgroups and Windows NT. MS-DOS is a single-user, single-tasking 16-bit operating system. Windows provides a graphical operating environment for DOS-based PCs that offers drop-down menus, icons and mixed text. Windows for Workgroups allows Windows users to share files, data and printers. Windows NT is a true 32-bit operating system designed to run on computers based on Intel 80386, 80486 and Pentium chips as well as most RISC architectures and multiprocessor systems.

Applications software includes Word (word processing); Excel (spreadsheet); Powerpoint (graphics); and Project (project management products). Office combines these basic business applications into a single offering. Languages include BASIC and C++. Databases include the FoxPro, Access and SQL Server relational database management systems. Consumer products include Works, an integrated software program, and Publisher, an entry-level desktop publishing tool, as well as assorted entertainment, educational and other offerings for the home.

The Microsoft Mouse, a handheld pointing device, is the company's principal hardware product. Publishing activities include computer-oriented books.

Important Developments

Jul. '95—During the fourth quarter of fiscal 1994-5, Microsoft recorded a $46 million ($0.05 a share) charge to reflect costs associated with its termination of an agreement to acquire Intuit, a leading developer of personal finance, tax preparation and small business accounting software.

Jun. '95—The U.S. Appeals Court in Washington, D.C., reinstated a 1994 antitrust settlement agreement between the company and the Justice Department. The agreement had been rejected by a federal district judge in February 1995.

Capitalization

Long Term Debt: None (6/95).

Per Share Data ($)   (Year Ended Jun. 30)

	1995	1994	1993	1992	1991	1990
Tangible Bk. Val.	NA	7.66	5.75	3.96	2.54	1.76
Cash Flow	NA	2.27	1.80	1.38	0.95	0.60
Earnings	2.32	1.88	1.58	1.20	0.82	0.52
Dividends	Nil	Nil	Nil	Nil	Nil	Nil
Payout Ratio	Nil	Nil	Nil	Nil	Nil	Nil
Prices - High	109¼	65⅛	49	47½	37⅜	18
- Low	58¼	39	35¼	32⅞	16¼	9⅜
P/E Ratio - High	47	35	31	39	45	35
- Low	25	21	22	27	20	18

Income Statement Analysis (Million $)

	1994	%Chg	1993	%Chg	1992	%Chg	1991
Revs.	4,649	24%	3,753	36%	2,759	50%	1,843
Oper. Inc.	1,963	34%	1,464	33%	1,097	54%	714
Depr.	237	72%	138	37%	101	51%	67.0
Int. Exp.	2.0	100%	1.0	-50%	2.0	-56%	4.5
Pretax Inc.	1,722	23%	1,401	35%	1,041	55%	671
Eff. Tax Rate	33%	—	32%	—	32%	—	31%
Net Inc.	1,146	20%	953	35%	708	53%	463

Balance Sheet & Other Fin. Data (Million $)

	1994	1993	1992	1991	1990	1989
Cash	3,614	2,290	1,345	686	449	301
Curr. Assets	4,312	2,850	1,770	1,029	720	469
Total Assets	5,363	3,805	2,640	1,644	1,105	721
Curr. Liab.	913	563	447	293	187	159
LT Debt	Nil	Nil	Nil	Nil	Nil	Nil
Common Eqty.	4,450	3,242	2,193	1,351	919	562
Total Cap.	4,450	3,242	2,193	1,351	919	562
Cap. Exp.	278	239	318	275	159	92.0
Cash Flow	1,383	1,091	809	530	326	196

Ratio Analysis

	1994	1993	1992	1991	1990	1989
Curr. Ratio	4.7	5.1	4.0	3.5	3.9	3.0
% LT Debt of Cap.	Nil	Nil	Nil	Nil	Nil	Nil
% Net Inc.of Revs.	24.7	25.4	25.7	25.1	23.6	21.2
% Ret. on Assets	25.0	29.1	32.5	33.4	30.1	27.9
% Ret. on Equity	29.8	34.6	39.3	40.4	37.1	36.1

Dividend Data (No cash has been paid. A two-for-one stock split was effected in May 1994.)

Data as orig. reptd.; bef. results of disc. opers. and/or spec. items. Per share data adj. for stk. divs. as of ex-div. date. E-Estimated. NA-Not Available. NM-Not Meaningful. NR-Not Ranked.

Office—One Microsoft Way, Redmond, WA 98052-6399. **Tel**—(206) 882-8080. **Chrmn & CEO**—W. H. Gates III. **CFO**—M. W. Brown. **Secy**—W. H. Neukom. **Investor Contact**—Raymond B. Ferguson. **Dirs**—P. G. Allen, W. H. Gates III, R. Hackborn, D. F. Marquardt, R. D. O'Brien, W. G. Reed, Jr., J. A. Shirley. **Transfer Agent**—First Interstate Bank, Calabasas, CA. **Incorporated** in Washington in 1981; reincorporated in Delaware in 1986. **Empl**-15,257. **S&P Analyst:** Peter C. Wood, CFA

02-OCT-95

Industry:
Electronics/Electric

Summary: Micron Technology is a leading manufacturer of semiconductor memories and other semiconductor components, board-level products and personal computers.

S&P Opinion: Hold (★★★)	Recent Price • 79⅜	Yield • 0.3%
	52 Wk Range • 94¾-15¼	12-Mo. P/E • 20.1

Quantitative Evaluations

Outlook
(1 Lowest—5 Highest)
• 3+

Fair Value
• 86¼

Risk
• **High**

Earn./Div. Rank
• B

Technical Eval.
• **Bullish** since 10/92

Rel. Strength Rank
(1 Lowest—99 Highest)
• 83

Insider Activity
• **Favorable**

Earnings vs. Previous Year
▲=Up ▼=Down ▶=No Change

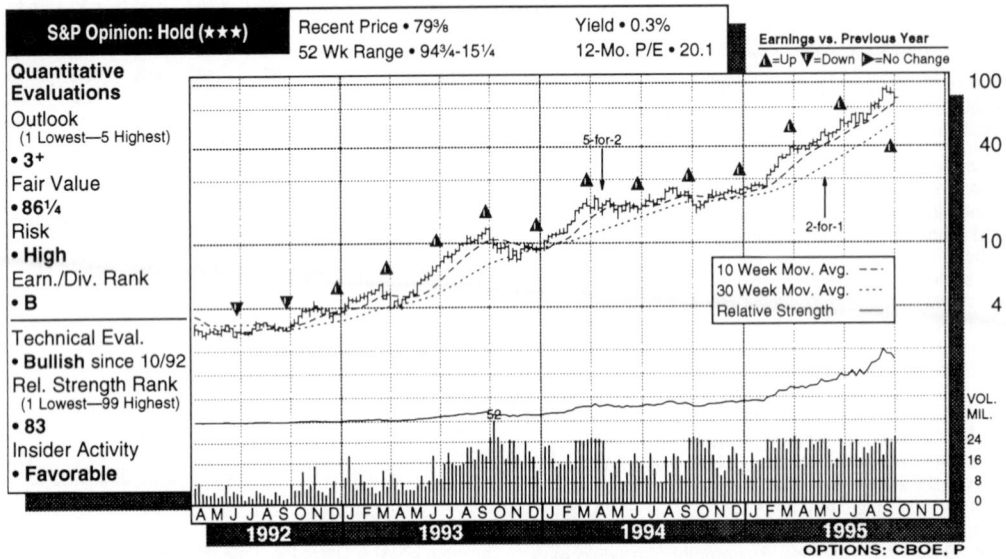

10 Week Mov. Avg. —
30 Week Mov. Avg. ····
Relative Strength —

OPTIONS: CBOE, P

Overview - 02-OCT-95

Sales are expected to double in fiscal 1996, reflecting continued strong PC demand. This brisk demand has created supply shortages for DRAM, a problem that should be exacerbated by the release of Windows 95. This new operating system from Microsoft boosts the amount of DRAM required on a typical PC. These factors are likely to leave DRAM capacity tight over at least the next six to 12 months, fueling strong sales growth for vendors. MU is also transitioning to a smaller chip design and larger wafers, both of which are expected to increase its capacity significantly. Margins should narrow, reflecting price pressures, MU's transition to 16MB DRAM production from 4MB DRAM and as PC's comprise a greater percentage of sales. Well controlled operating costs should lead to a 66% gain in EPS to $6.55 a share.

Valuation - 02-OCT-95

Micron's shares have been in a strong uptrend, buoyed by favorable industry conditions and stable DRAM prices. While these favorable conditions could persist over the next six to 12 months, we believe the shares will only be a market performer over this time frame, due to potential profit taking and concerns about pending DRAM capacity additions that could come on stream by the second half of 1996. This new supply could exert pressure on DRAM prices, which historically have fallen 30% annually, and ultimately impact earnings. As a result, we view the shares as adequately valued at current prices.

Key Stock Statistics

S&P EPS Est. 1996	6.55	Tang. Bk. Value/Share	7.65
P/E on S&P Est. 1996	12.1	Beta	1.92
Dividend Rate/Share	0.20	Shareholders	3,100
Shs. outstg. (M)	206.1	Market cap. (B)	$ 16.4
Avg. daily vol. (M)	6.318	Inst. holdings	58%
		Insider holdings	NA

Value of $10,000 invested 5 years ago: $ 410,788

Fiscal Year Ending Aug. 31

	1995	% Change	1994	% Change	1993	% Change
Revenues (Million $)						
1Q	535.0	67%	320.1	144%	131.0	17%
2Q	628.5	61%	390.5	121%	176.4	38%
3Q	761.2	79%	426.4	98%	214.9	64%
4Q	1,028	109%	491.6	61%	306.0	126%
Yr.	2,953	81%	1,629	97%	828.3	64%
Income (Million $)						
1Q	159.3	136%	67.55	NM	2.70	NM
2Q	183.5	112%	86.76	NM	9.04	NM
3Q	220.2	111%	104.3	NM	29.49	NM
4Q	281.0	98%	141.9	126%	62.84	NM
Yr.	844.0	111%	400.5	NM	104.1	NM
Earnings Per Share ($)						
1Q	0.76	132%	0.33	NM	0.01	NM
2Q	0.86	106%	0.42	NM	0.04	NM
3Q	1.02	106%	0.50	NM	0.15	NM
4Q	1.30	94%	0.67	115%	0.31	NM
Yr.	3.95	107%	1.91	NM	0.52	NM

Next earnings report expected: mid December

Business Summary - 02-OCT-95

Micron Technology designs, manufactures and markets semiconductors, board-level and system-level products, and personal computers.

The company's largest product line is dynamic random access memories (DRAMs), which accounted for 73% of sales in fiscal 1994. DRAMs are the most widely used semiconductor memory components in computer systems. The primary product in fiscal 1994 was the 4 megabit DRAM. MU is currently pursuing internal qualification of its 16 megabit DRAM, and is beginning to transfer the 64 megabit DRAM from the pilot line to the manufacturing area. Specialty DRAM memory products are also produced.

MU also produces static random access memories (SRAMs), which accounted for 8% of sales in fiscal 1994. SRAMs perform memory functions similar to those of DRAMs, but at faster speeds.

The company manufactures and markets a variety of memory intensive board-level products, all of which utilize semiconductor memory components. They accounted for 7% of sales in fiscal 1994.

In April 1995, MU formed Micron Electronics, Inc., a publicly traded company (NASDAQ, MUEI), in which it owns 79%. MUEI, which will manufacture personal computers and workstations, is the result of the merger between two of MU's subsidiaries and ZEOS International Ltd. Sales of personal computers accounted for 8% of MU's sales in fiscal 1994.

In November 1991, MU established a new subsidiary to design and develop new technologies relating to flat panel display technologies.

In November 1993, the company began selling semiconductor testers.

R&D spending increased to $128.8 million (4.4% of sales) in fiscal 1995, from $83.4 million (5.1%) in fiscal 1994.

Export sales represented 29% of net sales in fiscal 1994 (latest available), down from 30% in fiscal 1993.

Important Developments

Jul. '95—MU commenced construction of its new manufacturing complex, located in Lehi, Utah. Initial construction will focus on an 8-inch wafer fabrication facility, with the initial ramp of wafer production targeted for the fall of 1996.

Jun. '95—The company announced engineering samples of its Burst Extended Data-Out (EDO) DRAMs, a lower cost alternative to other high-speed memory technologies. High volume production is scheduled for the fourth quarter of 1995.

Capitalization

Long Term Debt: $129,400,000 (8/31/95).

Per Share Data ($)

(Year Ended Aug. 31)

	1995	1994	1993	1992	1991	1990
Tangible Bk. Val.	NA	4.91	3.19	2.67	2.65	2.62
Cash Flow	NA	2.78	1.07	0.50	0.45	0.35
Earnings	3.95	1.92	0.52	0.03	0.03	0.03
Dividends	0.15	0.06	0.01	0.01	Nil	Nil
Payout Ratio	4%	3%	2%	29%	Nil	Nil
Prices - High	94¾	22½	12¾	4½	3⅞	3¼
- Low	21¼	9	3⅝	2⅝	1⅞	1⅜
P/E Ratio - High	24	12	25	NM	NM	NM
- Low	5	5	5	NM	NM	NM

Income Statement Analysis (Million $)

	1994	%Chg	1993	%Chg	1992	%Chg	1991
Revs.	1,629	97%	828	64%	506	19%	425
Oper. Inc.	801	190%	276	163%	105	13%	93.0
Depr.	181	65%	110	21%	91.0	12%	81.4
Int. Exp.	5.8	-29%	8.2	-5%	8.6	-23%	11.2
Pretax Inc.	626	NM	163	NM	10.0	67%	6.0
Eff. Tax Rate	36%	—	36%	—	31%	—	14%
Net Inc.	401	NM	104	NM	7.0	40%	5.0

Balance Sheet & Other Fin. Data (Million $)

	1994	1993	1992	1991	1990	1989
Cash	433	186	73.0	68.0	77.0	161
Curr. Assets	793	440	227	213	198	279
Total Assets	1,530	966	724	706	697	625
Curr. Liab.	274	211	106	98.0	101	70.0
LT Debt	125	54.4	61.6	69.6	74.1	39.7
Common Eqty.	1,049	640	511	495	484	477
Total Cap.	1,228	740	609	598	590	547
Cap. Exp.	370	156	99	86.0	121	244
Cash Flow	582	214	98.0	86.0	66.0	141

Ratio Analysis

	1994	1993	1992	1991	1990	1989
Curr. Ratio	2.9	2.1	2.1	2.2	2.0	4.0
% LT Debt of Cap.	10.2	7.3	10.1	11.6	12.6	7.3
% Net Inc.of Revs.	24.6	12.6	1.3	1.2	1.5	23.8
% Ret. on Assets	32.1	12.1	0.9	0.7	0.7	20.0
% Ret. on Equity	47.4	17.7	1.3	1.0	1.0	26.6

Dividend Data —The company declared its initial cash dividend in September 1991.

Amt. of Div. $	Date Decl.	Ex-Div. Date	Stock of Record	Payment Date
0.050	Sep. 23	Sep. 26	Sep. 30	Oct. 24 '94
0.050	Dec. 19	Dec. 29	Jan. 05	Feb. 03 '95
2-for-1	Mar. 27	May. 23	May. 04	May. 22 '95
0.050	Mar. 27	May. 30	Jun. 05	Jun. 14 '95
0.050	Aug. 01	Aug. 09	Aug. 11	Aug. 21 '95

Data as orig. reptd.; bef. results of disc. opers. and/or spec. items. Per share data adj. for stk. divs. as of ex-div. date. E-Estimated. NA-Not Available. NM-Not Meaningful. NR-Not Ranked.

Office—2805 E. Columbia Rd., Boise, ID 83706-9698. **Tel**—(208) 368-4000. **Chrmn, CEO & Pres**—S. R. Appleton. **Vice Chrman**—T. A. Lowrey. **VP-Fin, CFO & Secy**—W. G. Stover, Jr. **Investor Contact**—Kipp A. Bedard. **Dirs**— S. R. Appleton, J. M. Hess, T. A. Lowrey, R. A. Lothrop, T. T. Nicholson, A. T. Noble, D. J. Simplot, J. R. Simplot, G. C. Smith, W. G. Stover, Jr. **Transfer Agent & Registrar**—West One Bank, Idaho, Boise. **Incorporated** in Delaware in 1984 (successor to a company incorporated in Idaho in 1978). **Empl**-5,400. **S&P Analyst:** John D. Coyle, CFA

Millipore Corp.

NYSE Symbol **MIL**
In S&P 500

02-SEP-95

Industry:
Electronics/Electric

Summary: Millipore manufactures and markets products used to analyze and purify fluids. Customers are primarily in the pharmaceutical, biotechnology, electronics and other industries.

S&P Opinion: Hold (★★★)		
Recent Price • 35⅝	Yield • 0.9%	
52 Wk Range • 37-22⅞	12-Mo. P/E • 25.7	

Earnings vs. Previous Year
▲=Up ▼=Down ▶=No Change

Quantitative Evaluations

Outlook
(1 Lowest—5 Highest)
• **2+**

Fair Value
• **34⅜**

Risk
• **Low**

Earn./Div. Rank
• **B+**

Technical Eval.
• **Bullish** since 2/95

Rel. Strength Rank
(1 Lowest—99 Highest)
• **59**

Insider Activity
• **Neutral**

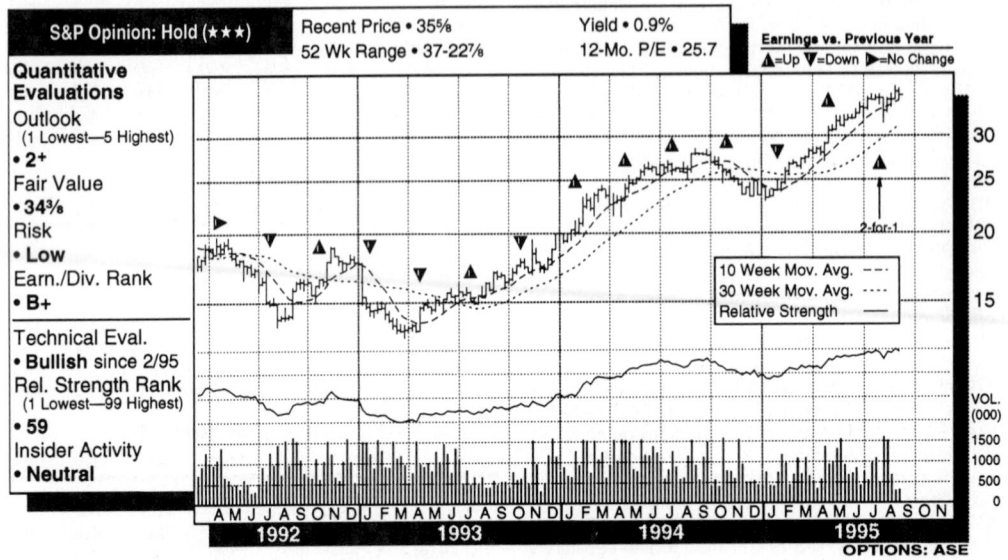

10 Week Mov. Avg. ----
30 Week Mov. Avg. ·····
Relative Strength ——

2-for-1

OPTIONS: ASE

Overview - 01-SEP-95

Strong demand for filtration products from the electronics/industrial markets should provide the company with significant top-line growth in 1995. Sales to the pharmaceutical/biotechnology sector, MIL's largest market (48% of 1994 sales), gained strength during the first half of 1995, and this trend should continue throughout 1995. Additionally, demand from the microelectronics industry, particularly in Asia/Pacific markets, continues to generate impressive revenue growth for the company, aided by a weak dollar. Margins are expected to expand on the increased sales volume and efficiencies. The company has been repurchasing its stock quite aggressively (about 12,000,000 shares on a post-split basis were purchased since late 1994), and per-share profits will benefit from ongoing and expanding share repurchase programs.

Valuation - 01-SEP-95

The shares have appreciated significantly thus far in 1995, and currently trade at a relatively high price/earnings ratio. Despite strong EPS growth forecast for 1995, this growth rate is not likely to be sustained in the long term. We believe that the shares warrant a P/E above that of the S&P 500, but recent price levels suggest limited room for appreciation over the next six to twelve months. Long-term investors may accumulate the stock at current prices.

Key Stock Statistics

S&P EPS Est. 1995	1.85	Tang. Bk. Value/Share	4.79
P/E on S&P Est. 1995	19.3	Beta	0.91
S&P EPS Est. 1996	2.05	Shareholders	4,000
Dividend Rate/Share	0.32	Market cap. (B)	$ 1.6
Shs. outstg. (M)	44.8	Inst. holdings	86%
Avg. daily vol. (M)	0.138	Insider holdings	NA

Value of $10,000 invested 5 years ago: $ 28,692

Fiscal Year Ending Dec. 31

	1995	% Change	1994	% Change	1993	% Change
Revenues (Million $)						
1Q	141.4	19%	119.0	13%	105.2	-47%
2Q	150.5	21%	124.7	9%	114.6	-39%
3Q	—	—	123.6	10%	111.8	-44%
4Q	—	—	130.1	14%	113.7	-41%
Yr.	—	—	497.3	12%	445.4	-43%
Income (Million $)						
1Q	20.68	35%	15.29	55%	9.84	-36%
2Q	22.05	25%	17.57	31%	13.41	177%
3Q	—	—	17.17	46%	11.80	-9%
4Q	—	—	9.58	-31%	13.96	104%
Yr.	—	—	59.61	22%	48.99	23%
Earnings Per Share ($)						
1Q	0.45	67%	0.27	54%	0.17	-36%
2Q	0.49	58%	0.31	29%	0.24	167%
3Q	E0.45	48%	0.31	45%	0.21	-11%
4Q	E0.46	130%	0.20	-20%	0.25	108%
Yr.	E1.85	70%	1.09	25%	0.88	24%

Next earnings report expected: mid October

Millipore Corp.

02-SEP-95

Business Summary - 01-SEP-95

Millipore Corp. is prominent in the field of membrane separations technology, developing and manufacturing products that are used primarily for the analysis and purification of fluids. Its markets include electronics/industrial, pharmaceutical/biotechnology, university/government and medical/health care. In mid-1994, the company sold its Waters Chromatography business (1993 sales of over $300 million) and its non-membrane bioscience instrument business.

MIL's products are based on a variety of membranes and certain other technologies, and effect separations, largely through physical and chemical methods. For analytical applications, Millipore's products are used to gain knowledge about a molecule, compound or micro-organism by detecting, identifying and quantifying the relevant components of a sample. For purification applications, its products are used in manufacturing and research operations to isolate and purify specific components or to remove contaminants.

The principal separation technologies used by the company are based on membrane filters, and certain chemistries, resins and enzyme immunoassays. Some of Millipore's newer membrane materials also use affinity, ion-exchange or electrical charge mechanisms for separation. MIL offers over 3,000 products, most of which are listed in its catalogs and sold as standard items, systems or devices.

About 64% of 1994 sales were to foreign markets, including Europe (31%) and Asia/Pacific (32%).

Important Developments

Feb. '95—Directors approved the use of an additional $50 million for the continuation of the company's stock repurchase program.
Jan. '95—MIL restated a net gain from discontinued operations of $5 million (recorded in the third quarter of 1994) to a net loss of $3.4 million. The action was taken following a re-evaluation of the fair market value of preferred stock MIL received as part of the sale of its Biosearch division in 1994.
Dec. '94—A net charge of $0.35 a share was recorded in 1994's fourth quarter for the settlement of a lawsuit related to the sale of MIL's process water business in 1989.
Sep. '94—MIL completed a tender offer via which it purchased 7,541,076 common shares at $28.625 a share (both adjusted). Subsequently, directors authorized the company to repurchase up to $100 million of its common shares in the open market.

Capitalization

Long Term Debt: $123,721,000 (6/95).

Per Share Data ($)

(Year Ended Dec. 31)

	1994	1993	1992	1991	1990	1989
Tangible Bk. Val.	4.67	8.19	7.61	8.14	7.36	6.72
Cash Flow	1.60	1.30	1.31	1.61	1.02	1.39
Earnings	1.09	0.88	0.71	1.08	0.50	0.95
Dividends	0.29	0.28	0.25	0.24	0.22	0.19
Payout Ratio	27%	31%	36%	22%	43%	21%
Prices - High	28½	20⅛	21	24	18⅝	18¾
- Low	19¼	13	13⅝	14⅞	12⅛	12⅝
P/E Ratio - High	26	23	30	22	37	20
- Low	18	15	19	14	24	13

Income Statement Analysis (Million $)

	1994	%Chg	1993	%Chg	1992	%Chg	1991
Revs.	497	12%	445	-43%	777	4%	748
Oper. Inc.	118	24%	95.0	-6%	101	-11%	114
Depr.	27.6	16%	23.8	-30%	34.0	16%	29.2
Int. Exp.	7.9	-41%	13.3	-18%	16.3	8%	15.1
Pretax Inc.	76.9	22%	63.2	23%	51.5	-34%	77.9
Eff. Tax Rate	23%	—	23%	—	23%	—	23%
Net Inc.	59.6	22%	49.0	23%	39.9	-34%	60.4

Balance Sheet & Other Fin. Data (Million $)

	1994	1993	1992	1991	1990	1989
Cash	30.2	40.6	70.5	76.3	55.2	57.4
Curr. Assets	259	357	430	442	412	376
Total Assets	528	703	787	784	734	651
Curr. Liab.	158	120	207	191	187	130
LT Debt	100	102	103	102	103	104
Common Eqty.	221	461	453	478	435	407
Total Cap.	322	563	556	581	538	511
Cap. Exp.	21.0	24.5	44.9	48.1	68.3	56.7
Cash Flow	87.2	72.8	73.9	89.6	56.5	77.6

Ratio Analysis

	1994	1993	1992	1991	1990	1989
Curr. Ratio	1.6	3.0	2.1	2.3	2.2	2.9
% LT Debt of Cap.	31.2	18.1	18.6	17.6	19.2	20.4
% Net Inc.of Revs.	12.0	11.0	5.1	8.1	4.0	8.0
% Ret. on Assets	10.8	6.6	5.1	7.9	4.0	8.6
% Ret. on Equity	19.8	10.7	8.6	13.2	6.6	13.7

Dividend Data

Cash has been paid each year since 1966. A dividend reinvestment plan is available.

Amt. of Div. $	Date Decl.	Ex-Div. Date	Stock of Record	Payment Date
0.150	Sep. 15	Oct. 07	Oct. 14	Oct. 21 '94
0.150	Dec. 08	Dec. 23	Dec. 30	Jan. 27 '95
0.150	Feb. 09	Mar. 20	Mar. 24	Apr. 21 '95
0.080	Jun. 08	Jun. 21	Jun. 23	Jul. 21 '95
2-for-1	Jun. 08	Jul. 24	Jun. 23	Jul. 21 '95

Data as orig. reptd.; bef. results of disc. opers. and/or spec. items. Per share data adj. for stk. divs. as of ex-div. date. E-Estimated. NA-Not Available. NM-Not Meaningful. NR-Not Ranked.

Office—80 Ashby Rd., Bedford, MA 01730. **Tel**—(617) 275-9200. **Chrmn, Pres & CEO**—J. A. Gilmartin. **VP-CFO & Treas**—M. P. Carroll. **Investor Contact**—Geoffrey E. Helliwell. **Dirs**—C.D. Baker, S.C. Butler, J.A. Gilmartin, M. Hoffman Jr., G.D. Laubach, S. Muller, T.O. Pyle, J.F. Reno. **Transfer Agent & Registrar**—First National Bank of Boston. **Incorporated** in Massachusetts in 1954. **Empl**- 3,117. **S&P Analyst:** Philip J. Birbara

Minnesota Mining

NYSE Symbol **MMM**
In S&P 500

24-SEP-95

Industry:
Conglomerate/diversified

Summary: MMM is a highly diversified manufacturer of industrial, commercial, healthcare and consumer products that share similar technological, manufacturing and marketing resources.

S&P Opinion: Hold (★★★)	Recent Price • 55¼
	52 Wk Range • 62⅛-50⅜

Yield • 3.4%
12-Mo. P/E • 16.5

Quantitative Evaluations

Outlook
(1 Lowest—5 Highest)
• **3⁻**

Fair Value
• **55⅛**

Risk
• **Low**

Earn./Div. Rank
• **A+**

Technical Eval.
• **Bullish** since 8/95

Rel. Strength Rank
(1 Lowest—99 Highest)
• **24**

Insider Activity
• **Neutral**

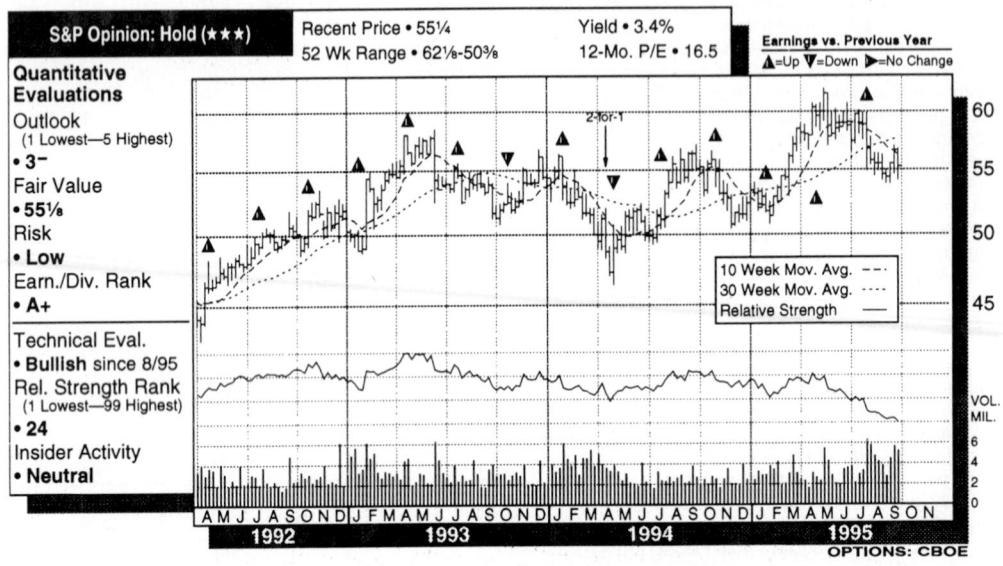

Earnings vs. Previous Year
▲=Up ▼=Down ▶=No Change

10 Week Mov. Avg. -----
30 Week Mov. Avg. ·······
Relative Strength ———

VOL.
MIL.

OPTIONS: CBOE

Overview - 22-SEP-95

MMM should continue to benefit from international sales, which increased 10% in the first half of 1995, and were well balanced throughout all geographical segments. Currency translation gains, which added 9% to revenue growth in the second quarter, will decrease as the dollar gains strength. Domestic unit sales were up only 1% in the quarter, restricted by recent softness in the economy. However, we expect an increase of about 4% for the remainder of the year. Although the company is increasing its efforts to cut costs, this may be offset by rising raw materials prices. EPS should increase about 10% in 1995.

Valuation - 22-SEP-95

The shares have declined slightly from their 1995 high, reflecting disappointing second quarter results. Earnings expectations have been revised downward to reflect sluggish projected domestic unit sales growth (now put at about 10% for the year). In addition, despite cost-cutting efforts, margins are being squeezed by higher raw materials prices. In light of these fundamentals, and with the shares currently trading at about 16X our 1995 estimate, we believe that the shares will be only average performers for the balance of the year.

Key Stock Statistics

S&P EPS Est. 1995	3.45	Tang. Bk. Value/Share	17.36
P/E on S&P Est. 1995	16.0	Beta	0.67
S&P EPS Est. 1996	3.95	Shareholders	33,900
Dividend Rate/Share	1.88	Market cap. (B)	$ 23.2
Shs. outstg. (M)	420.2	Inst. holdings	66%
Avg. daily vol. (M)	0.922	Insider holdings	NA

Value of $10,000 invested 5 years ago: $ 16,693

Fiscal Year Ending Dec. 31

	1995	% Change	1994	% Change	1993	% Change
Revenues (Million $)						
1Q	4,087	13%	3,632	3%	3,517	2%
2Q	4,135	10%	3,772	7%	3,540	NM
3Q	—	—	3,820	10%	3,481	-2%
4Q	—	—	3,855	11%	3,482	3%
Yr.	—	—	15,079	8%	14,020	1%
Income (Million $)						
1Q	376.0	23%	306.0	-7%	330.0	15%
2Q	353.0	3%	343.0	4%	331.0	3%
3Q	—	—	341.0	8%	316.0	-7%
4Q	—	—	332.0	16%	286.0	-1%
Yr.	—	—	1,322	5%	1,263	2%
Earnings Per Share ($)						
1Q	0.90	25%	0.72	-5%	0.76	8%
2Q	0.84	4%	0.81	7%	0.76	4%
3Q	E0.87	7%	0.81	10%	0.74	NM
4Q	E0.84	6%	0.79	19%	0.66	NM
Yr.	E3.45	10%	3.13	8%	2.91	3%

Next earnings report expected: late October

Business Summary - 22-SEP-95

Minnesota Mining's diverse product lines are separated into three major business segments, which contributed to 1994 results as follows:

	Sales	Profits
Industrial & Consumer	39%	44%
Information, Imaging & Electronic	31%	13%
Life Sciences	30%	43%

International sales accounted for 50% of the total in 1994, up from 49% in 1993.

The Industrial and Consumer segment develops technologies for pressure-sensitive adhesives, specialty tapes, coated and nonwoven abrasives and specialty chemicals. The sector is organized into five groups: Abrasive, Chemical and Film Products; Automotive Systems; Consumer Markets and Office Markets; and Tape.

The Information, Imaging and Electronic segment serves rapidly changing markets in audio, video and data recording; graphic communications; information storage, output and transfer; telecommunications; electronics and electrical products.

The Life Sciences segment's major technologies include adhesives, substrates, extrusion/coating, nonwoven materials, specialty polymers and resins, optical systems, drug delivery and electro-mechanical devices. The segment is organized into three groups: Medical Products; Pharmaceuticals, Dental and Personal Care Products; and Traffic and Personal Safety Products.

Research and development constitute an important part of MMM's activities, as it seeks to derive 30% of annual sales from products introduced within the past four years. R&D spending was equal to 7.0% of sales in 1994, versus 7.4% in 1993.

In February 1995, directors authorized the repurchase of up to 8 million common shares. About 11 million shares were purchased under a February 1994 authorization. In the 1994 first quarter, MMM recorded a $35 million ($0.05 a share) charge related to a proposed global settlement of breast implant litigations.

Important Developments

Sep. '95—MMM signed a joint development agreement with Chromagen Inc. The two companies will develop chemistries for the quantitative analysis of commercially important biological materials.
Aug. '95—The company signed an agreement with CNS Inc., making MMM the exclusive distributor of CNS Breathe Right nasal strips outside the U.S. and Canada.

Capitalization

Long Term Debt: $1,231,000,000 (6/95).

Per Share Data ($) (Year Ended Dec. 31)

	1994	1993	1992	1991	1990	1989
Tangible Bk. Val.	16.04	15.17	15.06	14.36	13.90	12.07
Cash Flow	5.50	5.16	5.11	4.64	4.71	4.38
Earnings	3.13	2.91	2.83	2.63	2.96	2.80
Dividends	1.76	1.66	1.60	1.56	1.46	1.30
Payout Ratio	56%	57%	57%	59%	49%	47%
Prices - High	57⅛	58½	53½	48¾	45¾	41
- Low	46⅜	48⅝	42¾	39⅛	36⅞	30⅛
P/E Ratio - High	18	20	19	19	15	15
- Low	15	17	15	15	12	11

Income Statement Analysis (Million $)

	1994	%Chg	1993	%Chg	1992	%Chg	1991
Revs.	15,079	8%	14,020	NM	13,883	4%	13,340
Oper. Inc.	3,254	9%	2,985	NM	2,984	5%	2,843
Depr.	1,003	3%	976	-3%	1,004	14%	884
Int. Exp.	87.0	74%	50.0	-34%	76.0	-22%	97.0
Pretax Inc.	2,154	8%	2,002	3%	1,947	4%	1,877
Eff. Tax Rate	36%	—	35%	—	35%	—	37%
Net Inc.	1,322	5%	1,263	2%	1,236	7%	1,154

Balance Sheet & Other Fin. Data (Million $)

	1994	1993	1992	1991	1990	1989
Cash	491	656	722	502	591	887
Curr. Assets	6,928	6,363	6,209	5,585	5,729	5,382
Total Assets	13,496	12,197	11,955	11,083	11,079	9,776
Curr. Liab.	3,605	3,282	3,241	3,236	3,339	2,721
LT Debt	1,031	796	687	764	760	885
Common Eqty.	6,734	6,512	6,599	6,293	6,110	5,378
Total Cap.	8,321	7,684	7,600	7,372	7,282	6,668
Cap. Exp.	1,148	1,112	1,318	1,326	1,337	1,187
Cash Flow	2,325	2,239	2,240	2,038	2,089	1,944

Ratio Analysis

	1994	1993	1992	1991	1990	1989
Curr. Ratio	1.9	1.9	1.9	1.7	1.7	2.0
% LT Debt of Cap.	12.4	10.4	9.0	10.4	10.4	13.3
% Net Inc.of Revs.	8.8	9.0	8.9	8.7	10.0	10.4
% Ret. on Assets	10.4	10.6	10.7	10.4	12.6	13.4
% Ret. on Equity	20.2	19.5	19.2	18.6	22.9	22.9

Dividend Data —Dividends have been paid since 1916 and increased for the past 37 years. A dividend reinvestment plan is available.

Amt. of Div. $	Date Decl.	Ex-Div. Date	Stock of Record	Payment Date
0.440	Nov. 14	Nov. 18	Nov. 25	Dec. 12 '94
0.470	Feb. 13	Feb. 17	Feb. 24	Mar. 12 '95
0.470	May. 09	May. 15	May. 19	Jun. 12 '95
0.470	Aug. 15	Aug. 23	Aug. 25	Sep. 12 '95

Data as orig. reptd.; bef. results of disc. opers. and/or spec. items. Per share data adj. for stk. divs. as of ex-div. date. E-Estimated. NA-Not Available. NM-Not Meaningful. NR-Not Ranked.

Office—3M Center, St. Paul, MN 55144. **Tel**—(612) 733-1110. **Chrmn & CEO**—L. D. DeSimone. **SVP-Fin**—G. Agostini. **SVP & Secy**—A. D. Levi. **Investor Contact**—Jon Greer (612-736-1915). **Dirs**—E. A. Brennan, L. D. DeSimone, L. E. Eaton, H. A. Hummerly, J. R. Junkins, R. A. Mitsch, A. E. Murray, A. L. Peters, R. L. Ridgway, F. Shrontz, F. A. Smith, L. W. Sullivan. **Transfer Agent & Registrar**—Norwest Bank Minnesota, South St. Paul. **Incorporated** in Delaware in 1929. **Empl**- 85,166. **S&P Analyst**: Mike Cavanaugh

Mobil Corp.

NYSE Symbol **MOB**
In S&P 500

14-AUG-95 Industry:
Oil and Gas

Summary: This worldwide integrated petroleum company and leading chemicals maker maintains an aggressive exploration program and focuses on high growth retail markets.

S&P Opinion: Accumulate (★★★★)

| Recent Price • 96⅛ | Yield • 3.8% |
| 52 Wk Range • 102-76⅝ | 12-Mo. P/E • 21.4 |

Earnings vs. Previous Year
▲=Up ▼=Down ▶=No Change

Quantitative Evaluations

Outlook
(1 Lowest—5 Highest)
• **2+**

Fair Value
• **86½**

Risk
• **Low**

Earn./Div. Rank
• **B+**

Technical Eval.
• **Bearish** since 5/95

Rel. Strength Rank
(1 Lowest—99 Highest)
• **28**

Insider Activity
• **Neutral**

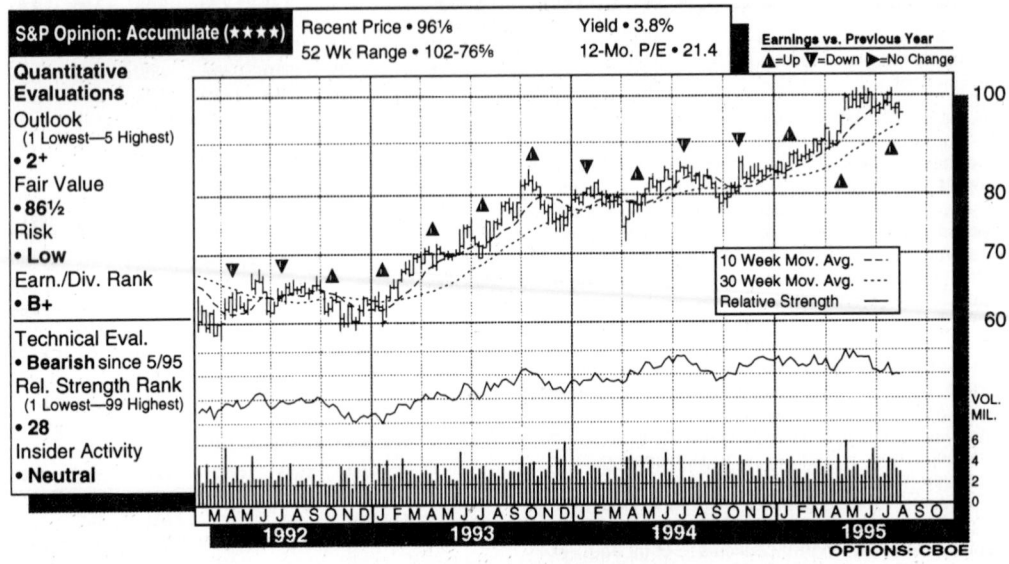

10 Week Mov. Avg. ---
30 Week Mov. Avg. ·····
Relative Strength ——

OPTIONS: CBOE

Overview - 11-AUG-95

Profits in 1995 should rebound from 1994's weak level, reflecting strong chemical segment profits, higher average oil prices, and the benefits of a recent ongoing restructuring that will yield $1 billion of annual cost savings. MOB has a greater concentration of refining and marketing assets in Pacific Rim markets than that of other major oil companies, and this focus will be important over the next several years. Although refining margins are relatively narrow, we anticipate refining results will benefit from the recent drop in feedstock prices, and stronger demand for refined products in the U.S. and Europe. A strong balance sheet and cash generating capacity will support expansion of international exploration in the Danish and U.K. sectors of the North Sea, and Nigeria.

Valuation - 11-AUG-95

MOB has registered one of the strongest performances in its industry by focusing on profitable exploration and marketing activities. Strong chemical segment earnings, expected to continue through mid-1996, should boost the shares. In addition, an excellent balance sheet and impressive cash generating capability should attract investors. Weaker oil prices over the past two months and excess production of natural gas have caused us to reduce our estimates for 1995 earnings. However, we believe the fundamentals are strong for Mobil, and with commodity prices relatively low, MOB, with only a 19% debt to total capital ratio, will likely pursue acquisitions aggressively.

Key Stock Statistics

S&P EPS Est. 1995	6.45	Tang. Bk. Value/Share	43.02
P/E on S&P Est. 1995	14.9	Beta	0.66
S&P EPS Est. 1996	7.30	Shareholders	192,700
Dividend Rate/Share	3.70	Market cap. (B)	$ 38.0
Shs. outstg. (M)	395.7	Inst. holdings	55%
Avg. daily vol. (M)	0.737	Insider holdings	NA

Value of $10,000 invested 5 years ago: $ 19,699

Fiscal Year Ending Dec. 31

	1995	% Change	1994	% Change	1993	% Change
Revenues ()						
1Q	17,627	18%	14,948	NM	14,880	-1%
2Q	—	—	16,047	NM	16,040	6%
3Q	—	—	16,739	7%	15,680	-3%
4Q	—	—	19,023	13%	16,870	-3%
Yr.	—	—	66,757	5%	63,474	NM
Income ()						
1Q	636.0	19%	535.0	9%	490.0	NM
2Q	706.0	NM	198.0	-66%	579.0	127%
3Q	—	—	503.0	-24%	666.0	61%
4Q	—	—	523.0	50%	349.0	-32%
Yr.	—	—	1,759	-16%	2,084	59%
Earnings Per Share ()						
1Q	1.57	20%	1.31	10%	1.19	NM
2Q	1.75	NM	0.46	-67%	1.41	135%
3Q	—	—	1.23	-25%	1.63	63%
4Q	E1.64	28%	1.28	52%	0.84	-33%
Yr.	E6.45	51%	4.28	-16%	5.07	62%

Next earnings report expected: late October

Mobil Corp.

Business Summary - 14-AUG-95

Mobil is a major integrated international oil company with a large presence in chemicals. Segment profit contributions in recent years were:

Profits	1994	1993
U.S. exploration & production	6%	14%
U.S. marketing & refining	12%	6%
Foreign expl. & prod.	46%	49%
Foreign market. & refin.	31%	30%
Chemicals	5%	1%

In 1994, worldwide net crude and natural gas liquids production averaged 854,000 bbl. a day, up from 838,000 b/d in 1993; the U.S. accounted for 35% of 1994 production. Net natural gas production was 4.67 Bcf a day (4.61), of which 33% was produced in the U.S. Natural gas represents more than half of the company's worldwide reserves and production. Refinery runs totaled 2,094,000 b/d (2,100,000), and petroleum product sales 3,075,000 b/d (2,934,000). Mobil's concentrates on high margin products where it is a leader, including synthetic lubricants and premium gasolines.

Net proved reserves at 1994 year-end stood at 3,444 million bbl. of crude and natural gas liquids, up from 3,343 million bbl. at 1993 year-end. Net proved reserves of natural gas at 1994 year-end totaled 17,675 Bcf (17,683).

Mobil Chemical makes and markets basic petrochemicals, plastic-packaging films and consumer plastics such as Hefty brands. Specialty products include synthetic lubricant base stocks and additives for fuels and lubricants. A new aromatics complex in Singapore began operation in 1994 to supply feedstocks for nylon and polyester production in the Asia-Pacific region.

Important Developments

Jul. '95—Operating income in the 1995 second quarter totaled $706 million, up 11% from the 1994 period. Chemical prices rose in all businesses, and sales volumes increased, reflecting capacity additions; segment earnings soared to $186 million, frc:n $174 million. Refining and marketing profits dropped, following the introduction of reformulated gasoline (RFG) and the decision by several states to drop out of the RFG program. Exploration and producing income was little changed, as higher volumes and U.S. crude oil prices offset lower gas prices in the U.S. and internationally. Earlier, in May '95, Mobil announced a major restructuring of its staff support services unit and refining and marketing operations, in which it will eliminate 4,700 positions. Mobil estimated annual cost savings at over $1 billion.

Capitalization

Long Term Debt: $4,714,000,000 (3/95).
Minority Interest: $73,000,000.
ESOP Conv. Preferred Stock: $745,000,000.

Per Share Data () (Year Ended Dec. 31)

	1994	1993	1992	1991	1990	1989
Tangible Bk. Val.	42.61	42.74	41.06	43.42	42.11	39.51
Cash Flow	12.06	11.66	10.11	11.13	11.21	10.50
Earnings	4.28	5.07	3.13	4.65	4.60	4.40
Dividends	3.40	3.25	3.20	3.13	2.83	2.55
Payout Ratio	79%	64%	102%	67%	61%	58%
Prices - High	87 1/8	84 3/4	69 3/4	73 1/8	69 1/2	63 1/4
- Low	72	59 1/2	57 7/8	55 1/8	55 7/8	45 1/4
P/E Ratio - High	20	17	22	16	15	14
- Low	17	12	18	12	12	10

Income Statement Analysis ()

	1994	%Chg	1993	%Chg	1992	%Chg	1991
Revs.	58,995	4%	56,576	NM	56,877	1%	56,042
Oper. Inc.	6,611	2%	6,467	12%	5,755	-11%	6,459
Depr.	3,098	18%	2,629	-5%	2,780	7%	2,589
Int. Exp.	498	36%	366	-40%	612	-17%	733
Pretax Inc.	3,678	-8%	4,015	40%	2,875	-29%	4,025
Eff. Tax Rate	52%	—	48%	—	55%	—	52%
Net Inc.	1,759	-16%	2,084	59%	1,308	-32%	1,920

Balance Sheet & Other Fin. Data ()

	1994	1993	1992	1991	1990	1989
Cash	531	827	303	870	1,138	1,541
Curr. Assets	11,181	11,069	10,956	12,401	13,231	11,920
Total Assets	41,542	40,585	40,561	42,187	41,665	39,080
Curr. Liab.	13,418	12,203	12,629	13,602	13,653	11,216
LT Debt	4,714	5,027	5,042	4,715	4,298	5,317
Common Eqty.	16,873	17,017	16,374	17,422	17,021	16,274
Total Cap.	24,572	25,024	24,719	25,930	25,382	25,389
Cap. Exp.	3,825	3,192	4,470	4,175	3,577	2,752
Cash Flow	4,799	4,654	4,028	4,448	4,549	4,304

Ratio Analysis

	1994	1993	1992	1991	1990	1989
Curr. Ratio	0.8	0.9	0.9	0.9	1.0	1.1
% LT Debt of Cap.	19.2	20.1	20.4	18.2	16.9	20.9
% Net Inc.of Revs.	3.0	3.7	2.3	3.4	3.3	3.6
% Ret. on Assets	4.3	5.1	3.2	4.6	4.8	4.7
% Ret. on Equity	10.1	12.1	7.4	10.8	11.3	11.3

Dividend Data —Dividends have been paid since 1902. A dividend reinvestment plan is available. A poison pill stock purchase rights plan was adopted in 1986.

Amt. of Div. $	Date Decl.	Ex-Div. Date	Stock of Record	Payment Date
0.850	Jul. 29	Aug. 02	Aug. 08	Sep. 12 '94
0.850	Oct. 28	Nov. 01	Nov. 07	Dec. 12 '94
0.850	Jan. 27	Jan. 31	Feb. 06	Mar. 10 '95
0.925	Apr. 28	May. 08	May. 12	Jun. 12 '95
0.925	Jul. 28	Aug. 03	Aug. 07	Sep. 11 '95

Data as orig. reptd.; bef. results of disc. opers. and/or spec. items. Per share data adj. for stk. divs. as of ex-div. date. E-Estimated. NA-Not Available. NM-Not Meaningful. NR-Not Ranked.

Office—3225 Gallows Rd., Fairfax, VA 22037-0001. **Tel**—(703) 846-3000. **Chrmn, Pres & CEO**—L. A. Noto. **Secy**—Caroline M. Devine **Treas**—W. R. Arnheim. **Investor Contact**—David F. Michael. **Dirs**—L. M. Branscomb, D. V. Fites, P. J. Hoenmans, A. F. Jacobson, S. C. Johnson, H. L. Kaplan, W. J. Kennedy III, J. R. Munro, L. A. Noto, A. L. Peters, E. A. Renna, C. S. Sanford, Jr., R. G. Schwartz, R. O. Swanson. **Transfer Agent & Registrar**—Mellon Securities Trust Co., NYC. **Incorporated** in New York in 1882; reincorporated in Delaware in 1976. **Empl**-58,500. **S&P Analyst:** Raymond J. Deacon

Monsanto Co.

NYSE Symbol **MTC**
In S&P 500

20-SEP-95

Industry:
Chemicals

Summary: This leading chemical company produces agricultural pesticides, industrial chemicals, plastics, fibers, pharmaceuticals, and low calorie sweeteners.

S&P Opinion: Accumulate (★★★★)

Recent Price • 102¾	Yield • 2.7%
52 Wk Range • 104⅛-66½	12-Mo. P/E • 17.0

Quantitative Evaluations

Outlook
(1 Lowest—5 Highest)
• **1+**

Fair Value
• **85⅛**

Risk
• **Low**

Earn./Div. Rank
• **A-**

Technical Eval.
• **Bearish** since 7/95

Rel. Strength Rank
(1 Lowest—99 Highest)
• **70**

Insider Activity
• **Neutral**

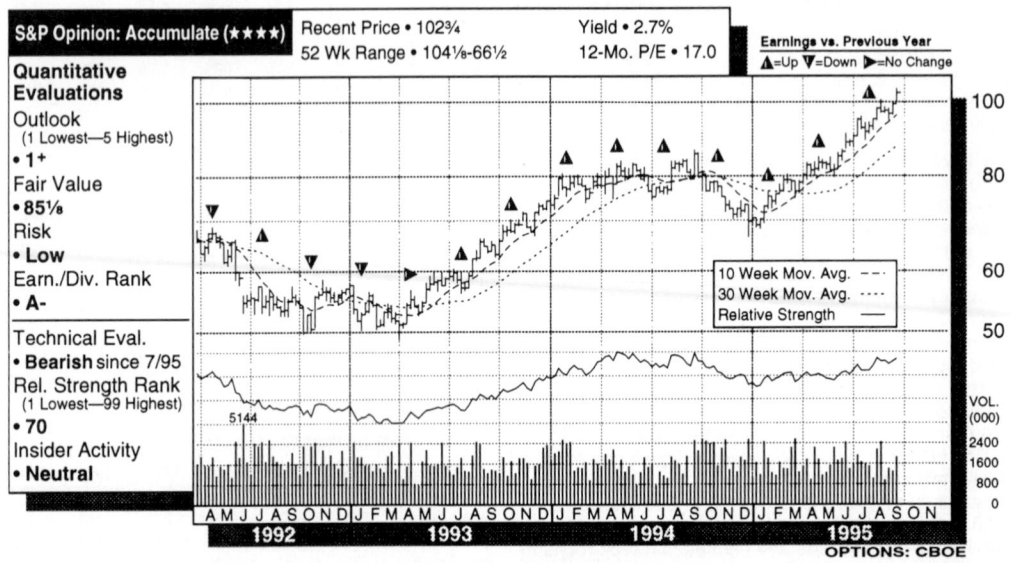

Earnings vs. Previous Year
▲=Up ▼=Down ▶=No Change

10 Week Mov. Avg. — · —
30 Week Mov. Avg. · · · · ·
Relative Strength ———

OPTIONS: CBOE

Overview - 20-SEP-95

We see agricultural earnings continuing to advance in 1996 on further growth of Roundup herbicide, boosted by the expected increase in U.S. crop acreage, and a rebound by the consumer business, while Posilac BST may turn profitable on higher sales. Assuming healthier U.S. auto and durable goods markets, chemicals margins will also be boosted by falling raw material costs. Profits of the Searle drug unit should further rise on expected growth of newer products (Daypro, Ambien) and benefits of intense cost controls. NutraSweet profits may again decline modestly as lower prices resulting from the 1992 patent expiration offset cost reductions, but Kelco (purchased in early 1995) will improve profitability on the absence of one-time acquisition related costs.

Valuation - 20-SEP-95

MTC's stock has been a strong performer in 1995, rising about 45% year to date. The stock has benefited from perceptions that the new CEO will be more aggressive in dealing with underperforming businesses, such as plastics, and in reducing costs. Approvals for new biotechnology products and a better profit performance by Searle have also boosted the stock. The shares remain attractive based on the 1996 EPS estimate and longer term prospects. The dividend has been raised annually for the past 22 consecutive years, a record that should continue in 1996.

Key Stock Statistics

S&P EPS Est. 1995	6.20	Tang. Bk. Value/Share	14.90
P/E on S&P Est. 1995	16.6	Beta	1.31
S&P EPS Est. 1996	7.00	Shareholders	56,600
Dividend Rate/Share	2.76	Market cap. (B)	$ 11.8
Shs. outstg. (M)	115.3	Inst. holdings	64%
Avg. daily vol. (M)	0.287	Insider holdings	NA

Value of $10,000 invested 5 years ago: $ 21,550

Fiscal Year Ending Dec. 31

	1995	% Change	1994	% Change	1993	% Change
Revenues (Million $)						
1Q	2,318	16%	2,001	3%	1,941	-2%
2Q	2,482	9%	2,269	2%	2,230	9%
3Q	—	—	1,912	3%	1,849	-2%
4Q	—	—	2,090	11%	1,882	NM
Yr.	—	—	8,272	5%	7,902	2%
Income (Million $)						
1Q	229.0	18%	194.0	38%	141.0	-3%
2Q	290.0	12%	258.0	29%	200.0	111%
3Q	—	—	116.0	22%	95.00	107%
4Q	—	—	54.00	-7%	58.00	NM
Yr.	—	—	622.0	26%	494.0	NM
Earnings Per Share ($)						
1Q	2.02	24%	1.63	39%	1.17	NM
2Q	2.51	15%	2.19	32%	1.66	113%
3Q	E0.95	-4%	0.99	27%	0.78	100%
4Q	E0.72	41%	0.51	4%	0.49	NM
Yr.	E6.20	17%	5.32	30%	4.10	NM

Next earnings report expected: mid October

Business Summary - 20-SEP-95

Monsanto is a leading chemical concern. Contributions by business segment in 1994 were:

	Sales	Profits
Agricultural products	27%	48%
Chemicals	45%	31%
NutraSweet	8%	14%
Pharmaceuticals	20%	7%

Foreign operations in 1994 accounted for 35% of sales and 49% of operating income.

Agricultural products consist of herbicides (including Lasso, Roundup, and Avadex) for crop protection, seeds, and Ortho lawn and garden products. In November 1993, the FDA approved MTC's bovine somatotropin growth hormone (Posilac).

Chemicals include nylon and acrylic fibers for carpet, apparel and industrial uses, plastics (ABS, SAN), Saflex interlayer, polymer modifiers, rubber processing chemicals, functional fluids, speciality resins and polyethylene products, and phosphates for industrial, cleaning, and food uses.

NutraSweet consists of NutraSweet aspartame low-calarie sweeteners, Equal and Canderel brands table top sweeteners, and Simplesse all natural fat substitute products.

Searle's pharmaceuticals include anti-infectives (Maxaquin), anti-inflammatory (Daypro, Arthrotec), cardiovascular (Calan), fertility control, and gastrointestinal (Cytotec) drugs, and Ambien sleep aid.

Important Developments

Sep. '95—MTC expected a significant gain in the third quarter from an insurance settlement.
Jul. '95—MTC acquired the women's health care business of the Syntex unit of Roche Holding. The business has annual sales of $100 million. MTC also entered into an agreement in which a major Japanese pharmaceutical company will co-develop Searl's oral anti-platelet agent in Japan. Both transactions are expected to contributed to income immediately. Separately, record earnings in the second quarter reflected record agricultural and pharmaceutical profits. Chemical profits declined modestly due to weaker demand and higher raw material costs. The contribution by Kelco (acquired in February 1995) continued to meet expectations. MTC acquired the Kelco specialty chemicals unit of Merck & Co. for $1.075 billion. Kelco is the leading producer of hydrocollids, with 1994 revenues of over $300 million. The acquisition is expected to be neutral to slightly dilutive in the first year, and to contribute to earnings in the second year.
May '95—MTC received final approval for Roundup Ready soybean seeds. MTC expected to begin selling the seeds in 1996.

Capitalization

Long Term Debt: $1,696,000,000 (6/95).

Per Share Data ($)

(Year Ended Dec. 31)

	1994	1993	1992	1991	1990	1989
Tangible Bk. Val.	16.26	14.37	16.10	19.23	21.18	17.08
Cash Flow	9.80	8.67	4.73	8.02	9.65	9.91
Earnings	5.32	4.10	-1.01	2.33	4.23	5.02
Dividends	2.47	2.30	2.20	2.04	1.90	1.65
Payout Ratio	46%	56%	NM	85%	44%	32%
Prices - High	86½	75	71¼	76	60⅛	62⅛
- Low	66½	48⅞	49¾	46	38¾	40¼
P/E Ratio - High	16	18	NM	33	14	12
- Low	13	12	NM	20	9	8

Income Statement Analysis (Million $)

	1994	%Chg	1993	%Chg	1992	%Chg	1991
Revs.	8,272	5%	7,902	2%	7,763	-12%	8,864
Oper. Inc.	1,486	14%	1,299	-7%	1,392	-20%	1,739
Depr.	523	-5%	550	-23%	710	-2%	723
Int. Exp.	141	NM	141	-24%	185	-4%	193
Pretax Inc.	895	23%	729	NM	-162	NM	458
Eff. Tax Rate	31%	—	32%	—	NM	—	32%
Net Inc.	622	26%	494	NM	-125	NM	296

Balance Sheet & Other Fin. Data (Million $)

	1994	1993	1992	1991	1990	1989
Cash	507	273	729	189	204	253
Curr. Assets	3,883	3,672	4,060	3,711	3,513	3,248
Total Assets	8,891	8,640	9,085	9,227	9,236	8,604
Curr. Liab.	2,435	2,295	2,548	2,175	2,190	1,922
LT Debt	1,405	1,502	1,423	1,877	1,652	1,471
Common Eqty.	2,948	2,855	3,005	3,654	4,089	3,941
Total Cap.	4,418	4,411	4,493	6,043	6,381	6,033
Cap. Exp.	409	437	586	591	750	607
Cash Flow	1,145	1,044	584	1,019	1,246	1,343

Ratio Analysis

	1994	1993	1992	1991	1990	1989
Curr. Ratio	1.6	1.6	1.6	1.7	1.6	1.7
% LT Debt of Cap.	31.8	34.1	31.7	31.1	25.9	24.4
% Net Inc.of Revs.	7.5	6.3	NM	3.3	6.1	7.8
% Ret. on Assets	7.2	5.7	NM	3.2	6.3	8.1
% Ret. on Equity	21.8	17.2	NM	7.7	13.9	17.9

Dividend Data —Dividends have been paid since 1925. A dividend reinvestment plan is available. A new "poison pill" stock purchase right was adopted in 1990.

Amt. of Div. $	Date Decl.	Ex-Div. Date	Stock of Record	Payment Date
0.630	Oct. 28	Nov. 04	Nov. 10	Dec. 12 '94
0.630	Jan. 27	Feb. 06	Feb. 10	Mar. 10 '95
0.690	Apr. 28	May. 08	May. 12	Jun. 12 '95
0.690	Jul. 28	Aug. 09	Aug. 11	Sep. 12 '95

Data as orig. reptd.; bef. results of disc. opers. and/or spec. items. Per share data adj. for stk. divs. as of ex-div. date.
E-Estimated. NA-Not Available. NM-Not Meaningful. NR-Not Ranked.

Office—800 North Lindbergh Blvd., St. Louis, MO 63167. **Tel**—(314) 694-1000. **Chrmn & CEO**—R. B. Shapiro. **SVP & CFO**—R. B. Hoffman. **SVP & Secy**—R. W. Duesenberg. **Investor Contact**—Robert Merritt. **Dirs**—J.T. Bok, R. M. Heyssel, G. S. King, P. Leder, H. M. Love, R. J. Mahoney, F. A. Metz, Jr., B. Mickel, J. F. M. Peters, N. L. Reding, J. S. Reed, W. D. Ruckelshaus, R. B. Shapiro, J. B. Slaughter. **Transfer Agent & Registrar**—First National Bank of Boston. **Incorporated** in Delaware in 1933. **Empl**-29,354. **S&P Analyst:** Richard O'Reilly, CFA

Moore Corp.

NYSE Symbol **MCL**
In S&P 500

05-AUG-95 Industry:
Office Equipment

Summary: Moore Corp. is a major producer of business forms and related items, and also provides database management products and services, direct marketing products, and custom packaging.

S&P Opinion: Avoid (★★)	Recent Price • 21½	Yield • 4.4%
	52 Wk Range • 23½-16¾	12-Mo. P/E • 7.5

Quantitative Evaluations

Outlook
  (1 Lowest—5 Highest)
• **4+**

Fair Value
• **22⅜**

Risk
• **Low**

Earn./Div. Rank
• **B-**

Technical Eval.
• **Bearish** since 6/95

Rel. Strength Rank
  (1 Lowest—99 Highest)
• **22**

Insider Activity
• **NA**

Earnings vs. Previous Year
▲=Up ▼=Down ▶=No Change

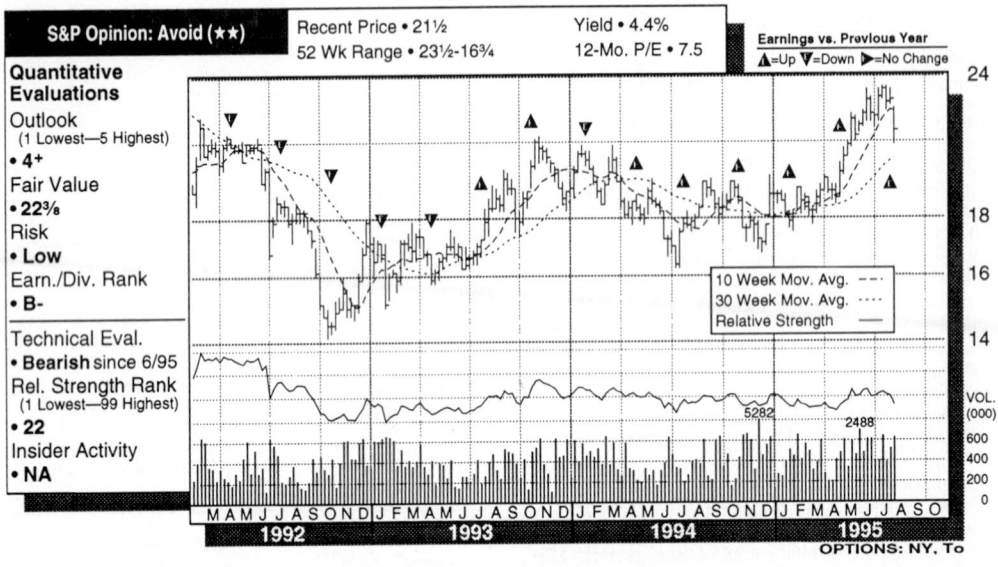

10 Week Mov. Avg. – – –
30 Week Mov. Avg. ·······
Relative Strength ——

5282   2488

VOL. (000)

OPTIONS: NY, To

Overview - 04-AUG-95

Modest sales growth from current operations in 1995 is largely due to paper price increases. Unit sales of business forms will continue to fall due to technological change emphasizing electronic forms in place of preprinted ones. With continuing restructuring efforts and cost reductions, operating income should rise before any unusual charges and with higher investment income and a $1.47 a share gain on the sale of a 35% interest in Toppan-Moore during 1995, net income should advance. MCL's hostile takeover offer for Wallace Computer Services is a rich offer which will result in earnings dilution for at least the first year and $40 million per year of goodwill amortization which will be a drag on earnings for 20 years.

Valuation - 04-AUG-95

MCL is a company in transition. Its mature paper forms markets are shrinking and growth in electronic forms and services, as well as customer communications services, has not picked up the slack. The hostile takeover offer for Wallace Computer Services is intended to hasten the transition. Wallace has managed only 6% a year compounded five-year annual growth in earnings, yet MCL is paying 23 times estimated current year earnings. Furthermore, in one swoop, MCL will move from cash rich to leveraged. While the dividend should remain secure, the company will have less flexibility to contend with future challenges and initially substantial earnings dilution is likely.

Key Stock Statistics

S&P EPS Est. 1995	2.75	Tang. Bk. Value/Share	13.53
P/E on S&P Est. 1995	7.8	Beta	1.39
S&P EPS Est. 1996	1.00	Shareholders	8,700
Dividend Rate/Share	0.94	Market cap. (B)	$ 2.1
Shs. outstg. (M)	99.6	Inst. holdings	40%
Avg. daily vol. (M)	0.141	Insider holdings	NA

Value of $10,000 invested 5 years ago: $ 9,812

Fiscal Year Ending Dec. 31

	1995	% Change	1994	% Change	1993	% Change
Revenues (Million $)						
1Q	649.4	6%	613.8	4%	592.9	-5%
2Q	629.5	10%	574.0	NM	569.5	-5%
3Q	—	—	583.9	3%	566.0	-5%
4Q	—	—	629.8	5%	600.3	-2%
Yr.	—	—	2,401	3%	2,329	-4%
Income (Million $)						
1Q	181.5	NM	26.26	13%	23.20	-8%
2Q	33.50	32%	25.44	21%	20.97	91%
3Q	—	—	30.50	85%	16.50	51%
4Q	—	—	39.20	NM	-138.2	180%
Yr.	—	—	121.4	NM	-77.60	NM
Earnings Per Share ($)						
1Q	1.82	NM	0.26	13%	0.23	-12%
2Q	0.34	31%	0.26	24%	0.21	91%
3Q	E0.34	—	0.31	82%	0.17	55%
4Q	E0.25	—	0.39	NM	-1.39	NM
Yr.	E2.75	—	1.22	NM	-0.78	NM

Next earnings report expected: early November

Business Summary - 04-AUG-95

Moore Corp. is a leading multinational producer of business forms, operating in 59 countries with over 100 manufacturing plants. Contributions by geographic area in 1994 (profit in million $):

	Sales	Profits
United States	60.8%	$105.1
Europe	14.3%	13.6
Other	17.0%	14.7
Canada	7.8%	7.9

Business forms and forms-based systems are MCL's primary focus and accounted for 79% of sales and $104.2 million of operating income. A variety of forms are manufactured, including handwritten types and complex forms for computers, optical scanners and other data processing equipment, and multi-part interleaved carbon or carbonless forms. MCL also produces a complete line of form handling equipment, including registers, tractors, detachers and decollators.

During 1994, the company acquired a 20% interest in JetForm Corp. for $18.7 million, announced a strategic alliance with Electronic Data Systems, and announced plans to take a 60% interest in a $20 million venture to market business forms and information handling solutions in China.

The remaining 21% of sales and $37.2 million of operating income in 1994 was contributed by customer communication services which includes creation and production of personalized mail, direct marketing program development, database management and segmentation services, response analysis services, and mail production outsourcing services.

Through its strategic customer services program, MCL assumes and manages the complete business forms needs of large organizations using electronic links to track usage. Small customers are served by traditional distribution methods.

Important Developments

Aug. '95—On August 2, MCL commenced a hostile cash tender offer for any or all of the outstanding shares of Wallace Computer Services (WCS) at US$56 per share or a total of $1.3 billion. With some $600 million in sales, WCS makes business forms, labels and provides value-added services focusing on newer technologies and electronic applications related to its products. MCL indicated that it would finance the acquisition using its $557 million cash hoard and borrow the balance.

Apr. '95—MCL's first quarter earnings reflect a net gain of $1.47 a share from the sale of 35% of its 45% interest in its Toppan Moore Japanese joint venture to Toppan Printing for $350 million.

Capitalization

Long Term Debt: $74,200,000 (6/95).
Minority Interest: $11,300,000.

Per Share Data ($) (Year Ended Dec. 31)

	1994	1993	1992	1991	1990	1989
Tangible Bk. Val.	13.53	13.01	14.62	15.84	15.64	14.74
Cash Flow	2.06	0.09	0.86	1.80	2.10	2.89
Earnings	1.22	-0.78	-0.02	0.91	1.27	2.15
Dividends	0.94	0.94	0.94	0.94	0.94	0.88
Payout Ratio	77%	NM	NM	104%	75%	41%
Prices - High	20⅞	21¼	22⅛	28½	30¼	33¾
- Low	16¼	15	14⅛	19	21⅝	24⅞
P/E Ratio - High	17	NM	NM	31	24	16
- Low	13	NM	NM	21	17	12

Income Statement Analysis (Million $)

	1994	%Chg	1993	%Chg	1992	%Chg	1991
Revs.	2,401	3%	2,329	-4%	2,433	-2%	2,492
Oper. Inc.	255	18%	217	15%	188	-9%	207
Depr.	83.4	-4%	86.5	-11%	97.6	12%	86.9
Int. Exp.	13.1	-24%	17.2	27%	13.5	2%	13.2
Pretax Inc.	166	NM	-95.0	NM	26.0	-81%	137
Eff. Tax Rate	26%	—	NM	—	101%	—	35%
Net Inc.	121	NM	-78.0	NM	-2.0	NM	88.0

Balance Sheet & Other Fin. Data (Million $)

	1994	1993	1992	1991	1990	1989
Cash	267	262	312	267	279	277
Curr. Assets	1,010	1,010	1,063	1,095	1,180	1,151
Total Assets	2,031	1,974	2,007	2,117	2,166	2,008
Curr. Liab.	447	451	366	332	410	376
LT Debt	77.0	68.0	32.0	59.0	56.0	40.0
Common Eqty.	1,365	1,313	1,476	1,585	1,538	1,441
Total Cap.	1,508	1,446	1,611	1,755	1,724	1,610
Cap. Exp.	77.0	82.0	91.0	120	166	127
Cash Flow	205	9.0	85.0	175	200	271

Ratio Analysis

	1994	1993	1992	1991	1990	1989
Curr. Ratio	2.3	2.2	2.2	3.3	2.9	3.1
% LT Debt of Cap.	5.1	4.7	2.0	3.3	3.3	2.5
% Net Inc.of Revs.	5.1	NM	NM	3.5	4.4	7.4
% Ret. on Assets	6.1	NM	NM	4.1	5.7	10.4
% Ret. on Equity	9.1	NM	NM	5.6	8.0	14.7

Dividend Data (Dividends have been paid since 1934. A new dividend reinvestment plan was approved in February 1994. A "poison pill" stock purchase rights plan was adopted in 1990. Payments are in U.S. funds, subject to 15% Canadian tax.)

Amt. of Div. $	Date Decl.	Ex-Div. Date	Stock of Record	Payment Date
0.235	Aug. 03	Aug. 29	Sep. 02	Oct. 03 '94
0.235	Nov. 03	Nov. 28	Dec. 02	Jan. 03 '95
0.235	Feb. 15	Feb. 27	Mar. 03	Apr. 03 '95
0.235	Apr. 28	May. 26	Jun. 02	Jul. 05 '95
0.235	Jul. 26	Aug. 30	Sep. 01	Oct. 02 '95

Data as orig. reptd.; bef. results of disc. opers. and/or spec. items. Per share data adj. for stk. divs. as of ex-div. date. E-Estimated. NA-Not Available. NM-Not Meaningful. NR-Not Ranked.

Office—1 First Canadian Place, Toronto, ON, Canada M5X 1G5. **Tel**—(416) 364-2600. **Chrmn, Pres & CEO**—R. Braun. **SVP-CFO**—S. A. Holinski. **VP-Secy**—J. M. Wilson. **Treas & Investor Contact**—Shoba Khetrapal. **Dirs**—J. D. Allan, R. Braun, D. H. Burney, E. H. Crawford, S. A. Dawe, J. D. Farley, A. R. Haynes, J. P. Lerman, C. E. Lindholm, C. E. Ritchie. **Transfer Agents**—R-M Trust Co., Toronto, Montreal, Vancouver, Winnipeg, Calgary; Chemical Mellon Shareholder Services, NYC. **Incorporated** in Ontario in 1938. **Empl-** 19,890. **S&P Analyst:** Joshua M. Harari, CFA

Morgan (J.P.) & Co.

NYSE Symbol **JPM**
In S&P 500

08-AUG-95 Industry:
Banking

Summary: This bank holding company emphasizes asset management and servicing, portfolio management, finance and advisory services, asset and liability management, and sales and trading.

S&P Opinion: Accumulate (★★★★)	Recent Price • 72⅜	Yield • 4.1%
	52 Wk Range • 74⅞-55⅛	12-Mo. P/E • 13.4

Quantitative Evaluations

Outlook
(1 Lowest—5 Highest)
• **4+**

Fair Value
• **72¾**

Risk
• **Low**

Earn./Div. Rank
• **B+**

Technical Eval.
• **Bullish** since 2/95

Rel. Strength Rank
(1 Lowest—99 Highest)
• **48**

Insider Activity
• **Neutral**

Earnings vs. Previous Year
▲=Up ▼=Down ▶=No Change

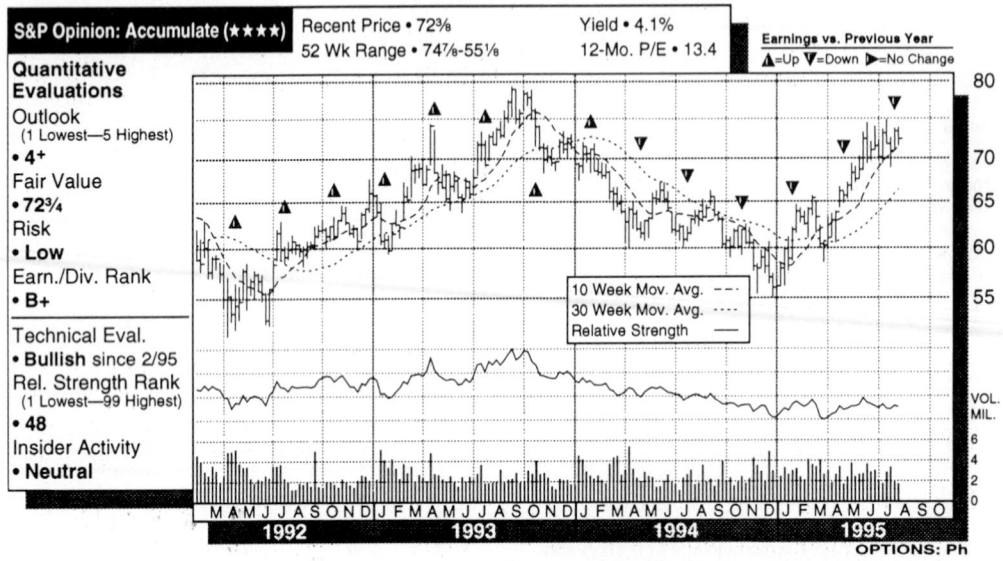

10 Week Mov. Avg. ---
30 Week Mov. Avg. ·····
Relative Strength —

VOL. MIL.

OPTIONS: Ph

Overview - 08-AUG-95

Earnings are expected to rebound in 1995 on improved asset/liability management experience and a recent turnaround in revenues from trading activities. Aided by diversification efforts, trading revenues in the first half of 1995 continued to improve, year to year, as strong results from debt instruments, foreign exchange, and equities and commodities trading offset weakness in revenues from swaps and other interest rate contracts. Improvements to JPM's cost structure are also expected as 1995 unfolds following an expense management program initiated in the first quarter of the year. Credit quality remains unparalleled, with the allowance for loan losses at 6.1 times the level of nonperforming assets and no loan loss provision expected for 1995.

Valuation - 08-AUG-95

The shares of this global financial intermediary modestly outpaced the broader market in the first seven months of 1995. While overall revenues remained flat through the second quarter, diversification efforts effectively reversed a downtrend in trading revenues experienced throughout 1994. With an improving revenue picture and expense growth moderation plan in place, the shares are expected to outperform in the next 12 to 18 months. On a side note, JPM is also seen as one of the primary benefactors should the Glass-Steagall Act be repealed or reformed, which would allow expanded securities underwriting and dealing activities.

Key Stock Statistics

S&P EPS Est. 1995	6.20	Tang. Bk. Value/Share	47.19
P/E on S&P Est. 1995	11.7	Beta	1.10
S&P EPS Est. 1996	7.10	Shareholders	28,900
Dividend Rate/Share	3.00	Market cap. (B)	$ 13.6
Shs. outstg. (M)	187.6	Inst. holdings	65%
Avg. daily vol. (M)	0.472	Insider holdings	NA

Value of $10,000 invested 5 years ago: $ 20,357

Fiscal Year Ending Dec. 31

	1995	% Change	1994	% Change	1993	% Change
Revenues (Million $)						
1Q	3,358	19%	2,831	-2%	2,884	18%
2Q	3,346	13%	2,957	NM	2,945	10%
3Q	—	—	3,048	-2%	3,124	15%
4Q	—	—	3,079	3%	2,988	24%
Yr.	—	—	11,915	NM	11,941	17%
Income (Million $)						
1Q	255.0	-26%	345.0	-20%	432.0	44%
2Q	315.0	-10%	350.0	-19%	431.0	12%
3Q	—	—	327.0	-30%	468.0	17%
4Q	—	—	193.0	-51%	392.0	77%
Yr.	—	—	1,215	-29%	1,723	52%
Earnings Per Share ($)						
1Q	1.27	-25%	1.69	-22%	2.16	44%
2Q	1.56	-10%	1.73	-18%	2.12	9%
3Q	E1.62	—	1.63	-29%	2.30	14%
4Q	E1.75	—	0.96	-50%	1.92	30%
Yr.	E6.20	—	6.02	-29%	8.48	23%

Next earnings report expected: mid October

Morgan (J.P.) & Co.

08-AUG-95

Business Summary - 08-AUG-95

This holding company owns Morgan Guaranty Trust, the fourth largest bank in the U.S. JPM's global business activities are divided into five major sectors: Asset Management and Servicing (investment management, private banking, exchange-traded product brokerage, securities and cash services, and Euroclear operations); Equity Investments; Finance and Advisory; Asset and Liability Management; and Sales and Trading. Revenues and pretax income in 1994 were:

	Revs.	Pretax Inc.
Asset management/servicing	29%	17%
Finance and advisory	20%	5%
Sales and trading	23%	7%
Equity investments	11%	30%
Asset/liability management	17%	41%

International operations accounted for 43% of net income in 1994 (75% in 1993).

During 1994, average earning assets of $134.4 billion (up from $126.9 billion in 1993) were divided: domestic loans 6%, foreign loans 12%, investment securities 15%, trading account assets 29%, other temporary investments 35% and other 3%. Average sources of funds were non-interest bearing liabilities 20%, interest-bearing deposits 23%, trading account liabilities 11%, short-term borrowings 31%, long-term debt 3%, equity 6% and other 6%.

At December 31, 1994, nonperforming assets totaled $220 million (1.00% of loans and related assets), down from $295 million (1.21%). The reserve for loan losses was 5.12% of loans, versus 4.75%. Net charge-offs were 0.11% of average loans in 1994, versus 0.38% in 1993.

At June 30, 1995, the Tier 1 capital ratio (estimated) was 8.7%, versus 9.6% at December 31, 1994. The total capital ratio (estimated) was 12.9%, versus 14.2%.

Important Developments

May '95—The company agreed to sell its global custody business, including custody-related securities lending and U.S. and U.K. custody operations, to Bank of New York Co. for an undisclosed amount. The sale relates to more than $800 billion of client assets and is part of JPM's strategy to free up resources to focus on core global banking activities.

Apr. '95—JPM noted that results in the first quarter of 1995 included a special charge of $55 million ($33 million after tax), or $0.17 a share, related to an expense management program initiated to moderate the growth of expenses.

Capitalization

Long Term Debt: $9,092,000,000 (6/95).
Adjust. Rate Cum. Pfd. Stock: $244,000,000.
Variable Cum. Pfd. Stock: $250,000,000.

Per Share Data ($)

(Year Ended Dec. 31)

	1994	1993	1992	1991	1990	1989
Tangible Bk. Val.	46.73	48.50	34.30	29.41	25.29	21.78
Earnings	6.02	8.48	6.92	5.63	3.99	-7.04
Dividends	2.79	2.48	2.23	2.03	1.86	1.70
Payout Ratio	46%	29%	32%	36%	47%	NM
Prices - High	72	79⅜	70½	70½	47¼	48⅛
- Low	55⅛	59⅜	51½	40½	29⅝	34
P/E Ratio - High	12	9	10	13	12	NM
- Low	9	7	7	7	7	NM

Income Statement Analysis (Million $)

	1994	%Chg	1993	%Chg	1992	%Chg	1991
Net Int. Inc.	1,981	12%	1,772	4%	1,708	15%	1,484
Tax Equiv. Adj.	120	-13%	138	-14%	161	-7%	173
Non Int. Inc.	3,536	-15%	4,176	63%	2,562	1%	2,531
Loan Loss Prov.	Nil	—	Nil	—	55.0	38%	40.0
% Exp/Op Revs.	66%	—	59%	—	64%	—	59%
Pretax Inc.	1,825	-32%	2,691	54%	1,749	18%	1,485
Eff. Tax Rate	33%	—	36%	—	21%	—	25%
Net Inc.	1,215	-29%	1,723	25%	1,382	24%	1,114
% Net Int. Marg.	1.56%	—	1.51%	—	1.78%	—	1.77%

Balance Sheet & Other Fin. Data (Million $)

	1994	1993	1992	1991	1990	1989
Earning Assets:						
Money Mkt.	90,542	76,094	44,827	35,939	32,740	33,964
Inv. Securities	22,657	19,547	21,511	22,180	18,541	16,294
Com'l Loans	4,243	5,694	4,990	4,639	5,266	7,000
Other Loans	17,837	18,686	21,448	23,158	22,296	21,650
Total Assets	154,917	133,888	102,941	103,468	93,103	88,964
Demand Deposits	4,460	5,520	3,983	4,313	6,642	5,491
Time Deposits	38,625	34,882	28,536	32,663	30,915	33,667
LT Debt	6,802	5,276	5,443	5,395	4,723	4,690
Common Eqty.	9,074	9,365	6,572	5,574	4,695	4,001

Ratio Analysis

	1994	1993	1992	1991	1990	1989
% Ret. on Assets	0.7	1.5	1.1	1.0	0.8	NM
% Ret. on Equity	12.9	21.3	22.5	21.3	16.7	NM
% Loan Loss Resv.	4.8	4.8	4.8	5.1	6.7	9.1
% Loans/Deposits	51.3	60.3	81.3	75.2	73.4	73.2
% Equity to Assets	5.3	6.8	5.1	4.7	4.4	5.2

Dividend Data

(Dividends have been paid since 1892. A dividend reinvestment plan is available.)

Amt. of Div. $	Date Decl.	Ex-Div. Date	Stock of Record	Payment Date
0.680	Sep. 14	Sep. 20	Sep. 26	Oct. 14 '94
0.750	Dec. 14	Dec. 20	Dec. 27	Jan. 13 '95
0.750	Mar. 08	Mar. 14	Mar. 20	Apr. 14 '95
0.750	Jun. 14	Jun. 22	Jun. 26	Jul. 14 '95

Data as orig. reptd.; bef. results of disc opers. and/or spec. items. Per share data adj. for stk. divs. as of ex-div. date. E-Estimated. NA-Not Available. NM-Not Meaningful. NR-Not Ranked.

Formed—in 1969; Bank incorporated in New York in 1864. **Office**—60 Wall St., New York, NY 10260-0060. **Tel**—(212) 483-2323. **Chrmn, Pres & CEO**—D. A. Warner III. **CFO**—J. T. Flynn. **Secy**—B. S. Stokes. **Investor Contact**—Ann B. Patton (212) 648-9446. **Dirs**—M. Feldstein, H. H. Gray, J. R. Houghton, J. L. Ketelsen, W. S. Lee, R. G. Mendoza, L. R. Raymond, R. D. Simmons, J. G. Smale, K. F. Viermetz, R. B. Wagner, D. A. Warner III, D. Weatherstone, D. C. Yearley. **Transfer Agent & Registrar**—First Chicago Trust Co. of New York, Jersey City, NJ. **Empl**-16,267. **S&P Analyst:** Stephen R. Biggar

Morgan Stanley Group

NYSE Symbol MS Options on Phila In S&P 500

Price	Range	P–E Ratio	Dividend	Yield	S&P Ranking	Beta
Oct. 12'95	1995					
94¾	99¾–57¾	16	1.28	1.4%	B+	2.11

Summary

Morgan Stanley Group is a global firm providing a wide range of financial services to corporations, governments, financial institutions and individual investors. Its businesses include securities underwriting, distribution and trading, mergers, acquisitions, restructurings, real estate, project finance, merchant banking and global custody. Directors and employees own about 40% of the common stock.

Current Outlook

Earnings for fiscal 1996 are projected at $7.85 a share, up from the $6.90 estimated for the 10-month fiscal year ending November 30, 1995.

The minimum expectation is for the dividend to continue at $0.32 a share.

Morgan is one of the securities industry's most consistently profitable firms. MS is a leading factor in the highly profitable mergers and acquisitions business, which is experiencing a rebound. Underwriting revenues are anticipated to recover beginning in 1995's third quarter. We anticipate that trading income will improve, mainly due to fixed-income trading gains resulting from a projected drop in interest rates. Asset management fees should continue to increase. Margins may remain under pressure, as the company has added to staff overseas to position itself for increased globalization of markets. Stock buybacks will aid share earnings.

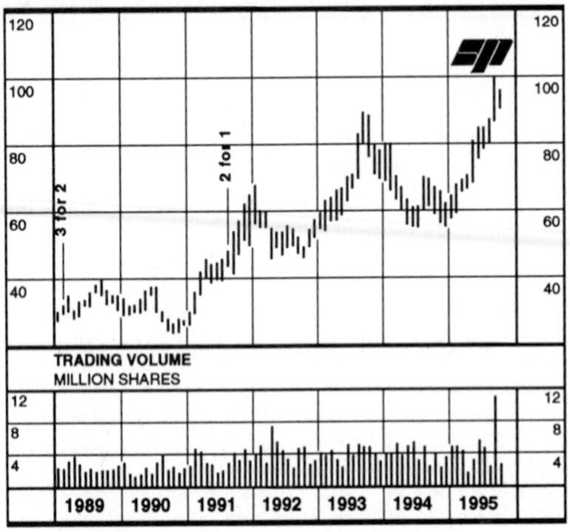

[1]Total Revenues (Million $)

Quarter:	1994–5	1993–4	1992–3	1991–2
Feb.	---	2,292	2,187	1,858
May	[2]3,518	2,262	2,489	2,099
Aug.	2,902	2,485	2,419	1,629
Nov.	---	2,337	2,081	1,795
	---	9,376	9,176	7,382

Total revenues for the six months ended August 31, 1995, rose 22% from those of the six months ended July 31, 1994. Investment banking revenues rose 33%, trading income gained 42%, commissions rose 13%, interest and dividends were 18% higher and asset management and administration fees advanced 8.2%. With interest costs up 24%, net revenues advanced 20%. Other costs were 12% higher, and pretax earnings increased 50%. After taxes at 31.7%, versus 35.0%, net income was up 58%, to $375 million, from $238 million.

[1]Common Share Earnings ($)

Quarter:	1994–5	1993–4	1992–3	1991–2
Feb.	---	1.27	2.40	1.62
May	[2]2.33	1.31	2.77	1.36
Aug.	2.45	1.30	2.20	1.26
Nov.	E2.12	0.29	2.18	1.68
	E6.90	4.18	9.59	5.90

Important Developments

Sep. '95— The company said that its significant market share in the mergers and acquisitions market, combined with improved debt and equity underwriting volumes, contributed to the growth of investment banking revenues in the August 1995 quarter.

Next earnings report expected in mid-December.

Per Share Data ($)

Yr. End Jan. 31[3]	1995	1994	1993	1992	1991	1990	1989	1988	1987	1986
Tangible Bk. Val.	**49.62**	49.00	37.71	30.13	24.49	23.93	19.09	13.48	10.53	7.46
Earnings	**4.18**	9.59	5.90	5.93	3.37	5.61	5.13	3.00	2.81	[4]1.78
Dividends	**1.200**	1.080	0.955	0.795	0.750	0.500	0.317	0.267	0.117	Nil
Payout Ratio	**29%**	11%	16%	13%	22%	9%	6%	9%	4%	Nil
Calendar Years	**1994**	1993	1992	1991	1990	1989	1988	1987	1986	1985
Prices—High	**80⅜**	NA	67⅞	65	37¾	39¾	28⁵⁄₁₆	28⅝	27⁵⁄₁₆	NA
Low	**55**	NA	45⅞	26	23⁹⁄₁₆	27⁷⁄₁₆	15⁹⁄₁₆	12¾	20⁷⁄₁₆	NA
P/E Ratio—	**19–13**	NA	12–8	11–4	11–7	7–5	6–3	10–4	10–7	NA

Data as orig. reptd. Adj. for stk. divs. of 100% Aug. 1991, 50% Feb. 1989. **1.** Quarters ended Apr., Jul., Oct. & Jan. of the foll. cal. yr. prior to 1994-5. **2.** Four mos. **3.** Prior to 1993, yr. ended Dec. 31 of the preceding year. **4.** Based on pro forma shs. outstanding. E-Estimated. NA-Not Available.

Morgan Stanley Group Inc.

Income Data (Million $)

Year Ended Jan. 31[1]	Commis-sions	Int. Inc.	Total Revs.	Int. Exp.	% Exp./ Op. Revs.	Net Bef. Taxes	Eff. Tax Rate	Net Inc.	% Return On		
									Revs.	Assets	[2]Equity
1995	**449**	**6,406**	**9,376**	**5,875**	**93.7**	**594**	**33.5%**	**395**	**4.2**	**0.4**	**8.8**
1994	393	5,660	9,176	5,020	86.9	1,200	34.5%	786	8.6	0.9	23.7
1993	312	4,814	7,382	4,362	89.3	793	35.7%	510	6.9	0.7	17.6
1992	271	4,181	6,785	3,925	88.6	772	38.5%	475	7.0	0.8	21.4
1991	275	3,894	5,870	3,711	92.0	470	42.5%	270	4.6	0.5	13.8
1990	250	3,519	5,831	3,378	87.3	738	40.0%	443	7.6	0.9	27.9
1989	230	2,029	4,109	1,905	84.5	637	38.0%	395	9.6	1.1	32.6
1988	297	1,421	3,148	1,380	88.4	364	36.6%	231	7.3	0.8	25.2
1987	216	1,063	2,463	1,035	86.9	323	37.6%	201	8.2	0.9	32.0
1986	154	938	1,795	900	89.8	183	42.2%	106	5.9	0.7	38.4

Balance Sheet Data (Million $)

Jan. 31[1]	Total Assets	Cash Items	Rec.	Secs. Owned	Sec. Borrowed	Due Brokers & Cust.	Other Liabs.	Capitalization		
								Debt	[2]Equity	Total
1995	**116,694**	**4,626**	**63,433**	**47,109**	**63,256**	**12,541**	**27,528**	**8,814**	**3,736**	**13,369**
1994	97,242	2,587	53,696	39,844	52,235	12,060	21,668	6,810	3,649	11,279
1993	80,353	3,558	40,390	35,662	48,206	8,306	16,448	3,960	2,813	7,394
1992	63,709	3,827	20,438	26,576	38,710	6,691	12,477	2,837	2,272	5,830
1991	53,526	2,275	17,520	23,393	31,790	5,434	12,749	1,382	1,781	3,553
1990	53,276	872	26,940	16,392	34,768	2,950	12,794	743	1,771	2,764
1989	40,051	1,623	28,765	8,924	26,335	4,002	7,299	815	1,337	2,414
1988	29,663	1,242	20,099	7,678	18,257	3,360	6,353	556	1,001	1,694
1987	29,190	459	18,605	9,511	20,074	3,396	4,541	381	786	1,178
1986	15,794	201	10,410	5,015	8,760	3,290	3,257	172	302	486

Data as orig. reptd. **1.** Prior to 1993, yr. ended Dec. 31 of the preceding year. **2.** Common; as reptd. by co.

Business Summary

Morgan Stanley Group is a major securities firm whose main subsidiary, Morgan Stanley & Co., is a leading investment banking company. Revenues in recent fiscal years were derived as follows:

	1994–5	1993–4	1992–3
Investment banking	26%	30%	32%
Principal transactions...	36%	39%	36%
Commissions	13%	10%	10%
Net Interest and dividends...............	15%	15%	15%
Asset mgmt./other	10%	6%	7%

Foreign operations accounted for 65% of net revenues and 11% of pretax earnings in 1994-5.

The company provides a broad range of sales, trading and research services to suppliers of capital worldwide and ranks as one of the largest dealers in equity and fixed-income securities. MS is a primary dealer in U.S. Government securities and a member of the major U.S. securities and commodities exchanges.

Through its investment banking division, MS provides advice to, and raises capital for, a variety of domestic and international clients. The company participates in the underwriting of public offerings of debt, equity and other securities. The company provides advisory services and is active in corporate merger, acquisition, defense, divestiture and reorganization transactions. MS provides advice and other services related to real estate. MS also manages assets for individuals, as well as pension and profit-sharing funds.

At May 31, 1995, Morgan Stanley & Co.'s net capital, as defined, totaled $733 million, which was $558 million in excess of the regulatory minimum requirement.

Dividend Data

Dividends were initiated in 1986.

Amt. of Divd. $	Date Decl.	Ex-divd. Date	Stock of Record	Payment Date
0.30	Nov. 16	Nov. 21	Nov. 28	Dec. 15'94
0.32	Feb. 28	Mar. 7	Mar. 13	Mar. 24'95
0.32	Jun. 28	Jul. 6	Jul. 10	Jul. 27'95
0.32	Sep. 26	Oct. 4	Oct. 9	Oct. 26'95

Capitalization

Long Term Debt: $8,726,000,000 (5/95).

Preferred Stock: $819,000,000, incl. $136 million conv. into com. at $35.88 per sh.

Common Stock: 76,778,494 shs. ($1 par).
Institutions hold about 60%, incl. a portion of 40% owned by directors & employees.
Shareholders of record: 1,350.

Office—1251 Ave. of the Americas, New York, NY 10020. **Tel**—(212) 703-4000. **Chrmn**—R. B. Fisher. **Pres**—J. J. Mack. **Secy**—J. M. Clark. **CFO**—P. N. Duff. **Investor Contact**—Charles B. Hintz. **Dirs**—B. M. Biggs, D. B. Burke, D. Cheney, R. B. Fisher, S. P. Gilbert, P. F. Karches, J. J. Mack, R. W. Matschullat, A. E. Murray, P. F. Oreffice, P. J. Rizzo, D. Walker. **Transfer Agent & Registrar**—First Chicago Trust Co. of New York, Jersey City, N.J. **Incorporated** in Delaware in 1975. **Empl**—9,685.

Morrison Knudsen

NYSE Symbol **MRN**
In S&P 500

07-NOV-95   **Industry:**
Building

Summary: This leading general contractor provides design, engineering, construction, contract mining, and management services worldwide.

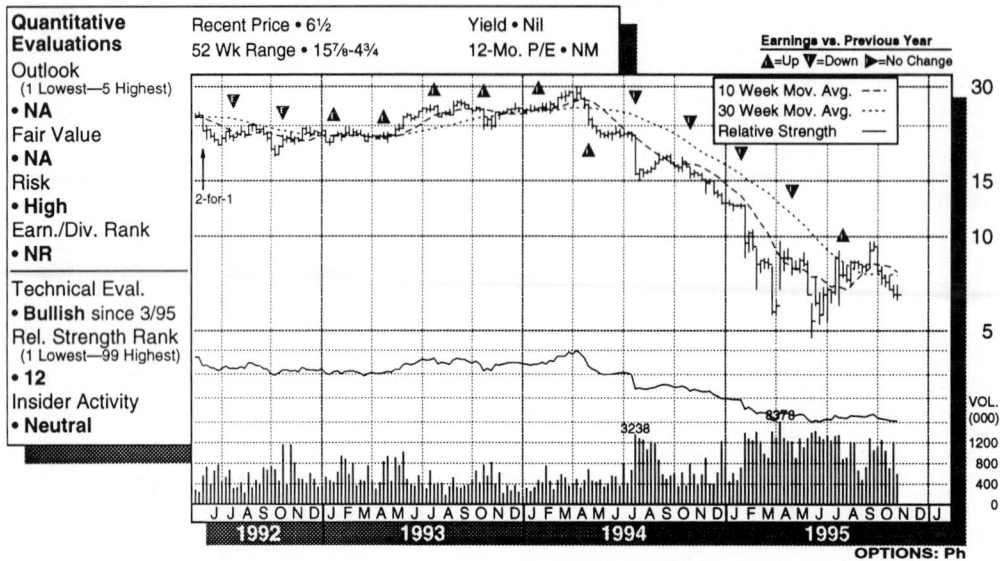

Quantitative Evaluations

Outlook
(1 Lowest—5 Highest)
• **NA**

Fair Value
• **NA**

Risk
• **High**

Earn./Div. Rank
• **NR**

Technical Eval.
• **Bullish** since 3/95

Rel. Strength Rank
(1 Lowest—99 Highest)
• **12**

Insider Activity
• **Neutral**

Recent Price • 6½
52 Wk Range • 15⅞-4¾

Yield • Nil
12-Mo. P/E • NM

Earnings vs. Previous Year
▲=Up ▼=Down ►=No Change

10 Week Mov. Avg. – – –
30 Week Mov. Avg. ⋯⋯
Relative Strength —

2-for-1

OPTIONS: Ph

Business Profile - 07-NOV-95

Following 1994's huge loss, MRN decided to focus on its engineering and construction segment and to dispose of its non-core businesses. In June, MRN sold its 46% stake in MK Gold Co.; in October, it disposed of its troubled transit operations, which accounted for most of the 1994 loss. MRN also plans to sell its 65% MK Rail stake. In August, MRN and its lenders restructured its existing indebtedness; in September, MRN said it had settled substantially all shareholder litigation.

Operational Review - 07-NOV-95

Revenues in the six months ended June 30, 1995, rose 18%, year to year. Operating income of $16.8 million contrasted with a loss of $62.1 million. After higher legal and interest expenses, and income taxes, versus a tax benefit, the net loss from continuing operations narrowed to $32.3 million ($0.98 a share) from $49.5 million ($1.53). Results exclude the operations of MK Rail, as well as MRN's gain on that unit's May 1994 IPO.

Stock Performance - 03-NOV-95

In the past 30 trading days, MRN's shares have declined 30%, compared to a 2% rise in the S&P 500. Average trading volume for the past five days was 116,620 shares, compared with the 40-day moving average of 236,643 shares.

Key Stock Statistics

Dividend Rate/Share	Nil	Shareholders	6,000
Shs. outstg. (M)	33.0	Market cap. (B)	$0.215
Avg. daily vol. (M)	0.168	Inst. holdings	57%
Tang. Bk. Value/Share	0.33	Insider holdings	NA
Beta	0.99		

Value of $10,000 invested 5 years ago: $ 3,479

Fiscal Year Ending Dec. 31

	1995	% Change	1994	% Change	1993	% Change
Revenues (Million $)						
1Q	517.2	-4%	541.3	-3%	560.2	10%
2Q	633.8	7%	591.4	-10%	655.4	25%
3Q	—	—	735.5	NM	733.8	26%
4Q	—	—	636.1	-18%	773.1	16%
Yr.	—	—	2,504	-8%	2,723	19%
Income (Million $)						
1Q	-19.88	NM	9.65	22%	7.88	17%
2Q	-12.39	NM	-40.47	NM	8.21	18%
3Q	—	—	-3.20	NM	9.25	NM
4Q	—	—	-315.6	NM	10.43	52%
Yr.	—	—	-349.6	NM	35.77	166%
Earnings Per Share ($)						
1Q	-0.60	NM	0.30	15%	0.26	18%
2Q	-0.37	NM	-1.24	NM	0.27	17%
3Q	—	—	-0.10	NM	0.30	NM
4Q	—	—	-9.64	NM	0.33	43%
Yr.	—	—	-10.75	NM	1.15	161%

Next earnings report expected: NA

Morrison Knudsen

Business Summary - 07-NOV-95

Morrison Knudsen's continuing operations are conducted through its engineering and construction (E&C) segment. Following a $350 million net loss in 1994, reflecting losses in connection with certain construction and transit projects, MRN decided to focus on its core E&C business and exit non-core business segments. The company decided to sell its 65% stake in its MK Rail unit in March 1995, and classified MK Rail as a discontinued operation. In June 1995, the company sold its 46.4% stake in MK Gold Co. for $22.5 million in cash. MRN completed the divestiture of its transit segment in October 1995. Contributions by industry segment in 1994 (profit in million $):

	Revs.	Profit
Engineering & construction	80%	-82.2
MK Rail	15%	-31.1
Transit	5%	-224.7

U.S. government agencies provided 22%, 22%, and 23% of revenues in 1994, 1993 and 1992, respectively.

MRN engages in all types of general construction work including industrial, heavy, civil and marine, mechanical, pipeline, building, and underground, and renders design services in practically all engineering disciplines. Markets for its services also include nuclear and fossil-fueled power plants, environmental and hazardous waste abatement services, operations and maintenance services for commercial and military facilities, design and construction management of mine facilities, and operation of coal, lignite and precious metal mines under long-term contracts.

Backlog of all uncompleted E&C contracts at December 31, 1994, totaled $2.43 billion, versus $3.05 billion a year earlier.

Important Developments

Oct. '95—MRN expected to record additional reserves in 1995's third quarter to cover costs and accounting charges arising from the October 1995 divestiture of its transit operations. Specific amounts were not disclosed.

Sep. '95—MRN said it had settled all outstanding securities class actions and all but one associated derivative action. The settlement provides for payments of $35 million by MRN's insurance carriers to the plaintiffs, the issuance of 2,976,923 MRN common shares to the plaintiff class and the implementation of certain corporate governance procedures.

Aug. '95—MRN and its bank lenders agreed to a restructuring of MRN's existing debt. MRN issued warrants to buy 14,029,391 common shares at $6.75 a share to the lenders in connection with the restructuring.

Capitalization

Long Term Debt: $1,400,000 (6/95).

Per Share Data ($) (Year Ended Dec. 31)

	1994	1993	1992	1991	1990	1989
Tangible Bk. Val.	0.37	11.72	11.42	13.46	11.69	10.99
Cash Flow	-9.20	2.37	1.44	2.54	2.86	2.65
Earnings	-10.75	1.15	0.44	1.30	1.45	1.41
Dividends	Nil	0.80	0.80	0.74	0.74	0.74
Payout Ratio	Nil	70%	182%	60%	51%	52%
Prices - High	29⅞	27⅛	28⅝	30⅜	30¼	24¼
- Low	12¼	19⅜	17⅞	18⅞	15¼	18⅜
P/E Ratio - High	NM	24	65	23	21	17
- Low	NM	17	41	15	10	13

Income Statement Analysis (Million $)

	1994	%Chg	1993	%Chg	1992	%Chg	1991
Revs.	2,532	-6%	2,702	19%	2,270	16%	1,964
Oper. Inc.	-314	NM	53.0	112%	25.0	-49%	49.0
Depr.	50.5	34%	37.7	25%	30.2	-10%	33.7
Int. Exp.	11.7	NM	3.3	-73%	12.3	-23%	16.0
Pretax Inc.	-441	NM	62.8	157%	24.4	-58%	57.9
Eff. Tax Rate	NM	—	42%	—	44%	—	39%
Net Inc.	-349	NM	35.8	167%	13.4	-62%	35.1

Balance Sheet & Other Fin. Data (Million $)

	1994	1993	1992	1991	1990	1989
Cash	79.0	92.0	178	255	195	10.0
Curr. Assets	866	793	681	643	630	476
Total Assets	1,273	1,226	1,104	1,034	931	726
Curr. Liab.	1,005	690	613	374	396	391
LT Debt	47.0	10.0	Nil	193	185	3.0
Common Eqty.	58.0	407	376	385	276	251
Total Cap.	162	450	408	610	490	287
Cap. Exp.	74.1	52.2	35.7	66.0	49.0	58.0
Cash Flow	-298	73.4	43.7	68.8	67.9	60.8

Ratio Analysis

	1994	1993	1992	1991	1990	1989
Curr. Ratio	0.9	1.2	1.1	1.7	1.6	1.2
% LT Debt of Cap.	29.2	2.2	0.1	31.7	37.7	0.9
% Net Inc.of Revs.	NM	1.3	0.6	1.8	2.1	1.5
% Ret. on Assets	NM	3.0	1.2	3.2	4.1	4.3
% Ret. on Equity	NM	9.0	3.4	9.8	12.9	13.4

Dividend Data —Dividends were resumed in 1973 and were omitted in February 1995. A "poison pill" stock purchase right was adopted in 1986.

Amt. of Div. $	Date Decl.	Ex-Div. Date	Stock of Record	Payment Date
0.200	Nov. 11	Nov. 17	Nov. 23	Jan. 03 '95

Data as orig. reptd.; bef. results of disc. opers. and/or spec. items. Per share data adj. for stk. divs. as of ex-div. date. E-Estimated. NA-Not Available. NM-Not Meaningful. NR-Not Ranked.

Office—Morrison-Knudsen Plaza (P.O. Box 73), Boise, ID 83729. **Tel**—(208) 386-5000. **Chrmn**—R. S. Miller, Jr. **Pres & CEO**—R. A. Tinstman. **EVP & CFO**—D. M. Slavich. **EVP & Secy**—S. G. Hanks. **Treas & Investor Contact**—Douglas L. Brigham. **Dirs**—J. Arrillaga, L. E. Fox, C. B. Hemmeter, P. S. Lynch, R. A. McCabe, R. S. Miller, Jr., I. C. Peden, G. R. Roche, J. W. Rogers, Jr., R. S. Tinstman. **Principal Transfer Agent & Registrar**—Chemical Trust Co. of California, SF. **Co-Transfer Agent & Co-Registrar**—West One Bancorp, Boise. **Reincorporated** in Delaware in 1932 and 1985. **Empl**-12,819. **S&P Analyst:** N. Rosenberg

Morton International

NYSE Symbol **MII**
In S&P 500

09-AUG-95 **Industry:** Chemicals

Summary: Morton International derives the major portion of its sales and earnings from specialty chemicals, and the balance from automotive inflatable restraint systems and salt.

S&P Opinion: Accumulate (★★★★)

Recent Price • 30⅜
52 Wk Range • 32-25¾

Yield • 1.7%
12-Mo. P/E • 15.5

Quantitative Evaluations

Outlook
(1 Lowest—5 Highest)
• **4+**

Fair Value
• 32⅞

Risk
• **Low**

Earn./Div. Rank
• **B+**

Technical Eval.
• **Bullish** since 4/95

Rel. Strength Rank
(1 Lowest—99 Highest)
• **55**

Insider Activity
• **NA**

Earnings vs. Previous Year
▲=Up ▼=Down ▶=No Change

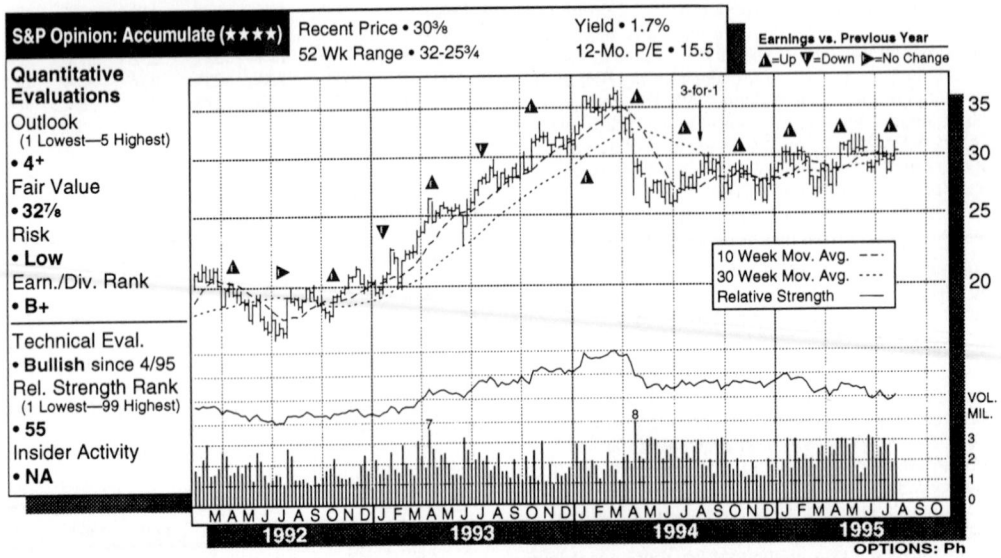

10 Week Mov. Avg. - - -
30 Week Mov. Avg. ·······
Relative Strength ——

OPTIONS: Ph

Overview - 09-AUG-95

We expect Morton's airbag sales to climb about 20% in fiscal 1996, to almost $1.5 billion, with much of the growth to come from additional U.S. demand, including redesigned Ford models and new programs with General Motors and Toyota. MII will also begin to supply Nissan with airbags for vehicles sold in Japan. Selling prices for airbags are expected to continue to decline, largely offset by cost reductions. Sales of specialty chemicals should continue to grow as a result of healthier worldwide economies. Price increases and positive currency exchange rates will help offset the adverse impact of higher chemical raw material costs. The salt business will likely be hurt by lower volumes for ice control salt as a result of high customer inventories following the mild winter weather in early calendar 1995.

Valuation - 09-AUG-95

The stock has been a lackluster performer since early 1994, in part due to the slowdown in the growth of the U.S. economy and auto markets, and despite the upbeat earnings outlook for the company. Given the very strong longer-term growth prospects for the chemical and airbag businesses, and the stock's current earnings multiple, we feel that the shares are attractive for purchase. The weaker performance expected for the higher-margin salt business in fiscal 1996 has been largely discounted by investors. A possible stock buyback program may give a lift to the shares.

Key Stock Statistics

S&P EPS Est. 1996	2.25	Tang. Bk. Value/Share	8.55
P/E on S&P Est. 1996	13.5	Beta	1.05
Dividend Rate/Share	0.52	Shareholders	10,200
Shs. outstg. (M)	148.0	Market cap. (B)	$ 4.6
Avg. daily vol. (M)	0.466	Inst. holdings	67%
		Insider holdings	NA

Value of $10,000 invested 5 years ago: $ 21,724

Fiscal Year Ending Jun. 30

	1995	% Change	1994	% Change	1993	% Change
Revenues (Million $)						
1Q	745.5	20%	619.6	15%	538.0	13%
2Q	836.2	21%	690.9	27%	545.0	7%
3Q	921.0	14%	808.3	25%	648.3	17%
4Q	841.6	15%	730.8	26%	578.2	14%
Yr.	3,355	18%	2,850	23%	2,310	13%
Income (Million $)						
1Q	61.90	44%	42.90	—	—	—
2Q	72.70	35%	53.70	52%	35.40	2%
3Q	89.90	26%	71.30	44%	49.40	20%
4Q	69.60	19%	58.60	NM	9.60	-72%
Yr.	294.1	30%	226.5	78%	126.9	-12%
Earnings Per Share ($)						
1Q	0.41	43%	0.29	21%	0.24	1%
2Q	0.49	37%	0.36	53%	0.23	-1%
3Q	0.60	27%	0.47	46%	0.32	15%
4Q	0.46	18%	0.39	NM	0.06	-73%
Yr.	1.96	30%	1.51	76%	0.86	-12%

Next earnings report expected: mid October

Business Summary - 09-AUG-95

Morton International, a diversified chemical company formed by the July 1989 spinoff of the commercial businesses of Thiokol Corp. (formerly Morton Thiokol Inc.), has interests in three major areas. Contributions by segment in fiscal 1995:

	Sales	Profits
Specialty chemicals	47%	39%
Salt	16%	21%
Automotive safety products	37%	40%

Foreign operations accounted for 20% of sales and 19% of profits in fiscal 1994.

Specialty chemicals include adhesives and specialty polymers (flexible packaging and industrial adhesives, water-based polymers, thermoplastic polyurethanes and advanced materials used by the food packaging, construction, graphic arts, industrial, automotive and consumer goods markets); coatings (automotive and industrial finishes, coil coatings, highway markings, powder coatings, and liquid colorants used by automotive, appliance, furniture and equipment manufacturers, and highway marking contractors); electronic materials (photoresists and solder masks used in the manufacture of printed circuit boards); and specialty chemical products (sodium borohydride, biocides, plastic additives, polymers and sealants, specialty dyes and organic specialties) used by the paper, construction, plastics and petroleum industries.

Salt is marketed under the Morton and Windsor brands for human and animal consumption; residential, municipal and industrial water conditioning; highway and residential ice control; food and meat processing; and industrial manufacturing and chemical processing.

Automotive safety products consist of gas generators (inflators) and modules for use in driver-side and passenger-side airbag passive restraint systems.

Important Developments

Jul. '95—MII said it was pleased with its fiscal fourth quarter, which ended strongly after a slow start. Specialty chemicals had solid results in June in contrast to weak April sales and despite continuing raw material pricing pressures. Airbag sales growth of 19% in the fourth quarter was less than in previous quarters as a result of lower auto production levels. Including a $2.4 million pretax charge for the elimination of 324 positions, profits also grew 19%. Full-year sales for airbags were up 31%, and profits climbed 38%. Sales of the salt business in fiscal 1995 declined 1% as reduced demand for ice control salt from a mild winter offset growth in other product lines and early season customer ice control inventory fill-up.

Capitalization

Long Term Debt: $198,600,000 (3/95).

Per Share Data ($)

(Year Ended Jun. 30)

	1995	1994	1993	1992	1991	1990
Tangible Bk. Val.	NA	7.23	5.80	5.90	5.07	4.43
Cash Flow	NA	2.43	1.62	1.68	1.58	1.46
Earnings	1.96	1.51	0.86	0.98	0.95	0.93
Dividends	0.55	0.37	0.32	0.32	0.31	0.29
Payout Ratio	28%	25%	37%	32%	33%	31%
Prices - High	32	37¼	33½	21⅝	19½	15⅞
- Low	26¼	25½	19⅛	16⅞	12⅞	11⅛
P/E Ratio - High	16	25	39	22	20	17
- Low	13	17	22	17	14	12

Income Statement Analysis (Million $)

	1994	%Chg	1993	%Chg	1992	%Chg	1991
Revs.	2,850	23%	2,310	13%	2,044	7%	1,906
Oper. Inc.	495	33%	371	8%	344	8%	319
Depr.	138	21%	114	12%	102	11%	92.0
Int. Exp.	27.8	-18%	33.7	NM	33.8	-7%	36.4
Pretax Inc.	358	79%	200	-13%	231	8%	214
Eff. Tax Rate	37%	—	37%	—	38%	—	36%
Net Inc.	227	79%	127	-12%	145	5%	138

Balance Sheet & Other Fin. Data (Million $)

	1994	1993	1992	1991	1990	1989
Cash	58.7	45.3	35.0	60.9	86.7	53.0
Curr. Assets	996	866	816	758	730	557
Total Assets	2,463	2,239	2,111	1,926	1,814	1,364
Curr. Liab.	557	525	491	410	406	301
LT Debt	199	218	223	256	261	44.0
Common Eqty.	1,400	1,200	1,223	1,103	1,008	901
Total Cap.	1,653	1,474	1,554	1,454	1,345	1,017
Cap. Exp.	220	202	200	164	111	132
Cash Flow	364	241	247	230	211	155

Ratio Analysis

	1994	1993	1992	1991	1990	1989
Curr. Ratio	1.8	1.6	1.7	1.8	1.8	1.9
% LT Debt of Cap.	12.0	14.8	14.3	17.6	19.4	4.3
% Net Inc.of Revs.	7.9	5.5	7.1	7.3	8.2	6.9
% Ret. on Assets	9.6	5.8	7.2	7.4	8.5	NA
% Ret. on Equity	17.4	10.4	12.4	13.1	14.1	NA

Dividend Data

(The company or predecessor companies have paid dividends since 1925. Quarterly dividends for MII were initiated in 1989.)

Amt. of Div. $	Date Decl.	Ex-Div. Date	Stock of Record	Payment Date
0.110	Oct. 27	Nov. 21	Nov. 28	Dec. 12 '94
0.110	Jan. 26	Feb. 21	Feb. 27	Mar. 13 '95
0.110	Apr. 27	May. 23	May. 30	Jun. 12 '95
0.130	Jun. 22	Aug. 24	Aug. 28	Sep. 11 '95

Data as orig. reptd.; bef. results of disc. opers. and/or spec. items. Per share data adj. for stk. divs. as of ex-div. date. E-Estimated. NA-Not Available. NM-Not Meaningful. NR-Not Ranked.

Office—100 North Riverside Plaza, Chicago, IL 60606-1596. **Tel**—(312) 807-2000. **Chrmn & CEO**—S. J. Stewart. **VP-Secy**—P. M. Phelps. **VP-CFO**—T. F. McDevitt. **VP-Investor Contact**—Nancy Hobor. **Dirs**—R. M. Barford, W. T. Creson, D. C. Fill, F. W. Luerssen, E. J. Mooney, C. A. Sanders, G. A. Schaefer, S. J. Stewart, R. W. Stone, R. C. Tower. **Transfer Agent & Registrar**—First Chicago Trust Co. of New York, Jersey City, N.J. **Incorporated** in Indiana in 1989. **Empl**-13,100. **S&P Analyst:** Richard O'Reilly, CFA

Motorola, Inc.

NYSE Symbol **MOT**
In S&P 500

10-OCT-95

Industry:
Electronics/Electric

Summary: A leading supplier of cellular telephone systems, semiconductors, two-way radios and paging equipment, Motorola also sells information systems and other electronics products.

S&P Opinion: Accumulate (★★★★)	Recent Price • 68¾	Yield • 0.6%
	52 Wk Range • 82½-50⅞	12-Mo. P/E • 22.3

Quantitative Evaluations

Outlook
(1 Lowest—5 Highest)
• **4+**

Fair Value
• **75**

Risk
• **Average**

Earn./Div. Rank
• **A**

Technical Eval.
• **Bullish** since 5/95

Rel. Strength Rank
(1 Lowest—99 Highest)
• **21**

Insider Activity
• **Neutral**

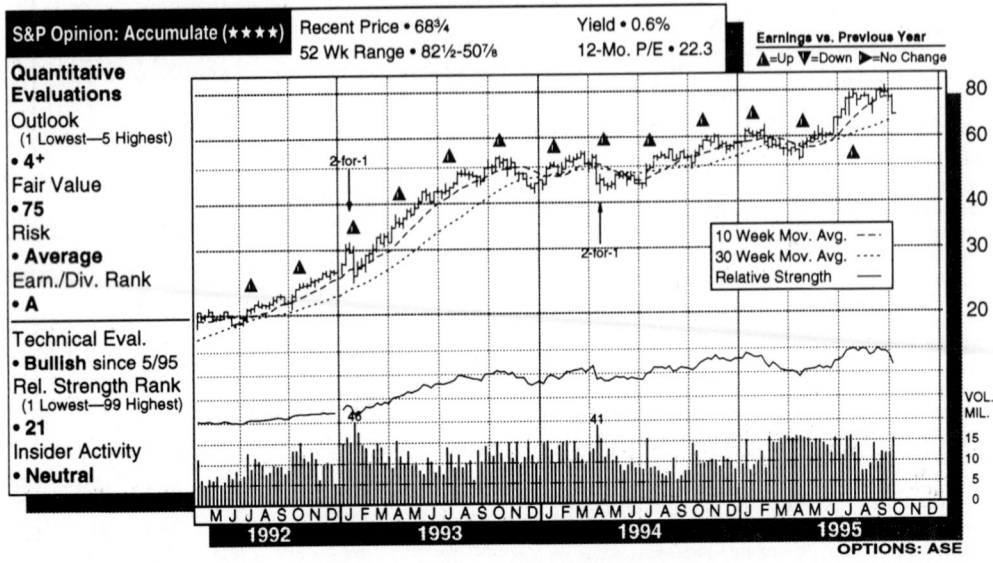

Earnings vs. Previous Year
▲=Up ▼=Down ▶=No Change

10 Week Mov. Avg. ---
30 Week Mov. Avg. ·····
Relative Strength —

OPTIONS: ASE

Overview - 10-OCT-95

Sales for the balance of 1995 and into 1996 are projected to advance approximately 20%, led by strong demand for cellular phones and related infrastructure equipment, semiconductors and pagers. However, this growth rate is down from previous years, reflecting some slowing in cellular phone sales in the U.S. Nevertheless, worldwide demand should remain strong, as should cellular infrastructure sales. Prospects are also bright for the semiconductor group, reflecting continued strong orders and ongoing capacity additions designed to meet this demand. Paging sales should benefit from strong international demand and new product introductions. Gross margins are expected to narrow, reflecting ongoing price competition and higher costs and depreciation related to the capacity additions. This erosion is expected to be offset by well controlled costs.

Valuation - 10-OCT-95

We have lowered our opinion of the shares to accumulate from strong buy after management cautioned of a slowdown in its U.S. cellular phone operations in its third quarter earnings announcement. We are also concerned about several other issues that could curtail near term EPS growth, including pricing pressures on cellular phones, higher cost associated with semiconductor capacity additions and product transition issues. As a result of this uncertainty, we believe a less aggressive stance is now in order and recommend that investors selectively accumulate the shares.

Key Stock Statistics

S&P EPS Est. 1995	3.14	Tang. Bk. Value/Share	16.92
P/E on S&P Est. 1995	21.9	Beta	0.87
S&P EPS Est. 1996	3.90	Shareholders	39,600
Dividend Rate/Share	0.40	Market cap. (B)	$ 40.7
Shs. outstg. (M)	589.8	Inst. holdings	62%
Avg. daily vol. (M)	2.566	Insider holdings	NA

Value of $10,000 invested 5 years ago: $ 49,442

Fiscal Year Ending Dec. 31

	1995	% Change	1994	% Change	1993	% Change
Revenues (Million $)						
1Q	6,011	28%	4,693	29%	3,626	18%
2Q	6,877	26%	5,439	38%	3,937	25%
3Q	6,851	21%	5,660	28%	4,408	30%
4Q	—	—	6,453	29%	4,993	35%
Yr.	—	—	22,245	31%	16,963	28%
Income (Million $)						
1Q	372.0	25%	298.0	46%	204.0	63%
2Q	481.0	31%	367.0	64%	224.0	57%
3Q	496.0	31%	380.0	50%	254.0	97%
4Q	—	—	515.0	51%	340.0	88%
Yr.	—	—	1,560	53%	1,022	77%
Earnings Per Share ($)						
1Q	0.61	20%	0.51	40%	0.36	55%
2Q	0.80	27%	0.63	56%	0.40	50%
3Q	0.81	25%	0.65	48%	0.44	83%
4Q	E0.92	6%	0.87	50%	0.58	73%
Yr.	E3.14	18%	2.65	49%	1.78	65%

Next earnings report expected: mid October

Motorola, Inc.

Business Summary - 10-OCT-95

Motorola is a diversified manufacturer of electronic products. Industry segment contributions (profits in millions) in 1994 were:

	Sales	Profits
General systems	35%	$1,214
Semiconductors	28%	996
Communications	24%	589
Government & space technology products	3%	-55
Other products	10%	156

International operations accounted for 44% of sales and 40% of operating profits in 1994.

The General Systems segment primarily develops, manufactures, sells, installs and services cellular infrastructure and cellular telephone subscriber units. The Motorola Computer Group, within this segment, develops, manufactures, sells and services multi-function computer systems and board level products, together with operating systems and system enablers. The segment also includes the Network Ventures Division and Personal Communications Systems Division.

The Semiconductor Products segment manufactures a broad line of semiconductor devices for both consumer and industrial applications.

The Communications Products segment is composed of the Land Mobile Products Sector and the Paging Products and Wireless Data Group. These groups provide mobile and portable FM two-way radio and radio paging communications.

The Government and Space Technology Group is engaged in the design, development and production of electronic systems and products for U.S. government projects. The Group's Satellite Communications Division is developing the IRIDIUM satellite-based communication system.

The Other Products segment includes the Automotive, Energy and Controls Group.

Important Developments

Sep. '95—PCS PrimeCo. announced that it selected MOT to supply CDMA infrastructure equipment in five of its U.S. Personal Communications Services (PCS) regional markets. The equipment includes radio base stations and switches. The company also announced that GTE Mobilnet has selected its cell site and switch equipment for its new PCS network. Separately, the company exercised its option to purchase a 230-acre parcel of land in Goochland County, Va. MOT said it expected to begin development of a wafer fabrication complex at this location in 1996, with semiconductor production set to begin in 1998.

Capitalization

Long Term Debt: $1,961,000,000 (9/30/95).

Per Share Data ($)

(Year Ended Dec. 31)

	1994	1993	1992	1991	1990	1989
Tangible Bk. Val.	15.39	11.40	9.54	8.76	8.08	7.29
Cash Flow	5.21	3.76	2.95	2.54	2.46	2.21
Earnings	2.65	1.78	1.08	0.86	0.95	0.96
Dividends	0.27	0.22	0.20	0.19	0.19	0.19
Payout Ratio	10%	12%	18%	22%	20%	20%
Prices - High	61 1/8	53 3/4	26 5/8	17 7/8	22 1/8	15 5/8
- Low	42 1/8	24 3/8	16 1/8	11 1/2	12 1/4	9 7/8
P/E Ratio - High	23	30	25	21	23	16
- Low	16	14	15	13	13	10

Income Statement Analysis (Million $)

	1994	%Chg	1993	%Chg	1992	%Chg	1991
Revs.	22,245	31%	16,963	28%	13,303	17%	11,341
Oper. Inc.	4,119	45%	2,848	45%	1,968	20%	1,636
Depr.	1,525	30%	1,170	17%	1,000	13%	886
Int. Exp.	207	7%	194	-6%	207	13%	184
Pretax Inc.	2,437	60%	1,525	91%	800	31%	613
Eff. Tax Rate	36%	—	33%	—	28%	—	26%
Net Inc.	1,560	53%	1,022	77%	576	27%	454

Balance Sheet & Other Fin. Data (Million $)

	1994	1993	1992	1991	1990	1989
Cash	1,059	1,244	930	533	577	433
Curr. Assets	8,925	6,713	5,218	4,487	4,452	3,915
Total Assets	17,536	13,498	10,629	9,375	8,742	7,686
Curr. Liab.	5,917	4,389	3,335	3,063	3,048	2,751
LT Debt	1,127	1,360	1,258	954	792	755
Common Eqty.	9,096	6,409	5,144	4,630	4,257	3,803
Total Cap.	10,732	8,202	6,632	5,780	5,252	4,741
Cap. Exp.	3,320	2,187	1,386	1,317	1,371	1,218
Cash Flow	3,085	2,192	1,576	1,340	1,289	1,148

Ratio Analysis

	1994	1993	1992	1991	1990	1989
Curr. Ratio	1.5	1.5	1.6	1.5	1.5	1.4
% LT Debt of Cap.	10.5	16.6	19.0	16.5	15.1	15.9
% Net Inc.of Revs.	7.0	6.0	4.3	4.0	4.6	5.2
% Ret. on Assets	9.8	8.4	5.7	5.0	6.0	6.9
% Ret. on Equity	19.7	17.4	11.7	10.2	12.3	13.8

Dividend Data —Dividends have been paid since 1942. A "poison pill" rights plan was adopted in 1988.

Amt. of Div. $	Date Decl.	Ex-Div. Date	Stock of Record	Payment Date
0.100	Nov. 01	Dec. 09	Dec. 15	Jan. 16 '95
0.100	Feb. 07	Mar. 09	Mar. 15	Apr. 13 '95
0.100	May. 03	Jun. 13	Jun. 15	Jul. 14 '95
0.100	Aug. 01	Sep. 13	Sep. 15	Oct. 13 '95
0.100	Oct. 02	Dec. 13	Dec. 15	Jan. 17 '96

Data as orig. reptd.; bef. results of disc. opers. and/or spec. items. Per share data adj. for stk. divs. as of ex-div. date. E-Estimated. NA-Not Available. NM-Not Meaningful. NR-Not Ranked.

Office—1303 E. Algonquin Rd., Schaumburg, IL 60196. **Tel**—(708) 576-5000. **Chrmn**—W. J. Weisz. **Vice Chrmn & CEO**—G. L. Tooker. **Pres & COO**—C. B. Galvin. **Exec VP & CFO**—C. F. Koenemann. **VP & Secy**—R. H. Weise. **Investor Contact**—Calvin Stuart. **Dirs**—E. Bloch, D. R. Clare, W. C. Doud, H. L. Fuller, C. B. Galvin, R. W. Galvin, J. T. Hickey, A. P. Jones, D. R. Jones, W. E. Massey, J. F. Mitchell, T. J. Murrin, J. E. Pepper Jr., S. C. Scott III, G. L. Tooker, G. L. Tucker, W. J. Weisz, B. K. West. **Transfer Agent & Registrar**—Harris Trust & Savings Bank, Chicago. **Incorporated** in Illinois in 1928; reincorporated in Delaware in 1973. **Empl**-132,000. **S&P Analyst:** John D. Coyle, CFA

NBD Bancorp

NYSE Symbol **NBD**
In S&P 500

17-AUG-95 Industry:
Banking

Summary: This bank holding company, the 18th largest in the U.S., recently agreed to combine its operations with those of First Chicago Corp. in a merger of equals.

| S&P Opinion: Hold (★★★) | Recent Price • 35 | Yield • 3.8% |
| | 52 Wk Range • 36-26¾ | 12-Mo. P/E • 9.6 |

Earnings vs. Previous Year
▲=Up ▼=Down ▶=No Change

Quantitative Evaluations

Outlook
(1 Lowest—5 Highest)
• **4⁻**

Fair Value
• **37**

Risk
• **Low**

Earn./Div. Rank
• **A**

Technical Eval.
• **Bearish** since 3/95

Rel. Strength Rank
(1 Lowest—99 Highest)
• **60**

Insider Activity
• **NA**

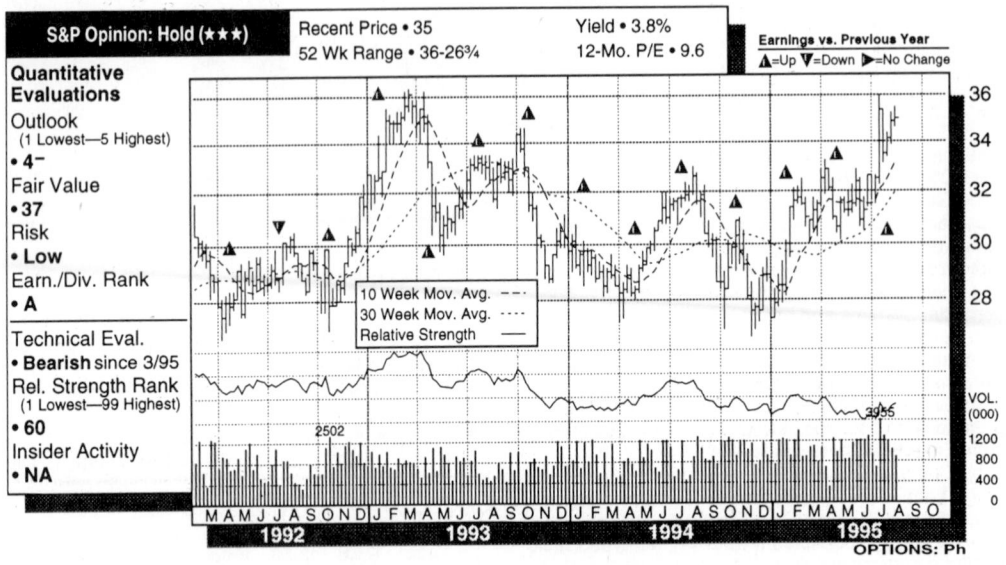

10 Week Mov. Avg. — — —
30 Week Mov. Avg. ·······
Relative Strength ——————

OPTIONS: Ph

Overview - 17-AUG-95

NBD's above-average credit quality and well-controlled expenses should lead to modestly higher earnings in 1995. The recent acquisitions of AmeriFed Financial and Deerbank Corp. have provided a boost to loan volume. The net interest margin, down 26 basis points in the first half of 1995, should level off in the latter half of 1995 as interest rates stabilize. Continued pressure on noninterest income, reflecting weak mortgage activity, will likely be offset by tightly controlled expenses. Despite a declining level of chargeoffs, the loan loss provision may rise moderately on substantial growth in the loan portfolio. Nonperforming loans accounted for only 0.56% of total loans and leases at June 30, 1995, evidence of NBD's strong asset quality.

Valuation - 17-AUG-95

The shares, which have lagged the major regional bank group for much of 1995, recently received a modest boost following news of a proposed merger with First Chicago Corp. The opportunity for cost savings, due to the geographic overlap of the two companies, could be significant, but uncertainty exists over whether such savings can be achieved and in what time frame. In any case, we would hold the shares at current levels until evidence is clear that the merged company is able to generate superior returns.

Key Stock Statistics

S&P EPS Est. 1995	3.65	Tang. Bk. Value/Share	22.18
P/E on S&P Est. 1995	9.6	Beta	1.25
S&P EPS Est. 1996	4.00	Shareholders	26,000
Dividend Rate/Share	1.32	Market cap. (B)	$ 5.4
Shs. outstg. (M)	155.0	Inst. holdings	48%
Avg. daily vol. (M)	0.226	Insider holdings	NA

Value of $10,000 invested 5 years ago: $ 20,174

Fiscal Year Ending Dec. 31

	1995	% Change	1994	% Change	1993	% Change
Revenues (Million $)						
1Q	1,008	30%	773.9	-5%	811.9	—
2Q	1,049	25%	837.3	4%	802.0	—
3Q	—	—	899.7	13%	799.4	—
4Q	—	—	950.0	20%	794.7	—
Yr.	—	—	3,461	8%	3,208	-5%
Income (Million $)						
1Q	140.9	15%	122.9	7%	115.1	16%
2Q	143.4	6%	135.2	10%	122.7	35%
3Q	—	—	147.6	18%	125.2	NM
4Q	—	—	141.5	19%	119.0	6%
Yr.	—	—	547.3	14%	481.8	43%
Earnings Per Share ($)						
1Q	0.88	14%	0.77	8%	0.71	8%
2Q	0.91	8%	0.84	11%	0.76	29%
3Q	E0.93	NM	0.93	21%	0.77	22%
4Q	E0.94	3%	0.91	23%	0.74	6%
Yr.	E3.65	6%	3.45	16%	2.98	41%

Next earnings report expected: mid October

NBD Bancorp

Business Summary - 17-AUG-95

NBD Bancorp, the 18th largest U.S. bank holding company, is the parent of NBD Bank, N.A., the largest bank in Michigan, and NBD Indiana, Inc. It also operates banks in Illinois, Ohio and Florida. The Michigan bank accounted for 67% of assets and 71% of net income in 1994. NBD concentrates on corporate banking, with a recent focus on small and mid-sized companies, retail banking and trust services. Trust activities include the management or administration of more than $103 billion in assets. NBD also serves as investment advisor to The Woodward Funds, a mutual fund family covering a wide variety of investment objectives with $6 billion in assets as of 1994 year-end.

In 1994, average earning assets of $40.0 billion (up from $36.4 billion in 1993) were divided: commercial loans 36%, real estate construction loans 2%, consumer loans 18%, residential mortgage loans 7%, foreign and other loans 4%, investment securities 31% and other 2%. Average sources of funds were demand deposits 14%, savings deposits 18%, money market deposits 12%, time deposits 20%, foreign deposits 6%, short-term borrowings 15%, long-term debt 5%, equity 8% and other 2%.

At year-end 1994, nonperforming loans were $180 million (0.62% of loans and related assets), down from $269 million (1.05%) a year earlier. The allowance for loan losses was 1.49% of loans and related assets at year-end 1994, versus 1.66% at December 31, 1993. Net chargeoffs in 1994 were 0.15% of average loans and leases, against 0.46% in 1993.

At June 30, 1995, Tier 1 and total capital was 7.99% and 12.25%, respectively, versus 8.44% and 12.50% at year-end 1994.

Important Developments

Jul. '95—NBD and First Chicago Corp. (NYSE; FNB) signed a definitive agreement providing for a merger of equals. Following the proposed stock transaction, it is expected that NBD and FNB shareholders will hold 49.9% and 50.1%, respectively, of the common equity of the combined company, which will be named First Chicago NBD Corp. With $120 billion in assets, the combined entity will have dominant market share position in Illinois, Michigan and Indiana. The transaction is expected to be completed in the first quarter of 1996, subject to regulatory and shareholder approvals.

Jul. '95—The company acquired Deerbank Corp. (assets of $760 million) of Deerfield, Ill., for about 3.3 million common shares.

Capitalization

Long Term Debt: $3,012,177,000 (6/95).

Per Share Data ($)

(Year Ended Dec. 31)

	1994	1993	1992	1991	1990	1989
Tangible Bk. Val.	21.11	19.96	18.34	18.22	17.00	15.51
Earnings	3.45	2.98	2.11	2.49	2.50	2.39
Dividends	1.17	1.08	1.02	0.93	0.89	0.75
Payout Ratio	34%	36%	48%	37%	36%	31%
Prices - High	33	36⅜	33⅛	30⅛	24	23⅝
- Low	26¾	28⅝	26¾	20¾	16¼	16⅛
P/E Ratio - High	10	12	16	12	10	10
- Low	8	10	13	8	6	7

Income Statement Analysis (Million $)

	1994	%Chg	1993	%Chg	1992	%Chg	1991
Net Int. Inc.	1,625	4%	1,558	3%	1,510	50%	1,008
Tax Equiv. Adj.	63.6	-12%	72.0	-11%	81.0	5%	77.0
Non Int. Inc.	548	-6%	585	11%	528	60%	330
Loan Loss Prov.	52.0	-57%	120	-47%	228	138%	96.0
% Exp/Op Revs.	58%	—	60%	—	63%	—	61%
Pretax Inc.	814	16%	702	49%	472	23%	383
Eff. Tax Rate	33%	—	31%	—	28%	—	24%
Net Inc.	547	14%	482	43%	338	15%	293
% Net Int. Marg.	4.22%	—	4.48%	—	4.39%	—	4.17%

Balance Sheet & Other Fin. Data (Million $)

	1994	1993	1992	1991	1990	1989
Earning Assets:						
Money Mkt.	1,153	1,114	975	1,172	992	916
Inv. Securities	12,423	10,392	10,902	8,078	7,014	6,442
Com'l Loans	15,889	14,080	13,845	9,979	9,024	8,433
Other Loans	13,341	11,471	11,298	7,743	7,278	6,920
Total Assets	47,111	40,776	40,937	29,513	26,747	25,771
Demand Deposits	6,731	6,668	6,672	3,882	3,944	3,878
Time Deposits	26,498	23,153	24,329	18,310	17,302	15,928
LT Debt	2,385	1,435	939	450	223	265
Common Eqty.	3,292	3,249	2,941	2,089	1,860	1,674

Ratio Analysis

	1994	1993	1992	1991	1990	1989
% Ret. on Assets	1.3	1.2	0.9	1.0	1.1	1.1
% Ret. on Equity	16.6	15.4	11.8	14.3	15.4	16.2
% Loan Loss Resv.	1.5	1.7	1.7	1.5	1.5	1.5
% Loans/Deposits	88.0	85.7	81.1	79.9	76.7	77.5
% Equity to Assets	7.5	7.8	7.3	7.2	6.9	6.6

Dividend Data —Dividends have been paid since 1935. A dividend reinvestment plan is available.

Amt. of Div. $	Date Decl.	Ex-Div. Date	Stock of Record	Payment Date
0.300	Jun. 20	Jul. 14	Jul. 20	Aug. 10 '94
0.300	Sep. 19	Oct. 14	Oct. 20	Nov. 10 '94
0.330	Dec. 19	Jan. 13	Jan. 20	Feb. 10 '95
0.330	Mar. 20	Apr. 12	Apr. 19	May. 10 '95
0.330	Jun. 19	Jul. 18	Jul. 20	Aug. 10 '95

Data as orig. reptd.; bef. results of disc opers. and/or spec. items. Per share data adj. for stk. divs. as of ex-div. date. E-Estimated. NA-Not Available. NM-Not Meaningful. NR-Not Ranked.

Office—611 Woodward Ave., Detroit, MI 48226. **Tel**—(313) 225-1000. **Chrmn & CEO**—V. G. Istock. **Pres & COO**—T. H. Jeffs II. **EVP, CFO & Treas**—P. S. Jones. **SVP & Secy**—D. T. Lis. **Investor Contact**—M. Renee Ahee. **Dirs**—T. E. Adderley, J. K. Baker, D. H. Barden, S. Buschmann, B. B. Butcher, J. W. Day, M. A. Fay, C. T. Fisher III, A. R. Glancy III, D. J. Gormley, J. L. Hudson, Jr., V. G. Istock, T. H. Jeffs II, J. E. Lobbia, R. A. Manoogian, W. T. McCormick, Jr., I. Rose, R. C. Stempel, P. W. Stroh, O. J. Wade. **Transfer Agent & Registrar**—State Street Bank and Trust Co., Boston. **Incorporated** in Delaware in 1972. Founded in 1933. **Empl**-17,800. **S&P Analyst:** Stephen R. Biggar

NACCO Industries

NYSE Symbol **NC**
In S&P 500

08-SEP-95 Industry: Machinery

Summary: One of the world's leading manufacturers of forklift trucks, this company also makes appliances, through Hamilton Beach/Proctor-Silex, and is a U.S. lignite producer.

S&P Opinion: Accumulate (★★★★)	Recent Price • 58	Yield • 1.2%
	52 Wk Range • 64-46%	12-Mo. P/E • 8.5

Quantitative Evaluations

Outlook
(1 Lowest—5 Highest)
• **NA**

Fair Value
• **NA**

Risk
• **Low**

Earn./Div. Rank
• **B+**

Technical Eval.
• **Bearish** since 4/95

Rel. Strength Rank
(1 Lowest—99 Highest)
• **20**

Insider Activity
• **Unfavorable**

Earnings vs. Previous Year
▲=Up ▼=Down ▶=No Change

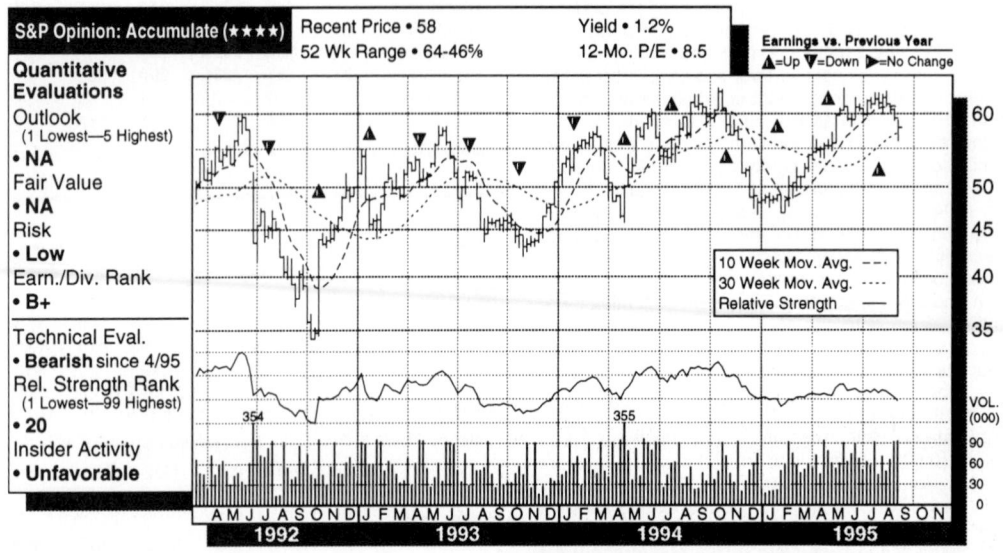

10 Week Mov. Avg. ----
30 Week Mov. Avg. ·····
Relative Strength ——

VOL. (000)

Overview - 08-SEP-95

Forklift volume should advance in 1995, paced by accelerating demand in Europe and Asia. Sales of service parts should increase. Margins will benefit from higher prices. An offset will be higher engineering, warranty and marketing expense, and costs for components sourced in Japan. While coal volume is expected to slip, reflecting plant shutdowns for maintenance and inroads by hydropower, profits will benefit from increased royalty income. Appliance volume will be flat, although the mix will shift to premium-grade products. Margins will benefit from higher productivity and improved scheduling and inventory control. Prices should increase moderately. At the Kitchen Collection, contributions from newly opened stores will offset lower results at mature sites. Aiding earnings will be lower interest expense and tax rates.

Valuation - 08-SEP-95

The rally in the shares of this forklift and appliance manufacturer stalled in mid-1995 amid mounting concern that NC was fast approaching peak-of-cycle profit levels. With NC trading at a large discount to the average stock, we believe there is continued room for capital appreciation. However, we recently downgraded the shares from strong buy to accumulate as the Street's profit expectations have reached levels that NC will have difficulty meeting. Another minor negative is the recent rebound of the dollar against the mark and yen as this serves to enhance the cost position of NC's leading competitors in the forklift market.

Key Stock Statistics

S&P EPS Est. 1995	6.60	Tang. Bk. Value/Share	NM
P/E on S&P Est. 1995	8.8	Beta	1.82
S&P EPS Est. 1996	7.30	Shareholders	1,500
Dividend Rate/Share	0.72	Market cap. (B)	$0.526
Shs. outstg. (M)	9.0	Inst. holdings	44%
Avg. daily vol. (M)	0.018	Insider holdings	NA

Value of $10,000 invested 5 years ago: $ 11,322

Fiscal Year Ending Dec. 31

	1995	% Change	1994	% Change	1993	% Change
Revenues (Million $)						
1Q	502.4	31%	383.3	11%	344.0	8%
2Q	517.6	18%	436.9	22%	358.7	3%
3Q	—	—	480.3	20%	401.7	2%
4Q	—	—	564.4	27%	445.1	5%
Yr.	—	—	1,865	20%	1,549	5%
Income (Million $)						
1Q	12.81	NM	2.77	NM	-0.01	NM
2Q	14.73	60%	9.19	NM	-0.20	NM
3Q	—	—	11.01	NM	2.05	-79%
4Q	—	—	22.30	129%	9.75	-19%
Yr.	—	—	45.27	NM	11.59	-52%
Earnings Per Share ($)						
1Q	1.43	NM	0.31	—	Nil	—
2Q	1.64	59%	1.03	NM	-0.02	NM
3Q	E1.55	26%	1.23	NM	0.23	-79%
4Q	E1.98	-20%	2.49	128%	1.09	-19%
Yr.	E6.60	30%	5.06	NM	1.30	-52%

Next earnings report expected: mid October

Business Summary - 08-SEP-95

Contributions to operating profits (in millions) by business segment in recent years were:

	1994	1993	1992
Forklift trucks	$65.8	$39.6	$44.3
Appliances	25.3	11.8	19.3
Coal	48.6	45.2	41.6
Retail	5.4	4.8	4.4
Bellaire	-0.1	-0.1	-0.1

NACCO Materials Handling Group owns 97% of Hyster-Yale Materials Handling, Inc., one of the world's leading manufacturers of electric and internal combustion engine forklift trucks. Overseas sales accounted for 30% of revenues in 1994. Service parts generate 18% of forklift revenues. In 1994, NC sold 55,751 forklift trucks, up from 43,879 in 1993.

Hamilton Beach/Proctor-Silex, Inc. (80% owned) is one of the leading producers of small electric appliances in North America. Motor-driven products such as blenders, food processors, mixers and electric knives are sold primarily under the Hamilton Beach name, while heat-generating appliances such as toasters, irons and coffeemakers are sold under the Proctor-Silex brand.

North American Coal is a leading producer of lignite. In 1994, it sold 27.2 million tons of lignite, up from 26.5 million in 1993. Some 76% of volume is sold to electric utilities. Reserves at 1994 year-end totaled 2.2 billion tons (including 145 million tons of bituminous coal). Bellaire Corp. has the residual liability related to certain closed mines.

Kitchen Collection operates 119 factory outlet stores in 37 states, specializing in kitchenware and small electric appliances.

Important Developments

Jun. '95—The order backlog for NACCO Materials Handling Group at June 30, 1995, totaled 26,100 units, up 18.6% from the 22,000 unit backlog a year earlier. The order backlog was 25,200 units at March 31, 1995. During 1995's second quarter, NC's unit sales of forklifts increased 17%, year to year, in North America, 34% in Europe and 74% in Asia.

Capitalization

Long Term Debt: $698,008,000 (6/95) of subsid. debt not guaranteed by parent, incl. approx. $140.1 million of lease obligs.
Minority Interest: $41,720,000.
Class A Common Stock: 7,251,265 shs. ($1 par). Officers & directors own 10%.
Class B Common Stock: 1,714,089 shs. ($1 par); 10 votes per sh.; limited transferability; conv. sh.-for-sh. into Cl. A stock.
Officers & directors own 24%.

Per Share Data ($)

(Year Ended Dec. 31)

	1994	1993	1992	1991	1990	1989
Tangible Bk. Val.	31.21	26.39	-26.83	-16.24	-17.00	-16.95
Cash Flow	13.70	9.61	9.89	9.33	10.10	11.15
Earnings	5.06	1.30	2.71	2.31	3.49	6.08
Dividends	0.68	0.65	0.63	0.62	0.60	0.57
Payout Ratio	13%	50%	24%	27%	17%	9%
Prices - High	64	58¼	60	56⅞	70½	56
- Low	45¾	42	34¼	29	22	31¼
P/E Ratio - High	13	45	22	25	20	9
- Low	9	32	13	13	6	5

Income Statement Analysis (Million $)

	1994	%Chg	1993	%Chg	1992	%Chg	1991
Revs.	1,865	20%	1,549	5%	1,482	8%	1,369
Oper. Inc.	215	26%	171	2%	168	4%	162
Depr.	77.3	4%	74.3	16%	63.8	2%	62.3
Int. Exp.	63.4	-9%	69.6	6%	65.8	-14%	76.3
Pretax Inc.	78.5	NM	24.7	-43%	43.5	45%	30.0
Eff. Tax Rate	39%	—	55%	—	45%	—	32%
Net Inc.	45.3	NM	11.6	-52%	24.1	18%	20.5

Balance Sheet & Other Fin. Data (Million $)

	1994	1993	1992	1991	1990	1989
Cash	20.0	29.0	34.0	52.0	101	172
Curr. Assets	587	505	496	532	658	702
Total Assets	1,694	1,642	1,664	1,608	1,722	1,680
Curr. Liab.	481	397	331	374	409	462
LT Debt	483	563	653	631	722	723
Common Eqty.	279	236	240	350	353	301
Total Cap.	802	840	934	1,016	1,111	1,030
Cap. Exp.	53.0	55.0	85.0	60.0	94.0	167
Cash Flow	123	85.9	87.9	82.8	89.7	99

Ratio Analysis

	1994	1993	1992	1991	1990	1989
Curr. Ratio	1.2	1.3	1.5	1.4	1.6	1.5
% LT Debt of Cap.	60.1	67.0	70.0	62.1	65.0	70.2
% Net Inc.of Revs.	2.4	0.7	1.6	1.5	2.2	4.5
% Ret. on Assets	2.7	0.7	1.5	1.2	1.8	4.3
% Ret. on Equity	17.6	4.9	8.1	5.8	9.5	19.7

Dividend Data —Dividends have been paid since 1947.

Amt. of Div. $	Date Decl.	Ex-Div. Date	Stock of Record	Payment Date
0.170	Aug. 10	Aug. 26	Sep. 01	Sep. 15 '94
0.170	Nov. 09	Nov. 25	Dec. 01	Dec. 15 '94
0.170	Feb. 08	Feb. 23	Mar. 01	Mar. 15 '95
0.180	May. 10	May. 25	Jun. 01	Jun. 15 '95
0.180	Aug. 09	Aug. 30	Sep. 01	Sep. 15 '95

Office—5875 Landerbrook Drive, Mayfield Heights, OH 44124-4017. **Tel**—(216) 449-9600. **Chrmn, Pres & CEO**—A. M. Rankin Jr. **VP & Secy**—C. A. Bittenbender. **Sr VP-CFO**—F. B. O'Brien. **Investor Contact**—B. Kenyon. **Dirs**—O. Brown II, J. J. Dwyer, R. M. Gates, L. J. Hendrix Jr., D. W. LaBarre, A. M. Rankin Jr., I. M. Ross, J. C. Sawhill, B. T. Taplin, F. E. Taplin Jr. **Transfer Agent & Registrar**—Society Investment Management & Trust Services, Cleveland. **Incorporated** in Ohio in 1913; reincorporated in Delaware in 1986. **Empl**-11,086. **S&P Analyst:** Stephen R. Klein

Nalco Chemical

NYSE Symbol **NLC**
In S&P 500

05-OCT-95

Industry:
Chemicals

Summary: This company is the world's largest producer of special-ized service chemicals used in water and waste treatment and indus-trial processes.

S&P Opinion: Hold (★★★)	

Recent Price • 34¼	Yield • 3.0%
52 Wk Range • 38⅜-31¼	12-Mo. P/E • 24.8

Quantitative Evaluations

Outlook
(1 Lowest—5 Highest)
• **2⁻**

Fair Value
• **32⅝**

Risk
• **Low**

Earn./Div. Rank
• **A**

Technical Eval.
• **Bullish** since 8/95

Rel. Strength Rank
(1 Lowest—99 Highest)
• **21**

Insider Activity
• **Neutral**

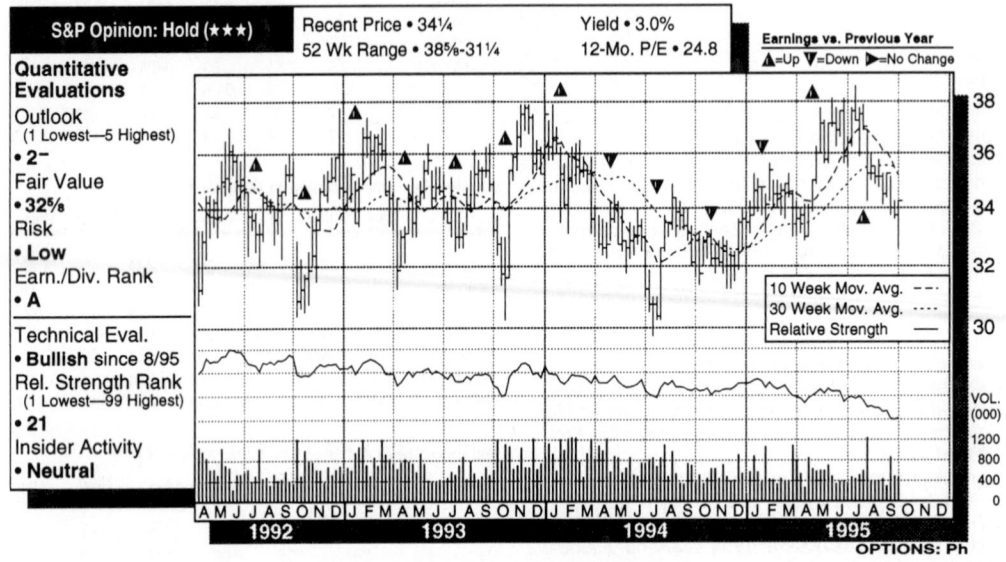

Earnings vs. Previous Year
▲=Up ▼=Down ▶=No Change

10 Week Mov. Avg. – – –
30 Week Mov. Avg. ·····
Relative Strength —

VOL.
(000)

OPTIONS: Ph

Overview - 05-OCT-95

S&P sees sales for ongoing businesses in late 1995 and 1996 continuing to advance at a high-single-digit pace, led by continued good gains in foreign markets for water treatment and process chemicals. Currency exchange rates may become less favorable. Domestic sales growth will likely remain modest, assuming a pickup in industrial activity. Margins should also fully benefit from the restructuring moves implemented since 1994, including employment reductions. We ex-pect that the Exxon venture will begin to post a profit improvement in 1996 after disappointing results during 1995. Share earnings will also be boosted by a contin-uing stock buyback program.

Valuation - 05-OCT-95

The stock of this specialty chemicals company at the end of the third quarter was virtually unchanged, year to date, continuing the lackluster performance of re-cent years mirroring weak earnings. The domestic water treatment industry is experiencing only modest growth as the market matures. We see a better EPS performance in 1995 and 1996 due to healthier eco-nomic conditions in the European and Pacific regions, benefits of a restructuring program, and contributions from the new petroleum chemicals venture with Exxon Corp. Nevertheless, with the shares selling at a higher multiple than those of other chemical companies, we only recommend holding current positions.

Key Stock Statistics

S&P EPS Est. 1995	2.15	Tang. Bk. Value/Share	5.95
P/E on S&P Est. 1995	15.9	Beta	0.96
S&P EPS Est. 1996	2.40	Shareholders	6,000
Dividend Rate/Share	1.00	Market cap. (B)	$ 2.2
Shs. outstg. (M)	67.5	Inst. holdings	73%
Avg. daily vol. (M)	0.118	Insider holdings	NA

Value of $10,000 invested 5 years ago: $ 15,959

Fiscal Year Ending Dec. 31

	1995	% Change	1994	% Change	1993	% Change
Revenues (Million $)						
1Q	315.4	-6%	336.2	NM	339.0	4%
2Q	326.8	-7%	352.0	1%	347.5	2%
3Q	—	—	343.4	-3%	354.0	1%
4Q	—	—	314.0	-10%	348.9	-3%
Yr.	—	—	1,346	-3%	1,389	1%
Income (Million $)						
1Q	37.80	12%	33.80	-4%	35.10	6%
2Q	37.10	12%	33.10	-13%	38.10	5%
3Q	—	—	7.50	-81%	38.70	11%
4Q	—	—	22.70	-44%	40.80	NM
Yr.	—	—	97.10	-36%	152.7	5%
Earnings Per Share ($)						
1Q	0.51	13%	0.45	-2%	0.46	7%
2Q	0.51	16%	0.44	-12%	0.50	4%
3Q	E0.56	NM	0.07	-87%	0.52	16%
4Q	E0.57	97%	0.29	-47%	0.55	2%
Yr.	E2.15	72%	1.25	-38%	2.03	7%

Next earnings report expected: late October

Nalco Chemical

Business Summary - 05-OCT-95

NLC is a producer of specialty chemicals and services. Contributions to sales by business segment:

	1994	1993
Water & waste treatment	26%	24%
Process chemicals	27%	25%
Petroleum chemicals	6%	10%
International	41%	41%

Foreign operations accounted for 36% of sales and 7% of operating profits in 1994.

NLC's service chemicals and services are generally designed to help customers maintain a high level of operating performance and efficiency or improve the quality of their products. Water and waste treatment chemicals are used for water clarification, water pollution control, energy conservation, and the control of corrosion, scale, foam, microbial activity and air emissions in industrial, utility, commercial, institutional and municipality boiler, cooling and process systems. Process chemicals are used during manufacturing processes to protect equipment and facilitate production in such industries as pulp and paper, steel, metals, mining and mineral processing, automotive, electronics, transportation, and food and beverage. Superabsorbent polymers are used for consumer disposable diapers. Petroleum chemicals are used in oil and natural gas drilling and production; enhanced oil recovery; pipeline and transmission systems; and petroleum refining and petrochemical processing (including refined product additives).

Important Developments

Jul. '95—Excluding the businesses transferred to the energy chemicals joint venture with Exxon Co. (formed in September 1994), second quarter sales rose 8%, year to year, reflecting double-digit gains in Europe, Latin America and the Pacific regions.

Feb. '95—Earnings in the second half of 1994 included after-tax charges totaling $54.0 million ($0.70 a share, fully diluted) for expenses related to the formation of the energy chemicals venture and for a restructuring of manufacturing and support operations. NLC reduced its employee count by some 1,300 (about 20%), including 900 now employed by the Exxon joint venture. The venture includes NLC's U.S. petroleum chemicals division, certain of NLC's international petroleum chemical operations, and Exxon's energy chemicals business. It will have annual revenues of $450 million.

Dec. '94—Directors authorized the repurchase of 2 million NLC common shares. Since 1992, NLC has repurchased 4 million common shares.

Capitalization

Long Term Debt: $245,500,000 (6/95).

ESOP Conv. Preferred Stock: $193,300,000.

Per Share Data ($)

(Year Ended Dec. 31)

	1994	1993	1992	1991	1990	1989
Tangible Bk. Val.	5.95	6.04	6.41	2.74	3.04	2.73
Cash Flow	2.54	3.27	3.02	2.75	2.45	2.08
Earnings	1.25	2.03	1.90	1.78	1.71	1.51
Dividends	0.95	0.88	0.84	0.83	0.76	0.68
Payout Ratio	76%	44%	44%	47%	43%	43%
Prices - High	37⅞	37⅞	40⅞	42¼	30⅝	25
- Low	29¾	30¼	30⅜	26⅛	22	17¼
P/E Ratio - High	30	19	22	24	18	17
- Low	24	15	16	15	13	11

Income Statement Analysis (Million $)

	1994	%Chg	1993	%Chg	1992	%Chg	1991
Revs.	1,346	-3%	1,389	1%	1,375	11%	1,237
Oper. Inc.	332	-5%	349	3%	340	15%	296
Depr.	89.2	3%	86.5	9%	79.4	15%	69.1
Int. Exp.	21.8	-21%	27.5	-32%	40.3	44%	27.9
Pretax Inc.	176	-30%	250	5%	238	7%	222
Eff. Tax Rate	45%	—	39%	—	39%	—	38%
Net Inc.	97.0	-37%	153	6%	145	7%	135

Balance Sheet & Other Fin. Data (Million $)

	1994	1993	1992	1991	1990	1989
Cash	45.0	78.0	222	212	120	130
Curr. Assets	362	375	522	518	406	387
Total Assets	1,282	1,212	1,351	1,324	1,037	938
Curr. Liab.	274	190	208	262	176	169
LT Debt	245	252	414	394	282	214
Common Eqty.	518	529	567	330	256	244
Total Cap.	846	861	1,097	1,014	816	720
Cap. Exp.	126	118	131	137	115	86.0
Cash Flow	175	228	214	194	174	157

Ratio Analysis

	1994	1993	1992	1991	1990	1989
Curr. Ratio	1.3	2.0	2.5	2.0	2.3	2.3
% LT Debt of Cap.	29.0	29.3	37.7	38.9	34.6	29.7
% Net Inc.of Revs.	7.2	11.0	10.5	10.9	10.8	11.2
% Ret. on Assets	7.8	12.0	10.8	11.4	13.5	13.9
% Ret. on Equity	16.6	26.1	24.8	42.4	49.3	32.9

Dividend Data

Dividends have been paid since 1928. A dividend reinvestment plan is available. An amended "poison pill" stock purchase rights plan was adopted in 1989.

Amt. of Div. $	Date Decl.	Ex-Div. Date	Stock of Record	Payment Date
0.240	Oct. 21	Nov. 14	Nov. 18	Dec. 09 '94
0.240	Dec. 16	Feb. 13	Feb. 20	Mar. 10 '95
0.250	Apr. 20	May. 15	May. 19	Jun. 09 '95
0.250	Jun. 15	Aug. 16	Aug. 18	Sep. 08 '95

Data as orig. reptd.; bef. results of disc. opers. and/or spec. items. Per share data adj. for stk. divs. as of ex-div. date. E-Estimated. NA-Not Available. NM-Not Meaningful. NR-Not Ranked.

Office—One Nalco Center, Naperville, IL 60563-1198. **Tel**—(708) 305-1000. **Chrmn, Pres & CEO**—E. J. Mooney Jr. **VP-Secy**—S. J. Gioimo. **VP-CFO**—W. E. Buchholz. **Investor Contact**—Dwight Grimestad. **Dirs**—H. G. Bernthal, J. L. Ballesteros, H. Corless, H. M. Dean, J. P. Frazee Jr., A. L. Kelly, F. A. Krehbiel, E. J. Mooney Jr., C. W. Parry, W. A. Pogue, J. J. Shea. **Transfer Agent & Registrar**—First Chicago Trust Co. of New York, Jersey City, N.J. **Incorporated** in Delaware in 1928. **Empl**-5,601. **S&P Analyst:** Richard O'Reilly, CFA

National City

NYSE Symbol **NCC**
In S&P 500

05-OCT-95 Industry: Banking

Summary: A planned merger with Integra Financial will boost assets of this diversified financial services company to $50 billion.

S&P Opinion: Accumulate (★ ★ ★ ★)

Recent Price • 30⅞
52 Wk Range • 31¾-23¾

Yield • 4.2%
12-Mo. P/E • 10.8

Quantitative Evaluations

Outlook
(1 Lowest—5 Highest)
• **4⁻**

Fair Value
• **31⅝**

Risk
• **Low**

Earn./Div. Rank
• **A-**

Technical Eval.
• **Bearish** since 6/95

Rel. Strength Rank
(1 Lowest—99 Highest)
• **71**

Insider Activity
• **Neutral**

Earnings vs. Previous Year
▲=Up ▼=Down ▶=No Change

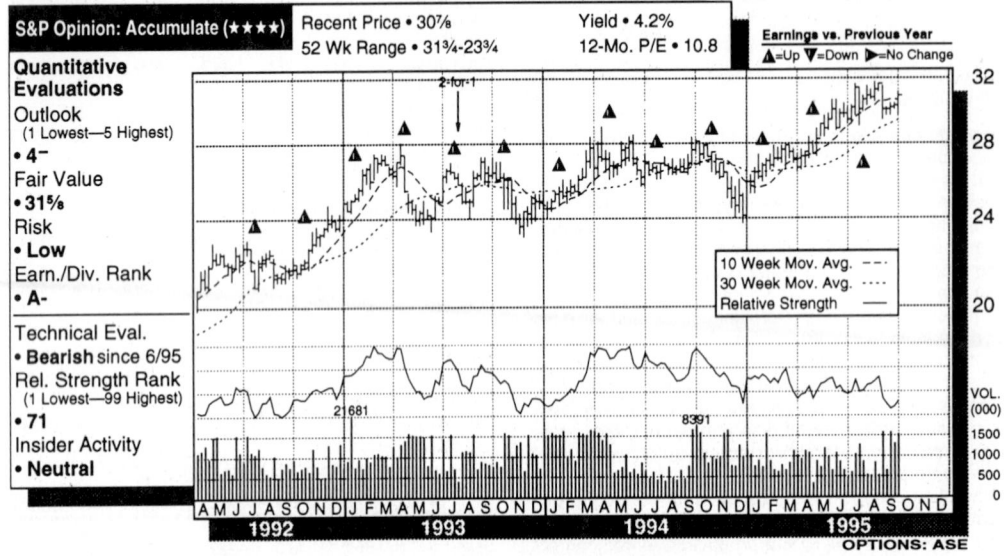

10 Week Mov. Avg. — —
30 Week Mov. Avg. ······
Relative Strength ——

OPTIONS: ASE

Overview - 05-OCT-95

NCC is currently the third largest bank holding company headquartered in Ohio. Earnings are expected to grow 10% in 1996, on higher net interest income from strong loan growth. EPS in the first half of 1995 rose 12%, year to year, reflecting 16% loan growth, which was particularly strong in the consumer and commercial segments, and the benefit of a share repurchase program. Asset quality improved; the ratio of nonperforming assets to loans and other real estate owned fell to 0.56%, from 0.76%; reserves were 1.93% of total loans. During the second quarter, the company acquired acquired Raffensperger, Hughes & Co., Inc., Indiana's largest full-service investment banking and brokerage firm, making it the first bank in the region with authority to deal in corporate debt and equity securities. The acquisition of Pittsburgh-based Integra Financial is planned.

Valuation - 05-OCT-95

The shares have lagged both the regional bank indices and the broader market thus far in 1995, which may reflect in part a view that subsequent to its planned acquisition of Integra Financial, NCC will be less likely to be an acquisition target itself, as well as concern over possible earnings dilution. However, with a P/E of 9.6X estimated 1996 EPS, a growth rate of 10%, a dividend yield over 4%, and a leading position in its marketplace, we see NCC's stock as worth accumulating for the long-term.

Key Stock Statistics

S&P EPS Est. 1995	2.93	Tang. Bk. Value/Share	17.25
P/E on S&P Est. 1995	10.5	Beta	1.18
S&P EPS Est. 1996	3.20	Shareholders	21,700
Dividend Rate/Share	1.32	Market cap. (B)	$ 4.6
Shs. outstg. (M)	147.3	Inst. holdings	57%
Avg. daily vol. (M)	0.325	Insider holdings	NA

Value of $10,000 invested 5 years ago: $ 20,524

Fiscal Year Ending Dec. 31

	1995	% Change	1994	% Change	1993	% Change
Revenues (Million $)						
1Q	797.7	17%	683.6	4%	658.3	10%
2Q	850.2	20%	707.0	5%	670.9	-4%
3Q	—	—	727.7	9%	669.0	-2%
4Q	—	—	787.0	12%	703.7	-13%
Yr.	—	—	2,905	8%	2,702	-3%
Income (Million $)						
1Q	111.0	7%	103.8	9%	95.32	38%
2Q	112.5	6%	105.8	3%	102.4	20%
3Q	—	—	108.4	6%	102.7	15%
4Q	—	—	111.4	8%	103.6	15%
Yr.	—	—	429.4	6%	404.0	16%
Earnings Per Share ($)						
1Q	0.72	14%	0.63	12%	0.57	13%
2Q	0.74	10%	0.67	10%	0.61	20%
3Q	E0.73	6%	0.69	13%	0.61	13%
4Q	E0.74	4%	0.71	15%	0.62	14%
Yr.	E2.93	9%	2.70	12%	2.41	15%

Next earnings report expected: mid October

National City

Business Summary - 05-OCT-95

Based on assets of $32.1 billion at December 31, 1994, National City Corp. was the third largest bank holding company headquartered in Ohio, operating 10 commercial banks with 614 banking offices in Ohio, Kentucky and southern Indiana. It also has subsidiaries engaged providing trust services, mortgage banking, merchant banking, venture capital, item processing and insurance.

Gross loans receivable amounted to $23.0 billion at December 31, 1994, up from $21.3 billion a year earlier, divided as follows:

	1994	1993
Commercial & industrial	38%	41%
Consumer & other	31%	27%
Residential mortgage	18%	19%
Commercial mortgage	11%	11%
Construction	2%	2%

The reserve for loan losses at year-end 1994 was $469.0 million (2.04% of loans receivable), compared to $443.4 million (2.08%) a year earlier. Net charge-offs during 1994 totaled $63.5 million (0.36% of average loans), versus $84.3 million (0.43%). Nonperforming assets at December 31, 1994, amounted to $128.5 million (0.40% of total assets), down from $209.2 million (0.67%) a year earlier.

Total deposits of $24.5 billion at December 31, 1994 consisted of time deposits for individuals 30%, noninterest bearing demand deposits 22%, insured money market accounts 20%, savings and NOW accounts 19%, overseas deposits 7%, and other time deposits 2%. On a tax-equivalent basis, the average yield on interest-earning assets in 1994 was 7.60% (7.48% in 1993), while the average rate paid on interest-bearing liabilities was 3.55% (3.26%), for a net spread of 4.05% (4.22%).

Important Developments

Aug. '95—NCC agreed to acquire NYSE-listed Integra Financial Corp. (ITG), a $15 billion bank holding company based in Pittsburgh, by exchanging two common shares for each of ITG's 16.4 million shares. The transaction is valued at $2.1 billion (1.96X book value). The combined company will have assets of $50 billion, deposits of $35 billion and stockholders' equity of $4 billion. The transaction, which is subject to regulatory and shareholder approval, is expected to close in the 1996 second quarter.

Capitalization

Long Term Debt: $993,186,000 (6/95).

Per Share Data ($)

(Year Ended Dec. 31)

	1994	1993	1992	1991	1990	1989
Tangible Bk. Val.	16.36	16.15	14.54	12.00	11.46	12.43
Earnings	2.70	2.41	2.09	1.81	1.93	2.17
Dividends	1.18	1.06	0.94	0.94	0.94	0.87
Payout Ratio	44%	44%	45%	52%	49%	40%
Prices - High	29	28⅛	24⅞	21⅛	20	20¾
- Low	23¾	23⅛	18	14	11⅜	15⅜
P/E Ratio - High	11	12	12	12	10	10
- Low	9	10	9	8	6	7

Income Statement Analysis (Million $)

	1994	%Chg	1993	%Chg	1992	%Chg	1991
Net Int. Inc.	1,237	3%	1,200	4%	1,153	24%	931
Tax Equiv. Adj.	29.5	-17%	35.7	-15%	42.0	-7%	45.0
Non Int. Inc.	853	7%	800	10%	726	30%	560
Loan Loss Prov.	79.4	-15%	93.1	-28%	129	-32%	191
% Exp/Op Revs.	66%	—	66%	—	68%	—	66%
Pretax Inc.	618	8%	571	23%	464	49%	311
Eff. Tax Rate	31%	—	29%	—	25%	—	26%
Net Inc.	429	6%	404	16%	347	50%	231
% Net Int. Marg.	4.65%	—	4.80%	—	4.65%	—	4.60%

Balance Sheet & Other Fin. Data (Million $)

	1994	1993	1992	1991	1990	1989
Earning Assets:						
Money Mkt.	681	1,219	1,331	1,505	683	903
Inv. Securities	4,395	5,166	5,499	4,411	3,962	3,989
Com'l Loans	8,884	8,657	8,337	7,025	7,333	7,229
Other Loans	14,151	12,629	10,401	8,492	8,614	8,002
Total Assets	32,114	31,068	28,964	24,170	23,743	22,972
Demand Deposits	5,332	5,215	4,819	3,573	3,677	3,444
Time Deposits	19,140	17,848	17,766	14,752	14,644	13,820
LT Debt	744	510	645	644	554	397
Common Eqty.	2,414	2,565	2,300	1,729	1,609	1,507

Ratio Analysis

	1994	1993	1992	1991	1990	1989
% Ret. on Assets	1.4	1.4	1.2	1.0	1.0	1.2
% Ret. on Equity	17.1	16.1	15.3	12.9	15.0	18.6
% Loan Loss Resv.	2.0	2.1	2.0	1.9	1.6	1.7
% Loans/Deposits	94.1	92.3	83.0	84.7	87.0	88.2
% Equity to Assets	7.8	8.1	7.6	7.2	6.8	6.7

Dividend Data

—Cash has been paid in each year since 1936. A dividend reinvestment plan is available.

Amt. of Div. $	Date Decl.	Ex-Div. Date	Stock of Record	Payment Date
0.300	Oct. 03	Oct. 06	Oct. 13	Nov. 01 '94
0.320	Jan. 03	Jan. 09	Jan. 13	Feb. 01 '95
0.330	Jul. 03	Jul. 11	Jul. 13	Aug. 01 '95
0.330	Oct. 02	Oct. 11	Oct. 13	Nov. 01 '95

Data as orig. reptd.; bef. results of disc opers. and/or spec. items. Per share data adj. for stk. divs. as of ex-div. date. E-Estimated. NA-Not Available. NM-Not Meaningful. NR-Not Ranked.

Office—National City Center, 1900 East Ninth St., Cleveland, OH 44114. **Tel**—(216) 575-2000. **Chrmn, Pres & CEO**—D. A. Daberko. **EVP & CFO**—R. G. Siefers. **SVP & Secy**—D. L. Zoeller. **SVP, Treas & Investor Contact**—Thomas A. Richlovsky (216-575-2126). **Dirs**—S. H. Austin, J. M. Biggar, C. H. Bowman, E. B. Brandon, J. G. Breen, D. Collins, D. A. Daberko, R. E. Disbrow, D. E. Evans, O. N. Frenzel III, B. P. Healy, J. H. Lemieux, A. S. Miles, W. R. Robertson, S. A. Stitle, M. Weiss. **Transfer Agent & Registrar**—National City Bank, Cleveland. **Incorporated** in Delaware in 1973; bank chartered in 1865. **Empl**-20,306. **S&P Analyst:** Thomas C. Ferguson

National Semiconductor

NYSE Symbol **NSM**
In S&P 500

20-SEP-95

Industry:
Electronics/Electric

Summary: This company is a leading manufacturer of a broad line of semiconductors, including analog, digital and mixed-signal integrated circuits.

S&P Opinion: Hold (★★★)	Recent Price • 29¾	Yield • Nil
	52 Wk Range • 33⅞-14⅜	12-Mo. P/E • 13.9

Earnings vs. Previous Year
▲=Up ▼=Down ▶=No Change

Quantitative Evaluations

Outlook
(1 Lowest—5 Highest)
• **5⁺**

Fair Value
• **35¾**

Risk
• **Average**

Earn./Div. Rank
• **B-**

Technical Eval.
• **Bullish** since 9/95

Rel. Strength Rank
(1 Lowest—99 Highest)
• **73**

Insider Activity
• **Unfavorable**

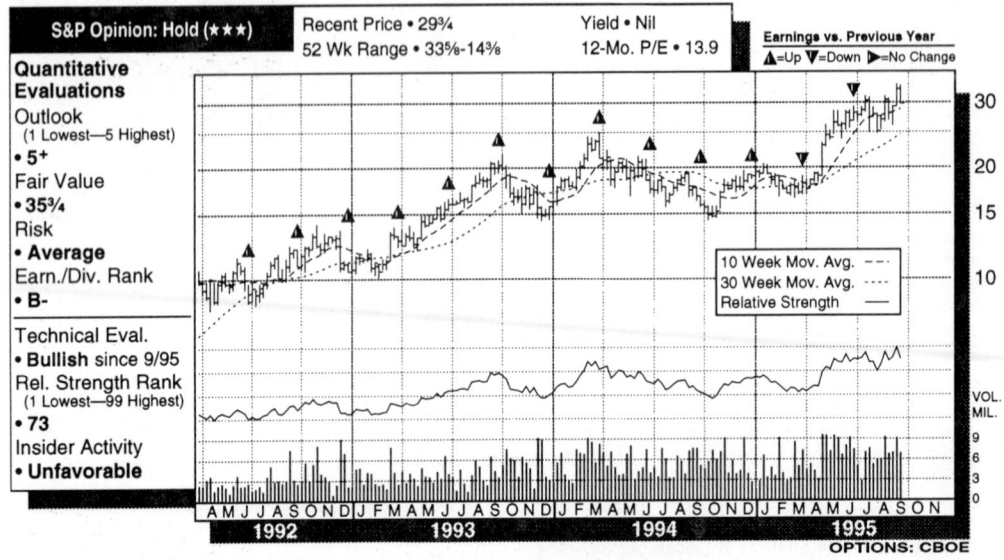

10 Week Mov. Avg. ----
30 Week Mov. Avg. ·······
Relative Strength ——

OPTIONS: CBOE

Overview - 20-SEP-95

Sales in fiscal 1996 are projected to increase approximately 25%. NSM is beginning to benefit from a strategic focus on more value-added offerings versus traditional commodity products. Specifically, the company should continue to experience strong demand for analog and mixed signal products in key communications, networking and personal systems markets. Capacity additions are also on track to help meet pent-up demand. Somewhat offsetting will be lower sales of older commodity products, especially bipolar lines. Opearing margins are expected to widen, as a more profitable product mix offsets higher operating expenses. The tax rate is expected to reach 25%, up from 20% in fiscal 1995. EPS on a fully diluted basis is expected to reach $2.45 a share ($2.60 primary), versus last year's $1.92 ($2.02).

Valuation - 20-SEP-95

We continue to see positive signs from NSM, mainly first quarter sales that increased 26% from a year earlier and 4% sequentially. While this rate of growth is still well below the 35%-40% industry growth rate expected for calendar 1995, the improved performance is encouraging. NSM's focus on the higher margin, value-added segment of the market is beginning to reap benefits and should allow it to achieve sales growth comparable to industry growth levels over the next six to 18 months. Nevertheless, we believe this improving outlook has already been discounted in the stock, and we would not recommend adding to positions at this time.

Key Stock Statistics

S&P EPS Est. 1996	2.60	Tang. Bk. Value/Share	10.05
P/E on S&P Est. 1996	11.4	Beta	1.71
S&P EPS Est. 1997	3.05	Shareholders	13,000
Dividend Rate/Share	Nil	Market cap. (B)	$ 3.8
Shs. outstg. (M)	123.7	Inst. holdings	84%
Avg. daily vol. (M)	1.529	Insider holdings	NA

Value of $10,000 invested 5 years ago: $ 41,034

Fiscal Year Ending May 31

	1996	% Change	1995	% Change	1994	% Change
Revenues (Million $)						
1Q	698.8	26%	553.8	NM	558.9	18%
2Q	—	—	584.4	NM	582.4	18%
3Q	—	—	571.4	5%	544.7	11%
4Q	—	—	669.8	10%	609.4	9%
Yr.	—	—	2,379	4%	2,295	14%
Income (Million $)						
1Q	73.50	25%	59.00	13%	52.20	—
2Q	—	—	67.00	10%	60.70	—
3Q	—	—	57.00	-11%	63.80	137%
4Q	—	—	81.20	-1%	82.40	78%
Yr.	—	—	264.2	2%	259.1	99%
Earnings Per Share ($)						
1Q	0.56	27%	0.44	13%	0.39	129%
2Q	E0.65	27%	0.51	11%	0.46	70%
3Q	E0.60	40%	0.43	-10%	0.48	153%
4Q	E0.80	29%	0.62	-2%	0.63	80%
Yr.	E2.60	29%	2.02	2%	1.98	102%

Next earnings report expected: early December

National Semiconductor

20-SEP-95

Business Summary - 18-SEP-95

National Semiconductor is a leading manufacturer of semiconductor components, including analog intensive, digital and mixed-signal complex integrated circuits. Revenues by product line in fiscal 1995 were:

	1995
Analog/mixed signal	56%
Bipolar/CMOS	22%
Discretes, microcontrollers & customized ICs	22%

The company is a leading supplier of analog and mixed signal products, serving broad-based markets such as the industrial and consumer markets and more narrowly defined markets such as Ethernet Local Area Networks (LANs) and automotive. Products which process analog information, convert analog to digital or convert digital to analog are considered analog and mixed signal. Analog devices control continuously variable functions (such as light, color, sound and power) and are used in automotive, telecommunications, audio/video and many industrial applications. The company's analog products include high performance operational amplifiers, power management circuits, data acquisition circuits and voltage regulators.

NSM also sells bipolar and complimentary metal oxide silicon (CMOS) logic and memory products, which are more mature products serving broad markets in data processing, switching equipment and personal computing.

Other product offerings include discretes, low density microcontrollers and customized integrated circuits.

International operations accounted for 57% of sales in 1994-5, versus 56% in 1993-4.

During fiscal 1995, the company acquired Comlinear, Inc., a producer of analog circuits. NSM also became a majority owner in a joint venture in Shanghai, Peoples' Republic of China (PRC). The joint venture will produce integrate circuit boards for telecommunications and other enterprises within the PRC.

Important Developments

Sep. '95—NSM said it will place privately $225 million in convertible subordinated notes due 2002, plus up to $33.75 million in notes to cover over-allotments. Proceeds will be used to expand manufacturing capacity and for general corporate purposes. Separately, NSM sold its Ethernet adapter card business to Microdyne Corp. Terms of the transaction were not disclosed.

Aug. '95—The company announced a $600 million expansion at its South Portland, Maine, facility for its eight-inch wafer manufacturing plant. The investment is part of a $1.3 billion investment by NSM in new manufacturing facilities.

Capitalization

Long Term Debt: $118,000,000 (8/27/95).

$3.25 Depositary Conv. Pfd. Stk.: 3,450,000 shs. ($50 liquid. value); ea. conv. into 3.5273 com.; represents 0.10 sh. of $32.50 conv. pfd. stk.

Per Share Data ($)

(Year Ended May 31)

	1995	1994	1993	1992	1991	1990
Tangible Bk. Val.	10.31	7.60	4.92	3.90	5.14	6.70
Cash Flow	3.50	3.36	2.36	0.28	0.17	1.34
Earnings	2.02	1.98	0.98	-1.98	-1.55	-0.38
Dividends	Nil	Nil	Nil	Nil	Nil	Nil
Payout Ratio	Nil	Nil	Nil	Nil	Nil	Nil
Cal. Yrs.	1994	1993	1992	1991	1990	1989
Prices - High	25	21¾	14⅛	9	8⅞	10
- Low	14⅜	10⅛	6⅜	3⅞	3	6¾
P/E Ratio - High	12	11	14	NM	NM	NM
- Low	7	5	7	NM	NM	NM

Income Statement Analysis (Million $)

	1995	%Chg	1994	%Chg	1993	%Chg	1992
Revs.	2,379	4%	2,295	14%	2,014	17%	1,718
Oper. Inc.	495	10%	449	55%	290	76%	165
Depr.	185	11%	167	4%	160	NM	160
Int. Exp.	6.7	103%	3.3	-25%	4.4	29%	3.4
Pretax Inc.	329	8%	304	103%	150	NM	-116
Eff. Tax Rate	20%	—	15%	—	13%	—	NM
Net Inc.	264	2%	259	99%	130	NM	-119

Balance Sheet & Other Fin. Data (Million $)

	1995	1994	1993	1992	1991	1990
Cash	467	467	332	159	193	129
Curr. Assets	1,178	1,016	842	595	613	625
Total Assets	2,236	1,748	1,477	1,149	1,191	1,378
Curr. Liab.	686	577	506	473	417	427
LT Debt	82.5	15.0	37.0	34.0	20.0	64.0
Common Eqty.	1,234	933	540	414	533	692
Total Cap.	1,509	1,139	892	588	693	895
Cap. Exp.	479	271	234	189	110	182
Cash Flow	438	408	273	30.0	18.0	138

Ratio Analysis

	1995	1994	1993	1992	1991	1990
Curr. Ratio	1.7	1.8	1.7	1.3	1.5	1.5
% LT Debt of Cap.	5.5	1.3	4.2	5.8	2.9	7.2
% Net Inc.of Revs.	11.1	11.3	6.5	NM	NM	NM
% Ret. on Assets	13.3	15.2	9.8	NM	NM	NM
% Ret. on Equity	23.4	31.3	23.4	NM	NM	NM

Dividend Data —No common dividends have ever been paid. A "poison pill" stock purchase rights plan was adopted in 1988.

Data as orig. reptd.; bef. results of disc. opers. and/or spec. items. Per share data adj. for stk. divs. as of ex-div. date. E-Estimated. NA-Not Available. NM-Not Meaningful. NR-Not Ranked.

Office—2900 Semiconductor Drive, Santa Clara, CA 95052-8090. **Tel**—(408) 721-5000. **Chrmn, Pres & CEO**—G. F. Amelio. **VP-Fin & CFO**—D. Macleod. **VP-Secy**—J. M. Clark III. **Investor Contact**—James Foltz. **Dirs**—G. F. Amelio, G. P. Arnold, R. Beshar, M. A. Maidique, E. R. McCracken, J. T. O'Rourke, C. E. Sporck, D. E. Weeden. **Transfer Agent & Registrar**—First National Bank of Boston. **Incorporated** in Delaware in 1959. **Empl**-22,400. **S&P Analyst:** John D. Coyle, CFA

Nat'l Service Industries

NYSE Symbol **NSI**
In S&P 500

01-OCT-95

Industry: Conglomerate/diversified

Summary: This diversified company has interests in lighting equipment, textile rentals and specialty chemicals, and to a lesser extent, operates insulation and envelope businesses.

S&P Opinion: Hold (★★★)	Recent Price • 29¼	Yield • 3.8%
	52 Wk Range • 31¼-24⅞	12-Mo. P/E • 15.2

Earnings vs. Previous Year
▲=Up ▼=Down ▶=No Change

Quantitative Evaluations

Outlook
(1 Lowest—5 Highest)
• **2+**

Fair Value
• **28¾**

Risk
• **Low**

Earn./Div. Rank
• **A**

Technical Eval.
• **Bearish** since 8/95

Rel. Strength Rank
(1 Lowest—99 Highest)
• **34**

Insider Activity
• **NA**

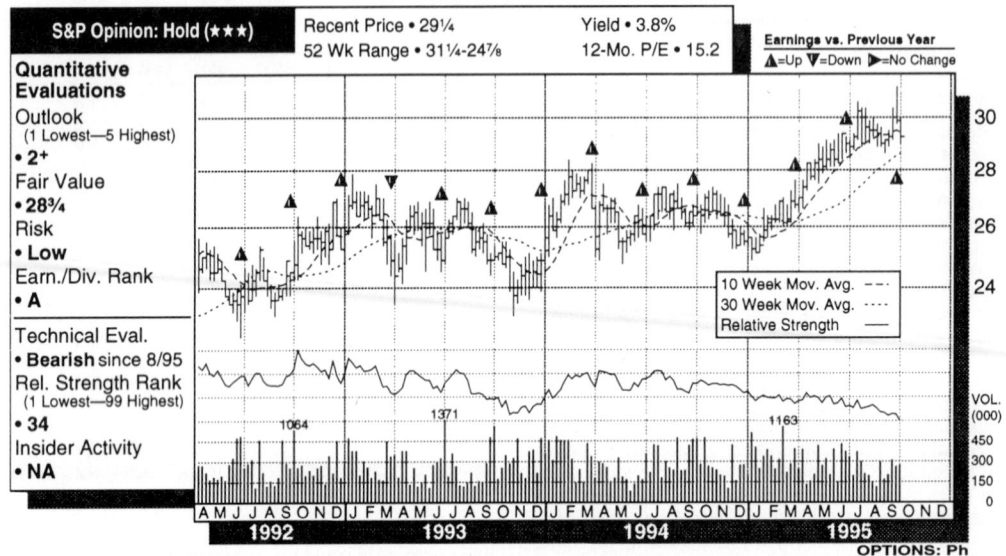

10 Week Mov. Avg. – – –
30 Week Mov. Avg. ⋯⋯⋯
Relative Strength ——

1992   1993   1994   1995

OPTIONS: Ph

Overview - 26-SEP-95

Revenue growth should continue through 1996 as the company invests heavily in its sales and marketing programs, despite the absence of sales from the marketing services business, which was divested in September 1994. The lighting equipment business is expected to improve profitability with the execution of its North American manufacturing and distribution strategy. Recent initiatives to improve operating performance in the textile rental business, which reversed a trend of declining profits in the third quarter of fiscal 1995, should continue to strengthen future results. The specialty chemical business, which was weak in fiscal 1995, should benefit with progress in its European operations. Higher net income should result with the operating improvements, which should offset expected less favorable economic conditions.

Valuation - 26-SEP-95

The shares of this diversified company have trended upward during 1995. However, the stock appears to be fairly valued based on its expected growth, and it is currently trading close to its historical price/earnings ratio. An increase in the stock repurchase program from two million to four million shares a year could improve future EPS results. With a high dividend yield and relatively low volatility, the stock is attractive to investors looking for high income and a low level of risk.

Key Stock Statistics

S&P EPS Est. 1996	2.10	Tang. Bk. Value/Share	12.91
P/E on S&P Est. 1996	13.9	Beta	0.46
Dividend Rate/Share	1.12	Shareholders	8,000
Shs. outstg. (M)	48.3	Market cap. (B)	$ 1.4
Avg. daily vol. (M)	0.053	Inst. holdings	60%
		Insider holdings	NA

Value of $10,000 invested 5 years ago: $ 13,240

Fiscal Year Ending Aug. 31

	1995	% Change	1994	% Change	1993	% Change
Revenues (Million $)						
1Q	481.0	5%	459.9	6%	434.0	8%
2Q	465.8	6%	439.3	3%	427.0	9%
3Q	505.8	5%	481.0	5%	460.0	11%
4Q	518.0	3%	501.6	4%	484.0	14%
Yr.	1,971	5%	1,882	4%	1,805	10%
Income (Million $)						
1Q	21.11	10%	19.17	3%	18.59	5%
2Q	17.58	8%	16.27	11%	14.63	-7%
3Q	25.63	12%	22.93	12%	20.51	39%
4Q	29.79	22%	24.33	14%	21.39	2%
Yr.	94.10	14%	82.70	10%	75.12	1%
Earnings Per Share ($)						
1Q	0.43	10%	0.39	3%	0.38	6%
2Q	0.36	9%	0.33	10%	0.30	-6%
3Q	0.53	15%	0.46	12%	0.41	3%
4Q	0.62	27%	0.49	14%	0.43	2%
Yr.	1.93	16%	1.67	10%	1.52	1%

Next earnings report expected: late December

Nat'l Service Industries

01-OCT-95

Business Summary - 08-AUG-95

National Service Industries conducts operations through six divisions. Contributions by business segment in fiscal 1994 were:

	Revs.	Profits
Lighting equipment	40%	35%
Textile rental	29%	34%
Chemical	18%	25%
Other	13%	6%

The lighting equipment division, through Lithonia Lighting (the North American U.S. manufacturer of lighting equipment) and other units, produces fluorescent fixtures for commercial, industrial, and institutional applications, high-intensity discharge fixtures for industrial and commercial use and outdoor lighting, downlighting, track lighting, vandal-resistant fixtures, emergency lighting, lighting and dimming controls and manufactured wiring systems.

The textile division, including National Linen Service, rents table linen, bed linens, towels, uniforms, operating room packs and dust control materials.

The chemical division manufactures chemical products used primarily in maintenance, sanitation and water treatment. Products include soaps, detergents, waxes and disinfectants.

Other divisions distribute insulation materials, provide insulation contract services, envelopes and filing systems and provide sales aids for the carpet industry.

Important Developments

Jun. '95—The lighting equipment division acquired Infranor-Canada, Inc., a small high-performance outdoor lighting products company. Production also began in the division's new facility in Monterrey, Mexico. Separately, NSI said it had repurchased about 947,000 shares during the current fiscal year.

Mar. '95—The board of directors increased the company's standing authority to purchase shares from the previous two million shares per fiscal year to the current four million shares. Earlier, in September 1994, the company completed the sale of its marketing services division for a small gain. The divestiture of the division was expected to remove about $30 million from anticipated fiscal 1995 sales, and negligibly impact profits.

Capitalization

Long Term Debt: $26,807,000 (5/95).

Per Share Data ($)

(Year Ended Aug. 31)

	1995	1994	1993	1992	1991	1990
Tangible Bk. Val.	NA	12.49	11.63	12.06	11.67	12.62
Cash Flow	NA	2.89	2.47	2.40	1.67	2.78
Earnings	1.93	1.67	1.52	1.50	0.65	2.02
Dividends	1.11	1.07	1.03	0.99	0.97	0.90
Payout Ratio	58%	64%	68%	66%	149%	45%
Prices - High	30⅞	28⅜	27⅞	27	28¼	28¾
- Low	24⅞	24¾	23⅛	22½	19	22⅛
P/E Ratio - High	16	17	18	18	43	14
- Low	13	15	15	15	29	11

Income Statement Analysis (Million $)

	1994	%Chg	1993	%Chg	1992	%Chg	1991
Revs.	1,882	4%	1,805	10%	1,634	2%	1,602
Oper. Inc.	204	13%	181	7%	169	4%	163
Depr.	60.5	28%	47.4	6%	44.7	-11%	50.2
Int. Exp.	3.7	-26%	5.0	84%	2.7	-30%	3.8
Pretax Inc.	132	10%	120	3%	117	139%	49.0
Eff. Tax Rate	37%	—	37%	—	37%	—	34%
Net Inc.	82.7	10%	75.1	1%	74.1	130%	32.2

Balance Sheet & Other Fin. Data (Million $)

	1994	1993	1992	1991	1990	1989
Cash	61.0	21.0	110	88.0	125	129
Curr. Assets	608	557	568	549	576	570
Total Assets	1,107	1,088	1,042	1,012	962	888
Curr. Liab.	251	244	210	198	142	134
LT Debt	26.9	28.4	28.4	31.4	27.5	20.8
Common Eqty.	727	704	683	661	675	613
Total Cap.	833	817	804	792	804	736
Cap. Exp.	42.5	82.2	49.8	58.4	82.9	66.5
Cash Flow	143	123	119	82.0	137	127

Ratio Analysis

	1994	1993	1992	1991	1990	1989
Curr. Ratio	2.4	2.3	2.7	2.8	4.0	4.3
% LT Debt of Cap.	3.2	3.5	3.5	4.0	3.4	2.8
% Net Inc.of Revs.	4.4	4.2	4.5	2.0	6.1	6.2
% Ret. on Assets	7.6	7.1	7.2	3.3	10.8	11.1
% Ret. on Equity	11.6	10.8	11.0	4.8	15.4	16.2

Dividend Data

Dividends have been paid since 1937. A "poison pill" stock purchase right was adopted in 1988.

Amt. of Div. $	Date Decl.	Ex-Div. Date	Stock of Record	Payment Date
0.270	Sep. 21	Sep. 23	Sep. 29	Oct. 10 '94
0.280	Dec. 21	Dec. 23	Dec. 30	Jan. 10 '95
0.280	Mar. 17	Mar. 21	Mar. 27	Apr. 05 '95
0.280	Jun. 21	Jun. 28	Jun. 30	Jul. 12 '95
0.280	Sep. 20	Sep. 27	Sep. 29	Oct. 10 '95

Data as orig. reptd.; bef. results of disc. opers. and/or spec. items. Per share data adj. for stk. divs. as of ex-div. date. E-Estimated. NA-Not Available. NM-Not Meaningful. NR-Not Ranked.

Office—1420 Peachtree St. N.E., Atlanta, GA 30309. **Tel**—(404) 853-1000. **Chrmn, CEO & Investor Contact**—D. Raymond Riddle. **Pres**—D. W. Hubble. **SVP-Fin**—J. R. Hipps. **Treas**—J. Enis. **Secy**—K. Murphy. **Dirs**—J. L. Clendenin, J. Hill, Jr., R. M. Holder, Jr., D. W. Hubble, F. R. Johnson, J. C. Kennedy, D. R. Keough, B. D. Langton, D. Levy, B. Marcus, J. G. Medlin, Jr., D. R. Riddle, B. L. Seigel, E. Zaban. **Transfer Agent & Registrar**—Wachovia Bank & Trust Co., Winston-Salem, NC. **Incorporated** in Delaware in 1928. **Empl**- 22,200. **S&P Analyst:** Philip Birbara

NationsBank Corp.

07-AUG-95 Industry:
Banking

Summary: This bank holding company, the third largest in the U.S., with assets of $184 billion, operates offices in nine states and the District of Columbia.

S&P Opinion: Accumulate (★★★★)	Recent Price • 57⅜	Yield • 3.5%
	52 Wk Range • 57¾-43⅜	12-Mo. P/E • 9.1

Quantitative Evaluations

Outlook
(1 Lowest—5 Highest)
• **5⁻**

Fair Value
• **65¾**

Risk
• **Low**

Earn./Div. Rank
• **A-**

Technical Eval.
• **Bearish** since 1/95

Rel. Strength Rank
(1 Lowest—99 Highest)
• **58**

Insider Activity
• **NA**

Earnings vs. Previous Year
▲=Up ▼=Down ▶=No Change

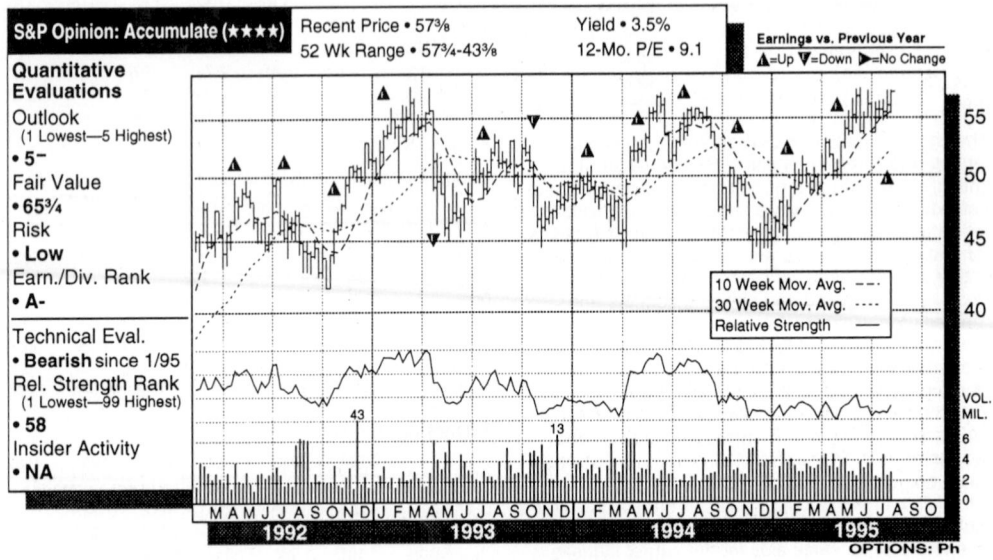

10 Week Mov. Avg. – – –
30 Week Mov. Avg. ·······
Relative Strength ——

OPTIONS: Ph

Overview - 07-AUG-95

Loan growth should continue at a strong pace (10% to 12%) in 1995, led by gains in the commercial and residential mortgage portfolio. Pressures on the net interest margin, resulting from a less favorable funding mix, should begin to ease later in 1995, leading to expected growth in net interest income of about 5%. An increased contribution from noninterest income, aided by gains in mortgage servicing and investment banking income, and operating expense control measures should also help NB achieve its 1995 earnings growth target of at least 12%. Asset quality has strengthened, with nonperforming assets down 23%, year to year, to $1.099 billion at June 30, 1995. The allowance for loan losses has declined somewhat to the 1.95% level, and may trend even lower to 1.70% before provisions are increased.

Valuation - 07-AUG-95

Above average earnings growth in 1995, resulting from healthy loan growth in the company's service territory, acquisitions, strong credit quality and rising fee-based income, should continue to propel the shares higher. A share repurchase program authorized in late 1994 will also benefit earnings comparisons. Trading at less than eight times the 1996 earnings estimate of $7.50 a share, a discount to the regional bank group and below the expected earnings growth rate, the shares are attractive for above-average appreciation in the year ahead.

Key Stock Statistics

S&P EPS Est. 1995	6.85	Tang. Bk. Value/Share	35.32
P/E on S&P Est. 1995	8.4	Beta	2.05
S&P EPS Est. 1996	7.50	Shareholders	105,800
Dividend Rate/Share	2.00	Market cap. (B)	$ 15.6
Shs. outstg. (M)	271.4	Inst. holdings	66%
Avg. daily vol. (M)	0.589	Insider holdings	NA

Value of $10,000 invested 5 years ago: $ 15,528

Fiscal Year Ending Dec. 31

	1995	% Change	1994	% Change	1993	% Change
Revenues (Million $)						
1Q	3,796	23%	3,092	30%	2,375	-13%
2Q	—	—	3,146	31%	2,408	-2%
3Q	—	—	3,346	27%	2,641	3%
4Q	—	—	3,529	19%	2,968	36%
Yr.	—	—	13,113	26%	10,392	5%
Income (Million $)						
1Q	443.0	6%	417.0	48%	281.0	-9%
2Q	467.0	7%	437.0	43%	306.0	22%
3Q	—	—	431.0	26%	341.0	-3%
4Q	—	—	405.0	9%	373.0	59%
Yr.	—	—	1,690	30%	1,301	14%
Earnings Per Share ($)						
1Q	1.60	5%	1.52	37%	1.11	-13%
2Q	1.71	8%	1.58	32%	1.20	20%
3Q	E1.75	—	1.55	17%	1.33	-5%
4Q	E1.80	—	1.46	7%	1.37	49%
Yr.	E6.85	—	6.12	22%	5.00	9%

Next earnings report expected: mid October

NationsBank Corp.

Business Summary - 07-AUG-95

On December 31, 1991, NCNB, the seventh largest banking organization in the U.S. and the largest in the Southeast, merged with C&S/Sovran Corp., the 12th largest in the U.S., and changed its name to NationsBank. The company is now the third largest U.S. bank holding company, with total assets of $184 billion at June 30, 1995. NB serves its customer base through three lines of business--the General Bank, the Institutional Group, and Financial Services. The General Bank serves consumers and small businesses through 1,855 banking offices in nine states and the District of Columbia. Specialized businesses including mortgage, bank card, and trust and mutual funds are also housed in the General Bank. The Institutional Group serves corporate customers by providing products and services including lending, investment banking, trading and treasury management. Financial Services contains nonbank businesses, primarily consumer finance and commercial finance units.

During 1994, average earning assets of $148.4 billion ($119.2 billion in 1993) were divided: commercial loans 35%, residential mortgage 10%, home equity 2%, consumer loans 14%, other loans 3%, investment securities 19%, trading account assets 7%, and other short-term assets 10%. Average sources of funds were noninterest-bearing deposits 12%, consumer deposits 38%, other time deposits 7%, short-term borrowings 29%, long-term debt 5%, equity 6%, and other 3%.

At December 31, 1994, nonperforming assets totaled $1.1 billion (1.10% of loans and related assets), down from $1.8 billion (1.92%) a year earlier. The reserve for loan losses was 2.11% of loans (2.36%). Net chargeoffs in 1994 were 0.33% of average loans and related assets (0.51%).

Important Developments

Jul. '95—NB announced a definitive agreement to purchase South Florida-based CSF Holdings, parent of Citizens Federal Bank (assets of $4 billion), for $516 million in cash. The transaction is expected to close around 1995 year-end.

Jun. '95—The company announced a definitive agreement to purchase Miami, Fla.-based Intercontinental Bank (assets of $1.1 billion) for $208 million in NB common stock.

Jun. '95—NationsBank agreed to sell its corporate trust business, which includes bond trustee, registrar, paying agent and escrow services, to Bank of New York for an undisclosed amount.

Capitalization

Long Term Debt: $9,816,000,000 (3/95).
Preferred Stock: $110,000,000.

Per Share Data ($) (Year Ended Dec. 31)

	1994	1993	1992	1991	1990	1989
Tangible Bk. Val.	33.24	31.02	26.86	21.88	20.79	20.95
Earnings	6.12	5.00	4.60	0.76	3.40	4.62
Dividends	1.88	1.64	1.51	1.48	1.42	1.10
Payout Ratio	31%	33%	33%	195%	42%	24%
Prices - High	$57\frac{3}{8}$	58	$53\frac{3}{8}$	$42\frac{3}{4}$	$47\frac{1}{4}$	55
- Low	$43\frac{3}{8}$	$44\frac{1}{2}$	$39\frac{5}{8}$	$21\frac{1}{2}$	$16\frac{7}{8}$	27
P/E Ratio - High	9	12	12	56	14	12
- Low	7	9	9	28	5	6

Income Statement Analysis (Million $)

	1994	%Chg	1993	%Chg	1992	%Chg	1991
Net Int. Inc.	5,211	12%	4,673	14%	4,098	8%	3,799
Tax Equiv. Adj.	94.0	9%	86.0	-7%	92.0	-35%	141
Non Int. Inc.	2,597	24%	2,101	10%	1,913	10%	1,742
Loan Loss Prov.	310	-28%	430	-40%	715	-55%	1,582
% Exp/Op Revs.	62%	—	65%	—	68%	—	76%
Pretax Inc.	2,555	28%	1,991	43%	1,396	NM	109
Eff. Tax Rate	34%	—	35%	—	18%	—	NM
Net Inc.	1,690	30%	1,301	14%	1,145	NM	202
% Net Int. Marg.	3.58%	—	4.00%	—	4.10%	—	3.82%

Balance Sheet & Other Fin. Data (Million $)

	1994	1993	1992	1991	1990	1989
Earning Assets:						
Money Mkt.	23,212	19,133	6,110	2,436	1,052	3,580
Inv. Securities	25,825	29,054	24,729	24,879	15,894	16,170
Com'l Loans	48,109	43,538	34,478	31,164	18,937	17,735
Other Loans	55,580	50,166	38,236	37,944	18,540	16,984
Total Assets	169,604	157,686	118,059	110,319	65,285	66,191
Demand Deposits	21,380	20,719	17,701	16,270	8,939	8,439
Time Deposits	79,090	70,394	65,026	71,805	41,283	40,137
LT Debt	8,488	7,648	3,066	2,876	1,697	1,466
Common Eqty.	10,900	9,771	7,695	6,145	2,958	2,712

Ratio Analysis

	1994	1993	1992	1991	1990	1989
% Ret. on Assets	1.0	0.9	1.0	0.2	0.6	0.8
% Ret. on Equity	16.3	14.8	15.9	2.7	12.0	20.5
% Loan Loss Resv.	2.1	2.3	2.0	2.3	1.8	1.4
% Loans/Deposits	103.2	102.8	87.9	78.5	73.9	70.8
% Equity to Assets	6.2	6.3	6.1	5.4	4.5	3.8

Dividend Data (Dividends have been paid since 1903. A dividend reinvestment plan is available.)

Amt. of Div. $	Date Decl.	Ex-Div. Date	Stock of Record	Payment Date
0.460	Jul. 27	Aug. 29	Sep. 02	Sep. 23 '94
0.500	Oct. 26	Nov. 28	Dec. 02	Dec. 22 '94
0.500	Jan. 25	Feb. 27	Mar. 03	Mar. 24 '95
0.500	Apr. 26	May. 26	Jun. 02	Jun. 23 '95
0.500	Jul. 26	Aug. 30	Sep. 01	Sep. 22 '95

Data as orig. reptd.; bef. results of disc opers. and/or spec. items. Per share data adj. for stk. divs. as of ex-div. date. E-Estimated. NA-Not Available. NM-Not Meaningful. NR-Not Ranked.

Office—NationsBank Corporate Center, Charlotte, NC 28255. **Tel**—(704) 386-5000. **Chrmn & CEO**—H. L. McColl, Jr. **Pres**—K. D. Lewis. **Vice Chrmn & CFO**—J. H. Hance, Jr. **Investor Contact**—Susan C. Carr. **Dirs**—R. W. Allen, W. M. Barnhardt, T. M. Belk, T. E. Capps, R. E. Cartledge, C. W. Coker, T. G. Cousins, A. T. Dickson, W. F. Dowd, Jr., A. L. Ellis, P. Fulton, L. L. Gellerstedt, Jr., T. L. Guzzle, E. B. Ingram, W. W. Johnson, H. L. McColl, Jr., B. Mickel, J. J. Murphy, J. C. Slane, J. W. Snow, M. R. Spangler, R. H. Spilman, W. W. Sprague, Jr., R. Townsend, J. M. Ward, M. Weintraub. **Transfer Agent**—Chemical Bank, NYC. **Incorporated** in North Carolina in 1968. **Empl**-59,633. **S&P Analyst:** Stephen R. Biggar

20-SEP-95 | **Industry:** Auto/Truck mfrs. | **Summary:** This company is a leading manufacturer of medium and heavy-duty trucks and school bus chassis and produces diesel engines for sale to original equipment manufacturers.

S&P Opinion: Avoid (★★)	Recent Price • 12⅞ Yield • Nil
	52 Wk Range • 17½-12⅛ 12-Mo. P/E • 9.3

Quantitative Evaluations

Outlook
(1 Lowest—5 Highest)
• **4**

Fair Value
• **14¼**

Risk
• **Average**

Earn./Div. Rank
• **C**

Technical Eval.
• **Bullish** since 9/95

Rel. Strength Rank
(1 Lowest—99 Highest)
• **5**

Insider Activity
• **Neutral**

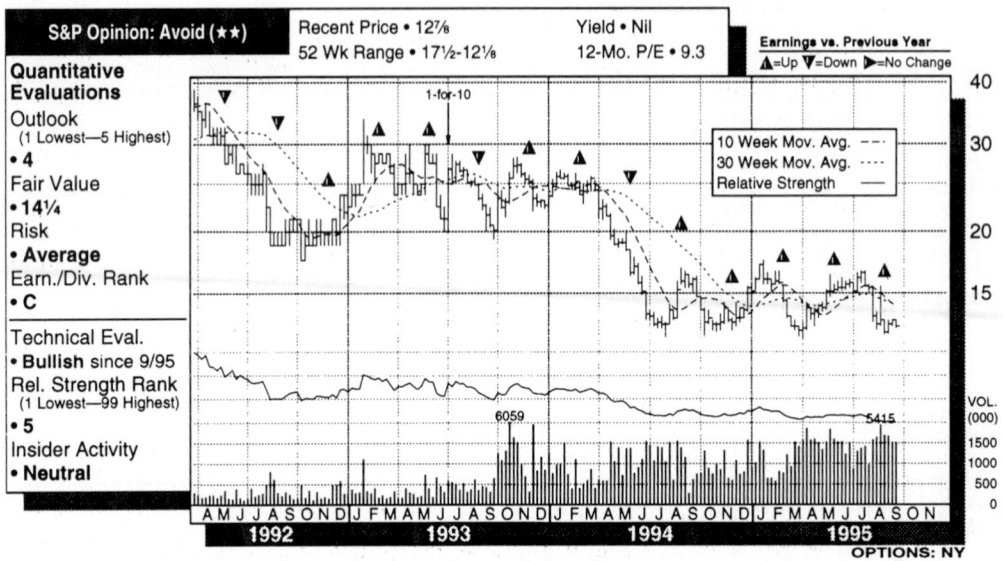

Earnings vs. Previous Year
▲=Up ▼=Down ▶=No Change

10 Week Mov. Avg. – – –
30 Week Mov. Avg. ·······
Relative Strength ——

1-for-10

OPTIONS: NY

Overview - 20-SEP-95

Although the overall heavy-duty truck order backlog in North America remains strong, cancellations exceeded new orders in August for the first time in recent memory. While sales should remain reasonably strong over the next few quarters, heavy truck shipments are expected to decline in 1996. Engine sales should flatten in 1996 as the medium and light duty truck markets stabilize, and parts sales may continue their recent flat trend. Overall, the company's prospects for 1996 will reflect the strength of the general economy. The modest decline we envision could turn into a cyclical decline if the economy weakens further. In such a case, margins could erode and earnings would be severely penalized by a drop in capacity utilization.

Valuation - 20-SEP-95

The shares of this leading truck manufacturer broke down recently as net new orders for heavy trucks turned negative in August for the first time in recent memory. The selloff reflects fears of the beginning of a cyclical decline in truck demand. Though NAV has bolstered its financial position through the issuance of equity in recent years, the firm remains vulnerable to the potential negative impact of a cyclical decline in truck sales which we think may now be unfolding. We advise lightening up on positions in anticipation of a further decline ahead.

Key Stock Statistics

S&P EPS Est. 1995	1.70	Tang. Bk. Value/Share	8.43
P/E on S&P Est. 1995	7.6	Beta	1.35
S&P EPS Est. 1996	1.50	Shareholders	88,300
Dividend Rate/Share	Nil	Market cap. (B)	$0.931
Shs. outstg. (M)	75.2	Inst. holdings	45%
Avg. daily vol. (M)	0.516	Insider holdings	NA

Value of $10,000 invested 5 years ago: $ 3,322

Fiscal Year Ending Oct. 31

	1995	% Change	1994	% Change	1993	% Change
Revenues (Million $)						
1Q	1,416	24%	1,139	10%	1,033	15%
2Q	1,640	18%	1,392	12%	1,238	35%
3Q	1,514	21%	1,251	11%	1,123	22%
4Q	—	—	1,548	19%	1,300	14%
Yr.	—	—	5,330	14%	4,694	21%
Income (Million $)						
1Q	23.00	44%	16.00	NM	2.00	NM
2Q	46.00	100%	23.00	53%	15.00	NM
3Q	39.00	95%	20.00	NM	-312.0	NM
4Q	—	—	43.00	95%	22.00	NM
Yr.	—	—	102.0	NM	-273.0	NM
Earnings Per Share ($)						
1Q	0.21	75%	0.12	NM	-0.19	NM
2Q	0.52	148%	0.21	-34%	0.32	NM
3Q	0.43	153%	0.17	NM	-9.99	NM
4Q	E0.54	10%	0.49	75%	0.28	NM
Yr.	E1.70	72%	0.99	NM	-8.63	NM

Next earnings report expected: early December

Navistar International

Business Summary - 19-SEP-95

Navistar is the largest producer of medium- and heavy-duty trucks (Classes 5-8) in North America. Contributions to sales in recent fiscal years:

	1994	1993	1992
Medium trucks	32%	35%	40%
Heavy trucks	42%	40%	34%
Parts	14%	14%	16%
Engines	12%	11%	10%

NAV delivered 91,600 medium and heavy-duty trucks in fiscal 1994, up from 79,800 in fiscal 1993. NAV's share of the North American medium and heavy-duty truck market was 27.0% in fiscal 1994, versus 27.6% in fiscal 1993. NAV is the leading supplier of school bus chassis in the U.S. and has a minority stake in American Transportation Corp., a manufacturer of school bus bodies. Service is provided and products are distributed through a network of 951 dealers and outlets in the U.S. and Canada. NAV exports trucks to more than 70 nations. In fiscal 1994 NAV exported 5,100 trucks (5.6% of total deliveries), versus 5,300 units (6.6%) in fiscal 1993.

All Navistar trucks are equipped with diesel engines. Medium-duty trucks, accounting for two-thirds of truck sales, are powered with NAV-built engines, while engines for NAV's heavy-duty trucks are primarily produced by outside suppliers. In fiscal 1994, NAV sold 130,600 engines (67.9% of total engine output), up from 118,200 units (67.4%) in fiscal 1993, to original equipment manufacturers for use in pick-up trucks and vans. NAV also sells engine blocks and cylinder blocks to original equipment manufacturers.

Navistar Financial Corp. finances new retail sales of Navistar trucks, dealers' inventories and used trucks produced by various manufacturers. In fiscal 1994, NAV financed 93% of dealer inventories and 15% of retail sales of NAV vehicles.

Important Developments

Aug. '95—In the quarter ended July 31, 1995, shipments of medium and heavy trucks and school bus chassis were 25,500 units and mid-range diesel engine shipments were 38,800, up 21% and 11% respectively, year to year. Service parts sales were unchanged at $178 million. NAV noted that it had seen some slowdown in industrywide truck orders recently, but that the order backlog remained sizable. NAV believes that the slowdown reflects customer uncertainty, but that it expected good sales levels in fiscal 1996.

Capitalization

Total Debt: $939,000,000 (7/95).
Cum. Conv. Pfd. & Pref. Stk.: $244,000,000.
Class B Common Stock: 24,676,976 shs. ($0.10 par). Convertible sh. for sh. into ord. common held by Navistar Retiree Supplemental Trust.

Per Share Data ($)

(Year Ended Oct. 31)

	1994	1993	1992	1991	1990	1989
Tangible Bk. Val.	3.16	2.16	-10.90	-2.90	7.60	26.40
Cash Flow	1.94	-6.50	-3.90	-4.90	1.00	4.60
Earnings	0.99	-8.63	-7.00	-7.70	-1.60	2.30
Dividends	Nil	Nil	Nil	Nil	Nil	Nil
Payout Ratio	Nil	Nil	Nil	Nil	Nil	Nil
Prices - High	26⅝	33¾	41¼	42½	46¼	70
- Low	12¼	19¼	17½	21¼	20	32½
P/E Ratio - High	27	NM	NM	NM	NM	30
- Low	12	NM	NM	NM	NM	14

Income Statement Analysis (Million $)

	1994	%Chg	1993	%Chg	1992	%Chg	1991
Revs.	5,305	13%	4,694	21%	3,875	12%	3,460
Oper. Inc.	289	17%	247	NM	20.0	NM	-6.0
Depr.	72.0	-4%	75.0	-3%	77.0	8%	71.0
Int. Exp.	91.0	-13%	105	-5%	111	-17%	134
Pretax Inc.	158	NM	-440	NM	-144	NM	-161
Eff. Tax Rate	35%	—	NM	—	NM	—	NM
Net Inc.	102	NM	-272	NM	-146	NM	-164

Balance Sheet & Other Fin. Data (Million $)

	1994	1993	1992	1991	1990	1989
Cash	557	421	335	295	275	395
Curr. Assets	NA	NA	NA	NA	NA	NA
Total Assets	5,056	5,060	3,627	3,443	3,795	3,609
Curr. Liab.	1,810	1,338	1,152	1,145	1,579	1,731
LT Debt	696	1,194	1,291	865	682	496
Common Eqty.	544	501	93.0	332	570	664
Total Cap.	1,513	1,969	1,629	1,442	1,497	1,410
Cap. Exp.	92.0	124	55.0	77.0	182	118
Cash Flow	145	-226	-99.0	-122	26.0	118

Ratio Analysis

	1994	1993	1992	1991	1990	1989
Curr. Ratio	NA	NA	NA	NA	NA	NA
% LT Debt of Cap.	46.0	60.6	79.3	60.0	45.6	35.2
% Net Inc.of Revs.	1.9	NM	NM	NM	NM	2.1
% Ret. on Assets	2.0	NM	NM	NM	NM	2.8
% Ret. on Equity	14.0	NM	NM	NM	NM	9.1

Dividend Data —Dividends on the common were omitted in 1981.

Data as orig. reptd.; bef. results of disc. opers. and/or spec. items. Per share data adj. for stk. divs. as of ex-div. date.
E-Estimated. NA-Not Available. NM-Not Meaningful. NR-Not Ranked.

Office—455 North Cityfront Plaza Drive, Chicago, IL 60611. **Tel**—(312) 836-2000. **Chrmn**—J. C. Cotting. **Pres & CEO**—J. R. Horne. **Secy**—S. K. Covey. **VP-CFO**—R. C. Lannert. **Investor Contact**—Carmen Corbett. **Dirs**—J. R. Anderson, W. F. Andrews, W. W. Booth, A. F. Brimmer, R. F. Celeste, J. D. Correnti, J. C. Cotting, W. C. Craig, J. E. Dempsey, M. Garst, C. Haggerty, A. G. Hansen, J. R. Horne, R. C. Lannert, J. Laskowski. **Transfer Agent**—Harris Trust & Savings Bank, Chicago. **Registrar**—First National Bank of Chicago. **Incorporated** in New Jersey in 1918; reincorporated in Delaware in 1965. **Empl**-14,909. **S&P Analyst:** Joshua M. Harari, CFA

New York Times

ASE Symbol NYT.A Options on Pacific (Jan-Apr-Jul-Oct) In S&P 500

Price	Range	P–E Ratio	Dividend	Yield	S&P Ranking	Beta
Jul. 31'95	1995					
25½	26⅛–20⅛	11	0.56	2.2%	B+	0.82

Summary

This diversified communications company publishes The New York Times and the Boston Globe newspapers, 28 smaller-city newspapers and consumer magazines. It also operates radio and television stations, has equity holdings in newsprint and paper mills, and syndicates news and features. The Women's Magazine division was sold in August 1994.

Current Outlook

Earnings for 1995 are projected at $1.40 a share, versus 1994's $2.05 (including net capital gains of $0.99). A gain to $1.60 is seen for 1996.
The $0.14 quarterly dividend is the minimum expected.
Lower revenues in 1995 will reflect the absence of the Women's Magazine division. Revenues from ongoing operations are expected to advance, however, on stronger print and broadcast advertising. Despite sharply higher newsprint costs, operating efficiencies and rising cover prices will compensate. Net interest income will advance, and equity in earnings of the forest products group will climb. Lower net income will reflect the absence of capital gains. Share earnings comparisons will benefit from fewer shares outstanding.

Revenues (Million $)

Quarter:	1995	1994	1993	1992
Mar.	571	590	455	440
Jun.	610	636	484	448
Sep.		527	446	430
Dec.		605	636	468
		2,358	2,020	1,774

Revenues in the first half of 1995 declined 3.5%, year to year. Costs and expenses also fell; operating earnings advanced 19%. With a 16% drop in interest expense, and after taxes at 46.9%, versus 48.2%, and sharply higher equity in earnings of affiliates, net income climbed 36%. Share earnings, on fewer shares, climbed 49%, to $0.73, from $0.49.

Common Share Earnings ($)

Quarter:	1995	1994	1993	1992
Mar.	0.28	0.17	0.14	0.17
Jun.	0.45	0.32	0.28	0.19
Sep.	E0.20	1.16	d0.04	d0.43
Dec.	E0.27	0.41	d0.11	d0.05
	E1.40	2.05	0.07	d0.14

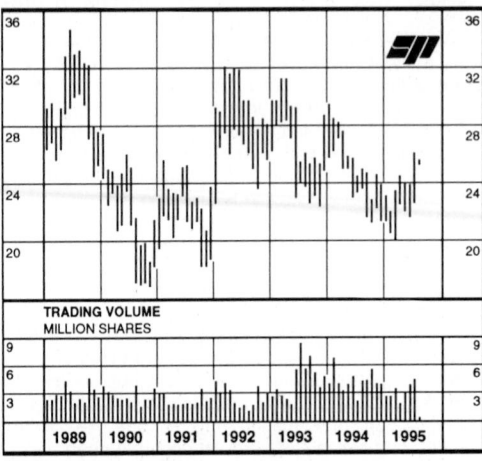

TRADING VOLUME
MILLION SHARES

Important Developments

Jul. '95— NYT said it had repurchased 2 million Class A common shares, at a cost of $45.7 million, in the first half of 1995. During 1994, 10 million shares were purchased for $235.2 million.

Jun. '95— As part of a long-term plan to increase ownership of media and electronic information properties, the company acquired WTKR-TV, a CBS affiliate serving the Norfolk-Portsmouth-Newport News TV market in Virginia.

Apr. '95— NYT raised the newsstand price of the metropolitan edition of the Sunday Times to $2.50, from $2.00, and raised the seven-day home delivery price to $6.70, from $6.10. Earlier price hikes announced for northeast and national editions ranged from 13% to 33%.

Next earnings report expected in late October.

Per Share Data ($)

Yr. End Dec. 31	1994	1993	1992	1991	1990	1989	1988	1987	1986	1985
Tangible Bk. Val.	NA	1.57	NA	6.90	6.30	5.94	4.12	3.13	2.55	0.92
Cash Flow	NA	1.13	NM	1.54	1.81	1.62	2.82	2.72	2.31	2.02
Earnings[1]	2.05	0.07	d0.14	0.61	0.85	0.87	2.00	1.96	1.63	1.45
Dividends	0.56	0.56	0.56	0.56	0.54	0.50	0.46	0.40	0.33	0.29
Payout Ratio	27%	NM	NM	94%	64%	57%	23%	20%	20%	20%
Prices—High	29½	31¼	32⅛	25⅝	27½	34⅝	32¾	49⅝	42	25½
Low	21¼	22⅜	22⅝	18¼	16⅞	24⅜	24⅜	24¾	23¼	17⅝
P/E Ratio—	14–10	NM	NM	42–30	32–20	40–28	16–12	25–13	26–14	18–12

Data as orig. reptd. Adj. for stk. divs. of 100% Oct. 1986. 1. Bef. results of disc. ops. of +2.54 in 1989, +0.08 in 1988. d-Deficit. E-Estimated. NM-Not Meaningful. NA-Not Available.

The New York Times Company

Income Data (Million $)

Year Ended Dec. 31	Revs.	Oper. Inc.	% Oper. Inc. of Revs.	Cap. Exp.	Depr.	Int. Exp.	[4]Net Bef. Taxes	Eff. Tax Rate	[5]Net Inc.	% Net Inc. of Revs.	Cash Flow
[1]1993	2,020	216	10.7	80	89.3	30.9	49	87.6%	6	0.3	95
[1]1992	1,774	NA	NA	47	NA	[3]26.1	Nil	NM	[6]d11	NM	NM
1991	1,703	186	10.9	40	72.4	32.4	69	31.6%	47	2.8	NM
1990	1,777	203	11.4	121	73.6	41.4	114	43.2%	65	3.6	138
[1]1989	1,769	228	12.9	230	58.8	55.2	132	48.5%	68	3.9	127
[2]1988	1,700	318	18.7	278	66.5	46.1	253	36.3%	161	9.5	227
1987	1,690	354	20.9	218	62.4	31.9	286	44.0%	160	9.5	223
1986	1,565	327	20.9	103	54.9	29.1	256	48.3%	[6]132	8.5	187
[1]1985	1,394	259	18.6	110	45.6	24.5	215	45.9%	116	8.3	162
1984	1,230	214	17.4	74	37.3	7.9	186	46.2%	100	8.1	137

Balance Sheet Data (Million $)

Dec. 31	Cash	Assets	Curr. Liab.	Ratio	Total Assets	% Ret. on Assets	Long Term Debt	Common Equity	Total Cap.	% LT Debt of Cap.	% Ret. on Equity
1993	42	493	554	0.9	3,215	0.2	460	1,599	2,258	20.4	0.4
1992	119	433	399	1.1	1,995	NA	207	1,000	1,396	14.8	NA
1991	85	389	438	0.9	2,128	2.2	213	1,073	1,578	13.5	4.4
1990	32	338	430	0.8	2,150	3.0	319	1,056	1,669	19.1	6.1
1989	76	374	435	0.9	2,188	3.3	337	1,064	1,700	19.9	7.1
1988	13	331	470	0.7	1,915	9.0	378	873	1,414	26.7	19.3
1987	76	319	311	1.0	1,712	10.3	391	823	1,359	28.8	21.0
1986	26	233	322	0.7	1,405	9.7	217	705	1,045	20.7	20.3
1985	8	215	280	0.8	1,296	10.7	274	586	975	28.1	21.5
1984	81	247	194	1.3	869	12.2	75	485	639	11.7	22.3

Data as orig. reptd. **1.** Refl. merger or acq. **2.** Excl. disc. ops. **3.** Net of interest income. **4.** Incl. equity in earns. of nonconsol. subs. **5.** Bef. disc. ops. **6.** Refl. acctg. change. d-Deficit. NA-Not Available. NM-Not Meaningful.

Business Summary

The New York Times Company diversified interests in newspapers, magazines, broadcasting, information services and forest products. Contributions by business segment in 1994 were:

	Revs.	Profits (mil. $)
Newspapers	83%	$196.1
Magazines	12%	19.2
Broadcasting/Information Services	5%	25.0

The New York Times newspaper derives 65% of its daily circulation in New York City and its suburbs, and 35% nationally and internationally. Average circulation in the six months ended September 30, 1994, was 1,114,905 copies daily and 1,724,708 Sunday. The Boston Globe, New England's largest newspaper, had circulation of 506,545 daily and 811,100 Sunday. Other interests include 28 regional newspapers, a wholesale newspaper distribution business in the New York City area, a 50% interest in the International Herald Tribune, and 13 consumer magazines.

Broadcasting properties include six TV stations (WNEP-TV, serving the Wilkes-Barre-Scranton area of Pennsylvania; WQAD-TV, serving the "Quad-Cities" area of Illinois and Iowa; KFSM-TV in Fort Smith, Ark.; WHNT-TV in Huntsville, Ala.; WREG-TV in Memphis); WTKR-TV, serving the Norfolk, Va. area; and two radio stations (WQXR AM & FM in NYC). Minority interests are held in two Canadian newsprint mills and in a supercalendered paper mill in Maine.

Dividend Data

Cash dividends have been paid on the Class A and Class B shares since 1958. A dividend reinvestment plan is available for Class A shares.

Amt. of Divd. $	Date Decl.	Ex-divd. Date	Stock of Record	Payment Date
0.14	Nov. 17	Nov. 25	Dec. 1	Dec. 15'94
0.14	Feb. 16	Mar. 1	Mar. 7	Mar. 24'95
0.14	May 18	May 31	Jun. 6	Jun. 23'95
0.14	Jul. 20	Aug. 31	Sep. 5	Sep. 22'95

Capitalization

Long Term Debt: $588,842,000 (3/95).

$5.50 Cum. Pref. Stk.: 17,837 shs. ($100 par).

Class A Common Stock: 96,577,496 ltd. voting shs. ($0.10 par).
Some 28% is closely held.
Institutions hold 50%.
Shareholders: 17,245 of record.

Class B Common Stock: 430,178 shs. ($0.10 par).
Some 86% is closely held.

Office—229 W. 43rd St., New York, NY 10036. **Tel**—(212) 556-1234. **Chrmn & CEO**—A. O. Sulzberger. **Pres & COO**—L. R. Primis. **Secy**—Laura J. Corwin. **SVP & CFO**—D. L. Gorham. **VP & Investor Contact**—Nancy Nielsen (212-556-4317). **Dirs**—J. F. Akers, R. L. Gelb, L. V. Gerstner, Jr., M. S. Heiskell, A. L. Higginbotham, Jr., R. S. Holmberg, R. A. Lawrence, G. B. Munroe, C. H. Price II, G. L. Shinn, D. M. Stewart, A. O. Sulzberger, J. P. Sulzberger, W. O. Taylor, C. R. Vance. **Transfer Agent & Registrar**—First Chicago Trust Co. of New York, NYC. **Incorporated** in New York in 1896. **Empl**—12,800.

Newell Co.

NYSE Symbol **NWL**
In S&P 500

24-AUG-95

Industry:
Housewares

Summary: This leading high-volume, brand-name consumer products firm has grown through acquisitions; major product lines include housewares, home furnishings, office products, and hardware.

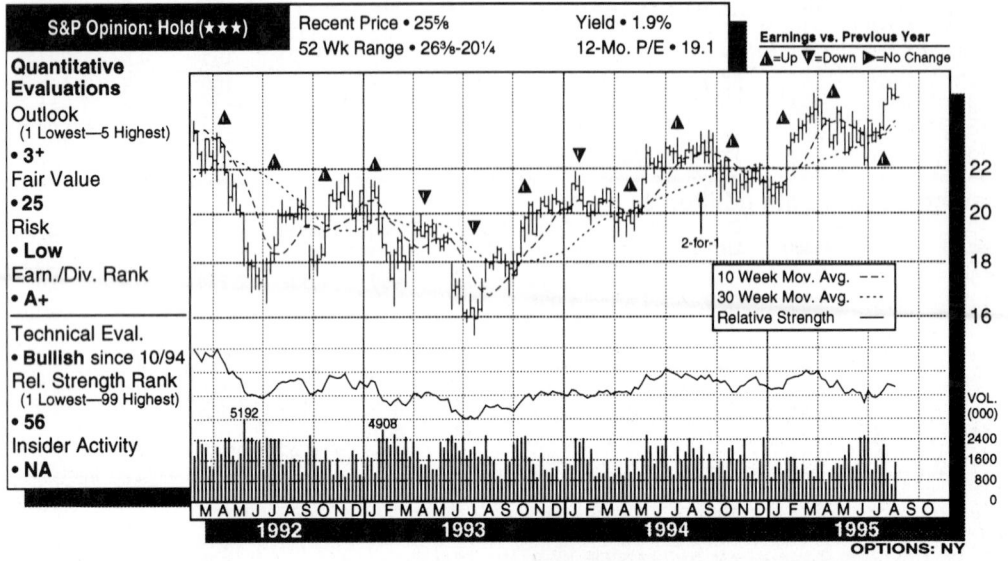

S&P Opinion: Hold (★★★)	Recent Price • 25%	Yield • 1.9%
	52 Wk Range • 26⅜-20¼	12-Mo. P/E • 19.1

Quantitative Evaluations

Outlook
(1 Lowest—5 Highest)
• **3+**

Fair Value
• **25**

Risk
• **Low**

Earn./Div. Rank
• **A+**

Technical Eval.
• **Bullish** since 10/94

Rel. Strength Rank
(1 Lowest—99 Highest)
• **56**

Insider Activity
• **NA**

Earnings vs. Previous Year
▲=Up ▼=Down ▶=No Change

10 Week Mov. Avg. ---
30 Week Mov. Avg. ·····
Relative Strength —

OPTIONS: NY

Overview - 24-AUG-95

Sales could top $2.5 billion in 1995, up 21% from the 1994 level. Approximately 5% of sales growth should come from higher volume from existing operations, reflecting new product introductions, expanded distribution through new store openings at Wal-Mart and Home Depot, and increased share at existing distribution outlets. The remainder of the gain will reflect 1994 acquisitions, including Faber-Castell (a maker of writing instruments), HFI (window coverings), and Corning Inc.'s European consumer business. Despite operating efficiencies arising from the integration of these businesses into existing operations, full-year margins could contract somewhat, reflecting a less favorable product mix. Interest charges will be higher, reflecting the acquisitions, but results should benefit from a lower tax rate.

Valuation - 24-AUG-95

The stock of this leading high-volume consumer manufacturer appears fully valued, given a projected growth rate of 10% to 15%. The shares are currently trading at a premium to the market multiple. With this valuation, we feel that the stock has only limited upside potential in the near-term. However, we continue to like the shares for the long-term. NWL is rapidly expanding its offerings through acquisitions and new product launches; benefiting from distribution synergies as it increases its product offerings; and increasing market share through mass merchandisers, including Wal-Mart and Home Depot.

Key Stock Statistics

S&P EPS Est. 1995	1.45	Tang. Bk. Value/Share	3.19
P/E on S&P Est. 1995	17.7	Beta	1.50
S&P EPS Est. 1996	1.65	Shareholders	10,300
Dividend Rate/Share	0.48	Market cap. (B)	$ 4.1
Shs. outstg. (M)	158.2	Inst. holdings	71%
Avg. daily vol. (M)	0.250	Insider holdings	NA

Value of $10,000 invested 5 years ago: $ 25,502

Fiscal Year Ending Dec. 31

	1995	% Change	1994	% Change	1993	% Change
Revenues (Million $)						
1Q	556.6	25%	443.5	33%	334.2	8%
2Q	621.3	26%	493.5	32%	372.7	17%
3Q	—	—	553.2	21%	456.7	14%
4Q	—	—	584.7	21%	481.4	14%
Yr.	—	—	2,075	26%	1,645	13%
Income (Million $)						
1Q	36.10	15%	31.50	14%	27.74	1%
2Q	54.93	25%	43.98	27%	34.50	-2%
3Q	—	—	58.00	22%	47.63	11%
4Q	—	—	62.10	12%	55.46	-4%
Yr.	—	—	195.6	18%	165.3	1%
Earnings Per Share ($)						
1Q	0.23	15%	0.20	14%	0.17	-3%
2Q	0.35	25%	0.28	27%	0.22	-4%
3Q	E0.44	19%	0.37	21%	0.31	11%
4Q	E0.43	10%	0.39	11%	0.35	-4%
Yr.	E1.45	17%	1.24	18%	1.05	NM

Next earnings report expected: mid October

Business Summary - 24-AUG-95

Newell is a manufacturer and full-service marketer of high-volume consumer products serving the needs of volume purchasers. For 25 years, acquisitions have been the company's primary vehicle for growth. In the 1990s alone, it has completed 10 major acquisitions, representing $1.5 billion in incremental sales. Sales by major divisions in recent years were:

	1994	1993	1992
Housewares	33%	32%	35%
Home Furnishings	31%	26%	11%
Office Products	18%	21%	19%
Hardware	17%	20%	22%
Sold Businesses	---	1%	12%

The housewares segment includes Mirro and WearEver, producers of aluminum cookware, bakeware and kitchen utensils; Anchor Hocking Glass, a producer of tabletop glassware and oven bakeware; Anchor Hocking Plastics, a producer of microwave cookware and food storage containers; Goody and Ace, producers of hair accessories; and Newell Europe (formerly Corning's European consumer operations), a producer of Pyrex, Pyroflam, Visions and Vitri glassware in Europe.

The home furnishings segment includes window furnishings, consisting of Levolor, a producer of window coverings, and Newell Window furnishings, a manufacturer of window shades, drapery hardware, window treatments and accessories; Intercraft, the world's largest supplier of ready-made picture frames; Lee/Rowan, a manufacturer of coated wire storage and organization products; and Dorfile and System Works, producers of laminated particleboard storage systems for the closet, kitchen, garage, laundry and basement.

Office products consists of Sanford, a maker of markers and writing instruments; Eberhard Faber, a producer of wood-cased pencils and rolling ball pens; Stuart Hall, a manufacturer of school and office supplies and stationery; and Newell Office Products, and Rogers and Keene, makers of desktop and office accessories.

Hardware products include EZ Paintr, a maker of painting accessories; Amerock, a producer of cabinet hardware; BernzOmatic, a manufacturer of hand torches; and Bulldog home hardware products.

Important Developments

Jul. '95—NWL attributed a 26% increase in sales and a 25% rise in net income in the 1995 second quarter to acquisitions made during in 1994. Separately, it signed a definitive agreement to acquire Berol Corp., an international maker and marketer of writing instruments.

Capitalization

Long Term Debt: $408,216,000 (3/95).

Per Share Data ($)
(Year Ended Dec. 31)

	1994	1993	1992	1991	1990	1989
Tangible Bk. Val.	2.79	2.96	3.41	3.69	2.93	2.49
Cash Flow	1.70	1.46	1.39	1.19	1.11	1.01
Earnings	1.24	1.05	1.05	0.90	0.84	0.71
Dividends	0.39	0.35	0.30	0.30	0.25	0.21
Payout Ratio	31%	33%	29%	33%	30%	30%
Prices - High	23⅞	21½	26½	22⅞	17¾	12⅝
- Low	18⅞	15⅜	16½	11½	8⅞	6⅜
P/E Ratio - High	19	20	25	25	21	18
- Low	15	15	16	13	11	9

Income Statement Analysis (Million $)

	1994	%Chg	1993	%Chg	1992	%Chg	1991
Revs.	2,075	26%	1,645	13%	1,452	30%	1,119
Oper. Inc.	415	22%	340	13%	301	32%	228
Depr.	72.5	13%	64.3	19%	53.9	54%	35.1
Int. Exp.	30.0	57%	19.1	-6%	20.4	24%	16.4
Pretax Inc.	329	19%	276	NM	278	49%	187
Eff. Tax Rate	41%	—	40%	—	41%	—	40%
Net Inc.	196	19%	165	1%	163	46%	112

Balance Sheet & Other Fin. Data (Million $)

	1994	1993	1992	1991	1990	1989
Cash	14.9	2.9	28.0	26.3	50.3	38.8
Curr. Assets	918	676	595	286	375	380
Total Assets	2,488	1,953	1,570	1,040	871	871
Curr. Liab.	784	599	375	164	181	231
LT Debt	409	218	177	177	89.0	100
Common Eqty.	1,125	979	859	606	500	444
Total Cap.	1,552	1,197	1,036	810	622	578
Cap. Exp.	66.0	59.0	77.6	57.1	36.6	48.7
Cash Flow	268	230	217	147	139	121

Ratio Analysis

	1994	1993	1992	1991	1990	1989
Curr. Ratio	1.2	1.1	1.6	1.7	2.1	1.6
% LT Debt of Cap.	26.4	18.2	17.1	21.8	14.4	17.3
% Net Inc.of Revs.	9.4	10.1	11.2	10.0	9.4	7.6
% Ret. on Assets	8.8	9.4	11.3	11.5	11.6	9.0
% Ret. on Equity	18.6	17.9	20.1	19.8	21.3	22.3

Dividend Data
—Dividends have been paid each year since 1946.

Amt. of Div. $	Date Decl.	Ex-Div. Date	Stock of Record	Payment Date
2-for-1	Aug. 03	Sep. 02	Aug. 15	Sep. 01 '94
0.100	Nov. 03	Nov. 15	Nov. 21	Dec. 05 '94
0.100	Feb. 07	Feb. 13	Feb. 17	Mar. 03 '95
0.120	May. 11	May. 15	May. 19	Jun. 05 '95
0.120	Aug. 09	Aug. 14	Aug. 16	Sep. 01 '95

Data as orig. reptd.; bef. results of disc. opers. and/or spec. items. Per share data adj. for stk. divs. as of ex-div. date. E-Estimated. NA-Not Available. NM-Not Meaningful. NR-Not Ranked.

Office—29 East Stephenson St., Freeport, IL 61032-0943. **Tel**—(815) 235-4171. **Vice Chrmn & CEO**—W. P. Sovey. **Pres**—T. A. Ferguson, Jr. **VP-Fin**—W. T. Alldredge. **VP & Secy**—R. H. Wolff. **Investor Contact**—Ross A. Porter, Jr. **Dirs**—A. F. Doody, G. H. Driggs, D. C. Ferguson (Chrmn), T. A. Ferguson, Jr., R. L. Katz, J. J. McDonough, E. C. Millett, A. P. Newell, H. B. Pearsall, W. P. Sovey. **Transfer Agent & Registrar**—First Chicago Trust Co., NYC. **Incorporated** in Delaware in 1970. **Empl**-20,000. **S&P Analyst:** Elizabeth Vandeventer

Newmont Mining

NYSE Symbol **NEM**
In S&P 500

20-SEP-95

Industry:
Mining/Diversified

Summary: Newmont Mining owns 89.2% of Newmont Gold Co. (NGC), one of the world's leading gold producers, with operations in Nevada, Peru and Uzbekistan, and projects in Indonesia.

S&P Opinion: Hold (★★★)

| Recent Price • 44¾ | Yield • 1.1% |
| 52 Wk Range • 46¾-33⅛ | 12-Mo. P/E • 36.7 |

Earnings vs. Previous Year
▲=Up ▼=Down ▶=No Change

Quantitative Evaluations

Outlook
(1 Lowest—5 Highest)
• **1**+

Fair Value
• **29⅞**

Risk
• **Average**

Earn./Div. Rank
• **B**

Technical Eval.
• **Bearish** since 4/95

Rel. Strength Rank
(1 Lowest—99 Highest)
• **30**

Insider Activity
• **Neutral**

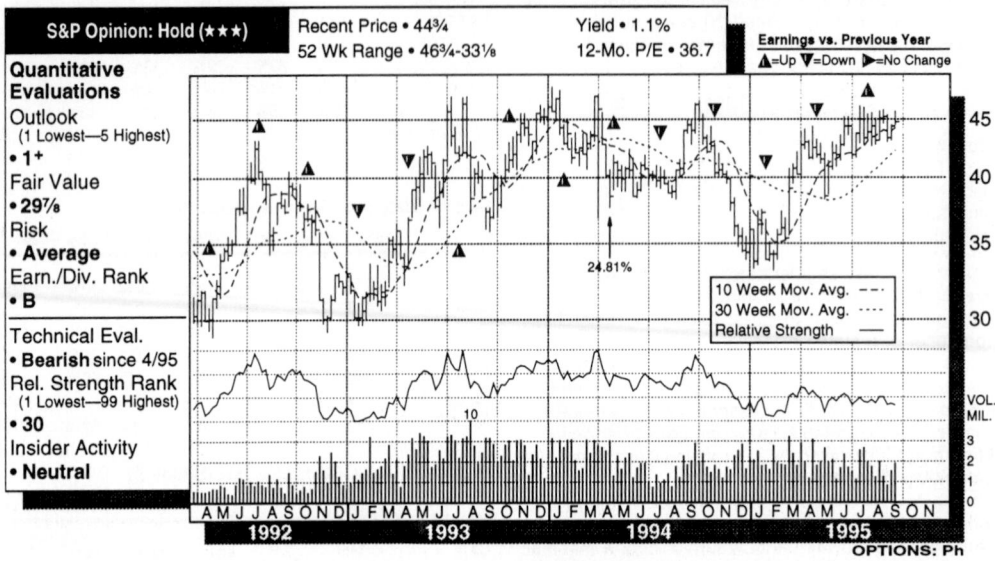

24.81%

10 Week Mov. Avg. − − −
30 Week Mov. Avg. ·······
Relative Strength ——

VOL.
MIL.

A M J J A S O N D J F M A M J J A S O N D J F M A M J J A S O N D J F M A M J J A S O N
1992   1993   1994   1995

OPTIONS: Ph

Overview - 20-SEP-95

Gold production in 1995 at the Carlin property in Nevada is expected to be flat, reflecting the closure of three mills. Start-up problems at Carlin's new refractory ore plant, which processes deeper ore, should be corrected during 1995's second half providing for good production gains in 1996. Production will be sharply higher at Yanacocha (38%-owned), reflecting the opening of a new mine in late 1994. Helping to lift overall production levels will be the start up of the Zarafshan project in Uzbekistan in mid-1995. Operating costs, which were higher in 1995's first half, should fall as Carlin's refractory plant operates more efficiently and increased volumes are derived from lower-cost properties. Gold prices are expected to be flat. Distorting comparisons is the $0.75 a share gain on the sale of Southern Peru Copper.

Valuation - 20-SEP-95

Shares of this major gold producer in 1995 rebounded sharply from 1994's selloff but remain locked in a trading range. Flat gold prices has served to offset good news on the production front. NEM's Newmont Gold unit is experiencing good volume growth at its 38%-owned Yanacocha property in Peru and is expected to shortly boost its holdings to 51%. A major gold recovery project in Uzbekistan came on line in 1995's second half and in 1996 production begins at a major property in Indonesia. However, with the odds favoring continued low inflation and flat gold prices, we think NEM only will be an average performer near term.

Key Stock Statistics

S&P EPS Est. 1995	1.30	Tang. Bk. Value/Share	4.48
P/E on S&P Est. 1995	34.4	Beta	-0.22
S&P EPS Est. 1996	1.25	Shareholders	6,000
Dividend Rate/Share	0.48	Market cap. (B)	$ 3.8
Shs. outstg. (M)	86.2	Inst. holdings	75%
Avg. daily vol. (M)	0.284	Insider holdings	NA

Value of $10,000 invested 5 years ago: $ 12,679

Fiscal Year Ending Dec. 31

	1995	% Change	1994	% Change	1993	% Change
Revenues (Million $)						
1Q	134.5	-10%	149.8	8%	138.1	-12%
2Q	145.1	4%	139.3	-11%	157.3	NM
3Q	—	—	150.1	-16%	178.1	14%
4Q	—	—	158.2	-2%	160.8	14%
Yr.	—	—	597.4	-6%	634.3	3%
Income (Million $)						
1Q	15.59	-28%	21.59	72%	12.55	-71%
2Q	67.76	NM	17.32	-56%	39.54	62%
3Q	—	—	20.42	-20%	25.66	40%
4Q	—	—	16.66	-2%	16.92	NM
Yr.	—	—	76.12	-20%	94.67	4%
Earnings Per Share ($)						
1Q	0.14	-30%	0.20	100%	0.10	-81%
2Q	0.74	NM	0.16	-62%	0.42	44%
3Q	E0.20	5%	0.19	-24%	0.25	16%
4Q	E0.22	47%	0.15	-1%	0.15	NM
Yr.	E1.30	86%	0.70	-24%	0.92	-12%

Next earnings report expected: late October

Newmont Mining

Business Summary - 20-SEP-95

Newmont Mining, through 89.2%-owned Newmont Gold (NGC), is one of the world's leading gold producers, with operations in Nevada and Peru and development projects in Uzbekistan and Indonesia. NGC's equity in gold production was 1.67 million oz. in 1994, and is projected to rise from 1995's estimated 1.9 million oz. to 2.5 million oz. in 1997. Its equity in gold reserves was 26.1 million oz. at year-end 1994, versus 26.0 million oz. at year-end 1993.

NGC produced 1.56 million oz. of gold in 1994 from its facilities in Carlin (Nev.), against 1.67 million oz. in 1993. In September 1994, NGC completed a $349 million sale and leaseback agreement for a new roaster, which should reach its design capacity by late 1995, to oxidize the deeper, refractory ores that will increasingly be phased into production. Reserves at year-end 1994 were estimated at 18.5 million oz., versus 17.8 million oz. a year earlier.

NGC's 38%-owned Yanacocha gold venture (Peru) produced 305,000 oz. in 1994; reserves totaled 4 million oz. The Zarafshan-Newmont 50/50 gold venture in Uzbekistan is expected to produce 2.5 million oz. of gold for NGC's account over a 17-year period from leaching ore stockpiles. Operating costs are expected to be some $150/oz. during the early years. Production began in June 1995 and is scheduled reach a rate of some 450,000 oz./year in 1996, half of which will be NGC's share. In November 1994, site preparation began at the Minahasa gold mine (80% owned) on the Indonesian island of Sulawesi. The $130 million project is expected to produce 1.8 million oz. at average cash operating costs of $150/oz. over 13 years. Output is scheduled for early 1996 at a rate of 140,000 oz./year. Reserves at Minahasa were 2.1 million oz. at year-end 1994. NGC's 80%-owned Batu Hijau prospect (Indonesia) has mineralized material containing 14.7 million oz. of gold, 27.6 million oz. of silver and 11.2 billion lbs. of copper. Production is not expected to commence until 1999.

Important Developments

Jul. '95—Net income for 1995's second quarter included a $72 million ($0.75 a share) gain from the sale of NGC's 11% stake in Southern Peru Copper Corp. Partly offsetting was a $15.1 million ($0.16 a share) charge, reflecting the writedown of the Ivanoe property and additions to reclamation reserves.

Mar. '95—Newmont Gold won a preliminary ruling in the Peruvian courts, paving the way for it to lift its stake in Yanacocha to 51%. NGC continues to account for operations on a 38% equity basis, pending final court approval.

Capitalization

Long Term Debt: $597,118,000 (6/95).
Minority Interest: $86,504,000.
5.5% Perpetual Preferred Stock: $287,500,000; conv. into com. at $36.395 a sh. Privately held.

Per Share Data ($)

(Year Ended Dec. 31)

	1994	1993	1992	1991	1990	1989
Tangible Bk. Val.	4.48	4.05	2.84	2.34	1.30	-2.37
Cash Flow	1.76	2.21	2.20	2.23	3.00	2.36
Earnings	0.70	0.92	1.04	1.11	1.99	1.54
Dividends	0.48	0.48	0.48	0.48	0.48	0.48
Payout Ratio	69%	52%	46%	43%	24%	31%
Prices - High	48 1/8	47 1/8	43 1/8	35 1/4	43 7/8	39 7/8
- Low	33 7/8	29 5/8	29	26 1/2	25 3/8	25 3/8
P/E Ratio - High	69	51	41	32	22	26
- Low	48	32	28	24	13	16

Income Statement Analysis (Million $)

	1994	%Chg	1993	%Chg	1992	%Chg	1991
Revs.	597	-6%	634	3%	613	-2%	623
Oper. Inc.	160	-23%	207	1%	204	-14%	237
Depr.	91.0	-18%	111	12%	99	5%	94.0
Int. Exp.	10.0	-52%	21.0	40%	15.0	15%	13.0
Pretax Inc.	54.0	-56%	124	23%	101	-25%	135
Eff. Tax Rate	NM	—	15%	—	2.80%	—	21%
Net Inc.	76.0	-20%	95.0	4%	91.0	-3%	94.0

Balance Sheet & Other Fin. Data (Million $)

	1994	1993	1992	1991	1990	1989
Cash	174	88.0	309	35.0	149	19.0
Curr. Assets	370	229	409	187	274	183
Total Assets	1,657	1,186	1,215	818	951	1,302
Curr. Liab.	153	110	243	235	267	318
LT Debt	594	192	177	112	302	964
Common Eqty.	386	342	241	201	110	-199
Total Cap.	1,347	913	830	462	600	937
Cap. Exp.	402	249	213	94.0	74.0	126
Cash Flow	151	189	188	188	253	199

Ratio Analysis

	1994	1993	1992	1991	1990	1989
Curr. Ratio	2.4	2.1	1.7	0.8	1.0	0.6
% LT Debt of Cap.	44.1	21.0	21.3	24.3	50.3	NM
% Net Inc.of Revs.	12.7	14.9	14.8	15.1	24.7	22.2
% Ret. on Assets	5.3	7.9	8.9	10.7	14.9	9.9
% Ret. on Equity	20.9	27.1	40.1	60.6	NM	NM

Dividend Data —Dividends have been paid since 1934. A dividend reinvestment plan is available. A "poison pill" stock purchase rights plan was amended in 1990.

Amt. of Div. $	Date Decl.	Ex-Div. Date	Stock of Record	Payment Date
0.120	Nov. 16	Nov. 18	Nov. 25	Dec. 07 '94
0.120	Jan. 25	Feb. 02	Feb. 08	Mar. 08 '95
0.120	May. 17	May. 25	Jun. 01	Jun. 12 '95
0.120	Jul. 19	Jul. 31	Aug. 02	Sep. 06 '95

Data as orig. reptd.; bef. results of disc. opers. and/or spec. items. Per share data adj. for stk. divs. as of ex-div. date. E-Estimated. NA-Not Available. NM-Not Meaningful. NR-Not Ranked.

Office—1700 Lincoln St., Denver, CO 80203. **Tel**—(303) 863-7414. **Chrmn, Pres & CEO**—R. C. Cambre. **SVP-CFO**—W. W. Murdy. **VP-Secy**—T. J. Schmitt. **VP-Investor Contact**—Jack H. Morris. **Dirs**—R. I. J. Agnew, J. P. Bolduc, R. C. Cambre, J. P. Flannery, T. A. Holmes, R. A. Plumbridge, M. A. Qureshi, M. K. Reilly, W. I. M. Turner Jr. **Transfer Agent & Registrar**—Chemical Bank, NYC. **Incorporated** in Delaware in 1921. **Empl**-2,835. **S&P Analyst:** Stephen R. Klein

Niagara Mohawk Power

NYSE Symbol **NMK**
In S&P 500

31-AUG-95 **Industry:** Util.-Diversified

Summary: Niagara Mohawk supplies electricity (85% of 1994 revenues) and gas (15%) to major cities in western New York, and a large area in the northern part of the state.

S&P Opinion: Sell (★)	Recent Price • 14½	Yield • 9.0%
	52 Wk Range • 15⅜-12	12-Mo. P/E • 20.1

Quantitative Evaluations

Outlook (1 Lowest—5 Highest)
• **3+**

Fair Value
• **14½**

Risk
• **Low**

Earn./Div. Rank
• **B**

Technical Eval.
• **Bearish** since 11/93

Rel. Strength Rank (1 Lowest—99 Highest)
• **4**

Insider Activity
• **Neutral**

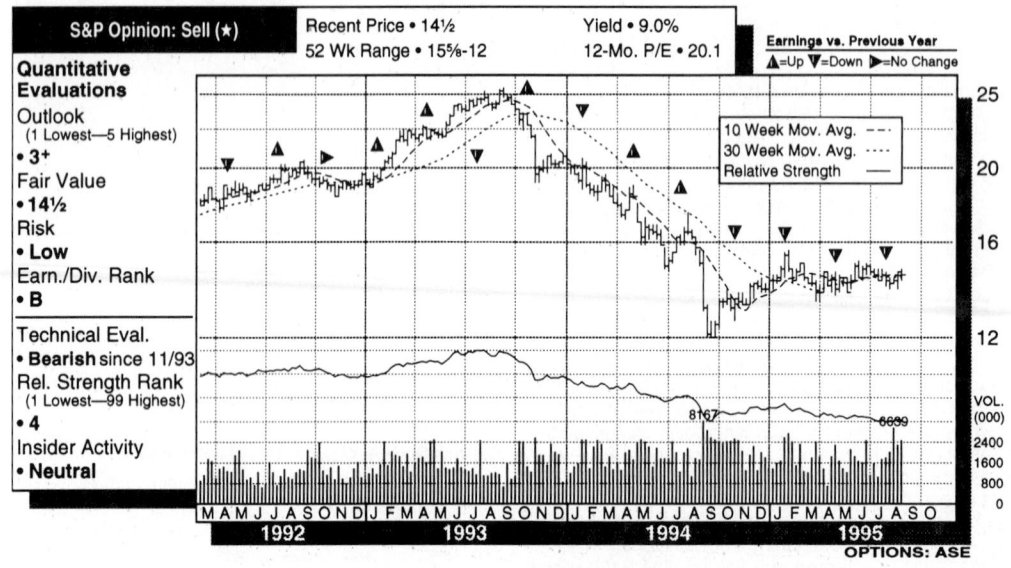

Earnings vs. Previous Year
▲=Up ▼=Down ▶=No Change

10 Week Mov. Avg. ---
30 Week Mov. Avg. ....
Relative Strength ——

VOL. (000)

OPTIONS: ASE

Overview - 30-AUG-95

A gas rate hike and savings from work force reductions as well as other efforts to cut costs may be more than offset in 1995 by several negative factors. These include a reduction in electric rates, an increase in preferred dividend requirements, and softening in the regional economy. Somewhat offsetting poor earnings comparisons will be the absence of 1994's $0.89-a-share onetime charge to reduce the work force. Of greatest concern over the long run is the company's inability to get relief from high-cost unregulated generator power contracts mandated by state regulators. Issues impeding earnings progress, including liabilities for environmental remediation, a possible negative tax adjustment and recovery of costs eliminated in the April rate case also remain unresolved.

Valuation - 30-AUG-95

NMK's stock has rebounded poorly from the steep decline the utility group experienced in 1993-1994, and a sizeable recovery does not seem likely, given the April rate decision that weakens its ability to recover cost increases. A soft local economy is also restricting the company's ability to carry out a financing program to lower borrowing costs and meet environmental regulations. While the dividend yield is somewhat above average, unresolved problems due to excess generating capacity in the region and NMK's inability to obtain related regulatory relief indicate that a dividend rollback is likely and an omission possible.

Key Stock Statistics

S&P EPS Est. 1995	1.50	Tang. Bk. Value/Share	14.25
P/E on S&P Est. 1995	9.7	Beta	0.57
S&P EPS Est. 1996	1.50	Shareholders	105,900
Dividend Rate/Share	1.12	Market cap. (B)	$ 1.8
Shs. outstg. (M)	144.3	Inst. holdings	44%
Avg. daily vol. (M)	1.319	Insider holdings	NA

Value of $10,000 invested 5 years ago: $ 12,728

Fiscal Year Ending Dec. 31

	1995	% Change	1994	% Change	1993	% Change
Revenues (Million $)						
1Q	1,125	-9%	1,236	9%	1,136	10%
2Q	938.8	-4%	979.7	5%	929.3	5%
3Q	—	—	918.8	4%	880.0	7%
4Q	—	—	1,018	3%	988.2	3%
Yr.	—	—	4,152	6%	3,933	6%
Income (Million $)						
1Q	118.7	-14%	138.4	9%	127.0	24%
2Q	54.49	-19%	67.56	3%	65.33	-9%
3Q	—	—	48.38	NM	48.60	20%
4Q	—	—	-77.42	NM	30.96	-26%
Yr.	—	—	177.0	-35%	271.8	6%
Earnings Per Share ($)						
1Q	0.75	-18%	0.92	7%	0.86	26%
2Q	0.31	-26%	0.42	2%	0.41	-11%
3Q	E0.23	-15%	0.27	-7%	0.29	26%
4Q	E0.21	NM	-0.61	NM	0.16	-33%
Yr.	E1.50	50%	1.00	-42%	1.71	6%

Next earnings report expected: late October

Niagara Mohawk Power

Business Summary - 30-AUG-95

Niagara Mohawk supplies electricity (85% of 1994 revenues) and gas (15%) to nearly 1.6 million customers in a large area of western and upstate New York and some parts of southern Ontario. Electric revenues by customer class in recent years:

	1994	1993	1992	1991
Residential	35%	35%	35%	34%
Commercial	36%	37%	37%	36%
Industrial	18%	17%	20%	19%
Other	11%	11%	8%	11%

Power sources in 1994 were coal 15%, oil 3%, nuclear 18%, hydro 8%, natural gas 2%, and purchased power 54%. Peak load in 1994 was 6,458 mw, and system capability totaled 8,026 mw, for a capacity margin of 20%.

NMK owns 100% of the Nine Mile Point 1 nuclear unit and 41% of the Nine Mile Point 2 unit. In 1987, NMK wrote off $755.0 million ($5.94 a share) of disallowed costs and $78.0 million ($0.61 a share) for construction delays. Nine Mile Point 2 began operating commercialy in April 1988. In January 1995, NML sold HYDRA-CO, an unregulated generating subsidiary; proceeds of $207 million cash were used to repay $200 million of short term debt.

Annual expenditures for construction and nuclear fuel were $490.1 million in 1994. The company estimates costs for these items in 1995 at under $380 million (to be funded by cash from operations), and $406 million, $358 million, $410 million and $358 million for the respective years 1996 through 1999.

Important Developments

Jul. '95—In reporting 1995 first half earnings, NMK noted that purchases of electricity from unregulated generators were continuing to pressure its prices. NMK is required by law to purchase unregulated generator power at prices in excess of its internal cost of production, and in greater volumes than it needs; it expects payments to unregulated generators to exceed $1 billion in 1995. The company reported share earnings for the 1995 six months of $1.06, down from $1.34 a year earlier due the negative impact on sales of warmer than normal weather, and to the loss of an electric revenue adjustment mechanism that allowed it to recover revenue shortfalls in future periods. The revenue reduction amounted to $39 million in the 1994 first half under an April 1995 New York Public Service Commission rate agreement. Expenses to repair storm damage were also a factor in the earnings decline.
Feb. '95—The company charged $0.89 a share against 1994 earnings to cover workforce reductions.

Capitalization

Long Term Debt: $3,455,933,000 (6/95).
Red. Preferred Stock: $251,700,000.
Cum. Preferred Stock.: $290,000,000.

Per Share Data ($)

(Year Ended Dec. 31)

	1994	1993	1992	1991	1990	1989
Tangible Bk. Val.	14.25	14.39	15.25	14.73	13.53	13.17
Earnings	1.00	1.71	1.61	1.49	0.30	0.78
Dividends	1.09	0.95	0.76	0.32	Nil	0.60
Payout Ratio	109%	56%	47%	21%	Nil	77%
Prices - High	20⅝	25½	20½	18	14¾	15
- Low	12	18⅞	17½	12¾	11¾	10¾
P/E Ratio - High	21	15	13	12	49	19
- Low	12	11	11	9	39	14

Income Statement Analysis (Million $)

	1994	%Chg	1993	%Chg	1992	%Chg	1991
Revs.	4,152	6%	3,933	6%	3,702	9%	3,383
Depr.	308	11%	277	1%	274	6%	259
Maint.	203	-14%	236	4%	226	NM	228
Fxd. Chgs. Cov.	1.8	-21%	2.3	8%	2.2	8%	2.0
Constr. Credits	9.1	-43%	16.0	-24%	21.0	11%	19.0
Eff. Tax Rate	40%	—	35%	—	38%	—	36%
Net Inc.	177	-35%	272	6%	256	5%	243

Balance Sheet & Other Fin. Data (Million $)

	1994	1993	1992	1991	1990	1989
Gross Prop.	10,485	10,109	9,642	9,180	8,703	8,324
Cap. Exp.	485	519	490	518	422	406
Net Prop.	7,036	6,877	6,666	6,439	6,219	6,041
Capitalization:						
LT Debt	3,298	3,259	3,491	3,325	3,313	3,249
% LT Debt	52	53	56	56	57	57
Pfd.	546	413	460	503	532	558
% Pfd.	8.70	6.70	7.40	8.50	9.20	9.70
Common	2,462	2,456	2,240	2,116	1,955	1,915
% Common	39	40	36	36	34	34
Total Cap.	7,565	7,442	6,947	6,643	6,431	5,961

Ratio Analysis

	1994	1993	1992	1991	1990	1989
Oper. Ratio	89.6	86.7	85.8	84.5	85.7	85.8
% Earn. on Net Prop.	6.2	7.8	8.0	8.3	7.4	6.9
% Ret. on Revs.	4.3	6.9	6.9	7.2	2.6	5.2
% Ret. On Invest.Cap	6.1	7.7	8.0	8.3	6.1	7.5
% Return On Com.Eqty	5.8	10.2	10.1	10.0	2.1	5.6

Dividend Data

—Following their omission in August 1989, common dividends were reinstated with the July 1991 declaration. Dividends had been maintained on the preferred shares.

Amt. of Div. $	Date Decl.	Ex-Div. Date	Stock of Record	Payment Date
0.280	Jul. 28	Aug. 02	Aug. 08	Aug. 31 '94
0.280	Oct. 27	Nov. 01	Nov. 07	Nov. 30 '94
0.280	Jan. 26	Jan. 31	Feb. 06	Feb. 28 '95
0.280	Apr. 13	Apr. 25	May. 01	May. 31 '95
0.280	Jul. 27	Aug. 03	Aug. 07	Aug. 31 '95

Data as orig. reptd.; bef. results of disc opers. and/or spec. items. Per share data adj. for stk. divs. as of ex-div. date.
E-Estimated. NA-Not Available. NM-Not Meaningful. NR-Not Ranked.

Office—300 Erie Boulevard West, Syracuse, NY 13202. **Tel**—(315) 474-1511. **Chrmn & CEO**—W. E. Davis. **Pres & COO**—A. J. Budney Jr. **Secy**—K. A. Rice. **VP-Treas**—A. W. Roos. **Investor Contact**—Leon T. Mazur (315-428-5876). **Dirs**—W. F. Allyn, L. Burkhardt III, D. M. Costle, E. M. Davis, W. E. Davis, W. J. Donlon, E. W. Duffy, J. G. Haehl Jr., B. G. Hill, H. A. Panasci Jr., P. M. Peterson, D. B. Riefler, S. B. Schwartz, J. G. Wick. **Transfer Agent & Registrar**—The Bank of New York, NYC. **Incorporated** in New York in 1937. Empl-9,200. **S&P Analyst:** Jane Collin

NICOR Inc.

NYSE Symbol **GAS**
In S&P 500

19-SEP-95

Industry:
Utilities-Gas

Summary: This holding company's Northern Illinois Gas subsidiary is one of the largest U.S. natural gas distributors. NICOR is also involved in containerized shipping.

S&P Opinion: Hold (★★★)	Recent Price • 27¾	Yield • 4.6%	**Earnings vs. Previous Year**
	52 Wk Range • 28½-21¾	12-Mo. P/E • 14.3	▲=Up ▼=Down ▶=No Change

Quantitative Evaluations

Outlook
(1 Lowest—5 Highest)
• **1+**

Fair Value
• **21¼**

Risk
• **Low**

Earn./Div. Rank
• **B+**

Technical Eval.
• **Bearish** since 6/95

Rel. Strength Rank
(1 Lowest—99 Highest)
• **65**

Insider Activity
• **NA**

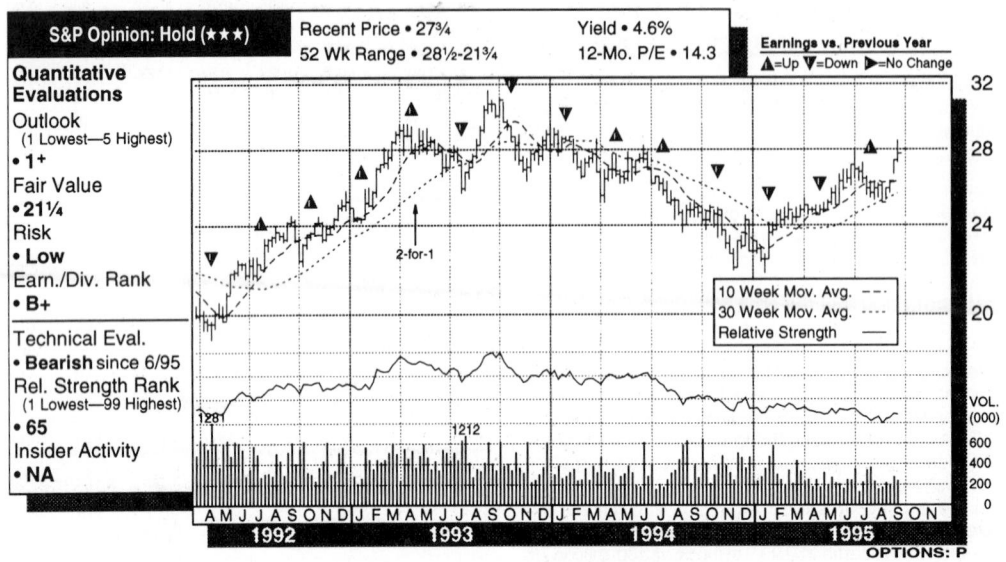

OPTIONS: P

Overview - 19-SEP-95

Although results should benefit from improved operating performance in both the gas distribution and shipping segments, earnings should decrease in 1995, as higher capital spending at Northern Illinois Gas exceeds typical levels, causing interest expense and depreciation charges to rise. A significantly higher tax rate will also depress earnings. Full-year results will be further penalized by depressed first half earnings, reflecting the impact of warmer weather. A share repurchase program should partially mitigate the negative impact on EPS.

Valuation - 19-SEP-95

Like those of others in its industry, NICOR's shares fell substantially in 1994, ending the year down over 25% from their 1993 high. The shares have appreciated over 20% since the beginning of 1995. The dividend was recently raised 1.6%, and the shares are currently yielding about 4.6%. Depressed earnings in the 1995 second half will limit further appreciation. The shares are trading at 13X to 14X estimated 1996 EPS of $2.05. Based on NICOR's near-term prospects, the stock is fully valued, and should be only an average market performer over the next six to 12 months. However, with a secure and rising dividend, the shares are an attractive holding for total return.

Key Stock Statistics

S&P EPS Est. 1995	1.90	Tang. Bk. Value/Share	13.19
P/E on S&P Est. 1995	14.6	Beta	0.19
S&P EPS Est. 1996	2.05	Shareholders	43,500
Dividend Rate/Share	1.28	Market cap. (B)	$ 1.4
Shs. outstg. (M)	50.5	Inst. holdings	50%
Avg. daily vol. (M)	0.047	Insider holdings	NA

Value of $10,000 invested 5 years ago: $ 15,969

Fiscal Year Ending Dec. 31

	1995	% Change	1994	% Change	1993	% Change
Revenues (Million $)						
1Q	609.8	-22%	780.0	16%	673.0	16%
2Q	246.9	-8%	268.0	-4%	278.0	7%
3Q	—	—	166.0	-11%	186.0	NM
4Q	—	—	395.5	-26%	538.0	-8%
Yr.	—	—	1,609	-4%	1,674	4%
Income (Million $)						
1Q	40.90	-20%	51.30	11%	46.40	16%
2Q	17.10	8%	15.90	-5%	16.70	-5%
3Q	—	—	7.50	-18%	9.20	-20%
4Q	—	—	34.70	-7%	37.20	-6%
Yr.	—	—	109.5	NM	109.4	1%
Earnings Per Share ($)						
1Q	0.80	-16%	0.95	14%	0.83	19%
2Q	0.34	13%	0.30	3%	0.29	-6%
3Q	E0.15	7%	0.14	-13%	0.16	-20%
4Q	E0.61	-9%	0.67	-1%	0.68	-3%
Yr.	E1.90	-8%	2.07	5%	1.97	3%

Next earnings report expected: late October

Business Summary - 19-SEP-95

NICOR is a diversified energy company engaged in the purchase, storage, distribution, transportation and sale of natural gas; fully containerized liner shipping; and the servicing of heating and cooling systems. Its oil and gas exploration and development business was sold in 1993. Segment contributions in 1994 (profits in million $) were:

	Revs.	Profits
Gas distribution	90%	$179.1
Shipping	10%	18.6
Other	Nil	-4.0

The Northern Illinois Gas subsidiary serves more than 1.8 million customers in an area in excess of 17,000 sq. mi., covering 544 communities in northern Illinois. Gas sales volume in 1994 totaled 288.7 Bcf, down from 303.4 Bcf in 1993. Gas transported for others totaled 211.1 Bcf, versus 185.4 Bcf in 1993. Degree days in 1994 were 5,851, versus 6,172 in 1993, versus a norm of 6,177 days. As of December 31, 1994, the company operated seven underground gas storage facilities. On an annual basis, GAS cycles about 130 Bcf in and out of storage.

Shipping operations, conducted by Tropical Shipping, consist of transportation of containerized freight between Florida and 22 ports in the Caribbean, Central America and Mexico. Most of Tropical's markets rely heavily on imports for food, construction materials, and other essentials. Operations are subject to seasonal fluctuations related to tourist and agricultural activity. In 1993, through a joint venture with Compagnie Generale Maritime of France, the unit began providing services to five ports in the Eastern Caribbean. Twenty-foot equivalent units shipped in 1994 came to 95,900, up from 93,800 in 1994. GAS owned 14 ships at 1994 and 1993 year-end.

Important Developments

May '95—Northern Illinois Gas filed with the Illinois Commerce Commission for a 4.4%, $73 million general rate increase. The company is seeking a rate of return on original-cost rate base of 10.67%, reflecting a 12.95% cost of common equity. It considers the increase needed to recover costs associated with enhancements to the underground storage and delivery system, other capital costs, and rising operating costs. The filing also proposes revisions to some services provided to commercial and industrial customers. The commission has up to 11 months to decide the case.

Capitalization

Long Term Debt: $459,100,000 (6/95).
Preferred & Preference Stock: $8,900,000.

Per Share Data ($)

(Year Ended Dec. 31)

	1994	1993	1992	1991	1990	1989
Tangible Bk. Val.	13.25	13.04	12.76	12.29	11.68	11.06
Cash Flow	4.03	3.72	4.12	3.89	3.86	3.78
Earnings	2.07	1.97	1.91	1.86	1.93	1.99
Dividends	1.26	1.22	1.17	1.12	1.06	1.00
Payout Ratio	60%	62%	61%	60%	55%	50%
Prices - High	29¼	31⅝	25¾	23¾	23½	23
- Low	21⅞	24⅛	19	19½	17⅜	14⅞
P/E Ratio - High	14	16	13	13	12	12
- Low	11	12	10	10	9	7

Income Statement Analysis (Million $)

	1994	%Chg	1993	%Chg	1992	%Chg	1991
Revs.	1,609	-4%	1,674	4%	1,612	6%	1,516
Oper. Inc.	297	NM	295	-8%	322	5%	307
Depr.	103	6%	97.0	-22%	124	5%	118
Int. Exp.	40.1	-4%	41.7	-11%	47.0	11%	42.2
Pretax Inc.	161	-2%	164	4%	158	NM	158
Eff. Tax Rate	32%	—	33%	—	31%	—	31%
Net Inc.	110	NM	109	NM	108	NM	109

Balance Sheet & Other Fin. Data (Million $)

	1994	1993	1992	1991	1990	1989
Cash	42.3	62.1	40.0	75.9	100	82.9
Curr. Assets	418	509	529	488	515	529
Total Assets	2,210	2,222	2,339	2,280	2,180	2,137
Curr. Liab.	600	584	694	578	546	543
LT Debt	459	459	417	458	422	392
Common Eqty.	683	704	712	704	676	655
Total Cap.	1,375	1,404	1,561	1,617	1,621	1,580
Cap. Exp.	172	142	174	209	174	150
Cash Flow	212	205	231	225	224	224

Ratio Analysis

	1994	1993	1992	1991	1990	1989
Curr. Ratio	0.7	0.9	0.8	0.8	0.9	1.0
% LT Debt of Cap.	33.4	32.7	26.7	28.3	26.0	24.8
% Net Inc.of Revs.	6.8	6.5	6.7	7.2	7.4	7.4
% Ret. on Assets	5.1	4.9	4.8	4.9	5.3	5.7
% Ret. on Equity	16.1	15.3	15.3	15.6	17.0	18.9

Dividend Data

Dividends have been paid since 1954. A dividend reinvestment plan is available.

Amt. of Div. $	Date Decl.	Ex-Div. Date	Stock of Record	Payment Date
0.315	Sep. 14	Sep. 26	Sep. 30	Nov. 01 '94
0.315	Dec. 14	Dec. 23	Dec. 30	Feb. 01 '95
0.320	Mar. 14	Mar. 27	Mar. 31	May. 01 '95
0.320	Jun. 14	Jun. 28	Jun. 30	Aug. 01 '95
0.320	Sep. 13	Sep. 27	Sep. 29	Nov. 01 '95

Data as orig. reptd.; bef. results of disc. opers. and/or spec. items. Per share data adj. for stk. divs. as of ex-div. date. E-Estimated. NA-Not Available. NM-Not Meaningful. NR-Not Ranked.

Office—1844 Ferry Rd., Naperville, IL 60563-9600. **Tel**—(708) 305-9500. **Chrmn & CEO**—R. G. Cline. **Pres**—T. L. Fisher. **SVP & Secy**—D. L. Cyranoski. **Treas**—D. W. Lohrentz. **Investor Contact**—Randy Horn. **Dirs**— R. M. Beavers, Jr., J. H. Birdsall III, W. H. Clark, R. G. Cline, T. L. Fisher, J. E. Jones, D. J. Keller, C. S. Locke, S. R. Petersen, D. R. Toll, P. A. Wier. **Transfer Agent & Registrar**—Harris Trust & Savings Bank, Chicago. **Incorporated** in Illinois in 1953. **Empl**-3,400. **S&P Analyst:** Ronald J. Gross

NIKE, Inc.

NYSE Symbol **NKE**
In S&P 500

01-AUG-95 | Industry: Leather/shoes | **Summary:** NIKE is one of the world's largest suppliers of high-quality athletic footwear and athletic apparel.

| **S&P Opinion: Accumulate (★★★★)** | Recent Price • 91⅝ | Yield • 1.1% |
| | 52 Wk Range • 92¾-58⅛ | 12-Mo. P/E • 16.8 |

Quantitative Evaluations

Outlook
  (1 Lowest—5 Highest)
• **2**
Fair Value
• **80¾**
Risk
• **Low**
Earn./Div. Rank
• **A-**

Technical Eval.
• **Bullish** since 5/95
Rel. Strength Rank
  (1 Lowest—99 Highest)
• **77**
Insider Activity
• **NA**

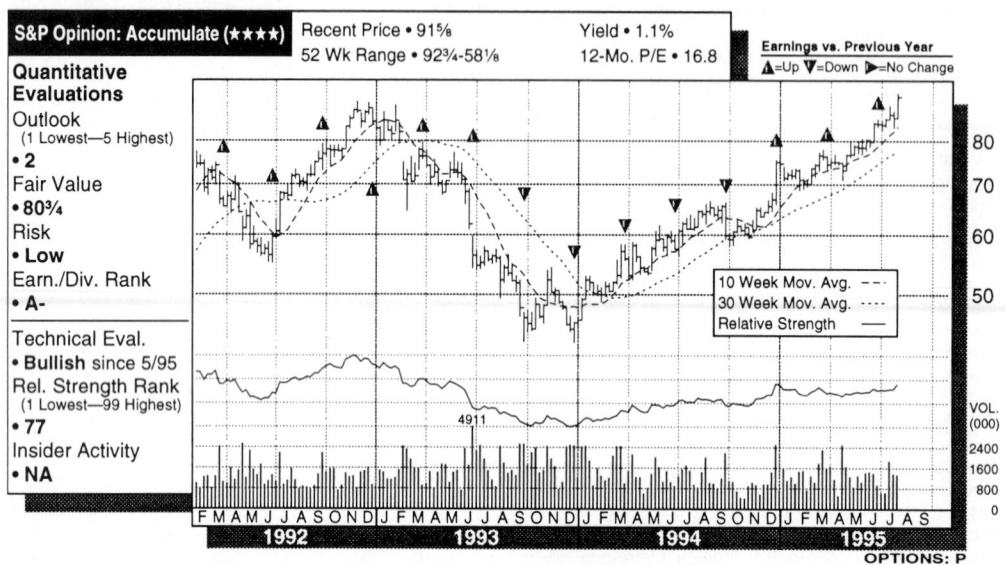

Earnings vs. Previous Year
▲=Up ▼=Down ▶=No Change

10 Week Mov. Avg. ---
30 Week Mov. Avg. ·····
Relative Strength ——

VOL. (000)

OPTIONS: P

Overview - 01-AUG-95

Sales should continue to improve in fiscal 1995-96; however, it is not likely that revenue growth will match 1994-95's 26% gain. Greater demand for athletic footwear and apparel as well as improved economies throughout the world, especially in Europe, should drive sales growth. In the U.S., demand for basketball shoes, increased market share, and enthusiasm for new athletic shoe styles should propel sales growth. Areas expected to show the greatest gains include cross training, women's fitness, children's and outdoor footwear, and related apparel. Margins should widen on higher volume, ongoing benefits of more diversified sourcing in Southeast Asia, tighter inventory controls, and more efficient expenditures on marketing and advertising. Share earnings will benefit from fewer outstanding shares, reflecting a $450 million, three-year share repurchase program approved in July 1993.

Valuation - 01-AUG-95

Although these shares are extremely volatile, patient investors have seen their investment in NIKE more than triple in the past five years. After reaching a high of 90 1/4 at the end of 1992, NIKE's stock nosedived, hitting a recent low of 43 1/8 in early 1994. Since then, however, the shares have recouped most of this loss, reflecting strong earnings gains in fiscal 1994-95 and expectations of good growth in 1995-96. We continue to recommend investors accumulate this stock for above-average appreciation.

Key Stock Statistics

S&P EPS Est. 1996	6.25	Tang. Bk. Value/Share	20.78
P/E on S&P Est. 1996	14.7	Beta	1.52
Dividend Rate/Share	1.00	Shareholders	3,900
Shs. outstg. (M)	72.2	Market cap. (B)	$ 6.5
Avg. daily vol. (M)	0.263	Inst. holdings	51%
		Insider holdings	NA

Value of $10,000 invested 5 years ago: $ 36,569

Fiscal Year Ending May 31

	1995	% Change	1994	% Change	1993	% Change
Revenues (Million $)						
1Q	1,170	6%	1,108	NM	1,098	16%
2Q	1,054	31%	805.8	-8%	876.0	18%
3Q	1,125	29%	871.8	-10%	972.0	12%
4Q	1,412	41%	1,004	2%	983.3	16%
Yr.	4,761	26%	3,790	-4%	3,931	15%
Income (Million $)						
1Q	106.0	-7%	114.1	—	—	—
2Q	84.94	62%	52.30	-31%	76.05	24%
3Q	95.35	51%	63.24	-29%	89.47	8%
4Q	113.4	64%	69.16	-10%	76.91	9%
Yr.	399.7	34%	298.8	-18%	365.0	11%
Earnings Per Share ($)						
1Q	1.43	-4%	1.49	-7%	1.60	7%
2Q	1.16	68%	0.69	-30%	0.98	22%
3Q	1.29	52%	0.85	-27%	1.16	7%
4Q	1.56	68%	0.93	-7%	1.00	9%
Yr.	5.44	37%	3.96	-16%	4.74	10%

Next earnings report expected: mid September

NIKE, Inc.

01-AUG-95

Business Summary - 01-AUG-95

NIKE, Inc. designs, develops and markets worldwide a broad variety of high-quality footwear and apparel products for a wide range of sport, athletic and leisure activities. Nike also produces high-quality classic footwear sold under the brand name Cole Haan, sells various plastic products through Tetra Plastics, and makes headwear with licensed team logos through its Sports Specialties division. In early 1995, the company acquired Montreal-based Canstar Sports Inc., the world's largest hockey equipment maker for $395 million (U.S.).

Approximately 64% of fiscal 1994-95 sales were made in the U.S., the same amount as in fiscal 1993-94. About 76% of domestic sales were footwear, 14% apparel, and 10% other brands. Products were sold to approximately 14,000 retail accounts in the U.S. The Footlocker is NIKE's largest customer, accounting for approximately 14% of total sales in 1993-94. International sales accounted for 36% of total sales in 1994-95, the same as in the preceding fiscal year. About 72% of international sales were footwear and 28% apparel. Products are sold abroad through a mix of independent distributors, licensees, subsidiaries and branch offices in about 82 countries.

NIKE believes that its research and development efforts form the cornerstone of its past and future success. During 1993-94, NIKE spent approximately $24.6 million on research and development.

Approximately 40% of NIKE's apparel is produced in the U.S., with the remainder made in Asia and South America. All footwear except Cole Haan is produced offshore, primarily in Asia.

Important Developments

Jul. '95—NIKE attributed strength in its fourth quarter earnings to sales increases of 142%, 47%, 39%, 29% and 28% of other footwear brands, domestic apparel, domestic athletic footwear, international apparel, and international footwear. Operating income surged 58% on lower selling, general and administrative expenses as a percent of sales. Separately, NIKE announced that worldwide orders scheduled for delivery between June and November 1995 totaled a record $2.5 billion, 35% higher than last year's. The company also said that as of May 31, 1995, it had bought a total of 4.9 million shares of Class B common stock for $283 million, in conjunction with the $450 million, three-year repurchase program approved in July 1993.

Capitalization

Long Term Debt: $10,565,000 (5/95).

$0.10 Red. Preferred Stock: 300,000 shs. ($1 par); red. at par. Held by Nissho Iwai American Corp.

Class A Common Stock: 26,679,057 shs. (no par); conv. sh.-for-sh. into Cl. B; elects 75% of dirs. P. H. Knight holds about 94% (5/94).

Class B Common Stock: 46,590,625 shs. (no par); P. H. Knight holds about 34% (5/94).

Shareholders of record: 7,092 (5/94).

Per Share Data ($)

(Year Ended May 31)

	1995	1994	1993	1992	1991	1990
Tangible Bk. Val.	NA	21.64	19.62	16.17	12.19	9.38
Cash Flow	NA	4.91	5.52	4.92	4.23	3.44
Earnings	5.44	3.96	4.74	4.30	3.77	3.21
Dividends	0.90	0.80	0.70	0.58	0.48	0.35
Payout Ratio	17%	20%	15%	13%	13%	11%
Cal. Yrs.	1994	1993	1992	1991	1990	1989
Prices - High	76½	89¼	90¼	75¾	47⅞	34⅝
- Low	46¼	43⅛	55	35⅛	24	12⅝
P/E Ratio - High	14	23	19	18	13	11
- Low	9	11	12	8	6	4

Income Statement Analysis (Million $)

	1994	%Chg	1993	%Chg	1992	%Chg	1991
Revs.	3,790	-4%	3,931	16%	3,402	13%	3,004
Oper. Inc.	579	-14%	672	13%	593	15%	516
Depr.	71.5	18%	60.4	27%	47.7	38%	34.5
Int. Exp.	15.6	-94%	265	NM	31.3	2%	30.8
Pretax Inc.	491	-17%	595	14%	522	13%	462
Eff. Tax Rate	39%	—	39%	—	37%	—	38%
Net Inc.	299	-18%	365	11%	329	15%	287

Balance Sheet & Other Fin. Data (Million $)

	1994	1993	1992	1991	1990	1989
Cash	519	291	260	120	90.0	86.0
Curr. Assets	1,770	1,621	1,388	1,280	838	638
Total Assets	2,374	2,187	1,873	1,708	1,095	825
Curr. Liab.	562	453	421	628	273	216
LT Debt	12.4	15.0	69.5	30.0	25.9	34.1
Common Eqty.	1,741	1,646	1,332	1,033	784	562
Total Cap.	1,772	1,691	1,401	1,072	814	601
Cap. Exp.	95.0	97.0	106	165	87.0	42.0
Cash Flow	370	425	377	321	260	182

Ratio Analysis

	1994	1993	1992	1991	1990	1989
Curr. Ratio	3.2	3.6	3.3	2.0	3.1	3.0
% LT Debt of Cap.	0.7	0.9	5.0	2.8	3.2	5.7
% Net Inc.of Revs.	7.9	9.3	9.7	9.6	10.9	9.8
% Ret. on Assets	13.3	17.9	18.4	20.4	25.3	21.7
% Ret. on Equity	17.9	24.5	27.8	31.5	36.0	34.2

Dividend Data (Dividends have been paid since 1984.)

Amt. of Div. $	Date Decl.	Ex-Div. Date	Stock of Record	Payment Date
0.200	Aug. 19	Sep. 02	Sep. 09	Oct. 03 '94
0.250	Nov. 18	Dec. 05	Dec. 09	Jan. 03 '95
0.250	Feb. 06	Mar. 06	Mar. 10	Apr. 03 '95
0.250	May. 19	Jun. 06	Jun. 09	Jul. 05 '95

Data as orig. reptd.; bef. results of disc. opers. and/or spec. items. Per share data adj. for stk. divs. as of ex-div. date. E-Estimated. NA-Not Available. NM-Not Meaningful. NR-Not Ranked.

Office—One Bowerman Drive, Beaverton, OR 97005-6453. **Tel**—(503) 671-6453. **Chrmn & CEO**—P. H. Knight. **Pres**—T. E. Clarke. **VP-CFO**—R. S. Falcone. **Secy**—J. E. Jaqua. **Dirs**—W. J. Bowerman, T. E. Clarke, J. K. Conway, R. D. DeNunzio, R. K. Donahue, D. J. Hayes, D. G. Houser, J. E. Jaqua, P. H. Knight, K. Ohmae, R. A. Pfeiffer Jr., C. W. Robinson, J. R. Thompson Jr. **Transfer Agent & Registrar**—First Chicago Trust Co. of New York, NYC. **Incorporated** in Oregon in 1968. **Empl**-9,500. **S&P Analyst:** Elizabeth Vandeventer

NorAm Energy Corp.

NYSE Symbol **NAE**
In S&P 500

12-SEP-95

Industry:
Utilities-Gas

Summary: This company (formerly Arkla, Inc.) is engaged in the distribution and transmission, including gathering and storage, of natural gas in the central U.S.

S&P Opinion: Hold (★★★)		
Recent Price • 7⅛	Yield • 3.9%	
52 Wk Range • 7¼-5⅛	12-Mo. P/E • 23.8	

Earnings vs. Previous Year
▲=Up ▼=Down ▶=No Change

Quantitative Evaluations

Outlook
(1 Lowest—5 Highest)
• **1+**

Fair Value
• **5¾**

Risk
• **Average**

Earn./Div. Rank
• **B**

Technical Eval.
• **Bullish** since 4/95

Rel. Strength Rank
(1 Lowest—99 Highest)
• **60**

Insider Activity
• **Neutral**

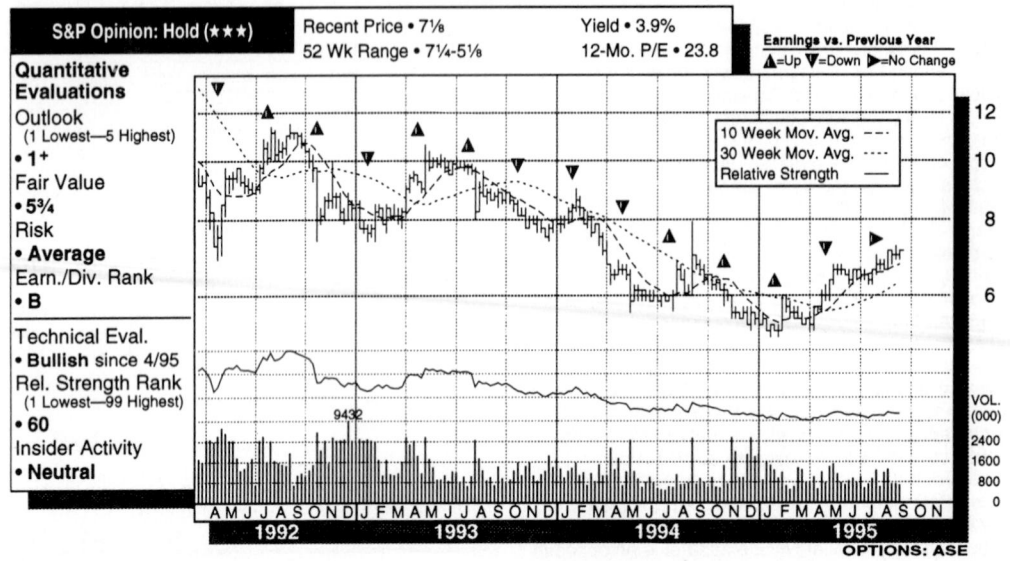

10 Week Mov. Avg. - - -
30 Week Mov. Avg. · · · ·
Relative Strength —

VOL. (000)
2400
1600
800
0

AMJJASOND 1992 JFMAMJJASOND 1993 JFMAMJJASOND 1994 JFMAMJJASON 1995

OPTIONS: ASE

Overview - 12-SEP-95

Recent efforts have been concentrated on closing the earnings gap between pipeline actual and allowed rates of return on assets, resulting in significant increases in operating income over the past two years. The recent "spindown" of gathering facilities into a separate non-regulated subsidiary should enable the company to be more aggressive in the provison of services to customers, and to anticipate changes in the marketplace. Results should also benefit from a new rate structure that allows for better cost recovery and reduces sensitivity to weather, and from development of the Perryville, La., hub. The hub's attractive geographic location could lead to strong profit growth. Distribution profits should increase in 1995 on higher gas sales, customer growth of 1%, and cost containment. Continuing efforts to reduce debt will likely lead to lower interest expense.

Valuation - 12-SEP-95

The stock, up somewhat from its recent lows, continues to reflect the current poor price environment for natural gas. Demand has returned to more normal levels, after a warm winter, but supply has been more than adequate. Consequently, it is unlikely that there will be a significant near-term rally in gas prices. As a result, the stock should not experience substantial price improvement in the near future. With a relatively high payout ratio, it is not likely that the dividend will be raised. However, the dividend yield is somewhat higher than that of NAE's peer group.

Key Stock Statistics

S&P EPS Est. 1995	0.38	Tang. Bk. Value/Share	1.15
P/E on S&P Est. 1995	18.8	Beta	0.70
S&P EPS Est. 1996	0.43	Shareholders	3,700
Dividend Rate/Share	0.28	Market cap. (B)	$0.883
Shs. outstg. (M)	123.9	Inst. holdings	41%
Avg. daily vol. (M)	0.174	Insider holdings	NA

Value of $10,000 invested 5 years ago: $ 3,547

Fiscal Year Ending Dec. 31

	1995	% Change	1994	% Change	1993	% Change
Revenues (Million $)						
1Q	888.2	-19%	1,092	8%	1,011	22%
2Q	565.8	6%	535.5	-13%	613.4	18%
3Q	—	—	460.5	NM	457.1	-2%
4Q	—	—	713.1	-18%	868.0	-6%
Yr.	—	—	2,801	-5%	2,950	7%
Income (Million $)						
1Q	52.00	-6%	55.49	-28%	76.71	NM
2Q	-7.07	NM	-6.38	NM	-7.99	NM
3Q	—	—	-21.66	NM	-24.56	NM
4Q	—	—	23.84	NM	-4.22	NM
Yr.	—	—	51.29	28%	39.94	NM
Earnings Per Share ($)						
1Q	0.41	-7%	0.44	-28%	0.61	NM
2Q	-0.07	NM	-0.07	NM	-0.08	NM
3Q	E-0.12	NM	-0.19	NM	-0.22	NM
4Q	E0.16	-11%	0.18	NM	-0.05	NM
Yr.	E0.38	6%	0.36	38%	0.26	NM

Next earnings report expected: early November

NorAm Energy Corp.

Business Summary - 12-SEP-95

NorAm Energy (formerly Arkla, Inc.) is engaged in transmission and distribution of natural gas in the central U.S. In 1992, it began a plan to improve the level and quality of earnings, reposition itself to better compete and succeed in the post-FERC Order 636 regulatory environment, and strengthen its financial condition through the sale of assets not central to the pipeline or distribution segments. Revenue contributions in recent years were:

	1994	1993	1992
Natural gas sales	92%	94%	92%
Gas transportation	6%	4%	4%
Chemical and petroleum	-	1%	3%
Other	2%	1%	1%

Arkla, Entex and Minnegasco provide gas distribution services to 2.7 million customers in six central states extending from the Gulf Coast to Minnesota. Together, the three units comprise the third largest U.S. gas distribution system. In September 1994, the company's distribution properties and certain related pipeline assets in Kansas were sold to UtiliCorp United Inc. Combined gas sales and transportation volumes in 1994 amounted to 524.2 Bcf, up from 518.0 Bcf in 1993.

The company's pipeline business is conducted through NorAm Gas Transmission (located primarily in Arkansas and Oklahoma), which operates 6,400 miles of transmission lines; Mississippi River Transmission, which operates a 2,200 mile interstate pipeline system with access to the St. Louis, Mo., and southeastern Illinois markets; and NorAm Energy Services markets natural gas. Gas throughput in 1994 totaled 996.9 Bcf, up from 930.7 Bcf in 1993.

In October 1992, the Resolution Trust Corp. sued NAE as the successor-in-interest to Entex, Inc. for the failure of University Savings Association. The suit was settled in November 1994, leading to a pretax charge of $3.3 million.

In February 1995, upon receipt of FERC approval, NAE completed the transfer, or "spindown," of its 3,000 miles of gathering facilities into a separate wholly owned subsidiary, NorAm Field Services Corp. Gathering facilities unaffiliated with a pipeline are not subject to FERC regulation.

Important Developments

Aug. '95—NAE issued $200 million of 7.50% notes, due August 1, 2000. Separately, Minnegasco filed for a 4.2% rate increase with the Minnesota Public Utilities Commission.

Capitalization

Long Term Debt: $1,323,674,000 (6/95).

$3 Conv. Exch. Pfd. Stk.: 2,600,000 shs. ($50 liquid. pref.); conv. into com. at $28.625 a sh.

Per Share Data ($)

		(Year Ended Dec. 31)				
	1994	1993	1992	1991	1990	1989
Tangible Bk. Val.	0.75	0.56	0.09	2.54	5.59	4.75
Cash Flow	1.59	1.50	1.22	1.73	3.03	0.92
Earnings	0.36	0.26	-0.01	0.09	1.10	-0.80
Dividends	0.28	0.28	0.48	1.08	1.08	1.08
Payout Ratio	78%	108%	NM	NM	98%	NM
Prices - High	9	10⅝	12⅜	20¼	27¼	27¾
- Low	5¼	7⅜	6⅞	9¾	18½	20
P/E Ratio - High	25	41	NM	NM	25	NM
- Low	15	28	NM	NM	17	NM

Income Statement Analysis (Million $)

	1994	%Chg	1993	%Chg	1992	%Chg	1991
Revs.	2,801	-5%	2,950	8%	2,744	-1%	2,779
Oper. Inc.	418	17%	358	6%	339	-19%	418
Depr.	152	NM	151	NM	151	-21%	190
Int. Exp.	171	-1%	173	-7%	187	-6%	198
Pretax Inc.	86.0	NM	86.0	NM	19.0	-46%	35.0
Eff. Tax Rate	40%	—	54%	—	67%	—	48%
Net Inc.	51.0	28%	40.0	NM	6.0	-67%	18.0

Balance Sheet & Other Fin. Data (Million $)

	1994	1993	1992	1991	1990	1989
Cash	17.6	14.9	26.2	38.3	44.4	13.3
Curr. Assets	409	548	527	675	981	763
Total Assets	3,561	3,728	4,111	4,970	5,114	3,886
Curr. Liab.	896	903	975	1,621	1,602	1,332
LT Debt	1,414	1,629	1,783	1,551	1,450	1,162
Common Eqty.	587	578	583	886	1,155	580
Total Cap.	2,390	2,563	2,672	2,962	3,308	2,354
Cap. Exp.	170	146	135	356	817	567
Cash Flow	195	183	149	200	271	78.0

Ratio Analysis

	1994	1993	1992	1991	1990	1989
Curr. Ratio	0.5	0.6	0.5	0.4	0.6	0.6
% LT Debt of Cap.	59.2	63.6	66.7	52.4	43.8	49.4
% Net Inc.of Revs.	1.8	1.4	0.2	0.6	4.3	NM
% Ret. on Assets	1.4	1.0	0.1	0.4	2.1	NM
% Ret. on Equity	8.8	5.5	NM	1.0	10.2	NM

Dividend Data

—Dividends have been paid since 1953. A dividend reinvestment plan is available.

Amt. of Div. $	Date Decl.	Ex-Div. Date	Stock of Record	Payment Date
0.070	Jul. 13	Aug. 16	Aug. 22	Sep. 15 '94
0.070	Nov. 16	Nov. 21	Nov. 28	Dec. 15 '94
0.070	Feb. 08	Feb. 14	Feb. 21	Mar. 15 '95
0.070	May. 09	May. 16	May. 22	Jun. 15 '95
0.070	Jul. 17	Aug. 17	Aug. 21	Sep. 15 '95

Office—1600 Smith St., Houston, TX 77002. **Tel**—(713) 654-5100. **Chrmn, Pres & CEO**—T. M. Honea. **SVP & Treas**—W. H. Kelly. **SVP & Secy**—H. Gentry, Jr. **Investor Contact**—R. Burkhalter. **Dirs**—M. B. Bracy, J. E. Chenoweth, O. H. Croswell, W. A. DeRoeck, M. P. Foret, J. P. Gover, J. M. Grant, R. C. Hanna, W. J. Hart, T. M. Honea, M. Jones, S. Moncrief, L. C. Wallace. **Transfer Agents**—Norwest Bank Minnesota, South St. Paul, Minn.; Worthen Trust Co., Little Rock, Ark. **Registrars**—First Commercial Bank, Little Rock; Norwest Bank Minnesota. **Incorporated** in Delaware in 1928. **Empl**-6,840. **S&P Analyst:** Michael C. Barr

Nordstrom, Inc.

NASDAQ Symbol **NOBE**
In S&P 500

30-AUG-95

Industry:
Retail Stores

Summary: This Seattle-based specialty retailer of apparel and accessories, widely known for its emphasis on service, has expanded beyond the West Coast and operates 55 specialty stores.

S&P Opinion: Hold (★★★)	Recent Price • 40⅛	Yield • 1.2%
	52 Wk Range • 49¾-35	12-Mo. P/E • 17.4

Quantitative Evaluations

Outlook
(1 Lowest—5 Highest)
• **4−**

Fair Value
• **43%**

Risk
• **Average**

Earn./Div. Rank
• **A+**

Technical Eval.
• **Bullish** since 3/95

Rel. Strength Rank
(1 Lowest—99 Highest)
• **27**

Insider Activity
• **Neutral**

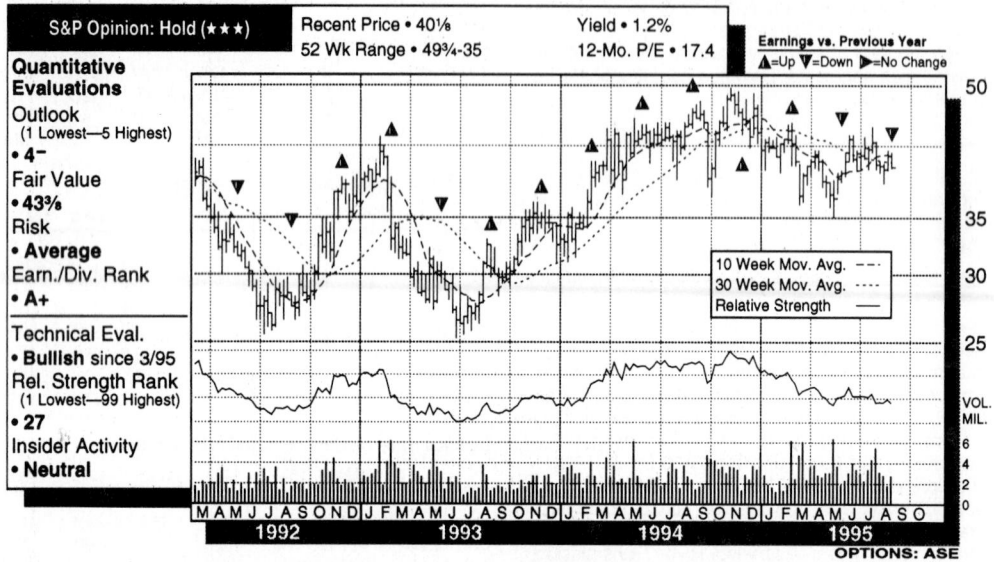

Earnings vs. Previous Year
▲=Up ▼=Down ▶=No Change

10 Week Mov. Avg. – – –
30 Week Mov. Avg. ·······
Relative Strength ——

VOL. MIL.

1992   1993   1994   1995

OPTIONS: ASE

Overview - 29-AUG-95

Sales gains for 1995-96 are projected at about 8%, with modest same store sales improvement of 2%, mostly in the second half. Gross margins should remain about level, as a stronger second half outweighs narrower gross margins in the first half. Expense ratios should also remain about level, leveraged off the higher volume from four new store openings. Over the longer term, square footage gains of 8% annually over the next few years enhance the company's earnings potential. A share buyback program of $100 million of the company's outstanding common stock has been authorized. Although the company plans additional borrowings to finance the share buyback, it remains conservatively financed.

Valuation - 29-AUG-95

The shares of this retail company are quite volatile. Because of its emphasis on service, the company's cost structure is higher than other apparel retailers. As a result, income is leveraged to same store sales gains, which were up only slightly in the first half of 1995-96. Although we anticipate healthier sales gains in the second half, earnings should be about flat with last year. But increased square footage, systems enhancements, and new stores coming on stream should boost earnings by about 16% next year. Until sales gains pick up, however, we remain neutral on the shares.

Key Stock Statistics

S&P EPS Est. 1996	2.45	Tang. Bk. Value/Share	16.55
P/E on S&P Est. 1996	16.4	Beta	1.90
S&P EPS Est. 1997	2.85	Shareholders	71,500
Dividend Rate/Share	0.50	Market cap. (B)	$ 3.3
Shs. outstg. (M)	82.3	Inst. holdings	55%
Avg. daily vol. (M)	0.515	Insider holdings	NA

Value of $10,000 invested 5 years ago: $ 11,424

Fiscal Year Ending Jan. 31

	1996	% Change	1995	% Change	1994	% Change
Revenues (Million $)						
1Q	815.6	7%	762.0	10%	695.6	5%
2Q	1,149	6%	1,080	6%	1,018	7%
3Q	—	—	862.0	12%	769.4	4%
4Q	—	—	1,191	8%	1,107	4%
Yr.	—	—	3,894	8%	3,590	5%
Income (Million $)						
1Q	27.68	-13%	31.97	183%	11.30	-48%
2Q	53.87	-15%	63.02	48%	42.65	2%
3Q	—	—	38.08	50%	25.46	9%
4Q	—	—	69.88	15%	61.02	22%
Yr.	—	—	203.0	45%	140.4	3%
Earnings Per Share ($)						
1Q	0.34	-13%	0.39	179%	0.14	-46%
2Q	0.65	-16%	0.77	48%	0.52	2%
3Q	E0.48	4%	0.46	48%	0.31	7%
4Q	E0.98	15%	0.85	15%	0.74	21%
Yr.	E2.45	NM	2.47	44%	1.71	2%

Next earnings report expected: early November

Business Summary - 29-AUG-95

Nordstrom is a specialty retailer, selling primarily full lines of medium-to-upscale apparel, shoes and accessories for women, men and children. At January 31, 1995, it was operating 55 large specialty stores and one smaller specialty store, 19 clearance and off-price stores, a men's boutique and leased shoe departments in 12 stores in Hawaii and Guam. Total square footage aggregated 10.0 million at 1994-95 year-end. Sales per square foot of selling space increased to $395 in 1994-95, from $383 in 1993-94.

Sales in 1994-95 were derived as follows:

Women's apparel & accessories	58%
Shoes	20%
Men's apparel & furnishings	16%
Children's apparel & accessories	4%
Other	2%

Nordstrom stores feature a wide selection of style, size and color in each merchandise category. Emphasis is placed on fashion and customer service. The company also places importance on store design and fixturing to enhance its merchandise presentations. The company operates 19 clearance centers under the name "Nordstrom Rack" that serve as outlets for clearance merchandise from the company's large specialty stores. The Racks also purchase merchandise directly from manufacturers.

The company launched its direct sales division with its first catalog mailed January 1994. Additional mailings will occur about every other month. The company is also testing interactive television shopping.

Important Developments

Aug. '95—Management said that second quarter 1995-96 results were disappointing, reflecting weak sales. Same store sales in the quarter rose only 0.4% from a year earlier. Directors authorized the repurchase of up to $100 million of the company's common stock. Additional borrowings will be required to fund the stock purchases. The company is scheduled to open two new department stores in the third quarter of 1995-96 and one new rack store. This, combined with two new department stores in the first quarter, completes the store opening schedule for 1995. A total of eight new stores are planned in 1996 and 1997. NOBE plans to spend over $750 million on capital projects during the next three years, of which $100 million will be allocated to refurbishing existing stores.

Capitalization

Long Term Debt: $339,768,000 (4/30/95), incl. lease obligs.

Per Share Data ($) (Year Ended Jan. 31)

	1995	1994	1993	1992	1991	1990
Tangible Bk. Val.	16.34	14.22	12.83	11.48	10.11	8.99
Cash Flow	3.82	2.97	2.92	2.83	2.47	2.27
Earnings	2.47	1.71	1.67	1.66	1.42	1.41
Dividends	0.39	0.34	0.32	0.31	0.30	0.28
Payout Ratio	16%	20%	19%	19%	21%	20%
Cal. Yrs.	1994	1993	1992	1991	1990	1989
Prices - High	49¾	43½	42¾	53	39¼	42½
- Low	31	25¼	25½	22	17¼	29¾
P/E Ratio - High	20	25	26	32	28	30
- Low	13	15	15	13	12	21

Income Statement Analysis (Million $)

	1995	%Chg	1994	%Chg	1993	%Chg	1992
Revs.	3,987	11%	3,590	5%	3,422	8%	3,180
Oper. Inc.	475	68%	283	NM	283	3%	274
Depr.	111	8%	103	NM	102	7%	95.5
Int. Exp.	39.1	-4%	40.8	-16%	48.3	-15%	56.5
Pretax Inc.	336	45%	231	4%	222	2%	217
Eff. Tax Rate	40%	—	39%	—	39%	—	38%
Net Inc.	203	45%	140	2%	137	NM	136

Balance Sheet & Other Fin. Data (Million $)

	1995	1994	1993	1992	1991	1990
Cash	32.5	91.2	29.1	14.7	24.7	33.1
Curr. Assets	1,398	1,315	1,220	1,178	1,090	1,011
Total Assets	2,397	2,177	2,053	2,042	1,903	1,707
Curr. Liab.	690	627	511	554	552	490
LT Debt	298	336	441	502	479	441
Common Eqty.	1,344	1,167	1,052	939	826	733
Total Cap.	1,642	1,550	1,542	1,488	1,351	1,218
Cap. Exp.	232	125	71.0	147	200	173
Cash Flow	314	243	239	231	201	185

Ratio Analysis

	1995	1994	1993	1992	1991	1990
Curr. Ratio	2.0	2.1	2.4	2.1	2.0	2.1
% LT Debt of Cap.	18.1	21.7	28.6	33.8	35.4	36.2
% Net Inc.of Revs.	5.1	3.9	4.0	4.3	4.0	4.3
% Ret. on Assets	8.9	6.6	6.7	6.9	6.4	7.1
% Ret. on Equity	16.2	12.7	13.7	15.4	14.8	16.7

Dividend Data —Cash has been paid in each year since 1971.

Amt. of Div. $	Date Decl.	Ex-Div. Date	Stock of Record	Payment Date
0.100	Aug. 16	Aug. 25	Aug. 31	Sep. 15 '94
0.100	Nov. 15	Nov. 23	Nov. 30	Dec. 15 '94
0.125	Feb. 21	Feb. 27	Mar. 03	Mar. 15 '95
0.125	May. 16	May. 24	May. 31	Jun. 15 '95
0.125	Aug. 15	Aug. 29	Aug. 31	Sep. 15 '95

Data as orig. reptd.; bef. results of disc. opers. and/or spec. items. Per share data adj. for stk. divs. as of ex-div. date. E-Estimated. NA-Not Available. NM-Not Meaningful. NR-Not Ranked.

Office—1501 Fifth Ave., Seattle, WA 98101-1603. **Tel**—(206) 628-2111. **Co-Chrmn**—R. Johnson & J. Whitacre. **Secy**—Karen E. Purpur. **Exec VP, Treas & Investor Contact**—John A. Goesling. **Dirs**—P. M. Condit. D. W. Gittinger, J. F. Harrigan, C. A. Lynch, A. McLaughlin, J. A. McMillan, B. A. Nordstrom, J. F. Nordstrom, J. N. Nordstrom, A. E. Osborne Jr., W. D. Ruckelshaus, E. C. Vaughan. **Transfer Agent & Registrar**—First Interstate Bank of California. **Incorporated** in Washington in 1946. **Empl**-40,000. **S&P Analyst:** Karen J. Sack CFA

Norfolk Southern

NYSE Symbol **NSC**
In S&P 500

30-AUG-95 **Industry:** Railroads

Summary: This company operates a 14,600-mile rail system and provides household relocation and high-value product motor carrier services.

S&P Opinion: Hold (★★★)	Recent Price • 70⅛	Yield • 2.9%
	52 Wk Range • 75-58½	12-Mo. P/E • 13.4

Quantitative Evaluations

Outlook
(1 Lowest—5 Highest)
• **2⁻**

Fair Value
• **64⅜**

Risk
• **Low**

Earn./Div. Rank
• **A**

Technical Eval.
• **Bullish** since 1/95

Rel. Strength Rank
(1 Lowest—99 Highest)
• **51**

Insider Activity
• **Neutral**

Earnings vs. Previous Year ▲=Up ▼=Down ►=No Change

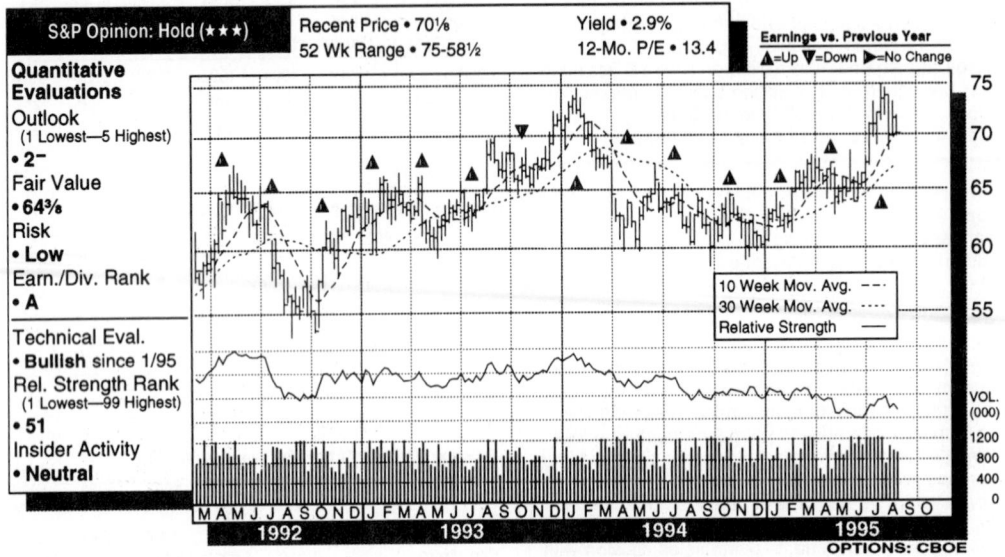

10 Week Mov. Avg. - - -
30 Week Mov. Avg. ·····
Relative Strength —

OPTIONS: CBOE

Overview - 30-AUG-95

Coal traffic in 1995 may be flat. A mild winter, excess stockpiles at domestic utilities and the displacement of coal by nuclear power generation will offset stronger export and metallurgical coal markets. Intermodal traffic should post strong gains, reflecting new services with connecting lines and an agreement with Hanjin Shipping. Domestic trailer movements will be hurt by increased truck competition. Auto volumes will be flat (in a down year for the industry) as NSC benefits from the startup of new Toyota and BMW plants. Grain volumes will benefit from increased shipments to poultry producers and a stronger export market. Margins should widen, reflecting reduced trackwork and increased asset and labor productivity. Improvement in high value motor carrier services will be offset by reduced contributions from relocation services.

Valuation - 30-AUG-95

In July the shares of this leading transportation firm tested the upper level of their two-year trading range. Investors rushed into rail stocks after a series of acquisitions drove home the point that rail issues were misvalued. Additionally, the economy didn't fall off a cliff in the third quarter, despite the abrupt slowdown in the Spring. With the Federal Reserve lowering interest rates and the industry's fundamentals better than ever, investors took a shine to rail issues. While we believe NSC is one of the best managed railroad firms, we recently downgraded the shares as rail shares have acquired a speculative tinge.

Key Stock Statistics

S&P EPS Est. 1995	5.45	Tang. Bk. Value/Share	36.37
P/E on S&P Est. 1995	12.9	Beta	0.92
S&P EPS Est. 1996	5.90	Shareholders	52,400
Dividend Rate/Share	2.08	Market cap. (B)	$ 9.4
Shs. outstg. (M)	131.0	Inst. holdings	61%
Avg. daily vol. (M)	0.191	Insider holdings	NA

Value of $10,000 invested 5 years ago: $ 20,534

Fiscal Year Ending Dec. 31

	1995	% Change	1994	% Change	1993	% Change
Revenues (Million $)						
1Q	1,139	6%	1,077	-3%	1,116	2%
2Q	1,190	2%	1,161	NM	1,170	2%
3Q	—	—	1,171	8%	1,089	-8%
4Q	—	—	1,172	8%	1,085	-7%
Yr.	—	—	4,581	3%	4,460	-3%
Income (Million $)						
1Q	170.7	18%	144.9	4%	138.9	NM
2Q	181.2	2%	178.5	15%	155.2	7%
3Q	—	—	168.3	77%	95.00	-35%
4Q	—	—	176.1	10%	159.4	24%
Yr.	—	—	667.8	22%	548.7	-2%
Earnings Per Share ($)						
1Q	1.29	23%	1.05	6%	0.99	2%
2Q	1.38	6%	1.30	17%	1.11	8%
3Q	E1.40	13%	1.24	80%	0.69	-33%
4Q	E1.38	5%	1.31	14%	1.15	26%
Yr.	E5.45	11%	4.90	24%	3.94	NM

Next earnings report expected: late October

Norfolk Southern

Business Summary - 30-AUG-95

Norfolk Southern Corp. was formed through the 1982 merger of Norfolk & Western Railway and Southern Railway. Contributions to operating profits (in millions) by business segment were:

	1994	1993	1992
Railroad	$1,043	$915	$926
Motor carrier	22	-55	-40

Rail service is provided over 14,500 miles in 20 southern and midwestern states and the Province of Ontario. About two-thirds of traffic handled originates on NSC's system. In 1994, the railroad transported 122.3 billion ton-miles of freight, versus 111.6 billion ton-miles in 1993. The average revenue generated per carload in 1994 was $884, versus $900 in 1993. Coal, coke and iron ore are the largest traffic sources, generating 33.2% of freight revenues in 1994. NSC handled 123.2 million tons of coal on its line in 1994; 20% was export volume. Other important traffic groups are chemicals (13.5% of freight revenues in 1994), paper and forest products (13.3%), automotive (11.4%) and intermodal (11.2%). Triple Crown Services Co. is a joint venture with Conrail that moves intermodal freight over certain routes.

North American Van Lines (NAVL) provides relocation services (7.1% of consolidated revenues), which involves the transportation of household goods for corporate accounts, and military and international relocations. NAVL's high-value products division (7.4% of revenues) specializes in the movement of office products and sensitive equipment, exhibits and displays. Customized Logistics Services provides integrated logistics services.

Pocahontas Land Corp. (1.5% of total revenues) manages more than 800,000 acres of coal, natural gas and timberland properties in six states.

Important Developments

Jul. '95—Pretax income for 1995's second quarter was reduced by $7.0 million to cover costs related to the planned closing of two car repair shops. Offsetting was a $5.3 million pretax reversal of rail retirement supplemental annuity taxes following a favorable settlement with the Internal Revenue Services.

Apr. '95—NSC entered into an agreement with Hanjin Shipping Co. of Korea, one of the world's largest containership operators, to handle all of Hanjin's international cargo east of the Mississippi. NSC said the seven-year pact is worth some $150 million in total revenues.

Capitalization

Long Term Debt: $1,612,600,000 (6/95).
Minority Interests: $51,800,000.

Per Share Data ($)

(Year Ended Dec. 31)

	1994	1993	1992	1991	1990	1989
Tangible Bk. Val.	35.19	33.36	30.16	28.64	31.57	30.44
Cash Flow	7.86	6.84	6.75	2.78	5.73	5.47
Earnings	4.90	3.94	3.94	0.20	3.43	3.48
Dividends	1.92	1.86	1.80	1.60	1.52	1.38
Payout Ratio	39%	47%	46%	NM	43%	39%
Prices - High	74¾	72⅜	67½	65¾	47¼	41¼
- Low	58½	59¼	53¼	39¾	35	30¼
P/E Ratio - High	15	18	17	NM	14	12
- Low	12	15	14	NM	10	9

Income Statement Analysis (Million $)

	1994	%Chg	1993	%Chg	1992	%Chg	1991
Revs.	4,642	3%	4,516	-3%	4,662	5%	4,451
Oper. Inc.	1,519	12%	1,360	2%	1,330	13%	1,173
Depr.	404	NM	406	2%	397	4%	381
Int. Exp.	139	-6%	148	-3%	152	6%	144
Pretax Inc.	1,049	17%	899	3%	875	NM	144
Eff. Tax Rate	36%	—	39%	—	36%	—	79%
Net Inc.	668	22%	549	-2%	558	NM	30.0

Balance Sheet & Other Fin. Data (Million $)

	1994	1993	1992	1991	1990	1989
Cash	307	258	378	465	625	581
Curr. Assets	1,338	1,564	1,397	1,469	1,747	1,710
Total Assets	10,588	10,520	10,401	10,148	10,523	10,244
Curr. Liab.	1,132	1,198	1,183	1,341	1,372	1,207
LT Debt	1,548	1,482	1,566	1,300	1,030	694
Common Eqty.	4,685	4,621	4,233	4,093	4,912	5,169
Total Cap.	8,494	8,286	8,508	8,056	8,718	8,634
Cap. Exp.	713	669	716	713	697	652
Cash Flow	1,072	954	954	411	929	953

Ratio Analysis

	1994	1993	1992	1991	1990	1989
Curr. Ratio	1.2	1.3	1.2	1.1	1.3	1.4
% LT Debt of Cap.	18.2	17.9	18.4	16.1	11.8	8.0
% Net Inc.of Revs.	14.4	12.2	12.0	0.7	12.0	13.4
% Ret. on Assets	6.5	5.3	5.5	0.3	5.6	6.1
% Ret. on Equity	14.6	12.5	13.5	0.7	11.5	12.1

Dividend Data

—Dividends were paid by Norfolk & Western Railway since 1901 and Southern Railway since 1943. A dividend reinvestment plan is available.

Amt. of Div. $	Date Decl.	Ex-Div. Date	Stock of Record	Payment Date
0.480	Jul. 06	Aug. 01	Aug. 05	Sep. 10 '94
0.480	Oct. 24	Oct. 31	Nov. 04	Dec. 10 '94
0.520	Jan. 24	Jan. 30	Feb. 03	Mar. 10 '95
0.520	Apr. 25	May. 01	May. 05	Jun. 10 '95
0.520	Jul. 25	Aug. 02	Aug. 04	Sep. 11 '95

Data as orig. reptd.; bef. results of disc. opers. and/or spec. items. Per share data adj. for stk. divs. as of ex-div. date. E-Estimated. NA-Not Available. NM-Not Meaningful. NR-Not Ranked.

Office—Three Commercial Place, Norfolk, VA 23510-2191. **Tel**—(804) 629-2680. **Chrmn & Pres**—D. R. Goode. **EVP-Fin**—H. C. Wolf. **Secy**—D. M. Martin. **Investor Contact**—Deborah H. Noxon. **Dirs**—G. L. Baliles, G. R. Carter, L. E. Coleman, D. R. Goode, T. M. Hahn, Jr., L. Hilliard, E. B. Leisenring, Jr., A. B. McKinnon, R. E. McNair, J. M. O'Brien, H. W. Pote. **Transfer Agent & Registrar**—Bank of New York, NYC. **Incorporated** in Virginia in 1980. **Empl**-27,168. **S&P Analyst:** Stephen R. Klein

13-OCT-95

Industry:
Util.-Diversified

Summary: This electric and gas utility serves Minnesota and the upper Midwest, and will be the 10th largest electric utility in the U.S. after it merges with Wisconsin Energy in late 1996.

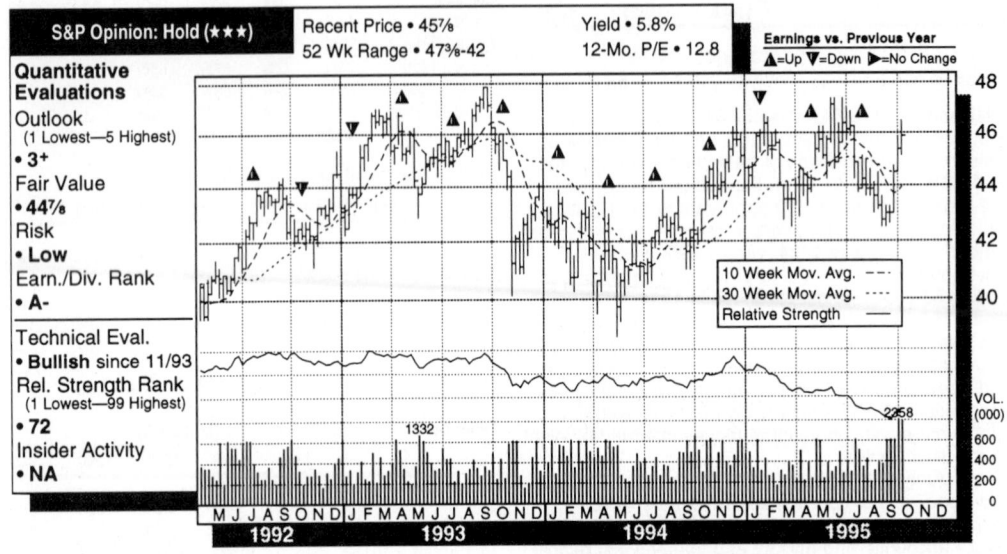

S&P Opinion: Hold (★★★)

Recent Price • 45⅞	Yield • 5.8%
52 Wk Range • 47⅜-42	12-Mo. P/E • 12.8

Earnings vs. Previous Year
▲=Up ▼=Down ▶=No Change

Quantitative Evaluations

Outlook
(1 Lowest—5 Highest)
• **3+**

Fair Value
• **44⅞**

Risk
• **Low**

Earn./Div. Rank
• **A-**

Technical Eval.
• **Bullish** since 11/93

Rel. Strength Rank
(1 Lowest—99 Highest)
• **72**

Insider Activity
• **NA**

10 Week Mov. Avg. — — —
30 Week Mov. Avg. ·········
Relative Strength ——

VOL. (000)

1332

2258

600
400
200
0

M J J A S O N D J F M A M J J A S O N D J F M A M J J A S O N D J F M A M J J A S O N D
1992 1993 1994 1995

Overview - 13-OCT-95

Share earnings should benefit in 1995 from higher electricity sales, along with continued growth in the company's service economy, and ongoing programs to reduce operating costs. Although we also expect a boost from increasing contributions from the company's nonutility, energy-related businesses, overall results are likely to be quite modest in the absence of 1994's one-time gain of $0.08. NSP is among the lowest cost energy producers in its service area. Following the proposed merger-of-equals with Wisconsin Energy, we expect that the roughly $2 billion in cost savings over 10 years will enhance the competitive of the new company, Primergy, particularly as it lowers retail electric power rates in 1996 and beyond. Divestiture of existing gas and non-utility operations is a possibility.

Valuation - 13-OCT-95

NSP's share price has lagged the pace of the S&P Electric Utilities Index in 1995 to date, following an above average performance in 1994 and in early 1995 due to investors' anticipation of lower interest rates and good earnings growth. While we expect better pricing of NSP shares over the long term, the high-dividend-paying, safe-haven shares are likely to remain average performers until the merger with Wisconsin Energy receives final approvals from regulators, and until regulators allocate net cost savings between ratepayers and shareholders following the merger.

Key Stock Statistics

S&P EPS Est. 1995	3.50	Tang. Bk. Value/Share	28.26
P/E on S&P Est. 1995	13.1	Beta	0.36
S&P EPS Est. 1996	3.60	Shareholders	85,200
Dividend Rate/Share	2.70	Market cap. (B)	$ 3.1
Shs. outstg. (M)	67.7	Inst. holdings	28%
Avg. daily vol. (M)	0.288	Insider holdings	NA

Value of $10,000 invested 5 years ago: $ 16,303

Fiscal Year Ending Dec. 31

	1995	% Change	1994	% Change	1993	% Change
Revenues (Million $)						
1Q	661.2	-3%	683.4	7%	640.8	14%
2Q	589.7	1%	582.0	7%	545.3	9%
3Q	—	—	612.3	4%	588.0	12%
4Q	—	—	608.8	-1%	616.0	8%
Yr.	—	—	2,487	3%	2,404	11%
Income (Million $)						
1Q	68.19	2%	66.80	23%	54.48	23%
2Q	59.81	13%	52.81	47%	35.89	15%
3Q	—	—	76.07	27%	59.90	8%
4Q	—	—	48.80	-9%	53.70	80%
Yr.	—	—	243.5	15%	211.7	32%
Earnings Per Share ($)						
1Q	0.97	3%	0.94	16%	0.81	29%
2Q	0.84	14%	0.74	48%	0.50	16%
3Q	E1.00	-8%	1.09	14%	0.96	16%
4Q	E0.69	1%	0.68	-9%	0.75	79%
Yr.	E3.50	1%	3.46	15%	3.02	31%

Next earnings report expected: mid November

Business Summary - 29-SEP-95

Northern States Power and subsidiaries provide electric and gas service to a population of some three million in sections of Minnesota, Wisconsin, Michigan and North and South Dakota. The Minneapolis-St. Paul metropolitan area comprised 61% of 1994 electric retail revenues and 56% of gas revenues. Electricity totaled 91% of operating revenues in 1994 and gas 9%. Contributions to electric revenues in recent years:

	1994	1993	1992	1991
Residential	36%	33%	33%	34%
Small comm'l & ind'l	18%	17%	17%	17%
Large comm'l & ind'l	44%	40%	39%	38%
Other	2%	10%	11%	11%

Sources of electric generation in 1994 were 47% coal, 28% nuclear, 21% purchased and interchange, and 4% hydro and other. Peak demand in 1994 was 7,101 mw, and capability at peak was 8,817 mw, for a capacity margin of 19%. Gas sales totaled 85,677 MMcf, down from 88,644 MMcf in 1993.

NSP has spent $700 million on capitalized environmental improvements to its facilities since 1968, and expects to incur roughly $15 million out of a $383 million capital budget for 1995 to comply with environmental regulations. Fuel costs for the company's three existing nuclear units are expected to total $51 million in 1995 and $267 million of the $1.9 billion in outlays projected for 1996 through 1999. Remaining expenditures through 1999 are for a number of smaller utility projects. NSP expects to fund 60% and 90%, respectively, for capital budgets internally.

NSP plans to investment further in unregulated businesses. Non-regulated businesses were 14% of 1994 earnings per share.

Important Developments

Sep. '95—NSP's non-regulated energy business for 1995 is expected to fall below the year ago level due to higher costs from a rise in project development activities, and reflecting the sale of several operating contracts to Pacific Gas & Electric. Also in September, shareholders approved the pooling-of-interests merger with Wisconsin Energy Corp. (WEC), in which NSP shares would be converted into 1.626 shares of common stock of Primergy, the resulting company, and each outstanding share of WEC common would be exchanged on a share-for-share basis. Based on the exchange ratio and NSP's current dividend, the pro forma dividend for Primergy would be $1.62 a share. NSP expects its policy of yearly dividend increases to continue prior to the merger, which, pending approvals, it expects to complete late in 1996.

Capitalization

Long Term Debt: $1,465,599,000 (6/95).
Cum. Preferred Stock: $240,469,000.

Per Share Data ($)

(Year Ended Dec. 31)

	1994	1993	1992	1991	1990	1989
Tangible Bk. Val.	28.26	27.24	25.86	25.16	24.37	23.76
Earnings	3.46	3.02	2.31	3.02	2.79	3.24
Dividends	2.63	2.57	2.49	2.40	2.29	2.20
Payout Ratio	76%	85%	108%	79%	82%	68%
Prices - High	47	47⅞	45⅜	44	40½	40
- Low	38¾	40⅛	38½	31¾	28⅜	30¼
P/E Ratio - High	14	16	20	15	15	12
- Low	11	13	17	11	10	9

Income Statement Analysis (Million $)

	1994	%Chg	1993	%Chg	1992	%Chg	1991
Revs.	2,487	3%	2,404	11%	2,160	-2%	2,201
Depr.	274	3%	265	12%	236	4%	228
Maint.	170	6%	161	-11%	181	2%	178
Fxd. Chgs. Cov.	3.5	3%	3.4	16%	3.0	-15%	3.5
Constr. Credits	12.3	-4%	12.8	-16%	15.2	31%	11.6
Eff. Tax Rate	35%	—	38%	—	35%	—	36%
Net Inc.	244	15%	212	32%	161	-22%	207

Balance Sheet & Other Fin. Data (Million $)

	1994	1993	1992	1991	1990	1989
Gross Prop.	8,109	7,776	7,349	6,979	6,703	6,476
Cap. Exp.	409	362	428	350	323	313
Net Prop.	4,274	4,214	4,126	3,997	3,955	3,896
Capitalization:						
LT Debt	1,463	1,292	1,300	1,234	1,240	1,263
% LT Debt	41	39	41	40	40	41
Pfd.	240	240	275	301	301	301
% Pfd.	6.70	7.10	8.60	9.70	9.80	9.90
Common	1,897	1,827	1,622	1,577	1,527	1,486
% Common	53	54	51	51	50	49
Total Cap.	4,624	4,336	4,168	4,049	4,004	3,956

Ratio Analysis

	1994	1993	1992	1991	1990	1989
Oper. Ratio	87.6	87.4	88.1	86.1	86.0	84.6
% Earn. on Net Prop.	7.3	7.3	6.3	7.7	7.3	7.9
% Ret. on Revs.	9.8	8.8	7.5	9.4	9.3	11.2
% Ret. On Invest.Cap	7.8	7.5	6.4	7.8	7.5	8.2
% Return On Com.Eqty	12.4	11.4	9.1	12.2	11.8	13.9

Dividend Data

Dividends have been paid since 1910. A dividend reinvestment plan is available.

Amt. of Div. $	Date Decl.	Ex-Div. Date	Stock of Record	Payment Date
0.660	Aug. 24	Sep. 22	Oct. 03	Oct. 20 '94
0.660	Dec. 14	Dec. 30	Jan. 06	Jan. 20 '95
0.660	Mar. 27	Apr. 03	Apr. 07	Apr. 20 '95
0.675	Jun. 28	Jul. 11	Jul. 13	Jul. 20 '95
0.675	Sep. 13	Sep. 28	Oct. 02	Oct. 20 '95

Data as orig. reptd.; bef. results of disc opers. and/or spec. items. Per share data adj. for stk. divs. as of ex-div. date. E-Estimated. NA-Not Available. NM-Not Meaningful. NR-Not Ranked.

Office—414 Nicollet Mall, Minneapolis, MN 55401. **Tel**—(612) 330-5500. **Chrmn & CEO**—J. J. Howard. **Pres**—E. M. Theisen. **VP & CFO**—E. J. McIntyre. **Investor Contact**—Edmund J. Hall. **Dirs**—H. L. Bretting, D. A. Christensen, W. J. Driscoll, D. L. Haakenstad, J. J. Howard, A. F. Jacobson, R. M. Kovacevich, D. W. Leatherdale, J. E. Pearson, G. M. Pieschel, M. R. Preska, A. P. Sampson, E. M. Theisen. **Transfer Agent**—Company's office. **Registrar**—Norwest Bank Minnesota, Minneapolis. **Incorporated** in Minnesota in 1909. **Empl**-7,690. **S&P Analyst:** Jane Collin

Northern Telecom

NYSE Symbol **NT**
In S&P 500

28-AUG-95

Industry:
Telecommunications

Summary: This company (52%-owned by BCE Inc.) is Canada's largest telecommunications equipment manufacturer, and is second only to AT&T in North America.

S&P Opinion: Hold (★★★)		
Recent Price • 36½	Yield • 1.2%	
52 Wk Range • 41-31¼	12-Mo. P/E • 22.1	

Quantitative Evaluations

Outlook
(1 Lowest—5 Highest)
• **2⁻**

Fair Value
• **35⅜**

Risk
• **Low**

Earn./Div. Rank
• **B**

Technical Eval.
• **Bearish** since 5/95

Rel. Strength Rank
(1 Lowest—99 Highest)
• **24**

Insider Activity
• **NA**

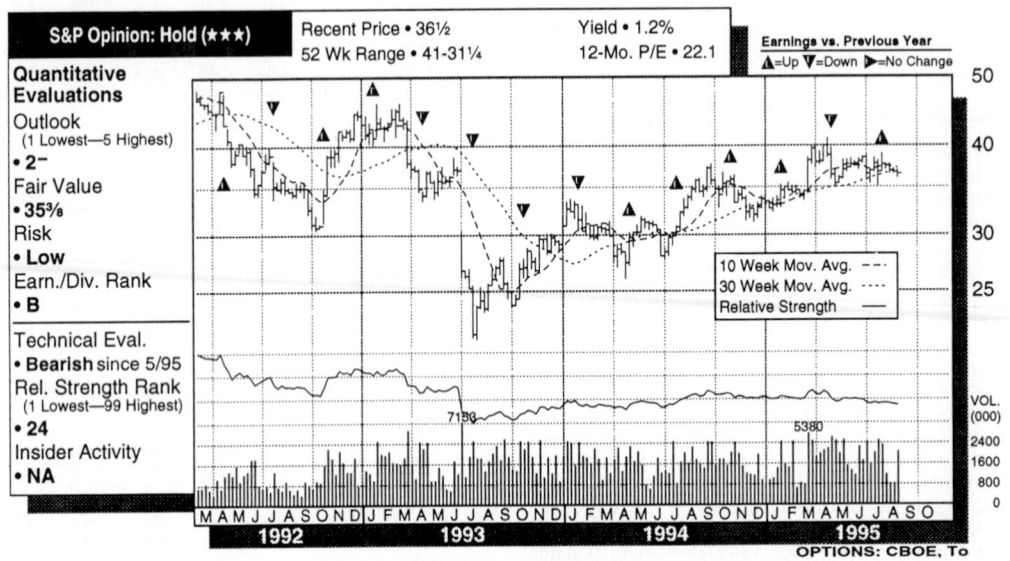

Earnings vs. Previous Year
▲=Up ▼=Down ▶=No Change

10 Week Mov. Avg. – – –
30 Week Mov. Avg. · · · ·
Relative Strength —

VOL. (000)

OPTIONS: CBOE, To

Overview - 28-AUG-95

Revenue growth in 1995 will continue to be driven by the wireless and enterprise networking product lines. The company expects wireless equipment to account for 25% of total sales by 2000, up from 10% in 1994. Increased penetration of international markets, particularly in the Asia-Pacific and Latin American regions, will also aid growth. NT is also seeking growth in the U.S. personal communications services (PCS) market. Successful bidders in recently completed FCC auctions for U.S. PCS licenses are in the process of choosing vendors to supply equipment to build networks; however, competition will be fierce. Although margins are beginning to benefit from earlier restructuring efforts, they will continue to be restricted by pricing pressures, high R&D spending, and costs to penetrate international markets.

Valuation - 28-AUG-95

The shares fell sharply in April, on disappointing first quarter earnings. Alhtough second quarter earnings were better than expected, the shares were little changed. International sales are increasing, but sales in Canada continue to decline, as telephone companies in that country have scaled back their capital spending plans. NT still faces tough competition, but we believe that growth in wireless and international sales and improved margins will enhance future results. We recommend holding the shares for capital appreciation.

Key Stock Statistics

S&P EPS Est. 1995	1.90	Tang. Bk. Value/Share	10.06
P/E on S&P Est. 1995	19.2	Beta	0.95
S&P EPS Est. 1996	2.36	Shareholders	10,200
Dividend Rate/Share	0.44	Market cap. (B)	$ 9.3
Shs. outstg. (M)	253.6	Inst. holdings	26%
Avg. daily vol. (M)	0.241	Insider holdings	NA

Value of $10,000 invested 5 years ago: $ 16,697

Fiscal Year Ending Dec. 31

	1995	% Change	1994	% Change	1993	% Change
Revenues (Million $)						
1Q	2,247	12%	1,999	3%	1,942	2%
2Q	2,442	15%	2,123	14%	1,868	-4%
3Q	—	—	2,003	7%	1,880	-7%
4Q	—	—	2,749	12%	2,458	-3%
Yr.	—	—	8,874	9%	8,148	-3%
Income (Million $)						
1Q	62.00	-30%	88.00	16%	75.90	-27%
2Q	80.00	111%	38.00	NM	-1,026	NM
3Q	—	—	57.00	NM	-33.70	NM
4Q	—	—	225.0	112%	106.0	-59%
Yr.	—	—	408.0	NM	-878.0	NM
Earnings Per Share ($)						
1Q	0.24	-31%	0.35	17%	0.30	-27%
2Q	0.31	107%	0.15	NM	-4.13	NM
3Q	E0.55	150%	0.22	NM	-0.13	NM
4Q	E0.80	-9%	0.88	110%	0.42	-59%
Yr.	E1.90	19%	1.60	NM	-3.54	NM

Next earnings report expected: late October

Business Summary - 28-AUG-95

Northern Telecom Ltd. is the largest manufacturer of telecommunications equipment in Canada, and the second largest (next to AT&T) in North America. Revenues sources in recent years were:

	1994	1993
Central office switching	44%	46%
Multimedia comm. systems	28%	27%
Transmission equip't	11%	9%
Cable & outside plant prods	7%	12%
Wireless	10%	6%

U.S. operations accounted for 55% of revenues and 73% of operating earnings in 1994, Canada for 13% and 19%, and Europe for 17% and 7%. NT is moving to penetrate markets in the Caribbean, Asia-Pacific and Latin American regions. These markets contributed 15% of revenues and less than 1% of operating earnings for 1994.

NT's principal customers are telephone companies in Canada and the U.S. Central office switching equipment is used to interconnect access lines with transmission facilities to provide local or long-distance telecommunications service. Through its multimedia communications unit, NT also provides private switching systems to businesses, including private branch exchanges (PBXs), key systems, data communications systems, and telephone sets. Transmission equipment is used for the actual transport of the voice, data, image or video communications. Cable and outside plant products include twisted-pair telephone wires, fiber-optic cables, terminals for cable connection, and modular connection systems.

Bell-Northern Research Ltd., 70% owned (Bell Canada owns the balance), is Canada'a largest industrial R&D organization and is active in all phases of telecommunications research.

Important Developments

Aug. '95—NT signed a three-year development and supply contract with Concert, a joint venture between MCI and British Telecommunications. Separately, GTE will deploy 25,000 NT Millenium intelligent pay phones over the next three years.

Jul. '95—The company received two multi-year contracts worth $450 million to provide personal communications services equipment.

Mar. '95—The company signed a letter of intent to be the primary supplier for the video transport backbone serving Pacific Bell's hybrid fiber-coax network. Separately, NT signed a $200 million contract to upgrade Ameritech's digital switching systems.

Capitalization

Long Term Debt: $1,555,000,000 (3/95).

Minority Interest: $122,000,000.

Red. Cum. Pfd. Stk.: $73,000,000.

Per Share Data ($) (Year Ended Dec. 31)

	1994	1993	1992	1991	1990	1989
Tangible Bk. Val.	9.93	7.03	8.75	14.97	13.24	11.14
Cash Flow	3.22	-1.66	4.09	4.01	3.25	2.87
Earnings	1.60	-3.54	2.17	2.03	1.80	1.47
Dividends	0.36	0.36	0.34	0.32	0.30	0.28
Payout Ratio	22%	NM	16%	16%	17%	19%
Prices - High	37¾	46	49¼	46¼	29⅝	24⅛
- Low	26	21⅜	30½	26¼	22⅛	14¼
P/E Ratio - High	24	NM	23	23	16	16
- Low	16	NM	14	13	12	10

Income Statement Analysis (Million $)

	1994	%Chg	1993	%Chg	1992	%Chg	1991
Revs.	8,874	9%	8,148	-3%	8,409	3%	8,183
Oper. Inc.	829	9%	762	-44%	1,369	4%	1,316
Depr.	408	-13%	470	NM	474	-2%	485
Int. Exp.	195	-30%	278	11%	251	14%	221
Pretax Inc.	569	NM	-1,069	NM	756	6%	710
Eff. Tax Rate	28%	—	NM	—	28%	—	28%
Net Inc.	408	NM	-877	NM	548	6%	515

Balance Sheet & Other Fin. Data (Million $)

	1994	1993	1992	1991	1990	1989
Cash	1,059	138	90.0	183	105	170
Curr. Assets	5,355	4,812	4,155	3,779	3,224	3,125
Total Assets	8,785	9,485	9,379	9,534	6,842	6,375
Curr. Liab.	3,195	4,147	3,409	3,607	2,114	2,165
LT Debt	1,507	1,512	1,147	1,161	798	816
Common Eqty.	3,355	3,014	3,967	3,676	3,224	2,696
Total Cap.	5,293	4,954	5,681	5,498	4,688	4,130
Cap. Exp.	389	471	572	514	442	370
Cash Flow	812	-413	1,010	981	788	691

Ratio Analysis

	1994	1993	1992	1991	1990	1989
Curr. Ratio	1.7	1.2	1.2	1.0	1.5	1.4
% LT Debt of Cap.	28.5	30.5	20.2	21.1	17.0	19.8
% Net Inc.of Revs.	4.6	NM	6.5	6.3	6.8	6.2
% Ret. on Assets	4.4	NM	5.8	6.3	6.9	6.1
% Ret. on Equity	12.6	NM	14.0	14.3	14.7	13.7

Dividend Data —Dividends have been paid since 1974. A dividend reinvestment plan is available. Payments are in U.S. funds, before 15% Canadian non-resident tax.

Amt. of Div. $	Date Decl.	Ex-Div. Date	Stock of Record	Payment Date
0.090	Jul. 28	Sep. 02	Sep. 09	Sep. 30 '94
0.090	Nov. 17	Dec. 05	Dec. 09	Dec. 30 '94
0.090	Feb. 23	Mar. 03	Mar. 09	Mar. 31 '95
0.110	Apr. 27	Jun. 06	Jun. 09	Jun. 30 '95
0.110	Jul. 27	Sep. 06	Sep. 08	Sep. 29 '95

Data as orig. reptd.; bef. results of disc. opers. and/or spec. items. Per share data adj. for stk. divs. as of ex-div. date. E-Estimated. NA-Not Available. NM-Not Meaningful. NR-Not Ranked.

Office—2920 Matheson Blvd. East, Mississauga, ON, Canada L4W 4M7. **Tel**—(905) 238-7000. **Chrmn**—D. J. Schuenke. **Pres & CEO**—J. C. Monty. **SVP & CFO**—P. W. Currie. **Secy**—P. J. Chilibeck. **Dirs**— R. M. Barford, F. C. Carlucci, J. V. R. Cyr, G. V. Dirvin, L. Y. Fortier, R. S. Hurlbut, B. Kennedy, G. A. Kenney-Wallace, B. K. Kuhn, E. P. Lougheed, J. C. Monty, P. F. Oreffice, D. J. Schuenke, S. H. Smith, Jr., L. R. Wilson. **U.S. Transfer Agent & Registrar**—Chemical Bank, NYC. **Incorporated** in Canada in 1914. **Empl**-57,054. **S&P Analyst:** Kevin J. Gooley

Northrop Grumman

NYSE Symbol **NOC**
In S&P 500

02-OCT-95

Industry:
Aerospace

Summary: This company manufactures military aircraft and commercial aircraft subsystems. It also performs electronics and system integration and provides data systems and services.

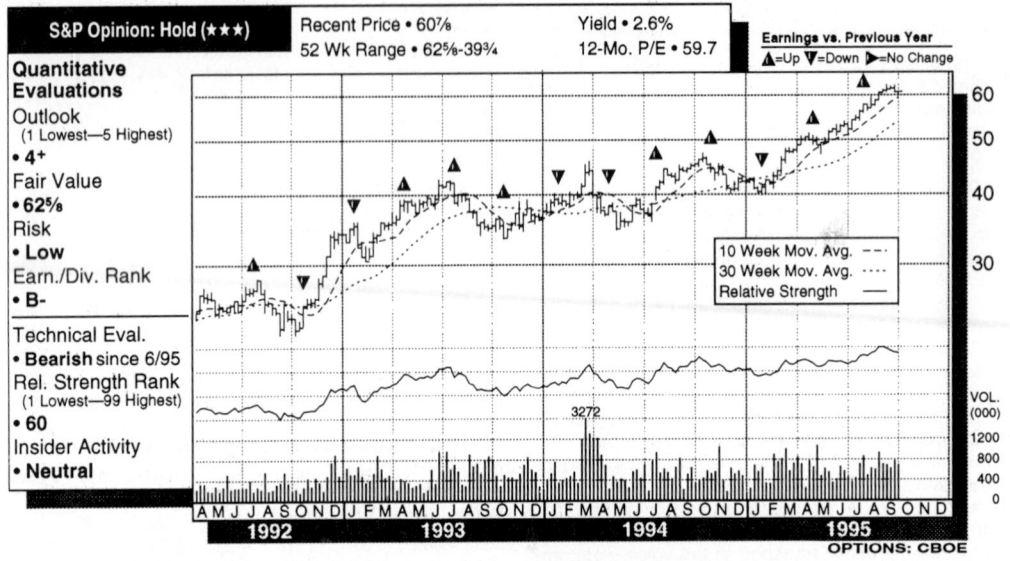

| S&P Opinion: Hold (★★★) | Recent Price • 60⅞ | Yield • 2.6% |
| | 52 Wk Range • 62⅝-39¾ | 12-Mo. P/E • 59.7 |

Earnings vs. Previous Year
▲=Up ▼=Down ▶=No Change

Quantitative Evaluations

Outlook
(1 Lowest—5 Highest)
• **4+**

Fair Value
• **62⅝**

Risk
• **Low**

Earn./Div. Rank
• **B-**

Technical Eval.
• **Bearish** since 6/95

Rel. Strength Rank
(1 Lowest—99 Highest)
• **60**

Insider Activity
• **Neutral**

10 Week Mov. Avg. -- --
30 Week Mov. Avg. · · · ·
Relative Strength ——

3272

VOL.
(000)

OPTIONS: CBOE

Overview - 02-OCT-95

Revenues for 1995 are likely to be up moderately from the $6.7 billion achieved in 1994. Aircraft sales may advance slightly, despite lower revenues on the B-2 program, due to commercial subcontracting and work on the C-17 program. Electronics segment revenues should rise sharply with the full inclusion of such programs as JSTARS and E-2C. Information systems revenues will also benefit from inclusion of a number of Grumman programs for 12 months. Missiles sales will be lower. Overall operating margins should begin to benefit from restructuring moves. Although higher interest costs and nonrecurring pension charges will restrain earnings growth, the absence of $282 million of early retirement program expenses will boost income.

Valuation - 02-OCT-95

Shares are up substantiallly since early 1995. As a major subcontractor to Boeing, the company is expected to benefit from a pickup in aircraft orders. There is also hope that Congress will approve long lead funding for three more B-2s--the minimum number necessary to maintain production of the bomber for another year. Such an action may lead to future purchases. In September 1995, the House supported funding for the B-2, but the Senate did not; voting was very close. Congress is expected to settle the issue in conference this fall. Given the uncertainty regarding the B-2 program (which provides approximately 25% of total revenues), we view the shares as fairly valued at 11 times our estimate of 1996 earnings.

Key Stock Statistics

S&P EPS Est. 1995	4.90	Tang. Bk. Value/Share	NM
P/E on S&P Est. 1995	12.4	Beta	1.84
S&P EPS Est. 1996	5.70	Shareholders	11,200
Dividend Rate/Share	1.60	Market cap. (B)	$ 3.0
Shs. outstg. (M)	49.4	Inst. holdings	62%
Avg. daily vol. (M)	0.145	Insider holdings	NA

Value of $10,000 invested 5 years ago: $ 44,437

Fiscal Year Ending Dec. 31

	1995	% Change	1994	% Change	1993	% Change
Revenues (Million $)						
1Q	1,617	33%	1,218	-4%	1,275	-2%
2Q	1,759	4%	1,686	29%	1,312	-9%
3Q	—	—	1,927	58%	1,220	-6%
4Q	—	—	1,880	50%	1,256	-17%
Yr.	—	—	6,711	33%	5,063	-9%
Income (Million $)						
1Q	54.00	4%	52.00	NM	52.00	10%
2Q	79.00	22%	65.00	23%	53.00	4%
3Q	—	—	39.00	50%	26.00	NM
4Q	—	—	-121.0	NM	-35.00	NM
Yr.	—	—	35.00	-64%	96.00	-21%
Earnings Per Share ($)						
1Q	1.10	5%	1.05	-4%	1.09	9%
2Q	1.59	20%	1.33	19%	1.12	4%
3Q	E1.05	33%	0.79	46%	0.54	NM
4Q	E1.16	NM	-2.45	NM	-0.73	NM
Yr.	E4.90	NM	0.72	-64%	1.99	-22%

Next earnings report expected: mid October

Business Summary - 02-OCT-95

Northrop Grumman Corp. operates in the aerospace industry. Contributions by segment (profits in millions) in 1994:

	Sales	Profits
Military & commerc. aircraft	67%	$463
Electr. & sys. integration	23%	122
Data systems and other	5%	14
Missiles & unmanned vehicle systems	5%	-18

Sales to the U.S. government accounted for 82% of the total in 1994, versus 89% in 1993.

NOC's major aircraft program is the B-2 stealth bomber, with total production of 20 aircraft expected to end in 1997. The company also modifies the B-707s that carry the Joint Surveillance and Target Attack Radar System (JSTARS), and manufactures airframes for the E-2C early warning aircraft. In addition, it is the major subcontractor on the F/A-18 multi-mission plane. Commercial aircraft products include engine nacelle systems, integrated tail sections and other structures for nineteen aircraft programs.

Electronics and system integration segment is composed of surveillance and battle management, electronics and information warfare, electronics and readiness support, and precision weapons. Major programs include E-8 JSTARS, E-2C Hawkeye, the GAM precision weapon for the B-2, and the BAT "brilliant" antiarmor submunition.

Data systems and services division applies systems integration and service expertise to internal operations as well as external customers. Activities include records management, image processing, computing skill and technical services.

The primary product of the missiles segment, the Tri-Service Standoff Attack Missile (TSSAM), was cancelled in February 1995.

Important Developments

Sep. '95—Northrop Grumman merged three of its major retirement plans to cut costs and improve its competitive position. The company said the move will reduce 1995 net income by $15 million.
Jul. '95—The backlog as of June 30, 1995, totaled $10.9 billion, versus $12.1 billion a year earlier.
Apr. '95—The company signed a long-term agreement with Boeing for continued production of major sections of Boeing's 747, 757 and 767 airliners.
Feb. '95—The Defense Department cancelled the Tri-Service Standoff Attack Missile program, for which NOC was the prime contractor.

Capitalization

Long Term Debt: $1,496,000,000 (6/95).

Per Share Data ($)

(Year Ended Dec. 31)

	1994	1993	1992	1991	1990	1989
Tangible Bk. Val.	-9.16	26.78	26.31	25.04	21.94	18.56
Cash Flow	6.19	6.45	5.96	9.33	8.45	2.98
Earnings	0.72	1.99	2.56	5.69	4.48	-1.71
Dividends	1.60	1.60	1.20	1.20	1.20	1.20
Payout Ratio	NM	80%	47%	21%	27%	NM
Prices - High	47⅜	42⅝	34⅞	31¼	20¼	29¾
- Low	34½	30½	22½	16½	13¾	16
P/E Ratio - High	66	21	14	5	5	NM
- Low	48	15	9	3	3	NM

Income Statement Analysis (Million $)

	1994	%Chg	1993	%Chg	1992	%Chg	1991
Revs.	6,711	33%	5,062	-9%	5,550	-3%	5,694
Oper. Inc.	750	73%	433	11%	389	-26%	523
Depr.	269	26%	214	34%	160	-6%	171
Int. Exp.	109	187%	38.0	-19%	47.0	-41%	80.0
Pretax Inc.	65.0	-62%	170	-6%	180	-35%	277
Eff. Tax Rate	46%	—	44%	—	33%	—	3.20%
Net Inc.	35.0	-64%	96.0	-21%	121	-55%	268

Balance Sheet & Other Fin. Data (Million $)

	1994	1993	1992	1991	1990	1989
Cash	17.0	100	230	203	173	5.0
Curr. Assets	2,431	1,560	1,760	1,807	1,785	1,747
Total Assets	6,047	2,939	3,162	3,128	3,094	3,196
Curr. Liab.	1,964	1,079	1,406	1,196	1,214	1,655
LT Debt	1,633	160	160	470	691	551
Common Eqty.	1,290	1,322	1,254	1,182	1,033	875
Total Cap.	2,939	1,529	1,464	1,685	1,811	1,508
Cap. Exp.	134	135	123	117	121	187
Cash Flow	304	310	281	440	397	140

Ratio Analysis

	1994	1993	1992	1991	1990	1989
Curr. Ratio	1.2	1.4	1.3	1.5	1.5	1.1
% LT Debt of Cap.	55.6	10.5	10.9	27.9	38.1	36.5
% Net Inc.of Revs.	0.5	1.9	2.2	4.7	3.8	NM
% Ret. on Assets	0.8	3.1	3.8	8.6	6.7	NM
% Ret. on Equity	2.7	7.3	9.9	24.2	22.1	NM

Dividend Data

—Dividends have been paid since 1951. A reinvestment plan is available.

Amt. of Div. $	Date Decl.	Ex-Div. Date	Stock of Record	Payment Date
0.400	Nov. 17	Nov. 21	Nov. 28	Dec. 10 '94
0.400	Feb. 15	Feb. 21	Feb. 27	Mar. 11 '95
0.400	May. 17	May. 23	May. 30	Jun. 10 '95
0.400	Aug. 16	Aug. 24	Aug. 28	Sep. 09 '95

Office—1840 Century Park East, Los Angeles, CA 90067-2199. **Tel**—(310) 553-6262. **Chrmn, Pres & CEO**—K. Kresa. **VP & CFO**—R. B. Waugh, Jr. **VP & Secy**—S. M. Gibbons. **Investor Contact**—J. Gaston Kent, Jr. (310-201-3423). **Dirs**—J. R. Borsting, J. T. Chain, Jr. J. Edwards, B. C. Jordan, K. Kresa, A. L. Peters, J. E. Robson, R. M. Rosenberg, W. F. Schmied, B. Scowcroft, J. B. Slaughter, W. C. Solberg, R. J. Stegemeier. **Transfer Agent & Registrar**—Chemical Bank, NYC. **Incorporated** in California in 1939; reincorporated in Delaware in 1985. **Empl**-42,400. **S&P Analyst:** Joe Victor Shammas

Norwest Corp.

NYSE Symbol **NOB**
In S&P 500

20-OCT-95

Industry:
Banking

Summary: This bank holding company owns banks in 15 primarily upper Midwest states, and has substantial consumer finance and mortgage banking operations nationwide.

S&P Opinion: Accumulate (★★★★)	Recent Price • 32⅞	Yield • 3.0%
	52 Wk Range • 33-21	12-Mo. P/E • 12.2

Quantitative Evaluations

Outlook
(1 Lowest—5 Highest)
• **3+**

Fair Value
• **32½**

Risk
• **Low**

Earn./Div. Rank
• **A-**

Technical Eval.
• **Bullish** since 12/94

Rel. Strength Rank
(1 Lowest—99 Highest)
• **74**

Insider Activity
• **Neutral**

Earnings vs. Previous Year
▲=Up ▼=Down ▶=No Change

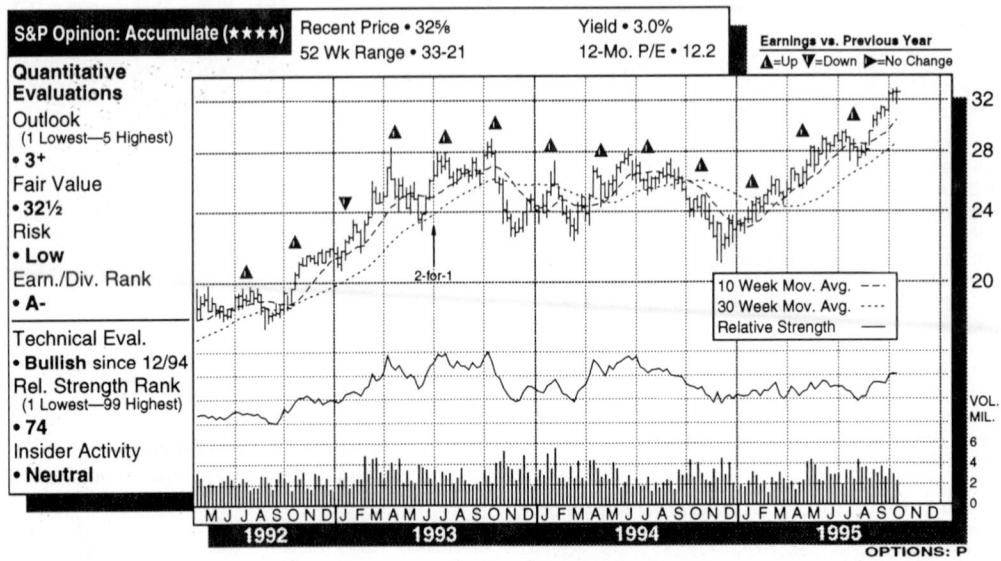

10 Week Mov. Avg. ---
30 Week Mov. Avg. ·····
Relative Strength —

2-for-1

1992 1993 1994 1995

OPTIONS: P

Overview - 19-OCT-95

Healthy gains in average earning assets, reflecting acquisitions and a dynamic service territory, should continue to fuel profits into 1996. A higher provision for loan losses will be needed to cover anticipated growth in the loan portfolio. Pressure on net interest margins from increased funding costs (due to higher debt levels and deposit prices) should be mitigated by a better mix of earning assets. Improved core noninterest income has been masked by losses in the securities portfolio, but NOB has used the opportunity to reinvest proceeds from securities sales at higher yields. Credit quality has been improving, with the level of nonperforming assets to total assets declining and the allowance for loan losses now at 650% of nonperforming loans.

Valuation - 19-OCT-95

With a 1.43% return on assets and 22.3% return on equity in the 1995 third quarter, NOB continues to generate some of the best returns on shareholder value in our regional bank group. Interest in the shares, which have performed only in line with the broader market thus far in 1995, should begin to pick up as investors focus on bank stocks that have the most promising prospects in a slower growth environment. With earnings expected to climb an average 13% over the next two years, the shares, trading at 10 times the 1996 earnings estimate, are attractive for accumulation.

Key Stock Statistics

S&P EPS Est. 1995	2.80	Tang. Bk. Value/Share	12.91
P/E on S&P Est. 1995	11.7	Beta	1.65
S&P EPS Est. 1996	3.15	Shareholders	17,400
Dividend Rate/Share	0.96	Market cap. (B)	$ 10.5
Shs. outstg. (M)	325.3	Inst. holdings	57%
Avg. daily vol. (M)	0.617	Insider holdings	NA

Value of $10,000 invested 5 years ago: $ 34,312

Fiscal Year Ending Dec. 31

	1995	% Change	1994	% Change	1993	% Change
Revenues (Million $)						
1Q	1,685	18%	1,427	14%	1,254	10%
2Q	1,840	26%	1,461	10%	1,331	16%
3Q	1,966	30%	1,510	16%	1,300	10%
4Q	—	—	1,634	17%	1,392	19%
Yr.	—	—	6,032	14%	5,277	14%
Income (Million $)						
1Q	216.8	14%	190.5	27%	150.2	23%
2Q	234.3	16%	202.0	25%	161.1	26%
3Q	245.2	21%	203.0	21%	167.3	25%
4Q	—	—	204.9	17%	175.0	26%
Yr.	—	—	800.4	22%	653.6	26%
Earnings Per Share ($)						
1Q	0.66	12%	0.59	20%	0.49	32%
2Q	0.68	11%	0.61	17%	0.52	27%
3Q	0.70	13%	0.62	13%	0.55	25%
4Q	E0.76	21%	0.63	11%	0.57	185%
Yr.	E2.80	14%	2.45	15%	2.13	50%

Next earnings report expected: mid January

Business Summary - 19-OCT-95

Norwest Corp. is the 12th largest U.S. bank holding company (based on assets of $66.6 million at June 30, 1995), with 619 branches in 15 primarily upper Midwest states. Banking services include corporate and community banking, capital management, data processing and credit card services. Subsidiaries also engage in mortgage banking, consumer finance, equipment leasing, agricultural finance, commercial finance, securities brokerage and investment banking, insurance agency services, data processing, trust services and venture capital investments. There are 3,024 branches and affiliates in all 50 states, all 10 Canadian provinces, and internationally. Operating earnings (in millions) in recent years were derived as follows:

	1994	1993	1992	1991
Banking	$507.1	$397.2	$227.7	$246.0
Norwest Financial	222.5	200.1	159.0	123.5
Norwest Mortgage	70.8	56.3	53.4	31.4

Average earning assets of $49.9 billion in 1994 (up from $46.2 billion in 1993) were divided: commercial loans 19%, real estate loans 23%, consumer loans 19%, investment securities 27%, assets held for sale 11%, and temporary investments 1%. Average sources of funds were interest-bearing deposits 48%, non-interest-bearing deposits 16%, short-term borrowings 12%, long-term debt 14%, equity 7%, and other 3%.

At year-end 1994, nonperforming assets were $218 million (0.4% of total assets), down from $320 million (0.6%) a year earlier. Net chargeoffs totaled $193 million (0.64% of average loans and leases) in 1994, versus $178 million (0.67%) in 1993. The allowance for credit losses was 2.42% of year-end loans and leases in 1994 (2.74%).

Important Developments

Jul. '95—NOB signed a definitive agreement to acquire Reno, Nev.-based Amfed Financial Inc. (assets of $1.58 billion) in a stock transaction valued at about $197 million.

Jun. '96—The company signed a definitive agreement to acquire Liberty National Bank of Austin, Texas (assets of $147 million), for an undisclosed amount.

May '95—Norwest signed a definitive agreement to acquire Foothill Group in a stock transaction valued at about $441 million. A total of 16,415,890 common shares are expected to be issued in the transaction. Separately, it agreed to acquire State National Bank of El Paso, Texas ($1.1 billion), for an undisclosed amount.

Capitalization

Long Term Debt: $12,686,300,000 (9/95).
Preferred Stock: $302,000,000.

Per Share Data ($) (Year Ended Dec. 31)

	1994	1993	1992	1991	1990	1989
Tangible Bk. Val.	10.79	11.04	9.69	8.63	7.02	6.83
Earnings	2.45	2.13	1.42	1.48	1.36	1.26
Dividends	0.76	0.64	0.54	0.47	0.42	0.38
Payout Ratio	31%	30%	38%	32%	31%	30%
Prices - High	28¼	29	22⅛	18½	11⅞	12⅛
- Low	21	20⅝	16⅝	9⅜	6¾	8
P/E Ratio - High	12	14	16	13	9	10
- Low	9	10	12	6	5	6

Income Statement Analysis (Million $)

	1994	%Chg	1993	%Chg	1992	%Chg	1991
Net Int. Inc.	2,804	18%	2,376	14%	2,078	27%	1,632
Tax Equiv. Adj.	29.0	-12%	33.0	—	NA	—	34.0
Non Int. Inc.	1,718	22%	1,406	21%	1,166	20%	972
Loan Loss Prov.	165	18%	140	-48%	267	-17%	322
% Exp/Op Revs.	68%	—	75%	—	NA	—	69%
Pretax Inc.	1,181	26%	938	56%	603	27%	475
Eff. Tax Rate	32%	—	30%	—	27%	—	16%
Net Inc.	800	22%	654	49%	440	10%	399
% Net Int. Marg.	5.67%	—	5.59%	—	NA	—	5.11%

Balance Sheet & Other Fin. Data (Million $)

	1994	1993	1992	1991	1990	1989
Earning Assets:						
Money Mkt.	765	637	597	428	635	NA
Inv. Securities	14,837	11,322	11,764	11,225	6,734	4,906
Com'l Loans	9,155	7,674	7,473	6,444	6,438	5,903
Other Loans	29,695	26,290	23,612	17,360	14,103	11,970
Total Assets	59,316	50,782	46,657	38,502	30,626	24,335
Demand Deposits	9,283	8,339	6,785	5,700	4,095	3,194
Time Deposits	27,141	24,234	21,919	19,739	16,029	12,012
LT Debt	9,186	6,802	4,481	3,579	2,905	2,557
Common Eqty.	3,334	3,227	2,798	2,246	1,523	1,278

Ratio Analysis

	1994	1993	1992	1991	1990	1989
% Ret. on Assets	1.5	1.3	1.0	1.1	1.1	1.1
% Ret. on Equity	22.6	20.9	12.4	18.9	20.4	20.2
% Loan Loss Resv.	2.1	3.7	2.5	2.6	2.0	1.6
% Loans/Deposits	103.6	124.3	104.8	89.8	97.6	111.8
% Equity to Assets	6.2	6.2	NA	5.6	5.2	5.2

Dividend Data —Dividends have been paid since 1939. A dividend reinvestment plan is available. Poison pill stock purchase rights were issued in 1988.

Amt. of Div. $	Date Decl.	Ex-Div. Date	Stock of Record	Payment Date
0.210	Oct. 25	Oct. 31	Nov. 04	Dec. 01 '94
0.210	Jan. 24	Jan. 30	Feb. 03	Mar. 01 '95
0.210	Apr. 25	May. 01	May. 05	Jun. 01 '95
0.240	Jul. 25	Aug. 02	Aug. 04	Sep. 01 '95

Data as orig. reptd.; bef. results of disc opers. and/or spec. items. Per share data adj. for stk. divs. as of ex-div. date. E-Estimated. NA-Not Available. NM-Not Meaningful. NR-Not Ranked.

Office—Norwest Center, Sixth and Marquette, Minneapolis, MN 55479. **Tel**—(612) 667-1234. **Chrmn**—L. P. Johnson. **Pres & CEO**—R. M. Kovacevich. **EVP & CFO**—J. T. Thornton. **SVP & Secy**—L. A. Holschuh. **VP & Investor Contact**—Robert S. Strickland. **Dirs**—D. A. Christensen, G. J. Ford, P. M. Grieve, C. M. Harper, N. B. Hart, W. A. Hodder, G. C. Howe, L. P. Johnson, R. C. King, R. M. Kovacevich, R. S. Levitt, R. D. McCormick, C. H. Milligan, J. E. Pearson, I. M. Rolland, S. E. Watson, M. W. Wright. **Transfer Agent & Registrar**—Norwest Bank Minnesota, N.A., Minneapolis. **Incorporated** in Delaware in 1929. **Empl**-38,836. **S&P Analyst:** Stephen R. Biggar

Novell, Inc.

NASDAQ Symbol **NOVL**
In S&P 500

20-SEP-95

Industry:
Data Processing

Summary: Novell's NetWare local area network operating system is the de facto standard. With the 1994 acquisition of WordPerfect Corp., NOVL became a major provider of PC software.

S&P Opinion: Accumulate (★★★★)	Recent Price • 19	Yield • Nil
	52 Wk Range • 23¼-14⅛	12-Mo. P/E • 23.8

Earnings vs. Previous Year
▲=Up ▼=Down ▶=No Change

Quantitative Evaluations

Outlook
(1 Lowest—5 Highest)
• **5⁻**

Fair Value
• **26¼**

Risk
• **Average**

Earn./Div. Rank
• **B+**

Technical Eval.
• **Bullish** since 8/95

Rel. Strength Rank
(1 Lowest—99 Highest)
• **48**

Insider Activity
• **Neutral**

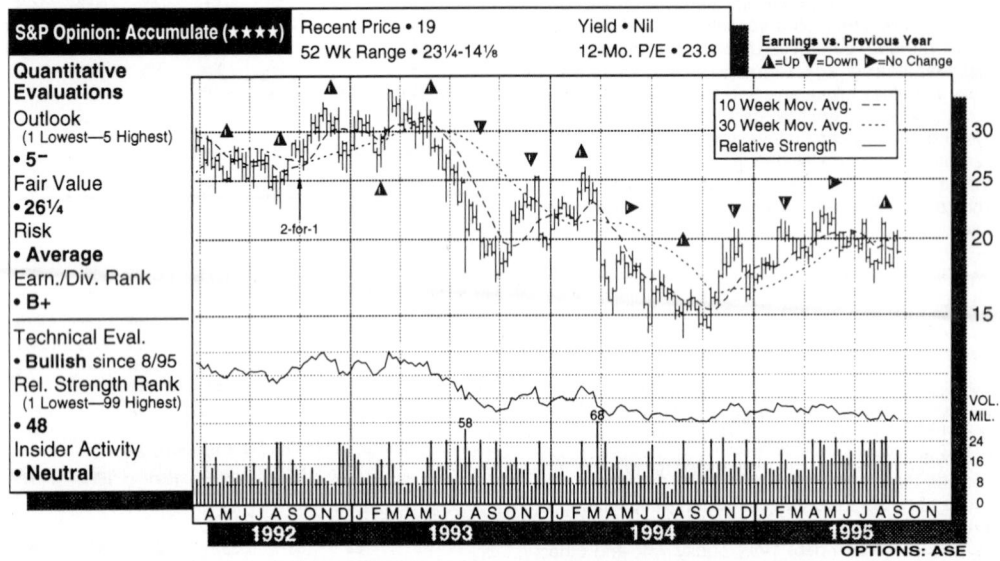

10 Week Mov. Avg. ---
30 Week Mov. Avg. ····
Relative Strength —

OPTIONS: ASE

Overview - 20-SEP-95

Sales are expected to rise through fiscal 1996, as the company's leading market share positions it to benefit from continued rapid growth of the LAN market. NetWare 4, the network operating system for larger and more complex networks, continues to sell well. The company's PerfectOffice suite of business software applications is well positioned to continue gaining market share, despite a slowdown in the third quarter of fiscal 1994-95 owing to anticipation of the release of the new Windows 95 operating system. Margins should widen slightly on a more favorable product mix, volume efficiencies and well controlled expenses. Earnings are expected to benefit from the higher sales and wider margins.

Valuation - 20-SEP-95

The shares are off from their 1993 peak, reflecting earnings disappointments due to a transition to the latest version of NetWare, disruptions from assimilation of acquisitions, and fears over competition in the LAN operating system market. However, NOVL's position in LAN operating systems remains formidable, recent acquisitions appear to be mostly integrated, and new upgrades of major application products should help to resume stable earnings growth. The stock has risen thus far in 1995; however, much uncertainty over Novell's prospects remains factored into the price. With the profit gains we project, the stock should outperform the market in the months ahead.

Key Stock Statistics

S&P EPS Est. 1995	1.05	Tang. Bk. Value/Share	NM
P/E on S&P Est. 1995	18.1	Beta	1.94
S&P EPS Est. 1996	1.25	Shareholders	9,800
Dividend Rate/Share	Nil	Market cap. (B)	$ 7.3
Shs. outstg. (M)	369.1	Inst. holdings	47%
Avg. daily vol. (M)	5.686	Insider holdings	NA

Value of $10,000 invested 5 years ago: $ 49,032

Fiscal Year Ending Oct. 31

	1995	% Change	1994	% Change	1993	% Change
Revenues (Million $)						
1Q	493.2	1%	488.3	88%	260.2	27%
2Q	529.5	-1%	534.9	91%	280.7	25%
3Q	537.9	10%	488.9	79%	272.8	12%
4Q	—	—	486.0	57%	309.2	19%
Yr.	—	—	1,998	78%	1,123	20%
Income (Million $)						
1Q	81.52	-14%	94.46	33%	70.88	36%
2Q	95.87	NM	96.36	20%	80.46	31%
3Q	102.0	NM	-4.47	NM	-255.4	NM
4Q	—	—	20.37	-70%	68.91	NM
Yr.	—	—	206.7	NM	-35.16	NM
Earnings Per Share ($)						
1Q	0.22	-15%	0.26	13%	0.23	35%
2Q	0.26	NM	0.26	NM	0.26	30%
3Q	0.27	NM	-0.01	NM	-0.80	NM
4Q	E0.30	NM	0.06	-73%	0.22	-4%
Yr.	E1.05	88%	0.56	NM	-0.11	NM

Next earnings report expected: mid December

Business Summary - 20-SEP-95

Novell, Inc. designs, manufactures, markets and services network operating system software, general purpose operating system products and application software, development tools and related products. Networking offerings are based on proprietary network operating system software (NetWare) that lets networked PCs share resources such as hard disk storage, printers and communication devices, communicate with other networked PCs, and access minicomputer and mainframe host computers.

The NetWare Systems Group features the NetWare operating system, which is compatible with all current versions of the DOS, Windows, OS/2, UNIX and Macintosh operating systems, and is independent of underlying network architecture and hardware. Multi-user application programs written for these operating systems run without modification on LANs supported by the NetWare operating system. The NetWare family of operating systems includes NetWare 2, designed for small businesses, offices and work groups; NetWare 3, a full-featured, 32-bit enterprisewide connectivity tool for large departments and corporations; and NetWare 4, which provides advanced networking features, such as directory services, and enhanced security, administration and management capabilities. The company also offers network monitoring, diagnostic and management products; communications and connectivity software; selected strategic hardware; and message and electronic mail products.

Through its UNIX Systems Group, NOVL provides a full suite of UNIX operating system and UNIX connectivity products. Its AppWare Systems Group provides tools and technologies for the development of network-aware applications.

Following the June 1994 acquisition of WordPerfect Corp., the company gained a major presence in the business applications, workgroup applications, electronic publishing, and consumer product software markets. Its PerfectOffice suite of business applications (shipped in December 1994) has established a market presence.

Important Developments

Sep. '95—NOVL signed a definitive agreement to sell its UNIX business to Santa Cruz Operation (SCO) for about 6.1 million SCO common shares valued at about $67 million, plus a future revenue stream not to exceed $84 million net present value.

Dec. '94—In the fiscal 1994 fourth quarter, Novell recorded restructuring charges totaling $61,084,000 ($0.11 a share, after taxes). In the third quarter, it recorded a $120 million charge ($0.22 a share) to reflect costs associated with the acquisition of WordPerfect (for 59 million common shares) and the purchase of Borland International's Quattro Pro business.

Capitalization

Long Term Debt: None (7/29/95).

Minority Interests: $16,531,000.

Per Share Data ($)

	1994	1993	1992	1991	1990	1989
Tangible Bk. Val.	4.08	3.58	3.12	2.08	1.42	0.89
Cash Flow	0.80	0.02	0.90	0.62	0.39	0.23
Earnings	0.56	-0.11	0.81	0.55	0.34	0.19
Dividends	Nil	Nil	Nil	Nil	Nil	Nil
Payout Ratio	Nil	Nil	Nil	Nil	Nil	Nil
Prices - High	26¼	35¼	33½	32⅜	8½	4¾
- Low	13¾	17	22½	7⅝	3⅜	3
P/E Ratio - High	47	NM	41	59	25	26
- Low	25	NM	28	14	10	16

(Year Ended Oct. 31)

Income Statement Analysis (Million $)

	1994	%Chg	1993	%Chg	1992	%Chg	1991
Revs.	1,998	78%	1,123	20%	933	46%	640
Oper. Inc.	547	25%	436	13%	386	57%	246
Depr.	86.4	107%	41.7	45%	28.7	44%	20.0
Int. Exp.	NA	—	0.4	-30%	0.6	-32%	0.9
Pretax Inc.	297	186%	104	-72%	377	52%	248
Eff. Tax Rate	31%	—	134%	—	34%	—	35%
Net Inc.	207	NM	-35.0	NM	249	54%	162

Balance Sheet & Other Fin. Data (Million $)

	1994	1993	1992	1991	1990	1989
Cash	862	664	545	347	255	130
Curr. Assets	1,453	1,052	866	553	402	270
Total Assets	1,963	1,344	1,097	726	494	347
Curr. Liab.	463	230	149	118	94.0	54.0
LT Debt	Nil	Nil	0.5	1.2	2.4	57.0
Common Eqty.	1,487	1,103	938	599	398	236
Total Cap.	1,501	1,113	947	608	401	293
Cap. Exp.	73.5	70.2	69.9	86.9	28.1	43.2
Cash Flow	293	7.0	278	182	108	60.0

Ratio Analysis

	1994	1993	1992	1991	1990	1989
Curr. Ratio	3.1	4.6	5.8	4.7	4.3	5.0
% LT Debt of Cap.	Nil	Nil	0.1	0.2	0.6	19.5
% Net Inc.of Revs.	10.3	NM	26.7	25.4	19.0	11.5
% Ret. on Assets	11.6	NM	26.9	26.4	21.8	15.6
% Ret. on Equity	14.8	NM	31.9	32.3	29.0	24.3

Dividend Data —No cash has been paid.

Data as orig. reptd.; bef. results of disc. opers. and/or spec. items. Per share data adj. for stk. divs. as of ex-div. date. E-Estimated. NA-Not Available. NM-Not Meaningful. NR-Not Ranked.

Office—122 East 1700 South, Provo, UT 84606. **Tel**—(801) 429-7000. **Chrmn, Pres & CEO**—R. J. Frankenberg. **CFO**—J. R. Tolonen. **COO**—M. M. Burnside. **SVP & Secy**—D. R. Bradford. **Investor Contact**—Peter Troop (408-473-8361). **Dirs**—A. C. Ashton, B. W. Bastain, E. R. Bond, R. J. Frankenberg, J. L. Messman, K. S. Rekhi, L. W. Sonsini, I. R. Wilson, J. A. Young. **Transfer Agent & Registrar**—Mellon Bank, Pittsburgh. **Incorporated** in Delaware in 1983. **Empl**-7,599. **S&P Analyst:** Peter C. Wood, CFA

Nucor Corp.

NYSE Symbol **NUE**
In S&P 500

18-SEP-95 **Industry:** Steel-Iron

Summary: Nucor is the fourth largest U.S. steelmaker, and operates the largest U.S. minimill. It is currently gaining market share in flat roll sheet and strip steel.

S&P Opinion: Accumulate (★★★★)

Recent Price • 46	Yield • 0.6%
52 Wk Range • 71⅜-42½	12-Mo. P/E • 14.4

Quantitative Evaluations

Outlook
(1 Lowest—5 Highest)
• **2⁻**

Fair Value
• **49½**

Risk
• **Average**

Earn./Div. Rank
• **A**

Technical Eval.
• **Bearish** since 7/95

Rel. Strength Rank
(1 Lowest—99 Highest)
• **5**

Insider Activity
• **Unfavorable**

Earnings vs. Previous Year
▲=Up ▼=Down ▶=No Change

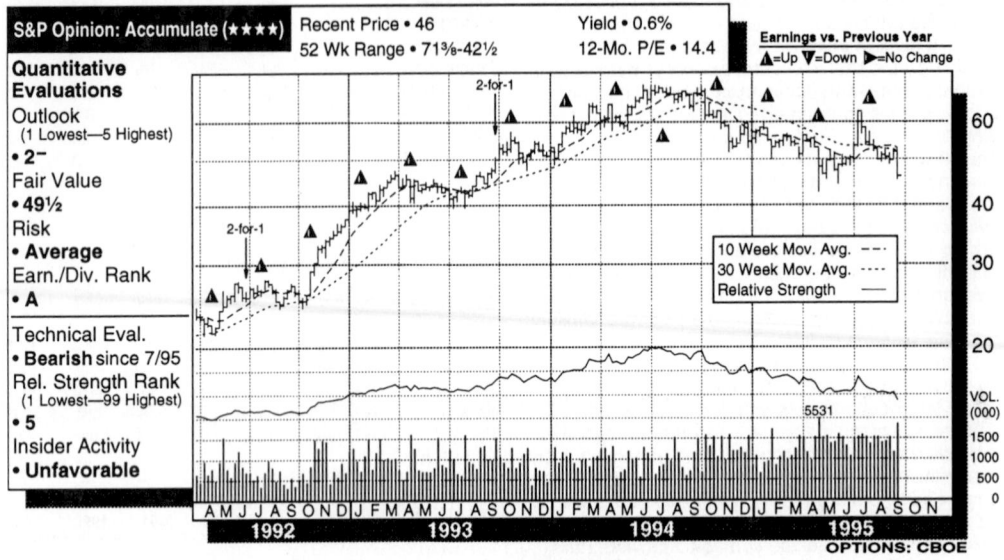

10 Week Mov. Avg. ---
30 Week Mov. Avg. ·····
Relative Strength —

OPTIONS: CBOE

Overview - 18-SEP-95

We expect a 10% sales gain in 1996, reflecting lower imports, rebuilding of inventories by service centers and higher prices for carbon flat roll steel. Increased capacity utilization at the flat roll mills, an improved product mix and only moderate increases in scrap costs will lift profits in 1996. Due to the ongoing inventory drawdown in flat roll steel, earnings comparisons may not turn positive until 1996's second quarter. Long-term sales and profit growth will be enhanced by NUE's entrance into the markets for wide flange beams and flat-rolled steel. Also, the ultimate success of NUE's iron carbide plant and joint ventures to develop new technologies for direct steelmaking and scrap substitutes will boost future earnings.

Valuation - 15-SEP-95

Although NUE's stock has fallen 16% through mid September, we are keeping our accumulate rating on the stock. We recently lowered our estimates for 1995 and 1996 to $3.05 and $3.70, respectively, but still think the shares are oversold on a P/E basis. The market is treating NUE just like the other carbon steelmakers that are currently out of favor. NUE is in a class by itself compared to the integrated carbon steelmakers. Besides having a broader product range, lower costs and substantially greater growth prospects, NUE has far more stable earnings and much less financial leverage vis a vis the other steelmakers. The market's distorted view of NUE creates an excellent opportunity to accumulate a dynamic industrial company.

Key Stock Statistics

S&P EPS Est. 1995	3.05	Tang. Bk. Value/Share	14.29
P/E on S&P Est. 1995	15.1	Beta	0.69
S&P EPS Est. 1996	3.70	Shareholders	38,000
Dividend Rate/Share	0.28	Market cap. (B)	$ 4.0
Shs. outstg. (M)	87.4	Inst. holdings	69%
Avg. daily vol. (M)	0.450	Insider holdings	NA

Value of $10,000 invested 5 years ago: $ 31,416

Fiscal Year Ending Dec. 31

	1995	% Change	1994	% Change	1993	% Change
Revenues (Million $)						
1Q	841.7	30%	649.7	33%	489.8	26%
2Q	880.2	19%	740.1	31%	564.9	45%
3Q	—	—	786.4	34%	587.3	39%
4Q	—	—	799.4	31%	611.8	46%
Yr.	—	—	2,976	32%	2,254	39%
Income (Million $)						
1Q	67.31	93%	34.88	60%	21.74	34%
2Q	69.93	41%	49.68	63%	30.42	75%
3Q	—	—	64.52	85%	34.81	70%
4Q	—	—	77.55	112%	36.54	45%
Yr.	—	—	226.6	83%	123.5	56%
Earnings Per Share ($)						
1Q	0.77	93%	0.40	60%	0.25	32%
2Q	0.80	40%	0.57	63%	0.35	75%
3Q	E0.69	-7%	0.74	85%	0.40	70%
4Q	E0.79	-11%	0.89	112%	0.42	45%
Yr.	E3.05	17%	2.60	83%	1.42	55%

Next earnings report expected: mid October

Business Summary - 15-SEP-95

Nucor is primarily a producer of steel and steel products, including hot-rolled and cold-finished steel shapes, steel joists and girders, wide flange beams, heavy structural steel products, steel deck and steel grinding balls.

Production in 1994 totaled 7,007,000 tons, up from 5,749,000 tons in 1993. Steel sales in 1994 came to 5,980,000 tons (4,937,000 tons). Some 15% of production was used internally. The average cost of scrap was $145 a ton in 1994, $125 a ton in 1993, $100 a ton in 1992 and $110 a ton in 1991.

NUE's Crawfordsville flat-rolled steel mill began operations in the second half of 1989, and became profitable in June 1990. The mill uses a new process for casting a thin slab 2 inches thick and 52 inches wide. In 1992, the company completed construction and began operation of a second thin slab cast mill near Hickman, Ark. At 1994's year end combined capacity at the two mills was 3,800,000 tons.

Four steel mills located in South Carolina, Nebraska, Texas and Utah produce bar, light structural carbon and alloy products.

Vulcraft produces steel joists, joist girders and steel deck for nonresidential construction markets. Joist production in 1994 was 487,000 tons, versus 417,000 tons in 1993. Steel deck sales were 207,000 tons, versus 170,000 tons in 1993.

Sales of cold finished steel products totaled 239,000 tons in 1994, versus 213,000 tons in 1993.

Through Nucor-Yamato Steel Co. (51% owned), NUE produces wide flange beams and heavy structural steel products. Operations began in the second half of 1988. Shipments of finished and semi-finished products exceeded 1,600,000 tons in 1994, versus shipments in excess of 1,200,000 tons in 1993. In 1993, NUE completed an expansion that increased annual capacity to 1,800,000 tons and enabled the mill to make jumbo wide flange beams up to 40 inches in depth.

Important Developments

Sep. '95—NUE stated that it would have difficulty in matching 1994's third quarter earnings due to reduced demand and prices for flat rolled steel. The company noted that price cuts had resulted in increased orders and said that prices might be stabilizing. NUE added that it was still too early to determine whether it could achieve full year estimates of $3.26 a share.
Mar. '95—NUE announced plans to build a new 1,800,000 tons per year thin slab steel mill in Berkeley County, South Carolina. The new mill is expected to cost $500 million and will produce hot and cold rolled sheet steel. Full operations are expected to begin by early 1997. The addition of the new mill will increase Nucor's capacity to 10,000,000 tons per year.

Capitalization

Long Term Debt: $136,850,000 (7/95).
Minority Interest: $187,955,340.

Per Share Data ($) (Year Ended Dec. 31)

	1994	1993	1992	1991	1990	1989
Tangible Bk. Val.	12.84	10.36	9.04	8.24	7.59	6.83
Cash Flow	4.41	2.83	2.04	1.83	1.86	1.58
Earnings	2.60	1.42	0.91	0.75	0.88	0.68
Dividends	0.18	0.16	0.14	0.13	0.12	0.11
Payout Ratio	7%	11%	15%	17%	14%	16%
Prices - High	72	57¼	40	22⅜	20½	16⅞
- Low	48¾	38	21	14¼	12⅛	11¼
P/E Ratio - High	28	40	44	30	23	25
- Low	19	27	23	19	14	17

Income Statement Analysis (Million $)

	1994	%Chg	1993	%Chg	1992	%Chg	1991
Revs.	2,976	32%	2,254	39%	1,619	11%	1,465
Oper. Inc.	528	63%	323	45%	223	18%	189
Depr.	158	30%	122	25%	97.8	4%	93.6
Int. Exp.	14.6	2%	14.3	59%	9.0	NM	2.6
Pretax Inc.	357	91%	187	60%	117	22%	96.0
Eff. Tax Rate	37%	—	34%	—	33%	—	33%
Net Inc.	22.7	-82%	124	57%	79.2	22%	64.7

Balance Sheet & Other Fin. Data (Million $)

	1994	1993	1992	1991	1990	1989
Cash	102	27.0	26.0	38.0	52.0	33.0
Curr. Assets	639	468	365	334	315	280
Total Assets	2,002	1,829	1,490	1,182	1,038	1,034
Curr. Liab.	382	350	272	229	226	194
LT Debt	173	352	247	73.0	29.0	156
Common Eqty.	1,123	902	784	712	653	584
Total Cap.	1,535	1,428	1,190	930	813	840
Cap. Exp.	185	364	379	218	57.0	130
Cash Flow	384	246	177	158	160	134

Ratio Analysis

	1994	1993	1992	1991	1990	1989
Curr. Ratio	1.7	1.3	1.3	1.5	1.4	1.4
% LT Debt of Cap.	11.3	24.7	20.7	7.8	3.5	18.6
% Net Inc.of Revs.	7.6	5.5	4.9	4.4	5.1	4.6
% Ret. on Assets	11.8	7.4	5.9	5.8	7.2	5.8
% Ret. on Equity	22.4	14.6	10.6	9.5	12.1	10.3

Dividend Data —Cash dividends have been paid since 1973. A dividend reinvestment plan is available.

Amt. of Div. $	Date Decl.	Ex-Div. Date	Stock of Record	Payment Date
0.045	Sep. 14	Sep. 26	Sep. 30	Nov. 11 '94
0.045	Dec. 19	Dec. 23	Dec. 30	Feb. 10 '95
0.070	Mar. 02	Mar. 27	Mar. 31	May. 12 '95
0.070	Jun. 15	Jun. 28	Jun. 30	Aug. 11 '95
0.070	Sep. 15	Sep. 27	Sep. 29	Nov. 10 '95

Data as orig. reptd.; bef. results of disc. opers. and/or spec. items. Per share data adj. for stk. divs. as of ex-div. date. E-Estimated. NA-Not Available. NM-Not Meaningful. NR-Not Ranked.

Office—2100 Rexford Rd., Charlotte, NC 28211. **Tel**—(704) 366-7000. **Chrmn & CEO**—F. K. Iverson. **Pres**—J. D. Correnti. **Vice Chrmn, CFO, Secy & Treas**—S. Siegel. **Dirs**—H. D. Aycock, J. D. Correnti, J. W. Cunningham, F. K. Iverson, S. Siegel. **Transfer Agent & Registrar**—First Union National Bank, Charlotte. **Incorporated** in Delaware in 1958. **Empl**-5,900. **S&P Analyst:** Leo Larkin

NYNEX Corp.

NYSE Symbol **NYN**
In S&P 500

24-OCT-95 | **Industry:** Telecommunications

Summary: NYNEX operates the fifth largest local exchange telephone business in the U.S., serving the majority of telephone customers in New York State and the New England states.

S&P Opinion: Hold (★★★)	Recent Price • 48⅛	Yield • 4.9%
	52 Wk Range • 48¾-35⅞	12-Mo. P/E • 19.8

Quantitative Evaluations

Outlook (1 Lowest—5 Highest)
• **2⁺**

Fair Value
• **46**

Risk
• **Low**

Earn./Div. Rank
• **B+**

Technical Eval.
• **Bearish** since 8/95

Rel. Strength Rank (1 Lowest—99 Highest)
• **74**

Insider Activity
• **Unfavorable**

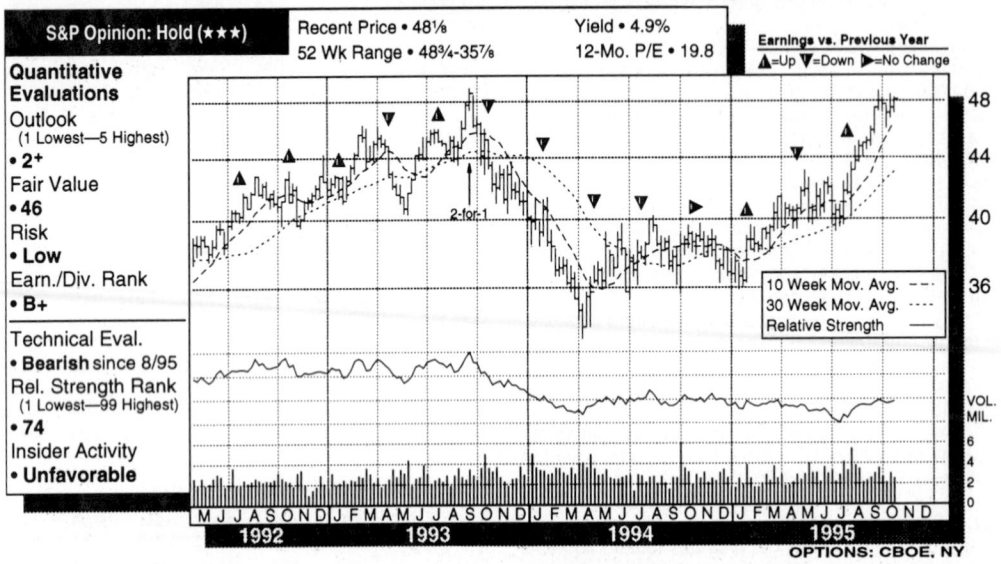

Earnings vs. Previous Year
▲=Up ▼=Down ▶=No Change

10 Week Mov. Avg. – – –
30 Week Mov. Avg. ·····
Relative Strength ——

VOL. MIL.

OPTIONS: CBOE, NY

Overview - 24-OCT-95

The company's core telephone operations will continue to be impacted by fierce competition. However, a new regulatory plan recently enacted by New York regulators gives NYN more flexibility to adjust prices to meet competition. The plan also allows the company to keep earnings improvements from enhanced productivity and operating efficiencies. The company's cellular operations have underperformed those of its peers in the past, but should benefit from alliances with Bell Atlantic, AirTouch Communications and U S WEST. Investments in international ventures will continue to dilute earnings over the near term, but will enhance the company's long-term growth prospects. In addition, NYN and Bell Atlantic recently completed a joint $100 million investment in CAI Wireless, which will allow NYN to enter the video services market sooner. Our 1995 estimate includes $0.43 of nonrecurring charges.

Valuation - 24-OCT-95

The shares have been trading at a discount to the company's peer group, reflecting fierce competition within its operating territory. Proposed federal legislation would eventually allow the Bell companies into the long-distance market; the House and Senate bills are now being reconciled in conference committee. The company's international investments, cellular alliances and New York regulatory plan should improve future earnings prospects. Due to competitive pressures, we expect the shares to be a market performer in the near-term; however, with a healthy dividend yield, the shares offer adequate total return prospects.

Key Stock Statistics

S&P EPS Est. 1995	2.80	Tang. Bk. Value/Share	13.61
P/E on S&P Est. 1995	17.2	Beta	0.71
S&P EPS Est. 1996	3.42	Shareholders	936,500
Dividend Rate/Share	2.36	Market cap. (B)	$ 20.4
Shs. outstg. (M)	427.3	Inst. holdings	38%
Avg. daily vol. (M)	0.510	Insider holdings	NA

Value of $10,000 invested 5 years ago: $ 14,755

Fiscal Year Ending Dec. 31

	1995	% Change	1994	% Change	1993	% Change
Revenues (Million $)						
1Q	3,354	2%	3,273	NM	3,302	2%
2Q	3,496	6%	3,312	-2%	3,364	2%
3Q	3,238	-3%	3,331	NM	3,330	NM
4Q	—	—	3,391	NM	3,393	3%
Yr.	—	—	13,307	NM	13,408	2%
Income (Million $)						
1Q	250.2	-14%	290.6	-12%	331.1	-2%
2Q	240.8	NM	1.20	-100%	340.2	3%
3Q	342.9	13%	302.5	1%	298.3	-7%
4Q	—	—	198.3	NM	-1,241	NM
Yr.	—	—	792.6	NM	-272.4	NM
Earnings Per Share ($)						
1Q	0.59	-16%	0.70	-13%	0.80	-3%
2Q	0.56	NM	Nil	—	0.82	2%
3Q	0.80	11%	0.72	NM	0.72	-7%
4Q	E0.85	81%	0.47	NM	-3.00	NM
Yr.	E2.80	48%	1.89	NM	-0.66	NM

Next earnings report expected: late January

NYNEX Corp.

Business Summary - 24-OCT-95

NYNEX is the nation's fifth largest telephone holding company, based on 1994 U.S. access lines, providing local telephone service to 16.6 million access lines in seven Northeast states. Over 83% of operating revenues are generated by NYN's telephone subsidiaries.

In July 1995, NYN and Bell Atlantic (BEL) merged their cellular operations, now known as Bell Atlantic NYNEX Mobile (BANM). Initially, NYN will own 37.65% and Bell Atlantic will own 62.35%, and NYN will have the right to purchase an additional 2.35% interest for $500 million. However, the venture is managed as a 50/50 partnership. The venture is the second largest cellular carrier in the U.S. in terms of potential customers and has a presence in seven of the top 20 U.S. markets. BANM, either directly or through partnerships, provides cellular mobile communications services primarily within the companies' service areas in the Northeastern and Eastern U.S. As of September 30, 1995, BANM was serving some 2,973,000 cellular customers.

In October 1994, NYN and BEL agreed to form a national wireless partnership with AirTouch Communications (ATI) and U S WEST (USW); the partnership builds on the proposed merger of NYN's and BEL's cellular assets. Separately, USW and ATI have agreed to form a cellular joint venture which will have operations in 21 states. The four companies formed a partnership, 50%-owned by the NYN/BEL partnership, which successfully bid for 11 PCS (personal communications services) licenses in the recent FCC auction. The licenses will complement the four companies' existing cellular assets. A second entity will be formed which will provide services for the companies' cellular operations as well as the PCS operations. This company will develop technical standards for the wireless operations, develop a national branding and marketing strategy, and create a national distribution network.

Other subsidiaries provide staff support services and various operational support activities, primarily for the telephone companies; publish directories and provide related services; provide communication networks and services outside the U.S.; build and operate fiber-based cable television and telephony networks in the U.K; and provide financial services. NYN also jointly owns, with the other Bell holding companies, Bell Communications Research, which provides technical assistance and consulting services to the companies.

Important Developments

Sep. '95—The new regulatory plan approved by New York state regulators took effect September 1. As part of the plan, NYN will freeze basic telephone rates for seven years and will cut other charges by $100 million in the first 12 months.

Capitalization

Long Term Debt: $7,759,100,000 (12/94).

Per Share Data ($) (Year Ended Dec. 31)

	1994	1993	1992	1991	1990	1989
Tangible Bk. Val.	20.26	20.28	23.38	22.27	22.74	23.65
Cash Flow	8.20	5.48	9.34	7.42	8.22	7.93
Earnings	1.89	-0.66	3.20	1.49	2.39	2.05
Dividends	2.36	3.54	2.32	2.28	2.28	2.18
Payout Ratio	125%	NM	73%	153%	95%	106%
Prices - High	41⅜	NM	44¼	40⅜	45½	46
- Low	33¼	NM	34⅝	33½	33⅝	32⅝
P/E Ratio - High	22	NM	14	27	19	22
- Low	18	NM	11	22	14	16

Income Statement Analysis (Million $)

	1994	%Chg	1993	%Chg	1992	%Chg	1991
Revs.	13,307	NM	13,408	2%	13,155	NM	13,229
Depr.	2,641	4%	2,534	NM	2,518	5%	2,398
Maint.	3,040	-5%	3,194	15%	2,779	-15%	3,252
Constr. Credits	NA	—	30.8	NM	30.6	7%	28.6
Eff. Tax Rate	28%	—	NM	—	30%	—	24%
Net Inc.	793	NM	-271	NM	1,311	118%	601

Balance Sheet & Other Fin. Data (Million $)

	1994	1993	1992	1991	1990	1989
Gross Prop.	35,467	33,969	33,078	31,654	30,515	30,274
Net Prop.	20,623	20,250	19,973	19,915	19,729	19,465
Cap. Exp.	3,012	2,717	2,450	2,499	2,493	2,421
Total Cap.	20,035	19,259	20,474	19,572	19,521	19,616
Fxd. Chgs. Cov.	2.6	0.3	3.7	2.0	2.8	2.5
Capitalization:						
LT Debt	7,785	6,938	7,018	6,833	6,945	6,465
Pfd.	Nil	Nil	Nil	Nil	Nil	Nil
Common	8,581	8,416	9,724	9,120	9,149	9,369

Ratio Analysis

	1994	1993	1992	1991	1990	1989
% Ret. on Revs.	6.0	NA	10.0	4.5	7.0	6.1
% Ret. On Invest.Cap	7.5	2.0	10.0	6.8	8.4	7.7
% Return On Com.Eqty	9.3	NM	13.9	6.6	10.3	8.6
% Earn. on Net Prop.	7.1	2.5	9.8	7.1	8.4	7.7
% LT Debt of Cap.	47.6	45.2	41.9	42.8	43.2	40.8
Capital. % Pfd.	Nil	Nil	Nil	Nil	Nil	Nil
Capital. % Common	52.4	54.8	58.1	57.2	56.8	59.2

Dividend Data —Dividends were initiated in 1984. A dividend reinvestment plan is available. A "poison pill" stock purchase rights plan was adopted in 1989.

Amt. of Div. $	Date Decl.	Ex-Div. Date	Stock of Record	Payment Date
0.590	Sep. 22	Sep. 26	Sep. 30	Nov. 01 '94
0.590	Dec. 15	Dec. 23	Dec. 30	Feb. 01 '95
0.590	Mar. 16	Mar. 27	Mar. 31	May. 01 '95
0.590	Jun. 15	Jun. 28	Jun. 30	Aug. 01 '95
0.590	Sep. 21	Oct. 05	Oct. 10	Nov. 01 '95

Data as orig. reptd.; bef. results of disc. opers. and/or spec. items. Per share data adj. for stk. divs. as of ex-div. date. E-Estimated. NA-Not Available. NM-Not Meaningful. NR-Not Ranked.

Office—1095 Avenue of the Americas, New York, NY 10036. **Tel**—(212) 395-2121. **Chrmn & CEO**—I. G. Seidenberg. **EVP & CFO**—A. Z. Senter. **VP & Treas**—C. P. Turner. **EVP-Secy**—R. F. Burke. **Investor Contact**—Allen F. Pattee. **Dirs**—J. Brademas, R. W. Bromery, R. L. Carrion, J. J. Creedon, W. C. Ferguson, S. P. Goldstein, H. L. Kaplan, E. T. Kennan, E. E. Phillips, F. V. Salemo, I. G. Seidenberg, W. V. Shipley, J. R. Strafford. **Transfer Agent & Registrar**—First National Bank of Boston. **Incorporated** in Delaware in 1983. **Empl**-70,600. **S&P Analyst:** Kevin J. Gooley

31-JUL-95 | Industry: Oil and Gas

Summary: Occidental is a worldwide oil and natural gas production company with large interests in chemicals and gas transmission.

S&P Opinion: Hold (★★★)

Recent Price • 22½	Yield • 4.4%
52 Wk Range • 24⅜-18	12-Mo. P/E • 23.7

Quantitative Evaluations

Outlook
(1 Lowest—5 Highest)
• **1**

Fair Value
• **20**

Risk
• **Low**

Earn./Div. Rank
• **B-**

Technical Eval.
• **Bearish** since 7/95

Rel. Strength Rank
(1 Lowest—99 Highest)
• **26**

Insider Activity
• **Neutral**

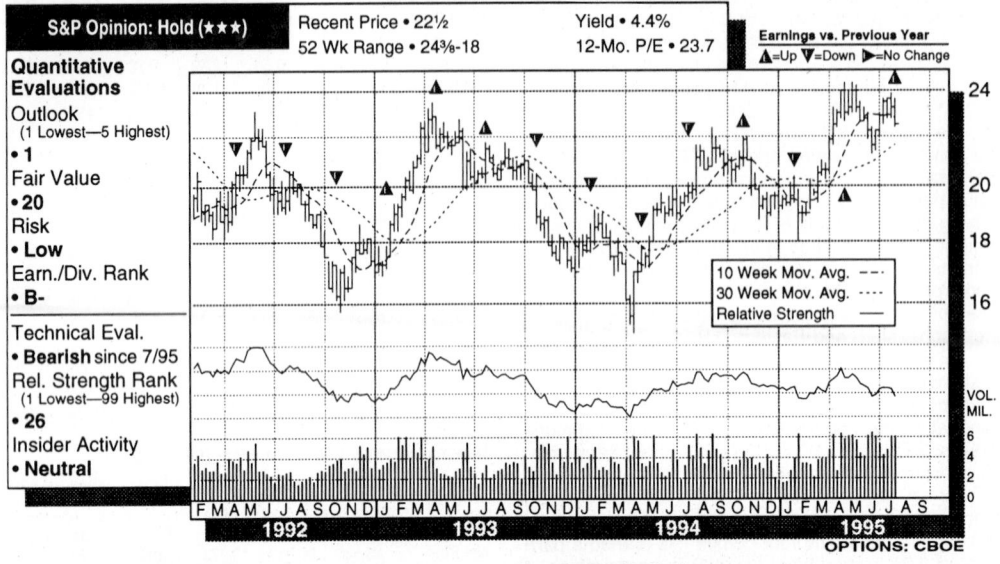

Earnings vs. Previous Year
▲=Up ▼=Down ▶=No Change

10 Week Mov. Avg. – – –
30 Week Mov. Avg. · · · ·
Relative Strength ——

VOL. MIL.

OPTIONS: CBOE

Overview - 31-JUL-95

Earnings in 1995 and beyond should benefit from a sharp rise in chemical prices and an improved outlook for oil production. Projects in Venezuela and Qatar are expected to lead to a substantial increase in OXY's international reserve base, and management is planning to participate in 40 exploratory wells in 1995, 20 of which are wildcat wells. Though production levels will rise, the company may feel the bite of dropping oil prices in the second half of the year, since OPEC may decide to increase production, which would result in lower prices. Increased demand for gas should buoy the shares, however. Strong cash flow, bolstered by high caustic chemical and chlorine prices should lead to reduced debt costs. Earnings should exceed the dividend for the first time in 14 years.

Valuation - 27-JUL-95

The shares have gained some momentum thus far in 1995, as chemical segment profits continue to soar, with higher levels of demand and little additional industry capacity being added. We expect the trend of higher chemical earnings to continue through 1995, and see long-term benefits from higher levels of cash flow being generated. The company intends to reduce debt by $1 billion over the next two years. And the sale of a polyvinyl chloride resins plant to Borden Chemicals & Plastics L.P. will provide funding for projects in Bangladesh and Ireland. Longer-term, we expect further oil and gas discoveries to lead the shares higher. However, necessary restructuring moves and debt reduction moves should cause the shares to trade in a narrow range during 1995.

Key Stock Statistics

S&P EPS Est. 1995	1.59	Tang. Bk. Value/Share	10.16
P/E on S&P Est. 1995	14.2	Beta	1.01
S&P EPS Est. 1996	1.90	Shareholders	379,800
Dividend Rate/Share	1.00	Market cap. (B)	$ 7.1
Shs. outstg. (M)	317.3	Inst. holdings	55%
Avg. daily vol. (M)	1.099	Insider holdings	NA

Value of $10,000 invested 5 years ago: $ 11,445

Fiscal Year Ending Dec. 31

	1995	% Change	1994	% Change	1993	% Change
Revenues (Million $)						
1Q	2,714	29%	2,106	-3%	2,169	7%
2Q	2,679	24%	2,162	8%	2,011	NM
3Q	—	—	2,404	25%	1,916	-10%
4Q	—	—	2,564	27%	2,020	-13%
Yr.	—	—	9,236	14%	8,116	-4%
Income (Million $)						
1Q	178.0	NM	-40.00	NM	83.00	NM
2Q	187.0	NM	-19.00	NM	75.00	29%
3Q	—	—	23.00	NM	-101.0	NM
4Q	—	—	Nil	—	17.00	21%
Yr.	—	—	-36.00	NM	74.00	-41%
Earnings Per Share ($)						
1Q	0.49	NM	-0.19	NM	0.26	NM
2Q	0.51	NM	-0.12	NM	0.21	17%
3Q	E0.39	—	0.01	NM	-0.36	NM
4Q	E0.20	—	-0.06	NM	0.02	-60%
Yr.	E1.59	—	-0.36	NM	0.12	-71%

Next earnings report expected: mid October

Occidental Petroleum

31-JUL-95

Business Summary - 31-JUL-95

Occidental is a worldwide oil and natural gas exploration and production company with major chemical holdings. Chemical operations are conducted through the OxyChem unit, which makes basic chemicals, petrochemicals, polymers and plastics and some agricultural products. OXY's MidCon Corp. is a natural gas transmission concern. OXY sold its coal business in 1993.

Earnings (million $)	1994	1993
Oil & gas	$27	$278
Natural gas transmission	276	426
Chemicals	350	173

Production totaled 237,000 bbl. of crude oil per day in 1994, up from 216,000 bbl. per day in 1993 (including natural gas liquids), and 673 MMcf of natural gas per day in 1994, versus 652 MMcf per day in 1993. Natural gas transportation volumes decreased slightly in 1994, while sales volumes decreased about 17%. Proved reserves at 1994 year end were 918 million bbl. of oil and 2,333 Bcf of gas.

OxyChem operates 38 chemical product manufacturing facilities in the United States, and 14 in eight foreign countries, with the most significant foreign plants located in Brazil. Chemical segment results have recently been buoyed by capacity additions over the past few years. Industry operating problems, strong demand growth, and limited industry capacity increases have resulted in sharply higher prices and margins within the segment.

Important Developments

Jul. '95—OXY announced its second quarter net income rose to $187 million ($0.51 a share), from a net loss of $19 million ($0.12) the prior year, mainly on strength in chemical segment results. Chemical earnings soared to $354 million, from $65 million, with margins improving for PVC, caustic soda and petrochemicals. Results for 1995 include a $40 million pretax gain from the sale of a PVC facility in Louisiana. Higher crude oil production and prices helped oil and gas earnings to rise to $79 million, versus $25 million the prior year. However, offsetting these gains was a $109 million litigation charge, as well as lower natural gas prices in the U.S. which resulted from mild weather and higher than normal U.S. storage levels. Higher transport margins drove a modest improvement in natural gas transmission earnings.

Capitalization

Long Term Debt: Approx. $5,300,000,000 (6/95).
Minority Interest: $6,000,000.
$3.00 Cum. Conv. Pfd. Stock: 26,495,824 shs. ($50 liquid pref.), conv. into CanadianOxy com. shs.

Per Share Data ($)

(Year Ended Dec. 31)

	1994	1993	1992	1991	1990	1989
Tangible Bk. Val.	9.88	11.07	11.33	14.33	13.73	21.67
Cash Flow	2.48	2.99	3.24	3.95	-2.37	4.59
Earnings	-0.36	0.12	0.41	1.25	-5.80	0.92
Dividends	1.00	1.00	1.00	1.00	2.50	2.50
Payout Ratio	NM	833%	244%	81%	NM	271%
Prices - High	22⅜	23½	23⅛	25⅜	30¼	31
- Low	15⅛	16⅞	15¾	16½	17¾	25⅛
P/E Ratio - High	NM	NM	56	20	NM	34
- Low	NM	NM	38	13	NM	27

Income Statement Analysis (Million $)

	1994	%Chg	1993	%Chg	1992	%Chg	1991
Revs.	9,236	14%	8,116	-4%	8,494	-16%	10,096
Oper. Inc.	1,539	22%	1,266	7%	1,180	-29%	1,668
Depr.	882	NM	878	3%	856	6%	806
Int. Exp.	589	NM	591	-10%	659	-27%	902
Pretax Inc.	109	-50%	218	-33%	325	-67%	986
Eff. Tax Rate	131%	—	66%	—	60%	—	61%
Net Inc.	-36.0	NM	74.0	-41%	126	-67%	379

Balance Sheet & Other Fin. Data (Million $)

	1994	1993	1992	1991	1990	1989
Cash	129	157	90.0	276	364	303
Curr. Assets	2,258	1,934	2,245	2,968	4,451	3,974
Total Assets	17,989	17,123	17,877	16,115	19,743	20,741
Curr. Liab.	2,201	2,048	2,290	2,778	4,314	3,605
LT Debt	6,114	6,047	5,806	5,925	7,992	8,217
Common Eqty.	3,132	3,383	3,440	4,300	4,069	5,856
Total Cap.	13,142	12,406	11,287	10,527	13,022	15,205
Cap. Exp.	1,103	1,007	765	954	1,336	1,272
Cash Flow	770	913	979	1,178	-691	1,237

Ratio Analysis

	1994	1993	1992	1991	1990	1989
Curr. Ratio	1.0	0.9	1.0	1.1	1.0	1.1
% LT Debt of Cap.	46.5	48.7	51.4	56.3	61.4	54.0
% Net Inc.of Revs.	NM	0.9	1.5	3.8	NM	1.3
% Ret. on Assets	NM	0.4	0.7	2.1	NM	1.2
% Ret. on Equity	NM	1.0	3.2	8.8	NM	4.1

Dividend Data

(A dividend reinvestment plan is available. A "poison pill" stock purchase right was adopted in 1986.)

Amt. of Div. $	Date Decl.	Ex-Div. Date	Stock of Record	Payment Date
0.250	Jul. 14	Sep. 02	Sep. 09	Oct. 15 '94
0.250	Nov. 10	Dec. 05	Dec. 09	Jan. 15 '95
0.250	Feb. 09	Mar. 06	Mar. 10	Apr. 15 '95
0.250	Apr. 28	Jun. 08	Jun. 12	Jul. 15 '95
0.250	Jul. 13	Sep. 07	Sep. 11	Oct. 15 '95

Data as orig. reptd.; bef. results of disc. opers. and/or spec. items. Per share data adj. for stk. divs. as of ex-div. date.
E-Estimated. NA-Not Available. NM-Not Meaningful. NR-Not Ranked.

Office—10889 Wilshire Blvd., Los Angeles, CA 90024. **Tel**—(310) 208-8800. **Chrmn & Pres**—R. R. Irani. **EVP & CFO**—A. R. Leach. **VP & Investor Contact**—Kenneth J. Huffman (212-603-8183). **Dirs**—A. Gore, Sr., A. Groman, J. R. Hirl, R. R. Irani, J. W. Kluge, D. R. Laurance, I. W. Maloney, G. O. Nolley, J. F. Riordan, R. Segovia, A. D. Syriani, R. Tomich. **Transfer Agents & Registrars**—Chemical Trust Co. of California; Chemical Trust Co., NYC; Montreal Trust Co. **Incorporated** in California in 1920; reincorporated in Delaware in 1986. **Empl**-19,860. **S&P Analyst:** Raymond J. Deacon

Ogden Corp.

NYSE Symbol **OG**
In S&P 500

05-AUG-95

Industry:
Conglomerate/diversified

Summary: Ogden is a leading global service company focusing on entertainment, aviation, waste-to-energy, power generation and water/wastewater treatment services.

S&P Opinion: Hold (★★★)	Recent Price • 23⅛	Yield • 5.4%
	52 Wk Range • 23⅜-17¾	12-Mo. P/E • 18.4

Quantitative Evaluations

Outlook
(1 Lowest—5 Highest)
• **5**⁻

Fair Value
• **25¼**

Risk
• **Low**

Earn./Div. Rank
• **B+**

Technical Eval.
• **Bearish** since 7/95

Rel. Strength Rank
(1 Lowest—99 Highest)
• **61**

Insider Activity
• **Neutral**

Earnings vs. Previous Year
▲=Up ▼=Down ▶=No Change

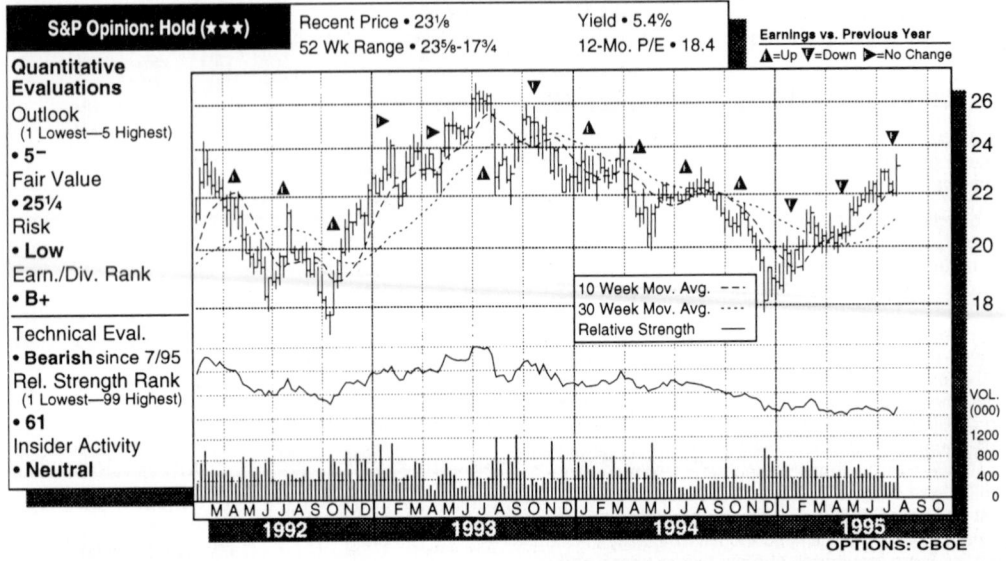

10 Week Mov. Avg. ---
30 Week Mov. Avg. ·····
Relative Strength —

VOL. (000)

OPTIONS: CBOE

Overview - 04-AUG-95

Revenues are expected to rise about 5% in 1995. A much stronger performance is anticipated for entertainment services, which was hurt by the baseball and hockey players' strikes in 1994. Growth is also seen for aviation services, reflecting greater passenger traffic and worldwide expansion efforts. Substantially lower construction activity for waste-to-energy facilities should result in a decline in project revenues, although gains are expected to continue for existing plants. Margins were under pressure early in the year from high levels of development costs, but improvement is expected as the year progresses.

Valuation - 04-AUG-95

Our estimate for 1995 includes a one-time charge of $0.20 a share recorded in the second quarter; excluding the charge, our full year estimate would be $1.70. With annual operating earnings growth of around 10% seen for this year and 1996, the shares have a deserved below-market P/E and appear fairly valued. We advise holding the shares, which offer an attractive yield of between 5% and 6%. Ogden should benefit longer term from the increased emphasis being placed on its core entertainment, aviation and project services, with the greatest growth expected to come from the entertainment area. OG also plans to accelerate the divestiture of non-core activities over the next 12 months.

Key Stock Statistics

S&P EPS Est. 1995	1.50	Tang. Bk. Value/Share	12.21
P/E on S&P Est. 1995	15.4	Beta	1.32
S&P EPS Est. 1996	1.90	Shareholders	12,700
Dividend Rate/Share	1.25	Market cap. (B)	$ 1.1
Shs. outstg. (M)	48.8	Inst. holdings	60%
Avg. daily vol. (M)	0.072	Insider holdings	NA

Value of $10,000 invested 5 years ago: $ 10,309

Fiscal Year Ending Dec. 31

	1995	% Change	1994	% Change	1993	% Change
Revenues (Million $)						
1Q	503.5	5%	479.3	5%	458.5	11%
2Q	539.3	2%	527.7	2%	516.2	20%
3Q	—	—	546.7	1%	540.9	18%
4Q	—	—	556.5	6%	523.8	12%
Yr.	—	—	2,110	3%	2,039	15%
Income (Million $)						
1Q	12.29	-20%	15.33	11%	13.82	1%
2Q	10.28	-42%	17.64	10%	16.09	9%
3Q	—	—	18.74	27%	14.72	-15%
4Q	—	—	16.12	-8%	17.49	15%
Yr.	—	—	67.83	9%	62.13	2%
Earnings Per Share ($)						
1Q	0.25	-29%	0.35	9%	0.32	NM
2Q	0.21	-48%	0.40	8%	0.37	9%
3Q	E0.54	—	0.43	26%	0.34	-15%
4Q	E0.50	—	0.37	-8%	0.40	14%
Yr.	E1.50	—	1.55	8%	1.43	1%

Next earnings report expected: late October

Ogden Corp.

Business Summary - 04-AUG-95

Ogden Corp. is one of the world's largest and most comprehensive service management organizations. It also builds and operates mass-burn resource recovery facilities. Segment contributions in 1994 were:

	Revs.	Profits
Services:		
Aviation	19.6%	---
Entertainment	11.6%	---
Environmental	6.7%	---
Technology	10.1%	---
Facility Management	16.9%	---
Other	0.5%	---
Total Services	65.4%	32.4%
Projects	34.6%	67.6%

The services group provides ground services, catering and fueling of aircraft at domestic and foreign airports; facility management, concert promotions, food, beverage and novelty concession services and maintenance services at entertainment facilities; environmental, infrastructure and energy consulting, engineering and design services; a broad range of technology and scientific solutions for public and private industry, including the development and manufacture of commercial technology products; and facility management, housekeeping, security and other support services for office facilities. Customers include airlines, transportation terminals, sports arenas, stadiums, banks, owners and tenants of office buildings, state, local and federal governments, universities and other institutions, and large industrial organizations.

The projects segment builds and operates solid waste resource recovery plants utilizing the mass-burn technology of Martin GmbH of Germany. As of March 1995, OG had 27 projects in operation, with one more project under construction. The company is also pursuing opportunities to develop independent power projects that utilize fuels other than waste and to operate and maintain water and wastewater processing facilities.

Important Developments

Aug. '95—Ogden recorded an after-tax charge of $9.6 million ($0.20 a share) in 1995's second quarter for the write-off of receivables and related costs in connection with a project for the assembly and installation of telecommunications equipment and a reduction in the carrying value of certain other inventory.

Capitalization

Long Term Debt: $2,054,981,000 (3/95), incl. $85 million of 6% debs. conv. into com. at $39.077 a sh., and $63.65 million of 5.75% debs. conv. into com. at $41.772 a sh.

Minority Interest: $9,770,000.

$1.875 Part. Pfd. Stock: 52,000 shs. ($1 par); ea. conv. into 5.97626 com. shs.

Per Share Data ($)

(Year Ended Dec. 31)

	1994	1993	1992	1991	1990	1989
Tangible Bk. Val.	10.15	9.23	9.28	9.29	9.72	10.54
Cash Flow	3.63	3.40	2.94	2.66	2.48	2.60
Earnings	1.55	1.43	1.41	1.33	1.31	1.68
Dividends	1.25	1.25	1.25	1.25	1.25	1.25
Payout Ratio	81%	88%	89%	94%	96%	75%
Prices - High	24³/₈	27	24³/₈	23¹/₄	32⁷/₈	34³/₄
- Low	17³/₄	21¹/₂	17¹/₈	17⁵/₈	15	25¹/₂
P/E Ratio - High	16	19	17	17	25	21
- Low	11	15	12	13	11	15

Income Statement Analysis (Million $)

	1994	%Chg	1993	%Chg	1992	%Chg	1991
Revs.	2,084	2%	2,039	15%	1,769	13%	1,568
Oper. Inc.	314	-1%	318	9%	291	12%	259
Depr.	90.5	6%	85.6	30%	66.0	16%	57.1
Int. Exp.	140	1%	138	7%	129	3%	125
Pretax Inc.	139	10%	126	12%	113	9%	104
Eff. Tax Rate	44%	—	45%	—	40%	—	37%
Net Inc.	67.8	9%	62.1	2%	60.8	6%	57.6

Balance Sheet & Other Fin. Data (Million $)

	1994	1993	1992	1991	1990	1989
Cash	309	203	216	129	127	130
Curr. Assets	996	NA	NA	NA	NA	NA
Total Assets	3,645	3,313	3,192	2,846	2,693	2,598
Curr. Liab.	513	NA	NA	NA	NA	279
LT Debt	2,047	1,947	2,003	1,782	1,682	1,681
Common Eqty.	596	485	480	477	483	440
Total Cap.	2,936	2,694	2,693	2,372	2,254	2,168
Cap. Exp.	120	116	69.0	111	196	331
Cash Flow	158	148	127	114	106	103

Ratio Analysis

	1994	1993	1992	1991	1990	1989
Curr. Ratio	1.9	NA	NA	NA	NA	NA
% LT Debt of Cap.	69.7	72.3	74.4	75.1	74.6	77.5
% Net Inc.of Revs.	3.3	3.0	3.4	3.7	3.6	4.9
% Ret. on Assets	1.8	1.9	2.0	2.1	2.0	2.8
% Ret. on Equity	11.9	12.8	12.7	11.9	11.7	15.4

Dividend Data (Dividends were resumed in 1972.)

Amt. of Div. $	Date Decl.	Ex-Div. Date	Stock of Record	Payment Date
0.313	Nov. 17	Dec. 08	Dec. 14	Jan. 05 '95
0.313	Jan. 19	Mar. 08	Mar. 14	Apr. 04 '95
0.313	May. 26	Jun. 12	Jun. 14	Jul. 05 '95
0.313	Jul. 13	Sep. 12	Sep. 14	Oct. 05 '95

Data as orig. reptd.; bef. results of disc. opers. and/or spec. items. Per share data adj. for stk. divs. as of ex-div. date. E-Estimated. NA-Not Available. NM-Not Meaningful. NR-Not Ranked.

Office—2 Pennsylvania Plaza, New York, NY 10121. **Tel**—(212) 868-6100. **Chrmn**—Ralph E. Ablon. **Vice Chrmn**—A. Zaleznik. **Pres & CEO**—R. Richard Ablon. **SVP-CFO & Treas**—P. G. Husby. **VP & Secy**—K. Ritch. **VP & Investor Contact**—Nancy R. Christal. **Dirs**—R. E. Ablon, R. R. Ablon, D. M. Abshire, C. G. Caras, N. G. Einspruch, A. Kappas, T. A. Kramer, M. P. Monet, J. D. Moyers, H. A. Neal, S. S. Penner, J. Sainz, F. Seitz, R. E. Smith, H. F. O. Volcker, A. Zaleznik. **Transfer Agent & Registrar**—Chemical Bank, NYC. **Incorporated** in Delaware in 1939. **Empl**- 45,000.
S&P Analyst: Michael V. Pizzi

Ohio Edison

NYSE Symbol **OEC**
In S&P 500

23-AUG-95 Industry: Utilities-Electric

Summary: This Akron-based electric utility serves 1.1 million customers in Ohio and western Pennsylvania. Steel and other heavy industry manufacturing dominate its industrial base.

S&P Opinion: Hold (★★★)	Recent Price • 22	Yield • 6.9%
	52 Wk Range • 22⅝-17⅝	12-Mo. P/E • 10.9

Earnings vs. Previous Year
▲=Up ▼=Down ▶=No Change

Quantitative Evaluations

Outlook
(1 Lowest—5 Highest)
• **2+**

Fair Value
• **20½**

Risk
• **Low**

Earn./Div. Rank
• **B**

Technical Eval.
• **Bullish** since 1/95

Rel. Strength Rank
(1 Lowest—99 Highest)
• **38**

Insider Activity
• **NA**

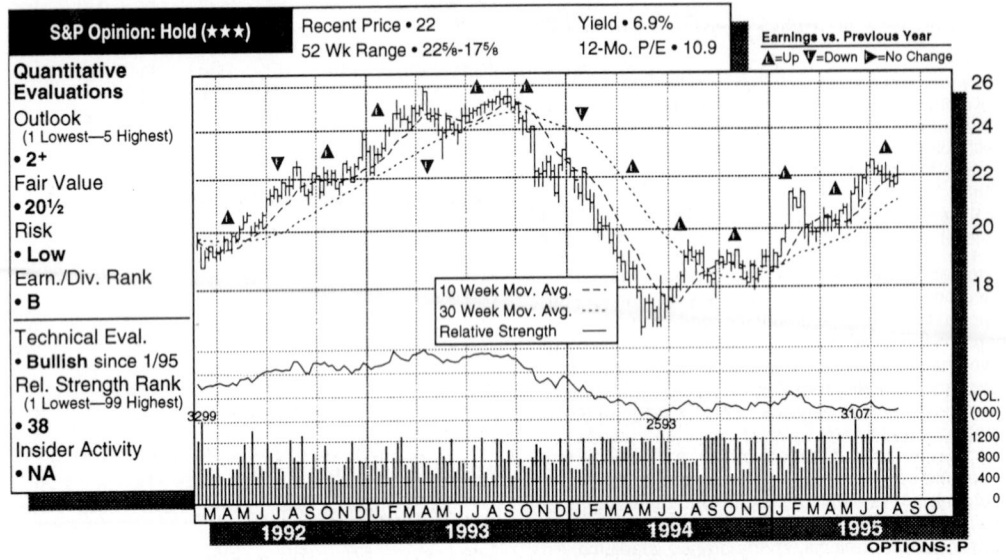

10 Week Mov. Avg. ----
30 Week Mov. Avg. ······
Relative Strength ——

OPTIONS: P

Overview - 23-AUG-95

Share earnings should increase modestly in 1995, reflecting slightly higher revenues on growth in electricity sales due to continued strength within the company's service territory and an increase in sales to other utilities. Economic development and energy efficiency rate discounts to some industrial customers are restraining revenue growth, but margins should widen on cost savings from reductions in the workforce, lower interest costs and efforts to control expenses. The company's long-term debt as a percentage of total capital at a level of about 51% is only slightly above the norm for an electric utility. Although OEC is a high cost producer in the region, a freeze on rate increases until 1999 bolsters its competitive position.

Valuation - 18-AUG-95

The shares have advanced 20% this year, in part due to a run up this Spring in anticipation of the Federal Reserve raising interest rates. In addition, the company's ongoing cost cutting efforts are beginning to bear fruit. Earnings growth is gaining momentum and should continue to do so for the remainder of the year due to high air-conditioning use, particularly in the third quarter. Lower interest costs and moderation in construction projects should help raise OEC's cash generating ability and secure the dividend. We do not expect a dividend hike until the payout ratio has moved closer to the low 70% level.

Key Stock Statistics

S&P EPS Est. 1995	2.03	Tang. Bk. Value/Share	15.41
P/E on S&P Est. 1995	10.8	Beta	0.77
S&P EPS Est. 1996	2.08	Shareholders	145,600
Dividend Rate/Share	1.50	Market cap. (B)	$ 3.3
Shs. outstg. (M)	152.6	Inst. holdings	36%
Avg. daily vol. (M)	0.163	Insider holdings	NA

Value of $10,000 invested 5 years ago: $ 14,117

Fiscal Year Ending Dec. 31

	1995	% Change	1994	% Change	1993	% Change
Revenues (Million $)						
1Q	587.7	-2%	601.3	1%	593.2	NM
2Q	593.8	1%	585.4	4%	563.3	NM
3Q	—	—	614.4	-2%	624.5	4%
4Q	—	—	567.1	-4%	588.8	2%
Yr.	—	—	2,368	NM	2,370	2%
Income (Million $)						
1Q	71.60	5%	67.93	1%	67.22	-8%
2Q	77.05	4%	74.04	NM	74.55	25%
3Q	—	—	88.23	NM	88.22	11%
4Q	—	—	73.34	NM	-205.5	NM
Yr.	—	—	303.5	NM	24.52	-91%
Earnings Per Share ($)						
1Q	0.46	5%	0.44	10%	0.40	-11%
2Q	0.50	4%	0.48	7%	0.45	25%
3Q	E0.59	2%	0.58	7%	0.54	10%
4Q	E0.48	2%	0.47	NM	-1.38	NM
Yr.	E2.03	3%	1.97	NM	0.01	-99%

Next earnings report expected: mid October

Business Summary - 23-AUG-95

Ohio Edison Co. and its wholly owned subsidiary Pennsylvania Power Co. serve the highly industrialized areas of northern Ohio and western Pennsylvania. Electric revenue contributions in recent years were:

	1994	1993	1992	1990
Residential	37%	37%	36%	35%
Commercial	37%	27%	27%	27%
Industrial	26%	25%	26%	26%
Other	10%	11%	11%	12%

Sources of electric generation in 1994 were 76% coal and 24% nuclear. Peak demand in 1994 was 5,744 mw and system capability at peak totaled 5,980 mw, for a capacity margin of 3.9%. The Clean Air Act Amendments of 1990 require significant emissions reductions from coal-fired generating units. The company estimates capital expenditures for environmental compliance at $70 million a year through 1999.

Costs for construction totaled $227 million in 1994, largely to improve existing plant and to build transmission and distribution lines, substations and other related additions. The company estimates construction costs for 1995 through 1999 at $800 million, including $180 million in 1995. OEC is not currently adding any new base load facilities.

OEC has access to 35% of the Perry 1 nuclear station and 42% of the Beaver Valley 2 nuclear unit. In March 1989, the PUC of Ohio issued an order that finalized the prudency disallowance for the two plants. As a result, the company wrote the Beaver Valley asset down $245 million and, late in 1993, recorded a $366 million write off of the Perry 2 nuclear unit.

Important Developments

Jul. '95—OEC attributed improved second quarter earnings to a 9.1% increase in total kilowatt-hour sales and lower operating andmaintenance expenses. Industrial sales rose 3.8%, commercial sales 1.1% and residential sales were basically flat. Sales to other utilities rose 46%. In February, OEC trimmed its workforce by 227 employees, part of ongoing efforts to reduce costs and strengthen its financial position. The company expects the cutbacks and shutdown of two old units at the Burger plant to reduce annual operating expenses by about $13 million annually. A rate stabilization and service area development program approved by Ohio regulators in 1992 freezes OEC's base electric rates at least until 1999.

Capitalization

Long Term Debt: $2,822,225,000 (6/95).
Subsidiary Preferred Stock: $65,905,000.
Red. Pfd. & Pref. Stock: $25,000,000.
Cum. Preferred Stock: $277,335,000.

Per Share Data ($) (Year Ended Dec. 31)

	1994	1993	1992	1991	1990	1989
Tangible Bk. Val.	15.13	14.63	15.11	15.01	16.15	16.28
Earnings	1.97	0.01	1.70	1.60	1.67	2.18
Dividends	1.50	1.50	1.50	1.50	1.73	1.96
Payout Ratio	76%	NM	88%	94%	104%	90%
Prices - High	22¾	26	24	20½	23⅞	24
- Low	16½	21	18¾	16⅜	15⅞	18⅝
P/E Ratio - High	12	NM	14	13	14	11
- Low	8	NM	11	10	10	9

Income Statement Analysis (Million $)

	1994	%Chg	1993	%Chg	1992	%Chg	1991
Revs.	2,368	NM	2,370	2%	2,332	-1%	2,359
Depr.	221	1%	218	-4%	226	-4%	236
Maint.	NA	—	NA	—	NA	—	NA
Fxd. Chgs. Cov.	2.5	7%	2.4	1%	2.3	5%	2.2
Constr. Credits	5.2	4%	5.0	-17%	6.0	-45%	11.0
Eff. Tax Rate	38%	—	69%	—	34%	—	39%
Net Inc.	304	NM	24.5	-91%	277	5%	265

Balance Sheet & Other Fin. Data (Million $)

	1994	1993	1992	1991	1990	1989
Gross Prop.	8,745	8,610	8,489	8,346	8,239	8,052
Cap. Exp.	258	257	253	236	271	258
Net Prop.	5,835	5,878	5,938	5,985	6,049	6,082
Capitalization:						
LT Debt	3,167	3,039	3,122	3,243	3,105	3,074
% LT Debt	54	54	53	54	51	51
Pfd.	368	302	414	420	417	444
% Pfd.	6.30	5.00	7.00	7.00	6.90	7.30
Common	2,317	2,243	2,408	2,372	2,545	2,566
% Common	40	40	41	39	42	42
Total Cap.	7,875	7,687	6,787	6,878	6,854	6,794

Ratio Analysis

	1994	1993	1992	1991	1990	1989
Oper. Ratio	76.5	77.8	77.6	76.7	77.1	74.8
% Earn. on Net Prop.	9.5	8.9	8.8	9.1	8.4	9.0
% Ret. on Revs.	12.8	1.0	11.9	11.2	12.7	16.8
% Ret. On Invest.Cap	7.4	4.1	8.2	8.3	7.5	8.3
% Return On Com.Eqty	12.4	11.4	10.8	9.9	9.9	13.0

Dividend Data —Dividends have been paid since 1930. A dividend reinvestment plan is available.

Amt. of Div. $	Date Decl.	Ex-Div. Date	Stock of Record	Payment Date
0.375	Jul. 19	Sep. 01	Sep. 08	Sep. 30 '94
0.375	Nov. 15	Dec. 01	Dec. 07	Dec. 30 '94
0.375	Feb. 21	Mar. 01	Mar. 07	Mar. 31 '95
0.375	May. 16	Jun. 01	Jun. 07	Jun. 30 '95
0.375	Jul. 18	Sep. 06	Sep. 08	Sep. 29 '95

Data as orig. reptd.; bef. results of disc opers. and/or spec. items. Per share data adj. for stk. divs. as of ex-div. date. E-Estimated. NA-Not Available. NM-Not Meaningful. NR-Not Ranked.

Office—76 South Main St., Akron, OH 44308. **Tel**—(216) 384-5100. **Pres & CEO**—W. R. Holland. **SVP & CFO**—H. P. Burg. **Secy**—N. C. Brink. **Treas & Investor Contact**—Richard H. Marsh. **Dirs**—D. C. Blasius, H. P. Burg, R. H. Carlson, R. M. Carter, C. A. Cartwright, W. R. Holland, R. L. Loughhead, G. H. Meadows, P.J. Powers, C. W. Rainger, G. M. Smart, J. T. Williams. **Transfer Agent & Registrar**—Co.'s office. **Incorporated** in Ohio in 1930. **Empl**-4,929. **S&P Analyst:** Jane Collin

ONEOK Inc.

NYSE Symbol **OKE**
In S&P 500

12-SEP-95 | **Industry:** Utilities-Gas

Summary: OKE operates a natural gas utility in Oklahoma, and also engages in nonutility energy-related activities, including oil and gas exploration and natural gas liquids extraction.

S&P Opinion: Hold (★★★)	Recent Price • 22¼	Yield • 5.0%
	52 Wk Range • 23⅞-15⅞	12-Mo. P/E • 14.5

Earnings vs. Previous Year
▲=Up ▼=Down ▶=No Change

Quantitative Evaluations

Outlook
(1 Lowest—5 Highest)
• **2+**

Fair Value
• **21⅜**

Risk
• **Low**

Earn./Div. Rank
• **B**

Technical Eval.
• **Bearish** since 9/95

Rel. Strength Rank
(1 Lowest—99 Highest)
• **44**

Insider Activity
• **Neutral**

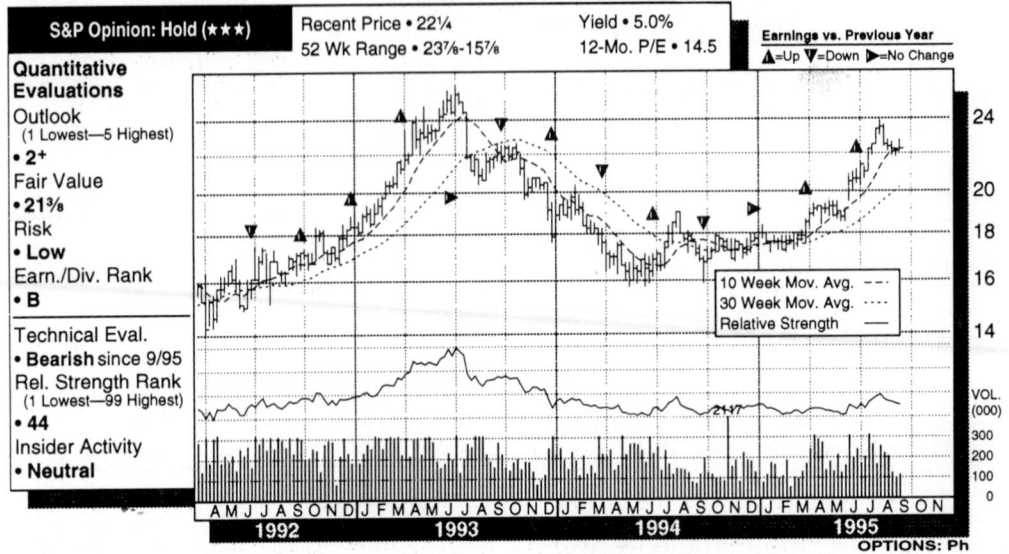

10 Week Mov. Avg. – –
30 Week Mov. Avg. · · · ·
Relative Strength —

VOL. (000)

OPTIONS: Ph

Overview - 12-SEP-95

Profits from utility operations should increase slightly in fiscal 1995 and beyond, reflecting improved margins and customer growth. Natural gas liquids processing should continue to increase its contribution to the bottom line as a result of additional sales volumes and improved margins. Exploration and production profits should edge up fractionally, due to increased natural gas liquids and gas sales from recently acquired properties, increased oil prices, and lower depreciation and depletion expenses. In recognition of increasing competitive conditions in the industrial gas market, OKE has restructured and reduced its rates for large industrial customers, with revenue losses associated with the restructuring being shifted to the general system core customers.

Valuation - 12-SEP-95

Although this company is largely a utility, the shares began a downtrend in mid-1993, as a drop in oil prices led to depressed gas processing margins. The stock price decline was extended as interest rates began to rise. The shares, now trading at about 14X estimated fiscal 1996 EPS of $1.60, have appreciated about 25% since the beginning of calendar 1995. Based on this appreciation, the stock is likely to be only an average performer over the next 12 months. Over the next several years, the dividend growth rate is expected to significantly trail EPS growth, as OKE tries to bring its payout ratio down to about 75%. However, with a current yield of 5.0%, the shares remain an attractive holding for total return.

Key Stock Statistics

S&P EPS Est. 1995	1.55	Tang. Bk. Value/Share	13.86
P/E on S&P Est. 1995	14.4	Beta	0.03
S&P EPS Est. 1996	1.60	Shareholders	12,300
Dividend Rate/Share	1.12	Market cap. (B)	$0.605
Shs. outstg. (M)	27.0	Inst. holdings	48%
Avg. daily vol. (M)	0.029	Insider holdings	NA

Value of $10,000 invested 5 years ago: $ 18,936

Fiscal Year Ending Aug. 31

	1995	% Change	1994	% Change	1993	% Change
Revenues (Million $)						
1Q	166.3	-6%	177.2	11%	159.4	3%
2Q	287.4	-3%	295.4	-6%	314.0	18%
3Q	304.5	60%	190.5	1%	188.0	25%
4Q	—	—	129.3	NM	128.2	20%
Yr.	—	—	792.4	NM	789.1	17%
Income (Million $)						
1Q	7.79	NM	7.81	30%	6.00	7%
2Q	28.29	7%	26.39	-15%	31.23	34%
3Q	9.04	59%	5.69	107%	2.75	6%
4Q	—	—	-3.71	NM	-1.55	NM
Yr.	—	—	36.18	-6%	38.42	18%
Earnings Per Share ($)						
1Q	0.29	NM	0.29	32%	0.22	5%
2Q	1.05	7%	0.98	-16%	1.17	34%
3Q	0.33	57%	0.21	110%	0.10	NM
4Q	E-0.12	NM	-0.14	NM	-0.06	NM
Yr.	E1.55	16%	1.34	-6%	1.43	18%

Next earnings report expected: early October

ONEOK Inc.

Business Summary - 12-SEP-95

ONEOK Inc. (formerly Oklahoma Natural Gas) is a diversified energy company engaged in natural gas utility operations in Oklahoma and nonutility energy-related activities, including oil and gas exploration and production. Segment contributions (profits in millions) in fiscal 1994 were:

	Revs.	Profits
Gas utility	78%	$87.9
Gas processing	13%	6.6
Oil & gas production	3%	0.7
Contract drilling	1%	-2.4
Other	5%	-0.8

Gas utility operations are conducted principally by Oklahoma Natural Gas Co., which distributes gas to about 715,000 customers in 292 communities in Oklahoma, with Oklahoma City and Tulsa the largest markets, and at wholesale to other distributors serving 44 Oklahoma communities. Gas sales volume in fiscal 1994 totaled 136.7 Bcf, down from 145.9 Bcf in fiscal 1993. Degree days in fiscal 1994 came to 3,874, down from 3,953 in fiscal 1993.

The ONEOK Exploration Co. and ONEOK Resources Co. subsidiaries are engaged in oil and gas exploration, development and production. At fiscal 1994 year-end, proved reserves amounted to 32.4 Bcf of gas and 2.3 million bbl. of oil. Other nonutility operations include extraction and sale of natural gas liquids, contract drilling of oil and gas wells (sold in fiscal 1994), gas marketing and operation of a parking garage.

Important Developments

Jun. '95—The Oklahoma Corporation Commission approved a $14.9 million rate increase for Oklahoma Natural Gas Co. The settlement includes a change in the company's gas pricing that will result in a significant reduction in gas costs for residential and commercial customers. Also, rates for Oklahoma Natural's 35 largest industrial customers will be restructured and maximum rates will be reduced. The settlement also provides for limited (up to 10%) rate recovery for large industrial customer revenue losses, and a temperature normalization adjustment clause. As part of the agreement, Oklahoma Natural will not apply for a general rate increase for two years.

Apr. '95—The company sold its Caney River Transmission Co. unit, which owned OKE's 25% partnership interest in the Ozark Gas Transmission System, to NGC Corp. for $44.8 million.

Capitalization

Long Term Debt: $350,969,000 (5/95).
Cum. Preferred Stock: $9,000,000.

Per Share Data ($) (Year Ended Aug. 31)

	1994	1993	1992	1991	1990	1989
Tangible Bk. Val.	13.88	13.63	13.28	13.03	12.51	12.11
Earnings	1.34	1.43	1.21	1.33	1.21	1.29
Dividends	1.11	1.06	0.96	0.82	0.74	0.47
Payout Ratio	83%	74%	79%	62%	62%	37%
Prices - High	$20\frac{3}{8}$	$26\frac{1}{4}$	19	$16\frac{7}{8}$	$16\frac{1}{2}$	17
- Low	$15\frac{3}{4}$	$17\frac{5}{8}$	14	$12\frac{1}{2}$	$11\frac{7}{8}$	$9\frac{1}{4}$
P/E Ratio - High	15	18	16	13	14	13
- Low	12	12	12	9	10	7

Income Statement Analysis (Million $)

	1994	%Chg	1993	%Chg	1992	%Chg	1991
Revs.	792	NM	789	17%	677	-2%	689
Depr.	50.8	6%	48.0	3%	46.8	23%	38.2
Maint.	6.4	-8%	7.0	6%	6.6	3%	6.4
Fxd. Chgs. Cov.	2.7	4%	2.6	NM	2.5	-19%	3.1
Constr. Credits	0.6	13%	0.5	12%	0.5	30%	0.4
Eff. Tax Rate	37%	—	35%	—	37%	—	38%
Net Inc.	36.2	-6%	38.4	18%	32.6	-9%	35.9

Balance Sheet & Other Fin. Data (Million $)

	1994	1993	1992	1991	1990	1989
Gross Prop.	1,218	1,196	1,124	1,047	952	897
Cap. Exp.	74.0	86.0	70.0	111	69.0	43.0
Net Prop.	737	752	684	663	591	561
Capitalization:						
LT Debt	363	376	381	283	216	144
% LT Debt	49	50	51	44	39	30
Pfd.	9.0	9.0	9.0	9.0	9.0	9.0
% Pfd.	1.20	1.20	1.20	1.40	1.60	1.90
Common	370	363	354	347	333	334
% Common	50	49	48	54	60	69
Total Cap.	940	944	926	821	731	651

Ratio Analysis

	1994	1993	1992	1991	1990	1989
Oper. Ratio	91.0	90.4	90.4	90.9	91.4	90.1
% Earn. on Net Prop.	9.7	10.8	9.6	10.0	10.0	10.4
% Ret. on Revs.	4.6	4.9	4.8	5.2	4.9	5.9
% Ret. On Invest.Cap	7.5	8.1	7.4	8.0	8.3	9.0
% Return On Com.Eqty	9.7	10.6	9.2	10.4	9.8	11.1

Dividend Data —Common dividends, omitted in March 1988, were resumed in January 1989. A dividend reinvestment plan is available. A poison pill stock purchase rights plan was adopted in 1988.

Amt. of Div. $	Date Decl.	Ex-Div. Date	Stock of Record	Payment Date
0.280	Oct. 20	Oct. 25	Oct. 31	Nov. 15 '94
0.280	Jan. 19	Jan. 25	Jan. 31	Feb. 15 '95
0.280	Apr. 20	Apr. 24	Apr. 28	May. 15 '95
0.280	Jul. 20	Jul. 27	Jul. 31	Aug. 15 '95

Data as orig. reptd.; bef. results of disc opers. and/or spec. items. Per share data adj. for stk. divs. as of ex-div. date. E-Estimated. NA-Not Available. NM-Not Meaningful. NR-Not Ranked.

Office—100 West Fifth St., Tulsa, OK 74103. **Tel**—(918) 588-7000. **Chrmn, Pres & CEO**—L. W. Brummett. **VP, CFO & Treas**—J. D. Neal. **VP & Secy**—L. W. Neal. **Investor Contact**—Weldon Watson. **Dirs**—W. M. Bell, L. W. Brummett, D. R. Cummings, W. L. Ford, J. M. Graves, S. J. Jatras, B. H. Mackie, D. A. Newsom, G. D. Parker, J. D. Scott, J. E. Tyree, G. R. Williams, S. L. Young. **Transfer Agent & Registrar**—Liberty National Bank & Trust Co. of Oklahoma City. **Incorporated** in Delaware in 1933. **Empl**-2,061. **S&P Analyst:** Ronald J. Gross

Oracle Systems

NASDAQ Symbol **ORCL**

In S&P 500

05-AUG-95

Industry: Data Processing

Summary: Oracle supplies computer software products used for database management, applications development and decision support, as well as end-user and other applications.

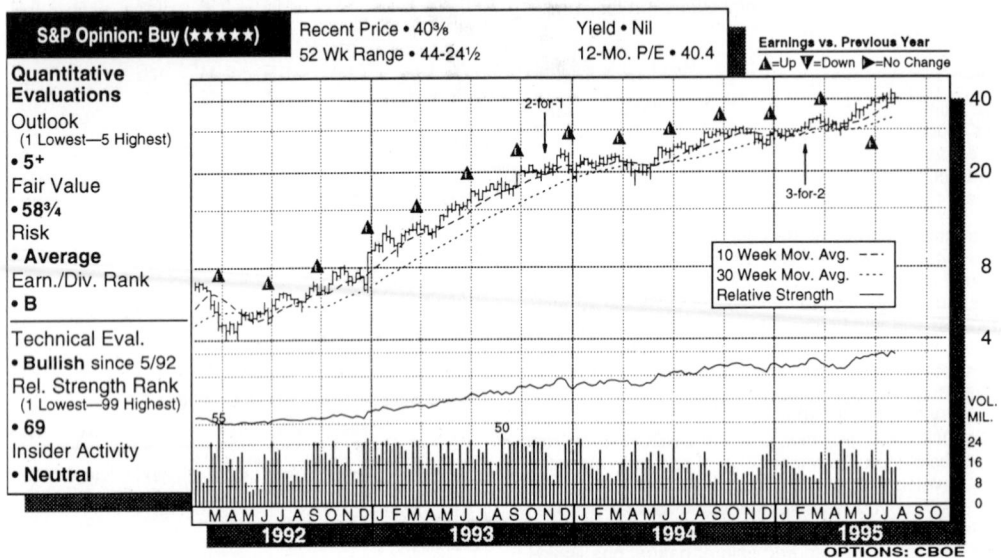

S&P Opinion: Buy (★★★★)	Recent Price • 40%	Yield • Nil
	52 Wk Range • 44-24½	12-Mo. P/E • 40.4

Quantitative Evaluations

Outlook (1 Lowest—5 Highest)
• **5+**

Fair Value
• **58¾**

Risk
• **Average**

Earn./Div. Rank
• **B**

Technical Eval.
• **Bullish** since 5/92

Rel. Strength Rank (1 Lowest—99 Highest)
• **69**

Insider Activity
• **Neutral**

Earnings vs. Previous Year
▲=Up ▼=Down ▶=No Change

10 Week Mov. Avg. – – –
30 Week Mov. Avg. – · – ·
Relative Strength ———

OPTIONS: CBOE

Overview - 03-AUG-95

Revenues should continue to increase strongly in 1995-96, reflecting strong demand for Oracle's relational database management system, aided by new releases of application products, strength in tools for the Windows market, ongoing strong demand for services, and continued expansion of the worldwide economies. Products for the UNIX and desktop environments (which now account for 90% of total revenues) should continue to show the most rapid growth. Margins are expected to widen on volume efficiencies, ongoing cost controls, and higher interest income. Earnings should benefit from the higher revenues and wider margins.

Valuation - 03-AUG-95

Earnings should rise an impressive 40% for the year ending May 31, 1996, from fiscal 1995 levels. The database software segment is growing rapidly as organizations cope with managing and utilizing the massive data stored on their computer systems. Oracle's leadership position and growing market share bode well; the core database server business is strong, applications software revenues should continue to grow rapidly, the database tools business should increase, and there is an ongoing need for additional services. The strong earnings growth we expect should help the stock outperform the market in the coming months.

Key Stock Statistics

S&P EPS Est. 1996	1.40	Tang. Bk. Value/Share	1.73
P/E on S&P Est. 1996	28.8	Beta	1.84
Dividend Rate/Share	Nil	Shareholders	400
Shs. outstg. (M)	431.2	Market cap. (B)	$ 17.4
Avg. daily vol. (M)	3.073	Inst. holdings	64%
		Insider holdings	NA

Value of $10,000 invested 5 years ago: $ 51,815

Fiscal Year Ending May 31

	1995	% Change	1994	% Change	1993	% Change
Revenues (Million $)						
1Q	556.5	40%	398.0	30%	307.0	25%
2Q	670.3	48%	452.2	28%	353.0	24%
3Q	722.3	50%	482.8	30%	370.0	28%
4Q	1,018	52%	668.1	41%	472.6	101%
Yr.	2,967	48%	2,001	33%	1,503	28%
Income (Million $)						
1Q	61.20	64%	37.36	—	—	—
2Q	93.87	51%	62.13	86%	33.49	147%
3Q	104.8	50%	69.75	139%	29.16	74%
4Q	181.7	59%	114.5	66%	69.11	140%
Yr.	441.5	56%	283.7	100%	141.7	129%
Earnings Per Share ($)						
1Q	0.14	68%	0.08	NM	0.02	NM
2Q	0.21	52%	0.14	83%	0.08	130%
3Q	0.24	50%	0.16	140%	0.07	67%
4Q	0.41	58%	0.26	66%	0.16	135%
Yr.	1.00	56%	0.64	100%	0.32	123%

Next earnings report expected: late September

Oracle Systems

Business Summary - 03-AUG-95

Oracle Systems Corporation develops, markets and supports computer software products used for database management, network communications, applications development and end-user applications. Its principal product is the ORACLE relational database management system (DBMS). The company offers its products, along with related database design, consulting, training and support services, worldwide.

The ORACLE relational DBMS, which runs on a broad range of massively parallel, mainframes, minicomputers, workstations and personal computers, gives users the ability to define, retrieve, manipulate and control data stored on multiple computers using the industry standard SQL language.

A variety of applications development and CASE products, which increase programmer productivity, are sold as add-ons to the ORACLE relational DBMS.

The company also offers an integrated family of end-user financial applications, including general ledger, purchasing, payables, assets, receivables and revenue accounting programs, and end-user manufacturing applications. These application products use the ORACLE relational DBMS and related development and decision support tools.

Oracle offers consulting, education and systems integration services to assist customers in the design and development of applications based on company products.

Important Developments

Jun. '95—Total revenues in the fourth quarter of fiscal 1995 increased 52%, year to year, aided by a 57% advance in service revenues and a 52% gain in license revenues. Oracle gained market share in its core database server business -- server license revenues rose 70% year to year. Application license revenues rose 115%, from fiscal 1994's fourth quarter, aided by new products. Margins widened on the greater volume, despite a less favorable revenue mix and higher sales and marketing costs. After taxes at 33.0% in each period, net income rose 59%.

Jan. '95—During the second quarter of fiscal 1994-5, the company completed the acquisition of Digital Equipment Corp.'s Rdb database, CDD/Repository and the DBA Workcenter suite of database administration tools, and all corresponding support business, for $108 million in cash. Oracle also shipped its Cooperative Development Environment 2, the next generation of products for client/server application development and data access.

Capitalization

Long Term Debt: $81,721,000 (5/95).

Per Share Data ($) (Year Ended May 31)

	1995	1994	1993	1992	1991	1990
Tangible Bk. Val.	NA	1.73	1.24	1.04	0.84	0.99
Cash Flow	NA	0.79	0.45	0.26	0.11	0.37
Earnings	1.00	0.64	0.32	0.14	-0.03	0.29
Dividends	Nil	Nil	Nil	Nil	Nil	Nil
Payout Ratio	Nil	Nil	Nil	Nil	Nil	Nil
Cal. Yrs.	1994	1993	1992	1991	1990	1989
Prices - High	31	25⅛	9½	5½	9½	8⅝
- Low	17½	8⅞	4	1¹³/₁₆	1⅝	3⅛
P/E Ratio - High	31	39	30	39	NM	30
- Low	17	14	12	13	NM	11

Income Statement Analysis (Million $)

	1994	%Chg	1993	%Chg	1992	%Chg	1991
Revs.	2,001	33%	1,503	28%	1,178	15%	1,028
Oper. Inc.	485	63%	297	80%	165	104%	81.0
Depr.	65.2	16%	56.2	10%	50.9	-7%	54.5
Int. Exp.	6.9	-23%	9.0	-52%	18.6	-23%	24.0
Pretax Inc.	423	94%	218	127%	96.0	NM	-13.0
Eff. Tax Rate	33%	—	35%	—	36%	—	NM
Net Inc.	284	100%	142	129%	62.0	NM	-12.0

Balance Sheet & Other Fin. Data (Million $)

	1994	1993	1992	1991	1990	1989
Cash	465	358	177	101	50.0	49.0
Curr. Assets	1,076	842	641	586	569	337
Total Assets	1,595	1,184	956	858	787	460
Curr. Liab.	682	551	406	479	284	178
LT Debt	82.8	86.4	95.9	18.0	89.1	33.5
Common Eqty.	741	528	435	345	388	231
Total Cap.	862	623	541	369	499	276
Cap. Exp.	251	41.3	46.6	60.7	89.3	68.4
Cash Flow	349	198	112	42.0	153	101

Ratio Analysis

	1994	1993	1992	1991	1990	1989
Curr. Ratio	1.6	1.5	1.6	1.2	2.0	1.9
% LT Debt of Cap.	9.6	13.9	17.7	4.9	17.9	12.1
% Net Inc.of Revs.	14.2	9.4	5.2	NM	12.1	14.0
% Ret. on Assets	20.4	13.2	6.7	NM	18.6	22.6
% Ret. on Equity	44.6	29.2	15.6	NM	37.5	43.9

Dividend Data (No cash dividends have been paid. However, stock dividends have been distributed over the years, the most recent being a three-for-two stock split, effected in February 1995. A "poison pill" stock purchase rights plan was adopted in 1990.)

Amt. of Div. $	Date Decl.	Ex-Div. Date	Stock of Record	Payment Date
3-for-2	Jan. 24	Feb. 23	Feb. 06	Feb. 22 '95

Data as orig. reptd.; bef. results of disc. opers. and/or spec. items. Per share data adj. for stk. divs. as of ex-div. date. E-Estimated. NA-Not Available. NM-Not Meaningful. NR-Not Ranked.

Office—500 Oracle Parkway, Redwood Shores, CA 94065. **Tel**—(415) 506-7000. **Chrmn**—J. A. Abrahamson. **Pres & CEO**—L. J. Ellison. **EVP & CFO**—J. O. Henley. **SVP & Secy**—R. L. Ocampo, Jr. **Investor Contact**—Catherine Buan. **Dirs**—J. A. Abrahamson, M. J. Boskin, J. Costello, L. J. Ellison, J. Kemp, D. L. Lucas, R. P. McKenna, D. W. Yocam. **Transfer Agent & Registrar**—Harris Trust & Savings Bank, Chicago. **Reincorporated** in Delaware in 1987. **Empl**- 14,830. **S&P Analyst:** Peter C. Wood, CFA

Oryx Energy

NYSE Symbol **ORX**
In S&P 500

01-NOV-95 | **Industry:** Oil and Gas | **Summary:** Oryx is one of the world's largest independent oil and natural gas producers.

S&P Opinion: Avoid (★★)	Recent Price • 11⅛	Yield • Nil
	52 Wk Range • 14⅞-9⅞	12-Mo. P/E • 7.0

Quantitative Evaluations

Outlook
(1 Lowest—5 Highest)
• **1**

Fair Value
• **6**

Risk
• **Average**

Earn./Div. Rank
• **NR**

Technical Eval.
• **Bullish** since 10/95

Rel. Strength Rank
(1 Lowest—99 Highest)
• **20**

Insider Activity
• **Neutral**

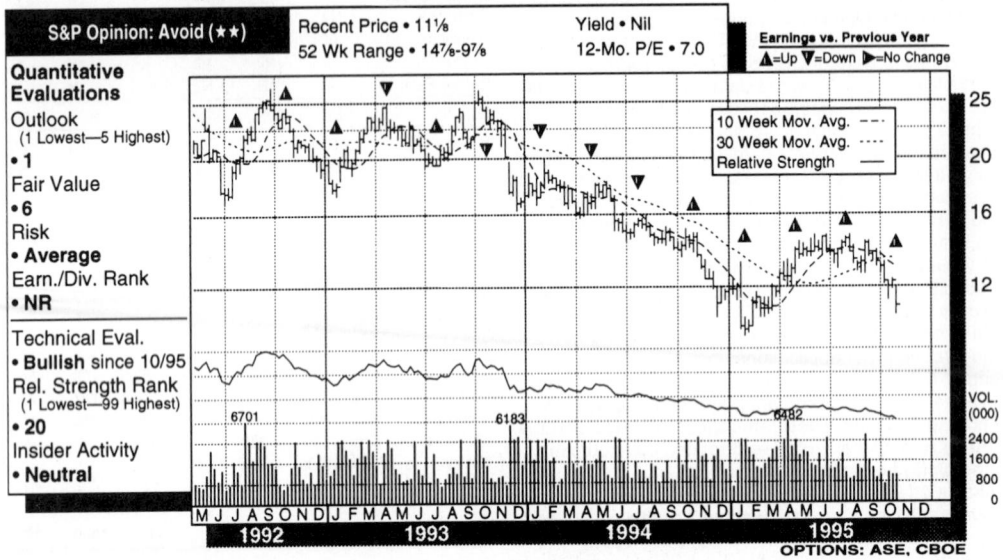

Earnings vs. Previous Year
▲=Up ▼=Down ▶=No Change

10 Week Mov. Avg. – – –
30 Week Mov. Avg. ·······
Relative Strength ——

OPTIONS: ASE, CBOE

Overview - 01-NOV-95

Revenues should fall modestly over the near term as a result of asset sales and lower domestic natural gas prices. However, we expect to see expense levels drop following a recent accounting change and successful restructuring efforts. Longer-term profitability will benefit only slightly from efforts to reduce debt over the next two years. We see considerable upside potential from exploration in Kazakhstan, although the risks with this project are formidable. Indonesian exploration should boost cash flow, and we expect this strong cash flow to lead to further exploration in the region. However, with gas prices not expected to show major gains with markets well supplied and with oil prices expected to remain stable, Oryx's earnings will remain disappointing.

Valuation - 01-NOV-95

The shares have traded in a narrow range after hitting an all-time low in February 1995, reflecting uncertainty about ORX's future. We believe the stock will underperform the market in both 1995 and 1996, given our expectations for cash flow and earnings over the next two years. We are forecasting steadily higher natural gas prices through 1996 as a result of increased demand. However, asset sales will lead to lower production. Meanwhile, the near-term outlook for oil prices will depend on the timing of Iraq's return to world markets, which would undoubtedly lead to a short-term drop in oil prices. Longer term, we believe oil prices should hover around $19/bbl., at which level ORX's assets would be undervalued at the current stock price.

Key Stock Statistics

S&P EPS Est. 1995	1.51	Tang. Bk. Value/Share	NM
P/E on S&P Est. 1995	7.4	Beta	1.40
S&P EPS Est. 1996	0.70	Shareholders	36,800
Dividend Rate/Share	Nil	Market cap. (B)	$ 1.2
Shs. outstg. (M)	104.4	Inst. holdings	66%
Avg. daily vol. (M)	0.201	Insider holdings	NA

Value of $10,000 invested 5 years ago: $ 2,887

Fiscal Year Ending Dec. 31

	1995	% Change	1994	% Change	1993	% Change
Revenues (Million $)						
1Q	293.0	13%	260.0	-8%	283.0	-15%
2Q	285.0	12%	255.0	-8%	278.0	-24%
3Q	345.0	26%	273.0	3%	264.0	-34%
4Q	—	—	284.0	24%	229.0	-22%
Yr.	—	—	1,072	2%	1,054	-24%
Income (Million $)						
1Q	13.00	NM	-60.00	NM	-7.00	NM
2Q	25.00	NM	-7.00	NM	4.00	100%
3Q	108.0	NM	-12.00	NM	-45.00	NM
4Q	—	—	14.00	NM	-45.00	NM
Yr.	—	—	-65.00	NM	-93.00	NM
Earnings Per Share ($)						
1Q	0.13	NM	-0.62	NM	-0.08	NM
2Q	0.25	NM	-0.08	NM	0.03	NM
3Q	1.04	NM	-0.13	NM	-0.48	NM
4Q	E0.09	-36%	0.14	NM	-0.48	NM
Yr.	E1.51	NM	-0.68	NM	-1.01	NM

Next earnings report expected: NA

Oryx Energy

01-NOV-95

Business Summary - 01-NOV-95

Oryx Energy Company (formerly Sun Exploration and Production) acquires, explores for, produces and markets crude oil and condensate, natural gas and natural gas liquids. The company, which was spun off by Sun Co. in 1988, is the managing general partner of 98%-owned Sun Energy Partners, L.P., which conducts ORX's U.S. exploration and production business. Contributions (profits in millions) in 1994 were:

	Revs.	Profits
U.S.	57%	$152
U.K.	33%	82
Indonesia	8%	-5
Other	2%	-19

Net production in 1994 averaged 127,500 barrels per day of crude oil and condensate (117,200 in 1993) and 600,000 Mcf per day of natural gas (603,000). At December 31, 1994, estimated net proved reserves were 474 million bbl. of oil (508 million) and 1,520 Bcf of natural gas (1,881 Bcf). During 1994, ORX replaced only 80% of its oil and gas equivalent production with new reserves, versus its five-year average of 124%. Its exploration and development portfolio consists of both frontier projects and mature fields, in which ORX is pioneering advanced technologies, including horizontal and subsalt drilling and three-dimensional geological analysis.

The 1994 finding, development and acquisition cost was $4.76 per equivalent bbl. of oil and natural gas, down from $5.53 the year before.

Exploration will focus on prospects that offer shorter cycle-time projects in the Gulf of Mexico, as ORX is committed to reducing long-term debt in 1995. The company will also emphasize high-grading its asset base and de-emphasizing assets with low margins and limited growth potential.

Important Developments

Oct. '95—Net income for 1995's third quarter was $107 million, or $1.03 per share, including a $106 million net gain on the sale of assets. Oil volume decreased by 22,000 barrels per day, and discretionary cash flow per share was $0.72, versus $0.88 in the year-earlier period. Natural gas prices on a worldwide basis were about 6% lower, although the average price received for U.K. gas rose to $2.27, from $2.10. Operating costs fell in the period, due in part to lower volumes produced and to a drop in exploration expenses, to $14 million, from $33 million.

Capitalization

Long Term Debt: $1,167,000,000 (6/95).
Cum. Conv. Preference Stock: 1,009,394 shs. ($1 par).

Per Share Data ($)

(Year Ended Dec. 31)

	1994	1993	1992	1991	1990	1989
Tangible Bk. Val.	-3.82	6.57	8.05	6.23	7.81	14.17
Cash Flow	2.10	3.14	5.88	6.70	8.02	4.08
Earnings	-0.68	-1.01	0.74	0.08	2.26	0.51
Dividends	Nil	0.40	0.80	1.20	1.20	1.20
Payout Ratio	Nil	NM	108%	593%	44%	233%
Prices - High	20	26¼	27¼	40⅜	54⅞	46¼
- Low	10⅝	16¼	16¾	22	34¾	25½
P/E Ratio - High	NM	NM	37	NM	24	91
- Low	NM	NM	23	NM	15	50

Income Statement Analysis (Million $)

	1994	%Chg	1993	%Chg	1992	%Chg	1991
Revs.	1,082	NM	1,080	-15%	1,275	-14%	1,484
Oper. Inc.	424	-3%	438	-19%	544	-10%	607
Depr. Depl. & Amort.	271	-33%	403	-9%	444	-16%	529
Int. Exp.	162	NM	163	-13%	187	-14%	217
Pretax Inc.	-99	NM	-107	NM	-4.0	NM	-52.0
Eff. Tax Rate	NM	—	NM	—	NM	—	NM
Net Inc.	-65.0	NM	-93.0	NM	73.0	NM	19.0

Balance Sheet & Other Fin. Data (Million $)

	1994	1993	1992	1991	1990	1989
Cash	10.0	10.0	10.0	10.0	81.0	16.0
Curr. Assets	195	205	275	397	1,184	406
Total Assets	2,107	3,624	3,738	4,405	5,252	4,185
Curr. Liab.	532	324	586	453	1,245	386
LT Debt	1,546	1,741	1,489	2,341	2,267	1,509
Common Eqty.	-346	676	817	534	622	1,485
Total Cap.	1,420	3,099	3,012	3,806	3,848	3,610
Cap. Exp.	281	453	372	527	1,631	428
Cash Flow	205	305	508	535	799	430

Ratio Analysis

	1994	1993	1992	1991	1990	1989
Curr. Ratio	0.4	0.6	0.1	0.9	1.0	1.1
% LT Debt of Cap.	108.9	56.2	49.4	61.5	58.9	41.8
% Ret. on Assets	NM	NM	1.6	0.4	5.3	1.3
% Ret. on Equity	NM	NM	8.7	1.0	24.9	3.5

Dividend Data —Common dividends, initiated in 1988, were omitted in 1994. A "poison pill" stock purchase rights plan was adopted in 1990.

Data as orig. reptd.; bef. results of disc opers. and/or spec. items. Per share data adj. for stk. divs. as of ex-div. date. E-Estimated. NA-Not Available. NM-Not Meaningful. NR-Not Ranked.

Office—13155 Noel Rd., Dallas, TX 75240-5067. **Tel**—(214) 715-4000. **Chrmn, Pres & CEO**—R. L. Keiser. **Exec VP & CFO**—E. W. Moneypenny. **Secy**—W. C. Lemmer. **Investor Contact**—John O'Keefe. **Dirs**—J. W. Box, W. E. Bradford, R. B. Gill, D. S. Hollingsworth, R. L. Keiser, E. W. Moneypenny, C. H. Pistor Jr., P. R. Seegers, I. L. White-Thomson. **Transfer Agent & Registrar**—Chemical Bank, NYC. **Incorporated**—in Delaware in 1971. **Empl**-1,200. **S&P Analyst:** Raymond J. Deacon

Outboard Marine

NYSE Symbol **OM**
In S&P 500

05-OCT-95

Industry:
Leisure/Amusement

Summary: OM is a major global manufacturer and marketer of marine engines, boats and accessories, mainly for recreational use. Major brand names include Johnson, Evinrude and Chris-Craft.

S&P Opinion: Avoid (★★)	Recent Price • 21½	Yield • 1.8%
	52 Wk Range • 24⅞-17⅜	12-Mo. P/E • 8.1

Quantitative Evaluations

Outlook
(1 Lowest—5 Highest)
• **2⁻**

Fair Value
• **19¾**

Risk
• **Average**

Earn./Div. Rank
• **B-**

Technical Eval.
• **Bullish** since 7/95

Rel. Strength Rank
(1 Lowest—99 Highest)
• **75**

Insider Activity
• **NA**

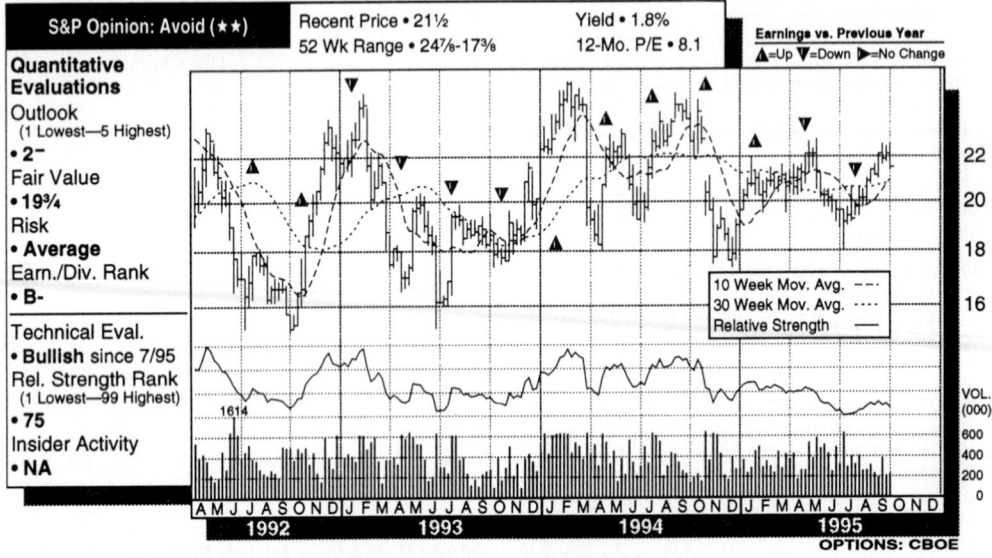

Earnings vs. Previous Year
▲=Up ▼=Down ▶=No Change

10 Week Mov. Avg. – – –
30 Week Mov. Avg. · · · ·
Relative Strength —

OPTIONS: CBOE

Overview - 04-OCT-95

We expect OM to achieve double-digit sales growth in fiscal 1995, helped by the sharp increases recorded in the first half of the year. However, we are concerned about the prospect of consumers becoming more cautious in their spending patterns. Therefore, we anticipate slower growth in fiscal 1996, due to the slowdown in the economy and declining consumer confidence. Additional cost savings from OM's restructuring program in both fiscal 1995 and 1996 are likely to be offset by investments in such areas as product development, marketing, and plant improvements. Also, further use of tax credits is expected. With a normalized tax rate, we estimate per share earnings in fiscal 1995 and 1996 at about $1.55 and $1.70, respectively.

Valuation - 04-OCT-95

Due to likely concern about consumer spending and the prospect of OM being near the peak of its earnings cycle, we advise avoiding these shares. We look for OM's long-term position in the marine market to be helped by investments made in product development and marketing during fiscal 1995 and 1996. Both OM and other marine companies are facing the prospect of tighter environmental requirements for new boat engines, starting within the next several years. We expect that will at least initially lead to higher engine costs for consumers, and could modestly dampen sales levels for manufacturers such as OM. However, the effect is likely to be eased by a lengthy phase-in period.

Key Stock Statistics

S&P EPS Est. 1995	2.20	Tang. Bk. Value/Share	8.85
P/E on S&P Est. 1995	9.8	Beta	1.75
S&P EPS Est. 1996	2.35	Shareholders	5,300
Dividend Rate/Share	0.40	Market cap. (B)	$0.445
Shs. outstg. (M)	20.0	Inst. holdings	78%
Avg. daily vol. (M)	0.053	Insider holdings	NA

Value of $10,000 invested 5 years ago: $ 9,607

Fiscal Year Ending Sep. 30

	1995	% Change	1994	% Change	1993	% Change
Revenues (Million $)						
1Q	242.6	27%	190.8	7%	178.0	-8%
2Q	318.8	21%	263.5	-4%	274.5	4%
3Q	329.6	4%	318.2	8%	295.4	NM
4Q	—	—	305.3	7%	286.4	-9%
Yr.	—	—	1,078	4%	1,035	-3%
Income (Million $)						
1Q	-3.10	NM	-9.30	NM	-18.90	NM
2Q	18.00	-6%	19.10	NM	1.00	-44%
3Q	28.00	NM	28.00	NM	-104.1	NM
4Q	—	—	10.70	NM	-43.00	NM
Yr.	—	—	48.50	NM	-165.0	NM
Earnings Per Share ($)						
1Q	-0.16	NM	-0.47	NM	-0.97	NM
2Q	0.90	-5%	0.95	NM	0.05	-50%
3Q	1.39	NM	1.40	NM	-5.31	NM
4Q	E0.07	-87%	0.53	NM	-2.19	NM
Yr.	E2.20	-9%	2.42	NM	-8.42	NM

Next earnings report expected: early November

Outboard Marine

Business Summary - 04-OCT-95

Outboard Marine is a major manufacturer of marine products, including outboard motors, stern-drive engines and boats. Nonmarine businesses were sold in 1989. In fiscal 1994, the U.S. accounted for about 75% of net sales.

The company is the world's largest maker of outboard motors, with models ranging from 2.3-horsepower portables to 300-horsepower V-8s designed to power large offshore fishing and performance boats. Its outboards are sold under the Johnson and Evinrude brands. Also, OM and AB Volvo Penta are partners in a joint venture to produce stern drive and inboard marine power systems. Other products include replacement parts and accessories; services include boat rentals and financing.

OM is also one of the largest U.S. boat companies. Since 1986, it has acquired all or part of more than a dozen boat manufacturers. Boats ranging from aluminum canoes to large cruisers are offered; brands or product lines include Chris-Craft, Four Winns, Grumman, Haines Hunter, Javelin, Lowe, Princecraft, Quest, Roughneck, Ryds, Sea Nymph, Seabird, Seaswirl, Springbok, Stacer, Stratos, Sunbird, and Suncruiser.

In fiscal 1993, OM had restructuring charges of about $7.40 a share. This followed restructuring charges totaling $1.70 a share in fiscal 1991 and $0.85 in fiscal 1990. In addition, there were other special items in these years' results. Earlier, in 1989, OM sold its nonmarine businesses, which included Cushman vehicles and Lawn-Boy power mowers.

Important Developments

Jul. '95—In fiscal 1995's third quarter, OM reported flat earnings compared with the year-earlier quarter on a 3.4% sales increase. The company attributed the slower growth versus the first two quarters of fiscal 1995 to the slowdown in the broader U.S. economy and declining consumer confidence. As a result of the softer sales, OM and its dealers had excess inventory and the company had adjusted its production schedules and staffing to work inventory levels down.
Jul. '95—The company and FICHT GmbH of Kirchseeon, Germany, announced they had formed a strategic alliance for the development and worldwide manufacturing and marketing of high pressure fuel injection systems and other technologies.

Capitalization

Long Term Debt: $177,300,000 (6/95), incl. about $74.8 million of conv. debs.

Per Share Data ($)   (Year Ended Sep. 30)

	1994	1993	1992	1991	1990	1989
Tangible Bk. Val.	8.85	6.44	17.38	17.27	21.13	25.38
Cash Flow	4.63	-5.58	3.16	-0.94	-0.51	4.77
Earnings	2.42	-8.42	0.10	-4.42	-3.98	1.09
Dividends	0.40	0.40	0.40	0.50	0.80	0.80
Payout Ratio	17%	NM	400%	NM	NM	74%
Prices - High	25⅞	25¼	26⅝	19⅜	28¼	46
- Low	17⅜	15¼	15⅛	11½	9	25
P/E Ratio - High	11	NM	NM	NM	NM	42
- Low	7	NM	NM	NM	NM	23

Income Statement Analysis (Million $)

	1994	%Chg	1993	%Chg	1992	%Chg	1991
Revs.	1,078	4%	1,035	-3%	1,065	8%	984
Oper. Inc.	90.0	88%	48.0	-48%	92.0	163%	35.0
Depr.	44.0	-21%	55.6	-8%	60.7	-10%	67.6
Int. Exp.	15.1	-24%	19.8	4%	19.0	-39%	31.1
Pretax Inc.	53.0	NM	-159	NM	13.0	NM	-105
Eff. Tax Rate	9.20%	—	NM	—	85%	—	NM
Net Inc.	49.0	NM	-164	NM	1.9	NM	-85.9

Balance Sheet & Other Fin. Data (Million $)

	1994	1993	1992	1991	1990	1989
Cash	80.0	104	143	80.0	15.0	20.0
Curr. Assets	430	425	555	501	589	753
Total Assets	817	792	997	957	1,105	1,254
Curr. Liab.	234	251	232	252	288	282
LT Debt	178	183	198	133	158	233
Common Eqty.	209	161	455	463	558	643
Total Cap.	387	344	653	596	716	876
Cap. Exp.	68.2	50.0	40.6	36.1	61.1	88.6
Cash Flow	93.0	-108	63.0	-18.0	-10.0	92.0

Ratio Analysis

	1994	1993	1992	1991	1990	1989
Curr. Ratio	1.8	1.7	2.4	2.0	2.0	2.7
% LT Debt of Cap.	46.0	53.2	30.4	22.3	22.0	26.6
% Net Inc.of Revs.	4.5	NM	0.2	NM	NM	1.4
% Ret. on Assets	6.0	NM	0.2	NM	NM	1.8
% Ret. on Equity	26.1	NM	0.4	NM	NM	3.4

Dividend Data —Dividends have been paid since 1937. A dividend reinvestment plan is available. A "poison pill" stock purchase rights plan was adopted in 1986 and amended in 1990.

Amt. of Div. $	Date Decl.	Ex-Div. Date	Stock of Record	Payment Date
0.100	Nov. 03	Dec. 12	Dec. 16	Dec. 30 '94
0.100	Jan. 19	Feb. 06	Feb. 10	Feb. 24 '95
0.100	Apr. 19	May. 08	May. 12	May. 26 '95
0.100	Jul. 25	Aug. 09	Aug. 11	Aug. 25 '95

Data as orig. reptd.; bef. results of disc. opers. and/or spec. items. Per share data adj. for stk. divs. as of ex-div. date.
E-Estimated. NA-Not Available. NM-Not Meaningful. NR-Not Ranked.

Office—100 Sea-Horse Drive, Waukegan, IL 60085. **Tel**—(708) 689-6200. **Chrmn, Pres & CEO**—H. W. Bowman. **Treas**—C. R. Sachs. **Secy**—H. Malovany. **Investor Contact**—Stan R. Main. **Dirs**—F. Borman, H. W. Bowman, W. C. France, Jr., U. T. Kuechle, R. T. Lindgren, J. W. Marriott, Jr., R. J. Stegemeier, C. D. Strang, R. T. Teerlink. **Transfer Agent & Registrar**—First Chicago Trust Co. of NY. **Incorporated** in Delaware in 1936. **Empl**-8,500. **S&P Analyst:** Michael V. Pizzi

Owens-Corning Fiberglas

NYSE Symbol **OCF**
In S&P 500

02-OCT-95

Industry:
Building

Summary: This leading manufacturer of glass fiber products also makes other construction and industrial products. Foreign operations account for about 25% of sales.

S&P Opinion: Accumulate (★★★★)

Recent Price • 44⅝	Yield • Nil	
52 Wk Range • 47⅛-27¾	12-Mo. P/E • 10.7	

Quantitative Evaluations

Outlook
(1 Lowest—5 Highest)
• **1+**

Fair Value
• 24¾

Risk
• **Low**

Earn./Div. Rank
• **B-**

Technical Eval.
• **Bearish** since 4/95

Rel. Strength Rank
(1 Lowest—99 Highest)
• **79**

Insider Activity
• **NA**

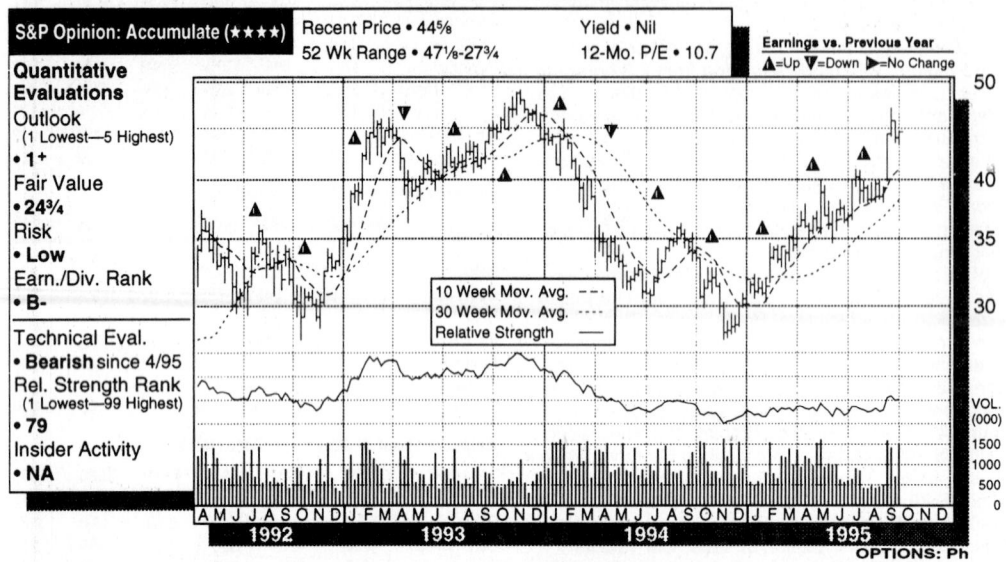

Earnings vs. Previous Year
▲=Up ▼=Down ▶=No Change

10 Week Mov. Avg. – – –
30 Week Mov. Avg. ·····
Relative Strength —

VOL. (000)

OPTIONS: Ph

Overview - 29-SEP-95

Sales should be solidly higher in 1995, benefiting from increased volume and more favorable pricing in both operating segments. The gains will reflect better economic conditions in Europe, recent acquisitions, an aggressive policy of geographic expansion and new product introductions. Operating margins are likely to benefit from restructuring efforts undertaken in 1994. Earnings comparisons will also be aided by the absence of $117 million of pretax charges for productivity initiatives and other cost reduction actions (including $89 million of restructuring charges), and will receive a further boost from an improving balance sheet. Primary EPS will be based on a larger number of shares, following debt conversion in the first half of 1995. OCF's strong position in its markets and commitment to foreign expansion brighten long-term prospects.

Valuation - 02-OCT-95

After falling for much of 1994 on investor nervousness about rising domestic interest rates, the shares have rebounded strongly since late 1994, as interest rate prospects brightened; a strong bounce was also received after OCF's September 1995 settlement regarding coverage for asbestos claims. Although U.S. business could be slowed by a moderating economy, the recent drop in long-term interest rates is likely to boost the capital spending outlook as 1995 progresses. With results also expected to benefit from better international conditions and measures taken to improve operations, the shares should appreciate from their recent trading range of about 9X our 1996 EPS projection.

Key Stock Statistics

S&P EPS Est. 1995	4.40	Tang. Bk. Value/Share	NM
P/E on S&P Est. 1995	10.1	Beta	2.48
S&P EPS Est. 1996	4.85	Shareholders	7,500
Dividend Rate/Share	Nil	Market cap. (B)	$ 2.3
Shs. outstg. (M)	50.7	Inst. holdings	76%
Avg. daily vol. (M)	0.302	Insider holdings	NA

Value of $10,000 invested 5 years ago: $ 17,761

Fiscal Year Ending Dec. 31

	1995	% Change	1994	% Change	1993	% Change
Revenues (Million $)						
1Q	844.0	25%	677.0	4%	651.0	4%
2Q	877.0	3%	852.0	13%	754.0	3%
3Q	—	—	936.0	19%	785.0	NM
4Q	—	—	886.0	18%	754.0	3%
Yr.	—	—	3,351	14%	2,944	2%
Income (Million $)						
1Q	33.00	NM	-67.00	NM	-9.00	NM
2Q	63.00	40%	45.00	36%	33.00	50%
3Q	—	—	53.00	10%	48.00	50%
4Q	—	—	43.00	30%	33.00	175%
Yr.	—	—	74.00	-30%	105.0	46%
Earnings Per Share ($)						
1Q	0.71	NM	-1.52	NM	-0.20	NM
2Q	1.25	21%	1.03	36%	0.76	46%
3Q	E1.32	11%	1.19	9%	1.09	45%
4Q	E1.12	14%	0.98	31%	0.75	150%
Yr.	E4.40	159%	1.70	-29%	2.40	43%

Next earnings report expected: mid October

Business Summary - 02-OCT-95

Owens-Corning Fiberglas is the world's leading manufacturer of glass fiber materials, many of which are marketed under the FIBERGLAS trademark. Company products are used in the home improvement, construction, transportation, marine, aerospace, energy, appliance, packaging and electronics industries. Contributions by industry segment in 1994 were:

	Sales	Profits
Building products	68%	63%
Industrial materials	32%	37%

International operations accounted for 24% of sales and 15% of profits in 1994, versus 24% and 7%, respectively, in 1993.

The building products segment operates primarily in North America and Europe, and has a growing presence in Latin America and Asia/Pacific, through joint venture and licensee relationships. The division sells a variety of building and home improvement products in the areas of insulation; roofing materials; and windows/patio doors and other specialty products for the home exterior.

The industrial materials segment operates primarily in North America, with subsidiaries in Europe and Latin America and affiliates and licensees around the world. The division is the world's leading producer of glass fiber materials used in composites. Composites are fabricated material systems made up of two or more components used in various applications to replace traditional materials such as aluminum, wood and steel. The global composites industry has expanded to include more than 40,000 end-use products.

Important Developments

Sep. '95—The company reached a $330 million settlement with a major insurer regarding non-products coverage for asbestos claims. The unidentified insurance company also granted OCF the right to purchase additional insurance through 2007. OCF noted that the settlement substantially confirmed its $600 million of insurance for asbestos claims. Through the second quarter of 1995, OCF had paid a total of $1.68 billion to settle asbestos-related lawsuits; Owens-Corning no longer produces asbestos.

May '95—OCF completed the private placement of four million shares of 6.5% monthly income preferred securities, each convertible into OCF common stock at $43.80 a share. Proceeds of $200 million less issuance costs were to be used to repay borrowings.

Apr. '95—Following a call for redemption of $149.8 million of the company's 8% junior subordinated debentures, all $173 million (including $23.2 million not called) of its outstanding 8% debentures were converted into common stock at $29.75 a share, resulting in the issuance of 5.8 million shares.

Capitalization

Long Term Debt: $883,000,000 (6/95).

Per Share Data ($)

				(Year Ended Dec. 31)		
	1994	1993	1992	1991	1990	1989
Tangible Bk. Val.	-18.80	-21.90	-25.69	-28.14	-11.06	-13.23
Cash Flow	4.34	4.82	4.53	-9.36	5.09	7.35
Earnings	1.70	2.40	1.68	-12.58	1.78	4.08
Dividends	Nil	Nil	Nil	Nil	Nil	Nil
Payout Ratio	Nil	Nil	Nil	Nil	Nil	Nil
Prices - High	46	49⅛	39¾	35½	26½	36⅞
- Low	27¾	34⅜	22⅜	15	13⅝	22¼
P/E Ratio - High	27	20	24	NM	15	9
- Low	16	14	13	NM	8	5

Income Statement Analysis (Million $)

	1994	%Chg	1993	%Chg	1992	%Chg	1991
Revs.	3,351	14%	2,944	2%	2,878	3%	2,783
Oper. Inc.	461	24%	372	6%	352	16%	304
Depr.	118	12%	105	-15%	123	-7%	132
Int. Exp.	94.0	6%	89.0	-19%	110	-16%	131
Pretax Inc.	132	-13%	152	45%	105	NM	-752
Eff. Tax Rate	44%	—	31%	—	31%	—	NM
Net Inc.	74.0	-30%	105	46%	72.0	NM	-514

Balance Sheet & Other Fin. Data (Million $)

	1994	1993	1992	1991	1990	1989
Cash	59.0	3.0	2.0	3.0	7.0	29.0
Curr. Assets	930	827	658	619	711	816
Total Assets	3,274	3,013	2,126	2,106	1,807	1,924
Curr. Liab.	1,073	876	535	448	653	791
LT Debt	1,037	898	1,018	1,148	1,086	1,201
Common Eqty.	-679	-868	-1,007	-1,075	-349	-434
Total Cap.	351	29.0	10.0	72.0	749	791
Cap. Exp.	258	164	130	96.0	121	125
Cash Flow	192	210	195	-382	214	310

Ratio Analysis

	1994	1993	1992	1991	1990	1989
Curr. Ratio	0.9	0.9	1.2	1.4	1.1	1.0
% LT Debt of Cap.	290.5	NM	NM	NM	145.0	NM
% Net Inc.of Revs.	2.2	3.6	2.5	NM	2.4	5.7
% Ret. on Assets	2.3	4.1	3.4	NM	4.0	9.8
% Ret. on Equity	NM	NM	NM	NM	NM	NM

Dividend Data —Common dividends were omitted in 1986. A poison pill stock purchase rights plan was adopted in 1986.

Data as orig. reptd.; bef. results of disc. opers. and/or spec. items. Per share data adj. for stk. divs. as of ex-div. date. E-Estimated. NA-Not Available. NM-Not Meaningful. NR-Not Ranked.

Office—Fiberglas Tower, Toledo, OH 43659. **Tel**—(419) 248-8000. **Chrmn & CEO**—G. H. Hiner. **SVP & CFO**—D. W. Devonshire. **SVP & Secy**—C. L. Campbell. **VP & Treas**—M. I. Miller. **Investor Contact**—Bradford C. Oelman. **Dirs**—N. P. Blake, Jr., W. W. Colville, C. E. Exley, Jr., L. Hilliard, G. H. Hiner, T. Holdsworth, J. M. Huntsman, Jr., W. W. Lewis, D. T. McGovern, F. C. Moseley, Jr., W. A. Reynolds. **Transfer Agent & Registrar**—Chemical Bank, NYC. **Incorporated** in Delaware in 1938. **Empl**-17,000. **S&P Analyst:** Michael W. Jaffe

PECO Energy

NYSE Symbol **PE**
In S&P 500

02-NOV-95

Industry:
Util.-Diversified

Summary: PECO Energy (formerly Philadelphia Electric) is an electric and gas utility primarily serving Philadelphia and its surrounding suburbs and two counties in northeastern Maryland.

S&P Opinion: Hold (★★★)	Recent Price • 29⅝	Yield • 5.8%
	52 Wk Range • 30⅛-23⅞	12-Mo. P/E • 11.0

Earnings vs. Previous Year
▲=Up ▼=Down ▶=No Change

Quantitative Evaluations

Outlook
(1 Lowest—5 Highest)
• **3+**

Fair Value
• **29⅝**

Risk
• **Low**

Earn./Div. Rank
• **B**

Technical Eval.
• **Bullish** since 9/95

Rel. Strength Rank
(1 Lowest—99 Highest)
• **84**

Insider Activity
• **Neutral**

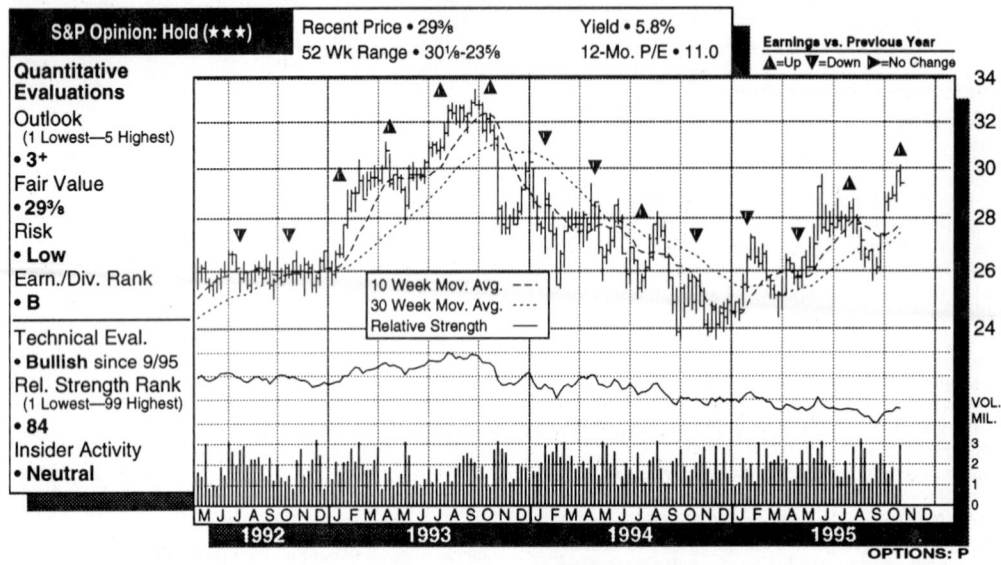

10 Week Mov. Avg. – – –
30 Week Mov. Avg. - - -
Relative Strength ——

VOL.
MIL.

OPTIONS: P

Overview - 25-OCT-95

Share earnings for 1995 should reflect higher energy sales, particularly for bulk power, along with the absence of 1994's $0.66-a-share workforce reduction charge, a full year of cost savings from this program, and other cost control efforts. The company has targeted $75 million of cost reductions (pretax) for administrative and general overhead budgets that could help boost earnings a modest 5% this year. A modest rate increase will allow the company to recover new accounting costs for retiree health and welfare benefits as well. Growth from businesses gearing up to participate in the expanding national wholesale power market and in natural gas brokering add to prospects for 1996.

Valuation - 25-OCT-95

This well-managed utility's market performance does not yet reflect the influence of its solid cash-flow position, an improving balance sheet, strong plant operating performance, and aggressive actions to enhance its competitive position. We expect PE shares would be more strongly supported if its consumer rates were more competitive. For the future, an offsetting factor is the Pennsylvania Public Utility Commission's conservative stance on wholesale wheeling, which would limit PE's exposure to competition from out of state. A 7.4% increase in the dividend in October adds to the stock's long term appeal, but a merger penalty may restrain valuations over the short term.

Key Stock Statistics

S&P EPS Est. 1995	2.65	Tang. Bk. Value/Share	19.41
P/E on S&P Est. 1995	11.1	Beta	0.49
S&P EPS Est. 1996	2.75	Shareholders	190,200
Dividend Rate/Share	1.74	Market cap. (B)	$ 6.6
Shs. outstg. (M)	221.9	Inst. holdings	38%
Avg. daily vol. (M)	0.351	Insider holdings	NA

Value of $10,000 invested 5 years ago: $ 17,761

Fiscal Year Ending Dec. 31

	1995	% Change	1994	% Change	1993	% Change
Revenues (Million $)						
1Q	1,059	-6%	1,128	5%	1,071	NM
2Q	985.6	4%	951.5	6%	901.7	NM
3Q	1,125	8%	1,041	-3%	1,073	8%
4Q	—	—	919.5	-2%	941.8	-4%
Yr.	—	—	4,041	1%	3,988	NM
Income (Million $)						
1Q	152.0	-5%	159.4	-2%	162.4	84%
2Q	153.6	32%	116.1	8%	107.7	14%
3Q	184.3	NM	22.20	-88%	181.7	28%
4Q	—	—	129.1	-7%	138.9	-10%
Yr.	—	—	426.7	-28%	590.7	23%
Earnings Per Share ($)						
1Q	0.66	-1%	0.67	-1%	0.68	106%
2Q	0.67	40%	0.48	12%	0.43	23%
3Q	0.80	NM	0.06	-92%	0.77	31%
4Q	0.52	-5%	0.55	-5%	0.58	-8%
Yr.	E2.65	51%	1.76	-28%	2.45	29%

Next earnings report expected: late January

PECO Energy

Business Summary - 02-NOV-95

PECO Energy (formerly Philadelphia Electric) provides electric (90% of 1994 revenues) and gas (10%) service to a population of some 3.7 million in southeastern Pennsylvania, and through a subsidiary to two northeastern Maryland counties. Electric revenues by customer class:

	1994	1993	1992	1991
Residential	38%	38%	36%	37%
Large comm'l/ind'l	32%	32%	34%	35%
Small comm'l/ind'l	20%	19%	19%	18%
Other	10%	11%	11%	10%

Sources of generation in 1994 were nuclear 60%, coal 17%, purchased 13%, oil 5%, hydro 3%, and other 2%. Peak demand in 1994 was 7,227 mw and net generating capacity was 8,956 mw, for a capacity margin of 19%. Nuclear generation uses the company's lowest-cost fuel.

In 1988, PE wrote off $463.3 million ($1.59 a share) of disallowed costs for its Limerick 1 plant and, in 1990, wrote off $250 million ($1.18 a share) of disallowed Limerick 2 costs and other charges. Settlement of appeals from an April 1990 rate case approved in 1991 permits PE to retain net proceeds of off-system sales of 399 mw of capacity found to excessive by the PUC. PE also has a 42.5% interest in and operates the Peach Bottom nuclear station.

In June 1995, PE sold its Maryland retail electric subsidiary, Conowingo Power Co., to Delmarva Power (NYSE: DEW) for $150 million and a ten-year contract for PE to sell power to Delmarva.

Important Developments

Nov. '95—On November 1, PE said it had withdrawn its offer to acquire PP&L Resources (NYSE: PPL) and said it would take no further action after PPL announced it was not interested in a combination. On October 23, PE had raised its offer to acquire PP&L Resources through an exchange of one PPL common share for 0.921 shares of Peco common, up from an exchange of 0.865 of its common stock offered August 14. The new bid valued PPL shares at $27.50 each, versus the earlier $24. The offer was to have expired November 3. PPL had anticipated cost savings from the merger of $2 billion and an $860 million rate reduction (given approvals) for both companies over 10 years. PPL had rejected the initial proposal on September 6.

Capitalization

Long Term Debt: $4,313,900,000 (9/95).
Minority Interest: $221,300,000.
Red. Cum. Preferred Stock: $92,700,000.
Cum. Preferred Stock: $277,400,000.

Per Share Data ($)

					(Year Ended Dec. 31)	
	1994	1993	1992	1991	1990	1989
Tangible Bk. Val.	19.41	19.06	18.11	17.57	16.56	17.57
Earnings	1.76	2.45	1.90	2.15	0.07	2.36
Dividends	1.55	1.43	1.33	1.23	1.45	2.20
Payout Ratio	88%	58%	70%	57%	NM	93%
Prices - High	30	33½	26¾	26	23½	24½
- Low	23⅝	25½	22⅝	17½	14½	19⅛
P/E Ratio - High	17	14	14	12	NM	10
- Low	13	10	12	8	NM	8

Income Statement Analysis (Million $)

	1994	%Chg	1993	%Chg	1992	%Chg	1991
Revs.	4,041	1%	3,988	NM	3,962	NM	3,976
Depr.	442	4%	425	3%	414	3%	401
Maint.	328	-10%	364	3%	354	7%	332
Fxd. Chgs. Cov.	2.3	-16%	2.8	30%	2.1	-5%	2.3
Constr. Credits	22.2	-7%	23.8	15%	20.7	-10%	23.0
Eff. Tax Rate	37%	—	38%	—	32%	—	38%
Net Inc.	427	-28%	591	23%	479	-10%	535

Balance Sheet & Other Fin. Data (Million $)

	1994	1993	1992	1991	1990	1989
Gross Prop.	15,247	14,905	14,489	14,089	13,784	13,632
Cap. Exp.	571	568	594	507	541	1,038
Net Prop.	11,003	10,958	10,901	10,822	10,833	10,994
Capitalization:						
LT Debt	4,900	5,019	5,355	5,583	6,011	5,963
% LT Debt	51	51	53	55	58	56
Pfd.	370	609	654	738	753	974
% Pfd.	3.80	6.20	6.50	7.20	7.20	9.10
Common	4,303	4,263	4,022	3,892	3,625	3,745
% Common	44	43	40	38	35	35
Total Cap.	13,394	13,663	11,335	11,360	11,390	11,733

Ratio Analysis

	1994	1993	1992	1991	1990	1989
Oper. Ratio	79.5	74.0	73.9	72.8	79.3	76.2
% Earn. on Net Prop.	7.6	9.5	9.5	10.0	7.0	7.6
% Ret. on Revs.	10.6	14.8	12.1	13.4	2.9	17.3
% Ret. On Invest.Cap	6.3	8.4	8.7	9.7	6.0	9.6
% Return On Com.Eqty	9.1	13.1	10.6	12.5	0.4	13.5

Dividend Data

—Dividends have been paid since 1902. A dividend reinvestment plan is available.

Amt. of Div. $	Date Decl.	Ex-Div. Date	Stock of Record	Payment Date
0.405	Oct. 24	Nov. 03	Nov. 09	Dec. 16 '94
0.405	Jan. 30	Feb. 15	Feb. 22	Mar. 31 '95
0.405	Apr. 12	May. 18	May. 24	Jun. 30 '95
0.405	Jul. 24	Aug. 21	Aug. 23	Sep. 29 '95
0.435	Oct. 23	Nov. 13	Nov. 15	Dec. 20 '95

Data as orig. reptd.; bef. results of disc opers. and/or spec. items. Per share data adj. for stk. divs. as of ex-div. date. E-Estimated. NA-Not Available. NM-Not Meaningful. NR-Not Ranked.

Office—2301 Market St., Philadelphia, PA 19103. **Tel**—(215) 841-4000. **Chrmn**—J. F. Paquette Jr. **Pres & CEO**—C. A. McNeill Jr. **VP-CFO**—K. G. Lawrence. **Secy**—K. K. Dodd. **Investor Contact**—Lisa Ewbank. **Dirs**—S. W. Catherwood, M. W. D'Alessio, R. G. Gilmore, R. H. Glanton, J. A. Hagen, N. G. Harris, J. C. Ladd, E. J. Levit, K. R. McKee, J. J. McLaughlin, C. A. McNeill Jr., J. M. Palms, J. F. Paquette Jr., R. Rubin, R. Subin. **Transfer Agent & Registrar**—First Chicago Trust Co. of New York, Jersey City, NJ. **Incorporated** in Pennsylvania in 1929. **Empl**-7,187. **S&P Analyst:** Jane Collin

PNC Bank

NYSE Symbol **PNC**

In S&P 500

01-SEP-95

Industry: Banking

Summary: This bank holding company, which owns banks in Pennsylvania, Indiana, Kentucky, Ohio and Delaware, recently agreed to acquire New Jersey-based Midlantic Corp.

S&P Opinion: Hold (★★★)

| Recent Price • 25½ | Yield • 5.3% |
| 52 Wk Range • 28¼-20 | 12-Mo. P/E • 12.5 |

Earnings vs. Previous Year
▲=Up ▼=Down ▶=No Change

Quantitative Evaluations

Outlook
(1 Lowest—5 Highest)
• **2⁻**

Fair Value
• **23⅜**

Risk
• **Low**

Earn./Div. Rank
• **B**

Technical Eval.
• **Bearish** since 7/95

Rel. Strength Rank
(1 Lowest—99 Highest)
• **55**

Insider Activity
• **Favorable**

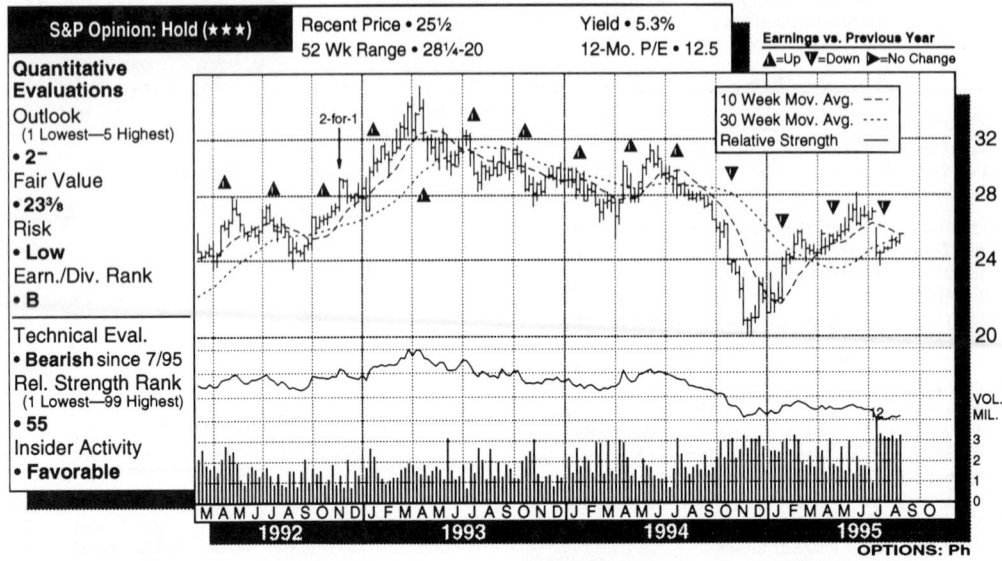

10 Week Mov. Avg. ---
30 Week Mov. Avg. ......
Relative Strength —

OPTIONS: Ph

Overview - 01-SEP-95

Net interest income is expected to decline at least 15% in 1995, reflecting a downsized investment portfolio following the sale of fixed-rate securities in an attempt to reduce interest rate sensitivity. With the early 1995 purchase of interest rate caps and pay-fixed swaps, the company has mitigated the impact of higher interest rates on net interest income. PNC has also taken steps to further diversify its revenue base; the recent acquisition of BlackRock Financial is expected to add about 20% to investment and trust income on an annualized basis. Capital levels are strong, and with the allowance for credit losses at 312% of nonperforming loans, a provision for loan losses is not expected in 1995. Earnings comparisons in 1995 will be hurt by an approximate $190 million pretax charge to integrate the operations of Midlantic.

Valuation - 01-SEP-95

Investors greeted the proposed acquisition of Midlantic Corp. with little enthusiasm, reflecting fears of dilution. In addition, at twice book value, the purchase price is at the upper end of the valuations for recent bank takeovers. On the bright side, the transaction, when coupled with the purchase of Chemical Banking's southern and central New Jersey branches, will give PNC second largest market share in the New Jersey and Philadelphia areas, as well as provide a much needed source of deposit funding and less reliance on wholesale funds. The shares remain a hold until evidence materializes that the acquisitions will contribute meaningfully to earnings.

Key Stock Statistics

S&P EPS Est. 1995	2.40	Tang. Bk. Value/Share	19.20
P/E on S&P Est. 1995	10.6	Beta	1.44
S&P EPS Est. 1996	2.75	Shareholders	43,900
Dividend Rate/Share	1.40	Market cap. (B)	$ 6.0
Shs. outstg. (M)	230.1	Inst. holdings	48%
Avg. daily vol. (M)	1.087	Insider holdings	NA

Value of $10,000 invested 5 years ago: $ 16,787

Fiscal Year Ending Dec. 31

	1995	% Change	1994	% Change	1993	% Change
Revenues (Million $)						
1Q	1,261	8%	1,163	8%	1,074	1%
2Q	1,308	13%	1,155	16%	994.9	NM
3Q	—	—	1,239	17%	1,056	6%
4Q	—	—	1,129	11%	1,022	-2%
Yr.	—	—	4,684	13%	4,146	NM
Income (Million $)						
1Q	125.7	-39%	205.7	10%	187.0	49%
2Q	137.0	-27%	187.9	11%	169.1	33%
3Q	—	—	188.0	-14%	217.7	64%
4Q	—	—	28.53	-83%	171.4	19%
Yr.	—	—	610.1	-18%	745.3	41%
Earnings Per Share ($)						
1Q	0.54	-38%	0.87	10%	0.79	34%
2Q	0.59	-25%	0.79	11%	0.71	20%
3Q	E0.62	-22%	0.79	-14%	0.92	53%
4Q	E0.65	NM	0.12	-83%	0.72	18%
Yr.	E2.40	-7%	2.57	-18%	3.14	33%

Next earnings report expected: mid October

Business Summary - 01-SEP-95

PNC Bank Corp. (formerly PNC Financial) is the 13th largest bank holding company in the U.S. It offers a full range of banking products and services through its Corporate Banking, Retail Banking, Investment Management and Trust, and Investment Banking units. Retail banking services are provided through the 604 branches of its subsidiary banks in Pennsylvania, Kentucky, Ohio, Delaware and Massachusetts. PNC Mortgage Bank operates nearly 100 mortgage origination offices nationwide. Corporate banking provides financing, liquidity, cash management and other financial services to businesses and government entities. Investment management and trust operations are sizable, with some $213 billion (more than $50 billion discretionary) of trust assets under administration. Investment banking activities include underwriting, direct investment services and full service brokerage.

During 1994, average earning assets of $57.2 billion ($47.3 billion in 1993) were divided: commercial loans 21%, real estate loans 20%, consumer loans 15%, other loans 2%, investment securities 39%, and temporary investments and other assets 3%. Average sources of funds were non-interest bearing deposits 10%, savings and money market deposits 15%, time deposits 21%, other interest bearing deposits 7%, short-term borrowings 19%, long-term debt 19%, equity 7%, and other 2%.

At year-end 1994, nonperforming assets were $446 million (1.25% of related assets), against $554 million (1.65%) a year earlier. The allowance for loan losses stood at $1.0 billion (2.83% of loans), versus $972 million (2.92%). Net chargeoffs during 1994 were 0.29% of average loans, versus 0.66%.

Important Developments

Jul. '95—PNC signed a definitive agreement to acquire Midlantic Corp. (Nasdaq; MIDL) in a transaction whereby each MIDL common share would be exchanged for 2.05 PNC common shares; a total of about 48 million PNC shares would be issued. The combination would create the 12th largest bank holding company in the U.S. with total assets of about $76 billion. The acquisition is expected to be completed by 1995 year-end, PNC plans to record a pretax charge of about $190 million to cover expenses for merging the acquired operations.

Mar. '95—The company signed a definitive agreement to acquire the central and southern New Jersey branch franchise of Chemical Banking Corp. (NYSE: CHL), including 84 branches and retail core deposits of $2.9 billion, for $504 million. Separately, PNC acquired BlackRock Financial Management L.P., a fixed-income management firm, for about $240 million.

Capitalization

Notes & Debentures: $8,995,000,000 (6/95).
Preferred Stock: $19,000,000 (liquid. value).

Per Share Data ($) (Year Ended Dec. 31)

	1994	1993	1992	1991	1990	1989
Tangible Bk. Val.	15.80	18.34	15.96	15.27	13.41	14.83
Earnings	2.57	3.14	2.36	1.98	0.37	1.99
Dividends	1.31	1.17	1.06	1.06	1.06	1.03
Payout Ratio	51%	37%	45%	54%	290%	52%
Prices - High	31⅝	36⅜	29¼	24⅛	22⅛	24½
- Low	20	27	23⅛	9½	7⅞	19¼
P/E Ratio - High	12	12	12	12	60	12
- Low	8	9	10	5	22	10

Income Statement Analysis (Million $)

	1994	%Chg	1993	%Chg	1992	%Chg	1991
Net Int. Inc.	1,936	6%	1,829	10%	1,657	15%	1,435
Tax Equiv. Adj.	33.5	-15%	39.5	-8%	42.8	-27%	59.0
Non Int. Inc.	931	-1%	945	40%	673	-9%	742
Loan Loss Prov.	60.1	-71%	204	-37%	324	-24%	428
% Exp/Op Revs.	61%	—	55%	—	61%	—	57%
Pretax Inc.	902	-19%	1,117	44%	778	42%	548
Eff. Tax Rate	32%	—	33%	—	32%	—	29%
Net Inc.	610	-18%	745	41%	529	36%	390
% Net Int. Marg.	3.40%	—	3.95%	—	4.03%	—	3.73%

Balance Sheet & Other Fin. Data (Million $)

	1994	1993	1992	1991	1990	1989
Earning Assets:						
Money Mkt.	NA	856	1,165	1,868	1,835	553
Inv. Securities	20,921	23,060	20,742	14,173	12,189	12,867
Com'l Loans	12,445	12,463	11,751	12,211	14,870	15,965
Other Loans	23,689	20,845	14,358	13,936	13,488	12,852
Total Assets	64,145	62,080	51,380	44,892	45,534	45,661
Demand Deposits	6,992	7,057	5,889	5,095	5,380	5,096
Time Deposits	28,019	26,058	23,580	24,924	26,664	25,024
LT Debt	11,754	2,585	1,018	1,287	1,319	715
Common Eqty.	4,375	4,305	3,712	3,280	2,561	2,780

Ratio Analysis

	1994	1993	1992	1991	1990	1989
% Ret. on Assets	1.0	1.5	1.2	0.9	0.2	0.9
% Ret. on Equity	14.1	18.8	15.5	14.0	2.5	13.6
% Loan Loss Resv.	2.8	2.9	3.5	3.1	2.8	2.2
% Loans/Deposits	102.5	100.6	87.6	84.8	86.2	93.3
% Equity to Assets	7.1	7.9	7.6	6.4	6.0	6.5

Dividend Data —Dividends were paid by the bank's predecessors in each year since the 1860s. A dividend reinvestment plan is available.

Amt. of Div. $	Date Decl.	Ex-Div. Date	Stock of Record	Payment Date
0.350	Oct. 06	Oct. 11	Oct. 17	Oct. 24 '94
0.350	Jan. 06	Jan. 09	Jan. 16	Jan. 24 '95
0.350	Apr. 06	Apr. 10	Apr. 17	Apr. 24 '95
0.350	Jul. 06	Jul. 13	Jul. 17	Jul. 24 '95

Data as orig. reptd.; bef. results of disc opers. and/or spec. items. Per share data adj. for stk. divs. as of ex-div. date. E-Estimated. NA-Not Available. NM-Not Meaningful. NR-Not Ranked.

Office—One PNC Plaza, Fifth Avenue and Wood Street, Pittsburgh, PA 15265. **Tel**—(412) 762-3900. **Chrmn & CEO**—T. H. O'Brien. **Pres**—J. E. Rohr. **EVP-Fin & Admin**—W. E. Gregg Jr. **SVP & CFO**—R. L. Haunschild. **VP-Investor Contact**—William H. Callihan. **Dirs**—R. N. Clay, W. G. Copeland, G. A. Davidson Jr., C. G. Grefenstette, T. Marshall, W. C. McClelland, D. I. Moritz, T. H. O'Brien, J. H. Randolph, J. E. Rohr, R. H. Ross, V. A. Sarni, R. P. Simmons, T. J. Usher, M. A. Washington, H. H. Wehmeier. **Transfer Agent & Registrar**—Chemical Bank, NYC. **Empl**-21,000. **S&P Analyst:** Stephen R. Biggar

PPG Industries

NYSE Symbol **PPG**
In S&P 500

09-AUG-95

Industry:
Coatings, paint, varnishes

Summary: PPG is a leading manufacturer of coatings and resins, flat and fiber glass, and industrial and specialty chemicals.

S&P Opinion: Accumulate (★★★★)	Recent Price • 45¼	Yield • 2.7%
	52 Wk Range • 46⅜-33¾	12-Mo. P/E • 12.9

Earnings vs. Previous Year
▲=Up ▼=Down ▶=No Change

Quantitative Evaluations

Outlook
(1 Lowest—5 Highest)
• **4+**

Fair Value
• **46⅝**

Risk
• **Low**

Earn./Div. Rank
• **A-**

Technical Eval.
• **Bullish** since 12/94

Rel. Strength Rank
(1 Lowest—99 Highest)
• **61**

Insider Activity
• **Neutral**

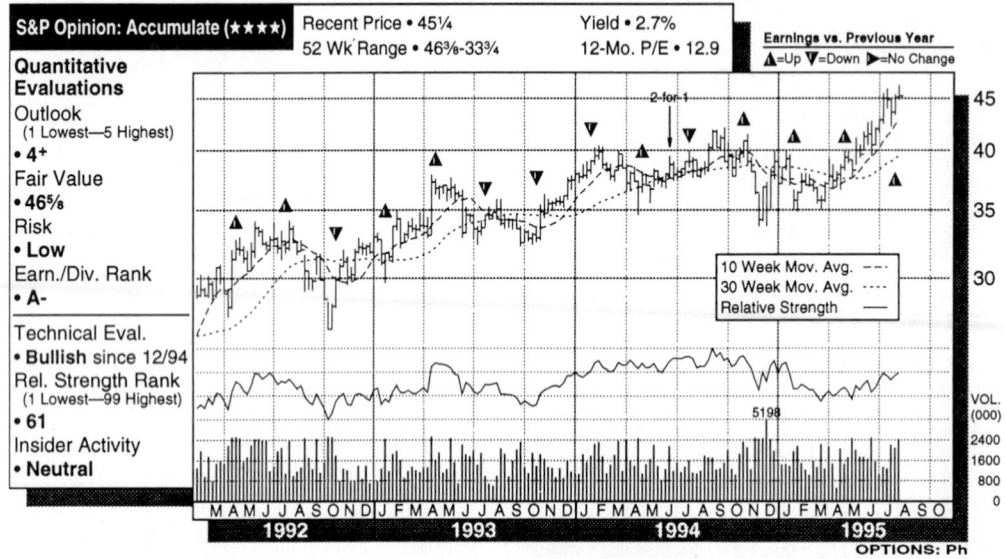

10 Week Mov. Avg. ---
30 Week Mov. Avg. ....
Relative Strength —

5198

VOL.
(000)
2400
1600
800
0

1992   1993   1994   1995

OPTIONS: Ph

Overview - 04-AUG-95

We see earnings for this diversified manufacturer continuing to advance in 1995 and 1996 with the moderately growing U.S. economy and as automobile and construction markets for glass and coatings strengthen. Results in Europe (PPG's second largest market) are also expected to advance on better economic conditions. Pricing for flat and fiber glass should continue to improve with high industry operating rates, while chemicals profits will advance on the dramatic rise in caustic soda prices since early 1994 and continuing gains in specialty products. Earnings in all segments will also be boosted by continued productivity and cost reduction programs. Share earnings comparisons will be helped by fewer shares outstanding.

Valuation - 09-AUG-95

The shares have been strong in recent months, reaching new highs in July, partly due to renewed optimism regarding the U.S. economy. PPG's strategy of focusing on expanding international operations while remaining a low-cost producer in its glass and commodity chemicals operations enhances long-term prospects. With the U.S. economy expected to grow at a modest pace, European markets rebounding, and glass and chlor-alkali prices moving up, the shares are attractive at 12 times our estimated EPS for 1995. Moreover, dividends have grown steadily over the past 23 years and the shares currently provide an attractive yield of 2.6%.

Key Stock Statistics

S&P EPS Est. 1995	3.70	Tang. Bk. Value/Share	12.50
P/E on S&P Est. 1995	12.2	Beta	1.09
S&P EPS Est. 1996	4.00	Shareholders	33,400
Dividend Rate/Share	1.20	Market cap. (B)	$ 9.3
Shs. outstg. (M)	206.2	Inst. holdings	52%
Avg. daily vol. (M)	0.393	Insider holdings	NA

Value of $10,000 invested 5 years ago: $ 27,039

Fiscal Year Ending Dec. 31

	1995	% Change	1994	% Change	1993	% Change
Revenues (Million $)						
1Q	1,741	18%	1,477	2%	1,447	NM
2Q	1,870	16%	1,619	6%	1,524	NM
3Q	—	—	1,575	12%	1,405	-2%
4Q	—	—	1,660	20%	1,378	-2%
Yr.	—	—	6,331	10%	5,754	-1%
Income (Million $)						
1Q	219.2	80%	121.9	11%	110.1	40%
2Q	216.8	125%	96.20	-9%	106.2	NM
3Q	—	—	145.5	NM	24.80	-62%
4Q	—	—	151.0	180%	53.90	-21%
Yr.	—	—	514.6	74%	295.0	-8%
Earnings Per Share ($)						
1Q	1.06	86%	0.57	10%	0.52	41%
2Q	1.06	130%	0.46	-8%	0.50	NM
3Q	E0.79	—	0.68	NM	0.11	-63%
4Q	E0.79	—	0.72	182%	0.25	-20%
Yr.	E3.70	—	2.43	75%	1.39	-8%

Next earnings report expected: mid October

PPG Industries

Business Summary - 09-AUG-95

PPG, a diversified manufacturer, derived 1994 sales and operating income as follows:

	Sales	Profits
Glass	38%	33%
Coatings & resins	42%	52%
Chemicals	20%	23%
Other	Nil	-8%

International business contributed 32% of sales and 20% of operating profits in 1994.

PPG is one of the world's largest producers of flat glass and fabricated glass. Major markets include original and replacement glass for automobiles, commercial and residential construction, aircraft transparencies, furniture and glass products for various industrial uses. PPG is the world's second largest producer of continuous strand and chopped strand fiber glass, including plastic reinforcement yarns and industrial and decorative yarns, for transportation, construction, electronics, recreational and industrial uses.

PPG produces protective and decorative coatings for the automotive, appliance, container, industrial equipment and architectural markets, metal pretreatments and adhesives and sealants for the automotive industry.

PPG is a leading worldwide producer of chlorine and caustic soda, vinyl chloride monomer and chlorinated solvents. Specialty chemicals include silica compounds, surfactants, photochromic lenses, and fine chemicals (optical resins, pool and water treatment chemicals, phosgene derivatives and flame retardants). In January 1995, PPG completed its departure from the medical electronics business.

Important Developments

Jul. '95—Second quarter 1995 sales growth of 16% showed continuing benefits of stronger pricing, particularly in commodity chemicals, fiber glass, and flat glass, as well as some volume gain in North America. The ongoing European economic expansion also contributed to higher sales. Profits for the coatings business were adversely affected by higher raw material costs, despite higher sales. The company said that its strong performance in the 1995 first half, despite softening North American auto production and housing starts, reflects the strategic diversity of its portfolio. PPG has completed nearly 25% of a 10 million share repurchase program initiated in late April.

Capitalization

Long Term Debt: $652,800,000 (6/95).
Minority Interest: $76,800,000.

Per Share Data ($)

(Year Ended Dec. 31)

	1994	1993	1992	1991	1990	1989
Tangible Bk. Val.	12.35	11.57	12.72	12.50	12.00	10.49
Cash Flow	3.93	2.95	3.16	2.60	3.72	3.41
Earnings	2.43	1.39	1.51	0.95	2.22	2.09
Dividends	1.12	1.29	0.94	0.86	0.82	0.74
Payout Ratio	46%	93%	62%	91%	37%	35%
Prices - High	42⅛	38⅛	34¼	29¾	27⅝	23
- Low	33¾	29¾	25	20¾	17¼	18½
P/E Ratio - High	17	27	23	31	12	11
- Low	14	21	17	22	8	9

Income Statement Analysis (Million $)

	1994	%Chg	1993	%Chg	1992	%Chg	1991
Revs.	6,331	10%	5,754	-1%	5,814	2%	5,673
Oper. Inc.	1,329	27%	1,048	1%	1,036	13%	918
Depr.	318	-4%	331	-6%	352	NM	351
Int. Exp.	91.0	-17%	109	-26%	148	-12%	169
Pretax Inc.	856	57%	544	NM	542	53%	354
Eff. Tax Rate	38%	—	43%	—	40%	—	42%
Net Inc.	515	75%	295	-8%	319	59%	201

Balance Sheet & Other Fin. Data (Million $)

	1994	1993	1992	1991	1990	1989
Cash	62.0	112	61.0	38.0	59.0	65.0
Curr. Assets	2,168	2,026	1,951	2,173	2,217	2,056
Total Assets	5,894	5,652	5,662	6,056	6,108	5,645
Curr. Liab.	1,425	1,281	1,253	1,341	1,471	1,338
LT Debt	773	774	872	1,163	1,186	1,178
Common Eqty.	2,557	2,473	2,699	2,655	2,547	2,282
Total Cap.	3,703	3,568	4,103	4,369	4,263	3,941
Cap. Exp.	NA	253	279	299	564	572
Cash Flow	832	626	671	553	798	758

Ratio Analysis

	1994	1993	1992	1991	1990	1989
Curr. Ratio	1.5	1.6	1.6	1.6	1.5	1.5
% LT Debt of Cap.	20.9	21.7	21.3	26.6	27.8	29.9
% Net Inc.of Revs.	8.1	5.1	5.5	3.6	7.9	8.1
% Ret. on Assets	9.1	5.2	5.5	3.3	8.2	8.6
% Ret. on Equity	20.8	11.4	11.9	7.7	19.9	20.6

Dividend Data (Dividends have been paid since 1899. A dividend reinvestment plan is available. A revised "poison pill" stock purchase rights plan was adopted in 1988.)

Amt. of Div. $	Date Decl.	Ex-Div. Date	Stock of Record	Payment Date
0.280	Jul. 22	Aug. 04	Aug. 10	Sep. 12 '94
0.290	Oct. 20	Nov. 04	Nov. 10	Dec. 12 '94
0.290	Jan. 19	Feb. 14	Feb. 21	Mar. 10 '95
0.290	Apr. 24	May. 04	May. 10	Jun. 12 '95
0.300	Jul. 20	Aug. 08	Aug. 10	Sep. 12 '95

Data as orig. reptd.; bef. results of disc. opers. and/or spec. items. Per share data adj. for stk. divs. as of ex-div. date. E-Estimated. NA-Not Available. NM-Not Meaningful. NR-Not Ranked.

Office—One PPG Place, Pittsburgh, PA 15272. **Tel**—(412) 434-3131. **Chrmn & CEO**—J. E. Dempsey. **Secy**—H. K. Linge. **SVP-Fin**—W. H. Hernandez. **Investor Contact**—Douglas B. Atkinson. **Dirs**—E. B. Davis Jr., J. E. Dempsey, S. C. Gault, A. J. Krowe, S. C. Mason, H. A. McInnes, R. Mehrabian, V. A. Sarni, D. G. Vice, D. R. Whitwam. **Transfer Agent & Registrar**—Chemical Bank, NYC. **Incorporated** in Pennsylvania in 1883. **Empl**-30,800. **S&P Analyst:** Richard O'Reilly, CFA

STOCK REPORTS

PACCAR Inc

NASDAQ Symbol **PCAR**
In S&P 500

20-SEP-95   Industry:
Auto/Truck mfrs.

Summary: This leading producer of heavy-duty trucks also manufactures equipment for the oil and gas and construction industries, and distributes auto parts in five states.

S&P Opinion: Avoid (★★)	

Recent Price • 51	Yield • 2.0%
52 Wk Range • 54⅝-40	12-Mo. P/E • 8.6

Quantitative Evaluations

Outlook
(1 Lowest—5 Highest)
• **4+**

Fair Value
• **53⅞**

Risk
• **Low**

Earn./Div. Rank
• **B+**

Technical Eval.
• **Bearish** since 8/94

Rel. Strength Rank
(1 Lowest—99 Highest)
• **38**

Insider Activity
• **Favorable**

Earnings vs. Previous Year
▲=Up ▼=Down ▶=No Change

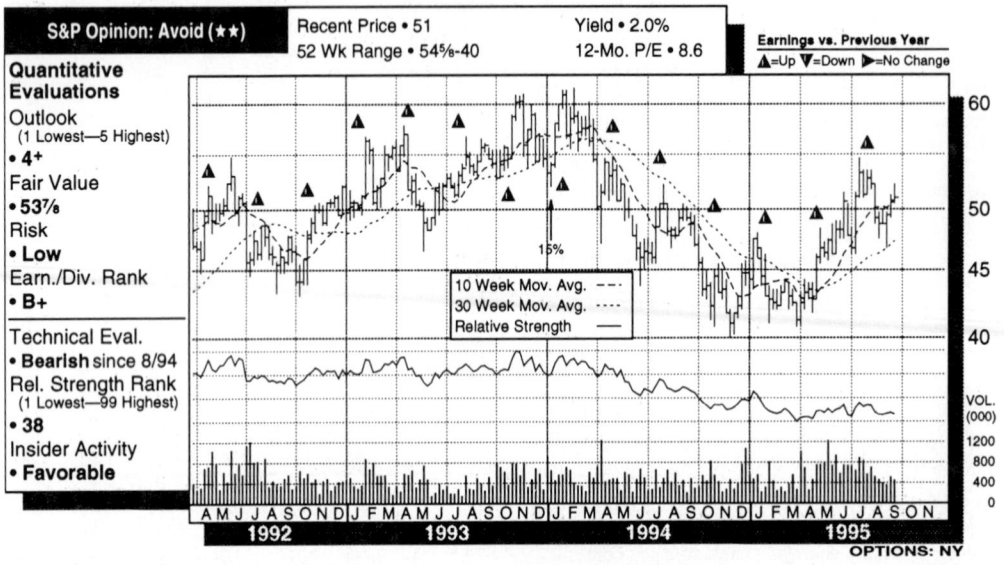

10 Week Mov. Avg. ----
30 Week Mov. Avg. ·····
Relative Strength ——

OPTIONS: NY

Overview - 20-SEP-95

Although the overall heavy-duty truck order backlog in North America remains strong, cancellations exceeded new orders in August for the first time in recent memory. While sales should remain reasonably strong over the next few quarters, heavy truck shipments are expected to decline in 1996. The longer term outlook is cloudy as several years of very strong sales have left little pent up demand. With little pent up demand, the modest decline we envision could turn into a cyclical decline if the general economy weakens further. In such a case, margins would erode and earnings would be severely penalized by a drop in capacity utilization. During such periods, PCAR normally suffers less than its competitors because it is less vertically integrated.

Valuation - 20-SEP-95

We downgraded the shares to avoid as net new orders for heavy trucks turned negative in August for the first time in recent memory. We expect that fears that a cyclical decline may be unfolding will affect the shares. Even without a deep cyclical decline, the stock market has traditionally been reluctant to reward heavy industrials with more than a modest multiple of peak year earnings. We believe that 1995 will be the peak earnings year for this cycle and that a multiple expansion is unlikely. Trading at 8.5 times expected 1995 earnings, the shares are likely to mark time before declining in 1996 when earnings are expected to drop.

Key Stock Statistics

S&P EPS Est. 1995	5.85	Tang. Bk. Value/Share	32.63
P/E on S&P Est. 1995	8.7	Beta	1.24
S&P EPS Est. 1996	5.00	Shareholders	3,300
Dividend Rate/Share	1.00	Market cap. (B)	$ 2.0
Shs. outstg. (M)	38.9	Inst. holdings	42%
Avg. daily vol. (M)	0.085	Insider holdings	NA

Value of $10,000 invested 5 years ago: $ 17,249

Fiscal Year Ending Dec. 31

	1995	% Change	1994	% Change	1993	% Change
Revenues (Million $)						
1Q	1,130	15%	986.3	30%	761.4	29%
2Q	1,207	13%	1,071	28%	838.0	46%
3Q	—	—	1,115	26%	884.1	29%
4Q	—	—	1,114	24%	895.4	22%
Yr.	—	—	4,285	27%	3,379	31%
Income (Million $)						
1Q	54.30	25%	43.60	59%	27.40	154%
2Q	65.10	29%	50.60	54%	32.80	195%
3Q	—	—	53.20	46%	36.50	101%
4Q	—	—	57.10	25%	45.50	81%
Yr.	—	—	204.5	44%	142.2	118%
Earnings Per Share ($)						
1Q	1.40	25%	1.12	59%	0.70	153%
2Q	1.67	28%	1.30	54%	0.84	194%
3Q	E1.40	2%	1.37	46%	0.94	100%
4Q	E1.38	-6%	1.47	26%	1.17	82%
Yr.	E5.85	11%	5.26	44%	3.66	118%

Next earnings report expected: mid October

PACCAR Inc

Business Summary - 19-SEP-95

PACCAR Inc is the second largest producer of heavy-duty trucks in the U.S., accounting for 22% of registrations in 1994. Contributions to pretax profits (in millions) by business segment in recent years were:

	1994	1993	1992
Truck manufacturing	$299	$194	$78
Auto parts	4	2	-5
Financial services	58	40	26
Other	4	9	8

Truck manufacturing generated 89.6% of revenues in 1994. Trucks are marketed in the U.S. under the Peterbilt and Kenworth names and in the U.K. under the Foden plate. PCAR also derives a small portion of sales from medium-duty trucks. Vehicles are also produced in Canada and Australia, and in Mexico through VILPAC S.A. (55% owned). The company sold about 53,000 trucks worldwide in 1994, versus 44,000 in 1993, through a network of 290 independent dealers in the U.S. and 36 overseas.

The auto parts segment (3.8% of revenues) involves the distribution of auto parts and accessories and minor auto repair and maintenance work through some 121 Al's Auto Supply and Grand Auto stores in California, Washington, Nevada, Idaho and Alaska.

Financial services (4.6% of revenues) include PACCAR Financial Corp., which provides wholesale and retail financing for trucks and trailers produced by the company and others. PACCAR Leasing manages a full-service lease fleet of more than 7,800 trucks and trailers and 492 railcars for the Soo Line R.R.

Other operations (2.1% of revenues) include the manufacture of oilfield extraction pumps, sold under the Trico and Kobe names, and winches used in the logging, construction and oilfield industries.

Important Developments

Aug. '95—PCAR acquired full ownership of VILPAC, its Mexican subsidiary which manufactures Kenworth trucks for distribution in Mexico. Previously, PCAR owned 55% of VILPAC, which has produced Kenworth heavy-duty class 8 tractors for the Mexican market in Mexicali, Baja California for 36 years.

Jul. '95—U.S. retail sales for Peterbilt and Kenworth's Class 8 trucks for 1995's first six months were 21,034 units, up 8.3% from the 19,430 trucks sold in the year-earlier period. Through June, PCAR's Peterbilt unit held an 8.7% share of the Class 8 market, while its Kenworth brand held an 11.5% market share.

Capitalization

Total Debt: $1,872,600,000 (6/95).
Minority Interest: $25,600,000.

Per Share Data ($)

	1994	1993	1992	1991	1990	1989
Tangible Bk. Val.	29.56	27.86	26.02	25.82	25.46	25.10
Cash Flow	6.88	5.12	2.90	2.29	2.90	7.30
Earnings	5.26	3.66	1.68	1.02	1.59	6.00
Dividends	3.00	2.00	1.13	0.96	0.87	2.17
Payout Ratio	57%	55%	67%	94%	53%	36%
Prices - High	61¾	61⅛	54¾	43¾	39¾	45⅝
- Low	40	46½	41½	27¼	23¼	32⅞
P/E Ratio - High	12	17	33	43	25	8
- Low	8	13	25	27	15	5

Income Statement Analysis (Million $)

	1994	%Chg	1993	%Chg	1992	%Chg	1991
Revs.	4,490	27%	3,542	30%	2,735	17%	2,339
Oper. Inc.	471	44%	326	76%	185	39%	133
Depr.	63.2	11%	56.7	20%	47.2	-4%	49.2
Int. Exp.	NA	—	NA	—	NA	—	96.0
Pretax Inc.	320	45%	220	139%	92.0	92%	48.0
Eff. Tax Rate	36%	—	35%	—	29%	—	18%
Net Inc.	205	44%	142	118%	65.0	63%	40.0

Balance Sheet & Other Fin. Data (Million $)

	1994	1993	1992	1991	1990	1989
Cash	553	459	465	496	478	555
Curr. Assets	NA	NA	NA	NA	NA	NA
Total Assets	3,928	3,291	2,809	2,738	2,906	3,067
Curr. Liab.	NA	NA	NA	NA	NA	NA
LT Debt	631	460	240	219	325	485
Common Eqty.	1,175	1,108	1,038	1,032	1,019	1,007
Total Cap.	1,838	1,567	1,278	1,251	1,344	1,492
Cap. Exp.	81.0	109	100	51.0	80.0	71.0
Cash Flow	268	199	112	89.0	115	295

Ratio Analysis

	1994	1993	1992	1991	1990	1989
Curr. Ratio	NA	NA	NA	NA	NA	NA
% LT Debt of Cap.	34.3	29.3	18.7	17.5	24.2	32.5
% Net Inc.of Revs.	4.6	4.0	2.4	1.7	2.3	6.9
% Ret. on Assets	5.7	4.7	2.4	1.4	2.2	8.3
% Ret. on Equity	17.9	13.3	6.3	3.9	6.4	25.7

Dividend Data —Cash has been paid in each year since 1943. A "poison pill" stock purchase rights plan was adopted in 1990.

Amt. of Div. $	Date Decl.	Ex-Div. Date	Stock of Record	Payment Date
2.000	Dec. 13	Dec. 19	Dec. 23	Jan. 05 '95
0.250	Dec. 13	Feb. 13	Feb. 17	Mar. 02 '95
0.250	Apr. 26	May. 12	May. 18	Jun. 05 '95
0.250	Jul. 25	Aug. 17	Aug. 21	Sep. 05 '95
0.250	Sep. 19	Nov. 16	Nov. 20	Dec. 05 '95

Data as orig. reptd.; bef. results of disc. opers. and/or spec. items. Per share data adj. for stk. divs. as of ex-div. date. Revs. in Income Statement Analysis incl. finl. svcs. E-Estimated. NA-Not Available. NM-Not Meaningful. NR-Not Ranked.

Office—777 106th Ave. N.E., Bellevue, WA 98004. **Incorporated**—in Washington in 1924; reincorporated in Delaware in 1972. **Tel**—(206) 455-7400. **Chrmn & CEO**—C. M. Pigott. **Pres**—D. J. Hovind. **VP & Secy**—G. G. Morie. **Treas & Investor Contact**—J. Waggoner. **Dirs**—R. P. Cooley, J. M. Fluke, Jr., C. H. Hahn. H. J. Haynes, D. J. Hovind, C. M. Pigott, J. C. Pigott, M. C. Pigott, J. W. Pitts, M. A. Tembreull, J. H. Wiborg. **Transfer Agent**—First Chicago Trust Co. of New York, Jersey City, N.J. **Empl**-14,600. **S&P Analyst:** Joshua M. Harari, CFA

Pacific Enterprises

NYSE Symbol **PET**
In S&P 500

16-AUG-95 Industry:
Utilities-Gas

Summary: This Los Angeles-based utility holding company's principal area of service is Southern and Central California.

S&P Opinion: Hold (★★★)	Recent Price • 23¼	Yield • 5.8%
	52 Wk Range • 26⅜-20	12-Mo. P/E • 11.2

**Quantitative
Evaluations**

Outlook
(1 Lowest—5 Highest)
• **2⁺**

Fair Value
• **21½**

Risk
• **Low**

Earn./Div. Rank
• **B-**

Technical Eval.
• **Bearish** since 7/95

Rel. Strength Rank
(1 Lowest—99 Highest)
• **24**

Insider Activity
• **Neutral**

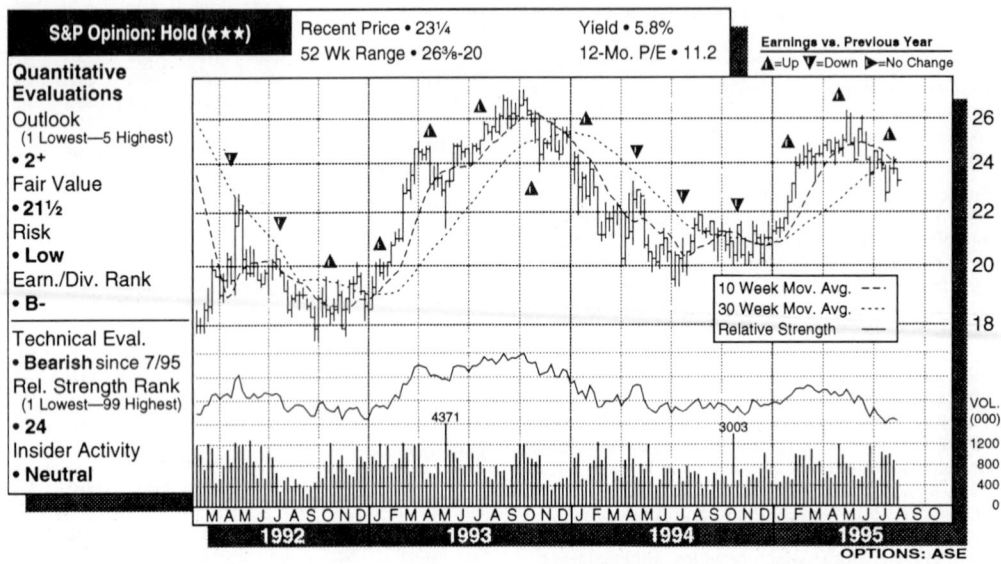

Earnings vs. Previous Year
▲=Up ▼=Down ▶=No Change

10 Week Mov. Avg. – – –
30 Week Mov. Avg. ····
Relative Strength ——

OPTIONS: ASE

Overview - 11-AUG-95

Earnings for 1995 should benefit from an expected improvement in the Southern California economy, which
should result in rate base growth in the neighborhood
of 2.0%, while the population in the company's service
area should continue to grow. An increase in the allowed return on equity to 12% should enhance earnings growth in 1995. Efforts to cut costs should benefit
margins, allowing PET to continue to earn in excess of
its allowed rate of return. Strong levels of cash flow
will permit expansion into non-regulated business and
reduce the debt burden over the next several years.
Restricting earnings growth will be sharply reduced
opportunities in the large-volume utility electric generation market, since customers are increasingly becoming price sensitive and are able to switch from one
fuel source to another.

Valuation - 16-AUG-95

The shares have been rising on expectations that demand for natural gas will return to more normal levels,
following an exceptionally mild winter. As interest rates
rose during 1994, the shares languished. However, investors are have begun to return to utility stocks. We
see the shares of PET as a solid income generating
investment vehicle. However, regulatory changes now
make gas utilities responsible for storage of their gas,
and the shares have taken on the characteristics of
the commodity to a large degree. We anticipate gas
prices will rise modestly during the remainder of 1995,
while the long-term demand outlook appears more
favorable.

Key Stock Statistics

S&P EPS Est. 1995	2.10	Tang. Bk. Value/Share	14.51
P/E on S&P Est. 1995	11.1	Beta	0.68
S&P EPS Est. 1996	2.15	Shareholders	43,100
Dividend Rate/Share	1.36	Market cap. (B)	$ 2.0
Shs. outstg. (M)	84.6	Inst. holdings	53%
Avg. daily vol. (M)	0.184	Insider holdings	NA

Value of $10,000 invested 5 years ago: $ 6,397

Fiscal Year Ending Dec. 31

	1995	% Change	1994	% Change	1993	% Change
Revenues (Million $)						
1Q	626.0	-11%	705.0	-9%	773.0	3%
2Q	599.0	-8%	651.0	NM	652.0	NM
3Q	—	—	591.0	-9%	649.0	3%
4Q	—	—	717.0	-13%	825.0	-6%
Yr.	—	—	2,664	-8%	2,899	NM
Income (Million $)						
1Q	45.00	18%	38.00	NM	38.00	NM
2Q	45.00	7%	42.00	NM	42.00	NM
3Q	—	—	42.00	-22%	54.00	64%
4Q	—	—	50.00	6%	47.00	31%
Yr.	—	—	172.0	-5%	181.0	33%
Earnings Per Share ($)						
1Q	0.51	19%	0.43	-4%	0.45	10%
2Q	0.51	9%	0.47	-4%	0.49	26%
3Q	E0.51	9%	0.47	-20%	0.59	55%
4Q	E0.57	-2%	0.58	12%	0.52	24%
Yr.	E2.10	8%	1.95	-5%	2.06	29%

Next earnings report expected: early November

Pacific Enterprises

Business Summary - 16-AUG-95

Pacific Enterprises (formerly Pacific Lighting) distributes natural gas in Southern California, including Los Angeles, and parts of central California, through its Southern California Gas (SoCalGas) unit, the largest U.S. gas distributor. In a restructuring designed to focus on utility operations, PET completed the divestiture of its retailing and oil and gas exploration and production operations in January 1993. Gas revenues by customer group in recent years were derived:

	1994	1993	1992
Residential	63%	60%	56%
Commercial/industrial	29%	31%	32%
Utility electric gen.	4%	5%	7%
Wholesale & other	4%	4%	5%

Gas throughput of 1,020 Bcf in 1994, up from 965 Bcf in 1993, was divided: 35% commercial and industrial, 25% residential, 26% electric generation, and 14% wholesale. About 65% of gas deliveries in 1994 were customer-owned gas, up from 64% in 1993. At 1994 year end, customers served totaled 4,694,358, up from 4,670,787 a year earlier. The weighted average rate base at year end was $2,862 million, up from $2,769 million. In 1995, SoCalGas is authorized to earn a 9.67% (9.22% in 1994) rate of return on rate base and a 12.0% (11.00%) rate of return on common equity. SoCalGas provides a gas storage service; during 1993, SoCalGas stored about 24 Bcf of customer-owned gas.

Other activities include operation of an interstate and offshore natural gas pipeline, and building and operating electricity generating plants fueled by renewable energy sources, including gas.

Important Developments

Aug. '95—In 1995's second quarter, net income rose to $45 million ($0.51 a share, after preferred dividends), from $42 million ($0.47) in the 1994 period, due primarily to the improved profitability of SoCalGas. Utility income rose to $50 million, from $43 million, as a result of a higher allowed return on equity and cost savings. Earnings were reduced by a $4 million after-tax reserve, established pending settlement of a power sales contract at an alternative energy subsidiary. There was a slight decrease in the rate base in the period.

Capitalization

Long Term Debt: $1,409,000,000 (3/95).
Subsidiary Preferred Stock: $195,000,000.
Preferred Stock: $218,000,000.

Per Share Data ($)

	1994	1993	1992	1991	1990	1989
Tangible Bk. Val.	14.31	12.19	9.44	19.74	23.76	27.55
Cash Flow	4.87	5.08	4.76	4.02	4.49	8.47
Earnings	1.95	2.06	1.60	-1.45	-0.86	3.05
Dividends	1.26	0.60	0.44	2.62	3.48	3.48
Payout Ratio	65%	29%	28%	NM	NM	122%
Prices - High	24½	27⅜	27⅜	43⅜	52	53¾
- Low	19¼	18½	17⅜	23¼	34¼	37⅛
P/E Ratio - High	13	13	17	NM	NM	18
- Low	10	9	11	NM	NM	12

(Year Ended Dec. 31)

Income Statement Analysis (Million $)

	1994	%Chg	1993	%Chg	1992	%Chg	1991
Revs.	2,664	-8%	2,899	NM	2,900	-56%	6,599
Oper. Inc.	650	-3%	671	3%	649	28%	509
Depr.	239	-2%	243	3%	236	-40%	393
Int. Exp.	132	-7%	142	-13%	163	-29%	230
Pretax Inc.	321	1%	317	20%	265	NM	-35.0
Eff. Tax Rate	43%	—	40%	—	46%	—	NM
Net Inc.	182	-5%	191	34%	143	NM	-81.0

Balance Sheet & Other Fin. Data (Million $)

	1994	1993	1992	1991	1990	1989
Cash	287	152	432	103	187	309
Curr. Assets	1,323	1,264	1,547	1,966	2,181	2,158
Total Assets	5,445	5,596	5,414	6,701	7,291	7,326
Curr. Liab.	1,146	1,463	1,165	1,526	2,213	2,122
LT Debt	1,550	1,394	1,915	2,381	1,998	1,816
Common Eqty.	1,210	1,026	711	1,441	1,680	1,911
Total Cap.	3,400	3,127	3,245	4,793	4,665	4,789
Cap. Exp.	249	327	329	537	654	640
Cash Flow	399	409	356	289	314	550

Ratio Analysis

	1994	1993	1992	1991	1990	1989
Curr. Ratio	1.2	0.9	1.3	1.3	1.0	1.0
% LT Debt of Cap.	45.6	44.6	59.0	49.7	42.8	37.9
% Net Inc.of Revs.	6.8	6.6	4.9	NM	NM	3.2
% Ret. on Assets	3.3	3.3	2.3	NM	NM	2.9
% Ret. on Equity	14.3	18.2	10.9	NM	NM	10.2

Dividend Data

Dividends on the common stock, omitted in February 1992, were resumed in May, 1993. A "poison pill" stock purchase rights plan was adopted in 1989.

Amt. of Div. $	Date Decl.	Ex-Div. Date	Stock of Record	Payment Date
0.320	Jun. 07	Jul. 14	Jul. 20	Aug. 15 '94
0.320	Oct. 11	Oct. 14	Oct. 20	Nov. 15 '94
0.320	Jan. 03	Jan. 13	Jan. 20	Feb. 15 '95
0.340	Apr. 04	Apr. 13	Apr. 20	May. 15 '95
0.340	Jun. 06	Jul. 18	Jul. 20	Aug. 15 '95

Data as orig. reptd.; bef. results of disc. opers. and/or spec. items. Per share data adj. for stk. divs. as of ex-div. date.
E-Estimated. NA-Not Available. NM-Not Meaningful. NR-Not Ranked.

Office—555 West Fifth St., Los Angeles, CA 90013. **Tel**—(213) 895-5000. **Co-Chrmn**—W. B. Wood & R. D. Farman. **CEO**—W. B. Wood. **Pres & COO**—R. D. Farman. **CFO**—L. A. Levitin. **Secy**—T. C. Sanger. **Treas**—L. A. Levitin. **Investor Contact**—Clem Teng. **Dirs**—H. H. Bertea, H. L. Carter, R. D. Farman, W. D. Godbold, Jr., I. E. Lozano, Jr., H. M. Messmer, Jr., P. A. Miller, R. J. Stegemeier, R. C. Siciliano, D. L. Walker, W. B. Wood. **Transfer Agent & Registrar**—Chemical Bank, NYC. **Incorporated** in California in 1907. **Empl**-8,500. **S&P Analyst:** Raymond J. Deacon

Pacific Gas & Electric

NYSE Symbol **PCG**
In S&P 500

31-OCT-95

Industry: Util.-Diversified

Summary: This California-based electric and gas utility, one of the largest in the U.S., owns the two-unit Diablo Canyon nuclear facility.

S&P Opinion: Avoid (★★)	Recent Price • 30	Yield • 6.6%
	52 Wk Range • 30⅝-22	12-Mo. P/E • 11.1

Quantitative Evaluations

Outlook
(1 Lowest—5 Highest)
• **3⁺**

Fair Value
• **29⅞**

Risk
• **Low**

Earn./Div. Rank
• **B**

Technical Eval.
• **Bullish** since 4/95

Rel. Strength Rank
(1 Lowest—99 Highest)
• **62**

Insider Activity
• **Favorable**

Earnings vs. Previous Year
▲=Up ▼=Down ▶=No Change

10 Week Mov. Avg. — ·—
30 Week Mov. Avg. ·······
Relative Strength ——

OPTIONS: ASE

Overview - 31-OCT-95

Share earnings in 1995 should benefit from cost savings from work force reductions, other cost control efforts, a reduction in one-time charges and a higher contribution from Diablo Canyon, due to a high capacity utilization rate as a refueling outage is scheduled at only one unit. Both Diablo Canyon units had refueling outages during 1994. However, these positive factors will be partially offset by lower rates from power produced at these two low-cost nuclear generating stations under an agreement recently approved by the California PUC. We expect earnings for 1996 to be under pressure from a rate-based decrease in revenues, continuing one-time charges, and highly competitive markets.

Valuation - 31-OCT-95

PCG's shares have recently outperformed S&P's Utility Index and, since the end of 1994, have risen 24%, compared with a 28% gain for the S&P 500, as investors correctly anticipated good earnings growth on high capacity utilitization rates for the nuclear generating stations, low fuel prices and a greater than expected throughput on a pipeline expansion from Canada. Expectations of lower interest rates may continue to boost the shares in 1995. However, longer term, PCG's comparatively high rates, a strong consumer-oriented regulatory environment and only modest economic growth in its service area may limit growth in earnings and the dividend rate, and restrain future advances in the stock.

Key Stock Statistics

S&P EPS Est. 1995	2.90	Tang. Bk. Value/Share	20.25
P/E on S&P Est. 1995	10.3	Beta	0.59
S&P EPS Est. 1996	3.00	Shareholders	230,000
Dividend Rate/Share	1.96	Market cap. (B)	$ 12.6
Shs. outstg. (M)	424.4	Inst. holdings	41%
Avg. daily vol. (M)	0.496	Insider holdings	NA

Value of $10,000 invested 5 years ago: $ 19,318

Fiscal Year Ending Dec. 31

	1995	% Change	1994	% Change	1993	% Change
Revenues (Million $)						
1Q	2,307	-8%	2,514	2%	2,464	2%
2Q	2,448	NM	2,440	NM	2,464	-2%
3Q	2,645	-7%	2,855	-3%	2,947	5%
4Q	—	—	2,638	-3%	2,707	6%
Yr.	—	—	10,447	-1%	10,582	3%
Income (Million $)						
1Q	328.7	39%	236.9	-7%	255.7	-8%
2Q	405.5	68%	241.4	-2%	245.4	-27%
3Q	377.6	-11%	425.6	20%	356.1	1%
4Q	—	—	103.5	-50%	208.4	1%
Yr.	—	—	1,007	-5%	1,066	-9%
Earnings Per Share ($)						
1Q	0.73	40%	0.52	-7%	0.56	-8%
2Q	0.92	74%	0.53	NM	0.53	-29%
3Q	0.85	-11%	0.96	22%	0.79	1%
4Q	E0.40	90%	0.21	-53%	0.45	2%
Yr.	E2.90	31%	2.21	-5%	2.33	-10%

Next earnings report expected: mid January

Pacific Gas & Electric

Business Summary - 31-OCT-95

Pacific Gas & Electric, one of the largest investor-owned gas and electric utilities in the U.S., provides electricity and related services to some 4.4 million customers and gas to roughly 3.5 million in northern and central California. Electricity accounted for 77% of 1994 revenues, and gas 23%. Electric revenues in recent years:

	1994	1993	1992	1991
Residential	38%	38%	37%	37%
Commercial	37%	38%	38%	37%
Industrial	14%	15%	16%	16%
Other	11%	9%	9%	10%

Sources of electric generation in 1994 were natural gas/oil 34%, nuclear 18%, hydro 9%, geothermal 7%, and other (purchased power) 32%. Capability in 1994 totaled 18,768 mw and peak load was 15,334 mw, for a capacity margin of 18%. Gas sales in 1994 were 306,930 MMcf, down from 430,718 MMcf in 1993.

PCG's assumes a significant portion of the operating risk of its two-unit 2,160 mw Diablo Canyon facility under a 1988 rate case settlement that establishes a price for each kilowatt hour generated, rather than for recovery of costs, as in traditional ratemaking.

As part of its goal to divest its interest in the oil and gas exploration and production business, in April 1994, PCG's PG&E Enterprises sold its Dalen Corp. unit for $455 million, for a minimal gain.

Important Developments

Oct. '95—Directors authorized filing an application with the California Public Utilities Commission to establish a holding company. If approved, PCG would transfer its interests in the gas pipeline company and unregulated business including independent power production to the holding company. In August, the Federal Energy Commission approved PCG's open access wholesale transmission tariffs. Effective July 1, the tariffs offer eligible customers the same or comparable wholesale transmission service that PSG provides for wholesale sales. PCG is developing an electronic bulletin board for users to view transmission service, availability and rates, and to advertise transmission rights for sale or purchase. In late May, the California Public Utilities Commission (CPUC) approved an agreement among PCG and the CPUC's Division of Ratepayer Advocates, the State Attorney General's office and a group of consumer organizations to reduce the PCG's rates at its nuclear plants by $2.1 billion over the next five years.

Capitalization

Long Term Debt: $8,250,722,000 (6/95).

Red. Cum. Preferred Stock: $137,500,000.

Cum. Preferred Stock: $732,995,000.

Per Share Data ($)

(Year Ended Dec. 31)

	1994	1993	1992	1991	1990	1989
Tangible Bk. Val.	20.06	18.67	18.48	18.17	17.65	17.17
Earnings	2.21	2.33	2.58	2.24	2.10	1.90
Dividends	1.96	1.88	1.76	1.64	1.52	1.40
Payout Ratio	89%	81%	68%	73%	72%	74%
Prices - High	35	36¾	34⅝	32⅝	25⅝	22
- Low	21⅜	31¾	29	24	20	17¼
P/E Ratio - High	16	16	13	15	12	12
- Low	10	14	11	11	10	9

Income Statement Analysis (Million $)

	1994	%Chg	1993	%Chg	1992	%Chg	1991
Revs.	10,447	-1%	10,582	3%	10,296	5%	9,778
Depr.	1,397	6%	1,316	8%	1,221	7%	1,141
Maint.	457	3%	443	-9%	485	-8%	525
Fxd. Chgs. Cov.	3.2	-8%	3.4	3%	3.3	8%	3.1
Constr. Credits	32.0	-73%	120	44%	83.6	99%	42.0
Eff. Tax Rate	45%	—	46%	—	43%	—	45%
Net Inc.	1,007	-5%	1,065	-9%	1,171	14%	1,026

Balance Sheet & Other Fin. Data (Million $)

	1994	1993	1992	1991	1990	1989
Gross Prop.	31,668	30,919	29,268	27,144	25,543	23,523
Cap. Exp.	1,107	1,842	2,352	1,771	1,517	1,423
Net Prop.	19,399	19,683	18,761	17,671	17,076	15,990
Capitalization:						
LT Debt	8,675	9,292	8,379	8,249	7,786	7,824
% LT Debt	48	50	48	49	48	48
Pfd.	870	883	938	987	1,101	1,152
% Pfd.	4.80	4.70	5.30	5.80	6.70	7.00
Common	8,635	8,446	8,283	7,681	7,506	7,455
% Common	48	45	47	45	46	45
Total Cap.	22,475	23,011	19,855	19,057	18,407	18,309

Ratio Analysis

	1994	1993	1992	1991	1990	1989
Oper. Ratio	84.4	83.3	82.2	82.5	82.0	81.1
% Earn. on Net Prop.	8.4	9.2	10.1	9.9	10.1	10.2
% Ret. on Revs.	9.6	10.1	11.4	10.5	10.4	10.5
% Ret. On Invest.Cap	7.7	8.6	10.1	9.7	9.8	9.6
% Return On Com.Eqty	11.1	12.0	13.7	12.3	11.9	11.1

Dividend Data

—Dividends have been paid since 1919. A dividend reinvestment plan is available.

Amt. of Div. $	Date Decl.	Ex-Div. Date	Stock of Record	Payment Date
0.490	Oct. 20	Dec. 09	Dec. 15	Jan. 15 '95
0.490	Jan. 23	Mar. 09	Mar. 15	Apr. 15 '95
0.490	May. 22	Jun. 13	Jun. 15	Jul. 15 '95
0.490	Jul. 21	Sep. 13	Sep. 15	Oct. 15 '95
0.490	Oct. 20	Dec. 13	Dec. 15	Jan. 15 '96

Data as orig. reptd.; bef. results of disc opers. and/or spec. items. Per share data adj. for stk. divs. as of ex-div. date.
E-Estimated. NA-Not Available. NM-Not Meaningful. NR-Not Ranked.

Office—77 Beale St., San Francisco, CA 94177. **Tel**—(415) 973-7000. **Chrmn & CEO**—S. T. Skinner. **Pres & COO**—R. D. Glynn, Jr. **SVP-CFO**—R. R. Smith. **Treas**—K. M. Harvey. **Secy**—L. H. Everett. **Investor Contact**—Angela M. Comstock. **Dirs**—R. A. Clarke, H. M. Conger, W. S. Davila, D. M. Lawrence, R. B. Madden, G. A. Maneatis, M. S. Metz, W. F. Miller, R. Q. Morgan, J. B. M. Place, S. T. Reeves, C. E. Reichardt, J. C. Sawhill, A. Seelenfreund, S. T. Skinner, B. L. William. **Transfer Agent**—Company's office. **Incorporated**—in California in 1905. **Empl**-21,000. **S&P Analyst:** Jane Collin

Pacific Telesis

NYSE Symbol **PAC**
In S&P 500

27-OCT-95 **Industry:** Telecommunications

Summary: Pacific Telesis provides local telephone service in parts of California and Nevada.

| S&P Opinion: Avoid (★★) | Recent Price • 29¾ | Yield • 7.3% |
| | 52 Wk Range • 32⅛-25⅝ | 12-Mo. P/E • 11.8 |

Quantitative Evaluations

Outlook
(1 Lowest—5 Highest)
• **1+**

Fair Value
• **25½**

Risk
• **Low**

Earn./Div. Rank
• **B+**

Technical Eval.
• **Bullish** since 6/95

Rel. Strength Rank
(1 Lowest—99 Highest)
• **65**

Insider Activity
• **Favorable**

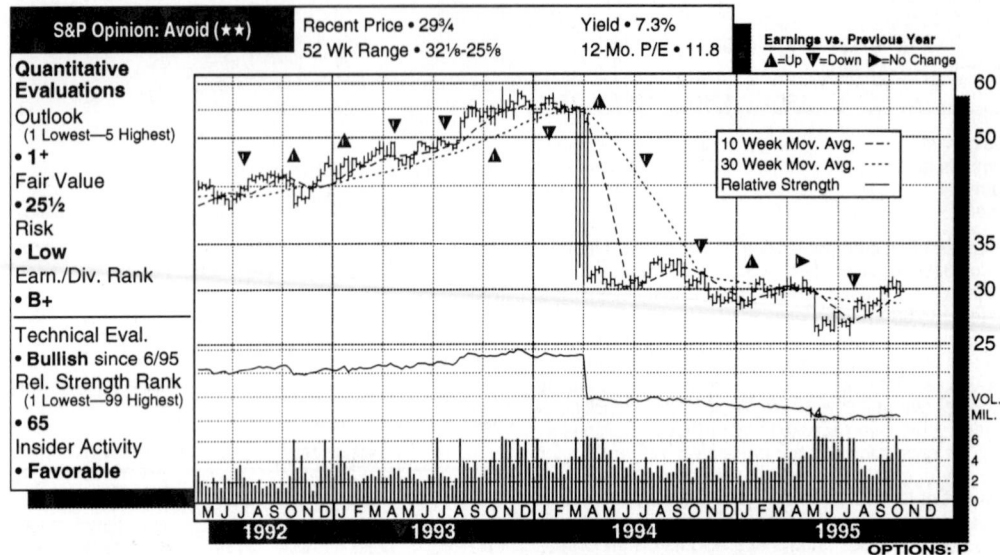

Earnings vs. Previous Year
▲=Up ▼=Down ▶=No Change

10 Week Mov. Avg. – – –
30 Week Mov. Avg. ·······
Relative Strength ——

OPTIONS: P

Overview - 27-OCT-95

Revenues and earnings are expected to decline in 1995, reflecting intense competition in California's local toll market and required rate reductions. In addition, California regulators will open the state's entire local market to competition in January 1996. In the long-term, investment in network infrastructure will improve competitive positioning and allow for provision of advanced services. Aggressive cost control efforts and work force reductions will aid margins, but significant earnings growth is not anticipated in the near-term. Plans to provide PCS (personal communications services) within PAC's markets offer potential for rapidly growing revenues, while leveraging the underlying wireline network asset base. However, the cost of winning licenses and building systems may depress earnings for several years.

Valuation - 27-OCT-95

Despite their healthy yield, we recommend that investors avoid the shares, as weak near-term earnings growth prospects may limit capital appreciation potential. The opening of the California market to competition in 1995 has led to market share losses, with revenues and earnings suffering as a result. In the long-term, investments in infrastructure upgrades and PCS may provide growth opportunities, but the shares are unlikely to reflect these possibilities until earnings visibility is clearer. Meanwhile, costs associated with these investments are likely to preclude dividend increases.

Key Stock Statistics

S&P EPS Est. 1995	2.45	Tang. Bk. Value/Share	11.25
P/E on S&P Est. 1995	12.1	Beta	0.85
S&P EPS Est. 1996	2.50	Shareholders	759,300
Dividend Rate/Share	2.18	Market cap. (B)	$ 12.7
Shs. outstg. (M)	428.4	Inst. holdings	41%
Avg. daily vol. (M)	1.214	Insider holdings	NA

Value of $10,000 invested 5 years ago: NA

Fiscal Year Ending Dec. 31

	1995	% Change	1994	% Change	1993	% Change
Revenues (Million $)						
1Q	2,254	-2%	2,294	-9%	2,525	4%
2Q	2,231	-1%	2,256	-12%	2,578	3%
3Q	2,275	-2%	2,329	-10%	2,602	4%
4Q	—	—	2,356	3%	2,297	-8%
Yr.	—	—	9,235	NM	9,244	-7%
Income (Million $)						
1Q	282.0	NM	282.0	NM	2.00	-99%
2Q	260.0	-6%	278.0	-4%	291.0	NM
3Q	275.0	-12%	314.0	-3%	323.0	13%
4Q	—	—	262.0	NM	-405.0	NM
Yr.	—	—	1,136	-41%	1,910	67%
Earnings Per Share ($)						
1Q	0.67	NM	0.67	—	Nil	—
2Q	0.61	-6%	0.65	-8%	0.71	-1%
3Q	0.64	-14%	0.74	-4%	0.77	8%
4Q	E0.53	-15%	0.62	NM	-0.96	NM
Yr.	E2.45	-9%	2.68	NM	0.46	-84%

Next earnings report expected: mid January

Pacific Telesis

Business Summary - 27-OCT-95

Pacific Telesis is the sixth largest U.S. telephone holding company, based on U.S. access lines. Its telephone subsidiaries furnish local telephone service through 15,298,000 access lines in California and Nevada.

PAC plans to spend $16 billion over the next seven years to upgrade its California telephone network for the provision of advanced services. The investment is expected to be primarily internally funded as cash flows benefit from improved efficiencies and stringent cost control efforts. The upgrade is part of an effort to improve the company's position as its markets become more competitive. The California Public Utility Commission ordered the local toll service market in that state opened to competition in January 1995. In connection with the introduction of toll competition, the CPUC ordered rate rebalancing, effective January 1, 1995, to raise PAC's local service rates closer to costs while providing reductions in toll rates.

Pacific Bell Directory publishes white and yellow pages and specialized directories for the telephone units.

PAC and the six other Bell companies jointly own Bell Communications Research, which provides technical assistance and consulting services to the companies.

On April 1, 1994, PAC completed the spinoff of its 86% interest in its domestic and international cellular and paging operations and the domestic vehicle location operations in a share-for-share tax-free distribution to its shareholders of record March 21. An initial public offering of a 14% stake in the new company, AirTouch Communications (formerly PacTel Corp.), was completed in December 1993.

Important Developments

Sep. '95—PAC will accelerate construction of its advanced communications network in the San Francisco Bay area in response to competitive pressures. PAC will scale back deployment in the rest of the state, instead relying more heavily on wireless cable technology to provide basic cable television services.
Jul. '95—The California Public Utilities Commission voted to open the local telephone market to competition on January 1, 1996.
Apr. '95—PAC agreed to acquire Cross Country Wireless Inc., a cable television company, for $120 million in stock.
Mar. '95—In FCC auctions for broadband PCS licenses, the company won two licenses, including the Los Angeles and San Franisco markets, for a total of $696 million. PAC hopes to begin PCS market trials in 1996. Dilution is expected beginning in 1995, and will likely increase in 1997 with the establishment of commercial services. Separately, the company formed a joint venture with Bell Atlantic and NYNEX to create and deliver nationally branded home entertainment, information and interactive services.

Capitalization

Long Term Debt: $5,232,000,000 (9/95).

Per Share Data ($)

(Year Ended Dec. 31)

	1994	1993	1992	1991	1990	1989
Tangible Bk. Val.	11.25	17.28	18.95	17.97	16.68	17.23
Cash Flow	6.89	4.65	7.43	7.21	7.29	7.50
Earnings	2.68	0.46	2.83	2.58	2.59	3.02
Dividends	2.18	2.18	2.18	2.14	2.02	1.88
Payout Ratio	81%	NM	77%	83%	78%	62%
Prices - High	58	59¼	47	49⅞	51½	51⅛
- Low	28¼	43¼	36⅞	38½	36¼	30⅜
P/E Ratio - High	22	NM	17	19	20	17
- Low	11	NM	13	15	14	10

Income Statement Analysis (Million $)

	1994	%Chg	1993	%Chg	1992	%Chg	1991
Revs.	9,235	NM	9,244	-7%	9,935	NM	9,895
Depr.	1,787	3%	1,736	-6%	1,854	NM	1,868
Maint.	NA	—	1,739	38%	1,264	-10%	1,407
Constr. Credits	NA	—	NA	—	31.0	3%	30.0
Eff. Tax Rate	37%	—	5.00%	—	35%	—	38%
Net Inc.	1,136	NM	191	-83%	1,142	13%	1,015

Balance Sheet & Other Fin. Data (Million $)

	1994	1993	1992	1991	1990	1989
Gross Prop.	26,565	26,607	27,221	26,036	26,531	25,475
Net Prop.	16,114	16,646	17,337	17,117	17,160	17,079
Cap. Exp.	1,684	1,800	2,381	2,207	2,059	1,896
Total Cap.	11,803	14,513	17,318	17,370	17,279	17,551
Fxd. Chgs. Cov.	4.9	1.3	4.5	3.8	3.6	4.7
Capitalization:						
LT Debt	4,897	5,129	5,299	5,504	5,611	5,325
Pfd.	Nil	Nil	127	117	93.0	66.0
Common	5,233	7,786	8,251	7,729	7,401	7,888

Ratio Analysis

	1994	1993	1992	1991	1990	1989
% Ret. on Revs.	12.3	2.1	11.5	10.3	10.6	12.9
% Ret. On Invest.Cap	12.1	4.5	9.8	9.5	9.9	10.3
% Return On Com.Eqty	17.5	2.4	14.2	13.2	13.7	15.4
% Earn. on Net Prop.	9.4	12.5	8.8	8.7	9.4	10.3
% LT Debt of Cap.	48.3	39.7	38.8	41.2	42.8	40.1
Capital. % Pfd.	Nil	Nil	0.9	0.9	0.7	0.5
Capital. % Common	51.7	60.3	60.3	57.9	56.5	59.4

Dividend Data

—Dividends were initiated in 1984. A dividend reinvestment plan is available.

Amt. of Div. $	Date Decl.	Ex-Div. Date	Stock of Record	Payment Date
0.545	Sep. 23	Sep. 29	Oct. 05	Nov. 01 '94
0.545	Dec. 16	Dec. 23	Dec. 30	Feb. 01 '95
0.545	Mar. 24	Apr. 05	Apr. 11	May. 01 '95
0.545	Jun. 23	Jul. 07	Jul. 11	Aug. 01 '95
0.545	Sep. 22	Oct. 05	Oct. 10	Nov. 01 '95

Office—130 Kearny St., San Francisco, CA 94018. **Tel**—(415) 394-3000. **Chrmn, Pres & CEO**—P. J. Quigley. **EVP & Secy**—R. W. Odgers. **EVP, Treas & CFO**—W. E. Downing. **Investor Contact**—Jeffrey A. Heyser. **Dirs**—W. P. Clark, H. E. Gallegos, D. E. Guinn, F. C. Herringer, I. J. Houston, M. S. Metz, L. E. Platt, P. J. Quigley, T. Rembe, S. D. Ritchey, R. M. Rosenberg. **Transfer Agent & Registrar**—Bank of Boston. **Incorporated** in Nevada in 1983. **Empl**-51,590. **S&P Analyst:** Kevin J. Gooley

STOCK REPORTS

PacifiCorp

NYSE Symbol **PPW**
In S&P 500

06-SEP-95

Industry:
Utilities-Electric

Summary: This major electric utility holding company also has interests in telecommunications and financial services. Electric operations serve customers in seven western states.

S&P Opinion: Hold (★★★)	Recent Price • 18¼	Yield • 5.9%
	52 Wk Range • 19⅞-15⅞	12-Mo. P/E • 12.2

Earnings vs. Previous Year
▲=Up ▼=Down ▶=No Change

Quantitative Evaluations

Outlook
(1 Lowest—5 Highest)
• **2⁻**

Fair Value
• **17½**

Risk
• **Low**

Earn./Div. Rank
• **B+**

Technical Eval.
• **Bullish** since 8/95

Rel. Strength Rank
(1 Lowest—99 Highest)
• **28**

Insider Activity
• **NA**

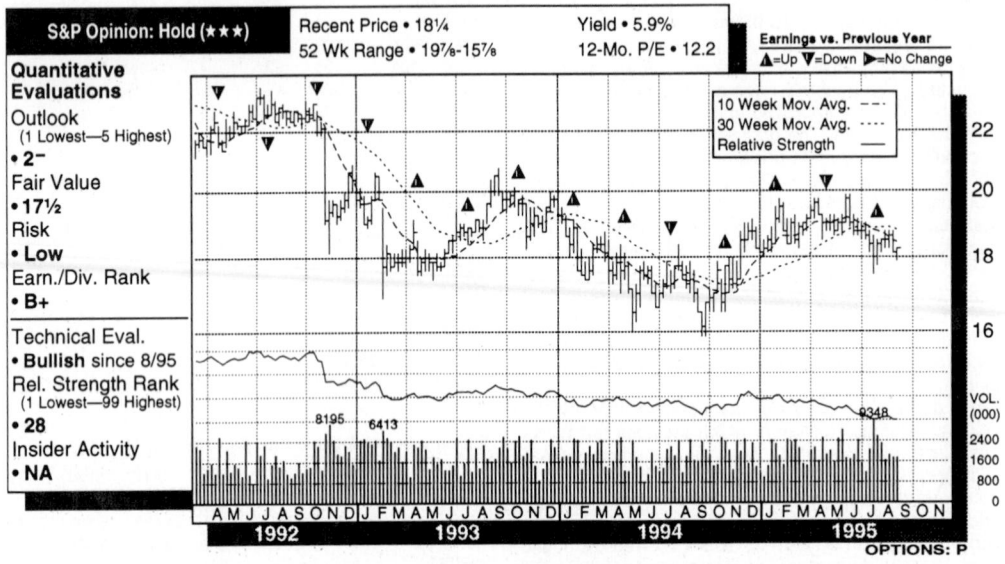

10 Week Mov. Avg. – – –
30 Week Mov. Avg. ·····
Relative Strength —

8195   6413   9348

VOL. (000)

OPTIONS: P

Overview - 31-AUG-95

Share earnings for 1995 should benefit from a continuation of modest growth in kwh sales combined with greater availability of low-cost hydro-power and natural gas. We expect other electric utility costs to be well controlled, but a slight increase in interest costs and the number of shares outstanding may restrain overall earnings growth. Earnings comparisons will also reflect a gain of about $0.13 a share from the sale of the Alascom unit, against a one-time gain totaling $0.06 in 1994. Assuming demand for power from municipal customers remains soft in 1996, earnings will be comparatively flat next year, despite an ongoing acquisition of rural telephone exchanges in western states.

Valuation - 06-SEP-95

PacifiCorp's shares are nearly unchanged from the 1994 year end level due to investors' expectations of only modest revenue and earnings growth in coming periods. However, this third lowest cost electricity producer in the U.S. is investing in new business ventures, including marketing electric power, developing and operating non-regulated generating facilities, and expanding its telecommunications base. Given weak earnings growth, a dividend increase is unlikely. Still, the shares are likely to hold their value in a market downturn.

Key Stock Statistics

S&P EPS Est. 1995	1.49	Tang. Bk. Value/Share	11.22
P/E on S&P Est. 1995	12.2	Beta	0.27
S&P EPS Est. 1996	1.53	Shareholders	14,900
Dividend Rate/Share	1.08	Market cap. (B)	$ 5.2
Shs. outstg. (M)	284.3	Inst. holdings	35%
Avg. daily vol. (M)	0.353	Insider holdings	NA

Value of $10,000 invested 5 years ago: $ 11,523

Fiscal Year Ending Dec. 31

	1995	% Change	1994	% Change	1993	% Change
Revenues (Million $)						
1Q	854.2	-1%	865.3	NM	862.0	11%
2Q	807.9	-3%	836.1	3%	809.2	5%
3Q	—	—	915.0	6%	861.7	5%
4Q	—	—	890.1	1%	879.2	1%
Yr.	—	—	3,507	3%	3,412	5%
Income (Million $)						
1Q	114.8	-5%	120.5	7%	112.5	NM
2Q	93.50	5%	89.30	-3%	91.90	39%
3Q	—	—	131.8	25%	105.2	8%
4Q	—	—	126.4	12%	113.1	NM
Yr.	—	—	468.0	11%	422.7	181%
Earnings Per Share ($)						
1Q	0.37	-5%	0.39	3%	0.38	NM
2Q	0.29	4%	0.28	-7%	0.30	36%
3Q	E0.41	-5%	0.43	23%	0.35	9%
4Q	E0.42	2%	0.41	11%	0.37	NM
Yr.	E1.49	-1%	1.51	8%	1.40	NM

Next earnings report expected: late October

Business Summary - 06-SEP-95

PacifiCorp (formerly Pacific Power & Light) owns electric and telephone utilities and engages in nonregulated ventures in telecommunications and finance. PPW acquired Utah Power & Light Co. in 1993 and also sold its 82% stake in NERCO Inc., a natural resources unit. Revenue and profits contributions from continuing operations in 1994 were:

	Revs.	Profits
Electric	76%	83%
Telecommunications	20%	17%
Other	4%	NM

Electric utility services are provided in Utah, Oregon, Wyoming, Washington, Idaho, California and Montana. Revenues by customer class in 1994 were: residential 27%, industrial 27%, commercial 22% and wholesale & other 24%. Energy sources in 1994 were 79% coal, 5% hydro, 14% purchased power and 2% other. Peak system load in 1994 was 7,174 mw, and capacity at peak was 8,903 mw, for a capacity margin of 19%.

Pacific Telecom, Inc. (87%-owned) provides long-distance telecommunication services in Alaska and local service in nine states. The unit is seeking to expand its local telephone operations through acquisitions.

PacifiCorp Financial Services, Inc., which PPW has been reducing in size since 1989, took aftertax writedowns of $115 million in 1992. PPW intends to continue reduction of the unit in an orderly manner.

Important Developments

Aug. '95—PPW closed the sale of Alascom, Inc. to AT&T for $291 million cash and a $75 million transition payment. Proceeds were used to repay short term debt from the acquisition of transmission lines in Colorado.

Aug. '95—PPW reported a 1% decrease in earnings in the six months ended June 30. The contribution from electric operations was 29% lower due to a $32 million settlement with the IRS. Also, a decline in prices and volumes due to competition in wholesale markets, lower industrial demand and mild weather penalized results. Lower costs for power partly offset the decline. Telecommunications earnings grew 11% due to newly acquired assets in Colorado, an upward revision of exchange revenues and growth in existing exchange and cellular business. Other businesses improved as well.

Mar. '95—PPW agreed to acquire the 13% minority interest in Pacific Telecom (5.3 million shares) it does not already own for $30 a share.

Capitalization

Long Term Debt: $3,855,000,000 (6/95).
Minority Interest: $110,000,000.
Red. Cum. Preferred Stock: $219,000,000.
Cum. Preferred Stock: $367,400,000.

Per Share Data ($)

(Year Ended Dec. 31)

	1994	1993	1992	1991	1990	1989
Tangible Bk. Val.	11.34	11.04	10.12	12.43	11.78	11.68
Earnings	1.51	1.40	0.42	1.86	1.85	1.81
Dividends	1.08	1.20	1.14	1.47	1.41	1.35
Payout Ratio	72%	85%	273%	80%	79%	75%
Prices - High	19½	20¾	25¼	25¼	23⅞	23⅛
- Low	15⅞	16⅞	18⅛	20⅜	17½	16⅝
P/E Ratio - High	13	15	60	14	13	13
- Low	11	12	43	11	9	9

Income Statement Analysis (Million $)

	1994	%Chg	1993	%Chg	1992	%Chg	1991
Revs.	3,507	3%	3,412	5%	3,242	-19%	4,007
Depr.	424	5%	405	-11%	453	-21%	576
Maint.	292	-2%	297	3%	288	-9%	315
Fxd. Chgs. Cov.	3.0	7%	2.8	57%	1.8	-40%	2.9
Constr. Credits	14.5	4%	13.9	-14%	16.2	-47%	30.6
Eff. Tax Rate	35%	—	31%	—	38%	—	29%
Net Inc.	468	11%	423	182%	150	-70%	507

Balance Sheet & Other Fin. Data (Million $)

	1994	1993	1992	1991	1990	1989
Gross Prop.	12,583	12,073	11,309	12,963	11,617	10,748
Cap. Exp.	789	742	694	912	763	606
Net Prop.	8,446	8,210	7,858	9,129	8,103	7,548
Capitalization:						
LT Debt	3,768	4,028	4,349	5,195	4,672	4,395
% LT Debt	48	51	55	55	55	56
Pfd.	694	691	722	742	628	526
% Pfd.	8.80	8.80	9.00	7.80	7.40	6.60
Common	3,460	3,263	2,908	3,512	3,208	3,007
% Common	44	41	37	37	38	38
Total Cap.	9,935	9,910	9,161	10,838	9,907	9,293

Ratio Analysis

	1994	1993	1992	1991	1990	1989
Oper. Ratio	79.0	78.7	81.1	74.7	73.8	74.1
% Earn. on Net Prop.	8.9	9.1	8.0	11.8	12.7	12.9
% Ret. on Revs.	13.3	12.4	4.6	12.7	12.5	12.5
% Ret. On Invest.Cap	7.5	7.7	5.7	9.4	9.7	10.4
% Return On Com.Eqty	12.8	12.4	3.5	14.1	14.3	15.0

Dividend Data —Dividends have been paid since 1950. The quarterly dividend was cut 30% to $0.27 a share in May 1993. A dividend reinvestment plan is available.

Amt. of Div. $	Date Decl.	Ex-Div. Date	Stock of Record	Payment Date
0.270	Aug. 10	Oct. 17	Oct. 21	Nov. 15 '94
0.270	Nov. 09	Jan. 17	Jan. 23	Feb. 15 '95
0.270	Feb. 08	Apr. 17	Apr. 21	May. 15 '95
0.270	May. 10	Jul. 19	Jul. 21	Aug. 15 '95
0.270	Aug. 09	Oct. 18	Oct. 20	Nov. 15 '95

Data as orig. reptd.; bef. results of disc opers. and/or spec. items. Per share data adj. for stk. divs. as of ex-div. date. E-Estimated. NA-Not Available. NM-Not Meaningful. NR-Not Ranked.

Office—700 N. E. Multnomah, Portland, OR 97232-4116. **Tel**—(503) 731-2000. **Chrmn**—K. R. McKennon. **Pres & CEO**—F. W. Buckman. **VP-Secy**—S. A. Nofziger. **SVP & CFO**—R. T. O'Brien. **Investor Contact**—Chris Hunter. **Dirs**—K. A. Braun, F. W. Buckman, C. T. Conover, R. C. Edgley, J. C. Hampton, N. E. Karras, K. R. McKennon, R. G. Miller, V. R. Topham, D. M. Wheeler, N. Wilgenbusch, P. I. Wold. **Transfer Agent & Registrar**—Company's office. **Incorporated** in Maine in 1910; reincorporated in Oregon in 1989. **Empl**-13,635. **S&P Analyst:** Jane Collin

Pall Corp.

NYSE Symbol **PLL**
In S&P 500

24-SEP-95 **Industry:** Machinery

Summary: Pall is the leading producer of fine disposable filters and other fluid clarification equipment for the healthcare, aeropower and fluid processing industries.

S&P Opinion: Accumulate (★★★★)

Recent Price • 20%	Yield • 2.0%
52 Wk Range • 24-15¾	12-Mo. P/E • 19.8

Quantitative Evaluations

Outlook
(1 Lowest—5 Highest)
• 5+

Fair Value
• 26¾

Risk
• Low

Earn./Div. Rank
• A

Technical Eval.
• **Bullish** since 7/95

Rel. Strength Rank
(1 Lowest—99 Highest)
• 12

Insider Activity
• NA

Earnings vs. Previous Year
▲=Up ▼=Down ▶=No Change

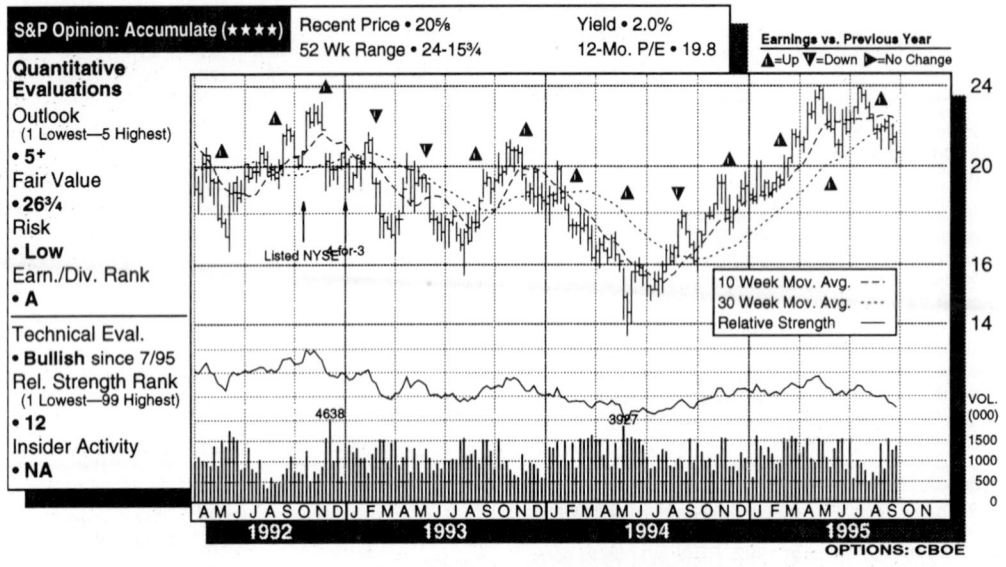

10 Week Mov. Avg. - - -
30 Week Mov. Avg. ......
Relative Strength —

OPTIONS: CBOE

Overview - 22-SEP-95

Sales should grow solidly in fiscal 1996, primarily from expanding domestic and international demand for fluid processing products. Aeropower and healthcare sales should rise moderately. Stronger gains could result from improvement in the German economy and expansion into Asia's growing markets (especially China). Margins should widen, as benefits of restructuring efforts are realized. In the long term, Pall sees stronger blood filter sales, including greater blood filter sales to blood banks; expansion in Asia for new fluid processing products; some growth in aeropower products (on increasing market share); and a move into the high-end filtration and separations markets, aided by the acquisition of Filtron Technology.

Valuation - 22-SEP-95

Pall's shares have been trending upward since the recent-year bottom in May 1994. Although we believe the share price will plateau near term, PLL's fundamentals are solid. The company should easily meet its stated goal of double-digit sales growth, reflecting increased backlogs, acquisitions, new products and continued expansion in Asia. Earnings should continue to grow, aided by a restructuring and capital expenditure program. After a recently completed $50 million stock repurchase program, along with yearly dividend increases, PLL should provide solid total return in the near and longer term.

Key Stock Statistics

S&P EPS Est. 1996	1.20	Tang. Bk. Value/Share	5.62
P/E on S&P Est. 1996	17.2	Beta	1.42
Dividend Rate/Share	0.42	Shareholders	4,400
Shs. outstg. (M)	114.4	Market cap. (B)	$ 2.4
Avg. daily vol. (M)	0.265	Inst. holdings	64%
		Insider holdings	NA

Value of $10,000 invested 5 years ago: $ 19,803

Fiscal Year Ending Jul. 31

	1995	% Change	1994	% Change	1993	% Change
Revenues (Million $)						
1Q	159.2	12%	141.9	-4%	148.0	7%
2Q	192.8	14%	169.7	2%	167.0	NM
3Q	217.3	22%	177.8	3%	173.0	-2%
4Q	253.5	20%	211.4	6%	198.9	-3%
Yr.	822.8	17%	700.8	2%	687.2	NM
Income (Million $)						
1Q	13.31	20%	11.07	NM	10.98	50%
2Q	26.48	20%	22.03	NM	3.26	-83%
3Q	33.51	20%	27.82	11%	25.00	-8%
4Q	45.92	21%	38.00	-3%	39.08	6%
Yr.	119.2	21%	98.92	26%	78.31	-13%
Earnings Per Share ($)						
1Q	0.12	20%	0.10	11%	0.09	50%
2Q	0.23	21%	0.19	NM	0.03	-82%
3Q	0.29	21%	0.24	9%	0.22	-4%
4Q	0.40	21%	0.33	-3%	0.34	6%
Yr.	1.04	21%	0.86	26%	0.68	-12%

Next earnings report expected: early December

Pall Corp.

24-SEP-95

Business Summary - 22-SEP-95

Pall Corporation makes fine filters and other fluid clarification devices for the removal of solid, liquid and gaseous contaminants from a variety of liquids and gases. Contributions in fiscal 1994 were:

	Sales	Profits
Healthcare	50%	65%
Aeropower	26%	20%
Fluid processing	24%	15%

Customers in the Western Hemisphere accounted for 43% of sales and 50% of operating profit in fiscal 1994, European customers for 40% and 42% and Pacific Rim customers for 17% and 8%.

Healthcare products include filters for direct use with hospital patients to protect against contamination in intravenous and other fluids, transfused blood and breathing gases; in diagnosis of human, animal and plant disease; for the production of drugs and biologicals; and for producing yeast- and bacteria-free water, beverages and food products. The company also makes electronic filter test instruments. In 1993, American Red Cross Blood Services named Pall as its exclusive supplier for high-efficiency leukocyte depletion filters.

Aeropower products include fuel filters, lubrication oil filters, hydraulic system filters and manifolds. Filters are sold to makers of military vehicles and equipment, naval vessels and aircraft-related equipment, as well as to producers and users of industrial machinery and mobile equipment.

Fluid processing involves the removal of contaminants from liquids and gases in process streams, the retention and recirculation of catalysts and the minimization of hazardous waste. Major markets served include microelectronics, magnetic, optical recording and transmission media, film, fiber, paint, chemicals, petrochemicals, gas and oil, and electric power. In 1992, Pall Advanced Separations Systems (PASS) was established as an operating divison in this segment; it has since expanded its activities into power generation and battery separators. In January 1995, PLL acquired Filtron, Inc., a maker of ultrafiltration membranes and cassettes.

Important Developments

Sep. '95—Commenting on fiscal 1995's fourth quarter, Pall said that 25% sales increases in both the Aeropower and Fluid Processing segments led PLL's strong revenue growth. PLL added that sales growth in Asia/Australia, Europe and the U.S. was 31%, 25% and 12%, respectively.

Capitalization

Long Term Debt: $68,814,000 (7/95).

Per Share Data ($)
(Year Ended Jul. 31)

	1995	1994	1993	1992	1991	1990
Tangible Bk. Val.	NA	4.71	4.42	4.51	3.98	3.67
Cash Flow	NA	1.20	0.98	1.07	0.96	0.80
Earnings	1.04	0.86	0.68	0.77	0.69	0.57
Dividends	0.50	0.36	0.31	0.26	0.21	0.18
Payout Ratio	48%	42%	46%	33%	31%	32%
Prices - High	24	20¼	21⅝	24⅛	21	12½
- Low	18⅜	13⅝	15⅝	16½	11¼	8¾
P/E Ratio - High	23	24	32	31	30	22
- Low	18	16	23	21	16	15

Income Statement Analysis (Million $)

	1994	%Chg	1993	%Chg	1992	%Chg	1991
Revs.	701	2%	687	NM	685	4%	657
Oper. Inc.	180	6%	170	NM	170	8%	157
Depr.	39.5	12%	35.2	2%	34.4	8%	31.9
Int. Exp.	8.8	-6%	9.4	-21%	11.9	-34%	18.1
Pretax Inc.	135	30%	104	-17%	126	9%	116
Eff. Tax Rate	27%	—	25%	—	29%	—	31%
Net Inc.	99	26%	78.3	-13%	90.2	13%	79.9

Balance Sheet & Other Fin. Data (Million $)

	1994	1993	1992	1991	1990	1989
Cash	89.0	107	101	59.0	81.0	129
Curr. Assets	470	470	483	385	415	433
Total Assets	960	902	913	774	786	707
Curr. Liab.	257	278	259	203	261	269
LT Debt	54.1	24.5	59.0	51.6	56.3	40.4
Common Eqty.	587	543	546	488	441	374
Total Cap.	673	596	640	561	516	432
Cap. Exp.	73.4	62.6	56.2	58.3	81.8	62.9
Cash Flow	138	114	125	112	93.0	82.0

Ratio Analysis

	1994	1993	1992	1991	1990	1989
Curr. Ratio	1.8	1.7	1.9	1.9	1.6	1.6
% LT Debt of Cap.	8.0	4.1	9.2	9.2	10.9	9.4
% Net Inc.of Revs.	14.1	11.4	13.2	13.2	11.7	11.6
% Ret. on Assets	10.7	8.6	10.7	10.2	8.9	8.9
% Ret. on Equity	17.6	14.4	17.5	17.1	16.2	16.3

Dividend Data

—With the exception of fiscal 1971 through fiscal 1973, cash has been paid since 1958. In 1989, a "poison pill" stock purchase rights plan was adopted. A dividend reinvestment plan is available.

Amt. of Div. $	Date Decl.	Ex-Div. Date	Stock of Record	Payment Date
0.093	Oct. 03	Oct. 07	Oct. 14	Oct. 28 '94
0.105	Jan. 09	Jan. 13	Jan. 20	Feb. 03 '95
0.105	Apr. 18	Apr. 24	Apr. 28	May. 12 '95
0.105	Jul. 14	Jul. 20	Jul. 24	Aug. 04 '95

Data as orig. reptd.; bef. results of disc. opers. and/or spec. items. Per share data adj. for stk. divs. as of ex-div. date. E-Estimated. NA-Not Available. NM-Not Meaningful. NR-Not Ranked.

Office—2200 Northern Blvd., East Hills, NY 11548. **Tel**—(516) 484-5400. **Fax**—(516) 484-3529. **Chrmn & CEO**—E. Krasnoff. **Pres, Treas & CFO**—J. Hayward-Surry. **Exec VP & COO**—D. T. D. Williams. **Secy**—P. Schwartzman. **Investor Contact**—Jan Phillipsborn. **Dirs**—A. B. Appel, U. Haynes Jr., J. Hayward-Surry, A. Krasnoff, E. Krasnoff, E. W. Martin Jr., D. B. Pall, C. F. Seibert, H. Shelley, A. B. Slifka, J. D. Watson, D. T. D. Williams. **Transfer Agent & Registrar**—Wachovia Bank of North Carolina, Winston-Salem. **Incorporated** in New York in 1946. **Empl**- 6,200. **S&P Analyst:** Robert E. Friedman

Panhandle Eastern

NYSE Symbol **PEL**
In S&P 500

24-SEP-95

Industry:
Utilities-Gas

Summary: This company owns and operates a major natural gas pipeline network serving the Midwest and Northeast, and is engaged in the marketing of natural gas and related energy services.

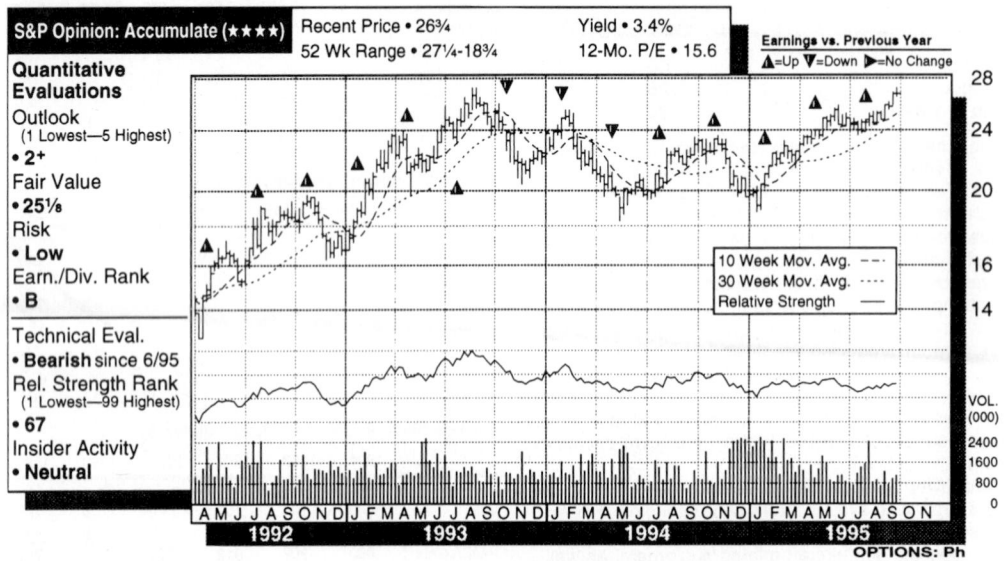

S&P Opinion: Accumulate (★★★★)

Recent Price • 26¾	Yield • 3.4%
52 Wk Range • 27¼-18¾	12-Mo. P/E • 15.6

Earnings vs. Previous Year
▲=Up ▼=Down ▶=No Change

Quantitative Evaluations

Outlook
(1 Lowest—5 Highest)
• **2+**

Fair Value
• **25⅛**

Risk
• **Low**

Earn./Div. Rank
• **B**

Technical Eval.
• **Bearish** since 6/95

Rel. Strength Rank
(1 Lowest—99 Highest)
• **67**

Insider Activity
• **Neutral**

10 Week Mov. Avg. ---
30 Week Mov. Avg. ·····
Relative Strength ——

VOL. (000)

OPTIONS: Ph

Overview - 22-SEP-95

Natural gas transmission earnings in 1995 should increase, aided by contributions from the completion of several new projects and tight controls on operating expenses. Results should be bolstered by significant growth in the market and supply service group, reflecting the December 1994 Associated Natural Gas merger, higher natural gas processing margins and volumes, partially offset by mild weather in 1995's first half. Relatively high margins at National Methanol Company should continue to contribute to the significant increase in equity earnings from unconsolidated affiliates. In the long term, pipeline earnings should grow as a result of capital projects, new services, penetration into new market areas, and the expansion of PEL's market and supply services activities.

Valuation - 22-SEP-95

PEL's shares fell significantly during 1994. However, the stock managed to finish the year with a partial rebound. The shares are up about 37% since the beginning of 1995, and are currently trading at about 12 to 13 times 1996 estimated earnings of $2.15 a share. The dividend was recently raised about 7.1%, and the shares are currently yielding about 3.0%. Based on PEL's near-term prospects, and despite the recent increase in stock price, PEL should continue to outperform the market over the next 6-12 months.

Key Stock Statistics

S&P EPS Est. 1995	1.90	Tang. Bk. Value/Share	11.99
P/E on S&P Est. 1995	14.1	Beta	1.18
S&P EPS Est. 1996	2.15	Shareholders	31,400
Dividend Rate/Share	0.90	Market cap. (B)	$ 4.0
Shs. outstg. (M)	149.7	Inst. holdings	66%
Avg. daily vol. (M)	0.205	Insider holdings	NA

Value of $10,000 invested 5 years ago: $ 12,119

Fiscal Year Ending Dec. 31

	1995	% Change	1994	% Change	1993	% Change
Revenues (Million $)						
1Q	1,232	7%	1,148	87%	612.6	-10%
2Q	1,283	12%	1,145	100%	573.8	18%
3Q	—	—	1,124	151%	447.5	-21%
4Q	—	—	1,168	140%	487.0	-30%
Yr.	—	—	4,585	116%	2,121	-13%
Income (Million $)						
1Q	84.10	30%	64.80	-7%	69.50	15%
2Q	67.50	20%	56.10	63%	34.40	197%
3Q	—	—	51.10	100%	25.60	-64%
4Q	—	—	53.20	186%	18.60	-58%
Yr.	—	—	225.2	52%	148.1	-21%
Earnings Per Share ($)						
1Q	0.56	27%	0.44	-31%	0.64	14%
2Q	0.45	18%	0.38	23%	0.31	182%
3Q	E0.39	15%	0.34	62%	0.21	-68%
4Q	E0.50	39%	0.36	125%	0.16	-61%
Yr.	E1.90	26%	1.51	17%	1.29	-26%

Next earnings report expected: mid October

Panhandle Eastern

Business Summary - 22-SEP-95

Panhandle Eastern Corporation is a holding company engaged primarily in the interstate transportation and storage of natural gas and in the gathering, processing, marketing and intrastate transportation of natural gas, natural gas liquids (NGLs) and crude oil.

PEL's natural gas transmission group consists of four interstate pipeline subsidiaries: Panhandle Eastern Pipe Line Co., Trunkline Gas Co., Texas Eastern Transmission Corp. and Algonquin Gas Transmission Co. Through these subsidiaries, the company owns and operates a 26,000-mile pipeline network that delivers gas from most major producing regions of North America to customers throughout the midwestern, mid-Atlantic and New England states.Operating profit contributions (in millions) by subsidiary were:

	1994	1993	1992
Texas Eastern	$264.8	$182.0	$277.8
Algonquin Gas	65.9	56.0	47.9
Panhandle Eastern	145.6	119.8	101.3
Trunkline Gas	47.7	53.3	49.7

Services relating to the gathering, processing, marketing and intrastate transportation of natural gas, natural gas liquids (NGLs) and crude oil are provided by PEL's market and supply services group. This group operates primarily through Associated Natural Gas Corp., which was merged with PEL in December 1994, Centana Energy Corp. and their subsidiaries.

Through its subsidiaries, PEL owns interests in a partnership operating a cogeneration facility and in a joint venture that owns and operates a chemical-grade methanol plant. Other activities include the regasification and sale of imported liquefied natural gas, nonregulated marketing of natural gas in the national market, an investment in cogeneration operations and interests in TEPPCO Partners, L.P., which transports liquid petroleum products, and National Methanol Co. 1Source Corp. provides comprehensive information products and services for the energy industry.

Important Developments

Sep. '95—Associated Natural Gas Corp. (ANGC) agreed to purchase Continental Energy Marketing Ltd., a Calgary, Alberta-based natural gas marketing company. Terms were not disclosed.

Aug. '95—ANGC signed a letter of intent to purchase substantially all of Snyder Oil Corp.'s remaining Wattenberg gas system in Weld County, Colorado, for $63.5 million. The transaction is expected to close in October 1995. Separately, ANGC's affiliate, Centana Gathering Co., purchased the Wharton Gas Plant and Gathering System in Wharton County, Texas, from Warrior Gas Co., Comstock Natural Gas, Inc., and SND Energy Co., Inc., for an undisclosed sum.

Capitalization

Long Term Debt: $2,373,700,000 (6/95).

Per Share Data ($)   (Year Ended Dec. 31)

	1994	1993	1992	1991	1990	1989
Tangible Bk. Val.	11.35	9.54	8.31	7.21	6.27	16.21
Cash Flow	3.24	3.26	3.68	3.14	-0.09	3.84
Earnings	1.51	1.29	1.74	0.86	-2.63	0.97
Dividends	0.84	0.80	0.80	0.80	1.40	2.00
Payout Ratio	56%	62%	46%	102%	NM	251%
Prices - High	25½	27¼	19¾	16½	29¾	30¾
- Low	18¼	16¾	12⅞	9⅞	10⅜	20½
P/E Ratio - High	17	21	11	19	NM	32
- Low	12	13	7	11	NM	21

Income Statement Analysis (Million $)

	1994	%Chg	1993	%Chg	1992	%Chg	1991
Revs.	4,585	116%	2,121	-9%	2,342	-5%	2,454
Oper. Inc.	858	12%	767	1%	757	11%	680
Depr.	257	13%	227	9%	209	-7%	225
Int. Exp.	250	-8%	273	-11%	307	-8%	333
Pretax Inc.	387	54%	251	-26%	340	95%	174
Eff. Tax Rate	42%	—	41%	—	45%	—	51%
Net Inc.	225	52%	148	-22%	189	122%	85.0

Balance Sheet & Other Fin. Data (Million $)

	1994	1993	1992	1991	1990	1989
Cash	33.0	18.0	3.0	11.0	48.0	237
Curr. Assets	811	524	792	814	939	1,160
Total Assets	7,508	6,731	6,399	6,177	6,069	6,266
Curr. Liab.	946	847	1,035	1,278	1,323	1,679
LT Debt	2,364	1,923	2,506	2,267	2,484	2,754
Common Eqty.	2,035	1,666	1,439	1,333	1,138	1,415
Total Cap.	5,583	4,765	4,589	4,162	4,168	4,282
Cap. Exp.	555	299	263	230	400	311
Cash Flow	482	375	398	310	-8.0	276

Ratio Analysis

	1994	1993	1992	1991	1990	1989
Curr. Ratio	0.9	0.6	0.8	0.6	0.7	0.7
% LT Debt of Cap.	42.3	40.3	54.6	54.5	59.6	64.3
% Net Inc.of Revs.	4.9	7.0	8.1	3.5	NM	2.5
% Ret. on Assets	2.8	2.1	3.0	1.2	NM	1.3
% Ret. on Equity	11.0	9.3	13.6	6.3	NM	5.3

Dividend Data —Dividends have been paid since 1937. A dividend reinvestment plan is available. A "poison pill" stock purchase right was adopted in 1986.

Amt. of Div. $	Date Decl.	Ex-Div. Date	Stock of Record	Payment Date
0.210	Oct. 26	Nov. 04	Nov. 11	Dec. 15 '94
0.210	Jan. 25	Feb. 09	Feb. 15	Mar. 15 '95
0.225	Apr. 26	May. 09	May. 15	Jun. 15 '95
0.225	Jul. 26	Aug. 10	Aug. 14	Sep. 15 '95

Data as orig. reptd.; bef. results of disc. opers. and/or spec. items. Per share data adj. for stk. divs. as of ex-div. date. E-Estimated. NA-Not Available. NM-Not Meaningful. NR-Not Ranked.

Office—5400 Westheimer Court, P.O. Box 1642, Houston, TX 77251-1642. **Tel**—(713) 627-5400. **Chrmn**—D. R. Hendrix. **Vice Chrmn**—G. L. Mazanec. **Pres & CEO**—P. M. Anderson. **Sr VP & CFO**—J. B. Hipple. **VP & Secy**—R. W. Reed. **Treas**—B. A. Williamson. **Investor Contact**—Gregg E. McBride (713) 627-4600. **Dirs**—P. M. Anderson, M. Carroll, R. Cizik, C. W. Duncan Jr., H. E. Ekblom, W. T. Esrey, A. M. Gray, D. R. Hendrix, H. S. Hook, L. E. Linbeck Jr., G. L. Mazanec, R. S. O'Connor. **Transfer Agent & Registrar**—Continental Stock Transfer & Trust Co., NYC. **Incorporated** in Delaware in 1929; reincorporated in Delaware in 1981. **Empl**- 5,500. **S&P Analyst**: Ronald J. Gross

Parker Hannifin

NYSE Symbol **PH**
In S&P 500

23-OCT-95

Industry:
Machinery

Summary: Parker Hannifin is a worldwide supplier of components for fluid power systems to a wide range of industrial and aerospace markets.

S&P Opinion: Accumulate (★★★★)	Recent Price • 34	Yield • 2.1%
	52 Wk Range • 41½-27⅝	12-Mo. P/E • 10.8

Quantitative Evaluations

Outlook
(1 Lowest—5 Highest)
• **3+**

Fair Value
• **32⅛**

Risk
• **Low**

Earn./Div. Rank
• **B+**

Technical Eval.
• **Bearish** since 8/95

Rel. Strength Rank
(1 Lowest—99 Highest)
• **17**

Insider Activity
• **NA**

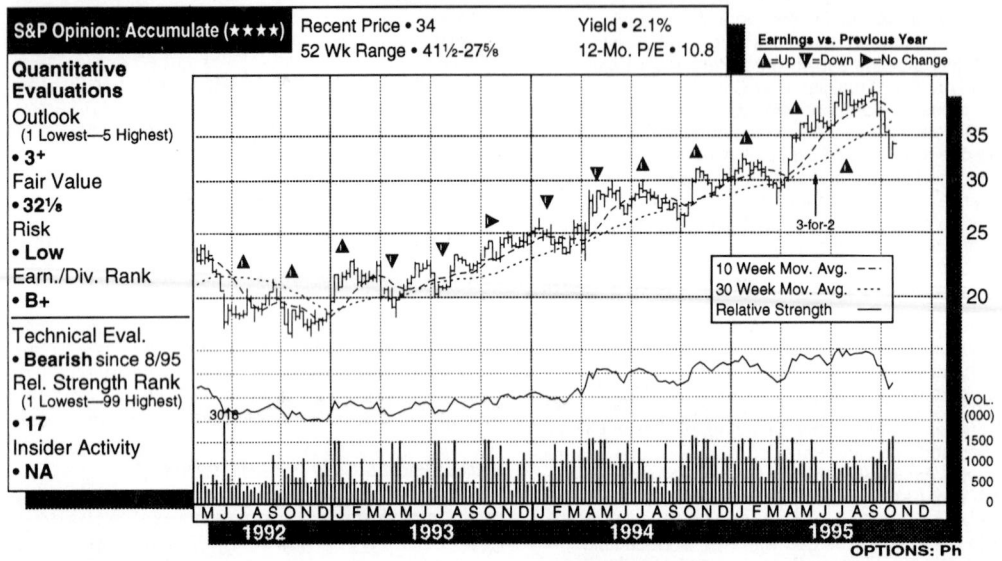

Earnings vs. Previous Year
▲=Up ▼=Down ▶=No Change

10 Week Mov. Avg. ---
30 Week Mov. Avg. ....
Relative Strength —

3-for-2

1992 1993 1994 1995

VOL. (000)

OPTIONS: Ph

Overview - 23-OCT-95

We anticipate a 15% revenue gain for fiscal 1996, versus fiscal 1995's 25% rate of growth, reflecting a plateauing in the North American industrial unit and less rapid economic growth in Europe. The rate of growth in the aerospace segment should improve from the fiscal 1995 level. Sales gains will also reflect acquisitions. Continued high operating rates, greater parts sales in aerospace, and flat raw material costs should lead to widening margins and higher operating income. Assuming only a small increase in interest costs and a level tax rate, earnings should rise again in fiscal 1996. Acquisitions, introduction of new products, gains in market share, and a cyclical upturn in the aerospace business should lead to increased long-term sales and profits.

Valuation - 23-OCT-95

After a sharp decline beginning in late September, the shares rebounded only 13% through late October. The stock had risen 38% through mid-September, but announcements by cyclical companies such as Caterpillar that third quarter earnings comparisions would be unfavorable, together with softness in PH's September orders, put great pressure on the stock price. Nevertheless, we are maintaining our accumulate rating. We believe that the weaker order pattern is temporary, and are confident that the company can still earn $3.30 a share for fiscal 1996. At current levels, the stock offers good value; the market overreaction provides an opportunity to buy the shares at an attractive price.

Key Stock Statistics

S&P EPS Est. 1996	3.30	Tang. Bk. Value/Share	14.62
P/E on S&P Est. 1996	10.3	Beta	1.02
Dividend Rate/Share	0.72	Shareholders	35,600
Shs. outstg. (M)	74.0	Market cap. (B)	$ 2.5
Avg. daily vol. (M)	0.321	Inst. holdings	74%
		Insider holdings	NA

Value of $10,000 invested 5 years ago: $ 23,730

Fiscal Year Ending Jun. 30

	1996	% Change	1995	% Change	1994	% Change
Revenues (Million $)						
1Q	839.0	18%	712.5	17%	607.4	NM
2Q	—	—	738.2	25%	592.2	NM
3Q	—	—	879.7	30%	677.3	12%
4Q	—	—	884.0	26%	699.3	2%
Yr.	—	—	3,214	25%	2,576	3%
Income (Million $)						
1Q	57.38	31%	43.65	172%	16.07	—
2Q	—	—	41.08	192%	14.06	-4%
3Q	—	—	65.86	NM	-19.08	NM
4Q	—	—	67.65	66%	40.82	110%
Yr.	—	—	218.2	NM	52.18	-20%
Earnings Per Share ($)						
1Q	0.77	31%	0.59	168%	0.22	NM
2Q	E0.72	29%	0.56	190%	0.19	-3%
3Q	E0.89	NM	0.89	NM	-0.26	NM
4Q	E0.92	NM	0.92	64%	0.56	110%
Yr.	E3.30	11%	2.96	NM	0.71	-20%

Next earnings report expected: mid January

Business Summary - 23-OCT-95

Parker Hannifin makes motion control products, including fluid power systems, electromechanical controls and related components. Products are sold through direct sales employees and more than 6,000 distributors. Contributions in fiscal 1995 were:

	Sales	Profits
Industrial	83%	85%
Aviation/Space/Marine	17%	15%

Repair and replacement components account for about half of total sales. Operations outside of North America accounted for 27% of sales and 20% of operating profit in fiscal 1995.

The product lines of the industrial unit cover most of the components of motion control systems. The Motion and Control Group makes hydraulic and precision metering pumps, power units, control valves, accumulators, cylinders, actuators and hydrostatic steering components. The Filtration Group makes filters to remove contaminants from fuel, air, oil water and other fluids in industrial, process and other applications. The Fluid Connectors Group makes connectors, tube and hose fittings, hoses and couplers that transmit fluid. The Seal Group makes sealing devices, gaskets and packing that ensure leak-proof connections. The Automotive and Refrigeration Group makes components for use in industrial and automotive air conditioning and refrigeration systems, including pressure regulators, solenoid valves, expansion valves, filter-dryers and hose assemblies.

The principal products of the aerospace segment are hydraulic, pneumatic and fuel systems and components that are utilized on virtually every domestic commercial, military and general aviation aircraft.

Backlog at June 30, 1995 was approximately $1.0 billion, verus $852.5 million a year earlier. About 79% of the backlog was scheduled for delivery in the next twelve months.

Important Developments

Oct. '95—PH reported fiscal 1996 first quarter EPS of $0.77, on an 18% sales increase, versus $0.59 in the fiscal 1995 period. Nearly half of the sales gain resulted from acquisitions in the previous 12 months. The company said sales benefited from its diverse product lines and breath of global markets. It noted that North American industrial product demand had begun to ease, as anticipated. PH added that although some customers had adjusted delivery schedules, business volume was strong enough to enable it to operate within more sustainable production schedules. Backlog at the end of the quarter stood at $1.0 billion, up from $869.9 million a year earlier.

Capitalization

Long Term Debt: $236,784,000 (9/95).

Per Share Data ($)

(Year Ended Jun. 30)

	1995	1994	1993	1992	1991	1990
Tangible Bk. Val.	14.69	12.46	14.00	11.98	12.15	11.89
Cash Flow	4.11	2.26	2.39	2.29	2.18	2.77
Earnings	2.96	0.71	0.89	0.88	0.82	1.51
Dividends	1.02	0.65	0.64	0.62	0.61	0.59
Payout Ratio	34%	92%	72%	71%	75%	39%
Prices - High	41	30⅛	25⅜	24⅛	20⅝	21⅞
- Low	27⅝	22⅝	18⅝	17⅜	15⅛	12⅜
P/E Ratio - High	14	42	28	27	25	14
- Low	9	32	19	20	18	8

Income Statement Analysis (Million $)

	1995	%Chg	1994	%Chg	1993	%Chg	1992
Revs.	3,214	25%	2,576	3%	2,489	5%	2,376
Oper. Inc.	502	51%	333	18%	283	5%	270
Depr.	120	6%	113	3%	110	7%	103
Int. Exp.	31.0	-18%	37.8	-20%	47.1	-10%	52.2
Pretax Inc.	348	NM	112	4%	108	3%	105
Eff. Tax Rate	37%	—	54%	—	40%	—	40%
Net Inc.	218	NM	52.2	-20%	65.0	3%	63.0

Balance Sheet & Other Fin. Data (Million $)

	1995	1994	1993	1992	1991	1990
Cash	63.9	81.6	160	100	39.0	22.0
Curr. Assets	1,246	1,018	1,056	1,056	1,019	1,129
Total Assets	2,302	1,913	1,964	1,921	1,890	1,996
Curr. Liab.	653	504	468	359	358	438
LT Debt	237	257	378	447	477	512
Common Eqty.	1,192	966	933	934	943	938
Total Cap.	1,453	1,232	1,329	1,402	1,469	1,504
Cap. Exp.	152	100	91.0	85.0	112	126
Cash Flow	127	165	175	166	158	203

Ratio Analysis

	1995	1994	1993	1992	1991	1990
Curr. Ratio	1.9	2.0	2.3	2.9	2.8	2.6
% LT Debt of Cap.	16.3	20.9	28.5	31.9	32.4	34.0
% Net Inc.of Revs.	6.8	2.0	2.6	2.7	2.4	4.5
% Ret. on Assets	10.3	2.7	3.3	3.3	3.1	5.6
% Ret. on Equity	20.2	5.0	7.0	6.7	6.3	12.4

Dividend Data
—Dividends have been paid since 1949. A poison pill stock purchase rights plan was adopted in 1987.

Amt. of Div. $	Date Decl.	Ex-Div. Date	Stock of Record	Payment Date
0.250	Oct. 26	Nov. 14	Nov. 18	Dec. 02 '94
0.250	Feb. 02	Feb. 17	Feb. 24	Mar. 03 '95
0.270	Apr. 13	May. 12	May. 18	Jun. 02 '95
3-for-2	Apr. 13	Jun. 02	May. 18	Jun. 01 '95
0.180	Jul. 13	Aug. 22	Aug. 24	Sep. 01 '95

Data as orig. reptd.; bef. results of disc. opers. and/or spec. items. Per share data adj. for stk. divs. as of ex-div. date. E-Estimated. NA-Not Available. NM-Not Meaningful. NR-Not Ranked.

Office—17325 Euclid Ave, Cleveland, OH 44112. Tel—(216) 531-3000. Chrmn—P. S. Parker. Pres & CEO—D. E. Collins. VP-Fin—M. J. Hiemstra. VP & Secy—J. D. Whiteman. Treas & Investor Contact—Timothy K. Pistell. Dirs—J. G. Breen, D. E. Collins, P, C. Ely, Jr., A. H. Ford, K. M. Hudson, F. A. LePage, P. W. Likins, P. S. Parker, A. L. Rayfield, P. G. Schloemer, W. R. Schmitt, W. Seipp, D. W. Sullivan. Transfer Agent & Registrar—Society National Bank, Cleveland. Incorporated in Ohio in 1938. Empl-30,590. S&P Analyst: Leo Larkin

Penney (J.C.)

NYSE Symbol **JCP**
In S&P 500

24-SEP-95

Industry:
Retail Stores

Summary: J.C. Penney is one of the largest U.S. retailers through its department stores and catalog operations. Penney also operates a chain of drug stores.

S&P Opinion: Hold (★★★)	Recent Price • 48⅞	Yield • 3.9%
	52 Wk Range • 52⅞-39⅞	12-Mo. P/E • 12.3

Quantitative Evaluations

Outlook
(1 Lowest—5 Highest)
• **3⁻**

Fair Value
• **48½**

Risk
• **Low**

Earn./Div. Rank
• **A-**

Technical Eval.
• **Bullish** since 5/95

Rel. Strength Rank
(1 Lowest—99 Highest)
• **56**

Insider Activity
• **NA**

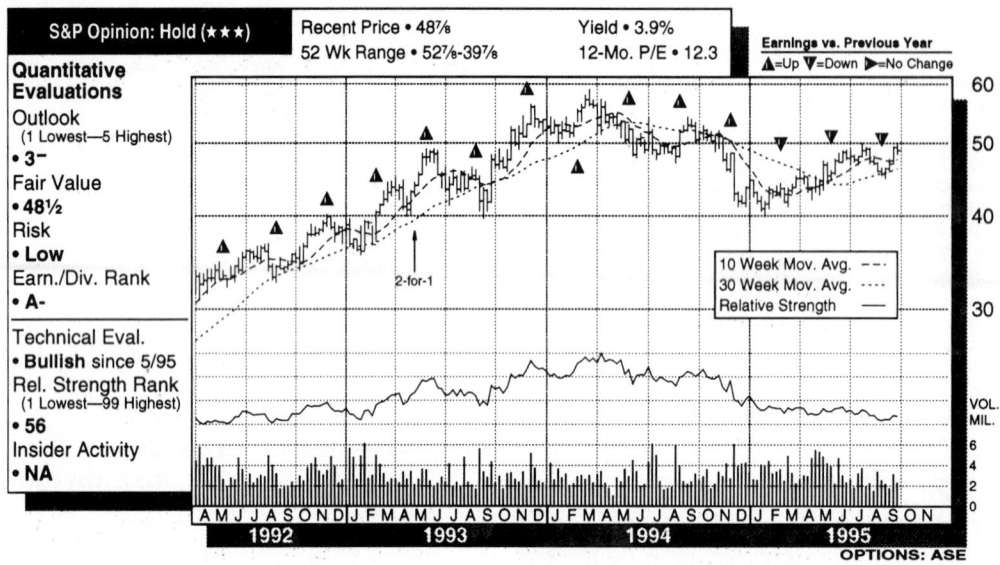

Earnings vs. Previous Year
▲=Up ▼=Down ▶=No Change

10 Week Mov. Avg. ---
30 Week Mov. Avg. ····
Relative Strength —

2-for-1

1992 1993 1994 1995

OPTIONS: ASE

Overview - 28-AUG-95

Sales for 1995-96 should show modest increases in comparable-store sales of some 2%, mostly in the second half. Gross margins should narrow, reflecting continued competitive pricing and only a modest increase in volume. SG&A expenses, although well controlled, could increase over 3%, about the same percentage of sales as a year earlier. Operating income could decline by some 4% to 5%. Interest expense will continue to increase as the company uses debt financing to fund its second 10 million share stock repurchase plan. The company's strong cash flow will be used for its $600 million annual capital expenditure program over the next three years. Earnings could resume an uptrend in 1996-7 with stronger sales gains.

Valuation - 31-AUG-95

The share price has moved up from the lows of earlier this year on expectations of improved sales in the second half. But competitive pricing and only modest sales gains will keep a lid on earnings. We do not anticipate earnings to resume growth until 1996-97 as sales pick up and new stores come on stream. As a result, we expect the shares to track the market in the near term. However, with the company's strong cash flow, healthy dividend yield and 10 million share buyback program, the downside risk is limited.

Key Stock Statistics

S&P EPS Est. 1996	4.05	Tang. Bk. Value/Share	22.31
P/E on S&P Est. 1996	12.1	Beta	0.96
S&P EPS Est. 1997	4.50	Shareholders	53,000
Dividend Rate/Share	1.92	Market cap. (B)	$ 11.0
Shs. outstg. (M)	225.8	Inst. holdings	73%
Avg. daily vol. (M)	0.485	Insider holdings	NA

Value of $10,000 invested 5 years ago: $ 17,041

Fiscal Year Ending Jan. 31

	1996	% Change	1995	% Change	1994	% Change
Revenues (Million $)						
1Q	4,367	NM	4,350	10%	3,964	5%
2Q	4,435	5%	4,242	7%	3,963	5%
3Q	—	—	5,149	9%	4,735	9%
4Q	—	—	6,639	5%	6,321	4%
Yr.	—	—	20,380	7%	18,983	5%
Income (Million $)						
1Q	156.0	-30%	223.0	30%	172.0	26%
2Q	116.0	-12%	132.0	18%	112.0	40%
3Q	—	—	274.0	24%	221.0	19%
4Q	—	—	428.0	-3%	439.0	17%
Yr.	—	—	1,057	12%	944.0	21%
Earnings Per Share ($)						
1Q	0.63	-28%	0.88	29%	0.68	26%
2Q	0.46	-12%	0.52	18%	0.43	41%
3Q	E1.06	-5%	1.11	26%	0.88	17%
4Q	E1.90	7%	1.78	-1%	1.80	16%
Yr.	E4.05	-6%	4.29	13%	3.79	20%

Next earnings report expected: mid November

Penney (J.C.)

Business Summary - 08-SEP-95

J.C. Penney operates 1,233 department stores in 50 states and Puerto Rico that include catalog departments. The company also operates 552 freestanding sales centers and 526 drug stores.

At January 28, 1995, the company was operating 1,233 J.C. Penney stores with sales per square foot in 1994-5 of $159, up from $146 in 1993-4. These stores are primarily in premier regional shopping centers in the suburbs. The company was also operating 552 freestanding sales centers and merchants. Catalog sales totaled $3.8 billion in 1994-5, and accounted for 19% of total retail sales.

The company has created a merchandise development organization to build private label brands into a coordinated merchandising collection to compete with national brands. The strategy focuses on developing well-priced, fashionable, coordinated apparel and home lines. Private label names include, Worthington brand for career women, Original Arizona Jean Company, Stafford Executive suits and Classic Traditions, a home furnishings collection.

Drug stores, operating under the Thrift Drug Center names, totaled 526 stores at 1994-5 year end. Sales per gross square foot averaged $243. These units accounted for 7.6% of total retail sales in 1994-5.

J.C. Penney Life Insurance Co. markets life, health and credit insurance through direct response. At the end of 1994-5, there were 7.5 million policies and certificates in force. J.C. Penney National Bank offers Visa and MasterCard credit cards; about 497,000 credit cards were active at the end of 1994-5.

Important Developments

Aug. '95—J.C. Penney received approval from the U.S. Bankruptcy Court to acquire seven Woodward & Lothrop stores in a joint bid with May Department Stores for a total of 24 stores from the bankrupt retailer for about $589 million. JCP said it planned to keep a tight rein on expenses in the second half of the year. Inventories are in line with expectations due to accelerated promotional activity in the second quarter, up 2.8% from a year earlier. Management also said that sales of fall merchandise, particularly apparel, have been encouraging. Gross margins in the second quarter decreased, reflecting summer clearance of store and catalog merchandise. SG&A expenses declined as a percentage of sales. The company has purchased 5.3 million common shares year-to-date as part of a ten million share repurchase program.

Capitalization

Long Term Debt: $3,167,000,000 (4/29/95).
ESOP 7.9% Preferred Stock: $630,000,000. Conv. into 11.8 million com. shs.

Per Share Data ($)

(Year Ended Jan. 31)

	1995	1994	1993	1992	1991	1990
Tangible Bk. Val.	23.27	21.59	20.04	15.02	15.86	15.16
Cash Flow	5.65	5.10	4.46	2.33	3.56	4.28
Earnings	4.29	3.79	3.15	0.99	2.29	3.16
Dividends	1.68	1.80	1.32	1.32	1.32	1.12
Payout Ratio	38%	47%	42%	134%	58%	35%
Cal. Yrs.	1994	1993	1992	1991	1990	1989
Prices - High	59	40¼	40¼	29⅛	37⅞	36⅝
- Low	41	25⅜	25⅜	21¼	18¾	25¼
P/E Ratio - High	14	63	13	30	16	12
- Low	10	8	8	22	8	8

Income Statement Analysis (Million $)

	1995	%Chg	1994	%Chg	1993	%Chg	1992
Revs.	21,706	11%	19,578	3%	19,085	10%	17,295
Oper. Inc.	2,292	18%	1,943	6%	1,825	23%	1,485
Depr.	323	2%	316	3%	308	-2%	314
Int. Exp.	320	11%	289	-11%	324	NM	327
Pretax Inc.	1,699	9%	1,554	23%	1,259	169%	468
Eff. Tax Rate	38%	—	39%	—	38%	—	44%
Net Inc.	1,057	12%	944	21%	777	194%	264

Balance Sheet & Other Fin. Data (Million $)

	1995	1994	1993	1992	1991	1990
Cash	261	173	397	111	137	408
Curr. Assets	9,468	8,565	6,970	6,695	6,799	7,539
Total Assets	16,202	14,788	13,563	12,520	12,325	12,698
Curr. Liab.	4,481	3,883	3,077	2,409	2,662	3,400
LT Debt	3,335	2,929	3,171	3,354	3,135	2,755
Common Eqty.	5,292	5,096	4,486	3,504	3,697	3,649
Total Cap.	9,989	9,307	8,707	8,335	8,550	8,232
Cap. Exp.	550	480	453	515	637	519
Cash Flow	1,340	1,220	1,052	544	842	1,042

Ratio Analysis

	1995	1994	1993	1992	1991	1990
Curr. Ratio	2.1	2.2	2.3	2.8	2.6	2.2
% LT Debt of Cap.	33.4	31.5	36.4	40.2	36.7	33.5
% Net Inc.of Revs.	4.9	4.8	4.1	1.5	3.3	4.7
% Ret. on Assets	6.9	6.6	5.9	2.1	4.7	6.5
% Ret. on Equity	19.9	18.8	17.5	6.4	15.0	22.4

Dividend Data —Dividends have been paid since 1922. A dividend reinvestment plan is available. A new "poison pill" stock purchase rights plan was adopted in 1990.

Amt. of Div. $	Date Decl.	Ex-Div. Date	Stock of Record	Payment Date
0.420	Sep. 14	Oct. 03	Oct. 10	Nov. 01 '94
0.420	Nov. 09	Jan. 04	Jan. 10	Feb. 01 '95
0.480	Mar. 08	Apr. 04	Apr. 10	May. 01 '95
0.480	May. 22	Jul. 06	Jul. 10	Aug. 01 '95
0.480	Sep. 13	Oct. 05	Oct. 10	Nov. 01 '95

Data as orig. reptd.; bef. results of disc. opers. and/or spec. items. Per share data adj. for stk. divs. as of ex-div. date. E-Estimated. NA-Not Available. NM-Not Meaningful. NR-Not Ranked.

Office—6501 Legacy Dr., Plano, TX 75024-3698. **Tel**—(214) 431-1000. **Chrmn**—W. R. Howell. **Vice Chrmn & CEO**—J. E. Oesterreicher. **Pres & COO**—W. B. Tygart. **EVP-CFO**—R. E. Northam. **Investor Contact**—Wynn C. Watkins. **Dirs**—M. A. Burns, C. H. Chandler, W. R. Howell, V. E. Jordan Jr., G. Nigh, J. E. Oesterreicher. J. C. Pfeiffer, A. W. Richards, C. S. Sanford, W. B. Tygart, J. D. Williams. **Registrar & Transfer Agent**—Chemical Bank, NYC. **Incorporated** in Delaware in 1924. **Empl**- 202,000. **S&P Analyst:** Karen J. Sack, CFA

Pennzoil Co.

NYSE Symbol **PZL**
In S&P 500

31-OCT-95

Industry:
Oil and Gas

Summary: This company, the leading U.S. marketer of lubricants, also engages in crude oil and natural gas development and owns the Jiffy Lube auto service business.

S&P Opinion: Avoid (★★)	Recent Price • 36⅝	Yield • 2.7%
	52 Wk Range • 52⅞-34⅝	12-Mo. P/E • NM

Earnings vs. Previous Year
▲=Up ▼=Down ▶=No Change

Quantitative Evaluations

Outlook
(1 Lowest—5 Highest)
• **1**⁻

Fair Value
• **24⅝**

Risk
• **Low**

Earn./Div. Rank
• **B-**

Technical Eval.
• **Bullish** since 7/95

Rel. Strength Rank
(1 Lowest—99 Highest)
• **11**

Insider Activity
• **Neutral**

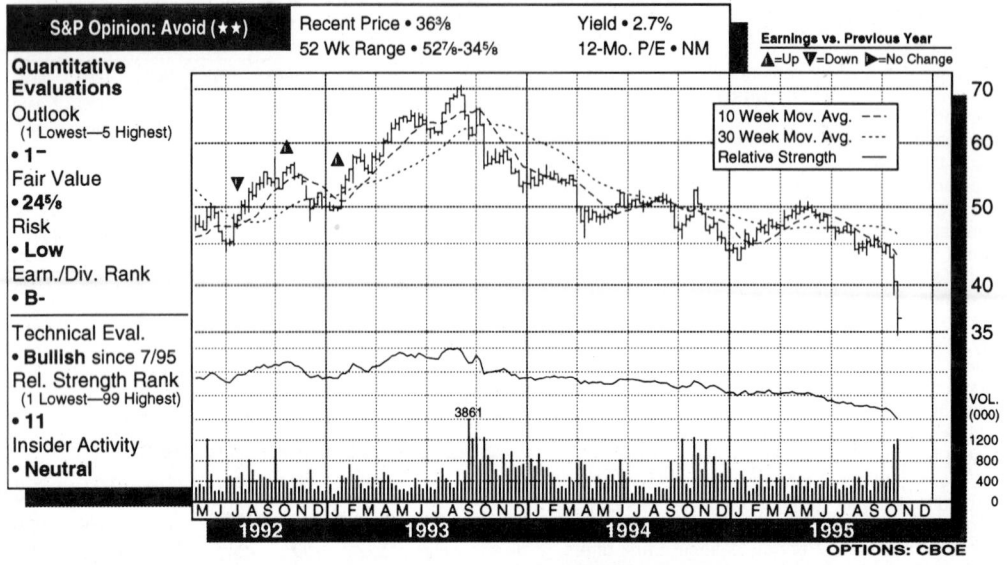

10 Week Mov. Avg. - - -
30 Week Mov. Avg. · · · ·
Relative Strength —

3861

VOL.
(000)

OPTIONS: CBOE

Overview - 31-OCT-95

Pennzoil hopes to revive earnings by cutting the dividend and undertaking cost reduction programs on a company-wide basis. Oil and natural gas sales volumes should increase, and we project modest improvement in average natural gas prices through 1996, as well as stable oil prices through 1996, barring any surprise from the November OPEC meeting. Operating profits in 1995 have been hurt by low domestic natural gas prices, offsetting Jiffy Lube's increasing contributions. Anticipated restructuring moves and asset write-downs may have a positive impact on future cash flow and earnings, allowing the company to boost exploration activities, and Caspian Sea exploration may provide considerable upside. However, competitive markets and slow growth in demand should restrain profits at the lubricants unit.

Valuation - 31-OCT-95

Following the 67% reduction in the dividend, the shares fell sharply, after trending lower over the past several months, mainly as a result of fears that OPEC might boost its production quota and that lower natural gas prices were on the horizon. Recent increases in demand for natural gas in the U.S. have been largely overshadowed by excess supplies that have resulted from mild weather. Pennzoil's plan to cut expense levels, faced with low gas prices, is likely to be met with scepticism, until the company can begin to generate consistent earnings. Longer-term, PZL's focus on overseas exploration should pay off.

Key Stock Statistics

S&P EPS Est. 1995	-5.84	Tang. Bk. Value/Share	25.80
P/E on S&P Est. 1995	NM	Beta	0.49
S&P EPS Est. 1996	1.15	Shareholders	20,000
Dividend Rate/Share	1.00	Market cap. (B)	$ 1.7
Shs. outstg. (M)	46.3	Inst. holdings	58%
Avg. daily vol. (M)	0.187	Insider holdings	NA

Value of $10,000 invested 5 years ago: $ 5,737

Fiscal Year Ending Dec. 31

	1995	% Change	1994	% Change	1993	% Change
Revenues (Million $)						
1Q	635.3	2%	622.1	-4%	650.5	19%
2Q	646.6	NM	651.8	-5%	685.2	16%
3Q	600.0	-5%	631.7	-4%	655.9	9%
4Q	—	—	657.4	-17%	790.8	28%
Yr.	—	—	2,563	-8%	2,782	18%
Income (Million $)						
1Q	2.74	-74%	10.74	-50%	21.53	NM
2Q	-4.79	NM	16.81	-51%	34.24	NM
3Q	-275.3	NM	-299.8	NM	12.04	15%
4Q	—	—	-11.49	NM	92.44	NM
Yr.	—	—	-283.7	NM	160.2	NM
Earnings Per Share ($)						
1Q	0.06	—	--	—	--	—
2Q	-0.10	—	--	—	--	—
3Q	-5.95	NM	-6.51	NM	1.79	NM
4Q	E0.15	NM	-0.25	NM	2.01	NM
Yr.	E-5.84	NM	-6.16	NM	3.80	NM

Next earnings report expected: early February

Business Summary - 30-OCT-95

Pennzoil is a diversified energy company that explores for, develops and produces oil and natural gas and manufactures and markets refined products. It also produces sulphur, and participates in the quick lube industry through Jiffy Lube International, Inc. Other income comes mainly from investment income and securities transactions. Operating profits (in millions $) in recent years were:

	1994	1993
Oil & gas production	-$4.9	$159.2
Motor oil & auto parts	41.8	90.0
Sulphur	-57.4	-20.8
Quick lube (franchise)	2.8	-17.6
Other	55.6	253.7

In 1994, net crude oil, condensate and natural gas liquids production averaged 68,709 bbl. a day, natural gas produced for sale 716,962 Mcf a day, refinery runs 58,703 b/d, and petroleum product sales 80,586 b/d. Worldwide proved crude oil reserves at year-end 1994 totaled 191 million bbl., versus 164 million bbl. a year earlier. Natural gas reserves at year-end 1994 were 1,545 Bcf (1,491 Bcf). PZL has been divesting nonstrategic properties.

During 1994, the company incurred $554 in non-recurring charges, including a $388 million pretax charge associated with the resolution of an IRS dispute related to the $3 billion Texaco settlement in 1988. PZL also incurred a $50 million charge on the sale of domestic sulphur assets.

Important Developments

Oct. '95—Pennzoil announced it will adopt a program to reduce general and administrative (G&A) costs by $40 million annually, noting the impact of continued low natural gas prices. Previously this year, the company said it would cut $35 million in G&A costs in the oil and gas division. The company believes most of these cost reductions will be completed by 1996's first quarter. Simultaneously, PZL also cut the quarterly dividend from $0.75 to $0.25. Also in October, the company said third quarter results reflected a $265 million (after-tax) charge to write down oil and gas properties.

Sep. '95—Pennzoil Exploration Co., a wholly-owned subsidiary of PZL, acquired an 87.5% working interest in the South-West Gebel El-Zeit concession in the southern Gulf of Suez offshore Egypt. Seismic acquisition will take place in early 1996. Pennzoil will be the operator for the farm-in agreement, which will require a minimum of $3 million in exploration expenditures over the next three years.

Capitalization

Long Term Debt: $1,970,833,000 (6/95).

Per Share Data ($) (Year Ended Dec. 31)

	1994	1993	1992	1991	1990	1989
Tangible Bk. Val.	26.11	32.80	28.99	28.79	31.10	35.23
Cash Flow	5.55	12.76	6.04	4.19	7.43	11.33
Earnings	-6.16	3.80	0.43	-1.05	2.37	6.06
Dividends	3.00	3.00	3.00	3.00	3.00	3.00
Payout Ratio	NM	79%	702%	NM	129%	50%
Prices - High	56⅜	70¾	57½	76½	89½	88⅞
- Low	43	49⅜	43⅛	52⅛	61¾	71⅝
P/E Ratio - High	NM	19	NM	NM	38	15
- Low	NM	13	NM	NM	26	12

Income Statement Analysis (Million $)

	1994	%Chg	1993	%Chg	1992	%Chg	1991
Revs.	2,475	NM	2,477	11%	2,223	-12%	2,527
Oper. Inc.	423	-10%	472	49%	317	-4%	329
Depr.	539	43%	378	66%	228	8%	211
Int. Exp.	486	154%	191	-18%	233	-9%	255
Pretax Inc.	-504	NM	219	NM	-1.0	NM	-77.0
Eff. Tax Rate	NM	—	27%	—	NM	—	NM
Net Inc.	-283	NM	160	NM	17.0	NM	-42.0

Balance Sheet & Other Fin. Data (Million $)

	1994	1993	1992	1991	1990	1989
Cash	25.0	947	21.0	112	266	469
Curr. Assets	728	1,544	646	783	835	1,018
Total Assets	4,716	4,886	4,457	5,231	5,261	4,882
Curr. Liab.	677	821	774	709	706	389
LT Debt	2,251	2,056	1,893	2,284	2,275	1,786
Common Eqty.	1,204	1,506	1,180	1,165	1,252	1,282
Total Cap.	3,827	3,867	3,488	4,255	4,425	4,365
Cap. Exp.	473	485	1,172	238	373	336
Cash Flow	255	538	245	169	294	411

Ratio Analysis

	1994	1993	1992	1991	1990	1989
Curr. Ratio	1.1	1.9	0.8	1.1	1.2	2.6
% LT Debt of Cap.	58.8	53.2	54.3	53.7	51.4	40.9
% Net Inc.of Revs.	NM	6.5	0.8	NM	4.3	11.9
% Ret. on Assets	NM	3.2	0.4	NM	1.8	5.0
% Ret. on Equity	NM	11.3	1.5	NM	7.0	17.0

Dividend Data —Dividends have been paid since 1925. A dividend reinvestment plan is available. A new poison pill stock purchase rights plan was adopted in 1988.

Amt. of Div. $	Date Decl.	Ex-Div. Date	Stock of Record	Payment Date
0.750	Nov. 04	Nov. 23	Nov. 30	Dec. 15 '94
0.750	Feb. 03	Feb. 22	Feb. 28	Mar. 15 '95
0.750	Apr. 27	May. 24	May. 31	Jun. 15 '95
0.750	Aug. 02	Aug. 29	Aug. 31	Sep. 15 '95
0.250	Oct. 25	Nov. 28	Nov. 30	Dec. 15 '95

Data as orig. reptd.; bef. results of disc. opers. and/or spec. items. Per share data adj. for stk. divs. as of ex-div. date. E-Estimated. NA-Not Available. NM-Not Meaningful. NR-Not Ranked.

Office—Pennzoil Place, P.O. Box 2967, Houston, TX 77252-2967. **Tel**—(713) 546-4000. **Chrmn, Pres & CEO**—J. L. Pate. **Secy**—L. F. Condit. **GVP-Fin & Treas**—D. P. Alderson, II. **Investor Contact**—Greg Panagos. **Dirs**—H. H. Baker, Jr., W. J. Bovaird, W. L. Lyons Brown, Jr., E. H. Cockrell, H. H. Cullen, A. Fanjul, B. Lawrence, J. L. Pate, B. Scowcroft, C. Wagner, Jr. **Transfer Agents**—Co.'s office; R-M Trust Co., Toronto. **Registrars**—KeyCorp Shareholder Services, Houston; R-M Trust Co., Toronto. **Incorporated** in Pennsylvania in 1889; reincorporated in Delaware in 1968. **Empl**-9,901. **S&P Analyst:** Raymond J. Deacon

Peoples Energy

NYSE Symbol **PGL**
In S&P 500

31-OCT-95

Industry:
Utilities-Gas

Summary: PGL operates two natural gas distribution utilities in Illinois, serving about one million customers in Chicago and 54 communities in the northeastern part of the state.

S&P Opinion: Hold (★★★)	Recent Price • 28⅞	Yield • 6.3%
	52 Wk Range • 29½-23⅜	12-Mo. P/E • 16.2

Earnings vs. Previous Year
▲=Up ▼=Down ▶=No Change

Quantitative Evaluations

Outlook
(1 Lowest—5 Highest)
• **1⁻**

Fair Value
• **26¼**

Risk
• **Low**

Earn./Div. Rank
• **B+**

Technical Eval.
• **Bearish** since 6/95

Rel. Strength Rank
(1 Lowest—99 Highest)
• **78**

Insider Activity
• **NA**

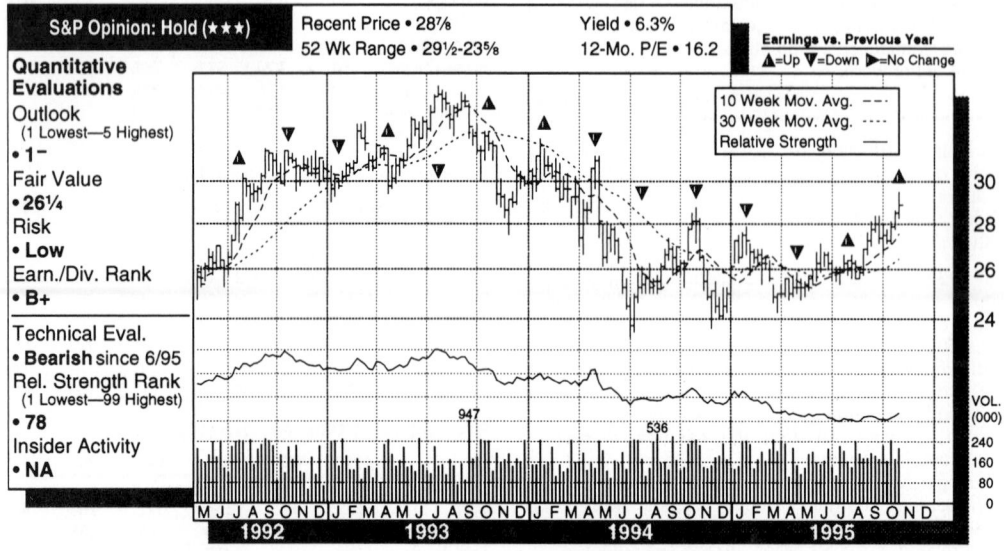

10 Week Mov. Avg. – – –
30 Week Mov. Avg. · · · · ·
Relative Strength ——

Overview - 31-OCT-95

Income should rise in fiscal 1996 as margins widen despite a delay in rate relief until at least late 1995. In the absence of extreme weather, overtime costs have been held down, and work force reductions are contributing to productivity gains. Although spaceheating is likely to remain PGL's largest market, development of the natural gas vehicle, cogeneration and gas air conditioning markets should contribute significantly to long-term gas throughput growth. Proximity to several major interstate pipeline systems provides a very low cost of gas, enabling the company to compete effectively with alternate fuel sources. Non-regulated activities, especially a partnership to provide district energy services to the McCormick Place Convention Center, will become increasingly important.

Valuation - 31-OCT-95

As with most utility shares, PGL stock tends to track interest rate movements, with recent strength reflecting generally declining rates. Recently reported fourth quarter fiscal 1995 results (covering the normally slow summer months) showed a smaller loss than last year, as increased gas deliveries and lower uncollectible expense outweighed increases in interest, taxes and other operation and maintenance expenses. With a higher than average yield, there is some room for a further advance in the price of the stock.

Key Stock Statistics

S&P EPS Est. 1996	2.00	Tang. Bk. Value/Share	19.21
P/E on S&P Est. 1996	14.4	Beta	0.78
Dividend Rate/Share	1.80	Shareholders	30,500
Shs. outstg. (M)	34.9	Market cap. (B)	$0.995
Avg. daily vol. (M)	0.041	Inst. holdings	37%
		Insider holdings	NA

Value of $10,000 invested 5 years ago: $ 16,223

Fiscal Year Ending Sep. 30

	1995	% Change	1994	% Change	1993	% Change
Revenues (Million $)						
1Q	307.0	-19%	379.0	NM	376.0	9%
2Q	424.4	-26%	575.0	10%	522.0	19%
3Q	187.2	-10%	207.0	-8%	224.0	12%
4Q	114.7	-4%	119.0	-13%	136.0	19%
Yr.	1,033	-19%	1,279	2%	1,259	15%
Income (Million $)						
1Q	25.13	-36%	38.99	26%	31.06	NM
2Q	45.82	-5%	48.40	-4%	50.64	15%
3Q	4.56	75%	2.60	-47%	4.89	-53%
4Q	-13.36	NM	-15.60	NM	-13.22	NM
Yr.	62.15	-16%	74.40	1%	73.38	4%
Earnings Per Share ($)						
1Q	0.72	-36%	1.12	26%	0.89	-1%
2Q	1.31	-6%	1.39	-4%	1.45	12%
3Q	0.13	86%	0.07	-50%	0.14	-53%
4Q	-0.38	NM	-0.45	NM	-0.38	NM
Yr.	1.78	-16%	2.13	NM	2.11	2%

Next earnings report expected: late January

Business Summary - 31-OCT-95

Peoples Energy Corporation is a holding corporation for two public utilities, The Peoples Gas Light and Coke Co., which serves customers in Chicago, and North Shore Gas Co., which supplies users in 54 suburbs north of the city. Peoples Gas has approximately 842,000 residential, commercial and industrial retail sales and transportation customers, while North Shore Gas has more than 129,000 customers.

Subsidiaries also include Peoples District Energy Corp., which provides heating and cooling services to large Chicago buildings; Peoples NGV Corp., which provides fueling services for gas powered fleet vehicles; and Peoples Energy Services Corp., whose initial business is the sale and distribution of carbon monoxide detectors. Revenues in recent fiscal years were derived as follows:

	1994	1993	1992
Residential	74%	74%	72%
Commercial	13%	12%	12%
Industrial	3%	3%	3%
Other	10%	11%	13%

Gas volumes sold and transported in fiscal 1994 totaled 278,430,000 Mcf, versus 277,614,000 Mcf in fiscal 1993. The number of customers averaged 970,590 in fiscal 1994, up slightly from 968,855 in fiscal 1993.

Sources of gas include connections to four interstate pipelines, supplies drawn from storage, and synthetic natural gas.

The Peoples Gas Light and Coke Co. and North Shore Gas Co. units are subject to regulation by the Illinois Commerce Commission.

Peoples District Energy Corp., a wholly owned subsidiary, is a 50% participant with Trigen-Peoples District Energy Corp. in a partnership formed to provide heating and cooling services to the McCormick Place exposition and convention center in Chicago, Illinois (under a 28-year contract with the Metropolitan Pier and Exposition Authority), and other large buildings near McCormick Place. Neither the partnership nor any of its partners is regulated as a public utility.

In September 1994, PGL's utility subsidiaries began a major project to reengineer their operations, to increase efficiency and cost-effectiveness.

Capital spending for fiscal 1995 was projected at about $94 million, up about $7.2 million from the fiscal 1994 level. Estimated expenditures include the continuation of a cast iron main replacement program, and $10 million for computers and office equipment.

Important Developments

Oct. '95—Earnings in fiscal 1995 declined mostly because of last winter's mild weather; the seasonal loss incurred during the fourth quarter narrowed on increased gas deliveries and lower uncollectibles.

Capitalization

Long Term Debt: $621,874,000 (6/95).

Per Share Data ($)

(Year Ended Sep. 30)

	1995	1994	1993	1992	1991	1990
Tangible Bk. Val.	NA	18.39	18.05	17.72	16.95	16.61
Earnings	1.78	2.13	2.11	2.06	2.05	2.07
Dividends	2.25	1.80	1.77	1.75	1.70	1.64
Payout Ratio	126%	84%	84%	85%	83%	79%
Prices - High	29½	32⅛	35	31⅝	28¼	26½
- Low	24¼	23⅜	27½	24⅜	21¾	20
P/E Ratio - High	17	15	17	15	14	13
- Low	14	11	13	12	11	10

Income Statement Analysis (Million $)

	1994	%Chg	1993	%Chg	1992	%Chg	1991
Revs.	1,279	2%	1,259	15%	1,097	NM	1,104
Depr.	64.7	6%	60.8	6%	57.3	3%	55.4
Maint.	37.9	6%	35.7	-3%	36.8	NM	36.7
Fxd. Chgs. Cov.	1.7	-31%	2.4	-57%	5.7	4%	5.4
Constr. Credits	Nil	—	Nil	—	0.2	83%	0.1
Eff. Tax Rate	27%	—	29%	—	28%	—	28%
Net Inc.	74.4	1%	73.4	4%	70.4	5%	67.0

Balance Sheet & Other Fin. Data (Million $)

	1994	1993	1992	1991	1990	1989
Gross Prop.	2,019	1,951	1,844	1,747	1,668	1,593
Cap. Exp.	87.2	132	118	102	103	135
Net Prop.	1,342	1,318	1,244	1,181	1,134	1,085
Capitalization:						
LT Debt	626	528	490	493	502	453
% LT Debt	49	46	44	46	47	45
Pfd.	Nil	Nil	12.9	16.8	20.7	25.9
% Pfd.	Nil	Nil	1.10	1.60	1.90	2.50
Common	641	628	616	555	543	528
% Common	51	54	55	52	51	53
Total Cap.	1,497	1,393	1,356	1,286	1,286	1,227

Ratio Analysis

	1994	1993	1992	1991	1990	1989
Oper. Ratio	92.0	91.0	90.2	90.5	91.2	91.3
% Earn. on Net Prop.	7.7	8.8	8.8	9.1	9.2	9.9
% Ret. on Revs.	5.8	5.8	6.4	6.1	5.8	6.6
% Ret. On Invest.Cap	8.5	8.7	8.9	9.1	9.2	10.2
% Return On Com.Eqty	7.6	11.8	12.0	12.2	12.6	15.3

Dividend Data —Dividends have been paid since the 1981 restructuring. A dividend reinvestment plan is available.

Amt. of Div. $	Date Decl.	Ex-Div. Date	Stock of Record	Payment Date
0.450	Dec. 07	Dec. 13	Dec. 19	Jan. 13 '95
0.450	Feb. 01	Mar. 13	Mar. 17	Apr. 14 '95
0.450	May. 03	Jun. 20	Jun. 22	Jul. 14 '95
0.450	Sep. 07	Sep. 20	Sep. 22	Oct. 14 '95

Data as orig. reptd.; bef. results of disc opers. and/or spec. items. Per share data adj. for stk. divs. as of ex-div. date. E-Estimated. NA-Not Available. NM-Not Meaningful. NR-Not Ranked.

Office—130 E. Randolph Dr., Chicago, IL 60601-6207. Tel—(312) 240-4000. Chrmn & CEO—R. E. Terry. Pres—J. B. Hasch. Secy, Treas & Investor Contact—Emmet P. Cassidy. Dirs—P. S. J. Cafferty, F. A. Cole, J. B. Hasch, F. C. Langenberg, H. J. Livingston, Jr., W. G. Mitchell, E. L. Neal, M. S. Reeves, R. E. Terry, R. P. Toft, A. R. Velasquez. Transfer Agent & Registrar—Harris Trust & Savings Bank, Chicago. Incorporated in Illinois in 1855; reincorporated in Illinois in 1967. Empl-3,278. S&P Analyst: Michael C. Barr

Pep Boys

NYSE Symbol **PBY**
In S&P 500

06-SEP-95 Industry:
Retail Stores

Summary: Pep Boys, a major automotive parts and accessories re-tailer, and offers maintenance and parts installation services. PBY should be operating over 500 stores by 1995-96 year-end.

S&P Opinion: Buy (★★★★)	Recent Price • 28⅛	Yield • 0.7%
	52 Wk Range • 36⅞-24⅜	12-Mo. P/E • 21.3

Quantitative Evaluations

Outlook
(1 Lowest—5 Highest)
• **5⁻**

Fair Value
• 36½

Risk
• **Average**

Earn./Div. Rank
• **A+**

Technical Eval.
• **Bearish** since 2/94

Rel. Strength Rank
(1 Lowest—99 Highest)
• **45**

Insider Activity
• **NA**

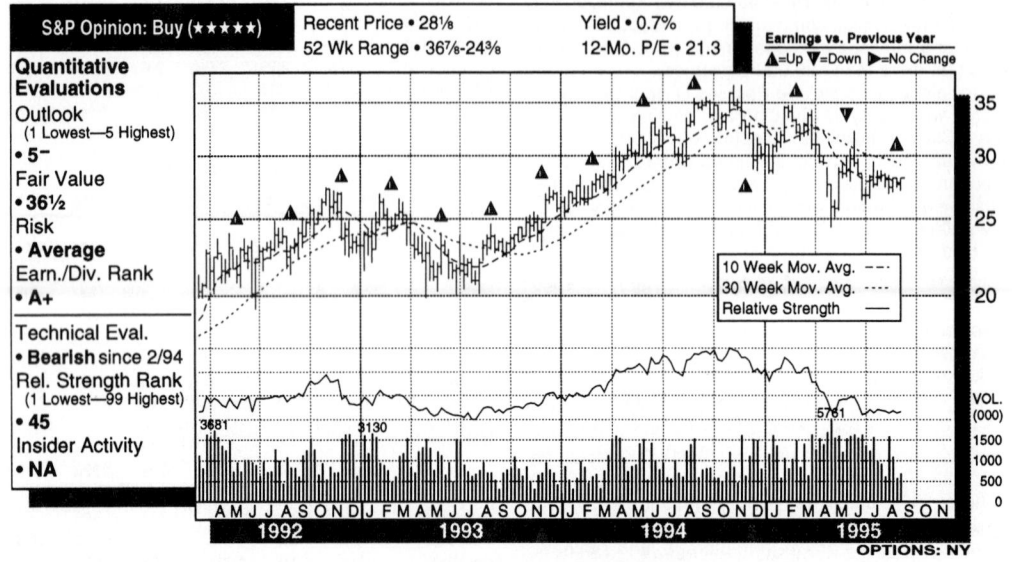

Earnings vs. Previous Year
▲=Up ▼=Down ▶=No Change

10 Week Mov. Avg. - - -
30 Week Mov. Avg. ....
Relative Strength ——

VOL. (000)
1500
1000
500
0

A M J J A S O N D J F M A M J J A S O N D J F M A M J J A S O N D J F M A M J J A S O N
1992   1993   1994   1995

OPTIONS: NY

Overview - 06-SEP-95

Higher revenues in the remainder of 1995-96 should result from the addition of over 50 stores, the maturing of stores opened in the prior fiscal year, and an expected overall rise in comparable-store sales for the year despite a decline in the first half. Future results will also be enhanced by an aging but still growing vehicle population, the continued rise in miles driven per vehicle, and the phase-in in 1995 and 1996 of new federally mandated emissions inspections at the states level. Longer term growth prospects will get a boost from the addition of PARTS USA stores and expansion into Puerto Rico, with the opening of the company's first Pep Boys store of a total of six planned for Puerto Rico in 1995-96.

Valuation - 06-SEP-95

PBY's unstimulating first half results, due to extremely hot weather combined with sagging consumer spending, have caused its shares to trade in a relatively narrow range. Despite this short-term digression, Pep Boys will continue to accelerate its store addition program and should also benefit from further consolidation of the retail auto aftermarket. Earnings will return to their normal growth pattern for the rest of the year, and we project earnings to grow at an annualized rate of about 20% over the next five years. We view this as a buying opportunity for one of the few quality operators in the fragmented automotive parts retailing industry.

Key Stock Statistics

S&P EPS Est. 1996	1.55	Tang. Bk. Value/Share	9.89
P/E on S&P Est. 1996	18.1	Beta	0.79
S&P EPS Est. 1997	1.95	Shareholders	3,800
Dividend Rate/Share	0.19	Market cap. (B)	$ 1.8
Shs. outstg. (M)	61.6	Inst. holdings	59%
Avg. daily vol. (M)	0.230	Insider holdings	NA

Value of $10,000 invested 5 years ago: $ 24,649

Fiscal Year Ending Jan. 31

	1996	% Change	1995	% Change	1994	% Change
Revenues (Million $)						
1Q	361.2	7%	338.0	13%	299.0	8%
2Q	410.8	11%	370.4	13%	329.1	7%
3Q	—	—	363.2	15%	316.0	6%
4Q	—	—	335.7	13%	296.8	9%
Yr.	—	—	1,407	13%	1,241	7%
Income (Million $)						
1Q	16.20	-8%	17.56	31%	13.44	24%
2Q	25.23	7%	23.52	23%	19.10	15%
3Q	—	—	20.64	18%	17.44	18%
4Q	—	—	18.29	18%	15.53	26%
Yr.	—	—	80.01	22%	65.51	20%
Earnings Per Share ($)						
1Q	0.27	-7%	0.29	32%	0.22	16%
2Q	0.41	5%	0.39	26%	0.31	15%
3Q	E0.44	29%	0.34	21%	0.28	17%
4Q	E0.37	23%	0.30	20%	0.25	25%
Yr.	E1.55	17%	1.32	25%	1.06	18%

Next earnings report expected: mid November

Business Summary - 30-AUG-95

The Pep Boys - Manny, Moe & Jack is engaged primarily in the retail sale of automotive parts and accessories; automotive maintenance and service; and installation of parts. As of year-end 1994-95, the company was operating a chain of 435 Pep Boys stores in 32 states, compared with 386 a year earlier.

In fiscal 1994-95, about 86% of revenues and 92% of gross profits were generated from merchandise sales, while 14% of sales and 8% of gross profits were derived from service and installation.

The company's stores occupied 8.9 million square feet of retail space at the end of fiscal 1994-95, up 15% from 7.8 million square feet a year earlier. In fiscal 1995-96, the company expects to open 50 of its typical 22,000 square foot supercenter stores with 11 service bays. The company also intends to open 25 PARTS USA stores, the prototype of which was opened late in fiscal 1994-95. PARTS USA stores will range from 10,000 to 13,000 square feet and will not have any service bays. PARTS USA stores will be built in "Do-it-yourself" neighborhoods that would not be able to support a superstore with service bays.

Each store carries the same basic product line, with variations based on the number and type of cars registered in different markets. A full line of a store's inventory includes about 24,000 items. A PARTS USA store will carry only 22,000 items, reflecting the absence of tires. Products include tires; batteries; new and rebuilt parts for domestic and imported cars (including shock absorbers, struts, ignition parts, mufflers and exhaust pipes, oil and air filters, belts and hoses, and brake parts); chemicals (including oil, antifreeze, polishes, additives, cleansers and paints); car radios and speakers; and car, truck and van accessories (including seat covers, alarms, floor mats, gauges, mirrors and booster cables).

Important Developments

Aug. '95—The company said it anticipates opening 54 new units, 37 supercenters and 17 PARTS USA stores, during the second half of 1995-96.
Jul. '95—Pep Boys said it opened its first store in Puerto Rico (Fajardo), a 22,000-square-foot supercenter that features 11 service bays and stocks approximately 26,000 automotive and related items. The company expects to open five additional units in Puerto Rico during the remainder of 1995-96 and ultimately believes the market can support 25-30 stores.

Capitalization

Long Term Debt: $359,612,000 (7/95), incl. $86.25 million of sub. notes conv. into com. at $41 per sh.

Per Share Data ($) (Year Ended Jan. 31)

	1995	1994	1993	1992	1991	1990
Tangible Bk. Val.	9.53	9.11	8.40	6.79	6.20	5.63
Cash Flow	2.05	1.69	1.50	1.28	1.17	1.04
Earnings	1.32	1.06	0.90	0.69	0.67	0.63
Dividends	0.21	0.15	0.14	0.13	0.12	0.11
Payout Ratio	16%	14%	15%	18%	17%	17%
Cal. Yrs.	1994	1993	1992	1991	1990	1989
Prices - High	36⅞	27⅜	27⅜	19½	17¼	17¼
- Low	25⅛	19⅞	15⅛	8⅜	8½	10½
P/E Ratio - High	28	26	30	28	26	27
- Low	19	19	17	12	13	17

Income Statement Analysis (Million $)

	1995	%Chg	1994	%Chg	1993	%Chg	1992
Revs.	1,407	13%	1,241	7%	1,156	15%	1,002
Oper. Inc.	193	21%	160	15%	139	19%	117
Depr.	44.4	14%	39.1	7%	36.7	10%	33.4
Int. Exp.	27.8	32%	21.0	NM	21.0	-18%	25.7
Pretax Inc.	126	20%	105	23%	85.6	41%	60.5
Eff. Tax Rate	37%	—	37%	—	36%	—	36%
Net Inc.	80.0	22%	65.5	20%	54.6	40%	38.9

Balance Sheet & Other Fin. Data (Million $)

	1995	1994	1993	1992	1991	1990
Cash	11.7	12.1	11.6	14.4	15.1	14.3
Curr. Assets	411	342	327	259	260	187
Total Assets	1,291	1,079	968	857	819	676
Curr. Liab.	289	249	223	177	168	117
LT Debt	381	253	209	279	286	228
Common Eqty.	586	548	510	379	345	312
Total Cap.	1,002	829	745	680	651	559
Cap. Exp.	184	135	78.0	66.0	106	88.0
Cash Flow	124	105	91.3	72.3	65.4	58.0

Ratio Analysis

	1995	1994	1993	1992	1991	1990
Curr. Ratio	1.4	1.4	1.5	1.5	1.5	1.6
% LT Debt of Cap.	38.0	30.5	28.1	41.1	43.9	40.7
% Net Inc.of Revs.	5.7	5.3	4.7	3.9	4.2	4.4
% Ret. on Assets	6.7	6.4	5.7	4.6	5.0	5.5
% Ret. on Equity	14.0	12.4	11.8	10.7	11.4	11.9

Dividend Data —Dividends have been paid since 1950. A dividend reinvestment plan is available. A "poison pill" stock purchase right was issued in 1987.

Amt. of Div. $	Date Decl.	Ex-Div. Date	Stock of Record	Payment Date
0.042	Sep. 08	Oct. 03	Oct. 10	Oct. 24 '94
0.042	Nov. 30	Jan. 03	Jan. 09	Jan. 23 '95
0.047	Mar. 31	Apr. 04	Apr. 10	Apr. 24 '95
0.047	May. 31	Jul. 06	Jul. 10	Jul. 24 '95

Data as orig. reptd.; bef. results of disc. opers. and/or spec. items. Per share data adj. for stk. divs. as of ex-div. date.
E-Estimated. NA-Not Available. NM-Not Meaningful. NR-Not Ranked.

Office—3111 West Allegheny Ave., Philadelphia, PA 19132. **Tel**—(215) 229-9000. **Chrmn & Pres**—M. G. Leibovitz. **Sr VP, CFO, Treas & Investor Contact**—Michael J. Holden. **Sr VP & Secy**—F. A. Stampone. **Dirs**—L. K. Black, P. Hutchinson, B. J. Korman, J. R. Leaman Jr., M. G. Leibovitz, M. D. Pryor, L. Rosenfeld, B. Strauss, M. H. Tanenbaum, D. V. Wachs. **Transfer Agent & Registrar**—American Stock Transfer & Trust Co., NYC. **Incorporated** in Pennsylvania in 1925. **Empl**-16,000. **S&P Analyst:** Philip D. Wohl

PepsiCo

NYSE Symbol **PEP**
In S&P 500

25-OCT-95

Industry:
Beverages

Summary: PepsiCo is a worldwide producer of branded beverage products and snack foods, and a leading operator and franchisor of restaurants with its Pizza Hut, Taco Bell and KFC chains.

S&P Opinion: Accumulate (★★★★)

Recent Price • 52%	Yield • 1.5%	
52 Wk Range • 53½-33%	12-Mo. P/E • 21.7	

Quantitative Evaluations

Outlook
(1 Lowest—5 Highest)
• **4+**

Fair Value
• **54**

Risk
• **Low**

Earn./Div. Rank
• **A+**

Technical Eval.
• **Bullish** since 9/95

Rel. Strength Rank
(1 Lowest—99 Highest)
• **83**

Insider Activity
• **Neutral**

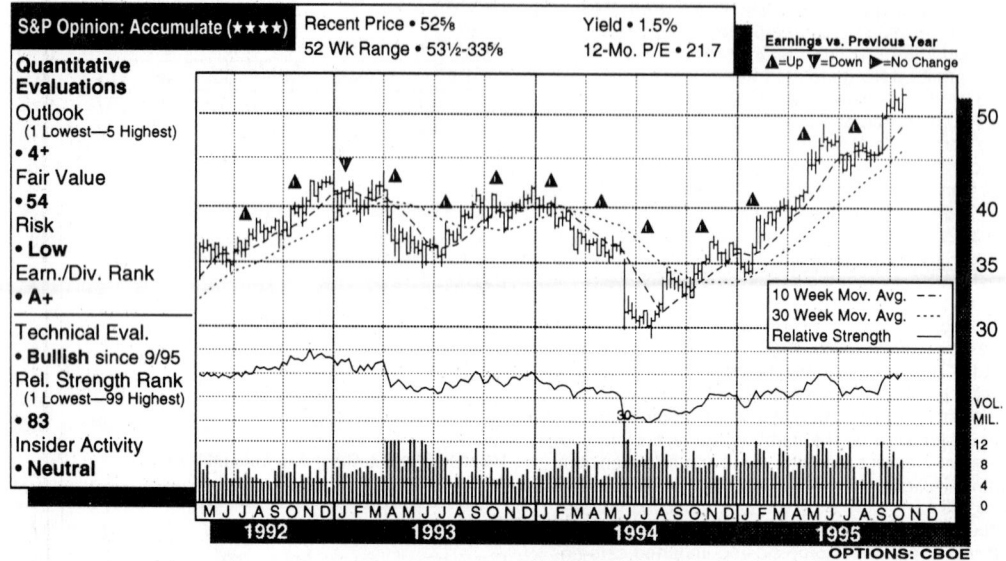

Earnings vs. Previous Year
▲=Up ▼=Down ▶=No Change

10 Week Mov. Avg. ---
30 Week Mov. Avg. ····
Relative Strength ——

VOL.
MIL.

OPTIONS: CBOE

Overview - 20-OCT-95

Annual sales growth of approximately 10% is seen through 1996. For 1995, projected beverage profit growth of about 14% should be driven by an approximate 5% increase in unit case volume and higher selling prices. Snack food profits should grow by about 7% to 10%, led primarily by volume growth and recent cost-cutting efforts. Restaurant profits are seen rising by about 15% in 1995, led by aggressive menu updates. Cash flows generated from cost cutting actions and future restaurant unit sales are likely to go toward share repurchases, which should contribute to 10% to 14% annual earnings per share growth through 1996.

Valuation - 20-OCT-95

Given our expectation of low double-digit annual earnings per share growth through 1996, the shares are attractive at current levels. The shares have made substantial recovery since mid-1994, helped by a sustained earnings rebound for the recently-troubled restaurant division. With restaurant profits up 16% in 1995's first nine months, we believe that investors may begin to once again look to the company as a well rounded growth company. Increasing reliance on restaurant franchising (versus unit ownership) should free up a significant amount of cash, which will likely be used to invest in more-profitable beverage and snack divisions, and for stock repurchases. These low-risk shares should stay in favor in the slow U.S. economic environment.

Key Stock Statistics

S&P EPS Est. 1995	2.45	Tang. Bk. Value/Share	NM
P/E on S&P Est. 1995	21.5	Beta	1.38
S&P EPS Est. 1996	2.80	Shareholders	107,000
Dividend Rate/Share	0.80	Market cap. (B)	$ 41.3
Shs. outstg. (M)	787.5	Inst. holdings	60%
Avg. daily vol. (M)	1.665	Insider holdings	NA

Value of $10,000 invested 5 years ago: $ 26,881

Fiscal Year Ending Dec. 31

	1995	% Change	1994	% Change	1993	% Change
Revenues (Million $)						
1Q	6,191	8%	5,729	13%	5,092	13%
2Q	7,286	11%	6,557	11%	5,890	15%
3Q	7,693	9%	7,064	12%	6,316	14%
4Q	—	—	9,123	18%	7,722	14%
Yr.	—	—	28,472	14%	25,021	14%
Income (Million $)						
1Q	321.1	14%	282.8	9%	260.4	11%
2Q	487.2	9%	446.5	5%	426.8	13%
3Q	616.8	14%	541.4	18%	458.2	9%
4Q	—	—	513.3	16%	442.5	67%
Yr.	—	—	1,784	12%	1,588	22%
Earnings Per Share ($)						
1Q	0.40	14%	0.35	9%	0.32	10%
2Q	0.61	11%	0.55	4%	0.53	13%
3Q	0.77	13%	0.68	21%	0.56	6%
4Q	E0.67	5%	0.64	16%	0.55	72%
Yr.	E2.45	10%	2.22	13%	1.96	22%

Next earnings report expected: early February

Business Summary - 24-OCT-95

PepsiCo's diversified interests include beverages, snack foods and restaurants. Business segment contributions in 1994 (excluding unusual charges):

	Revs.	Profits
Beverages	34%	37%
Snack foods	29%	41%
Restaurants	37%	22%

International operations accounted for 29% of sales and 19% of operating profits in 1994.

Beverage operations consist primarily of the production and distribution (to franchised bottlers) of soft drinks and soft drink concentrates. Principal brands include Pepsi-Cola, Diet Pepsi, Mountain Dew, Slice, Mug, and outside the U.S., 7UP and Diet 7UP. Products are available in approximately 160 countries and territories. PEP is also a major bottler of these products.

Food products operations are conducted domestically through Frito-Lay, which produces the best-selling line of snack foods in the U.S., including Fritos brand corn chips, Lay's and Ruffles brand potato chips, Doritos and Tostitos brands tortilla chips, Chee-tos brand cheese flavored snacks, Rold Gold pretzels, and Sunchips brand multigrain snacks. PepsiCo Foods International produces snack foods and other food products outside the U.S.

Restaurant chains include Pizza Hut, Taco Bell and KFC. At 1994 year-end, the three chains had an aggregate of 26,799 units, including 13,194 franchised/licensed units, 12,742 company units and 863 joint venture units. Of the total, 7,348 were located outside the U.S.

Important Developments

Oct. '95—PEP reported a 10% increase in operating profits in 1995's first half, year to year. Beverage profits rose 14%, led by higher U.S. bottler case sales and increased prices. Snack food profits were up 5%, as strong domestic volume growth offset the negative impact of adverse economic conditions in Mexico. Restaurant profits rose 16%, as a 40% increase for Pizza Hut (5% higher domestic same store sales, introduction of Stuffed Crust pizza) and a 13% increase for KFC (4% greater domestic same store sales) outweighed an 11% decline for Taco Bell (4% lower same store sales). Separately, as of October 16, 1995, PEP had repurchased 9.5 million shares year to date, and said it expected to repurchase 1% to 2% of its shares in 1995 and annually for the next few years.

Capitalization

Long Term Debt: $8,690,700,000 (9/9/95).

Per Share Data ($) (Year Ended Dec. 31)

	1994	1993	1992	1991	1990	1989
Tangible Bk. Val.	-1.25	-1.99	-2.01	-0.49	-1.19	-2.00
Cash Flow	4.18	3.69	3.09	2.60	2.46	2.09
Earnings	2.22	1.96	1.61	1.35	1.37	1.13
Dividends	0.70	0.61	0.51	0.46	0.38	0.32
Payout Ratio	32%	31%	31%	34%	28%	28%
Prices - High	41⅛	43⅝	43⅜	35⅝	27⅞	22
- Low	29¼	34½	30½	23½	18	12⅝
P/E Ratio - High	19	22	27	26	20	19
- Low	13	18	19	17	13	11

Income Statement Analysis (Million $)

	1994	%Chg	1993	%Chg	1992	%Chg	1991
Revs.	28,472	14%	25,021	14%	21,970	12%	19,608
Oper. Inc.	4,778	11%	4,312	15%	3,754	14%	3,302
Depr.	1,577	12%	1,405	18%	1,189	18%	1,009
Int. Exp.	645	13%	573	-2%	586	-5%	616
Pretax Inc.	2,664	10%	2,423	28%	1,899	14%	1,670
Eff. Tax Rate	33%	—	35%	—	31%	—	35%
Net Inc.	1,784	12%	1,588	22%	1,302	21%	1,080

Balance Sheet & Other Fin. Data (Million $)

	1994	1993	1992	1991	1990	1989
Cash	1,488	1,856	2,058	2,036	1,816	1,534
Curr. Assets	5,072	5,164	4,842	4,566	4,081	3,551
Total Assets	24,792	23,706	20,951	18,775	17,143	15,127
Curr. Liab.	5,270	6,575	4,324	3,722	4,771	3,692
LT Debt	8,841	7,443	7,965	7,806	5,900	6,076
Common Eqty.	6,856	6,339	5,356	5,545	4,904	3,891
Total Cap.	17,669	15,789	15,003	14,422	11,747	10,824
Cap. Exp.	2,253	2,008	1,583	1,524	1,180	944
Cash Flow	3,361	2,993	2,491	2,089	1,966	1,661

Ratio Analysis

	1994	1993	1992	1991	1990	1989
Curr. Ratio	1.0	0.8	1.1	1.2	0.9	1.0
% LT Debt of Cap.	50.0	47.1	53.1	54.1	50.2	56.1
% Net Inc.of Revs.	6.3	6.3	5.9	5.5	6.1	5.9
% Ret. on Assets	7.4	7.1	6.5	6.0	6.8	6.9
% Ret. on Equity	27.2	27.2	23.7	20.7	24.8	25.5

Dividend Data

—Dividends have been paid since 1952. A dividend reinvestment plan is available.

Amt. of Div. $	Date Decl.	Ex-Div. Date	Stock of Record	Payment Date
0.180	Nov. 17	Dec. 05	Dec. 09	Jan. 01 '95
0.180	Feb. 23	Mar. 06	Mar. 10	Mar. 31 '95
0.200	May. 03	Jun. 06	Jun. 09	Jun. 30 '95
0.200	Jul. 27	Sep. 06	Sep. 08	Sep. 29 '95

Data as orig. reptd.; bef. results of disc. opers. and/or spec. items. Per share data adj. for stk. divs. as of ex-div. date. E-Estimated. NA-Not Available. NM-Not Meaningful. NR-Not Ranked.

Office—700 Anderson Hill Rd., Purchase, NY 10577. **Tel**—(914) 253-2000. **Chrmn & CEO**—D. W. Calloway, Sr. **Vice Chrmn**—R. A. Enrico. **EVP-CFO**—R. G. Dettmer. **SVP-Secy**—E. V. Lahey, Jr. **Investor Contact**—Margaret D. Moore. **Dirs**—J. F. Akers, R. E. Allen, D. W. Calloway, R. A. Enrico, J. J. Murphy, A. E. Pearson, S. P. Rockefeller, R. B. Smith, R. H. Stewart III, F. A. Thomas, P. R. Vagelos, A. R. Weber. **Transfer Agent**—Bank of Boston. **Incorporated** in Delaware in 1919; reincorporated in North Carolina in 1986. **Empl-** 471,000. **S&P Analyst:** Kenneth A. Shea

Perkin-Elmer

NYSE Symbol **PKN**
In S&P 500

26-OCT-95

Industry:
Specialty instruments

Summary: Perkin-Elmer is the leading worldwide producer of analytical instruments and life science systems.

S&P Opinion: Accumulate (★★★★)	Recent Price • 36 Yield • 1.9%
	52 Wk Range • 38-25¼ 12-Mo. P/E • 22.1

Quantitative Evaluations

Outlook
(1 Lowest—5 Highest)
• **3+**

Fair Value
• **36⅞**

Risk
• **Low**

Earn./Div. Rank
• **B-**

Technical Eval.
• **Bearish** since 6/95

Rel. Strength Rank
(1 Lowest—99 Highest)
• **61**

Insider Activity
• **NA**

Earnings vs. Previous Year
▲=Up ▼=Down ▶=No Change

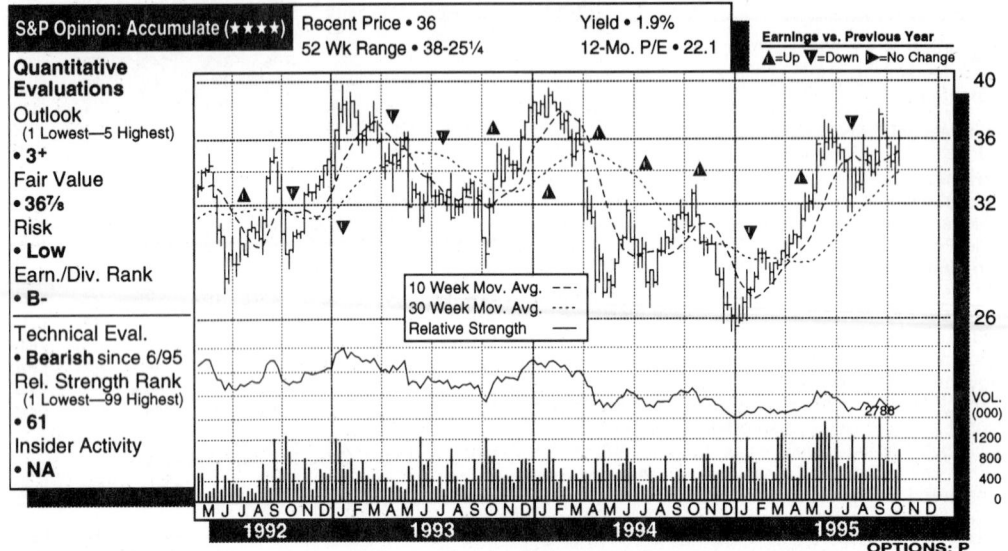

10 Week Mov. Avg. - - -
30 Week Mov. Avg. ⋯⋯
Relative Strength —

VOL. (000)

OPTIONS: P

Overview - 26-OCT-95

Revenues should increase 10% in fiscal 1996, led by life sciences, which should benefit from growth in the biotechnology industry and PKN's aggressive investment in this portion of its business. Analytical instrument sales should rise moderately. Demand should be particularly strong in Europe. In the U.S., sales should be driven by a maturing economy, greater enforcement of environmental regulations and new food labeling requirements. A rebound in demand from the pharmaceutical industry is also likely, due to the failure of health care legislation to pass. However, growth in Japan is likely to be modest. Margins should benefit from greater productivity, the restructuring announced in the fourth quarter and the absence of one-time charges of $0.04 a share. Fewer shares outstanding will aid per-share earnings.

Valuation - 26-OCT-95

Management of this leading instrument company is committed to enhancing shareholder value by dramatically increasing the profits of its core instrument business and rapidly expanding its life sciences operation. The company is currently implementing a restructuring that will reduce its costs by $20 million annually in fiscal 1996 and $25 million annually thereafter. In addition, the company has indicated that further restructuring actions are planned. The election of a new Chairman, President and CEO is likely to ensure that further aggressive steps will be taken to enhance profitability. These actions should lead to continued appreciation of the shares.

Key Stock Statistics

S&P EPS Est. 1996	1.95	Tang. Bk. Value/Share	7.24
P/E on S&P Est. 1996	18.5	Beta	1.07
Dividend Rate/Share	0.68	Shareholders	9,700
Shs. outstg. (M)	42.1	Market cap. (B)	$ 1.5
Avg. daily vol. (M)	0.138	Inst. holdings	73%
		Insider holdings	NA

Value of $10,000 invested 5 years ago: $ 18,219

Fiscal Year Ending Jun. 30

	1996	% Change	1995	% Change	1994	% Change
Revenues (Million $)						
1Q	264.4	7%	247.3	2%	243.3	-3%
2Q	—	—	261.0	2%	256.8	-5%
3Q	—	—	274.6	4%	263.5	2%
4Q	—	—	280.6	8%	260.9	13%
Yr.	—	—	1,064	4%	1,024	1%
Income (Million $)						
1Q	17.60	18%	14.94	10%	13.56	-14%
2Q	—	—	17.09	-23%	22.11	NM
3Q	—	—	36.68	80%	20.40	NM
4Q	—	—	-1.80	NM	17.90	193%
Yr.	—	—	66.88	-10%	73.98	NM
Earnings Per Share ($)						
1Q	0.41	17%	0.35	17%	0.30	15%
2Q	E0.46	15%	0.40	-20%	0.50	9%
3Q	E0.51	-41%	0.86	91%	0.45	NM
4Q	E0.57	NM	-0.04	NM	0.41	105%
Yr.	E1.95	24%	1.57	-5%	1.66	NM

Next earnings report expected: mid January

Business Summary - 26-OCT-95

Perkin-Elmer is the world leader in the developing, manufacturing and distributing life science and analytical instrument systems.

The company develops, manufactures, markets, sells and services analytical instrument systems. These include biochemical analytical instrument systems, consisting of instruments and associated consumable products for life science research and related applications. These automated systems are used for synthesis amplification, purification, isolation, analysis and sequencing of nucleic acids, proteins and other biological molecules. Other instruments include analytical instrument systems for determining the composition and molecular structure of chemical substances and measuring the concentration of materials in a sample.

Through a joint venture, Perkin-Elmer Sciex Instruments, the company is engaged in the manufacture and sale of mass spectrometry instrument systems.

The company also manufactures, markets and services on-line, real time, process analysis systems to monitor process quality and environmental purity.

PKN's instruments are used by private industry, educational and research institutions and governmental entities for fundamental research, applied industrial research, quality control, medical research, hospital clinical testing, pollution analysis and drug identification.

International business accounted for 63% of revenues in fiscal 1995 and $119.2 million of operating income.

During the fourth quarter of fiscal 1995 the company took a restructuring charge of $18.6 million ($0.44 a share) to reduce the cost structure in its analytical instruments business by $20 million in fiscal 1996 and $25 million annually in succeeding years. During the third quarter of fiscal 1995, the company sold its 7% equity interest in Silicon Valley Group, Inc., resulting in a pretax gain of $20.8 million ($0.40 a share after taxes).

The company announced in July 1993 that it was discontinuing its material sciences group.

Important Developments

Oct. '95—PKN said that something in the area of $50 million to $100 million in costs needed to come out of its analytical business over the next two to three years.

Oct. '95—The company said that first quarter fiscal 1996 sales and orders rose, year to year, in every major geographic area, with Europe the strongest. Life science sales rose 17% from the prior year, while analytical instrument revenues were flat. It said that the impact from the fourth quarter restructuring was small.

Capitalization

Long Term Debt: $29,200,000 (9/95).

Per Share Data ($) (Year Ended Jun. 30)

	1995	1994	1993	1992	1991	1990
Tangible Bk. Val.	7.24	6.76	1.98	9.08	7.80	11.77
Cash Flow	2.52	2.61	0.39	2.70	0.82	1.82
Earnings	1.57	1.66	0.54	1.72	-0.08	1.10
Dividends	0.68	0.68	0.68	0.68	0.68	0.68
Payout Ratio	43%	41%	126%	40%	NM	62%
Prices - High	37¼	39½	39¾	36	34⅜	24⅞
- Low	25¾	26½	28½	27¼	21⅜	18⅝
P/E Ratio - High	24	24	74	21	NM	23
- Low	16	16	53	16	NM	17

Income Statement Analysis (Million $)

	1995	%Chg	1994	%Chg	1993	%Chg	1992
Revs.	1,064	4%	1,024	1%	1,011	11%	911
Oper. Inc.	132	-5%	139	8%	129	5%	123
Depr.	40.7	-5%	42.7	3%	41.3	23%	33.7
Int. Exp.	8.2	15%	7.1	-46%	13.1	-31%	19.0
Pretax Inc.	82.3	-8%	89.0	102%	44.0	-44%	78.0
Eff. Tax Rate	19%	—	17%	—	44%	—	25%
Net Inc.	66.9	-10%	74.0	NM	24.5	-58%	58.8

Balance Sheet & Other Fin. Data (Million $)

	1995	1994	1993	1992	1991	1990
Cash	73.0	25.0	30.0	12.0	19.0	11.0
Curr. Assets	602	515	475	491	471	537
Total Assets	893	885	851	801	752	853
Curr. Liab.	374	378	374	372	380	351
LT Debt	34.1	34.3	7.0	57.0	54.0	60.0
Common Eqty.	305	290	307	305	262	391
Total Cap.	339	325	314	362	320	451
Cap. Exp.	28.9	34.5	28.4	29.5	32.2	26.3
Cash Flow	108	117	66.0	92.0	27.0	73.0

Ratio Analysis

	1995	1994	1993	1992	1991	1990
Curr. Ratio	1.6	1.4	1.3	1.3	1.2	1.5
% LT Debt of Cap.	10.1	10.6	2.3	15.6	17.0	13.3
% Net Inc.of Revs.	6.3	7.2	2.4	6.4	NM	5.3
% Ret. on Assets	7.5	8.5	2.6	7.6	NM	5.5
% Ret. on Equity	22.5	24.8	6.9	20.7	NM	10.3

Dividend Data —Dividends were initiated in 1971. A dividend reinvestment plan is available. A "poison pill" stock purchase rights plan was adopted in 1989.

Amt. of Div. $	Date Decl.	Ex-Div. Date	Stock of Record	Payment Date
0.170	Nov. 18	Nov. 25	Dec. 01	Jan. 03 '95
0.170	Feb. 15	Feb. 23	Mar. 01	Apr. 03 '95
0.170	Apr. 21	May. 25	Jun. 01	Jul. 03 '95
0.170	Aug. 17	Aug. 30	Sep. 01	Oct. 02 '95

Data as orig. reptd.; bef. results of disc. opers. and/or spec. items. Per share data adj. for stk. divs. as of ex-div. date. E-Estimated. NA-Not Available. NM-Not Meaningful. NR-Not Ranked.

Office—761 Main Ave., Norwalk, CT 06859-0001. **Tel**—(203) 762-1000. **Chrmn, Pres & CEO**—T. L. White. **VP-Fin, CFO**—S. O. Jaeger. **VP-Treas**—R. L. Seegal. **VP & Secy**—W. B. Sawch. **VP & Investor Contact**—Julianne Grace (203-761-5400). **Dirs**—J. F. Abely Jr., R. H. Ayers, J. Belingard, R. H. Hayes, G. N. Kelley, D. R. Melville, B. R. Roberts, J. S. Scott, C. W. Slayman, O. R. Smith, R. F. Tucker, T. L. White. **Transfer Agent & Registrar**—First National Bank of Boston. **Incorporated** in New York in 1939. **Empl**-5,890. **S&P Analyst:** Paul H. Valentine, CFA

Pfizer Inc.

NYSE Symbol **PFE**
In S&P 500

14-SEP-95

Industry:
Drugs-Generic and OTC

Summary: Earnings of this leading producer of ethical drugs, hospital products, animal health items and nonprescription medications should benefit from a strong new drug pipeline.

S&P Opinion: Buy (★★★★)	Recent Price • 47	Yield • 2.2%
	52 Wk Range • 51⅝-32	12-Mo. P/E • 20.8

Earnings vs. Previous Year
▲=Up ▼=Down ▶=No Change

Quantitative Evaluations

Outlook
(1 Lowest—5 Highest)
• **2+**

Fair Value
• **43¾**

Risk
• **High**

Earn./Div. Rank
• **A-**

Technical Eval.
• **Bullish** since 5/95

Rel. Strength Rank
(1 Lowest—99 Highest)
• **34**

Insider Activity
• **Unfavorable**

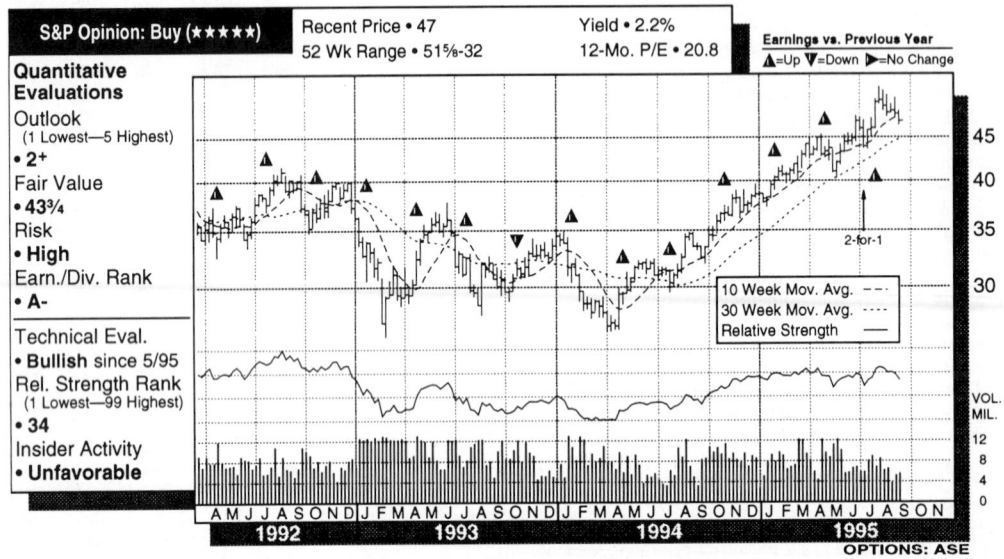

2-for-1

10 Week Mov. Avg. – – –
30 Week Mov. Avg. ·······
Relative Strength ——

VOL.
MIL.

1992 1993 1994 1995

OPTIONS: ASE

Overview - 14-SEP-95

Another good sales gain is expected for 1996, paced by continued brisk demand for PFE's strong product portfolio, which includes Norvasc and Cardura cardiovasculars, Diflucan antifungal, Zithromax anti-infective, Zoloft antidepressant and Glucotrol XL treatment for diabetes (sales of these six products rose 57% in the 1995 second quarter). New products under regulatory review, such as Enable antiarthritic and Zyrtec low-sedating antihistamine, should also boost volume. Gains are also seen for hospital products, consumer health care, and animal health lines. The company is engaged is discussions concerning the possible sale of its food science business.

Valuation - 14-SEP-95

The shares have been in a robust uptrend since the spring of 1994, although recent negative publicity caused some weakness in the stock. In late August, federal health officials issued a warning against short-acting Procardia, an older PFE heart drug. The company has taken strong exception to studies behind the warning, which did not apply to its newer Procardia XL and Norvasc calcium channel blockers. PFE has one of the strongest new drug pipelines in the industry, with over $5 billion in invested in R&D over the past decade. Potential blockbusters include Enable antiarthritic, Zyrtec anti-allergy, and Dofetilide anti-arrhythmia agent. We continue to recommend purchase of the shares.

Key Stock Statistics

S&P EPS Est. 1995	2.45	Tang. Bk. Value/Share	6.36
P/E on S&P Est. 1995	19.2	Beta	1.57
S&P EPS Est. 1996	2.85	Shareholders	61,500
Dividend Rate/Share	1.04	Market cap. (B)	$ 30.3
Shs. outstg. (M)	634.2	Inst. holdings	66%
Avg. daily vol. (M)	1.234	Insider holdings	NA

Value of $10,000 invested 5 years ago: $ 30,794

Fiscal Year Ending Dec. 31

	1995	% Change	1994	% Change	1993	% Change
Revenues (Million $)						
1Q	2,403	21%	1,983	6%	1,867	6%
2Q	2,482	29%	1,923	10%	1,749	3%
3Q	—	—	2,075	11%	1,873	2%
4Q	—	—	2,300	16%	1,989	2%
Yr.	—	—	8,281	11%	7,478	3%
Income (Million $)						
1Q	420.4	13%	370.7	13%	329.0	11%
2Q	316.3	23%	257.2	1%	253.8	15%
3Q	—	—	336.5	NM	-214.2	NM
4Q	—	—	334.0	16%	288.9	4%
Yr.	—	—	1,298	97%	657.5	-40%
Earnings Per Share ($)						
1Q	0.68	14%	0.59	17%	0.51	15%
2Q	0.50	19%	0.42	6%	0.39	20%
3Q	E0.65	19%	0.54	NM	-0.32	NM
4Q	E0.63	17%	0.54	20%	0.45	8%
Yr.	E2.45	17%	2.09	104%	1.02	-37%

Next earnings report expected: mid October

Pfizer Inc.

Business Summary - 14-SEP-95

Pfizer is a leading ethical pharmaceutical producer, with important positions in hospital products, animal health items, nonprescription medications and food ingredients. Segment contributions from ongoing businesses in 1994 were:

	Sales	Profits
Health care	84%	95%
Animal health	7%	2%
Consumer	5%	2%
Food science	4%	1%

Foreign operations contributed 47% of sales and 33% of profits in 1994. R&D spending equaled 13.8% of sales in 1994 (13.0% in 1993).

Health care products include cardiovascular drugs (29% of 1994 sales) such as Procardia XL, Norvasc, Minipress and Cardura; anti-infectives (21%), including Diflucan, Unasyn, Sulperazon, Vibramycin and Zithromax; Zoloft antidepressant (9%); and Feldene antiarthritic (4%). Other compounds include Sinequan psychotherapeutic, Diabinese and Glucotrol antidiabetes agents, and Reactine low-sedating antihistamine. A number of hospital products are also sold, including orthopedic, surgical and cardiac devices. The R&D pipeline contains drugs for arthritis, cardiac arrhythmias, psychosis and other disorders.

The animal health product line, enlarged through the January 1995 acquisition of SmithKline Beecham's animal health division, includes feed additives, vaccines, antibiotics, antihelmintics and other veterinary products.

Important consumer products are Ben-Gay ointment, Visine eye drops, Desitin ointment, Pacquin hand cream, Plax dental plaque removing rinse, Unisom sleep aid and Barbasol shave cream. Food science products consist of proprietary brand name ingredients sold to the food processing industry.

Important Developments

Aug. '95—The National Heart, Blood and Lung Institute issued a warning to doctors with regard to Pfizer's short-acting Procardia heart drug. The company took strong exception to the studies behind the warning, which does not apply to its newer Procardia XL and Norvasc heart drugs. New Pfizer drugs pending FDA review include Enable anti-arthritic, Zyrtec for allergies; Zoloft for the added indication of obsessive-compulsive disorder; and a pediatric form of Zithromax anti-infective. An additional 15 drugs are in late stages of development, including new treatments for infections, breast cancer, male erectile dysfunction, Alzheimer's disease and other ailments.

Capitalization

Long Term Debt: $611,200,000 (7/95).
Minority Interest: $44,800,000.

Per Share Data ($)

(Year Ended Dec. 31)

	1994	1993	1992	1991	1990	1989
Tangible Bk. Val.	6.88	6.02	7.26	7.63	7.71	6.86
Cash Flow	2.56	1.42	2.01	1.42	1.51	1.30
Earnings	2.09	1.02	1.63	1.07	1.20	1.01
Dividends	0.94	0.84	0.74	0.66	0.60	0.55
Payout Ratio	45%	82%	46%	60%	49%	53%
Prices - High	39¾	37⅞	43½	43⅛	20½	19
- Low	26⅝	26¼	32⅝	18⅜	13⅝	13½
P/E Ratio - High	19	37	27	40	17	19
- Low	13	26	20	17	11	13

Income Statement Analysis (Million $)

	1994	%Chg	1993	%Chg	1992	%Chg	1991
Revs.	8,281	11%	7,478	3%	7,230	4%	6,950
Oper. Inc.	2,248	18%	1,906	13%	1,686	15%	1,471
Depr.	289	14%	254	-2%	260	9%	238
Int. Exp.	142	17%	121	4%	116	-16%	138
Pretax Inc.	1,862	119%	851	-45%	1,535	63%	944
Eff. Tax Rate	30%	—	23%	—	29%	—	23%
Net Inc.	1,298	97%	658	-40%	1,094	52%	722

Balance Sheet & Other Fin. Data (Million $)

	1994	1993	1992	1991	1990	1989
Cash	2,019	1,177	1,704	1,548	1,068	1,058
Curr. Assets	5,788	4,733	5,385	4,808	4,436	4,505
Total Assets	11,099	9,331	9,590	9,635	9,052	8,325
Curr. Liab.	4,826	3,444	3,217	3,421	3,117	2,912
LT Debt	604	571	571	397	193	191
Common Eqty.	4,324	3,865	4,719	5,026	5,092	4,536
Total Cap.	5,179	4,665	5,472	5,742	5,666	5,062
Cap. Exp.	672	634	674	594	548	457
Cash Flow	1,588	912	1,353	960	1,019	882

Ratio Analysis

	1994	1993	1992	1991	1990	1989
Curr. Ratio	1.2	1.4	1.7	1.4	1.4	1.5
% LT Debt of Cap.	11.7	12.2	10.4	6.9	3.4	3.8
% Net Inc.of Revs.	15.7	8.8	15.1	10.4	12.5	12.0
% Ret. on Assets	12.8	7.0	11.5	7.7	9.2	8.5
% Ret. on Equity	32.0	15.4	22.6	14.3	16.7	15.4

Dividend Data —Dividends have been paid since 1901. A dividend reinvestment plan is available. A poison pill stock purchase rights plan was adopted in 1987.

Amt. of Div. $	Date Decl.	Ex-Div. Date	Stock of Record	Payment Date
0.470	Oct. 27	Nov. 04	Nov. 11	Dec. 15 '94
0.520	Jan. 26	Feb. 06	Feb. 10	Mar. 16 '95
0.520	Apr. 27	May. 08	May. 12	Jun. 15 '95
2-for-1	Apr. 27	Jul. 03	Jun. 01	Jun. 30 '95
0.260	Jun. 22	Aug. 02	Aug. 04	Sep. 21 '95

Data as orig. reptd.; bef. results of disc. opers. and/or spec. items. Per share data adj. for stk. divs. as of ex-div. date. E-Estimated. NA-Not Available. NM-Not Meaningful. NR-Not Ranked.

Office—235 E. 42nd St., New York, NY 10017. **Tel**—(212) 573-2323. **Chrmn & CEO**—W. C. Steere, Jr. **Vice Chrmn**—E. C. Bessey. **EVP & CFO**—H. A. McKinnell. **SVP & Secy**—C. L. Clemente. **Investor Contact**—J. R. Gardner. **Dirs**—E. C. Bessey, M. A. Burns, G. J. Fippinger, G. B. Harvey, C. J. Horner, S. O. Ikenberry, T. G. Labrecque, J. T. Lynn, P. A. Marks, E. T. Pratt, Jr., F. D. Raines, F. G. Rohatyn, W. C. Steere, Jr., J.-P. Valles. **Transfer Agent**—Co. office. **Registrar**—Mellon Securities Trust Co., NYC. **Incorporated** in Delaware in 1942. **Empl**-40,800. **S&P Analyst:** H.B. Saftlas

STOCK REPORTS

Phelps Dodge

NYSE Symbol **PD**
In S&P 500

15-AUG-95

Industry:
Mining/Diversified

Summary: Phelps Dodge is one of the world's largest copper producer, the largest North American producer of truck wheels and rims and one of the world's largest producers of carbon black.

S&P Opinion: Accumulate (★★★★)

| Recent Price • 63⅞ | Yield • 2.8% |
| 52 Wk Range • 70½-51⅞ | 12-Mo. P/E • 9.0 |

Earnings vs. Previous Year
▲=Up ▼=Down ▶=No Change

Quantitative Evaluations

Outlook
(1 Lowest—5 Highest)
• **3+**

Fair Value
• **65**

Risk
• **Average**

Earn./Div. Rank
• **B**

Technical Eval.
• **Bearish** since 7/95

Rel. Strength Rank
(1 Lowest—99 Highest)
• **54**

Insider Activity
• **NA**

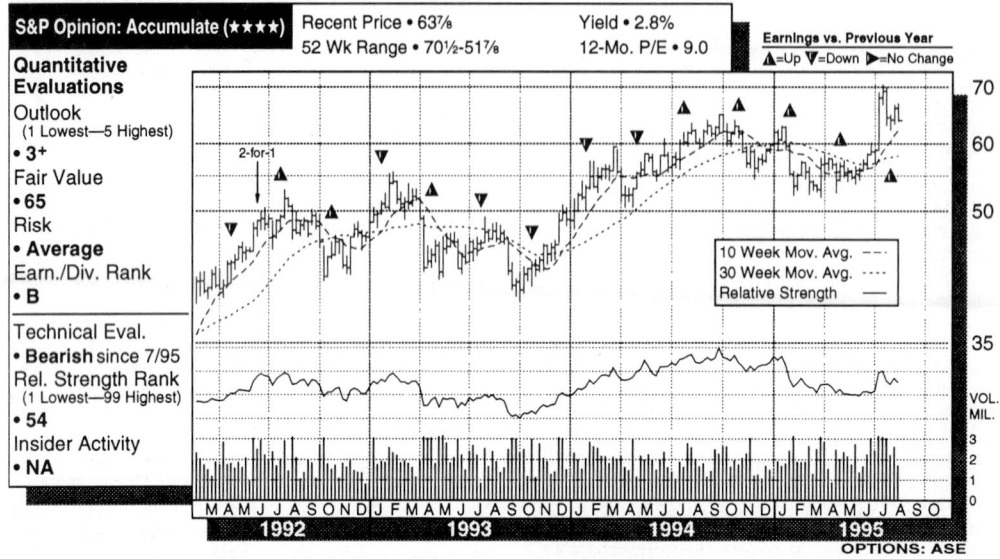

10 Week Mov. Avg. ---
30 Week Mov. Avg. .....
Relative Strength ——

OPTIONS: ASE

Overview - 15-AUG-95

Copper volumes in 1995 will increase significantly reflecting contributions from the new Candelaria mine in Chile and the completion of the Southside expansion at Morenci in 1995's second half. Unit costs should drop in 1995's second half after being hurt by lower mill throughput at Morenci due to harder ores. While copper prices will be higher, PD's extensive use of hedging will keep copper price realizations below spot market levels. An improved performance is seen for carbon black reflecting higher prices and volumes and the 1994 acquisition of a Spanish producer. Accuride should benefit from strong demand from North American truck builders. Interest costs will increase as PD is no longer capitalizing Candelaria-related debt. The effective tax rate will be higher.

Valuation - 15-AUG-95

Shares of this leading copper producer reached record highs in July as investors now anticipate firm copper prices well into next year. Despite PD's strong performance, the shares remain undervalued at nearly a 50% discount to the market multiple. With the completition of the Candelaria mine in late 1994, PD has ample cash flow to fund the 5,000,000 share (7%) buyback program launched in March and make additional hikes in the dividend rate. Profits should remain at high levels in 1996 even should copper prices slide since PD has hedged a large portion of its production at $0.95/lb. or greater.

Key Stock Statistics

S&P EPS Est. 1995	9.25	Tang. Bk. Value/Share	33.19
P/E on S&P Est. 1995	6.9	Beta	0.95
S&P EPS Est. 1996	8.75	Shareholders	11,500
Dividend Rate/Share	1.80	Market cap. (B)	$ 4.5
Shs. outstg. (M)	69.5	Inst. holdings	83%
Avg. daily vol. (M)	0.473	Insider holdings	NA

Value of $10,000 invested 5 years ago: $ 26,634

Fiscal Year Ending Dec. 31

	1995	% Change	1994	% Change	1993	% Change
Revenues ()						
1Q	1,034	49%	694.3	4%	666.7	13%
2Q	1,024	31%	780.4	24%	629.8	-5%
3Q	—	—	813.7	26%	646.7	-4%
4Q	—	—	1,001	53%	652.7	NM
Yr.	—	—	3,289	27%	2,596	NM
Income ()						
1Q	185.3	NM	48.60	-19%	60.30	16%
2Q	159.5	147%	64.60	40%	46.30	-30%
3Q	—	—	94.20	137%	39.70	-66%
4Q	—	—	63.60	53%	41.60	-36%
Yr.	—	—	271.0	44%	187.9	-38%
Earnings Per Share ()						
1Q	2.61	NM	0.69	-19%	0.85	15%
2Q	2.28	151%	0.91	38%	0.66	-30%
3Q	E2.20	65%	1.33	138%	0.56	-67%
4Q	E2.16	143%	0.89	51%	0.59	-37%
Yr.	E9.25	143%	3.81	43%	2.66	-38%

Next earnings report expected: mid October

Business Summary - 14-AUG-95

Phelps Dodge is one of the world's largest copper producer operating mines in the United States and Chile. PD also has interests in manufacturing and industrial processes. Contributions (in $ millions) to operating profits by business segment:

	1994	1993	1992
Copper/mining	$326.4	$227.2	$366.0
Industrial	106.1	129.1	85.2

In 1994 PD accounted for more than 25% of total U.S. copper production. Total copper production worldwide in 1994 was 572,800 tons (net of minority interests), versus 547,700 tons in 1993. Some 47% of production in 1994 was through the low-cost solution extraction/electrowinning process. At 1994 year-end PD had commercially recoverable copper reserves of 10.6 million tons. PD's copper operations include mining, concentrating, smelting, refining and rod production. PD produced 683,500 tons of copper rod in 1994 of which one-third was sold to an affiliated company. PD also smelts, refines and produces copper for others on a toll basis.

As a byproduct of its copper activities, PD produced in 1994 some 65,000 ounces of gold, 1,270,000 ounces of silver, 743,000 lbs. of molybdenum and 1,090,000 tons of sulfuric acid. PD also operates a fluospar mine in South Africa, has a 44.6% stake in a lead, zinc, copper and silver mine in South Africa and a 16.3% stake in Southern Peru Copper Corp.

Phelps Dodge's Industrial operations include Phelps Dodge Magnet Wire, the world's leading producer of insulated magnet wire for use in motors, generators and transformers; Columbian Chemicals Co., one of the world's largest producer of carbon black; Accuride Corp., the largest producer in North America of steel wheels and rims for trucks, buses and trailers and Hudson International Conductors, a manufacturer of specialty, high-performance conductors and alloys.

Important Developments

Aug. '95—Through August 4 the company repurchased 1,433,000 of its common shares for $78.7 million ($54.92 each) under a 5,000,000 share buyback plan (7.1% of PD's total) authorized in March. Separately in August PD agreed to acquire AZCO Mining's Sanchez copper project in Arizona and its 70% stake in the Piedras Verde copper deposit in Mexico for $40 million.

Capitalization

Long Term Debt: $624,800,000 (6/95).
Minority Interest: $67,300,000.

Per Share Data () (Year Ended Dec. 31)

	1994	1993	1992	1991	1990	1989
Tangible Bk. Val.	28.87	26.35	25.69	24.24	21.94	17.02
Cash Flow	6.56	5.23	6.51	5.85	8.40	5.64
Earnings	3.81	2.66	4.28	3.93	6.56	3.80
Dividends	1.69	1.65	1.61	1.50	1.50	6.43
Payout Ratio	44%	62%	38%	38%	23%	167%
Prices - High	65	55⅝	53	39⅝	35⅞	39⅜
- Low	47⅝	39⅛	32	26¼	23⅛	25¾
P/E Ratio - High	17	21	12	10	5	10
- Low	13	15	7	7	4	7

Income Statement Analysis ()

	1994	%Chg	1993	%Chg	1992	%Chg	1991
Revs.	3,289	27%	2,596	NM	2,579	6%	2,434
Oper. Inc.	753	52%	496	-12%	565	4%	545
Depr.	195	7%	182	16%	157	17%	134
Int. Exp.	57.3	5%	54.5	15%	47.4	NM	47.5
Pretax Inc.	384	31%	294	-29%	416	3%	404
Eff. Tax Rate	27%	—	36%	—	28%	—	33%
Net Inc.	271	44%	188	-38%	302	11%	273

Balance Sheet & Other Fin. Data ()

	1994	1993	1992	1991	1990	1989
Cash	287	256	251	182	162	13.0
Curr. Assets	1,208	987	990	818	839	691
Total Assets	4,134	3,721	3,441	3,051	2,827	2,505
Curr. Liab.	650	540	541	477	490	479
LT Debt	622	547	374	382	403	432
Common Eqty.	2,188	2,022	1,972	1,859	1,683	1,350
Total Cap.	3,119	2,918	2,662	2,434	2,221	1,869
Cap. Exp.	376	428	318	366	292	219
Cash Flow	466	370	458	406	582	395

Ratio Analysis

	1994	1993	1992	1991	1990	1989
Curr. Ratio	1.9	1.8	1.8	1.7	1.7	1.4
% LT Debt of Cap.	20.0	18.8	14.0	15.7	18.2	23.1
% Net Inc.of Revs.	8.2	7.2	11.7	11.2	17.3	9.9
% Ret. on Assets	6.9	5.2	9.2	9.2	17.1	9.5
% Ret. on Equity	12.9	9.4	15.7	15.3	30.1	17.9

Dividend Data — A "poison pill" stock purchase rights plan was amended in 1989.

Amt. of Div. $	Date Decl.	Ex-Div. Date	Stock of Record	Payment Date
0.412	Jul. 29	Aug. 15	Aug. 19	Sep. 08 '94
0.450	Nov. 02	Nov. 14	Nov. 18	Dec. 08 '94
0.450	Feb. 01	Feb. 13	Feb. 17	Mar. 08 '95
0.450	May. 03	May. 15	May. 19	Jun. 08 '95
0.450	Jul. 28	Aug. 16	Aug. 18	Sep. 08 '95

Data as orig. reptd.; bef. results of disc. opers. and/or spec. items. Per share data adj. for stk. divs. as of ex-div. date. E-Estimated. NA-Not Available. NM-Not Meaningful. NR-Not Ranked.

Office—2600 N. Central Ave., Phoenix, AZ 85004-3014. **Tel**—(602) 234-8100. **Chrmn, Pres & CEO**—D. C. Yearley. **SVP & CFO**—T. M. St. Clair. **VP & Secy**—W. C. Tubman. **VP & Investor Contact**—Thomas M. Foster. **Dirs**—E. L. Addison, R. N. Burt, P. W. Douglas, W. A. Franke, P. Hazen, M. L. Knowles, R. D. Krebs, S. J. Morcott, G. R. Parker, D. C. Yearley. **Transfer Agent & Registrar**—Chemical Bank, NYC. **Incorporated** in New York in 1885. **Empl**-15,498. **S&P Analyst:** Stephen R. Klein

Philip Morris

NYSE Symbol **MO**
In S&P 500

23-OCT-95

Industry: Tobacco

Summary: Philip Morris is the world's largest cigarette producer, the largest U.S. food processor (Kraft Foods), and the second largest U.S. brewer (Miller Brewing).

S&P Opinion: Buy (★★★★★)	Recent Price • 85⅝	Yield • 4.7%
	52 Wk Range • 86-55¾	12-Mo. P/E • 13.7

Earnings vs. Previous Year
▲=Up ▼=Down ▶=No Change

Quantitative Evaluations

Outlook (1 Lowest—5 Highest)
• **5+**

Fair Value
• **99⅝**

Risk
• **Low**

Earn./Div. Rank
• **A+**

Technical Eval.
• **Bullish** since 8/94

Rel. Strength Rank (1 Lowest—99 Highest)
• **85**

Insider Activity
• **Neutral**

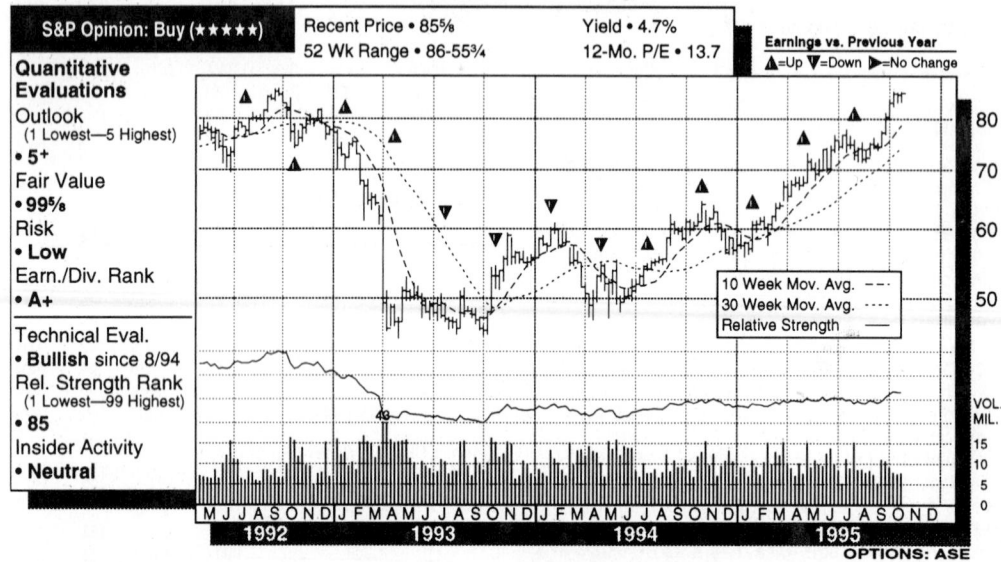

10 Week Mov. Avg. – – –
30 Week Mov. Avg. ····
Relative Strength ——

OPTIONS: ASE

Overview - 23-OCT-95

U.S. tobacco profits are expected to grow at an approximate 10% annual pace through 1996, driven primarily by an improving product mix shift to full-priced, premium brands (principally Marlboro) and cost cutting. International tobacco profits are expected to rise by 15% to 20% through 1996, driven by higher volumes in new and existing markets and higher selling prices. Food and beer profits are expected to grow more modestly, led by an improved U.S. business mix and international expansion. Reduced interest expense and continued aggressive stock repurchases should allow earnings per share to advance at strong rates through 1996. Further divestments of underperforming businesses are likely, which could enhance our near-term earnings estimates.

Valuation - 23-OCT-95

Given our bullish earnings growth projections, MO's relatively modest market valuation, and an attractive 4%-plus dividend yield, we believe MO offers investors compelling total return prospects in the current slow economic environment. Although tobacco industry risks are above average, we believe the industry's legal and regulatory environment in the near term may become more favorable. Our belief stems from the new Republican-controlled Congress's stance on easing regulatory burdens on business, and recent judgments that may make lawsuits brought by a handful of states against the U.S. tobacco industry seeking recovery for alleged tobacco-related illnesses more difficult.

Key Stock Statistics

S&P EPS Est. 1995	6.55	Tang. Bk. Value/Share	NM
P/E on S&P Est. 1995	13.1	Beta	1.66
S&P EPS Est. 1996	7.60	Shareholders	154,300
Dividend Rate/Share	4.00	Market cap. (B)	$ 71.9
Shs. outstg. (M)	840.0	Inst. holdings	61%
Avg. daily vol. (M)	1.577	Insider holdings	NA

Value of $10,000 invested 5 years ago: $ 25,445

Fiscal Year Ending Dec. 31

	1995	% Change	1994	% Change	1993	% Change
Revenues (Million $)						
1Q	13,300	4%	12,730	1%	12,570	6%
2Q	17,129	27%	13,530	3%	13,160	2%
3Q	16,689	22%	13,670	9%	12,580	NM
4Q	—	—	13,840	12%	12,320	-3%
Yr.	—	—	53,780	6%	50,621	1%
Income (Million $)						
1Q	1,363	16%	1,171	-4%	1,218	11%
2Q	1,410	14%	1,232	17%	1,053	-22%
3Q	1,433	17%	1,230	27%	971.0	-25%
4Q	—	—	1,092	NM	339.0	-72%
Yr.	—	—	4,725	32%	3,568	-28%
Earnings Per Share ($)						
1Q	1.60	19%	1.34	-3%	1.38	15%
2Q	1.67	18%	1.42	18%	1.20	-19%
3Q	1.71	20%	1.42	28%	1.11	-23%
4Q	E1.57	24%	1.27	NM	0.38	-72%
Yr.	E6.55	20%	5.45	34%	4.06	-26%

Next earnings report expected: late January

Business Summary - 23-OCT-95

Philip Morris is the largest cigarette company in the world and a major food and beer producer. Segment contributions in 1994:

	Revs.	Profits
Tobacco	44%	62%
Food	49%	32%
Brewing	6%	4%
Financial & real estate	1%	2%

International operations accounted for approximately 45% of sales (including U.S. exports) and 26% of operating profits in 1994.

Philip Morris U.S.A., with 45% of the U.S. cigarette market, accounted for 17% of total company sales and 31% of operating profits in 1994. Major brands include Marlboro, Benson & Hedges, Merit, Virginia Slims and Cambridge. MO is a defendant in a number of product-liability suits related to cigarettes. Philip Morris International's share of the world market in 1994 (excluding U.S.) was approximately 11%.

Kraft Foods is the largest processor and marketer in the U.S. of packaged grocery, coffee, cheese and processed meat products. Kraft Foods International produces a wide variety of similar products that are manufactured and marketed in Europe, Canada, Latin America and the Asia/Pacific region. Food products include Post cereals; Jell-O desserts; Maxwell House coffee; Velveeta, Cracker Barrel and Churny cheeses; Oscar Mayer meat products; and Claussen pickles.

Miller Brewing (No. 2 U.S. brewer) holds nearly 23% of the domestic beer market. Brands include High Life, Lite, Genuine Draft, Lowenbrau, and Meister Brau. Miller also imports more than 20 brands from six countries, including Molson and Foster's Lager.

Important Developments

Oct. '95—During the first nine months of 1994, domestic tobacco profits increased 12%, year to year, primarily reflecting higher selling prices and a favorable product mix shift toward full-priced brands (principally Marlboro). International tobacco profits rose 20%, driven by greater volume and favorable currency movements. Food profits rose 4% (7% excluding divestments), aided by volume gains and cost reductions for domestic operations and cost reduction efforts for international operations. Beer profits rose 8%, benefiting from volume growth of premium-priced brands, particularly its new Red Dog product. Separately, MO continued to repurchase its shares under an existing 3-year, $6 billion program; it bought 21.6 million shares during the first nine months at a cost of $1.5 billion.

Capitalization

Long Term Debt: $13,324,000,000 (9/95).

Per Share Data ($)
(Year Ended Dec. 31)

	1994	1993	1992	1991	1990	1989
Tangible Bk. Val.	-8.20	-9.30	-6.72	-6.69	-7.70	-6.58
Cash Flow	7.33	5.90	7.09	5.80	5.26	4.41
Earnings	5.45	4.06	5.45	4.24	3.83	3.18
Dividends	3.03	2.60	2.35	1.91	1.55	1.25
Payout Ratio	56%	64%	43%	45%	40%	39%
Prices - High	64½	77⅝	86⅝	81¾	52	45¾
- Low	47¼	45	69½	48¼	36	25
P/E Ratio - High	12	19	16	19	14	14
- Low	9	11	13	11	9	8

Income Statement Analysis (Million $)

	1994	%Chg	1993	%Chg	1992	%Chg	1991
Revs.	53,776	6%	50,621	1%	50,095	4%	48,064
Oper. Inc.	11,080	11%	9,939	-14%	11,550	10%	10,515
Depr.	1,631	1%	1,611	9%	1,484	3%	1,438
Int. Exp.	1,288	-13%	1,478	-2%	1,513	-11%	1,696
Pretax Inc.	8,216	33%	6,196	-28%	8,608	23%	6,971
Eff. Tax Rate	43%	—	42%	—	43%	—	44%
Net Inc.	4,725	32%	3,568	-28%	4,939	26%	3,927

Balance Sheet & Other Fin. Data (Million $)

	1994	1993	1992	1991	1990	1989
Cash	184	182	1,021	126	146	118
Curr. Assets	NA	NA	NA	NA	NA	NA
Total Assets	52,649	51,205	50,014	47,384	46,569	38,528
Curr. Liab.	NA	NA	NA	NA	NA	NA
LT Debt	14,975	15,021	14,265	14,200	16,108	14,685
Common Eqty.	12,786	11,627	12,563	12,512	11,947	9,571
Total Cap.	31,156	29,715	29,716	29,186	30,753	26,264
Cap. Exp.	1,726	1,592	1,573	1,562	1,355	1,246
Cash Flow	6,356	5,179	6,423	5,365	4,865	4,088

Ratio Analysis

	1994	1993	1992	1991	1990	1989
Curr. Ratio	NA	NA	NA	NA	NA	NA
% LT Debt of Cap.	48.1	50.6	48.0	48.7	52.4	55.9
% Net Inc.of Revs.	8.8	7.0	9.9	8.2	8.0	7.6
% Ret. on Assets	9.2	7.1	10.3	8.4	8.3	7.8
% Ret. on Equity	39.2	29.8	40.0	32.2	32.9	34.1

Dividend Data
—Dividends have been paid since 1928. A dividend reinvestment plan is available. A "poison pill" stock purchase rights plan was adopted in 1989.

Amt. of Div. $	Date Decl.	Ex-Div. Date	Stock of Record	Payment Date
0.825	Nov. 23	Dec. 09	Dec. 15	Jan. 10 '95
0.825	Mar. 01	Mar. 09	Mar. 15	Apr. 10 '95
0.825	May. 31	Jun. 13	Jun. 15	Jul. 10 '95
1.000	Aug. 30	Sep. 13	Sep. 15	Oct. 10 '95

Data as orig. reptd.; bef. results of disc. opers. and/or spec. items. Per share data adj. for stk. divs. as of ex-div. date.
E-Estimated. NA-Not Available. NM-Not Meaningful. NR-Not Ranked.

Office—120 Park Ave., New York, NY 10017. **Tel**—(212) 880-5000. **Chrmn & CEO**—G. C. Bible. **SVP-CFO**—H. G. Storr. **VP-Secy**—G. P. Holsenbeck. **Investor Contact**—Michael Kenny. **Dirs**—E. E. Bailey, G. C. Bible, M. H. Bring, H. Brown, W. H. Donaldson, J. Evans, R. E. R. Huntley, R. Murdoch, J. D. Nichols, R. D. Parsons, R. S. Penske, J. S. Reed, H. G. Storr, S. M. Wolf. **Transfer Agents & Registrars**—First Chicago Trust Co. of New York, NYC. **Incorporated** in Virginia in 1919. **Empl**-165,000. **S&P Analyst:** Kenneth A. Shea

Phillips Petroleum

NYSE Symbol **P**
In S&P 500

31-OCT-95

Industry:
Oil and Gas

Summary: Phillips is an integrated oil and gas company. It also makes plastics and petrochemicals and is the largest U.S. producer of natural gas liquids.

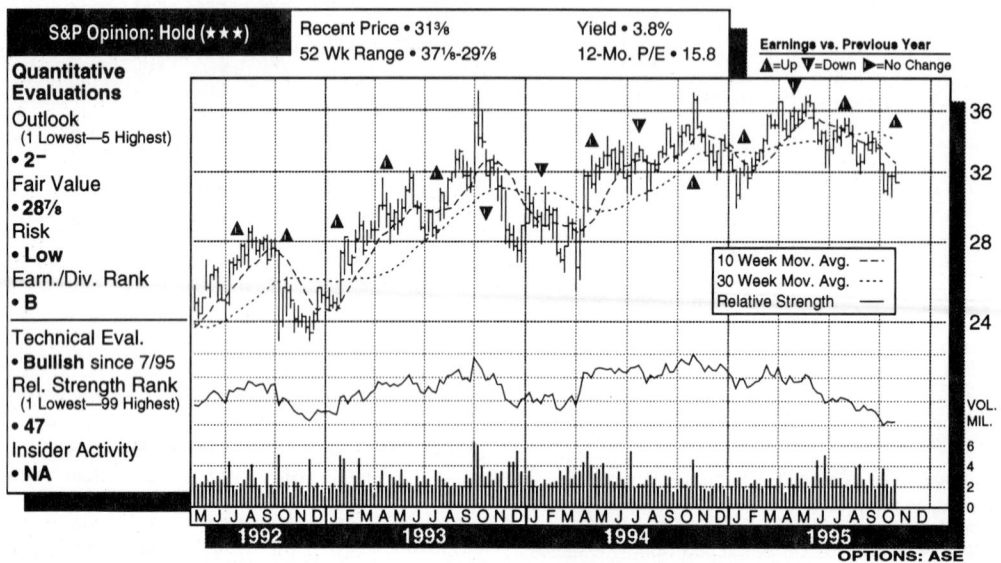

S&P Opinion: Hold (★★★)	

Recent Price • 31⅜	Yield • 3.8%
52 Wk Range • 37⅛-29⅞	12-Mo. P/E • 15.8

Earnings vs. Previous Year
▲=Up ▼=Down ▶=No Change

Quantitative Evaluations

Outlook
(1 Lowest—5 Highest)
• **2-**

Fair Value
• **28⅞**

Risk
• **Low**

Earn./Div. Rank
• **B**

Technical Eval.
• **Bullish** since 7/95

Rel. Strength Rank
(1 Lowest—99 Highest)
• **47**

Insider Activity
• **NA**

10 Week Mov. Avg. – – –
30 Week Mov. Avg. ·····
Relative Strength ——

VOL. MIL.

OPTIONS: ASE

Overview - 31-OCT-95

Revenues will rise in the near-term, as increased volumes offset lower prices. Operating profits are also expected to show modest improvement. The company is aggressively developing its holdings in the Gulf of Mexico, where P has made a substantial sub-salt discovery in the Mahogany field, in which P has a 37.5% net interest. South China Sea and Norwegian production should plateau over the next several years, however further discoveries in the Gulf of Mexico sub-salt should make up for the short-fall. Chemical earnings should taper off in late 1995 and into 1996, though additional paraxylene capacity in Puerto Rico and elsewhere bodes well for the future. Debt reduction will remain a priority, and cost controls are an important aspect of further business restructuring efforts.

Valuation - 31-OCT-95

The shares have recently retreated, as a result of weak fundamentals for commodity prices. We believe Phillips' shares should perform as well as the market in the remainder of 1995, barring any surprises from the November OPEC meeting. Our forecast for gradually rising natural gas prices through 1996 is the reason we rate the stock a hold at current levels, though it currently appears overvalued on a P/E basis relative to the domestic integrated oil group. Strong cash flow, primarily from increased chemical capacity, will allow Phillips to accept attractive oil and gas exploration projects which should buoy the shares.

Key Stock Statistics

S&P EPS Est. 1995	2.05	Tang. Bk. Value/Share	11.80
P/E on S&P Est. 1995	15.3	Beta	1.00
S&P EPS Est. 1996	2.20	Shareholders	69,500
Dividend Rate/Share	1.22	Market cap. (B)	$ 8.4
Shs. outstg. (M)	262.2	Inst. holdings	54%
Avg. daily vol. (M)	0.500	Insider holdings	NA

Value of $10,000 invested 5 years ago: $ 15,745

Fiscal Year Ending Dec. 31

	1995	% Change	1994	% Change	1993	% Change
Revenues (Million $)						
1Q	3,124	8%	2,884	-5%	3,029	12%
2Q	3,636	21%	2,995	-7%	3,230	6%
3Q	3,369	2%	3,315	5%	3,170	2%
4Q	—	—	3,017	5%	2,880	-7%
Yr.	—	—	12,211	NM	12,309	3%
Income (Million $)						
1Q	111.0	-13%	127.0	108%	61.00	NM
2Q	113.0	49%	76.00	-38%	123.0	23%
3Q	136.0	14%	119.0	190%	41.00	-59%
4Q	—	—	162.0	NM	39.00	-73%
Yr.	—	—	484.0	98%	245.0	-9%
Earnings Per Share ($)						
1Q	0.43	-12%	0.49	113%	0.23	NM
2Q	0.42	45%	0.29	-38%	0.47	24%
3Q	0.52	16%	0.45	181%	0.16	-61%
4Q	E0.68	10%	0.62	NM	0.08	-86%
Yr.	E2.05	11%	1.85	97%	0.94	-10%

Next earnings report expected: late January

McGraw Hill

Phillips Petroleum

31-OCT-95

Business Summary - 31-OCT-95

Phillips explores for and produces crude oil and natural gas worldwide, markets refined products in the U.S., and manufactures chemicals. Earnings by segment in recent years were divided:

	1994	1993
U.S. exploration/production	35%	43%
Foreign expl. & prod.	11%	23%
Refining, Marketing & Transp.	18%	11%
Gas and gas liquids	Nil	7%
Chemicals	36%	16%

In 1994, crude oil production averaged 206,000 bbl. a day (203,000 in 1993), natural gas production 1.41 Bcf a day (1.36), natural gas liquids 14,000 b/d (13,000), crude oil refined (U.S.) 317,000 b/d (278,000), and petroleum products sold 547,000 b/d (506,000). Worldwide crude oil proved reserves at year-end 1994 amounted to 703 billion barrels, while proved natural gas reserves stood at 5,030 Bcf. Natural gas liquids proved reserves equaled 178 million barrels. Phillips replaced 149% of its production during 1994. The 1995 capital budget calls for spending of $1.4 billion, up from 1994's $1.2 billion.

In February 1994, P announced a restructuring of its refining, marketing and chemical (downstream) activities into two divisions: Phillips 66 Co., which will include refining, marketing and transportation, and Phillips Chemical Co., for natural gas liquids, chemicals and plastics. Important initiatives for 1995 include sub-salt exploration in the Gulf of Mexico, where nearly one-quarter of the exploration budget will be directed. Chinese and North Sea exploration will also be two areas of focus, and further expansion of petrochemical capacity in Puerto Rico is planned. Additional olefin and plastic capacity will also be added.

Important Developments

Oct. '95—Operating income fell to $151 million in the third quarter, up from $141 million the prior year, and down from the second quarter's $178 million. Narrower refining and marketing margins hurt third quarter comparisons, despite refineries operating at near capacity. Exploration & production earnings fell as a result of an 18% decline in the average U.S. natural gas price, although natural gas production was up 7%, and crude oil output rose 9%. Improved margins for ethylene and polyethylene drove sharply higher earnings from the chemical segment.

Sep. '95—Phillips said start-up natural gas volumes from its Judy/Joanne project at J-Block in the U.K. North Sea may be delayed or lower than estimated. The company said the long term economics of the project remain favorable, but delays in production will affect net earnings and cash flows in the near term.

Capitalization

Long Term Debt: $2,876,000,000 (9/95).
Minority Interest: $351,000,000.

Per Share Data ($)

(Year Ended Dec. 31)

	1994	1993	1992	1991	1990	1989
Tangible Bk. Val.	11.29	10.28	10.37	10.61	10.51	8.74
Cash Flow	4.89	3.98	4.13	5.03	5.33	5.96
Earnings	1.85	0.94	1.04	0.38	2.18	0.90
Dividends	1.12	1.12	1.12	1.12	1.03	1.02
Payout Ratio	61%	119%	108%	297%	49%	114%
Prices - High	37¼	37⅜	28⅞	29½	31⅛	30⅛
- Low	25½	24½	22	21⅞	22½	19⅛
P/E Ratio - High	20	40	28	78	14	33
- Low	14	26	21	58	10	21

Income Statement Analysis (Million $)

	1994	%Chg	1993	%Chg	1992	%Chg	1991
Revs.	12,211	NM	12,309	3%	11,933	-5%	12,604
Oper. Inc.	1,752	25%	1,407	-5%	1,486	2%	1,461
Depr.	794	NM	795	-1%	804	-33%	1,208
Int. Exp.	265	-8%	289	-26%	392	-18%	479
Pretax Inc.	852	58%	538	5%	511	13%	451
Eff. Tax Rate	43%	—	55%	—	47%	—	78%
Net Inc.	484	98%	245	-9%	270	176%	98.0

Balance Sheet & Other Fin. Data (Million $)

	1994	1993	1992	1991	1990	1989
Cash	193	119	131	114	670	708
Curr. Assets	2,465	2,193	2,349	2,459	3,322	2,876
Total Assets	11,436	10,868	11,468	11,473	12,130	11,256
Curr. Liab.	2,441	2,271	2,517	2,603	2,910	2,706
LT Debt	3,106	3,208	3,718	3,876	3,839	3,939
Common Eqty.	2,953	2,688	2,698	2,757	2,719	2,132
Total Cap.	7,354	7,159	7,438	7,828	7,841	7,792
Cap. Exp.	1,154	1,132	1,254	1,406	1,383	872
Cash Flow	1,278	1,040	1,074	1,306	1,327	1,452

Ratio Analysis

	1994	1993	1992	1991	1990	1989
Curr. Ratio	1.0	1.0	0.9	0.9	1.1	1.1
% LT Debt of Cap.	42.2	44.8	50.0	49.5	49.0	50.6
% Net Inc.of Revs.	4.0	2.0	2.3	0.8	4.0	1.8
% Ret. on Assets	4.3	2.2	2.4	0.8	4.5	1.9
% Ret. on Equity	17.2	9.1	9.9	3.6	21.7	10.3

Dividend Data

Dividends have been paid since 1934. A dividend reinvestment plan is available. A new "poison pill" stock purchase rights plan was adopted in 1989.

Amt. of Div. $	Date Decl.	Ex-Div. Date	Stock of Record	Payment Date
0.280	Oct. 10	Oct. 31	Nov. 04	Dec. 01 '94
0.280	Jan. 09	Jan. 30	Feb. 03	Mar. 01 '95
0.305	Apr. 10	May. 01	May. 05	Jun. 01 '95
0.305	Jul. 10	Aug. 02	Aug. 04	Sep. 01 '95
0.305	Oct. 09	Nov. 01	Nov. 03	Dec. 01 '95

Data as orig. reptd.; bef. results of disc. opers. and/or spec. items. Per share data adj. for stk. divs. as of ex-div. date. E-Estimated. NA-Not Available. NM-Not Meaningful. NR-Not Ranked.

Office—Phillips Bldg., Bartlesville, OK 74004. **Tel**—(918) 661-6600. **Chrmn & CEO**—W. W. Allen. **Pres & COO**—J. J. Mulva. **SVP & CFO**—T. C. Morris. **Secy**—D. J. Billam. **VP & Investor Contact**—E. K. Grigsby, 630 Fifth Ave, New York, NY 10111 (212-397-9766). **Dirs**—W. W. Allen, N. R. Augustine, G. B. Beitzel, D. L. Boren, C. L. Bowerman, R. E. Chappell, Jr., L. S. Eagleburger, J. B. Edwards, L. D. Horner, E. D. Kenna, J. J. Mulva, N. L Tobias, V. J. Tschinkel, K. C. Turner, J. L. Whitmire. **Transfer Agents & Registrars**—Chemical Bank, NYC; Montreal Trust Co., Toronto. **Incorporated** in Delaware in 1917. **Empl**-18,400. **S&P Analyst:** Raymond J. Deacon

Pioneer Hi-Bred International

NASDAQ Symbol **PHYB**

In S&P 500

24-OCT-95

Industry:
Food

Summary: This company is the leading North American breeder and producer of hybrid seed corn, with an approximate 45% North American market share.

S&P Opinion: Hold (★★★)

Recent Price • 47	Yield • 1.7%
52 Wk Range • 50½-30½	12-Mo. P/E • 21.8

Quantitative Evaluations

Outlook
(1 Lowest—5 Highest)
• **2+**

Fair Value
• **44⅜**

Risk
• **Low**

Earn./Div. Rank
• **B+**

Technical Eval.
• **Bullish** since 11/94

Rel. Strength Rank
(1 Lowest—99 Highest)
• **78**

Insider Activity
• **Neutral**

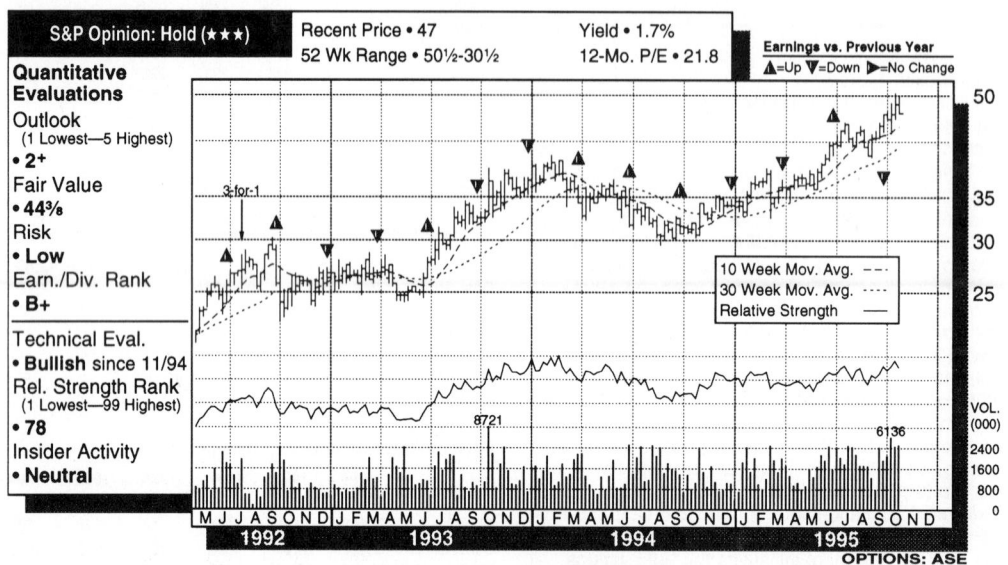

Earnings vs. Previous Year
▲=Up ▼=Down ▶=No Change

3-for-1

10 Week Mov. Avg. ---
30 Week Mov. Avg. ······
Relative Strength ——

8721

6136

VOL. (000)

MJJASONDJFMAMJJASONDJFMAMJJASONDJFMAMJJASOND
1992 1993 1994 1995

OPTIONS: ASE

Overview - 24-OCT-95

Net sales are expected to rise by 10% to 15% in fiscal 1996, led by a good rebound in North American planted corn acreage, increased seed corn market share, and modestly higher average prices. Margins should benefit from the above factors, and push net income up by 15% to 20%. With fewer shares outstanding following recent aggressive share buybacks, earnings per share could climb to $2.60 in fiscal 1996. Longer-term prospects are also bright, reflecting the company's dominant position in the highly profitable seed corn supplier market. Future returns on shareholders equity should hover at about 20% annually despite a relatively low amount of debt outstanding.

Valuation - 24-OCT-95

Despite our expectations of a strong rebound in earnings per share for fiscal 1996, we expect the shares to be only an average market performer in the near-term due principally to the stock's already strong upward movement in 1995. At their current multiple of 18 times fiscal 1996's $2.60 EPS estimate, the shares are trading at a significant premium to most of its peers, as well as the S&P 500. However, based upon the company's bright future, as well as past performance of consistent earnings growth, we do advise longer term investors to selectively accumulate these high-quality shares upon any share weakness.

Key Stock Statistics

S&P EPS Est. 1996	2.60	Tang. Bk. Value/Share	9.96
P/E on S&P Est. 1996	18.1	Beta	1.38
Dividend Rate/Share	0.80	Shareholders	3,500
Shs. outstg. (M)	84.1	Market cap. (B)	$ 4.0
Avg. daily vol. (M)	0.755	Inst. holdings	56%
		Insider holdings	NA

Value of $10,000 invested 5 years ago: $ 35,134

Fiscal Year Ending Aug. 31

	1995	% Change	1994	% Change	1993	% Change
Revenues (Million $)						
1Q	69.00	3%	66.67	-2%	68.00	26%
2Q	277.0	11%	250.0	60%	156.6	-12%
3Q	1,049	1%	1,039	12%	930.9	13%
4Q	137.0	11%	123.5	-34%	187.5	-8%
Yr.	1,532	4%	1,479	10%	1,343	6%
Income (Million $)						
1Q	-48.00	NM	-43.85	NM	-38.81	NM
2Q	9.00	-44%	16.15	NM	-15.20	NM
3Q	272.0	4%	260.3	14%	228.6	16%
4Q	-50.00	NM	-19.97	NM	-37.16	NM
Yr.	183.0	-14%	212.7	55%	137.4	-10%
Earnings Per Share ($)						
1Q	-0.57	NM	-0.49	NM	-0.43	NM
2Q	0.11	-39%	0.18	NM	-0.17	NM
3Q	3.23	10%	2.94	16%	2.53	16%
4Q	-0.59	NM	-0.23	NM	-0.42	NM
Yr.	2.16	-10%	2.40	57%	1.53	-9%

Next earnings report expected: mid January

Pioneer Hi-Bred International

24-OCT-95

Business Summary - 24-OCT-95

Pioneer Hi-Bred International is the leading North American breeder and producer of hybrid seed corn. It also breeds and produces hybrid sorghum, soybean, forage and other seeds. In addition, the company provides computer-based data services for farmers and agribusiness and produces genetically engineered microorganisms for crop and livestock production.

Contributions (profits in millions) in fiscal 1994 were:

	Sales	Profits
Corn	80%	$383.4
Soybeans	9%	7.5
Other	11%	-21.1

Operations outside North America contributed 29% of net sales and 28% of operating profits in fiscal 1994.

Based on company estimates, Pioneer seed corn accounted for 44.9% of the total North American market in fiscal 1994. The company is also believed to have a leading position of the soybean seed market, with an estimated 16.4% share. In fiscal 1994, the company spennt $113.7 million on R&D, up 8% from the level of fiscal 1993.

The seed business is highly seasonal, with substantially all sales made in December through May. Operations during the first and fourth quarters of the fiscal year are often unprofitable.

Pioneer owns 24 conditioning plants for commercial seed corn. The plants can handle 57,940 bushels of ear corn per hour, on average, and condition 15,100 units per hour. In a normal year, seed conditioning is completed by early February.

Important Developments

Oct. '95—Pioneer said results in fiscal 1995 were encouraging in light of the nearly 10% reduction in U.S. corn acreage during the year, which reflected a government set-aside program and extremely wet fields in much of the Midwest. Also challenging the company's profitability during the year was abundant supplies of seed corn after the bountiful 1994 harvest, which led to very aggressive pricing in North America. PHYB said that it held its North Anerica hybrid seed corn market share at approximately 45%. Management also said that it looked forward to a strong year in fiscal 1996, relecting in part Pioneer's overall good supply of high quality seed, and expectations of significantly increased corn acreage in the spring of 1996.

Capitalization

Long Term Debt: $14,000,000 (5/95).
Minority Interest: $10,000,000.

Per Share Data ($)

(Year Ended Aug. 31)

	1995	1994	1993	1992	1991	1990
Tangible Bk. Val.	NA	9.96	8.92	8.54	7.28	6.92
Cash Flow	NA	3.08	2.10	2.25	1.77	1.32
Earnings	2.16	2.40	1.53	1.68	1.15	0.78
Dividends	0.71	0.65	0.50	0.40	0.39	0.39
Payout Ratio	33%	27%	33%	24%	34%	50%
Prices - High	50½	40½	38¾	30¼	24¾	15⅞
- Low	32½	29½	24⅛	19¾	11⅞	10⅜
P/E Ratio - High	23	17	25	18	22	20
- Low	15	12	16	12	10	13

Income Statement Analysis (Million $)

	1994	%Chg	1993	%Chg	1992	%Chg	1991
Revs.	1,479	10%	1,343	6%	1,262	12%	1,125
Oper. Inc.	362	9%	331	12%	295	20%	245
Depr.	60.1	16%	52.0	NM	51.7	-8%	56.3
Int. Exp.	11.3	-37%	17.8	8%	16.5	-26%	22.3
Pretax Inc.	347	56%	223	-7%	239	42%	168
Eff. Tax Rate	39%	—	38%	—	36%	—	38%
Net Inc.	213	55%	137	-10%	152	46%	104

Balance Sheet & Other Fin. Data (Million $)

	1994	1993	1992	1991	1990	1989
Cash	135	92.0	97.6	62.4	48.4	54.5
Curr. Assets	742	717	703	605	538	474
Total Assets	1,253	1,221	1,216	1,086	1,006	914
Curr. Liab.	232	261	286	295	294	221
LT Debt	65.6	68.1	73.9	67.4	18.9	16.5
Common Eqty.	881	825	799	681	649	627
Total Cap.	954	900	885	754	672	650
Cap. Exp.	80.0	100	75.0	59.0	77.0	92.0
Cash Flow	273	189	204	160	126	131

Ratio Analysis

	1994	1993	1992	1991	1990	1989
Curr. Ratio	3.2	2.7	2.5	2.1	1.8	2.1
% LT Debt of Cap.	6.9	7.6	8.4	8.9	2.8	2.5
% Net Inc.of Revs.	14.4	10.2	12.1	9.3	7.5	9.4
% Ret. on Assets	17.5	11.3	13.2	10.1	7.6	9.2
% Ret. on Equity	25.4	17.0	20.6	15.8	11.5	13.7

Dividend Data

—Cash has been paid each year since 1935. A dividend reinvestment plan is available.

Amt. of Div. $	Date Decl.	Ex-Div. Date	Stock of Record	Payment Date
0.170	Dec. 13	Dec. 20	Dec. 27	Jan. 10 '95
0.170	Mar. 14	Mar. 21	Mar. 27	Apr. 07 '95
0.200	Jun. 13	Jun. 22	Jun. 26	Jul. 07 '95
0.200	Sep. 12	Sep. 21	Sep. 25	Oct. 06 '95

Data as orig. reptd.; bef. results of disc. opers. and/or spec. items. Per share data adj. for stk. divs. as of ex-div. date. E-Estimated. NA-Not Available. NM-Not Meaningful. NR-Not Ranked.

Office—700 Capital Square, 400 Locust St., Des Moines, IA 50309. **Tel**—(515) 248-4800. **Chrmn**—T. N. Urban. **Pres & CEO**—C. S. Johnson. **Treas**—D. G. Dollison. **SVP & CFO**—J. L. Chicoine. **Investor Contact**—James Ansorge. **Dirs**—N. Y. Bekavac, C. R. Brenton, P. Cuatrecasas, R. A. Goldberg, F. S. Hubbell, C. S. Johnson, L. Kaufmann, F. W. McFarlan, O. J. Newlin, R. P. Seifert, T. N. Urban, V. Walbot, H. S. Wallace, F. W. Weitz, H. H. F. Wijffels. **Transfer Agent & Registrar**—First National Bank of Boston. **Incorporated** in Iowa in 1926. **Empl**-4,800. **S&P Analyst:** Kenneth A. Shea

Pitney Bowes

NYSE Symbol **PBI**
In S&P 500

20-SEP-95

Industry:
Office Equipment

Summary: This company is the world's largest manufacturer of mailing systems. It also provides copying and facsimile systems, facility management services and lease financing.

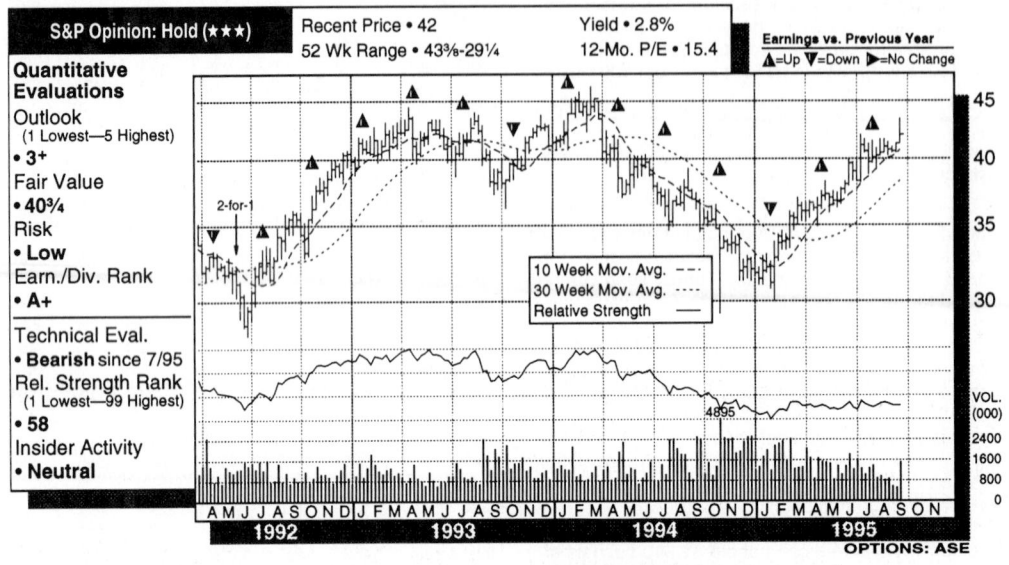

S&P Opinion: Hold (★★★)		
Recent Price • 42	Yield • 2.8%	
52 Wk Range • 43⅜-29¼	12-Mo. P/E • 15.4	

Quantitative Evaluations

Outlook
(1 Lowest—5 Highest)
• **3+**

Fair Value
• **40¾**

Risk
• **Low**

Earn./Div. Rank
• **A+**

Technical Eval.
• **Bearish** since 7/95

Rel. Strength Rank
(1 Lowest—99 Highest)
• **58**

Insider Activity
• **Neutral**

Earnings vs. Previous Year
▲=Up ▼=Down ▶=No Change

10 Week Mov. Avg. ---
30 Week Mov. Avg. ······
Relative Strength —

OPTIONS: ASE

Overview - 20-SEP-95

Revenues should continue to rise in the second half of 1995, driven primarily by increased rental and facilities management revenues. New mailing products targeted at the fast growing small business market are expected to enhance revenues, while the facilities management business should continue its double-digit growth. International penetration, particularly in countries like China, could also be additive to revenue growth during 1995. Gross margins will likely remain under pressure, as the less profitable facilities management business continues to grow as a percent of sales. Operating costs should remain well controlled, owing to recent restructuring actions including the sales of PBI's Monarch Marking Systems and Dictaphone Corp. subsidiaries. Earnings should reach $2.70 a share.

Valuation - 20-SEP-95

The shares have recovered nicely since early 1995, following a disappointing 1994 which saw the stock price fall from its high of 46 3/8 to below 30. The rebound is the result of cost-cutting efforts, dividend increases, a share buyback program, and restructuring actions which included the sale of the Dictaphone and Monarch subsidiaries. In addition, management's renewed operational focus should allow for the resumption of double-digit earnings growth in 1995. We continue to believe that the shares are a worthwhile holding based on their total return potential.

Key Stock Statistics

S&P EPS Est. 1995	2.70	Tang. Bk. Value/Share	10.85
P/E on S&P Est. 1995	15.6	Beta	1.30
S&P EPS Est. 1996	2.90	Shareholders	31,200
Dividend Rate/Share	1.20	Market cap. (B)	$ 6.4
Shs. outstg. (M)	151.5	Inst. holdings	76%
Avg. daily vol. (M)	0.186	Insider holdings	NA

Value of $10,000 invested 5 years ago: $ 20,451

Fiscal Year Ending Dec. 31

	1995	% Change	1994	% Change	1993	% Change
Revenues (Million $)						
1Q	839.9	-4%	876.8	5%	833.4	3%
2Q	862.6	-10%	954.9	9%	874.4	5%
3Q	—	—	806.4	-6%	861.2	NM
4Q	—	—	900.5	-8%	973.9	5%
Yr.	—	—	3,271	-8%	3,543	3%
Income (Million $)						
1Q	95.99	4%	91.86	12%	82.06	22%
2Q	98.35	NM	98.62	13%	87.31	18%
3Q	—	—	85.32	24%	69.03	-13%
4Q	—	—	94.42	-18%	114.8	21%
Yr.	—	—	348.4	-1%	353.2	13%
Earnings Per Share ($)						
1Q	0.63	9%	0.58	12%	0.52	24%
2Q	0.65	5%	0.62	13%	0.55	20%
3Q	E0.67	24%	0.54	26%	0.43	-10%
4Q	E0.75	23%	0.61	-15%	0.72	20%
Yr.	E2.70	22%	2.21	NM	2.22	13%

Next earnings report expected: late October

Pitney Bowes

Business Summary - 20-SEP-95

Pitney Bowes operates in two industry segments. Contributions in 1994 were as follows:

	Revs.	Profits
Business equipment & services	79%	65%
Financial services	21%	35%

Foreign operations contributed 16% of revenues and 1% of operating profits in 1994.

Business equipment and services includes mailing, copying and facsimile systems and facilities management services.

Mailing systems include postage meters, parcel registers, mailing machines, manifest systems, letter and parcel scales, mail openers, mailroom furniture, folders and paper and handling equipment. Copying systems include a wide range of copying systems and supplies. Facsimile systems include a variety of facsimile systems and supplies.

The company provides facilities management services for a variety of business support functions, including mail and reprographics management, high volume automated mail center management and related activities. In October 1993, PBI acquired NYSE-listed Ameriscribe (ACR), a provider of financial printing and related services.

The financial services segment (consolidated since 1988) provides lease financing for PBI's products, as well as financial services for commercial and industrial markets. In March 1993, the company began phasing out the leasing of non-PBI products outside the U.S.

In October 1994, PBI took a $93.2 million charge for costs related to 2,000 employee reductions and for the hiring of 850 new employees with enhanced skills. These actions reflect a refinement of PBI's strategic focus, which will now primarily include concentration on core businesses and the introduction of new and advanced products.

Important Developments

Aug. '95—PBI announced that it had completed the sale of its Dictaphone Corp. subsidiary and related worldwide operations for $450 million in cash, to an affiliate of Stonington Partners Inc. Earlier, in June, the company sold its Monarch Marking Systems subsidiary for about $127 million in cash, to a new company formed by Paxar Corp. and Odyssey Partners L.P. The proceeds of both sales will be used to pay down debt incurred from a stock repurchasing program, and other corporate uses.

Capitalization

Long Term Debt: $1,051,528,000 (6/95).
$2 Conv. Preferred Stk.: 954 shs. ($50 par); red. at $50; ea. conv. into 12.12 com. shs.
$2.12 Conv. Pref. Stk.: 103,017 shs. (no par); red. at $28; ea. conv. into 8 com. shs.

Per Share Data ($)   (Year Ended Dec. 31)

	1994	1993	1992	1991	1990	1989
Tangible Bk. Val.	10.05	10.35	9.59	10.34	9.06	8.12
Cash Flow	3.91	3.86	3.53	3.29	2.68	2.36
Earnings	2.21	2.22	1.96	1.80	1.30	1.14
Dividends	1.04	0.90	0.78	0.68	0.60	0.52
Payout Ratio	47%	41%	39%	38%	46%	45%
Prices - High	46⅜	44½	41	32¾	26¾	27⅜
- Low	29¼	36¼	28	19	13½	20½
P/E Ratio - High	21	20	21	18	21	24
- Low	13	16	14	11	10	18

Income Statement Analysis (Million $)

	1994	%Chg	1993	%Chg	1992	%Chg	1991
Revs.	3,271	-8%	3,543	3%	3,434	3%	3,332
Oper. Inc.	999	-3%	1,028	4%	987	5%	943
Depr.	268	2%	263	5%	251	5%	238
Int. Exp.	194	4%	187	-18%	227	-12%	258
Pretax Inc.	567	-1%	575	16%	495	7%	462
Eff. Tax Rate	39%	—	39%	—	37%	—	38%
Net Inc.	348	-1%	353	13%	312	8%	288

Balance Sheet & Other Fin. Data (Million $)

	1994	1993	1992	1991	1990	1989
Cash	76.0	56.0	73.0	118	80.0	61.0
Curr. Assets	2,084	1,937	1,839	1,936	1,799	1,699
Total Assets	7,400	6,794	6,499	6,381	6,061	5,611
Curr. Liab.	3,978	3,273	3,097	2,995	2,889	2,271
LT Debt	802	877	1,048	1,095	1,136	1,411
Common Eqty.	1,742	1,869	1,650	1,796	1,584	1,422
Total Cap.	3,001	3,158	3,037	3,385	3,170	3,305
Cap. Exp.	346	292	225	250	323	300
Cash Flow	616	616	563	526	427	374

Ratio Analysis

	1994	1993	1992	1991	1990	1989
Curr. Ratio	0.5	0.6	0.6	0.6	0.6	0.7
% LT Debt of Cap.	26.7	27.8	34.5	32.3	35.8	42.7
% Net Inc.of Revs.	10.7	10.0	9.1	8.6	6.5	6.3
% Ret. on Assets	5.0	5.3	4.9	4.6	3.5	3.5
% Ret. on Equity	19.7	20.0	18.2	16.9	13.7	13.4

Dividend Data —Dividends have been paid since 1934. A dividend reinvestment plan is available. A "poison pill" stock purchase right was adopted in 1986.

Amt. of Div. $	Date Decl.	Ex-Div. Date	Stock of Record	Payment Date
0.260	Nov. 14	Nov. 18	Nov. 25	Dec. 12 '94
0.300	Feb. 13	Feb. 17	Feb. 24	Mar. 12 '95
0.300	Apr. 10	May. 22	May. 26	Jun. 12 '95
0.300	Jul. 10	Aug. 23	Aug. 25	Sep. 12 '95

Data as orig. reptd.; bef. results of disc. opers. and/or spec. items. Per share data adj. for stk. divs. as of ex-div. date. E-Estimated. NA-Not Available. NM-Not Meaningful. NR-Not Ranked.

Office—World Headquarters, Stamford, CT 06926-0700. **Tel**—(203) 356-5000. **Chrmn, Pres & CEO**—G. B. Harvey. **Vice Chrmn**— M. J. Critelli, M. C. Breslawsky. **VP-Fin & Treas**—C. F. Adimando. **Investor Contact**—Ernest J. Jackson (203-351-6349). **Dirs**—L. G. Alvarado, M. C. Breslawsky, W. E. Butler, C. G. Campbell, M. J. Critelli, J. C. Emery, Jr., G. B. Harvey, C. E. Hugel, D. T. Kimball, L. D. Nunery, P. S. Sewell, A. R. Taylor. **Transfer Agent & Registrar**—Chemical Bank, NYC. **Incorporated** in Delaware in 1920. **Empl**-32,792. **S&P Analyst:** Mike Cavanaugh

Pittston Services Group

NYSE Symbol **PZS**
In S&P 500

10-SEP-95 **Industry:** Air Transport

Summary: Pittston Services Group operates Burlington Air Freight and Brink's armored car and home security services.

S&P Opinion: Buy (★★★★★)	Recent Price • 25¾	Yield • 0.8%
	52 Wk Range • 30⅞-22½	12-Mo. P/E • 11.9

Quantitative Evaluations

Outlook
(1 Lowest—5 Highest)
• **5⁻**

Fair Value
• **31**

Risk
• **Average**

Earn./Div. Rank
• **B**

Technical Eval.
• **Bearish** since 11/94

Rel. Strength Rank
(1 Lowest—99 Highest)
• **46**

Insider Activity
• **NA**

Earnings vs. Previous Year
▲=Up ▼=Down ▶=No Change

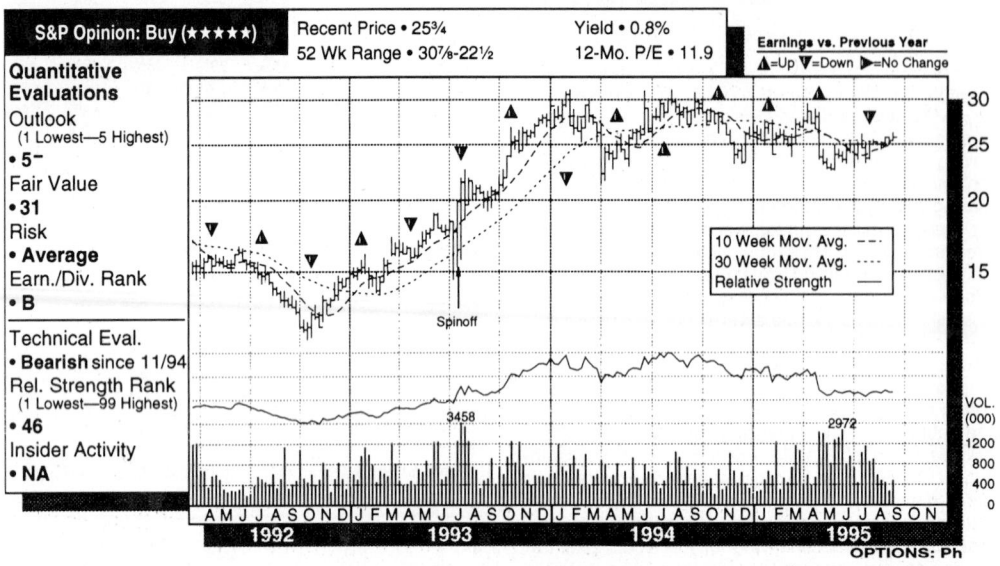

10 Week Mov. Avg. – – –
30 Week Mov. Avg. ·······
Relative Strength ——

Spinoff

3458   2972

VOL. (000)
1200
800
400
0

OPTIONS: Ph

Overview - 08-SEP-95

Growth in air freight volume in 1995 will be paced by strong gains in international markets. While North American growth will slow, Burlington will experience market-share gains, aided by its recent fleet expansion and shrinking cargo space at passenger airlines. Rates are expected to be flat in the U.S. but improve overseas. Margins will benefit from increased productivity and increased fuel efficiency. Brink's will benefit from strong demand for ATM servicing, currency processing, armored car and coin wrapping services. Contributions from international affiliates will be mixed, with improvement in Brazil and recent acquisitions in France offsetting continued weakness in Mexico. Home security services will be aided by more subscribers in established markets and expansion into new territories.

Valuation - 08-SEP-95

The shares of this air freight, armored car and home security concern have staged a partial recovery. As the U.S. economy awoke from its second quarter nap, investors have become more confident that PZS can get back on its growth track. Moreover, Burlington Air now derives 55% of its revenues from its international business, which climbed 32% in 1995's second quarter. The long-term picture for the Brink's commercial and home security services is excellent. The company continues its stock buyback program, repurchasing 120,000 shares at $23.33 during 1995's second quarter. We urge continued buying of PZS at these levels.

Key Stock Statistics

S&P EPS Est. 1995	2.25	Tang. Bk. Value/Share	6.08
P/E on S&P Est. 1995	11.4	Beta	NA
S&P EPS Est. 1996	2.65	Shareholders	5,800
Dividend Rate/Share	0.20	Market cap. (B)	$ 1.1
Shs. outstg. (M)	41.7	Inst. holdings	88%
Avg. daily vol. (M)	0.088	Insider holdings	NA

Value of $10,000 invested 5 years ago: $ 12,779

Fiscal Year Ending Dec. 31

	1995	% Change	1994	% Change	1993	% Change
Revenues (Million $)						
1Q	503.3	22%	411.0	13%	363.8	13%
2Q	527.6	15%	457.4	20%	380.2	10%
3Q	—	—	483.7	21%	400.4	10%
4Q	—	—	520.2	22%	424.7	11%
Yr.	—	—	1,872	19%	1,569	-24%
Income (Million $)						
1Q	13.60	29%	10.51	94%	5.41	90%
2Q	19.97	-6%	21.29	94%	10.97	122%
3Q	—	—	25.01	63%	15.31	74%
4Q	—	—	23.03	49%	15.43	45%
Yr.	—	—	79.85	69%	47.13	74%
Earnings Per Share ($)						
1Q	0.36	29%	0.28	87%	0.15	-25%
2Q	0.53	-5%	0.56	87%	0.30	-3%
3Q	E0.70	6%	0.66	61%	0.41	3%
4Q	E0.66	8%	0.61	49%	0.41	-2%
Yr.	E2.25	7%	2.11	65%	1.28	-3%

Next earnings report expected: late October

Pittston Services Group

Business Summary - 08-SEP-95

In 1993, Pittston Co. split its common stock into two classes. Pittston Services Group Common Stock was formed to track the results of the company's air freight, armored car and home security services. Contributions (in millions) to operating profits in recent years were:

	1994	1993	1992
Air freight	$69.2	$38.0	$15.1
Armored car	39.7	35.0	30.4
Home security	32.4	26.4	16.5

Burlington Air Express (BAX) is a leading U.S. air freight carrier, specializing in heavy freight, and provides logistics services, ocean freight forwarding and customs brokerage services. In 1994, BAX derived 53% of its revenues from international transactions. BAX provides service to 112 countries through 488 shipping stations. In North America, BAX utilizes a fleet of 31 leased aircraft having nightly lift capacity of 2.4 million lbs. BAX purchases space on commercial airlines for movements. In 1994, BAX moved 1.25 billion lbs. of cargo, up from 1.02 billion lbs. in 1993.

Brink's, the largest provider of armored car services in North America, operates a fleet of 1,800 vehicles. Principal customers include banks, brokerage firms and the U.S. Government. International affiliates (accounting for 38% of revenues) operate 4,300 armored vehicles in 47 countries. Brink's also provides air courier services, currency and deposit processing and coin wrapping services, maintains automated teller machines and provides software for deposit processing and vault management.

Brink's Home Security (BHS) is the second largest provider of home security, fire and medical alert services in the U.S. At 1994 year-end, BHS had 318,000 subscribers in 28 states and parts of Canada.

Important Developments

Jun. '95—Total subscribers for Brink's Home Security at June 30 were 346,540, up 20% from 289,618 accounts a year earlier. The net number of service terminations during 1995's first six months was 9,851 (or 2.8% of the subscriber base), versus 7,920 accounts (2.7%) in the 1994 period. Brink's reported that it had opened a new branch operation in Norfolk, VA.

Jun. '95—During 1995's second quarter, Pittston repurchased 120,000 of its common shares for $2.8 million ($23.33 each). The company has authority remaining to repurchase an additional 873,900 PZS shares (or 2.1% of its total).

Capitalization

Long Term Debt: $56,660,000 (6/95).
Cum. Conv. Prfd.: $1,526,000.

Per Share Data ($)

(Year Ended Dec. 31)

	1994	1993	1992	1991	1990	1989
Tangible Bk. Val.	5.95	3.98	2.93	2.28	6.41	5.23
Cash Flow	3.54	2.57	3.22	0.77	2.44	1.13
Earnings	2.11	1.28	1.32	-0.77	1.24	0.10
Dividends	0.20	0.25	0.25	0.20	0.20	0.15
Payout Ratio	9%	20%	19%	NM	16%	148%
Prices - High	31¼	29¾	19	21¼	22⅛	22¼
- Low	21⅜	13⅝	11⅜	14	15⅝	16⅞
P/E Ratio - High	15	23	14	NM	18	NM
- Low	10	11	9	NM	13	NM

Income Statement Analysis (Million $)

	1994	%Chg	1993	%Chg	1992	%Chg	1991
Revs.	1,875	19%	1,572	-24%	2,073	7%	1,946
Oper. Inc.	180	37%	131	-7%	141	13%	125
Depr.	53.8	13%	47.8	-32%	70.4	22%	57.7
Int. Exp.	6.3	-28%	8.8	-21%	11.1	-30%	15.9
Pretax Inc.	125	58%	79.0	1%	78.0	NM	-37.0
Eff. Tax Rate	36%	—	41%	—	37%	—	NM
Net Inc.	80.0	70%	47.0	-4%	49.0	NM	-29.0

Balance Sheet & Other Fin. Data (Million $)

	1994	1993	1992	1991	1990	1989
Cash	40.7	32.2	52.4	59.6	40.2	26.4
Curr. Assets	386	289	422	399	352	289
Total Assets	941	807	1,322	1,240	1,120	984
Curr. Liab.	333	282	414	371	334	285
LT Debt	50.0	58.0	91.0	72.0	111	92.0
Common Eqty.	456	378	341	317	480	424
Total Cap.	540	470	452	407	611	530
Cap. Exp.	80.4	76.0	101	79.0	97.0	54.0
Cash Flow	134	94.9	120	28.8	97.8	42.7

Ratio Analysis

	1994	1993	1992	1991	1990	1989
Curr. Ratio	1.2	1.0	1.0	1.1	1.1	1.0
% LT Debt of Cap.	9.2	12.4	20.2	17.7	18.1	17.4
% Net Inc.of Revs.	4.3	3.0	2.4	NM	2.5	0.2
% Ret. on Assets	9.1	NA	3.8	NM	4.4	0.4
% Ret. on Equity	19.1	NA	14.9	NM	10.2	0.9

Dividend Data

—Dividends for Pittston Services Group Common Stock are paid from earnings of the Services Group.

Amt. of Div. $	Date Decl.	Ex-Div. Date	Stock of Record	Payment Date
0.050	Nov. 07	Nov. 10	Nov. 17	Dec. 01 '94
0.050	Feb. 03	Feb. 09	Feb. 15	Mar. 01 '95
0.050	May. 05	May. 09	May. 15	Jun. 01 '95
0.050	Jul. 07	Aug. 11	Aug. 15	Sep. 01 '95

Data as orig. reptd.; bef. results of disc. opers. and/or spec. items. Per share data adj. for stk. divs. as of ex-div. date. E-Estimated. NA-Not Available. NM-Not Meaningful. NR-Not Ranked.

Office—100 First Stamford Place, Stamford, CT 06912-0070. **Tel**—(203) 978-5200. **Chrmn & Pres**—J. C. Farrell. **Vice Chrmn**—D. L. Marshall. **VP & Secy**—A. F. Reed. **VP, Treas & Investor Contact**—James B. Hartough. **Dirs**—R. G. Ackerman, M. J. Anton, J. R. Barker, J. L. Broadhead, W. F. Craig, J. C. Farrell, C. F. Haywood, E. G. Jordan, D. L. Marshall, R. H. Spilman, R. G. Stone Jr., A. H. Zimmerman. **Transfer Agent & Registrar**—Chemical Bank, NYC. **Incorporated** in Delaware in 1930; reincorporated in Virginia in 1986. **Empl**- 15,100. **S&P Analyst:** Stephen R. Klein

Placer Dome

NYSE Symbol PDG Options on Phila & Toronto (Mar-Jun-Sep-Dec) In S&P 500

Price	Range	P–E Ratio	Dividend	Yield	S&P Ranking	Beta
Aug. 22'95	1995					
26⅝	29½–18⅜	NM	¹0.30	¹1.1%	B–	0.04

Summary

This company is one of the world's largest gold producers, with gold properties located in North America, Latin America and the South Pacific. It also produces silver, copper and molybdenum. Profits should improve significantly in 1995's second half following completion of the Dome mine expansion in July and commencement of copper production in June at the 50%-owned Zaldivar mine in Chile.

Current Outlook

Profits for 1995 are estimated at $0.45 a share (after a $0.07 charge), versus $0.44 (including $0.03 of non-recurring income) in 1994.

Dividends are expected to be maintained at US$0.07½ quarterly (before 15% Canadian tax) .

Gold volumes should rebound in 1995's second half following the completion of the Dome mine expansion at mid-year. Partly offsetting will be lower recovery rates at the Detour Lake and Golden Sunlight mines. The commencement of copper production at the 50% Zaldivar mine in June will be a major plus. While gold and silver prices are expected to be flat, molybdenum prices will be sharply higher. Limiting profitability will be high exploration costs related to the Vasilkovskoye despoit in Kazakhstan. Also hurting comparisons will be the write down of PDG's investment in Tempo Technology Corp.

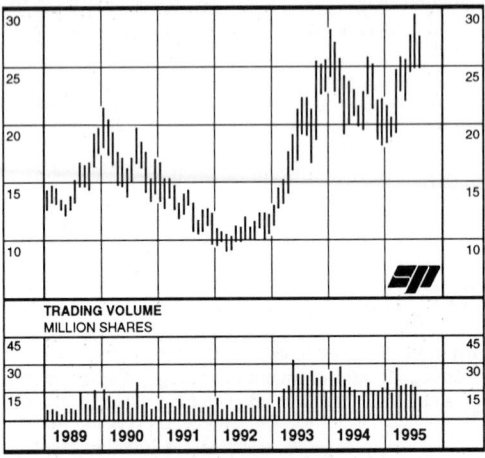

TRADING VOLUME
MILLION SHARES

Sales (Million U.S. $)

Quarter:	1995	1994	1993	1992
Mar.	236	216	213	248
Jun.	235	242	234	259
Sep.		210	219	264
Dec.		231	251	249
		899	917	1,020

Sales for 1995's first half rose 2.8%, year to year. Net income was off 80% to $0.05 a share from $0.25.

Common Share Earnings (U.S. $)

Quarter:	1995	1994	1993	1992
Mar.	0.16	0.16	0.05	0.05
Jun.	d0.11	0.09	0.08	0.10
Sep.	E0.20	0.08	0.06	0.14
Dec.	E0.20	0.11	0.26	0.18
	E0.45	0.44	0.45	0.47

Important Developments

Jul. '95— Net income for 1995's second quarter was reduced by $17 million ($0.07 a share) to reflect the writedown of PDG's entire investment in Tempo Technology Corp. Tempo is developing a process to manufacture synthetic industrial diamonds.

Jun. '95— Copper production commenced at the Zaldivar mine (50%-owned) in Chile. The $600 million Zaldivar mine is expected to produce some 275 million pounds of copper annually by 1997.

May '95— PDG allowed its $304 million offer for all common shares of International Musto Resources, whose assets include a 50% stake in one of the world's largest undeveloped gold-copper deposits, to lapse.

Next earnings report expected in late October.

Per Share Data (U.S. $)

Yr. End Dec. 31	1994	⁵1993	1992	1991	1990	1989	1988	²1987	1986	1985
Tangible Bk. Val.	6.41	6.36	6.15	6.26	7.45	7.04	6.78	5.21	³4.86	NA
Cash Flow	1.01	1.15	1.26	d0.24	0.90	0.83	1.42	1.03	NA	NA
Earnings⁴	0.44	0.45	0.47	d1.02	0.27	0.41	0.97	0.56	0.35	0.24
Dividends	0.270	0.260	0.260	0.262	0.257	0.259	0.126	0.076	0.101	0.115
Payout Ratio	61%	58%	55%	NM	96%	63%	13%	14%	29%	48%
Prices—High	28¼	25⅝	12⅜	16¾	21½	19¾	15¾	21⅜	NA	NA
Low	18⅛	11¼	9	9⅝	13⅜	12⅛	10⅞	10⅞	NA	NA
P/E Ratio—	64–41	57–25	26–19	NM	81–50	48–30	16–11	38–19	NA	NA

Data as orig. reptd.; prior to 1987 pro forma data as reptd. in Information Circular dated Jul. 10, 1987. Conv. to U.S. $ at year-end exch. rates. **1.** In U.S. funds, bef. 15% Canadian tax on nonresidents. **2.** Reflects merger or acquisition. **3.** As of Mar. 31, 1987. **4.** Bef. results of disc. opers. of +0.02 in 1991, +0.43 in 1990, +0.05 in 1989. **5.** Refl. acctg. change. d-Deficit. E-Estimated. NM-Not Meaningful. NA-Not Available.

Income Data (Million U.S. $)

Year Ended Dec. 31	Revs.	Oper. Inc.	% Oper. Inc. of Revs.	Cap. Exp.	Depr.	Int. Exp.	Net Bef. Taxes	Eff. Tax Rate	[4]Net Inc.	% Net Inc. of Revs.	Cash Flow
1994	899	286	31.8	434	136	20.0	[3]199	33.2%	105	11.7	241
[5]1993	917	276	30.1	147	167	22.0	[3]157	12.1%	107	11.7	274
1992	1,020	321	31.5	236	187	20.0	[3]155	15.5%	111	10.9	298
1991	969	d87	NM	226	185	24.9	d238	NM	d242	NM	d57
[1]1990	931	270	29.0	481	148	22.7	[3]159	40.2%	63	6.8	211
[1]1989	781	204	26.2	522	100	12.2	[3]201	36.9%	96	12.3	196
1988	661	205	31.1	380	102	9.4	[3]308	17.9%	220	33.3	322
[2]1987	641	169	26.4	122	103	16.2	[3]162	10.6%	[5]122	19.0	225
1986	520	NA	NA	NA	NA	20.4	[3]111	21.6%	71	13.6	NA

Balance Sheet Data (Million U.S. $)

Dec. 31	Cash	Assets	Curr. Liab.	Ratio	Total Assets	% Ret. on Assets	Long Term Debt	Common Equity	Total Cap.	% LT Debt of Cap.	% Ret. on Equity
1994	312	565	177	3.2	2,246	4.7	225	1,529	1,907	11.8	6.9
1993	777	994	153	6.5	2,228	5.0	243	1,514	1,904	12.8	7.2
1992	477	757	201	3.8	2,067	5.1	69	1,459	1,673	4.1	7.5
1991	623	885	235	3.8	2,291	NM	250	1,481	1,879	13.3	NM
1990	785	1,000	241	4.1	2,662	2.5	310	1,761	2,204	14.1	3.7
1989	577	1,143	254	4.5	2,449	4.1	160	1,654	1,960	8.1	5.9
1988	637	874	135	6.5	2,190	11.1	138	1,590	1,855	7.4	15.6
1987	289	449	112	4.0	1,664	NA	37	1,143	1,516	2.5	NA

Data as orig. reptd.; prior to 1987 pro forma data as reptd. in information circular dated Jul. 10, 1987. Prior to 1991 conv. to U.S. $ at year-end exch. rates. **1.** Excl. disc. opers. **2.** Reflects merger or acquisition. **3.** Incl. equity in earns. of nonconsol. subs. **4.** Bef. results of disc. opers. **5.** Reflects accounting change. d-Deficit. NM-Not Meaningful. NA-Not Available.

Business Summary

Placer Dome and its units are mainly engaged in exploration for and production of gold, and also produce silver, copper and molybdenum. Its share of proven and probable reserves as of year-end 1994 was estimated at 19.8 million oz. of gold, after production of 1,721,000 oz. in 1994.

Placer Dome Canada operates the Campbell Mine, Dome Mine and Detour Lake Mine, all in Ontario, which produced 323,170, 175,017 and 124,549 oz. of gold, respectively, in 1994. Sigma Mines and Kiena Gold Mines, both in Quebec, produced 85,145 and 83,044 oz., respectively. In March 1995, new capacity at Dome will increase its output to an annual rate of 315,000 oz. Other operations include the Endako molybdenum mine (B.C.).

Placer Dome U.S. (PDUS) manages Bald Mountain (Nev.) and Golden Sunlight Mines (Mont.), which produced 120,289 and 50,097 oz. of gold, respectively, in 1994. In February 1995, milling operations were resumed at Golden Sunlight after having been ceased in June 1994 due to ground movement. The 60%-owned Cortez Gold Mines (Nev.) produced 41,765 oz. for PDG's account. In March 1995, all litigation regarding its 60%-owned Pipeline deposit on the Cortez property was resolved, whereby Gold Fields Mining Co. received $30 million, while PDUS got legal title to GFMC's mining claims, which contain 40% of the deposit.

Placer Dome Latin America is responsible for PDG's activities in South and Central America. The 50%-owned La Coipa gold/silver mine (Chile) produced 116,319 oz. of gold and 5.7 million oz. of silver in 1994 for PDG's account. At year-end 1994, PDG's share of the mineral resource at its 70%-owned Las Cristinas property (Venezuela) was estimated at 6.0 million oz. of gold.

Other major gold mines are held by 75.4%-owned Placer Pacific (PP). PDG's share of 1994 output from PP's Misima mine (80% owned) in Papua New Guinea (PNG) was 203,468 oz. The Porgera mine (25%-owned by PP) also in PNG produced 194,674 oz. for PDG's account. PP's Australian gold mines are 70%-owned Kidston Gold Mines, which produced 110,290 oz. as PDG's share in 1994; and 60%-owned Granny Smith (91,089 oz.).

Dividend Data

Predecessor companies paid dividends since 1920. Payments by Placer Dome were initiated in mid-1987. In January, 1990 PDG adopted a "poison pill" stock purchase right. Dividends are in U.S. funds, before 15% tax on U.S. residents:

Amt. of Divd. $	Date Decl.	Ex–divd. Date	Stock of Record	Payment Date
0.07½	Sep. 21	Nov. 14	Nov. 18	Dec. 19'94
0.07½	Feb. 24	Mar. 6	Mar. 10	Mar. 27'95
0.07½	May 8	May 22	May 26	Jun. 26'95
0.07½	Jul. 20	Aug. 23	Aug. 25	Sep. 25'95

Capitalization

Long Term Debt: US$414,000,000 (6/95).

Minority Interests: US$143,000,000.

Common Shares: 238,958,217 shs. (no par). Institutions hold about 36%. Shareholders of record: 22,103.

Offices—Suite 1600, Bentall IV, 1055 Dunsmuir St., Vancouver, BC V7X 1P1. **Tel**—(604) 682-7082. **Chrmn**—R. M. Franklin. **Pres & CEO**—M. Willson. **SVP & CFO**—I. G. Austin. **VP & Secy**—J. A. Eckersley. **Investor Contact**—Earl Dunlop. **Dirs**—T. A. Buell, P. A. Cherniavsky, G. B. Coulombe, R. M. Franklin, H. J. McDonald, A. R. McFarland, C. L. Michel, B. C. Ryan, V. F. Taylor III, J. M. Willson, W. G. Wilson. **Transfer Agents & Registrars**—R-M Trust Co., Toronto, Vancouver, Montreal, Calgary; Bank of New York, NYC; Coopers & Lybrand, Sydney, Australia. **Incorporated** in Canada in 1987. **Empl**—7,004.

Information has been obtained from sources believed to be reliable, but its accuracy and completeness are not guaranteed.   Stephen R. Klein

Polaroid Corp.

NYSE Symbol **PRD**
In S&P 500

23-OCT-95 Industry: Leisure/Amusement

Summary: This large instant photography company is making a major effort to develop new digital electronic imaging products.

S&P Opinion: Avoid (★★)	Recent Price • 42	Yield • 1.4%
	52 Wk Range • 45⅛-29	12-Mo. P/E • 72.4

Earnings vs. Previous Year
▲=Up ▼=Down ▶=No Change

Quantitative Evaluations

Outlook
(1 Lowest—5 Highest)
• **4⁻**

Fair Value
• **44½**

Risk
• **Low**

Earn./Div. Rank
• **B**

Technical Eval.
• **Bullish** since 12/94

Rel. Strength Rank
(1 Lowest—99 Highest)
• **62**

Insider Activity
• **Neutral**

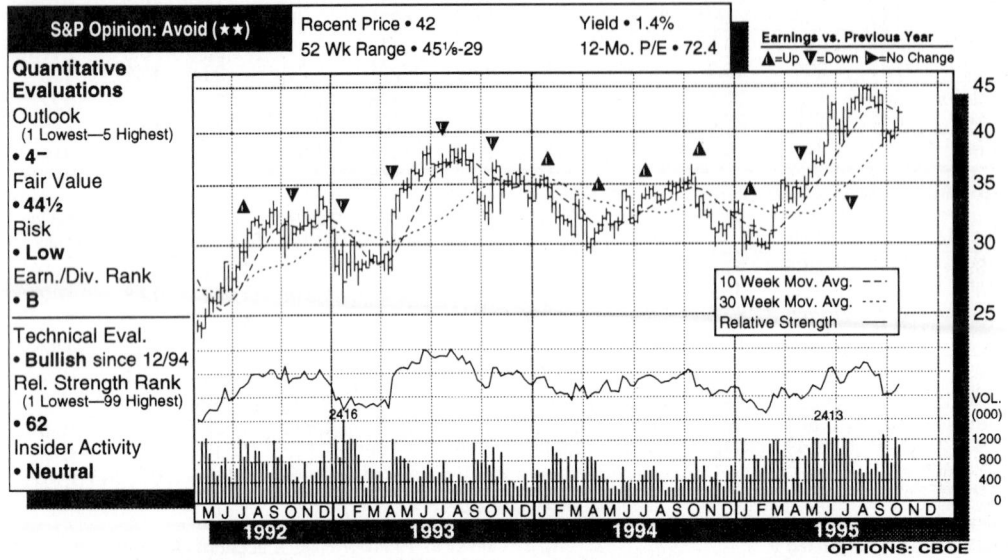

10 Week Mov. Avg. - - -
30 Week Mov. Avg. ·····
Relative Strength ——

OPTIONS: CBOE

Overview - 23-OCT-95

We expect PRD's sales in the year ahead to be bolstered by growing sales to newer markets such as China, and by increased promotional spending directed at U.S. consumers. Thus far in 1995, PRD's sales have been hurt by a strategic shift in which dealers received a lower level of promotional incentives, and reduced their inventory levels of PRD products. Going forward, sales to dealers should largely depend on the extent to which PRD can stimulate retail demand through promotions aimed directly at consumers. Also, we expect PRD's 1996 profits to be helped by cost reduction efforts. Long term, PRD is seeking to make a transition toward greater emphasis on higher-resolution digital imaging products. In 1996, spending on such products is likely to be a major drain on earnings, but less than it is expected to be in 1995.

Valuation - 23-OCT-95

We advise investors to avoid the stock of this major photography company. We are concerned that there may be future shortfalls in revenues and earnings from PRD's traditional U.S. instant photography business. Also, PRD's ability to turn its digital research efforts into profits remains a question. With a new CEO from outside the company likely to be appointed soon, we expect that PRD may accelerate future efforts to cut costs, but we don't see this, or a recent upward revision in our fourth quarter earnings estimate, as enough to enthuse about the stock.

Key Stock Statistics

S&P EPS Est. 1995	0.55	Tang. Bk. Value/Share	17.46
P/E on S&P Est. 1995	76.4	Beta	0.72
S&P EPS Est. 1996	2.60	Shareholders	12,100
Dividend Rate/Share	0.60	Market cap. (B)	$ 1.9
Shs. outstg. (M)	45.2	Inst. holdings	80%
Avg. daily vol. (M)	0.206	Insider holdings	NA

Value of $10,000 invested 5 years ago: $ 10,282

Fiscal Year Ending Dec. 31

	1995	% Change	1994	% Change	1993	% Change
Revenues (Million $)						
1Q	409.6	-11%	462.6	-1%	468.5	9%
2Q	572.5	-3%	587.3	3%	569.9	2%
3Q	580.0	NM	576.7	8%	533.9	4%
4Q	—	—	685.9	2%	672.6	4%
Yr.	—	—	2,313	3%	2,245	4%
Income (Million $)						
1Q	-75.80	NM	1.40	NM	-23.50	NM
2Q	22.90	-22%	29.20	2%	28.60	-19%
3Q	23.70	-19%	29.30	18%	24.90	-10%
4Q	—	—	57.30	46%	39.20	32%
Yr.	—	—	117.2	73%	67.90	-31%
Earnings Per Share ($)						
1Q	-1.66	NM	0.03	NM	-0.50	NM
2Q	0.50	-19%	0.62	2%	0.61	-18%
3Q	0.51	-18%	0.62	17%	0.53	-10%
4Q	E1.19	-3%	1.23	48%	0.83	32%
Yr.	E0.55	-78%	2.49	72%	1.45	-30%

Next earnings report expected: early February

Polaroid Corp.

Business Summary - 23-OCT-95

Polaroid designs, manufactures and markets worldwide a variety of products, primarily in fields involving the recording of instant images. PRD's long-term strategy includes using cash flow from its traditional instant photography business to support development of newer digital or electronic imaging products. In 1994, international sales accounted for 50% of PRD's total, up from 47% in 1993.

PRD's products include instant photographic cameras and films, electronic recording imaging devices, videotapes, conventional films and light polarizing filters and lenses. In 1994, PRD sold 6.4 million instant cameras worldwide, up from 4.9 million in 1993. In 1993, PRD introduced a single-use 35mm camera called Sidekick in the U.S.

In addition to family and recreational use, PRD's photography products are used in fields such as real estate and jewelry sales, insurance, architecture, construction, theme park concessions and education.

A variety of PRD products are aimed at technical and industrial customers. Included are many types of film and a broad range of application-specific imaging systems targeted for market areas such as science and medicine; office and presentation products; identification and documentation; and professional photography.

Capital expenditures totaled $147 million in 1994, and are expected to be about $165 million in 1995.

Important Developments

Oct. '95— During 1995's first nine months, PRD's U.S. sales were down 15%, year to year, partly due to a strategic change in PRD's marketing approach. PRD's dealers are receiving less promotional or pricing incentives than they have in the past, and PRD is planning to place a greater emphasis on promotional efforts which are directed at consumers. PRD is looking for consumer-directed promotions to boost demand in 1995's fourth quarter. Other steps in a PRD plan to enhance profitability include accelerating sales in newer overseas markets, selling some real estate, and consolidating manufacturing facilities. In 1995's first quarter, PRD incurred a restructuring charge of about $1.10 a share after-tax, largely related to a workforce reduction. Also, PRD is expected to name a new CEO within the next several months.

Capitalization

Long Term Debt: $547,000,000 (9/95).

Per Share Data ($) (Year Ended Dec. 31)

	1994	1993	1992	1991	1990	1989
Tangible Bk. Val.	18.79	16.39	17.33	15.80	4.15	2.86
Cash Flow	5.01	3.60	3.92	13.70	3.89	3.48
Earnings	2.49	1.45	2.06	12.54	2.20	1.96
Dividends	0.60	0.60	0.60	0.60	0.60	0.60
Payout Ratio	24%	41%	28%	4%	27%	28%
Prices - High	36¾	38¾	35	29	48¼	50⅜
- Low	29¼	25¾	23⅝	19⅝	20¼	35⅛
P/E Ratio - High	15	27	17	2	22	26
- Low	12	18	11	1	9	18

Income Statement Analysis (Million $)

	1994	%Chg	1993	%Chg	1992	%Chg	1991
Revs.	2,313	3%	2,245	4%	2,152	4%	2,071
Oper. Inc.	319	12%	286	-6%	303	-9%	332
Depr.	118	18%	100	12%	89.1	4%	85.5
Int. Exp.	56.3	-7%	60.5	-12%	68.5	5%	65.3
Pretax Inc.	161	58%	102	-37%	163	-85%	1,083
Eff. Tax Rate	27%	—	33%	—	39%	—	37%
Net Inc.	117	72%	68.0	-31%	99	-86%	684

Balance Sheet & Other Fin. Data (Million $)

	1994	1993	1992	1991	1990	1989
Cash	229	139	190	245	198	279
Curr. Assets	1,489	1,414	1,351	1,340	1,240	1,346
Total Assets	2,317	2,212	2,008	1,889	1,701	1,777
Curr. Liab.	602	580	562	645	631	704
LT Debt	566	602	637	472	514	602
Common Eqty.	864	767	809	773	208	149
Total Cap.	1,430	1,370	1,446	1,245	1,070	1,073
Cap. Exp.	147	166	202	176	121	95.0
Cash Flow	235	168	188	738	201	200

Ratio Analysis

	1994	1993	1992	1991	1990	1989
Curr. Ratio	2.5	2.4	2.4	2.1	2.0	1.9
% LT Debt of Cap.	39.6	44.0	44.1	37.9	48.0	56.1
% Net Inc.of Revs.	5.1	3.0	4.6	33.0	7.7	7.6
% Ret. on Assets	5.2	3.2	5.2	38.5	8.9	9.1
% Ret. on Equity	14.5	8.6	12.8	133.7	64.6	25.5

Dividend Data —Dividends have been paid since 1952. A dividend reinvestment plan is available. A "poison pill" stock purchase rights plan was adopted in 1986.

Amt. of Div. $	Date Decl.	Ex-Div. Date	Stock of Record	Payment Date
0.150	Oct. 25	Nov. 18	Nov. 25	Dec. 24 '94
0.150	Jan. 31	Feb. 17	Feb. 24	Mar. 25 '95
0.150	May. 16	May. 22	May. 26	Jun. 24 '95
0.150	Jul. 25	Aug. 23	Aug. 25	Sep. 23 '95

Data as orig. reptd.; bef. results of disc. opers. and/or spec. items. Per share data adj. for stk. divs. as of ex-div. date. E-Estimated. NA-Not Available. NM-Not Meaningful. NR-Not Ranked.

Office—549 Technology Square, Cambridge, MA 02139. **Tel**—(617) 386-2000. **Chrmn, Pres & CEO**—I. M. Booth. **EVP & CFO**—W. J. O'Neill Jr. **VP & Secy**—R. F. deLima. **Investor Contact**—Philip Ruddick. **Dirs**—I. M. Booth, Y. T. Feng, R. Gomory, F. S. Jones, J. W. Loose, J. D. Mahoney, A. F. Moschner, H. Necarsulmer, K. H. Olsen, L. Pollack, C. P. Slichter, R. Z. Sorenson, D. C. Staley, A. M. Zeien. **Transfer Agent & Registrar**—First National Bank of Boston. **Incorporated** in Delaware in 1937. **Empl**-12,104. **S&P Analyst:** Tom Graves, CFA

Potlatch Corp.

NYSE Symbol **PCH**
In S&P 500

25-JUL-95 — Industry: Paper/Products

Summary: This integrated forest products concern is a major producer of wood products and also has interests in coated printing paper, bleached paperboard and consumer products.

S&P Opinion: Hold (★★★)

Recent Price • 42⅝ Yield • 3.8%
52 Wk Range • 44¼-35½ 12-Mo. P/E • 14.6

Earnings vs. Previous Year
▲=Up ▼=Down ▶=No Change

Quantitative Evaluations

Outlook
(1 Lowest—5 Highest)
• **3+**

Fair Value
• **42**

Risk
• **Low**

Earn./Div. Rank
• **B+**

Technical Eval.
• **Bullish** since 7/95

Rel. Strength Rank
(1 Lowest—99 Highest)
• **27**

Insider Activity
• **Favorable**

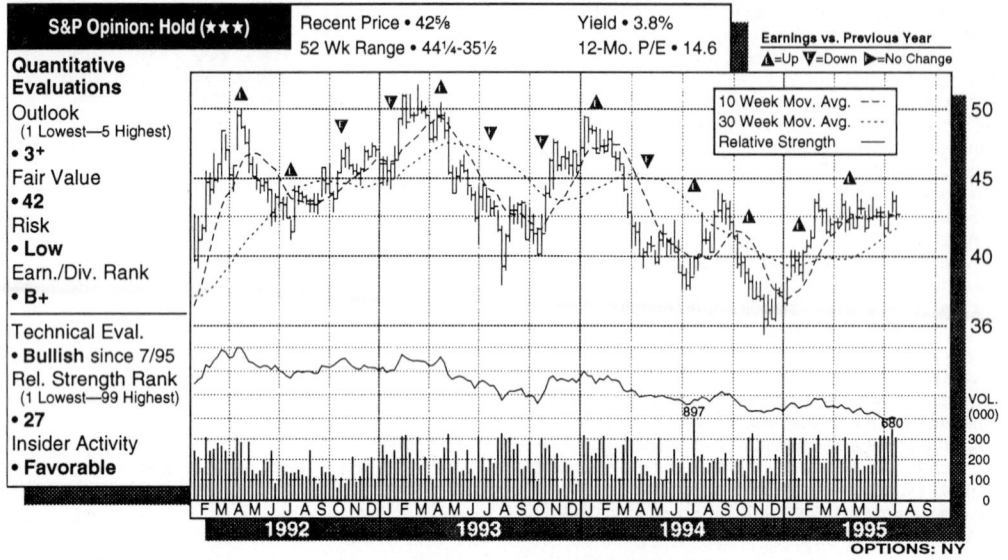

10 Week Mov. Avg. ---
30 Week Mov. Avg. ····
Relative Strength —

OPTIONS: NY

Overview - 24-JUL-95

Sales should be solidly higher in 1995, as recovering worldwide economies have generated increased demand and much higher prices for coated paper and bleached board products. A tight supply picture and favorable export markets should enable PCH's paper markets to remain strong despite a moderating U.S. economy. Wood products sales are likely to be slightly lower, hurt by first half demand and pricing weakness related to a sluggish U.S. housing market. However, a substantial mid-year decline in interest rates is likely to boost housing and wood products markets as the year progresses. A considerable improvement in operating margins is likely, on the surge in paper pricing and, to a lesser extent, improved manufacturing efficiencies. Those factors should far outweigh the impact of higher pulp costs and the early year wood products troubles.

Valuation - 24-JUL-95

After declining throughout much of 1994, PCH's shares enjoyed a nice bounce from late 1994 into early 1995, but have had little movement since that time. Potlatch's erratic stock performance has been related to conflicting conditions in its two industry segments over that period of time. Given our forecast of continued strength in PCH's pulp and paper segment and a pick-up in wood products markets, the company's upcoming earnings prospects are quite favorable. However, despite our optimism about Potlatch's earnings outlook, the company's shares seem fairly priced in their recent trading range of 9 to 10X our 1996 estimate.

Key Stock Statistics

S&P EPS Est. 1995	3.50	Tang. Bk. Value/Share	31.49
P/E on S&P Est. 1995	12.2	Beta	1.22
S&P EPS Est. 1996	4.50	Shareholders	3,500
Dividend Rate/Share	1.60	Market cap. (B)	$ 1.2
Shs. outstg. (M)	29.2	Inst. holdings	48%
Avg. daily vol. (M)	0.094	Insider holdings	NA

Value of $10,000 invested 5 years ago: $ 14,138

Fiscal Year Ending Dec. 31

	1995	% Change	1994	% Change	1993	% Change
Revenues (Million $)						
1Q	394.6	8%	365.3	1%	361.5	8%
2Q	397.2	15%	345.1	6%	326.6	NM
3Q	—	—	373.3	10%	338.2	NM
4Q	—	—	387.5	13%	342.5	6%
Yr.	—	—	1,471	7%	1,369	3%
Income (Million $)						
1Q	23.53	NM	5.31	-76%	22.16	40%
2Q	23.90	NM	6.05	119%	2.76	-92%
3Q	—	—	10.74	NM	-2.18	NM
4Q	—	—	26.89	72%	15.60	48%
Yr.	—	—	49.00	28%	38.34	-51%
Earnings Per Share ($)						
1Q	0.81	NM	0.18	-76%	0.76	38%
2Q	0.81	NM	0.21	133%	0.09	-92%
3Q	E0.91	—	0.37	NM	-0.07	NM
4Q	E0.97	—	0.92	74%	0.53	47%
Yr.	E3.50	—	1.68	28%	1.31	-52%

Next earnings report expected: mid October

Potlatch Corp.

Business Summary - 24-JUL-95

Potlatch grows and harvests timber, and manufactures wood products, printing papers and other pulp-based products. Segment contributions in 1994 (profits in millions) were:

	Sales	Profits
Wood products	37%	$160
Printing papers	28%	40
Other pulp-based products	35%	-53

Export sales, of which 85% consisted of paperboard, accounted for 9.0% of total sales in 1994.

During 1994, PCH produced 408 million board feet of lumber, 298 million square feet of plywood, 1.1 billion square feet of oriented strand board, and 67 million square feet of particleboard. Wood products are manufactured at facilities in Arkansas, Idaho and Minnesota, and are marketed through the company's sales offices primarily to wholesalers for nationwide distribution.

At facilities in Minnesota, PCH produces high-quality coated free-sheet printing papers used in annual reports, catalogs, art reproductions and advertising. Printing papers are sold primarily to paper merchants for distribution. In 1994, PCH produced 341,000 tons of printing papers.

Other pulp-based products include bleached kraft pulp and paperboard, tissue, towels and napkins. Bleached kraft paperboard produced by the company is used for the packaging of milk and other foods, pharmaceuticals and toiletries and for paper cups and paper plates. PCH is the leading producer of private-label tissue products on the West Coast. During 1994, PCH produced 816,000 tons of pulp, 549,000 tons of paperboard, and 135,000 tons of tissue paper.

Potlatch owns some 1.5 million acres of timberland in Idaho, Arkansas and Minnesota. In 1994, the company's lands provided approximately 59% of its sawlogs and plywood logs, and 35% of raw materials, including those used for pulp and oriented strand board.

Important Developments

Jul. '95—In reporting continued strong year over year earnings gains in the second quarter of 1995, the company said that it remained optimistic about the second half of the year, given the current favorable market trends for its pulp-based products. Although sales and earnings had weakened in the wood products segment in recent quarters, Potlatch said it had just begun to see some improvement in those markets.

Capitalization

Long Term Debt: $576,643,000 (6/95).

Per Share Data ($)

(Year Ended Dec. 31)

	1994	1993	1992	1991	1990	1989
Tangible Bk. Val.	30.79	31.47	32.79	31.51	30.93	28.74
Cash Flow	5.77	5.04	6.39	5.13	6.39	7.39
Earnings	1.68	1.31	2.71	1.92	3.41	4.79
Dividends	1.57	1.52	1.42	1.34	1.23	1.08
Payout Ratio	93%	116%	53%	70%	36%	23%
Prices - High	49½	51⅞	50	47	44½	38⅝
- Low	35½	38¼	36¾	27¾	23	30¾
P/E Ratio - High	29	40	18	24	13	8
- Low	21	29	14	14	7	6

Income Statement Analysis (Million $)

	1994	%Chg	1993	%Chg	1992	%Chg	1991
Revs.	1,471	7%	1,369	3%	1,327	7%	1,237
Oper. Inc.	248	20%	206	-13%	236	11%	212
Depr.	120	10%	109	2%	107	15%	93.0
Int. Exp.	53.9	2%	52.6	2%	51.5	19%	43.3
Pretax Inc.	76.0	17%	65.0	-48%	125	47%	85.0
Eff. Tax Rate	36%	—	41%	—	37%	—	35%
Net Inc.	49.0	29%	38.0	-52%	79.0	41%	56.0

Balance Sheet & Other Fin. Data (Million $)

	1994	1993	1992	1991	1990	1989
Cash	56.0	8.0	13.0	22.0	1.7	221
Curr. Assets	371	308	324	310	292	516
Total Assets	2,081	2,067	1,999	1,892	1,708	1,686
Curr. Liab.	229	179	184	196	206	191
LT Debt	633	707	634	563	392	459
Common Eqty.	920	920	956	915	896	829
Total Cap.	1,705	1,767	1,815	1,696	1,502	1,495
Cap. Exp.	104	202	180	267	318	155
Cash Flow	169	147	186	149	185	211

Ratio Analysis

	1994	1993	1992	1991	1990	1989
Curr. Ratio	1.6	1.7	1.8	1.6	1.4	2.7
% LT Debt of Cap.	37.2	40.0	34.9	33.2	26.1	30.7
% Net Inc.of Revs.	3.3	2.8	5.9	4.5	7.9	11.1
% Ret. on Assets	2.4	1.9	4.0	3.1	5.8	8.5
% Ret. on Equity	5.3	4.1	8.4	6.2	11.4	17.6

Dividend Data (Dividends have been paid since 1939. A dividend reinvestment plan is available.)

Amt. of Div. $	Date Decl.	Ex-Div. Date	Stock of Record	Payment Date
0.390	Jul. 28	Aug. 11	Aug. 17	Sep. 06 '94
0.400	Sep. 16	Nov. 09	Nov. 16	Dec. 05 '94
0.400	Jan. 26	Feb. 08	Feb. 14	Mar. 06 '95
0.400	Mar. 03	May. 10	May. 16	Jun. 05 '95

Data as orig. reptd.; bef. results of disc. opers. and/or spec. items. Per share data adj. for stk. divs. as of ex-div. date. E-Estimated. NA-Not Available. NM-Not Meaningful. NR-Not Ranked.

Office—One Maritime Plaza, San Francisco, CA 94111. **Tel**—(415) 576-8800. **Chrmn & CEO**—J. M. Richards. **Pres**—L. P. Siegel. **SVP-Fin**—G. E. Pfautsch. **Treas**—G. L. Zuehlke. **Secy**—Betty R. Fleshman. **Dirs**—R. A. Clarke, K. T. Derr, A. F. Jacobson, G. F. Jewett Jr., R. B. Madden, R. M. Morrow, V. W. Piasecki, T. Rembe, J. M. Richards, R. F. Richards, R. M. Rosenberg, R. G. Schwartz, C. R. Weaver, F. T. Weyerhaeuser, W. T. Weyerhaeuser. **Transfer Agent & Registrar**—Harris Trust & Savings Bank, Chicago. **Incorporated** in Delaware in 1955. **Empl**-6,700. **S&P Analyst:** Michael W. Jaffe

Praxair, Inc.

NYSE Symbol **PX**
In S&P 500

31-OCT-95 Industry:
Chemicals

Summary: This company is the largest producer of industrial gases in North and South America and one of the largest worldwide. It also provides ceramic and metallic coatings.

S&P Opinion: Accumulate (★★★★)	Recent Price • 26⅞	Yield • 1.2%
	52 Wk Range • 29-18¾	12-Mo. P/E • 15.3

Quantitative Evaluations

Outlook
(1 Lowest—5 Highest)
• **3+**

Fair Value
• **26⅝**

Risk
• **Average**

Earn./Div. Rank
• **NR**

Technical Eval.
• **Bullish** since 11/93

Rel. Strength Rank
(1 Lowest—99 Highest)
• **54**

Insider Activity
• **NA**

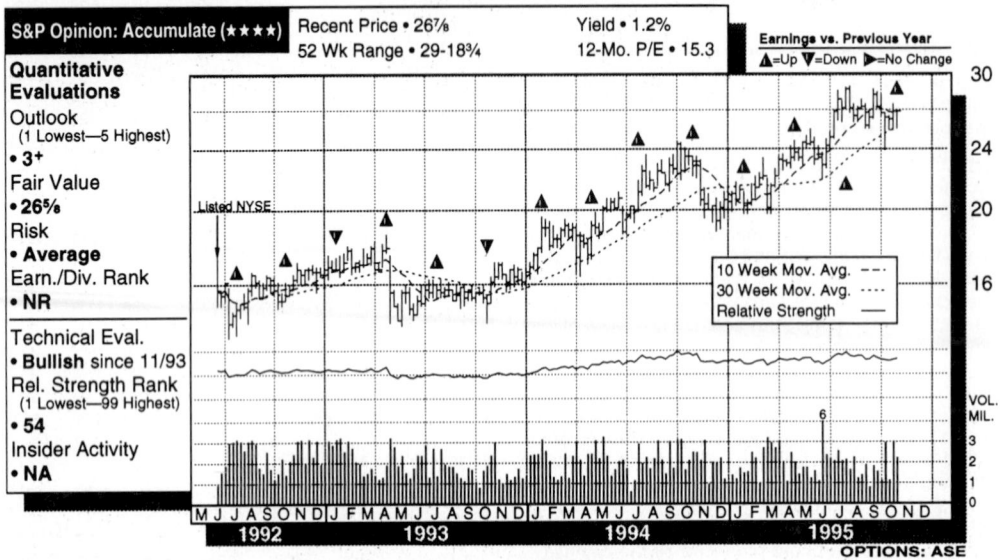

Earnings vs. Previous Year
▲=Up ▼=Down ▶=No Change

10 Week Mov. Avg. - - -
30 Week Mov. Avg. ·····
Relative Strength —

OPTIONS: ASE

Overview - 31-OCT-95

We expect sales of this supplier of industrial gases (as currently constituted) to advance about 10% in 1996, on continued worldwide volume growth for gases, reflecting good economic conditions. Recent acquisitions of U.S. packaged gases company will also contribute to gains. We believe that high operating rates for the U.S. gases industry will lead to a more favorable pricing environment for the next few years. First half earnings comparisons will be limited by unfavorable exchange rates for the Brazilian Real. The proposed acquisition of CBI Industries, if successful, is expected to be neutral to earnings in 1996, but additive thereafter. PX plans to repay much of the debt associated with the acquisition.

Valuation - 31-OCT-95

The shares have pulled back from their August 1995 record high, reflecting a general softness in chemicals issues, with increased investor concerns regarding a cyclical decline for the industry. The proposed $2.1 billion purchase of CBI Industries has also raised concerns. However, if completed, the acquisition will give PX potential for greater sales growth and significant cost savings, helping it achieve annual earnings growth of about 15% for the next several years. Fundamentals of the industrial gases industry should continue to improve, with demand growth faster than that of the overall economy, and selling prices trending higher. The stock, trading at about 15X our 1995 EPS estimate, is attractive, based on PX's favorable outlook.

Key Stock Statistics

S&P EPS Est. 1995	1.80	Tang. Bk. Value/Share	7.06
P/E on S&P Est. 1995	14.9	Beta	NA
S&P EPS Est. 1996	2.00	Shareholders	53,700
Dividend Rate/Share	0.32	Market cap. (B)	$ 3.7
Shs. outstg. (M)	138.5	Inst. holdings	70%
Avg. daily vol. (M)	0.504	Insider holdings	NA

Value of $10,000 invested 5 years ago: NA

Fiscal Year Ending Dec. 31

	1995	% Change	1994	% Change	1993	% Change
Revenues (Million $)						
1Q	756.0	24%	611.0	3%	594.0	-9%
2Q	788.0	22%	645.0	4%	623.0	-6%
3Q	795.0	8%	733.0	21%	608.0	-7%
4Q	—	—	722.0	18%	613.0	-4%
Yr.	—	—	2,711	11%	2,438	-6%
Income (Million $)						
1Q	65.00	55%	42.00	27%	33.00	6%
2Q	67.00	22%	55.00	45%	38.00	19%
3Q	64.00	25%	51.00	59%	32.00	-3%
4Q	—	—	55.00	38%	40.00	NM
Yr.	—	—	203.0	42%	143.0	70%
Earnings Per Share ($)						
1Q	0.46	53%	0.30	20%	0.25	4%
2Q	0.47	21%	0.39	39%	0.28	17%
3Q	0.44	22%	0.36	50%	0.24	-4%
4Q	E0.43	10%	0.39	34%	0.29	NM
Yr.	E1.80	24%	1.45	37%	1.06	66%

Next earnings report expected: mid January

Business Summary - 31-OCT-95

Praxair, Inc. is the largest producer of industrial gases in North and South America, and also provides wear- and corrosion-resistant coatings. The company was spun off to Union Carbide Corp. shareholders in June 1992. Contributions in 1994 by geographical area were:

	Sales	Profits
U.S.	46%	44%
South America	22%	30%
Europe	16%	15%
Canada, Mexico and Asia	16%	11%

The industrial gases business involves the production, distribution and sale of atmospheric gases (oxygen, nitrogen, argon and rare gases), hydrogen, helium, acetylene, specialty gases, and equipment for the production of industrial gases. Atmospheric gases are produced through air separation processes, primarily cryogenic, while other gases are produced by various methods. PX has also developed non-cryogenic air separation processes. Major customers include aerospace, chemicals, electronics, food processing, health care, glass, metal fabrication, petroleum, primary metals, and pulp and paper concerns.

Industrial gases are supplied to customers through three basic methods: on-site/pipeline (24% of total 1994 sales), merchant (39%) and packaged (28%). The company has about 124 cryogenic air separation plants in the U.S. and about 185 plants worldwide.

S.A. White Martins (52% owned) is the leading producer of industrial gases in Brazil. White Martins has most of its business in merchant and packaged gases, with about a 70% share of the Brazilian market.

The Surface Technologies business (7% of 1994 sales) applies metallic and ceramic coatings to parts and equipment provided by customers, including those in the aircraft engine, paper, petrochemical, metals, printing and textile industries. Other businesses (2% of 1994 sales) include the sale of cylinders and products related to industrial gases.

Important Developments

Oct. '95—PX offered to acquire CBI Industries, Inc. (CBI) for $32 a share in cash or stock, for a total cost (including equity and debt) of $2.1 billion. The company said that if its offer is rejected by CBI, it may make a cash offer directly to CBI shareholders. CBI, with 1994 sales of $1.9 billion, is a leading supplier of industrial gases, including carbon dioxide. Separately, PX said its record third quarter earnings reflected strong industrial gases demand, productivity gains, and acquisitions in packaged gases and Surface Technologies.

Capitalization

Long Term Debt: $936,000,000 (9/95).

Minority Interest: $381,000,000.

Per Share Data ($)
(Year Ended Dec. 31)

	1994	1993	1992	1991	1990	1989
Tangible Bk. Val.	5.43	4.22	3.69	NA	NA	NA
Cash Flow	3.40	2.93	2.52	NA	NA	NA
Earnings	1.45	1.06	0.64	0.84	0.85	0.31
Dividends	0.28	0.25	0.13	NA	NA	NA
Payout Ratio	19%	24%	20%	NA	NA	NA
Prices - High	24⅝	18⅝	17½	NA	NA	NA
- Low	16¼	14⅛	13⅝	NA	NA	NA
P/E Ratio - High	17	18	27	NA	NA	NA
- Low	11	13	21	NA	NA	NA

Income Statement Analysis (Million $)

	1994	%Chg	1993	%Chg	1992	%Chg	1991
Revs.	2,711	11%	2,438	-6%	2,604	5%	2,469
Oper. Inc.	737	24%	592	-12%	675	10%	612
Depr.	273	8%	253	2%	247	5%	236
Int. Exp.	112	4%	108	-53%	230	30%	177
Pretax Inc.	346	44%	240	45%	166	-20%	207
Eff. Tax Rate	24%	—	20%	—	22%	—	33%
Net Inc.	203	42%	143	70%	84.0	-21%	107

Balance Sheet & Other Fin. Data (Million $)

	1994	1993	1992	1991	1990	1989
Cash	63.0	34.0	24.0	82.0	73.0	NA
Curr. Assets	840	691	691	824	763	NA
Total Assets	3,520	3,255	3,344	3,451	3,027	2,714
Curr. Liab.	889	831	1,210	1,862	497	NA
LT Debt	893	967	669	176	1,275	1,242
Common Eqty.	839	635	544	650	645	527
Total Cap.	2,286	2,099	1,774	1,208	2,176	2,046
Cap. Exp.	326	240	333	417	363	243
Cash Flow	476	396	331	343	318	218

Ratio Analysis

	1994	1993	1992	1991	1990	1989
Curr. Ratio	0.9	0.8	0.6	0.4	1.5	NA
% LT Debt of Cap.	39.1	45.9	37.7	14.6	58.6	60.7
% Net Inc.of Revs.	7.5	5.9	3.2	4.3	5.0	2.1
% Ret. on Assets	5.9	4.3	NA	3.3	4.2	1.6
% Ret. on Equity	27.2	24.0	NA	16.5	20.5	8.6

Dividend Data
—Dividends were initiated in 1992. A dividend reinvestment plan is available.

Amt. of Div. $	Date Decl.	Ex-Div. Date	Stock of Record	Payment Date
0.070	Oct. 25	Dec. 01	Dec. 07	Dec. 15 '94
0.080	Jan. 24	Mar. 01	Mar. 07	Mar. 15 '95
0.080	Apr. 19	Jun. 01	Jun. 07	Jun. 15 '95
0.080	Jul. 25	Sep. 06	Sep. 08	Sep. 15 '95
0.080	Oct. 24	Dec. 05	Dec. 07	Dec. 15 '95

Data as orig. reptd.; bef. results of disc. opers. and/or spec. items. Per share data adj. for stk. divs. as of ex-div. date. E-Estimated. NA-Not Available. NM-Not Meaningful. NR-Not Ranked.

Office—39 Old Ridgebury Rd., Danbury, CT 06810-5113. **Tel**—(203) 794-3000. **Chrmn & CEO**—H. W. Lichtenberger. **Pres**—E. G. Hotard. **VP & CFO**—J. A. Clerico. **VP & Secy**—D. H. Chaifetz. **Investor Contact**—Scott S. Cunningham. **Dirs**—A. Achaval, J. A. Clerico, J. J. Creedon, C. F. Fetterolf, D. F. Frey, C. W. Gargalli, E. G. Hotard, R. L. Kuehn, Jr., H. W. Lichtenberger, B. F. Payton, G. J. Ratcliffe, Jr., H. M. Watson, Jr. **Transfer Agent & Registrar**—Bank of New York, NYC. **Incorporated** in Delaware in 1988. **Empl**-17,780. **S&P Analyst:** Richard O'Reilly, CFA

Premark International

NYSE Symbol **PMI**
In S&P 500

19-SEP-95

Industry:
Housewares

Summary: Premark makes plastic products under the Tupperware name, commercial food equipment and consumer/decorative products, including West Bend small appliances.

S&P Opinion: Accumulate (★★★★)

Recent Price • 53¼	Yield • 2.0%
52 Wk Range • 54¾-38½	12-Mo. P/E • 14.2

Quantitative Evaluations

Outlook
(1 Lowest—5 Highest)
• **3+**

Fair Value
• **53**

Risk
• **Low**

Earn./Div. Rank
• **B+**

Technical Eval.
• **Bullish** since 3/95

Rel. Strength Rank
(1 Lowest—99 Highest)
• **48**

Insider Activity
• **Neutral**

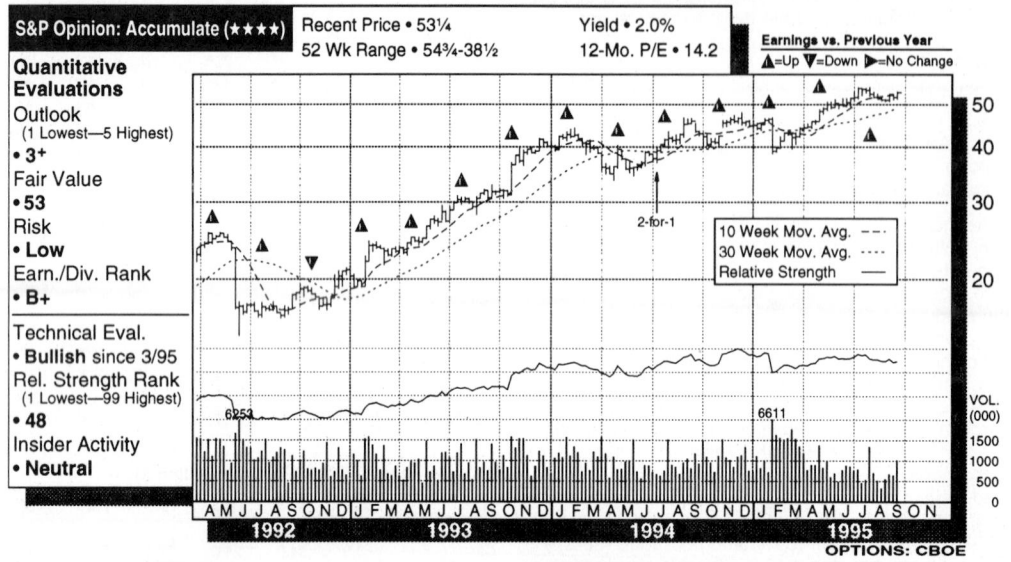

Earnings vs. Previous Year
▲=Up ▼=Down ▶=No Change

2-for-1

10 Week Mov. Avg. ---
30 Week Mov. Avg. ·····
Relative Strength ——

6253 6611

VOL. (000)

1992 1993 1994 1995

OPTIONS: CBOE

Overview - 18-SEP-95

Sales should continue in an uptrend in 1995, with gains at all divisions. Sales of Tupperware should increase in the high single-digit range, reflecting higher demand in Europe, the U.S. and Latin America as a result of new products and an increased sales force. Sales should also improve in the Asia Pacific region. Sales of food equipment could improve on stronger European economies. Consolidated sales will also be boosted by higher demand for West Bend appliances, mainly reflecting new products. Sales of Ralph Wilson laminated plastic products, Hartco Flooring and Florida Tile could be under some pressure from increased competition. Despite a one-time charge at West Bend, margins should widen on higher volume at most divisions, cost control efforts, and the absence of warranty expenses at Ralph Wilson plastics. Share earnings comparisons will benefit from fewer outstanding shares.

Valuation - 18-SEP-95

Since Premark underwent a major restructuring in 1992, earnings have been in a healthy uptrend. Earnings for the first half of 1995 were higher than estimated, and we expect the company will continue to report good earnings progress for the remainder of the year and into 1996. Results will be aided mainly by strong demand for Tupperware and food equipment in overseas markets. The shares, which have risen considerably over the past few years, appear undervalued to us, given the company's growth prospects, and should be accumulated.

Key Stock Statistics

S&P EPS Est. 1995	4.05	Tang. Bk. Value/Share	12.47
P/E on S&P Est. 1995	13.1	Beta	1.65
S&P EPS Est. 1996	4.40	Shareholders	25,000
Dividend Rate/Share	1.08	Market cap. (B)	$ 3.3
Shs. outstg. (M)	61.1	Inst. holdings	73%
Avg. daily vol. (M)	0.158	Insider holdings	NA

Value of $10,000 invested 5 years ago: $ 39,670

Fiscal Year Ending Dec. 31

	1995	% Change	1994	% Change	1993	% Change
Revenues (Million $)						
1Q	849.7	6%	801.6	14%	706.0	4%
2Q	889.9	7%	831.3	9%	763.2	4%
3Q	—	—	824.3	11%	744.8	4%
4Q	—	—	993.6	13%	883.2	7%
Yr.	—	—	3,451	11%	3,097	5%
Income (Million $)						
1Q	46.50	23%	37.80	84%	20.50	7%
2Q	67.10	18%	56.90	39%	41.00	39%
3Q	—	—	40.90	24%	32.90	NM
4Q	—	—	89.90	21%	74.60	47%
Yr.	—	—	225.5	31%	172.5	NM
Earnings Per Share ($)						
1Q	0.71	26%	0.57	57%	0.36	14%
2Q	1.06	23%	0.86	41%	0.61	30%
3Q	E0.74	19%	0.62	27%	0.49	NM
4Q	E1.54	14%	1.35	22%	1.11	43%
Yr.	E4.05	19%	3.39	32%	2.57	NM

Next earnings report expected: late October

Business Summary - 18-SEP-95

Premark International manufactures and markets consumer and commercial products under well known brand names. Business segment contributions in 1994:

	Sales	Profits
Tupperware	39%	56%
Food equipment	33%	23%
Consumer/decorative products	28%	21%

Sales in the U.S. accounted for 55% of all sales in 1994 and 42% of operating profits; in Europe, 27% and 39%; in Asia Pacific, 11% and 14%; in Latin America, 4.5% and 4.8%; and in Canada, 2.3% and 0.4%.

Tupperware manufactures and sells, directly to the consumer through independent distributors, a broad line of molded plastic food storage and serving containers, as well as educational toys and personal care and home products. Important products include Tuppertoys educational toys, Bell tumblers, Modular Mates stackable storage containers, Wonderlier and Servalier bowls, Tupperware microwave cookware, and One Touch canisters. In 1994, sales in foreign countries represented approximately 82% of total Tupperware revenues.

The food equipment group, which includes Hobart, Wolf and Vulcan-Hart, produces commercial food preparation equipment, including food mixers, slicers, cutters, meat saws and grinders; weighing and wrapping equipment and related systems; baking and cooking equipment such as ovens, ranges, fryers, griddles and broilers; refrigeration equipment; and warewashers. In 1994, sales in foreign countries represented approximately 39% of total food equipment sales.

The decorative products division consists of the Ralph Wilson division (decorative plastic laminates used on cabinetry, countertops, vanities, store fixtures and furniture); Hartco (prefinished oak and maple flooring and moldings); and Florida Tile (ceramic wall and floor tile). The consumer products division consists of West Bend (small electric appliances and stainless steel cookware); and Precor (home physical fitness equipment).

Important Developments

Aug. '95—Directors authorized the repurchase of up to 6 million PMI common shares.
Jul. '95—PMI attributed its strong second-quarter earnings to profit gains of 22%, 20% and 19% at the consumer and decorative products, food equipment and Tupperware divisions, respectively. Profitability was especially driven by strong Tupperware results in Latin America, good momentum of food equipment in the U.S., the absence of Wilsonart warranty expenses, and favorable foreign exchange rates.

Capitalization

Long Term Debt: $197,600,000 (7/1/95).

Per Share Data ($)

(Year Ended Dec. 31)

	1994	1993	1992	1991	1990	1989
Tangible Bk. Val.	12.44	9.86	8.17	10.21	9.19	10.06
Cash Flow	5.34	4.09	2.62	3.25	2.22	2.13
Earnings	3.39	2.58	0.07	1.63	0.82	1.12
Dividends	0.64	0.54	0.48	0.42	0.42	0.39
Payout Ratio	19%	21%	NM	26%	50%	34%
Prices - High	48	41⅞	25⅝	20⅜	15½	21
- Low	33⅝	19⅛	14⅞	8⅛	6⅜	14¾
P/E Ratio - High	14	16	NM	13	19	19
- Low	10	7	NM	5	8	13

Income Statement Analysis (Million $)

	1994	%Chg	1993	%Chg	1992	%Chg	1991
Revs.	3,451	11%	3,097	5%	2,946	5%	2,816
Oper. Inc.	447	25%	359	-2%	365	19%	308
Depr.	130	27%	102	-39%	168	63%	103
Int. Exp.	23.8	-26%	32.1	-9%	35.1	-37%	55.7
Pretax Inc.	311	35%	230	NM	34.0	-79%	160
Eff. Tax Rate	28%	—	25%	—	86%	—	36%
Net Inc.	226	31%	173	NM	5.0	-95%	102

Balance Sheet & Other Fin. Data (Million $)

	1994	1993	1992	1991	1990	1989
Cash	121	140	72.0	88.0	41.0	97.0
Curr. Assets	1,274	1,139	1,001	1,037	1,026	1,046
Total Assets	2,358	2,117	1,959	2,034	2,034	1,757
Curr. Liab.	921	888	750	780	659	605
LT Debt	122	168	274	279	496	254
Common Eqty.	972	812	710	836	758	801
Total Cap.	1,105	989	995	1,196	1,323	1,116
Cap. Exp.	148	146	141	98.0	303	103
Cash Flow	355	275	173	205	141	150

Ratio Analysis

	1994	1993	1992	1991	1990	1989
Curr. Ratio	1.4	1.3	1.3	1.3	1.6	1.7
% LT Debt of Cap.	11.1	17.0	27.6	23.3	37.5	22.8
% Net Inc.of Revs.	6.5	5.6	0.2	3.6	1.9	3.0
% Ret. on Assets	10.1	8.5	0.2	5.0	2.9	4.6
% Ret. on Equity	25.3	22.6	0.6	12.8	7.0	10.1

Dividend Data —Dividends were initiated in 1987. A "poison pill" stock purchase rights plan was adopted in 1989.

Amt. of Div. $	Date Decl.	Ex-Div. Date	Stock of Record	Payment Date
0.200	Aug. 03	Sep. 12	Sep. 16	Oct. 04 '94
0.200	Nov. 02	Dec. 08	Dec. 14	Jan. 06 '95
0.200	Mar. 03	Mar. 10	Mar. 16	Apr. 03 '95
0.270	May. 03	Jun. 14	Jun. 16	Jul. 05 '95
0.270	Aug. 02	Sep. 13	Sep. 15	Oct. 04 '95

Data as orig. reptd.; bef. results of disc. opers. and/or spec. items. Per share data adj. for stk. divs. as of ex-div. date. E-Estimated. NA-Not Available. NM-Not Meaningful. NR-Not Ranked.

Office—1717 Deerfield Rd., Deerfield, IL 60015. **Tel**—(708) 405-6000. **Chrmn & CEO**—W. L. Batts. **Pres**—J. M. Ringler. **Sr VP & CFO**—L. B. Skatoff. **Sr VP & Secy**—J. M. Costigan. **Investor Contact**—Christine Hanneman. **Dirs**—W. L. Batts, W. O. Bourke, R. M. Davis, L. C. Elam, E. V. Goings, C. J. Grum, J. E. Luecke, B. Marbut, J. B. McKinnon, D. R. Parker, R. M. Price, J. M. Ringler, J. D. Stoney. **Transfer Agent & Registrar**—Chemical Bank, NYC. **Incorporated** in Delaware in 1986. **Empl**-24,000. **S&P Analyst:** Elizabeth Vandeventer

Price/Costco, Inc.

NASDAQ Symbol **PCCW**
In S&P 500

01-NOV-95

Industry: Retail Stores

Summary: Price/Costco operates more than 240 membership warehouses in the U.S. and Canada. It also has units in the U.K. and Mexico.

S&P Opinion: Hold (★★★)	Recent Price • 17	Yield • Nil
	52 Wk Range • 18¾-12	12-Mo. P/E • 25.0

Quantitative Evaluations

Outlook (1 Lowest—5 Highest)
• **5+**

Fair Value
• **24%**

Risk
• **Average**

Earn./Div. Rank
• **NR**

Technical Eval.
• **Bullish** since 10/95

Rel. Strength Rank (1 Lowest—99 Highest)
• **49**

Insider Activity
• **Unfavorable**

Earnings vs. Previous Year
▲=Up ▼=Down ▶=No Change

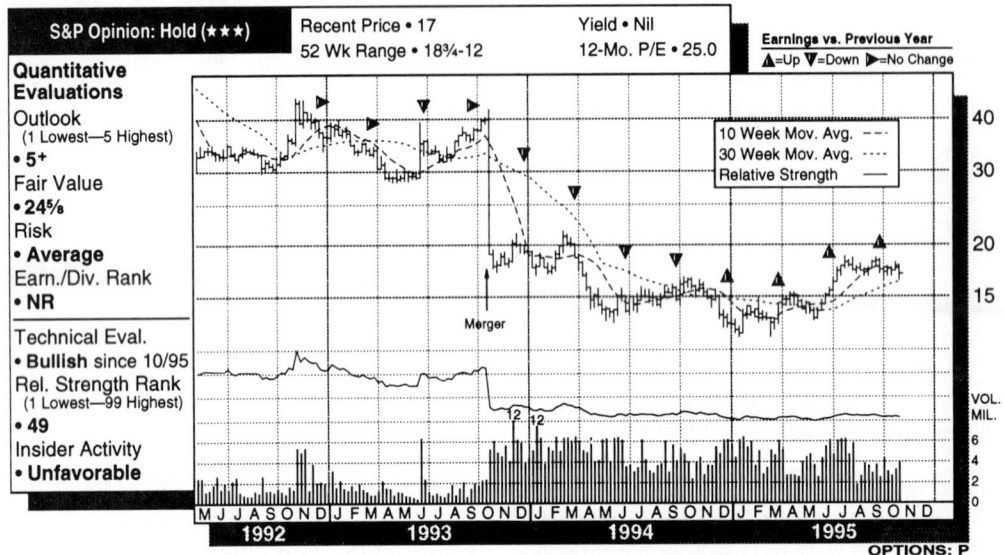

10 Week Mov. Avg. – – –
30 Week Mov. Avg. ·····
Relative Strength ——

Merger

VOL. MIL.

OPTIONS: P

Overview - 01-NOV-95

Sales should increase moderately in fiscal 1996, reflecting modest gains in same-store sales and 20 additional warehouses; membership fees should be up only slightly. Gross margins should widen marginally, as price increases are controlled; low prices remain PCCW's competitive advantage in the overcrowded retail marketplace. Selling, general and administrative expenses should decrease as a percentage of sales. Interest expense could rise, as borrowings are used to fund a store expansion program. In the long-term, a larger base of warehouse clubs and expansion overseas should continue to boost earnings. Consolidation in the warehouse club sector has resulted in the concentration of business in the hands of fewer players, resulting in a decline in head-to-head competition that has plagued the industry in the past.

Valuation - 01-NOV-95

The shares appear to be fully valued at current levels. PCCW moved up in price earlier in the year as same store sales strengthened. Recently, the shares have been trading in a narrow range. We believe that the shares will track the market in the near-term. PCCW remains a successful survivor in the warehouse club industry with ample opportunities to open new units domestically and abroad and we would retain the shares for capital appreciation.

Key Stock Statistics

S&P EPS Est. 1996	1.25	Tang. Bk. Value/Share	7.49
P/E on S&P Est. 1996	13.6	Beta	NA
Dividend Rate/Share	Nil	Shareholders	13,800
Shs. outstg. (M)	195.0	Market cap. (B)	$ 3.3
Avg. daily vol. (M)	0.646	Inst. holdings	58%
		Insider holdings	NA

Value of $10,000 invested 5 years ago: NA

Fiscal Year Ending Aug. 31

	1995	% Change	1994	% Change	1993	% Change
Revenues (Million $)						
1Q	4,030	9%	3,681	8%	3,423	12%
2Q	4,307	5%	4,098	10%	3,736	12%
3Q	3,825	6%	3,616	8%	3,348	8%
4Q	6,014	18%	5,086	9%	4,648	7%
Yr.	18,247	11%	16,481	9%	15,155	10%
Income (Million $)						
1Q	48.53	NM	-36.94	NM	44.33	-2%
2Q	64.77	8%	59.71	-14%	69.03	-4%
3Q	32.62	11%	29.44	-13%	33.95	-30%
4Q	71.33	22%	58.69	-23%	75.94	-1%
Yr.	217.2	96%	110.9	-50%	223.3	-8%
Earnings Per Share ($)						
1Q	0.22	NM	-0.17	NM	0.20	NM
2Q	0.31	15%	0.27	-13%	0.31	NM
3Q	0.17	21%	0.14	-13%	0.16	-24%
4Q	0.35	30%	0.27	-21%	0.34	NM
Yr.	1.05	106%	0.51	-50%	1.01	-6%

Next earnings report expected: mid December

Price/Costco, Inc.

01-NOV-95

Business Summary - 01-NOV-95

At September 3, 1995, Price/Costco operated a chain of 236 cash and carry membership warehouses. The company spun off its commercial real estate operations and certain other assets to shareholders effective August 29, 1994.

Clubs offer low prices on a limited selection of national brand merchandise and selected private label products in a wide range of merchandise categories. A typical warehouse format averages about 120,000 sq. ft. Rapid inventory turnover, combined with operating efficiencies achieved by volume purchasing in a no-frills, self-service warehouse facility, enables the company to operate profitably at significantly lower gross margins than traditional retailers. PCCW generally receives cash from the sale of a substantial portion of its inventory at mature warehouse operations before it is required to pay vendors, even though the company often pays early to obtain payment discounts.

The company has two primary types of membership: Business and Gold Star (individual) members. Businesses (including individuals) with a resale or business license may become Business members by paying an annual $35 fee. Gold Star membership is $35 annually. At August 28, 1994, Price/Costco had 3.4 million Business memberships and 6.4 million Gold Star memberships.

In January 1995, PCCW exchanged 23 million shares tendered by shareholders for Price Enterprises Inc. (PREN) shares on a one-for-one basis. The company sold to PREN the 3.8 million PREN shares it held, for a $45.9 million secured note.

Important Developments

Oct. '95—For the 53 weeks ended September 3, 1995, net sales totaled $17.9 billion, up 11% from the prior 52 weeks. On a comparable warehouse basis, sales increased 2% in fiscal 1995. The company reported income from continuing operations of $217.2 million ($1.05 a share) in fiscal 1995, compared to $110.9 million ($0.51) in fiscal 1994. Excluding the $80.0 million ($0.36) merger and restructuring charges in fiscal 1994, income from continuing operations would have been $190.9 million ($0.87). The company opened a net increase of 19 warehouses in fiscal 1995, ending the year with 236 units. About eleven to twelve new locations will be added by year-end 1995. In addition, PCCW owns a 50% interest in Price Club Mexico, which currently operates 13 warehouses in Mexico.

Capitalization

Long Term Debt: $1,094,615,000 (9/95).
Minority Interest: $50,838,000.

Per Share Data ($)

(Year Ended Aug. 31)

	1995	1994	1993	1992	1991	1990
Tangible Bk. Val.	NA	7.56	8.08	16.29	14.58	12.49
Cash Flow	NA	1.14	NA	3.37	3.35	2.78
Earnings	1.05	0.51	1.01	2.61	2.68	2.47
Dividends	Nil	Nil	Nil	Nil	Nil	Nil
Payout Ratio	Nil	Nil	Nil	Nil	Nil	Nil
Prices - High	18¾	21⅝	42¼	55	58½	48¼
- Low	12	12½	17⅛	29½	37¾	26½
P/E Ratio - High	18	42	NM	21	22	20
- Low	11	25	12	11	14	11

Income Statement Analysis (Million $)

	1994	%Chg	1993	%Chg	1992	%Chg	1991
Revs.	16,476	7%	15,464	10%	14,097	17%	12,042
Oper. Inc.	503	5%	477	3%	465	14%	407
Depr.	139	24%	112	26%	89.0	24%	72.0
Int. Exp.	57.6	25%	46.1	30%	35.5	37%	26.0
Pretax Inc.	204	-45%	370	-8%	401	11%	361
Eff. Tax Rate	46%	—	40%	—	40%	—	39%
Net Inc.	111	-50%	223	-8%	242	11%	219

Balance Sheet & Other Fin. Data (Million $)

	1994	1993	1992	1991	1990	1989
Cash	63.0	210	376	NA	NA	NA
Curr. Assets	1,534	1,389	1,388	NA	NA	NA
Total Assets	4,236	3,940	3,577	2,986	2.0	1,740
Curr. Liab.	1,647	1,258	1,106	NA	NA	NA
LT Debt	795	813	814	500	200	234
Common Eqty.	1,685	1,797	1,594	1,430	988	778
Total Cap.	2,581	2,674	2,461	NA	NA	NA
Cap. Exp.	477	533	636	342	NA	NA
Cash Flow	250	335	332	291	NA	NA

Ratio Analysis

	1994	1993	1992	1991	1990	1989
Curr. Ratio	0.9	1.1	1.3	NA	NA	NA
% LT Debt of Cap.	30.8	30.4	33.1	NA	NA	NA
% Net Inc.of Revs.	0.7	1.4	1.7	1.8	1.8	1.8
% Ret. on Assets	2.7	5.9	7.4	8.7	9.3	9.0
% Ret. on Equity	6.4	13.2	16.0	18.1	27.6	21.1

Dividend Data —The company does not intend to pay dividends in the foreseeable future.

Data as orig. reptd.; bef. results of disc. opers. and/or spec. items. Per share data adj. for stk. divs. as of ex-div. date.
E-Estimated. NA-Not Available. NM-Not Meaningful. NR-Not Ranked.

Office—10809 120th Ave. N.E., Kirkland, WA 98033. **Tel**—(206) 803-8100. **Chrmn**—H. Brotman. **Pres & CEO**—J. D. Sinegal. **EVP, CFO & Investor Contact**—Richard A. Galanti (206-803-8256). **Dirs**—D. Bernard, J. H. Brotman, R. D. DiCerchio, H. E. James, J. P. Kinloch, J. K. Kornwasser, R. M. Libenson, M. G. Lynn, J. W. Meisenbach, P. A. Peterson, J. D. Sinegal. **Transfer Agent & Registrar**—First Interstate Bank of Washington, LA. **Incorporated** in Delaware in 1993. **Empl**-47,000. **S&P Analyst:** Karen. J. Sack, CFA

Procter & Gamble

NYSE Symbol **PG**
In S&P 500

STOCK REPORTS

19-SEP-95

Industry:
Household Products

Summary: This leading consumer products company markets household and personal care products in more than 140 countries.

S&P Opinion: Accumulate (★★★★)	Recent Price • 75⅛	Yield • 2.1%	
	52 Wk Range • 75½-58¼	12-Mo. P/E • 20.2	

Quantitative Evaluations

Outlook
(1 Lowest—5 Highest)
• **2+**

Fair Value
• **71¾**

Risk
• **Low**

Earn./Div. Rank
• **A-**

Technical Eval.
• **Bullish** since 8/95

Rel. Strength Rank
(1 Lowest—99 Highest)
• **68**

Insider Activity
• **Neutral**

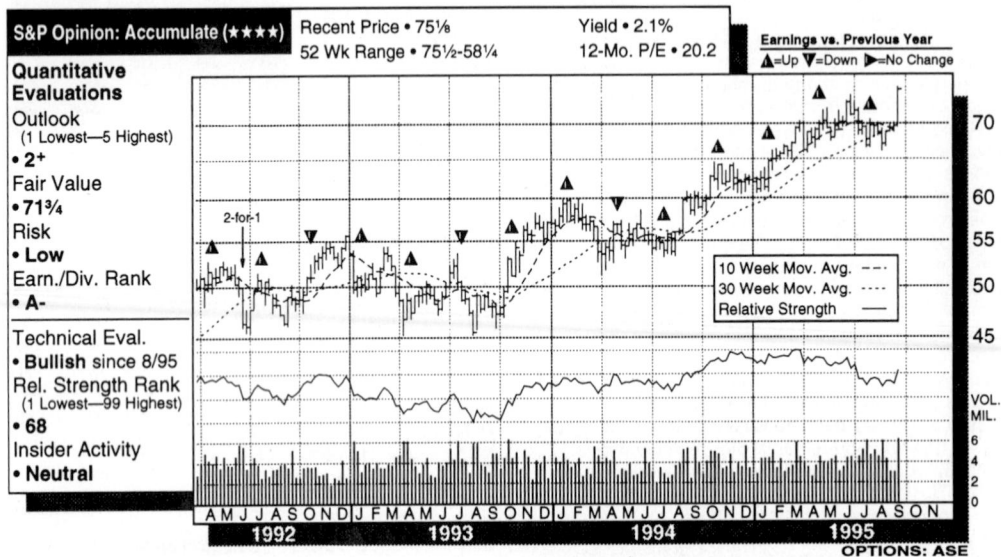

Earnings vs. Previous Year
▲=Up ▼=Down ▶=No Change

10 Week Mov. Avg. ---
30 Week Mov. Avg. .....
Relative Strength ——

OPTIONS: ASE

Overview - 19-SEP-95

Volume should remain in a solid uptrend in fiscal 1996, fueled by international unit volume growth, acquisitions and higher sales of personal products. Despite pricing pressures in the U.S. and Europe, particularly from private-label brands, and higher marketing costs aimed at supporting new products and increasing or maintaining share, margins should widen on a lower overall cost structure. Margins should also be aided by a continuing shift in sales mix to higher-margin personal care and beauty care products. More favorable currency exchange rates could boost sales and earnings growth. Over the next five years, earnings growth should outpace sales growth. Profits are expected to rise about 12% - 14% annually.

Valuation - 19-SEP-95

Over the past years, PG's shares have trended upward on steady and fairly predictable earnings growth. The shares are currently trading at the low end of the historical price earnings multiple, based on estimated earnings of $4.30 a share for the fiscal year to end June 1996. This implies that these shares could appreciate in the low double-digit range over the next year, barring any unforeseen catastrophe. We recommend that risk-adverse investors who are focused on a longer-term, buy-and-hold strategy and are looking for above-average appreciation potential, along with stable yearly increases in dividends, continue to accumulate shares of this industry leader.

Key Stock Statistics

S&P EPS Est. 1996	4.30	Tang. Bk. Value/Share	5.87
P/E on S&P Est. 1996	17.5	Beta	0.95
S&P EPS Est. 1997	5.00	Shareholders	202,000
Dividend Rate/Share	1.60	Market cap. (B)	$ 51.4
Shs. outstg. (M)	687.4	Inst. holdings	48%
Avg. daily vol. (M)	0.965	Insider holdings	NA

Value of $10,000 invested 5 years ago: $ 24,066

Fiscal Year Ending Jun. 30

	1995	% Change	1994	% Change	1993	% Change
Revenues (Million $)						
1Q	8,161	8%	7,564	-4%	7,880	9%
2Q	8,467	9%	7,788	NM	7,840	4%
3Q	8,312	12%	7,441	1%	7,350	-2%
4Q	8,494	13%	7,503	2%	7,365	3%
Yr.	33,434	10%	30,296	NM	30,433	4%
Income (Million $)						
1Q	792.0	18%	670.0	55%	431.0	-20%
2Q	750.0	15%	653.0	11%	590.0	13%
3Q	631.0	8%	584.0	13%	516.0	9%
4Q	472.0	16%	406.0	NM	-1,218	NM
Yr.	2,645	20%	2,211	NM	269.0	-86%
Earnings Per Share ($)						
1Q	1.12	18%	0.95	67%	0.57	-25%
2Q	1.06	15%	0.92	14%	0.81	11%
3Q	0.88	33%	0.66	-10%	0.73	9%
4Q	0.65	16%	0.56	NM	-1.83	NM
Yr.	3.71	20%	3.09	NM	0.25	-90%

Next earnings report expected: late October

Procter & Gamble

Business Summary - 28-AUG-95

Procter & Gamble markets a wide range of personal care and consumer household products. In July 1991, it acquired Revlon Inc.'s worldwide Max Factor and Betrix lines of cosmetics and fragrances, and in mid-1994 it acquired Giorgio of Beverly Hills from Avon. In early 1993, the company sold its commercial pulp business and exited the 100%-juice business. Contributions by business segment in fiscal 1994 were:

	Sales	Profits
Laundry/cleaning products	32%	39%
Personal care products	55%	51%
Food & beverage products	11%	10%
Pulp & chemicals	2%	--

International business contributed 52% of sales and 31% of net income in fiscal 1994.

Among the more popular laundry and cleaning brands are Bold, Bounce, Cascade, Cheer, Comet, Dash, Downy, Era, Gain, Ivory Snow, Ivory Liquid, Mr. Clean, Solo, Spic and Span, Tide and Top Job.

Personal care products include Camay, Ivory, Safeguard and Zest bar soaps; Bounty, Charmin, Puffs and White Cloud paper tissue products; Pampers and Luvs disposable diapers; Always feminine hygiene products; Sure, Secret and Old Spice deodorants; Crest toothpaste; Scope mouthwash; Head & Shoulders, Pantene, Pert and Vidal Sasson hair care products; Oil of Olay, Noxzema, Cover Girl, Max Factor and Clearasil skin care products; Pepto-Bismol and the Vicks line of cough and cold medicines; and pharmaceuticals. Disposable diapers accounted for 15% of total sales in fiscal 1994.

Food items include Crisco oil, Duncan Hines cake mixes, Folgers coffee, Tender Leaf tea, Jif peanut butter, Pringles potato chips and Hawaiian Punch and Sunny Delight juice drinks.

Other products include chemicals.

Important Developments

Aug. '95—PG said that North American sales in fiscal 1995 increased 7%, year to year, on a 6% rise in volume; profits rose 9%. Sales in Europe, the Middle East and Africa were up 13%, on a volume increase of 15%, while earnings surged 22%. In Asia, sales increased 15% on a 24% volume increase, while profits rose 40%. Sales in Latin America fell 3%, primarily due to the impact of the peso devaluation, on a 6% rise in volume, while net income was up 48%.

Capitalization

Long Term Debt: $5,157,000,000 (3/95).
Preferred Stock: $1,919,000,000.

Per Share Data ($)

(Year Ended Jun. 30)

	1995	1994	1993	1992	1991	1990
Tangible Bk. Val.	5.97	7.19	5.20	4.75	4.23	5.67
Cash Flow	5.53	4.75	1.92	3.97	3.39	3.36
Earnings	3.71	3.09	0.25	2.62	2.46	2.25
Dividends	1.40	1.32	1.10	1.02	0.98	0.88
Payout Ratio	38%	43%	449%	39%	39%	39%
Prices - High	74¼	64⅝	58⅞	55¾	47¾	45⅝
- Low	60⅝	51¼	45¼	45⅛	38	30⅞
P/E Ratio - High	20	21	NM	21	19	20
- Low	16	17	NM	17	15	14

Income Statement Analysis (Million $)

	1995	%Chg	1994	%Chg	1993	%Chg	1992
Revs.	33,434	10%	30,296	NM	30,433	4%	29,362
Oper. Inc.	NA	—	5,432	26%	4,301	14%	3,777
Depr.	1,253	10%	1,134	NM	1,140	25%	910
Int. Exp.	488	1%	482	-16%	577	8%	535
Pretax Inc.	4,000	20%	3,346	NM	349	NM	349
Eff. Tax Rate	34%	—	34%	—	23%	—	35%
Net Inc.	2,645	20%	2,211	NM	269	-86%	1,872

Balance Sheet & Other Fin. Data (Million $)

	1995	1994	1993	1992	1991	1990
Cash	2,178	2,656	2,322	1,776	1,384	1,407
Curr. Assets	10,842	9,988	9,975	9,366	8,435	7,644
Total Assets	28,125	25,535	24,935	24,025	20,468	18,487
Curr. Liab.	8,648	8,040	8,287	7,642	6,733	5,417
LT Debt	5,161	4,980	5,174	5,223	4,111	3,588
Common Eqty.	8,676	8,677	7,308	7,085	5,741	6,518
Total Cap.	16,281	14,159	12,798	15,777	13,157	12,364
Cap. Exp.	2,146	1,841	1,911	1,911	1,979	1,300
Cash Flow	3,796	3,243	1,307	2,688	2,542	2,325

Ratio Analysis

	1995	1994	1993	1992	1991	1990
Curr. Ratio	1.3	1.2	1.2	1.2	1.3	1.4
% LT Debt of Cap.	31.7	35.2	40.4	33.1	31.2	29.0
% Net Inc.of Revs.	7.9	7.3	0.9	6.4	6.6	6.7
% Ret. on Assets	9.9	8.7	1.1	8.5	9.2	8.9
% Ret. on Equity	32.7	26.3	2.0	27.7	28.0	25.7

Dividend Data

—Dividends have been paid since 1891. A dividend reinvestment plan is available.

Amt. of Div. $	Date Decl.	Ex-Div. Date	Stock of Record	Payment Date
0.350	Oct. 11	Oct. 17	Oct. 21	Nov. 15 '94
0.350	Jan. 10	Jan. 13	Jan. 20	Feb. 15 '95
0.350	Apr. 11	Apr. 17	Apr. 21	May. 15 '95
0.400	Jul. 11	Jul. 19	Jul. 21	Aug. 15 '95

Data as orig. reptd.; bef. results of disc. opers. and/or spec. items. Per share data adj. for stk. divs. as of ex-div. date.
E-Estimated. NA-Not Available. NM-Not Meaningful. NR-Not Ranked.

Office—1 Procter & Gamble Plaza, Cincinnati, OH 45202. **Tel**—(513) 983-1100. **Chrmn & CEO**—J. E. Pepper. **Pres**—D. I. Jager. **SVP & CFO**—E. G. Nelson. **Secy**—T. L. Overbey. **Investor Contact**—G. A. Dowdell. **Dirs**—D. M. Abshire, E. L. Artzt, N. R. Augustine, D. R. Beall, G. F. Brunner, R. B. Cheney, H. Einsmann, R. J. Ferris, J. T. Gorman, D. I. Jager, J. R. Junkins, C. R. Lee, L. Martin, J. E. Pepper, J. G. Smale, J. F. Smith, Jr., R. Snyderman, R. D. Storey, M. v. N. Whitman. **Transfer Agent**—Co. itself. **Registrar**—PNC Bank, Ohio, Cincinnati. **Incorporated** in Ohio in 1905. **Empl**-96,500. **S&P Analyst:** Elizabeth Vandeventer

Providian Corp.

NYSE Symbol **PVN**
In S&P 500

24-AUG-95   **Industry:** Insurance

Summary: Providian Corp. is one of the largest stockholder-owned insurance companies, providing life, health, and property-casualty insurance, annuities and other investments.

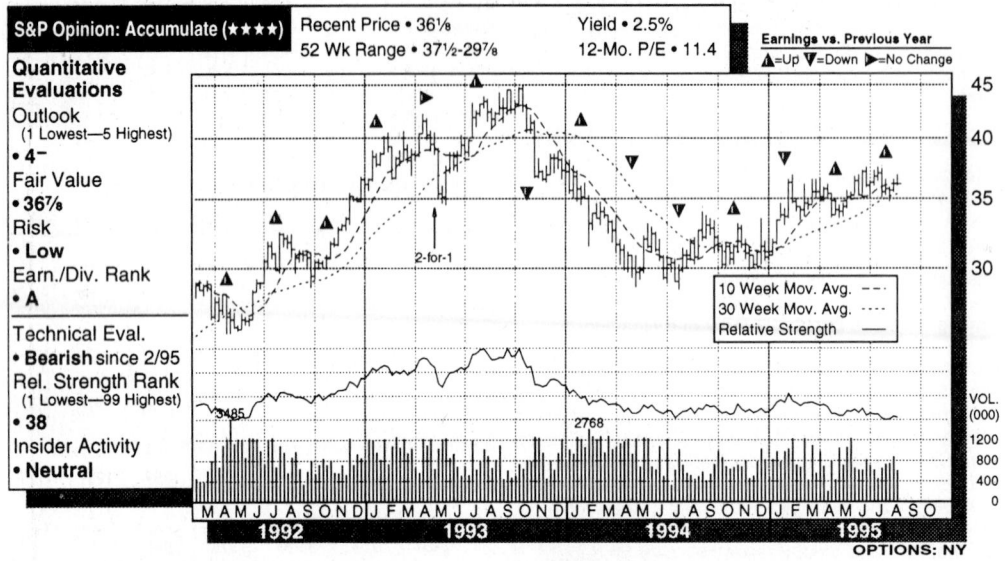

S&P Opinion: Accumulate (★★★★)

Recent Price • 36⅛
52 Wk Range • 37½-29⅞

Yield • 2.5%
12-Mo. P/E • 11.4

Earnings vs. Previous Year
▲=Up ▼=Down ►=No Change

Quantitative Evaluations

Outlook
(1 Lowest—5 Highest)
• **4-**

Fair Value
• **36⅞**

Risk
• **Low**

Earn./Div. Rank
• **A**

Technical Eval.
• **Bearish** since 2/95

Rel. Strength Rank
(1 Lowest—99 Highest)
• **38**

Insider Activity
• **Neutral**

2-for-1

10 Week Mov. Avg. — - —
30 Week Mov. Avg. ········
Relative Strength ——

VOL.
(000)
1200
800
400
0

OPTIONS: NY

Overview - 24-AUG-95

Operating earnings should continue to advance in coming periods as life operations benefit from increased demand for retirement and savings products. Resulting strong cash flow will lead to increased net investment income, although relatively lower investment yields will temper growth. Improved health profits are predicated on a continuation of favorable morbidity experience. P-C profits have improved amid tighter underwriting standards and better auto claims experience, but further improvement will depend on better pricing. Capital Management (formerly Accumulation and Investment Group) results will benefit from greater demand for annuities, and from a pick-up in sales of guaranteed investment contracts (GICs), but margins on spread-based products will remain under pressure until the effect of relatively lower short and intermediate interest rates makes its way through the portfolio.

Valuation - 24-AUG-95

After a lackluster performance during much of 1994 amid the negative effects of higher interest rates, these interest-sensitive shares have rebounded somewhat during 1995. Although margins in some spread-based businesses may come under pressure, near term, until these liabilities reprice under a relatively lower interest rate environment, PVN is well positioned long term. Trading at only 9 times our 1995 operating earnings estimate of $4.00 a share (which excludes realized investment gains or losses), the shares are still modestly valued.

Key Stock Statistics

S&P EPS Est. 1995	4.00	Tang. Bk. Value/Share	22.11
P/E on S&P Est. 1995	9.0	Beta	1.67
S&P EPS Est. 1996	4.40	Shareholders	19,000
Dividend Rate/Share	0.90	Market cap. (B)	$ 3.5
Shs. outstg. (M)	95.3	Inst. holdings	73%
Avg. daily vol. (M)	0.165	Insider holdings	NA

Value of $10,000 invested 5 years ago: $ 15,784

Fiscal Year Ending Dec. 31

	1995	% Change	1994	% Change	1993	% Change
Revenues (Million $)						
1Q	797.5	14%	698.3	-3%	717.0	—
2Q	856.4	15%	745.3	2%	732.9	—
3Q	—	—	762.3	8%	706.7	—
4Q	—	—	753.2	4%	727.7	1%
Yr.	—	—	2,959	3%	2,884	1%
Income (Million $)						
1Q	71.13	11%	64.01	-3%	65.84	NM
2Q	84.16	3%	81.70	-11%	91.53	18%
3Q	—	—	86.11	17%	73.76	-17%
4Q	—	—	69.08	-25%	91.54	1%
Yr.	—	—	300.9	-7%	322.7	NM
Earnings Per Share ($)						
1Q	0.72	16%	0.62	-3%	0.64	NM
2Q	0.88	7%	0.82	-8%	0.89	17%
3Q	—	—	0.87	23%	0.71	-18%
4Q	—	—	0.70	-21%	0.89	1%
Yr.	E4.00	32%	3.02	-3%	3.12	NM

Next earnings report expected: early November

Providian Corp.

24-AUG-95

Business Summary - 23-AUG-95

Providian Corp. (formerly Capital Holding Corp.) ranks among the largest U.S. stock life insurance companies, providing life, annuity, accident and health, and property-casualty insurance through several affiliated companies. It also owns First Deposit Corp., which owns a consumer bank engaged principally in issuing credit cards.

Contributions to pretax earnings (in million $) in recent years:

	1994	1993	1992
Agency group	$183.1	$189.6	$185.7
Direct response	116.4	110.5	90.2
Capital Management	136.6	134.1	120.1
Banking	150.0	117.7	93.5

The Agency Group markets individual life and health products principally through home service agents. Providian Direct Response markets life and health products using television, print media and direct mail, and also markets personal lines property-casualty insurance.

The Capital Management Group markets spread and fee-based investment products (including guaranteed investment contracts and an array of annuities) to individuals and institutions. This group also manages PVN's invested assets. The Banking Group offers consumer loans, issues credit cards, and other banking services.

Important Developments

Jul. '95—PVN's year-to-year pretax segment profit comparisons for the first half of 1995 were mixed. Agency group pretax profits were off 2.1% due to adverse mortality experience in the life insurance area and to increased health claims activity; cost cuts and higher investment income helped stem the decline in this segment's earnings. Direct Response profits rose 11% amid tighter underwriting standards, contributions from new products, and cost cuts. Banking profits were up 26% on continued growth in receivables and wider margins. Capital Management pretax earnings slumped 15% as margins continued to come under pressure from higher interest rates. Share earnings were aided by a buyback program. During 1994, PVN reacquired over 4.3 million of its common shares. Though July, 1995, another 2.67 million shares were reacquired.

Capitalization

Long Term Debt: $754,296,000 (6/95).
Subsidiary Preferred Stock: $100,000,000.

Per Share Data ($)

(Year Ended Dec. 31)

	1994	1993	1992	1991	1990	1989
Tangible Bk. Val.	19.48	21.32	18.23	15.40	13.50	12.64
Oper. Earnings	3.75	3.32	3.18	2.89	2.58	2.23
Earnings	3.02	3.12	3.14	2.67	1.70	2.93
Dividends	0.80	0.73	0.66	0.60	0.54	0.50
Relative Payout	26%	23%	21%	23%	32%	17%
Prices - High	38⅛	44⅞	36¾	31⅞	27⅛	26⅛
- Low	28⅝	34½	26	17¼	13⅛	15⅝
P/E Ratio - High	13	14	12	12	16	9
- Low	9	11	8	6	8	5

Income Statement Analysis (Million $)

	1994	%Chg	1993	%Chg	1992	%Chg	1991
Life Ins. In Force	66,074	NM	65,987	13%	58,262	5%	55,642
Prem.Inc Life A&H	965	-7%	1,038	-2%	1,055	15%	918
Prem.Inc Cas/Prop	176	22%	144	3%	140	-2%	143
Net Invest. Inc.	1,612	10%	1,461	NM	1,454	-2%	1,480
Oth. Revs.	206	-19%	255	25%	204	57%	130
Total Revs.	2,959	3%	2,884	1%	2,853	7%	2,671
Pretax Inc.	440	-10%	487	8%	452	31%	346
Net Oper. Inc.	377	10%	342	5%	326	21%	270
Net Inc.	301	-7%	323	NM	322	29%	250

Balance Sheet & Other Fin. Data (Million $)

	1994	1993	1992	1991	1990	1989
Cash & Equiv.	881	702	1,068	841	891	1,021
Premiums Due	Nil	Nil	Nil	Nil	Nil	Nil
Inv. Assets Bonds	9,744	10,472	9,008	8,213	7,360	6,641
Inv. Assets Stock	557	427	450	535	503	555
Inv. Assets Loans	7,860	6,415	6,338	6,233	5,362	4,608
Inv. Assets Total	18,696	17,775	16,074	15,160	13,338	11,850
Deferred Policy Cost	1,491	1,373	1,312	1,225	1,154	1,041
Total Assets	23,613	22,929	20,588	18,873	16,669	14,970
Debt	694	589	589	611	386	330
Common Eqty.	2,122	2,393	1,948	1,655	1,403	1,366

Ratio Analysis

	1994	1993	1992	1991	1990	1989
Comb. Loss-Exp.Ratio	104.9	106.9	108.4	112.2	117.7	110.5
% Ret. on Revs.	10.2	11.2	11.3	9.4	6.4	11.0
% Ret. on Equity	13.3	14.6	17.5	15.8	11.3	21.0
% Invest. Yield	8.8	8.6	9.3	10.3	11.1	11.6

Dividend Data —Dividends have been paid since 1941. A dividend reinvestment plan is available. A "poison pill" stock purchase right was adopted in 1987.

Amt. of Div. $	Date Decl.	Ex-Div. Date	Stock of Record	Payment Date
0.200	Aug. 10	Aug. 26	Sep. 01	Sep. 15 '94
0.200	Nov. 08	Nov. 25	Dec. 01	Dec. 15 '94
0.225	Dec. 07	Feb. 23	Mar. 01	Mar. 15 '95
0.225	May. 05	May. 25	Jun. 01	Jun. 15 '95
0.225	Aug. 09	Aug. 30	Sep. 01	Sep. 15 '95

Data as orig. reptd.; bef. results of disc. opers. and/or spec. items. Per share data adj. for stk. divs. as of ex-div. date. E-Estimate. NA-Not Available. NM-Not Meaningful. NR-Not Ranked.

Office—400 West Market St., Louisville, KY 40202. **Tel**—(502) 560-2000. **Chrmn & CEO**— I. W. Bailey II. **Pres & COO**—S. J. Mehta. **SVP-Fin & CFO**—R. L. Walker. **Secy**—R. M. Slaven. **Investor Contact**—Jeffrey L. Rosen. **Dirs**—I. W. Bailey II, J. L. Clendenin, J. M. Cranor III, J. F. Decosimo, L. Everingham, R. V. Gilmartin, J. D. Grissom, W. Hill Jr., F. W. McFarlan, S. J. Mehta, M. R. Seger, L. D. Thompson. **Transfer Agent & Registrar**—First Chicago Trust Co. of New York, NYC. **Incorporated** in Delaware in 1969; Commonwealth Life Insurance incorporated in 1904. **Empl**-8,985. **S&P Analyst:** Catherine A. Seifert

STANDARD & POOR'S

Public Service Enterprise Group

STOCK REPORTS

NYSE Symbol **PEG**
In S&P 500

17-OCT-95

Industry:
Util.-Diversified

Summary: This holding company owns Public Service Electric and Gas (PSE&G), whose service area encompasses 70% of New Jersey, and invests in energy-related businesses.

S&P Opinion: Avoid (★★)		
Recent Price • 29¼	Yield • 7.4%	
52 Wk Range • 30¼-25	12-Mo. P/E • 11.2	

Quantitative Evaluations

Outlook
(1 Lowest—5 Highest)
• **1⁻**

Fair Value
• **25½**

Risk
• **Low**

Earn./Div. Rank
• **B+**

Technical Eval.
• **Bearish** since 9/95

Rel. Strength Rank
(1 Lowest—99 Highest)
• **66**

Insider Activity
• **Neutral**

Earnings vs. Previous Year
▲=Up ▼=Down ▶=No Change

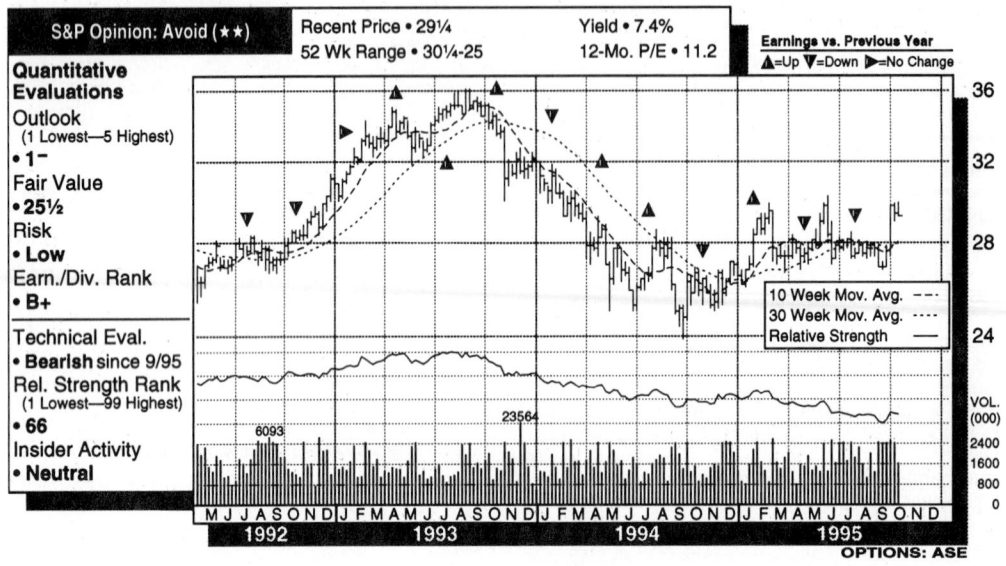

10 Week Mov. Avg. - - -
30 Week Mov. Avg. ·····
Relative Strength —

VOL.
(000)

OPTIONS: ASE

Overview - 13-OCT-95

Under pressure from its customers, PEG has lowered rates for three municipal electric companies and for its second largest utility, and is taking steps to lower its cost structure as well. Measures taken in recent years include exiting the real estate business, refinancing debt and preferred stock, increasing the use of lower-cost purchased power, reducing employee levels, and upgrading older facilities. Weather-related weakness in 1995 first half sales and revenues, and a rise in operating and maintenance expenses due to refueling outages at the Salem nuclear plants as well as downtime from a one-week stoppage at the Hope Creek nuclear plant in the third quarter are expected to hurt comparisons for the year. Future prospects may also be hurt by poor capacity utilization at its nuclear plants.

Valuation - 13-OCT-95

Given continued pressure on pricing in PEG's gas and electric utility markets, we expect earnings to fall in 1995, albeit modestly. Longer term, a lower cost structure and improved contributions from non-regulated businesses could allow a more positive trend in profitability. In the absence of major capital programs, we also anticipate steady cash flow to support continuation of PEG's above-average dividend yield. Still, given the poor plant utilization we expect in the next two years, the stock is not likely to be a good market performer in the next six to twelve months.

Key Stock Statistics

S&P EPS Est. 1995	2.70	Tang. Bk. Value/Share	20.93
P/E on S&P Est. 1995	10.8	Beta	0.57
S&P EPS Est. 1996	2.85	Shareholders	185,900
Dividend Rate/Share	2.16	Market cap. (B)	$ 7.1
Shs. outstg. (M)	244.7	Inst. holdings	35%
Avg. daily vol. (M)	0.503	Insider holdings	NA

Value of $10,000 invested 5 years ago: $ 15,090

Fiscal Year Ending Dec. 31

	1995	% Change	1994	% Change	1993	% Change
Revenues (Million $)						
1Q	1,674	-7%	1,794	13%	1,595	5%
2Q	1,329	4%	1,278	3%	1,246	5%
3Q	—	—	1,375	-2%	1,402	12%
4Q	—	—	1,468	NM	1,462	4%
Yr.	—	—	5,916	4%	5,706	7%
Income (Million $)						
1Q	212.6	-8%	230.1	10%	210.0	13%
2Q	110.7	-15%	129.9	8%	119.8	37%
3Q	—	—	187.2	-3%	192.2	39%
4Q	—	—	131.8	79%	73.50	-20%
Yr.	—	—	679.0	14%	595.5	18%
Earnings Per Share ($)						
1Q	0.87	-7%	0.94	6%	0.89	10%
2Q	0.45	-15%	0.53	8%	0.49	29%
3Q	E0.78	3%	0.76	-4%	0.79	34%
4Q	E0.60	11%	0.54	80%	0.30	-23%
Yr.	E2.70	-3%	2.78	12%	2.48	14%

Next earnings report expected: mid October

Public Service Enterprise Group

Business Summary - 13-OCT-95

Public Service Enterprise Group has two wholly owned subsidiaries: Public Service Electric and Gas Co. (PSE&G), which supplies electric and gas service to the most populous area in New Jersey and accounted for 91% of 1994 net income; and Enterprise Diversified Holdings Inc. (EDHI), whose nonutility businesses include oil and gas exploration and production and other unregulated energy investments.

Electric operations in 1994 accounted for 68% of total PSE&G revenues, and gas operations 32%. Contributions to electric utility revenues in recent years were:

	1994	1993	1992	1990
Residential	32%	33%	31%	32%
Commercial	47%	46%	47%	45%
Industrial	19%	20%	21%	19%
Other	1%	1%	1%	1%

Nuclear fuel comprised 45% of power generation in 1994, coal 19%, gas 7%, oil 2%, and purchased or interchanged power 27%. Peak demand in 1994 was 9,001 mw, and installed capacity at peak was 10,597 mw, for a reserve margin of 15%. PSE&G sold or transported 3.75 billion gas therms, versus 3.67 billion in 1993.

In February 1987, PSE&G's 95%-owned 1,067 mw Hope Creek nuclear plant began operating commercially, completing PSE&G's baseload construction for some 20 years. In 1994, utility plant additions, largely for improvements to existing power plants, transmission, and distribution and gas system facilities totaled $887 million, little changed from 1993's $890 million. Management expects to finance 1995 through 1999 construction outlays of $3.2 billion internally. The company's future generation strategy focuses on load management, conservation and upgrading older generating stations, with power purchases representing a lesser portion of capability.

Important Developments

Jul. '95—Revenues for the six months ended June 30, 1995 were down 2.3% from the year earlier period, due to the comparatively mild winter and and cool spring, and to lower gas prices and volumes, particularly in the residential sector. These declines were partly offset by lower maintenance expenses. With lower contributions from its non-utility businesses and a 19% increase in preferred dividend requirements, net income was off 10%.

Capitalization

Long Term Debt: $5,288,817,000 (6/95).
Subsid. Cum. Preferred Stock: $684,994,000.

Per Share Data ($)

(Year Ended Dec. 31)

	1994	1993	1992	1991	1990	1989
Tangible Bk. Val.	20.93	20.37	19.93	20.68	20.08	19.46
Earnings	2.78	2.48	2.17	2.43	2.56	2.62
Dividends	2.16	2.16	2.16	2.13	2.09	2.05
Payout Ratio	78%	83%	100%	88%	82%	78%
Prices - High	32	36⅛	31⅜	29⅜	29¾	29⅜
- Low	23⅞	30	25⅜	25¼	22½	23
P/E Ratio - High	12	14	14	12	12	11
- Low	9	12	12	10	9	9

Income Statement Analysis (Million $)

	1994	%Chg	1993	%Chg	1992	%Chg	1991
Revs.	5,916	4%	5,706	7%	5,357	5%	5,093
Depr.	630	5%	600	-7%	643	5%	613
Maint.	308	1%	304	-1%	308	-2%	315
Fxd. Chgs. Cov.	3.0	8%	2.8	17%	2.3	-13%	2.7
Constr. Credits	46.6	41%	33.1	7%	30.8	-32%	45.0
Eff. Tax Rate	31%	—	33%	—	32%	—	32%
Net Inc.	679	14%	596	18%	504	-7%	544

Balance Sheet & Other Fin. Data (Million $)

	1994	1993	1992	1991	1990	1989
Gross Prop.	16,245	15,577	14,858	14,219	13,837	12,960
Cap. Exp.	999	951	830	813	968	674
Net Prop.	11,098	10,804	10,471	10,183	9,874	9,337
Capitalization:						
LT Debt	5,234	5,209	5,031	5,182	4,722	4,348
% LT Debt	47	48	49	50	49	49
Pfd.	685	580	505	430	430	430
% Pfd.	6.10	5.30	4.90	4.10	4.50	4.80
Common	5,311	5,134	4,782	4,763	4,465	4,191
% Common	48	47	46	46	46	47
Total Cap.	14,548	14,158	12,473	12,549	11,654	10,904

Ratio Analysis

	1994	1993	1992	1991	1990	1989
Oper. Ratio	80.0	81.0	82.0	80.4	79.7	80.4
% Earn. on Net Prop.	10.6	10.4	9.4	10.0	10.1	10.2
% Ret. on Revs.	11.5	10.4	9.4	10.7	11.3	11.3
% Ret. On Invest.Cap	8.2	8.4	8.4	8.4	8.8	9.2
% Return On Com.Eqty	13.0	12.0	10.8	11.7	12.7	13.4

Dividend Data

Dividends have been paid since 1907. A dividend reinvestment plan is available.

Amt. of Div. $	Date Decl.	Ex-Div. Date	Stock of Record	Payment Date
0.540	Nov. 15	Dec. 01	Dec. 07	Dec. 31 '94
0.540	Feb. 21	Mar. 01	Mar. 07	Mar. 31 '95
0.540	May. 16	Jun. 01	Jun. 07	Jun. 30 '95
0.540	Jul. 19	Sep. 06	Sep. 08	Sep. 29 '95

Data as orig. reptd.; bef. results of disc opers. and/or spec. items. Per share data adj. for stk. divs. as of ex-div. date.
E-Estimated. NA-Not Available. NM-Not Meaningful. NR-Not Ranked.

Office—80 Park Plaza (P. O. Box 1171), Newark, NJ 07101-1171. **Tel**—(201) 430-7000. **Chrmn & Pres**—E. J. Ferland. **VP-CFO**—R. C. Murray. **Secy**—R. S. Smith. **Investor Contact**—Brian Smith. **Dirs**—L. R. Codey, E. H. Drew, T. J. D. Dunphy, R. R. Ferguson Jr., E. J. Ferland, R. V. Gilmartin, S. A. Jackson, I. Lerner, W. E. Marfuggi, M. M. Pfaltz, J. C. Pitney, R. J. Swift, J. S. Weston. **Transfer Agents**—Company's office; First Chicago Trust Co. of New York, NYC. **Registrars**—First Fidelity Bank, Newark; First Chicago Trust Co. of New York, NYC. **Incorporated** in New Jersey in 1924. **Empl**-11,919. **S&P Analyst:** Jane Collin

Pulte Corp.

NYSE Symbol **PHM**
In S&P 500

03-AUG-95

Industry:
Building

Summary: Through its Pulte Home unit, PHM builds moderately priced, single-family homes and condominiums, with operations in 24 states. It also has mortgage banking and finance units.

S&P Opinion: Accumulate (★★★★)	Recent Price • 26¾	Yield • 0.9%
	52 Wk Range • 30½-18⅛	12-Mo. P/E • 9.8

Earnings vs. Previous Year
▲=Up ▼=Down ▶=No Change

Quantitative Evaluations

Outlook
(1 Lowest—5 Highest)
• **4-**

Fair Value
• **28⅛**

Risk
• **Average**

Earn./Div. Rank
• **A-**

Technical Eval.
• **Bearish** since 7/95

Rel. Strength Rank
(1 Lowest—99 Highest)
• **32**

Insider Activity
• **NA**

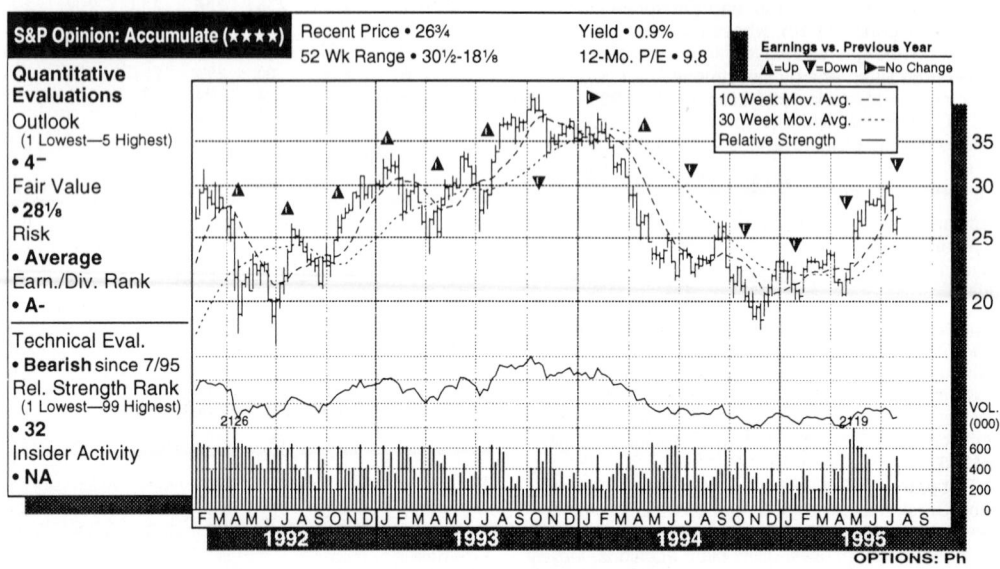

10 Week Mov. Avg. – – –
30 Week Mov. Avg. ·····
Relative Strength —

Overview - 03-AUG-95

Revenues should be moderately higher in 1995, as the mid-1995 drop in long-term interest rates has been stimulating a revival of homebuilding and mortgage banking operations, following early year sluggishness. The housing segment should also be assisted by continued geographic expansion and further investments in existing markets. The only division likely to report lower revenues is the financing segment, which is involved in a self-liquidation. Margins are likely to narrow on competitive homebuilding conditions, early year weakness in mortgage banking and the reduced activity in financing. However, the recent improvement in homebuilding and mortgage banking market conditions probably signals a bottoming of margins. PHM will also be assisted by some $10 million of pretax gains recorded in the first half of the year on the sale of ICM's remaining core mortgage servicing portfolio.

Valuation - 03-AUG-95

After following a steep downward path since late 1993, Pulte's shares have enjoyed a nice bounce since long-term interest rates started to decline in the spring of 1995. Although a moderating economy and weak employment picture could persuade potential home buyers to delay their purchases, we believe that industry conditions will continue to strengthen under the influence of lower interest rates. Given our forecast of improved earnings trends for Pulte, the shares should have room for further appreciation.

Key Stock Statistics

S&P EPS Est. 1995	1.80	Tang. Bk. Value/Share	26.26
P/E on S&P Est. 1995	14.9	Beta	1.90
S&P EPS Est. 1996	2.20	Shareholders	900
Dividend Rate/Share	0.24	Market cap. (B)	$0.732
Shs. outstg. (M)	27.0	Inst. holdings	59%
Avg. daily vol. (M)	0.085	Insider holdings	NA

Value of $10,000 invested 5 years ago: $ 25,294

Fiscal Year Ending Dec. 31

	1995	% Change	1994	% Change	1993	% Change
Revenues (Million $)						
1Q	332.9	-2%	340.6	8%	316.0	23%
2Q	485.5	13%	427.9	6%	405.0	28%
3Q	—	—	452.6	5%	431.7	21%
4Q	—	—	534.8	11%	480.5	9%
Yr.	—	—	1,756	8%	1,633	19%
Income (Million $)						
1Q	-0.43	NM	11.33	4%	10.87	14%
2Q	9.49	-40%	15.88	-30%	22.55	41%
3Q	—	—	17.93	-9%	19.74	-14%
4Q	—	—	17.24	-30%	24.61	3%
Yr.	—	—	62.37	-20%	77.77	8%
Earnings Per Share ($)						
1Q	-0.01	NM	0.40	3%	0.39	5%
2Q	0.34	-40%	0.57	-30%	0.81	37%
3Q	E0.65	—	0.65	-8%	0.71	-14%
4Q	E0.82	—	0.62	-29%	0.87	NM
Yr.	E1.80	—	2.24	-19%	2.78	5%

Next earnings report expected: late October

Pulte Corp.

Business Summary - 01-AUG-95

Pulte Corp. (formerly PHM Corp.) is a holding company for Pulte Home, a major homebuilder operating in 38 markets in 24 states. It also has mortgage banking and financing subsidiaries. Thrift operations were discontinued in 1994. Housing units sold (settlements) by region in recent years:

	1994	1993	1992	1991
North	2,003	1,863	1,651	1,082
South	2,734	2,050	1,632	1,512
Central	3,577	3,432	2,827	2,731
West	2,828	2,453	1,918	1,361

Pulte builds a wide variety of homes, including detached units, townhouses, condominiums and duplexes. Single-family detached homes represented 75% of total unit sales in 1994. At December 31, 1994, PHM was offering homes for sale in 357 subdivisions at prices ranging from $50,000 to over $600,000 (in 374 communities at June 30, 1995). In 224 of these subdivisions (63% of the total), prices ranged from $75,000 to $175,000. Backlog at the end of 1994 was $387 million, representing 2,287 units, down from $420 million, or 2,868 units, a year earlier; backlog increased to a company record $683 million (4,198 units) at June 30, 1995. Construction work on PHM's homes is generally performed by subcontractors under supervision of the company's on-site construction superintendents.

At 1994 year-end, Pulte owned about 20,000 lots in subdivisions in which homes were being constructed, and also had about 11,900 lots under option.

ICM Mortgage Corp. is a full service mortgage banker which arranges financing through the origination of mortgage loans to buyers of Pulte's homes and to the general public, and engages in the sale of such loans to outside investors. ICM had historically retained servicing rights to mortgage loans it originated, but implemented a new strategy in 1994 aimed at selling a substantial portion of its core portfolio (program completed in 1995's second quarter). ICM originated mortgage loans for 49% of the homes sold by PHM in 1994, which represented 41% of total ICM originations.

Important Developments

Jul. '95—Pulte recorded a 46% year over year increase in net new orders in the second quarter of 1995, to a company record $566 million (3,692 units).
Jul. '95—The company delivered a letter to UDC Homes, which indicated Pulte's interest in submitting a takeover proposal for UDC in opposition to UDC's mid-1995 agreement to be acquired by DMB Property Ventures L.P., a Phoenix real-estate investment and development company. UDC filed Chapter 11 bankruptcy proceedings in May 1995.

Capitalization

Long Term Debt: $551,981,000 (3/95).

Per Share Data ($)

(Year Ended Dec. 31)

	1994	1993	1992	1991	1990	1989
Tangible Bk. Val.	25.88	20.20	17.55	14.42	13.43	12.08
Cash Flow	NM	NM	NM	NM	NM	NM
Earnings	2.24	2.78	2.66	1.71	1.18	2.10
Dividends	0.24	0.24	0.24	0.12	0.12	0.12
Payout Ratio	11%	9%	9%	7%	10%	5%
Prices - High	38⅝	41⅜	31¾	25⅛	12½	18⅞
- Low	18⅛	23½	17¼	9¼	6	9½
P/E Ratio - High	17	15	12	15	11	9
- Low	8	8	6	5	5	5

Income Statement Analysis (Million $)

	1994	%Chg	1993	%Chg	1992	%Chg	1991
Revs.	1,756	8%	1,633	19%	1,370	13%	1,214
Oper. Inc.	NA	—	NA	—	NA	—	NA
Depr.	NA	—	NA	—	NA	—	NA
Int. Exp.	NA	—	NA	—	NA	—	NA
Pretax Inc.	104	-8%	113	45%	77.9	73%	44.9
Eff. Tax Rate	40%	—	31%	—	7.30%	—	5.20%
Net Inc.	62.4	-20%	77.8	8%	72.2	69%	42.6

Balance Sheet & Other Fin. Data (Million $)

	1994	1993	1992	1991	1990	1989
Cash	160	109	67.0	126	213	249
Curr. Assets	NA	NA	NA	NA	NA	NA
Total Assets	1,941	3,811	3,706	3,635	3,993	4,325
Curr. Liab.	NA	NA	NA	NA	NA	NA
LT Debt	563	876	1,202	1,751	2,220	2,536
Common Eqty.	711	556	481	357	316	306
Total Cap.	1,274	1,432	1,684	2,136	2,562	2,866
Cap. Exp.	NA	NA	NA	NA	6.5	8.9
Cash Flow	NM	NM	NM	NM	NM	NM

Ratio Analysis

	1994	1993	1992	1991	1990	1989
Curr. Ratio	NA	NA	NA	NA	NA	NA
% LT Debt of Cap.	44.2	61.2	71.4	82.0	86.7	88.5
% Net Inc.of Revs.	3.6	4.8	5.3	3.5	2.6	4.9
% Ret. on Assets	2.2	2.1	1.9	1.1	0.7	1.3
% Ret. on Equity	9.9	15.0	16.5	12.4	9.9	20.5

Dividend Data (Dividends have been paid since 1977.)

Amt. of Div. $	Date Decl.	Ex-Div. Date	Stock of Record	Payment Date
0.060	Jul. 15	Sep. 12	Sep. 16	Oct. 01 '94
0.060	Sep. 19	Dec. 12	Dec. 16	Jan. 03 '95
0.060	Mar. 06	Mar. 13	Mar. 17	Apr. 01 '95
0.060	May 12	Jun. 14	Jun. 16	Jul. 03 '95
0.060	Jul. 13	Sep. 13	Sep. 15	Oct. 02 '95

Data as orig. reptd.; bef. results of disc. opers. and/or spec. items. Per share data adj. for stk. divs. as of ex-div. date. E-Estimated. NA-Not Available. NM-Not Meaningful. NR-Not Ranked.

Office—33 Bloomfield Hills Pkwy., Suite 200, Bloomfield Hills, MI 48304. **Tel**—(313) 647-2750. **Chrmn**—W. J. Pulte. **Pres & CEO**—R. K. Burgess. **EVP & CFO**—M. D. Hollerbach. **Treas**—J. A. Weissenborn. **Investor Contact**—Harmon D. Smith. **Dirs**—H. P. Berkowitz, R. K. Burgess, J. Grosfeld, M. D. Hollerbach, W. J. Pulte, A. E. Schwartz, F. J. Sehn, G. A. Wiegers. **Transfer Agent & Registrar**—State St. Bank & Trust, Boston. **Incorporated** in Delaware in 1969; reincorporated in Michigan in 1985. **Empl**-3,400. **S&P Analyst:** Michael W. Jaffe

Quaker Oats

NYSE Symbol **OAT**
In S&P 500

08-AUG-95 **Industry:** Food

Summary: Quaker Oats is an international producer of brandname packaged food and beverage products.

S&P Opinion: Hold (★★★)	

Recent Price • 34¼   Yield • 3.3%
52 Wk Range • 42½–29¾   12-Mo. P/E • 5.7

Earnings vs. Previous Year
▲=Up ▼=Down ▶=No Change

Quantitative Evaluations

Outlook
(1 Lowest—5 Highest)
• **1⁻**

Fair Value
• **27⅞**

Risk
• **Average**

Earn./Div. Rank
• **A-**

Technical Eval.
• **Bullish** since 7/95

Rel. Strength Rank
(1 Lowest—99 Highest)
• **39**

Insider Activity
• **Neutral**

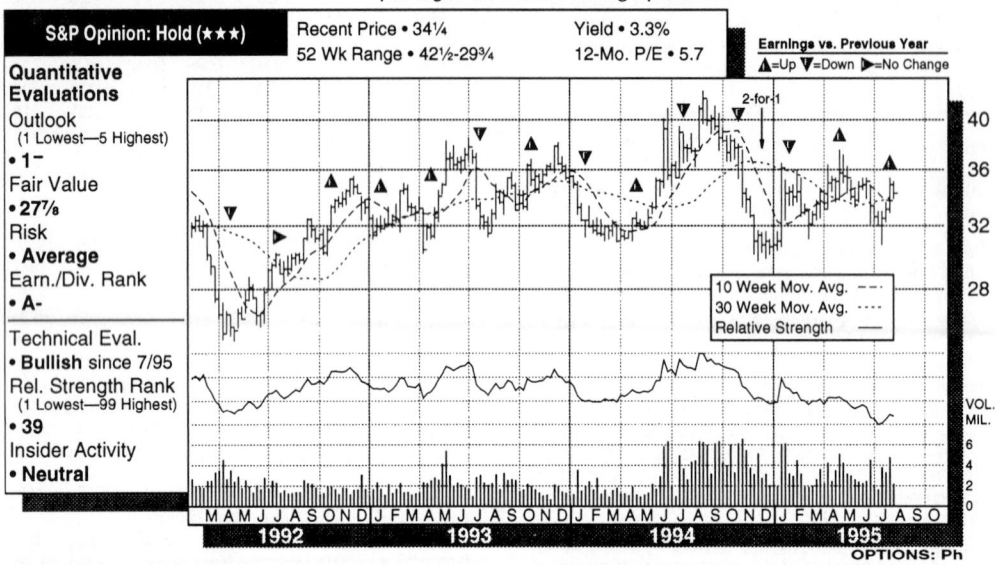

10 Week Mov. Avg. – – –
30 Week Mov. Avg. ·······
Relative Strength ——

2-for-1

VOL.
MIL.

1992   1993   1994   1995

OPTIONS: Ph

Overview - 08-AUG-95

The company is in the process of transitioning from a June fiscal year to a calendar year basis beginning on January 1, 1996. On a calendar 1995 and 1996 basis, and excluding extraordinary items, we project sales to rise at a mid single-digit annual pace, led primarily by broad-based unit volume growth and price increases. Earnings will likely be further pressured by a high level of marketing spending for new and existing products (principally cereals and beverages) and for international expansion; and substantially greater interest expense and amortization of goodwill resulting from the late 1994 acquisition of Snapple. Excluding special items, EPS are estimated at $1.10 for 1995 and $1.60 for 1996 (both calendar years).

Valuation - 08-AUG-95

Given our expectations of continued pressures on earnings per share through calendar 1996, we view this equity as neutral. Quaker's management has over the past year aggressively repositioned the company for increased profitability and earnings growth potential, but in doing so is penalizing current earnings due to: the absorption of operating losses and financing costs associated with the Snapple acquisition; foregone earnings from profitable food businesses that were sold to fund the Snapple deal; and a substantially greater amount of acquisition-related depreciation and amortization expenses. Although longer-term growth prospects may be enhanced by the business portfolio shakeup, we advise taking a wait-and-see approach to this equity due to its rich valuation (on a P/E basis).

Key Stock Statistics

S&P EPS Est. 1996	1.70	Tang. Bk. Value/Share	2.21
P/E on S&P Est. 1996	20.1	Beta	0.67
S&P EPS Est. 1997	1.45	Shareholders	33,600
Dividend Rate/Share	1.14	Market cap. (B)	$ 4.6
Shs. outstg. (M)	134.1	Inst. holdings	44%
Avg. daily vol. (M)	0.678	Insider holdings	NA

Value of $10,000 invested 5 years ago: $ 13,939

Fiscal Year Ending Jun. 30

	1995	% Change	1994	% Change	1993	% Change
Revenues (Million $)						
1Q	1,636	7%	1,534	3%	1,494	10%
2Q	1,508	11%	1,354	2%	1,333	NM
3Q	1,634	13%	1,449	7%	1,358	2%
4Q	1,587	-2%	1,618	5%	1,546	NM
Yr.	6,365	7%	5,955	4%	5,731	3%
Income (Million $)						
1Q	61.40	-33%	91.40	46%	62.50	47%
2Q	34.40	-20%	42.80	-27%	58.50	31%
3Q	366.1	NM	73.80	-7%	79.20	40%
4Q	344.2	NM	23.50	-75%	93.40	27%
Yr.	806.1	NM	231.5	-19%	286.8	16%
Earnings Per Share ($)						
1Q	0.45	-31%	0.65	62%	0.40	50%
2Q	0.25	-21%	0.32	-18%	0.39	33%
3Q	2.73	NM	0.54	3%	0.52	40%
4Q	2.57	NM	0.17	-74%	0.65	-6%
Yr.	6.00	NM	1.68	-15%	1.96	21%

Next earnings report expected: late October

Quaker Oats

Business Summary - 07-AUG-95

Quaker Oats is a major international producer and marketer of brandname packaged foods and beverages. Contributions by region in fiscal 1994 were:

	Sales	Profits
U.S.	68%	81%
Canada	4%	2%
Europe	19%	3%
Latin America/Pacific	9%	14%

Products include breakfast foods such as hot cereals (Quick and Old Fashioned Quaker Oats), ready-to-eat cereals (Cap'n Crunch, Life, 100% Natural, Oat Squares, Toasted Oatmeal), and waffles and syrups (Aunt Jemima); snacks (Quaker Chewy Granola and Quaker Rice Cakes); frozen pizza (Celeste), rice and pasta foods (Rice-A-Roni, Noodle Roni); and beverage products such as iced teas and fruit drinks (Snapple), and isotonic sports drinks (Gatorade).

Since December 1994, OAT acquired the Snapple Beverage Corp. (annual sales of $516 million), a producer of iced teas and fruit drinks, for $1.7 billion; and sold its European pet foods business ($760 million) for $700 million, its U.S. and Canadian pet food businesses ($540 million) for $725 million; its Mexican chocolate business ($100 million); and its canned bean and chili businesses ($180 million). Terms of these two sales were not disclosed.

Important Developments

Aug. '95—Excluding gains on divestitures, restructuring charges, and the cumulative effect of an accounting charge, OAT reported earnings per share of $1.15 for the fiscal year ended June 30, 1995, down from $2.16 in the prior year. Pretax gains generated from business divestments during fiscal 1995 totaled $1.17 billion ($5.20 per share), and included worldwide pet food, Van Camp's/Wolf Brand, Mexican chocolate and Dutch honey businesses. Fiscal 1995 pretax restructuring charges totaled $105.5 million ($0.48). Separately, management cited numerous factors for the shortfall in comparable earnings in fiscal 1995, including higher U.S. advertising and merchandising spending; volume shortfalls in hot cereals; and higher raw materials and manufacturing costs.

May '95—OAT said it would change its fiscal year end from June 30 to December 31, effective with the calendar year beginning January 1, 1996.

Capitalization

Long Term Debt: $1,107,300,000 (3/95).
ESOP $5.46 Cum. Conv. Preferred Stock: $100,000,000. Conv. into 1,282,051 com. shs.

Per Share Data ($)

(Year Ended Jun. 30)

	1995	1994	1993	1992	1991	1990
Tangible Bk. Val.	NA	-0.36	0.86	2.21	2.36	2.99
Cash Flow	NA	2.95	3.05	2.67	2.52	2.30
Earnings	6.00	1.68	1.96	1.63	1.52	1.46
Dividends	1.95	1.06	0.96	0.86	0.78	0.70
Payout Ratio	33%	63%	49%	52%	51%	47%
Prices - High	37½	42½	38½	37¼	37⅞	29¾
- Low	30⅜	29⅝	30¼	25⅛	23⅞	20½
P/E Ratio - High	6	25	20	23	25	20
- Low	5	18	15	15	16	14

Income Statement Analysis (Million $)

	1994	%Chg	1993	%Chg	1992	%Chg	1991
Revs.	5,955	4%	5,731	3%	5,576	2%	5,491
Oper. Inc.	774	7%	724	3%	702	7%	659
Depr.	171	9%	157	NM	156	3%	151
Int. Exp.	100	52%	66.0	-16%	79.0	-19%	97.0
Pretax Inc.	379	-19%	468	11%	422	2%	412
Eff. Tax Rate	39%	—	39%	—	41%	—	43%
Net Inc.	232	-19%	287	16%	248	5%	236

Balance Sheet & Other Fin. Data (Million $)

	1994	1993	1992	1991	1990	1989
Cash	140	61.0	95.0	30.0	18.0	24.0
Curr. Assets	1,254	1,068	1,256	1,258	1,481	1,598
Total Assets	3,043	2,816	3,040	3,016	3,326	3,222
Curr. Liab.	1,259	1,105	1,055	927	1,139	902
LT Debt	760	633	689	701	740	767
Common Eqty.	446	551	752	807	919	1,037
Total Cap.	1,303	1,285	1,888	1,974	2,087	2,230
Cap. Exp.	185	187	176	241	276	298
Cash Flow	399	440	400	383	353	338

Ratio Analysis

	1994	1993	1992	1991	1990	1989
Curr. Ratio	1.0	1.0	1.2	1.4	1.3	1.8
% LT Debt of Cap.	58.3	49.2	36.5	35.5	35.5	34.4
% Net Inc.of Revs.	3.9	5.0	4.4	4.3	4.6	3.5
% Ret. on Assets	8.0	10.1	8.3	7.4	7.1	6.6
% Ret. on Equity	46.6	41.9	31.9	26.7	23.4	17.8

Dividend Data (Dividends have been paid since 1906. A dividend reinvestment plan is available. A poison pill stock purchase rights plan was adopted in 1986.)

Amt. of Div. $	Date Decl.	Ex-Div. Date	Stock of Record	Payment Date
0.570	Sep. 14	Sep. 15	Sep. 21	Oct. 14 '94
2-for-1	Sep. 14	Dec. 06	Nov. 09	Dec. 05 '94
0.285	Nov. 09	Dec. 12	Dec. 16	Jan. 13 '95
0.285	Mar. 08	Mar. 13	Mar. 17	Apr. 17 '95
0.285	May. 10	Jun. 14	Jun. 16	Jul. 17 '95

Data as orig. reptd.; bef. results of disc. opers. and/or spec. items. Per share data adj. for stk. divs. as of ex-div. date. E-Estimated. NA-Not Available. NM-Not Meaningful. NR-Not Ranked.

Office—Quaker Tower, 321 North Clark St., Chicago, IL 60610. **Tel**—(312) 222-7111. **Chrmn & CEO**—W. D. Smithburg. **Pres & COO**—P. A. Marineau. **SVP & CFO**—R. S. Thomason. **SVP & Secy**—L. C. McKinney. **Investor Contact**—Margaret M. Eichman. **Dirs**—F. C. Carlucci, S. C. Cathcart, K. I. Chenault, J. C. Lewent, V. R. Loucks, Jr., T. C. MacAvoy, P. A. Marineau, L. C. McKinney, G. G. Michelson, W. J. Salmon, W. D. Smithburg, W. L. Weiss. **Transfer Agent & Registrar**—Harris Trust & Savings Bank, Chicago. **Incorporated** in New Jersey in 1901. **Empl**-20,000. **S&P Analyst:** Kenneth A. Shea

Ralston-Ralston Purina Group

NYSE Symbol **RAL**
In S&P 500

24-OCT-95

Industry: Food

Summary: This company is the world's largest producer of dry dog & cat foods (Purina), and dry cell battery products (Eveready, Energizer).

S&P Opinion: Accumulate (★★★★)

Recent Price • 60¼	Yield • 2.0%
52 Wk Range • 60¼-41¼	12-Mo. P/E • 32.7

Quantitative Evaluations

Outlook
(1 Lowest—5 Highest)
• **2+**

Fair Value
• **57⅛**

Risk
• **Low**

Earn./Div. Rank
• **B+**

Technical Eval.
• **Bearish** since 9/94

Rel. Strength Rank
(1 Lowest—99 Highest)
• **83**

Insider Activity
• **NA**

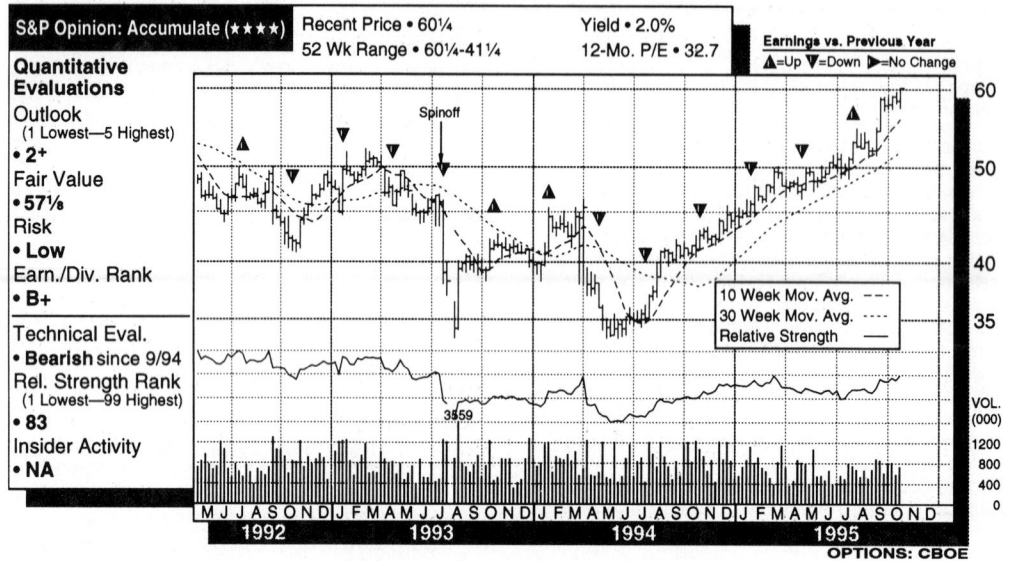

Earnings vs. Previous Year
▲=Up ▼=Down ▶=No Change

Spinoff

10 Week Mov. Avg. ---
30 Week Mov. Avg. ·····
Relative Strength —

3559

VOL. (000)

OPTIONS: CBOE

Overview - 20-OCT-95

Sales from ongoing operations are expected to rise at a low single-digit annual pace through fiscal 1995-96, driven principally by increased volumes for both major business segments. Operating margins should benefit from the recent shedding of unstrategic assets, as well as from additive acquisitions in core businesses. Pet food profits should rise at a high single-digit annual pace, helped by less-costly promotional practices and a more-profitable product & distributional channel mix. Battery profits should also trend higher, buoyed by growing global demand. Earnings per share from continuing operations should rise at an approximate 10% annual pace through fiscal 1995-96.

Valuation - 20-OCT-95

Given our expectation of rising earnings per share from continuing operations through fiscal 1995-96, these low-risk shares are attractive at current levels for above average gains ahead. The shares have risen sharply since mid-1994, helped by improving investor sentiment toward this former conglomerate in the wake of management's recent shedding of low-return businesses. Also, a pronounced investor rotation since mid-1994 toward defensive issues, like RAL, in the midst of a slow U.S. economy has boosted the stock. We expect these factors to help push the shares even higher in coming months.

Key Stock Statistics

S&P EPS Est. 1995	2.85	Tang. Bk. Value/Share	NM
P/E on S&P Est. 1995	21.1	Beta	NA
S&P EPS Est. 1996	3.25	Shareholders	28,200
Dividend Rate/Share	1.20	Market cap. (B)	$ 6.3
Shs. outstg. (M)	105.9	Inst. holdings	54%
Avg. daily vol. (M)	0.146	Insider holdings	NA

Value of $10,000 invested 5 years ago: NA

Fiscal Year Ending Sep. 30

	1995	% Change	1994	% Change	1993	% Change
Revenues (Million $)						
1Q	1,514	-12%	1,724	2%	1,691	-17%
2Q	1,282	-15%	1,507	6%	1,417	-24%
3Q	1,860	52%	1,223	-10%	1,360	-27%
4Q	—	—	1,304	-10%	1,448	-28%
Yr.	—	—	5,759	-3%	5,915	-24%
Income (Million $)						
1Q	106.4	-20%	133.4	NM	132.3	1%
2Q	53.90	-26%	73.30	-11%	82.60	-4%
3Q	68.20	34%	50.90	-18%	62.30	-18%
4Q	—	—	-26.50	NM	64.10	129%
Yr.	—	—	231.1	-32%	341.3	6%
Earnings Per Share ($)						
1Q	1.02	-20%	1.27	55%	0.82	-28%
2Q	0.50	-26%	0.68	-4%	0.71	-7%
3Q	0.62	35%	0.46	-6%	0.49	-28%
4Q	E0.71	NM	-0.31	NM	0.52	136%
Yr.	E2.85	34%	2.12	-17%	2.56	-9%

Next earnings report expected: early November

Ralston-Ralston Purina Group

Business Summary - 23-OCT-95

Ralston-Ralston Purina Group (RAL) common stock represents the remaining operations of Ralston Purina Co. following the July 1995 disposal of its fresh bakery products business (Ralston-Continental Baking Group; CBG), and the March 1994 spinoff of the company's consumer foods and resorts operations businesses (Ralcorp; RAH). RAL is a diversified holding company whose principal interests include pet food, battery products, and protein supplement products.

Ralston Purina Pet Products produces and sells dog and cat foods under the Purina name, including Dog Chow, Cat Chow and numerous other brand names. The division operates 19 pet food plants worldwide.

Eveready Battery Co. produces and sells primary batteries, rechargeable batteries and battery-powered lighting products in the U.S. and worldwide, principally under the Eveready and Energizer labels.

The Soy Protein products segment produces dietary soy protein, fiber food ingredients and polymer products for use in the food processing industry, among others.

The Ralston Purina International segment consists primarily of the business of producing Chow brand formula feed and animal health products in 63 facilities outside the U.S.

In April 1995, RAL terminated negotiations to sell its international agribusiness to PM Holdings Corporation.

Important Developments

Jul. '95—Operating profit for pet foods during fiscal 1995's first nine months increased on higher volume and favorable product mix and ingredient costs, partially offset by cost reduction spending. Battery products' operating profit, exclusive of restructuring charges, was flat as improvements in the Asia Pacific region were offset by first quarter declines in the domestic market due to lower sales to the warehouse class of trade. Battery segment results during the first nine months were also favorably impacted by foreign currency exchange rates. Soy Protein product profits benefited from strong volume in food protein products, increased productivity, and lower raw material costs. Separately, RAL sold its Continental Baking Co. subsidiary to Interstate Bakeries Corp. for 16,923,077 IBC common shares and $220 million in cash.

Capitalization

Long Term Debt: $1,538,500,000 (6/95).
ESOP 6.75% Red. Preferred Stock: $463,400,000.

Per Share Data ($)

	(Year Ended Sep. 30)					
	1994	1993	1992	1991	1990	1989
Tangible Bk. Val.	-1.70	-1.55	-4.07	-0.90	-3.40	-1.54
Cash Flow	4.00	4.42	5.21	5.33	4.99	4.14
Earnings	2.12	2.56	2.82	3.34	3.23	2.66
Dividends	1.20	1.20	1.20	1.04	0.90	0.81
Payout Ratio	57%	47%	43%	31%	27%	29%
Prices - High	46⅜	52⅛	58⅞	60⅛	54⅛	50¾
- Low	33½	33½	40⅞	46	38⅞	39⅜
P/E Ratio - High	22	22	21	18	17	19
- Low	16	15	14	14	12	15

Income Statement Analysis (Million $)

	1994	%Chg	1993	%Chg	1992	%Chg	1991
Revs.	5,759	-3%	5,915	-24%	7,752	5%	7,376
Oper. Inc.	946	NM	939	-12%	1,068	-4%	1,109
Depr.	190	-1%	192	-25%	255	15%	221
Int. Exp.	191	-9%	211	-13%	243	16%	209
Pretax Inc.	451	-10%	502	-7%	542	-16%	648
Eff. Tax Rate	49%	—	43%	—	41%	—	40%
Net Inc.	231	-19%	284	-12%	321	-18%	392

Balance Sheet & Other Fin. Data (Million $)

	1994	1993	1992	1991	1990	1989
Cash	112	57.0	60.0	158	112	381
Curr. Assets	1,662	1,621	1,780	1,676	1,587	1,821
Total Assets	3,791	4,294	5,151	4,632	4,395	4,382
Curr. Liab.	1,520	1,370	1,745	1,194	1,340	1,316
LT Debt	1,252	1,732	2,111	2,071	1,961	1,791
Common Eqty.	340	436	655	784	585	832
Total Cap.	1,902	2,553	3,133	3,180	2,809	2,833
Cap. Exp.	267	291	376	404	470	264
Cash Flow	402	456	554	592	580	526

Ratio Analysis

	1994	1993	1992	1991	1990	1989
Curr. Ratio	1.1	1.2	1.0	1.4	1.2	1.4
% LT Debt of Cap.	65.8	67.8	67.4	65.1	69.8	63.2
% Net Inc.of Revs.	4.0	4.8	4.1	5.3	5.6	5.3
% Ret. on Assets	5.6	NA	6.8	8.7	9.5	8.8
% Ret. on Equity	54.1	NA	43.1	54.4	56.2	37.5

Dividend Data

—Dividends have been paid since 1934. A dividend reinvestment plan is available. A "poison pill" stock purchase right was adopted in 1986.

Amt. of Div. $	Date Decl.	Ex-Div. Date	Stock of Record	Payment Date
0.300	Sep. 23	Nov. 08	Nov. 15	Dec. 09 '94
0.300	Feb. 09	Feb. 14	Feb. 21	Mar. 10 '95
0.300	Mar. 23	May. 16	May. 22	Jun. 09 '95
0.300	May. 25	Aug. 17	Aug. 21	Sep. 08 '95
0.300	Sep. 29	Nov. 16	Nov. 20	Dec. 08 '95

Data as orig. reptd.; bef. results of disc. opers. and/or spec. items. Per share data adj. for stk. divs. as of ex-div. date. E-Estimated. NA-Not Available. NM-Not Meaningful. NR-Not Ranked.

Office—Checkerboard Square, St. Louis, MO 63164-0001. **Tel**—(314) 982-1000. **Chrmn, CEO & Pres**—W. P. Stiritz. **VP-CFO**—J. R. Elsesser. **VP-Secy**—J. M. Neville. **Investor Contact**—Michael Grabel. **Dirs**—D. R. Banks, J. H. Biggs, T. A. Burtis, D. Danforth Jr., W. H. Danforth, D. C. Farrell, M. D. Ingram, J. F. McDonnell, K. D. Ortega, W. P. Stiritz. **Transfer Agents**—Company's office; Boatmen's Trust Co., St. Louis. **Registrar**—Boatmen's Trust Co., St. Louis. **Incorporated** in Missouri in 1894. **Empl**-32,589. **S&P Analyst:** Kenneth A. Shea

Raychem Corp.

NYSE Symbol **RYC**
In S&P 500

08-SEP-95

Industry:
Electronics/Electric

Summary: This company primarily produces high-performance plastic and elastomer products and systems for customers in various industries.

Quantitative Evaluations

Outlook
(1 Lowest—5 Highest)
• **2+**

Fair Value
• **42½**

Risk
• **Average**

Earn./Div. Rank
• **B-**

Technical Eval.
• **Bullish** since 7/95

Rel. Strength Rank
(1 Lowest—99 Highest)
• **73**

Insider Activity
• **Neutral**

Recent Price • 44%   Yield • 0.7%
52 Wk Range • 45-32%   12-Mo. P/E • NM

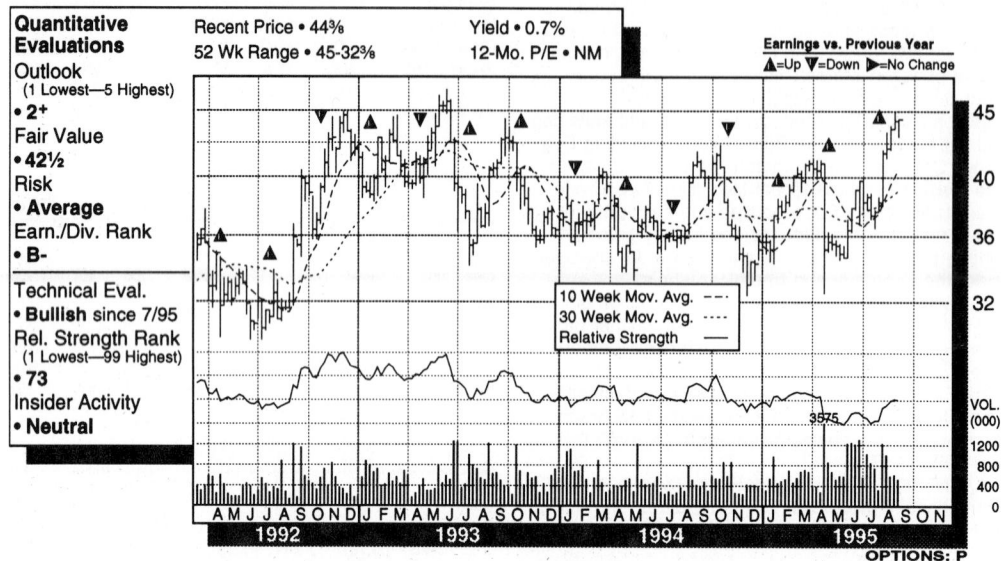

Earnings vs. Previous Year
▲=Up ▼=Down ▶=No Change

10 Week Mov. Avg. - - -
30 Week Mov. Avg. · · · ·
Relative Strength —

OPTIONS: P

Business Profile - 08-SEP-95

This company uses its expertise in materials science, product design and process engineering to produce products such as electronic interconnection systems, temperature maintenance systems, and telephone and cable TV accessories. Raychem serves several industries. Over 50% of revenues come from infrastructure-building projects, offering opportunities in the Pacific Rim, Latin America and Eastern Europe.

Operational Review - 08-SEP-95

Based on a preliminary report, revenues rose about 5% in fiscal 1995. Sales growth was partly offset by the loss of income from Raynet (now operated as a joint venture). Results were penalized by charges of $140.7 million related to the Ericsson Raynet joint venture, restructuring programs, and equity in losses of affiliated companies. A loss of $0.49 a share (excluding charges totaling $0.18) replaced income of $0.04.

Stock Performance - 01-SEP-95

In the past 30 trading days, RYC's shares have increased 18%, compared to a 2% rise in the S&P 500. Average trading volume for the past five days was 103,680 shares, compared with the 40-day moving average of 147,663 shares.

Key Stock Statistics

Dividend Rate/Share	0.32	Shareholders	7,700
Shs. outstg. (M)	43.9	Market cap. (B)	$ 2.0
Avg. daily vol. (M)	0.140	Inst. holdings	80%
Tang. Bk. Value/Share	17.30	Insider holdings	NA
Beta	1.44		

Value of $10,000 invested 5 years ago: $ 14,753

Fiscal Year Ending Jun. 30

	1995	% Change	1994	% Change	1993	% Change
Revenues (Million $)						
1Q	390.7	10%	355.4	2%	348.0	14%
2Q	382.5	8%	353.8	NM	352.0	7%
3Q	368.8	2%	361.3	11%	324.0	4%
4Q	411.1	5%	391.0	8%	361.1	3%
Yr.	1,531	5%	1,462	5%	1,386	7%
Income (Million $)						
1Q	-48.33	NM	6.41	70%	3.76	-50%
2Q	20.00	NM	1.66	-49%	3.26	NM
3Q	10.90	NM	1.07	138%	0.45	-92%
4Q	-4.01	NM	-7.45	NM	0.45	NM
Yr.	-21.45	NM	1.68	-79%	7.93	NM
Earnings Per Share ($)						
1Q	-1.12	NM	0.15	67%	0.09	-53%
2Q	0.45	NM	0.04	-50%	0.08	NM
3Q	0.25	NM	0.02	100%	0.01	-93%
4Q	-0.09	NM	-0.17	NM	0.01	NM
Yr.	-0.49	NM	0.04	-79%	0.19	NM

Next earnings report expected: mid October

Raychem Corp.

Business Summary - 08-SEP-95

Raychem Corporation produces high-performance products based on materials science for customers in several industries. Contributions by business segment in fiscal 1994 (operating profits in millions, before provision for restructuring and divestitures) were:

	Sales	Profits
Electronics	36%	$88.1
Industrial	31%	77.8
Telecommunications	29%	76.5
Raynet	4%	-100.4

International operations accounted for 62% of sales and $134 million of operating profits in fiscal 1994.

The electronics segment includes electrical and electronic interconnection systems, wire and cable, heat-shrinkable insulation, circuit protection devices, connectors, fiber optics, heating devices and fluid fittings for the electronics, transportation, aerospace and defense markets.

The industrial segment consists of electric heat-tracing systems, power cable accessories, electric insulation products, heat-shrinkable sleeves and coatings for pipeline protection, cathodic protection products and leak detection systems.

The telecommunications segment supplies a wide variety of products for telephone operating companies and cable television providers, including accessories, closures, sealing products, connectors and telephone cable terminal blocks.

In October 1994, the company formed with Ericsson a telecommunications joint venture that assumed operation of Raychem's startup Raynet subsidiary. The venture will design, make and market fiber-optic access network systems worldwide. For the first five to eight years of operation, subject to certain conditions, substantially all profits up to $156 million will be allocated to Raychem; thereafter, Ericsson will receive 51% and Raychem 49% of the profits. Ericsson's share of the venture's losses was capped at $25 million for the fiscal year ending June 30, 1995.

Important Developments

Jun. '95—The company announced plans to reorganize its joint venture with Ericsson, in order to cut costs and sharpen focus on certain products, markets and customers. Changes include the consolidation of certain administrative functions, and the relocation of some manufacturing operations to Ericsson's Swedish facilities.

Capitalization

Long Term Debt: $263,552,000 (6/95).

Per Share Data ($)
(Year Ended Jun. 30)

	1995	1994	1993	1992	1991	1990
Tangible Bk. Val.	NA	17.04	16.47	17.77	17.05	18.96
Cash Flow	NA	2.03	2.03	1.58	1.51	-1.15
Earnings	-0.49	0.04	0.19	-0.43	-0.63	-3.12
Dividends	0.32	0.32	0.32	0.32	0.32	0.32
Payout Ratio	NM	NM	168%	NM	NM	NM
Prices - High	41⅜	42⅜	46¾	44⅞	36⅞	35½
- Low	32½	32⅜	34⅛	29⅞	21¼	15¾
P/E Ratio - High	NM	NM	NM	NM	NM	NM
- Low	NM	NM	NM	NM	NM	NM

Income Statement Analysis (Million $)

	1994	%Chg	1993	%Chg	1992	%Chg	1991
Revs.	1,462	5%	1,386	7%	1,296	4%	1,250
Oper. Inc.	140	-13%	161	28%	126	17%	108
Depr.	86.2	11%	77.9	NM	78.1	-2%	79.5
Int. Exp.	22.0	-19%	27.0	-5%	28.4	1%	28.1
Pretax Inc.	34.0	-15%	40.0	90%	21.0	NM	-3.0
Eff. Tax Rate	95%	—	80%	—	180%	—	NM
Net Inc.	2.0	-75%	8.0	NM	-17.0	NM	-23.0

Balance Sheet & Other Fin. Data (Million $)

	1994	1993	1992	1991	1990	1989
Cash	78.0	134	149	99	137	153
Curr. Assets	736	715	776	660	724	673
Total Assets	1,399	1,332	1,393	1,235	1,271	1,173
Curr. Liab.	324	315	335	259	456	315
LT Debt	245	234	230	233	31.0	29.0
Common Eqty.	733	690	715	652	690	734
Total Cap.	1,009	955	1,005	937	776	816
Cap. Exp.	104	90.0	93.0	137	115	101
Cash Flow	88.0	86.0	61.0	56.0	-41.0	105

Ratio Analysis

	1994	1993	1992	1991	1990	1989
Curr. Ratio	2.3	2.3	2.3	2.6	1.6	2.1
% LT Debt of Cap.	24.2	24.5	22.9	24.9	4.0	3.6
% Net Inc.of Revs.	0.1	0.6	NM	NM	NM	3.4
% Ret. on Assets	0.1	0.6	NM	NM	NM	3.2
% Ret. on Equity	0.2	1.1	NM	NM	NM	5.1

Dividend Data —Dividends have been paid since 1977.

Amt. of Div. $	Date Decl.	Ex-Div. Date	Stock of Record	Payment Date
0.080	Jul. 21	Aug. 04	Aug. 10	Sep. 14 '94
0.080	Oct. 18	Nov. 03	Nov. 09	Dec. 14 '94
0.080	Jan. 18	Feb. 02	Feb. 08	Mar. 08 '95
0.080	Apr. 19	May. 11	May. 17	Jun. 14 '95
0.080	Jul. 19	Aug. 07	Aug. 09	Sep. 13 '95

Data as orig. reptd.; bef. results of disc. opers. and/or spec. items. Per share data adj. for stk. divs. as of ex-div. date.
E-Estimated. NA-Not Available. NM-Not Meaningful. NR-Not Ranked.

Office—300 Constitution Dr., Menlo Park, CA 94025-1164. **Tel**—(415) 361-4180. **Chrmn**—R. A. Kashnow (effective 10/1/95). **Secy**—R. J. Vizas. **SVP & CFO**—R. J. Simms. **Investor Contact**—Scott F. Wylie (415-361-7855). **Dirs**—P. M. Cook, R. Dulude, J. F. Gibbons, J. P. McTague, D. O. Morton, I. Stein, C. J. Yansouni. **Transfer Agent & Registrar**—Harris Trust & Savings Bank, Chicago. **Incorporated** in California in 1957; reincorporated in Delaware in 1987. **Empl**-10,000. **S&P Analyst:** Mike Cavanaugh

Raytheon Co.

NYSE Symbol **RTN**
In S&P 500

17-SEP-95

Industry:
Electronics/Electric

Summary: Raytheon manufactures air defense missiles, radar systems and other military electronics products. It also produces power and industrial plants, aircraft and major appliances.

| S&P Opinion: Accumulate (★★★★) | Recent Price • 83⅞ | Yield • 1.8% |
| | 52 Wk Range • 84⅛-60¾ | 12-Mo. P/E • 13.9 |

Earnings vs. Previous Year
▲=Up ▼=Down ►=No Change

Quantitative Evaluations

Outlook
(1 Lowest—5 Highest)
• **1+**

Fair Value
• **65⅝**

Risk
• **Low**

Earn./Div. Rank
• **A+**

Technical Eval.
• **Bullish** since 1/95

Rel. Strength Rank
(1 Lowest—99 Highest)
• **54**

Insider Activity
• **Neutral**

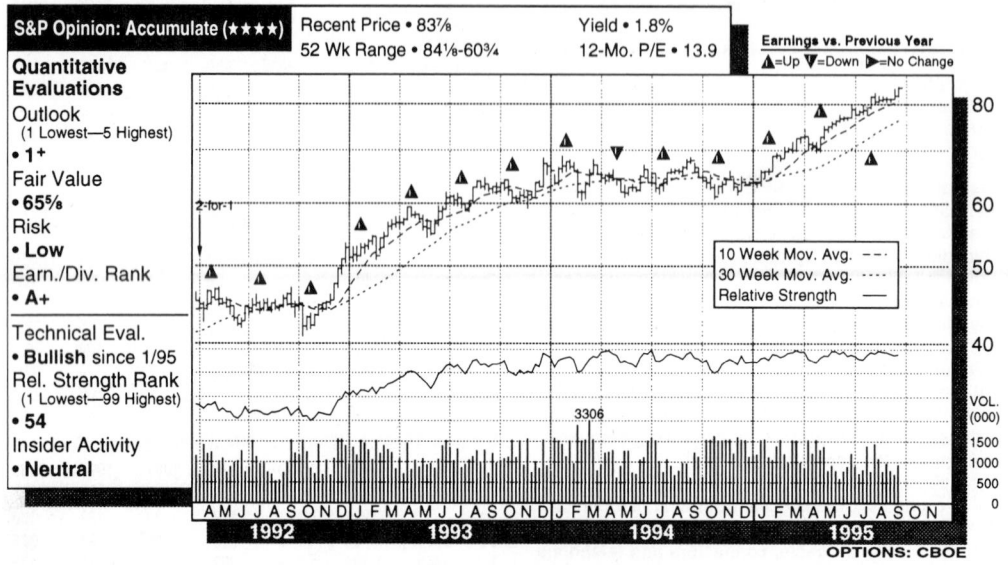

OPTIONS: CBOE

Overview - 15-SEP-95

Revenues in 1995 are expected to climb more than 15% from those of 1994, reflecting several acquisitions. Excluding E-Systems, Raytheon's most significant purchase, electronics revenues would be unchanged as higher commercial electronics sales should offset eroding defense electronics sales. In the commercial segments, gains are projected to come mainly from aircraft products. The slowing economy will restrain revenue growth from appliances and engineering and construction services (excluding possible SIVAM contributions). Nevertheless, a 1994 restructuring program and strict cost control should result in improved margins from commercial activities. The net interest charge is expected to increase, but a stock buyback program will boost EPS.

Valuation - 15-SEP-95

The shares have climbed substantially since early 1995 in response to defense industry consolidation, including RTN's acquisition of E-Systems, and the award of several major contracts. The company's long-term outlook is favorable, with a rising backlog, despite budget cuts. As a leading missile producer, Raytheon will likely benefit from Congressional plans to develop a national missile defense. In addition, engineering and construction, aircraft and appliances are all expected to generate increased sales and earnings. Given Raytheon's growth prospects and the modest P/E multiple of the stock, we view the shares as attractive.

Key Stock Statistics

S&P EPS Est. 1995	6.40	Tang. Bk. Value/Share	25.84
P/E on S&P Est. 1995	13.1	Beta	0.41
S&P EPS Est. 1996	7.00	Shareholders	22,000
Dividend Rate/Share	1.50	Market cap. (B)	$ 10.2
Shs. outstg. (M)	122.0	Inst. holdings	74%
Avg. daily vol. (M)	0.180	Insider holdings	NA

Value of $10,000 invested 5 years ago: $ 27,853

Fiscal Year Ending Dec. 31

	1995	% Change	1994	% Change	1993	% Change
Revenues (Million $)						
1Q	2,387	3%	2,315	5%	2,204	3%
2Q	2,816	11%	2,527	12%	2,258	-3%
3Q	—	—	2,443	10%	2,223	NM
4Q	—	—	2,729	8%	2,517	5%
Yr.	—	—	10,013	9%	9,201	2%
Income (Million $)						
1Q	173.9	NM	7.00	-96%	157.5	10%
2Q	195.5	2%	192.2	7%	179.3	8%
3Q	—	—	192.0	12%	170.8	9%
4Q	—	—	205.7	11%	185.4	9%
Yr.	—	—	596.9	-14%	693.0	9%
Earnings Per Share ($)						
1Q	1.41	NM	0.05	-96%	1.16	8%
2Q	1.60	12%	1.43	8%	1.32	7%
3Q	E1.65	14%	1.45	15%	1.26	9%
4Q	E1.74	8%	1.61	18%	1.37	9%
Yr.	E6.40	42%	4.51	-12%	5.11	8%

Next earnings report expected: mid October

Raytheon Co.

Business Summary - 15-SEP-95

Raytheon is a diversified manufacturer of electronic equipment and components. Contributions by segment in 1994 were:

	Sales	Profits
Electronics	41%	54%
Engineering & constr.	28%	21%
Aircraft products	17%	18%
Major appliances	14%	7%

The U.S. government accounted for 39% of total sales in 1994, including purchases made on behalf of foreign governments (7%). International sales provided 20% of the total.

In defense electronics, the company produces ground-based and airborne missiles (incl. Patriot, Hawk, Sidewinder, Sparrow, Stinger, AMRAAM, Standard, and Maverick), radar systems, electronic countermeasures, guidance and firecontrol systems, sonar, communications equipment and microwave components. Commercial electronics products are used in environmental monitoring, communications, air traffic control and transportation systems. D.C. Heath and Co. publishes textbooks and educational software.

The engineering and construction segment designs and constructs electricity generating fossil fuel and nuclear plants, petroleum refining, petrochemical, and other types of heavy industrial plants. Raytheon also produces paving and mixing equipment and provides technical services and operations.

Raytheon Aircraft Co. includes Beech Aircraft, a leading manufacturer of general aviation aircraft, and Raytheon Corporate Jets, which makes the Hawker 800 and 1000 medium-size business jets.

Household and commercial appliances include refrigerators, freezers, ovens, ranges, cooktops, dishwashers, washers and dryers, air conditioners, furnaces and heat pumps. Products are sold under the Amana, Speed Queen, Caloric and Modern Maid brand names.

Important Developments

Jul. '95—RTN expressed confidence that a contract suspension imposed by a Brazilian Federal judge on its SIVAM contract would be lifted. The $1.3 billion contract, signed in May 1995, is to develop and install a surveillance system designed to assist the Brazilian government in protecting the environment.
Jun. '95—The Beech MkII was selected as the primary training aircraft for the Air Force and Navy. The 20 year program has an estimated potential value of $7 billion, and additional strong foreign sales potential.
May '95—Raytheon acquired E-Systems, Inc. for $2.3 billion in cash. E-Systems, with 1994 sales of $2 billion, makes electronic systems and products, primarily for military applications.

Capitalization

Total Debt: $3,593,216,000 (7/2/95).

Per Share Data ($)

(Year Ended Dec. 31)

	1994	1993	1992	1991	1990	1989
Tangible Bk. Val.	25.84	27.94	27.89	24.30	20.55	17.70
Cash Flow	6.58	7.23	6.97	6.79	6.59	6.14
Earnings	4.51	5.11	4.72	4.48	4.27	4.01
Dividends	1.45	1.05	1.33	1.23	1.20	1.10
Payout Ratio	32%	21%	28%	28%	28%	27%
Prices - High	68⅞	68½	53½	44⅛	35⅝	42½
- Low	60½	50½	40⅝	32⅞	28⅞	32¼
P/E Ratio - High	15	13	11	10	8	11
- Low	13	10	9	7	7	8

Income Statement Analysis (Million $)

	1994	%Chg	1993	%Chg	1992	%Chg	1991
Revs.	10,013	9%	9,201	2%	9,058	-2%	9,274
Oper. Inc.	1,353	12%	1,207	NM	1,196	6%	1,128
Depr.	275	-4%	287	-5%	302	-1%	306
Int. Exp.	49.0	53%	32.0	-33%	48.0	-48%	92.0
Pretax Inc.	900	-14%	1,047	10%	956	10%	873
Eff. Tax Rate	34%	—	34%	—	34%	—	32%
Net Inc.	597	-14%	693	9%	635	7%	592

Balance Sheet & Other Fin. Data (Million $)

	1994	1993	1992	1991	1990	1989
Cash	202	190	89.0	138	138	99
Curr. Assets	4,985	4,609	3,776	3,748	3,603	3,104
Total Assets	7,395	7,258	6,015	6,087	6,119	5,338
Curr. Liab.	3,283	2,910	2,137	2,716	3,146	2,822
LT Debt	24.5	24.4	25.3	39.3	46.4	46.0
Common Eqty.	3,928	4,298	3,843	3,323	2,847	2,426
Total Cap.	3,953	4,322	3,869	3,363	2,893	2,472
Cap. Exp.	267	310	308	349	391	414
Cash Flow	872	980	937	898	861	810

Ratio Analysis

	1994	1993	1992	1991	1990	1989
Curr. Ratio	1.5	1.6	1.8	1.4	1.1	1.1
% LT Debt of Cap.	0.6	0.6	0.7	1.2	1.6	1.9
% Net Inc.of Revs.	6.0	7.5	7.0	6.4	6.0	6.0
% Ret. on Assets	8.5	10.5	10.4	9.6	9.7	10.6
% Ret. on Equity	15.2	17.1	17.6	19.0	21.2	23.4

Dividend Data

Dividends have been paid since 1964. A dividend reinvestment plan is available. A poison pill stock purchase rights plan was adopted in 1986.

Amt. of Div. $	Date Decl.	Ex-Div. Date	Stock of Record	Payment Date
0.375	Sep. 29	Oct. 03	Oct. 10	Oct. 31 '94
0.375	Dec. 20	Jan. 03	Jan. 09	Jan. 30 '95
0.375	Mar. 22	Apr. 04	Apr. 10	May. 01 '95
0.375	Jun. 28	Jul. 06	Jul. 10	Jul. 31 '95

Data as orig. reptd.; bef. results of disc. opers. and/or spec. items. Per share data adj. for stk. divs. as of ex-div. date. E-Estimated. NA-Not Available. NM-Not Meaningful. NR-Not Ranked.

Office—141 Spring St., Lexington, MA 02173. Tel—(617) 862-6600. Chrmn & CEO—D. J. Picard. EVP & CFO—P. D'Angelo. SVP & Secy—C. L. Hoffmann. Investor Contact—Michele C. Heid (617-860-2303). Dirs—C. F. Adams, F. H. Burr, F. Colloredo-Mansfeld, T. L. Eliot, Jr., B. B. Hauptfuhrer, R. D. Hill, L. D. Kozlowski, J. N. Land, Jr., A. L. Lawson, T. L. Phillips, D. J. Picard, W. B. Rudman, J. J. Sisco, A. M. Zeien. Transfer Agent & Registrar—State Street Bank & Trust Co., Boston. Incorporated in Delaware in 1928. Empl- 74,400. S&P Analyst: Joe Victor Shammas

Reebok International

NYSE Symbol **RBK**
In S&P 500

13-OCT-95   Industry:
Leather/shoes

Summary: Reebok is a leading producer of athletic footwear and apparel sold in the U.S. and overseas.

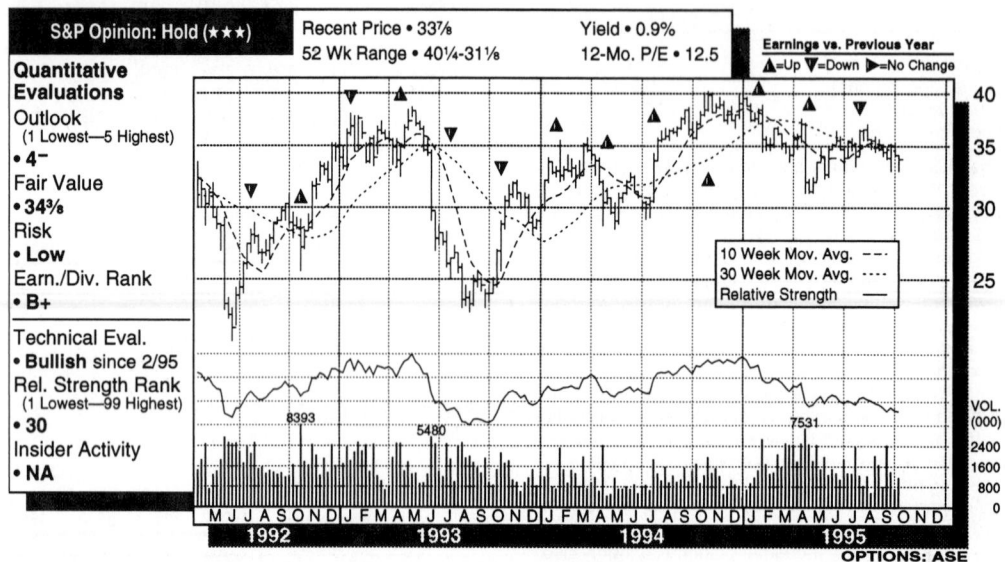

| S&P Opinion: Hold (★★★) | Recent Price • 33⅞ | Yield • 0.9% |
| | 52 Wk Range • 40¼-31⅛ | 12-Mo. P/E • 12.5 |

Quantitative Evaluations

Outlook
(1 Lowest—5 Highest)
• **4⁻**

Fair Value
• **34⅜**

Risk
• **Low**

Earn./Div. Rank
• **B+**

Technical Eval.
• **Bullish** since 2/95

Rel. Strength Rank
(1 Lowest—99 Highest)
• **30**

Insider Activity
• **NA**

Earnings vs. Previous Year
▲=Up ▼=Down ▶=No Change

10 Week Mov. Avg. ---
30 Week Mov. Avg. ·····
Relative Strength —

OPTIONS: ASE

Overview - 13-OCT-95

Sales should rise somewhat in 1995 following a strong recovery in 1994. Sales in the U.S. will increase slightly on market share gains, a rebound in demand for basketball shoes, higher demand for Rockports, and increased growth of casual outdoor footwear (e.g. hiking boots). Overseas sales will benefit from greater volume in China, improved European economies and expanded distribution of Rockport shoes. Margins could be hurt by higher marketing costs as a percent of sales and a one-time pretax charge of $18 million ($0.14 a share) to streamline operations. Share earnings will benefit from fewer shares outstanding.

Valuation - 13-OCT-95

After outperforming the market in 1994's second half, Reebok's shares have trended downward for most of 1995. We attribute the stock's depressed performance mainly to several quarters of disappointing results. In response to these lackluster results, especially when compared with ongoing strong results at Reebok's main competitor Nike, major institutional investors in Reebok recently publicly questioned the ability of Reebok's management to competitively run the company. While Reebok has announced several initiatives to return operations into a growth mode, we remain skeptical, given past profit enhancement attempts by the company. As a result, we are retaining a neutral opinion on these shares for the time being.

Key Stock Statistics

S&P EPS Est. 1995	2.60	Tang. Bk. Value/Share	11.42
P/E on S&P Est. 1995	13.0	Beta	1.72
S&P EPS Est. 1996	3.35	Shareholders	8,300
Dividend Rate/Share	0.30	Market cap. (B)	$ 2.6
Shs. outstg. (M)	78.4	Inst. holdings	70%
Avg. daily vol. (M)	0.209	Insider holdings	NA

Value of $10,000 invested 5 years ago: $ 19,119

Fiscal Year Ending Dec. 31

	1995	% Change	1994	% Change	1993	% Change
Revenues (Million $)						
1Q	935.5	9%	857.4	4%	825.0	4%
2Q	788.7	2%	776.8	18%	657.6	-6%
3Q	—	—	937.2	16%	808.5	-6%
4Q	—	—	709.2	18%	602.6	-9%
Yr.	—	—	3,280	13%	2,894	-4%
Income (Million $)						
1Q	65.92	NM	65.79	-3%	67.77	9%
2Q	21.40	-58%	51.01	24%	41.03	-10%
3Q	—	—	84.66	32%	63.93	-14%
4Q	—	—	53.03	5%	50.69	NM
Yr.	—	—	254.5	14%	223.4	95%
Earnings Per Share ($)						
1Q	0.80	4%	0.77	4%	0.74	10%
2Q	0.26	-57%	0.60	30%	0.46	-6%
3Q	E0.83	-18%	1.01	36%	0.74	-8%
4Q	E0.71	11%	0.64	8%	0.59	NM
Yr.	E2.60	-14%	3.02	19%	2.53	104%

Next earnings report expected: mid October

Reebok International

Business Summary - 05-OCT-95

Reebok designs, develops and markets footwear and apparel for men, women and children. RBK has three major operating units: Reebok, the specialty business group (which focuses on non-Reebok and non-athletic brands) and licensing. In 1993, the company sold Boston Whaler and Ellesse.

The Reebok U.S. operations include apparel (4.6% of total 1994 sales) and all sports, fitness and casual footwear products (44%) sold in the U.S. under the Reebok, Weebok and Boks trademarks, except certain golf shoes. Reebok International, headquartered in the U.K., markets footwear products and apparel (39%) abroad, with subsidiaries throughout Europe, Asia, Latin America and Canada, and through distributors and joint ventures in more than 120 countries.

The specialty business group includes the Rockport brand, the BOKS casual footwear line, the company's Reebok brand outdoor products and Avia. Rockport (9.8%) designs, develops and markets lightweight and comfortable casual, dress and fitness walking shoes. Avia (3.8%) designs, develops and markets athletic footwear and apparel under the Avia brand. The specialty business group is also responsible for the company's golf products, including the Greg Norman line of golf shoes, and retail operations. RBK operates concept stores in Boston, Mass., New York City and Santa Monica, Calif., and approximately 50 factory outlet-type stores.

The licensing division seeks to expand RBK's strategic trademarks. Leading trademarks include THE PUMP, REEBOK, BLACKTOP and ABOVE THE RIM.

The majority of RBK's footwear is manufactured through independent contractors in Southeast Asia. Foot Locker, a specialty chain of retail stores with various affiliates, is a substantial customer, although it accounted for less than 10% of the company's 1994 sales.

Important Developments

Sep. '95—RBK sold $100 million of 6 3/4% debentures due September 15, 2005. Net proceeds were earmarked to repay short-term indebtedness incurred in order to redeem in full on September 15, 1995, the $100 million aggregate principal amount of the company's 9 3/8% debentures due 1998.

Jul. '95—RBK reported that orders as of the end of the second quarter were up 5.9% from last year, reflecting a 22% increase in international orders. Separately, RBK took a one-time, after-tax charge of $11.3 million ($0.14 a share) for severance and other related costs associated with the streamlining of certain segments of its operations. RBK said it planned to reduce selling, general and administrative expenses by $75 milion in 1996 as a result of this streamlining.

Capitalization

Long Term Debt: $237,528,000 (6/95).
Minority Interest: $27,718,000 (6/95).

Per Share Data ($) (Year Ended Dec. 31)

	1994	1993	1992	1991	1990	1989
Tangible Bk. Val.	12.24	10.12	9.38	9.05	8.71	7.42
Cash Flow	3.40	2.81	1.53	2.59	1.72	1.65
Earnings	3.02	2.53	1.24	2.37	1.54	1.53
Dividends	0.30	0.30	0.30	0.30	0.30	0.30
Payout Ratio	10%	12%	23%	12%	19%	20%
Prices - High	40¼	38⅝	35⅝	35⅛	20	19⅝
- Low	28⅜	23	21⅜	10¾	8⅛	11⅛
P/E Ratio - High	13	15	29	15	13	13
- Low	9	9	17	5	5	7

Income Statement Analysis (Million $)

	1994	%Chg	1993	%Chg	1992	%Chg	1991
Revs.	3,280	13%	2,894	-4%	3,023	11%	2,734
Oper. Inc.	453	8%	419	NM	417	-3%	429
Depr.	32.2	28%	25.2	-7%	27.2	24%	22.0
Int. Exp.	16.5	-34%	25.0	24%	20.1	-32%	29.4
Pretax Inc.	417	12%	372	44%	258	-34%	390
Eff. Tax Rate	37%	—	38%	—	56%	—	40%
Net Inc.	254	14%	223	94%	115	-51%	235

Balance Sheet & Other Fin. Data (Million $)

	1994	1993	1992	1991	1990	1989
Cash	84.0	79.0	105	85.0	227	171
Curr. Assets	1,337	1,127	1,060	1,027	1,030	784
Total Assets	1,649	1,392	1,345	1,431	1,403	1,166
Curr. Liab.	506	396	386	424	294	203
LT Debt	132	134	116	170	106	110
Common Eqty.	991	847	839	824	997	844
Total Cap.	1,144	995	960	1,006	1,109	963
Cap. Exp.	61.8	26.6	36.5	37.7	24.1	18.4
Cash Flow	287	249	142	257	197	189

Ratio Analysis

	1994	1993	1992	1991	1990	1989
Curr. Ratio	2.6	2.8	2.7	2.4	3.5	3.9
% LT Debt of Cap.	11.5	13.5	12.1	16.9	9.5	11.4
% Net Inc.of Revs.	7.8	7.7	3.8	8.6	8.2	9.6
% Ret. on Assets	17.0	16.9	8.3	18.4	13.7	15.6
% Ret. on Equity	28.1	27.4	13.9	29.0	19.1	22.7

Dividend Data —Dividends were initiated in 1987.

Amt. of Div. $	Date Decl.	Ex-Div. Date	Stock of Record	Payment Date
0.075	Oct. 04	Dec. 08	Dec. 14	Jan. 04 '95
0.075	Dec. 15	Mar. 09	Mar. 15	Apr. 05 '95
0.075	May. 02	Jun. 13	Jun. 15	Jul. 06 '95
0.075	Jul. 20	Sep. 11	Sep. 13	Oct. 04 '95

Data as orig. reptd.; bef. results of disc. opers. and/or spec. items. Per share data adj. for stk. divs. as of ex-div. date. E-Estimated. NA-Not Available. NM-Not Meaningful. NR-Not Ranked.

Office—100 Technology Center Drive, Stoughton, MA 02072. **Tel**—(617) 341-5000. **Fax**—(617) 341-5087. **Chrmn, CEO & Pres**—P.B. Fireman. **EVP-CFO**—P. R. Duncan. **VP & Investor Contact**—Kate Burnham (617-341-7298). **Dirs**—J. E. Barad, J. H. Duerden, P. R. Duncan, P. B. Fireman, D. E. Gill, W. F. Glavin, B. M. Lee Sr., R. G. Lesser, W. M. Marcus, R. Meers, G. Nunes, J. A. Quelch. **Transfer Agent & Registrar**—First National Bank of Boston. **Incorporated** in Massachusetts in 1979. **Empl**-6,500. **S&P Analyst:** Elizabeth Vandeventer

Republic New York

NYSE Symbol **RNB**
In S&P 500

30-AUG-95

Industry:
Banking

Summary: This bank holding company engages in retail and commercial banking and in private banking primarily in metropolitan New York, Florida and abroad.

S&P Opinion: Hold (★★★)		
Recent Price • 54½	Yield • 2.6%	
52 Wk Range • 58¾-41⅞	12-Mo. P/E • 12.0	

Quantitative Evaluations

Outlook
(1 Lowest—5 Highest)
• **5+**

Fair Value
• **64⅜**

Risk
• **Low**

Earn./Div. Rank
• **B+**

Technical Eval.
• **Bearish** since 8/95

Rel. Strength Rank
(1 Lowest—99 Highest)
• **53**

Insider Activity
• **Neutral**

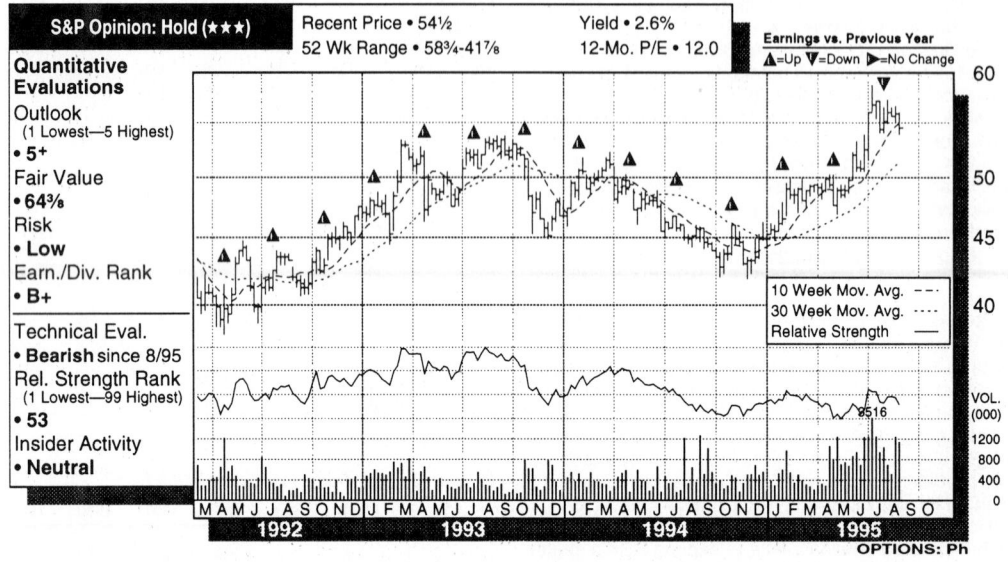

Earnings vs. Previous Year
▲=Up ▼=Down ▶=No Change

10 Week Mov. Avg. ‒ ‒ ‒
30 Week Mov. Avg. ....
Relative Strength ‒‒‒

OPTIONS: Ph

Overview - 30-AUG-95

As RNB's focus remains on depositor safety, funds will continue to be invested primarily in lower-risk assets. The net interest margin widened further in the second quarter of 1995 as a result of the highly liquid balance sheet, a trend that should continue following efforts to reduce holdings of longer-term investment securities to insulate net interest income from interest rate changes. RNB has been placing increasing emphasis on expanding fee income sources, particularly the domestic private banking business and mutual fund operations, which should offset a difficult environment for trading operations. With the reserve for loan losses at a hefty 593% of nonaccrual loans, the loan loss provision is expected to decline further in 1995.

Valuation - 30-AUG-95

Relatively modest revenue growth assumptions remain the primary reason for our tepid appraisal of the shares. Net interest income remains substantially insulated from changes in interest rates following a realignment of the investment portfolio in mid-1994, but the expectation of flat loan volume will restrain earnings. The recent launch of a corporate-wide project to improve operating efficiencies and reduce costs, however, will benefit long-term results. After rebounding from a late 1994 oversold condition, the shares are only expected to track market averages until earnings gains materialize.

Key Stock Statistics

S&P EPS Est. 1995	4.65	Tang. Bk. Value/Share	37.97
P/E on S&P Est. 1995	11.7	Beta	1.41
S&P EPS Est. 1996	6.75	Shareholders	3,000
Dividend Rate/Share	1.44	Market cap. (B)	$ 2.9
Shs. outstg. (M)	52.3	Inst. holdings	52%
Avg. daily vol. (M)	0.220	Insider holdings	NA

Value of $10,000 invested 5 years ago: $ 18,340

Fiscal Year Ending Dec. 31

	1995	% Change	1994	% Change	1993	% Change
Revenues (Million $)						
1Q	711.0	21%	588.9	3%	572.5	-2%
2Q	703.5	15%	609.7	8%	566.9	-1%
3Q	—	—	652.8	11%	589.8	NM
4Q	—	—	708.3	18%	599.3	2%
Yr.	—	—	2,560	10%	2,328	NM
Income (Million $)						
1Q	87.51	10%	79.78	16%	68.75	14%
2Q	11.09	-86%	79.43	6%	74.93	17%
3Q	—	—	91.42	18%	77.61	15%
4Q	—	—	89.38	12%	79.93	20%
Yr.	—	—	340.0	13%	301.2	16%
Earnings Per Share ($)						
1Q	1.48	7%	1.38	17%	1.18	13%
2Q	0.02	-99%	1.35	4%	1.30	20%
3Q	E1.55	NM	1.55	16%	1.34	16%
4Q	E1.60	6%	1.51	9%	1.38	21%
Yr.	E4.65	-20%	5.79	11%	5.20	18%

Next earnings report expected: mid October

Republic New York

Business Summary - 30-AUG-95

Republic New York Corp., the 23rd largest bank holding company in the U.S., owns Republic National Bank of New York, which provides a variety of banking and financial services worldwide to corporations, financial institutions, governmental units and individuals through 34 branches in New York City and Westchester and Rockland counties, as well as several foreign branches and representative offices. Through 49%-owned Safra Republic Holdings, Republic National Bank also offers a range of private banking services to wealthy individuals. RNB also owns Republic Bank for Savings, a New York state chartered savings bank that grants mortgages on residential real property primarily in New York State, which operates through 24 offices in the New York City area and eight offices in Florida. A high proportion of assets is held in liquid investments. Precious metals trading is important, as are factoring and currency trading operations. International operations accounted for 59% and 50% of 1994 assets and net income, respectively.

In 1994, average earning assets of $33.4 billion ($32.6 billion in 1992) were divided: domestic loans 20%, international loans 10%, investment securities 39%, trading account assets 3%, and other short-term assets 28%. Average sources of funds were: international deposits 29%, domestic savings and time deposits 21%, noninterest-bearing deposits 4%, short-term borrowings 14%, long-term debt 12%, shareholders' equity 6%, and other 14%.

At year-end 1994, nonperforming assets were $81.6 million (0.92% of loans), down from $118.2 million (1.24%) a year earlier. The allowance for loan losses was 3.58% of loans, versus 3.28%. Net chargeoffs during 1994 were 0.12% of average loans, compared with 0.15% in 1993.

At June 30, 1995, the company had estimated Tier 1 and total capital ratios of 16.80% and 28.40%, respectively, up from 16.17% and 27.49% at year-end 1994.

Important Developments

May '95—RNB began the implementation phase of a companywide project to improve operating efficiencies and reduce costs. The company expects to achieve pretax cost savings of not less than $75 million per year in operating expenses within 14 months. Savings will be made in personnel and nonpersonnel areas resulting from general efficiencies, process redesign, vendor management, restructuring and consolidation of operations and automation. A related pretax restructuring charge of $120 million, primarily for severance costs, was recorded in the second quarter of 1995.

Capitalization

Long Term Debt: $3,953,995,000 (6/95).
Cum. Preferred Stock: $747,500,000.

Per Share Data ($)

(Year Ended Dec. 31)

	1994	1993	1992	1991	1990	1989
Tangible Bk. Val.	37.38	41.57	32.71	29.60	26.61	23.44
Earnings	5.79	5.20	4.42	3.95	3.62	0.03
Dividends	1.32	1.08	1.00	0.95	0.88	0.85
Payout Ratio	23%	21%	23%	24%	24%	NM
Prices - High	52¼	53¾	48¼	47¼	35	34½
- Low	41⅞	44⅜	38	31⅜	24⅞	28½
P/E Ratio - High	9	10	11	12	10	NM
- Low	7	9	9	8	7	NM

Income Statement Analysis (Million $)

	1994	%Chg	1993	%Chg	1992	%Chg	1991
Net Int. Inc.	846	4%	814	13%	720	24%	581
Tax Equiv. Adj.	35.5	14%	31.0	-3%	32.0	NM	32.0
Non Int. Inc.	371	-4%	388	33%	291	9%	267
Loan Loss Prov.	19.0	-78%	85.0	-29%	120	94%	62.0
% Exp/Op Revs.	58%	—	52%	—	53%	—	57%
Pretax Inc.	492	9%	451	30%	347	20%	288
Eff. Tax Rate	31%	—	33%	—	26%	—	21%
Net Inc.	340	13%	301	16%	259	14%	227
% Net Int. Marg.	2.64%	—	2.60%	—	2.51%	—	2.27%

Balance Sheet & Other Fin. Data (Million $)

	1994	1993	1992	1991	1990	1989
Earning Assets:						
Money Mkt.	15,366	8,851	12,771	9,056	8,768	9,315
Inv. Securities	11,440	14,950	12,331	9,667	7,643	5,638
Com'l Loans	2,884	2,839	2,181	2,117	2,353	1,984
Other Loans	6,076	6,765	5,975	6,664	6,880	4,698
Total Assets	41,068	39,494	37,146	31,221	29,597	25,467
Demand Deposits	1,816	1,563	1,316	1,049	1,111	991
Time Deposits	20,910	21,239	19,787	19,334	18,875	15,534
LT Debt	4,987	4,855	4,633	3,120	2,416	2,521
Common Eqty.	1,967	2,191	1,707	1,541	1,374	1,063

Ratio Analysis

	1994	1993	1992	1991	1990	1989
% Ret. on Assets	0.8	0.8	0.8	0.7	0.6	0.1
% Ret. on Equity	21.9	21.8	20.6	19.4	19.3	0.2
% Loan Loss Resv.	3.6	3.3	3.0	2.7	2.6	4.4
% Loans/Deposits	39.2	41.7	38.0	42.0	45.1	39.8
% Equity to Assets	3.4	3.3	3.3	3.4	3.0	2.8

Dividend Data —Dividends have been paid since 1975.

Amt. of Div. $	Date Decl.	Ex-Div. Date	Stock of Record	Payment Date
0.330	Jul. 22	Sep. 09	Sep. 15	Oct. 01 '94
0.330	Oct. 20	Dec. 09	Dec. 15	Jan. 01 '95
0.360	Jan. 18	Mar. 09	Mar. 15	Apr. 01 '95
0.360	Apr. 20	Jun. 13	Jun. 15	Jul. 01 '95
0.360	Jul. 19	Sep. 13	Sep. 15	Oct. 01 '95

Data as orig. reptd.; bef. results of disc opers. and/or spec. items. Per share data adj. for stk. divs. as of ex-div. date.
E-Estimated. NA-Not Available. NM-Not Meaningful. NR-Not Ranked.

Office—452 Fifth Ave., New York, NY 10018. Tel—(212) 525-6100. **Chrmn & CEO**—W. H. Weiner. **Pres**—J. C. Keil. **EVP, Treas & Investor Contact**—Thomas F. Robards. **SVP & Secy**—W. F. Rosenblum, Jr. **Dirs**—K. Andersen, A. S. Corwen, C. S. Dwek, E. Ginsberg, N. Hasson, M. Hirsch, J. C. Keil, P. Kimmelman, L. Lieberman, W. C. MacMillen, Jr., P. J. Mansbach, M. F. Mertz, J. L. Morice, E. D. Morris, J. L. Norwood, J. A. Pancetti, J. Perez de Cuellar, V. S. Portera, W. M. Rabinowitz, W. P. Rogers, D. C. Schlein, J. Tawil, W. H. Weiner, P. White. **Transfer Agent & Registrar**—American Stock Transfer & Trust Co., NYC. **Incorporated** in Maryland in 1973. **Empl**-5,500. **S&P Analyst:** Stephen R. Biggar

Reynolds Metals

NYSE Symbol RLM Options on Pacific (Feb-May-Aug-Nov) In S&P 500

Price	Range	P–E Ratio	Dividend	Yield	S&P Ranking	Beta
Jul. 26'95	1995					
57⅞	63⅜–46¼	13	1.20	2.1%	B–	1.11

Summary

The second largest U.S. aluminum producer, Reynolds fabricates aluminum products for a wide variety of industries. For future growth and profit potential, RLM is targeting six strategic markets: packaging, consumer products, aluminum cans, transportation, building and construction, and infrastructure. Earnings should advance substantially in 1995 on higher fabricated aluminum products prices.

Current Outlook

Earnings for 1995 are estimated at $5.75 a share, up from 1994's $1.42 (after a $0.92 one-time gain). Earnings for 1996 are projected at $7.50.

Dividends were increased 20%, to $0.30 quarterly from $0.25, with the July 1995 payment.

Sales for 1995 are likely to rise significantly on increases in aluminum prices and shipments. Aluminum consumption now exceeds output, as world economic growth outweighs massive aluminum exports from Russia and gradual restarts of idled aluminum industry capacity. While RLM began to benefit from higher fabricated products prices in the last half of 1994, the positive effect should be fully realized in 1995. Despite absence of 1994's gain, earnings should advance sharply. Continued strength of global aluminum demand in 1996 would lead to further profits gains.

Net Sales (Million $)

Quarter:	1995	1994	1993	1992
Mar.	1,651	1,254	1,231	1,284
Jun.	1,864	1,455	1,356	1,490
Sep.	---	1,531	1,336	1,473
Dec.	---	1,639	1,346	1,346
	---	5,879	5,269	5,593

First-half 1995 sales jumped 30%, year to year, on higher demand for RLM's products and stronger prices. With good cost control and taxes of $83 million versus a tax credit of $6 million, net income was $193 million, in contrast to a net loss of $9 million. Share earnings were $2.64 (on 19% more shares assuming conversion of preferred stock), against a loss of $0.41 (after preferred dividends, but not assuming conversion of preferred).

Common Share Earnings ($)

Quarter:	1995	1994	1993	1992
Mar.	1.13	d0.46	d0.55	0.09
Jun.	1.51	0.05	d0.38	0.42
Sep.	E1.56	0.86	d0.47	0.21
Dec.	E1.55	0.97	d3.98	d2.55
	E5.75	1.42	d5.38	d1.83

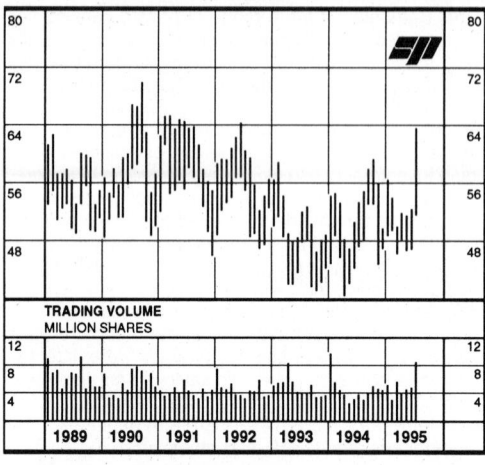

TRADING VOLUME
MILLION SHARES

1989 1990 1991 1992 1993 1994 1995

Important Developments

May '95— Capital expenditures of $85 million in the 1995 first quarter included $34 million for operating needs. The rest was for continuing performance improvement and strategic investment projects, including modernization of can manufacturing facilities; improvements at the can sheet facility in Alabama; a new wheel facility in Wisconsin; expansion of foil rolling capacity at a facility in Kentucky; and equipment upgrades. Capital spending for all of 1995 is expected to total $575 million, of which some 35% will be for operating requirements. In addition to those projects where expenditures were made in the first quarter, others include participation in the construction of foreign can plants; expansion at a plastic film plant in Virginia; and a $12 million expansion that will more than double annual capacity by early 1996 at a fabricated aluminum auto components plant in Indiana.

Next earnings report expected in late October.

Per Share Data ($)

Yr. End Dec. 31	1994	1993	1992	[1]1991	[1]1990	1989	[1]1988	1987	1986	1985
Tangible Bk. Val.	27.39	25.38	32.35	49.66	49.22	45.24	37.77	29.69	26.39	22.33
Cash Flow	6.19	d0.59	2.93	7.07	8.64	12.65	12.44	7.37	5.73	d3.17
Earnings[2]	1.42	d5.38	d1.83	2.60	5.01	[3]9.20	[3]9.01	[3]3.95	[3]2.04	d6.96
Dividends	1.000	1.200	1.800	1.800	1.800	1.700	0.900	0.575	0.500	0.500
Payout Ratio	70%	NM	NM	70%	36%	19%	10%	15%	25%	NM
Prices—High	59⅜	58⅞	64⅜	65⅜	70	62¾	58	61¾	26½	20⅝
Low	40⅜	41⅛	47	46	48½	49	34	20¼	18¼	15⅛
P/E Ratio—	42–28	NM	NM	25–18	14–10	7–5	6–4	16–5	13–9	NM

Data as orig. reptd. Adj. for stk. div. of 100% Jul. 1987. **1.** Reflects merger or acquisition. **2.** Bef. spec. items of -10.73 in 1992, +0.38 in 1987, +2.05 in 1986, +0.14 in 1985. **3.** Ful. dil.: 9.06 in 1989, 8.35 in 1988, 3.67 in 1987, 1.94 in 1986. d-Deficit. NM-Not Meaningful. E-Estimated.

Income Data (Million $)

Year Ended Dec. 31	Revs.	Oper. Inc.	% Oper. Inc. of Revs.	Cap. Exp.	Depr.	Int. Exp.	[1]Net Bef. Taxes	Eff. Tax Rate	[2]Net Inc.	% Net Inc. of Revs.	Cash Flow
1994	5,879	506	8.6	404	295	[5]156	190	36.0%	122	2.1	382
1993	5,269	254	4.8	385	287	[5]159	d515	NM	d322	NM	d35
1992	5,593	462	8.3	302	284	[5]167	d195	NM	[4]d109	NM	175
[3]1991	5,730	592	10.3	398	265	[5]161	220	30.1%	154	2.7	419
[3]1990	6,022	829	13.8	936	214	[5]96	422	29.7%	297	4.9	511
1989	6,143	1,003	16.3	555	200	122	758	29.8%	533	8.7	733
[3]1988	5,567	936	16.8	287	184	148	659	26.8%	482	8.7	666
1987	4,284	539	12.6	176	170	140	265	24.3%	201	4.7	366
1986	3,639	358	9.8	130	162	137	187	45.4%	[4]102	2.8	251
1985	3,416	239	7.0	220	165	139	d358	NM	d298	NM	d137

Balance Sheet Data (Million $)

Dec. 31	Cash	Assets	Curr. Liab.	Ratio	Total Assets	% Ret. on Assets	Long Term Debt	Common Equity	Total Cap.	% LT Debt of Cap.	% Ret. on Equity
1994	434	2,322	1,425	1.6	7,461	1.7	1,848	1,767	4,303	43.0	5.1
1993	19	1,590	1,181	1.3	6,709	NM	1,990	1,623	3,769	52.8	NM
1992	80	1,757	1,185	1.5	6,897	NM	1,798	2,060	4,024	44.7	NM
1991	67	1,780	1,016	1.8	6,685	2.3	1,854	2,960	5,219	35.5	5.2
1990	90	1,816	974	1.9	6,527	4.9	1,742	2,928	5,094	34.2	10.6
1989	71	1,763	982	1.8	5,556	9.6	1,166	2,684	4,257	27.4	21.6
1988	331	1,864	1,155	1.6	5,032	10.3	1,321	2,040	3,630	36.4	26.5
1987	110	1,452	782	1.9	4,314	4.5	1,611	1,600	3,298	48.8	12.9
1986	185	1,407	815	1.7	3,709	2.8	1,231	1,190	2,638	46.6	8.1
1985	27	1,276	855	1.5	3,647	NM	1,256	999	2,427	51.8	NM

Data as orig. reptd. 1. Incl. equity in earns. of nonconsol. subs. 2. Bef. spec. items. 3. Reflects merger or acquisition. 4. Reflects accounting change. 5. Net of int. inc. d-Deficit. NM-Not Meaningful.

Business Summary

Reynolds is a major integrated aluminum manufacturer, and produces plastic and paper products. Segments (operating income in millions) in 1994:

	Sales	Oper. Inc.
Production & processing	48%	$2
Finished products & other....	52%	255

Production of primary and reclaimed aluminum in 1994 was 792,000 and 409,000 metric tons, respectively. At year-end 1994, primary and reclaimed capacity was 998,000 and 491,000 tons, respectively.

RLM makes printed foil, paper and film laminates; specialty cartons; plastic containers and lids; printing cylinders and engravings; and foil, paper and plastic products for the foodservice market.

Consumer products include Reynolds Wrap aluminum foil, Diamond foil and plastic products, Reynolds plastic wrap, freezer paper and oven bags, Reynolds CUT-RITE wax paper and sandwich bags, Reynolds Baker's Choice bake cups, and Presto bags and wraps.

RLM operates 20 aluminum beverage can plants with an annual capacity of about 21 billion cans. It also designs and builds can-making equipment.

RLM serves the auto and truck market with cast aluminum wheels, wheel stock, door intrusion beams, bumper systems, drive shaft tubes, heat exchanger tubing, fin stock and body sheet.

A leading producer of aluminum, vinyl and composite materials for construction, RLM provides siding, windows, doors, roofing, wall panels, shutters, soffit, fascia, raincarriers, trim and gutter coil.

RLM also serves the emerging infrastructure market, which includes the construction and renovation of bridges, highways, mass transit systems and water treatment facilities around the world.

Dividend Data

Dividends have been paid since 1942. A dividend reinvestment plan is available. A "poison pill" stock purchase rights plan was adopted in 1987.

Amt. of Divd. $	Date Decl.	Ex-divd. Date	Stock of Record	Payment Date
0.25	Aug. 19	Sep. 1	Sep. 8	Oct. 3'94
0.25	Nov. 18	Nov. 25	Dec. 1	Jan. 3'95
0.25	Feb. 17	Feb. 27	Mar. 3	Apr. 3'95
0.30	May 19	May 26	Jun. 2	Jul. 3'95

Capitalization

Long Term Debt: $1,868,000,000 (6/95).

7% Pfd. Stk.: 11,000,000 shs. ($47.25 stated val.); ea. conv. into 0.82 com. to 12/31/97, when mand. conv. into one com.; red. for com. aft. 12/31/96.

Common Stock: 63,160,000 shs. (no par).
Institutions hold about 82%.
Shareholders of record: 10,439.

Office—6601 West Broad St., Richmond, VA 23261-7003. **Tel**—(804) 281-2000. **Chrmn & CEO**—R. G. Holder. **Pres**—J. J. Sheehan. **Vice Chrmn**—Y. M. Brandt, R. N. Reynolds. **EVP-CFO**—H. S. Savedge Jr. **VP-Secy**—D. M. Jones. **VP-Treas & Investor Contact**—Julian H. Taylor. **Dirs**—P. C. Barron, W. O. Bourke, Y. M. Brandt, J. R. Hall, R. L. Hintz, R. G. Holder, W. H. Joyce, M. B. Mangum, D. L. Moore, R. N. Reynolds, J. M. Ringler, H. S. Savedge Jr., J. J. Sheehan, R. J. Vlasic, J. B. Wyatt. **Transfer Agent & Registrar**—Mellon Securities Trust Co., Pittsburgh, PA. **Incorporated** in Delaware in 1928. **Empl**—29,100.

Information has been obtained from sources believed to be reliable, but its accuracy and completeness are not guaranteed. A. M. Sorrentino, CFA

Rite Aid

NYSE Symbol **RAD**
In S&P 500

31-OCT-95

Industry:
Retail Stores

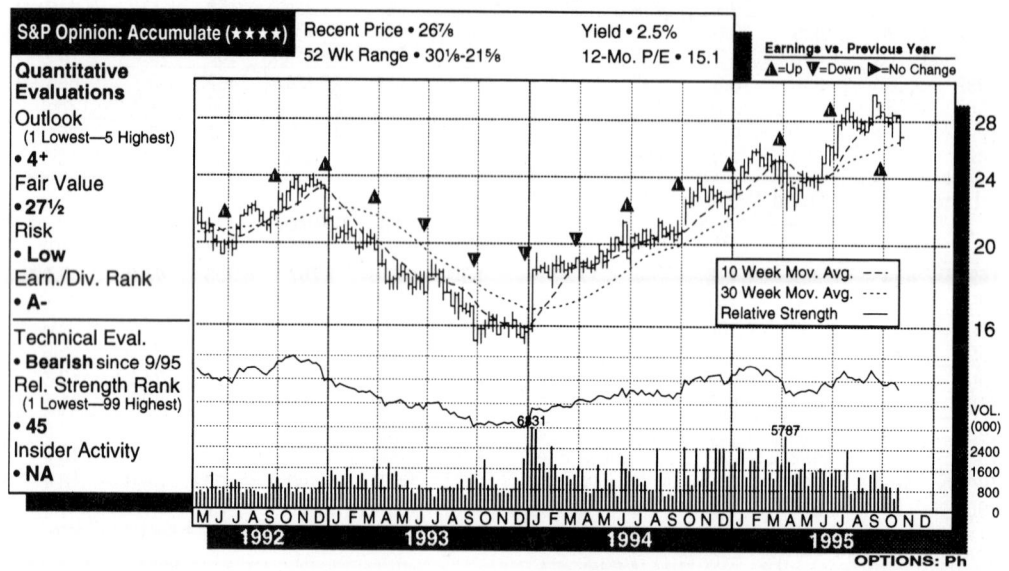

Summary: Rite Aid operates the largest chain of retail drug stores in the U.S., with over 2,700 units. The company has divested its non-drug store related businesses.

S&P Opinion: Accumulate (★★★★)

Recent Price • 26⅞	Yield • 2.5%
52 Wk Range • 30⅛-21⅞	12-Mo. P/E • 15.1

Earnings vs. Previous Year
▲=Up ▼=Down ▶=No Change

Quantitative Evaluations

Outlook
(1 Lowest—5 Highest)
• **4+**

Fair Value
• **27½**

Risk
• **Low**

Earn./Div. Rank
• **A-**

Technical Eval.
• **Bearish** since 9/95

Rel. Strength Rank
(1 Lowest—99 Highest)
• **45**

Insider Activity
• **NA**

10 Week Mov. Avg. ---
30 Week Mov. Avg. ······
Relative Strength —

VOL.
(000)

OPTIONS: Ph

Overview - 31-OCT-95

Strong sales gains are anticipated for FY 96 (Feb.), reflecting solid gains in same store sales, the addition of new stores and continued growth in prescription sales. Gross margins should widen, reflecting the increased buying power from the larger number of stores and the integration of the 224 units acquired from Perry Drug Stores, Inc. Somewhat offsetting will be cost pressures from third party payment plans. Expense ratios should begin to decline, benefiting from the closure of unprofitable units and both the elimination of labor expenses and improved efficiencies in newly acquired stores. The company is using the proceeds from the sale of its specialty retailing businesses to pay down debt, fund its aggressive capital expenditure program and repurchase shares.

Valuation - 27-OCT-95

The share price has remained in a trading range in the past few months. New and larger stores, the elimination of underperforming units and increased use of technology should boost earnings over the next few years. We anticipate earnings per share gains of 13% to 15% over the next few years and recommend the shares for accumulation. This company will be the beneficiary of the consolidation in the drug store industry through numerous acquisitions and aggressive store expansion, reaping the benefits from the economies of scale.

Key Stock Statistics

S&P EPS Est. 1996	1.90	Tang. Bk. Value/Share	8.63
P/E on S&P Est. 1996	14.1	Beta	1.06
S&P EPS Est. 1997	2.15	Shareholders	9,000
Dividend Rate/Share	0.68	Market cap. (B)	$ 2.3
Shs. outstg. (M)	83.8	Inst. holdings	87%
Avg. daily vol. (M)	0.154	Insider holdings	NA

Value of $10,000 invested 5 years ago: $ 18,897

Fiscal Year Ending Feb. 28

	1996	% Change	1995	% Change	1994	% Change
Revenues (Million $)						
1Q	1,355	29%	1,051	5%	1,000	2%
2Q	1,328	28%	1,035	6%	973.2	-1%
3Q	—	—	1,094	8%	1,009	NM
4Q	—	—	1,354	26%	1,077	-3%
Yr.	—	—	4,534	12%	4,059	NM
Income (Million $)						
1Q	38.38	13%	33.98	7%	31.64	-4%
2Q	30.91	14%	27.12	26%	21.58	-21%
3Q	—	—	26.93	30%	20.67	-22%
4Q	—	—	53.25	NM	-47.67	NM
Yr.	—	—	141.3	NM	26.21	-80%
Earnings Per Share ($)						
1Q	0.46	15%	0.40	11%	0.36	-5%
2Q	0.37	16%	0.32	28%	0.25	-19%
3Q	E0.36	13%	0.32	39%	0.23	-23%
4Q	E0.71	13%	0.63	NM	-0.54	NM
Yr.	E1.90	14%	1.67	NM	0.30	-80%

Next earnings report expected: mid December

Business Summary - 31-OCT-95

Rite Aid operates the largest chain of drug stores in the U.S., comprising 2,829 stores in 23 eastern states and the District of Columbia at March 4, 1995. Pharmacy volume accounted for 53.1% of FY 95 (Feb.) drug store revenues. Third party transactions accounted for some 58% of pharmacy sales. Private label products generated some 15% of nonprescription volume.

The company introduced a new 10,000 square foot store design, about 25% larger than the previous store prototype. These stores have expanded merchandise assortments to include convenience foods and a full line of cosmetic and fragrance sections. Rite-Aid has added one hour photo processing labs and at year-end operated 166 of these departments. The company sells about 1,200 private label products.

The company also operates Eagle Managed Care Corp., a subsidiary that markets prescription plans and sells other managed care health services to large employers and government sponsored employee benefit programs. Eagle accounted for $125 million in prescription revenues at Rite Aid stores.

As part of a restructuring plan announced January 4, 1994, the company sold its specialty operations, bought back stock, and closed 200 underperforming drug stores and write off other assets. As a result, the company recorded a pretax charge of $149 million ($1.03 a share) in the fourth quarter of FY 94. The assets sold include 96 ADAP and Auto Palace automotive parts stores, the Encore deep discount book chain with 98 units, Concord Custom Cleaners, operating 168 dry cleaning outlets in 11 southeastern and midwestern states, and Sera-Tec, which has 33 specialized plasma collection centers.

On February 16, 1994, directors announced a share buyback program of up to 5 million common shares. During FY 95, the company repurchased 1,847,798 common shares.

Important Developments

Sep. '95—Same store sales increased 6.8% in the second quarter of FY 96 (Feb.). During the second quarter, the company added 51 drug stores, including 30 locations acquired from Pathmark in August, and closed or sold 183 stores. RAD also sold its nursing home pharmacy business. The proceeds of $85.3 million from the sales will be used to offset future lease obligations. The company relocated or expanded 42 stores into the new, larger prototype. At the end of the quarter, the company operated 2,704 drug stores. RAD plans to develop 300 new prototype stores each year for the next three years. During the past six months, the company has opened 117 of these large 10,000 sq. ft. stores and plans to open 205 in the second half of FY 96.

Capitalization

Long Term Debt: $967,808,000 (9/2/95).

Per Share Data ($)

(Year Ended Feb. 28)

	1995	1994	1993	1992	1991	1990
Tangible Bk. Val.	9.00	9.63	10.11	9.16	7.42	6.57
Cash Flow	2.64	1.17	2.40	2.29	2.41	1.82
Earnings	1.67	0.30	1.51	1.43	1.30	0.99
Dividends	0.62	0.60	0.56	0.51	0.46	0.42
Payout Ratio	37%	200%	37%	36%	36%	43%
Cal. Yrs.	1994	1993	1992	1991	1990	1989
Prices - High	24	21½	24⅛	23⅞	19⅜	20⅝
- Low	15¾	15¼	19¼	17¼	14¾	14¾
P/E Ratio - High	14	72	16	17	15	21
- Low	9	51	13	12	11	15

Income Statement Analysis (Million $)

	1995	%Chg	1994	%Chg	1993	%Chg	1992
Revs.	4,534	12%	4,059	NM	4,085	9%	3,748
Oper. Inc.	357	19%	300	-8%	326	3%	318
Depr.	82.7	8%	76.3	-2%	78.2	4%	75.2
Int. Exp.	42.3	47%	28.7	-13%	32.9	-19%	40.8
Pretax Inc.	231	NM	46.0	-79%	215	6%	202
Eff. Tax Rate	39%	—	43%	—	38%	—	39%
Net Inc.	141	NM	26.0	-80%	132	6%	124

Balance Sheet & Other Fin. Data (Million $)

	1995	1994	1993	1992	1991	1990
Cash	7.1	17.4	5.4	27.4	25.9	14.5
Curr. Assets	1,373	1,125	1,092	1,013	945	849
Total Assets	2,473	1,989	1,875	1,734	1,667	1,539
Curr. Liab.	577	362	281	290	237	216
LT Debt	806	613	489	428	585	542
Common Eqty.	1,012	955	1,036	951	774	704
Total Cap.	1,895	1,627	1,595	1,445	1,430	1,323
Cap. Exp.	183	169	125	88.0	157	177
Cash Flow	224	103	211	199	201	151

Ratio Analysis

	1995	1994	1993	1992	1991	1990
Curr. Ratio	2.4	3.1	3.9	3.5	4.0	3.9
% LT Debt of Cap.	42.5	37.7	30.7	29.6	40.9	41.0
% Net Inc.of Revs.	3.1	0.6	3.2	3.3	3.1	2.6
% Ret. on Assets	6.4	1.4	7.3	7.1	6.7	5.5
% Ret. on Equity	14.5	2.7	13.3	14.0	14.5	12.2

Dividend Data

Dividends have been paid since 1968. A dividend reinvestment plan is available. A "poison pill" stock purchase right was issued in 1989.

Amt. of Div. $	Date Decl.	Ex-Div. Date	Stock of Record	Payment Date
0.170	Jan. 05	Jan. 09	Jan. 16	Feb. 23 '95
0.170	Apr. 05	Apr. 18	Apr. 24	May. 01 '95
0.170	Jul. 11	Jul. 20	Jul. 24	Jul. 31 '95
0.170	Oct. 10	Oct. 19	Oct. 23	Oct. 30 '95

Data as orig. reptd.; bef. results of disc. opers. and/or spec. items. Per share data adj. for stk. divs. as of ex-div. date. E-Estimated. NA-Not Available. NM-Not Meaningful. NR-Not Ranked.

Office—30 Hunter Lane, Camp Hill, PA 17011 (P.O. Box 3165, Harrisburg, PA 17105). **Tel**—(717) 761-2633. **Chrmn & CEO**—M. L. Grass. **Pres & COO**—T. J. Noonan. **VP-Secy**—W. M. Knievel. **EVP, CFO & Investor Contact**—Frank Bergonzi. **Dirs**—F. C. Brown, A. Grass, M. L. Grass, P. Neivert, T. J. Noonan, L. N. Stern, H. Taub, P. R. Tisch, G. Tsai Jr. **Transfer Agent & Registrar**—Harris Trust Co. of New York, NYC. **Incorporated** in Delaware in 1968. **Empl**-36,700. **S&P Analyst:** Karen J. Sack, CFA

Roadway Services

NASDAQ Symbol **ROAD**
In S&P 500

31-JUL-95
Industry: Trucking

Summary: This company provides a broad range of transportation services, including national and regional general freight trucking, package delivery and air freight services.

S&P Opinion: Avoid (★★)

| Recent Price • 50¼ | Yield • 2.8% |
| 52 Wk Range • 64½-42 | 12-Mo. P/E • 67.0 |

Quantitative Evaluations

Outlook
(1 Lowest—5 Highest)
• **1⁻**

Fair Value
• **40⅝**

Risk
• **Low**

Earn./Div. Rank
• **A-**

Technical Eval.
• **Bullish** since 4/95

Rel. Strength Rank
(1 Lowest—99 Highest)
• **53**

Insider Activity
• **Unfavorable**

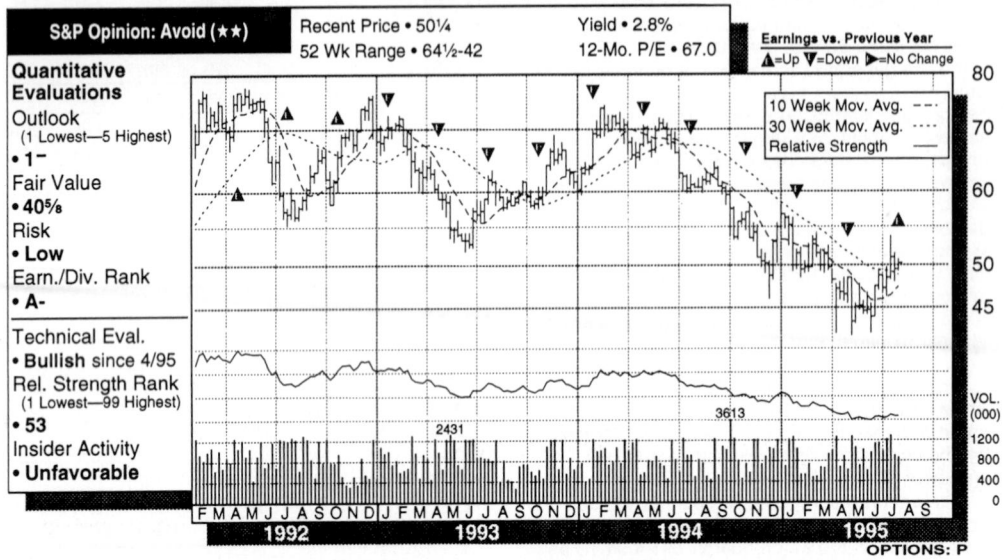

Earnings vs. Previous Year
▲=Up ▼=Down ▶=No Change

10 Week Mov. Avg. ---
30 Week Mov. Avg. ·····
Relative Strength —

OPTIONS: P

Overview - 31-JUL-95

Profits for Roadway Express in 1995 are expected to make a limited recovery from last year's depressed levels, which were hurt by losses incurred during the Teamsters' strike, a charge to realign its terminal network and employee relocation costs. Margins will remain under pressure as a lull in the economy contributed to a rate war during 1995's first half. ROAD's regional carriers may post a flat year as strong operating gains are offset by costs to develop new information technologies and costs to consolidate Spartan Express' two operating divisions. Roadway Package Service should post higher profits, reflecting territorial expansion and higher rates. The deregulation of intrastate trucking should help RPS target overnight ground delivery business. Losses at Roadway Global Air will be comparable to 1994's level, despite a solid revenue gain.

Valuation - 31-JUL-95

The shares of this multi-modal transportation have been attempting to build a base after undergoing a major price adjustment since 1994. Roadway's entry into air freight is seen depressing profits in 1995 by $1.50 a share, with no prospects for earnings at this unit until 1998. The heavy capital requirements for its fledgling air cargo unit and other businesses has forced ROAD to borrow money for the first time in 25 years. While ROAD's management is steering the firm in the right direction, we would avoid the shares, which at current prices, have discounted a stronger recovery than we think can be delivered.

Key Stock Statistics

S&P EPS Est. 1995	1.75	Tang. Bk. Value/Share	22.75
P/E on S&P Est. 1995	28.7	Beta	1.00
S&P EPS Est. 1996	3.40	Shareholders	7,300
Dividend Rate/Share	1.40	Market cap. (B)	$ 2.0
Shs. outstg. (M)	39.1	Inst. holdings	45%
Avg. daily vol. (M)	0.274	Insider holdings	NA

Value of $10,000 invested 5 years ago: $ 13,573

Fiscal Year Ending Dec. 31

	1995	% Change	1994	% Change	1993	% Change
Revenues (Million $)						
1Q	1,087	6%	1,024	20%	856.0	7%
2Q	1,097	18%	930.2	NM	939.3	17%
3Q	—	—	1,092	11%	983.9	18%
4Q	—	—	1,527	11%	1,377	21%
Yr.	—	—	4,572	10%	4,156	16%
Income (Million $)						
1Q	5.85	-63%	15.91	-21%	20.26	-34%
2Q	-2.00	NM	-21.73	NM	27.32	-16%
3Q	—	—	11.65	-60%	29.04	-12%
4Q	—	—	13.73	-68%	42.71	-17%
Yr.	—	—	19.56	-84%	119.3	-19%
Earnings Per Share ($)						
1Q	0.15	-63%	0.40	-22%	0.51	-35%
2Q	-0.05	NM	-0.55	NM	0.69	-16%
3Q	E0.70	—	0.30	-59%	0.74	-11%
4Q	E0.95	—	0.35	-68%	1.08	-17%
Yr.	E1.75	—	0.50	-83%	3.02	-19%

Next earnings report expected: late September

Business Summary - 31-JUL-95

Roadway Services is a transportation holding company with subsidiaries providing long-haul less-than-truckload (LTL) service, regional LTL carriage, domestic and international air freight, small-package and expedited-delivery services and custom logistics services.

Roadway Express is the nation's third largest general freight motor carrier. It specializes in long-haul LTL shipments and offers direct service to all 50 states, Canada and parts of Mexico. Indirect service also is provided to South America, Europe, Asia and Australia. Roadway, which operates through a network of 577 terminals, handled 7,037,000 tons of freight in 1994, compared with 7,860,000 tons in 1993.

Roadway Regional Group provides short-haul LTL freight services through four carriers. Viking Freight System operates 48 terminals in eight western states; Spartan Express, operating through two divisions, operates 74 terminals in 17 central and southern states; Coles Express serves 11 New England and Middle Atlantic states through 25 terminals and Central Freight Lines operates through 85 terminals in eight Southwestern and Midwestern states.

Roadway Package System (RPS) specializes in the transport of shipments weighing under 150 lbs. focusing on the business-to-business segment. RPS, which provides service to 96% of the U.S. population and also to 86% of the Canadian market through a network of 317 terminals.

Roadway Global Air provides air cargo service in North America, Europe, Asia and Australia through a network of 77 air logistics centers plus 154 agents.

Other operations include Roberts Express, which provides expedited delivery for time-sensitive freight, and Roadway Logistics Systems, which provides custom logistics services, including transportation, routing, scheduling and warehousing.

Important Developments

Jul. '95—ROAD reported that 1995 second quarter net income was reduced by $0.03 a share, reflecting costs to consolidate Spartan Express' southern and central divisions. In an unrelated development, profits for 1994's fourth quarter were reduced by $0.35 a share to reflect the settlement of a tax dispute concerning the tax status of independent contractors at Roadway Package System.

Apr. '95—Roadway Global Air (RGA) entered an agreement with American International Freight (AIF) whereby RGA would share a portion of its Indiana sortation hub with AIF and in return AIF would make space available to RGA on its aircraft.

Capitalization

Long Term Debt: None (3/95).

Per Share Data ($) (Year Ended Dec. 31)

	1994	1993	1992	1991	1990	1989
Tangible Bk. Val.	23.30	24.04	23.51	20.51	17.85	16.02
Cash Flow	5.86	8.08	8.10	7.31	6.94	6.03
Earnings	0.50	3.02	3.73	3.27	3.05	2.44
Dividends	1.40	1.35	1.25	1.15	1.10	1.10
Payout Ratio	NM	45%	34%	35%	36%	45%
Prices - High	74¼	72½	77¾	61¾	43	43¼
- Low	46	51¾	55¼	38	27¼	27¾
P/E Ratio - High	NM	24	21	19	14	18
- Low	NM	17	15	12	9	11

Income Statement Analysis (Million $)

	1994	%Chg	1993	%Chg	1992	%Chg	1991
Revs.	4,572	10%	4,156	16%	3,578	13%	3,177
Oper. Inc.	262	-35%	403	-2%	410	14%	360
Depr.	211	6%	200	16%	173	10%	157
Int. Exp.	NA	—	NA	—	Nil	—	Nil
Pretax Inc.	52.0	-76%	214	-14%	250	17%	214
Eff. Tax Rate	63%	—	44%	—	41%	—	40%
Net Inc.	20.0	-83%	119	-19%	147	16%	127

Balance Sheet & Other Fin. Data (Million $)

	1994	1993	1992	1991	1990	1989
Cash	37.0	112	316	227	145	150
Curr. Assets	643	619	677	550	442	417
Total Assets	1,949	1,846	1,660	1,489	1,341	1,273
Curr. Liab.	697	578	495	454	419	401
LT Debt	Nil	Nil	Nil	Nil	Nil	Nil
Common Eqty.	1,015	1,047	1,021	890	778	718
Total Cap.	1,059	1,105	1,062	940	831	793
Cap. Exp.	300	310	211	203	201	198
Cash Flow	231	319	320	284	271	236

Ratio Analysis

	1994	1993	1992	1991	1990	1989
Curr. Ratio	0.9	1.1	1.4	1.2	1.1	1.0
% LT Debt of Cap.	Nil	Nil	Nil	Nil	Nil	Nil
% Net Inc.of Revs.	0.4	2.9	4.1	4.0	4.0	3.6
% Ret. on Assets	1.0	6.8	9.3	8.9	9.2	7.8
% Ret. on Equity	1.9	11.6	15.3	15.2	16.0	13.8

Dividend Data (Cash has been paid each year since 1956. A dividend reinvestment plan is available.)

Amt. of Div. $	Date Decl.	Ex-Div. Date	Stock of Record	Payment Date
0.350	Aug. 12	Oct. 07	Oct. 14	Nov. 01 '94
0.350	Nov. 11	Jan. 09	Jan. 13	Feb. 01 '95
0.350	Feb. 08	Apr. 07	Apr. 14	May. 01 '95
0.350	May. 10	Jul. 12	Jul. 14	Aug. 01 '95

Data as orig. reptd.; bef. results of disc. opers. and/or spec. items. Per share data adj. for stk. divs. as of ex-div. date. E-Estimated. NA-Not Available. NM-Not Meaningful. NR-Not Ranked.

Office—1077 Gorge Blvd., P.O. Box 88, Akron, OH 44309-0088. **Tel**—(216) 384-8184. **Chrmn & CEO**—J. M. Clapp. **Pres**—D. J. Sullivan. **VP-Treas**—J. P. Chandler. **SVP-Fin & Secy**—D. A. Wilson. **Dirs**—G. B. Beitzel, R. A. Chenoweth, J. M. Clapp, N. C. Harbert, C. R. Longsworth, R. E. Mercer, G. J. Roush, D. J. Sullivan, W. Sword, H. M. Watson Jr., S. R. Werner. **Transfer Agent & Registrar**—KeyCorp Shareholder Services, Cleveland. **Incorporated** in Delaware in 1954. **Empl**-50,600. **S&P Analyst:** Stephen R. Klein

Rockwell International

NYSE Symbol **ROK**
In S&P 500

31-JUL-95 | Industry: Aerospace

Summary: Rockwell is a leading producer of space systems, including the Space Shuttle, makes military and commercial electronics products and produces automotive and graphics systems.

S&P Opinion: Accumulate (★★★★)

| Recent Price • 45¾ | Yield • 2.4% |
| 52 Wk Range • 48-33½ | 12-Mo. P/E • 13.9 |

Quantitative Evaluations

Outlook
(1 Lowest—5 Highest)
• 3

Fair Value
• 44

Risk
• Low

Earn./Div. Rank
• A-

Technical Eval.
• **Neutral** since 7/95

Rel. Strength Rank
(1 Lowest—99 Highest)
• 40

Insider Activity
• **Neutral**

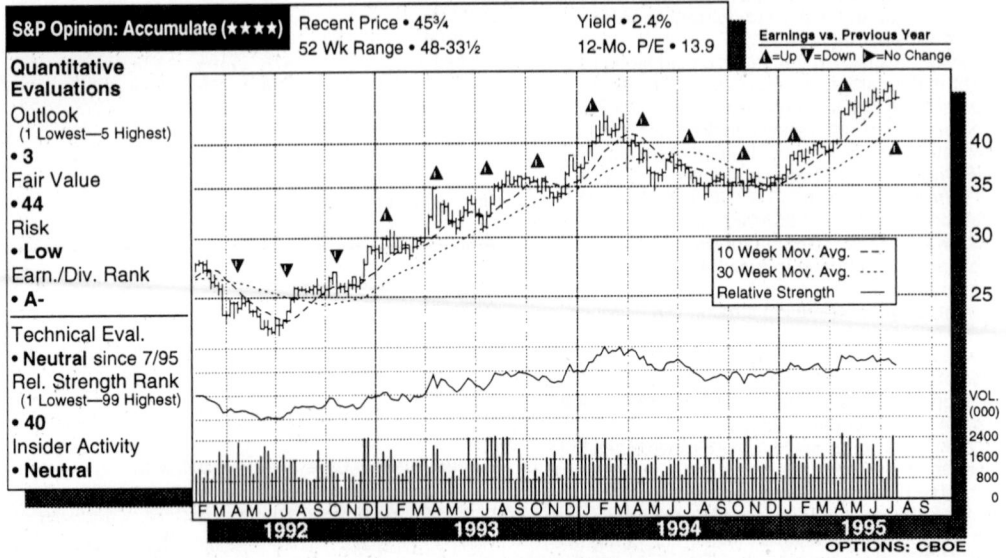

Earnings vs. Previous Year
▲=Up ▼=Down ►=No Change

10 Week Mov. Avg. — —
30 Week Mov. Avg. ·····
Relative Strength —

VOL. (000)
2400
1600
800
0

1992 1993 1994 1995

OPTIONS: CBOE

Overview - 31-JUL-95

Revenues for fiscal 1996 are projected to increase robustly from those estimated for 1995, largely reflecting the inclusion of Reliance Electric. The electronics division should also benefit from roughly 20% growth in the telecommunications business. Excluding acquisitions, revenues from aerospace, automotive and graphics are forecast to be about unchanged from 1995 levels, reflecting reduced spending by NASA, a weaker automotive market, and competitive pressures in the graphics business. Overall company margins should widen, reflecting improvement in telecommunications, defense electronics, light vehicles, and aerospace operations. Increased debt associated with recent acquisitions and greater capital expenditures will result in higher interest charges.

Valuation - 31-JUL-95

ROK shares are up substantially since late 1994, well ahead of the strong stock market. The company has been reducing its dependence on the shrinking defense market and aggressively expanding into commercial and international markets. Furthermore, recent acquisitions, such as Reliance Electric, have augmented that shift. With Rockwell participating in many high-growth commercial markets and developing products based on emerging technologies, this trend is expected to continue. Strong long-term earnings expansion is forecast to follow the top line growth. Consequently, at current levels of about 12 times estimated fiscal 1996 earnings, we view ROK shares as attractive for long term value.

Key Stock Statistics

S&P EPS Est. 1995	3.40	Tang. Bk. Value/Share	6.93
P/E on S&P Est. 1995	13.5	Beta	0.63
S&P EPS Est. 1996	3.75	Shareholders	132,000
Dividend Rate/Share	1.08	Market cap. (B)	$ 9.9
Shs. outstg. (M)	216.6	Inst. holdings	37%
Avg. daily vol. (M)	0.303	Insider holdings	NA

Value of $10,000 invested 5 years ago: $ 22,698

Fiscal Year Ending Sep. 30

	1995	% Change	1994	% Change	1993	% Change
Revenues (Million $)						
1Q	2,623	NM	2,601	4%	2,489	-3%
2Q	3,361	22%	2,762	3%	2,694	-2%
3Q	3,452	20%	2,873	2%	2,813	4%
4Q	—	—	2,889	2%	2,844	-2%
Yr.	—	—	11,123	3%	10,840	NM
Income (Million $)						
1Q	164.7	10%	149.5	17%	127.8	4%
2Q	191.4	24%	154.7	13%	136.9	38%
3Q	197.0	19%	164.9	12%	147.2	20%
4Q	—	—	165.0	10%	150.0	9%
Yr.	—	—	634.1	13%	561.9	16%
Earnings Per Share ($)						
1Q	0.76	12%	0.68	17%	0.58	7%
2Q	0.88	26%	0.70	11%	0.63	40%
3Q	0.90	22%	0.74	12%	0.66	20%
4Q	E0.86	—	0.75	10%	0.68	10%
Yr.	E3.40	—	2.87	13%	2.55	18%

Next earnings report expected: early November

Rockwell International

Business Summary - 21-JUL-95

Rockwell International is a diversified company serving commercial and aerospace markets. Business segment contributions in fiscal 1994 were:

	Sales	Profits
Electronics	45%	56%
Aerospace	24%	30%
Automotive	25%	11%
Graphics	6%	3%

Foreign operations provided 35% of sales in fiscal 1994. Sales to the U.S. government (DOD and NASA) accounted for 35% of the total.

Through Allen-Bradley, the company is a leader in plant floor automation. Products include programmable controllers, sensing devices and communications networks. The electronics division also manufactures products for avionics, telecommunications and defense.

The company is a prime contractor for the Space Shuttle orbiter and their main engines, and is involved in the power system for the space station. It also provides parts and service for the B-1B bomber and several Boeing jets.

Automotive components sold for heavy- and medium-duty trucks, buses and heavy-duty off-highway vehicles includes axles, brakes and braking systems, transmissions, clutches and driveline components. Light-vehicle products include sunroofs, doors, access control systems, steel wheels, suspension systems and auto electronics.

The Graphics Group manufactures high-speed printing presses for newspaper and commercial printing. Three out of four U.S. daily newspapers are printed on Rockwell presses.

Important Developments

Jul. '95—Rockwell agreed to acquire the wafer fabrication facilty of United Technologies, which should add $50 million in annual revenues. Separately, the company announced plans to invest $200 million to expand its own semiconductor manufacturing capacity.
Jun. '95—ROK acquired the Aerostructure Components and Defense businesses of AeroSpace Technologies of Australia (ASTA) Limited. In April, Rockwell purchased the automotive window regulator business of Dura Automotive Systems Inc. In January, the company acquired Reliance Electric Co., a maker of industrial automation equipment, with 1993 sales of $1.6 billion. Reliance's telecommunications operations are under agreement to be resold for $475 million.

Capitalization

Long Term Debt: $1,778,000,000 (6/95).
Conv. Preferred Stock: $1,400,000.
Class A Common Stock: 34,928,078 shs. ($1 par); 10 votes per sh.; limited transferability; conv. sh.-for-sh. into com. Employees own 41%.
Shareholders of Record: 57,750 (11/94).

Per Share Data ($) (Year Ended Sep. 30)

	1994	1993	1992	1991	1990	1989
Tangible Bk. Val.	11.77	9.69	8.80	13.98	12.58	11.50
Cash Flow	5.11	4.79	4.65	5.14	5.10	5.28
Earnings	2.87	2.55	2.16	2.57	2.56	2.87
Dividends	1.02	0.96	0.92	0.86	0.80	0.75
Payout Ratio	36%	38%	43%	33%	31%	26%
Prices - High	$44\frac{1}{8}$	$38\frac{1}{2}$	$29\frac{3}{8}$	$29\frac{1}{4}$	$28\frac{3}{4}$	$27\frac{1}{8}$
- Low	$33\frac{1}{2}$	$27\frac{7}{8}$	$22\frac{1}{4}$	$22\frac{3}{4}$	$20\frac{1}{2}$	$19\frac{3}{4}$
P/E Ratio - High	15	15	13	11	11	9
- Low	12	11	10	9	8	7

Income Statement Analysis (Million $)

	1994	%Chg	1993	%Chg	1992	%Chg	1991
Revs.	11,123	3%	10,840	NM	10,910	-9%	11,927
Oper. Inc.	1,530	8%	1,418	7%	1,327	-17%	1,600
Depr.	494	NM	491	-12%	558	-7%	601
Int. Exp.	97.0	-7%	104	-3%	107	-21%	135
Pretax Inc.	1,021	13%	904	16%	778	-24%	1,024
Eff. Tax Rate	38%	—	38%	—	38%	—	41%
Net Inc.	634	13%	562	16%	483	-20%	601

Balance Sheet & Other Fin. Data (Million $)

	1994	1993	1992	1991	1990	1989
Cash	628	773	603	504	411	332
Curr. Assets	4,928	4,946	4,889	4,823	4,775	4,367
Total Assets	9,861	9,885	9,731	9,479	9,738	8,939
Curr. Liab.	3,020	2,991	3,112	3,322	3,843	3,482
LT Debt	831	1,028	1,035	740	553	552
Common Eqty.	3,350	2,950	2,771	4,216	4,177	3,968
Total Cap.	4,187	3,984	3,813	5,662	5,422	5,187
Cap. Exp.	568	433	386	484	538	609
Cash Flow	1,128	1,053	1,041	1,202	1,244	1,349

Ratio Analysis

	1994	1993	1992	1991	1990	1989
Curr. Ratio	1.6	1.7	1.6	1.5	1.2	1.3
% LT Debt of Cap.	19.8	25.8	27.2	13.1	10.2	10.6
% Net Inc.of Revs.	5.7	5.2	4.4	5.0	5.0	5.9
% Ret. on Assets	6.5	5.7	5.1	6.4	6.8	8.3
% Ret. on Equity	20.2	19.6	14.1	14.6	15.7	19.6

Dividend Data (Dividends have been paid since 1948. A dividend reinvestment plan is available.)

Amt. of Div. $	Date Decl.	Ex-Div. Date	Stock of Record	Payment Date
0.270	Nov. 02	Nov. 07	Nov. 14	Dec. 05 '94
0.270	Feb. 01	Feb. 07	Feb. 13	Mar. 06 '95
0.270	May. 03	May. 09	May. 15	Jun. 05 '95
0.270	Jul. 10	Aug. 10	Aug. 14	Sep. 11 '95

Data as orig. reptd.; bef. results of disc. opers. and/or spec. items. Per share data adj. for stk. divs. as of ex-div. date. E-Estimated. NA-Not Available. NM-Not Meaningful. NR-Not Ranked.

Office—2201 Seal Beach Boulevard (PO Box 4250), Seal Beach, CA 90740-8250. **Tel**—(310) 797-3311. **Chrmn & CEO**—D. R. Beall. **COO**—K. M. Black, D. H. Davis, Jr. **SVP-Fin & CFO**—W. M. Barnes. **SVP & Secy**—W. J. Calise, Jr. **VP & Treas**—L. H. Cramer. **Investor Contact**—Tom J. Joyce (412-565-7436). **Dirs**—L. Allen, Jr., D. R. Beall, R. M. Bressler, J. J. Creedon, D. H. Davis Jr., R. C. Duke, J. L. Estrin, W. H. Gray III, J. C. LaForce, Jr., W. T. McCormick, Jr., J. D. Nichols, B. M. Rockwell, W. S. Sneath, J. F. Toot, Jr. **New York Transfer Agent & Registrar**—Mellon Bank, Pittsburgh and NYC. **Incorporated** in Delaware in 1928. **Empl**-71,891. **S&P Analyst:** Joe Victor Shammas

Rohm & Haas

NYSE Symbol **ROH**
In S&P 500

26-JUL-95 | **Industry:** Chemicals | **Summary:** This company is an important producer of chemicals, plastics, pesticides and related products.

| S&P Opinion: Hold (★★★) | Recent Price • 57 | Yield • 2.9% |
| | 52 Wk Range • 68½-49½ | 12-Mo. P/E • 14.8 |

Earnings vs. Previous Year
▲=Up ▼=Down ▶=No Change

Quantitative Evaluations

Outlook
(1 Lowest—5 Highest)
• **4−**

Fair Value
• **58**

Risk
• **Low**

Earn./Div. Rank
• **B+**

Technical Eval.
• **Bearish** since 5/95

Rel. Strength Rank
(1 Lowest—99 Highest)
• **38**

Insider Activity
• **Unfavorable**

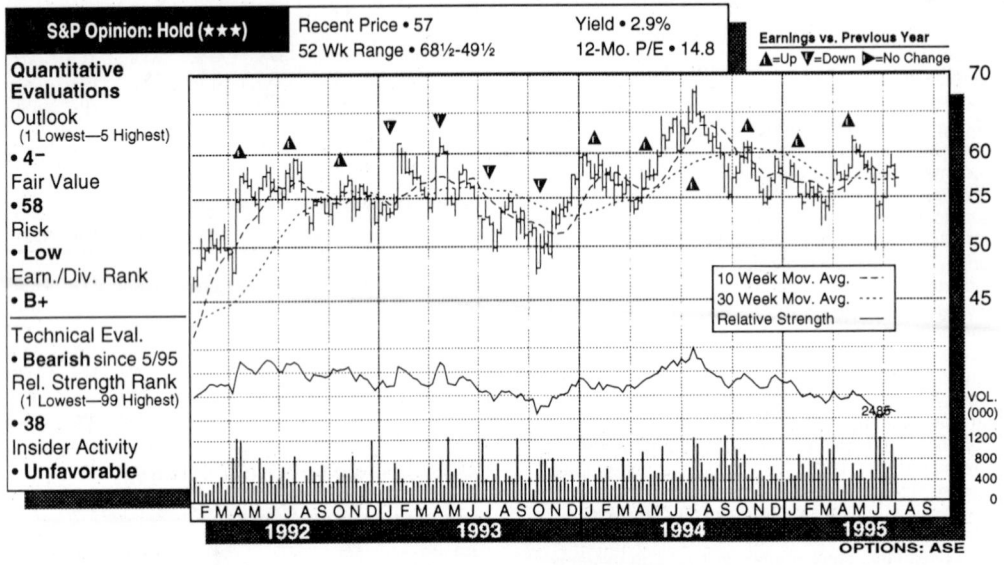

10 Week Mov. Avg. ---
30 Week Mov. Avg. ····
Relative Strength —

OPTIONS: ASE

Overview - 25-JUL-95

We are projecting that sales of this major producer of chemicals and plastics products will rise about 10% in 1995, reflecting growth in its European and Asian markets for the polymers, plastics and specialty chemicals segments. Currency exchange rates are anticipated to be positive. North American markets may show only modest growth due to the slowdown in economic activity since the first quarter. New capacity for acrylic acid monomer started up in June, relieving tight supplies of this material. Rising selling prices are expected to largely offset the adverse impact of higher raw material costs. Profits will also benefit from aggressive cost reductions designed to keep overhead costs flat. Capital spending is projected at about $400 million in 1995.

Valuation - 25-JUL-95

We recommend holding the shares of this major chemicals producer which are selling at about 14 times our EPS estimate for 1995. The shares declined in mid-July after ROH reported lower than expected second quarter earnings due to the slowdown in the U.S. business and as well as higher manufacturing costs. We believe that the company will benefit from the pick-up in economic activity which we expect to begin late in 1995. The recent completion of new acrylic acid manufacturing capacity will relieve supply shortages for this key product and also bodes well for the company's longer term prospects. Dividends have been raised for 17 consecutive years.

Key Stock Statistics

S&P EPS Est. 1995	4.10	Tang. Bk. Value/Share	19.69
P/E on S&P Est. 1995	13.9	Beta	1.26
S&P EPS Est. 1996	5.00	Shareholders	4,900
Dividend Rate/Share	1.64	Market cap. (B)	$ 3.9
Shs. outstg. (M)	67.7	Inst. holdings	73%
Avg. daily vol. (M)	0.167	Insider holdings	NA

Value of $10,000 invested 5 years ago: $ 18,991

Fiscal Year Ending Dec. 31

	1995	% Change	1994	% Change	1993	% Change
Revenues (Million $)						
1Q	985.0	15%	856.0	4%	826.0	16%
2Q	1,042	10%	944.0	7%	884.0	13%
3Q	—	—	874.0	9%	799.0	-1%
4Q	—	—	860.0	13%	760.0	NM
Yr.	—	—	3,534	8%	3,269	7%
Income (Million $)						
1Q	79.00	18%	67.00	14%	59.00	4%
2Q	87.00	-8%	95.00	51%	63.00	-15%
3Q	—	—	55.00	NM	-21.00	NM
4Q	—	—	47.00	81%	26.00	NM
Yr.	—	—	264.0	110%	126.0	-28%
Earnings Per Share ($)						
1Q	1.14	19%	0.96	14%	0.84	-2%
2Q	1.26	-8%	1.37	52%	0.90	-20%
3Q	E0.85	—	0.78	NM	-0.34	NM
4Q	E0.85	—	0.68	94%	0.35	NM
Yr.	E4.10	—	3.79	118%	1.74	-31%

Next earnings report expected: mid October

Business Summary - 18-JUL-95

Rohm and Haas is a diversified producer of chemicals and allied products. Contributions in 1994:

	Sales	Income
Polymers, resins & monomers	47%	55%
Plastics	18%	19%
Performance chemicals	23%	13%
Agricultural chemicals	12%	13%

International operations accounted for 44% of sales and 42% of income in 1994.

Polymers, resins and monomers (including opaque polymers, emulsions, modifiers, water-soluble polymers and acrylate and methacrylate monomers) are produced for paints, coatings, inks, textile and paper coatings, detergents, adhesives, sealants, water treatment, nonwoven materials, construction products and leather products.

The plastics group consists of additives, impact modifiers and processing aids for plastics; Plexiglas acrylic resins, plastic sheeting and molding powders; and polycarbonate sheeting.

Performance chemicals include biocides for industrial, household cleaning and personal care products; ion exchange and fluid process chemicals for water treatment and food and chemical processing; additives for petroleum products and lubricants; and electronic chemicals and encapsulating materials for printed wiring boards and semiconductors.

Agricultural chemicals include fungicides, herbicides, insecticides and spray adjuvants, primarily for specialty crops and fruits and vegetables.

Important Developments

Jul. '95—ROH said that lower second quarter earnings reflected a slowdown in the U.S. economy, higher manufacturing costs and costs associated with monomer production problems. North American volumes fell 9% and raw material costs were 30% higher than in the 1994 second quarter. ROH accelerated plans to bring on-stream a new 220 million pound acrylic acid expansion in late June. Combined European and Pacific regions sales were up 23% on a 10% volume increase.
Apr. '95—ROH announced plans to increase its annual worldwide emulsion capacity by 730 million pounds (30%) by the end of 1997. The increase includes the construction of three new plants and capacity expansions at five other sites at a total cost of about $100 million. Separately, first quarter 1995 earnings included a charge of $0.25 a share for remediation clean-up costs.

Capitalization

Long Term Debt: $647,000,000 (3/95).
$2.75 Cum. Preferred Stock: 2,671,722 shs.

Per Share Data ($) (Year Ended Dec. 31)

	1994	1993	1992	1991	1990	1989
Tangible Bk. Val.	20.11	17.37	16.93	18.72	17.26	18.84
Cash Flow	7.21	5.09	5.62	5.30	5.49	4.90
Earnings	3.79	1.74	2.53	2.45	3.10	2.65
Dividends	1.44	1.36	1.28	1.24	1.22	1.16
Payout Ratio	38%	78%	51%	51%	39%	44%
Prices - High	68½	62	59⅝	48½	37	37½
- Low	53¼	47¼	42¾	32¾	24¼	28¾
P/E Ratio - High	18	36	24	20	12	14
- Low	14	27	17	13	8	12

Income Statement Analysis (Million $)

	1994	%Chg	1993	%Chg	1992	%Chg	1991
Revs.	3,545	8%	3,278	7%	3,072	11%	2,773
Oper. Inc.	717	28%	560	-2%	569	29%	442
Depr.	231	2%	226	11%	203	11%	183
Int. Exp.	60.0	NM	60.0	-44%	107	67%	64.0
Pretax Inc.	407	110%	194	-26%	261	9%	240
Eff. Tax Rate	35%	—	35%	—	33%	—	32%
Net Inc.	264	110%	126	-28%	174	7%	163

Balance Sheet & Other Fin. Data (Million $)

	1994	1993	1992	1991	1990	1989
Cash	127	35.0	91.0	208	65.0	150
Curr. Assets	1,440	1,200	1,257	1,141	1,009	1,011
Total Assets	3,861	3,524	3,445	2,897	2,702	2,455
Curr. Liab.	932	701	713	535	585	577
LT Debt	629	690	699	718	598	359
Common Eqty.	1,486	1,305	1,292	1,231	1,233	1,311
Total Cap.	2,402	2,289	2,274	2,224	1,991	1,670
Cap. Exp.	339	382	283	265	412	385
Cash Flow	488	344	373	340	366	326

Ratio Analysis

	1994	1993	1992	1991	1990	1989
Curr. Ratio	1.5	1.7	1.8	2.1	1.7	1.8
% LT Debt of Cap.	26.2	30.1	30.7	32.3	30.0	21.5
% Net Inc.of Revs.	7.4	3.8	5.7	5.9	7.3	6.6
% Ret. on Assets	7.1	3.6	5.4	5.8	8.0	7.5
% Ret. on Equity	18.4	9.1	13.1	13.2	16.3	14.0

Dividend Data (Dividends have been paid since 1927.)

Amt. of Div. $	Date Decl.	Ex-Div. Date	Stock of Record	Payment Date
0.370	Jul. 25	Aug. 01	Aug. 05	Sep. 01 '94
0.370	Oct. 13	Oct. 31	Nov. 04	Dec. 01 '94
0.370	Feb. 06	Feb. 13	Feb. 17	Mar. 01 '95
0.370	May. 01	May. 08	May. 12	Jun. 01 '95
0.410	Jul. 24	Aug. 02	Aug. 04	Sep. 01 '95

Data as orig. reptd.; bef. results of disc. opers. and/or spec. items. Per share data adj. for stk. divs. as of ex-div. date.
E-Estimated. NA-Not Available. NM-Not Meaningful. NR-Not Ranked.

Office—100 Independence Mall West, Philadelphia, PA 19106-2399. Tel—(215) 592-3000. Chrmn & CEO—J. L. Wilson. Pres—J. P. Mulroney. Secy—G. P. Granoff. Treas—A. F. Smith. VP-CFO—F. W. Shaffer. Investor Contact—T. J. Suess. Dirs—G. B. Beitzel, D. B. Burke, E. G. Graves, J. A. Henderson, J. H. McArthur, P. F. Miller Jr., S. O. Moose, J. P. Mulroney, R. E. Naylor Jr., G. S. Omenn, R. H. Schmitz, A. Schriesheim, M. C. Whittington, J. L. Wilson. Transfer Agent & Registrar—Wachovia Bank of North Carolina, Winston-Salem. Incorporated in Delaware in 1917. Empl-12,211. S&P Analyst: Richard O'Reilly, CFA

Rowan Companies

NYSE Symbol **RDC**
In S&P 500

28-JUL-95 | **Industry:** Oil and Gas

Summary: Rowan performs contract oil and natural gas drilling. RDC also provides contract aviation services and operates a steel mill, makes heavy equipment and builds drilling rigs.

S&P Opinion: Buy (★★★★★)

| Recent Price • 7¼ | Yield • Nil |
| 52 Wk Range • 8¾-5⅜ | 12-Mo. P/E • NM |

Earnings vs. Previous Year
▲=Up ▼=Down ▶=No Change

Quantitative Evaluations

Outlook
(1 Lowest—5 Highest)
• 1

Fair Value
• 5¼

Risk
• **Average**

Earn./Div. Rank
• C

Technical Eval.
• **Bullish** since 3/95

Rel. Strength Rank
(1 Lowest—99 Highest)
• 17

Insider Activity
• **Neutral**

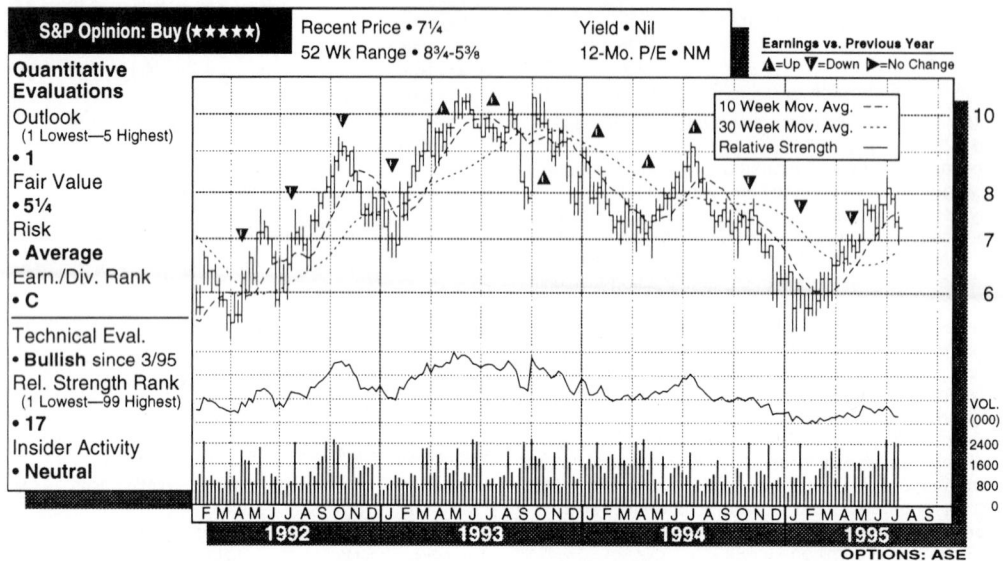

10 Week Mov. Avg. – – –
30 Week Mov. Avg. ....
Relative Strength ——

OPTIONS: ASE

Overview - 28-JUL-95

For 1995, RDC is expected to show a loss, primarily as a result of a slow improvement in drilling segment results. Natural gas prices weakened in 1994, due mostly to mild weather and excess supply. This led to delays in exploration projects, causing lower rig fleet utilization for Rowan. However, we believe U.S. natural gas drilling will continue to rebound in 1995, and rising gas usage will stimulate exploration activity. The lack of suitable rigs in the North Sea, and Rowan's expertise in harsh-environment areas bode well for the company. In order to leverage its position in domestic gas markets, RDC is expanding its turnkey drilling contract services. Longer-term earnings power has been enhanced by the February 1994 acquisition of Marathon LeTourneau, which manufactures drilling rigs and industrial equipment.

Valuation - 28-JUL-95

In 1992 and 1993, RDC shares advanced along with gas prices while in 1994 the stock's drop corresponded with that of gas prices. Natural gas markets should rebound by late 1995, once gas fundamentals begin to improve as a result of tighter supplies and increased drawdown levels. The 3-D seismic measurement of reserves, and other technologies now allow integrated oil companies to pursue smaller deposits economically, and with the number of suitable offshore rigs falling, we believe day rates are poised to advance further in 1995. We are particularly optimistic about the shares for 1995's second half.

Key Stock Statistics

S&P EPS Est. 1995	-0.14	Tang. Bk. Value/Share	5.00
P/E on S&P Est. 1995	NM	Beta	0.77
S&P EPS Est. 1996	0.25	Shareholders	3,800
Dividend Rate/Share	Nil	Market cap. (B)	$0.601
Shs. outstg. (M)	84.4	Inst. holdings	85%
Avg. daily vol. (M)	0.502	Insider holdings	NA

Value of $10,000 invested 5 years ago: $ 6,444

Fiscal Year Ending Dec. 31

	1995	% Change	1994	% Change	1993	% Change
Revenues (Million $)						
1Q	92.80	-8%	100.7	37%	73.54	37%
2Q	117.4	11%	105.4	28%	82.09	41%
3Q	—	—	129.2	21%	106.6	51%
4Q	—	—	102.9	13%	90.93	35%
Yr.	—	—	438.2	24%	353.2	41%
Income (Million $)						
1Q	-21.74	NM	-5.96	NM	-13.51	-38%
2Q	-3.71	NM	-5.86	NM	-8.20	-42%
3Q	—	—	5.64	-31%	8.18	NM
4Q	—	—	-16.82	NM	0.27	NM
Yr.	—	—	-22.99	NM	-13.26	NM
Earnings Per Share ($)						
1Q	-0.26	NM	-0.07	NM	-0.18	NM
2Q	-0.04	NM	-0.07	NM	-0.11	NM
3Q	E0.06	—	0.07	-30%	0.10	NM
4Q	E0.11	—	-0.20	—	Nil	—
Yr.	E-0.14	—	-0.27	NM	-0.17	NM

Next earnings report expected: mid October

Rowan Companies

Business Summary - 26-JUL-95

Rowan primarily provides contract drilling services in offshore domestic and foreign waters and onshore in the U.S. It also provides contract and charter aviation services and, following the February 1994 acquisition of Marathon LeTourneau, RDC produces steel, manufactures heavy equipment and makes oil rigs. Business segment contributions (profits in million $) in 1994:

	Revs.	Profits
Drilling	56%	$0.2
Aviation	22%	4.6
Manufacturing	22%	7.7

RDC owns 20 offshore rigs, including three heavy-duty Gorilla jack-ups, 17 deep water jack-ups, one semi-submersible, and three submersible barge rigs. Work is done primarily in the Gulf of Mexico and the North Sea. Some work is done in Canada and Latin America. Worldwide offshore utilization averaged 85% in 1994, unchanged from 1993. The company has 17 land rigs, seven of which were "mothballed" at March 31, 1995.

Weak prices for natural gas in 1994's second half led to lower utilization rates for the company's rigs in the Gulf of Mexico. North Sea activity showed some improvement, and overall rig utilization reached 84%, up from 67% in 1993, although day rates were lower.

The Era Aviation, Inc. unit operates a fleet of 89 helicopters, of which 49 were based in Alaska and 40 in the Gulf of Mexico area, and 17 fixed wing aircraft that were based in Alaska. RDC has a 49% interest in the helicopter unit of KLM Royal Dutch Airlines. Flight services are heavily dependent upon helicopter activities for oil and natural gas exploration and production.

The company also manufactures cranes, loaders and trucks used in coal, gold, copper, iron ore and other mines, and a mini-steel mill. The marine group has built over one-third of all mobile offshore jack-up drilling rigs, including all 20 operated by the company.

Important Developments

Jul. '95—Rowan Companies noted that the second quarter was its strongest in the last five years. Drilling division results showed improvement throughout the quarter, and there was a marginal profit during June. The offshore rig fleet had a 100% utilization rate, as of July. In addition, aviation is realizing a normal seasonal increase and the manufacturing division is operating profitably, and the company said the outlook continues to be favorable. The company expects a return to profitability in the third quarter.

Apr. '95—RDC said it plans to build the world's largest bottom supported mobile offshore drilling unit for use in the North Sea. The cost is estimated at $135 million.

Capitalization

Long Term Debt: $248,352,000 (6/95).

Per Share Data ($) (Year Ended Dec. 31)

	1994	1993	1992	1991	1990	1989
Tangible Bk. Val.	5.21	5.44	5.08	6.06	6.63	6.58
Cash Flow	-0.33	0.49	-0.31	0.19	0.72	0.19
Earnings	-0.27	-0.17	-1.01	-0.53	0.03	-0.52
Dividends	Nil	Nil	Nil	Nil	Nil	Nil
Payout Ratio	Nil	Nil	Nil	Nil	Nil	Nil
Prices - High	9¼	10¾	9⅜	11⅜	15⅞	11⅞
- Low	5¾	6⅝	4⅝	4¾	9⅞	5⅝
P/E Ratio - High	NM	NM	NM	NM	NM	NM
- Low	NM	NM	NM	NM	NM	NM

Income Statement Analysis (Million $)

	1994	%Chg	1993	%Chg	1992	%Chg	1991
Revs.	438	24%	353	41%	250	-8%	272
Oper. Inc.	49.4	-17%	59.3	NM	0.7	-98%	29.9
Depr.	50.8	-2%	51.9	NM	51.4	-2%	52.7
Int. Exp.	27.5	8%	25.4	-3%	26.3	23%	21.4
Pretax Inc.	-22.5	NM	-13.5	NM	-73.3	NM	-38.0
Eff. Tax Rate	NM	—	NM	—	NM	—	NM
Net Inc.	-23.0	NM	-13.3	NM	-73.8	NM	-38.7

Balance Sheet & Other Fin. Data (Million $)

	1994	1993	1992	1991	1990	1989
Cash	111	117	30.0	235	108	131
Curr. Assets	254	216	103	303	179	184
Total Assets	805	765	684	896	739	738
Curr. Liab.	58.0	44.0	42.0	177	45.0	50.0
LT Debt	249	207	213	221	154	163
Common Eqty.	442	460	376	445	486	479
Total Cap.	695	672	594	671	645	649
Cap. Exp.	33.0	22.0	40.0	58.0	60.0	23.0
Cash Flow	27.8	38.7	-22.4	13.9	52.4	14.0

Ratio Analysis

	1994	1993	1992	1991	1990	1989
Curr. Ratio	4.4	4.9	2.5	1.7	4.0	3.7
% LT Debt of Cap.	35.7	30.8	35.9	32.9	23.8	25.2
% Net Inc.of Revs.	NM	NM	NM	NM	0.7	NM
% Ret. on Assets	NM	NM	NM	NM	0.3	NM
% Ret. on Equity	NM	NM	NM	NM	0.4	NM

Dividend Data (Common dividends were omitted in 1986 after having been paid since 1964. In February 1992, directors declared one preferred stock purchase right for each common share outstanding on or after March 11, 1992.)

Data as orig. reptd.; bef. results of disc. opers. and/or spec. items. Per share data adj. for stk. divs. as of ex-div. date. E-Estimated. NA-Not Available. NM-Not Meaningful. NR-Not Ranked.

Office—5450 Transco Tower, 2800 Post Oak Blvd., Houston, TX 77056-6196. **Tel**—(713) 621-7800. **Chrmn & Pres**—C. R. Palmer. **VP-Fin & Treas**—E. E. Thiele. **Secy**—M.H. Hay. **VP-Investor Contact**—W. C. Provine. **Dirs**—R. E. Bailey, H. O. Boswell, H. E. Lentz, C. R. Palmer, W. P. Schmoe, C. P. Siess Jr., P. Simonis, C. W. Yeargain. **Transfer Agent & Registrar**—American Stock Transfer & Trust Co., NYC. **Incorporated** in Delaware in 1947. **Empl**-3,457. **S&P Analyst:** Raymond J. Deacon

Royal Dutch Petroleum

NYSE Symbol **RD**

In S&P 500

28-AUG-95

Industry:
Oil and Gas

Summary: Royal Dutch owns 60% of the Royal Dutch/"Shell" Group, a leading factor in the oil, natural gas and chemical industries. Shell Oil is a major U.S. integrated petroleum company.

S&P Opinion: Accumulate (★★★★)

| Recent Price • 120 | Yield • 3.8% |
| 52 Wk Range • 128⅜-104⅞ | 12-Mo. P/E • 13.2 |

Earnings vs. Previous Year
▲=Up ▼=Down ▶=No Change

Quantitative Evaluations

Outlook
(1 Lowest—5 Highest)
• **2+**

Fair Value
• **109½**

Risk
• **Low**

Earn./Div. Rank
• **A**

Technical Eval.
• **Bullish** since 7/95

Rel. Strength Rank
(1 Lowest—99 Highest)
• **23**

Insider Activity
• **NA**

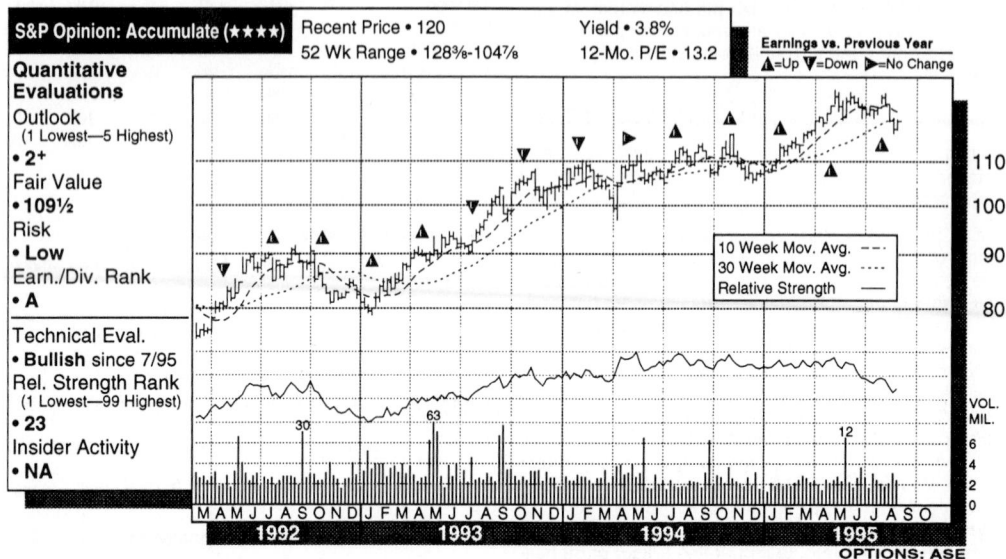

10 Week Mov. Avg. — - -
30 Week Mov. Avg. - - - -
Relative Strength ——

Overview - 24-AUG-95

Profits are expected to trend higher in 1995 and 1996, as the group repositions its substantial worldwide asset base in the high growth sectors of the industry. Recently soaring chemical profits have boosted already strong cash flow. During the next two years, we expect refined product margins to rebound, fueling earnings growth. Consumption of refined products is increasing, particularly in the Pacific Rim where the group has a preeminent market share. Furthermore, the group is foreseen gaining a leading market position in the development of China's huge refined product market. Refined product fundamentals are firming in Europe while in the U.S. petroleum product usage is strong. Also, stable commodity prices should benefit earnings through year-end 1995.

Valuation - 24-AUG-95

The shares will benefit from modestly rebounding refined product fundamentals and cash dividends should trend higher in coming years. Excess industry capacity will be offset by stronger refined products demand in the U.S. and Europe. On a cash flow and earnings basis, the shares typically trade at a premium to the group of international integrated oils, and we believe a stabilizing dollar should help to boost the shares. We are optimistic that OPEC will maintain production discipline, though there is some confusion in the markets following a recent Saudi cabinet reshuffling. In addition, we believe strengthening fundamentals for natural gas will benefit the shares over the next two years.

Key Stock Statistics

S&P EPS Est. 1995	8.70	Tang. Bk. Value/Share	NM
P/E on S&P Est. 1995	13.8	Beta	0.83
S&P EPS Est. 1996	9.30	Shareholders	500,000
Dividend Rate/Share	4.51	Market cap. (B)	$ 64.3
Shs. outstg. (M)	536.1	Inst. holdings	28%
Avg. daily vol. (M)	0.465	Insider holdings	NA

Value of $10,000 invested 5 years ago: $ 19,531

Fiscal Year Ending Dec. 31

	1995	% Change	1994	% Change	1993	% Change
Revenues (Million $)						
1Q	15,586	19%	13,106	-8%	14,183	10%
2Q	17,009	23%	13,774	-2%	14,074	8%
3Q	—	—	14,732	NM	14,596	10%
4Q	—	—	15,316	7%	14,252	-10%
Yr.	—	—	56,898	NM	57,105	4%
Income (Million $)						
1Q	1,209	44%	838.0	—	—	—
2Q	1,228	103%	605.0	—	—	—
3Q	—	—	758.0	—	—	—
4Q	—	—	1,559	—	—	—
Yr.	—	—	3,760	32%	2,858	-18%
Earnings Per Share ($)						
1Q	2.38	43%	1.66	NM	1.66	NM
2Q	2.42	102%	1.20	14%	1.05	-22%
3Q	E1.95	31%	1.49	3%	1.44	-17%
4Q	E1.95	-36%	3.03	148%	1.22	-26%
Yr.	E8.70	18%	7.37	37%	5.37	-16%

Next earnings report expected: early November

Royal Dutch Petroleum

Business Summary - 28-AUG-95

Royal Dutch Petroleum owns 60% of the Royal Dutch/ Shell Group; the other 40% is owned by Shell Transport & Trading Co. The Group ranks with Exxon as the leading factors in the petroleum industry. The Group also produces and trades in petrochemicals, coal and metals. It owns Shell Oil Co. (U.S.) and a 79% interest in Shell Canada. Recent operating profits by segment (in million Netherlands guilder):

	1994	1993	1992
Exploration & Prod.	923	1,200	1,117
Manufacturing, marine and marketing	1,251	1,057	746
Chemicals	204	(245)	(134)
Coal	(75)	19	(13)
Metals	30	(57)	(25)
Other	(14)	9	(5)

In 1994, the Group's crude oil production averaged 2,194,000 b/d; crude oil purchases totaled 5,307,000 b/d; natural gas sales 7.3 billion cubic feet a day; refinery processing intakes 3,669,000 b/d; and crude and oil product sales 9,341,000 b/d. Net proved reserves at the end of 1994, including the share of reserves of associated companies, stood at 8,945 million barrels of crude oil and natural gas liquids (9,124 in 1993) and 48,707 (50,453) billion cubic feet of natural gas. In 1994, net additions to reserves of oil and gas were equivalent to 78% of crude oil and liquids production and 32% of natural gas production. Group capital expenditures and exploration expense for 1994 totaled $10.5 billion, up from $9.5 billion in 1993.

Important Developments

Jul. '95—Net income for 1995's second quarter rose 104%, reflecting a 99% increase in exploration and production operating profits, due to higher average oil prices, which offset sharply lower natural gas prices. Meanwhile, manufacturing, marine and marketing results continued to be weak, with refining margins remaining at low relative levels. Chemical profits rose sharply (333%), benefiting from changes to the cost structure and a rise in volumes. The firm believes that the second half of the year will be marked by somewhat weaker chemical demand. Cash flow from operating activities amounted to $3.9 billion, versus $1.9 billion the prior year. Excluding non-recurring items, operating income climbed 192%.

Capitalization

Long Term Debt: $4,734,000,000 (6/95).
Minority Interest: $1,871,000,000.
4% Cum. Preference Stock: 1,500 shares (1,000 guilder par).
Ordinary Share Capital: 536,074,088 shs. (5 guilder par).
U.S. institutions hold about 28%.
Shareholders of record: about 325,000.

Per Share Data ($) (Year Ended Dec. 31)

	1994	1993	1992	1991	1990	1989
Tangible Bk. Val.	62.83	57.74	58.03	60.44	60.17	53.58
Cash Flow	15.09	12.25	13.83	12.44	14.28	13.29
Earnings	7.37	5.37	6.38	5.23	7.78	7.58
Dividends	4.51	4.01	4.19	3.76	3.59	3.27
Payout Ratio	61%	75%	66%	72%	46%	43%
Prices - High	116¾	108⅛	91⅝	86¼	87	77⅝
- Low	96⅞	78¾	74¾	73	70½	56⅞
P/E Ratio - High	16	20	14	16	11	10
- Low	13	15	12	14	9	8

Income Statement Analysis (Million $)

	1994	%Chg	1993	%Chg	1992	%Chg	1991
Revs.	56,898	NM	57,104	-2%	57,975	-6%	61,618
Oper. Inc.	8,937	10%	8,123	-4%	8,453	-2%	8,643
Depr.	4,138	12%	3,710	-6%	3,932	2%	3,854
Int. Exp.	716	-12%	811	-11%	911	NM	917
Pretax Inc.	6,089	17%	5,212	-7%	5,614	-3%	5,813
Eff. Tax Rate	34%	—	45%	—	37%	—	52%
Net Inc.	3,760	32%	2,858	-18%	3,480	24%	2,817

Balance Sheet & Other Fin. Data (Million $)

	1994	1993	1992	1991	1990	1989
Cash	6,960	5,754	5,145	5,277	5,108	3,900
Curr. Assets	21,534	18,854	19,152	20,269	22,215	17,359
Total Assets	64,711	59,898	60,491	63,320	63,859	54,116
Curr. Liab.	16,862	14,802	15,090	16,420	18,178	12,905
LT Debt	3,572	3,675	4,223	4,025	2,689	2,674
Common Eqty.	33,684	30,954	31,110	32,402	32,253	28,723
Total Cap.	42,968	41,019	41,803	43,949	42,916	38,767
Cap. Exp.	5,776	4,936	4,779	6,420	6,023	5,328
Cash Flow	8,088	6,568	7,412	6,671	7,657	7,126

Ratio Analysis

	1994	1993	1992	1991	1990	1989
Curr. Ratio	1.3	1.3	1.3	1.2	1.2	1.3
% LT Debt of Cap.	8.3	9.0	10.1	9.2	6.3	6.9
% Net Inc.of Revs.	6.9	5.0	6.0	4.6	6.5	8.0
% Ret. on Assets	6.3	4.7	5.6	4.4	7.0	7.8
% Ret. on Equity	12.2	9.2	11.0	8.7	13.6	14.8

Dividend Data

Dividends were initiated in 1894. An interim dividend from each year's earnings is normally paid in October of that year and a final dividend is paid in June of the following year.

Amt. of Div. $	Date Decl.	Ex-Div. Date	Stock of Record	Payment Date
1.860	—	Sep. 19	Sep. 23	Oct. 07 '94
2.653	—	May. 19	May. 25	Jun. 09 '95

Data as orig. reptd.; bef. results of disc. opers. and/or spec. items. Per share data adj. for stk. divs. as of ex-div. date. Earnings data is based on RD's participation in Group net income at varying exchange rates. E-Estimated. NA-Not Available. NM-Not Meaningful. NR-Not Ranked.

Office—Carel van Bylandtlaan 30, 2596 HR The Hague, The Netherlands. **Tel**—31-70-377 4540. **Pres**—C. A. J. Herkstroeter. **Managing Dirs**—H. de Ruiter, M. A. van den Bergh. **U. S. Investor Contact**—J. C. Grapsi. (Tel. 212-261-5660). **Supervisory Dirs**—L. C. van Wachem (Chrmn), T. C. Braakman, K. V. Cassani, J. H. Choufoer, J. M. H. van Engelshoven, J. D. Hooglandt, K. O. Pohl. **Transfer Agent & Registrar for 5 guilder shares**—Shell Oil Co., Houston, Texas. **Incorporated** in Holland in 1890. **Empl**-106,000. **S&P Analyst:** Raymond J. Deacon

Rubbermaid Inc.

NYSE Symbol **RBD**

In S&P 500

24-AUG-95

Industry:
Housewares

Summary: This company manufactures a broad line of plastic and rubber products for the home, specialty, office and commercial markets.

S&P Opinion: Hold (★★★)		

Recent Price • 30

52 Wk Range • 34¼-25⅜

Yield • 1.7%

12-Mo. P/E • 23.6

Earnings vs. Previous Year

▲=Up ▼=Down ▶=No Change

Quantitative Evaluations

Outlook
(1 Lowest—5 Highest)
• **1⁻**

Fair Value
• **26½**

Risk
• **Low**

Earn./Div. Rank
• **A+**

Technical Eval.
• **Bearish** since 2/95

Rel. Strength Rank
(1 Lowest—99 Highest)
• **38**

Insider Activity
• **Neutral**

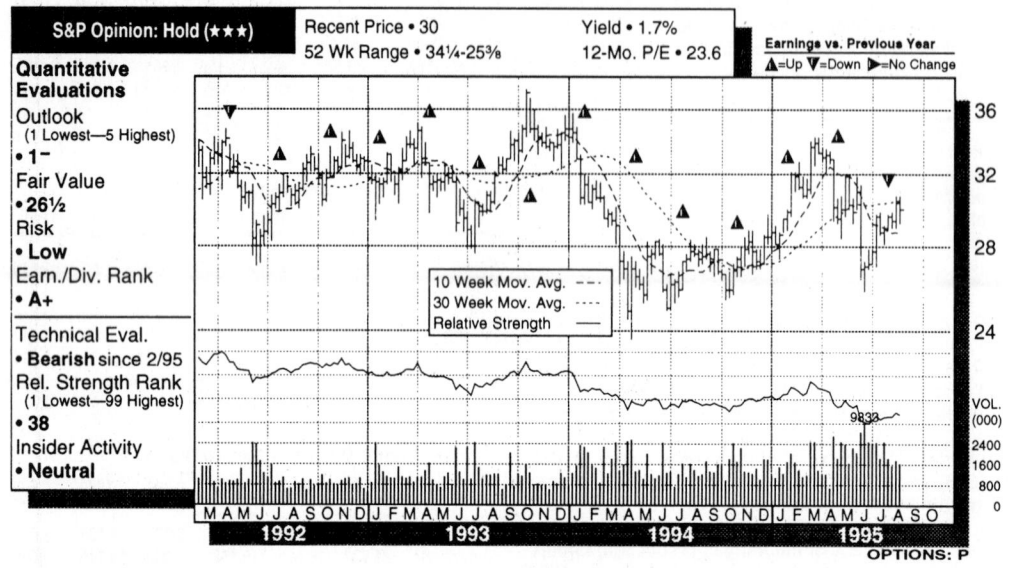

10 Week Mov. Avg. ---
30 Week Mov. Avg. ·····
Relative Strength ——

VOL. (000)

2400
1600
800
0

OPTIONS: P

Overview - 24-AUG-95

Volume from ongoing operations should continue to improve in 1995, reflecting steady demand for RBD's extensive product line. New product introductions (about 30% of each year's sales are generated by products introduced in the past five years) should continue to boost volume growth, as should acquisitions in 1994 and 1995, including Carex, Empire Brushes, Ausplay and Injectaplastic. Increased exposure overseas through joint ventures, licensing agreements and establishment of overseas manufacturing bases add to volume gains. The company hopes to derive 25% of revenues from outside the U.S. by 2000. Despite higher prices and productivity improvements, margins could be under pressure from higher resin prices. For the long-term, earnings are expected to rise 14% to 15% annually.

Valuation - 24-AUG-95

This well-known company is currently having difficulty in maintaining its historical growth rate. This stems mainly from weak consumer spending and substantially higher resin costs that RBD has been unable to fully pass on to customers. These problems may be temporary, however, and by the second half of 1995, some of the company's historical growth mnay resume. RBD expects volume to be boosted by higher consumer spending, and wider margins should result from productivity improvements. However, we recommend that investors only hold the shares for now.

Key Stock Statistics

S&P EPS Est. 1995	1.35	Tang. Bk. Value/Share	8.22
P/E on S&P Est. 1995	22.2	Beta	1.52
S&P EPS Est. 1996	1.85	Shareholders	15,400
Dividend Rate/Share	0.50	Market cap. (B)	$ 4.8
Shs. outstg. (M)	160.9	Inst. holdings	46%
Avg. daily vol. (M)	0.310	Insider holdings	NA

Value of $10,000 invested 5 years ago: $ 17,542

Fiscal Year Ending Dec. 31

	1995	% Change	1994	% Change	1993	% Change
Revenues (Million $)						
1Q	563.9	15%	491.6	2%	484.0	8%
2Q	556.8	5%	531.1	9%	488.5	9%
3Q	—	—	580.3	13%	515.2	9%
4Q	—	—	566.3	20%	472.9	9%
Yr.	—	—	2,169	11%	1,960	9%
Income (Million $)						
1Q	54.14	7%	50.62	2%	49.62	87%
2Q	28.81	-49%	56.15	11%	50.58	16%
3Q	—	—	66.76	11%	60.38	15%
4Q	—	—	54.60	7%	50.84	15%
Yr.	—	—	228.1	8%	211.4	27%
Earnings Per Share ($)						
1Q	0.34	6%	0.32	3%	0.31	94%
2Q	0.18	-49%	0.35	9%	0.32	19%
3Q	E0.45	10%	0.41	11%	0.37	12%
4Q	E0.38	12%	0.34	6%	0.32	14%
Yr.	E1.35	-5%	1.42	8%	1.32	27%

Next earnings report expected: mid October

Rubbermaid Inc.

24-AUG-95

Business Summary - 24-AUG-95

Rubbermaid manufactures plastic and rubber products for the consumer (79% of 1994 sales) and commercial markets (21%).

The home products division makes bathware, cleaning products, decorative coverings, food storage containers, gadgets, home organizers, household containers, mailboxes, microwave cookware, recycling products, refuse containers, sinkware, storage containers, indoor casual furniture, brushes, tableware and toolboxes.

The seasonal products division produces sporting goods products, automotive accessories and lawn and garden products. The casual outdoor furniture business was sold in late 1994.

The juvenile products division includes Little Tikes Co., which manufactures children's toys and furniture. Through Iron Mountain Forge, RBD also produces commercial playgrounds.

The commercial products division manufactures buckets; carts; foodservice storage and transporting items; maintenance products; material-handling products; mopping systems; odor control products; recycling and refuse containers; stock watering tanks; and tableware.

Through Carex Inc., acquired in 1994, RBD manufactures and markets healthcare products, including ambulatory aids and bath safety products to assist aging and physically challenged people.

The office products division makes bulletin boards, chairmats, cleaning products, clothing care items, desk and computer accessories, modular office furniture, office organizers, recycling containers and wastebaskets.

International sales accounted for 12.1% of total sales in 1994 (10.5% in 1993) and 7.2% of operating earnings (5.8%). The company distributes most of its products worldwide either through exports from plants in the U.S., Mexico, Canada or Europe or through licensing agreements. Main international operations include Rubbermaid de Mexico; Rubbermaid Europe; a 51% interest in a joint venture with Richell Corp., one of Japan's leading housewares manufacturers; a 50% interest in a joint venture with Royal Plastics Group of Canada; and Injectaplastic.

Important Developments

Jul. '95—RBD attributed a 5% increase in 1995 second sales to a 5% price hike. Margins contracted considerably, especially at the home products division, reflecting a 100% rise in resin costs over the past year. Results also reflected the absence of a non-operating gain. The company expects results to improve in the second half of 1995, aided by higher sales reflecting marketing initiatives and new products, and by productivity gains.

Capitalization

Long Term Debt: $16,524,000 (6/95).

Per Share Data ($)

(Year Ended Dec. 31)

	1994	1993	1992	1991	1990	1989
Tangible Bk. Val.	8.00	7.05	6.16	5.53	4.80	4.06
Cash Flow	2.00	1.82	1.48	1.41	1.25	1.16
Earnings	1.42	1.32	1.04	1.02	0.90	0.79
Dividends	0.46	0.40	0.35	0.31	0.27	0.23
Payout Ratio	33%	31%	34%	31%	30%	29%
Prices - High	35¾	37⅜	37⅜	38¼	22½	18⅞
- Low	23⅝	27⅝	27	18½	15½	12½
P/E Ratio - High	25	28	36	38	25	24
- Low	17	21	26	18	17	16

Income Statement Analysis (Million $)

	1994	%Chg	1993	%Chg	1992	%Chg	1991
Revs.	2,169	11%	1,960	9%	1,805	8%	1,667
Oper. Inc.	450	6%	426	17%	364	14%	319
Depr.	93.7	16%	80.9	16%	69.9	11%	62.7
Int. Exp.	7.2	-8%	7.8	3%	7.6	-9%	8.3
Pretax Inc.	367	7%	342	28%	267	2%	263
Eff. Tax Rate	38%	—	38%	—	37%	—	38%
Net Inc.	228	8%	211	26%	167	2%	163

Balance Sheet & Other Fin. Data (Million $)

	1994	1993	1992	1991	1990	1989
Cash	151	194	122	153	77.0	97.0
Curr. Assets	927	830	700	664	603	516
Total Assets	1,709	1,513	1,327	1,245	1,114	915
Curr. Liab.	296	259	223	246	235	202
LT Debt	11.6	19.4	20.3	27.8	39.2	50.3
Common Eqty.	1,286	1,130	988	886	768	598
Total Cap.	1,297	1,150	1,010	943	837	684
Cap. Exp.	118	142	135	123	104	86.0
Cash Flow	322	292	237	225	199	171

Ratio Analysis

	1994	1993	1992	1991	1990	1989
Curr. Ratio	3.1	3.2	3.1	2.7	2.6	2.5
% LT Debt of Cap.	0.9	1.7	2.0	2.9	4.7	7.3
% Net Inc.of Revs.	10.5	10.8	9.2	9.8	9.4	8.7
% Ret. on Assets	14.1	14.9	13.0	13.8	13.6	13.7
% Ret. on Equity	18.9	20.0	17.8	19.7	20.2	21.0

Dividend Data

—Dividends have been paid since 1941. A dividend reinvestment plan is available.

Amt. of Div. $	Date Decl.	Ex-Div. Date	Stock of Record	Payment Date
0.112	Jun. 28	Aug. 08	Aug. 12	Sep. 01 '94
0.125	Oct. 25	Nov. 04	Nov. 11	Dec. 01 '94
0.125	Jan. 12	Feb. 06	Feb. 10	Mar. 01 '95
0.125	Apr. 25	May. 08	May. 12	Jun. 01 '95
0.125	Jun. 27	Aug. 09	Aug. 11	Sep. 01 '95

Data as orig. reptd.; bef. results of disc. opers. and/or spec. items. Per share data adj. for stk. divs. as of ex-div. date. E-Estimated. NA-Not Available. NM-Not Meaningful. NR-Not Ranked.

Office—1147 Akron Rd., Wooster, OH 44691-6000. **Tel**—(216) 264-6464. **Chrmn & CEO**—W. R. Schmitt. **Pres**—C. A. Carroll. **SVP & CFO**—G. C. Weigand. **SVP & Secy**—J. A. Morgan. **SVP & Investor Contact**—Richard D. Gates. **Dirs**—T. H. Barrett, C. A. Carroll, R. O. Ebert, S. C. Gault, R. M. Gerrity, K. N. Horn, W. D. Marohn, S. A. Minter, J. Nicholson, P. G. Schloemer, W. R. Schmitt, G. R. Sullivan. **Transfer Agent & Registrar**—Bank of Boston. **Incorporated** in Ohio in 1920. **Empl**-12,939. **S&P Analyst:** Elizabeth Vandeventer

03-AUG-95   Industry:
Textiles

Summary: Russell is a vertically integrated manufacturer and marketer of leisure apparel, athletic uniforms and woven fabrics.

S&P Opinion: Hold (★★★)	Recent Price • 28⅝	Yield • 1.7%	Earnings vs. Previous Year
	52 Wk Range • 32⅝-26½	12-Mo. P/E • 14.8	▲=Up ▼=Down ▶=No Change

Quantitative Evaluations

Outlook
(1 Lowest—5 Highest)
• **4⁻**

Fair Value
• **29¾**

Risk
• **Low**

Earn./Div. Rank
• **A-**

Technical Eval.
• **Bullish** since 3/95

Rel. Strength Rank
(1 Lowest—99 Highest)
• **33**

Insider Activity
• **Neutral**

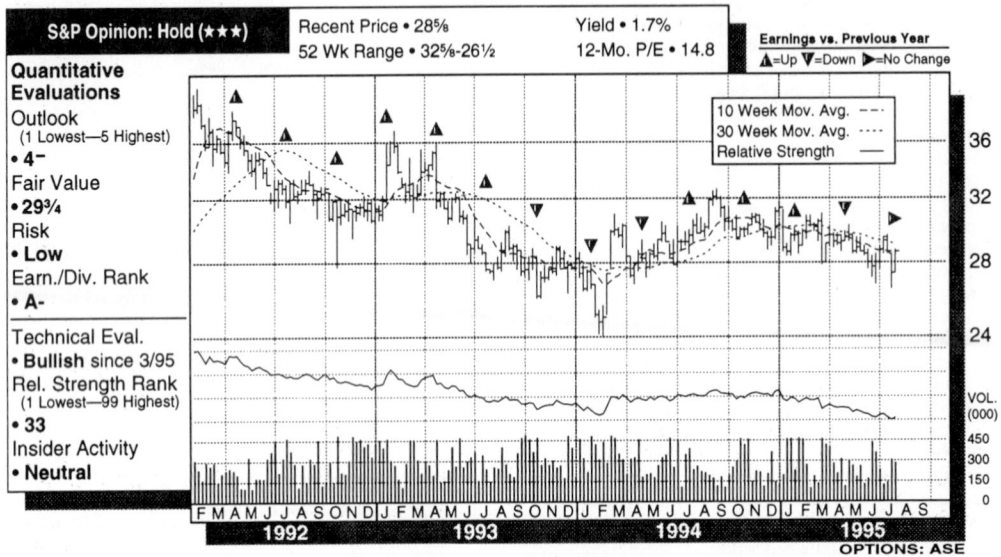

OPTIONS: ASE

Overview - 03-AUG-95

Sales in 1995 should improve moderately on higher volume of knit apparel, Cross Creek apparel, and increased penetration into European and Latin American markets. A potential acquisition could further boost sales. Sales at the Russell Athletic and Licensed products divisions (about 25% of the company's consolidated sales) could be under some pressure, reflecting low order rates in the first quarter from department stores. Sales at these divisions could also be hurt by competitive pricing. Overall margins could decline somewhat. Price increases in the second half of 1994 and early 1995 are not likely to fully offset higher cotton and polyester price increases that occurred in 1994.

Valuation - 03-AUG-95

These shares have been trading in a narrow range since mid-1994, due to pressures on margins arising from competitive pricing and higher raw material prices. This is a very competitive niche in the apparel industry. RML's major competitors - V.F. Corp. and Fruit of the Loom - both entered the licensed apparel area in 1995 via acquisitions, and are battling head on for market share. To compound problems, industrywide growth for both athletic and licensed apparel, once thought to be high growth areas, has slowed. Meanwhile, demand for activewear made by athletic footwear makers is booming. As a result of this uncertain outlook, we are retaining a neutral opinion on these shares for now.

Key Stock Statistics

S&P EPS Est. 1995	2.00	Tang. Bk. Value/Share	14.89
P/E on S&P Est. 1995	14.3	Beta	1.45
S&P EPS Est. 1996	2.20	Shareholders	13,000
Dividend Rate/Share	0.48	Market cap. (B)	$ 1.1
Shs. outstg. (M)	39.0	Inst. holdings	48%
Avg. daily vol. (M)	0.044	Insider holdings	NA

Value of $10,000 invested 5 years ago: $ 11,789

Fiscal Year Ending Dec. 31

	1995	% Change	1994	% Change	1993	% Change
Revenues (Million $)						
1Q	248.3	7%	232.1	13%	204.6	4%
2Q	268.7	10%	243.5	16%	209.1	12%
3Q	—	—	317.1	19%	266.6	3%
4Q	—	—	305.5	22%	250.4	-3%
Yr.	—	—	1,098	18%	930.8	4%
Income (Million $)						
1Q	12.23	-9%	13.37	-17%	16.03	4%
2Q	12.71	NM	12.72	NM	12.70	2%
3Q	—	—	24.20	NM	-3.76	NM
4Q	—	—	28.54	18%	24.13	-21%
Yr.	—	—	78.83	61%	49.10	-40%
Earnings Per Share ($)						
1Q	0.31	-6%	0.33	-15%	0.39	5%
2Q	0.32	NM	0.32	3%	0.31	3%
3Q	E0.62	—	0.60	NM	-0.09	NM
4Q	E0.75	—	0.71	20%	0.59	-20%
Yr.	E2.00	—	1.96	65%	1.19	-40%

Next earnings report expected: mid October

Russell Corp.

Business Summary - 03-AUG-95

Russell Corp. (formerly Russell Mills) is a vertically integrated designer, manufacturer and marketer of activewear, licensed sports apparel, athletic uniforms, better knit shirts and a comprehensive line of lightweight woven fabrics. Over 90% of the company's total revenues are derived from completed apparel, with the balance from woven fabrics. In early 1994, RML acquired DeSoto Mills, Inc., a sock producer, and the trademarks and licenses of Chalk Line.

Under the RUSSELL ATHLETIC label, the Athletic division, believed to be the largest U.S. manufacturer of athletic uniforms, supplies uniforms nationwide to professional, collegiate, high school and other teams, as well as to individuals. RML also provides activewear under the RUSSELL ATHLETIC LABEL.

Under the JERZEES label and private labels, the Knit Apparel division produces a wide variety of knitted apparel, including fleece sportswear such as sweatshirts, sweatpants and lightweight sportswear. In 1993, the company signed an exclusive licensing agreement to produce a line of women's and children's activewear under the "chic" brand name.

The Fabrics division designs and markets quality woven fabrics of cotton and blends of cotton and synthetic fibers in a wide variety of patterns, colors and constructions for sale primarily to apparel manufacturers.

Cross Creek Apparel (acquired in 1988) designs and markets high-quality knit products, including placket, turtleneck and rugby shirts. Russell Corp. U.K. (1989) produces fleece garments and T-shirts for the U.K. and Europe. The Game Inc., a wholly owned subsidiary as of December 23, 1993, is a wholesale distributor of high-quality, licensed collegiate and professional caps and apparel.

Important Developments

Jul. '95—Although second quarter 1995 sales rose 10%, year to year, led by increased demand for the company's core activewear offerings, net income fell 1.8%, to $12.5 million from $12.7 million. RML attributed this decline to competitive pricing pressures and increases in raw material prices. Looking ahead, the company said that it believed that superior product and customer service would be primary tools to combat prevailing competitive pricing pressures. The company also said that escalating raw material prices had subsided.

Capitalization

Long Term Debt: $209,382,000 (7/2/95).

Per Share Data ($) (Year Ended Dec. 31)

	1994	1993	1992	1991	1990	1989
Tangible Bk. Val.	14.89	13.80	13.38	11.79	10.68	9.45
Cash Flow	3.63	2.78	3.44	2.76	2.93	2.66
Earnings	1.96	1.19	1.99	1.38	1.65	1.57
Dividends	0.42	0.39	0.34	0.32	0.32	0.28
Payout Ratio	21%	33%	17%	23%	19%	18%
Prices - High	32⅝	36⅞	40⅜	36¼	31	26½
- Low	24	26	27¾	19¾	16	15⅝
P/E Ratio - High	17	31	20	26	19	17
- Low	12	22	14	14	10	10

Income Statement Analysis (Million $)

	1994	%Chg	1993	%Chg	1992	%Chg	1991
Revs.	1,098	18%	931	4%	899	12%	805
Oper. Inc.	213	8%	198	-3%	204	24%	165
Depr.	67.0	3%	65.3	9%	59.7	5%	56.6
Int. Exp.	19.4	15%	16.9	7%	15.8	-13%	18.1
Pretax Inc.	128	58%	81.0	-38%	130	43%	91.0
Eff. Tax Rate	38%	—	39%	—	37%	—	37%
Net Inc.	78.8	60%	49.1	-40%	82.2	45%	56.8

Balance Sheet & Other Fin. Data (Million $)

	1994	1993	1992	1991	1990	1989
Cash	4.1	3.9	6.1	13.4	13.2	75.6
Curr. Assets	511	474	428	327	334	327
Total Assets	1,047	1,017	965	818	795	721
Curr. Liab.	201	196	142	71.7	84.8	59.8
LT Debt	144	163	186	180	191	205
Common Eqty.	629	588	570	503	456	402
Total Cap.	824	800	810	737	703	656
Cap. Exp.	39.0	84.0	111	90.0	116	80.0
Cash Flow	146	114	142	113	118	109

Ratio Analysis

	1994	1993	1992	1991	1990	1989
Curr. Ratio	2.5	2.4	3.0	4.6	3.9	5.5
% LT Debt of Cap.	17.5	20.4	22.9	24.5	27.2	31.2
% Net Inc.of Revs.	7.2	5.3	9.1	7.1	9.5	9.4
% Ret. on Assets	7.7	5.0	9.2	7.0	9.0	10.1
% Ret. on Equity	13.1	8.5	15.2	11.7	15.7	17.2

Dividend Data (Dividends have been paid since 1963. A dividend reinvestment plan is available. A "poison pill" stock purchase rights plan was adopted in 1989.)

Amt. of Div. $	Date Decl.	Ex-Div. Date	Stock of Record	Payment Date
0.100	Jul. 27	Aug. 02	Aug. 08	Aug. 22 '94
0.120	Oct. 26	Nov. 01	Nov. 07	Nov. 22 '94
0.120	Jan. 25	Jan. 31	Feb. 06	Feb. 20 '95
0.120	Apr. 26	May. 02	May. 08	May. 22 '95
0.120	Jul. 26	Aug. 03	Aug. 07	Aug. 21 '95

Data as orig. reptd.; bef. results of disc. opers. and/or spec. items. Per share data adj. for stk. divs. as of ex-div. date. E-Estimated. NA-Not Available. NM-Not Meaningful. NR-Not Ranked.

Office—1 Lee St., Alexander City, AL 35010-0272. **Tel**—(205) 329-4000. **Chrmn, Pres & CEO**—J. C. Adams. **Exec VP-CFO**—J. D. Nabors. **Secy**—S. R. Forehand. **Investor Contact**—Tony Meyer. **Dirs**—J. C. Adams, H. M. Bloom, R. G. Bruno, H. S. Howell, G. Ireland II, C. T. Johnson III, J. D. Nabors, C. V. Nalley III, B. Russell, J. R. Thomas, J. A. White. **Transfer Agents & Registrars**—First Alabama Bank of Montgomery; Wachovia Bank of North Carolina, Winston-Salem. **Incorporated** in Alabama in 1902. **Empl**-16,640. **S&P Analyst:** Elizabeth Vandeventer

Ryan's Family Steak Houses

NASDAQ Symbol **RYAN**

In S&P 500

26-JUL-95

Industry:
Food serving

Summary: This company owns and franchises about 200 restaurants, largely in the southeastern U.S. A large portion of sales is derived from a self-service Mega Bar.

S&P Opinion: Accumulate (★★★★)	Recent Price • 7	Yield • Nil
	52 Wk Range • 8½-5⅜	12-Mo. P/E • 12.1

Earnings vs. Previous Year
▲=Up ▼=Down ▶=No Change

Quantitative Evaluations

Outlook
(1 Lowest—5 Highest)
• 3⁻

Fair Value
• 7

Risk
• **Average**

Earn./Div. Rank
• **B+**

Technical Eval.
• **Bearish** since 7/95

Rel. Strength Rank
(1 Lowest—99 Highest)
• **16**

Insider Activity
• **Neutral**

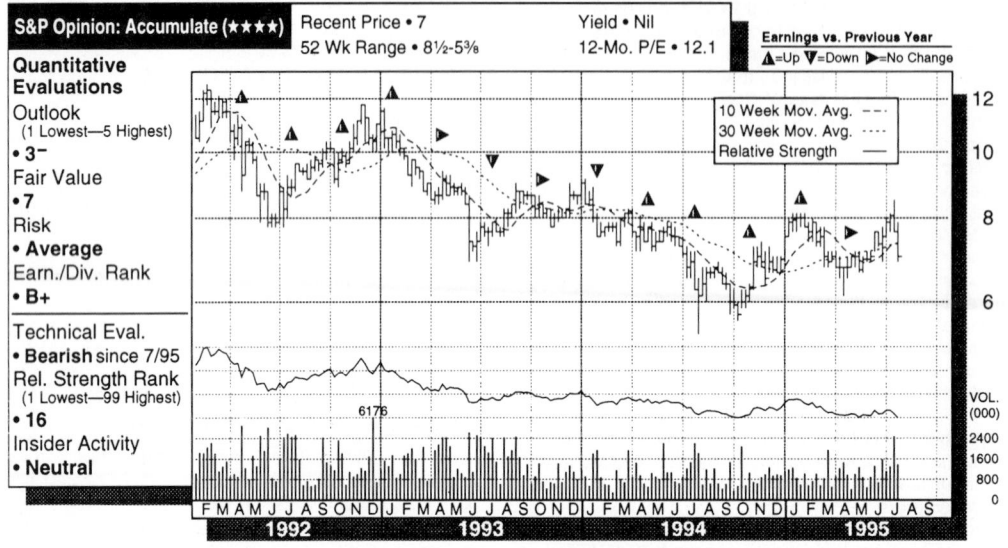

10 Week Mov. Avg. — — —
30 Week Mov. Avg. · · · · ·
Relative Strength ——

6176

VOL. (000)
2400
1600
800
0

F M A M J J A S O N D | J F M A M J J A S O N D | J F M A M J J A S O N D | J F M A M J J A S
1992 | **1993** | **1994** | **1995**

Overview - 26-JUL-95

We expect that RYAN's sales growth in 1995 will come largely from more restaurants being open. The number of company-operated units is expected to increase by about 22. Also, at the flagship Ryan's chain, we look for sales to be bolstered by growing use of a scatter format with the self-service Mega Bar, which already accounts for a majority of unit sales. With the scatter (multi-location) format, customers' access to the Mega Bar should generally be easier, particularly at busy times. An increase in marketing expenditures should also help comparable-unit sales. However, we expect RYAN's overall profit margins to narrow, including pressure from labor costs. RYAN's franchise revenues in 1995 should be helped by the absence of a royalty non-payment issue, which had a modest adverse impact on RYAN's earnings in 1994.

Valuation - 26-JUL-95

We view the stock of this restaurant company as having appeal for capital gains, based on the prospect of at least modest earnings growth in the year ahead. We look for investor support to grow if our projections of improved comparable-unit sales and higher profits materialize. We view the prospect of improved earnings momentum as more than offsetting concerns about prospective labor cost pressure, and rising competition from other casual dining chains. Longer-term, the company's efforts to develop several new restaurant concepts add some speculative appeal to the stock.

Key Stock Statistics

S&P EPS Est. 1995	0.60	Tang. Bk. Value/Share	5.18
P/E on S&P Est. 1995	11.7	Beta	1.03
S&P EPS Est. 1996	0.65	Shareholders	9,800
Dividend Rate/Share	Nil	Market cap. (B)	$0.381
Shs. outstg. (M)	53.4	Inst. holdings	58%
Avg. daily vol. (M)	0.361	Insider holdings	NA

Value of $10,000 invested 5 years ago: $ 9,180

Fiscal Year Ending Dec. 31

	1995	% Change	1994	% Change	1993	% Change
Revenues (Million $)						
1Q	117.3	10%	106.9	18%	90.39	7%
2Q	131.4	14%	114.8	13%	101.3	11%
3Q	—	—	115.0	10%	104.1	14%
4Q	—	—	111.5	14%	98.10	14%
Yr.	—	—	448.2	14%	393.9	12%
Income (Million $)						
1Q	7.31	NM	7.27	2%	7.16	40%
2Q	9.06	3%	8.83	11%	7.93	-6%
3Q	—	—	7.84	6%	7.40	-5%
4Q	—	—	6.61	9%	6.05	-14%
Yr.	—	—	30.54	7%	28.54	NM
Earnings Per Share ($)						
1Q	0.14	NM	0.14	8%	0.13	NM
2Q	0.17	6%	0.16	7%	0.15	-6%
3Q	E0.16	—	0.15	7%	0.14	NM
4Q	E0.13	—	0.12	9%	0.11	-15%
Yr.	E0.60	—	0.57	8%	0.53	NM

Next earnings report expected: mid October

Ryan's Family Steak Houses

26-JUL-95

Business Summary - 26-JUL-95

Ryan's Family Steak Houses is an operator and franchisor of restaurants, located mainly in the Southeast. In 1994, the Ryan's chain, including franchises, had systemwide sales totaling about $499 million, up 11% from the year before. Also, in 1994, average sales for company-owned restaurants open at least 18 months declined about 0.5%, following a 2.7% drop in 1993.

In the Ryan's chain, the number of units in operation at the end of recent years was:

	1994	1993	1992	1991
Company-owned	210	194	165	142
Franchised	30	34	35	35

The Ryan's company-owned restaurants are free-standing units with seating capacity for about 300 to 500 persons. The menu includes a self-service Mega Bar, plus traditional "steak house" entrees, such as steaks, hamburgers, chicken, and seafood. The Mega Bar, which generates a sizable portion of sales, includes salad items, soups, cheeses, rolls, and a variety of hot meats and vegetables. Since 1993, RYAN has been rolling out a scatter Mega Bar format, which includes five food service locations intended to provide easier customer access and more food variety. At year-end 1994, scatter bars had been installed in about 105 company-operated restaurants. Also, all entree purchases include the opportunity to visit a bakery bar, which features various dessert selections.

In 1995, a net increase of about 18 company-operated Ryan's units is expected. RYAN is now testing several new casual dining concepts, and is likely to have about five such units open by year-end 1995. Also, at June 28, 1995, RYAN had notes payable totaling $67.5 million.

Important Developments

Jul. '95—In 1995's first quarter, comparable-unit sales at company-operated restaurants increased 3%, following a less than 1% rise in the prior quarter. RYAN's sales are getting a boost from the rollout of a new "scatter" Mega Bar format, which is intended to offer customers easier access and more food variety. As of June 28, 1995, 166 of RYAN's company-operated restaurants had this format. Also, in the second quarter there was a net addition of four company-operated restaurants in the Ryan's chain. However, profit margins narrowed at company units, largely due to higher labor costs. RYAN has been seeking to improve service levels by adding personnel, and has also boosted some training efforts. In addition, RYAN is now testing three new restaurant concepts, including one that features Southwestern food.

Capitalization

Long Term Debt: None (6/95).

Per Share Data ($)

	1994	1993	1992	1991	1990	1989
Tangible Bk. Val.	5.04	4.47	3.93	3.35	2.89	2.43
Cash Flow	0.89	0.83	0.78	0.65	0.66	0.57
Earnings	0.57	0.53	0.53	0.44	0.46	0.41
Dividends	Nil	Nil	Nil	Nil	Nil	Nil
Payout Ratio	Nil	Nil	Nil	Nil	Nil	Nil
Prices - High	9⅛	11⅝	12⅝	10¼	8½	9
- Low	5⅜	6⅞	7¾	5⅜	3⅞	5⅛
P/E Ratio - High	16	22	24	23	18	22
- Low	9	13	15	12	8	13

(Year Ended Dec. 31)

Income Statement Analysis (Million $)

	1994	%Chg	1993	%Chg	1992	%Chg	1991
Revs.	449	13%	396	13%	352	18%	299
Oper. Inc.	65.6	8%	61.0	4%	58.6	22%	48.2
Depr.	17.4	8%	16.1	18%	13.7	20%	11.4
Int. Exp.	2.7	85%	1.5	11%	1.3	-14%	1.5
Pretax Inc.	48.0	6%	45.3	NM	45.3	22%	37.1
Eff. Tax Rate	36%	—	37%	—	38%	—	37%
Net Inc.	30.5	7%	28.5	NM	28.3	21%	23.3

Balance Sheet & Other Fin. Data (Million $)

	1994	1993	1992	1991	1990	1989
Cash	0.7	1.9	1.7	2.6	2.6	0.4
Curr. Assets	9.0	9.5	6.0	6.3	6.1	3.1
Total Assets	380	334	275	238	205	165
Curr. Liab.	100	84.9	55.7	50.3	43.1	28.1
LT Debt	Nil	Nil	Nil	Nil	Nil	Nil
Common Eqty.	269	239	210	177	152	127
Total Cap.	280	249	219	187	162	137
Cap. Exp.	66.7	71.3	54.2	43.9	46.1	32.0
Cash Flow	47.9	44.6	42.0	34.7	34.6	29.9

Ratio Analysis

	1994	1993	1992	1991	1990	1989
Curr. Ratio	0.1	0.1	0.1	0.1	0.1	0.1
% LT Debt of Cap.	Nil	Nil	Nil	Nil	Nil	Nil
% Net Inc.of Revs.	6.8	7.2	8.0	7.8	8.8	8.9
% Ret. on Assets	8.6	9.4	11.0	10.5	13.0	14.0
% Ret. on Equity	12.0	12.7	14.6	14.1	17.2	18.4

Dividend Data (The company does not expect to pay cash dividends in the foreseeable future, but plans rather to retain available funds for expansion.)

Data as orig. reptd.; bef. results of disc. opers. and/or spec. items. Per share data adj. for stk. divs. as of ex-div. date. E-Estimated. NA-Not Available. NM-Not Meaningful. NR-Not Ranked.

Office—405 Lancaster Ave., P.O. Box 100, Greer, SC 29652. Tel—(803) 879-1000. Chrmn, Pres & CEO—C. D. Way. EVP—G. E. McCranie. VP-Fin & CFO—F. T. Grant, Jr. Secy & Investor Contact—Janet J. Gleitz. Dirs—J. D. Cockman, B. L. Edwards, B. S. MacKenzie, G. E. McCranie, H. K. Roberts, Jr., J. M. Shoemaker, Jr., C. D. Way. Transfer Agent—Wachovia Bank of North Carolina, N. A., Winston-Salem. Incorporated in South Carolina in 1977. Empl-15,000. S&P Analyst: Tom Graves, CFA

Ryder System

NYSE Symbol **R**
In S&P 500

25-SEP-95

Industry:
Auto rental/service

Summary: Ryder is the largest U.S. lessor of trucks and a leading hauler of automobiles. It also provides contract carriage and logistics services and school bus transportation.

| S&P Opinion: Accumulate (★★★★) | Recent Price • 25⅝ | Yield • 2.3% |
| | 52 Wk Range • 26⅞-19⅞ | 12-Mo. P/E • 12.8 |

Earnings vs. Previous Year
▲=Up ▼=Down ►=No Change

Quantitative Evaluations

Outlook
(1 Lowest—5 Highest)
• **3⁻**

Fair Value
• **25**

Risk
• **Low**

Earn./Div. Rank
• **B**

Technical Eval.
• **Bearish** since 7/95

Rel. Strength Rank
(1 Lowest—99 Highest)
• **58**

Insider Activity
• **NA**

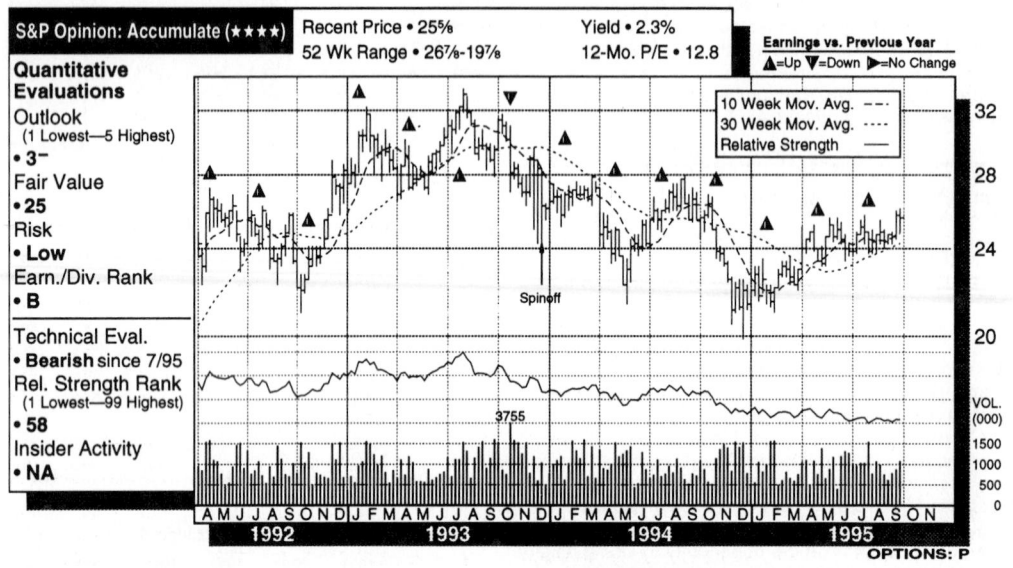

10 Week Mov. Avg. ---
30 Week Mov. Avg. ····
Relative Strength ——

Spinoff

3755

VOL. (000)

OPTIONS: P

Overview - 25-SEP-95

Full-service leasing profits in 1995 will benefit from internal growth and the acquisition of Lend Lease Trucks. International revenues will be aided by recent acquisitions. Margins may narrow, restricted by lower rates under new contracts. Margins for commercial truck rentals may narrow, as slower economic growth contributes to excess industry capacity. Consumer truck rentals will be flat, reflecting housing activity. Despite the benefits of recent restructuring efforts and a better workers' compensation experience, auto hauling profits may slip, reflecting flat volumes and the effects of September's strike. Strong gains are anticipated from student transportation services. Logistics services will be aided by a rise in the number of companies outsourcing these activities. Higher interest costs will be balanced by increased equipment gains.

Valuation - 25-SEP-95

The shares of this leading truck lessor have continued to creep upward in 1995 but remain locked in a two-year bear market. Despite solid profit growth from its truck leasing and transportation businesses, investors have been indifferent to Ryder's stock, apparently put off by the cyclical nature of its business. Though the third quarter strike against Ryder's auto hauling division is likely to penalize 1995 comparisons, we think investors will focus on the 1996 environment, which we view constructively. Ryder's long-term outlook is bright as it enjoys a leadership position in the rapidly expanding market for logistics.

Key Stock Statistics

S&P EPS Est. 1995	2.05	Tang. Bk. Value/Share	10.91
P/E on S&P Est. 1995	12.5	Beta	1.25
S&P EPS Est. 1996	2.40	Shareholders	19,600
Dividend Rate/Share	0.60	Market cap. (B)	$ 2.0
Shs. outstg. (M)	78.9	Inst. holdings	87%
Avg. daily vol. (M)	0.172	Insider holdings	NA

Value of $10,000 invested 5 years ago: NA

Fiscal Year Ending Dec. 31

	1995	% Change	1994	% Change	1993	% Change
Revenues (Million $)						
1Q	1,233	15%	1,072	7%	1,000	-19%
2Q	1,324	13%	1,176	9%	1,080	-19%
3Q	—	—	1,195	14%	1,044	-19%
4Q	—	—	1,243	14%	1,094	-18%
Yr.	—	—	4,686	11%	4,217	-19%
Income (Million $)						
1Q	26.58	12%	23.74	19%	19.95	15%
2Q	51.49	3%	49.84	22%	40.74	8%
3Q	—	—	41.96	79%	23.49	-29%
4Q	—	—	37.99	24%	30.54	2%
Yr.	—	—	153.5	34%	114.7	-3%
Earnings Per Share ($)						
1Q	0.34	13%	0.30	30%	0.23	15%
2Q	0.65	2%	0.64	25%	0.51	9%
3Q	E0.50	-6%	0.53	77%	0.30	-27%
4Q	E0.56	17%	0.48	23%	0.39	8%
Yr.	E2.05	5%	1.95	36%	1.43	NM

Next earnings report expected: mid October

Ryder System

Business Summary - 25-SEP-95

Contributions to operating profits (in millions) by business segment in recent years were:

	1994	1993
Vehicle leasing & services	$389.1	$335.8
Automotive carriers	49.9	31.8
Other	0.3	-0.1

Ryder is the world's largest full-service truck lessor, managing a fleet of 83,100 vehicles in the U.S. and Canada and 9,973 vehicles in the U.K., Germany, Poland and Mexico. Under a full-service lease, the company provides vehicles, maintenance and supplies, while customers furnish drivers and control dispatching. Ryder also performs maintenance services on more than 32,000 non-leased vehicles.

The company is the U.S. leader in commercial truck rentals, with a fleet of some 41,000 vehicles. Ryder is the second largest consumer truck rental company in the U.S., having a fleet of 34,000 vehicles at 4,800 company locations and independent dealers.

Ryder's dedicated logistics division provides integrated supply chain management, including the transportation, warehousing and purchase of raw materials through delivery of finished products. At 1994 year-end, Ryder had contracts with nearly 500 firms.

Ryder's public transportation unit manages or operates 89 public transit systems in 29 states, is the second largest provider of student transportation services, operating 7,753 school buses in 20 states, and maintains 17,500 public transit vehicles in 28 states.

The company is the largest U.S. hauler of light trucks and automobiles. In 1994, it transported 6.3 million new automobiles and trucks, up from 5.9 million vehicles in 1993. GM accounted for 54% of auto group sales in 1994.

Important Developments

Sep. '95—Ryder said it plans to appeal the decision by the National Labor Relations Board to reject its bid to halt the Teamsters' strike against three of its auto hauling units. Ryder also said it is pursuing the civil suit against the Teamsters filed in the U.S. District Court of Alexandria, Va. claiming damages of some $1.0 million for each day of the strike. The Teamsters' strike, which began on September 7, concerns the union's right to handle all of Ryder's auto business including that performed by R's non-union and non-Teamster carriers.

Capitalization

Long Term Debt: $2,254,083,000 (6/95).

Per Share Data ($)

				(Year Ended Dec. 31)		
	1994	1993	1992	1991	1990	1989
Tangible Bk. Val.	14.33	12.81	18.23	17.47	18.04	18.22
Cash Flow	9.46	8.44	9.07	8.92	9.20	8.67
Earnings	1.95	1.43	1.43	0.75	0.96	0.58
Dividends	0.60	0.60	0.60	0.60	0.60	0.60
Payout Ratio	31%	42%	42%	80%	62%	103%
Prices - High	28	33½	28⅞	21⅝	23⅜	31⅛
- Low	19⅞	24¼	19⅝	14	12¼	19¾
P/E Ratio - High	14	23	20	29	24	54
- Low	10	17	14	19	13	34

Income Statement Analysis (Million $)

	1994	%Chg	1993	%Chg	1992	%Chg	1991
Revs.	4,686	11%	4,217	-19%	5,192	3%	5,061
Oper. Inc.	1,000	14%	879	-7%	941	NM	933
Depr.	592	9%	543	-5%	574	-5%	603
Int. Exp.	145	16%	125	-29%	176	-15%	206
Pretax Inc.	261	24%	210	6%	199	73%	115
Eff. Tax Rate	41%	—	45%	—	41%	—	43%
Net Inc.	154	34%	115	-3%	118	79%	66.0

Balance Sheet & Other Fin. Data (Million $)

	1994	1993	1992	1991	1990	1989
Cash	76.0	57.0	72.0	72.0	101	104
Curr. Assets	759	601	1,235	1,319	1,282	1,486
Total Assets	5,014	4,258	4,930	5,080	5,502	5,938
Curr. Liab.	1,093	969	1,142	1,185	1,444	1,545
LT Debt	1,795	1,375	1,529	1,777	1,923	2,193
Common Eqty.	1,129	990	1,375	1,288	1,328	1,387
Total Cap.	3,494	2,892	3,452	3,585	3,828	4,185
Cap. Exp.	1,769	1,175	1,035	580	795	1,129
Cash Flow	745	654	681	659	688	670

Ratio Analysis

	1994	1993	1992	1991	1990	1989
Curr. Ratio	0.7	0.6	1.1	1.1	0.9	1.0
% LT Debt of Cap.	51.4	47.5	44.3	49.6	50.2	52.4
% Net Inc.of Revs.	3.3	2.7	2.3	1.3	1.6	1.0
% Ret. on Assets	3.3	2.5	2.3	1.2	1.5	0.9
% Ret. on Equity	14.4	9.3	8.0	4.2	5.4	3.2

Dividend Data —Dividends were resumed in 1976. A dividend reinvestment plan is available. A "poison pill" stock purchase rights plan was adopted in 1986.

Amt. of Div. $	Date Decl.	Ex-Div. Date	Stock of Record	Payment Date
0.150	Oct. 21	Nov. 14	Nov. 18	Dec. 20 '94
0.150	Feb. 17	Feb. 27	Mar. 03	Mar. 20 '95
0.150	May. 05	May. 22	May. 26	Jun. 20 '95
0.150	Aug. 18	Aug. 30	Sep. 01	Sep. 20 '95

Data as orig. reptd.; bef. results of disc. opers. and/or spec. items. Per share data adj. for stk. divs. as of ex-div. date. E-Estimated. NA-Not Available. NM-Not Meaningful. NR-Not Ranked.

Office—3600 N.W. 82nd Ave., Miami, FL 33166. **Tel**—(305) 593-3726. **Chrmn, Pres & CEO**—M. A. Burns. **Sr Exec VP-Fin & CFO**—E. A. Huston. **Secy**—H. J. Chozianin. **Investor Contact**—R. Tromberg. **Dirs**—A. H. Bernstein, M. A. Burns, J. L. Dionne, E. T. Foote II, J. A. Georges, V. E. Jordan Jr., D. T. Kearns, L. M. Martin, J. W. McLamore, P. J. Rizzo, H. B. Waldron, A. O. Way, M. H. Willes. **Transfer Agent & Registrar**—First National Bank of Boston. **Incorporated** in Florida in 1955. **Empl**-43,654. **S&P Analyst:** Stephen R. Klein

SBC Communications Inc.

NYSE Symbol SBC Options on Pacific (Jan-Apr-Jul-Oct) In S&P 500

Price	Range	P–E Ratio	Dividend	Yield	S&P Ranking	Beta
Jul. 31'95	1995					
48⅛	49–39⅝	17	1.66	3.4%	A	0.51

Summary

SBC Communications (formerly Southwestern Bell) has diversified beyond its core telephone operations through investments in cellular telephone service, cable television and international ventures.

Current Outlook

Earnings for 1995 are estimated at $3.05, versus $2.74 earned in 1994.

The quarterly dividend was raised 5.1%, to $0.41½ from $0.39½ with the May 1995 payment.

The company is positioning itself for growth by expanding its core network operations strengths to new market opportunities and by working with regulators to reduce its regulatory burden. In 1995, about one-third of net income will be generated by SBC's investments outside its core telephone operations. Growth will be led by the cellular operations which we believe are among the best run in the nation. Although the bulk of earnings growth will come from diversified operations, core telephone operations should continue to post moderate earnings increases. The company should be able to maintain revenue growth despite emerging competition.

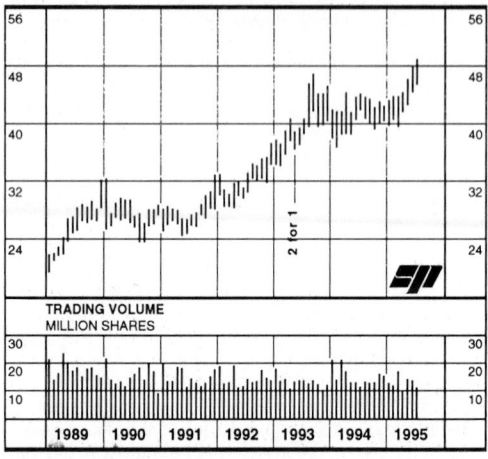

TRADING VOLUME
MILLION SHARES

Revenues (Billion $)

Quarter:	1995	1994	1993	1992
Mar.	2.88	2.65	2.46	2.29
Jun.	2.99	2.76	2.54	2.39
Sep.	---	3.00	2.80	2.62
Dec.	---	3.21	2.90	2.72
	---	11.62	10.69	10.02

Revenues for the six months ended June 30, 1995, rose 8.4%, year to year, reflecting solid gains at the telephone unit and strong cellular growth. Margins widened, aided by cost control efforts. Net income advanced 13%. Share earnings were $1.38, versus $1.24.

Common Share Earnings ($)

Quarter:	1995	1994	1993	1992
Mar.	0.65	0.59	0.51	0.44
Jun.	0.73	0.64	0.56	0.51
Sep.	E0.86	0.80	0.68	0.64
Dec.	E0.81	0.71	0.64	0.59
	E3.05	2.74	2.39	2.17

Important Developments

May '95— SBC's Texas operations will move from rate of return regulation to price regulation on September 1, 1995. In April 1995, SBC, Ameritech, BellSouth and Walt Disney agreed to form a video and interactive services venture.

Mar. '95— In the first phase of FCC auctions for broadband personal communications services (PCS) licenses, SBC placed winning bids in Little Rock, Tulsa and Memphis.

Feb. '95— SBC purchased a 40% equity stake in VTRI, a privately-owned telecommunications holding company in Chile, for $316.6 million. In October 1994, SBC formed a marketing alliance with GTE Corp., which essentially allows each company to compete as an additional cellular brand on the other's cellular network. The alliance will extend SBC's wireless reach to more of its wireline operating territory and increase traffic generated on its network by GTE.

Next earnings report expected in mid-October.

Per Share Data ($)

Yr. End Dec. 31	1994	1993	1992	1991	1990	1989	1988	1987	1986	1985
Tangible Bk. Val.	**9.37**	10.70	13.03	12.13	11.85	11.42	11.59	11.07	12.59	12.13
Cash Flow	**6.13**	5.74	5.24	4.87	4.65	4.97	4.84	NA	NA	NA
Earnings[1]	**2.74**	2.39	2.17	1.93	1.84	1.82	1.77	1.74	1.71	1.67
Dividends	**1.563**	1.498	1.450	1.410	1.360	1.285	1.220	1.137	1.050	0.984
Payout Ratio	57%	63%	67%	73%	74%	71%	69%	65%	61%	59%
Prices—High	**44⅜**	47	37⅜	32¹⁵⁄₁₆	32⅜	32³⁄₁₆	21⁵⁄₁₆	22¾	19⁷⁄₁₆	14¾
Low	**36¾**	34³⁄₁₆	28⁵⁄₁₆	24½	23⅜	19⁷⁄₁₆	16½	13¾	13³⁄₁₆	11⁷⁄₁₆
P/E Ratio—	**16–13**	20–14	17–13	17–13	18–13	18–11	12–9	13–8	11–8	9–7

Data as orig. reptd. Adj. for stk. div. of 100% May 1993, 200% May 1987. **1.** Bef. spec. item(s) of -3.80 in 1993, -0.27 in 1991. NA-Not Available.

SBC Communiccations Inc.

Income Data (Million $)

Year Ended Dec. 31	Revs.	Depr.	Maint.	Oper. Ratio	[1]Fxd. Chgs. Cover.	Constr. Credits	Eff. Tax Rate	[2]Net Inc.	% Return On Revs.	% Return On Invest. Capital	[3]Com. Equity	Cash Flow
1994	11,619	2,038	NA	82.7%	4.44	NA	32.3%	1,649	14.2	13.0	20.7	3,687
1993	10,690	2,007	NA	83.6%	5.15	NA	30.3%	1,435	13.4	11.1	19.2	3,442
1992	10,015	1,842	NA	83.7%	4.53	NA	30.4%	1,302	13.0	9.7	14.3	3,144
1991	9,332	1,765	1,535	82.4%	4.02	34.1	29.7%	1,157	12.4	9.2	13.0	2,922
1990	9,113	1,691	1,553	82.3%	3.76	26.1	28.5%	1,101	12.1	9.1	12.9	2,792
1989	8,730	1,891	1,450	81.4%	3.60	14.8	26.1%	1,093	12.5	9.3	12.9	2,984
1988	8,453	1,845	1,469	81.0%	3.42	15.3	24.8%	1,060	12.5	9.1	12.7	2,905
1987	8,003	1,650	1,439	80.8%	4.11	27.2	34.2%	1,047	13.1	8.9	13.0	NA
1986	7,902	1,387	1,600	81.2%	4.47	42.3	41.0%	1,023	12.9	9.2	13.3	NA
1985	7,925	1,302	1,612	81.5%	4.40	54.5	39.7%	996	12.6	9.4	13.7	NA

Balance Sheet Data (Million $)

Dec. 31	Gross Prop.	Capital Expend.	Net Prop.	% Earn. on Net Prop.	Total Cap.	LT Debt	% LT Debt	Pfd.	% Pfd.	Com.	% Com.
1994	29,256	2,350	17,317	11.6	16,893	5,848	41.2	Nil	Nil	8,356	58.8
1993	28,171	2,221	17,092	10.3	15,885	5,459	41.8	Nil	Nil	7,609	58.2
1992	26,978	2,144	16,899	9.8	19,044	5,716	38.1	Nil	Nil	9,304	61.9
1991	25,755	1,826	16,510	10.0	18,622	5,675	39.0	Nil	Nil	8,859	61.0
1990	24,670	1,778	16,322	10.0	18,224	5,483	39.0	Nil	Nil	8,581	61.0
1989	24,529	1,483	16,078	10.0	18,051	5,456	39.5	Nil	Nil	8,367	60.5
1988	23,651	1,222	16,304	9.7	17,792	5,039	37.2	Nil	Nil	8,504	62.8
1987	23,085	1,484	16,740	9.2	18,138	5,649	40.8	Nil	Nil	8,191	59.2
1986	21,911	1,970	16,727	9.0	16,892	4,912	38.6	Nil	Nil	7,818	61.4
1985	20,524	2,090	16,140	9.3	16,212	5,001	40.3	Nil	Nil	7,397	59.7

Data as orig. reptd. 1. Times int. exp. (pretax basis). 2. Bef. spec. items. 3. As reptd. by co. NA-Not Available.

Business Summary

SBC Communications (formerly Southwestern Bell) is the eighth largest telephone holding company in the U.S. Its telephone subsidiary provides wireline local telephone service in five southwestern states to 13.6 million access lines. SBC also provides cellular telephone service in its home markets and certain other markets nationwide; at June 30, 1995, it operated systems serving 3.2 million subscribers.

In January 1994, SBC acquired two cable television systems in the Washington, D.C., metropolitan area for $650 million. In May, SBC filed a request with Maryland regulators for authority to provide telephone service to customers in Montgomery County over its cable network.

Other subsidiaries publish and sell advertising for classified directories, and market a variety of telecommunications systems and products. The company also owns a minority interest in Bell Communications Research, which provides technical assistance and consulting services to local telephone companies.

International operations include a 10% interest in Teléfonos de México, cable and telecommunications operations in the U.K., and Australian directory services.

Finances

In October 1994, SBC agreed to invest $626 million in a joint venture with Compagnie Generale des Eaux (CGE). The investment will give SBC an effective 10% stake in a nationwide French cellular system plus a minority interest in other mobile communications businesses. SBC sees strong growth potential from the investment as French cellular penetration lags that of other major European countries; in addition, the investment positions SBC to take advantage of the opening of the French telephone market to competition by 1998. Through the joint venture, CGE will invest $247 million for a 10% stake in SBC's Washington D.C./Baltimore cellular operations.

Dividend Data

Dividends were initiated in 1984. A dividend reinvestment plan is available. A "poison pill" stock purchase rights plan was adopted in 1989.

Amt of Divd. $	Date Decl.	Ex-divd. Date	Stock of Record	Payment Date
0.39½	Sep. 30	Oct. 4	Oct. 11	Nov. 1'94
0.39½	Dec. 20	Jan. 4	Jan. 10	Feb. 1'95
0.41½	Mar. 31	Apr. 4	Apr. 10	May 1'95
0.41½	Jun. 30	Jul. 6	Jul. 10	Aug. 1'95

Capitalization

Long Term Debt: $5,559,500,000 (3/95).

Common Stock: 607,746,811 shs. ($1 par).
Institutions hold 37%.
Shareholders of record: 963,355.

Office—175 E. Houston, San Antonio, TX 78205. Tel—(210) 821-4105. Chrmn & CEO—E. E. Whitacre Jr. SVP, Treas & CFO—D. E. Kiernan. Secy—J. M. Sahm. Investor Contact—Sallie Westbrook. Dirs—C. C. Barksdale, J. E. Barnes, J. S. Blanton, A. A. Busch III, R. R. Cardenas, M. K. Eby Jr., T. C. Frost, J. T. Hay, B. R. Inman, C. F. Knight, S. C. Mobley, H. M. Monroe Jr., C. Slim Helú, P. P. Upton, E. E. Whitacre Jr. Transfer Agent & Registrar—The Bank of New York, NYC. Incorporated in Delaware in 1983. Empl—58,750.

SCEcorp

NYSE Symbol **SCE**
In S&P 500

24-AUG-95 | **Industry:** Utilities-Electric

Summary: SCEcorp is the holding company for Southern California Edison. Its nonutility division is engaged in electric power generation, financial investments and real estate development.

S&P Opinion: Hold (★★★)	Recent Price • 16¾	Yield • 6.0%
	52 Wk Range • 18-12⅝	12-Mo. P/E • 10.4

Quantitative Evaluations

Outlook
(1 Lowest—5 Highest)
• **2⁺**

Fair Value
• **16**

Risk
• **Low**

Earn./Div. Rank
• **B+**

Technical Eval.
• **Bearish** since 12/94

Rel. Strength Rank
(1 Lowest—99 Highest)
• **30**

Insider Activity
• **Neutral**

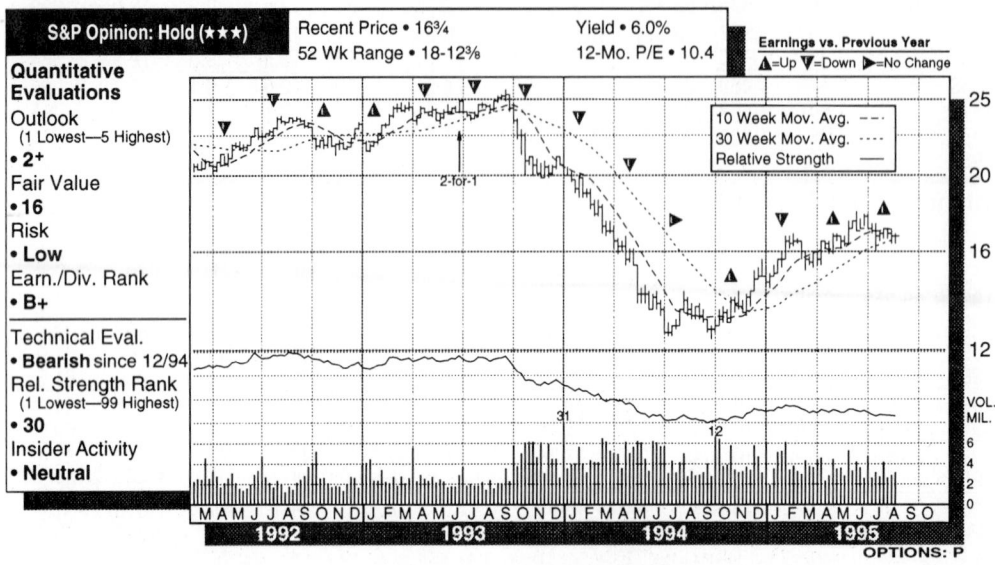

Earnings vs. Previous Year
▲=Up ▼=Down ▶=No Change

10 Week Mov. Avg. - - -
30 Week Mov. Avg. ·······
Relative Strength ——

2-for-1

OPTIONS: P

Overview - 24-AUG-95

Share earnings should benefit in 1995 from a higher return on equity authorized last November. Partially offsetting is a rate cut under a provisional general rate case agreement, but cost controls and the absence of modest one-time charges from headcount reduction programs at the utility should help cushion its negative impact on results. Over the long term, SCE's high rates will present a challenge as competition heats up in the electric utility industry. However, continuing cost reduction efforts and the June 1994 dividend cut enhance SCE's pricing flexibility. Rising profits from the unregulated Mission Energy unit should continue to add to long-term prospects.

Valuation - 24-AUG-95

The shares have recovered about 25% of their value since the precipitous decline that began in late 1993 and mirrored the market's perception that a dividend cut was imminent as well as concerns about rising competition within the electric utility industry. These concerns were accentuated when the California PUC issued a direct access proposal in April 1994 which would, in stages, allow all electricity users within the state to choose their electricity suppliers by the year 2002. The California PUC has yet to issue its final plan for the restructuring of the industry at the retail level; a statewide pooling of power resources being considered would limit the utility's growth potential. SCE's dividend payout is below average for the utilities group, and a dividend increase is not expected.

Key Stock Statistics

S&P EPS Est. 1995	1.65	Tang. Bk. Value/Share	13.13
P/E on S&P Est. 1995	10.2	Beta	0.51
S&P EPS Est. 1996	1.70	Shareholders	153,000
Dividend Rate/Share	1.00	Market cap. (B)	$ 7.5
Shs. outstg. (M)	446.0	Inst. holdings	32%
Avg. daily vol. (M)	0.586	Insider holdings	NA

Value of $10,000 invested 5 years ago: $ 12,371

Fiscal Year Ending Dec. 31

	1995	% Change	1994	% Change	1993	% Change
Revenues (Million $)						
1Q	1,822	4%	1,747	-2%	1,785	4%
2Q	1,861	NM	1,878	6%	1,768	NM
3Q	—	—	2,678	10%	2,424	-5%
4Q	—	—	2,042	11%	1,845	-6%
Yr.	—	—	8,345	7%	7,821	-2%
Income (Million $)						
1Q	153.6	16%	132.0	-11%	148.9	-5%
2Q	159.9	13%	142.0	NM	141.1	-11%
3Q	—	—	273.0	29%	211.3	-22%
4Q	—	—	134.0	-3%	137.8	-9%
Yr.	—	—	681.0	7%	639.0	-14%
Earnings Per Share ($)						
1Q	0.34	13%	0.30	-9%	0.33	-7%
2Q	0.36	13%	0.32	NM	0.32	-10%
3Q	E0.53	-13%	0.61	30%	0.47	-23%
4Q	E0.42	40%	0.30	-3%	0.31	-9%
Yr.	E1.65	9%	1.52	6%	1.43	-14%

Next earnings report expected: mid October

Business Summary - 24-AUG-95

SCEcorp was formed in 1988 as the holding company for Southern California Edison, now its main subsidiary. SCE provides electric service to an area with a population of nearly 11 million people. Electric revenues by customer class in recent years were:

	1994	1993	1992	1991
Residential	36%	36%	36%	35%
Commercial	37%	37%	37%	37%
Industrial	13%	13%	14%	16%
Other	14%	14%	13%	12%

Power sources in 1994 were oil/natural gas 26%, nuclear 20%, coal 13%, hydro 4%, and purchased 37%. Purchased power will likely represent a similar portion of power sources in the future. Peak demand in 1994 was 18,044 mw; capacity at peak totaled 20,615 mw, for a capacity reserve margin of 20%.

SCE owns 75% of the San Onofre 2 and 3 nuclear units. The San Onofre 1 plant was permanently retired in December 1992. SCE also has a 15.8% interest in the three-unit Palo Verde nuclear station. In November 1994, the California PUC increased the return on common equity for SCE's utility from 11% to 12.1% for 1995, reversing a five-year decline.

Capital expenditures totaled $1.1 billion in 1994, down from $1.3 billion in 1993. SCEcorp forecasts construction project expenditures of $4.9 billion for 1995 through 1999 to upgrade existing facilities.

The Mission Group, SCE's nonutility subsidiary, is a leading developer, owner and operator of independent, nonregulated power facilities. It invests in electric power projects and real estate development and has interests totaling 2,124 mw in 36 foreign and U.S. power plants.

Important Developments

Jul. '95—SCEcorp reported a rise in year-to-date earnings to $0.70 a share from $0.61 a year earlier that reflects 7% lower fuel costs, a 7.8% reduction in other operating and maintenance expenses and fewer shares outstanding. Results include contributions of $0.08 and $0.05 from Mission Energy in the respective periods. In January, directors authorized repurchase of up to $150 million (2%) of SCE's common stock.
Jul. '95—The company created a new business unit that will consolidate transmission planning, contracting and operating functions. SCE is separating its generation, transmission and distribution to enhance accountability for costs and revenues. In March, SCE froze rates for residential and small business customers through 1996. It plans to offer business customers flexible pricing options beginning in 1996, and is working to cut electricity prices 25% by the year 2000.

Capitalization

Long Term Debt: $6,884,357,000 (6/95).
Subsid. Cum. Pfd. & Pref. Stock: $646,255,000.

Per Share Data ($) (Year Ended Dec. 31)

	1994	1993	1992	1991	1990	1989
Tangible Bk. Val.	12.76	12.45	12.49	12.11	11.85	11.40
Earnings	1.52	1.43	1.66	1.61	1.80	1.78
Dividends	1.11	1.42	1.39	1.35	1.31	1.27
Payout Ratio	73%	99%	84%	84%	73%	71%
Prices - High	20½	25¾	23⅞	23¾	20⅛	20½
- Low	12⅜	19⅞	20⅛	18	16¾	15½
P/E Ratio - High	13	18	14	15	11	12
- Low	8	14	12	11	9	9

Income Statement Analysis (Million $)

	1994	%Chg	1993	%Chg	1992	%Chg	1991
Revs.	8,345	7%	7,821	-2%	7,984	6%	7,502
Depr.	945	2%	922	14%	807	6%	764
Maint.	332	-9%	363	NM	362	-5%	382
Fxd. Chgs. Cov.	2.9	12%	2.6	-17%	3.1	7%	2.9
Constr. Credits	28.0	-22%	36.0	-3%	37.0	32%	28.0
Eff. Tax Rate	40%	—	36%	—	39%	—	38%
Net Inc.	681	7%	639	-14%	739	5%	703

Balance Sheet & Other Fin. Data (Million $)

	1994	1993	1992	1991	1990	1989
Gross Prop.	20,127	19,441	18,652	17,523	16,916	16,376
Cap. Exp.	1,137	1,259	844	986	905	838
Net Prop.	12,417	12,303	11,937	11,184	11,220	11,281
Capitalization:						
LT Debt	6,347	6,459	6,320	5,745	5,291	5,283
% LT Debt	48	50	49	48	47	47
Pfd.	721	634	637	558	569	583
% Pfd.	5.50	4.90	4.90	4.70	5.00	5.20
Common	6,144	5,948	5,954	5,681	5,503	5,289
% Common	47	46	46	47	48	47
Total Cap.	18,305	17,476	15,618	13,260	12,532	12,234

Ratio Analysis

	1994	1993	1992	1991	1990	1989
Oper. Ratio	84.4	84.4	83.2	83.6	82.6	83.1
% Earn. on Net Prop.	10.5	10.0	11.0	11.0	11.1	10.3
% Ret. on Revs.	8.2	8.2	9.3	9.4	10.9	11.3
% Ret. On Invest.Cap	7.0	7.1	8.6	10.1	11.3	11.5
% Return On Com.Eqty	11.3	10.7	12.5	12.5	14.5	15.0

Dividend Data —Dividends have been paid since 1909. SCE cut the dividend to $0.25 from $0.355 in June 1994.

Amt. of Div. $	Date Decl.	Ex-Div. Date	Stock of Record	Payment Date
0.250	Sep. 15	Sep. 29	Oct. 05	Oct. 31 '94
0.250	Nov. 18	Dec. 29	Jan. 05	Jan. 31 '95
0.250	Feb. 17	Mar. 30	Apr. 05	Apr. 30 '95
0.250	May. 19	Jun. 30	Jul. 05	Jul. 30 '95

Data as orig. reptd.; bef. results of disc opers. and/or spec. items. Per share data adj. for stk. divs. as of ex-div. date.
E-Estimated. NA-Not Available. NM-Not Meaningful. NR-Not Ranked.

Office—2244 Walnut Grove Ave., Rosemead, CA 91770. **Tel**—(818) 302-2222. **Chrmn & CEO**—J. E. Bryson. **SVP, Treas & CFO**—A. J. Fohrer. **Secy**—K. S. Stewart. **Investor Contact**—Jackson P. Horne. **Dirs**—H. P. Allen, N. Barker, Jr., J. E. Bryson, C. C. Frost, W. B. Gerken, J. C. Hanley, C. F. Huntsinger, C. D. Miller, L. G. Nogales, J. J. Pinola, J. M. Rosser, H. T. Segerstrom, E. L. Shannon, Jr., R. H. Smith, D. M. Tellep, J. D. Watkins, E. Zapanta. **Transfer Agent & Registrar**—Co.'s office. **Incorporated** in California in 1909. **Empl**-17,074. **S&P Analyst:** Jane Collin

SAFECO Corp.

NASDAQ Symbol **SAFC**
In S&P 500

31-JUL-95 | **Industry:** Insurance | **Summary:** Mainly a property-casualty insurer, SAFECO also engages in life, health and surety insurance, real estate, investment management and commercial credit.

| **S&P Opinion: Hold (★★★)** | Recent Price • 59¼ | Yield • 3.6% |
| | 52 Wk Range • 59⅞-46¾ | 12-Mo. P/E • 11.1 |

Quantitative Evaluations

Outlook
(1 Lowest—5 Highest)
• **4⁻**

Fair Value
• **58¼**

Risk
• **Low**

Earn./Div. Rank
• **A-**

Technical Eval.
• **Bullish** since 7/95

Rel. Strength Rank
(1 Lowest—99 Highest)
• **49**

Insider Activity
• **Neutral**

Earnings vs. Previous Year
▲=Up ▼=Down ▶=No Change

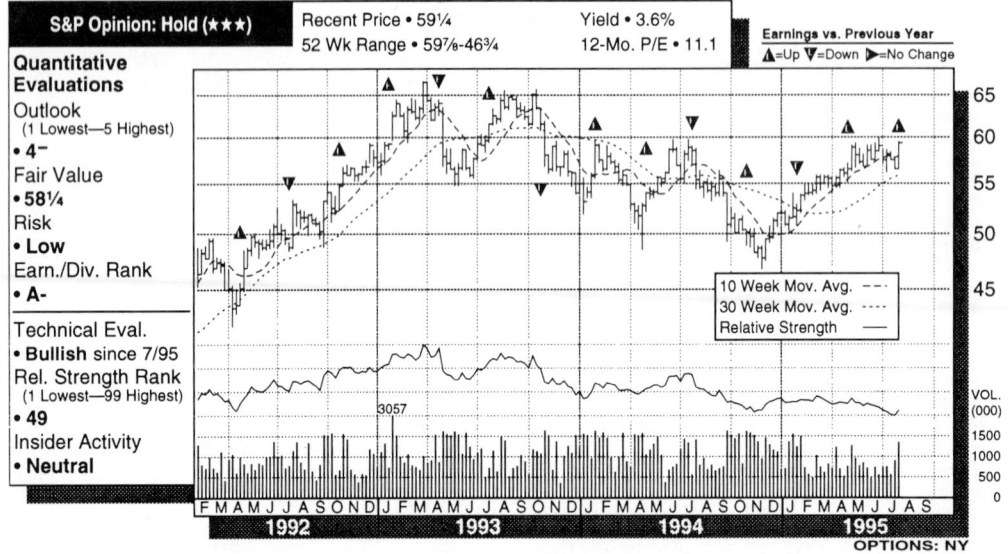

10 Week Mov. Avg. – – –
30 Week Mov. Avg. ·····
Relative Strength —

OPTIONS: NY

Overview - 31-JUL-95

Property-casualty (p-c) written premiums will likely rise 7%-10% in 1995, amid better pricing and/or modest growth in most lines. Underwriting results will be mixed, however. The favorable underwriting trends seen in late 1994 in SAFC's core personal auto line deteriorated somewhat during 1995's first half, as both the severity and frequency of claims increased. However, SAFC's commitment to write personal auto insurance at a time when others are withdrawing from this line aids prospects for market share growth. Underwriting results in the homeowners' line (SAFC's second largest) have been plagued by heavy catastrophe losses, but premium rate hikes and higher insurance-to-value ratios should help mitigate the adverse claim trends. Though commercial lines' pricing remains competitive, selective growth and stringent underwriting have yielded above-average results.

Valuation - 31-JUL-95

After a lackluster performance during the latter part of 1994 amid concerns over the negative effects of rising interest rates and over the adequacy of premium pricing and loss reserves, the shares have rebounded nicely in 1995 and now trade at about 11 times our 1995 operating earnings estimate (which excludes realized investment gains or losses) of $5.30 a share. Despite this seemingly low multiple, the shares are actually trading at the upper end of their historical P/E range. In light of their recent appreciation (aided by the decline in interest rates), the shares are fairly valued, near term.

Key Stock Statistics

S&P EPS Est. 1995	5.30	Tang. Bk. Value/Share	50.45
P/E on S&P Est. 1995	11.2	Beta	1.17
S&P EPS Est. 1996	6.10	Shareholders	5,600
Dividend Rate/Share	2.12	Market cap. (B)	$ 3.7
Shs. outstg. (M)	63.0	Inst. holdings	74%
Avg. daily vol. (M)	0.179	Insider holdings	NA

Value of $10,000 invested 5 years ago: $ 18,480

Fiscal Year Ending Dec. 31

	1995	% Change	1994	% Change	1993	% Change
Revenues (Million $)						
1Q	897.5	5%	857.8	2%	837.3	NM
2Q	984.7	14%	864.6	-2%	885.2	7%
3Q	—	—	901.8	NM	897.0	—
4Q	—	—	912.9	NM	907.4	10%
Yr.	—	—	3,537	NM	3,517	7%
Income (Million $)						
1Q	65.21	16%	56.03	-23%	72.50	-15%
2Q	102.7	14%	90.05	-30%	129.4	NM
3Q	—	—	72.51	-23%	93.79	17%
4Q	—	—	95.79	-26%	130.3	26%
Yr.	—	—	314.4	-26%	425.9	37%
Earnings Per Share ($)						
1Q	1.04	17%	0.89	1%	0.88	-30%
2Q	1.63	14%	1.43	-3%	1.48	NM
3Q	—	—	1.15	17%	0.98	-14%
4Q	—	—	1.52	-1%	1.54	5%
Yr.	E5.30	—	4.99	2%	4.88	13%

Next earnings report expected: late October

Business Summary - 31-JUL-95

SAFECO is a holding company whose subsidiaries engage in property-casualty, life and health insurance throughout the U.S. Other interests include real estate, commercial credit and investment management. Contributions by business segment in 1994 were:

	Revs.	Net Inc.
Property-casualty	82%	68%
Life & health	11%	28%
Real estate	4%	2%
Other	3%	2%

Property-casualty insurance is the company's principal line of business. Through independent agents, most major lines of personal and commercial p-c coverage are offered in nearly all states. Gross p-c premiums written in 1994 amounted to $2.28 billion ($2.13 billion in 1993), of which personal auto accounted for 44%, homeowners 18%, other personal lines 6%, commercial lines 26%, surety 4% and other lines 2%.

The life and health companies provide a broad range of individual and group products, pension programs and annuities, offered through independent agents in all states and the District of Columbia.

SAFECO Properties Inc. is the parent of Winmar Co., a real estate subsidiary involved primarily in the development and management of regional shopping centers and office buildings. SAFECO Credit provides commercial credit and leasing services. SAFECO Asset Management is the investment adviser for the SAFECO family of mutual funds, variable annuity portfolios, and for outside pension accounts. At December 31, 1994, assets under management totaled $2.5 billion ($2.4 billion in 1993).

Important Developments

Jul. '95—SAFECO noted that net written premium growth of 7.7% during the first six months of 1995 reflected a 7.4% rise in personal lines writings, 7.5% higher commercial lines premiums, and a 21% uptick in surety premiums. Underwriting results improved, amid somewhat lower catastrophe losses of $90 million (including $28 million in claims from the second quarter storms in Dallas and a $25 million increase in earthquake loss estimates in the first quarter), versus $106 million (including $88 million in losses from the January 1994 California earthquake).

Capitalization

Total Debt: $1,251,073,000. (6/95).

Per Share Data ($)

(Year Ended Dec. 31)

	1994	1993	1992	1991	1990	1989
Tangible Bk. Val.	44.95	44.09	38.97	35.40	31.50	29.27
Oper. Earnings	4.58	4.88	4.33	3.78	4.31	4.17
Earnings	4.99	6.77	4.96	4.14	4.41	4.75
Dividends	2.37	1.72	1.56	1.42	1.28	1.14
Relative Payout	47%	25%	31%	34%	29%	24%
Prices - High	59¾	66¾	59⅜	48¾	42⅜	39¾
- Low	46¾	53⅞	42	31¼	25⅛	23⅛
P/E Ratio - High	12	10	14	12	10	10
- Low	9	8	10	8	6	6

Income Statement Analysis (Million $)

	1994	%Chg	1993	%Chg	1992	%Chg	1991
Life Ins. In Force	NA	—	NA	—	NA	—	NA
Prem.Inc Life A&H	277	-9%	306	-7%	329	—	NA
Prem.Inc Cas/Prop	2,053	6%	1,930	10%	1,754	—	NA
Net Invest. Inc.	992	4%	952	5%	903	7%	847
Oth. Revs.	215	-35%	329	6%	309	-7%	332
Total Revs.	3,537	NM	3,517	7%	3,295	5%	3,148
Pretax Inc.	390	-32%	577	43%	403	42%	283
Net Oper. Inc.	288	-6%	307	13%	272	15%	237
Net Inc.	314	-26%	426	37%	311	20%	260

Balance Sheet & Other Fin. Data (Million $)

	1994	1993	1992	1991	1990	1989
Cash & Equiv.	293	278	274	248	229	206
Premiums Due	419	401	336	327	326	296
Inv Assets Bonds	9,611	10,830	9,722	8,544	7,482	6,421
Inv. Assets Stock	855	910	919	864	725	773
Inv. Assets Loans	472	453	442	415	390	311
Inv. Assets Total	13,467	12,641	11,477	10,272	9,052	7,953
Deferred Policy Cost	389	367	346	310	291	263
Total Assets	15,902	14,807	13,252	11,907	10,553	9,279
Debt	983	918	839	824	784	765
Common Eqty.	2,829	2,774	2,448	2,221	1,976	1,851

Ratio Analysis

	1994	1993	1992	1991	1990	1989
Comb. Loss-Exp.Ratio	103.8	99.5	104.1	NA	NA	NA
% Ret. on Revs.	8.9	8.7	8.2	7.5	8.9	9.4
% Ret. on Equity	11.2	11.8	11.6	11.3	14.2	15.4
% Invest. Yield	7.6	7.9	8.3	8.8	9.0	9.2

Dividend Data (Cash has been paid each year since 1933.)

Amt. of Div. $	Date Decl.	Ex-Div. Date	Stock of Record	Payment Date
0.490	Aug. 03	Oct. 03	Oct. 07	Oct. 24 '94
0.490	Nov. 02	Dec. 30	Jan. 06	Jan. 23 '95
0.490	Feb. 02	Apr. 03	Apr. 07	Apr. 24 '95
0.530	May. 04	Jul. 05	Jul. 07	Jul. 24 '95

Data as orig. reptd.; bef. results of disc. opers. and/or spec. items. Per share data adj. for stk. divs. as of ex-div. date. E-Estimate. NA-Not Available. NM-Not Meaningful. NR-Not Ranked.

Office—SAFECO Plaza, Seattle, WA 98185. **Tel**—(206) 545-5000. **Chrmn, Pres & CEO**—R. H. Eigsti. **EVP-CFO**—B. A. Dickey. **VP-Secy**—R. A. Pierson. **Dirs**—P. J. Campbell, R. S. Cline, B. A. Dickey, R. H. Eigsti, J. W. Ellis, W. P. Gerberding, D. G. Graham Jr., J. Green III, C. Knudsen, W. G. Reed Jr., J. M. Runstad, P. W. Skinner, G. H. Weyerhaeuser, W. R. Wiley. **Transfer Agent**—First Chicago Trust Co., NYC. **Registrar**—Morgan Guaranty Trust Co., NYC. **Incorporated** in Washington in 1929. **Empl**-7,300. **S&P Analyst:** Catherine A. Seifert

Safety-Kleen Corp.

NYSE Symbol **SK**
In S&P 500

12-OCT-95

Industry:
Pollution Control

Summary: This company provides services to aid automotive service stations, manufacturers and other industrial customers in the cleaning and maintenance of small parts and other equipment.

S&P Opinion: Hold (★★★)	Recent Price • 14⅝	Yield • 2.5%
	52 Wk Range • 18⅛-12⅞	12-Mo. P/E • 16.3

Quantitative Evaluations

Outlook
(1 Lowest—5 Highest)
• **5⁻**

Fair Value
• **17⅝**

Risk
• **Average**

Earn./Div. Rank
• **B+**

Technical Eval.
• **Bullish** since 7/95

Rel. Strength Rank
(1 Lowest—99 Highest)
• **33**

Insider Activity
• **Favorable**

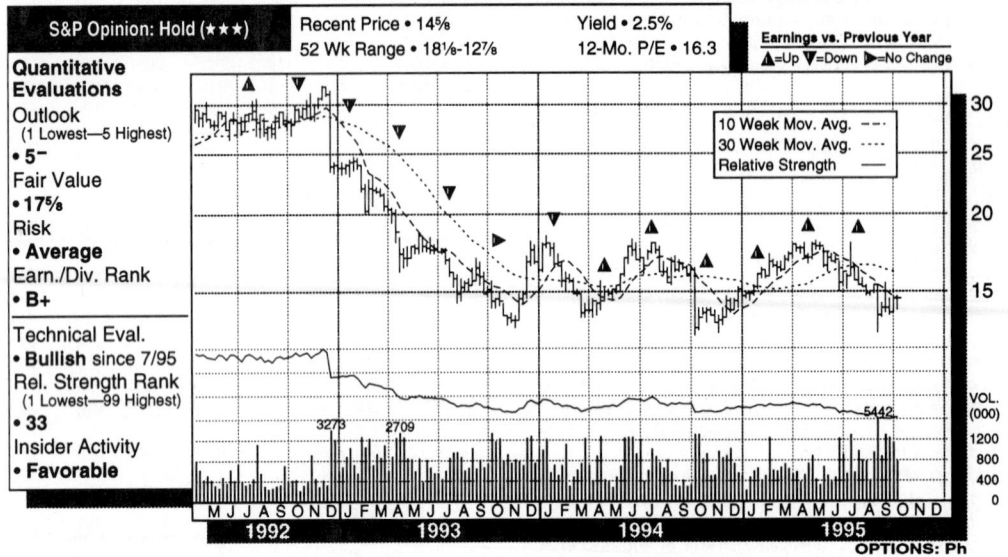

Earnings vs. Previous Year
▲=Up ▼=Down ▶=No Change

10 Week Mov. Avg. ---
30 Week Mov. Avg. ····
Relative Strength —

OPTIONS: Ph

Overview - 12-OCT-95

Revenues should continue to rise moderately through 1996, reflecting growth in the parts cleaner service stemming from market share gains and expansion efforts. Revenues are also seen advancing in the industrial fluid recovery and oil recovery service segments. Margins, which were hurt in 1995's third period by increased costs resulting from unscheduled fuel-burning outages, are expected to recover in the fourth quarter and during 1996 on increased installations of the new cyclonic parts cleaner (which requires less frequent servicing), higher pricing in selected markets and a reduction in imaging services startup losses. SK expects to have all 250,000 of its parts cleaner machines converted to its new, more efficient equipment by mid-1996. Long-term prospects are enhanced by expansion into other services, although growth will be restricted by waste minimization efforts.

Valuation - 12-OCT-95

The stock is likely to be only a market performer in the near term, as the company continues to retrench following disappointing results in recent years. Despite favorable customer reception for the new cyclonic parts cleaner machine, the unscheduled fuel-burning outages, which affected three of the company's four cement plants in the third quarter, are unpredictable and could impact future results. With the shares trading at 17X our $0.85 EPS estimate for 1995, and 15X our $0.95 projection for 1996, a multiple close to that of the market, we suggest holding for potential long-term appreciation.

Key Stock Statistics

S&P EPS Est. 1995	0.85	Tang. Bk. Value/Share	4.98
P/E on S&P Est. 1995	17.2	Beta	0.96
S&P EPS Est. 1996	0.95	Shareholders	7,300
Dividend Rate/Share	0.36	Market cap. (B)	$0.830
Shs. outstg. (M)	57.8	Inst. holdings	62%
Avg. daily vol. (M)	0.229	Insider holdings	NA

Value of $10,000 invested 5 years ago: $ 7,957

Fiscal Year Ending Dec. 31

	1995	% Change	1994	% Change	1993	% Change
Revenues (Million $)						
1Q	194.6	10%	176.8	-3%	181.8	5%
2Q	203.2	11%	183.3	-3%	189.3	3%
3Q	197.5	8%	182.1	NM	182.1	-2%
4Q	—	—	249.0	3%	242.3	-4%
Yr.	—	—	791.3	NM	795.5	NM
Income (Million $)						
1Q	12.07	24%	9.71	12%	8.64	-29%
2Q	12.13	6%	11.47	9%	10.49	-28%
3Q	11.13	-9%	12.21	110%	5.81	-6%
4Q	—	—	16.71	NM	-126.3	NM
Yr.	—	—	50.09	NM	-101.3	NM
Earnings Per Share ($)						
1Q	0.21	24%	0.17	13%	0.15	-29%
2Q	0.21	5%	0.20	11%	0.18	-28%
3Q	0.19	-10%	0.21	110%	0.10	NM
4Q	E0.24	-17%	0.29	NM	-2.19	NM
Yr.	E0.85	-2%	0.87	NM	-1.76	NM

Next earnings report expected: early February

Safety-Kleen Corp.

Business Summary - 11-OCT-95

Safety-Kleen provides fluid recovery services to about 400,000 customers, primarily generators of small quantities of hazardous waste fluids. At the end of 1994, it operated 236 branch facilities, 12 solvent recycling centers, three fuel blending facilities for cement kilns and two used-oil re-refining plants. Revenues by business segment in recent years were:

	1994	1993
Automotive/retail repair services	30%	31%
Industrial services	28%	27%
Oil recovery services	15%	14%
Other services	16%	18%
European operations	11%	10%

The company's core parts cleaner service business consists of a service representative's placing parts cleaner equipment and solvent with a customer and (at regular service intervals) cleaning and maintaining the equipment, delivering clean solvent for use in degreasing small parts and removing the dirty solvent. Substantially all fluid wastes collected are recycled into solvents for re-use or into fuel for the cement manufacturing industry. Parts cleaner services are provided mainly to the automotive/retail repair sector, including service stations and car and truck dealers. At September 9, 1995, the company had 613,251 parts cleaners in service, up from 580,044 a year earlier.

Envirosystems services involve the collection and recycling of waste solvent and other waste fluids from customers that generate larger quantities of such wastes than those collected by the fluid recovery service. The oil recovery service collects used lubricating oils from automobile and truck dealers, garages, oil change outlets, service stations, industrial plants and other businesses and either re-refines the oil into reusable lubricating oil or processes it into fuel for use in industrial furnaces.

Important Developments

Sep. '95—SK said its 1995 third quarter earnings were reduced by approximately $1 million due to new supply agreements with two cement plants and unscheduled fuel burning outages at three of its four plants. Results were hurt by high waste processing and disposal costs, including the costs for disposal of waste-derived fuel that resulted from the fuel burning outages at cement kilns used as the primary outlets for such fuels.

Capitalization

Long Term Debt: $298,492,000 (9/9/95).

Per Share Data ($)

(Year Ended Dec. 31)

	1994	1993	1992	1991	1990	1989
Tangible Bk. Val.	4.89	4.44	6.32	6.26	6.62	4.43
Cash Flow	1.96	-0.62	2.09	1.79	1.93	1.51
Earnings	0.87	-1.76	0.78	0.90	1.05	0.91
Dividends	0.36	0.36	0.34	0.32	0.27	0.24
Payout Ratio	41%	NM	43%	35%	27%	26%
Prices - High	18½	24¾	32¼	37⅞	29⅞	25⅞
- Low	12¾	13⅛	22⅝	22	18¼	15⅞
P/E Ratio - High	21	NM	41	42	28	28
- Low	15	NM	29	24	17	17

Income Statement Analysis (Million $)

	1994	%Chg	1993	%Chg	1992	%Chg	1991
Revs.	791	NM	796	NM	795	14%	695
Oper. Inc.	162	19%	136	-22%	175	18%	148
Depr.	63.1	-4%	65.8	-13%	75.7	48%	51.2
Int. Exp.	17.6	59%	11.1	-37%	17.7	-5%	18.7
Pretax Inc.	85.0	NM	-168	NM	74.3	-11%	83.3
Eff. Tax Rate	41%	—	NM	—	39%	—	38%
Net Inc.	50.0	NM	-100	NM	45.3	-12%	51.6

Balance Sheet & Other Fin. Data (Million $)

	1994	1993	1992	1991	1990	1989
Cash	21.0	17.4	30.6	20.0	33.2	23.6
Curr. Assets	191	194	189	182	170	139
Total Assets	1,016	995	1,006	904	719	538
Curr. Liab.	166	149	141	128	103	82.0
LT Debt	284	289	301	244	122	138
Common Eqty.	396	363	492	464	430	261
Total Cap.	750	713	852	763	603	443
Cap. Exp.	88.0	96.0	149	182	166	133
Cash Flow	113	-36.0	121	103	101	77.0

Ratio Analysis

	1994	1993	1992	1991	1990	1989
Curr. Ratio	1.2	1.3	1.3	1.4	1.7	1.7
% LT Debt of Cap.	37.9	40.5	35.3	31.9	20.3	31.2
% Net Inc.of Revs.	6.3	NM	5.7	7.4	9.4	9.6
% Ret. on Assets	5.0	NM	4.7	6.3	8.4	9.8
% Ret. on Equity	13.2	NM	9.4	11.5	15.3	19.1

Dividend Data —Cash payments began in 1979. A "poison pill" stock purchase rights plan was adopted in 1988.

Amt. of Div. $	Date Decl.	Ex-Div. Date	Stock of Record	Payment Date
0.090	Nov. 11	Dec. 09	Dec. 15	Dec. 29 '94
0.090	Feb. 03	Mar. 10	Mar. 16	Mar. 30 '95
0.090	May. 12	Jun. 13	Jun. 15	Jun. 29 '95
0.090	Aug. 18	Sep. 12	Sep. 14	Sep. 28 '95

Data as orig. reptd.; bef. results of disc. opers. and/or spec. items. Per share data adj. for stk. divs. as of ex-div. date. E-Estimated. NA-Not Available. NM-Not Meaningful. NR-Not Ranked.

Office—1000 N Randall Rd., Elgin, IL 60123-7857. **Tel**—(708) 697-8460. **Chrmn**—D. W. Brinckman. **Pres & CEO**—J. G. Johnson, Jr. **SVP-Fin, Secy & Investor Contact**—Robert W. Willmschen, Jr (708-468-2002). **Treas**—L. M. Rudnick. **Dirs**—D. W. Brinckman, R. T. Farmer, R. A. Gwillim, E. D. Jannotta, J. G. Johnson, Jr., K. G. Otzen, P. D. Schrage, M. Williams, W. G. Wood. **Transfer Agent & Registrar**—First Chicago Trust Co. of N.Y., Jersey City, NJ. **Incorporated** in Wisconsin in 1963. **Empl**-6,600. **S&P Analyst:** Stewart Scharf

St. Jude Medical

NASDAQ Symbol **STJM**
In S&P 500

23-AUG-95

Industry:
Medical equipment/
supply

Summary: The world's leading maker of mechanical heart valves, with over 60% of the worldwide market, STJM also produces cardiac pacemakers through its Pacesetter division.

S&P Opinion: Accumulate (★★★★)	

Recent Price • 57¼	Yield • Nil
52 Wk Range • 60⅜-32½	12-Mo. P/E • 30.0

Quantitative Evaluations

Outlook
(1 Lowest—5 Highest)
• **3+**

Fair Value
• **57¼**

Risk
• **Low**

Earn./Div. Rank
• **B+**

Technical Eval.
• **Bullish** since 7/94

Rel. Strength Rank
(1 Lowest—99 Highest)
• **71**

Insider Activity
• **Neutral**

Earnings vs. Previous Year
▲=Up ▼=Down ▶=No Change

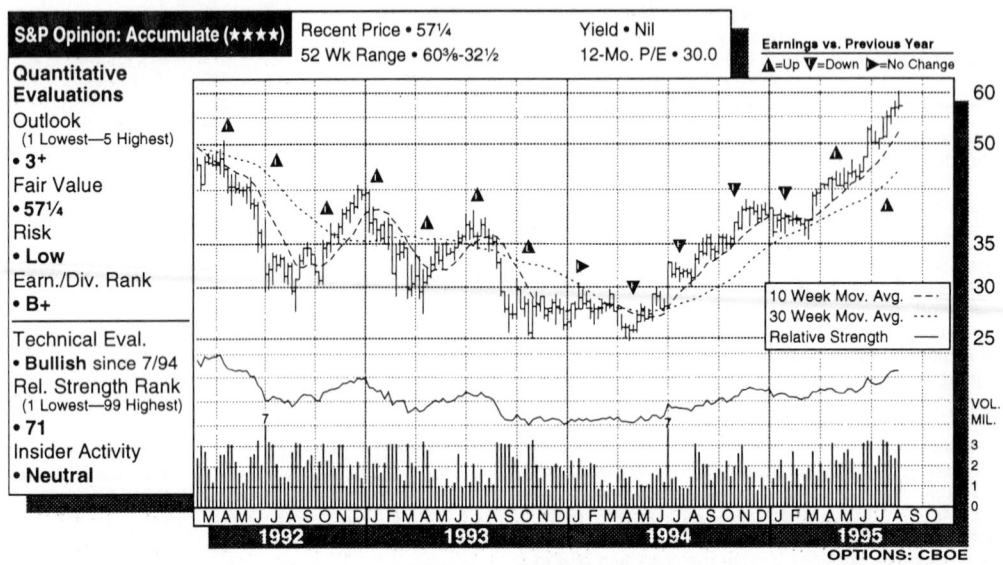

10 Week Mov. Avg. — —
30 Week Mov. Avg. ·····
Relative Strength —

OPTIONS: CBOE

Overview - 23-AUG-95

Bolstered by the full-year inclusion of the Pacesetter cardiac pacemaker business (acquired in September 1994), sales are expected to reach $720 million in 1995, up from 1994's $360 million. Pacesetter sales are being augmented by new products such as the Trilogy, Microny, Paragon and Phoenix pacers. New products are also bolstering sales of the company's heart valves and cardiac assist products. Despite a projected rise in the tax rate, earnings in 1995 should benefit from the greater volume and increased in-house production of heart valve components. Fueled by new products, expanded markets and productivity enhancements, further earnings progress is seen for 1996.

Valuation - 23-AUG-95

Like most health care issues, the shares have been strong performers over the past 12 months, reflecting renewed investor confidence in the medical sector, improving earnings and benefits from the Pacesetter acquisition. Pacesetter has established a leadership position in the $2.45 billion cardiac rhythm management market, which is expected to grow to $4 billion by the end of this decade. STJM is also expanding its commanding position in heart valves through new mechanical and tissue valve products. Company valves have a long-standing reputation for excellence, as attested by their successful implantation in more than 590,000 patients to date. The shares are recommended for long-term appreciation.

Key Stock Statistics

S&P EPS Est. 1995	2.80	Tang. Bk. Value/Share	4.72
P/E on S&P Est. 1995	20.4	Beta	1.05
S&P EPS Est. 1996	3.15	Shareholders	4,800
Dividend Rate/Share	Nil	Market cap. (B)	$ 2.6
Shs. outstg. (M)	46.6	Inst. holdings	64%
Avg. daily vol. (M)	0.590	Insider holdings	0%

Value of $10,000 invested 5 years ago: $ 24,443

Fiscal Year Ending Dec. 31

	1995	% Change	1994	% Change	1993	% Change
Revenues (Million $)						
1Q	180.5	171%	66.69	-2%	68.20	13%
2Q	185.6	178%	66.74	NM	66.90	17%
3Q	—	—	62.47	6%	58.95	1%
4Q	—	—	163.8	179%	58.60	-9%
Yr.	—	—	359.6	42%	252.6	5%
Income (Million $)						
1Q	30.58	15%	26.54	-9%	29.19	17%
2Q	33.12	26%	26.20	-9%	28.84	16%
3Q	—	—	24.49	-6%	25.97	3%
4Q	—	—	2.00	-92%	25.64	-3%
Yr.	—	—	79.23	-28%	109.6	8%
Earnings Per Share ($)						
1Q	0.65	14%	0.57	-7%	0.61	17%
2Q	0.70	25%	0.56	-8%	0.61	17%
3Q	E0.71	37%	0.52	-5%	0.55	4%
4Q	E0.74	NM	0.04	-93%	0.55	NM
Yr.	E2.80	66%	1.69	-27%	2.32	9%

Next earnings report expected: mid October

St. Jude Medical

Business Summary - 23-AUG-95

St. Jude Medical, Inc. is the world's largest maker of mechanical heart valves, accounting for an estimated 62% of the worldwide mechanical valve market. The sales base was boosted over 2.5-fold with the purchase of the Pacesetter cardiac pacemaker division of Siemens AG in September 1994. Sales and profits broke down geographically in 1994 as follows:

	Sales	Profits
U.S. and Canada	70%	67%
Europe	30%	33%

European sales include exports to Africa and the Middle East. All other exports are included in U.S. sales. R&D spending equaled 5.8% of sales in 1994, versus 4.3% in 1993.

The main heart valve product is a bileaflet prosthetic heart valve with four basic components: two leaflets, the valve body, and the sewing cuff. The company receives pyrolytic carbon components for its heart valves from CarboMedics Inc. under a long-term supply contract. Under its agreement with CarboMedics, STJM will be able to produce 48% of its valves from its own components in 1995, 80% in 1996 and 100% by 1999. Worldwide industry heart valve procedures totaled nearly 200,000 in 1994, of which 70% were mechanical valves and 30% porcine or tissue valves. Tissue valves, sold under the BioImplant name, are used in cases where mechanical valve replacement is contraindicated. The company is also doing R&D on new tissue valves. Other products include an annuloplasty ring, an intra-aortic balloon pump and related products.

Pacesetter, based in Sylmar, Calif., with European operations near Stockholm, Sweden, is the world's second largest maker of bradycardia pacemakers, with an estimated 25% share of the market. Its products, sold under the Microny, Solus, Phoenix, Trilogy, Synchrony and other names, had sales of about $400 million in the 12 months through September 1994.

Important Developments

Aug. '95—The FDA granted STJM clearance to begin clinical trials of a new steroid active fixation pacemaker lead called the Tendril. The steroid, situated in the lead's helix tip, is intended to supress the body's inflammatory response to a foreign substance, thereby promoting lower pacing thresholds. Earlier, in June, the FDA approved three new Trilogy pacemakers that feature the company's new PDx diagnostic and programming software with twice the memory capacity of previous versions.

Capitalization

Long Term Debt: $205,000,000 (6/95).

Per Share Data ($)

	1994	1993	1992	1991	1990	1989
Tangible Bk. Val.	11.88	10.43	9.03	6.90	5.10	3.68
Cash Flow	1.87	2.42	2.20	1.90	1.44	1.14
Earnings	1.69	2.32	2.12	1.75	1.35	1.07
Dividends	0.30	0.40	0.30	Nil	Nil	Nil
Payout Ratio	18%	17%	14%	Nil	Nil	Nil
Prices - High	41	42¼	55½	55½	36½	25¼
- Low	24¾	25	27½	30¼	18½	9⅝
P/E Ratio - High	24	18	26	32	27	24
- Low	15	11	13	17	14	9

(Year Ended Dec. 31)

Income Statement Analysis (Million $)

	1994	%Chg	1993	%Chg	1992	%Chg	1991
Revs.	360	42%	253	5%	240	14%	210
Oper. Inc.	148	9%	136	8%	126	17%	108
Depr.	8.3	84%	4.5	25%	3.6	-50%	7.2
Int. Exp.	3.7	—	Nil	—	Nil	—	Nil
Pretax Inc.	106	-27%	145	7%	136	20%	113
Eff. Tax Rate	26%	—	25%	—	26%	—	26%
Net Inc.	79.0	-28%	110	8%	102	21%	84.0

Balance Sheet & Other Fin. Data (Million $)

	1994	1993	1992	1991	1990	1989
Cash	137	369	339	263	179	121
Curr. Assets	434	450	416	330	241	171
Total Assets	920	527	470	375	278	202
Curr. Liab.	113	40.9	39.0	28.5	22.2	14.4
LT Debt	255	Nil	Nil	Nil	Nil	Nil
Common Eqty.	552	484	429	345	254	186
Total Cap.	807	486	431	347	256	187
Cap. Exp.	18.8	16.4	11.7	7.4	9.3	6.8
Cash Flow	88.0	114	105	91.0	69.0	54.0

Ratio Analysis

	1994	1993	1992	1991	1990	1989
Curr. Ratio	3.9	11.0	10.7	11.6	10.9	11.9
% LT Debt of Cap.	31.6	Nil	Nil	Nil	Nil	Nil
% Net Inc.of Revs.	22.0	43.4	42.4	40.0	36.9	34.4
% Ret. on Assets	10.9	22.2	24.0	25.6	26.9	29.4
% Ret. on Equity	15.3	24.3	26.2	28.0	29.3	32.1

Dividend Data —Cash dividends were terminated with the acquisition of Pacesetter in September 1994. Prior to omission, dividends were paid at a rate of $0.10 quarterly. The last payment was in August 1994.

Amt. of Div. $	Date Decl.	Ex-Div. Date	Stock of Record	Payment Date
0.100	Jul. 21	Aug. 04	Aug. 10	Aug. 24 '94

Data as orig. reptd.; bef. results of disc. opers. and/or spec. items. Per share data adj. for stk. divs. as of ex-div. date. E-Estimated. NA-Not Available. NM-Not Meaningful. NR-Not Ranked.

Office—One Lillehei Plaza, St. Paul, MN 55117. **Tel**—(612) 483-2000. **Chrmn, Pres & CEO**—R. A. Matricaria. **VP-Fin & CFO**—S. L. Wilson. **Investor Contact**—Paul Vetter (612-481-7773). **Dirs**—F. A. Ehmann, T. H. Garrett III, K. G. Langone, L. A. Lehmkuhl, R. A. Matricaria, W. R. Miller, C. V. Owens, W. L. Sembrowich, R. G. Stoll, G. R. Wilensky. **Transfer Agent**—American Stock Transfer & Trust Co., Brooklyn. **Incorporated** in Minnesota in 1976. **Empl-**2,248. **S&P Analyst:** H. B. Saftlas

St. Paul Companies

NYSE Symbol **SPC**
In S&P 500

25-AUG-95 Industry:
Insurance

Summary: SPC owns St. Paul Fire & Marine Insurance (the 15th largest property-liability insurer in the U.S.), Minet Group (an insurance broker), and 77% of John Nuveen & Co.

S&P Opinion: Buy (★★★★)	Recent Price • 49½	Yield • 3.2%
	52 Wk Range • 51⅞-39⅜	12-Mo. P/E • 9.0

Quantitative Evaluations

Outlook
(1 Lowest—5 Highest)
• **2+**

Fair Value
• **47½**

Risk
• **Low**

Earn./Div. Rank
• **A-**

Technical Eval.
• **Bullish** since 2/94

Rel. Strength Rank
(1 Lowest—99 Highest)
• **40**

Insider Activity
• **NA**

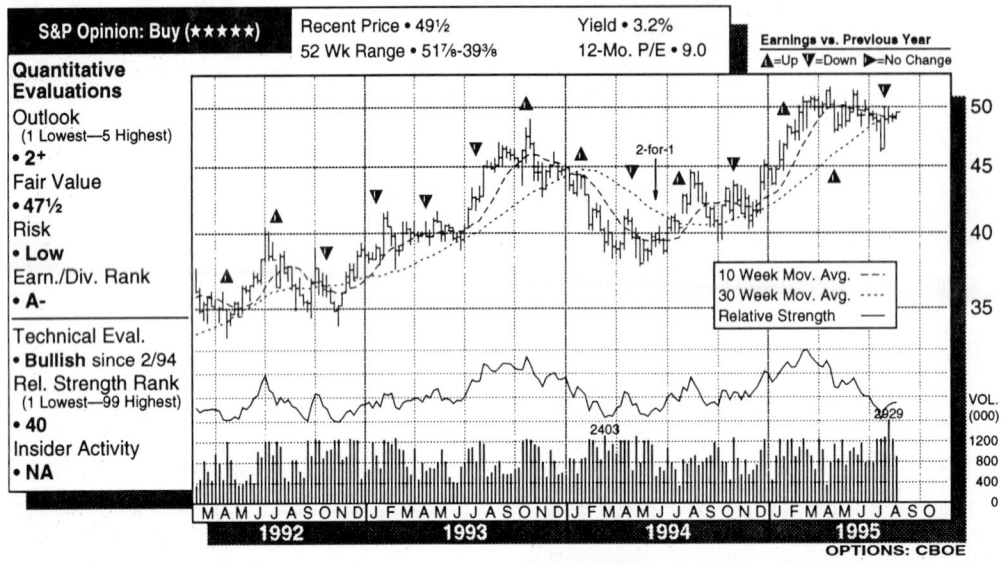

Earnings vs. Previous Year
▲=Up ▼=Down ▶=No Change

10 Week Mov. Avg. ---
30 Week Mov. Avg. ....
Relative Strength —

VOL. (000)

OPTIONS: CBOE

Overview - 25-AUG-95

Written premiums during 1995 will likely advance 10%-12%, as increased volume and/or better pricing in personal lines and reinsurance will be offset by competitive pricing in certain casualty lines. SPC's strong market position in certain lines, such as medical malpractice (where it is the number one underwriter) should offer a certain degree of insulation from price competition. A shift in business mix away from subpar lines such as workers' compensation will aid long-term underwriting results, but may mask an otherwise strong written premium growth trend. Despite heavy second quarter 1995 storm losses, an easing of the heavy catastrophe losses that impaired profitability in 1994 should aid year-to-year comparisons in 1995. Steps taken to increase underwriting efficiency will also aid margins. A firming of insurance pricing would aid results in the insurance brokerage segment.

Valuation - 25-AUG-95

After a lackluster performance during much of 1994 amid the negative effects of rising interest rates and heavy catastrophe losses, the shares have recovered most of their lost ground. Despite the recent appreciation, the shares trade at less than 10 times our 1995 operating earnings estimate of $5.00 a share (which excludes realized investment gains or losses). Given SPC's above-average premium growth trend, underwriting record, and return on equity, expansion of the P/E multiple is warranted.

Key Stock Statistics

S&P EPS Est. 1995	5.00	Tang. Bk. Value/Share	35.60
P/E on S&P Est. 1995	9.9	Beta	0.83
S&P EPS Est. 1996	5.70	Shareholders	7,600
Dividend Rate/Share	1.60	Market cap. (B)	$ 4.2
Shs. outstg. (M)	84.5	Inst. holdings	84%
Avg. daily vol. (M)	0.311	Insider holdings	NA

Value of $10,000 invested 5 years ago: $ 20,445

Fiscal Year Ending Dec. 31

	1995	% Change	1994	% Change	1993	% Change
Revenues (Million $)						
1Q	1,267	9%	1,164	4%	1,114	—
2Q	1,331	14%	1,165	9%	1,069	—
3Q	—	—	1,199	9%	1,105	—
4Q	—	—	1,173	NM	1,172	6%
Yr.	—	—	4,701	5%	4,460	NM
Income (Million $)						
1Q	110.6	72%	64.44	-27%	88.03	-17%
2Q	113.0	-12%	127.8	18%	108.5	-24%
3Q	—	—	129.8	-8%	141.4	NM
4Q	—	—	120.8	35%	89.69	NM
Yr.	—	—	442.8	4%	427.6	NM
Earnings Per Share ($)						
1Q	1.27	74%	0.73	-28%	1.01	-17%
2Q	1.30	-13%	1.49	19%	1.25	-24%
3Q	—	—	1.51	-8%	1.64	NM
4Q	—	—	1.40	37%	1.02	NM
Yr.	E5.00	-2%	5.12	4%	4.92	NM

Next earnings report expected: late October

Business Summary - 25-AUG-95

St. Paul Companies is a management company engaged, through subsidiaries, in providing property-liability insurance and insurance-related products and services to commercial and personal customers. The company's principal subsidiary is St. Paul Fire & Marine Insurance Co., which ranks as the 15th largest property-liability insurer in the U.S. St. Paul Re is the eighth largest reinsurance underwriter in the U.S. and sells reinsurance worldwide.

Contributions to 1994 revenue and pretax income (in million $):

	Revs.	Pretax Income
Underwriting	88%	$561
Investment banking	5%	72
Brokerage & other	7%	-10

The company writes most lines of property-liability insurance. Of the $3.62 billion in written premiums in 1994 ($3.18 billion in 1993), specialized commercial accounted for 30%, personal and business insurance 21%, medical services 19% (SPC is the largest medical liability insurer in the U.S.), reinsurance 14%, standard commercial 11%, and international 5%.

London-based Minet Group, the tenth largest insurance broker in the world, engages in wholesale and retail insurance and reinsurance brokering and risk advisory services in the U.S. and abroad.

John Nuveen & Co., 77%-owned as of year end 1994, underwrites and trades municipal bonds and tax exempt unit investment trusts; and markets tax-exempt open-end and closed-end bond funds. At year end 1994, assets under management totaled $29.7 billion.

Important Developments

Jul. '95—SPC said that the increase in first half 1995 operating earnings to $2.47 a share from $1.92 in the 1994 interim reflected 12% growth in revenues amid solid premium and investment income growth. Margins were aided by lower catastrophe losses and well-contained underwriting expenses. Quarterly results were mixed, though, due to much higher first quarter 1995 storm losses. Separately, in May, SPC sold publicly 4.14 million shares of 6% monthly income preferred securities (MIPS). The MIPS have a liquidation preference of $50 a share, and are convertible into common at $59 a share.

Capitalization

Total Debt: $628,178,000 (3/95).
Ser. B Conv. Preferred Stock: $145,709,000.

Per Share Data ($) (Year Ended Dec. 31)

	1994	1993	1992	1991	1990	1989
Tangible Bk. Val.	29.14	32.12	24.74	24.10	19.85	18.75
Oper. Earnings	4.78	4.44	-3.28	4.39	4.22	3.46
Earnings	5.12	4.92	-2.84	4.68	4.29	4.06
Dividends	2.63	1.40	1.36	1.30	1.20	1.10
Payout Ratio	51%	28%	NM	28%	28%	27%
Prices - High	45½	49	40⅜	37⅛	33	31¾
- Low	37¾	37½	33¼	28½	23½	21½
P/E Ratio - High	9	10	NM	8	8	8
- Low	7	8	NM	6	5	5

Income Statement Analysis (Million $)

	1994	%Chg	1993	%Chg	1992	%Chg	1991
Premium Income	3,412	7%	3,178	1%	3,143	NM	3,146
Net Invest. Inc.	695	5%	661	NM	666	-1%	676
Oth. Revs.	595	-4%	621	-10%	690	30%	530
Total Revs.	4,701	5%	4,460	NM	4,499	3%	4,352
Pretax Inc.	564	8%	523	NM	-224	NM	528
Net Oper. Inc.	414	7%	387	NM	-256	NM	381
Net Inc.	443	4%	428	NM	-232	NM	405

Balance Sheet & Other Fin. Data (Million $)

	1994	1993	1992	1991	1990	1989
Cash & Equiv.	230	200	195	189	174	185
Premiums Due	2,000	1,813	1,759	1,761	1,676	1,179
Inv Assets Bonds	8,829	9,148	8,361	7,833	7,405	6,828
Inv. Assets Stock	861	847	725	687	591	773
Inv. Assets Loans	Nil	Nil	Nil	Nil	Nil	Nil
Inv. Assets Total	11,163	11,256	9,577	8,973	8,468	8,107
Deferred Policy Cost	324	295	280	293	286	264
Total Assets	17,496	17,149	13,597	12,982	12,204	11,030
Debt	623	640	567	487	460	263
Common Eqty.	2,733	3,005	2,202	2,533	2,196	2,349

Ratio Analysis

	1994	1993	1992	1991	1990	1989
Prop&Cas Loss	72.1	72.5	85.6	75.2	73.2	75.7
Prop&Cas Expense	30.2	32.0	32.2	29.4	30.0	30.5
Prop&Cas Comb.	102.3	104.5	117.8	104.6	103.2	106.2
% Ret. on Revs.	9.4	9.6	NM	9.3	9.8	10.5
% Return on Equity	15.4	16.4	NM	16.9	17.0	18.4

Dividend Data —Dividends have been paid since 1872. A dividend reinvestment plan is available. A "poison pill" stock purchase right was adopted in 1989.

Amt. of Div. $	Date Decl.	Ex-Div. Date	Stock of Record	Payment Date
0.375	Aug. 02	Sep. 26	Sep. 30	Oct. 17 '94
0.375	Nov. 01	Dec. 23	Dec. 30	Jan. 17 '95
0.400	Feb. 07	Mar. 27	Mar. 31	Apr. 17 '95
0.400	May. 02	Jun. 28	Jun. 30	Jul. 17 '95
0.400	Aug. 01	Sep. 27	Sep. 29	Oct. 17 '95

Data as orig. reptd.; bef. results of disc. opers. and/or spec. items. Per share data adj. for stk. divs. as of ex-div. date.
E-Estimated. NA-Not Available. NM-Not Meaningful. NR-Not Ranked.

Office—385 Washington St., St. Paul, MN 55102. **Tel**—(612) 221-7911. **Chrmn & Pres**—D. W. Leatherdale. **EVP-CFO**—P. A. Thiele. **VP-Secy**—B. A. Backberg. **VP-Treas & Investor Contact**—James L. Boudreau. **Dirs**—M. R. Bonsignore, J. H. Dasburg, W. J. Driscoll, P. M. Grieve, R. James, W. H. Kling, D. W. Leatherdale, B. K. MacLaury, I. A. Martin, G. D. Nelson, A. M. Pampusch, G. Sprenger, P. A. Thiele. **Transfer Agent & Registrar**—First Chicago Trust Co., NYC. **Incorporated** in Minnesota in 1853; reincorporated in 1968. **Empl**-12,900. **S&P Analyst:** Catherine A. Seifert

Salomon Inc

NYSE Symbol **SB**
In S&P 500

07-AUG-95 | **Industry:** Securities

Summary: Salomon Inc owns Salomon Brothers, a worldwide investment banker, market maker and research firm. Quarterly earnings are highly variable.

S&P Opinion: No Opinion	Recent Price • 36⅞	Yield • 1.7%
	52 Wk Range • 44⅜-32¼	12-Mo. P/E • NM

Earnings vs. Previous Year
▲=Up ▼=Down ▶=No Change

Quantitative Evaluations

Outlook
(1 Lowest—5 Highest)
• **2+**

Fair Value
• **33¼**

Risk
• **Low**

Earn./Div. Rank
• **B**

Technical Eval.
• **Bearish** since 6/95

Rel. Strength Rank
(1 Lowest—99 Highest)
• **18**

Insider Activity
• **NA**

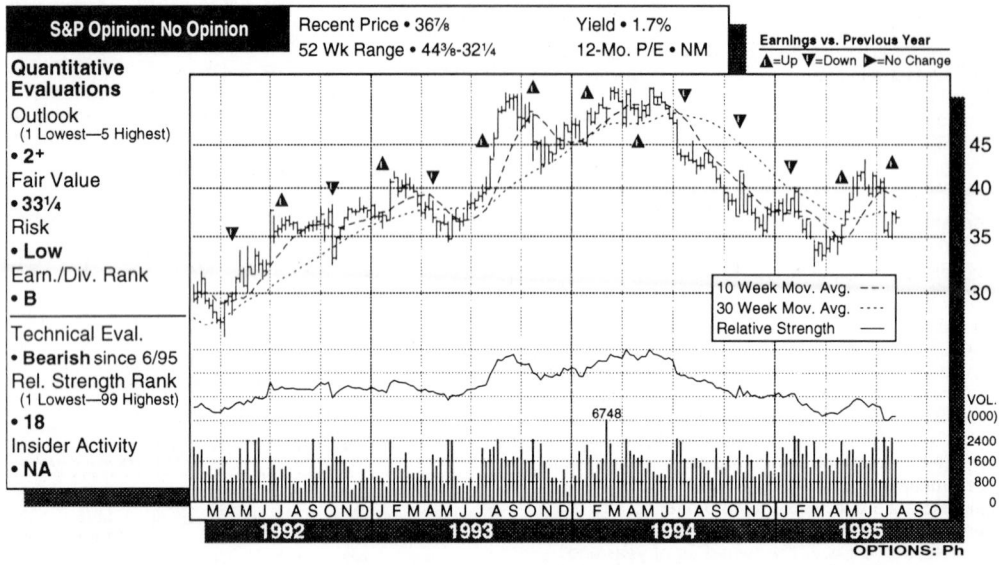

10 Week Mov. Avg. — — —
30 Week Mov. Avg. · · · · ·
Relative Strength ——

6748

VOL. (000)
2400
1600
800
0

MAMJJASOND 1992 | JFMAMJJASOND 1993 | JFMAMJJASOND 1994 | JFMAMJJASO 1995

OPTIONS: Ph

Overview - 07-AUG-95

With the caveat that the company's earnings outlook is subject to a high degree of uncertainty, given its history of volatile results, it appears that 1996 will show distinct improvement over 1995. The most important positive factor is a projected decline in interest rates, accompanied by an upward sloping yield curve. SB's fortunes are closely tied to the bond market, and in the projected interest rate environment, arbitrage opportunities will be more plentiful. Lower rates should also stimulate the company's investment banking business. In addition, management is reducing head count, and is also modifying the compensation system, in an effort to control costs while retaining talented employees.

Valuation - 07-AUG-95

The shares trade in a range of 75% to 140% of year-end book value. Book value is the preferred valuation measure to use, because SB is highly liquid and its assets and liabilities are marked to market on a daily basis. The more commonly employed P/E is subject to distortion. At market tops, the P/E is unrealistically low, because earnings are inflated, while at market bottoms, the P/E may be meaningless if the company is losing money. Based on the most recent closing price, the shares were trading at a modest premium to book value. Legendary investor Warren Buffet has a large stake in SB.

Key Stock Statistics

S&P EPS Est. 1995	2.15	Tang. Bk. Value/Share	28.88
P/E on S&P Est. 1995	17.2	Beta	0.93
S&P EPS Est. 1996	3.60	Shareholders	13,500
Dividend Rate/Share	0.64	Market cap. (B)	$ 3.9
Shs. outstg. (M)	106.2	Inst. holdings	73%
Avg. daily vol. (M)	0.554	Insider holdings	NA

Value of $10,000 invested 5 years ago: $ 17,547

Fiscal Year Ending Dec. 31

	1995	% Change	1994	% Change	1993	% Change
Revenues (Million $)						
1Q	2,068	17%	1,770	11%	1,590	-18%
2Q	1,950	52%	1,280	-51%	2,590	10%
3Q	—	—	1,700	-9%	1,860	6%
4Q	—	—	1,528	-45%	2,760	29%
Yr.	—	—	6,278	-29%	8,800	7%
Income (Million $)						
1Q	81.00	23%	66.00	NM	-65.00	NM
2Q	-60.00	NM	-204.0	NM	433.0	105%
3Q	—	—	-104.0	NM	20.00	NM
4Q	—	—	-157.0	NM	476.0	NM
Yr.	—	—	-399.0	NM	864.0	57%
Earnings Per Share ($)						
1Q	0.59	23%	0.48	NM	-0.76	NM
2Q	-0.73	NM	-2.08	NM	3.75	125%
3Q	E1.50	—	-1.20	NM	0.01	NM
4Q	E0.79	—	-1.65	NM	4.33	NM
Yr.	E2.15	—	-4.31	NM	7.34	76%

Next earnings report expected: early October

Salomon Inc

Business Summary - 07-AUG-95

Salomon Inc operates through Salomon Brothers and Phibro Energy, Inc. Pretax earnings (in million $; before corporate expense) by segment in recent years were:

	1994	1993	1992
Client-driven	-$636	$1,159	$276
Proprietary trading	-49	416	1,416
Other	99	-61	-241

Salomon Brothers is an international investment banking, market making and research concern, serving corporations, state and local governments, sovereign and provincial governments and their agencies, supra-national organizations, central banks and other financial institutions. It is a major dealer in government securities in New York, London, Frankfurt, and Tokyo.

Phibro Energy is a major global trader of crude oil. It also trades natural gas, metals, plastics, coal, coke, fertilizer and soft commodities such as coffee, cocoa, grains and sugar. Phibro Energy USA owns and operates three oil refineries in the U. S. Gulf Coast region.

Trading is integral to the company's profitability. Financial and energy positions are marked to market. Because market prices fluctuate considerably, operating results are subject to considerable volatility.

At March 31, 1995, Salomon Brothers had net capital of $1,178 million, $1,139 million in excess of regulatory requirements.

Important Developments

Jul. '95—Salomon said proprietary trading showed a pretax loss of $93 million in the 1995 second quarter, versus a pretax profit of $239 million in the first quarter. Fixed income revenues improved significantly in the quarter, benefiting from increased volumes in global bond markets.

Capitalization

Term Debt: $15,239,000,000 (3/95), excl. $2,971,000,000 of CMOs.
9% Conv. Preferred Stock: $700,000,000. Held by affiliates of Berkshire Hathaway, Inc.
Preferred Stock: $312,000,000.

Per Share Data ($)

(Year Ended Dec. 31)

	1994	1993	1992	1991	1990	1989
Tangible Bk. Val.	28.88	36.93	30.50	26.80	24.04	22.71
Cash Flow	NA	NA	NA	NA	2.79	3.89
Earnings	-4.31	7.34	4.18	3.90	2.08	3.26
Dividends	0.64	0.64	0.64	0.64	0.64	0.64
Payout Ratio	NM	9%	15%	16%	29%	19%
Prices - High	53¾	51⅞	39	37	27	29⅜
- Low	35	34⅜	26⅝	20¾	20	20½
P/E Ratio - High	NM	7	9	9	13	9
- Low	NM	5	6	5	10	6

Income Statement Analysis (Million $)

	1994	%Chg	1993	%Chg	1992	%Chg	1991
Commissions	336	18%	285	41%	202	-5%	213
Int. Inc.	5,902	-1%	5,989	19%	5,046	-14%	5,867
Total Revs.	6,278	-29%	8,799	7%	8,196	-11%	9,175
Int. Exp.	4,892	6%	4,600	6%	4,324	-23%	5,638
Pretax Inc.	-830	NM	1,465	39%	1,056	15%	919
Eff. Tax Rate	NM	—	41%	—	48%	—	45%
Net Inc.	-398	NM	864	57%	550	8%	507

Balance Sheet & Other Fin. Data (Million $)

	1994	1993	1992	1991	1990	1989
Total Assets	172,732	184,835	159,459	97,402	109,877	118,250
Cash Items	3,539	908	620	643	1,252	371
Receivables	69,350	58,548	66,871	32,569	46,098	37,852
Secs. Owned	103,311	118,923	84,398	54,661	52,900	71,229
Sec. Borrowed	78,579	97,890	88,417	40,393	42,888	62,716
Due Brokers & Cust.	6,815	5,997	3,973	4,159	5,763	4,569
Other Liabs.	64,618	60,117	49,321	34,935	45,906	38,117
Capitalization:						
Debt	18,228	15,500	13,440	13,900	11,797	9,283
Equity	3,480	4,319	3,496	3,203	2,823	2,865
Total	21,708	20,831	17,748	17,915	15,320	12,848

Ratio Analysis

	1994	1993	1992	1991	1990	1989
% Ret. on Revs.	NM	9.8	6.7	5.5	3.4	5.2
% Ret. on Assets	NM	0.5	0.4	0.5	0.3	0.5
% Ret. on Equity	NM	20.7	14.4	14.4	8.8	14.9

Dividend Data

(Dividends have been paid since 1960. A dividend reinvestment plan is available. A poison pill stock purchase rights plan was adopted in 1988.)

Amt. of Div. $	Date Decl.	Ex-Div. Date	Stock of Record	Payment Date
0.160	Sep. 09	Sep. 13	Sep. 19	Oct. 01 '94
0.160	Dec. 07	Dec. 13	Dec. 19	Jan. 03 '95
0.160	Mar. 01	Mar. 09	Mar. 15	Apr. 01 '95
0.160	Jun. 08	Jun. 15	Jun. 19	Jul. 01 '95

Data as orig. reptd.; bef. results of disc opers. and/or spec. items. Per share data adj. for stk. divs. as of ex-div. date. E-Estimated. NA-Not Available. NM-Not Meaningful. NR-Not Ranked.

Office—Seven World Trade Center, New York, NY 10048. **Tel**—(212) 783-7000. **Chrmn & CEO**—R. E. Denham. **EVP**—D. C. Maughan. **CFO**—J. H. Bailey. **Secy**—A. S. Olshin. **VP & Investor Contact**—Jeffrey Smith (212-783-7597). **Dirs**—D. O. Andreas, W. E. Buffett, C. M. Fagin, A. J. Hall, G. B. Horowitz, D. C. Maughan, W. F. May, C. T. Munger, R. G. Zeller. **Transfer Agent & Registrar**—First Chicago Trust Co. of New York, Jersey City, NJ. **Incorporated** in Delaware in 1960. **Empl**-9,077. **S&P Analyst:** Paul L. Huberman, CFA

Santa Fe Energy Resources

NYSE Symbol **SFR**
In S&P 500

25-OCT-95

Industry:
Oil and Gas

Summary: This independent crude oil and natural gas company engages in exploration, development and production, primarily in the U.S., but also in Argentina and Indonesia.

S&P Opinion: Hold (★★★)

| Recent Price • 8⅞ | Yield • Nil |
| 52 Wk Range • 10⅝-7⅞ | 12-Mo. P/E • 98.6 |

Quantitative Evaluations

Outlook
(1 Lowest—5 Highest)
• **1** ⁻

Fair Value
• **5½**

Risk
• **Low**

Earn./Div. Rank
• **NR**

Technical Eval.
• **Bearish** since 10/95

Rel. Strength Rank
(1 Lowest—99 Highest)
• **38**

Insider Activity
• **NA**

Earnings vs. Previous Year
▲=Up ▼=Down ▶=No Change

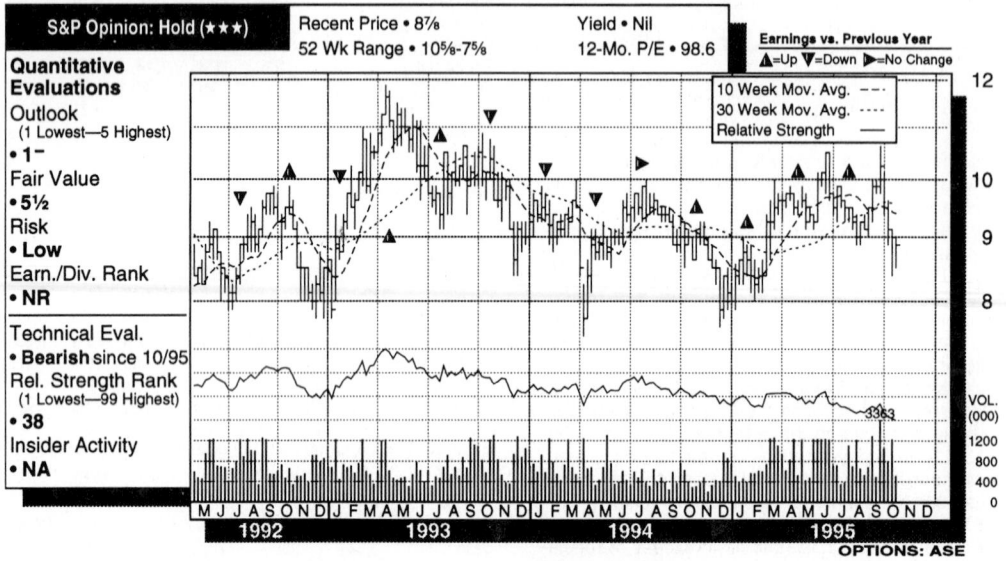

10 Week Mov. Avg. — · —
30 Week Mov. Avg. · · · ·
Relative Strength ——

OPTIONS: ASE

Overview - 19-OCT-95

A 1993 restructuring led to a substantial loss, but profitability was restored in 1994. Revenues and income should continue to improve in 1995, as shown by an upturn in the year's first nine months, aided by the completion of the restructuring program. The program reduced long term debt through refinancings, cut production costs, eliminated staff positions, and included the disposition of assets. SFR intends to stabilize gas production, during periods of price weakness such as occurred earlier in 1995, while increasing oil production to capitalize on price upsurges, and continue its oil hedging program. Capital spending, which has been increased for offshore interests, will be directed toward high-return projects, both domestic and international. SFR's Gulf of Mexico efforts, for example, have been rewarded with success.

Valuation - 19-OCT-95

Santa Fe's shares, after moving up from their lows of late 1994 and early 1995, have retreated from the highs attained in the spring of 1995, which reflected the turnaround in the company's position brought about by the completion of its restructuring. Revenues and income were boosted by recent higher prices received for the company's predominantly heavy oil. While this oil price trend has stabilized, the climb in income should continue for the foreseeable future and, with a more focused asset base, provide ongoing support for the company's stock. However, at current prices the shares still are not undervalued and, in the absence of a dividend, should be viewed as a hold.

Key Stock Statistics

S&P EPS Est. 1995	0.12	Tang. Bk. Value/Share	3.74
P/E on S&P Est. 1995	74.0	Beta	0.45
S&P EPS Est. 1996	0.25	Shareholders	50,200
Dividend Rate/Share	Nil	Market cap. (B)	$0.824
Shs. outstg. (M)	90.3	Inst. holdings	55%
Avg. daily vol. (M)	0.179	Insider holdings	NA

Value of $10,000 invested 5 years ago: NA

Fiscal Year Ending Dec. 31

	1995	% Change	1994	% Change	1993	% Change
Revenues (Million $)						
1Q	98.60	9%	90.30	-22%	115.3	47%
2Q	109.7	10%	99.7	-14%	116.3	19%
3Q	111.1	7%	103.6	NM	102.7	-20%
4Q	--	—	97.80	-5%	102.6	-17%
Yr.	--	—	391.4	-10%	436.9	2%
Income (Million $)						
1Q	3.60	NM	-2.50	NM	-0.40	NM
2Q	7.60	85%	4.10	3%	4.00	122%
3Q	7.00	-36%	11.00	NM	2.40	-67%
4Q	—	—	4.50	NM	-83.10	NM
Yr.	—	—	17.10	NM	-77.10	NM
Earnings Per Share ($)						
1Q	Nil	—	-0.05	NM	-0.02	NM
2Q	0.04	100%	0.02	NM	0.02	100%
3Q	0.04	-50%	0.08	NM	0.01	-83%
4Q	E0.04	NM	0.01	NM	-0.95	NM
Yr.	E0.12	100%	0.06	NM	-0.94	NM

Next earnings report expected: mid February

Santa Fe Energy Resources

Business Summary - 25-OCT-95

Santa Fe Energy Resources, Inc. engages in exploration, development and production of oil and natural gas in most of the major producing basins in the continental U.S. and in certain areas abroad. The bulk of domestic crude oil production is in California and Texas; natural gas production comes mainly from the Gulf of Mexico, New Mexico and Texas. Overseas production is in Argentina and Indonesia. The company has disposed of substantially all non-core properties, including natural gas gathering and processing assets. About 75% of 1994 revenues were derived from oil. Contributions (in millions) by segment in 1994 were:

	Revs.	Oper. Inc.
Domestic	$346.7	$90.3
International	44.7	-2.3

A substantial portion of oil production comes from mature fields; 69% of domestic proved crude oil and liquids reserves and 54% of average daily domestic production are attributable to the Midway-Sunset field in California, where nearly all reserves are heavy oil, the production of which depends on enhanced oil recovery involving sophisticated recovery methods, including steam injection. During 1994, SFR spent $130 million on capital programs, with $190 million budgeted for 1995.

At December 31, 1994, estimated proved reserves totaled 258 million bbl. of crude oil and 242 Bcf of natural gas, versus 248 million bbl. of oil and 263 Bcf of gas a year earlier. The present value of estimated future net cash flows from proved reserves (discounted at 10%) was $740 million, versus $502 million at 1993 year-end.

In 1994, average crude oil production was 57,600 bbl. per day (66,700 b/d in 1993). Natural gas production was 136,300 Mcf/d (165,400 Mcf/d).

In October 1993, SFR initiated a restructuring program that included the concentration of capital spending on core operating areas, the disposition of non-core assets, the elimination of the quarterly common cash dividend and an evaluation of the company's capital and cost structures.

Important Developments

Oct. '95—Crude oil and liquids production increased 3.1% in 1995's third quarter over the prior quarter, while natural gas production was up 8%. The company expects continued production growth for the remainder of 1995. SFE benefits from an ongoing oil hedging program; gas will be hedged during November and December, and during 1996.

Capitalization

Long Term Debt: $344,400,000 (9/95).

$1.40 Conv. Pfd. Stock: 5,000,000 shs. ($20 liquid. pref.); ea. conv. into 1.3913 com. shs.

$.732 Conv. Pfd. Stock: 10,700,000 shs.($8.875 liquid. pref.); ea. conv. into 0.8474 com. shs.

Per Share Data ($)

(Year Ended Dec. 31)

	1994	1993	1992	1991	1990	1989
Tangible Bk. Val.	3.67	3.56	4.63	3.49	3.35	3.17
Cash Flow	1.41	1.87	1.78	1.96	2.00	1.60
Earnings	0.06	-0.94	-0.07	0.29	0.28	0.03
Dividends	Nil	0.12	0.16	0.16	0.12	NA
Payout Ratio	Nil	NM	NM	55%	45%	NA
Prices - High	10	11⅞	9⅞	16¾	22⅜	NA
- Low	7½	7¾	7	7	13¾	NA
P/E Ratio - High	NM	NM	NM	58	80	NA
- Low	NM	NM	NM	24	49	NA

Income Statement Analysis (Million $)

	1994	%Chg	1993	%Chg	1992	%Chg	1991
Revs.	391	-11%	437	2%	428	13%	380
Oper. Inc.	168	-6%	178	-7%	191	11%	172
Depr. Depl. & Amort.	121	-52%	252	73%	146	36%	107
Int. Exp.	27.5	-40%	45.8	-18%	55.6	18%	47.3
Pretax Inc.	23.0	NM	-149	NM	-1.0	NM	33.0
Eff. Tax Rate	26%	—	NM	—	NM	—	43%
Net Inc.	17.1	NM	-77.1	NM	-1.4	NM	18.5

Balance Sheet & Other Fin. Data (Million $)

	1994	1993	1992	1991	1990	1989
Cash	53.7	4.8	83.8	28.2	47.7	34.2
Curr. Assets	157	173	205	100	145	135
Total Assets	1,071	1,077	1,337	912	911	905
Curr. Liab.	126	166	172	97.0	130	213
LT Debt	350	405	493	441	417	350
Common Eqty.	332	324	417	225	216	202
Total Cap.	910	853	1,108	772	737	653
Cap. Exp.	139	151	536	174	107	NA
Cash Flow	127	168	141	125	124	102

Ratio Analysis

	1994	1993	1992	1991	1990	1989
Curr. Ratio	1.2	1.0	1.2	1.0	1.1	0.6
% LT Debt of Cap.	38.5	47.5	44.5	57.1	56.6	53.5
% Ret. on Assets	1.6	NM	NM	2.0	1.7	NA
% Ret. on Equity	1.6	NM	NM	8.4	6.9	NA

Dividend Data —Dividends on the common stock, begun in 1990, were omitted in 1993. A poison pill stock purchase rights plan, adopted in 1990, expired in December 1991.

Data as orig. reptd.; bef. results of disc opers. and/or spec. items. Per share data adj. for stk. divs. as of ex-div. date. E-Estimated. NA-Not Available. NM-Not Meaningful. NR-Not Ranked.

Office—1616 South Voss, Suite 1000, Houston, TX 77057. **Tel**—(713) 507-5000. **Chrmn, Pres & CEO**—J. L. Payne. **SVP & CFO**—R. G Whaling. **Secy**—M. A. Older. **Investor Contact**—Kathy E. Hager. **Dirs**—W. E. Greehey, M. N. Klein, R. D. Krebs, A. V. Martini, M. A. Morphy, J. L. Payne, R. F. Richards, M. J. Shapiro, R. F. Vagt, K. D. Wriston. **Transfer Agent & Registrar**—First Chicago Trust Co. of New York, Jersey City, NJ. **Incorporated** in Delaware in 1971. **Empl**-647. **S&P Analyst:** Michael C. Barr

Santa Fe Pacific Gold

NYSE Symbol **GLD** Options on ASE & CBOE (Mar-Jun-Sep-Dec) In S&P 500

Price	Range	P–E Ratio	Dividend	Yield	S&P Ranking	Beta
Aug. 21'95	1995					
12⅞	14–8⅞	32	[1]0.05	[1]0.4%	NR	NA

Summary

Formerly a subsidiary of Santa Fe Pacific Corp. (SFX), this company is one of the largest gold mining concerns in North America. Its three U.S. gold mines in Nevada and California produced 936,310 ounces in 1994, and had year-end proven and probable reserves of 15.4 million oz. In its initial public offering on June 15, 1994, GLD sold 18,000,000 common shares at $14 each; the shares were listed on the NYSE. In September, SFX spun off to its shareholders its remaining 85.4% interest in GLD.

Business Summary

Santa Fe Pacific Gold is one of North America's largest gold mining concerns. The company produced 936,310 ounces of gold at average cash costs of $184/oz. in 1994. Its three open-pit gold mines are located in Humboldt County, Nev. (the Twin Creeks mine and the Lone Tree mine) and in Imperial County, Calif. (the Mesquite mine). GLD also evaluates precious metal prospects elsewhere in the U.S. and in Canada, Latin America, central Asia, Australia, the southwest Pacific and Africa. It has been involved in the exploration and development of gold properties since the early 1980s.

At year-end 1994, reserves were 250.4 million tons of ore grading 0.061 oz./ton, which contained 15,363,000 oz. of gold, including 10,013,000 oz. at the Twin Creeks mine, 4,051,000 at the Lone Tree mine, and 1,299,000 at the Mesquite mine. GLD is one of the largest holders of mineral rights in the western U.S., controlling 6.89 millon acres of mineral rights, including 1.95 million in northern Nevada where the U.S.'s major gold area is located.

The Twin Creeks mine is believed by GLD to be North America's third-largest primary gold mine and in 1994 was one of the nation's lowest-cost gold producers. It produced a record 501,891 oz. at cash costs of $174/oz. in 1994, and is expected to produce 425,000-435,000 oz. at $170-$180/oz. in 1995. GLD is building a $250 million plant over a five-year period to process refractory reserves, which should extend mine life to about 14 years from eight years. The project involves the start-up of two autoclaves (high pressure/high temperature vessels used to oxidize refractory ore) scheduled to begin operation in 1997 and 1999.

Gold production at the Lone Tree mine was a record 226,911 oz. in 1994 at cash costs of $210/oz. In February 1994, GLD completed a sulfide processing plant to treat higher-grade refractory ore. Consequently, the mine's estimated life will be extended to 2006. Separately, test results indicated that recoveries from low-grade refractory ore, using heap leaching methods, were running

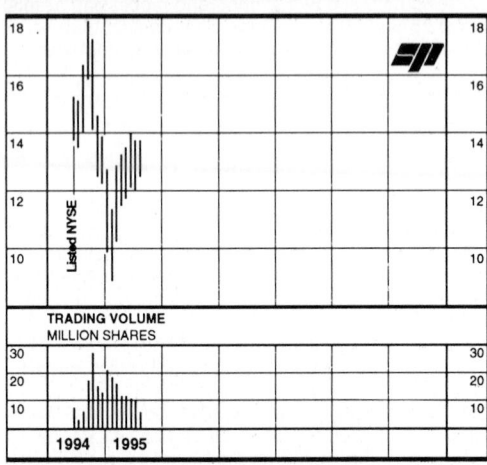

TRADING VOLUME
MILLION SHARES

less than expected. GLD has identified a proprietary process that appears to boost recovery rates. Until testing is completed, this category of ore will be stockpiled. Thus, output will be reduced to some 185,000-195,000 oz. in 1995.

The Mesquite mine had gold production in 1994 totaling 207,508 oz. at cash costs of $180/oz. At about 200,000 oz. of gold per year, the mine is projected to last through 1999.

Important Developments

Jul. '95— Directors approved the Mule Canyon gold project in Nevada. Estimated to contain 1.1 million ounces of gold, Mule Canyon will cost an estimated $129 million to bring into production by early 1997. The annual production rate will be 110,000 to 150,000 oz. Separately, directors authorized construction of a $46 million flotation circuit at Lone Tree designed to provide incremental production of 85,000 to 90,000 ounces by 1997.

Next earnings report expected in late October.

Per Share Data ($)

Yr. End Dec. 31	[2]1994	[2]1993
Tangible Bk. Val.	3.97	[3]3.53
Cash Flow	1.09	0.84
Earnings[4]	0.46	0.34
Dividends	Nil	NA
Payout Ratio	Nil	NA
Prices—High	17⅞	NA
Low	12¼	NA
P/E Ratio—	39–27	NA

Data as reptd. in prospectus dated Jun. 15, 1994. **1.** See Dividend Data. **2.** Pro forma. **3.** As reptd. by Co. as of Mar. 31, 1994, pro forma as adjusted. **4.** Bef. results of disc. opers. of +1.27 in 1993. NA-Not Available.

Santa Fe Pacific Gold Corporation

Income Data (Million $)

Year Ended Dec. 31	Revs.	Oper. Inc.	% Oper. Inc. of Revs.	Cap. Exp.	Depr.	Int. Exp.	Net Bef. Taxes	Eff. Tax Rate	Net Inc.	% Net Inc. of Revs.	Cash Flow
1994	376	160	42.6	95	76.5	9.20	76.7	26.1%	[2]56.7	15.1	133
[1]1993	316	133	42.1	NA	62.8	7.33	64.1	32.6%	43.2	13.7	106

Balance Sheet Data (Million $)

Dec. 31	Cash	Assets	Curr. Liab.	Ratio	Total Assets	% Ret. on Assets	Long Term Debt	Common Equity	Total Cap.	% LT Debt of Cap.	% Ret. on Equity
1994	34.2	155	76	2.0	858	6.2	90	522	720	12.5	14.4
[3]1993	21.8	NA	NA	NA	NA	NA	135	463	NA	NA	NA

Data as reptd. in prospectus dated Jun. 15, 1994. **1.** Pro forma. **2.** Bef. results of disc. opers. **3.** As of Mar. 31, 1994, pro forma as adjusted. NA-Not Available.

Total Revenues (Million $)

Quarter:	1995	1994	[1]1993
Mar.	84.7	84.3	---
Jun.	85.4	93.5	---
Sep.		95.9	---
Dec.		101.9	---
	375.6	315.7	

Total revenues for 1995's first half fell 4.3%, year to year reflecting a 4.7% decline in gold volumes. The average price realized increased 1.5% to $402/oz. from $396/oz. Operating profits slid 17% reflecting higher mining costs at Mesquite as GLD processes more refractory ores and increased administrative costs reflecting GLD's status as a publicly-traded company. After sharply lower interest costs, pretax income was off 13%. After taxes at 28.5%, versus 27.2%, net income fell 15%. Share earnings were $0.18 (on 15% more shares), versus $0.24.

Common Share Earnings ($)

Quarter:	1995	1994	[1]1993
Mar.	0.09	0.12	---
Jun.	0.09	0.12	---
Sep.		0.10	---
Dec.		0.12	---
		0.46	0.34

Finances

In May 1995 directors authorized development of the Trenton Canyon Project. Located in Nevada, the Trenton mine will employ heap leach technology to produce some 50,000 to 80,000 oz. of gold annually. Average cash costs were estimated at $210 to $220 per ounce. Production is expected to commence in late 1996. The property, containing some 517,000 ounces of gold, should produce gold over a seven-year period.

In its initial public offering on June 15, 1994, Santa Fe Pacific Gold, a wholly-owned subsidiary of Santa Fe Pacific Gold Corp. (SFX), sold 18,000,000 common shares (12,000,000 in the U.S. and 6,000,000 outside the U.S.) at $14 each through underwriters led by Goldman, Sachs & Co., Merrill Lynch & Co., and S.G. Warburg & Co. An additional 1,200,000 shares were sold through exercise of underwriters' over-allotment options. Net proceeds totaled $250.3 million, of which $228.4 million was used to repay debt. The IPO reduced SFX's ownership of GLD to 85.4% from 100%. On September 30, 1994, SFX spun off its entire 85.4% interest to its shareholders of record September 12, with one GLD share distributed for each 1.666634 SFX shares held.

On June 25, 1993, the company acquired the gold assets (including 3.8 million ounces of gold reserves) of Hanson Natural Resources Co., an affiliate of Hanson plc, in exchange for all of its coal and aggregates assets. In the exchange, GLD received the Chimney Creek mine, the Mesquite mine, two late-stage exploration projects in Nevada and Montana, and other gold prospects in North America and Chile. The exchange has enabled GLD to focus its operations exclusively on gold mining. Following the exchange, GLD consolidated the operations of the Rabbit Creek mine with the Chimney Creek mine, forming the Twin Creeks mine.

GLD completed the Lone Tree Sulfide Expansion under budget and ahead of schedule in February 1994. The $109 million project allows for the milling of high-grade oxide ores and the processing of refractory ores through a mill with a pressure oxidation circuit.

Dividend Data

GLD initiated annual dividend payments at $0.05 a share in June 1995.

Amt. of Divd. $	Date Decl.	Ex–divd. Date	Stock of Record	Payment Date
0.05	May 25	May 30	Jun. 5	Jun. 30'95

Capitalization

Long Term Debt: $130,000,000 (6/95).

Common Stock: 131,356,000 shs. ($0.01 par).
Institutions hold about 57%.
Shareholders of record: 68,000.

---

1. Pro forma.

Office—6200 Uptown Blvd. NE, Albuquerque, NM 87110. **Tel**—(505) 880-5300. **Chrmn & Pres**—P. M. James. **VP-CFO**—D. A. Smith. **Secy**—W. Jarke. **Investor Contact**—Gina Wilson. **Dirs**—J. T. Curry, D. W. Gentry, P. M. James, R. D. Krebs, G. B. Munroe, J. H. Sisco, R. J. Stoehr, R. T. Zitting. **Transfer Agent & Registrar**—Harris Trust and Savings Bank, Chicago, Ill. **Incorporated** in Delaware in 1983. **Empl**—1,635.

Stephen R. Klein

Sara Lee

NYSE Symbol **SLE**
In S&P 500

30-OCT-95   **Industry:**
Food

Summary: Sara Lee is a diversified producer of branded food products (meats, fresh and frozen baked goods, and coffee products), and personal apparel and household care products.

S&P Opinion: Accumulate (★★★★)

Recent Price • 29⅛	Yield • 2.6%
52 Wk Range • 30⅝-24	12-Mo. P/E • 17.5

Quantitative Evaluations

Outlook
(1 Lowest—5 Highest)
• **4+**

Fair Value
• **31**

Risk
• **Low**

Earn./Div. Rank
• **A**

Technical Eval.
• **Bullish** since 10/94

Rel. Strength Rank
(1 Lowest—99 Highest)
• **60**

Insider Activity
• **Neutral**

Earnings vs. Previous Year
▲=Up ▼=Down ▶=No Change

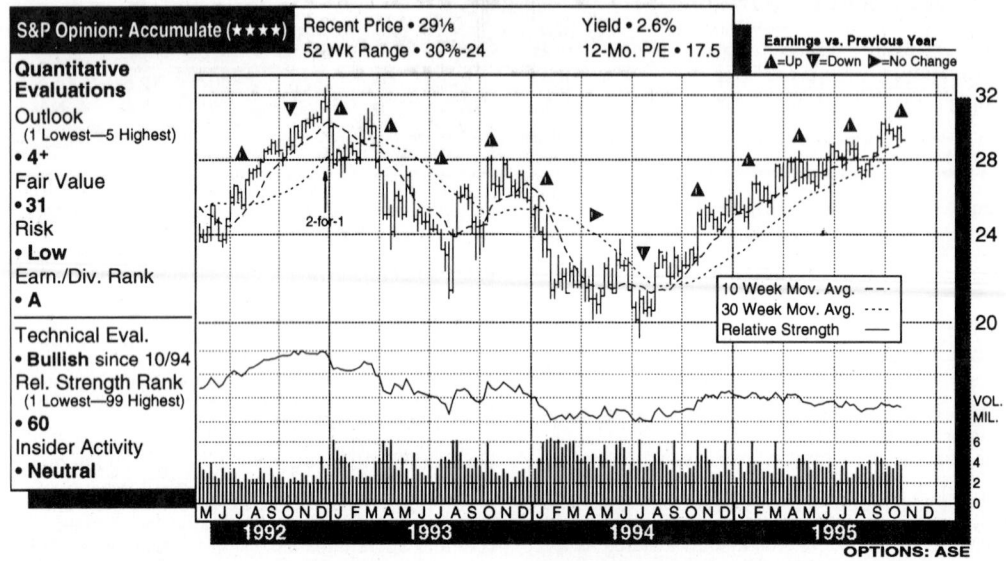

10 Week Mov. Avg. ---
30 Week Mov. Avg. ....
Relative Strength ——

OPTIONS: ASE

Overview - 30-OCT-95

Sales are projected to climb at an approximate 10% rate in fiscal 1996, led primarily by broad-based unit volume growth, product mix improvement, and acquisition contributions. Operating profits are seen growing in line with sales in fiscal 1996, reflecting low double-digit profit gains for all major segments, with the possible exception of Coffee and Grocery, which faces challenging profit comparisons over the next few quarters. With only an anticipated modest rise in net interest expense, lower currency hedging expense, and a stable effective tax rate, we see earnings per share growth of 14%, to $1.85 in fiscal 1996.

Valuation - 30-OCT-95

Given our favorable earnings growth forecast in fiscal 1996, we view the shares of this well-diversified, global producer of consumer necessities as attractive at current levels for both near-term and longer-term gains. The shares fell out of favor in early 1993, mostly due to profit-taking pressures following substantial appreciation the prior two years, and from a profit slowdown for SLE's important personal products division. However, aggressive management restructuring actions since that time has led to the division's turnaround, helping total profit growth to resume at a good pace. We expect the stock to extend its recent upward trend well into 1996.

Key Stock Statistics

S&P EPS Est. 1996	1.85	Tang. Bk. Value/Share	NM
P/E on S&P Est. 1996	15.7	Beta	0.79
Dividend Rate/Share	0.76	Shareholders	95,600
Shs. outstg. (M)	484.1	Market cap. (B)	$ 14.1
Avg. daily vol. (M)	0.738	Inst. holdings	47%
		Insider holdings	NA

Value of $10,000 invested 5 years ago: $ 19,875

Fiscal Year Ending Jun. 30

	1996	% Change	1995	% Change	1994	% Change
Revenues (Million $)						
1Q	4,656	9%	4,290	13%	3,796	6%
2Q	—	—	4,648	16%	4,010	4%
3Q	—	—	4,193	14%	3,664	11%
4Q	—	—	4,588	13%	4,066	6%
Yr.	—	—	17,719	14%	15,536	7%
Income (Million $)						
1Q	186.0	13%	165.0	6%	155.0	9%
2Q	—	—	252.0	7%	236.0	7%
3Q	—	—	166.0	9%	152.0	NM
4Q	—	—	221.0	NM	-309.0	NM
Yr.	—	—	804.0	NM	234.0	-67%
Earnings Per Share ($)						
1Q	0.37	12%	0.33	6%	0.31	11%
2Q	E0.57	12%	0.51	6%	0.48	9%
3Q	E0.38	15%	0.33	10%	0.30	NM
4Q	E0.53	18%	0.45	NM	-0.65	NM
Yr.	E1.85	14%	1.62	NM	0.44	-69%

Next earnings report expected: late January

Sara Lee

Business Summary - 30-OCT-95

Sara Lee makes a variety of branded foods and personal and household care products. Segment contributions in fiscal 1995 were:

	Sales	Profits
Packaged foods:		
Packaged meats & bakery	34%	24%
Coffee & grocery	16%	24%
Packaged consumer prod.:		
Personal products	40%	41%
Household & pers'l care	10%	11%

The Packaged meats division makes and sells pork, poultry, and beef products to supermarkets, warehouse clubs and other customers in the U.S., Europe, and Mexico. Brands include Ball Park, Best's, Kahn's, Hillshire Farm, and Mr. Turkey. The Bakery division produces fresh and frozen Sara Lee brand baked goods and specialty items throughout the U.S., U.K., France, Mexico, Australia, and many Pacific Rim countries. Foodservice business is conducted principally under the PYA/Monarch name. Coffee and Grocery products (Douwe Egberts coffee, Pickwick tea) are sold principally in Europe.

Consumer products include such personal products as hosiery (Hanes, L'eggs, Sheer Energy, Underalls, Dim, Pretty Polly, Razzamatazz); activewear (Beefy-T, Champion, Hanes Her Way); underwear and intimate apparel (Bali, Dim, Hanes, Playtex); and household and personal care items (Kiwi shoecare, Sanex skin-care products).

Foreign operations in fiscal 1995 accounted for 40% of sales (31% Western/Central Europe; 7% Asia Pacific/Latin America; 2% other) and 45% of pretax profits (36% Western/Central Europe; 6% Asia Pacific/Latin America; 3% other).

Important Developments

Oct. '95—Fiscal 1996 first quarter operating profit for Packaged Meats & Bakery rose 11%, led by increased sales of higher-margin products and acquisition contributions. Coffee & Grocery profits advanced 26%, reflecting increased coffee selling prices the favorable effect of stronger foreign currencies relative to the U.S. dollar, and an acquisition. Personal Products profits rose 12%, reflecting an increased emphasis on higher-margin products. Household & Personal care profits advanced 10%, as higher sales, profits and margins for core products offset lower results for the division's direct selling operations. The effective tax rate in the quarter eased to 34% from 35%. Management said that the company was positioned for sustained growth throughout fiscal 1996.

Capitalization

Long Term Debt: $1,873,000,000 (9/30/95).

Minority Interest: $526,000,000.

Auction Preferred Stock: $300,000,000.

ESOP Convertible Preferred Stock: $330,000,000.

Per Share Data ($)

(Year Ended Jun. 30)

	1995	1994	1993	1992	1991	1990
Tangible Bk. Val.	NM	NM	7.32	6.37	4.76	4.23
Cash Flow	2.74	1.56	2.45	2.51	1.71	1.52
Earnings	1.62	0.44	1.40	1.54	1.08	0.96
Dividends	0.67	0.63	0.56	0.61	0.46	0.40
Payout Ratio	41%	142%	40%	41%	44%	43%
Prices - High	29⅛	26	32⅜	31⅛	29⅛	16¾
- Low	24¼	19⅜	21	21	14⅞	12⅛
P/E Ratio - High	18	59	23	22	27	17
- Low	15	44	15	17	14	13

Income Statement Analysis (Million $)

	1995	%Chg	1994	%Chg	1993	%Chg	1992
Revs.	17,719	14%	15,536	7%	14,580	10%	13,243
Oper. Inc.	2,010	10%	1,834	9%	1,686	11%	1,518
Depr.	606	7%	568	9%	522	11%	472
Int. Exp.	243	29%	188	16%	162	-6%	172
Pretax Inc.	1,219	NM	389	-64%	1,082	-8%	1,174
Eff. Tax Rate	34%	—	40%	—	35%	—	35%
Net Inc.	804	NM	234	-67%	704	-7%	761

Balance Sheet & Other Fin. Data (Million $)

	1995	1994	1993	1992	1991	1990
Cash	202	189	325	198	125	169
Curr. Assets	4,928	4,469	3,976	3,695	2,920	2,868
Total Assets	12,431	11,665	10,862	9,989	8,122	7,636
Curr. Liab.	4,844	4,919	4,269	3,300	2,526	2,483
LT Debt	1,817	1,496	1,164	1,389	1,399	1,524
Common Eqty.	3,939	3,326	3,551	3,055	2,215	1,949
Total Cap.	6,882	5,963	5,888	5,913	5,174	4,816
Cap. Exp.	480	628	728	509	640	673
Cash Flow	1,372	778	1,190	1,194	791	699

Ratio Analysis

	1995	1994	1993	1992	1991	1990
Curr. Ratio	1.0	0.9	0.9	1.1	1.2	1.2
% LT Debt of Cap.	26.4	25.0	19.8	23.5	27.0	31.6
% Net Inc.of Revs.	4.5	1.5	4.8	5.7	4.3	4.1
% Ret. on Assets	6.7	2.0	6.7	8.3	6.8	6.6
% Ret. on Equity	21.2	6.1	19.2	27.0	23.4	24.3

Dividend Data

Dividends have been paid since 1946. A dividend reinvestment plan is available. A "poison pill" stock purchase right was adopted in 1988.

Amt. of Div. $	Date Decl.	Ex-Div. Date	Stock of Record	Payment Date
0.170	Oct. 27	Nov. 25	Dec. 01	Jan. 01 '95
0.170	Jan. 26	Feb. 23	Mar. 01	Apr. 01 '95
0.170	Apr. 27	May. 25	Jun. 01	Jul. 01 '95
0.170	Jun. 29	Aug. 30	Sep. 01	Oct. 01 '95
0.190	Oct. 26	Nov. 29	Dec. 01	Jan. 01 '96

Data as orig. reptd.; bef. results of disc. opers. and/or spec. items. Per share data adj. for stk. divs. as of ex-div. date.
E-Estimated. NA-Not Available. NM-Not Meaningful. NR-Not Ranked.

Office—3 First National Plaza, Chicago, IL 60602-4260. Tel—(312) 726-2600. Chrmn & CEO—J. H. Bryan. Vice Chrmn—M. E. Murphy. SVP & CFO—Judith A. Sprieser. SVP & Secy—G. H. Newman. VP & Investor Contact—Janet E. Bergman (312-558-4966). Dirs—P. A. Allaire, F. H. Andriessen, J. H. Bryan, D. L. Burnham, C. W. Coker, W. D. Davis, H. F. Jacobson, A. F. Jacobson, V. E. Jordan, Jr., J. L. Ketelsen, H. B. van Liemt, J. D. Manley, C. S. McMillan, N. M. Minow, M. E. Murphy, Sir Arvi H. Parbo, R. L. Ridgway, R. L. Thomas. Transfer Agent—Co. itself. Registrar—First National Bank of Chicago. Incorporated in Maryland in 1941. Empl-149,000. S&P Analyst: Kenneth A. Shea

Schering-Plough

NYSE Symbol **SGP**
In S&P 500

28-SEP-95

Industry:
Drugs-Generic and
OTC

Summary: This company is a leading producer of prescription and OTC pharmaceuticals, and has important interests in sun care, animal health and foot care products.

S&P Opinion: Accumulate (★★★★)	Recent Price • 50⅝	Yield • 2.2%
	52 Wk Range • 51-34⅛	12-Mo. P/E • 23.0

Quantitative Evaluations

Outlook
(1 Lowest—5 Highest)
• **4+**

Fair Value
• **51¼**

Risk
• **Low**

Earn./Div. Rank
• **A+**

Technical Eval.
• **Bullish** since 5/92

Rel. Strength Rank
(1 Lowest—99 Highest)
• **91**

Insider Activity
• **Neutral**

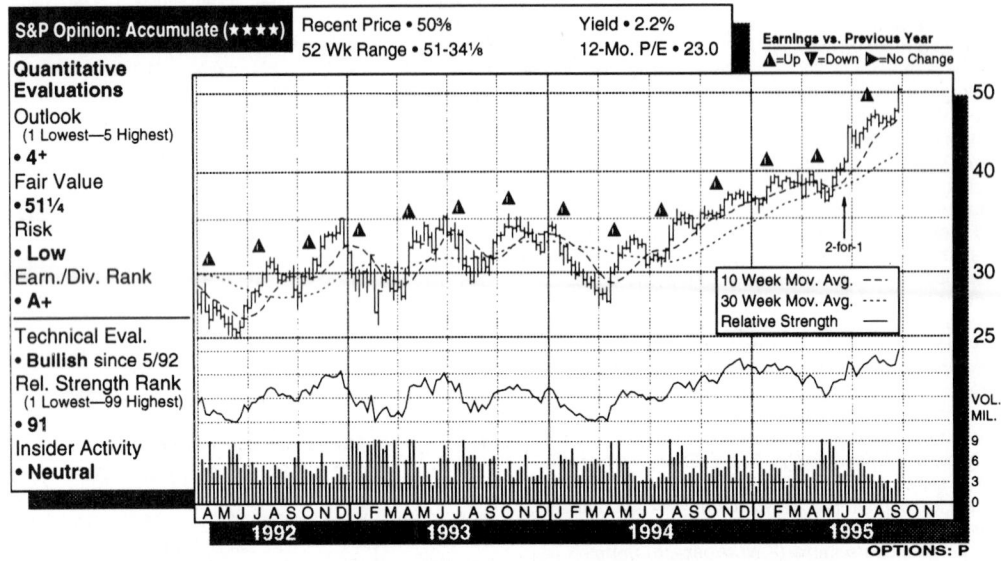

Earnings vs. Previous Year
▲=Up ▼=Down ▶=No Change

2-for-1

10 Week Mov. Avg. ---
30 Week Mov. Avg. ····
Relative Strength —

VOL. MIL.

1992 1993 1994 1995

OPTIONS: P

Overview - 28-SEP-95

Sales are expected to post further growth in 1996. Despite continuing competitive pricing in global pharmaceutical markets and further generic erosion in the Proventil and Theo-Dur lines, volume should benefit from strong gains in newer lines such as Claritin and Claritin-D nonsedating antihistamine agents (leading drugs in the antihistamine market), Eulexin and Intron A anticancer and anti-infective agents, Cedax antibiotic and Leucomax white blood cell stimulant. Margins should be well maintained, on improved volume and cost efficiencies. With fewer shares outstanding, EPS should reach $3.15, from $2.80 indicated for 1995 (before charges of $0.45 associated with the discontinued Wesley-Jessen division).

Valuation - 28-SEP-95

Like those of other leading pharmaceutical companies, the shares have been in a sustained uptrend in recent months, as renewed investor confidence in the drug group reflects a friendlier regulatory environment in Washington and improving industry fundamentals. SGP's mix of popular prescription drugs and OTC medications, its highly productive R&D program, and strict controls over operating costs and expenses, have enabled it to achieve wide margins and strong earnings growth in recent years. These factors should continue to spur earnings in coming years. The shares (which split two for one in June) merit accumulation for above-average long-term total return.

Key Stock Statistics

S&P EPS Est. 1995	2.80	Tang. Bk. Value/Share	4.36
P/E on S&P Est. 1995	18.0	Beta	0.86
S&P EPS Est. 1996	3.15	Shareholders	37,900
Dividend Rate/Share	1.16	Market cap. (B)	$ 19.5
Shs. outstg. (M)	372.3	Inst. holdings	64%
Avg. daily vol. (M)	0.862	Insider holdings	NA

Value of $10,000 invested 5 years ago: $ 26,948

Fiscal Year Ending Dec. 31

	1995	% Change	1994	% Change	1993	% Change
Revenues (Million $)						
1Q	1,244	7%	1,162	7%	1,090	7%
2Q	1,333	12%	1,190	6%	1,123	10%
3Q	—	—	1,126	6%	1,062	4%
4Q	—	—	1,180	11%	1,066	7%
Yr.	—	—	4,657	7%	4,341	7%
Income (Million $)						
1Q	278.6	10%	253.2	13%	223.5	16%
2Q	276.1	15%	240.7	13%	213.2	15%
3Q	—	—	224.3	12%	199.4	14%
4Q	—	—	203.8	8%	188.9	13%
Yr.	—	—	922.0	12%	825.0	15%
Earnings Per Share ($)						
1Q	0.75	15%	0.65	16%	0.57	18%
2Q	0.74	18%	0.63	15%	0.54	18%
3Q	E0.67	15%	0.59	14%	0.51	17%
4Q	E0.64	17%	0.54	11%	0.49	17%
Yr.	E2.80	16%	2.41	14%	2.11	17%

Next earnings report expected: mid October

Schering-Plough

Business Summary - 28-SEP-95

Schering-Plough Corporation is a leading manufacturer of prescription and OTC pharmaceuticals, and has interests in sun care, animal health and foot care products. Contributions by business segment in 1994 were:

	Sales	Profits
Pharmaceutical products	86%	88%
Health care products	14%	12%

Foreign operations accounted for 45% of sales and 35% of profits in 1994. R&D equaled 13.3% of sales both in 1994 and 1993.

Respiratory drugs (accounting for 31% of 1994 sales) include Claritin nonsedating antihistamine and Claritin-D, a combination decongestant; Theo-Dur, Proventil and Uni-Dur asthma treatments; and Vancenase allergy nasal products and Vanceril asthma inhaler. Anti-infectives and anticancer products (20%) consist of Intron-A (alpha-2 interferon), which is marketed for various anticancer and antiviral indications; Cedax, a third generation cephalosporin antibiotic; Eulexin, a treatment for prostatic cancer; Leucomax, a granulocyte macrophage colony stimulating factor; and Netromycin, an aminoglycoside antibiotic.

Dermatological products (11%) include high potency steroids such as Diprolene and Diprosone; Elocon, a topical steroid cream and ointment; and Lotrisone, a topical antifungal and anti-inflammatory cream. Cardiovasculars (7%) consist of Imdur, an oral nitrate; Nitro-Dur, a transdermal nitroglycerin patch for angina pectoris; Normodyne, an anti-hypertensive; and K-Dur, a potassium supplement. Other products products (17%), include Losec antiulcer drug (marketed overseas), Fibre Trim diet aid products, animal health items and other drugs.

Health care products encompass OTC medicines (6%) such as Afrin nasal spray, Chlor-Trimeton allergy tablets, Coricidin and Drixoral cold medications, Correctal laxative, and Gyne-Lotrimin for vaginal yeast infections; foot care items (5%) sold under Dr. Scholl's and other names; and Coppertone and other sun care products (3%).

Important Developments

Sep. '95—SGP projected 1995 EPS at slightly over $2.80. The chairman, R.P. Luciano, expressed confidence that the company can continue to produce at least low-to-mid double digit EPS growth for 1996 and 1997. Earlier, in June, SGP sold its Wesley-Jessen contact lens business for $47.5 million in cash.

Capitalization

Long Term Debt: $186,300,000 (6/95).

Per Share Data ($)

(Year Ended Dec. 31)

	1994	1993	1992	1991	1990	1989
Tangible Bk. Val.	3.78	3.61	3.53	2.86	4.31	3.94
Cash Flow	2.82	2.44	2.10	1.77	1.49	1.27
Earnings	2.41	2.11	1.80	1.51	1.25	1.05
Dividends	0.99	0.87	0.75	0.63	0.53	0.44
Payout Ratio	41%	41%	42%	40%	42%	43%
Prices - High	38	35½	35⅛	33⅝	25⅜	21½
- Low	27¼	25⅞	25	20⅜	18½	13⅞
P/E Ratio - High	16	17	19	22	20	21
- Low	11	12	14	14	15	13

Income Statement Analysis (Million $)

	1994	%Chg	1993	%Chg	1992	%Chg	1991
Revs.	4,657	7%	4,341	7%	4,056	12%	3,616
Oper. Inc.	1,407	14%	1,234	10%	1,124	12%	1,003
Depr.	158	24%	127	6%	120	4%	115
Int. Exp.	68.0	11%	61.0	-14%	71.0	-8%	77.0
Pretax Inc.	1,213	13%	1,078	13%	954	11%	861
Eff. Tax Rate	24%	—	24%	—	25%	—	25%
Net Inc.	922	12%	825	15%	720	11%	646

Balance Sheet & Other Fin. Data (Million $)

	1994	1993	1992	1991	1990	1989
Cash	161	429	529	927	920	935
Curr. Assets	1,739	1,901	2,013	2,102	2,000	2,047
Total Assets	4,326	4,317	4,157	4,013	4,103	3,614
Curr. Liab.	2,029	2,132	1,969	1,528	1,530	1,214
LT Debt	186	182	184	754	183	186
Common Eqty.	1,574	1,582	1,597	1,346	2,081	1,955
Total Cap.	2,006	1,940	1,980	2,286	2,436	2,271
Cap. Exp.	272	365	403	339	243	186
Cash Flow	1,080	952	840	760	674	571

Ratio Analysis

	1994	1993	1992	1991	1990	1989
Curr. Ratio	0.9	0.9	1.0	1.4	1.3	1.7
% LT Debt of Cap.	9.3	9.4	9.3	33.0	7.5	8.2
% Net Inc.of Revs.	19.8	19.0	17.8	17.9	17.0	14.9
% Ret. on Assets	21.8	19.8	17.7	16.7	14.8	13.4
% Ret. on Equity	59.6	52.7	49.2	39.9	28.3	25.9

Dividend Data

—Dividends have been paid since 1952. A new poison pill stock purchase rights plan was adopted in 1989. A dividend reinvestment plan is available.

Amt. of Div. $	Date Decl.	Ex-Div. Date	Stock of Record	Payment Date
0.510	Oct. 25	Oct. 31	Nov. 04	Nov. 29 '94
0.510	Jan. 24	Jan. 30	Feb. 03	Feb. 28 '95
0.580	Apr. 04	May. 01	May. 05	May. 30 '95
2-for-1	Apr. 04	Jun. 12	May. 05	Jun. 09 '95
0.290	Jun. 27	Aug. 02	Aug. 04	Aug. 29 '95

Data as orig. reptd.; bef. results of disc. opers. and/or spec. items. Per share data adj. for stk. divs. as of ex-div. date. E-Estimated. NA-Not Available. NM-Not Meaningful. NR-Not Ranked.

Office—One Giralda Farms, Madison, NJ 07940-1000. **Tel**—(201) 822-7000. **Chrmn & CEO**—R. P. Luciano. **Pres**—R. J. Kogan. **VP & Secy**—K. A. Quinn. **VP & Treas**—J. L. Wyszomierski. **SVP & Investor Contact**—Geraldine U. Foster. **Dirs**—H. A. D'Andrade, H. W. Becherer, D. C. Garfield, R. E. Herzlinger, R. J. Kogan, R. P. Luciano, H. B. Morley, C. E. Mundy, R de J. Osborne, P. F. Russo, W. A. Schreyer, R. F. W. van Oordt, R. J. Ventres, J. Wood. **Transfer Agent & Registrar**—Bank of New York, NYC. **Incorporated** in New Jersey in 1970. **Empl**-21,200. **S&P Analyst:** H.B. Saftlas

Schlumberger Ltd.

NYSE Symbol **SLB**
In S&P 500

31-OCT-95

Industry:
Oil and Gas

Summary: This worldwide leader in wellsite and drilling services to the oil and natural gas industry also manufactures meters and measurement instruments.

S&P Opinion: Accumulate (★★★★)

Recent Price • 59½	Yield • 2.5%
52 Wk Range • 69⅝-50	12-Mo. P/E • 22.5

Earnings vs. Previous Year
▲=Up ▼=Down ▶=No Change

Quantitative Evaluations

Outlook
(1 Lowest—5 Highest)
• **1+**

Fair Value
• **52⅛**

Risk
• **Low**

Earn./Div. Rank
• **B+**

Technical Eval.
• **Bearish** since 7/95

Rel. Strength Rank
(1 Lowest—99 Highest)
• **30**

Insider Activity
• **Neutral**

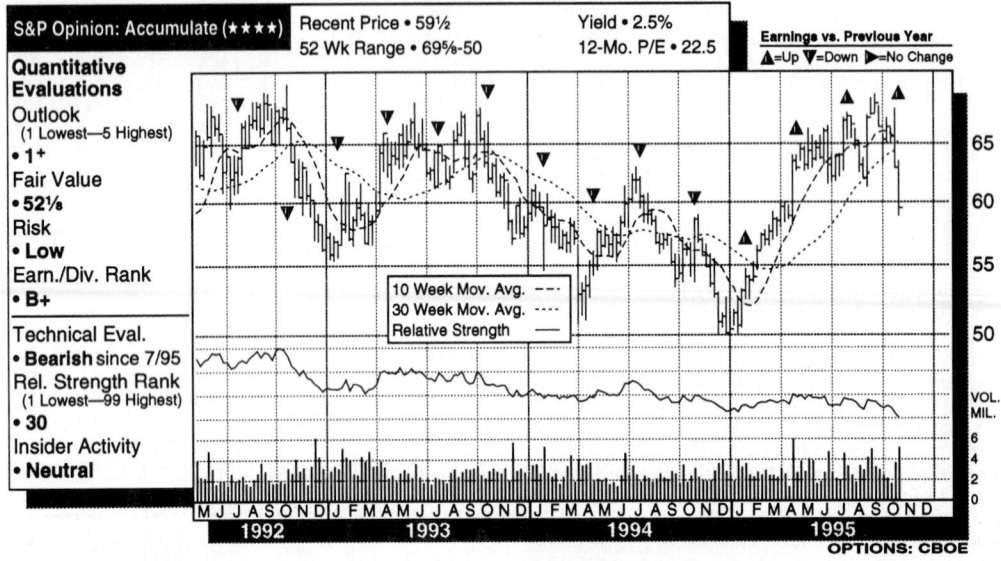

10 Week Mov. Avg. ---
30 Week Mov. Avg. ....
Relative Strength —

OPTIONS: CBOE

Overview - 31-OCT-95

Growth in Schlumberger's earnings has resulted from the success of new products that are boosting market share. We believe that future earnings will be aided by robust growth in oilfield service revenues, and by wider margins. Marine seismic revenues should grow, in large part reflecting SLB's success in winning lucrative North Sea contracts. Sharply higher day rates and rig utilization for the Sedco Forex rig fleet should continue through 1996. Measurement & Systems should show strong growth through 1996, on high levels of demand for metering equipment and systems in Europe, as well as improved results for the smart card business. We also believe that Platform Express, SLB's latest well-logging tool, will gain rapid acceptance.

Valuation - 31-OCT-95

We believe that SLB ranks as one of the best plays in the oil service field, which is being helped by higher spending by the major integrated oils, and increased outsourcing. A strong balance sheet and excellent cash generating capacity enhance the outlook for the shares. We forecast stable oil prices and rising gas prices into 1996, although OPEC's worries about shrinking market share will likely lead to somewhat increased production. Barring any major surprises at OPEC's November meeting, oil prices will average $18.50 a barrel in 1996, up from our 1995 $18.00 a barrel forecast. Growing demand for measurement products from developing countries will make an important contribution in coming years.

Key Stock Statistics

S&P EPS Est. 1995	2.72	Tang. Bk. Value/Share	14.42
P/E on S&P Est. 1995	21.9	Beta	1.09
S&P EPS Est. 1996	3.30	Shareholders	27,000
Dividend Rate/Share	1.50	Market cap. (B)	$ 14.8
Shs. outstg. (M)	241.9	Inst. holdings	60%
Avg. daily vol. (M)	0.653	Insider holdings	NA

Value of $10,000 invested 5 years ago: $ 13,743

Fiscal Year Ending Dec. 31

	1995	% Change	1994	% Change	1993	% Change
Revenues (Million $)						
1Q	1,786	9%	1,640	1%	1,624	5%
2Q	1,877	15%	1,639	-6%	1,745	12%
3Q	1,941	19%	1,637	-2%	1,665	4%
4Q	—	—	1,781	2%	1,746	7%
Yr.	—	—	6,697	NM	6,705	6%
Income (Million $)						
1Q	146.8	21%	121.5	-9%	133.2	-15%
2Q	166.9	35%	123.4	-24%	163.0	-9%
3Q	168.8	24%	136.6	-16%	162.7	-6%
4Q	—	—	154.7	25%	124.0	-20%
Yr.	—	—	536.1	-8%	582.8	-12%
Earnings Per Share ($)						
1Q	0.61	22%	0.50	-9%	0.55	-15%
2Q	0.69	35%	0.51	-24%	0.67	-9%
3Q	0.70	25%	0.56	-16%	0.67	-7%
4Q	E0.72	13%	0.64	25%	0.51	-20%
Yr.	E2.72	23%	2.21	-8%	2.40	-13%

Next earnings report expected: late January

Schlumberger Ltd.

Business Summary - 31-OCT-95

Schlumberger is a world leader in providing drilling services and fully computerized wireline and interpretation services to the petroleum industry. It also makes computer-aided systems and electronic products. The Sedco Forex unit operates 40 offshore and 34 land drilling rigs. Segment contributions in 1994 were:

	Revs.	Profits
Oilfield services	65%	87%
Measurement & systems	35%	23%

Geco-Prakla provides acquisition, processing and interpretation, of land, transition zone and marine seismic data. Dowell provides cementing, stimulation, coiled tubing and drilling fluids services to enhance well productivity. SLB has a leading wireline services market share throughout the major exploration regions of the world. It also offers measurement-while-drilling and logging-while-drilling services.

The measurement and systems segment has five business units: electricity, water and gas management, as well as electronic transactions and automatic test equipment. Products include electricity meters and equipment for power distribution, transformers, network protection systems, water and gas meters, and electronic payment systems. The group also produces computer aided engineering, design and manufacturing systems, semiconductor testing systems, and smart cards.

Important Developments

Oct. '95—EPS in the 1995 third quarter climbed 25%, year to year, spurred by market share gains and growth outside of North America. A 23% jump in measurement and systems revenues reflected strong demand for products and services at the electronic transactions, gas management and automatic test equipment segments. Improved European economic conditions and higher levels of Far East shipments outweighed weaker demand in Mexico for water management services, leading to a 7% revenue gain. Oilfield revenues in North America were higher, outpacing the increase in drilling rig count. The Sedco Forex contract drilling unit benefited from improved North Sea and West Africa operations and higher rig utilization (66%, versus 63%). Dowell's 18% revenue gain resulted from greater activity in Latin America. Anadrill's 29% revenue rise was primarily due to a 63% increase in directional drilling revenues. Schlumberger noted it was very pleased with the acceptance of its new Platform Express well logging tool, which allows more accurate evaluation of reservoirs and reduces the time required for logging operations.

Capitalization

Long Term Debt: $408,464,000 (9/95).

Per Share Data ($)   (Year Ended Dec. 31)

	1994	1993	1992	1991	1990	1989
Tangible Bk. Val.	13.95	13.54	15.16	14.22	11.98	11.04
Cash Flow	5.39	5.45	5.53	6.03	4.58	3.84
Earnings	2.21	2.40	2.75	3.42	2.40	1.77
Dividends	1.20	1.20	1.20	1.20	1.20	1.20
Payout Ratio	54%	50%	44%	35%	50%	68%
Prices - High	63	68⅞	70⅝	74	69⅞	50½
- Low	50	55⅜	52⅝	50½	43½	32
P/E Ratio - High	29	29	26	22	29	29
- Low	23	23	19	15	18	18

Income Statement Analysis (Million $)

	1994	%Chg	1993	%Chg	1992	%Chg	1991
Revs.	6,697	NM	6,705	6%	6,332	3%	6,145
Oper. Inc.	1,373	NM	1,373	NM	1,373	1%	1,358
Depr.	776	5%	739	10%	671	7%	627
Int. Exp.	63.0	-9%	69.0	-10%	77.0	-25%	102
Pretax Inc.	617	-7%	664	-11%	748	-24%	982
Eff. Tax Rate	13%	—	12%	—	12%	—	17%
Net Inc.	536	-8%	583	-12%	662	-19%	816

Balance Sheet & Other Fin. Data (Million $)

	1994	1993	1992	1991	1990	1989
Cash	1,232	1,186	1,345	1,466	1,324	1,353
Curr. Assets	3,824	3,476	3,453	3,566	3,247	3,031
Total Assets	8,322	7,917	7,007	6,854	6,176	5,482
Curr. Liab.	2,787	2,568	2,211	2,472	2,435	2,147
LT Debt	394	447	374	341	332	292
Common Eqty.	4,583	4,406	4,231	3,853	3,255	2,898
Total Cap.	4,977	4,853	4,605	4,194	3,587	3,190
Cap. Exp.	783	691	809	921	675	549
Cash Flow	1,312	1,322	1,333	1,442	1,090	913

Ratio Analysis

	1994	1993	1992	1991	1990	1989
Curr. Ratio	1.4	1.4	1.6	1.4	1.3	1.4
% LT Debt of Cap.	7.9	9.2	8.1	8.1	9.2	9.2
% Net Inc.of Revs.	8.0	8.7	10.4	13.3	10.7	9.0
% Ret. on Assets	6.6	7.8	9.5	12.5	9.8	7.6
% Ret. on Equity	12.0	13.4	16.3	22.9	18.5	14.9

Dividend Data —Dividends have been paid since 1957.

Amt. of Div. $	Date Decl.	Ex-Div. Date	Stock of Record	Payment Date
0.300	Oct. 19	Dec. 13	Dec. 19	Jan. 06 '95
0.300	Jan. 25	Feb. 21	Feb. 27	Apr. 07 '95
0.375	Apr. 24	May. 26	Jun. 02	Jul. 03 '95
0.375	Jul. 19	Aug. 30	Sep. 01	Oct. 02 '95
0.375	Oct. 18	Dec. 14	Dec. 18	Jan. 05 '96

Data as orig. reptd.; bef. results of disc. opers. and/or spec. items. Per share data adj. for stk. divs. as of ex-div. date. E-Estimated. NA-Not Available. NM-Not Meaningful. NR-Not Ranked.

Offices—277 Park Ave., New York, NY 10172. **Tel**—(212) 350-9400. **Chrmn & CEO**—D. E. Baird. **EVP-Fin & CFO**—A. Lindenauer. **Secy**—D. S. Browning. **Investor Contact**—S. Crook. **Dirs**—D. E. Ackerman, D. E. Baird, P. Faurre, Sir Denys Henderson, A. Levy-Lang, W. T. McCormick, Jr., D. Primat, N. Seydoux, L. G. Stuntz, S. Ullring, E. Umene, A. de Vitry. **Transfer Agent & Registrar**—First National Bank of Boston. **Incorporated** in Netherlands Antilles in 1956. **Empl**-48,000. **S&P Analyst:** Raymond J. Deacon

Scientific-Atlanta

NYSE Symbol **SFA**
In S&P 500

17-AUG-95

Industry: Specialty instruments

Summary: This company manufactures broadband communications equipment, test and measurement instruments, and defense electronic systems.

S&P Opinion: Hold (★★★)

Recent Price • 21¼	Yield • 0.3%
52 Wk Range • 24⅞-17½	12-Mo. P/E • 25.6

Quantitative Evaluations

Outlook
(1 Lowest—5 Highest)
• **4+**

Fair Value
• **21⅝**

Risk
• **Average**

Earn./Div. Rank
• **B+**

Technical Eval.
• **Bullish** since 6/95

Rel. Strength Rank
(1 Lowest—99 Highest)
• **15**

Insider Activity
• **Neutral**

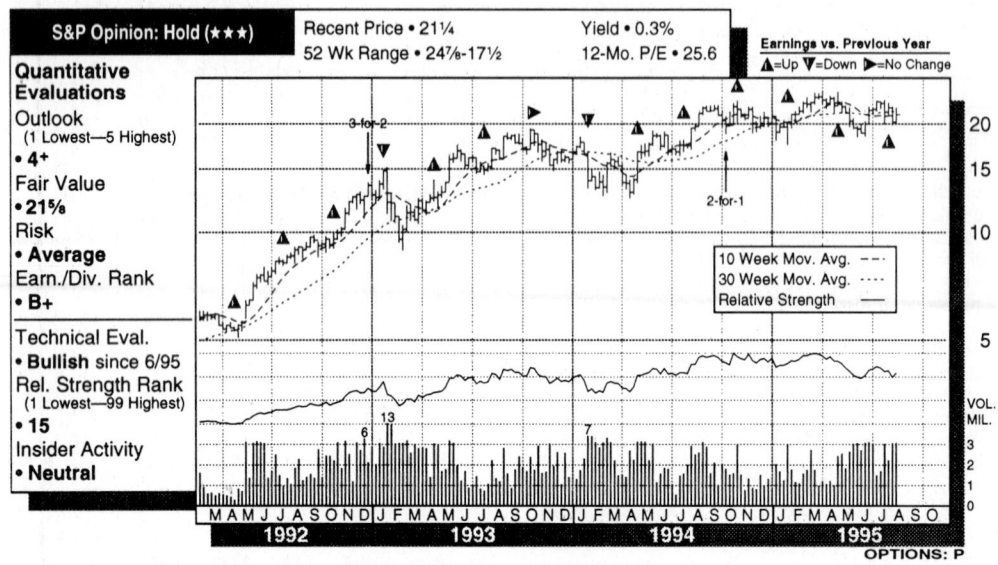

Earnings vs. Previous Year
▲=Up ▼=Down ▶=No Change

10 Week Mov. Avg. ---
30 Week Mov. Avg. ····
Relative Strength —

OPTIONS: P

Overview - 17-AUG-95

Revenues should increase rapidly again in fiscal 1996, as orders and backlog continue to reach record levels. Broadband communications sales are expected to show strong growth, benefiting from increased capital spending by cable operators and local telephone companies seeking to provide broadband video, voice and data services. Sales of satellite products should rise moderately, aided by growth in foreign markets. Sales of electronic equipment may continue to be restricted by slowdowns in government spending. Margins will be stable over the next several quarters, as progress in a margin improvement program will be offset by costs associated with increased production of set-top terminals.

Valuation - 17-AUG-95

The shares have been trading in a narrow range for the past year. Future results should benefit from an increasing focus on international business; the company's stated goal is to derive more than 50% of total revenues from international operations by the end of the decade. The company's major challenge is to profitably manage its explosive growth while ensuring it has enough capacity to meet soaring customer demand. We recommend holding the shares pending the outcome of the current telecommunications reform bill in Congress.

Key Stock Statistics

S&P EPS Est. 1996	1.14	Tang. Bk. Value/Share	5.78
P/E on S&P Est. 1996	18.6	Beta	1.78
Dividend Rate/Share	0.06	Shareholders	6,000
Shs. outstg. (M)	76.7	Market cap. (B)	$ 1.6
Avg. daily vol. (M)	0.645	Inst. holdings	84%
		Insider holdings	NA

Value of $10,000 invested 5 years ago: $ 27,787

Fiscal Year Ending Jun. 30

	1995	% Change	1994	% Change	1993	% Change
Revenues (Million $)						
1Q	232.3	36%	170.3	NM	171.0	34%
2Q	277.4	56%	178.0	-76%	730.6	NM
3Q	313.5	54%	204.1	11%	184.1	26%
4Q	323.3	25%	259.4	38%	188.6	9%
Yr.	1,147	41%	811.6	11%	730.6	26%
Income (Million $)						
1Q	12.10	69%	7.15	—	—	—
2Q	15.01	NM	-4.58	NM	1.40	-37%
3Q	15.67	32%	11.91	73%	6.90	72%
4Q	20.70	NM	20.55	116%	9.50	22%
Yr.	63.50	81%	35.02	42%	24.67	51%
Earnings Per Share ($)						
1Q	0.16	68%	0.09	NM	0.09	171%
2Q	0.19	NM	-0.06	NM	0.02	-43%
3Q	0.21	35%	0.15	72%	0.09	64%
4Q	0.27	2%	0.26	112%	0.13	14%
Yr.	0.83	84%	0.45	36%	0.33	43%

Next earnings report expected: late October

Business Summary - 17-AUG-95

Scientific-Atlanta supplies broadband communications equipment, cable television electronics, satellite-based network systems, and electronic instrumentation products.

SFA's broadband communications products consist of a range of products for the cable television (CATV) industry, including headend systems to receive and process television signals, distribution and transmission equipment, and set-top terminals that allow subscribers to receive CATV signals and are "headend" addressable for conditional subscriber access. The company also manufactures equipment for transmitting compact-disc quality music programming via satellite and cable. SFA is the leading supplier of broadband networks to the cable industy and the second largest provider of subscriber equipment. Sales of set-top terminals accounted for 21% of revenues in fiscal 1994.

Satellite network products include satellite earth stations, very-small-aperture terminal (VSAT) satellite networks, direct broadcast radio systems and transportable communications terminals for maritime or land-based applications. The company also develops services and applications that can be utilized by customers on their satellite-based systems.

Other business areas include acoustic and electronic signal processing systems and instrumentation systems used to design and test microwave antennas and components.

SFA has actively sought to increase its penetration of international markets; international sales represented 33% of total sales in fiscal 1994.

Important Developments

Jun. '95—Southern Multimedia Communications, Inc., a subsidiary of US WEST, named SFA as a key supplier for upgrading a 12,000-mile cable network in the metropolitan Atlanta area. SFA will supply receivers, stereo encoders and modulators for the headends as well as amplifiers for the distribution network.
Apr. '95—SFA received a contract for up to $150 million over three years from Pacific Telesis for equipment for its interactive video network. In addition, SFA received a contract from Optus Vision to supply equipment for the development of a broadband digital telephony and home entertainment network in Australia. Separately, SFA shipped more than 300 headend systems to cable operators to deliver the Sega Channel.
Mar. '95—Ameritech ordered about $400 million of analog and digital set-top terminals and remote controls from the company over five years. Separately, SFA and Siemens AG agreed to jointly develop and market telephone services over cable television lines.

Capitalization

Long Term Debt: $800,000 (6/95).

Per Share Data ($)
(Year Ended Jun. 30)

	1995	1994	1993	1992	1991	1990
Tangible Bk. Val.	NA	5.14	4.63	4.19	3.98	3.99
Cash Flow	NA	0.73	0.59	0.46	0.26	0.82
Earnings	0.83	0.46	0.33	0.24	0.02	0.63
Dividends	0.08	0.06	0.06	0.05	0.05	0.05
Payout Ratio	9%	13%	18%	23%	344%	8%
Prices - High	24⅞	20¼	19⅜	13¾	6	9¾
- Low	17½	12½	8⅞	5⅛	3⅞	3
P/E Ratio - High	30	44	59	54	NM	15
- Low	21	27	27	22	NM	5

Income Statement Analysis (Million $)

	1994	%Chg	1993	%Chg	1992	%Chg	1991
Revs.	812	11%	731	26%	581	18%	494
Oper. Inc.	87.8	78%	49.3	46%	33.7	34%	25.1
Depr.	20.9	9%	19.1	19%	16.1	-4%	16.8
Int. Exp.	1.1	15%	0.9	63%	0.6	-49%	1.1
Pretax Inc.	51.5	57%	32.9	52%	21.7	NM	1.5
Eff. Tax Rate	32%	—	25%	—	25%	—	31%
Net Inc.	35.0	42%	24.7	52%	16.3	NM	1.1

Balance Sheet & Other Fin. Data (Million $)

	1994	1993	1992	1991	1990	1989
Cash	123	104	91.0	112	91.0	80.0
Curr. Assets	505	406	343	311	310	294
Total Assets	640	524	441	394	389	356
Curr. Liab.	202	130	112	87.0	87.0	74.0
LT Debt	1.1	1.4	1.7	2.0	2.3	2.6
Common Eqty.	396	353	300	282	279	257
Total Cap.	397	354	307	288	285	268
Cap. Exp.	34.9	24.0	18.5	19.9	27.4	15.6
Cash Flow	55.9	43.7	32.4	17.9	57.6	49.5

Ratio Analysis

	1994	1993	1992	1991	1990	1989
Curr. Ratio	2.5	3.1	3.1	3.6	3.6	4.0
% LT Debt of Cap.	0.2	0.4	0.6	0.7	0.8	1.0
% Net Inc.of Revs.	4.3	3.4	2.8	0.2	7.2	6.6
% Ret. on Assets	6.0	4.9	3.9	0.3	12.1	11.0
% Ret. on Equity	9.3	7.3	5.6	0.4	16.7	15.0

Dividend Data —Dividends were initiated in 1976. A "poison pill" stock purchase rights plan was adopted in 1987.

Amt. of Div. $	Date Decl.	Ex-Div. Date	Stock of Record	Payment Date
0.030	Aug. 25	Sep. 01	Sep. 08	Oct. 06 '94
2-for-1	Aug. 25	Oct. 06	Sep. 08	Oct. 05 '94
0.015	Nov. 11	Nov. 23	Nov. 30	Dec. 14 '94
0.015	Feb. 23	Mar. 01	Mar. 07	Mar. 22 '95
0.015	May. 17	May. 25	Jun. 01	Jun. 21 '95

Data as orig. reptd.; bef. results of disc. opers. and/or spec. items. Per share data adj. for stk. divs. as of ex-div. date.
E-Estimated. NA-Not Available. NM-Not Meaningful. NR-Not Ranked.

Office—One Technology Parkway, South, Norcross, GA 30092-2967. **Tel**—(404) 903-5000. **Chrmn**—J. V. Napier. **Pres & CEO**—J. F. McDonald. **SVP-CFO & Treas**—H. A. Wagner. **SVP-Secy**—W. E. Eason Jr. **Investor Contact**—Robert S. Meyers. **Dirs**—M. H. Antonini, W. E. Kassling, W. B. King, M. B. Mangum, A. L. McDonald, J. F. McDonald, D. J. McLaughlin, J. V. Napier, S. Topol. **Transfer Agent & Registrar**—Bank of New York, NYC. **Incorporated** in Georgia in 1951. **Empl**-4,000. **S&P Analyst:** Alan Aaron

Scott Paper

NYSE Symbol **SPP**
In S&P 500

20-SEP-95

Industry:
Household Products

Summary: Scott has reached a definitive agreement to be acquired by Kimberly-Clark in a stock transaction, creating the second largest household products company in the U.S.

S&P Opinion: Accumulate (★★★★)

Recent Price • 49⅛	Yield • 0.8%
52 Wk Range • 51⅝-29¾	12-Mo. P/E • 16.5

Quantitative Evaluations

Outlook
(1 Lowest—5 Highest)
• **2+**

Fair Value
• **46⅝**

Risk
• **Low**

Earn./Div. Rank
• **B**

Technical Eval.
• **Bearish** since 1/95

Rel. Strength Rank
(1 Lowest—99 Highest)
• **48**

Insider Activity
• **NA**

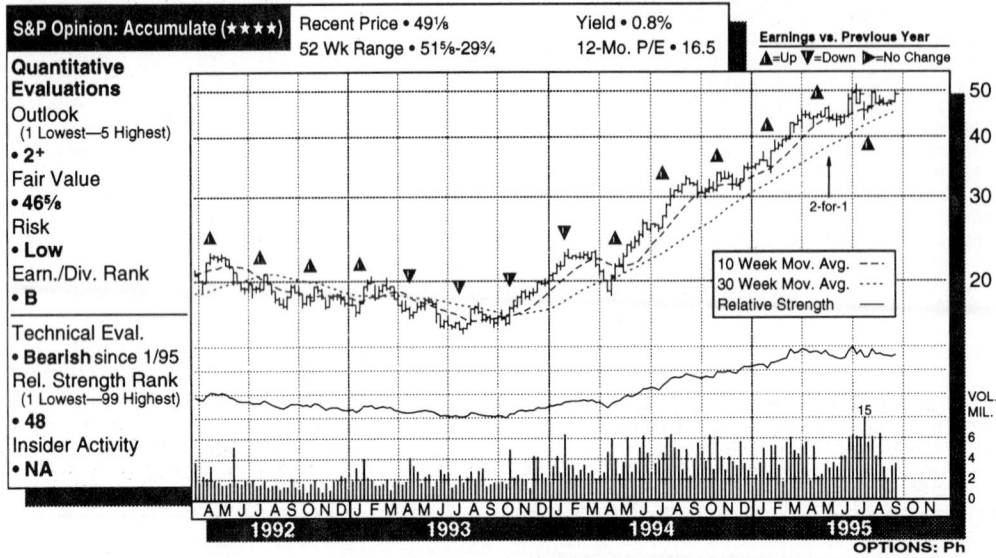

Earnings vs. Previous Year
▲=Up ▼=Down ►=No Change

2-for-1

10 Week Mov. Avg. - - - -
30 Week Mov. Avg. ....
Relative Strength ——

VOL.
MIL.

OPTIONS: Ph

Overview - 20-SEP-95

Assuming that the planned takeover by Kimberly-Clark is completed as expected in the final quarter of 1995, the combined firm is likely to have solidly higher sales in 1996. Sales growth should be driven by Scott's strong European marketing organization, the broader product mixture of the merged company and the recent uptrend in consumer tissue pricing. The merged firm should garner much shelf space through the combination of SPP's value-priced lines and KMB's premium products. On top of cost savings generated by Scott's recent restructuring program, margins of the combined firm should benefit from actions taken to eliminate redundant overhead costs, consolidate workforces and streamline manufacturing facilities. Our 1996 earnings forecast for the combined firm, operating under the KMB name, is $5.00 a share.

Valuation - 20-SEP-95

Scott's shares have risen sharply since the spring of 1994, on enthusiasm over new management and its overhaul of the company, and rumors that SPP was being readied for a takeover which was borne out with Kimberly-Clark's takeover offer in July 1995. Although the shares have been flat since the merger agreement, as investors were less optimistic about KMB's earnings outlook, we believe the KMB shares received in the takeover will generate above-market returns. Our enthusiasm is related to the complementary nature of the firms' product lines and distribution organizations, and considerable cost savings to be generated through the integration of operations.

Key Stock Statistics

S&P EPS Est. 1995	3.15	Tang. Bk. Value/Share	10.39
P/E on S&P Est. 1995	15.6	Beta	1.48
Dividend Rate/Share	0.40	Shareholders	34,400
Shs. outstg. (M)	151.7	Market cap. (B)	$ 7.3
Avg. daily vol. (M)	0.598	Inst. holdings	73%
		Insider holdings	NA

Value of $10,000 invested 5 years ago: $ 22,620

Fiscal Year Ending Dec. 31

	1995	% Change	1994	% Change	1993	% Change
Revenues (Million $)						
1Q	1,003	21%	828.7	-28%	1,156	-4%
2Q	1,058	16%	914.3	-24%	1,209	NM
3Q	—	—	877.3	-26%	1,180	-5%
4Q	—	—	960.8	-20%	1,205	-2%
Yr.	—	—	3,581	-25%	4,749	-3%
Income (Million $)						
1Q	96.90	NM	25.20	7%	23.50	-48%
2Q	145.5	NM	40.20	71%	23.50	-50%
3Q	—	—	60.60	146%	24.60	-20%
4Q	—	—	130.8	NM	-360.7	NM
Yr.	—	—	264.1	NM	-289.1	NM
Earnings Per Share ($)						
1Q	0.64	NM	0.17	6%	0.16	-48%
2Q	0.96	NM	0.27	69%	0.16	-49%
3Q	E0.75	88%	0.40	142%	0.17	-20%
4Q	E0.80	-9%	0.88	NM	-2.44	NM
Yr.	E3.15	78%	1.77	NM	-1.95	NM

Next earnings report expected: mid October

Business Summary - 20-SEP-95

Scott Paper, which is the world's largest producer of sanitary tissue products, reached a definitive agreement in July 1995, to be acquired by Kimberly-Clark. In the year prior to the merger announcement, Scott had been involved in a massive restructuring program, under which SPP was placing focus strictly on its core tissue business. Geographic contributions in 1994 (pretax profits in million $) were:

	Sales	Profits
U.S.	61%	$349.7
Europe	31%	121.6
Pacific & Latin America	8%	42.0

Personal care and cleaning products include bathroom and facial tissue, paper towels, baby wipes, premoistened cleansing cloths, table napkins, soaps, toilet seat covers, industrial garments, environmental cleaning and wiping products and bathroom dispensers. These products are sold under the Scott name, and under other company tradenames. Products sold directly to consumers are marketed through supermarkets, drugstores and mass merchandisers, and away-from-home products are sold through distributors to manufacturing, lodging, office building, foodservice, healthcare and public facilities.

Important Developments

Jul. '95—SPP signed a definitive agreement to be acquired by Kimberly-Clark Corp. (KMB), with Scott shareholders to receive 0.765 KMB common shares for each SPP share held (0.780 if the pending spinoff of Kimberly's tobacco papers business precedes the merger). The combination would create the second largest household and personal care products company in the U.S. and the world's leading tissue manufacturer. The merger was expected to be completed in 1995's fourth quarter, subject to approval by shareholders of both companies and regulatory authorities. Wayne R. Sanders would continue as chairman and CEO of KMB, while Albert J. Dunlap, who holds those titles at Scott, would resign from the firm and serve as a board advisor. KMB's more familiar brand names include Kleenex, Kotex, New Freedom, Huggies, Pull-Ups and Hi-Dri. Kimberly's quarterly dividend of $0.45 a share will be the continuing payment of the combined company. Prior to the merger agreement, Scott had been involved in a program to sell non-strategic business assets (implemented after SPP's new management team was put in place in April 1994), with proceeds of about $2.4 billion derived through mid-1995; the largest transaction had been the December 1994 sale of the S.D. Warren printing and publishing unit to a South African investment group for $1.6 billion. The restructuring also included the elimination of about one-third of SPP's workforce.

Capitalization

Long Term Debt: $1,210,300,000 (7/1/95).

Per Share Data ($) (Year Ended Dec. 31)

	1994	1993	1992	1991	1990	1989
Tangible Bk. Val.	11.54	10.59	13.65	13.44	14.77	14.01
Cash Flow	3.14	-0.06	2.93	1.80	3.23	4.58
Earnings	1.77	-1.95	1.13	-0.47	1.01	2.55
Dividends	0.40	0.40	0.40	0.40	0.40	0.40
Payout Ratio	23%	NM	35%	NM	40%	16%
Prices - High	35⅜	20⅝	23	23⅜	25¾	26¼
- Low	18⅝	15½	17¼	14¾	15	19¼
P/E Ratio - High	20	NM	20	NM	26	10
- Low	11	NM	15	NM	15	8

Income Statement Analysis (Million $)

	1994	%Chg	1993	%Chg	1992	%Chg	1991
Revs.	3,581	-25%	4,749	-3%	4,886	-2%	4,977
Oper. Inc.	606	-2%	621	-6%	659	-2%	670
Depr.	205	-27%	281	6%	266	-21%	335
Int. Exp.	202	5%	192	-7%	207	-17%	250
Pretax Inc.	414	NM	-342	NM	235	NM	-82.0
Eff. Tax Rate	34%	—	NM	—	25%	—	NM
Net Inc.	264	NM	-288	NM	167	NM	-70.0

Balance Sheet & Other Fin. Data (Million $)

	1994	1993	1992	1991	1990	1989
Cash	1,114	134	142	185	114	49.0
Curr. Assets	2,309	1,610	1,392	1,481	1,733	1,407
Total Assets	5,626	6,625	6,300	6,493	6,901	5,746
Curr. Liab.	1,930	1,770	1,516	1,510	1,595	1,306
LT Debt	1,093	2,366	2,031	2,333	2,455	1,678
Common Eqty.	1,745	1,569	2,018	1,982	2,175	2,061
Total Cap.	3,190	4,276	4,468	4,745	5,139	4,302
Cap. Exp.	NA	458	330	315	815	791
Cash Flow	468	-8.0	433	265	475	672

Ratio Analysis

	1994	1993	1992	1991	1990	1989
Curr. Ratio	1.2	0.9	0.9	1.0	1.1	1.1
% LT Debt of Cap.	34.3	55.3	45.5	49.2	47.8	39.0
% Net Inc.of Revs.	7.4	NM	3.4	NM	2.8	7.4
% Ret. on Assets	4.3	NM	2.6	NM	2.3	6.9
% Ret. on Equity	15.8	NM	8.3	NM	7.0	18.7

Dividend Data —Dividends have been paid since 1915. A dividend reinvestment plan is available. A "poison pill" stock purchase rights plan was adopted in 1986.

Amt. of Div. $	Date Decl.	Ex-Div. Date	Stock of Record	Payment Date
0.200	Oct. 21	Nov. 17	Nov. 23	Dec. 10 '94
0.200	Feb. 03	Feb. 13	Feb. 17	Mar. 10 '95
2-for-1	Apr. 19	May. 15	Apr. 28	May. 12 '95
0.100	Apr. 19	May. 19	May. 25	Jun. 10 '95
0.100	Jul. 27	Aug. 16	Aug. 18	Sep. 10 '95

Data as orig. reptd.; bef. results of disc. opers. and/or spec. items. Per share data adj. for stk. divs. as of ex-div. date. E-Estimated. NA-Not Available. NM-Not Meaningful. NR-Not Ranked.

Office—Scott Center, 2650 N. Military Trail, Suite 300, Boca Raton, FL 33431. **Tel**—(407) 989-2300. **Chrmn & CEO**—A. J. Dunlap. **VP, Treas & CFO**—B. L. Anderson. **SVP & Secy**—J. P. Murtagh. **Investor Contact**—Michael D. Masseth. **Dirs**—W. A. Andres, G. E. Beaux, M. C. Davis, A. J. Dunlap, J. F. Fort, P. Harf, H. G. Kristol, R. K. Lochridge, G. L. Roubos. **Transfer Agent & Registrar**—First Chicago Trust Co., Jersey City, NJ. **Incorporated** in Pennsylvania in 1922. **Empl**-15,100. **S&P Analyst:** Michael W. Jaffe

Seagram Co.

NYSE Symbol **VO**
In S&P 500

07-SEP-95

Industry: Beverages

Summary: Seagram is a leading global producer of distilled spirits, wines, and fruit juices. In June 1995, it acquired an 80% interest in entertainment concern MCA, Inc.

S&P Opinion: Hold (★★★)		
Recent Price • 37¼	Yield • 1.6%	
52 Wk Range • 38¼-25½	12-Mo. P/E • 3.7	

Quantitative Evaluations

Outlook
(1 Lowest—5 Highest)
• **1**

Fair Value
• **28½**

Risk
• **Average**

Earn./Div. Rank
• **A-**

Technical Eval.
• **Bearish** since 8/95

Rel. Strength Rank
(1 Lowest—99 Highest)
• **55**

Insider Activity
• **Neutral**

Earnings vs. Previous Year
▲=Up ▼=Down ▶=No Change

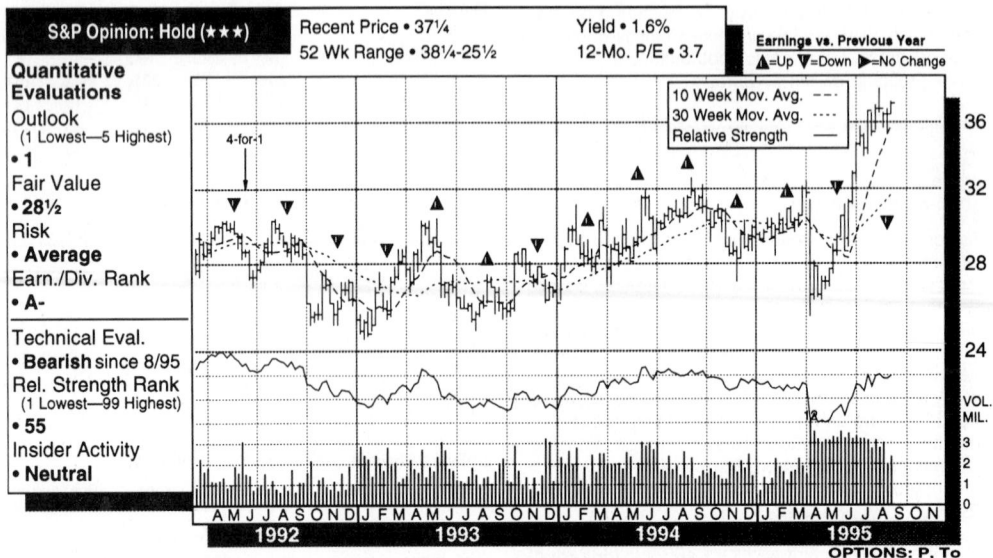

10 Week Mov. Avg. ----
30 Week Mov. Avg. ......
Relative Strength ——

4-for-1

OPTIONS: P, To

Overview - 07-SEP-95

Gross revenues for fiscal 1995-96 will be substantially above those of 1994-95, due primarily to the inclusion of MCA's operations as of June 1995. Revenues for VO's beverages operations are expected to advance at at high single-digit pace, helped by the acquisition of the Dole fruit juice business, and selling price increases. Earnings comparisons over the near term will be negatively impacted by VO's April 1995 sale of virtually its entire DuPont holdings, partially offset by rising contributions from the recently-acquired MCA and Dole fruit juice businesses. Substantially greater acquisition-related depreciation and amortization expenses will also restrain near-term profits. Earnings per share are seen reaching $1.20 in 1995-96, and $1.65 in 1996-97.

Valuation - 07-SEP-95

The shares have rebounded strongly in recent months, following their precipitous drop earlier in the year when the company sold 95% of its DuPont common stock holdings (for about $8.8 billion), which had provided VO a steady stream of dividends and unremitted earnings. With the funds, VO acquired an 80% stake in the entertainment company MCA, Inc. for $5.7 billion. Although the company's earnings visibility is less certain than before, given the volatile entertainment business, we believe that long-term growth prospects are enhanced. The company's balance sheet is strong, which should bolster future prospects. The stock is a worthwhile holding for most investors.

Key Stock Statistics

S&P EPS Est. 1996	1.20	Tang. Bk. Value/Share	20.37
P/E on S&P Est. 1996	31.0	Beta	0.92
S&P EPS Est. 1997	1.65	Shareholders	8,700
Dividend Rate/Share	0.60	Market cap. (B)	$ 13.5
Shs. outstg. (M)	372.2	Inst. holdings	29%
Avg. daily vol. (M)	0.571	Insider holdings	NA

Value of $10,000 invested 5 years ago: $ 18,216

Fiscal Year Ending Jan. 31

	1996	% Change	1995	% Change	1994	% Change
Revenues (Million $)						
1Q	1,282	6%	1,211	1%	1,195	-3%
2Q	1,883	30%	1,448	NM	1,441	2%
3Q	—	—	1,513	7%	1,417	-2%
4Q	—	—	2,227	12%	1,985	-1%
Yr.	—	—	6,399	6%	6,038	-1%
Income (Million $)						
1Q	59.00	-70%	197.0	22%	162.0	6%
2Q	89.00	-60%	224.0	32%	170.0	56%
3Q	—	—	199.0	NM	-100.0	NM
4Q	—	—	191.0	11%	172.0	NM
Yr.	—	—	811.0	114%	379.0	-20%
Earnings Per Share ($)						
1Q	0.16	-70%	0.53	23%	0.43	5%
2Q	0.24	-60%	0.60	30%	0.46	59%
3Q	E0.35	-34%	0.53	NM	-0.27	NM
4Q	E0.45	-13%	0.52	30%	0.40	NM
Yr.	E1.20	-45%	2.18	114%	1.02	-19%

Next earnings report expected: late November

Seagram Co.

Business Summary - 07-SEP-95

Seagram Co. is one of the world's largest producers and marketers of distilled spirits and wines, with affiliates and joint ventures in 41 countries.

Contributions by business segment in 1994-95 were:

	Revs.	Profits
Spirits & wines	76%	88%
Fruit juices, coolers & mixers	24%	12%

The Seagram Spirits and Wine group produces and markets, in the aggregate, more than 225 brands of distilled spirits and some 210 brands of wines, champagnes, ports and sherries, sold in more than 150 countries.

The Seagram Beverage group, which includes Tropicana Products, Inc., and The Seagram Beverage Co., is a leading producer of branded fruit juices, juice beverages, and alcoholic beverage products. In May 1995, VO acquired the Dole worldwide juice and juice beverages business from Dole Food Co., Inc., for about $240 million.

In April 1995, VO sold to E. I. du Pont Nemours and Co. (DD) 156,000,000 shares of DD common stock owned by VO in a transaction valued at approximately $8.8 billion. VO retained 8.2 million DD shares, or about 1.5% of DD's shares outstanding. In June 1995, VO acquired from Matsushita Electric Industrial Co., an 80% interest in MCA, Inc. for $5.7 billion in cash. MCA has business interests in the areas of motion pictures, television, music, publishing and theme parks.

VO holds a 14.9% interest in Time Warner Inc., the world's largest media and entertainment company.

Important Developments

Aug. '95—During fiscal 1995-96's second quarter, VO reported an 11% increase in EBITDA (earnings before interest, taxes, depreciation and amortization expenses) for its beverages operations, aided by strong growth for spirits and wine operations in developing countries (Asia Pacific and Latin America), and the inclusion of the Dole fruit juice business (acquired in May 1995). Partial period (6/5-6/30) EBITDA profits from MCA of $66 million were also recorded in the second quarter.

Jun. '95—VO acquired from Matsushita Electric Industrial Co. an 80% interest in Matsushita's MCA, Inc., subsidiary, for $5.704 billion in cash. Matsushita retained the remaining 20% interest in MCA. MCA (estimated 1994 revenues of $4.8 billion) has business interests in the areas of motion pictures (Universal Pictures), television, music, publishing and theme parks.

Capitalization

Long Term Debt: $2,638,000,000 (4/30/95).

Per Share Data ($)

(Year Ended Jan. 31)

	1995	1994	1993	1992	1991	1990
Tangible Bk. Val.	10.58	9.28	9.09	13.01	11.72	10.04
Cash Flow	2.67	1.46	1.70	2.32	2.37	2.15
Earnings	2.18	1.02	1.26	1.92	2.01	1.84
Dividends	0.58	0.56	0.54	0.50	0.46	0.35
Payout Ratio	27%	55%	43%	26%	23%	19%
Cal. Yrs.	1994	1993	1992	1991	1990	1989
Prices - High	32⅝	30⅜	30⅞	29½	23½	22⅞
- Low	26¼	24½	25⅛	20⅜	18⅛	15⅛
P/E Ratio - High	15	30	25	15	12	12
- Low	12	24	20	11	9	8

Income Statement Analysis (Million $)

	1995	%Chg	1994	%Chg	1993	%Chg	1992
Revs.	5,563	6%	5,227	NM	5,214	-1%	5,278
Oper. Inc.	909	-1%	920	NM	926	2%	910
Depr.	184	11%	166	1%	164	9%	150
Int. Exp.	408	16%	351	3%	341	-1%	345
Pretax Inc.	1,000	82%	550	-15%	650	-32%	952
Eff. Tax Rate	19%	—	31%	—	27%	—	24%
Net Inc.	811	114%	379	-20%	474	-35%	727

Balance Sheet & Other Fin. Data (Million $)

	1995	1994	1993	1992	1991	1990
Cash	157	131	116	266	131	138
Curr. Assets	4,176	3,794	3,836	4,327	3,970	3,289
Total Assets	12,956	11,718	10,104	11,876	11,477	10,213
Curr. Liab.	4,091	2,996	2,003	1,896	3,130	2,491
LT Debt	2,841	3,053	2,559	3,013	2,038	2,011
Common Eqty.	5,509	5,001	4,930	6,483	5,952	5,357
Total Cap.	8,377	8,295	7,689	9,684	8,166	7,538
Cap. Exp.	172	163	168	215	309	206
Cash Flow	995	545	638	877	891	828

Ratio Analysis

	1995	1994	1993	1992	1991	1990
Curr. Ratio	1.0	1.3	1.9	2.3	1.3	1.3
% LT Debt of Cap.	33.9	36.8	33.3	31.1	25.0	26.7
% Net Inc.of Revs.	14.6	7.3	9.1	13.8	15.0	15.8
% Ret. on Assets	6.6	3.5	4.3	6.2	7.0	7.2
% Ret. on Equity	15.4	7.6	8.4	11.6	13.5	13.9

Dividend Data —Dividends have been paid since 1937. Payments are in U.S. funds, subject to 15% Canadian tax to U.S. residents.

Amt. of Div. $	Date Decl.	Ex-Div. Date	Stock of Record	Payment Date
0.150	Aug. 31	Sep. 09	Sep. 15	Sep. 30 '94
0.150	Nov. 30	Dec. 09	Dec. 15	Dec. 30 '94
0.150	Feb. 15	Mar. 09	Mar. 15	Mar. 30 '95
0.150	May. 31	Jun. 13	Jun. 15	Jun. 30 '95
0.150	Aug. 30	Sep. 13	Sep. 15	Sep. 29 '95

Data as orig. reptd.; bef. results of disc. opers. and/or spec. items. Per share data adj. for stk. divs. as of ex-div. date. Revs. in Income Statement Analysis excl. excise taxes. E-Estimated. NA-Not Available. NM-Not Meaningful. NR-Not Ranked.

Office—1430 Peel St., Montreal, QC, Canada H3A 1S9. **Tel**—(514) 849-5271. **Chrmn**—E. M. Bronfman. **Co-Chrmn**—C. R. Bronfman. **Pres & CEO**—E. Bronfman Jr. **Sr EVP**—S. E. Banner. **Secy & Investor Contact**—M. C. L. Hallows. **Dirs**—S. E. Banner, M. W. Barrett, C. R. Bronfman, E. M. Bronfman, E. Bronfman Jr., S. Bronfman II, D. M. Culver, W. G. Davis, P, Desmarais, D. L. Johnston, E. L. Kolber, M. Josee Kravis, E. F. McDonnell, C. E. Medland, J. L. Weinberg, J. S. Weimberg. **Transfer Agents & Registrars**—Chemical Bank, NYC; R-M Trust Co., Montreal, Toronto, Calgary & Vancouver. **Incorporated** in Canada in 1928. **Empl**-16,100. **S&P Analyst:** Kenneth A. Shea

Sears, Roebuck

NYSE Symbol **S**
In S&P 500

13-SEP-95

Industry:
Retail Stores

Summary: Sears operates more than 1,800 stores, offering home appliances, electronics and apparel. Freestanding units sell home furniture and automobile parts and tires.

S&P Opinion: Buy (★★★★)		
Recent Price • 34½	Yield • 2.6%	
52 Wk Range • 61¼-29⅜	12-Mo. P/E • 6.9	

Earnings vs. Previous Year
▲=Up ▼=Down ▶=No Change

Quantitative Evaluations

Outlook
(1 Lowest—5 Highest)
• **NA**

Fair Value
• **NA**

Risk
• **Average**

Earn./Div. Rank
• **B-**

Technical Eval.
• **Bullish** since 7/95

Rel. Strength Rank
(1 Lowest—99 Highest)
• **5**

Insider Activity
• **NA**

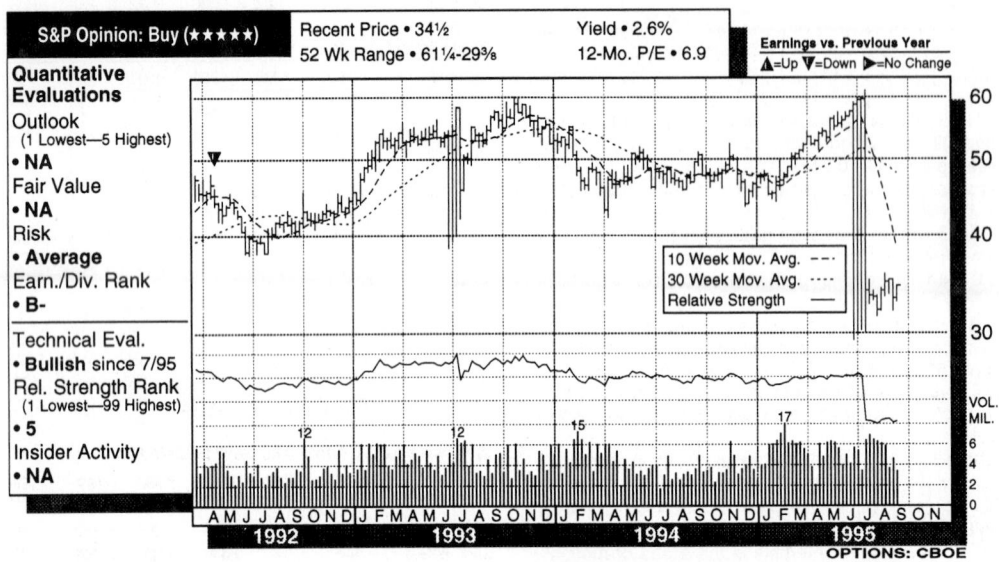

10 Week Mov. Avg. – – –
30 Week Mov. Avg. ·······
Relative Strength —

OPTIONS: CBOE

Overview - 13-SEP-95

Revenues at the merchandise group should increase about 6% to 7% in 1995, aided by the remodeling of units and 3% to 4% same-store sales gains. Gross margins should narrow, reflecting continued pressure on prices of low-margin electronics and appliances. The home group accounts for over half of company revenues. Higher-margin apparel sales should improve some 7% to 8%. Costs and expenses should continue to decline as a percentage of sales, reflecting successful cost cutting and improved logistics. The company spun off its 80%-owned Allstate subsidiary to shareholders in mid-1995 and sold its Homart real estate unit. Sears's strategy entails remodeling its mall stores, increasing its assortment of apparel, opening freestanding hardware and furniture stores and lowering its cost structure. Acquisitions of chains in the automotive parts and servicing business are a distinct possibility.

Valuation - 13-SEP-95

Sears continues to gain marketshare in an overall weak retail sales environment. Its operating strategies should keep earnings growing at about 15% annually over the next two years. The company spun off its stake in Allstate to shareholders at the end of June; absent Allstate, the company's earnings growth will be more consistent and share price less volatile. With the dividend yield of about 2.7%, the shares are a worthwhile purchase for total return.

Key Stock Statistics

S&P EPS Est. 1995	2.50	Tang. Bk. Value/Share	26.27
P/E on S&P Est. 1995	13.8	Beta	1.09
S&P EPS Est. 1996	2.85	Shareholders	262,600
Dividend Rate/Share	0.92	Market cap. (B)	$ 13.9
Shs. outstg. (M)	389.5	Inst. holdings	73%
Avg. daily vol. (M)	0.941	Insider holdings	NA

Value of $10,000 invested 5 years ago: NA

Fiscal Year Ending Dec. 31

	1995	% Change	1994	% Change	1993	% Change
Revenues (Million $)						
1Q	7,449	-40%	12,440	10%	11,298	-5%
2Q	8,204	-38%	13,151	8%	12,157	-4%
3Q	—	—	13,342	5%	12,719	NM
4Q	—	—	15,626	7%	14,664	-2%
Yr.	—	—	54,559	7%	50,838	-3%
Income (Million $)						
1Q	124.0	NM	-103.0	NM	317.0	144%
2Q	218.0	-58%	513.0	-53%	1,094	NM
3Q	—	—	347.0	-24%	453.9	NM
4Q	—	—	487.0	-11%	544.6	NM
Yr.	—	—	1,244	-48%	2,409	NM
Earnings Per Share ($)						
1Q	0.30	NM	-0.28	NM	0.82	141%
2Q	0.54	-58%	1.30	-55%	2.86	—
3Q	E0.57	-34%	0.87	-24%	1.15	NM
4Q	E1.10	-11%	1.23	-12%	1.39	NM
Yr.	E2.50	-20%	3.12	-50%	6.22	NM

Next earnings report expected: mid October

Sears, Roebuck

Business Summary - 13-SEP-95

This major retailer operates more than 1,940 stores. The company spun off its 80.3% stake in The Allstate Corp. to shareholders on June 30, 1995.

In early 1993, Sears announced a plan to streamline the merchandise group by discontinuing its money-losing catalog operations, closing unprofitable stores, and offering an early retirement program. The company is focusing on its three core retail operations: apparel; home, including home appliances and electronics, home improvement and furniture; and automotive, including Sears Auto Centers and Western Auto. The company implemented a $4 billion store remodeling program intended to create a dominant position in each of the major departments in the multi-line stores. At year-end 1994, merchandising operations included 800 department stores, with 412 large-size stores and 379 medium-sized stores. There were 1,140 free-standing stores, including 633 Western Auto stores, 72 Homelife furniture centers, 80 hardware stores and 285 dealer stores. Revenues per selling square foot totaled $340, up from $321 in 1993. Foreign operations are conducted through Sears Canada, a 61.1% owned subsidiary, and 75.2%-owned Sears Mexico.

The Homart Development Co. subsidiary owns, manages or is a partner in regional malls with assets of $2.2 billion. The sale of Homart is expected to be completed in the third quarter of 1995. Sears has two joint ventures with IBM: Prodigy Services Co., an online information service; and Advantis, a provider of networking technology.

Dean Witter, Discover & Co. was spun off to shareholders in June 1993; Coldwell Banker Residential Services and the Sears Mortgage Banking Group were sold in 1993.

Important Developments

Jul. '95—Revenues from the merchandise group increased 5.0%, year to year, in the second quarter of 1995; same-store sales rose 3.2%. Improved selling and administrative expenses as a percentage of sales were partially offset by lower gross margin percentage. Domestic gross margins declined to 26.7% of sales in the second quarter from 27.4% a year earlier, reflecting the competitive retail climate. Domestic credit operations benefited from continued growth in the receivables portfolio. International operations, which consist of merchandising and credit operations in Canada and Mexico, posted a loss of $2 million, compared with a loss of $1 million a year ago. Sears distributed its 80.3% ownership in The Allstate Corp. on June 30, 1995.

Capitalization

Long Term Debt: $9,008,000,000 (4/95), including cap. leases.
Preferred Stock: $325,000,000.

Per Share Data ($)

	1994	1993	1992	1991	1990	1989
Tangible Bk. Val.	26.18	28.80	25.94	38.70	35.77	38.15
Cash Flow	NM	NM	NM	NM	NM	NM
Earnings	3.16	6.22	-7.02	3.71	2.60	4.12
Dividends	1.60	1.60	2.00	2.00	2.00	2.00
Payout Ratio	51%	26%	NM	54%	77%	47%
Prices - High	55⅛	60⅛	48	43½	41⅞	48⅛
- Low	42⅛	38½	37	24⅜	22	36½
P/E Ratio - High	17	10	NM	12	16	12
- Low	13	6	NM	7	8	9

(Year Ended Dec. 31)

Income Statement Analysis (Million $)

	1994	%Chg	1993	%Chg	1992	%Chg	1991
Revs.	54,559	7%	50,838	-3%	52,345	-9%	57,242
Oper. Inc.	NA	—	NA	—	NA	—	NA
Depr.	NA	—	NA	—	NA	—	NA
Int. Exp.	1,340	-12%	1,531	-2%	1,559	-53%	3,309
Pretax Inc.	1,712	-39%	2,810	NM	-4,680	NM	1,471
Eff. Tax Rate	21%	—	14%	—	NM	—	13%
Net Inc.	1,244	-48%	2,409	NM	-2,566	NM	1,279

Balance Sheet & Other Fin. Data (Million $)

	1994	1993	1992	1991	1990	1989
Cash	1,421	1,864	2,627	5,984	5,217	3,281
Curr. Assets	NA	NA	NA	NA	NA	NA
Total Assets	91,896	90,808	83,533	106,434	96,253	86,972
Curr. Liab.	NA	NA	NA	NA	NA	NA
LT Debt	9,713	10,265	11,467	17,680	12,493	9,443
Common Eqty.	9,240	10,103	9,212	13,863	12,824	13,622
Total Cap.	22,448	24,263	22,240	31,868	25,316	23,498
Cap. Exp.	1,120	670	967	1,228	1,219	1,040
Cash Flow	NM	NM	NM	NM	NM	NM

Ratio Analysis

	1994	1993	1992	1991	1990	1989
Curr. Ratio	NA	NA	NA	NA	NA	NA
% LT Debt of Cap.	43.3	42.3	51.6	55.5	49.3	40.2
% Net Inc.of Revs.	2.3	4.7	NM	2.2	1.6	2.7
% Ret. on Assets	1.4	2.7	NM	1.3	1.0	1.8
% Ret. on Equity	12.5	24.5	NM	9.5	6.7	10.9

Dividend Data

Dividends have been paid since 1935. A dividend reinvestment plan is available.

Amt. of Div. $	Date Decl.	Ex-Div. Date	Stock of Record	Payment Date
0.400	Nov. 09	Nov. 23	Nov. 30	Jan. 03 '95
0.400	Feb. 07	Feb. 22	Feb. 28	Apr. 03 '95
0.400	May. 11	May. 24	May. 31	Jul. 03 '95
Stk.	Jun. 20	Jul. 13	Jun. 30	Jul. 12 '95
0.230	Aug. 09	Aug. 29	Aug. 31	Oct. 02 '95

Data as orig. reptd.; bef. results of disc. opers. and/or spec. items. Per share data adj. for stk. divs. as of ex-div. date. E-Estimated. NA-Not Available. NM-Not Meaningful. NR-Not Ranked. Bk. val. on front incl. Allstate.

Office—3333 Beverly Road B 5, Hoffman Estates,ILL 60174. **Tel**—(708) 286-2500. **Chrmn & CEO**—A. C. Martinez. **SVP Fin**—A. J. Lacy. **SVP & Secy**—D. Shute. **Investor Contact**—Harry E. Wren (708-286-1468). **Dirs**—H. Adams, Jr., W. L. Batts, J. W. Cozad, W. E. LaMothe, A. C. Martinez, M. A. Miles, S. C. Mobley, N. C. Reynolds, C. B. Rogers, Jr., D. H. Rumsfeld, D. A. Terrell. **Transfer Agent & Registrar**— First Chicago Trust Co. of New York, NYC. **Incorporated** in New York in 1906. **Empl**-358,780. **S&P Analyst:** Karen J. Sack, CFA

01-SEP-95

Industry:
Services

Summary: This company is the world's largest funeral and cemetary concern, with 2,550 funeral service locations, 247 cemeteries and 110 crematories in North America, Europe and Australia.

S&P Opinion: Hold (★★★)	

Recent Price • 35⅛	Yield • 1.3%
52 Wk Range • 35⅜-24⅛	12-Mo. P/E • 21.5

Quantitative Evaluations

Outlook
(1 Lowest—5 Highest)
• **4+**

Fair Value
• **35¼**

Risk
• **Low**

Earn./Div. Rank
• **A-**

Technical Eval.
• **Bullish** since 6/94

Rel. Strength Rank
(1 Lowest—99 Highest)
• **70**

Insider Activity
• **Neutral**

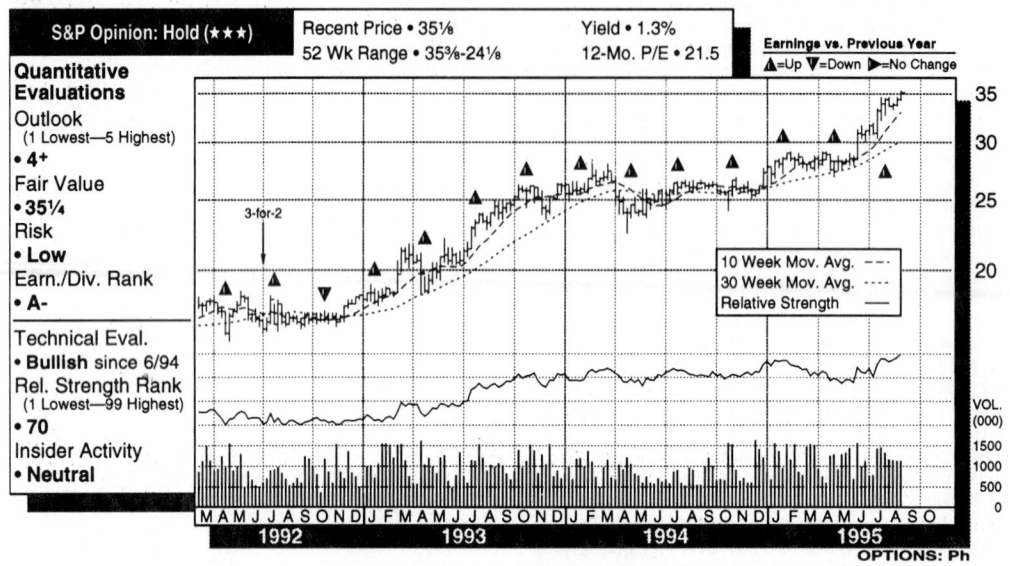

Earnings vs. Previous Year
▲=Up ▼=Down ▶=No Change

10 Week Mov. Avg. — — —
30 Week Mov. Avg. - - - -
Relative Strength ———

3-for-2

VOL. (000)
1500
1000
500
0

OPTIONS: Ph

Overview - 01-SEP-95

SRV has generated impressive revenue and profit growth in recent years, boosted by an aggressive acquisition program. Acquisitions in 1994 added about $260 million to annual revenues. Revenues in 1995 will also benefit from contributions from Service Corp. International plc (established in 1994), a subsidiary that is the largest single provider of funeral services in a market that includes England, Northern Ireland, Scotland and Wales. Profits in 1995 may suffer from lower margins associated with newly acquired funeral home operations, but economies of scale should allow for substantial growth in coming years.

Valuation - 01-SEP-95

The long-term earnings outlook is bright, aided by strong fundamentals underlying the death services industry. The company's rapid acquisition pace should generate substantial revenue momentum as smaller funeral service providers are consolidated into SRV's expanding network, but margins may contract while new operations are absorbed. In addition, the balance sheet shows nearly $1.6 billion of long term debt. We believe that the shares should not command a premium P/E multiple to that of the S&P 500, and that they will be only market performers over the next six to 12 months. However, the stock remains a sound long-term holding, reflecting the company's position as world leader in the death services industry.

Key Stock Statistics

S&P EPS Est. 1995	1.72	Tang. Bk. Value/Share	4.23
P/E on S&P Est. 1995	20.4	Beta	0.99
S&P EPS Est. 1996	2.05	Shareholders	8,700
Dividend Rate/Share	0.44	Market cap. (B)	$ 3.4
Shs. outstg. (M)	96.3	Inst. holdings	80%
Avg. daily vol. (M)	0.240	Insider holdings	NA

Value of $10,000 invested 5 years ago: $ 37,582

Fiscal Year Ending Dec. 31

	1995	% Change	1994	% Change	1993	% Change
Revenues (Million $)						
1Q	348.1	33%	261.3	16%	224.4	12%
2Q	353.6	35%	262.9	21%	217.1	16%
3Q	—	—	277.8	31%	211.4	15%
4Q	—	—	315.2	28%	246.3	23%
Yr.	—	—	1,117	24%	899.2	16%
Income (Million $)						
1Q	47.38	27%	37.45	28%	29.25	16%
2Q	40.64	35%	30.20	24%	24.33	22%
3Q	—	—	28.60	44%	19.81	16%
4Q	—	—	34.80	17%	29.70	22%
Yr.	—	—	131.1	27%	103.1	19%
Earnings Per Share ($)						
1Q	0.49	11%	0.44	19%	0.37	12%
2Q	0.42	20%	0.35	21%	0.29	12%
3Q	E0.38	15%	0.33	43%	0.23	5%
4Q	E0.45	15%	0.39	11%	0.35	9%
Yr.	E1.72	14%	1.51	22%	1.24	10%

Next earnings report expected: late October

Service Corp. Int'l

Business Summary - 01-SEP-95

Service Corporation International is the world's largest provider of death care services and products. At June 30, 1995, it operated 1,561 funeral homes (including 674 acquired in 1994), 245 cemeteries (28) and 110 crematories (24) in North America, Australia and Europe. It also provides capital financing to independent funeral home and cemetery operators. Business segment contributions in 1994 were:

	Revs.	Oper. Profits
Funeral	67%	65%
Cemetery	31%	32%
Financial services	2%	3%

Company funeral homes perform all professional services related to funerals, including the use of funeral facilities and motor vehicles. They sell caskets, burial vaults, cremation receptacles, flowers, and burial garments, and certain homes also operate crematories. The funeral homes allow customers to select prearranged funeral services. The death rate tends to be somewhat higher in the winter months, during which funeral homes generally experience a greater volume of business.

SRV's cemeteries sell cemetery interment rights (including mausoleum spaces and lawn crypts) and certain merchandise (including stone and bronze memorials and burial vaults), and perform interment and cemetery maintenance services. Certain cemeteries also operate crematories.

Wholly owned Provident Services Inc. provides capital financing for funeral home or cemetery acquisitions, and construction loans for funeral home or cemetery improvement and expansion.

Important Developments

Aug. '95—SRV acquired a 51% stake in Omnium de Gestion et de Financement SA (OGF), which in turn owns 65% of Pompes Funebres Generales SA (PFG), for a net cost of $425 million. The company subsequently made public offers to acquire the remaining stakes in OGF and PFG, which, on a combined basis, form the largest funeral service entity in Europe, with more than 950 locations.

Jul. '95—The company agreed to acquire the remaining interest in Service Corp. International Canada, which owns and operates 74 funeral homes and three cemetaries throughout Canada, for about $60 million. Earlier, in June, SRV agreed to acquire Gibraltar Mausoleum Corp., an owner an operator of 23 funeral homes and 54 cemetaries in 12 states, for 3,286,759 common shares, $99 million in cash, and the assumption of $54 million of debt.

Capitalization

Long Term Debt: $1,579,918,000 (6/95).
SCI Finance $3.125 Series A Term Conv.
Shares: 3,450,000 shs. ($50 stated value). Ea. conv. into 1.6617 SRV com. (NYSE: SRV PrT).

Per Share Data ($)

	(Year Ended Dec. 31)					
	1994	1993	1992	1991	1990	1989
Tangible Bk. Val.	4.07	5.19	3.41	3.85	4.61	6.35
Cash Flow	2.09	1.68	1.57	1.39	1.15	0.92
Earnings	1.51	1.24	1.13	1.03	0.85	0.65
Dividends	0.42	0.40	0.39	0.37	0.37	0.35
Payout Ratio	28%	32%	34%	39%	43%	54%
Prices - High	28	26⅜	18¾	18⅜	16⅛	14⅝
- Low	22½	17⅞	15⅝	13½	8¾	8½
P/E Ratio - High	19	21	17	18	19	23
- Low	15	14	14	13	10	13

Income Statement Analysis (Million $)

	1994	%Chg	1993	%Chg	1992	%Chg	1991
Revs.	1,117	24%	899	16%	772	20%	643
Oper. Inc.	341	33%	257	18%	217	28%	169
Depr.	51.0	37%	37.1	9%	34.1	32%	25.9
Int. Exp.	80.1	34%	59.6	10%	54.4	26%	43.1
Pretax Inc.	219	27%	173	24%	139	28%	109
Eff. Tax Rate	40%	—	41%	—	38%	—	33%
Net Inc.	131	27%	103	19%	86.5	18%	73.4

Balance Sheet & Other Fin. Data (Million $)

	1994	1993	1992	1991	1990	1989
Cash	218	21.0	31.0	38.0	18.0	37.0
Curr. Assets	592	312	259	237	180	179
Total Assets	5,162	3,683	2,611	2,123	1,654	1,601
Curr. Liab.	472	141	107	80.2	66.8	58.3
LT Debt	1,330	1,062	980	787	577	486
Common Eqty.	1,197	885	683	616	434	558
Total Cap.	2,937	2,094	1,762	1,472	1,073	1,094
Cap. Exp.	81.0	60.0	67.0	38.0	30.0	26.0
Cash Flow	182	140	121	99	81.2	66.5

Ratio Analysis

	1994	1993	1992	1991	1990	1989
Curr. Ratio	1.3	2.2	2.4	2.9	2.7	3.1
% LT Debt of Cap.	45.3	50.7	55.6	53.5	53.8	44.4
% Net Inc.of Revs.	11.7	11.5	11.2	11.4	11.3	10.3
% Ret. on Assets	2.8	3.1	3.6	3.7	4.0	3.1
% Ret. on Equity	12.0	12.6	13.2	13.4	12.5	8.7

Dividend Data

—Dividends were initiated in 1973. A poison pill stock purchase rights plan was adopted in 1988.

Amt. of Div. $	Date Decl.	Ex-Div. Date	Stock of Record	Payment Date
0.105	Aug. 11	Oct. 07	Oct. 14	Oct. 28 '94
0.105	Nov. 10	Jan. 10	Jan. 17	Jan. 31 '95
0.110	Feb. 16	Apr. 07	Apr. 14	Apr. 28 '95
0.110	May. 11	Jul. 12	Jul. 14	Jul. 28 '95
0.110	Aug. 10	Oct. 12	Oct. 16	Oct. 31 '95

Data as orig. reptd.; bef. results of disc. opers. and/or spec. items. Per share data adj. for stk. divs. as of ex-div. date. E-Estimated. NA-Not Available. NM-Not Meaningful. NR-Not Ranked.

Office—1929 Allen Pkwy., Houston, TX 77019. **Tel**—(713) 522-5141. **Chrmn & CEO**—R. L. Waltrip. **Pres & COO**—L. W. Heiligbrodt. **SVP, CFO & Investor Contact**—George R. Champagne. **Dirs**—A. L. Coelho, D. M. Conway, J. Finkelstein, A. J. Foyt, Jr., J. J. Gavin, Jr., J. H. Greer, L. W. Heiligbrodt, B. D. Hunter, J. W. Mecom, Jr., C. H. Morris, Jr., S. W. Rizzo, E. H. Thornton, Jr., R. L. Waltrip, W. B. Waltrip, E. E. Williams. **Transfer Agent & Registrar**—Society National Bank, Houston. **Incorporated** in Texas in 1962. **Empl**-12,619. **S&P Analyst:** Robert M. Gold

Shared Medical Systems

NASDAQ Symbol **SMED**

In S&P 500

15-AUG-95

Industry:
Data Processing

Summary: Shared Medical is a leading provider of computer-based information systems and related services to hospitals, clinics and physician groups.

S&P Opinion: Hold (★★★)	Recent Price • 38⅞	Yield • 2.2%
	52 Wk Range • 42¾-23⅛	12-Mo. P/E • 24.5

Quantitative Evaluations

Outlook
(1 Lowest—5 Highest)
• **1+**

Fair Value
• **30⅛**

Risk
• **Average**

Earn./Div. Rank
• **B+**

Technical Eval.
• **Neutral** since 6/95

Rel. Strength Rank
(1 Lowest—99 Highest)
• **30**

Insider Activity
• **Unfavorable**

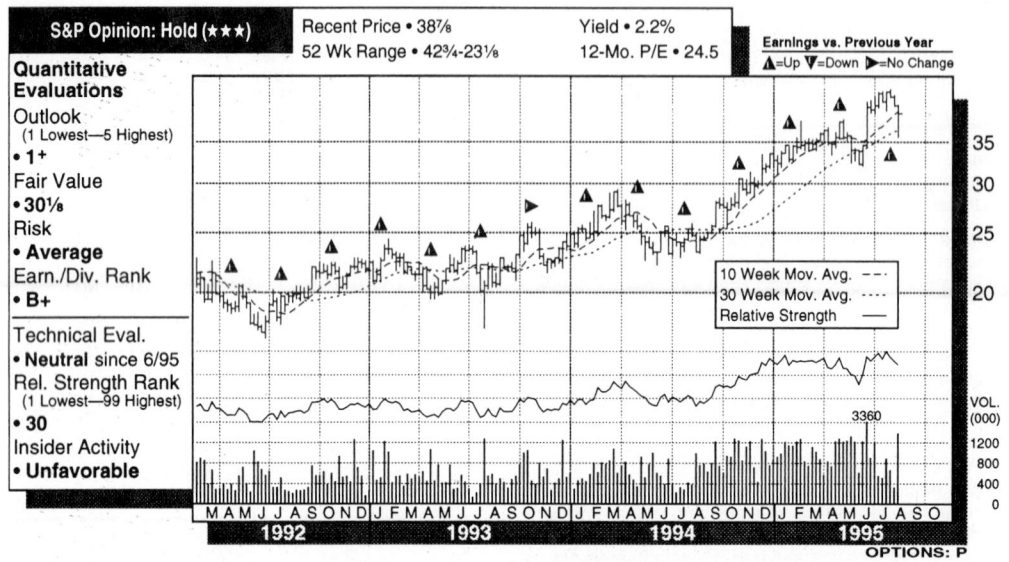

Earnings vs. Previous Year
▲=Up ▼=Down ▶=No Change

10 Week Mov. Avg. - - -
30 Week Mov. Avg. ·····
Relative Strength —

OPTIONS: P

Overview - 15-AUG-95

Revenues are expected to increase through 1996, reflecting continued demand for SMED's products in the hospital systems market (which accounts for about 70% of revenues), growth in international markets, and acquisition related benefits. Margins are expected to be maintained, as volume efficiencies and cost controls offset pricing pressures and a less favorable revenue mix. Changes in the delivery of health care services, including the advent of managed care and the vertical integration of services at multiple treatment locations, will demand more complex and specific health care information systems. Continued major investment in R&D, however, will restrict earnings gains over the next several years.

Valuation - 15-AUG-95

Despite our bullish outlook for earnings growth through 1996, the shares appear to be fairly valued at current levels, following a sharp rise since mid-1994. The stock rightly commands a premium valuation to the market P/E, reflecting accelerating revenue growth, the high visibility of earnings and a conservative balance sheet. However, although we believe that the shares will continue to maintain their premium, underlying earnings growth remains under 15%. As a result, we expect the shares to perform only in line with the market in coming months.

Key Stock Statistics

S&P EPS Est. 1995	1.70	Tang. Bk. Value/Share	8.68
P/E on S&P Est. 1995	22.9	Beta	0.75
S&P EPS Est. 1996	1.90	Shareholders	5,600
Dividend Rate/Share	0.84	Market cap. (B)	$0.889
Shs. outstg. (M)	23.1	Inst. holdings	61%
Avg. daily vol. (M)	0.222	Insider holdings	NA

Value of $10,000 invested 5 years ago: $ 37,120

Fiscal Year Ending Dec. 31

	1995	% Change	1994	% Change	1993	% Change
Revenues ()						
1Q	145.3	16%	125.2	7%	117.2	4%
2Q	155.3	17%	132.6	7%	124.2	6%
3Q	—	—	138.8	12%	123.7	7%
4Q	—	—	154.2	13%	136.2	9%
Yr.	—	—	550.8	10%	501.3	7%
Income ()						
1Q	9.59	12%	8.54	13%	7.54	11%
2Q	9.68	13%	8.56	9%	7.85	10%
3Q	—	—	8.93	24%	7.19	NM
4Q	—	—	9.06	7%	8.44	16%
Yr.	—	—	35.10	13%	31.01	9%
Earnings Per Share ()						
1Q	0.41	11%	0.37	12%	0.33	10%
2Q	0.41	11%	0.37	9%	0.34	10%
3Q	E0.43	13%	0.38	23%	0.31	NM
4Q	E0.44	13%	0.39	5%	0.37	16%
Yr.	E1.70	13%	1.51	12%	1.35	9%

Next earnings report expected: late October

Shared Medical Systems

Business Summary - 15-AUG-95

Shared Medical Systems Corporation provides computer-based information processing systems and associated services to the health care industry.

The company's products are made available to hospitals of all types (urban, teaching, suburban, rural and specialty), proprietary hospital companies, not-for-profit multihospital groups and integrated health networks. Products are also offered to healthcare organizations such as clinics, physician groups, medical schools, public health departments, and home health organizations. These products include a full range of financial, patient management, clinical, ambulatory, and decision support software systems that use diverse computing and networking technologies ranging from remote processing to distributed processing systems to onsite turnkey systems. SMED also provides a variety of professional services related to the information systems business, such as system installation and support and client education.

SMED's markets are generally acute-care hospitals, usually with more than 100 beds, multi-entity health care corporations, integrated health networks, physician groups, and other healthcare providers. Historically, the company's primary market has been in the U.S., with hospital contracts in 47 states, the District of Columbia and Puerto Rico. SMED also has contracts in 12 European countries, including the U.K., Ireland, Germany, Spain, France, Italy and Portugal.

Although the number of acute-care hospital beds has declined slightly in recent years, demand for integrated information systems in the health care industry has grown with the emergence of multi-entity healthcare organizations and integrated health networks, increases in information required by the government and private insurers, additional medical services provided by health care organizations, and needs related to HMOs and PPOs. In addition, cost containment pressures on healthcare providers, insurers and employers require sophisticated information systems and services.

Important Developments

Jun. '95—The company acquired the business and assets of Professional Datacare (PDC) from the National Health Systems' North West Regional Health Authority in the U.K., for about $8,500,000. PDC provides various financial processing services in the U.K.
Sep. '30—SMED acquired GTE Health Systems Inc. (GTEHS) and its MedSeries4 product line from GTE Information Services, for about $17 million. GTEHS provides hospital information systems to the health care industry.

Capitalization

Long Term Obligs.: $4,300,000 (6/95).

Per Share Data ()

(Year Ended Dec. 31)

	1994	1993	1992	1991	1990	1989
Tangible Bk. Val.	8.68	8.71	8.27	7.89	7.69	7.45
Cash Flow	2.62	2.45	2.32	2.39	2.22	1.84
Earnings	1.51	1.35	1.24	1.11	1.01	0.79
Dividends	0.84	0.84	0.84	0.84	0.84	0.84
Payout Ratio	56%	62%	67%	76%	83%	106%
Prices - High	34½	26	24⅜	23⅜	18⅜	19⅜
- Low	22⅛	17½	16⅞	13⅞	12	12
P/E Ratio - High	23	19	20	21	18	25
- Low	15	13	14	13	12	15

Income Statement Analysis ()

	1994	%Chg	1993	%Chg	1992	%Chg	1991
Revs.	550	10%	501	7%	468	7%	438
Oper. Inc.	84.0	8%	78.0	13%	69.0	NM	69.0
Depr.	25.8	2%	25.4	3%	24.7	-15%	29.0
Int. Exp.	1.4	7%	1.4	22%	1.1	9%	1.0
Pretax Inc.	57.5	11%	51.7	15%	45.0	14%	39.5
Eff. Tax Rate	39%	—	40%	—	37%	—	36%
Net Inc.	35.1	13%	31.0	9%	28.4	12%	25.3

Balance Sheet & Other Fin. Data ()

	1994	1993	1992	1991	1990	1989
Cash	21.2	35.8	30.9	27.3	10.7	18.3
Curr. Assets	177	166	156	151	140	133
Total Assets	380	341	306	293	286	278
Curr. Liab.	117	92.8	87.9	82.0	82.2	75.1
LT Debt	5.0	6.4	2.3	4.2	4.4	4.8
Common Eqty.	219	198	187	177	172	168
Total Cap.	246	227	205	198	193	188
Cap. Exp.	20.3	24.9	18.4	21.6	22.6	22.5
Cash Flow	60.9	56.4	53.1	54.3	45.0	42.1

Ratio Analysis

	1994	1993	1992	1991	1990	1989
Curr. Ratio	1.5	1.8	1.8	1.8	1.7	1.8
% LT Debt of Cap.	2.0	2.8	1.1	2.1	2.3	2.6
% Net Inc.of Revs.	6.4	6.2	6.1	5.8	5.6	4.7
% Ret. on Assets	9.7	9.5	9.5	8.7	8.1	6.5
% Ret. on Equity	16.8	16.1	15.6	14.5	13.4	10.9

Dividend Data

—Cash has been paid each year since 1977. A poison pill stock purchase rights plan was adopted in 1991.

Amt. of Div. $	Date Decl.	Ex-Div. Date	Stock of Record	Payment Date
0.210	Jun. 14	Jun. 24	Jun. 30	Jul. 15 '94
0.210	Sep. 07	Sep. 26	Sep. 30	Oct. 14 '94
0.210	Dec. 06	Dec. 23	Dec. 31	Jan. 13 '95
0.210	Mar. 06	Mar. 27	Mar. 31	Apr. 14 '95
0.210	Jun. 07	Jun. 28	Jun. 30	Jul. 14 '95

Data as orig. reptd.; bef. results of disc. opers. and/or spec. items. Per share data adj. for stk. divs. as of ex-div. date. E-Estimated. NA-Not Available. NM-Not Meaningful. NR-Not Ranked.

Office—51 Valley Stream Parkway, Malvern, PA 19355. Tel—(610) 219-6300. Chrmn—R. J. Macaleer. Pres & CEO—M. S. Cadwell. VP-Fin, Treas & Investor Contact—Terrence W. Kyle. Secy—J. C. Kelly. Dirs—M. S. Cadwell, R. K. Denworth, Jr., F. W. DeTurk, R. J. Macaleer, J. S. Rubin, J. S. Weston. Transfer Agent—Chemical Bank, NYC. Incorporated in Delaware in 1969. Empl-4,370. S&P Analyst: Peter C. Wood, CFA

Shawmut National

NYSE Symbol **SNC**
In S&P 500

30-AUG-95

Industry: Banking

Summary: This bank holding company, the third largest in New England, has reached a definitive agreement to be acquired by Fleet Financial Group in a stock transaction.

S&P Opinion: Hold (★★★)	Recent Price • 31¾	Yield • 2.8%
	52 Wk Range • 32½-16⅜	12-Mo. P/E • 12.6

Quantitative Evaluations

Outlook
(1 Lowest—5 Highest)
• **1⁻**

Fair Value
• **26½**

Risk
• **Average**

Earn./Div. Rank
• **B-**

Technical Eval.
• **Bearish** since 7/95

Rel. Strength Rank
(1 Lowest—99 Highest)
• **69**

Insider Activity
• **Unfavorable**

Earnings vs. Previous Year
▲=Up ▼=Down ▶=No Change

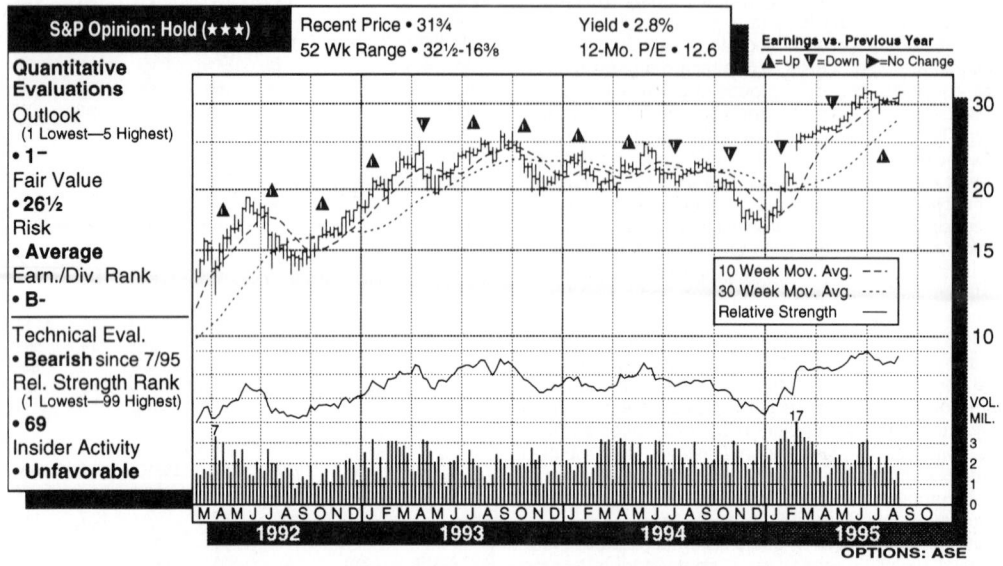

10 Week Mov. Avg. – – –
30 Week Mov. Avg. · · · ·
Relative Strength ——

OPTIONS: ASE

Overview - 29-AUG-95

Net interest income is expected to be flat in 1995 as modest loan growth is offset by continued pressure on the net interest margin in the current interest rate environment. A focus on higher yielding loan sectors, particularly asset-based and consumer instalment lending, has resulted in a better asset mix and will improve the position of the company's loan portfolio going forward. Credit quality continues to strengthen, and the provision for credit losses was eliminated in 1994's second quarter. With reserves at 242% of nonperforming loans, little or no provision for losses is expected in 1995. Noninterest income should increase on growing sales of financial products following an expansion of the investment services group. Earnings comparisons in 1995 will benefit from the absence of substantial merger and restructuring charges.

Valuation - 29-AUG-95

After rising strongly following news of the proposed merger with Fleet Financial, the shares, given that they are now linked to the prospects of Fleet, are not expected to outperform the overall market. Currently trading at about a 7% discount to the acquisition price, the shares are a worthwhile hold for modest capital appreciation until the merger is completed, which is expected in the fourth quarter of 1995. It should be noted that the transaction, which has been approved by the shareholders of both Shawmut and Fleet, still faces regulatory approval.

Key Stock Statistics

S&P EPS Est. 1995	2.60	Tang. Bk. Value/Share	17.04
P/E on S&P Est. 1995	12.2	Beta	2.01
Dividend Rate/Share	0.88	Shareholders	30,300
Shs. outstg. (M)	128.7	Market cap. (B)	$ 4.1
Avg. daily vol. (M)	0.354	Inst. holdings	50%
		Insider holdings	NA

Value of $10,000 invested 5 years ago: $ 20,893

Fiscal Year Ending Dec. 31

	1995	% Change	1994	% Change	1993	% Change
Revenues (Million $)						
1Q	676.7	24%	546.0	15%	474.8	-16%
2Q	725.8	28%	568.5	17%	484.9	-2%
3Q	—	—	584.5	21%	483.8	NM
4Q	—	—	626.3	28%	487.9	NM
Yr.	—	—	2,316	20%	1,931	-5%
Income (Million $)						
1Q	62.60	-19%	77.30	NM	-16.50	NM
2Q	82.60	NM	-18.70	NM	56.26	NM
3Q	—	—	85.30	20%	71.10	NM
4Q	—	—	93.50	-30%	133.6	NM
Yr.	—	—	237.4	-3%	244.6	NM
Earnings Per Share ($)						
1Q	0.47	-24%	0.62	NM	-0.22	NM
2Q	0.61	NM	-0.19	NM	0.56	NM
3Q	E0.70	3%	0.68	-6%	0.72	NM
4Q	E0.82	11%	0.74	-46%	1.36	NM
Yr.	E2.60	39%	1.87	-23%	2.44	NM

Next earnings report expected: mid October

Business Summary - 30-AUG-95

Shawmut National Corp., formed through the 1988 merger of Hartford National Corp. and Shawmut Corp., operates through a network of more than 300 branches in Massachusetts, Connecticut, New Hampshire and Rhode Island. It provides a range of corporate, commercial, correspondent and individual banking services to consumers, small businesses and middle-market and large corporations, including a specialization in credit and cash management services for insurance companies. Investment services are also important, and Shawmut has mortgage banking operations.

During 1994, average earning assets were $28.6 billion (up from $26.9 billion the year before), consisting of loans 62%, investment securities 36%, and other 2%. Sources of funds were: noninterest-bearing deposits 15%, savings and other interest-bearing deposits 28%, time deposits 18%, short-term borrowings 27%, long-term debt 4%, equity 7%, and other 1%.

At year-end 1994, the loan portfolio consisted of commercial and industrial loans 38%, commercial real estate 16%, residential real estate 30%, and other consumer loans 16%.

Nonperforming assets at 1994 year end were $242 million (1.31% of loans and related assets), down from $437 million (2.48%) a year earlier. The reserve for loan losses of $542 million was 2.93% of loans, versus $669 million (3.80%) at the end of 1993. Net chargeoffs during 1994 were 0.76% of average loans, against 1.72% in 1993.

Important Developments

Aug. '95—The company and Fleet Financial Group (NYSE: FLT) announced details of their divestiture proposal, which calls for $3.2 billion of deposits in Massachusetts, Connecticut, Rhode Island and New Hampshire to be divested in connection with their planned merger. Earlier, in June, shareholders of Shawmut approved the proposed merger with Fleet in a transaction whereby each SNC common share would be exchanged for 0.8922 of a FLT common share. The merger would create the ninth largest U.S. bank holding company, with assets of $81 billion and leading deposit share in Connecticut, Maine, Massachusetts, New Hampshire and Rhode Island. The transaction remains subject to regulatory approval and is expected to be completed in the fourth quarter of 1995.

Capitalization

Long Term Debt: $2,339,441,000 (6/95).
Preferred Stock: $303,185,000.

Per Share Data ($)

	1994	1993	1992	1991	1990	1989
Tangible Bk. Val.	15.44	15.92	14.09	13.62	15.70	18.63
Earnings	1.87	2.44	0.60	-2.35	-1.84	-1.77
Dividends	0.82	0.50	Nil	Nil	0.75	1.40
Payout Ratio	44%	21%	Nil	Nil	NM	NM
Prices - High	25	26⅜	19½	10⅞	21	29¾
- Low	16⅜	17⅞	8⅞	2⅞	4	17½
P/E Ratio - High	13	11	33	NM	NM	NM
- Low	9	7	15	NM	NM	NM

Income Statement Analysis (Million $)

	1994	%Chg	1993	%Chg	1992	%Chg	1991
Net Int. Inc.	1,068	15%	925	12%	825	12%	737
Tax Equiv. Adj.	11.4	-13%	13.0	-13%	15.0	-35%	23.0
Non Int. Inc.	378	4%	364	-7%	392	-13%	451
Loan Loss Prov.	3.0	-90%	29.0	-85%	190	-59%	466
% Exp/Op Revs.	74%	—	79%	—	84%	—	80%
Pretax Inc.	372	57%	237	NM	78.0	NM	-168
Eff. Tax Rate	36%	—	NM	—	27%	—	NM
Net Inc.	237	-3%	245	NM	57.0	NM	-170
% Net Int. Marg.	3.77%	—	4.03%	—	4.16%	—	3.77%

Balance Sheet & Other Fin. Data (Million $)

	1994	1993	1992	1991	1990	1989
Earning Assets:						
Money Mkt.	776	28.0	750	199	594	118
Inv. Securities	9,992	8,991	6,078	5,094	4,347	4,089
Com'l Loans	7,006	6,321	5,822	4,891	5,335	6,921
Other Loans	11,553	9,479	9,504	9,683	10,227	12,725
Total Assets	32,399	27,245	25,288	22,816	23,703	27,855
Demand Deposits	5,161	4,587	4,572	4,289	4,596	4,680
Time Deposits	15,585	10,710	11,838	12,224	14,959	14,085
LT Debt	2,022	759	810	660	676	699
Common Eqty.	2,019	1,625	1,304	1,005	1,157	1,363

Ratio Analysis

	1994	1993	1992	1991	1990	1989
% Ret. on Assets	0.8	1.0	0.3	NM	NM	NM
% Ret. on Equity	11.2	16.2	4.5	NM	NM	NM
% Loan Loss Resv.	2.9	4.0	5.6	6.9	6.1	3.8
% Loans/Deposits	89.5	103.3	93.4	88.3	79.6	104.7
% Equity to Assets	6.3	5.6	5.1	4.7	5.3	6.3

Dividend Data —The common dividend was reinstated in 1993, after having been omitted in January 1991.

Amt. of Div. $	Date Decl.	Ex-Div. Date	Stock of Record	Payment Date
0.200	Sep. 22	Sep. 29	Oct. 05	Oct. 15 '94
0.220	Dec. 16	Dec. 29	Jan. 05	Jan. 15 '95
0.220	Mar. 23	Mar. 30	Apr. 05	Apr. 15 '95
0.220	Jun. 21	Jun. 30	Jul. 05	Jul. 15 '95

Data as orig. reptd.; bef. results of disc opers. and/or spec. items. Per share data adj. for stk. divs. as of ex-div. date.
E-Estimated. NA-Not Available. NM-Not Meaningful. NR-Not Ranked.

Offices—777 Main St., Hartford, CT 06115; One Federal St., Boston, MA 02211. **Tels**—(203) 728-2000; (617) 292-2000. **Chrmn & CEO**—J. B. Alvord. **Pres & COO**—G. S. Overstrom. **CFO**—S. Lester. **EVP & Secy**—R. A. Guenter. **Investor Contact**—Thomas R. Rice (203-986-4872). **Dirs**—J. B. Alvord, S. B. Brown, J. T. Collins, F. Colloredo-Mansfeld, B. M. Fox, R. J. Matura, G. S. Overstrom, L. D. Rice, M. Segall, S. O. Thier, P. R. Tregurtha, W. Wilde. **Transfer Agent**—Chemical Bank, NYC. **Incorporated** in Massachusetts in 1988. **Empl**-9,565. **S&P Analyst:** Stephen R. Biggar

Sherwin-Williams

NYSE Symbol **SHW**
In S&P 500

04-AUG-95

Industry:
Coatings, paint,
varnishes

Summary: Sherwin-Williams is the largest U.S. producer of paints, and is also a major seller of wallcoverings and related products.

S&P Opinion: Hold (★★★)	Recent Price • 36⅞	Yield • 1.7%	
	52 Wk Range • 38-29¾	12-Mo. P/E • 16.3	

Quantitative Evaluations

Outlook
(1 Lowest—5 Highest)
• **3**

Fair Value
• **35⅜**

Risk
• **Low**

Earn./Div. Rank
• **A**

Technical Eval.
• **Bearish** since 5/95

Rel. Strength Rank
(1 Lowest—99 Highest)
• **46**

Insider Activity
• **Unfavorable**

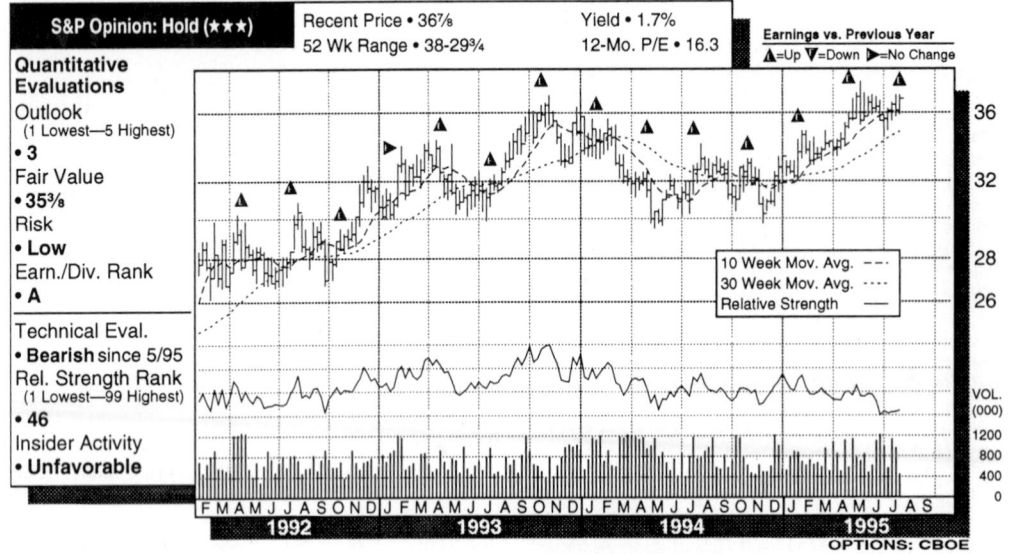

Earnings vs. Previous Year
▲=Up ▼=Down ▶=No Change

10 Week Mov. Avg. — · —
30 Week Mov. Avg. · · · · ·
Relative Strength ——

OPTIONS: CBOE

Overview - 04-AUG-95

Sales are likely to remain in an uptrend for the remainder of 1995, with mid- to upper-single-digit percentage gains expected in the Paint Stores segment, and low-single-digit increases in the Coatings segment. Increased selling prices, volume gains and manufacturing efficiencies will continue to minimize the effect of higher raw material costs. Sales and profits should benefit as SHW solidifies its position as the leading U.S. paint manufacturing entity. The company's sensitivity to the home construction and resale markets may restrict earnings growth in the event of an economic slowdown. However, EPS comparisons should benefit from a six million share repurchase program.

Valuation - 04-AUG-95

The shares of this leading paint and coatings manufacturer have trended higher over the past several quarters, despite the threat of a slowdown in home sales and construction, which could restrict earnings growth. We expect results in 1995 to benefit from improved margins, lower interest expense and new business in the coatings segment. A share repurchase program could further buoy the share price. However, due to the uncertainty of economic conditions, we view SHW as a market performer.

Key Stock Statistics

S&P EPS Est. 1995	2.35	Tang. Bk. Value/Share	11.17
P/E on S&P Est. 1995	15.7	Beta	1.25
S&P EPS Est. 1996	2.65	Shareholders	12,300
Dividend Rate/Share	0.64	Market cap. (B)	$ 3.1
Shs. outstg. (M)	85.2	Inst. holdings	63%
Avg. daily vol. (M)	0.162	Insider holdings	NA

Value of $10,000 invested 5 years ago: $ 23,555

Fiscal Year Ending Dec. 31

	1995	% Change	1994	% Change	1993	% Change
Revenues (Million $)						
1Q	716.8	12%	639.2	3%	618.3	4%
2Q	904.7	3%	880.5	7%	824.2	7%
3Q	—	—	876.7	5%	838.8	9%
4Q	—	—	703.6	5%	668.0	10%
Yr.	—	—	3,100	5%	2,949	7%
Income (Million $)						
1Q	18.73	21%	15.51	12%	13.81	19%
2Q	73.21	6%	69.16	14%	60.61	13%
3Q	—	—	71.23	11%	64.37	15%
4Q	—	—	30.68	16%	26.43	13%
Yr.	—	—	186.6	13%	165.2	14%
Earnings Per Share ($)						
1Q	0.22	29%	0.17	13%	0.15	15%
2Q	0.85	6%	0.80	18%	0.68	13%
3Q	E0.89	—	0.83	15%	0.72	14%
4Q	E0.39	—	0.36	20%	0.30	15%
Yr.	E2.35	—	2.15	16%	1.85	13%

Next earnings report expected: mid October

Business Summary - 04-AUG-95

Sherwin-Williams is the largest producer and distributor of paints and varnishes in the U.S. and also manufactures several allied products. Business segment contributions in 1994 were:

	Sales	Profits
Paint Stores	64.1%	40.3%
Coatings	35.5%	57.4%
Other	0.5%	2.3%

At December 31, 1994, the Paint Stores segment consisted of 2,046 stores operating in 48 states, P.R. and Canada. Paint and related products, including wallcoverings, floorcoverings, window treatments, industrial maintenance products and finishes and assorted tools, are marketed by store personnel and direct sales representatives to the do-it-yourself, professional painting, industrial maintenance and home building markets and to manufacturers of products requiring a factory finish. In 1993, SHW began a long-term project to re-merchandise its paint stores to provide a more appealing customer shopping experience and increase efficiency of store personnel.

The Coatings segment manufactures, distributes and sells paints, varnishes, lacquers and allied products under the Sherwin-Williams, Dutch Boy, Kem-Tone, Martin Senour, Cuprinol, Acme, Krylon and other brand names. The Consumer Brands division distributes these products through unaffiliated home centers, mass merchandisers, independent dealers and distributors. The Automotive division sells vehicle finish and refinish products through some 139 branches supported by a direct sales staff and through jobbers and wholesale distributors. The Specialty division sells paint applicators, aerosol products and coatings through SHW's paint stores, as well as unaffiliated merchandisers and distribution channels. Transportation Services are provided for the company and other customers. International operations are conducted through subsidiaries, joint ventures and licensees.

Other businesses consist of real estate operations related to the Paint Stores and Coatings units.

Important Developments

Apr. '95—The company said it expects to add approximately 50 new stores in 1995, bringing the total number in operation at year end to about 2,100. SHW also said it would complete its store remerchandising program, which involved redecorating and replacing some equipment. The remerchandising program had slowed new openings for several years.

Feb. '95—SHW acquired all the outstanding shares of FLR Paints Inc., a manufacturer of a wide variety of specialty stains, sealers and coatings, with significant distribution in Florida and the southeastern United States.

Capitalization

Long Term Debt: $20,752,000 (3/95).

Per Share Data ($)
(Year Ended Dec. 31)

	1994	1993	1992	1991	1990	1989
Tangible Bk. Val.	11.17	10.37	8.80	8.27	7.34	7.59
Cash Flow	3.00	2.62	2.37	2.13	2.00	1.77
Earnings	2.15	1.85	1.63	1.45	1.41	1.26
Dividends	0.56	0.50	0.44	0.42	0.38	0.35
Payout Ratio	25%	27%	27%	29%	27%	28%
Prices - High	35¾	37½	32⅞	27¾	21	17⅞
- Low	29½	29⅞	25⅜	17⅝	15	12½
P/E Ratio - High	17	20	20	19	15	14
- Low	14	16	16	12	11	10

Income Statement Analysis (Million $)

	1994	%Chg	1993	%Chg	1992	%Chg	1991
Revs.	3,100	5%	2,949	7%	2,748	8%	2,541
Oper. Inc.	383	13%	340	10%	310	13%	275
Depr.	73.7	7%	68.8	4%	66.3	11%	59.9
Int. Exp.	3.2	-51%	6.5	-24%	8.6	-30%	12.3
Pretax Inc.	299	13%	264	17%	226	14%	199
Eff. Tax Rate	38%	—	38%	—	36%	—	36%
Net Inc.	187	13%	165	14%	145	13%	128

Balance Sheet & Other Fin. Data (Million $)

	1994	1993	1992	1991	1990	1989
Cash	251	270	168	101	99	202
Curr. Assets	1,189	1,151	988	887	824	846
Total Assets	1,962	1,915	1,730	1,612	1,504	1,375
Curr. Liab.	597	568	506	488	432	433
LT Debt	20.0	38.0	60.0	72.0	138	105
Common Eqty.	1,053	1,033	906	868	764	668
Total Cap.	1,074	1,089	982	1,040	1,000	866
Cap. Exp.	78.7	63.0	68.8	51.0	64.4	66.9
Cash Flow	260	234	NA	188	174	153

Ratio Analysis

	1994	1993	1992	1991	1990	1989
Curr. Ratio	2.0	2.0	2.0	1.8	1.9	2.0
% LT Debt of Cap.	1.9	3.5	6.1	6.9	13.8	12.1
% Net Inc.of Revs.	6.0	5.6	NA	5.0	5.4	5.1
% Ret. on Assets	9.8	9.1	8.6	8.2	8.5	8.3
% Ret. on Equity	18.3	17.0	16.2	15.6	17.1	17.2

Dividend Data
(Cash has been paid each year since 1979. A dividend reinvestment plan is available. A "poison pill" stock purchase rights plan was adopted in 1989.)

Amt. of Div. $	Date Decl.	Ex-Div. Date	Stock of Record	Payment Date
0.140	Jul. 20	Aug. 22	Aug. 26	Sep. 09 '94
0.140	Oct. 19	Nov. 14	Nov. 18	Dec. 02 '94
0.160	Feb. 15	Feb. 21	Feb. 27	Mar. 13 '95
0.160	Apr. 26	May. 22	May. 26	Jun. 09 '95
0.160	Jul. 19	Aug. 23	Aug. 25	Sep. 08 '95

Data as orig. reptd.; bef. results of disc. opers. and/or spec. items. Per share data adj. for stk. divs. as of ex-div. date. E-Estimated. NA-Not Available. NM-Not Meaningful. NR-Not Ranked.

Office—101 Prospect Ave., N.W., Cleveland, OH 44115-1075. **Tel**—(216) 566-2000. **Chrmn & CEO**—J. G. Breen. **Pres**—T. A. Commes. **SVP-Fin, Treas & CFO**—L. J. Pitorak. **VP & Secy**—L. E. Stellato. **VP & Investor Contact**—Conway G. Ivy. **Dirs**—J. M. Biggar, J. G. Breen, L. Carter, T. A. Commes, D. E. Evans, R . W. Mahoney, W. G. Mitchell, A. M. Mixon, III, H. O. Petrauskas, R. E. Schey, R. K. Smucker. **Transfer Agent & Registrar**—Society National Bank, Cleveland. **Incorporated** in Ohio in 1884. **Empl**-17,900. **S&P Analyst:** Maureen C. Carini

Shoney's, Inc.

NYSE Symbol **SHN**
In S&P 500

25-SEP-95

Industry:
Food serving

Summary: Operations of this major restaurant company include the flagship Shoney's chain and the Captain D's seafood chain. Several other businesses are to be divested.

| S&P Opinion: Avoid (★★) | Recent Price • 12¼ | Yield • Nil |
| | 52 Wk Range • 15⅞-9⅛ | 12-Mo. P/E • 11.6 |

Quantitative Evaluations

Outlook
(1 Lowest—5 Highest)
• 5⁻

Fair Value
• 14⅜

Risk
• **Average**

Earn./Div. Rank
• **B**

Technical Eval.
• **Bullish** since 8/94

Rel. Strength Rank
(1 Lowest—99 Highest)
• **60**

Insider Activity
• **Neutral**

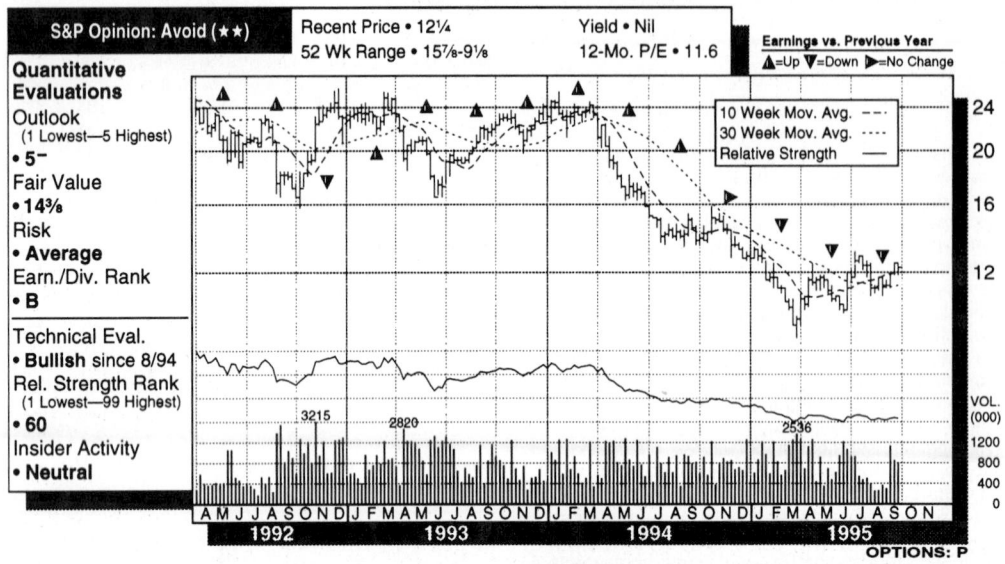

OPTIONS: P

Overview - 25-SEP-95

We expect SHN's fiscal 1995 earnings to be hurt by recent weakness in comparable-unit sales, plus spending aimed at improving operating results. Also, SHN's income statement is likely to include various unusual items, including one-time charges related to SHN's planned restructuring, and an impact from the sale of businesses which are now being treated as discontinued operations. Such items are largely excluded from our fiscal 1995 earnings estimate. Longer term, we look for earnings from continuing operations to be helped by some cost reductions, restaurant remodelings, the closing of weaker units, employee training efforts, and the use of asset sale proceeds to reduce debt. With SHN's proposed acquisition of TPI Enterprises Inc., we look for cost cutting efforts to offset at least part of the initial EPS dilution we expect.

Valuation - 25-SEP-95

In view of recent disappointing sales and reduced earnings estimates, we are now advising investors to avoid the stock of this restaurant company. We look for restructuring efforts and debt retirement to help SHN generate profit improvement in fiscal 1996. Also, the presence of a new chairman/CEO could generate some investor interest in the stock. However, we are concerned about the prospect of earnings weakness in fiscal 1995's fourth quarter, and by the competitive position of the flagship Shoney's chain. We see Shoney's facing both price discounting from fast-food chains, and rapid unit expansion by casual dining restaurant companies.

Key Stock Statistics

S&P EPS Est. 1995	0.66	Tang. Bk. Value/Share	NM
P/E on S&P Est. 1995	18.6	Beta	1.67
S&P EPS Est. 1996	0.90	Shareholders	8,300
Dividend Rate/Share	Nil	Market cap. (B)	$0.508
Shs. outstg. (M)	41.5	Inst. holdings	44%
Avg. daily vol. (M)	0.156	Insider holdings	NA

Value of $10,000 invested 5 years ago: $ 10,315

Fiscal Year Ending Oct. 31

	1995	% Change	1994	% Change	1993	% Change
Revenues (Million $)						
1Q	310.4	-8%	339.2	7%	317.7	7%
2Q	253.2	-9%	277.5	6%	262.8	2%
3Q	253.9	-10%	281.9	3%	274.1	7%
4Q	—	—	267.6	-6%	285.4	14%
Yr.	—	—	1,166	2%	1,140	7%
Income (Million $)						
1Q	8.01	-44%	14.20	17%	12.11	35%
2Q	6.20	-63%	16.86	12%	15.12	9%
3Q	8.17	-53%	17.25	4%	16.57	8%
4Q	—	—	14.27	NM	14.21	NM
Yr.	—	—	62.59	8%	58.01	NM
Earnings Per Share ($)						
1Q	0.19	-44%	0.34	13%	0.30	43%
2Q	0.15	-63%	0.41	11%	0.37	19%
3Q	0.20	-52%	0.42	2%	0.41	21%
4Q	E0.12	-66%	0.35	NM	0.35	NM
Yr.	E0.66	-57%	1.52	6%	1.44	NM

Next earnings report expected: late December

Business Summary - 25-SEP-95

Shoney's, Inc. is an operator and franchiser of restaurants. At August 6, 1995, SHN's businesses included 1,850 restaurants, of which 799 were company-owned units and 1,051 were franchises. In fiscal 1994, there was a net addition of 13 restaurants. As part of a restructuring announced in early 1995, SHN is looking to divest various operations, including its Lee's restaurant business.

Sales of company-operated restaurants accounted for 76% of SHN's total revenues in fiscal 1994, while about 20% came from food distribution and manufacturing operations, 3% from franchise fees, and about 2% from other sources.

As of August 6, 1995, SHN had 907 family restaurants operating under the Shoney's name, including 375 company-owned units. In addition, SHN's Captain D's chain had 634 restaurants, of which 332 were company owned. A third chain, Lee's Famous Recipe Chicken, included 275 restaurants, of which 60 were company owned. Also, there were 34 restaurants (32 company-owned) operating under the Pargo's, Fifth Quarter, or BarbWire's names.

Other SHN operations include Mike Rose Foods, Inc., a private-label manufacturer of salad dressings, dry batter, biscuit mixes and condiments for the food-service industry; and a sizable commissary business. In November 1991, SHN completed the sale of its Shoney's Inn division for $1.1 million, plus a portion of future revenues, and the potential for other future consideration.

At August 6, 1995, SHN's balance sheet included reserve liabilities of $67.9 million related to settlement of a discrimination lawsuit. Also, in 1988, SHN completed a recapitalization that included the payment of a special dividend ($16 a share in cash and $4 a share principal amount of 12% debentures) to stockholders.

Important Developments

Sep. '95—SHN signed a letter of intent to acquire TPI Enterprises Inc., a major franchisee in the Shoney's and Captain D's Seafood chains. Terms call for SHN to issue 0.28 of a SHN common share, plus a partial warrant, for each of TPI's approximately 20.4 million common shares outstanding. TPI operates 188 Shoney's and 69 Captain D's restaurants. Earlier, in May 1995, C. Stephen Lynn, became chairman and CEO of SHN. Mr. Lynn had been chairman and CEO of restaurant company Sonic Corp. since 1986. Also, SHN is seeking to implement a restructuring which would include divesting its Lee's Famous Recipe Chicken, and Mike Rose Foods businesses. As part of its restructuring, SHN is looking to significantly improve the performance and growth of its flagship Shoney's restaurant business.

Capitalization

Long Term Debt: $437,419,601 (8/6/95).

Per Share Data ($)

(Year Ended Oct. 31)

	1994	1993	1992	1991	1990	1989
Tangible Bk. Val.	-3.32	-5.16	-7.48	-6.63	-8.39	-9.60
Cash Flow	2.57	2.43	0.32	1.88	1.67	1.41
Earnings	1.52	1.44	-0.65	0.94	0.76	0.50
Dividends	Nil	Nil	Nil	Nil	Nil	Nil
Payout Ratio	Nil	Nil	Nil	Nil	Nil	Nil
Prices - High	25⅝	25⅝	27¼	24¼	16¾	13¼
- Low	12⅝	16½	15¾	10½	9¼	7¾
P/E Ratio - High	17	18	NM	26	22	27
- Low	8	11	NM	11	12	16

Income Statement Analysis (Million $)

	1994	%Chg	1993	%Chg	1992	%Chg	1991
Revs.	1,155	2%	1,136	7%	1,059	7%	990
Oper. Inc.	170	-3%	175	5%	166	5%	158
Depr.	43.4	9%	40.0	1%	39.6	5%	37.7
Int. Exp.	42.1	-6%	44.9	-15%	52.6	-19%	64.7
Pretax Inc.	98.2	5%	93.4	NM	-46.4	NM	59.3
Eff. Tax Rate	36%	—	38%	—	NM	—	36%
Net Inc.	62.6	8%	58.0	NM	-26.6	NM	38.0

Balance Sheet & Other Fin. Data (Million $)

	1994	1993	1992	1991	1990	1989
Cash	4.2	7.8	4.3	4.7	4.2	7.9
Curr. Assets	95.0	107	79.4	64.9	52.8	61.3
Total Assets	558	528	469	429	400	400
Curr. Liab.	197	245	181	122	115	92.0
LT Debt	414	390	461	543	579	635
Common Eqty.	-136	-209	-289	-264	-320	-357
Total Cap.	293	189	170	298	279	302
Cap. Exp.	95.0	82.8	58.6	56.0	48.5	35.4
Cash Flow	106	98.0	13.0	75.7	65.3	53.4

Ratio Analysis

	1994	1993	1992	1991	1990	1989
Curr. Ratio	0.5	0.4	0.4	0.5	0.5	0.7
% LT Debt of Cap.	141.4	205.8	270.7	181.8	207.3	210.4
% Net Inc.of Revs.	5.4	5.1	NM	3.8	3.2	2.2
% Ret. on Assets	11.5	11.4	NM	9.0	7.3	4.7
% Ret. on Equity	NM	NM	NM	NM	NM	NM

Dividend Data —Paid each year since 1971, dividends were discontinued following a large special distribution in mid-1988.

Data as orig. reptd.; bef. results of disc. opers. and/or spec. items. Per share data adj. for stk. divs. as of ex-div. date. E-Estimated. NA-Not Available. NM-Not Meaningful. NR-Not Ranked.

Office—1727 Elm Hill Pike, P.O. Box 1260, Nashville, TN 37202. Tel—(615) 391-5201. Chrmn & CEO—C. S. Lynn. Pres—C. E. Porter. Sr Exec VP, CFO, & Investor Contact—W. Craig Barber. Treas & Secy—F. E. McDaniel Jr. Dirs—D. C. Bottorff, T. H. Henry Jr., C. F. Hoover, V. B. Jackson, C. S. Lynn, D. W. Maddox, W. N. Rasmussen, A. Schoenbaum, R. T. Shircliff, B. F. Skinner, J. R. Thomas II, C. Turner Jr. Transfer Agent & Registrar—Harris Trust & Savings Bank, Chicago. Incorporated in Tennessee in 1968. Empl-30,000. S&P Analyst: Tom Graves, CFA

Sigma-Aldrich Corp.

NASDAQ Symbol **SIAL**
In S&P 500

15-OCT-95

Industry:
Chemicals

Summary: This company makes and distributes a wide range of bi-ochemicals, organic chemicals, chromatography products, and diagnostic reagents. It also produces metal components.

S&P Opinion: Hold (★★★)	Recent Price • 45¼	Yield • 0.8%
	52 Wk Range • 51¾-31	12-Mo. P/E • 18.9

Quantitative Evaluations

Outlook
(1 Lowest—5 Highest)
• **2+**

Fair Value
• **45¾**

Risk
• **Low**

Earn./Div. Rank
• **A+**

Technical Eval.
• **Bullish** since 3/95

Rel. Strength Rank
(1 Lowest—99 Highest)
• **22**

Insider Activity
• **Neutral**

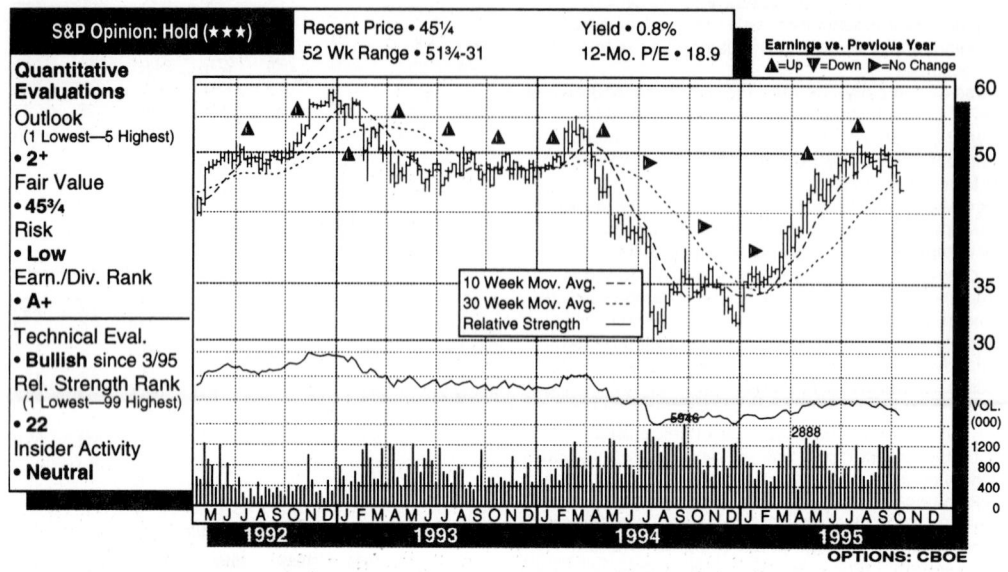

Earnings vs. Previous Year
▲=Up ▼=Down ▶=No Change

10 Week Mov. Avg. ---
30 Week Mov. Avg. ·····
Relative Strength ——

OPTIONS: CBOE

Business Profile - 22-AUG-95

This company produces and distributes an extensive line of biochemical, organic and chromatography products for research and diagnostic purposes, and also makes metal struts and other components. Long term growth prospects are tied to the introduction of both new products and applications designed to keep pace with technological developments in the field of research. Major capital investments in the past several years provides additional production and distribution capacity.

Operational Review - 22-AUG-95

Net sales for the six months ended June 30, 1995, advanced 16%, year to year, due to a stronger world economy and less uncertainty regarding health-care reform in the U.S. Chemical sales rose 17%, aided by sales improvements in global markets and favorable currency exchange rates; metal sales rose 14%. Net income was up 17%, to $66,225,000 ($1.33 a share) from $56,703,000 ($1.14).

Stock Performance - 13-OCT-95

In the past 30 trading days, SIAL's shares have declined 5%, compared to a 4% rise in the S&P 500. Average trading volume for the past five days was 232,120 shares, compared with the 40-day moving average of 213,067 shares.

Key Stock Statistics

Dividend Rate/Share	0.36	Shareholders	2,600
Shs. outstg. (M)	49.9	Market cap. (B)	$ 2.3
Avg. daily vol. (M)	0.224	Inst. holdings	60%
Tang. Bk. Value/Share	15.87	Insider holdings	NA
Beta	1.29		

Value of $10,000 invested 5 years ago: $ 16,310

Fiscal Year Ending Dec. 31

	1995	% Change	1994	% Change	1993	% Change
Revenues (Million $)						
1Q	244.8	17%	208.5	16%	180.0	7%
2Q	243.3	15%	212.4	16%	183.8	13%
3Q	—	—	217.4	14%	190.8	15%
4Q	—	—	212.9	15%	184.8	17%
Yr.	—	—	851.2	15%	739.4	13%
Income (Million $)						
1Q	32.74	10%	29.73	11%	26.90	12%
2Q	33.48	24%	26.98	NM	26.89	12%
3Q	—	—	27.03	1%	26.71	7%
4Q	—	—	26.61	NM	26.58	18%
Yr.	—	—	110.3	3%	107.2	12%
Earnings Per Share ($)						
1Q	0.66	10%	0.60	11%	0.54	12%
2Q	0.67	24%	0.54	NM	0.54	12%
3Q	—	—	0.54	NM	0.54	8%
4Q	—	—	0.53	NM	0.53	15%
Yr.	—	—	2.21	3%	2.15	12%

Next earnings report expected: late October

Sigma-Aldrich Corp.

Business Summary - 30-AUG-95

Sigma-Aldrich Corp. is engaged in two lines of business: the production and sale of biochemicals, organic and inorganic chemicals, diagnostic reagents, chromatography products and related products; and the manufacture and sale of metal components for strut, cable tray, pipe support and telecommunication systems and electrical enclosures. Segment contributions in 1994:

	Sales	Profits
Chemical products	81%	86%
Metal products	19%	14%

The company distributes 76,000 chemical products (with 5,000 added in 1994) for use primarily in research and development, in the diagnosis of disease, and as specialty chemicals for manufacturing. In laboratory applications, its products are used in biochemistry, synthetic chemistry, quality control and testing, immunology, hematology, pharmacology, microbiology, neurology and endocrinology and in studies of life processes. Diagnostic products are used to detect liver and kidney diseases, heart attacks and metabolic disorders. Supelco Inc. (acquired in May 1993) is a global supplier of chromatography products used in chemical research and production.

Sigma also offers approximately 60,000 esoteric chemicals as a special service to customers that screen them for potential applications. Esoterics account for less than 1% of total sales.

Of the 76,000 products listed in the company's catalogs, it produced about 35,000 (accounting for 45% of the 1994 net sales of chemical products). The remainder were purchased from many outside sources. In 1994, foreign purchases accounted for about 30% of chemical products' net sales.

In the metals business, B-Line Systems makes and markets a line of products for use in electrical, mechanical and telecommunications applications. These products include strut, cable tray and pipe support systems, and telecommunication racks and cable runways. Wholly owned Circle A W Products Co. (acquired in 1993) produces metal enclosure boxes used to protect electric meters, fuse and circuit breaker boards. These subsidiaries market worldwide over 25,000 metal products (with 250 added in 1994).

Important Developments

Jul. '95—SIAL said that its results for the first half of 1995 reflected a continuing strong demand for its products because of a growing world economy and less uncertainty regarding health care in the U.S. The company expected that profit margins for the rest of 1995 would be consistent with the first half.

Capitalization

Long Term Debt: $14,344,000 (6/95).

Per Share Data ($) (Year Ended Dec. 31)

	1994	1993	1992	1991	1990	1989
Tangible Bk. Val.	14.04	11.87	10.28	8.86	7.42	6.04
Cash Flow	2.95	2.75	2.47	2.12	1.91	1.62
Earnings	2.21	2.15	1.92	1.60	1.44	1.30
Dividends	0.34	0.23	0.26	0.23	0.21	0.19
Payout Ratio	15%	11%	14%	14%	14%	14%
Prices - High	55¼	58	59¼	53½	37⅞	29¾
- Low	30	44½	41⅝	27¾	25	21⅞
P/E Ratio - High	25	27	31	33	25	23
- Low	14	21	22	17	17	17

Income Statement Analysis (Million $)

	1994	%Chg	1993	%Chg	1992	%Chg	1991
Revs.	851	15%	739	13%	654	11%	589
Oper. Inc.	210	6%	198	10%	180	14%	158
Depr.	36.7	24%	29.7	8%	27.4	6%	25.8
Int. Exp.	2.9	19%	2.4	-55%	5.4	-33%	8.0
Pretax Inc.	170	2%	166	13%	147	19%	124
Eff. Tax Rate	35%	—	35%	—	35%	—	36%
Net Inc.	110	3%	107	12%	95.5	20%	79.8

Balance Sheet & Other Fin. Data (Million $)

	1994	1993	1992	1991	1990	1989
Cash	9.7	10.3	44.9	28.1	6.6	9.7
Curr. Assets	502	451	416	391	341	284
Total Assets	852	753	616	597	546	472
Curr. Liab.	105	111	66.2	70.9	92.9	99
LT Debt	14.5	17.3	18.7	69.3	70.8	61.5
Common Eqty.	700	591	512	441	368	299
Total Cap.	714	608	543	520	448	367
Cap. Exp.	72.0	102	30.9	26.1	32.5	51.7
Cash Flow	147	137	123	106	95.0	80.0

Ratio Analysis

	1994	1993	1992	1991	1990	1989
Curr. Ratio	4.8	4.0	6.3	5.5	3.7	2.9
% LT Debt of Cap.	2.0	2.8	3.5	13.3	15.8	16.7
% Net Inc.of Revs.	13.0	14.5	14.6	13.5	13.5	14.5
% Ret. on Assets	13.7	15.6	15.7	14.0	14.0	15.3
% Ret. on Equity	17.1	19.4	20.0	19.7	21.3	23.5

Dividend Data —Cash has been paid each year since 1970.

Amt. of Div. $	Date Decl.	Ex-Div. Date	Stock of Record	Payment Date
0.090	Nov. 08	Dec. 09	Dec. 15	Jan. 03 '95
0.090	Feb. 21	Feb. 23	Mar. 01	Mar. 15 '95
0.090	May. 02	May. 25	Jun. 01	Jun. 15 '95
0.090	Aug. 15	Aug. 30	Sep. 01	Sep. 15 '95

Data as orig. reptd.; bef. results of disc. opers. and/or spec. items. Per share data adj. for stk. divs. as of ex-div. date. E-Estimated. NA-Not Available. NM-Not Meaningful. NR-Not Ranked.

Office—3050 Spruce St., St. Louis, MO 63103. **Tel**—(314) 771-5765. **Chrmn & CEO**—C. T. Cori. **Pres & COO**—D. R. Harvey. **VP-Secy**—T. M. Tallarico. **VP-CFO & Treas**—P. A. Gleich. **Contr & Investor Contact**—Kirk A. Richter. **VP & Treas**—T. M. Tallarico. **Dirs**—C. T. Cori, D. R. Harvey, R. J. Hurst, D. M. Kipnis, A. E. Newman, W. C. O'Neil, Jr., J. W. Sandweiss, D. D. Spatz, T. N. Urban. **Transfer Agent**—Boatmen's Trust Co., St. Louis. **Incorporated** in Delaware in 1975. **Empl**- 5,500. **S&P Analyst:** Richard O'Reilly, CFA

Silicon Graphics

NYSE Symbol **SGI**
In S&P 500

29-AUG-95

Industry:
Data Processing

Summary: This company manufactures workstations, servers and supercomputers that incorporate interactive 3-D graphics, digital media and multiprocessing technologies.

S&P Opinion: Accumulate (★★★★)	Recent Price • 42⅞	Yield • Nil
	52 Wk Range • 45⅝-23⅜	12-Mo. P/E • 33.5

Quantitative Evaluations

Outlook
(1 Lowest—5 Highest)
• **5+**

Fair Value
• **60%**

Risk
• **Average**

Earn./Div. Rank
• **B-**

Technical Eval.
• **Bearish** since 8/95

Rel. Strength Rank
(1 Lowest—99 Highest)
• **48**

Insider Activity
• **Neutral**

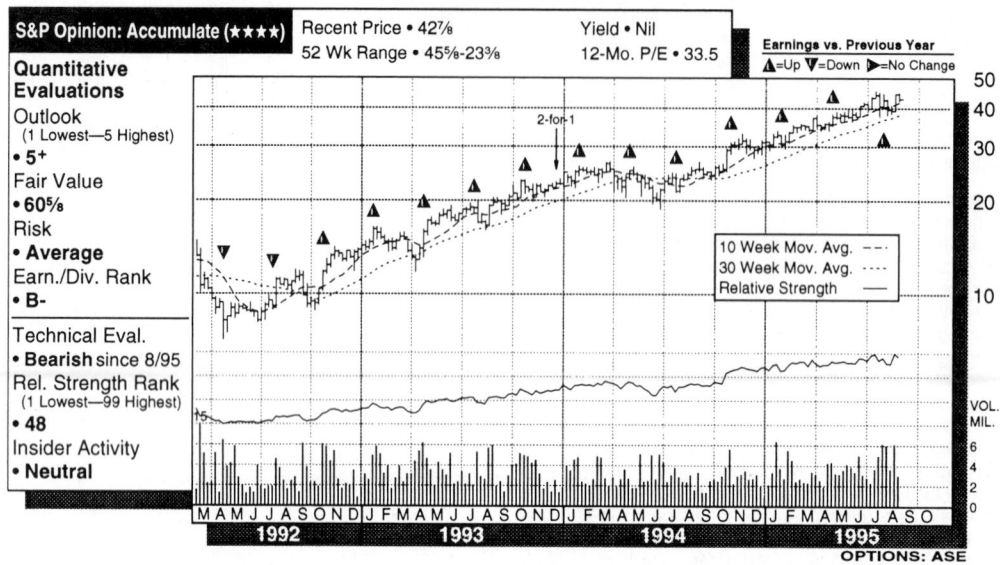

Earnings vs. Previous Year
▲=Up ▼=Down ▶=No Change

10 Week Mov. Avg. — - —
30 Week Mov. Avg. - - - -
Relative Strength ———

OPTIONS: ASE

Overview - 28-AUG-95

We are projecting total revenue growth of about 45% in fiscal 1996, as SGI is experiencing strong demand for its visual computing products in all geographies and product lines. Two areas worth noting are the high-end supercomputing line, where SGI is enjoying great success against weakened competition, and in low-end desktop systems, where it is growing much faster than the corporate average. Gross margins, which have exceeded the company's 50%-52% target range in the past several quarters, should narrow as more aggressive pricing actions are implemented. In addition, operating margins have been well above SGI's 11%-13% target. This target should be met as SGI ramps up infrastructure spending to support its growth. Our $1.85 EPS estimate for fiscal 1996 is based on 12% more shares outstanding.

Valuation - 28-AUG-95

Despite the strong price gains since mid-1994, the shares of this dominant visual computing vendor remain attractive based on the excellent growth prospects in its core workstation business. In addition, several joint ventures, including those with Time Warner and AT&T for video server and operating system software, and two recent software acquisitions, should be additive to longer-term EPS and share price prospects. Because the shares are valued well below our two-to-three year projected EPS growth rate of 30%-40%, we recommend that they be accumulated for their above-average capital gains potential.

Key Stock Statistics

S&P EPS Est. 1996	1.85	Tang. Bk. Value/Share	6.37
P/E on S&P Est. 1996	23.2	Beta	1.67
S&P EPS Est. 1997	2.40	Shareholders	1,800
Dividend Rate/Share	Nil	Market cap. (B)	$ 6.6
Shs. outstg. (M)	158.6	Inst. holdings	73%
Avg. daily vol. (M)	0.915	Insider holdings	NA

Value of $10,000 invested 5 years ago: $ 58,628

Fiscal Year Ending Jun. 30

	1995	% Change	1994	% Change	1993	% Change
Revenues (Million $)						
1Q	427.4	42%	301.6	31%	231.1	26%
2Q	524.0	41%	370.4	37%	270.2	15%
3Q	552.0	47%	376.3	39%	270.7	30%
4Q	653.2	51%	433.3	36%	319.3	33%
Yr.	2,228	50%	1,482	36%	1,091	26%
Income (Million $)						
1Q	41.84	63%	25.74	—	—	—
2Q	53.89	48%	36.34	65%	21.98	31%
3Q	64.23	83%	35.10	73%	20.24	NM
4Q	52.75	21%	43.50	34%	32.39	NM
Yr.	224.9	60%	140.7	60%	87.69	NM
Earnings Per Share ($)						
1Q	0.27	59%	0.17	79%	0.09	NM
2Q	0.34	42%	0.24	55%	0.15	35%
3Q	0.40	74%	0.23	64%	0.14	NM
4Q	0.30	7%	0.28	30%	0.22	NM
Yr.	1.28	41%	0.91	52%	0.60	NM

Next earnings report expected: late October

Business Summary - 28-AUG-95

Silicon Graphics, Inc. manufactures a family of workstation, server and supercomputer systems that incorporate interactive three-dimensional graphics, digital media and multiprocessing supercomputing technologies. Sales outside North America accounted for 47% of revenues in fiscal 1994.

The company's graphics computer systems range from the Indigo series of desktop workstations, including the Indy desktop workstation, to the Onyx and POWER Onyx systems, a family of advanced graphics supercomputers. In addition, the Challenge and POWER Challenge systems range from entry-level single-processor servers to enterprise-wide symmetric multiprocessing supercomputers.

Workstations are used primarily by technical, scientific and creative professionals to simulate, analyze, develop and display complex 3-D objects and phenomena. Servers are general-purpose computers with the same computational performance as workstations, but without the graphics capabilities. The company's supercomputing servers, which were introduced in July 1994, are meant to replace or augment aging mainframe computers in compute-intensive engineering, animation and scientific environments.

SGI's computers all use RISC microprocessors developed by MIPS Technologies, a wholly owned subsidiary acquired in June 1992. The company's products are generally binary-compatible, allowing software to be run without modification across the entire product line. In October 1994, MIPS and two semiconductor partners, NEC Electronics and Toshiba America Electronic Components, announced the company's next-generation microprocessor design, the MIPS R10000.

All of the company's hardware products use IRIX, an enhanced version of UNIX, as their operating system software. Approximately 1,900 application software programs are available for use on SGI workstations.

Important Developments

Jul. '95—SGI unveiled Indigo2 IMPACT, a new line of 3D graphics and imaging workstations that feature customized third-party software solutions. The list price of a lower-end model starts at $35,000.
Jun. '95—SGI acquired leading animation software vendors Alias Research, Inc. (fiscal 1994 revenues of $38 million) and Wavefront Technologies (1993 revenues of $17.8 million). SGI issued common stock valued at about $630 million, including $460 million for Alias and $170 million for Wavefront. Separately, the company unveiled its Silicon Exchange initiative, an integrated solution set of software and hardware for financial service institutions.

Capitalization

Long Term Debt: $287,267,000 (6/95).
Conv. Preferred Stock: $33,996,000; held by NKK Corp.

Per Share Data ($)

(Year Ended Jun. 30)

	1995	1994	1993	1992	1991	1990
Tangible Bk. Val.	NA	6.37	4.56	3.60	3.97	3.02
Cash Flow	NA	1.45	0.98	-0.54	0.68	0.68
Earnings	1.28	0.91	0.60	-1.10	0.36	0.43
Dividends	Nil	Nil	Nil	Nil	Nil	Nil
Payout Ratio	Nil	Nil	Nil	Nil	Nil	Nil
Prices - High	45⅝	33⅛	24¾	14⅞	12¼	10¼
- Low	29⅛	18¾	11¾	7⅛	5⅝	4½
P/E Ratio - High	36	36	41	NM	33	24
- Low	23	21	20	NM	15	11

Income Statement Analysis (Million $)

	1994	%Chg	1993	%Chg	1992	%Chg	1991
Revs.	1,482	36%	1,091	26%	867	58%	550
Oper. Inc.	277	54%	180	104%	88.2	18%	74.8
Depr.	84.2	54%	54.8	-14%	63.4	103%	31.3
Int. Exp.	8.3	184%	2.9	5%	2.8	-14%	3.2
Pretax Inc.	198	58%	125	NM	-102	NM	48.0
Eff. Tax Rate	29%	—	30%	—	NM	—	31%
Net Inc.	141	60%	88.0	NM	-117	NM	33.0

Balance Sheet & Other Fin. Data (Million $)

	1994	1993	1992	1991	1990	1989
Cash	401	155	183	196	86.0	94.0
Curr. Assets	1,024	676	578	480	298	238
Total Assets	1,519	946	758	642	364	291
Curr. Liab.	356	268	217	116	83.0	46.0
LT Debt	230	26.0	27.3	27.8	36.4	87.8
Common Eqty.	887	600	446	329	210	157
Total Cap.	1,151	660	507	523	281	245
Cap. Exp.	89.4	83.6	67.0	47.2	29.6	23.3
Cash Flow	224	142	-60.3	62.5	54.3	26.6

Ratio Analysis

	1994	1993	1992	1991	1990	1989
Curr. Ratio	2.8	2.5	2.7	4.1	3.6	5.1
% LT Debt of Cap.	20.0	3.9	5.4	5.3	13.0	35.9
% Net Inc.of Revs.	9.5	8.0	NM	6.0	7.7	4.4
% Ret. on Assets	11.1	10.0	NM	6.1	9.5	4.6
% Ret. on Equity	18.3	16.3	NM	10.8	16.9	7.6

Dividend Data —No dividends have ever been paid. The shares were split two-for-one in December 1993 and February 1992.

Data as orig. reptd.; bef. results of disc. opers. and/or spec. items. Per share data adj. for stk. divs. as of ex-div. date. E-Estimated. NA-Not Available. NM-Not Meaningful. NR-Not Ranked.

Office—2011 N. Shoreline Blvd., Mountain View, CA 94039-7311. **Tel**—(415) 960-1980. **Chrmn, Pres & CEO**—E. R. McCracken. **Pres & COO**—T. A. Jermoluk. **Sr VP-Fin & CFO**—S. J. Meresman. **Secy**—W. L. Kelly. **Investor Contact**—Marilyn Lattin. **Dirs**—R. R. Bishop, A. F. Jacobson, T. A. Jermoluk, C. R. Kramlich, E. R. McCracken, J. A. McDivitt, M.W. Perry, L. Shapiro, J. G. Treybig. **Transfer Agent & Registrar**—First National Bank of Boston. **Incorporated** in California in 1981; reincorporated in Delaware in 1990. **Empl**-4,400. **S&P Analyst:** John D. Coyle, CFA

Snap-on Inc.

NYSE Symbol **SNA**
In S&P 500

03-AUG-95 Industry:
Building

Summary: Snap-on Inc. (formerly Snap-on Tools) is the largest manufacturer and distributor of hand tools, storage units and diagnostic equipment for professional mechanics and industry.

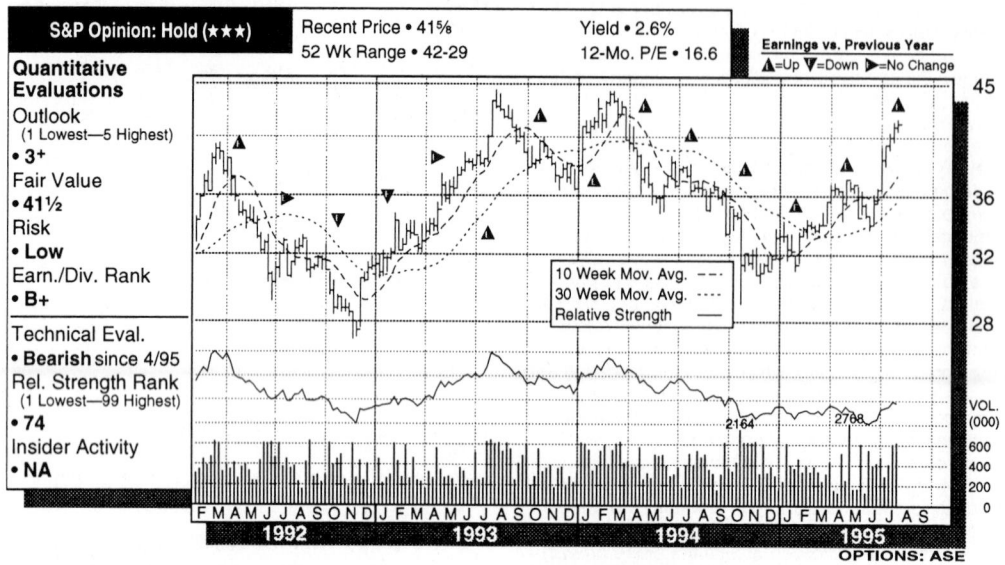

S&P Opinion: Hold (★★★)	Recent Price • 41⅝	Yield • 2.6%
	52 Wk Range • 42-29	12-Mo. P/E • 16.6

Quantitative Evaluations

Outlook
(1 Lowest—5 Highest)
• **3+**

Fair Value
• **41½**

Risk
• **Low**

Earn./Div. Rank
• **B+**

Technical Eval.
• **Bearish** since 4/95

Rel. Strength Rank
(1 Lowest—99 Highest)
• **74**

Insider Activity
• **NA**

Earnings vs. Previous Year
▲=Up ▼=Down ▶=No Change

10 Week Mov. Avg. - - -
30 Week Mov. Avg. · · · ·
Relative Strength —

OPTIONS: ASE

Overview - 03-AUG-95

Sales should rise in 1996, reflecting growth in tool demand related to a projected increase in the automotive aftermarket for vehicle repair services. The increased demand for repairs will be stimulated by the imposition of new vehicle emissions inspection standards in most states. Repair shops will need to upgrade their equipment to detect and repair failing vehicles. Emerging emissions standards in other parts of the world should provide market opportunities in the next few years. Operating profits will benefit from price increases to offset materials cost increases and modest cost savings as the company continues to fine tune its warehouse and regional distribution centers. Despite higher interest expense, increased earnings are expected.

Valuation - 03-AUG-95

Although we expect earnings to rise in 1995 and 1996, and we expect SNA to benefit from the eventual introduction of new emissions standards, we are concerned by ongoing delays in the start-up of new state testing programs. A congressional threat to reopen the Clean Air Act of 1990 resulted in delay and changes by the U.S. EPA in the methods to implement the new testing standard. It appears that the result will be a larger market for emissions test, diagnostic and repair equipment, however, the timing of that revenue stream may be further delayed. Because of this uncertainty, we rate SNA stock a hold despite a modest valuation of about 13 times projected 1996 earnings.

Key Stock Statistics

S&P EPS Est. 1995	2.70	Tang. Bk. Value/Share	16.65
P/E on S&P Est. 1995	15.4	Beta	0.66
S&P EPS Est. 1996	3.00	Shareholders	9,300
Dividend Rate/Share	1.08	Market cap. (B)	$ 1.7
Shs. outstg. (M)	40.1	Inst. holdings	78%
Avg. daily vol. (M)	0.120	Insider holdings	NA

Value of $10,000 invested 5 years ago: $ 15,325

Fiscal Year Ending Dec. 31

	1995	% Change	1994	% Change	1993	% Change
Revenues (Million $)						
1Q	309.1	3%	298.8	10%	270.7	20%
2Q	326.8	9%	298.8	10%	272.7	17%
3Q	—	—	278.4	3%	271.1	20%
4Q	—	—	318.4	NM	317.5	6%
Yr.	—	—	1,194	6%	1,132	15%
Income (Million $)						
1Q	26.46	16%	22.83	23%	18.50	NM
2Q	29.72	14%	26.10	17%	22.36	14%
3Q	—	—	22.71	11%	20.54	35%
4Q	—	—	26.68	9%	24.41	91%
Yr.	—	—	98.31	15%	85.81	30%
Earnings Per Share ($)						
1Q	0.62	15%	0.54	23%	0.44	NM
2Q	0.73	20%	0.61	17%	0.52	13%
3Q	E0.63	—	0.53	10%	0.48	33%
4Q	E0.72	—	0.62	7%	0.58	93%
Yr.	E2.70	—	2.30	14%	2.02	29%

Next earnings report expected: mid October

Snap-on Inc.

Business Summary - 01-AUG-95

Snap-on Inc. (formerly Snap-on Tools) manufactures a line of 15,000 high-quality professional mechanic tools, diagnostic equipment and tool chests. Sales by product category in recent years were as follows:

	1994	1993	1992
Hand tools	38%	37%	43%
Power tools	7%	7%	8%
Tool storage	11%	11%	13%
Diagnostics/shop	44%	45%	36%

Hand tools include wrenches, screwdrivers, sockets, pliers and similar items. Power tools include pneumatic impact wrenches, air ratchets, power drills, sanders and polishers. Tool storage refers to tool chests and roll cabinets. Electronic tools and shop equipment include automotive diagnostic equipment, wheel balancing and aligning equipment, and battery chargers. The addition of Sun Electric and Balco in recent years expanded SNA's electronic diagnostic and emissions test equipment.

Products are sold to mechanics, industrial accounts and foreign distributors for use in automotive service, manufacturing and other repair and maintenance. Special custom tools are also made.

Tools and equipment are sold to more than 5,000 dealers worldwide and industrial products are sold by some 540 company salesmen. Dealers operate out of walk-in vans that carry a product inventory. In 1994, dealers, industrial customers and foreign distributors accounted for 82%, 17% and 1% of sales, respectively, versus 83%, 15% and 2% in 1993. About 21% of sales and 22% of profits were derived from foreign countries.

Important Developments

Jun. '95—The company increased its ownership of EDGE Diagnostics from 30% to 90% and will acquire all remaining equity within four years. EDGE is a developer of software and firmware that facilitate the diagnosis of sophisticated vehicle computer systems and ensure compliance with environmental, safety and fuel efficiency regulations. Separately, on May 1, 1995 the company substantially completed the repurchase of $100 million of common stock in the open market by purchase of a block of 1.9 million shares. A total of 2.8 million shares were repurchased under the $100 million authorization.

Capitalization

Long Term Debt: $114,076,000 (6/95).

Per Share Data ($)

(Year Ended Dec. 31)

	1994	1993	1992	1991	1990	1989
Tangible Bk. Val.	16.62	15.28	15.67	15.46	15.42	13.93
Cash Flow	3.00	2.76	2.16	2.36	3.04	3.08
Earnings	2.30	2.02	1.56	1.75	2.45	2.55
Dividends	1.08	1.08	1.08	1.08	1.08	1.04
Payout Ratio	47%	53%	69%	62%	44%	41%
Prices - High	44³/₈	44¹/₂	40	34¹/₂	38	41⁷/₈
- Low	29	30¹/₂	27	27³/₈	26¹/₄	28⁷/₈
P/E Ratio - High	19	22	26	20	16	16
- Low	13	15	17	16	11	11

Income Statement Analysis (Million $)

	1994	%Chg	1993	%Chg	1992	%Chg	1991
Revs.	1,254	5%	1,193	14%	1,047	12%	938
Oper. Inc.	188	5%	179	27%	141	-5%	149
Depr.	30.1	-5%	31.8	25%	25.5	NM	25.6
Int. Exp.	10.8	-4%	11.2	88%	6.0	14%	5.3
Pretax Inc.	154	13%	136	24%	110	-8%	119
Eff. Tax Rate	36%	—	37%	—	40%	—	38%
Net Inc.	98.0	14%	86.0	30%	66.0	-10%	73.0

Balance Sheet & Other Fin. Data (Million $)

	1994	1993	1992	1991	1990	1989
Cash	9.0	6.7	59.0	10.9	6.6	5.1
Curr. Assets	873	855	838	667	675	565
Total Assets	1,235	1,219	1,177	915	908	778
Curr. Liab.	238	308	322	177	237	179
LT Debt	109	100	93.1	7.2	7.3	7.7
Common Eqty.	766	702	665	653	636	573
Total Cap.	882	809	763	660	656	591
Cap. Exp.	41.8	33.2	21.1	23.4	44.1	71.4
Cash Flow	128	118	91.0	99	125	127

Ratio Analysis

	1994	1993	1992	1991	1990	1989
Curr. Ratio	3.7	2.8	2.6	3.8	2.9	3.1
% LT Debt of Cap.	12.4	12.3	12.2	1.1	1.1	1.3
% Net Inc.of Revs.	7.8	7.2	6.3	7.8	10.2	11.2
% Ret. on Assets	8.0	7.1	6.3	7.9	11.9	14.5
% Ret. on Equity	13.3	12.5	10.0	11.2	16.6	19.4

Dividend Data (Dividends have been paid since 1939. A "poison pill" stock purchase rights plan was adopted in 1987.)

Amt. of Div. $	Date Decl.	Ex-Div. Date	Stock of Record	Payment Date
0.270	Oct. 28	Nov. 14	Nov. 18	Dec. 09 '94
0.270	Jan. 27	Feb. 13	Feb. 17	Mar. 10 '95
0.270	Apr. 28	May. 15	May. 19	Jun. 09 '95
0.270	Jun. 23	Aug. 17	Aug. 21	Sep. 11 '95

Data as orig. reptd.; bef. results of disc. opers. and/or spec. items. Per share data adj. for stk. divs. as of ex-div. date. E-Estimated. NA-Not Available. NM-Not Meaningful. NR-Not Ranked.

Office—2801 80th St., Kenosha, WI 53141-1410. Tel—(414) 656-5200. Chrmn & Pres—R. A. Cornog. VP-Secy—S. F. Marrinan. SVP & CFO—D. J. Huml. Treas & Investor Contact—Denis J. Loverine. Dirs—D. W. Brinckman, B. S. Chelberg, R. A. Cornog, R. J. Decyk, R. F. Farley, A. L. Kelly, G. W. Mead, E. H. Rensi, J. H. Schnabel. Transfer Agent & Registrar—Harris Trust & Savings Bank, Chicago. Incorporated in Delaware in 1930. Empl-9,000. S&P Analyst: Joshua M. Harari, CFA

Sonat Inc.

NYSE Symbol **SNT**
In S&P 500

31-AUG-95 **Industry:**
Utilities-Gas

Summary: This energy company operates a natural gas pipeline serving eight southeastern states and, to a lesser extent, is involved in oilfield services and exploration and production.

S&P Opinion: Hold (★★★)	Recent Price • 31⅜ Yield • 3.4%
	52 Wk Range • 33½-26 12-Mo. P/E • 24.3

Quantitative Evaluations

Outlook
(1 Lowest—5 Highest)
• **1⁻**

Fair Value
• **26⅜**

Risk
• **Low**

Earn./Div. Rank
• **B**

Technical Eval.
• **Bullish** since 11/94

Rel. Strength Rank
(1 Lowest—99 Highest)
• **58**

Insider Activity
• **NA**

Earnings vs. Previous Year
▲=Up ▼=Down ▶=No Change

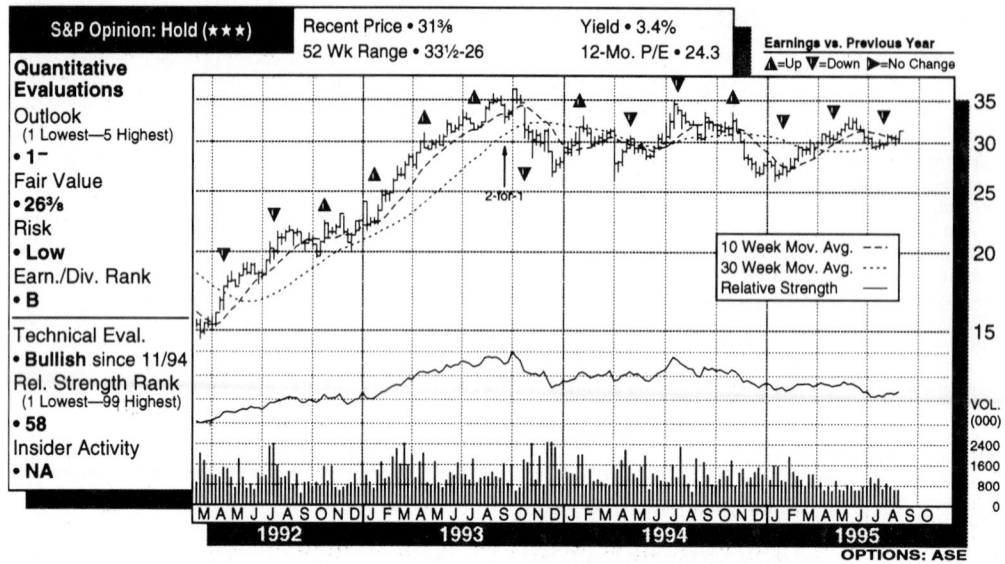

10 Week Mov. Avg. ---
30 Week Mov. Avg. ·····
Relative Strength ——

2-for-1

VOL.
(000)

OPTIONS: ASE

Overview - 31-AUG-95

Pipeline profits should improve in 1995, on expansion of service into Florida and Georgia in May 1994 and the March 1995 startup of Citrus Corp.'s Phase III project (despite a sharp drop in allowance for funds used during construction that will result from completion of the project). A customer settlement, also filed in March and supported by many SNT customers, will resolve outstanding rate and transition costs and lead to more competitive rates. Gas marketing profits will rise on growth in gas demand later in 1995. However, gas marketing margins will remain narrow, restricted by stiff competition, although the company intends to emphasize profitable services. Weak natural gas prices will restrict energy production profit growth but allow acquisition of additional reserves at attractive prices.

Valuation - 31-AUG-95

SNT's shares have held up well despite continuing weakness in natural gas prices, even advancing since the beginning of the year. Recent asset sales have raised funds to pay down short term debt and enhance future cash flow, which was already strong. With a sizable pipeline project that began service to Florida in March 1995 operating at a very high utilization rate, and the flexibility to further expand its pipeline system into attractive gas growth markets in the Southeast, the company has favorable prospects. However, the shares, trading at 20X projected 1995 EPS of $1.55, remain a hold.

Key Stock Statistics

S&P EPS Est. 1995	1.55	Tang. Bk. Value/Share	16.25
P/E on S&P Est. 1995	20.2	Beta	0.59
S&P EPS Est. 1996	1.80	Shareholders	12,700
Dividend Rate/Share	1.08	Market cap. (B)	$ 2.7
Shs. outstg. (M)	86.4	Inst. holdings	71%
Avg. daily vol. (M)	0.136	Insider holdings	NA

Value of $10,000 invested 5 years ago: $ 16,364

Fiscal Year Ending Dec. 31

	1995	% Change	1994	% Change	1993	% Change
Revenues (Million $)						
1Q	431.2	-10%	479.5	-4%	496.9	18%
2Q	480.6	16%	415.0	16%	356.5	20%
3Q	—	—	411.8	27%	324.5	8%
4Q	—	—	467.6	-17%	563.2	20%
Yr.	—	—	1,774	2%	1,741	17%
Income (Million $)						
1Q	37.62	-24%	49.61	-28%	68.92	61%
2Q	17.34	-50%	34.54	-73%	125.9	NM
3Q	—	—	35.29	74%	20.29	-5%
4Q	—	—	21.96	-56%	49.99	22%
Yr.	—	—	141.4	-47%	265.1	163%
Earnings Per Share ($)						
1Q	0.44	-23%	0.57	-29%	0.80	60%
2Q	0.20	-50%	0.40	-73%	1.45	NM
3Q	E0.45	13%	0.40	74%	0.23	-6%
4Q	E0.46	84%	0.25	-56%	0.57	20%
Yr.	E1.55	-4%	1.62	-47%	3.05	160%

Next earnings report expected: late October

Sonat Inc.

Business Summary - 31-AUG-95

Sonat Inc. (formerly Southern Natural Resources) and its subsidiaries operate in the energy industry through its exploration and production and natural gas transmission and marketing segments. Operating income by segment in recent years were as follow:

	1994	1993	1992
Exploration and Production	38%	37%	26%
Natural Gas Transmission and Marketing	59%	62%	72%
Other	3%	1%	3%

The company is engaged in the exploration for and the acquisition, development and production of oil and natural gas in the U.S. through Sonat Exploration Co. Sonat Exploration's strategy is to acquire gas properties with significant development potential. Since this strategy was implemented in 1988, Sonat Exploration's reserves have grown six-fold to 1.6 tcfe at December 31, 1994. Proved reserves totaled 1,367,300,000 Mcf of natural gas and 31,627,000 bbl. of oil at 1994 year end. Net sales volumes in 1994 consisted of 182,000,000 Mcf of natural gas, 4,155,000 bbl. of oil and condensate and 1,227,000 bbl. of natural gas liquids.

Sonat participates in the natural gas transmission and marketing business through Southern Natural Gas Co., Citrus Corp. (50% owned) and Sonat Marketing Co. Southern Natural Gas Co. operates an interstate pipeline system serving markets in seven states in the Southeast. Total volume transported in 1994 was 886 bcf. Citrus Corp. owns Southern and Florida Gas Transmission, which is the principal supplier of natural gas to Florida. Total 1994 volume was 325 bcf. Sonat Marketing Co. markets the majority of the natural gas production of Sonat Exploration. Adding the Sonat Exploration volumes has enabled it to expand its presence in Gulf Coast, Midwest and Northeast markets and to begin building a significant base of sales of natural gas acquired from unaffiliated producers. Total natural gas equivalent sales volumes rose to 482 bcf in 1994 from 285 bcf in 1993.

Important Developments

Jul. '95—SNT announced the sale of its 11,252,300 share investment in Sonat Offshore Drilling Inc. in an underwritten secondary offering for $340 million; the company netted approximately $210 million in cash. Separately, the company reported fractionally lower revenues for the first six months of 1995, compared to 1994. Lower natural gas prices of $1.48 per Mcf versus $2.03 per Mcf led to decreased revenues and income for the period. Net income was also restricted by the sale of properties, a loss related to the company's sale of its investment in Baker Hughes preferred stock, and a gain on the termination of certain long-term gas sales contracts.

Capitalization

Long Term Debt: $1,070,433,000 (3/95).

Per Share Data ($) (Year Ended Dec. 31)

	1994	1993	1992	1991	1990	1989
Tangible Bk. Val.	16.11	15.64	13.62	12.14	13.58	13.66
Cash Flow	4.58	5.66	3.79	3.47	3.66	3.33
Earnings	1.62	3.05	1.17	0.91	1.30	1.33
Dividends	1.08	1.04	1.00	1.00	1.00	1.00
Payout Ratio	67%	34%	85%	110%	77%	75%
Prices - High	34⅞	9¼	24⅛	23¾	28	25¼
- Low	26	2⅜	14½	15½	21½	14⅜
P/E Ratio - High	22	12	21	26	22	19
- Low	16	8	12	17	17	11

Income Statement Analysis (Million $)

	1994	%Chg	1993	%Chg	1992	%Chg	1991
Revs.	1,774	2%	1,741	17%	1,484	4%	1,421
Oper. Inc.	484	5%	459	5%	436	3%	424
Depr.	258	14%	226	NM	225	20%	187
Int. Exp.	87.0	-4%	91.0	-22%	116	-15%	137
Pretax Inc.	157	-57%	368	169%	137	37%	100
Eff. Tax Rate	10%	—	28%	—	26%	—	23%
Net Inc.	141	-47%	265	162%	101	29%	78.0

Balance Sheet & Other Fin. Data (Million $)

	1994	1993	1992	1991	1990	1989
Cash	9.0	11.0	58.0	24.0	22.0	15.0
Curr. Assets	387	464	649	632	643	682
Total Assets	3,531	3,214	3,165	3,208	3,196	3,084
Curr. Liab.	570	633	448	484	535	606
LT Debt	963	741	1,176	1,315	1,086	928
Common Eqty.	1,392	1,363	1,172	1,043	1,165	1,123
Total Cap.	2,543	2,297	2,556	2,552	2,507	2,331
Cap. Exp.	448	516	226	478	592	426
Cash Flow	399	491	326	298	313	272

Ratio Analysis

	1994	1993	1992	1991	1990	1989
Curr. Ratio	0.7	0.7	1.4	1.3	1.2	1.1
% LT Debt of Cap.	37.9	32.3	46.0	51.5	43.3	39.8
% Net Inc.of Revs.	8.0	15.2	6.8	5.5	7.3	6.1
% Ret. on Assets	4.2	8.3	3.2	2.4	3.5	3.5
% Ret. on Equity	10.3	20.8	9.1	7.1	9.5	9.8

Dividend Data —Dividends have been paid since 1936. A dividend reinvestment plan is available. A "poison pill" stock purchase rights plan was adopted in 1986.

Amt. of Div. $	Date Decl.	Ex-Div. Date	Stock of Record	Payment Date
0.270	Jul. 28	Aug. 25	Aug. 31	Sep. 14 '94
0.270	Oct. 27	Nov. 23	Nov. 30	Dec. 14 '94
0.270	Jan. 26	Feb. 22	Feb. 28	Mar. 14 '95
0.270	Apr. 27	May. 24	May. 31	Jun. 14 '95
0.270	Jul. 27	Aug. 29	Aug. 31	Sep. 14 '95

Data as orig. reptd.; bef. results of disc. opers. and/or spec. items. Per share data adj. for stk. divs. as of ex-div. date. E-Estimated. NA-Not Available. NM-Not Meaningful. NR-Not Ranked.

Office—AmSouth-Sonat Tower, Birmingham, AL 35203. **Tel**—(205) 325-3800. **Chrmn, Pres & CEO**—R. L. Kuehn, Jr. **VP-Fin & Treas**—T. W. Barker, Jr. **VP & Secy**—Beverley T. Krannich. **Investor Contact**—Bruce L. Connery. **Dirs**—W. O. Bourke, J. J. Creedon, R. C. Goizueta, R. L. Kuehn, Jr., C. Marshall, B. F. Payton, J. J. Phelan, Jr., J. J. Richardson, D. G. Russell, L. E. Smart, A. M. Tocklin, J. B. Williams, J. B. Wyatt. **Transfer Agent & Registrar**—Chemical Bank, NYC. **Incorporated** in Delaware in 1935. **Empl**-1,800. **S&P Analyst:** Michael C. Barr

Southern Co.

NYSE Symbol **SO**
In S&P 500

24-AUG-95

Industry:
Utilities-Electric

Summary: This major utility holding company, serving much of the southeastern U.S., has diversified its power sources through its 45.7% interest in the two-unit Vogtle nuclear project.

S&P Opinion: Hold (★★★)	Recent Price • 21⅞	Yield • 5.7%
	52 Wk Range • 22⅞-17	12-Mo. P/E • 13.5

Quantitative Evaluations

Outlook
(1 Lowest—5 Highest)
• **2⁻**

Fair Value
• **19¾**

Risk
• **Low**

Earn./Div. Rank
• **A-**

Technical Eval.
• **Bullish** since 10/94

Rel. Strength Rank
(1 Lowest—99 Highest)
• **28**

Insider Activity
• **Neutral**

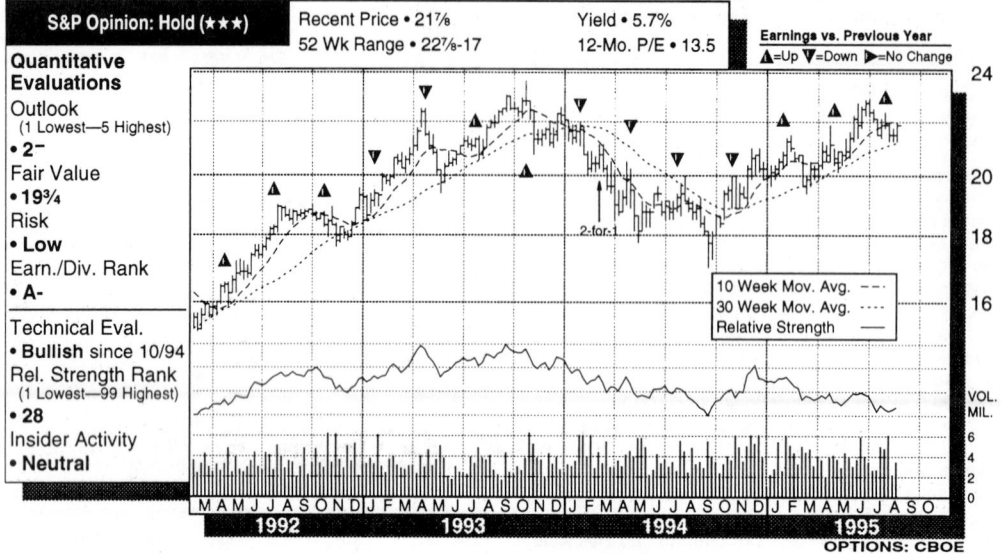

Earnings vs. Previous Year
▲=Up ▼=Down ▶=No Change

10 Week Mov. Avg. ---
30 Week Mov. Avg. ·····
Relative Strength —

OPTIONS: CBOE

Overview - 23-AUG-95

Share earnings in 1995 year should benefit from modestly higher demand for electricity as the southeastern economies in the company's service territory continue to grow. Results should also benefit from the absence of net one-time charges totaling $0.06 a share, including a $0.09 charge to reduce the workforce, and a full year's effect of expense savings from the cutback. Earnings comparisons are not likely to be affected by a gain on the fourth and final sale of the Scherer Unit 4 capacity, since it will be equal to the gain recognized in 1994. The company's cash flow in 1995 should remain at a healthy level. In addition, Southern Company's comparatively modest long term debt is not likely to exceed 45% of total capitalization. Given continued efficiencies from steady growth in kilowatt hours sales, the moderate uptrend in earnings should persist in 1996.

Valuation - 23-AUG-95

Shares have risen about 7% so far in 1995, an average performance compared to the mature utility industry group as a whole. As with most of the publicly held electric companies, SO's market performance is dependent on investors' expectations for interest rates. Given additional Fed easing in 1995, SO's stock price should continue to move up in line with its peers. While the stock yield is below-average, dividend hikes over the next few years should exceed the average for the industry. The company is well positioned within this increasingly competitive industry due to its low rates for industrial customers.

Key Stock Statistics

S&P EPS Est. 1995	1.65	Tang. Bk. Value/Share	12.58
P/E on S&P Est. 1995	13.3	Beta	0.41
S&P EPS Est. 1996	1.71	Shareholders	234,900
Dividend Rate/Share	1.22	Market cap. (B)	$ 14.3
Shs. outstg. (M)	665.5	Inst. holdings	30%
Avg. daily vol. (M)	0.712	Insider holdings	NA

Value of $10,000 invested 5 years ago: $ 21,074

Fiscal Year Ending Dec. 31

	1995	% Change	1994	% Change	1993	% Change
Revenues (Million $)						
1Q	1,929	NM	1,932	5%	1,840	2%
2Q	2,184	6%	2,069	NM	2,068	3%
3Q	—	—	2,381	-10%	2,636	10%
4Q	—	—	1,915	-2%	1,945	4%
Yr.	—	—	8,297	-2%	8,489	5%
Income (Million $)						
1Q	206.3	45%	142.0	-20%	177.0	-4%
2Q	268.0	5%	256.0	2%	250.0	12%
3Q	—	—	416.0	-6%	442.0	9%
4Q	—	—	175.0	32%	133.0	-6%
Yr.	—	—	989.0	-1%	1,002	5%
Earnings Per Share ($)						
1Q	0.31	41%	0.22	-21%	0.28	-5%
2Q	0.40	3%	0.39	-1%	0.39	13%
3Q	E0.65	2%	0.64	-7%	0.69	8%
4Q	E0.29	7%	0.27	29%	0.21	-7%
Yr.	E1.65	9%	1.52	-3%	1.57	4%

Next earnings report expected: late October

Business Summary - 23-AUG-95

The Southern Company is a utility holding company whose subsidiaries, Alabama Power, Georgia Power, Gulf Power, Mississippi Power, and Savannah Electric & Power (acquired 1988), serve over 3.4 million retail customers in the Southeast. Electric revenues by customer class:

	1994	1993	1992	1991
Residential	32%	32%	30%	30%
Commercial	29%	27%	27%	26%
Industrial	27%	26%	26%	26%
Other	12%	15%	17%	18%

The textiles, chemical and paper industry comprised roughly one-third of SO's industrial customer base, which accounted for 36% of total 1994 energy sales. In 1994, SO system's peak load was 25,937 mw and system capability at peak totaled 29,513 mw, for a capacity margin of 12%. Power requirements were derived from coal 71%, nuclear 18%, hydro 4%, oil/gas 1%, and purchased power 6%.

The company estimates capital expenditures for ongoing construction programs of $1.4 billion in 1995, $1.3 billion in 1996 and $1.3 billion in 1997. They include construction of combustion turbine peaking units to add about 1,100 megawatts by 1997, and significant outlays for transmission and distribution facilities as well as to upgrade existing generating plants to extend their useful lives. Outlays for construction projects in 1994 totaled $1.5 billion. SO expects to continue to make significant investments in subsidiaries related to its core business to provide sustainable earnings growth in the future.

To comply with emissions limits set by the Clean Air Act Amendments of 1990, SO estimates systemwide compliance-related construction expenditures of about $275 million through 1995. Additional compliance-related construction costs during the period 1996 through 2000 are estimated at between $450 million and $800 million.

Important Developments

Jul. '95—The company reported a 16% rise in earnings per share for the six months ended June 30, 1995, to $0.71 from $0.61 a year earlier. The increase reflected the absence of a 1994 one-time net charge to income for workforce reductions of $0.06 and 2.5% more shares outstanding. SO noted that retail customer demand rose 3.4%, including growth of 2.5% for residential consumers and 4.1% for the industrial sector.

Capitalization

Long Term Debt: $7,242,629,000 (3/95).
Subsidiary Pfd. Stock: $1,332,203,000.

Per Share Data ($)

(Year Ended Dec. 31)

	1994	1993	1992	1991	1990	1989
Tangible Bk. Val.	12.46	11.79	11.05	10.72	10.57	10.54
Earnings	1.52	1.57	1.51	1.39	0.96	1.34
Dividends	1.18	1.14	1.10	1.07	1.07	1.07
Payout Ratio	78%	73%	73%	77%	112%	80%
Prices - High	22⅛	23⅝	19⅝	17⅜	14¾	14⅞
- Low	17	18½	15¼	12⅞	11½	11
P/E Ratio - High	15	15	13	13	15	11
- Low	11	12	10	9	12	8

Income Statement Analysis (Million $)

	1994	%Chg	1993	%Chg	1992	%Chg	1991
Revs.	8,297	-2%	8,489	5%	8,073	NM	8,050
Depr.	821	4%	793	3%	768	NM	763
Maint.	660	1%	653	7%	613	-4%	637
Fxd. Chgs. Cov.	3.3	-18%	4.0	40%	2.9	9%	2.6
Constr. Credits	29.0	32%	22.0	NM	22.0	-29%	31.0
Eff. Tax Rate	39%	—	35%	—	37%	—	34%
Net Inc.	989	-1%	1,002	5%	953	9%	876

Balance Sheet & Other Fin. Data (Million $)

	1994	1993	1992	1991	1990	1989
Gross Prop.	30,694	28,947	27,955	27,313	26,809	26,532
Cap. Exp.	1,536	1,441	1,105	1,123	1,185	1,346
Net Prop.	21,117	20,013	16,489	16,609	16,811	16,998
Capitalization:						
LT Debt	7,593	7,411	7,241	7,992	8,458	8,575
% LT Debt	44	45	46	49	51	51
Pfd.	1,432	1,333	1,359	1,333	1,358	1,400
% Pfd.	8.30	8.10	8.60	8.20	8.20	8.30
Common	8,186	7,684	7,234	6,976	6,783	6,861
% Common	48	47	46	43	41	41
Total Cap.	23,063	22,358	16,791	17,305	17,662	17,947

Ratio Analysis

	1994	1993	1992	1991	1990	1989
Oper. Ratio	79.3	79.2	78.2	78.4	79.6	78.5
% Earn. on Net Prop.	8.3	9.7	10.6	10.4	9.6	9.5
% Ret. on Revs.	11.9	11.8	11.8	10.9	7.6	11.3
% Ret. On Invest.Cap	7.6	9.3	10.5	10.2	8.6	9.7
% Return On Com.Eqty	12.5	13.4	13.4	12.7	8.9	12.5

Dividend Data

—Dividends have been paid since 1948. A dividend reinvestment plan is available.

Amt. of Div. $	Date Decl.	Ex-Div. Date	Stock of Record	Payment Date
0.295	Jul. 18	Jul. 26	Aug. 01	Sep. 06 '94
0.295	Oct. 17	Nov. 01	Nov. 07	Dec. 06 '94
0.305	Jan. 16	Jan. 31	Feb. 06	Mar. 06 '95
0.305	Apr. 17	Apr. 25	May. 01	Jun. 06 '95
0.305	Jul. 17	Aug. 03	Aug. 07	Sep. 06 '95

Data as orig. reptd.; bef. results of disc opers. and/or spec. items. Per share data adj. for stk. divs. as of ex-div. date. E-Estimated. NA-Not Available. NM-Not Meaningful. NR-Not Ranked.

Office—64 Perimeter Center East, Atlanta, GA 30346. Tel—(404) 393-0650. Chrmn, CEO & Pres—A. W. Dahlberg. Secy—T. Chisholm. VP-Fin—W. L. Westbrook. Investor Contact—Carl West (212-269-8842). Dirs—J. C. Adams, A. D. Correll, A. W. Dahlberg, P. J. DeNicola, J. Edwards, J.M. Farley, H. A. Franklin, B. S. Gordon, L. G. Hardman III, E. B. Harris, W. A. Parker Jr., G. J. St. Pe, W. J. Rushton III, G. M. Shatto, H. Stockham. Transfer Agent & Registrar—Company's office. Incorporated in Delaware in 1945. Empl-27,826. S&P Analyst: Jane Collin

STANDARD & POOR'S
STOCK REPORTS

Southwest Airlines

NYSE Symbol **LUV**
In S&P 500

01-OCT-95

Industry:
Air Transport

Summary: This airline, with operating costs among the lowest in the industry, provides low-fare, high-frequency service to markets primarily in the midwestern, southwestern and western U.S.

S&P Opinion: Accumulate (★★★★)

Recent Price • 25⅛
52 Wk Range • 29⅞-15½

Yield • 0.2%
12-Mo. P/E • 24.4

Quantitative Evaluations

Outlook
(1 Lowest—5 Highest)
• **4+**

Fair Value
• **26¼**

Risk
• **Average**

Earn./Div. Rank
• **B+**

Technical Eval.
• **Bullish** since 5/95

Rel. Strength Rank
(1 Lowest—99 Highest)
• **22**

Insider Activity
• **Unfavorable**

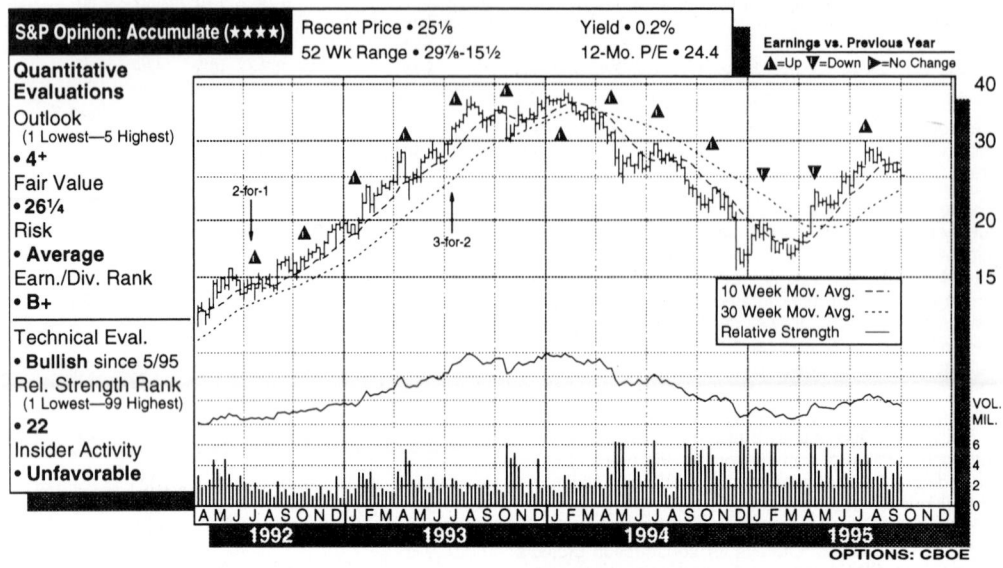

Earnings vs. Previous Year
▲=Up ▼=Down ▶=No Change

10 Week Mov. Avg. — · —
30 Week Mov. Avg. - - - -
Relative Strength —

VOL.
MIL.

OPTIONS: CBOE

Overview - 27-SEP-95

Revenues should rise fairly strongly in 1995. Traffic is expected to grow robustly, reflecting strong industry conditions as well as current fleet expansion plans (currently at about 12%). Yields are projected to benefit from higher fares and a reduction in promotional discounting, which was needed to establish several new markets. Margins should hold steady with the company's traditionally strong expense control and improvements in aircraft scheduling and passenger ticketing. Interest expense should increase slightly.

Valuation - 27-SEP-95

LUV shares have rebounded in recent months following a steep and steady decline since early 1994. Fueling the stock's growth have been favorable industry traffic growth, higher average fares and lower promotional expenses from a slower rate of expansion into new markets. Competition is heating up in certain western markets, but Southwest, the low-cost leader is still able to generate an acceptable profit on these routes, unlike most of its competitors. Similarly, while the 1996 expansion into Florida might be difficult given the importance of the area to a large number of airlines, Southwest should ultimately profit. We view the shares of this growth airline as attractive at 16 times our estimate of 1996 earnings.

Key Stock Statistics

S&P EPS Est. 1995	1.20	Tang. Bk. Value/Share	9.13
P/E on S&P Est. 1995	20.9	Beta	1.55
S&P EPS Est. 1996	1.60	Shareholders	10,700
Dividend Rate/Share	0.04	Market cap. (B)	$ 3.6
Shs. outstg. (M)	143.8	Inst. holdings	47%
Avg. daily vol. (M)	0.604	Insider holdings	NA

Value of $10,000 invested 5 years ago: $ 47,808

Fiscal Year Ending Dec. 31

	1995	% Change	1994	% Change	1993	% Change
Revenues (Million $)						
1Q	621.0	NM	619.4	24%	499.0	33%
2Q	738.2	12%	661.1	16%	568.0	36%
3Q	—	—	685.3	10%	621.0	39%
4Q	—	—	626.2	3%	608.6	36%
Yr.	—	—	2,592	13%	2,297	36%
Income (Million $)						
1Q	11.83	-72%	41.85	68%	24.93	85%
2Q	59.72	2%	58.52	40%	41.89	78%
3Q	—	—	58.62	20%	48.83	82%
4Q	—	—	20.34	-47%	38.37	41%
Yr.	—	—	179.3	16%	154.3	70%
Earnings Per Share ($)						
1Q	0.08	-71%	0.28	65%	0.17	70%
2Q	0.41	3%	0.40	38%	0.29	74%
3Q	E0.44	10%	0.40	21%	0.33	77%
4Q	E0.27	93%	0.14	-46%	0.26	35%
Yr.	E1.20	-2%	1.22	16%	1.05	62%

Next earnings report expected: late October

Southwest Airlines

Business Summary - 25-JUL-95

Southwest Airlines is a major domestic airline that provides shorthaul, high frequency, point-to-point, low fare service to 44 cities, primarily in the midwestern, southwestern and western states.

Operating data (including Morris Air in 1993) in recent years (passenger- and seat-miles in billions):

	1994	1993	1992
Rev. pass-miles	21.61	18.83	13.79
Avail. seat-miles	32.12	27.51	21.37
Load factor %	67.3	68.4	64.5
Rev. per RPM (cents)	11.56	11.77	11.78
Cost per ASM (cents)	7.08	7.25	7.03

Southwest has maintained a cost advantage by increasing asset utilization. The point-to-point route system, as compared to hub-and-spoke, provides for more direct routings for shorthaul customers and, therefore, minimizes stops, connections, delays, and total trip time. Aircraft are scheduled to minimize the amount of time the aircraft is at the gate, generally less than 20 minutes, thereby reducing the number of aircraft and gate facilities that would otherwise be required.

Also enhancing Southwest's ability to sustain high productivity and reliable ontime performance is a preference to serve satellite or downtown airports; consequently, the airline avoids many congested hub airports. In addition, by using only one type of aircraft, the company drastically simplifies scheduling, maintenance, flight operations and training activities.

At December 31, 1994, the Southwest fleet consisted of 199 Boeing 737 aircraft, with an average age of 7.6 years. In addition, there were commitments to acquire 118 more B-737s through 2004.

Important Developments

Jul. '95—Passenger traffic increased 6.7%, year to year, in the first five months of 1995. Capacity was up 13.8%, and the load factor was 64.2%, against 68.5%.
Mar. '95—The company began participating in the SABRE Travel Information Network computer reservations system (CRS). In May 1994, certain CRSs disabled their automated ticketing function for Southwest travel.
Jan. '95—Southwest reached an agreement with its pilots union. The 10-year contract call for the payment of stock options in exchange for, among other things, maintaining current pay rates for the first five years, with 3% raises in three of the final five years.

Capitalization

Long Term Debt: $675,949,000 (3/95).

Per Share Data ($)

(Year Ended Dec. 31)

	1994	1993	1992	1991	1990	1989
Tangible Bk. Val.	8.65	7.38	6.16	4.97	4.79	4.47
Cash Flow	2.26	1.94	1.41	0.89	0.98	1.06
Earnings	1.22	1.05	0.65	0.21	0.37	0.53
Dividends	0.04	0.04	0.04	0.03	0.03	0.03
Payout Ratio	3%	4%	5%	16%	9%	6%
Prices - High	39	37⅝	19⅞	11⅝	6⅝	6⅞
- Low	15½	18⅛	10¾	5½	4¼	4⅜
P/E Ratio - High	32	36	31	56	18	13
- Low	13	17	17	26	12	8

Income Statement Analysis (Million $)

	1994	%Chg	1993	%Chg	1992	%Chg	1991
Revs.	2,592	13%	2,297	36%	1,685	28%	1,314
Oper. Inc.	470	8%	434	49%	291	95%	149
Depr.	153	17%	131	21%	108	25%	86.2
Int. Exp.	53.4	-9%	58.5	NM	58.9	34%	43.9
Pretax Inc.	300	15%	260	77%	147	NM	44.0
Eff. Tax Rate	40%	—	41%	—	38%	—	39%
Net Inc.	179	16%	154	69%	91.0	NM	26.9

Balance Sheet & Other Fin. Data (Million $)

	1994	1993	1992	1991	1990	1989
Cash	175	296	411	261	88.0	146
Curr. Assets	315	432	506	340	158	204
Total Assets	2,823	2,576	2,293	1,837	1,471	1,415
Curr. Liab.	522	479	368	260	225	196
LT Debt	583	639	699	617	327	354
Common Eqty.	1,239	1,054	854	629	605	587
Total Cap.	2,055	1,877	1,687	1,351	1,041	1,060
Cap. Exp.	789	530	533	341	318	262
Cash Flow	333	285	199	113	127	144

Ratio Analysis

	1994	1993	1992	1991	1990	1989
Curr. Ratio	0.6	0.9	1.4	1.3	0.7	1.0
% LT Debt of Cap.	28.4	34.1	41.4	45.7	31.4	33.4
% Net Inc.of Revs.	6.9	6.7	5.4	2.0	4.0	7.0
% Ret. on Assets	6.6	6.3	4.2	1.6	3.3	5.4
% Ret. on Equity	15.6	16.0	11.8	4.4	8.1	12.8

Dividend Data —Dividends were initiated in 1976. A "poison pill" stock purchase rights plan was adopted in 1986.

Amt. of Div. $	Date Decl.	Ex-Div. Date	Stock of Record	Payment Date
0.010	Jul. 22	Aug. 30	Sep. 06	Sep. 27 '94
0.010	Nov. 18	Nov. 30	Dec. 06	Jan. 03 '95
0.010	Jan. 24	Feb. 27	Mar. 03	Mar. 28 '95
0.010	May. 19	May. 26	Jun. 02	Jun. 27 '95
0.010	Jul. 28	Sep. 01	Sep. 06	Sep. 27 '95

Data as orig. reptd.; bef. results of disc. opers. and/or spec. items. Per share data adj. for stk. divs. as of ex-div. date. E-Estimated. NA-Not Available. NM-Not Meaningful. NR-Not Ranked.

Office—P.O. Box 36611, Dallas, TX 75235-1611. **Tel**—(214) 904-4000. **Chrmn, Pres & CEO**—H. D. Kelleher. **EVP & Secy**—C. C. Barrett. **VP & CFO**—G. C. Kelly. **Dirs**—S. E. Barshop, G. H. Bishop, C. W. Crockett, W. P. Hobby Jr., T. C. Johnson, H. D. Kelleher, R. W. King, W. M. Mischer Sr., J. M. Morris. **Transfer Agent & Registrar**—Continental Stock Transfer & Trust Co., NYC. **Incorporated** in Texas in 1967. **Empl-** 16,818. **S&P Analyst:** Joe Victor Shammas

Springs Industries

NYSE Symbol **SMI**
In S&P 500

27-AUG-95 | Industry: Home Furnishings

Summary: SMI is a major manufacturer of home furnishings, finished fabrics and industrial fabrics.

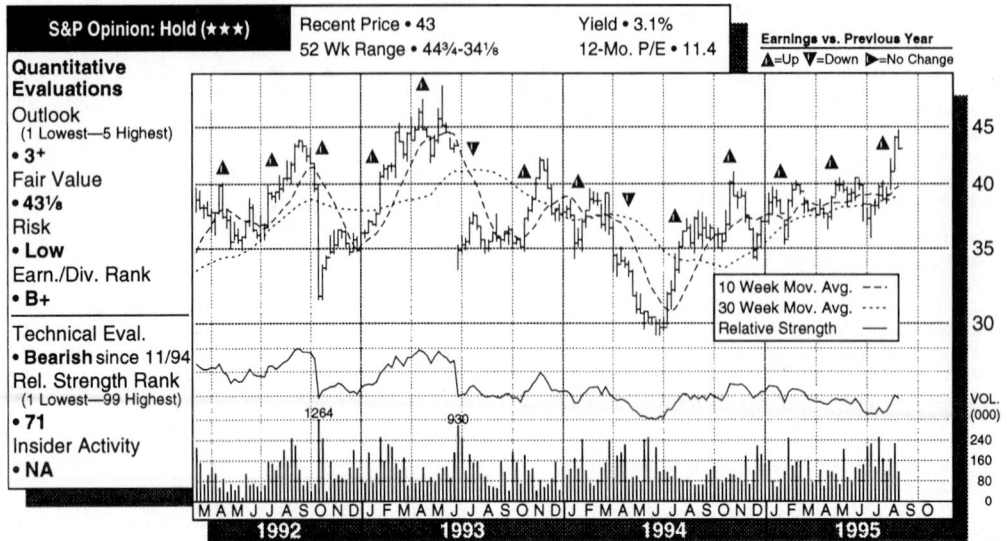

S&P Opinion: Hold (★★★)	Recent Price • 43	Yield • 3.1%
	52 Wk Range • 44¾-34⅛	12-Mo. P/E • 11.4

Quantitative Evaluations

Outlook
(1 Lowest—5 Highest)
• **3+**

Fair Value
• **43⅛**

Risk
• **Low**

Earn./Div. Rank
• **B+**

Technical Eval.
• **Bearish** since 11/94

Rel. Strength Rank
(1 Lowest—99 Highest)
• **71**

Insider Activity
• **NA**

Earnings vs. Previous Year
▲=Up ▼=Down ▶=No Change

10 Week Mov. Avg. - - - -
30 Week Mov. Avg. ·······
Relative Strength ———

Overview - 25-AUG-95

Sales should advance 5% to 7% in 1995, reflecting the recent acquisition of Dundee Mills and Dawson Home Fashions. The home products division will benefit from the recent introduction of the Liz Claiborne at Home line, and from good demand for accessory products, such as bedding products, and window hardware. The industrial fabrics division should be aided by strong demand for fiberglass used in electronics products. Full-year margins are expected to contract somewhat, restricted by the inability to fully pass on higher raw material prices. although some of this pressure could be alleviated toward the end of 1995 by higher selling prices. In the long-term, operations will benefit from NAFTA, which will open new tariff-free markets in North America for SMI's products.

Valuation - 25-AUG-95

The shares have appreciated substantially since the end of 1994, despite stagnant flat sales at existing operations and margin pressures resulting from weak volume and higher raw material prices. We have therefore lowered our opinion on the stock to neutral. At its current price, and based on our EPS projections for 1995 and 1996, we believe that the shares are fully valued, and are not likely to outperform the market in the near-term.

Key Stock Statistics

S&P EPS Est. 1995	3.75	Tang. Bk. Value/Share	32.20
P/E on S&P Est. 1995	11.5	Beta	1.39
S&P EPS Est. 1996	4.10	Shareholders	3,200
Dividend Rate/Share	1.32	Market cap. (B)	$0.866
Shs. outstg. (M)	20.1	Inst. holdings	40%
Avg. daily vol. (M)	0.031	Insider holdings	NA

Value of $10,000 invested 5 years ago: $ 13,912

Fiscal Year Ending Dec. 31

	1995	% Change	1994	% Change	1993	% Change
Revenues (Million $)						
1Q	483.1	NM	485.2	-3%	502.0	8%
2Q	532.7	3%	515.3	6%	483.9	NM
3Q	—	—	535.3	4%	514.5	4%
4Q	—	—	533.2	2%	522.7	-2%
Yr.	—	—	2,069	2%	2,023	2%
Income (Million $)						
1Q	9.87	70%	5.80	-37%	9.16	71%
2Q	14.39	10%	13.08	46%	8.95	-20%
3Q	—	—	19.61	43%	13.67	3%
4Q	—	—	23.73	53%	15.48	6%
Yr.	—	—	62.23	32%	47.26	6%
Earnings Per Share ($)						
1Q	0.55	67%	0.33	-35%	0.51	70%
2Q	0.78	7%	0.73	46%	0.50	-21%
3Q	E1.10	NM	1.10	43%	0.77	3%
4Q	E1.32	-1%	1.34	54%	0.87	6%
Yr.	E3.75	7%	3.50	32%	2.65	6%

Next earnings report expected: mid October

Springs Industries

Business Summary - 13-JUN-95

Springs Industries is a leading maker of home furnishings, finished fabrics and industrial fabrics. Industry segment contributions in 1994 were:

	Sales	Profits
Home furnishings	71%	72%
Specialty fabrics	29%	28%

The home furnishings group produces sheets, pillowcases, bedspreads, comforters, soft window treatments, various bath products and juvenile novelties, sold primarily under the trademarks Springmaid, Wamsutta, Wondercale, Supercale, Andre Richard, Pacific, Custom Designs, Performance, Wabasso and Texmade labels, and private labels. It also produces decorative window products, including drapery hardware, blinds and window shades sold under the trademarks Graber, Fashion Pleat, CrystalPleat and Bali. In 1992, SMI sought to expand this division outside the U.S. by buying the marketing and distribution operations of C. S. Brooks Canada and the Griffiths-Kerr division of Canada-based Finlayson Enterprises, Ltd.

The specialty fabrics business includes a broad range of fabrics sold to apparel manufacturers and to the decorative home furnishings and the home sewing markets. Major brand names include Springmaid, Wamsutta and Ultrasuede. The specialty fabrics business also includes industrial fabrics, consisting of fiberglass industrial fabrics for use in printed electronic circuit boards, reinforced plastic applications, and as a substrate for coating and laminating processes; industrial fabrics for the printing and electrical industries; fabrics for antiballistic vests, sporting goods and various other end-uses; and protective and fire-retardant fabrics.

Important Developments

Jun. '95—SMI closed its acquisition of shower curtain and bath accessories producer Dawson Home Fashions Inc. for an undisclosed amount of cash. In May, Springs completed the acquisition of Dundee Mills Inc., a towel and baby products manufacturer, for $120 million in cash and stock. SMI had earlier announced that it was reorganizing into three operating groups intended to strengthen customer service, align assets and productive capacity more closely with marketing, and focus on costs. The new groups will include bedding, bath, and diversified (which will consist of industrial products, finished fabrics, and window fashions). Dundee and Dawson were to be included in the bath group.

Capitalization

Long Term Debt: $261,786,000 (4/1/95).
Class A Common Stock: 9,777,411 shs. ($0.25 par).
Class B Common Stock: 7,830,375 ($0.25 par); 4 votes per sh.; divd. 10% below Cl. A.; conv. sh.-for-sh. into Cl. A; 99% closely held.

Per Share Data ($)

(Year Ended Dec. 31)

	1994	1993	1992	1991	1990	1989
Tangible Bk. Val.	33.20	30.89	33.47	32.39	32.05	33.08
Cash Flow	7.98	7.03	6.87	5.77	3.72	7.43
Earnings	3.50	2.65	2.50	1.53	-0.39	3.64
Dividends	1.20	1.20	1.20	1.20	1.20	1.20
Payout Ratio	34%	45%	47%	78%	NM	33%
Prices - High	41	49	43⅞	36¼	39½	45¼
- Low	29¼	33½	30½	21¼	16⅞	30½
P/E Ratio - High	12	18	18	24	NM	12
- Low	8	13	12	14	NM	8

Income Statement Analysis (Million $)

	1994	%Chg	1993	%Chg	1992	%Chg	1991
Revs.	2,069	2%	2,023	2%	1,976	5%	1,890
Oper. Inc.	216	8%	200	5%	191	23%	155
Depr.	79.7	2%	78.1	NM	77.7	3%	75.2
Int. Exp.	29.3	-3%	30.3	-4%	31.4	-3%	32.3
Pretax Inc.	107	27%	84.0	5%	80.0	60%	50.0
Eff. Tax Rate	42%	—	44%	—	44%	—	45%
Net Inc.	62.2	32%	47.3	6%	44.5	64%	27.1

Balance Sheet & Other Fin. Data (Million $)

	1994	1993	1992	1991	1990	1989
Cash	1.0	3.0	4.0	6.0	5.0	6.0
Curr. Assets	617	627	603	596	588	607
Total Assets	1,289	1,292	1,250	1,251	1,201	1,188
Curr. Liab.	244	273	275	266	231	252
LT Debt	265	293	274	288	260	228
Common Eqty.	584	543	588	569	561	585
Total Cap.	880	864	896	902	865	878
Cap. Exp.	93.0	88.0	80.0	137	118	119
Cash Flow	142	125	122	102	66.0	132

Ratio Analysis

	1994	1993	1992	1991	1990	1989
Curr. Ratio	2.5	2.3	2.2	2.2	2.5	2.4
% LT Debt of Cap.	30.2	33.9	30.5	31.9	30.1	25.9
% Net Inc.of Revs.	3.0	2.3	2.3	1.4	NM	3.4
% Ret. on Assets	4.8	3.7	3.6	2.2	NM	5.6
% Ret. on Equity	11.0	8.4	7.7	4.8	NM	11.5

Dividend Data —Dividends have been paid since 1898.

Amt. of Div. $	Date Decl.	Ex-Div. Date	Stock of Record	Payment Date
0.300	Aug. 18	Sep. 12	Sep. 16	Sep. 30 '94
0.300	Dec. 12	Dec. 16	Dec. 22	Jan. 03 '95
0.300	Feb. 16	Mar. 06	Mar. 10	Mar. 24 '95
0.300	May. 01	Jun. 14	Jun. 16	Jun. 30 '95
0.330	Aug. 17	Sep. 13	Sep. 15	Sep. 29 '95

Data as orig. reptd.; bef. results of disc. opers. and/or spec. items. Per share data adj. for stk. divs. as of ex-div. date. E-Estimated. NA-Not Available. NM-Not Meaningful. NR-Not Ranked.

Office—205 North White St., Fort Mill, SC 29715. Tel—(803) 547-1500. Chrmn & CEO—W. Y. Elisha. EVP & CFO—S. P. Kelbley. VP & Secy—C. P. Dorsett. VP, Treas & Investor Contract—James F. Zahrn. Dirs—J. F. Akers, C. C. Bowles, J. L. Clendenin, L. S. Close, C. W. Coker, W. Y. Elisha, D. M. Krausse, J. H. McArthur, A. Papone, R. B. Smith, S. H. Smith Jr., S. Turley. Transfer Agent & Registrar—Wachovia Bank of North Carolina, Winston-Salem. Incorporated in South Carolina in 1895. Empl- 20,300. S&P Analyst: Elizabeth Vandeventer

STANDARD & POOR'S
STOCK REPORTS

Sprint Corp.

NYSE Symbol **FON**
In S&P 500

26-OCT-95 | **Industry:** Telecommunications | **Summary:** Sprint is the only major U.S. telephone company with local, long-distance and wireless operations.

| S&P Opinion: Hold (★★★) | Recent Price • 37¾ | Yield • 2.6% |
| | 52 Wk Range • 38¼-25⅞ | 12-Mo. P/E • 13.9 |

Quantitative Evaluations

Outlook
(1 Lowest—5 Highest)
• **4+**

Fair Value
• **40⅛**

Risk
• **Low**

Earn./Div. Rank
• **B**

Technical Eval.
• **Bearish** since 6/95

Rel. Strength Rank
(1 Lowest—99 Highest)
• **87**

Insider Activity
• **Neutral**

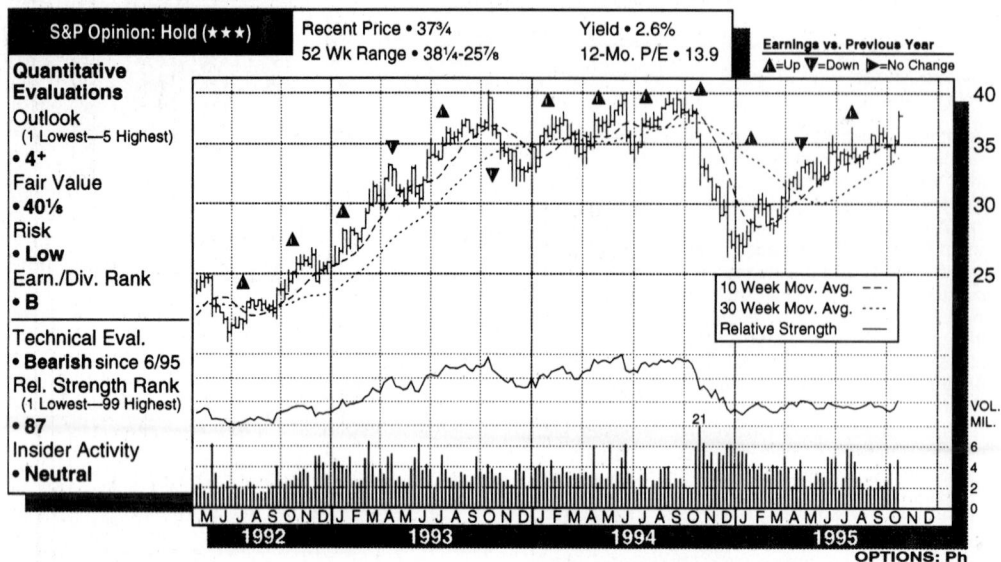

Earnings vs. Previous Year
▲=Up ▼=Down ▶=No Change

10 Week Mov. Avg. ----
30 Week Mov. Avg. ·······
Relative Strength ——

VOL. MIL.

OPTIONS: Ph

Overview - 26-OCT-95

Through alliances with other industry players, FON is seeking to capitalize on the opening of telecommunications markets worldwide and leverage its position as the only major full service telecom carrier in the U.S. An alliance with cable companies will allow FON to offset any marketshare loss if the Baby Bells are allowed into the long-distance market with additional revenues from competitive local telephone operations and new wireless operations; however, significant costs associated with developing these operations may limit near-term earnings gains. If approved by regulators, a proposed alliance with the French and German telephone companies would position FON to benefit from the rapidly growing demand for global telecommunications services. FON will also spin off its fast growing cellular telephone operations in early 1996.

Valuation - 26-OCT-95

The shares have risen sharply in 1995 on strong earnings gains and an agreement in principle regarding the terms of a planned sale of a 20% stake to France Telecom and Deutsche Telekom. FON's cable alliance positions it to benefit from the opening of telecommunications markets in the U.S., while completion of the proposed alliance with the French and German carriers would position it for the opening of worldwide markets as well as provide a significant portion of the cash required to fund the cable venture's ambitious plans. However, the shares are vulnerable if the foreign alliance falls through.

Key Stock Statistics

S&P EPS Est. 1995	2.75	Tang. Bk. Value/Share	11.91
P/E on S&P Est. 1995	13.7	Beta	0.45
S&P EPS Est. 1996	2.84	Shareholders	82,800
Dividend Rate/Share	1.00	Market cap. (B)	$ 13.2
Shs. outstg. (M)	348.6	Inst. holdings	59%
Avg. daily vol. (M)	0.692	Insider holdings	NA

Value of $10,000 invested 5 years ago: $ 12,278

Fiscal Year Ending Dec. 31

	1995	% Change	1994	% Change	1993	% Change
Revenues (Million $)						
1Q	3,272	8%	3,033	12%	2,718	23%
2Q	3,366	7%	3,150	12%	2,801	23%
3Q	3,442	6%	3,234	13%	2,868	23%
4Q	—	—	3,244	9%	2,981	24%
Yr.	—	—	12,662	11%	11,368	9%
Income (Million $)						
1Q	224.3	-1%	227.4	NM	-11.30	NM
2Q	245.7	12%	219.6	33%	165.1	76%
3Q	268.5	17%	230.1	68%	136.7	19%
4Q	—	—	206.6	9%	190.1	61%
Yr.	—	—	883.7	84%	480.6	13%
Earnings Per Share ($)						
1Q	0.64	-2%	0.65	NM	-0.03	NM
2Q	0.70	11%	0.63	31%	0.48	12%
3Q	0.76	15%	0.66	69%	0.39	-25%
4Q	E0.65	10%	0.59	7%	0.55	4%
Yr.	E2.75	9%	2.53	82%	1.39	-28%

Next earnings report expected: late January

Sprint Corp.

Business Summary - 20-OCT-95

Sprint is the second largest independent local telephone service carrier in the U.S. and the third largest long-distance carrier. Contributions in 1994:

	Sales	Income
Long-distance services	52%	34%
Local services	34%	57%
Cellular services	5%	5%
Complementary businesses	9%	4%

The long-distance operation's market share at the end of 1994 was about 9% share of of the U.S. market. At December 31, 1994, local telephone units served over 6.4 million access lines in 19 states. Cellular telephone service was provided to 1,039,989 subscribers in properties covering a population base of 20.5 million (as adjusted for percentage ownership).

Complementary businesses include directory publishing and distribution of telecommunications, electrical and security alarm products.

In June 1994, FON agreed to form an alliance with France Telecom and Deutsche Telekom. Each carrier would have exclusivity over the partnership's services within its home market, while services would be provided elsewhere by a global operating group (50% owned by FON) and a European operating group (33% owned). Under the agreement (revised in June 1995), the French and German companies would spend about $4.1 billion (versus $4.2 billion under the original plan) to purchase a combined 20% stake in FON in a two-part transaction.

Important Developments

Oct. '95—The European Competition Commission reached an agreement in principle allowing the proposed Phoenix joint venture of Sprint, Deutsche Telekom and France Telecom. The Commission is expected to make a final decision by next summer. FCC and shareholder approval are still required.
Jun. '95—Sprint, France Telecom and Deutsche Telekom finalized the terms under which the foreign carriers will buy a 20% stake in Sprint for $3.5 billion.
Mar. '95—The first phase of FCC auctions for broadband personal communications services (PCS) licenses was completed. FON's joint venture with cable operators Tele-Communications Inc., Comcast Corp. and Cox Cable won licenses in 29 U.S. major trading areas for $2.1 billion. The venture will provide a broad range of communications services. The cable companies plan to upgrade their systems to allow for delivery of broadband telephone services marketed under the Sprint brand. Capital expenditures for development of local service and PCS systems are expected to be at a high level in 1995.

Capitalization

Long Term Debt: $5,473,500,000 (9/95).
Red. Preferred Stock: $32,700,000.

Per Share Data ($)

(Year Ended Dec. 31)

	1994	1993	1992	1991	1990	1989
Tangible Bk. Val.	10.96	9.26	12.75	11.54	10.30	9.42
Cash Flow	6.77	5.35	7.35	7.04	6.21	6.14
Earnings	2.53	1.39	1.93	1.68	1.43	1.72
Dividends	1.00	1.00	1.00	1.00	1.00	0.97
Payout Ratio	40%	72%	52%	60%	70%	56%
Prices - High	40⅛	40¼	26¾	31½	46⅜	43¾
- Low	26⅛	25½	20¾	21¼	20⅝	22
P/E Ratio - High	16	29	14	19	32	25
- Low	10	18	11	13	14	13

Income Statement Analysis (Million $)

	1994	%Chg	1993	%Chg	1992	%Chg	1991
Revs.	12,662	11%	11,368	23%	9,230	5%	8,780
Oper. Inc.	3,266	25%	2,609	16%	2,248	3%	2,177
Depr.	1,478	9%	1,359	14%	1,192	2%	1,164
Int. Exp.	407	-10%	452	14%	395	-6%	421
Pretax Inc.	1,404	81%	776	18%	656	8%	607
Eff. Tax Rate	36%	—	38%	—	35%	—	32%
Net Inc.	884	84%	481	13%	427	16%	368

Balance Sheet & Other Fin. Data (Million $)

	1994	1993	1992	1991	1990	1989
Cash	123	207	109	74.0	119	115
Curr. Assets	2,189	1,978	1,444	1,618	1,777	1,509
Total Assets	14,936	14,149	10,188	10,464	10,553	9,821
Curr. Liab.	3,055	3,069	2,507	2,326	2,438	2,279
LT Debt	4,605	4,571	3,535	3,696	3,974	3,747
Common Eqty.	4,525	3,918	2,814	2,519	2,296	2,073
Total Cap.	10,426	9,711	7,339	7,910	7,896	7,416
Cap. Exp.	2,016	1,595	1,151	1,244	1,566	1,730
Cash Flow	2,359	1,839	1,617	1,529	1,389	1,284

Ratio Analysis

	1994	1993	1992	1991	1990	1989
Curr. Ratio	0.7	0.6	0.6	0.7	0.7	0.7
% LT Debt of Cap.	44.2	47.1	48.2	46.7	50.3	50.5
% Net Inc.of Revs.	7.0	4.2	4.6	4.2	3.7	4.8
% Ret. on Assets	6.0	3.5	4.1	3.5	3.0	3.7
% Ret. on Equity	20.7	12.1	15.8	15.0	13.8	18.2

Dividend Data —Dividends have been paid since 1939. A dividend reinvestment plan is available. A new "poison pill" stock purchase rights plan was adopted in 1989.

Amt. of Div. $	Date Decl.	Ex-Div. Date	Stock of Record	Payment Date
0.250	Oct. 11	Dec. 02	Dec. 08	Dec. 29 '94
0.250	Feb. 21	Mar. 03	Mar. 09	Mar. 31 '95
0.250	Apr. 18	Jun. 02	Jun. 08	Jun. 30 '95
0.250	Aug. 08	Sep. 05	Sep. 07	Sep. 29 '95
0.250	Oct. 03	Dec. 04	Dec. 06	Dec. 28 '95

Data as orig. reptd.; bef. results of disc. opers. and/or spec. items. Per share data adj. for stk. divs. as of ex-div. date.
E-Estimated. NA-Not Available. NM-Not Meaningful. NR-Not Ranked.

Office—2330 Shawnee Mission Pkwy., Westwood, KS 66205 (P.O. Box 11315, Kansas City, MO 64112). **Tel**—(913) 624-3000. **Chrmn & CEO**—W. T. Esrey. **Exec VP-CFO**—A. B. Krause. **VP-Secy**—D. A. Jensen. **Investor Contact**—Greg Block. **Dirs**—D. Ausley, W. L. Batts, R. M. Davis, W. T. Esrey, D. J. Hall, P. H. Henson, H. S. Hook, R. E. R. Huntley, R. T. LeMay, L. Koch Lorimer, C. H. Price II, F. E. Reed, C. E. Rice, S. Turley. **Transfer Agents & Registrars**—United Missouri Bank, Kansas City, MO; Chemical Bank, NYC. **Incorporated** in Kansas in 1938. **Empl**-50,500. **S&P Analyst:** Kevin J. Gooley

Stanley Works

NYSE Symbol **SWK**
In S&P 500

06-SEP-95

Industry:
Building

Summary: Stanley Works is a worldwide producer of tools, hardware and specialty hardware for home improvement, consumer, industrial and professional use.

S&P Opinion: Hold (★★★)	Recent Price • 44⅝	Yield • 3.2%
	52 Wk Range • 44⅞-34⅞	12-Mo. P/E • 15.7

Earnings vs. Previous Year
▲=Up ▼=Down ▶=No Change

Quantitative Evaluations

Outlook
(1 Lowest—5 Highest)
• **3-**

Fair Value
• **44⅝**

Risk
• **Low**

Earn./Div. Rank
• **B+**

Technical Eval.
• **Bullish** since 12/94

Rel. Strength Rank
(1 Lowest—99 Highest)
• **79**

Insider Activity
• **Neutral**

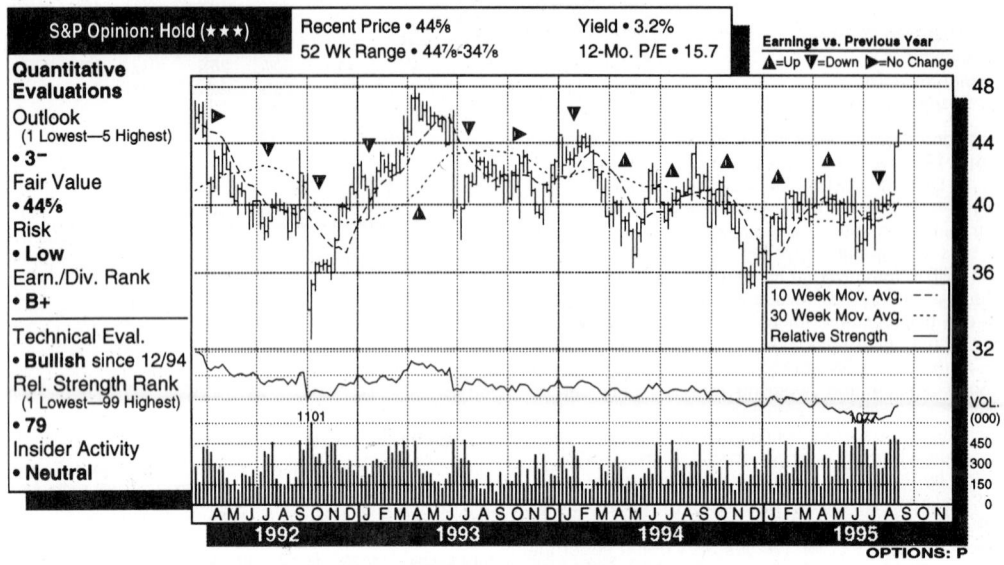

10 Week Mov. Avg. — - —
30 Week Mov. Avg. - - - -
Relative Strength ——

OPTIONS: P

Overview - 06-SEP-95

Sales are expected to be slightly higher in 1995, boosted mostly by strength in U.S. industrial markets and growth in European sales. The level of sales growth is likely to be restricted by the slowing domestic economy, which has brought about sluggish orders in retail and construction markets, although the recent drop in long-term interest rates could spark those areas in the latter part of the year. Margins are likely to be little changed. Cost reduction efforts and lower charges for environmental expenses and facility closings should aid the bottom line, but are likely to be offset by the impact of lower than budgeted sales levels and costs of closing and integrating mechanics tool facilities.

Valuation - 06-SEP-95

The company's shares, which fell sharply upon its June 1995 announcement that orders were slowing in certain important markets, have surged since Stanley unveiled an aggressive growth and cost cutting strategy in the following month. Despite Stanley's strong commitment to growth initiatives, the moderating U.S. economy and sluggish retail markets are likely to hinder SWK's operating performance in upcoming periods. Given those modest expectations, SWK shares appear fairly valued in their recent trading range.

Key Stock Statistics

S&P EPS Est. 1995	2.90	Tang. Bk. Value/Share	13.22
P/E on S&P Est. 1995	15.4	Beta	1.11
S&P EPS Est. 1996	3.15	Shareholders	17,600
Dividend Rate/Share	1.44	Market cap. (B)	$ 2.0
Shs. outstg. (M)	44.4	Inst. holdings	67%
Avg. daily vol. (M)	0.136	Insider holdings	NA

Value of $10,000 invested 5 years ago: $ 13,818

Fiscal Year Ending Dec. 31

	1995	% Change	1994	% Change	1993	% Change
Revenues (Million $)						
1Q	643.3	10%	585.7	6%	553.4	10%
2Q	655.5	4%	628.8	11%	565.2	NM
3Q	—	—	632.6	10%	576.3	4%
4Q	—	—	663.8	15%	578.2	-3%
Yr.	—	—	2,511	10%	2,273	2%
Income (Million $)						
1Q	28.70	12%	25.60	11%	23.00	31%
2Q	31.50	-7%	33.70	25%	27.00	-6%
3Q	—	—	32.20	29%	25.00	-2%
4Q	—	—	33.80	92%	17.60	-33%
Yr.	—	—	125.3	35%	92.60	-6%
Earnings Per Share ($)						
1Q	0.65	14%	0.57	12%	0.51	34%
2Q	0.71	-5%	0.75	25%	0.60	-5%
3Q	E0.72	NM	0.72	29%	0.56	NM
4Q	E0.82	8%	0.76	95%	0.39	-33%
Yr.	E2.90	4%	2.80	36%	2.06	-4%

Next earnings report expected: mid October

Business Summary - 06-SEP-95

The Stanley Works makes hand tools and hardware products for the home improvement, consumer, industrial and professional markets. Contributions by industry segment in 1994 were:

	Sales	Profits
Tools	75%	79%
Hardware	12%	12%
Specialty hardware	13%	9%

International operations accounted for 28% of sales and 21% of operating income in 1994. The company's operations abroad are principally in the European Economic Community. Other important areas are Canada, the Far East, Australia and Latin America.

Consumer tools include hand tools such as measuring instruments, planes, hammers, knives, wrenches, sockets, screwdrivers, saws, chisels, boring tools, masonry, tile and drywall tools, and paint preparation and application tools. The company also makes industrial and mechanics' tools and high-density industrial storage and retrieval systems. Engineered tools include air, hydraulic and fastening tools and fasteners.

The hardware segment makes hinges, hasps, brackets, bolts and latches; closet hardware, organizer systems and shelving; screen and storm door hardware, and hardware for sliding, folding and pocket doors; and residential door hardware, mirrors and mirrored closet doors.

Specialty hardware includes residential door systems such as original and replacement garage and entry doors; power-operated doors and gates; and home automation products, including garage door openers and electronic controls.

A large portion of SWK's products are sold through home centers and mass merchandisers in the U.S.

Important Developments

Jul. '95—In reporting a 6.5% year-to-year decline in net income for the second quarter of 1995, on a 4.2% gain in sales, Stanley said that the disappointing results reflected a sudden decrease in orders within U.S. consumer and construction related markets. SWK attributed the weakening order activity to both soft retail markets and the effort by some retailers to reduce inventory levels. Stanley also outlined its new growth initiatives, which include an assessment of its business and organizational strategies to optimize future performance, as well as activities targeted at expanding its markets and geographic reach. SWK said that to ensure that resources are available to institute the growth strategies, it planned to take $150 million out of its cost structure by the end of 1997. Although it expected to record restructuring charges for the growth initiatives, the extent and timing were unknown.

Capitalization

Long Term Debt: $396,300,000 (6/95).

Per Share Data ($)

(Year Ended Dec. 31)

	1994	1993	1992	1991	1990	1989
Tangible Bk. Val.	13.04	11.40	11.47	12.55	14.38	13.15
Cash Flow	4.21	3.47	3.51	3.62	3.94	4.00
Earnings	2.80	2.06	2.15	2.31	2.53	2.71
Dividends	1.38	1.34	1.28	1.22	1.14	1.02
Payout Ratio	49%	65%	60%	58%	44%	37%
Prices - High	44⅞	47⅞	48⅛	44	40	39¼
- Low	34⅞	37⅞	32½	26	26⅜	27½
P/E Ratio - High	16	23	22	19	16	14
- Low	12	18	15	11	10	10

Income Statement Analysis (Million $)

	1994	%Chg	1993	%Chg	1992	%Chg	1991
Revs.	2,511	10%	2,273	2%	2,218	13%	1,962
Oper. Inc.	330	22%	271	NM	270	2%	266
Depr.	63.3	NM	63.1	1%	62.4	2%	61.4
Int. Exp.	33.6	5%	32.0	-3%	33.1	-13%	38.0
Pretax Inc.	202	36%	148	-6%	158	NM	157
Eff. Tax Rate	38%	—	37%	—	38%	—	39%
Net Inc.	125	34%	93.0	-5%	98.0	3%	95.0

Balance Sheet & Other Fin. Data (Million $)

	1994	1993	1992	1991	1990	1989
Cash	69.3	43.7	81.1	58.3	94.7	55.4
Curr. Assets	889	759	779	744	744	760
Total Assets	1,701	1,577	1,608	1,548	1,494	1,491
Curr. Liab.	422	357	330	309	282	284
LT Debt	387	377	438	397	398	416
Common Eqty.	744	681	696	706	697	674
Total Cap.	1,146	1,094	1,189	1,159	1,152	1,146
Cap. Exp.	66.0	70.0	65.0	92.0	78.0	84.0
Cash Flow	189	156	161	157	166	174

Ratio Analysis

	1994	1993	1992	1991	1990	1989
Curr. Ratio	2.1	2.1	2.4	2.4	2.6	2.7
% LT Debt of Cap.	33.8	34.5	36.8	34.2	34.6	36.3
% Net Inc.of Revs.	5.0	4.1	4.4	4.8	5.4	6.0
% Ret. on Assets	7.7	5.9	6.2	6.0	7.3	8.1
% Ret. on Equity	17.6	13.6	14.0	12.9	15.9	17.1

Dividend Data —Dividends have been paid each year since 1877. A dividend reinvestment plan is available.

Amt. of Div. $	Date Decl.	Ex-Div. Date	Stock of Record	Payment Date
0.350	Aug. 31	Sep. 06	Sep. 12	Sep. 30 '94
0.350	Oct. 26	Nov. 28	Dec. 02	Dec. 30 '94
0.350	Mar. 01	Mar. 07	Mar. 13	Mar. 31 '95
0.350	May. 31	Jun. 08	Jun. 12	Jun. 30 '95
0.360	Aug. 30	Sep. 07	Sep. 11	Sep. 30 '95

Data as orig. reptd.; bef. results of disc. opers. and/or spec. items. Per share data adj. for stk. divs. as of ex-div. date. E-Estimated. NA-Not Available. NM-Not Meaningful. NR-Not Ranked.

Office—1000 Stanley Dr., New Britain, CT 06053. **Tel**—(203) 225-5111. **Chrmn & CEO**—R. H. Ayers. **Pres & COO**—R. A. Hunter. **VP & Secy**—S. S. Weddle. **VP & CFO**—R. Huck. **Investor Contact**—Patricia R. McLean (203-827-3833). **Dirs**—R. H. Ayers, S. B. Brown, E. R. Fiedler, M. L. Jackson, J. G. Kaiser, E. S. Kraus, G. A. Lorch, W. J. McNerney, G. G. Michelson, J. S. Scott, H. E. Uyterhoeven, W. W. Williams. **Transfer Agent & Registrar**—Mellon Securities Trust Co., Ridgefield Park, N.J. **Incorporated** in Connecticut in 1852. **Empl**-20,000. **S&P Analyst:** Michael W. Jaffe

31-JUL-95

Industry:
Containers

Summary: Primarily a manufacturer of corrugated containers, Stone also markets paperboard and corrugating medium to others, and is a major newsprint producer.

| S&P Opinion: Accumulate (★★★★) | Recent Price • 21⅝ | Yield • 2.8% |
| | 52 Wk Range • 24⅝-14⅝ | 12-Mo. P/E • 9.0 |

Quantitative Evaluations

Outlook
(1 Lowest—5 Highest)
• **5**

Fair Value
• **25⅝**

Risk
• **Average**

Earn./Div. Rank
• **C**

Technical Eval.
• **Bullish** since 1/94

Rel. Strength Rank
(1 Lowest—99 Highest)
• **57**

Insider Activity
• **Neutral**

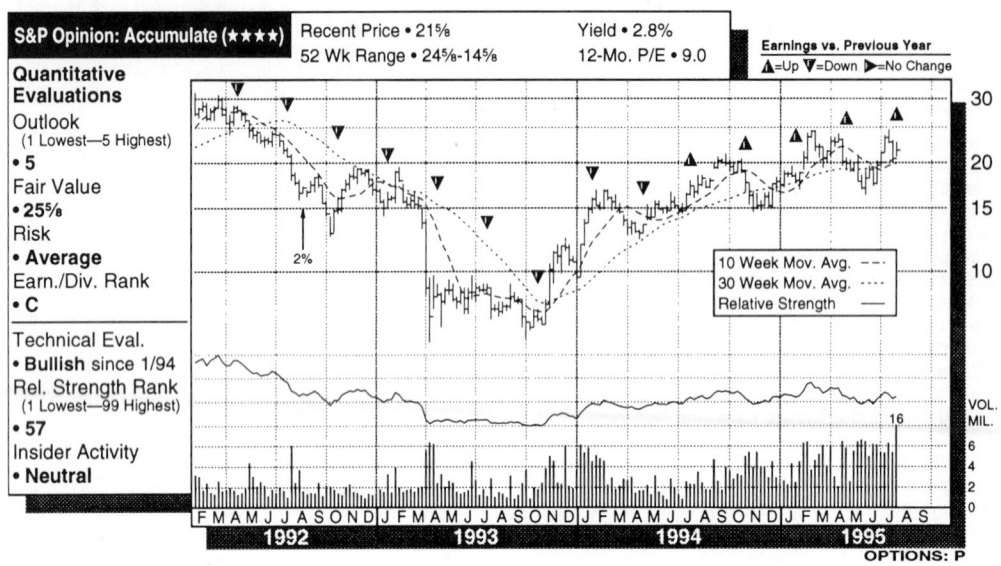

Earnings vs. Previous Year
▲=Up ▼=Down ▶=No Change

10 Week Mov. Avg. ---
30 Week Mov. Avg. ····
Relative Strength ——

OPTIONS: P

Overview - 31-JUL-95

Sales should be strongly higher in 1995, with recovering global economies generating increased demand and steep prices for nearly all of STO's paper grades. Although a moderating U.S. economy and substantial industry capacity coming on line cause worries about containerboard and corrugated container operations (Stone's major businesses), producers should be able to maintain volume and pricing levels through an increased reliance on solid export markets. Stone's business could also benefit from the recent drop in long-term interest rates, which is likely to spark the domestic economy. Despite the continued impact of high recycled fiber costs (although prices started to decline in mid-1995) and elevated levels of interest charges, Stone should be highly profitable in 1995, marking its first year of earnings since 1990.

Valuation - 31-JUL-95

Stone's volatile shares have appreciated strongly since late 1993. The initial gains were related to Stone's ability to stave off bankruptcy after making a highly leveraged acquisition at the time of the last industry peak in early 1989, while more recent appreciation reflected the upturn in industry conditions which has allowed STO to return to profitability. Although containerboard producers have recently fallen out of favor because of economic and capacity worries, we believe STO's earnings growth will continue, and its stock has room for some further appreciation.

Key Stock Statistics

S&P EPS Est. 1995	5.65	Tang. Bk. Value/Share	NM
P/E on S&P Est. 1995	3.8	Beta	2.32
S&P EPS Est. 1996	6.75	Shareholders	6,500
Dividend Rate/Share	0.60	Market cap. (B)	$ 2.0
Shs. outstg. (M)	90.6	Inst. holdings	72%
Avg. daily vol. (M)	1.876	Insider holdings	NA

Value of $10,000 invested 5 years ago: $ 10,374

Fiscal Year Ending Dec. 31

	1995	% Change	1994	% Change	1993	% Change
Revenues (Million $)						
1Q	1,819	41%	1,291	-1%	1,306	-4%
2Q	1,964	45%	1,354	7%	1,268	-8%
3Q	—	—	1,482	19%	1,243	-15%
4Q	—	—	1,621	30%	1,243	-7%
Yr.	—	—	5,749	14%	5,060	-8%
Income (Million $)						
1Q	96.80	NM	-78.90	NM	-62.70	NM
2Q	131.0	NM	-50.80	NM	-71.60	74%
3Q	—	—	-28.90	NM	-99.2	127%
4Q	—	—	29.80	NM	-85.80	13%
Yr.	—	—	-128.8	NM	-319.2	NM
Earnings Per Share ($)						
1Q	1.04	NM	-0.99	NM	-0.91	NM
2Q	1.42	NM	-0.58	NM	-1.03	NM
3Q	E1.54	—	-0.38	NM	-1.42	NM
4Q	E1.65	—	0.31	NM	-1.23	NM
Yr.	E5.65	—	-1.60	NM	-4.59	NM

Next earnings report expected: late October

Stone Container

Business Summary - 31-JUL-95

Stone Container manufactures corrugated containers and sells paperboard and corrugating medium to others. The March 1989 acquisition of Consolidated-Bathurst also made Stone a major newsprint producer. Business segment contributions (profits in millions) in 1994 were:

	Sales	Profits
Paperboard & packaging	73%	$354
White paper, pulp & other	27%	25

Canada accounted for 16% of sales in 1994 and Europe for 11%.

The company is the leading U.S. manufacturer of containerboard and corrugated containers. During 1994, STO produced 4,694,000 short tons of containerboard and shipped 54.1 billion square feet of corrugated containers. It is also the leading producer of kraft paper and bags and sacks. STO produced 517,000 short tons of kraft paper in 1994 and shipped 654,000 short tons of paper bags and sacks. In addition, the company is a major European supplier of boxboard, folding cartons and related items; in 1994, it produced 102,000 short tons of boxboard and other paperboard and shipped 97,000 short tons of folding cartons and partitions.

Stone is a major producer of newsprint, uncoated groundwood paper (used in advertising materials, magazines, directories and computer printers) and market pulp. In 1994, the company produced 1,279,000 short tons of newsprint, 536,000 short tons of uncoated groundwood paper and 800,000 short tons of market pulp.

Wood products include lumber, plywood and veneer. STO produced 602 million board feet of lumber and 404 million square feet of plywood and veneer during 1994.

Important Developments

Apr. '95—Stone announced incremental capacity projects at seven of its 12 U.S. containerboard mills. Scheduled for completion between December 1995 and October 1996, the projects would add a total of 704 tons per day to STO's linerboard and corrugating medium capacity (or 2.8% of STO's total mill capacity).

Capitalization

Long Term Debt: $4,636,200,000 (3/95).
Minority Interest: $226,000,000.
$1.75 Ser. E Cum. Conv. Exch. Pfd. Stk.: 4,600,000 shs. ($0.01 par).

Per Share Data ($)

				(Year Ended Dec. 31)		
	1994	1993	1992	1991	1990	1989
Tangible Bk. Val.	-3.90	-6.59	0.78	5.55	4.67	4.02
Cash Flow	2.47	0.27	1.29	3.55	5.75	8.11
Earnings	-1.60	-4.59	-2.50	-0.77	1.56	4.67
Dividends	Nil	Nil	0.36	0.71	0.71	0.71
Payout Ratio	Nil	Nil	NM	NM	45%	15%
Prices - High	21⅛	19½	32	25½	24¾	35⅝
- Low	9⅝	6⅜	12½	8⅞	8	21¾
P/E Ratio - High	NM	NM	NM	NM	16	8
- Low	NM	NM	NM	NM	5	5

Income Statement Analysis (Million $)

	1994	%Chg	1993	%Chg	1992	%Chg	1991
Revs.	5,749	14%	5,060	-8%	5,521	3%	5,384
Oper. Inc.	616	90%	324	-31%	468	-19%	576
Depr.	359	3%	347	29%	269	-2%	274
Int. Exp.	461	5%	438	NM	434	-9%	479
Pretax Inc.	-162	NM	-462	NM	-194	NM	-12.0
Eff. Tax Rate	NM	—	NM	—	NM	—	NM
Net Inc.	-128	NM	-318	NM	-170	NM	-49.0

Balance Sheet & Other Fin. Data (Million $)

	1994	1993	1992	1991	1990	1989
Cash	109	247	58.9	64.1	53.9	22.9
Curr. Assets	1,817	1,753	1,679	1,685	1,586	1,687
Total Assets	7,005	6,837	6,682	6,903	6,690	6,254
Curr. Liab.	1,032	944	939	915	1,147	1,073
LT Debt	4,432	4,268	4,105	4,046	3,681	3,537
Common Eqty.	533	471	1,070	1,521	1,447	1,335
Total Cap.	5,683	5,623	5,590	5,883	5,438	5,102
Cap. Exp.	233	150	281	430	552	502
Cash Flow	218	20.0	92.0	224	352	496

Ratio Analysis

	1994	1993	1992	1991	1990	1989
Curr. Ratio	1.8	1.9	1.8	1.8	1.4	1.6
% LT Debt of Cap.	78.0	75.9	73.4	68.8	67.7	69.3
% Net Inc.of Revs.	NM	NM	NM	NM	1.7	5.4
% Ret. on Assets	NM	NM	NM	NM	1.5	6.6
% Ret. on Equity	NM	NM	NM	NM	6.9	23.8

Dividend Data (Cash dividends on the common, which had been omitted in July 1992, have been resumed with a $0.15 quarterly declaration on July 25, 1995. A $2.1875 a share dividend on STO's preferred stock, payable on August 15, 1995, fully satisfies arrearages. A "poison pill" stock purchase rights plan was adopted in 1988.)

Amt. of Div. $	Date Decl.	Ex-Div. Date	Stock of Record	Payment Date
0.150	Jul. 25	Aug. 22	Aug. 24	Sep. 13 '95

Data as orig. reptd.; bef. results of disc. opers. and/or spec. items. Per share data adj. for stk. divs. as of ex-div. date.
E-Estimated. NA-Not Available. NM-Not Meaningful. NR-Not Ranked.

Office—150 North Michigan Ave., Chicago, IL 60601. Tel—(312) 346-6600. Chrmn, Pres & CEO—R. W. Stone. Exec VP-CFO & Investor Contact—Arnold F. Brookstone. VP-Secy—L. T. Lederer. Dirs—R. A. Giesen, J. J. Glasser, J. M. Greenberg, G. D. Kennedy, H. C. Miller Jr., J. D. Nichols, J. K. Pearlman, R. J. Raskin, A. Stone, A. J. Stone, I. N. Stone, J. H. Stone, R. W. Stone. Transfer Agent & Registrar—First National Bank of Chicago. Incorporated in Illinois in 1945; reincorporated in Delaware in 1987. Empl-29,100. S&P Analyst: Michael W. Jaffe

Stride Rite

NYSE Symbol **SRR**
In S&P 500

04-OCT-95 | **Industry:** Leather/shoes

Summary: Stride Rite is a leading marketer of quality children's and adults' footwear sold under the Stride Rite, Sperry Top-Sider and Keds names.

S&P Opinion: Avoid (★★)	Recent Price • 11⅛	Yield • 3.4%
	52 Wk Range • 14½-9⅝	12-Mo. P/E • 48.4

Quantitative Evaluations

Outlook
(1 Lowest—5 Highest)
• **1⁻**

Fair Value
• **9½**

Risk
• **Average**

Earn./Div. Rank
• **A-**

Technical Eval.
• **Bullish** since 12/94

Rel. Strength Rank
(1 Lowest—99 Highest)
• **36**

Insider Activity
• **Neutral**

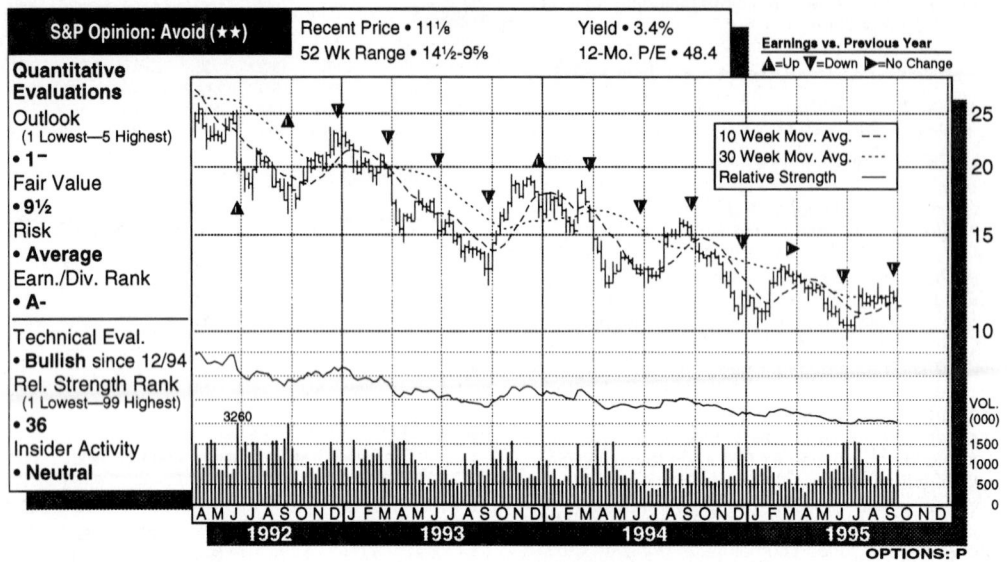

Earnings vs. Previous Year
▲=Up ▼=Down ▶=No Change

10 Week Mov. Avg. ---
30 Week Mov. Avg. ······
Relative Strength —

3260

VOL. (000)

OPTIONS: P

Overview - 04-OCT-95

Sales should recover somewhat in fiscal 1996, up from fiscal 1995's depressed levels. Demand for Keds could be slightly stronger, as the company emphasizes providing a product line that is more responsive to apparel trends. Demand for Sperry Top-Siders should continue to be strong. Sales growth will also benefit from higher contributions from international revenues and from the Boston Footwear Group. Sales of children's shoes are expected to rise only slightly; however, revenue from the company-run children's footwear stores should rise considerably on new store openings. Despite a less profitable mix, as the company skews its sales mix to less profitable retailing, margins are expected to widen on the higher volume.

Valuation - 29-SEP-95

After reaching a high of 31 7/8 early in 1992, shares of Stride Rite have trended downward as the company entered a period of disappointing sales and earnings. Results in fiscal 1994 were especially hurt by higher than expected startup costs at a new distribution center, which caused many customers to cancel orders. While we believe most of these problems have now been alleviated, results in fiscal 1995 will be even lower than those reported in fiscal 1994, on weak demand for Keds mainly due to ongoing weakness in the women's apparel sector. We expect some pick-up in fiscal 1996, although results could remain substantially below those reported in the late 1980s and early 1990s. In sum, we would avoid these shares for now.

Key Stock Statistics

S&P EPS Est. 1995	0.21	Tang. Bk. Value/Share	5.66
P/E on S&P Est. 1995	53.0	Beta	1.60
S&P EPS Est. 1996	0.60	Shareholders	5,100
Dividend Rate/Share	0.38	Market cap. (B)	$0.557
Shs. outstg. (M)	49.5	Inst. holdings	65%
Avg. daily vol. (M)	0.172	Insider holdings	NA

Value of $10,000 invested 5 years ago: $ 8,654

Fiscal Year Ending Nov. 30

	1995	% Change	1994	% Change	1993	% Change
Revenues (Million $)						
1Q	134.8	10%	122.1	-13%	140.8	1%
2Q	144.4	-11%	161.7	-2%	164.5	-4%
3Q	139.1	-10%	155.0	-7%	166.5	-1%
4Q	—	—	85.14	-23%	111.1	3%
Yr.	—	—	523.9	-10%	582.9	NM
Income (Million $)						
1Q	4.97	2%	4.85	-68%	15.18	-11%
2Q	4.00	-48%	7.68	-60%	19.36	-11%
3Q	3.49	-59%	8.51	-54%	18.37	-11%
4Q	—	—	-1.24	NM	7.42	NM
Yr.	—	—	19.80	-67%	60.33	-2%
Earnings Per Share ($)						
1Q	0.10	NM	0.10	-67%	0.30	-9%
2Q	0.08	-47%	0.15	-61%	0.38	-10%
3Q	0.07	-59%	0.17	-53%	0.36	-10%
4Q	E-0.04	NM	-0.02	NM	0.15	NM
Yr.	E0.21	-48%	0.40	-66%	1.19	NM

Next earnings report expected: mid January

Business Summary - 04-OCT-95

Stride Rite is the leading marketer of quality children's footwear in the U.S., and a major marketer of athletic and casual footwear for children and adults.

The company manufactures products in its own facilities in the U.S. and in the Dominican Republic, and imports products from overseas.

SRR markets children's footwear, designed primarily for consumers between the ages of six months and 12 years, under the trademarks Stride Rite and Keds. Children's and adults' marine shoes and outdoor recreational and casual footwear are marketed under the company's Sperry Top-Sider trademark. Casual and athletic footwear is marketed under the Keds, Pro-Keds and Grasshoppers trademarks.

Footwear is distributed through independent retail stores including Stride Rite Bootery stores, department stores, sporting goods stores, marinas, and company-owned stores, including bootery stores, manufacturers' outlet stores, a Keds store, a new concept store called Great Feet, and children's footwear departments in department stores. The company's largest single customer accounted for less than 6% of consolidated net sales for in fiscal 1994.

At the end of fiscal 1994, the company operated 136 Stride Rite Bootery stores, one retail store for Keds brand products, one new concept store called Great Feet, 103 leased shoe departments in department stores, and 11 manufacturers' outlet stores for Stride Rite, Keds and Sperry Top-Sider.

In January 1995, SRR acquired University Brands and its trademarks (Toddler University, Kids University, Street Hot, etc.) from Genesco Inc. The new brands were to be marketed by wholly owned Boston Footwear Group Inc., which markets children's and adult's footwear products. The acquisition was a part of a growth strategy to enhance the company's portfolio of premium children's footwear brands.

Important Developments

Sep. '95—SRR attributed its fiscal 1995 first nine months sales decline of 4.7% and profit decline of 41% to a 14% decrease in sales of Keds. The decline at Keds was partially offset by a 15% increase in sales of Sperry Top-Siders, a 22% rise in international sales, and a 5% increase at the Boston Footwear Group, a newly formed business unit organized to market Grasshoppers and other branded footwear. Sales of children's shoes to independent retailers declined 5%, while sales at company-run children's stores were up 16%. mainly owing to new store openings. Comparable store sales declined 2.5%. Looking ahead, the company said that with the current retail environment still weak, it was expecting to report a loss in the fourth quarter. On the upside, however, the company said it was expecting fiscal 1996's first half to be stronger than fiscal 1995's first half.

Capitalization

Long Term Debt: $1,667,000 (9/1/95).

Per Share Data ($)

	1994	1993	1992	1991	1990	1989
Tangible Bk. Val.	5.74	5.81	5.12	4.64	3.54	3.09
Cash Flow	0.57	1.31	1.30	1.36	1.14	0.94
Earnings	0.40	1.19	1.19	1.28	1.05	0.86
Dividends	0.38	0.35	0.31	0.25	0.20	0.17
Payout Ratio	95%	29%	26%	20%	18%	20%
Prices - High	18⅞	23⅛	31⅞	30¼	15¼	15⅛
- Low	10½	12⅛	16⅜	13⅜	9¾	6½
P/E Ratio - High	47	19	27	24	14	18
- Low	26	10	14	10	9	8

(Year Ended Nov. 30)

Income Statement Analysis (Million $)

	1994	%Chg	1993	%Chg	1992	%Chg	1991
Revs.	524	-10%	583	NM	586	2%	574
Oper. Inc.	47.0	-56%	107	-12%	122	12%	109
Depr.	8.5	36%	6.3	17%	5.4	28%	4.2
Int. Exp.	0.5	20%	0.4	-6%	0.5	-27%	0.7
Pretax Inc.	33.0	-66%	98.0	-2%	100	-7%	108
Eff. Tax Rate	39%	—	38%	—	39%	—	39%
Net Inc.	19.8	-67%	60.3	-2%	61.5	-7%	66.0

Balance Sheet & Other Fin. Data (Million $)

	1994	1993	1992	1991	1990	1989
Cash	76.0	104	98.2	88.4	32.9	24.8
Curr. Assets	331	344	345	301	235	220
Total Assets	397	412	384	332	266	252
Curr. Liab.	94.0	100	98.3	78.0	66.7	64.4
LT Debt	1.7	2.5	3.3	4.2	5.0	5.8
Common Eqty.	293	302	272	240	181	167
Total Cap.	302	312	285	254	199	187
Cap. Exp.	8.5	33.9	3.7	3.5	2.7	4.3
Cash Flow	28.3	66.6	66.9	70.2	59.8	50.6

Ratio Analysis

	1994	1993	1992	1991	1990	1989
Curr. Ratio	3.5	3.4	3.5	3.9	3.5	3.4
% LT Debt of Cap.	0.6	0.8	1.2	1.6	2.5	3.1
% Net Inc.of Revs.	3.8	10.3	10.5	11.5	10.8	10.2
% Ret. on Assets	4.9	15.2	17.3	21.9	22.0	18.7
% Ret. on Equity	6.7	21.1	24.2	31.1	32.7	30.8

Dividend Data

Dividends have been paid since 1955. A dividend reinvestment plan is available. A "poison pill" stock purchase rights plan was adopted in 1987.

Amt. of Div. $	Date Decl.	Ex-Div. Date	Stock of Record	Payment Date
0.095	Oct. 28	Nov. 22	Nov. 29	Dec. 15 '94
0.095	Feb. 10	Feb. 22	Feb. 28	Mar. 15 '95
0.095	May. 05	May. 23	May. 30	Jun. 15 '95
0.095	Aug. 03	Aug. 28	Aug. 30	Sep. 15 '95

Data as orig. reptd.; bef. results of disc. opers. and/or spec. items. Per share data adj. for stk. divs. as of ex-div. date. E-Estimated. NA-Not Available. NM-Not Meaningful. NR-Not Ranked.

Office—5 Cambridge Center, Cambridge, MA 02142. **Tel**—(617) 491-8800. **Chrmn, Pres & CEO**—R. C. Siegel. **VP-Treas & Investor Contact**—J. M. Kelliher. **Secy & Clerk**—K. K. Crider. **Dirs**—D. R. Gant, T. Levitt, M. A. McKenna, R. L. Seelert, R. C. Siegel, M. J. Slosberg, W. P. Tippett, J. S. Wagner. **Transfer Agent & Registrar**—First National Bank of Boston. **Incorporated** in Massachusetts in 1919. **Empl**-3,700. **S&P Analyst:** Elizabeth Vandeventer

Sun Co.

NYSE Symbol **SUN**
In S&P 500

06-NOV-95

Industry:
Oil and Gas

Summary: Sun Co. is primarily a petroleum refiner and marketer serving much of the Northeast and the Midwest through its Sunoco brand.

S&P Opinion: Hold (★★★)	Recent Price • 29 Yield • 3.4% 52 Wk Range • 32⅞-24¾ 12-Mo. P/E • 16.4

Quantitative Evaluations

Outlook
(1 Lowest—5 Highest)
• **2⁻**

Fair Value
• **27⅜**

Risk
• **Low**

Earn./Div. Rank
• **NR**

Technical Eval.
• **Bearish** since 5/95

Rel. Strength Rank
(1 Lowest—99 Highest)
• **83**

Insider Activity
• **NA**

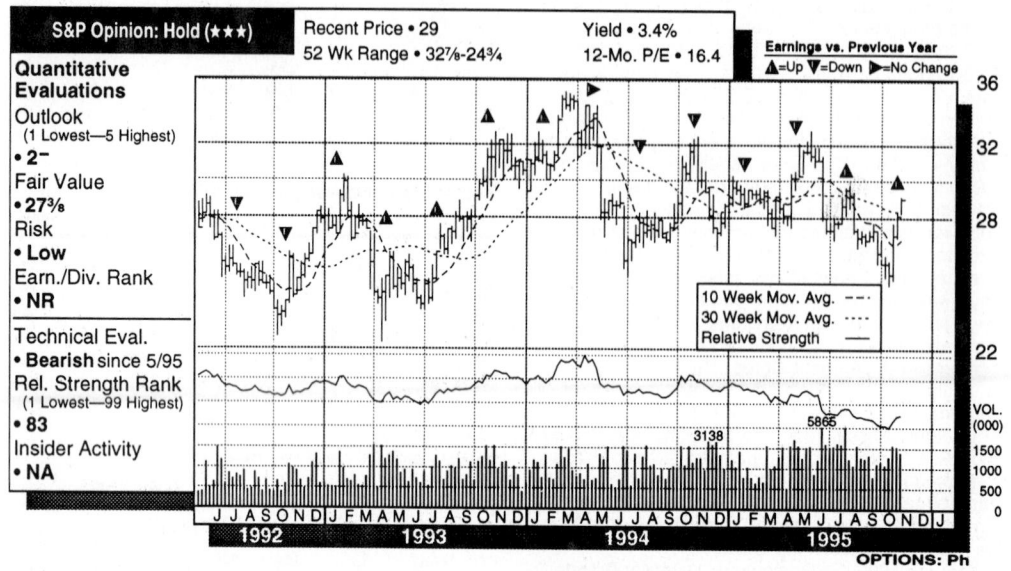

Earnings vs. Previous Year
▲=Up ▼=Down ▶=No Change

10 Week Mov. Avg. ---
30 Week Mov. Avg. ····
Relative Strength —

OPTIONS: Ph

Overview - 06-NOV-95

Branded marketing profits should rebound in 1995, since we expect refining margins will see an upturn from recent historically low levels seen during early 1995, as gasoline prices recover from the introduction of reformulated gasoline (RFG). Current price levels for RFG have left refiners unable to pass on the $0.05 to $0.07 per gallon higher production costs to consumers. The conversion of 200 Atlantic stations to SUNOCO in 1995 should boost refined product sales volumes, and further conversions are anticipated. Costs to convert the stations, as well as temporary closings, will have a negative impact on branded marketing results in the short term. Strong petrochemical and coal earnings will begin to taper off by 1995's final quarter.

Valuation - 06-NOV-95

The shares have underperformed the market during 1995, reflecting uncertainty about the profitability of the company's refining and marketing system. Meanwhile, recent restructuring moves, including a 44% cut in the dividend, the issuance of depository shares, and a Dutch auction stock repurchase, have led to earnings volatility. Yet the company's shares will be buoyed by the moderate improvement in refining & marketing margins we are forecasting to occur through 1996, due principally to increased utilization of refineries in the Northeast. Interest in chemical segment earnings is likely to waver in 1996, as product demand diminishes.

Key Stock Statistics

S&P EPS Est. 1995	2.41	Tang. Bk. Value/Share	16.92
P/E on S&P Est. 1995	12.0	Beta	1.09
S&P EPS Est. 1996	2.25	Shareholders	59,000
Dividend Rate/Share	1.00	Market cap. (B)	$ 2.2
Shs. outstg. (M)	75.5	Inst. holdings	81%
Avg. daily vol. (M)	0.324	Insider holdings	NA

Value of $10,000 invested 5 years ago: $ 10,063

Fiscal Year Ending Dec. 31

	1995	% Change	1994	% Change	1993	% Change
Revenues (Million $)						
1Q	2,588	25%	2,070	-10%	2,304	-5%
2Q	2,915	30%	2,250	-8%	2,439	-6%
3Q	2,415	-12%	2,730	15%	2,384	-14%
4Q	—	—	1,631	-29%	2,290	-13%
Yr.	—	—	7,702	6%	7,297	-30%
Income (Million $)						
1Q	-7.00	NM	34.00	-3%	35.00	NM
2Q	109.0	NM	12.00	-83%	70.00	—
3Q	78.00	63%	48.00	-58%	114.0	NM
4Q	—	—	3.00	-95%	64.00	94%
Yr.	—	—	97.00	-66%	283.0	NM
Earnings Per Share ($)						
1Q	-0.07	NM	0.32	NM	0.32	NM
2Q	1.02	NM	0.11	-83%	0.66	—
3Q	0.87	93%	0.45	-58%	1.07	NM
4Q	E0.59	NM	0.03	-95%	0.60	94%
Yr.	E2.41	165%	0.91	-66%	2.65	NM

Next earnings report expected: mid January

Business Summary - 06-NOV-95

SUN is primarily a petroleum refiner and marketer serving much of the Northeast and Midwest through its Sunoco brand. In 1992, it began narrowing its overseas oil and gas activities to North Sea production. SUN sold its remaining 55% ownership stake in its Suncor Canadian during 1995 for $770 million. The company also intends to dispose of interests in coal, real estate and leasing operations. Earnings (in millions) in recent years were derived as follows:

	1994	1993
Fuels	$64	$43
Lubricants	12	18
Chemicals	32	13
Logistics	46	56
International production	60	73
Canada (Suncor)	45	33

In 1994, international production averaged 29,000 bbl. of oil per day (28,000 b/d in 1993) and 46,000 Mcf daily of natural gas (56,000). Oil production at Suncor averaged 10,800 b/d (10,100), natural gas 119,000 Mcf/d (116,000), and synthetic oil 70,700 b/d (60,500). Reserves at 1994 year-end included 78 million bbl. of oil (65 million) and 689,000,000 Mcf of natural gas (601,000,000). Canadian oil reserves represented 51% of total oil reserves and 86% of total natural gas reserves.

Refining capacity at December 31, 1994, totaled 847,000 b/d. U.S. refined product sales totaled 677,500 b/d in 1994 (595,600 b/d in 1993). Refinery utilization in 1994 was 86% (90%). Gasoline sales in 1994 were some 44% (45%) of total sales, middle distillate heating oil 18% (16%), and other 38% (39%). Canadian refined product sales were 84,500 b/d in 1994 (81,900).

Important Developments

Oct. '95—Operating income in the 1995 third quarter rose to $78 million, up from $55 million a year earlier. The company attributed the improvement to efficiencies achieved at its refineries, which ran in excess of 95% of total capacity, and strong demand for the majority of its products.

Sep. '95—Sun announced that after evaluating the bids received for its Toledo refining and marketing system it had decided to retain the system and strengthen it. The system includes a 125,000 barrel-per-day refinery in Toledo, Ohio, and a products pipeline running both east and north from the refinery; and eleven petroleum products terminals. SUN has undertaken a plan to improve the efficiency of the system, and increase its profitability.

Capitalization

Long Term Debt: $888,000,000 (6/95).

Per Share Data ($)

	1994	1993	1992	1991	1990	1989
Tangible Bk. Val.	17.07	18.10	17.37	25.41	30.83	30.50
Cash Flow	4.26	6.02	0.68	3.28	6.46	4.76
Earnings	0.91	2.65	-2.98	-1.25	1.86	0.92
Dividends	1.80	1.80	1.80	1.80	1.80	1.80
Payout Ratio	198%	68%	NM	NM	96%	196%
Prices - High	35¼	32¾	30¾	35¾	41⅞	43¼
- Low	25⅛	22¼	22½	25¾	25¾	31⅜
P/E Ratio - High	39	12	NM	NM	23	47
- Low	28	8	NM	NM	14	34

Income Statement Analysis (Million $)

	1994	%Chg	1993	%Chg	1992	%Chg	1991
Revs.	7,702	6%	7,297	-15%	8,626	-15%	10,184
Oper. Inc.	562	-16%	671	NM	221	-67%	670
Depr.	359	NM	359	-8%	389	-19%	480
Int. Exp.	97.0	20%	81.0	-16%	97.0	-13%	112
Pretax Inc.	155	-66%	453	NM	-431	NM	-128
Eff. Tax Rate	15%	—	32%	—	NM	—	NM
Net Inc.	97.0	-66%	283	NM	-316	NM	-131

Balance Sheet & Other Fin. Data (Million $)

	1994	1993	1992	1991	1990	1989
Cash	117	118	179	366	298	416
Curr. Assets	1,508	1,277	1,331	1,694	2,503	2,368
Total Assets	6,465	5,900	6,071	7,143	9,000	8,699
Curr. Liab.	1,915	1,505	1,746	1,965	2,613	2,429
LT Debt	1,073	726	792	853	1,459	1,377
Common Eqty.	1,863	1,984	1,896	2,696	3,274	3,254
Total Cap.	3,606	3,451	3,347	4,625	6,028	5,912
Cap. Exp.	848	612	530	674	788	763
Cash Flow	456	642	72.0	348	690	509

Ratio Analysis

	1994	1993	1992	1991	1990	1989
Curr. Ratio	0.8	0.8	0.8	0.9	1.0	1.0
% LT Debt of Cap.	29.8	21.0	23.7	18.4	24.2	23.3
% Net Inc.of Revs.	1.3	3.9	NM	NM	1.7	1.0
% Ret. on Assets	1.6	4.7	NM	NM	2.3	1.1
% Ret. on Equity	5.0	14.6	NM	NM	6.1	3.0

Dividend Data —Dividends have been paid since 1904. A dividend reinvestment plan is available.

Amt. of Div. $	Date Decl.	Ex-Div. Date	Stock of Record	Payment Date
0.450	Oct. 06	Nov. 04	Nov. 10	Dec. 09 '94
0.450	Jan. 05	Feb. 07	Feb. 13	Mar. 10 '95
0.450	Apr. 06	May. 04	May. 10	Jun. 09 '95
0.250	Jun. 13	Aug. 08	Aug. 10	Sep. 08 '95
0.250	Oct. 05	Nov. 08	Nov. 10	Dec. 08 '95

Data as orig. reptd.; bef. results of disc. opers. and/or spec. items. Per share data adj. for stk. divs. as of ex-div. date. E-Estimated. NA-Not Available. NM-Not Meaningful. NR-Not Ranked.

Office—Ten Penn Center, 1801 Market St., Philadelphia, PA 19103-1699. **Tel**—(215) 977-3000. **Chrmn, Pres & CEO**—R. H. Campbell. **SVP & CFO**—R. M. Aiken, Jr. **Secy**—D. J. Ainsworth. **Investor Contact**—K. Turner. **Dirs**—R. H. Campbell, R. E. Cartledge, R. E. Cawthorn, M. J. Evans, T. P. Gerrity, J. G. Kaiser, R. D. Kennedy, T. W. Langfitt, R. A. Pew, A. E. Piscopo, W. F. Pounds, A. B. Trowbridge. **Transfer Agents & Registrars**—Co. itself; Montreal Trust Co., Calgary, Canada. **Incorporated** in New Jersey in 1901; reincorporated in Pennsylvania in 1971. **Empl**-14,500. **S&P Analyst:** Raymond J. Deacon

Sun Microsystems

NASDAQ Symbol **SUNW**
In S&P 500

31-OCT-95

Industry:
Data Processing

Summary: Sun makes high-performance computer workstations for engineering, scientific, commercial and technical markets. Sun also sells network servers and operating system software.

S&P Opinion: Buy (★★★★★)	Recent Price • 76⅝ Yield • Nil 52 Wk Range • 76⅝-29⅞ 12-Mo. P/E • 18.9

Quantitative Evaluations

Outlook
(1 Lowest—5 Highest)
• **4+**

Fair Value
• **88⅝**

Risk
• **Average**

Earn./Div. Rank
• **B**

Technical Eval.
• **Bearish** since 6/95

Rel. Strength Rank
(1 Lowest—99 Highest)
• **99**

Insider Activity
• **Neutral**

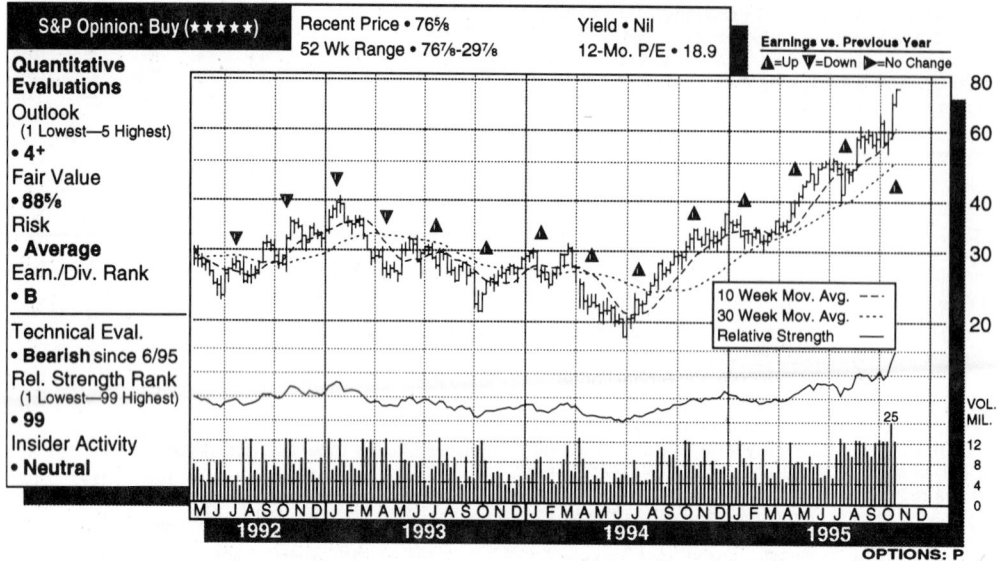

Earnings vs. Previous Year
▲=Up ▼=Down ►=No Change

10 Week Mov. Avg. ‑ ‑ ‑
30 Week Mov. Avg. ‑‑‑‑
Relative Strength ——

VOL. MIL.

OPTIONS: P

Overview - 31-OCT-95

Revenues are forecast to grow approximately 20% during fiscal 1996, owing to a new and more powerful product line-up, strong contributions from Internet-related products and Sun's continued success in penetrating new commercial markets with client-server solutions. Gross margins are likely to trend slightly higher, as Sun should benefit from higher sales of more richly configured systems. While expense growth could outpace revenue growth in the first half of the year, owing to efforts to build up Sun's commercial enterprise infrastructure, these efforts should ease in the second half. EPS comparisons should be helped by a 12 million share buyback plan, of which 8.4 million shares were purchased during the first quarter. Sun's goal is to achieve compound earnings growth of 15% over any three-year period.

Valuation - 31-OCT-95

We continue to recommend buying the shares, as we expect strong sales and earnings comparisons through fiscal 1997. Sun is currently benefiting from growth opportunities in new markets like commercial client-server and the Internet. These efforts are proving to be additive to both revenues and gross margins and should fuel earnings growth of some 15%-20% over the next several years. We also believe there is further upside potential to our estimates for both fiscal 1996 and 1997. Against this favorable backdrop and based on the reasonable valuation, we continue to recommend that investors buy the shares.

Key Stock Statistics

S&P EPS Est. 1996	5.10	Tang. Bk. Value/Share	19.99
P/E on S&P Est. 1996	15.0	Beta	1.63
S&P EPS Est. 1997	6.00	Shareholders	5,200
Dividend Rate/Share	Nil	Market cap. (B)	$ 7.5
Shs. outstg. (M)	95.6	Inst. holdings	82%
Avg. daily vol. (M)	3.712	Insider holdings	NA

Value of $10,000 invested 5 years ago: $ 44,420

Fiscal Year Ending Jun. 30

	1996	% Change	1995	% Change	1994	% Change
Revenues (Million $)						
1Q	1,485	17%	1,273	33%	960.5	12%
2Q	—	—	1,475	30%	1,131	8%
3Q	—	—	1,505	26%	1,196	5%
4Q	—	—	1,648	17%	1,403	11%
Yr.	—	—	5,902	26%	4,690	9%
Income (Million $)						
1Q	84.70	120%	38.43	131%	16.61	NM
2Q	—	—	81.62	86%	43.82	28%
3Q	—	—	107.6	87%	57.48	11%
4Q	—	—	128.2	65%	77.91	2%
Yr.	—	—	355.8	82%	195.8	25%
Earnings Per Share ($)						
1Q	0.85	113%	0.40	150%	0.16	NM
2Q	E1.25	51%	0.83	80%	0.46	100%
3Q	E1.45	33%	1.09	82%	0.60	28%
4Q	E1.55	23%	1.26	54%	0.82	14%
Yr.	E5.10	41%	3.61	79%	2.02	36%

Next earnings report expected: mid January

Business Summary - 31-OCT-95

Sun Microsystems is a leading supplier of networked computing products including workstations, servers, software, micrprocessors and a full range of services and support. Computer systems are used mainly for commercial and technical applications. Net revenues by geographic area in recent fiscal years were:

	1995	1994	1993
U.S.	49%	49%	52%
Europe	26%	26%	26%
Rest of World	25%	25%	22%

Sun's workstations range from low cost X-terminals to high performance color graphics systems. Current desktops include the low-end SPARC Xterminal 1, the low-end color SPARCstation 4 and SPARCstation 5, and the high-performance SPARCstation 20 series. The company's servers can be used for file sharing, enabling users to access data distributed across multiple storage devices and networks, or as compute resources, to distribute compute-intensive applications across multiple processors. Servers include the low end SPARCstation 4 and 5 for small workgroups, the SPARCserver 20 and SPARCserver 1000 for mid-range needs and the high-end SPARCcenter 2000 for enterprise-wide solutions. Netra servers offer specialized capabilities such as system management or Internet Functionality.

The UNIX operating system is the foundation for Sun's open systems approach, while it utilizes and licenses its own own SPARC (Scalable Processor ARChitecture) microprocessor.

Software offerings include Solaris, an open client-server UNIX system software envioronment offeredon SPARC and Intel platforms. In January 1995, the company introduced Solstice, a suite of software products that manages large heterogenous networks that utilize distributed computing technologies.

R&D costs expensed in fiscal 1995 equaled 8.8% of net revenues, versus 9.7% in fiscal 1994.

Important Developments

Sep. '95—Intuit, the world's largest personal financial software provider, selected Sun systems as the primary technology platform for its Automated Financial Services applications network and national call centers that provide customer service. The company also chose Sun's SunScreen network security solution as the strategic security platform to link various banks' accounting networks with its Quicken Online home banking service.

Capitalization

Long Term Liabilities: $50,386,000 (10/01/95).

Per Share Data ($)

(Year Ended Jun. 30)

	1995	1994	1993	1992	1991	1990
Tangible Bk. Val.	NA	17.35	16.09	14.85	12.58	10.01
Cash Flow	NA	4.59	3.70	3.82	3.99	3.13
Earnings	3.61	2.02	1.49	1.71	1.85	1.21
Dividends	Nil	Nil	Nil	Nil	Nil	Nil
Payout Ratio	Nil	Nil	Nil	Nil	Nil	Nil
Prices - High	51½	37⅝	41	36⅛	38⅝	37¼
- Low	29⅞	18¼	21⅛	22½	20¾	15
P/E Ratio - High	14	19	28	21	21	31
- Low	8	9	14	13	11	12

Income Statement Analysis (Million $)

	1994	%Chg	1993	%Chg	1992	%Chg	1991
Revs.	4,690	9%	4,309	20%	3,589	11%	3,221
Oper. Inc.	526	11%	473	NM	477	-8%	516
Depr.	248	7%	232	8%	215	-3%	221
Int. Exp.	21.8	-38%	34.9	-23%	45.2	-9%	49.4
Pretax Inc.	283	26%	224	-12%	255	-10%	284
Eff. Tax Rate	31%	—	30%	—	32%	—	33%
Net Inc.	196	25%	157	-9%	173	-9%	190

Balance Sheet & Other Fin. Data (Million $)

	1994	1993	1992	1991	1990	1989
Cash	883	1,139	1,220	834	394	54.0
Curr. Assets	2,305	2,272	2,148	1,801	1,297	880
Total Assets	2,898	2,768	2,672	2,326	1,779	1,269
Curr. Liab.	1,148	947	839	713	493	463
LT Debt	116	154	313	351	359	143
Common Eqty.	1,628	1,643	1,485	1,213	927	662
Total Cap.	1,745	1,797	1,798	1,564	1,286	805
Cap. Exp.	213	196	186	192	213	205
Cash Flow	444	389	389	411	295	164

Ratio Analysis

	1994	1993	1992	1991	1990	1989
Curr. Ratio	2.0	2.4	2.6	2.5	2.6	1.9
% LT Debt of Cap.	6.7	8.6	17.4	22.5	27.9	17.7
% Net Inc.of Revs.	4.2	3.6	4.8	5.9	4.5	3.4
% Ret. on Assets	7.2	5.7	6.8	9.1	7.3	5.7
% Ret. on Equity	12.5	9.9	12.6	17.5	13.4	11.2

Dividend Data —No cash dividends have been paid. A "poison pill" stock purchase rights plan was adopted in May 1989.

Data as orig. reptd.; bef. results of disc. opers. and/or spec. items. Per share data adj. for stk. divs. as of ex-div. date. E-Estimated. NA-Not Available. NM-Not Meaningful. NR-Not Ranked.

Office—2550 Garcia Ave., Mountain View, CA 94043-1100. **Tel**—(415) 960-1300. **Chrmn & CEO**—S. G. McNealy. **VP & CFO**—M. Lehman. **VP & Secy**—M. H. Morris. **Dirs**—L. J. Doerr, J. Estrin, R. J. Fisher, W. R. Hearst III, R. L. Long, S. G. McNealy, M. K. Oshman, A. M. Spence. **Transfer Agent & Registrar**—Bank of Boston. **Incorporated** in California in 1982. **Empl**-14,500. **S&P Analyst:** John D. Coyle, CFA

SunTrust Banks

NYSE Symbol **STI**
In S&P 500

17-OCT-95

Industry:
Banking

Summary: This bank holding company, the 20th largest in the U.S., operates more than 650 full-service branch offices in Florida, Georgia, Tennessee and Alabama.

S&P Opinion: Hold (★★★)	Recent Price • 66⅞	Yield • 2.2%
	52 Wk Range • 67¾-46⅜	12-Mo. P/E • 14.0

Quantitative Evaluations

Outlook
(1 Lowest—5 Highest)
• **2+**

Fair Value
• **63⅞**

Risk
• **Low**

Earn./Div. Rank
• **A+**

Technical Eval.
• **Bullish** since 12/94

Rel. Strength Rank
(1 Lowest—99 Highest)
• **76**

Insider Activity
• **Neutral**

Earnings vs. Previous Year
▲=Up ▼=Down ▶=No Change

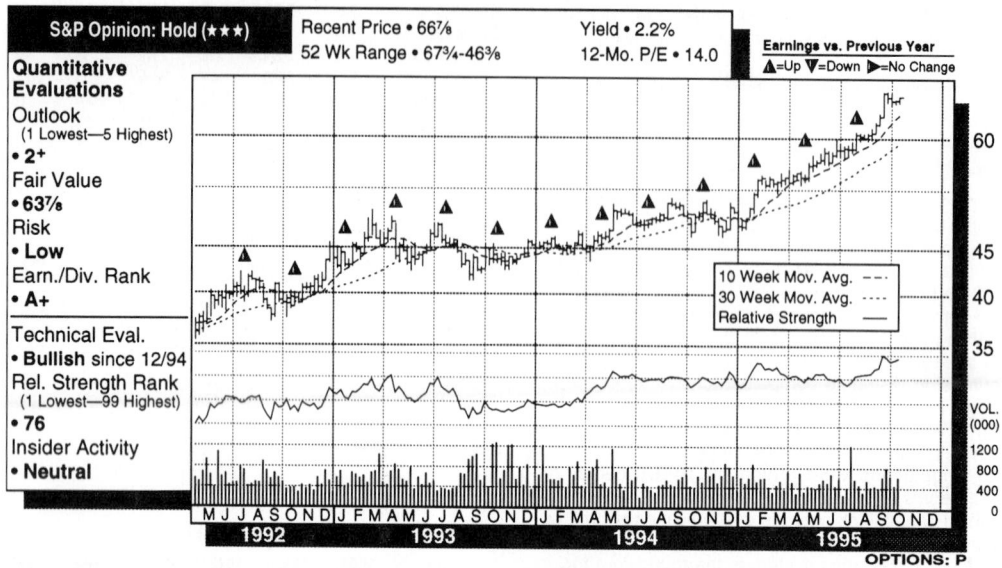

10 Week Mov. Avg. ---
30 Week Mov. Avg. ·····
Relative Strength ——

OPTIONS: P

Overview - 13-OCT-95

Loan growth has accelerated in recent periods, as STI's regional service territory remains among the healthiest in the nation. The net interest margin declined somewhat more than expected in the third quarter of 1995, reflecting a shift to more expensive sources of funds. But given the flat to falling interest rate environment expected in the quarters ahead, the margin should begin to stabilize, leading to a more pronounced contribution from loan growth. Credit quality continues to improve, as nonperforming loans of $174.3 million at September 30, 1995, fell 16% from a year earlier. With reserves built to 397% of nonperforming loans, provisions should continue to decline. Softness in noninterest income remains a concern, but a focus on controlling noninterest expense should offset this to some extent.

Valuation - 13-OCT-95

The share price has increased about 38% thus far in 1995, somewhat less than the average regional bank but well above the S&P 500. Results should benefit from reasonably strong loan growth from an attractive service territory and stabilizing margins, although pressure on noninterest income will dampen the overall improvement in earnings. Based on projected earnings growth and an average dividend yield, the shares appear adequately valued at 12 times the 1996 earnings estimate of $5.35 a share. Since SunTrust is periodically mentioned as a potential takeover target, the shares may have appeal for speculators.

Key Stock Statistics

S&P EPS Est. 1995	4.95	Tang. Bk. Value/Share	32.67
P/E on S&P Est. 1995	13.5	Beta	1.30
S&P EPS Est. 1996	5.35	Shareholders	29,000
Dividend Rate/Share	1.44	Market cap. (B)	$ 7.6
Shs. outstg. (M)	114.2	Inst. holdings	51%
Avg. daily vol. (M)	0.098	Insider holdings	NA

Value of $10,000 invested 5 years ago: $ 34,048

Fiscal Year Ending Dec. 31

	1995	% Change	1994	% Change	1993	% Change
Revenues (Million $)						
1Q	903.4	18%	767.2	NM	774.4	-3%
2Q	932.7	17%	798.3	4%	770.8	-2%
3Q	—	—	825.8	7%	772.8	1%
4Q	—	—	860.9	12%	770.7	2%
Yr.	—	—	3,252	5%	3,089	NM
Income (Million $)						
1Q	136.0	7%	127.1	10%	115.5	15%
2Q	140.9	7%	131.5	11%	118.7	15%
3Q	143.7	9%	131.9	10%	120.3	15%
4Q	—	—	132.3	11%	119.2	13%
Yr.	—	—	522.7	10%	473.7	15%
Earnings Per Share ($)						
1Q	1.18	13%	1.04	16%	0.90	15%
2Q	1.22	12%	1.09	16%	0.94	15%
3Q	1.26	14%	1.11	16%	0.96	16%
4Q	E1.28	13%	1.13	16%	0.97	14%
Yr.	E4.95	13%	4.37	16%	3.77	15%

Next earnings report expected: early January

SunTrust Banks

Business Summary - 13-OCT-95

SunTrust Banks was formed through the 1985 merger of SunBanks (Florida) and Trust Co. of Georgia; it subsequently acquired Third National Corp. (Tennessee and Alabama). With about $42.7 billion in assets at December 31, 1994, the company is the 20th largest bank holding company in the U.S., with 15 banks in Florida, 11 in Georgia, five in Tennessee and one in Alabama. Trust operations are among the largest in the Southeast. Other operations include mortgage banking, factoring, discount brokerage, credit related insurance, data processing, corporate finance and credit cards.

Contributions of the subsidiary banks ($ million) in 1994 were:

	Net Inc.	Return on Assets
SunBanks	$279.5	1.37%
Trust Co. of Ga.	210.8	1.62%
Third Nat'l	81.5	1.29%

Average earning assets during 1994 of $36.1 billion (up from $34.0 billion in 1993) were divided: loans 73%, investment securities 25%, other short-term investments 2%. Average sources of funds were non-interest bearing deposits 17%, NOW/money market 24%, savings deposits 11%, time deposits 24% (average deposits of $30.9 billion were up 4.0%), short-term borrowings 10%, long-term debt 2%, equity 7%, and other 5%.

At year-end 1994, nonperforming assets were $275 million (0.96% of loans and other real estate owned), down from $411 million (1.61%) a year earlier. The reserve for loan losses was 2.27% of loans, versus 2.22%. Domestic net chargeoffs during 1994 were 0.23% of average loans, against 0.46% in 1993.

The company owns 24,133,248 shares of common stock of Coca-Cola Co., which had a market value of about $1.36 billion at March 31, 1995.

Important Developments

Sep. '95—STI said it signed a definitive agreement to acquire Ponte Vedra Banking Corp. ($87 million in assets), which operates four offices in the Ponte Vedra, Jacksonville Beach and Atlantic Beach areas of Florida. Financial terms of the transaction were not disclosed.
Jun. '95—The company said it signed a definitive agreement to acquire Key Biscayne Bankcorp Inc. and its Key Biscayne Bank & Trust unit (assets of $145 million) for an undisclosed amount. Earlier, in May, STI completed the acquisition of Peoples State Bank of New Port Richey, Fla. ($124 million), for $16.9 million in cash and stock.

Capitalization

Long Term Debt: $1,002,000,000 (9/95).

Per Share Data ($)   (Year Ended Dec. 31)

	1994	1993	1992	1991	1990	1989
Tangible Bk. Val.	27.80	27.79	20.17	18.48	16.73	14.84
Earnings	4.37	3.77	3.28	2.90	2.75	2.61
Dividends	1.32	1.16	1.03	0.94	0.86	0.78
Payout Ratio	30%	31%	31%	32%	31%	30%
Prices - High	51⅜	49⅝	45⅝	40	24¼	26⅞
- Low	43½	41⅜	33½	20½	16½	19¾
P/E Ratio - High	12	13	14	14	9	10
- Low	10	11	10	7	6	8

Income Statement Analysis (Million $)

	1994	%Chg	1993	%Chg	1992	%Chg	1991
Net Int. Inc.	1,620	3%	1,572	4%	1,515	12%	1,352
Tax Equiv. Adj.	55.7	-11%	62.7	-9%	68.6	-10%	76.0
Non Int. Inc.	703	-3%	726	10%	658	9%	601
Loan Loss Prov.	138	-27%	189	-14%	220	7%	206
% Exp/Op Revs.	59%	—	60%	—	61%	—	61%
Pretax Inc.	782	12%	701	19%	589	17%	503
Eff. Tax Rate	33%	—	32%	—	30%	—	26%
Net Inc.	523	10%	474	15%	413	11%	371
% Net Int. Marg.	4.60%	—	4.80%	—	5.11%	—	4.83%

Balance Sheet & Other Fin. Data (Million $)

	1994	1993	1992	1991	1990	1989
Earning Assets:						
Money Mkt.	1,095	1,204	1,920	1,987	1,165	1,642
Inv. Securities	9,319	10,644	8,384	7,257	6,012	4,643
Com'l Loans	9,552	8,570	8,158	7,570	7,907	7,322
Other Loans	18,996	16,722	14,740	14,144	14,404	14,058
Total Assets	42,709	40,728	36,649	34,554	33,411	31,044
Demand Deposits	7,654	7,611	6,935	5,944	5,848	5,529
Time Deposits	24,565	22,875	21,909	22,044	20,978	19,433
LT Debt	930	630	545	475	480	485
Common Eqty.	3,453	3,610	2,704	2,546	2,305	2,089

Ratio Analysis

	1994	1993	1992	1991	1990	1989
% Ret. on Assets	1.3	1.3	1.2	1.1	1.1	1.2
% Ret. on Equity	14.8	16.5	15.8	15.2	16.0	16.9
% Loan Loss Resv.	2.3	2.2	2.0	1.7	1.6	1.6
% Loans/Deposits	88.6	83.0	79.0	77.1	82.4	84.6
% Equity to Assets	8.5	8.9	7.7	7.4	7.1	6.7

Dividend Data —Dividends were initiated in 1985. A dividend reinvestment plan is available.

Amt. of Div. $	Date Decl.	Ex-Div. Date	Stock of Record	Payment Date
0.360	Nov. 08	Nov. 25	Dec. 01	Dec. 15 '94
0.360	Feb. 16	Feb. 23	Mar. 01	Mar. 15 '95
0.360	Apr. 18	May. 25	Jun. 01	Jun. 15 '95
0.360	Aug. 22	Aug. 30	Sep. 01	Sep. 15 '95

Data as orig. reptd.; bef. results of disc opers. and/or spec. items. Per share data adj. for stk. divs. as of ex-div. date. E-Estimated. NA-Not Available. NM-Not Meaningful. NR-Not Ranked.

Office—25 Park Place, N.E., Atlanta, GA 30303; P.O. Box 4418, Atlanta, GA 30302. **Tel**—(404) 588-7711. **Chrmn & CEO**—J. B. Williams. **Pres**—L. P. Humann. **EVP & CFO**—J. W. Spiegel. **Investor Contact**—James C. Armstrong. **Dirs**—J. H. Brown, J. D. Camp Jr., W. M. Cason, R. C. Goizueta, T. M. Hahn Jr., D. H. Hughes, L. P. Humann, J. L. Lanier Jr., H. G. Pattillo, S. L. Probasco Jr., R. W. Scherer, J. W. Tucker Jr., J. B. Williams, J. H. Williams. **Transfer Agent**—Trust Company Bank, Atlanta. **Incorporated** in Georgia in 1984. **Empl**-19,408. **S&P Analyst:** Stephen R. Biggar

Supervalu Inc.

NYSE Symbol **SVU**
In S&P 500

25-OCT-95 | Industry:
Food

Summary: This company, one of the largest food wholesalers in the U.S., also operates 300 supermarkets under various names and formats.

S&P Opinion: Avoid (★★)	Recent Price • 30%	Yield • 3.2%
	52 Wk Range • 31⅛-22	12-Mo. P/E • 52.8

Quantitative Evaluations

Outlook
(1 Lowest—5 Highest)
• **4−**

Fair Value
• **32%**

Risk
• **Low**

Earn./Div. Rank
• **A**

Technical Eval.
• **Bearish** since 8/95

Rel. Strength Rank
(1 Lowest—99 Highest)
• **63**

Insider Activity
• **NA**

Earnings vs. Previous Year
▲=Up ▼=Down ▶=No Change

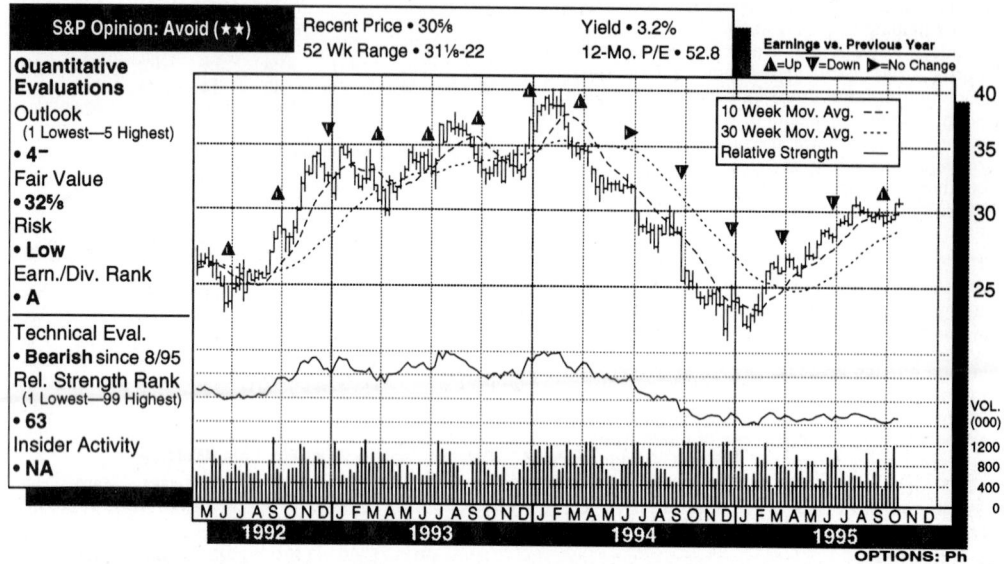

10 Week Mov. Avg. – – –
30 Week Mov. Avg. ·······
Relative Strength ——

VOL.
(000)
1200
800
400
0

1992 | 1993 | 1994 | 1995

OPTIONS: Ph

Overview - 25-OCT-95

Sales should decline in FY 96 (Feb.), as a result of the closing of units. Operating profits at the food distribution segment should improve, reflecting greater productivity. Retail store operating income should also increase, aided by the closure of unprofitable stores. However, these gains will be offset by much higher interest and corporate expense. Charges related to a restructuring program should increase to $0.20 to $0.25 a share in FY 96, from $0.13 in FY 95. Early benefits from the program should offset expenses in FY 97. Equity in earnings of ShopKo should improve, with easy comparisons. In the long term, SVU's reengineering program should put earnings on a growth track.

Valuation - 25-OCT-95

The shares have rebounded from the lows seen earlier in 1995. We believe that although SVU is moving ahead with its restructuring project, the resumption of earnings growth is a long way off. In addition to the costs invested in reengineering, major projects of this size often take longer to reap benefits than management anticipates. The shares should underperform the market in coming months. However, the 3.3% yield and the possible sale of the company's stake in Shopko (worth about $2.70 a share) provide some downside protection.

Key Stock Statistics

S&P EPS Est. 1996	2.45	Tang. Bk. Value/Share	9.58
P/E on S&P Est. 1996	12.5	Beta	0.67
S&P EPS Est. 1997	2.75	Shareholders	8,600
Dividend Rate/Share	0.98	Market cap. (B)	$ 2.1
Shs. outstg. (M)	68.2	Inst. holdings	70%
Avg. daily vol. (M)	0.161	Insider holdings	NA

Value of $10,000 invested 5 years ago: $ 12,456

Fiscal Year Ending Feb. 28

	1996	% Change	1995	% Change	1994	% Change
Revenues (Million $)						
1Q	4,973	NM	4,991	2%	4,876	49%
2Q	3,779	NM	3,774	2%	3,704	50%
3Q	—	—	3,908	6%	3,670	24%
4Q	—	—	3,891	6%	3,687	-4%
Yr.	—	—	16,564	4%	15,937	27%
Income (Million $)						
1Q	45.95	-9%	50.61	NM	51.08	11%
2Q	33.28	NM	33.52	-8%	36.24	12%
3Q	—	—	-84.12	NM	45.24	23%
4Q	—	—	43.33	-18%	52.61	5%
Yr.	—	—	43.33	-77%	185.3	13%
Earnings Per Share ($)						
1Q	0.66	-7%	0.71	NM	0.71	11%
2Q	0.49	4%	0.47	-8%	0.51	13%
3Q	E0.61	NM	-1.18	NM	0.63	24%
4Q	E0.69	13%	0.61	-16%	0.73	4%
Yr.	E2.45	NM	0.61	-76%	2.58	12%

Next earnings report expected: late December

Supervalu Inc.

Business Summary - 25-OCT-95

Supervalu Inc. (formerly Super Valu Stores) is one of the largest U.S. food wholesalers, following its late 1992 acquisition of Wetterau Inc. The company serves 4,600 retail stores in 48 states. SVU operated 296 retail food stores at the end of FY 95 (Feb.). It also has a 46% interest in ShopKo Stores, following that unit's 1991 initial public stock offering. ShopKo operated 128 discount stores in 15 states at the end of FY 95. Sales and operating profit by business segment (in millions) in FY 95 were:

	Sales	Profits
Wholesale foods	$14.8	$257.5
Retail foods	$ 4.2	$(104.3)

A $244 million restructuring of operations was announced in the third quarter of FY 95. Charges were for the sale, closure and restructuring of certain retail businesses, and for a fundamental change in business processes (the ADVANTAGE project). SVU aims to create a more efficient, low cost logistics network; to develop marketing capabilities for independent retailers; and to adopt a new approach to pricing.

In addition to supplying merchandise, the company offers retail stores a wide variety of support services, including advertising, promotional and merchandising assistance, computerised inventory control and many other services.

SVU's 296 retail stores operate under several formats and names, including Cub Foods, Hornbacher's, Scott's Foods, bigg's, Save-a-Lot and Twin Valu.

As of October 31, 1992, the company acquired Wetterau Inc. for $647 million and the assumption of $460 million in debt.

Important Developments

Sep. '95—Sales in the distribution segment were $3.4 billion in the second quarter of FY 96 (Feb.), level with a year earlier. Sales were hurt by last year's facility consolidation and the soft retail environment. Operating earnings were $78.5 million, down from $78.8 million last year. Expenses from the company's wholesale realignment project, ADVANTAGE, totaled $5.0 million, of which $4.0 million was charged to the food distribution segment. Excluding these expenses, earnings in the distribution segment would have increased 4.7%. Operating earnings in the retail food operations were $10.5 million, versus $6.6 million last year, benefiting from the bigg's acquisition and the elimination of operating losses from underperforming stores. SVU has repurchased over 3.6 million common shares under a December 1994 five million share authorization.

Capitalization

Long Term Debt: $1,462,784,000 (6/95), incl. $249.9 million of capital lease obligs.

Preferred Stock: 5,908 shs. ($1,000 stated value).

Per Share Data ($)

(Year Ended Feb. 28)

	1995	1994	1993	1992	1991	1990
Tangible Bk. Val.	9.58	11.68	9.75	14.35	13.01	11.59
Cash Flow	3.39	5.00	4.28	4.27	3.88	3.61
Earnings	0.61	2.58	2.31	2.78	2.06	1.97
Dividends	1.14	0.85	0.76	0.71	0.65	0.59
Payout Ratio	188%	33%	33%	24%	31%	30%
Cal. Yrs.	1994	1993	1992	1991	1990	1989
Prices - High	40⅛	37⅞	34⅞	30¼	29	30⅛
- Low	22	29½	23⅜	21⅝	21¾	22⅝
P/E Ratio - High	66	15	15	11	14	15
- Low	36	11	10	8	11	11

Income Statement Analysis (Million $)

	1995	%Chg	1994	%Chg	1993	%Chg	1992
Revs.	16,564	4%	15,937	27%	12,568	18%	10,632
Oper. Inc.	553	2%	543	26%	431	22%	352
Depr.	199	14%	174	23%	141	27%	111
Int. Exp.	138	12%	123	41%	87.1	16%	75.1
Pretax Inc.	16.0	-95%	294	14%	259	-20%	323
Eff. Tax Rate	NM	—	37%	—	36%	—	36%
Net Inc.	43.0	-77%	185	12%	165	-21%	208

Balance Sheet & Other Fin. Data (Million $)

	1995	1994	1993	1992	1991	1990
Cash	4.8	2.8	1.8	1.5	2.7	2.2
Curr. Assets	1,646	1,563	1,574	1,163	1,144	1,081
Total Assets	4,305	4,042	4,064	2,484	2,615	2,429
Curr. Liab.	1,447	1,224	1,326	745	998	951
LT Debt	1,460	1,263	1,347	608	577	561
Common Eqty.	1,187	1,270	1,135	1,031	979	870
Total Cap.	2,653	2,638	2,568	1,690	1,591	1,473
Cap. Exp.	298	240	152	158	262	223
Cash Flow	242	359	305	319	292	270

Ratio Analysis

	1995	1994	1993	1992	1991	1990
Curr. Ratio	1.1	1.3	1.2	1.6	1.1	1.1
% LT Debt of Cap.	55.0	47.9	52.5	36.0	36.3	38.1
% Net Inc.of Revs.	0.3	1.2	1.3	2.0	1.3	1.3
% Ret. on Assets	1.1	4.6	5.0	8.3	6.1	6.2
% Ret. on Equity	3.6	15.4	15.2	21.1	16.8	17.9

Dividend Data —Dividends have been paid since 1936. A new poison pill stock purchase rights plan was adopted in 1989.

Amt. of Div. $	Date Decl.	Ex-Div. Date	Stock of Record	Payment Date
0.235	Oct. 12	Nov. 25	Dec. 01	Dec. 15 '94
0.235	Nov. 21	Feb. 23	Mar. 01	Mar. 15 '95
0.235	Apr. 13	May. 25	Jun. 01	Jun. 15 '95
0.245	Jun. 28	Aug. 30	Sep. 01	Sep. 15 '95
0.245	Oct. 11	Nov. 29	Dec. 01	Dec. 15 '95

Data as orig. reptd.; bef. results of disc. opers. and/or spec. items. Per share data adj. for stk. divs. as of ex-div. date. E-Estimated. NA-Not Available. NM-Not Meaningful. NR-Not Ranked.

Office—11840 Valley View Rd., Eden Prairie, MN 55344 (PO Box 990, Minneapolis, MN 55440). **Tel**—(612) 828-4000. **Chrmn, Pres & CEO**—M. W. Wright. **EVP & CFO**—J. Girard. **Secy**—Teresa H. Johnson. **VP & Investor Contact**—Kris Sundberg (612-828-4441). **Dirs**—H. Cain, S. I. D'Agostino, E. C. Gage, V. H. Heath, W. A. Hodder, G. L. Keith, Jr., R. L. Knowlton, C. M. Lillis, H. K. Perlmutter, C. F. St. Mark, W. R. Wallin, M. W. Wright. **Transfer Agent & Registrar**—Norwest Bank Minnesota, South St. Paul. **Incorporated** in Delaware in 1925. **Empl**-43,500. **S&P Analyst:** Karen J. Sack, CFA

Sysco Corp.

NYSE Symbol **SYY**
In S&P 500

30-OCT-95

Industry:
Food

Summary: Sysco is the largest marketer and distributor of foodservice products in the U.S., serving more than 255,000 customers nationwide.

S&P Opinion: Accumulate (★★★★)	Recent Price • 29⅝	Yield • 1.5%
	52 Wk Range • 31⅜-24⅛	12-Mo. P/E • 20.7

Quantitative Evaluations

Outlook
(1 Lowest—5 Highest)
• **2+**

Fair Value
• **28⅛**

Risk
• **Low**

Earn./Div. Rank
• **A+**

Technical Eval.
• **Bullish** since 12/94

Rel. Strength Rank
(1 Lowest—99 Highest)
• **77**

Insider Activity
• **Neutral**

Earnings vs. Previous Year
▲=Up ▼=Down ▶=No Change

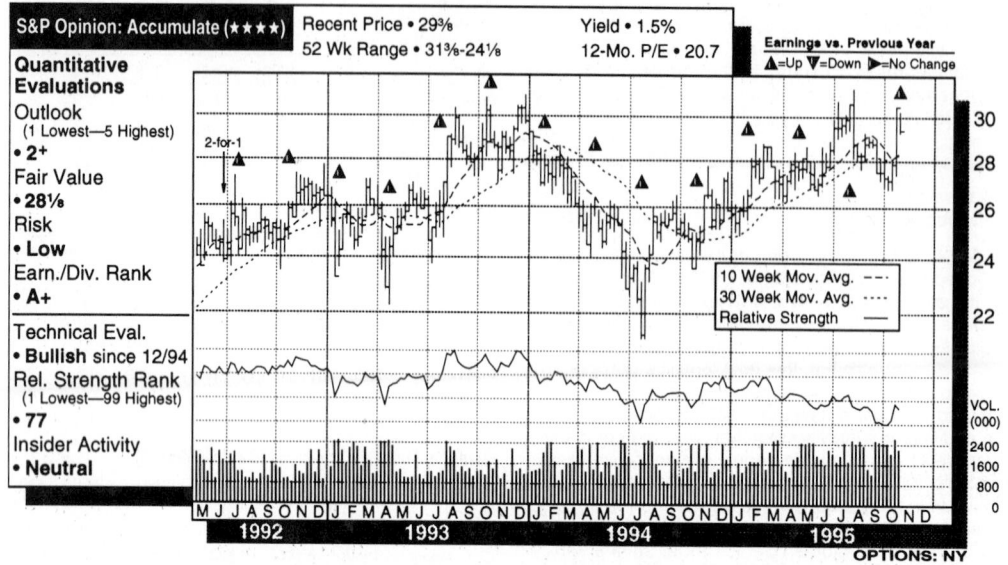

10 Week Mov. Avg. – – –
30 Week Mov. Avg. ·····
Relative Strength ——

OPTIONS: NY

Overview - 30-OCT-95

Sales are expected to grow at a 10% - 12% rate in fiscal 1996, reflecting high single-digit volume growth and, to a lesser extent, acquisition contributions and food inflation. Our volume expectations assume further 3% annual growth in the approximate $129 billion U.S. foodservice distribution market. Operating margins should benefit from further productivity enhancements and ongoing facility expansion and upgrading, which should allow pretax profits to grow at a slightly higher rate than sales. Ongoing stock buybacks should contribute to annual earnings per share growth of approximately 15% over the next few years. Finances are sound, which bolsters growth prospects.

Valuation - 30-OCT-95

Given our expectation of steady, fairly predictable annual earnings per share growth of about 15% over the next few years, we view the shares as attractive at current levels for both near-term and longer-term gains. The shares are especially attractive in times of economic weakness, given the company's relatively low business risk, strong finances and long history of consistent earnings and dividend growth. The shares have been good performers since mid-1994 due to such factors, and we anticipate further gains in the coming months. Longer-term prospects are also bright, reflecting Sysco's dominant position in the steadily growing U.S. foodservice distribution industry.

Key Stock Statistics

S&P EPS Est. 1996	1.60	Tang. Bk. Value/Share	6.26
P/E on S&P Est. 1996	18.4	Beta	1.07
S&P EPS Est. 1997	1.85	Shareholders	21,100
Dividend Rate/Share	0.44	Market cap. (B)	$ 5.4
Shs. outstg. (M)	182.8	Inst. holdings	61%
Avg. daily vol. (M)	0.570	Insider holdings	NA

Value of $10,000 invested 5 years ago: $ 19,695

Fiscal Year Ending Jun. 30

	1996	% Change	1995	% Change	1994	% Change
Revenues (Million $)						
1Q	3,292	10%	2,983	10%	2,710	12%
2Q	—	—	3,007	13%	2,666	11%
3Q	—	—	2,966	10%	2,685	12%
4Q	—	—	3,162	10%	2,882	2%
Yr.	—	—	12,118	11%	10,943	9%
Income (Million $)						
1Q	66.17	13%	58.37	21%	48.06	7%
2Q	—	—	63.55	14%	55.56	15%
3Q	—	—	52.79	16%	45.69	7%
4Q	—	—	77.12	14%	67.44	2%
Yr.	—	—	251.8	16%	216.8	7%
Earnings Per Share ($)						
1Q	0.36	13%	0.32	23%	0.26	8%
2Q	E0.40	14%	0.35	17%	0.30	15%
3Q	E0.34	17%	0.29	16%	0.25	9%
4Q	E0.50	19%	0.42	14%	0.37	6%
Yr.	E1.60	16%	1.38	17%	1.18	9%

Next earnings report expected: mid January

Business Summary - 30-OCT-95

Sysco Corporation distributes a wide range of food and related products to approximately 255,000 customers within the foodservice or away-from-home-eating industry throughout the U.S. Sales contributions by type of customer in recent fiscal years were:

	1995	1994	1993
Restaurants	60%	60%	60%
Hospital & nursing homes	12%	13%	13%
Schools & colleges	7%	7%	7%
Hotels & motels	6%	6%	6%
Other	15%	14%	14%

Traditional foodservice products distributed by the company to businesses and organizations include a full line of frozen foods, such as meats, fully prepared entrees, fruits, vegetables and desserts, and a full line of canned and dry goods. In addition, Sysco's broader line of product offerings includes such items as fresh meat, imported specialties and fresh produce. The company also provides a wide variety of nonfood items, including paper products (disposable napkins, plates and cups); tableware (china and silverware); restaurant and kitchen equipment and supplies; medical/surgical supplies; and cleaning supplies. Products include both nationally branded merchandise and items packed under Sysco's private label. No single traditional foodservice customer accounted for as much as 5% of the company's total sales in fiscal 1995.

Sysco's SYGMA Network subsidiary specializes in customized service to chain restaurants, whose sales consist of a variety of food products necessitated by the increasingly broad menus of chain restaurants. No chain restaurant customer accounted for as much as 3% of total sales in fiscal 1995.

The company estimates that it purchases from more than thousands of independent sources, none of which represents more than 5% of its purchases.

Important Developments

Oct. '95—SYY's real sales growth, after adjusting for food price inflation of 3%, was 7.4% in fiscal 1996's first quarter. Fiscal 1996's first quarter earnings per share also benefited from a slight increase in the operating margin (3.6% versus 3.5%) and a reduction in SYY's effective tax rate (39.0% versus 39.7%). Management said that it was pleased with the company's financial results, and noted that SYY's sales continued to build during the final month of the quarter, creating the momentum for an additional sales record in the week ended October 7. Separately, SYY said that its new Hartford, Connecticut "fold-out" facility that opened in early summer was exceeding original expectations.

Capitalization

Long Term Debt: $541,556,000 (4/1/95).

Per Share Data ($)

(Year Ended Jun. 30)

	1995	1994	1993	1992	1991	1990
Tangible Bk. Val.	6.26	5.33	4.72	4.25	3.48	2.73
Cash Flow	2.09	1.76	1.59	1.46	1.34	1.18
Earnings	1.38	1.18	1.08	0.93	0.83	0.73
Dividends	0.40	0.32	0.26	0.17	0.12	0.10
Payout Ratio	29%	27%	24%	18%	14%	14%
Prices - High	31⅜	29¼	31	27⅜	23¾	19¼
- Low	24⅞	21⅛	22¼	20⅝	15	12⅞
P/E Ratio - High	23	25	29	29	28	26
- Low	18	18	21	22	18	18

Income Statement Analysis (Million $)

	1995	%Chg	1994	%Chg	1993	%Chg	1992
Revs.	12,118	11%	10,942	9%	10,022	13%	8,893
Oper. Inc.	586	15%	509	10%	464	11%	418
Depr.	131	22%	107	13%	95.0	-5%	100
Int. Exp.	38.6	3%	37.6	-7%	40.3	-12%	45.6
Pretax Inc.	418	14%	368	11%	332	18%	282
Eff. Tax Rate	40%	—	41%	—	39%	—	39%
Net Inc.	2.5	-99%	217	7%	202	17%	172

Balance Sheet & Other Fin. Data (Million $)

	1995	1994	1993	1992	1991	1990
Cash	1,339	86.7	68.8	74.4	70.2	56.0
Curr. Assets	1,787	1,600	1,420	1,240	1,144	1,047
Total Assets	3,095	2,812	2,530	2,302	2,160	1,992
Curr. Liab.	945	847	746	655	612	574
LT Debt	542	539	494	489	543	583
Common Eqty.	1,404	1,241	1,137	1,057	919	771
Total Cap.	2,151	1,965	1,784	1,646	1,548	1,418
Cap. Exp.	202	161	128	134	135	182
Cash Flow	383	324	297	272	246	214

Ratio Analysis

	1995	1994	1993	1992	1991	1990
Curr. Ratio	1.9	1.9	1.9	1.9	1.9	1.8
% LT Debt of Cap.	25.2	27.4	27.7	29.7	35.1	41.1
% Net Inc.of Revs.	2.1	2.0	2.0	2.0	1.9	1.7
% Ret. on Assets	8.5	8.1	8.4	7.7	7.4	6.8
% Ret. on Equity	19.1	18.2	18.5	17.4	18.1	18.7

Dividend Data

Dividends have been paid since 1970. A "poison pill" stock purchase rights plan was adopted in 1986.

Amt. of Div. $	Date Decl.	Ex-Div. Date	Stock of Record	Payment Date
0.090	Sep. 01	Oct. 24	Oct. 28	Nov. 18 '94
0.110	Dec. 23	Jan. 23	Jan. 27	Feb. 17 '95
0.110	Feb. 08	Apr. 24	Apr. 28	May. 12 '95
0.110	May. 10	Jul. 26	Jul. 28	Aug. 18 '95
0.110	Sep. 01	Oct. 25	Oct. 27	Nov. 17 '95

Data as orig. reptd.; bef. results of disc. opers. and/or spec. items. Per share data adj. for stk. divs. as of ex-div. date. E-Estimated. NA-Not Available. NM-Not Meaningful. NR-Not Ranked.

Office—1390 Enclave Parkway, Houston, TX 77077-2099. **Tel**—(713) 584-1390. **Chrmn**—J. F. Woodhouse. **Pres & CEO**—B. M. Lindig. **VP, Treas & Investor Contact**—Diane S. Day. **VP & Secy**—La Dee G. Riker. **Dirs**—J. W. Anderson, J. F. Baugh, C. G. Campbell, C. H. Cotros, F. A. Godchaux III, J. Golden, D. J. Keller, B. M. Lindig, R. G. Merrill, D. H. Pegler Jr., F. H. Richardson, P. S. Sewell, A. J. Swenka, T. B. Walker Jr., J. F. Woodhouse. **Transfer Agent & Registrar**—First National Bank of Boston. **Incorporated** in Delaware in 1969. **Empl**- 28,100. **S&P Analyst:** Kenneth A. Shea

TJX Companies

NYSE Symbol **TJX**
In S&P 500

14-SEP-95

Industry:
Retail Stores

Summary: TJX primarily operates off-price apparel specialty stores and an off-price women's apparel mail-order catalog business.

S&P Opinion: Hold (★★★)	Recent Price • 12½	Yield • 4.5%
	52 Wk Range • 23¼-11⅛	12-Mo. P/E • 44.6

Quantitative Evaluations

Outlook
(1 Lowest—5 Highest)
• **4−**

Fair Value
• **13¼**

Risk
• **Average**

Earn./Div. Rank
• **B**

Technical Eval.
• **Bearish** since 9/95

Rel. Strength Rank
(1 Lowest—99 Highest)
• **8**

Insider Activity
• **NA**

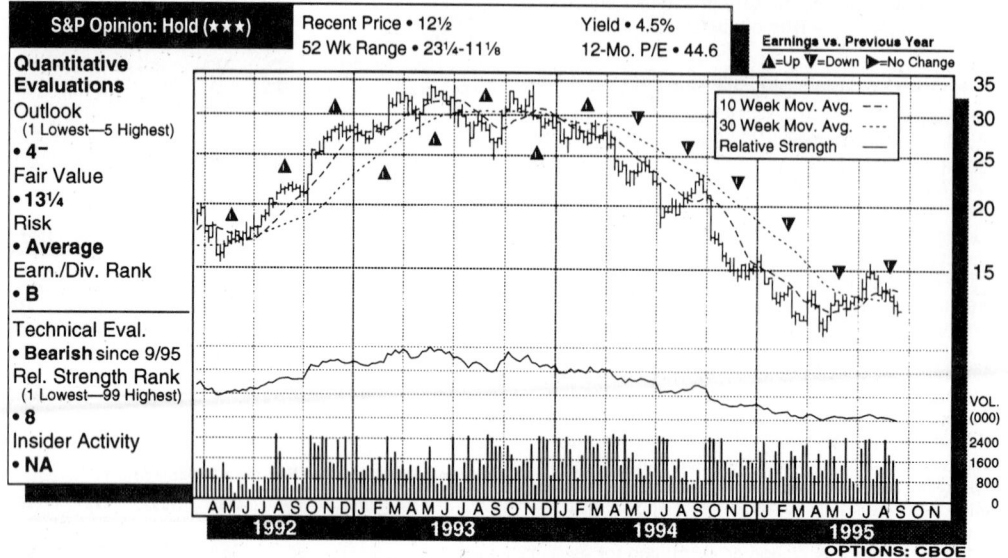

Earnings vs. Previous Year
▲=Up ▼=Down ▶=No Change

10 Week Mov. Avg. ---
30 Week Mov. Avg. ....
Relative Strength —

VOL. (000)

OPTIONS: CBOE

Overview - 14-SEP-95

Sales should increase moderately in 1995-96, mostly in the second half. The company plans to add some 40 to 45 T. J. Maxx stores, 12 Winners stores and 10 HomeGoods units. Gross margins should widen on the higher sales and better inventory management. Expense ratios should be well controlled. Operating income should increase at T. J. Maxx and remain flat at Chadwick's, while Winners should continue to achieve strong gains in operating profit. The sale of Hit or Miss, a money-losing operation, is a plus. International expansion bodes well for the long term. The company's U.K. venture, T.K. Maxx, with five stores and plans to double its size in 1995, is a prelude to expanding the off-price retail concept overseas. Aggressive expansion of Winners in understored Canada is another positive.

Valuation - 14-SEP-95

The share price has leveled off from the sharp decline that began in April. Weak sales gains and high markdowns have characterized apparel sales from 1994 through the first half of 1995; an excess of retail outlets and more competitive pricing at department stores have hurt earnings. We anticipate that these same factors will continue to restrict earnings gains for the balance of 1995. The sale of Hit or Miss is a plus, eliminating a loss and enabling management to focus on the company's more viable businesses. TJX has increased its long-term debt significantly during this period of weak earnings and peak inventories.

Key Stock Statistics

S&P EPS Est. 1996	0.90	Tang. Bk. Value/Share	5.61
P/E on S&P Est. 1996	13.9	Beta	1.66
S&P EPS Est. 1997	1.10	Shareholders	28,000
Dividend Rate/Share	0.56	Market cap. (B)	$0.905
Shs. outstg. (M)	72.4	Inst. holdings	83%
Avg. daily vol. (M)	0.352	Insider holdings	NA

Value of $10,000 invested 5 years ago: $ 9,719

Fiscal Year Ending Jan. 31

	1996	% Change	1995	% Change	1994	% Change
Revenues (Million $)						
1Q	911.6	7%	851.0	8%	785.6	17%
2Q	848.9	-2%	866.7	3%	841.0	12%
3Q	—	—	1,012	5%	959.7	14%
4Q	—	—	1,113	7%	1,040	4%
Yr.	—	—	3,843	6%	3,627	11%
Income (Million $)						
1Q	8.07	-58%	19.37	-15%	22.66	50%
2Q	7.71	-59%	18.80	-28%	25.99	37%
3Q	—	—	32.79	-31%	47.72	18%
4Q	—	—	11.67	-62%	30.68	5%
Yr.	—	—	82.62	-35%	127.1	22%
Earnings Per Share ($)						
1Q	0.09	-63%	0.24	-14%	0.28	27%
2Q	0.08	-65%	0.23	-30%	0.33	27%
3Q	E0.40	-5%	0.42	-31%	0.61	15%
4Q	E0.33	136%	0.14	-64%	0.39	3%
Yr.	E0.90	-13%	1.03	-36%	1.62	16%

Next earnings report expected: mid November

TJX Companies

Business Summary - 14-SEP-95

The TJX Companies consists of T. J. Maxx, Hit or Miss, Chadwick's of Boston, Winners Apparel and HomeGoods. In 1989, the company changed its name from Zayre Corp. following a major restructuring that included Zayre's acquisition of the minority interest in 83%-owned TJX Cos.

Sales and operating income (in millions) in 1994-95 were derived as follows:

	Sales	Profits
Off-price family apparel	80%	$208
Off-price women's specialty	9%	-5
Off-price catalog	11%	6

The T. J. Maxx chain operated 551 stores at January 28, 1995. It sells a broad range of brand name family apparel, related accessories, women's shoes, domestics and giftware at prices 20% to 60% below department and specialty stores.

The Hit or Miss off-price women's apparel chain operated 490 stores at the end of 1994-95; in August 1995, the company agreed to sell the Hit or Miss operations. Chadwick's of Boston is an off-price mail order company. Winners Apparel Ltd. is a rapidly growing Canadian off-price family apparel chain operating 37 stores. TJX also operates 15 HomeGoods off-price home fashion stores.

In 1988, the company sold its 388-unit Zayre discount department store division to Ames Department Stores. It remains contingently liable for the leases of most of the former Zayre stores still operated by Ames and has available $13.1 million in reserves to meet this liability. TJX also has $140.3 million in capital loss carryforwards.

Important Developments

Aug. '95—The company is selling its Hit or Miss division to a group including Hit or Miss management for $3 million in cash and a $10 million, seven-year note. TJX plans to shut 69 Hit or Miss stores prior to the closing, which is anticipated to be in September. The sale is expected to result in an after-tax loss of $31.7 million; the operating results of Hit or Miss are classified as discontinued operations. Management said that with the exception of Winners Apparel Ltd., sales in the second qurter of 1995-96 were below expectations. During the second quarter, the company completed a $200 million long-term debt financing. In 1994-95, the company repurchased 1.1 million common shares as part of a $100 million share repurchase program.

Capitalization

Long Term Debt: $433,600,000 (7/29/95).
8% Cum. Conv. Preferred Stock: 250,000 shs. ($100 stated value); conv. into com. at $21 a sh.
6.25% Cum. Conv. Preferred Stock: 1,650,000 shs. ($1 par); ea. conv. into 1.9277 com. shs.

Per Share Data ($)

(Year Ended Jan. 31)

	1995	1994	1993	1992	1991	1990
Tangible Bk. Val.	5.64	5.30	4.13	2.33	2.43	1.83
Cash Flow	2.07	2.52	2.20	1.81	1.68	1.71
Earnings	1.03	1.62	1.40	1.00	1.06	1.16
Dividends	0.54	0.38	0.46	0.57	0.44	3.90
Payout Ratio	53%	23%	33%	57%	42%	36%
Cal. Yrs.	1994	1993	1992	1991	1990	1989
Prices - High	29⅜	34¼	29	20⅜	17¾	30⅛
- Low	14¼	24½	15⅜	9⅝	8¾	13⅞
P/E Ratio - High	29	91	21	20	17	26
- Low	14	65	11	10	8	12

Income Statement Analysis (Million $)

	1995	%Chg	1994	%Chg	1993	%Chg	1992
Revs.	3,843	6%	3,627	11%	3,261	18%	2,758
Oper. Inc.	244	-18%	297	13%	262	28%	205
Depr.	76.5	14%	67.2	7%	62.7	11%	56.5
Int. Exp.	26.2	36%	19.2	-28%	26.6	-3%	27.3
Pretax Inc.	142	-33%	211	22%	173	43%	121
Eff. Tax Rate	42%	—	40%	—	40%	—	42%
Net Inc.	83.0	-35%	127	22%	104	49%	70.0

Balance Sheet & Other Fin. Data (Million $)

	1995	1994	1993	1992	1991	1990
Cash	42.0	58.0	107	67.0	83.0	54.0
Curr. Assets	1,046	882	821	656	631	563
Total Assets	1,638	1,427	1,305	1,105	1,047	949
Curr. Liab.	758	592	576	485	401	369
LT Debt	239	211	180	307	309	296
Common Eqty.	498	482	398	261	271	228
Total Cap.	880	836	729	621	646	580
Cap. Exp.	128	126	112	90.0	79.0	67.0
Cash Flow	152	187	163	127	122	117

Ratio Analysis

	1995	1994	1993	1992	1991	1990
Curr. Ratio	1.4	1.5	1.4	1.4	1.6	1.5
% LT Debt of Cap.	27.2	25.2	24.7	49.5	47.7	51.0
% Net Inc.of Revs.	2.2	3.5	3.2	2.5	3.0	3.5
% Ret. on Assets	514.0	9.3	8.4	6.5	7.4	5.5
% Ret. on Equity	15.5	27.3	29.8	26.4	29.7	16.8

Dividend Data —Dividends were initiated in 1980. A "poison pill" stock purchase right issued in 1989 was redeemed in early 1994 at $0.01 per right.

Amt. of Div. $	Date Decl.	Ex-Div. Date	Stock of Record	Payment Date
0.140	Sep. 21	Nov. 04	Nov. 10	Dec. 01 '94
0.140	Jan. 27	Feb. 03	Feb. 09	Mar. 02 '95
0.140	Apr. 04	May. 05	May. 11	Jun. 01 '95
0.140	Jun. 06	Aug. 08	Aug. 10	Aug. 31 '95
0.140	Sep. 07	Nov. 07	Nov. 09	Nov. 30 '95

Data as orig. reptd.; bef. results of disc. opers. and/or spec. items. Per share data adj. for stk. divs. as of ex-div. date. E-Estimated. NA-Not Available. NM-Not Meaningful. NR-Not Ranked.

Office—770 Cochituate Rd., Framingham, MA 01701. **Tel**—(508) 390-1000. **Chrmn**—S. L. Feldberg. **Pres & CEO**—B. Cammarata. **SVP-Fin & CFO**—D. G. Campbell. **VP, Treas & Investor Contact**—Steven Wishner. **VP & Secy**—J. H. Meltzer. **Dirs**—B. Cammarata, S. H. Feldberg, S. L. Feldberg, A. F. Loewy, J. M. Nelson, R. F. Shapiro, W. B. Shire, B. S. Stern, F. H. Wiley, A. Zaleznik. **Transfer Agent & Registrar**—State Street Bank & Trust Co., Boston. **Incorporated** in Delaware in 1962. **Empl**-36,000. **S&P Analyst:** Karen J. Sack, CFA

TRW Inc.

NYSE Symbol **TRW**
In S&P 500

27-AUG-95

Industry:
Auto parts/equipment

Summary: TRW provides high technology products and services to the automotive, space and defense, and information systems markets.

S&P Opinion: Accumulate (★★★★)	Recent Price • 77⅞		Yield • 2.6%
	52 Wk Range • 82⅝-61¾		12-Mo. P/E • 12.3

Earnings vs. Previous Year
▲=Up ▼=Down ▶=No Change

Quantitative Evaluations

Outlook
(1 Lowest—5 Highest)
• **3+**

Fair Value
• **76⅜**

Risk
• **Low**

Earn./Div. Rank
• **B+**

Technical Eval.
• **Bearish** since 7/95

Rel. Strength Rank
(1 Lowest—99 Highest)
• **41**

Insider Activity
• **Neutral**

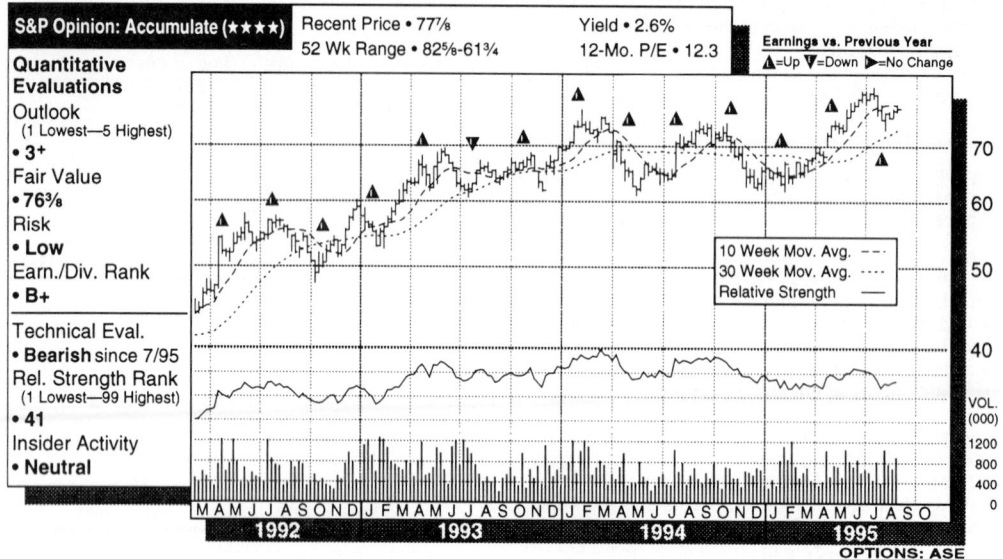

10 Week Mov. Avg. ---
30 Week Mov. Avg. ·····
Relative Strength —

VOL. (000)

OPTIONS: ASE

Overview - 25-AUG-95

Sales and profits should rise strongly again in 1996. Automotive operations will benefit from gains in vehicle production in Europe, and increased installation of airbags, remote keyless entry systems, engine valves and rack and pinion power steering in North America and Europe. Domestic operations should benefit from improvements in efficiency and growing business with Japanese automakers assembling vehicles in the U.S. The space and defense segment appears to have successfully negotiated the transition to lower government defense spending by focusing on civilian and commercial projects. The information systems segment is back on track and moving forward on an initiative to provide timelier, more accurate and more useful credit reporting information.

Valuation - 25-AUG-95

TRW is well positioned to capitalize on its status as a space and defense technology leader providing innovative products to civilian and commercial markets. The technology transfer to automotive applications has helped fuel 20% annual growth in TRW's content per vehicle produced worldwide since 1985. TRW's content amounted to $110 per vehicle in 1994, when some 45 million vehicles were produced worldwide. The next major initiative is establishment of a satellite-driven global cellular telephone system called Odyssey. Despite attractive prospects and although trading near its all-time high, the stock remains modestly valued at about 10 times our 1996 earnings estimate, and is a worthwhile portfolio addition.

Key Stock Statistics

S&P EPS Est. 1995	6.75	Tang. Bk. Value/Share	17.81
P/E on S&P Est. 1995	11.5	Beta	1.21
S&P EPS Est. 1996	7.35	Shareholders	31,300
Dividend Rate/Share	2.00	Market cap. (B)	$ 5.1
Shs. outstg. (M)	65.1	Inst. holdings	59%
Avg. daily vol. (M)	0.168	Insider holdings	NA

Value of $10,000 invested 5 years ago: $ 19,127

Fiscal Year Ending Dec. 31

	1995	% Change	1994	% Change	1993	% Change
Revenues (Million $)						
1Q	2,596	20%	2,159	6%	2,029	NM
2Q	2,712	17%	2,317	15%	2,011	-7%
3Q	—	—	2,164	14%	1,903	-6%
4Q	—	—	2,447	22%	2,005	-4%
Yr.	—	—	9,087	14%	7,948	-4%
Income (Million $)						
1Q	114.7	79%	64.10	26%	51.00	38%
2Q	123.1	42%	86.60	57%	55.00	-44%
3Q	—	—	81.80	60%	51.00	-35%
4Q	—	—	100.2	58%	63.60	-40%
Yr.	—	—	332.7	51%	220.1	13%
Earnings Per Share ($)						
1Q	1.74	79%	0.97	23%	0.79	36%
2Q	1.84	38%	1.33	56%	0.85	-3%
3Q	E1.42	13%	1.26	64%	0.77	12%
4Q	E1.75	17%	1.49	52%	0.98	4%
Yr.	E6.75	34%	5.05	49%	3.39	10%

Next earnings report expected: mid October

Business Summary - 25-AUG-95

TRW is a leader in auto parts, space and defense systems and information systems. Segment contributions in 1994:

	Sales	Profits
Automotive parts	62%	64%
Space and defense	31%	23%
Information systems	7%	13%

TRW designs, manufactures and sells four major automotive product lines for cars, trucks, buses, and off-highway vehicles: occupant restraint systems; steering and suspension systems; engine valves and valve train parts; and electrical and electronic products and controls. Parts are sold primarily to the original equipment market. Key growth areas include inflatable restraints (airbags), engine valves, power rack and pinion steering systems, and remote keyless entry systems. TRW expects to ship some 13 million airbag units in 1995, compared with 9.5 million in 1994 and 4.6 million in 1993. The growth in airbags is being fueled by increased U.S. sales of passenger-side airbags in cars and driver-side airbags in light trucks in the U.S., and increased foreign shipments for both occupant positions. Further growth in the next few years should be derived from addition of side-impact airbags and development of smart airbags which can modify deployment depending upon the size and position of the occupant and speed of the vehicle.

Space and defense includes spacecraft; propulsion systems; electro-optical and instrument systems; spacecraft payloads; lasers; space and defense mission software and systems engineering support services; communications systems, avionics systems, and other electronic technologies for space, defense and commercial applications.

Information systems includes consumer credit information, real estate information and services, and information systems engineering.

Important Developments

Jul. '95—TRW said that it would immediately appeal a directed verdict by a Phoenix court judge in favor of Talley Industries in TRW's airbag licensing lawsuit against Talley. A federal jury awarded $138 million in accelerated royalty payments to Talley after the judge dismissed claims by TRW that Talley had defaulted on a 1989 airbag license agreement which included a five-year non-compete clause. The $138 million award represents the present value of the estimated royalties which would be paid by TRW through 2001, the end of the 12-year agreement.

Capitalization

Long Term Debt: $709,000,000 (3/95).
Minority Interest: $65,000,000.
Conv. Serial Pfd. Stock II: $12,000,000.

Per Share Data ($)

(Year Ended Dec. 31)

	1994	1993	1992	1991	1990	1989
Tangible Bk. Val.	17.92	13.26	10.94	15.62	18.61	16.09
Cash Flow	12.28	10.46	9.39	4.10	9.64	10.05
Earnings	5.05	3.39	3.09	-2.30	3.39	4.31
Dividends	1.94	1.88	1.82	1.80	1.74	1.72
Payout Ratio	38%	55%	59%	NM	50%	39%
Prices - High	77½	70¼	60¼	46¼	51¾	49⅞
- Low	61	52½	41	34½	31⅜	41¼
P/E Ratio - High	15	21	19	NM	15	12
- Low	12	15	13	NM	9	10

Income Statement Analysis (Million $)

	1994	%Chg	1993	%Chg	1992	%Chg	1991
Revs.	9,087	14%	7,948	-4%	8,311	5%	7,913
Oper. Inc.	1,125	18%	953	-1%	967	19%	811
Depr.	476	4%	458	17%	392	NM	392
Int. Exp.	112	-23%	146	-17%	176	-12%	200
Pretax Inc.	535	49%	359	3%	348	NM	-128
Eff. Tax Rate	38%	—	39%	—	44%	—	NM
Net Inc.	333	51%	220	13%	194	NM	-139

Balance Sheet & Other Fin. Data (Million $)

	1994	1993	1992	1991	1990	1989
Cash	109	79.0	66.0	75.0	72.0	114
Curr. Assets	2,215	1,994	2,116	2,262	2,237	2,295
Total Assets	5,636	5,336	5,458	5,635	5,555	5,259
Curr. Liab.	1,986	1,826	2,012	1,982	1,947	1,794
LT Debt	694	870	941	1,213	1,042	1,063
Common Eqty.	1,812	1,523	1,404	1,671	1,893	1,734
Total Cap.	2,954	2,707	2,642	3,402	3,472	3,310
Cap. Exp.	506	482	530	537	587	452
Cash Flow	808	677	585	251	588	611

Ratio Analysis

	1994	1993	1992	1991	1990	1989
Curr. Ratio	1.1	1.1	1.1	1.1	1.1	1.3
% LT Debt of Cap.	24.3	32.1	35.6	35.7	30.0	32.1
% Net Inc.of Revs.	3.7	2.8	2.3	NM	2.5	3.6
% Ret. on Assets	6.0	4.0	3.5	NM	3.8	5.4
% Ret. on Equity	19.8	14.9	12.4	NM	11.4	15.9

Dividend Data —Dividends have been paid since 1936. A dividend reinvestment plan is available. A new "poison pill" stock purchase rights plan was adopted in 1988.

Amt. of Div. $	Date Decl.	Ex-Div. Date	Stock of Record	Payment Date
0.500	Jul. 27	Aug. 08	Aug. 12	Sep. 15 '94
0.500	Oct. 26	Nov. 04	Nov. 11	Dec. 15 '94
0.500	Dec. 14	Feb. 06	Feb. 10	Mar. 15 '95
0.500	Apr. 26	May. 08	May. 12	Jun. 15 '95
0.500	Jul. 26	Aug. 09	Aug. 11	Sep. 15 '95

Data as orig. reptd.; bef. results of disc. opers. and/or spec. items. Per share data adj. for stk. divs. as of ex-div. date.
E-Estimated. NA-Not Available. NM-Not Meaningful. NR-Not Ranked.

Office—1900 Richmond Rd., Cleveland, OH 44124. **Tel**—(216) 291-7000. **Chrmn & CEO**—J. T. Gorman. **Pres & COO**—P. S. Hellman. **EVP & CFO**—R. D. Sugar. **EVP-Secy**—M. A. Coyle. **Investor Contact**—Thomas A. Myers. **Dirs**—M. H. Armacost, R. B. Cheney, M. Feldstein, R. M. Gates, J. T. Gorman, C. H. Hahn, G. H. Heilmeier, P. S. Hellman, K. N. Horn, E. B. Jones, W. S. Kiser, J. T. Lynn, L. M. Martin, J. D. Ong, R. W. Pogue. **Transfer Agents**—First Chicago Trust Co. of New York, Jersey City, NJ; Company's office. **Registrars**—First Chicago Trust Co. of New York, Jersey City, NJ; National City Bank, Cleveland. **Incorporated** in Ohio in 1916. **Empl-** 64,200. **S&P Analyst:** Joshua M. Harari, CFA

Tandem Computers

NYSE Symbol **TDM**
In S&P 500

07-AUG-95

Industry:
Data Processing

Summary: Tandem is a manufacturer of continuously available multi-processing servers and fault tolerant Unix systems. Its UB Networks unit offers networking hardware and software solutions.

S&P Opinion: Accumulate (★★★★)	Recent Price • 12¾	Yield • Nil
	52 Wk Range • 19¾-12	12-Mo. P/E • 9.4

Quantitative Evaluations

Outlook
(1 Lowest—5 Highest)
• **4-**

Fair Value
• **13½**

Risk
• **Average**

Earn./Div. Rank
• **C**

Technical Eval.
• **Bearish** since 11/94

Rel. Strength Rank
(1 Lowest—99 Highest)
• **4**

Insider Activity
• **Neutral**

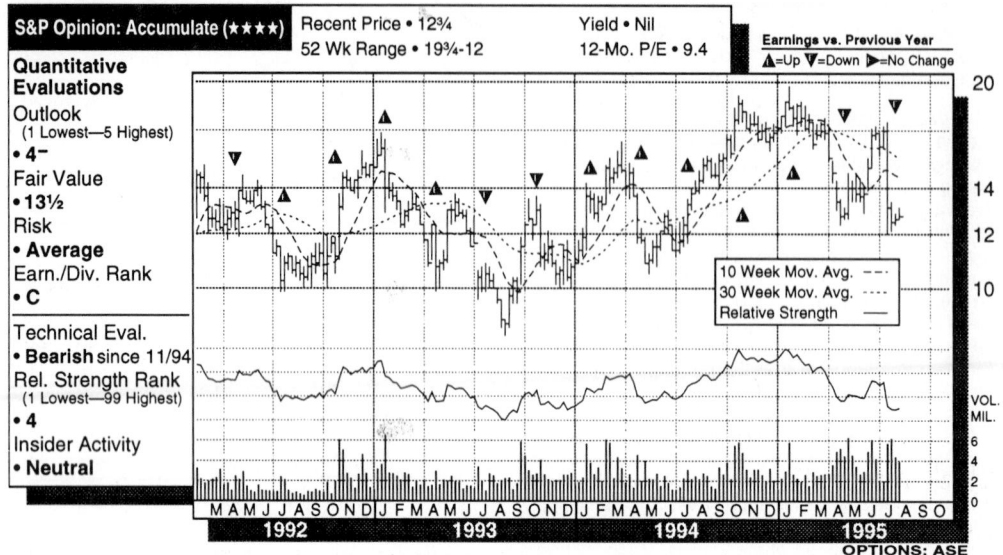

Earnings vs. Previous Year
▲=Up ▼=Down ▷=No Change

10 Week Mov. Avg. ---
30 Week Mov. Avg. ·····
Relative Strength —

OPTIONS: ASE

Overview - 07-AUG-95

Tandem's prospects for the balance of fiscal 1995 and into fiscal 1996 should improve, versus the disappointing results of recent quarters. Unit growth for the company's new family of servers, which offer substantial price/performance improvements over earlier versions, continues to be strong. While the company has experienced some product transition issues in these lines that led to lower than expected earnings, the underlying demand should ultimately lead to the resumption of double-digit revenue growth. Gross margins are expected to narrow through fiscal 1996, reflecting ongoing price pressures, but operating costs should be well controlled. The tax rate is expected to increase from depressed levels seen in recent quarters.

Valuation - 07-AUG-95

Despite the recent selloff in the shares, we are retaining our accumulate opinion on Tandem. The shares represent a good value at current levels, as the company is prudently focused on delivering increased price/performance characteristics in its product line every 15 to 18 months. This is the right strategy which, with proper execution, should allow Tandem to profitably exploit its niche of providing fault tolerant computing in mission critical applications. Based on our $1.55 EPS estimate for fiscal 1996, the shares remain attractive and are recommended for investors seeking above-average capital appreciation over the next 12 months.

Key Stock Statistics

S&P EPS Est. 1995	1.29	Tang. Bk. Value/Share	8.80
P/E on S&P Est. 1995	9.9	Beta	1.59
S&P EPS Est. 1996	1.55	Shareholders	6,500
Dividend Rate/Share	Nil	Market cap. (B)	$ 1.5
Shs. outstg. (M)	116.3	Inst. holdings	76%
Avg. daily vol. (M)	1.688	Insider holdings	NA

Value of $10,000 invested 5 years ago: $ 5,543

Fiscal Year Ending Sep. 30

	1995	% Change	1994	% Change	1993	% Change
Revenues (Million $)						
1Q	534.6	12%	475.5	-2%	484.0	6%
2Q	515.9	7%	484.1	-6%	517.7	3%
3Q	594.4	9%	543.9	14%	475.6	-5%
4Q	—	—	604.4	9%	553.9	-4%
Yr.	—	—	2,108	4%	2,031	NM
Income (Million $)						
1Q	35.23	41%	24.90	NM	5.14	NM
2Q	21.69	-16%	25.78	132%	11.10	26%
3Q	30.84	-36%	48.51	NM	-549.5	NM
4Q	—	—	71.00	NM	3.19	-88%
Yr.	—	—	170.2	NM	-530.1	NM
Earnings Per Share ($)						
1Q	0.30	36%	0.22	NM	0.05	NM
2Q	0.18	-22%	0.23	130%	0.10	11%
3Q	0.26	-40%	0.43	NM	-4.88	NM
4Q	E0.55	—	0.62	NM	0.03	-88%
Yr.	E1.29	—	1.50	NM	-4.72	NM

Next earnings report expected: late October

Business Summary - 07-AUG-95

Tandem Computers designs and manufactures continuously available parallel processing servers and fault-tolerant UNIX systems for critical business computing. The company is also a leading provider of networking products. International business represented 46% of revenues in both fiscal 1994 and 1993.

TDM's NonStop systems and servers are designed to provide continuous operation, distributed processing, data integrity and modular expandability. They feature multiple independent processors and nonshared memory. During 1993, the company introduced the Himalaya line of NonStop servers, which offered greatly improved price performance over previous products. The Himalya line incorporates reduced instruction set computing (RISC) microprocessors from MIPS Technologies, a subsidiary of Silicon Graphics. These products also incorporate the NonStop Kernal operating system, which is designed to keep applications running through any single failure. For example, if a processor fails, work is redirected to other processors in the system.

The Integrity FT systems family is designed to extend fault tolerance to the market for UNIX software-based systems and is also based on RISC technology. The company also offers a complete line of non-fault-tolerant UNIX systems, the Integrity NR series, including the entry level Indy and Indigo workstations, which are resold by it under an agreement with Silicon Graphics.

In January 1995, TDM introduced new generations of its Himalaya and Integrity servers that offer a 33% to a 300% improvement over older models at comparable prices.

The company's UB Networks subsidiary (formerly Ungermann-Bass) provides a full-line of networking products including modular and stackable hubs, high speed concentrators, internetworking products and adapter cards.

The company's systems are used worldwide in a number of governmental agencies and in over 25 industries, including manufacturing, banking, communications, financial services, retail and transportation.

Important Developments

Jul. '95—The company signed a letter of intent with a major computer company to jointly develop and manufacture servers for the Microsoft Windows NT segment of the market.
Jun. '95—TDM was chosen by Woolworth Corp. to develop and run the latter's data warehouse and decision support system. Separately, the company entered into a strategic relationship with Sweden-based Ericsson, that will integrate Tandem computing solutions for UNIX systems into Ericsson's future UNIX applications. The supply pact is expected to total $30 million.

Capitalization

Long Term Debt: $76,735,000 (6/95).

Per Share Data ($)

(Year Ended Sep. 30)

	1994	1993	1992	1991	1990	1989
Tangible Bk. Val.	8.07	6.30	9.47	9.79	9.62	7.80
Cash Flow	2.94	-3.50	1.26	1.84	2.23	2.22
Earnings	1.50	-4.72	-0.38	0.33	1.13	1.17
Dividends	Nil	Nil	Nil	Nil	Nil	Nil
Payout Ratio	Nil	Nil	Nil	Nil	Nil	Nil
Prices - High	19⅛	16⅞	15⅞	17⅝	30⅛	26⅜
- Low	10½	8½	9⅞	9⅛	8⅞	14¾
P/E Ratio - High	13	NM	NM	53	27	23
- Low	7	NM	NM	28	8	13

Income Statement Analysis (Million $)

	1994	%Chg	1993	%Chg	1992	%Chg	1991
Revs.	2,108	4%	2,031	NM	2,037	6%	1,922
Oper. Inc.	320	162%	122	-51%	249	12%	222
Depr.	163	19%	137	-23%	179	10%	163
Int. Exp.	13.0	-17%	15.7	-11%	17.6	-13%	20.3
Pretax Inc.	181	NM	-462	NM	-32.0	NM	57.0
Eff. Tax Rate	6.10%	—	NM	—	NM	—	39%
Net Inc.	170	NM	-529	NM	-41.0	NM	35.0

Balance Sheet & Other Fin. Data (Million $)

	1994	1993	1992	1991	1990	1989
Cash	124	125	149	115	91.0	197
Curr. Assets	928	851	988	873	863	863
Total Assets	1,762	1,685	2,045	1,932	1,877	1,619
Curr. Liab.	737	862	631	511	495	441
LT Debt	86.0	86.0	94.0	93.0	96.0	107
Common Eqty.	939	737	1,237	1,248	1,203	989
Total Cap.	1,025	823	1,415	1,421	1,383	1,177
Cap. Exp.	153	146	125	138	301	136
Cash Flow	333	-392	138	198	242	225

Ratio Analysis

	1994	1993	1992	1991	1990	1989
Curr. Ratio	1.3	1.0	1.6	1.7	1.7	2.0
% LT Debt of Cap.	8.4	10.5	6.6	6.6	6.9	9.1
% Net Inc.of Revs.	8.1	NM	NM	1.8	6.5	7.2
% Ret. on Assets	9.8	NM	NM	1.8	6.8	7.9
% Ret. on Equity	20.1	NM	NM	2.8	10.9	12.5

Dividend Data (No cash dividends have been paid. A "poison pill" stock purchase right was adopted in 1985.)

Data as orig. reptd.; bef. results of disc. opers. and/or spec. items. Per share data adj. for stk. divs. as of ex-div. date.
E-Estimated. NA-Not Available. NM-Not Meaningful. NR-Not Ranked.

Office—19333 Vallco Parkway, Cupertino, CA 95014-2599. **Tel**—(408) 285-6000. **Chrmn**—T. J. Perkins. **Pres & CEO**—J. G. Treybig. **SVP & CFO**—D. J. Rynne. **VP & Secy**—J. T. Parry. **Investor Contact**—Pete Selda. **Dirs**—J. F. Bennett, M. Collins, C. Fraser, F. P. Johnson, Jr., R. C. Marshall, T. J. Perkins, V. S. Shirley, R. G. Stone, Jr., W. SyCip, J. G. Treybig, T. I. Unterberg, W. B. Wriston. **Transfer Agent & Registrar**—First National Bank of Boston. **Incorporated** in California in 1974; reincorporated in Delaware in 1980. **Empl**-8,466. **S&P Analyst:** John D. Coyle, CFA

Tandy Corp.

NYSE Symbol **TAN**
In S&P 500

06-SEP-95

Industry:
Retail Stores

Summary: This leading retailer of consumer electronic products operates about 4,700 owned and 2,000 franchised Radio Shack stores and other outlets.

S&P Opinion: Buy (★★★★)

Recent Price • 61	Yield • 1.2%
52 Wk Range • 63⅝-40⅞	12-Mo. P/E • 20.0

Quantitative Evaluations

Outlook
(1 Lowest—5 Highest)
• **4⁻**

Fair Value
• **62¼**

Risk
• **Low**

Earn./Div. Rank
• **B**

Technical Eval.
• **Bullish** since 7/95

Rel. Strength Rank
(1 Lowest—99 Highest)
• **70**

Insider Activity
• **NA**

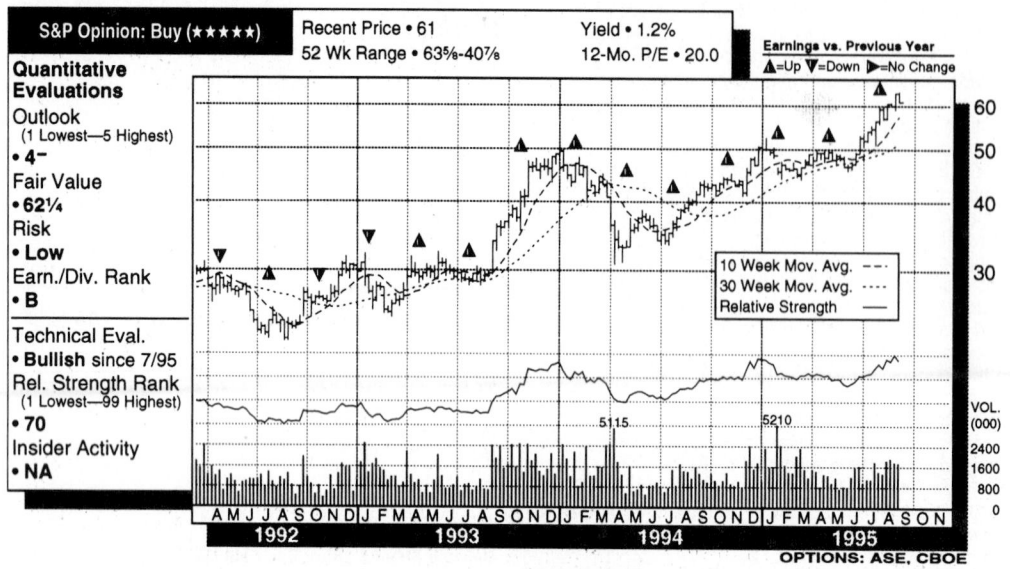

Earnings vs. Previous Year
▲=Up ▼=Down ▶=No Change

10 Week Mov. Avg. ---
30 Week Mov. Avg. ·····
Relative Strength —

OPTIONS: ASE, CBOE

Overview - 06-SEP-95

We expect sales and earnings growth to accelerate over the next several quarters, paced by double-digit same-store sales at core Radio Shack stores and an aggressive expansion plan that will add 100 new stores in 1995. Tandy will focus on its Computer City and Incredible Universe superstores, which have performed above expectations. As these high-volume, low-price stores account for a greater percentage of total sales, gross margins will narrow, but the increased volume and greater expense efficiencies should allow sales gains to flow through to earnings. The closing of unprofitable mall stores and the sale of credit accounts and extended service contracts will let the company capitalize on its core retailing strengths.

Valuation - 06-SEP-95

The shares recently reached new highs. Results in the first half of 1995 benefited from improving same-store sales, the divestiture of unprofitable mall stores, and the sale of the company's credit business. Although aggressive price-cutting among intensely competitive consumer electronics retailers will restrict margins, Tandy should be able to offset this by reducing its cost structure. The repurchase of common shares will aid EPS comparisons. We expect earnings to grow about 25% for the balance of 1995. With the shares trading at a P/E below our estimated growth rate, we recommend purchase.

Key Stock Statistics

S&P EPS Est. 1995	3.65	Tang. Bk. Value/Share	22.43
P/E on S&P Est. 1995	16.7	Beta	1.60
S&P EPS Est. 1996	4.35	Shareholders	33,700
Dividend Rate/Share	0.72	Market cap. (B)	$ 4.0
Shs. outstg. (M)	65.2	Inst. holdings	72%
Avg. daily vol. (M)	0.379	Insider holdings	NA

Value of $10,000 invested 5 years ago: $ 17,171

Fiscal Year Ending Dec. 31

	1995	% Change	1994	% Change	1993	% Change
Revenues (Million $)						
1Q	1,227	24%	992.0	15%	865.0	1%
2Q	1,185	17%	1,009	20%	843.0	-1%
3Q	--	—	1,119	19%	940.0	4%
4Q	--	—	1,823	25%	1,455	10%
Yr.	--	—	4,944	20%	4,103	—
Income (Million $)						
1Q	38.95	-7%	41.80	3%	40.67	-3%
2Q	37.96	10%	34.42	8%	31.74	-60%
3Q	—	—	46.19	9%	42.56	21%
4Q	—	—	101.9	26%	80.66	187%
Yr.	—	—	224.3	15%	195.6	NM
Earnings Per Share ($)						
1Q	0.55	4%	0.53	6%	0.50	19%
2Q	0.55	25%	0.44	16%	0.38	12%
3Q	E0.75	27%	0.59	13%	0.52	30%
4Q	E1.80	31%	1.37	33%	1.03	NM
Yr.	E3.65	25%	2.91	17%	2.48	—

Next earnings report expected: mid October

Business Summary - 06-SEP-95

Tandy Corporation is a retailer of consumer electronics and personal computers. In July 1993, its computer manufacturing operations, including four plants in the U.S. and one in Scotland, and marketing operations in the U.S., Canada and Europe were sold to AST Research.

At December 31, 1994, Radio Shack, the largest operating division, had 4,598 company-owned stores throughout the U.S. in major malls, strip centers and individual store fronts, primarily in metropolitan markets. The company also had a network of 2,005 dealer/franchise stores to service smaller communities. In addition, Radio Shack had 67 international dealers. Company-owned stores average approximately 2,350 sq. ft. and carry an assortment of electronic parts and accessories, audio/video equipment, cellular and conventional telephones, scanners, electronic toys and personal computers.

At December 31, 1994, the Tandy Name Brand Retail Group consisted of 306 VideoConcepts, McDuff and The Edge in Electronics retail outlets that sold name brand TVs, audio equipment, PCs and other electronic products and appliances. In line with a business restructuring plan to close or convert 233 of these stores, on January 3, 1995, the Tandy Name Brand division was dissolved and the continuing stores became part of a new specialty retail group of the Radio Shack division.

At the end of 1994, the company was also operating 69 Computer City stores, including four in Europe and three in Canada. The Computer City chain operates in a supercenter format (carrying over 5,000 products) and features name brand computers and related products. The division also operates nine Incredible Universe stores that are 160,000 to 200,000 sq. ft. in size and offer a broad selection of consumer electronics and appliances.

Important Developments

Sep. '95—Tanday reported August 1995 sales totaling $443.8 million, up 27%, year to year. Same-store sales rose 7%, reflecting continued strength in the Radio Shack business, and the launch of Windows 95.

Capitalization

Long Term Debt: $148,863,000 (6/95).

Per Share Data ($) (Year Ended Dec. 31)

	1994	1993	1992	1991	1990	1989
Tangible Bk. Val.	23.28	22.87	21.00	18.12	19.06	18.73
Cash Flow	3.61	3.10	0.49	3.38	3.85	4.67
Earnings	2.91	2.48	0.02	2.24	2.58	3.54
Dividends	0.63	0.60	0.30	0.60	0.60	0.60
Payout Ratio	22%	24%	NM	27%	23%	16%
Prices - High	50⅝	50¾	31¾	31¾	36½	41⅛
- Low	30¾	24⅝	22¼	22¼	23⅜	23½
P/E Ratio - High	17	20	NM	14	14	12
- Low	11	10	NM	10	9	7

Income Statement Analysis (Million $)

	1994	%Chg	1993	%Chg	1992	%Chg	1991
Revs.	4,991	20%	4,160	87%	2,228	-53%	4,742
Oper. Inc.	440	4%	423	160%	163	-63%	435
Depr.	84.8	6%	79.9	116%	37.0	-64%	103
Int. Exp.	30.0	-24%	39.7	56%	25.5	-57%	59.4
Pretax Inc.	360	16%	311	NM	33.0	-89%	300
Eff. Tax Rate	38%	—	37%	—	89%	—	39%
Net Inc.	224	14%	196	NM	4.0	-98%	184

Balance Sheet & Other Fin. Data (Million $)

	1994	1993	1992	1991	1990	1989
Cash	206	213	84.0	106	186	135
Curr. Assets	2,556	2,160	1,954	2,340	2,262	2,485
Total Assets	3,244	3,219	3,151	3,165	3,078	3,240
Curr. Liab.	1,206	1,032	880	784	711	1,172
LT Debt	153	187	307	358	428	253
Common Eqty.	1,370	1,481	1,346	1,388	1,747	1,723
Total Cap.	2,004	2,137	2,223	2,349	2,337	2,045
Cap. Exp.	181	129	55.0	123	139	113
Cash Flow	270	236	38.0	270	301	382

Ratio Analysis

	1994	1993	1992	1991	1990	1989
Curr. Ratio	2.1	2.1	2.2	3.0	3.2	2.1
% LT Debt of Cap.	7.7	8.7	13.8	15.2	18.3	12.3
% Net Inc.of Revs.	4.5	4.7	0.2	3.9	4.4	6.5
% Ret. on Assets	7.3	6.1	NM	6.5	6.6	10.4
% Ret. on Equity	13.6	10.5	NM	11.9	11.7	17.3

Dividend Data —Dividends, omitted in 1959, were reinstated in 1986.

Amt. of Div. $	Date Decl.	Ex-Div. Date	Stock of Record	Payment Date
0.150	Aug. 02	Sep. 26	Oct. 01	Oct. 21 '94
0.180	Dec. 16	Dec. 23	Jan. 01	Jan. 21 '95
0.180	Feb. 23	Mar. 27	Apr. 01	Apr. 21 '95
0.180	May. 24	Jun. 28	Jul. 01	Jul. 21 '95
0.180	Jul. 31	Sep. 27	Oct. 01	Oct. 21 '95

Data as orig. reptd.; bef. results of disc. opers. and/or spec. items. Per share data adj. for stk. divs. as of ex-div. date. E-Estimated. NA-Not Available. NM-Not Meaningful. NR-Not Ranked.

Office—1800 One Tandy Center, Fort Worth, Texas 76102. **Tel**—(817) 390-3700. **Chrmn & Pres**—J. V. Roach. **SVP & CFO**—D. H. Hughes. **SVP & Secy**—H. C. Winn. **VP & Treas**—L. K. Jensen. **Investor Contact**—Martin Moad. **Dirs**—J. I. Cash, Jr., D. R. Ecton, L. F. Kornfeld Jr., J. L. Messman, W. G. Morton, Jr., T. G. Plaskett, J. V. Roach, W. T. Smith, A. J. Stein, W. E. Tucker, J. L. Upchurch, J. A. Wilson. **Transfer Agent & Registrar**—First National Bank of Boston. **Incorporated** in New Jersey in 1899; reincorporated in Delaware in 1967. **Empl**-45,800. **S&P Analyst:** Maureen C. Carini

Tektronix, Inc.

NYSE Symbol **TEK**
In S&P 500

26-OCT-95

Industry:
Specialty instruments

Summary: Tektronix is the world's leading producer of oscilloscopes. It also has a position in printers, X terminals and television systems.

S&P Opinion: Accumulate (★★★★)	Recent Price • 58⅝	Yield • 1.0%
	52 Wk Range • 61⅞-31⅜	12-Mo. P/E • 21.2

Quantitative Evaluations

Outlook
(1 Lowest—5 Highest)
• **2+**

Fair Value
• **56½**

Risk
• **Average**

Earn./Div. Rank
• **B-**

Technical Eval.
• **Bullish** since 3/95

Rel. Strength Rank
(1 Lowest—99 Highest)
• **92**

Insider Activity
• **Neutral**

Earnings vs. Previous Year
▲=Up ▼=Down ▶=No Change

10 Week Mov. Avg. – – –
30 Week Mov. Avg. · · · ·
Relative Strength —

OPTIONS: ASE, P

Overview - 26-OCT-95

Sales for 1995-96 should increase more than 20%, aided by stronger worldwide economic conditions and well-received new product introductions. The largest gains should be achieved by color printing and imaging, which is especially benefiting from strong demand for its Phaser line of printers aimed at the office market. Video systems should experience higher sales, due to new products and a stronger broadcasting market. Network displays should continue to benefit from the company's leading position in X terminals. A long-delayed turnaround in the measurement business should gain further momentum, led by new products and strong industry sales. Margins should widen on the higher volume and well controlled costs. A stock repurchase program should extend the gain in share earnings.

Valuation - 26-OCT-95

Tektronix's shares have performed strongly in 1995, as earnings have exceeded expectations. Investors now view the company as revitalized, due to the success of new product introductions over the past several years. The company now generates 60% of its product revenue from products introduced over the past two years, up from 22% in 1991. The recovery in the company's core measurement business is also welcomed following years of depressed demand. These factors should continue to allow for strong earnings that should lead to further appreciation in the shares.

Key Stock Statistics

S&P EPS Est. 1996	3.40	Tang. Bk. Value/Share	19.17
P/E on S&P Est. 1996	17.2	Beta	1.09
Dividend Rate/Share	0.60	Shareholders	4,500
Shs. outstg. (M)	33.5	Market cap. (B)	$ 2.0
Avg. daily vol. (M)	0.114	Inst. holdings	75%
		Insider holdings	NA

Value of $10,000 invested 5 years ago: $ 37,876

Fiscal Year Ending May 31

	1996	% Change	1995	% Change	1994	% Change
Revenues (Million $)						
1Q	401.0	27%	314.7	8%	290.1	-5%
2Q	—	—	350.3	10%	317.2	-5%
3Q	—	—	367.2	10%	332.8	7%
4Q	—	—	439.5	16%	377.9	7%
Yr.	—	—	1,472	12%	1,318	1%
Income (Million $)						
1Q	22.67	42%	15.94	64%	9.73	—
2Q	—	—	18.18	59%	11.46	36%
3Q	—	—	21.72	40%	15.48	70%
4Q	—	—	25.47	6%	24.01	NM
Yr.	—	—	81.31	34%	60.68	NM
Earnings Per Share ($)						
1Q	0.68	31%	0.52	63%	0.32	52%
2Q	E0.77	31%	0.59	59%	0.37	32%
3Q	E0.90	29%	0.70	37%	0.51	70%
4Q	E1.05	28%	0.82	3%	0.80	NM
Yr.	E3.40	29%	2.63	32%	2.00	NM

Next earnings report expected: mid December

Tektronix, Inc.

Business Summary - 26-OCT-95

Tektronix is a leading supplier of electronic products and systems in the areas of test and measurement, computer graphics and communications. Sales by product line in the past two fiscal years:

	1994-95	1993-94
Measurement	50%	51%
Color printing & imaging	31%	24%
Video systems	12%	11%
Network displays	6%	7%
Other	1%	7%

Foreign sales accounted for 49% of revenues in fiscal 1994-95.

The oscilloscope is the company's primary measurement product. Oscilloscopes measure an electrical event and display the measurement on the screen of a cathode ray tube. Other instrument products include logic analyzers, digitizers, curve tracers and a modular line of general purpose test instruments.

Color printing and imaging sales are led by the company line of color Phaser printers aimed at the office market.

Video systems primarily consist of television systems products that include vectorscopes, waveform monitors, picture monitors, signal generators, demodulators and correctors, used primarily by the television industry to test and display the quality of video signals. Television routing and switching equipment is also made. Communications products also include cable and fiber optic testers and data communications analyzers.

Network displays sales primarily consist of the company's line of X terminals.

Important Developments

Sep. '95—TEK said that during the first quarter of 1995-96, sales growth was led by a 36% increase at the color printing and imaging division. Demand for its Phaser 340 solid ink printers was especially strong. Demand for Profile video disk recorder and Grass Valley Network Display products led the 29% increase in sales at the video and networking division. Sales at the measurement business division rose 19%, paced by strong increases in tools and communication test equipment. In addition, international sales increased 30%, while domestic sales rose 22%. Margins widened, as effective cost controls more than offset declining gross margins as TEK continued to sell more of its products through alternative distribution channels, continued to experience the short-term impact of early shipments of the Phaser 340 color printer, and benefited from the impact of increased systems integration sales.

Capitalization

Long Term Debt: $153,756,000 (8/95).

Per Share Data ($)

(Year Ended May 31)

	1995	1994	1993	1992	1991	1990
Tangible Bk. Val.	19.17	14.93	13.34	14.73	14.42	12.94
Cash Flow	3.94	3.80	0.16	2.90	4.22	-0.67
Earnings	2.63	2.00	-1.94	0.67	1.66	-3.19
Dividends	0.60	0.60	0.60	0.60	0.60	0.60
Payout Ratio	23%	30%	NM	90%	36%	NM
Cal. Yrs.	1994	1993	1992	1991	1990	1989
Prices - High	40½	27⅞	22⅞	30⅞	19¼	24¼
- Low	23⅝	20⅛	16½	16	11⅝	16⅛
P/E Ratio - High	15	14	NM	46	12	NM
- Low	9	10	NM	24	7	NM

Income Statement Analysis (Million $)

	1995	%Chg	1994	%Chg	1993	%Chg	1992
Revs.	1,472	12%	1,318	1%	1,302	NM	1,297
Oper. Inc.	152	6%	143	5%	136	3%	132
Depr.	40.7	-26%	54.9	-13%	63.1	-4%	65.6
Int. Exp.	10.1	1%	10.0	-3%	10.3	-9%	11.3
Pretax Inc.	110	28%	86.0	NM	-99.0	NM	30.0
Eff. Tax Rate	26%	—	29%	—	NM	—	34%
Net Inc.	81.2	34%	60.7	NM	-58.0	NM	20.0

Balance Sheet & Other Fin. Data (Million $)

	1995	1994	1993	1992	1991	1990
Cash	32.0	43.0	30.0	18.0	33.0	71.0
Curr. Assets	651	591	516	447	461	523
Total Assets	1,210	991	985	877	900	973
Curr. Liab.	381	276	334	295	309	340
LT Debt	105	104	70.0	84.0	89.0	175
Common Eqty.	603	469	435	440	428	385
Total Cap.	708	574	505	530	548	591
Cap. Exp.	102	70.3	57.8	66.0	68.0	97.0
Cash Flow	122	116	5.0	85.0	123	-19.0

Ratio Analysis

	1995	1994	1993	1992	1991	1990
Curr. Ratio	1.7	2.0	1.5	1.5	1.5	1.5
% LT Debt of Cap.	14.8	18.2	13.9	15.9	16.3	29.7
% Net Inc.of Revs.	5.5	4.6	NM	1.5	3.6	NM
% Ret. on Assets	7.4	6.2	NM	2.2	5.1	NM
% Ret. on Equity	15.2	13.5	NM	4.5	11.9	NM

Dividend Data —Dividends have been paid since 1972.

Amt. of Div. $	Date Decl.	Ex-Div. Date	Stock of Record	Payment Date
0.150	Sep. 21	Oct. 03	Oct. 07	Oct. 24 '94
0.150	Dec. 15	Jan. 13	Jan. 20	Feb. 06 '95
0.150	Mar. 15	Apr. 07	Apr. 14	May. 01 '95
0.150	Jun. 21	Jul. 12	Jul. 14	Jul. 31 '95
0.150	Sep. 20	Oct. 04	Oct. 06	Oct. 23 '95

Data as orig. reptd.; bef. results of disc. opers. and/or spec. items. Per share data adj. for stk. divs. as of ex-div. date. E-Estimated. NA-Not Available. NM-Not Meaningful. NR-Not Ranked.

Office—26600 S.W. Parkway (P.O. Box 1000, M/S 63-858), Wilsonville, OR 97070-1000. **Tel**—(503) 627-7111. **Chrmn, Pres & CEO**—J. J. Meyer. **VP-CFO**—C. W. Neun. **VP & Secy**—J. P. Karalis. **Treas & Investor Contact**—Douglas Shafer. **Dirs**—A. G. Ames, P. E. Bragdon, P. C. Ely, Jr., A. M. Gleason, W. R. Hicks, K. R. McKennon, M. A. McPeak, J. J. Meyer, J. E. Vollum, W. D. Walker. **Transfer Agent & Registrar**—First Chicago Trust Co. of New York, Jersey City, NJ. **Incorporated** in Oregon in 1946. **Empl**-7,730. **S&P Analyst:** Paul H. Valentine, CFA

Tele-Communications

NASDAQ Symbol TCOMA (Incl. in Nat'l Market) Options on ASE In S&P 500

Price	Range	P-E Ratio	Dividend	Yield	S&P Ranking	Beta
Aug. 7'95	1995					
26¼	26½–17¼	NM	None	None	NR	1.62

Summary

This leading cable TV system operator sold 17% of its international business in a May 1995 IPO, and plans to issue a new class of common stock to track the performace of Liberty Media. In July 1995, TCI agreed to purchase Viacom's cable systems, serving 1.2 million subscribers.

Current Outlook

A net loss of about $0.37 a share is anticipated for 1995. Another deficit is likely in 1996.

No common cash dividend has been paid, and none is likely within the next several years.

Revenues in 1995 and 1996 will be boosted significantly by acquisitions. Heavier spending on capital improvements and sharply higher noncash charges and interest expense will hurt bottom line comparisons in each year. Preferred dividend requirements began in 1995, and the number of shares outstanding will increase during the year.

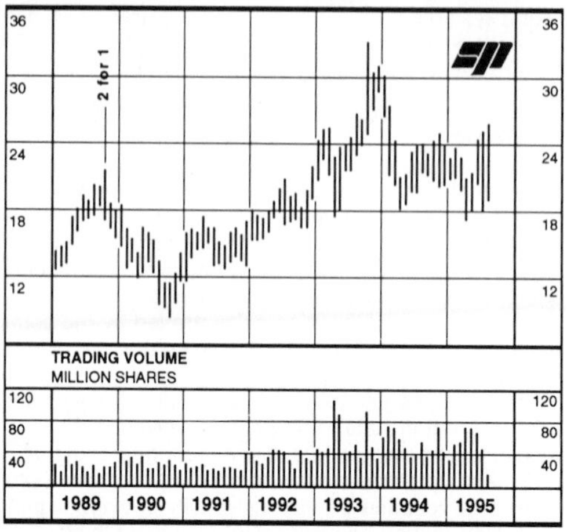

Revenues (Million $)

Quarter:	1995	1994	1993	1992
Mar.	1,524	1,060	1,018	856
Jun.		1,081	1,042	879
Sep.		1,286	1,044	896
Dec.		1,509	1,049	943
		4,936	4,153	3,574

Revenues in the quarter ended March 31, 1995, advanced 44%, year to year, boosted by acquisitions. Costs and expenses climbed 63%, and operating earnings fell 23%. Operating cash flow rose to $464 million, from $450 million. After other items, including interest expense (35% higher), a net loss of $53 million replaced net income of $32 million.

Common Share Earnings ($)

Quarter:	1995	1994	1993	1992
Mar.	d0.08	0.07	0.11	d0.05
Jun.		0.01	0.07	0.04
Sep.		0.04	d0.13	0.06
Dec.		d0.02	d0.07	d0.12
	Ed0.37	0.09	d0.02	d0.08

Important Developments

Jul. '95— TCI agreed to acquire from Viacom cable systems serving 1.2 million subscribers, in a transaction valued at $2.25 billion ($1,875 per subscriber). Under the agreement, the company will assume about $1.7 billion in debt, and will pay $350 million in cash. Viacom shareholders will receive 5% preferred stock in the acquired cable company, convertible into TCI common stock in five years. The transaction should be completed in early 1996.

May '95— The company sold a 17% stake in its international unit in an IPO valued at $380 million. TCI retained 91% voting power. The transaction was part of a restructuring approved by directors in February 1995, under which the company also plans to distribute to shareholders a new class of common intended to track and reflect the performance of Liberty Media. Directors decided not to issue additional classes of stock to reflect the performance of other business groups.

Next earnings report due in mid-August.

Per Share Data ($)

Yr. End Dec. 31	1994	1993	1992	[1]1991	[1]1990	[1]1989	[1]1988	[1,2]1987	[1,2]1986	[1,2]1985
Tangible Bk. Val.	**d11.24**	d15.75	d11.42	d10.23	d12.60	d10.60	d5.49	d5.25	d2.46	d0.59
Cash Flow	**1.38**	2.01	1.45	1.63	1.01	0.76	1.14	0.95	0.58	0.43
Earnings[3]	**0.09**	d0.02	d0.08	d0.28	d0.81	d0.73	0.15	0.02	0.24	0.04
Dividends	**Nil**	Nil	Nil	Nil	Nil	Nil	Nil	Nil	Nil	Nil
Payout Ratio	**Nil**	Nil	Nil	Nil	Nil	Nil	Nil	Nil	Nil	Nil
Prices—High	**30¼**	33¼	22	17½	18½	21⅝	14	15⅛	9¾	6½
Low	**18¼**	17½	15⅜	11⅝	8⅜	12⅝	10¼	7⅝	5⅞	3¾
P/E Ratio—	**NM**	NM	NM	NM	NM	NM	90–66	NM	40–24	NM

Data as orig. reptd. Adj. for stk. divs. of 100% Oct. 1989, 50% Aug. 1987, 100% Jul. 1986. **1.** Refl. merger or acq. **2.** Refl. acctg. change. **3.** Bef. results of disc. ops. of -0.04 in 1992. d-Deficit. E-Estimated. NM-Not Meaningful.

Income Data (Million $)

Year Ended Dec. 31[1]	Revs.	Oper. Inc.	% Oper. Inc. of Revs.	Cap. Exp.	Depr.	Int. Exp.	[4]Net Bef. Taxes	Eff. Tax Rate	[5]Net Inc.	% Net Inc. of Revs.	Cash Flow
1994	4,936	1,488	30.1	1,264	700	785	169	68.6%	55	1.1	747
1993	4,153	1,817	43.8	1,020	880	731	166	101.2%	d7	NM	871
[3]1992	3,574	1,614	45.2	1,209	650	718	172	87.2%	d19	NM	616
1991	3,827	1,491	39.0	694	687	877	d9	NM	d102	NM	585
1990	3,625	1,326	36.6	990	646	918	d326	NM	d287	NM	359
1989	3,026	1,094	36.2	1,511	525	817	d335	NM	d257	NM	268
1988	2,282	872	38.2	1,061	382	574	99	44.0%	56	2.5	438
[2]1987	1,709	643	37.6	872	285	357	58	75.4%	6	0.3	291
[2]1986	646	278	43.0	1,198	123	161	118	39.5%	72	11.2	196
[2]1985	577	233	40.4	191	111	135	d2	NM	10	1.8	121

Balance Sheet Data (Million $)

Dec. 31	Cash	Assets	Curr. Liab.	Ratio	Total Assets	% Ret. on Assets	Long Term Debt	Common Equity	Total Cap.	% LT Debt of Cap.	% Ret. on Equity
1994	74.0	NA	2,399	NA	19,528	0.3	9,956	2,971	16,969	58.7	1.7
1993	1.0	NA	1,777	NA	16,520	NM	8,904	2,112	14,629	60.9	NM
1992	34.0	NA	1,300	NA	13,164	NM	9,640	1,486	11,808	81.6	NM
1991	35.0	NA	1,242	NA	13,010	NM	9,286	1,439	11,585	80.2	NM
1990	31.0	NA	814	NA	12,310	NM	9,300	622	11,265	82.6	NM
1989	19.0	NA	1,402	NA	11,432	NM	7,356	908	9,705	75.8	NM
1988	20.4	NA	1,151	NA	8,574	0.7	5,440	1,206	7,279	74.7	5.3
1987	78.7	NA	617	NA	6,296	0.1	4,642	787	5,589	83.1	0.7
1986	20.2	NA	305	NA	4,008	2.5	2,773	716	3,619	76.6	13.2
1985	2.0	NA	172	NA	1,751	0.6	1,167	374	1,559	74.9	3.2

Data as orig. reptd. **1.** Refl. merger or acq. **2.** Refl. acctg. change. **3.** Excl. disc ops. **4.** Inc. equity in earns. of nonconsol. subs. **5.** Bef. results of disc. opers. d-Deficit. NM-Not Meaningful. NA-Not Available.

Business Summary

Tele-Communications, Inc. (TCI) is the largest U.S. owner and operator of cable television systems. It also has a number of equity holdings in other cable operators and cable programmers, including Turner Broadcasting System and The Discovery Channel. In August 1994, it reacquired Liberty Media, which had been spun off in 1991, in a tax-free exchange of stock. Liberty has interests in a number of cable programming services, and in cable systems serving more than 3.2 million subscribers. In February 1995, Liberty Media and Comcast acquired QVC Programming Holdings; Liberty holds a 42.6% interest.

As of mid-May 1995, TCI owned systems serving more than 12,700,000 subscribers throughout the U.S. and Puerto Rico. In partnership with cable system operators and others, the company is deploying and testing a wide range of new technologies and services. TCI is also actively expanding cable, programming and telephone services in a number of international markets. It expects to be serving the majority of customers with state-of-the-art fiber optic cable systems by the end of 1997. Capital spending about equal to 1994's $1.26 billion is seen for 1995.

Dividend Data

No cash dividends have been paid. The shares (both classes) were split two for one in 1989, three for two in 1987 and two for one in 1986.

Finances

In June 1995, TCI agreed to acquire United Video Satellite in exchange for stock valued at over $700 million. United Video, a leading producer of electronic cable-TV progam guides, would become a publicly traded company subsidiary.

In a February 1995 public offering, 17 million Class A common shares were sold at $21 each, for net proceeds of $350 million.

In January 1995, the company acquired TeleCable Corp. in exchange for 41,666,667 Class A common shares and $300 million of convertible preferred stock (total value about $1.6 billion). TeleCable serves 740,000 subscribers in 15 states.

Capitalization

Total Debt: $11,162,000,000 (12/94).

$5.50 Series D Preferred Stk.: 1,000,000 shs. (no par); ea. conv. into 10 Cl. A com.

Class A Common Stock: 571,690,775 shs. (2/95) ($1 par); 1 vote per sh.
Institutions hold 66%.
Shareholders: 8,802.

Class B Common Stock: 85,114,800 shs. ($1 par); 10 votes per sh.; 69% closely held.
Officers and directors have 44% voting control.
Shareholders: 671.

Office—5619 DTC Parkway, Englewood, CO 80111-3000. **Tel**—(303) 267-5500. **Chrmn**—B. Magness. **Pres & CEO**—J. C. Malone. **SVP, Treas & Investor Contact**—Bernard W. Schotters. **Secy**—P. J. O'Brien. **Dirs**—D. F. Fisher, J. W. Gallivan, J. H. Kern, B. Magness, K. Magness, J. C. Malone, R. A. Naify. **Transfer Agents & Registrars**—First Security Bank of Utah, Salt Lake City; Bank of New York, NYC. **Incorporated** in Delaware in 1968. **Empl**—24,000.

Information has been obtained from sources believed to be reliable, but its accuracy and completeness are not guaranteed. William H. Donald

Teledyne

NYSE Symbol **TDY**
In S&P 500

01-AUG-95

Industry:
Conglomerate/diversified

Summary: This international conglomerate serves customers through 18 companies focused in four areas: aviation and electronics, specialty metals, industrial, and consumer products.

S&P Opinion: Hold (★★★)	Recent Price • 23½	Yield • 1.7%
	52 Wk Range • 27⅜-15⅜	12-Mo. P/E • 9.8

Quantitative Evaluations

Outlook
(1 Lowest—5 Highest)
• **1**

Fair Value
• **20½**

Risk
• **Average**

Earn./Div. Rank
• **NR**

Technical Eval.
• **Bearish** since 2/95

Rel. Strength Rank
(1 Lowest—99 Highest)
• **16**

Insider Activity
• **Neutral**

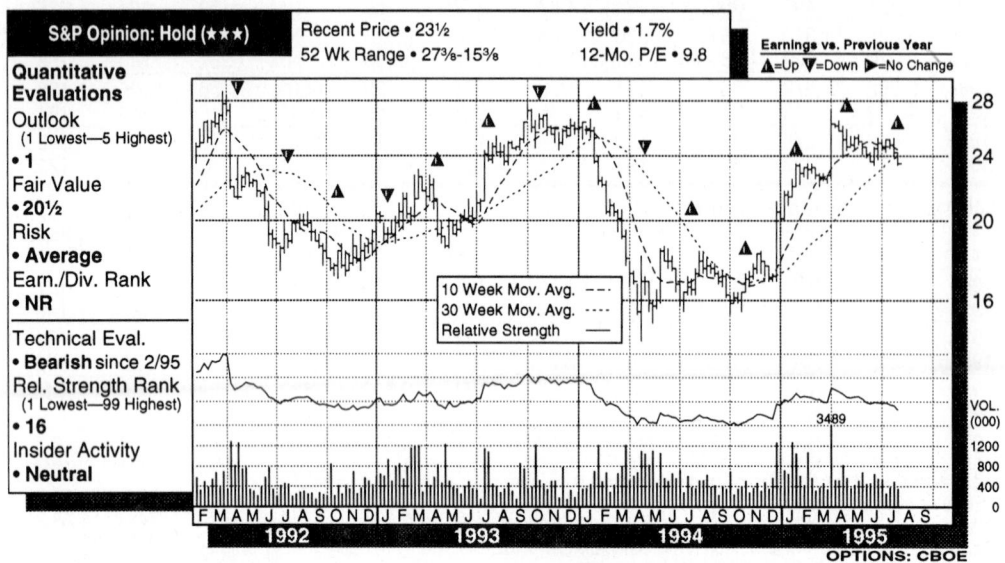

Earnings vs. Previous Year
▲=Up ▼=Down ▶=No Change

10 Week Mov. Avg. ‑ ‑ ‑
30 Week Mov. Avg. ·····
Relative Strength ——

3489

VOL. (000)

OPTIONS: CBOE

Overview - 01-AUG-95

Sales for 1995 are likely to rise more than 10% from those of 1994. The primary sources of growth will be the aviation and electronics and specialty metals divisions, which should benefit from a recovery in the aerospace market. Otherwise, sales of this diversified manufacturer will benefit from general expansion of the U.S. economy. Also boosting 1995 sales is a large contract to supply power generators to the Air Force. A substantial reorganization and rationalization of units in the past year should result in improved segment operating margins. In addition, earnings will benefit from a $50 million nonrecurring gain from the sale of the Electronic Systems business.

Valuation - 01-AUG-95

TDY's share price has risen above the range it maintained for most of 1994. This initially reflected the WHX Corp. $22 a share December 1994 offer; however, the stock has continued to climb after the offer was rejected. We attribute much of the recent strength to a dramatic improvement in earnings. This company, which had not been able to achieve a meager 3% return on sales in any of the past five years, has since posted three consecutive quarters of favorable earnings. We believe the current earnings momentum is sustainable given recent reorganization and cost cutting efforts (and a renewed emphasis to increase shareholder value). Accordingly, we view TDY shares as moderately attractive at 11 times our estimate of 1996 earnings.

Key Stock Statistics

S&P EPS Est. 1995	2.75	Tang. Bk. Value/Share	4.48
P/E on S&P Est. 1995	8.5	Beta	0.93
S&P EPS Est. 1996	2.10	Shareholders	13,000
Dividend Rate/Share	0.40	Market cap. (B)	$ 1.3
Shs. outstg. (M)	55.7	Inst. holdings	48%
Avg. daily vol. (M)	0.076	Insider holdings	NA

Value of $10,000 invested 5 years ago: $ 4,151

Fiscal Year Ending Dec. 31

	1995	% Change	1994	% Change	1993	% Change
Revenues (Million $)						
1Q	625.5	9%	572.9	-10%	636.5	-11%
2Q	706.7	19%	595.8	-5%	624.4	-16%
3Q	—	—	578.1	-3%	597.9	-16%
4Q	—	—	644.4	2%	632.9	-12%
Yr.	—	—	2,391	-4%	2,492	-14%
Income (Million $)						
1Q	64.30	NM	-55.10	NM	33.80	186%
2Q	32.60	196%	11.00	36%	8.10	9%
3Q	—	—	19.30	27%	15.20	-7%
4Q	—	—	16.40	4%	15.70	51%
Yr.	—	—	-8.40	NM	72.80	59%
Earnings Per Share ($)						
1Q	1.16	NM	-0.99	NM	0.61	190%
2Q	0.59	NM	0.19	27%	0.15	7%
3Q	E0.50	—	0.35	30%	0.27	-7%
4Q	E0.50	—	0.30	7%	0.28	47%
Yr.	E2.75	—	-0.15	NM	1.32	59%

Next earnings report expected: mid October

Business Summary - 01-AUG-95

Teledyne is an international conglomerate that serves customers through 18 operating companies focused in four business segments: aviation & electronics, specialty metals, industrial equipment and consumer products. Contributions by segment (profits in millions) in 1994 were:

	Sales	Profits
Aviation and electronics	40%	$-2.2
Specialty metals	31%	28.6
Industrial	15%	13.5
Consumer	14%	22.2

Manufacturing operations are predominantly located in the U.S. Exports represented 16% of 1994 sales (versus 15% in 1993), and the U.S. government accounted for 32% (39%).

Aviation and electronics products include aircraft engines (TDY makes half the general aviation piston engines in the U.S.), airframe structures, remotely piloted aerial vehicles, target drone systems, and equipment and subsystems for spacecraft and avionics. Other products include semiconductors, relays, aircraft-monitoring and control systems, and military electronic equipment.

Specialty metals include zirconium, titanium, high-temperature nickel based alloys, high-speed and tool steels, tungsten and molybdenum.

The industrial segment is comprised of companies that are involved in the design and/or manufacture of combat vehicles, diesel engines, crash fire rescue vehicles, material handling equipment, machine tools, dies and consumable tooling.

The consumer segment manufactures shower massages, water and air purification systems, swimming pool and spa heaters and dental supplies, and provides other products and services.

Important Developments

Jul. '95—Teledyne announced that revenues from continuing operations rose 28%, year to year, in the second quarter of 1995. Results by segment were: aviation and electronics jumped 52%; specialty metals climbed 19%; industrial products rose 9.4%; and consumer products advanced 1.7%. Separately, the new Piper Aircraft Co. emerged from bankruptcy with TDY holding 25% ownership and an option to purchase an additional 25%.

May '95—Teledyne was awarded a $164 million contract to build the military's new Tier II Plus Unmanned Aerial Vehicle. The reconnaissance system program could eventually be worth more than $500 million.

May '95—R. LaBow, chairman of WHX Corp., succeeded in becoming a director of Teledyne after WHX failed to acquire the company in December 1994 for $22 cash per share.

Capitalization

Long Term Debt: $359,400,000 (3/95).

Series E Cum. Pfd. Stock: $8,300,000 (3/95).

Per Share Data ($)

(Year Ended Dec. 31)

	1994	1993	1992	1991	1990	1989
Tangible Bk. Val.	4.48	4.60	7.55	7.69	8.94	41.49
Cash Flow	1.11	2.63	2.26	1.06	2.88	4.47
Earnings	-0.15	1.32	0.83	-0.46	1.25	2.71
Dividends	Nil	0.80	0.80	0.80	0.80	0.80
Payout Ratio	Nil	61%	96%	NM	64%	29%
Prices - High	26⅝	27¾	28¾	24⅜	72¾	76⅛
- Low	14¼	18½	17	14⅞	12	63½
P/E Ratio - High	NM	21	35	NM	58	28
- Low	NM	14	20	NM	10	23

Income Statement Analysis (Million $)

	1994	%Chg	1993	%Chg	1992	%Chg	1991
Revs.	2,391	-4%	2,492	-14%	2,888	-10%	3,207
Oper. Inc.	237	32%	180	-8%	195	-8%	211
Depr.	70.0	-4%	73.0	-8%	79.0	-6%	84.0
Int. Exp.	43.5	-4%	45.1	-20%	56.2	-9%	61.9
Pretax Inc.	-4.0	NM	113	30%	87.0	NM	-32.0
Eff. Tax Rate	NM	—	36%	—	47%	—	NM
Net Inc.	-8.0	NM	73.0	59%	46.0	NM	-25.0

Balance Sheet & Other Fin. Data (Million $)

	1994	1993	1992	1991	1990	1989
Cash	30.0	155	231	196	186	236
Curr. Assets	758	804	960	1,141	1,103	1,056
Total Assets	1,478	1,478	1,536	1,719	1,666	3,447
Curr. Liab.	466	448	472	636	532	462
LT Debt	357	357	450	497	511	571
Common Eqty.	273	281	441	454	524	2,327
Total Cap.	630	637	947	1,017	1,083	2,949
Cap. Exp.	65.0	81.0	70.0	98.0	113	145
Cash Flow	62.0	146	125	59.0	160	248

Ratio Analysis

	1994	1993	1992	1991	1990	1989
Curr. Ratio	1.6	1.8	2.0	1.8	2.1	2.3
% LT Debt of Cap.	56.6	56.0	47.5	48.9	47.2	19.4
% Net Inc.of Revs.	NM	2.9	1.6	NM	2.0	4.3
% Ret. on Assets	NM	4.8	2.8	NM	2.7	3.5
% Ret. on Equity	NM	20.2	10.3	NM	4.9	6.8

Dividend Data (Dividends, initiated in 1987, were omitted January 27, 1994. Payments were resumed in March 1995, together with $0.15 of a new 8% preferred stock. A "poison pill" stock purchase rights plan was adopted in January 1995.)

Amt. of Div. $	Date Decl.	Ex-Div. Date	Stock of Record	Payment Date
Stk.	Jan. 26	Feb. 09	Feb. 15	Mar. 08 '95
0.100	Jan. 26	Feb. 09	Feb. 15	Mar. 08 '95
Stk.	Apr. 26	May. 02	May. 08	May. 24 '95
0.100	Apr. 26	May. 02	May. 08	May. 24 '95
Stk.	Jul. 26	Aug. 17	Aug. 21	Sep. 15 '95
0.100	Jul. 26	Aug. 17	Aug. 21	Sep. 15 '95

Data as orig. reptd.; bef. results of disc. opers. and/or spec. items. Per share data adj. for stk. divs. as of ex-div. date. E-Estimated. NA-Not Available. NM-Not Meaningful. NR-Not Ranked.

Office—2049 Century Park East, Los Angeles, CA 90067-3101. **Tel**—(310) 277-3311. **Chrmn & CEO**—W. P. Rutledge. **Pres & COO**—D. B. Rice. **Secy**—J. R. Nelson. **CFO & Treas**—D. J. Grant. **Investor Contact**—Roseanne O'Brien (310-551-4265). **Dirs**—F. V. Cahouet, D. C. Creel, G. Kozmetsky, R. LaBow, D. B. Rice, G. A. Roberts, W. P. Rutledge, F. Sarofim, H. E. Singleton. **Transfer Agent & Registrar**—Chemical Bank, NYC. **Incorporated** in Delaware in 1960. **Empl**-18,000. **S&P Analyst:** Joe Victor Shammas

Tellabs, Inc.

NASDAQ Symbol TLAB (Incl. in Nat'l Market) In S&P 500

Price	Range	P–E Ratio	Dividend	Yield	S&P Ranking	Beta
Oct. 16'95	1995					
35⅛	52¾–23½	31	None	None	B	0.98

Summary

This company designs, manufactures, markets and services voice and data equipment used in public and private communications networks worldwide. Strong sales of digital systems led to sharply higher earnings in recent periods.

Current Outlook

Earnings for 1995 are projected to reach $1.20 a share, versus 1994's $0.80 (adjusted). For 1996, earnings are estimated at $1.50.

Initiation of cash dividends is not anticipated in the near-future.

Revenues are expected to grow strongly through 1996, reflecting higher sales of SONET-based TITAN digital cross-connect and Martis DXX systems. Revenues should also benefit from potential telecom reform legislation which would open markets to new participants. Margins should remain stable, as the higher volume and manufacturing efficiencies offset possible pricing pressures and an increasing level of research and development expenditures. Net interest income will continue to grow due to higher operating cash flows and the absence of long-term debt. Following a stable tax rate, per-share earnings will reflect a rising number of shares outstanding.

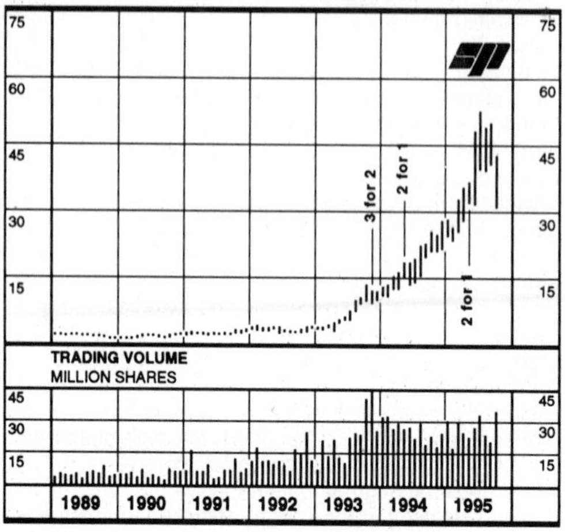

Net Sales (Million $)

Quarter:	1995	1994	1993	1992
Mar.	142.2	99.5	64.7	56.5
Jun.	159.9	123.0	71.5	55.8
Sep.	151.8	123.0	77.1	58.8
Dec.	---	148.6	107.2	87.6
	---	494.2	320.5	258.6

Net sales for the nine months ended September 30, 1995, advanced 31%, year to year, led by international gains and higher TITAN digital cross-connect and Martis DXX systems revenues. Pretax income rose 74%. After taxes at 29.0%, versus 26.0%, net income was up 67%, to $77,500,000 ($0.85 a share), from $46,314,000 ($0.51, as adjusted for the two-for-one stock split in May 1995).

Common Share Earnings ($)

Quarter:	1995	1994	1993	1992
Mar.	0.25	0.12	0.05	0.04
Jun.	0.30	0.19	0.06	0.03
Sep.	0.30	0.20	0.07	0.02
Dec.	E0.35	0.29	0.17	0.12
	E1.20	0.80	0.35	0.20

Important Developments

Sep. '95— Tellabs announced that it signed a two-year contract extension for its SONET-based TITAN 5500 digital cross-connect system with LDDS Worldcom. The agreement, which is estimated to be worth more than $25 million, also covers deployment of TLAB's recently introduced OC-12 SONET interface for the TITAN system.

Next earnings report expected in late January.

Per Share Data ($)

Yr. End Dec. 31	1994	[1]1993	1992	1991	1990	1989	1988	1987	1986	1985
Tangible Bk. Val.	**2.85**	1.87	2.02	1.80	1.70	1.59	1.49	1.34	1.20	1.10
Cash Flow	**1.01**	0.47	0.30	0.19	0.22	0.20	0.25	0.19	0.16	0.13
Earnings[2]	**0.80**	0.35	0.20	0.09	0.11	0.10	0.18	0.14	0.11	0.09
Dividends	**Nil**	Nil	Nil	Nil	Nil	Nil	Nil	Nil	Nil	Nil
Payout Ratio	**Nil**	Nil	Nil	Nil	Nil	Nil	Nil	Nil	Nil	Nil
Prices—High	**28**	13⁹⁄₁₆	4⅜	3⅝	2½	2½	2⅝	3¼	2½	3⅜
Low	**10¹⁵⁄₁₆**	3⅛	2⅝	2	1⅜	1⅜	1⅞	1⅝	1⅝	1½
P/E Ratio—	**35–14**	39–9	22–13	43–24	24–13	26–15	15–11	23–12	23–15	38–16

Data as orig. reptd. Adj. for stk. divs. of 100% May 1995, 100% May 1994, 50% Nov. 1993. **1.** Refl. merger or acq. **2.** Bef. spec. item of +0.02 in 1993. E-Estimated.

Income Data (Million $)

Year Ended Dec. 31	Revs.	Oper. Inc.	% Oper. Inc. of Revs.	Cap. Exp.	Depr.	Int. Exp.	Net Bef. Taxes	Eff. Tax Rate	[2]Net Inc.	% Net Inc. of Revs.	Cash Flow
1994	494	119	24.1	23.0	19.5	1.77	97.8	26.0%	72.4	14.6	91.9
[1]1993	320	43	13.4	40.1	10.7	0.49	35.8	14.9%	[3]30.5	9.5	41.2
1992	259	25	9.6	18.8	8.6	0.13	19.2	12.0%	16.9	6.5	25.5
1991	213	14	6.4	7.2	8.4	0.42	7.0	5.6%	6.6	3.1	15.0
1990	211	17	7.8	13.9	8.3	0.87	10.7	24.5%	8.1	3.8	16.4
1989	181	19	10.3	15.4	8.2	0.52	9.3	24.5%	7.1	3.9	15.3
1988	155	20	12.6	10.9	5.5	0.33	17.6	23.3%	13.5	8.7	18.9
1987	136	18	13.4	8.8	4.4	0.39	16.7	34.4%	10.7	7.9	15.1
1986	116	15	13.1	5.0	3.8	0.58	13.4	36.0%	8.4	7.3	12.2
1985	100	11	11.3	9.6	3.0	0.49	10.6	34.2%	7.0	7.0	10.0

Balance Sheet Data (Million $)

Dec. 31	Cash	Assets	Curr. Liab.	Ratio	Total Assets	% Ret. on Assets	Long Term Debt	Common Equity	Total Cap.	% LT Debt of Cap.	% Ret. on Equity
1994	74.7	221	82	2.7	390	20.1	2.85	293	297	1.0	29.0
1993	45.6	176	112	1.6	329	11.1	2.85	207	210	1.4	16.0
1992	49.4	144	35	4.1	211	8.4	3.77	167	174	2.2	10.6
1991	44.3	128	32	4.0	186	3.6	3.99	145	154	2.6	4.7
1990	38.5	111	32	3.4	172	4.9	4.18	130	139	3.0	6.4
1989	42.4	106	27	3.9	158	4.7	4.36	120	131	3.3	6.1
1988	44.8	97	19	5.2	141	10.1	4.41	112	122	3.6	12.7
1987	52.3	94	17	5.6	131	8.7	4.92	104	114	4.3	10.9
1986	38.4	87	14	6.3	116	7.6	5.44	93	103	5.3	9.4
1985	24.5	77	11	7.2	106	6.9	5.95	86	95	6.3	8.4

Data as orig. reptd. **1.** Refl. merger or acq. **2.** Bef. spec. item in 1993. **3.** Refl. acctg. change.

Business Summary

Tellabs, Inc. designs, manufactures, markets and services voice and data equipment used worldwide by telephone companies, interexchange carriers, government and businesses. Its products include network access products, data communication systems and digital systems.

Network access products include digital signal processing (DSP) products, special service products and local access products such as high bit rate digital subscriber line (HDSL) products. DSP products include echo cancellers, voice compression products, or T-coders, and a channel service unit used to terminate and provide test access for T1 facilities. Special service products include line amplifiers, terminating devices, signaling equipment and systems, and loop treatment equipment. The company also sells a line of voice conferencing and alerting systems and a series of products with remote alignment and diagnostic maintenance capabilities. Network access products accounted for 26% of sales in 1994 (35% in 1993).

Data communication systems include statistical multiplexers, packet switches, T1 multiplexers and network management systems. Such products provide cost-effective data transmission by concentrating multiple synchronous or asynchronous channels over owned or leased lines, and allow provisioning and management of networks composed of the company's data communication prod-

ucts. Data communication systems accounted for 27% of sales in 1994 (21% in 1993).

The digital systems product family consists of state-of-the-art digital cross-connect systems, which are intelligent electronic switching devices that operate under software control and are typically used to manage high-speed digital traffic over the telephone network. Such products accounted for 46% of sales in 1994 (42% in 1993).

Products are sold in both domestic and international marketplaces to Bell Operating Companies (26% of total sales in 1994), independent telephone companies (7%), interexchange carriers (16%), local telephone administrations, local exchange carriers, original equipment manufacturers, cellular companies, competitive access providers, system integrators, government agencies and business end-users (collectively 17%). International sales accounted for 34% of total sales in 1994.

Dividend Data

No cash dividends have been paid. Two-for-one stock splits were effected in May 1994 and May 1995.

Capitalization

Long Term Debt: $2,850,000 (9/95).

Common Stock: 88,420 010 shs. ($0.01 par).
Institutions hold about 72%.
Shareholders of record: 1,685 (2/94).

Office—4951 Indiana Ave., Lisle, IL 60532. **Tel**—(708) 969-8800. **Pres & CEO**—M. J. Birck. **Exec VP, CFO, Treas & Investor Contact**—Peter A. Guglielmi (708) 378-6111. **VP & Secy**—C. C. Gavin. **Dirs**—M. J. Birick, J. D. Foulkes, P. A. Guglielmi, B. J. Jackman, F. A. Krehbiel, R. P. Reuss, W. F. Souders, T. H. Thompson. **Transfer Agent**—Harris Trust & Savings Bank, Chicago. **Incorporated** in Delaware in 1992. **Empl**—2,585.

Information has been obtained from sources believed to be reliable, but its accuracy and completeness are not guaranteed. Alan Aaron

Temple-Inland

NYSE Symbol **TIN**
In S&P 500

28-SEP-95

Industry:
Containers

Summary: This major producer of corrugated containers and containerboard also makes market pulp, paperboard and building products, and has expanded into financial services as well.

S&P Opinion: Hold (★★★)

| Recent Price • 52⅜ | Yield • 2.3% |
| 52 Wk Range • 56¾-41½ | 12-Mo. P/E • 13.8 |

Earnings vs. Previous Year
▲=Up ▼=Down ▶=No Change

Quantitative Evaluations

Outlook
(1 Lowest—5 Highest)
• **5+**

Fair Value
• **63¾**

Risk
• **Low**

Earn./Div. Rank
• **B+**

Technical Eval.
• **Bearish** since 9/95

Rel. Strength Rank
(1 Lowest—99 Highest)
• **57**

Insider Activity
• **NA**

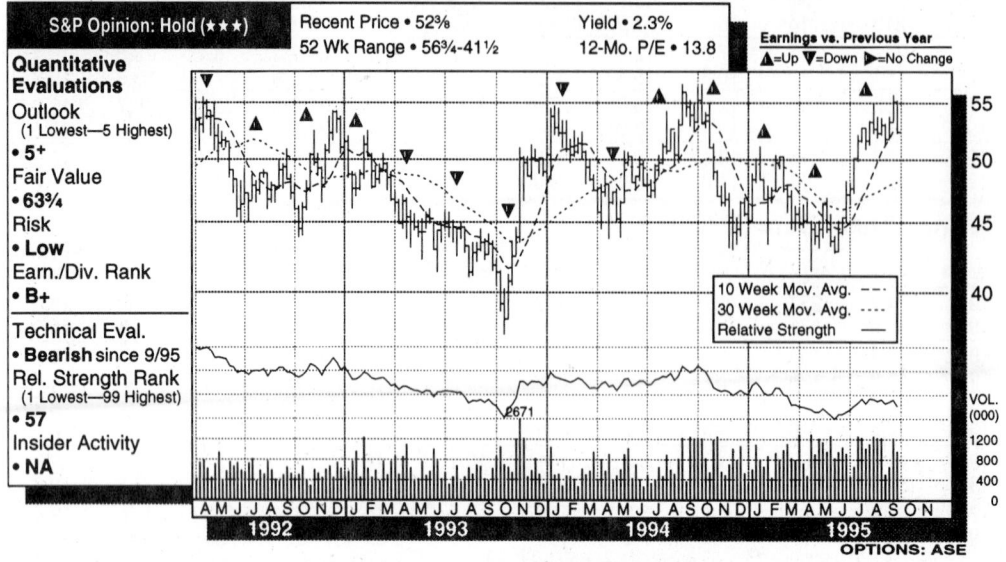

10 Week Mov. Avg. ---
30 Week Mov. Avg. ·····
Relative Strength ——

VOL. (000)
1200
800
400
0

A M J J A S O N D J F M A M J J A S O N D J F M A M J J A S O N D J F M A M J J A S O N
1992   1993   1994   1995

OPTIONS: ASE

Overview - 28-SEP-95

Sales should be solidly higher in 1995, on increased shipment volume and steep prices for corrugated boxes, although the moderating U.S. economy has recently slowed demand in the sector. Despite tougher trends, prices should be supported by extensive industry downtime and strong export markets. Bleached paperboard sales should be modestly higher, but building products sales have been hurt by low lumber prices, although the mid-1995 drop in interest rates should provide some assistance to the segment. Margins should widen sharply on the higher containerboard prices, the recent plunge in recycled paper costs (following a period of steep increases) and the positive impact of the current interest rate environment on the financial services segment. Those factors should far outweigh higher log costs in wood products and start-up costs from a bleached paperboard expansion.

Valuation - 28-SEP-95

TIN shares bounced off their late 1994 lows, on investor excitement about rapidly improving conditions in the containerboard area. Although demand subsequently weakened in that area, the shares have maintained their uptrend on enthusiasm about falling raw materials prices in containerboard, TIN's new bleached paperboard machine and strong conditions in financial services. However, while we remain optimistic about Temple's earnings outlook and believe that some of the company's trouble spots will be aided by the lower interest rate environment, the shares seem fairly valued in their recent trading range.

Key Stock Statistics

S&P EPS Est. 1995	5.10	Tang. Bk. Value/Share	33.53
P/E on S&P Est. 1995	10.3	Beta	1.48
S&P EPS Est. 1996	6.25	Shareholders	8,100
Dividend Rate/Share	1.20	Market cap. (B)	$ 3.0
Shs. outstg. (M)	56.1	Inst. holdings	70%
Avg. daily vol. (M)	0.175	Insider holdings	NA

Value of $10,000 invested 5 years ago: $ 16,963

Fiscal Year Ending Dec. 31

	1995	% Change	1994	% Change	1993	% Change
Revenues (Million $)						
1Q	834.7	18%	706.3	3%	682.8	4%
2Q	889.0	23%	725.1	3%	702.6	3%
3Q	—	—	755.0	11%	681.0	1%
4Q	—	—	751.1	12%	669.4	-4%
Yr.	—	—	2,938	7%	2,736	NM
Income (Million $)						
1Q	58.30	155%	22.90	-18%	28.00	-20%
2Q	72.90	174%	26.60	27%	20.90	-56%
3Q	—	—	33.10	190%	11.40	-71%
4Q	—	—	48.80	NM	7.00	-72%
Yr.	—	—	131.4	95%	67.35	-54%
Earnings Per Share ($)						
1Q	1.04	154%	0.41	-18%	0.50	-21%
2Q	1.30	171%	0.48	26%	0.38	-55%
3Q	E1.36	131%	0.59	181%	0.21	-70%
4Q	E1.40	61%	0.87	NM	0.12	-74%
Yr.	E5.10	117%	2.35	94%	1.21	-54%

Next earnings report expected: mid October

Temple-Inland

Business Summary - 28-SEP-95

Temple-Inland has interests in paper, packaging, building products and financial services. Segment contributions (profits in millions) in 1994 were:

	Revs.	Profits
Container/containerboard	49%	$102.0
Bleached paperboard	10%	-22.1
Building products	19%	132.6
Other mfg. activities	1%	1.5
Financial services	21%	56.3

The company makes containerboard that it converts into a complete line of corrugated boxes and containers. In 1994, about 84% of containerboard produced was converted into corrugated containers at its box manufacturing facilities. A nationwide network of box plants produces a wide range of products from commodity brown boxes to intricate die-cut containers that can be printed with multicolor graphics. As of 1994 year-end, approximately 48% of box shipments were being sold directly to the food industry. TIN also makes multi-wall bulk containers.

Bleached paperboard, linerboard, bristols and market pulp produced by TIN are used by other paper companies and by producers that buy paper in roll lots and convert it into items such as paper cups and plates, file folders, cartons and paperback book covers.

TIN sells lumber, plywood, particleboard, gypsum wallboard, hardboard siding and fiberboard sheathing, primarily in the Southeast and Southwest.

Financial services include savings and loan activities, mortgage banking, land development and insurance. Guaranty Federal Bank, F.S.B., operates 123 branches in Texas. At 1994 year-end, mortgage banking operations were servicing $10.1 billion in loans.

The company owns 1.9 million acres of timberland in Texas, Louisiana, Georgia and Alabama.

Important Developments

Aug. '95—TIN signed a letter of intent to acquire a 50% interest in Caraustar Industries' Standard Gypsum unit, which would be operated as a joint venture between TIN and Caraustar. It was believed that Temple will eventually obtain a 100% stake in Standard.
Jul. '95—The company reported that during the second quarter of 1995, its Evadale, Tex., bleached paper mill experienced the start-up of its new fiber line and new paper machine, under a $500 million expansion and modernization program that was nearing completion. However, the mill was to begin a recovery boiler rebuild in August, which would limit total production from the facility for 90 days. TIN noted that the boiler rebuild and other start-up activities would continue to penalize earnings of the bleached paperboard group for the rest of the year, with the full benefits of the expansion becoming available in 1996.

Capitalization

Long Term Debt: $1,517,700,000 (7/1/95).

Per Share Data ($)

(Year Ended Dec. 31)

	1994	1993	1992	1991	1990	1989
Tangible Bk. Val.	31.83	30.64	29.55	27.89	26.37	22.02
Cash Flow	6.07	4.76	5.75	5.43	6.81	6.08
Earnings	2.35	1.21	2.65	2.51	4.20	3.75
Dividends	1.02	1.00	0.96	0.88	0.80	0.58
Payout Ratio	43%	83%	36%	35%	19%	15%
Prices - High	56¾	52½	57½	51½	38⅝	35½
- Low	43	37¼	43⅞	28½	24⅛	23⅜
P/E Ratio - High	24	43	22	21	9	9
- Low	18	31	17	11	6	6

Income Statement Analysis (Million $)

	1994	%Chg	1993	%Chg	1992	%Chg	1991
Revs.	2,938	7%	2,736	NM	2,713	8%	2,507
Oper. Inc.	545	19%	459	4%	443	13%	392
Depr.	208	6%	197	15%	172	6%	162
Int. Exp.	176	-3%	181	50%	121	41%	86.0
Pretax Inc.	193	101%	96.0	-46%	177	6%	167
Eff. Tax Rate	32%	—	30%	—	17%	—	17%
Net Inc.	131	96%	67.0	-54%	147	7%	138

Balance Sheet & Other Fin. Data (Million $)

	1994	1993	1992	1991	1990	1989
Cash	315	165	125	171	180	93.0
Curr. Assets	NA	NA	NA	NA	NA	NA
Total Assets	12,251	11,959	10,766	10,068	7,834	7,249
Curr. Liab.	NA	NA	NA	NA	NA	NA
LT Debt	1,531	1,267	2,569	997	652	1,502
Common Eqty.	1,783	1,700	1,633	1,532	1,439	1,259
Total Cap.	3,477	3,083	4,542	2,828	2,400	3,069
Cap. Exp.	483	354	370	387	328	273
Cash Flow	339	264	319	300	377	336

Ratio Analysis

	1994	1993	1992	1991	1990	1989
Curr. Ratio	NA	NA	NA	NA	NA	NA
% LT Debt of Cap.	44.0	41.1	56.6	35.3	27.2	49.0
% Net Inc.of Revs.	4.5	2.5	5.4	5.5	9.7	9.8
% Ret. on Assets	1.1	0.6	1.4	1.5	3.1	3.9
% Ret. on Equity	7.5	4.0	9.3	9.3	17.3	17.7

Dividend Data

Dividends were initiated in 1984. A dividend reinvestment plan is available. A poison pill stock purchase rights plan was adopted in 1989.

Amt. of Div. $	Date Decl.	Ex-Div. Date	Stock of Record	Payment Date
0.270	Nov. 07	Nov. 25	Dec. 01	Dec. 15 '94
0.270	Feb. 03	Feb. 23	Mar. 01	Mar. 15 '95
0.270	May. 05	May. 25	Jun. 01	Jun. 15 '95
0.300	Aug. 04	Aug. 30	Sep. 01	Sep. 15 '95

Data as orig. reptd.; bef. results of disc. opers. and/or spec. items. Per share data adj. for stk. divs. as of ex-div. date.
E-Estimated. NA-Not Available. NM-Not Meaningful. NR-Not Ranked.

Office—303 South Temple Drive, Diboll, TX 75941. **Tel**—(409) 829-5511. **Chrmn & CEO**—C. J. Grum. **CFO**—K. M. Jastrow II. **VP & Secy**—M. R. Warner. **Investor Contact**—Doyle R. Simons. **Dirs**—P. M. Anderson, R. Cizik, A. M. Frank, C. J. Grum, B. R. Inman, H. A. Sklenar, W. P. Stern, A. Temple III, C. Temple, L. E. Temple. **Transfer Agent & Registrar**—First Chicago Trust Co. of New York, Jersey City, NJ. **Incorporated** in Delaware in 1983. **Empl**-15,000. **S&P Analyst**: Michael W. Jaffe

Tenet Healthcare

NYSE Symbol **THC**
In S&P 500

13-OCT-95 **Industry:** Health Care Centers

Summary: This California-based company owns and operates 83 acute care hospitals and related healthcare businesses in the U.S. and overseas.

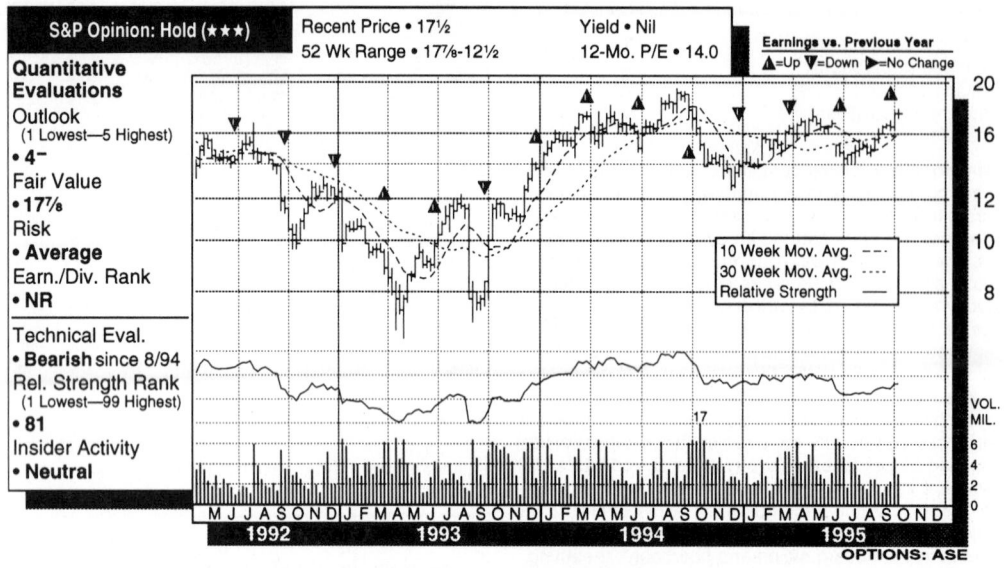

S&P Opinion: Hold (★★★)	Recent Price • 17½	Yield • Nil
	52 Wk Range • 17⅞-12½	12-Mo. P/E • 14.0

Earnings vs. Previous Year
▲=Up ▼=Down ▶=No Change

Quantitative Evaluations

Outlook
(1 Lowest—5 Highest)
• **4⁻**

Fair Value
• **17⅞**

Risk
• **Average**

Earn./Div. Rank
• **NR**

Technical Eval.
• **Bearish** since 8/94

Rel. Strength Rank
(1 Lowest—99 Highest)
• **81**

Insider Activity
• **Neutral**

10 Week Mov. Avg. – – –
30 Week Mov. Avg. · · · ·
Relative Strength ——

1992 1993 1994 1995

VOL.
MIL.

OPTIONS: ASE

Overview - 13-OCT-95

The domestic hospital market has been under substantial pressure from cost-conscious purchasers of health care services, including HMOs seeking to reduce their costs associated with hospital stays. As a result, the industry has been rapidly consolidating in order to gain economies of scale and reduce operating overhead. Tenet has identified those hospitals with deteriorating operating margins, and has been successful in improving the performance of these facilities. These moves should begin to positively impact earnings in the coming quarters. During the first quarter of fiscal 1996, EPS of $0.29 (before gains of $0.30 from the sale of facilities) met expectations, and we continue to anticipate full-year operating EPS of $1.35. In addition, the expected sale of noncore assets will help improve the balance sheet.

Valuation - 13-OCT-95

Based on our 1995-6 EPS estimate of $1.35 (before nonrecurring gains of $0.30), the shares appear to be fairly valued at recent levels. THC has been addressing many problem areas, but near-term results may be volatile, as it focuses on emerging domestic opportunities and continues to identify potential cost savings from the merger of NME and AMI. The integration of AMI appears to be going well, and the company hopes to realize about $60 million in annual cost savings in 1995-6, with the bulk expected during the second half of the year. We expect the stock to trade in a narrow range until earnings visibility improves.

Key Stock Statistics

S&P EPS Est. 1996	1.65	Tang. Bk. Value/Share	9.93
P/E on S&P Est. 1996	10.6	Beta	1.68
Dividend Rate/Share	Nil	Shareholders	16,200
Shs. outstg. (M)	200.0	Market cap. (B)	$ 3.4
Avg. daily vol. (M)	0.571	Inst. holdings	49%
		Insider holdings	NA

Value of $10,000 invested 5 years ago: $ 10,061

Fiscal Year Ending May 31

	1996	% Change	1995	% Change	1994	% Change
Revenues (Million $)						
1Q	1,284	94%	662.8	-14%	775.0	-18%
2Q	—	—	638.8	-17%	770.0	-17%
3Q	—	—	660.5	-8%	720.3	-23%
4Q	—	—	1,356	93%	701.8	-27%
Yr.	—	—	3,318	12%	2,967	-21%
Income (Million $)						
1Q	118.3	85%	64.03	NM	-100.9	NM
2Q	—	—	46.22	-24%	61.18	17%
3Q	—	—	48.90	-46%	90.72	68%
4Q	—	—	35.30	NM	11.28	NM
Yr.	—	—	194.4	-10%	215.9	35%
Earnings Per Share ($)						
1Q	0.59	55%	0.38	NM	-0.32	NM
2Q	E0.33	22%	0.27	-27%	0.37	16%
3Q	E0.36	24%	0.29	-47%	0.55	67%
4Q	E0.37	118%	0.17	143%	0.07	NM
Yr.	E1.65	50%	1.10	-15%	1.29	34%

Next earnings report expected: late December

Tenet Healthcare

13-OCT-95

Business Summary - 29-SEP-95

Tenet Healthcare Corp., formed through the March 1995 merger of National Medical Enterprises (NME) and American Medical International (AMI), operates general hospitals and related healthcare facilities, serving primarily urban areas in 13 states and holds investments in other healthcare companies.

At fiscal 1995 year-end, Tenet operated 70 domestic general hospitals with 15,451 beds. These facilities are located in California (23), Texas (11), Florida (10), Louisiana (6), Missouri (4) and eight other states (16). THC also operates six physical rehabilitation hospitals and five phychiatric facilities, which are located on the same campus as, or nearby, Tenet's general hospitals. In addition, the company operates various ancillary healthcare facilities, including outpatient surgery centers, home healthcare programs, ambulatory, occupational and rural healthcare clinics, a health maintenance organization (HMO), a preferred provider organization (PPO) and a managed care insurance company.

At the start of fiscal 1995, the company continued to operate as a discontinued business 54 freestanding psychiatric hospitals, residential treatment centers and substance abuse recovery facilities. By the end of the year, Tenet had sold or closed all but two of the facilities. In addition, during fiscal 1995, THC sold its management services division, which managed psychiatric, substance abuse and rehabilitation hospitals and units for third parties and for Tenet.

Tenet has decided to focus on its core business of operating domestic hospitals and is divesting its international operations (5% of revenues). In June 1995, Tenet sold its two Singapore hospitals to Parkway Holdings for $243 million (net). The company has agreed to sell its 52% stake in Australian Medical Enterprises (a publicly-traded Australian healthcare company), and anticipates the sale of its 40% interest in the Bumrungrad Medical Center in Thailand and its 30% interest in the Subang Jaya Medical Centre in Malaysia prior to the end of the second quarter of fiscal 1996.

Important Developments

Aug. '95—Tenet acquired Mercy+Baptist Medical Center, an 808 bed acute care hospital in New Orleans, for undisclosed terms.
Jul. '95—THC engaged Perot Systems Corp. for consulting and technology services expected to generate cost savings of $100 million over seven years. Perot will help merge the technical environments of NME and AMI, and will provide information systems to improve quality and efficiency at THC's hospitals.
Jun. '95—The company sold two hospitals and related healthcare businesses in Singapore to Parkway Holdings Ltd., for $243 million (net).

Capitalization

Long Term Debt: $3,500,000,000 (5/95).

Per Share Data ($)

(Year Ended May 31)

	1995	1994	1993	1992	1991	1990
Tangible Bk. Val.	9.93	7.95	10.56	10.03	10.08	7.97
Cash Flow	2.20	2.15	1.97	1.68	2.59	2.37
Earnings	1.10	1.29	0.96	0.77	1.73	1.52
Dividends	Nil	0.12	0.48	0.46	0.40	0.36
Payout Ratio	Nil	9%	50%	60%	25%	23%
Cal. Yrs.	1994	1993	1992	1991	1990	1989
Prices - High	19½	14⅜	18⅛	25⅞	20⅛	19½
- Low	12½	6½	9⅝	12⅝	14⅝	10¾
P/E Ratio - High	18	11	19	34	12	13
- Low	11	5	10	16	8	7

Income Statement Analysis (Million $)

	1995	%Chg	1994	%Chg	1993	%Chg	1992
Revs.	3,318	12%	2,967	-21%	3,762	-5%	3,951
Oper. Inc.	623	17%	534	-8%	581	-10%	644
Depr.	195	36%	143	-15%	168	8%	156
Int. Exp.	138	86%	74.0	-16%	88.0	-16%	105
Pretax Inc.	338	-6%	360	32%	272	14%	239
Eff. Tax Rate	40%	—	40%	—	36%	—	41%
Net Inc.	194	-10%	216	35%	160	20%	133

Balance Sheet & Other Fin. Data (Million $)

	1995	1994	1993	1992	1991	1990
Cash	294	373	239	200	197	170
Curr. Assets	1,624	1,444	1,068	1,097	941	935
Total Assets	7,918	3,697	4,173	4,236	4,060	3,807
Curr. Liab.	1,356	1,640	913	874	595	686
LT Debt	3,273	223	892	1,066	1,140	1,361
Common Eqty.	1,986	1,320	1,752	1,674	1,762	1,257
Total Cap.	5,560	1,668	2,961	3,072	3,289	2,992
Cap. Exp.	264	185	306	509	403	494
Cash Flow	389	359	328	289	415	379

Ratio Analysis

	1995	1994	1993	1992	1991	1990
Curr. Ratio	1.2	0.9	1.2	1.3	1.6	1.4
% LT Debt of Cap.	58.9	13.4	30.1	34.7	34.7	45.5
% Net Inc.of Revs.	5.9	7.3	4.3	3.4	7.3	6.2
% Ret. on Assets	3.4	5.5	3.8	3.3	6.7	6.1
% Ret. on Equity	11.8	14.1	9.4	7.9	17.6	20.0

Dividend Data —Dividends, initiated in 1973, were omitted in late 1993. The most recent cash dividend was $0.12 in September 1993.

Data as orig. reptd.; bef. results of disc. opers. and/or spec. items. Per share data adj. for stk. divs. as of ex-div. date.
E-Estimated. NA-Not Available. NM-Not Meaningful. NR-Not Ranked.

Office—2700 Colorado Ave. (P.O. Box 4070), Santa Monica, CA 90411. Tel—(310) 998-8000. Chrmn & CEO—J. C. Barbakow. Pres & COO—M. H. Focht. SVP & Secy—S. M. Brown. SVP & Treas—M. Andersons. Investor Contact—Paul J. Russell. Dirs—M. J. DeWald, J. C. Barbakow, B. B. Bratter, J. T. Casey, P. de Wetter, E. Egbert, M. H. Focht, R. A. Hay, L. P. Korn, J. P. Livingston, R. W. O'Leary, T. J. Pritzker, R. S. Schweiker. Transfer Agent & Registrar—Bank of New York, NYC. Incorporated in California in 1968; reincorporated in Nevada in 1976. Empl-69,050. S&P Analyst: Robert M. Gold

Tenneco Inc.

NYSE Symbol **TEN**
In S&P 500

21-SEP-95

Industry:
Conglomerate/diversified

Summary: This diversified holding company has interests in natural gas pipeline operations; auto parts; construction and farm equipment; packaging products; and shipbuilding.

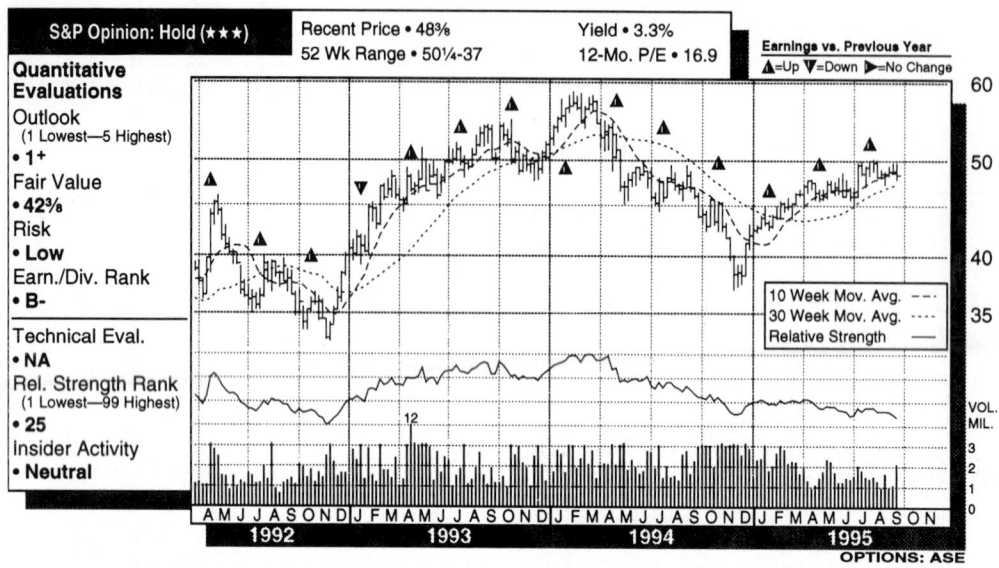

S&P Opinion: Hold (★★★)	Recent Price • 48%	Yield • 3.3%
	52 Wk Range • 50¼-37	12-Mo. P/E • 16.9

Earnings vs. Previous Year
▲=Up ▼=Down ▶=No Change

Quantitative Evaluations

Outlook
(1 Lowest—5 Highest)
• **1+**

Fair Value
• **42⅝**

Risk
• **Low**

Earn./Div. Rank
• **B-**

Technical Eval.
• **NA**

Rel. Strength Rank
(1 Lowest—99 Highest)
• **25**

Insider Activity
• **Neutral**

10 Week Mov. Avg. — - —
30 Week Mov. Avg. ‥‥‥
Relative Strength —

OPTIONS: ASE

Overview - 21-SEP-95

This diversified company has embarked on a program to redeploy assets into more profitable ventures. TEN is moving away from its energy businesses, as shown by the recent agreement to sell its 50% interest in the Kern River gas pipeline. Reduction of its stake in Case to 21% through three stock offerings has helped TEN reduce overall cyclicality, as has the sale of its Albright & Wilson chemicals division. Proceeds from those sales have given TEN the financial flexibility to pursue its strategy based on a 15% return on investment goal. Operating initiatives include expansion into non-regulated areas, and an improved product mix in the automotive, shipbuilding and paperboard packaging businesses. We expect investment in non-dilutive acquisitions, particularly abroad, to continue. TEN has been reducing its debt to total equity ratio in recent periods, which also adds to long-term prospects.

Valuation - 21-SEP-95

A $500 million share repurchase program initiated in December 1994 has helped raise TEN's stock price since the beginning of the year, along with strong earnings prospects for future periods as this largely industrial supplier monetizes its assets to promote earnings growth. However, with the buyback program nearly 70% complete and the 12-month trailing P/E at around 17, the shares are becoming more vulnerable to disappointing economic news, including the possibility of any weakening in its defense business.

Key Stock Statistics

S&P EPS Est. 1995	4.00	Tang. Bk. Value/Share	13.69
P/E on S&P Est. 1995	12.1	Beta	1.10
S&P EPS Est. 1996	4.60	Shareholders	112,000
Dividend Rate/Share	1.60	Market cap. (B)	$ 8.5
Shs. outstg. (M)	178.3	Inst. holdings	69%
Avg. daily vol. (M)	0.334	Insider holdings	NA

Value of $10,000 invested 5 years ago: $ 10,273

Fiscal Year Ending Dec. 31

	1995	% Change	1994	% Change	1993	% Change
Revenues (Million $)						
1Q	2,163	-29%	3,049	-6%	3,250	1%
2Q	2,198	-33%	3,258	-6%	3,482	1%
3Q	—	—	3,049	-3%	3,150	NM
4Q	—	—	2,818	-17%	3,376	2%
Yr.	—	—	12,174	-8%	13,255	NM
Income (Million $)						
1Q	153.0	26%	121.0	64%	74.00	111%
2Q	185.0	15%	161.0	45%	111.0	122%
3Q	—	—	150.0	29%	116.0	152%
4Q	—	—	209.0	39%	150.0	NM
Yr.	—	—	641.0	42%	452.0	NM
Earnings Per Share ($)						
1Q	0.84	27%	0.66	43%	0.46	109%
2Q	1.05	19%	0.88	40%	0.63	97%
3Q	E0.92	14%	0.81	27%	0.64	129%
4Q	E1.28	12%	1.14	37%	0.83	NM
Yr.	E4.00	15%	3.49	35%	2.59	NM

Next earnings report expected: late October

Business Summary - 21-SEP-95

Contributions of this diversified holding company's industry segments in 1994 were:

	Revs.	Profits
Pipelines	20%	30%
Farm & construction equip.	32%	24%
Automotive	16%	16%
Shipbuilding	14%	15%
Packaging	18%	15%

Tenneco Gas Inc. transports or sells through its 19,300-mile interstate pipeline roughly 16% of all natural gas consumed in the U.S. Its multiple line system begins in the gas-producing regions of Texas and Louisiana including the Gulf of Mexico, and extends to New England and Chicago. It also holds interests in Kern River Transmission Co. (50%) and Iroquois Gas Transmission Co. (30%), and has growing interests in nonregulated businesses that offer higher potential returns on investment.

Tenneco Automotive makes and sells original equipment and aftermarket auto parts worldwide. Its Walker Manufacturing unit produces exhaust systems; Monroe Auto Equipment makes shocks and struts and other ride-control components. Growth strategies include expansion in India, China and other high growth Far East regions, and in Europe. Late in 1994, it acquired Gillet Group, a leading European maker of auto exhaust equipment.

Packaging Corp. of America is the leading U.S. producer of food containers made of clear plastic, aluminum foil and molded fiber, and the largest supplier of corrugated containers. Newport News Shipbuilding designs, builds, overhauls and repairs a full range of nuclear-powered and conventional ships for defense and commercial markets.

TEN holds a 21% interest in Case Corp., a leading manufacturer of both farm and construction equipment. TEN has reduced its stake in Case from 100% through three public stock offerings since June 1994.

Important Developments

Sep. '95—TEN said it entered into an agreement to sell its 50% stake in the Kern River gas pipeline to Questar Pipeline Co., a subsidiary of Questar Corp., for $225 million. The Williams Cos., which owns the remaining 50%, has the right of first refusal as regards the agreement.

Capitalization

Long Term Debt: $3,309,000,000 (6/95).
Cum. Red. Preferred Stock: $129,000,000.

Per Share Data ($)   (Year Ended Dec. 31)

	1994	1993	1992	1991	1990	1989
Tangible Bk. Val.	13.67	12.78	5.21	18.07	23.92	22.82
Cash Flow	5.88	5.69	-0.83	-1.03	8.29	8.47
Earnings	3.49	2.59	-4.85	-5.62	4.37	4.46
Dividends	1.60	1.60	1.60	2.80	3.12	3.04
Payout Ratio	46%	62%	NM	NM	70%	68%
Prices - High	58¾	55	46	52	71	64¼
- Low	37	39⅛	31¼	27⅜	40	46⅞
P/E Ratio - High	17	21	NM	NM	16	14
- Low	11	15	NM	NM	9	11

Income Statement Analysis (Million $)

	1994	%Chg	1993	%Chg	1992	%Chg	1991
Revs.	12,174	-8%	13,255	NM	13,139	-4%	13,662
Oper. Inc.	1,681	16%	1,455	8%	1,348	94%	696
Depr.	429	-16%	509	-12%	579	3%	563
Int. Exp.	568	-21%	718	-20%	902	-14%	1,045
Pretax Inc.	972	53%	636	NM	-606	NM	-682
Eff. Tax Rate	31%	—	23%	—	NM	—	NM
Net Inc.	641	42%	451	NM	-682	NM	-673

Balance Sheet & Other Fin. Data (Million $)

	1994	1993	1992	1991	1990	1989
Cash	405	218	111	231	147	276
Curr. Assets	3,895	5,417	6,283	6,968	7,945	7,523
Total Assets	12,542	15,373	16,584	18,696	19,034	17,381
Curr. Liab.	3,054	4,910	5,680	6,848	7,234	6,201
LT Debt	3,570	4,799	6,400	6,837	5,976	5,573
Common Eqty.	2,900	2,592	1,321	2,765	3,367	3,277
Total Cap.	8,396	8,941	9,272	10,972	11,057	10,507
Cap. Exp.	736	587	595	894	920	663
Cash Flow	1,058	960	-119	-126	1,031	1,075

Ratio Analysis

	1994	1993	1992	1991	1990	1989
Curr. Ratio	1.3	1.1	1.1	1.0	1.1	1.2
% LT Debt of Cap.	42.5	54.0	69.0	62.3	54.0	53.0
% Net Inc.of Revs.	5.3	3.4	NM	NM	3.9	4.1
% Ret. on Assets	4.3	2.8	NM	NM	3.1	3.4
% Ret. on Equity	21.8	22.3	NM	NM	16.6	17.6

Dividend Data —Dividends have been paid since 1948. A dividend reinvestment plan is available. A "poison pill" stock purchase right was adopted in 1988.

Amt. of Div. $	Date Decl.	Ex-Div. Date	Stock of Record	Payment Date
0.400	Oct. 04	Nov. 18	Nov. 25	Dec. 13 '94
0.400	Jan. 10	Feb. 17	Feb. 24	Mar. 14 '95
0.400	May. 09	May. 22	May. 26	Jun. 13 '95
0.400	Jul. 11	Aug. 23	Aug. 25	Sep. 12 '95

Data as orig. reptd.; bef. results of disc. opers. and/or spec. items. Per share data adj. for stk. divs. as of ex-div. date. E-Estimated. NA-Not Available. NM-Not Meaningful. NR-Not Ranked.

Office—Tenneco Building (PO Box 2511) Houston, TX 77252. Tel—(713) 757-2131. Chrmn, Pres & CEO—D. G. Mead. SVP & CFO—R. T. Blakely. VP & Secy—K. A. Stewart. Treas—K. R. Osar. Investor Contact—Jack Lascar. Dirs—M. Andrews, W. M. Blumenthal, M. K. Eickhoff, P. T. Flawn, H. U. Harris, Jr., B. K. Johnson, J. B. McCoy, D. G. Mead, J. J. Sisco, W. L. Weiss, C. R. Wharton, Jr. Transfer Agent & Registrar—First Chicago Trust Co. of New York, Jersey City, N.J. Incorporated in Delaware in 1947. Empl-55,000. S&P Analyst: Raymond J. Deacon

Texaco Inc.

NYSE Symbol **TX**
In S&P 500

15-AUG-95 Industry: Oil and Gas

Summary: Texaco is a leading international oil and natural gas company engaged in exploration, refining and marketing operations.

S&P Opinion: Hold (★★★)	Recent Price • 64¾	Yield • 4.9%
	52 Wk Range • 69⅝-58⅛	12-Mo. P/E • 14.3

Quantitative Evaluations

Outlook
(1 Lowest—5 Highest)
• **1+**

Fair Value
• **56⅝**

Risk
• **Low**

Earn./Div. Rank
• **B**

Technical Eval.
• **Bullish** since 4/94

Rel. Strength Rank
(1 Lowest—99 Highest)
• **25**

Insider Activity
• **NA**

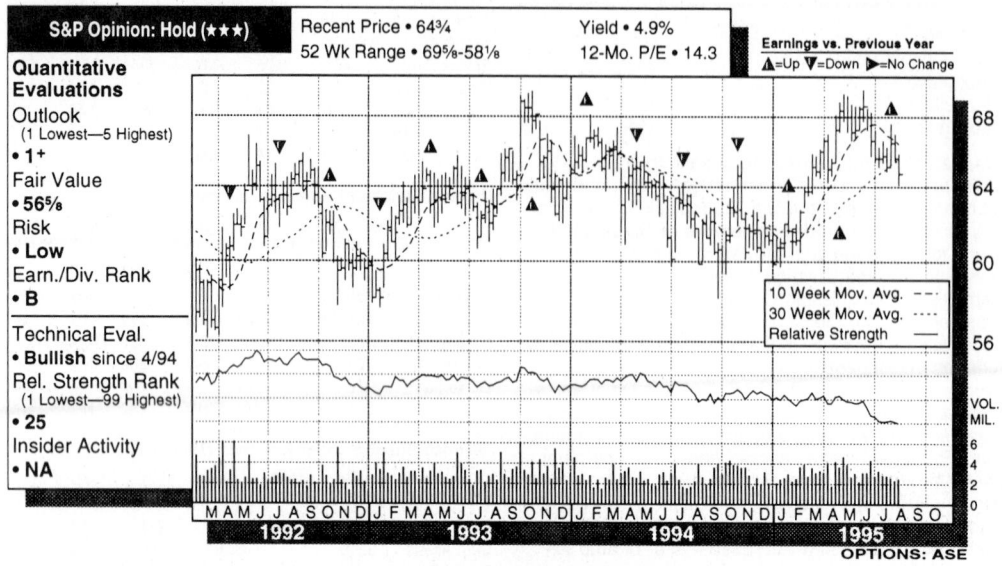

Earnings vs. Previous Year
▲=Up ▼=Down ▶=No Change

10 Week Mov. Avg. - - -
30 Week Mov. Avg. ·····
Relative Strength ——

VOL.
MIL.

OPTIONS: ASE

Overview - 11-AUG-95

Earnings in 1995 should rebound from 1994's depressed levels. We expect the company's 50% owned Caltex subsidiary to fuel long-term earnings growth. Caltex concentrates on refining and marketing in the Pacific Rim, where robust economies will continue to expand. Also, the fundamental outlook for the company's worldwide natural gas business is promising, as demand for gas increases, and foreign exploration activities speed up. Gas should continue to garner market share from coal and crude oil for the foreseeable future. An anticipated upturn in refining margins in 1995 should boost earnings as well. Texaco's concentrated exploration program and aggressive cost cutting measures are undermined to some degree by a relatively high level of debt.

Valuation - 15-AUG-95

Though now off somewhat from the high reached in May, Texaco's shares have rebounded in 1995 as the company's focus on core businesses has shown signs of success. A restructuring program is continuing that will lower lifting and overhead expenses. Earnings are foreseen increasing about 18% in 1995, on an operating basis. This level of earnings growth will lead investors to value the stock at about 16 times earnings, and 5.5 times cash flow per share. An increased capital spending budget for 1995 will focus on a promising Pacific Rim and Latin American asset base, and strong prospects in the North Sea. The stock, with an attractive yield, is an appealing long-term holding.

Key Stock Statistics

S&P EPS Est. 1995	4.30	Tang. Bk. Value/Share	37.04
P/E on S&P Est. 1995	15.1	Beta	0.68
S&P EPS Est. 1996	4.70	Shareholders	200,000
Dividend Rate/Share	3.20	Market cap. (B)	$ 16.9
Shs. outstg. (M)	259.7	Inst. holdings	60%
Avg. daily vol. (M)	0.475	Insider holdings	NA

Value of $10,000 invested 5 years ago: $ 14,682

Fiscal Year Ending Dec. 31

	1995	% Change	1994	% Change	1993	% Change
Revenues ()						
1Q	8,585	19%	7,230	-10%	8,061	-4%
2Q	—	—	7,865	-8%	8,591	-7%
3Q	—	—	8,725	5%	8,276	-15%
4Q	—	—	8,718	5%	8,317	-12%
Yr.	—	—	32,540	-2%	33,245	-10%
Income ()						
1Q	301.0	49%	202.0	-27%	278.0	20%
2Q	262.0	128%	115.0	-63%	309.0	105%
3Q	—	—	281.0	-11%	317.0	NM
4Q	—	—	381.0	9%	349.0	12%
Yr.	—	—	979.0	-22%	1,259	24%
Earnings Per Share ()						
1Q	1.10	59%	0.69	-30%	0.98	22%
2Q	0.95	171%	0.35	-68%	1.11	127%
3Q	E1.10	12%	0.98	-13%	1.13	NM
4Q	E1.15	-19%	1.42	14%	1.25	13%
Yr.	E4.30	25%	3.43	-23%	4.47	27%

Next earnings report expected: late October

Texaco Inc.

Business Summary - 15-AUG-95

Texaco is a major integrated oil company. TX has extensive international interests, including the 50%-owned Caltex group of companies (Chevron Corp. holds the remaining 50%). Caltex operates in 58 countries, primarily east of Suez, Egypt, including some of the world's fastest growing economies. In December 1988, TX and Saudi Arabian Oil Co. formed a U.S.-based joint venture called Star Enterprise, which refines, distributes and markets Texaco-branded petroleum products in 26 East and Gulf Coast states and the District of Columbia. TX is developing exploration and production projects in West Africa, the Partitioned Neutral Zone between Saudi Arabia and Kuwait, Colombia, China, Indonesia, Russia, Australia and the U.K. sector of the North Sea. TX is also active in the Gulf of Mexico. Chemical operations were sold in April 1994.

Profit contributions	1994	1993
U.S. exploration & production	32%	34%
Intl. exploration & production	20%	22%
U.S. manufacturing & marketing	20%	15%
Intl. manufacturing & marketing	28%	29%

In 1994, net production of crude oil and natural gas liquids (including interests in nonsubsidiary companies) averaged 783,000 bbl. a day (728,000 b/d in 1993), natural gas sales 3.4 Bcf a day (3.0 Bcf), refinery input 1,453,000 b/d (1,470,000 b/d), and petroleum product sales 2,352,000 b/d (2,334,000 b/d). Net proved reserves at the end of 1994 were 2,684 million bbl. of crude oil and natural gas liquids (2,685 million bbl. a year earlier) and 6,193 Bcf of natural gas (6,110 Bcf). Additions to reserves in 1994 equaled 112% of oil and gas production.

Important Developments

Jul. '95—Texaco reported that higher oil prices and a rise in international oil and gas production, as well as improvements in the Latin American marketing business, boosted second quarter operating income to $262 million ($0.95 a share) from $115 million ($0.35). Sharply lower natural gas prices and relatively low industry refining margins restrained further gains.
May '95—Texaco and British Petroleum received approvals necessary to award construction contracts for developent of the Erskine field in the U.K. North Sea. Production is expected to begin in late 1997. Estimated recoverable reserves stand at more than 330 Bcf of gas and 75 MMbls of condensate. Texaco also announced the sale of its Pekin Energy ethanol unit for $167 million.

Capitalization

Long Term Debt: $5,645,000,000 (3/95).
Minority Interest: $606,000,000.
Preferred Stock: $300,000,000.
ESOP Conv. Preferred Stock: $509,000,000.

Per Share Data ()

(Year Ended Dec. 31)

	1994	1993	1992	1991	1990	1989
Tangible Bk. Val.	35.51	35.26	34.27	35.08	33.57	32.07
Cash Flow	10.13	10.53	9.82	10.65	11.56	15.56
Earnings	3.43	4.47	3.53	4.61	5.18	9.12
Dividends	3.20	3.20	3.20	3.20	3.05	10.00
Payout Ratio	93%	72%	91%	69%	58%	114%
Prices - High	68⅛	69½	66⅞	70	68½	59
- Low	58⅛	57⅝	56⅛	55½	55	48½
P/E Ratio - High	20	16	19	15	13	6
- Low	17	13	16	12	11	5

Income Statement Analysis ()

	1994	%Chg	1993	%Chg	1992	%Chg	1991
Revs.	32,540	-2%	33,245	-10%	36,812	-1%	37,271
Oper. Inc.	2,668	12%	2,390	-7%	2,581	3%	2,503
Depr.	1,735	11%	1,568	-4%	1,627	4%	1,560
Int. Exp.	511	NM	508	-10%	565	-9%	624
Pretax Inc.	1,248	5%	1,189	-10%	1,323	-8%	1,436
Eff. Tax Rate	18%	—	NM	—	22%	—	8.80%
Net Inc.	979	-22%	1,259	24%	1,012	-22%	1,294

Balance Sheet & Other Fin. Data ()

	1994	1993	1992	1991	1990	1989
Cash	464	536	482	883	829	2,320
Curr. Assets	6,019	6,865	5,611	6,581	7,256	7,730
Total Assets	25,505	26,626	25,992	26,182	25,975	25,636
Curr. Liab.	5,015	4,756	4,225	6,290	6,968	6,409
LT Debt	5,564	6,157	6,441	5,173	4,485	4,714
Common Eqty.	9,216	9,132	8,867	9,068	8,667	8,498
Total Cap.	16,802	18,130	17,972	16,848	15,700	15,560
Cap. Exp.	2,050	1,844	2,076	2,346	2,270	1,975
Cash Flow	2,623	2,726	2,540	2,751	3,006	4,011

Ratio Analysis

	1994	1993	1992	1991	1990	1989
Curr. Ratio	1.2	1.4	1.3	1.0	1.0	1.2
% LT Debt of Cap.	33.1	34.0	35.8	30.7	28.6	30.3
% Net Inc.of Revs.	3.0	3.8	2.7	3.5	3.5	7.4
% Ret. on Assets	3.8	4.8	3.9	5.0	5.7	8.9
% Ret. on Equity	9.7	12.9	10.2	13.4	15.9	28.1

Dividend Data

—A revised "poison pill" stock purchase rights plan was adopted in 1989. A share repurchase program was initiated in July 1994.

Amt. of Div. $	Date Decl.	Ex-Div. Date	Stock of Record	Payment Date
0.800	Jul. 22	Aug. 02	Aug. 08	Sep. 09 '94
0.800	Oct. 28	Nov. 02	Nov. 08	Dec. 09 '94
0.800	Jan. 27	Feb. 01	Feb. 07	Mar. 10 '95
0.800	Apr. 21	May. 01	May. 05	Jun. 09 '95
0.800	Jul. 28	Aug. 04	Aug. 08	Sep. 08 '95

Data as orig. reptd.; bef. results of disc. opers. and/or spec. items. Per share data adj. for stk. divs. as of ex-div. date. E-Estimated. NA-Not Available. NM-Not Meaningful. NR-Not Ranked.

Office—2000 Westchester Ave., White Plains, NY 10650. **Tel**—(914) 253-4000. **Chrmn & CEO**—A. C. DeCrane, Jr. **Vice Chrmn**—A. J. Krowe. **SVP & CFO**—W. C. Bousquette. **VP & Secy**—C. B. Davidson. **VP & Investor Contact**—Elizabeth P. Smith. **Dirs**—R. A. Beck, J. Brademas, W. C. Butcher, E. M. Carpenter, A. C. DeCrane, Jr., F. G. Jenifer, A. J. Krowe, T. S. Murphy, C. H. Price II, R. B. Smith, W. C. Steere, Jr., T. A. Vanderslice, W. Wrigley. **Transfer Agents**—Co.'s office; Mellon Securities Transfer Services, NYC. **Incorporated** in Delaware in 1926 (original co. in 1902). **Empl**-32,514. **S&P Analyst:** Raymond J. Deacon

Texas Instruments

NYSE Symbol **TXN**
In S&P 500

17-OCT-95

Industry:
Electronics/Electric

Summary: Texas Instruments, one of the world's largest manufacturers of semiconductors, also produces defense electronics, software and calculators.

S&P Opinion: Accumulate (★★★★)	Recent Price • 72%	Yield • 1.0%
	52 Wk Range • 83¾-33%	12-Mo. P/E • 14.1

Quantitative Evaluations

Outlook
(1 Lowest—5 Highest)
• **5+**

Fair Value
• **88%**

Risk
• **Average**

Earn./Div. Rank
• **B**

Technical Eval.
• **Bullish** since 2/95

Rel. Strength Rank
(1 Lowest—99 Highest)
• **24**

Insider Activity
• **Unfavorable**

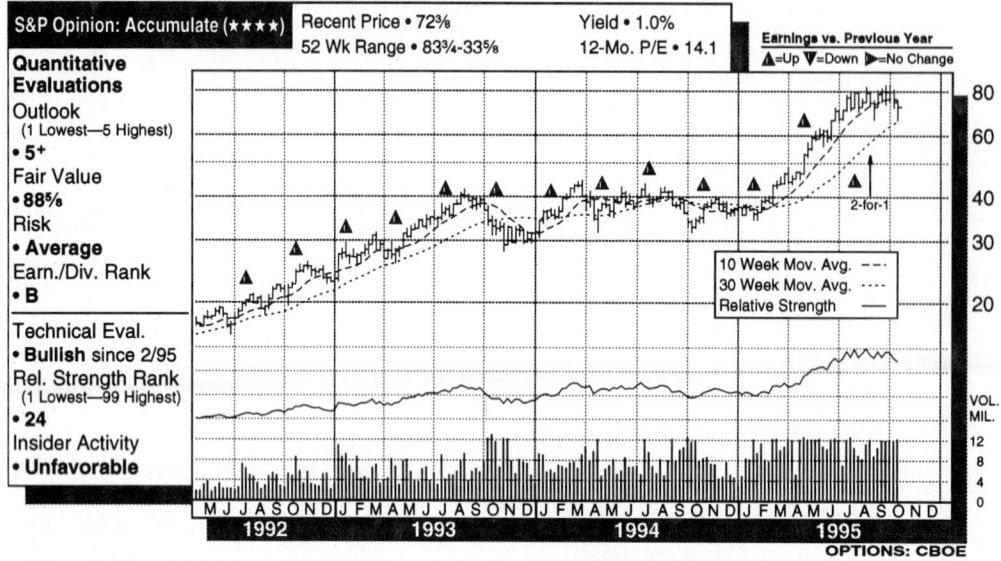

Earnings vs. Previous Year
▲=Up ▼=Down ▶=No Change

10 Week Mov. Avg. ---
30 Week Mov. Avg. ·····
Relative Strength ——

2-for-1

VOL. MIL.

1992 1993 1994 1995

OPTIONS: CBOE

Overview - 13-OCT-95

Revenues are likely to advance more than 30% in 1995's fourth quarter and some 25% in 1996, led by broad-based strength in the semiconductor industry. The company is benefiting from secular growth trends in key semiconductor product categories, most notably DRAM and digital signal processors (DSPs). Demand for DRAM is being fueled by strong demand for personal computers, while the recent release of Windows 95 is signficantly boosting the standard memory configuration of a typical unit. The company should also experience strong growth for DSPs, where it is the industry leader, fueled by growing demand for multimedia products. Margins may narrow as supply and demand converge in late 1996 and as manufacturing capacity is added, but well controlled operating costs will allow for above average EPS growth.

Valuation - 13-OCT-95

We continue to believe that shares of TXN will outperform the market over the next 6 to 12 months, reflecting strong industry fundamentals and the low valuation based on our 1996 earnings estimate. The use of semiconductors is proliferating in a number of applications as well as in most emerging countries. This broader penetration should lead to a more normal supply/demand balance versus the boom/bust cycles the industry has experienced in previous years. We believe TXN will be a major beneficiary of this industry-wide strength. Moreover, we see strong sales and earnings visibility in key product categories.

Key Stock Statistics

S&P EPS Est. 1995	5.67	Tang. Bk. Value/Share	18.94
P/E on S&P Est. 1995	12.8	Beta	1.69
S&P EPS Est. 1996	6.70	Shareholders	29,100
Dividend Rate/Share	0.68	Market cap. (B)	$ 13.2
Shs. outstg. (M)	187.9	Inst. holdings	77%
Avg. daily vol. (M)	2.464	Insider holdings	NA

Value of $10,000 invested 5 years ago: $ 44,062

Fiscal Year Ending Dec. 31

	1995	% Change	1994	% Change	1993	% Change
Revenues (Million $)						
1Q	2,862	17%	2,449	30%	1,884	11%
2Q	3,238	29%	2,510	19%	2,105	13%
3Q	3,425	33%	2,574	19%	2,161	14%
4Q	—	—	2,782	17%	2,374	19%
Yr.	—	—	10,315	21%	8,523	15%
Income (Million $)						
1Q	230.0	72%	134.0	58%	85.00	113%
2Q	278.0	51%	184.0	64%	112.0	56%
3Q	289.0	55%	186.0	27%	146.0	156%
4Q	—	—	188.0	40%	134.0	72%
Yr.	—	—	691.0	45%	476.0	93%
Earnings Per Share ($)						
1Q	1.20	71%	0.71	58%	0.44	154%
2Q	1.44	49%	0.96	64%	0.59	62%
3Q	1.48	53%	0.97	26%	0.77	166%
4Q	E1.54	56%	0.99	39%	0.71	78%
Yr.	E5.67	56%	3.64	43%	2.53	103%

Next earnings report expected: mid January

Business Summary - 13-OCT-95

Texas Instruments produces a variety of electrical and electronics products. Contributions by industry segment (profits in million $) in 1994 were:

	Revs.	Profits
Components	66%	$1,101
Defense electronics	17%	172
Digital products	16%	62
Metallurgical materials	1%	-8

Foreign operations accounted for 49% of revenues and 17% of profits in 1994. Sales to the U.S. government (primarily defense electronics) accounted for 12% of the total.

Components consist of semiconductor integrated circuits (such as microprocessors/microcontrollers, application processors, memories, and digital and linear circuits), semiconductor discrete devices, semiconductor subassemblies (such as custom modules for specific applications), and electrical and electronic control devices. In addition, the company has a portfolio of patents that generates substantial income.

Defense electronics include radar systems, navigation systems, infrared surveillance and fire control systems, defense suppression missiles, missile guidance and control systems, and electronic warfare systems.

Digital products include software development productivity tools, integrated enterprise information solutions, notebook computers, printers, electronic calculators and learning aids, and custom engineering and manufacturing services. Multiuser minicomputer systems and services operations were sold in the fourth quarter of 1992.

Metallurgical materials include clad metals, precision-engineered parts and connectors.

Important Developments

Oct. '95—The company said it expects the growth of the worldwide semiconductor market in 1995 to approximate 40%, the third consecutive year of strong growth.
Sep. '95—TXN introduced its Extensa notebook computer family, a line of value-priced notebooks targeted at the retail marketplace.
Jul. '95—TXN said it is ramping up production of advanced microprocessors in its newest facility in Dallas, Tex. and is planning to accelerate construction of the second phase of this facility for future generations of microprocessors and digital signal processors. This will result in the commencement of production in late 1996, several months ahead of the previous schedule.

Capitalization

Long Term Debt: $886,000,000 (9/95).

Per Share Data ($)   (Year Ended Dec. 31)

	1994	1993	1992	1991	1990	1989
Tangible Bk. Val.	16.40	12.75	8.92	8.13	11.23	12.05
Cash Flow	7.10	5.73	4.81	0.90	2.85	4.16
Earnings	3.64	2.53	1.25	-2.70	-0.46	1.52
Dividends	0.46	0.36	0.36	0.36	0.36	0.36
Payout Ratio	13%	14%	28%	NM	NM	23%
Prices - High	44¾	42⅛	26⅛	23⅞	22	23⅜
- Low	30½	22⅞	15	13	11¼	14⅛
P/E Ratio - High	12	17	21	NM	NM	15
- Low	8	9	12	NM	NM	9

Income Statement Analysis (Million $)

	1994	%Chg	1993	%Chg	1992	%Chg	1991
Revs.	10,315	21%	8,523	15%	7,440	10%	6,784
Oper. Inc.	1,748	30%	1,345	31%	1,030	NM	341
Depr.	665	8%	617	1%	610	3%	590
Int. Exp.	58.0	5%	55.0	-4%	57.0	-3%	59.0
Pretax Inc.	1,042	50%	696	89%	369	NM	-303
Eff. Tax Rate	34%	—	32%	—	33%	—	NM
Net Inc.	691	45%	476	93%	247	NM	-408

Balance Sheet & Other Fin. Data (Million $)

	1994	1993	1992	1991	1990	1989
Cash	1,290	888	859	601	412	637
Curr. Assets	4,017	3,314	2,626	2,381	2,305	2,446
Total Assets	6,989	5,993	5,185	5,009	5,048	4,804
Curr. Liab.	2,199	2,001	1,665	1,568	1,479	1,303
LT Debt	808	694	909	896	715	618
Common Eqty.	3,039	2,315	1,473	1,335	1,837	1,964
Total Cap.	3,847	3,009	2,856	2,851	3,073	3,102
Cap. Exp.	1,076	730	429	504	909	863
Cash Flow	1,356	1,073	820	147	466	707

Ratio Analysis

	1994	1993	1992	1991	1990	1989
Curr. Ratio	1.8	1.7	1.6	1.5	1.6	1.9
% LT Debt of Cap.	21.0	23.1	31.8	31.4	23.3	19.9
% Net Inc.of Revs.	6.7	5.6	3.3	NM	NM	4.5
% Ret. on Assets	10.5	8.1	4.8	NM	NM	6.3
% Ret. on Equity	25.6	23.2	14.9	NM	NM	13.6

Dividend Data—Dividends have been paid since 1962. A "poison pill" stock purchase right was adopted in 1988.

Amt. of Div. $	Date Decl.	Ex-Div. Date	Stock of Record	Payment Date
0.250	Dec. 02	Dec. 21	Dec. 28	Jan. 30 '95
0.250	Mar. 16	Mar. 30	Apr. 05	Apr. 24 '95
0.340	Jun. 15	Jun. 26	Jun. 28	Jul. 24 '95
2-for-1	Jun. 15	Aug. 21	Jul. 21	Aug. 18 '95
0.170	Sep. 21	Oct. 02	Oct. 04	Oct. 23 '95

Data as orig. reptd.; bef. results of disc. opers. and/or spec. items. Per share data adj. for stk. divs. as of ex-div. date.
E-Estimated. NA-Not Available. NM-Not Meaningful. NR-Not Ranked.

Office—13500 North Central Expressway (P.O. Box 655474), Dallas, TX 75265. **Tel**—(214) 995-2011. **Chrmn, Pres & CEO**—J. R. Junkins. **SVP, Treas & CFO**—W. A. Aylesworth. **SVP & Secy**—R. J. Agnich. **Investor Contact**—Max Post (214-995-3773). **Dirs**—J. R. Adams, D. L. Boren, J. B. Busey IV, G. W. Fronterhouse, J. R. Junkins, W. S. Lee, W. B. Mitchell, G. M. Shatto, W. P. Weber, C. K. Yeutter. **Transfer Agent & Registrar**—Harris Trust and Savings Bank, Chicago. **Incorporated** in Delaware in 1938. **Empl**-56,333. **S&P Analyst:** John D. Coyle, CFA

Texas Utilities

NYSE Symbol **TXU**
In S&P 500

25-OCT-95

Industry:
Utilities-Electric

Summary: This Dallas-based utility holding company provides electricity and related services to a growing, diversified residential and industrial manufacturing base primarily in Texas.

S&P Opinion: Accumulate (★★★★)

| Recent Price • 36½ | Yield • 5.5% |
| 52 Wk Range • 36⅝-30⅛ | 12-Mo. P/E • NM |

Earnings vs. Previous Year
▲=Up ▼=Down ▶=No Change

Quantitative Evaluations

Outlook
(1 Lowest—5 Highest)
• **1+**

Fair Value
• **32⅞**

Risk
• **Low**

Earn./Div. Rank
• **B+**

Technical Eval.
• **Bullish** since 5/94

Rel. Strength Rank
(1 Lowest—99 Highest)
• **77**

Insider Activity
• **NA**

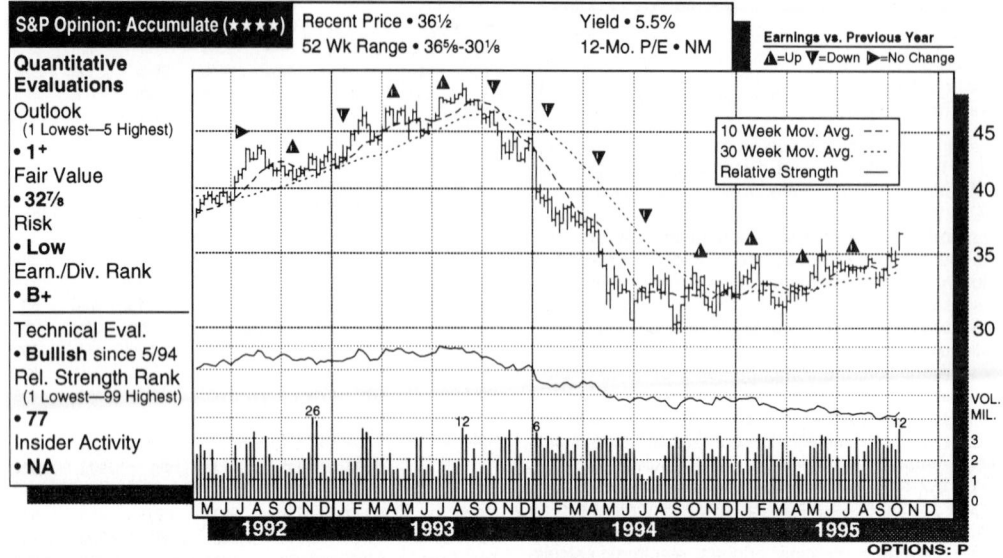

10 Week Mov. Avg. – – –
30 Week Mov. Avg. ......
Relative Strength —

OPTIONS: P

Overview - 25-OCT-95

A loss from operations is forthcoming in 1995, due to a $3.55 a share charge to write down non-performing assets, primarily partially completed coal plants and coal reserves that are no longer needed. Excluding the non-cash charge, we expect 1995 earnings to rise some 17%, to $2.80, reflecting continued customer growth, particularly in the residential segment, and cost reduction activities. In 1996, earnings should benefit from continued productivity gains, cost saving efforts and significant debt refinancings. Share repurchase should also add to per share results. Over the longer term, TXU benefits from a high level of energy-using industries--such as banking, insurance, communications, electronics and aerospace manufacturers--in its service area.

Valuation - 25-OCT-95

Investors' concerns about pending regulatory issues and growing competition from independent power producers has limited gains in TXU's common stock and, despite an upturn on restructuring news, the shares remain well below their 1993 peak. The recent writedown, taken to use the company's strong cash flows to enhance future earnings, reduces risk from potentialy stranded assets under deregulation. A lower dividend also allows greater flexibility in price-setting and new opportunistic investments. A $250 million share repurchase program adds to the company's appeal as a worthwhile total return holding over the long term.

Key Stock Statistics

S&P EPS Est. 1995	-0.75	Tang. Bk. Value/Share	28.22
P/E on S&P Est. 1995	NM	Beta	0.25
S&P EPS Est. 1996	3.00	Shareholders	107,000
Dividend Rate/Share	2.00	Market cap. (B)	$ 8.2
Shs. outstg. (M)	225.8	Inst. holdings	49%
Avg. daily vol. (M)	1.015	Insider holdings	NA

Value of $10,000 invested 5 years ago: $ 16,411

Fiscal Year Ending Dec. 31

	1995	% Change	1994	% Change	1993	% Change
Revenues (Million $)						
1Q	1,244	-4%	1,301	14%	1,142	8%
2Q	1,354	-5%	1,430	14%	1,256	5%
3Q	1,776	4%	1,702	-5%	1,786	21%
4Q	—	—	1,230	-2%	1,250	6%
Yr.	—	—	5,664	4%	5,435	11%
Income (Million $)						
1Q	75.41	13%	66.75	-56%	153.1	79%
2Q	148.0	1%	146.2	-10%	162.7	4%
3Q	-441.7	NM	294.3	NM	51.67	-82%
4Q	—	—	35.58	NM	1.21	-99%
Yr.	—	—	542.8	47%	368.7	-40%
Earnings Per Share ($)						
1Q	0.33	10%	0.30	-57%	0.70	75%
2Q	0.66	2%	0.65	-12%	0.74	1%
3Q	-1.96	NM	1.30	NM	0.23	-83%
4Q	E0.22	38%	0.16	NM	0.01	-97%
Yr.	E-0.75	NM	2.40	45%	1.66	-42%

Next earnings report expected: late January

Texas Utilities

Business Summary - 24-OCT-95

Texas Utilities is a holding company whose main subsidiary is Texas Utilities Electric Co. TXU provides electric service to the north central, eastern and western parts of the state, with a population of about 5,730,000. The company serves the cities of Dallas, Fort Worth and Midland. Electric revenues in recent years:

	1994	1993	1992	1991
Residential	43%	41%	41%	42%
Commercial	29%	28%	29%	28%
Industrial	17%	16%	17%	17%
Other	11%	15%	13%	13%

Sources of power in 1994 were lignite coal 37%, gas 34%, nuclear 16%, and purchased power 13%. Peak load in 1994 was 18,173 mw and capability totaled 22,493 mw, for a capacity margin of 21%. TXU added 2,300 mw of nuclear capability through its wholly owned two-unit Comanche Peak facility when it began operating Unit 1 and common facilities commercially in 1990. Unit 2 began operating commercially in 1993. In 1993 TXU incurred a $1.32-a-share charge largely to resolve regulatory disallowances for Comanche Peak design and construction costs, and fuel issues. In January 1995, the Court of Appeals for the Third District of Texas affirmed an earlier disallowance of $472 million, but reversed and remanded to the Texas PUC $909 million of prior disallowances related to reacquisition of a minority ownership stake in Comanche. The Court of Appeals also ruled that tax benefits generated by costs not allowed in rates must be used to cut customer rates. TXU believes the rate treatment could violate IRS normalization rules and require payments to the IRS of up to $1.3 billion. TXU has appealed the decision in the Texas Supreme Court. In April 1994, the Texas PUC granted TXU a final revised rate hike of $449 million (9.0%).

Capital projects in 1994 totaled $436 million and are budgeted at $400 million a year over the next three years. TXU is considering alternative uses for its investment ($807 million as of 1994 year end) in an incomplete lignite-fueled 750 mw plant, including exempt wholesale generation, different locations for the plant or sale of the facilities, some of which may not provide complete recovery of its investment.

Important Developments

Oct. '95—Directors lowered the quarterly common stock dividend 35% to $0.50 a share. TXU plans to use its strong cash flows to buy back long-term debt and preferred and common stock over the next three years, and fund attractive investment opportunities.

Capitalization

Long Term Debt: $8,146,794,000 (6/95).
Subsidiary Preferred Stock: $1,156,326,000.

Per Share Data ($) (Year Ended Dec. 31)

	1994	1993	1992	1991	1990	1989
Tangible Bk. Val.	28.74	29.29	30.06	29.55	34.38	34.26
Earnings	2.40	1.66	2.88	-1.98	4.40	4.44
Dividends	3.08	3.08	3.04	3.00	2.96	2.92
Payout Ratio	128%	186%	106%	NM	67%	66%
Prices - High	43⅛	49¾	43¾	43	39	37½
- Low	29⅝	41⅝	37	34⅛	32	27¾
P/E Ratio - High	18	30	15	NM	9	8
- Low	12	25	13	NM	7	6

Income Statement Analysis (Million $)

	1994	%Chg	1993	%Chg	1992	%Chg	1991
Revs.	5,664	4%	5,435	11%	4,908	NM	4,893
Depr.	550	25%	440	5%	421	-4%	437
Maint.	305	-13%	350	16%	301	-3%	309
Fxd. Chgs. Cov.	2.0	16%	1.8	-14%	2.0	NM	0.2
Constr. Credits	22.0	-92%	263	-13%	304	-16%	364
Eff. Tax Rate	33%	—	29%	—	22%	—	45%
Net Inc.	543	47%	369	-40%	619	NM	-409

Balance Sheet & Other Fin. Data (Million $)

	1994	1993	1992	1991	1990	1989
Gross Prop.	24,001	23,722	22,994	21,902	20,715	19,137
Cap. Exp.	444	871	1,137	1,232	1,454	1,812
Net Prop.	17,669	17,818	17,484	16,768	17,280	15,989
Capitalization:						
LT Debt	7,888	8,380	7,932	7,951	7,381	6,417
% LT Debt	50	51	50	51	47	46
Pfd.	1,258	1,480	1,328	1,433	1,434	1,337
% Pfd.	8.00	9.00	8.40	9.20	9.20	9.50
Common	6,490	6,571	6,591	6,284	6,828	6,330
% Common	42	40	42	40	44	45
Total Cap.	19,168	19,823	17,613	17,228	17,496	15,881

Ratio Analysis

	1994	1993	1992	1991	1990	1989
Oper. Ratio	76.5	78.2	76.3	76.8	76.1	76.1
% Earn. on Net Prop.	7.5	6.7	6.8	6.7	6.5	6.8
% Ret. on Revs.	9.6	6.8	12.6	NM	18.7	18.0
% Ret. On Invest.Cap	7.0	6.0	7.9	2.4	9.0	8.8
% Return On Com.Eqty	8.3	5.6	9.6	NM	12.9	13.0

Dividend Data —Dividends have been paid since 1917. A dividend reinvestment plan is available.

Amt. of Div. $	Date Decl.	Ex-Div. Date	Stock of Record	Payment Date
0.770	Nov. 18	Dec. 01	Dec. 07	Jan. 03 '95
0.770	Feb. 17	Mar. 03	Mar. 09	Apr. 03 '95
0.770	May. 19	Jun. 02	Jun. 08	Jul. 03 '95
0.770	Aug. 18	Sep. 05	Sep. 07	Oct. 02 '95
0.500	Oct. 16	Dec. 05	Dec. 07	Jan. 02 '96

Data as orig. reptd.; bef. results of disc opers. and/or spec. items. Per share data adj. for stk. divs. as of ex-div. date. E-Estimated. NA-Not Available. NM-Not Meaningful. NR-Not Ranked.

Office—1601 Bryan Tower, Dallas, TX 75201. **Tel**—(214) 812-4600. **Chrmn**—J. Farrington. **CEO & Pres**—E. Nye. **Secy**—P. B. Tinkham. **VP-CFO**—H. J. Gibbs. **Investor Contact**—Bob Shapard. **Dirs**—J. W. Evans, J. Farrington, B. H. Friedman, W. M. Griffin, K. Laday, M. N. Maxey, J. A. Middleton, E. Nye, C. R. Perry, H. H. Richardson. **Transfer Agent & Registrar**—Texas Utilities Shareholder Services, Dallas. **Incorporated** in Texas in 1945. **Empl**-10,798. **S&P Analyst:** Jane Collin

Textron Inc.

NYSE Symbol **TXT**
In S&P 500

29-JUL-95

Industry:
Conglomerate/diversified

Summary: This diversified company has operations in manufacturing and financial services.

| **S&P Opinion: Accumulate (★★★★)** | Recent Price • 65¾ | Yield • 2.4% |
| | 52 Wk Range • 66½-46½ | 12-Mo. P/E • 12.8 |

Quantitative Evaluations

Outlook
(1 Lowest—5 Highest)
• **3**

Fair Value
• **61¾**

Risk
• **Low**

Earn./Div. Rank
• **A**

Technical Eval.
• **Bullish** since 2/95

Rel. Strength Rank
(1 Lowest—99 Highest)
• **74**

Insider Activity
• **Unfavorable**

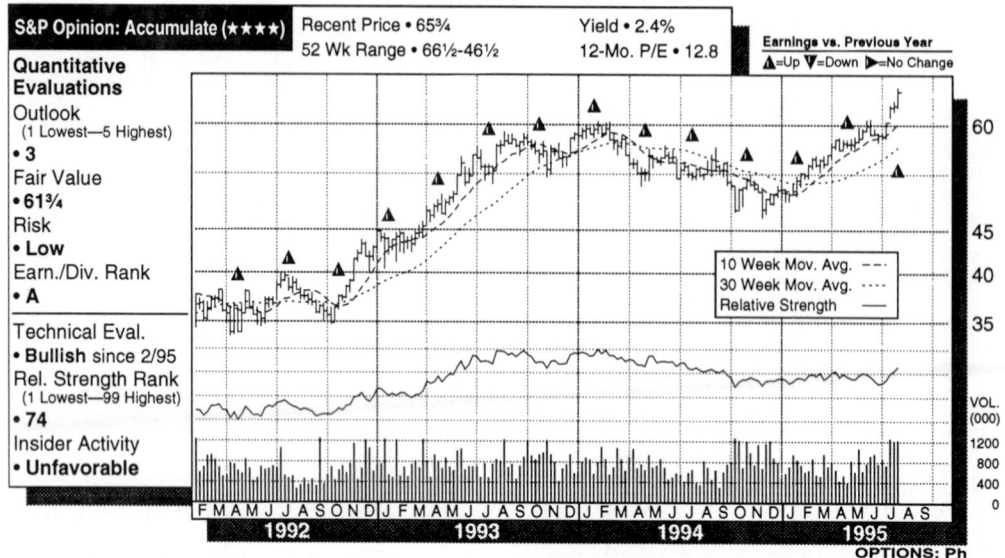

Earnings vs. Previous Year
▲=Up ▼=Down ▶=No Change

10 Week Mov. Avg. - - -
30 Week Mov. Avg. ······
Relative Strength ——

VOL. (000)

OPTIONS: Ph

Overview - 28-JUL-95

Revenues in 1995 are expected to be essentially unchanged from those of 1994, as growth in continuing businesses offsets the absence of sales from Lycoming Turbine Engine and Homelite. Strong order trends should translate into greater aircraft sales. Industrial revenues are projected to grow with the slowly expanding economy. Financial services should continue to benefit from recent marketing efforts. Somewhat offsetting will be lower automotive sales, due to a slowdown in that industry. Systems and components sales are also likely to remain under pressure. Margins are expected to widen on manufacturing efficiencies, well-controlled costs and lower chargeoffs in financial services. A stock repurchase program should aid share earnings.

Valuation - 28-JUL-95

TXT shares are expected to continue their recent rebound as concerns about the surge in claims experienced at Paul Revere begin to fade. The company should succeed in its aggressive efforts to improve earnings of Paul Revere's disability business. The stock should also benefit from the breadth of the recovery in the aerospace market; demand for Bell and Cessna products should continue to grow, both domestically and internationally. In addition, rising income from other segments will lead to another year of earnings improvement for Textron. A relatively low multiple, continued steady earnings growth and a significant dividend yield should further allow the shares to advance.

Key Stock Statistics

S&P EPS Est. 1995	5.45	Tang. Bk. Value/Share	17.01
P/E on S&P Est. 1995	12.1	Beta	1.07
S&P EPS Est. 1996	5.95	Shareholders	27,000
Dividend Rate/Share	1.56	Market cap. (B)	$ 5.6
Shs. outstg. (M)	85.1	Inst. holdings	73%
Avg. daily vol. (M)	0.259	Insider holdings	NA

Value of $10,000 invested 5 years ago: $ 31,195

Fiscal Year Ending Dec. 31

	1995	% Change	1994	% Change	1993	% Change
Revenues (Million $)						
1Q	2,387	NM	2,408	11%	2,165	9%
2Q	2,502	NM	2,517	12%	2,253	4%
3Q	—	—	2,381	7%	2,233	10%
4Q	—	—	2,377	-2%	2,427	12%
Yr.	—	—	9,683	7%	9,078	9%
Income (Million $)						
1Q	109.0	9%	100.0	21%	82.80	19%
2Q	121.0	10%	110.0	17%	94.30	17%
3Q	—	—	111.0	12%	99.5	19%
4Q	—	—	112.0	9%	102.5	13%
Yr.	—	—	433.0	14%	379.1	17%
Earnings Per Share ($)						
1Q	1.25	14%	1.10	20%	0.92	16%
2Q	1.40	15%	1.22	16%	1.05	15%
3Q	E1.40	—	1.23	12%	1.10	17%
4Q	E1.40	—	1.26	12%	1.13	11%
Yr.	E5.45	—	4.80	14%	4.21	15%

Next earnings report expected: mid October

Textron Inc.

Business Summary - 27-JUN-95

Textron is a diversified company with operations in manufacturing and financial services. Contributions in sales and operating income in 1994 were:

	Sales	Profits
Aircraft	23%	19%
Automotive	16%	13%
Industrial	14%	14%
Systems and components	16%	9%
Finance	17%	32%
Paul Revere	14%	13%

Foreign sales accounted for 14% of revenues and 20% of income in 1994. Exports represented 12% of revenues, and sales to the U.S. government totaled 17%.

Aircraft consists of Bell Helicopter, a leading international helicopter company serving commercial and military markets, and Cessna Aircraft, the world's largest light and mid-size business jet company.

The automotive segment is a leading global full-service supplier of automotive interior and exterior plastic components.

The industrial segment is comprises of three major business groups: fastening systems, golf and turf-care equipment and diversified products.

The systems and components businesses manufacture various products and components primarily for the commercial aerospace and defense industries.

Finance consists of Avco Financial Service, a multinational consumer finance company, and Textron Financial Corp., a diversified commerical finance company that finances the sale of Textron and third-party products.

Paul Revere, which is 83%-owned, is the leading provider of individual non-cancellable disability insurance in the United States and Canada.

Important Developments

Mar. '95—The company announced that its Cessna subsidiary planned to re-enter the general aviation market. Plans call for it to build 2,000 single-engine airplanes annually, which could add $300 million in revenues for the company.

Feb. '95—TXT announced an 11% dividend increase to $0.39 a share from $0.35 and said that its board had authorized the purchase of an additional 5 million shares of common stock, doubling the company's share repurchase program. It added that 3.7 million shares had been repurchased under the existing 5 million share authorization. Earlier the company said that its fourth quarter earnings benefited from growth in both manufacturing and financial services, although earnings at Paul Revere declined 41%.

Capitalization

Total Debt: $9,364,000,000 (12/94).
Cum. Conv. Preferred Stock: $16,600,000.

Per Share Data ($)   (Year Ended Dec. 31)

	1994	1993	1992	1991	1990	1989
Tangible Bk. Val.	15.52	14.36	12.13	22.04	18.78	16.15
Cash Flow	9.21	6.49	6.63	5.95	5.64	5.41
Earnings	4.80	4.21	3.66	3.42	3.18	3.02
Dividends	1.40	1.24	1.12	1.03	1.00	1.00
Payout Ratio	29%	29%	30%	30%	30%	33%
Prices - High	60⅝	58⅞	44⅞	40¼	27⅝	29⅜
- Low	46½	40⅜	33⅝	24¼	18¾	22⅝
P/E Ratio - High	13	14	12	12	9	10
- Low	10	10	9	7	6	7

Income Statement Analysis (Million $)

	1994	%Chg	1993	%Chg	1992	%Chg	1991
Revs.	9,681	7%	9,075	9%	8,344	7%	7,823
Oper. Inc.	1,815	22%	1,483	-3%	1,530	5%	1,455
Depr.	398	93%	206	-22%	264	18%	223
Int. Exp.	665	NM	668	-10%	742	-2%	754
Pretax Inc.	754	23%	614	17%	527	6%	495
Eff. Tax Rate	41%	—	38%	—	39%	—	40%
Net Inc.	433	14%	379	17%	324	8%	300

Balance Sheet & Other Fin. Data (Million $)

	1994	1993	1992	1991	1990	1989
Cash	49.0	26.2	31.0	50.0	66.0	29.0
Curr. Assets	NA	NA	NA	NA	NA	NA
Total Assets	20,925	19,658	18,367	15,737	14,892	13,790
Curr. Liab.	NA	NA	NA	NA	NA	NA
LT Debt	8,137	7,789	7,543	6,219	6,449	5,942
Common Eqty.	2,866	2,763	2,467	2,905	2,637	2,520
Total Cap.	11,019	10,569	10,030	9,147	9,111	8,489
Cap. Exp.	302	252	217	156	191	240
Cash Flow	830	584	588	521	502	482

Ratio Analysis

	1994	1993	1992	1991	1990	1989
Curr. Ratio	NA	NA	NA	NA	NA	NA
% LT Debt of Cap.	73.8	73.7	75.2	68.0	70.8	70.0
% Net Inc.of Revs.	4.5	4.2	3.9	3.8	3.6	3.6
% Ret. on Assets	2.2	2.0	1.9	1.9	2.0	2.0
% Ret. on Equity	15.6	14.4	11.9	10.7	11.2	10.7

Dividend Data (Dividends have been paid since 1942. A dividend reinvestment plan is available. A "poison pill" stock purchase rights plan was adopted in 1987.)

Amt. of Div. $	Date Decl.	Ex-Div. Date	Stock of Record	Payment Date
0.350	Jul. 27	Sep. 02	Sep. 09	Oct. 01 '94
0.350	Oct. 27	Dec. 05	Dec. 09	Jan. 01 '95
0.390	Feb. 22	Mar. 06	Mar. 10	Apr. 01 '95
0.390	May. 24	Jun. 06	Jun. 09	Jul. 01 '95
0.390	Jul. 26	Sep. 13	Sep. 15	Oct. 01 '95

Data as orig. reptd.; bef. results of disc. opers. and/or spec. items. Per share data adj. for stk. divs. as of ex-div. date. E-Estimated. NA-Not Available. NM-Not Meaningful. NR-Not Ranked.

Office—40 Westminster St. (P.O. Box 878), Providence, RI 02903. **Tel**—(401) 421-2800. **Chrmn & CEO**—J. F. Hardymon. **Pres & COO**—L. B. Campbell. **EVP & CFO**—S. L. Key. **EVP & Secy**—R. A. McWhirter. **Investor Contact**—Mary F. Lovejoy. **Dirs**—H. J. Arnelle, L. B. Campbell, R. S. Dickson, B. F. Dolan, J. F. Hardymon, W. C. Hayes III, J. D. Macomber, B. S. Preiskel, S. F. Segnar, J. H. Sisco, J. W. Snow, M. D. Walker, T. B. Wheeler. **Transfer Agent & Registrar**—First Chicago Trust Company of New York, NYC. **Incorporated** in Rhode Island in 1928; reincorporated in Delaware in 1967. **Empl**- 53,000. **S&P Analyst:** Paul H. Valentine, CFA

Thomas & Betts

NYSE Symbol **TNB**
In S&P 500

27-AUG-95 Industry:
Electronics/Electric

Summary: This company is a leading manufacturer of electrical and electronic components.

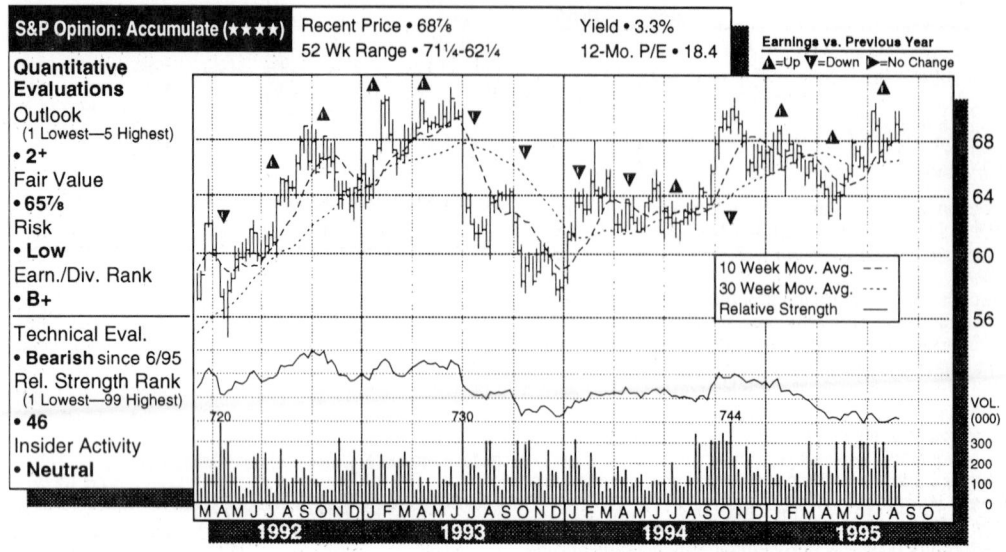

S&P Opinion: Accumulate (★★★★)	Recent Price • 68⅞	Yield • 3.3%
	52 Wk Range • 71¼-62¼	12-Mo. P/E • 18.4

Earnings vs. Previous Year
▲=Up ▼=Down ▶=No Change

Quantitative Evaluations

Outlook
(1 Lowest—5 Highest)
• **2⁺**

Fair Value
• **65⅞**

Risk
• **Low**

Earn./Div. Rank
• **B+**

Technical Eval.
• **Bearish** since 6/95

Rel. Strength Rank
(1 Lowest—99 Highest)
• **46**

Insider Activity
• **Neutral**

10 Week Mov. Avg. ----
30 Week Mov. Avg. ·······
Relative Strength ——

Overview - 25-AUG-95

Sales are expected to increase approximately 8% in 1996. Growth should be led by a 15% increase in sales of electronic products, which are benefiting from strong sales to the automotive industry, good connector demand and further market penetration. Electrical sales should grow approximately 8%, reflecting economic growth, market share gains from the company's Signature Service program, and higher prices. Sales to utility markets are only expected to increase 2%, restrained by weak capital spending in the industry. Margins should benefit from a better pricing environment and a projected $12 million savings from the restructuring announced in the third quarter of 1994.

Valuation - 25-AUG-95

The shares have begun a modest recovery from a selloff in July when investors became concerned that weakness in certain segments of the economy would hurt future results. While Thomas & Betts has experienced some softness in its business this year, we believe results over the next several quarters will meet or exceed expectations. That should allow the shares to continue their advance. In addition, the shares continue to be modestly priced relative to the market on a historical basis, and the dividend, which is expected to be increased over the next several quarters, provides a yield of about 3.3%. The shares are ranked "accumulate."

Key Stock Statistics

S&P EPS Est. 1995	4.00	Tang. Bk. Value/Share	12.82
P/E on S&P Est. 1995	17.2	Beta	0.71
S&P EPS Est. 1996	4.70	Shareholders	4,000
Dividend Rate/Share	2.24	Market cap. (B)	$ 1.4
Shs. outstg. (M)	19.7	Inst. holdings	76%
Avg. daily vol. (M)	0.032	Insider holdings	NA

Value of $10,000 invested 5 years ago: $ 17,002

Fiscal Year Ending Dec. 31

	1995	% Change	1994	% Change	1993	% Change
Revenues (Million $)						
1Q	302.6	22%	248.3	-7%	267.1	3%
2Q	298.1	14%	261.7	-1%	264.8	NM
3Q	—	—	277.4	3%	268.5	NM
4Q	—	—	288.8	5%	275.5	6%
Yr.	—	—	1,076	NM	1,076	2%
Income (Million $)						
1Q	16.68	63%	10.26	-22%	13.22	NM
2Q	18.84	48%	12.77	4%	12.24	-19%
3Q	—	—	-40.72	NM	13.20	-22%
4Q	—	—	19.57	20%	16.26	-14%
Yr.	—	—	1.89	-97%	54.91	8%
Earnings Per Share ($)						
1Q	0.85	57%	0.54	-23%	0.70	NM
2Q	0.96	43%	0.67	3%	0.65	-19%
3Q	E1.06	NM	-2.11	NM	0.70	-22%
4Q	E1.17	17%	1.00	16%	0.86	-15%
Yr.	E4.00	NM	0.10	-97%	2.91	7%

Next earnings report expected: late October

Business Summary - 25-AUG-95

Thomas & Betts designs, manufactures and markets a broad line of electrical and electronic connectors, components and related products for worldwide electrical and electronic markets.

The company's electrical construction components connect, terminate, protect and manage raceways, wires and cables for the distribution of electrical power. These products include fittings and accessories for electrical raceways, fastening products, terminals, power connectors, switch and outlet boxes, covers and accessories, floor boxes, metal framing, ground rods and clamps, products for outdoor security, roadway and adverse and hazardous location lighting, circuit brakers, safety switches and metal centers. In North America, the company's components are sold through distributors and retail outlets such as home centers and mass merchants. These products accounted for 49% of the company's sales in 1994.

The company's electronic/OEM components segment is a worldwide designer, manufacturer and marketer of electronic connectors, flexible interconnects, flat cable, premises wiring management components and other components. These products accounted for 23% of sales in 1994.

Other products and components are comprised of heating products, transmission poles and towers, telecommunications components and other components. These products accounted for 28% of sales in 1994.

Foreign operations accounted for 22% of sales and an $8.9 million pretax profit in 1994.

During 1994, the company made several acquisitions with combined annualized sales of $105 million at a cost totaling $72 million. It also acquired a 29% interest in Leviton Manufacturing Co. In July 1994, it sold its Vitramon subsidiary for $184 million.

Important Developments

Jul. '95—TNB said that during the second quarter its worldwide sales of electrical construction and maintenance components rose 16%. While the pace of these sales slowed somewhat in April and May after a strong first quarter, June saw a return to strong sales growth. Electronic/OEM components sales grew 18%. The other products and components segment had a 6% increase in sales. The company said it is focusing on international expansion and actively seeking a major acquisition in Europe.

Capitalization

Long Term Debt: $346,050,000 (7/95).

Per Share Data ($)

(Year Ended Dec. 31)

	1994	1993	1992	1991	1990	1989
Tangible Bk. Val.	11.72	9.00	7.93	19.75	18.85	17.74
Cash Flow	2.87	5.99	5.64	4.90	4.89	4.85
Earnings	0.10	2.91	2.72	2.84	2.84	3.16
Dividends	2.24	2.24	2.24	2.21	2.09	1.96
Payout Ratio	NM	77%	82%	78%	73%	62%
Prices - High	71¼	72	69	60⅞	61½	55¾
- Low	58⅛	57	54¾	45	40¼	46
P/E Ratio - High	NM	25	25	21	22	18
- Low	NM	20	20	16	14	15

Income Statement Analysis (Million $)

	1994	%Chg	1993	%Chg	1992	%Chg	1991
Revs.	1,076	NM	1,076	2%	1,051	86%	566
Oper. Inc.	168	3%	163	-6%	173	59%	109
Depr.	53.5	-8%	57.9	6%	54.7	56%	35.1
Int. Exp.	26.9	-11%	30.2	-10%	33.4	169%	12.4
Pretax Inc.	0.5	-99%	78.4	12%	69.8	3%	68.0
Eff. Tax Rate	NM	—	30%	—	27%	—	29%
Net Inc.	1.9	-97%	54.9	8%	50.9	5%	48.5

Balance Sheet & Other Fin. Data (Million $)

	1994	1993	1992	1991	1990	1989
Cash	122	104	98.0	101	90.0	98.0
Curr. Assets	534	489	463	335	337	336
Total Assets	1,208	1,133	1,117	600	586	564
Curr. Liab.	280	205	199	152	167	160
LT Debt	320	394	420	68.3	48.8	57.6
Common Eqty.	553	481	463	363	351	336
Total Cap.	887	899	893	440	409	401
Cap. Exp.	59.1	38.6	47.4	40.3	47.9	44.9
Cash Flow	55.0	113	106	83.5	83.3	82.4

Ratio Analysis

	1994	1993	1992	1991	1990	1989
Curr. Ratio	1.9	2.4	2.3	2.2	2.0	2.1
% LT Debt of Cap.	36.0	43.8	47.1	15.5	11.9	14.4
% Net Inc.of Revs.	0.2	5.1	4.8	8.6	8.1	9.9
% Ret. on Assets	0.2	4.9	5.7	8.2	8.4	10.1
% Ret. on Equity	0.4	11.6	11.8	13.5	14.1	16.5

Dividend Data —Dividends have been paid since 1934. A dividend reinvestment plan is available.

Amt. of Div. $	Date Decl.	Ex-Div. Date	Stock of Record	Payment Date
0.560	Sep. 07	Sep. 12	Sep. 16	Oct. 03 '94
0.560	Nov. 02	Dec. 12	Dec. 16	Jan. 03 '95
0.560	Feb. 01	Feb. 28	Mar. 06	Apr. 03 '95
0.560	May. 03	Jun. 14	Jun. 16	Jul. 03 '95

Data as orig. reptd.; bef. results of disc. opers. and/or spec. items. Per share data adj. for stk. divs. as of ex-div. date.
E-Estimated. NA-Not Available. NM-Not Meaningful. NR-Not Ranked.

Office—1555 Lynnfield Road, Memphis, Tennessee 38119. **Tel**—(901) 682-7766. **Chrmn & CEO**—T. K. Dunnigan. **Pres**—C. R. Moore. **VP-Fin**—R. P. Babcock. **Secy**—J. H. Way. **Investor Contact**—Robert V. Berry. **Dirs**—R. B. Carey, Jr., E. H. Drew, T. K. Dunnigan, J. K. Hauswald, T. W. Jones, R. A. Kenkel, K. R. Masterson, C. R. Moore, J. D. Parkinson, Jr., I. M. Ross, W. H. Waltrip. **Transfer Agent & Registrar**—First Chicago Trust Co. of New York, NYC. **Incorporated** in New Jersey in 1917. **Empl**-7,400. **S&P Analyst:** Paul H. Valentine, CFA

Time Warner

NYSE Symbol **TWX**
In S&P 500

26-SEP-95

Industry:
Filmed Entertainment

Summary: Time Warner is the world's largest media/entertainment company, with major interests in publishing, music, filmed entertainment, and cable television systems and programming.

| S&P Opinion: Accumulate (★★★★) | Recent Price • 40⅝ | Yield • 0.9% |
| | 52 Wk Range • 45⅞-31½ | 12-Mo. P/E • NM |

Quantitative Evaluations

Outlook
(1 Lowest—5 Highest)
• **NA**

Fair Value
• **NA**

Risk
• **Low**

Earn./Div. Rank
• **B-**

Technical Eval.
• **Bearish** since 7/95

Rel. Strength Rank
(1 Lowest—99 Highest)
• **18**

Insider Activity
• **Neutral**

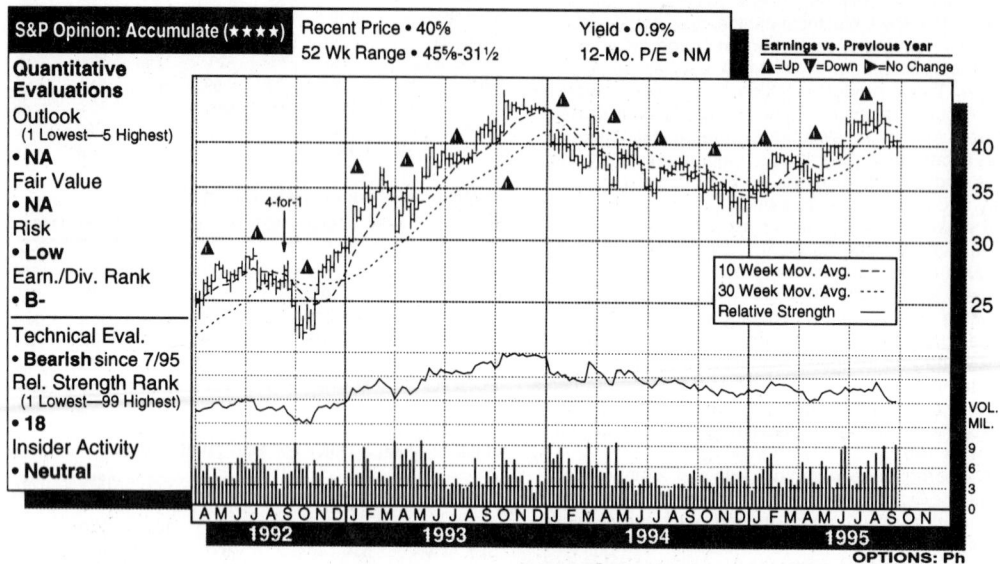

Earnings vs. Previous Year
▲=Up ▼=Down ▶=No Change

4-for-1

10 Week Mov. Avg. ---
30 Week Mov. Avg. ····
Relative Strength —

OPTIONS: Ph

Overview - 26-SEP-95

Wholly owned publishing and music segments should report healthy revenue gains and double digit earnings growth for 1995, helped by operating efficiencies. Higher equity earnings will reflect a strong rebound in cable system operations, and gains from cable programming. Entertainment operations will reflect startup costs of the new WB Network, but comparisons will benefit from a number of boxoffice hits. Interest costs will be lower. In the first half of 1995 the company raised $1.3 billion for debt reduction. The outlook for 1996 is positive. Revenue and earnings growth should continue for each business segment, with cable and filmed entertainment showing particular strength. Higher noncash charges and expanded programming for the WB Network will restrict the improvement in profitability.

Valuation - 26-SEP-95

The shares reacted negatively to the news of the planned TBS merger, reflecting the market's disappointment with the amount of dilution, and concern that TWX may be forced to pay USW handsomely to drop its suit contesting the proposed merger. TWX may also have to pay other large TBS owners (Comcast Corp. and Continental Cablevision) a premium for their shares. We believe the market has already discounted all the negatives dogging the stock, and that sentiment will soon turn positive as investors begin to concentrate on the favorable long-term implications of the proposed merger.

Key Stock Statistics

S&P EPS Est. 1995	-0.03	Tang. Bk. Value/Share	NM
P/E on S&P Est. 1995	NM	Beta	1.47
S&P EPS Est. 1996	0.10	Shareholders	300
Dividend Rate/Share	0.36	Market cap. (B)	$ 15.4
Shs. outstg. (M)	386.2	Inst. holdings	57%
Avg. daily vol. (M)	1.898	Insider holdings	NA

Value of $10,000 invested 5 years ago: $ 14,248

Fiscal Year Ending Dec. 31

	1995	% Change	1994	% Change	1993	% Change
Revenues (Million $)						
1Q	1,817	17%	1,558	—	—	—
2Q	1,907	14%	1,667	—	—	—
3Q	—	—	1,884	-59%	4,620	42%
4Q	—	—	2,287	17%	1,960	-47%
Yr.	—	—	7,396	-49%	14,544	11%
Income (Million $)						
1Q	-47.00	NM	-51.00	NM	-15.00	NM
2Q	-8.00	NM	-20.00	NM	-45.00	NM
3Q	—	—	-32.00	NM	-111.0	NM
4Q	—	—	12.00	71%	7.00	-90%
Yr.	—	—	-91.00	NM	-164.0	NM
Earnings Per Share ($)						
1Q	-0.13	NM	-0.14	NM	-0.33	NM
2Q	-0.03	NM	-0.06	NM	-0.13	NM
3Q	E-0.01	NM	-0.09	NM	-0.30	NM
4Q	E0.15	NM	0.02	NM	-0.01	NM
Yr.	E-0.03	NM	-0.27	NM	-0.75	NM

Next earnings report expected: mid October

Business Summary - 25-SEP-95

Time Warner is the world's largest media and entertainment company. Effective January 1, 1994, it deconsolidated Time Warner Entertainment Co. (TWE), a 74.5%-owned partnership that owns its filmed entertainment, theme park, cable programming and cable system operations. Joint-venture partner U S West owns 25.5% of TWE.

Publishing operations include 24 magazines; among them are Time, Sports Illustrated, Life, People, Fortune, Money, Southern Living, Sunset, Entertainment Weekly, and Parenting. Book operations include Little, Brown & Co., Warner Books, Book-of-the-Month Club, Time Life Inc., Oxmoor House and Sunset Books.

Music recording and publishing include the Warner, Elektra and Atlantic labels. TWX owns 50% of Columbia House Co., the largest music and video club in North America.

Filmed entertainment operations include Warner Bros. (WB) and Lorimar Television, which produce and distribute theatrical films, television programming and home videos. WB Consumer Products includes licensing, studio store, toys, and interactive entertainment. Six Flags Entertainment Corp. (49% owned) is the largest U.S. regional theme-park company. Time Warner Cable is the second largest U.S. cable system operator, with more than 7.5 million subscribers at the end of 1994. Cable programming consists of Home Box Office (HBO), the largest U.S. pay TV service, and Cinemax.

Important Developments

Sep. '95—TWX and Turner Broadcasting System (TBS) agreed to merge, creating the world's largest media company. Under terms of the agreement, TWX will issue up to 178 million common shares. Subject to certain conditions, Liberty Media, a subsidiary of TeleCommunications Inc. and owner of 21% of TBS, has agreed to vote its TBS shares for the merger. The complex transaction is expected to close in 1996, subject to various regulatory approvals and shareholders approvals. After the merger announcement, U S West, owner of 25.5% of TWE, asked the Delaware Chancery Court to prevent the merger on the grounds that it violates non-compete covenants between USW and TWX. TBS is a leading supplier of entertainment and news through its ownership of the world's largest film and animation libraries and of TV networks in the U.S., Latin America, Europe and Asia. TBS's operations also include motion picture, animation and TV production, theatrical film distribution, home video, TV syndication, licensing and merchandising, publishing and professional sports.

Capitalization

Long Term Debt: $9,001,000,000 (3/95).

Per Share Data ($) (Year Ended Dec. 31)

	1994	1993	1992	1991	1990	1989
Tangible Bk. Val.	2.66	3.25	4.40	6.05	1.57	5.11
Cash Flow	0.88	0.38	1.70	1.45	1.53	1.17
Earnings	-0.27	-0.75	-1.46	-2.40	-3.42	-1.09
Dividends	0.35	0.31	0.26	0.26	0.25	0.25
Payout Ratio	NM	NM	NM	NM	NM	NM
Prices - High	44¼	46⅞	29⅝	31¼	31¼	45¾
- Low	31½	28¾	21½	19½	16⅝	26
P/E Ratio - High	NM	NM	NM	NM	NM	NM
- Low	NM	NM	NM	NM	NM	NM

Income Statement Analysis (Million $)

	1994	%Chg	1993	%Chg	1992	%Chg	1991
Revs.	7,396	12%	6,581	-50%	13,070	9%	12,021
Oper. Inc.	1,074	14%	942	-60%	2,374	12%	2,127
Depr.	437	3%	424	-64%	1,172	6%	1,109
Int. Exp.	769	10%	698	-4%	729	-20%	912
Pretax Inc.	89.0	10%	81.0	-75%	320	NM	52.0
Eff. Tax Rate	202%	—	303%	—	73%	—	290%
Net Inc.	-91.0	NM	-163	NM	86.0	NM	-99.0

Balance Sheet & Other Fin. Data (Million $)

	1994	1993	1992	1991	1990	1989
Cash	282	200	942	199	172	234
Curr. Assets	2,817	2,534	5,117	3,890	3,946	3,834
Total Assets	16,716	16,892	27,366	24,889	25,337	24,791
Curr. Liab.	2,972	2,225	3,912	3,576	3,651	3,270
LT Debt	8,839	9,291	10,068	8,716	11,184	10,838
Common Eqty.	1,008	1,230	1,635	2,242	360	1,172
Total Cap.	12,687	13,659	22,025	19,730	20,135	20,140
Cap. Exp.	164	198	574	527	574	522
Cash Flow	333	142	630	417	352	275

Ratio Analysis

	1994	1993	1992	1991	1990	1989
Curr. Ratio	0.9	1.1	1.3	1.1	1.1	1.2
% LT Debt of Cap.	69.7	68.0	45.7	44.2	55.5	53.8
% Net Inc.of Revs.	NM	NM	0.7	NM	NM	NM
% Ret. on Assets	NM	NM	0.3	NM	NM	NM
% Ret. on Equity	NM	NM	NM	NM	NM	NM

Dividend Data —Dividends paid since 1930. A dividend reinvestment plan is available. A poison pill stock purchase rights plan was adopted in January 1994.

Amt. of Div. $	Date Decl.	Ex-Div. Date	Stock of Record	Payment Date
0.090	Nov. 17	Nov. 28	Dec. 02	Dec. 15 '94
0.090	Jan. 19	Feb. 23	Mar. 01	Mar. 15 '95
0.090	May. 18	May. 25	Jun. 01	Jun. 15 '95
0.090	Jul. 20	Aug. 30	Sep. 01	Sep. 15 '95

Data as orig. reptd.; bef. results of disc. opers. and/or spec. items. Per share data adj. for stk. divs. as of ex-div. date.
E-Estimated. NA-Not Available. NM-Not Meaningful. NR-Not Ranked.

Office—75 Rockefeller Plaza, New York, NY 10019. **Tel**—(212) 484-8000. **Chrmn & CEO**—G. M. Levin. **Pres**—R. Parsons. **SVP & CFO**—R. J. Bressler. **Secy**—A. B. Ecker. **Investor Contact**—Joan Nicolais Sumner (212-484-8718). **Dirs**—M. Adelson, L. B. Buttenwieser, E. S. Finkelstein, B. S. Greenough, C. A. Hills, D. T. Kearns, G. M. Levin, H. Luce III, R. Mark, M. A. Miles, J. R. Munro, R. D. Parsons, D. S. Perkins, R. S. Troubh, F. T. Vincent, Jr. **Transfer Agent & Registrar**—Chemical Bank, NYC. **Incorporated** in New York in 1922; reincorporated in Delaware in 1983. **Empl**-50,000. **S&P Analyst:** William H. Donald

Times Mirror

NYSE Symbol TMC Options on NYSE In S&P 500

Price	Range	P–E Ratio	Dividend	Yield	S&P Ranking	Beta
Jul. 31'95	1995					
28¾	33½–17¼	33	0.24	0.8%	B–	1.25

Summary

This major information company is primarily a publisher of newspapers, professional information and magazines. As part of a major restructuring, TMC discontinued television broadcasting in 1993, and separated from its cable TV operations in January 1995 by transfering them to Cox Cable Communications, then spinning off 20% of the new cable company to TMC shareholders. Beginning in the second quarter of 1995, TMC reduced the $0.27 quarterly cash dividend on the publicly held common stock to $0.06. In July, 1995 the New York City edition of Newsday was shut down.

Current Outlook

Earnings from continuing operations for 1995 are projected at roughly $0.30 a share, versus the $0.98 from continuing operations reported for 1994. About $0.65 is estimated for 1996.

The $0.06 quarterly dividend, which was reduced from $0.27 in the second quarter of 1995, is expected to be maintained.

Revenues from continuing operations are expected to grow less than 6% in 1995. Profitability will be strained by revamped pricing strategies at Matthew Bender, development costs, and higher newsprint prices. Net income will also be reduced by substantial restructuring and other charges that the company expects to incur in the second half. Preferred dividends will be about $47 million.

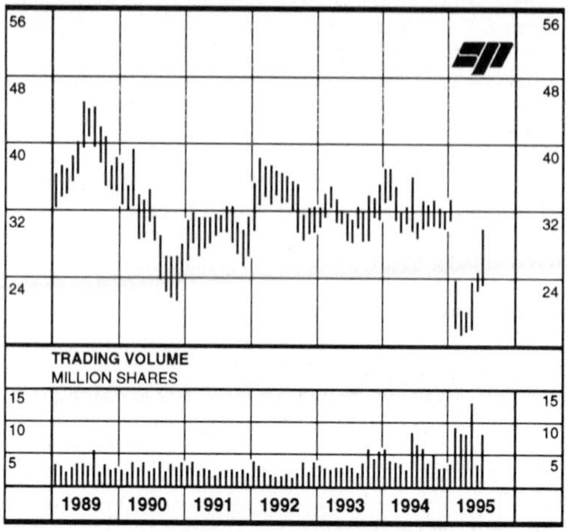

Total Revenues (Million $)

Quarter:	1995	1994	1993	1992
Mar.	774	734	868	866
Jun.	843	808	903	911
Sep.		859	924	914
Dec.		957	1,019	1,011
		3,357	3,714	3,702

Revenues from continuing operations for the 1995 first half rose 4.9%, year to year. Operating profit fell 24%. After interest income (net) of $1.1 million, versus interest expense (net) of $33.5 million and taxes, income from continuing operations rose 3.9%. After preferred dividends, share earnings were $0.19, down from $0.31. Income from discontinued operations equaled $13.84, versus $0.22.

Common Share Earnings ($)

Quarter:	1995	1994	1993	1992
Mar.	0.08	0.06	0.21	0.26
Jun.	0.11	0.25	0.31	0.34
Sep.	E0.02	0.31	0.57	0.32
Dec.	E0.09	0.36	0.18	d0.48
	E0.30	0.98	1.27	0.44

Important Developments

Jul. '95— TMC continued its massive restructuring with the closing of the New York City edition of Newsday. Among other cost-reduction and profit improvement measures, the company also plans to reduce employees by more than 1,000 in 1995, including 700 at the Los Angeles Times. TMC said it does not plan to sell any of its companies.

Jan. '95— TMC merged its cable operations into Cox Cable Communications (CCC). In return, TMC received $1.364 billion and TMC shareholders, other than the Chandler Trusts, received about 20% of the stock of CCC, or 0.6 share, valued at $10.45. The Trusts received nonvoting preferred stock in the new TMC. New TMC common stock was issued to all shareholders. Dividends on the new TMC common were initiated at a $0.24 annual rate, versus the old annual rate of $1.08 a share.

Next earnings report expected in late October.

Per Share Data ($)

Yr. End Dec. 31	1994	1993	1992	1991	1990	1989[1]	1988[1]	1987[1]	1986[1]	1985
Tangible Bk. Val.	**8.56**	6.33	4.35	6.90	5.61	5.16	4.17	2.92	2.75	3.34
Cash Flow	**2.30**	3.26	2.33	2.54	3.29	3.96	4.08	3.33	4.32	3.02
Earnings[2]	**0.98**	1.27	0.44	0.64	1.40	2.30	2.58	2.06	3.16	1.75
Dividends	**Nil**	1.08	1.08	1.08	1.08	1.00	0.92	0.82	0.75	0.68
Payout Ratio	**Nil**	85%	245%	169%	77%	43%	36%	40%	24%	37%
Prices—High	**37⅛**	35¼	38⅜	32⅝	39⅜	45	40¼	52⅞	36⅞	29½
Low	**28¾**	28¼	28½	25½	21¼	32⅜	29	30⅛	25⅛	19
P/E Ratio—	**38–29**	28–22	87–65	51–40	28–15	20–14	16–11	26–15	12–8	17–11

Data as orig. reptd. Adj. for stk. divs. of 100% Jan. 1988 (Series C), 100% Feb. 1984. **1.** Refl. merger or acq. **2.** Bef. results of disc. opers of +1.19 in 1993 and spec. item of -0.96 in 1992. d-Deficit. E-Estimated.

Income Data (Million $)

Year Ended Dec. 31	Revs.	Oper. Inc.	% Oper. Inc. of Revs.	Cap. Exp.	Depr.	Int. Exp.	Net Bef. Taxes	Eff. Tax Rate	[4]Net Inc.	% Net Inc. of Revs.	Cash Flow
1994	3,357	464	13.8	128	170	70.6	[2]248	49.0%	126	3.8	296
[5]1993	3,714	632	17.0	229	256	85.6	302	45.6%	164	4.4	420
[1]1992	3,702	622	16.8	198	243	78.5	[2]120	52.5%	[3]57	1.5	300
1991	3,614	550	15.2	209	252	90.9	[2]166	50.6%	82	2.3	327
1990	3,621	614	17.0	340	244	94.2	[2]307	41.2%	180	5.0	424
[1]1989	3,475	712	20.5	452	215	77.4	[2]494	39.6%	298	8.6	513
[1]1988	3,259	662	20.3	332	194	69.2	[2]542	38.8%	332	10.2	526
[1]1987	3,080	680	22.1	251	165	59.5	[2]495	46.2%	266	8.7	432
[1]1986	2,920	640	21.9	304	150	65.0	[2]680	40.0%	[3]408	14.0	558
1985	2,947	639	21.7	252	173	62.7	[2]461	48.6%	237	8.0	410

Balance Sheet Data (Million $)

Dec. 31	Cash	Assets	Curr. Liab.	Ratio	Total Assets	% Ret. on Assets	Long Term Debt	Common Equity	Total Cap.	% LT Debt of Cap.	% Ret. on Equity
1994	81.9	1,533	1,486	1.0	4,265	2.8	246	1,957	2,335	10.6	6.5
1993	5.0	1,217	1,162	1.0	4,606	3.7	795	1,899	2,975	26.7	9.1
1992	24.8	903	902	1.0	4,327	1.4	1,114	1,701	2,951	37.8	3.2
1991	34.0	839	665	1.3	4,052	2.0	978	1,884	3,119	31.4	4.3
1990	37.0	860	692	1.2	4,193	4.4	1,068	1,917	3,255	32.8	9.5
1989	38.0	824	695	1.2	3,947	8.0	892	1,877	3,022	29.5	16.7
1988	37.0	771	472	1.6	3,476	10.1	877	1,687	2,802	31.3	21.1
1987	20.0	683	389	1.8	3,122	8.8	878	1,454	2,536	34.6	19.4
1986	32.0	659	459	1.4	2,929	14.5	836	1,300	2,288	36.5	35.9
1985	27.0	645	638	1.0	2,701	9.3	721	974	1,903	37.9	21.9

Data as orig. reptd. **1.** Refl. merger or acq. **2.** Incl. equity in earns. of nonconsol. subs. **3.** Refl. acctg. change. **4.** Bef. spec. item(s) and results of disc. ops. **5.** Excl. disc. ops.

Business Summary

Contributions by business segment in 1994 were:

	Revs.	Profits
Newspaper publishing.........	61%	54%
Professional information	30%	48%
Consumer media	9%	−2%

Newspaper publishing includes the Los Angeles Times, the Baltimore Sun, Newsday, the Hartford (Conn.) Courant, the Call-Chronicle Newspapers of Allentown, Pa., and seven community newspapers in Connecticut and California. Combined average circulation in 1994 was 2,509,555 daily and 3,289,573 Sunday.

Through Matthew Bender, Richard D. Irwin, CRC Press, Mosby-Year Book and Harry N. Abrams, TMC publishes law, medical, business, economics and art books. TMC also publishes nine consumer magazines that rank it the sixth largest such publisher in the U.S. and five trade magazines, road maps, telephone directories and recording charts. Jeppesen Sanderson produces aeronautical charts, pilot training materials, computerized flight plans and weather briefings. TMC is also a leading provider of courseware for industrial training through Kaset Inc., Learning International and Zenger-Miller.

Cable television operations were sold in January, 1995. TMC sold its four television stations in 1993.

Dividend Data

Dividends have been paid since 1892. A dividend reinvestment plan is available. Payments on the Series A and Series C shares:

Amt. of Divd. $	Date Decl.	Ex-divd. Date	Stock of Record	Payment Date
0.27	Jun. 2	Aug. 22	Aug. 26	Sep. 10'94
0.27	Sep. 1	Nov. 21	Nov. 28	Dec. 10'94
0.27	Dec. 2	Feb. 15	Feb. 22	Mar. 10'95
0.06	Mar. 2	May 22	May 26	Jun. 10'95
0.06	Jun. 7	Aug. 23	Aug. 25	Sep. 10'95

Capitalization

Long Term Debt: $247,603,000 (3/95).

Preferred Stock: $762 million stated value ($1 par); mandatory conv. of 16,563.000 shs. of Ser. B preferred into one sh. ea. of Ser. A common after 1/31/98.

Series A Common Stock: 82,924,000 shs. ($1 par).

Series C Common Stock: 29,166,000 shs. ($1 par); 10 votes per sh.; transfer restricted; conv. sh.-for-sh. into Series A.

The Chandler family group owns 19% of the Series A common & 68% of the Series C.

Institutions hold about 47% of the Series A and Series C, combined.

Shareholders of record: 5,098.

Office—Times Mirror Square, Los Angeles, CA 90053. **Tel**—(213) 237-3700. **Chrmn, Pres & CEO**—R. F. Erburu. **VP-CFO**—J. F. Guthrie. **Secy**—O. J. Williams. **Treas**—A. L. Ross. **Investor Contact**—Jean M. Jarvis (213) 237-3955. **Dirs**—C. M. Armstrong, G. G. Babcock, D. R. Beall, J. E. Bryson, B. Chandler, O. Chandler, R. F. Erburu, C. W. Frye Jr., D. A. Laventhol, A. E. Osborne Jr., J. A. Payden, W. Stinehart Jr., H. M. Williams, W. B. Williamson, E. Zapanta. **Transfer Agent & Registrar**—First Interstate Bank of California, Los Angeles. **Incorporated** in California in 1884; reincorporated in Delaware in 1986. **Empl**—26,936.

Information has been obtained from sources believed to be reliable, but its accuracy and completeness are not guaranteed.   William H. Donald

Timken Co.

NYSE Symbol **TKR**
In S&P 500

04-OCT-95

Industry:
Machinery

Summary: Timken is a leading manufacturer of highly engineered bearings and alloy steels for the auto, machinery, railroad, aerospace and agricultural industries.

S&P Opinion: Hold (★★★)	Recent Price • 42⅝	Yield • 2.5%
	52 Wk Range • 48-31½	12-Mo. P/E • 12.5

Quantitative Evaluations

Outlook
(1 Lowest—5 Highest)
• **1+**

Fair Value
• **36¼**

Risk
• **Low**

Earn./Div. Rank
• **B**

Technical Eval.
• **Bearish** since 5/95

Rel. Strength Rank
(1 Lowest—99 Highest)
• **27**

Insider Activity
• **Neutral**

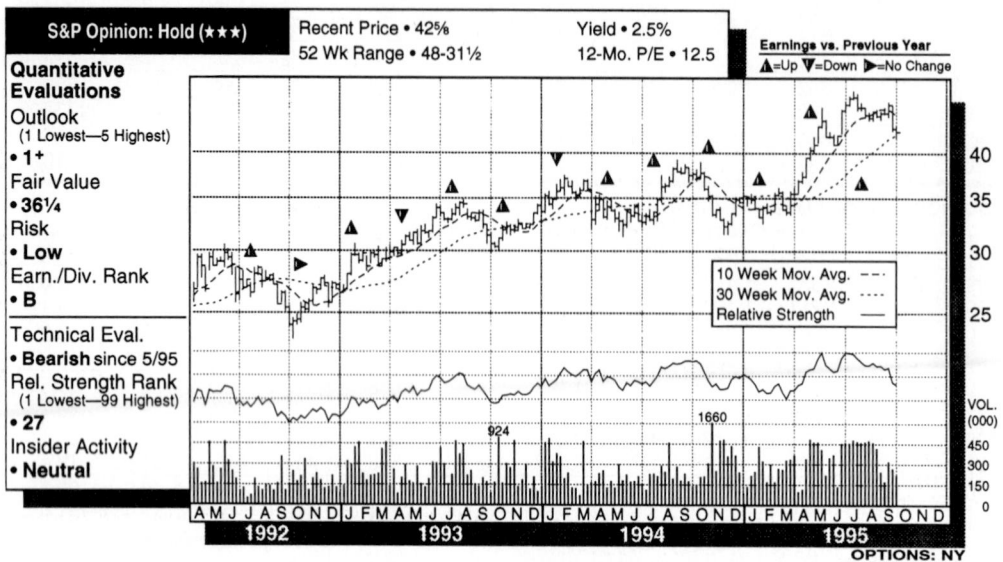

Earnings vs. Previous Year
▲=Up ▼=Down ▶=No Change

10 Week Mov. Avg. – –
30 Week Mov. Avg. · · ·
Relative Strength —

VOL.
(000)

OPTIONS: NY

Overview - 04-OCT-95

Based on our assumption of 2.6% GDP growth, we anticipate a 9% gain in sales for 1996, reflecting a projected rise in volume and prices in both segments. Bearings sales will benefit from a favorable shift in mix and a likely upturn in the aerospace industry. Steel sales will continue to rise as a result of lower imports and stable demand from capital goods producing industries. Continued high capacity utilization, a better mix in bearings, less rapidly rising scrap costs and higher steel prices should lift gross profits. Aided further by cost cutting and lower interest expense, earnings should rise again in 1996. An improved product mix in bearings, acquisitions and the benefits of restructuring will boost long-term sales and earnings.

Valuation - 04-OCT-95

Although TKR's shares are attractive at 9.2X our $4.85 earnings estimate for 1996 and about 5.2X our cash flow per share estimate of $8.55, we are maintaining our hold rating on the shares near term. Through late September, TKR has risen 27%, versus a 24% gain for the S&P 500. Given this strong price action and an increasingly negative psychology toward cyclicals, we think there is little upside potential from current price levels. Accordingly, we are not recommending accumulation of the shares for now. We would consider upgrading our rating if the shares decline on a market pullback and there is no change in our positive outlook for earnings.

Key Stock Statistics

S&P EPS Est. 1995	3.70	Tang. Bk. Value/Share	22.04
P/E on S&P Est. 1995	11.5	Beta	0.95
S&P EPS Est. 1996	4.85	Shareholders	50,000
Dividend Rate/Share	1.08	Market cap. (B)	$ 1.3
Shs. outstg. (M)	31.2	Inst. holdings	69%
Avg. daily vol. (M)	0.052	Insider holdings	NA

Value of $10,000 invested 5 years ago: $ 18,756

Fiscal Year Ending Dec. 31

	1995	% Change	1994	% Change	1993	% Change
Revenues (Million $)						
1Q	568.9	22%	466.5	11%	422.0	NM
2Q	585.8	19%	494.0	12%	441.2	5%
3Q	—	—	466.3	15%	405.5	NM
4Q	—	—	503.5	15%	439.5	10%
Yr.	—	—	1,930	13%	1,709	4%
Income (Million $)						
1Q	34.28	NM	7.75	144%	3.18	-35%
2Q	31.24	51%	20.63	116%	9.56	184%
3Q	—	—	14.29	NM	-0.45	NM
4Q	—	—	25.79	NM	-29.96	NM
Yr.	—	—	68.46	NM	-17.67	NM
Earnings Per Share ($)						
1Q	1.10	NM	0.25	150%	0.10	-38%
2Q	1.00	49%	0.67	116%	0.31	182%
3Q	E0.70	52%	0.46	NM	-0.01	NM
4Q	E0.90	8%	0.83	NM	-0.97	—
Yr.	E3.70	67%	2.21	NM	-0.57	NM

Next earnings report expected: late October

Timken Co.

Business Summary - 04-OCT-95

Timken Co. is the world's largest producer of tapered roller bearings, with about 130 tapered bearing types in some 26,000 combinations. Contributions in 1994 were:

	Sales	Profits
Bearings	68%	62%
Steel	32%	38%

International operations accounted for 21% of sales and 21% of operating income in 1994.

Tapered roller anti-friction bearings reduce friction where shafts, gears or wheels are used. They consist of four components: the cone or inner race, the cup or outer race, the tapered rollers that roll between the cup and the cone and the cage, which serves as a retainer and maintains proper spacing between the rollers. The four components are made and sold in a wide variety of configurations and sizes. TKR's bearings are used in general industry and a wide variety of products, including passenger cars, aircraft, trucks, railroad cars and locomotives, machine tools, rolling mills, and farm and construction equipment. With the 1990 acquisition of MBP Corp., TKR makes super-precision ball and roller bearings for high-precision applications.

Steel products include carbon and alloy seamless tubing, carbon and alloy steel solid bars and various solid shapes, tool steels and other custom-made specialty steel products. A principal use for TKR's steel is in its bearings operations. Sales are also made to other anti-friction bearing companies and to the aircraft, automotive, forging, oil and gas well-drilling, tooling and steel warehouse industries.

Backlog at December 31, 1994, totaled $880 million, up from $520 million at December 31, 1993.

Important Developments

Jul. '95—TKR reported share earnings of $1.00 on a 19% increase in sales for 1995's second quarter, versus $0.67 a year earlier. Sales in the bearings unit increased 19%, to $399.8 million from $337.0 million a year earlier; operating income rose to $34.2 million from $21.3 million in 1994. Steel sales advanced to $186.0 million, up 18% from $157.0 million in 1994's first quarter; operating profit increased to $24.1 million from $20.8 million a year earlier. The company attributed the strong earnings performance for the quarter and six months ended June 30, 1995, to continued market expansion, productivity gains and slightly improved pricing. It said that it achieved higher volume in all markets, including soft markets such as aerospace and oil and gas.

Capitalization

Long Term Debt: $150,797,000 (6/95).

Per Share Data ($)

(Year Ended Dec. 31)

	1994	1993	1992	1991	1990	1989
Tangible Bk. Val.	20.66	19.31	29.12	30.78	33.16	34.87
Cash Flow	6.07	3.28	3.94	2.47	5.23	4.59
Earnings	2.21	-0.57	0.15	-1.21	1.85	1.88
Dividends	1.00	1.00	1.00	1.00	0.98	0.92
Payout Ratio	45%	NM	NM	NM	52%	51%
Prices - High	39¼	34⅞	30½	30	36¼	39¼
- Low	31¼	26½	23⅛	20⅝	20	25½
P/E Ratio - High	18	NM	NM	NM	20	21
- Low	14	NM	NM	NM	11	14

Income Statement Analysis (Million $)

	1994	%Chg	1993	%Chg	1992	%Chg	1991
Revs.	1,930	13%	1,709	4%	1,642	NM	1,647
Oper. Inc.	258	38%	187	15%	163	9%	149
Depr.	119	NM	118	4%	114	5%	109
Int. Exp.	28.0	-11%	31.3	1%	30.9	8%	28.7
Pretax Inc.	111	NM	-21.0	NM	13.0	NM	-42.0
Eff. Tax Rate	39%	—	NM	—	67%	—	NM
Net Inc.	68.5	NM	-17.7	NM	4.5	NM	-36.0

Balance Sheet & Other Fin. Data (Million $)

	1994	1993	1992	1991	1990	1989
Cash	12.1	5.3	7.9	2.0	23.0	42.0
Curr. Assets	657	586	556	562	658	608
Total Assets	1,859	1,790	1,738	1,759	1,815	1,566
Curr. Liab.	479	432	390	414	419	248
LT Debt	151	181	173	135	114	48.0
Common Eqty.	733	685	985	1,019	1,075	1,065
Total Cap.	884	866	1,247	1,256	1,301	1,220
Cap. Exp.	114	89.0	136	146	181	92.0
Cash Flow	188	101	119	73.0	157	135

Ratio Analysis

	1994	1993	1992	1991	1990	1989
Curr. Ratio	1.4	1.4	1.4	1.4	1.6	2.4
% LT Debt of Cap.	17.1	20.9	13.9	10.7	8.7	3.9
% Net Inc.of Revs.	35.0	NM	0.3	NM	3.2	3.6
% Ret. on Assets	3.7	NM	0.3	NM	3.3	3.4
% Ret. on Equity	9.6	NM	0.4	NM	5.3	5.2

Dividend Data

Dividends have been paid since 1921. A dividend reinvestment plan is available.

Amt. of Div. $	Date Decl.	Ex-Div. Date	Stock of Record	Payment Date
0.250	Nov. 04	Nov. 15	Nov. 21	Dec. 09 '94
0.270	Feb. 02	Feb. 13	Feb. 20	Mar. 10 '95
0.270	Apr. 18	May. 15	May. 19	Jun. 05 '95
0.270	Aug. 04	Aug. 16	Aug. 18	Sep. 05 '95

Data as orig. reptd.; bef. results of disc. opers. and/or spec. items. Per share data adj. for stk. divs. as of ex-div. date. E-Estimated. NA-Not Available. NM-Not Meaningful. NR-Not Ranked.

Office—1835 Dueber Ave., S.W., Canton, OH 44706. Tel—(216) 438-3000. Chrmn—W. R. Timken Jr. CEO & Pres—J. F. Toot Jr. V-P Fin—G. E. Little. Investor Contact—Thomas A. Kirkpatrick. Dirs—R. Anderson, S. C. Gault, J. C. La Force, Jr., R. W. Mahony, J. W. Pilz, J. M. Timken Jr., W. R. Timken Jr., F. Toot, Jr., M. D. Walker, C. H. West, A. W. Whitehouse. Transfer Agents—First Chicago Trust Co. of New York, NYC; Co.'s office. Registrars—First Chicago Trust Co. of New York, NYC.; United National Bank & Trust Co., Canton, Ohio. Incorporated in Ohio in 1904. Empl-16,202. S&P Analyst: Leo Larkin

31-JUL-95

Industry:
Insurance

Summary; This financial services holding company derives most of its earnings from life and health insurance operations. Other subsidiaries manage and market a series of mutual funds.

S&P Opinion: Hold (★★★)	Recent Price • 38⅞	Yield • 3.0%
	52 Wk Range • 44½-32⅜	12-Mo. P/E • 10.4

Earnings vs. Previous Year
▲=Up ▼=Down ▶=No Change

Quantitative Evaluations

Outlook
(1 Lowest—5 Highest)
• 3⁻

Fair Value
• 37⅞

Risk
• Low

Earn./Div. Rank
• A+

Technical Eval.
• **Bullish** since 7/95

Rel. Strength Rank
(1 Lowest—99 Highest)
• 28

Insider Activity
• NA

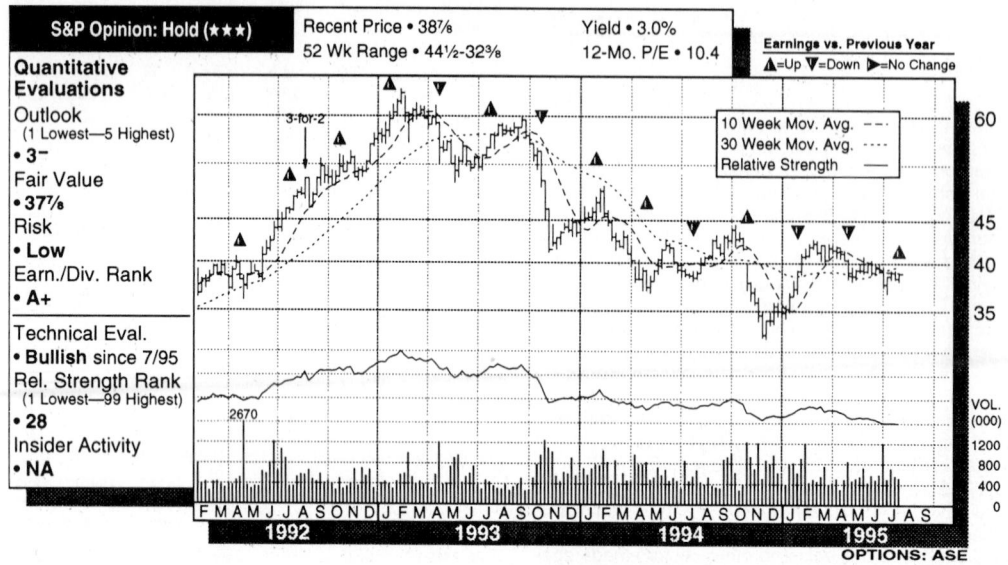

10 Week Mov. Avg. — —
30 Week Mov. Avg. ·····
Relative Strength —

3-for-2

2670

VOL. (000)

1992 1993 1994 1995

OPTIONS: ASE

Overview - 31-JUL-95

The growth in earnings seen for 1995 is skewed by the negative effects of low interest rates on investment income and the drop in health premiums that hurt results in 1994. Earnings growth in TMK's core individual life and health lines is predicated on continued cost controls. Individual health operating results will likely be mixed, as confusion over health care reform and increased competition hurt Medicare supplemental policy sales. Persistency rates in some individual life lines have been favorable in recent years. Because improved persistency rates lead to an attendant drop in policy acquisition costs, a continuation of this trend would aid margin growth. Growth in assets under management, combined with well contained costs, will fuel growth in asset management profits. Investment income will remain under pressure by relatively low interest rates, but asset writedowns are unlikely.

Valuation - 31-JUL-95

After a lackluster performance during most of 1994 due to the negative effects of higher interest rates, the shares have rebounded somewhat during 1995. Despite their recent appreciation, the shares currently trade at just over 9 times our operating earnings estimate (which excludes realized investment gains or losses) of $4.15 a share for 1995. However, given the uncertainty surrounding TMK's core Medicare supplemental policy sales, we believe the shares are fairly valued in the near term.

Key Stock Statistics

S&P EPS Est. 1995	4.15	Tang. Bk. Value/Share	11.45
P/E on S&P Est. 1995	9.4	Beta	1.04
S&P EPS Est. 1996	4.50	Shareholders	8,200
Dividend Rate/Share	1.16	Market cap. (B)	$ 2.8
Shs. outstg. (M)	71.6	Inst. holdings	58%
Avg. daily vol. (M)	0.117	Insider holdings	NA

Value of $10,000 invested 5 years ago: $ 12,229

Fiscal Year Ending Dec. 31

	1995	% Change	1994	% Change	1993	% Change
Revenues (Million $)						
1Q	530.2	6%	498.7	-5%	525.0	3%
2Q	527.0	13%	464.4	-15%	543.3	6%
3Q	—	—	463.3	-13%	531.2	—
4Q	—	—	496.2	-14%	577.1	12%
Yr.	—	—	1,923	-12%	2,177	6%
Income (Million $)						
1Q	68.62	-9%	75.60	3%	73.50	15%
2Q	70.02	8%	64.90	-17%	78.25	18%
3Q	—	—	65.00	NM	64.40	-5%
4Q	—	—	63.77	-26%	85.87	28%
Yr.	—	—	269.0	-4%	279.6	5%
Earnings Per Share ($)						
1Q	0.96	-7%	1.03	51%	0.68	-19%
2Q	0.98	9%	0.90	-14%	1.05	17%
3Q	—	—	0.90	5%	0.86	-8%
4Q	—	—	0.89	-23%	1.16	27%
Yr.	E4.15	—	3.72	-1%	3.76	5%

Next earnings report expected: late October

Torchmark Corp.

31-JUL-95

Business Summary - 26-JUL-95

Torchmark Corp. is a holding company whose principal subsidiaries are Liberty National Life Insurance Co., Globe Life and Accident Insurance Co., United American Insurance Co., Family Service Life Insurance Co., United Investors Life Insurance Co., Waddell & Reed, Inc., and Torch Energy Advisors. Revenue sources in recent years:

	1994	1993
Life insurance premiums	31%	26%
Health insurance premiums	40%	37%
Other premiums	1%	6%
Net investment income	17%	17%
Financial services	7%	6%
Energy & other	4%	8%

Through subsidiaries, TMK offers a full line of non-participating ordinary individual life products and health insurance (primarily Medicare supplemental coverage). Fixed and variabel annuities are also offered. The subsidiaries are licensed to sell insurance in all 50 states, the District of Columbia, Puerto Rico, Guam, the Virgin Islands, and Canada. Distribution is through home service agents, independent and general agents and direct solicitation. Annualized premiums in force at year-end 1994 were $1.6 billion, of which Medicare supplemental accounted for 36%, traditional life 28%, interest-sensitive life 11%, term and other 11%, other health 7%, and cancer 7%. Annuity deposits at year end 1994 were $1.5 billion, of which 54% were fixed and 46% variable.

Waddell & Reed, Inc. markets and manages mutual funds under the following names: United Group of Mutual Funds (16 funds), Waddell & Reed Fund (five funds), TMK/United Fund (nine funds) and Torchmark Fund (two funds). At year-end 1994, assets under management totaled $14.5 billion. Torch Energy Advisors (held for sale) manages oil and gas investments.

Important Developments

Jun. '95—TMK said it expects the sale of Torch Energy Advisors Inc. to be completed in the third quarter of 1995. TMK also remarked that progress was being made in executing a definitive purchase agreement. In its second quarter earnings report, TMK said it entered into a preliminary agreement to sell its energy management subsidiary for $115 million.

Capitalization

Long Term Debt: $792,851,000 (3/95).
Monthly Income Pfd. Stock: $193,063,000.

Per Share Data ($)

(Year Ended Dec. 31)

	1994	1993	1992	1991	1990	1989
Tangible Bk. Val.	9.40	16.77	14.47	13.47	11.52	10.41
Oper. Earnings	3.81	3.69	3.59	3.10	2.82	2.59
Earnings	3.72	3.76	3.58	3.13	2.85	2.59
Dividends	1.12	1.08	1.07	1.00	0.93	0.83
Payout Ratio	30%	29%	30%	32%	33%	32%
Prices - High	49½	64¾	58⅜	39½	38¼	39⅛
- Low	32⅜	41⅛	36	30⅞	25⅜	20
P/E Ratio - High	13	17	16	13	13	15
- Low	9	11	10	10	9	8

Income Statement Analysis (Million $)

	1994	%Chg	1993	%Chg	1992	%Chg	1991
Life Ins. In Force	74,835	22%	61,367	5%	58,306	4%	56,111
Premium Income Life	602	8%	556	2%	544	4%	524
Prem.Inc A & H	768	-4%	800	NM	798	4%	770
Premium Income Other	19.0	-86%	137	22%	112	56%	72.0
Net Invest. Inc.	330	-11%	372	-3%	383	5%	364
Total Revs.	1,923	-12%	2,177	6%	2,046	6%	1,932
Pretax Inc.	387	-12%	441	6%	418	10%	381
Net Oper. Inc.	275	1%	272	2%	266	9%	243
Net Inc.	269	-4%	280	6%	265	8%	246

Balance Sheet & Other Fin. Data (Million $)

	1994	1993	1992	1991	1990	1989
Cash & Equiv.	70.0	110	68.9	63.9	56.1	53.0
Premiums Due	224	153	131	95.0	81.0	108
Inv Assets Bonds	4,505	4,762	4,193	3,889	3,597	3,091
Inv. Assets Stock	32.0	41.0	54.0	38.0	40.0	27.0
Inv. Assets Loans	202	154	152	151	146	190
Inv. Assets Total	5,236	5,441	4,926	4,542	4,100	3,507
Deferred Policy Cost	1,017	902	904	1,028	1,024	942
Total Assets	8,404	7,646	6,770	6,161	5,536	4,921
Debt	793	792	498	667	529	498
Common Eqty.	1,243	1,416	1,115	1,078	943	894

Ratio Analysis

	1994	1993	1992	1991	1990	1989
% Ret. on Revs.	14.0	12.8	13.0	12.8	12.8	12.9
% Ret. on Assets	3.4	3.9	4.1	4.2	4.4	4.5
% Ret. on Equity	20.2	21.8	23.9	23.8	24.2	24.1
% Invest. Yield	7.1	7.2	8.1	8.4	9.2	9.2

Dividend Data (Cash has been paid each year since 1933.)

Amt. of Div. $	Date Decl.	Ex-Div. Date	Stock of Record	Payment Date
0.280	Jul. 29	Oct. 03	Oct. 09	Nov. 01 '94
0.280	Nov. 04	Dec. 30	Jan. 06	Feb. 01 '95
0.280	Mar. 03	Apr. 03	Apr. 07	May. 01 '95
0.280	May. 09	Jul. 05	Jul. 07	Aug. 01 '95
0.290	Jul. 27	Oct. 04	Oct. 06	Nov. 01 '95

Data as orig. reptd.; bef. results of disc. opers. and/or spec. items. Per share data adj. for stk. divs. as of ex-div. date.
E-Estimated. NA-Not Available. NM-Not Meaningful. NR-Not Ranked.

Office—2001 Third Avenue South, Birmingham, AL 35233. **Tel**—(205) 325-4200. **Chrmn & CEO**—R. K. Richey. **Vice Chrmn**—K. A. Tucker. **Investor Contact**—M. Klyce. **Dirs**—J. P. Bryan, J. M. Farley, L. T. Hagopian, C. B. Hudson, J. L. Lanier Jr., H. T. McCormick, J. W. Morris, G. J. Records, R. K. Richey, Y. G. Samford Jr., K. A. Tucker. **Transfer Agent & Registrar**—First Chicago Trust Co. of New York, NYC. **Incorporated** in Alabama in 1929; reincorporated in Delaware in 1979. **Empl**-6,270. **S&P Analyst:** Catherine A. Seifert

STANDARD & POOR'S
STOCK REPORTS

Toys "R" Us

NYSE Symbol **TOY**
In S&P 500

29-AUG-95 **Industry:** Retail Stores

Summary: This company is the world's largest toy retailer, with more than 920 locations, and also operates a children's retail clothing business, with over 200 stores.

S&P Opinion: Hold (★★★)

Recent Price • 27 | 52 Wk Range • 39-23¾ | Yield • Nil | 12-Mo. P/E • 15.8

Quantitative Evaluations
Outlook
(1 Lowest—5 Highest)
• **4−**
Fair Value
• **28⅛**
Risk
• **Average**
Earn./Div. Rank
• **B+**

Technical Eval.
• **Bearish** since 7/95
Rel. Strength Rank
(1 Lowest—99 Highest)
• **27**
Insider Activity
• **Neutral**

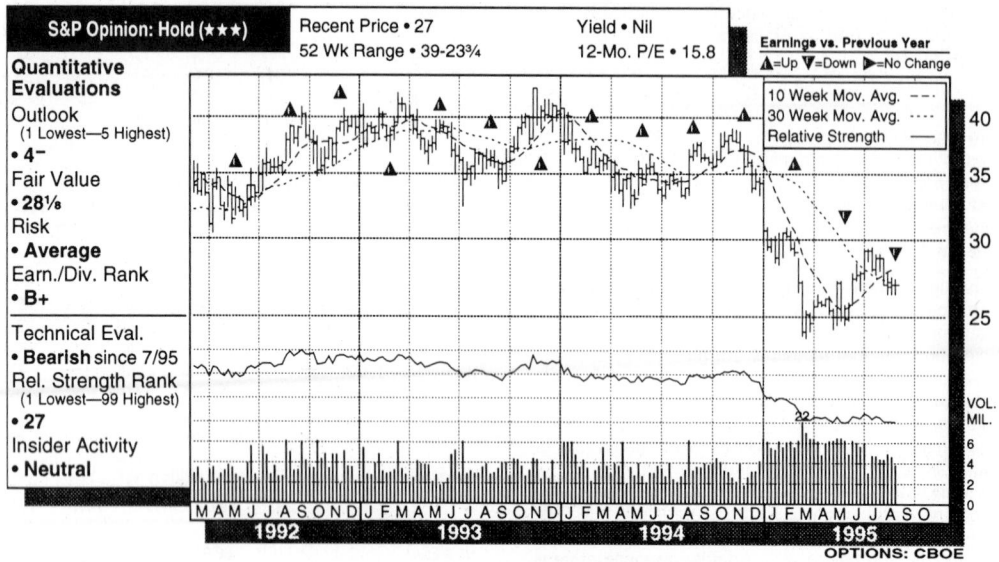

Earnings vs. Previous Year
▲=Up ▼=Down ▶=No Change

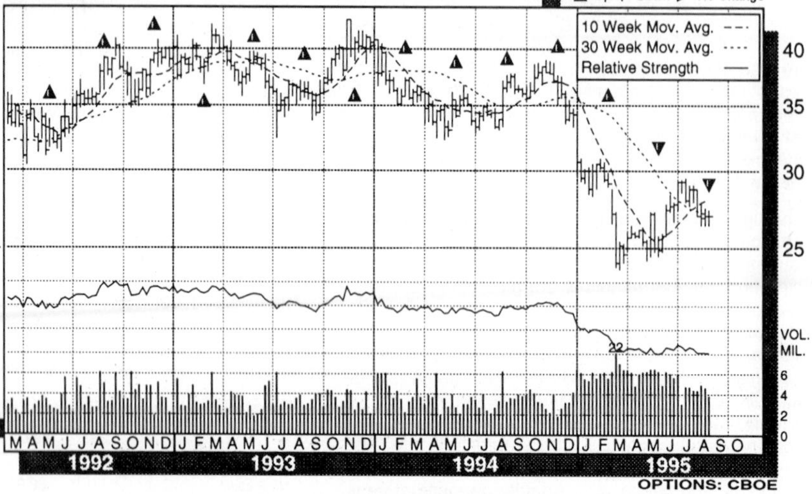
10 Week Mov. Avg.
30 Week Mov. Avg.
Relative Strength
40
35
30
25
VOL. MIL.
6
4
2
0
22
M A M J J A S O N D J F M A M J J A S O N D J F M A M J J A S O N D J F M A M J J A S O
1992
1993
1994
1995

OPTIONS: CBOE

Overview - 29-AUG-95

Revenue growth in 1995-6 should be fueled by the addition of some 35 toy stores and 15 to 20 remodels in the U.S. and 50 international stores, as well as 10 new Kids stores. Gross margins should remain under pressure from competitive pricing. SG&A expenses will increase as a percentage of sales due to costs related to increasing customer service and higher advertising expenditures. Operating profits at the U.S. toy division could decline slightly from last year's, while the international division should show gains. A modest operating profit increase is anticipated in the Kids division. The company's balance sheet is strong. Share earnings will benefit from a $1 billion stock repurchase program, about two-thirds of which has been completed.

Valuation - 29-AUG-95

Declining same-store sales in 1995 have kept the share price near its lows. In an attempt to regain market share lost to discounters and other retailers, the company is beefing up service, increasing advertising and remaining sharply price competitive. New video products will not be introduced until the fourth quarter, and it is unclear whether consumers will be in a spending mood. Until then, there are few new "hot" products to drive sales. As a result, we anticipate flat earnings in 1995-6. Over the longer term, however, new video product introductions, more attractive stores with improved service and international growth should boost profitability.

Key Stock Statistics

S&P EPS Est. 1996	1.85	Tang. Bk. Value/Share	12.26
P/E on S&P Est. 1996	14.6	Beta	1.19
S&P EPS Est. 1997	2.20	Shareholders	27,200
Dividend Rate/Share	Nil	Market cap. (B)	$ 7.5
Shs. outstg. (M)	276.4	Inst. holdings	65%
Avg. daily vol. (M)	0.876	Insider holdings	NA

Value of $10,000 invested 5 years ago: $ 11,289

Fiscal Year Ending Jan. 31

	1996	% Change	1995	% Change	1994	% Change
Revenues (Million $)						
1Q	1,493	2%	1,462	14%	1,286	10%
2Q	1,614	11%	1,452	10%	1,317	5%
3Q	—	—	1,631	13%	1,449	8%
4Q	—	—	4,200	8%	3,893	14%
Yr.	—	—	8,746	10%	7,946	11%
Income (Million $)						
1Q	18.44	-51%	37.58	6%	35.44	25%
2Q	15.84	-58%	38.01	7%	35.51	9%
3Q	—	—	47.37	26%	37.46	2%
4Q	—	—	408.8	9%	374.6	10%
Yr.	—	—	531.8	10%	483.0	10%
Earnings Per Share ($)						
1Q	0.07	-46%	0.13	8%	0.12	20%
2Q	0.06	-54%	0.13	8%	0.12	9%
3Q	E0.12	-29%	0.17	31%	0.13	8%
4Q	E1.60	10%	1.46	15%	1.27	11%
Yr.	E1.85	NM	1.85	13%	1.63	11%

Next earnings report expected: mid November

Business Summary - 29-AUG-95

Toys "R" Us, Inc. operates the world's largest chain of toy specialty retail stores. At January 28, 1995, it operated 618 Toys "R" Us toy stores in 47 states and Puerto Rico and in 239 international locations. The company also operated 204 Kids "R" Us children's clothing stores.

In 1994, the company significantly expanded its catalog program with a Spring catalog and two new and one expanded holiday toy catalogs. The strategy stresses development of strong consumer recognition through the use of advertising that promotes broad selection and everyday low prices. The company continues to test various specialty shops within each store. In 1994, Toys added 130 Books "R" Us shops, bringing the total to more than 300. In addition, the company added 20 Lego, 20 Stuffed Animal and five Learning Center shops in existing stores. In 1995, about 100 stores will add Learning Centers. Enhancing customer service has also been a priority for the company.

Kids "R" Us clothing stores, ranging in size from 18,000 to 21,500 sq. ft., apply merchandising policies similar to those in the Toys "R" Us stores--everyday low pricing on name brands, full assortments and liberal refund policies.

The company uses a computer inventory system that allows management to constantly monitor current activity and inventory in each region and each store. This allows allocation of the proper amount of merchandise to each store and keeps stores adequately stocked at all times.

Important Developments

Aug. '95—The company's U.S. toy stores experienced a comparable-store sales decrease of less than 1% in the second quarter of 1995-6 and a 5% drop in the first half. Sharper pricing and strong promotions in the basic business aided sales in the second quarter. Internationally, only Spain and Japan experienced comparable-store increases. Sales in Japan have been helped by the 32-bit video machines released by Sega and Sony in late 1994. Same-store sales declined at Kids, reflecting weak industrywide apparel sales. Management said that the decline in first-half earnings was anticipated in light of a worldwide decline in the video business and very strong sales a year earlier. The company plannned to open a total of 35 toy stores in the U.S. and about 50 internationally and ten Kids stores. Since January 1994, the company has repuchased 21 million common shares.

Capitalization

Long Term Debt: $828,405,000 (4/29/95).

Per Share Data ($)

	1995	1994	1993	1992	1991	1990
Tangible Bk. Val.	12.26	10.87	9.86	8.39	7.11	5.95
Cash Flow	2.41	2.08	1.87	1.49	1.37	1.32
Earnings	1.85	1.63	1.47	1.15	1.11	1.09
Dividends	Nil	Nil	Nil	Nil	Nil	Nil
Payout Ratio	Nil	Nil	Nil	Nil	Nil	Nil
Cal. Yrs.	1994	1993	1992	1991	1990	1989
Prices - High	40⅞	42⅞	41	36	35	26¾
- Low	29⅝	32⅜	30⅜	22	19⅞	16
P/E Ratio - High	22	26	28	31	32	25
- Low	16	20	21	19	18	15

(Year Ended Jan. 31)

Income Statement Analysis (Million $)

	1995	%Chg	1994	%Chg	1993	%Chg	1992
Revs.	8,746	10%	7,924	11%	7,169	17%	6,124
Oper. Inc.	1,073	12%	954	11%	858	25%	684
Depr.	161	21%	133	12%	119	18%	101
Int. Exp.	90.9	14%	79.6	3%	77.5	11%	70.1
Pretax Inc.	844	9%	773	12%	689	28%	539
Eff. Tax Rate	37%	—	38%	—	37%	—	37%
Net Inc.	532	10%	483	10%	438	29%	340

Balance Sheet & Other Fin. Data (Million $)

	1995	1994	1993	1992	1991	1990
Cash	370	792	764	445	35.0	41.0
Curr. Assets	2,531	2,708	2,385	1,927	1,404	1,338
Total Assets	6,571	6,150	5,323	4,548	3,582	3,075
Curr. Liab.	2,137	2,075	1,588	1,594	1,228	1,100
LT Debt	785	724	671	391	195	173
Common Eqty.	3,429	3,148	2,889	2,426	2,046	1,705
Total Cap.	4,434	4,075	3,735	2,954	2,355	1,975
Cap. Exp.	586	557	422	549	486	374
Cash Flow	693	616	557	440	405	387

Ratio Analysis

	1995	1994	1993	1992	1991	1990
Curr. Ratio	1.2	1.3	1.5	1.2	1.1	1.2
% LT Debt of Cap.	17.7	17.8	18.0	13.2	8.3	8.8
% Net Inc.of Revs.	6.1	6.1	6.1	5.5	5.9	6.7
% Ret. on Assets	8.5	8.5	8.8	8.3	9.8	11.4
% Ret. on Equity	16.4	16.1	16.4	15.1	17.3	20.6

Dividend Data —No cash dividends have ever been paid.

Data as orig. reptd.; bef. results of disc. opers. and/or spec. items. Per share data adj. for stk. divs. as of ex-div. date.
E-Estimated. NA-Not Available. NM-Not Meaningful. NR-Not Ranked.

Office—461 From Rd., Paramus, NJ 07652. **Tel**—(201) 262-7800. **Chrmn**—C. Lazarus. **Vice Chrmn & CEO**—M. Goldstein. **Vice Chrmn & Pres**—R. C. Nakasone. **Sr VP & CFO**—L. Lipschitz. **VP & Treas**—J. Kimmins. **Dirs**—R. A. Bernhard, M. Goldstein, M. S. Gould, S. S. Kenny, C. Lazarus, R. Mark, H. Moore, R.C. Nakasone, N. M. Schneider, H. M. Wit. **Transfer Agent & Registrar**—American Stock Transfer & Trust Co., NYC. **Incorporated** in Delaware in 1928. **Empl**-55,000. **S&P Analyst:** Karen J. Sack, CFA

Transamerica Corp.

NYSE Symbol **TA**
In S&P 500

22-AUG-95

Industry:
Insurance

Summary: This diversified financial services organization is involved primarily in life insurance and finance-related operations. It is also the second largest lessor of containers.

S&P Opinion: Hold (★★★)

| Recent Price • 63¾ | Yield • 3.1% |
| 52 Wk Range • 64⅞-46¼ | 12-Mo. P/E • 11.0 |

Earnings vs. Previous Year
▲=Up ▼=Down ▶=No Change

Quantitative Evaluations

Outlook
(1 Lowest—5 Highest)
• **NA**

Fair Value
• **NA**

Risk
• **NA**

Earn./Div. Rank
• **B**

Technical Eval.
• **NA**

Rel. Strength Rank
(1 Lowest—99 Highest)
• **63**

Insider Activity
• **Neutral**

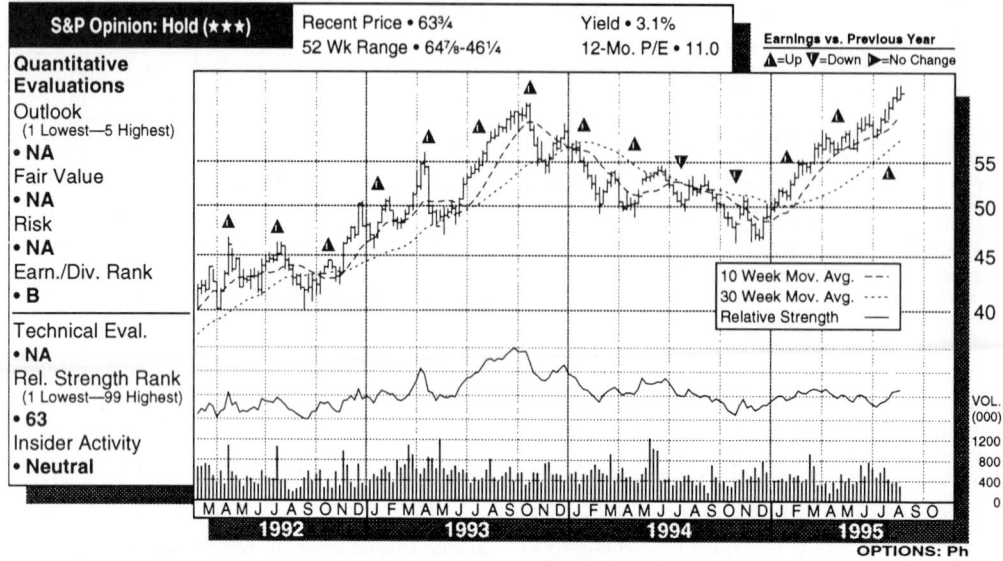

10 Week Mov. Avg. — · —
30 Week Mov. Avg. · · · ·
Relative Strength —————

VOL.
(000)
1200
800
400
0

MAMJJASONDJFMAMJJASONDJFMAMJJASONDJFMAMJJASO
1992 1993 1994 1995

OPTIONS: Ph

Overview - 22-AUG-95

The forecast of higher operating earnings in coming periods is predicated upon continued strong life insurance operations. While TA's mainstay will continue to be its array of traditional life products, two targeted niches--individual annuities and long-term care--will aid long-term prospects. Increased competition and a slowdown in mortgage refinancing activity will keep real estate profits under pressure in 1995. Growth in receivables (due to acquisitions and branch expansions) should offset margin pressures due to competitive pressures in consumer lending. Receivables growth and favorable spreads will aid commercial lending profits. Leasing profits will trend upward, aided by contributions from the 1994 Tiphook acquisition, and by stronger economies in the U.S. and certain overseas markets. Share repurchases (including a 7.2 million buyback made in 1994) wil aid per share comparisons.

Valuation - 22-AUG-95

After a lackluster performance during 1994 due to the negative effects of higher interest rates, these interest-sensitive shares have rebounded considerably so far in 1995; and now trade at about 11 times our 1995 operating earnings estimate of $5.70 a share (versus $5.25 of operating earnings reported in 1994, both before realized investment gains or losses). Despite TA's favorable long term prospects, the shares are trading at the upper end of their valuation range and are fairly valued, near term.

Key Stock Statistics

S&P EPS Est. 1995	5.70	Tang. Bk. Value/Share	38.73
P/E on S&P Est. 1995	11.2	Beta	1.15
S&P EPS Est. 1996	6.25	Shareholders	53,700
Dividend Rate/Share	2.00	Market cap. (B)	$ 4.4
Shs. outstg. (M)	68.6	Inst. holdings	62%
Avg. daily vol. (M)	0.069	Insider holdings	0%

Value of $10,000 invested 5 years ago: $ 18,384

Fiscal Year Ending Dec. 31

	1995	% Change	1994	% Change	1993	% Change
Revenues (Million $)						
1Q	1,421	15%	1,235	7%	1,150	NM
2Q	—	—	1,363	11%	1,229	NM
3Q	—	—	1,371	13%	1,210	-2%
4Q	—	—	1,385	11%	1,245	-9%
Yr.	—	—	5,355	11%	4,833	-3%
Income (Million $)						
1Q	96.30	-7%	103.7	13%	91.80	29%
2Q	117.8	11%	105.7	-15%	123.9	27%
3Q	—	—	104.9	-25%	139.0	59%
4Q	—	—	113.6	18%	95.90	10%
Yr.	—	—	427.9	-5%	450.5	31%
Earnings Per Share ($)						
1Q	1.33	3%	1.29	19%	1.08	23%
2Q	1.63	22%	1.34	-10%	1.49	27%
3Q	—	—	1.40	-18%	1.70	63%
4Q	—	—	1.43	22%	1.17	15%
Yr.	E5.70	4%	5.46	NM	5.44	32%

Next earnings report expected: late October

Transamerica Corp.

22-AUG-95

Business Summary - 18-AUG-95

This major financial services company is engaged primarily in insurance and finance-related activities. Contributions to operating income (in millions):

	1994	1993
Life insurance	$250.2	$215.7
Insurance brokerage	Nil	10.2
Real estate services	56.0	84.3
Consumer lending	90.4	93.1
Commercial lending	53.7	-4.0
Leasing	63.6	53.6
Asset management	8.3	0.3

The Transamerica Life Companies market an array of life insurance (including term and universal), annuity (like fixed, variable and structured settlement), group pension, and life/health reinsurance products. Premiums and equivalents totaled $1.5 billion in 1994, of which reinsurance contributed 33%, interest sensitive policy charges 28%, individual life insurance 21%, group pension 8%, and other 10%.

Transamerica Financial Services is one of the leading independent consumer finance companies in the U.S., based on $4.1 billion of net finance receivables outstanding at year-end 1994. Transamerica Commercial Finance provides inventory, asset-based and insurance premium financing and is one of the leading commercial finance firms in North America, with $3.4 billion in receivables outstanding at year-end 1994. Real estate services include real estate tax, information and other services.

TA sold its 21% equity interest in Sedgwick Group, a London-based insurance broker, in April 1994. The sale of Transamerica Insurance Group (TA's property-casualty unit) was completed in 1993.

Important Developments

Jun. '95—TA's board authorized the repurchase of 2 million common shares. During 1994, TA reacquired 7.2 million of its common shares at an average cost of $53.70 a share. Since year end 1994, TA completed a number of transactions. In April it acquired the home equity loan portfolio of ITT Corp's (NYSE:ITT) consumer finance unit for $1.03 billion. In May, it sold its Criterion Investment Management Co. unit ($10 billion in assets under management) for gross proceeds of $60 million.

Feb. '95—During 1994 TA, completed a number of transactions. In December, it sold its mutual fund unit to a division of John Hancock Mutual Funds for $100 million. In April, it sold its 21% equity interest in London-based insurance broker Sedgwick Group. In March, it acquired the container division of London-based Tiphook plc for about [S]722 million, becoming the second largest lessor of containers.

Capitalization

Long Term Debt: $9,149,000,000 (6/95).

Minority Interest: $200,000,000.

Preferred Stock: $315,100,000.

Per Share Data ($)

(Year Ended Dec. 31)

	1994	1993	1992	1991	1990	1989
Tangible Bk. Val.	28.48	31.98	29.86	29.04	28.83	28.11
Oper. Earnings	5.25	5.12	4.05	1.10	3.11	3.65
Earnings	5.46	5.44	4.11	1.14	3.29	4.18
Dividends	2.00	2.00	2.00	1.98	1.94	1.90
Payout Ratio	37%	37%	49%	174%	59%	45%
Prices - High	57⅝	62⅜	50½	40	44⅝	48
- Low	46¼	45⅝	37⅛	29⅝	23¼	32¾
P/E Ratio - High	11	11	12	35	14	11
- Low	8	8	9	26	7	8

Income Statement Analysis (Million $)

	1994	%Chg	1993	%Chg	1992	%Chg	1991
Life Ins. In Force	NA	—	NA	—	306,800	6%	288,852
Premium Income Life	1,495	19%	1,256	-21%	1,590	10%	1,440
Prem.Inc A & H	Nil	—	Nil	—	Nil	—	Nil
Premium Income Other	Nil	—	19.7	-32%	29.0	-98%	1,920
Net Invest. Inc.	1,783	2%	1,750	9%	1,600	-10%	1,777
Total Revs.	5,355	11%	4,833	-3%	4,988	-27%	6,815
Pretax Inc.	690	15%	601	7%	560	NM	143
Net Oper. Inc.	413	-3%	425	26%	338	NM	96.0
Net Inc.	428	-5%	451	31%	343	NM	99

Balance Sheet & Other Fin. Data (Million $)

	1994	1993	1992	1991	1990	1989
Cash & Equiv.	64.0	93.0	22.0	43.0	40.0	74.0
Premiums Due	2,610	2,015	885	1,621	1,535	1,444
Inv Assets Bonds	21,037	19,616	18,546	18,546	1,703	14,884
Inv. Assets Stock	427	466	342	615	401	397
Inv. Assets Loans	868	890	948	1,020	1,074	1,163
Inv. Assets Total	22,496	20,972	18,294	20,181	18,548	16,444
Deferred Policy Cost	2,481	1,929	1,706	1,754	1,724	1,590
Total Assets	40,394	36,051	32,298	33,682	31,784	29,840
Debt	7,489	5,681	6,511	7,000	6,641	6,960
Common Eqty.	2,602	2,939	2,875	2,801	2,792	2,704

Ratio Analysis

	1994	1993	1992	1991	1990	1989
% Ret. on Revs.	8.0	9.3	6.9	1.5	4.0	4.9
% Ret. on Assets	1.1	1.3	1.1	0.3	0.9	1.2
% Ret. on Equity	15.0	14.7	11.3	3.1	9.1	12.2
% Invest. Yield	8.2	8.9	9.1	9.2	9.4	9.4

Dividend Data —Dividends have been paid since 1934. A dividend reinvestment plan is available. A "poison pill" stock purchase right was adopted in 1986.

Amt. of Div. $	Date Decl.	Ex-Div. Date	Stock of Record	Payment Date
0.500	Sep. 15	Sep. 29	Oct. 05	Oct. 31 '94
0.500	Dec. 15	Dec. 23	Dec. 30	Jan. 31 '95
0.500	Mar. 16	Mar. 30	Apr. 05	Apr. 28 '95
0.500	Jun. 15	Jun. 30	Jul. 05	Jul. 31 '95

Data as orig. reptd.; bef. results of disc. opers. and/or spec. items. Per share data adj. for stk. divs. as of ex-div. date.
E-Estimated. NA-Not Available. NM-Not Meaningful. NR-Not Ranked.

Office—600 Montgomery St., San Francisco, CA 94111. **Tel**—(415) 983-4000. **Chrmn**—J. R. Harvey. **Pres & CEO**—F. C. Herringer. **VP-CFO & Secy**—E. H. Grubb. **VP-Treas**—R. R. Lindberg. **VP-Investor Contact**—Ron Petrunoff. **Dirs**— M. DuBain, S. L. Ginn, J. R. Harvey, F. C. Herringer, G. E. Moore, T. Rembe, C. Rice, C. R. Schwab, F. N. Shumway, P. V. Ueberroth. **Transfer Agent & Registrar**—First Chicago Trust Co. of New York, NYC. **Incorporated** in Delaware in 1928. **Empl**-10,800. **S&P Analyst:** Catherine A. Seifert

Travelers Inc.

NYSE Symbol **TRV**
In S&P 500

24-OCT-95

Industry:
Finance

Summary: This holding company offers investment services through Smith Barney Inc., consumer finance services, and an array of life and property-casualty insurance through the Travelers.

S&P Opinion: Accumulate (★★★★)

Recent Price • 50½	Yield • 1.6%
52 Wk Range • 55-30⅜	12-Mo. P/E • 10.9

Earnings vs. Previous Year
▲=Up ▼=Down ▶=No Change

Quantitative Evaluations

Outlook
(1 Lowest—5 Highest)
• **3+**

Fair Value
• **50½**

Risk
• **Low**

Earn./Div. Rank
• **B+**

Technical Eval.
• **Bullish** since 7/95

Rel. Strength Rank
(1 Lowest—99 Highest)
• **44**

Insider Activity
• **Favorable**

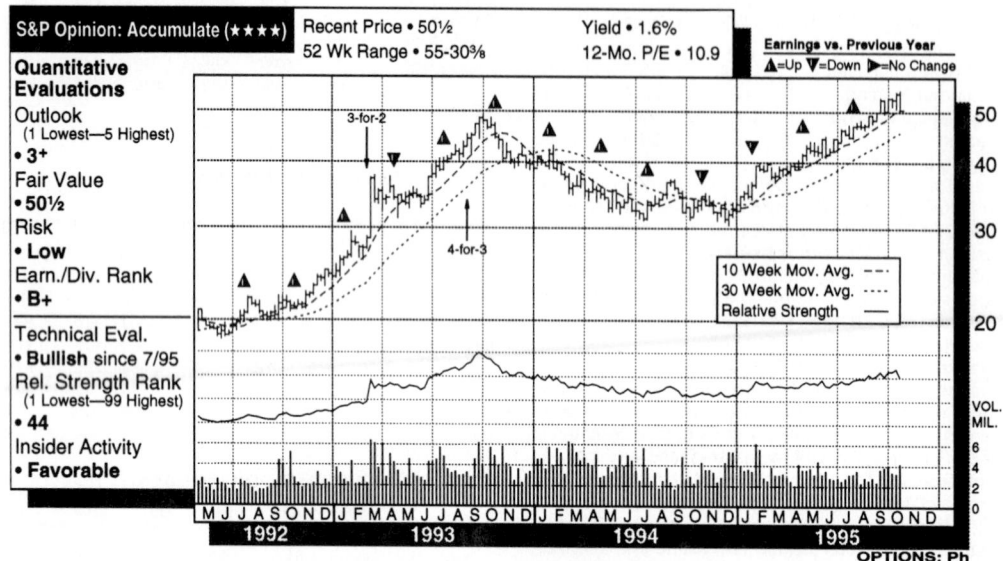

10 Week Mov. Avg. – – –
30 Week Mov. Avg. ·······
Relative Strength ——

OPTIONS: Ph

Overview - 23-OCT-95

Operating earnings growth in 1995 is predicated on sustained growth at Smith Barney. After an interest rate driven slowdown in investor activity in 1994, profit comparisons in 1995 will be aided by a lower interest rate environment (which has helped fuel much of the recent stock market activity). With much of the charge-offs and asset writedowns required to integrate the Travelers acquisition already undertaken, profit comparisons from most insurance operations will improve in 1995. An easing of interest rates would aid margins here, and in the consumer finance area. TRV's decision to use most of the proceeds from the sale of its interest in MetraHealth to bolster the capital base of its life insurance unit enhances that division's competitive stance. Stock repurchases, including the 6.8 million shares reacquired since the beginning of 1995, will aid per share comparisons.

Valuation - 24-OCT-95

After plummeting during 1994 along with most interest-sensitive issues, TRV shares have been in a steady uptrend during most of 1995. Thanks to a more favorable interest rate environment and broad based favorable earnings prospects, this trend will likely continue. Despite their appreciation, the shares remain attractively valued at just over 10 times our 1996 operating earnings estimate. We would look for a pullback of 10% from current levels as an opportunity to add to positions.

Key Stock Statistics

S&P EPS Est. 1995	4.50	Tang. Bk. Value/Share	18.44
P/E on S&P Est. 1995	11.2	Beta	2.16
S&P EPS Est. 1996	5.00	Shareholders	33,000
Dividend Rate/Share	0.80	Market cap. (B)	$ 15.8
Shs. outstg. (M)	319.1	Inst. holdings	73%
Avg. daily vol. (M)	0.750	Insider holdings	NA

Value of $10,000 invested 5 years ago: NA

Fiscal Year Ending Dec. 31

	1995	% Change	1994	% Change	1993	% Change
Revenues (Million $)						
1Q	4,676	-2%	4,769	NM	1,302	—
2Q	4,172	-9%	4,601	NM	1,284	—
3Q	4,512	-4%	4,714	134%	2,016	—
4Q	—	—	4,381	100%	2,195	73%
Yr.	—	—	18,465	172%	6,797	33%
Income (Million $)						
1Q	368.9	9%	339.8	64%	207.0	-6%
2Q	377.0	18%	320.5	72%	186.4	25%
3Q	481.4	45%	331.3	28%	258.7	57%
4Q	—	—	333.9	12%	297.9	35%
Yr.	—	—	1,326	39%	951.0	26%
Earnings Per Share ($)						
1Q	1.10	12%	0.98	10%	0.89	-8%
2Q	1.12	20%	0.93	22%	0.76	13%
3Q	1.45	49%	0.97	-6%	1.03	42%
4Q	—	—	0.99	-17%	1.19	23%
Yr.	E4.50	17%	3.86	NM	3.88	16%

Next earnings report expected: late January

Business Summary - 23-OCT-95

Travelers Group Inc. (formerly Primerica Corp. from 1988 to 1993) is a diversified financial services holding company. On December 31, 1993, TRV acquired the 73% of Travelers Corp. it did not already own for stock worth about $3.5 billion and subsequently changed its name. Contributions to revenues in recent years:

	1994	1993
Investment services	31%	52%
Life insurance services	38%	23%
Prop.-Cas. insurance services	25%	5%
Consumer finance & other	6%	20%

Investment services consist of Smith Barney Inc., an investment banking and securities brokerage firm (formerly Smith Barney Shearson); and a 99% interest in RCM Capital Management. Mutual fund manager American Capital Management & Research was sold in December 1994. Assets under management at year-end 1994 were $115.5 billion.

Insurance services include life, accident and health, and property and casualty insurance, and auto service contract insurance. Travelers Life and Annuities and Primerica Financial Services and its affiliates underwrite individual life insurance and market annuities and mutual funds. At year-end 1994, life insurance in force totaled $384 billion. Property-casualty insurance is underwritten by Travelers. Net written premiums totaled $5.4 billion in 1994 and consisted of an array of personal and commercial lines coverage.

Consumer finance services include real estate-secured loans, personal loans, credit cards and other personal loans. Net consumer finance receivables were $6.7 billion at year-end 1994.

Important Developments

Oct. '95—TRV, on October 2, completed the sale of MetraHealth Companies to United HealthCare Corp. (NYSE:UNH) for $1.65 billion in cash and stock. MetraHealth is a managed healthcare company formed in January 1995 through the combination of TRV's and Metropolitan Life Insurance Co's. group health insurance units. TRV received $831 million in cash for its 48.25% stake in MetraHealth; and could receive up to an additional $169 million in contingency payments. TRV plans to post a $100 million pretax gain on the sale in the fourth quarter. Also, effective September 29, 1995 TRV spun off its Transport Holdings life/health insurer to shareholders by distributing one Transport Class A common share for every 200 TRV common shares held.

Capitalization

Long Term Debt: $8,613,000,000 (6/95).
Preferred Stock: $800,000,000.

Per Share Data ($)

(Year Ended Dec. 31)

	1994	1993	1992	1991	1990	1989
Tangible Bk. Val.	18.44	19.45	11.47	8.62	6.40	5.60
Earnings	3.86	3.88	3.34	2.14	1.64	1.43
Dividends	0.57	0.49	0.36	0.22	0.18	0.14
Payout Ratio	15%	13%	11%	10%	11%	10%
Prices - High	43⅛	49½	25	20⅛	18⅞	15
- Low	30⅜	24⅛	17⅞	10⅞	8½	10⅛
P/E Ratio - High	11	13	7	9	12	10
- Low	8	6	5	5	5	7

Income Statement Analysis (Million $)

	1994	%Chg	1993	%Chg	1992	%Chg	1991
Premium Income	7,590	NM	1,480	-13%	1,694	-5%	1,783
Inv. Inc.	3,637	NM	718	19%	605	-12%	688
Oth. Revs.	7,238	57%	4,599	63%	2,826	-32%	4,138
Total Revs.	18,465	172%	6,797	33%	5,125	-22%	6,608
Int. Exp.	1,284	82%	707	5%	674	-23%	876
% Exp/Op Revs.	90%	—	78%	—	81%	—	89%
Pretax Inc.	2,149	41%	1,523	28%	1,188	50%	791
Eff. Tax Rate	38%	—	36%	—	36%	—	36%
Net Inc.	1,326	39%	951	26%	756	58%	479

Balance Sheet & Other Fin. Data (Million $)

	1994	1993	1992	1991	1990	1989
Receivables	12,256	10,477	3,220	3,263	Nil	Nil
Cash & Invest.	40,347	43,725	3,618	3,696	3,522	3,511
Loans	6,746	6,216	5,655	6,772	8,301	7,348
Total Assets	115,297	101,360	23,397	21,561	19,689	17,955
Capitalization:						
Debt	9,555	9,526	6,584	8,044	7,022	6,276
Equity	7,840	8,526	3,929	3,280	2,859	2,603
Total	18,333	18,052	10,813	11,323	9,881	8,878
Price Times Book HI	2.3	2.5	2.1	2.3	3.0	2.7
Price Times Book LO	1.6	1.2	1.5	1.3	1.3	1.8

Ratio Analysis

	1994	1993	1992	1991	1990	1989
% Ret. on Revs.	7.2	14.0	14.8	7.2	6.0	5.1
% Ret. on Assets	1.2	1.5	3.4	2.3	2.0	1.8
% Ret. on Equity	15.2	15.5	20.8	15.6	13.7	12.7
Loans/Equity	0.8	1.0	1.6	1.8	2.9	2.8

Dividend Data —Dividends were initiated in 1986.

Amt. of Div. $	Date Decl.	Ex-Div. Date	Stock of Record	Payment Date
0.150	Oct. 26	Nov. 01	Nov. 07	Nov. 23 '94
0.200	Jan. 25	Jan. 31	Feb. 06	Feb. 24 '95
0.200	Apr. 26	May. 02	May. 08	May. 26 '95
0.200	Jul. 26	Aug. 03	Aug. 07	Aug. 25 '95
Stk.	Aug. 25	Oct. 03	Sep. 11	Oct. 02 '95

Data as orig. reptd.; bef. results of disc opers. and/or spec. items. Per share data adj. for stk. divs. as of ex-div. date.
E-Estimated. NA-Not Available. NM-Not Meaningful. NR-Not Ranked.

Offices—388 Greenwich St., New York, NY. 10013. **Tel**—(212) 891-8900. **Chrmn & CEO**—S. I. Weill. **Vice Chrmn**—R. I. Lipp, J. J. Plumeri. **Pres & COO**—J. Dimon. **VP-CFO**—H. G. Miller. **VP-Secy**—C. O. Prince III. **Treas**—J. T. Fadden. **Investor Contacts**—Mary McDermott, Barbara Yastine. **Dirs**—C. M. Armstrong, K. J. Bialkin, E. H. Budd, J. A. Califano Jr., D. D. Danforth, R. F. Daniell, J. Dimon, L. B. Disharoon, G. R. Ford, R. F. Greenhill, A. D. Jordan, R. I. Lipp, D. C. Mecum, A. E. Pearson, F. J. Tasco, L. J. Wachner, S. I. Weill, J. R. Wright Jr., A. Zankel. **Transfer Agent & Registrar**—First National Bank of Boston. **Incorporated** in Delaware in 1968. **Empl**-53,400. **S&P Analyst:** Catherine A. Seifert

Tribune Co.

NYSE Symbol **TRB**
In S&P 500

26-SEP-95

Industry:
Publishing

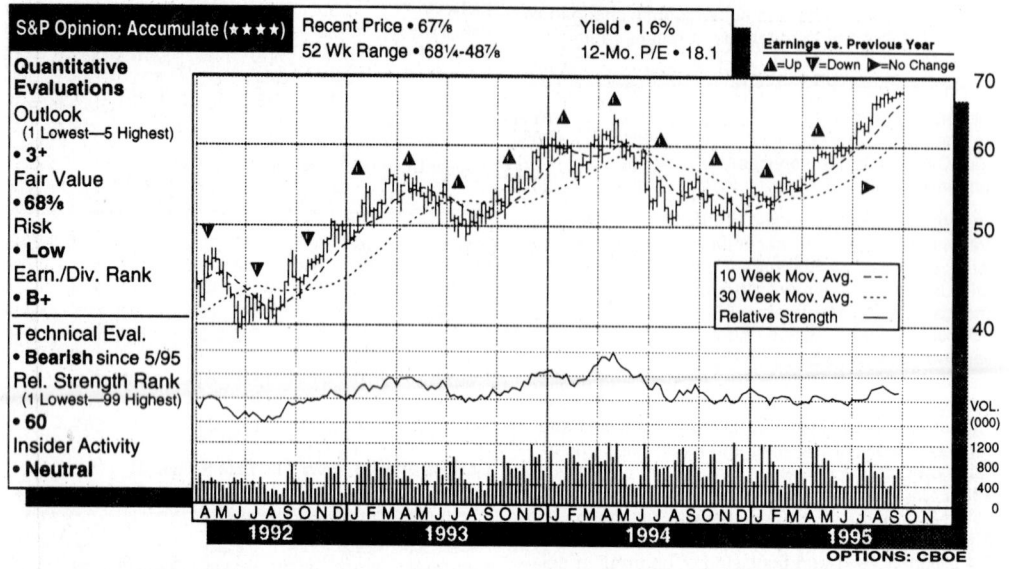

Summary: Tribune is engaged in newspaper publishing, broadcasting and entertainment; since 1993, it has also been rapidly expanding educational book and electronic publishing.

S&P Opinion: Accumulate (★★★★)

| Recent Price • 67⅞ | Yield • 1.6% |
| 52 Wk Range • 68¼-48⅞ | 12-Mo. P/E • 18.1 |

Quantitative Evaluations

Outlook
(1 Lowest—5 Highest)
• **3+**

Fair Value
• **68⅞**

Risk
• **Low**

Earn./Div. Rank
• **B+**

Technical Eval.
• **Bearish** since 5/95

Rel. Strength Rank
(1 Lowest—99 Highest)
• **60**

Insider Activity
• **Neutral**

Earnings vs. Previous Year
▲=Up ▼=Down ▶=No Change

10 Week Mov. Avg. – – –
30 Week Mov. Avg. ·····
Relative Strength ——

OPTIONS: CBOE

Overview - 26-SEP-95

A moderate increase in revenues is seen for 1995, on growth in each business segment, despite lost revenues from the delayed opening of the Major League Baseball season. Margins will be restricted by sharply higher newsprint prices, but profitability will be aided by improved business conditions, cost controls and other factors. Despite expected continued startup costs, New Media/Education group operating profits will strengthen. Capital gains are likely to be lower, but net income will benefit from equity in earnings, versus equity in losses, and interest costs will be lower. Revenue growth should continue into 1996 and, in the absence of negative surprises, margins should widen.

Valuation - 26-SEP-95

The shares should outperfom the market over the next 12 months, despite investor fears related to the impact of rising newsprint costs on publishers. A healthy outlook for advertising-supported media puts the company in a favorable position. The company is currently benefiting from its 53% equity interest in the major Canadian newsprint maker, QUNO Corp., but it may sell all or most of that investment. The market's perception of Tribune is enhanced by the fact that its thrust into new media and educational publishing has been profitable since the program's start in 1993.

Key Stock Statistics

S&P EPS Est. 1995	3.95	Tang. Bk. Value/Share	NM
P/E on S&P Est. 1995	17.2	Beta	0.88
S&P EPS Est. 1996	4.50	Shareholders	4,600
Dividend Rate/Share	1.12	Market cap. (B)	$ 4.4
Shs. outstg. (M)	65.1	Inst. holdings	53%
Avg. daily vol. (M)	0.115	Insider holdings	NA

Value of $10,000 invested 5 years ago: $ 16,101

Fiscal Year Ending Dec. 31

	1995	% Change	1994	% Change	1993	% Change
Revenues (Million $)						
1Q	532.8	10%	482.8	11%	435.0	-8%
2Q	591.8	3%	573.8	11%	517.4	-7%
3Q	—	—	513.3	5%	486.7	-8%
4Q	—	—	591.1	15%	513.8	-7%
Yr.	—	—	2,155	10%	1,953	-7%
Income (Million $)						
1Q	67.96	70%	40.07	35%	29.65	90%
2Q	82.13	-3%	85.03	37%	62.29	38%
3Q	—	—	47.83	24%	38.60	14%
4Q	—	—	69.12	19%	58.08	38%
Yr.	—	—	242.1	28%	188.6	38%
Earnings Per Share ($)						
1Q	0.96	81%	0.53	39%	0.38	124%
2Q	1.19	NM	1.19	37%	0.87	38%
3Q	E0.75	17%	0.64	25%	0.51	11%
4Q	E1.05	9%	0.96	20%	0.80	40%
Yr.	E3.95	19%	3.32	30%	2.56	41%

Next earnings report expected: mid October

Business Summary - 26-SEP-95

Tribune Company is engaged in publishing newspapers, educational books and information in print and digital formats, television and radio broadcasting, and entertainment. Segment contributions in 1994 were:

	Revs.	Profits
Publishing	60%	68%
Broadcasting & entertainment	35%	31%
New media/education	5%	1%

The company publishes six daily newspapers with combined average daily circulation in 1994 of 1,370,000 and Sunday circulation of 2,027,000. Properties include The Chicago Tribune, The Fort Lauderdale Sun-Sentinel, The Orlando Sentinel, The Daily Press and The Times-Herald in Newport News and The Times-Advocate in Escondido. As part of a strategy begun in 1993 to place greater emphasis on educational book and electronic publishing, Tribune acquired Compton's Multimedia Publishing Group, Contemporary Books and The Wright Group.

Tribune is the fourth largest TV group broadcaster, with eight independent TV stations, in Chicago (WGN-TV), New York (WPIX-TV), Philadelphia (WPHL-TV), Denver (KWGN-TV), New Orleans (WGNO-TV), Atlanta (WGNX-TV), Los Angeles (KTLA-TV), and Boston (WLVI-TV,). It also owns five radio stations: WGN-AM, Chicago; WQCD-FM, New York; and KVOD-FM, KOSI-FM & KEZW-AM, Denver.

Entertainment and programming services are provided through Independent Network News, Tribune Entertainment Co. and the Chicago Cubs. A 34% equity interest is held in QUNO Corp., a major newsprint manufacturer.

Important Developments

Sep. '95—Tribune announced that it is exploring ways to reduce or sell all of its shareholdings in QUNO Corp., a Canadian newsprint producer. Prior to an initial public offering in February 1993, TRB owned 100% of QUNO; it currently holds common shares and convertible securities that, combined, amount to 53% of the equity of QUNO.

Aug. '95—TRB exercised its first equity option and will invest $12 million to acquire a 12.5% limited partnership interest in The Warner Bros. Television Network (WB). TRB has additional options to acquire up to a 25% interest in The WB. Separately, TRB agreed to acquire KTTY-TV, located in San Diego and affiliated with The WB, for $70.5 million.

Capitalization

Long Term Debt: $497,439,000 (6/95).

ESOP $7.75 Conv. Preferred Stock: 1,531,084 shs. (no par); ea. conv. into four com.

Per Share Data ($)

(Year Ended Dec. 31)

	1994	1993	1992	1991	1990	1989
Tangible Bk. Val.	6.40	4.77	3.44	-1.77	-3.42	1.13
Cash Flow	5.40	4.11	3.97	3.78	0.65	4.66
Earnings	3.32	2.56	1.82	1.94	-1.22	3.17
Dividends	1.04	0.96	0.96	0.96	0.96	0.88
Payout Ratio	31%	38%	53%	50%	NM	26%
Prices - High	64½	61¼	50⅝	48⅜	48¼	63⅛
- Low	48⅞	48	38⅝	33⅛	31¼	36⅜
P/E Ratio - High	19	24	28	25	NM	20
- Low	15	19	21	17	NM	11

Income Statement Analysis (Million $)

	1994	%Chg	1993	%Chg	1992	%Chg	1991
Revs.	2,155	10%	1,953	-7%	2,096	3%	2,035
Oper. Inc.	512	12%	459	12%	411	1%	406
Depr.	115	12%	103	-26%	140	18%	119
Int. Exp.	20.6	-20%	25.8	-51%	52.7	-19%	65.1
Pretax Inc.	429	29%	332	42%	233	-4%	242
Eff. Tax Rate	44%	—	43%	—	41%	—	41%
Net Inc.	242	28%	189	38%	137	-4%	142

Balance Sheet & Other Fin. Data (Million $)

	1994	1993	1992	1991	1990	1989
Cash	21.8	18.5	16.8	17.0	13.6	27.7
Curr. Assets	544	491	574	589	618	657
Total Assets	2,786	2,536	2,752	2,795	2,826	3,051
Curr. Liab.	530	505	680	599	616	631
LT Debt	411	511	741	898	999	881
Common Eqty.	1,262	1,040	871	504	415	728
Total Cap.	1,894	1,695	1,720	1,920	1,962	2,194
Cap. Exp.	92.0	76.0	130	94.0	149	243
Cash Flow	339	273	258	244	43.0	338

Ratio Analysis

	1994	1993	1992	1991	1990	1989
Curr. Ratio	1.0	1.0	0.8	1.0	1.0	1.0
% LT Debt of Cap.	21.7	30.1	43.1	46.8	50.9	40.1
% Net Inc.of Revs.	11.2	9.7	6.5	7.0	NM	9.9
% Ret. on Assets	9.1	7.0	4.9	5.0	NM	8.4
% Ret. on Equity	19.5	17.6	13.9	27.1	NM	25.3

Dividend Data —Payments on the publicly held shares began in 1983. A poison pill preferred stock purchase rights plan was adopted in 1987. A dividend reinvestment plan is available.

Amt. of Div. $	Date Decl.	Ex-Div. Date	Stock of Record	Payment Date
0.260	Oct. 25	Nov. 17	Nov. 23	Dec. 08 '94
0.280	Feb. 21	Feb. 28	Mar. 06	Mar. 16 '95
0.280	May. 09	May. 19	May. 25	Jun. 08 '95
0.280	Jul. 25	Aug. 29	Aug. 31	Sep. 14 '95

Data as orig. reptd.; bef. results of disc. opers. and/or spec. items. Per share data adj. for stk. divs. as of ex-div. date. E-Estimated. NA-Not Available. NM-Not Meaningful. NR-Not Ranked.

Office—435 North Michigan Ave., Chicago, IL 60611. **Tel**—(312) 222-9100. **Chrmn**—C. T. Brumback. **Pres & CEO**—J. W. Madigan. **Sr VP & CFO**—D. C. Grenesko. **VP & Secy**—S. J. Gradowski. **VP & Treas**—D. J. Granat. **VP & Investor Contact**—Joseph A. Hays. **Dirs**—C. T. Brumback, S. R. Cook, J. C. Dowdle, D. E. Hernandez, R. E. LaBlanc, J. W. Madigan, N. H. Maynard, A. J. McKenna, K. Miller, N. N. Minow, J. J. O'Connor, D. H. Rumsfeld, A. R. Weber. **Transfer Agent & Registrar**—First Chicago Trust Co. of New York, Jersey City, N.J. **Incorporated** in Illinois in 1861; reincorporated in Delaware in 1968. **Empl**-10,500. **S&P Analyst:** William H. Donald

Trinova Corp.

NYSE Symbol **TNV**
In S&P 500

18-OCT-95 Industry:
Machinery

Summary: Trinova is a worldwide manufacturer of engineered components and systems for industry.

S&P Opinion: Accumulate (★★★★)

Recent Price • 29½	Yield • 2.4%
52 Wk Range • 38¾-23½	12-Mo. P/E • 9.8

Quantitative Evaluations

Outlook
(1 Lowest—5 Highest)
• **4+**

Fair Value
• **30⅞**

Risk
• **Average**

Earn./Div. Rank
• **B-**

Technical Eval.
• **Bearish** since 5/95

Rel. Strength Rank
(1 Lowest—99 Highest)
• **8**

Insider Activity
• **Neutral**

Earnings vs. Previous Year
▲=Up ▼=Down ▶=No Change

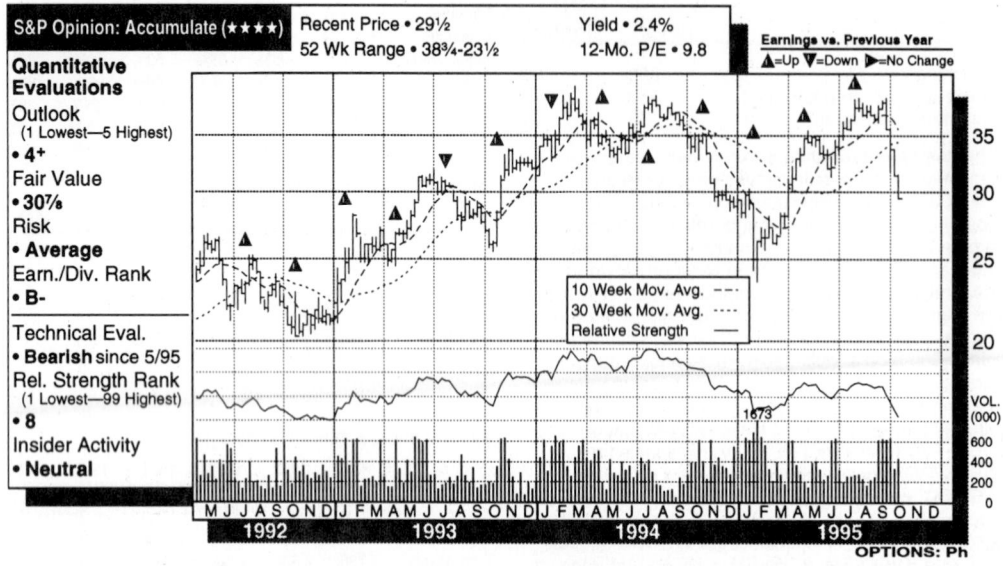

10 Week Mov. Avg. ----
30 Week Mov. Avg. ····
Relative Strength ——

OPTIONS: Ph

Overview - 18-OCT-95

Based upon our forecast for 2.6% GDP growth in the U. S. and continued economic growth in Europe, we look for a 9.0% rise in sales for 1996. The acquisition of Electronic Systems Division together with steady economic growth will boost sales in the industrial unit. An upturn in aerospace should lead to another gain in that unit. The automotive segment sales will be even with 1995 as new programs begin. Continued high capacity utilization, stable raw material costs and only minimal costs for integrating Electronic Systems will outweigh a small increase in interest expense and a higher tax rate. Accordingly, earnings should rise in 1996. Internal improvement, acquisitions, aggressive debt reduction and a large award from Ford Motor should boost longer-term sales and profits.

Valuation - 18-OCT-95

TNV's shares have been quite volatile in 1995. Following a downward revision in analyst earnings estimates in late January, TNV's shares dropped some 17% before stabilizing at about $25 a share in early February. The shares then rose 55% through late August as earnings gains exceeded expectations. Subsequently, the stock declined to the $31 level by early October, with general weakness in cyclical issues the principal reason for the decline. Based upon its attractive multiple on 1996's projected earnings and continued progress in strengthening the balance sheet, we are maintaining our accumulate rating on the stock.

Key Stock Statistics

S&P EPS Est. 1995	3.20	Tang. Bk. Value/Share	12.14
P/E on S&P Est. 1995	9.2	Beta	1.61
S&P EPS Est. 1996	3.50	Shareholders	11,300
Dividend Rate/Share	0.72	Market cap. (B)	$0.850
Shs. outstg. (M)	28.8	Inst. holdings	79%
Avg. daily vol. (M)	0.104	Insider holdings	NA

Value of $10,000 invested 5 years ago: $ 14,189

Fiscal Year Ending Dec. 31

	1995	% Change	1994	% Change	1993	% Change
Revenues (Million $)						
1Q	498.6	13%	439.8	3%	429.0	1%
2Q	501.6	9%	460.9	10%	419.8	-4%
3Q	—	—	437.6	11%	393.3	-2%
4Q	—	—	456.4	14%	401.7	-7%
Yr.	—	—	1,795	9%	1,644	-3%
Income (Million $)						
1Q	22.59	70%	13.27	136%	5.63	NM
2Q	33.28	72%	19.32	NM	-9.12	NM
3Q	—	—	15.13	60%	9.46	NM
4Q	—	—	18.13	NM	4.54	-25%
Yr.	—	—	65.86	NM	10.51	-27%
Earnings Per Share ($)						
1Q	0.77	67%	0.46	130%	0.20	NM
2Q	1.11	68%	0.66	NM	-0.32	NM
3Q	E0.62	19%	0.52	58%	0.33	NM
4Q	E0.70	13%	0.62	NM	0.16	-24%
Yr.	E3.20	42%	2.26	NM	0.37	-27%

Next earnings report expected: mid October

Trinova Corp.

Business Summary - 18-OCT-95

Trinova is a worldwide manufacturer of engineered components and systems for industry. Contributions in 1994:

	Sales	Profits
Industrial	54%	54%
Aerospace & defense	17%	17%
Automotive	29%	29%

Foreign operations accounted for 35% of sales and 28% of operating profit in 1994.

Industrial products include all pressure ranges of hose and fittings; adapters; self-sealing couplings; and molded and extruded and co-extruded plastic products. The Vickers, Inc., unit makes electronic, electrohydraulic, pneumatic and hydraulic control devices; piston and vane pumps and motors; servovalves and controls; electric motors and drives; computer numerical controls; and test and simulation equipment.

Aerospace & defense includes hose, fittings, couplings, swivels, V-Band couplings, fuel-handling products, high-pressure tube fittings, hydraulic motors and motor packages, motor pumps and generator packages, electrohydraulic and electromechanical actuators, and fixed and variable-displacement fuel pumps.

Automotive includes air conditioning, power steering, oil and transmission cooler and fuel line components and systems, body side moldings, bumper nerf strips, window frames, instrument panels, consoles, engine covers, bumper beams, engine components and height sensors.

Worldwide sales by product class in 1994: fluid connectors (36%); pumps and motors (17%); hydraulic and electronic controls (15%); plastic products (21%); and miscellaneous components and systems (11%).

Important Developments

Sep. '95—TNV and Cincinnati Milacron (NYSE, CMZ) jointly announced a letter of intent for the purchase of Milacron's Electronic Systems Division (ESD) for $105 million in cash, subject to post closing adjustments. ESD's sales in 1995 were estimated at $90 million. ESD produces computer controls for machine tools and plastics machinery. The transaction was expected to close by 1995's year end.
Jul. '95—TNV reported share earnings of $1.11 on a 9% increase in revenues for 1995's second quarter, versus $0.66 a year earlier. Sales and earnings for the quarter and six months reached record levels. The company attributed the strong performance to sales gains and initiatives to improve manufacturing and distribution processes.

Capitalization

Long Term Debt: $235,814,000 (6/95), incl. $100 million of debs. due 2002, conv. into com. at $52.50 a sh.

Per Share Data ($)

(Year Ended Dec. 31)

	1994	1993	1992	1991	1990	1989
Tangible Bk. Val.	11.11	8.91	12.34	13.11	21.22	19.75
Cash Flow	4.11	2.55	2.71	-4.32	3.86	2.84
Earnings	2.26	0.37	0.51	-6.52	1.51	0.98
Dividends	0.68	0.68	0.68	0.68	0.68	0.67
Payout Ratio	30%	184%	133%	NM	42%	67%
Prices - High	40	33¾	26¾	27½	29⅜	30⅜
- Low	28½	21	19¼	15⅜	14⅞	21
P/E Ratio - High	18	91	52	NM	19	31
- Low	13	57	38	NM	10	21

Income Statement Analysis (Million $)

	1994	%Chg	1993	%Chg	1992	%Chg	1991
Revs.	1,795	9%	1,644	-3%	1,696	NM	1,681
Oper. Inc.	202	29%	157	30%	121	66%	73.0
Depr.	60.8	-2%	61.8	NM	62.2	NM	62.0
Int. Exp.	21.1	-17%	25.5	-3%	26.3	NM	26.5
Pretax Inc.	101	NM	17.0	-29%	24.0	NM	-194
Eff. Tax Rate	35%	—	39%	—	40%	—	NM
Net Inc.	66.0	NM	11.0	-21%	14.0	NM	-183

Balance Sheet & Other Fin. Data (Million $)

	1994	1993	1992	1991	1990	1989
Cash	27.9	20.5	26.0	27.0	25.0	23.0
Curr. Assets	540	487	547	573	671	738
Total Assets	1,001	972	1,017	1,070	1,314	1,361
Curr. Liab.	289	325	368	450	429	416
LT Debt	235	246	239	177	196	204
Common Eqty.	320	253	353	375	599	651
Total Cap.	563	505	628	583	839	895
Cap. Exp.	55.0	55.0	52.0	86.0	77.0	98.0
Cash Flow	127	72.0	77.0	-121	117	97.0

Ratio Analysis

	1994	1993	1992	1991	1990	1989
Curr. Ratio	1.9	1.5	1.5	1.3	1.6	1.8
% LT Debt of Cap.	41.8	48.8	38.0	30.4	23.3	22.8
% Net Inc.of Revs.	3.7	0.6	0.9	NM	2.3	1.7
% Ret. on Assets	6.6	1.1	1.4	NM	3.7	2.4
% Ret. on Equity	22.8	3.5	4.0	NM	7.9	5.1

Dividend Data —Dividends have been paid since 1933. A dividend reinvestment plan is available. A new "poison pill" stock purchase rights plan was adopted in 1989.

Amt. of Div. $	Date Decl.	Ex-Div. Date	Stock of Record	Payment Date
0.170	Oct. 27	Nov. 08	Nov. 15	Dec. 15 '94
0.180	Jan. 26	Feb. 14	Feb. 21	Mar. 15 '95
0.180	Apr. 20	May. 09	May. 15	Jun. 15 '95
0.180	Jul. 27	Aug. 11	Aug. 15	Sep. 15 '95

Data as orig. reptd.; bef. results of disc. opers. and/or spec. items. Per share data adj. for stk. divs. as of ex-div. date. E-Estimated. NA-Not Available. NM-Not Meaningful. NR-Not Ranked.

Office—3000 Strayer, Maumee, OH 43537-0050. **Tel**—(419) 867-2200. **Chrmn, Pres & CEO**—D. F. Allen. **VP-Secy**—J. M. Oathout. **VP-CFO**—D. M. Risley. **VP & Investor Contact**—Warren N. Bimblick. **Dirs**—D. F. Allen, P. Crawford, J. C. Farrell, D. R. Goode, P. Ormond, J. P. Reilly, R. H. Spilman, W. R. Timken Jr. **Transfer Agent & Registrar**—First Chicago Trust Co. of New York, NYC. **Incorporated** in Ohio in 1916. **Empl**-15,024.
S&P Analyst: Leo Larkin

Tyco International Ltd.

NYSE Symbol **TYC**
In S&P 500

25-OCT-95

Industry:
Building

Summary: This leading manufacturer of fire protection systems also makes disposable medical products, flow control products, electrical and electronic components and packaging materials.

S&P Opinion: Accumulate (★★★★)	Recent Price • 62½	Yield • 0.6%
	52 Wk Range • 63¼-43⅝	12-Mo. P/E • 20.8

Quantitative Evaluations

Outlook
(1 Lowest—5 Highest)
• **5⁺**

Fair Value
• **85⅞**

Risk
• **Low**

Earn./Div. Rank
• **B+**

Technical Eval.
• **Bullish** since 8/95

Rel. Strength Rank
(1 Lowest—99 Highest)
• **69**

Insider Activity
• **Neutral**

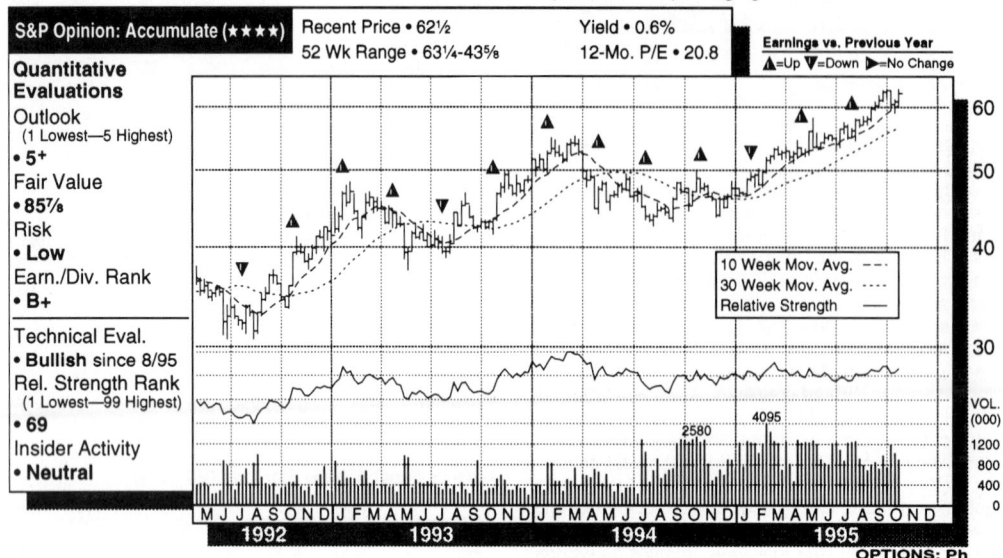

Earnings vs. Previous Year
▲=Up ▼=Down ▶=No Change

10 Week Mov. Avg. - - -
30 Week Mov. Avg. ·····
Relative Strength —

VOL. (000)

OPTIONS: Ph

Overview - 25-OCT-95

Sales growth should exceed 10% in fiscal 1996, with double-digit gains expected in all operating segments. Sales gains should be driven by stable global economies, Tyco's aggressive efforts to secure leading market positions and a continued focus on geographic expansion. Margins should widen on the increased sales, efficiencies derived through TYC's extensive capital investment program and a reduction of overhead costs through a streamlining of operations. Particular gains are likely in the fire protection area, where the company should be aided by a shift in service mix toward more profitable service and inspection and retrofit jobs, as well as its investments in Asia, where results are expected to turn profitable. Tyco's bottom line will also benefit from the absence of a $0.41-a-share charge for merger and transaction costs related to the Kendall acquisition.

Valuation - 25-OCT-95

The company's shares have resumed an upward path since the latter part of 1994, driven by expectations of ongoing worldwide economic strength, Tyco's favorable earnings reports and investor enthusiasm about the acquisition of Kendall International. Given our belief that global economies will remain relatively healthy in the foreseeable future, we anticipate solid earnings growth through fiscal 1996 and expect continued appreciation in the company's shares. Tyco could also experience an expansion of its P/E ratio, as the Kendall acquisition reduces its vulnerability to economic cycles.

Key Stock Statistics

S&P EPS Est. 1996	4.00	Tang. Bk. Value/Share	8.30
P/E on S&P Est. 1996	15.6	Beta	0.81
Dividend Rate/Share	0.40	Shareholders	5,100
Shs. outstg. (M)	76.4	Market cap. (B)	$ 4.7
Avg. daily vol. (M)	0.188	Inst. holdings	85%
		Insider holdings	NA

Value of $10,000 invested 5 years ago: $ 13,029

Fiscal Year Ending Jun. 30

	1996	% Change	1995	% Change	1994	% Change
Revenues (Million $)						
1Q	1,216	15%	1,054	33%	790.0	-2%
2Q	—	—	1,098	37%	802.9	5%
3Q	—	—	1,135	40%	809.9	9%
4Q	—	—	1,248	45%	860.1	8%
Yr.	—	—	4,535	39%	3,263	5%
Income (Million $)						
1Q	65.66	23%	53.40	95%	27.45	NM
2Q	—	—	26.62	-10%	29.69	15%
3Q	—	—	64.96	101%	32.33	22%
4Q	—	—	71.63	104%	35.10	NM
Yr.	—	—	216.6	74%	124.6	72%
Earnings Per Share ($)						
1Q	0.86	19%	0.72	20%	0.60	13%
2Q	E0.95	171%	0.35	-45%	0.64	10%
3Q	E1.04	22%	0.85	21%	0.70	23%
4Q	E1.15	22%	0.94	24%	0.76	NM
Yr.	E4.00	39%	2.87	6%	2.70	71%

Next earnings report expected: mid January

Tyco International Ltd.

25-OCT-95

Business Summary - 25-OCT-95

Tyco International Ltd. (formerly Tyco Laboratories) is the world's largest manufacturer and installer of fire protection systems and a leading producer of disposable medical products, packaging materials, flow control products and electrical and electronic components. Industry segment contributions in fiscal 1995 were:

	Sales	Pretax Profits
Fire protection	38%	17%
Flow control products	22%	17%
Electrical & electronic components	9%	15%
Disposable & specialty products	31%	51%

Operations outside North America accounted for 28% of sales and 9% of income from operations in fiscal 1995. Tyco operates in more than 50 countries worldwide.

The company is the world's largest fire protection contractor. It designs, fabricates, installs and services automatic sprinkler and fire suppression systems in buildings and other installations.

Flow control products consist of pipe, fittings, valves, meters and related products, which are used to transport, control and measure the flow of liquids and gases.

The electrical and electronic components segment manufactures underwater communications cable, cable assemblies, printed circuit boards, electrical conduit and related components. It also assembles backplanes for the electronics industry.

The disposable and specialty products segment primarily produces medical supplies, adhesive products and tapes, disposable medical products, laminated and coated products, technical products, extrusion coated polyester yarns and woven fabrics, and polyethylene film and packaging. It also markets a variety of home healthcare products. Disposable medical products operations were significantly expanded through the October 1994 acquisition of Kendall International (purchased for $1.4 billion in Tyco stock).

Important Developments

Oct. '95—Tyco declared a two-for-one stock split, to be distributed on November 14, 1995.

Oct. '95—The company reported a 23% year-to-year earnings gain for the first quarter of fiscal 1996 (a 19% EPS gain on more shares), as sales rose 15%. Tyco experienced sales and earnings gains in all operating segments, with the strongest growth in its fire protection and flow control segments. Tyco added that it was optimistic about upcoming prospects and, to achieve sustained growth, would focus on less economically sensitive businesses, shift its service mix in the fire protection and flow control divisions, continue its acquisition program and invest in technology necessary to improve its position in all segments.

Capitalization

Long Term Debt: $506,417,000 (6/95).

Per Share Data ($)

(Year Ended Jun. 30)

	1995	1994	1993	1992	1991	1990
Tangible Bk. Val.	8.30	4.63	1.88	2.44	0.98	5.83
Cash Flow	4.63	4.14	2.96	3.49	3.98	NA
Earnings	2.87	2.70	1.58	2.06	2.57	2.90
Dividends	0.40	0.50	0.29	0.45	0.35	0.31
Payout Ratio	14%	19%	19%	22%	14%	11%
Prices - High	58¼	55¼	51¾	42⅝	52¼	65¾
- Low	46½	42⅞	37⅜	30⅝	8	37⅛
P/E Ratio - High	20	20	33	21	20	23
- Low	16	16	24	15	11	13

Income Statement Analysis (Million $)

	1995	%Chg	1994	%Chg	1993	%Chg	1992
Revs.	4,535	39%	3,263	5%	3,115	2%	3,066
Oper. Inc.	618	98%	312	11%	282	8%	261
Depr.	133	101%	66.2	5%	63.1	-5%	66.5
Int. Exp.	63.0	40%	45.0	-11%	50.5	-20%	63.3
Pretax Inc.	385	92%	201	56%	129	-2%	131
Eff. Tax Rate	44%	—	38%	—	44%	—	28%
Net Inc.	217	74%	125	74%	72.0	-24%	95.0

Balance Sheet & Other Fin. Data (Million $)

	1995	1994	1993	1992	1991	1990
Cash	66.0	6.2	32.9	32.1	22.7	15.8
Curr. Assets	1,452	1,048	1,133	1,107	1,098	732
Total Assets	3,381	2,416	2,459	2,452	2,393	1,417
Curr. Liab.	1,085	811	869	833	855	513
LT Debt	506	413	562	535	609	270
Common Eqty.	1,635	1,079	920	1,041	905	607
Total Cap.	2,151	1,506	1,490	1,602	1,538	904
Cap. Exp.	119	73.0	80.0	68.0	67.0	55.0
Cash Flow	350	191	135	162	182	NA

Ratio Analysis

	1995	1994	1993	1992	1991	1990
Curr. Ratio	1.3	1.3	1.3	1.3	1.3	1.4
% LT Debt of Cap.	23.5	27.4	37.7	33.4	39.6	29.8
% Net Inc.of Revs.	4.8	3.8	2.3	3.1	3.8	5.7
% Ret. on Assets	6.6	5.1	3.0	3.9	NA	8.5
% Ret. on Equity	14.4	12.5	7.4	9.8	NA	21.7

Dividend Data

—Dividends were initiated in 1975. A dividend reinvestment plan is available.

Amt. of Div. $	Date Decl.	Ex-Div. Date	Stock of Record	Payment Date
0.100	Dec. 15	Dec. 27	Jan. 03	Feb. 01 '95
0.100	Mar. 16	Mar. 29	Apr. 04	May. 01 '95
0.100	Jun. 15	Jul. 03	Jul. 06	Aug. 01 '95
0.100	Sep. 14	Sep. 28	Oct. 02	Nov. 01 '95
2-for-1	Oct. 20	Nov. 15	Oct. 30	Nov. 14 '95

Data as orig. reptd.; bef. results of disc. opers. and/or spec. items. Per share data adj. for stk. divs. as of ex-div. date. E-Estimated. NA-Not Available. NM-Not Meaningful. NR-Not Ranked.

Office—One Tyco Park, Exeter, NH 03833. **Tel**—(603) 778-9700. **Chrmn, Pres & CEO**—L. D. Kozlowski. **VP & CFO**—M. Swartz. **Secy**—J. M. Berman. **VP & Investor Contact**—David P. Brownell. **Dirs**—J. M. Berman, R. S. Bodman, J. F. Fort, S. W. Foss, R. A. Gilleland, P. M. Hampton, L. D. Kozlowski, F. E. Walsh Jr. **Transfer Agent & Registrar**—Mellon Bank, Pittsburgh. **Incorporated** in Massachusetts in 1962. **Empl**-32,000. **S&P Analyst:** Michael W. Jaffe

USX-Marathon Group

NYSE Symbol **MRO**
In S&P 500

15-AUG-95

Industry:
Oil and Gas

Summary: USX-Marathon, the energy operations of USX Corp., engages in worldwide exploration and production and domestic refining and marketing.

S&P Opinion: Accumulate (★★★★)

Recent Price • 20¼	Yield • 3.4%
52 Wk Range • 20¾-15¾	12-Mo. P/E • 18.4

Quantitative Evaluations

Outlook
(1 Lowest—5 Highest)
• **1+**

Fair Value
• **16⅛**

Risk
• **Low**

Earn./Div. Rank
• **NR**

Technical Eval.
• **Bearish** since 4/95

Rel. Strength Rank
(1 Lowest—99 Highest)
• **53**

Insider Activity
• **NA**

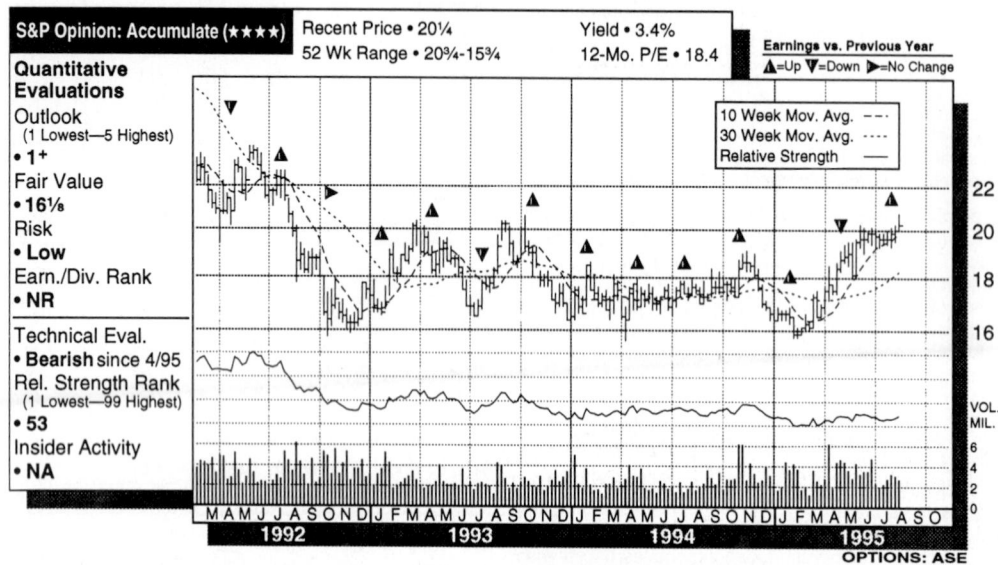

Earnings vs. Previous Year
▲=Up ▼=Down ▶=No Change

10 Week Mov. Avg. – – –
30 Week Mov. Avg. ·······
Relative Strength ——

OPTIONS: ASE

Overview - 11-AUG-95

Earnings should fall slightly in 1995, as lower natural gas prices offset greater oil and gas volumes.
Near-term operating earnings should decline, reflecting narrower margins and higher costs associated with replacing reserves. MRO has boosted oil and gas volumes, and strong cash flow is being utilized to cut the high debt level. Property sales will allow the company to focus on its highly profitable international upstream operations, which have benefited from ongoing expense reductions. We expect refining margins to continue to improve through 1995, after they narrowed sharply in 1994 on overhanging supply caused by warm winter weather and the introduction of reformulated gasoline. An interest in a joint venture in Russia may benefit long-term results if Russia's parliament legalizes production sharing contracts.

Valuation - 11-AUG-95

Weak refining and downstream margins have reversed course recently and should boost the shares in spite of weak natural gas near-term fundamentals. Higher production volumes of crude oil and gas will partly offset the impact of the current downturn in natural gas prices. MRO may have to take an inventory valuation charge during 1995's second half, since oil prices have dropped nearly three dollars a barrel from the level seen during the second quarter. A number of international projects make the stock an attractive holding at current levels, especially with strong current cash flow being used to reduce debt.

Key Stock Statistics

S&P EPS Est. 1995	0.95	Tang. Bk. Value/Share	11.11
P/E on S&P Est. 1995	21.3	Beta	NA
S&P EPS Est. 1996	1.30	Shareholders	130,000
Dividend Rate/Share	0.68	Market cap. (B)	$ 6.0
Shs. outstg. (M)	297.2	Inst. holdings	62%
Avg. daily vol. (M)	0.565	Insider holdings	NA

Value of $10,000 invested 5 years ago: $ 6,935

Fiscal Year Ending Dec. 31

	1995	% Change	1994	% Change	1993	% Change
Revenues ()						
1Q	3,337	21%	2,747	-7%	2,954	NM
2Q	3,528	14%	3,105	NM	3,103	-4%
3Q	—	—	3,497	17%	2,983	-12%
4Q	—	—	3,408	17%	2,922	-10%
Yr.	—	—	12,757	7%	11,962	-6%
Income ()						
1Q	77.00	-30%	110.0	NM	31.00	29%
2Q	108.0	50%	72.00	NM	21.00	-88%
3Q	—	—	102.0	NM	30.00	25%
4Q	—	—	37.00	NM	-88.00	-27%
Yr.	—	—	321.0	NM	-6.00	NM
Earnings Per Share ()						
1Q	0.26	-32%	0.38	NM	0.10	25%
2Q	0.37	48%	0.25	NM	0.07	-89%
3Q	E0.25	—	0.35	NM	0.10	25%
4Q	E0.07	—	0.12	NM	-0.31	NM
Yr.	E0.95	—	1.10	NM	-0.04	NM

Next earnings report expected: late October

USX-Marathon Group

Business Summary - 15-AUG-95

USX Corp.-Marathon Group represents the energy operations of USX Corp.(formerly U.S. Steel), one of the largest U.S. steel manufacturers. MRO is involved primarily in worldwide oil and natural gas exploration and production and domestic refining and marketing.

Oper. Profits (Million $)	1994	1993
Exploration & production	$210	$80
Refining, mkt. & trans.	287	407
Special items and other	87	-241

In 1994, worldwide crude oil production averaged 172,000 bbl. per day (156,000 b/d in 1993), natural gas production totaled 1,014,000 Mcf per day (937,000 Mcf/d). International oil output represented some 36% of total crude production while domestic output accounted for 71%. Total natural gas output was divided 59% domestic, 41% overseas. Refined product sales were 743,000 b/d (726,000 b/d), all of which were in the U.S. Proved reserves at 1994 year end were 795,000,000 bbl. of oil (842,000,000 bbl. in 1993) and 3,654 Bcf of natural gas (3,748 Bcf).

In 1994, MRO completed its Brae Lock production platform and SAGE gas transportation and marketing system in the United Kingdom. As a result, gas and crude oil volumes should rise 20% in 1995. In December 1993, MRO brought on stream its East Brae field in the U.K. sector of the North Sea. Marathon also has extensive exposure in the Gulf of Mexico.

The refining system is composed of a five-facility refining complex designed to convert low-cost, high-sulfur, heavy crude oil into high-value gasoline and diesel fuels. A network of 51 terminals in the Midwest and South serve 2,331 independently owned Marathon-brand gasoline service stations.

Important Developments

Jul. '95—Net income in 1995's second quarter rose to $108 million ($0.37 a share) from $72 million ($0.25) a year earlier. Excluding a favorable inventory market valuation adjustment in the 1995 period, and tax credits, operating income amounted to $251 million, up from $63 million. Greater crude oil volumes and higher oil prices led to an increase in domestic exploration and production profits, while soaring international upstream profits were due chiefly to higher liquid hydrocarbon prices and volumes, and expense reductions. Profits in refining, marketing and transportation climbed, reflecting improved refined product margins and volumes.

Capitalization

Long Term Debt: $4,058,000,000 (3/95).
Cum. Conv. Preferred Stock: $78,000,000.

Per Share Data ()

(Year Ended Dec. 31)

	1994	1993	1992	1991	1990	1989
Tangible Bk. Val.	11.01	10.57	11.35	12.44	13.14	13.25
Cash Flow	3.61	2.48	3.23	3.12	5.95	5.47
Earnings	1.10	-0.04	0.37	-0.31	1.94	1.49
Dividends	0.68	0.68	1.22	0.70	NM	NM
Payout Ratio	62%	NM	330%	NM	NM	NM
Prices - High	19⅛	20⅝	24¾	33⅛	NA	NA
- Low	15⅝	16⅜	15¾	20⅞	NA	NA
P/E Ratio - High	17	NM	67	NM	NA	NA
- Low	14	NM	43	NA	NA	NA

Income Statement Analysis ()

	1994	%Chg	1993	%Chg	1992	%Chg	1991
Revs.	10,215	2%	10,035	-10%	11,127	-10%	12,313
Oper. Inc.	1,305	46%	892	-25%	1,197	-3%	1,236
Depr.	721	NM	723	-11%	812	-7%	874
Int. Exp.	384	-1%	389	8%	359	-12%	407
Pretax Inc.	476	NM	-55.0	NM	201	NM	65.0
Eff. Tax Rate	33%	—	NM	—	46%	—	209%
Net Inc.	321	NM	-6.0	NM	109	NM	-71.0

Balance Sheet & Other Fin. Data ()

	1994	1993	1992	1991	1990	1989
Cash	28.0	185	35.0	200	193	490
Curr. Assets	1,737	1,598	1,934	2,153	2,357	2,381
Total Assets	10,951	10,806	11,141	11,644	11,931	12,622
Curr. Liab.	1,712	1,668	2,278	2,467	2,527	2,148
LT Debt	3,983	4,239	3,743	4,084	3,986	4,586
Common Eqty.	3,163	3,032	3,257	3,215	3,542	3,387
Total Cap.	8,676	8,572	8,307	8,856	9,091	10,162
Cap. Exp.	753	910	1,193	960	1,000	1,033
Cash Flow	1,036	711	915	796	1,519	1,408

Ratio Analysis

	1994	1993	1992	1991	1990	1989
Curr. Ratio	1.0	1.0	0.8	0.9	0.9	1.1
% LT Debt of Cap.	45.9	49.5	45.1	46.1	43.8	45.1
% Net Inc.of Revs.	3.1	NM	1.0	NM	3.8	3.8
% Ret. on Assets	2.9	NM	0.9	NM	4.1	3.3
% Ret. on Equity	10.2	NM	3.0	NM	13.9	11.4

Dividend Data (Dividends were initiated in 1991. A dividend reinvestment plan is available.)

Amt. of Div. $	Date Decl.	Ex-Div. Date	Stock of Record	Payment Date
0.170	Jul. 26	Aug. 01	Aug. 05	Sep. 10 '94
0.170	Oct. 25	Oct. 31	Nov. 04	Dec. 10 '94
0.170	Jan. 31	Feb. 10	Feb. 16	Mar. 10 '95
0.170	Apr. 25	May. 11	May. 17	Jun. 10 '95
0.170	Jul. 25	Aug. 14	Aug. 16	Sep. 09 '95

Data as orig. reptd.; bef. results of disc. opers. and/or spec. items. Per share data adj. for stk. divs. as of ex-div. date.
E-Estimated. NA-Not Available. NM-Not Meaningful. NR-Not Ranked.

Office—USX Corp., 600 Grant St., Pittsburgh, PA 15219-4776. Tel—(412) 433-1121. Marathon Oil—5555 San Felipe Rd., P.O. Box 3128, Houston, TX 77253-3128. Tel—(713) 629-6600. Chrmn & CEO—C. A. Corry. Pres & Vice Chrmn-Marathon Group—V. G. Beghini. Secy—W. F. Schwind Jr. EVP-CFO—R. M. Hernandez. VP-Investor Contact—Charles D. Williams. Dirs—N. A. Armstrong, V. G. Beghini, J. G. Brown, C. A. Corry, J. H. Filer, J. A. D. Geier, R. M. Hernandez, C. R. Lee, P. E. Lego, J. F. McGillicuddy, J. M. Richman, D. M. Roderick, J. W. Snow, D. R. Whitwam, D. C. Yearley. Transfer Agent—USX Corp., 600 Grant St., Pittsburgh, Pa. Registrar—Mellon Bank, Pittsburgh. Incorporated in New Jersey in 1901; reincorporated in Delaware in 1965. Empl-21,914. S&P Analyst: Raymond J. Deacon

UNUM Corp.

NYSE Symbol **UNM**
In S&P 500

22-AUG-95   Industry:
Insurance

Summary: UNUM offers a broad range of disability, health and life insurance and group pension products. The company is a leading provider of group long term disability insurance.

S&P Opinion: Hold (★★★)	Recent Price • 47⅜	Yield • 2.2%
	52 Wk Range • 50-35⅛	12-Mo. P/E • 23.3

Quantitative Evaluations

Outlook
(1 Lowest—5 Highest)
• **2⁻**

Fair Value
• **43¾**

Risk
• **Average**

Earn./Div. Rank
• **NR**

Technical Eval.
• **Bearish** since 7/95

Rel. Strength Rank
(1 Lowest—99 Highest)
• **52**

Insider Activity
• **NA**

Earnings vs. Previous Year
▲=Up ▼=Down ▶=No Change

10 Week Mov. Avg. - - -
30 Week Mov. Avg. · · · ·
Relative Strength ——

OPTIONS: ASE

Overview - 17-AUG-95

The rebound in operating earnings seen for 1995 is skewed by $192.4 million of additional reserves (taken to counter adverse individual disability claim trends) that hurt results in 1994. The decision to stop selling fixed-price, noncancellable individual disability insurance is positive, but near-term results will be hurt by the disruptive effects of restructuring this line. UNM is still a dominant underwriter of disability insurance--with a more than one-third share of the group long-term disability (LTD) market--and is therefore afforded a certain degree of pricing control. Expansion into supplemental insurance products will also aid results. UNM's decision in mid-1995 to liquidate its common stock portfolio and reinvest the proceeds in investment grade bonds should reduce balance sheet volatility. Repurchases of 7.6 million shares in 1993 and 1994 will aid per-share comparisons.

Valuation - 17-AUG-95

After a dismal performance during much of 1994 amid the negative effects of higher interest rates and adverse claim development in its individual disability lines, UNM's shares have rebounded nicely so far in 1995. Although we believe UNM's market dominance and high degree of specialization merits a slightly higher P/E multiple than that of a standard lines insurer, the shares are fairly valued near term at 12 times our aggressive 1995 operating earnings estimate of $3.90 a share (before realized investment gains or losses), in light of the somewhat diminished profit outlook in some key disability lines.

Key Stock Statistics

S&P EPS Est. 1995	3.90	Tang. Bk. Value/Share	28.07
P/E on S&P Est. 1995	12.1	Beta	1.18
S&P EPS Est. 1996	4.30	Shareholders	25,300
Dividend Rate/Share	1.06	Market cap. (B)	$ 3.5
Shs. outstg. (M)	72.6	Inst. holdings	75%
Avg. daily vol. (M)	0.139	Insider holdings	0%

Value of $10,000 invested 5 years ago: $ 21,703

Fiscal Year Ending Dec. 31

	1995	% Change	1994	% Change	1993	% Change
Revenues (Million $)						
1Q	955.1	9%	877.4	7%	822.6	27%
2Q	1,156	25%	928.0	9%	854.6	32%
3Q	—	—	890.5	5%	850.3	28%
4Q	—	—	927.8	7%	869.5	29%
Yr.	—	—	3,624	7%	3,397	29%
Income (Million $)						
1Q	63.40	-18%	77.10	1%	76.00	28%
2Q	88.90	4%	85.30	6%	80.80	28%
3Q	—	—	-61.70	NM	72.10	13%
4Q	—	—	54.00	-35%	83.10	33%
Yr.	—	—	154.7	-50%	312.0	25%
Earnings Per Share ($)						
1Q	0.87	-15%	1.02	6%	0.96	9%
2Q	1.22	7%	1.14	12%	1.02	9%
3Q	—	—	-0.84	NM	0.91	-4%
4Q	—	—	0.75	-31%	1.08	16%
Yr.	E3.90	87%	2.09	-47%	3.96	7%

Next earnings report expected: early November

Business Summary - 18-AUG-95

UNUM Corp. is the holding company for UNUM Life Insurance Co., formed in 1986 when Union Mutual converted from a mutual to a stock company. UNM offers a broad line of disability, health and life insurance and group pension products. Contributions to pretax income (in millions) were:

	1994	1993	1992
Employee benefits	$257.8	$239.1	$222.5
Related businesses	60.3	57.3	53.4
Colonial Cos.	62.7	70.4	60.5
Individual disability	-188.2	69.0	44.6
Retirement products	25.7	21.1	6.7
Corporate & other	-19.7	3.4	10.8

The Employee Benefits segment markets group disability, group life and specialty insurance products. The segment's principal product, accounting for 67% of its 1994 premiums, is group long-term disability insurance. Group term life and accidental death insurance products are also sold. The company also sells a flexible benefits product through which its various policies may be combined.

Related Businesses include Commercial Life Insurance Co., which markets disability, group life, travel and accidental death products; UNUM Ltd., a provider of group long-term disability in the U.K.; and LTD Reinsurance, a specialty reinsurer. The Colonial Companies (acquired in 1993) market life and health products, mainly through payroll deduction.

Individual Disability products, which had been sold on a noncancellable basis, are being discontinued. A new line of individual disability products is being introduced.

The Retirement Products segment markets tax-sheltered annuities to non-profit organizations and offers long-term care insurance to employer groups and other healthcare sponsors.

Important Developments

Jun. '95—UNM unveiled a new individual disability product to replace its traditional non-cancellable individual disability product. After a $192.4 million reserve boost taken to cover adverse claim trends in the individual disability line impaired profitability in 1994, UNM stopped selling fixed-price, noncancellable individual disability policies in the U.S. First half 1995 results included an additional $3.2 million net charge for final costs associated with discontinuing this product. UNM also made a $108.6 million net addition to certain other disability and life insurance reserves during 1995's second quarter.

Capitalization

Long Term Debt: $180,800,000 (3/95).

Per Share Data ($)

	(Year Ended Dec. 31)					
	1994	1993	1992	1991	1990	1989
Tangible Bk. Val.	26.45	27.67	24.93	22.10	18.63	17.09
Oper. Earnings	1.67	3.55	3.35	2.95	2.60	1.86
Earnings	2.09	3.96	3.70	3.08	2.69	1.94
Dividends	0.92	0.76	0.63	0.49	0.38	0.29
Payout Ratio	44%	19%	17%	16%	14%	15%
Prices - High	58	60⅛	54⅜	40½	28⅝	24½
- Low	35⅛	47¾	32	20¾	16⅛	13⅜
P/E Ratio - High	28	15	15	13	11	13
- Low	23	12	9	7	6	7

Income Statement Analysis (Million $)

	1994	%Chg	1993	%Chg	1992	%Chg	1991
Life Ins. In Force	145,426	12%	130,323	32%	98,657	16%	84,794
Premium Income Life	504	6%	477	29%	370	15%	322
Prem.Inc A & H	2,207	12%	1,972	43%	1,376	8%	1,270
Premium Income Other	21.3	-17%	25.7	-20%	32.1	33%	24.2
Net Invest. Inc.	770	-3%	790	1%	779	NM	773
Total Revs.	3,624	7%	3,397	29%	2,641	9%	2,421
Pretax Inc.	199	-57%	460	36%	338	29%	262
Net Oper. Inc.	NA	—	NA	—	225	15%	196
Net Inc.	155	-50%	312	25%	249	21%	205

Balance Sheet & Other Fin. Data (Million $)

	1994	1993	1992	1991	1990	1989
Cash & Equiv.	232	205	195	203	166	133
Premiums Due	190	166	142	130	106	85.0
Inv Assets Bonds	7,868	7,433	6,837	6,309	5,535	4,779
Inv. Assets Stock	628	730	572	545	466	464
Inv. Assets Loans	1,417	1,611	1,830	2,006	2,142	2,243
Inv. Assets Total	10,434	10,096	9,516	9,147	8,450	7,650
Deferred Policy Cost	1,035	879	568	482	401	350
Total Assets	13,127	12,437	11,214	10,668	9,514	8,556
Debt	182	129	75.8	50.0	75.7	Nil
Common Eqty.	1,915	2,103	1,687	1,468	1,237	1,213

Ratio Analysis

	1994	1993	1992	1991	1990	1989
% Ret. on Revs.	4.3	9.2	9.4	8.5	8.5	8.0
% Ret. on Assets	1.2	2.6	2.3	2.0	2.0	1.9
% Ret. on Equity	7.7	15.2	15.8	15.1	15.1	12.3
% Invest. Yield	7.5	7.9	8.4	8.8	9.0	9.2

Dividend Data —Dividend were initiated in 1987. A dividend reinvestment plan is available. A new "poison pill" stock purchase right was adopted in 1992.

Amt. of Div. $	Date Decl.	Ex-Div. Date	Stock of Record	Payment Date
0.240	Jul. 18	Jul. 19	Jul. 25	Aug. 19 '94
0.240	Oct. 13	Oct. 25	Oct. 31	Nov. 18 '94
0.240	Jan. 13	Jan. 24	Jan. 30	Feb. 17 '95
0.265	Apr. 11	Apr. 18	Apr. 24	May. 19 '95
0.265	Jul. 14	Jul. 27	Jul. 31	Aug. 18 '95

Data as orig. reptd.; bef. results of disc. opers. and/or spec. items. Per share data adj. for stk. divs. as of ex-div. date. Historical EPS data includes realized inv. gains & losses; estimates do not. E-Estimated. NA-Not Available. NM-Not Meaningful. NR-Not Ranked.

Office—2211 Congress St., Portland, ME 04122. **Tel**—(207) 770-2211. **Chrmn & CEO**—J. F. Orr III. **Sr VP-CFO**—R. N. Hook. **Secy**—K. J. Tierney. **VP-Investor Contact**—Kent W. Mohnkern (207) 770-4330. **Dirs**—G. O. Averyt, K. S. Axelson, R. E. Dillon Jr., G. H. Gillespie, R. E. Goldsberry, D. W. Harward, G. J. Mitchell, C. A. Montgomery, J. L. Moody Jr., J. F. Orr III, L. R. Pugh, L. D. Rice, J. W. Rowe. **Transfer Agent & Registrar**—First Chicago Trust Co.of New York, NYC. **Incorporated** in Delaware in 1985. **Empl**- 7,200. **S&P Analyst:** Catherine A. Seifert

USF&G Corp.

NYSE Symbol **FG**
In S&P 500

17-AUG-95 Industry: Insurance

Summary: USF&G is the 25th largest property-casualty insurer in the U.S., offering an array of commercial and personal lines coverage. To a lesser degree, life insurance is also offered.

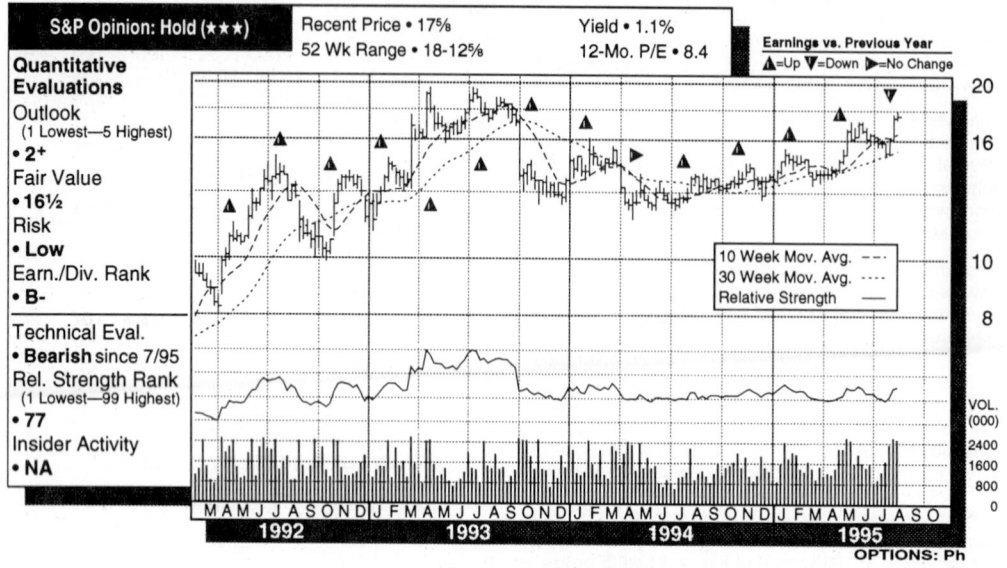

S&P Opinion: Hold (★★★)		
Recent Price • 17⅞	Yield • 1.1%	
52 Wk Range • 18-12⅝	12-Mo. P/E • 8.4	

Quantitative Evaluations

Outlook
(1 Lowest—5 Highest)
• **2+**

Fair Value
• **16½**

Risk
• **Low**

Earn./Div. Rank
• **B-**

Technical Eval.
• **Bearish** since 7/95

Rel. Strength Rank
(1 Lowest—99 Highest)
• **77**

Insider Activity
• **NA**

Earnings vs. Previous Year
▲=Up ▼=Down ▶=No Change

10 Week Mov. Avg. ---
30 Week Mov. Avg. ......
Relative Strength —

VOL. (000)

OPTIONS: Ph

Overview - 17-AUG-95

The decline in operating earnings projected for 1995 is skewed by $281 million of special tax credits that helped boost results in 1994. That aside, the positive effects of a multi-year restructuring plan, together with improved underwriting results, should improve operating earnings in 1995. While written premium levels will decline by around 5%-10%, this is largely due to a reduced exposure to certain loss-ridden lines such as workers' compensation. Still, intense price competition in many of FG's core lines (like general liability) will limit near term premium growth. However, attempts to venture into more specialized (and less price-competitive) lines of business, like nonstandard auto via the acquisition of Victoria Financial, enhance long term prospects. Investment income growth will be modest, reflecting a shift to higher quality, lower yielding securities.

Valuation - 17-AUG-95

After a mixed performance during much of 1994 due to the negative effects of rising interest rates and higher industry-wide catastrophe losses, FG shares have rebounded during 1995 and now trade at approximately 13 times our 1995 operating earnings estimate of $1.35 a share (which excludes realized investment gains or losses). Although the positive effects of a multi-year restructuring aid FG's long term prospects, the shares are fairly valued near term in light of the company's declining (near term) premium base and average underwriting record.

Key Stock Statistics

S&P EPS Est. 1995	1.35	Tang. Bk. Value/Share	12.04
P/E on S&P Est. 1995	13.1	Beta	1.02
S&P EPS Est. 1996	1.55	Shareholders	33,700
Dividend Rate/Share	0.20	Market cap. (B)	$ 2.0
Shs. outstg. (M)	110.7	Inst. holdings	42%
Avg. daily vol. (M)	0.629	Insider holdings	NA

Value of $10,000 invested 5 years ago: $ 9,389

Fiscal Year Ending Dec. 31

	1995	% Change	1994	% Change	1993	% Change
Revenues (Million $)						
1Q	795.0	4%	766.0	-12%	875.0	—
2Q	—	—	791.0	-4%	820.0	—
3Q	—	—	811.0	7%	755.0	-25%
4Q	—	—	853.0	7%	799.0	NM
Yr.	—	—	3,221	NM	3,249	-11%
Income (Million $)						
1Q	49.00	113%	23.00	NM	23.00	NM
2Q	46.00	-37%	73.00	192%	25.00	NM
3Q	—	—	74.00	NM	20.00	82%
4Q	—	—	62.00	5%	59.00	NM
Yr.	—	—	232.0	83%	127.0	NM
Earnings Per Share ($)						
1Q	0.42	NM	0.13	NM	0.13	NM
2Q	0.35	-51%	0.72	NM	0.15	NM
3Q	—	—	0.72	NM	0.10	NM
4Q	—	—	0.57	4%	0.55	NM
Yr.	E1.35	-37%	2.14	130%	0.93	NM

Next earnings report expected: late October

Business Summary - 16-AUG-95

USF&G Corp. (formerly U.S. Fidelity & Guaranty) derives most of its earnings from property-casualty insurance operations. Products are sold primarily through a network of about 3,800 independent agents in the U.S. Revenue sources:

	1994	1993	1992
Prop.-cas. premiums:			
Commercial	37%	37%	41%
Fidelity-surety	4%	4%	3%
Personal	18%	21%	22%
Reinsurance	12%	9%	4%
Life ins. premiums	5%	4%	3%
Net invest. inc.	23%	23%	22%
Other	1%	2%	5%

Property-casualty premiums written totaled $2.3 billion in 1994 ($2.4 billion in 1993), of which personal lines accounted for 25%, reinsurance 18%, commercial auto 16%, general liability 15%, commercial property 14%, workers' compensation 6%, and fidelity and surety 6%. Life insurance in force at 1994 year end was $10.6 billion, of which individual permanent equaled 54%, and term 46%.

At March 31, 1995, the $10.6 billion investment portfolio was comprised of 83% bonds, 9% mortgages and real estate (net of reserves), 3% short-term investments, 1% equities, and 4% other.

Important Developments

May '95—FG completed its acquisition of Victoria Financial Corp. (NASDAQ:VICF) for $59 million of common stock, or about $13.85 per VICR share. The final purchase price was somewhat higher than earlier estimates of $55.3 million due to the subsequent appreciation of FG's stock price. The purchase of this regional, nonstandard auto insurer marks FG's entree into the market for substandard or high risk auto insurance. At September 30, 1994 VICR had shareholders' equity of $27.2 million.

Apr. '95—The company acquired Discover Re Managers, Inc. for approximately 5.4 million common shares plus options to purchase an additional 700,000 common shares. Discover Re offers insurance and related services to the alternative risk transfer market.

Capitalization

Total Debt: $632,000,000 (3/95).

$4.10 Conv. Exch. Preferred Stock: 4,000,000 shs. ($50 par); ea. conv. into 1.192 com. shs.

$10.25 Ser. B Cum. Conv. Preferred Stock: 1,300,000 shs. ($50 par); ea. conv. into 8.316 com. shs.

Per Share Data ($)　　　　　(Year Ended Dec. 31)

	1994	1993	1992	1991	1990	1989
Tangible Bk. Val.	10.86	12.42	8.87	9.53	10.78	19.79
Oper. Earnings	2.00	NA	-1.91	-2.60	-1.48	1.57
Earnings	2.14	0.93	-0.16	-2.15	-5.71	1.21
Dividends	0.15	0.20	0.20	0.20	2.44	2.80
Payout Ratio	7%	22%	NM	NM	NM	231%
Prices - High	16⅛	19⅝	15	12½	30⅜	34
- Low	11⅝	11⅛	7⅛	5⅝	7	28¼
P/E Ratio - High	8	21	NM	NM	NM	28
- Low	5	12	NM	NM	NM	23

Income Statement Analysis (Million $)

	1994	%Chg	1993	%Chg	1992	%Chg	1991
Premium Income	2,435	NM	2,456	-7%	2,637	-17%	3,187
Net Invest. Inc.	743	NM	749	-8%	817	-7%	877
Oth. Revs.	43.0	-2%	44.0	-24%	58.0	-17%	70.0
Total Revs.	3,221	NM	3,249	-11%	3,660	-11%	4,134
Pretax Inc.	-49.0	NM	99	183%	35.0	NM	-140
Net Oper. Inc.	NA	—	NA	—	-111	NM	-181
Net Inc.	232	83%	127	NM	35.0	NM	-143

Balance Sheet & Other Fin. Data (Million $)

	1994	1993	1992	1991	1990	1989
Cash & Equiv.	67.0	17.0	25.0	87.0	221	280
Premiums Due	697	656	725	897	891	708
Inv. Assets Bonds	8,631	9,205	9,723	10,283	8,364	8,173
Inv. Assets Stock	70.0	135	171	521	459	1,638
Inv. Assets Loans	349	302	186	283	269	363
Inv. Assets Total	10,421	11,377	11,346	12,167	11,239	11,012
Deferred Policy Cost	495	435	466	504	536	458
Total Assets	13,774	14,335	11,864	14,456	13,910	13,604
Debt	401	211	238	277	333	291
Common Eqty.	1,038	1,056	815	868	1,005	1,807

Ratio Analysis

	1994	1993	1992	1991	1990	1989
Prop&Cas Loss	73.1	75.4	82.0	84.1	81.9	76.5
Prop&Cas Expense	35.0	33.7	34.9	33.1	32.9	32.8
Prop&Cas Comb.	108.1	109.1	116.9	117.2	114.8	109.3
% Ret. on Revs.	7.2	3.9	1.0	NM	NM	2.5
% Return on Equity	17.8	8.4	NM	NM	NM	5.5

Dividend Data—Common dividends have been paid since 1939. A dividend reinvestment plan is available. A "poison pill" stock purchase right was adopted in 1987.

Amt. of Div. $	Date Decl.	Ex-Div. Date	Stock of Record	Payment Date
0.050	Sep. 28	Oct. 11	Oct. 17	Oct. 31 '94
0.050	Dec. 19	Jan. 03	Jan. 09	Jan. 31 '95
0.050	Feb. 01	Apr. 04	Apr. 10	Apr. 28 '95
0.050	Apr. 26	Jul. 13	Jul. 17	Jul. 31 '95
0.050	Jul. 26	Oct. 13	Oct. 17	Oct. 31 '95

Data as orig. reptd.; bef. results of disc. opers. and/or spec. items. Per share data adj. for stk. divs. as of ex-div. date. Historical EPS data includes realized gains and losses; estimates do not. E-Estimated. NA-Not Available. NM-Not Meaningful. NR-Not Ranked.

Office—100 Light St., Baltimore, MD 21202. **Tel**—(410) 547-3000. **Chrmn, CEO & Pres**—N. P. Blake Jr. **EVP-CFO**—D. L. Hale. **VP & Treas**—R. P. Campagna. **Investor Contact**—Jennifer Macke. **Dirs**—H. F. Baldwin, M. J. Birck, N. P. Blake, Jr., G. L. Bunting Jr., R. E. Davis, D. F. Frey, R. E. Gregory Jr., R. J. Hurst, W. G. Lewellen, H. A. Rosenberg, Jr., L. P. Scriggins, A. M. Whittemore. **Transfer Agent & Registrar**—First Chicago Trust Co. of New York, NYC. **Incorporated** in Maryland in 1896. **Empl**-6,300. **S&P Analyst:** Catherine A. Seifert

UST Inc.

NYSE Symbol **UST**
In S&P 500

22-OCT-95

Industry:
Tobacco

Summary: This company is a leading producer of moist smokeless tobacco products marketed under such leading brand names as Copenhagen and Skoal.

S&P Opinion: Hold (★★★)	Recent Price • 29⅞	Yield • 4.4%
	52 Wk Range • 32⅝-25⅞	12-Mo. P/E • 14.4

Quantitative Evaluations

Outlook
(1 Lowest—5 Highest)
• **5+**

Fair Value
• **34⅛**

Risk
• **Low**

Earn./Div. Rank
• **A+**

Technical Eval.
• **Bullish** since 10/95

Rel. Strength Rank
(1 Lowest—99 Highest)
• **65**

Insider Activity
• **Neutral**

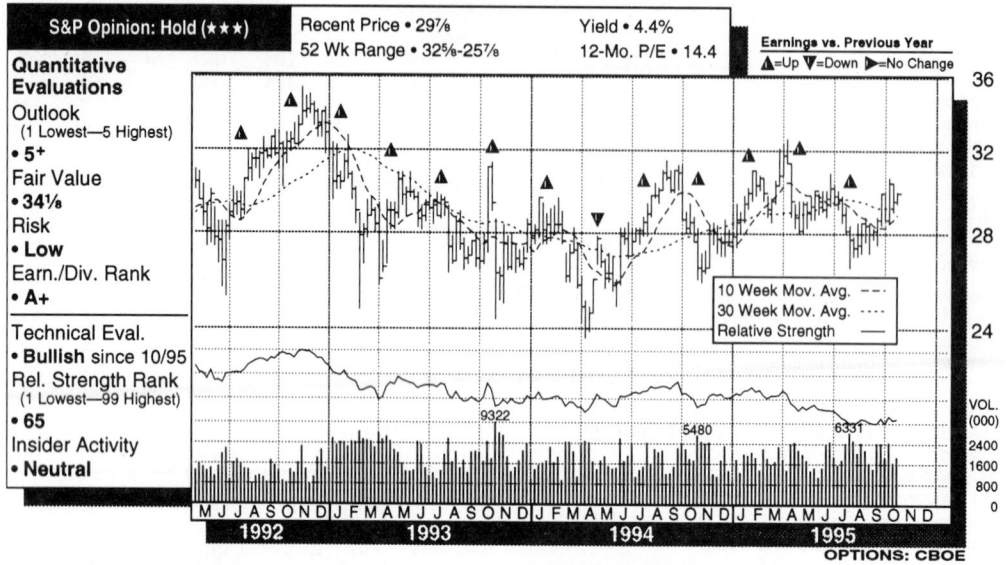

Earnings vs. Previous Year
▲=Up ▼=Down ▶=No Change

10 Week Mov. Avg. ---
30 Week Mov. Avg. ····
Relative Strength —

OPTIONS: CBOE

Overview - 20-OCT-95

In the likely absence of significantly higher near-term federal excise taxes on tobacco products or alcoholic beverages, net sales should continue to grow about 10% a year through 1996, primarily reflecting higher selling prices for the company's moist smokeless tobacco products, and to lesser extent, modestly higher (1% to 2%) unit volumes. Operating margins are expected to benefit from the increased prices, and from improved productivity. Earnings per share gains in the low double-digits are expected, assuming continued aggressive share repurchases (3% to 5% a year). Skoal Flavor Packs, a new tobacco product targeted at smokers, is currently being rolled out.

Valuation - 20-OCT-95

Given the recent slowdown in unit volume growth for UST's important moist smokeless tobacco products, we expect that profit growth will slow in the near-term from the 15% to 20% annual gains recorded in the recent past. Management has responded to the challenge by replacing management at its tobacco segment, and is in the midst of rolling out a new product (Skoal Flavor Packs) in the hope of rejuvenating its volume growth. Although it is too early to tell whether UST's recent actions will accelerate volume gains, we expect that earnings per share through 1996 will still grow at a double-digit rate. Although tobacco stocks in general carry an above-average amount of risk, we recommend holding the shares based on their relatively high dividend yield, strong balance sheet, and historically high returns on invested capital.

Key Stock Statistics

S&P EPS Est. 1995	2.15	Tang. Bk. Value/Share	2.05
P/E on S&P Est. 1995	13.9	Beta	1.08
S&P EPS Est. 1996	2.45	Shareholders	13,100
Dividend Rate/Share	1.30	Market cap. (B)	$ 5.8
Shs. outstg. (M)	195.2	Inst. holdings	55%
Avg. daily vol. (M)	0.399	Insider holdings	NA

Value of $10,000 invested 5 years ago: $ 23,353

Fiscal Year Ending Dec. 31

	1995	% Change	1994	% Change	1993	% Change
Revenues (Million $)						
1Q	306.1	9%	280.4	6%	265.0	12%
2Q	340.2	10%	310.2	11%	279.9	6%
3Q	334.3	8%	310.4	11%	279.0	2%
4Q	—	—	322.1	12%	286.7	5%
Yr.	—	—	1,223	10%	1,110	6%
Income (Million $)						
1Q	99.2	12%	88.76	-14%	103.6	48%
2Q	109.9	10%	99.5	11%	89.84	15%
3Q	110.0	10%	100.3	13%	88.70	5%
4Q	—	—	98.95	14%	86.80	9%
Yr.	—	—	387.5	5%	368.9	18%
Earnings Per Share ($)						
1Q	0.49	17%	0.42	-11%	0.47	52%
2Q	0.55	15%	0.48	17%	0.41	17%
3Q	0.55	15%	0.48	17%	0.41	8%
4Q	E0.56	14%	0.49	20%	0.41	14%
Yr.	E2.15	15%	1.87	9%	1.71	21%

Next earnings report expected: mid January

Business Summary - 20-OCT-95

UST Inc. (formerly U.S. Tobacco) is the leading U.S. manufacturer of smokeless tobacco (snuff and chewing tobacco); imports and sells other tobacco products; and produces and sells wine. Segment contributions (profits in million $) in 1994 were:

	Sales	Profits
Tobacco	86%	$653.7
Wine	7%	8.8
Other	7%	1.5

Smokeless tobacco products include Copenhagen and Skoal, the world's two largest selling brands of moist smokeless tobacco. Moist brands also include Skoal Long Cut and Skoal Bandits. Other tobacco products carry the Bruton, CC, Red Seal, and WB Cut tradenames. The company sells tobacco products throughout the U.S., principally to chain stores and tobacco and grocery wholesalers. In 1986, federal legislation was enacted regulating smokeless tobacco products by requiring health warning notices on smokeless tobacco packages and advertising, and prohibiting the advertising of smokeless tobacco products on electronic media.

Wines consist of premium varietal and blended wines dominated by Washington state-produced Chateau Ste. Michelle and Columbia Crest and two premium-quality California wines: Conn Creek and Villa Mt. Eden.

In March 31, 1993, UST sold the distribution rights for Zig Zag cigarette papers and related products for $39 million in cash, plus additional consideration based on future earnings over 10 years. None of its other remaining businesses (including pipes and international operations) constitute a material portion of operations.

Important Developments

Oct. '95—During 1995's first nine months, operating income advanced 10%, year to year, on a 9% rise in sales. After a lower effective tax rate of 39.0%, versus 39.5% (the benefit of which was offset in part by substantially greater net interest expense), net income rose 11%. Earnings per share increased 15%, to $1.59 on 4.2% fewer shares, from $1.38. Higher selling prices of moist smokeless tobacco products was the principal factor behind the greater company sales and profits, as domestic unit volume for moist smokeless tobacco in the first nine months rose only 0.5%, to 471.8 million cans. The company's Wine segment also posted a sales gain in the period, while sales for the Other segment were lower.

Capitalization

Long Term Debt: $125,000,000 (6/95).

Per Share Data ($) (Year Ended Dec. 31)

	1994	1993	1992	1991	1990	1989
Tangible Bk. Val.	1.79	2.20	2.38	2.22	2.19	2.19
Cash Flow	2.00	1.83	1.51	1.28	1.07	0.89
Earnings	1.87	1.71	1.41	1.18	0.98	0.82
Dividends	1.12	0.96	0.80	0.66	0.55	0.46
Payout Ratio	60%	56%	54%	52%	52%	53%
Prices - High	31½	32¾	35⅜	34	18¼	15⅜
- Low	23⅝	24⅜	25¼	16⅜	12⅜	9¾
P/E Ratio - High	17	19	25	29	19	19
- Low	13	14	18	14	13	12

Income Statement Analysis (Million $)

	1994	%Chg	1993	%Chg	1992	%Chg	1991
Revs.	1,198	11%	1,080	7%	1,013	15%	880
Oper. Inc.	669	13%	591	13%	524	17%	446
Depr.	28.2	9%	25.9	10%	23.6	6%	22.3
Int. Exp.	4.6	NM	1.2	70%	0.7	7%	0.7
Pretax Inc.	641	6%	602	20%	503	18%	426
Eff. Tax Rate	40%	—	39%	—	38%	—	38%
Net Inc.	388	5%	369	18%	313	18%	266

Balance Sheet & Other Fin. Data (Million $)

	1994	1993	1992	1991	1990	1989
Cash	50.7	25.3	36.4	41.5	46.6	54.6
Curr. Assets	382	335	330	305	266	280
Total Assets	741	706	674	657	623	636
Curr. Liab.	161	107	81.2	95.5	68.7	92.1
LT Debt	125	40.0	Nil	Nil	3.1	6.8
Common Eqty.	362	463	517	483	474	482
Total Cap.	492	511	563	534	530	544
Cap. Exp.	27.7	54.5	34.0	41.5	26.9	35.8
Cash Flow	416	395	336	288	243	207

Ratio Analysis

	1994	1993	1992	1991	1990	1989
Curr. Ratio	2.4	3.1	4.1	3.2	3.9	3.0
% LT Debt of Cap.	25.4	7.8	Nil	Nil	0.6	1.2
% Net Inc.of Revs.	32.4	34.1	30.9	30.2	29.7	28.4
% Ret. on Assets	54.7	54.2	47.0	41.8	35.9	31.0
% Ret. on Equity	96.3	76.5	62.5	55.8	47.3	40.9

Dividend Data

—Dividends have been paid since 1912. A dividend reinvestment plan is available.

Amt. of Div. $	Date Decl.	Ex-Div. Date	Stock of Record	Payment Date
0.280	Oct. 27	Nov. 29	Dec. 05	Dec. 15 '94
0.325	Dec. 15	Feb. 27	Mar. 03	Mar. 15 '95
0.325	May. 02	May. 30	Jun. 05	Jun. 15 '95
0.325	Jul. 26	Aug. 31	Sep. 05	Sep. 15 '95

Data as orig. reptd.; bef. results of disc. opers. and/or spec. items. Per share data adj. for stk. divs. as of ex-div. date. E-Estimated. NA-Not Available. NM-Not Meaningful. NR-Not Ranked.

Office—100 West Putnam Ave., Greenwich, CT 06830. **Tel**—(203) 661-1100. **Chrmn, Pres & CEO**—V. A. Gierer Jr. **EVP & CFO**—J. J. Bucchignano. **VP & Secy**—J. P. Nelson. **Investor Contact**—Mark Rozelle. **Dirs**—L. F. Bantle, J. J. Bucchignano, J. W. Chapin, E. H. DeHority Jr., V. A. Gierer Jr., P. X. Kelley, A. H. Leader, R. L. Rossi, S. R. Stuart, J. P. Warwick. **Transfer Agent & Registrar**—First National Bank of Boston. **Incorporated** in New Jersey in 1911; reincorporated in Delaware in 1986. **Empl**- 3,817. **S&P Analyst:** Kenneth A. Shea

USX-U.S. Steel Group

NYSE Symbol **X**
In S&P 500

22-SEP-95

Industry:
Steel-Iron

Summary: This company, USX Corp.'s steel segment, is the largest U.S. integrated steelmaker.

S&P Opinion: Hold (★★★)	Recent Price • 33	Yield • 3.1%
	52 Wk Range • 43-29¼	12-Mo. P/E • 8.0

Quantitative Evaluations

Outlook
(1 Lowest—5 Highest)
• **5⁻**

Fair Value
• **45½**

Risk
• **Average**

Earn./Div. Rank
• **NR**

Technical Eval.
• **Bearish** since 7/95

Rel. Strength Rank
(1 Lowest—99 Highest)
• **18**

Insider Activity
• **NA**

Earnings vs. Previous Year
▲=Up ▼=Down ▶=No Change

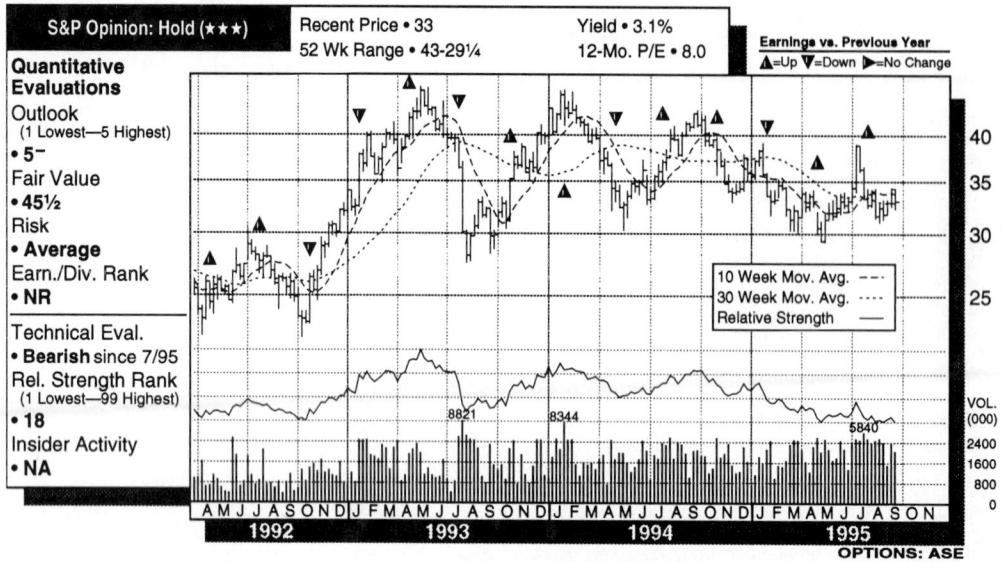

10 Week Mov. Avg. ---
30 Week Mov. Avg. ....
Relative Strength —

8821 8344 5840

VOL. (000)
2400
1600
800
0

40
35
30
25

A M J J A S O N D J F M A M J J A S O N D J F M A M J J A S O N D J F M A M J J A S O N
1992   1993   1994   1995

OPTIONS: ASE

Overview - 22-SEP-95

Assuming GDP growth of 2.6% in 1996, we anticipate a 10% rise in sales on increased volume and higher prices for steel, coke and coal products. The gain in steel will mainly reflect a rebound in sheet prices and continued strength in plate and oil country tubular goods. With lower exports and increased shipments to capital goods markets, the mix will improve in 1996. Coke and coal sales should increase, as a result of greater demand from other domestic steelmakers. Aided by only a small increase in raw material costs, higher levels of equity income and lower interest costs, net income and earnings should rise again in 1996. Long term sales and profits should rise on an upturn in demand for oil country tubular goods, an improved product mix, asset sales, lower interest costs and investment in technology joint ventures.

Valuation - 22-SEP-95

Although X's sales are attractive based on 1996's projected earnings, we are maintaining our hold ranking on the shares for the near-term. This is due mostly to the negative stock market psychology toward cyclical issues in general and steel stocks in particular. Through late September, X's shares are down 11%, versus a 24% increase in the S&P 500 and an 11% decline in the S&P Steel Stock Index. Given the negative price action and the prospects for improvement in 1996, we believe there is little downside from current levels. On the other hand, it is too early to turn positive and accumulate the shares. We prefer the sidelines for now.

Key Stock Statistics

S&P EPS Est. 1995	3.65	Tang. Bk. Value/Share	12.72
P/E on S&P Est. 1995	9.0	Beta	NA
S&P EPS Est. 1996	4.75	Shareholders	83,300
Dividend Rate/Share	1.00	Market cap. (B)	$ 2.6
Shs. outstg. (M)	81.7	Inst. holdings	61%
Avg. daily vol. (M)	0.459	Insider holdings	NA

Value of $10,000 invested 5 years ago: NA

Fiscal Year Ending Dec. 31

	1995	% Change	1994	% Change	1993	% Change
Revenues (Million $)						
1Q	1,577	14%	1,384	15%	1,208	3%
2Q	1,623	6%	1,534	7%	1,427	13%
3Q	—	—	1,505	5%	1,429	12%
4Q	—	—	1,643	6%	1,548	25%
Yr.	—	—	6,066	8%	5,612	13%
Income (Million $)						
1Q	74.00	NM	-35.00	NM	10.00	NM
2Q	81.00	45%	56.00	NM	-336.0	NM
3Q	—	—	90.00	173%	33.00	NM
4Q	—	—	90.00	-27%	124.0	NM
Yr.	—	—	201.0	NM	-169.0	NM
Earnings Per Share ($)						
1Q	0.89	NM	-0.56	NM	0.13	NM
2Q	0.99	52%	0.65	NM	-5.71	NM
3Q	E0.85	-23%	1.11	171%	0.41	NM
4Q	E0.92	-17%	1.11	-34%	1.67	NM
Yr.	E3.65	55%	2.35	NM	-2.96	NM

Next earnings report expected: late October

Business Summary - 18-SEP-95

The U.S. Steel Group consists of USX Corp.'s steel segment (USS), the largest U.S. domestic integrated steel producer, and related businesses. Contributions in 1994 were:

	Sales	Profits
Steel & related	98%	76%
Other	2%	24%

The steel and related unit consists mostly of the production and sale of a wide range of steel mill products, taconite pellets and coke.

In 1994, raw steel production totaled 11.7 million tons (11.3 million in 1993), coke production was 6.8 million tons (6.4).

USS's raw steel making facilities operated at 97.4% of capacity in 1994 (95.6% in 1993). The continuous casting rate was 100% in 1994 and 1993. Steel shipments were 10.6 million tons in 1994 (10.0 million). Iron ore pellet shipments were 16.2 million tons in 1994, versus 15.9 million tons in 1993. Coal shipments were 7.7 million tons in 1994, versus 11.0 million tons in 1993.

Steel mill products include sheet, strip and tin mill products (77% of 1994 shipments), plates and other steel mill products (17%), tubular products (6%).

Steel shipments by major market in 1994 were as follows: service centers (26%), converters (23%), transportation (19%), containers (9%), construction (7%), exports (4%) and all other (12%).

The other businesses includes operations in real estate, fencing products, leasing and financial activities and a majority interest in a titanium metal products company.

U.S. Steel Group participates in several joint ventures that are accounted for under the equity method: Double Eagle Steel Coating Co., USS-POSCO Industries, USS/Kobe Steel Co., Worthington Specialty Processing, Transtar Inc., PRO-TEC Coating Co. and National-Oilwell.

Important Developments

Aug. '95—USX Corp. announced that it will call for redemption all the outstanding shares of its adjustable rate preferred stock on September 29, 1995.
Jul. '95— X said that it will build a $50 million coated steel processing line at its Fairfield Works plant. The line will be capable producing 260,000 tons annually of zinc and zinc aluminum sheet products. Production was expected to begin in late 1996.
May '95—USX Corp. and Armco Inc. signed a letter of intent for the sale of jointly owned National-Oilwell partnership. Terms of the sale, expected to close in the 1995 third quarter, were not disclosed.

Capitalization

Long Term Debt: $1,147,000,000 (6/95).
Preferred Stock: $32,000,000.

Per Share Data ($) (Year Ended Dec. 31)

	1994	1993	1992	1991	1990	1989
Tangible Bk. Val.	11.25	7.22	3.18	32.01	40.62	38.03
Cash Flow	6.52	1.93	0.25	-5.02	11.44	16.13
Earnings	2.35	-2.96	-4.92	-10.00	6.00	10.17
Dividends	1.00	1.00	1.00	0.50	NM	NM
Payout Ratio	43%	34%	NM	NM	NM	NM
Prices - High	45⅝	46	34⅜	30¼	NA	NA
- Low	30¼	27½	22⅛	20	NA	NA
P/E Ratio - High	19	NM	NM	NM	NA	NA
- Low	13	NM	NM	NA	NA	NA

Income Statement Analysis (Million $)

	1994	%Chg	1993	%Chg	1992	%Chg	1991
Revs.	6,066	8%	5,612	13%	4,947	2%	4,864
Oper. Inc.	627	14%	549	NM	85.0	124%	38.0
Depr.	314	NM	314	9%	288	14%	253
Int. Exp.	160	-52%	336	78%	189	-2%	192
Pretax Inc.	248	NM	-209	NM	-393	NM	-755
Eff. Tax Rate	19%	—	NM	—	NM	—	NM
Net Inc.	201	NM	-168	NM	-270	NM	-506

Balance Sheet & Other Fin. Data (Million $)

	1994	1993	1992	1991	1990	1989
Cash	20.0	79.0	22.0	79.0	70.0	296
Curr. Assets	1,780	1,575	1,321	1,292	1,541	1,217
Total Assets	6,480	6,616	6,251	5,627	5,582	5,499
Curr. Liab.	1,267	1,621	1,263	1,193	1,020	1,177
LT Debt	1,432	1,540	2,132	1,848	1,404	1,393
Common Eqty.	913	585	222	1,667	2,219	1,968
Total Cap.	2,441	2,162	2,395	3,577	3,738	3,448
Cap. Exp.	248	198	298	432	574	399
Cash Flow	490	124	14.0	-255	585	831

Ratio Analysis

	1994	1993	1992	1991	1990	1989
Curr. Ratio	1.4	1.0	1.0	1.1	1.5	1.0
% LT Debt of Cap.	58.7	71.2	89.0	51.7	37.6	40.4
% Net Inc.of Revs.	3.3	NM	NM	NM	5.1	8.3
% Ret. on Assets	3.0	NM	NM	NM	5.4	9.4
% Ret. on Equity	22.8	NM	NM	NM	14.3	30.3

Dividend Data —Common stock dividends are based primarily on long-term earnings and cash flow capabilities of the U.S. Steel Group, as well as on the policies of publicly traded steel companies. A dividend reinvestment plan is available.

Amt. of Div. $	Date Decl.	Ex-Div. Date	Stock of Record	Payment Date
0.250	Oct. 25	Oct. 31	Nov. 04	Dec. 10 '94
0.250	Jan. 31	Feb. 10	Feb. 16	Mar. 10 '95
0.250	Apr. 25	May. 11	May. 17	Jun. 10 '95
0.250	Jul. 25	Aug. 14	Aug. 16	Sep. 09 '95

Data as orig. reptd.; bef. results of disc. opers. and/or spec. items. Per share data adj. for stk. divs. as of ex-div. date.
E-Estimated. NA-Not Available. NM-Not Meaningful. NR-Not Ranked.

Office—600 Grant St., Pittsburgh, PA 15219-4776. **Tel**—(412) 433-1121. **Chrmn & CEO**—T. J. Usher. **Vice Chrmn & CFO**—R. M. Hernandez. **Secy**—D. A. Sandman. **Pres U.S. Steel Group**—P. J. Wilhelm. **Investor Contact**—Charles D. Williams. **Dirs**—N. A. Armstrong, V. G. Beghini, J. G. Brown, C. A. Corry, J. A. Geier, R. M. Hernandez, C. R. Lee, P. E. Lego, R. Marshall, J. F. McGillicuddy, J. M. Richman, S. E. Schofield, J. W. Snow, T. J. Usher, D. C. Yearley. **Transfer Agent**—Co.'s office. **Registrar**—Mellon Bank, Pittsburgh. **Incorporated** in New Jersey in 1901; reincorporated in Delaware in 1965. **Empl**-21,310. **S&P Analyst:** Leo Larkin

Unicom

NYSE Symbol **UCM**
In S&P 500

31-AUG-95

Industry:
Utilities-Electric

Summary: This electric utility holding company (formerly Commonwealth Edison) serves more than 3.3 million customers in the diverse economy of northern Illinois.

S&P Opinion: Hold (★★★)	Recent Price • 28¼	Yield • 5.6%
	52 Wk Range • 28⅜-20%	12-Mo. P/E • 11.2

Quantitative Evaluations

Outlook
(1 Lowest—5 Highest)
• **3+**

Fair Value
• **27⅝**

Risk
• **Low**

Earn./Div. Rank
• **B**

Technical Eval.
• **Bullish** since 12/94

Rel. Strength Rank
(1 Lowest—99 Highest)
• **60**

Insider Activity
• **NA**

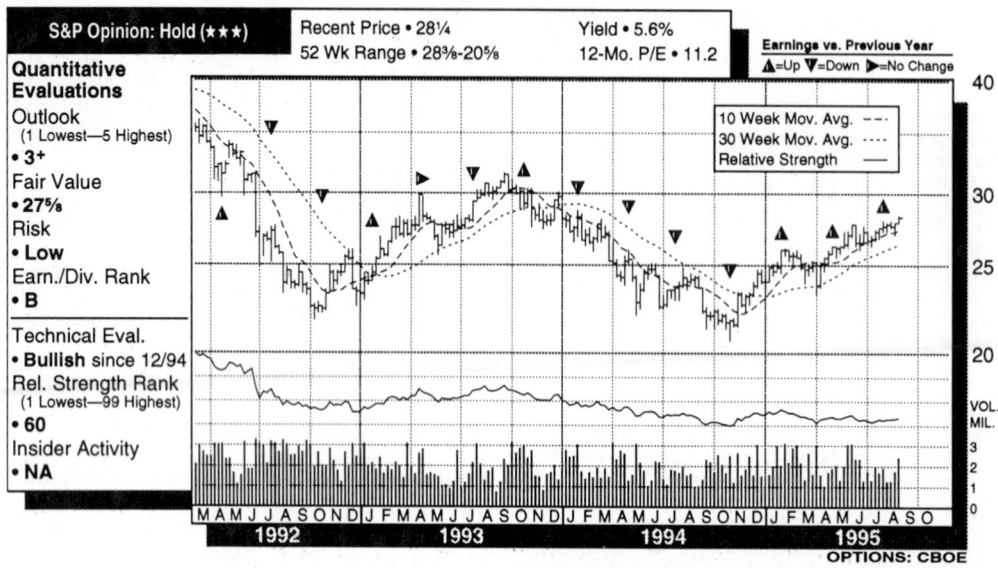

Earnings vs. Previous Year
▲=Up ▼=Down ▶=No Change

10 Week Mov. Avg. ---
30 Week Mov. Avg. ····
Relative Strength —

OPTIONS: CBOE

Overview - 31-AUG-95

Share earnings comparisons for 1995 should benefit from a rate increase, the absence of charges totaling $0.25 for work force reductions and a writedown of uranium properties, and cost savings resullting from the 1994 cut in the work force. A 5.2% rate increase, based in part on a determination that UCM's Byron and Braidwood nuclear plants are now 100% used and useful, became effective January 15, 1995. A higher capacity utilization rate for the Quad-Cities nuclear station adds to prospects for the future.

Valuation - 31-AUG-95

The shares have risen 18% since the end of 1994, reflecting renewed investor confidence in UCM's ability to improve cash flows and maintain its dividend. The company has completed a number of restructuring moves since slashing the dividend 44% in 1992, including the adoption of a holding company format that will help it add new, non-regulated businesses. However, as a comparatively high-cost electricity generator, UCM needs to reduce operating and maintenance costs further to ensure continued viability. Although the shares are likely to perform well while interest rates are falling, new commitments are not advisable at this time.

Key Stock Statistics

S&P EPS Est. 1995	2.66	Tang. Bk. Value/Share	25.15
P/E on S&P Est. 1995	10.6	Beta	0.46
S&P EPS Est. 1996	2.86	Shareholders	182,000
Dividend Rate/Share	1.60	Market cap. (B)	$ 6.1
Shs. outstg. (M)	214.6	Inst. holdings	59%
Avg. daily vol. (M)	0.333	Insider holdings	NA

Value of $10,000 invested 5 years ago: $ 11,481

Fiscal Year Ending Dec. 31

	1995	% Change	1994	% Change	1993	% Change
Revenues (Million $)						
1Q	1,578	4%	1,525	3%	1,483	4%
2Q	1,560	9%	1,432	NM	1,431	NM
3Q	—	—	1,855	NM	1,872	10%
4Q	—	—	1,465	NM	474.1	-68%
Yr.	—	—	6,278	19%	5,260	-13%
Income (Million $)						
1Q	88.60	72%	51.57	-24%	67.47	NM
2Q	108.9	NM	-7.86	NM	75.09	-29%
3Q	—	—	263.7	-8%	287.1	22%
4Q	—	—	78.59	NM	-327.0	NM
Yr.	—	—	354.9	NM	102.7	-80%
Earnings Per Share ($)						
1Q	0.41	141%	0.17	-26%	0.23	NM
2Q	0.51	NM	-0.11	NM	0.27	-34%
3Q	E1.35	10%	1.23	-3%	1.27	25%
4Q	E0.39	5%	0.37	NM	-1.60	NM
Yr.	E2.66	60%	1.66	NM	0.17	-92%

Next earnings report expected: mid October

Business Summary - 31-AUG-95

Unicom (formerly Commonwealth Edison) is an electric utility holding company that serves 3.3 million customers in Chicago and northern Illinois. The company owns and operates the largest network of nuclear plants in the U.S. Contributions to electric revenues by customer class in recent years were:

	1994	1993	1992	1991
Residential	37%	38%	37%	38%
Small commercial & industrial	32%	31%	32%	31%
Large commercial & industrial	23%	23%	24%	23%
Other	8%	8%	7%	8%

Fuel sources of generation in 1994 were nuclear 71%, coal 25%, oil 1% and natural gas 3%. Peak demand in 1994 was 17,928 mw, and system capability at time of peak totaled 22,074 mw, for a capacity margin of 24%.

UCM's construction program for 1995-7 encompasses improvements to existing nuclear and other electric production, transmission and distribution facilities. The program is budgeted at $920 million for 1995, $930 million for 1996, and $900 million for 1997. The company plans to meet expected growth in demand through demand-side management programs, non-utility generation or power purchases, and does not anticipate adding new generating capacity.

Unicom Enterprises, an unregulated subsidiary, provides district cooling services to office and other buildings in Chicago through Unicom Thermal, a development stage company. It is not expected to make a material contribution to UCM in the near future.

Under a November 1993 settlement, the company cut its annual rates about $339 million and began refunding $1.26 billion to customers for temporarily reduced rates through October 1994.

Important Developments

Jul. '95—The company reported a 6.1% increase in revenues in the first half of 1995, reflecting a 5.2% rate increase effective January 14, 1995. Comparisons benefited from the absence of $19 million ($0.09 a share) of pension expense from early retirement programs, and $34 million ($0.16) to write down the carrying value of investments in uranium-related properties. The rate increase is being collected subject to a refund as a result of subsequent judicial action affecting $139 million of operating revenues through June 30, 1995. UCM is appealing the order.

Jan. '95—The Illinois Commerce Commission allowed UCM a 5.2% rate increase as of January 14, 1995.

Capitalization

Long Term Debt: $7,315,700,000 (6/95).
Red. Cum. Pref. Stock: $289,200,000.
Cum. Pfd. & Pref. Stock: $508,100,000.

Per Share Data ($)

(Year Ended Dec. 31)

	1994	1993	1992	1991	1990	1989
Tangible Bk. Val.	25.15	25.02	26.43	26.72	29.63	32.46
Earnings	1.66	0.17	2.08	0.08	0.22	2.83
Dividends	1.60	1.60	2.30	3.00	3.00	3.00
Payout Ratio	96%	NM	111%	NM	NM	106%
Prices - High	28¾	31⅝	40⅛	42⅝	37⅞	40¾
- Low	20⅝	22⅞	21¾	33⅝	27¼	32⅛
P/E Ratio - High	17	NM	19	NM	NM	14
- Low	12	NM	10	NM	NM	11

Income Statement Analysis (Million $)

	1994	%Chg	1993	%Chg	1992	%Chg	1991
Revs.	6,278	19%	5,260	-13%	6,026	-4%	6,276
Depr.	887	3%	863	3%	835	1%	825
Maint.	561	-4%	582	-1%	588	12%	527
Fxd. Chgs. Cov.	1.8	59%	1.1	-43%	2.0	32%	1.5
Constr. Credits	42.0	11%	38.0	3%	37.0	16%	32.0
Eff. Tax Rate	40%	—	26%	—	34%	—	79%
Net Inc.	355	NM	103	-80%	514	NM	95.0

Balance Sheet & Other Fin. Data (Million $)

	1994	1993	1992	1991	1990	1989
Gross Prop.	26,947	26,760	26,291	25,164	24,963	24,436
Cap. Exp.	997	1,102	1,216	1,212	959	1,051
Net Prop.	17,323	17,892	15,283	15,003	15,506	15,783
Capitalization:						
LT Debt	7,886	7,872	7,948	7,123	7,306	6,964
% LT Debt	56	56	55	52	50	47
Pfd.	800	751	755	797	866	896
% Pfd.	5.70	5.30	5.20	5.80	6.00	6.10
Common	5,448	5,422	5,708	5,738	6,345	6,923
% Common	39	39	40	42	44	47
Total Cap.	19,236	14,792	15,188	14,469	15,373	15,667

Ratio Analysis

	1994	1993	1992	1991	1990	1989
Oper. Ratio	82.7	92.3	80.1	79.0	82.5	76.6
% Earn. on Net Prop.	6.2	2.3	7.9	8.6	5.9	8.5
% Ret. on Revs.	5.7	2.0	8.5	1.5	2.4	12.1
% Ret. On Invest.Cap	5.4	0.5	7.8	5.0	4.9	8.3
% Return On Com.Eqty	6.5	0.8	7.7	0.3	0.7	8.6

Dividend Data —Dividends have been paid since 1890. A dividend reinvestment plan is available.

Amt. of Div. $	Date Decl.	Ex-Div. Date	Stock of Record	Payment Date
0.400	Sep. 08	Sep. 26	Sep. 30	Nov. 01 '94
0.400	Dec. 08	Dec. 23	Dec. 30	Feb. 01 '95
0.400	Mar. 09	Mar. 27	Mar. 31	May. 01 '95
0.400	May. 24	Jun. 28	Jun. 30	Aug. 01 '95

Office—10 South Dearborn St. (P.O. Box 767), Chicago, IL 60690-0767. **Tel**—(312) 394-4321. **Chrmn**—J. J. O'Connor. **Pres**—S. K. Skinner. **VP & CFO**—J. C. Bukovski. **Secy**—D. A. Scholz. **Investor Contact**—Kathryn M. Houtsma. **Dirs**—J. Allard, J. W. Compton, S. L. Gin, D. P. Jacobs, E. D. Janotta, G. E. Johnson, E. A. Mason, J. J. O'Connor, F. A. Olson, S. K. Skinner, L. W. Zech Jr. **Transfer Agent & Registrar**—First Chicago Trust Co. of New York, Jersey City, NJ, and Chicago. **Incorporated** in Illinois in 1913. **Empl**-18,451. **S&P Analyst:** Jane Collin

Unilever N.V.

NYSE Symbol **UN**
In S&P 500

19-SEP-95

Industry:
Household Products

Summary: This company and Unilever PLC constitute a vast international organization that is a world leader in brand name consumer goods, mainly foods, detergents and toiletries.

| S&P Opinion: Hold (★★★) | Recent Price • 125 | Yield • 2.7% |
| | 52 Wk Range • 137¼-109⅛ | 12-Mo. P/E • 13.4 |

Quantitative Evaluations

Outlook
(1 Lowest—5 Highest)
• **4⁻**

Fair Value
• **136½**

Risk
• **Low**

Earn./Div. Rank
• **A**

Technical Eval.
• **Bearish** since 3/95

Rel. Strength Rank
(1 Lowest—99 Highest)
• **23**

Insider Activity
• **NA**

Earnings vs. Previous Year
▲=Up ▼=Down ▶=No Change

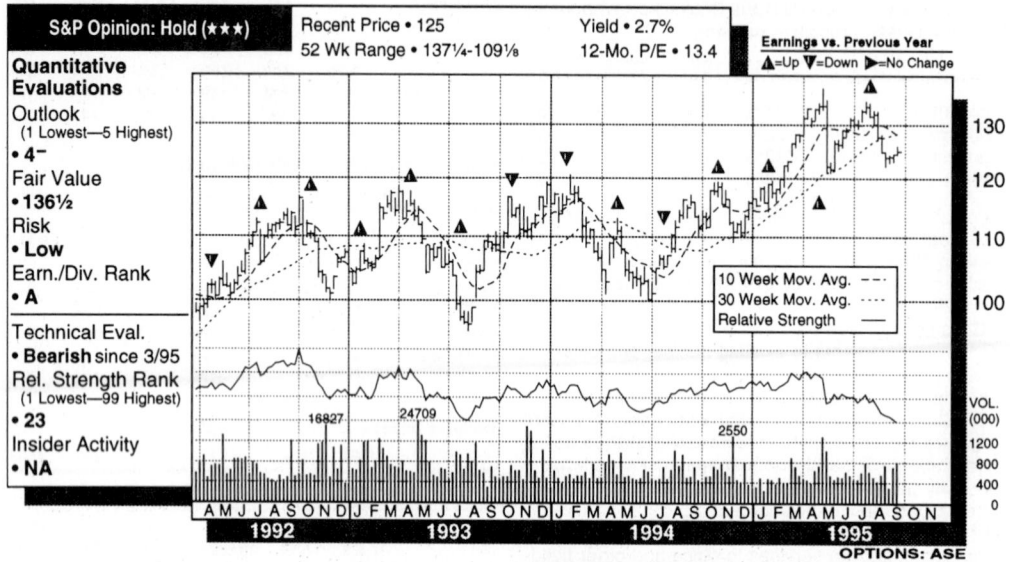

- 10 Week Mov. Avg. - - -
- 30 Week Mov. Avg. - - -
- Relative Strength ———

16827 24709 2550

VOL. (000)
1200
800
400
0

| A M J J A S O N D | J F M A M J J A S O N D | J F M A M J J A S O N D | J F M A M J J A S O N |
| 1992 | 1993 | 1994 | 1995 |

OPTIONS: ASE

Overview - 19-SEP-95

Sales should continue to trend upward in 1995. Sales in Europe, UN's largest market, and in North America, the second largest market, should rise moderately on acquisitions, higher volume of existing products, new fragrances and cosmetics introductions, and higher demand for specialty chemicals. Sales in the rest of the world should show the fastest growth on higher penetration into untapped markets. Despite ongoing pricing pressures for detergents and roll-out costs for new products, operating margins could improve on higher sales in profitable emerging growth markets. Interest charges may be higher. Cash flows should permit additional acquisitions. A declining dollar versus the guilder would increase dollar-denominated earnings.

Valuation - 19-SEP-95

Despite Unilever's leading market positions in many consumer products worldwide and vast opportunities for growth in emerging markets, we are maintaining a neutral stance on this company for now. We feel many investors are concerned about Unilever's ability to maintain share in the U.S. and Europe without spending a considerable amount on advertising and promotions. There are also concerns about the near-term future of the company's detergent business in Europe. This business suffered a major setback in 1994 when it was discovered that a new detergent formulation was damaging particular fabrics. At this date, the European detergent division is only beginning to regain market share.

Key Stock Statistics

S&P EPS Est. 1995	9.65	Tang. Bk. Value/Share	NM
P/E on S&P Est. 1995	13.0	Beta	0.77
S&P EPS Est. 1996	10.40	Shareholders	78,800
Dividend Rate/Share	3.33	Market cap. (B)	$ 20.1
Shs. outstg. (M)	160.0	Inst. holdings	16%
Avg. daily vol. (M)	0.128	Insider holdings	NA

Value of $10,000 invested 5 years ago: $ 16,787

Fiscal Year Ending Dec. 31

	1995	% Change	1994	% Change	1993	% Change
Revenues (Million $)						
1Q	10,902	7%	10,172	5%	9,675	-3%
2Q	12,235	5%	11,650	9%	10,647	-5%
3Q	—	—	11,737	10%	10,649	-4%
4Q	—	—	11,860	9%	10,907	-5%
Yr.	—	—	45,419	8%	41,878	-4%
Income (Million $)						
1Q	475.0	3%	463.0	5%	440.0	-1%
2Q	652.0	10%	591.0	3%	573.0	-4%
3Q	—	—	693.0	10%	629.0	NM
4Q	—	—	639.0	108%	307.0	-50%
Yr.	—	—	2,386	22%	1,949	-15%
Earnings Per Share ($)						
1Q	1.69	8%	1.57	NM	1.56	1%
2Q	2.33	15%	2.03	-3%	2.10	4%
3Q	E2.78	12%	2.49	13%	2.21	-8%
4Q	E2.85	17%	2.44	124%	1.09	-50%
Yr.	E9.65	13%	8.53	23%	6.96	-15%

Next earnings report expected: mid November

Unilever N.V.

Business Summary - 19-SEP-95

Unilever NV and Unilever PLC constitute a diversified international group of businesses operating as a single entity with identical boards of directors and linked by a series of agreements which equalize dividends payable and other shareholder rights. The group makes branded consumer goods, primarily foods, detergents, and personal products. There is also a specialty chemicals operation. Segment contributions in 1994:

	Sales	Profits
Foods:		
Oil & dairy-based foods	15.5%	15.6%
Meals & meal components	13.0%	10.3%
Ice cream, beverages, & snacks	12.9%	16.0%
Professional food	10.9%	4.5%
Total foods	52.3%	46.3%
Detergents	22.0%	19.6%
Personal products	14.6%	18.6%
Specialty chemicals	8.7%	12.8%
Other operations	2.4%	2.7%

Products and services are provided in over 80 countries. The geographic distribution of Group sales (and operating profits) in 1994 was: Europe 53% (51%), North America 20% (19%), and rest of the world 27% (30%).

UN acquired 22 businesses in 1994 for $895 million, and disposed of 18 companies for proceeds of $200 million. The acquired companies will add some $1.6 billion to sales, annually. Capital expenditures for 1994 were about $2.2 billion, versus 1993's $2.1 billion.

Important Developments

Aug. '95—Commenting on its first half 1995 results, UN said that sales and profits rose 5.4% and 62%, respectively, in North America; and 13% and 22% in the rest of the world. While sales rose 2.0% in Europe, profits were off 7.3%, reflecting a 19% decline in the first quarter. UN attributed the improvement in North America to higher volume of detergents, personal products, and ice cream. Results in the rest of the world benefited from strong performances in India and South America. Looking ahead, UN said results in the second half of 1995 would most likely match those in the first half. However, the geographic mix of the results could be different, with some easing in North America. The impact of exchange rates on UN's reporting currencies would also remain significant.

Capitalization

Net Debt: $4,127,000,000 (6/95).

Minority Interest: $527,000,000.

Ordinary Stock: Fl. 1,114,908 equivalent to 278,727,000 ordinary shares Fl. 4 par. Ordinary shares of Unilever N.V. alone number 160,041,250. Each New York share is equiv. to one ordinary sh.

Per Share Data ($)

(Year Ended Dec. 31)

	1994	1993	1992	1991	1990	1989
Tangible Bk. Val.	NA	NA	NA	NA	NA	NA
Cash Flow	NA	NA	NA	NA	NA	NA
Earnings	8.53	6.96	8.16	7.23	7.06	6.02
Dividends	2.75	2.68	2.77	2.56	2.40	2.06
Payout Ratio	32%	38%	34%	35%	34%	34%
Prices - High	120⅝	119¼	116¾	106⅝	91	84¾
- Low	100⅛	95½	97	73¾	72⅛	57¾
P/E Ratio - High	14	17	14	15	13	14
- Low	12	14	12	10	10	10

Income Statement Analysis (Million $)

	1994	%Chg	1993	%Chg	1992	%Chg	1991
Revs.	45,419	8%	41,878	-4%	43,719	7%	40,767
Oper. Inc.	4,977	27%	3,918	-17%	4,742	7%	4,439
Depr.	1,121	11%	1,013	3%	986	7%	922
Int. Exp.	537	2%	526	-16%	627	-21%	792
Pretax Inc.	3,648	25%	2,915	-19%	3,591	14%	3,154
Eff. Tax Rate	32%	—	30%	—	34%	—	33%
Net Inc.	2,386	22%	1,949	-15%	2,286	13%	2,028

Balance Sheet & Other Fin. Data (Million $)

	1994	1993	1992	1991	1990	1989
Cash	2,327	1,731	2,204	1,838	1,609	854
Curr. Assets	15,337	13,133	13,140	13,834	13,654	11,539
Total Assets	28,393	24,735	24,267	25,394	24,737	20,618
Curr. Liab.	11,029	10,200	10,054	10,530	10,418	9,388
LT Debt	3,230	2,176	2,548	3,158	3,383	2,384
Common Eqty.	8,188	6,813	6,789	6,367	5,389	4,262
Total Cap.	12,233	10,091	10,795	10,991	10,174	7,966
Cap. Exp.	2,185	2,031	1,678	1,978	2,104	1,734
Cash Flow	3,499	2,950	3,262	2,943	2,788	2,351

Ratio Analysis

	1994	1993	1992	1991	1990	1989
Curr. Ratio	1.4	1.3	1.3	1.3	1.3	1.2
% LT Debt of Cap.	26.4	21.6	23.6	28.7	33.3	29.9
% Net Inc.of Revs.	5.3	4.7	5.2	5.0	5.0	4.9
% Ret. on Assets	9.0	7.9	9.2	8.1	8.7	8.3
% Ret. on Equity	31.7	28.5	34.6	34.4	40.9	33.8

Dividend Data —The company normally pays an interim dividend from a year's earnings around December of that year and a final dividend around the next May.

Amt. of Div. $	Date Decl.	Ex-Div. Date	Stock of Record	Payment Date
0.734	—	Nov. 18	Nov. 25	Dec. 21 '94
2.600	—	May. 04	May. 10	Jun. 02 '95

Data as orig. reptd.; bef. results of disc. opers. and/or spec. items. Per share data adj. for stk. divs. as of ex-div. date. Quarterly data based on varying exch. rates; quarters will not add to yr. end totals. E-Estimated. NA-Not Available. NM-Not Meaningful. NR-Not Ranked.

Office—Weena 455 (P.O. Box 760) 3000 DK Rotterdam, The Netherlands. **U. S. Investor Contact**—Mike Miller, Unilever United States, 390 Park Ave., New York, NY 10022. **Tel**—(212) 906-4695. **Dirs**—M. Tabaksblat (Chrmn), Sir Michael Perry (Vice Chrmn), J. I. W. Anderson, R. D. Brown, A. Burgmans, A. C. Butler, H. Eggerstedt, N. W. A. FitzGerald, A. S. Ganguly, C. M. Jemmett, A. Kemner, O. O. H. Muller, J. Peelen, R. Phillips. **Secys**—J. W. B. Westerburgen, S. G. Williams. **Transfer Agent**—New York Shares-Morgan Guaranty Trust Co., NYC. **Registrar**—Morgan Guaranty Trust Co., NYC. **Incorporated** in the Netherlands in 1927. **Empl**-304,000. **S&P Analyst:** Elizabeth Vandeventer

Union Camp

NYSE Symbol **UCC**
In S&P 500

07-AUG-95 Industry:
Paper/Products

Summary: This major producer of paper, paperboard and packaging also has interests in wood products and chemicals.

| **S&P Opinion: Accumulate (★★★★)** | Recent Price • 56 | Yield • 2.9% |
| | 52 Wk Range • 61¼-44⅜ | 12-Mo. P/E • 12.2 |

Quantitative Evaluations

Outlook
(1 Lowest—5 Highest)
• **4+**

Fair Value
• **61¾**

Risk
• **Low**

Earn./Div. Rank
• **B**

Technical Eval.
• **Bearish** since 6/95

Rel. Strength Rank
(1 Lowest—99 Highest)
• **41**

Insider Activity
• **Favorable**

Earnings vs. Previous Year
▲=Up ▼=Down ▶=No Change

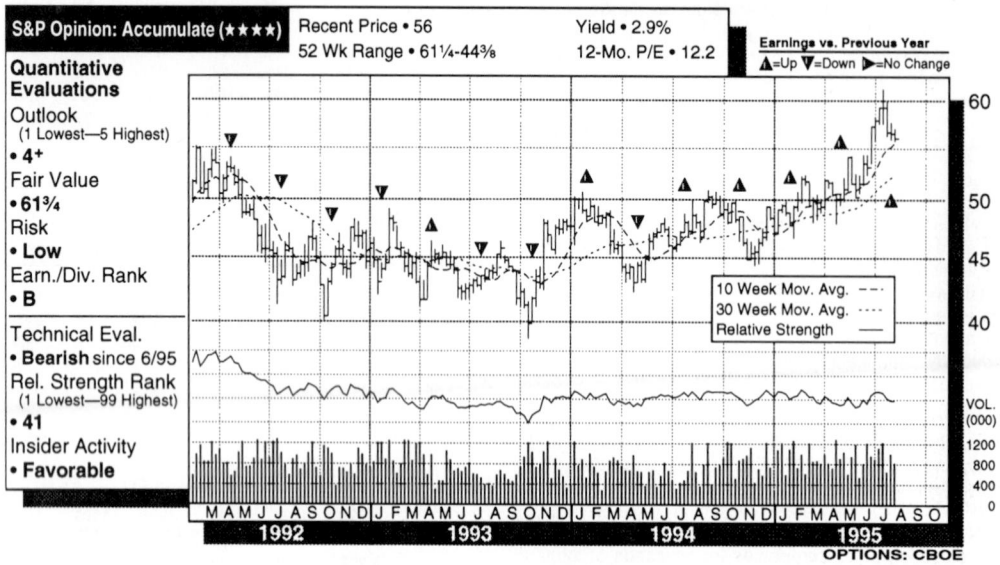

10 Week Mov. Avg. – – –
30 Week Mov. Avg. ·····
Relative Strength ——

VOL.
(000)

1992 1993 1994 1995

OPTIONS: CBOE

Overview - 07-AUG-95

Sales are expected to be considerably higher in 1995, as stronger global economies should continue to generate solid demand and steep prices in the paper and packaging segments. Despite worries about the moderating U.S. economy, limited industry capacity expansion in recent years (with the exception of substantial capacity now coming on line in containerboard) and strong export markets should allow volume and pricing levels to be maintained. Healthy demand for UCC's chemical products should also boost top line growth, and although wood products shipments should remain solid, lower prices are likely to result in a sales decline in the segment. Margins should widen considerably, on the very favorable pricing trends for paper and packaging, along with UCC's ongoing efforts to optimize manufacturing efficiency. Some margin weakness in wood products should have little impact.

Valuation - 07-AUG-95

UCC's shares have appreciated solidly in the past year on exceptional conditions in its main business segments, but the shares have still lagged those of many in the company's peer group. Despite some worries about the slowing U.S. economy, we expect industry strength to continue through 1996, with lower interest rates possibly providing some further spark. Based on our forecast of a more than quadrupling of earnings in 1995 and additional growth in 1996, further stock appreciation appears warranted, with the shares recently trading at around 6 to 7X our 1996 EPS estimate.

Key Stock Statistics

S&P EPS Est. 1995	7.60	Tang. Bk. Value/Share	25.68
P/E on S&P Est. 1995	7.4	Beta	0.93
S&P EPS Est. 1996	8.50	Shareholders	9,300
Dividend Rate/Share	1.64	Market cap. (B)	$ 3.9
Shs. outstg. (M)	70.1	Inst. holdings	80%
Avg. daily vol. (M)	0.190	Insider holdings	NA

Value of $10,000 invested 5 years ago: $ 18,409

Fiscal Year Ending Dec. 31

	1995	% Change	1994	% Change	1993	% Change
Revenues (Million $)						
1Q	1,021	29%	790.1	4%	761.5	NM
2Q	1,109	34%	827.2	5%	786.5	NM
3Q	—	—	856.3	10%	778.7	NM
4Q	—	—	922.2	16%	793.8	7%
Yr.	—	—	3,396	9%	3,120	2%
Income (Million $)						
1Q	105.0	NM	11.27	-10%	12.52	NM
2Q	133.1	NM	25.91	72%	15.09	-35%
3Q	—	—	21.73	NM	4.88	-77%
4Q	—	—	58.32	NM	17.55	36%
Yr.	—	—	117.2	134%	50.04	17%
Earnings Per Share ($)						
1Q	1.50	NM	0.16	-11%	0.18	NM
2Q	1.90	NM	0.37	68%	0.22	-33%
3Q	E2.05	—	0.31	NM	0.07	-77%
4Q	E2.15	—	0.83	NM	0.25	32%
Yr.	E7.60	—	1.67	132%	0.72	18%

Next earnings report expected: late October

Business Summary - 07-AUG-95

UCC is an integrated producer of paper and paperboard products, packaging, wood products and chemicals. Segment contributions in 1994 (profits before non-recurring charge) were:

	Sales	Profits
Paper & paperboard	33%	52%
Packaging	41%	7%
Wood products	9%	22%
Chemicals	17%	19%

UCC produced 3,412,000 tons of paper and paperboard in 1994--59% unbleached and 41% bleached. Unbleached kraft paper produced by the company is used mainly in the manufacture of multiwall bags, while unbleached kraft linerboard is used in corrugated shipping containers. Bleached uncoated free sheet is sold in roll and sheet form for conversion into envelopes and forms, and for use in business and printing papers. Other products include bleached bristol grades used in greeting cards and book covers.

Packaging products include multiwall bags used to package cement, insulation, feed, fertilizer, chemicals and mineral products; and specialty bags and plastic packaging. The company also makes corrugated and solid fibre containers used to ship and store canned, bottled and packaged products, and produces folding cartons used for shelf packaging.

UCC owns or controls 1,558,000 acres of timberland in the Southeast. In 1994, it obtained 34% of its requirements from its own timberlands. Company mills have the capacity to produce 485 million board feet of lumber, 240 million sq. ft. of plywood, and 100 million sq. ft. of particleboard annually.

In the chemicals area, the company owns a 68% stake in Bush Boake Allen, a producer of flavors, fragrances and aroma chemicals. The segment also includes the Chemical Products division, which makes chemicals derived from the pulping process, used in inks, coatings and adhesives.

Important Developments

Jul. '95—The company recorded a five-fold year over year increase in earnings in the second quarter of 1995, on a 34% sales gain. Union attributed the substantial improvement to a favorable pricing climate, both domestically and overseas, and to significant production gains in its mill operations. Those factors led to record results in the company's fine paper, packaging and chemicals operations. Union added that it remained confident in its markets and business, even if a pause in the overall economy dampens near-term growth rates.

Jul. '95—Directors authorized a five million share stock repurchase program.

Capitalization

Long Term Debt: $1,240,063,000 (3/95).

Per Share Data ($) (Year Ended Dec. 31)

	1994	1993	1992	1991	1990	1989
Tangible Bk. Val.	25.68	25.41	26.93	27.38	27.81	25.19
Cash Flow	5.30	4.20	4.03	4.82	6.52	7.32
Earnings	1.67	0.72	0.61	1.80	3.35	4.35
Dividends	1.56	1.56	1.56	1.56	1.54	1.42
Payout Ratio	93%	218%	255%	87%	45%	33%
Prices - High	50⅞	49⅛	55⅛	51½	39¾	41⅜
- Low	42¼	38¾	40⅛	34⅝	30½	33½
P/E Ratio - High	30	68	90	29	12	10
- Low	25	54	66	19	9	8

Income Statement Analysis (Million $)

	1994	%Chg	1993	%Chg	1992	%Chg	1991
Revs.	3,396	9%	3,120	2%	3,064	3%	2,967
Oper. Inc.	542	19%	455	-5%	477	-2%	486
Depr.	253	4%	243	2%	238	14%	209
Int. Exp.	131	-2%	133	-11%	150	4%	144
Pretax Inc.	195	95%	100	54%	65.0	-68%	200
Eff. Tax Rate	37%	—	50%	—	35%	—	38%
Net Inc.	117	134%	50.0	16%	43.0	-66%	125

Balance Sheet & Other Fin. Data (Million $)

	1994	1993	1992	1991	1990	1989
Cash	13.0	38.0	68.0	61.0	52.0	56.0
Curr. Assets	951	911	1,024	910	860	721
Total Assets	4,777	4,685	4,739	4,698	4,400	3,417
Curr. Liab.	884	909	892	765	643	367
LT Debt	1,252	1,245	1,290	1,348	1,222	693
Common Eqty.	1,836	1,816	1,882	1,936	1,911	1,755
Total Cap.	3,758	3,644	3,725	3,912	3,722	3,030
Cap. Exp.	325	323	220	483	1,026	563
Cash Flow	371	293	280	334	447	504

Ratio Analysis

	1994	1993	1992	1991	1990	1989
Curr. Ratio	1.1	1.0	1.1	1.2	1.3	2.0
% LT Debt of Cap.	33.3	34.2	34.6	34.5	32.8	22.9
% Net Inc.of Revs.	3.5	1.6	1.4	4.2	8.1	10.8
% Ret. on Assets	2.5	1.1	0.9	2.7	5.9	9.2
% Ret. on Equity	6.4	2.7	2.2	6.4	12.7	18.1

Dividend Data (Dividends have been paid since 1940. A dividend reinvestment plan is available.)

Amt. of Div. $	Date Decl.	Ex-Div. Date	Stock of Record	Payment Date
0.390	Oct. 25	Nov. 28	Dec. 02	Dec. 13 '94
0.390	Jan. 31	Feb. 27	Mar. 03	Mar. 13 '95
0.410	Apr. 25	May. 26	Jun. 02	Jun. 13 '95
0.410	Jun. 27	Aug. 30	Sep. 01	Sep. 13 '95

Data as orig. reptd.; bef. results of disc. opers. and/or spec. items. Per share data adj. for stk. divs. as of ex-div. date. E-Estimated. NA-Not Available. NM-Not Meaningful. NR-Not Ranked.

Office—1600 Valley Rd., Wayne, NJ 07470. **Tel**—(201) 628-2000. **Chrmn & CEO**—W. C. McClelland. **Pres & COO**—J. H. Ballengee. **Vice-Chrmn & CFO**—J. M. Reed. **VP & Secy**—D. R. Soutendijk. **Investor Contact**—Timothy McKenna. **Dirs**—J. H. Ballengee, G. D. Busbee, R. E. Cartledge, Sir Colin R. Corness, R. D. Kennedy, G. E. MacDougal, W. C. McClelland, A. D. McLaughlin, J. T. Mills, J. M. Reed, G. J. Sella, Jr., T. D. Simmons. **Transfer Agent**—Bank of New York, NYC. **Incorporated** in Virginia in 1956. **Empl**-19,000. **S&P Analyst:** Michael W. Jaffe

Union Carbide

NYSE Symbol **UK**
In S&P 500

18-AUG-95 **Industry:**
Chemicals

Summary: This company is a leading producer of petrochemicals, plastics, solvents and resins, and specialty chemicals, including ethylene oxide and its derivatives and polyethylene resins.

S&P Opinion: Accumulate (★★★★)	Recent Price • 36½	Yield • 2.1%
	52 Wk Range • 39½-25½	12-Mo. P/E • 7.7

Quantitative Evaluations

Outlook
(1 Lowest—5 Highest)
• **4+**

Fair Value
• 38⅛

Risk
• **Average**

Earn./Div. Rank
• **NR**

Technical Eval.
• **Bearish** since 5/95

Rel. Strength Rank
(1 Lowest—99 Highest)
• **59**

Insider Activity
• **Neutral**

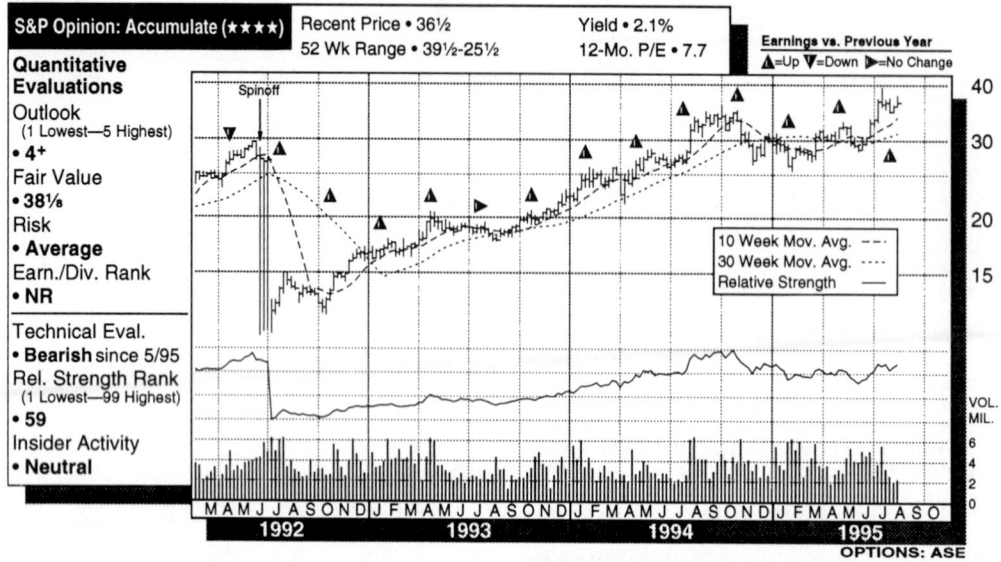

Earnings vs. Previous Year
▲=Up ▼=Down ▶=No Change

10 Week Mov. Avg. ---
30 Week Mov. Avg. ····
Relative Strength —

VOL. MIL.

OPTIONS: ASE

Overview - 18-AUG-95

Sales and earnings will climb sharply in 1995, reflecting much higher prices for polyethylene resins and ethylene glycol. Polyethylene prices and margins will soften during the second half as a result of the U.S. economic slowdown and customer inventory reductions, but should firm in 1996 on tighter supply/demand conditions. The less cyclical solvents, specialty chemicals and technology licensing businesses should continue to do well. Several major capacity additions and European joint ventures will be completed during 1995, offsetting the absence of equity income from the divested UCAR joint venture. Profitability will benefit further from UK's cost reduction program, which has reached $575 million a year. Share earnings will also be boosted by UK's aggressive stock repurchase program.

Valuation - 18-AUG-95

This stock has been strong for the past few months, reflecting renewal optimism regarding the outlook for petrochemical industry and the favorable EPS outlook for the company. At current modest multiples, the shares are attractive in view of our positive outlook for the commodity chemicals industry. We expect that the industry's supply/demand balance will remain tight through 1996, ensuring healthy profit margins for polyethylene and ethylene glycol. Longer term prospects are enhanced by the formation this year of two European joint ventures in polyethylene and the planned startups of several major capacity expansions.

Key Stock Statistics

S&P EPS Est. 1995	5.75	Tang. Bk. Value/Share	10.00
P/E on S&P Est. 1995	6.3	Beta	0.94
S&P EPS Est. 1996	6.00	Shareholders	55,000
Dividend Rate/Share	0.75	Market cap. (B)	$ 4.9
Shs. outstg. (M)	137.3	Inst. holdings	70%
Avg. daily vol. (M)	0.427	Insider holdings	NA

Value of $10,000 invested 5 years ago: $ 19,803

Fiscal Year Ending Dec. 31

	1995	% Change	1994	% Change	1993	% Change
Revenues (Million $)						
1Q	1,453	29%	1,126	-6%	1,193	NM
2Q	1,541	31%	1,177	-5%	1,244	-1%
3Q	—	—	1,252	11%	1,130	-9%
4Q	—	—	1,310	22%	1,073	-10%
Yr.	—	—	4,865	5%	4,640	-5%
Income (Million $)						
1Q	230.0	NM	63.00	50%	42.00	NM
2Q	228.0	NM	73.00	78%	41.00	14%
3Q	—	—	96.00	153%	38.00	73%
4Q	—	—	157.0	NM	44.00	132%
Yr.	—	—	389.0	136%	165.0	39%
Earnings Per Share ($)						
1Q	1.57	NM	0.39	39%	0.28	4%
2Q	1.59	NM	0.44	83%	0.24	NM
3Q	E1.40	130%	0.61	165%	0.23	64%
4Q	E1.19	18%	1.01	NM	0.26	117%
Yr.	E5.75	136%	2.44	144%	1.00	32%

Next earnings report expected: mid October

Business Summary - 18-AUG-95

Union Carbide is a diversified producer of chemicals and plastics used in paints, adhesives, films, household and personal care, textiles, automotive, agricultural and food products, and oil and gas industries. The company is the world's largest producer of ethylene oxide and derivatives, used for antifreeze and polyester fibers and films, and one of the largest manufacturers of polyethylene, used in films, bags, bottles and electrical insulation.

Foreign operations accounted for 27% of sales and 21% of operating income in 1994.

Chemicals and plastics includes polyolefins (32% of 1994 sales: linear low- and high density polyethylene, post-consumer recycled plastics, specialty polymers, and UNIPOL technology licensing for polyethylene and polypropylene); industrial chemicals (26%: ethylene oxide/glycol and derivatives, including polyethylene glycols, surfactants, deicing fluids, heat transfer fluids, amines, lubricants, and solvents); solvents and emulsions systems (27%: alcohols, ketones, esters, acrylics, vinyl acetate, latexes, and thickeners); and speciality polymers and products (15%: biocides, water soluble resins, solvents, coatings resins, plastic additives and modifiers, catalysts, molecular sieves, separation systems, and adsorbents).

In February 1989, UK paid $425 million to settle all litigation arising from the 1984 leak of methyl isocyanate gas at Bhopal, India, with 51%-owned Union Carbide India Ltd. also paying the rupee equivalent of $45 million. In May 1986, all claims in U.S. Federal Court against UK were dismissed.

Important Developments

Aug. '95—UK said that it would sell all or nearly all of its 8.9 million shares (25% interest) in UCAR Int'l Inc., as part of UCAR's initial public offering. UK expected to realize proceeds of about $200 million from the sale, resulting in a significant gain for UK in the third quarter. First quarter 1995 earnings included a gain of $154 million ($0.95 a share) from the sale of half of UK's 50% interest in UCAR, partly offset by charges of totaling $0.88 a share.

Jul. '95—The second quarter 1995 earnings improvement was driven by higher prices and demand for many of UK's products. Average prices for most products rose, despite some weakening of polyethylene prices in June. Directors authorized the repurchase of up to 10 million additional common shares. Share repurchases in the first half totaled 11.4 million shares at a cost of about $325 million.

Capitalization

Long Term Debt: $898,000,000 (3/95).

Minority Interest: $24,000,000.

ESOP 8.8% Preferred Stock: $147,000,000.

Per Share Data ($)

(Year Ended Dec. 31)

	1994	1993	1992	1991	1990	1989
Tangible Bk. Val.	10.19	9.19	8.68	16.60	17.72	16.39
Cash Flow	4.24	2.85	2.98	1.20	5.56	7.61
Earnings	2.44	1.00	0.76	-1.06	2.19	4.07
Dividends	0.75	0.75	0.88	1.00	1.00	1.00
Payout Ratio	31%	75%	114%	NM	41%	25%
Prices - High	35⅞	23⅛	29⅝	22⅝	24⅞	33¼
- Low	21½	16	10¾	15⅜	14⅛	22¾
P/E Ratio - High	15	23	39	NM	11	8
- Low	9	16	14	NM	6	6

Income Statement Analysis (Million $)

	1994	%Chg	1993	%Chg	1992	%Chg	1991
Revs.	4,865	5%	4,640	-5%	4,872	NM	4,877
Oper. Inc.	766	34%	572	-2%	584	8%	542
Depr.	274	NM	276	-6%	293	2%	287
Int. Exp.	93.0	11%	84.0	-49%	164	-33%	245
Pretax Inc.	526	116%	243	48%	164	NM	-167
Eff. Tax Rate	26%	—	32%	—	27%	—	NM
Net Inc.	389	136%	165	39%	119	NM	-115

Balance Sheet & Other Fin. Data (Million $)

	1994	1993	1992	1991	1990	1989
Cash	109	108	171	64.0	127	142
Curr. Assets	1,614	1,429	1,579	2,641	2,930	2,787
Total Assets	5,028	4,689	4,941	6,826	8,733	8,546
Curr. Liab.	1,285	1,196	1,477	2,432	2,539	2,328
LT Debt	899	931	1,113	1,160	2,340	2,080
Common Eqty.	1,509	1,428	1,238	2,239	2,373	2,383
Total Cap.	2,567	2,474	2,488	3,801	5,992	5,703
Cap. Exp.	409	395	359	400	744	785
Cash Flow	653	431	395	152	784	1,071

Ratio Analysis

	1994	1993	1992	1991	1990	1989
Curr. Ratio	1.3	1.2	1.1	1.1	1.2	1.2
% LT Debt of Cap.	35.0	37.6	44.7	30.5	41.3	36.5
% Net Inc.of Revs.	8.0	3.6	2.4	NM	4.0	6.6
% Ret. on Assets	8.2	3.2	2.0	NM	3.8	6.7
% Ret. on Equity	26.3	11.0	5.7	NM	13.7	26.8

Dividend Data —A dividend reinvestment plan is available. A "poison pill" stock purchase right was adopted in 1989.

Amt. of Div. $	Date Decl.	Ex-Div. Date	Stock of Record	Payment Date
0.188	Jul. 27	Aug. 15	Aug. 19	Sep. 01 '94
0.188	Oct. 26	Nov. 08	Nov. 15	Dec. 01 '94
0.188	Jan. 25	Feb. 09	Feb. 15	Mar. 01 '95
0.188	Apr. 26	May. 12	May. 18	Jun. 01 '95
0.188	Jul. 26	Aug. 16	Aug. 18	Sep. 01 '95

Data as orig. reptd.; bef. results of disc. opers. and/or spec. items. Per share data adj. for stk. divs. as of ex-div. date. E-Estimated. NA-Not Available. NM-Not Meaningful. NR-Not Ranked.

Office—39 Old Ridgebury Rd., Danbury, CT 06817-0001. **Tel**—(203) 794-2000. **Chrmn**—R. D. Kennedy. **Pres & CEO**—W. H. Joyce. **VP & CFO**—G. E. Playford. **VP & Secy**—J. E. Geoghan. **Investor Contact**—D. N. Thold. **Dirs**—J. J. Creedon, C. F. Fetterolf, J. E. Geoghan, R. E. Gut, J. M. Hester, V. E. Jordan, Jr., W. H. Joyce, R. D. Kennedy, R. L. Kuehn, Jr., R. L. Ridgway, W. S. Sneath. **Transfer Agent**—Co.'s offices. **Registrar**—Chemical Bank, NYC. **Incorporated** in New York in 1917. **Empl**-12,004. **S&P Analyst:** Richard O'Reilly, CFA

Union Electric

NYSE Symbol **UEP**
In S&P 500

21-AUG-95

Industry:
Utilities-Electric

Summary: Union Electric, Missouri's largest electric utility, provides electric service to a population of over 2.6 million in Missouri and Illinois.

S&P Opinion: Hold (★★★)	Recent Price • 35¼	Yield • 6.9%
	52 Wk Range • 38¼-32¾	12-Mo. P/E • 12.6

Earnings vs. Previous Year
▲=Up ▼=Down ▶=No Change

Quantitative Evaluations

Outlook
(1 Lowest—5 Highest)
• **2+**

Fair Value
• **32½**

Risk
• **Low**

Earn./Div. Rank
• **A-**

Technical Eval.
• **Bullish** since 7/95

Rel. Strength Rank
(1 Lowest—99 Highest)
• **20**

Insider Activity
• **NA**

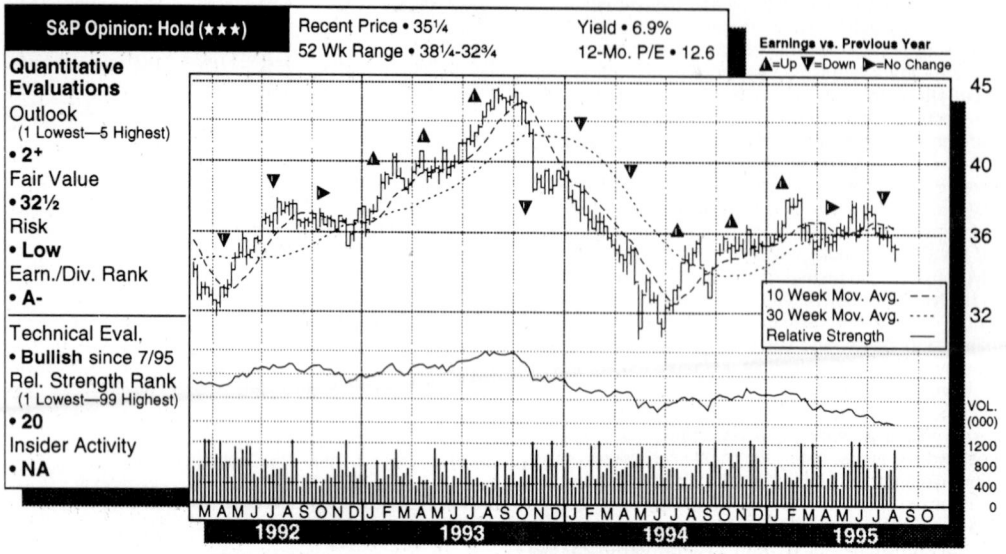

10 Week Mov. Avg. - - -
30 Week Mov. Avg. ····
Relative Strength —

Overview - 18-AUG-95

Share earnings in 1995 should benefit from an increase in commercial and industrial sales due to a strengthened local economy, as reflected in part by retooling at local automobile factories, continued operating cost containment, and a reduction in the preferred dividend requirement. However, these benefits should be partially offset by lower residential usage as weather patterns return to more normal levels. Also, fuel costs can be expected to increase and interest expense will be higher. In the long-term, UEP is well positioned for an increase in competition for wholesale power business, as it charges its industrial customers rates that are 13% below the national average. A proposed merger with CIPSCO Inc., to be completed by year-end 1996, is projected to realize $570 million in savings for the combined utility over 10 years.

Valuation - 18-AUG-95

UEP shares have recovered from the lows reached in mid-1994 and have remained in a narrow trading range over the course of the last ten months. Earnings are not estimated to equal last year's and it is unlikely that the shares will appreciate much in the short term, even with the merger announcement. As the result of a recent 2.5% dividend increase, the stock currently has a dividend yield of 6.9%, which is slightly above the industry average. At current price levels, the shares are trading at 12-times 1995 estimated earnings, and appear to be fully valued. However, the healthy yield makes these shares attractive on a total return basis.

Key Stock Statistics

S&P EPS Est. 1995	2.85	Tang. Bk. Value/Share	22.05
P/E on S&P Est. 1995	12.4	Beta	0.44
S&P EPS Est. 1996	2.95	Shareholders	119,900
Dividend Rate/Share	2.44	Market cap. (B)	$ 3.6
Shs. outstg. (M)	102.1	Inst. holdings	28%
Avg. daily vol. (M)	0.142	Insider holdings	0%

Value of $10,000 invested 5 years ago: $ 17,575

Fiscal Year Ending Dec. 31

	1995	% Change	1994	% Change	1993	% Change
Revenues (Million $)						
1Q	447.1	2%	438.9	-3%	453.0	5%
2Q	513.6	-4%	532.9	4%	512.2	2%
3Q	—	—	677.2	-2%	689.3	5%
4Q	—	—	407.0	-1%	411.5	-3%
Yr.	—	—	2,056	NM	2,066	3%
Income (Million $)						
1Q	38.22	NM	38.23	-14%	44.20	39%
2Q	76.03	-22%	97.39	12%	86.85	29%
3Q	—	—	166.5	3%	161.3	-3%
4Q	—	—	18.66	NM	4.82	-87%
Yr.	—	—	320.8	8%	297.2	-2%
Earnings Per Share ($)						
1Q	0.34	NM	0.34	-15%	0.40	43%
2Q	0.71	-23%	0.92	12%	0.82	32%
3Q	E1.60	NM	1.60	4%	1.54	-4%
4Q	E0.20	33%	0.15	NM	0.01	-97%
Yr.	E2.85	-5%	3.01	9%	2.77	-2%

Next earnings report expected: late October

Business Summary - 18-AUG-95

Union Electric, the largest electric utility in Missouri, provides electric service to a population of 2.6 million in Missouri and Illinois. Natural gas purchased from non-affiliated pipeline companies is distributed in 90 Missouri communities and in Alton, Illinois, and vicinity. The service area covers about 24,500 sq. mi. and includes metropolitan St. Louis. About 96% of 1994 revenues came from electric sales, with the remainder from gas, steam and water. Contributions to electric revenues in recent years were:

	1994	1993	1992	1991
Residential	41%	42%	39%	41%
Commercial	36%	35%	35%	34%
Industrial	19%	19%	21%	20%
Other	4%	4%	5%	5%

In 1994, residential customers accounted for 33% of kwh sales, and their average usage fell 2.9%, lowering the average bill to $816, from $839.

In 1994, UEP sold 31,975 kwh of electricity, up 1.3% from 1993. Total electric customers in 1994 rose 1.0%, to 1,121,987, from 1,111,184 in 1993.

The company's generating facilities consist of four coal-fired plants, two hydro plants, two oil and natural gas-powered plants, one pumped storage facility and the Callaway nuclear plant. Callaway has an assumed 40 year life, expiring in 2024. Decommissioning costs are estimated at $383 million. UEP's fuel mix in 1994 was 64% coal, 29% nuclear, and the rest hydro and other. Peak demand was 7,430 mw; system capability at the time of peak was 8,469 mw, for a 12.3% capacity margin.

The company is engaged in a construction program under which expenditures averaging approximately $290 million are anticipated during each of the next five years. Capital expenditures for compliance with the Clean Air Act are included in the construction program. UEP does not anticipate a need for additional base load electric generating capacity until after 2013. During the five year period ended 1994, gross additions to the property of UEP, including allowance for funds used during construction and excluding nuclear fuel, were approximately $1.3 billion (including $314 million in 1994) and property retirements were $197 million. In addition to the funds required for construction during the 1995-99 period, $248 million will be required to repay long term debt and preferred stock.

Important Developments

Aug. '95—UEP and CIPSCO Inc. agreed to merge in a transaction valued at $1.2 billion; UEP shareholders will receive one share of common in the new holding company for each share of UEP.

Capitalization

Long Term Debt: $1,783,844,000 (3/95).
Red. Cum. Preferred Stock: $676,000.
Cum. Preferred Stock: $218,497,000.

Per Share Data ($)

(Year Ended Dec. 31)

	1994	1993	1992	1991	1990	1989
Tangible Bk. Val.	21.64	20.98	20.75	20.32	19.49	18.84
Earnings	3.01	2.77	2.83	3.01	2.74	2.61
Dividends	2.40	2.34	2.26	2.18	2.10	2.02
Payout Ratio	80%	84%	80%	72%	77%	77%
Prices - High	39½	44⅝	38¾	38⅝	30	28⅝
- Low	30¾	35¾	31¾	28½	24⅝	23
P/E Ratio - High	13	16	14	11	11	11
- Low	10	13	11	9	9	9

Income Statement Analysis (Million $)

	1994	%Chg	1993	%Chg	1992	%Chg	1991
Revs.	2,056	NM	2,066	3%	2,015	-4%	2,097
Depr.	226	3%	220	3%	214	5%	204
Maint.	198	4%	190	2%	187	10%	170
Fxd. Chgs. Cov.	4.4	7%	4.1	1%	4.1	1%	4.0
Constr. Credits	11.0	-8%	12.0	50%	8.0	-11%	9.0
Eff. Tax Rate	39%	—	38%	—	39%	—	41%
Net Inc.	321	8%	297	-2%	303	-6%	322

Balance Sheet & Other Fin. Data (Million $)

	1994	1993	1992	1991	1990	1989
Gross Prop.	8,454	8,344	8,062	7,753	7,512	7,310
Cap. Exp.	345	304	323	263	256	213
Net Prop.	5,345	5,265	5,201	5,119	5,121	5,118
Capitalization:						
LT Debt	1,823	1,767	1,660	1,730	1,948	2,107
% LT Debt	42	42	41	43	47	49
Pfd.	219	219	219	219	219	228
% Pfd.	5.10	5.20	5.40	5.40	5.20	5.30
Common	2,269	2,206	2,164	2,106	2,021	1,954
% Common	53	53	54	52	48	46
Total Cap.	5,834	5,731	5,071	5,046	5,135	5,202

Ratio Analysis

	1994	1993	1992	1991	1990	1989
Oper. Ratio	78.1	80.1	79.6	77.0	77.4	76.8
% Earn. on Net Prop.	8.5	7.9	8.0	9.4	8.9	9.1
% Ret. on Revs.	15.6	14.4	15.0	15.3	14.5	14.2
% Ret. On Invest.Cap	7.9	7.8	8.6	9.5	9.1	8.5
% Return On Com.Eqty	13.8	13.0	13.7	15.0	14.2	14.0

Dividend Data —Dividends have been paid since 1953. A dividend reinvestment plan is available.

Amt. of Div. $	Date Decl.	Ex-Div. Date	Stock of Record	Payment Date
0.595	Jul. 15	Sep. 01	Sep. 08	Sep. 30 '94
0.610	Oct. 14	Dec. 01	Dec. 07	Dec. 29 '94
0.610	Feb. 10	Mar. 02	Mar. 08	Mar. 31 '95
0.610	Apr. 25	Jun. 01	Jun. 07	Jun. 30 '95
0.610	Jul. 21	Sep. 01	Sep. 06	Sep. 29 '95

Data as orig. reptd.; bef. results of disc opers. and/or spec. items. Per share data adj. for stk. divs. as of ex-div. date. E-Estimated. NA-Not Available. NM-Not Meaningful. NR-Not Ranked.

Office—1901 Chouteau Ave., St Louis, MO 63103. **Tel**—(314) 621-3222. **Pres & CEO**—C. W. Mueller. **Secy**—J. C. Thompson. **Treas**—J. E. Birdsong. **Investor Contact**—Carlin C. Scanlan (314) 554-2902. **Dirs**—W. E. Cornelius, T. A. Hays, T. H. Jacobsen, R. A. Liddy, J. P. MacCarthy, P. L. Miller, Jr., C. W. Mueller, R. H. Quenon, H. Saligman, J. M. Weakley. **Transfer Agent & Registrar**—Co.'s office. **Incorporated** in Missouri in 1922. **Empl**- 6,266. **S&P Analyst:** Michael C. Barr

Union Pacific

NYSE Symbol **UNP**
In S&P 500

25-SEP-95

Industry:
Railroads

Summary: The proposed acquisition of Southern Pacific for $4.1 billion in cash and stock would make UNP the nation's largest railroad. UNP plans to spin off its oil and gas unit in 1996.

S&P Opinion: Hold (★★★)	Recent Price • 67⅛	Yield • 2.6%
	52 Wk Range • 69½-43¾	12-Mo. P/E • 30.1

Quantitative Evaluations

Outlook
(1 Lowest—5 Highest)
• **2⁻**

Fair Value
• **64¼**

Risk
• **Low**

Earn./Div. Rank
• **A-**

Technical Eval.
• **Bearish** since 8/95

Rel. Strength Rank
(1 Lowest—99 Highest)
• **68**

Insider Activity
• **Neutral**

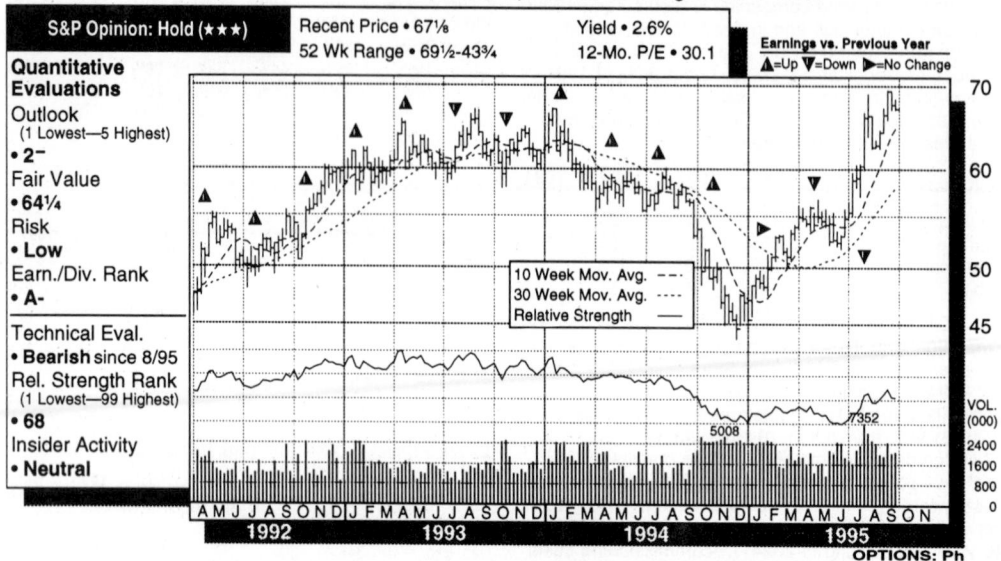

Earnings vs. Previous Year
▲=Up ▼=Down ▶=No Change

10 Week Mov. Avg. – – –
30 Week Mov. Avg. · · · ·
Relative Strength —

OPTIONS: Ph

Overview - 22-SEP-95

In August 1995, UNP reclassified its natural resources unit as discontinued to reflect plans to sell a minority stake in 1995 followed by a complete spinoff to shareholders in 1996. Higher profits from from continuing operations are seen for 1995, entirely reflecting higher rail profits. The improvement in rail operations primarily reflects the acquisition of the remaining 70% of Chicago and North Western. Excluding merger-related gains, UNP will benefit from increased shipments export corn and greater movements of western coal, metals and minerals. Intermodal traffic may slip as truckers slash rates to regain marketshare. Overnite is expected to post sharply lower profits as competitive pressure on rates and a shift in mix to loner-haul freight hurt margins. UNP's recently acquired 25% stake in Southern Pacific will be slightly dilutive.

Valuation - 22-SEP-95

The shares of this rail and trucking firm have climbed sharply since mid-1995, initially reflecting the rally in the rail group and later responding to plans to spin off the firm's natural resources unit and acquire Southern Pacific Rail. Our profit estimates for 1995 and 1996 exclude the resources unit, which we value at about $20 per UNP share and only a 25% equity interest in Southern Pacific Rail. We think UNP's plan to acquire the remaining 75% of RSP for 38.1 million common shares plus $585 million in cash stands a good chance of winning regulatory approval. However, we are neutral on UNP as the stock now fully reflects these developments.

Key Stock Statistics

S&P EPS Est. 1995	3.20	Tang. Bk. Value/Share	22.48
P/E on S&P Est. 1995	21.0	Beta	1.30
S&P EPS Est. 1996	4.40	Shareholders	62,500
Dividend Rate/Share	1.72	Market cap. (B)	$ 13.8
Shs. outstg. (M)	205.4	Inst. holdings	66%
Avg. daily vol. (M)	0.465	Insider holdings	NA

Value of $10,000 invested 5 years ago: $ 20,655

Fiscal Year Ending Dec. 31

	1995	% Change	1994	% Change	1993	% Change
Revenues (Million $)						
1Q	1,664	-11%	1,860	2%	1,830	5%
2Q	1,874	-6%	1,988	8%	1,848	4%
3Q	—	—	1,958	3%	1,901	3%
4Q	—	—	1,992	NM	1,982	3%
Yr.	—	—	7,798	3%	7,561	4%
Income (Million $)						
1Q	130.0	-54%	285.0	74%	164.0	13%
2Q	150.0	-34%	228.0	15%	198.0	-4%
3Q	—	—	210.0	94%	108.0	-42%
4Q	—	—	235.0	NM	235.0	22%
Yr.	—	—	958.0	36%	705.0	-3%
Earnings Per Share ($)						
1Q	0.63	-55%	1.39	74%	0.80	13%
2Q	0.73	-34%	1.11	16%	0.96	-5%
3Q	E0.95	-7%	1.02	92%	0.53	-42%
4Q	E0.89	-22%	1.14	NM	1.14	21%
Yr.	E3.20	-31%	4.66	36%	3.43	-4%

Next earnings report expected: mid October

Union Pacific

25-SEP-95

Business Summary - 22-SEP-95

Profit contributions (in $ millions) from continuing operations by business segment in recent years were:

	1994	1993	1992
Railroad	$1,173	$1,042	$1,031
Natural resources	351	382	315
Trucking	67	69	57
Waste services	---	-5	8
Other	4	1	-6

The Union Pacific R.R. is the third largest U.S. railroad (based on mileage). The propsed merger with Southern Pacific Rail would make it the nation's largest railroad. Its 17,500 mile system links the Pacific and Gulf Coasts with the Midwest. UPRR handled 5.0 million carloads in 1994 yielding average revenue of $1,045 per unit, versus 4.6 million carloads in 1993 at $1,055. In 1994, chemicals generated 21.1% of freight revenues, coal 18.9% and intermodal 15.6%. The operating ratio in 1994 was 77.9%, versus 79.1%. In June 1995, UNP completed the acquisition of Chicago & North Western, a 5,500-mile midwestern railroad.

In August 1995, UNP revealed plans to sell a 15.5% stake in its natural resource operations followed by a spinoff of the remaining subsidiary shares to UNP stockholders by mid-1996. Natural resources activities include the production of oil and gas, coal and trona. At 1994 year-end, the company had reserves of 154.7 million bbl. of oil and gas liquids and 2.13 trillion cubic feet of natural gas. UNP also produces coal, collects royalties and has interests in a trona deposit.

Overnite Transportation provides motor freight service nationwide and in parts of Canada and Mexico through a network of 173 service centers. Overnite handled 5.22 million tons of freight in 1994 (87% less-than-truckload cargo). Skyway Freight Systems arranges time-definite logistics services.

In January 1995, USPCI, Inc., a waste management concern, was sold to Laidlaw Inc. for $225 million.

Important Developments

Sep. '95—UNP purchased through a public tender offer a 25% stake in Southern Pacific Rail Corp. for $976 million. Subject to approval by RSP shareholders and regulatory clearance (seen by mid-1995), Union Pacific would pay $585 million in cash and issue 38,073,000 common shares for the balance of RSP's outstanding common shares. RSP, which operates a 14,600 mile railroad in 15 states, earned $248 million in 1994 on revenues of $3.1 billion. The proposed merger with RSP would make UNP the nation's largest rail operator.

Capitalization

Long Term Debt: $6,173,000,000 (6/95).

Per Share Data ($)

(Year Ended Dec. 31)

	1994	1993	1992	1991	1990	1989
Tangible Bk. Val.	20.36	17.38	16.43	14.02	14.62	12.82
Cash Flow	9.55	7.77	7.71	3.74	6.56	5.38
Earnings	4.66	3.43	3.57	0.31	3.09	2.81
Dividends	1.66	1.54	1.42	1.30	1.18	1.11
Payout Ratio	36%	45%	40%	414%	38%	38%
Prices - High	67⅛	67	60½	51¾	39⅞	40½
- Low	43¾	56⅞	44⅜	32⅝	30⅝	31⅝
P/E Ratio - High	14	20	17	NM	13	14
- Low	9	17	12	NM	10	11

Income Statement Analysis (Million $)

	1994	%Chg	1993	%Chg	1992	%Chg	1991
Revs.	7,798	3%	7,561	4%	7,294	4%	7,029
Oper. Inc.	2,501	10%	2,282	8%	2,119	9%	1,939
Depr.	1,005	13%	892	6%	843	22%	691
Int. Exp.	337	NM	335	-9%	369	-6%	394
Pretax Inc.	1,419	23%	1,155	5%	1,101	NM	112
Eff. Tax Rate	33%	—	39%	—	34%	—	43%
Net Inc.	958	36%	705	-3%	728	NM	64.0

Balance Sheet & Other Fin. Data (Million $)

	1994	1993	1992	1991	1990	1989
Cash	121	113	245	144	169	187
Curr. Assets	1,822	1,382	1,381	1,168	1,255	1,255
Total Assets	15,942	15,001	14,098	13,326	13,078	12,459
Curr. Liab.	2,505	2,089	2,084	1,868	1,814	1,868
LT Debt	4,090	4,069	3,989	3,913	3,883	3,837
Common Eqty.	5,131	4,885	4,639	4,163	4,277	3,911
Total Cap.	12,077	11,630	11,004	10,206	10,417	9,821
Cap. Exp.	1,597	1,520	1,525	1,191	1,229	1,137
Cash Flow	1,963	1,597	1,571	755	1,234	1,138

Ratio Analysis

	1994	1993	1992	1991	1990	1989
Curr. Ratio	0.7	0.7	0.7	0.6	0.7	0.7
% LT Debt of Cap.	33.9	35.0	36.3	38.3	37.3	39.1
% Net Inc.of Revs.	12.8	9.3	10.0	0.9	8.9	9.2
% Ret. on Assets	6.2	4.8	5.3	0.5	4.8	5.1
% Ret. on Equity	19.1	14.8	16.5	1.5	15.1	15.1

Dividend Data —Dividends have been paid since 1900.

Amt. of Div. $	Date Decl.	Ex-Div. Date	Stock of Record	Payment Date
0.430	Jul. 28	Sep. 08	Sep. 14	Oct. 03 '94
0.430	Nov. 17	Dec. 08	Dec. 14	Jan. 03 '95
0.430	Feb. 23	Mar. 09	Mar. 15	Apr. 03 '95
0.430	May. 25	Jun. 12	Jun. 14	Jul. 03 '95
0.430	Jul. 27	Sep. 11	Sep. 13	Oct. 02 '95

Data as orig. reptd.; bef. results of disc. opers. and/or spec. items. Per share data adj. for stk. divs. as of ex-div. date. E-Estimated. NA-Not Available. NM-Not Meaningful. NR-Not Ranked.

Office—Martin Tower, Eighth and Eaton Aves., Bethlehem, PA 18018. Tel—(610) 861-3200. Chrmn & CEO—D. Lewis. Pres—R. K. Davidson. VP & Secy—J. L. Swantak. VP, Treas & Investor Contact—Gary M. Stuart. Dirs—R. Bauman, R. Cheney, E. V. Conway, R. K. Davidson, S. F. Eccles, E. T. Gerry, Jr., W. H. Gray III, J. R. Hope, L. M. Jones, D. Lewis, R. J. Mahoney, C. B. Malone, L. W. Mathews III, J. Messman, J. R. Meyer, T. A. Reynolds, Jr., J. D. Robinson III, R. W. Roth, R. D. Simmons. Transfer Agent & Registrar—First Chicago Trust Co. of New York, Jersey City, NJ. Incorporated in Utah in 1969; R.R. incorporated in 1897. Empl-46,900. S&P Analyst: Stephen R. Klein

Unisys Corp.

NYSE Symbol **UIS**
In S&P 500

20-OCT-95

Industry:
Data Processing

Summary: Unisys is a leading worldwide supplier of information services and technology solutions to more than 60,000 customers in 100 countries.

S&P Opinion: Hold (★★★)		
Recent Price • 7⅜	Yield • Nil	
52 Wk Range • 11¾-7⅜	12-Mo. P/E • NM	

Quantitative Evaluations

Outlook
(1 Lowest—5 Highest)
• 1⁻

Fair Value
• 6½

Risk
• Average

Earn./Div. Rank
• B-

Technical Eval.
• **Neutral** since 10/95

Rel. Strength Rank
(1 Lowest—99 Highest)
• 17

Insider Activity
• **Neutral**

Earnings vs. Previous Year
▲=Up ▼=Down ▶=No Change

10 Week Mov. Avg. ---
30 Week Mov. Avg. ·····
Relative Strength ——

OPTIONS: ASE

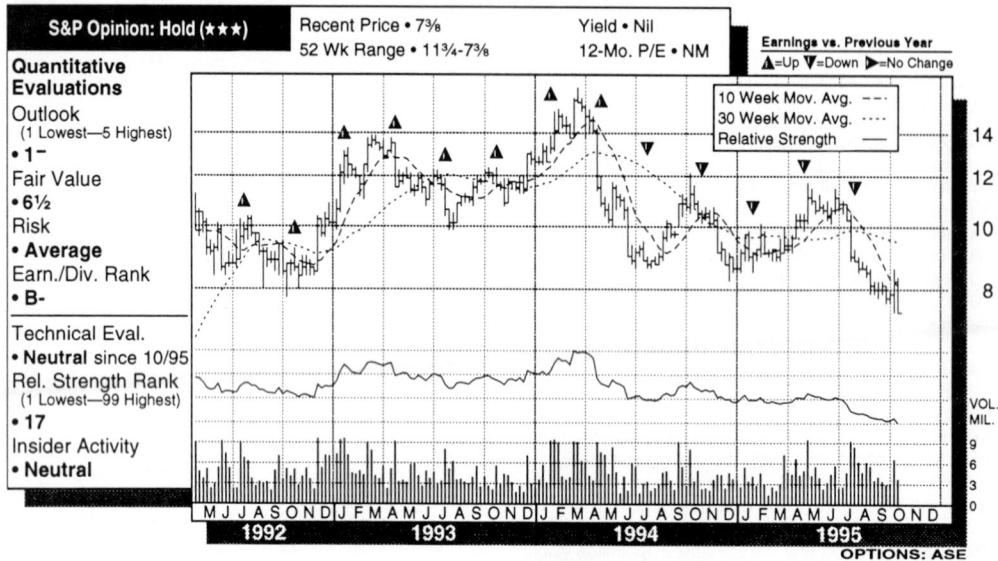

Overview - 19-OCT-95

Revenues should grow approximately 10% in 1996, led by the newly formed information services segment, which has been growing at a 20% annual rate and should continue that brisk pace of growth. Higher revenues from global support services should be led by desktop services, network integration and multivendor support. Computer systems growth is likely to be modest. Profitability should be restored as a result of benefits from realignment of the company's operations, aggressive cost reductions and the absence of charges related to the realignment. The possibility exists that management will seek to enhance shareholder value by selling or spinning off certain operations.

Valuation - 19-OCT-95

Unisys has disappointed investors in 1995 as an anticipated turnaround failed to materialize. The shares staged a brief rally in mid-October on the announcement that the company would realign its operations, but quickly sold off in concert with other technology stocks. We remain cautious toward the shares, pending release of third quarter earnings, which could prove disappointing. However, favorable operating trends in the information service business and certain other operations and plans for aggressive cost reductions could cause us to upgrade our recommendation once third quarter earnings are reported.

Key Stock Statistics

S&P EPS Est. 1995	-1.30	Tang. Bk. Value/Share	NM
P/E on S&P Est. 1995	NM	Beta	1.76
S&P EPS Est. 1996	0.30	Shareholders	45,000
Dividend Rate/Share	Nil	Market cap. (B)	$ 1.3
Shs. outstg. (M)	171.4	Inst. holdings	41%
Avg. daily vol. (M)	0.767	Insider holdings	NA

Value of $10,000 invested 5 years ago: $ 6,500

Fiscal Year Ending Dec. 31

	1995	% Change	1994	% Change	1993	% Change
Revenues (Million $)						
1Q	1,407	-17%	1,689	-11%	1,908	-5%
2Q	1,496	-17%	1,799	-7%	1,927	-8%
3Q	—	—	1,788	-1%	1,807	-13%
4Q	—	—	2,124	1%	2,101	-7%
Yr.	—	—	7,400	-4%	7,743	-8%
Income (Million $)						
1Q	32.10	-53%	67.70	19%	56.80	18%
2Q	39.80	-20%	49.90	-52%	103.0	17%
3Q	—	—	42.90	-49%	84.10	44%
4Q	—	—	-52.30	NM	117.7	16%
Yr.	—	—	108.2	-70%	361.6	22%
Earnings Per Share ($)						
1Q	0.02	-90%	0.21	31%	0.16	45%
2Q	0.06	-50%	0.12	-73%	0.44	26%
3Q	E-0.13	NM	0.08	-76%	0.33	94%
4Q	E-1.25	NM	-0.48	NM	0.53	23%
Yr.	E-1.30	NM	-0.07	NM	1.46	38%

Next earnings report expected: late October

Unisys Corp.

Business Summary - 19-OCT-95

Unisys is a leading worldwide provider of integration services, systems, software and related services. Revenue sources in recent years were:

	1994	1993
Services & systems integration	27%	21%
Enterprise systems & servers	19%	21%
Equipment maintenance	18%	18%
Custom defense systems	16%	20%
Departmental servers & desktop systems	10%	10%
Software	10%	10%

International operations provided 40% of revenues in 1994; government agencies contributed 22%.

Services and systems integration includes systems integration, outsourcing services, information planning, application development and education. Enterprise systems and servers comprise a complete line of small to large processors and related communication and peripheral products, such as printers, storage devices and document handling equipment. Equipment maintenance includes preventive maintenance, spare parts and other repair activities. Departmental servers and desktop systems include UNIX servers, workstations, personal computers and terminals. UIS offers both application and systems software. Custom defense systems, which had revenues of $1.4 billion in 1994, were sold to Loral Corp. in May 1995 for $862 million.

In February 1995, the company acquired TopSystems Int'l, a European-based developer of object-oriented and open-application tools for the client/server marketplace.

In November 1994, UIS introduced a complete line of high performance servers based on Intel's Pentium microprocessor technology and a new series of full-featured notebook systems.

Important Developments

Oct. '95—The company announced that it would dismantle its matrix management structure and form three distinct businesses, each with its own sales force. The three new businesses will be information services, global support services and computer services. The company also said it will continue its aggressive cost reductions, and that its goal from the realignment is to trim at least $400 million from the current cost structure by the end of 1996. A significant charge against earnings will be taken in the fourth quarter of 1995 in connection with this initiative.

Capitalization

Long Term Debt: $1,873,500,000 (6/95).

$3.75 Cum. Conv. Series A Pfd. Stk.: 28,405,186 shs. ($50 liquid. pref.); ea. conv. into 1.67 com.

Cum. Conv. Series B & C Pfd. Stk.: $150,000,000; divd. at 9.5%; conv. into 4.6% of com.; held by Mitsui & Co.

Per Share Data ($)

(Year Ended Dec. 31)

	1994	1993	1992	1991	1990	1989
Tangible Bk. Val.	-0.63	-0.98	-3.45	-5.72	2.41	5.52
Cash Flow	1.69	3.47	4.30	-4.98	0.25	-0.97
Earnings	-0.07	1.46	1.06	-9.37	-3.45	-4.71
Dividends	Nil	Nil	Nil	Nil	0.50	1.00
Payout Ratio	Nil	Nil	Nil	Nil	NM	NM
Prices - High	16½	13⅞	11¾	7	17⅛	30½
- Low	8¼	9⅞	4⅛	2⅛	1¾	12⅜
P/E Ratio - High	NM	10	11	NM	NM	NM
- Low	NM	7	4	NM	NM	NM

Income Statement Analysis (Million $)

	1994	%Chg	1993	%Chg	1992	%Chg	1991
Revs.	7,400	-4%	7,743	-8%	8,422	-3%	8,687
Oper. Inc.	791	-26%	1,066	-15%	1,251	NM	123
Depr.	300	-10%	332	-37%	530	-25%	711
Int. Exp.	204	-16%	242	-29%	341	-16%	408
Pretax Inc.	153	-70%	503	15%	436	NM	-1,287
Eff. Tax Rate	29%	—	28%	—	32%	—	NM
Net Inc.	108	-70%	362	22%	296	NM	-1,392

Balance Sheet & Other Fin. Data (Million $)

	1994	1993	1992	1991	1990	1989
Cash	885	951	809	814	403	9.0
Curr. Assets	3,142	3,200	3,868	4,296	4,870	5,083
Total Assets	7,324	7,519	7,509	8,432	10,289	10,751
Curr. Liab.	2,509	2,366	3,044	3,663	4,210	3,537
LT Debt	1,864	2,025	2,173	2,695	2,495	3,248
Common Eqty.	1,034	1,017	666	436	1,907	2,453
Total Cap.	4,469	4,720	4,465	4,863	6,079	7,214
Cap. Exp.	226	197	252	248	460	615
Cash Flow	288	572	704	-803	40.0	-153

Ratio Analysis

	1994	1993	1992	1991	1990	1989
Curr. Ratio	1.3	1.4	1.3	1.2	1.2	1.4
% LT Debt of Cap.	41.7	42.9	48.7	55.4	41.0	45.0
% Net Inc.of Revs.	1.5	4.7	3.5	NM	NM	NM
% Ret. on Assets	1.5	4.7	2.2	NM	NM	NM
% Ret. on Equity	NM	31.2	31.6	NM	NM	NM

Dividend Data —Common dividends were omitted in September 1990, after having been paid since 1895. Preferred dividends were reinstated in January 1993, following suspension in February 1991. In February 1994, UIS retired the $80 million preferred stock dividend arrearage on the Series A shares with an $80 million payment. A "poison pill" stock purchase rights plan was adopted in 1986.

Data as orig. reptd.; bef. results of disc. opers. and/or spec. items. Per share data adj. for stk. divs. as of ex-div. date. E-Estimated. NA-Not Available. NM-Not Meaningful. NR-Not Ranked.

Office—Township Line and Union Meetings Roads, Blue Bell, PA 19424. **Tel**—(215) 986-4011. **Chrmn & CEO**—J. A. Unruh. **VP-CFO**—G. T. Robson. **Secy**—B. Jones. **VP & Treas**—S. C. Riesenfeld. **VP & Investor Contact**—J. F. McHale. **Dirs**—J. P. Bolduc, J. J. Duderstadt, G. D. Fosler, M. R. Goodes, E. A. Huston, K. A. Macke, T. E. Martin, R. McClements Jr., A. E. Schwartz, J. A. Unruh. **Transfer Agent & Registrar**—Harris Trust Co. of New York, NYC. **Incorporated** in Michigan in 1905; reincorporated in Delaware in 1984. **Empl**-46,300. **S&P Analyst:** Paul H. Valentine, CFA

United HealthCare

NYSE Symbol **UNH**
In S&P 500

12-AUG-95

Industry:
Health Care Centers

Summary: This leading provider of health care services owns and operates a national network of HMOs and also provides specialty managed care services.

S&P Opinion: Accumulate (★★★★)	Recent Price • 41½	Yield • 0.1%
	52 Wk Range • 55⅝-34⅛	12-Mo. P/E • 21.2

Quantitative Evaluations

Outlook
(1 Lowest—5 Highest)
• **5⁻**

Fair Value
• **52**

Risk
• **Average**

Earn./Div. Rank
• **B**

Technical Eval.
• **Bullish** since 7/95

Rel. Strength Rank
(1 Lowest—99 Highest)
• **25**

Insider Activity
• **Neutral**

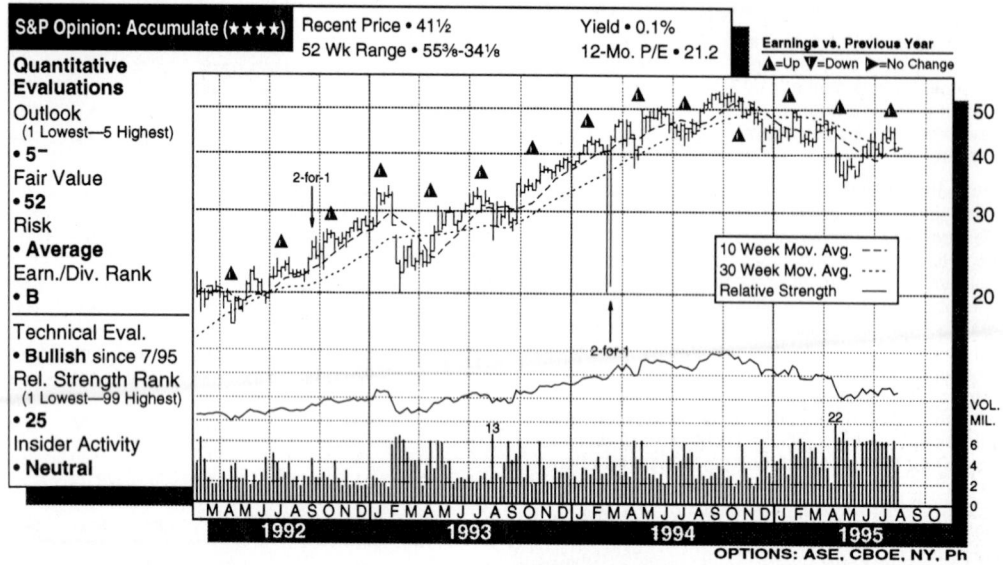

Earnings vs. Previous Year
▲=Up ▼=Down ▶=No Change

10 Week Mov. Avg. - - -
30 Week Mov. Avg. · · · ·
Relative Strength ——

OPTIONS: ASE, CBOE, NY, Ph

Overview - 11-AUG-95

Boosted by accelerated Medicaid and Medicare enrollment, "same-store" membership growth in 1995 should approach 20%. Going forward, enrollment and premium revenue should advance in the range of 15%-20% annually, aided by penetration into new markets and an increased number of services. The anticipated conversion of MetraHealth members into HMO plans could raise enrollment growth in excess of 20% a year. Revenues will also benefit from greater amounts of management fees. Margins should stablize in the second half of 1995, but we remain concerned about potential margin erosion in 1996 due to MetraHealth's large indemnity (fee-for-service) business and bloated operating environment.

Valuation - 11-AUG-95

Based on our 1996 EPS forecast of $3.00, representing an approximate 36% rise from 1995's estimate, the shares of UNH are attractive at recent levels. Management is confident that the MetraHealth merger will add to earnings from the outset. With about 9.7 million MetraHealth lives in fee-for-service health plans, the company has the opportunity to convert a large number of individuals into its HMOs. Our primary concern regarding the transaction remains margin compression, as the higher costs related to MetraHealth's indemnity business may be combined with ongoing price competition in the HMO sector. United's balance sheet will remain strong after the merger, with no long term debt and cash of about $2.3 billion.

Key Stock Statistics

S&P EPS Est. 1995	2.20	Tang. Bk. Value/Share	14.42
P/E on S&P Est. 1995	18.9	Beta	1.46
S&P EPS Est. 1996	3.00	Shareholders	3,400
Dividend Rate/Share	0.03	Market cap. (B)	$ 7.2
Shs. outstg. (M)	173.2	Inst. holdings	97%
Avg. daily vol. (M)	1.288	Insider holdings	NA

Value of $10,000 invested 5 years ago: $ 137,431

Fiscal Year Ending Dec. 31

	1995	% Change	1994	% Change	1993	% Change
Revenues (Million $)						
1Q	1,104	55%	713.5	23%	580.2	73%
2Q	1,158	23%	939.5	50%	627.1	79%
3Q	—	—	956.8	47%	649.3	77%
4Q	—	—	969.0	44%	670.8	73%
Yr.	—	—	3,769	49%	2,527	75%
Income (Million $)						
1Q	89.43	39%	64.26	49%	43.00	72%
2Q	89.88	71%	52.66	15%	45.85	66%
3Q	—	—	80.84	61%	50.15	71%
4Q	—	—	84.24	52%	55.57	72%
Yr.	—	—	288.1	48%	194.6	70%
Earnings Per Share ($)						
1Q	0.51	28%	0.40	48%	0.27	42%
2Q	0.51	70%	0.30	3%	0.29	49%
3Q	E0.57	—	0.46	44%	0.32	52%
4Q	E0.61	—	0.48	35%	0.36	54%
Yr.	E2.20	—	1.64	32%	1.24	51%

Next earnings report expected: early November

United HealthCare

Business Summary - 11-AUG-95

United HealthCare Corporation is a national leader in health care management. At the end of 1994, it was serving more than 3 million members through owned and managed health plans, and provided specialty managed care products and services to more than 23 million participating lives through employers, employee groups, insurers, HMO operators and other health care payors and providers. Contributions in 1994 were:

	Revenues	Profits
Owned health plans	89.1%	66.7%
Managed plans/specialty managed care services	12.1%	24.9%
Corporate/eliminations	-1.2%	8.4%

At June 30, 1995, the company was operating 21 owned and managed health plans whose combined enrollment amounted to 3,980,000 members. Some 70% of enrollees were in owned plans and 30% in managed plans. By payor source, enrollment at June 30, 1995, was divided as follows: commercial 86%, Medicaid 9%, and Medicare 5%.

UNH provides, for both owned and managed health plans, computerized management information systems, claims processing, marketing, contracting, financial and accounting services. For management services provided to health plans, it receives fees based on a percentage of gross revenues and may receive additional fees based on performance.

Specialty managed care services offered by the company include care management and benefit administration services, transplant services, workers' compensation and disability management services, mental health/substance abuse programs, and geriatric care management. At 1994 year-end, specialty services were provided to 23 million participants, 81% of whom were not enrolled in one of the company's owned health plans.

Important Developments

Jun. '95—United agreed to acquire The MetraHealth Companies Inc. (McLean, Virginia) for total consideration of $1.65 billion, consisting of $1.15 billion in cash and $500 million of 5.75% convertible preferred stock. MetraHealth, formed in early 1995 through the combination of the group health care businesses of Metropolitan Life Insurance Co. and The Travelers Insurance Co., provides health coverage to about 10.1 million persons, including about 5.25 million in fee-for-service plans, 2.55 million in point-of-service plans, 1.89 million in preferred provider organizations (PPOs) and 450,000 in HMOs. MetraHealth also provides specialty care programs to about 18 million individuals.

Capitalization

Long Term Liabilities: $20,545,000 (6/95).
Minority Interest: $6,374,000.

Per Share Data ($)

(Year Ended Dec. 31)

	1994	1993	1992	1991	1990	1989
Tangible Bk. Val.	14.42	4.92	3.80	2.07	0.94	0.51
Cash Flow	2.01	1.54	1.02	0.71	0.68	0.25
Earnings	1.64	1.24	0.82	0.60	0.32	0.16
Dividends	0.03	0.02	0.01	0.01	0.01	Nil
Payout Ratio	2%	1%	1%	1%	2%	Nil
Prices - High	55⅜	39⅜	29¼	19⅝	6	3¼
- Low	37¼	20	17⅛	5	1 15/16	1¼
P/E Ratio - High	34	32	35	33	18	20
- Low	23	16	21	8	6	8

Income Statement Analysis (Million $)

	1994	%Chg	1993	%Chg	1992	%Chg	1991
Revs.	3,769	49%	2,527	75%	1,442	70%	847
Oper. Inc.	570	62%	352	72%	205	59%	129
Depr.	64.1	40%	45.7	69%	27.0	89%	14.3
Int. Exp.	2.2	95%	1.1	18%	0.9	-25%	1.3
Pretax Inc.	468	53%	305	72%	177	55%	114
Eff. Tax Rate	38%	—	36%	—	35%	—	34%
Net Inc.	288	48%	195	71%	114	52%	74.8

Balance Sheet & Other Fin. Data (Million $)

	1994	1993	1992	1991	1990	1989
Cash	1,654	250	242	251	113	152
Curr. Assets	1,908	431	320	301	142	175
Total Assets	3,489	1,494	994	574	293	237
Curr. Liab.	664	513	333	235	139	103
LT Debt	24.3	0.7	0.4	3.4	7.0	58.3
Common Eqty.	2,795	959	656	319	126	50.0
Total Cap.	2,825	971	658	331	145	127
Cap. Exp.	79.6	55.3	22.4	15.1	2.7	3.7
Cash Flow	352	240	141	89.2	44.6	21.5

Ratio Analysis

	1994	1993	1992	1991	1990	1989
Curr. Ratio	2.9	0.8	1.0	1.3	1.0	1.7
% LT Debt of Cap.	0.9	0.1	0.1	1.0	4.8	46.0
% Net Inc.of Revs.	7.6	7.7	7.9	8.8	5.6	3.3
% Ret. on Assets	11.2	15.0	14.1	16.4	10.9	6.2
% Ret. on Equity	14.9	23.0	22.7	32.2	34.5	48.0

Dividend Data (Annual dividend payments of $0.03 a share (not adjusted) have been made since 1990. The most recent payment was on April 15. 1995, to shareholders of record April 3.)

Amt. of Div. $	Date Decl.	Ex-Div. Date	Stock of Record	Payment Date
2-for-1 Split	Aug. 12	Sep. 16	Sep. 01	Sep. 15 '92
0.030	Feb. 16	Mar. 26	Apr. 01	Apr. 16 '93
2-for-1	Feb. 11	Mar. 11	Feb. 23	Mar. 10 '94
0.030	Feb. 11	Mar. 25	Apr. 01	Apr. 15 '94
0.030	Feb. 15	Mar. 28	Apr. 03	Apr. 15 '95

Data as orig. reptd.; bef. results of disc. opers. and/or spec. items. Per share data adj. for stk. divs. as of ex-div. date. E-Estimated. NA-Not Available. NM-Not Meaningful. NR-Not Ranked.

Office—300 Opus Center, 9900 Bren Road East, Minnetonka, MN 55343. **Tel**—(612) 936-1300. **Chrmn, Pres & CEO**—W. W. McGuire. **VP, Treas, CFO & Investor Contact**—David P. Koppe (612-992-5341). **Secy**—K. H. Roche. **Dirs**—W. C. Ballard, Jr., G. B. Borkow, R. T. Burke, R. K. Ditmore, J. A. Johnson, T. H. Kean. D. W. Leatherdale, E. J. McCormack, W. W. McGuire, J. L. Seiberlich, W. G. Spears, G. R. Wilensky. **Transfer Agent & Registrar**—Norwest Bank Minnesota, Minneapolis. **Incorporated** in Minnesota in 1977. **Empl**- 9,600. **S&P Analyst:** Robert M. Gold

U.S. Bancorp

NASDAQ Symbol **USBC**
In S&P 500

16-AUG-95 | Industry: Banking

Summary: The bank holding company, which operates banks in Oregon, Washington, Northern California, Nevada and Idaho, recently agreed to acquire West One Bancorp in a stock transaction.

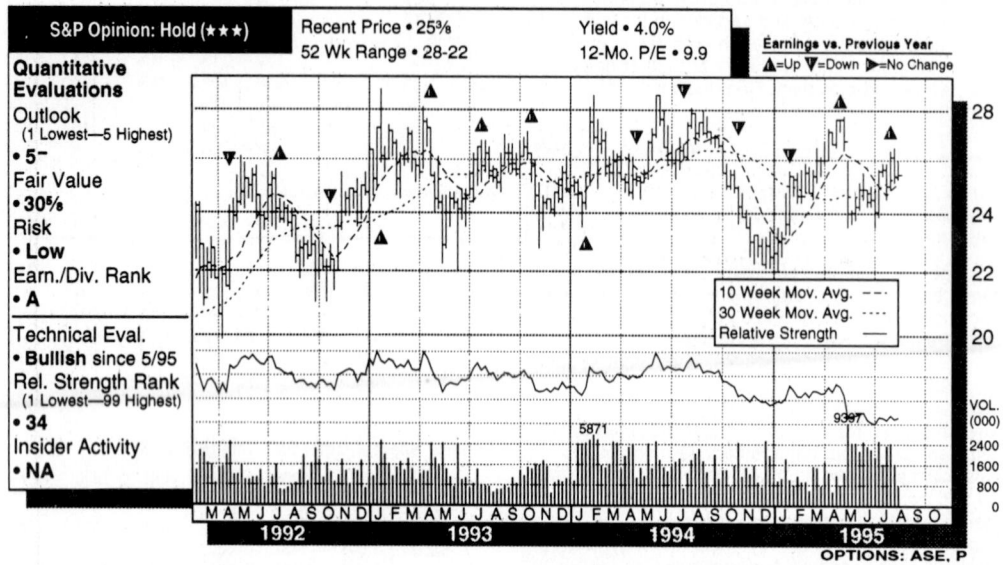

| S&P Opinion: Hold (★★★) | Recent Price • 25⅝ | Yield • 4.0% |
| | 52 Wk Range • 28-22 | 12-Mo. P/E • 9.9 |

Earnings vs. Previous Year
▲=Up ▼=Down ▶=No Change

Quantitative Evaluations

Outlook
(1 Lowest—5 Highest)
• **5⁻**

Fair Value
• **30⅝**

Risk
• **Low**

Earn./Div. Rank
• **A**

Technical Eval.
• **Bullish** since 5/95

Rel. Strength Rank
(1 Lowest—99 Highest)
• **34**

Insider Activity
• **NA**

10 Week Mov. Avg. – – –
30 Week Mov. Avg. · · · ·
Relative Strength ——

OPTIONS: ASE, P

Overview - 16-AUG-95

Modest growth in the company's regional service territory is expected to lead to a 6% to 9% increase in loans for 1995, excluding the pending acquisition of West One, although earning assets will likely remain relatively flat due to a runoff in the securities portfolio. Despite lackluster growth in the deposit base, margins are not expected to stray much from the 5.45% level achieved in 1995's second quarter, leading to modest net interest income gains. Noninterest income has trended lower in recent periods, reflecting the divestiture of non-strategic businesses, but should stabilize over the next few quarters as the company focuses on its remaining core revenue generators. An early 1994 restructuring program has largely succeeded in bringing the efficiency ratio down to the previously targeted 59% level.

Valuation - 16-AUG-95

Following the pending acquisition of West One Bancorp, USBC will have the largest deposit share in Oregon and Idaho and third largest in Washington and Nevada. While the largely in-market acquisition has obvious benefits for the longer term, it will be slightly dilutive in 1996. USBC has made great strides in reducing its efficiency ratio and is now able to turn its attention to the task of building revenues. But with its service territory expected to generate only modest loan growth in the year ahead, the shares, trading at nine times estimated 1996 earnings of $2.85 a share, appear fairly valued.

Key Stock Statistics

S&P EPS Est. 1995	2.70	Tang. Bk. Value/Share	17.12
P/E on S&P Est. 1995	9.4	Beta	1.53
S&P EPS Est. 1996	2.85	Shareholders	15,500
Dividend Rate/Share	1.00	Market cap. (B)	$ 2.5
Shs. outstg. (M)	98.2	Inst. holdings	52%
Avg. daily vol. (M)	0.302	Insider holdings	NA

Value of $10,000 invested 5 years ago: $ 17,928

Fiscal Year Ending Dec. 31

	1995	% Change	1994	% Change	1993	% Change
Revenues (Million $)						
1Q	508.8	13%	451.2	-5%	472.9	-3%
2Q	517.0	9%	473.8	-2%	484.9	NM
3Q	—	—	518.2	3%	504.3	8%
4Q	—	—	493.0	-2%	503.4	NM
Yr.	—	—	1,936	-1%	1,966	2%
Income (Million $)						
1Q	66.55	NM	-28.47	NM	61.49	31%
2Q	69.97	36%	51.34	-19%	63.56	19%
3Q	—	—	62.74	-5%	65.84	58%
4Q	—	—	65.88	-2%	67.06	1%
Yr.	—	—	151.5	-41%	258.0	24%
Earnings Per Share ($)						
1Q	0.65	NM	-0.32	NM	0.59	23%
2Q	0.68	39%	0.49	-20%	0.61	13%
3Q	E0.68	13%	0.60	-5%	0.63	58%
4Q	E0.70	11%	0.63	-2%	0.64	2%
Yr.	E2.70	93%	1.40	-43%	2.47	20%

Next earnings report expected: late October

Business Summary - 15-AUG-95

U.S. Bancorp is a regional multibank holding company headquartered in Portland, Ore. Activities are concentrated in the Pacific Northwest, but there are also operations throughout the Far West and, to a lesser extent, the rest of the U.S. and in British Columbia. Principal subsidiaries include Oregon's largest bank in terms of deposits, U.S. Bank of Oregon (172 locations), and Washington's third largest bank, U.S. Bank of Washington (164). The company also operates banking units in Northern California (65), Nevada (29) and Idaho (11). Other financial services businesses include mortgage banking, lease financing, consumer and commercial finance including credit cards, discount brokerage, investment advisory services, and insurance agency and credit life insurance services.

Average earning assets of $18.6 billion in 1994 ($18.2 billion in 1993) consisted of loans 79%, investment securities 16%, money market investments 2%, and other 3%. Average sources of funds were noninterest-bearing deposits 18%, interest-bearing deposits 54%, short-term borrowings 12%, long-term debt 5%, equity 8%, and other 3%.

At 1994 year end, the allowance for loan losses was $305.8 million (1.96% of loans and leases), compared with $270.2 million (1.91%) a year earlier. Net loan chargeoffs in 1994 were $70.1 million ($82.1 million in 1993), or 0.48% (0.60%) of average loans outstanding. As of December 31, 1994, nonperforming assets totaled $204.8 million (1.31% of loans and related assets), versus $252.1 million (1.77%) a year earlier.

On a tax-equivalent basis, the yield on average interest-earning assets in 1994 was 8.13% (8.07% in 1993), while the cost of funds supporting those assets was 2.78% (2.78%), for a net interest margin of 5.35% (5.29%).

Important Developments

May '95—The company signed a definitive agreement to merge with West One Bancorp (Nasdaq: WEST), which had total assets of $8.7 billion and 223 branches at March 31, 1995, in a transaction whereby each WEST common share would be exchanged for 1.47 shares of USBC. With about $30 billion in assets, the combined entity would be among the 30 largest banking organizations in the U.S. and hold the largest deposit share position in Oregon and Idaho, third largest in Washington and Nevada and fourth largest in Northern California. The transaction is expected to be completed by 1995 year end and be accretive to earnings in 1997.

Capitalization

Long Term Debt: $890,338,000 (6/95).
Preferred Stock: $150,000,000.

Per Share Data ($) — (Year Ended Dec. 31)

	1994	1993	1992	1991	1990	1989
Tangible Bk. Val.	16.58	16.77	14.95	14.38	13.22	11.80
Earnings	1.40	2.47	2.05	2.01	2.04	1.69
Dividends	0.94	0.85	0.76	0.71	0.61	0.51
Payout Ratio	67%	34%	37%	35%	30%	30%
Prices - High	28⅝	28⅞	26⅝	23¾	18⅛	18¼
- Low	22⅛	22	19⅞	11¾	9⅞	10½
P/E Ratio - High	20	12	13	12	9	11
- Low	16	9	10	6	5	6

Income Statement Analysis (Million $)

	1994	%Chg	1993	%Chg	1992	%Chg	1991
Net Int. Inc.	962	4%	928	8%	860	12%	768
Tax Equiv. Adj.	32.9	-6%	34.9	-5%	36.7	-21%	46.6
Non Int. Inc.	464	-13%	532	20%	443	21%	367
Loan Loss Prov.	107	15%	93.0	-31%	134	7%	125
% Exp/Op Revs.	75%	—	66%	—	65%	—	63%
Pretax Inc.	216	-44%	384	28%	300	9%	275
Eff. Tax Rate	30%	—	33%	—	31%	—	29%
Net Inc.	152	-41%	258	24%	208	6%	196
% Net Int. Marg.	5.34%	—	5.29%	—	5.18%	—	4.93%

Balance Sheet & Other Fin. Data (Million $)

	1994	1993	1992	1991	1990	1989
Earning Assets:						
Money Mkt.	568	512	916	586	434	585
Inv. Securities	2,774	3,413	3,015	1,680	1,602	2,212
Com'l Loans	8,204	7,371	7,039	7,392	7,484	6,727
Other Loans	7,550	7,648	7,230	6,984	5,881	4,897
Total Assets	21,816	21,415	20,741	18,875	17,613	16,975
Demand Deposits	4,022	3,910	3,479	2,617	2,431	2,429
Time Deposits	11,027	11,601	11,947	10,699	10,103	9,003
LT Debt	995	1,052	1,329	1,221	673	610
Common Eqty.	1,627	1,668	1,481	1,412	1,197	1,054

Ratio Analysis

	1994	1993	1992	1991	1990	1989
% Ret. on Assets	0.7	1.3	1.1	1.1	1.0	1.0
% Ret. on Equity	8.6	15.8	14.5	14.7	16.3	15.1
% Loan Loss Resv.	1.9	1.8	1.8	1.6	1.5	1.3
% Loans/Deposits	104.7	96.8	92.5	108.0	106.6	101.7
% Equity to Assets	7.7	7.6	7.2	7.3	6.4	6.6

Dividend Data

Cash has been paid each year since 1899. A dividend reinvestment plan is available.

Amt. of Div. $	Date Decl.	Ex-Div. Date	Stock of Record	Payment Date
0.220	Apr. 19	Jun. 06	Jun. 10	Jul. 01 '94
0.250	Aug. 18	Sep. 02	Sep. 09	Oct. 03 '94
0.250	Nov. 17	Dec. 05	Dec. 09	Jan. 03 '95
0.250	Feb. 16	Mar. 06	Mar. 10	Apr. 03 '95
0.250	Apr. 20	Jun. 06	Jun. 09	Jul. 03 '95

Data as orig. reptd.; bef. results of disc opers. and/or spec. items. Per share data adj. for stk. divs. as of ex-div. date. E-Estimated. NA-Not Available. NM-Not Meaningful. NR-Not Ranked.

Office—111 S.W. Fifth Ave., P.O. Box 8837, Portland, OR 97208. **Tel**—(503) 275-6111. **Chrmn & CEO**—G. B. Cameron. **EVP & CFO**—S. P. Erwin. **EVP & Secy**—R. D. Geddes. **SVP & Investor Contact**—Donald F. Bowler (503-275-5702). **Dirs**—R. L. Breezley, G. B. Cameron, F. G. Drake, J. Green III, R. S. Miller, Jr., P. A. Redmond, N. S. Rogers, A. V. Smith, B. R. Whiteley. **Transfer Agent & Registrar**—U.S. Bancorp c/o First Chicago Trust Co. of New York, Jersey City, NJ. **Organized** in Oregon in 1968; U.S. National Bank of Oregon chartered in 1891. **Empl**-9,780. **S&P Analyst:** Stephen R. Biggar

U.S. Healthcare, Inc.

NASDAQ Symbol **USHC**
In S&P 500

13-SEP-95

Industry:
Health Care Centers

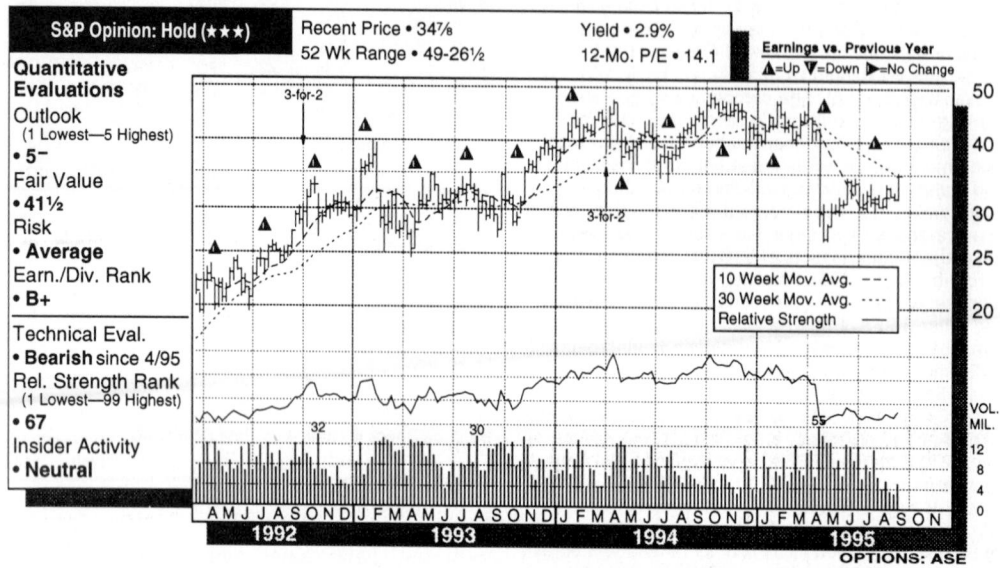

Summary: This leading managed healthcare provider serves about 1.9 million members through its HMOs in the mid-Atlantic, Greater New York and New England regions.

S&P Opinion: Hold (★★★)		
Recent Price • 34⅞		Yield • 2.9%
52 Wk Range • 49-26½		12-Mo. P/E • 14.1

Quantitative Evaluations

Outlook
(1 Lowest—5 Highest)
• **5⁻**

Fair Value
• **41½**

Risk
• **Average**

Earn./Div. Rank
• **B+**

Technical Eval.
• **Bearish** since 4/95

Rel. Strength Rank
(1 Lowest—99 Highest)
• **67**

Insider Activity
• **Neutral**

Earnings vs. Previous Year
▲=Up ▼=Down ▶=No Change

10 Week Mov. Avg. ---
30 Week Mov. Avg. ····
Relative Strength —

OPTIONS: ASE

Overview - 13-SEP-95

Paced by strong commercial enrollment growth in existing markets, penetration into new geographical areas, and demand for the Quality Point-of-Service plan, revenues should continue to climb in 1995. Penetration of the Medicare segment is also expected to increase, and Medicaid growth will benefit from increased awareness at the state level of the cost-benefits of managed care services. However, margins will remain under pressure for the balance of 1995, reflecting the impact of certain strategies designed to build marketshare in competitive markets such as Philadelphia, New York and New Jersey. An ongoing share repurchase program should provide some support to EPS comparisons.

Valuation - 13-SEP-95

U.S. Healthcare's stock has been under pressure since April 1995, following the announcement of a strategy aimed at generating annual enrollment growth of 15% - 25% through 1996. The strategy includes a decision to allow the medical loss ratio (the percentage of medical costs to premium income) to expand in the range of 300 - 400 basis points from the 1994 level. Although we believe that long-term results will benefit, per-share profits in 1995 are likely to be flat to down moderately from 1994. As a result, we recently lowered our investment opinion to Hold, reflecting concerns over low earnings visibility and negative investor sentiment clouding the HMO sector in general.

Key Stock Statistics

S&P EPS Est. 1995	2.40	Tang. Bk. Value/Share	5.58
P/E on S&P Est. 1995	14.5	Beta	1.08
S&P EPS Est. 1996	2.85	Shareholders	3,100
Dividend Rate/Share	1.00	Market cap. (B)	$ 5.2
Shs. outstg. (M)	153.9	Inst. holdings	85%
Avg. daily vol. (M)	0.959	Insider holdings	NA

Value of $10,000 invested 5 years ago: NA

Fiscal Year Ending Dec. 31

	1995	% Change	1994	% Change	1993	% Change
Revenues (Million $)						
1Q	833.8	16%	716.0	12%	640.7	23%
2Q	866.7	19%	726.8	12%	650.2	22%
3Q	—	—	754.8	12%	674.2	20%
4Q	—	—	776.9	14%	680.1	19%
Yr.	—	—	2,975	12%	2,645	21%
Income (Million $)						
1Q	94.55	6%	89.34	42%	63.02	39%
2Q	93.06	NM	93.27	39%	67.18	43%
3Q	—	—	101.4	30%	78.25	63%
4Q	—	—	107.2	17%	91.22	53%
Yr.	—	—	391.1	31%	299.7	50%
Earnings Per Share ($)						
1Q	0.59	7%	0.55	41%	0.39	39%
2Q	0.59	2%	0.58	40%	0.41	44%
3Q	E0.60	-5%	0.63	31%	0.48	64%
4Q	E0.62	-7%	0.67	20%	0.56	53%
Yr.	E2.40	NM	2.42	32%	1.84	50%

Next earnings report expected: late October

Business Summary - 13-SEP-95

U.S. Healthcare Inc. provides comprehensive managed health care services through HMOs in Pennsylvania, New Jersey, New York, Delaware, Connecticut, Massachusetts, New Hampshire, Maryland, Georgia, Virginia, Rhode Island and the District of Columbia. At June 30, 1995, membership in the company's health plans totaled 1,903,000, up from 1,636,000 a year earlier.

The company's HMOs generally operate under the individual-practice model, whereby the HMO contracts with independent physicians who are broadly dispersed throughout a community and who care for patients in their own offices. Under fully insured HMO plans, members receive comprehensive medical coverage in exchange for a fixed monthly premium. The company offers plans with minimum out-of-pocket member expense and plans with lower premium rates and higher copayments. When an individual enrolls in a company HMO, he or she selects a primary-care physician (family and general practitioners, internists or pediatricians) from among those who have contracted with U.S. Healthcare. The primary care physician is responsible for making referrals to specialists.

In 1994, USHC launched its Quality Point-of-Service Program (QPOS), under which members can obtain comprehensive HMO benefits through participating providers or go directly, without referral, to any provider they choose, subject, among other things, to certain deductibles and coinsurance.

The company's HMO services are marketed primarily to employee groups. In addition to comprehensive primary-physician care, specialist care and hospital services, USHC makes available home health care and other outpatient services, dental plans, prescription drug plans, vision plans, employee assistance programs, wellness programs and a workers' compensation managed care program.

USHC also provides managed care administrative services to self-insured and other employees. Membership in employer-insured plans for which the company provides such services was 343,000 at June 30, 1995, up from 234,000 a year earlier.

Important Developments

Aug. '95—USHC announced plans to form a company with UNUM Corp. (Portland, Maine) and Zenith National Insurance (Woodland Hills, California) to market a fully integrated, 24-hour product which will combine managed health care, workers' compensation insurance and disability coverage in one package. The new entity will initially operate in New Jersey, Pennsylvania and New York.

Capitalization

Long Term Liabs.: $18,417,000 (6/95).
Class B Stock: 14,536,530 shs.; 50 votes ea.; conv. sh.-for-sh. into com.
L. Abramson holds 99.9%.

Per Share Data ($) (Year Ended Dec. 31)

	1994	1993	1992	1991	1990	1989
Tangible Bk. Val.	5.66	4.76	3.13	2.19	1.47	1.05
Cash Flow	2.57	1.96	1.33	0.99	0.52	0.21
Earnings	2.42	1.84	1.23	0.93	0.48	0.18
Dividends	0.72	0.39	0.27	0.16	0.10	0.06
Payout Ratio	30%	21%	22%	17%	21%	35%
Prices - High	49	40⅜	34⅛	20⅜	8⅞	4⅝
- Low	33¾	24½	17⅛	7	2⅞	1⁹⁄₁₆
P/E Ratio - High	20	22	28	22	18	26
- Low	14	13	14	8	6	9

Income Statement Analysis (Million $)

	1994	%Chg	1993	%Chg	1992	%Chg	1991
Revs.	2,974	12%	2,645	24%	2,129	28%	1,664
Oper. Inc.	681	30%	522	83%	285	35%	211
Depr.	23.9	28%	18.7	25%	15.0	54%	9.7
Int. Exp.	Nil	—	Nil	—	Nil	—	Nil
Pretax Inc.	657	30%	504	53%	330	34%	247
Eff. Tax Rate	41%	—	41%	—	39%	—	39%
Net Inc.	391	30%	300	50%	200	32%	151

Balance Sheet & Other Fin. Data (Million $)

	1994	1993	1992	1991	1990	1989
Cash	1,133	1,088	179	90.0	314	206
Curr. Assets	1,275	1,204	277	175	391	278
Total Assets	1,464	1,344	981	758	613	414
Curr. Liab.	542	558	463	401	374	245
LT Debt	Nil	Nil	Nil	Nil	Nil	Nil
Common Eqty.	906	770	505	347	234	164
Total Cap.	906	770	505	347	234	164
Cap. Exp.	27.2	40.9	43.2	17.1	44.9	18.3
Cash Flow	415	318	215	161	84.0	33.0

Ratio Analysis

	1994	1993	1992	1991	1990	1989
Curr. Ratio	2.4	2.2	0.6	0.4	1.0	1.1
% LT Debt of Cap.	Nil	Nil	Nil	Nil	Nil	Nil
% Net Inc.of Revs.	13.1	11.3	9.4	9.1	6.0	2.9
% Ret. on Assets	28.0	25.7	22.8	22.0	15.0	8.2
% Ret. on Equity	46.9	47.0	46.7	52.0	38.7	18.6

Dividend Data —Cash dividends are paid quarterly.

Amt. of Div. $	Date Decl.	Ex-Div. Date	Stock of Record	Payment Date
0.210	Aug. 03	Sep. 01	Sep. 08	Sep. 22 '94
0.210	Nov. 14	Dec. 02	Dec. 08	Dec. 22 '94
0.250	Feb. 07	Mar. 01	Mar. 07	Mar. 21 '95
0.250	May. 18	Jun. 01	Jun. 07	Jun. 21 '95
0.250	Aug. 17	Sep. 05	Sep. 07	Sep. 21 '95

Data as orig. reptd.; bef. results of disc. opers. and/or spec. items. Per share data adj. for stk. divs. as of ex-div. date.
E-Estimated. NA-Not Available. NM-Not Meaningful. NR-Not Ranked.

Office—980 Jolly Rd., P.O. Box 1109, Blue Bell, PA 19422-0770. **Tel**—(215) 628-4800. **Chrmn & CEO**—L. Abramson. **Pres**—M. Cardillo. **Pres**—J. Sebastianelli. **EVP & CFO**—C. C. Nicolaides. **Dirs**—L. Abramson, B. Cohen, J.S. Goodman, A. Misher, D.B. Soll, T.T. Weglicki. **Transfer Agent**—American Stock Transfer & Trust Co. NYC. **Incorporated** in Pennsylvania in 1982. **Empl**-4,268. **S&P Analyst:** Robert M. Gold

STOCK REPORTS

U. S. Surgical

NYSE Symbol **USS**
In S&P 500

19-SEP-95

Industry:
Medical equipment/
supply

Summary: USS is the world's leading producer of surgical stapling devices, as well as a major factor in disposable instruments used in minimally invasive laparoscopic surgical procedures.

S&P Opinion: Hold (★★★)	Recent Price • 24½ Yield • 0.3%
	52 Wk Range • 27¾-18¼ 12-Mo. P/E • 41.5

Quantitative Evaluations

Outlook
(1 Lowest—5 Highest)
• **4+**

Fair Value
• **26%**

Risk
• **Average**

Earn./Div. Rank
• **B+**

Technical Eval.
• **Bullish** since 7/95

Rel. Strength Rank
(1 Lowest—99 Highest)
• **51**

Insider Activity
• **NA**

Earnings vs. Previous Year
▲=Up ▼=Down ▶=No Change

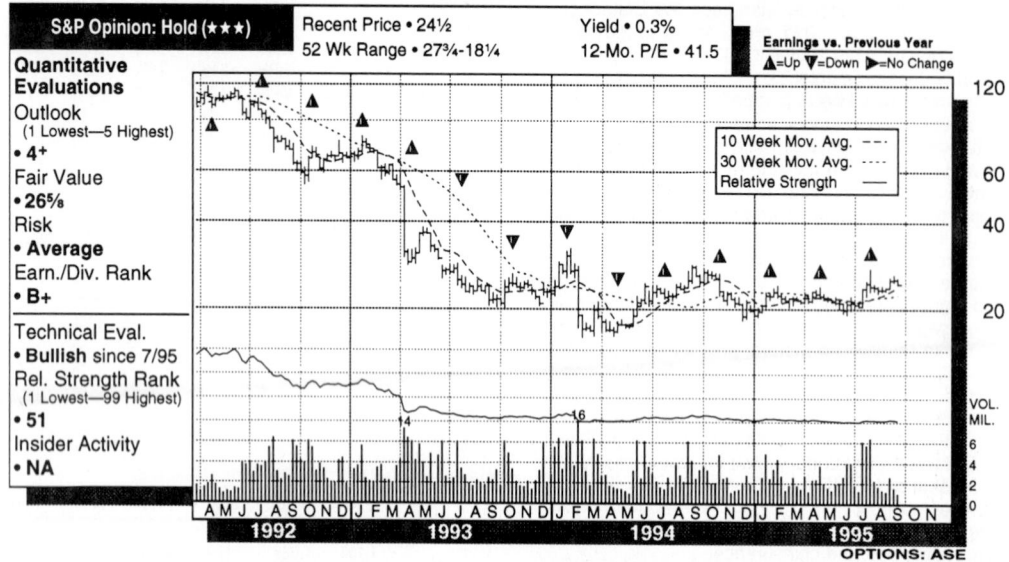

10 Week Mov. Avg. — – –
30 Week Mov. Avg. ·····
Relative Strength —

OPTIONS: ASE

Overview - 19-SEP-95

Sales are expected to rise about 10% in 1996, comparable to growth indicated for 1995. Despite ongoing cost consciousness in an increasingly managed care oriented hospital market and competition from Johnson & Johnson, sales should be bolstered by the full-year inclusion of a Japanese distributor, new laparoscopic and surgical stapling products, and acquisitions. Volume may also be augmented by new sole source agreements with large providers such as the one signed with Kaiser Permanente in May 1995. Despite a projected rise in the tax rate to about 33% from 23%, profitability should benefit from the better volume and restructuring moves, which should result in improved gross margins.

Valuation - 19-SEP-95

The shares perked up recently after a long period in the doldrums, buoyed by a strong second quarter and takeover rumors. However, sequential earnings growth over the near term may be less impressive, reflecting limited volume gains with more competitive hospital markets and less favorable foreign exchange. USS has seen its dominance in laparoscopic and surgical stapling products erode, as J&J's Ethicon division moved aggressively in each segment. The company raised $200 million by selling preferred shares in 1994; the shares require annual dividend payments of $19.6 million, and may be converted in the future into 8.9 million common shares. We maintain a neutral rating on the stock.

Key Stock Statistics

S&P EPS Est. 1995	0.90	Tang. Bk. Value/Share	8.13
P/E on S&P Est. 1995	27.2	Beta	1.98
S&P EPS Est. 1996	1.05	Shareholders	12,700
Dividend Rate/Share	0.08	Market cap. (B)	$ 1.4
Shs. outstg. (M)	57.0	Inst. holdings	51%
Avg. daily vol. (M)	0.319	Insider holdings	NA

Value of $10,000 invested 5 years ago: $ 18,463

Fiscal Year Ending Dec. 31

	1995	% Change	1994	% Change	1993	% Change
Revenues (Million $)						
1Q	240.6	6%	226.0	-31%	326.0	18%
2Q	263.6	14%	232.0	1%	229.0	-25%
3Q	—	—	234.2	-2%	238.0	-19%
4Q	—	—	226.5	-7%	244.0	-24%
Yr.	—	—	918.7	-11%	1,037	-13%
Income (Million $)						
1Q	14.40	NM	-7.90	NM	36.00	21%
2Q	19.10	139%	8.00	NM	-22.00	NM
3Q	—	—	13.20	NM	-14.30	NM
4Q	—	—	5.90	NM	-138.4	NM
Yr.	—	—	19.20	NM	-138.7	NM
Earnings Per Share ($)						
1Q	0.17	NM	-0.14	NM	0.61	24%
2Q	0.25	NM	0.05	NM	-0.39	NM
3Q	E0.23	53%	0.15	NM	-0.26	NM
4Q	E0.25	NM	0.02	NM	-2.46	NM
Yr.	E0.90	NM	0.08	NM	-2.48	NM

Next earnings report expected: late October

Business Summary - 19-SEP-95

U.S. Surgical is the world's leading maker of surgical staplers, a leader in the field of laparoscopic surgical instruments, and a recent entrant into the suture market. Foreign operations (including sales to international distributors) accounted for 46% of the total in 1994 (40% in 1993). R&D spending equaled 4.1% of sales in 1994 (4.9% in 1993).

USS is the leading producer of surgical stapling products, marketed under the Auto Suture name. The line includes disposable and reusable staplers, disposable surgical clip appliers, and presterilized disposable loading units for use with the reusable stapling instruments. These instruments enable surgeons to reduce blood loss, tissue trauma and operating time while joining internal tissue, reconstructing or sealing off organs, removing diseased tissue, occluding blood vessels, and closing skin.

The company is also a leader in laparoscopic surgical instruments. Laparoscopy, a minimally invasive surgical technique that requires incisions of less than one-half inch in diameter, is used extensively in gall bladder removals and is being applied to other procedures such as hernia repair, appendectomy and hysterectomy. It offers important reductions in patient trauma and hospital stays vis a vis conventional methods.

Suture products include both absorbable and non-absorbable sutures. USS's sutures are designed to come out of the package without kinking, and offer other competitive advantages. Suture needles are also offered.

Important Developments

Sep. '95—The company plans to shortly complete the planned acquisition of its Japanese distributor for about $61 million. The distributor has annualized sales of about $100 million, with a pretax margin of 15%. Also in September, USS won an important decision against Johnson & Johnson's Ethicon Endo Surgery division when a U.S. District Court dismissed a patent suit brought by Ethicon against USS. The suit related to certain surgical stapling products. In June, the company acquired the ChemoSite infusion port business (implantable vascular access systems) of Device Labs, Inc. In May, USS signed a sole source agreement to supply suture products to Kaiser Permanente. The agreement, covering all 16 hospitals in Kaiser's Northern California region, is expected to generate a total of $15 million in sales over five years.

Capitalization

Long Term Debt: $199,500,000 (6/95).
9.76% Series A Pfd. Stock: 177,400 shs. ($5 par); conv. into maximum of 8.9 million com. shs.

Per Share Data ($)

(Year Ended Dec. 31)

	1994	1993	1992	1991	1990	1989
Tangible Bk. Val.	7.03	7.89	10.61	6.30	4.62	3.60
Cash Flow	1.66	-0.99	3.03	2.09	1.32	1.11
Earnings	0.08	-2.48	2.32	1.58	0.89	0.66
Dividends	0.08	0.24	0.30	0.29	0.24	0.17
Payout Ratio	100%	NM	13%	17%	25%	27%
Prices - High	32½	79½	134½	116⅜	35⅞	15⅜
- Low	15⅞	19⅞	53¾	31¼	12⅛	7⅝
P/E Ratio - High	NM	NM	58	74	41	23
- Low	NM	NM	23	20	14	12

Income Statement Analysis (Million $)

	1994	%Chg	1993	%Chg	1992	%Chg	1991
Revs.	919	-11%	1,037	-13%	1,197	42%	844
Oper. Inc.	140	37%	102	-59%	250	45%	172
Depr.	89.4	7%	83.2	97%	42.3	44%	29.4
Int. Exp.	18.2	-35%	28.0	90%	14.7	23%	12.0
Pretax Inc.	33.0	NM	-136	NM	193	48%	130
Eff. Tax Rate	41%	—	NM	—	28%	—	30%
Net Inc.	19.0	NM	-138	NM	139	52%	91.2

Balance Sheet & Other Fin. Data (Million $)

	1994	1993	1992	1991	1990	1989
Cash	11.3	0.9	2.5	2.7	3.0	1.9
Curr. Assets	440	465	517	386	219	147
Total Assets	1,104	1,171	1,168	742	461	327
Curr. Liab.	184	217	163	122	90.0	58.0
LT Debt	249	505	395	252	131	97.0
Common Eqty.	462	444	590	330	225	168
Total Cap.	919	954	1,005	619	371	269
Cap. Exp.	47.0	216	272	145	72.0	44.0
Cash Flow	94.0	-56.0	181	121	69.0	52.0

Ratio Analysis

	1994	1993	1992	1991	1990	1989
Curr. Ratio	2.4	2.1	3.2	3.2	2.4	2.5
% LT Debt of Cap.	27.0	53.0	39.3	40.6	35.3	36.0
% Net Inc.of Revs.	2.1	NM	11.6	10.8	9.0	8.9
% Ret. on Assets	1.7	NM	14.2	14.7	11.5	10.3
% Ret. on Equity	0.9	NM	29.5	31.9	23.0	20.4

Dividend Data —Cash dividends were initiated in 1985.

Amt. of Div. $	Date Decl.	Ex-Div. Date	Stock of Record	Payment Date
0.020	Nov. 18	Nov. 25	Dec. 01	Dec. 09 '94
0.020	Feb. 10	Feb. 23	Mar. 01	Mar. 10 '95
0.020	May. 12	May. 25	Jun. 01	Jun. 09 '95
0.020	Aug. 11	Aug. 30	Sep. 01	Sep. 08 '95

Data as orig. reptd.; bef. results of disc. opers. and/or spec. items. Per share data adj. for stk. divs. as of ex-div. date.
E-Estimated. NA-Not Available. NM-Not Meaningful. NR-Not Ranked.

Office—150 Glover Ave., Norwalk, CT 06856. **Tel**—(203) 845-1000. **Chrmn & Pres**—L. C. Hirsch. **SVP & CFO**—H. M. Rosenkrantz. **Secy**—P. Komenda. **VP & Investor Contact**—Marianne Scipione (203-845-1404). **Dirs**—J. A. Bogardus, Jr., J. K. Blake, T. R. Bremer, L. C. Hirsch, T. Josefsen, D. L. King, W. F. May, H. M. Rosenkrantz, M. Scipione, J. R. Silber. **Transfer Agent & Registrar**—First Chicago Trust Co. of New York, NYC. **Reincorporated** in Delaware in 1990. **Empl**-5,952. **S&P Analyst:** H. B. Saftlas

U S WEST

NYSE Symbol **USW**
In S&P 500

31-OCT-95 **Industry:** Telecommunications

Summary: The seventh largest U.S. telephone holding company, USW also has investments in cellular telephone, cable television, and international communications operations.

S&P Opinion: Accumulate (★★★★)	Recent Price • 47¼	Yield • 4.6%
	52 Wk Range • 48⅞-28⅜	12-Mo. P/E • 16.0

Quantitative Evaluations

Outlook (1 Lowest—5 Highest)
• **1⁻**

Fair Value
• **40⅞**

Risk
• **Low**

Earn./Div. Rank
• **B+**

Technical Eval.
• **Bearish** since 8/95

Rel. Strength Rank (1 Lowest—99 Highest)
• **73**

Insider Activity
• **NA**

Earnings vs. Previous Year
▲=Up ▼=Down ▶=No Change

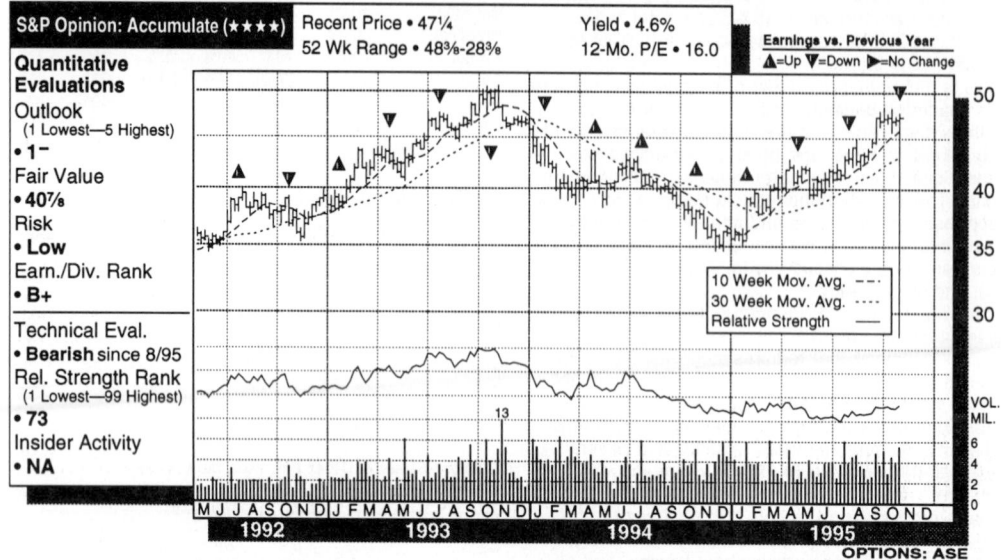

10 Week Mov. Avg. — – –
30 Week Mov. Avg. ∙∙∙∙
Relative Strength —

OPTIONS: ASE

Overview - 31-OCT-95

A targeted stock plan will divide the company's equity into two stock classes, but USW will remain one corporation legally. The Communications Group will comprise local telephone operations, and will continue to pay the current dividend. The Media Group will comprise cable, wireless, international and directory publishing operations, and will pay no dividend. The targeted stock will begin trading in November 1995. The Communications Group should benefit from a recent Justice Department ruling recommending the company be allowed to offer long-distance service outside its region. The Media Group has positioned itself to benefit from the opening of communications markets, and should continue its rapid growth. Separately, USW suspended pending FCC applications to deploy video dialtone. It still plans to deploy the service, but wants first to examine alternative technologies.

Valuation - 31-OCT-95

We believe that USW's three-pronged growth strategy positions it well for coming changes in the telecommunications market. Once issued, both target stock classes should benefit. The company's strategy includes upgrading its core network to provide advanced services; moving to compete in the operating territories of other telephone companies through wireless and cable operations; and investing in international ventures for growth opportunities. With a healthy dividend and strong growth prospects, the shares are attractive for total return.

Key Stock Statistics

S&P EPS Est. 1995	2.70	Tang. Bk. Value/Share	12.34
P/E on S&P Est. 1995	17.5	Beta	0.60
S&P EPS Est. 1996	2.80	Shareholders	816,000
Dividend Rate/Share	2.14	Market cap. (B)	$ 22.1
Shs. outstg. (M)	470.8	Inst. holdings	44%
Avg. daily vol. (M)	0.870	Insider holdings	NA

Value of $10,000 invested 5 years ago: NA

Fiscal Year Ending Dec. 31

	1995	% Change	1994	% Change	1993	% Change
Revenues (Million $)						
1Q	2,828	7%	2,641	5%	2,510	NM
2Q	2,894	7%	2,708	7%	2,542	NM
3Q	2,964	7%	2,765	7%	2,576	NM
4Q	—	—	2,839	6%	2,666	NM
Yr.	—	—	10,953	6%	10,294	NM
Income (Million $)						
1Q	330.0	2%	324.0	10%	295.7	-7%
2Q	318.0	-15%	375.0	29%	291.2	NM
3Q	325.0	2%	318.0	NM	-375.1	NM
4Q	—	—	409.0	55%	264.1	-13%
Yr.	—	—	1,426	200%	475.9	-60%
Earnings Per Share ($)						
1Q	0.70	-4%	0.73	3%	0.71	-8%
2Q	0.67	-19%	0.83	19%	0.70	-1%
3Q	0.69	-1%	0.70	NM	-0.90	NM
4Q	E0.64	-28%	0.89	44%	0.62	-15%
Yr.	E2.70	-14%	3.14	178%	1.13	-60%

Next earnings report expected: mid January

Business Summary - 31-OCT-95

U S WEST is the seventh largest U.S. telephone holding company, based on 1994 U.S. access lines. Telephone operations provide local telephone and exchange access service to 14.7 million customer access lines in 14 states.

U S WEST NewVector Group provides mobile communications services. At September 30, 1995, the company had 1.3 million cellular telephone customers (adjusted for ownership). USW and AirTouch Communications have reached an agreement to form a cellular joint venture which will be 30%-owned by USW and will have operations in 21 states. Initially, the cellular operations will operate as separate entities under a joint management company; after USW has received waivers from certain regulatory restrictions the properties will be combined. USW expects the arrangement to contribute to earnings in 1995. The companies will also form a 50/50 joint venture to pursue additional wireless opportunities.

In September 1993, USW completed a strategic alliance with Time Warner Entertainment (TWE), investing $2.5 billion for a 25.51% stake in TWE. USW has an option to acquire up to an additional 6.3% interest. The venture planned to spend up to $5 billion to upgrade TWE's cable television systems to provide two-way, switched communications, entertainment and information services.

Other subsidiaries conduct advertising and directory publishing, business development and international operations, including cellular, directory, international cable and infrastructure projects.

The company owns jointly, with the six other regional Bell holding companies, Bell Communications Research, which provides technical assistance and consulting services to the companies.

Important Developments

Oct. '95—The Justice Department filed a motion with the U.S. District Court in support of the company's proposal to provide long-distance service outside its 14 state operating region to customers who sign up for the company's planned local telephone services. Separately, Time Warner filed a countersuit against U S WEST; the company had filed suit to block the merger of Time Warner and Turner Broadcasting System in Delaware chancery court in September.
Mar. '95—In FCC auctions for PCS (personal communications services) licenses, USW, as part of a national wireless partnership with AirTouch Communications (ATI), Bell Atlantic and NYNEX, bid a total of $1.1 billion for 11 markets, including Chicago, Dallas and Miami. The partnership builds on USW's joint venture with ATI. The partnership will be 50%-owned by the USW/ATI venture.

Capitalization

Long Term Debt: $5,144,000,000 (9/95).

Per Share Data ($) (Year Ended Dec. 31)

	1994	1993	1992	1991	1990	1989
Tangible Bk. Val.	15.73	13.29	19.51	22.84	22.92	21.05
Cash Flow	7.67	5.60	7.43	6.06	7.89	7.65
Earnings	3.14	1.13	2.86	1.38	3.11	3.01
Dividends	2.14	2.14	2.11	2.06	1.97	1.85
Payout Ratio	68%	189%	74%	149%	63%	61%
Prices - High	46¼	50¾	40	40¾	40½	40⅜
- Low	34⅝	37¾	32⅞	33¾	32⅜	28⅜
P/E Ratio - High	15	45	14	30	13	13
- Low	11	33	11	24	10	9

Income Statement Analysis (Million $)

	1994	%Chg	1993	%Chg	1992	%Chg	1991
Revs.	10,953	6%	10,294	NM	10,281	-3%	10,577
Depr.	2,052	5%	1,955	3%	1,890	NM	1,876
Maint.	NA	—	NA	—	NA	—	1,426
Constr. Credits	NA	—	NA	—	NA	—	NA
Eff. Tax Rate	38%	—	36%	—	31%	—	25%
Net Inc.	1,426	NM	394	-67%	1,179	113%	553

Balance Sheet & Other Fin. Data (Million $)

	1994	1993	1992	1991	1990	1989
Gross Prop.	31,014	29,161	28,786	27,248	26,851	25,750
Net Prop.	13,997	13,232	18,712	18,064	18,103	17,413
Cap. Exp.	2,597	2,449	2,598	2,654	2,559	2,186
Total Cap.	14,688	13,000	17,539	21,181	20,720	19,395
Fxd. Chgs. Cov.	5.7	2.7	3.7	1.9	3.4	3.2
Capitalization:						
LT Debt	5,101	5,423	6,737	7,629	7,175	7,248
Pfd.	51.0	Nil	Nil	Nil	Nil	Nil
Common	7,382	5,861	8,268	9,587	9,240	8,071

Ratio Analysis

	1994	1993	1992	1991	1990	1989
% Ret. on Revs.	13.0	4.6	11.5	5.2	12.0	11.5
% Ret. On Invest.Cap	19.6	7.8	9.5	6.3	9.6	9.5
% Return On Com.Eqty	10.3	Nil	13.2	5.7	13.7	14.2
% Earn. on Net Prop.	12.1	6.4	10.2	9.5	10.5	10.2
% LT Debt of Cap.	40.7	48.1	44.9	44.3	43.7	47.3
Capital. % Pfd.	0.4	Nil	Nil	Nil	Nil	Nil
Capital. % Common	58.9	51.9	55.1	55.7	56.3	52.7

Dividend Data —Dividends were initiated in 1984. A poison pill stock purchase right was adopted in 1989. A dividend reinvestment plan is available.

Amt. of Div. $	Date Decl.	Ex-Div. Date	Stock of Record	Payment Date
0.535	Dec. 02	Jan. 13	Jan. 20	Feb. 01 '95
0.535	Apr. 07	Apr. 12	Apr. 19	May. 01 '95
0.535	Apr. 07	Apr. 12	Apr. 19	May. 01 '95
0.535	Jul. 07	Jul. 18	Jul. 20	Aug. 01 '95
0.535	Oct. 10	Oct. 18	Oct. 20	Nov. 01 '95

Office—7800 East Orchard Rd., Englewood, CO 80111-2526. **Tel**—(303) 793-6500. **Chrmn, Pres & CEO**—R. D. McCormick. **EVP & CFO**—J. M. Osterhoff. **EVP & Secy**—C. P. Russ III. **Investor Contacts**—Communications: Sara Stratton; Media: Carolyn Crawford. **Dirs**—D. Cheney, R. Diaz-Oliver, G. A. Dove, A. D. Gilmour, P. M. Grieve, S. M. Hufstedler, A. F. Jacobson, R. D. McCormick, M. C. Nelson, F. Popoff, G. L. Ryland, J. O. Williams, D. Yankelovich. **Transfer Agent & Registrar**—Boston Financial Data Services, Quincy, MA. **Incorporated** in Colorado in 1983. **Empl**-61,505. **S&P Analyst:** Kevin J. Gooley

USAir Group

NYSE Symbol **U**
In S&P 500

15-AUG-95 Industry:
Air Transport

Summary: This holding company's principal subsidiary, USAir, operates scheduled service to more than 150 cities in the U.S., Canada, France, Germany and elsewhere.

S&P Opinion: Hold (★★★)		

Recent Price • 8¼
52 Wk Range • 14-3⅞

Yield • Nil
12-Mo. P/E • NM

Earnings vs. Previous Year
▲=Up ▼=Down ▶=No Change

Quantitative Evaluations

Outlook
(1 Lowest—5 Highest)
• 1

Fair Value
• 4⅛

Risk
• **High**

Earn./Div. Rank
• C

Technical Eval.
• **Bearish** since 6/95

Rel. Strength Rank
(1 Lowest—99 Highest)
• 3

Insider Activity
• **NA**

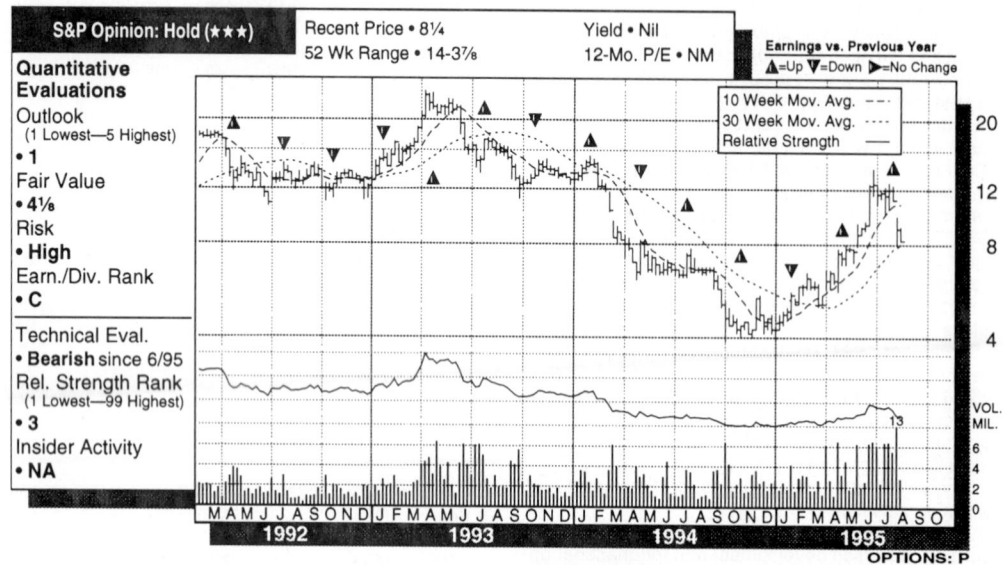

10 Week Mov. Avg. – – –
30 Week Mov. Avg. ......
Relative Strength ——

OPTIONS: P

Overview - 15-AUG-95

Revenues in 1995 are likely to be up moderately from those of 1994. The average fare is forecast to increase, reflecting significantly less competition from low-fare carriers (arising primarily from the elimination of Continental's Lite operations). However, traffic should remain about the same, despite the robust industry growth, due to scheduled reductions in service and comparison with last year's strong second half. Unit operating expenses will decline with the implementation of cost-cutting initiatives. Consequently, modest operating income may be achieved for the full year. Interest expense is expected to increase, resulting in a net loss, before one-time gains.

Valuation - 15-AUG-95

A strong airline sector and word that three of USAir's unions have tentatively agreed to pay cuts contributed to the recent recovery in the stock price. The rebound ended abruptly when USAir terminated wage concession negotiations with the unions, saying some issues proved unsolvable. With one of the highest cost structures in the industry, the company needs to secure further cost reductions to achieve sustained profitability. Wage concessions are the most likely avenue for these savings. Consequently, we expect volatility in the stock price to reflect news in this area. USAir returned to profitability in the second quarter, but second-quarter results typically have been the company's best. With fewer gains from the sale of assets expected, we do not see a return to full-year profitability.

Key Stock Statistics

S&P EPS Est. 1995	-0.04	Tang. Bk. Value/Share	NM
P/E on S&P Est. 1995	NM	Beta	1.69
Dividend Rate/Share	Nil	Shareholders	36,900
Shs. outstg. (M)	62.2	Market cap. (B)	$0.529
Avg. daily vol. (M)	1.581	Inst. holdings	37%
		Insider holdings	NA

Value of $10,000 invested 5 years ago: $ 2,486

Fiscal Year Ending Dec. 31

	1995	% Change	1994	% Change	1993	% Change
Revenues ()						
1Q	1,763	5%	1,686	-2%	1,716	4%
2Q	1,983	6%	1,880	4%	1,816	7%
3Q	—	—	1,751	NM	1,749	3%
4Q	—	—	1,681	-7%	1,802	10%
Yr.	—	—	6,997	-1%	7,083	6%
Income ()						
1Q	-96.88	NM	-196.7	NM	-61.03	-45%
2Q	112.9	NM	13.81	137%	5.83	NM
3Q	—	—	-180.1	NM	-177.6	68%
4Q	—	—	-322.0	NM	-116.5	-54%
Yr.	—	—	-684.9	NM	-349.4	NM
Earnings Per Share ()						
1Q	-1.91	NM	-3.64	NM	-1.65	NM
2Q	1.47	NM	-0.09	NM	-0.23	NM
3Q	E-0.75	NM	-3.32	NM	-3.33	NM
4Q	E-0.35	NM	-5.63	NM	-2.29	NM
Yr.	E-0.04	NM	-12.73	NM	-7.68	NM

Next earnings report expected: late October

USAir Group

Business Summary - 15-AUG-95

USAir Group, Inc. is a holding company whose principal subsidiary is USAir, Inc., the sixth largest U.S. air carrier. Other subsidiaries include Allegheny Airlines, Piedmont Airlines and Jetstream International Airlines.

As of January 1995, USAir provided regularly scheduled jet service to more than 150 cities in the U.S., Canada, Bermuda, the Caribbean, Mexico, Germany and France. Service to the U.K. is provided by code-sharing partner British Airways. Primary hubs are at Pittsburgh, Charlotte, Philadelphia and Baltimore/Washington.

Operating data for USAir in recent years (passenger- and seat-miles in billions):

	1994	1993	1992
Rev. pass.-miles	37.94	35.22	35.10
Avail. seat-miles	61.03	59.49	59.67
Load factor (%)	62.2	59.2	58.8
Rev. per RPM (cents)	15.61	17.27	16.49
Cost per ASM (cents)	11.02	11.09	10.83

A total of 10 regional carriers (including Allegheny, Piedmont and Jetstream) operate under the name "USAir Express." At January 4, 1995, USAir Express carriers served 185 airports.

At December 31, 1994, the USAir fleet consisted of 424 aircraft: six B-727s, 220 B-737s, 27 B-757s, nine B-767s, 31 MD-80s, 72 DC-9s, 40 F-100s and 19 F-28s. On order were 55 aircraft, the majority for delivery after 1999. The three regional subsidiaries operated 111 turboprops.

Important Developments

Jul. '95—The company said it was ending discussions with its unions on a wage concession package and will be concentrating on reducing labor costs through traditional collective bargaining. USAir said it still intends to achieve the labor cost savings it needs to sustain profitability. Earlier, the carrier noted that it will approach $400 million in cost reductions this year and that it expects to surpass its goal of $500 million next year.
Jul. '95—USAir reported a 3.4% increase in traffic for the first six months of 1995. Capacity rose 1.9%, and load factor was 63.3%, up from 62.3%.

Capitalization

Long Term Debt: $2,927,841,000 (3/95).
$92.50 Conv. Preferred Stock Series A: 358,000 shs. ($1,000 liquid. pref.); conv. into com. at $39.55 a sh.; owned by Berkshire Hathaway.
Conv. Preferred Stock Series F: 30,000 shs.($10,000 liquid. pref.); conv. into com. at $19.50 a sh.; owned by British Airways Plc.
Conv. Preferred Stock Series T: 10,000 shs.; conv. into com. at $20.50 and $26.40 a sh.; owned by British Airways Plc.
$4.375 Depositary Preferred Stock: 4,263,000 shs. ($50 liquid. pref.); conv. into 2.4925 com.; represents 0.01 sh. of $437.50 Ser. B cum. pfd. stk.

Per Share Data ()

(Year Ended Dec. 31)

	1994	1993	1992	1991	1990	1989
Tangible Bk. Val.	-18.71	-21.36	-23.11	7.24	15.43	25.07
Cash Flow	-6.90	-1.90	-6.94	-0.86	-3.35	4.29
Earnings	-12.73	-7.68	-13.88	-7.62	-10.89	-1.73
Dividends	Nil	Nil	Nil	Nil	0.09	0.12
Payout Ratio	Nil	Nil	Nil	Nil	NM	NM
Prices - High	15⅜	24¾	18⅜	24½	33¾	54¾
- Low	3⅞	11⅛	10½	7	12⅝	30⅝
P/E Ratio - High	NM	NM	NM	NM	NM	NM
- Low	NM	NM	NM	NM	NM	NM

Income Statement Analysis ()

	1994	%Chg	1993	%Chg	1992	%Chg	1991
Revs.	6,997	-1%	7,083	6%	6,686	3%	6,514
Oper. Inc.	113	-85%	753	NM	97.0	35%	72.0
Depr.	350	10%	318	-2%	326	5%	310
Int. Exp.	284	14%	250	NM	249	-4%	259
Pretax Inc.	-684	NM	-348	NM	-600	NM	-414
Eff. Tax Rate	NM	—	NM	—	NM	—	NM
Net Inc.	-684	NM	-348	NM	-600	NM	-304

Balance Sheet & Other Fin. Data ()

	1994	1993	1992	1991	1990	1989
Cash	452	368	296	320	408	15.0
Curr. Assets	1,117	1,178	988	1,029	1,253	936
Total Assets	6,808	6,878	6,595	6,454	6,574	6,069
Curr. Liab.	2,260	2,237	2,433	1,943	1,892	1,578
LT Debt	2,895	2,444	2,265	2,115	2,263	1,468
Common Eqty.	-1,142	-425	-168	1,105	1,434	1,893
Total Cap.	2,757	2,990	2,667	3,902	4,239	4,075
Cap. Exp.	180	816	440	499	1,245	1,078
Cash Flow	-412	-104	-325	-39.0	-149	189

Ratio Analysis

	1994	1993	1992	1991	1990	1989
Curr. Ratio	0.5	0.5	0.4	0.5	0.7	0.6
% LT Debt of Cap.	105.0	81.7	84.9	54.2	53.4	36.0
% Net Inc.of Revs.	NM	NM	NM	NM	NM	NM
% Ret. on Assets	NM	NM	NM	NM	NM	NM
% Ret. on Equity	NM	NM	NM	NM	NM	NM

Dividend Data —Common dividends, paid since 1980, were omitted in 1990. Preferred dividends were omitted in September 1994. A "poison pill" stock purchase rights plan was adopted in 1989.

Data as orig. reptd.; bef. results of disc. opers. and/or spec. items. Per share data adj. for stk. divs. as of ex-div. date.
E-Estimated. NA-Not Available. NM-Not Meaningful. NR-Not Ranked.

Office—2345 Crystal Dr., Arlington, VA 22227. **Tel**—(703) 418-5306. **Chrmn & CEO**—S. E. Schofield. **Pres & COO**—F. L. Salizzoni. **Exec VP & Secy**—J. T. Lloyd. **Sr VP & CFO**—J. W. Harper. **Investor Contact**—Laura F. Smith (703) 418-5009. **Dirs**—W. E. Buffett, E. I. Colodny, M. J. DeVito, G. J. W. Goodman, J. W. Harris, E. A. Horrigan Jr., R. LeBuhn, Sir Colin Marshall, R. P. Maynard, J. G. Medlin Jr., H. M. Merriman, C. T. Munger, F. L. Salizzoni, S. E. Schofield, R. W. Smith, D. M. Stevens. **Transfer Agent & Registrar**—Chemical Bank, NYC. **Incorporated** in Delaware in 1937. **Empl**-45,500. **S&P Analyst:** Joe Victor Shammas

United Technologies

NYSE Symbol **UTX**
In S&P 500

09-AUG-95

Industry:
Aerospace

Summary: United Technologies is a major producer of aircraft jet engines, helicopters, flight systems, air conditioning equipment, elevators and escalators, and automotive products.

S&P Opinion: Accumulate (★★★★)	Recent Price • 83⅝	Yield • 2.4%
	52 Wk Range • 84⅞-55	12-Mo. P/E • 15.6

Earnings vs. Previous Year
▲=Up ▼=Down ▶=No Change

Quantitative Evaluations

Outlook
(1 Lowest—5 Highest)
• **3+**

Fair Value
• **81¾**

Risk
• **Low**

Earn./Div. Rank
• **B**

Technical Eval.
• **Bullish** since 12/94

Rel. Strength Rank
(1 Lowest—99 Highest)
• **68**

Insider Activity
• **NA**

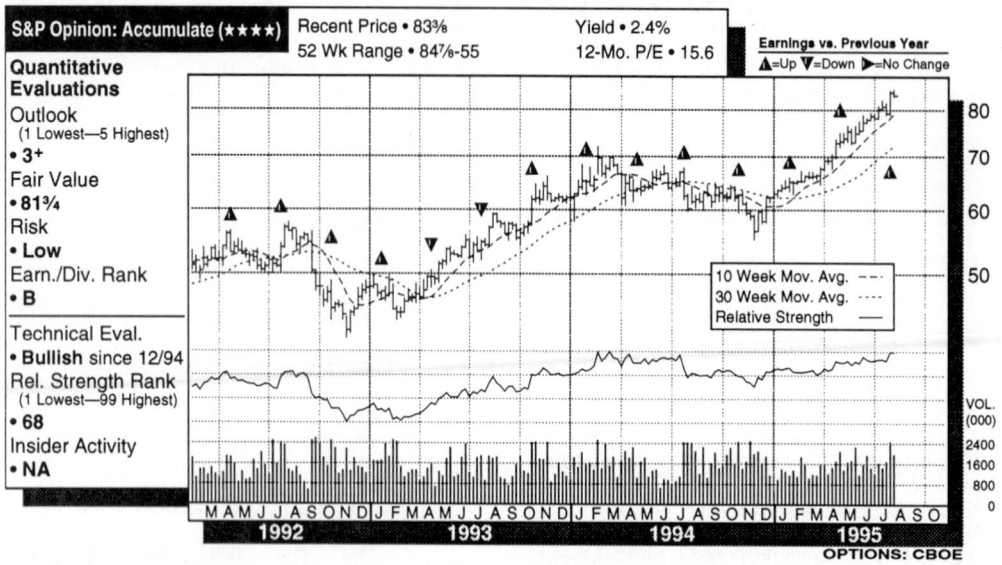

10 Week Mov. Avg. ---
30 Week Mov. Avg. ---
Relative Strength —

OPTIONS: CBOE

Overview - 09-AUG-95

Revenues for 1995 are expected to increase, reflecting improvement in commercial activities. Otis will benefit from expansion in international markets and a greater emphasis on maintenance activities. Carrier should profit from new products and improving world economies. Gains are expected at UT Automotive from the trend toward increased electrical content per vehicle. Higher spare parts revenues and greater deliveries of commercial aircraft engines should slightly outweigh lower military sales at Pratt & Whitney. However, flight systems sales are expected to fall with reduced U.S. government defense spending. Nevertheless, earnings should benefit from strong cost reduction efforts, foreign exchange translation gains, asset sales, and the absence of restructuring charges.

Valuation - 09-AUG-95

Management has been effective at improving efficiency and freeing assets. Consequently, operating margins have improved significantly in recent years. With revenues of $21 billion, each 1% of margin improvement translates into increased earnings of about $1.00 per share; at current levels, operating margin still has room to grow. Productivity gains, combined with continued robust sales growth, will lead to increased earnings over the next few years. With its P/E multiple near the industry average, we view UTX shares as attractive.

Key Stock Statistics

S&P EPS Est. 1995	5.70	Tang. Bk. Value/Share	25.77
P/E on S&P Est. 1995	14.6	Beta	1.20
S&P EPS Est. 1996	6.35	Shareholders	28,000
Dividend Rate/Share	2.00	Market cap. (B)	$ 10.3
Shs. outstg. (M)	123.4	Inst. holdings	79%
Avg. daily vol. (M)	0.406	Insider holdings	NA

Value of $10,000 invested 5 years ago: $ 18,482

Fiscal Year Ending Dec. 31

	1995	% Change	1994	% Change	1993	% Change
Revenues (Million $)						
1Q	5,344	10%	4,838	NM	4,864	-6%
2Q	5,840	6%	5,489	-1%	5,570	-3%
3Q	—	—	5,253	2%	5,128	-5%
4Q	—	—	5,675	3%	5,519	-4%
Yr.	—	—	21,197	NM	21,081	-4%
Income (Million $)						
1Q	135.0	101%	67.00	5%	64.00	-32%
2Q	218.0	32%	165.0	27%	130.0	-12%
3Q	—	—	188.0	20%	157.0	25%
4Q	—	—	165.0	21%	136.0	NM
Yr.	—	—	585.0	20%	487.0	NM
Earnings Per Share ($)						
1Q	1.03	106%	0.50	16%	0.43	-37%
2Q	1.65	34%	1.23	29%	0.95	-14%
3Q	E1.52	—	1.41	22%	1.16	23%
4Q	E1.50	—	1.26	29%	0.98	NM
Yr.	E5.70	—	4.40	25%	3.53	NM

Next earnings report expected: late October

Business Summary - 09-AUG-95

United Technologies Corp. produces and sells high technology products and services. Contributions by segment in 1994 were:

	Revs.	Profits
Pratt & Whitney	27%	25%
Carrier	23%	18%
Otis	22%	27%
Flight systems	15%	18%
Automotive	13%	12%

Non-U.S. operations accounted for 39% of revenues in 1994, while exports contributed another 14%. U.S. government business comprised 18% of sales.

Pratt & Whitney is a leading maker of engines and spare parts for commercial, general aviation and military aircraft. Sales to Boeing accounted for 21% and to McDonnell Douglas for 8% of 1994 P & W revenues. P & W also makes rocket motors and provides maintenance and overhaul services.

Carrier makes heating, air conditioning and refrigeration systems. Commercial products accounted for 46% of the segment's sales in 1994, and residential products for 33%.

Otis is the leading producer of elevators and escalators. In 1994, maintenance and repair work accounted for 50% of division revenues, new equipment for 36%, and modernization services for 13%.

Flight systems include Sikorsky helicopters for military and commercial operations, and Hamilton Standard aircraft and space controls and parts. The Norden radar and electronic systems unit was sold to Westinghouse in 1994.

UT Automotive produces wiring systems, electromechanical and hydraulic devices and electric motors.

Important Developments

Jul. '95—The company said all five of its business segments achieved double-digit year-to-year operating income growth in the second quarter, paced by international market expansion and productivity improvements.

Jul. '95—Pratt & Whitney said its PT6A-68 engine was chosen to power the aircraft the Air Force will use as its primary trainer for pilots. Separately, P&W's PW150 engine was chosen to power the de Havilland Dash 8 Series 400 regional airliner.

Jun. '95—Sikorsky announced the launch of full scale development of the S-92 Helibus. First flight for the medium-lift utility helicopter is scheduled for 1998 and certification is expected in 2000.

Capitalization

Long Term Debt: $1,753,000,000 (6/95).

Minority Interest: $400,000,000 (12/94).

Series A ESOP 7.38% Prefd. Stock: $905,000,000. 13,633,513 shs. (liq. pref. $65 per sh.). Conv. sh.-for-sh. into com. Entitled to 1.3 votes per sh.

Per Share Data ($)

(Year Ended Dec. 31)

	1994	1993	1992	1991	1990	1989
Tangible Bk. Val.	24.69	23.10	21.29	21.37	31.89	28.17
Cash Flow	10.29	9.99	6.86	-2.62	11.71	10.16
Earnings	4.40	3.53	-0.05	-8.91	5.91	5.34
Dividends	1.90	1.80	1.90	1.80	1.80	1.60
Payout Ratio	43%	51%	NM	NM	31%	28%
Prices - High	72	66⅛	57⅞	54½	62½	57⅜
- Low	55	43¾	41½	42⅛	40⅛	39⅞
P/E Ratio - High	16	19	NM	NM	11	11
- Low	13	12	NM	NM	7	7

Income Statement Analysis (Million $)

	1994	%Chg	1993	%Chg	1992	%Chg	1991
Revs.	21,161	NM	21,081	-4%	22,032	5%	20,953
Oper. Inc.	2,108	7%	1,975	92%	1,028	-13%	1,178
Depr.	793	-3%	815	-4%	852	12%	764
Int. Exp.	294	5%	280	-16%	334	-18%	409
Pretax Inc.	1,076	18%	909	NM	200	NM	-890
Eff. Tax Rate	36%	—	37%	—	39%	—	NM
Net Inc.	585	20%	487	NM	35.0	NM	-1,020

Balance Sheet & Other Fin. Data (Million $)

	1994	1993	1992	1991	1990	1989
Cash	386	421	354	523	201	267
Curr. Assets	8,228	7,706	8,101	8,931	9,012	8,507
Total Assets	15,624	15,618	15,928	15,985	15,918	14,598
Curr. Liab.	6,553	6,920	7,037	6,577	5,951	6,376
LT Debt	1,885	1,939	2,358	2,903	2,902	1,960
Common Eqty.	3,752	3,598	3,370	3,961	5,343	4,739
Total Cap.	6,572	6,259	6,411	7,555	9,002	7,381
Cap. Exp.	759	846	920	1,193	1,208	1,251
Cash Flow	1,356	1,259	845	-318	1,415	1,308

Ratio Analysis

	1994	1993	1992	1991	1990	1989
Curr. Ratio	1.3	1.1	1.2	1.4	1.5	1.3
% LT Debt of Cap.	28.7	31.0	36.8	38.4	32.2	26.6
% Net Inc.of Revs.	2.8	2.3	0.2	NM	3.5	3.6
% Ret. on Assets	3.8	3.1	0.2	NM	4.9	5.3
% Ret. on Equity	15.5	12.0	NM	NM	14.2	14.9

Dividend Data (Dividends have been paid since 1936.)

Amt. of Div. $	Date Decl.	Ex-Div. Date	Stock of Record	Payment Date
0.500	Aug. 01	Aug. 15	Aug. 19	Sep. 10 '94
0.500	Oct. 31	Nov. 14	Nov. 18	Dec. 10 '94
0.500	Feb. 06	Feb. 17	Feb. 24	Mar. 10 '95
0.500	Apr. 25	May. 15	May. 19	Jun. 10 '95
0.500	Jul. 31	Aug. 16	Aug. 18	Sep. 10 '95

Data as orig. reptd.; bef. results of disc. opers. and/or spec. items. Per share data adj. for stk. divs. as of ex-div. date. E-Estimated. NA-Not Available. NM-Not Meaningful. NR-Not Ranked.

Office—United Technologies Building, Hartford, CT 06101. **Tel**—(203) 728-7000. **Chrmn**—R. F. Daniell. **Pres & CEO**—G. David. **VP & Treas**—F. C. Flynn, Jr. **VP & Secy**—W. H. Trachsel. **Investor Contact**—Angelo J. Messina (203-728-7575). **Dirs**—H. H. Baker, Jr., A. H. Chayes, R. F. Daniell, G. David, R. F. Dee, C. W. Duncan, Jr., P. G. Gyllenhammar, G. D. Hines, C. R. Lee, R. H. Malott, H. A. Wagner, J. G. Wexler. **Transfer Agent & Registrar**—First Chicago Trust Co. of New York, NYC. **Incorporated** in Delaware in 1934. **Empl**-171,500. **S&P Analyst:** Joe Victor Shammas

Unocal Corp.

NYSE Symbol **UCL**
In S&P 500

03-AUG-95 Industry:
Oil and Gas

Summary: Unocal is an integrated crude oil and natural gas company with interests in chemicals, geothermal energy and minerals.

| S&P Opinion: Accumulate (★★★★) | Recent Price • 28 | Yield • 2.9% |
| | 52 Wk Range • 30⅛-25¼ | 12-Mo. P/E • 54.9 |

Quantitative Evaluations

Outlook
(1 Lowest—5 Highest)
• **1**

Fair Value
• **21⅞**

Risk
• **Low**

Earn./Div. Rank
• **B**

Technical Eval.
• **Bearish** since 7/95

Rel. Strength Rank
(1 Lowest—99 Highest)
• **27**

Insider Activity
• **Neutral**

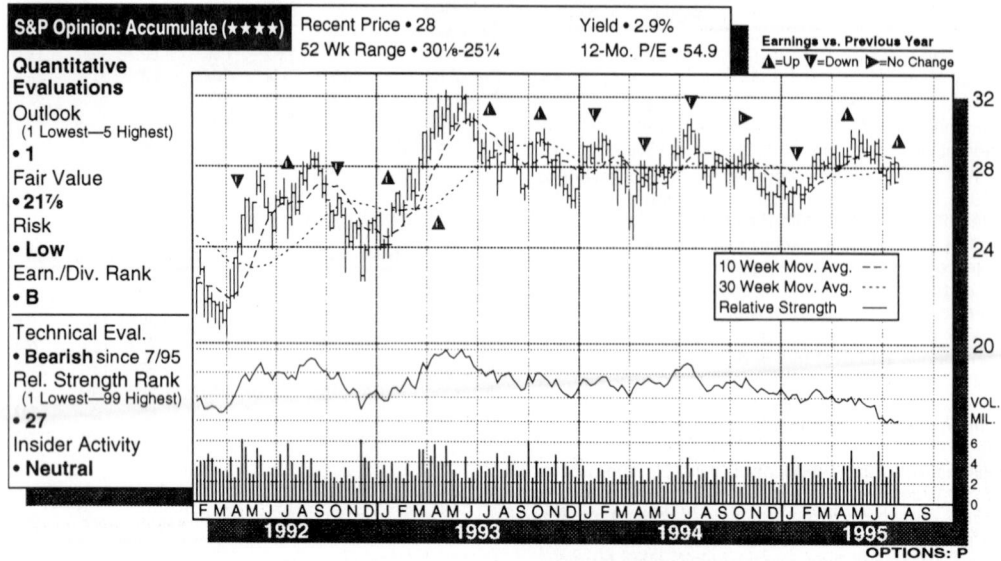

Earnings vs. Previous Year
▲=Up ▼=Down ▶=No Change

10 Week Mov. Avg. – – –
30 Week Mov. Avg. ·······
Relative Strength ——

OPTIONS: P

Overview - 03-AUG-95

Profits should trend higher in 1995 and beyond, reflecting improved refined product margins, greater product sales and healthy chemical and fertilizer segment results. Strong demand for natural gas from the Pacific Rim and the company's strategy of becoming the low-cost producer in the region bodes well for future results. With demand for reformulated gasoline (RFG) poised to soar in California, due to federally imposed mandates, Unocal should be able to capitalize on its refineries which are currently geared toward RFG production. We believe neighboring states will not have sufficient RFG capacity to export significant quantities into California, which should result in improved margins on RFG in the state.

Valuation - 03-AUG-95

The shares have traded in a narrow range in 1995, as weak natural gas prices have kept a damper on earnings prospects. UCL's strategy of becoming the low-cost producer of natural gas in Asia is expected to pay off in coming years. We believe the benefits of experience there will give the company an advantage. UCL's downstream operations in California have been hurt in recent periods by weaker than expected refining margins and scheduled maintenance. However, we are optimistic about prospects in California. Expansion into car wash and convenience store operations will lead to improved margins through 1996. We believe that currently low natural gas prices will improve by year-end, driving share price growth.

Key Stock Statistics

S&P EPS Est. 1995	1.35	Tang. Bk. Value/Share	9.56
P/E on S&P Est. 1995	20.7	Beta	0.68
Dividend Rate/Share	0.80	Shareholders	44,500
Shs. outstg. (M)	245.4	Market cap. (B)	$ 7.1
Avg. daily vol. (M)	0.703	Inst. holdings	66%
		Insider holdings	NA

Value of $10,000 invested 5 years ago: $ 11,030

Fiscal Year Ending Dec. 31

	1995	% Change	1994	% Change	1993	% Change
Revenues (Million $)						
1Q	1,960	7%	1,830	-17%	2,200	-8%
2Q	2,290	13%	2,020	NM	2,040	-22%
3Q	—	—	—	—	1,910	-23%
4Q	—	—	1,984	3%	1,930	-19%
Yr.	—	—	7,965	-1%	8,080	-18%
Income (Million $)						
1Q	74.00	37%	54.00	-62%	141.0	NM
2Q	78.00	56%	50.00	-43%	88.00	33%
3Q	—	—	60.00	-14%	70.00	NM
4Q	—	—	-68.00	NM	44.00	-57%
Yr.	—	—	124.0	-64%	343.0	75%
Earnings Per Share ($)						
1Q	0.27	23%	0.22	-60%	0.55	NM
2Q	0.28	33%	0.21	-36%	0.33	18%
3Q	E0.34	—	0.25	NM	0.25	NM
4Q	E0.45	—	-0.32	NM	0.14	-64%
Yr.	E1.35	—	0.36	-72%	1.27	69%

Next earnings report expected: early November

Unocal Corp.

Business Summary - 03-AUG-95

Unocal is an integrated petroleum and natural gas company engaged in worldwide exploration and production and domestic refining and marketing. It is also the world's largest producer of geothermal energy. The company has been extensively restructuring its operations. The UNO-VEN joint venture, formed in 1989 with the Venezuela national oil company, represents the company's interests in its Chicago refinery and related assets. UCL is streamlining its California geothermal operations. Divestitures of mineral and chemical properties are planned.

Profits	1994	1993
Exploration & production	66%	62%
Refin., market. & trans.	21%	25%
Chemicals	8%	6%
Geothermal	5%	7%

Net crude oil and condensate production in 1994 averaged 260,000 barrels a day (246,000 in 1993), natural gas production 1,766 million cubic feet a day (1,580 Mmcf), natural gas liquids 22,000 b/d (20,000 b/d), input to crude oil processing units 295,000 b/d (288,000 b/d) and sales of petroleum products 316,000 b/d (345,000 b/d). The company produced 7.5 million megawatt-hours of geothermal energy during 1994.

Net proved reserves at 1994 year-end were 697 million barrels of crude oil and condensate (764 million bbl.) and 6,911 billion cubic feet of natural gas (6,632 Bcf). In 1995, UCL will concentrate its spending on natural gas in North America and Southeast Asia.

Important Developments

Jul. '95—UCL reported second quarter earnings of $78 million, or $0.28 per share. Excluding nonrecurring items, income from operations was $101 million, or $0.37 a share, versus $74 million ($0.27). A 3% rise in natural gas production and 17% higher oil prices boosted exploration and production profits to $105 million from $89 milion a year ago. '76 Products Co. (refining & marketing) incurred another loss with weak West Coast refining margins persisting, though there was an improvement from first quarter levels following the completion of refinery maintenance. Agricultural products earnings rose to $58 million from $15 million, benefiting from strong nitrogen fertilizer sales prices and volumes. Meanwhile, carbon and minerals' earnings rose to $17 million from $10 million mainly on improved lanthanide earnings. Capital expenditures increased 30%, year to year.

Capitalization

Long Term Debt: $3,771,000,000 (6/95).
$3.50 Cum. Conv. Preferred Stock: 10,250,000 shs. ($50 liquid. pref.); conv. into 1.626 com.

Per Share Data ($)

(Year Ended Dec. 31)

	1994	1993	1992	1991	1990	1989
Tangible Bk. Val.	9.43	10.84	10.88	10.50	10.87	9.83
Cash Flow	4.27	5.27	4.80	4.14	5.54	5.00
Earnings	0.36	1.27	0.75	0.31	1.71	1.53
Dividends	0.80	0.73	0.70	0.70	0.70	0.55
Payout Ratio	NM	57%	93%	225%	41%	36%
Prices - High	30¾	32⅝	28⅞	29½	34½	31¼
- Low	24⅜	23½	20¼	20⅝	24⅝	18⅝
P/E Ratio - High	85	26	39	95	20	20
- Low	68	19	27	67	14	12

Income Statement Analysis (Million $)

	1994	%Chg	1993	%Chg	1992	%Chg	1991
Revs.	6,904	-5%	7,261	-18%	8,895	-8%	9,685
Oper. Inc.	1,348	-16%	1,611	6%	1,523	4%	1,458
Depr.	947	-2%	963	NM	964	7%	899
Int. Exp.	308	-8%	334	-19%	413	-5%	435
Pretax Inc.	294	-52%	611	73%	354	62%	218
Eff. Tax Rate	58%	—	44%	—	43%	—	64%
Net Inc.	124	-64%	343	75%	196	168%	73.0

Balance Sheet & Other Fin. Data (Million $)

	1994	1993	1992	1991	1990	1989
Cash	148	205	157	175	130	348
Curr. Assets	1,528	1,578	1,660	1,896	2,071	1,993
Total Assets	9,337	9,254	9,452	9,836	9,762	9,257
Curr. Liab.	1,257	1,196	1,436	1,543	1,846	1,475
LT Debt	3,461	3,468	3,546	4,563	4,047	3,887
Common Eqty.	2,302	2,616	2,618	2,464	2,550	2,300
Total Cap.	6,919	7,472	7,596	7,928	7,711	7,512
Cap. Exp.	1,272	1,249	959	1,470	1,316	1,050
Cash Flow	1,035	1,270	1,143	972	1,298	1,169

Ratio Analysis

	1994	1993	1992	1991	1990	1989
Curr. Ratio	1.2	1.3	1.2	1.2	1.1	1.4
% LT Debt of Cap.	50.0	46.4	46.7	57.6	52.5	51.7
% Net Inc.of Revs.	1.8	4.7	2.2	0.8	3.8	3.6
% Ret. on Assets	1.3	3.7	2.0	0.7	4.2	3.8
% Ret. on Equity	3.6	11.7	7.0	2.9	16.5	16.0

Dividend Data (Dividends have been paid since 1916. A dividend reinvestment plan is available.)

Amt. of Div. $	Date Decl.	Ex-Div. Date	Stock of Record	Payment Date
0.200	Sep. 26	Oct. 04	Oct. 11	Nov. 10 '94
0.200	Dec. 05	Jan. 04	Jan. 10	Feb. 10 '95
0.200	Mar. 27	Apr. 04	Apr. 10	May. 10 '95
0.200	May. 22	Jul. 06	Jul. 10	Aug. 10 '95

Data as orig. reptd.; bef. results of disc. opers. and/or spec. items. Per share data adj. for stk. divs. as of ex-div. date. E-Estimated. NA-Not Available. NM-Not Meaningful. NR-Not Ranked.

Office—1201 West Fifth St. (P.O. Box 7600), Los Angeles, CA 90051. **Tel**—(213) 977-7600. **Chrmn & CEO**—R. C. Beach. **Pres**—J. F. Imle Jr. **CFO**—N. Schmale. **VP-Secy**—D. P. Codon. **Investor Contacts**—T. R. Brunet--LA (213) 977-6188; W. S. Schneider--NYC (212) 582-2520. **Dirs**—J. W. Amerman, R. C. Beach, M. G. Becket, J. W. Creighton, M. R. Currie, F. C. Herringer, J. F. Imle Jr., D. P. Jacobs, N. E. Schmale, R. J. Stegemeier, C. R. Weaver, J. S. Whisler, M. v. N. Whitman. **Transfer Agents & Registrars**—Chemical Trust Co. of California, Los Angeles; Chemical Bank, NYC. **Incorporated** in California in 1890; reincorporated in Delaware in 1983. **Empl**-13,127. **S&P Analyst:** Raymond J. Deacon

Upjohn Co.

NYSE Symbol **UPJ**
In S&P 500

23-AUG-95

Industry:
Drugs-Generic and OTC

Summary: This pharmaceutical company plans to merge with Swedish drugmaker Pharmacia AB through a tax-free exchange of stock.

S&P Opinion: Accumulate (★★★★)

Recent Price • 39⅝	Yield • 3.4%
52 Wk Range • 40⅛-29⅞	12-Mo. P/E • 14.0

Quantitative Evaluations

Outlook
(1 Lowest—5 Highest)
• **1+**

Fair Value
• **31¾**

Risk
• **Low**

Earn./Div. Rank
• **A**

Technical Eval.
• **Bearish** since 2/95

Rel. Strength Rank
(1 Lowest—99 Highest)
• **87**

Insider Activity
• **NA**

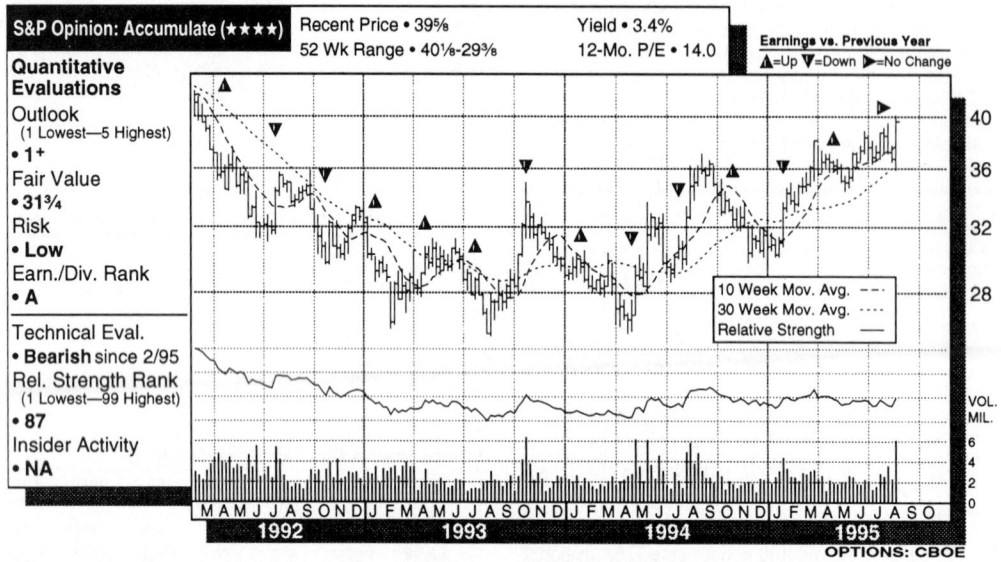

Earnings vs. Previous Year
▲=Up ▼=Down ▶=No Change

10 Week Mov. Avg. — · —
30 Week Mov. Avg. · · · ·
Relative Strength ——

OPTIONS: CBOE

Overview - 23-AUG-95

Based on current operations, sales are expected to decline in 1995 from 1994's $3.3 billion. Despite indicated gains in Depo-Provera contraceptive and several other lines, overall drug sales are expected to suffer from further generic erosion in Xanax and Halcion psychotherapeutics, Ansaid antiarthritic and Micronase antidiabetic. Despite cost control efforts, profitability is expected to be hurt by lower volume and a rise in the tax rate to about 29% from 24%. However, EPS comparisons will benefit from fewer shares outstanding, and from a gain of $0.15 associated with the termination of a co-marketing alliance.

Valuation - 23-AUG-95

In August 1995, after years of rumors about a takeover or merger, Upjohn agreed to merge with Swedish drugmaker Pharmacia AB via a tax-free exchange of stock. The company will benefit from Pharmacia's diverse portfolio of drugs and European base of operations, while Pharmacia will gain expanded access in the U.S., the world's largest pharmaceutical market. The combined concern, to be called Pharmacia & Upjohn (P&U), had 1994 pro forma sales of nearly $7 billion, and earnings of $835 million. The merger is expected to generate cost synergies in excess of $500 million, of which 85% should be realized by the end of 1996. P&U should enjoy accelerated EPS growth in coming years.

Key Stock Statistics

S&P EPS Est. 1995	2.80	Tang. Bk. Value/Share	12.77
P/E on S&P Est. 1995	14.2	Beta	1.21
S&P EPS Est. 1996	2.75	Shareholders	46,600
Dividend Rate/Share	1.48	Market cap. (B)	$ 7.4
Shs. outstg. (M)	172.8	Inst. holdings	66%
Avg. daily vol. (M)	1.500	Insider holdings	0%

Value of $10,000 invested 5 years ago: $ 12,846

Fiscal Year Ending Dec. 31

	1995	% Change	1994	% Change	1993	% Change
Revenues (Million $)						
1Q	808.7	1%	800.7	-12%	912.3	5%
2Q	850.8	4%	818.7	-8%	894.6	1%
3Q	—	—	809.2	-8%	877.9	-2%
4Q	—	—	846.5	-9%	926.3	-6%
Yr.	—	—	3,275	-9%	3,611	NM
Income (Million $)						
1Q	151.6	22%	123.9	-19%	152.4	11%
2Q	115.9	-2%	118.1	-6%	125.3	1%
3Q	—	—	139.9	NM	-30.07	NM
4Q	—	—	107.2	-32%	156.9	2%
Yr.	—	—	489.1	22%	402.5	-26%
Earnings Per Share ($)						
1Q	0.85	21%	0.70	-18%	0.85	12%
2Q	0.66	NM	0.66	-6%	0.70	1%
3Q	E0.70	-11%	0.79	NM	-0.19	NM
4Q	E0.59	-2%	0.60	-32%	0.88	2%
Yr.	E2.80	2%	2.75	23%	2.24	-26%

Next earnings report expected: mid October

Upjohn Co.

Business Summary - 23-AUG-95

Upjohn produces prescription drugs, over-the-counter products and animal health items. The Asgrow Seed subsidiary (sales of $221 million in 1994) was sold in January 1995 for about $300 million.

Foreign operations accounted for 41% of sales and 17% of pretax earnings in 1994. R&D spending equaled 18.5% of sales in 1994, versus 18.3% in 1993.

Pharmaceuticals include reproductive and women's health drugs (16% of total 1994 revenues) such as Ogen estrogen replacement therapy, Depo-Provera injectable contraceptive, Provera progestin and Caverject for erectile dysfunction; central nervous system agents (14%) such as Xanax anti-anxiety and Halcion sleeping agent; steroids, anti-inflammatory and analgesic drugs (13%), which include Motrin and Ansaid antiarthritics and Medrol anti-inflammatory and anti-allergy treatment; anti-infectives (13%) such as Lincocin, Cleocin and Vantin; and animal health (10%) items such as feed additives and growth promotants. Other products (34%) include: Orinase, Tolinase, Micronase and Glynase antidiabetics; Rogaine topical minoxidil for male pattern baldness and female hair loss; and nonprescription items such as Kaopectate for diarrhea and Unicap vitamins. U.S. patents have expired on Ansaid, Xanax, Halcion and Micronase.

Important Developments

Aug. '95—The company and Swedish drugmaker Pharmacia AB signed a definitive agreement to merge via a tax-free exchange of stock. Each Upjohn common share would be exchanged for 1.45 shares of a new company, to be called Pharmacia & Upjohn (P&U). Pharmacia shareholders would receive one P&U share for each Class A or Class B Pharmacia share held. Upon completion of the merger, P&U would have about 504 million shares outstanding, equally divided between current Pharmacia and Upjohn shareholders. On a pro forma basis, P&U had 1994 sales of $7 billion, with EPS of $1.66. It would have sales in excess of $500 million in each of six key therapeutic areas. P&U's annual R&D spending would exceed $1 billion, with plans for 28 new product introductions and line extensions over the next three years. P&U plans to pay initial quarterly dividends of $0.27 a share. The transaction, subject to approval by shareholders of each concern and certain other conditions, is expected to be completed in November.

Capitalization

Long Term Debt: $782,205,000 (6/95), incl. guarantee of $267 million of ESOP debt.

Per Share Data ($)

(Year Ended Dec. 31)

	1994	1993	1992	1991	1990	1989
Tangible Bk. Val.	13.66	11.94	11.49	9.89	8.54	9.44
Cash Flow	3.69	3.17	3.98	3.76	3.16	2.29
Earnings	2.75	2.24	3.04	2.96	2.48	1.67
Dividends	1.48	1.11	1.76	1.21	1.00	0.91
Payout Ratio	54%	50%	57%	40%	40%	54%
Prices - High	37⅛	35	45⅞	49¼	44⅝	42⅛
- Low	25¾	25⅝	29⅝	34¾	33	27⅝
P/E Ratio - High	13	16	15	17	18	25
- Low	9	11	10	12	13	17

Income Statement Analysis (Million $)

	1994	%Chg	1993	%Chg	1992	%Chg	1991
Revs.	3,345	-8%	3,653	NM	3,669	7%	3,426
Oper. Inc.	763	-10%	845	-2%	862	NM	860
Depr.	163	NM	163	-2%	166	17%	142
Int. Exp.	36.7	-22%	47.2	12%	42.3	28%	33.0
Pretax Inc.	643	31%	490	-30%	700	-3%	720
Eff. Tax Rate	24%	—	18%	—	22%	—	25%
Net Inc.	489	22%	402	-27%	547	2%	537

Balance Sheet & Other Fin. Data (Million $)

	1994	1993	1992	1991	1990	1989
Cash	502	292	240	188	216	247
Curr. Assets	2,130	1,945	1,915	1,722	1,632	1,513
Total Assets	5,162	4,816	4,605	4,147	3,668	3,247
Curr. Liab.	1,119	1,058	1,139	1,039	842	851
LT Debt	796	802	678	570	550	256
Common Eqty.	2,365	2,071	2,005	1,734	1,506	1,736
Total Cap.	3,283	2,969	2,772	2,802	2,577	2,178
Cap. Exp.	252	324	295	258	247	242
Cash Flow	640	553	701	667	567	426

Ratio Analysis

	1994	1993	1992	1991	1990	1989
Curr. Ratio	1.9	1.8	1.7	1.7	1.9	1.8
% LT Debt of Cap.	24.2	27.0	24.5	20.4	21.3	11.8
% Net Inc.of Revs.	14.6	11.0	14.9	15.7	15.1	10.7
% Ret. on Assets	9.8	8.6	12.5	13.8	13.5	9.8
% Ret. on Equity	21.5	19.2	26.8	32.5	28.1	17.5

Dividend Data—Dividends have been paid since 1909. A dividend reinvestment plan is available. A poison pill stock purchase rights plan was adopted in 1986.

Amt. of Div. $	Date Decl.	Ex-Div. Date	Stock of Record	Payment Date
0.370	Sep. 20	Oct. 04	Oct. 11	Nov. 01 '94
0.370	Dec. 20	Jan. 04	Jan. 10	Feb. 01 '95
0.370	Mar. 21	Apr. 05	Apr. 11	May. 01 '95
0.370	Jun. 19	Jul. 07	Jul. 11	Aug. 01 '95

Data as orig. reptd.; bef. results of disc. opers. and/or spec. items. Per share data adj. for stk. divs. as of ex-div. date. E-Estimated. NA-Not Available. NM-Not Meaningful. NR-Not Ranked.

Office—7000 Portage Rd., Kalamazoo, MI 49001. **Tel**—(616) 323-4000. **Chrmn & CEO**—J. L. Zabriskie. **Pres**—L. S. Smith. **SVP & CFO**—R. C. Salisbury. **SVP & Secy**—K. M. Cyrus. **Treas**—S. J. Aschleman. **Investor Contact**—Barbara L. Guiness (616-323-5918). **Dirs**—R. H. Brown, F. C. Carlucci, M. K. Eickhoff, A. M. Gotto Jr., D. F. Grisham, L. C. Hoff, G. Kenney-Wallace, W. E. LaMothe, J. R. Mitchell, W. D. Mulholland, W. U. Parfet, L. S. Smith, J. L. Zabriskie. **Transfer Agent & Registrar**—Harris Trust and Savings Bank, Chicago, Ill. **Incorporated** in Delaware in 1958. **Empl**-16,500. **S&P Analyst:** H.B. Saftlas

USLIFE Corp.

NYSE Symbol **USH**
In S&P 500

26-SEP-95

Industry:
Insurance

Summary: This holding company mainly provides individual and group life and health insurance products. Other subsidiaries engage in real estate and investment advisory activities.

S&P Opinion: Hold (★★★)	Recent Price • 30⅛	Yield • 3.1%
	52 Wk Range • 31⅞-20⅝	12-Mo. P/E • 10.6

Quantitative Evaluations

Outlook
(1 Lowest—5 Highest)
• **3⁻**

Fair Value
• **30⅝**

Risk
• **Low**

Earn./Div. Rank
• **B+**

Technical Eval.
• **Bearish** since 7/95

Rel. Strength Rank
(1 Lowest—99 Highest)
• **63**

Insider Activity
• **Favorable**

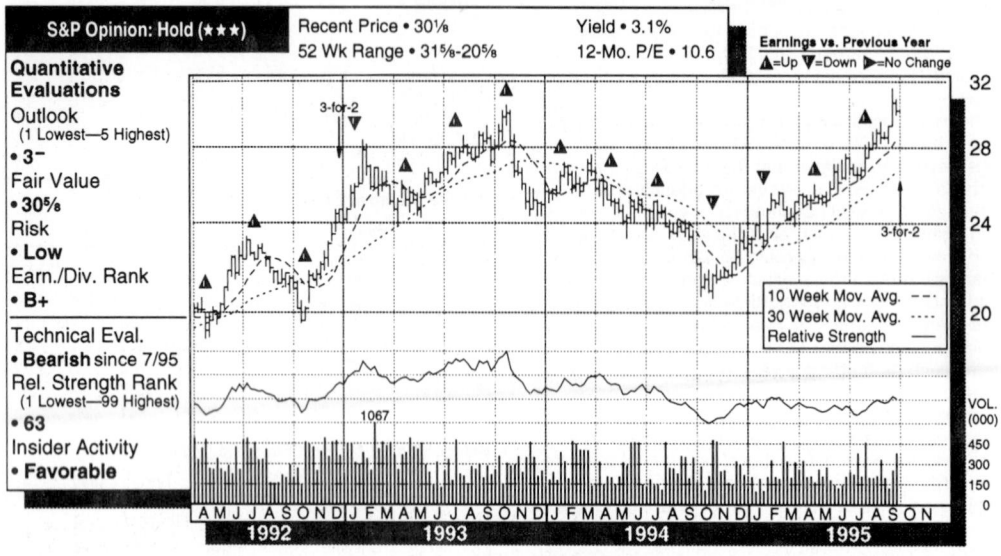

Earnings vs. Previous Year
▲=Up ▼=Down ▶=No Change

10 Week Mov. Avg. – – –
30 Week Mov. Avg. ·······
Relative Strength —

Overview - 26-SEP-95

Higher earnings are seen in coming periods, predicated upon continued strength in the individual life and annuities segments. After falling sharply in 1994 amid a planned reduction in sales taken to better balance the product mix, individual annuity sales growth may resume in 1995, albeit at a slower pace. It is assumed that individual annuities will retain their tax-deferred status. Longer term, growth here may be hampered by the looming competitive threat posed by banks and other financial institutions. Revenue growth in the group health indemnity line may be difficult amid an industry-wide shift into managed care, but recently implemented steps such as the joint venture with HIP may help USH recapture some heretofore lost premium revenue. An easing of interest rates will help margins in most lines, but may limit investment income growth.

Valuation - 26-SEP-95

These interest-sensitive shares underperformed the broader market during 1994 due to an upturn in interest rates. So far in 1995, the shares have recovered and are trading close to their 52-week high, amid hopes interest rates will continue to trend downward. As a result of their recent appreciation, the shares, which now trade at more than 10 times our aggressive operating earnings estimate for 1995, are at the upper end of their valuation range. Longer term, we would look for a pullback of 15% from current levels as an opportunity to accumulate the shares. the shares were split 3-for-2 in late September.

Key Stock Statistics

S&P EPS Est. 1995	2.93	Tang. Bk. Value/Share	33.66
P/E on S&P Est. 1995	10.3	Beta	1.17
S&P EPS Est. 1996	3.20	Shareholders	8,100
Dividend Rate/Share	0.93	Market cap. (B)	$ 1.0
Shs. outstg. (M)	34.4	Inst. holdings	70%
Avg. daily vol. (M)	0.048	Insider holdings	NA

Value of $10,000 invested 5 years ago: $ 18,495

Fiscal Year Ending Dec. 31

	1995	% Change	1994	% Change	1993	% Change
Revenues (Million $)						
1Q	418.8	7%	390.7	2%	382.8	—
2Q	443.2	3%	428.9	5%	407.1	—
3Q	—	—	413.8	4%	397.5	—
4Q	—	—	417.8	1%	412.7	5%
Yr.	—	—	1,651	3%	1,600	5%
Income (Million $)						
1Q	24.29	3%	23.62	15%	20.46	17%
2Q	26.17	8%	24.16	2%	23.73	20%
3Q	—	—	25.51	-4%	26.53	33%
4Q	—	—	22.89	-13%	26.43	112%
Yr.	—	—	96.19	NM	97.16	40%
Earnings Per Share ($)						
1Q	0.70	2%	0.69	14%	0.60	17%
2Q	0.75	8%	0.70	2%	0.69	20%
3Q	—	—	0.73	-5%	0.77	32%
4Q	—	—	0.67	-14%	0.77	115%
Yr.	E2.93	5%	2.79	-2%	2.83	39%

Next earnings report expected: late October

Business Summary - 20-SEP-95

USLIFE is a holding company that mainly provides individual and group life and health insurance products through subsidiaries. Subsidiaries are also engaged in investment advisory, broker-dealer, real estate and data processing and administrative services.

Through its life insurance subsidiaries, USH offers individual life insurance and annuity policies, group life and health insurance with particular emphasis on small groups, and credit insurance. Several life subsidiaries also offer products designed for funding pension, profit sharing and other qualified plans. At year-end 1994, life insurance in force totaled $142 billion, of which individual life accounted for 61%, group 21%, credit 6%, and other 12%. In 1994, total life premiums accounted for 51% of total premiums, and health for 49%. Individual life (including credit life) accounted for 63% of total life premiums, and group health 86% of total health premiums. Despite regional concentrations, several subsidiaries conduct business in all states.

Real estate activities are conducted through USLIFE Realty Corp. and its subsidiary, USLIFE Real Estate Service Corp. USLIFE Advisers Inc. and USLIFE Equity Sales Corp., a registered broker-dealer, engage in investment activities.

Important Developments

Jul. '95—USH noted that pretax operating profits for the first half of 1995 rose 6.8%, year to year, on a fractional rise in premiums. These results reflect growth in the core individual life insurance line, partly offset by a pretax loss in the group health area as USH de-emphasizes its small group major medical business. Segment highlights include an 11% rise in individual life pretax profits, reflecting improved mortality and persistency and growth in investment income. Improved first quarter underwriting trends offset weaker secondquarter results and led to a 63% rise in group life pretax operating profits. Total life insurance segment pretax profits increased 14%, to $106.8 million from $93.7 million. Total health insurance pretax profits plunged 85%, to $1.1 million from $7.4 million, primarily reflecting a $1.7 million pretax loss (versus a year earlier profit of $3.8 million) in the group health area.

Feb. '95—USH formed USLIFE Financial Institution Marketing Group, Inc., to capitalize on growing opportunities to sell its life insurance products through various other financial institutions.

Capitalization

Long Term Debt: $349,425,000 (6/95).
Conv. Preferred Stock: $541,000.

Per Share Data ($)
(Year Ended Dec. 31)

	1994	1993	1992	1991	1990	1989
Tangible Bk. Val.	25.63	28.41	26.36	28.68	26.85	24.78
Oper. Earnings	2.81	2.67	2.09	2.18	1.90	1.81
Earnings	2.79	2.83	2.03	2.15	1.90	2.06
Dividends	0.84	0.81	0.76	0.71	0.66	0.63
Payout Ratio	30%	28%	37%	33%	35%	30%
Prices - High	27⅝	30½	25½	21¼	20⅛	21⅜
- Low	20⅝	23⅞	17⅜	12	10⅜	15⅛
P/E Ratio - High	10	11	13	10	11	10
- Low	7	8	9	6	5	7

Income Statement Analysis (Million $)

	1994	%Chg	1993	%Chg	1992	%Chg	1991
Life Ins. In Force	141,682	13%	125,012	9%	115,000	7%	107,868
Premium Income Life	495	9%	455	7%	427	4%	409
Prem.Inc A & H	471	-4%	489	-2%	500	16%	432
Premium Income Other	Nil		Nil		Nil		Nil
Net Invest. Inc.	461	4%	445	7%	414	14%	362
Total Revs.	1,651	3%	1,600	5%	1,529	11%	1,383
Pretax Inc.	147	-3%	152	46%	104	-6%	111
Net Oper. Inc.	97.0	5%	92.0	35%	68.0	-11%	76.0
Net Inc.	96.0	-1%	97.0	39%	70.0	-7%	75.0

Balance Sheet & Other Fin. Data (Million $)

	1994	1993	1992	1991	1990	1989
Cash & Equiv.	180	178	184	176	161	147
Premiums Due	53.7	52.3	39.8	32.9	29.7	28.6
Inv. Assets Bonds	5,067	4,820	4,259	3,511	2,798	2,545
Inv. Assets Stock	5.0	9.0	20.0	24.0	25.0	26.0
Inv. Assets Loans	603	643	672	720	728	738
Inv. Assets Total	5,724	5,523	5,022	4,322	3,629	3,393
Deferred Policy Cost	793	742	706	649	605	598
Total Assets	7,004	6,740	6,095	5,329	4,573	4,336
Debt	349	349	349	249	349	349
Common Eqty.	877	965	890	969	928	929

Ratio Analysis

	1994	1993	1992	1991	1990	1989
% Ret. on Revs.	5.8	6.1	4.6	5.4	5.6	6.7
% Ret. on Assets	1.4	1.5	1.2	1.5	1.5	1.9
% Ret. on Equity	10.4	10.5	7.8	7.9	7.4	8.7
% Invest. Yield	7.9	8.4	8.9	9.1	9.2	9.3

Dividend Data —Dividends have been paid since 1951. A dividend reinvestment plan is available. A "poison pill" stock purchase rights plan was adopted in 1986.

Amt. of Div. $	Date Decl.	Ex-Div. Date	Stock of Record	Payment Date
0.330	Oct. 25	Nov. 08	Nov. 15	Dec. 01 '94
0.330	Jan. 24	Feb. 08	Feb. 14	Mar. 01 '95
0.330	Apr. 25	May. 09	May. 15	Jun. 01 '95
0.350	Jul. 25	Aug. 11	Aug. 15	Sep. 01 '95
3-for-2	Jul. 25	Sep. 25	Sep. 01	Sep. 22 '95

Data as orig. reptd.; bef. results of disc. opers. and/or spec. items. Per share data adj. for stk. divs. as of ex-div. date.
E-Estimated. NA-Not Available. NM-Not Meaningful. NR-Not Ranked.

Office—125 Maiden Lane, New York, NY 10038. **Tel**—(212) 709-6000. **Chrmn**—G. E. Crosby, Jr. **Pres & CEO**—W. A. Simpson. **Vice Chrmn & CFO**—G. F. Henderson. **VP, Secy & Investor Contact**—R. G. Hohn. **Dirs**— K. Black, Jr., W. J. Catacosinos, G. E. Crosby, Jr., A. L. D'Alton, C. A. Davis, J. R. Galvin, R. E. Grant, G. F. Henderson, T. H. Lenagh, R. H. Osborne, E. W. Pyne, J. W. Riehm, C. S. Ruisi, F. R. Saul, R. L. Shafer, W. G. Sharwell, W. A. Simpson, B. W. Sprinkel, P. C. Walker. **Transfer Agent & Registrar**—Chemical Bank, NYC. **Incorporated** in New York in 1850; reincorporated in 1966. **Empl**-2,140. **S&P Analyst:** Catherine A. Seifert

V. F. Corp.

NYSE Symbol **VFC**
In S&P 500

29-SEP-95 Industry:
Textiles

Summary: This global apparel company produces jeans, decorated knitwear and sportswear, intimate apparel, children's playwear and specialty apparel under some 25 well-known brand names.

S&P Opinion: Hold (★★★)

Recent Price • 49⅝
52 Wk Range • 57⅛-44¼

Yield • 2.7%
12-Mo. P/E • 11.3

Quantitative Evaluations

Outlook
(1 Lowest—5 Highest)
• **2+**

Fair Value
• **47¼**

Risk
• **Low**

Earn./Div. Rank
• **A-**

Technical Eval.
• **Bearish** since 9/95

Rel. Strength Rank
(1 Lowest—99 Highest)
• **16**

Insider Activity
• **Neutral**

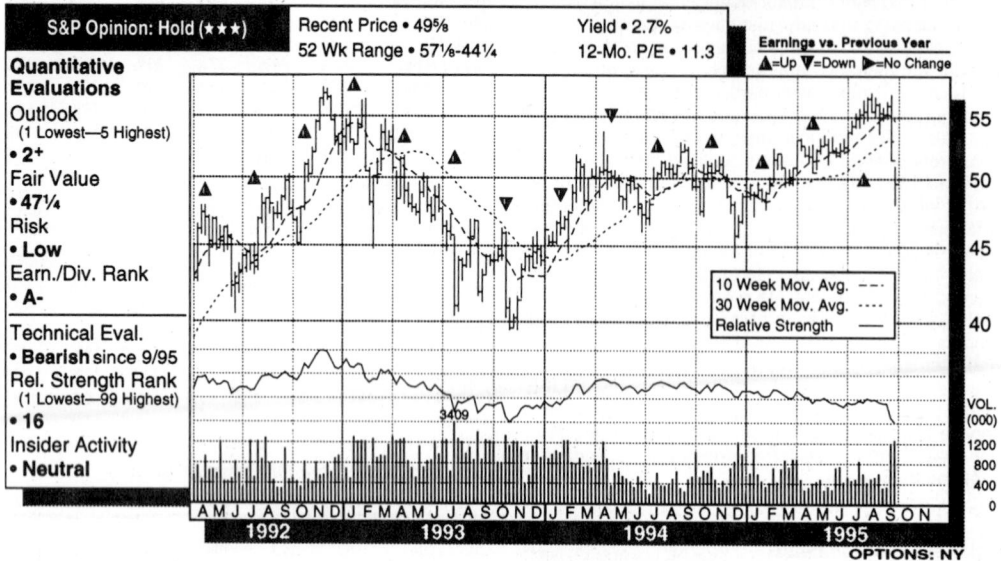

Earnings vs. Previous Year
▲=Up ▼=Down ►=No Change

10 Week Mov. Avg. - - -
30 Week Mov. Avg. ·······
Relative Strength ——

OPTIONS: NY

Overview - 29-SEP-95

Sales should continue to rise in 1995, with gains at all divisions. Sales will not be as strong as previously estimated, however, reflecting the sluggish apparel retail environment in the summer and a non-existent back-to-school season. Weaker operating margins in the second quarter are expected to hurt full-year margins. As a result of weak sales in late summer 1995, VFC has curtailed production in order to control inventories, and will thus incur various overhead expenses without the volume to offset these expenses. Full-year earnings will also be hurt by a one-time $0.10-a-share charge to close one of the jeans plants in Europe. Over the longer term, however, VFC hopes to grow consolidated sales and net income at least 10% annually.

Valuation - 29-SEP-95

These shares recently came under pressure when the company announced in mid-September that full-year earnings would be lower than expected due to the weak retail environment for basic clothing. As a result, we lowered our opinion on the stock to a hold. Until there are some signs that demand for apparel is picking up, at least for basic apparel, we feel these shares are likely to trade in a narrow range. The stock is still appealing over the longer term, however. VFC is one of the premier companies in the apparel industry with strong share positions in the various markets it serves. It has excelled in developing state-of-the art manufacturing and distribution systems, and is one of the most technologically advanced companies in its industry.

Key Stock Statistics

S&P EPS Est. 1995	4.00	Tang. Bk. Value/Share	13.03
P/E on S&P Est. 1995	12.4	Beta	1.36
S&P EPS Est. 1996	4.80	Shareholders	8,200
Dividend Rate/Share	1.36	Market cap. (B)	$ 3.3
Shs. outstg. (M)	63.8	Inst. holdings	80%
Avg. daily vol. (M)	0.276	Insider holdings	NA

Value of $10,000 invested 5 years ago: $ 18,488

Fiscal Year Ending Dec. 31

	1995	% Change	1994	% Change	1993	% Change
Revenues (Million $)						
1Q	1,188	6%	1,123	10%	1,017	24%
2Q	1,272	7%	1,186	13%	1,053	23%
3Q	—	—	1,373	19%	1,153	2%
4Q	—	—	1,289	17%	1,098	7%
Yr.	—	—	4,972	15%	4,320	13%
Income (Million $)						
1Q	57.95	10%	52.90	NM	52.73	21%
2Q	65.24	11%	58.92	6%	55.73	21%
3Q	—	—	87.80	14%	76.82	NM
4Q	—	—	74.92	23%	61.14	-13%
Yr.	—	—	274.5	11%	246.4	4%
Earnings Per Share ($)						
1Q	0.89	10%	0.81	-2%	0.83	14%
2Q	1.01	12%	0.90	6%	0.85	10%
3Q	E0.90	-33%	1.34	14%	1.18	-9%
4Q	E1.20	4%	1.15	22%	0.94	-20%
Yr.	E4.00	-5%	4.20	11%	3.80	-4%

Next earnings report expected: mid October

Business Summary - 29-SEP-95

V. F. Corporation is an international basic apparel company. As part of its strategy to diversify, VFC acquired H. H. Cutler Company and Nutmeg Industries, both major manufacturers of apparel imprinted with the names and logos of professional sports teams, for a total consideration of $507 million in early 1994. Segment contributions in 1994 were:

	Sales	Profits
Jeanswear	51%	64%
Decorated knitwear	13%	6%
Intimate apparel	15%	10%
Playwear	7%	6%
Specialty apparel	14%	13%

International operations accounted for 15% of sales and 14% of operating income in 1994.

The jeanswear division produces and sells denim products under the Lee, Riders, Wrangler, Rustler and Girbaud names in both the U.S., where it has a 30% share, and overseas. The decorated knitwear division includes Bassett-Walker, a leading manufacturer of knitted, fleeced activewear; Nutmeg Industries and H. H. Cutler, both manufacturers of licensed sports apparel; and JanSport, an imprinter of purchased activewear and T-shirts with various college logos.

The intimate apparel division includes Vanity Fair, Vassarette, Barbizon and the intimate apparel divisions in Europe. The playwear division consists of Healthtex, a children's apparel company; the children's playwear and sleepwear operations of H. H. Cutler; and the preschool sizes of Lee and Wrangler in the U.S. The specialty apparel business group includes occupational apparel, made by Red Kap; Jantzen, a producer of swimwear and sportswear for men and women; and JanSport backpacks and daypacks.

Important Developments

Sep. '95—VFC announced that its second half earnings would be significantly lower than consensus estimates due to a weak back to school season, typically a high volume period for the company. VFC blamed the weakness on hot weather in most of the country and a change in consumer buying patterns. The company said consumers tend to buy closer to need today, versus ahead of time. As a result of this weakness, VFC said it was curtailing some production in order to control inventories, which would in turn hurt operating margins, especially in the third quarter. VFC also said that it was taking a cautious approach towards the fourth quarter, and had reduced its previous expectations.

Capitalization

Long Term Debt: $615,673,000 (7/1/95).
Red. Preferred Stock: $61,382,000; conv. into approx. 1.65 mil. com. shs.; held by ESOP.

Per Share Data ($) (Year Ended Dec. 31)

	1994	1993	1992	1991	1990	1989
Tangible Bk. Val.	12.82	15.07	10.07	8.94	6.94	6.69
Cash Flow	6.66	5.75	5.82	4.34	3.06	4.12
Earnings	4.20	3.80	3.97	2.75	1.35	2.72
Dividends	1.30	1.22	1.11	1.02	1.00	0.91
Payout Ratio	31%	32%	28%	37%	74%	30%
Prices - High	53¾	56½	57½	41½	34¼	38⅜
- Low	44¼	39½	38½	17⅝	11⅝	27¾
P/E Ratio - High	13	15	14	15	25	14
- Low	11	10	10	6	9	10

Income Statement Analysis (Million $)

	1994	%Chg	1993	%Chg	1992	%Chg	1991
Revs.	4,972	15%	4,320	13%	3,824	30%	2,952
Oper. Inc.	697	25%	558	4%	538	36%	395
Depr.	159	26%	126	17%	108	19%	91.0
Int. Exp.	80.3	10%	72.7	2%	71.1	4%	68.6
Pretax Inc.	456	14%	400	6%	376	43%	263
Eff. Tax Rate	40%	—	38%	—	37%	—	39%
Net Inc.	275	12%	246	4%	237	47%	161

Balance Sheet & Other Fin. Data (Million $)

	1994	1993	1992	1991	1990	1989
Cash	60.0	152	86.0	162	62.0	36.0
Curr. Assets	1,551	1,500	1,366	1,071	824	874
Total Assets	3,336	2,877	2,712	2,127	1,853	1,890
Curr. Liab.	912	660	684	511	351	325
LT Debt	517	528	768	583	585	638
Common Eqty.	1,734	1,547	1,154	938	823	820
Total Cap.	2,335	2,151	1,985	1,591	1,535	1,535
Cap. Exp.	133	209	207	111	110	125
Cash Flow	429	368	341	248	175	267

Ratio Analysis

	1994	1993	1992	1991	1990	1989
Curr. Ratio	1.7	2.3	2.0	2.1	2.3	2.7
% LT Debt of Cap.	22.1	24.5	38.7	36.7	38.1	41.5
% Net Inc.of Revs.	5.5	5.7	6.2	5.5	3.1	6.9
% Ret. on Assets	8.9	8.5	9.7	8.1	4.4	10.4
% Ret. on Equity	16.5	17.3	21.9	17.7	9.5	20.1

Dividend Data

Dividends have been paid since 1941. A dividend reinvestment plan is available. A "poison pill" stock purchase right was adopted in 1988.

Amt. of Div. $	Date Decl.	Ex-Div. Date	Stock of Record	Payment Date
0.340	Oct. 19	Dec. 05	Dec. 09	Dec. 19 '94
0.340	Feb. 14	Mar. 06	Mar. 10	Mar. 20 '95
0.340	Apr. 18	Jun. 06	Jun. 09	Jun. 19 '95
0.340	Jul. 19	Sep. 06	Sep. 08	Sep. 18 '95

Data as orig. reptd.; bef. results of disc. opers. and/or spec. items. Per share data adj. for stk. divs. as of ex-div. date.
E-Estimated. NA-Not Available. NM-Not Meaningful. NR-Not Ranked.

Office—1047 North Park Rd., Wyomissing, PA 19610. **Tel**—(610) 378-1151. **Chrmn & CEO**—L. R. Pugh. **Pres**—M. J. McDonald. **VP-Fin & CFO**—G. G. Johnson. **VP-Secy**—Lori M. Tarnoski. **Investor Contact**—Cindy Knoebel (212) 782-0276. **Dirs**—R. D. Buzzell, E. E. Crutchfield Jr., U. Fairbairn, B. S. Feigin, R. S. Hillas, L. C. Holt Jr., R. J. Hurst, R. F. Longbine, M. J. McDonald. W. E. Pike, L. R. Pugh, M. R. Sharp, L. D. Walker. **Transfer Agent & Registrar**-First Chicago Trust Co. of New York, Jersey City, N.J. **Incorporated** in Pennsylvania in 1899. **Empl**-68,000. **S&P Analyst:** Elizabeth Vandeventer

Varity Corp.

NYSE Symbol **VAT**
In S&P 500

01-SEP-95

Industry:
Auto parts/equipment

Summary: Following the 1994 sale of Massey Ferguson Group, VAT remains a maker of automotive brake products and diesel engines. It owns 46% of Hayes Wheels International.

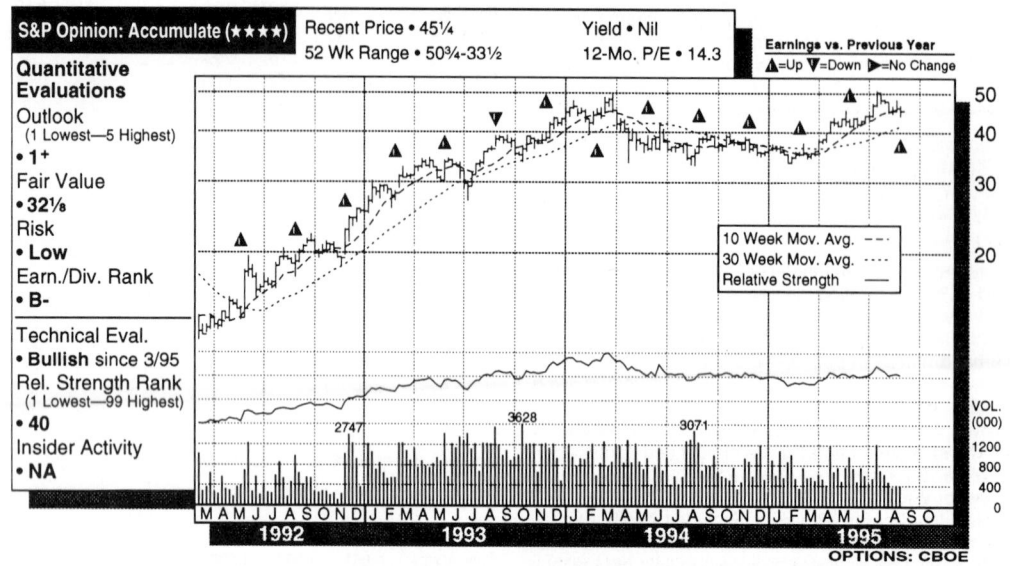

S&P Opinion: Accumulate (★★★★)	Recent Price • 45¼	Yield • Nil
	52 Wk Range • 50¾-33½	12-Mo. P/E • 14.3

Quantitative Evaluations

Outlook
(1 Lowest—5 Highest)
• **1+**

Fair Value
• **32⅛**

Risk
• **Low**

Earn./Div. Rank
• **B-**

Technical Eval.
• **Bullish** since 3/95

Rel. Strength Rank
(1 Lowest—99 Highest)
• **40**

Insider Activity
• **NA**

Earnings vs. Previous Year
▲=Up ▼=Down ▶=No Change

10 Week Mov. Avg. ― ―
30 Week Mov. Avg. ·····
Relative Strength ―

OPTIONS: CBOE

Overview - 01-SEP-95

Higher sales in fiscal 1995-96 will reflect greater market penetration in anti-lock brakes and strong global demand for diesel engines. Aided by higher profits from Perkins and Kelsey-Hayes, equity in income of Hayes Wheels, lower interest expense, and a continued low tax rate, operating earnings should advance strongly before an expected $10 million to $25 million charge to restructure the foundation brakes unit. To meet its long-term goal of doubling sales by 2000, VAT is positioning itself in the global marketplace as a total brake system supplier for motor vehicles, and as a maker of diesel engines focused on agricultural, industrial and construction equipment markets. VAT has signed many long-term diesel engine supply agreements in foreign markets, and is expanding its book of four-wheel anti-lock brake system orders.

Valuation - 01-SEP-95

Our accumulate recommendation on VAT reflects the company's focus on the fast-growing anti-lock brake sector and its high exposure to foreign markets via Perkins diesel engines. The company should continue to grow, even if there is a mild slowdown in the North American market. VAT's 46% stake in Hayes Wheel should also aid results as the global aluminum wheel market continues to expand. The shares, attractively valued at about 11X estimated fiscal 1996-97 EPS, offer a sensible long-term investment for investors seeking modest exposure to foreign markets and participation in secular growth opportunities.

Key Stock Statistics

S&P EPS Est. 1996	3.65	Tang. Bk. Value/Share	12.74
P/E on S&P Est. 1996	12.4	Beta	0.88
S&P EPS Est. 1997	4.05	Shareholders	34,200
Dividend Rate/Share	Nil	Market cap. (B)	$ 1.9
Shs. outstg. (M)	40.8	Inst. holdings	87%
Avg. daily vol. (M)	0.082	Insider holdings	NA

Value of $10,000 invested 5 years ago: $ 18,100

Fiscal Year Ending Jan. 31

	1996	% Change	1995	% Change	1994	% Change
Revenues (Million $)						
1Q	595.3	18%	505.8	-22%	645.0	-22%
2Q	572.4	11%	517.4	-22%	660.9	-26%
3Q	—	—	605.0	-13%	692.2	-18%
4Q	—	—	639.6	-12%	727.7	-11%
Yr.	—	—	2,268	-17%	2,726	-19%
Income (Million $)						
1Q	33.70	35%	25.00	127%	11.00	NM
2Q	32.70	43%	22.80	42%	16.10	14%
3Q	—	—	32.70	47%	22.20	111%
4Q	—	—	36.60	36%	27.00	141%
Yr.	—	—	117.1	53%	76.30	128%
Earnings Per Share ($)						
1Q	0.80	45%	0.55	175%	0.20	NM
2Q	0.78	56%	0.50	47%	0.34	-8%
3Q	E1.00	37%	0.73	26%	0.58	152%
4Q	E1.07	27%	0.84	42%	0.59	157%
Yr.	E3.65	40%	2.61	45%	1.80	NM

Next earnings report expected: late November

Varity Corp.

Business Summary - 01-SEP-95

After its 1994 sale of Massey Ferguson, Varity Corp. (formerly Massey-Ferguson) is now a producer of automotive products and diesel engines. Contributions (profits in millions) in 1994-5 were:

	Sales	Profits
Automotive products	61%	$116
Engines	39%	68

The U.S. accounted for 56% of sales in 1994-5, Europe for 39%, and other 5%.

Automotive products includes The Kelsey-Hayes Group (K-H) and Dayton Walther. K-H manufactures original equipment two- and four-wheel anti-lock braking systems (ABS), electromechanical sensors, power door lock actuators, hubs, drums, disc brake rotors and disc and drum brakes. Based on awarded contracts, K-H expects its North Amercian four-wheel ABS market share to rise to 31% by 1997, from about 21% in 1994. Dayton Walther offers wheel end components for medium and heavy trucks and trailers, including hubs, cast spoke wheels, brake drums and rotors, hydraulic disc brake components and in-wheel parking brakes. VAT owns 46% of Hayes Wheels International, which is a global supplier of cast and fabricated aluminum and fabricated steel wheels.

Perkins produces diesel engines in the 5- to 2,500-horsepower range, which are used by some 600 manufacturers of tractors, construction machinery, materials-handling equipment, generators, cars, trucks, boats and tanks. Major customers include Caterpillar, Chrysler, AGCO, Vickers, Volvo Penta, GKN, Renault and Ingersoll Rand.

In 1994, VAT sold Massey Ferguson farm tractors to AGCO Corp. for $310 million and 500,000 AGCO shares.

Important Developments

Aug. '95—In the fiscal 1995-96 first half, automotive products sales rose 3.9%, year to year. Brake systems operating profit margins increased to 9.9% from 8.8%, while heavy duty brakes operated at breakeven, versus a small loss. Engine sales rose 33% and operating profit margins expanded to 8.6% from 7.7% of sales. VAT expects to take a charge of between $10 million and $25 million in the second half to restructure the foundation brakes unit. VAT will implement modern manufacturing techniques now in use on anti-lock brake production lines. The charge will account for employee termination costs and plant writedowns.

May '95—VAT discontinued Pacoma Hydraulik GmbH, a hydraulic cylinder maker. No gain or loss was recognized on the planned disposal.

Capitalization

Long Term Debt: $163,600,000 (7/95).

Cdn. $1.625 Cum. Red. Conv. Exch. Pfd. Cl. II Stock: 2,001,000 shs. (liq. pref. Cdn. $25); ea. conv. into 0.3333 com.

Per Share Data ($)

(Year Ended Jan. 31)

	1995	1994	1993	1992	1991	1990
Tangible Bk. Val.	11.72	7.58	1.11	-5.12	6.45	15.66
Cash Flow	4.38	3.62	4.45	-3.92	7.12	6.28
Earnings	2.61	1.80	0.56	-7.87	3.40	3.50
Dividends	Nil	Nil	Nil	Nil	Nil	Nil
Payout Ratio	Nil	Nil	Nil	Nil	Nil	Nil
Cal. Yrs.	1994	1993	1992	1991	1990	1989
Prices - High	50⅛	45⅜	25⅞	30	40	33¾
- Low	33	25	12⅛	10½	17½	20
P/E Ratio - High	19	25	46	NM	12	10
- Low	13	14	22	NM	5	6

Income Statement Analysis (Million $)

	1995	%Chg	1994	%Chg	1993	%Chg	1992
Revs.	2,268	-17%	2,726	-19%	3,375	7%	3,169
Oper. Inc.	224	29%	173	-41%	294	43%	205
Depr.	78.0	16%	67.0	-34%	102	3%	99
Int. Exp.	27.0	-44%	48.0	-68%	150	-11%	168
Pretax Inc.	141	58%	89.0	98%	45.0	NM	-164
Eff. Tax Rate	17%	—	14%	—	26%	—	NM
Net Inc.	117	54%	76.0	130%	33.0	NM	-177

Balance Sheet & Other Fin. Data (Million $)

	1995	1994	1993	1992	1991	1990
Cash	190	113	154	224	178	302
Curr. Assets	734	944	1,009	1,532	1,337	1,430
Total Assets	1,824	2,028	2,087	3,180	2,975	2,982
Curr. Liab.	556	826	915	1,441	1,177	1,055
LT Debt	163	186	305	864	617	792
Common Eqty.	748	593	273	216	507	387
Total Cap.	947	820	866	1,380	1,426	1,503
Cap. Exp.	155	155	106	118	145	634
Cash Flow	193	133	117	-98.0	177	134

Ratio Analysis

	1995	1994	1993	1992	1991	1990
Curr. Ratio	1.3	1.1	1.1	1.1	1.1	1.4
% LT Debt of Cap.	17.3	22.6	35.2	62.6	43.2	52.7
% Net Inc.of Revs.	5.2	2.8	1.0	NM	2.8	3.9
% Ret. on Assets	6.2	3.1	1.1	NM	3.4	3.7
% Ret. on Equity	17.5	13.4	5.5	NM	18.6	22.3

Dividend Data —No common dividends have been paid since 1977. A poison pill stock purchase rights plan was adopted in 1994.

Data as orig. reptd.; bef. results of disc. opers. and/or spec. items. Per share data adj. for stk. divs. as of ex-div. date. E-Estimated. NA-Not Available. NM-Not Meaningful. NR-Not Ranked.

Office—672 Delaware Ave., Buffalo, NY 14209. **Tel**—(716) 888-8000. **Chrmn & CEO**—V. A. Rice. **Vice Chrmn**—V. D. Laurenzo. **COO**—J. A. Gilroy. **SVP & CFO**—N. D. Arnold. **VP & Secy**—K. L. Walker. **VP & Treas**—F. J. Chapman. **VP & Investor Contact**—Kevin C. Shanahan. **Dirs**—P. M. F. Cheng, W. A. Corbett, T. N. Davidson, R. M. Gates, L. F. Kahl, V. D. Laurenzo, W. D. McKeough, B. Nicholson, V. A. Rice, W. S. Rustand, W. R. Teschke, R. H. Warrender. **Transfer Agent & Registrar**—Mellon Securities Trust Co., NYC. **Incorporated** in Canada in 1891; reincorporated in Delaware in 1991. **Empl**-10,511. **S&P Analyst:** Joshua M. Harari, CFA

Viacom Inc.

ASE Symbol **VIA.B**
In S&P 500

16-AUG-95

Industry:
Filmed Entertainment

Summary: This major entertainment company now includes various businesses of Paramount Communications and Blockbuster Entertainment, which were acquired by VIA in 1994.

S&P Opinion: Hold (★★★)	Recent Price • 48	Yield • Nil
	52 Wk Range • 52⅛-32⅛	12-Mo. P/E • 22.6

Earnings vs. Previous Year
▲=Up ▼=Down ▶=No Change

Quantitative Evaluations

Outlook
(1 Lowest—5 Highest)
• **NA**

Fair Value
• **NA**

Risk
• **NA**

Earn./Div. Rank
• **NR**

Technical Eval.
• **Bearish** since 8/95

Rel. Strength Rank
(1 Lowest—99 Highest)
• **50**

Insider Activity
• **NA**

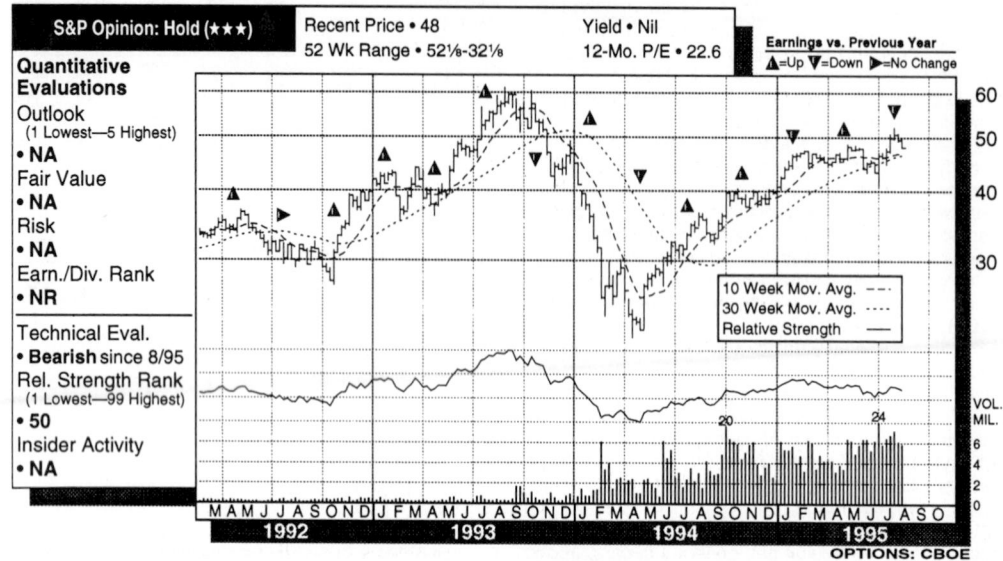

10 Week Mov. Avg. – – –
30 Week Mov. Avg. ·······
Relative Strength ——

VOL.
MIL.

1992 1993 1994 1995

OPTIONS: CBOE

Overview - 16-AUG-95

VIA's size and scope was greatly increased by the 1994 acquisitions of Paramount Communications and Blockbuster Entertainment. Following strong pro forma growth from the movie, cable network and video retail businesses in 1995's first half, we expect comparisons to be more difficult in the year ahead. In part, this is because VIA will be lapping the remarkable 1994-95 success of Forrest Gump. However, VIA's overall 1996 growth prospects are favorable, helped by strong demand for TV network advertising time. Per share earnings are being restrained by interest expense, non-cash goodwill amortization, and the issuance of more than 250 million shares in 1994. Asset divestitures are being used to reduce debt.

Valuation - 16-AUG-95

Based on expected earnings improvement and cash flow generation, we view VIA's stock as being adequately priced. Because of the sizable non-cash expense (e.g. goodwill related to acquisitions) on VIA's income statement, we believe that the stock is better valued on the basis of a cash flow measure, rather than reported earnings per share (EPS). In both 1995 and 1996, we expect VIA's annual earnings to include about $0.73 a share in non-cash goodwill expense related to its 1994 acquisitions, which leads to an adjusted EPS estimate for 1996 of $2.38. Over the long-term, VIA's asset value should be boosted by continuing efforts to find cross-promotional opportunities and overlaps between its businesses.

Key Stock Statistics

S&P EPS Est. 1995	0.90	Tang. Bk. Value/Share	NM
P/E on S&P Est. 1995	53.3	Beta	1.35
S&P EPS Est. 1996	1.65	Shareholders	40,600
Dividend Rate/Share	Nil	Market cap. (B)	$ 17.5
Shs. outstg. (M)	359.8	Inst. holdings	42%
Avg. daily vol. (M)	2.208	Insider holdings	NA

Value of $10,000 invested 5 years ago: NA

Fiscal Year Ending Dec. 31

	1995	% Change	1994	% Change	1993	% Change
Revenues ()						
1Q	2,696	NM	878.0	86%	471.0	9%
2Q	2,865	66%	1,728	NM	496.0	10%
3Q	—	—	2,131	NM	508.0	8%
4Q	—	—	2,777	NM	530.0	4%
Yr.	—	—	7,363	NM	2,005	8%
Income ()						
1Q	63.60	NM	-431.6	NM	70.63	NM
2Q	53.00	-80%	264.6	NM	41.63	NM
3Q	—	—	335.1	NM	30.90	-31%
4Q	—	—	-34.70	NM	26.33	126%
Yr.	—	—	130.5	-23%	169.5	156%
Earnings Per Share ()						
1Q	0.13	NM	-3.59	NM	0.59	NM
2Q	0.10	-94%	1.69	NM	0.35	NM
3Q	E0.35	—	1.45	NM	0.25	-32%
4Q	E0.32	—	-0.14	NM	0.11	10%
Yr.	E0.90	—	0.25	-81%	1.30	136%

Next earnings report expected: mid November

Viacom Inc.

Business Summary - 11-AUG-95

Viacom Inc. is a diversified entertainment and communications company. The 1994 acquisitions of Paramount Communications (PCI) and Blockbuster Entertainment (BV) added various entertainment and publishing operations. Viacom's cable programming businesses include three U.S. advertiser-supported basic cable programming services (MTV: Music Television, Nickelodeon and VH-1/Video Hits One), and three premium subscription TV programming services (Showtime, The Movie Channel and Flix). Viacom also has equity interests in the ad-supported USA and Comedy Central cable services, owns 100% of MTV Europe, has a revenue-sharing interest in MTV Asia, and has interests in various other overseas programming ventures. In addition, Viacom operates a pay-per-view event distribution business and a home satellite programming service.

The Paramount acquisition includes the distribution of movies and TV shows, five theme parks, and movie theaters. PCI assets related to Madison Square Garden in New York were sold by VIA for $1.0 billion in March 1995. Also, Viacom owns, operates, or controls about 12 television stations, and 12 radio stations. The PCI publishing business includes Simon & Schuster and Macmillan Publishing Company. The BV business includes large video and music retail chains, and majority equity interests in Spelling Entertainment Group and Discovery Zone, Inc. Also, VIA is looking to spin off ownership of its cable TV systems business, which serves about 1.2 million customers.

Important Developments

Aug. '95—VIA is looking to sell its 78% equity interest in Spelling Entertainment Group., which is a producer and distributor of filmed entertainment. Also, VIA has announced a multi-step transaction in which ownership of its cable TV systems would be spun off, and the business would subsequently be acquired by Tele-Communications Inc. As a result of the cable TV transaction, about $1.7 billion of debt would leave VIA's balance sheet. Earlier in 1995, VIA completed a $1.0 billion sale of various assets related to Madison Square Garden (MSG) in New York. The MSG assets, which were part of VIA's 1994 acquisition of entertainment and pubblishing company Paramount Communications, included an arena and two professional sports teams.

Capitalization

Long Term Debt: $10,036,600,000 (3/31/95.
5% Conv. Pref. Stk.: 32,000,000 shs.; sold to NYNEX Corp. for $1.2 billion.
Class A Common Stock: 74,705,702 shs. ($0.01 par) (ASE: VIA) (4/30/95). National Amusements, controlled by S. Redstone, owns about 61%.
Nonvoting Class B Common Stock: 285,117,311 shs. ($0.01 par). (4/30/95).

Per Share Data ()

(Year Ended Dec. 31)

	1994	1993	1992	1991	1990	1989
Tangible Bk. Val.	-15.39	-10.45	-11.95	-13.16	-18.03	-16.60
Cash Flow	1.23	2.07	1.23	0.21	-0.13	1.77
Earnings	0.25	1.30	0.55	-0.41	-0.84	1.07
Dividends	Nil	Nil	Nil	Nil	Nil	Nil
Payout Ratio	Nil	Nil	Nil	Nil	Nil	Nil
Prices - High	45	67½	44	35⅜	29⅝	32⅝
- Low	21¾	37⅛	28⅛	23½	15⅝	15¼
P/E Ratio - High	NM	52	80	NM	NM	31
- Low	NM	29	51	NM	NM	14

Income Statement Analysis ()

	1994	%Chg	1993	%Chg	1992	%Chg	1991
Revs.	7,363	NM	2,005	8%	1,865	9%	1,712
Oper. Inc.	824	72%	478	11%	429	12%	382
Depr.	216	133%	92.8	14%	81.5	16%	70.1
Int. Exp.	536	NM	155	-21%	196	-34%	299
Pretax Inc.	395	32%	299	98%	151	NM	-4.0
Eff. Tax Rate	71%	—	43%	—	56%	—	NM
Net Inc.	131	-22%	169	156%	66.0	NM	-47.0

Balance Sheet & Other Fin. Data ()

	1994	1993	1992	1991	1990	1989
Cash	598	1,882	48.4	28.7	43.1	12.4
Curr. Assets	5,255	2,686	797	718	654	591
Total Assets	28,274	6,417	4,317	4,188	4,028	3,753
Curr. Liab.	4,131	966	911	876	799	713
LT Debt	10,402	2,441	2,423	2,321	2,537	2,283
Common Eqty.	10,592	918	757	699	366	456
Total Cap.	22,194	5,159	3,179	3,020	2,903	2,739
Cap. Exp.	365	135	110	57.0	76.0	57.0
Cash Flow	271	250	148	24.0	-14.0	189

Ratio Analysis

	1994	1993	1992	1991	1990	1989
Curr. Ratio	1.3	2.8	0.9	0.8	0.8	0.8
% LT Debt of Cap.	46.9	47.3	76.2	76.8	87.4	83.4
% Net Inc.of Revs.	1.8	8.5	3.5	NM	NM	9.1
% Ret. on Assets	0.6	3.2	1.6	NM	NM	3.4
% Ret. on Equity	0.8	18.7	9.1	NM	NM	28.6

Dividend Data (No cash dividends have been paid since Viacom's predecessor was acquired in 1987 by National Amusements, Inc. In 1990, one share of nonvoting common stock (otherwise identical to ordinary common) was distributed for each common share held.)

Data as orig. reptd.; bef. results of disc. opers. and/or spec. items. Per share data adj. for stk. divs. as of ex-div. date.
E-Estimated. NA-Not Available. NM-Not Meaningful. NR-Not Ranked.

Office—200 Elm St., Dedham, MA 02026. **Tel**—(617) 461-1600. **Chrmn**—S. M. Redstone. **Pres & CEO**—F. J. Biondi, Jr. **SVP & CFO**—G. S. Smith, Jr. **SVP & Treas**—V. A. Clarke. **Shareholder Relations**—212-258-6700. **EVP & Secy**—P. P. Dauman. **Dirs**—G. S. Abrams, S. R. Berrard, F. J. Biondi, Jr., P. P. Dauman, W. C. Ferguson, H. W. Huizenga, G. D. Johnson, Jr., K. H. Miller, B. D. Redstone, S. M. Redstone, S. Redstone, F. V. Salerno, W. Schwartz. **Transfer Agent & Registrar**—First Chicago Trust Co. of New York, NYC. **Incorporated** in Delaware in 1986. **Empl**-70,000. **S&P Analyst:** Tom Graves, CFA

WMX Technologies

NYSE Symbol **WMX**
In S&P 500

20-SEP-95

Industry:
Pollution Control

Summary: This company is a leading international provider of environmental, engineering and construction, industrial and related services.

S&P Opinion: Hold (★★★)			

Recent Price • 30⅜
52 Wk Range • 32½-24½

Yield • 2.0%
12-Mo. P/E • 20.0

Earnings vs. Previous Year
▲=Up ▼=Down ▶=No Change

Quantitative Evaluations

Outlook
(1 Lowest—5 Highest)
• **4⁻**

Fair Value
• **30¾**

Risk
• **Low**

Earn./Div. Rank
• **A-**

Technical Eval.
• **Bearish** since 7/95

Rel. Strength Rank
(1 Lowest—99 Highest)
• **36**

Insider Activity
• **Neutral**

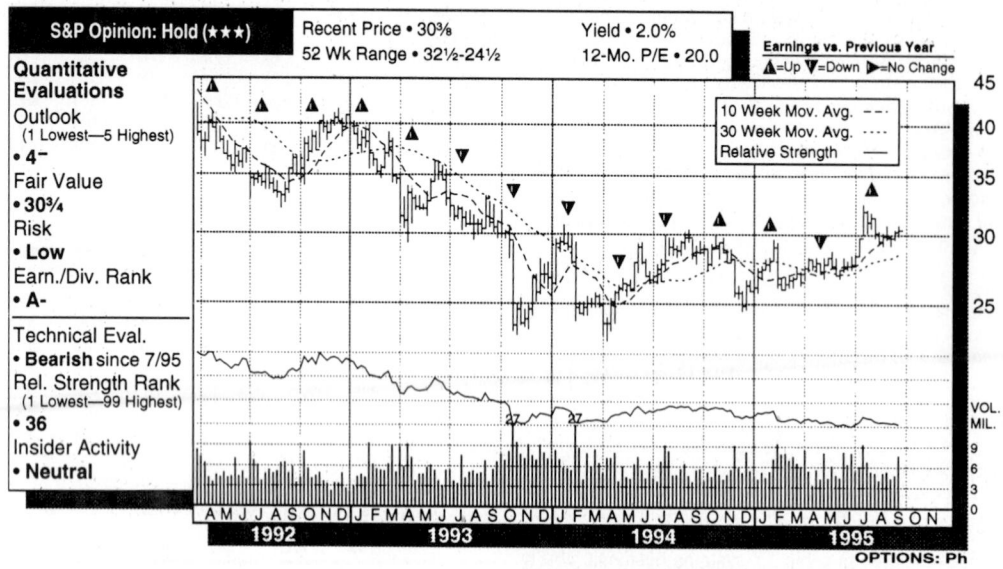

10 Week Mov. Avg. – – –
30 Week Mov. Avg. ·······
Relative Strength ——

VOL.
MIL.

AMJJASOND|JFMAMJJASOND|JFMAMJJASOND|JFMAMJJASON
1992   1993   1994   1995

OPTIONS: Ph

Overview - 19-SEP-95

WMX should experience moderate gains for its domestic solid waste business in 1995 reflecting the opening of new landfills, higher volumes at existing sites and price increases. Recycling profits will increase sharply reflecting acquisitions and higher materials prices (through mid-year). Lower contributions are seen from international operations reflecting competitive pressure on prices and lower volumes in France and Italy. Hazardous waste profits will be hurt by reduced event volumes and lower prices. Contributions from Wheelabrator should increase reflecting expansion of that firm's water treatment business. Rust will benefit from increased engineering and construction work. Distorting comparisons will be the first quarter charge of $0.19 to revalue certain hazardous waste assets.

Valuation - 19-SEP-95

The shares of this leading environmental services concern have been an average market performer in 1995. After trading at a substantial premium to the market multiple in the early 1990s, WMX now carries a more reasonable valuation. Investors have scaled back growth expectations and now view the waste management industry as a semi-cyclical one. With interests in all aspects of environmental services plus a substantial international presence, WMX's earnings are less cyclical than many of its peers. Currently trading at a slight premium to the market multiple, we consider WMX to be fairly valued.

Key Stock Statistics

S&P EPS Est. 1995	1.65	Tang. Bk. Value/Share	1.24
P/E on S&P Est. 1995	18.4	Beta	1.47
S&P EPS Est. 1996	2.05	Shareholders	70,400
Dividend Rate/Share	0.60	Market cap. (B)	$ 14.5
Shs. outstg. (M)	484.9	Inst. holdings	60%
Avg. daily vol. (M)	1.112	Insider holdings	NA

Value of $10,000 invested 5 years ago: $ 9,537

Fiscal Year Ending Dec. 31

	1995	% Change	1994	% Change	1993	% Change
Revenues (Million $)						
1Q	2,605	14%	2,284	7%	2,135	6%
2Q	2,856	12%	2,552	11%	2,291	5%
3Q	—	—	2,603	12%	2,323	3%
4Q	—	—	2,658	11%	2,387	8%
Yr.	—	—	10,097	11%	9,136	5%
Income (Million $)						
1Q	101.3	-38%	162.6	-18%	199.3	4%
2Q	219.1	8%	203.1	-7%	217.7	-34%
3Q	—	—	212.9	NM	-127.2	NM
4Q	—	—	205.8	26%	162.9	-11%
Yr.	—	—	784.4	73%	452.8	-51%
Earnings Per Share ($)						
1Q	0.21	-38%	0.34	-17%	0.41	5%
2Q	0.45	7%	0.42	-7%	0.45	-32%
3Q	E0.50	14%	0.44	NM	-0.26	NM
4Q	E0.49	17%	0.42	24%	0.34	-8%
Yr.	E1.65	2%	1.62	74%	0.93	-50%

Next earnings report expected: mid October

WMX Technologies

Business Summary - 19-SEP-95

WMX Technologies, Inc. (formerly Waste Management, Inc.) is a leading international provider of comprehensive waste management services, as well as engineering and construction, industrial and related services. Revenue and profit breakdown for 1994:

	Revs.	Profits
Solid waste	49%	60%
Hazardous waste	6%	5%
Engineering, construction & industrial	16%	6%
Energy, water treatment & air quality	13%	16%
International	16%	13%

Through Waste Management, Inc. (WMI), WMX collects, processes and disposes of solid waste in 48 states, the District of Columbia, four Canadian provinces and Mexico. In 1994, operations in California, Florida and Pennsylvania accounted for about 30% of WMI's revenues. At the end of 1994, WMI served about 1.0 million commercial and industrial customers and 11.8 million households, and also operated 134 landfills and 129 transfer stations in North America. Operations also include recycling and medical and infectious waste management services.

Chemical Waste Management is a leading provider of comprehensive hazardous waste management services in the U.S. Operations include chemical waste transportation, treatment, resource recovery and disposal services, which are provided principally to commercial and industrial customers. Rust International furnishes engineering, construction, environmental and infrastructure consulting, hazardous and radioactive substance remediation and other services.

Wheelabrator Technologies Inc. (57% owned) is a leading developer of facilities for and provider of services to the trash-to-energy and other markets, and also provides water and air quality control services. Waste Management International (56% owned) provides environmental services primarily in Europe, Australia and Asia.

Important Developments

Aug. '95—WMX acquired 15 materials recyling facilities from New England CR Inc. for an undisclosed amount.

Aug. '95—Wheelabrator Technologies (WTI) (57%-owned) said it was negotiating the purchase of a 90 million gallon/day wastewater plant from the City of Wilmington (DE). In July WTI bought the Franklin, OH wastewater plant for $6.8 million.

Jul. '95—WMX lifted its interest in Rust International to 60% from 56% with the purchase of that firm's publicly-held shares for $51 million.

Capitalization

Long Term Debt: $6,585,138,000 (6/95).
Minority Interest: $1,478,772,000.

Per Share Data ($)

(Year Ended Dec. 31)

	1994	1993	1992	1991	1990	1989
Tangible Bk. Val.	1.51	1.44	3.14	3.30	3.70	3.72
Cash Flow	3.44	2.57	3.31	2.43	2.54	2.08
Earnings	1.62	0.93	1.86	1.23	1.49	1.22
Dividends	0.60	0.58	0.50	0.42	0.35	0.29
Payout Ratio	37%	62%	27%	34%	24%	24%
Prices - High	$30\frac{3}{4}$	$40\frac{1}{4}$	$46\frac{5}{8}$	$44\frac{3}{8}$	$45\frac{1}{2}$	$35\frac{7}{8}$
- Low	$22\frac{5}{8}$	23	32	$32\frac{5}{8}$	$28\frac{5}{8}$	$20\frac{3}{8}$
P/E Ratio - High	19	43	25	36	31	29
- Low	14	25	17	27	19	17

Income Statement Analysis (Million $)

	1994	%Chg	1993	%Chg	1992	%Chg	1991
Revs.	10,097	11%	9,136	5%	8,661	15%	7,551
Oper. Inc.	2,658	13%	2,362	3%	2,304	11%	2,067
Depr.	880	10%	797	12%	714	20%	593
Int. Exp.	445	11%	401	29%	311	11%	280
Pretax Inc.	1,529	76%	867	-38%	1,398	36%	1,028
Eff. Tax Rate	39%	—	41%	—	34%	—	41%
Net Inc.	784	73%	453	-51%	921	52%	606

Balance Sheet & Other Fin. Data (Million $)

	1994	1993	1992	1991	1990	1989
Cash	142	126	68.0	222	233	107
Curr. Assets	3,089	2,778	2,508	2,145	1,905	1,086
Total Assets	17,539	16,264	14,114	12,572	10,518	6,405
Curr. Liab.	3,180	2,678	2,380	2,114	1,916	1,242
LT Debt	6,044	6,146	4,313	3,783	3,140	1,504
Common Eqty.	4,541	4,159	4,320	4,133	3,673	2,738
Total Cap.	13,040	12,129	10,317	9,096	7,861	4,745
Cap. Exp.	1,456	2,163	1,963	1,587	2,714	1,375
Cash Flow	1,665	1,249	1,635	1,199	1,211	957

Ratio Analysis

	1994	1993	1992	1991	1990	1989
Curr. Ratio	1.0	1.0	1.1	1.0	1.0	0.9
% LT Debt of Cap.	46.4	50.7	41.8	41.6	39.9	31.7
% Net Inc.of Revs.	7.8	5.0	10.6	8.0	11.8	12.6
% Ret. on Assets	4.6	3.0	6.9	5.2	8.2	9.8
% Ret. on Equity	17.8	10.8	21.9	15.5	21.7	22.6

Dividend Data —Dividends were initiated in 1976. A dividend reinvestment plan is available.

Amt. of Div. $	Date Decl.	Ex-Div. Date	Stock of Record	Payment Date
0.150	Aug. 09	Sep. 15	Sep. 21	Oct. 06 '94
0.150	Nov. 15	Dec. 15	Dec. 21	Jan. 05 '95
0.150	Jan. 30	Mar. 16	Mar. 22	Apr. 06 '95
0.150	May. 12	Jun. 19	Jun. 21	Jul. 06 '95
0.150	Aug. 08	Sep. 18	Sep. 20	Oct. 05 '95

Data as orig. reptd.; bef. results of disc. opers. and/or spec. items. Per share data adj. for stk. divs. as of ex-div. date. E-Estimated. NA-Not Available. NM-Not Meaningful. NR-Not Ranked.

Office—3003 Butterfield Rd., Oak Brook, IL 60521. **Tel**—(708) 572-8800. **Chrmn & CEO**—D. L. Buntrock. **Pres**—P. B. Rooney. **SVP, CFO, Treas**—J. E. Koenig. **SVP & Secy**—H. A. Getz. **Investor Contact**—Melissa White. **Dirs**—H. J. Arnelle, H. H. Baker, Jr., D. L. Buntrock, P. S. J. Cafferty, J. E. Dempsey, J. B. Edwards, D. F. Flynn, P. H. Huizenga, P. Pedersen, J. R. Peterson, P. B. Rooney, A. B. Trowbridge. **Transfer Agent & Registrar**—Harris Trust & Savings Bank, Chicago. **Incorporated** in Delaware in 1968. **Empl**-74,400. **S&P Analyst:** Stephen R. Klein

Wachovia Corp.

STOCK REPORTS

NYSE Symbol **WB**
In S&P 500

17-OCT-95

Industry:
Banking

Summary: This bank holding company, the 21st largest in the U.S., operates more than 490 branches in North Carolina, South Carolina and Georgia.

S&P Opinion: Hold (★★★)	Recent Price • 45	Yield • 3.2%
	52 Wk Range • 45¼-31⅞	12-Mo. P/E • 13.0

Quantitative Evaluations

Outlook
(1 Lowest—5 Highest)
• **3+**

Fair Value
• **43⅞**

Risk
• **Low**

Earn./Div. Rank
• **A-**

Technical Eval.
• **Bullish** since 1/95

Rel. Strength Rank
(1 Lowest—99 Highest)
• **88**

Insider Activity
• **Neutral**

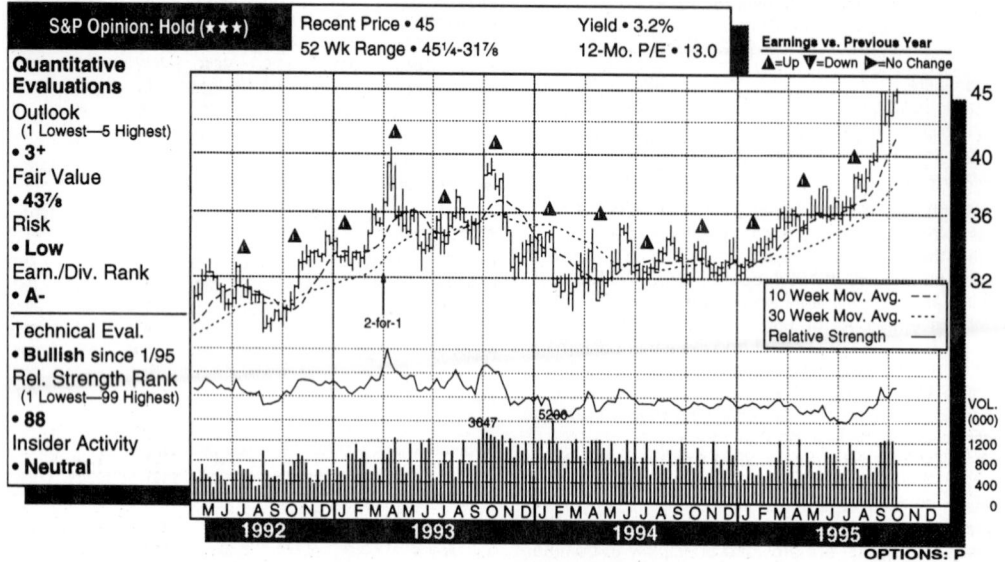

Earnings vs. Previous Year
▲=Up ▼=Down ▶=No Change

10 Week Mov. Avg. − − −
30 Week Mov. Avg. ·······
Relative Strength —

2-for-1

3647   5266

VOL.
(000)
1200
800
400
0

M J J A S O N D J F M A M J J A S O N D J F M A M J J A S O N D J F M A M J J A S O N D
1992   1993   1994   1995

OPTIONS: P

Overview - 17-OCT-95

Healthy loan demand in both the commercial and consumer categories in WB's service territory should continue to boost the level of average earning assets into 1996, although competitive pricing will likely lead to only modest growth in net interest income. Proceeds from the recent sale of the mortgage servicing portfolio are being reinvested in businesses with higher growth potential. Asset quality has improved, with nonperforming assets down 31%, year to year, to $75.4 million at September 30, 1995, and the reserve for loan losses at 710% of nonperforming loans at that date. A focus on cost containment and a reorganization of the delivery network to more closely align services with customers should favorably impact results.

Valuation - 17-OCT-95

The shares have performed in line with the average regional bank and outpaced the broader S&P 500 index thus far in 1995. Interest expense continued to rise at double the pace of interest income in the first nine months of 1995, blunting the impact of strong loan growth in the company's economically attractive service territory and highlighting the negative effect higher interest rates have had on its operations. On the plus side, a recent realignment of corporate, consumer, investment management and trust functions to strengthen development and delivery of services and provide more focus on each market should begin to produce favorable results.

Key Stock Statistics

S&P EPS Est. 1995	3.55	Tang. Bk. Value/Share	20.75
P/E on S&P Est. 1995	12.7	Beta	1.12
S&P EPS Est. 1996	3.80	Shareholders	28,700
Dividend Rate/Share	1.44	Market cap. (B)	$ 7.7
Shs. outstg. (M)	170.4	Inst. holdings	55%
Avg. daily vol. (M)	0.267	Insider holdings	NA

Value of $10,000 invested 5 years ago: $ 26,649

Fiscal Year Ending Dec. 31

	1995	% Change	1994	% Change	1993	% Change
Revenues (Million $)						
1Q	848.8	25%	679.3	-1%	689.5	-4%
2Q	969.2	34%	723.3	7%	674.9	-5%
3Q	957.2	26%	759.4	11%	682.4	-1%
4Q	—	—	808.0	15%	703.7	8%
Yr.	—	—	2,970	8%	2,750	-1%
Income (Million $)						
1Q	142.2	14%	124.8	3%	121.6	15%
2Q	162.9	21%	134.1	9%	123.1	13%
3Q	151.3	10%	138.0	11%	124.4	14%
4Q	—	—	142.1	16%	123.0	12%
Yr.	—	—	539.1	10%	492.1	14%
Earnings Per Share ($)						
1Q	0.83	15%	0.72	3%	0.70	13%
2Q	0.94	21%	0.78	10%	0.71	13%
3Q	0.88	10%	0.80	13%	0.71	13%
4Q	E0.90	8%	0.83	17%	0.71	11%
Yr.	E3.55	13%	3.13	11%	2.83	13%

Next earnings report expected: mid January

Wachovia Corp.

17-OCT-95

Business Summary - 13-OCT-95

Wachovia Corp. (formerly First Wachovia) was formed in 1985 through the merger of Wachovia Corp. and First Atlanta Corp., parent of the second largest bank in Georgia. In December 1991, South Carolina National Corp., the largest bank in South Carolina, was acquired. Based on total assets of $42.9 billion at June 30, 1995, WB was the 21st largest bank holding company in the U.S. It has 216 banking offices in North Carolina, 127 in Georgia, and 150 in South Carolina. Among important business areas are trust services ($17.1 billion of assets under management), credit card operations and depository operations. Strengths in corporate banking include cash management services. Nonbank subsidiaries engage in mortgage banking, brokerage services, leasing and insurance.

During 1994, average earning assets of $32.8 billion (up from $29.8 billion in 1993) consisted of commercial loans 28%, commercial mortgages 10%, residential mortgages 11%, retail loans 22%, construction loans 2%, investment securities 23%, trading assets 2% and other 2%. Average sources of funds were interest-free deposits 15%, demand deposits 9%, savings, money market deposits and CDs 35%, foreign time deposits 1% (total deposits were $22.3 billion), short-term borrowings 17%, long-term debt 12%, equity 8%, and other 3%.

At year-end 1994, nonperforming assets were $101 million (0.39% of loans and related assets), down from $155 million (0.67%) a year earlier. The reserve for loan losses was 1.57% of loans, versus 1.76%. Net chargeoffs during 1994 of $70.4 million were 0.29% of average loans, versus $67.4 million (0.31%) in 1993.

At September 30, 1995, Tier 1 capital was estimated at 9.3%, versus 9.3% at 1994 year-end; total capital was estimated at 12.9%, compared with 12.7%.

Important Developments

Oct. '95—WB noted that earnings for the first nine months of 1995 included an after-tax gain of $47.4 million ($0.27 a share) from the sale of its $9 billion residential mortgage loan servicing portfolio to GE Capital Mortgage Services Inc., and after-tax securities losses of $16.7 million ($0.10) from the restructuring of maturities in the available-for-sale securities portfolio.

Capitalization

Long Term Debt: $5,065,726,000 (6/95).

Per Share Data ($)

(Year Ended Dec. 31)

	1994	1993	1992	1991	1990	1989
Tangible Bk. Val.	18.77	17.61	15.58	13.84	13.23	12.12
Earnings	3.13	2.83	2.51	1.34	2.13	1.94
Dividends	1.23	1.11	1.00	0.92	0.82	0.70
Payout Ratio	39%	39%	40%	69%	39%	36%
Prices - High	35⅜	40½	34¾	30	22⅝	22¾
- Low	30⅛	31⅞	28¼	20¼	16¼	15½
P/E Ratio - High	11	14	14	22	11	12
- Low	10	11	11	15	8	8

Income Statement Analysis (Million $)

	1994	%Chg	1993	%Chg	1992	%Chg	1991
Net Int. Inc.	1,324	3%	1,284	2%	1,255	7%	1,169
Tax Equiv. Adj.	100	1%	99	25%	79.0	-17%	95.0
Non Int. Inc.	604	-4%	628	13%	555	13%	490
Loan Loss Prov.	72.0	-23%	93.0	-22%	119	-59%	293
% Exp/Op Revs.	54%	—	57%	—	58%	—	63%
Pretax Inc.	761	11%	688	15%	596	112%	281
Eff. Tax Rate	29%	—	28%	—	27%	—	18%
Net Inc.	539	10%	492	14%	433	88%	230
% Net Int. Marg.	4.34%	—	4.64%	—	4.75%	—	4.50%

Balance Sheet & Other Fin. Data (Million $)

	1994	1993	1992	1991	1990	1989
Earning Assets:						
Money Mkt.	1,098	1,492	1,565	2,399	1,663	1,692
Inv. Securities	7,723	7,879	6,486	6,265	3,779	3,598
Com'l Loans	10,376	8,843	8,442	8,505	7,307	6,703
Other Loans	15,515	14,134	12,644	12,112	9,329	8,594
Total Assets	39,188	36,526	33,367	33,158	26,271	24,050
Demand Deposits	5,663	6,144	5,627	4,758	4,988	4,377
Time Deposits	17,406	17,209	17,749	18,248	13,225	13,010
LT Debt	4,790	590	439	171	113	171
Common Eqty.	3,287	3,018	2,775	2,484	1,929	1,740

Ratio Analysis

	1994	1993	1992	1991	1990	1989
% Ret. on Assets	1.5	1.5	1.4	0.7	1.2	1.2
% Ret. on Equity	17.4	17.1	16.7	9.3	16.4	16.5
% Loan Loss Resv.	1.6	1.8	1.8	1.8	1.1	1.1
% Loans/Deposits	112.2	98.4	90.2	89.6	91.3	87.8
% Equity to Assets	8.4	8.5	8.2	7.7	7.6	7.3

Dividend Data —Dividends were paid by the predecessor Wachovia Corp. since 1936 and by First Atlanta since 1866. A dividend reinvestment plan is available.

Amt. of Div. $	Date Decl.	Ex-Div. Date	Stock of Record	Payment Date
0.330	Oct. 28	Nov. 02	Nov. 08	Dec. 01 '94
0.330	Jan. 27	Feb. 02	Feb. 08	Mar. 01 '95
0.330	Apr. 28	May. 02	May. 08	Jun. 01 '95
0.360	Jul. 28	Aug. 03	Aug. 07	Sep. 01 '95

Data as orig. reptd.; bef. results of disc opers. and/or spec. items. Per share data adj. for stk. divs. as of ex-div. date. E-Estimated. NA-Not Available. NM-Not Meaningful. NR-Not Ranked.

Offices—301 North Main St., Winston-Salem, NC 27150; 191 Peachtree St., N.E., Atlanta, GA 30303. **Tels**—(910) 770-5000; (404) 332-5000. **Chrmn**—J. G. Medlin, Jr. **Pres & CEO**—L. M. Baker, Jr. **EVP & CFO**—R. S. McCoy, Jr. **EVP & Treas**—R. B. Roberts. **Investor Contact**—James C. Mabry. **Dirs**—L. M. Baker, Jr., R. C. Barkley, Jr., C. C. Bowles, J. L. Clendenin, L. M. Gressette, Jr., T. K. Hearn, Jr., W. H. Hipp, R. M. Holder, Jr., D. R. Hughes, F. K. Iverson, J. W. Johnston, J. G. Medlin, Jr., W. Robertson, H. J. Russell, S. H. Smith, Jr., C. M. Taylor. **Transfer Agent**—Wachovia Bank of North Carolina, N.A., Winston-Salem. **Incorporated** in North Carolina in 1985. **Empl**-15,707. **S&P Analyst:** Stephen R. Biggar

Wal-Mart Stores

NYSE Symbol **WMT**
In S&P 500

26-JUL-95 | Industry: Retail Stores

Summary: Wal-Mart is the largest retailer in the U.S., operating a chain of discount department stores, wholesale clubs and combination discount stores and supermarkets.

S&P Opinion: Accumulate (★★★★)

| Recent Price • 27½ | Yield • 0.7% |
| 52 Wk Range • 27½-20½ | 12-Mo. P/E • 23.1 |

Quantitative Evaluations

Outlook
(1 Lowest—5 Highest)
• **5⁻**

Fair Value
• **32¼**

Risk
• **Low**

Earn./Div. Rank
• **A+**

Technical Eval.
• **Bullish** since 5/95

Rel. Strength Rank
(1 Lowest—99 Highest)
• **59**

Insider Activity
• **Neutral**

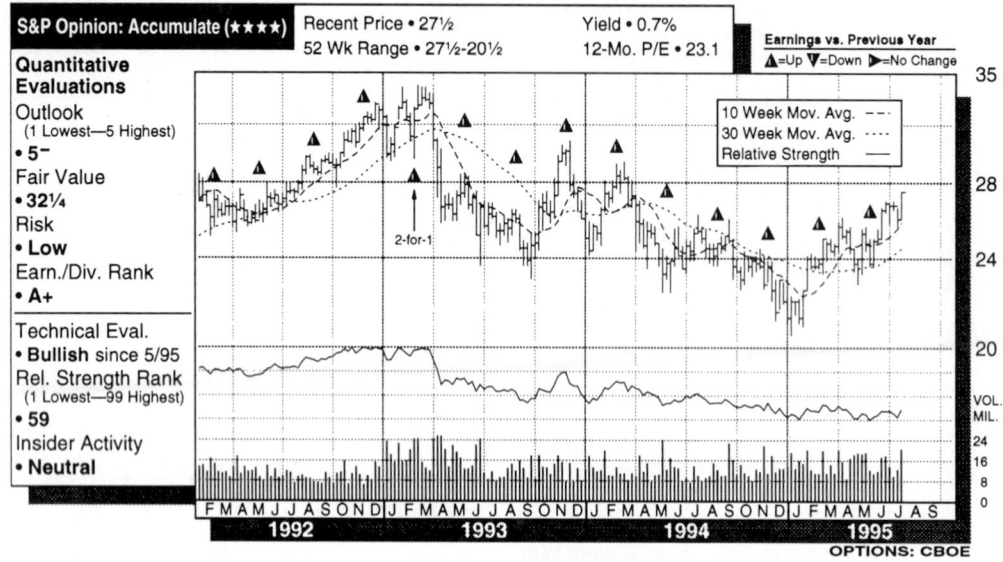

Earnings vs. Previous Year
▲=Up ▼=Down ▶=No Change

10 Week Mov. Avg. – – –
30 Week Mov. Avg. ·······
Relative Strength ——

OPTIONS: CBOE

Overview - 26-JUL-95

Same-store sales at discount stores should increase some 6% in 1995-96, while same-store sales at Sam's should begin to show modest increases. Higher volume and continued efforts to pare operating costs should accommodate an aggressive pricing posture. Further out, the supercenter format, which includes groceries and general merchandise, is the key to the company's long-term growth. The company operates over 160 of these units, generating over $60 million per unit annually. International expansion through joint ventures in China, Hong Kong and South America enhances the company's long-term growth prospects. Expansion plans in Mexico, which is a profitable market for Wal-Mart, have been slowed by the crisis in that country's economy.

Valuation - 26-JUL-95

After trending down for two years, the share price is up from the lows of earlier this year, boosted by a solid first quarter in 1995-96; same-store sales at Sam's Clubs were up 2.9%. We believe that the P/E contraction that resulted from investors discounting a lower earnings growth rate for this retailing giant has run its course and the multiple should range from 16 to 18. Focusing on international growth, notably in Canada, Latin America and Asia, and its supercenter general merchandise and supermarket format, Wal-Mart is on track for solid earnings gains over the next few years. This is an opportune time to buy this growth stock as it comes back into favor.

Key Stock Statistics

S&P EPS Est. 1996	1.40	Tang. Bk. Value/Share	5.71
P/E on S&P Est. 1996	19.6	Beta	1.14
S&P EPS Est. 1997	1.60	Shareholders	259,300
Dividend Rate/Share	0.20	Market cap. (B)	$ 62.0
Shs. outstg. (M)	2297.3	Inst. holdings	31%
Avg. daily vol. (M)	2.880	Insider holdings	NA

Value of $10,000 invested 5 years ago: $ 25,202

Fiscal Year Ending Jan. 31

	1996	% Change	1995	% Change	1994	% Change
Revenues (Million $)						
1Q	20,440	16%	17,690	27%	13,920	19%
2Q	—	—	19,942	23%	16,237	25%
3Q	—	—	20,418	21%	16,827	23%
4Q	—	—	24,448	20%	20,361	19%
Yr.	—	—	82,494	22%	67,345	21%
Income (Million $)						
1Q	553.4	11%	498.5	11%	450.6	16%
2Q	—	—	564.8	14%	495.9	18%
3Q	—	—	588.1	13%	518.7	18%
4Q	—	—	1,030	19%	868.0	16%
Yr.	—	—	2,681	15%	2,333	17%
Earnings Per Share ($)						
1Q	0.24	9%	0.22	10%	0.20	18%
2Q	E0.28	—	0.25	14%	0.22	22%
3Q	E0.29	—	0.26	13%	0.23	21%
4Q	E0.59	—	0.45	18%	0.38	15%
Yr.	E1.40	—	1.17	15%	1.02	17%

Next earnings report expected: mid August

Business Summary - 26-JUL-95

Wal-Mart is the largest retailer in the U.S., through the operation of 1,990 Wal-Mart discount department stores, 428 Sam's Clubs, 143 supercenters and 123 Wal-Mart Canada stores at January 31, 1995. The company operates operates 63 Wal-Mart stores, 11 supercenters, and 22 Sam's Clubs in Mexico and three Value Clubs in Hong Kong. Units are set to open in Argentina, China and Brazil.

The average Wal-Mart discount store is 84,000 sq. ft. in size; store sizes range from 30,000 to 200,000 sq. ft. Wal-Mart stores are organized with 36 departments and offer a wide variety of merchandise, about 27% of which is soft goods and 26% hardware, housewares, auto supplies and small appliances. Nationally advertised merchandise accounts for a majority of sales. WMT markets limited lines of merchandise under brand names including "Sam's American Choice." The company also operates Wal-Mart Supercenters in 19 states, averaging 173,000 sq. ft. and selling grocery items in addition to general merchandise.

Sam's Clubs are membership-only, cash-and-carry wholesale warehouses operating in 49 states and Puerto Rico, averaging 120,000 sq. ft.

In 1990, Wal-Mart acquired McLane Co., a provider of retail and grocery distribution services. In 1992, Wal-Mart purchased Western Merchandisers, Inc., a wholesale distributor of books and pre-recorded music.

Important Developments

May '95—Same-store sales in the first quarter of 1995-96 rose 6.2%. The Wal-Mart division had sales of $14.5 billion; operating profit rose 17% to $1.1 billion. Sales at Sam's were $4.4 billion, up 6%; operating profit rose 18% to $122 million. Sales at the international division totaled $602 million, up 389%; there was an operating loss of $10.5 million, versus breakeven results a year earlier. Capital expenditure plans for 1995-96 approximate $3.2 billion within the U.S., including the opening of 100 new discount stores and about 100 Supercenters. About 85 of the new supercenters would be relocations or expansions of existing discount stores. International expansion is planned in Hong Kong and China through a joint venture to open warehouse clubs and discount stores. New retail square footage in 1995-96 should approximate 34 million square feet.

Capitalization

Long Term Debt: $9,709,000,000 (1/95), incl. $1,838,000,000 of capital lease obligations.

Per Share Data ($) (Year Ended Jan. 31)

	1995	1994	1993	1992	1991	1990
Tangible Bk. Val.	5.54	4.68	3.81	3.04	2.35	1.74
Cash Flow	1.63	1.37	1.14	0.91	0.72	0.60
Earnings	1.17	1.02	0.87	0.70	0.57	0.48
Dividends	0.17	0.13	0.10	0.08	0.07	0.06
Payout Ratio	15%	13%	11%	12%	12%	12%
Cal. Yrs.	1994	1993	1992	1991	1990	1989
Prices - High	29¼	34⅛	33	30	18⅜	11¼
- Low	21	23	25⅛	14¼	10⅛	7½
P/E Ratio - High	25	33	38	43	32	24
- Low	18	23	29	20	18	16

Income Statement Analysis (Million $)

	1995	%Chg	1994	%Chg	1993	%Chg	1992
Revs.	82,494	22%	67,345	21%	55,484	26%	43,887
Oper. Inc.	5,120	17%	4,389	21%	3,615	25%	2,892
Depr.	1,070	30%	822	31%	627	32%	475
Int. Exp.	776	33%	582	44%	403	33%	302
Pretax Inc.	4,262	15%	3,692	17%	3,166	24%	2,553
Eff. Tax Rate	37%	—	37%	—	37%	—	37%
Net Inc.	2,681	15%	2,333	17%	1,995	24%	1,608

Balance Sheet & Other Fin. Data (Million $)

	1995	1994	1993	1992	1991	1990
Cash	45.0	20.0	12.0	31.0	13.0	13.0
Curr. Assets	15,338	12,115	10,198	8,575	6,415	4,713
Total Assets	32,819	26,441	20,565	15,443	11,389	8,198
Curr. Liab.	9,973	7,406	6,754	5,004	3,990	2,845
LT Debt	9,709	7,960	4,845	3,278	1,899	1,273
Common Eqty.	12,726	10,752	8,759	6,990	5,366	3,966
Total Cap.	22,846	19,035	13,811	10,440	7,398	5,353
Cap. Exp.	3,734	4,371	4,043	1,805	1,388	955
Cash Flow	3,751	3,155	2,622	2,084	1,638	1,345

Ratio Analysis

	1995	1994	1993	1992	1991	1990
Curr. Ratio	1.5	1.6	1.5	1.7	1.6	1.7
% LT Debt of Cap.	42.5	41.8	35.1	31.4	25.7	23.8
% Net Inc.of Revs.	3.3	3.5	3.6	3.7	4.0	4.2
% Ret. on Assets	9.1	9.9	11.1	12.0	13.1	14.8
% Ret. on Equity	22.8	23.9	25.3	26.0	27.6	30.8

Dividend Data (Dividends were initiated in 1973.)

Amt. of Div. $	Date Decl.	Ex-Div. Date	Stock of Record	Payment Date
0.042	Aug. 11	Aug. 30	Sep. 06	Oct. 03 '94
0.042	Nov. 10	Nov. 29	Dec. 05	Jan. 05 '95
0.050	Mar. 09	Mar. 15	Mar. 21	Apr. 14 '95
0.050	Jun. 01	Jun. 08	Jun. 12	Jul. 10 '95

Data as orig. reptd.; bef. results of disc. opers. and/or spec. items. Per share data adj. for stk. divs. as of ex-div. date. E-Estimated. NA-Not Available. NM-Not Meaningful. NR-Not Ranked.

Office—702 Southwest 8th St. (P.O. Box 116), Bentonville, AR 72716. **Tel**—(501) 273-4000. **Chrmn**—S. R. Walton. **Pres & CEO**—D. D. Glass. **Vice Chrmn & COO**—D. G. Soderquist. **Secy**—R. K. Rhoads. **Dirs**—P. R. Carter, J. A. Cooper Jr., R. H. Dedman, D. D. Glass, F. S. Humphries, F. K. Iverson, E. A. Sanders, J. Shewmaker, D. G. Soderquist, J. T. Walton, S. R. Walton. **Transfer Agent & Registrar**—Boatmen's Trust Co., St. Louis, Mo. **Incorporated** in Delaware in 1969. **Empl**-622,000. **S&P Analyst:** Karen J. Sack, CFA

Walgreen Co.

NYSE Symbol **WAG**

In S&P 500

01-AUG-95
Industry: Retail Stores

Summary: Walgreen is the largest retail drug chain in revenues in the U.S. The company operates over 2,000 drug stores in 30 states and Puerto Rico.

S&P Opinion: Hold (★★★)	Recent Price • 53	Yield • 1.5%
	52 Wk Range • 53¾-35¼	12-Mo. P/E • 20.9

Quantitative Evaluations

Outlook
(1 Lowest—5 Highest)
• 1

Fair Value
• 44

Risk
• Low

Earn./Div. Rank
• A+

Technical Eval.
• Bearish since 7/95

Rel. Strength Rank
(1 Lowest—99 Highest)
• 54

Insider Activity
• Unfavorable

Earnings vs. Previous Year
▲=Up ▼=Down ▶=No Change

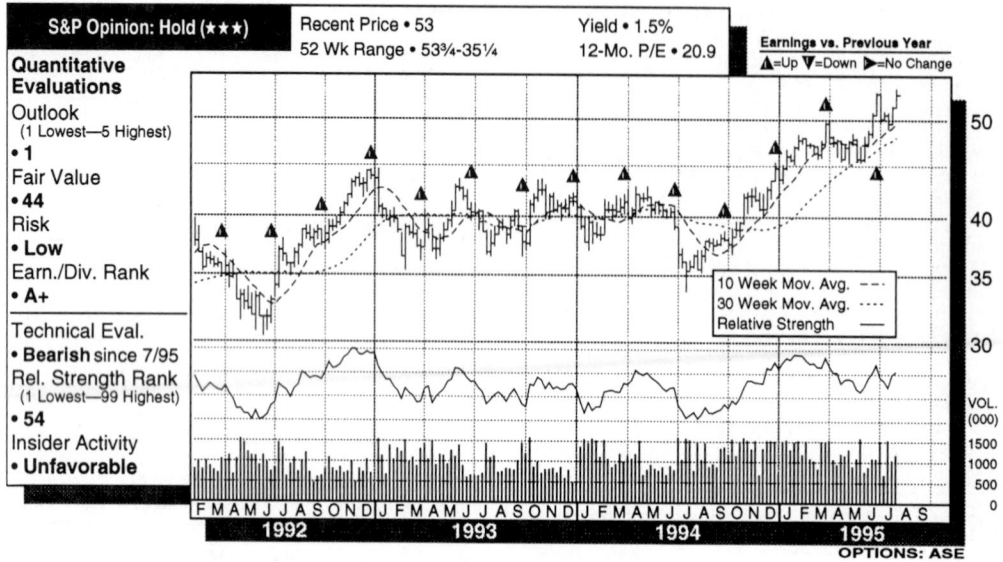

- 10 Week Mov. Avg. - - -
- 30 Week Mov. Avg. ·······
- Relative Strength ——

OPTIONS: ASE

Overview - 01-AUG-95

Sales growth in fiscal 1996 is projected at 12%, fueled by continued strong gains for prescription sales. Market share gains should continue as the company expands its store base by about 200 units. WAG plans to enter several new markets in the next few years. Competitive pricing and third-party programs will restrict gross margins, but expense ratios should improve, reflecting cost containment and better inventory management. Annual earnings per share growth should approximate 13% over the next few years. In the long term, continuing productivity advances, superior pharmacy operations and new store growth should sustain WAG's strong industry position. The company is conservatively financed, with no long-term debt. With ample cash flow generation, internal funds will be used for capital expenditures. A 2-for-1 common stock split will be paid on August 8.

Valuation - 28-JUL-95

With the uncertainty surrounding health care reform legislation eliminated, and strong sales gains, particularly in prescriptions, the share price has risen dramatically since late 1994. As one of the premier drug chains in a rapidly consolidating drug store business, the company's shares trade at a higher multiple than other drug store chains. At the current level, however, the shares appear fully valued, and we anticipate that they will only track the market in the next six months.

Key Stock Statistics

S&P EPS Est. 1995	2.60	Tang. Bk. Value/Share	14.17
P/E on S&P Est. 1995	20.4	Beta	0.96
S&P EPS Est. 1996	2.95	Shareholders	29,900
Dividend Rate/Share	0.78	Market cap. (B)	$ 6.4
Shs. outstg. (M)	123.1	Inst. holdings	56%
Avg. daily vol. (M)	0.245	Insider holdings	NA

Value of $10,000 invested 5 years ago: $ 24,631

Fiscal Year Ending Aug. 31

	1995	% Change	1994	% Change	1993	% Change
Revenues (Million $)						
1Q	2,406	14%	2,118	11%	1,915	12%
2Q	2,807	12%	2,499	11%	2,258	11%
3Q	2,617	12%	2,336	12%	2,085	11%
4Q	—	—	2,283	12%	2,037	11%
Yr.	—	—	9,235	11%	8,295	11%
Income (Million $)						
1Q	53.99	22%	44.21	10%	40.26	14%
2Q	111.6	14%	97.62	16%	84.21	9%
3Q	78.99	11%	71.02	10%	64.40	14%
4Q	—	—	69.08	18%	58.31	13%
Yr.	—	—	281.9	15%	245.3	11%
Earnings Per Share ($)						
1Q	0.44	22%	0.36	13%	0.32	10%
2Q	0.90	14%	0.79	18%	0.67	8%
3Q	0.64	12%	0.57	10%	0.52	13%
4Q	E0.62	—	0.56	19%	0.47	15%
Yr.	E2.60	—	2.28	15%	1.98	11%

Next earnings report expected: early October

Walgreen Co.

01-AUG-95

Business Summary - 28-JUL-95

Walgreen is the largest U.S. retail drug store chain in terms of revenues. At August 31, 1994, it had 1,968 drug stores in operation in 30 states and Puerto Rico, with the largest concentrations in Florida (326), Illinois (313) and Texas (189). Drug stores averaged $4.7 million in sales per unit ($473 per sq. ft.). More than two-thirds of the stores have been opened or remodeled in the past five years.

In fiscal 1994, prescriptions accounted for 41% of sales, nonprescription drugs for 13%, general merchandise 24%, liquor and beverages 9%, cosmetics and toiletries 9%, and tobacco products 4%. The company's pharmacy continues to be a growing part of the business. WAG filled nearly 148 million prescriptions in fiscal 1994.

Recent technological advances include satellite linkage to all stores and facilities, point-of-sale scanning and implementation of the strategic inventory management system (SIMS), uniting all elements of the purchasing, distribution and sales cycle. This will reduce inventory, improve in-stock positions, and provide quicker reaction to sales trends. Intercom is an on-line pharmacy system that links all stores with headquarters and one another.

The company has invested more than $1 billion over the past five years in new and remodeled stores, new distribution centers and store technology. Capital spending for fiscal 1995 is expected to be about $300 million.

In 1992, a pharmacy mail service division, Walgreen Healthcare Plus, began operations. Expansion into this business gives the company a full service approach to pharmaceutical care.

Sales of peripheral businesses have enabled WAG to focus entirely on the operations of drug stores. In 1988, a family restaurant chain was sold to Marriott Corp., and in August 1989, the company sold its private label manufacturing operations.

Important Developments

Jun. '95—WAG reported year-to-year sales gains of 12% for the third quarter of fiscal 1995; same-store pharmacy sales advanced 14%. Pharmacy now accounts for 43% of total sales, and could provide 50% by the end of the decade. The company opened or relocated 140 stores in the first nine months of fiscal 1995; about 200 stores are planned for the full fiscal year. The company plans to enter two new markets in 1996 - Oklahoma City and Richmond - with 10 new stores in the first year; some 20 to 25 stores are planned for each of these markets. WAG plans to be operating 3,000 stores by the year 2000. The company began the rollout of its Intercom Plus advanced pharmacy computer and work-flow system. The system is expected to be chainwide by the end of 1996.

Capitalization

Long Term Debt: None (5/31/95).

Per Share Data ($)

(Year Ended Aug. 31)

	1994	1993	1992	1991	1990	1989
Tangible Bk. Val.	12.79	11.20	10.02	8.78	7.70	6.69
Cash Flow	3.24	2.83	2.53	2.26	1.98	1.77
Earnings	2.28	1.98	1.78	1.58	1.42	1.25
Dividends	0.68	0.60	0.52	0.46	0.40	0.34
Payout Ratio	30%	30%	29%	29%	28%	27%
Prices - High	45¾	44⅝	44½	38⅝	26⅝	25⅛
- Low	33¾	35⅜	30⅜	24⅝	20	15
P/E Ratio - High	20	23	25	24	19	20
- Low	15	18	17	16	14	12

Income Statement Analysis (Million $)

	1994	%Chg	1993	%Chg	1992	%Chg	1991
Revs.	9,235	11%	8,295	11%	7,475	11%	6,733
Oper. Inc.	574	12%	511	13%	451	11%	405
Depr.	118	13%	105	14%	92.1	9%	84.3
Int. Exp.	3.1	-54%	6.8	-58%	16.2	-15%	19.1
Pretax Inc.	458	14%	400	13%	353	13%	312
Eff. Tax Rate	39%	—	39%	—	38%	—	38%
Net Inc.	282	15%	245	11%	221	13%	195

Balance Sheet & Other Fin. Data (Million $)

	1994	1993	1992	1991	1990	1989
Cash	108	121	226	135	214	226
Curr. Assets	1,673	1,463	1,439	1,247	1,187	1,083
Total Assets	2,909	2,535	2,374	2,095	1,914	1,681
Curr. Liab.	1,051	884	889	684	632	545
LT Debt	11.0	17.0	31.0	136	163	168
Common Eqty.	1,574	1,379	1,233	1,081	947	823
Total Cap.	1,758	1,569	1,462	1,393	1,266	1,124
Cap. Exp.	290	185	145	202	192	121
Cash Flow	400	350	313	279	245	218

Ratio Analysis

	1994	1993	1992	1991	1990	1989
Curr. Ratio	1.6	1.7	1.6	1.8	1.9	2.0
% LT Debt of Cap.	0.6	1.1	2.1	9.8	12.9	14.9
% Net Inc.of Revs.	3.1	3.0	3.0	2.9	2.9	2.9
% Ret. on Assets	10.4	10.0	9.9	9.7	9.7	9.7
% Ret. on Equity	19.1	18.8	19.1	19.2	19.7	20.1

Dividend Data (Dividends have been paid since 1933. A dividend reinvestment plan is available.)

Amt. of Div. $	Date Decl.	Ex-Div. Date	Stock of Record	Payment Date
0.170	Jul. 13	Aug. 16	Aug. 22	Sep. 12 '94
0.195	Oct. 12	Nov. 07	Nov. 14	Dec. 12 '94
0.195	Jan. 11	Feb. 15	Feb. 22	Mar. 11 '95
0.195	Apr. 13	May. 16	May. 22	Jun. 12 '95
2-for-1	Jul. 12	Aug. 09	Jul. 24	Aug. 08 '95

Data as orig. reptd.; bef. results of disc. opers. and/or spec. items. Per share data adj. for stk. divs. as of ex-div. date. E-Estimated. NA-Not Available. NM-Not Meaningful. NR-Not Ranked.

Office—200 Wilmot Rd., Deerfield, IL 60015. **Tel**—(708) 940-2500. **Chrmn & CEO**—C. R. Walgreen III. **Pres**—L. D. Jorndt. **Vice Chrmn & CFO**—C. D. Hunter. **Secy**—J. A. Oettinger. **Investor Contact**—John M. Palizza. **Dirs**—T. Dimitriou, J. J. Howard, C. D. Hunter, L. D. Jorndt, C. Reed, J. B. Schwemm, W. H. Springer, M. M. von Ferstel, C. R. Walgreen III. **Transfer Agent & Registrar**—Harris Trust & Savings Bank, Chicago. **Incorporated** in Illinois in 1909. **Empl**-62,000. **S&P Analyst:** Karen J. Sack, CFA

STOCK REPORTS

Warner-Lambert

NYSE Symbol **WLA**
In S&P 500

11-SEP-95

Industry:
Drugs-Generic and
OTC

Summary: This company is a leading producer of prescription pharmaceuticals and OTC medications, with interests in gums and mints and other consumer products.

S&P Opinion: Accumulate (★★★★)

| Recent Price • 92½ | Yield • 2.8% |
| 52 Wk Range • 92½-73 | 12-Mo. P/E • 17.6 |

Quantitative Evaluations

Outlook
(1 Lowest—5 Highest)
• **2⁻**

Fair Value
• **84⅝**

Risk
• **Low**

Earn./Div. Rank
• **A-**

Technical Eval.
• **Bearish** since 9/94

Rel. Strength Rank
(1 Lowest—99 Highest)
• **67**

Insider Activity
• **Neutral**

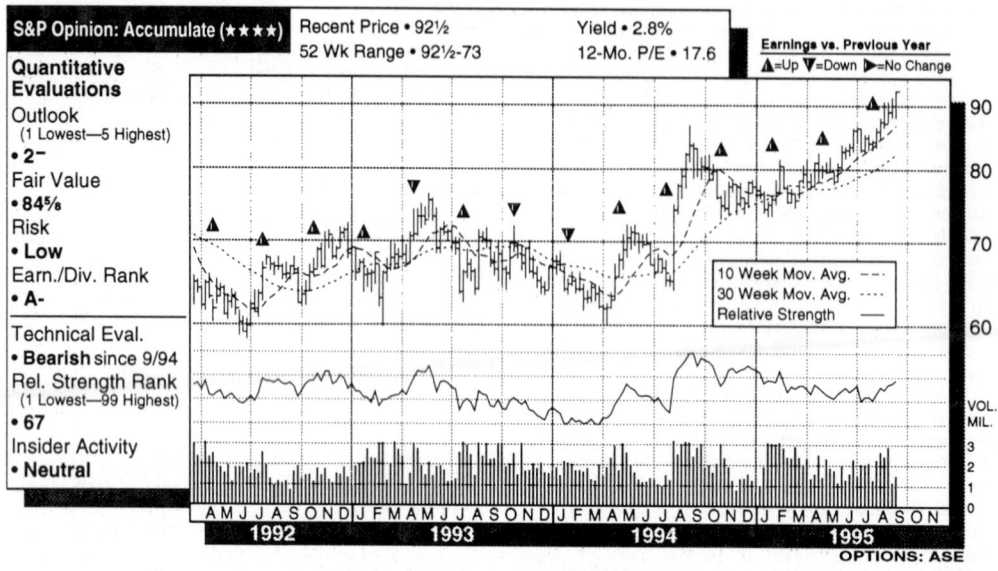

Earnings vs. Previous Year
▲=Up ▼=Down ▶=No Change

10 Week Mov. Avg. ---
30 Week Mov. Avg. ····
Relative Strength —

VOL. MIL.

1992 1993 1994 1995

OPTIONS: ASE

Overview - 11-SEP-95

Sales advance modestly in 1996. Despite continued pricing pressures in global drug markets and generic erosion in Lopid cholesterol-lowering drug, pharmaceutical sales should rise, aided by gains for Accupril antihypertensive, Dilantin and Neurontin anti-epileptic agents, and Cognex (for Alzheimer's disease). New products such as a planned launch of Listerine toothpaste and an OTC version of Zantac for heartburn should boost consumer products sales. Despite a likely increase in the tax rate, profitability should benefit from cost streamlining measures, and comparisons will be aided by the absence of losses from the devaluation of the Mexican peso.

Valuation - 11-SEP-95

The shares have appreciated about 20% in the past six months, buoyed by continued strength in the drug sector and by investor interest in WLA as a takeover candidate. Renewed merger speculation was triggered by the purchase of Marion Merrell Dow by Hoechst AG and the forthcoming merger of Upjohn and Pharmacia AB. Despite a recent slowing of quarterly earnings, profit growth should accelerate in coming years, aided by the planned divestiture of non-strategic businesses and by new products. The company believes that its drug pipeline has the potential to add $2 billion to annual sales and over $2 to EPS over the next five to seven years. The shares remain attractive for total return.

Key Stock Statistics

S&P EPS Est. 1995	5.45	Tang. Bk. Value/Share	10.72
P/E on S&P Est. 1995	17.0	Beta	0.96
S&P EPS Est. 1996	5.90	Shareholders	43,000
Dividend Rate/Share	2.60	Market cap. (B)	$ 12.5
Shs. outstg. (M)	134.8	Inst. holdings	77%
Avg. daily vol. (M)	0.426	Insider holdings	NA

Value of $10,000 invested 5 years ago: $ 18,778

Fiscal Year Ending Dec. 31

	1995	% Change	1994	% Change	1993	% Change
Revenues (Million $)						
1Q	1,605	9%	1,473	11%	1,332	2%
2Q	1,800	16%	1,552	7%	1,450	6%
3Q	—	—	1,671	13%	1,479	3%
4Q	—	—	1,721	12%	1,534	4%
Yr.	—	—	6,417	11%	5,794	4%
Income (Million $)						
1Q	201.4	6%	190.4	40%	136.1	-17%
2Q	201.0	2%	196.7	4%	189.9	7%
3Q	—	—	169.2	9%	155.9	-5%
4Q	—	—	137.6	NM	-196.0	NM
Yr.	—	—	694.0	143%	285.0	-56%
Earnings Per Share ($)						
1Q	1.50	6%	1.42	41%	1.01	-17%
2Q	1.49	1%	1.47	5%	1.40	6%
3Q	E1.35	7%	1.26	9%	1.16	-5%
4Q	E1.11	9%	1.02	NM	-1.46	NM
Yr.	E5.45	5%	5.17	145%	2.11	-56%

Next earnings report expected: mid October

McGraw Hill

Business Summary - 11-SEP-95

Warner-Lambert produces ethical drugs, over-the-counter (OTC) pharmaceuticals, and consumer products. Segment contributions in 1994 were:

	Sales	Profits
Pharmaceuticals	32%	42%
Consumer health care	46%	42%
Gums & mints	22%	16%

International operations represented 54% of sales and 50% of profits in 1994.

Pharmaceuticals include ethical drugs, biologicals and diagnostic products, capsules and hospital products. Products include Meclomen nonsteroidal anti-inflammatory agent, Procan SR and Manoplax cardiovasculars, Centrax tranquilizer, Lopid lipid (fat) regulator, Accupril and Dilzem antihypertensives, Cognex for Alzheimer's disease, Dilantin and Neurontin epilepsy treatments, Comprecin antibacterial, Doryx antibiotic and Cholybar cholesterol-lowering candy bar. Branded generics and empty hard gelatin drug capsules are also sold.

Consumer health care products include nonprescription items such as Listerine oral antiseptic, Listermint mouthwash, Bromo-Seltzer antacid-analgesic, Halls cough tablets, Rolaids antacid, Benadryl cold medication, and Replens vaginal moisturizer; Schick and Wilkinson Sword razors and blades; and Tetra home aquarium products. WLA also has a joint venture with British drugmaker Glaxo Wellcome to market OTC drugs.

Gums and mints include Dentyne, Trident, Freshen-Up, Bubblicious, Mondo, Cinn-A-Burst and Mint-A-Burst gums; and Clorets, Dynamints and Certs mints.

R&D spending equaled 7.1% of sales in 1994, versus 8.0% in 1993.

Important Developments

Sep. '95—The company and LeukoSite, Inc. signed a second collaborative agreement to develop and commercialize anti-inflammatory drugs. Separately, positive clinical results were released on Troglitazone, a new drug to reduce insulin dependency in patients with Type II diabetes. The drug is being developed with Sankyo Co. of Japan. In June, WLA agreed to sublicense fedotozine, a new treatment for irritable bowel syndrome and related ailments, to Glazo Wellcome. In July, an FDA advisory committee recommended approval for an OTC version of Glaxo's Zantac. Upon full FDA approval, the product will be marketed by a joint venture of WLA and Glaxo.

Capitalization

Long Term Debt: $435,800,000 (6/95).

Per Share Data ($) (Year Ended Dec. 31)

	1994	1993	1992	1991	1990	1989
Tangible Bk. Val.	10.67	8.02	10.14	7.52	9.24	7.34
Cash Flow	6.53	3.37	5.93	2.06	4.50	3.82
Earnings	5.17	2.11	4.78	1.05	3.61	3.05
Dividends	2.44	2.28	2.04	1.76	1.52	1.28
Payout Ratio	47%	108%	43%	168%	42%	42%
Prices - High	86¾	76⅜	79¼	82¼	70⅜	59⅜
- Low	60	59¾	58⅜	61¼	49⅝	37¼
P/E Ratio - High	17	36	17	78	19	19
- Low	12	28	12	59	14	12

Income Statement Analysis (Million $)

	1994	%Chg	1993	%Chg	1992	%Chg	1991
Revs.	6,417	11%	5,794	4%	5,598	11%	5,059
Oper. Inc.	1,192	21%	985	NM	989	16%	852
Depr.	181	6%	170	9%	156	15%	136
Int. Exp.	103	41%	72.8	-18%	88.9	32%	67.6
Pretax Inc.	1,005	NM	319	-63%	858	NM	222
Eff. Tax Rate	22%	—	11%	—	25%	—	36%
Net Inc.	694	144%	285	-56%	644	NM	141

Balance Sheet & Other Fin. Data (Million $)

	1994	1993	1992	1991	1990	1989
Cash	465	441	718	536	306	253
Curr. Assets	2,515	2,219	2,176	1,844	1,559	1,367
Total Assets	5,533	4,828	4,077	3,602	3,261	2,860
Curr. Liab.	2,353	2,016	1,333	1,250	1,101	1,031
LT Debt	535	546	565	448	307	303
Common Eqty.	1,816	1,390	1,529	1,171	1,402	1,130
Total Cap.	2,461	2,005	2,145	1,656	1,890	1,596
Cap. Exp.	406	347	334	326	240	219
Cash Flow	875	455	799	276	605	518

Ratio Analysis

	1994	1993	1992	1991	1990	1989
Curr. Ratio	1.1	1.1	1.6	1.5	1.4	1.3
% LT Debt of Cap.	21.7	27.5	26.3	27.0	16.2	19.0
% Net Inc.of Revs.	10.8	4.9	11.5	2.8	10.3	9.8
% Ret. on Assets	13.4	6.4	16.7	4.1	15.9	14.9
% Ret. on Equity	43.2	19.6	47.6	10.9	38.4	38.9

Dividend Data—Dividends have been paid since 1926. A dividend reinvestment plan is available. A poison pill stock purchase rights plan was adopted in 1988.

Amt. of Div. $	Date Decl.	Ex-Div. Date	Stock of Record	Payment Date
0.610	Jul. 26	Aug. 01	Aug. 05	Sep. 09 '94
0.610	Oct. 25	Oct. 31	Nov. 04	Dec. 09 '94
0.650	Jan. 24	Jan. 30	Feb. 03	Mar. 10 '95
0.650	Apr. 25	May. 01	May. 05	Jun. 09 '95
0.650	Jul. 25	Aug. 02	Aug. 04	Sep. 08 '95

Data as orig. reptd.; bef. results of disc. opers. and/or spec. items. Per share data adj. for stk. divs. as of ex-div. date. E-Estimated. NA-Not Available. NM-Not Meaningful. NR-Not Ranked.

Office—201 Tabor Rd., Morris Plains, NJ 07950. **Tel**—(201) 540-2000. **Chrmn & CEO**—M. R. Goodes. **Pres & COO**—L. J. R. de Vink. **VP & CFO**—E. J. Larini. **Secy**—R. G. Paltiel. **Investor Contact**—George Shields. **Dirs**—B. C. Ames, D. C. Clark, L. J. R. de Vink, J. A. Georges, M. R. Goodes, W. H. Gray III, W. R. Howell, L. D. Leffall, Jr., P. S. Longe, A. Mandl, L. G. Rawl, M. I. Sovern, J. D. Williams. **Transfer Agent & Registrar**—First Chicago Trust Co. of New York, NYC. **Incorporated** in Delaware in 1920. **Empl**-36,000. **S&P Analyst:** H.B. Saftlas

Wells Fargo

NYSE Symbol **WFC**
In S&P 500

28-SEP-95 Industry: Banking

Summary: This bank holding company, the 17th largest in the U.S., owns the second largest bank in California. Branch banking constitutes the largest portion of WFC's business.

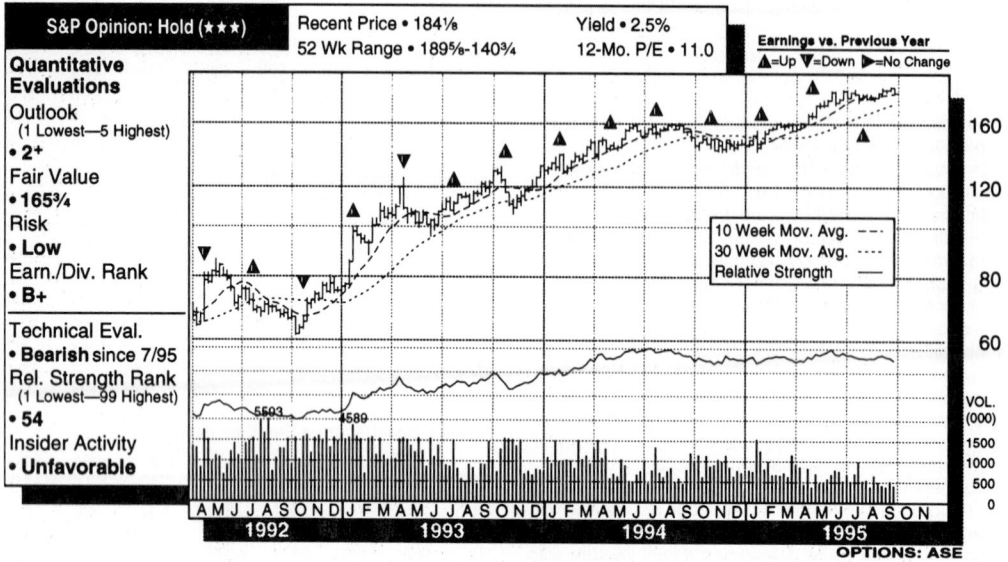

S&P Opinion: Hold (★★★)

Recent Price • 184⅛
52 Wk Range • 189⅝–140¾

Yield • 2.5%
12-Mo. P/E • 11.0

Earnings vs. Previous Year
▲=Up ▼=Down ▶=No Change

Quantitative Evaluations

Outlook
(1 Lowest—5 Highest)
• **2+**

Fair Value
• **165¾**

Risk
• **Low**

Earn./Div. Rank
• **B+**

Technical Eval.
• **Bearish** since 7/95

Rel. Strength Rank
(1 Lowest—99 Highest)
• **54**

Insider Activity
• **Unfavorable**

10 Week Mov. Avg. — –
30 Week Mov. Avg. ....
Relative Strength —

VOL. (000)

OPTIONS: ASE

Overview - 28-SEP-95

Despite an improving California economy that has led to better business conditions and increased demand in nearly all loan categories, net interest income is expected to be stagnant in 1995, following a strategic decision to sell about $4 billion of one-to-four family first mortgages in the second and third quarters, resulting in a drop in earning assets. An expected loss on the sale will penalize noninterest income, although fee-based products and mutual fund management fees should continue to rise. Much of the EPS gain expected for 1995 will come from lower credit costs (WFC recorded no loan loss provisions in the 1995 first half) and fewer shares outstanding (following a share repurchase program). A $100 million gain from the sale of a joint venture has been factored into the earnings forecast.

Valuation - 28-SEP-95

The shares, up 29% thus far in 1995, have underperformed the average regional bank but modestly outperformed the broader market, as an expectation of flat to declining interest rates has aided bank stocks in general. Per-share earnings should rise in 1995, on gains on investments, reduced loan loss provisions, and fewer shares outstanding, but long-term revenue growth remains a challenge. With only modestly higher earnings expected for 1996, the shares appear adequately valued at about nine times estimated EPS.

Key Stock Statistics

S&P EPS Est. 1995	19.00	Tang. Bk. Value/Share	61.35
P/E on S&P Est. 1995	9.7	Beta	1.45
S&P EPS Est. 1996	21.00	Shareholders	27,800
Dividend Rate/Share	4.60	Market cap. (B)	$ 9.0
Shs. outstg. (M)	48.3	Inst. holdings	61%
Avg. daily vol. (M)	0.087	Insider holdings	NA

Value of $10,000 invested 5 years ago: $ 30,926

Fiscal Year Ending Dec. 31

	1995	% Change	1994	% Change	1993	% Change
Revenues (Million $)						
1Q	1,267	6%	1,195	-3%	1,229	-8%
2Q	1,341	9%	1,231	2%	1,211	-8%
3Q	—	—	1,261	6%	1,189	-8%
4Q	—	—	1,278	4%	1,225	-2%
Yr.	—	—	4,965	2%	4,854	-7%
Income (Million $)						
1Q	233.0	15%	202.0	87%	108.0	-9%
2Q	232.0	13%	206.0	38%	149.0	82%
3Q	—	—	217.0	32%	165.0	NM
4Q	—	—	215.0	13%	190.0	NM
Yr.	—	—	841.0	37%	612.0	116%
Earnings Per Share ($)						
1Q	4.41	29%	3.41	98%	1.72	-18%
2Q	4.51	26%	3.57	45%	2.46	85%
3Q	E4.75	23%	3.86	41%	2.74	NM
4Q	E5.33	35%	3.96	25%	3.18	NM
Yr.	E19.00	29%	14.78	46%	10.10	127%

Next earnings report expected: mid October

Business Summary - 28-SEP-95

Wells Fargo & Co., the 17th largest U.S. bank holding company, owns California's second largest bank. Branch banking, conducted through 634 California locations, constitutes the largest portion of the company's business, offering a broad array of traditional consumer banking services, as well as credit card services, mutual funds and small business loans. Wholesale banking activities include commercial banking, wholesale services (operating and cash management products), international trade and foreign exchange services, real estate lending and capital market products. The Business and Investment Group concentrates on providing loans and other services for small businesses in California. WFC has agreed to sell its 50% interest in Wells Fargo Nikko Investment Advisors, which at year-end 1994 was the largest U.S. manager of index and other quantitatively structured funds. Nonbanking activities include leasing, mortgage banking, consumer and agricultural credit and credit life insurance.

Average earning assets in 1994 of $47.0 billion (up from $46.3 billion in 1993) consisted of commercial loans 15%, real estate loans 37%, consumer loans 17%, lease financing and foreign loans 3%, investment securities 27% and other 1%. Average sources of funds were noninterest-bearing deposits 17%, interest-bearing checking 9%, savings deposits 36%, time and foreign deposits 16%, short-term borrowings 5%, long-term debt 7%, equity 8% and other 2%.

At year-end 1994, nonperforming assets were $871 million (2.4% of total loans), down from $1.56 billion (4.7%) a year earlier. The allowance for loan losses was $2.08 billion (5.73% of total loans), versus $2.12 billion (6.41%) a year earlier. Net chargeoffs in 1994 were 0.70% of average loans, versus 1.44% in 1993.

At June 30, 1995, Tier 1 and total risk-based capital ratios were estimated at 8.60% and 12.50%, respectively, down from 8.73% and 12.78% at March 31, 1995. The decline primarily reflected the repurchase of 1,222,228 common shares during the second quarter of 1995.

Important Developments

Jun. '95—WFC and Nikko Securities Co. signed a definitive agreement to sell their joint venture interest in Wells Fargo Nikko Investment Advisors to Barclays PLC for a total of $440 million. The company expects to record a net gain of about $100 million on the sale.

Capitalization

Long Term Debt: $2,967,000,000 (6/95).
Preferred Stock: $489,000,000.

Per Share Data ($)

(Year Ended Dec. 31)

	1994	1993	1992	1991	1990	1989
Tangible Bk. Val.	51.08	50.63	40.70	33.61	37.20	41.18
Earnings	14.78	10.10	4.44	0.04	13.39	11.02
Dividends	4.00	2.25	2.00	3.50	3.90	3.30
Payout Ratio	27%	22%	45%	NM	29%	30%
Prices - High	160¾	133½	86⅜	98¾	86	87½
- Low	127⅛	74¾	56⅜	48	41¼	59
P/E Ratio - High	11	13	19	NM	6	8
- Low	9	7	13	NM	3	5

Income Statement Analysis (Million $)

	1994	%Chg	1993	%Chg	1992	%Chg	1991
Net Int. Inc.	2,610	-2%	2,657	-1%	2,691	7%	2,520
Tax Equiv. Adj.	NA	—	3.0	-40%	5.0	-75%	20.0
Non Int. Inc.	1,192	9%	1,093	8%	1,014	13%	895
Loan Loss Prov.	200	-64%	550	-55%	1,215	-9%	1,335
% Exp/Op Revs.	57%	—	58%	—	55%	—	59%
Pretax Inc.	1,454	40%	1,038	108%	500	NM	54.0
Eff. Tax Rate	42%	—	41%	—	43%	—	61%
Net Inc.	841	37%	612	116%	283	NM	21.0
% Net Int. Marg.	5.55%	—	5.74%	—	5.70%	—	5.17%

Balance Sheet & Other Fin. Data (Million $)

	1994	1993	1992	1991	1990	1989
Earning Assets:						
Money Mkt.	260	1,668	NA	NA	NA	11.0
Inv. Securities	11,608	13,058	9,338	3,833	1,387	1,738
Com'l Loans	9,492	8,124	9,381	12,440	15,800	15,544
Other Loans	26,855	24,975	27,512	31,659	33,176	26,183
Total Assets	53,374	52,513	52,537	53,547	56,199	48,737
Demand Deposits	10,145	9,719	9,190	8,216	8,130	8,003
Time Deposits	32,187	31,925	33,054	35,503	34,555	28,427
LT Debt	2,853	4,221	4,040	4,220	2,417	2,541
Common Eqty.	3,422	3,676	3,170	2,808	2,955	2,456

Ratio Analysis

	1994	1993	1992	1991	1990	1989
% Ret. on Assets	1.6	1.2	0.5	0.0	1.4	1.3
% Ret. on Equity	26.6	20.7	9.7	0.1	29.4	29.6
% Loan Loss Resv.	5.7	6.4	5.6	3.7	1.8	1.8
% Loans/Deposits	85.9	79.5	87.4	100.9	114.7	114.5
% Equity to Assets	5.8	5.3	4.6	4.8	4.6	4.1

Dividend Data —Dividends have been paid since 1936. A dividend reinvestment plan is available.

Amt. of Div. $	Date Decl.	Ex-Div. Date	Stock of Record	Payment Date
1.000	Oct. 18	Oct. 25	Oct. 31	Nov. 21 '94
1.150	Jan. 17	Jan. 25	Jan. 31	Feb. 21 '95
1.150	Apr. 18	Apr. 24	Apr. 28	May. 22 '95
1.150	Jul. 18	Jul. 27	Jul. 31	Aug. 21 '95

Data as orig. reptd.; bef. results of disc opers. and/or spec. items. Per share data adj. for stk. divs. as of ex-div. date.
E-Estimated. NA-Not Available. NM-Not Meaningful. NR-Not Ranked.

Office—420 Montgomery St., San Francisco, CA 94163. **Tel**—(415) 477-1000. **Chrmn & CEO**—P. Hazen. **Pres & COO**—W. F. Zuendt. **Vice Chrmn & CFO**—R. L. Jacobs. **Secy**— G. Rounsaville, Jr. **Investor Contact**—Cindy Koehn. **Dirs**—H. J. Arnelle, W. R. Breuner, W. S. Davila, R. S. Dezember, P. Hazen, R. K. Jaedicke, P. A. Miller, E. M. Newman, P. J. Quigley, C. E. Reichardt, D. B. Rice, S. G. Swenson, C. L. Tien, J. A. Young, W. F. Zuendt. **Transfer Agent & Registrar**—First Chicago Trust Co. of New York, Jersey City, NJ. **Incorporated** in California in 1968; reincorporated in Delaware in 1987; bank incorporated in 1899. **Empl**—19,493. **S&P Analyst:** Stephen R. Biggar

Wendy's International

NYSE Symbol **WEN**
In S&P 500

19-OCT-95

Industry:
Food serving

Summary: This company operates or franchises more than 4,400 Wendy's restaurants, over 90% of which are in the U.S.

S&P Opinion: Accumulate (★★★★)	Recent Price • 21⅛ Yield • 1.1%
	52 Wk Range • 22¾-13½ 12-Mo. P/E • 20.7

Quantitative Evaluations

Outlook
(1 Lowest—5 Highest)
• **3+**

Fair Value
• **20⅞**

Risk
• **Low**

Earn./Div. Rank
• **B+**

Technical Eval.
• **Bullish** since 2/95

Rel. Strength Rank
(1 Lowest—99 Highest)
• **62**

Insider Activity
• **Neutral**

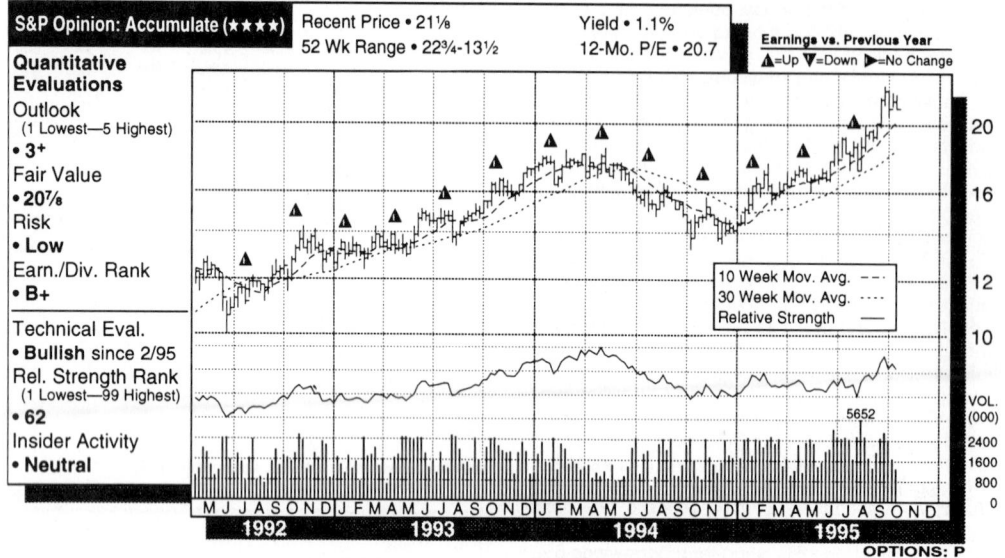

Earnings vs. Previous Year
▲=Up ▼=Down ▶=No Change

10 Week Mov. Avg. – – –
30 Week Mov. Avg. .....
Relative Strength ——

OPTIONS: P

Overview - 19-OCT-95

We expect WEN's sales growth in 1995 to be fueled by the presence of more company-operated units and by modest improvement in comparable-unit sales. We look for WEN to continue its successful strategy of offering a diversified menu, including both relatively low-cost items and special premium sandwiches. With higher volume, we expect a further widening of the restaurant operating profit margin. Systemwide (including franchises), we look for at least 400 restaurants to either open in 1995 or be under construction by year-end. Longer term, WEN is likely to accelerate its restaurant development in international markets. WEN's pending acquisition of the Tim Horton restaurant business is expected to add about $0.08 a share to earnings in the first year of ownership.

Valuation - 19-OCT-95

We recommend accumulation of these shares for capital gains. We expect investor support for the shares to be bolstered by the recent news of Wendy's intention to acquire a large breakfast-food chain. This acquisition should add to WEN's growth opportunities, both by adding outlets which combine features of its two restaurant concepts, and through stand-alone expansion of the Tim Horton business. Favorable aspects of the pending acquisition more than offset our concern about sales and profit weakness in 1995's second quarter, when WEN's earnings were boosted by an unusually low tax rate. In recognition of WEN's operating improvements and growth prospects, the stock has already more than quadrupled from its 1990 low.

Key Stock Statistics

S&P EPS Est. 1995	1.10	Tang. Bk. Value/Share	6.75
P/E on S&P Est. 1995	19.2	Beta	0.83
S&P EPS Est. 1996	1.30	Shareholders	57,000
Dividend Rate/Share	0.24	Market cap. (B)	$ 2.1
Shs. outstg. (M)	102.3	Inst. holdings	55%
Avg. daily vol. (M)	0.391	Insider holdings	NA

Value of $10,000 invested 5 years ago: $ 51,462

Fiscal Year Ending Dec. 31

	1995	% Change	1994	% Change	1993	% Change
Revenues (Million $)						
1Q	346.4	8%	319.8	3%	310.4	11%
2Q	379.6	3%	367.2	6%	345.2	2%
3Q	—	—	359.4	6%	338.9	7%
4Q	—	—	351.5	8%	325.7	6%
Yr.	—	—	1,398	6%	1,320	7%
Income (Million $)						
1Q	15.81	27%	12.49	27%	9.84	28%
2Q	40.10	20%	33.35	22%	27.35	22%
3Q	—	—	29.76	22%	24.48	23%
4Q	—	—	21.56	23%	17.59	20%
Yr.	—	—	97.16	23%	79.27	23%
Earnings Per Share ($)						
1Q	0.15	25%	0.12	20%	0.10	25%
2Q	0.38	19%	0.32	19%	0.27	23%
3Q	E0.31	7%	0.29	21%	0.24	20%
4Q	E0.26	24%	0.21	24%	0.17	21%
Yr.	E1.10	18%	0.93	21%	0.77	20%

Next earnings report expected: early November

Business Summary - 19-OCT-95

Wendy's International, Inc. owns and operates, and licenses others to operate, restaurants under the name Wendy's Old Fashioned Hamburgers. In 1994, WEN's average sales at domestic restaurants (including franchises) were $988,000, up about 2.3% from those the year before.

WEN's worldwide systemwide sales totaled $4.23 billion in 1994, up 7.7% from 1993's level. The number of units in operation at recent year-ends were as follows:

	1994	1993
Company-owned	1,264	1,224
Franchised	3,147	2,944
Total	4,411	4,168

In 1995, WEN is expected to either open or have under construction about 400 systemwide restaurants by year-end. At January 1, 1995 there were 65 units under construction.

Restaurant menus may vary somewhat, but major items include hamburgers, other types of sandwiches, french fries and a SuperBar buffet (introduced in 1987). In most markets, WEN has a Super Value Menu, which offers seven products at $0.99 each.

Franchise holders are required to pay the company a royalty of 4% of gross receipts. In addition, a technical assistance fee is typically required, which in the U.S., under newly executed franchise agreements, is $25,000 per restaurant.

Important Developments

Aug. '95—WEN reached an agreement in principle to acquire privately-owned Tim Hortons, which has more than 1,000 breakfast-oriented outlets (mostly franchises) in Canada. In the pooling-of-interest transaction, WEN would issue 16.2 million common shares and assume about $125 million (U.S) of debt. The acquisition is expected to be completed by early 1996. Excluding deal-related costs, WEN expects the acquisition to boost its overall earnings. In Canada, WEN and Tim Hortons already have combination units which feature both restaurant concepts, with certain common areas for customers. Meanwhile, in 1995's second quarter, WEN's systemwide sales (including franchises) were up 5.1%, year to year. However, pretax profit was up only slightly from the year-earlier level. WEN's overall earnings growth in the quarter primarily came from WEN having an unusually low tax rate in the 1995 period.

Capitalization

Long Term Debt: $140,949,000 (7/2/95), incl. $36.4 million of lease obligs.
Options: To buy 9,654,000 shs. at $5.13 to $18.06 ea. (1/1/95).

Per Share Data ($) (Year Ended Dec. 31)

	1994	1993	1992	1991	1990	1989
Tangible Bk. Val.	6.37	5.70	5.07	4.61	4.31	4.16
Cash Flow	1.59	1.41	1.25	1.08	0.97	0.83
Earnings	0.93	0.77	0.64	0.52	0.40	0.25
Dividends	0.24	0.24	0.24	0.24	0.24	0.24
Payout Ratio	26%	31%	37%	45%	60%	96%
Prices - High	18½	17⅜	14¼	11	7½	7
- Low	13¼	12⅜	9⅝	5⅞	3⅞	4½
P/E Ratio - High	20	23	22	21	19	28
- Low	14	16	15	11	10	18

Income Statement Analysis (Million $)

	1994	%Chg	1993	%Chg	1992	%Chg	1991
Revs.	1,370	5%	1,303	7%	1,220	16%	1,048
Oper. Inc.	199	13%	176	12%	157	16%	135
Depr.	68.1	4%	65.7	6%	61.7	10%	56.1
Int. Exp.	18.7	-13%	21.6	-4%	22.5	-3%	23.3
Pretax Inc.	149	28%	116	15%	101	29%	78.0
Eff. Tax Rate	35%	—	31%	—	36%	—	34%
Net Inc.	97.2	23%	79.3	23%	64.7	25%	51.7

Balance Sheet & Other Fin. Data (Million $)

	1994	1993	1992	1991	1990	1989
Cash	135	112	112	135	55.0	74.0
Curr. Assets	203	179	162	176	98.0	122
Total Assets	1,086	996	920	880	758	780
Curr. Liab.	207	143	128	133	109	129
LT Debt	145	201	234	240	168	179
Common Eqty.	681	601	529	478	447	429
Total Cap.	866	842	786	742	646	647
Cap. Exp.	142	117	120	69.0	42.0	39.0
Cash Flow	165	145	126	108	94.0	80.0

Ratio Analysis

	1994	1993	1992	1991	1990	1989
Curr. Ratio	1.0	1.2	1.3	1.3	0.9	0.9
% LT Debt of Cap.	16.7	23.8	29.7	32.3	26.0	27.7
% Net Inc.of Revs.	7.1	6.1	5.3	4.9	3.9	2.3
% Ret. on Assets	9.3	8.2	7.1	6.3	5.0	3.0
% Ret. on Equity	15.1	13.9	12.8	11.2	8.8	5.6

Dividend Data —Cash dividends were initiated in 1976. A dividend reinvestment plan is available. A "poison pill" stock purchase right was adopted in 1988.

Amt. of Div. $	Date Decl.	Ex-Div. Date	Stock of Record	Payment Date
0.060	Nov. 03	Nov. 07	Nov. 14	Nov. 29 '94
0.060	Feb. 23	Feb. 28	Mar. 06	Mar. 20 '95
0.060	May. 01	May. 05	May. 11	May. 25 '95
0.060	Aug. 03	Aug. 10	Aug. 14	Aug. 28 '95

Data as orig. reptd.; bef. results of disc. opers. and/or spec. items. Per share data adj. for stk. divs. as of ex-div. date. E-Estimated. NA-Not Available. NM-Not Meaningful. NR-Not Ranked.

Office—4288 West Dublin-Granville Rd., P.O. Box 256, Dublin, OH 43017-0256. **Tel**—(614) 764-3100. **Chrmn**—J. W. Near. **Pres, CEO & COO**—G. F. Teter. **Vice Chrmn & CFO**—J. K. Casey. **Investor Contacts**—Debbie J. Mitchell (614-764-3044) for analysts and portfolio managers; Marsha Gordon (614-764-3019) for general inquiries. **Dirs**—J. K. Casey, W. C. Hamner, E. S. Hayeck, J. Hill, T. F. Keller, R. E. Musick, J. W. Near, F. B. Nutter Sr., J. V. Pickett, F. R. Reed, T. R. Shackelford, G. F. Teter, R. D. Thomas. **Transfer Agent & Registrar**—American Stock Transfer & Trust Co., NYC. **Incorporated** in Ohio in 1969. **Empl**-44,000. **S&P Analyst:** Tom Graves, CFA

Western Atlas

NYSE Symbol **WAI**
In S&P 500

16-AUG-95 **Industry:** Oil and Gas

Summary: Western Atlas is one of the world's leading oilfield services and industrial technology companies.

S&P Opinion: Accumulate (★★★★)	Recent Price • 44 Yield • Nil
	52 Wk Range • 47⅝-35% 12-Mo. P/E • 26.3

Quantitative Evaluations

Outlook
(1 Lowest—5 Highest)
• **NA**

Fair Value
• **NA**

Risk
• **Low**

Earn./Div. Rank
• **NR**

Technical Eval.
• **Bearish** since 5/95

Rel. Strength Rank
(1 Lowest—99 Highest)
• **25**

Insider Activity
• **Neutral**

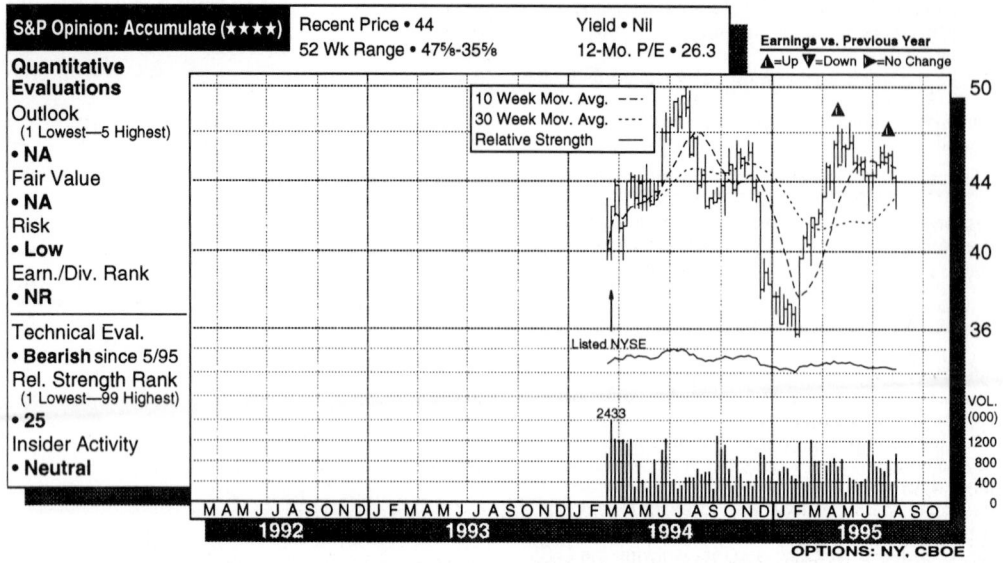

Earnings vs. Previous Year
▲=Up ▼=Down ▶=No Change

10 Week Mov. Avg. – – –
30 Week Mov. Avg. ·····
Relative Strength ——

Listed NYSE

2433

VOL. (000)

OPTIONS: NY, CBOE

Overview - 16-AUG-95

Revenues in 1995 should rise, reflecting acquisitions and increased market share. Higher average oil prices will give some support to oil and gas fundamentals. The industrial automation business segment should benefit from further U.S. economic growth and economic expansion abroad. However, a large portion of these gains will be postponed until 1996, when large backlogs will hit WAI's bottom line. The recent sale of WAI's seismic exploration products operations for $120 million will enable it to lower its debt burden and concentrate on its core competency as a service company. By focusing on bringing the latest technology and superior services to its customers, we expect WAI will garner additional market share, and we anticipate sustained growth over the next several years in the oilfield services segment.

Valuation - 16-AUG-95

The shares should continue to rise in 1995, buoyed by higher capital spending budget announcements and expanded exploration programs. Western Atlas' oil services business is poised to grow 13% a year, which leads us to believe a higher price/earnings multiple for the shares is warranted. With capital spending by the major integrated oil companies up some 14% in 1995, and with many poorer countries searching for partners to develop their reserves, we are maintaining our $60 12-month price target. The shares' performance is sensitive to changes in the outlook for the global economy, since earnings from the industrial automation segment are perceived as cyclical.

Key Stock Statistics

S&P EPS Est. 1995	1.85	Tang. Bk. Value/Share	14.51
P/E on S&P Est. 1995	23.8	Beta	NA
S&P EPS Est. 1996	2.20	Shareholders	NA
Dividend Rate/Share	Nil	Market cap. (B)	$ 2.3
Shs. outstg. (M)	53.0	Inst. holdings	85%
Avg. daily vol. (M)	0.144	Insider holdings	NA

Value of $10,000 invested 5 years ago: NA

Fiscal Year Ending Dec. 31

	1995	% Change	1994	% Change	1993	% Change
Revenues (Million $)						
1Q	505.9	1%	500.7	—	--	—
2Q	566.0	2%	555.6	—	--	—
3Q	—	—	559.9	—	--	—
4Q	—	—	549.5	—	--	—
Yr.	—	—	2,166	-2%	2,212	—
Income (Million $)						
1Q	19.19	17%	16.40	—	—	—
2Q	24.27	33%	18.21	—	—	—
3Q	—	—	21.58	—	—	—
4Q	—	—	21.58	—	—	—
Yr.	—	—	77.74	—	—	—
Earnings Per Share ($)						
1Q	0.36	3%	0.35	—	--	—
2Q	0.45	15%	0.39	—	--	—
3Q	E0.52	13%	0.46	—	--	—
4Q	E0.50	25%	0.40	—	--	—
Yr.	E1.85	16%	1.60	108%	0.77	—

Next earnings report expected: late October

Western Atlas

Business Summary - 16-AUG-95

Western Atlas operates in two business segments: oilfield information services and industrial automation. Both businesses were owned by Litton Industries, Inc. prior to their spinoff to Litton shareholders in March 1994. Segment contributions in 1994:

	Revs.	Profits
Oilfield services	55%	64%
Industrial automation	45%	36%

WAI operates in the high-technology sector of the oilfield information services industry. As a source of integrated reservoir description, the company is involved in worldwide seismic services and wireline logging for exploration, development and production of crude oil and natural gas. WAI purchased Halliburton's geophysical business in January 1994. The company also develops and markets computer workstation software products. Principal markets are in Europe, Africa, the Middle East and Southeast Asia, and to a lesser extent the U.S. About 68% of oilfield services revenues are derived from international markets, and more than half of oilfield services revenues are derived from geophysical services, such as seismic surveying.

The company is also an international supplier of industrial automation technologies, with emphasis on integrated manufacturing systems, automated data collection systems, and material handling and management systems. WAI supplies machining and assembly systems and precision grinding systems for the automotive industry, and automated data collection systems for manufacturing and distribution applications. In the material handling and management markets, the company is concentrating on the warehousing, distribution and manufacturing segments. Over 50% of the company's industrial automation revenues come from automotive machining and assembly orders, and 30% from the automated data collection business (30%).

Important Developments

Aug. '95—A division of Western Atlas was awarded a contract from two of China's largest auto makers for machining equipment used to manufacture six-cylinder diesel truck engines. Previously, in July, Western Atlas, together with The Expro Group and Nowsco, won a contract estimated at over $30 million to provide non-rig related oil and gas well services, on- and offshore in The Netherlands for two years.
Jun. '95—The company announced a joint venture to offer seismic, well-logging and integrated project services to local and international oil companies in the former Soviet Union.

Capitalization

Long Term Obligations: $529,686,000 (6/95).

Per Share Data ($)
(Year Ended Dec. 31)

	1994	1993	1992	1991	1990	1989
Tangible Bk. Val.	14.51	10.12	NA	NA	NA	NA
Cash Flow	5.51	4.93	NA	NA	NA	NA
Earnings	1.60	0.77	NA	NA	NA	NA
Dividends	Nil	NA	NA	NA	NA	NA
Payout Ratio	Nil	NA	NA	NA	NA	NA
Prices - High	50	NA	NA	NA	NA	NA
- Low	36¾	NA	NA	NA	NA	NA
P/E Ratio - High	31	NA	NA	NA	NA	NA
- Low	23	NA	NA	NA	NA	NA

Income Statement Analysis (Million $)

	1994	%Chg	1993	%Chg	1992	%Chg	1991
Revs.	2,166	-2%	2,212	—	NA	—	NA
Oper. Inc.	380	-7%	408	—	NA	—	NA
Depr.	190	-3%	195	—	NA	—	NA
Int. Exp.	60.0	-21%	75.6	—	NA	—	NA
Pretax Inc.	134	106%	65.2	—	NA	—	NA
Eff. Tax Rate	42%	—	42%	—	NA	—	NA
Net Inc.	77.7	113%	36.4	—	NA	—	NA

Balance Sheet & Other Fin. Data (Million $)

	1994	1993	1992	1991	1990	1989
Cash	42.1	57.5	NA	NA	NA	NA
Curr. Assets	994	999	NA	NA	NA	NA
Total Assets	2,404	2,447	NA	NA	NA	NA
Curr. Liab.	594	480	NA	NA	NA	NA
LT Debt	503	944	NA	NA	NA	NA
Common Eqty.	1,248	953	NA	NA	NA	NA
Total Cap.	1,775	1,897	NA	NA	NA	NA
Cap. Exp.	170	NA	NA	NA	NA	NA
Cash Flow	268	232	NA	NA	NA	NA

Ratio Analysis

	1994	1993	1992	1991	1990	1989
Curr. Ratio	1.7	2.1	NA	NA	NA	NA
% LT Debt of Cap.	28.3	49.8	NA	NA	NA	NA
% Net Inc.of Revs.	3.6	1.6	NA	NA	NA	NA
% Ret. on Assets	NM	NA	NA	NA	NA	NA
% Ret. on Equity	NM	NA	NA	NA	NA	NA

Dividend Data—In August, 1994 WAI adopted a "poison pill" stock purchase plan. The company is prohibited from paying dividends under the terms of its principal bank credit facility.

Data as orig. reptd.; bef. results of disc. opers. and/or spec. items. Per share data adj. for stk. divs. as of ex-div. date. E-Estimated. NA-Not Available. NM-Not Meaningful. NR-Not Ranked.

Office—360 North Crescent Drive, Beverly Hills, CA 90210 **Tel**—(310) 888-2500. **Chrmn & CEO**—A. J. Brann. **Vice Chrmn & CFO**—J. T. Casey. **VP-Investor Contact**—Dirk Koerber. **Dirs**—P. Bancroft III, A. J. Brann, J. T. Casey, W. C. Edwards, C. W. Gargalli, O. L. Hoch, S. B. Sample. **Transfer Agent & Registrar**—Chemical Trust Co. of California. **Incorporated** in Delaware. **Empl**-14,200. **S&P Analyst:** Raymond J. Deacon

Westinghouse Electric

NYSE Symbol **WX**

In S&P 500

25-AUG-95

Industry:
Electronics/Electric

Summary: Westinghouse has operations in power generation, electronic systems, transport temperature control, government and environmental services and broadcasting.

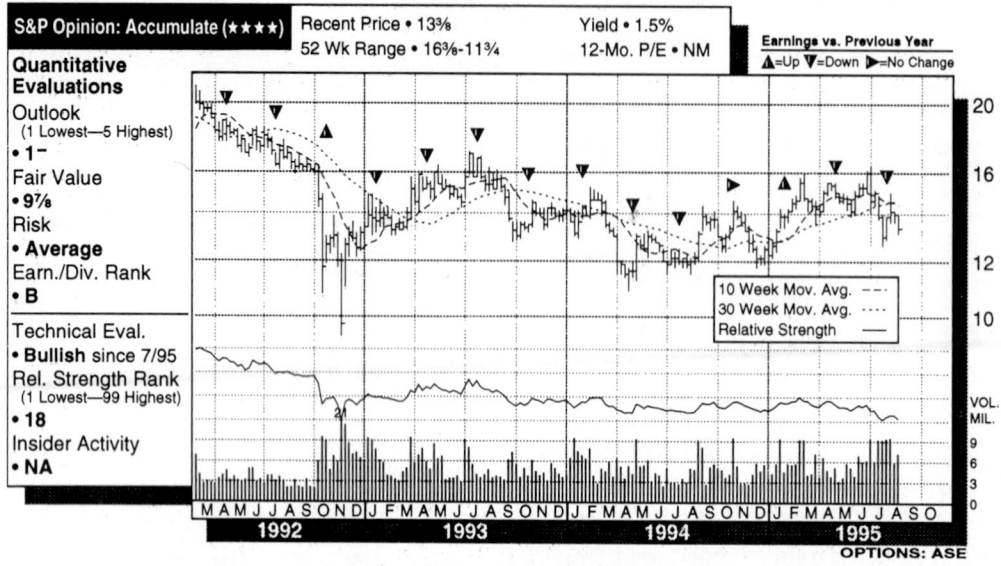

S&P Opinion: Accumulate (★★★★)	Recent Price • 13⅞	Yield • 1.5%
	52 Wk Range • 16⅜-11¾	12-Mo. P/E • NM

Quantitative Evaluations

Outlook
(1 Lowest—5 Highest)
• **1** ⁻

Fair Value
• **9⅞**

Risk
• **Average**

Earn./Div. Rank
• **B**

Technical Eval.
• **Bullish** since 7/95

Rel. Strength Rank
(1 Lowest—99 Highest)
• **18**

Insider Activity
• **NA**

Earnings vs. Previous Year
▲=Up ▼=Down ▶=No Change

10 Week Mov. Avg. — · —
30 Week Mov. Avg. · · · ·
Relative Strength —

OPTIONS: ASE

Overview - 25-AUG-95

Sales on continuing operations for 1996 are expected to increase approximately 60% in 1996, reflecting 12% growth on continuing businesses and the consolidation of CBS. Results will exclude the projected sales of businesses to raise $1.5 billion to $2.0 billion to reduce debt incurred with the planned purchase of CBS. Operating margins are likely to rise substantially due to continuing cost reductions on existing businesses and the consolidation of CBS, which has margins well in excess of WX's. However, sharply higher goodwill and interest expense will be more than offsetting and cause earnings to decline.

Valuation - 25-AUG-95

WX shares should outperform the market over the next six months as its long depressed businesses begin an important recovery and investors' react favorably to its purchase of CBS. The company's should report strong second half earnings due to a strengthening of revenues and benefits from aggressive cost reductions. While the CBS acquisition will initially dilute earnings, CBS should boost WX's price/earnings multiple because the acquisition should accelerate earnings growth and because broadcasting properties are viewed more favorably by investors than WX's existing businesses. However, our enthusiasm towards the shares is tempered by the initial dilution from the purchase of CBS.

Key Stock Statistics

S&P EPS Est. 1995	0.85	Tang. Bk. Value/Share	NM
P/E on S&P Est. 1995	15.7	Beta	1.17
S&P EPS Est. 1996	0.65	Shareholders	127,600
Dividend Rate/Share	0.20	Market cap. (B)	$ 4.9
Shs. outstg. (M)	358.0	Inst. holdings	39%
Avg. daily vol. (M)	1.788	Insider holdings	NA

Value of $10,000 invested 5 years ago: $ 4,544

Fiscal Year Ending Dec. 31

	1995	% Change	1994	% Change	1993	% Change
Revenues (Million $)						
1Q	2,024	16%	1,743	-14%	2,020	9%
2Q	2,296	9%	2,108	-2%	2,154	-1%
3Q	—	—	2,229	8%	2,060	NM
4Q	—	—	2,768	5%	2,641	13%
Yr.	—	—	8,848	NM	8,875	5%
Income (Million $)						
1Q	15.00	-58%	36.00	-39%	59.00	-9%
2Q	59.00	-21%	75.00	-11%	84.00	-18%
3Q	—	—	73.00	12%	65.00	-27%
4Q	—	—	-107.0	NM	-383.0	NM
Yr.	—	—	77.00	NM	-175.0	NM
Earnings Per Share ($)						
1Q	0.01	-86%	0.07	-50%	0.14	-26%
2Q	0.12	-25%	0.16	-20%	0.20	-33%
3Q	E0.29	93%	0.15	NM	0.15	-32%
4Q	E0.43	NM	-0.30	NM	-1.11	NM
Yr.	E0.85	NM	0.07	NM	-0.64	NM

Next earnings report expected: late October

Westinghouse Electric

Business Summary - 25-AUG-95

Westinghouse produces products and provides various services. Segment contributions (profits in millions) in 1994 were:

	Sales	Profits
Broadcasting	10%	$203
Electronic systems	28%	165
Government and environmental	4%	58
Thermo King	10%	130
Energy systems	14%	7
Power generation	19%	110
Knoll	6%	-67
WCI	3%	68
Other	6%	-27

The U.S. government accounted for 26% of sales from continuing operations in 1994. Foreign operations accounted for 11% of sales and 4.7% of operating profits in 1994.

Broadcasting consists of Group W, which primarily owns and operates radio and television stations. The electronic systems group produces advanced electronic systems for the U.S. Department of Defense and other government agencies. Government and environmental systems provides environmental services, including toxic, hazardous and radioactive waste services. Thermo King provides transport temperature control. Energy systems is a world leader in commercial nuclear power and process control systems. Power generation provides equipment for electrical power generation. Knoll produces office furniture. WCI develops residential communities.

Important Developments

Aug. '95—WX announced that it had agreed to acquire CBS Inc. Under terms of the agreement, which has been approved by the board of directors of each company, WX will acquire all the outstanding shares of CBS for $81 per share in cash plus certain additional limited consideration depending on the timing of the closing. The value of the transaction is expected to total $5.4 billion. Two banks have each committed to lend $1 billion and have agreed to arrange the remainder of the financing. Pending various approvals, the transaction is expected to be completed in late 1995 or early 1996. WX also announced that it planned to reduce the debt incurred in the transaction by selling businesses that would produce $1.5 billion to $2.0 billion in proceeds.

Capitalization

Long Term Debt: $1,566,000,000 (6/95).

Minority Interest: $34,000,000.

Depositary Shares: 68,890,000 shs. ($1 par); two series, subject to call provision; converts sh.-for-sh. into com. in 1995 and 1997. Represents fractional sh. of convertible preferred stk.

Per Share Data ($)

(Year Ended Dec. 31)

	1994	1993	1992	1991	1990	1989
Tangible Bk. Val.	1.53	·1.10	4.38	7.30	9.35	11.52
Cash Flow	0.90	0.24	1.70	-2.25	2.15	4.29
Earnings	0.07	-0.64	0.93	-3.46	0.91	3.16
Dividends	0.20	0.40	0.72	1.40	1.35	1.15
Payout Ratio	NM	NM	78%	NM	146%	36%
Prices - High	15¼	17⅛	21⅛	31	39⅜	38⅛
- Low	10⅞	12¾	9⅜	13¾	24¼	25⅝
P/E Ratio - High	NM	NM	20	NM	43	12
- Low	NM	NM	10	NM	27	8

Income Statement Analysis (Million $)

	1994	%Chg	1993	%Chg	1992	%Chg	1991
Revs.	8,848	NM	8,875	5%	8,447	-34%	12,794
Oper. Inc.	1,010	25%	807	-21%	1,017	-51%	2,092
Depr.	320	3%	311	15%	270	-29%	378
Int. Exp.	177	-20%	220	16%	189	-81%	998
Pretax Inc.	157	NM	-235	NM	536	NM	-1,095
Eff. Tax Rate	45%	—	NM	—	34%	—	NM
Net Inc.	77.0	NM	-174	NM	348	NM	-1,085

Balance Sheet & Other Fin. Data (Million $)

	1994	1993	1992	1991	1990	1989
Cash	338	637	739	1,244	1,523	2,281
Curr. Assets	4,720	4,774	3,965	NA	NA	NA
Total Assets	10,624	10,553	10,398	20,159	22,033	20,314
Curr. Liab.	3,709	3,925	3,957	NA	NA	NA
LT Debt	1,886	1,885	1,323	5,280	6,091	4,365
Common Eqty.	1,780	1,037	2,336	3,746	3,897	4,384
Total Cap.	3,708	2,964	3,700	9,880	10,229	9,320
Cap. Exp.	259	237	229	363	522	420
Cash Flow	347	86.0	590	-707	631	1,256

Ratio Analysis

	1994	1993	1992	1991	1990	1989
Curr. Ratio	1.3	1.2	1.0	NA	NA	NA
% LT Debt of Cap.	50.9	63.6	35.8	53.4	59.5	46.8
% Net Inc.of Revs.	0.9	NM	4.1	NM	2.1	7.2
% Ret. on Assets	0.7	NM	2.2	NM	1.3	4.9
% Ret. on Equity	1.9	NM	10.4	NM	6.5	22.5

Dividend Data

Dividends have been paid since 1935. A dividend reinvestment plan is available.

Amt. of Div. $	Date Decl.	Ex-Div. Date	Stock of Record	Payment Date
0.050	Jul. 27	Aug. 01	Aug. 06	Sep. 01 '94
0.050	Sep. 28	Oct. 31	Nov. 05	Dec. 01 '94
0.050	Jan. 25	Jan. 30	Feb. 04	Mar. 01 '95
0.050	Apr. 26	May. 01	May. 06	Jun. 01 '95
0.050	Jul. 26	Aug. 02	Aug. 05	Sep. 01 '95

Data as orig. reptd.; bef. results of disc. opers. and/or spec. items. Per share data adj. for stk. divs. as of ex-div. date.
E-Estimated. NA-Not Available. NM-Not Meaningful. NR-Not Ranked.

Office—Westinghouse Building, 11 Stanwix St., Pittsburgh, PA 15222-1384. **Tel**—(412) 244-2000. **Chrmn & CEO**—M. H. Jordan. **Pres**—G. M. Clark. **EVP & CFO**—F. G. Reynolds. **VP & Secy**—Angeline C. Straka. **Investor Contact**—Larry Bridge (412-642-3766). **Dirs**—F. C. Carlucci, R. E. Cawthorn, G. M. Clark, G. H. Conrades, W. C. Gray III, M. H. Jordan, D. T. McLaughlin, R. M. Morrow, R. R. Pivirotto, T. Stern, R. D. Walter. **Transfer Agents & Registrars**—First Chicago Trust Co., Jersey City, NJ. **Incorporated** in Pennsylvania in 1886. **Empl**-84,399. **S&P Analyst:** Paul Valentine, CFA

Westvaco Corp

NYSE Symbol **W**
In S&P 500

25-OCT-95

Industry:
Paper/Products

Summary: Westvaco is one of the largest integrated producers of bleached board and white printing and converting papers, as well as an important factor in linerboard and corrugated medium.

S&P Opinion: Accumulate (★★★★)	Recent Price • 28¾	Yield • 3.1%
	52 Wk Range • 31⅞-21⅛	12-Mo. P/E • 11.8

Quantitative Evaluations

Outlook
(1 Lowest—5 Highest)
• **4+**

Fair Value
• **29⅝**

Risk
• **Low**

Earn./Div. Rank
• **B**

Technical Eval.
• **Bearish** since 3/95

Rel. Strength Rank
(1 Lowest—99 Highest)
• **27**

Insider Activity
• **NA**

Earnings vs. Previous Year
▲=Up ▼=Down ▶=No Change

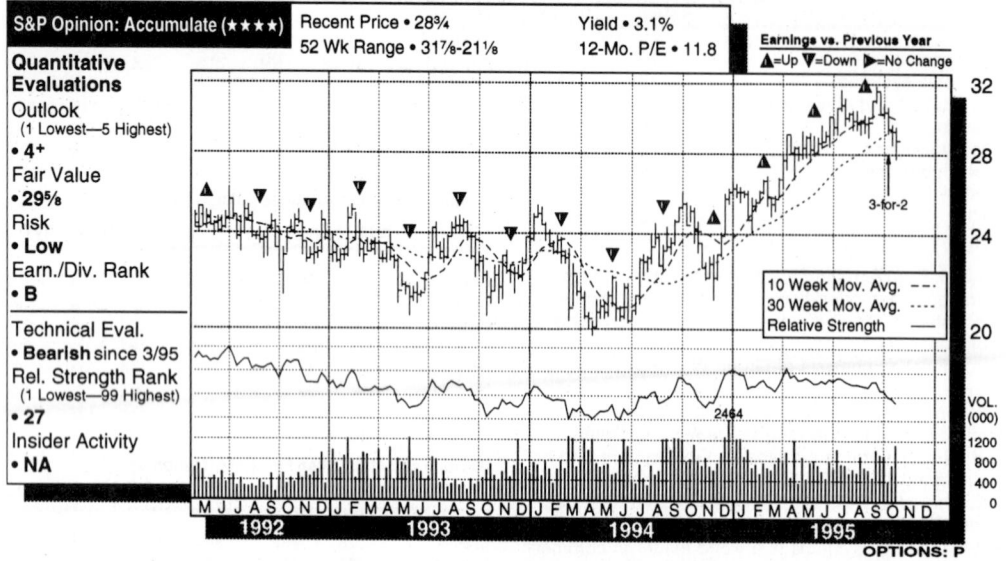

10 Week Mov. Avg. - - -
30 Week Mov. Avg. · · · ·
Relative Strength ——

3-for-2

2464

VOL. (000)

OPTIONS: P

Overview - 25-OCT-95

Assuming that W's planned sale of domestic box operations is completed, sales are likely to be relatively flat in fiscal 1996, as the loss of domestic box revenues is offset by gains in other product areas. Despite worries about the impact of slower economic trends, overall demand and pricing for Westvaco's products should remain favorable, benefiting from W's positioning in some of the industry's stronger sectors and limited capacity expansion in recent years. W's sales outlook should also be aided by its value-added products strategy and growing focus on foreign markets, while an expected economic rebound should further boost sales trends. Margins should continue to benefit from steep product prices and cost controls. Any loss of profits from domestic box operations should be offset by the beneficial use of proceeds from the transaction.

Valuation - 25-OCT-95

After appreciating strongly since early 1994, W's shares have been a part of the recent correction of paper industry stocks, which has been stimulated by worries that moderating industry trends could be signalling a nearing cycle peak. We dispute that line of thinking, given our belief that a rebound of global economies will extend the upcycle. We also favor Westvaco because of its differentiated products strategy, which makes it less susceptible to pricing cycles, and its presence in better positioned grades. With all of those factors leading us to believe that earnings growth will continue through fiscal 1996, we expect W's shares to resume their uptrend.

Key Stock Statistics

S&P EPS Est. 1995	2.80	Tang. Bk. Value/Share	19.83
P/E on S&P Est. 1995	10.3	Beta	1.01
S&P EPS Est. 1996	3.50	Shareholders	15,000
Dividend Rate/Share	0.88	Market cap. (B)	$ 2.9
Shs. outstg. (M)	101.5	Inst. holdings	62%
Avg. daily vol. (M)	0.149	Insider holdings	NA

Value of $10,000 invested 5 years ago: $ 17,063

Fiscal Year Ending Oct. 31

	1995	% Change	1994	% Change	1993	% Change
Revenues (Million $)						
1Q	741.7	28%	577.3	3%	561.0	4%
2Q	804.6	28%	626.4	8%	579.5	-2%
3Q	854.6	33%	641.3	9%	586.0	NM
4Q	—	—	762.5	23%	618.0	NM
Yr.	—	—	2,607	11%	2,345	NM
Income (Million $)						
1Q	49.32	NM	15.82	-24%	20.90	-23%
2Q	65.03	NM	16.28	-16%	19.44	-52%
3Q	80.15	NM	20.17	-10%	22.53	-37%
4Q	—	—	51.33	NM	-6.36	NM
Yr.	—	—	103.6	83%	56.51	-58%
Earnings Per Share ($)						
1Q	0.49	NM	0.16	-23%	0.21	-24%
2Q	0.65	NM	0.16	-20%	0.20	-51%
3Q	0.79	NM	0.20	-9%	0.22	-39%
4Q	E0.87	70%	0.51	NM	-0.06	NM
Yr.	E2.80	172%	1.03	82%	0.57	-59%

Next earnings report expected: mid November

Westvaco Corp

Business Summary - 25-OCT-95

Westvaco is one of the largest producers of paper and paperboard in the U.S. It converts paper and paperboard into various end-products, manufactures specialty chemicals, produces lumber and sells timber. In Brazil, the company is a major producer of paperboard and corrugated packaging. Segment contributions in fiscal 1994 were:

	Sales	Profits
Bleached paper, paperboard & packaging	64%	71%
Unbleached paper products	26%	15%
Chemicals	10%	14%

Sales outside the U.S. accounted for 19% of Westvaco's total sales in fiscal 1994.

The company produced 2,848,000 tons of paper, paperboard and market pulp in fiscal 1994, up from 2,626,000 tons in fiscal 1993. Westvaco makes bleached products at four domestic mills and markets them as pulp, printing-grade papers and board, envelopes, food containers, folding cartons and cartons for liquid products. Sales of printing-grade papers and board accounted for 40% of the total in fiscal 1994, while envelopes accounted for 11%.

Westvaco also manufactures unbleached products, marketed as corrugated shipping containers (14% of fiscal 1994 sales) and kraft paper and board (10%); in September 1995, W agreed to sell its 10 domestic corrugated box plants to Weyerhauser Co.

A $25 million printing and package converting facility in the Czech Republic is expected to begin operations in the fall of 1995. In addition, Westvaco has begun construction of its fourth Brazilian corrugated box plant, also scheduled to begin operations in the fall 1995.

Four plants produce specialty chemicals, including activated-carbon products, printing ink resins, lignin-based surfactants and tall oil derivatives.

At October 31, 1994, Westvaco owned about 1,453,000 acres of timberland in the U.S. and Brazil. During fiscal 1994, 36% of wood requirements were harvested from the company's own forests.

Important Developments

Sep. '95—The company reached an agreement to sell its container division, consisting of 10 domestic corrugated box plants, to Weyerhauser Co. No terms were disclosed. The sale of the division was not expected to have any impact on W's Brazilian box operations.
Aug. '95—In reporting continued strong sales and earnings growth in the third quarter of fiscal 1995, W said that despite moderating economic trends, demand for its products remained good. It added that, although backlogs had come down a bit from the unsustainably high levels of late 1994, they were still up 35% on a year over year basis at the end of the quarter.

Capitalization

Long Term Debt: $1,171,204,000 (7/95).

Per Share Data ($)

(Year Ended Oct. 31)

	1994	1993	1992	1991	1990	1989
Tangible Bk. Val.	18.48	18.18	17.84	17.21	16.53	15.27
Cash Flow	3.21	2.51	3.21	3.22	3.65	3.89
Earnings	1.03	0.57	1.37	1.40	1.93	2.30
Dividends	0.73	0.73	0.73	0.71	0.68	0.63
Payout Ratio	71%	129%	53%	51%	35%	27%
Prices - High	26½	25⅜	27½	26½	21	22¼
- Low	19¾	20	21⅜	17⅛	14⅝	17⅞
P/E Ratio - High	26	45	20	19	11	10
- Low	19	35	16	12	8	8

Income Statement Analysis (Million $)

	1994	%Chg	1993	%Chg	1992	%Chg	1991
Revs.	2,607	11%	2,345	NM	2,336	2%	2,301
Oper. Inc.	485	13%	429	-9%	471	-2%	481
Depr.	219	12%	195	7%	183	2%	179
Int. Exp.	115	NM	115	13%	102	2%	100
Pretax Inc.	162	74%	92.9	-55%	206	-9%	226
Eff. Tax Rate	36%	—	39%	—	34%	—	39%
Net Inc.	104	84%	56.5	-58%	136	NM	137

Balance Sheet & Other Fin. Data (Million $)

	1994	1993	1992	1991	1990	1989
Cash	75.0	57.0	191	172	184	185
Curr. Assets	631	609	671	624	668	624
Total Assets	3,983	3,928	3,704	3,462	3,332	2,961
Curr. Liab.	362	365	353	314	298	296
LT Debt	1,234	1,258	1,055	970	961	768
Common Eqty.	1,862	1,824	1,777	1,699	1,619	1,488
Total Cap.	3,621	3,563	3,351	3,148	3,034	2,665
Cap. Exp.	215	433	318	303	472	537
Cash Flow	323	252	319	317	357	378

Ratio Analysis

	1994	1993	1992	1991	1990	1989
Curr. Ratio	1.7	1.7	1.9	2.0	2.2	2.1
% LT Debt of Cap.	34.1	35.3	31.5	30.8	31.7	28.8
% Net Inc.of Revs.	4.0	2.4	5.8	6.0	7.8	9.8
% Ret. on Assets	2.6	1.5	3.8	4.0	6.0	8.1
% Ret. on Equity	5.6	3.1	7.8	8.2	12.1	15.9

Dividend Data—Dividends have been paid since 1892. A dividend reinvestment plan is available. A poison pill stock purchase rights plan was adopted in 1987.

Amt. of Div. $	Date Decl.	Ex-Div. Date	Stock of Record	Payment Date
0.275	Nov. 22	Nov. 30	Dec. 06	Jan. 02 '95
0.275	Feb. 28	Mar. 06	Mar. 10	Apr. 03 '95
0.275	May. 23	May. 26	Jun. 02	Jul. 03 '95
0.220	Aug. 22	Aug. 30	Sep. 01	Oct. 02 '95
3-for-2	Aug. 22	Oct. 03	Sep. 01	Oct. 02 '95

Data as orig. reptd.; bef. results of disc. opers. and/or spec. items. Per share data adj. for stk. divs. as of ex-div. date.
E-Estimated. NA-Not Available. NM-Not Meaningful. NR-Not Ranked.

Office—299 Park Ave., New York, NY 10171. **Tel**—(212) 688-5000. **Chrmn**—D. L. Luke III. **Pres & CEO**—J. A. Luke, Jr. **VP & Secy**—J. W. Hetherington. **Sr VP & CFO**—G. E. Cruser. **Investor Contact**—Roger A. Holmes. **Dirs**—J. C. Bierwirth, S. W. Bodman III, W. H. Brown, W. L. L. Brown, Jr., T. W. Cole, Jr., G. E. Cruser, D. L. Hopkins, Jr., D. L. Luke III, J. A. Luke, J. A. Luke, Jr., W. R. Miller, K. G. Peden, R. A. Zimmerman. **Transfer Agent & Registrar**—Bank of New York, NYC. **Incorporated** in Delaware in 1899. **Empl**-14,170. **S&P Analyst:** Michael W. Jaffe

Weyerhaeuser Co.

NYSE Symbol **WY**
In S&P 500

17-OCT-95

Industry:
Building

Summary: This company is the world's largest private owner of marketable softwood timber and a major producer of pulp and paper products.

S&P Opinion: Accumulate (★★★★)	Recent Price • 47⅝ Yield • 3.4%
	52 Wk Range • 50⅜–35¾ 12-Mo. P/E • 10.6

Quantitative Evaluations

Outlook
(1 Lowest—5 Highest)
• **4+**

Fair Value
• **49½**

Risk
• **Low**

Earn./Div. Rank
• **B+**

Technical Eval.
• **Bearish** since 7/95

Rel. Strength Rank
(1 Lowest—99 Highest)
• **66**

Insider Activity
• **Unfavorable**

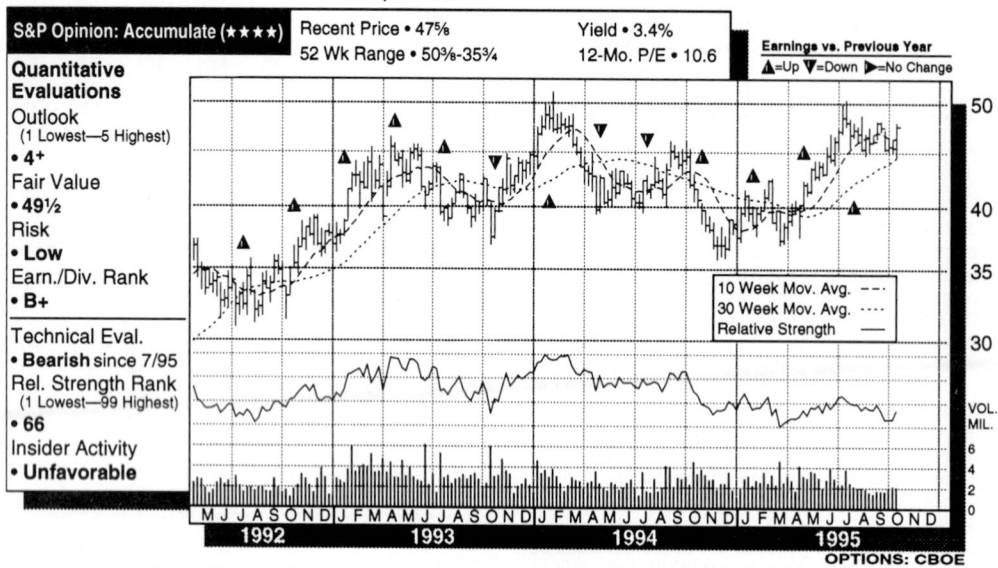

Earnings vs. Previous Year
▲=Up ▼=Down ▶=No Change

10 Week Mov. Avg. – – –
30 Week Mov. Avg. · · · ·
Relative Strength —

OPTIONS: CBOE

Overview - 17-OCT-95

Sales growth should continue through 1996, but at a moderating pace. Relatively healthy global economies and limited industry capacity expansion in recent years (with the exception of containerboard) should keep demand solid and prices high in most pulp and paper areas. Although we continue to anticipate a strengthening of economic conditions in upcoming periods, slower economic trends and inventory adjustments have eased box demand in recent months, and are likely to cause somewhat lower sales in that sector in 1996. Wood products sales, which are battling lower lumber prices generated by a sluggish period in homebuilding, should start to benefit from the recent interest rate stimulated revival of the housing market. Margins should be favorable, on initiatives put in place to improve production efficiencies and reduce overhead costs, and better wood products trends.

Valuation - 17-OCT-95

The shares have appreciated solidly to date in 1995, as WY has posted very strong earnings gains, but worries about the paper industry nearing its cyclical peak have stalled the shares since mid-year. While we share concern about the impact of the slowing U.S. economy on WY's business, we continue to forecast solid earnings growth through 1996. Our optimism centers on the belief that paper operations will remain firm, boosted in part by an expected economic rebound, and that a rejuvenated housing market will aid the wood products business. Given those factors, we feel that further stock appreciation is warranted.

Key Stock Statistics

S&P EPS Est. 1995	5.00	Tang. Bk. Value/Share	22.18
P/E on S&P Est. 1995	9.5	Beta	1.14
S&P EPS Est. 1996	6.00	Shareholders	24,100
Dividend Rate/Share	1.60	Market cap. (B)	$ 9.7
Shs. outstg. (M)	203.3	Inst. holdings	58%
Avg. daily vol. (M)	0.379	Insider holdings	NA

Value of $10,000 invested 5 years ago: $ 21,421

Fiscal Year Ending Dec. 31

	1995	% Change	1994	% Change	1993	% Change
Revenues (Million $)						
1Q	2,745	15%	2,386	2%	2,340	6%
2Q	3,074	18%	2,598	9%	2,388	2%
3Q	3,112	16%	2,681	20%	2,225	-5%
4Q	—	—	2,733	5%	2,591	11%
Yr.	—	—	10,398	9%	9,545	4%
Income (Million $)						
1Q	206.6	63%	126.6	-29%	177.4	105%
2Q	246.7	91%	128.9	-29%	181.5	95%
3Q	279.3	93%	144.4	117%	66.62	-38%
4Q	—	—	188.9	86%	101.7	19%
Yr.	—	—	588.7	12%	527.3	42%
Earnings Per Share ($)						
1Q	1.00	61%	0.62	-29%	0.87	102%
2Q	1.21	95%	0.62	-30%	0.89	98%
3Q	1.37	93%	0.71	122%	0.32	-40%
4Q	E1.42	56%	0.91	82%	0.50	19%
Yr.	E5.00	75%	2.86	11%	2.58	41%

Next earnings report expected: mid January

Weyerhaeuser Co.

17-OCT-95

Business Summary - 13-OCT-95

Weyerhaeuser is the world's largest timber products concern and is a major producer of pulp and paper. Contributions by business segment in 1994:

	Sales	Profits
Timberlands & wood products	48%	92%
Pulp & paper	39%	19%
Real estate	9%	1%
Financial services	2%	1%
Corporate & other	2%	-13%

Sales outside the U.S., including exports, accounted for 24% of total sales in 1994. A large portion of U.S. export sales was made to customers in Japan.

The company owns about 5.6 million acres of commercial forest land in the U.S., 51% of which is located in the South and the remaining 49% in the Pacific Northwest. WY also has long-term license arrangements in Canada covering about 17.8 million acres. The total timber inventory on these lands is about 246 million cunits (one cunit equals 100 cubic feet of solid wood), of which approximately 75% is softwood, the principal wood used for building construction. WY's wood products businesses produce and sell lumber, plywood and veneer, composite panels, oriented strand board, doors, logs, chips and timber to wholesalers, retailers and industrial users.

Products made by WY's pulp, paper and packaging segment include chemical wood pulp for world markets; newsprint, which is marketed to West Coast and Japanese newspaper publishers; coated and uncoated paper; linerboard, corrugating medium and corrugated shipping containers; and bleached paperboard used to produce liquid containers. The company also operates an extensive wastepaper collection system.

Other operations include real estate development and mortgage lending.

Important Developments

Oct. '95—The company reported that through September, it had repurchased a total of 4.9 million of its common shares under the 10 million share program authorized in April 1995.
Sep. '95—WY signed a letter of intent to purchase Westvaco Corp.'s corrugated container operations, consisting of 10 box plants (Weyerhauser currently owns 36 box plants). Terms were not disclosed.
Jul. '95—Weyerhauser noted that it embarked on a new series of business improvement plans in 1995's second quarter, which targets $650 million in pretax operating improvements by 1997 year-end. In April 1995, WY reported that the pulp and paper division's $1 billion facility modernization program (initiated in 1992) would be completed in 1995.

Capitalization

Long Term Debt: $4,270,000,000 (6/95).
Minority Interest: $106,000,000.

Per Share Data ($) (Year Ended Dec. 31)

	1994	1993	1992	1991	1990	1989
Tangible Bk. Val.	20.86	19.34	17.85	17.25	19.21	18.55
Cash Flow	5.46	4.87	4.23	1.99	4.34	3.85
Earnings	2.86	2.58	1.83	-0.50	1.87	1.56
Dividends	1.20	1.20	1.20	1.20	1.20	1.20
Payout Ratio	42%	47%	66%	NM	63%	77%
Prices - High	51¼	46½	39¼	30⅝	28⅜	32¾
- Low	35¾	36¼	26⅝	20⅛	17⅞	24½
P/E Ratio - High	18	18	21	NM	15	21
- Low	12	14	15	NM	9	16

Income Statement Analysis (Million $)

	1994	%Chg	1993	%Chg	1992	%Chg	1991
Revs.	10,398	9%	9,545	4%	9,219	6%	8,702
Oper. Inc.	1,754	21%	1,452	12%	1,294	15%	1,122
Depr.	534	13%	471	-4%	489	-2%	501
Int. Exp.	391	NM	388	-5%	410	-14%	478
Pretax Inc.	920	14%	808	44%	563	NM	-177
Eff. Tax Rate	36%	—	35%	—	34%	—	NM
Net Inc.	589	12%	527	42%	372	NM	-100

Balance Sheet & Other Fin. Data (Million $)

	1994	1993	1992	1991	1990	1989
Cash	112	160	524	616	215	261
Curr. Assets	NA	NA	NA	NA	NA	NA
Total Assets	13,007	12,638	18,158	16,928	16,356	15,976
Curr. Liab.	NA	NA	NA	NA	NA	NA
LT Debt	4,586	5,082	5,449	5,013	5,209	3,374
Common Eqty.	4,290	3,966	3,646	3,489	3,864	3,798
Total Cap.	9,965	10,062	9,949	8,592	9,988	8,689
Cap. Exp.	1,102	948	1,174	663	977	954
Cash Flow	1,123	998	861	400	883	786

Ratio Analysis

	1994	1993	1992	1991	1990	1989
Curr. Ratio	NA	NA	NA	NA	NA	NA
% LT Debt of Cap.	46.0	50.5	54.8	58.3	52.1	43.0
% Net Inc.of Revs.	5.7	5.5	4.0	NM	4.4	3.4
% Ret. on Assets	4.6	3.4	2.1	NM	2.5	2.2
% Ret. on Equity	14.3	13.8	10.4	NM	10.0	8.5

Dividend Data —Dividends have been paid since 1933. A dividend reinvestment plan is available. A "poison pill" stock purchase rights plan was adopted in 1986.

Amt. of Div. $	Date Decl.	Ex-Div. Date	Stock of Record	Payment Date
0.300	Oct. 12	Oct. 24	Oct. 28	Nov. 28 '94
0.300	Jan. 10	Jan. 23	Jan. 27	Feb. 27 '95
0.400	Apr. 20	May. 01	May. 05	May. 30 '95
0.400	Jul. 11	Jul. 26	Jul. 28	Aug. 28 '95
0.400	Oct. 11	Oct. 25	Oct. 27	Nov. 27 '95

Data as orig. reptd.; bef. results of disc. opers. and/or spec. items. Per share data adj. for stk. divs. as of ex-div. date. Ratios are affected by inclusion of non-forest products opers. E-Estimated. NA-Not Available. NM-Not Meaningful. NR-Not Ranked.

Office—Tacoma, WA 98477. **Tel**—(206) 924-2345. **Chrmn**—G. H. Weyerhaeuser. **Pres & CEO**—J. W. Creighton Jr. **SVP & CFO**—W. C. Stivers. **Secy**—S. McDade. **Investor Contact**—Richard J. Taggart. **Dirs**—W. H. Clapp, J. W. Creighton Jr., W. J. Driscoll, D. C. Frisbee, P. M. Hawley, E. B. Ingram, J. I. Kieckhefer, W. D. Ruckelshaus, R. H. Sinkfield, G. H. Weyerhaeuser. **Transfer Agent**—Chemical Bank, NYC. **Incorporated** in Washington in 1900. **Empl**-36,665. **S&P Analyst:** Michael W. Jaffe

Whirlpool Corp.

NYSE Symbol **WHR**
In S&P 500

25-AUG-95

Industry:
Electronics/Electric

Summary: Whirlpool is the world's second largest manufacturer of home appliances. Sears, Roebuck is its largest customer.

S&P Opinion: Hold (★★★)	Recent Price • 55⅛	Yield • 2.5%
	52 Wk Range • 58%-44%	12-Mo. P/E • 30.6

Earnings vs. Previous Year
▲=Up ▼=Down ▶=No Change

Quantitative Evaluations

Outlook
(1 Lowest—5 Highest)
• **2⁻**

Fair Value
• **52⅞**

Risk
• **Low**

Earn./Div. Rank
• **B**

Technical Eval.
• **Bullish** since 5/94

Rel. Strength Rank
(1 Lowest—99 Highest)
• **24**

Insider Activity
• **NA**

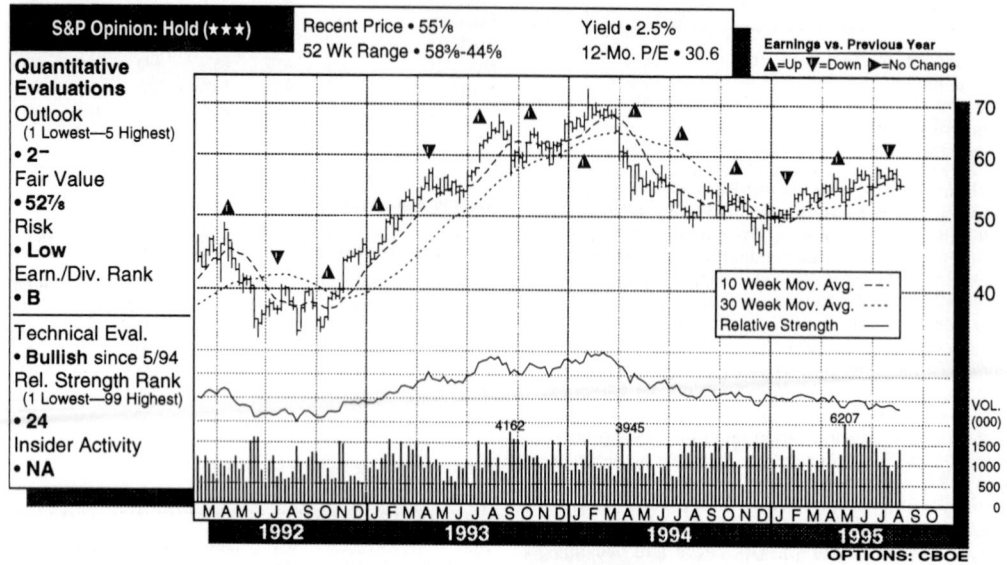

10 Week Mov. Avg. – – –
30 Week Mov. Avg. ·······
Relative Strength ——

VOL. (000)

OPTIONS: CBOE

Overview - 25-AUG-95

Revenues should continue to improve in 1995. Sales in overseas markets will benefit from expanded operations in Asia and Latin America. Volume in Europe could increase, on stronger economies there. However, volume is expected to rise only barely in North America, reflecting soft market demand. Full-year margins could be under some pressure, mainly reflecting soft shipments in North America and higher than expected start-up costs. Longer term, results should benefit from global expansion, efforts to reduce costs through a major restructuring plan announced in late 1994, further productivity improvements, and global integration. Share earnings comparisons will benefit from the absence of a $2.45 restructuring charge.

Valuation - 25-AUG-95

We are retaining a neutral opinion on this leading appliance maker over the near term. With industrywide appliance shipments estimated to decline this year, we feel any share appreciation will be limited. In addition, although the company had warned investors, second quarter results were disappointing, and mainly reflected soft industry conditions, a less profitable product mix, and intense competition. Whirlpool is optimistic that conditions will improve in the second half of 1995; however, we would rather see some evidence of this pick-up before re-recommending purchase of these shares. Over the long term, these shares should do well, as Whirlpool increasingly enters into untapped markets via partnerships with local companies.

Key Stock Statistics

S&P EPS Est. 1995	4.25	Tang. Bk. Value/Share	12.61
P/E on S&P Est. 1995	13.0	Beta	1.58
S&P EPS Est. 1996	4.90	Shareholders	11,800
Dividend Rate/Share	1.36	Market cap. (B)	$ 4.1
Shs. outstg. (M)	73.9	Inst. holdings	84%
Avg. daily vol. (M)	0.215	Insider holdings	NA

Value of $10,000 invested 5 years ago: $ 19,564

Fiscal Year Ending Dec. 31

	1995	% Change	1994	% Change	1993	% Change
Revenues (Million $)						
1Q	1,985	6%	1,870	3%	1,808	5%
2Q	2,115	3%	2,050	7%	1,912	4%
3Q	—	—	2,085	9%	1,909	NM
4Q	—	—	2,099	10%	1,904	4%
Yr.	—	—	8,104	8%	7,533	3%
Income (Million $)						
1Q	75.00	12%	67.00	NM	18.00	-49%
2Q	52.00	-38%	84.00	14%	74.00	40%
3Q	—	—	98.00	40%	70.00	27%
4Q	—	—	-91.00	NM	69.00	11%
Yr.	—	—	158.0	-32%	231.0	13%
Earnings Per Share ($)						
1Q	1.00	11%	0.90	NM	0.25	-50%
2Q	0.70	-36%	1.10	6%	1.04	39%
3Q	E1.35	4%	1.30	35%	0.96	23%
4Q	E1.20	NM	-1.20	NM	0.94	8%
Yr.	E4.25	102%	2.10	-34%	3.19	10%

Next earnings report expected: mid October

Whirlpool Corp.

Business Summary - 25-AUG-95

Whirlpool Corp. manufactures a full line of household appliances and other products for home and commercial use. Products are manufactured in 12 countries and marketed in more than 120. Growth in recent years has been aided by acquisitions, including the purchase of the appliance business of N.V. Philips Electronics of The Netherlands in the early 1990s. In Latin America and Asia, growth is primarily being fueled by partnerships with existing local appliance companies.

In November 1994, Whirlpool announced a restructuring of its North American and European operations, resulting in a before tax charge of $240 million. The restructuring was aimed at improving productivity in the U.S. and Europe by eliminating 3,200 employees, closing two plants, and reorganizing the European sales force. WHR expected to realize annual cost savings of $150 million by 1997.

Major appliances produced include home laundry equipment (32% of 1994 sales); home refrigeration and room air conditioning equipment (36%); and various other appliances (30%), including dishwashers and cooking equipment. Whirlpool Financial Corp., which provides financing for distributors and dealers, accounted for the remaining 2% of sales.

In 1994, 63% of total sales were made in North America. Major brands in the U.S. include Whirlpool, KitchenAid, Roper, Estate, and Coolerator. About 19% of 1994 consolidated sales were made to Sears, mainly under the Kenmore and Whirlpool names. Major brands in Canada are Inglis, Admiral, Speed Queen, Estate, Roper, Whirlpool and KitchenAid. About 30% of total sales were made by Whirlpool Europe, B.V. under the Algor, Bauknecht, Fides, Ignis, Laden, and Whirlpool brand names.

Other markets include Latin America and Asia. Approximately 4% of total sales were made in Latin America. Most sales in Latin America take place through three joint ventures in Brazil and through a wholly-owned subsidiary, Whirlpool Argentina. About 3% of total sales were made in Asia. As of early 1995, the company was involved in three joint ventures in China and two joint ventures in India.

Important Developments

Jul. '95—WHR's second quarter 1995 earnings before equity items fell 51%, year to year, on abrupt drops in home appliance industry shipments in the U.S. and Europe, a negative change in the product mix, intense competition, and higher than expected start-up costs. Separately, WHR received government approval to acquire a majority position in Shunde SMC Microwave Products Co., Ltd., China's largest producer of microwave ovens.

Capitalization

Long Term Debt: $1,016,000,000 (6/95).
Minority Interests: $166,000,000.

Per Share Data ($)

(Year Ended Dec. 31)

	1994	1993	1992	1991	1990	1989
Tangible Bk. Val.	13.38	12.63	11.50	8.70	14.21	15.44
Cash Flow	5.62	6.88	7.19	6.18	4.59	5.90
Earnings	2.10	3.19	2.90	2.45	1.04	2.70
Dividends	1.22	1.19	1.10	1.10	1.10	1.10
Payout Ratio	58%	37%	38%	45%	106%	41%
Prices - High	73½	68	48⅞	41	33½	33¼
- Low	44⅝	43¼	34½	19⅞	17½	24¼
P/E Ratio - High	35	21	17	17	32	12
- Low	21	14	12	8	17	9

Income Statement Analysis (Million $)

	1994	%Chg	1993	%Chg	1992	%Chg	1991
Revs.	8,104	8%	7,533	3%	7,301	8%	6,770
Oper. Inc.	904	8%	838	-6%	888	14%	779
Depr.	266	NM	266	-12%	302	16%	260
Int. Exp.	165	-4%	172	-24%	227	NM	229
Pretax Inc.	351	-10%	391	9%	359	20%	300
Eff. Tax Rate	50%	—	38%	—	43%	—	43%
Net Inc.	158	-32%	231	13%	205	21%	170

Balance Sheet & Other Fin. Data (Million $)

	1994	1993	1992	1991	1990	1989
Cash	72.0	88.0	66.0	42.0	80.0	141
Curr. Assets	3,078	2,708	2,740	2,920	2,900	2,889
Total Assets	6,655	6,047	6,118	6,445	5,614	5,354
Curr. Liab.	2,988	2,763	2,887	2,931	2,651	2,251
LT Debt	885	840	1,215	1,528	874	982
Common Eqty.	1,723	1,648	1,600	1,515	1,424	1,421
Total Cap.	2,924	2,747	3,028	3,211	2,641	2,809
Cap. Exp.	418	309	288	287	272	693
Cash Flow	424	497	507	430	319	409

Ratio Analysis

	1994	1993	1992	1991	1990	1989
Curr. Ratio	1.0	1.0	0.9	1.0	1.1	1.3
% LT Debt of Cap.	30.3	30.6	40.1	47.6	33.1	35.0
% Net Inc.of Revs.	1.9	3.1	2.8	2.5	1.1	3.0
% Ret. on Assets	2.5	3.7	3.3	2.8	1.3	4.3
% Ret. on Equity	9.3	13.9	13.1	11.6	5.1	13.6

Dividend Data —Dividends have been paid since 1929. A dividend reinvestment plan is available. A "poison pill" stock purchase right was adopted in 1988.

Amt. of Div. $	Date Decl.	Ex-Div. Date	Stock of Record	Payment Date
0.305	Aug. 16	Aug. 24	Aug. 30	Sep. 15 '94
0.305	Oct. 18	Nov. 25	Dec. 01	Dec. 31 '94
0.340	Feb. 21	Feb. 27	Mar. 03	Mar. 15 '95
0.340	Apr. 18	May. 12	May. 18	Jun. 15 '95
0.340	Aug. 15	Aug. 28	Aug. 30	Sep. 15 '95

Data as orig. reptd.; bef. results of disc. opers. and/or spec. items. Per share data adj. for stk. divs. as of ex-div. date. E-Estimated. NA-Not Available. NM-Not Meaningful. NR-Not Ranked.

Office—2000 North M-63, Benton Harbor, MI 49022-2692. **Tel**—(616) 923-5000. **Chrmn & CEO**—D. R. Whitwam. **Pres**—W. D. Marohn. **Secy**—D. F. Hopp. **Investor Contact**—Thomas C. Filstrup. **Dirs**—V. A. Bonomo, R. A. Burnett, H. Cain, A. D. Gilmour, K. J. Hempel, A. G. Langbo, W. D. Marohn, M. L. Marsh, P. L. Smith, P. G. Stern, J. D. Stoney, D. R. Whitwam. **Transfer Agent & Registrar**—Harris Trust & Savings Bank, Chicago. **Incorporated** in Delaware in 1955. **Empl**-39,000. **S&P Analyst:** Elizabeth Vandeventer

Whitman Corp.

NYSE Symbol **WH**

In S&P 500

18-OCT-95

Industry:
Beverages

Summary: Whitman is a diversified holding company with interests in soft drink bottling, automobile services, and refrigeration equipment manufacturing.

S&P Opinion: Accumulate (★★★★)	

Recent Price • 20⅞	Yield • 1.8%
52 Wk Range • 21⅝-15⅝	12-Mo. P/E • 17.3

Earnings vs. Previous Year
▲=Up ▼=Down ▶=No Change

Quantitative Evaluations

Outlook
(1 Lowest—5 Highest)
• **2⁻**

Fair Value
• **20¼**

Risk
• **Low**

Earn./Div. Rank
• **B**

Technical Eval.
• **Bearish** since 3/95

Rel. Strength Rank
(1 Lowest—99 Highest)
• **72**

Insider Activity
• **Neutral**

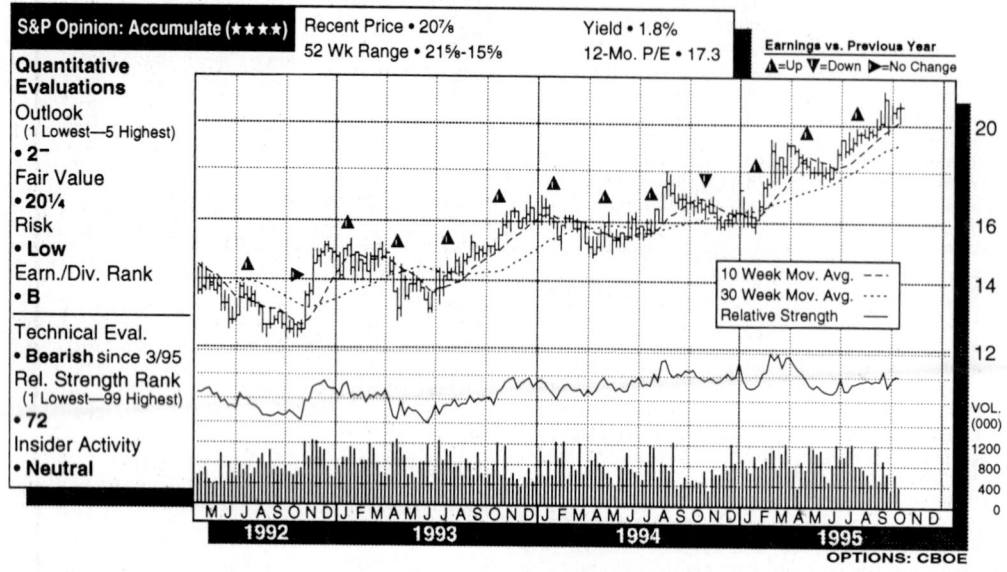

10 Week Mov. Avg. – – –
30 Week Mov. Avg. · · · ·
Relative Strength ——

OPTIONS: CBOE

Overview - 18-OCT-95

Total company sales are projected to rise at about a 10% annual pace through 1996, with gains in all major segments. Pepsi General profits are seen extending their uptrend as greater unit case volumes, higher prices, and an improving product mix outweigh a high level of investment spending related to expansion in Poland. Midas profits should grow modestly with strengthening domestic markets, despite a possible continuation of mixed international results. Hussmann profit growth will be challenging near-term, as difficult market conditions in Mexico may continue to offset benefits of productivity gains and an upgraded product line. Total company share earnings are seen growing 10% to 14% annually through 1996.

Valuation - 18-OCT-95

Given our expectation of steady, 10% to 14% annual EPS growth through 1996, the shares are attractive at current levels for above average gains. Our favorable view of WH stems from management's ability over the years to grow each of its three large, market-leading businesses. We expect management will continue to deploy the strong, dependable cash flows generated from these consumer-driven businesses to fund expansion overseas, pay down debt, and regularly boost its dividend. This strategy should over time lead to well above-average total return to shareholders. These low-risk shares, trading at about the multiple of the S&P 500, are especially attractive now for their defensive characteristics in a slow economic climate.

Key Stock Statistics

S&P EPS Est. 1995	1.30	Tang. Bk. Value/Share	0.30
P/E on S&P Est. 1995	16.1	Beta	1.08
S&P EPS Est. 1996	1.45	Shareholders	14,900
Dividend Rate/Share	0.38	Market cap. (B)	$ 2.2
Shs. outstg. (M)	104.8	Inst. holdings	71%
Avg. daily vol. (M)	0.103	Insider holdings	NA

Value of $10,000 invested 5 years ago: NA

Fiscal Year Ending Dec. 31

	1995	% Change	1994	% Change	1993	% Change
Revenues (Million $)						
1Q	594.4	9%	546.9	5%	522.5	5%
2Q	734.7	9%	673.5	6%	634.7	4%
3Q	827.1	12%	741.3	5%	703.7	6%
4Q	—	—	697.1	4%	668.8	8%
Yr.	—	—	2,659	5%	2,530	6%
Income (Million $)						
1Q	14.00	43%	9.80	17%	8.40	58%
2Q	38.00	6%	35.80	23%	29.10	15%
3Q	47.50	64%	29.00	-27%	39.80	14%
4Q	—	—	31.80	9%	29.10	10%
Yr.	—	—	106.4	NM	106.4	16%
Earnings Per Share ($)						
1Q	0.13	44%	0.09	13%	0.08	60%
2Q	0.36	6%	0.34	26%	0.27	12%
3Q	0.45	67%	0.27	-27%	0.37	12%
4Q	E0.36	20%	0.30	11%	0.27	8%
Yr.	E1.30	30%	1.00	1%	0.99	15%

Next earnings report expected: late November

Business Summary - 18-OCT-95

This diversified company makes consumer and commercial products. Business segment contributions in 1994 were:

	Sales	Profits
Pepsi General	47%	54%
Midas	20%	22%
Hussmann	33%	24%

Pepsi-Cola General Bottlers (PGB) produces and distributes soft drinks and non-alcoholic beverages, under exclusive franchises, in 12 states in the Midwest--a market of 25 million people. In 1994, 87% of PGB's volume was from Pepsi-Cola products. In mid-1994, PGB began to distribute Pepsi-Cola products in Poland.

Midas International provides automotive exhaust systems, suspension systems and brake services through 2,575 franchised and company-owned Midas shops in 14 countries. Revenues are derived primarily from the collection of an initial franchise fee and yearly royalties based on the franchisee's gross revenues. Midas also generates revenues from the sale of manufactured mufflers and tubing and from the resale of purchased parts (brakes, shocks and front-end alignment components) to its franchisees.

Hussmann Corp. produces merchandising and refrigeration systems for the world's food industry. Products include refrigerated display cases, commercial/industrial refrigeration systems, storage coolers, bottle coolers, walk-in coolers and HVAC equipment. Hussmann is the market leader in North America and has substantial operations in the U.K.

Important Developments

Oct. '95—Pepsi General profits increased 9% in 1995's first nine months, year to year, on 14% greater sales, as the benefits from higher case volumes and selling prices offset sizable losses and expenses associated with the start of business in Poland. Midas profits rose 8%, on 7% higher sales, primarily reflecting improved retail sales in the U.S. and the continuing benefit of new marketing and advertising programs. Hussmann profits declined 4%, on 5% higher sales, hurt by the devaluation of the Mexican peso and continued poor economic conditions in Mexico, which outweighed improved earnings from U.S. operations. Separately, WH said it invested over $200 million in capital spending, joint ventures and acquisitions during 1995's first nine months, more than double the year earlier level.

Capitalization

Long Term Debt: $868,700,000 (6/95).
Minority Interest: $217,600,000.

Per Share Data ($)

(Year Ended Dec. 31)

	1994	1993	1992	1991	1990	1989
Tangible Bk. Val.	0.27	-0.08	-0.61	-0.96	-2.20	-8.33
Cash Flow	1.92	1.88	1.73	1.41	0.14	2.71
Earnings	1.00	0.99	0.86	0.76	-0.68	1.87
Dividends	0.33	0.29	0.25	0.44	1.05	1.01
Payout Ratio	33%	29%	30%	59%	NM	54%
Prices - High	18	17	16⅜	27	29¾	38¼
- Low	14¾	12¾	12¼	11	17	27½
P/E Ratio - High	18	17	19	36	NM	20
- Low	15	13	14	14	NM	15

Income Statement Analysis (Million $)

	1994	%Chg	1993	%Chg	1992	%Chg	1991
Revs.	2,659	5%	2,530	6%	2,388	NM	2,393
Oper. Inc.	425	6%	401	9%	368	7%	343
Depr.	98.0	2%	96.0	2%	94.0	36%	69.0
Int. Exp.	71.0	-26%	96.0	-2%	98.0	-24%	129
Pretax Inc.	213	NM	212	24%	171	6%	162
Eff. Tax Rate	41%	—	43%	—	40%	—	44%
Net Inc.	106	NM	106	15%	92.0	15%	80.0

Balance Sheet & Other Fin. Data (Million $)

	1994	1993	1992	1991	1990	1989
Cash	71.0	93.0	133	105	80.0	102
Curr. Assets	708	691	671	654	898	1,056
Total Assets	2,135	2,103	2,063	2,123	3,347	3,718
Curr. Liab.	483	473	483	451	459	623
LT Debt	723	749	792	896	1,643	1,796
Common Eqty.	553	517	479	462	357	394
Total Cap.	1,497	1,506	1,501	1,581	2,738	2,971
Cap. Exp.	127	86.0	78.0	79.0	95.0	160
Cash Flow	204	202	186	149	-3.0	278

Ratio Analysis

	1994	1993	1992	1991	1990	1989
Curr. Ratio	1.5	1.5	1.4	1.4	2.0	1.7
% LT Debt of Cap.	48.3	49.8	52.7	56.7	60.0	60.4
% Net Inc.of Revs.	4.0	4.2	3.9	3.4	NM	5.7
% Ret. on Assets	5.1	5.1	4.4	2.9	NM	6.4
% Ret. on Equity	20.1	21.4	19.6	19.3	NM	30.5

Dividend Data

Dividends have been paid since 1950. A dividend reinvestment plan is available. A "poison pill" stock purchase rights plan was adopted in 1989.

Amt. of Div. $	Date Decl.	Ex-Div. Date	Stock of Record	Payment Date
0.085	Nov. 18	Dec. 05	Dec. 09	Jan. 01 '95
0.085	Feb. 17	Mar. 02	Mar. 08	Apr. 01 '95
0.095	May. 04	Jun. 06	Jun. 09	Jul. 01 '95
0.095	Aug. 18	Sep. 06	Sep. 08	Oct. 01 '95

Data as orig. reptd.; bef. results of disc. opers. and/or spec. items. Per share data adj. for stk. divs. as of ex-div. date.
E-Estimated. NA-Not Available. NM-Not Meaningful. NR-Not Ranked.

Office—3501 Algonquin Rd., Rolling Meadows, IL 60008. **Tel**—(708) 818-5000. **Chrmn & CEO**—B. S. Chelberg. **VP & Treas**—Kathleen R. Gannon. **VP & Secy**—W. B. Moore. **Investor Contact**—Charles Connolly. **Dirs**—B. S. Chelberg, R. G. Cline, J. W. Cozad, P. S. duPont IV, A. R. Dykes, H. Galland, J. Gilbert, Jr., V. B. Jackson, D. P. Jacobs, C. S. Locke. **Transfer Agent & Registrar**—First Chicago Trust Co. of New York, NYC. **Incorporated** in Delaware in 1962. **Empl**-15,271. **S&P Analyst:** Kenneth A. Shea

Willamette Industries

NASDAQ Symbol **WMTT**
In S&P 500

31-AUG-95 | **Industry:** Paper/Products | **Summary:** This integrated forest products company manufactures a wide variety of paper and building products and owns or controls 1.2 million acres of forests.

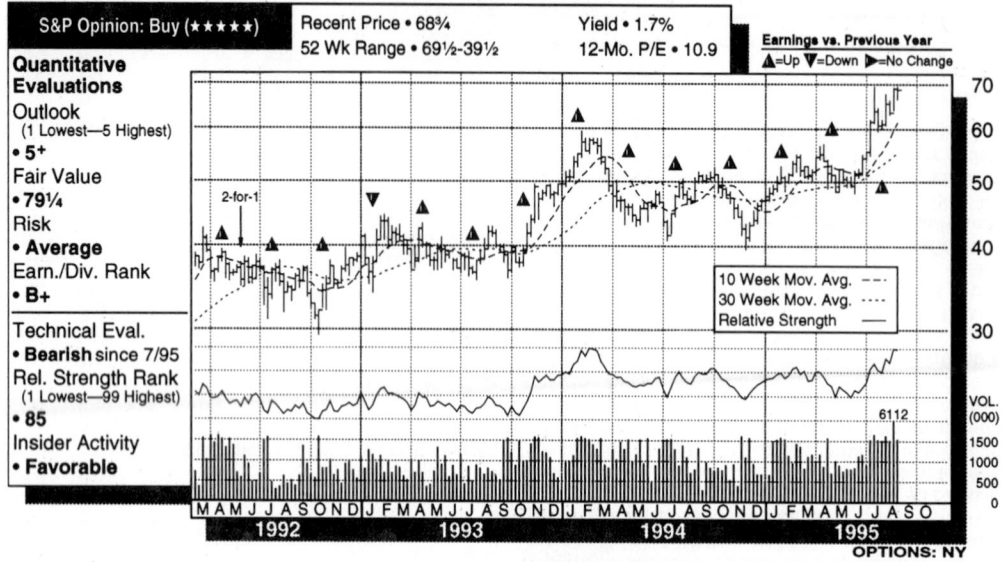

S&P Opinion: Buy (★★★★★)	Recent Price • 68¾
	52 Wk Range • 69½–39½

Yield • 1.7%
12-Mo. P/E • 10.9

Earnings vs. Previous Year
▲=Up ▼=Down ▶=No Change

Quantitative Evaluations

Outlook
(1 Lowest—5 Highest)
• **5+**

Fair Value
• **79¼**

Risk
• **Average**

Earn./Div. Rank
• **B+**

Technical Eval.
• **Bearish** since 7/95

Rel. Strength Rank
(1 Lowest—99 Highest)
• **85**

Insider Activity
• **Favorable**

2-for-1

10 Week Mov. Avg. -----
30 Week Mov. Avg. ......
Relative Strength ——

6112

VOL.
(000)
1500
1000
500
0

1992 1993 1994 1995

OPTIONS: NY

Overview - 31-AUG-95

Sales should be sharply higher in 1995, on solid demand and steep prices for most pulp, paper and packaging grades. The trends are related to relatively healthy global economies, along with limited industry capacity expansion in recent years. Although a moderating U.S. economy and substantial capacity coming on line threaten containerboard operations, industry totals should be helped by an increased reliance on exports and a likely economic spark provided by the recent drop in interest rates. The somewhat sluggish building products segment should improve as the year progresses, on the downturn in interest rates, curtailed industry production of lumber and reduced Canadian imports. Margins should widen significantly on the favorable pricing trends for paper and benefits of WMTT's ambitious capital spending program.

Valuation - 31-AUG-95

WMTT's stock fell out of investor favor for much of 1994, when tighter credit weakened trends in building materials markets. However, the shares have appreciated sharply since the latter part of that year, on a downtrend in interest rates and exceptional strength in the company's paper and packaging segment. Despite some nervousness about box operations, we continue to forecast solid earnings growth into 1996, with pulp and fine paper operations expected to remain quite strong and the building materials segment likely to show some improvement. Despite their run-up since late 1994, WMTT's shares still appear undervalued, trading recently at about 6X our 1996 EPS forecast.

Key Stock Statistics

S&P EPS Est. 1995	9.70	Tang. Bk. Value/Share	26.75
P/E on S&P Est. 1995	7.1	Beta	1.43
S&P EPS Est. 1996	11.00	Shareholders	6,100
Dividend Rate/Share	1.20	Market cap. (B)	$ 3.8
Shs. outstg. (M)	55.1	Inst. holdings	65%
Avg. daily vol. (M)	0.577	Insider holdings	NA

Value of $10,000 invested 5 years ago: $ 28,620

Fiscal Year Ending Dec. 31

	1995	% Change	1994	% Change	1993	% Change
Revenues (Million $)						
1Q	900.6	33%	679.7	7%	633.0	13%
2Q	1,004	38%	728.7	11%	654.1	10%
3Q	—	—	780.8	15%	677.1	9%
4Q	—	—	818.7	24%	658.0	10%
Yr.	—	—	3,008	15%	2,622	11%
Income (Million $)						
1Q	99.1	NM	32.89	6%	30.90	30%
2Q	134.4	NM	29.73	12%	26.57	8%
3Q	—	—	37.72	79%	21.11	5%
4Q	—	—	77.29	141%	32.10	142%
Yr.	—	—	177.6	60%	110.7	36%
Earnings Per Share ($)						
1Q	1.80	NM	0.60	7%	0.56	22%
2Q	2.44	NM	0.54	10%	0.49	9%
3Q	E2.66	NM	0.68	79%	0.38	3%
4Q	E2.80	99%	1.41	139%	0.59	146%
Yr.	E9.70	NM	3.23	60%	2.02	33%

Next earnings report expected: mid October

McGraw Hill

Willamette Industries

Business Summary - 31-AUG-95

Willamette Industries, Inc. grows and harvests timber and manufactures paper and building products. The company owns or controls 1.2 million acres of forests. Segment contributions in 1994 were:

	Sales	Profits
Paper	63%	34%
Building materials	37%	66%

Approximately 97% of the company's total output is sold domestically.

In 1994, the company accounted for 4.9% of U.S. production of bleached hardwood market pulp and for 5.9% of U.S. fine-paper production. Four Willamette paper mills manufactured 4.1% of the country's production of linerboard, corrugating medium and bag paper, all of which was used by company box and bag manufacturing plants or traded for their needs. Recycled fiber provides more than half of Willamette's fiber needs.

Six Willamette plants accounted for 5.8% of U.S. production of business forms in 1994. Corrugated containers are made at 32 facilities, accounting for 5.7% of U.S. production in 1994, while four bag plants produced 12% of the country's paper bags.

Willamette manufactured 7.0% of the plywood produced in the U.S. in 1994 at 10 plants, and its six sawmills produced 1.3% of U.S. lumber output. Lumber and plywood products are marketed through independent wholesalers and distributors. Five facilities produced 14.0% of 1994 U.S. particleboard output, and two plants accounted for 19.5% of the country's medium-density fiberboard production. Composite board products are sold nationwide through distributors, as well as directly to cabinet and furniture makers. The company also accounted for 26.2% of U.S. laminated beam production in 1994.

The company supplies 40% of its own long-term log needs, with the remainder purchased through government and private sales and open-market purchases.

Important Developments

Aug. '95—Directors authorized a $365 million expansion of WMTT's fine paper mill in Hawesville, Ky. (expected completion in 1998), subject to regulatory approvals. The board additionally authorized the repurchase of up to $100 million of Willamette common shares. In May 1995, WMTT acquired Mead Corp.'s fine paper mill in Kingsport, Tenn., while in April 1995, directors approved the $200 million construction of a new pulp mill in Hawesville, Ky. (which would replace an existing pulp mill in Hawesville). The Hawesville pulp project would bring the mill into compliance with all existing and foreseeable environmental regulations, and would allow for future expansion of production at the site.

Capitalization

Long Term Debt: $924,353,000 (6/95).

Per Share Data ($)

	1994	1993	1992	1991	1990	1989
Tangible Bk. Val.	25.22	22.91	21.27	19.52	19.42	17.72
Cash Flow	7.18	5.56	4.75	3.87	4.67	5.82
Earnings	3.23	2.02	1.52	0.90	2.55	3.76
Dividends	0.96	0.88	0.84	0.80	0.80	0.73
Payout Ratio	30%	44%	56%	89%	31%	19%
Prices - High	59½	50	42½	30⅜	28¾	27¾
- Low	39½	34	29	19⅜	14⅞	20½
P/E Ratio - High	18	25	28	34	11	7
- Low	12	18	19	22	6	5

(Year Ended Dec. 31)

Income Statement Analysis (Million $)

	1994	%Chg	1993	%Chg	1992	%Chg	1991
Revs.	3,008	15%	2,622	11%	2,372	18%	2,005
Oper. Inc.	584	29%	451	22%	371	26%	295
Depr.	217	12%	194	11%	174	15%	151
Int. Exp.	80.8	2%	79.2	7%	73.8	15%	64.0
Pretax Inc.	289	53%	189	47%	129	74%	74.0
Eff. Tax Rate	39%	—	42%	—	37%	—	38%
Net Inc.	178	60%	111	35%	82.0	78%	46.0

Balance Sheet & Other Fin. Data (Million $)

	1994	1993	1992	1991	1990	1989
Cash	12.8	9.5	9.0	2.2	21.1	11.4
Curr. Assets	605	533	481	439	402	349
Total Assets	3,033	2,805	2,527	2,219	1,965	1,604
Curr. Liab.	466	376	323	292	246	167
LT Debt	916	942	844	747	565	388
Common Eqty.	1,388	1,258	1,165	994	987	901
Total Cap.	2,535	2,398	2,191	1,912	1,717	1,437
Cap. Exp.	393	387	367	244	347	280
Cash Flow	395	305	255	197	237	296

Ratio Analysis

	1994	1993	1992	1991	1990	1989
Curr. Ratio	1.3	1.4	1.5	1.5	1.6	2.1
% LT Debt of Cap.	36.1	39.3	38.5	39.0	32.9	27.0
% Net Inc.of Revs.	5.9	4.2	3.4	2.3	6.8	10.1
% Ret. on Assets	6.1	4.1	3.3	2.2	7.3	12.6
% Ret. on Equity	13.4	9.1	7.3	4.6	13.7	23.2

Dividend Data —Cash has been paid each year since 1962.

Amt. of Div. $	Date Decl.	Ex-Div. Date	Stock of Record	Payment Date
0.240	Aug. 04	Aug. 23	Aug. 29	Sep. 14 '94
0.240	Nov. 10	Nov. 21	Nov. 28	Dec. 14 '94
0.270	Feb. 09	Feb. 21	Feb. 27	Mar. 14 '95
0.270	Apr. 27	May. 22	May. 29	Jun. 14 '95
0.300	Aug. 03	Aug. 24	Aug. 28	Sep. 14 '95

Data as orig. reptd.; bef. results of disc. opers. and/or spec. items. Per share data adj. for stk. divs. as of ex-div. date. E-Estimated. NA-Not Available. NM-Not Meaningful. NR-Not Ranked.

Office—3800 First Interstate Tower, 1300 S.W. Fifth Ave., Portland, OR 97201. **Tel**—(503) 227-5581. **Chrmn & CEO**—W. Swindells. **Pres**—S. R. Rogel (CEO effective Oct. 1). **Exec VP, CFO, Secy, Treas & Investor Contact**—J. A. Parsons. **Dirs**—C. M. Bishop Jr., G. K. Drummond, E. B. Hart, C. W. Knodell, P. N. McCracken, S. R. Rogel, S. J. Shelk Jr., R. M. Smelick, W. Swindells, S. C. Wheeler, B. R. Whiteley. **Transfer Agent & Registrar**—First Interstate Bank, Seattle. **Incorporated** in Oregon in 1906. **Empl**-12,260. **S&P Analyst:** Michael W. Jaffe

Williams Companies

NYSE Symbol **WMB**
In S&P 500

10-AUG-95

Industry:
Utilities-Gas

Summary: Williams owns and operates interstate natural gas and petroleum products pipeline systems, operates a national fiber-optic network and provides telecommunications services.

S&P Opinion: Accumulate (★★★★)		
Recent Price • 37⅛	Yield • 3.0%	
52 Wk Range • 37⅜-23½	12-Mo. P/E • 2.8	

Quantitative Evaluations

Outlook
(1 Lowest—5 Highest)
• **2+**

Fair Value
• **34⅝**

Risk
• **Low**

Earn./Div. Rank
• **B**

Technical Eval.
• **Bullish** since 5/92

Rel. Strength Rank
(1 Lowest—99 Highest)
• **60**

Insider Activity
• **NA**

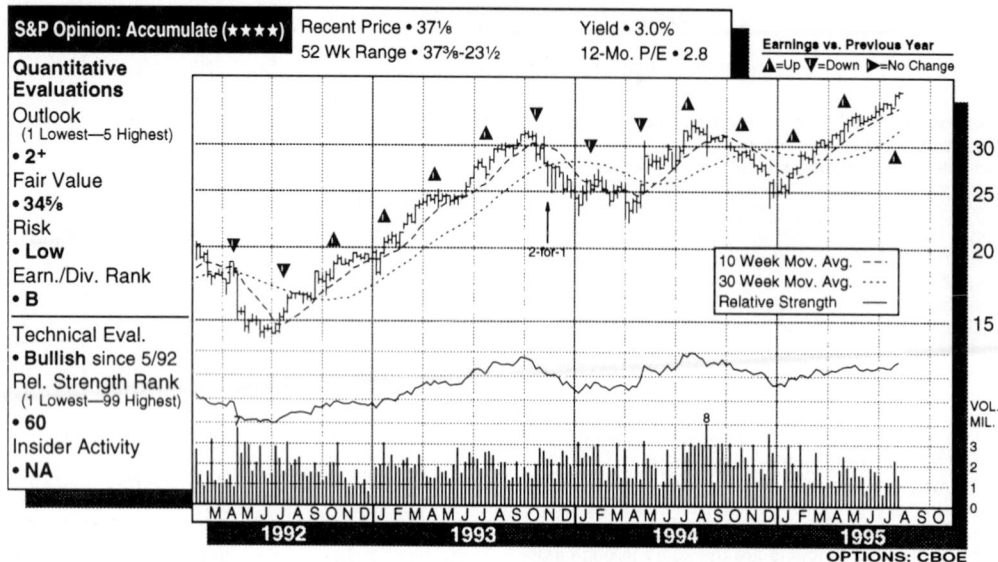

Earnings vs. Previous Year
▲=Up ▼=Down ▶=No Change

10 Week Mov. Avg. -- --
30 Week Mov. Avg. ......
Relative Strength ___

2-for-1

1992   1993   1994   1995

VOL. MIL.

OPTIONS: CBOE

Overview - 04-AUG-95

Earnings are expected to increase, following the divestiture of WilTel Network Services for after-tax proceeds totaling about $1.0 billion and the acquisition of Transco Energy Co. in a transaction valued at about $3.0 billion, including up to $431 million in cash. Earnings should benefit from the application of the remainder of the proceeds from the WilTel sale towards nonregulated businesses which should yield returns on investment in the 15%-20% range, versus 10%-15% for pipeline operations. Synergies associated with the Transco acquisition will lead to higher levels of profitability for Transco, and improved financial flexibility. With interest rates leveling off, and gas prices expected to turn up by year-end, earnings should rise at faster levels in 1996.

Valuation - 04-AUG-95

The shares have been in an uptrend since the December 1994 announcement that the Transco Energy acquisition would become effective in May. The acquisition will be additive to earnings in 1995. Growth in WilTel's remaining businesses and Williams' expanded pipeline transportation business will buoy the shares in 1995. An anticipated leveling off in interest rates during 1995 will make the shares more attractive, although mature markets for oil and natural gas in the U.S. may impede growth in transportation services. Expected favorable rate decisions could boost the shares in late 1995. We feel the stock is undervalued at current levels.

Key Stock Statistics

S&P EPS Est. 1995	2.45	Tang. Bk. Value/Share	27.11
P/E on S&P Est. 1995	15.2	Beta	0.97
S&P EPS Est. 1996	2.85	Shareholders	7,400
Dividend Rate/Share	1.08	Market cap. (B)	$ 3.7
Shs. outstg. (M)	101.3	Inst. holdings	72%
Avg. daily vol. (M)	0.293	Insider holdings	NA

Value of $10,000 invested 5 years ago: $ 23,773

Fiscal Year Ending Dec. 31

	1995	% Change	1994	% Change	1993	% Change
Revenues (Million $)						
1Q	958.0	148%	386.6	-49%	750.8	29%
2Q	947.4	126%	419.9	-23%	541.9	29%
3Q	—	—	467.3	-14%	541.8	-2%
4Q	—	—	477.3	-21%	603.7	-21%
Yr.	—	—	1,751	-28%	2,438	NM
Income (Million $)						
1Q	88.90	68%	52.80	-55%	118.0	199%
2Q	83.30	13%	74.00	185%	26.00	NM
3Q	—	—	55.60	NM	7.00	-62%
4Q	—	—	76.50	119%	35.00	-45%
Yr.	—	—	258.9	40%	185.0	44%
Earnings Per Share ($)						
1Q	0.88	83%	0.48	-63%	1.28	NM
2Q	0.79	14%	0.69	109%	0.33	NM
3Q	E0.48	—	0.51	NM	0.15	-6%
4Q	E0.29	—	0.77	60%	0.48	-25%
Yr.	E2.45	—	2.45	11%	2.20	76%

Next earnings report expected: mid October

Business Summary - 10-AUG-95

The Williams Companies is engaged in pipeline transportation of natural gas and petroleum products, natural gas gathering and processing, and nationwide telecommunications services. Segment contributions in 1994 were:

	Sales	Profits
Natural gas pipelines	26%	44%
Williams Field Services	33%	37%
Liquids pipeline/energy ventures	19%	14%
Williams Telecommunications	22%	5%

Northwest Pipeline owns and operates a 3,900 mile pipeline extending northwest from New Mexico to Washington. Williams Natural Gas is a 6,300 mile interstate pipeline system serving seven Midcontinent states. In 1994, combined throughput was 1,025 TBtu, up from 1,019 TBtu in 1993. At December 31, 1994, delivery capacity totaled 4.7 Bcf per day. WMB also holds a 50% interest in Kern River Gas Transmission Co. Williams Field Services owns and operates natural gas gathering and processing facilities, and natural gas properties and markets natural gas. Williams Pipe Line transports petroleum products, liquefied petroleum gas and crude oil in 11 Midwest states. Williams Energy Ventures provides price risk management, gas liquids marketing and electronic information services.

WilTel, Inc. is a telecommunications company providing customer-premises equipment and services nationwide and video communications products and services. In January 1995, the company sold WilTel's network services operations for $2.5 billion ($1.0 billion gain), but retained the telecommunications equipment and service business, as well as the Vyvx video transmission business.

Important Developments

Aug. '95—The company acquired Pekin Energy Co., a producer of fuel-grade and industrial ethanol and various co-products for $167,000,000.
Jul. '95—WMB reported second quarter income from continuing operations of $83.3 million, versus $57.9 million, as restated. Transco, whose operations were consolidated as of May 1, contributed $0.14 a share to net income. Earnings from Transco's Transcontinental Gas Pipe Line (TGPL) amounted to $45.4 million during the quarter. Also during the quarter, the company recorded a $16 million gain from the sale of WMB's interest in Texasgulf. Separately, WMB extended until August 31 its conditional offer to exchange up to $90,752,500 principal amount of its 9.60% Quarterly Income Capital Securities, due 2025,for up to all 3,630,100 shares of its $2.21 Cum. Pfd. stock.

Capitalization

Long Term Debt: $2,848,200,000 (3/95).
$2.21 Cum. Red. Preferred Stock: $100,000,000.

Per Share Data ($)
(Year Ended Dec. 31)

	1994	1993	1992	1991	1990	1989
Tangible Bk. Val.	15.46	15.75	13.75	12.81	12.29	12.16
Cash Flow	2.99	4.32	3.28	3.23	2.74	2.42
Earnings	2.45	2.24	1.25	1.17	0.79	0.59
Dividends	0.84	0.78	0.76	0.70	0.70	0.70
Payout Ratio	34%	35%	62%	59%	89%	120%
Prices - High	33⅜	31⅞	20½	19⅝	20⅜	22⅜
- Low	22⅛	17⅞	14	12¾	11⅝	14⅞
P/E Ratio - High	14	14	16	17	26	38
- Low	9	8	11	11	15	25

Income Statement Analysis (Million $)

	1994	%Chg	1993	%Chg	1992	%Chg	1991
Revs.	1,751	-28%	2,438	NM	2,448	17%	2,092
Oper. Inc.	465	-20%	584	29%	452	4%	436
Depr.	150	-29%	211	15%	184	7%	172
Int. Exp.	146	-12%	166	2%	162	NM	163
Pretax Inc.	247	-34%	377	119%	172	14%	151
Eff. Tax Rate	33%	—	38%	—	26%	—	27%
Net Inc.	165	-11%	185	45%	128	16%	110

Balance Sheet & Other Fin. Data (Million $)

	1994	1993	1992	1991	1990	1989
Cash	36.0	64.0	212	48.0	51.0	65.0
Curr. Assets	1,457	627	743	448	512	471
Total Assets	5,226	5,020	4,982	4,247	4,034	3,900
Curr. Liab.	1,474	733	978	687	717	713
LT Debt	1,308	1,605	1,683	1,540	1,368	1,285
Common Eqty.	1,406	1,624	1,268	1,070	1,017	998
Total Cap.	3,476	3,954	3,772	3,325	3,106	2,976
Cap. Exp.	326	529	586	317	254	198
Cash Flow	306	431	298	271	227	186

Ratio Analysis

	1994	1993	1992	1991	1990	1989
Curr. Ratio	1.0	0.9	0.8	0.7	0.7	0.7
% LT Debt of Cap.	37.6	40.6	44.6	46.3	44.0	43.2
% Net Inc.of Revs.	9.4	9.5	5.2	5.3	4.2	3.1
% Ret. on Assets	3.4	4.4	2.7	2.6	1.9	1.4
% Ret. on Equity	11.0	14.5	9.3	9.4	6.5	4.6

Dividend Data
(Dividends were resumed in 1974. A "poison pill" stock purchase right was adopted in 1986.)

Amt. of Div. $	Date Decl.	Ex-Div. Date	Stock of Record	Payment Date
0.210	Jul. 25	Aug. 22	Aug. 26	Sep. 19 '94
0.210	Sep. 15	Nov. 28	Dec. 02	Dec. 26 '94
0.270	Jan. 23	Feb. 27	Mar. 03	Mar. 27 '95
0.270	May. 18	May. 26	Jun. 02	Jun. 26 '95
0.270	Jul. 24	Aug. 23	Aug. 25	Sep. 18 '95

Data as orig. reptd.; bef. results of disc. opers. and/or spec. items. Per share data adj. for stk. divs. as of ex-div. date. E-Estimated. NA-Not Available. NM-Not Meaningful. NR-Not Ranked.

Office—One Williams Center, Tulsa, OK 74172. **Tel**—(918) 588-2000. **Chrmn, Pres & CEO**—K. E. Bailey. **SVP-Fin & CFO**—J. D. McCarthy. **Secy**—D. M. Higbee. **VP & Investor Contact**—Linda K. Lawson. **Dirs**—H. W. Andersen, K. E. Bailey, R. E. Bailey, G. A. Cox, T. H. Cruikshank, E. S. Duggan, R. J. LaFortune, J. C. Lewis, J. A. MacAllister, J. A. McClure, P. C. Meinig, K. A. Orr, G. R. Parker, J. H. Williams. **Transfer Agents & Registrars**—First Chicago Trust Co. of New York, NYC. **Incorporated** in Nevada in 1949; reincorporated in Delaware in 1987. Empl-8,227. **S&P Analyst:** Raymond J. Deacon

Winn-Dixie Stores

NYSE Symbol **WIN**
In S&P 500

11-AUG-95 Industry:
Retail Stores

Summary: Winn-Dixie, based in Jacksonville, Fla., is the largest supermarket operator in the highly competitive Sunbelt.

S&P Opinion: Hold (★★★)	Recent Price • 57	Yield • 3.0%
	52 Wk Range • 58-45⅞	12-Mo. P/E • 18.3

Quantitative Evaluations

Outlook
(1 Lowest—5 Highest)
• **2+**

Fair Value
• **51⅛**

Risk
• **Low**

Earn./Div. Rank
• **A+**

Technical Eval.
• **Bullish** since 10/94

Rel. Strength Rank
(1 Lowest—99 Highest)
• **31**

Insider Activity
• **Neutral**

Earnings vs. Previous Year
▲=Up ▼=Down ▶=No Change

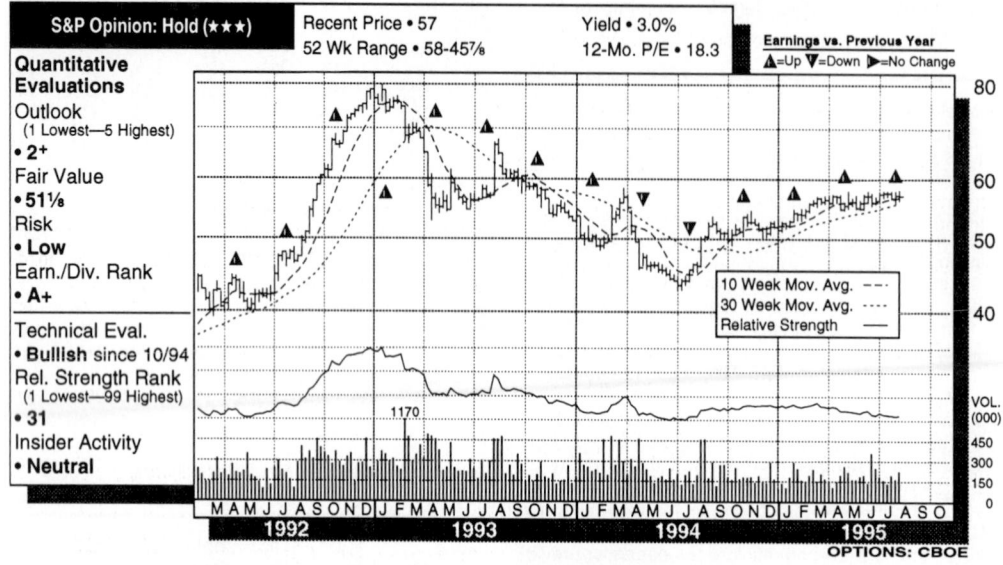

10 Week Mov. Avg. – – –
30 Week Mov. Avg. ·······
Relative Strength —

OPTIONS: CBOE

Overview - 11-AUG-95

Sales should advance about 8.5% in fiscal 1996 reflecting the acquisition of 25 Thriftway stores, and 75 new and 90 remodeled stores; same-store sales should increase by about 3%. The company plans to close about 65 smaller stores. Gross margins should widen, as larger stores and improved buying outweigh the impact of the company's everyday low price strategy. The higher margin product mix in larger stores, which include service departments and more general merchandise, boosts gross margins. Expense ratios should improve on the increased volume and efficiencies despite higher payroll costs in the larger stores. Interest expense should remain about level. The Thriftway acquisition should boost earnings per share by $0.10. Further acquisitions in the company's trade area or contiguous areas are a possibility.

Valuation - 11-AUG-95

The shares have traded in a narrow range so far this year. The company's aggressive store expansion and refurbishment program and the addition of 25 Thriftway stores should boost earnings per share by about 13% in fiscal 1996. The stock is amply valued to reflect this. We anticipate that the shares will track the market in the months to come. The company's balance sheet is one of the strongest in the supermarket industry. The dividend, currently yielding almost 3.0%, is raised frequently. These factors suggest little downside risk.

Key Stock Statistics

S&P EPS Est. 1996	3.50	Tang. Bk. Value/Share	14.26
P/E on S&P Est. 1996	16.3	Beta	0.93
Dividend Rate/Share	1.68	Shareholders	39,800
Shs. outstg. (M)	75.8	Market cap. (B)	$ 4.3
Avg. daily vol. (M)	0.033	Inst. holdings	16%
		Insider holdings	NA

Value of $10,000 invested 5 years ago: $ 20,458

Fiscal Year Ending Jun. 30

	1995	% Change	1994	% Change	1993	% Change
Revenues (Million $)						
1Q	2,590	5%	2,464	3%	2,390	3%
2Q	3,538	5%	3,381	4%	3,240	3%
3Q	2,776	5%	2,651	6%	2,504	3%
4Q	2,884	12%	2,585	-4%	2,691	12%
Yr.	11,788	6%	11,082	2%	10,832	5%
Income (Million $)						
1Q	40.00	11%	35.95	—	—	—
2Q	67.47	6%	63.78	1%	63.03	17%
3Q	56.94	9%	52.03	-9%	57.20	6%
4Q	67.73	5%	64.35	-22%	82.78	NM
Yr.	232.2	7%	216.1	-9%	236.4	9%
Earnings Per Share ($)						
1Q	0.54	12%	0.48	9%	0.44	26%
2Q	0.91	7%	0.85	4%	0.82	17%
3Q	0.76	9%	0.70	-7%	0.75	7%
4Q	0.90	3%	0.87	-21%	1.10	3%
Yr.	3.11	7%	2.90	-7%	3.11	10%

Next earnings report expected: early October

Winn-Dixie Stores

Business Summary - 11-AUG-95

Winn-Dixie is the largest food retailer in the Sunbelt, operating 1,159 stores in 13 Sunbelt states at June 29, 1994. The heaviest concentrations of stores are in Florida (439), North Carolina (129), Georgia (126), South Carolina (86), Alabama (84), Louisiana (78) and Texas (72). Store data at the end of recent fiscal years was:

	1994	1993	1992
Stores	1,159	1,151	1,189
Total store square footage (million)	40.7	39.0	38.6

The average supermarket contained about 35,100 sq. ft. at the end of fiscal 1994, up from 33,900 sq. ft. a year earlier. Some 234 stores exceed 44,000 sq. ft.; these stores account for over 61% of sales. Stores operate under the names Winn-Dixie, Marketplace, Buddies and Food Pavilion. Recent emphasis has been on constructing larger superstores and combination stores, and closing or enlarging older, smaller stores. The company's labor force is predominantly non-union.

WIN operates various support facilities for its stores, including 16 warehousing and distribution centers and a variety of manufacturing and processing plants. An unconsolidated subsidiary operates 14 stores in the Bahamas.

Important Developments

Jul. '95—Identical store sales rose 3.8% in the fourth quarter; average store sales increased 9.5% in the quarter. Identical store sales rose 3.0% in fiscal 1995 and average store sales increased 6.8%. Management said that the merging of Thriftway stores into the company's operations has been completed. The sales momentum should have a positive effect on fiscal 1996 operating results. During fiscal 1995, the company opened 108 new store locations, averaging 47,100 square feet and closed 92 stores, averaging 27,300 feet. An additional 86 stores were enlarged or remodeled. This includes Thriftway, Inc., a 25-store supermarket chain operating in Ohio and Kentucky, acquired for stock on March 26, 1995.

Capitalization

Long Term Debt: $82,528,000 of capital lease obligs. (4/95).

Per Share Data ($)

					(Year Ended Jun. 30)	
	1995	1994	1993	1992	1991	1990
Tangible Bk. Val.	NA	14.26	13.14	12.39	11.15	10.39
Cash Flow	NA	4.98	4.96	4.47	3.65	3.42
Earnings	3.11	2.90	3.11	2.82	2.20	1.93
Dividends	1.29	1.44	1.32	1.20	1.08	0.99
Payout Ratio	41%	50%	42%	43%	49%	51%
Prices - High	57⅞	58⅜	79¾	79½	41¼	38⅝
- Low	51⅛	42⅝	52¾	35¾	29¾	28⅜
P/E Ratio - High	19	20	26	28	19	20
- Low	16	15	17	13	14	15

Income Statement Analysis (Million $)

	1994	%Chg	1993	%Chg	1992	%Chg	1991
Revs.	11,082	2%	10,832	5%	10,337	3%	10,074
Oper. Inc.	422	8%	391	8%	361	28%	282
Depr.	157	11%	141	11%	127	12%	113
Int. Exp.	14.3	-21%	18.1	-28%	25.2	17%	21.6
Pretax Inc.	348	-4%	364	11%	328	27%	259
Eff. Tax Rate	38%	—	35%	—	34%	—	34%
Net Inc.	216	-8%	236	9%	216	26%	171

Balance Sheet & Other Fin. Data (Million $)

	1994	1993	1992	1991	1990	1989
Cash	31.5	108	204	103	198	128
Curr. Assets	1,361	1,413	1,363	1,203	1,169	1,031
Total Assets	2,147	2,063	1,977	1,817	1,733	1,575
Curr. Liab.	873	869	813	767	742	635
LT Debt	85.0	87.0	90.0	97.0	83.0	72.0
Common Eqty.	1,057	985	952	860	813	783
Total Cap.	1,143	1,072	1,042	957	897	856
Cap. Exp.	278	209	164	179	133	140
Cash Flow	374	378	343	284	271	271

Ratio Analysis

	1994	1993	1992	1991	1990	1989
Curr. Ratio	1.6	1.6	1.7	1.6	1.6	1.6
% LT Debt of Cap.	7.5	8.1	8.7	10.1	9.3	8.5
% Net Inc.of Revs.	2.0	2.2	2.1	1.7	1.6	1.5
% Ret. on Assets	10.3	11.8	11.4	9.7	9.3	8.7
% Ret. on Equity	21.2	24.7	23.9	20.6	19.3	17.8

Dividend Data

(Dividends, which have been paid since 1934, are declared quarterly and paid monthly. A dividend reinvestment plan is available.)

Amt. of Div. $	Date Decl.	Ex-Div. Date	Stock of Record	Payment Date
0.130	Apr. 03	May. 09	May. 15	Jun. 01 '95
0.130	Apr. 03	Jun. 13	Jun. 15	Jul. 03 '95
0.140	Jul. 03	Jul. 13	Jul. 17	Aug. 01 '95
0.140	Jul. 03	Aug. 11	Aug. 15	Sep. 01 '95
0.140	Jul. 03	Sep. 13	Sep. 15	Oct. 02 '95

Data as orig. reptd.; bef. results of disc. opers. and/or spec. items. Per share data adj. for stk. divs. as of ex-div. date. E-Estimated. NA-Not Available. NM-Not Meaningful. NR-Not Ranked.

Office—5050 Edgewood Court, Jacksonville, FL 32254-3699. **Tel**—(904) 783-5000. **Chrmn & CEO**—A. Dano Davis. **Pres**—J. Kufeldt. **Secy**—J. W. Dixon. **VP-Fin & Investor Contact**—R. P. McCook. **Dirs**—A. M. Codina, A. Dano Davis, R. D. Davis, T. W. Davis, J. Kufeldt, R. D. Lovett, C. H. McKellar, D. F. Miller, C. T. Rider, C. P. Stephens. **Transfer Agent & Registrar**—First Union National Bank of North Carolina, Charlotte. **Incorporated** in Florida in 1928. **Empl**-112,000. **S&P Analyst:** Karen J. Sack, CFA

Woolworth Corp.

NYSE Symbol **Z**
In S&P 500

17-AUG-95 Industry:
Retail Stores

Summary: Woolworth operates some 8,629 general merchandise and specialty stores worldwide.

S&P Opinion: Hold (★★★)	Recent Price • 14	Yield • Nil
	52 Wk Range • 19⅝-13½	12-Mo. P/E • 50.0

Quantitative Evaluations

Outlook
(1 Lowest—5 Highest)
• **4-**

Fair Value
• **14**

Risk
• **Average**

Earn./Div. Rank
• **B+**

Technical Eval.
• **Bearish** since 8/95

Rel. Strength Rank
(1 Lowest—99 Highest)
• **10**

Insider Activity
• **Neutral**

Earnings vs. Previous Year
▲=Up ▼=Down ▶=No Change

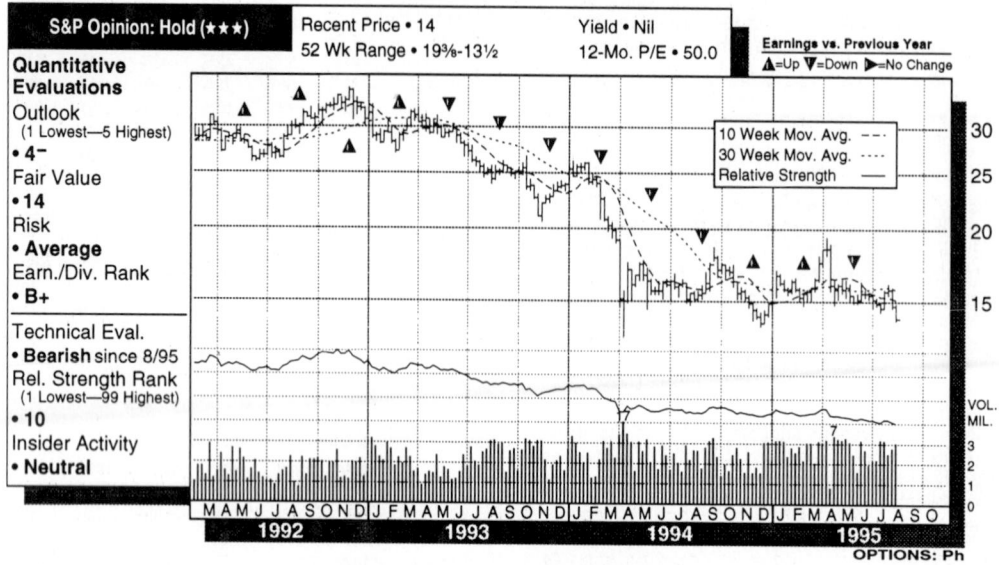

10 Week Mov. Avg. – – –
30 Week Mov. Avg. ·······
Relative Strength ——

OPTIONS: Ph

Overview - 17-AUG-95

Woolworth has gone through a major repositioning in the past few years. The company's business mix has shifted toward athletic footwear and apparel stores, and away from general merchandise formats, which should boost profit margin potential. The company reduced the size of its general merchandise chain by half and pared its Kinney shoe chain by one-third. Its Canadian Woolco stores were sold to Wal-Mart in early 1994; other small chains were also sold. The company has eliminated its dividend and cut back its capital expenditure program and is in the process of liquidating excess inventories. The company should begin to reap the benefits from these moves in the second half of 1995-96 and beyond. In addition, its general merchandise units in Germany (about 18% of revenues) should post improved operating profits in 1995-96.

Valuation - 17-AUG-95

The shares have remained in a narrow trading range in recent months. Weak consumer spending so far in 1995 has held down sales gains and prospects for earnings gains. We believe that the many initiatives taken by the new management team will begin to place earnings on a growth track by year-end. The company is narrowly focused on growing its profitable formats and lowering its cost structure to more acceptable levels. Improved technology and logistics should boost operating performance. The shares are a worthwhile holding for the longer term.

Key Stock Statistics

S&P EPS Est. 1996	0.65	Tang. Bk. Value/Share	9.18
P/E on S&P Est. 1996	21.5	Beta	1.13
S&P EPS Est. 1997	1.10	Shareholders	51,900
Dividend Rate/Share	Nil	Market cap. (B)	$ 1.9
Shs. outstg. (M)	132.5	Inst. holdings	51%
Avg. daily vol. (M)	0.552	Insider holdings	NA

Value of $10,000 invested 5 years ago: $ 5,457

Fiscal Year Ending Jan. 31

	1996	% Change	1995	% Change	1994	% Change
Revenues (Million $)						
1Q	1,794	2%	1,760	-18%	2,135	2%
2Q	1,922	2%	1,876	-18%	2,288	3%
3Q	—	—	2,097	-12%	2,387	-5%
4Q	—	—	2,560	-9%	2,816	-10%
Yr.	—	—	8,293	-14%	9,626	-3%
Income (Million $)						
1Q	-79.70	NM	-38.00	NM	-24.00	NM
2Q	-11.00	NM	-42.00	NM	-10.00	NM
3Q	—	—	37.00	NM	-350.0	NM
4Q	—	—	90.00	NM	-111.0	NM
Yr.	—	—	47.00	NM	-495.0	NM
Earnings Per Share ($)						
1Q	-0.60	NM	-0.29	NM	-0.18	NM
2Q	-0.09	NM	-0.32	NM	-0.08	NM
3Q	—	—	0.28	NM	-2.66	NM
4Q	—	—	0.69	NM	-0.84	NM
Yr.	E0.65	81%	0.36	NM	-3.76	NM

Next earnings report expected: mid November

Woolworth Corp.

Business Summary - 17-AUG-95

Woolworth Corp. (formerly F.W. Woolworth Co.) is a major retailer in the U.S. and abroad, operating over 8,629 retail stores, of which 7,558 are specialty units and 1,071 general merchandise stores. Segment contributions in fiscal 1994-95 were:

	Revs.	Profits
Specialty	61%	94%
General merchandise	39%	6%

The company has downsized its mature formats - Woolworth general merchandise stores and Kinney shoe stores - to fund new and developing specialty retailing formats, such as Foot Locker and Northern Reflections. The company's specialty stores consists of the following divisions: athletic footwear and apparel; specialty footwear; and Northern Reflections operated by Woolworth Canada. The company operated 1,828 Foot Locker stores and 595 Lady Foot Locker stores at the end of January 1995. Kinney consisted of 826 family shoe stores and leased departments at fiscal 1994-95 year-end. Champs Sports operated 539 stores and Northern Reflections women's casual sportswear 466 stores.

The general merchandise division consisted of 1,071 stores in the U.S., Canada and Germany at the end of 1994-95, mainly 812 general merchandise units, up from 962 units a year earlier. The company operates 194 low-priced apparel The Bargain! Shop stores in Canada. The Rx Place drug stores were sold in May 1995 for $37 million in cash and notes and its Kids Mart/Little Folks stores were sold in June 1995.

Important Developments

Aug. '95—Z said that second quarter and year-to-date results are on plan. The athletic footwear and apparel divisions continued to show strong increases in sales. As part of the company's ongoing initiatives to clear its stores of aged merchandise, higher levels of markdowns have been taken. So far, this inventory improvement program has resulted in 10% reductions in the U.S. and 6% worldwide, year-to-year. The company has reduced both borrowings and interest expense. In addition, the $100 million global cost reduction program, which includes the elimination of 2,000 positions, is proceeding according to plan. The company continued with its strategy of selling non-strategic assets. It completed the sale of Little Folk/Kids Mart and closed its Kanuba and Canary Island operations in Canada.

Capitalization

Long Term Debt: $571,000,000 (4/29/95), incl. capital lease obligations.
$2.20 Conv. Preferred Stock: 100,983 shs. ($1 par); conv. into 5.68 com. shs.

Per Share Data ($)

(Year Ended Jan. 31)

	1995	1994	1993	1992	1991	1990
Tangible Bk. Val.	9.15	9.05	14.44	14.22	16.78	14.78
Cash Flow	2.12	-1.81	4.03	1.56	4.22	4.12
Earnings	0.36	-3.76	2.14	-0.41	2.45	2.55
Dividends	0.74	1.16	1.12	1.08	1.04	0.94
Payout Ratio	NM	NM	52%	NM	43%	37%
Cal. Yrs.	1994	1993	1992	1991	1990	1989
Prices - High	26¼	32¾	35	36⅜	36½	36⅛
- Low	12⅞	20½	26	23½	22⅞	24⅛
P/E Ratio - High	73	NM	16	NM	15	14
- Low	36	NM	12	NM	9	9

Income Statement Analysis (Million $)

	1995	%Chg	1994	%Chg	1993	%Chg	1992
Revs.	8,293	-14%	9,626	-3%	9,962	NM	9,914
Oper. Inc.	466	77%	264	-66%	773	19%	650
Depr.	233	-9%	257	3%	249	-3%	256
Int. Exp.	110	31%	84.0	-11%	94.0	-5%	99
Pretax Inc.	96.0	NM	-797	NM	437	NM	-83.0
Eff. Tax Rate	51%	—	NM	—	36%	—	NM
Net Inc.	47.0	NM	-494	NM	280	NM	-53.0

Balance Sheet & Other Fin. Data (Million $)

	1995	1994	1993	1992	1991	1990
Cash	72.0	57.0	49.0	69.0	50.0	56.0
Curr. Assets	2,069	2,494	2,654	2,590	2,391	2,235
Total Assets	4,173	4,593	4,692	4,618	4,305	3,907
Curr. Liab.	1,710	2,081	1,658	1,592	1,436	1,299
LT Debt	309	336	372	425	269	306
Common Eqty.	1,353	1,344	2,054	2,025	2,334	2,069
Total Cap.	1,767	1,767	2,536	2,545	2,713	2,476
Cap. Exp.	218	359	333	387	396	317
Cash Flow	280	-237	529	203	551	530

Ratio Analysis

	1995	1994	1993	1992	1991	1990
Curr. Ratio	1.2	1.2	1.6	1.6	1.7	1.7
% LT Debt of Cap.	17.5	19.0	14.7	16.7	9.9	12.4
% Net Inc.of Revs.	0.6	NM	2.8	NM	3.2	3.7
% Ret. on Assets	1.1	NM	6.0	NM	7.7	8.8
% Ret. on Equity	3.5	NM	13.7	NM	14.4	16.8

Dividend Data —Prior to omission in April 1995, dividends had been paid since 1912. A dividend reinvestment plan is available. A "poison pill" stock purchase right was adopted in 1988.

Amt. of Div. $	Date Decl.	Ex-Div. Date	Stock of Record	Payment Date
0.290	Jan. 12	Jan. 26	Feb. 01	Mar. 01 '94
0.290	Apr. 13	Apr. 26	May. 02	Jun. 01 '94
0.150	Jul. 13	Jul. 26	Aug. 01	Sep. 01 '94
0.150	Oct. 12	Oct. 26	Nov. 01	Dec. 01 '94
0.150	Jan. 11	Jan. 26	Feb. 01	Mar. 01 '95

Data as orig. reptd.; bef. results of disc. opers. and/or spec. items. Per share data adj. for stk. divs. as of ex-div. date. E-Estimated. NA-Not Available. NM-Not Meaningful. NR-Not Ranked.

Office—233 Broadway, New York, NY 10279-0003. **Tel**—(212) 553-2000. **Chrmn & CEO**—R. N. Farah. **Pres & COO**—D. W. Hilpert. **Treas**—J. H. Cannon. **VP-Secy**—G. M. Bahler. **Dirs**—J. W. Adams, J. C. Bacot, R. N. Farah, H. Galland, P. H. Geier, Jr., J. Gilbert Jr., F. E. Hennig, D. W. Hilpert, S. H. Knox III, M. P. MacKimm, J. J. Mackowski, J. E. Preston, H. E. Sells. **Transfer Agents & Registrars**—First Chicago Trust Co. of New York; R-M Trust Co., Toronto. **Incorporated** in New York in 1911. **Empl**-119,000. **S&P Analyst:** Karen. J. Sack, CFA

Worthington Industries

NASDAQ Symbol **WTHG**

In S&P 500

01-NOV-95   Industry:
Steel-Iron

Summary: This leading processor of close-tolerance steel also manufactures steel castings, pressure cylinders, and custom plastic and precision metal parts.

S&P Opinion: Accumulate (★★★★)	Recent Price • 17⅛	Yield • 2.6%
	52 Wk Range • 23¼-16¾	12-Mo. P/E • 13.7

Quantitative Evaluations

Outlook
(1 Lowest—5 Highest)
• **5⁻**

Fair Value
• **21¼**

Risk
• **Average**

Earn./Div. Rank
• **A-**

Technical Eval.
• **Bearish** since 8/95

Rel. Strength Rank
(1 Lowest—99 Highest)
• **14**

Insider Activity
• **Favorable**

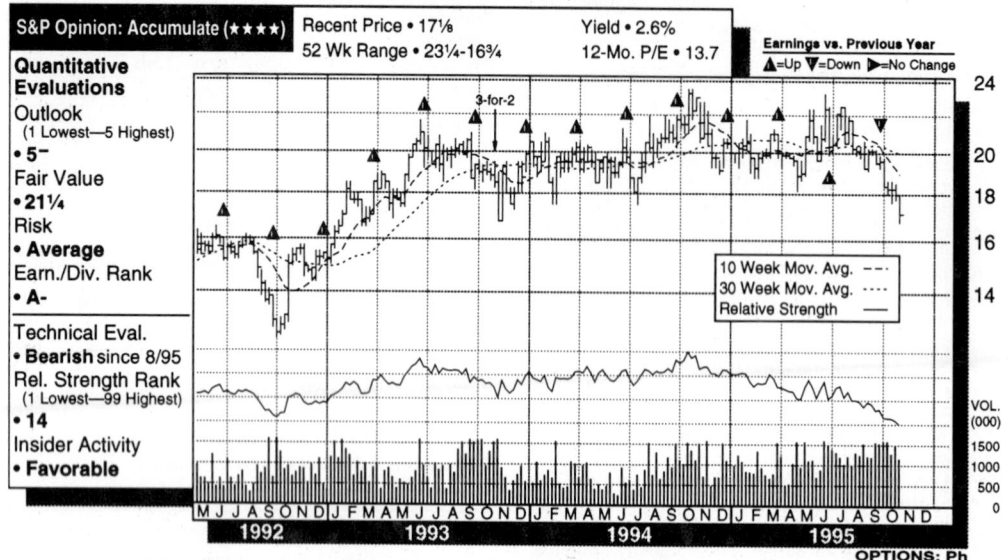

Earnings vs. Previous Year
▲=Up ▼=Down ▶=No Change

10 Week Mov. Avg. ---
30 Week Mov. Avg. .....
Relative Strength —

OPTIONS: Ph

Overview - 01-NOV-95

We anticipate a small decline in sales in 1995-96 reflecting lower pricing for processed steel products and flat sales at the other two units. We expect to see sales and earnings improve sequentially in 1995-96 but comparisons with 1994-95 will probably not be positive for any quarter. Most of the sequential improvement will come in 1995-96's second half as demand from the auto industry rebounds and boost prices for processed steel products. With lower operating profit along with lower equity earnings and higher interest expense, earnings for 1995-96 will trail 1994-95. Market share gains, consolidation of auto industry suppliers, a secular decline in material costs, contributions from the BHP Delta plant and acquisitions should boost long-term sales and earnings.

Valuation - 01-NOV-95

Although we project lower sales and earnings in 1995-96, we are maintaining our accumulate rating on WTHG's shares, based on the company's attractive valuation and excellent long-term prospects. Through early November 1995, the shares were down 16% since 1994's year end, versus a 26% gain in the S&P 500. Currently selling at about 15X our 1995-96 estimate, WTHG's multiple is low for a company with a demonstrated ability to achieve solid sales and earnings growth in a mature, cyclical industry. We think that the stock price reflects most of the bad news about earnings and the current weakness creates an opportunity to accumulate the shares at an attractive level.

Key Stock Statistics

S&P EPS Est. 1996	1.15	Tang. Bk. Value/Share	6.50
P/E on S&P Est. 1996	14.9	Beta	0.58
Dividend Rate/Share	0.44	Shareholders	9,200
Shs. outstg. (M)	90.7	Market cap. (B)	$ 1.5
Avg. daily vol. (M)	0.279	Inst. holdings	56%
		Insider holdings	NA

Value of $10,000 invested 5 years ago: $ 18,937

Fiscal Year Ending May 31

	1996	% Change	1995	% Change	1994	% Change
Revenues (Million $)						
1Q	325.7	-6%	346.3	19%	289.9	16%
2Q	—	—	363.3	23%	295.9	13%
3Q	—	—	370.1	15%	323.1	17%
4Q	—	—	403.9	7%	376.2	15%
Yr.	—	—	1,484	15%	1,285	15%
Income (Million $)						
1Q	21.51	-15%	25.45	28%	19.90	—
2Q	—	—	28.26	46%	19.41	31%
3Q	—	—	28.65	45%	19.74	26%
4Q	—	—	34.32	33%	25.80	13%
Yr.	—	—	116.7	38%	84.85	28%
Earnings Per Share ($)						
1Q	0.24	-14%	0.28	27%	0.22	50%
2Q	E0.27	-13%	0.31	48%	0.21	26%
3Q	E0.30	-6%	0.32	45%	0.22	27%
4Q	E0.34	-11%	0.38	31%	0.29	14%
Yr.	E1.15	-11%	1.29	37%	0.94	27%

Next earnings report expected: mid December

Worthington Industries

01-NOV-95

Business Summary - 01-NOV-95

Worthington Industries, Inc. processes flat-rolled steel, manufactures pressure cylinders, and makes a broad line of cast steel products and precision parts. Sales and profits in 1994-5 were derived as follows:

	Sales	Profits
Processed steel products	70%	73%
Custom plastic products	20%	13%
Cast products	10%	14%

Processed steel products buys coils of wide, open tolerance sheet steel from major steel mills and processes it to the custom order of more than 1,700 industrial customers in the automotive, appliance, electrical, machinery, communication, leisure time and other industries. It also produces disposable and reusable steel and aluminum cylinders, sold primarily to producers and distributors of refrigerant gases, and refillable steel and aluminum cylinders, used to hold liquefied petroleum gas.

Custom products includes the manufacture of injection molded plastic components parts and assemblies, primarily for customers in automotive original equipment markets. Sales are also made to appliance, lawn equipment and houseware manufacturers. Custom products also includes the manufacture of precision metal components for power steering, transmission, brake and other mechanical systems.

Cast products manufactures a broad line of cast steel products ranging in size from 100 pounds to 30 tons. The products are sold to the railroad, mass transit, construction and off-highway markets.

WTHG participates in five joint ventures that are accounted for by the equity method: Worthington Armstrong, Worthington Specialty Processing, TWB Co., London Industries, Acerex and S. A. de C.V. WTHG has a 28% equity interest in Rouge Steel.

Important Developments

Sep. '95— WTHG reported share earnings of $0.24 on a 5.9% decline in sales for the first quarter of FY 96 (May), versus $0.28 a year earlier. The company attributed the lower earnings to slower economic activity which caused weakness in both volume and pricing. Decreased selling prices and the reduction of more expensive inventory caused a contraction in gross margins. Sales and profits fell in processed steel products due to weakening in auto demand; sales in custom products were flat while sales rose in the cast products units. WTHG stated that orders had improved beginning in August and that the slowdown was temporary. The company added that it was still optimistic and expected earnings to improve for the rest of the year.

Capitalization

Long Term Debt: $83,146,000 (8/95).

Per Share Data ($) (Year Ended May 31)

	1995	1994	1993	1992	1991	1990
Tangible Bk. Val.	6.49	5.56	4.80	4.35	4.00	3.84
Cash Flow	1.66	1.30	1.07	0.93	0.77	0.85
Earnings	1.29	0.94	0.74	0.63	0.50	0.61
Dividends	0.40	0.36	0.33	0.30	0.27	0.25
Payout Ratio	31%	38%	0%	49%	54%	41%
Cal. Yrs.	1994	1993	1992	1991	1990	1989
Prices - High	23½	21⅝	17⅝	15⅝	11	11⅜
- Low	17½	15	12⅜	9⅛	8⅜	9⅛
P/E Ratio - High	18	23	24	25	22	18
- Low	14	16	17	14	17	15

Income Statement Analysis (Million $)

	1995	%Chg	1994	%Chg	1993	%Chg	1992
Revs.	1,484	15%	1,285	15%	1,116	15%	974
Oper. Inc.	188	24%	152	10%	138	17%	118
Depr.	34.1	5%	32.4	11%	29.2	9%	26.9
Int. Exp.	6.0	100%	3.0	-12%	3.4	-23%	4.4
Pretax Inc.	187	38%	136	30%	105	21%	87.0
Eff. Tax Rate	38%	—	37%	—	37%	—	36%
Net Inc.	117	38%	84.9	28%	66.2	19%	55.5

Balance Sheet & Other Fin. Data (Million $)

	1995	1994	1993	1992	1991	1990
Cash	2.0	13.3	17.6	6.0	9.0	50.0
Curr. Assets	452	413	364	311	276	313
Total Assets	917	799	686	622	564	561
Curr. Liab.	179	181	147	131	107	133
LT Debt	53.5	54.1	55.6	57.3	59.0	42.5
Common Eqty.	590	504	433	389	355	344
Total Cap.	720	617	539	490	455	426
Cap. Exp.	61.5	47.0	29.1	45.1	63.3	54.6
Cash Flow	151	117	95.4	82.4	68.4	76.0

Ratio Analysis

	1995	1994	1993	1992	1991	1990
Curr. Ratio	2.5	2.3	2.5	2.4	2.6	2.3
% LT Debt of Cap.	7.4	8.8	10.3	11.7	13.0	10.0
% Net Inc.of Revs.	7.9	6.6	5.9	5.7	5.1	6.0
% Ret. on Assets	13.6	11.4	10.1	9.3	8.0	9.9
% Ret. on Equity	21.3	18.1	16.0	14.9	12.8	16.7

Dividend Data

Cash has been paid in each year since 1968. A dividend reinvestment plan is available.

Amt. of Div. $	Date Decl.	Ex-Div. Date	Stock of Record	Payment Date
0.100	Nov. 16	Dec. 01	Dec. 07	Dec. 30 '94
0.100	Feb. 24	Mar. 06	Mar. 11	Mar. 27 '95
0.110	May. 24	Jun. 08	Jun. 12	Jun. 26 '95
0.110	Aug. 17	Aug. 24	Aug. 28	Sep. 25 '95

Data as orig. reptd.; bef. results of disc. opers. and/or spec. items. Per share data adj. for stk. divs. as of ex-div. date. E-Estimated. NA-Not Available. NM-Not Meaningful. NR-Not Ranked.

Office—1205 Dearborn Drive, Columbus, OH 43085. **Tel**—(614) 438-3210.   **Chrmn**—J. H. McConnell. **CEO**—J. P. McConnell. **Pres & COO**—D. H. Malenick. **VP & CFO**—D. G. Barger, Jr. **Secy**—C. D. Minor. **Investor Contact**—Jeff Bradley. **Dirs**— C. R. Carson, J. E. Fisher, J. F. Havens, R. J. Klein, P. A. Klisares, K. S. LeVeque, D. H. Malenick, J. H. McConnell, J. P. McConnell, R. B. McCurry, C. D. Minor, G. B. Mitchell, J. Petropoulos. **Transfer Agent & Registrar**—First National Bank of Boston. **Incorporated** in Ohio in 1955; reincorporated in Delaware in 1986. **Empl**-8,200. **S&P Analyst:** Leo Larkin

Wrigley (Wm.) Jr.

NYSE Symbol **WWY**

In S&P 500

31-OCT-95

Industry: Food

Summary: This company is the world's largest producer of chewing gum, with about 50% of the U.S. market. The Wrigley family controls 51% of the supervoting Class B stock.

S&P Opinion: Hold (★★★)	Recent Price • 47⅛	Yield • 1.4%
	52 Wk Range • 51¼-42⅞	12-Mo. P/E • 25.8

Earnings vs. Previous Year
▲=Up ▼=Down ▶=No Change

Quantitative Evaluations

Outlook
(1 Lowest—5 Highest)
• **1⁻**

Fair Value
• 41½

Risk
• **Low**

Earn./Div. Rank
• **A+**

Technical Eval.
• **Bullish** since 9/95

Rel. Strength Rank
(1 Lowest—99 Highest)
• **45**

Insider Activity
• **Neutral**

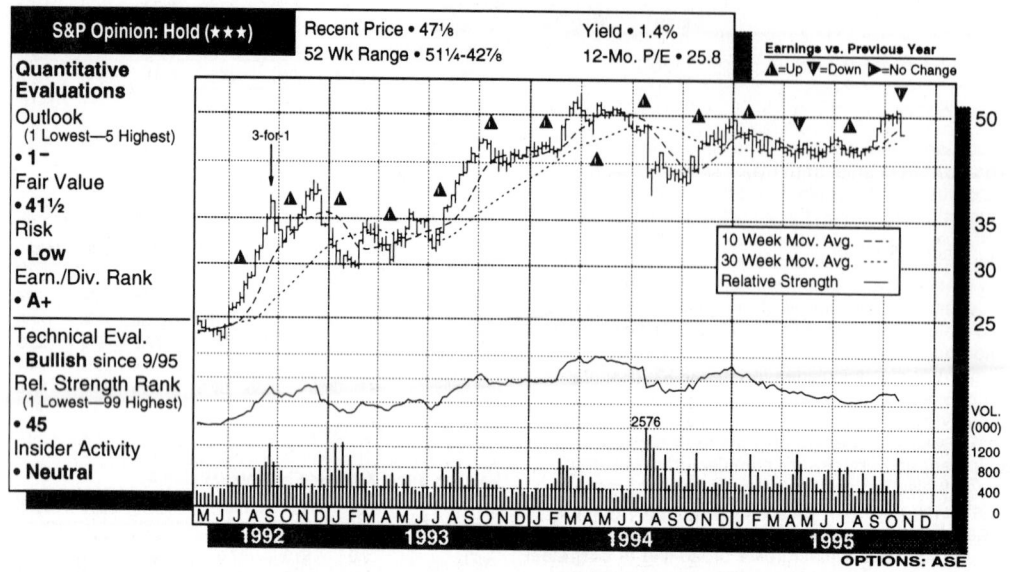

10 Week Mov. Avg. ---
30 Week Mov. Avg. ·····
Relative Strength —

OPTIONS: ASE

Overview - 31-OCT-95

Net sales are projected to rise about 10% annually through 1996, driven principally by unit volume growth of 5% to 10% in international markets, and about 1% to 2% in the U.S., and to a lesser degree, selective selling price increases. Operating margins should be sustained at their relatively high level, as manufacturing efficiencies help offset a mix shift toward less-profitable international sales, as well as continued heavy marketing spending associated with expansion abroad. Higher foreign tax credits may allow a slight easing in the effective tax rate in 1995. Overall, we expect EPS (excluding special items) to advance at a 10% to 15% annual rate through 1996.

Valuation - 31-OCT-95

Despite our bullish earnings outlook for the company through 1996, the stock appears to be fairly valued at current levels. In recent years, WWY shares have commanded a large premium relative to the P/E multiple of the S&P 500 Index (25% to 75%), reflecting WWY's steady, mid-teen EPS growth and low risk profile during this time period. The shares are currently in the middle of this range, and, given our expectations of a slight slowing of EPS gains, we thus foresee only average performance over the next six to 12 months. However, these high-quality shares remain suitable for long-term investors seeking above-average capital appreciation with relatively low risk.

Key Stock Statistics

S&P EPS Est. 1995	1.92	Tang. Bk. Value/Share	6.70
P/E on S&P Est. 1995	24.5	Beta	0.93
S&P EPS Est. 1996	2.15	Shareholders	24,100
Dividend Rate/Share	0.68	Market cap. (B)	$ 5.5
Shs. outstg. (M)	116.1	Inst. holdings	25%
Avg. daily vol. (M)	0.116	Insider holdings	NA

Value of $10,000 invested 5 years ago: $ 29,802

Fiscal Year Ending Dec. 31

	1995	% Change	1994	% Change	1993	% Change
Revenues (Million $)						
1Q	410.2	8%	378.6	14%	332.0	7%
2Q	470.6	11%	423.0	10%	386.2	14%
3Q	431.5	7%	404.1	12%	360.5	7%
4Q	—	—	390.9	12%	349.5	16%
Yr.	—	—	1,597	12%	1,429	11%
Income (Million $)						
1Q	55.28	-27%	75.94	79%	42.36	42%
2Q	63.90	10%	58.35	9%	53.56	20%
3Q	58.29	-5%	61.62	25%	49.11	19%
4Q	—	—	34.62	16%	29.86	17%
Yr.	—	—	230.5	32%	174.9	18%
Earnings Per Share ($)						
1Q	0.48	-26%	0.65	81%	0.36	13%
2Q	0.55	10%	0.50	9%	0.46	21%
3Q	0.50	-6%	0.53	26%	0.42	20%
4Q	E0.39	30%	0.30	15%	0.26	18%
Yr.	E1.92	-3%	1.98	32%	1.50	18%

Next earnings report expected: late January

Wrigley (Wm.) Jr.

Business Summary - 26-OCT-95

Wrigley is the world's largest manufacturer of chewing gum, accounting for about 50% of total chewing gum sales volume in the U.S. Principal products include Wrigley's Spearmint, Doublemint, Juicy Fruit, Big Red and Winterfresh. Other products include Freedent, Orbit, Hubba Bubba (bubble gum) and Extra. Chewing gum accounts for over 90% of total sales and earnings.

By geographical area, sales and profit contributions in 1994 were derived as follows:

	Sales	Profits
U.S.	55%	50%
Europe	33%	30%
Asia, Pacific & Other	12%	20%

Three associated domestic companies produce certain other products. Amurol Products Co. primarily manufactures novelty gum products and, to a lesser extent, hard candies and mints. L.A. Dreyfus Co. makes chewing gum base for Wrigley and other customers, as well as industrial coatings and adhesives. Northwestern Flavors, Inc. processes flavorings and refines mint oil for Wrigley and for food-related industries. The Wrico Packaging division produces a large portion of the company's domestic printed and other wrapping supplies. Major markets abroad include Australia, Canada, Germany, the Philippines, Taiwan and the U.K. WWY brands are sold in 121 countries and territories.

Important Developments

Oct. '95—WWY attributed its 9% year to year increase in net sales during 1995's first nine months primarily to international volume gains, currency translation gains due to a relatively weaker U.S. dollar, and selective selling price increases. Excluding 1994's non-recurring gain of $24.8 million ($0.21 per share) from the sale of property in Singapore, earnings during the first nine months of 1995 rose $6.3 million, or about 4%.
Jan. '95—WWY's 12% sales increase in 1994 reflected 9% greater unit volume growth of chewing gum, and higher selling prices. In North America, U.S. unit volumes of Wrigley brands rose 3%, led by new Winterfresh product contributions. Overseas, unit volume climbed 15%, on strong shipments in Eastern and Central Europe, the U.K. and Germany.

Capitalization

Long Term Debt: None (6/95).
Class B Common Stock: 24,853,659 shs. (no par). 10 votes per sh.; ea. conv. into one com.; restricted transferability.
The Wrigley family controls 51%.
Stockholders: 24,078.

Per Share Data ($)

(Year Ended Dec. 31)

	1994	1993	1992	1991	1990	1989
Tangible Bk. Val.	5.92	4.94	4.27	3.95	3.42	2.91
Cash Flow	2.33	1.80	1.52	1.34	1.22	1.11
Earnings	1.98	1.50	1.27	1.09	1.00	0.90
Dividends	0.90	0.75	0.62	0.55	0.49	0.45
Payout Ratio	45%	50%	49%	50%	49%	50%
Prices - High	53⅞	46⅛	39⅞	27	19¾	18
- Low	38⅛	29½	22⅛	16⅜	14⅝	11⅞
P/E Ratio - High	27	31	31	25	20	20
- Low	19	20	17	15	15	13

Income Statement Analysis (Million $)

	1994	%Chg	1993	%Chg	1992	%Chg	1991
Revs.	1,597	12%	1,429	11%	1,287	12%	1,149
Oper. Inc.	331	9%	303	22%	249	10%	227
Depr.	41.1	19%	34.6	16%	29.8	4%	28.7
Int. Exp.	149	NM	1.5	29%	1.2	-15%	1.4
Pretax Inc.	353	27%	279	20%	232	12%	208
Eff. Tax Rate	35%	—	37%	—	36%	—	38%
Net Inc.	231	32%	175	17%	149	16%	129

Balance Sheet & Other Fin. Data (Million $)

	1994	1993	1992	1991	1990	1989
Cash	230	190	182	145	114	109
Curr. Assets	623	502	449	403	357	308
Total Assets	979	815	711	625	564	499
Curr. Liab.	210	159	149	127	127	148
LT Debt	Nil	Nil	Nil	Nil	Nil	Nil
Common Eqty.	688	575	499	463	401	343
Total Cap.	704	598	512	471	410	351
Cap. Exp.	87.0	63.1	66.7	45.2	45.5	45.4
Cash Flow	272	209	178	157	144	131

Ratio Analysis

	1994	1993	1992	1991	1990	1989
Curr. Ratio	3.0	3.2	3.0	3.2	2.8	2.1
% LT Debt of Cap.	Nil	Nil	Nil	Nil	Nil	Nil
% Net Inc.of Revs.	14.4	12.2	11.5	11.2	10.6	10.7
% Ret. on Assets	25.7	23.0	22.3	21.7	22.1	22.7
% Ret. on Equity	36.5	32.6	31.0	29.8	31.6	32.8

Dividend Data —For many years quarterly dividends have been supplemented by a substantial year-end extra. Dividends have been paid since 1913. A dividend reinvestment plan is available. Payments on the common and Class B common in the past 12 months were:

Amt. of Div. $	Date Decl.	Ex-Div. Date	Stock of Record	Payment Date
0.140	Mar. 09	Apr. 10	Apr. 17	May. 01 '95
0.140	Jun. 14	Jul. 13	Jul. 17	Aug. 01 '95
0.170	Aug. 18	Oct. 11	Oct. 13	Nov. 01 '95
.37 Ext.	Oct. 24	Nov. 29	Dec. 01	Dec. 15 '95
0.170	Oct. 24	Jan. 10	Jan. 15	Feb. 01 '96

Data as orig. reptd.; bef. results of disc. opers. and/or spec. items. Per share data adj. for stk. divs. as of ex-div. date.
E-Estimated. NA-Not Available. NM-Not Meaningful. NR-Not Ranked.

Office—410 North Michigan Ave., Chicago, IL 60611. **Tel**—(312) 644-2121. **Pres & CEO**—W. Wrigley. **VP & Treas**—D. Petrovich. **Investor Contact**—Christopher J. Perille. **Dirs**—C. F. Allison III, L. P. Bell, R. P. Billingsley, R. D. Ewers, G. E. Gardner, P. S. Pritzker, R. K. Smucker, W. Wrigley, W. Wrigley, Jr. **Transfer Agent & Registrar**—First Chicago Trust Co. of New York, NYC. **Incorporated** in Delaware in 1927. **Empl**-7,000.
S&P Analyst: Kenneth A. Shea

Xerox Corp.

NYSE Symbol **XRX**
In S&P 500

08-NOV-95

Industry:
Office Equipment

Summary: Xerox serves the document processing market worldwide, offering a complete line of copiers, electronic printers, and other office and computer equipment.

S&P Opinion: Accumulate (★★★★)	Recent Price • 132	Yield • 2.3%
	52 Wk Range • 138½-90⅝	12-Mo. P/E • 16.3

Quantitative Evaluations

Outlook
(1 Lowest—5 Highest)
• **1+**

Fair Value
• **116⅞**

Risk
• **Low**

Earn./Div. Rank
• **B-**

Technical Eval.
• **Bullish** since 8/95

Rel. Strength Rank
(1 Lowest—99 Highest)
• **67**

Insider Activity
• **Neutral**

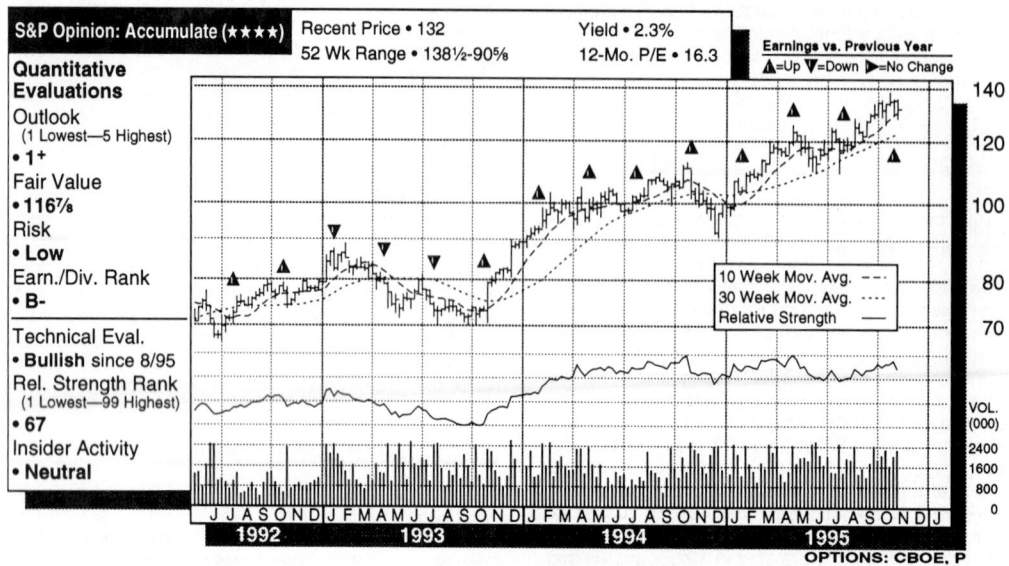

Earnings vs. Previous Year
▲=Up ▼=Down ▶=No Change

10 Week Mov. Avg. ----
30 Week Mov. Avg. ......
Relative Strength ——

OPTIONS: CBOE, P

Overview - 08-NOV-95

Sales growth in 1996 is expected to reach double-digit levels, spurred by improving worldwide economies, new product introductions, strong demand for digital products, color copiers and printers, and a growing facilities management business. Gross margins should continue to widen, although at a less rapid pace, reflecting further cost reductions and a more favorable product and geographical mix. Favorable currency translations helped revenue growth in the first nine months of 1995 and should continue to be additive in future quarters, reflecting the continued weakness of the dollar against European currencies. Additional personnel reductions should contribute to strong earnings comparisons.

Valuation - 08-NOV-95

The shares are currently below the record high established in October 1995, but the company's positive fundamentals remain intact. XRX continues to pursue productivity initiatives, mainly through staff cuts, and it is enjoying good success in high growth markets like digital publishing and color copying and printing. Continuing efforts to disengage from the financial services businesses are providing a sharper focus on core document processing operations and should strengthen the balance sheet as these units are sold. The net result should be continued EPS gains, the possibility of shareholder-oriented actions such as a dividend hike, and the potential for above-average share appreciation.

Key Stock Statistics

S&P EPS Est. 1995	8.80	Tang. Bk. Value/Share	36.73
P/E on S&P Est. 1995	15.0	Beta	1.35
S&P EPS Est. 1996	10.45	Shareholders	71,200
Dividend Rate/Share	3.00	Market cap. (B)	$ 13.8
Shs. outstg. (M)	107.5	Inst. holdings	84%
Avg. daily vol. (M)	0.395	Insider holdings	NA

Value of $10,000 invested 5 years ago: $ 29,501

Fiscal Year Ending Dec. 31

	1995	% Change	1994	% Change	1993	% Change
Revenues (Million $)						
1Q	3,770	15%	3,271	1%	3,230	-24%
2Q	4,054	13%	3,584	4%	3,430	-24%
3Q	4,027	11%	3,636	4%	3,490	-30%
4Q	—	—	4,597	13%	4,080	-20%
Yr.	—	—	15,088	6%	14,230	-24%
Income (Million $)						
1Q	147.0	12%	131.0	17%	112.0	NM
2Q	238.0	43%	167.0	64%	102.0	-18%
3Q	236.0	28%	185.0	7%	173.0	43%
4Q	—	—	311.0	NM	-576.0	NM
Yr.	—	—	794.0	NM	-189.0	NM
Earnings Per Share ($)						
1Q	1.23	17%	1.05	6%	0.99	-3%
2Q	2.07	58%	1.31	52%	0.86	-23%
3Q	2.03	26%	1.61	7%	1.50	40%
4Q	E3.47	26%	2.76	NM	-5.62	NM
Yr.	E8.80	31%	6.73	NM	-2.46	NM

Next earnings report expected: mid February

Xerox Corp.

Business Summary - 08-NOV-95

Xerox is a leading manufacturer of copiers and a range of other document processing products. Efforts to disengage from financial services businesses are continuing. Foreign operations provided 48% of document processing revenue in 1994. Revenues by product category in recent years were:

	1994	1993
Black & white copiers	62%	63%
Digital products	22%	20%
Other products	10%	11%
Paper	5%	5%

The company sells a broad range of black & white and color copiers and duplicators. Xerox digital products include the DocuTech digital publishing system, which scans hard copy and converts it to digital documents directly from networked personal computers. XRX also offers a complete line of electronic laser printers. Other products include ink-jet and electrostatic printers, facsimile products, scanners; PC and workstation software; and integrated systems solutions. XRX's facilities management business provides printing, publishing, and duplicating and related services.

In February 1995, the company increased its stake in England-based Rank Xerox to 80% from 67%. Rank Xerox makes and markets products and supplies in more than 80 countries in Europe, Asia and Africa, and owns a 50% interest in Fuji Xerox.

Xerox Credit Corp., the sole financial services business XRX will retain, provides equipment financing. Insurance includes Talegen Holdings (formerly Crum and Forster), Ridge Reinsurance Ltd. and Xerox Financial Services, Inc. In July 1995, XRX completed the sale of Viking Insurance Holdings, Inc. to Guaranty National Corp. for about $103 million in cash. In June 1995, XRX sold its Financial Services Life Insurance Co. to General American Life Insurance Co. In April 1995, the company sold Constitution Re Corp. to Exor America Inc. for $421 million.

Employment has declined by 11,400 since year-end 1993, reflecting a restructuring program announced in December 1993. XRX achieved pretax cost reductions of $350 million in 1994, expects to achieve $700 million in 1995, and more thereafter.

Important Developments

Nov. '95—XRX introduced two new printer series, the Xerox DocuPrint Continuous Feed Series family and the Xerox DocuPrint IPS Series, which, according to International Data Corp., opens an incremental market opportunity for XRX of about $1 billion.

Capitalization

Long Term Debt: $8,837,000,000 (9/95).
Minority Interest: $748,000,000.
Preferred Stock: $767,000,000.

Per Share Data ($)

(Year Ended Dec. 31)

	1994	1993	1992	1991	1990	1989
Tangible Bk. Val.	36.73	35.35	36.27	36.93	35.44	33.95
Cash Flow	12.93	3.76	3.66	11.20	12.84	14.25
Earnings	6.73	-2.46	-3.32	3.91	5.51	6.56
Dividends	3.00	3.00	3.00	3.00	3.00	3.00
Payout Ratio	45%	NM	NM	76%	53%	43%
Prices - High	112¾	90	82¼	69¾	58⅞	69
- Low	87¾	69⅞	66½	35¼	29	54⅜
P/E Ratio - High	17	NM	NM	18	11	11
- Low	13	NM	NM	9	5	8

Income Statement Analysis (Million $)

	1994	%Chg	1993	%Chg	1992	%Chg	1991
Revs.	16,831	4%	16,193	-5%	17,040	2%	16,745
Oper. Inc.	1,961	37%	1,434	180%	512	-68%	1,615
Depr.	681	4%	655	-11%	739	6%	695
Int. Exp.	714	-5%	755	-12%	862	5%	821
Pretax Inc.	1,558	NM	-226	NM	171	-82%	963
Eff. Tax Rate	35%	—	NM	—	162%	—	36%
Net Inc.	794	NM	-188	NM	-255	NM	454

Balance Sheet & Other Fin. Data (Million $)

	1994	1993	1992	1991	1990	1989
Cash	1,058	1,796	657	797	1,407	1,219
Curr. Assets	NA	NA	NA	NA	NA	NA
Total Assets	38,585	38,750	34,051	31,658	31,495	30,088
Curr. Liab.	NA	NA	NA	NA	NA	NA
LT Debt	7,780	7,386	8,105	6,247	7,108	7,511
Common Eqty.	4,177	3,972	3,875	5,140	5,051	5,035
Total Cap.	13,214	12,627	13,256	12,870	13,595	13,807
Cap. Exp.	389	470	582	498	444	436
Cash Flow	1,402	381	398	1,063	1,210	1,419

Ratio Analysis

	1994	1993	1992	1991	1990	1989
Curr. Ratio	NA	NA	NA	NA	NA	NA
% LT Debt of Cap.	58.9	59.5	61.1	48.5	52.3	54.4
% Net Inc.of Revs.	4.7	NM	NM	2.7	3.6	4.2
% Ret. on Assets	2.0	NM	NM	1.4	2.0	2.6
% Ret. on Equity	17.5	NM	NM	7.2	10.3	13.3

Dividend Data

—Dividends have been paid since 1930. A dividend reinvestment plan is available.

Amt. of Div. $	Date Decl.	Ex-Div. Date	Stock of Record	Payment Date
0.750	Oct. 10	Nov. 28	Dec. 02	Jan. 01 '95
0.750	Feb. 06	Feb. 27	Mar. 03	Apr. 01 '95
0.750	May. 18	May. 26	Jun. 02	Jul. 01 '95
0.750	Jul. 10	Aug. 30	Sep. 01	Oct. 01 '95
0.750	Oct. 09	Nov. 29	Dec. 01	Jan. 01 '96

Data as orig. reptd.; bef. results of disc. opers. and/or spec. items. Per share data adj. for stk. divs. as of ex-div. date.
E-Estimated. NA-Not Available. NM-Not Meaningful. NR-Not Ranked.

Office—800 Long Ridge Rd. (P.O. Box 1600), Stamford, CT 06904-1600. **Tel**—(203) 968-3000. **Chrmn & CEO**—P. A. Allaire. **EVP & CFO**—B. D. Romeril. **VP, Secy & Treas**—E. M. Filter. **Investor Contacts**—Clark K. Robson, Charles K. Wessendorf. **Dirs**—P. A. Allaire, R. A. Beck, B. R. Inman, V. E. Jordan, Jr., Y. Kobayashi, H. Kopper, R. S. Larsen, J. D. Macomber, G. J. Mitchell, N. J. Nicholas, Jr., J. E. Pepper, M. R. Seger, T. C. Theobald. **Transfer Agent and Registrar**—The First National Bank of Boston. **Incorporated** in New York in 1906. **Empl**-85,600. **S&P Analyst:** Ronald J. Gross

Yellow Corp.

NASDAQ Symbol **YELL**

In S&P 500

31-JUL-95

Industry: Trucking

Summary: This firm operates the nation's largest long-haul less-than-truckload (LTL) motor carrier and, through acquisitions, has recently established a presence in the regional LTL market.

S&P Opinion: Hold (★★★)	Recent Price • 15⅝	Yield • Nil
	52 Wk Range • 24⅜-15⅜	12-Mo. P/E • 15.3

Quantitative Evaluations

Outlook (1 Lowest—5 Highest)
• **4⁻**

Fair Value
• **16**

Risk
• **Average**

Earn./Div. Rank
• **B-**

Technical Eval.
• **Bullish** since 4/95

Rel. Strength Rank (1 Lowest—99 Highest)
• **3**

Insider Activity
• **NA**

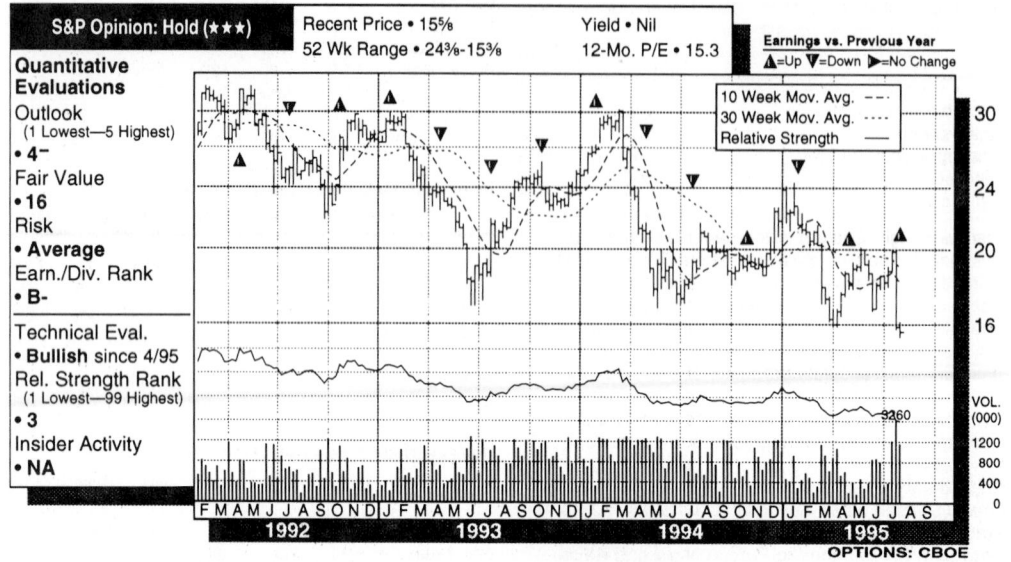

Earnings vs. Previous Year
▲=Up ▼=Down ▶=No Change

10 Week Mov. Avg. – – –
30 Week Mov. Avg. ····
Relative Strength ——

OPTIONS: CBOE

Overview - 31-JUL-95

YELL should move back into the black in 1995 as comparisons benefit from the absence of strike-related losses incurred at Yellow Freight System in 1994 and severe winter weather. Limiting YELL's performance will be severe rate discounting pressure as truckers try to recapture freight lost during last year's strike. Increased used of part-time dock workers and the restructuring of its linehaul operations to permit greater shipment of freight via rail piggyback service will be offset by higher wages. While the restructuring of Preston's service has attracted shippers with shorter transit times, pressure on rates and higher labor costs will limit profitability. Saia should post higher profits, reflecting the consolidation of Smalley and system expansion. Interest costs will be higher.

Valuation - 31-JUL-95

The mid-year rebound in the shares of this leading trucker proved short-lived. While other motor carriers have continued to rebound despite dismal second quarter results, YELL plunged to new lows in July after suspending its generous $0.235 quarterly dividend payment. We think YELL made the right decision eliminating its dividend since it bolsters its chances be a survivor in the treacherous less-than-truckload freight market. While YELL paints a gloomy picture for 1995's second half, hinting at losses, we believe the economy is on the mend and that rate discounting pressure will subside. With the bad news out, YELL should be an average market performer.

Key Stock Statistics

S&P EPS Est. 1995	0.50	Tang. Bk. Value/Share	16.40
P/E on S&P Est. 1995	31.3	Beta	1.29
S&P EPS Est. 1996	1.30	Shareholders	3,400
Dividend Rate/Share	Nil	Market cap. (B)	$0.439
Shs. outstg. (M)	28.1	Inst. holdings	80%
Avg. daily vol. (M)	0.303	Insider holdings	NA

Value of $10,000 invested 5 years ago: $ 7,164

Fiscal Year Ending Dec. 31

	1995	% Change	1994	% Change	1993	% Change
Revenues (Million $)						
1Q	765.0	2%	748.2	24%	602.2	6%
2Q	773.8	31%	592.2	-19%	732.9	29%
3Q	—	—	769.3	NM	761.7	33%
4Q	—	—	757.9	NM	759.7	36%
Yr.	—	—	2,867	NM	2,857	26%
Income (Million $)						
1Q	3.20	NM	-6.38	NM	-1.75	NM
2Q	1.04	NM	-21.88	NM	-1.89	NM
3Q	—	—	13.20	26%	10.47	-9%
4Q	—	—	11.21	-6%	11.97	85%
Yr.	—	—	-3.85	NM	18.80	-54%
Earnings Per Share ($)						
1Q	0.11	NM	-0.23	NM	-0.06	NM
2Q	0.04	NM	-0.78	NM	-0.07	NM
3Q	E0.10	—	0.47	27%	0.37	-10%
4Q	E0.25	—	0.40	-7%	0.43	87%
Yr.	E0.50	—	-0.14	NM	0.67	-54%

Next earnings report expected: mid October

Yellow Corp.

Business Summary - 31-JUL-95

Yellow Corp. is a holding company for a family of motor carriers that offer long-haul and regional less-than-truckload (LTL) freight services and logistics services. Contributions to revenues (in millions) in recent years:

	1994	1993
Yellow Freight System	$2,221	$2,358
Preston Trucking	417	338
Saia Motor Freight	138	102
Smalley Transportation	40	32
CSI/Reeves	36	25
Logistics/other	15	2

Yellow Freight System is the nation's largest LTL freight motor carrier. Yellow provides direct service throughout the 50 states, Puerto Rico, Canada and Mexico. Shipments moving between Europe and the U.S. are handled through an arrangement with Royal Frans Maas Group.

Preston Trucking provides regional LTL freight service in the Northeast and Upper Midwest. Saia Motor Freight Line, operating through a network of 28 terminals, specializes in overnight and second-day delivery of LTL freight in nine southeastern states. Service to North and South Carolina is being initiated in 1995. Smalley Transportation, (consolidated into Saia on January 1, 1995) provides LTL service in Florida and Georgia. WestEx (acquired in November 1994) provides overnight freight service in Arizona, New Mexico and parts of Texas and Nevada. Service to California was initiated in 1995.

Yellow Logistics offers a full range of logistics services including warehousing, transportation, information systems, distribution and packaging. In July 1995, YELL agreed to sell CSI/Reeves, Inc., a provider of transportation and specialized services for the carpet industry, to U.S. Xpress for an undisclosed sum.

In October 1994, Yellow Freight System restructured its linehaul operations to allow for a substantial increase in freight shipped using rail intermodal service. This change was made possible under the new Teamsters' contract signed in June.

Important Developments

Jul. '95—Citing the need to maintain a strong balance sheet and conserve capital for needed investments in technology and service enhancements, directors suspended YELL's $0.235 quarterly dividend payment.
Apr. '95—YELL's WestEx unit initiated service into California with the opening of a freight terminal in the Los Angeles area. YELL said WestEx will be able to provide full coverage to California by the end of 1995's third quarter.

Capitalization

Long Term Debt: $278,299,000 (3/95).

Per Share Data ($) (Year Ended Dec. 31)

	1994	1993	1992	1991	1990	1989
Tangible Bk. Val.	16.40	17.31	17.28	16.94	16.69	15.24
Cash Flow	4.63	5.38	5.68	5.39	6.83	4.93
Earnings	-0.14	0.67	1.46	0.95	2.31	0.65
Dividends	0.94	0.94	0.94	0.94	0.82	0.73
Payout Ratio	NM	140%	64%	99%	35%	113%
Prices - High	30¼	29⅞	32⅜	33½	31¼	32⅞
- Low	16¾	16⅞	21¾	23¾	18¾	23⅞
P/E Ratio - High	NM	45	22	35	14	51
- Low	NM	25	15	25	8	37

Income Statement Analysis (Million $)

	1994	%Chg	1993	%Chg	1992	%Chg	1991
Revs.	2,867	NM	2,857	26%	2,263	-3%	2,344
Oper. Inc.	145	-29%	204	1%	201	10%	182
Depr.	134	2%	132	12%	118	-6%	125
Int. Exp.	18.4	4%	17.7	45%	12.2	-14%	14.2
Pretax Inc.	-3.0	NM	35.0	-46%	65.0	63%	40.0
Eff. Tax Rate	NM	—	47%	—	37%	—	34%
Net Inc.	-3.8	NM	18.8	-54%	41.0	54%	26.7

Balance Sheet & Other Fin. Data (Million $)

	1994	1993	1992	1991	1990	1989
Cash	24.9	20.7	32.3	12.7	8.3	4.4
Curr. Assets	403	379	274	270	270	266
Total Assets	1,307	1,266	1,061	1,098	1,116	1,082
Curr. Liab.	376	342	255	288	290	269
LT Debt	240	214	123	146	164	187
Common Eqty.	461	486	485	476	469	439
Total Cap.	755	760	681	705	723	714
Cap. Exp.	183	77.0	86.0	110	169	193
Cash Flow	0.3	151	159	151	193	142

Ratio Analysis

	1994	1993	1992	1991	1990	1989
Curr. Ratio	1.1	1.1	1.1	0.9	0.9	1.0
% LT Debt of Cap.	31.8	28.2	18.1	20.7	22.6	26.1
% Net Inc.of Revs.	NM	0.7	1.8	1.1	2.8	0.8
% Ret. on Assets	NM	1.6	3.8	2.4	6.0	1.8
% Ret. on Equity	NM	3.9	8.5	5.6	14.6	4.4

Dividend Data (Cash dividends were suspended in July 1995 after being paid since 1958. A "poison pill" stock purchase right was distributed in 1986.)

Amt. of Div. $	Date Decl.	Ex-Div. Date	Stock of Record	Payment Date
0.235	Jul. 21	Jul. 26	Aug. 01	Aug. 15 '94
0.235	Oct. 20	Oct. 25	Oct. 31	Nov. 14 '94
0.235	Jan. 31	Feb. 07	Feb. 13	Feb. 27 '95
0.235	Apr. 19	Apr. 25	May. 01	May. 15 '95

Data as orig. reptd.; bef. results of disc. opers. and/or spec. items. Per share data adj. for stk. divs. as of ex-div. date. E-Estimated. NA-Not Available. NM-Not Meaningful. NR-Not Ranked.

Office—10777 Barkley Ave., Overland Park, KS 66207. **Tel**—(913) 967-4300. **Chrmn**—G. E. Powell Jr. **Pres & CEO**—G. E. Powell III. **SVP-Secy**—W. F. Martin Jr. **SVP-CFO**—H. A. Trucksess III. **VP-Treas & Investor Contact**—Phillip A. Spangler. **Dirs**—K. E. Agthe, M. R. Armstrong, H. M. Dean, D. H. Hughes, R. T. LeMay, J. C. McKelvey, G. E. Powell Jr., G. E. Powell III, W. L. Trubeck. **Transfer Agent & Registrar**—Mellon Securities Trust Co., Pittsburgh. **Incorporated** in Indiana in 1950; reincorporated in Delaware in 1983. **Empl-33,400. S&P Analyst:** Stephen R. Klein

Zenith Electronics

NYSE Symbol **ZE**
In S&P 500

09-AUG-95 Industry:
Electronics/Electric

Summary: This major producer of television sets and VCRs also makes picture tubes, cable products and other electronic components.

S&P Opinion: Avoid (★★)

Recent Price • 8⅝	Yield • Nil
52 Wk Range • 14⅛-6⅞	12-Mo. P/E • NM

Earnings vs. Previous Year
▲=Up ▼=Down ▶=No Change

Quantitative Evaluations

Outlook
(1 Lowest—5 Highest)
• **NA**

Fair Value
• **NA**

Risk
• **Average**

Earn./Div. Rank
• **C**

Technical Eval.
• **Bullish** since 3/95

Rel. Strength Rank
(1 Lowest—99 Highest)
• **62**

Insider Activity
• **NA**

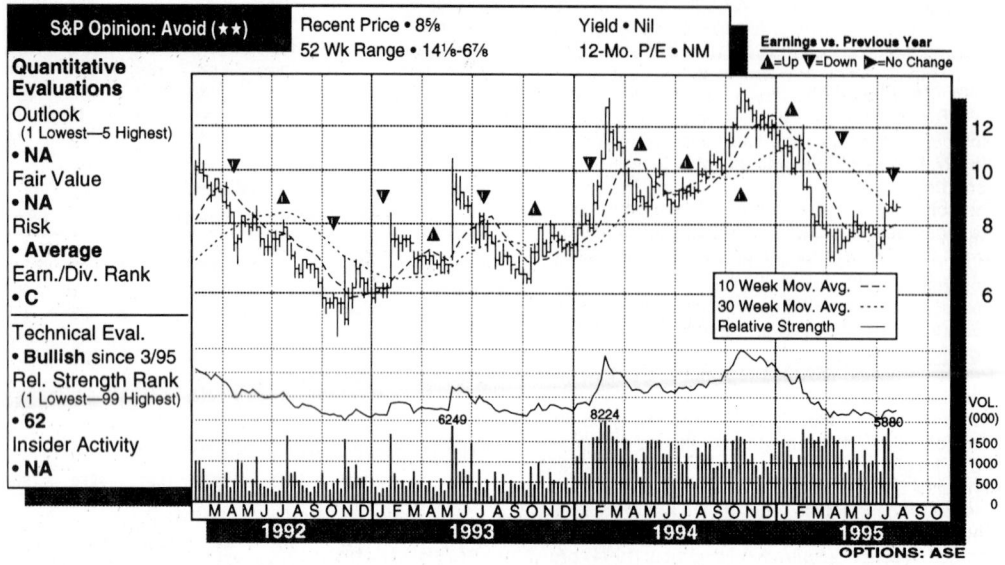

10 Week Mov. Avg. - - -
30 Week Mov. Avg. ....
Relative Strength ——

OPTIONS: ASE

Overview - 09-AUG-95

Sales should grow approximately 15% in 1996. Television sales should benefit from stronger industry conditions and a closer working relationship with LG Electronics, which is acquiring a majority position in the company. Network systems should experience sharply higher sales due to pent-up demand for cable decoder boxes and wider acceptance of analog systems. The initial shipment of digital video disc systems should provide incremental revenues. International sales should rise significantly as the company begins to globalize operations. Profitability should be restored due to continuing aggressive cost reductions and the absence of $18 million in restructuring charges. Interest expense should be lower due to the recent investment by LG Electronics.

Valuation - 07-AUG-95

We believe that ZE's shares will underperform the market over the near-term due to continuing losses caused by weak industry conditions. However, longer-term, television sales have proven resilient in the past and should recover and network systems sales should be strong in 1996. In addition, the acquisition of a majority interest by LG Electronics (Goldstar), the introduction of digital video disc systems in early 1996 and the arrival of High Definition Television in early 1997 bode well. Lastly, a worldwide shortage of picture tube capacity and the company's position as a low cost producer should also be positives, as should the impact of continuing cost reduction efforts.

Key Stock Statistics

S&P EPS Est. 1995	-1.65	Tang. Bk. Value/Share	4.53
P/E on S&P Est. 1995	NM	Beta	1.09
S&P EPS Est. 1996	0.50	Shareholders	16,500
Dividend Rate/Share	Nil	Market cap. (B)	$0.405
Shs. outstg. (M)	47.0	Inst. holdings	45%
Avg. daily vol. (M)	0.494	Insider holdings	NA

Value of $10,000 invested 5 years ago: $ 6,764

Fiscal Year Ending Dec. 31

	1995	% Change	1994	% Change	1993	% Change
Revenues (Million $)						
1Q	262.1	-12%	297.1	2%	291.0	10%
2Q	284.6	-5%	299.0	9%	274.7	-2%
3Q	—	—	419.4	39%	301.8	-4%
4Q	—	—	453.5	26%	361.2	-6%
Yr.	—	—	1,469	20%	1,228	-1%
Income (Million $)						
1Q	-24.30	NM	-11.90	NM	-21.80	-24%
2Q	-45.30	NM	-8.40	NM	-24.70	63%
3Q	—	—	9.40	NM	-14.50	-65%
4Q	—	—	-3.30	NM	-36.00	77%
Yr.	—	—	-14.20	NM	-97.00	NM
Earnings Per Share ($)						
1Q	-0.53	NM	-0.32	NM	-0.72	NM
2Q	-0.97	NM	-0.20	NM	-0.79	NM
3Q	E-0.25	—	0.21	NM	-0.44	NM
4Q	E0.10	—	-0.07	NM	-1.04	NM
Yr.	E-1.65	—	-0.34	NM	-3.01	NM

Next earnings report expected: mid October

Zenith Electronics

Business Summary - 09-AUG-95

Zenith Electronics manufactures consumer electronic products and components.

The company designs, develops and manufactures video products, including color television sets and other consumer products, along with parts and accessories for such products. These products, as well as purchased video cassette recorders, are sold principally to retail dealers and wholesale distributors.

ZE's video products business also includes color picture tubes that are produced for and sold to other manufacturers; cable and subscription television products which are sold primarily to cable television operators.

The company, together with AT&T and other partners, has been selected by the U.S. government to provide the standard for a high definition television (HDTV) broadcast system for the U.S.

In April 1994, ZE sold its switch mode power supply business. During 1993, it sold its monochrome video monitor business.

The company's major competitors are foreign-owned global giants, generally with greater worldwide television volume and overall resources. In an effort to increase market share or achieve higher production volumes, ZE's competitiors have aggressively lowered their selling prices in the past several years.

Foreign sales accounted for 7.1% of revenues and produced a pretax loss of $6.1 million in 1994.

Important Developments

Aug. '95—The company announced that in conjunction with Barley Participaoes LTDA it was establishing a new color television assembly operation in Brazil as a means to enter the Brazilian market.

Jul. '95—LG Electronics, Inc., a South Korean concern, announced that it will purchase for $10 per share 16.5 million newly issued shares of ZE common stock and 18.619 million shares from ZE shareholders in a tender offer. Together with the 1.45 million ZE shares LG Electronics currently holds, upon the successful completion of these transactions LG Electronics will own 57.7% of the outstanding common stock of ZE. The tender offer commenced on July 24, 1995, and is scheduled to expire on September 19, 1995. The transaction is subject to the completion of a successful tender offer, ZE shareholder approval, certain governmental and regulatory approvals and the satisfaction of customary closing conditions.

Capitalization

Long Term Debt: $215,500,000 (7/95), incl. $67 million of 8.5% debs. due 2000, conv. into com. at $9.76 a sh., and $115 million of 6.25% debs. due 2011, conv. into com. at $31.25 a sh.

Per Share Data ($)

(Year Ended Dec. 31)

	1994	1993	1992	1991	1990	1989
Tangible Bk. Val.	5.00	4.25	6.94	10.60	12.32	14.90
Cash Flow	0.35	-1.91	-2.31	-0.48	-0.50	0.88
Earnings	-0.34	-3.01	-3.59	-1.79	-1.95	-0.64
Dividends	Nil	Nil	Nil	Nil	Nil	Nil
Payout Ratio	Nil	Nil	Nil	Nil	Nil	Nil
Prices - High	14⅛	10½	11⅛	9⅜	13⅝	21½
- Low	7	5¾	5	5⅛	4	11½
P/E Ratio - High	NM	NM	NM	NM	NM	NM
- Low	NM	NM	NM	NM	NM	NM

Income Statement Analysis (Million $)

	1994	%Chg	1993	%Chg	1992	%Chg	1991
Revs.	1,469	20%	1,228	-1%	1,244	-6%	1,322
Oper. Inc.	-14.9	NM	-41.0	NM	-48.0	NM	-4.0
Depr.	28.8	-19%	35.4	-6%	37.7	NM	37.9
Int. Exp.	15.9	3%	15.5	13%	13.7	10%	12.4
Pretax Inc.	-15.0	NM	-97.0	NM	-121	NM	-51.0
Eff. Tax Rate	NM	—	NM	—	NM	—	NM
Net Inc.	-14.0	NM	-97.0	NM	-105	NM	-52.0

Balance Sheet & Other Fin. Data (Million $)

	1994	1993	1992	1991	1990	1989
Cash	9.0	21.0	6.0	36.0	56.0	176
Curr. Assets	471	396	390	483	511	696
Total Assets	654	559	579	687	724	918
Curr. Liab.	243	237	219	229	231	369
LT Debt	182	170	150	150	151	151
Common Eqty.	228	152	210	309	342	398
Total Cap.	410	322	360	458	493	549
Cap. Exp.	58.9	26.1	32.6	36.7	32.4	34.1
Cash Flow	14.6	-61.6	-68.2	-13.7	-13.5	23.5

Ratio Analysis

	1994	1993	1992	1991	1990	1989
Curr. Ratio	1.9	1.7	1.8	2.1	2.2	1.9
% LT Debt of Cap.	44.4	52.7	41.6	32.6	30.7	27.5
% Net Inc.of Revs.	NM	NM	NM	NM	NM	NM
% Ret. on Assets	NM	NM	NM	NM	NM	NM
% Ret. on Equity	NM	NM	NM	NM	NM	NM

Dividend Data (Dividends were omitted in 1982 after having been paid since 1939. A "poison pill" stock purchase rights plan was adopted in 1986.)

Data as orig. reptd.; bef. results of disc. opers. and/or spec. items. Per share data adj. for stk. divs. as of ex-div. date. E-Estimated. NA-Not Available. NM-Not Meaningful. NR-Not Ranked.

Office—1000 Milwaukee Ave., Glenview, IL 60025. **Tel**—(708) 391-7000. **Chrmn & CEO**—J. K. Pearlman. **Pres**—A. F. Moschner. **SVP-Fin & CFO**—K. B. Benson. **Secy**—D. S. Levin. **VP, Treas & Investor Contact**—W. C. McNitt III. **Dirs**—H. G. Beckner, T. K. Brooker, D. H. Cohen, I. S. Gordon, C. Marshall, G. M. McCarthy, A. McNally IV, A. F. Moschner, J. K. Pearlman, P. S. Willmott. **Transfer Agent & Registrar**—Bank of New York, NYC. **Incorporated** in Delaware in 1958. **Empl**- 22,500. **S&P Analyst:** Paul H. Valentine, CFA

Zurn Industries

NYSE Symbol **ZRN**
In S&P 500

24-SEP-95

Industry:
Machinery

Summary: This company is a leading provider of products and services for alternate energy and power plants, and water quality control systems. ZRN also makes Lynx golf equipment.

Quantitative Evaluations

Outlook
(1 Lowest—5 Highest)
- **4+**

Fair Value
- **26¾**

Risk
- **Low**

Earn./Div. Rank
- **B+**

Technical Eval.
- **Bearish** since 4/95

Rel. Strength Rank
(1 Lowest—99 Highest)
- **86**

Insider Activity
- **Favorable**

Recent Price • 25⅛
52 Wk Range • 26-16¾

Yield • 1.6%
12-Mo. P/E • 25.6

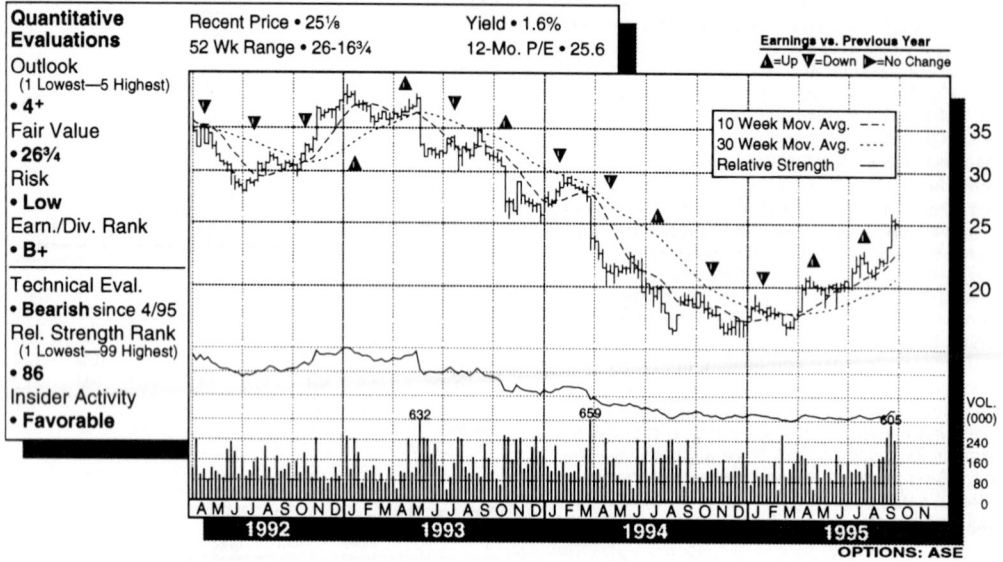

Business Profile - 22-SEP-95

Zurn is now focusing on international markets for its power systems segment; 1994-5 segment revenues amounted to only one-third of the 1993-4 total, reflecting a depressed domestic independent power market. Profitability has been improving at the water control segment, aided by sales of plumbing products, for which market share is growing. Backlog has soared at Lynx Golf since the January 1995 introduction of the new Black Cat irons.

Operational Review - 22-SEP-95

Revenues in 1995-6's first three months rose 7.0%, mostly due to sharp sales increases from a new line of irons in the Lynx Golf segment, which more than offset declines in Water Control sales from project start-up delays. Operating income soared 107%, reflecting higher plumbing prices in the Water Control segment, and improved economies of scale from volume increases in the Lynx Golf unit. After higher other expenses, net income surged 140%, to $4,649,000, from $1,944,000.

Stock Performance - 22-SEP-95

In the past 30 trading days, ZRN's shares have increased 20%, compared to a 5% rise in the S&P 500. Average trading volume for the past five days was 60,180 shares, compared with the 40-day moving average of 54,133 shares.

Key Stock Statistics

Dividend Rate/Share	0.40	Shareholders	5,300
Shs. outstg. (M)	12.3	Market cap. (B)	$0.310
Avg. daily vol. (M)	0.077	Inst. holdings	74%
Tang. Bk. Value/Share	18.07	Insider holdings	NA
Beta	0.98		

Value of $10,000 invested 5 years ago: $ 7,392

Fiscal Year Ending Mar. 31

	1996	% Change	1995	% Change	1994	% Change
Revenues (Million $)						
1Q	122.3	7%	114.4	-60%	288.8	102%
2Q	—	—	112.2	-48%	215.5	21%
3Q	—	—	114.5	-20%	142.7	-25%
4Q	—	—	122.1	-12%	138.7	-12%
Yr.	—	—	463.2	-41%	785.7	17%
Income (Million $)						
1Q	4.65	140%	1.94	NM	-16.63	NM
2Q	—	—	2.47	-64%	6.83	10%
3Q	—	—	1.36	-72%	4.92	-28%
4Q	—	—	3.55	NM	-9.00	NM
Yr.	—	—	9.32	NM	-13.88	NM
Earnings Per Share ($)						
1Q	0.38	138%	0.16	NM	-1.34	NM
2Q	—	—	0.20	-64%	0.55	10%
3Q	—	—	0.11	-73%	0.40	-31%
4Q	—	—	0.29	NM	-0.73	NM
Yr.	—	—	0.76	NM	-1.12	NM

Next earnings report expected: late October

Zurn Industries

Business Summary - 22-SEP-95

Zurn Industries primarily makes products and provides services for power plants and water quality control systems. Segment contributions in 1994-5 (profits in million $):

	Sales	Profits
Power systems	35%	-$4.8
Water control	50%	28.4
Lynx Golf	7%	-12.4
Other technologies	8%	3.6

Power systems designs, constructs and operates alternate energy and combined-cycle power plants, builds steam generators and waste heat energy recovery and incineration systems, and produces equipment and fans to control emissions of solid particulate and gaseous pollutants. Major contracts are generally with project financed entities.

The water control group manufactures and builds a wide variety of systems and products used in nonresidential construction and by government agencies to control and treat water and wastewater. Products and services include engineering and construction of water resource and water quality control systems, engineered concrete products, water treatment systems and equipment, wastewater controls and automatic fire sprinkler systems.

Lynx Golf makes and distributes premium golf clubs and accessories, including Boom Boom metal woods and Parallax irons.

The other technologies area includes both a standard line and highly engineered couplings, clutches and brakes for a variety of power transmission applications in the metals, petrochemical, mining and paper industries.

Important Developments

Aug. '95—Zurn said it appealed an adverse decision regarding a power plant construction contract. If all issues are lost, ZRN is potentially liable for up to an additional $22.1 million, an amount which, to date, has not been reserved.

Jun. '95—Zurn reduced its quarterly dividend 55%, from $0.22 a share, to $0.10. ZRN said flexibility is needed to make large investments in U.S. and overseas power plant projects, as well as to expand product development and production capabilities in the plumbing products unit of ZRN's Water Control segment.

Capitalization

Long Term Debt: $9,089,000 (6/95).

Per Share Data ($) (Year Ended Mar. 31)

	1995	1994	1993	1992	1991	1990
Tangible Bk. Val.	17.74	17.86	20.04	18.79	20.13	18.47
Cash Flow	1.54	-0.26	3.05	1.83	3.44	3.21
Earnings	0.76	-1.12	2.20	0.91	2.46	2.28
Dividends	1.10	0.88	0.88	0.88	0.82	0.72
Payout Ratio	145%	NM	40%	96%	33%	32%
Cal. Yrs.	1994	1993	1992	1991	1990	1989
Prices - High	29¾	40¾	39⅜	41⅜	51⅛	44¼
- Low	16¾	25⅛	27¾	29½	29⅝	25¾
P/E Ratio - High	39	NM	18	45	21	19
- Low	22	NM	13	32	12	11

Income Statement Analysis (Million $)

	1995	%Chg	1994	%Chg	1993	%Chg	1992
Revs.	463	-41%	786	18%	665	11%	597
Oper. Inc.	18.2	-50%	36.6	-15%	43.3	17%	37.0
Depr.	9.7	-9%	10.7	NM	10.6	-8%	11.5
Int. Exp.	4.1	23%	3.3	38%	2.4	-16%	2.9
Pretax Inc.	13.0	NM	-23.5	NM	40.8	127%	18.0
Eff. Tax Rate	30%	—	NM	—	33%	—	36%
Net Inc.	9.3	NM	-13.9	NM	27.5	139%	11.5

Balance Sheet & Other Fin. Data (Million $)

	1995	1994	1993	1992	1991	1990
Cash	54.8	65.4	90.6	69.7	41.6	39.0
Curr. Assets	298	332	366	321	314	281
Total Assets	415	448	490	441	437	395
Curr. Liab.	143	171	182	149	154	136
LT Debt	10.0	11.0	18.7	15.8	11.0	12.7
Common Eqty.	219	222	249	237	251	228
Total Cap.	229	233	268	253	272	249
Cap. Exp.	8.9	9.2	14.3	9.9	8.9	15.0
Cash Flow	19.0	-3.2	38.1	23.0	43.0	39.9

Ratio Analysis

	1995	1994	1993	1992	1991	1990
Curr. Ratio	2.1	1.9	2.0	2.1	2.0	2.1
% LT Debt of Cap.	4.2	4.7	7.0	6.2	4.0	5.1
% Net Inc.of Revs.	2.0	NM	4.1	1.9	4.4	4.7
% Ret. on Assets	2.2	NM	5.9	2.6	7.4	7.5
% Ret. on Equity	4.2	NM	11.4	4.7	12.8	13.0

Dividend Data —Dividends have been paid since 1964. A dividend reinvestment plan is available. A poison pill stock purchase rights plan was adopted in 1986.

Amt. of Div. $	Date Decl.	Ex-Div. Date	Stock of Record	Payment Date
0.220	Aug. 05	Sep. 12	Sep. 16	Oct. 15 '94
0.220	Oct. 24	Dec. 12	Dec. 16	Jan. 15 '95
0.220	Jan. 23	Mar. 13	Mar. 17	Apr. 15 '95
0.100	Jun. 08	Jun. 15	Jun. 19	Jul. 15 '95
0.100	Aug. 04	Sep. 13	Sep. 15	Oct. 15 '95

Data as orig. reptd.; bef. results of disc. opers. and/or spec. items. Per share data adj. for stk. divs. as of ex-div. date. E-Estimated. NA-Not Available. NM-Not Meaningful. NR-Not Ranked.

Office—One Zurn Place, Erie, PA 16514-2000. **Tel**—(814) 452-2111. **Chrmn & CEO**—R. R. Womack. **SVP & CFO**—J.R. Mellett. **Secy**—D. Haines. **Investor Contact**—Stephen P. Adams. **Dirs**—Z. Baird, W. E. Butler, E. J. Campbell, A. S. Cartwright, R.D. Neary, D. W. Wallace, R. R. Womack. **Transfer Agent & Registrar**—KeyCorp Securities Services, Inc, Cleveland. **Incorporated** in Pennsylvania in 1932. **Empl**- 2,430. **S&P Analyst:** Robert E. Friedman